W9-CNO-933

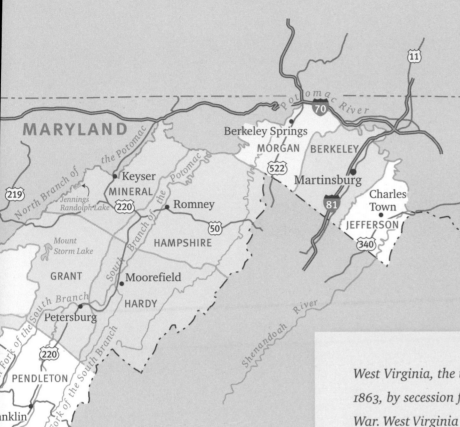

VANIA

MARYLAND

the Potomac

North Branch of the Potomac

Keyser

MINERAL

Jennings Randolph Lake

Romney

South Branch of the Potomac

HAMPSHIRE

Mount Storm Lake

GRANT

Moorefield

South Branch

HARDY

Petersburg

PENDLETON

South Fork of the South Branch

anklin

North Fork of the South Branch

Berkeley Springs

MORGAN

BERKELEY

Martinsburg

Charles Town

JEFFERSON

Potomac River

Shenandoah River

RGINIA

219

220

50

220

70

11

522

81

340

West Virginia, the thirty-fifth state, was created June 20, 1863, by secession from Virginia at the height of the Civil War. West Virginia has a total area of 24,282 square miles, contained within an irregular shape defined by 1,170 miles of border. Known as the Mountain State, West Virginia has the highest average elevation of any state east of the Mississippi. Spruce Knob, at 4,861 feet above sea level, is the highest point in West Virginia, and Harpers Ferry, at 247 feet, is the lowest. There are fifty-five counties in West Virginia, 549 miles of interstate highways, and more than 36,000 miles of other public roads. Largely rural, West Virginia has six cities with populations over 25,000 and none over 60,000. Altogether, there were 1,808,350 West Virginians at the time of the 2000 Census.

West Virginia's independent-minded citizens cherish the state slogan, "Mountaineers are always free." The West Virginia Encyclopedia is their book.

THE WEST VIRGINIA ENCYCLOPEDIA

The **West Virginia** Encyclopedia

Edited by KEN SULLIVAN

Deborah J. Sonis, *Managing Editor*

THE WEST VIRGINIA HUMANITIES COUNCIL

Copyright 2006, by the
West Virginia Humanities Council.

All rights reserved.

This book may not be reproduced in
whole or in part, in any form (except as
permitted by the U.S. Copyright Law and
except by reviewers for the public press),
without the written permission of the
publisher.

Set in Charter and Meta types by
Keystone Typesetting, Inc.
Printed in the United States of America
by Thomson-Shore, Inc.

This book is printed on acid-free paper.
Library of Congress Control Number:
2006921612
ISBN 0-9778498-0-5

West Virginia Humanities Council
1310 Kanawha Boulevard, East
Charleston, West Virginia 25301

10 9 8 7 6 5 4 3 2 1

The West Virginia Encyclopedia is published through the generous support of the following financial contributors:

The West Virginia Humanities Council
The State of West Virginia
The Katharine B. Tierney Charitable Foundation
U.S. Department of Housing & Urban Development
The West Virginia Historical Education Foundation
The Bernard McDonough Foundation
West Virginia Celebration 2000
Columbia Natural Resources

Verizon
Cabot Oil & Gas Corporation
McJunkin Corporation
University of Charleston
United Bank
Bowles Rice McDavid Graff & Love
Columbia Gas Transmission
The Daywood Foundation
The Greater Kanawha Valley Foundation
The Herscher Foundation
The John Deaver Drinko Academy, Marshall University
West Virginia American Water Company

The Union Carbide Foundation
The Bernard H. & Blanche E. Jacobson Foundation
Concord University
American Electric Power
Betty Gardner Bailey
The Bluefield Area Foundation

EDITORIAL STAFF

Ken Sullivan	*Editor*
Deborah J. Sonis	*Managing Editor*
Cheryl R. Marsh	*Project Coordinator*
Judie Smith	*Copy Editor*
Nancy Adams	*Writer*
C. Belmont Keeney	*Researcher*
Paul H. Rakes	*Researcher*
Annette Cipriani	*Data Input*
Carol Nutter	*Data Input*
Barbara Phillips	*Data Input*
Kaitlin Mehle	*Intern*
Anna Sale	*Intern*
Cindy Brown	*Fact Checker*
Tina S. Holmes	*Proofreader*
Fred Kameny	*Indexer*
Richard Hendel	*Designer*

ON THE EIGHTH DAY

God, in a playful mood,
Piled up West Virginia,
Then patted her down again.
Pile, pinch, press, punch,
On a hunch he left her
That way.

And it was good.

—Phyllis Wilson Moore

CONTENTS

Introduction xi

The West Virginia Encyclopedia 1

Acknowledgments 821

Our writers & photographers 823

Illustration credits 839

Sidebar credits 843

Common & scientific names of the
   West Virginia species included in this book 845

Bibliography & citations 853

Index 895

INTRODUCTION

If you were making the book of West Virginia, what would you put in it?

Consider the entire state as you ponder the question, the whole rumpled expanse of this great place, from the wind-blown heights of Spruce Knob to the low elevations of the eastern and western river valleys. Think of the mountains in between, Gauley, Sewell, Flat Top, Back Allegheny and the Allegheny Front, and Cheat Mountain, the grandest of them all, and many more. Think also of the rivers, the Elk; the Kanawha and Little Kanawha; the Guyandotte, known to its own people as the Guyan; the Monongahela; the Cheat; the Potomac, with its north and south branches and even north and south forks of the South Branch; the broad Ohio; the Big Sandy and its Tug Fork; the Blackwater and the Bluestone; the beautiful, free-flowing Greenbrier, and all the others.

Think then of the underlying geology, a buried trove of mineral resources worth far more than a king's ransom, underpinning our rugged landscape and shaping so much of our history. Think of the endless forest which was here in the beginning and which crept back over the course of the 20th century to cover most of the state once again. It was said that a squirrel might travel from the Potomac to the Ohio without touching the ground in the old days, and—with forests having reclaimed nearly four-fifths of our land—it seems almost possible again.

Think of the entirety of West Virginia's flora and fauna as you consider that energetic squirrel tree-topping from east to west. Among his fellow game animals—and yes, we eat squirrel in West Virginia, preferably with gravy and biscuits—there are 50 species, including mammals, birds, fish, and at least one amphibian. There are 63 mammal species in all, game and non-game, 178 species of fish, and literally countless species of insects. There are 321 species of birds, more than were present 75 years ago. The number of plant species exceeds 2,300, native and exotic. Nature's abundant variety is a blessing to West Virginians, and most of us live close enough to nature that we can lift up our eyes to the wooded hills at any time of the day.

And think, certainly, of the people, the 1.8 million of us who make up the Mountain State population today and the millions who preceded us. Think of the great undifferentiated mass of us, rolling to the Carolina beaches in the summer and jamming the highways on fall weekends to go see the Mountaineers play (or the Thundering Herd or any of a dozen smaller college teams). You will find a good number of us in the woods a little later in the fall, deer hunting, or skiing the mountainsides in the winter. Spring brings ramp suppers and fishing season, and the first of the craft and music festivals.

We enjoy the company of other West Virginians on such occasions. We are apt to sing "Country Roads" when we get together, enthusiastically if not always well. We take pride in the things that set us apart, but in most ways we are much like other Americans: Working steady, driving the best car we can afford, and sheltering our family in the most comfortable housing we can secure. We are rightly proud of these accomplishments, too, for sometimes it seems that West Virginians have to work a little harder for the good things.

Think also of the individual people, from Governor Mac-Corkle to Anne Bailey; Senators Davis and Elkins; Cornstalk and his foe, Andrew Lewis; and labor agitator Mother Jones and Don Chafin, high sheriff of Logan County. Remember Phil Conley and Jim Comstock, who published their own West Virginia encyclopedias some decades ago; the novelist Davis Grubb and our great poet, Louise McNeill; Chief Logan and Captain Bull; A. James Manchin and Senator Byrd, and the other colorful figures who populate our history and the daily news.

Consider as well the ones who passed this way before us, the prehistoric Adena and the other mysterious ancient peoples, and the various nations of Indians who contested our ancestors for possession of these mountains, particularly the fierce Shawnee. Think of the settlers, fierce enough themselves, the Scotch-Irish and others from the British Isles, the Germans who came at about the same time, and the African-Americans who came early if unwillingly. Think then of the great immigration waves of the late 19th and early 20th centuries, bringing Italians, Jews, Hungarians, and others to West Virginia's mines and mills and bustling towns.

Study the cultural tapestry these various forebears left us. Although West Virginia is by many measures today among the least diverse states as regards racial and ethnic makeup, nonetheless we celebrate a variety that reaches well beyond the mountaineer culture for which we are best known. We have a Lebanese festival in West Virginia, an Irish festival, an India festival, at least two Italian festivals, and several generic "international" festivals. The onion-shaped domes of the Eastern Orthodox religion gleam in McDowell and Mercer counties on our southern border, in the capital city, and in the Northern Panhandle. Muslims worship in a fine mosque near Charleston, its builders including families whose ancestors came here generations ago. These and other cultures provide leaven and spice to our traditional mountain ways—though West Virginians of every background may be expected to step a little livelier when the fiddler takes up his bow.

And think of our history as you consider West Virginia, the great story of exploration and settlement of the mountain frontier, the subsequent filling out of the territory, then the establishment of ourselves as a distinct place and people. Eventually —"after many long and weary years of insult and injustice," as our first governor said at his 1863 inauguration—we declared ourselves a separate state in the Union. In time the new state became one of the nation's industrial centers, and lately we have had to work our way through the challenging problems of industrial decline.

You must not pass over the bad things as you consider West Virginia. Remember the Buffalo Creek flood, and the fearful disasters at Monongah and Farmington and the dozens of other mine explosions that came between—and before and after— those two. Think of the hard-fought labor wars that stopped the trains at Martinsburg and the aluminum smelters at Ravenswood, and required the dispatching of federal troops to Blair Mountain. Remember the cooling tower collapse at Willow Island and the hundreds of tunnel workers lost to silicosis at Hawks Nest. Think of recurring poverty and the health problems too many of our people struggle against, and the times we find ourselves on the wrong end of some national list. Some misfortunes we brought on ourselves, some were the work of others, and some were acts of nature. But all helped forge our identities as West Virginians, and certainly they must be remembered.

It is a long, complex story. West Virginia has been a state for almost a century and a half, and we have nearly as much history before statehood as after. And keep in mind that we date history only from the time of first contact between white explorers and the native people: It was recorded as history, after all, only because there was some literate person on hand to write it down. And of course there was much that happened before that, in the untold but eventful ages before the first scribe appeared to make a record. So think also of prehistory, unavailable in the written record but inscribed on the land itself in myriad archeological sites.

Think, finally, of the very finest place you know in West Virginia.

Maybe for you that means looking up at Seneca Rocks from the banks of the North Fork; or the grand view from Harpers Ferry that Thomas Jefferson said was worth traveling across the Atlantic to see; or the Tug Fork slipping down between Kentucky and West Virginia, in the stream's lonesome middle stretches where no road will take you. Or maybe it is something our people have built, perhaps glorious Old Main at Bethany College, which has earned the rare designation of national historic landmark; or the state capitol, its dome recently re-gilded and worth a trip itself; or German Street in Shepherdstown; or the spectacular New River Gorge Bridge. Perhaps it is a private place of your own people, maybe a Doddridge County homeplace or a fishing camp somewhere on Elk River—"up Elk," as we say here at the mouth of the river in Charleston. There are thousands of such retreats in West Virginia, rarely fancy but all beautiful to the families who cherish them.

After thinking long and hard you may concur in the late Jim Comstock's wry assessment, that West Virginia is "a great state for the state it's in."

But what would you put in the book of West Virginia?

That was the question we confronted in planning *The West Virginia Encyclopedia*. Our answer now lies before you. You will find articles in these pages on the mountains and rivers, other articles on the 55 counties and all the cities and towns of any size, dozens more on history and prehistory, and still others on geology, geography, literature, folklore, the fine arts and the folk arts, as well as botany and the other natural and physical sciences.

You will find hundreds of biographies in *The West Virginia Encyclopedia*, of the notable individuals who made the Mountain State what it is today. They come from politics and business, of course, but also from entertainment, sports, religion, education, literature and other fields. Mostly they are "dead white men," as the feminist saying goes, but we have made a deliberate effort to be inclusive. You will find many, many strong West Virginia women in these pages, as well as Indians, African-Americans, immigrants, and other minorities who have contributed to our history while being too often overlooked in our history books. We have even included a few people from elsewhere who spent time among us and made a big impression—George Washington and John Kennedy, for example, and the engineer Claudius Crozet, who served with Napoleon before coming to build roads in our mountains.

It is not all of West Virginia, to be sure. It is impossible to pack all that between the covers of a book, despite our motto, "All there is to know about West Virginia." But we are proud to offer an extensive sample. In almost 2,200 articles by nearly 600 writers we think we have something to say concerning just about everything West Virginians want to know about their favorite place.

The dream of a West Virginia encyclopedia goes way back with me, beginning during my years as editor of *Goldenseal* magazine. *Goldenseal*, as you may know, is the folklife quarterly published at the West Virginia Division of Culture and History. I got a graduate education in West Virginia while working at *Goldenseal.* I learned the state's story, traveled the byways of every county, and developed a network of writers and photographers. What I learned, above all, is that West Virginia is a place with a strong and fine sense of itself. West Virginians are proud of their state. They are attached to West Virginia, ready to share their knowledge of it, and eager to learn more themselves.

In 18 years at *Goldenseal*, I worked with a small staff to compile thousands of pages of West Virginiana. I remain proud of what we accomplished. Today *Goldenseal* is routinely cited in scholarly articles and books, and entire books have been made of its own articles. But like any other collection of magazines, the 30-plus volumes of *Goldenseal* edited by me and others amount to an unstructured accretion of information and not a systematic reference. And that is what I came to want to make, a systematic, authoritative West Virginia reference book.

I brought the idea to the West Virginia Humanities Council when I came here in 1997, and it was the Humanities Council that provided the wherewithal to compile and publish *The West Virginia Encyclopedia*. A surprising amount of money—more than a million dollars by the time you read these words in print—was raised or applied from the Council's resources. I thank the board of directors for its support and patience and the staff for its forbearance during this book's long gestation. Our Council made progress on other fronts while the *Encyclopedia* was in the works, but there must have been times when I appeared consumed and distracted by what we came to call our flagship project.

By 1998 we had *The West Virginia Encyclopedia* seriously under way. We made the basic organizational decisions early on, determining that our book would be arranged alphabetically and employ freelancers rather than staff writers. We have done everything we can to improve ease of use, cross-referencing most articles and providing a full index at the back. We hope *The West Virginia Encyclopedia* becomes a browser, as readers drift from item to item or follow a particular interest trail. We want our book in libraries and schools, of course, and on the desks of researchers—but most of all we want it in the hands of ordinary, curious West Virginians. We will be delighted if it becomes the state's foremost coffee-table book.

Several other state and regional encyclopedias have been done in recent years, and we learned all we could from them. I visited editor John Kleber of the *Kentucky Encyclopedia* early on and found him to be generous in advice. We looked in particular at other books from our book designer, Rich Hendel, including the handsome *Encyclopedia of New York City* published by Yale University Press in 1995. I involved myself with the *Encyclopedia of Appalachia*, serving on the editorial board of that book which proceeded on a schedule similar to ours. I found reassurance in the collaboration, particularly in much good-natured commiseration with *Encyclopedia of Appalachia* editor Rudy Abramson.

The big question of what to put in the big book required much thought. We initially brainstormed with Council board and staff, producing among ourselves a list of several hundred topics. Then we hit the road, organizing meetings at several places, including Charleston, Flatwoods, Elkins, Glen Ferris, and Berkeley Springs. We never burdened those freewheeling sessions with the label of focus groups, but that was the general idea. Our method was to gather a dozen or so collaborators at each place, people whom we had reason to think were knowledgeable about their area or West Virginia as a whole. We put them up overnight and picked their brains all the next day, recording the conversation just as it came from their lips.

We sought experts in many fields for these meetings, and one of the most satisfying aspects of the project was to discover the depth of expertise available in West Virginia. It was a pleasure to work with the wildlife professionals at the Elkins office of the Division of Natural Resources, for example, with the geologists at the West Virginia Geological and Economic Survey at Mount Chateau, and with other specialists across the state. I am sure that we called on the scholarly resources of every college in West Virginia. Obviously, we had decided by that time to expand the contents of the *Encyclopedia* beyond the humanities, while keeping it true to the essential humanities enterprise of harvesting knowledge broadly and disseminating it as widely as possible.

Through the group discussions and countless individual conversations, we gradually built up a list of more than 2,000 topics. These are basically the topics you will find in these pages, though we continued to hone the list, adding items, deleting others, and combining still others. While perhaps more art than science, our selection process was nonetheless fruitful. The final mix represents the good ideas of many people.

There were endless questions of style to be addressed in putting together *The West Virginia Encyclopedia*. We have not included a usage section, since we have tried generally to follow commonly available stylebooks, including the *Chicago Manual of Style*, *Words into Type*, and the *American Heritage Dictionary*.

We admit to a few eccentricities not to be found in any of the guidebooks. On the theory that all the best places are to be found inside our own borders, for example, our policy has been to omit "West Virginia" after the names of places within the state. For major towns and cities we put merely the place name: thus Beckley, not Beckley, West Virginia; Weirton, not Weirton, West Virginia, and so on. Smaller places are located by adding the county name: Jumping Branch, Summers County; St. Joseph, Marshall County; and so on. Of course, hundreds of articles deal with the time before there was a West Virginia. Our usual practice is to use the term "Western Virginia," with the "W" capitalized (though sometimes we use "present West Virginia" or "(West) Virginia" more or less interchangeably), for the area that became West Virginia in 1863. Our goal in every case was clarity of communication, while allowing for a range of expression by our writers. We have tried to preserve as much style and grace as possible, avoiding the most ruthless abbreviations: You will not find the postal abbreviation "WV" in the text of this book, for example.

Our practice in naming biographical articles has been to use the individual's popular name or nickname in the title, while giving the full name in the first sentence. Thus we have an article titled "Devil Anse Hatfield," identifying him as Anderson Hatfield in the text that follows. We similarly have articles titled "Chuck Yeager," "Little Sleepy Glenn," and "Cousin Abe Lilly." Where no nickname applies, we use the name most commonly associated with the person, frequently the whole name or the first name and middle initial. Ordinarily we give the formal name for high-ranking officials, such as governors and U.S. senators, with exceptions where the individuals themselves preferred the informality of nicknames—thus "Bob Wise" for the governor and "Jay Rockefeller" for the senator.

We have worked hard to avoid errors in *The West Virginia Encyclopedia*. In the course of fact checking we have second-guessed our long-suffering writers countless times as we raised and resolved thousands of questions regarding the contents of this book. Nonetheless, some mistakes and inaccuracies probably survived. With 2,200 articles and nearly a million words of text, how could it be otherwise? No doubt, we got some things wrong at the outset, and other information, accurate at first, has been rendered inaccurate by intervening change. We ask your help in correcting mistakes. This book represents only the visible part of a large encyclopedic database, which we continue to refine. Please help us get it right.

You will find an acknowledgments section elsewhere in the *Encyclopedia*, but I'd be remiss in closing this introduction without recognizing the contribution of Managing Editor Debby Sonis. This book would not have been possible without at least one other person who felt as stubbornly passionate about it as I, and Ms. Sonis is that person. Her passion translated into long hours, endless patience in working with legions of freelancers, and a fierce insistence on getting the details right.

I thank other staffers as well: Cheryl Marsh, who managed the database and located thousands of photos; Judie Smith, our copy editor and fact checker; Nancy Adams, researcher and journeyman writer during the critical middle years of the project; historians Chuck Keeney and Paul Rakes, graduate students (now Ph.D.'s) who worked as researchers and also contributed articles to the book; and Anna Sale, who did fine work as a summer intern. Cindy Brown (now Rubenstein) worked here as well, and Annette Cipriani and Kaitlin Mehle helped as needed. We especially remember Barbara Phillips, who died during our project.

Need I say, in conclusion, that our book is addressed primarily to West Virginians? This is not to say that we don't value other readers. We believe *The West Virginia Encyclopedia* is the best available introduction to West Virginia, and we hope that it helps newcomers get acquainted. We welcome your interest, and we welcome you to this book and to our great state. You will find a lot of inside chatter in these pages, most meaningful to West Virginians, but there is nothing here that we aren't proudly willing to share.

But as indicated before, I learned years ago that West Virginians have a strong sense of themselves and a passionate attachment to their state. Mountaineers are a settled people, by and large, knowing their place in the world and glad to be there. These are special qualities, worth encouraging in today's homogenized society. And that is what we want to do with *The West Virginia Encyclopedia*, to validate and encourage the qualities that set West Virginia apart and make it special. Thus, you may consider this book a celebration as well as a documentation. We wanted to compile the best possible West Virginia reference, of course, and we believe we have done so. Ultimately, though, our aim was to cater to the deep and abiding interest that West Virginians have in their home and neighbors. That was what guided us as we decided what to put into our book of West Virginia.

We took a lot of satisfaction in the work, as you may imagine. In leaving the project one long-term staffer commented that it was the most important job she had ever had. I took it to mean that she thought she had been able to contribute to something of lasting value and genuine importance. I am sure we all agreed. It is a rare opportunity we have had, and we are grateful for the privilege.

Ken Sullivan

A

Abolitionism

From the 1830s through the Civil War, the abolitionists worked to emancipate all slaves within the United States. During the religious movement known as the Second Great Awakening, evangelical Christianity gained popular appeal in the Northern states, calling for an end to sinful practices and perpetuating a vision of a better human society. Such could not be achieved, claimed some evangelicals, in a country that tolerated slavery. As the size of the United States greatly expanded during the mid-1800s, the debate over slavery in the new territories helped turn this religious movement into a moral and political crusade.

In what is now West Virginia, abolitionists quietly fought this crusade in the early decades of the movement. The debate quickened as the Civil War approached. In 1857 the town of Ceredo, on the banks of the Ohio River in Wayne County, was founded by northern abolitionists led by Eli Thayer. The townspeople helped fugitive slaves slip across the river where they might find sanctuary at nearby Quaker Bottom (later Proctorville), Ohio, and eventually find safe passage to Canada. Z. D. Ramsdell was another prominent Ceredo abolitionist who allegedly helped fugitives in the same capacity.

Historical evidence suggests that the majority of Western Virginians supported emancipation of the slaves. The different viewpoints between Eastern and Western Virginia were due largely to the contrasting economic and social developments of the regions. Slave-based agriculture did not thrive on the rugged farms and in the colder climate of Western Virginia. Many Western Virginians had little contact with slavery, and the religious denominations of the many Scotch-Irish and German settlers of Western Virginia typically condemned the institution. In Eastern Virginia, the economic ties with slavery were too strong to allow for any sizable abolitionist sentiment.

Yet Western Virginians generally opposed extreme abolitionism. Perhaps the best example of the Western Virginian view on slavery comes from the "Ruffner Pamphlet," published in 1847. Henry Ruffner of Kanawha County proposed gradual emancipation and attacked slavery on economic, rather than moral, grounds. This moderate viewpoint claimed that, "Slavery is demonstrated to be not only unprofitable, but deeply injurious to the public prosperity."

Although most Western Virginians supported Ruffner's moderate approach, the most famous example of radical abolitionism in America occurred in Western Virginia, pushing the boundaries of anti-slavery radicalism. John Brown, attempting to incite a slave rebellion, seized the federal arsenal at Harpers Ferry on October 16, 1859. After the attempted uprising failed, Brown was tried and hanged for treason. John Brown's raid sharpened the already strong divisions between North and South, leading the nation ever closer to Civil War.

During the Civil War, prominent Western Virginians became more outspoken against slavery as the statehood movement grew. At the West Virginia Constitutional Convention, the issue of emancipation was hotly debated. Among those calling for emancipation were Robert Hager, Granville Parker, and Gordon Battelle. Others such as Waitman T. Willey and Chester Hubbard were willing to accept emancipation but did not press the issue. Those who opposed the abolitionists included John J. Jackson, John J. Davis, John S. Carlile, and Sherrard Clemens.

Abraham Lincoln and the Congress refused to grant statehood unless an emancipation clause was added to the new state constitution. In February 1863, Willey proposed an amendment to the state constitution that mandated that all slaves under 21 years old as of July 4, 1863, would be freed upon reaching that age. After the approval of the Willey Amendment, the voters of Western Virginia ratified the constitution by a vote of 28,321 to 572. Thus, abolitionism within the statehood movement proved significant in the formation of West Virginia.

See also John Brown, Henry Ruffner, Slavery, Underground Railroad, Willey Amendment

C. Belmont Keeney
West Virginia Humanities Council

Patch Adams

Physician Hunter Doherty "Patch" Adams, controversial founder of the Gesundheit! Institute in Pocahontas County, was born May 26, 1945 in Washington. Since 1971, Adams has promoted an alternative vision of health care: traditional medicine and holistic healing integrated with art, recreation, nature, and fun. In his public appearances, he wears clown clothes and employs slapstick to advertise his message.

In 1963, Adams spent two weeks in a psychiatric facility being treated for depression. After the experience, Adams resolved to live a happier life and spread joy to others. In 1967, he graduated from George Washington University, and he received his M.D. from the Medical College of Virginia in 1971. In 1979, he moved to Washington and began raising money to build a hospital that would offer free care, which he named the Gesundheit! Institute. In 1980, he bought the property for the hospital, a 310-acre farm near Droop Mountain in Pocahontas County.

In 1998, the release of the movie *Patch Adams* brought national fame to Adams. The movie, based on his autobiography *Gesundheit!*, starred Robin Williams.

Adams' critics question the institute's finances. After more than 20 years, the hospital is still a dream. Adams lives in Arlington, Virginia, and lectures about humor, health care, wellness, and creativity.

Adena

The prehistoric Adena culture developed with the beginnings of horticulture about 2,500 years ago within the Ohio River Valley and along major tributaries such as the Kanawha, Scioto, and Kentucky rivers. The word refers to a culture rather than to a particular ethnic group. The archeological evidence suggests that many language or ethnic groups made the artifacts that today we recognize as part of the widespread Adena culture. The Adena were characterized by widespread trade and use of exotic artifacts in complex mortuary rituals involving mound building and geometric earthworks. People of the Adena culture left their enduring mark on the region with these works, which survive today at Moundsville, South Charleston, and other places.

Evidence for long-distance trading among people at this early period comes from the excavation of the many burial mounds that dot the valleys and river confluences of the Ohio River watershed. Navigable rivers connected small, isolated villages into trade networks that moved artifacts from their sources in the Gulf Coast (marine shell), Upper Midwest (copper), and Appalachian (mica, ceramics) regions to communities throughout present southwestern West Virginia, northern Kentucky, and southern Ohio. Items such as stone pipes, copper gorgets, bracelets, finger rings, and pieces of mica fashioned into headdress or hair ornaments have been recovered throughout the area.

Only certain men and women were

This bird carving is an Adena artifact.

buried in the large log-lined tombs characteristic of Adena mounds. These were covered with earth to create a crypt within the mound. New interments were either added to existing mounds, or new mounds were started nearby to create clusters of mounds. Such clusters were documented in the Charleston region more than 150 years ago. Most people, however, were cremated, and their ashes interred in the mound or elsewhere.

Other than mortuary mounds, Adena people also created large circular, rectangular, or hexagonal earthworks by digging ditches and using the excavated soil to build a surrounding berm of earth. It is known that these were not defensive sites, but the activities that occurred within them are largely undocumented since so few contained artifacts of any kind. Their cleaned interiors suggest a ritual use for such places, perhaps as ceremonial dance grounds or meeting places where villagers from isolated settlements came together.

Recent excavations indicate that Adena communities survived by hunting and gathering, supplemented by growing domesticated plants such as goosefoot, maygrass, and sunflower. Typically, settlements consisted of one or two circular houses, about 30 feet to 50 feet in diameter, with a central fireplace, and storage pits. Associated refuse indicates a short period of occupation, perhaps only a couple of years, before a settlement was abandoned and a new one established. Interestingly, few settlements contain any of the kinds of exotic artifacts found in burial contexts, suggesting the high value placed on these traded items, their significant role in ritual life, and their separation from everyday activities.

These early mound builders were the ancestors of the Hopewell Indians who also developed extensive exchange about 300 years later in much the same region. The reasons for the decline of both trade networks are unknown. Analysis of the stylistic decoration of Adena artifacts has not revealed any apparent connection to any modern Indian groups. Population movements after the end of the Adena period into and out of the Ohio River Valley during the last 2,000 years have obscured any possible ethnic or genetic connections to American Indians of the later period. The mounds and earthworks that are still preserved are the most visible remains of this complex society of ancient Native America.

See also Archeology, Prehistoric People

James P. Fenton
Lexington, Kentucky

Don W. Dragoo, *Mounds for the Dead: An Analysis of the Adena Culture,* Annals of the Carnegie Museum, 1963; William S. Webb and Raymond S. Baby, *The Adena People, No. 2,* 1957.

Walter Aegerter

Photographer Walter Aegerter, born in Helvetia, July 8, 1894, was the youngest son of Gottfried and Marianna Dubach Aegerter, who immigrated from Switzerland to Helvetia, Randolph County, in 1885. Walter made his living as a farmer but took up amateur photography as a young man, learning the trade from his father. By the 1890s, the Aegerters were turning out dozens of photographs of local families and the community, using the contemporary glass dry-plate technology. At his death, Aegerter left a large collection of hundreds of images documenting life in this small, Swiss German settlement between the years 1890 and 1930. The glass plate negatives survive to this day, and many photographs are housed at the West Virginia State Archives in Charleston and the West Virginia and Regional History Collection at West Virginia University. Aegerter died in Upshur County, May 28, 1965.

See also Helvetia

David Sutton
Webster, New Hampshire

David H. Sutton, *One's Own Hearth Is Like Gold: A History of Helvetia, West Virginia,* 1990.

African Methodist Episcopal Church

The African Methodist Episcopal Church originated in 1787 when black worshipers, led by Richard Allen and Absalom Jones, left the mixed-race Methodist Episcopal Church in Philadelphia to establish the Bethel A.M.E. Church of Philadelphia, the mother church of the denomination. The A.M.E. Church in doctrine and polity largely agrees with the Methodist Episcopal Church. Its Book of Discipline is modeled after practices in the original Methodist Episcopal Church. Minor differences have developed over the years. A.M.E. bishops have more power than their counterparts in the Methodist Episcopal Church, for example, but the main difference remains racial identity.

The African Methodist Episcopal Church sent missionaries to aid slaves in Western Virginia immediately following John Brown's raid on Harpers Ferry in 1859. Throughout the Civil War, additional workers moved south on the heels of Union soldiers. Between 1870 and 1926, numerous A.M.E. churches were organized throughout West Virginia.

Socially and politically active, the denomination rapidly gained membership in the South following the Civil War. When the Wheeling District of the Pittsburgh Conference assembled in Charleston in May 1907, Rev. S. B. West, presiding elder of the Wheeling District, asked for a separate West Virginia Conference in his annual address. The process moved forward the next year when, in May 1908, West presented a bill calling for a separate West Virginia Conference to the

General Conference held at Norfolk, Virginia. The bill, with a single amendment that left Jefferson County attached to the Virginia Conference, was adopted, making West Virginia a separate conference attached to the Third Episcopal District. When the conference was organized in October 1908, members appointed Rev. W. R. Derrick as presiding bishop, S. B. West as secretary, and W. R. Derrick, J. Harris, and H. E. Tyler as presiding elders.

The number of West Virginia A.M.E. churches, along with church membership, grew in the first decades of the 20th century but began to decline in the mid-1930s. In 1906, there were 35 churches with 1,002 members in West Virginia. In 1919, 33 churches had a membership of 1,325. Churches and membership increased by 1926, to a total of 64 churches and 2,298 members. By 1936, the number of African Methodist Episcopal churches in West Virginia declined to 40. As of 2002, there were 23 churches belonging to the Third Episcopal District located in West Virginia. These churches remain a vital presence in the state, providing spiritual, social, and economic support to their communities.

See also African-American Heritage

Connie Park Rice
West Virginia University

Howard D. Gregg, *History of the African Methodist Episcopal Church,* 1980; C. Eric Lincoln and Lawrence H. Mamiya, *The Black Church in the African American Experience,* 1990.

African Zion Baptist Church

The African Zion Baptist Church, a center of worship for Malden's black community, organized as a formal congregation in 1852, and the present building was built two decades later. Known then as the Kanawha Salines, Malden held West

African Zion Baptist Church.

Virginia's largest concentration of slaves, numbering more than 1,500 and tending the town's booming saltworks. Gen. Lewis Ruffner gave the land, money, and materials for construction of the one-room church building. Services began there in 1872 and continued well into the 20th century. African Zion is the state's oldest black Baptist church and is recognized as the mother church for all of West Virginia's black Baptists.

Its most famous congregant was educator Booker T. Washington, who had come as a boy to the Kanawha Valley when freed from slavery. After graduation from Hampton Normal Institute in Virginia in 1876, Washington returned to live in Malden, teaching Sunday School at African Zion. Washington clerked and married his first wife, Fannie Smith, at the church in 1881 before leaving for Tuskegee. Until his death in 1915, Washington kept his membership in the church.

African Zion's architectural style is typical for the Southern church: simple, unadorned, even spartan. Essentially unchanged since the 1870s, the wood-frame church is a rectangular, front gable design with two tall windows with segmental arch hoods on each side. A short steeple crowns the roof above the front door. Special ceremonies still occur in the sanctuary.

Today, the church is part of an African-American heritage nucleus in the middle of Malden. "Fresh Start Salt Village," a replica of the postbellum salt-worker's living conditions, features a reproduction of Washington's cabin (the original sat approximately 50 yards to the northwest), a combination schoolhouse-church, and a museum. The African Zion Baptist Church was named to the National Register of Historic Places in 1974.

See also African-American Heritage, Malden, Booker T. Washington

Garrett C. Jeter
Charleston

African-American Coal Miners

African-Americans played a key role in the growth of West Virginia's coal industry. Blacks from rural areas of the upper south, mainly Virginia, helped to lay track for the three major railroads that opened up the bituminous fields: the Chesapeake & Ohio, the Norfolk & Western, and the Virginian. It was work on the C&O, at the Great Bend Tunnel in Greenbrier County, that produced the black folk hero John Henry.

As each railroad completed lines through the region, contingents of black railroad men remained behind to work in the coal mines. They were later joined by growing numbers of blacks who went directly into the mines. While blacks from the nearby states of Virginia, Kentucky, and Tennessee dominated the migration to West Virginia during the early period, the advent of World War I brought growing numbers of migrants from the Deep South states of Alabama, Georgia, and Mississippi.

From the turn of the century through the early 1930s, African-Americans made up between 20 percent and 26 percent of the total coal mining labor force in southern West Virginia. They also gradually increased their numbers in the mines in northern West Virginia, but they would remain a much smaller percentage of the total there. Coal companies actively recruited black workers, but black men and women also established their own kin and friendship networks, and helped to facilitate their own movement into the coal towns.

During the Great Depression of the 1930s, blacks shouldered a disproportionate share of the unemployment and hard times. Their percentage in the state's coal mining labor force dropped from more than 22 percent in 1930 to about 17 percent in 1940. The Depression and World War II also unleashed new technological and social forces that transformed the coal industry, and stimulated massive out-migration in the postwar years. Loading machines rapidly displaced miners during the 1940s and '50s. Black miners recall that the mine management always put the first loading machines where blacks were working, meaning that black miners were the first to lose their jobs.

As the state's black coal mining labor force declined, racial discrimination persisted in all facets of life. In 1961, according to the West Virginia Human Rights Commission, most of the state's public accommodations—restaurants, motels, hotels, swimming pools, and medical facilities—discriminated against blacks. By the late 20th century African-American miners had dropped to less than three percent of the work force, and as blacks lost coal mining jobs, they found few alternative employment opportunities.

See also African-American Heritage, Coal Industry

Joe William Trotter Jr.
Carnegie Mellon University
Ronald L. Lewis, *Black Coal Miners in America: Race, Class, and Community Conflict, 1780–1980,* 1987; Jack Salzman, ed., *Encyclopedia of African American Culture and History,* 1996; Joe William Trotter Jr., *Coal, Class, and Color: Blacks in Southern West Virginia, 1915–32,* 1990.

African-American Education

Early black education in West Virginia developed through a combination of forces: self-help efforts; the aid and support of benevolent white people; support from the U.S. Freedmen's Bureau and missionary associations; and the activities of public school officials. By the middle of the 20th century, on the eve of desegregation, the state's African-American schools had become a well-functioning, effective system.

When the first West Virginia legislature met in 1863, it agreed to educate "free colored children," but the proposition was left unfunded. With the condition that white and black children should not be taught in the same schools, West Virginia's second constitution in 1872 affirmed the state's commitment to the education of African-American children. Although most school boards cooperated, court action sometimes had to be undertaken or threatened to force some to provide the needed support for black education.

Sumner School, the first school for black children in West Virginia, a self-help effort, opened in Parkersburg in 1862. After 1865, education for West Virginia's black citizens was undertaken wherever there were enough students. Schools were under way in 18 communities by 1868, including Parkersburg, Wheeling, Clarksburg, Charleston, Lewisburg, Martinsburg, Charles Town, and Malden. These early schools were held wherever space could be found, sometimes in homes and churches. In some instances the schools were private and served both adults and children.

Among the major difficulties was the dearth of teachers. In the beginning, whites served, as did black teachers from neighboring states, particularly Ohio. The first formal effort to train black teachers in West Virginia came at Storer College in Harpers Ferry. The college was begun in 1865 by the Freewill Baptist Church. In 1881 the state agreed to contract with Storer to train African-American teachers. Until the state's black land grant college, West Virginia Colored Institute (now West Virginia State University), was founded in 1891, Storer College was the only institution in the state preparing blacks for the teaching profession. Later, Bluefield Colored Institute (now Bluefield State College), established in 1895, joined the other two in this mission. These institutions also provided secondary education.

As the railroads and mines drew more black people into West Virginia in the late 19th and early 20th centuries, the need for public education increased. Initially, the school law permitted the establishment of a black school wherever there were 30 black students between the ages of six and 21. Over the years, this number was reduced until a school could be started with 10 students of school age. With this reduction in the number required, elementary schools sprang up in many areas. One of the earliest was the Clarksburg School, for which a construction bid was accepted in 1868. Statewide, there were 207 black schools and 278 teachers serving 7,886 students in 1902. By 1924, there were 453 elementary and junior high schools.

Black high school education began slowly. The first institution to offer such instruction was the Sumner School in Parkersburg, which added high school courses to its curriculum in 1885. This was followed by high schools in Clarksburg, Charleston, and Huntington. By 1923, the number of black high schools had increased to 21. In some cases, cooperative arrangements allowed African-American students to cross county lines to attend high school; for example Preston County students attended in Monongalia County. In other instances students either ended their education at the eighth grade, boarded with families in areas where there were high schools, or daily traveled long distances by train, bus, or streetcar.

In addition to black public education, several private educational efforts were attempted. Storer College continued in Harpers Ferry until 1956; St. Phillips Academy was operated for a time by St. Phillips Episcopal Church in Charles Town; the Baptist State Association operated a school at Hilltop in Fayette County; and Catholics operated St. Peter Claver in Huntington.

In 1919 the state created the position of state supervisor of Negro schools and appointed a Negro Board of Education. In 1933 assistant superintendents of Negro education were appointed in counties having 50 or more black teachers. In addition to the push for more voice in the operation of their schools, blacks also struggled for adequate buildings and materials, for equal salaries for teachers, and for a full nine-month school year.

By 1950, the West Virginia public school system provided separate education for more than 19,000 of the state's black youth, grades 1–12. Included were schools for black students in institutional settings, including the deaf and blind. Higher education through the baccalaureate level was available at Bluefield State College and West Virginia State. Academics were enriched by strong extracurricular offerings such as dramatics, music, art, various clubs, and athletics. Statewide competitions, tournaments, and exhibitions helped to knit together black communities across West Virginia. The black colleges, elementary and junior and senior high schools, and their administrators and teachers are remembered and honored by their alumni for helping them to develop a strong educational background, basic values, community spirit, and lifelong friendships.

When the 1954 *Brown v. Board of Education* Supreme Court decision ended segregated schools in the United States, West Virginia began dismantling its system of black education. By the mid-1960s, the process was essentially complete, with African-American students and teachers participating in integrated public schools.

See also African-American Heritage, Storer College

Ancella R. Bickley
Charleston

Ancella R. Bickley, *History of the West Virginia State Teachers' Association*, 1979; Joel E. Hight, "History of Negro Secondary Education in McDowell County West Virginia," M.E. thesis, University of Cincinnati, 1946.

African-American Heritage

West Virginia was a product of the Civil War. When Virginia seceded from the Union, Western Virginians soon formed a new state. Although Booker T. Washington and others made the journey across the mountains, West Virginia did not become a general refuge for slaves and free blacks. The state's first constitution provided for the phasing out of slavery, but only the ratification of the 13th Amendment in 1865 completely abolished slavery in West Virginia. Although the state's constitutional convention of 1872 guaranteed the vote, it denied African-Americans the right to serve on juries; approved the segregationist clause that "white and colored shall not be taught in the same school"; and sanctioned a racially stratified and unequal society that would persist.

As the state industrialized following Reconstruction, many Southern blacks moved to West Virginia and made the complicated transition from agriculture to life in the coal towns. The state's black population increased from 25,800 in 1880 to more than 64,000 in 1910, and to nearly 115,000 in 1930. The expansion of the coal industry underlay this dynamic population growth. Blacks made up more than 20 percent of West Virginia's total mining labor force from the 1890s through the early 20th century.

As the African-American population increased, so did racial hostility. In 1919, for example, a white mob lynched two black miners at Chapmanville, Logan County. During the early 1920s, chapters of the Ku Klux Klan emerged in Logan, Mercer, and Kanawha counties and elsewhere. Moreover, racial injustice before the law also prevailed, as in several cases of black men accused of crimes against whites, especially charges of rape. In 1922, for example, Governor Morgan denied a plea for clemency and permitted a black man, Leroy Williams, to hang for rape of a white woman despite evidence suggesting his innocence.

As elsewhere, African-Americans developed a variety of institutional and political responses to inequality. As early as 1872, they urged the adoption of a provision that would permit black men to serve on juries in the state's courts of law. Membership in black religious organizations (predominantly the Baptist and African Methodist Episcopal churches) climbed from less than 15,000 before World War I to nearly 33,000 in 1926. Membership in black fraternal orders and mutual benefit societies reached about 32,000 before declining during the late 1920s. The emergence of West Virginia branches and affiliates of the National Association for the Advancement of Colored People and Marcus Garvey's Universal Negro Improvement Association, as well as the McDowell County Colored Republican Organization and the black *McDowell Times* weekly newspaper, rounded out the institutional life of blacks in West Virginia before the onslaught of the Great Depression.

In 1918, three black men were elected

Coming to the new state

"My mother's husband, who was the stepfather of my brother John and myself, did not belong to the same owners as did my mother. In fact, he seldom came to our plantation. I remember seeing him there perhaps once a year, that being about Christmas time. In some way, during the war, by running away and following the Federal soldiers, it seems, he found his way into the new state of West Virginia. As soon as freedom was declared, he sent for my mother to come to the Kanawha Valley, in West Virginia. What little clothing and few household goods we had were placed in a cart, but the children walked the greater portion of the distance, which was several hundred miles.

"I do not think any of us ever had been very far from the plantation, and the taking of a long journey into another state was quite an event. The parting from our former owners and the members of our own race on the plantation was a serious occasion. . . . We were several weeks making the trip, and most of the time we slept in the open air and did our cooking over a log fire out of doors. One night I recall that we camped near an abandoned log cabin, and my mother decided to build a fire in that for cooking, and afterward to make a 'pallet' on the floor for our sleeping. Just as the fire had gotten well started a large black snake fully a yard and a half long dropped down the chimney and ran out on the floor. Of course we at once abandoned that cabin. Finally we reached our destination —a little town called Malden, which is about five miles from Charleston, the present capital of the state."

—Booker T. Washington *Up From Slavery* (1901)

to the state legislature: Charleston attorney T. G. Nutter; Keystone attorney Harry J. Capehart; and coal miner John V. Coleman of Fayette County. By 1930, African-Americans claimed two state colleges (West Virginia State and Bluefield State); a tuberculosis sanitarium; homes for the deaf, blind, aged, and infirm; schools for delinquent youth; a Bureau of Negro Welfare and Statistics; and an expanding number of public elementary, junior high, and high schools.

After receiving the vote along with white women in 1920, black women increased their influence in the political life of the state. In 1927, when the black legislator E. Howard Harper died in office, his wife, Minnie Buckingham Harper, served the remainder of his term. Mrs. Harper was the first black woman to become a member of a legislative body in the United States. Memphis Tennessee Garrison, the school teacher and civil rights activist, was among the prominent black women in the institutional, social, and political life of the state. During the 1920s, she initiated the NAACP's national Christmas Seal campaign, and later won the association's coveted Madame C. J. Walker Gold Medal for her work.

The Depression and rapid mechanization of coal production undercut the black mining labor force after World War II. The percentage of black miners dropped steadily to about 12 percent in 1950, 6.6 percent in 1960, and 5.2 percent in 1970. By 1980, African-Americans made up less than 3 percent of the state's coal miners.

African-Americans in West Virginia did not sit quietly as the times changed around them. They used the 1954 U.S. Supreme Court school desegregation decision to push for full access to the state's schools, colleges, and universities, but the fruits of integration were sometimes bitter. Much was lost as the tradition of all-black public institutions gradually came to an end. Bluefield State College and West Virginia State University became predominantly white institutions by the mid-1970s. Local school boards closed one black high school after another, bringing to an end one of the major public institutions in black life during the era of Jim Crow. As R. Charles Byers, professor of education at West Virginia State University, states, the fall of black high schools was a "heart-breaking" development.

African-Americans responded to declining economic and social conditions in a variety of ways. Many moved to the large metropolitan areas of the Northeast and Midwest, including Cleveland, Chicago, Detroit, and New York. Others moved to the nearby upper South and border cities such as Washington. Some moved as far west as California. Indicative of the rapid out-migration of West Virginia blacks, the African-American population dropped from a peak of 117,700 in 1940 to 65,000 in 1980, a decline from 6 percent to 3 percent of the total state population. Still, other West Virginia blacks remained behind and sought to make a living in the emerging new order.

Partly because of disappointment with integration, African-Americans in the Mountain State struggled to maintain black churches, fraternal orders, social clubs, civil rights and political organizations, and the black press. Formed in the 1950s, the *West Virginia Beacon Journal* replaced the *McDowell Times* as the preeminent organ of black public opinion in the state. In 1988, the First Baptist Church of Charleston hosted the First Annual Conference on West Virginia's Black History. Spearheaded by the Alliance for the Collection, Preservation, and Dissemination of West Virginia's Black History, the conference continued into the next decade, featuring a variety of papers, speeches, and comments on the state's black heritage and committed to African-American institutions, values, and beliefs.

Joe William Trotter Jr.
Carnegie Mellon University

Ronald L. Lewis, *Black Coal Miners in America: Race, Class, and Community Conflict, 1780–1980*, 1987; Joe William Trotter Jr., *Coal, Class, and Color: Blacks in Southern West Virginia, 1915–32*, 1990; Trotter, "West Virginia," in Jack Salzman, ed., *Encyclopedia of African American Culture and History*, 1996.

Agriculture

The first settlers in West Virginia were adventurous individuals and families seeking a new life in a new land. Little was understood of elevations and mean rainfall, but the cool mountains and fertile valleys attracted a variety of hardy pioneers. These first arrivals possessed or quickly learned frontier ways. They needed woodsmen skills to harvest timber and build houses, barns, and other buildings. They trapped and hunted for food and skins. They gathered fruit, nuts, roots, and the sap from maple trees.

As land was cleared for growing corn, wheat, and buckwheat and for grazing animals, gathering and hunting became less essential to meeting the family's needs. Goods acquired by hunting, trapping, and gathering continued to be of value for trade, but domestic grains, fruits, and the products of domestic animals gained in importance. Various areas of present West Virginia went through these stages of development in the late 1700s and early 1800s.

By the time of the Civil War farms and orchards were well developed statewide. Cattlemen were improving their herds with superior breeding stock, and some larger operators had established patterns of winter feeding on home farms and summer grazing on well identified mountain pastures. When ready for slaughter, cattle were driven to eastern market centers because rail lines were mostly lacking.

The Civil War brought crushing setbacks, but with the cessation of hostility and the attainment of statehood agriculture recovered and rapidly made up for earlier losses. By 1869, West Virginia had 40,000 farms totaling 8.6 million acres. The number of farms and acreage of improved land increased steadily during the next decade. Thereafter the number of farms continued to increase, but the total farm acreage at the end of the 19th century was about the same as in the 1860s. By 1900 there were nearly 100,000 farms in West Virginia, occupying more than

A Tucker County hayfield.

8.9 million acres. Pasture and hay land made up most of the farm acreage, but farmers grew thousands of acres of corn, small grains, soybeans, and potatoes on land later deemed unsuitable for row and grain crops. Sales were largely confined to local markets.

The number of farms peaked at 102,000 in 1940, and dropped steadily thereafter. The number remained at about 20,000 with an average size of 175 acres for the last three decades of the 20th century. Gross farm production had an annual value of about $400 million at century's end.

Many of the soils in the state are steeply sloping and tend to be shallow, acidic, and deficient in available phosphorus. As early as the late 19th century progressive farmers used rock phosphate, bone meal, and lime to increase crop yield and quality. Since the mid-20th century farmers have used soil tests and corrected mineral deficiencies. Most crop land and much of the pasture land are no longer severely deficient in essential nutrients.

West Virginia has always been primarily a livestock producing state. Land on steep slopes is best suited to producing pasture and hay. A half-century ago the value of livestock, dairy, poultry, and crops each made up about one-fourth of total agricultural value. Since then, dairy enterprises and crop production have diminished somewhat and beef cattle numbers have remained relatively constant.

Poultry production increased rapidly in the late 20th century as processors moved into West Virginia and entered into production contracts with farmers. At century's end, poultry generated more than half of the total value of agricultural production. Commercial broiler production started in the 1930s in several South Branch Valley counties, reaching 100,000 broilers in 1935 and increasing steadily for the next four decades. The state produced about 20 million broilers in 1980, increasing rapidly to more than 90 million at the end of the century. Turkey production has doubled since 1980 to the present level of about 4.5 million birds per year. As with broilers, turkey production predominates in Hardy, Pendleton, Grant, and Hampshire counties. Currently, almost all egg production is for home consumption.

Dairy farming saw many changes in the 20th century. Most visible was the shift from mixed and cross-bred herds early in the century to several European breeds, including Holstein, Ayrshire, Jersey, Guernsey, and a few others, and then overwhelmingly to Holsteins by century's end. Artificial insemination and embryo transfer, scientific feeding, and the use of nutritional supplements and hormones were among the factors leading to an increase in yearly milk production per cow from less than 5,000 pounds in 1900 to more than 15,000 pounds in 2000. At the same time, improved equipment for milking and feed handling reduced labor needs. National overproduction resulted, and many West Virginia dairymen found it impossible to compete. As the industry shifted westward, the number of dairy producers in West Virginia steadily declined, with many farmers taking advantage of a federal herd buyout in the 1980s. The number of dairy cows fell from about 34,000 in 1985 to about 24,000 in 1990, and milk production fell from 382 million pounds to 270 million pounds.

The beef cattle industry historically has been the most stable agricultural enterprise. Cattle numbers peaked during World War II at 628,000 head, compared with 440,000 to 480,000 during the 1990s. Production is spread over the state, with greatest concentrations in counties along and east of the Allegheny range. Other pockets of high concentration are in Mason, Jackson, and Wood counties along the Ohio River and in the central counties of Harrison, Lewis, and Upshur. Cow-calf operations and summer grazing programs are the most common and widespread livestock enterprises. Mountain pastures have long been a prized asset to the cattle industry.

The state has always been a leader in livestock marketing. Extension Service marketing specialists held the first graded feeder calf sale in America at Jackson's Mill in the early 1930s. Producers now sell their cattle and other livestock at about a dozen licensed livestock markets around the state, with about five of these markets accounting for a high percentage of the livestock sold. Modern communications supplement the sales effort. Using a system of "tele-auctions" buyers on the telephone compete with each other and local buyers for uniform truckload lots of graded cattle.

Sheep numbers peaked in the late 19th century with more than 800,000 head in flocks distributed over most of the state. Numbers have declined steadily, and currently most of the 40,000 to 60,000 sheep in the state are concentrated in Pendleton, Pocahontas, Randolph, and a few adjoining counties.

Hog numbers also peaked early and have declined for many years. As a commercial hog industry developed outside of West Virginia, swine production on small farms became less attractive. Currently Berkeley, Hampshire, and Hardy are leading counties in hog production and are also leading corn producers.

Most West Virginia farmland produces grass. Nearly half of the 3.7 million acres of farmland in the state is devoted to permanent pastures. In addition, livestock producers use nearly half of the 1.3 million acres of cropland for rotation pasture. They harvest hay from about 85 percent of the remainder.

Hay acreage has been consistently high, peaking at about 840,000 acres in the early 1940s when cattle numbers peaked. In the 1990s hay production accounted for about 500,000 acres annually. Alfalfa hay acreage peaked at 140,000 acres in the 1950s and total production at 330,000 tons in the mid-1980s. Alfalfa is best adapted to deep limestone influenced soils. As dairy cow numbers declined there has been a corresponding reduction of alfalfa production.

Corn and small grains once grew on much of the acreage now devoted to hay and pasture. At the end of the 19th century West Virginia farmers grew 1.2 million acres of corn and wheat. It wasn't until the formation of the USDA Soil Conservation Service in the 1930s that more appropriate land use prevailed. Farmers reserved their best land for corn and small grain and allowed steeper land to remain in semi-permanent hay or pasture. The healed gullies seen today are a reminder of a former time when soil erosion was a severe and unsightly problem on steep crop land.

Nowadays, about 40 percent of the corn crop is harvested by chopping the entire plant and storing as silage for use as animal feed. An important benefit of corn silage over corn for grain is that it produces nearly twice as much feed because the whole plant is used. A few counties produce most of the corn. Sixty percent to 70 percent of corn production for both grain and silage occurs in Jefferson, Berkeley, Hardy, Monroe, Preston, and Mason counties. Only Jefferson County regularly harvests more than one million bushels and produces more corn than is used in the county.

Except for wartime, small grain production has steadily declined for a century. While still important on individual farms, wheat, oats, and barley provide a small portion of total farm income. Preston County leads the state in oats, and Jefferson leads in wheat and barley.

Farmers grew the highest acreage of soybeans early in the 20th century, mostly for hay. Currently, growers produce soybeans for a cash market mostly in the Eastern Panhandle and Ohio Valley.

Burley tobacco has been an important cash crop for farmers in a few southwestern counties since West Virginia became a state. In recent years Mason has displaced Lincoln as the leading tobacco producer. Other major tobacco counties are Putnam, Cabell, Jackson, and Monroe, with smaller acreages in Roane and Wirt. In the early 1900s annual leaf production exceeded 14 million pounds. With production quotas established in the 1930s to stabilize prices and with more recent health concerns, the amount of tobacco grown in West Virginia has declined. Recently, growers have produced less than three million pounds of leaf per year. Alternative crops are being sought which will provide acceptable income.

The Eastern Panhandle counties of Berkeley, Hampshire, Jefferson, and Morgan account for nearly 95 percent of apple and peach production. These counties also produce almost all of the nectarines, cherries, plums, and pears. Commercial orchards expanded rapidly during and following World War II, largely in response to the presence of processing and marketing facilities in and near the Panhandle. Production had declined by about half at the end of the 20th century, to about 125 million pounds of apples and 13 million pounds of peaches per year. Growers sell most of the peaches as fresh fruit. Early in the 20th century growers sold more than half of their apples as fresh fruit. Now they sell slightly more than 20 percent for fresh use and the remainder to food processors. Ninety percent of apple trees set before 1965 were on standard rootstocks, but now 90 percent of new plantings are on dwarf or semi-dwarf rootstocks.

Production of small fruit (raspberries, blackberries, strawberries, blueberries) is of small magnitude and occurs all over the state to supply local markets. Grape production has increased somewhat, largely for wine making. There are about a dozen wineries, spread generally throughout the state. Each has several acres of grapes and buys additional grapes from West Virginia growers. By law, 75 percent of their wine must be from grapes grown in the state.

New and non-traditional enterprises such as trout and other fish production and organic crop production are increasing in importance. A growing array of small enterprises produce fruit, potatoes and other vegetables, herbs, cut flowers, bedding plants, ginseng, black walnuts, sorghum molasses, and countless other products primarily for local markets. Growers sell these products on the farm, at the courthouse square in some counties, at one of about 20 farmers markets, or at more than 200 roadside stands.

Farmers belong to a variety of organizations, the West Virginia Farm Bureau being the largest. Other organizations include the West Virginia Cattlemen's Association, West Virginia State Horticultural Society, and the West Virginia Soil Conservation Districts. In addition, there are numerous local livestock marketing alliances and farm supply associations and recently formed organic and nonorganic produce buying and selling organizations.

The 20th century brought dramatic changes to the nature of farming in the mountain state. At the close of the century West Virginia farmers were as deeply involved with meeting environmental and health concerns as they had been with production practices and erosion control a few decades earlier. Almost all farms with concentrations of animals were using some aspect of nutrient and animal waste plans to ensure wise land husbandry. Programs were in place for nutrient and waste management and for pesticide use certification. In addition producer-run voluntary programs in the livestock industry and for organic farms encouraged acceptance in the marketplace.

Charles Sperow
Morgantown

West Virginia Agricultural Statistics Service, Annual Bulletin, 1999. West Virginia Department of Agriculture and U.S.D.A., 2000.

Department of Agriculture

The West Virginia Department of Agriculture promotes the state's agricultural industry and works to ensure the safety of agricultural products sold in the state. The commissioner of agriculture, one of the executive branch's constitutional officers, directs the department.

In 1891, the legislature set up the four-member State Board of Agriculture to plan agricultural programs and publish information. In 1911, the legislature passed a bill to create the Department of Agriculture and the office of commissioner of agriculture. A year later, the Board of Agriculture disbanded. Elected in 1912, the first commissioner was directed to promote agriculture as an industry and encourage the organization of agricultural and horticultural groups.

In 1913, the legislature assigned to the commissioner the responsibility to regulate farm products. In the 1920s and 1930s, the Department of Agriculture, guided by new state laws, acted to assist farmers in marketing. One early project was the state apple packing plant in Inwood, Berkeley County, established in 1920. The Department of Agriculture also helped farmers set standards for their products, especially vegetables, small fruits, poultry, eggs, lambs, and wool. Consumer protection later became one of the department's primary responsibilities, after the legislature assigned it the authority to enforce the state's pure food laws.

The Department of Agriculture has many responsibilities: 1) to prevent, control, and eradicate animal and poultry diseases; 2) to inspect commercial slaughterhouses; 3) to regulate pesticides; 4) to detect and control plant diseases; 5) to distribute agricultural information, including the monthly *Market Bulletin*, circulation 60,000; 6) to enforce laws to protect the public food supply; and 7) to support rural development initiatives. The state Department of Agriculture works cooperatively with the U.S. Department of Agriculture on some matters, particularly meat and poultry inspections and detection and control of plant diseases.

The department employs more than 200 people. Besides the commissioner's state capitol office, the department maintains facilities at the Guthrie Agricultural Center in Sissonville in Kanawha County; a water quality laboratory in Moorefield, Hardy County; offices in Inwood; and field offices and farmers' markets throughout the state.

In 2000, Gus R. Douglass, a Mason County native, was elected to his ninth four-year term as commissioner of agriculture. He has served in statewide office longer than any other person. As commissioner, he sits on the Board of Public Works, the Air Quality Board, the State Soil Conservation Committee, and State Forestry Commission.

See also Agriculture, Constitutional Officers

Nancy Ray Adams
Pine Mountain Settlement School

Charles H. Ambler and Festus P. Summers, *West Virginia, The Mountain State,* 1958; William D. Barns, *The West Virginia State Grange, The First Century, 1873–1973,* 1973; *West Virginia Blue Book,* 1998.

Air National Guard

The West Virginia Air National Guard was founded after World War II. Lt. Col. James K. McLaughlin organized the 167th Fighter Squadron in Charleston, and it was recognized by federal authorities on March 7, 1947. The 167th's first P-47D Thunderbolt fighter planes were delivered from Wright-Patterson Air Force Base. The Thunderbolts were soon replaced with the famous P-51D Mustangs.

The squadron was called to active duty during the Korean War in 1950 and moved to Godman Air Force Base in Kentucky as part of the 123rd Fighter Group. Twelve 167th pilots served in Korea and two died there, Roma Fogelsong and Lee Harper. Maj. Woodford Sutherland was killed after a training flight in Florida when his parked P-51 was hit by another Mustang in 1951. Tragedy struck again when a C-47 transport filled with 167th personnel going to attend Sutherland's funeral crashed near Kanawha (now Yeager) Airport, killing 21.

The 167th was reorganized during 1953 and moved to Martinsburg in late 1955, where it later received jet fighters, F-86H Sabres. Prior to this move the 130th Troop Carrier Squadron was formed from a cadre of 167th men who would remain in Charleston. Early in its history the 130th furnished SA-16 amphibious planes and crews assigned to help invade Cuba had the 1961 Bay of Pigs landing succeeded. The 130th operated the C-119 transports from 1963 until 1975, when they received C-130Es.

West Virginia Air National Guard on a 1989 exercise.

The 167th in Martinsburg lost its fighter jets on April 1, 1961, and began operating C-119s as an Aeromedical Transport Squadron. C-121G Super Constellations replaced the 119s in July of 1963, and the unit flew supply missions to Vietnam using C-121Cs. Almost phased out in 1967 and 1971, the 167th was rescued by Sen. Robert C. Byrd and given C130As. During the Gulf War the 167th Tactical Airlift Group was in charge of "Operation Volant Pine" in Europe, the command unit of the five Air National Guard units. Simultaneously, the 130th flew combat support missions in the Middle East.

The 130th now operates eight C-130Hs from Yeager Airport and has about 800 personnel. The 167th remains in Martinsburg, with about 1,200 personnel and 12 C-130H aircraft. In 1998 the 167th was named top C-130 unit in the air force.

See also Aviation

Jack H. Smith
South Charleston

Jack H. Smith, *West Virginia Air Power: A Pictorial History of the 130th and 167th Tactical Airlift Groups*, 1992.

Akro Agate Company

The Akro Agate Company of Clarksburg was a world leader in manufacturing glass marbles. Organized in Akron, Ohio, in 1911 the firm relocated to Clarksburg in 1914 because of the availability of glass sand and cheap natural gas for fuel. The Chinese Checker craze of the 1930s and '40s helped make the marbles very profitable, with more than 2,000,000 made per week. Beginning in the 1930s a line of pressed glass vases, floral ware, and colorful glass containers was produced. Miniature glass children's dishes, including tea pots, cups, saucers, and other pieces, were sold as inexpensively boxed sets when World War II limited the availability of metal for toys. The marbles and multicolored pressed articles in similar

hues are sought by collectors today. Pressed products can sometimes be identified by the trademark of the letter A with a crow flying through it. The firm, located off South Chestnut Street, ceased production in 1951.

See also Clarksburg, Glass Industry, Marbles

Dean Six
West Virginia Museum of American Glass
Edwin Sweeney, "Marbles and Pressed Glass: Remembering Akro Agate of Clarksburg," *Goldenseal,* Summer 1984.

Alderson Baptist Academy

Founded by Miss Emma Alderson in Greenbrier County, 1901.

See Alderson-Broaddus College.

Alderson Federal Prison Camp

Alderson Federal Prison Camp opened in 1927 as the Federal Industrial Institution for Women. Its first warden was Mary B. Harris. The prison complex is located near Alderson on the Greenbrier River in Summers County.

Prior to the construction of Alderson Federal Prison Camp, there was no federal women's prison. Women who had committed federal violations were incarcerated in separate sections of penitentiaries for men, state prisons, jails, and houses of correction throughout the United States. Few of these facilities were modern, and they offered few if any programs for the rehabilitation of women prisoners.

The Alderson prison was established in large part through the effort and inspiration of Mabel Walker Willebrandt, the first woman appointed U.S. assistant attorney general in charge of federal felons. The recreational hall at Alderson was named after Willebrandt. The prison architecture resembles that of a college campus.

The federal Industrial Institution for

Women later became the Federal Reformatory for Women, and in November 1988 the name was changed to Alderson Federal Prison Camp. Alderson was the first federal institution for female offenders, and is now the largest minimum-security facility in the federal prison system. The prison employs 195 full-time staff members, and has a capacity of 677 inmates. Inmates represent every state and several foreign countries. Over the years, the prison has housed some famous female inmates including singer Billie Holiday, radio propagandists Axis Sally and Tokyo Rose, Charles Manson cult member Lynette "Squeaky" Fromme, and Martha Stewart.

The prison is fully accredited by the American Correctional Association, Commission on Accreditation for Correction.

Stephen D. Trail
Hinton

Alderson-Broaddus College

As its hyphenated name suggests, Alderson-Broaddus College has gone through some permutations during its long history, including several changes in name and location. The college has been in four different places and has had seven name changes in the 130 years of its existence. Only in 1932 did the Philippi college settle on the name it now holds.

The roots of Alderson-Broaddus extend back to post-Civil War Virginia, and to the personal efforts of Edward Jefferson Willis, peripatetic adventurer, war hero, and devout Baptist layman. In 1871, at the prompting of local Baptist congregations, Willis founded the Winchester Female Institute in Winchester, Virginia, the ancestor of Broaddus College. From this point the college has hewn steadfastly to its American Baptist identity. In 1875 the name was changed to Broaddus Female College in honor of Baptist preacher William F. Broaddus. In 1876, Willis moved the school across the mountains to Clarksburg, in response to a depressed economy in Virginia. In 1894, Broaddus accepted its first male students and in 1909 moved to Philippi.

Miss Emma Alderson founded Alderson Academy in Alderson, Greenbrier County, in 1901. Coeducational from the start, the Academy announced an enrollment of 40 students its first year, and 107 students had enrolled by the end of the year. In 1911 the name was changed to Alderson Baptist Academy, and in 1919 to Alderson Baptist Academy and Junior College. In 1932 the Academy merged with Broaddus College and moved to the Philippi campus. The Great Depression had put both institutions in dire financial straits, and the West Virginia Baptist Convention ordered the merger of the two. Out of this marriage came Alderson-

Broaddus College, the name the school holds to this day.

The tiny college, whose early Philippi campus consisted of just three major buildings, struggled during the 1930s and World War II. The Depression drained the college's finances, while the war took away male students. The end of the war, however, brought better times and an influx of GI Bill students. Enrollment increased significantly and with it the college's finances. In 1945, A-B established the first baccalaureate nursing program in West Virginia.

In 1950, a young pastor, Richard E. Shearer, accepted the offer of the board of trustees to assume the presidency of Alderson-Broaddus College. At 30 he was thought to be the youngest college president in the country. Under Shearer the fortunes of the college improved dramatically, ushering in two decades of growth. It was during Shearer's 32-year tenure that the modern campus and identity emerged.

The 1950s saw the construction of the Pickett Library-Funkhouser Auditorium, the Benedum Residence Hall, and Broaddus Hospital. The decade was capped, in 1959, by the achievement of accreditation from the North Central Association of Colleges and Schools. This signal event was made known to students, faculty, and staff when Dr. Shearer, an avid amateur pilot, tossed a doll out of his airplane while flying over campus. Excited students, intercepting the doll as it floated down by parachute, read this message emblazoned on its chest: "We Made It!"

The 1960s and 1970s witnessed continued growth with the addition of eight new campus structures. Through the commitment and vision of Dr. Hu Myers, a revered Barbour County physician, the college established in 1968 the first baccalaureate physician assistant program in the country. Building on the successful nursing program, this underscored the growing importance of the health sciences at Alderson-Broaddus. Rising from the ashes of historic Old Main Hall, destroyed by fire in 1978, was New Main, which opened in 1980 at a cost of $2 million.

The 1990s were another time of fundamental change for the institution. Having weathered wars, depressions, and social upheavals, Alderson-Broaddus now confronted sweeping social and economic changes. During this time the institution carried out its most successful capital campaign, which brought more than $12 million into college coffers. The money helped bring upgrades to the computer system, comprehensive renovations to three of the four residence halls, and the building of the Erickson Alumni Center. The college also had its share of setbacks. Undoubtedly the greatest was the temporary loss of accreditation of the Physician

Assistant Program in 1995 and the extensive restructuring and downsizing of the program that followed. Although accreditation was restored in 1996, it was clear that A-B could no longer depend so heavily on the health sciences. By the end of the decade a newly streamlined college was beginning to implement a new set of educational programs—distance learning, professional training, and adult education.

Some things don't change, however. Alderson-Broaddus College continues to enjoy a strong denominational identity as an American Baptist institution, and a continuing commitment to a values-based liberal arts education. This is the identity which, despite all the changes, links the college with all its institutional ancestors.

See also Baptists, Philippi

Kim Smucker
Alderson-Broaddus College

Richard Withers and Martha Rose Roy, *Light on the Hill: A Pictorial History of Alderson-Broaddus College,* 1995.

Allegheny Front

The Allegheny Front is a bold southeast-facing escarpment of resistant Pocono and Pottsville sandstone two to three miles wide, extending along an irregular line from Keyser to Bramwell. East of the front is the Ridge and Valley Province, and to the west are the wedge-like Allegheny Mountains and the Allegheny Plateau. Unbroken slopes of 1,000 feet are not uncommon to the front.

The Allegheny Front is marked by an irregular line of high elevations. From 3,500 feet west of Keyser the front rises steadily to 4,861 feet at Spruce Knob, the highest point in the state. In this general region along the eastern segment of the Pendleton-Randolph county line, the front is offset ten to 12 miles to the northwest, west of the Greenbrier River, and then follows southwesterly along the line of Shavers (4,193 feet), Back Allegheny (4,840 feet), and Droop (3,136 feet) mountains. Southwest of Droop Mountain the front is broken into spur-like projections with elevations up to 3,500 feet. Near Alderson the front lies athwart the Greenbrier River, making a ten- to 12-mile jog southeast to Little Mountain (2,800 feet), and is even more pronounced with ridges to the east higher at 4,000 feet. About 12 miles southwest of the New River, the front near Princeton is again offset some six to seven miles to the northwest, and the face of the escarpment is eroded into finger-like projections that extend to the valley of the Bluestone River. The Allegheny Front exits the state near Bramwell with elevations of 3,000 feet.

Wind and water gaps through the escarpment have influenced human and animal movement along specific routes,

and its physical nature was not attractive to human settlement, though Spruce Knob, Cass Scenic Railroad, and Droop Mountain Battlefield are attractions now associated with the Allegheny Front.

See also Allegheny Mountains, Geography

Howard G. Adkins
Ona

Delorme, *West Virginia Atlas and Gazetteer,* 1997; Nevin M. Fenneman, *Physiography of Eastern United States,* 1938.

Allegheny Lodge

Minnehaha Springs, on State Route 92 in Pocahontas County, was once the site of a popular resort and hunting lodge. In 1912, J. A. Viquesney and H. M. Lockridge organized the Allegheny Sportsmen's Association. Membership included many prominent West Virginians, among them Governor Glasscock and former Governor MacCorkle. The association acquired 5,000 acres of land, which it stocked with fish and game. In 1913, Allegheny Lodge was erected on the land, its facade reminiscent of a Southern plantation house. Twin stairways curved up to a columned veranda on the first floor, covered by a second-floor porch, which was covered in turn by a railed roof. Gabled dormers projected on each side, with a white-railed widow's walk at the top of the building.

In 1926, Harry R. Wyllie of Huntington, owner of the H. R. Wyllie China Company, purchased the lodge and grounds for use as a private estate. Also in 1926, an imposing stone wall and gateposts were built at the front entrance, and a handsome wooden gate was installed. In later years the lodge passed through the hands of many owners. Sometimes it was used as a private estate. Other owners operated it as a resort hotel. Famous visitors, including author Pearl S. Buck and Olympic gold medal skier Jean Claude Killy, were guests there. On October 17, 1983, the lodge building burned to the ground. The stone entryway is still standing.

See also Minnehaha Springs

Leona Gwinn Brown
Daniels

Leona G. Brown, "Allegheny Lodge," *Goldenseal,* Fall 1991.

Allegheny Mountain, Battle of

The December 13, 1861, Battle of Allegheny Mountain in Pocahontas County was one of the bloodiest conflicts of the Civil War's first year. More than a month after an October 3 battle at Camp Bartow (known as the Battle of Greenbrier River), the Confederate army stationed at that point withdrew to winter quarters atop the summit of Allegheny Mountain. Possibly believing the Confederates to be demoralized, Union Gen. Robert H. Milroy led a force of about 1,900 troops in an attack on the Confederate brigade which numbered about 1,200 men.

Milroy's advance skirmished with a Confederate scouting party at Camp Bartow on December 12. Early on the following morning, Milroy divided his troops into two columns in an effort to attack both flanks of the Confederate camp simultaneously. The first column marched up the Staunton-Parkersburg Turnpike, arrived near daybreak on the Confederate right, and attacked. The battle raged for several hours before the Federals were forced to withdraw. Shortly after the conclusion of fighting on the right of the camp, the second Union column arrived and attacked the Confederate left. This attack was also unsuccessful. Total Union casualties were 140 killed or wounded and two missing. Confederate casualties were 128 killed or wounded and 34 captured or missing.

Ironically, the Confederate brigade had received orders to withdraw a few days earlier. The failed attack, however, convinced Confederate Gen. W. W. Loring to leave Col. Edward Johnson's force at Camp Allegheny through the winter of 1861–62.

See also Civil War

Joe Geiger
Huntington
Joe Geiger, "Holding the Line: Confederate Defense of the Parkersburg-Staunton Turnpike in the Fall of 1861," Marshall University, M.A. thesis, 1995; Boyd Stutler, *West Virginia in the Civil War,* 1966.

Allegheny Mountains

The Allegheny Mountains form a high region running from the Elk (4,345 feet) and Gauley (4,571 feet) mountains in Pocahontas and Randolph counties northward to the state line. The Alleghenies are marked on the east by the line of Back Allegheny (4,840 feet), Shavers (4,193 feet), and Allegheny Front (3,200 feet) mountains, and on the west by the line of Rich (3,660 feet), Laurel (2,915 feet), and Chestnut (2,600 feet) mountains. The Allegheny Mountains make up about 12 percent of West Virginia's total area, mostly in Preston, Tucker, and Randolph counties.

The Allegheny Mountains are higher than the Allegheny Plateau to the west. The mountains themselves are plateau-like with closely spaced broad summits and flat horizons. The mild folds of the bedrock throughout the mountains generally control the erosional forms, producing a weak, trellis-like stream pattern of narrow valleys similar to the well-developed broad valleys of the Ridge and Valley Province to the east. In the north the valley strips are some 300 to 500 feet deep, and in extreme cases along the Cheat River up to 1,000 feet deep, whereas in the broken ranges in the south valley depths of 1,000 feet are not uncommon.

The surface of the region consists of rolling to steeply ridged hills. In Preston and Tucker counties the average elevation is close to 3,000 feet, and Randolph, where two-thirds of the county is in slopes steeper than 20 percent, may be referred to as entirely mountainous.

Settlement in the Allegheny Mountains dates from 1753, when the Eckarly brothers settled on the Cheat River near Kingwood. In the river valleys and on the more gentle slopes the early settlers raised livestock, buckwheat, corn, and other essentials of a pioneer life. The first real economic boost came when the Baltimore & Ohio Railroad crossed the region in 1852. By the turn of the next century, the timbering of virgin stands of red spruce above 2,500 feet elevation and of northern hardwoods, between 2,000 and 2,500 feet, and coal mining fueled a boom economy. Elkins (1,920 feet), Kingwood (1,863 feet), Terra Alta (2,559 feet), Parsons (1,652 feet), Piedmont (935 feet), and Davis (the highest town in West Virginia at 3,100 feet) are the largest towns in the mountains.

Elevation has a direct effect on the climate of the Allegheny Mountains. The January average temperature of 28 degrees F. at Terra Alta is the lowest in the state. The mean annual snowfall for the region is about 60 inches, with more than 100 inches falling on the southern margins of Cheat Mountain and Back Allegheny Mountain at the Snowshoe ski resort. Another fact of the Allegheny region is heavy rainfall. Pickens, located at about 2,700 feet on the western slope of Turkeybone Mountain, has an average annual rainfall of about 70 inches.

At the rugged and high southern end of the Allegheny Mountains are the headwaters of the Gauley, Elk, Little Kanawha, Tygart, Cheat, and Greenbrier rivers. The Cheat River flows northward through the heart of the Allegheny Mountains to a confluence with the Monongahela just north of the state line in Pennsylvania.

The Seneca Trail, one of the principal Indian trails in North America, followed Seneca Creek across the Allegheny Front, then crossed in succession Spruce, Rich, Middle, Shavers, and Cheat mountains to the present location of Elkins. This is the route now followed by U.S. 33 and State Route 55. With elevations of 3,000 to 3,500 feet not uncommon, it includes some of the highest and most scenic stretches of highway in West Virginia.

From southern Preston County, U.S. 219 crosses Backbone and Cheat mountains, follows the Tygart Valley, then crosses through gaps or skirts around the edges of Elk (4,345 feet), Valley (3,846 feet), Middle (3,993 feet), Gauley (4,571 feet), Red Lick (4,686 feet), and Elk (3,760 feet) mountains before exiting the region. (There are two Elk mountains, one

in Randolph County and the other in Pocahontas.) U.S. 50 follows Friendship Gap across Laurel Mountain at about 2,500 feet above sea level. State Route 7 through Terra Alta crosses Briery Mountain at almost 3,000 feet. Farther to the north, the Allegheny Mountains are more plateau-like where Interstate 68 crosses between Coopers Rock and Hazleton. The elevations between these two points average about 2,000 feet, but vary as ridges are crossed.

Several natural recreation areas are associated with the Allegheny Mountains, including the Dolly Sods Wilderness Area, Canaan Valley, Blackwater Falls and Canyon, Snowshoe, and the Monongahela National Forest.

See also Geography

Howard G. Adkins
Ona
Delorme, *West Virginia Atlas and Gazetteer,* 1997; Nevin M. Fenneman, *Physiography of Eastern United States,* 1938.

Allegheny Plateau

The Allegheny Plateau makes up about half of the Appalachian Mountains and most of West Virginia. Near the Ohio River the maximum elevations of the Allegheny Plateau are about 1,000 feet above sea level, increasing eastward to more than 4,000 feet as the Allegheny Front is approached. All streams on the Allegheny Plateau follow an irregular dendritic or tree-like pattern, eventually draining to the Ohio River. The plateau is dissected with razorback ridges, held up by strong sandstone like the Pottsville, and youthful valleys cut deep into shale.

Throughout their history the Appalachians have been repeatedly uplifted. As streams such as the Little Kanawha, Elk, Guyandotte, New, Monongahela, and others were rejuvenated with the uplifts, meanders became entrenched, with valley slopes steeper below than above and often at grades of 35 to 40 degrees. The plateau is so minutely and deeply dissected that valley bottoms are almost always narrow.

Valleys are the primary locations of human activities, and settlement follows the creeks and rivers. All the streams except the New River originate on the plateau. The New, older than the plateau itself, cuts through the plateau in a gorge averaging 1,000 feet deep.

The Allegheny Plateau is rich in natural resources. It is covered with regrowth forests of central hardwoods. Another resource is coal, first reported in 1742 on the Coal River in present Boone County. The coming of railroads in the 19th century made the coal accessible, and mining, with its coal towns, company stores, and burgeoning work force, transformed the region. Petroleum and natural gas are widespread. The natural gas and glass sand of near pure silica content supported a glass industry that remains in several plateau counties, including Cabell, Wood, Hancock, Lewis, and Ritchie.

With a surface more rugged than any region east of the Rockies, the plateau does not have much good farm land. The dominant agricultural land use is related to livestock, including the production of grass and hay. Tobacco is a specialty crop of the plateau, with 95 percent of the state's total raised in six plateau counties, centering on Mason and Putnam. About 83 percent of the state's population and all cities with a population more than 10,000, excepting Bluefield and Martinsburg, are in the Allegheny Plateau.

See also Geography

Howard G. Adkins
Ona

Nevin M. Fenneman, *Physiography of Eastern United States*, 1938; Charles B. Hunt, *Physiography of the United States*, 1967.

Allegheny Trail

For nearly 300 miles, the Allegheny Trail traverses eastern West Virginia's most inspiring scenery. Stretching from the state's southeastern border with Virginia, a few miles east of Peterstown, Monroe County, to the Mason-Dixon Line near Morgantown, this hiking trail passes through several national forests, numerous state parks and forests, and private lands.

Connected at its southern end to the Appalachian Trail on Peters Mountain, the Allegheny Trail heads northeastward along the West Virginia-Virginia border for close to 50 miles. Turning northward, it crosses Pocahontas, Randolph, Tucker, and Preston counties on its way to Pennsylvania. The trail proceeds by way of the Greenbrier River, Glady Fork, Canaan Valley, and the Blackwater Canyon.

The Allegheny Trail is West Virginia's longest trail. Conceived by members of the West Virginia Scenic Trails Association, construction of the pathway began in the 1970s. The route continues to be built and maintained primarily by members of the organization.

Leonard M. Adkins
Catawba, Virginia

Allegheny Woodrat

The Allegheny woodrat is a North American rodent, present in West Virginia but considered rare and threatened. It differs from similarly sized non-native Norway and black rats primarily by its hairy tail that is dark on top and light underneath. Large eyes, large ears, silky fur, and a blunt nose also characterize the Allegheny woodrat.

The Allegheny woodrat lives in rocky areas including cliffs and caves. It is a herbivore, preferring fruits, berries, nuts, and seeds. Primarily nocturnal, this species is active year-round, supplementing seasonal food sources in the winter with

Allegheny Woodrat.

stores of nuts and other vegetation. Its nest is built of finely shredded bark and other materials, and the woodrat strategically places large piles of leaves and other forest litter around the nest site. It is thought these debris piles serve to alert the woodrat of approaching predators.

Historically, the Allegheny woodrat has been found from southern New York to northern Alabama and west to Indiana. Although it is found throughout the state, the Allegheny woodrat is on the rare species list of the West Virginia Division of Natural Resources. The Allegheny woodrat is not federally protected, but rapid declines in population throughout its range have prompted most states with Allegheny woodrats to declare them as endangered, threatened, or species of concern.

See also Fauna

Amy Donaldson Arnold
Ivydale

Steven Bryan Castleberry, "Conservation and Management of the Allegheny Woodrat in the Central Appalachians," Ph.D. dissertation, West Virginia University, 2000.

Walter Allen

Walter Allen, a coal miner from Dry Branch, Kanawha County, was the only person to be convicted of treason in the trials following the famous Miners' March in August–September, 1921. The armed miners, who had set out to unionize Logan and Mingo counties, were turned back at the Battle of Blair Mountain.

Allen, 41 at the time of the march, was tried in late summer of 1922 in Jefferson County in the same courthouse where John Brown had been tried. Witnesses testified persuasively about Allen's leadership: that he spoke at a mass meeting of miners on the lawn of the state capitol prior to the march; that he led the miners at Dry Branch when they voted to take part in the march; that he recruited miners from other camps; and that he obtained weapons, served on the marchers' finance committee, and was seen participating in many phases throughout the march.

A jury found Allen guilty on September 16. He was sentenced to ten years in the state penitentiary but was freed on $15,000 bond pending appeal. On De-

cember 16, 1922, county officials reported Allen had defaulted in his surety. He was never heard from again. An important aspect of the trial is that the detailed, lengthy testimony by leaders of both sides in the mine war has provided an invaluable and colorful historical record of the march.

See also Battle of Blair Mountain, Miners' March, Mine Wars

Lon Savage
Salem, Virginia

Lon Savage, *Thunder in the Mountains: The West Virginia Mine War 1920–21*, 1990.

Allied Artists of West Virginia

Allied Artists of West Virginia is a statewide nonprofit organization of painters, sculptors, print makers, and creative craftspeople. The group's purpose is to encourage artists to hold exhibits, to foster art in general, and to further interest in art. Active membership is open to professional and amateur artists who are residents of West Virginia. Acceptance into the group is through jurying of the prospective member's work, which takes place twice a year. Former members who now reside outside of the state are members-at-large.

Charleston lawyer Arthur Dayton began the Charleston Art Association in 1930, and the group exhibited that year in the Charleston library. The next year, Dayton changed the name to Allied Artists of West Virginia. The group's 1938 exhibit was its first to be juried. Today, Allied Artists of West Virginia has more than 200 members and holds juried exhibits every other year, in even-numbered years. In addition to the biennial exhibit traditionally held at the old Sunrise Art Museum, the organization also exhibits in the Frankenberger Gallery at the University of Charleston. Additionally, various businesses frequently offer space.

Alpha Psi Omega

Alpha Psi Omega, the collegiate dramatics honorary fraternity, was founded August 12, 1925, at Fairmont State Normal School, now Fairmont State College. The Masquers, the college drama club, under the direction of Paul F. Opp of the English faculty, created the Alpha cast (chapter) of APO to honor student excellence in theater and to promote theater education. The fraternity's national faculty officers included E. Turner Stump of Marshall College (now Marshall University) as president, and Opp as secretary and editor of the APO publication, *The Playbill*. The national office was with Opp at Fairmont State.

In 1929 Alpha Psi Omega created both Delta Psi Omega, a junior college branch, chartering 53 colleges the first year, and the National (now International) Thespian Society, the high school dramatics honorary. Opp, at the suggestion of an

APO member from Casper, Wyoming, developed the Thespians. He was assisted by Ernest Bavely and by East Fairmont High School dramatics director Harry Leeper, both Monongah natives and former Fairmont State students. The Thespians' publication, *The High School Thespian* (now *Dramatics* magazine) was edited by Leeper. He also designed the insignia, which is still in use. The second and third Thespian troupes (chapters) were at Fairmont Senior High School and East Fairmont High School.

The offices of APO, DPO, and the Thespians moved from Fairmont State to Canada in the fall of 1929, as Opp took leave to pursue a doctorate at the University of Toronto. In 1930, Bavely became the Thespians' national secretary, moving the national office to Weir High School, Weirton, where he taught. Two years later Bavely moved the headquarters to Cincinnati, where it remains. Bavely was Thespians national secretary until his death in 1950. When Opp came back to Fairmont State, the headquarters for APO, DPO, and *The Playbill* returned to Fairmont, where it remained until Opp's 1966 retirement as secretary and editor.

Alpha Psi Omega now lists 640 casts in the United States and abroad. Delta Psi Omega lists 285 casts. The International Thespian Society lists 3,200 troupes with an aggregate membership of nearly 2 million. The Junior Thespians have 222 troupes.

See also Fairmont State University

JoAnn Lough
Fairmont State University

Alpine Lake

The 2,300-acre Alpine Lake Resort and Conference Center is located northeast of Terra Alta, in Preston County. The private development, managed by the Alpine Lake Property Owners Association, includes 345 residences, a 150-acre lake, motel, restaurant, meeting rooms, fitness center, 18-hole golf course, cross-country ski trails, and tennis courts. The facilities are open to the public.

The resort started as a hunting and fishing camp in the 1930s. Arlie Hull, who lived near Terra Alta, owned the property. He created a five-acre lake, stocked it with bass, and bought adjoining land. In the early 1960s, a group of Preston County businessmen bought the 1,000-acre camp and named it Mountaintop Vacationland. To secure the loan, the group sold memberships in the development. They built a lodge, manager's house, cabins, campground, and a swimming pool. In 1969, Morgantown industrialist J. W. Ruby and his wife, Hazel, whose company was named Mountaintop Development Co., bought the camp. The Rubys renamed the camp Alpine Lake, expanded the resort, and drew up a residential community plan. They offered lots for sale, first to charter members and then to the public. In 1980, Mountaintop Development deeded Alpine Lake to the property owners' association.

Charles Henry Ambler

A key figure in applying modern approaches to the study and writing of West Virginia history, Charles Henry Ambler was born in New Matamoras, Ohio, August 12, 1876. He grew up in St. Marys, West Virginia, and from 1894 to 1900 he taught school in Pleasants County. He coupled that experience with study at West Liberty Normal School. He served as sheriff of Pleasants County in 1900 and 1901. In 1901 he entered West Virginia University, which awarded him an A.B. in social sciences in 1904 and an M.A. in 1905. Ambler then enrolled at the University of Wisconsin, where one of his mentors was Frederick Jackson Turner, famous for his frontier thesis of American history.

After completing his doctorate in 1908, Ambler taught history and political science at Randolph-Macon College in Virginia until 1917. For the next 30 years he was a member of the WVU history department, and from 1929 to 1946 he served as chairman. Among his enduring legacies was the creation of the West Virginia and Regional History Collection in the university library.

In his prodigious research and prolific writings, Ambler explored numerous topics that had received but scant attention from professional or amateur historians. Prominent among his works relating to the era before West Virginia became a state were *Sectionalism in Virginia from 1776 to 1861*; *George Washington and the West*; *A History of Transportation in the Ohio Valley*; and others dealing with Thomas Ritchie, John Floyd, and Robert M. T. Hunter, who were influential in Virginia political affairs. Other books, including *Francis H. Pierpont: Union War Governor of Virginia and Father of West Virginia* and *Waitman Thomas Willey: Orator, Churchman, Humanitarian*, reflected Ambler's interest in the Civil War and West Virginia statehood, as did such edited volumes as Anna Pierpoint Siviter's *Recollections of War and Peace* and *Debates and Proceedings of the First Constitutional Convention of West Virginia*.

Ambler was honored with the presidency of the Mississippi Valley Historical Association in 1942–43 and numerous other recognitions. From 1951 to 1955 he represented Monongalia County in the state legislature. He died August 31, 1957.

See also History of West Virginia

Otis K. Rice
WVU Institute of Technology

American Electric Power

Headquartered in Columbus, American Electric Power is one of the nation's largest investor-owned electric utilities, serving nearly three million customers in seven states. About 500,000 of those customers live in West Virginia, where the company operates through its subsidiary, Appalachian Power Company. For several years after 1996 Appalachian Power Company and other AEP subsidiaries operated under the AEP name. Appalachian Power Company, often called Apco, has operated under its own name since 2004, reestablishing a familiar corporate identity. The company serves about half of West Virginia households, mostly in the southern counties.

West Virginia is home to AEP's largest generating facility—the giant coal-fired John E. Amos Plant, located on the Kanawha River west of Charleston. When operating at full capacity, the 2.9-million-kilowatt Amos Plant uses 27,600 tons of West Virginia coal each day. The company has five other coal-fired generating stations in West Virginia. In addition it operates mining subsidiaries and a fleet of towboats and barges, based at Lakin, Mason County. In all, AEP employs more than 3,700 West Virginians.

American Electric Power is a contributor to *The West Virginia Encyclopedia*.

See also Appalachian Power Company

James E. Casto
Herald-Dispatch

American Legion

The American Legion was founded in Paris by members of the American Expeditionary Force in March, 1919. It is composed of men and women who were members of the armed forces of the United States, serving honorably in active duty during times of war. The Department of West Virginia began after World War I, at a meeting held in Charleston on May 2, 1919, and was perfected at a convention in Charleston on October 15–16, 1919. At century's end it had 114 posts in the state and a membership over 27,000. Permanent headquarters are maintained in Charleston with the department adjutant in charge. The official department publication, *West Virginia Legionnaire*, was established in April 1925 and is edited by the department adjutant.

A women's affiliate, the American Legion Auxiliary, Department of West Virginia, was organized at Grafton on July 20–21, 1922. The charter was signed September 29, 1922. At the time of organization there were 14 units with a total membership of 1,011. There are now 81 units in the state with more than 10,000 members. Wives, mothers, sisters, daughters, granddaughters, great-granddaughters, grandmothers, and steprelatives of Legion members or deceased veterans are eligible to join the Auxiliary. Women veterans may join the Auxiliary, as well as the Legion itself. The principal work of the Auxiliary is for veterans' welfare in hospitals, veteran homes, or for other veterans and veteran's families with special needs.

Both organizations have programs for youth, including Boys' State, Rhododendron Girls State, King-for-a-Day, scholarship programs, and American flag programs. Both the Legion and the Auxiliary are active in legislation for veterans and in encouraging respect for the flag. The Auxiliary has an annual distribution of poppies, made by veterans in hospitals, in exchange for donations to be used for the welfare of veterans.

Eileen Cain Stanley
Kenna

Amphibians and Reptiles

West Virginia has 87 known species of amphibians and reptiles, including 34 species of salamanders, three species of toads, 11 species of frogs, 13 species of turtles, six species of lizards, and 20 species of snakes.

Most amphibians have moist glandular skin, and all deposit gelatinous-covered eggs in water or in terrestrial sites such as rotting logs, under rocks, or underground. Their sensitive integument and eggs make them susceptible to pollutants in water and soil, as well as changes in moisture and temperature.

Salamanders are found in ponds, streams, and on wooded hillsides. In West Virginia they range in size from the hellbender, which can be nearly 24 inches in length, to the diminutive four-toed salamander, which is about four inches long. Two species, the West Virginia spring salamander and the Cheat Mountain salamander, are endemic to the Mountain State, occurring only here. The West Virginia spring salamander is known to occur only in General Davis Cave in Greenbrier County, and the Cheat Mountain salamander occurs in the five eastern, mountainous counties of Randolph, Pocahontas, Tucker, Pendleton, and Grant. The Cheat Mountain salamander is the only amphibian in the state on the federal list of threatened and endangered species. No reptiles are listed.

Three species of toads are known to inhabit the state. The American toad and Fowler's toad are relatively common, but the spadefoot toad is seldom seen because of its secretive nature of remaining underground, only surfacing to mate and deposit eggs during heavy rains. Frogs are found from the lowest elevations to the highest. They range in size from the tiny cricket frog to the bullfrog. Frogs are put into two groups, tree frogs and true frogs. Tree frogs include the common spring peeper and five other species. In addition to the bullfrog, there are four other species of true frogs in West Virginia.

Reptiles (turtles, lizards, and snakes) come in a variety of shapes but all share common characteristics such as epidermal scales and an egg with embryonic membrane. Their skin and eggs allow them to live in more adverse habitats than amphibians. The box turtle is the most terrestrial turtle in the state. The wood turtle (only known to occur in the Eastern Panhandle) is frequently seen on land. Some aquatic species such as the spotted turtle (also only known to occur in the Eastern Panhandle) have limited ranges. Other aquatic species such as the snapping turtle are common throughout the Mountain State.

Lizards resemble salamanders, but unlike salamanders have scales and ear openings. The most common lizards are the fence lizard and the five-lined skink (sometimes locally known as the blue-tailed lizard). Lizards range in size from the ground skink (four inches long) to the broadhead skink (up to 12 inches long).

Of the 22 species of snakes known to occur in West Virginia, only two, the timber rattlesnake and the northern copperhead, are venomous. Most species encountered by people are not venomous. There are three species of black snakes in the state, the black racer, black rat snake, and black kingsnake. The most uncommon snake is the pine snake. Only one specimen of this species has been recorded in the state (Monroe County in 1910).

There is concern among biologists of an apparent worldwide decline of some amphibian species. West Virginia is not immune from such declines. Recent surveys in known sites for Blanchard's cricket frog along the Ohio River and for the upland chorus frog in Monroe and Greenbrier counties indicate that the Blanchard's cricket frog may no longer occur in West Virginia and the upland chorus frog may not be in these southeastern counties. Still, West Virginia has a rich representation of amphibians and reptiles that fit into valuable ecological niches. They represent a major component of our hidden biodiversity.

See also Fauna

Thomas K. Pauley
Marshall University

N. B. Green and T. K. Pauley, *Amphibians and Reptiles in West Virginia*, 1987.

Amtrak

Concerned with the elimination of passenger service by private railroad companies, Congress in 1970 passed the National Passenger Railroad Act. The act created Amtrak, a semi-public passenger rail service. Originally operating over 24,000 miles of track, Amtrak trains served most major cities via specific routes that varied frequently depending on track conditions. Amtrak operates its trains over the tracks of the major railroad companies. Initially plagued by antiquated equipment and poor service, Amtrak improved its trains after the mid-1970s. Ridership increased, although the question of Amtrak's survival remained a recurrent issue into the 21st century.

Amtrak operates two trains through West Virginia, both traveling from Washington to Chicago by different routes. The Cardinal operates via the old Chesapeake & Ohio line from Covington, Virginia, through Charleston to Huntington, and the Capitol Limited follows the old Baltimore & Ohio through Harpers Ferry and Martinsburg in northeastern West Virginia. The Capitol Limited was a continuation into the Amtrak era of a well-known B&O train. The Cardinal was a totally new train, although it initially followed the route and schedule of the New York Central's James Whitcomb Riley, which operated from Cincinnati to Chicago prior to 1971.

Previously two other Amtrak trains served West Virginia, the Blue Ridge from Washington to Parkersburg and the Hilltopper over the Norfolk & Western main line from Petersburg, Virginia, to Catlettsburg, Kentucky. Saddled with inconvenient schedules and poor performance, neither train lasted long.

See also Railroads

Robert L. Frey
Miamisburg, Ohio

Harold A. Edmonson, *Journey to Amtrak*, 1972.

An American Vendetta

An American Vendetta was a collection of articles by Theron C. Crawford concerning the Hatfield-McCoy Feud of 1882–90. The articles were originally written for the *New York World* newspaper, and published as a book in 1889. Crawford arrived in Logan County in 1888, and was led from Charleston to Logan County by John B. Floyd, a state senator. The pair arrived during the third week of October

From T. C. Crawford's An American Vendetta.

and stayed at Devil Anse Hatfield's home one night.

Crawford's articles contained the first known interview with Hatfield. During his conversation with Crawford, Hatfield stressed that he wanted peace with the McCoy family but would not disarm and would not surrender to law officers without guarantees of his family's safety. Crawford described Hatfield as "a jovial old pirate." Crawford's lurid writing, his awkward attempt to re-create mountain dialect, and the accompanying illustrations of menacing and sometimes slouching and unkempt mountaineers did much to create the hillbilly stereotype.

See also Devil Anse Hatfield, Hatfield-McCoy Feud

Robert Y. Spence
Logan

Andrews Methodist Episcopal Church

The first Mother's Day observance took place at Andrews Methodist Episcopal Church in Grafton, May 10, 1908, the anniversary of Anna Maria Reeves Jarvis's death. Jarvis, whose humanitarian efforts were well known in Taylor County, had worked at Andrews Methodist Episcopal Church for 30 years. She had dreamed of establishing a day to honor mothers, a dream later realized through the advocacy of her daughter, also named Anna.

Located on East Main Street, the two-story red brick structure sits on a cut-stone foundation. From 1873 to 1966, church services were held at Andrews Methodist Church, which was named for Bishop Edward Gayer Andrews from New York state, who was present at the church's dedication, March 16, 1873. In 1966, the United Methodist conference merged the congregation with St. Paul's Methodist and West Main Street Methodist churches, forming the Church of the Good Shepherd.

In 1962, citizens formed the International Mother's Day Shrine Commission. They established the shrine in the parlor at Andrews Methodist Episcopal Church. After the three Methodist congregations merged, Andrews was no longer used regularly as a church. The shrine commission restored the church and opened the entire structure as a shrine in the late 1960s. In 1970, the church was listed on the National Register of Historic Places, and in 1992 became a National Historic Landmark, one of only 15 in West Virginia.

The shrine contains many original church furnishings and displays of Jarvis family photographs and papers. The building is open from April 15 to October 31, and a Mother's Day service is held each year.

See also Anna Jarvis, Mother's Day
Howard H. Wolfe, *Mother's Day and the Mother's Day Church,* 1962.

The Ironworkers' Noontime.

Thomas Anshutz

Artist Thomas Pollock Anshutz, born in Newport, Kentucky, October 5, 1851, used West Virginia settings and subjects in crafting a reputation as one of the foremost American painters in the realist style. Although he was raised in Kentucky, he reportedly lived in Wheeling, the native city of his mother, Abigail Pollock, from 1868 to 1872, and returned on occasion as a visitor with his wife, Effie Schriver Russell, also from Wheeling. Anshutz studied at the National Academy of Design in New York and went on to become head of the painting department at the Pennsylvania Academy of the Fine Arts.

His most famous paintings include *The Ironworkers' Noontime* (1880), depicting Wheeling nail factory workers on a lunch break, and *Steamboat on the Ohio* (1896), a composite painting inspired by cyanotype photographs that Anshutz had taken during preparatory studies, a method he often used. *Farmer and His Son Harvesting* (1879) is also known to represent the landscape of the Wheeling area. Although much of Anshutz's work involved portraits and beach scenes, his realistic industrial paintings inspired the term "Ashcan School" for the style of painting practiced by a number of his notable students such as John Sloan, Robert Henri, and William Glackens. Other landscapes by Anshutz include scenes along the Shenandoah and Potomac rivers. Anshutz died in Pennsylvania, June 16, 1912.

Larry Sonis
Arlington, Texas
John A. Cuthbert, *Early Art and Artists in West Virginia,* 2000.

Anthony Correctional Center

Located at Neola in Greenbrier County, the Anthony Correctional Center is a minimum-security facility for young adults, primarily ages 18 to 21. The center's goal is to rehabilitate its inmates through vocational training, academic classes, individual and group counseling, a work program, and job placement services. Young adults are sent to Anthony instead of serving a prison sentence, often as the result of a plea bargain.

All inmates receive an individual program plan, which must be completed before they can leave the center. Most inmates complete the program in six months, but others take longer. An inmate who repeatedly breaks the center's rules may have to appear before a judge, who may impose the original sentence. From July 1998 to June 1999, 86 percent of the inmates successfully completed the center's programs and were not imprisoned again.

The facility, completed in 1966, was originally used by the federal government as a Job Corps Center. In 1970, the West Virginia Department of Public Institutions (now Division of Corrections) leased the facility for use as a correctional center for juvenile males. The center began accepting adult males in 1980 and females in 1985. The state bought the property in 1995.

Anthony Correctional Center can house 220 offenders. In 2001, the center began housing adult male prisoners in its diagnostic unit due to overcrowding in the regional and county jails. The center also began accepting adult female prisoners who are eligible for or are nearing parole.

Antiquities Commission

The West Virginia Antiquities Commission was established by the legislature on March 6, 1965. The commission was created to identify and oversee the development of important historic sites, "or other objects of archaeological or historic interest." The creation of the commission, which preceded by one year the National Historic Preservation Act, reflected the state's interest in preserving cultural and historical resources. The board, composed of six to nine members, made significant progress in the preservation of sites, such as Grave Creek Mound and Independence Hall. In 1977, the legislature abolished the commission and created the Department of Culture and History. The Historic Preservation Section assumed the duties and responsibilities of the Antiquities Commission, with the Archives and History Commission serving as a review board.

Joe Geiger
Huntington

Appalachia

The Appalachian Mountains rise like a spine down the back of the eastern United States, forming a distinct geographic, social, and political region that has come to be called Appalachia. At least since the turn of the 20th century this region of stark beauty, cultural diversity, and economic contrasts has fascinated Americans and has played a major role in how we see ourselves as a nation and how we relate to the land and to each other. West Virginia lies at the heart of this region, and is the only state wholly included within its boundaries. As the rest of America has struggled to define Appalachia and the Appalachian experience, popular images of this enigmatic region have fallen for good and ill on the Mountain State.

Geographically, the Appalachian mountain system extends southwest from New York state to northern Alabama. It is a region of topographic variety, reaching from the lofty Blue Ridge Mountains in the east to the rugged Appalachian Plateaus of West Virginia and Kentucky to the west. In the middle lies a fertile ridge and valley district split by great river drainages such as the Shenandoah, the James, the New, and the Tennessee. From prehistoric times a diverse people of mixed races and cultures inhabited the region, drawn together by their common relationship to the land. During the colonial period the mountains served as a barrier to the expansion of European settlement to the west, and after the Revolutionary War a backcountry economy and society survived in more remote parts of the region long after the passing of the frontier.

It was the survival of this backcountry society that eventually led urban Americans, struggling to find a national identity after the Civil War, to define Appalachia as a separate region inhabited by a distinct sub-culture. Writing for new national magazines such as *Harper's*, *Atlantic*, and *Cosmopolitan*, journalists

Appalachia

I am Appalachia. In my veins
Runs fierce mountain pride; the hill-fed streams
Of passion; and, stranger, you don't know me!
You've analyzed my every move — you still
Go away shaking your head. I remain
Enigmatic. How can you find rapport with me —
You, who never stood in the bowels of hell,
Never felt a mountain shake and open its jaws
To partake of human sacrifice?
You, who never stood on a high mountain,
Watching the sun unwind its spiral rays;
Who never searched the glens for wild flowers,
Never picked mayapples or black walnuts; never ran
Wildly through the woods in pure delight,
Nor dangled your feet in a lazy creek?
You, who never danced to wild sweet notes,
Outpouring of nimble-fingered fiddlers;
Who never just "sat a spell," on a porch,
Chewing and whittling; or hearing in pastime
The deep-throated bay of chasing hounds
And hunters shouting with joy, "he's treed!"
You, who never once carried a coffin
To a family plot high up on a ridge
Because mountain folk know it's best to lie
Where breezes from the hills whisper, "you're home";
You, who never saw from the valley that graves on a hill
Bring easement of pain to those below?
I tell you, stranger, hill folk know
What life is all about; they don't need pills
To tranquilize the sorrow and joy of living.
I am Appalachia: and, stranger,
Though you've studied me, you still don't know.

—Muriel Miller Dressler

traveled into the mountains in search of local color material that might interest urban middle-class readers. An overwhelmingly rural place conveniently close to eastern cities, the region provided a dramatic landscape upon which to cast stories of violence and passion among a rustic people whose lifestyle contrasted markedly with urban perceptions of the national experience. Eventually these writers created a literary image of the mountains as a place inhabited by moonshiners, feudists, and other primitive folk.

By the turn of the 20th century the idea of Appalachia as "a strange land inhabited by a peculiar people" had crystallized in the popular mind. More than just a mountain range, Appalachia had become a distinct sub-region within America but somehow not of it. Implicit in the idea of Appalachia was the assumption that geography had isolated the region from the historical forces that shaped the rest of the modernizing nation. Appalachia was a "land where time stood still." Like a mammoth in ice, the mountains had preserved therein an earlier stage of American civilization with all of its pastoral and savage qualities. For a nation conscious of the progress of its history, Appalachia became a counterpoint to

contemporary definitions of the good life. If one valued modernization, Appalachia was a problem, a region in need of development and uplift. If one questioned modernity, the folk culture of Appalachia was a treasure to be preserved and protected from the surge of the mainstream. The region itself became an American symbol that could mean different things to different observers.

Ironically, at the same time that the idea of Appalachia was becoming part of the national consciousness, the region itself was undergoing the same process of economic change that was sweeping the rest of the country. The arrival of railroads, coal mines, and logging operations propelled mountaineers, like other Americans, into the machine age, expanding opportunities for public employment and integrating mountain communities into the consumer culture. Like other Americans, mountaineers struggled to maintain traditional values in the new order, but because of popular stereotypes, Appalachian resistance to industrial "progress" was often portrayed as backwardness or a cultural propensity for violence. Unlike other parts of the nation, the process of transformation left the region sucked of its wealth of natural resources and many of its people under-educated and dependent. The collapse of the new industrial order in the 1920s, during a regional depression foreshadowing the hard times awaiting the nation in the next decade, left much of Appalachia impoverished. Thousands of families returned to the land and to traditional patterns of life. Appalachia's poverty, however, was not the result of its geography or culture but of the process of development itself.

After World War II, socio-economic conditions in the mountains continued to define Appalachia as part of the "other America." When millions of mountain migrants fled to the cities in search of jobs, they joined a growing population of inner-city Americans who were bypassed by the arrival of the affluent society of the 1950s. Following the victory of John Kennedy in the 1960 West Virginia presidential primary, a swarm of journalists descended upon the region to document its economic distress. Once again Appalachia was discovered as a place outside the current of American progress, and President Kennedy promised to do something to assist the mountain poor. An image of Appalachia as a place in need reinforced older images of the mountains as a land of violence and folk culture, and a spate of new government and private programs sought to assimilate the region into the mainstream. Appalachia became an important battleground in the War on Poverty, and because it was at the heart of the region, West Virginia received millions of dollars of federal support.

The rediscovery of Appalachian poverty and the creation of the Appalachian Regional Commission to coordinate development also stirred the growth of regional identity within the mountains and a renaissance of interest in Appalachian culture, literature, and heritage. Today the folk arts, music, and crafts provide pride, continuity, and connection for a people and a region swept up in rapid change. For the nation, Appalachia continues to serve as a symbol of our continuing efforts to define America and to search for the good life in an ever-changing world.

See also Appalachian Mountains, Appalachian Regional Commission

Ronald D. Eller
University of Kentucky

Ronald D. Eller, *Miners, Millhands and Mountaineers: The Industrialization of the Appalachian South, 1880–1930,* 1982; Henry Shapiro, *Appalachia on our Mind: The Southern Mountains and Mountaineers in the American Consciousness,* 1978; John Alexander Williams, *Appalachia: A History,* 2002.

Appalachian Basin

Long before our mountains were formed, the Appalachian geosyncline existed as a low-lying basin, mostly to entirely covered by a shallow sea. This continued throughout the Paleozoic Era, from about 570 million to 240 million years ago. The basin continued to subside through that tremendously long stretch of time, and to receive sediment from adjacent lands to the west and east. The lands to the east were the dominant source of sediment to the subsiding basin (geosyncline), as those lands were being intermittently raised by continental collisions between the North American and European-African plates; this uplifting accelerated erosion. With time and the tremendous pressures of burial and later mountain building, the thousands of feet of sediment became rock, containing the great mineral wealth of today's Appalachia.

The size of the Appalachian geosyncline fluctuated somewhat during the 330 million years of its existence, but generally it ranged from what is now New York in the north to Georgia and Alabama in the south. The Appalachian Basin encompasses much of present Pennsylvania and Maryland, all of West Virginia, and parts of Ohio, Virginia, Kentucky, and Tennessee. The geologic strata that occur in that area were deposited as sediments of mud, sand, silt, lime muds, and peat that today are sedimentary rocks such as sandstone, siltstone, shale, limestone, and coal beds.

The sedimentary rocks deposited in that widespread, long-enduring basin contain considerable mineral deposits and fossil fuel deposits. The term "Appalachian Basin" is commonly used among fossil fuel prospectors and developers to refer to the portion of that ancient sedimentary basin that now contains those fossil fuels and other minerals such as salt and salt brines. Other sedimentary basins occur in other parts of the United States and around the world, and are the sources of the world's fossil fuel supplies, along with other important mineral resources.

The mineral resources of the Appalachian Basin were recognized early in the region's settlement history, and in fact were used to some extent by the native tribes. Natural occurrences of saltwater springs and seeps were used by Indians and early European settlers alike, and natural oil and gas seeps were recorded by early explorers. Coal was dug and used locally by blacksmiths and others before commercial mines were opened. The Appalachian Basin resources began to be developed in earnest in the mid- and late-1800s and fueled the Industrial Revolution in the United States with oil, gas, and coal deposits, including the high-quality coals needed for production of steel.

In West Virginia, the Appalachian Basin produces natural gas, oil, and coal. In 2002, West Virginia was the nation's second-leading coal producer. The commercial coal beds occur only in strata deposited during the Pennsylvanian Period of geologic time, while oil and gas deposits are found in strata from throughout the Paleozoic Era. The large chemical industry of the Kanawha Valley at and near Charleston originated with development of the natural salt brine deposits.

See also Geology

Ron Mullennex
Bluefield

Raymond E. Janssen, *Earth Science: A Handbook on the Geology of West Virginia,* 1973.

Appalachian Bible College

Originally named Appalachian Bible Institute, this nondenominational, independent Christian college was established in 1950 by Rev. Robert Guelich, pastor and founder of Independent Baptist Church of Pettus, Raleigh County, and Rev. Lester E. Pipkin. The 120-acre campus sits at the junction of State Route 16 and U.S. 19, near Beckley in the community of Bradley. Eleven major buildings compose the campus, including a combined chapel and music hall, administration-library-dining complex, women's dormitory, men's dormitory, classroom building, and gymnasium-conference center.

The school first took impetus in the late 1940s, when Guelich and a deacon in his church, John R. Price, saw the need for a Bible school in southern West Virginia. At the time, students in Guelich's church who wanted to take Bible classes had to travel 135 miles over mountainous roads to attend a Bible institute near Pikeville, Kentucky. Guelich persuaded Rev. Pipkin, who lived in Minnesota, to relocate to West Virginia to help with the proposed school. They converted a vacant two-story building in the Boone County town of Sylvester into a dormitory, dining hall, and office, and furnished it with war surplus materials. Classrooms were set up in the basement of Guelich's church in Pettus, four miles away. On September 5, 1950, the Appalachian Bible Institute opened with an enrollment of seven students. Pipkin served as the first president of what the students named "the longest campus in the world."

At the outset, the school's board of directors adopted principles that have guided its growth. The independent school's curriculum would emphasize Bible study and prepare students to serve in church-related ministries. The school would be frugal and support its mission with help from churches and individual Christians.

During the early years, Pettus Independent Baptist Church paid most of the school's expenses, and transported students in the church bus from classrooms to the dormitory. In 1953, the institute graduated six students in its first class. The school continued to attract students and faculty. By 1954, with a student body of 40, it needed more space.

With the help and financial support of FayRal Development Corp., a business group from Fayette and Raleigh counties, the school bought a 95-acre farm near Bradley, in Raleigh County. The new campus opened in the fall of 1956.

The institute continued to grow. In 1978, the board of directors changed the school's name to Appalachian Bible College, which reflects the four-year degree curriculum chosen by most students. The school is accredited by the North Central Association of Colleges and Schools Commission on Institutions of Higher Education, and the Accrediting Association of Bible Colleges. In 2000, school enrollment was 300, representing 33 states and 10 countries. One-third of the students were from West Virginia. Gifts from churches and individuals subsidize tuition rates. Graduates serve as missionaries, pastors, ministers of music, Christian school teachers, and counselors for independent Baptist and Bible churches.

Fern Hanlin Coberly, *Appalachian Bible College, 1950–2000, Because Life is for Service,* 2000.

Appalachian Corridor Highways

Development of West Virginia's Appalachian Corridor highways began in 1965, when U.S. Sen. Jennings Randolph helped to create the Appalachian Regional Commission. The Appalachian Development Highway System was created under the Appalachian Regional Commission to attract industry and diversify the economic base by building good roads throughout the previously isolated region. Originally including 23 individual corridors designated alphabetically from A to W, the 3,285-mile system was designed to link the Interstate highways of the 13 Appalachian states. West Virginia's 424-mile system included six routes, designated D, E, G, H, L, and Q.

Corridor D (U.S. 50) was designed as an 82-mile four-lane highway from Ohio to I-77 at Parkersburg and on to I-79 at Clarksburg. While 72 miles were built from Parkersburg to Clarksburg by the late 1970s, lack of funding delayed the final segment westward from I-77 through Parkersburg and over the Ohio River. New construction to complete Corridor D into Ohio began in 2000.

Corridor E, completed in the late 1970s as U.S. 48 and redesignated in 1992 as Interstate 68, is a 32-mile link from I-79 near Morgantown eastward to I-70 near Hancock, Maryland.

Corridor G (U.S. 119) is a 79-mile route linking Kentucky near Williamson with I-64 at Charleston. Corridor G is also known as the Robert C. Byrd Freeway, because Byrd helped to secure a major part of the funding for it and other corridors. By the 1990s the four-lane highway was complete to Williamson, with construction under way in neighboring Kentucky.

Corridor H follows U.S. 33 from I-79 at Weston to Elkins and will move from there through the eastern mountains. The building of this road was controversial, arousing strong passions for and against. Decades of public debate and legal battles aired the essential question of whether previously isolated areas should be preserved or opened to development. Historic and environmental concerns for the remaining 100 miles were being addressed as construction on several sections began in 2000. The road will go from Elkins to Bismark, then south to Moorefield, where it will follow State Route 55 to the Virginia border. In Virginia motorists will travel via Route 55 to Interstate 81 at Strasburg.

Corridor L (U.S. 19) is a 70-mile link between I-77 near Beckley and I-79 near Sutton. Including the spectacular New River Gorge Bridge, the road was completed in the 1970s with four lanes only from U.S. 60 south. Continuing increases in traffic resulted in upgrading the remainder to four lanes, with the final segments from Summersville northward completed at the end of the 1990s.

Corridor Q (U.S. 460), a 27-mile route through Mercer County completed in the 1970s, connects via the Virginia portion of U.S. 460 to I-81.

West Virginia expects to complete Corridor D in 2006 and, depending on funding for the remainder of Corridor H, its entire Appalachian Highway system in 2018.

See also Appalachian Regional Commission

Carol Melling
Division of Highways

Appalachian Craftsmen, Inc.

Appalachian Craftsmen, Inc., was an economic development project arising from the War on Poverty. It was chartered in 1971 by the Southwestern Community Action Council and the Junior League of Huntington, and provided low-income artisans a means to earn money by making clothing, home decor, and stuffed toys. Formed in Lincoln County, the organization expanded to include residents of Cabell, Mason, and Wayne counties. Quilters in Upshur County were included when Mountain Artisans, a local sewing group, closed.

Sewers who wanted to supplement family income, but who could not leave home to do so, were provided training, fabric, and designs and were paid on a piece-rate basis. Marketing initially followed a sales party strategy, with a national network of women showing samples of the high-end clothing, quilts, home decorator items, and toys in their homes. Orders were filled by the rural artisans and shipped to the buyers.

Appalachian Craftsmen also sold nationwide through holiday shows, craft fairs, and to gift and clothing boutiques. A Huntington shop provided a local retail outlet. In 1979, a shop opened at the Greenbrier resort and, in 1980, another followed at the Homestead resort in Virginia. Appalachian Craftsmen returned almost $500,000 to more than 250 rural women. In 1984, sales declined due to the influx of foreign imports, and the organization closed in 1988.

See also Crafts Movement, Handcrafts
Carter T. Seaton
Huntington

Appalachian Mountains

The Appalachian Mountains extend from Alabama to Newfoundland, and westward from the Piedmont to the Midwest. Elevations range as high as 6,684 feet in North Carolina, 5,729 feet in Virginia, and 4,861 feet in West Virginia. The Alleghenies, one of the constituent ranges making up the Appalachians, traverse West Virginia, as does a short section of the Blue Ridge. West Virginia is the only state located wholly within the Appalachian Mountains.

In the Paleozoic Era, a mountainous land mass of old, strong, and highly complex rock was situated along the Atlantic Coast. The region is referred to as "Old Appalachia" and included the area that became the modern Blue Ridge and Piedmont. About 275 million years ago, in a mountain-building event known as the Appalachian Orogeny, the sediments produced by the erosion of Old Appalachia were raised from the bottom of an inland sea and produced the "Young Appalachians."

The Young Appalachians were worn down by stream erosion to a nearly level plain in the Mesozoic Era. At the close of the era, the Appalachians were again uplifted and many rivers, especially the New River, became entrenched. Since that time stream erosion has created in the east the present mountainous landscape of parallel ridges and valleys and in the west a dissected plateau where streams follow the slope in a dendritic or tree-like pattern. The mixture of youthful valleys and mature intervening high ground produces a difficult terrain, with 90 percent of West Virginia in slopes of more than 10 percent grade.

The last cataclysmic event to affect the Appalachian Mountains were glaciers in the great Ice Age. Glaciers did not extend into West Virginia, but when they blocked the northern outlets of the ancient Teays and Monongahela rivers the modern Ohio River was created. It became the major drainage system for the central Appalachian Mountains, including most of our state.

The major physiographic divisions of the Appalachian Mountains in West Virginia are (from east to west) the Blue Ridge, Ridge and Valley, and Allegheny Plateau. Between the Ridge and Valley and the Allegheny Plateau is the Allegheny Front, and between the Allegheny Front and the Allegheny Plateau in north central West Virginia are the rugged Allegheny Mountains. Near two-thirds of the state is within the Allegheny Plateau, lying to the west of the Allegheny Mountains, with another fifth within the Ridge and Valley.

West Virginia's climate and weather are affected by the lay of the land, with an average elevation of 1,500 feet and heights that extend upward to a maximum of 4,861 feet at Spruce Knob. Cold to mild winters and hot to cool summers prevail, with a mean annual temperature between 50 and 55 degrees. The average annual precipitation of about 43 to 45 inches is about evenly distributed throughout the year, though with considerable geographical variation. For example, Pickens receives an average of about 70 inches and Brandywine about 30 inches of precipitation yearly.

The mountainous terrain, mid-latitude location, and ample rainfall support a varied forest vegetation cover. About 80 percent of the state is covered with regrowth mixed hardwoods that include oak, hickory, poplar, maple, sycamore, cherry, and black walnut. The softwoods include spruce and white and Virginia pines. Some of America's best hardwood sawtimber is produced in the counties of the Allegheny Front, Allegheny Mountains, and Allegheny Plateau.

The Appalachian Mountains are not endowed with prime farm land. In West Virginia, the best agricultural land is in the Eastern Panhandle and Ohio River valley counties. Three-fourths of the market value of agriculture is concentrated in the Ridge and Valley, primarily in poultry, livestock, hay, and corn production. Tobacco is a specialty crop produced in several southwestern counties.

Topography affects the distribution of people in the Appalachian Mountains. In West Virginia, the population of about 1.8 million resides mostly in counties along the Ohio, Kanawha, New, and Monongahela rivers, and in the Eastern Panhandle in Berkeley and Jefferson counties. By census definition the state's population is predominantly rural with about two-thirds living outside urban and metropolitan places. The average density is 75 people per square mile, while that of surrounding states is several times greater.

See also Geography, Geology

Howard G. Adkins
Ona

Nevin M. Fenneman, *Physiography of Eastern United States*, 1938; Charles B. Hunt, *Physiography of the United States*, 1967; Raymond E. Janssen, *Earth Science: A Handbook on the Geology of West Virginia*, 1973.

Appalachian Orogeny

In geological terms, "orogeny" refers to the process of mountain building. The Appalachian Orogeny, previously called the Appalachian Revolution, describes the collective geological events that produced the belt of folded, faulted, and metamorphosed rock that stretches from Newfoundland to northern Alabama. All of West Virginia is included within this belt. It was produced during the ancient collision of the North American, European, and African continents.

The current Appalachian Mountains are an erosional remnant of mountains formed millions of years ago during the Appalachian Orogeny. These ancestral mountains were much more extensive and probably appeared something like today's Himalayas or Canadian Rockies. They were eroded nearly flat, then split in two during the opening of the Atlantic Ocean, so that rocks and structures of similar age can be found on both sides of the ocean, in North America, Europe, and Africa. In North America, these remnant structures were uplifted and eroded again to form the present Appalachians. They are pale by comparison to their rugged ancestors.

The Appalachian Orogeny is generally separated into three periods, referred to as the Taconic, Acadian, and Alleghenian orogenies. In West Virginia, the evidence for these three events is limited to the thick sedimentary rock units that were deposited in the basin that formed to the west of the mountains.

The Taconic Orogeny is named after the Taconic Mountains of New York. The Taconic Orogeny is thought to be the result of the collision of a volcanic arc with the east coast of North America. Extensive folding and metamorphism from New England to southeastern Pennsylvania is attributed to this event. In West Virginia, the evidence is limited to a great wedge of Ordovician and Silurian sedimentary rocks, including the Tuscarora Sandstone and the underlying red mudstones of the Juniata Formation, both of which are exposed on North Fork Mountain along U.S. 33 in Pendleton County. Seneca Rocks is a spectacular Tuscarora formation.

The Acadian Orogeny is named for Acadia, a historical term for the Canadian Maritime provinces, and resulted from deformed and metamorphosed sedimentary rocks. Extensive metamorphism and deformation in the Late Silurian and Devonian eras produced deposits of sedimentary rock often referred to as the Catskill Delta. In West Virginia, these sediments are exposed on U.S. 33 east of Elkins.

The Allegheny Orogeny is named after the high ridges of the Allegheny Mountains in Pennsylvania and West Virginia.

The evidence for this event is two-fold. The thick Pennsylvanian Era sediments of West Virginia, including most of the commercial coal beds, were deposited along the ancient coastal plain that flanked the highlands to the east. These sediments consist of alternating terrestrial and marine deposits and are found throughout West Virginia west of the Allegheny Front. The other evidence can be seen in the Ridge and Valley physiographic province, which displays sedimentary rock deposited during the previous two orogenic events that were folded and faulted during the Alleghenian event.

See also Appalachian Mountains, Geology

David Matchen
Geological & Economic Survey

Robert H. Dott Jr. and Donald R. Prothero, *Evolution of the Earth*, 1994; R.D. Hatcher Jr., W.A. Thomas, and G.W. Viele, eds., *The Appalachian-Ouachita Orogen in the United States*, 1989; John McPhee, "In Suspect Terrane," *Annals of the Former World*, 1998.

Appalachian Power Company

The Appalachian Power Company began in 1910 when a group of entrepreneurs decided that hydroelectric dams could be built on the New River in Virginia to supply electricity to the burgeoning coal country of southern West Virginia. The company built two dams in Virginia and an 88,000-volt transmission line to carry electricity across the mountains to West Virginia.

During the early 1920s, American Electric Power, then known as American Gas & Electric Power Company, began acquiring small companies in a half-dozen states, including West Virginia. In 1926, AG&E consolidated a dozen of these companies, including Appalachian Power, into a new subsidiary it called Appalachian Electric Power.

In the 1920s and 1930s, Appalachian's construction crews strung transmission lines across much of southern West Virginia. The crews lived in camps, slept in tents, and ate their meals from chuck wagons. Ox teams were used to drag steel for transmission towers up hills, where it was set in foundations dug by hand with picks and shovels or blasted out of solid rock. Interrupted by World War II, the construction program resumed after the war, and by 1949 electricity was available throughout the 21 counties the company served in southern West Virginia.

With a growing economy and an increasing number of customers, the company needed to expand its generating capacity. In the late 1940s and early 1950s, Appalachian and Ohio Power Company jointly constructed the Philip Sporn Plant on the Ohio River in Mason County. Construction of other coal-fired power plants followed. Originally founded to bring electricity to the coalfields of southern

West Virginia, Appalachian essentially reversed that process by using West Virginia coal to generate electricity and send it to the nation. "Coal by wire," some called it.

In a 1958 corporate reorganization, the company's name again became Appalachian Power Company, or Apco for short. The venerable corporate name was retired in 1996, when parent American Electric Power imposed a single corporate identity. In 2004, Appalachian Power Company resumed its own name, while retaining part of AEP.

See also American Electric Power

James E. Casto
Herald-Dispatch

Appalachian Regional Commission

The Appalachian Regional Commission was established by Congress in 1965 to bring almost 400 counties in Appalachia into the mainstream of the American economy. As defined by the Commission, the 200,000-square-mile region covers all of West Virginia and parts of 12 other states: Alabama, Georgia, Kentucky, Maryland, Mississippi, New York, North Carolina, Ohio, Pennsylvania, South Carolina, Tennessee, and Virginia.

President Lyndon Johnson signed the Appalachian Regional Development Act on March 9, 1965, but its origin can be traced back to President John F. Kennedy. During his pivotal primary campaign for president in West Virginia in 1960, Kennedy saw firsthand the despair in Appalachia, where one of every three families lived in poverty. The states' governors formed the Conference of Appalachian Governors in 1960, and Kennedy kept a campaign promise by inviting the group to meet with him and top federal officials in Washington. The President's Appalachian Regional Commission (PARC) was created, led by Franklin D. Roosevelt Jr. Following Kennedy's assassination in 1963, the PARC recommendations were delivered to President Johnson, who saw that they were quickly transformed into enabling legislation.

The ARC federal-state partnership is embodied in its membership—the 13 Appalachian governors plus one federal representative, or federal co-chairman, appointed by the president and subject to Senate confirmation. Each year the governors elect one of their number to serve as the states' co-chairman. The federal co-chairman has one vote on commission policy matters, and the governors, voting as a unit, share one vote. The commission appoints an executive director to head the ARC staff. Each governor names an alternate to handle ARC matters in his absence, and the states also employ a representative based in Washington who tracks ARC activities.

The ARC programs fall into two broad categories: (1) the Appalachian Development Highway System, a 3,285-mile corridor highway network intended to break the regional isolation created by mountainous terrain and thereby link Appalachian communities to national and international markets; and (2) an area development program to create a basis for sustained local economic growth. The development of six Appalachian Developmental Highways, or corridors, in West Virginia was the most visible accomplishment of the agency in the early years of its existence, complementing the new Interstate highway system that was built at about the same time.

The corridor from Morgantown east to the Maryland border in Preston County was converted to Interstate 68 but the others, all four-lane, limited-access expressways, remain part of the Appalachian corridor system. One connects Parkersburg to Clarksburg on U.S. 50; Corridor G stretches along U.S. 119 from Charleston southwest through Logan to Williamson and continues into Kentucky. Corridor L, which connects I-77 at Beckley to I-79 near Sutton via U.S. 19 through Summersville, includes a bridge over the New River that is the longest steel arch bridge in the United States. The other two are a short stretch of U.S. 460 through the state's southernmost region and the controversial and still unfinished Corridor H, already open from I-79 near Weston to Elkins and planned to extend to the Virginia border near Strasburg, Virginia. The Appalachian Development Highway System (ADHS) was 79 percent completed or under construction at the end of 1997 with 2,258.8 miles opened to traffic. The estimated cost of completion has been set at $8.5 billion in combined state and federal funding, with the federal share on a 70-30 matching basis exceeding $6.2 billion. Altogether the ARC spent $7.2 billion between 1965 and 1977, and $4.5 billion of that was on highways. West Virginia received the largest share of this highway money, $990.2 million. In October of 1998, Congress passed full reauthorization of ARC funding for the first time in 16 years, after passing a bill four months earlier that set aside $2.25 billion to speed up completion of the highway system.

See also Appalachia, Appalachian Corridor Highways

Tom D. Miller
Huntington

Michael Bradshaw, *The Appalachian Regional Commission: Twenty-five Years of Government Policy,* 1992.

Appalachian Regional Hospitals

Following the 1946 national coal strike, the United Mine Workers of America established a Welfare and Retirement Fund to meet the medical needs of miners, their families, and widowed spouses and orphans. The initial program used existing medical facilities. Then in the 1950s the UMW constructed a chain of hospitals as part of the program. Ten were constructed in the Appalachian region, with three hospitals in West Virginia, at Williamson, Man, and Beckley. The hospitals at Williamson and Beckley served as hubs in the interstate system.

The hospitals offered the best medical care available at the time. Accidents in the mines often resulted in spinal cord injuries. The hospitals constructed by the UMW, as well as other hospitals that had participated in the program earlier, gained fame for their advances in treating spinal cord injuries. The union hospitals often served as sites for research or instruction related to these injuries. The hospitals later added nursing schools. The medical program also pioneered intensive vocational rehabilitation programs.

Despite the union's initial enthusiasm for hospital construction, problems soon emerged. The UMW was not prepared for the financial burden and the day-to-day administration of the interstate hospital system, and in the 1960s announced that the chain would be closed. S. M. Kerr, a Presbyterian minister who had worked with the hospital chain in Kentucky, realized the crisis this would create for the rural mining counties. He persuaded the Board of National Missions of the United Presbyterian Church to step in to save the network in 1963. The board formed a nonprofit corporation, Appalachian Regional Hospitals, and bought the hospitals for $8 million using state and federal funds.

In the 1960s and '70s, ARH faced hard economic times and fell into debt. The number of working union miners continued to decline. In 1978, ARH announced it would close its Man hospital. The ARH hired a new administrator, Robert L. Johnson, who brought financial stability to the network by increasing efforts to collect bad debts and raising rates for services.

In 1986, Appalachian Regional Hospitals changed its name to Appalachian Regional Healthcare. As of 2001, the corporation operated nine hospitals, 22 clinics, and 12 home health agencies, and offered health-related services, including laboratory testing, radiological service, and sterile equipment supplies.

See also Miners Health Plan, United Mine Workers of America

Shae Davidson
The Plains, Ohio

Ivana Krajcinovic, *From Company Doctors to Managed Care: The United Mine Workers' Noble Experiment,* 1997.

The Appalachian Trail

The Appalachian Trail follows the crest of the Appalachian Mountains for more than 2,100 miles from Springer Mountain, Georgia, to Mount Katahdin, Maine. Although other people had put forth similar ideas, a 1921 magazine article by Benton MacKaye is generally regarded as having provided the impetus for the trail.

In October 1923, the first miles to be built for the Appalachian Trail were opened in Harriman-Bear Mountain State Park, New York. On August 14, 1937, the final section was constructed in central Maine. A remarkable aspect of the trail is that nearly every bit of effort expended on its behalf has been done by volunteers. Appalachian Trail Conference, the organization overseeing volunteer efforts, estimates that more than four million people annually enjoy some portion of the trail.

The trail comes in contact with southeastern West Virginia a few miles east of Peterstown, Monroe County. Traversing Peters Mountain along the West Virginia-Virginia border, it zigzags along the state line for close to 13 miles. This stretch offers commanding views of waves of Allegheny Mountain summits from Rice Field and Symms Gap Meadow. Before dropping off the mountain into Virginia, the trail passes the southern terminus of the Allegheny Trail, West Virginia's premier long-distance pathway.

In the Eastern Panhandle, the Appalachian Trail again follows a ridgeline weaving along the West Virginia-Virginia border, this time east of Charles Town. A little over seven of the 14 miles are located entirely in West Virginia. Stone foundations seen along the pathway are vestiges of fortifications from the Civil War. Dropping into the state, and passing pits and ditches from the charcoal producing days of the 1800s, the trail crosses the Shenandoah River and enters Harpers Ferry, headquarters of the Appalachian Trail Conference. The Appalachian Trail leaves West Virginia and enters Maryland by crossing the Potomac River.

See also Allegheny Trail

Leonard M. Adkins
Catawba, Virginia

Appalachian Volunteers

The Appalachian Volunteers were a government funded community development organization involved in many of the more controversial episodes of the War on Poverty in West Virginia. The organization was founded in 1963 as an offshoot of the Council of the Southern Mountains, headquartered at the time at Berea College, Kentucky. The AVs, as they were known, began as a group of students from Kentucky colleges who volunteered in one-room schools in East Kentucky. When President Johnson's War on Poverty geared up in 1965, the AVs received funding to expand their efforts.

AV activities in West Virginia began with the 1966 summer project, which in-

volved about 500 college students, more than 150 of whom were assigned to coal camps and rural settlements in southern West Virginia. AV staff, summer volunteers, and members of Volunteers in Service to America (VISTA) began organizing community meetings around issues such as inadequate schools, poor roads, and strip mining. Soon corrupt elections and unfair taxation were added to the list, and by 1967 several county antipoverty programs were taken over by grass-roots coalitions organized by the AVs and their allies. Local political leaders protested to the governor and to West Virginia's representatives in Washington. Funding was soon cut and political restrictions imposed.

However, the AV influence lived on for several years in the Fair Elections, strip mine control, and tax reform movements of the late '60s and early '70s, and in the candidacy of Paul Kaufman, a liberal state senator from Kanawha County who ran unsuccessfully for the Democrat nomination for governor in 1968. Perhaps the greatest impact was on the Black Lung and Miners for Democracy movements. Former Appalachian Volunteers helped a disabled miner from Cabin Creek, Arnold Miller, to become president of the United Mine Workers of America in 1972.

Although some moved to Washington with Miller when he took control of the union, several of the "outside agitator" AVs stayed on in West Virginia, working in law, health care, public broadcasting, and business.

See also VISTA, War on Poverty

Gibbs Kinderman
Marlinton

Appalachian Wage Agreement

During the 1920s and 1930s, the United Mine Workers of America was fighting for its existence. The unionized mines of Illinois and Indiana found it difficult to compete with nonunion operations in West Virginia and Kentucky. Wage cuts and declining coal prices left the industry in disarray by the 1930s, with excess production and too many mines and miners. In West Virginia the union had suffered losses in the Mine Wars of the early 20th century, culminating in the hard-fought strikes of the early 1920s.

The pro-labor legislation of Franklin Roosevelt's New Deal brought rebirth. UMWA President John L. Lewis sent hundreds of organizers into the coalfields claiming "the president wants you to join the union." Within a short time, most miners did. Now, with the coalfields highly unionized, Lewis hoped to stabilize the American coal industry by applying consistent union wage rates in all mines. For the first time, he was able to negotiate regional master agreements

that would not face the danger of cracking.

The pacesetter of the regional master agreements was the Appalachian Wage Agreement of 1933. Covering West Virginia and the surrounding region, the Appalachian agreement was re-negotiated at approximately two-year intervals until World War II. Lewis slowly brought all the regional agreements closer together, and by 1941 the power of the UMWA had eliminated the traditional wage differentials between the northern and southern coalfields. In obtaining uniform wages and organizing most of the mines, the union halted the practice of cutthroat competition by the reduction of wages. Lewis was moving toward a national labor agreement for the American coal industry, which finally occurred in 1950 as the National Bituminous Coal Wage Agreement.

See also Labor History, United Mine Workers of America

John David
WVU Institute of Technology

The Apple Butter Festival

Thousands of people flock to Berkeley Springs every Columbus Day weekend for the Apple Butter Festival. Founded in 1973, the two-day homecoming celebration begins with a Saturday morning parade from the high school through the town square and on to the old train station on Williams Street. The festival ends late Sunday afternoon. A successor to the once popular Tomato Festival, the Apple Butter Festival celebrates the orchard tradition of the surrounding countryside. It offers traditional entertainment, including a turtle race; beard and moustache contest; egg toss; decorated pumpkin contest; apple butter and baking contests; cider-making; hog calling, fiddling, and liars' competitions; quiltmaking; music contests and shows; theater; and a wide variety of food heavy with apple flavor. Vendors selling everything from ice cream to antiques line the streets of the historic town. Begun by members of the business community, the festival is a Chamber of Commerce event that has grown to have a major economic and social impact on the area. Berkeley Springs, the county seat of Morgan County, is best known for its mineral water baths which once attracted George Washington to relax there.

See also Berkeley Springs

Peggy Ross
Reedsville

Apples

West Virginia has produced two great apples, the first of which was the Grimes Golden, discovered about 1805 on the farm of Thomas Grimes at Fowlersville near Wellsburg, supposedly from a seed planted by Johnny Appleseed. Consid-

Golden Delicious apples.

ered by some to be the best frying apple ever, the Grimes Golden was commonly grown in home and commercial orchards until the early 1940s, when the Golden Delicious largely displaced it.

Anderson Mullins discovered the Golden Delicious, thought to be a chance offspring of a Grimes Golden, in 1912 in Clay County. The tree was purchased by Stark Brothers' Nursery, which built a cage around the tree and protected it for many years while propagating the Golden Delicious worldwide. This aromatic fruit is a fine eating apple and a good keeper, unexcelled as an all-purpose apple. The Golden Delicious is the second most popular apple in the country. Those grown in the West are larger, smoother, and more uniformly colored than the tastier, freckled Golden Delicious grown in West Virginia. Lawmakers named the Golden Delicious the West Virginia state apple in 1995.

Commercially, the growing of both apples and peaches takes place mostly in the Eastern Panhandle, where the Shenandoah Valley provides ideal climate and soil.

The growing of apples over the years has passed from standard-size apple trees growing 25 feet tall, to semi-dwarf apple trees growing 15 feet tall, to dwarf apple trees growing seven to nine feet tall and trained onto wires. The modern commercial apple orchard bears more than a little resemblance to a grape vineyard.

Unlike a bean or a pea, apples do not grow true from seed. Rather, skilled workers graft a bud of a desired variety onto a rootstock of another variety. The graft is chosen for its fruit, while the rootstock may be chosen for its sturdiness or other qualities. Thus, every commercially productive apple tree is a man-made union of two apple trees, producing the fruit of the grafted-on variety. New varieties

arise through chance or deliberate breeding and are themselves then propagated by grafting. A few dedicated people labor to keep the gene pool alive and the old apples growing. Carlos Manning is one such person, growing nearly 300 varieties in his nursery in Lester, Raleigh County.

Depressed prices, in part caused by imports of apple juice, make it difficult for all but growers of premium-priced specialty apples to survive. Two such growers excelled in recent years. Morgan Orchard in Monroe County raised some 50 varieties for the commercial market. Summit Point Raceway Orchards in Jefferson County, until recently owned by Barbara and William Scott, almost single-handedly created a grocery store market for the Nittany, a crisp, juicy, and flavorful keeping apple whose red skin with yellow blush was once considered unattractive. Both Morgan Orchard and Summit Point helped revive the York, a flattened, bi-colored crisp keeper that had just about vanished from commercial orchards.

Oddly, the Nittany had begun life as a West Virginian at the West Virginia University experimental farm at Kearneysville, Jefferson County. The Nittany came from good parents, probably a York open-pollinated by a Golden Delicious. Apple specialists at Kearneysville lost interest in the new variety and shipped it off to State College, Pennsylvania, where pomologists gave it a name that sounded good to their ears. Perhaps to make amends for promoting a fruit bearing the name of the mascot of Penn State University, the Scotts later took a genetic variant of a York apple and named it Mountaineer.

See also Golden Delicious, Grimes Golden, Orchards

Bob Schwarz
Charleston Gazette

John W. M. Appleton

Soldier and businessman John W. M. Appleton, born in Boston, April 1, 1832, was educated in Boston public schools and at Harvard. In the Civil War, Appleton, who was white, sought and received a commission as 2nd lieutenant in the famous 54th Massachusetts Infantry, a black regiment formed in Boston and led by Col. Robert G. Shaw. Promoted to captain and then major, Appleton led Company A into intense combat on the sea islands of South Carolina, Georgia, and Florida, where the 54th was assigned to capture Confederate coastal positions. He was twice wounded before being sent home to Boston, where, at the end of the war, he served as warden of the prison holding Confederate Vice President Alexander Stephens.

In 1865, Appleton moved to Kanawha County where he managed the Mill Creek Cannel Coal Company. During the next 50 years, he had a variety of business interests in West Virginia, including operating the Salt Sulphur Springs resort in Monroe County. He served in the West Virginia National Guard, rising to the rank of adjutant general. As adjutant general, Appleton's major contributions included compiling records of West Virginia's Civil War Union veterans and units and organizing the National Guard for service in the Spanish-American War. He died October 23, 1913, on his Monroe County farm after being injured by a runaway bull.

Kenneth R. Bailey
WVU Institute of Technology

Aracoma

Aracoma, perhaps meaning "a corn blossom," was the legendary daughter of Shawnee war leader Cornstalk, famous for his role in the 1774 Battle of Point Pleasant. Aracoma, according to Logan County tradition, married the white renegade Boling Baker, thought to have been a deserter from Gen. Edward Braddock's army that attempted to take Fort Duquesne in July 1755, during the French and Indian War.

Baker and Aracoma moved to what is now called Midelburg Island, in the Guyandotte River at the later site of the city of Logan. They were killed by white men led by John Breckenridge and William Madison during the Revolutionary War, perhaps in the spring of 1780 after Baker led Indians to steal horses from New River Valley settlers. The story has been made into an outdoor drama, presented annually at Chief Logan State Park. George W. L. Bickley's 1852 *History of the Settlement and Indian Wars of Tazewell County, Virginia* includes an early printed version of the legend of Aracoma. It is likely that this story, later used by Henry Clay Ragland in his *History of Logan County,* was embellished by the poet Thomas Dunn English in the 1850s.

Robert Y. Spence
Logan

Aracoma Hotel

Named after the Indian princess, Aracoma, legendary daughter of Chief Cornstalk, the Aracoma Hotel is a Logan landmark. Built in 1917 at a cost of $50,000 by Harvey Ghiz, a Syrian immigrant, the hotel was the largest downtown building erected during the wave of fireproof construction that followed Logan's great fire of January 1912. While preparing the ground for the foundation, wooden scrapers pulled by mules unearthed a bone and relic field roughly a block square that had been an Indian burial site.

The original four-story brick hotel, built in an architectural style known as Richardson Romanesque and trimmed in ornamental stone, fronted on Coal Street with an elaborate arched facade. Inside, there were 94 rooms, most with private shower baths. The Aracoma had electric elevators and fine woodwork, some of which remains.

In 1921 during the Mine Wars, women of the town set up an emergency food station in the lobby to supply meals and sundries to the troops, police, and other anti-union forces quartered in Logan. Notable guests at the hotel have included the Cincinnati Reds baseball team (1923), evangelist Billy Sunday (1923), Eleanor Roosevelt (1939), and John F. Kennedy and Edward Kennedy during the presidential primary campaign of 1960. Significant alterations over time include the loss of the arched entrance (the present entrance is at 201 Main Street) and the closing of the dining room.

The Aracoma remained in use as a hotel through the end of the 20th century.

See also Logan, Mine Wars

Paula D. White
Logan

Matthew Arbuckle

Captain Matthew Arbuckle, "large of stature and large of spirit," was born about 1741 in Scotland. He is listed as serving in the Augusta County, Virginia, militia in 1758–59, was a lieutenant in 1767, and commissioned captain of Botetourt County militia in 1770. He served as a gentleman justice of Botetourt County from its founding in 1769 until 1773.

A hunter and trapper, Arbuckle was probably the first white man to travel from Virginia to the Ohio other than as a prisoner of the Indians. In 1774 he built the stockade on Muddy Creek, Greenbrier County, now known as Arbuckle's Old Fort.

Commanding a company of Botetourt County militia he served as guide and chief scout for Gen. Andrew Lewis's 1774 march to Point Pleasant, contributing greatly to the defeat of the Indians led by Chief Cornstalk at the Battle of Point Pleasant. Later he built Fort Randolph at Point Pleasant. He was in command there when a mob of newly arrived and undisciplined militia, who had witnessed one of their number killed and scalped by the Indians, overcame their officers' and Arbuckle's attempts to maintain order and murdered the captive Cornstalk.

Soon after 1774, Arbuckle established his residence near Lewisburg, then known as Fort Savannah, and when the town was laid out in 1780 he was the first settler. In 1778 he was active in raising the siege of Fort Donnally, near Lewisburg. On retirement from active military service he farmed his extensive lands and served several public duties. In March of 1781 he was commissioned to lay out a route from Lewisburg to Warm Springs, Bath County. In June of that year, returning from the capital at Williamsburg, Arbuckle was caught in a violent storm near the banks of the Jackson River and killed by a falling tree. He left a widow and six strong sons.

See also Arbuckle's Fort, Battle of Point Pleasant

Joseph Crosby Jefferds Jr.
Charleston

Arbuckle's Fort

Arbuckle's Fort was a Revolutionary-era frontier fort located in Greenbrier County, one of many forts that helped white and African-American settlers to colonize Western Virginia. The fort stood on the property of John Keeney when it was built in the spring of 1774, under order of Capt. Matthew Arbuckle.

Captain Arbuckle's militia company occupied Arbuckle's Fort from the spring to the fall of 1774. In September 1774, Captain Arbuckle and his men left the fort to help guide Col. Andrew Lewis and the southwestern Virginia militia down the Kanawha River to Point Pleasant, where they fought in the Battle of Point Pleasant. Other militia companies occupied Arbuckle's Fort in 1776, 1777, and 1778. Although no large-scale attacks on this fort occurred, it was fired upon by Indian forces in 1774, and nearby settlers reported hearing gunshots near the fort in 1777. Spent lead shot has been recovered from archeological excavations conducted in 1997.

The excavations established that the fort was diamond-shaped, about 100 feet on a side, and consisted of a log stockade with bastions at the north and south ends. A blockhouse with a stone foundation and a central stone chimney was located inside the stockade. Large amounts of slag and unworked iron are evidence of a blacksmithing area inside the fort. Artifacts recovered from the archeological excavations include worn-out gun-flints and a letter seal that expressed the inhabitants' Revolutionary zeal by imprinting the word "Liberty."

Kim McBride
Kentucky Archeological Survey
Stephen McBride
McBride Preservation Services

Kim A. McBride and W. Stephen McBride, "Forting Up on the Greenbrier: Archaeological Investigations of Arbuckle's Fort," 1993; W. Stephen McBride, Kim A. McBride, and J. David McBride, "Frontier Defense of the Greenbrier and Middle New River Country," 1996.

Archeology

The first archeological excavation undertaken in West Virginia was at Grave Creek Mound at Moundsville in 1838. The second major site was recorded in the fall of 1846, when Ephraim G. Squier and Edwin H. Davis documented the Salt Rock petroglyphs along the Guyandotte River in Cabell County. Their report, published in 1848, was included in the first volume of the Smithsonian Institution's "Contributions to Knowledge" series, titled *Ancient Monuments of the Mississippi Valley*.

The early settlers believed a prehistoric race of people they called "Mound Builders" constructed the burial mounds and earthworks. The Mound Builders were viewed as an ancient race from Europe, Africa, or the Near East, who had vanished and been replaced by American Indians. Some early scholars believed the Mound Builders were one of the Lost Tribes of Israel.

In 1881, Congress gave $5,000 to the Smithsonian Institution to conduct archeological excavations relating to the prehistoric Mound Builders. Wills De Hass of Wheeling was put in charge of the project. He was replaced by Cyrus Thomas after one year. Col. P. W. Norris led the mound explorations for the Smithsonian

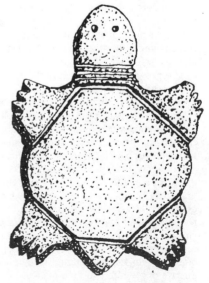

Turtle effigy stone tablet from Marshall County's Cresap Mound.

in the Kanawha Valley from 1882 to 1884. Norris dug a deep shaft into the Criel Mound in South Charleston, the second-largest mound in West Virginia, and found an individual buried with a copper headdress, six shell beads, and one flint knife.

The goal of the Smithsonian mound explorations was to settle the question of the identity of the Mound Builders. By 1890, more than 2,000 mounds and earthworks had been studied in the eastern United States. About 100 of these were in the Kanawha Valley. In 1894, Cyrus Thomas published *Report on the Mound Explorations of the Bureau of Ethnology* and proved the Mound Builders were not a vanished race but ancestors of American Indians. This publication marks the birth of modern American archeology.

During the late 1800s the Smithsonian continued to be active in West Virginia. Gerard Fowke published on numerous archeological sites in the eastern region and on artifacts in the Kanawha Valley. John P. MacLean investigated several sites on Blennerhassett Island, and Garrick Mallery described a pictograph and several petroglyph sites in West Virginia. During the early 1900s most of the published references to archeological sites came from county histories.

The 1930s saw the beginning of university involvement, reflecting the growth of the new field of descriptive anthropology. Charles Bache and Linton Satterwaite Jr., of the University of Pennsylvania, excavated the Beech Bottom Mound in Brooke County and published their findings in the *Museum Journal* in 1930. James B. Griffin visited several village sites and defined the Clover Phase in 1943.

After World War II, a group of amateur archeologists began working with Dr. Ralph Solecki and the Smithsonian Institution's River Basin Survey on the Bluestone Reservoir project. In 1949, Robert and William Athey, Joseph Essington, Elmer W. Fetzer, Oscar L. Mairs, and Delf Norona joined with Solecki and founded the West Virginia Archeological Society. In the same year they began publication of the *West Virginia Archeologist*.

By 1950, Sigfus Olafson, a Boone County geologist, began publishing articles on petroglyphs, the painted trees, Gabriel Arthur, and other subjects. West Virginia joined the Eastern States Archeological Federation, and Olafson eventually became president of both organizations.

While members of the Archeological Society were active in documenting and interpreting West Virginia's prehistory, they recruited professional archeologists James Kellar, Ralph Solecki, and Frank Setzler to conduct major investigations and excavations at Mount Carbon Stone Walls, Natrium Mound, and Welcome

Mound. During the 1950s the Carnegie Museum at Pittsburgh began its Upper Ohio Valley Archeological Survey, with extensive fieldwork conducted in northern West Virginia by William J. Mayer-Oakes and Don Dragoo. Many classic sites were excavated, including the Speidel Site, Watson Farm, Globe Hill, Cresap Mound, Dixon Rock Shelter, and Rohr Rock Shelter.

The West Virginia Archeological Society with the assistance of Dr. Paul H. Price, the state geologist, convinced the state legislature in 1960 to create the position of state archeologist. Dr. Edward V. McMichael was hired, and the West Virginia Geological and Economic Survey's Section of Archeology was created.

The 1960s were the golden years of West Virginia archeology. McMichael conducted major excavations at the Buffalo Site and Mount Carbon and with the assistance of society members conducted archeological surveys and test excavations throughout the state. Bettye J. Broyles received National Science Foundation grants to excavate at the St. Albans Site. The Section of Archeology began its own publication series and continued to publish extensively in the *West Virginia Archeologist*. By 1968, McMichael had published his *Introduction to West Virginia Archeology*, which continues to be the only major overview of West Virginia archeology. By 1970, McMichael had left the Geological Survey. Broyles replaced him and was eventually replaced by Daniel B. Fowler.

In 1965 the West Virginia Antiquities Commission was established, and archeology was included in its program. In 1966, Congress enacted the National Historic Preservation Act, which established the National Register of Historic Places, requiring each state to appoint a state historic preservation officer and a board to review grants. The Antiquities Com-

mission assumed these responsibilities in West Virginia.

After the passage of the Moss-Bennett Bill in 1974 federal agencies had to comply with the National Historic Preservation Act, and cultural resources management became the dominating force in West Virginia archeology. Cultural resources management, the practice of managing archeological and historic sites, involves excavating, analyzing, stabilizing, and documenting sites and structures that are endangered. Federal agencies responded to the new legislation by hiring professional archeologists and integrating cultural resources management into the federal planning process.

On July 1, 1977, the West Virginia Antiquities Commission was supplanted by the Archives and History Commission at the newly created West Virginia Department of Culture and History. The new department consolidated West Virginia's arts and history programs. Gradually, much of the responsibility for archeology was transferred to the historic preservation office at Culture and History. The West Virginia Geological and Economic Survey phased out its archeology program. Daniel B. Fowler, who served as state archeologist with the Geological and Economic Survey, moved to the Blennerhassett Historical Park Commission on May 21, 1979, and the survey's archeological collections were moved to Blennerhassett Museum in March 1984. The 1,600 boxes of artifacts and 73 boxes of associated documents were moved to the Delf Norona Museum in Moundsville on October 1, 1996.

During the 1980s and 1990s most professional archeological work in West Virginia was accomplished under federally funded cultural resources management projects, usually by out-of-state consulting firms. Professional archeologists working in West Virginia banded together to

---

Excavating the South Charleston mound

"The excavation in the mound was commenced twelve feet square at the top and sunk to the bottom, narrowing as it went down.

"In a very hard bed of mixed earth and ashes, about four feet from the top, were found two much decayed human skeletons, adult size, lying horizontally on their backs, with their heads to the south; and near the heads were several stone implements. At a depth of thirty-one feet from the top, a human skeleton was found lying with the head to the north; it had evidently been enclosed in a coffin or wrapping of bark. A thin sheet of hammered native copper was found in contact with the bones of the skull and had helped to preserve them. At this point the excavation was opened out to a diameter of about sixteen feet to give a better opportunity of finding and examining whatever might lie at the base of the mound. This disclosed the fact that the builders, after having first leveled, smoothed and packed the natural surface, covered it with a layer of bark, inner side up, and spread upon this a layer of fine, clear, white ashes, probably several inches thick, though now pressed down to little more than an inch. On this bed of ashes the bodies were laid, and probably covered with bark.

"Examination here brought to light ten other adult skeletons, all extended horizontally, five on each side of the central skeleton, with feet pointing towards, but not quite touching it."

—John P. Hale *History of the Great Kanawha Valley* (1891)

form the Council For West Virginia Archaeology, incorporated on October 8, 1985. Its members have earned at least a master's degree or equivalent and work in archeology or related fields.

In 1990, Congress passed the Native American Graves Protection and Repatriation Act, which had a major impact on American archeology. West Virginia has no federally recognized Native American tribes or Indian reservations, and none of the prehistoric skeletal remains recovered in the state can be associated with historic tribes. On September 14, 1990, the state historic preservation officer, William Drennen, entered into a memorandum of understanding with the West Virginia Committee on Native American Archaeological and Burial Policies which led to the Cotiga Mound Memorandum of Agreement. This agreement essentially gave the Native American Committee control over the Department of Highways excavation of an Indian burial mound in Mingo County. After several meetings the West Virginia Archeological Society, the Council For West Virginia Archaeology, and the United Cherokee Tribe of West Virginia filed a lawsuit against the state to rescind the agreement. The West Virginia Department of Transportation and the State Historic Preservation Office prevailed in the case, but the Cotiga excavations were opened to the public and many of the stipulations were reinterpreted to the benefit of archeologists.

While West Virginia University and Marshall University have archeology classes, there is no strong university program in prehistoric or historic archeology. The West Virginia University Institute for the History of Technology and Industrial Archaeology, founded by Dr. Emory Kemp, provides the state with an excellent program in industrial archeology.

As of January 2001, West Virginia had 10,211 recorded archeological sites and the number continues to increase. The number of in-state cultural resources management firms continues to grow, and there is a dramatic increase in highway archeology. More accurate cultural chronologies are being developed based on 450 radiocarbon dates for West Virginia and state of the art analysis techniques. Continued collaboration between the state's archeological organizations will ensure the future of West Virginia archeology into the new century.

See also Prehistoric People

Robert F. Maslowski
Milton

R. P. Stephen Davis Jr., *Bibliography of West Virginia Archaeology,* 1978; Edward V. McMichael, *Introduction to West Virginia Archaeology,* 1968; William J. Mayer-Oakes, *Prehistory of the Upper Ohio Valley: An Introductory Archeological Study,* Annals of Carnegie Museum, 1955.

Architects and Architecture

When West Virginia legislators first met in 1863, they appointed a committee to oversee the design of a state seal. According to the written description, one side depicts "A cultivated slope with the log farmhouse peculiar to this region." Peculiar to this region or not, log houses were certainly the prevalent building type from the earliest days of settlement until long afterward.

Logs weren't used only for houses. In July 1788, Francis Asbury wrote in his diary that he "had large congregations at Rehoboth." Now a lovingly preserved Methodist shrine, this small log church still stands, covered with a protective canopy, in Monroe County.

Log buildings ranged from the simple to the elaborate. Some were constructed from written specifications that might even include directions regarding the type of notching. Log construction persisted for many years in isolated parts of the state, as evidenced in 1872 in McDowell County, when commissioners ordered that a new courthouse, the county's second, be of log construction. Throughout the state, log buildings remain in excellent condition today, many covered from the beginning with clapboards.

Sawmills, brickyards, and quarries provided other building materials. In 1798, a visitor to Wheeling described Moses Shepherd's new dwelling as "one of the best built and handsomest stone houses . . . on this side of the mountains." With its graceful Georgian proportions and finely crafted details, Shepherd Hall or Monument Place, as it came to be called, would have been at home on either side of the mountains. It stood on the same site where Moses's father had built a log stockade, Fort Shepherd, a few decades before. Old Stone Church in Lewisburg, another late 18th-century building, tells eloquently of its significance by its very name.

By this time Samuel Washington had already built his own stone mansion, Harewood, in the Eastern Panhandle. In 1794 its beautifully paneled walls witnessed the wedding of Dolley Payne Todd and James Madison. Early in the 19th century, other Washington family members built even larger houses, of brick, near Harewood on tracts that a teenaged George Washington had originally surveyed for Lord Fairfax. Blakeley and Claymont Court still stand across from each other on the meandering Bullskin Run in Jefferson County.

Far to the south, mineral springs in Greenbrier and Monroe counties were already attracting visitors in the early 1800s. As at Berkeley Springs, health and pleasure seekers were first housed in log structures. By 1840 the management at Sweet Springs opened a new hostelry so

attractive that its design has often been attributed to Thomas Jefferson, even though it was built after his death. As it turns out, William B. Phillips, one of the talented builders at Jefferson's University of Virginia, designed and built the hotel which still stands. Sweet Springs was soon eclipsed by the phenomenal Grand Central Hotel at nearby White Sulphur.

Just before the Civil War, the state of Virginia began construction of the Trans-Allegheny Lunatic Asylum at Weston. When the hospital's main building was finally completed in 1880, its proponents bragged that it was the largest cut-stone building in the United States. No longer used as a hospital, the sprawling building still dominates its environs.

The Weston hospital was designed by Richard Snowden Andrews, a Baltimore architect, but other antebellum institutions looked westward for their architects. Cincinnati's James Keys Wilson provided Alexander Campbell with a Gothic Revival design for Bethany College in Brooke County. Begun in 1858 and completed in 1871, Old Main was a remarkable achievement for its time and place. It remains the centerpiece of one of America's most idyllic campuses.

Far to the east, the U.S. Armory at Harpers Ferry was not so idyllic, certainly not in October 1859 when John Brown attempted to seize it. His so-called "fort," the brick fire-engine house where he was captured, has been moved and rebuilt no fewer than four times, testament to its status as a shrine. Brown's action helped precipitate events that led to the formation of West Virginia, and some of these took place in another structure that the federal government had recently built. Wheeling's post office and custom house, a stone Renaissance Revival building, soon came to play a far more important role than architect Ammi B. Young could have anticipated, when it housed delegates who met in 1861 to create the new state. Now handsomely restored, it is known as West Virginia Independence Hall.

Another architectural testament to the separation of one state from the other lies close by. Cast-iron fronts of the List Building were fabricated in Wheeling, but at different times, since the building was erected in several stages. The base of one pilaster is labeled "Sweeneys & Co. Wheeling. Va.," while the base of the adjoining pilaster bears the label "Sweeney & Son. Wheeling W.Va."

Wheeling could build almost anything, thanks in great measure to its talented cadre of German craftsmen and builders. Known as the Nail City, it also became famous for its pressed, stamped-metal "Wheeling Ceilings." Rows and rows of townhouses still exist in Wheeling, the

Blakeley mansion, near Charles Town.

United Carbon Building, Charleston.

only city of any real urban character when West Virginia was created.

Three of the new state's first priorities were to provide for a state university, a state penitentiary, and to decide where to locate the capital. After alternating between Wheeling and Charleston, the latter city was finally selected as the permanent seat of government, and it soon began to grow accordingly. Charleston's 1870s Kanawha Presbyterian Church was designed by another Cincinnati architect, M. E. Anderson, and its interior is lit by richly colored stained-glass windows by Tiffany.

West Virginia University, located in Morgantown, has grown over the years to become a fascinating architectural amalgam. One of the earliest architects associated with the university was Elmer Forrest Jacobs, who also embellished Morgantown with some of its finest Victorian-era mansions and commercial structures. Jacobs was the first, and for many years the only, West Virginia member of the American Institute of Architects.

The original architect for the State Penitentiary, a grim, foreboding Gothic pile at Moundsville, is believed to have been Joseph Sinclair Fairfax. At the turn of the 20th century, Wheeling architects Franzheim and Giesey designed a huge addition. Ironically, West Virginia's state motto, Montani Semper Liberi, which translates as "Mountaineers [are] always free," appears high above the prison's battlemented entrance.

Edward Bates Franzheim, Millard F. Giesey, and their sometime partner Frederic F. Faris, were the state's leading architectural triumvirate for many years. Though their work centered in the Wheeling area, they designed a courthouse for

Mineral County, and did several buildings at the turn of the century in Marion County's overnight oil boomtown, Mannington.

Parkersburg, a city that had already grown rich on oil, was large enough to have its own architects. Parkersburg's Juliana and Ann streets contain the state's most concentrated grouping of Italianate, Second Empire, and Queen Anne mansions, all typical of upscale Victorian-era design. Many were designed by Richard H. Adair and William Howe Patton. H. Rus Warne, a Parkersburg native, practiced in his hometown only briefly before moving to Charleston. He became one of the state's most important early 20th-century architects, and founded a firm that still exists. Two of his most interesting and unusual commissions were for the 1907 Jamestown Exposition, held in Norfolk, Virginia. His colonial-revival West Virginia Building remains standing there, but his "Coal Column," an obelisk constructed of coal from 19 different West Virginia seams, is gone.

Huntington, Collis P. Huntington's planned town on the Ohio at the western terminus of his Chesapeake & Ohio Railway, became headquarters for many coal companies with the development of the southern coalfields. Its downtown skyline grew tall, and Fifth Avenue became a street of churches, where Gothic towers share honors with Romanesque arches and Ionic porticos.

With coal came the company town, the most maligned and most misunderstood category of West Virginia architecture. Castigated as monotonous, poorly constructed, and horribly located, some company towns were all of the above. Others were model communities. At Gary, in

McDowell County, the U.S. Coal and Coke Company maintained an in-house staff of architects and engineers who, among other duties, designed houses, churches, stores, and even baseball diamonds. No matter that the drawing of an onion dome for a proposed eastern Orthodox Church appears more like something from Vidalia than from Muscovy, the company tried earnestly to provide its work force with amenities far beyond basic requirements.

Many coal-company owners lived outside the state, and built palatial houses elsewhere with their West Virginia profits. One who stayed home was James E. Watson, who built High Gate in Fairmont. The state's most remarkable Tudor Revival mansion, it was designed by Philadelphia architect Horace Trumbauer. Bluefield architect Alex B. Mahood, trained at the Ecole des Beaux Arts in Paris, designed mansions for magnates of the southern coalfields, and embellished Bluefield's residential districts with some of the grandest Georgian Revival houses in the state. Bluefield is also home to a small building that is among West Virginia's architectural jewels. Sacred Heart Church is one of several projects during the 1920s that resulted from the inspired partnership of John J. Swint, Roman Catholic Bishop of West Virginia, and Edward J. Weber, architect of Pittsburgh. Wheeling's St. Joseph Cathedral, a magnificent stone edifice that takes its architectural cues from Lombard Romanesque churches of medieval Italy, is the capstone of their remarkable collaboration.

The Depression of the 1930s hit West Virginia hard. Yet, some of our most significant and important buildings were products of this pivotal decade. Cass

Gilbert's magnificent State Capitol in Charleston had been started in 1924, but was not completed until 1932. Its main wing follows the architectural pattern established by the U.S. Capitol, though its gilded dome rises five feet higher. Next door is the Executive Mansion, designed by Charleston architect Walter F. Martens.

With Eleanor Roosevelt's encouragement, the nation's first subsistence homestead project was created in West Virginia. The federal government purchased the Arthur family farm in Preston County. A number of houses, all with enough land for a vegetable garden, are still occupied by the families for whom they were built. Two other West Virginia communities were created under the same auspices, Eleanor in Putnam County and Tygart Valley Homesteads at Dailey in Randolph County.

Also during the Depression, a number of state parks were developed, with design assistance from the National Park Service and building assistance from the Civilian Conservation Corps (CCC). Log cabins, concession stands, picnic pavilions, stables, and other structures reflected the rustic flavor then deemed appropriate for park design. Pioneers of the olden days would have deplored the round logs, heavy chinking, and chopped-off ends of CCC work. After more than a half century, these "Lincoln Log" buildings in parks such as Babcock in Fayette County, Watoga in Pocahontas, and Lost River in Hardy, seem just right for their woodsy settings. Hawks Nest, in Fayette County, has several Depression-era buildings along with a 1960s lodge designed by the well-known Cambridge, Massachusetts, firm TAC: The Architects Collaborative. The lodge, an angular composition of poured-in-place concrete and brick, has yet to appear as comfortable in its spectacular natural setting as its 1930s companions.

Modern architecture in West Virginia has kept up the pace of excellence that earlier generations established. Walter Martens and his son, Robert, with help from Eliel Saarinen, gave Charleston's riverfront a superb International Style skyscraper just before World War II when the United Carbon Building was completed. A wing of the Huntington Museum of Art, built in 1968–70, is the last work of the internationally famous architect Walter Gropius. In 1975, Clarksburg opened a new public library designed by Marcel Breuer, adding another distinctive element to its architecturally rich downtown. In the 1980s, Michael Graves designed one of his signature buildings for the Erickson Alumni Center at West Virginia University. Perhaps the most unusual of the state's religious structures is in Marshall County, near Moundsville. At the end of one of West Virginia's most tortuous country roads stands a splendid vision of Indian Hindu architecture: the Hare Krishna Palace of Gold. Tenderly crafted in the 1970s by disciples of the faith using "how to" books, it incorporates marble, semi-precious stones, gold leaf, and stained glass. Charleston's brand new U.S. Courthouse by architects Skidmore, Owings & Merrill combines state-of-the-art functionality with a design based on one of the world's oldest architectural styles. Its huge lotus columns harken back to the time of the Pharaohs.

Architecture is alive and well in West Virginia. The framers of the state seal would be happy to know that many of the old log farmhouses peculiar to the region still stand, now alongside a myriad of buildings representing every conceivable type and style, and built of materials they could not have imagined.

S. Allen Chambers Jr.
Society of Architectural Historians

Art and Artists

The development of art in West Virginia followed similar lines to that of elsewhere in America. The earliest artistic activity was utilitarian in nature, including botanical and topographic documentation and decorative arts and crafts.

Portraiture emerged as soon as a sufficient population base existed. The Baltimore portrait artist John Drinker was active in what is now the Eastern Panhandle possibly as early as 1788 and eventually settled there. Joshua Johnson, the nation's earliest identified professional African-American painter, and Charles Peale Polk were among many itinerant portraitists who followed Drinker's lead in the ensuing decades. Another was Swiss immigrant David Boudon, who was in Wheeling by 1816. Other pioneer portrait artists of the Upper Ohio Valley region were painters Jarvis Hanks, John Hanna, and Charles Sullivan, and the sculptor John Airy. Hanks was among the first of his trade to visit the Kanawha Valley, where he was active by the mid-1820s. George Esten Cooke was one of several visiting portraitists who found clients in the fashionable mineral springs region of the state.

West Virginia's scenic beauty attracted the attention of landscape painters, including George Beck, as early as the 1790s. Harpers Ferry, in particular, became one of the most frequently painted towns in America during the early 19th century. The state's rugged interior was explored during the ensuing decades by several notable members of the so-called Hudson River School of American landscape painters, including T. Worthington Whittredge and William L. Sonntag.

Prominent native and resident artists of the antebellum and early statehood eras included Martinsburg's David Hunter Strother (1816–88), and Jefferson Countian David English Henderson (1832–87). Strother, also known as Porte Crayon, worked as a portrait painter during the late 1830s and 1840s before gaining employment as a writer and illustrator for *Harper's New Monthly Magazine* during the early 1850s. His work in the latter capacity made him one of the best known artists in the nation by the end of the decade. A protégé of Strother, Henderson worked as an illustrator and painter of portraits and Civil War subjects.

The flood of news illustrations depicting West Virginia that appeared nationally during the Civil War likely contributed to the new wave of landscape painters who visited the state, briefly for the most part, in the decades following the war. Included in this group were Alexander Wyant, Hugh Bolton Jones, and many others whose works reflected the newer and more intimate Barbizon esthetic in landscape art. Another, with family ties to Wheeling, was Thomas P. Anshutz, a prominent figure in American art history. Anshutz's famous painting of workers at a Wheeling nail factory, *Ironworkers' Noontime* (1880), is considered a pivotal work in the development of Social Realist painting in America.

The late 19th century witnessed the birth of several West Virginia artists who achieved national prominence. William Robinson Leigh (1866–1956) of Falling Waters, Berkeley County, painted many masterful portraits and landscapes based upon West Virginia subjects before earning recognition as one of the leading artists of the Old West. A Monongalia Countian, Blanche Lazzell (1878–1956), spent her life traveling back and forth between West Virginia and Provincetown, Massachusetts, where she became a prominent printmaker and abstract painter. Piedmont native Leslie Thrasher (1889–1936) gained fame as one of the nation's leading magazine cover illustrators, while Preston County's William Rudolf O'Donovan (1844–1920) achieved international renown as a sculptor of bust portraits and memorials.

Like their colleagues across the nation, West Virginia artists experimented with the divergent realist and abstract currents in vogue during the early and mid-20th century. In the Northern Panhandle, Virginia B. Evans was both an Impressionist and Abstract Expressionist painter, as well as a skillful designer of art deco glass. A cousin of Blanche Lazzell, Grace Martin Taylor, explored a wide range of modernist currents in her work as an artist and as a leading teacher in the Kanawha Valley, as did Katherine Burnside in Parkersburg. Clarksburg native James Edward Davis's progressive experiments with color and motion eventually led him to a pioneering role in the field of abstract filmmaking. These and other regional figures contributed to a flowering of artistic activity in the state during the mid-20th century which witnessed the birth of arts centers and museums across the state, many of which survive to the present.

John A. Cuthbert
WVU Libraries

Gabriel Arthur

Frontiersman Gabriel Arthur is believed to have been the first white person to see the Kanawha Valley, having visited the area with a band of Indians in 1674. Little is known of Arthur personally, other than he was a young man, possibly 19, when his great adventure began, and probably of English birth. He traveled with James Needham and others sent out by Abraham Wood from Fort Henry (present Petersburg, Virginia) to explore western lands. Needham was killed by an Indian guide, but Arthur traveled widely with the natives, possibly as their captive though he is said to have married an Indian woman. He ventured as far south as Spanish West Florida (present Alabama) and apparently participated in raiding the Shawnee in the Ohio Valley. Eventually he reached present West Virginia, following the Big Coal River to its mouth at the Kanawha River. Though in hostile Shawnee territory, the southern Indians with whom Arthur traveled were welcomed by local Moneton Indians, themselves perhaps a Shawnee remnant. Their large village was located at present St. Albans at the mouth of Big Coal River. Arthur's journey, which began in May 1673, ended with his return to Fort Henry with several Indians and a load of furs in June 1674.

See also Needham and Arthur Expedition

Arthurdale

Arthurdale, located in Preston County west of Kingwood, was the first of many experimental communities founded under the National Industrial Recovery Act of 1933. The act authorized $25 million in federal funds to create subsistence homesteads in the United States. The idea was to relocate impoverished families from industrial centers to government-planned communities. More than 100 New Deal communities were established between 1934 and 1944, three of which were in West Virginia.

The Arthurdale story began when First Lady Eleanor Roosevelt traveled to coal camps in northern West Virginia in August 1933. At Scotts Run and other places, she found families hard hit by the Depression and felt compelled to help. She developed a plan with government officials and relief organizations to relocate families from these destitute areas to a more rural setting.

By October 1933, the federal government had purchased a 1,200-acre farm from Richard Arthur, for whom the community was named. One hundred sixty-five houses were built by and for the homesteaders between 1934 and 1937. Each house had electricity, indoor plumbing, and enough land for a garden and livestock. Homesteaders paid a monthly rent which included utilities, on the un-

Architectural study of the first Arthurdale homestead.

derstanding that they could later buy their homes.

A school was constructed in 1935, based upon the principles of progressive education advanced by John Dewey and others. The curriculum stressed individualism and a hands-on approach, including handicrafts and the manual arts.

Employment was provided for the homesteaders in cooperative businesses such as communal farming, factory work, and cottage industries. The isolated nature of the community, weak consumer demand, and a small work force caused many of the businesses to shut down after a few years. As the American economy boomed during World War II and after, the issues of poverty and unemployment which had led to Arthurdale's creation faded from memory. In 1947, the federal government sold the homes and community buildings to the homesteaders. Eleanor Roosevelt continued to visit Arthurdale after the federal government liquidated the project.

Today, Arthurdale is a National Historic District. It is also a sizable unincorporated community, with about 700 residents and all but one of the original houses still standing. Arthurdale Heritage, Inc., was founded in 1985 to preserve the history of Arthurdale. A museum and research center are housed in five of the original structures, including a working 1930s homestead.

See also Eleanor, Great Depression, Tygart Valley Homesteads

Jennifer Bonnette
Arthurdale Heritage

Bryan Ward, ed., *A New Deal for America: Proceedings from a National Conference on New Deal Communities*, 1995.

The Artists' Excursion

The Baltimore & Ohio Railroad was completed from Baltimore to Wheeling in December 1852 and opened to the public the following year. Although revenues from hauling coal and other freight soon followed, the railroad was faced with competition from the Chesapeake & Ohio Canal and an uncertain future. One of the railroad executives, William Prescott Smith, decided to increase passenger traffic by promoting the tourism potential along the railroad line.

Smith pursued this goal by inviting many of the nation's prominent artists, photographers, and writers to take an excursion train from Baltimore to Wheeling. The train would stop along the route wherever the passengers wanted, and the cars were luxuriously furnished with just about anything the group needed, including a photographic darkroom.

The train left Camden Station in Baltimore early on the morning of June 1, 1858, with about 50 passengers. They included artist and writer David Hunter Strother, artists Thomas Rossiter, Thomas

The Artists' Excursion on the B&O.

Hicks, and Asher Durand, and *New York Times* editor Henry Jarvis Raymond.

After stopping several times in Maryland so the guests could take photographs, the train arrived at Harpers Ferry. The train then proceeded through Martinsburg to Berkeley Springs, where the passengers spent the night. Much of the area opened by the railroad was in what later became West Virginia. It was wild, beautiful, and unknown to most Americans. Many sites along the route were described by the excursionists, including Piedmont, Grafton, Altamont, Cranberry Summit, Cheat River, and Tygart's Valley River.

The group reached Wheeling on June 4 and returned to Baltimore the following day. The excursionists recorded their impressions in numerous photographs and sketches, the best-known being David Hunter Strother's "Artists' Excursion over the Baltimore & Ohio Rail Road," published with an article of his in *Harper's New Monthly Magazine* in June 1859.

See also Art and Artists, Baltimore & Ohio Railroad

William D. Theriault
Bakerton

Francis Asbury

Bishop Francis Asbury was born in Staffordshire, England, August 20 or 21, 1745. By 1770, Asbury was part of the growing Methodist movement. In 1771 he volunteered to come to America, and Methodist founder John Wesley appointed him one year later as one of his assistants in America. The Christmas Conference held in Baltimore in 1784 founded the Methodist Society in America, and Francis Asbury was appointed as its first superintendent. In that same year, a regular

Methodist Society was formed in Greenbrier County. In 1787, Asbury broke with English Methodists and established the Methodist Episcopal Church in America.

Asbury and the Methodists were part of the great revival known as the Great Awakening. Emotional gatherings drew large crowds, and denominations connected with the Great Awakening spread rapidly. This excitement led to a strong sense of evangelism, which pushed men such as Asbury westward. Records show that Asbury first set foot in present West Virginia on July 18, 1776, outside of Berkeley Springs. He notes in his journal that the area was "Good for the health, but most injurious to religion." He worked extensively in what is now the Eastern Panhandle, preaching and lecturing almost every day, before continuing farther into Western Virginia.

In 1785 or 1786, Rehoboth Church was built in what is now Monroe County. Bishop Asbury is said to have preached the dedication sermon. He later held sessions of the Methodist Greenbrier Conference at the church in 1792, 1793, and 1796. Eventually, Asbury crisscrossed much of the state and brought many people into the Methodist Church. Bishop Asbury died March 31, 1816.

See also Methodists, Rehoboth Church

Bil Lepp
South Charleston

L. C. Rudolph, *Francis Asbury*, 1966.

Harrison Ash

Lawman Harrison Ash apparently was born in Scott County, Virginia, May 26, 1853. He and his three brothers migrated to southern West Virginia at the turn of the century. The completion of the Chesapeake & Ohio Railroad in 1873 had brought big changes, and the local coal industry was booming. His brothers took advantage of the opportunities by opening saloons and working as merchants. Standing six-foot-four and weighing more than 275 pounds, Ash seemed tailor-made for the challenge of law enforcement in the rough coal and railroad towns.

Formerly a railroad detective and an agent for the Baldwin-Felts Detective Agency, Ash in about 1902 became chief of police at the New River Gorge town of Thurmond. The job was not an easy one. His duties included keeping peace in the saloons that lined the south side of the New River across from Thurmond. It was his responsibility to keep the ruffians, gamblers, and thieves who roamed the muddy streets of "Southside" from interfering with the respectable citizens and visitors of Thurmond proper. Ash used all necessary force in accomplishing his purposes and himself became part of the enduring folklore of violence and colorful mayhem associated with the Thurmond community. Legend maintains that he frequented the drinking establishments that he patrolled, and in his off hours he ran his own saloon.

Ash died December 12, 1924. The vision of Ash, in his uniform and Stetson hat and carrying a notched pistol, was long recalled in Fayette County.

See also Thurmond

Melody Bragg
National Mine Health and Safety Academy

Ashford General Hospital

In August 1942 the U.S. Army purchased the Greenbrier Hotel and 7,000 acres of surrounding countryside from the Chesapeake & Ohio Railway for $3.3 million, and began converting it into a military hospital for sick and wounded soldiers and airmen. Named for Army physician Col. Bailey K. Ashford (1873–1934), the new hospital received its first patients in November. Before Ashford General closed in mid-1946, more than 25,000 seriously ill and wounded patients—including many from West Virginia—had received treatment.

Ashford employed 45 doctors, 100 nurses, and 500 enlisted men. Assisting them were 200 WACs, 35 civilian nurses, some 500 civilian employees, and scores of Red Cross volunteers. Seven hundred German prisoners of war maintained the grounds and buildings. Families, friends, and good-hearted people from throughout West Virginia came to visit and help the men toward a speedy recovery. The recovering servicemen could use all of the famous resort's special facilities— swimming pool, golf courses, tennis courts, hiking and biking trails, and so on—and monthly dances with live entertainment were held. Today, few of The Greenbrier's visitors know of the vital role it played during World War II, but

"This country will require much work"

"We journeyed on through devious lonely wilds, where no food might be found, except what grew in the woods, or was carried with us. We met with two women who were going to see their friends, and to attend the quarterly meeting at Clarksburg. Near midnight we stopped at William Anglin's, who hissed his dogs at us; but the women were determined to get to quarterly meeting, so we went in. Our supper was tea. . . . I lay on the floor on a few deer skins with the fleas. That night our poor horses got no corn; and the next morning they had to swim across Monongahela. . . . O, how glad should I be of a plain, clean plank to lie on, as preferable to most of the beds; and where the beds are in a bad state, the floors are worse. The gnats are almost as troublesome here, as the mosquitoes in the lowlands of the sea-board. This country will require much work to make it tolerable."

—Francis Asbury *Journal* (1788)

those who were there have vivid recollections of Ashford General Hospital as a Shangri-la for wounded servicemen.

See also The Greenbrier

Louis E. Keefer
Reston, Virginia

Louis E. Keefer, "Ashford General Hospital: The Greenbrier Goes to War," *Goldenseal,* Fall 1993; Keefer, *Shangri-La for Wounded Soldiers: The Greenbrier as a World War II Army Hospital,* 1995.

Atheneum Prison

The Atheneum, Wheeling's Civil War military prison, located at the southeast corner of 16th (then John) and Market streets, was a four-story structure built in 1853–54 as a warehouse for the Crescent Manufacturing Company, a maker of boiler, sheet, and railway iron. The first and second floors were used by the company while the third and fourth were outfitted as a theater, which opened in January 1855. In 1856 a troupe presented "Uncle Tom's Cabin." The prison took its name from the theater, the Atheneum.

In the fall of 1861, after the Civil War began, two large rooms on the second floor of the building were rented by the government for use as winter quarters for secessionist prisoners held at Camp Carlile on Wheeling Island. The theater portion of the building was effectively closed by this action.

From October 1863 to October 1865, the entire building was rented for use as a military prison, barracks, and hospital. Called by some the "Lincoln Bastille," the Atheneum held Confederate prisoners captured in battle, civilians who refused to take the oath of allegiance, rebel spies, court-martialed soldiers, and those guilty of various other offenses such as bushwhacking. Eventually most of the prisoners were transferred to Camp Chase near Columbus, Ohio, so the number of people confined fluctuated from well over 100 to as few as 50 or 60.

After the war, the building contained a malt business and agriculture store. It burned down in October 1868. In modern times, the Pythian Building occupied the site but was demolished for a private park.

See also Civil War, Wheeling

Margaret Brennan
Wheeling Area Historical Society

Edward Phillips, *The Atheneum,* 1999.

Mary Meek Atkeson

Writer Mary Meek Atkeson was born February 23, 1884, on the family farm at Buffalo, Putnam County. She earned bachelor's and master's degrees at West Virginia University. Her master's thesis, titled *West Virginia Writers 1669–1913,* cataloged the work of 87 individuals. Further graduate study followed at the University of Missouri, where she also taught English during the academic year 1914–15. Returning to her home state, she taught at WVU and in 1919 completed a Ph.D. in Literature at Ohio State University. She was married to Blaine Free Moore.

Atkeson was the daughter of Thomas Clark Atkeson, first dean of the School of Agriculture at West Virginia University. Inheriting her interest in country life and agriculture from her father, Atkeson wrote, with him, *Pioneering in Agriculture* (1937). Other books included *The Woman on the Farm* (1924) and *The Shining Hours* (1927). Four of Atkeson's plays were published in a 1922 collection: "The Cross Roads Meetin' House," "Don't," "Will," and "The Good Old Days." Various stories, poems, and articles appeared in such publications as *Ladies' Home Journal, McCall's, The Country Gentleman, Good Housekeeping, The English Journal, The Penwoman,* and *The Farmer's Wife.* Mary Meek Atkeson was well known throughout the region as educator, author, and authority on country life and agriculture. Atkeson died on the family farm in Putnam County in 1971.

Barbara Smith
Philippi

Jim Comstock, *West Virginia Heritage Encyclopedia,* 1974.

George W. Atkinson

George Wesley Atkinson, tenth governor of West Virginia, was born in Charleston, June 29, 1845. His ancestors from Cumberland County, England, and County Armagh, Ireland, had settled in Virginia by

1750 and on the Ohio River by 1796. His parents were Col. James and Miriam Rader Atkinson. Other members of the accomplished family spelled the surname differently, including Thomas Clark Atkeson, the first dean of the School of Agriculture at West Virginia University and international leader of the Grange; Willis (William) Atkeson, governor of Georgia; and Mary Meek Atkeson, writer.

One of West Virginia's best-educated governors, Atkinson earned a master's degree and a Ph.D. from Ohio institutions, and studied law in Washington. He was twice married, to Ellen Eagan, with whom he had five children, and to Myra Camden. Before being elected governor, Atkinson served as Charleston postmaster, Wheeling newspaper editor, U.S. internal revenue agent, U.S. marshal, and congressman for the First District in northern West Virginia. He was a leader of the Methodists, the Masons, and the Republican Party.

Atkinson was elected governor in 1896, in an upset victory over Cornelius C. Watts of Charleston which ended 26 years of Democratic rule. As governor, Atkinson was a moderate progressive. He called for an eight-hour workday, the prohibition of the employment of children under 14 years of age, improved working conditions for women, and safety regulations in manufacturing and mining. The legislature failed to enact most of his proposals, but Atkinson continued to call for change. He championed high-quality public education, a permanent road system, and open and equal immigration, and he worked against corruption in politics and professional lobbying. He spoke against the racist Jim Crow legislation that neighboring states were succumbing to, noting that West Virginia "has never adopted a law which abridged the rights and privileges of any of its citizens."

The most serious issue facing Governor Atkinson was a state financial crisis arising from expanded services and low taxes. He proposed increased corporate taxes, among other measures, and in this was opposed by Republican boss Stephen B. Elkins. Senator Elkins eventually agreed to a tax increase but with concessions that split the reform wing of the party.

After serving as governor from 1897 to 1901, Atkinson became the U.S. district attorney for the Southern District of West Virginia and was then appointed by President Theodore Roosevelt as judge of the U.S. Court of Claims. Popular as a speaker on politics, economics, literature, history, and religion, the scholarly Atkinson wrote 11 books of poetry and non-fiction, including *History of Kanawha County* (1876), *After the Moonshiners* (1881), *Prominent Men of West Virginia* (1890), and *Bench and Bar of West Virginia* (1919).

In 1899, Atkinson composed his own epitaph and sent it to a friend. It read, "He tried to be honest; he would not lie; he never intentionally wronged his fellowmen; he sought on all occasions to lift up his fellows; he was a friend of the poor and the helpless; he never stole a dollar or a cent; and his purpose was ever to do what he could to make the world broader and better and nobler and grander because he lived in it."

It was never used. Governor Atkinson lived another quarter century. He died April 4, 1925, and is buried in Charleston. His monument in Spring Hill Cemetery gives his name and dates and four words more: "Christian - Statesman - Scholar - Gentleman."

Barbara Smith
Philippi

George W. Atkinson and Alvaro F. Gibbins, *Prominent Men of West Virginia,* 1890; James Morton Callahan, *History of West Virginia, Old and New,* 1923; John G. Morgan, *West Virginia Governors, 1863–1980,* 1980.

Attorney General

The attorney general is West Virginia's chief legal officer, serving as the adviser to all agency heads in the executive branch, including the governor. As chief legal officer he handles all court suits in which the state is a party and supervises the legal business of state agencies. His office gives written opinions on questions of law and constitutionality on request of the legislature, public officials, and county prosecuting attorneys.

The attorney general is an independent officer, one of the five so-called constitutional officers, who, with the governor, make up the executive branch of West Virginia state government. He has been elected by popular vote since the first constitution in 1863. Although originally this official served for only two years, as did the governor and other state elected officials, today he serves a four-year term and may be reelected to an unlimited number of terms.

The attorney general is a key figure in the operation of government. Not only does he represent the state in all claims against the state, but he also is charged with the power to initiate criminal proceedings on office authority alone. The attorney general serves on numerous boards, such as the Housing Development Board, the Board of Public Works, and the Public Land Corporation. The varied functions of the attorney general can be seen by the extensive organization chart of the office. Divisions include matters dealing with civil rights, antitrust, consumer protection, health and human resources, and public safety. There is even a division that handles tax, revenue, education, arts, and transportation.

As an independently elected officer, the attorney general is a strong political figure, sometimes contending with the governor and other members of the executive branch. The formal and informal powers of the attorney general have expanded in recent years, and sometimes the office is a stepping stone to the governor's office.

See also Constitutional Officers, Executive Branch

Evelyn L. Harris
Charleston

Auditor

The auditor is West Virginia's official bookkeeper, whose job is to ensure the legality of the payment of funds from the state treasurer. The auditor is independently elected, one of the five constitutional officers who, with the governor, make up the executive branch of West Virginia state government.

The auditor performs a great variety of functions in the day-to-day operation of government. Although most of his time is involved with financial record keeping, he also receives and collects certain taxes and fees, provides services for business corporations in the state, is a member of the Board of Public Works (with numerous statutory duties connected to that position), and maintains a savings bond program for state employees. Since the early 1960s, the auditor has been the West Virginia official responsible for administering the so-called "218 agreements" for the Social Security Administration, which are required for government employees to be eligible for social security coverage.

The auditor not only has responsibility for the accounting of state funds, but also has jurisdiction over the finances of county government. He oversees the receipt of taxes that county sheriffs collect for the state government. The auditor is also charged with collecting and distributing public utility taxes for both the state and the counties.

Most of the duties of the auditor do not require policy decisions but are rather of a technical and formal nature. However, the concern of the auditor for the financial accountability of public officials, boards, and county sheriffs makes this office important. He must issue a warrant approving any expenditure of state funds and ascertain that the funds are available. He can disallow proposed expenditures by state agencies as well as the legislature. He is really a controller of the money. The nature of his duties requires independence, making it necessary for the auditor to be elected, not appointed. This has been the case since the constitution of 1863. While the office is elective every four years, it has been held by the Glen Gainer family for two generations.

See also Constitutional Officers, Executive Branch

Evelyn L. Harris
Charleston

Audra State Park

The 355-acre Audra State Park is located south of Philippi between U.S. 119 and U.S. 250 in Barbour County. Its forests and rhododendron thickets border the Middle Fork River, which flows through the park. In spring, melting snow and rains feed the river's boulder-filled channel.

Land within the park has been used in various ways. As the town of Audra, it was home to five families, a gristmill, and sawmill in 1900. The Baltimore & Ohio Railroad owned the surrounding property. The B&O had purchased the land to block plans by another railroad to extend its operations from Tygart Junction, a few miles north. In the early 20th century, loggers timbered in the area. From 1919 to 1923, Barbour County 4-H clubs used the area as a camp.

By 1944, the state of West Virginia had purchased 311 acres for the park. It bought an additional 44 acres in 1961. After a caretaker was hired in 1950, the state began to construct parking lots bordered with stonework, a swimming area, and bathhouse. The park was a day-use facility until the early 1960s, when land was cleared for campsites. Today, the park includes hiking trails, 65 camping sites, a river beach, and swimming area.

Pictorial Histories Publishing Company, *Where People and Nature Meet,* 1988.

Auger Mining

Auger mining uses large-diameter drills mounted on mobile equipment to bore into a coal seam. Holes are horizontally drilled at regular intervals to depths of as much as 1,000 feet. As the cutting head of the auger bites into the coalface, the cut coal is carried out by the screw portion of the bit. Once the hole is mined to its required depth, the auger machine is moved a few feet and another hole is drilled. Auger mining is a relatively low cost method of coal mining and is practical in areas where the overburden (material covering the coal seam) is too thick to be removed economically or where the coal seam is too thin for underground mining.

Auger mining was introduced to the West Virginia coalfields in the 1940s. Today, auger mining continues to be used as a surface mining method in West Virginia, usually on contour surface mines where augers drill the last available coal from the highwall. A recent offshoot of auger mining is the development of highwall miners. Also operating from a surface mine bench, these machines take a larger, deeper cut and use a cutting head similar to those on continuous miner machines.

See also Surface Mining

David J. Kessler
Miners' Health Safety and Training

Augusta County, Virginia

Named for Augusta, Princess of Wales, Augusta County was created November 12, 1738. Frederick County, named for Augusta's husband, the Prince of Wales, was created by the same act, which stipulated that both counties were created from the western lands of Orange County.

The county government of Augusta County was organized in 1745. The western boundary of Augusta was defined as "the utmost limits of Virginia," which meant the Mississippi River in the west and the headwaters of the Mississippi in the northwest. From Augusta County whole states would be carved, including Kentucky, Ohio, Indiana, Illinois, Michigan, and Wisconsin, as well as the southwest corner of Pennsylvania and most of West Virginia.

In 1732, John Lewis settled near the present site of Staunton and built a dwelling that also incorporated a fort, which became Fort Lewis. By the 1750s traders were active in the Ohio Valley sector of Augusta County. In 1754, during the French and Indian War, the governor of Virginia established a fort on the present site of Pittsburgh and offered land to those who would enlist to fight. In 1758 the fort was named Fort Pitt. The jurisdiction of the Augusta County court was extended, and additional justices were appointed to meet at Fort Pitt. Land grants in the area were recorded in the county courthouse in Staunton. Pennsylvania also claimed the area around Fort Pitt and created its own county of Westmoreland, which caused friction between the two colonies.

Despite the Royal Proclamation of 1763, which followed the French and Indian War and prohibited settlement beyond the Appalachian divide, people moved into western Augusta County and encountered various tribes of Indians. To alleviate hostilities the government negotiated treaties with the Indians. By the Treaty of Hard Labor in 1768 the Cherokees gave up claims to land in western Augusta that is in present West Virginia. That same year under the Treaty of Fort Stanwix the Iroquois and other tribes relinquished all claims to land lying west of the Alleghenies between the Ohio and Tennessee rivers. This included a separate agreement of some 2,862 square miles north of Little Kanawha River and west of the Monongahela River, known as Indiana Territory and including present northwestern West Virginia. This area was the subject of land development schemes variously called Grand Ohio Company, Vandalia Company, and Walpole Company organized in the spring of 1769. Claiming the Trans-Allegheny region on the basis of its charter of 1609, the Indian treaties, and possession, Virginia successfully defended its rights to the territory. Nonetheless Indian resistance continued into the 1790s.

The District of West Augusta was created in 1776, and the same year some inhabitants of that district petitioned the Continental Congress to establish a separate state called Westsylvania. On November 6, 1776, the District of West Augusta was divided into three new Virginia counties: Yohogania, Ohio, and Monongalia, and the Westsylvania proposal lost support. In 1779 commissioners from Virginia and Pennsylvania met to settle the boundary between the two colonies. Pittsburgh and the surrounding area were ceded to Pennsylvania. The small portion of Yohogania County that remained in Virginia was added to Ohio County. Yohogania became extinct.

Botetourt County had been formed from the southern half of Augusta County in 1770, and two years later Fincastle County was created from western Botetourt. Effective January 1, 1777, Fincastle County became extinct, and the counties of Kentucky, Washington, and Montgomery were created from the same area. Plans to establish a new state of Franklin to include land that had been part of southwestern Augusta in present east Tennessee and surrounding areas, including parts of southern West Virginia, were defeated when Virginia let it be known that it would not approve. Kentucky County was divided into three counties (Fayette, Jefferson, and Lincoln) in 1780, and six additional counties were organized before the territory originally known as Kentucky County became the state of Kentucky with Virginia's blessing in 1792.

Meanwhile, George Rogers Clark had led a successful military expedition into the Illinois territory, and Illinois County was formed from Augusta County in 1778. In 1784, Virginia ceded its claim to the Northwest Territory including Illinois County. That territory became the states of Ohio, Indiana, Illinois, Wisconsin, and Michigan. By the acts of cession of 1784 and 1792, Virginia trimmed its western boundary to the Ohio River, thus reducing its size to the present territory of Virginia and West Virginia. Also, by 1792 all that remained of the original Augusta County was 968 square miles situated between the Blue Ridge and Allegheny mountains. Today, its boundaries unchanged since 1791, Augusta County is a thriving agricultural community with a diverse economic base and its county seat still at Staunton.

Louis H. Manarin
Richmond, Virginia

John Lewis Peyton, *History of Augusta County, Virginia,* 1882; Morgan Poitiaux Robinson, *Virginia Counties: Those Resulting from Virginia Legislation,* 1916; Joseph Addison Waddell, *Annals of Augusta County, Virginia,* 1902.

Augusta Heritage Center

The Augusta Heritage Center of Davis & Elkins College promotes activities pertaining to traditional and ethnic folklife, folk art, and crafts. Located in Elkins, the center attracts more than 2,000 people annually for intensive week-long programs, with thousands more attending public concerts, dances, and festivals. A year-round center with a staff of seven, Augusta sponsors field research and documentation projects within the state.

Augusta was begun in 1973 by a group of Randolph County women who were concerned about the preservation and conservation of traditional crafts. Originally the region was a part of Augusta County, Virginia, thus the name. Twenty-two students participated the first year. The program quickly added an emphasis on traditional performance arts and folklore. In 1981, Augusta was acquired and hosted by Davis & Elkins College. Throughout the next two decades, the offerings increased, adding various regional folk arts, traditional crafts, children and senior programs, and more performance venues, including the Augusta Heritage Festival.

Augusta is best known for its educational workshops. Begun in 1972, these have brought together master artists, musicians, dancers, craftspeople, and enthusiasts of all ages. Participants range from complete novices to professional artists, and come from nearly every state and several countries. The themes are not confined to West Virginia or Appalachia. Rather, they include vocal traditions, old-time music, blues, Cajun and Creole, Irish, French-Canadian, swing, guitars, dulcimers, and the folklore, crafts, food ways, and dance forms associated with these traditions. Augusta attracts top practitioners in all these fields, who impart their knowledge to workshop participants.

Augusta's mission includes documenting, promoting, and nurturing folk traditions. The West Virginia Folk Art Apprenticeship Program, established in 1989, helps to preserve West Virginia's traditions for future generations through funding of one-on-one apprenticeships. Augusta's research and documentation of folk artists have resulted in the production of more than 40 compact disks, audiocassettes, and video documentaries of West Virginia's traditions and culture. The Augusta Collection of Folk Culture at Davis & Elkins College's Booth Library offers scholars access to a large collection of field recordings, oral histories, historical concert tapes, and photographs. A large and very active website offers links to numerous individual artisans and musicians.

Gerald Milnes
Augusta Heritage Center

Averell's Raid

Averell's Raid of August 1863 was the first of three Union cavalry raids launched from West Virginia toward Confederate railroads and troop and supply concentrations in western Virginia during the latter half of 1863. The second raid in November culminated in a Union victory in the Battle of Droop Mountain, while the third, known as the Salem Raid, took place in December and resulted in partial destruction of the Virginia & Tennessee Railroad, a key Confederate communications link. The commander of all three raids, Brig. Gen. William Woods Averell (1832–1900), regarded the Salem Raid as the greatest success.

Averell in 1863 was a 31-year-old career officer, eight years out of West Point, where he was remembered more for his horsemanship than his academic performance. He had an adventurous early career, but as a field commander he had been less than successful. His posting to West Virginia amounted to a punishment for failures during the Chancellorsville campaign, and he would be removed from command again by Maj. Gen. Philip H. Sheridan for his performance in Sheridan's 1864 Shenandoah Valley campaign.

Averell's West Virginia command, consisting primarily of cavalry and mounted infantry from West Virginia and Pennsylvania, was ordered south from Moorefield on August 12, the objectives being to destroy saltpeter works near Franklin, to disperse Confederate troops from the Greenbrier Valley, and to capture the Virginia Supreme Court of Appeals library in Lewisburg for the new state of West Virginia. The raiders accomplished the first two objectives—destroying the works at Franklin on August 19 and forcing Confederate Gen. William L. "Mudwall" Jackson out of Pocahontas County on August 22. In addition they destroyed a supply base and another saltpeter works in nearby Virginia. But when Averell turned toward Lewisburg he encountered resistance. At Rocky Gap near White Sulphur Springs on August 26, he met a Confederate force commanded by Maj. Gen. Samuel Jones. After a two-day engagement, Averell withdrew, leaving Jones in command of the field. Despite considerable harassment from rebel guerrillas during his retreat, Averell reached Beverly on August 31, with his command intact but without the law books.

See also Civil War

John Alexander Williams
Appalachian State University
William Woods Averell, *Ten Years in the Saddle: The Memoirs of William Woods Averell,* Edward K. Eckert and Nicholas J. Amato, eds., 1978.

Aviation

Before World War I, aircraft were a novelty in West Virginia and most other places. The use of airplanes during the European war demonstrated the effectiveness of powered flight and brought legitimacy to aviation for commercial as well as military purposes. In 1921 three MB-2 twin-engine bombers and several smaller planes were brought to West Virginia from Langley, Virginia, to assist in putting down the Mine Wars. The planes landed on a makeshift grass airfield in Kanawha City, now a dense residential neighborhood of Charleston.

After 1920, aviation expanded rapidly in West Virginia. In 1922, the first Morgantown airport was built where the WVU Coliseum is now located. The present Morgantown Municipal Airport opened in 1939, three miles north of downtown. In 1923, Shepherd Field (now the Eastern West Virginia Regional Airport) opened in Martinsburg. Then in 1927, Wertz Field near Dunbar was constructed to serve Charleston and the Kanawha Valley. The 1930s saw construction of numerous airports. Tri-County Airport, now the Harrison-Marion Regional Airport at Bridgeport, began as a grass airstrip in 1935. By 1940 there were approximately 125 airfields in the state.

Wertz Field was closed during World War II to make room for a plant producing synthetic rubber for the war, and in 1947 Kanawha Airport was opened at Charleston. Three mountains were leveled to construct the airport, later renamed Yeager Airport for Gen. Chuck Yeager, West Virginia's World War II ace fighter pilot and the man who broke the sound barrier.

Today West Virginia has 32 airports, nine of which offer scheduled commercial air service. In addition to Morgantown, Harrison-Marion, and Yeager, the commercial airports are Tri-State Airport in Huntington (1952), Raleigh County Memorial Airport near Beckley (1952), Wood County Airport near Parkersburg (1946), Greater Cumberland Regional Airport at Wiley Ford (1946), Mercer County Airport near Princeton (1953), and the Greenbrier Valley Airport at Lewisburg (1968). General aviation airports, which serve mostly private planes, are becoming increasingly important throughout the state.

In 1939 a small airplane, a Stinson Reliant owned by All American Aviation, took off from Latrobe, Pennsylvania, hooking a mailbag suspended from poles and flying on to a waiting crowd in Morgantown. This was the inaugural flight for rural airmail service. This system of picking up and dropping off mail bags in flight at many small airports was soon discontinued, but the airline went on to greater success. All American changed its name to Allegheny Airlines in 1953 and in 1997 to US Airways. Today US Airways, which serves the entire Southeast from Charlotte, North Carolina, is the primary

DC-3 on the runway at Kanawha Airport, about 1950.

air carrier at seven of the nine commercial airports in West Virginia.

West Virginia has had aircraft industries since early in the 20th century. In 1927, Fokker Aircraft of America opened in Glen Dale, Marshall County. Pioneer airplane designer and manufacturer Anthony H. G. Fokker operated the plant constructing the F-10A, a popular three-engine commercial aircraft that competed with the Ford Tri-motor. Fokker, a German firm, is best known as the builder of the famous Fokker Tri-plane used by the Red Baron, Baron Von Richtofen, in World War I.

Today, aviation manufacturing takes place at a number of locations in West Virginia. Tiger Aircraft makes the classic Tiger sports plane at Martinsburg, and Sino Swearingen expects to produce the SJ30-2 business jet there as well. There is a thriving airport service industry at the Bridgeport airport, including Pratt & Whitney, Bombardier, and others. Lockheed Martin operates in nearby Clarksburg.

West Virginia's best known aviators include Rose Agnes Rolls Cousins, a participant in the World War II pilot training program at West Virginia State College and one of the early black women civilian pilots. Cousins and fellow West Virginia State student George Spencer "Spanky" Roberts graduated through the 1939 Civilian Pilot Training Act. Roberts, William Lee Hill, and John Lyman Whitehead went on to become Tuskegee Airmen. A member of the 302nd Fighter Squadron, the nation's first black flying unit, Roberts eventually became the commander of the 99th Pursuit Squadron.

Another West Virginian, Gen. James K. McLaughlin, flew the B-17 bomber and led the raid over Schweinfurt, Germany. This was the largest Allied daytime bombing raid during World War II. He returned to Charleston after the war and organized the 167th Fighter Squadron, which became the West Virginia Air National Guard. The 167th moved to Martinsburg in 1955, leaving behind the newly created 130th Troop Carrier Squadron in Charleston.

Yeager, a P-51 Mustang fighter pilot during World War II, is the most famous West Virginia aviator. Breaking the sound barrier in December 1953, he was immortalized in Tom Wolfe's 1980 book, *The Right Stuff,* and the later movie of the same title. Other notable West Virginia aviators include Stephen Coonts, a navy pilot during the Vietnam War and best-selling author. Among Coonts's books are *Flight of the Intruder* and *The Cannibal Queen,* the latter named for his 1942 Stearman open-cockpit biplane. Col. Ralph D. Albertazzi of Berkeley County flew Air Force One for President Nixon.

U.S. Sen. Jennings Randolph (1902–98), a flight enthusiast and true pioneer of aviation, sponsored the 1938 Civil Aeronautics Act, Federal Airport Act, and legislation creating the Civil Air Patrol, National Air and Space Museum, and National Aviation Day. Randolph's sponsorship of the Airways Development Act creating the Airport Trust Fund led to the current grant system for expansion of the nation's airports.

In 1978, Congress deregulated the airline industry and many government subsidies were eliminated. Airlines ceased operating unprofitable routes, including many flights to smaller cities. West Virginia airports have not fully recovered the commercial service resulting from these losses. West Virginia airports are served by the West Virginia Aeronautics Commission, which was formed by the legislature in 1947 to foster aviation. The Aeronautics Commission cooperates with Federal Aviation Administration officials on matters of concern to West Virginia aviation.

David W. Bott
Morgantown Municipal Airport

Babcock Lumber Company

Founded in Pittsburgh in 1887, Babcock Lumber Company was a major operator in West Virginia's early timber industry and continues in business today. In the early 1900s, Babcock was the largest producer of hardwood lumber in the world, cutting more than 400,000 board feet per day. With timber, coal, and agricultural operations stretching from Pennsylvania to Georgia, the Babcock Lumber & Boom Company bought Thompson Lumber Company at Davis, Tucker County, in 1907. The assets included a softwood sawmill capable of cutting 100,000 board feet per day, a hardwood sawmill, box factory, planing mill, 40 miles of railroad, and 46,000 acres of forest. The Davis operation employed 500 men at its peak and remained in business until 1924. Other enterprises included a stone quarry for local construction, coal mines to fuel the steam logging locomotives, and farms in Tucker County producing thousands of bushels of potatoes, as well as cattle, sheep, and swine.

Babcock also operated a double band sawmill at Landisburg, coal mines at Clifftop, coke ovens at Sewell, and a narrow-gauge railroad connecting these operations in Fayette County, from 1912 to 1924. Babcock State Park was later built on the timbered-out lands donated by the Babcock Lumber Company to the state. The company continues today in wood processing and wholesale distribution, its West Virginia operations including a sawmill at Belington, a truss manufacturing plant at Glenville, and a distribution center at Gassaway.

See also Babcock State Park

William N. Grafton
WVU Extension Service

Babcock State Park

Babcock State Park in Fayette County offers visitors an opportunity to explore an expansive second-growth forest bisected by mountain streams and sprawling colonies of rhododendron. The rich forest cover and deep canyons of Glade Creek and Manns Creek provide food and shelter for wildlife, including bobcat, raccoon, red and gray squirrels, deer mice, moles, shrews, weasels, red fox, deer, and wild turkey. Hundreds of species of wildflowers grow throughout the park, and well over a hundred species of birds reside there during the breeding season.

Babcock, one of the earliest state parks, covers 4,127 acres. It was opened on July 1, 1937, and built as a public works program during the Great Depression. The main facilities and trails were constructed between 1934 and 1937 by young workers employed through the Civilian Conservation Corps. The main park headquarters, 13 cabins, a horse stable, superintendent's house, a natural swimming pool, and picnic facilities were constructed from locally quarried stone and American chestnut trees killed by the chestnut blight. The door latches and other metal work were hand-forged on site by CCC workers. The landscape had been completely denuded of vegetation by disastrous fires that followed logging of the site. By the mid-1950s, the hillsides were again green, and the streams supported populations of native trout.

Several additional facilities were added beginning in the 1960s, including a 40-site campground, the 18-acre Boley Lake, and 13 more cabins. A modern in-ground pool was built in the 1970s because the water quality in Glade Creek had been degraded by acid mine drainage from strip mines. The famous Glade Creek gristmill was completed in 1976 from parts of two older mills in other parts of West Virginia.

See also Babcock Lumber Company, Glade Creek Mill, State Parks

Emily Grafton
Morgantown

Back-to-the-Land Movement

Whether it was the rebirth of rural life, the death rattle of the hippie era, or a blend of both, the back-to-the-land movement of the 1970s left a lasting mark on the West Virginia countryside. The lure of cheap land, the state's natural beauty, and a desire to live simple, genuine, peaceful lives in an era of burgeoning materialism brought thousands of new pioneers to West Virginia's farm counties.

Most of the newcomers came from outside the state, were in their 20s, were several generations removed from life on the farm, had at least some college education, and were willing—at first, at least—to endure hardship in their quest to live off the land. They settled in virtually every county, avoiding only the state's southern coalfields where the scars of mining were evident and farmsteads were scarce due to the dominance of corporate landowners.

In 1970, Lincoln County became an early magnet for the newcomers, who began streaming into the state by the hundreds after an article appeared in the third issue of *Mother Earth News*, a magazine encouraging the homestead movement. In the article, a new settler wrote of buying 79 acres of Lincoln County land for $2,700. The article was advertised in a series of radio spots, and the rush was on.

The movement quickly spread across the state, fueled by nationally distributed Strout Real Estate catalogs featuring photos of rural properties at bargain prices. Concentrations of back-to-the-land settlers sprang up in the Greenbrier Valley counties of Pocahontas, Greenbrier, Summers, and Monroe, and in the rolling hills and overgrown pastures of north-central counties such as Roane, Calhoun, Ritchie, and Gilmer. Health food stores and natural foods co-ops blossomed in communities such as Hamlin and Spencer, where the newcomers' presence was most visible.

While communes were frequently a part of the back-to-the-land movement in other states, where land prices were higher, they were rare and mostly short-lived in West Virginia. Here, most homesteaders acquired individual farms of their own. An exception was the Catholic Workers farm established five miles north of Hamlin in 1970 by Kansan Chuck Smith, a former Franciscan brother, and Wheeling native Sandy Adams. For six years, Smith and Adams published the *Green Revolution*, a newsletter encouraging rural communities and Christian ideals, and established a land trust to protect farmland from future development.

Response to the newcomers by long-

May Day is celebrated at a back-to-the-land community in Summers County.

established local residents varied from amused neighborliness to outright hostility, depending in part on the newcomers' willingness to accept advice and to respect, if not embrace, local customs. Overall, despite vast differences in background, point of view, and mode of dress, the new arrivals and their established neighbors got along surprisingly well. Numerous farmsteaders immersed themselves in mountain music and took up Appalachian craftmaking. Today, many of the state's best artisans and traditional musicians trace their West Virginia roots to the back-to-the-land movement of the 1970s.

Living off the land proved to be difficult, however. Some homesteaders sustained themselves in cottage industries, usually crafts, or by taking work off the farm. A few others kept their farmsteads intact by turning to a more lucrative but illegal pursuit, the cultivation of marijuana. Perhaps most of those who came to West Virginia to live off the land eventually moved off their farms. Many left the state.

Those who stayed helped breathe new life into the hills and hollows abandoned by the job-seeking sons, daughters, and grandchildren of local residents. Some became activists in social and environmental issues that arose in subsequent years, including surface mining, the building of freeway-style highways into rural areas, the creation of Stonewall Jackson Lake, and the proposed construction of a high-voltage power line across a scenic stretch of Summers and Monroe counties.

Some shifted their focus from subsistence farming to operating shops, inns, and restaurants in nearby communities, or working in nearby towns and cities as teachers, lawyers, health care providers, sawmill operators, social workers, and journalists, among other pursuits. Today former back-to-the-landers are productive, active citizens in many areas, some of them among the state's important opinion makers.

Rick Steelhammer
Charleston Gazette

The Bailes Brothers

The Bailes Brothers, among the best country music performers of the 1940s, were the first West Virginians to become *Grand Ole Opry* stars. Born and reared in Kanawha County, Kyle (1915–96), Johnnie (1918–89), Walter (1920–2000), and Homer (b. 1922) struggled with their widowed mother to survive the Depression, and became increasingly inspired by the music they heard on radio and in church. As musicians the four brothers rarely worked together, but usually as duets. They played a variety of stringed instruments, and all of them sang. Known for their sincere emotional style, the

Johnnie and Walter Bailes with fiddler Del Heck and "Little Evy" Thomas.

brothers composed many secular and sacred songs. After playing for several years on various West Virginia radio stations, they moved to WSM Nashville and the *Opry* in October 1944. The following year they began recording for Columbia and later King, with "Dust On the Bible" and "I Want to be Loved" being two of their best original songs. Later, Walter composed "Give Mother My Crown," which became a Flatt and Scruggs classic. Late in 1946, the Bailes Brothers moved to KWKH Shreveport. First Walter, and later Homer, left music for the ministry, but they all continued to perform intermittently over the years.

Abby Gail Goodnite
University of Rio Grande
Ivan M. Tribe, *Mountaineer Jamboree: Country Music in West Virginia*, 1984.

Cleve Bailey

Congressman Cleveland Monroe "Cleve" Bailey represented West Virginia's third congressional district for eight terms in the U.S. House of Representatives, 1945–47 and 1949–63. Born July 15, 1886, on a farm in Pleasants County, Bailey was educated at West Liberty State College and at Geneva College in Pennsylvania. Before entering public service, he was a teacher and school administrator in Clarksburg, Clarksburg city councilman, and Associated Press editor for the *Clarksburg Exponent*.

Bailey was appointed as the assistant state auditor in 1933. He served until Governor Neely appointed him director of the budget in 1941, and he remained in the latter post until entering Congress. A Democrat, Bailey first won a seat in Congress by defeating Edward G. Rohrbough, a Republican from Glenville, in 1944. Rohrbough came back to defeat him in 1946, but Bailey won again in 1948 and in the next six contests. A New Deal

liberal, Bailey's main focus as a congressman was protection of West Virginia industries and workers, especially from foreign competition, and increased federal support of education. Following his departure from Congress, a school in Oklahoma was named in Bailey's honor.

The old third district included West Virginia's central counties, from Harrison south to Fayette. Redistricting after the 1960 Census put Bailey's Clarksburg hometown in the first district, and Bailey was defeated by Congressman Arch Moore in 1962. Bailey died July 13, 1965, in Charleston. There is a bust of him in the state capitol in Charleston, the only congressman to be so honored.

Michael K. Wilson
Charleston
Michael K. Wilson, "Cleveland M. Bailey-Mountaineer Congressman," M.A. final project, Marshall University Graduate College, 1999.

R. D. Bailey

Judge Robert Darius "R. D." Bailey was born July 6, 1883, at Baileysville, Wyoming County. He served as Wyoming County prosecuting attorney, as Democrat state chairman, as a state senator, and ran unsuccessfully in 1928 and 1948 for governor in the Democrat primary. R. D. Bailey was judge of Mingo County circuit court from 1921 to 1928.

Bailey came into wide prominence as the judge of the Matewan Massacre trial in 1921, and during the later trial and conviction of Levi Lane and Clyde Beale for the murder of Rissie Purdue. In the latter case, the jury failed to recommend mercy, and a death sentence by hanging was mandatory. While Beale's appeal was pending at the state Supreme Court, Judge Bailey learned that Beale had been convicted on perjured testimony. Convinced that a miscarriage of justice had taken place in his court and despite orders from the Supreme Court, Bailey refused in 1927 and 1928 to set a date for Beale's hanging. The sentence was later commuted to life imprisonment, and in 1949 Beale was pardoned by Governor Patteson.

Bailey was the grandson of James Bailey, the founder of Baileysville. At the age of 18, R. D. Bailey became a deputy for Sheriff John Ball. He graduated from Valparaiso University in Indiana in 1909 and started his law practice in Baileysville, where he remained until 1920 when he was elected circuit judge. In 1922, he moved to Pineville and remained there the rest of his life. Bailey returned to the practice of law after his service as circuit judge. Judge Bailey died October 24, 1961. The R. D. Bailey Lake is named in his honor.

See also Matewan Massacre

Robert Beanblossom
Division of Natural Resources

Ballad of Mad Ann Bailey

Mad Ann, from the streets of London
    Town
Rides in a wamus shirt
And britches made of a red buck's skin
Instead of a linsey skirt.

Her coon tail cap is ringed with dust,
And her horse's flanks shine wet,
And the rowelled wounds in his black
    side sting
With the salty grime of sweat.

Her screams are cut with a cockney
    blur
But she gives the white alarm,
And she carries a flint lock rifle primed
In the crook of her muscled arm.

The scalps in her belt outfly the wind,
And the gravels whirl to flame.
Death! Death! To the copper-
    skinned....
Plague on the Shawnee name!

She curses the race who killed her
    man,
With oaths from an English slum.
She swears by the god of the border
    folk
And swigs from her jug of rum.

—Louise McNeill

Mad Anne Bailey

Pioneer Anne Bailey's place in West Virginia history is tied to an event that may not have happened. She is often credited with carrying gunpowder from Lewisburg to relieve a 1790 siege on Fort Lee at the site of present Charleston. Contemporary chroniclers make no mention of this siege, and subsequent historians consider the tale apocryphal. Nevertheless, "Mad Anne" Bailey remains a powerful symbol of the fortitude required of frontier women.

Bailey was born Anne Hennis in Liverpool, England, in 1742. How she came to Virginia is a subject of some debate; however, it is certain she lived in Staunton by 1761 and married Richard Trotter in 1765. After Richard was killed at the 1774 Battle of Point Pleasant, Anne became a scout and spent 11 years roaming the Western Virginia wilderness, relaying messages between frontier forts. About 1785, she married John Bailey, a Greenbrier County soldier, but she did not give up scouting.

Regardless of the veracity of the Fort Lee story, Anne Bailey's services to frontier settlements were invaluable. When the 1795 Treaty of Greenville ended the border wars between Indians and European settlers, Bailey continued her wanderer's life, carrying mail between Staunton and Gallipolis, Ohio. She has also been credited with driving livestock from the Shenandoah to the Kanawha Valley.

Bailey spent her last years in Gallipolis, living near her son, William Trotter. According to tradition, and in keeping with the many accounts of her eccentricities, she refused to live in William's house and built her own cabin from fence rails. She died in 1825.

Christine M. Kreiser
Clarksburg

Grace McCartney Hall, "Anne Bailey in West Virginia Tradition," *West Virginia History,* October 1955.

Boling Baker

The turncoat Boling Baker (birth and death dates unknown) was the legendary husband of Aracoma, the supposed daughter of Shawnee chief Cornstalk. Baker may have been a soldier in Gen. Edward Braddock's army during the disastrous assault on Fort Duquesne in July 1755 during the French and Indian War. Baker was evidently captured by Shawnees and accepted into the tribe. He had wed Aracoma and moved to Hatfield (or Midelburg) Island in present Logan by about 1760. He led a band of Shawnees to steal horses from the Bluestone River area in 1780 when smallpox ravaged Aracoma's village. His band was destroyed by frontiersmen led by William Madison and John Breckenridge in a battle on Hatfield Island. Historian Sigfus Olafson found the name "Boling Baker" among Kanawha County names for his census index of the year 1810. At that time Kanawha included part of present Logan County, but it is not known if the entire tale of Boling Baker is true. Baker may have written this inscription on a tree: "Boling Baker, his hand and knife, can't steal a horse to save his life."

See also Aracoma

Robert Y. Spence
Logan

Newton Diehl Baker

Statesman Newton Diehl Baker was born in Martinsburg, December 3, 1871. He earned a B.A. degree from Johns Hopkins University in 1892. After receiving a law degree from Washington and Lee University in 1894, Baker practiced law in Martinsburg. In 1896, he became private secretary to U.S. Postmaster General William L. Wilson, also a West Virginian. In 1897, Baker returned to Martinsburg to practice law. He moved to Cleveland, Ohio, in 1899. Serving as city solicitor from 1902 to 1912, Baker then spent four years as mayor.

Appointed by President Woodrow Wilson, Baker served as secretary of war from 1916 to 1921. After a successful show of force along the Mexican border, Baker oversaw U.S. involvement in World War I. Gen. John J. Pershing dealt with military decisions, while Baker built a large army and made provisions for supplies essential to winning the war. He helped bring the industry of war to his native West Virginia, including the Naval Ordnance Plant in South Charleston and one of the world's largest chemical complexes in Nitro.

Returning to the practice of law in 1921, Baker served as a director of the Cleveland Trust Company and the Baltimore & Ohio Railroad. In 1928, he became president of the Woodrow Wilson Foundation, and President Coolidge appointed Baker to the Permanent Court of Arbitration at The Hague. In 1929, President Hoover appointed Baker to the Law Enforcement Commission. Commanding Colonel of the Officers Reserve Corps, Baker also received the U.S. Distinguished Service Medal in 1929. In 1932, the Democrat Party considered Baker for nomination for president. He died in Cleveland, December 25, 1937.

Russ Barbour
Huntington

Clarence Cramer, *Newton D. Baker, a Biography,* 1961.

Bald Eagle

The bald eagle was adopted as the national symbol in 1782. At that time, this large bird was not uncommon, and there may have been more than 100,000 bald eagles in what would become the lower 48 states. However, only 417 nesting pairs could be found in 1963, and the species was declared endangered in the continental U.S. in 1969.

The adult bald eagle is distinctively colored with a dark brown body and wings and a white head and tail. The wingspan can reach seven feet. Young eagles are the size of adults, but are dark brown or mottled brown and white; they do not develop a white head and tail until they are four or five years old. Bald eagles mate for life. Two or three eggs are laid in late winter or early spring, and both adults share the responsibilities of raising the young. When they are 10 to 13 weeks old, the young leave the nest. Bald eagles often feed on fish, but they are opportunistic feeders and will feed on other types of meat, including carrion.

Although it is likely that bald eagles nested in present West Virginia when settlers arrived, the first nest was not documented until 1981. The number of nesting pairs has increased, and 16 active nests were observed in 2004. These nests were all located in the Potomac River drainage, and the 14 successful nests produced 25 eaglets that year. However, only 16 eaglets were observed in 2005. In 2001, the first nest outside the Eastern Panhandle was discovered when a pair of bald eagles established themselves on Blennerhassett Island in the Ohio River. Unfortunately, this pair abandoned the site early in the nesting season and although biologists suspect eagles are nesting in the Ohio River drainage, no nests had been confirmed as of 2005.

Because the number of eagles has increased in recent years, the U.S. Fish and Wildlife Service "downlisted" the bald eagle from endangered to threatened status in 1995. At the end of the 20th century approximately 4,500 pairs lived in the lower 48 states. If populations continue to increase, this bird may be removed from the list of threatened and endangered species in the near future.

Craig W. Stihler
Division of Natural Resources

The Baldwin-Felts Detective Agency

The Baldwin-Felts Detective Agency played a controversial role in the early years of the coal industry of southern West Virginia, enforcing public law in the coalfields at the direction of the coal operators who hired them. Their often brutal, repressive policies, especially toward union miners, contributed significantly to the violence of the period.

The agency was founded in the early 1890s by William G. Baldwin and Thomas L. Felts in Roanoke, Virginia, initially to contract as a private police force to protect railroads. It soon expanded to the coal industry and opened a second headquarters in Bluefield, West Virginia.

From the beginning, Baldwin-Felts agents were deputized by hard-pressed local sheriffs to maintain law and order, but coal operators increasingly used them to prevent organization of the miners by the United Mine Workers of America. The guards kept union sympathizers from entering the coal camps. They spied on miners, reporting those with union sympathies, their highly organized spy system extending even into the UMWA leadership. In 1902, they helped break a strike in the New River Field. Eventually, their overriding purpose in West Virginia was to prevent unionization of the miners.

More than 150 Baldwin-Felts guards—called "thugs" by the miners—sought to thwart the Paint Creek-Cabin Creek strike of 1912. Union members vigorously resisted. The ensuing violence resulted in the death of several guards, miners, and others.

During a 1920 UMWA organizing campaign along the Tug River, the agency again leaped to national attention in the Matewan Massacre of May 19. After the guards had evicted families from their homes, angry miners, led by Police Chief Sid Hatfield, killed seven detectives, including Al and Lee Felts, the founder's brothers. A jury acquitted all of the accused, such was the hatred of the detectives. On August 1, 1921, Baldwin-Felts agents gunned down Hatfield and deputy Ed Chambers at Welch, helping to incite a march on Mingo by more than 10,000 miners in September. The march and

A Baldwin-Felts agent at Glen Jean, Fayette County, 1902.

ensuing Battle of Blair Mountain were the culminating events of the Mine Wars.

Baldwin-Felts guards also were involved in the 1914 "Ludlow Massacre" in Colorado's coalfields, in which women and children were burned to death in a union tent colony. Three separate congressional investigations of labor violence in West Virginia and Colorado produced much negative publicity about the guard system. Partly because of that, use of Baldwin-Felts guards declined in the 1920s and ended in the 1930s. The agency closed after the deaths of Baldwin in 1936 and Felts a year later.

See also Battle of Blair Mountain, Matewan Massacre, Mine Wars

Lon Savage
Salem, Virginia

Richard Hadsell and William Coffey, "From Law and Order to Class Warfare: Baldwin-Felts Detectives in the Southern West Virginia Coal Fields," *West Virginia History*, Spring 1979; Lon Savage, *Thunder in the Mountains: The West Virginia Mine War 1920–21*, 1990.

Dr. Maggie Ballard

Physician Margaret Byrnside "Dr. Maggie" Ballard, Monroe County historian and country doctor, was born April 9, 1900, in Greenville to Isaac Newton Ballard and Kate May Walkup. She attended public schools in Monroe County and completed her undergraduate degree at West Virginia University. In 1926, she graduated from the University of Maryland School of Medicine, as one of the first women to complete the M.D. program there. For the next 43 years she practiced medicine in Baltimore.

Upon retirement Dr. Maggie returned to Monroe County where she actively pursued her interest in genealogy and lo-

cal history. She was one of the founders of the Monroe County Historical Society. For many years she participated in the Mountain State Art & Craft Fair at Cedar Lakes where she made and sold lye soap. Ballard's extensive collection of historical material was placed in the West Virginia and Regional History Collection at WVU upon her death, September 25, 1976.

Michael M. Meador
Abingdon, Virginia

Baltimore & Ohio Railroad

The Baltimore & Ohio played an important role in the creation of West Virginia. It was a major employer in towns such as Harpers Ferry, Martinsburg, Grafton, Parkersburg, Wheeling, and Clarksburg. The railroad's management eventually sided with the North during the Civil War, influencing many people in the northern part of the area that became West Virginia to support statehood in 1863. Once war started, the route of the rail line affected the shape of the new state.

The B&O was chartered in 1827 as Baltimore's answer to the westward construction of New York's Erie Canal and Pennsylvania's canal system. When passenger and freight operations began in May 1830, the B&O was the first common carrier railroad in the country. The B&O proved that steam locomotion was feasible, and by late 1831 the line had been completed to Harpers Ferry.

It was another decade before the B&O was completed to Cumberland (1842) and yet another decade before the line achieved the original objective of the founders—the Ohio River at Wheeling (1853). Several years later an alternate line from Grafton to Parkersburg was

A B&O steam locomotive at Wheeling, 1952.

completed. The rugged terrain through what is now West Virginia slowed the construction and increased the cost. It was necessary to sell stock subscriptions and bonds in England to finance the railroad. In the first decade of the company's history a substantial portion of its revenue came from passenger service. With the opening of the coal mines in the area around Cumberland and in the mountains west of that city, coal traffic to Baltimore became the major source of revenue.

John W. Garrett was president of the B&O during the Civil War period. John Brown stopped a B&O passenger train and occupied railroad property in his attack on the U.S. arsenal at Harpers Ferry in 1859. Col. Thomas J. "Stonewall" Jackson commanded VMI cadets at Brown's execution, and returned to Jefferson County as commander of Virginia forces at the outset of the Civil War. By the time Jackson withdrew from Harpers Ferry in June 1861, he had systematically looted the railroad. Tools and equipment were transported deep into the Confederacy and six locomotives were moved, part of the way over highways, to the Manassas Gap Railroad. The bridge over the Potomac was destroyed, and railroad equipment and rolling stock from Harpers Ferry to Martinsburg was damaged or destroyed.

The B&O continued to suffer extensive damage during the war. Nonetheless, dedicated employees, many living in West Virginia, reopened the line quickly and allowed the company to operate at a profit. By the time the Civil War ended the B&O was in a position to expand. This began with the construction of large wrought-iron bridges over the Ohio River at Wheeling and Parkersburg.

By a combination of leases and purchases the B&O reached Columbus, Ohio, Lake Erie, and Pittsburgh (from Cumberland) in 1871. Other lines took the B&O into Virginia at Lexington, to Philadelphia, and eventually to Chicago. At the end of the Civil War the B&O had operated 520 miles of railroad, but by 1884 it had expanded to 1,700 miles. Unfortunately, most of this expansion had been financed by borrowed money. Furthermore, the B&O had engaged in a series of rate wars with the Pennsylvania, the New York Central, and the Erie that reduced profits from its operations. Trouble was brewing.

The railroad industry in the 1870s underwent a significant struggle between management and labor. This peaked during the economic depression of the mid-1870s, when anti-union efforts and wage cuts increased significantly. A series of national strikes began in Martinsburg in 1877, when B&O employees seized control of the railroad. Local police and the state militia could not handle the situation. Federal troops were required to restore order, and the animosity lasted for many years.

Overexpansion and inadequate income were the major problems faced by the B&O in the late 19th century. The quality of maintenance and service began to decline rapidly. So did the traffic, much of it lost to competitors. In 1889, the B&O hauled 31 percent of the nation's Tidewater-bound soft coal; by 1896, it hauled only four percent. The decline in traffic and the depression of the mid-

1890s forced the B&O, along with many other railroads, into receivership.

The B&O recovered from receivership rapidly, partly because of the return of prosperity in the late 1890s, and it continued to expand, primarily by purchasing or by entering into operating agreements with other railroads. In West Virginia it added the Monongahela River Railroad (Fairmont to Clarksburg) in 1900, while in 1901 it began the process of acquiring the Ohio River Railroad from Wheeling through Parkersburg and Huntington to Kenova. In the 1920s, operating agreements were developed with the Morgantown & Kingwood Railroad and the Coal & Coke Railway (Elkins to Charleston), essentially completing its routes in West Virginia. All of these railroads were eventually incorporated into the B&O.

After a short period of control by the Pennsylvania Railroad in the first decade of the 20th century, Daniel Willard became president of the B&O in 1910, a position he would hold until 1941. Willard carried out a major modernization of the system which made the B&O one of the premier American railroads. In the 1920s, it averaged revenues of about $225 million a year with dividends up to six percent.

Then came the Great Depression, hitting the B&O harder than most railroads. Barely surviving receivership, the railroad recovered briefly during World War II and into the early 1950s, but the decline of coal mining along its lines and increasing competition from other railroads and highways placed the company in a weak financial position by 1960. Faced with mounting debt, in 1962 the B&O accepted merger overtures from the Chesapeake & Ohio while rejecting those from the New York Central. The absorption of the oldest common carrier proceeded slowly and was not finalized until 1973. The Chessie System was created that year, and today the B&O is part of the vast CSX transportation system.

See also Civil War, CSX, Railroad Strike of 1877, Railroads

Robert L. Frey
Miamisburg, Ohio

Edward Hungerford, *The Story of the Baltimore & Ohio Railroad: 1827–1927*, 1928; John F. Stover, *History of the Baltimore & Ohio Railroad*, 1987.

Harry Hill Bandholtz

Harry Hill Bandholtz, commander of the federal troops that intervened to end the West Virginia Mine Wars in 1921, was born in Michigan, December 18, 1864. Bandholtz graduated from West Point in 1890 and served with distinction in World War I.

Bandholtz was commander of the Military District of Washington in 1921 when President Harding ordered him to restore civil authority in southern West Virginia.

With a 2,000-man detachment from four U.S. Army regiments and 14 bombers commanded by the military aviation pioneer, Gen. Billy Mitchell, Bandholtz quickly reestablished law and order in the riotous coalfields without firing a shot. Bandholtz's smoothly executed double envelopment on September 3 and subsequent disarming of the combatants at the Battle of Blair Mountain effectively ended the Mine Wars. Neither side wished to exchange fire with federal soldiers. Bandholtz expressed disgust that West Virginia state and local government had allowed a labor dispute to escalate into one of America's largest civil insurrections. He died in Michigan, May 7, 1925.

See also Battle of Blair Mountain, Mine Wars, Billy Mitchell

C. Stuart McGehee
West Virginia State University
Clayton L. Laurie, "The United States Army and the Return to Normalcy in Labor Dispute Interventions: The Case of the West Virginia Coal Mine Wars, 1920–1921," *West Virginia History*, 1991; Lon Savage, *Thunder in the Mountains: The West Virginia Mine War 1920–21*, 1990.

Banjo

Scholars have suggested that West Virginia's banjo tradition arrived with black railroad workers, who left their mark in legend and in songs such as "John Henry," "John Hardy," and "Sandy Boys." Even earlier, in the 1840s, white minstrel performers began to tour river communities, performing a parody of black life and playing banjo music learned from black musicians on instruments not unlike ones found in Africa. These performers helped to spark a national fad for the banjo. This brought a revolution in banjo manufacture. Mountain musicians first played homemade instruments, but

Banjos made by Clay County craftsman Jenes Cottrell.

by the late 19th century mail-order banjos were common.

Minstrel musicians played in the clawhammer or stroke style, learned from slaves. A clawhammer player notes with his left hand, while the right hand is held in claw fashion. The index or middle finger strikes down on the strings and the thumb pulls on the fifth (or drone) string. The thumb may also drop down and catch notes on the second string. This is called "drop thumb" or "double noting." The banjo was also finger-picked in a variety of ways. These styles descend from late 19th-century parlor and classical music written for the banjo.

Today the dominant banjo sounds in West Virginia are clawhammer and the modern three-finger Scruggs-style bluegrass picking, popularized by Earl Scruggs while playing in the 1940s with Bill Monroe's Blue Grass Boys band. Louder banjos with resonator shells on the back were developed for bluegrass picking. The bluegrass banjo player takes solo breaks and plays highly developed back-up patterns or "licks" behind the fiddle, mandolin, and guitar, as musicians trade the lead. In old-time music, the fiddle and banjo usually attempt to blend for one sound, with the clawhammer banjo providing a syncopation to the fiddle lead.

West Virginia banjo playing came to new attention in the folk revival of the late 1960s and '70s. Banjo players Frank George and the late Oscar Wright and Elmer Bird were known for their clawhammer playing, and commercial recordings of their music were produced. The late Don Stover from Raleigh County came to national attention in the 1960s for his innovative finger-picking style while playing with the Lilly Brothers and his own bluegrass bands. A black clawhammer banjo style has also been identified, best represented by the late John Homer "Uncle Homer" Walker of Summers County and the late Clarence Tross of Hardy County.

The state also produced noted banjo makers, including the late Jenes Cottrell of Clay County, who fashioned banjos from parts of 1956 Buick automobile transmissions, and the late Andy Boarman of Berkeley County, who built "Dixie Grand" resonator banjos. Boarman was also well known for his classical style of banjo picking.

Paul Gartner
Sod

Cecelia Conway, *African Banjo Echoes in Appalachia: A Study of Folk Traditions*, 1995.

Banking

The early history of banking in West Virginia is closely tied to the banks of Virginia. Before the creation of our state in 1863, several banks chartered by Virginia had branches within the present bounds of West Virginia.

These included the Bank of Virginia at Richmond, incorporated in 1804 with a branch later established in Charleston. The Northwestern Bank of Virginia in Wheeling was chartered in 1817. It had branches in Parkersburg, Clarksburg, and Wellsburg. The Bank of the Valley in Virginia, chartered in Winchester in 1817, had branches in Charles Town, Romney, and Moorefield. The Merchants and Mechanics Bank in Wheeling was incorporated in 1834 and had branch offices in Morgantown and Point Pleasant. The Exchange Bank of Virginia in Norfolk was established in 1837, with branches in Weston and Lewisburg. There were private banks as well, operating without charter, and some residents relied on banks in neighboring states.

West Virginia passed no state banking laws until 1872. In the meantime, between 1863 and 1872, some of the old Virginia banks were transformed into national banks under 1864 federal banking legislation, and some closed. Under this legislation, the First National Bank of Parkersburg, formerly a branch of the Northwestern Bank of Virginia and now United Bank, became the first national bank in West Virginia in 1864. By the end of 1865, 13 banks had become national banks, including banks at Martinsburg, Wheeling, and elsewhere. On December 26, 1872, the legislature passed West Virginia's first general banking law. Numerous state banks were established before this act was repealed in 1881. From 1881 until 1901, banks were created under law governing joint stock companies.

The legislature created a state banking department in 1891, and authorized the governor to appoint a bank examiner. The agency's authority included state-chartered banks and similar institutions, but not national banks. Similar lines of authority apply today. The West Virginia Division of Banking oversees state-chartered financial institutions, which are also examined by federal authorities. All national banks are overseen by a bureau of the U.S. Treasury Department.

In 1891, there were 49 state banks and 22 national banks in West Virginia. The number peaked in 1924, with 225 state banks and 125 national banks, for a total of 350 banks. In 1933, after the Great Depression had taken its toll, there remained only 103 state banks and 78 national banks.

The Great Depression was the most disastrous event in West Virginia banking history. Bank failures began even before the stock market crash, as 13 banks closed in the late 1920s. Between the stock market crash in October 1929 and the end of 1933, 68 state banks and 25 national banks closed in West Virginia. Some communities were left without banks. Confidence was restored when Congress passed the Banking Act of 1933. This legislation

A bank note issued by the Bank of Charleston, 1861.

created the Federal Deposit Insurance Corporation to insure bank deposits.

Following the Depression, banking enjoyed an era of recovery that continued through World War II. Banks grew in strength, in part because of the demand for the state's resources, including coal, and for its chemicals and manufactured goods. Through the late 1940s and early 1950s, West Virginia banks also benefited from a national boom in consumer borrowing. Then, in the mid-1950s, another economic crisis hit West Virginia with the loss of mining jobs and mass migration from the coalfields. Some smaller banks were forced to close. Between 1960 and 1970, there was renewed growth in the West Virginia banking industry. The number of state banks and national banks increased, and deposits in both nearly doubled.

By this time, Mountain State banking had a distinctly dual character. Large banks operated in Charleston, Huntington, Wheeling, Weirton, and Parkersburg, as well as other cities and large towns. Smaller towns and less populous counties had their local banks, smaller but often thriving institutions. Branch banking was prohibited under a 1929 state law, protecting local institutions from the competition of metropolitan banks. The legislature confirmed the prohibition in 1972, but allowed banks to operate one off-premise site (either a walk-in or drive-up facility) within 2,000 feet of the main office.

The branch banking issue—as well as the related questions of mergers, bank-holding companies, and interstate banking—divided West Virginia bankers. Small bankers joined the Independent Bankers Association to oppose branch banking. Those who supported branch banking joined the Progressive Bankers Association. The West Virginia Bankers Association tried to take a neutral stance, but eventually supported branch banking.

As late as 1980, banks could not operate automated teller machines off their premises. Branch banking was still not allowed, nor could banks offer services beyond the traditional lending and deposit taking. Multi-bank holding companies and interstate banking did not exist in West Virginia. That year, Congress passed the Depository Institutions Deregulation and Monetary Control Act, which deregulated interest rates paid by banks and allowed savings and loan institutions and credit unions to offer many services previously offered only by banks. Under federal deregulation, there was more competition among banks. At the same time banks began to face competition from other financial institutions.

In 1982, Governor Rockefeller called for broad changes in the state banking system. Resulting legislation allowed the formation of bank-holding companies, so that one company could own several banks, but banks themselves were not allowed to merge, combine with, or consolidate into other West Virginia banks or banks from outside West Virginia. County-wide branch banking was allowed after June 7, 1984. After January 1, 1986, statewide branch banking was allowed.

Changes in state banking laws and federal deregulation brought a dramatic restructuring of banking in West Virginia. Large banks established bank-holding companies, acquiring smaller banks and eventually each other. Relaxation of interstate banking laws allowed out-of-state banks to acquire branches in West Virginia, and West Virginia banks to acquire branches in other states. A few very large banks emerged, and some of these were later acquired by banks outside the state. For example, Centurion Bancshares, including Charleston National and other banks, and Key Bancshares, including First Huntington and other banks, eventually became part of Bank One of Chicago. National Bank of Commerce became part of Huntington Banks of Columbus, Ohio. In 2000, One Valley Bank (formerly Kanawha Valley Bank), the largest bank in West Virginia, was acquired by BB&T, a North Carolina bank. Other large banks, including United and Wesbanco, have not merged with out-of-state banks.

The number of banks fell dramatically with the mergers and combinations. By 1990, West Virginia had 180 commercial banks and 15 savings institutions. In 2005, there were 66 commercial banks headquartered in West Virginia and six savings institutions. Control of West Virginia banking rested in fewer hands than previously, and some of the largest banks were headquartered outside the state. Bankers competed in a variety of fields, including insurance and brokerage services, that would have surprised their predecessors. More than $23 billion was on deposit in West Virginia financial institutions. Banks in West Virginia are regulated by the West Virginia Board of Banking and Financial Institutions and the state Division of Banking, and must comply with state and federal laws and regulations. Banks are represented by the West Virginia Bankers Association, and the West Virginia Association of Community Bankers.

Otis Rice and Stephen Brown, *A Centennial of Strength, West Virginia Banks,* 1991.

Baptists

West Virginia Baptists follow the same basic patterns of beliefs that have distinguished Baptists historically: the Bible as the sole authority for rule and practice; the belief in baptism by immersion for believers; the complete autonomy of each local congregation; the priesthood of every believer; the separation of church and state; and religious liberty.

The first Baptist church in present West Virginia was the Mill Creek Baptist Church in the Eastern Panhandle. Though it dissolved within a few years of its founding in the mid-1740s, it was a training station for several ministers who made their way over the mountains to do lasting work in Western Virginia. John Corbly and John, James, and Isaac Sutton were part of the Mill Creek Church and founders of the first two active Baptist churches west of the mountains, both of which continue to the present. Corbly and the Sutton brothers moved west, in part, because colonial Virginia's established church refused to license them to preach as Baptists.

Corbly settled in the Morgantown area about 1770 and gathered a congregation around him called the Forks-of-Cheat Baptist Church. His family was attacked by Indians on their way to church in May 1782. His wife and three of his children were killed in that attack, and two other children were scalped but lived. John Sutton helped form the Simpson Creek Baptist Church in Harrison County in about 1770. Baptist work in southern West Virginia began with the efforts of John Alderson Jr. in 1781.

By 1800, there were approximately 16 churches with 450 members within the boundaries of present West Virginia. Among the churches were 12 Particular Baptist (predestinarian), two General Baptist, one Seventh Day Baptist, and one Six Principle Baptist. Distances and rugged terrain dictated that for fellowship, mutual support, counseling of churches and ministers, and discipline of congregations, associations of churches in geographical proximity were needed. The first was the Greenbrier Association in 1800. By 1835, there were four associations with slightly more than 1,000 church members. By the time of the Civil War in 1861, there were six associations with almost 7,000 members.

The issue of slavery caused a division among Baptists nationally and in Western Virginia. In 1845, the Southern Baptist Convention was organized, and shortly thereafter Baptists primarily in the North organized themselves as the American Baptist Missionary Union. The Civil War brought a sharp decline in church membership and activity. Baptist churches were not only divided in loyalty, but numerous church buildings were damaged or destroyed, used as barracks for soldiers, for the storage of supplies, for prisons, and even as stables for horses.

By the end of the war, about two-thirds of West Virginia Baptist churches were aligned with the American (or Northern) Baptists and the remainder with the Southern Baptist Convention. The Baptist General Association of West Virginia, now known as the West Virginia Baptist Convention, was formed after the war in 1865. By 1869, the split between the Northern and Southern Baptists in the state was mended, and both Northern and Southern Baptists had united as the West Virginia Baptist Convention.

Baptist growth, like the general population of the new state of West Virginia, increased steadily following the war; there were approximately 250 churches in 1866 and 600 churches by 1900. After a slight drop in churches and membership during the Great Depression, Baptist growth reached its greatest numbers during the early 1950s—more than 800 churches.

By 2000, the West Virginia Baptist Convention, part of the American Baptist Churches in the USA, had a reported 463 churches and 108,087 adherents. Southern Baptists had 165 churches with a reported 43,606 adherents. Seventh Day Baptists have been influential in northern West Virginia where, for many years, they were closely related to Salem College. The black National Baptists have churches primarily in the southern counties, and Independent Baptists are found throughout the state.

West Virginia Baptists have had an emphasis on evangelism and missions throughout their history, along with an involvement in social concerns such as the prohibition of alcohol. Baptists were particularly involved with rural ministries, including a railroad chapel car ministry to mining and lumber camps in the early 1900s. Numerous churches were organized as a result of itinerant mission work. Special attention to foreign immigrants in the coalfields was also emphasized at the turn of the century. Baptists have been leaders in the field of Christian education through local churches and schools, the most notable Baptist institutions of higher education being Alderson-Broaddus College in Philippi and Salem College in Salem.

West Virginia Baptists have served the state and the nation in many capacities. Notable are Robert C. Byrd and Jennings Randolph, who have served in the U.S. Senate with distinction. Baptists who have served as governors of West Virginia include Howard Mason Gore and Clarence Watson Meadows.

In 1940, a West Virginia Baptist Historical Society was formed at the West Virginia Baptist Convention's annual meeting, and in 1981 the society occupied a vault and an adjoining room of the West Virginia Baptist Conference Center at Ripley.

George Truett Rogers
Terra Alta

Truett Rogers, *West Virginia Baptist History, The Convention Years, 1865–1965*, 1994; Rogers, *West Virginia Baptist History, The Early Years, 1770–1865*, 1990.

Waitman Barbe

Writer, newspaperman, and educator Waitman Barbe was born November 19, 1864, in Monongalia County. He was educated at West Virginia University, as well as Harvard, Oxford, and Denison universities. A well-known member of the WVU English department, Barbe also wrote poetry and literary criticism.

Barbe was managing editor of the Parkersburg *Daily State Journal* newspaper from 1889 to 1895, when he joined the WVU faculty. He was an accomplished poet. "The Song of the Centuries" (1888) is regarded as his first important poem, and the 1892 book *Ashes and Incense* secured his reputation. He later wrote books of poetic analysis, including *The Study of Poetry* (1905), *Famous Poems Explained* (1909), and *Great Poems Interpreted* (1913). During his years at the university, Barbe corresponded with many famous personalities, including Winston Churchill, Richard Harding Davis, Julia Ward Howe, William Dean Howells, Amy Lowell, and Owen Wister. Their responses to Barbe's questions, collected in the Waitman Barbe papers at the West Virginia and Regional History Collection at WVU, exemplify the depth and the breadth of Barbe's curiosity. Barbe died October 30, 1925.

Cheryl B. Torsney
West Virginia University

Barbour County

Barbour County was created from parts of Lewis, Harrison, and Randolph counties by an act of the Virginia legislature on March 3, 1843. The county was named for the distinguished Virginia jurist Philip Pendleton Barbour, as was the county seat, Philippi. Settlement began as early as 1780.

Barbour County has an area of 345.4 square miles and a 2000 population of 15,557. It is located on the Allegheny Plateau in north-central West Virginia. Its mountainous terrain is drained by the Buckhannon, the Middle Fork, and the Tygart Valley rivers. U.S. 119 and U.S. 250 run north and south the full length of the county, while U.S. 33 cuts across its southernmost tip. Barbour County is served by the Chessie System and the Western Maryland Railroad. It is bordered on the north by Taylor and Preston counties, on the east by Tucker and Randolph, on the south by Upshur, and on the west by Harrison. Laurel Mountain, the westernmost of the high Allegheny ridges, forms the eastern boundary of Barbour County.

Philippi, the county seat, has a population of 2,870. The town is located on the Tygart Valley River at the junction of U.S. 119 and U.S. 250, in the center of the county. Philippi's historic covered bridge carries U.S. 250 across the river. It was designed and built by Lemuel Chenoweth in 1852. Barbour has another covered bridge, as well, crossing the Buckhannon River at Carrollton.

Belington, the second-largest town in Barbour County, is located on U.S. 250 ten miles southeast of Philippi. It was named after John Bealin, who established a store there before the Civil War. It has a population of 1,788. Both Philippi and Belington were sites of battles during the first campaign of the Civil War.

Before dawn on June 3, 1861, what is generally considered the first land battle of the Civil War took place at Philippi as 3,000 federal troops under Col. Benjamin F. Kelley routed a newly recruited and poorly equipped Confederate contingent of about 800, commanded by Col. George A. Porterfield. While no one was killed during the brief encounter, both sides suffered casualties. The Battle of Belington or Laurel Mountain was a series of skirmishes that took place the following month, July 7–11, 1861. Federal troops under Brig. Gen. William S. Rosecrans attacked a nearly equal number of Confederates commanded by Brig. Gen. Robert S. Garnett and drove them from their positions on Laurel Mountain.

Until the late 20th century the economy of Barbour County was based primarily on its natural resources, including coal, gas, and timber, as well as agriculture. Historically, the county's agricultural production has come from family farms nestled among the mountains and along the river valleys. At the beginning of the 20th century there was a large

FAST FACTS ABOUT BARBOUR COUNTY

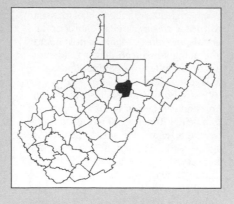

Founded: 1843

Land in square miles: 345.4

Population: 15,557

Percentage minorities: 2.6%

Percentage rural: 82.5%

Median age: 38.7

Percentage 65 and older: 15.6%

Birth rate per 1,000 population: 9.0

Median household income: $24,729

High school graduate or higher: 72.7%

Bachelor's degree or higher: 11.8%

Home ownership: 78.6%

Median home value: $56,100

This information is from the 2000 U.S. Census. In 2000, West Virginia as a whole had 5 percent minorities, a median age of 38.9, median household income of $29,696, and a 75.2 percent home ownership rate.

---

hardwood timber industry. Loggers soon exhausted the great stands of virgin timber, although second- and third-growth timber is still harvested annually. Logging and wood products remain important industries.

Oil and coal no longer contribute as greatly to the county's economy as they did a century ago. The oil reserves were largely depleted early in the 20th century, and the coal industry has experienced a decline since peak production of 3,895,803 tons in 1948. Today the largest employer in Barbour County is the public school system, with a total of nearly 350 full-time employees. Broaddus Hospital and Alderson-Broaddus College are the second- and third-largest employers respectively.

The history of Alderson-Broaddus College in Barbour County dates from 1909 when Broaddus Institute moved from Clarksburg to Philippi. It was merged with Alderson Academy in 1932 and became the four-year coeducational college it is today. The private Baptist school has recognized programs in nursing, the medical sciences, education, music, and the liberal arts. It was the first college in West Virginia to offer a four-year degree in nursing.

Among the prominent people of Barbour County were the Dayton and Woods families. The Daytons were active in the formation of West Virginia, while a member of the Woods family was a delegate to the Virginia secessionist convention in 1861 and voted for secession. U.S. District Judge Alston G. Dayton authored a historic legal decision in the 1907 *Hitchman* case, which sanctioned the yellow-dog contract and the use of court injunctions as anti-union devices during the period of the West Virginia Mine Wars. Under the leadership of Ruth Woods Dayton the two families joined in founding the Day-

wood Foundation, a philanthropic organization based in Charleston. Judge Ira Robinson was also an important West Virginia jurist. His house, Adaland, near Philippi, is now open to the public. Ida L. Reed composed hundreds of religious hymns, including "I Belong to the King." Howard Willis Smith was a noted artist and cartoonist, and Ted Cassidy played "Lurch" on the television comedy, *The Addams Family*.

James W. Daddysman
Alderson-Broaddus College

Barboursville

Barboursville, population 3,183, was chartered in 1813 and named for James Barbour, the governor of Virginia (1812–14). It was designated the county seat of Cabell County in 1814. Barboursville is located on the Guyandotte River and Interstate 64, near Huntington.

Union troops under Gen. Jacob Cox drove Confederate militia and cavalry out of the town during the Battle of Barboursville, July 14, 1861. Union forces remained in control of Barboursville for the remainder of the war. Barboursville was incorporated by an act of the state legislature on February 12, 1867. After the completion of the C&O Railway to Huntington, Barboursville no longer was the center of activity in Cabell County. Consequently, the courthouse was moved to Huntington in 1887.

On September 12, 1888, the Barboursville Seminary, later Barboursville College, opened in the former courthouse. In 1901, Morris Harvey, a Fayette County sheriff, businessman, and coal operator, and his wife, Rosa, donated $10,000 to the school. In recognition of this gift, the school's name was changed to Morris Harvey College. In 1935, the college was moved to Charleston, where it continues as the University of Charleston. The lower level of the former college was

used for a junior high school, and the buildings on the upper level became a state mental health facility. In 1981, Governor Rockefeller converted the upper buildings into the state's first and only veterans home.

The Huntington Mall, which is located within the boundaries of Barboursville, opened in February 1981.

Joseph Platania
Huntington

Barger Springs

Barger Springs, located in Summers County three miles south of Talcott, on the Big Bend of the Greenbrier River, was the site of a mineral spring resort from 1903 to 1929. The spring property was first developed commercially prior to the Civil War. Owner Isaac Carden established a lodging place for hunters and trappers, and constructed a row of log cabins for their use. Carden also had one of the first stores in the region at his spring.

Between the end of the Civil War and 1903, the property was farmed by William Barger, who had married into the Carden family. A springhouse was erected in 1868, but Barger did little to develop the site commercially. In 1903, the property was purchased by a company of 30 investors from nearby Hinton who divided the land into 30 lots for the building of vacation cottages, erected a new pavilion over the spring, and renamed their development Greenbrier Springs. In 1905, the company constructed a three-story wooden hotel near the spring for the accommodation of visitors. This hotel opened to the public in 1906. The resort at Barger Springs was popular with the local population as a place for swimming, fishing, and other outdoor activities. The hotel was closed in 1929, and the building was razed. Many private cottages are located on the former resort grounds, and in 1976 the spring pavilion was renovated.

Michael M. Meador
Abingdon, Virginia

Stan Cohen, *Historic Springs of the Virginias,* 1981; James H. Miller, *History of Summers County West Virginia,* 1908.

Gray Barker

Flying saucer investigator Gray Barker was born in Riffle, Braxton County, May 2, 1925. He grew up in Braxton County and spent most of his life in central West Virginia. After receiving a B.A. from Glenville State College in 1947, he taught school and became a booking agent for theaters in the area.

Barker became interested in unidentified flying objects in the 1950s after investigating the sightings of the Flatwoods Monster. He became acquainted with Albert K. Bender and Bender's theory of the "Men in Black." Barker published his best-known book, *They Knew Too Much About Flying Saucers,* in 1956. At various times Barker published flying saucer magazines and newsletters. Through these publications, he came in contact with people worldwide who were interested in UFOs, many of whom claimed to have been contacted by aliens.

In 1970, following the 1967 collapse of the Silver Bridge in Point Pleasant, Barker published his next book, *The Silver Bridge*. This publication related the popular legend of the Mothman sightings. Although he published many other books on strange phenomena, Barker is best known for these two books and a 1983 publication called *MIB, The Terror Among Us*, about the Men in Black. He was the subject of the 1995 video by Ralph Coon, *Whispers From Space*. For this production, Coon collected stories from various people who knew and worked with Barker.

After his death December 6, 1984, Barker's collection was acquired by the Clarksburg-Harrison Public Library and is housed there in the Gray Barker Room. When asked if he believed in flying saucers, Barker replied, "I am not sure, but anything that generates that volume of interest is worth collecting."

See also Flatwoods Monster, Mothman
Merle Moore
Webster Springs

Walter Barnes

Professor Walter Barnes, an early leader in the preservation of West Virginia folklore, was born July 29, 1880, in Barnesville, Ohio. He graduated in 1905 from West Virginia University, received an M.A. from Harvard in 1911, and a Ph.D. from New York University in 1930. Barnes taught and administered schools in Mineral and Harrison counties, and came to the English Department at Glenville State Normal School (now Glenville State College) in 1907. He served at Fairmont State Normal School (now Fairmont State University), 1914–28; was a member of the State Board of Education, 1914–20; and president of the West Virginia Education Association, 1921. After 1928, he taught at New York University.

While at Fairmont State, Barnes expanded his interest in folklore and its application to teaching, especially through ballads, songs, verses, jingles, and other verbal expressions, as well as folktales. In 1915, he founded the West Virginia Folklore Society along with John Harrington Cox and Robert Allen Armstrong of WVU. Although the Folklore Society became inactive in 1917, when Barnes retired back to Fairmont in 1950 he helped to revive it with Ruth Ann Musick of Fairmont State College and Patrick Gainer of WVU, and encouraged the establishment of *West Virginia Folklore* as its official publication. He served as the society's president until 1954 and its president emeritus until 1967.

Barnes was editor of the *West Virginia School Journal* and literary editor of the *West Virginia Review*. His books included *English in the Country School* (1913), *An Easy Primer* (1918), *Types of Children's Literature* (1920), *New Democracy in the Teaching of English* (1923), *The Children's Poets* (1924), *Boy's Life of Mark Twain* (1929), *English for American High Schools* (1931), *The Photoplay as Literature Art* (1936), *Contemporary Children's Poetry* (1938), and *The Teacher Speaks* (1949). Barnes died August 27, 1969, in Bradenton, Florida.

Judy Prozzillo Byers
Fairmont State University

The Barnette Case

The refusal of West Virginia school children to participate in compulsory flag-salute ceremonies resulted in the expansion of the constitutional protection for religious liberties for all Americans in the landmark 1943 case, *West Virginia State Board of Education v. Barnette*. Jehovah's Witnesses Walter Barnette, Lucy McClure, and Paul Stull sued when their children were expelled from the Kanawha County schools for their refusal to salute the flag. They claimed that requiring participation in the ceremony violated First Amendment freedom of speech and religion. Two years earlier, the U.S. Supreme Court had held, in an 8-1 decision in *Minersville School District v. Gobitis*, that such requirements did not violate the Constitution.

America's involvement in World War II made refusal to salute the flag especially unpopular, but Jehovah's Witnesses continued steadfast. Flag-salute confrontations between the sect and school officials occurred throughout America. In 1942, quoting extensively from the *Gobitis* decision, the West Virginia State Board of Education adopted flag-salute regulations. The Jehovah's Witnesses challenged the regulations and won at trial. The state appealed to the U.S. Supreme Court, which in the 6-3 *Barnette* decision struck down the laws of all states requiring schoolchildren to salute the flag.

Justice Robert Jackson wrote the Court's opinion. "The very purpose of a Bill of Rights," he contended, "was to withdraw certain subjects from the vicissitudes of political controversy, to place them beyond the reach of majorities and officials."

See also Catlette v. United States, Jehovah's Witnesses, Jehovah's Witnesses v. Pittsburgh Plate Glass Company
Chuck Smith
West Virginia State University
David R. Manwaring, *Render Unto Caesar: The Flag Salute Controversy*, 1962.

Barns

West Virginia barns present a wide variety of type, shape, style, and materials. The oldest barn styles, those built during the frontier period, are a visual historic

Log barns remain common in much of West Virginia.

record of westward expansion. West Virginia's earliest settlers, many of whom came to the South Branch of the Potomac, the Greenbrier, and other river valleys, constructed barns that show stylistic evidence of their builders' ethnic origins.

Three general barn types may be observed among the older barns along the eastern side of the state: the double-crib log barn, the "Pennsylvania" or "German bank barn," and the "English barn." Early settlers favored log barns because of the ease with which they could obtain the materials. As sawn boards became available, large, timber-framed bank barns, with their multi-level entrances, dotted the countryside in areas where people of German descent settled. Rectangular framed English-style barns may also be found, reflecting that ethnicity's place in early settlement. These barn types did not die out after the pioneer period, and many fine log barns were constructed until the early to mid-20th century. As one travels from east to west in the state, greater variation with less adherence to classic style may be observed in the structural aspects and overall shape of barns. Several 19th-century round barns have endured to the present.

West Virginia hill farms are likely to have more numerous, smaller barns than the "great barns" found in the larger river bottoms of the state, the gentler terrain of the Eastern Panhandle, and the western Ohio Valley. Like geography, age contributes to marked differences in styles because of newer construction materials. Traditional log, lumber, and stone components gave way to concrete, brick, blocks, and metal for foundations and walls, while asphalt-shingled and tin roofs replaced the more traditional wooden shingles or slate. Modern barns display more windows, owing to the greater availability and reasonable cost of glass, whereas older barns simply had hinged openings.

Barns are utilitarian buildings. Their shape and usefulness are determined by their function. Hay barns, tobacco barns, dairy barns, sheepfolds, and horse stables present varied reasons for design and shape. Today, due to advanced farming techniques, older barns may not be used in ways for which they were intended. As more and more people abandon agrarian lifestyles, obsolete barns simply become symbols of country life, while they are put to other, non-agrarian uses. Barns are now recognized American icons, and their presence is important for those who identify with our country's rural past.

Gerald Milnes
Augusta Heritage Center

Gerald C. Milnes, "The Barns of Pendleton County," *Goldenseal,* Spring 1998; Allen G. Noble, *The Old Barn Book: A Field Guide to North American Barns and Other Farm Structures,* 1996; Leroy G. Shultz, "The Barns of West Virginia," *Goldenseal,* April–September 1978.

William Wallace Barron

William Wallace Barron, West Virginia's 26th governor, achieved a remarkable record of legislative success during his term, brought national attention to Appalachia, and launched job programs in an era of high unemployment caused by mechanization of coal production. But his accomplishments were overshadowed by the fact that he was the first governor in state history to be indicted or convicted of a major crime. His troubles came not from a crime he committed while in office, but for bribing a jury foreman in a later case. He spent four years in a federal penitentiary.

A native of Elkins, Barron—known statewide as "Wally"—was born December 8, 1911, the son of Dr. Frederick Henry Barron and Mary Cuthbert Butler Barron. His father was a Presbyterian minister. He attended school in Elkins and Charleston, studied history and economics at Washington and Lee University, and received his law degree from West Virginia University in 1941. In 1936, he married Opal Marie Wilcox, a Pocahontas County native. They had three daughters.

In 1943, Barron enlisted in the U.S. Army. He was discharged as a sergeant in 1945. He served as mayor of Elkins, as a member of the House of Delegates, and as West Virginia attorney general. His election as governor came in 1960, a high-profile year for the Democratic Party. It was the year Massachusetts Sen. John F. Kennedy, whom Barron supported, defeated Minnesota Sen. Hubert Humphrey in the West Virginia primary. Barron pledged to "clean up the state," to work with a Democratic legislature, and to build a strong economy. He was a

Governor William Wallace Barron (1911–2002).

strong advocate of higher pay for teachers. Barron survived an allegation that he had offered $65,000 to an opponent to stay out of the race. The matter eventually was settled out of court.

In the end, Barron received 446,775 votes to 360,665 for Republican Harold Neely. The 26th governor took the oath of office secretly at 12:02 a.m. so he could immediately sign into law a one-cent consumers sales tax that predecessor Cecil Underwood had declined to sign. Barron's public swearing-in was held later, beneath the dome in the state capitol at noon, and attended by 2,700 persons. Personally reserved and a consensus builder, Barron was hospitable and friendly with friend and foe. Mrs. Barron earned the reputation of an outgoing, gracious, and active first lady.

The Barron administration's legislative record included establishment of a personal income tax and creation of a Human Rights Commission. He issued an executive order declaring state employees would be hired "regardless of race, creed, color or national origin." At the Southern Governors Conference at the Greenbrier, he firmly told Gov. George Wallace of Alabama that he would oppose "any and all statements . . . which would in any way promote or sanction discrimination."

Barron focused on jobs, oversaw the state's recovery from the 1961 flood that claimed 22 lives, and supervised allocation of north-south interstate highway mileage from Pennsylvania to Charleston. He traveled to Japan to promote West Virginia coal, shamed utility companies into dropping rate increases, positioned Green Bank as site of the world's largest movable radio telescope, and started the highly successful West Virginia Youth Science Camp. West Virginia celebrated its centennial in 1963. President Kennedy repaid a debt to his primary supporter and the people who

launched him toward the presidency by speaking before 10,000 people at the official ceremony June 20 in Charleston.

Highway construction was boosted with the passage of a $200 million bond issue in 1964, the final full year of Barron's term. He proclaimed that West Virginia had broken 14 economic records that year. He had centered economic development efforts in a new State Department of Commerce, headed by the man who would become his successor as governor, Hulett C. Smith of Beckley.

Governor Barron stepped down from office in early 1965, and opened a law office in Charleston. He was mentioned as a potential candidate for governor in 1968. In February 1968, however—in what became known as the "Valentine Day's Massacre"—Barron and five others were indicted by a federal grand jury on bribery-conspiracy charges relating to alleged "dummy corporations." Barron insisted he was innocent. The charges sketched an elaborate kickback scheme from persons doing business with the state.

At the August trial the prosecution alleged that documents signed by all six indicated they would "share equally in all profits." Five state vendors testified they sent checks to the dummy firms. The judge felt the governor's case was "on a little different basis than [those of] the other defendants," and seriously considered a directed verdict of acquittal on the basis the governor acted routinely in signing the agreements without intent of wrongdoing. The jury deliberated 18 hours. Their verdict read: Barron, innocent; the others, guilty.

In 1969, the Barrons moved to Florida. But in 1970, the state awakened to the news of a second indictment against the former governor, this one alleging the rigging of purchasing contracts. However, a Supreme Court decision in July nullified those indictments.

During the summer, stories began to surface in the press speculating that the jury in the original trial had voted 11-1 in favor of convicting Barron. The lone holdout was the jury foreman, Ralph Buckalew. The speculation ended in February 1971 when the former governor received a telephone call from a reporter, informing him a federal jury had indicted both Barron and Mrs. Barron on charges of bribing the foreman of the jury that acquitted Barron. The indictment claimed Mrs. Barron passed $25,000 in a brown paper bag to Mrs. Buckalew as a payoff. Buckalew immediately pleaded guilty. Mrs. Barron's name was dropped from the indictment, and Barron pleaded guilty to a new indictment of conspiracy, bribery, and obstruction of justice. He was sentenced to 25 years in prison and served four.

Barron later said he was convinced any verdict against him in the original trial would have been set aside on appeal and asserted the payoff scheme was the brainchild of his attorney. He said he received no money from any of the so-called business deals. He said he pleaded guilty in the second trial in order to get the indictment against his wife dropped. He felt had he testified in the original trial, he would have been found innocent anyway. He never denied the $25,000 paid the jury foreman. "You just don't know how hard it has been for me to live with that," he lamented.

Released from prison in 1975, Barron returned with a new sense of religious faith and a non-diminished love for West Virginia. He and Mrs. Barron spent several months a year in Mercer County before his death November 12, 2002, in Charlotte, North Carolina.

Jack Canfield
Charleston

John G. Morgan, *West Virginia Governors 1863–1980,* 1980.

Betty Bartholomew

Botanist Elizabeth Ann "Betty" Bartholomew was born June 14, 1912, in Wheeling. Much of her formal training was under naturalists P. D. Strausbaugh and Earl Core while she completed a study on the flora of Wirt County. In 1936, she earned a teacher's certificate and an A.B. in botany from West Virginia University, followed by a master's degree in 1947. Bartholomew began working for the university's botany department in 1938 and spent nearly 40 years there, retiring as WVU herbarium curator in 1977. She was instrumental in building the dried plant collection at WVU from 30,000 to 140,000 specimens, and she initiated a 2,000-plant seed collection.

Bartholomew led a simple life devoted to botanical studies, spending long hours on *Flora of West Virginia,* the monumental book by Strausbaugh, Core, and their associates. She died in Morgantown, March 14, 1985. The Elizabeth Ann Bartholomew Award of the Southern Appalachian Botanical Society is named in her honor.

William N. Grafton
WVU Extension Service

Annie Latham Bartlett

Artist Annie Virginia Latham Bartlett was born in Grafton, December 6, 1865, the daughter of Gen. George R. Latham and Caroline A. Thayer Latham. At the time of Annie's birth, her father was serving in the U.S. House of Representatives. He was among the first West Virginians to serve in Congress, which he left after a single term to become U.S. consul to Australia.

Annie Latham married Leonidas Bartlett in 1885. Following her son Frank's death during World War I, she entered the Maryland Institute at Baltimore at age 57 to study the fine arts as a "mental diversion." Her clay sculptures included conventional busts as well as figurines interpreting West Virginia's historic and cultural past, with such titles as "Madonna of the Hills" and "The Moonshiner." Her works won many awards and were exhibited at the New York World's Fair in 1939. Allen Eaton described Bartlett's work as a "unique individual product" in *Handicrafts of the Southern Highlands,* his monumental Depression era survey of Appalachian arts and crafts. Eaton noted that Bartlett had developed a process to harden clay without firing it, then painted and varnished her pieces to give the appearance of majolica or colored porcelain. Bartlett was also a painter and poet.

Annie Latham Bartlett died at her home in Buckhannon, April 21, 1948.

Noel W. Tenney
Tallmansville

Bartley Mine Disaster

On January 10, 1940, the Pond Creek No. 1 mine, at Bartley, McDowell County, exploded. The blast killed 91 miners, with another 47 escaping. Rescue teams worked five days to retrieve the bodies, but found no additional miners alive.

Pond Creek No. 1 was a deep shaft mine, operating in the Pocahontas No. 4 coal seam at a depth of nearly 600 feet. The mine was owned by the Pond Creek Pocahontas Coal Company, an Island Creek Coal Company affiliate. Investigators blamed methane gas for the fatal explosion, finding that the normally explosive coal dust, having been treated with rock dust or crushed lime, did not contribute to the blast. Most of the victims died instantly, though some asphyxiated following the explosion; two left farewell letters.

The mine disaster came only three months after a local school bus wreck cost the community six children. The Mullins family, whose daughter died in the bus wreck, lost a father and son in the mine. A monument erected by the United Mine Workers of America memorializes the dead miners.

See also Coal Mine Disasters

Baseball

In the first 20 years of the 20th century, professional baseball teams were organized in every area of West Virginia. The earliest town to have a team was Wheeling, which played several Midwestern cities in the Class B Central League from 1903 through 1912.

Fairmont, Clarksburg, and Piedmont played in the Class D Western Pennsylvania League in 1907. When the league folded a year later, Fairmont and Clarksburg switched to the Class D Pennsylvania-West Virginia League. Mannington spent less than half a season in professional ball, combining with Fairmont, Clarksburg, and Grafton to form the Class D West Virginia League in 1910. When the Grafton team disbanded on July 5, the league folded. Those early teams, which consisted mostly of local players, were not associated with the major leagues.

By 1920, 14 West Virginia cities and towns had spent time in professional baseball. They were Charleston, Clarksburg, Fairmont, Follansbee, Grafton, Huntington, Mannington, Martinsburg, Montgomery, Parkersburg, Piedmont, Point Pleasant, Wheeling, and Williamson. By the early 1930s, there were 11 teams, at Beckley, Bluefield, Charleston, Clarksburg, Fairmont, Huntington, Logan, Parkersburg, Welch, Wheeling, and Williamson.

In the early 1920s, future Hall of Fame members Hack Wilson and Lefty Grove played for Martinsburg of the Class D Blue Ridge League. In 1938–39, Stan Musial played for Williamson of the Class D Mountain State League. The minor-league boom of the late 1940s largely bypassed West Virginia. At that time, only Charleston, Bluefield, and Welch fielded teams.

Charleston entered professional baseball in 1910, calling its team the Statesmen. The Statesmen played in the Class D Virginia Valley League with Huntington, Point Pleasant, Parkersburg, Montgomery, and Ashland-Catlettsburg (Kentucky). It was the start of a busy and productive century of baseball in the capital city. After one year in the Virginia Valley League, Charleston participated in the Class D Mountain State League (1911–12) and the Class D Ohio State League (1913–16). In 1916, the city built Kanawha Park, a 3,500-seat wooden structure on the present site of Watt Powell Park, but spent the next 15 years without a pro team. In 1931, Charleston joined the Class C Middle Atlantic League (1931–42), a 12-city affiliation that included Beckley, Huntington, Fairmont, Clarksburg, and Wheeling.

By 1936, Charleston and Huntington were the Middle Atlantic League's lone remaining West Virginia cities. That year, Huntington's Walter Alston, a future Hall of Fame member, led the league with 35 home runs. Huntington dropped out after the '36 season, leaving Charleston as the league's only state representative. The other West Virginia cities offering professional baseball on the eve of World War II were Bluefield, Logan, Welch, and Williamson of the Class D Mountain State League.

Beginning with construction of 5,000-seat Watt Powell Park in 1949, Charleston began moving up the baseball ladder to the Class A Central League (1949–51), Class AAA American Association (1952–60), Class A Eastern League (1962–64), Class AAA International League (1961, 1971–83), and Class A South Atlantic

League (1987–present). Charleston's move to the American Association in 1952—the highest level ever for a West Virginia city — happened suddenly and unexpectedly. On June 23 of that year, the Toledo Mud Hens moved to the West Virginia capital, thereby thrusting Charleston into competition with Milwaukee, Kansas City, St. Paul, Louisville, Indianapolis, Minneapolis, and Columbus. As a member of the American Association in 1956, Charleston produced the only future Hall of Fame member in the city's long baseball history. Jim Bunning pitched for the team for three months before going to the Detroit Tigers.

By 2002, only Charleston, Bluefield, and Princeton had professional baseball teams. Except for a one-year absence in 1956, Bluefield has thrived as a member of the Appalachian Rookie League since 1946. The team produced major-league stars Cal Ripken Jr. and Eddie Murray. Nearby Princeton joined the league in 1988, its Devil Rays offering the Bluefield Orioles some cross-county competition. Huntington had a rookie team, the Cubs, from 1990 to 1994. The team, a Chicago Cubs affiliate, competed against Bluefield and Princeton and others in the Appalachian League.

Mike Whiteford
Charleston Gazette
Lloyd Johnson and Miles A. Wolff, *The Encyclopedia of Minor League Baseball*, 1993.

Basket Making

Traditional basket making in West Virginia has always relied on materials that could be found growing in the local area. Various indigenous plants useful for basketry materials include white oak, hickory, maple, elm, and yellow poplar trees; honeysuckle, Virginia creeper, wisteria, and grapevines; willows, straw, cattails, and other plants that have both strength and flexibility. White oak, rived into long thin pieces called splits, is the most common basket material, used to make a variety of different styles, shapes, and sizes.

While traditional basket makers are now rare, several different basket types continue to be made on a limited basis. These include rib, split, and wicker baskets. Rib baskets are made from a framework of a handle and rim, inset with ribs, and woven with thin splits. Split baskets have no such frame, but are constructed almost entirely from thin flat splits and include round, square, and rectangular shapes. Wicker baskets may be formed from naturally growing round materials such as willow or vines, or made from white oak that has been shaped into long flexible rods.

Baskets are named for their shape, size, and household use. Rib baskets may be called egg, butterfly, fanny, melon, or potato baskets; split baskets are often named for standard measures, such as pint, quart, and gallon; and wicker baskets sometimes are named for what they are used for, such as sewing or corn baskets.

From the late 1960s to the present, a public interest in traditional folklife and craft has vitalized basketry. The Cedar Lakes Craft Center and the Augusta Heritage Center offer classes in basketry, while Tamarack, MountainMade.com, and other services market crafts, thus encouraging the continuation of basket making.

See also Crafts Movement
Rachel Nash Law
Fayetteville
Rachel Nash Law and Cynthia W. Taylor, *Appalachian White Oak Basketmaking: Handing Down the Basket*, 1991.

Basketball Tournament

The West Virginia boys' high school basketball tournament began in Buckhannon on March 21, 1914. Since then more than 350 high schools have entered teams at some level of tournament play. Each spring the tournament city, Charleston in recent decades, takes on a holiday atmosphere as thousands of players and fans arrive from across the state.

The event was first sponsored by Wesleyan College, which at the time had West Virginia's largest and finest gymnasium. Invitations were issued to Elkins and Wheeling, each of which claimed basketball supremacy in 1914. Elkins High emerged triumphant and became the first school to earn the title "state champions." In 1915, Wesleyan athletic director Harry Stansbury contacted high schools all over West Virginia, inviting them to participate in an open tournament for the state basketball title. Fourteen teams answered the call, and the building of a sports tradition was under way.

The number of participating schools began to climb as basketball's popularity took hold. In 1922, the field of 64 was broken into "A" and "B" divisions, classified according to team strength rather than school size. Several different plans for structuring the event were used before the tournament was completely reorganized in 1933. Under the new plan sectional winners would advance to eight regional tournaments. The regional champions, the "State Eight," would then meet in the conclusive event. Since 1959, a three-class format has been used, based on school size, each class having eight teams in the tournament.

In 1939, after a 25-year run at Wesleyan College, the tournament was moved to Mountaineer Field House in Morgantown, which could better accommodate the growing crowds. Huntington's Memorial Field House was the site for the 1955 event, largely in response to the argument that the southern part of the state be given the opportunity to host the tournament. The annual affair alternated between Morgantown and Huntington until 1965, when Charleston's Civic Center made it a three-way rotation. Charleston has hosted the meet since 1972, with the exception of 1979–80 when it was held in Morgantown while the Charleston Civic Center coliseum was under construction.

The preeminent school in tournament history is Woodrow Wilson of Beckley. As of 2005, the Flying Eagles had won 15 state titles (all in the highest classification). Among schools still active, Wheeling Central is a distant second with eight, followed by Parkersburg with seven. Now closed by consolidation, Northfork's Blue Demons attracted national attention with eight consecutive Class AA crowns, and a total of 10 in a span of 18 years. Among the former giants that are no longer open, Wheeling won eight championships, Huntington seven, and Charleston six. Mullens, the only school to capture titles in three different classes, gathered seven of them before it was closed. Special mention must go to Hundred (1930) and Normantown (1945), small schools that won unclassified tournaments against all comers.

In 1919, the first state tournament for girls' high school basketball was held at Spencer. With growing opposition from many principals, some of whom expressed the view that basketball was not a suitable activity for young ladies, the girls' tournament did not survive the 1920s. Restoration of the event did not come until 1976. In the modern tournaments, the most successful schools have been Parkersburg in Class AAA (six championships) and Tucker County in Class AA (four championships). The Class A ranks have been dominated by Parkersburg Catholic with eight titles and Mercer Christian with seven.

See also Northfork Basketball, Sports
Tim L. Wyatt
Woodbridge, Virginia

Batboy

Batboy, along with Mothman and the Flatwoods Monster, is one of several bizarre creatures attributed to West Virginia. He was first reported by the *Weekly World News* in 1992, as having been found in a "previously uncharted cave east of Seneca Rocks." The sensationalist tabloid quoted a zoologist as speculating that Batboy was the offspring of creatures living deep in the earth, originally human, who had adapted to living in the dark. Batboy was described as standing two feet tall and weighing 19 pounds, with oversized amber eyes and ears "like satellite dishes." The newspaper published a picture meeting that description, later reproduced on a T-shirt used as a circulation premium.

Batboy, as depicted by the Weekly World News.

Batboy quickly found a cult following, and the *Weekly World News* published several other stories. Batboy was reported as having escaped from those who had found him in the cave, having been recaptured and escaping again, and having fallen in love. In 2000, he was reported as endorsing Al Gore for president of the United States. The popular story was made into an off-Broadway musical, which concluded its New York run in 2001 and moved into repertory theaters in other cities. *BatBoy*, the musical play, placed the story in the fictitious town of Hope Falls, West Virginia.

See also Flatwoods Monster, Mothman

Bath

See Berkeley Springs.

Bats

Although one out of every four mammal species is a bat and nearly 1,000 species of bats are known to exist, only 14 bat species have been found in West Virginia. These are the little brown bat, northern long-eared bat, Indiana bat, gray bat, small-footed bat, silver-haired bat, eastern pipistrelle, big brown bat, red bat, Seminole bat, hoary bat, evening bat, Virginia big-eared bat, and Rafinesque's big-eared bat. Nearly 70 percent of the world's bats feed on insects, as do all bats in the Mountain State.

Most bats in the state use caves at some point in their lives. Many hibernate in caves where they find cool, humid environments that stay above the freezing point all winter. Here, they lower their metabolism to conserve energy. In this way, they can survive the winter on fat accumulated in the fall before entering hibernation. Bats use an echo-location system to "see with their ears" and find their way in the dark.

Bats are common in all West Virginia counties, but some species such as the Virginia big-eared bats are localized to particular areas. More bats probably hibernate in Pendleton County than in any other county in the state.

The endangered Virginia big-eared bat is the only bat in West Virginia that raises its young, called pups, in caves. Other bats gather in warm areas, such as attics or hollow trees, to raise their pups. Most give birth to only one pup each year. The pups grow rapidly and are able to fly by the time they are three to four weeks old. Bats are relatively long-lived for mammals their size; some have lived more than 30 years.

Tree bats do not use caves at all. These bats live in trees where they hide among the foliage or in cracks in the bark. Because they do not hibernate in caves, these species may migrate south to avoid the cold of winter. Tree bats found in West Virginia include the red bat, hoary bat (West Virginia's largest bat), Seminole bat, and silver-haired bat.

Craig W. Stihler
Division of Natural Resources

Gordon Battelle

Minister Gordon Battelle played a role in the formation of West Virginia. Battelle was born in Newport, Ohio, November 14, 1814. He was educated at the Marietta Collegiate Institute (now Marietta College) in Ohio and the Allegheny College at Meadsville, Pennsylvania, where he received a B.A. degree in 1840. He taught at the Asbury Academy in Parkersburg, and then became the principal at the Northwestern Virginia Academy at Clarksburg.

Although he earned a reputation as an excellent teacher, his strong religious leanings led Battelle to be ordained a Methodist minister in 1847. Four years later, he left teaching and accepted a call as pastor of the Methodist Episcopal Church in Charleston. After two years, he moved to a similar position in Clarksburg, where in 1855 he was appointed as the presiding elder of the Clarksburg District of the Methodist Episcopal Church. Battelle was called to a church in Wheeling in 1859, where he became embroiled in the anti-slavery movement.

He was elected as a delegate to the first Constitutional Convention in 1861 and was instrumental in including a provision in the proposed constitution to support free public education. He failed, however, in having the abolition of slavery included in the final draft of the constitution. At the outbreak of the Civil War, he volunteered as chaplain to the First Virginia Volunteer Infantry and died of typhoid fever on August 7, 1862, in Washington.

Kenneth R. Bailey
WVU Institute of Technology

George J. Blazier, "The Pioneer Battelles and their Contributions to the Building of Ohio and West Virginia," *West Virginia History*, 1954.

Batts and Fallam Expedition

On September 1, 1671, Thomas Batts, Thomas Wood, and Robert Fallam set out from Petersburg, Virginia, with Indian guides to explore beyond the mountains. The colonists who had settled on the eastern seaboard knew very little about what was beyond the Appalachian Mountains. It was hoped a trade route across the continent could be discovered. Acting under a commission granted to Abraham Wood and authorized by the Virginia House of Burgesses, the Batts and Fallam group is credited with discovering Woods River, now called the New.

There is some speculation that the New River was actually discovered in 1654 by Abraham Wood, for whom it was first named, but the 1671 discovery is the first to be recorded. The explorers may have followed the river to the falls of the Kanawha in present Fayette County. Some suspect they went only as far as the border of West Virginia and Virginia. They ended their explorations because their Indian guides were afraid of the

---

Batts and Fallam discover the New River

"Sept. 16 [1671]. Our Indians . . . brought us some exceeding good Grapes and killed two turkies which were very welcome and with which we feasted ourselves and about ten of the clock set forward and after we had travelled about ten miles one of our Indians killed us a Deer and presently afterwards we had sight of a curious River like Apomatack River. Its course here was north and so as we suppose runs west about a certain curious mountain we saw westward. Here we had . . . our quarters, our course having been west. We understand the Mohecan Indians did here formerly live. It cannot be long, since we found corn stalks in the ground.

"Sept. 17. Early in the morning we went to seek some trees to mark, our Indians being impatient of longer stay by reason it was likely to be bad weather, and that it was so difficult to get provisions. We found four trees exceeding fit for our purpose that had been half bared by our Indians, standing after one the other. We first proclaimed the King in these words: 'Long live Charles the Second, by the grace of God King of England, Scotland, France, Ireland, and Virginia and of all the Territories thereunto belonging, Defender of the faith, etc.' firing some guns and went to the first tree which we marked . . . with a pair of marking irons for his sacred majesty."

—Robert Fallam *A Journey from Virginia to Beyond the Appalachian Mountains* (1671)

Indians who lived in this region. Woods River retained its name for at least 80 years. The Eman Bowen map published in 1749 is perhaps the earliest map calling it the New River. Land grants referencing the river issued in 1750, to the Harmons who settled in present West Virginia, were still calling it Woods River.

In 1763, in negotiations following the French and Indian War, the Batts and Fallam exploration was used in treaty negotiations to bolster England's claim to the Ohio Valley.

See also New River

W. Eugene Cox
National Park Service

Lewis P. Summers, *History of Southwest Virginia, 1746–1786, Washington County, 1777–1870,* 1989.

Beans and Cornbread

West Virginians of every social class enjoy a bowl of beans and cornbread from time to time, as the humble, high-fiber, high-protein dish moves up the food chain. The beans are pinto beans, called brown beans in some parts of the state. The bread is made the way cornbread is made throughout the Upper South, baked in cast iron with little or no sugar. The beans and bread are served hot from the kitchen, often with chopped or sliced onions on the side.

The simple meal requires hours of preparation. The dried beans are typically soaked overnight, then seasoned with salt and fatback pork and cooked through much of the next day. Pinto beans are not commonly grown in West Virginia and were not among our pioneer foods, but became available with the spread of stores as a cheap bulk or bagged commodity. Many mountaineers recall among their earliest memories the sight of a mother or grandmother picking over a pan of uncooked beans to remove the debris found in dried beans from the store. The beans were then rinsed in preparation for soaking.

Like biscuits and gravy, beans and cornbread are a folk food that have made the transition from family table to restaurant. Beans and cornbread, often very good, may now be found in restaurants across the state.

Ken Sullivan
West Virginia Humanities Council

Bear Rock Lakes

The Bear Rock Lakes Wildlife Management Area is located 13 miles east of Wheeling and two miles from the Dallas Pike interchange of Interstate 70, just off U.S. 40 near Valley Grove in Ohio County. The area is named for huge rocks found on its 242 acres. Four lakes, covering 16 acres, provide fishing for trout, catfish, muskie, large-mouth bass, and bluegill, as well as a home to waterfowl.

In 1936, the state purchased the initial three tracts of land totaling approximately 164 acres. In 1949, the West Virginia Conservation Commission constructed Baker Lake, 3.4 acres; Bear Lake, eight acres; Rock Lake, 4.1 acres; and Wood Pond, 0.5 acre. In 1950, the area was opened to fishing. Subsequent additions were 36 acres in 1968 and 43 acres in 1988. A handicapped accessible fishing pier was added to Wood Pond in 1988.

Woodlands of mixed hardwoods surround the lakes. Limited hunting is allowed for squirrel, raccoon, rabbit, and deer. Trapping permits are issued for beaver, raccoon, and muskrat. The area also includes 50 acres of cleared land and picnic facilities.

Beartown State Park

Beartown, a 107-acre state park, is located seven miles southwest of Hillsboro in Pocahontas County. One of the state's most unusual natural areas, Beartown is a world of stone, with rocks the size of houses and deep crevices the size of streets twisting among the rocks. A half-mile boardwalk on stilts allows visitors to view the spectacular sight.

Beartown's geologic history holds the clues to the unusual rock formation. The local cap rock consists of a 30-foot layer of Pocono sandstone underlain by softer shale. As the shale erodes, the support for the hard sandstone is worn down and it slumps downhill, causing cracks and fissures to develop. Sandstone breaks in regular fractures, so deep fissures develop and widen as the rocks continue to slip downhill.

Another feature of the sandstone is its many circular pits or cavities. The pits are caused by erosion as large grains of sand wash out until the more compact and resistant stone remains. Mice and birds nest in the small cavities. Some cavities are large enough for den sites. Beartown gets its name from black bears reputed to den in the rocks. The area around Beartown is rugged, and ice may remain in shady, rock-strewn valleys until July.

Norma Jean Kennedy-Venable
Morgantown

Tony Beaver

Tony Beaver is a West Virginia folk figure similar to Paul Bunyan. Margaret Prescott Montague, native poet and author, believed Tony and Paul were one and the same, a mythical super-lumberman appearing under different names in different parts of the country. Montague first collected the stories of his exploits from real lumbermen at the turn of the century. This folk hero's adventures were created by the West Virginia "woodhicks" as they tried to out-lie each other during evenings in the logging camps.

Tony Beaver had been born regular-size but throughout childhood he grew in a most outrageous manner. As a young man he naturally preferred the out-of-

doors. It was high on a mountain, up mythical "Eel River," that Tony built his lumbering camp.

Folks often sent Tony word, by a jaybird, that they desperately needed help. One winter it got so cold and snowy that they couldn't get outside for firewood. Tony just strolled out across those snowbanks and cut hundreds of tree tops, delivering firewood right down through the chimneys. Spring came slowly and planted crops failed until Tony put his efforts into growing one big "tater." It covered four acres of ground, and fed the entire population for several weeks.

See also Margaret Prescott Montague

Noel W. Tenney
Tallmansville

Beckley

Beckley, the county seat and largest town in Raleigh County, is situated in the central part of the county on a high plateau at an elevation of about 2,400 feet. Located near the intersection of three major highways (Interstates 64 and 77, and U.S. 19), Beckley developed from a small agricultural settlement into a commercial hub for the surrounding coalfields and now has an economy based primarily on retail, service, and tourism. Its 2000 population was 17,254.

The town was founded by Gen. Alfred P. Beckley. He named the town for his father, John Beckley, the first clerk of the U.S. House of Representatives and the first Librarian of Congress. The town of Beckley was established in 1838 by an act of the Virginia General Assembly that authorized Alfred Beckley to lay out a town on 30 acres of his property lying at the 23rd mile marker of the old Bluestone Road. In 1850, Raleigh County was created, and Beckley was named the county seat. Development was slow. During the Civil War both Union and Confederate forces occupied the community, and in 1863 Union troops shelled the town, killing a small girl.

Mining of Raleigh County's rich bituminous coal deposits began in the 1890s, and a branch of the C&O finally reached Beckley in 1901. The opening of the great Winding Gulf coalfield in 1907, virtually on Beckley's doorstep, spurred growth. After the Virginian Railway began building a new line in 1908 to the ports of Virginia, coal production doubled and then tripled within a few years.

Development of the coalfields brought an influx of population. The number of inhabitants rose from 342 in 1900 to 2,161 in 1910. Homes, businesses, schools, and churches were built. In 1906, Beckley's first theater, the Carter Opera House, opened with a production of *The Merry Widow*. Street paving began in 1916.

Beckley's fortunes fluctuated with those of the coal industry. While the city suffered less during the Depression of the 1930s than other parts of the state, coal prices declined and mines closed throughout southern West Virginia. World War II brought an increased demand for coal, but after the war shrinking markets and depleted coal seams created new hardships. Construction of the West Virginia Turnpike, completed from Charleston to Beckley and Princeton in the early '50s, provided an economic boost, and the energy crisis of the 1970s created new demands for coal. Coal production continued to be the mainstay of the region's economy into the 1980s, when increasing mechanization led to the loss of thousands of mining jobs. Beckley weathered the subsequent economic downturn more successfully than smaller communities. The city's location at the junction of two interstate highways acted as a magnet for new business investment, and in the 1990s Beckley again became one of the state's fastest-growing areas.

Beckley is the birthplace of two West Virginia governors, Clarence W. Meadows (1945–49) and Hulett C. Smith (1965–69). It is home to Mountain State University, founded as Beckley College in 1933, with the National Mine Health and Safety Academy and the Appalachian Bible College nearby. The city's four hospitals are Beckley Appalachian Regional Hospital, Raleigh General Hospital, the Veteran's Administration Regional Medical Center, and Pinecrest State Hospital. Beckley has three radio stations, a public television station, and a daily newspaper, the *Register-Herald*, with a circulation of 32,323. The area is served by one airline from the Raleigh County Memorial Airport.

The Beckley Exhibition Coal Mine is located at the city's New River Park, along with the Youth Museum of Southern West Virginia. Tamarack, a showcase for West Virginia arts and crafts, is located at a nearby turnpike exit. Grandview and Twin Falls state parks, Lake Stephens, and Winterplace ski resort are nearby. Theatre West Virginia produces two annual outdoor musical dramas at nearby Grandview, *Honey in the Rock* and *Hatfields & McCoys*. Wildwood, the home of Gen. Alfred Beckley, has been restored and is now operated as a house museum.

See also Alfred Beckley, John Beckley

Margo Stafford
Clarksburg

Alfred Beckley

City founder Alfred Beckley, born May 26, 1802, in Washington, was the only surviving child of John James Beckley and Maria Prince. The death of his father in 1807 made Beckley's early life economically precarious. With the assistance of President James Monroe, a family friend, he was appointed to West Point, graduating in 1823.

After a long legal battle Beckley in 1835 gained a clear title to 56,679 acres in what is now Raleigh County, land that his father had acquired decades before. He resigned from the army in 1836 and moved to his property with his wife, Amelia, the daughter of Neville Craig of Pittsburgh. The town of Beckley, originally called Raleigh Courthouse, grew up around Wildwood, the Beckley family home which remains a city landmark. Beckley was appointed a militia general in 1849. He later saw limited service with the Confederacy during the Civil War and was briefly imprisoned at Camp Chase, Ohio. Five of his sons served in the Civil War.

Beckley was joined at his holdings on the Bluestone Road by several members of his mother's family, the Princes, bringing another prominent Raleigh County surname to the area. He spent most of the remainder of his life developing his mill and landholdings. The town of Beckley, chartered in 1838, is based on his entrepreneurial efforts and was named in honor of his father. Alfred Beckley died May 26, 1888, at Wildwood.

See also Beckley, John Beckley

Gerard W. Gawalt
Library of Congress

Beckley College

See Mountain State University.

John Beckley

John James Beckley, born the son of obscure English parents, August 4, 1757, was sent to Virginia in 1769 as an indentured servant. Using his remarkable skills as a scribe and the opportunities presented by the American Revolution, Beckley moved from general clerical assistant to his master, John Clayton, to become a lawyer. In 1789, he became the first clerk of the U.S. House of Representatives, and first Librarian of Congress in 1802. While Congress met in New York, Beckley met Maria Prince, whom he married in 1790. A political ally of Thomas Jefferson, Beckley wrote many supportive essays, pamphlets, and a Jefferson campaign biography in 1800. Beckley sought to make his fortune in land speculation, and among other properties he acquired a large acreage in what is now Raleigh County, where his only surviving child, Alfred, established the town of Beckley. John Beckley died April 8, 1807.

See also Alfred Beckley

Gerard W. Gawalt
Library of Congress

Beckley Register-Herald

The *Register-Herald* is published seven mornings a week in Beckley, with an average circulation of 31,000. The newspaper's history dates back to 1880, when the *Raleigh County Index* was established by Edwin Prince, a Beckley merchant. In 1893, Robert A. Spencer acquired the paper and renamed it the *Raleigh Register*. After further changes in ownership and party affiliation, the *Register* settled down as a Democratic paper and remained so until it ceased publication in 1984. Meanwhile, county Republicans launched the *Raleigh Herald* in 1900.

In 1912, a local newspaper dynasty was born when Charles Hodel, who had previously been editor and manager of the *Herald* for 18 months, took over editorship of the *Register* and management of the corporation owning it. In the fall of 1921, the *Register* began publishing twice a week, and in 1923 a Sunday issue was added. In 1924, Beckley's first daily newspaper, the *Evening Post*, was established. In 1926, the backers of the *Post* bought the *Raleigh Herald* and combined the two, naming the publication the *Post-Herald*. In 1928, the *Register* also became a daily.

In September 1929, Hodel took over the *Post-Herald* while retaining the *Register*. The Beckley Newspapers Corporation was organized, now owning both papers. Hodel became president and general manager of the new corporation and publisher of both papers. Hodel's sons, Emile, John, and George followed him into the newspaper business. Emile became editor of the *Post Herald* in 1957. John became editor of the *Register* in 1962. Charles Hodel died in 1973, and George became president of Beckley Newspapers in 1965.

In 1976, Beckley Newspapers Corporation was sold to Clay Communications, a Charleston company publishing the *Charleston Daily Mail* and other papers. The evening *Register* was merged into the morning *Post-Herald* in 1984, with the combined paper named the *Register-Herald*. Clay Communications sold its newspapers, including the *Register-Herald* in 1987 to Lincoln Publishing Company, an affiliate of Thomson Newspapers. Community Newspaper Holdings of Alabama bought the paper in 2000.

Judie Smith
West Virginia Humanities Council

Jim Wood, *Raleigh County, West Virginia*, 1994.

Clair Bee

Clair Francis Bee, born March 2, 1896 in Pennsboro, Ritchie County, was a successful, innovative college basketball coach and widely published author of both technical basketball books and young adult fiction. Bee spent his childhood in Grafton, where he graduated from high school.

After an impressive start to his coaching career at Rider College in New Jersey, Bee became basketball coach at Long Island University, where he established the Blackbirds as a national power by winning the National Invitational Tournament in 1939 and 1941. Bee ended his college coaching career following the 1951 point-shaving scandals that devastated college basketball. He was crushed by the involvement of three of his players and took it as his personal failure as a coach and the failure of college basketball to instill better values in players.

In 1948, Bee wrote *Touchdown Pass*. The book, featuring Chip Hilton as a high school football player, sold more than 125,000 copies. Bee wrote 23 more books in the Chip Hilton series, which traced the athletic careers of Chip and his friends from Valley Falls through high school and college seasons in football, basketball, and baseball. Valley Falls was named for a place near Grafton, and State College was set in a small college town not unlike Morgantown.

Most critics claim that the best in the series was *Hoop Crazy*, published in 1950. The final Chip Hilton book, *Comeback Cagers*, was published in 1962. Through Chip, Bee taught a generation of young readers to be honest, stoical, modest, and to obey their parents and coaches. Chip exuded America's small-town values and a strong sense of group loyalty.

Clair Bee received numerous awards, including election to the Basketball Hall of Fame and the West Virginia Sportswriters Hall of Fame. He died May 20, 1983.

C. Robert Barnett
Marshall University
Rogers McAvoy, "Mr. Basketball: The Clair Bee Story," *Goldenseal*, Winter 1991.

Bee Hunting

The honey bee, although not native to West Virginia, was present in large numbers as a wild insect from the time of first settlement until bee populations were decimated by disease in the late 20th century. The bees, having been brought to North America in hives, soon escaped in significant numbers and often traveled ahead of westward-moving European settlers, swarming from tree to tree in the primeval forests.

Bee trees, valued for their store of honey and sometimes for the colony of bees, were avidly hunted by generations of West Virginians. This was made easier by the fact that bees typically travel in a straight "bee line" when returning home. Bee hunters would closely observe returning bees, sometimes lying on their backs to "skylight" the insects against the light of the sky as they left a water or nectar source. Once spotted, bees would be sighted as far as the eye could see, and the hunter would then advance to that point to await other home-bound bees. Eventually the bees were followed back to their tree, which was then cut and robbed of its sweet treasure.

The wild honey was a welcome addition to the diet of mountaineers, who often supplemented their agricultural pursuits by hunting and gathering. Some-

times the queen bee was saved as well, and a new domestic colony was started by the bee hunter. May and June were the preferred months for bee hunting.

Ken Sullivan
West Virginia Humanities Council

Bee Line March

In June 1775, the Continental Congress ordered the formation of two companies of Virginia riflemen to march to the aid of George Washington's forces at Boston. Washington recommended that Hugh Stephenson and Daniel Morgan command the two companies. Stephenson raised his company in the Shepherdstown area, while Morgan raised his around Winchester. As the companies were being raised, a rivalry ensued between the two commanders. Each wanted the privilege of leading the way, an honor to be given to the first to fill his company. Within a week both companies were filled, and after six weeks of preparation both were ready and eager to get to Boston. Stephenson and Morgan agreed that the two companies would rendezvous at nearby Frederick, Maryland, and march together to Boston. Stephenson arrived at Frederick only to find that Morgan, wanting to arrive at Boston first, had stolen a day's march. Stephenson's 98-man company left on July 17 and attempted to overtake their rivals, often marching 30 to 36 miles in a day, but were unable to do so. After marching 600 miles in 24 days, Stephenson's riflemen arrived at Cambridge, Massachusetts, and were placed in the defense of Roxbury. Morgan had arrived five days before. The extraordinary journey of the Virginians became known as the Bee Line March.

See also Berkeley County Riflemen
Lee R. Maddex
WVU Institute for the History of Technology
Millard Kessler Bushong, *Historic Jefferson County*, 1972; Danske Dandridge, *Historic Shepherdstown*, 1910.

Beech Fork Lake

Beech Fork Lake, located in Cabell and Wayne counties, was constructed by the U.S. Army Corps of Engineers and opened to the public in 1978. The lake was created by damming the Beech and Miller forks of Twelvepole Creek. Beech Fork Lake provides outdoor recreational opportunities and flood control, and consists of more than 720 acres of water with an additional 3,981 acres of land in adjoining Beech Fork State Park. There are boat rentals and a boat launch ramp, picnicking and playgrounds, and hiking trails. The dam and visitors center are located in Wayne County, at the town of Lavalette, while Beech Fork Lake State Park is in southwestern Cabell County.

Leslie Birdwell
Huntington

Beech Fork State Park

Beech Fork State Park, located on the border of Cabell and Wayne counties, opened in 1979 after the U.S. Army Corps of Engineers created a lake by constructing Beech Fork Dam near Lavalette.

In 1979, Governor Rockefeller recommended a $5.1 million appropriation in the state budget to build a lodge in the park. The amount was cut to $200,000 because legislators representing Cabell and Wayne counties said plans were not yet ready. After a 1992 study concluded that a $23 million plan for a lodge, cottages, and a golf course could not pay for itself, the 1994 legislature and Governor Caperton approved $92,761 for a study of more modest developments. In 1999, the park received funds for construction of six luxury cabins, a 50-meter swimming pool with bathhouse, and a snack stand. These facilities opened in 2000. The park consists of 3,981 acres and offers 275 campsites with electric hookups. A visitors center and the park headquarters are located at the Bowen entrance to the park, accessible from State Route 10 in Cabell County south of Huntington. The marina, a swimming beach, and other picnic and recreational facilities are located at the Lavalette entrance via State Route 152 in Wayne County.

See also State Parks

Tom D. Miller
Huntington

Mary Behner

Reformer Mary Behner was born March 14, 1906, in Xenia, Ohio. After graduating in 1928 from Wooster College, Behner, the daughter of a Presbyterian minister, hoped to become a foreign missionary. Instead, she accepted a position with the Board of National Missions of the Presbyterian Church, U.S.A., and began a

Social activist Mary Behner (1906–88).

home mission in West Virginia's northern coalfields.

From 1928 until 1937, Behner worked in the coal camps along Scotts Run, a few miles from Morgantown, where once-prosperous mining operations had fallen victim to the depressed coal market of the late 1920s. Thousands of families, including numerous immigrants and African-Americans, were stranded by changing economic tides.

Behner was shocked by the poverty she encountered, but she was not easily daunted. Armed with an iron will and abiding faith, Behner comforted mothers whose babies had died for want of milk, castigated coal operators for ignoring their workers' needs, and created educational and social outlets for young people. Her most visible contribution to Scotts Run was "The Shack," a former company store that Behner converted into a community center. Behner continued to support social justice and service projects after her 1937 marriage to David Christopher. Chief among her interests were programs that assisted children in need and those that fostered an appreciation for different cultures. Mary Behner Christopher died in Morgantown, March 15, 1988.

See also Scotts Run

Christine M. Kreiser
Clarksburg
Bettijane Burger, "Mary Elizabeth Behner Christopher, 1906–," *Missing Chapters II: West Virginia Women in History,* 1986.

Belgians

During the first decade of the 20th century, French was frequently spoken on the streets of such communities as South Charleston, the North View section of Clarksburg, and the small town of Salem. These neighborhoods shared a connection to the window-glass industry, and the people speaking French often were Walloons, or French-speaking Belgians. About 1900, changes in window-glass manufacture brought thousands of immigrants from the Charleroi area of Belgium just when the industry was expanding into West Virginia to take advantage of cheap natural gas and large deposits of silica sand. For a generation, window-glass factories, many of which were worker-owned cooperatives, relied heavily on these Belgian immigrants to provide the skills necessary to make West Virginia a national center of production.

West Virginia's Belgians came from an area economically similar to West Virginia. The Charleroi basin of the Hainaut province in Belgium was dependent upon coal mining, steel production, and window-glass manufacturing. The Belgians' new homes in north-central West Virginia and the Kanawha Valley must have felt familiar.

They left Europe because the Belgian glass factories were struggling in the 1880s and 1890s. Equally important, workers had limited opportunities to voice their concerns either politically or economically. Belgian glassworkers found in the United States an effective trade union to represent their workplace concerns and the means to build a vibrant political movement advocating democratic socialism. In fact, some of these Belgian enclaves, including Star City near Morgantown and Adamston (now part of Clarksburg), elected Socialist mayors in the years before World War I. Aside from politics, Belgian ethnic communities also became famous for the cuisine, musical groups, social clubs, and celebrations composing the unique Belgian cultural heritage.

The technological changes that had made skilled Belgian workers so valuable, however, soon gave way to newer technologies that turned window-glass manufacture from a skilled craft to a mass-production industry. By the end of the 1920s, a few large corporations dominated the industry and machines replaced most of the skilled craftsmen. One exception, window-glass cutters, continued to provide opportunities to a new generation of Belgian-Americans. More than 70 years later, the Belgian-American Heritage Society keeps alive the history and culture of this fascinating ethnic group.

See also Glass Industry

Ken Fones Wolf
West Virginia University
Frederick Barkey, *Cinderheads in the Hills: The Belgian Window Glass Workers of West Virginia,* 1988.

Bell Atlantic Corporation

See Verizon.

Belsnickling

Belsnickling, once common in parts of West Virginia, is an ancient mid-winter practice related to many similar winter solstice activities found in western countries. Of German origin, belsnickling is similar to mumming traditions as found in Anglo-Celtic countries (England, Scotland, Ireland). The term is an Anglicized version of two German words: Pels (fur) and Nicholas (St. Nicholas). Over time, pels Nicholas came to be pronounced belsnickle, and it simply means a furry St. Nicholas.

The practice of belsnickling (also called "pelsing") in West Virginia involves a group, dressed in masquerade, going from house to house visiting neighbors and having the inhabitants guess who they are. Sometimes mischief is involved, and often the belsnickles were given seasonal treats such as cider and cake. Some older people remember that they, as belsnickles, carried a switch and switched the hands of children who reached for the candy they offered. The belsnickle figure sometimes represented this darker presence, and it was common for parents to warn children to "be good or the belsnickle will get you." Belsnickling is rare in West Virginia today, but until the mid-20th century it was common in areas of early German settlement in the eastern side of the state.

Gerald Milnes
Augusta Heritage Center
Ruth H. Cline, "Belsnickles and Shanghais," *Journal of American Folklore,* April–June 1958; Gerald C. Milnes, "Old Christmas and Belsnickles," *Goldenseal,* Winter 1995.

Pinckney Benedict

Writer Pinckney Benedict was born in Lewisburg, April 11, 1964, the son of a prominent local family, and grew up on the family dairy farm in Greenbrier County. He earned a bachelor's degree from Princeton University in 1986 and an M.F.A. degree from the Writers' Workshop at the University of Iowa in 1988.

Benedict has published two collections of short stories, *Town Smokes* and *The Wrecking Yard,* and the novel *Dogs of God.* All three were named Notable Books by the *New York Times Book Review.* His stories and nonfiction have appeared in magazines and anthologies such as *Esquire, New Stories from the South, The Oxford Book of American Short Stories,* and the O. Henry Awards anthology. Benedict has received several awards, including Britain's Steinbeck Award, the *Chicago Tribune's* Nelson Algren Award, inclusion in the Pushcart Prize XXI anthology, and the Henfield Foundation's Transatlantic Review Awards.

His plays have received staged readings and performances at the Greenbrier Valley Theatre in Lewisburg. Several of his short stories have been adapted for short films and television in the U.S. and Europe. He completed a feature-length screenplay, an adaptation of *Four Days* by

Author Pinckney Benedict (1964–).

Canadian novelist John Buell. The film premiered at the 1999 Toronto International Film Festival and was distributed on video by Paramount. Additionally, he wrote the screenplay for *Dogs of God* for Gerard de Thame Films, London.

Pinckney Benedict is an associate professor of English at Hollins University in Roanoke, Virginia.

Judie Smith
West Virginia Humanities Council

Michael L. Benedum

Philanthropist Michael Late Benedum, born in Bridgeport, July 16, 1869, made a fortune in the oil and gas business, starting in his native state but expanding his operations to Illinois, Arkansas, Louisiana, and Texas, and eventually to Canada, Mexico, and overseas. In 1896, he married Sarah Lantz, and the following year they had their only child, Claude Worthington Benedum. With the outbreak of World War I, Claude joined the army and was sent to Camp Meade in Maryland, where he was stricken by influenza. His parents were notified and were at their son's bedside when he died in 1918 at age 20.

Today, Michael Benedum is remembered not so much for his successful exploits as an oil man but for his generosity. In 1944, he established the Claude Worthington Benedum Foundation, which remains a major philanthropic organization a half-century later.

Himself mostly self-educated, Benedum underwrote hundreds of college scholarships at dozens of colleges. Though he had been a resident of Pittsburgh for many years, he maintained close ties with his hometown and in 1953 spent $1.5 million to build the handsome Bridgeport Methodist Church. In 1957, he built the Bridgeport Civic Center.

When Benedum died on July 30, 1959, he left half of his fortune, said to total $100 million or more, to family members and the other half to the Claude Worthington Benedum Foundation. Today, the Pittsburgh-based charity continues his generosity and, honoring his wishes, directs much of its philanthropy to West Virginia.

James E. Casto
Herald-Dispatch
Sam T. Mallison, *The Great Wildcatter,* 1953.

Jesse Bennet

Physician Jesse Bennet, who performed the first cesarean section in America in 1794, later figured prominently in Mason County history. Bennet was born in Frankford, Pennsylvania, July 10, 1769. He studied medicine in Philadelphia under Dr. Benjamin Rush, a prominent early American physician and signer of the Declaration of Independence. Bennet was granted his medical degree in April 1791.

"To give service to my country"
"I don't think that what's happening in 'Nam will win any cause worth 150,000 human lives. That's my opinion. I'll express it here now, or later when I might be risking my neck in 'Nam. It's my obligation as part of a democracy to let my voice be heard.
"It is also my obligation to give service to my country. That's why I'm here—to help provide freedom for dissenting voices. That's one of the things which makes a country great. Only when a system is considered hopeless should a person leave it or work for its destruction.
"I believe in America. I believe that our process of government can respond to the people's needs—if we each will assume our responsibility. Too many of us jump to the last resort first—leaving or destroying the system."

—Tom Bennett *Peaceful Patriot* (1980)

Bennet decided to go west to practice medicine, settling in Rockingham County, Virginia. In the spring of 1793, he married Elizabeth Hogg. It was on his wife that Bennet successfully performed a cesarean section in 1794, without proper equipment and with no antiseptics. He also removed his wife's ovaries. Both mother and baby girl survived.

In 1797, Bennet, with his wife and daughter, moved to present Mason County, on the Ohio River about five miles north of Point Pleasant. They settled on land granted to father-in-law Peter Hogg for service in the French and Indian War. Bennet established a large practice and lived there the remainder of his life. He was influential in the formation of Mason County in 1804. Bennet was appointed major of the Mason County militia in 1804, and he represented Mason County in the Virginia General Assembly. He served as Army surgeon in the War of 1812.

Dr. Jesse Bennet died July 13, 1842.

Dorothy Poling, "Jesse Bennet, Pioneer Physician and Surgeon," *West Virginia History,* January 1951.

Louis Bennett Jr.

Military aviator Louis Bennett Jr. was West Virginia's only World War I fighter ace. He was the son of Louis Bennett Sr., the unsuccessful 1908 Democratic candidate for governor, and Sallie Maxwell Bennett. Born in Weston, September 22, 1894, Bennett died in France, August 24, 1918, of injuries sustained when his plane was shot down by German anti-aircraft fire. With 12 combat kills, including three aircraft and nine balloons, Bennett placed himself ninth on the World War I roster of aces. This record was accomplished in just ten days after assignment to his combat unit on August 14, and with only 41 hours of combat flying time.

While attending Yale, from which he graduated in 1917, Bennett conceived the idea of a flying corps based on the concept of the French Escadrille Lafayette. He hoped to command the unit in Europe. When Governor Cornwell provided $10,000 in state funds, Bennett left Yale and returned to West Virginia and formed the West Virginia Flying Corps, whose flyers were commissioned by the governor on July 26, 1917. But when the U.S. Army refused to accept Bennett's corps as a unit, his eagerness to participate in the war led him to enter flight school with the British Royal Air Force in Canada. He was serving with the RAF at the time of his death. Bennett's mother erected monuments in the U.S. and Europe to commemorate and memorialize his sacrifice.

L. Wayne Sheets
Charleston
L. Wayne Sheets, "Able Courage—The Monumental Sallie Maxwell Bennett," *Goldenseal,* Spring 2000.

Tom Bennett

Congressional Medal of Honor winner Thomas W. Bennett was a conscientious objector who received America's highest honor for his heroism as an army medic in Vietnam. He was born in Morgantown, April 7, 1947, and died in a battle at Chu Pa, Vietnam, February 11, 1969. Active in high school clubs, ecumenical church work, and the Boy Scouts, Bennett was a vocal opponent of the Vietnam War while a student at West Virginia University. Believing it was wrong to evade the draft while others had to serve, he volunteered as a noncombatant medic with the 1st Battalion, 14th Infantry. He was killed by gunfire while trying to drag a wounded soldier to safety and nominated by his commanding officer and soldiers for the Medal of Honor.

Named for Bennett are the WVU residence hall Bennett Tower; the Bennett House campus ecumenical center; and the Bennett Youth Center at Schofield Barracks, U.S. Army 14th and 25th Infantry Division, Hawaii.

Bonni V. McKeown
Capon Springs
Bonni V. McKeown, *Peaceful Patriot: The Story of Tom Bennett,* 1980.

Bens Run Earthworks

The prehistoric Bens Run earthworks were located on a terrace of the Ohio River between the present communities of Bens Run and Long Reach, in Tyler County. The earliest eyewitness account of the earthworks was from the 1808 journal of Lewis Summers, who described it as "an ancient encampment" with square trenches enclosing an area of ten acres. In 1818, the journal of Thom Nuttall described the earthworks as "a small square embankment containing near an acre, with only one or two openings or entrances."

Later accounts described an oval or rectangular area of approximately 400 acres enclosed by the remnants of two parallel walls of earth and stone, six to 12 feet high and 120 feet apart, approximately four miles in length. A cross wall was reported running from one long side of the enclosure to the other, with two additional interior walls extending south from the cross wall. Two earthen mounds were reported within the enclosure, and several more mounds were located nearby.

The Archeology Section of the West Virginia Geological and Economic Survey officially recorded the Bens Run earthworks in 1965. By that time, all visible remnants of the earthworks were gone, probably through repeated plowing, although one of the mounds remained. Archeological surveys conducted in the 1990s found no evidence of the enclosure. While it seems likely that there were earthworks at Bens Run, the true dimensions may never be known. The discrepancies in the accounts may be the result of embellishment and second-hand reports. Data for similar enclosures recorded in West Virginia and Ohio support the earlier, more conservative descriptions.

Darla S. Hoffman
Cultural Resource Analysts

Benwood Mine Disaster

At about 7:10 on Monday morning, April 28, 1924, the workday was just beginning at the Benwood coal mine south of Wheeling. As the miners went through their daily routine of preparing their work areas and undercutting the coal, an explosion ripped through the Wheeling Steel Corporation mine. Portions of the main entry were blocked by slate falls and debris.

Two fire bosses had reported the mine free of gas before the workers entered the portal to begin their shift. A miner found a roof fall about 22 feet from the room face. Thinking the fall had been examined by the fire boss he went over the fall toward his room and his open light ignited the firedamp, an explosive mixture of methane and air. In all probability the fall occurred after the fire boss had visited the area. The mine was dry and dusty—sprinkling and ventilation were poor—and the subsequent dust explosion carried to every area of the mine.

The rescue effort was slow, difficult, and dangerous. The first teams began

Berkeley Castle, a Berkeley Springs landmark.

digging soon after the disaster, but the destruction of the haulage ways and entries slowed the initial exploration. The possibility of deadly afterdamp, as the carbon monoxide that follows mine explosions is called, presented a serious threat to rescue workers. While the rescue teams worked, relatives kept a constant vigil outside the mine, but by Friday it became clear that 119 men were dead.

Jeffrey B. Cook
North Greenville College

Berkeley Castle

Colonel Samuel Taylor Suit of Suitland, Maryland, built Berkeley Castle as a summer cottage for his young bride, Rosa Pelham. The daughter of an Alabama congressman, Rosa was less than half Suit's age when they married. Construction began on the Morgan County landmark in 1885; Suit never lived to see it finished.

Perched on Warm Springs Ridge overlooking Berkeley Springs, Suit's cottage was the most extravagant example of the town's Victorian building boom. Famous for sophisticated friends and gala parties, Rosa eventually lost the castle to debt. She was forced out in 1902, returned in 1909, and lost the place permanently within a few years more. Since then, Berkeley Castle has gone through several hands.

Built of local stone, the castle has 13 rooms plus a basement. The great hall has a high ceiling, hardwood floor, and stone fireplaces at each end. A pine-paneled dining room on the main floor also has a fireplace. A wide stairway curves up to second-floor bedrooms and a paneled library. A narrow staircase leads to the turreted rooftop trimmed with crenelated battlements and offering a fabulous view of the town. Three crosses are sunk into the stone walls of the castle's three-story

tower. State Route 9 now cuts through the castle property; a stone gate tower is stranded on the opposite side of the highway. Berkeley Castle is on the National Register of Historic Places.

Jeanne Mozier
Berkeley Springs

Berkeley County

Berkeley County is located in the Eastern Panhandle. Berkeley borders Maryland to the north and Virginia to the south, with Jefferson and Morgan counties on the east and west. Its major streams are Back Creek and Opequon Creek. They drain into the Potomac River, which forms Berkeley County's northern border. The North Mountain divides the county into distinct eastern and western sections.

Berkeley originally took in all of present Berkeley and Jefferson counties and two-thirds of Morgan. It was carved off Frederick County, Virginia, in 1772. The county was named for Norborne Berkeley, a colonial governor of Virginia. Jefferson County was separated from Berkeley in 1801, and Berkeley reached its present size of 324.8 square miles when Morgan County was formed in 1820.

In the 1720s, settlers started coming into the area, which was the first part of West Virginia to be settled. Though Morgan Morgan is traditionally recognized as the first white settler, several families came in the late 1720s, ahead of him. John and Isaac Vanmeter were authorized in 1730 to bring settlers to take up 40,000 acres east of Opequon Creek, and Morgan Bryant and Alexander Ross were similarly authorized for 70,000 acres west of Opequon. John Vanmeter settled in the area and took up about 3,000 acres. Many of the settlers came from Pennsylvania, New York, and New Jersey. Samuel Taylor had a ferry operating across the Potomac River southeast of Shepherdstown by 1734. Morgan acquired his 1,000 acres west of present Bunker Hill on November 12, 1735.

Much of this same land was claimed by Lord Fairfax. By 1748, Fairfax established a land office and began selling land, including some that had already been sold by Joist Hite and others. Title confusion persisted until the conclusion of a lawsuit between Hite and Fairfax, settled after both men were dead.

Many of the early settlers were Quakers, who established a meeting house by 1738 west of present Martinsburg. Presbyterians established three churches at an early date, including one at Falling Waters at about 1730, one at Tuscarora in the 1740s, and the third at what is now Tomahawk by 1770. In 1743, Baptists from Maryland established a settlement and meeting house at Mill Creek, now Gerrardstown. There was also an official, state-supported Anglican Church. This

FAST FACTS ABOUT BERKELEY COUNTY

Founded: 1772

Land in square miles: 324.8

Population: 75,905

Percentage minorities: 7.3%

Percentage rural: 45.7%

Median age: 35.8

Percentage 65 and older: 11.2%

Birth rate per 1,000 population: 14.2

Median household income: $38,763

High school graduate or higher: 77.6%

Bachelor's degree or higher: 15.1%

Home ownership: 74.2%

Median home value: $99,700

This information is from the 2000 U.S. Census. In 2000, West Virginia as a whole had 5 percent minorities, a median age of 38.9, median household income of $29,696, and a 75.2 percent home ownership rate.

was the old English Church, established at Bunker Hill about 1740 by Morgan Morgan, Dr. John Briscoe, and Jacob Hite, son of Joist Hite.

During the French and Indian War, George Washington established forts throughout Berkeley County. Several of the forts are still standing. These were homes that had stockades built to fortify them. Between the French and Indian War and the Revolution, Adam Stephen purchased 255 acres in 1770 and laid out Martinsburg, which he named after Thomas Bryan Martin, a nephew of Lord Fairfax. The town was incorporated in 1778 and became the county seat.

Berkeley County is known for its limestone and the rich valley land along its many streams. Grist mills were established in the 1730s. Flour was hauled overland to Alexandria and Baltimore and carried by boat on the Potomac River and later the C&O Canal. The coming of the Baltimore & Ohio Railroad in 1842 brought employment and a cheap means of exporting products. Later, the B&O played a big role in Berkeley County becoming part of West Virginia, since it was important that the railroad stay in Union hands.

Berkeley County was a slave-owning area, with some large plantations of 100 slaves or more. The 1830 census listed 1,034 male slaves and 885 female slaves, along with 276 free Negroes, out of a total population of 10,518. Berkeley County was about 75 percent Confederate during the Civil War. Confusion remained about the status of Berkeley County and neighboring Jefferson County after the war. Both had voted to join West Virginia in 1863, but under questionable wartime conditions. Their inclusion in the new state was later confirmed by the U.S. Congress.

The Cumberland Valley Railroad, which ran from Pennsylvania to Virginia,

had reached Martinsburg by 1876. Apples had been a staple fruit since the colonial period, and in the 1890s John Miller, the son of a pioneer orchardman, developed a major commercial apple industry. With the coming of electricity in 1890, Martinsburg soon became a textile town. Two major brick plants and several limestone quarries opened in the early 20th century. By 1900, the county population was 19,469. Before the Civil War, Berkeley County had had many privately owned schools. After the Civil War, free education was established, initially on a segregated basis. There are three high schools now.

Shepherd Field started in 1923 and has grown into a major airport now known as the Eastern West Virginia Regional Airport. One of West Virginia's two Air National Guard units is stationed there. The 167th Fighter Squadron, which flew Sabre jets out of Martinsburg in the late 1950s, is now the 167th Airlift Wing. Tiger Aircraft manufactures small planes near the airport, and the Sino Swearingen company expects to build corporate jets there.

In the second half of the 20th century Berkeley County became one of the fastest growing sections of West Virginia. Major companies establishing operations there in the 1960s included 3M, General Motors, and Pet Milk, as well as the Internal Revenue Service. By 1968, Interstate 81 had been completed, crossing Berkeley County from Virginia to Maryland. In the 1970s, more industries came. A new 840-bed Veteran's Administration building replaced the Newton D. Baker Veterans Hospital. Corning Glass and DuPont Explosives established plants in Berkeley County. The population more than doubled in the last 30 years, from 36,356 in 1970 to 75,905 in 2000.

At the beginning of the 21st century Berkeley County is part of the Wash-

ington metropolitan area. Two large printing companies, Quad Graphics and Quebecor Printing, have joined other major employers. A big effort is being made to manage growth, maintaining something of the county's rural character and preserving the best of its historic architecture while accommodating an expanding economy.

Notable Berkeley Countians include Morgan Morgan (1688–1766) and Gen. Adam Stephen (1718–91), surgeon and soldier. Gen. William Darke (1736–1801) had a long military career and saw much action in fighting the Indians during the French and Indian War. He voted for the ratification of the U.S. Constitution during the Virginia ratifying convention in 1788. Adm. Charles Boarman (1795–1879) served on Lake Ontario during the War of 1812, commanded the Brooklyn Navy Yard from 1852 to 1855, and remained in the U.S. Navy through the Civil War. Newton Diehl Baker Jr. (1879–1921) was appointed in 1916 by President Woodrow Wilson as secretary of war. Charles James Faulkner Sr. (1806–84) was appointed minister to France by President James Buchanan in 1859. He served as chief of staff to Confederate Gen. Stonewall Jackson and was awarded the rank of lieutenant colonel. Faulkner defended West Virginia's claim to Berkeley and Jefferson counties before the U.S. Supreme Court. David Hunter Strother, whose pen name was Porte Crayon, (1810–88), was one of the foremost journalists and illustrators of his day. Artist William Robinson Leigh (1866–1955) was born in the Falling Waters area of Berkeley County.

See also Eastern Panhandle

Don C. Wood
Berkeley County Historical Society

Berkeley County Riflemen

The Berkeley County Riflemen were organized June 10, 1775, at Morgan's Spring, Berkeley County (now Jefferson County), by Capt. Hugh Stephenson of Shepherdstown, in response to a call for Revolutionary War soldiers by Gen. George Washington. These 100 volunteers, dressed in linsey-woolsey hunting shirts, leather leggings, and moccasins, were among the first Southern soldiers to go to the aid of Boston, then under attack from the British. Each man supplied his own uniform, weapon, equipment, and food. On July 17, the troop set out on horseback for Boston, making its famous Bee Line March of 600 miles in 24 days. Captain Stephenson reported to General Washington, who knew several of the men and welcomed them all, that they were "from the right bank of the Potomac."

Capt. Daniel Morgan, who once lived in Berkeley County, organized a troop of volunteers at nearby Winchester, Virginia. These soldiers, sometimes confused or combined with the Berkeley

County Riflemen, were known as Morgan's Riflemen. They left Winchester on July 15 and rushed on ahead despite an apparent agreement that the two companies would travel together. Morgan's Riflemen arrived in Boston five days before the Berkeley County group.

See also Bee Line March

R. F. Hendricks
Marietta, Georgia

Virgil A. Lewis, *History and Government of West Virginia,* 1912; "Morgan, Daniel," *Encyclopedia Americana,* International Edition, 1999.

Berkeley Springs

Berkeley Springs, the county seat of Morgan County, had a population of 663 in 2000. The Eastern Panhandle town was originally called Bath, after the English resort city of the same name, but in the early 1800s the post office name was changed to Berkeley Springs. The town still answers to both names, however, and the official name remains Bath.

The namesake mineral springs are five in number, the most prominent being the Fairfax Spring and the Gentlemen's Spring. They are thermal springs, flowing at a constant 69.8 degrees F. Their reputed healing powers have made Berkeley Springs long popular as a health spa.

Berkeley Springs was officially recognized in 1776 after the sixth Lord Fairfax deeded to Virginia 50 acres surrounding the springs. George Washington was among those to purchase property at Berkeley Springs, and the main thoroughfare is named for him. During the Revolutionary War, the town served as a haven for families and fighters, as well as the wounded. After the war, Berkeley Springs prospered as a resort. Many prominent figures, including steamboat inventor James Rumsey, bought property in the area. Rumsey also oversaw construction of spa buildings. Gen. Horatio Gates and Samuel and William Washington were among other property owners. During the Civil War, Stonewall Jackson based his forces in Berkeley Springs during an 1862 attack on Hancock, Maryland, just 10 miles to the north.

The major industries in Berkeley Springs today are tourism, schools and education, sand mining, furniture manufacturing, and arts and crafts, in roughly that order. In the 19th century, there was a tannery in Berkeley Springs, an aggravation to those in the business of entertaining the town's paying visitors. The Country Inn was constructed in 1932, and is still a mainstay of local tourism. Since 1974, the Apple Butter Festival has drawn in thousands of visitors each fall.

Stephanie Earls
Yakima, Washington

Berkeley Springs State Park

Berkeley Springs State Park is one of the oldest units in the West Virginia state

Berkeley Springs.

park system. The warm springs that give the park its name have attracted visitors from before the time of white settlement, and Berkeley Springs was established as a spa in colonial times. In 1748, 16-year-old George Washington visited the location as part of a surveying party and later returned many times. The spa enjoyed its greatest success after the building of the Baltimore & Ohio Railroad through the area in the 1840s. The 400-guest Strother Hotel was soon completed, and under various owners remained the center of Berkeley Springs hospitality until it burned in 1898.

The seven-acre park, originally called Bath Square, along with 50 surrounding acres, was conveyed to Virginia in 1776 by Lord Fairfax. Fourteen trustees were put in charge, selling lots to Washington, Gen. Horatio Gates, and others. The trustees retained control of the springs, which have remained public property since that time. The state of West Virginia assumed control in the mid-1920s, and the historic spa was transferred to the Department of Natural Resources in 1970. Today, the park is listed on the National Register of Historic Places. A Roman Bath house, constructed at the park in 1815 under the direction of James Rumsey, is the oldest public building in Morgan County.

See also Berkeley Springs

Stephanie Earls
Yakima, Washington

Berkeley Woolen Mills

Shortly after the outbreak of World War I in Europe, Howard H. Emmert established Berkeley Woolen Company in Martinsburg. Other principal stockholders were from Martinsburg, nearby Winchester, Virginia, and New York City. By December 1914, the company employed 185

men and 36 women. During World War I, workers manufactured cloth for the French army and uniforms and overcoats for the U.S. Army. With its wartime profits, Berkeley Woolen added new buildings that included a dye house and other improvements that enabled the company to double its capacity.

From the end of World War I to the 1930s, the company manufactured men's suits. During the late 1930s, topcoats and women's clothing were added to the line of products. Berkeley Woolen Company managed to keep its doors open throughout the Great Depression. In 1933, Berkeley employees walked out when management refused to recognize the United Textile Workers as the workers' bargaining agent. Hostilities escalated for several months until the National Labor Review Board intervened in early September. After several days of negotiations, Berkeley employees returned to work, thus ending the city's first textile strike.

The 1933 settlement generally favored the union, although problems continued. The following year, Berkeley Woolen's employees participated in another strike, as did workers at the city's other woolen mill and hosiery company. The work force had grown to 375. The second strike lasted for the better part of a year. Following this confrontation, working relations at the woolen mill remained relatively stable throughout the rest of the decade and into the 1940s.

In World War II, Berkeley Woolen once again manufactured clothing for the war effort. Profits soared, but the prosperity was short-lived. Soon after the war ended, the company began experiencing serious financial difficulties. The small plant could not compete against larger operations, and in 1949 the company closed its operation in Martinsburg. Within four years, Dunn Woolen, Martinsburg's other woolen manufacturer, also closed its doors, and woolen production was no longer a part of the city economy.

Jerra Jenrette
Edinboro University

Berries

Wild berries are valuable natural foods for wildlife and people alike. West Virginia has dozens of native berry plants, ranging from trees and shrubs to vines and herbs.

Blackberries, blueberries, huckleberries, strawberries, serviceberries, and raspberries are the most sought after by humans and wildlife. Strawberries and serviceberries are the first big treats of the season, ripening from early June through July. July and August are the best months for juicy, tart blackberries. These months are also best for raspberries (black, red, and wineberry). July through September is the time to search for glossy blueberries and for shiny huckleberries that grow on shrubs along forest margins, in open woods, and open mountaintops. Hundreds of people make annual forays to Dolly Sods, Spruce Knob, and nearby areas to pick blueberries. Late summer and early autumn are also the best time to search for the large drooping clusters of black elderberry to make into elderberry jelly. Late autumn is the time for wild grapes, persimmon, and cranberries. Even in winter one can still find the tasty red berries of teaberry or the bland two-eyed partridgeberry. Red cedar (juniper) berries have been used for centuries to flavor gin. Many other berries such as gooseberries, currants, mulberries, may-apple, and ground-cherry offer a variety of tastes during the growing season.

Not everything is edible. White or whitish fruits generally should be regarded as toxic and poisonous. Plants with whitish berries include poison ivy, poison sumac, doll's-eyes, white coral-berry, and mistletoe. Unripe (greenish) fruits of ground-cherry and may-apple are toxic. Seeds inside the pulpy fruits of cherries and pokeberry are poisonous. The red fruits of red elderberry are bitter and unpleasant. The bright red berries of bittersweet are also poisonous.

Berries of holly, jack-in-the-pulpit, Solomon's seal, trillium, blue cohosh, ginseng, and goldenseal provide colorful red, blue, and yellow berries to forests, gardens, homes, and medicine chests.

See also Flora

William N. Grafton
WVU Extension Service

Chu Berry

Musician Leon "Chu" Berry was born September 13, 1910, in Wheeling. He was one of the most highly regarded saxophonists of the Swing Era, ranking alongside Coleman Hawkins and Lester Young in the opinion of many jazz critics. He was inspired to take up tenor sax after Hawkins played in Wheeling with Fletcher Henderson's pioneer big band. At West Virginia State College, Berry performed with the Edwards Collegians and other regional groups.

Known for his full tone, breath control, and fleet playing on up-tempo numbers, Berry performed and recorded with major artists such as Henderson, Bessie Smith, Benny Carter, Teddy Wilson, and Roy Eldridge throughout the 1930s. He spent his last four years in Cab Calloway's big band alongside young trumpeter Dizzy Gillespie. After gigs, Berry and Gillespie joined the late-night jammers who gave birth to the new bebop style. Berry's more famous solos include records of *Ghost Of A Chance* with Calloway, *Hot Mallets* with Lionel Hampton, and *On the Sunny Side of the Street* with his own orchestra. He died at age 31 in a car crash near Conneaut, Ohio, October 30, 1941, while on the road with the Calloway band.

John Douglas
Berkeley Springs

Berry v. Fox

In the case *Berry v. Fox*, the West Virginia Supreme Court of Appeals overturned legislation providing debt relief to local government. On December 9, 1933, the West Virginia legislature in its second extraordinary session of the year had enacted a measure that provided for the state to assume the debt for all of the outstanding school and road bonds issued by its various subdivisions. This would have made money available to local authorities for current expenses during the hard times of the Great Depression.

This legislation was an indirect response to pressure from the Roosevelt administration upon state government to provide state funds to supplement the federal relief funds. Both the state and federal governments had made the transition in the 1932 election from the conservative economics of the prior Republican administrations to an active approach to the nation's economic woes. But the Supreme Court of Appeals in a 3–2 decision written by Judge Haymond Maxwell held that the legislature had violated Section 6 of Article X of the state constitution, which prohibited the state from "assum[ing], or becom[ing] responsible for the debts or liabilities of any county, city, township, corporation, or person." Four of the judges on the court were Republicans, elected from five to 10 years earlier.

The plaintiff, A. M. Berry, a resident and taxpayer of Salt Lick District in Braxton County, had filed suit in Kanawha County immediately after the passage of the act. He was represented by two business-oriented Charleston law firms. A mere 36 days elapsed from the passage of the act until the court's decision. If, as Democratic partisans argued, justice was denied in this case, it certainly was not delayed.

H. John Rogers
New Martinsville

Berwind Lake Wildlife Management Area

Berwind Lake Wildlife Management Area is in southern McDowell County, about 20 miles from Welch. Operated by the West Virginia Division of Natural Resources, Berwind is managed primarily for forest game including turkey, deer, squirrel, racoon, and grouse. Extensive day-use recreational facilities are provided, including hiking trails, picnicking facilities, and a swimming pool.

Berwind Lake WMA began in 1959 when the Conservation Commission (now Division of Natural Resources) opened a 20-acre lake on War Creek to public fishing. The lake remains a focal point and provides excellent fishing for warm-water species such as large-mouth bass, channel catfish, and bluegill. Trout are stocked monthly from February through May, and adult channel catfish are stocked in June of each year. In 1974, approximately 18,000 acres of the rugged mountain terrain surrounding the lake were leased by the state from the Berwind Land Company. The leased land is used for wildlife management and to provide hunting opportunities for southern West Virginia hunters.

Robert Beanblossom
Division of Natural Resources

Bethany College

Located in the village of Bethany, Brooke County, Bethany College came into existence through the granting of a charter by the Virginia General Assembly on March 2, 1840. From the beginning, it has been a four-year, baccalaureate-degree college, the oldest such institution in West Virginia. The college also granted earned and honorary master's degrees from 1858 to 1931.

Founder Alexander Campbell (1788–1866) was a noted educational and religious reformer and one of the principal founders of the Christian Church (Disciples of Christ) denomination. Campbell served as president of the college until his death in 1866, as well as treasurer and one of the six original faculty members.

Bethany College has maintained a strong liberal arts curriculum throughout its history. The college is non-sectarian and governed by an independent board of trustees. However, strong historical ties with the Disciples movement provide a continuing relationship with the denomination.

The campus is dominated by Old Main, designated a National Historic Landmark, and one of the finest examples of 19th-century Gothic Revival architecture in the country. Begun in 1858, work on the building was interrupted by the Civil War and completed in the years immediately after. Two wings were subsequently added, Commencement Hall in 1871 and Oglebay Hall (now Kirkpatrick Hall) in 1912. Also designated a National Historic Landmark is the Campbell mansion, located a half-mile from the campus. The mansion began as a farmhouse (1793) on land owned by Campbell's future father in-law and was expanded in several stages throughout Campbell's lifetime.

Campus life, originally dominated by literary societies, was leavened by the arrival of social fraternities in the 1850s. Delta Tau Delta national fraternity was founded at Bethany in 1858. Psi Chapter of Beta Theta Pi was established in 1860,

Old Main at Bethany College, a National Historic Landmark.

making it the oldest fraternity chapter in continuous existence at the college and in the state.

The sectional strife leading up to the Civil War and the founding of the state of West Virginia provided a tremendous challenge to Bethany. As the campus drew its students from both slave and free states, Campbell attempted to dampen rancor by prohibiting political discussions, but was forced to dismiss several abolitionists as a matter of campus discipline after an incident in 1855. However, by the time of the outbreak of the war, campus sympathies were strongly pro-Union. Campbell opposed war, but his eldest son, Alexander Campbell Jr., rose to the rank of colonel in the armies of the Confederacy. Campbell's nephew, Archibald Campbell, was the fiercely pro-Union editor of the *Wheeling Intelligencer*. Enrollment dropped to only 23 students in the 1862–63 academic year.

Women were first admitted as students on a provisional basis in 1877 and granted full status the following year. Women have served on the faculty since 1882 and on the board of trustees since 1900. International students were members of the first class in 1841 and make up approximately ten percent of the student body today. Minority students have been a part of the student body throughout the college's history.

The Great Depression took its toll on the campus. Enrollment declined and money was hard to come by. During World War II, the college participated in programs for the army air corps and the navy to train pilots and engineers, in part to compensate for the loss of enrollment because of the war effort. Returning veterans aided by the GI Bill boosted enrollment in 1946 to more than 800, causing a serious housing shortage in the village. The 1960s brought a great surge in enrollment, and a corresponding expansion of facilities, as the "baby boom" generation began to enter college. Enrollment peaked at 1,100 in the early 1970s and then fell back to approximately 750 by the end of the 1980s. Enrollment was nearly 900 in fall 2002.

Through the years, 18 individuals, including Campbell, have served as president of Bethany College. Among the most influential were T. E. Cramblet (1902–19) who presided over a major building boom in the first two decades of the 20th century; his son, W. H. Cramblet (1934–52), who shepherded the college through the Depression and the war years; Perry Epler Gresham (1953–72), who expanded the campus to meet the influx of the baby boomers; and Cecil H. Underwood (1972–75) the once and future governor of West Virginia. President D. Duane Cummins served from 1988 to 2002, and Patricia L. Poteat from 2002 to 2004. G. T. Smith became president in July 2004.

Among Bethany's benefactors over the years have been the Phillips family, originally from Pennsylvania, the Oglebay family of Wheeling, and the Renner family of Ohio. James A. Garfield, 20th president of the United States, was a member of the board of trustees. J. B. "Champ" Clark, Class of 1873, rose to the speakership of the U.S. House of Representatives. Other Bethany alumni have distinguished themselves in the arts, business, education, electronic and print journalism, industry, and science.

See also Alexander Campbell, Archibald W. Campbell, Christian Church (Disciples of Christ)

Gary Kappel
Bethany College

D. Duane Cummins, *The Disciples Colleges: A History,* 1987; Perry Gresham, *Campbell and the Colleges,* 1973; Lester McAllister, *Bethany: The First 150 Years,* 1991.

Joseph Lawton Beury

Coal operator Joseph Lawton Beury, born in Schuykill County, Pennsylvania, August 15, 1842, served as a Union captain during the Civil War though he was later known as "colonel" in the West Virginia coalfields. In 1873, he shipped the first coal from the New River Coalfield.

Beury learned mining in his father's Pennsylvania anthracite mines, and brought the knowledge with him to the new southern West Virginia coal industry. He moved with his new wife to the New River about 1872, establishing the town of Quinnimont and opening the New River Coal Company mine. He was ready to ship coal when the Chesapeake & Ohio Railroad arrived in September 1873. Beury left Quinnimont in 1876 to start the Fire Creek mines, also on New River, and later operated at Hawks Nest, Ansted, and other places. In 1884, he and others opened Mill Creek Coal & Coke, the first mine in the Flat Top area of the Pocahontas Coalfield. After 1880, he and his brothers began to buy up tracts of coal land, and he eventually became a major coal owner.

Colonel Joe Beury lived at his town of Beury in the New River Gorge, dying there on June 3, 1903. A stone obelisk at Quinnimont commemorates his role as a coal industry pioneer.

Ken Sullivan
West Virginia Humanities Council

Beverly

The Randolph County town of Beverly, population 696, is located where Files Creek joins the Tygart Valley River as it flows toward Elkins, six miles to the north. Previously known as Edmonton, the village became the first county seat of Randolph County upon the county's founding in 1787. It was renamed Beverly in honor of the governor of Virginia, Beverley Randolph, and chartered in 1790. Beverly was a political, economic, and social center of Randolph and surrounding counties until the loss of the county seat to Elkins in 1899.

Beverly, located on the Staunton-Parkersburg Turnpike, lay at a strategic highway junction. The Civil War, from the time of the nearby battle at Rich Mountain in 1861 to Rosser's Raid on the town in 1865, disrupted local life. Beverly suffered much damage in the course of the war, while serving as an important supply and command post for thousands of federal troops serving in eastern West Virginia.

Prominent citizens of Beverly include Lemuel Chenoweth, the builder of covered bridges including the Philippi Bridge, and Laura Jackson Arnold, the sister of Thomas J. "Stonewall" Jackson. Today, the town is the location of the Colonial Millworks and Bruce Hardwood Floors.

See also Randolph County

Donald L. Rice
Elkins

Phyllis Baxter and Donald L. Rice, *Historic Beverly, A Guide Book,* 1993; Albert S. Bosworth, *History of Randolph County,* 1975; Hu Maxwell, *The History of Randolph County,* 1898.

Ambrose Bierce

Writer Ambrose Bierce found the setting for some of his famous short stories in the mountains of Western Virginia. Arising like other writing of his from Civil War battles and the lives of the soldiers, they often concentrated on death in shocking form.

Born in Ohio, June 24, 1842, Bierce enlisted at age 18 in Company C, 9th Regiment of Indiana Volunteers, which came into Western Virginia during the first year of the Civil War. Many of his writings were influenced by his observations of

Southern dead at the Battle of Bartow

"They were honest and courageous foemen, having little in common with the political madmen who persuaded them to their doom and the literary bearers of false witness in the aftertime. They did not live through the period of honorable strife into the period of vilification—did not pass from the iron age to the brazen—from the era of the sword to that of the tongue and pen. Among them is no member of the Southern Historical Society. Their valor was not the fury of the non-combatant; they have no voice in the thunder of the civilians and the shouting. Not by them are impaired the dignity and infinite pathos of the Lost Cause. Give them, these blameless gentlemen, their rightful part in all the pomp that fills the circuit of the summer hills."

—Ambrose Bierce "A Bivouac of the Dead" (1903)

the war in the Tygart Valley, as the war's first battles and skirmishes occurred from Philippi to the Cheat and Allegheny mountains in Randolph and Pocahontas counties. An 1891 collection of his stories, *Tales of Soldiers and Civilians* (later also published as *In the Midst of Life*), depicts the dark side of the Civil War. One of its stories, "Horseman in the Sky," had as its locale the mountains of Western Virginia. This story, like most of his writings, had an unusual ending: A son, in a dream-like state, shoots his father from a horse posed on a cliff in the rugged mountain area.

In 1903, Bierce returned to Randolph and Pocahontas counties to revisit the locations where he had served in 1861–62. While staying at Travelers' Repose in Pocahontas County, he wrote "A Bivouac of the Dead," which touched upon the neglected graves of the Confederate dead on the old Battle of the Greenbrier battlefield near Bartow.

Ambrose Bierce, who spoke of the Allegheny Mountains as the "Delectable Mountains" and Western Virginia as an enchanted land, disappeared under mysterious circumstances during a 1913–14 trip to revolution-torn Mexico.

Donald L. Rice
Elkins

Charles Carpenter, "West Virginia People and Places," *The West Virginia Heritage Encyclopedia*, 1974; William McCann, ed., *Ambrose Bierce's Civil War*, 1956.

Big Ugly

Big Ugly Creek is a tributary of the Guyandotte River, running from its Boone County headwaters to its mouth near Harts. Apart from its uppermost reaches, Big Ugly Creek is located entirely within Lincoln County.

The tributaries of Big Ugly include Pigeonroost, Bobby, Laurel, Sulphur, and Lefthand creeks, and Broad Branch. The community of Leet is located on Big Ugly Creek, at the mouth of Laurel, and County Route 7 parallels the lower section of the creek. The Big Ugly Wildlife Management Area consists of 6,421 acres on tributaries north of the creek itself. The land is leased from private owners and managed by the West Virginia Division of Natural Resources. In addition to hunting, the wildlife management area offers rustic camping and a shooting range.

Big Ugly occupies the southeastern corner of Lincoln County, once a long journey from the county seat. Although the mouth of the creek was settled as early as 1801, the Big Ugly community in early times remained remote from more populous areas and developed its own independent ways. Its name, whose origin is uncertain, has been a source of humor over the years.

Big Sandy River

The late fiddler Ed Haley played a tune called "Three Forks of Sandy" that had three parts to it, one each for the Tug Fork, the Levisa Fork, and the Big Sandy main stream. The Tug Fork originates in McDowell County, while the Levisa and its tributaries rise no more than 20 miles away in southwest Virginia. The two forks flow generally northwestward and parallel to each other. They join at Louisa, Kentucky, to form the Big Sandy River, which then flows to the Ohio River at Catlettsburg. The valley is about 190 miles long and 80 miles wide, with the Tug Fork and then the Big Sandy forming the entire length of the West Virginia-Kentucky state line. Major towns on the Big Sandy watershed include Williamson and Kenova, as well as Pikeville, Louisa, and Catlettsburg, Kentucky.

This is an area of thick forest, rugged terrain, and bituminous coal mining, and a hotbed of Scotch-Irish, English, and German culture. Roads came slowly. For generations the most practical means of transportation and the main contact with the rest of the world was by river. The Big Sandy Valley saw some of the Civil War, with the battles of Middle Creek and John's Creek probably being the most memorable. The most famous event in the valley's history was the Hatfield-McCoy feud, which raged along Tug Fork in the 1880s.

Steamboat traffic proliferated roughly from the 1830s to the eve of World War II, bringing needed things to isolated areas, moving passengers and mail back and forth, and carrying out produce to be sold. Some were sternwheelers, and some had exposed sidewheels and were called "bat wings." Steamboats traveled the entire length of Big Sandy and up the Levisa as far as Pikeville. When the water was too low, poled wooden flats called "pushboats" took over and went as far upstream as Williamson, on the Tug Fork.

Temporary splash dams were built on the Russell Fork of Levisa and other tributaries, to form pools to collect logs so that they could be floated out when the dams were dynamited and the waters released. The logs were collected downstream. The late Capt. Jesse P. Hughes said he remembered being almost able to walk across the mouth of the Big Sandy entirely on log rafts at Catlettsburg. Many of these rafts were towed down the Ohio, some as far down as Cincinnati, where much of the lumber went into the building of the palatial steamboats that graced the Mississippi and Ohio during this period.

The late Bob Kennedy, of Kenova, said 25 steamboats were based up the Big Sandy before the railroads arrived. Both banks were lined with landings, wharfboats, and warehouses to handle the upriver commerce all the way to Pikeville, mile 88.5 above Louisa. Probably the largest steamboat was the *Argand*, but she operated only at high stages of water. Captain Hughes ran the sternwheel *Cricket* for many years. In later years there were three locks and dams on the Big Sandy and one each on the Tug and Levisa. The last log raft down the Big Sandy originated on the Levisa in about 1942 or '43 and actually passed through Lock 1 on that stream. Today, nine miles of the Big Sandy are commercially navigated.

The Norfolk & Western Railroad was built down the Tug Fork and Big Sandy in the late 1880s, connecting the valley by rail to the Midwest and to the coal-shipping docks of Norfolk. Thereafter, mining the region's rich deposits of bituminous coal became the main economic activity of the Big Sandy watershed, and it remains so today. Rail and highway transportation gradually displaced the riverboats.

See also Tug Fork

John Hartford
Madison, Tennessee
Carol Crowe-Carraco, *The Big Sandy*, 1979.

"Billy Richardson's Last Ride"

A popular train song commemorates the death of a locomotive engineer in the Kanawha Valley. Billy Richardson, an engineer on the Chesapeake & Ohio Railroad from 1878 to 1910, was known to run fast and on time. People along the C&O recalled that Richardson would wave and whistle as his train sped by, his long beard flying in the wind. The affable engineer developed a habit of leaning far out of the right cab window.

Richardson's usual run was from Hinton to Huntington and back. On December 14, 1910, he was running west toward Huntington. Passing through Scary, near St. Albans, Richardson blew the whistle and stuck his head out the window to look back. The mail crane, a track-side device from which trains snatched mail bags on the fly, hit Billy Richardson in the head, pounding his left temple. The fireman, Cecil Lively, brought the train into Huntington on time. Richardson died shortly after reaching the hospital there.

Not until 1926 was the engineer memorialized in song. N&W engineer Cleburne Meeks, who as a boy in Fayette County stood in his backyard every other day to wave at Billy Richardson, wrote the song lyrics to "Billy Richardson's Last Ride." Carson J. Robinson wrote the tune in 1926, and Vernon Dalhart recorded the song for seven different record companies.

Jim McGee
Louisville, Kentucky

Birch River

Birch River begins near Cowen and flows in a northwesterly direction for 36.6 miles through Webster, Nicholas, and Braxton counties before entering Elk River at Glendon. The area through which it passes is entirely rural and, for the most part, isolated. The first settler along the river was William Dodrill in 1799. He settled in upper Birch and founded the town of Boggs. There is extensive evidence of prehistoric habitation, though Indians did not occupy the area at the time of white settlement.

The final 17 miles of Birch, starting at what is known locally as the Cora Brown Bridge in Nicholas County, was included in the State Natural Streams Preservation Act by the 1975 West Virginia legislature. Birch was studied by the National Park Service in 1981–83 for inclusion in the National Wild and Scenic Rivers System. The agency concluded that the river, although eligible, did not qualify to be a federally administered component of the system. The Army Corps of Engineers studied Birch during 1966–71 for a possible reservoir site. The proposed dam would have been built 1.3 miles above the mouth of the river and would have inundated 11.8 miles of stream. The project was later deferred for restudy, and in November 1986 was deactivated.

Although Birch is a small stream, logs and log rafts were once floated down the river in the spring or anytime there was sufficient water flow. This occurred mainly in the period from 1880 to 1920. Timbering was done all along Birch. In 1909, the Birch Boom & Lumber Company built a sawmill near the mouth of the river at Glendon, and also built a boom across the river to snare logs that had been floated down the river. Mounds of rock that held the boom are still visible.

Birch drains an area of 143 square miles, and is the second-largest tributary of Elk River. It falls an average of 42 feet per mile, from its beginning at elevation 2,300 feet to its mouth at elevation 775 feet. This steep gradient makes Birch a fast-flowing stream, attractive to white-water boaters on its lower 17 miles during periods of high water. An eight-mile stretch of this lower section, from Big Run in Nicholas County to near Middle Run in Braxton County, is noted for an abundance of rocks, many of them large.

Skip Johnson
Sutton

Birds

Since publication of the first *West Virginia Encyclopedia* in 1929, the state has gone through many changes. As would be expected, birds and their environment have also experienced changes. The changes were not detrimental to every bird species and benefited many. In 1929, some people considered snowbirds and robins to be fare for the table, and hawks, eagles, and owls were usually considered varmints and sometimes even had bounties on them.

The wood duck was considered rare in 1929. Hunting regulations, habitat management, and artificial nest boxes have aided this species considerably. These beautiful waterfowl are a common sight today. Canada geese were noted as migrants. This bird is now a permanent resident in the state, sometimes a nuisance. In writing for the 1929 encyclopedia, Earle Brooks expressed concern that the one sighting of sandhill crane would be the last the state would ever see. While still not a common visitor to West Virginia, recent sightings have occurred. On the other hand, the northern bobwhite was considered a common species in 1929. Now this bird has nearly disappeared from our state. Wild turkeys were rare to nearly non-existent 70 years ago. Since the early 1970s, the Division of Natural Resources has successfully returned the wild turkey to every county. They are a major game species today.

Turkey vultures were primarily listed in the eastern section of the state, and black vultures were not even on the state list at the time of Brooks. Turkey vultures are now found over most of West Virginia, even in a good portion of the state in winter. The expansion of their range has been attributed to the large population of white-tailed deer. Wounded deer not found by hunters, road-killed deer, and winter-killed deer provide an ample food supply. This may also contribute to the presence of the more southern black vulture, which is now fairly common in the eastern counties.

Brooks described some birds of prey as being harmful while others were useful. Bird-eating hawks, such as the sharp-shinned and Cooper's hawks, were considered harmful. Soaring hawks, such as the broadwinged and red-tailed hawks, called buteos, were usually branded as chicken hawks and shot on sight. Newspaper accounts of bald and golden eagles usually dealt with how many were shot. Now that laws protect these birds and the pesticide DDT has been banned, these predators are in better shape. Red-shouldered hawks appear to be more common today than they were in 1929. Changes in habitat probably contribute to this situation. Thirteen bald eagle nests were reported in West Virginia in 2002. Attempts to reintroduce peregrine falcons in New River Gorge and near the Eastern Panhandle have had little success. Similar

Tree swallows.

programs for ospreys on the Ohio River and near Tygart Lake have been more successful.

Red-headed woodpeckers were common early in the 20th century. They are less common today, probably because of the introduction of the European starling. This aggressive import forces the woodpecker from preferred nest sites. Whip-poor-wills were common in 1929. They have nearly disappeared from much of the state. Brooks said as many as 25 species of sparrow could be found in every community in his day. This may not be true today. These are grassland-loving species, and our state has much more forest cover than in earlier times. Two others, the vesper sparrow and the American tree sparrow, were common seasonal visitors. Today, neither is. Purple martins were common in 1929, and tree swallows were rare. Habitat change and the influence of man appear to have reversed conditions, so that purple martins are now rare and tree swallows are common.

Loggerhead shrikes were common along the Ohio River in 1929 but now are seldom encountered in that area. They are found in the eastern part of the state but are considered a species of concern. Blue-winged warblers were not very common and golden-winged warblers were doing well. This situation appears to be reversing itself today. Brooks wrote that the Bewick's wren was far more common in West Virginia than in most of the country. Today, the Bewick's wren is a rare sight. Brooks did not even list two imports, the European starling and the house (English) sparrow, which today crowd out native species such as woodpeckers and bluebirds. In the 1980s, another import reached our state. The house finch, originally a western species, is now a part of most neighborhoods.

West Virginia claimed about 268 species and subspecies during the time of Brooks. Today the list stands at about 321. While some of the additional bird varieties may have resulted from reclassification, the major factor contributing to an increased figure is habitat change. These changes include a dramatic increase in forest cover. According to forestry officials, in 1922, West Virginia was 35 percent forested. In 1996, the state was 77 percent forested. Road building, surface mining for coal, housing developments, waterway impoundments, and the introduction of multiflora rose have all affected bird life. Some species benefit from these changes, while others are harmed. Elevation contributes to our variety of birds, and some elevations have decreased due to mining. We have an abundance of rivers and streams, and now many man-made lakes as well. Sizable lakes such as Burnsville, Bluestone, Summersville, and Stonewall Jackson offer resting areas for migrating waterfowl

as well as nesting habitat. Although there is less farmland today than in 1929, some parts of the state still provide this habitat. Properly reclaimed surface mines supply some grassland birds and brush-loving birds with a place to live. Future research will determine the lasting effects of urban development, mountaintop removal, and recent timbering practices.

Organizations such as the Brooks Bird Club, local Audubon chapters, raptor rehabilitation centers, and the nongame section of the state Division of Natural Resources all encourage the study of West Virginia birds. The Audubon Society has sponsored the Christmas Bird Count for nearly 100 years. In recent years about 15 of these surveys were done across the state. Counts of migrating birds of prey are conducted near Bluefield on East River Mountain and near Waiteville on Peters Mountain in the fall.

Learning to identify the birds around you can be a rewarding experience. The birds are your friends. Birds serve as a barometer of the health of our environment. Their troubles may become our troubles. The best way to learn about birds is to experience them firsthand. So get out in your own backyard and get to know your neighbors.

Jim Phillips
Pipestem State Park
Albert R. Buckelew Jr., *West Virginia Breeding Bird Atlas,* 1994; James W. Bullard, ed., *Birding Guide to West Virginia,* 1998; George A. Hall, *West Virginia Birds,* 1983.

John Peale Bishop

Critic John Peale Bishop, born in Charles Town, May 21, 1892, attended high school in Hagerstown, Maryland. He showed an early interest in art which was encouraged by his family. However, during an unexplainable but temporary spell of blindness at age 17, he decided to become a writer. His poem, "To a Woodland Pool," was published in 1912 in *Harpers Weekly.*

In 1913, Bishop entered Princeton, where he was a classmate of F. Scott Fitzgerald. His first book of poetry, *Green Fruit,* was published in 1917, the year he graduated. Commissioned an officer in the army, Bishop was stationed in Europe until 1919, when he was hired at *Vanity Fair* magazine, eventually becoming its managing editor (1920–22). Traveling abroad with his wife following their marriage in 1922, he remained for lengthy periods of time in France, returning to live in the United States in 1933. During their European period, Bishop established lifelong friendships with critic Allen Tate and poet Archibald MacLeish.

Bishop is credited with writing his finest criticism, essays, and reviews of poetry between 1933 and 1940. These works include "The South and Tradition," "Homage to Hemingway," and "The Sorrows of

Thomas Wolfe," and reviews of works by W. H. Auden, Ezra Pound, and others.

His 1931 book, *Many Thousands Gone,* a collection of interrelated stories, is set in a fictionalized 19th-century Charles Town. The title story won the prestigious Scribner's Prize. Following extended periods of illness, Bishop died April 4, 1944, in Hyannis, Massachusetts.

Debra K. Sullivan
Charleston Catholic High School

Van Bittner

Labor organizer Van Amberg Bittner, born March 20, 1885, was one of the United Mine Workers of America's most durable infighters for nearly 40 years beginning in 1911. A John L. Lewis loyalist, Bittner began his UMWA career as a local president in his home state of Pennsylvania. In northern West Virginia, he oversaw unsuccessful organizing strikes and led resistance to unionized operators' abrogation of their union contracts in 1924–25. He briefly organized miners on Scotts Run near Morgantown in 1931, undercutting the dissident West Virginia Mine Workers Union. Bittner's major organizing victories in the state came as District 17 president, capitalizing on the protections offered by New Deal labor legislation in 1933 and 1935. These successes made Bittner an influential figure within the state Democratic Party's New Deal faction.

In 1936, Van Bittner became midwestern director of the Committee on Industrial Organization's campaign to organize the steel industry, operating from Chicago. He split with Lewis over Lewis's abandonment of Franklin D. Roosevelt in 1940. Bittner's position within the CIO was secure, however, and he directed the abortive drive to organize southern industrial workers in 1946. Although Bittner embraced the UMWA policy of racial inclusiveness, his refusal to form alliances with integrationist groups and his rigid antiradicalism undermined the CIO's organizational unity, probably doing mortal damage to the southern campaign. He died July 19, 1949.

See also United Mine Workers of America

John Hennen
Morehead State University

Black Bear

The black bear is the state animal of West Virginia. It is a member of the family *Ursidae americanus,* which ranges from Alaska to Labrador to Florida and northern Mexico. Grizzlies and polar bears, the larger North American members of this family, are found far to our north and west.

Black bears are generally less than six feet long and stand two to three feet high at the shoulder. Adult males ordinarily weigh from 150 to 450 pounds, but some

The black bear is West Virginia's state animal.

West Virginia records exceed 600 pounds. Adult females vary from 100 to 300 pounds, depending upon nutrition during their early years of rapid growth. Here in West Virginia, the blond and cinnamon color phases found in western states are absent. Our bears are uniformly black, with brown muzzles. About five percent to 10 percent have white markings on their brisket, varying from a few flecks to distinct V's.

Before white settlement, bears were widespread throughout our region's hardwood forests. The population was evidently quite large, though no accurate numbers are available. Hunting seasons are regulated by calculating bear population in relation to the amount of forest in a county, which is based on the number of bears killed by hunters in past seasons. Our most popular bear hunting season, which allows the use of hounds during December, is based on a minimum average take of one bear per 20 square miles of forest. This would translate roughly as a density of one bear per four or five square miles (approximately 3,000 acres) of forestland. There is a non-dog season as well, and a bow hunting season in October and November.

The current bear population of West Virginia is estimated at 8,000 to 10,000. Total recorded mortalities of a little over 1,000 would indicate an expanding bear population. Bears have been observed in practically all of West Virginia, but are most prevalent in a crescent of counties from Tucker through Greenbrier and Monroe and westward across Kanawha and Boone.

See also Mammals

Joseph C. Rieffenberger
Division of Natural Resources

The Black Hand

The Black Hand was the name and symbol of an underworld society of Italian immigrants which during the first decades of the 20th century sought to extort money from other Italian immigrants. Thriving in Sicily in the late 19th century, the Black Hand came to the New World as part of the great migration to America's mines and factories. Soon the mysterious society operated in West Virginia.

The Black Hand intimidated victims by sending threatening letters, accompanied by crude drawings of a hand painted black. Italians are the largest ethnic group in West Virginia, and their businessmen were the most frequent targets. Sometimes, the Black Hand sought to exploit miners. Some victims refused to pay, fought back, and were left alone.

Trials at several county courthouses led to the eradication of the group. On February 11, 1923, eight members of the Black Hand were arrested in Harrison County. Their successful prosecution constituted one of the most famous trials in Clarksburg, the county seat. The trial capped a three-year period when several mysterious murders in the county involved alleged gangland vendettas.

John C. McKinney, a police chief and detective at Fairmont, was active in the investigations of the gang in Marion and Harrison counties. He authored a paper titled "Black Hand," in which he reports how Tusca Morris, prosecuting attorney in Marion County, helped eliminate the organization there. Frank Amos, who also served as prosecutor in Marion, acted against the group, as did Will Morris in Harrison County. William Cramer, the prosecuting attorney of Monongalia County, helped convict members of the Black Hand despite threats on his life.

Extortion victims testified at the trials. An immigrant, Francisco Beradelli, helped bring down the Black Hand in northern West Virginia by joining the organization and informing on its workings. In Marion County an Italian immigrant shot a Black Hander who tried to extort him. The law set the shooter free. There is no reported case in which those who resisted were punished by the Black Hand.

Norman Julian
Dominion Post

Black Knight Country Club

The Black Knight Country Club in Beckley was organized in 1928–29 when Col. Ernest Chilson, general manager and vice president of Raleigh Coal & Coke, offered more than 60 acres of company property for a golf course and clubhouse. The club's name came from the "Black Knight" trademark of the coal company. Raleigh Coal & Coke owned the club, and membership was limited to those prominent in coal and related industries. The clubhouse, designed by Chilson, was a three-story white cinder block building with Art Deco features. The nine-hole golf course was designed by noted golf architect Fred Findlay. Governor Conley attended the club's grand opening, May 31, 1929.

In 1938, noted golfer Sam Snead played an exhibition match at Black Knight. In 1950, Raleigh Coal & Coke ceased operations, and the club members purchased the club in April 1951. By 2000, the club included six tennis courts, pro shops for golf and tennis, an Olympic-sized swimming pool, a bathhouse with sunning and picnic area, outdoor terraces on the first and second floors of the clubhouse, and remodeled ballroom, dining rooms, kitchen, and bar. The Black Knight Country Club continues to be a center for local business and social gatherings, with many businesses in addition to coal now represented in its membership.

Lois C. McLean
Beckley

Black Lung Disease

Coal miner's pneumoconiosis, or black lung disease, results from the inhalation of coal dust. Human anatomy filters out the larger dust particles, but the smallest manage to reach the alveoli, or air sacs, of the lungs. These air sacs exchange gases with the blood. Over time, inhaling substantial quantities of coal particles causes the air sacs to lose elasticity and become weaker, contributing to emphysema. Deposits of dust-containing blood cells become permanently lodged in the lungs, restricting airflow and producing chronic bronchitis. A miner in the early stages of this disease may experience occasional shortness of breath and coughing that eventually increases in frequency. Later symptoms include wheezing and pressure or tightness in the chest. Because it curtails oxygenation of the blood, pneumoconiosis may result in high blood pressure, enlarged heart, heart attack, or acute pneumonia.

Some early 19th-century physicians and critics of industrialization noted the symptoms of what was then referred to as "miner's asthma." The disease increased dramatically with 20th-century mine mechanization, which increased the level of dust in mining. Unfortunately, x-ray techniques failed to provide an efficient tool for diagnosing the medical effects of coal dust in the lungs. Black lung was denied as a real disease until established by crusading doctors after mid-century. A 1954 scholarly article by West Virginia physician Joseph E. Martin Jr. insisted that black lung was indeed a progressive, terminal disease associated with exposure to coal dust. By the 1960s, a small group of doctors, especially Donald Rasmussen, conducted research, pioneered alternative forms of diagnosis, and offered mounting medical evidence of black lung as an occupational disease. Rasmussen and other activist physicians such as I. E. Buff and Hawey A. Wells Jr. joined with the rank-and-file miners of the Black Lung Association to educate miners, the public, and politicians about the disease. Legislation declaring black lung a compensatory injury passed the

West Virginia legislature in 1969 and became federal law later the same year.

See also Black Lung Movement, I. E. Buff, Donald Rasmussen

Paul H. Rakes
WVU Institute of Technology
Barbara Ellen Smith, *Digging Our Own Graves: Coal Miners and the Struggle Over Black Lung Disease,* 1987.

Black Lung Movement

The campaign to have coal miner's pneumoconiosis (black lung) proclaimed a compensatory injury galvanized the West Virginia coalfields in the late 1960s.

As coal mining expanded, more workers exhibited symptoms of "miner's asthma," as the disease was originally called. The higher levels of coal dust produced by 20th-century mine mechanization increased the frequency of the disease. Still, black lung went officially unacknowledged. Three studies by the U.S. Public Health Service between 1924 and 1945 failed to bring recognition of black lung as a debilitating condition. Even though Great Britain recognized coal-related pneumoconiosis as a compensatory injury in 1943, American mainstream medical opinion contended that miner's asthma reflected a normal condition of mine work and actually posed no serious problems. Some doctors pointed out that the disease failed to appear on x-rays, and some suggested that complaining workers were trying to obtain illegitimate compensation. More sympathetic doctors worked to establish reliable means of diagnosis.

From 1942 to 1968, miners at their union's national convention consistently requested that the United Mine Workers of America undertake the task of having black lung declared a compensable disease. An authoritarian union leadership ignored or sidetracked such demands until 1968, when UMWA President Tony Boyle supported a campaign for black lung recognition at the state level only. In November 1968, an explosion at Consolidation Coal's No. 9 mine at Farmington, Marion County, killed 78 miners, and a national television audience heard political officials and the UMWA president defend the company, even suggesting that disasters constituted an accepted risk in mining. Occurring within an era of social unrest, Farmington contributed to the growing belief that an entrenched system needed reform from below.

Miners in Fayette County enlisted the aid of physicians I. E. Buff and Donald Rasmussen to educate workers about the disease. In a series of local meetings, Buff encouraged miners to take matters into their own hands. Poverty War volunteers such as Craig Robinson, familiar with civil protest, joined in the call for grassroots action, and in December 1968 a small group of miners in Montgomery

---

Crusading for black lung reform

"Buff and Wells were great entertainers. I was shocked at what Buff would do. He would thunder out, 'Y'all got black lung and y'all gonna die!'

"It was an interesting act to try to follow. Wells was the one who had gotten the dry inflated lung tissue from Dr. Lorin Kerr and he would crunch this stuff up and let it fall to the floor and say, 'That is what is happening to your brothers' lungs.'

"Buff would come with an oxygen tank and mask and a white hat and black hat. He would tell the miners about the legislators, 'They wear their black hat when they talk to coal operators.' He would wear the oxygen tank and oxygen mask and roar this when talking to miners, 'This is what you will end up wearing.' That was quite an experience.

"In November 1968 the mine at Mannington blew up. This focused the whole country on the mine issue. It was obvious they needed laws to address safety and health of the coal miners nationwide. Legislation was needed for workers compensation to become more fair for the miners."

—Dr. Donald Rasmussen *Appalachia: Spirit Triumphant*

---

formed the Black Lung Association. The new association hired liberal attorney Paul Kaufman to supervise the drafting of a compensation bill and lobby it through the state legislature.

Support spread through the coalfields while the legislature met in early 1969. Black lung activists from across the state assembled at the Charleston Civic Center on January 26 where Congressman Ken Hechler and state legislator Warren McGraw joined Rasmussen, Buff, and Dr. Hawey A. Wells Jr. to encourage the gathering to act decisively. On February 18, 282 miners at a Raleigh County mine went on strike over the black lung issue, and within a few days the walkout spread throughout southern West Virginia. On February 26, 2,000 miners protesting at the capitol heard Governor Moore promise a new bill for a special session of the legislature. Ignoring Moore's offer, the protesters moved into the capitol to lobby for themselves. The House judiciary committee reported out a weak version of the bill and, in reaction, all the state's coal miners, over 40,000, stopped work. Under pressure from hundreds of coal miners at the capitol, the House and then the Senate passed a stronger bill.

Events in West Virginia made black lung a national issue as Congress engaged in producing the sweeping Coal Mine Health and Safety Act of 1969. The new law placed strict standards on respirable dust levels and provided federally financed compensation for miners disabled by black lung and the widows of anyone who had succumbed to the disease. More liberal eligibility regulations increased the unexpectedly high cost of the black lung program in 1972, approaching $1 billion per year. The implementation of a tonnage tax on coal was meant to reduce the burden on taxpayers, but evidence suggests that the federal treasury bore the major cost into the 1980s. The Reagan administration implemented stricter eligibility standards for new claimants in 1982, ending the presumption that any miner with 15 years' experience qualified regardless of

x-ray evidence. In the early 21st century, about 80,000 American miners and family members receive about $460 million in annual benefits.

See also Black Lung Disease, I. E. Buff, Donald Rasmussen

Paul H. Rakes
WVU Institute of Technology
Brit Hume, *Death in the Mines: Rebellion and Murder in the United Mine Workers,* 1971; Curtis Seltzer, *Fire in the Hole: Miners and Managers in the American Coal Industry,* 1985; Barbara Ellen Smith, *Digging Our Own Graves: Coal Miners and the Struggle Over Black Lung Disease,* 1987.

Sam Black

Country preacher Samuel Black, born in Greenbrier County, March 1813, was a Methodist circuit rider. He traveled through Greenbrier, Clay, Fayette, Nicholas, Webster, and Kanawha counties, spreading the word to more people than most other ministers of his day. Affectionately known as "Uncle Sam," he organized many congregations and helped build churches with money earned by selling socks and deerskin gloves made by women church members. He was ordained a deacon in 1844 and was a two-time delegate to the general conference from his church. He was also one of the 16 charter members of the West Virginia Methodist Conference. A white frame structure named Sam Black Church was erected in 1902 in Greenbrier County, in memory of Reverend Black. His name is written in large letters across the doorway of the building, and today the community is named Sam Black Church. Samuel Black died July 13, 1899.

Cathy Hershberger Miller
State Archives

W. E. Blackhurst

Author Warren Elmer "Tweard" Blackhurst was born October 10, 1904, in Arbovale, Pocahontas County. Educated at Glenville State Teachers College, he taught English and Latin at Green Bank High School from 1932 to 1964. He developed and taught the state's first conservation class, and supervised senior students in the planting of five acres of seedlings annually in the Monongahela National Forest.

Blackhurst wrote for magazines and newspapers on conservation and wildlife. His popular novels, which retold stories of Cass and the history of the timber boom years in the Greenbrier Valley, included *Riders of the Flood* (1954), which was his most successful book, *Sawdust In Your Eyes* (1963), *Of Men and A Mighty Mountain* (1965), and *Mixed Harvest* (1970). *Afterglow*, a collection of poetry and prose, was published posthumously in 1972. Blackhurst, instrumental in a citizens' group that lobbied for acquisition of land and equipment to establish the Cass Scenic Railroad State Park, was its first commentator in 1963. Between puffs on his pipe, he would give lessons on history, geology, and other aspects of the area during train rides up and down the mountain. He was also a popular public speaker, sharing the history and human interest of Pocahontas County with wit and insight. W. E. Blackhurst died October 5, 1970.

See also Cass

Louise Burner Flegel
Pine Knoll Shore, North Carolina

The Blackwater Chronicle

In June 1851, Philip Pendleton Kennedy, the prominent illustrator David Hunter Strother, who was Kennedy's cousin, and several others on a trout fishing expedition in Western Virginia ventured into the Blackwater region. The group's experiences were detailed in *The Blackwater Chronicle*, written by Kennedy and illustrated by Strother, also known as "Porte Crayon." This humorous treatment of a wilderness adventure makes abundant use of witty literary devices and classical allusions more in the vein of 18th-century authors than the journalistic style of Kennedy's 19th-century contemporaries.

The adventurers traveled southward from the headwaters of the North Branch Potomac by present Gormania, Grant County, and then across the high Alleghenies. Eventually they found the North Fork of the Blackwater River, following that into the Blackwater Canyon in present Tucker County. Here they did their fishing. In his description of the region, which the trekkers called "Canaan," Kennedy provides modern readers with a glimpse of a portion of present West Virginia that was then untouched by agriculture or industry. The classic book is regarded today as an important ecological document, as well as fine local color writing. *The Blackwater Chronicle* was originally published in 1853, two years after the trip, and reissued in 2002 by the West Virginia University Press.

Philip Pendleton Kennedy, *The Blackwater Chronicle: A Narrative of An Expedition Into the Land of Canaan in Randolph County, Virginia,* 1853.

Blackwater Falls.

Blackwater Falls

The Blackwater Falls are located on Blackwater River in Tucker County, near the town of Davis. The dark, tumbling waters plunge almost 60 feet over resistant sandstone of the Pennsylvanian Age, creating one of the most photographed sights in West Virginia. The falls are accessible from steps, and several viewing platforms allow visitors to enjoy the falls throughout the year.

The river enters Blackwater Falls State Park at an elevation of 3,040 feet. For the next 2.2 miles it is a wild river, dropping 57 feet at the main falls and then descending another 560 feet, before leaving the park. The river, geologically young, has carved the spectacular, deep, and almost vertical walls of Blackwater Canyon, which cuts through the surrounding plateau. Blackwater Lodge opened in 1956 on the south rim of the canyon, and a 65-site campground was opened in 1961. The state park, consisting of 1,688 acres, was established in 1937.

In 1851, Philip Pendleton Kennedy wrote an account of his visit to the Blackwater area, describing the impenetrable rhododendron thickets, rugged terrain, and wildlife he found. Kennedy's book was illustrated by his better-known cousin, David Hunter Strother ("Porte Crayon"). Strother revisited the Blackwater wilderness in the early 1870s. Timbered in the early 1900s and then ravaged by fires that burned the rich organic soil, the area suffered much environmental degradation. Today, much of the forest has grown back.

Blackwater Falls is the site of an annual spring wildflower walk and is known for its variety of bird life, including several kinds of thrushes and warblers, and other songbirds.

See also The Blackwater Chronicle, Blackwater River

Norma Jean Kennedy-Venable
Morgantown

Philip Pendleton Kennedy, *The Blackwater Chronicle: A Narrative of An Expedition Into the Land of Canaan in Randolph County, Virginia,* 1853; J. Lawrence Smith, *Blackwater Country,* 1972.

Blackwater River

The Blackwater River rises in the southwestern end of Canaan Valley in Tucker County at an elevation of 3,250 feet. Its flow is generally northeastward to its juncture with the Little Blackwater River and then southwestward to where it enters the Dry Fork of Cheat River near Hendricks, at an elevation of 1,705 feet. The Blackwater River is 31 miles long and drains an area of 142 square miles. In ascending order, its principal tributaries are Big and Tub runs, North Fork, Pendleton and Beaver creeks, Devils Run, Yellow Creek, Little Blackwater River, North Branch, Sand, Yoakum, Freeland, Club, and Mill runs. As it flows through Canaan Valley, the Blackwater meanders wildly and its flow is sluggish. Below Davis, the Blackwater River flows into Blackwater Falls State Park and drops 57 feet over the famous falls. It then begins a much straighter and more determined course as it carves out the picturesque Blackwater Canyon. Near the state park lodge, the canyon reaches a depth of 525 feet. The color of the Blackwater River is dark amber and is due largely to tannic acid from the abundance of hemlock and spruce trees in its drainage basin.

See also Blackwater Falls

Patricia Hissom
Davis

Blaine Island

Located in the Kanawha River at South Charleston, this large island was surveyed at 65 acres when bought by the Union Carbide company in 1927. It is more than a mile long.

There is evidence that the island was inhabited in prehistoric times. In 1780, Fleming Cobb, a pioneer scout and settler of what would later become South Charleston, planted at least two pear trees on Blaine Island that survived until the 20th century. Cobb inherited the island from his uncle, Thomas Upton, in the early 1790s. It is said Cobb killed the last Indian slain in this part of West Virginia, near Blaine Island. He traded the entire island to Charles Blaine for a flintlock rifle. In later years the island served as the Blaine family farm, producing the finest watermelons in the valley.

In the early 20th century, Blaine Island held a small amusement park and bathing beach on the upper end, a favorite summer getaway for Charlestonians. Near the middle of the island a rudimentary airfield was cleared and aviators gave exhibitions. Since its acquisition by Union Carbide the island has served as a chemical plant of great importance. During World War II, its defense role merited a 24-hour U.S. Coast Guard Patrol circling the island.

Richard A. Andre
Charleston

Jacob Beeson Blair

Congressman Jacob Beeson Blair was the first West Virginian to be told by President Abraham Lincoln of Lincoln's support of the admission of West Virginia into the United States. Blair was born in Parkersburg, April 11, 1821, and died in Salt Lake City, February 12, 1901.

Orphaned at an early age, Blair was apprenticed to be taught carpentry, but in 1842 began to study the law under his uncle, John Jay Jackson Sr. He was admitted to the bar in 1844. Shortly thereafter he was elected prosecuting attorney of Ritchie County. When the Civil War broke out in 1861, Blair was an ardent Unionist. He supported the Reorganized Government of Virginia and was serving in the U.S. House of Representatives when on New Year's Eve, 1862, he and his two congressional colleagues from the state met at the White House to discuss West Virginia's admission into the Union with the president. Eager for Lincoln's answer, Blair entered the White House the next morning through an open window and was informed of his decision.

Blair was reelected to Congress twice before being appointed minister to Costa Rica in 1868. His last 25 years were spent in Wyoming and Utah.

See also Formation of West Virginia
Bernard L. Allen
Conway, South Carolina

Blair Mountain, Battle Of

In August 1921, armed coal miners from the Kanawha Valley and the southern counties of Boone, Fayette, Mingo, McDowell, and Logan gathered at Marmet in Kanawha County. The miners proposed to march to Logan and Mingo counties to rescue union miners who had been jailed or mistreated in attempts to unionize the mines. Their efforts brought on the most spectacular confrontation in West Virginia's labor history, the culminating event in the era known as the Mine Wars.

While accurate figures are not available, sources estimate the number of miners who participated in the march at anywhere from 7,000 to 20,000. Many were veterans of World War I, and they organized themselves like an army division. The marchers had medical and supply units, posted guards when appropriate, and used passwords to weed out infiltrators. Marchers commandeered trains and other vehicles to take them to

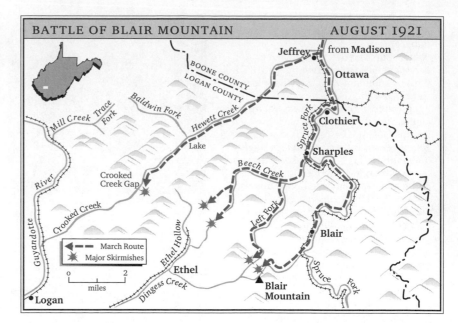

BATTLE OF BLAIR MOUNTAIN   **AUGUST 1921**

Logan County and confiscated supplies from company stores along the march.

State authorities, led by Governor Morgan, quickly organized a group of state police, volunteer militia companies, and coal company employees to keep the miners from invading Logan County. The opposing forces came together at Blair Mountain, near the Boone and Logan borders. The well-armed miners and their opponents battled along the ridge of Blair Mountain, resulting in several deaths. Like other statistics in this event, the exact numbers of killed and wounded are mere conjecture.

Morgan urgently requested federal intervention to end the bloodshed. President Warren G. Harding responded with 2,500 federal troops, including a bomber squadron under aviation pioneer Gen. William "Billy" Mitchell. The federal troops quickly brought the conflict to an end, and the miners returned home. Several hundred miners and their leaders were charged with various crimes from murder to treason. Most were given minor sentences, but serious attempts were made to punish William "Bill" Blizzard, one of the march leaders, who was charged with treason. He was tried in Charles Town, Lewisburg, and Fayetteville before the charges were eventually dropped.

The armed march and the Battle of Blair Mountain resulted in little or no gain for union miners, but the hostilities created by labor strife from the early 1900s to the 1920s color labor relations in West Virginia to the present.

See also Bill Blizzard, Mine Wars, Miners' March, Ephraim Franklin Morgan
Kenneth R. Bailey
WVU Institute of Technology

David A. Corbin, *Life, Work, and Rebellion in the Coal Fields: The Southern West Virginia Miners, 1880–1922,* 1981; Lon Savage, *Thunder in the Mountains, The West Virginia Mine War 1920–21,* 1990.

Blakeley

The house known as Blakeley is situated on the south side of County Route 13/3, facing across the small valley of the North Fork of Bullskin Run Creek near Charles Town in Jefferson County. It was constructed in 1820 by John A. Washington II as a two-story masonry building with a gable roof and two end chimneys. Basically Federal in style, it had eight rooms exclusive of two central hallways, one on each floor. In line to inherit Mount Vernon, the owner did not attempt to rival the grander Claymont Court built nearby by his brother, Bushrod Corbin Washington. John left Blakeley to John A. Washington III when he died in 1832.

Blakeley burned in November 1864. The roof was destroyed in this fire, as was much of the second floor except for the outer walls. Owner Richard B. Washington rebuilt the burned portion on the same plan as the original, replacing the wood roof with metal. The house remained in the Washington family for several decades before being purchased and rehabilitated in 1943 by Raymond J. Funkhouser.

Blakeley is important as the home to several prominent Jefferson County families and as a local example of historic rehabilitation as practiced in the earlier part of the 20th century. It was added to the National Register of Historic Places in 1980.

William D. Theriault
Bakerton

Florence Aby Blanchfield

Nurse Florence Aby Blanchfield was born in Shepherdstown, April 1, 1882. She attended business college at Pittsburgh, and in 1906 she graduated from the South Side Training School for Nurses in Pittsburgh. She received additional training at Johns Hopkins Hospital.

After several years as a civilian nurse, Blanchfield in 1917 enlisted in the Army Nurse Corps and served in France during World War I. After briefly returning to civilian life, she served at army hospitals in the United States and abroad, and in the surgeon general's office. As a lieutenant colonel commissioned in 1942, Blanchfield served as assistant to Col. Julia Flikke, superintendent of the Army Nurse Corps. She succeeded Flikke in 1943. Given serial number 1, Blanchfield then served in the temporary grade of full colonel. During World War II, she oversaw expansion of the corps from 1,000 to 57,000 nurses, the largest group ever to serve on active duty.

Blanchfield worked with Congresswoman Frances Payne Bolton to secure passage of the Army-Navy Nurses Act in 1947. As a result, the army and navy revised regulations, permitting women nurses to hold full rank and receive the rights, privileges, and pay afforded commissioned male officers. That year, Blanchfield became the first woman to hold a permanent commission in the regular army of the United States, receiving her commission from General Eisenhower. She received the Distinguished Service Medal in 1945, the International Red Cross's Florence Nightingale Medal in 1951, and the West Virginia Distinguished Service Medal in 1963.

Blanchfield retired in 1947 and died in Washington, May 12, 1971. Colonel Florence A. Blanchfield Army Community Hospital at Fort Campbell, Kentucky, was dedicated in her honor in 1982.

Russ Barbour
Huntington

Blenko Glass

Glass blower William John Blenko built his first factory in Milton in 1921. Born in England in 1854, Blenko was determined to introduce antique stained glass production into his adopted country.

Prior to his arrival in Cabell County, he made several failed attempts to establish his business. Blenko came to the U.S. in the 1890s, settling first in Kokomo, Indiana. While there, he became lifelong friends with Socialist leader Eugene V. Debs. Due to economic circumstances, Blenko was forced to return to England to continue his craft. In 1899, he returned to America and tried to set up shop in Point Marion, Pennsylvania. That effort failed, as did a later attempt in Clarksburg.

His first Milton plant, described as a shack by those who remember it, was known as the Eureka Art Glass Company. Blenko slept in a corner and lived on $3 a week. In 1923, he was joined by his son, William H., and daughter-in-law, Marian. His son was an able glassmaker and an even better salesman. Orders for the stained glass began to come in from the U.S. and Europe. The Great Depres-

Handblown glass from Blenko.

sion, however, nearly proved fatal to the business.

By 1930, William H. Blenko became convinced that diversification was the key to survival. The company began producing the decorative glassware for which it is most famous today. While stained glass production continued, the demand for decorative ware grew steadily. By the mid-1940s, Blenko glass was famous, having been featured in such publications as *Time, National Geographic, House Beautiful,* and *House and Garden.* Blenko stained glass can be found in the National Cathedral in Washington, the Cathedral of Rheims in France, the chapel of the U.S. Air Force Academy in Colorado, and many other places. Blenko also manufactures the prize for the annual Country Music Awards.

William John Blenko worked until his death in 1933 at the age of 78. William H. Blenko led the company until his death in 1969. He was succeeded by his son, William H. Blenko Jr., now chairman of the board. The current president of the company is his son, Richard Blenko.

See also Glass Industry

Rick Wilson
American Friends Service Committee

Harman Blennerhassett

Political adventurer Harman Blennerhassett was born October 8, 1764, at Hambledon, England, where his wealthy Irish parents were visiting. Blennerhassett's education included London's Westminster School and Trinity College, Dublin, and legal training at the Inns of Court, London, and at Dublin's King's Inns.

After inheriting the family estate in 1792, Blennerhassett embarked upon a fateful chain of decisions, joining in 1793 the secret Society of United Irishmen, which plotted the overthrow of English rule in Ireland, and wedding his niece,

Margaret Agnew, in 1794. He sold his property in 1795 before emigrating to America to escape arrest for his subversive activity and to avoid family friction over his marriage.

Landing August 1, 1796, at New York, the Blennerhassetts settled in 1798 on Belpre (later Blennerhassett) Island, in the Ohio River near present Parkersburg. In September 1800, their new home, an enormous Palladian structure, was completed, its rooms filled with imported furnishings. The mansion's beauty, romanticized by an island setting, was enhanced by nine acres of lawns and elaborately landscaped gardens.

By 1805, the Blennerhassetts accepted Aaron Burr's invitation to join his expedition to the Southwest. Many historians now believe this mysterious enterprise to have been against Spanish-ruled Texas, and not, as Burr's detractors maintained, a plot to separate the West from the United States. President Thomas Jefferson, however, ordered Burr and Blennerhassett's arrests late in 1806 on a charge of treason. Harman fled downriver, followed a few days later by his wife and children.

Soon Burr and Blennerhassett were captured and imprisoned in the Virginia State Penitentiary. Burr's subsequent acquittal freed Blennerhassett, who spent the rest of his life futilely attempting to rebuild his fortune. Returning impoverished to England in 1824, he died February 2, 1831, on Guernsey in the Channel Islands.

See also Blennerhassett Island, Burr Conspiracy

Ray Swick
Blennerhassett Island State Park
Ray Swick, *An Island Called Eden: An Historical Sketch of Blennerhassett Island near Parkersburg, West Virginia, 1798–1807,* 1996.

Blennerhassett Island

The Ohio River's most famous island, Blennerhassett, lies two miles west of Parkersburg. It is four miles long, and its 381 acres make it the river's fifth-largest island.

Blennerhassett was created sometime after A.D. 1300, when the river cut an additional channel north of the main channel. Located on a major stream furnishing food, water, and transportation, the island invited human settlement. Prehistoric Indians occupied the island until about 1680. They eventually cleared most of it to grow corn and lived in villages of structures covered with reed mats or bark. Twentieth-century excavations have revealed Blennerhassett Island to be one of the Midwest's richest archeological sites.

Blennerhassett's recorded history begins with a mention in the 1765 journal of the Indian trader George Croghan. A 1766 traveler noted the Delaware chief Nemacolin's cabin on the island which

Blennerhassett Mansion, re-created in 1991.

for that reason was called "Nemacolin's Island" in following years. It was also known as Belpre Island. The island was farmed by New Englanders during the Ohio Valley's 1791–95 Indian war. They erected two blockhouses for protection, transforming the island into a business center by building a store and two floating gristmills.

The island's most momentous chapter opened with the 1798 arrival of Harman and Margaret Blennerhassett, wealthy Irish aristocrats fleeing political persecution and personal scandal. Their years on the island, while brief, were charged with excitement and high style. The couple's mansion gained the reputation of the West's most beautiful home. In 1805–06, they allowed their estate to become headquarters for Aaron Burr's military expedition to the Southwest, an episode that raised the island to national renown and awarded it a permanent footnote in American history. Eventually it became the subject of a short story by Nathaniel Hawthorne, a poem by Walt Whitman, paintings of Eastern artists, and two New York operas. The Blennerhassetts fled the island when Burr's scheme collapsed.

Despite its notoriety, Blennerhassett Island led a sleepy farming existence until 1886 when a park, which lasted through 1912, was built on its upper end. The boxer "Gentleman Jim" Corbett competed at the park, as did the Cincinnati Reds, Brooklyn Dodgers, and Pittsburgh Pirates. As a 1920s moonshining center, Blennerhassett become the scene of occasional raids and bloody frays during Prohibition.

Today, Blennerhassett Island is a state historical park. With the reconstructed Blennerhassett mansion providing an elegant backdrop, the island welcomes 40,000 visitors a year.

See also Harman Blennerhassett

Ray Swick
Blennerhassett Island State Park

Margaret Agnew Blennerhassett

Margaret Agnew Blennerhassett, wife of Harman Blennerhassett, was born in the northern England town of Bishop Auckland in 1771. She lived from 1800 to 1806 in a grand 16-room mansion she and her husband had constructed on an Ohio River island near present Parkersburg. The Blennerhassetts attempted to bring refinement to the rugged frontier country. Margaret, a poet and skilled hostess, entertained her guests with music and dancing, readings in French, and recitations from Shakespeare. Tall and athletic, she was an accomplished horsewoman and strong enough to walk the 12 miles to Marietta. In 1805, she returned from Philadelphia with the smallpox vaccine, which she used to innoculate her own children and the children of local families. Following an ill-fated alliance with Aaron Burr, she and her family were forced to flee their island home in 1806. Margaret died in poverty in New York City, June 16, 1842. She and her son, Harman Jr., were reburied on Blennerhassett Island in 1996.

See also Harman Blennerhassett, Blennerhassett Island, Burr Conspiracy

Debra Conner
Parkersburg

Bill Blizzard

Unionist William "Bill" Blizzard was born September 19, 1892, the son of Timothy Blizzard and activist Sarah Rebecca "Mother" Blizzard. He became one of West Virginia's most influential and controversial labor leaders of the 20th century. Born on Cabin Creek, Kanawha County, Blizzard first became involved with the United Mine Workers of America during the bloody Paint Creek-Cabin Creek strike of 1912–13. During the next decade, he rose from the rank and file along with Frank Keeney and Fred Mooney.

In 1921, Blizzard played a key role in the Miners' March on Logan. While District 17 President Keeney and Secretary-treasurer Mooney managed events behind the scenes, Blizzard directed the actions of the miners in the front lines of the fighting at Blair Mountain. After the Battle of Blair Mountain, Blizzard was tried at Charles Town for treason and murder, but was defended by T. C. Townsend and found not guilty on both charges. However, the District 17 officials had lost favor with UMWA President John L. Lewis, and in 1924 Keeney and Mooney were forced to retire. Blizzard remained in the union but lost much of his influence.

Blizzard returned to prominence in 1931 when he led the UMWA's struggle against Keeney's West Virginia Mine Workers Union. Blizzard became a protegé of union leader Van Bittner and together they organized the entire state and turned the UMWA into a powerful political force. In 1945, Blizzard was appointed president of District 17 and served for 10 years. John L. Lewis forced Blizzard to resign after learning of a fistfight between Blizzard and Lewis's youngest brother, Raymond Lewis. Blizzard died of cancer July 31, 1958, denouncing John L. Lewis and the organization that he had spent his life serving.

See also Battle of Blair Mountain, Blizzard Treason Trial

C. Belmont Keeney
West Virginia Humanities Council

Mother Blizzard

Labor activist Sarah "Mother" Blizzard was born Sarah Rebecca Rogers, October 6, 1864, in Edmond, Fayette County. She spent her early life on the family farm and witnessed the advent of coal mining in southern West Virginia following the coming of the railroads in the 1870s and 1880s. Blizzard was deeply involved in the United Mine Workers of America, from the organization's early beginnings in the late 19th century. She encouraged her husband, Timothy Blizzard, and her children to participate in union activities. Her support for the 1902 coal strike led to her family's eviction from their home in Kilsyth, Fayette County.

The family resettled in the Cabin Creek district of Kanawha County, where Sarah Blizzard allowed striking miners to camp on her land during the violent 1912–13 Paint Creek-Cabin Creek strike. During the strike, she participated in the umbrella march with Mother Jones, whom she knew and to whom contemporaries often compared her; on this occasion the women armed themselves with umbrellas, Jones and Blizzard allegedly striking policemen with theirs. Blizzard also organized a group of women to sabotage a rail line, blocking the return of the armored Bull Moose Special to the miners' camp.

Remembered as "Mother" or "Ma"

Blizzard by the miners she helped to look after, Sarah Blizzard was the mother of UMW District 17 President Bill Blizzard and great-grandmother of UMW President Cecil Roberts. She died September 28, 1955.

See also Bill Blizzard, Bull Moose Special, Mine Wars, Mother Jones

Shae Davidson
The Plains, Ohio

Blizzard Treason Trial

The 1922 treason trial of labor leader Bill Blizzard followed the 1921 Battle of Blair Mountain. At the time of the battle Blizzard was president of United Mine Workers District 17's Subdistrict Two, based in St. Albans. The members of the subdistrict were known for their belligerence toward both company and UMW officials, and some observers (including Mother Jones) believed Blizzard's incendiary character would escalate the conflict. District 17 leaders Fred Mooney and Frank Keeney left the state during the battle in order to avoid arrest, but Blizzard remained. He played a decisive role in convincing the marchers to surrender once federal troops appeared upon the scene. The state accused several union leaders, including Blizzard, and many of the marchers with treason against the state of West Virginia and other charges, interpreting the miners' armed march as an insurrection against the state rather than an action directed against coal operators.

Prosecution and defense attorneys agreed to move the trials to Jefferson County, in the Eastern Panhandle far from the coalfields. Coal company attorneys composed the prosecution team. Thomas Townsend, former Kanawha County prosecuting attorney, led the defense. The prosecution chose to try Blizzard first, believing that the *State of West Virginia v. William Blizzard* was the strongest of the treason cases.

The trial centered on a discussion of Blizzard's location during the movement toward Blair Mountain. Prosecution witnesses claimed that Blizzard had shadowed the marchers, periodically requesting reports and issuing orders. The defense presented witnesses claiming that Blizzard had remained in Charleston during the crisis. Questions about the reliability of some prosecution witnesses, as well as Blizzard's role in convincing the miners to lay down their arms, led the jury to acquit him on the evening of May 27, 1922.

The treason trials, in the same courthouse where John Brown had been tried and condemned, depleted the union's treasury and crippled the organization for years to come. The United Mine Workers later supported Townsend, a Republican, in his failed 1932 run for gover-

Labor leader Sarah Rebecca "Mother" Blizzard (1864–1955).

nor, contributing to the Depression-era schism in the Democratic Party.

See also Battle of Blair Mountain, Bill Blizzard

Shae Davidson
The Plains, Ohio

David Alan Corbin, *Life, Work, and Rebellion in the Coal Fields: The Southern West Virginia Miners, 1880–1922*, 1981; Shae Davidson, "'The Boys'll Listen to Me:' The Labor Career of William Blizzard," M. A. thesis, Marshall University, 1998.

Bloch Brothers Tobacco Company

Mail Pouch Chewing Tobacco, perhaps West Virginia's most famous consumer product, was made by Bloch Brothers Tobacco Company. The company began with brothers Aaron and Samuel Bloch, who ran a small grocery and dry goods store in 1879 in Wheeling. They also had a small cigar factory on the second floor. Noticing that men chewed the cigar wrapper clippings, the Blochs conceived the idea of flavoring the scrap cuttings that were left over from cigar making and selling it in paper bags as chewing tobacco. The flood of 1884 destroyed the store, and the Blochs decided to focus exclusively on tobacco products.

The brothers were progressive employers. In 1890, many of their workers joined the Tobacco Workers Union, with which the company cooperated. Bloch Brothers had a health plan and established an eight-hour day and five-day week before these reforms were generally adopted. Aaron was succeeded by his brother, Samuel, as president in 1902. Samuel served until passing the company on to his son, Jesse A. Bloch, an influential state senator.

Jesse Bloch was president of the company from 1937 to 1947. During his tenure, the company expanded by acquiring the Pollack Crown stogie and the Penn

Tobacco Company. Jesse's son, Thomas, continued as head of the company, adding the firm of Christian Peper Tobacco Company and its line of pipe tobacco products to the mixtures being made in Wheeling. Bloch Brothers was sold in 1969 to the General Cigar and Tobacco Company, which became a division of Culbro in 1978. The company was acquired by the Helme Tobacco Company in 1983 and now uses the name Swisher International. Mail Pouch, described by tobacco chewers as drier and not as sweet as some other chewing tobaccos, remains a popular product.

See also Jesse A. Bloch

Katherine M. Jourdan
Indianapolis, Indiana

Jesse A. Bloch

Businessman and legislator Jesse A. Bloch was born in Wheeling, November 2, 1879, the year his father and uncle founded Bloch Brothers Tobacco Company. He entered the family business in 1900 and succeeded his father as president in 1937. A progressive Republican, Bloch was active in civic and political affairs. He served as a member of the House of Delegates in the 1910s and the state Senate in the 1920s. His achievements included introducing workers' compensation legislation and casting the decisive vote for ratification of the 19th Amendment (women's suffrage). His civic commitments included the Wheeling Housing Authority, Ohio Valley General Hospital, and the Boy Scouts.

Bloch married Jessie Thornton Moffat in 1905, and the couple had two children. Son Thomas carried on the family business tradition, succeeding his father as tobacco company president in 1947. Although the Blochs were one of Wheeling's original Jewish families, Jesse Bloch's parents had withdrawn from the Eoff Street Temple, and the family later became active in the Vance Memorial Presbyterian Church. Jesse Bloch died in Wheeling, January 17, 1951.

See also Bloch Brothers Tobacco Company

Deborah R. Weiner
Jewish Museum of Maryland

Blue Book

The *West Virginia Blue Book* is a West Virginia classic, present in public and private offices statewide and eagerly collected by many individuals. Published by the clerk of the state Senate, the *Blue Book* is a comprehensive record of all levels of government in West Virginia. John T. Harris of Parkersburg, who served a record 33 years as Senate clerk, produced the first volume and a revised edition in 1916 and was editor of 12 ensuing annual books. Harris died before the 1928 edition was completed. His wife was recorded as its publisher. Except for 1932,

1988, and 1990, annual editions have been printed every year since.

Although already commonly referred to as the *Blue Book* from the color of its cover, the volume was officially titled the *West Virginia Legislative Hand Book and Manual and Official Register* until the more familiar title was officially designated by Clerk Charles Lively of Lewis County in 1933. Harris was succeeded as editor by Lively and later Senate clerks, including some well-known Mountain State political figures. J. C. Dillon of Summers County edited the *Blue Book* in the late 1970s, and Logan's Todd C. Willis for most of the 1980s. Clerk Darrell E. Holmes of Kanawha County took over the task in 1989.

The *Blue Book* lists officers and employees of all state, county, and municipal governments, the legislature and courts, West Virginia's congressional delegation, federal agencies in the state, and all major institutions. Pictures and biographies of officials of the executive, legislative, and judicial branches, as well as the U.S. president, congressional representatives, federal district judges, and state chairs and officers of political parties are included in editions printed in odd-numbered years.

The *Blue Book* also includes the federal and state constitutions, directories of newspapers and broadcasting stations, zip codes, place names not covered by the postal directory, statewide election results, historical data about counties and municipalities, officers of clubs and organizations, plus a section dedicated to departmental, statistical, and general information. Language in the state budget requires that distribution of the *Blue Book* shall include 75 copies for each member of the Legislature, two copies for each high school and junior high school, and one copy for each elementary school within the state.

Karl C. Lilly III
State Senate

Blue Jacket

Blue Jacket was a Shawnee warrior and diplomat who worked to resist European expansion west of the Appalachians in the late 1700s. Myth and mystery obscure the facts of his life. West Virginia was long considered to be his birthplace, but this is uncertain. He may have actually been born in Pennsylvania, probably some time in the mid-1700s.

He is best known for his confrontations with armies led by Gen. Josiah Harmar and Gen. "Mad Anthony" Wayne. In October 1790, Blue Jacket joined Little Turtle in leading a multi-tribal confederacy to defeat Harmar at the head of the Maumee River. Then in August 1794, Indians suffered a pivotal defeat in the Battle of Fallen Timbers in Ohio, when Blue Jacket's warriors were defeated by General Wayne. This defeat removed the In-

dian threat from the Ohio Valley, ending the frontier wars in West Virginia.

After the battle, Blue Jacket, representing the Indian confederacy, signed the Treaty of Greenville, ceding half of what is now Ohio to the Americans. He remained a spokesman for the Shawnees, calling on Indians to reject the contaminating influences of whites, to restore native customs, and to abandon alcohol and the use of witchcraft. His exact death date is unknown, but estimates range from 1808 to 1810.

The controversy surrounding Blue Jacket stems from a belief that he was actually a white man named Marmaduke Van Swearingen, whose family lived near present Richwood. He was supposed to have been kidnapped as a teenager by the Shawnees, eventually becoming their famous chief. This story is widely accepted. Recently, however, scholars have challenged its accuracy, maintaining that Blue Jacket and Van Swearingen were actually separate individuals. DNA tests of Blue Jacket descendants and members of the Van Swearingen family reportedly support no connection between the two men.

See also Shawnee

Mary Lou Pratt
Huntington

John Sugden, *Blue Jacket: Warrior of the Shawnees*, 2000; "Blue Jacket," *American National Biography*, 1999.

Blue Ridge

The Blue Ridge, an Appalachian mountain range that stretches from eastern Pennsylvania to northern Georgia, crosses the easternmost tip of West Virginia. Its crest forms the boundary between Jefferson County, West Virginia, and Loudoun County, Virginia. Farther south in Virginia the Blue Ridge reaches elevations above 5,000 feet, but it reaches only 1,700 feet in West Virginia. The Shenandoah Valley separates the Blue Ridge from the Allegheny Mountains to the west. The oldest surface rocks in West Virginia, mostly sandstones, occur on the Blue Ridge. The very oldest is the Catoctin greenstone, a type of basalt that formed from 600-million-year-old lava flows that were altered by later geologic pressure.

The Blue Ridge was a formidable barrier to westward expansion during colonial times. Early European explorers such as John Lederer, Thomas Batts, and Robert Fallam penetrated the Blue Ridge in Virginia in the 1670s. However, most early explorations of the Blue Ridge and its passes in Virginia had little direct influence on the earliest settlement of West Virginia. The earliest settlements were primarily the result of explorations to the north, which found routes through the Blue Ridge in Pennsylvania, Maryland, and most notably, at a significant break in the Blue Ridge at Harpers Ferry. Here the

Shenandoah and Potomac rivers meet, cutting a dramatic gap through the mountain.

This gap, at 247 feet above sea level, is the lowest point in West Virginia. In 1702, the Swiss explorer Franz Louis Michel explored the Potomac region through the Harpers Ferry gap. In 1707, he created a map depicting the region. A Swiss associate, Baron Christopher de Graffenreid, produced a map of the area in 1712. These and other maps, along with tales told by Dutch and French traders of the fertile Shenandoah and South Branch valleys, lured German, English, and other immigrants into present Berkeley, Jefferson, Hampshire, and Hardy counties via Harpers Ferry and other northerly routes in the 1730s and 1740s. To the south, the Blue Ridge would remain a barrier, initially restricting immigration from eastern Virginia to a slow trickle. Consequently, the early settlers of West Virginia often did not come from eastern Virginia, but instead from Maryland, Pennsylvania, or New York. This pattern of immigration contributed to the social divisions that led to West Virginia statehood during the Civil War.

As transportation improved, the gap at Harpers Ferry became increasingly important for passage through the Blue Ridge. Both the Chesapeake & Ohio Canal and the Baltimore & Ohio Railroad were built through the gap. Control of the passage of goods and soldiers through the gap was a major objective of both Union and Confederate armies throughout the Civil War.

Historically, the mountain supported forests, small farms, resorts, and some mining of iron ore. Today, much of the Blue Ridge in West Virginia has been developed for residential use. Portions of the mountain are protected lands within Harpers Ferry National Historical Park and Shannondale Springs Wildlife Management Area. The famous Appalachian Trail follows a narrow corridor along the mountain's crest, and the trail's national headquarters is located in Harpers Ferry.

Rodney Bartgis
Nature Conservancy of West Virginia

Blue Sulphur Springs

Blue Sulphur Springs, located in Greenbrier County near Smoot, was the site of a mineral spring resort from 1834 until 1858, one of many in the Western Virginia mountains. The sulfur spring, which gives the site its name, was developed into a resort in 1834 when owner George Washington Buster built a large brick hotel, springhouse, cottages, and bathing facilities. Two hundred guests could be accommodated at the resort. The first mud baths in the United States were introduced there in the 1840s. Famous visitors to Blue Sulphur Springs included Andrew Jackson, Henry Clay, and Robert E. Lee. In 1858, the resort property was sold to the Western Virginia Baptist Association, which established Alleghany College there in 1860. During the Civil War the property was occupied by both armies. In 1864, Union troops burned down the resort buildings. Today only a pavilion remains over the spring.

Michael M. Meador
Abingdon, Virginia

Bluefield

Bluefield, incorporated in 1889, embodied the rapid growth of the southern West Virginia "smokeless" coalfields. Located in a broad valley between the headwaters of the Bluestone and East rivers along the Virginia border, the site was for 100 years the homestead of the Bailey and Davidson families. The decision of the Norfolk & Western Railway to locate its Pocahontas Division headquarters there in 1882 created the modern community. The N&W's natural gravity switching system made the Bluefield yards a model of efficiency and productivity. Around the railroad's offices, rail yard, and shops gathered banks, utilities, and the wholesale warehouses that stocked coal company stores in the booming Pocahontas Coalfield.

By 1910, Bluefield's population exceeded 10,000. Stately Federal Revival buildings in the downtown commercial district began to climb the hill southward toward East River Mountain, on whose slopes grew blue fields of chicory, the town's namesake. Bluefield's progressive 1921 city charter made it just the second city in the nation to adopt the city manager form of local government. By 1950, about 25,000 people lived in Bluefield, inducing adjoining Graham, Virginia, to change its name to Bluefield, Virginia. The 12-story West Virginian Hotel is the tallest building in West Virginia south of Charleston.

Bluefield's political Kee family—John, Jim, and Elizabeth—held West Virginia's Fifth Congressional District seat in Washington for 40 years. Hugh I. Shott built the *Bluefield Daily Telegraph* into a powerful media empire, and his WHIS radio, which began broadcasting in 1929, was an important leader in the early history of country music. Bluefield State College, a member of the state public college system, was founded in 1895 as Bluefield Colored Institute, and stands as evidence of the community's rich heritage of diversity. Mechanization of the coal industry and transportation changes, however, began inexorably to erode Bluefield's position of regional leadership, and the population dropped to 11,451 in 2000.

Bluefield is the largest city in Mercer County. At 2,655 feet, it is the highest incorporated community in West Virginia. Bluefield is known as "Nature's Air-Conditioned City," and civic officials distribute free lemonade on the infrequent

A 1950s Bluefield street scene.

days when the temperature exceeds 90 degrees. Both the South Bluefield residential neighborhood district and the central business district are listed on the National Register of Historic Places.

C. Stuart McGehee
West Virginia State University

C. Stuart McGehee, *Bluefield, West Virginia, 1889–1989: A Centennial History,* 1990; John Rankin, *Early History and Development of Bluefield,* 1976.

Bluefield Daily Telegraph

The *Bluefield Daily Telegraph,* circulation 20,000, serves Mercer, Monroe, and parts of Wyoming and Summers counties in West Virginia, and Tazewell, Buchanan, Bland, and Giles counties in neighboring Virginia.

In 1893, Bluefield had two newspapers, the *Bluefield Telegraph* and the *Daily Journal.* The *Journal* ceased daily publication in 1893 and closed altogether in 1895. That year, Hugh Ike Shott (1866–1953), a union linotype operator and conservative Republican originally from Staunton, Virginia, and two partners bought the *Bluefield Telegraph* and renamed it the *Bluefield Daily Telegraph.* The newspaper began publication under that name on January 16, 1896. On May 1, 1896, Shott bought out his partners. His newspaper advocated Republican doctrines and boasted of being "an acknowledged authority on matters pertaining to the Pocahontas-Flat Top Coal Field," according to the special edition of November 1, 1896.

Shott, who later served in Congress and the Senate, wrote and set the type for his front-page editorials, published under the heading, "Good Morning." In 1926, the Shott family started the *Sunset News-Observer,* an afternoon newspaper. At this point, the *Daily Telegraph* dropped

its Monday edition for several years, but eventually resumed Monday publication. The *Sunset News-Observer's* final edition was published March 31, 1972.

Shott's sons, Hugh I. Shott Jr. and James H. Shott, worked in the family business. In 1929, they helped launch radio station WHIS-AM, with the call letters taken from their father's initials. In 1955, under the leadership of James Shott, the family started television station WHIS, now WVVA-TV. After Hugh Shott Sr.'s death in 1953, Hugh Jr. became *Daily Telegraph* publisher.

The Shott family published the newspaper until January 1, 1985, when they sold it to Worrell Newspapers. On January 1, 1988, Thomson Newspapers purchased the newspaper. On September 1, 2000, Thomson sold the paper to Community Newspaper Holdings of Alabama.

See also Bluefield, Hugh I. Shott

William R. Archer
Bluefield

Bluefield State College

Created as Bluefield Colored Institute by the West Virginia legislature in 1895, Bluefield State College was the result of the demographic transformation produced by the industrialization of southern West Virginia. Thousands of African-Americans moved into mining and railroad jobs in Mercer, McDowell, Raleigh, and Fayette counties in the late 19th and early 20th centuries. Republican politicians successfully courted their vote by promising prompt attention to issues such as higher education for black West Virginians.

The school was situated on four acres in Bluefield, the largest city in the coalfields, within 100 miles of 70 percent of the Mountain State's black population. Storer College of Harpers Ferry supplied part of the first faculty to Bluefield, including Professor Hamilton Hatter, an African-American graduate of Bates College, who became the first administrator or principal. School officially began in January 1897 with 40 students.

In 1906, Principal Hatter was replaced by his assistant, Robert Page Sims, who led during three crucial decades as the school matured and grew in size, curriculum, and prominence. Enrollment climbed from 107 in 1910 to 281 in 1923 to 338 in 1925. In 1929, the state legislature changed the school's name to Bluefield Institute. And in 1931, the curriculum changes resulted in the adoption of the name Bluefield State Teachers College.

Between 1920 and 1927, the three buildings on campus were renovated, and a new classroom building was finished in 1930. Additional acreage was acquired, bringing the grounds to 22 acres.

Sims deserves much of the credit for the expansion of Bluefield State from a "high graded school" to a four-year institution with wide regional influence. It became a center of African-American culture, featuring appearances by poet Langston Hughes, historian John Hope Franklin, boxer Joe Louis, and musicians Fats Waller, Dizzy Gillespie, and Duke Ellington. Twice Bluefield State's Big Blues won national Negro College Athletic Association football championships in the late 1920s. Graduates of the school included Elizabeth Drewry, class of 1938, who became the first African-American woman elected to the state legislature.

In 1936, Sims stepped down, replaced by Henry Lake Dickason, who led the school for 16 years and presided over continued expansion and broadening of programs and physical facilities. New buildings were constructed, including a gymnasium in 1938. State lawmakers approved a bill in 1943 authorizing the name change to Bluefield State College. In 1947, Bluefield State was fully accredited by the American Association of Colleges of Teacher Education. Two years later, full accreditation was granted by the North Central Association.

In 1952, when Dickason retired, significant changes were under way in southern West Virginia. Dickason's successors, Gregory W. Whiting (1952–53 and 1957–58) and Stephen J. Wright (1953–57), presided over the college until Leroy Allen was named to the presidency in 1958. Allen, replaced in 1965, was to be the last black president of Bluefield State during the 20th century. After an interim term by E. J. Scrafford (1965–66), Wendell G. Hardway became president in 1966.

After the mid-century, racial desegregation and the changing population of the coalfields transformed the small residential black college into a different institution. The changes began in the late 1950s. The school shifted toward the role of a two-year and four-year commuter college for southern West Virginia, and those commuters were increasingly white. By 1963, the college had grown as its vocational training attracted hundreds of students, and enrollment was slightly less than 800 students. The last major physical expansion occurred in the 1960s, including the building of a new student union building in 1963 and a new gymnasium, finished in 1966.

Bluefield State was not untouched by the turbulence of the Vietnam War, urban riots, and general unrest of the 1960s. Tensions grew as only white presidents were appointed by state authorities. A 1968 bombing rocked the physical education building, and the administration closed the campus to the public and hired armed Pinkerton guards to patrol the grounds. President Hardway ordered the dorms closed, and they never reopened, ending Bluefield State's years as a historically black residential college.

Hardway, before leaving in 1973, approved a merger between Bluefield State and Concord College, forming a dual-campus regional college. The experiment failed, tensions flared, and the schools were separated once again. Billy Coffindaffer, who had become president in 1973, left the office in 1975. James Rowley served an interim term, and J. Wade Gilley assumed the presidency in 1976. Gilley left in 1978, and William H. Brothers served a brief period, before Jerold O. Dugger took over, serving for 10 years. Dugger in 1981 ended the football program, drawing protest from the alumni. Amid controversy, Dugger resigned in 1988, and after a brief interim by Chester L. Foster, he was succeeded by Greg Adkins, who served until 1993. Leonard Nelson was named acting president, and in June 1993 Robert Moore became president. He was replaced by Albert Walker in 2002, the first African-American president since 1965.

Redirecting the curriculum toward work force development programs and two-year vocational education helped enrollment grow to nearly 2,500 in the mid-1980s, and distance-learning programs and new centers in Beckley, Welch, and Lewisburg spread Bluefield State's service across southern West Virginia. Its 1995 centennial celebration highlighted Bluefield State College's historic mission with the theme "Strong Past, Dynamic Future." Community college functions were separated from Bluefield State upon the creation of New River Community and Technical College in 2004. The 2005 enrollment was 1,583.

C. Stuart McGehee
West Virginia State University

C. Stuart McGehee and Frank Wilson, *A Centennial History of Bluefield State College, 1895–1995*, 1995.

Bluegrass Music

Bluegrass music was developed in the 1930s by Kentucky mandolinist Bill Monroe, whose band was called the Blue Grass Boys in honor of his home state. The music combines acoustic guitar, mandolin, banjo, fiddle, and bass fiddle with close vocal harmonies. It draws heavily from the southern mountain instrumental and vocal traditions. It was also influenced by Southern blues, spirituals, church singing, and jazz.

This was a new concept in an era when country or "hillbilly" musicians performing in old-time string bands and jug bands sometimes compromised musical integrity for comic effect. With this new structured and serious approach to performance and the new significance given to the development of vocal harmonies, bluegrass became a high-energy music form. It has in turn had a dramatic impact on the subsequent directions and sounds of mainstream styles such as country, folk, and rock 'n' roll music, while being performed throughout the world.

West Virginia musicians were well represented during the 1940s and 1950s, the formative years of bluegrass, and continue to be today. The Lonesome Pine Fiddlers formed in Bluefield in 1938 with Ezra Cline, Curly Ray Cline, and Ned Cline. The Fiddlers performed with a variety of personnel, including Ray and Melvin Goins, until the mid-1960s. Curly Ray Cline eventually left the Fiddlers to play fiddle with the Stanley Brothers and then Ralph Stanley.

The Lilly Brothers of Raleigh County, with Everett on mandolin and Bea on guitar, introduced bluegrass to a new audience when they relocated to Boston in 1952, where they performed with Tex Logan and Don Stover as the Confederate Mountaineers. Before the move Everett also played as a member of the Foggy Mountain Boys, the Flatt and Scruggs band, in 1950, appearing on classic recordings such as "Somehow Tonight" and "'Tis Sweet to be Remembered." Stover played many years with the Lillys and is recognized as a banjo pioneer whose strong, clean style ranks him among the top players of any era.

Wilma Lee and Stoney Cooper, of Valley Head and Harman respectively, were a married couple who along with their band, the Clinch Mountain Clan, became stars of WWVA's *Wheeling Jamboree* in the late 1940s. In 1957, they became regulars on the *Grand Ole Opry*. With Stoney on fiddle and Wilma Lee playing guitar and banjo, they achieved commercial success in country music in the late 1950s and early 1960s.

Mercer County's Hazel Dickens played bass and sang harmony in the 1960s with the Greenbrier Boys. While better known for her solo folk singing, Dickens in 1994 was the first artist to be awarded the Merit Award for contribution to bluegrass music by the International Bluegrass Music Association. In 2001, she received a National Heritage Fellowship from the National Endowment for the Arts.

West Virginia's historically strong contingent of fiddlers is evident in bluegrass. Charlie Cline of Gilbert fiddled on some classic 1950s Bill Monroe instrumentals such as "Wheel Hoss" and even filled in on mandolin, Monroe's own instrument, when Monroe was injured in 1955. Joe Meadows performed for years with Jim and Jesse and the Virginia Boys in the 1970s. Buddy Griffin of Braxton County performed on fiddle and banjo with the Goins Brothers, and Boone County's James Price played fiddle with Ralph Stanley.

Important bands from the 1970s and '80s also had West Virginia contributors. Guitarist Dudley Connell of Scherr was a founding member of the Johnson Mountain Boys in 1978. Fiddler-mandolinist Tim O'Brien of Wheeling was a founding member of the contemporary bluegrass band Hot Rize in 1979 and continues to perform and produce with the major names in bluegrass music.

Perhaps the most enduring legacy of bluegrass in the Mountain State is its accessibility and status as a music of the people. Expensive equipment is not necessary and the instruments are easy to transport to gatherings where people play, share, and learn tunes. In the true oral tradition the young learn from the experienced players. Bluegrass is played in the home, at campsites, and at music festivals, affording many people the enrichment of firsthand musical experiences in their lives.

See also Curly Ray Cline, Lilly Brothers, Lonesome Pine Fiddlers

Mark Payne
West Virginia Humanities Council

Blues Revue

The magazine *Blues Revue*, published in Salem, is a popular blues publication. It covers the full spectrum of blues, from traditional acoustic to blues-rock, jazz, gospel, and zydeco.

The magazine was started by Bob Vorel, a Chicago native who moved from New England, where he had worked as a marine surveyor, to a 170-acre farm in Doddridge County in 1984. For a few years he made furniture, then turned his attention to music and blues guitar in particular. After a friend suggested the idea of publishing a blues newsletter, Vorel started the *Blues Revue Quarterly* in his former woodshop in 1991. He overcame problems presented by the remote location of his office through use of computers, fax machines, the Internet, and e-mail. In 1995, Vorel increased publication to bimonthly and shortened the magazine's name to *Blues Revue*. In 1998, Vorel moved the magazine's office from his farm to nearby Salem.

Blues Revue includes feature stories, interviews, artist updates, tributes, news, CD reviews, and commentaries. Vorel continues to serve as publisher and editor-in-chief. The magazine employs seven full-time staff members and also relies on freelance writers and musicians to write columns and articles. Circulation increased from 8,000 in 1992 to a worldwide subscription base of 31,000 in 2003.

Bluestone Dam and Lake

Bluestone Dam, located at Hinton, is one of the major flood control dams in West Virginia. It has the largest drainage area and flood storage capacity of any dam in the state. It is built across New River, one mile above its junction with the Greenbrier River and two miles below the confluence of New River and Bluestone River. Prior to the construction of the Bluestone Dam, flooding was a major problem on this great river system.

The Bluestone Dam on the New River near Hinton.

Bluestone Dam was authorized in 1935 by an executive order issued by President Franklin Roosevelt. Construction on the project began in 1942, but work was suspended in 1943 because of World War II. Work resumed in January 1946, and the dam was completed for operational purposes in January 1949, and totally completed in 1952. The approximate cost was $30 million.

With a drainage area of 4,565 square miles Bluestone Dam controls 44 percent of the river flow through the populous Kanawha Valley, which is downstream. It is a concrete gravity dam 165 feet high and 2,048 feet long, administered by the U.S. Army Corps of Engineers. Normal release of water from the Bluestone Lake is accomplished through 16 sluices in the base of the dam. The 790-foot spillway has 21 flood gates. There are also six sluiceways for hydroelectric power that have not been used in the early decades of the dam's history. The maximum discharge capacity is 430,000 square feet per second.

The dam contains 942,000 cubic yards of concrete and 7,800 tons of steel. Its lake has a summertime surface of 2,040 acres and is very popular with boaters, skiers, and fishermen. Bluestone State Park, located on the Bluestone River about three miles above the dam, provides lodging, camping, a restaurant, and recreational facilities.

The Bluestone Dam celebrated its 50th anniversary in 1999, when the Army Corps of Engineers estimated that the dam had prevented more than $1.6 billion in flood damages. Bluestone ended its first half-century with important improvements under way. The lake became a major supplier of public water in 1997, serving Hinton and Princeton and a large area between and around those two communities. Reinforcements were added to

the dam under the federal Dam Safety Assurance program, with the work continuing through the early years of the 21st century. Simultaneously, work began to add hydroelectric capacity to the dam, in a partnership between Hinton and other communities and private industry.

Michael M. Meador
Abingdon, Virginia
See also Bluestone River, Hydroelectricity, New River

Bluestone River

The Bluestone River rises from numerous springs on the northwest slope of East River Mountain in Tazewell County, Virginia. The river takes its name from the blue-grey color of the limestone that outcrops along the stream and its banks.

From the mountain, the river flows northeastward to Bluefield, Virginia. This part of the stream follows a generally straight course, with a few meanders. The Bluestone then turns sharply toward the northwest, crossing into West Virginia near Wolfe. In this section, the river cuts through several ridges and has numerous bends. From Wolfe it flows northeastward toward its mouth at New River. There are many more bends along the way, one of which enfolds Bramwell, the old "millionaires' town" built by the coal operators in Mercer County. It is likely that Mary Draper Ingles crossed the Bluestone in her escape from Indian captivity, near its confluence with the New.

The last stretch of the river, from Wolf Creek to its mouth, occupies the scenic Bluestone Gorge. This section had some level land, most now covered by Bluestone Lake. The dam is on New River just downstream from where Bluestone comes in, and it impounds long stretches of both rivers. The villages of Lilly and True were sacrificed for the lake, as was

Green Meador's place, once a campground for Union troops in the Civil War. Part of the river is included in Bluestone and Pipestem state parks. The parks are linked by the stretch of river designated as the Bluestone National Scenic River, administered by the National Park Service.

Eades Mill, at the junction of the Bluestone and Camp Creek, was an important gristmill. Bush Creek Falls, on a tributary, was the site of a woolen mill. There was a plan to build a flood control dam at Spanishburg, but it was never constructed. Most of the river is paralleled by roads. The Bluestone Turnpike once connected the New River road with a road at Flat Top, the latter road eventually reaching the Kanawha River by way of Paint Creek. The Bluestone Lumber Company built a railroad, now dismantled, down Brush Creek and along a part of the Bluestone. A hiking trail has been developed along parts of the river.

The total length of the Bluestone River is 86.7 miles. About 55 miles are in West Virginia. The river is slow-running in its upper stretches, with brisker water in the gorge below. The total fall of the Bluestone from source to mouth is 2,125 feet, an average of 24.5 feet per mile. The area of the Bluestone River watershed is 463.53 square miles. West Virginia towns along the river include Coopers, Bramwell, Flipping, Durhing, Montcalm, Rock, and Spanishburg. The major tributaries of Bluestone River are Brush Creek, Little Bluestone River, Camp Creek, Surveyors Branch, and Lorton Lick Creek.

See also Bluestone Dam and Lake

Raymond Thomas Hill
Athens

David B. Reger, West Virginia Geological Survey, *Mercer, Monroe, and Summers Counties,* 1926.

Bluestone State Park

Bluestone State Park, near Hinton, entered the West Virginia park system in 1955. Named for the Bluestone River, the park is located on the 2,000-acre Bluestone Lake, created by the Bluestone Dam, which impounds the New River and the Bluestone.

Bluestone State Park has a recreation building, a gift shop, and a playground. The park's heavily forested 2,155 acres are mountainous, with Old Mill and Meador campgrounds directly on the lake with good road access. A third camping spot, the East Shore campground, lies across the lake and is accessible only by water. A private concessionaire offers boat rentals and there are public boat ramps.

The lake and dam are run by the U.S. Army Corps of Engineers, which collaborates with state park officials and other authorities involved in the management of the area. The lake itself, the third-largest body of water in West Virginia, has three launching ramps and a marina where people may rent boats. Fishermen enjoy the lake for its crappie, bass, and bluegill. In the summer, water skiers trail long swirls in the blue waters.

Cliffs, waterfalls, and fine hiking trails draw visitors in all seasons. The paths are wide, covered with pine needles, and lined with rhododendron. This mountain lake retreat has 25 rental cabins with fireplaces and comfortable porches for guests viewing the lake and the mountains.

Maureen F. Crockett
St. Albans

Board of Control

West Virginia's institutions were controlled by 25 boards with 129 members when a 1909 joint legislative committee recommended eliminating the boards and consolidating management and fiscal controls under one agency. The 1909 West Virginia legislature created the Board of Control, a state agency, "with full power to manage, direct, and control" certain state institutions.

Initially, the Board of Control took over the state mental institutions, the three miners' hospitals, penal institutions, and schools for the deaf and blind at Romney. The board's scope was expanded greatly in 1911, when it was given responsibility to manage the state tuberculosis sanitarium at Terra Alta and the West Virginia Colored Orphans Home at Huntington. At the same time it was given control of the financial and business affairs of West Virginia University and 12 other state colleges and educational agencies. A number of city institutions, such as the Kings Daughters Hospital and City Hospital in Martinsburg, were included in the board's fiscal oversight responsibilities. By the early 1930s, 59 agencies of one type or another had been placed under the Board of Control.

As state government continued to grow, more specialized oversight agencies were created. In 1933, a state director of purchases was appointed and took over that responsibility from the Board of Control. In 1947, the business affairs for West Virginia University and the state colleges were transferred to the WVU Board of Governors and the State Board of Education, respectively. By the early 1950s, the Board of Control's responsibility had dwindled once more to care of the state mental health and penal institutions. A 1957 reorganization of state government transferred these remaining institutions to the new Department of Mental Health and to the Commissioner of Public Institutions. The Board of Control ceased to exist on June 30, 1957.

Kenneth R. Bailey
WVU Institute of Technology

Boarman Arts Center

The Boarman Arts Center is named for the Admiral Boarman House, built in Martinsburg in 1802. The building was sold in 1832 to Charles Boarman, a commodore in the U.S. Navy, who lived there with his family for more than 40 years.

The house was purchased in 1980 and restored. The Boarman Arts Center opened there in 1987 as a gallery and exhibition space for local artists. The original design included a retail shop on the first floor, with exhibition and classroom space on the second floor. The Boarman Arts Center now houses a studio space on the ground floor for artists-in-residence, with classrooms and exhibition space on the second floor.

The ArtSpace Open Studio gives local artists around-the-clock access to their own workspace in the Boarman Art Center. It also is a public forum, allowing visitors to view and talk with the artists at work. In addition to the ArtSpace project, the Boarman uses local artists and craftspeople to curate its season of exhibitions.

The Boarman Arts Center acquired Martinsburg's old federal building in May 2001. The group has begun a multi-year plan to ready its new quarters and move from the Boarman House.

Lakin Ray Cook
Clay Center for the Arts & Sciences

Bogs

Bogs are wetlands with an accumulation of peat derived from incomplete decomposition of plant remains. Low available oxygen, due to saturated conditions, and high acidity contribute to the incomplete decomposition. Sphagnum moss and sedges form the bulk of the peat in the state. More northerly bogs, outside West Virginia, often form around lakes. Bogs in the central Appalachians apparently have formed in depressions and as a result of stream levee formation. Behind these levees wet conditions persist, making ideal locations for sedges and sphagnum moss to thrive and for the deposition of peat. Cranberry Glades is an excellent example of this type of formation.

Bogs can form relatively quickly, as was documented by radiocarbon dating of peat in a shallow bog in the Canaan Valley area. This peat accumulation occurred in less than 50 years. Some bogs, such as Cranberry Glades, have more than 10 feet of peat, the result of 10,000 years of deposition. Pollen that has been preserved in West Virginia provides important clues to ancient times. Because of the slow and incomplete decomposition of peat and the protective coating of pollen grains, pollen may survive in these systems for thousands of years. Bogs in the central Appalachians have had cores removed and pollen from various depths analyzed. Analysis of pollen grains has revealed that West Virginia's climate has become wetter and warmer during the last 10,000 years, thus bogs act as "libraries" of historical climatic and vegetational change.

Many plants other than sedges and mosses occur in bogs, including grasses, bog goldenrod, cranberries, several showy orchids, blueberries, chokeberries, and unique insectivorous species such as pitcher plants and sundew. Most bogs in the state are restricted to higher elevations where there is ample precipitation and a cool climate. Good examples are Cranberry Glades, Pocahontas County; Cranesville Swamp, Preston County; and Alder Run Bog and Big Run Bog, Tucker County. In addition, there are numerous bogs in Canaan Valley.

Brian McDonald
Division of Natural Resources

Ivor F. Boiarsky

Legislator Ivor F. Boiarsky was born April 7, 1920, in Charleston, a son of Mose and Rae D. Boiarsky. He was educated at Brown University and the University of Virginia law school. He was married to Barbara Faith Polan and was president of Charleston Federal Savings and Loan Association as well as speaker of the House of Delegates at the time of his death. He was first elected to the House from Kanawha County in 1958 and was chairman of the House Finance Committee prior to his election as speaker in 1968.

As speaker of the House of Delegates, Boiarsky was co-author of the 1968 Modern Budget Amendment, which gave the governor greater control over the state's annual budget. Boiarsky also wanted the governor to have the authority to transfer funds between departments in state agencies, but that power still rests with the legislature. He was instrumental in creating a consolidated board for higher education in the state, the Board of Regents, that lasted a quarter-century before it was changed back to separate boards for the university system and the colleges.

During his brief three years as speaker, Boiarsky pushed the House of Delegates to 18- and 20-hour days that ultimately proved to be his downfall. He died March 12, 1971, at the age of 50, one day after a grueling debate on strip mining that lasted until 2:00 a.m.

Tom D. Miller
Huntington

Bollman Truss Bridge

Bollman truss bridges were the first successful all-iron railroad bridges used in the United States. More than 100 of these bridges were built between 1850 and 1870, mostly on the Baltimore & Ohio Railroad. Wendel Bollman, who was master of the road and responsible for the maintenance of track and structures, designed the iron bridge to replace poorly constructed wood and stone bridges on the B&O. The Bollman truss spans at Har-

pers Ferry were the largest and most impressive examples of this type of bridge.

Truss bridges were composed of individual groups of wood or iron members arranged in the form of a triangle. The Bollman truss span consisted of a series of simple king post trusses. Thus Bollman truss bridges had long runs of iron rods that gave them a "spiderweb" look.

In 1851, the "Winchester" span of the Harpers Ferry bridge was constructed to carry the Winchester & Potomac Railroad to a junction in mid-river with the B&O. In 1862, four Bollman truss spans were built from the Maryland side. Although damaged during the Civil War, they were repaired and new Bollman spans were added. The new Harpers Ferry bridge was completed in 1868. This magnificent bridge had eight Bollman truss spans of different lengths with the W&P junction in the river and a sharp curve onto the West Virginia bank at the west end. The bridge continued in use until 1894 when new bridges were constructed and some of the remaining Bollman trusses were converted to highway use. In March 1936, a flood destroyed the last Bollman spans at Harpers Ferry.

See also Bridges, Harpers Ferry

Robert L. Frey
Miamisburg, Ohio

Booger Hole

The peace of the Rush Fork Valley near Ivydale in northern Clay County was disrupted in the early 1900s, when a series of murders or disappearances earned the valley the colorful sobriquet of Booger Hole. Booger was local usage for "bogey" or "bogeyman."

Accounts vary as to the number of people who were killed in Booger Hole, but the estimates are generally between six and eight. They include Joe Clark, a clock repairman who lived at the local schoolhouse; John Henry, a Russian Jew and

peddler who is believed to be the first who entered Booger Hole and never left; Henry Hargis, alleged to have been killed for an inheritance; Lacy Ann Boggs, who supposedly was shot as she sat in her living room knitting and smoking her pipe; and Preston Tanner, a young man who was either killed or who died in his sleep, according to conflicting stories. Lacy Ann Boggs left a memorable quote in Booger Hole lore when she supposedly said she "could find Hargis's body before her pipe went out." It was sometime after that she herself was killed. The Preston Tanner episode ended the Booger Hole violence.

One version of how Booger Hole got its name is that an old stone mason who lived at the mouth of the valley grew tired of the violence and moved. Asked why, he said derisively that he was "leaving booger hole." Motorists on Interstate 79 pass near Booger Hole, which lies south of the highway between Wallback and Big Otter.

Ferrell Friend
Ivydale

Boone County

Boone County was formed March 11, 1847, from parts of Logan, Kanawha, and Cabell counties by an act of the Virginia legislature. It is located in the southern coalfields. It has an area of 506 square miles. Madison is the county seat, originally known as Boone Court House. Boone County was named for Daniel Boone, who lived in the neighboring Kanawha Valley in the late 18th century.

The topography is typical of the Allegheny Plateau, mountainous with little bottomland. Elevations vary from a low of 660 feet in the north to nearly 3,400 feet in the southeast. The land is heavily forested and rich in mineral resources. Boone is drained primarily by the Coal and Little Coal rivers, which converge outside the county and flow to the Kanawha River below Charleston.

FAST FACTS ABOUT BOONE COUNTY

Founded: 1847
Land in square miles: 506
Population: 25,535
Percentage minorities: 1.5%
Percentage rural: 87.9%
Median age: 38.8
Percentage 65 and older: 13.6%
Birth rate per 1,000 population: 14.5
Median household income: $25,669
High school graduate or higher: 64.0%
Bachelor's degree or higher: 7.2%
Home ownership: 78.9%
Median home value: $63,700

This information is from the 2000 U.S. Census. In 2000, West Virginia as a whole had 5 percent minorities, a median age of 38.9, median household income of $29,696, and a 75.2 percent home ownership rate.

The Boone County Courthouse.

The first permanent European settlements in present Boone County were likely made in the 1790s, though numerous explorers and hunting parties had previously visited the area. John Peter Salling, exploring in the region in 1742, discovered the coal deposits for which Coal River was named and which have provided generations of Boone Countians with their livelihood.

Prior to the Civil War, the young county remained sparsely populated and agricultural, with an 1850 population of 3,149. No major military actions occurred in the county during the Civil War, but there were numerous skirmishes and guerrilla raids. The population was divided in its loyalties, though most Boone County voters preferred secession when the question was put before Virginians in a May 1861 referendum. The 1860 census shows that out of about 750 families only 36 owned slaves. The first courthouse was burned by Union soldiers in September 1861 after a skirmish with Southern-sympathizing militia. The courthouse was not rebuilt until after the war.

Timber was the first major industry to come to Boone County, in the 1870s. Early timber companies included the W. M. Ritter Lumber Company, D. F. Mohler and Sons, Coal River Mining & Lumber Company, and the Boone Timber Company. Originally, the logs were floated down to mills on the Kanawha, and the industry expanded with the later arrival of the railroad. In 30 years the forests of Boone County were largely depleted. Today there are no stands of old-growth forest remaining, but logging remains important as second- and third-growth timber is taken from the county.

Boone County was one of the few places in Western Virginia where large-scale coal mining was undertaken before the coming of the railroad. Navigational improvements were made to the Coal River in the late 1850s, and substantial amounts of the region's valuable cannel coal were mined and shipped before these river improvements were largely lost in the great flood of 1861. The mining industry expanded greatly with the coming of the railroads after 1900. Coal quickly became the county's primary economic engine and major employer, with most other industries supporting the work of the mines.

The conditions under which the early miners worked were often less than satisfactory and sometimes brutal. This led to a series of labor-management conflicts known as the West Virginia Mine Wars. Boone County's part in the labor uprising was not as great as that of some surrounding counties, but several major events occurred in the county. During the 1921 armed miners' march, the striking miners twice gathered in Madison on their way toward Logan and Mingo counties. After the second meeting they continued south to confront Logan Sheriff Don Chafin's forces at the Battle of Blair Mountain on the Boone-Logan border. It was estimated that as many as 20,000 miners marched through Boone County to reach the battleground.

In recent years the number of miners has declined as mechanization and the shift to surface mining have reduced the need for labor. The Boone County population shrank from 33,173 in 1950 to 25,118 in 1970, then rose during the energy crisis to 30,447 in 1980. The 2000 population was 25,535. The number of coal miners employed in Boone County fell from 4,948 in 1950 to 2,425 in 2000, while the tonnage of coal extracted increased from approximately six million tons in 1950 to more than 32 million tons in 2000. During the same period the amount of surface mined coal increased from approximately 7 million to 16 million tons while the tonnage mined underground fell slightly. Boone County now produces more coal than any other county in West Virginia, and mining remains central to the economy and the psyche of Boone County.

The 1980s saw Boone County grow closer to Charleston with the completion of four-lane Corridor G (U.S. 119) from Madison to Charleston. Many residents began to commute to the Charleston area to work. These changes have been accompanied by a concerted effort to diversify the local economy, most notably in the field of tourism through the creation in the early 1980s of the Waterways water park and the opening of the Hatfield-McCoy Trail for all-terrain vehicles in 2002. Nonetheless, three of the five largest employers in Boone County remain related to the coal industry, the other top employers being the county school system and the Boone Memorial Hospital.

See also Battle of Blair Mountain, Daniel Boone, Coal River, Madison, Mine Wars

John E. Adkins
Wilbur Smith Associates
Boone County Genealogical Society, *Boone County, West Virginia, History,* 1990.

Daniel Boone

Frontiersman Daniel Boone, born October 22, 1734, near present Reading, Pennsylvania, lived several years in present West Virginia. In 1751, Boone's family resettled in North Carolina on the North Fork of the Yadkin River. He served as a teamster on the ill-fated 1755 Braddock campaign during the French and Indian War. He first visited Kentucky in 1767, where he hunted along the Big Sandy River. In 1775, he led a group of settlers associated with the Transylvania Company to the site of Boonesborough, Kentucky, cutting the Wilderness Road through Cumberland Gap. Later that year, he moved his own family to Kentucky.

When Kentucky was created as a county of Virginia in 1776, Boone became captain of militia, soon promoted to major. While engaged in the defense of the Kentucky settlements, he was captured by the Shawnee in February 1778 but escaped in June. He moved his family to Maysville in 1783, where he kept a tavern. Boone claimed thousands of acres, but because he did not properly enter his claims he was subjected to several ejectment suits in the 1780s. At his death he owned no land in Kentucky.

In 1788, Boone and his family settled near the mouth of the Kanawha River. He represented Kanawha County in the Virginia General Assembly in 1791 and won a contract to supply militia companies in Western Virginia. Never an acute businessman, Boone lost his contract and in

1792 moved to a site near present Charleston, then back to Kentucky in 1795. Following the issuance of an arrest warrant for debt by Mason County, (West) Virginia, authorities, he and his family moved to Missouri in 1799.

Daniel Boone died in the Femme Osage River Valley in Missouri, September 26, 1820, and was buried beside his wife, Rebecca, on the farm of his daughter, Jemima. In 1845, the Boones were disinterred and their remains were removed to Frankfort, Kentucky. Boone County, West Virginia, is named for the great pioneer.

Philip Sturm
Ohio Valley University
John Mack Faragher, *Daniel Boone, the Life and Legend of an American Pioneer,* 1992.

Arthur Ingraham Boreman

Arthur Ingraham (also spelled "Ingram") Boreman, West Virginia's first governor (1863–69), was born July 24, 1823, in Waynesburg, Pennsylvania. While still an infant, Boreman moved with his family to Middlebourne, Tyler County. Except for a brief period during which the family lived in Marshall County, he resided in Middlebourne for a decade and a half and received his schooling there. Then he studied law under the tutelage of an older brother and brother-in-law, James McNeill Stephenson, and was admitted to the bar in 1845. Shortly thereafter, Boreman moved to Parkersburg, the home of the Stephensons.

Parkersburg would remain Boreman's hometown for the remainder of his life. From there he was first elected to public office in 1855, when he was sent as a Whig to the General Assembly in Richmond. He served until Virginia's secession from the United States on April 17, 1861.

The decade of the 1860s was the most eventful of Boreman's political life. After Virginia's secession from the United States, he visited U.S. military officials in Cincinnati to seek protection for Unionists living in Parkersburg. In June 1861, he was elected president of the Second Wheeling Convention, which under his leadership voted to establish the Reorganized Government of Virginia, loyal to the Union and supplanting the secessionist government in Richmond. It was from Reorganized Virginia that Boreman and others secured the necessary constitutional approval for the creation of the state of West Virginia.

In October 1861, Boreman was elected to a circuit judgeship. On May 6–7, 1863, he attended the Constitutional Union Party Convention in Parkersburg and became its nominee to be governor of the new state. On May 28, 1863, he was elected to a two-year term without opposition. In his inaugural address in Wheeling on June 20, Governor Boreman asserted that he would assist in the founding of a

Governor Arthur Ingraham Boreman (1823–96).

system of public education throughout the state that would provide all children, regardless of economic level, schooling to prepare them for respectable positions in society. He backed his words with action during the next six years, during which he was reelected two times. A public school system was established, and with the aid of the Morrill Act, which had been enacted by the federal government in 1862, West Virginia University was created on February 7, 1867.

Boreman's primary business during the first 22 months of his governorship was steering the infant state through the remainder of the Civil War. It was not an easy task. Not everyone living within West Virginia's boundaries was loyal to the new state. Fifteen southern and central counties had not participated in the state's first election, and in an effort to retain control for the Radical Republicans, Boreman secured the passage of the voters' test oath law in February 1865. This divisive legislation denied the right to vote, to hold political office, to practice law, to teach, and to sue to those persons who could not prove their present and past loyalty to the Union. Such oaths effectively disenfranchised the many ex-Confederates in the new state, who were overwhelmingly Democrats. Thus the Republicans were assured of a majority in West Virginia in the first years after the war.

Governor Boreman found time to marry in 1864, wedding Laurane Tanner Bullock, a Wheeling widow and mother of two sons. The ceremony was performed by the Reverend Alexander Martin, who in 1867 became West Virginia University's first president. Boreman resigned as governor on February 26, 1869,

to be elected to the U.S. Senate by the state legislature.

As a senator and as a Republican, Boreman supported the ratification of the 15th Amendment to the U.S. Constitution, guaranteeing the right to vote regardless of race. Upon receiving word of its ratification, he telegramed Robert W. Simmons, the leader of the black community in Parkersburg, and a celebration was staged in that city in 1870. Five years later, Boreman's term as senator ended, and he returned to the private practice of law in his hometown. In 1884, he organized a relief effort to assist the victims of a devastating Ohio River flood. In 1888, he was once again elected to a circuit judgeship, a post he would hold until his death on April 19, 1896. His funeral was held in Parkersburg's Methodist Episcopal Church, North, where he had been a lay leader in the congregation. Boreman was survived by his wife, their two daughters, and two stepsons. He was buried in the Odd Fellows Cemetery in Parkersburg.

See also Formation of West Virginia, Reorganized Government of Virginia, Robert W. Simmons

Bernard L. Allen
Conway, South Carolina
Charles H. Ambler and Festus P. Summers, *West Virginia: The Mountain State,* 1958; John G. Morgan, *West Virginia Governors,* 1980; Isaiah A. Woodward, "Arthur Ingraham Boreman: A Biography." *West Virginia History,* July 1970, October 1970.

Botany

The first Caucasians to describe the plants of West Virginia traveled Indian trails, rivers, and mountaintops from the mid-1700s through the mid-1800s. Prominent botanists who explored early West Virginia included Peter Kalm, John Fraser, John Clayton, Frederick Pursh, Andre Michaux, Matthias Kin, Benjamin Barton, Constantine Rafinesque, and Thomas Nuttall. Asa Gray, who wrote the famous *Gray's Manual of Botany,* collected plants from Harpers Ferry to Tucker County, across Cheat Mountain and southward through the Greenbrier Valley and Mercer County, on his way to North Carolina in 1843.

Land speculators and surveyors such as George Washington, Daniel Boone, and Christopher Gist described trees and plants of commercial importance. Meshach Browning's book, *Forty-four Years of the Life of a Hunter,* describes the numerous glades of western Maryland and present West Virginia. Thomas Lewis, surveyor on the famous Fairfax Line of 1746, described the laurel swamp and huge spruce forests of Canaan Valley.

Charles F. Millspaugh was employed by West Virginia University from 1889 to 1894 to inventory botany resources and study agricultural weeds. His 1913 book, *The Living Flora of West Virginia,* de-

Ruellia, a perennial.

scribed 3,411 plants collected by him and others. Millspaugh was a close friend of Lawrence Nuttall, a New River coal operator, who collected nearly 1,000 flowering plant species near Nuttallburg and Keeneys Creek.

John Sheldon taught botany at WVU from 1903 to 1919 and made extensive plant collections. Perry D. Strausbaugh taught biology and botany at WVU from 1923 to 1948. He is noted for re-establishing the WVU herbarium, initiating summer botanical expeditions for students in all corners of the state, and as an excellent teacher. Among his accomplished students were Russell Brown, Elizabeth Bartholomew, and Weldon Boone. Boone completed a floristic study of Summers County and wrote a book titled *A History of Botany in West Virginia* in 1965. Bartholomew was the unofficial botanical ambassador for WVU, curator of the herbarium as it grew to 100,000 specimens, and longtime secretary of the Southern Appalachian Botanical Club.

Strausbaugh's career is closely entwined with that of Earl L. Core, one of his first students. They jointly wrote *Flora of West Virginia,* published in four parts from 1952 to 1964. This 1,079-page book listed nearly 2,000 flowering plants and ferns with descriptions, ranges, identification keys, and illustrations. Now a West Virginia classic, it was judged by many as the best flora book in the United States when it was published.

Core also was an excellent teacher. His students included Melvin Brown, William Lunk, Roland Guthrie, William Gillespie, and Ronald Fortney. Lunk produced many of the illustrations in Strausbaugh and Core's *Flora of West Virginia.* Gillespie wrote booklets on edible and poisonous plants of West Virginia and a book on the plant fossils of West Virginia. Dorothy Music and Dana Evans completed flora studies in the rugged terrain of southern West Virginia. Violet Phillips

taught botany at West Virginia Institute of Technology during the 1970s and 1980s, following her doctoral studies of plants found along New River.

Core organized the Southern Appalachian Botanical Club in 1936, serving as its president and editor of its journal, *Castanea.* He spearheaded efforts in field botany through the establishment of Core Arboretum on the WVU campus and the Terra Alta Biological Station in Preston County. As biology department chairman at WVU from 1948 to 1967 he created one of the nation's leading botany programs. Faculty members included Jesse Clovis, Charles Baer, Nelle Ammons, Roland Guthrie, Harold Bennett, and Roy Clarkson. Clarkson taught botany from the 1960s to the 1980s, was herbarium curator, completed his doctoral studies of the Monongahela National Forest, and wrote extensively. His book, *Tumult on the Mountains* (1964), is an excellent treatise on timbering the virgin forests during the late 1800s and early 1900s.

Kenneth Carvell and Robert L. Smith taught botany to their forestry students at WVU from the 1960s to the 1980s while writing many popular articles for newspapers and for *Wonderful West Virginia* magazine. William Grafton completed studies of the vegetation on New River while working for the WVU Extension Service. Later he collected several thousand plants for the herbarium from all parts of the state and was active in leading nature tours.

Marshall University started botany classes in 1890. Marshall's prominent botany teachers have included H. C. Darlington, Lewis Plymale, Donald Cox, Howard Mills, James Gillespie, Dan Evans, and Frank Gilliam. Darlington completed his doctoral dissertation on Cranberry Glades and loved to take people on nature tours of the boardwalk there. Frank Albert taught from 1927 to 1942 and made extensive collections that are now in the Marshall and WVU herbariums. The professors and their graduate students added greatly to the knowledge of the Ohio, Kanawha, and New River valleys, and southwestern West Virginia.

Other colleges left their marks as well. Meade McNeil of Concord College explored southeastern West Virginia, taught botany for three decades, and helped coordinate the WVU botanical expeditions with Earl Core. George Rossbach of West Virginia Wesleyan was an avid plant collector and enthusiastic teacher. His herbarium has been added to by Kathy Gregg, who has contributed several research studies on orchids of West Virginia. Steve Stephenson of Fairmont State College has contributed ecological studies of forest types, collected and written about fungi of the state, and authored the book, *Upland Forests of West Virginia.*

The Brooks family of French Creek in Upshur County produced four noted naturalists, including the brothers, Fred, A. B., and Earle. Fred worked primarily as an entomologist with the state and federal governments. His popular articles in the *West Virginia Review* created a wide following. A. B. is revered as the highly capable naturalist at Oglebay Park from 1928 to 1942. He wrote *Forestry and Wood Industries* (1911), the best historical account of our virgin forests. The Brooks Bird Clubs are named for A. B. Brooks. Earle Brooks wrote many articles on folklore and birds. Maurice Brooks (son of Fred) traveled extensively with his father and uncles to develop his knowledge of birds, salamanders, orchids, and ferns. His observations and research culminated in 37 years as a captivating teacher at WVU and the popular 1965 book, *The Appalachians.*

Contemporary botanists from nearby states have explored the Mountain State and left many noteworthy contributions. They included Per Axel Rydberg, who studied the high mountains such as Spruce Knob, Snowy, and North Fork mountains in the 1920s. Edgar Wherry, who botanized eastern West Virginia in the 1930s, made important finds about ferns and shale barren habitats. A. Allard spent vacations in Canaan Valley and nearby mountains during the 1940s, studying plant ecology and collecting plants. Allison Cusick specialized in sedges but has collected many county and state records from 1970 through the present, especially along the upper Ohio River. Tom Wieboldt has been a prolific collector in the southeastern counties since the 1980s. Larry Morse of the Nature Conservancy has studied plants of the Eastern Panhandle and higher mountains since the 1980s.

Botany has attracted the interest of many amateurs. Among them were Lawrence Nuttall, E. E. Hutton, Osbra Eye, and Fred Brooks. Joseph Harned, a pharmacist in Oakland, Maryland, explored the vegetation of western Maryland and adjacent West Virginia. His *Wild Flowers of the Alleghanies* was published in 1931. Hannibal Davis and his wife, Tyreeca, collected numerous plants throughout West Virginia and are recognized as the authorities on the genus Rubus, which includes blackberries and dewberries. Homer Duppstadt, a preacher from Pennsylvania, spent many days in the 1980s studying plants at the WVU herbarium. J. Lawrence Smith, a Methodist preacher, wrote *The Potomac Naturalist* in 1968 and other books, as well as numerous articles and newspaper columns.

The Nature Conservancy has become a major player in botany since the 1970s. Early presidents of the state chapter included Core, WVU ecologist Charles Baer, and Eleanor Bush, who contributed to the efforts to protect botanical areas such as

Cranesville Swamp, Dolly Sods, Rock Dome, North Fork Mountain, and Slaty Mountain. Professional staff has included Frank Pelurie, Paul Trianosky, and Rodney Bartgis. Bartgis studied Altona-Piedmont Marsh in Jefferson County and has explored and written articles on the botanical treasures of the Eastern Panhandle during the 1980s and 1990s.

After more than a century of organized work, challenges still remain for amateurs and professionals to explore and research the botanical resources of West Virginia. Will individuals step forward from the present generation to carry the lofty mantle of Millspaugh, Core, Davis, and Nuttall?

William N. Grafton
WVU Extension Service

Alexander Robinson Boteler

U.S. and Confederate Congressman Alexander Robinson Boteler was born in Shepherdstown, May 16, 1815. He was a farmer and a businessman, owning a hydraulic cement plant on the Potomac River near Pack Horse Ford at Shepherdstown. Boteler was elected to the U.S. House of Representatives as a Whig in 1859. A slave owner, he hoped to preserve both slavery and Virginia's place in the Union, but after Virginia seceded Boteler served in the Confederate Congress. He designed the seal of the Confederate States of America, which incorporated a likeness of George Washington.

Boteler served as a volunteer aide to Stonewall Jackson, while continuing in the Confederate Congress in Richmond. He counted Generals Turner Ashby and J. E. B. Stuart (whom he also served as an aide) as his friends. His Shepherdstown home, Fountain Rock, was burned to the ground in 1864 on orders of Union Gen. David Hunter, destroying several paintings by portrait artist Charles Willson Peale, Boteler's ancestor.

After the war, Boteler returned to Shepherdstown and ran unsuccessfully for Congress in 1872 and 1874 as an independent. He was a federal appointee under Presidents Arthur and Cleveland. He was a founder of Shepherd College and helped to bring the Shenandoah Valley Railroad (a predecessor to the Norfolk & Western, now the Norfolk Southern) through Shepherdstown.

Boteler was an artist and caricaturist of considerable ability and a witness to momentous times. He sketched the abolitionist John Brown after his capture at Harpers Ferry and interviewed Brown extensively. Boteler was an accomplished orator and maintained an interest in James Rumsey, the inventor of the steamboat. He produced a manuscript on Rumsey that he tried, unsuccessfully, to publish. He died May 8, 1892.

Charles S. Adams, ed., *Alexander Boteler, Wheel Horse of Whiggery, Stonewall's Courier*, 1998.

Bottled Water

West Virginia's spring waters have a long history, including the regular patronage of George Washington at Berkeley Springs. Mineral water was bottled at West Virginia springs in the 19th and early 20th centuries, including Capon Springs, Berkeley Springs, and Pence Springs. The bottled water industry was revived on a large scale in the late 20th century, with the national boom in bottled-water sales. Today West Virginia producers bottle both spring water and well water, and in one case even the recaptured water from the sap of sugar maple trees.

Our state's mineral springs and warm springs were originally valued for their reported health benefits, later becoming social gathering places. Resorts were developed at springs from the Eastern Panhandle to the southeastern region of the state. Drinking was often secondary to bathing in the spring waters, although both were believed therapeutic for a variety of medical conditions. Some springs were valued for their sulfur content, which makes their water unpalatable by today's standards.

In recent times, water from certain springs has been bottled and sold as a refreshing beverage. Quibell-brand water, which began to be bottled in 1987 from the water of Sweet Springs, helped to establish the reputation of West Virginia waters by competing with Perrier and the finest sparkling waters of the world. West Virginia waters frequently win the Berkeley Springs International Water Tasting event, which regularly draws entries from Europe and elsewhere.

The bottled-water market is highly competitive, particularly in the lucrative small bottle category. Commercial giants dominate retail shelf space for single-serving bottles, especially Dasani, a Coca-Cola product, and Pepsi's Aquafina. Local bottlers fare better in the market for larger sizes. Sales of five-gallon containers for home and office delivery have grown, as have sales of smaller shelf units at retail outlets, usually gallon bottles. Bulk water sales to large bottlers or grocery chains that bottle their own brands have likewise grown, in some cases exceeding the amount that the water producers themselves bottle. Long-established companies such as Tyler Mountain Water, which operates in West Virginia and Pennsylvania and has been a major supplier in the office-delivery market since the 1930s, have expanded their reach into the bottled-water market. Berkeley Club Beverages, also a major competitor, was established in 1934.

According to the state Bureau of Employment Programs there were 13 bottled-water plants in West Virginia in 2002, employing 158 workers. They produced nearly 13 million gallons of bottled water. Tyler Mountain Water and the West Virginia Spring Water Company of Berkeley Springs together produce more than half the state total. A third large operator, the Sweet Springs Valley Water Company, produces 2.5 million gallons yearly. Berkeley Club Beverages produces an additional 1.6 million gallons, with all the other companies dividing the remaining one-tenth of the total state production among themselves.

See also Mineral Springs

The Boundary of West Virginia

West Virginia's boundary is about 1,170 miles long, with 52 percent marked by rivers and streams, 31 percent by watershed divides and crest lines, and 17 percent defined by latitude and longitude. The boundary encloses an area of 24,282 square miles. The most observable feature of shape are two panhandles: one of eight counties extending eastward for about 100 miles, and the other of four counties extending northward for about 65 miles.

According to Article II of the state constitution the northwestern boundary "includes the bed, bank, and shores of the Ohio River," beginning at a point determined in 1779 by extending a line from the western end of the Mason-Dixon Line due north to the north bank of the Ohio River. From this point, just north of Chester, the state line runs downriver to Virginia Point at the mouth of Big Sandy River, a distance of about 277 miles. There are 12 border counties and 32 islands, including historic Blennerhassett Island and Wheeling Island, the most populated island in the Ohio River.

The southwestern boundary includes "so much of the . . . Big Sandy River as was formerly included in the Commonwealth of Virginia." This boundary line begins in McDowell County at the confluence of Fourpole Creek with the Tug Fork of the Big Sandy and extends about 114 miles down the Tug and Big Sandy to the Ohio River at Virginia Point, near Kenova. This boundary was fixed when Kentucky and West Virginia became states in 1792 and 1863, respectively.

West Virginia's most famous boundary is the Mason-Dixon Line, surveyed to settle a border shared at various points by Delaware, Maryland, (West) Virginia, and Pennsylvania. The better known east-west portion of the line was set at 39 degrees, 43 minutes, and 17.6 seconds, north latitude. In 1779, Virginia and Pennsylvania agreed that their boundary should be fixed as "that line commonly called Mason's and Dixon's line" extended due west five degrees of longitude from the Delaware River, and from that point another line was run northward to the north side of the Ohio River. These two straight lines define the square southwest corner of Pennsylvania, around which West Virginia wraps itself. The distances for these lines now dividing West Virginia and Pennsylvania are about 65 miles east-west, along the top of Preston, Monongalia, and part of Wetzel counties, and 55 miles south-north, up the eastern side of Marshall, Ohio, Brooke, and Hancock counties.

Virginia's land and water boundaries with Maryland were passed to West Virginia in 1863. However, with about 40 square miles between Preston County, West Virginia, and Garrett County, Maryland, in dispute, a commission appointed by the U.S. Supreme Court in 1910 established the boundary between the two counties and their respective states. It was to begin on the south bank of the North Branch of the Potomac River north of the Fairfax Stone and to run north to the Mason-Dixon Line. The 36-mile boundary thus created appears almost straight and vertical on the map, but has five slight east-west breaks. Beginning where this line intercepts the North Branch, the Maryland-West Virginia line follows the south bank of the river for 218 miles to the boundary with Virginia, near Harpers Ferry.

West Virginia's long eastern boundary, separating the old state from the new, follows the existing county lines separating 12 West Virginia counties and their Virginia neighbors. This boundary totals about 405 miles, running mostly along ridge tops. There have been boundary disputes between the two states: one involved Monroe, Giles, and Alleghany counties in 1956, and in 1997 the 16-mile boundary between Jefferson and Loudoun counties along the crest of the Blue Ridge was resolved by surveyors.

Rumors, legends, and tales abound about surveyors who missed the mark either because of whiskey, weather, terrain, or Indians, but the facts remain in their surveys that mark the boundary of West Virginia.

Howard G. Adkins
Ona

Bounty Lands

The French and Indian War, Dunmore's War, and the Revolutionary War placed a heavy financial burden on the often meager resources of the colony and state of Virginia. Virginia leaders turned to Virginia's extensive western lands between the Alleghenies and the Mississippi River, included in the colonial charter of 1609, as an alternative means of discharging wartime debts, including unpaid obligations to thousands of militiamen and their military officers. The distribution of these bounty lands has shaped landholding patterns in Virginia, Kentucky, and West Virginia down to the present.

As early as 1754, Governor Dinwiddie set aside 200,000 acres of land for men who served in the French and Indian War, with up to 400 acres to privates and increasing amounts, depending upon

rank, for officers. Many soldiers in need of ready cash sold their land rights for a fraction of their real worth, and speculators acquired thousands of acres, some in large tracts that remained intact for a century or more. George Washington, the commander of the Virginia Regiment during the French and Indian War, chose several prime tracts on the Ohio and Kanawha rivers in present West Virginia. One Kanawha tract was a few miles above Point Pleasant, which was expected to become the capital of Vandalia, a proposed 14th colony.

Bounty lands were sometimes caught in the uncertainties of the Virginia land system in which titles were insecure. Land disputes kept lawyers busy for decades and contributed to some of the worst features of land speculation, including an absentee land ownership that has often added to the social and economic woes of West Virginia.

Otis K. Rice
WVU Institute of Technology
Thomas Perkins Abernethy, *Western Lands and the American Revolution,* 1937; Roy Bird Cook, *Washington's Western Lands,* 1931; Otis K. Rice, *The Allegheny Frontier: West Virginia Beginnings, 1730–1830,* 1970.

Bourbon Democrats

The term "Bourbon" was once used to describe Democratic leaders who succeeded Republican Radicals and Carpetbaggers in Southern state governments in the years following the Civil War. The reference was not to corn whiskey but to the Bourbon kings of France, who, it was claimed, had learned nothing from the long and bitter years of the French Revolution and had instead endeavored to return to the practices that had produced the upheaval. In its Southern context, the term implied that the Democrats had learned nothing from the Civil War and were intent upon reclaiming political power, preventing blacks from voting and holding public office, maintaining white supremacy and white unity, and erasing every accomplishment of Reconstruction governments.

This fails to do justice to the flexibility of West Virginia Bourbons. The West Virginia Democrats who followed the Republican founders of the state included Governors Mathews, Jackson, Wilson, Fleming, and MacCorkle. These men were ready to adjust to changing political conditions and to the 13th, 14th, and 15th amendments to the federal Constitution, which conferred freedom, citizenship, and the right to vote and hold office upon former slaves. West Virginia Bourbons also came to terms with the new industrial character of the nation. However devoted they may have been to Southern, or traditional, American ideals, they were ready to attract industry to the state. In this respect, the step was not a giant one,

since West Virginians had clamored for decades for development of the state's resources and construction of suitable types of transportation.

In short, Bourbonism in West Virginia had a flexibility that stood for the retention of Southern values while coupling them with acceptance of the new industrial goals and necessities. After 1871, there came an increasing accommodation between political parties, which shared common goals, and also between races, so that "Jim Crow" racial discrimination in West Virginia was of a milder form than in the Deep South.

Otis K. Rice
WVU Institute of Technology
Charles H. Ambler and Festus P. Summers, *West Virginia: The Mountain State,* 1958; Otis K. Rice and Stephen W. Brown, *West Virginia: A History,* 1993.

Belle Boyd

Spy Marie Isabelle "Belle" Boyd was born May 9, 1843, in Martinsburg, the daughter of Benjamin R. Boyd, a merchant. In 1853, Mr. Boyd purchased land at the corner of Race and Spring streets and built the most architecturally significant Greek Revival mansion in Martinsburg.

Belle was sent to Mount Washington School in Baltimore in 1856, graduating at age 16. The Boyds moved from their Race Street mansion to the 500 block of South Queen Street in 1859. It was there on July 4, 1861, that Belle shot a Yankee soldier and started her spy career. She was imprisoned twice. She moved to Front Royal, Virginia, after being acquitted in the soldier's death. From Front Royal she carried news of Union plans to Confederate Gen. Stonewall Jackson during Jackson's successful 1862 Shenandoah Valley campaign. She returned to Martinsburg and continued to spy.

In 1864, Belle Boyd married Samuel Wylde Hardinge Jr. A former U.S. Navy officer who had been her captor, Hardinge had disgraced himself by falling under Boyd's influence and allowing an important prisoner to escape. The couple had one daughter before Hardinge died, probably in England between the end of 1865 and July 1866. Boyd married the second time in 1869 to John Swainston Hammond, and they had four children before divorcing in 1884. She married her third husband, Nathaniel High, in 1885.

Boyd wrote a book, *Belle Boyd in Camp and Prison,* while she was in London in 1865. It was republished many times. She made a living for her family as an actress. She died June 11, 1900, at Kilbourn, Wisconsin, where she is buried. Boyd's childhood house at 126 East Race Street in Martinsburg and the cottage in Front Royal, Virginia, are now museums.

Don C. Wood
Berkeley County Historical Society
Louis A. Sigaud, *Belle Boyd: Confederate Spy,* 1945.

Jennings Boyd

Coach Jennings Bryan Boyd, perhaps West Virginia's greatest high school basketball coach, was born August 1, 1933, in Buchanan County, Virginia. Boyd graduated from Northfork-Elkhorn High School in neighboring McDowell County in 1951 and received his teaching degree from Concord College. Returning to his alma mater (whose name had been shortened to Northfork High School) as a mathematics teacher and assistant coach, Boyd became head coach in 1966.

Under Boyd, the Northfork Blue Demons won eight consecutive AA state basketball championships from 1974 to 1981, an all-time state and national record, and a total of nine championships in 15 years. Boyd's up-tempo teams, famous for their fast breaks and transition offense, compiled a 102-5 home record on the high school's cozy, less-than-regulation, gymnasium court. He retired from coaching in 1981 after beating Dunbar 55-53 in his last state championship game, with a lifetime 446-83 (85 percent) record. Boyd retired from teaching in 1986 and served on both the McDowell County Board of Education and the county commission, where he was president in 1986. Boyd, West Virginia Coach of the Year in 1976, was inducted into the National High School Coaches Hall of Fame in 1983. He and his wife, the former Patricia Ann Romeo, had three sons. Jennings Boyd died at Welch, April 2, 2002.

See also Basketball Tournament

C. Stuart McGehee
West Virginia State University

Tony Boyle

Union official William Anthony "Tony" Boyle, born December 1, 1901, in Montana, went to work in the mines as a youth and soon became a labor activist. In 1940, he became president of United Mine Workers District 27 in Montana. UMW President John L. Lewis brought Boyle to Washington in 1947 as his assistant. Upon the retirement of Lewis in 1960, Boyle became vice president, then acting president. He was elected union president in 1963.

Lacking the charisma of Lewis, Boyle tried unsuccessfully to keep his predecessor's tight rein on union affairs. As the 1960s progressed, union miners agitated for local and district autonomy and the right to ratify national contracts. On the day following the mine disaster at Farmington, which killed 78 men on November 20, 1968, Boyle infuriated mine workers by telling newsmen: "As long as we mine coal, there is always this inherent danger. This happens to be one of the better companies, as far as cooperation with our union and safety is concerned."

Opposition mounted in early 1969 in the wake of strong demands that state and federal action be taken on black lung and mine safety. Boyle made it clear that since the Farmington disaster had little to do with black lung, the major emphasis of the UMWA would be on mine safety. This timid message sparked a strike of 40,000 West Virginia miners in defiance of Boyle. The agitation was further fueled by evidence of corruption within the union. At the end of May 1969, former ally Joseph A. "Jock" Yablonski startled the Boyle forces by announcing his candidacy for UMWA president in the December 1969 election. After a bitter campaign, Yablonski, his wife, and daughter were murdered on New Year's Eve 1969. Boyle was defeated by Arnold Miller in 1972.

Tony Boyle and three others were convicted and sentenced to life in prison for the Yablonski murders. He died May 31, 1985.

See also Black Lung Movement, Farmington Mine Disaster, United Mine Workers of America

Ken Hechler
Charleston

Nathan Cook Brackett

College founder Nathan Cook Brackett, the father of Storer College, was born July 28, 1836, in Phillips, Maine. He was a minister of the Free Will Baptist Church. Graduating from Dartmouth College in 1864, he joined the U.S. Christian Commission and was stationed in the Shenandoah Valley to assist both Union and Confederate soldiers and freed slaves.

After the war, Brackett served his church's mission to educate freed slaves by supervising 25 young female teachers from the North, scattered in Free Will Baptist schools throughout the valley from Harpers Ferry and Martinsburg to Lynchburg, Virginia. He proposed that his church's best service would be to equip blacks to teach other blacks, rather than relying only on missionary teachers from New England. The church leaders embraced the idea and raised the necessary funding to establish Storer College at Harpers Ferry. The college opened in October 1867, with Brackett as its first president.

Brackett retired from Storer's presidency in 1897, although he continued as treasurer until his death. Noted for his good humor and diplomacy, Brackett was respected by blacks and whites alike. He served on the Harpers Ferry Town Council and was for two years the superintendent of free schools there. He was a regent of the Bluefield Colored Institute (now Bluefield State College) for eight years, four as president of the board. Brackett died July 20, 1910, in Harpers Ferry.

See also African-American Education, Storer College

Barbara Rasmussen
Fairmont State University

Barbara Rasmussen, "Sixty-four Edited Letters of the Founders of Storer College," M.A. thesis, West Virginia University, 1986.

Braddock's Road

Braddock's Road traces the path of Maj. Gen. Edward Braddock, commander of British forces in the colonies, on his disastrous march to the Ohio Valley during the French and Indian War. In the spring of 1755, Braddock assembled an army of about 2,400 British regulars and colonial militia to attempt to force the French from Fort Duquesne, at present Pittsburgh.

Braddock's Road crosses what is now West Virginia's Eastern Panhandle. In order to move and supply his army, Braddock improved existing roads in present Jefferson, Berkeley, and Hampshire counties. Young George Washington, having traveled much of the same route the previous year when his own forces were defeated at Fort Necessity, Pennsylvania, served as an aide-de-camp to Braddock.

The army crossed some of the roughest terrain on the entire route in present West Virginia, as they traveled from Fort Enoch near Forks of Cacapon to the Potomac River ford at Fort Cox, about two miles west of Paw Paw. The soldiers crossed one mountain stream 19 times and another 20 times as they made their way over Spring Gap Mountain, Hampshire County.

Braddock was killed in fierce fighting before reaching Fort Duquesne, and the defeated army returned over the same route. Although Braddock's Road was abandoned years ago, traces of it can still be seen along various Eastern Panhandle county roads.

Tommy Swaim
Berkeley Springs

William H. Ansel Jr., *Frontier Forts along the Potomac and its Tributaries,* 1984; Walter Hough, *Braddock's Route through the Virginia Colony,* 1970.

J. G. Bradley

Industrialist Joseph Gardner "J. G." Bradley, born September 12, 1881, in New Jersey, came to West Virginia in 1904. A descendant of U.S. Sen. Simon Cameron of Pennsylvania, Abraham Lincoln's first secretary of war, and Justice Joseph P. Bradley of the U.S. Supreme Court, Bradley had just graduated from Harvard Law School when he became vice president of the Buffalo Creek & Gauley Railroad. He soon became president of the Elk River Coal & Lumber Company, which had been buying land in central West Virginia since 1896.

Controlling 36.5 percent of Clay County land, the Elk River Company was so significant to Clay County's economy that the county could not meet its obligations until the company paid its taxes. The coal company town of Widen and the former lumber town of Swandale, built by Bradley's company in the rugged eastern section of the county, and many colorful memories are his legacy to Clay County.

Bradley attracted capital investment from Massachusetts and Pennsylvania to his Clay County ventures. He was a director of the Dauphin Deposit Trust and the Harrisburg Trust Company, leading Pennsylvania banks. He was president of both the National Coal Association (1921–22), and the West Virginia Coal Association (1916–46). Bradley lived in an elegant estate at Dundon, near the town of Clay.

Staunchly antiunion, Bradley sought the loyalty of his work force by providing attractive houses, schools, and a variety of recreational resources, as well as an independent or "company" union. The onslaught of the Great Depression and organizing drives by the United Mine Workers resulted in strikes at Widen in 1933 and 1941, but both failed.

Following a prolonged, deadly strike in the early 1950s, Bradley sold the Widen mine in 1959. He returned to Massachusetts, dying there March 16, 1971.

See also Clay County, Widen

Lou Athey
Franklin & Marshall College
Betty Cantrell, Grace Phillips, and Helen Reed, "Widen: The Town J. G. Bradley Built," *Goldenseal,* January–March 1977; C. C. Stewart, "Strike Duty: A State Trooper Recalls Trouble in the Coalfields," *Goldenseal,* Winter 1995.

Ruby Bradley

Colonel Ruby Bradley was born near Spencer, December 9, 1907. She taught four years in one-room schools in Roane County. She became a nurse in 1933 and joined the Army Nurse Corps in 1934. She was serving in the Philippines when the Japanese bombed Pearl Harbor and captured three weeks later. She spent more than three years as a prisoner of war.

At Santo Tomas Internment Camp in Manila, Bradley and several other captive nurses established a clinic to care for the sick and wounded prisoners. Bradley assisted in over 230 major surgeries and delivered 13 American babies while a prisoner. When American troops liberated the camp in February 1945, Bradley weighed 86 pounds.

Bradley was a combat nurse in the Korean War, where she served on the front lines in evacuation hospitals. On one occasion, she refused to leave until she had loaded onto a plane all the sick and wounded while surrounded by Chinese snipers. She was the Eighth Army's chief nurse from 1950 to 1953. Bradley became a colonel in 1958. She retired from the army in 1963 but remained a nurse.

Colonel Bradley was one of the most decorated women in U.S. military history and the nation's most decorated female

veteran. Her record included 34 medals and citations of bravery, most notably two Legion of Merit medals, two Bronze Stars, and a U.N. Korean Service Medal with seven battle stars. Bradley left Korea with a full-dress honor guard ceremony, the first woman to receive such a salute. She also received the Florence Nightingale Medal from the International Red Cross. Her hometown of Spencer recognized her with a parade and many tributes during "Ruby Bradley Day" in September 1991.

Colonel Bradley died May 28, 2002, in a nursing home in Hazard, Kentucky. She is buried in Arlington National Cemetery.

David F. Matthews
Fairmont

Bramwell

Bramwell, near Bluefield in Mercer County, was incorporated in 1888. The town was named for its first postmaster, J. Herbert Bramwell, superintendent of the Flat Top Coal Company (later the Pocahontas Land Corporation), the land-leasing firm that established the town as its headquarters on a bend of the Bluestone River in 1885. Bramwell quickly became a business center for the Pocahontas Coalfield and a hub of southern West Virginia's financial network with the opening of the Bank of Bramwell in 1889. By 1909, the *Bluefield Daily Telegraph* had dubbed Bramwell the "Coalfield Capital."

In the town's bustling heyday, passenger trains stopped 14 times a day. Bramwell was home to numerous wealthy coal operators who built substantial late Victorian mansions there, including Edward Cooper, W. H. Thomas, Philip Goodwill, and Isaac T. Mann, the founder of the Bank of Bramwell and the Pocahontas Fuel Company. Once considered the "richest small town in America," Bramwell enjoyed an exclusive, prosperous status until the Bank of Bramwell closed in 1933 during the Great Depression.

A heightened awareness of Bramwell's historical and architectural significance began when the town was named to the National Register of Historic Places in 1983. The Bramwell Millionaire Garden Club inaugurated a popular series of annual tours of coal operators' homes, several of which had been restored by private homeowners. Several bed-and-breakfast establishments operate in Bramwell, and the Bramwell Foundation, a local nonprofit organization, works to secure and support the preservation of the historic district's architectural integrity. Bramwell had a population of 426 in 2000.

Beth Hager
Harrisburg, Pennsylvania
Beth A. Hager, "Millionaires' Town: The Houses and People of Bramwell," *Goldenseal,* Winter 1982.

Harry Brawley

Broadcaster Harry Morgan Brawley was born October 8, 1909, in Charleston. After contracting polio at age two, he succeeded in learning to walk but struggled with this disability for his entire life. He graduated from Charleston High School in 1927. Brawley attended Marshall College (now Marshall University) and then West Virginia University, where he graduated in 1930 with a B.S. in political science. He earned an M.A. in education at WVU in 1932. He taught history at Lincoln Junior High, 1932–35, and later at Charleston High School, pioneering the use of radio in teaching. In 1945, Brawley accepted a position as director of public affairs at Charleston radio station WCHS. He aired his first radio program for secondary schools, on the timely subject of the United Nations, in September 1945. He later founded the pioneering "School of the Air" and won a 1947 award for the series.

Brawley was instrumental in the formation of West Virginia educational television and later public radio, which are now West Virginia Public Broadcasting. He worked with his friend, the late Congressman Harley O. Staggers, to write federal legislation that became the Educational Television and Radio Amendments of 1969. This legislation permitted public broadcasting stations to purchase, through grants, the equipment necessary to get on the air.

In retirement, Brawley was known as an authority on Charleston history and developed several popular slide shows that were made into videotapes. He served on Charleston City Council from 1973 to 1987. Brawley Walkway in downtown Charleston was named in his honor in 1984. Harry Brawley died March 25, 1992.

Richard Fauss
State Archives
Harry M. Brawley, *Twenty Years On An Oasis in the Vast Wasteland,* 1981.

Braxton County

Braxton, the central county of West Virginia, was created in 1836 from Kanawha, Lewis, and Nicholas counties. It is named for Carter Braxton, a Virginia statesman and a signer of the Declaration of Independence. The geographic center of West Virginia is located in Braxton County, south of Flatwoods, about five miles southeast of Sutton and four miles west of Centralia, in the Elk River Wildlife Management Area. The first permanent white settlers in the county are believed to have been members of the Carpenter family, who settled at the mouth of Holly River in the 1780s.

Braxton's 519.7 square miles embrace the rolling central highlands of the state at elevations ranging from 760 feet to 2,180 feet. The county seat, Sutton, is

FAST FACTS ABOUT BRAXTON COUNTY

Founded: 1836

Land in square miles: 519.7

Population: 14,702

Percentage minorities: 2%

Percentage rural: 100%

Median age: 39.6

Percentage 65 and older: 15.8%

Birth rate per 1,000 population: 10.6

Median household income: $24,412

High school graduate or higher: 67.3%

Bachelor's degree or higher: 9.2%

Home ownership: 78.2%

Median home value: $59,300

This information is from the 2000 U.S. Census. In 2000, West Virginia as a whole had 5 percent minorities, a median age of 38.9, median household income of $29,696, and a 75.2 percent home ownership rate.

named for founder John D. Sutton, who gave one acre of ground in 1836 for a public square. Part of the town was burned on December 29, 1861, by withdrawing Confederate forces during the Civil War.

In addition to Sutton, other municipalities include Gassaway, Burnsville, and Flatwoods. Gassaway is named for Henry Gassaway Davis, a U.S. senator and industrialist. Gassaway was a major division point on Davis's Coal & Coke Railway, built between Charleston and Elkins in the early 1900s. It remained a railroad freight station until the depot was closed by CSX in 1988. From the early 1900s to the late 1950s, major shops were located at Gassaway for railroad cars and locomotives, and for repairing cabooses. Burnsville is named for John Burns, who operated the first sawmill in that section of the state. Flatwoods is a thriving complex of restaurants, motels, a factory outlet mall, and other businesses on Interstate 79.

Braxton County is bisected by Interstate 79. Four-lane U.S. 19, a busy north-south artery, connects with I-79 near Sutton and carries traffic to the West Virginia Turnpike (Interstate 77-64) at Beckley. Together, these roads funnel thousands of travelers through the county daily.

The principal streams are the Elk, Little Kanawha, Holly, Birch, and Little Birch rivers. The Elk flows for 40 miles through Braxton on its way to Charleston. In 1961, the Army Corps of Engineers completed a dam on Elk River at Sutton, impounding 1,520 surface acres of water at summer pool stage. Another dam was completed on the Little Kanawha River at Burnsville in 1978, impounding 968 acres. These two lakes and associated campgrounds have become popular recreational attractions. Bulltown Historic Area, which is part of the Burnsville Reservoir project, is the site of the massacre

of Captain Bull's band of Delaware Indians by frontiersmen in 1772 and of a Civil War skirmish in 1863. The Bulltown complex includes the 19th-century Cunningham-Skinner farm where Civil War troops camped; a section of the Weston &

Gauley Bridge Turnpike; the relocated St. Michael's Roman Catholic Church; and an interpretive center.

Other attractions include the 18,225-acre Elk River Wildlife Management Area, the 12,579-acre Burnsville Lake Wildlife Management Area, and 4-H Camp Holly Gray, which hosts regional horse shows.

Rural Braxton's population, never high, peaked at 23,973 in 1920 and was still more than 21,000 just prior to World War II. The number of Braxton Countians dropped below 14,000 in the 1970 census, following a decline that began in the 1950s. But Braxton is gaining population again, with the coming of new highways and new businesses. Its population was 14,702 in 2000.

The county's economy is founded on wood products, natural gas, conventions and tourism, and, until recent years, coal mining. The major employers are state and county government, utilities, John K. Skidmore Development, Inc., Meadows Stone & Paving, Go-Mart, and wood product manufacturers Weyerhaeuser, Appalachian Timber Services, Pioneer Division

The rolling hills of Braxton County.

of Coastal Lumber Company, and various sawmills. Medical services also employ many people. Braxton County Memorial Hospital, which opened in 1981, is a member of Camcare Health System.

There are six elementary schools, a middle school, and the consolidated Braxton County High School, which opened in 1969. There are public libraries at Sutton, Gassaway, and Burnsville. The county has two banks, City National Bank of West Virginia and Bank of Gassaway. Both have multiple branches in the county. Braxton County Airport, located three miles east of Sutton, has a 4,000-foot lighted runway.

Prominent personalities who were born in Braxton or grew up in the county include Adm. Chester R. Bender (1914–96), former U.S. Coast Guard commandant; Susanne Fisher (1903–91), Metropolitan Opera singer; and Danny Heater, who scored 135 points for Burnsville High School in a basketball game in 1960, setting a national single-game record.

Braxton has five individual structures on the National Register of Historic Places: the original Sutton High School, Windy Run School at Tesla, Gassaway train depot, the old bridge over the Little Kanawha at Burnsville, and the Cunningham Farmstead. Also on the register are the Sutton Downtown Historic District, the Bulltown Historic Area, which includes a ten-mile stretch of the Weston and Gauley Bridge Turnpike, and Civil War Union Trenches and Confederate Trenches.

See also Captain Bull, Carpenter Family, Sutton

Skip Johnson
Sutton

John D. Sutton, *History of Braxton County and Central West Virginia,* 1967; *West Virginia Blue Book,* 1997.

Braxton County Rune Stone

The Braxton County Rune Stone, also known as the Wilson Stone and Braxton County Tablet, was found by Blaine Wilson on April 10, 1931, on Triplett Fork, eight miles west of Gassaway. It is a piece of micaceous sandstone, 4 1/8 inches long, 3 3/16 inches wide, 13/16 inch thick, with an inscription very similar to the Grave Creek Tablet found at Grave Creek Mound at Moundsville in the spring of 1838. The inscription consists of three lines dividing three groups of characters with a cross at the bottom. Many of the characters are similar to the Grave Creek characters and follow the same sequence.

The state purchased the tablet nine years after Wilson found it and sent it to Dr. Emerson F. Greenman, an archeologist at the University of Michigan, for analysis. Upon completion of his detailed analysis he concluded, "It has not been demonstrated that the Wilson tablet is a fraud, but the preponderant evidence points in that direction." Today both the Grave Creek and Braxton County tablets are considered frauds by most professional archeologists. The Braxton tablet is owned by the West Virginia State Museum.

See also Archeology, Grave Creek Tablet
Robert F. Maslowski
Milton

Bretz Coke Ovens

The Bretz coke ovens, the last beehive coke ovens to operate in West Virginia, are located in Preston County a half-mile southwest of Masontown. The town of Bretz and the mining plant there were built by the West Virginia Coal Company about 1903, and were named for an official of the Morgantown & Kingwood Railroad. After purchasing this railroad in 1902, Stephen B. Elkins acquired Bretz in 1906, then built 400 beehive coke ovens there. His Elkins Coal & Coke Company put the ovens into full production in 1907, shipping the coke to the huge steel plant at Sparrows Point near Baltimore. In 1919, Bethlehem Steel Corporation acquired the Bretz property, but shut it down the following year and moved its coking operations to a modern byproduct facility in Baltimore. The Bretz mine and coke ovens were operated only intermittently, during periods of peak steel production, until 1953, when the Mercury Coal & Coke Company purchased the property. New coal handling equipment was installed, the ovens were refurbished, and the facility was put back into operation. It operated on a nearly full-time basis until 1981. As one of the last surviving beehive cokemaking operations in the nation, the Bretz coke ovens and mining plant were listed on the National Register of Historic Places in 1975 as the Elkins Coal & Coke Company Historic District.

Michael Edward Workman
WVU Institute for the History of Technology

Brick Industry

While bricks were made throughout West Virginia from the state's plentiful clay deposits, the historic heart of the industry was in the Northern Panhandle near particularly fine clay deposits around New Cumberland, Hancock County. Several entrepreneurial families, including the Porters, Atkinsons, Ballantynes, and Mackeys, recognized the economic benefits of the abundant local resources and bought clay and shale properties and the materials for hardening bricks. Firewood, which was considered by early brick makers to make the finest bricks, was used until the supply was depleted; then gas, and later coal, were used to fire or harden the bricks. Successive generations of these families started companies that operated flatboats, then keel boats, then sternwheelers, and later towboats and barges to ship bricks down the Ohio and Mississippi rivers and upstream to Pittsburgh and points east.

New Cumberland, located on a bend in the Ohio River that became known by rivermen as the Brickyard Bend, was the brick capital of the United States from about 1840 to 1910. In 1872, 11 million bricks were shipped via the Ohio River. After a railroad line was built through the area in 1886 by the Pennsylvania Railroad, 75 freight cars a day left New Cumberland loaded with brick and other clay products. While its arrival had been eagerly sought, the railroad with its increasingly high shipping costs played a role in the downfall of the local brick industry after World War I. As the clay deposits were mined out and synthetic paving and building materials replaced brick, West Virginia's national role in the brick industry ended.

Jeanne Grimm
Morgantown

Bridge Day

One of the most unusual events in America is Bridge Day, when tens of thousands of people gather at Fayetteville on the third Saturday of October to celebrate—and some to jump off—one of the world's great bridges. Several organizations, agencies, and individuals contribute to this event, officially sponsored by the Fayette County Chamber of Commerce. The preeminent attraction is the New River Gorge Bridge, the world's second-longest steel arch bridge. The bridge was completed on October 22, 1977. Northbound lanes of U.S. 19 have been closed for Bridge Day since 1980. Many people take advantage of this closure to walk the bridge and to view the spectacular fall colors of the New River Gorge far below. Participants may visit the many booths set up for this special day with food, displays, and exhibits. Parachutists jump from the bridge into the New River Gorge, the only day it is legally permissible to do so. Bridge Day is fast becoming a regional event, drawing crowds estimated at 80,000 people. Although canceled in 2001 because of security concerns following the September 11 terrorist attack, the festival resumed on an annual basis in 2002.

See also New River Gorge Bridge
W. Eugene Cox
National Park Service

Bridges

Bridges dot the landscape of mountainous West Virginia, carrying roads and railways over creeks and rivers. Pedestrian bridges carry sidewalks and the occasional footpath over obstacles of all sorts, and numerous overpasses were built along with West Virginia's modern highways. In the highway system alone

The East Huntington bridge spans the Ohio River.

there are more than 6,300 bridges, and there are many private pedestrian and auto bridges, as well as railroad bridges, throughout the state.

Bridges have been a feature of the landscape from the early days of European settlement, but the 19th century saw a legion of bridges built, from humble bridges built by non-professionals to monumental structures across major rivers. The earliest bridges were modest affairs constructed on a temporary basis. The first systematic building of bridges came with the construction of the turnpike roads authorized by the Virginia Board of Public Works. Many of the turnpike bridges were simple trestles, with their members exposed to the weather.

More familiar are the covered bridges, which were roofed and sided as protection against the weather. The covered bridge era began at the start of the 19th century and extended in West Virginia until the first decade of the 20th. The best-known covered bridge builder was Lemuel Chenoweth, who built numerous turnpike bridges. The record is incomplete, but at least a dozen major timber bridges are credited to him, including the famous 1852 Philippi bridge, and its sibling, the 1853 Barrackville bridge, both recently restored. Other notable covered bridges were erected across the state, including those at Marlinton, Caldwell, Cheat River, and the back-channel bridge at Wheeling Island.

With the advent of iron as a structural material, the all-timber covered bridges were displaced by the all-iron and later steel truss bridges, beginning with the Howe truss in which iron rods replaced tension members. This simple form had many advantages over the more traditional patterns, such as the all-timber Burr and Long trusses, and found wide application with 19th-century railroad bridges. The transformation from wood to iron bridges also marked the transformation from the "vernacular" or craft approach to formally designed bridges, proportioned by scientific methods in the hands of trained engineers.

Another vernacular bridge type was the stone arch bridge, such as the Van Meterford bridge in the Eastern Panhandle and bridges on the National Road in the Northern Panhandle. Because of their cost and the lack of skilled masons, stone bridges such as these did not blossom into a major type in the 19th century.

Among the very first use of iron for bridges were suspension trusses developed by Wendel Bollman and Albert Fink and widely employed on the Baltimore & Ohio Railroad. Fink's multispanned railway bridge at Fairmont attracted international attention with its three 205-foot spans. Later long-span railway bridges were built across the Ohio River at such places as Steubenville, Wheeling, Benwood, and Parkersburg. Also notable among mid-19th century works was the great Tray Run viaduct in cast iron, also by Fink, built near Rowlesburg in Preston County and recognized as a significant feature on the B&O from Baltimore to Wheeling.

For highway bridges, the widespread use of iron and later steel took the form of prefabricated bridges produced by many fabricating shops in the northeast United States. These so-called catalog bridges were erected throughout the state in large numbers, often under the direction of county commissioners.

By the end of the 19th century, reinforced concrete had become a rival of metal truss bridges for highway construction. West Virginia's most prolific builder of short- and medium-span concrete bridges was Frank Duff McEnteer of Clarksburg. During two decades ending in 1931, his Concrete Steel Bridge Company built more than 1,000 bridges in West Virginia and elsewhere. In contrast to McEnteer's more modest bridges, the monumental Fairmont High Level Bridge was under construction from 1918 to 1921.

The most famous of all of West Virginia's historic bridges is the 1849 Wheeling Suspension Bridge. This bridge spawned a number of early wire suspension bridges in Morgantown, Fairmont, Sutton, Charleston, and Guyandotte near Huntington. The suspension bridge tradition continues in West Virginia today, but in the form of cable-stayed bridges such as the spectacular single-pier bridges crossing the Ohio River at Weirton and Huntington. In cable-stayed bridges the support cables fan directly from the tower to the bridge deck, and not from a suspended cable.

West Virginia's best-known bridge of modern times is the steel arch New River Gorge bridge on U.S. 19 in Fayette County. Completed in 1977, the span soars 876 feet above the river and has a total road length of 3,030 feet. Set within a background of mountain vistas, the bridge serves as a major tourist attraction and is the site of the Bridge Day festival each October.

See also Cable-Stayed Bridges, Lemuel Chenoweth, Frank Duff McEnteer, New River Gorge Bridge, Philippi Covered Bridge, Wheeling Suspension Bridge

Emory L. Kemp
WVU Institute for the History of Technology
Stan Cohen, *West Virginia's Covered Bridges: A Pictorial Heritage,* 1992; Emory L. Kemp, *West Virginia's Historic Bridges,* 1984.

Brinkley Bridge

A Wayne County bridge entered West Virginia political lore during the 1960 presidential primary between John F. Kennedy and Hubert Humphrey. While covering the hotly contested campaign, NBC-TV newsman David Brinkley filmed a report at the old one-lane bridge across Twelvepole Creek on what was then U.S. 52 (now U.S. 152) just outside Wayne. Brinkley held his microphone down to the bridge's creaky wooden floorboards, and viewers nationwide heard them pop and groan as vehicles rumbled across. Built in 1907, the dilapidated bridge long had been the subject of complaint by those who had to use it.

Stung by Brinkley's report, state officials immediately ordered the bridge closed for repair. Soon it was reopened with a new floor and a fresh coat of silver paint. People in Wayne County had started calling it the "Brinkley Bridge." Why not make it official? some unknown soul suggested. So Brinkley was contacted and agreed to come back for ceremonies on June 17, 1961, at which time the bridge was named for him.

By 1970, the old bridge was again in bad shape and on September 22 of that year, it collapsed under the weight of an overloaded truck. The following year, a new replacement bridge was opened without the famous newsman's name. The Brinkley Bridge was no more.

James E. Casto
Herald-Dispatch

Broaddus College
See Alderson-Broaddus College.

Brook Trout

Brook trout are West Virginia's only native trout, known to many fishermen simply as "natives." State fishermen feel that this fish embodies the very essence of the Mountaineer spirit, inhabiting only cold, pristine streams of the high mountain valleys. In 1973, lawmakers chose the brook trout as the state fish of West Virginia.

The brook trout is West Virginia's state fish.

Many of the headwater streams of the Cheat, Greenbrier, Elk, Potomac, and Tygart rivers contain good brook trout populations. As of 2000, the longest brook trout was caught in the Lost River and measured 23.5 inches, and the heaviest was 7.19 pounds, caught in the Little River tributary of the Greenbrier.

The brook trout can be distinguished from both the rainbow and brown trout by light twisting lines across the back instead of brown or black spots, and the milky-white first ray of pectoral, pelvic, and anal fins. It feeds primarily on aquatic adult insects, terrestrial insects, and immature mosquitoes and gnats. Spawning takes place in autumn over a gravel substrate. Young brook trout emerge in spring, feeding primarily on subsurface, drifting larvae, and nymphs. The best time to fish for brook trout is in late April or May when the waters warm a little and the first good hatches of mayflies and other insects appear.

See also Fish

Kathleen Carothers Leo
Division of Natural Resources

Brooke County

Located in the Northern Panhandle, Brooke County is bounded on the north by Hancock County, on the south by Ohio County, by Pennsylvania on the east, and by the Ohio River and the state of Ohio on the west. The surface of Brooke County is mostly high rolling land, cut in every direction by deep ravines, along which flow rivulets and brooks. Most of Brooke's streams merge into Harmon, Buffalo, Cross, and Short creeks, and all drain west to the Ohio River. Bottomlands of varying widths border the Ohio.

At 92.5 square miles, Brooke is among the smallest counties in the state. Its average width is about seven miles and its length about 16 miles. The 2000 population was 25,447. Wellsburg, the county seat, is located on the Ohio River at an elevation of 635 feet above sea level. Brooke County is divided into five magisterial districts: Buffalo, Wellsburg, Cross Creek, Follansbee, and Weirton. The county's municipalities are Bethany, Follansbee, Weirton (part of which is also in Hancock County), Wellsburg, Beech Bottom, and Windsor Heights.

Brooke County was established under an act of the General Assembly of Virginia, passed November 30, 1796. The first county court meeting was held in Wellsburg, known as Charlestown at the time, on May 23, 1797. The county was formed from part of Ohio County and named in honor of Robert Brooke, governor of Virginia (1794–96). Brooke County was the 11th county created in the area that was to become West Virginia. It extended to the northernmost tip of the panhandle until 1848, when Hancock County was created from the northern half of Brooke.

Although there was Indian activity in the county, not much has been recorded. Richard "Greybeard" Wells erected a fort in northeastern Brooke County and maintained good relations with the natives. In contrast, in 1774, Daniel Greathouse and Joseph Tomlinson plus about 30 others massacred all of an Indian encampment, except for a little girl they kept as a prisoner. The dead were of Chief Logan's family and tribe, including Logan's sister. Logan, who bitterly memorialized the event in his famous speech, retaliated in a bloody campaign against white settlers, a precipitating factor in Dunmore's War.

Three prehistoric mounds were located at Beech Bottom, and one was found in what is now Follansbee. The last white man killed in Brooke County by the Indians was John Decker.

Indian trails, military roads, and the Ohio River served Brooke's early transportation needs, and by the 1870s the Pennsylvania Railroad's main line crossed east to west through Brooke County, on its way to St. Louis. The north-to-south Panhandle Railroad (now gone) made its first run February 28, 1878. Today, the county is served by two railroads. Brooke is also served by State Route 2, a main highway which parallels the Ohio River; State Routes 27 and 67, which cross the county from the east and join Route 2 at Wellsburg on the west; U.S. 22, going east and west at the county's northernmost boundary; plus State Route 88, beginning at State Route 27 and going south to Wheeling.

Brooke County is situated in the busy Ohio Valley. Between 1790 and the 1850s, the principal activities were agriculture, small specialty industries, some mining, and transportation. Gristmills ground local grain, and flour became a leading product, shipped on the Ohio River to New Orleans and elsewhere. The glass industry has one of the oldest continuous histories, beginning in the county in 1813. Coal mining started on a relatively small scale in the late 19th century and boomed in the 20th century, changing the face of the county. Coal, the river, and available flat bottomland brought steel, electricity, and chemicals to Brooke County. Today Brooke produces sheet metal and tin containers, plastic containers, coal, paper bags, tar and chemicals, electric power, glass and glassware, dairy products, and fruit. Sheet steel and tin plate plants and allied industries are located at Beech Bottom and Follansbee.

The Brooke County public library is in Wellsburg, with a branch in Follansbee. Brooke County's historical museum is in Wellsburg, housed in a structure built in 1795. There are nine primary schools, two middle schools, and one consolidated high school. In addition to these public schools, there are also two parochial schools. The county is home to Bethany College, which was established in 1840 by Alexander Campbell, a theologian, author, and founder of the Christian Church (Disciples of Christ). Two of West Virginia's 15 National Historic Landmarks are located at Bethany, the Campbell Mansion and Old Main at Bethany College.

Today there are more than 35 churches representing 21 denominations in Brooke County. St. John's, the first Episcopal church west of the Allegheny Mountains

FAST FACTS ABOUT BROOKE COUNTY

Founded: 1797
Land in square miles: 92.5
Population: 25,447
Percentage minorities: 2.1%
Percentage rural: 42.4%
Median age: 41.2
Percentage 65 and older: 18.3%
Birth rate per 1,000 population: 10.3
Median household income: $32,981
High school graduate or higher: 79.7%
Bachelor's degree or higher: 13.4%
Home ownership: 76.7%
Median home value: $67,000

This information is from the 2000 U.S. Census. In 2000, West Virginia as a whole had 5 percent minorities, a median age of 38.9, median household income of $29,696, and a 75.2 percent home ownership rate.

in what is now West Virginia, was erected on the Follansbee and Eldersville Road in 1793. An 1849 church building serves the congregation today.

For recreation, Brooke Hills Park offers fishing, swimming, golf, picnic shelters, games, and hiking. Castleman Run Lake, Cross Creek, Buffalo Creek, Short Creek, and the Ohio River are all popular with fishermen. Boating, speedboating, and water skiing draw many to the river, which is also a major commercial waterway. There is also the Highland Springs golf course. Community parks offer swimming, soccer, hockey, and other activities.

Brooke County has a long and proud past, with many old family names still represented in the area. Efforts are being made to preserve the past for the future.

A high percentage of the county's structures were constructed in the 1800s, and some are still standing from the 1790s, leading one to believe that those who built here intended to stay for a long time.

See also Bethany College, Greathouse Party Massacre, Wellsburg

Ruby A. Greathouse
Brooke County Historical Society
Phil Conley, *The West Virginia Encyclopedia*, 1929; Carlin F. Dodrill, Celia Vermillion, and William L. Young, *West Virginia Centennial Celebration, 1863–1963, Brooke County*, 1963; J. H. Newton, G. G. Nichols, and A. G. Sprankle, *History of the Pan-Handle; being historical collections of the counties of Ohio, Brooke, Marshall, and Hancock, West Virginia, with illustrations*, 1879.

A. B. Brooks

Alonzo Beecher Brooks, conservationist and nature educator, was born May 6, 1873, at French Creek. He attended local one-room schools, completed a business course at West Virginia Wesleyan College in 1900, and received a bachelor's degree in agriculture at West Virginia University in 1912. He married Nellie R. Coburn on June 22, 1899. Brooks was a surveyor, 1890–1902; for two years assistant clerk of Upshur County; served as forester for the West Virginia Geological Survey, 1910–1911, and for the West Virginia Experiment Station, 1911–1916; a forest pathologist in West Virginia and New York, for the U.S. Department of Agriculture, 1916–1921; and first chief state game warden for West Virginia, 1921–1928.

A. B. Brooks was part of a family of outstanding West Virginia naturalists, including his brothers, Fred and Earle, and nephew, Maurice. He is best remembered for his work as Oglebay Park naturalist, 1928–1942, where he established the Nature Leaders Training School in 1928. He wrote numerous publications related to forestry and natural history, most notably *Forestry and Wood Industries*, 1911, and *West Virginia Trees*, 1920. The Brooks Bird Club was named in his honor; Brooks Hall on WVU's main campus is a tribute to him and his brothers. Brooks returned to French Creek in 1942 and died May 16, 1944.

See also Botany, Maurice Brooks
George H. Breiding
Morgantown

Brooks Bird Club

The Brooks Bird Club, a national organization headquartered in Wheeling, was named to honor A. B. Brooks, the longtime naturalist at Wheeling's Oglebay Park. The club was formed in 1932 by John W. Handlan and a group of like-minded friends. It has published *The Redstart*, a quarterly journal, since 1933. There is a local chapter in Charleston.

The interests of the Brooks Bird Club extend beyond birds to a range of nature subjects. Each June, forays are held at locations in West Virginia where members and students can undertake intensive field studies. Classes and field work are led by club members knowledgeable in various subjects, including birds, fungi, butterflies, geology, wildflowers, trees, grasses, and herptiles.

In the late summer and early fall, club members run the Allegheny Front Migration Observatory, a bird-banding station in Grant County that has been operating for more than 40 years. Over the years the Brooks Bird Club has published a series of notable books, including the *Birding Guide to West Virginia* by James Bullard, *Birds of the Greater Kanawha Valley* by Charles Handley Sr., and *The West Virginia Breeding Bird Atlas* by Albert R. Buckelew Jr. and George A. Hall.

See also Birds, A. B. Brooks
Scott Shalaway
Cameron

Maurice Brooks

Born June 16, 1900, into a French Creek family whose name became synonymous with the study of natural history, Maurice Brooks became West Virginia's greatest naturalist. Father Fred, an entomologist, uncle A. B., the legendary naturalist at Wheeling's Oglebay Park, uncle Earle, and Maurice all devoted their lives to the study of the state's natural heritage.

Maurice Brooks graduated from West Virginia University in 1923 with a B.A. degree and in 1934 with an M.S. For several years he taught biology and English at Upshur County High School in Buckhannon. Then he served WVU as professor of biology from 1932 to 1938 and as professor of wildlife management from 1938 until his retirement in 1969.

Maurice Brooks was the first alumnus to receive an honorary doctorate from WVU. He received four other honorary doctorates and was an elected fellow of the American Ornithologists Union and the American Association for the Advancement of Science. In 1970, he received the Order of Vandalia, the highest honor WVU bestows, and in 1979, the *Charleston Gazette* named him "Man of the Year."

Brooks's legacy includes numerous scholarly publications, many newspaper and magazine articles, and two books, *The Appalachians* (1965) and *The Life of the Mountains* (1967). In the preface to *The Appalachians*, Roger Tory Peterson and John A. Livingston wrote, "To his friends and students he is, indeed, 'Dr. Appalachia.' No one knows these mountains more intimately. Although a professor of wildlife management at West Virginia University he is equally knowledgeable about orchids, salamanders, and wood warblers. He is typical of the new breed of all-round naturalists—in other words, an ecologist." Maurice Brooks died January 10, 1993.

Scott Shalaway
Cameron

Brookside Resort

Preston County resort built in 1880.
See Cathedral State Park.

William T. Brotherton Jr.

Attorney William T. Brotherton Jr. became the top official of two branches of state government—president of the state Senate and chief justice of the West Virginia Supreme Court of Appeals. Born April 17, 1926, to Charleston grocer William T. Brotherton and Kathryn Slack Brotherton, Brotherton received his undergraduate and law degrees from Washington and Lee University in Virginia. He was an assistant prosecuting attorney in Kanawha County for two years before serving in the House of Delegates from 1953 through 1965. His father had also served in the House, three consecutive terms beginning in 1935.

Brotherton was elected to the state Senate in 1964 and served until he was defeated in the 1980 Democratic primary election by Bob Wise, later congressman and governor. Brotherton chaired the judiciary committee of the House (1958–64) and Senate (1968–72) and was appointed to the rare dual role of judiciary chair and majority leader of both the House (1960–64) and Senate (1970–72). He began the 1973 legislative session in the first of four consecutive two-year terms as president of the Senate.

Brotherton defeated incumbent Supreme Court Justice Sam Harshbarger in the 1984 Democratic primary and went on to serve the state's highest court until he retired from the bench in 1995 following a massive heart attack. He was chief justice of the court in 1989 and 1994. Brotheron died April 6, 1997.

Karl C. Lilly III
State Senate

Izetta Jewell Brown

Izetta Jewell Brown, later Izetta Jewell Miller, was born Izetta Jewell Kenny in Hackettstown, New Jersey, November 24, 1883. She came to West Virginia in 1914 as the bride of Congressman William Gay Brown of Kingwood. Already a well-known actress and an activist for women's rights, during her West Virginia years Brown blazed the way for women in politics.

When her husband died in 1916, just three months after the birth of their daughter, she took over management of their Preston County farm and established a modern dairy operation. Active in farm organizations, she attended the first farm women's camp at Jackson's Mill and later served on a committee to improve wool production in the state.

Brown became the first woman to second a presidential nominee in a major party nominating convention as she seconded West Virginian John W. Davis for the Democratic nomination in 1920. She seconded Davis again in his successful quest for the nomination in 1924 and herself received an honorific nomination for vice president. She was the first woman south of the Mason-Dixon line to run for the U.S. Senate, as she battled Matthew Mansfield Neely for the Democratic nomination in 1922 and lost by only 6,000 votes. Brown lost to William E. Chilton in another narrow race in 1924.

In 1925, she married Hugh Miller, dean of the school of engineering at George Washington University. They moved to New York where she ran for Congress in 1930, became the commissioner of public welfare in Schenectady in 1931, and later served as a regional administrator with New Deal relief agencies, occasionally visiting West Virginia.

She died in La Jolla, California, in November 1978.

Jerry Bruce Thomas
Shepherd University

John Brown

Abolitionist John Brown, born May 9, 1800, was as responsible as any one person for the coming of the Civil War. His October 16, 1859, raid on Harpers Ferry galvanized the nation, further alienating North and South and drastically reducing any possible middle ground for compromise.

Unsuccessful at every occupation he had undertaken, by the 1850s Brown had committed himself to the violent abolition of slavery. He took an Old Testament view of his cause, believing that the great sin of human bondage must be purged from the land by the shedding of blood. In May 1856 he and his sons and followers killed five proslavery men in Kansas, and he later lost one of his sons in a similar raid.

At Chatham, Ontario, in 1858, Brown

John Brown, by David Hunter Strother.

met with supporters including Jefferson County native Martin Delany to plan for an armed insurrection of slaves in the South. In early 1859, he established himself and his followers on a Maryland farm near Harpers Ferry and in October carried out his raid on the U.S. arsenal there. Brown's plan was to issue government arms to slaves in the surrounding countryside, thereby enabling them to free themselves.

The raiders easily captured the arsenal and the town of Harpers Ferry, but in their military inexperience failed to capitalize on their initial success. The hoped-for slave uprising never materialized, and Brown's men soon were besieged by local militia and U.S. marines under the leadership of Col. Robert E. Lee. After a last stand in a small fire-engine house, Brown and his surviving followers surrendered. He had lost ten of his 18 men, and himself was wounded. They had killed four people in taking Harpers Ferry, ironically including Heyward Shepherd, a free African-American of the town.

John Brown was tried for murder, treason, and insurrection in the Jefferson County courthouse at Charles Town, convicted November 2, 1859, and hanged there on December 2. Maj. Thomas J. Jackson, later nicknamed "Stonewall," was among those commanding the Virginia forces standing guard at the execution.

Brown was instantly transformed into a demon in the Southern imagination and a martyr in the North. The song "John Brown's Body" was a favorite marching song of Union armies in the ensuing war, and (now with new words as the "Battle Hymn of the Republic") is still one of America's great patriotic songs. John Brown remains controversial a century and a half later, widely viewed as a murderous fanatic in an unquestionably good cause and a pivotal figure in the country's history. Harpers Ferry was made into a National Historic Park (originally Historic Monument) in 1944, and is the most visited historic site in West Virginia.

See also Harpers Ferry

Chauncey H. Browning

Jurist Chauncey Hoyt Browning was a member of the West Virginia Supreme Court of Appeals for the final 19 years of his life. Browning was born at Chauncey, Logan County, May 15, 1903, and graduated from Logan High School in 1920. He taught history and government there in 1924–25. He graduated from West Virginia University in 1924 and then from the WVU law school in 1927. In 1944, he was elected prosecuting attorney in Logan County and reelected in 1948. Browning was appointed state attorney general in February 1952. Five months later, he was appointed to the Supreme Court and later was elected to the unexpired term that ended December 31, 1960. In the election of 1960, he won a full 12-year term to the court. He was chief justice of that court in 1956, 1960, 1965, and 1970, but died of a heart attack still in office, June 24, 1971. His son, Chauncey H. Browning Jr., (b. 1934), was elected state attorney general in 1968 and served until 1985.

Robert Y. Spence
Logan

Meshach Browning

Backwoodsman Meshach Browning was born at Damascus, Maryland, in 1781, but spent most of his life on the Youghiogheny River watershed near Friendsville, Maryland. As a 16-year-old, he traveled to Wheeling and spent time in the bustling Ohio River frontier town before returning to western Maryland.

Browning's fame as a hunter is described in his autobiographical book, *Forty-four Years of the Life of a Hunter,* covering the period 1790–1835. His descriptions of the virgin forests, glades, and wildlife provide invaluable natural history information for western Maryland and neighboring (West) Virginia. He married Mary McMullen or McMilan in 1799 and together they raised 11 children. His book tells of personal trials and triumphs and the social and community events of the post-Revolutionary War era. Stories of living off the land and growing a garden and crops in the wilderness provide important historical perspectives.

Browning, a champion hunter, claimed he killed 2,000 deer, 400 bear, 50 panthers, several wolves, and many other animals to supply meat for his family and to sell for money. He occasionally hunted on Backbone Mountain and in the glades of Virginia, now Preston and Tucker counties, West Virginia.

Meshach Browning, who died in 1859, is buried in a small cemetery near Hoyes, Maryland, beside Maryland Route 42.

William N. Grafton
WVU Extension Service

Browns Island

Browns Island stands in the Ohio River opposite Weirton. It is 250 acres in area and four miles long. It has a rich prehistory and is most noted for the Browns Island Petroglyph, now permanently inundated by the Ohio River, and a small Adena mound. Traders spoke of passing the island on excursions down the Ohio River in 1765. Five years later, George Washington passed by the "long island" and remarked in his journal that it was "not very remarkable for length, breadth, or goodness." Richard Brown, a Revolutionary soldier, acquired the island, which had been part of a land grant awarded to Benjamin Johnston. Brown's family farmed and lived on the island, which was farmed into the 1900s. Everett Ferguson acquired the entire island in 1925 and sold it in 1946 to Weirton Ice and Coal Supply Company, operated by the immigrant entrepreneur, Michael Starvaggi.

In 1957, Weirton Steel purchased Browns Island for $40,000. Families used it for camping and picnics. In the 1970s, Weirton Steel planned to build a coke plant on the island. Prior to construction the island was cleared of vegetation and 57,000 tons of slag was added to provide a level area, 40 feet above the river. On December 15, 1972, as men prepared to make the ovens operational, they noted a gas leak and reported it. Minutes later the basement exploded, killing 19 men and injuring ten others. It was the worst industrial accident in Weirton's history. The accident slowed the start of coking operations, which began in May 1973. The plant stayed in operation for ten years, until coke became cheaper for the steel company to buy than to produce. Today there is a storage plant on the island for Weirton Steel.

See also Weirton, Weirton Steel

Jane Kraina
Weirton

Jane Kraina, "In Time and the River: The Story of Browns Island," *Goldenseal,* Winter 1989; Jack Welch, *History of Hancock County: Virginia and West Virginia,* 1963.

The Bruen Lands Feud

In 1846, the heirs of Matthias Bruen of New York City inherited 200,000 acres of a 1796 Western Virginia land grant, extending through the present counties of Putnam, Kanawha, Jackson, and Roane.

Attempts to manage the Bruen lands resulted in violence and bitterness, upsetting the peace of the area for generations.

The problem originated in the deplorable land records of Virginia, including faulty surveys and overlapping titles. Apparently Bruen land agents had already sold a number of farm sites to northern settlers by 1845. At about the same time, other land agents had also contracted to sell off a nearby tract that bordered on Bruen. They were responsible for a mass migration to Jackson County of families from the Clinch River area of southwestern Virginia. A dispute arose over their land titles that was never entirely settled. Differences were aggravated by conflicting Northern and Southern sympathies during the Civil War and partisan political differences.

Killings were associated with the feud. In 1877, long after the Clinch River settlers had established their Jackson County homesteads, Bruen agents reappeared in the area accompanied by U.S. Deputy Marshal Nathan Cunningham. The settlers were notified that the land they were on was part of the Bruen survey, and they were officially informed that they had only a short time to vacate. The settlers formed an armed vigilante committee, and when the marshal returned to enforce the order he was ambushed, shot, and killed. His brother, Dan Cunningham, also a lawman, then took up the cause and carried it on for many years.

Unconfirmed local tradition states that the vigilantes managed to intimidate their neighbors and local peace officers and attempted to protect their property by forming a Ku Klux Klan group. For years after, whenever an occasional barn burned or someone's livestock broke out, it was usually blamed on the Bruen lands feud.

See also Dan Cunningham

Bill Wintz
St. Albans

Brush Creek Falls

Brush Creek Falls, located in Mercer County ten miles north of Princeton on the Eads Mill Road, is a natural landmark and historic manufacturing site. The spectacular falls, which drop 29 feet, are located in a deep canyon one mile above where Brush Creek flows into the Bluestone River. Jimmy D. Johnson established a water-powered mill at the site about 1880 and built a three-storied structure. An overshot water wheel powered machinery to grind grain and manufacture yarn and woolen blankets. In 1896, George Sturdevant and John W. Johnson purchased the factory, and in 1904 they constructed new buildings with machinery powered by a water-driven turbine. In 1909, their partnership was dissolved, the factory ceased to oper-

ate, and the buildings were torn down. The property has not been commercially developed since then and is now owned by a conservation group.

Michael M. Meador
Abingdon, Virginia

Kyle McCormick, *The Story of Mercer County,* 1957.

Pearl S. Buck

Author Pearl Comfort (Sydenstricker) Buck, the first American woman to receive the Nobel Prize for Literature (1938), was born June 26, 1892, in Hillsboro, Pocahontas County, in the home of her maternal grandparents. This house, now the Pearl S. Buck Birthplace Museum, was for the young girl growing up abroad with her missionary parents "a symbol of security and peace in a world where there was neither security nor peace." It figures prominently in the early chapters of *The Exile,* Buck's fine biography of her mother, which gives a vivid account of life in the Greenbrier Valley in the mid-19th century.

Buck spent much of her childhood in China, where she learned Chinese almost as early as English. She returned to the U.S. in 1910 to attend Randolph-Macon Woman's College, graduating in 1914. She went back to China as a teacher for the Presbyterian Board of Foreign Missions. In 1917, she married another missionary, John Lossing Buck, an agricultural specialist. Her travels with him to Chinese farming villages provided the settings for many of her best novels.

The next decade brought important changes to her life. Buck gave birth to her only biological child, a daughter, Carol, whose mental retardation was a lifelong source of sorrow. Pearl and Lossing enrolled as graduate students at Cornell University, where she earned a master's

Author Pearl S. Buck (1892–1973).

degree in English. She also began submitting writings for publication, in part to earn money to care for Carol and their newly adopted daughter, Janice.

Her literary career was launched with the publication of *East Wind: West Wind* in 1930. The following year brought worldwide acclaim with the appearance of *The Good Earth*, winner of the 1932 Pulitzer Prize. From then until her death, Buck wrote prolifically, publishing more than 100 works of fiction and non-fiction. Her major achievement as a writer was in introducing Asia and its people to readers in Europe and North America, but she wrote on American topics as well.

In 1934, Buck moved permanently to the U.S. She divorced Lossing Buck in 1935 and married her publisher, Richard Walsh, who became her partner in many humanitarian efforts. Together they adopted eight children, several of them of mixed-race, and worked tirelessly to improve Asian-American relations. Buck became well-known as an advocate for civil rights, women's rights, and the needs of the handicapped. Her most lasting humanitarian legacies are Welcome House, the agency she founded in 1949 to oversee adoption of mixed-race children, and the Pearl S. Buck Foundation, established in 1964 to care for Amerasian children in their home countries. Buck died March 6, 1973, in Danby, Vermont.

Buck's ties with her native state remained strong even in the last decade of her life. In *My Mother's House*, a small book written to help raise funds for the Birthplace Museum, she paid tribute to the house her mother had described so lovingly: "For me it was a living heart in the country I knew was my own but which was strange to me until I returned to the house where I was born. For me that house was a gateway to America."

See also Literature

Elizabeth Johnston Lipscomb
Randolph-Macon Woman's College
Pearl S. Buck, *My Mother's House*, 1965; Peter Conn, *Pearl S. Buck: A Cultural Biography*, 1996.

Buckhannon

Buckhannon, the county seat of Upshur County, is located on the Buckhannon River at the juncture of U.S. 33, U.S. 119, and State Route 20. It was established in 1816 and first chartered in 1852. The 2000 population was 5,725. Buckhannon is the home of the West Virginia Strawberry Festival and West Virginia Wesleyan College.

John and Samuel Pringle, deserters from British-American forces at Fort Pitt, settled the area in the mid-1760s. The two brothers lived in a hollow sycamore tree a few miles away from present Buckhannon. The site of the original tree has now been designated Pringle Tree Park, and a hollow sycamore tree, a natural descendant of the Pringles' tree, still stands there today. According to one account,

the Pringle brothers named the Buckhannon River after a Delaware Indian named Buckongehanon or Buckongahelas, and the town was named for the river. However, some historians attribute the origin of the name to a missionary named John Buchanon who explored the area in the late 1700s. A statue of Buckongahelas and his son Mahonegon, erected in 2000, stands in Buckhannon's Jawbone Park.

Buckhannon's major employers include St. Joseph's Hospital, West Virginia Wesleyan College, the Upshur County Board of Education, Union Drilling, and Trus Joist, a wood products manufacturer. The town has one newspaper, the *Record Delta*.

Buckhannon has been home to several notable people including Col. George R. Latham, a member of the U.S. House of Representatives and U.S. consulate to Australia (1867–70); Daniel D. T. Farnsworth, second governor of West Virginia (1869) and member of the West Virginia House of Delegates and Senate; and Laura Jackson Arnold, sister of Confederate Maj. Gen. T. J. "Stonewall" Jackson. Buckhannon is the hometown of writers Stephen Coonts and Jayne Anne Phillips. West Virginia Poet Laureate Irene McKinney teaches at West Virginia Wesleyan.

See also Upshur County

Kim Howard
French Creek
Jim Comstock, *The West Virginia Heritage Encyclopedia*, 1976; W. B. Cutright, *History of Upshur County*, 1977.

Buckhannon Highways Garage

The massive stone highways garage west of Buckhannon, a familiar landmark on U.S. 33, is part of a maintenance complex that covers more than 18 acres. The main structure, constructed of native sandstone, was built in 1941 by prison labor. It is 2,052 feet long with walls four feet thick. The stone is laid on footers 10 feet wide and six feet deep, reinforced with steel rails. Twenty-six thousand cubic yards of cut stone was used in the construction. The masonry work required 51,300 bags of cement, and there are 1,770 cubic yards of concrete in the foundation. It has 70,000 square feet of floor space and a ceiling height of 54 feet. The windows required 50,000 glass blocks. It is heated by radiant floor heat.

The main building is used as a shop to repair large equipment and as a warehouse, which supplies parts and supplies to the 10 districts of the Division of Highways throughout the state. A smaller building, the administration building that houses offices for the director and staff, was also built in 1941. There are five other buildings in the complex, which were built later and are of less importance.

Jack Catalano
Division of Highways

Buckhannon River

The Buckhannon River is the namesake of the city of Buckhannon and the principal waterway of Upshur County. It provides public drinking water for much of Upshur County. Historically, the river provided power for gristmills and river sand for a variety of purposes. The Buckhannon River has always been a source of entertainment and recreation. At the turn of the 20th century, tour boats navigated the river, and swimmers, rafters, boaters, and fisherman still enjoy the stream today.

The Buckhannon River forms near Pickens, from three tributaries known as the Left and Right forks and the Left Fork of Right Fork. The forks converge to form the main river just inside the Upshur County line, and the Buckhannon River then travels north through the Upshur communities of Alton, Sago, Buckhannon, and Hall. Nearly 47 miles long, the Buckhannon River empties into the Tygart Valley River near Carrolton in Barbour County. The elevation at the headwaters of the Buckhannon is 3,750 feet, dropping to 1,310 feet at its mouth. In addition to the Left and Right forks, the main tributaries include Big Sand Run, Fink Run, and French Creek. The river, which begins as a cold-water trout stream in Randolph County and changes to a warm-water stream farther north on its course, is considered by fishermen to be one of the best muskie streams in the state. Bass, walleye, and native brook trout also inhabit its waters.

According to local belief, the river was named after Delaware Indian war leader Buckongahelas (or Buckongehanon).

See also Buckhannon, Buckongahelas

Kim Howard
French Creek

Buckongahelas

Buckongahelas (or Buckongehanon), born about 1725, was a Delaware Indian war leader for whom, some believe, the Buckhannon River was named. Buckongahelas was among the Indian allies of the British during the Revolutionary War, raiding American settlements on the frontier. He was among the Indians who attacked Wheeling during the first siege of Fort Henry in 1777. After the Revolution he moved westward and out of the history of Western Virginia. He signed the Treaty of Greenville (Ohio, 1795); the Fort Wayne Treaty (Indiana, 1803); and Vincennes Treaty (Indiana, 1804). He died in Indiana when he was about 80 years old in May 1805.

According to legend, Buckongahelas had a son named Mahonegon who was killed by Capt. William White in 1773, igniting major Indian hostilities in the Buckhannon area. According to the lore, years later, Buckongahelas avenged his son's death by killing White. A 1927 historical novel, *The Scout of the Buckonge-*

hanon by J. C. McWhorter, depicts the story of Buckongahelas and the early white settlers of the area. A statue of Buckongahelas and his fallen son, crafted by Buckhannon sculptor Ross Straight, was erected in Buckhannon's Jawbone Park in 2000. Roadside historic markers attribute the city's name to the Indian leader.

See also Buckhannon, Buckhannon River

Kim Howard
French Creek

J. C. McWhorter, *The Scout of the Buckongehanon,* 1927; Lucullus Virgil McWhorter, *The Border Settlers of Northwestern Virginia,* 1915.

I. E. Buff

Occupational health crusader Dr. Isadore E. Buff was born in Utica, New York, August 27, 1908. He moved to Charleston with his parents later that year. He graduated from the University of Louisville School of Medicine in 1931.

A cardiologist, Buff was the first physician to complain that the death certificates of coal miners frequently listed the cause of death as a heart attack when he contended that pneumoconiosis—black lung disease—placed such a burden on the heart that it was the precipitating cause. Long before others spoke out, Buff was thundering that half of the state's 40,000 coal miners had black lung and were being denied workers' compensation. Early on, the *Charleston Gazette* chastised him editorially. Then he took on the United Mine Workers for failing to include any coverage of lung disease in their contract.

In the late 1960s, Buff was joined by Drs. Donald L. Rasmussen and Hawey A. Wells Jr. in organizing a series of coalfield rallies. Buff, an accomplished showman, was the star performer. He was one of the key forces behind liberalizing the state workers' compensation law to cover pneumoconiosis and the Federal Coal Mine Health and Safety Act of 1969, which put a ceiling on the amount of coal dust allowed in the mines and provided compensation for black lung victims. Buff died in Charleston, March 14, 1974.

See also Black Lung Movement

Ken Hechler
Charleston

Buffalo Academy

The Buffalo Academy, located at Buffalo, Putnam County, was founded in 1849 by a company of local citizens. The two-story, four-room building in the Greek Revival style was built from bricks made on the site. George Rossetter, later president of Marietta College, was the first principal.

Buffalo Academy offered a liberal education in the classics and ancient and modern languages, as well as science, literature, and religion. The school drew students from up and down the Ohio and Kanawha valleys. It flourished until the Civil War, when many of the young men entered the service. The school was closed and the building was used by both armies as a headquarters, barracks, and at times a hospital. After the war, Buffalo Academy required extensive repairs before the school could be reopened. During the 1920s, it was incorporated into the county school system and later served as part of Buffalo High School until 1952.

The empty building remained in a state of disrepair until the Buffalo Historical Society formed in 1989, for the purpose of restoring it. Today the Buffalo Academy is on the National Register of Historic Places with neighboring buildings as part of the Buffalo Town Square Historic District.

Bill Wintz
St. Albans

Buffalo Archeological Site

The Buffalo archeological site is located on the east bank of the Kanawha River near the town of Buffalo, Putnam County. The site is listed on the National Register of Historic Places. It encompasses at least four time periods in one Late Archaic village (4000–1000 B.C.), one Middle Woodland village (A.D. 390–530), and at least two overlapping Fort Ancient villages (A.D. 1300–1600).

After many years of amateur archeological activity, systematic excavations were conducted between 1963 and 1965 by Edward V. McMichael, an archeologist with the West Virginia Geological and Economic Survey. The excavations revealed at least two overlapping oval stockades of the Fort Ancient period, with more than 40 houses surrounding a central plaza. Approximately 15 percent of the site was excavated, uncovering 562 burials and tens of thousands of ceramic, stone, shell, and bone artifacts.

The predominant burial orientation (84 percent) was with the head to the east; 53 percent of those buried were lying flat on their backs; and 71 percent of the burials were located within houses. Children and young adults were most likely to be buried with ceremonial grave goods, but unlike Ohio Fort Ancient sites none of the burials at Buffalo had complete pots as grave offerings. Several exotic marine shell gorgets, such as the Buffalo Mask, indicate contact with Mississippian peoples in the Southeast. The presence of copper artifacts, glass trade beads, and extended burials places the latest village within the Protohistoric period, about A.D. 1600.

The Late Archaic component of the Buffalo site represented the remains of a temporary campsite consisting of several shallow fire, cooking, and refuse pits, and flint processing areas. Study of the Buffalo archeological site resulted in the identification of two new projectile point types, Buffalo Expanding Stem and Buffalo Straight Stem.

See also Archeology, Buffalo Mask

Darla S. Hoffman
Cultural Resource Analysts

Buffalo Creek Flood

One of the country's worst mining-related disasters occurred February 26, 1972, on Buffalo Creek in Logan County. At approximately 8 a.m., a coal waste dam collapsed on the Middle Fork of Buffalo Creek, releasing 132 million gallons of water, coal refuse, and silt into the narrow mountain valley. Within two minutes, the black wave plowed downstream into two other coal waste dams and a burning coal refuse pile. In the next three hours, the rampaging water demolished or partially destroyed the 17 communities downstream. Saunders was hit first, followed by Pardee, Lorado, Craneco, Lundale, Stowe, Crites, Latrobe, Robinette, Amherstdale, Becco, Fanco, Riley, Braeholm, Accoville, Crown, and Kistler.

In the end, 125 people, including entire families, were killed; 1,000 people were injured; 507 houses and 44 mobile homes were destroyed, 273 houses were severely damaged, and 663 houses were partially damaged; and 4,000 of the 5,000 residents of Buffalo Creek were left homeless. Residents of the closely knit coal towns were dispersed. Some eventually rebuilt, but others never returned. Some communities vanished.

Buffalo Mining Company, a division of the Pittston Company, owned and operated the three coal waste dams. The dams were constructed to hold coal waste and water from the company's coal preparation plant on Buffalo Creek, about one-half mile north of Saunders.

At the time, the state Public Service Commission was responsible for overseeing impoundments that blocked streams. A state investigation found that neither Pittston nor the previous owner that had built a dam on Middle Fork had submitted dam construction plans to the PSC for approval. For years, Buffalo Creek residents had been concerned about whether the dams posed a danger to them. Surveys and inspections by officials from the U.S. Geological Survey and the state Department of Natural Resources had concluded that the dams might be susceptible to washouts.

After the flood, state and federal investigations found that the flood was caused by improper construction of the coal waste dams. The Governor's Ad Hoc Commission of Inquiry found that "The Pittston Company, through its officials, has shown flagrant disregard for the safety of residents of Buffalo Creek and other persons who live near coal-refuse impoundments." Pittston officials blamed the flood on the

After the Buffalo Creek flood.

3.7 inches of rain that fell in the three days before February 26, and called the disaster "an act of God."

After the flood, 645 survivors and family members of flood victims filed suit against Pittston. In 1974, the suit was settled for $13.5 million, an average of $13,000 for each plaintiff after legal fees. The state of West Virginia also filed suit against Pittston, asking for $100 million to compensate it for damage to state property and losses to residents. In 1977, Governor Moore accepted a $1 million settlement in the suit. In 1988, after years of legal procedures, the state was forced to reimburse $9.5 million to the U.S. Army Corps of Engineers for flood recovery work.

The Buffalo Creek Flood prompted Congress and the West Virginia legislature to pass new laws regulating dam construction and maintenance.

Nancy Ray Adams
Pine Mountain Settlement School
Kai T. Erikson, *Everything in its Path*, 1976; "The Buffalo Creek Flood and Disaster," *Official Report from the Governor's Ad Hoc Commission of Inquiry*, August 1972.

Buffalo Creek & Gauley Railroad

The Buffalo Creek & Gauley Railroad was built in 1904 from Widen to Dundon, Clay County, where it connected to the Coal & Coke Railroad (later B&O). The railroad's owner, Elk River Coal & Lumber Company, operated a mine at Widen. In 1916, the company built a sawmill at Swandale, and a logging railroad to serve it. The organizations were part of the Clay County empire of legendary industrialist J. G. Bradley.

By the early 1960s, the Buffalo Creek & Gauley was well known for its all-steam operations, rare by that time. The company was sold to Clinchfield Coal Company in 1958, the sawmill to Georgia-Pacific in 1963, and the steam locomo-

tives were retired. Since the Widen mine closed, the railroad has been used intermittently, most recently as part of the coal-hauling Elk River Railroad in the late 1990s. Five of the Buffalo Creek & Gauley steam locomotives are preserved, but none are in West Virginia.

George Deike
Cass

Buffalo Lake

Located eight miles south of Clarksburg, in Harrison County, 55-acre Buffalo Lake is the centerpiece of the Buffalo Lake Recreation Area. The 600-acre recreational area is open during the day for fishing, boating, and picnicking. In 1955, the town of Clarksburg constructed the lake to serve as a backup reservoir to its municipal water supply. The lake, fed by Buffalo Creek and natural springs, was never used for Clarksburg's water supply. In 1958, the Clarksburg Park Board developed the lake into a public recreation area.

Buffalo Lake is stocked with channel catfish and three types of trout. Paddle boats and aqua cycles are available for use on the lake. On the surrounding grounds are picnic tables and a shelter. In 1998, the lake was closed for swimming because Canada geese were fouling the water.

Buffalo Mask

The Buffalo Mask, from the Buffalo prehistoric site in Putnam County, is one of the most famous examples of engraved marine shell gorgets found in West Virginia. Marine shell gorgets were produced throughout the Southeast from about A.D. 1000 until the 1600s. Many found their way into neighboring regions through trade or intermarriage. In West Virginia, more than 60 marine shell gorgets have been found at late prehistoric

or near-historic villages of the Fort Ancient culture.

A gorget is an ornament of stone, shell, or metal strung on a leather cord and hung around the neck or gorge. Most marine shell gorgets were made from whelk shells found only along the Gulf and Atlantic coasts. A shell was cut into the rough form, the edges smoothed, and the surface engraved. Mask gorgets, bearing the features of a face, were always engraved on the convex, outer surface of the shell, while round gorgets were engraved on the concave, inner surface.

Many styles of gorgets were made throughout the Southeast. Most of the designs found on marine shell gorgets reflect elements in the mythology of historic Indian groups such as the Creek, Choctaw, and Cherokee. In West Virginia, the most commonly found styles are the mask gorget and the round rattlesnake gorget. The rattlesnake gorget was traditionally associated with women and children. Mask gorgets were traditionally associated with males and children. The "weeping eye" motif found on some mask gorgets is thought to represent tears, or the markings of a bird of prey, or Thunderbird.

See also Archeology, Buffalo Archeological Site, Prehistoric People

Darla S. Hoffman
Cultural Resource Analysts
Janet G. Brashler and Ron W. Moxley, "Late Prehistoric Engraved Shell Gorgets of West Virginia," *West Virginia Archeologist,* Spring 1990; Darla S. Hoffman, "From the Southeast to Fort Ancient: A Survey of Shell Gorgets in West Virginia," *West Virginia Archeologist,* Spring and Fall 1997.

Buffington Island

Buffington Island is situated in the Ohio River near Ravenswood. Its first inhabitants, prehistoric Indians, favored the island for its unusually high elevation above the river. It first appeared in written records in the late 1700s under the name Amberson Island, probably from an association with the squatter John Amberson (or Emerson), whose attempts to establish a government for local settlers were ended by the use of American troops in 1785. The island's permanent name derives from its first resident owner, Joel Buffington. In 1797, Buffington purchased the island, which is 150 acres and one and a half miles long. Tradition holds that the island was an Underground Railroad station.

During the Civil War, Confederate Gen. John Hunt Morgan's daring 1863 raid across Indiana and Ohio came to an end at Buffington Island. To escape back across the Ohio, Morgan chose nearby Buffington's Ford, one of the river's finest crossings. Overtaken there by federal troops, local militia, and three U.S. Navy gunboats, on July 19 he turned and fought his pursuers on the Ohio mainland adjacent to the island. The Battle of Buffington Island scattered Morgan's forces and spilled over onto the island when a number of his men crossed its head to reach the ford leading to the West Virginia shore. The deployment of the gunboats was the only naval action involving hostile fire ever to take place in West Virginia waters.

Buffington Island also served as the base of operations for the last of the Ohio River pirates, John Lockwood. He robbed vessels wrecked or stranded on the island's treacherous shoals, a practice that ended in 1863 when he was arrested for murder. Buffington Island's subsequent history has been quieter. Mostly it has been used for farming. During the late 19th and early 20th centuries, it was a popular picnic spot, and it entered the news in the late 1970s as one of four islands briefly misplaced into Ohio by a U.S. Geological Survey map. In 1993, Buffington Island's preservation, long threatened by sand and gravel dredgers, was assured when it became part of the Ohio River Islands National Wildlife Refuge.

See also Ohio River Islands National Wildlife Refuge

Ray Swick
Blennerhassett Island State Park
Myron J. Smith Jr., "Gunboats at Buffington: The U.S. Navy and Morgan's Raid, 1863," *West Virginia History,* Winter 1983.

The Bull Moose Special

The Bull Moose Special was an armored train deployed by the coal operators during the Paint Creek-Cabin Creek Strike of 1912–14. The train's name derived from the fact that the men who commissioned it were tied to the Progressive Party of West Virginia, nicknamed the Bull Moose Party after the national party's presidential candidate, Theodore Roosevelt. Outfitted at the C&O Railroad shops in Huntington, the train originally consisted of a locomotive, a passenger car, and an iron-plated baggage car equipped with two machine guns. The Special operated during the fall and winter of 1912, escorting other trains hauling nonunion workers into the strike district. Its most notorious trip came in February 1913, when the train was used to attack a tent colony of strikers at the Paint Creek community of Holly Grove.

The attack was triggered on February 7 when strikers from Holly Grove fired on a company ambulance and attacked the store at nearby Mucklow. Later that night, Kanawha County Sheriff Bonner Hill, Paint Creek coal operator Quinn Morton, a number of deputies, mine guards, and C&O Railway police boarded the Bull Moose Special armed with arrest warrants for unnamed persons. As the darkened train approached Holly Grove, two blasts from the engine's whistle ap-

parently signaled the beginning of machine gun and rifle fire from the Bull Moose Special into the tents of sleeping miners and their families. Several people were wounded, but only one striker, Cesco Estep, was killed. Estep was trying to get his son and pregnant wife to safety. In revenge, the enraged strikers attacked the mine guards' camp at Mucklow two days later.

See also Mine Wars, Paint Creek-Cabin Creek Strike

Fred A. Barkey
Marshall University Graduate College

Bulltown

Bulltown was named for Captain Bull, a Delaware Indian chief who settled there on the banks of the Little Kanawha River in the summer or fall of 1765 with five families of relatives to escape the warfare afflicting other frontier areas. The Bulltown Indians made salt from nearby salt springs and traded this commodity to white settlers. They remained on friendly terms with the whites until 1772, when the Adam Stroud family was killed at the mouth of Stroud Creek, on the nearby Gauley River. While Shawnee from Ohio probably killed the Strouds, local whites accused the Bulltown Indians and, in retaliation, massacred them. If Captain Bull escaped, he may have been killed in 1781 by other white fighters, or he may have lived until the 1790s.

Bulltown later developed into a local industrial center as a white community, with gristmills by the 1820s and prosperous saltworks by the 1830s. Salt was carried to larger towns to be traded or sold. There was a tannery by 1850, using the abundant salt and water. During the Civil War, Union and Confederate troops occupied Bulltown from June 1861 until April 1865 because the Weston & Gauley Bridge Turnpike crossed the Little Kanawha River on a covered bridge at this site. The Battle of Bulltown took place on October 1–3, 1863. Guerrilla units also fought around Bulltown.

The U.S. Army Corps of Engineers now owns Bulltown as part of its Burnsville Reservoir and manages it as the Bulltown Historic Area.

See also Captain Bull

Barbara J. Howe
West Virginia University

Lew Burdette

Pitcher Selva Lewis "Lew" Burdette Jr., an outstanding major league baseball player who spent most of his career with the Milwaukee Braves, was born November 22, 1926, in Nitro, near Charleston. An excellent football and basketball player at Nitro High School, Burdette did not play baseball because the school did not have a team. He learned to pitch in 1944 with the American Viscose Rayon Company team the summer after his high

Pitcher Lew Burdette (1926–).

school graduation. Burdette signed his first professional contract with the New York Yankees in 1946, but did not become a regular until 1952 as a member of the Boston Braves. In 1949, he married Mary Ann Shelton, a Charleston telephone operator.

Burdette at six feet and 180 pounds was a control pitcher. His best years were with the Milwaukee Braves from 1957 through 1961, when he won from 17 to 21 games each season and led the National League in a number of categories. In 1957, Burdette had a 17-9 win loss record and won three games in the World Series to lead the Braves to victory over the Yankees, four games to three. Following the World Series he returned to Nitro on October 4 for "Lew Burdette Day." He won 20 games in 1958 and 21 games in 1959. Burdette led the league in wins in 1959, and in strikeouts from 1959 to 1961.

The last stop in Burdette's baseball career was with the California Angels in 1967. In 18 major league seasons, he had won 203 games and lost 144. When he retired from baseball he worked in developing cable television in Florida where he has lived since 1954.

C. Robert Barnett
Marshall University
The Baseball Encyclopedia, 10th ed., 1996; David Driver, "The Pride of Nitro," *Goldenseal,* Fall 1998; Jack R. Stanton, "Lew Burdette," in David Porter, ed., *The Biographical Dictionary of American Sports: Baseball,* 1999.

Burial Customs

The bodies of the earliest settlers were buried wherever and whenever needed, often with little ceremony and sometimes under duress. Graves were often unmarked or poorly marked, perhaps even disguised because of possible Indian desecration. Regular burial customs were established as the settlements matured.

The earliest burial containers were

hollowed-out logs, followed by simple coffins made at home or by a local craftsman. Coffins were often constructed ahead of time, but graves were not dug until just before the burying. Graves were commonly dug by volunteers, especially in the family graveyards and country church yards that dot the West Virginia countryside. This custom still survives in rural areas, long after commercial undertakers have taken over other parts of the burial ritual. In early times, men built the coffin and dug the grave. Women washed and clothed the body, lined the coffin, cleaned the home, and prepared food for the wake. Planks, tables, or even ironing boards were used as cooling boards.

Wakes were common, during which family and neighbors sat with the body until the burial. Care was taken to ward off bugs and rats and cats, the latter believed capable of stealing the soul of the dead. Early hours of the wake were typified by the wailing and weeping of attending females. After cameras were available, photos were taken of the deceased lying in the coffin, often surrounded by family members. Although Irish families provided their dead with loose-fitting shrouds, most mountain people were buried in their own best clothing.

In warm weather, camphor was used plentifully as a preservative and deodorant. Weights of various kinds were placed on the corpse to keep it from swelling, and eyelids were commonly weighted with coins. Burial took place as soon as possible, especially in summer. During the winter the corpse might be kept in a homemade coffin in a barn or other outbuilding until the ground thawed. Often bodies were buried but the funeral postponed until later, when a minister was available. Because many preachers traveled extensive territories, "funeralizing" might be held only once a year, preferably on Memorial Day and often in the graveyard rather than the church. The service or "sarvis" tree was so named because its blooms appeared in late spring, in time to decorate these funeral services.

Wealthy families sent out black-edged invitations to the wake and funeral. Mourning or prayer cards, still in fashion in many parts of rural Appalachia, were distributed at the wake or the funeral. These cards often included a photo of the deceased along with favorite quotations or verses of Scripture. Mourning jewelry, such as a locket enclosing photos or a lock of hair, might be worn by family members and close friends. Hair albums and graveyard quilts were not uncommon and are still prepared by traditionalists.

Modern interpretations of old traditions may be found in such practices as newspaper memorial photos and verbal tributes. Family cemeteries may be seen in countless West Virginia locations, many of them still used for burials. Others have fallen into disuse as families have separated and land has changed ownership. Traditional customs have been replaced piecemeal, as modern funeral directors have taken over more and more of the old rituals. By the middle of the 20th century, corpses were commonly prepared for burial at the funeral home but they were still returned to the family home for a traditional wake. By century's end, short "visitations" at funeral parlors had replaced wakes and the funeral was held there or at a church, as burial rituals became increasingly abbreviated and impersonal.

See also Cemeteries

Barbara Smith
Philippi

James K. Crissman, *Death and Dying in Central Appalachia*, 1994.

Burning Springs

The Burning Springs were located on the eastern side of the Kanawha River eight and a half miles above the mouth of Elk River. These springs were discovered in 1773 by Capt. Matthew Arbuckle, the Reverend J. Alderson, and John and Peter Van Bibber. The springs were included in a 1775 survey of 250 acres for Generals George Washington and Andrew Lewis in consideration of military service performed by Washington. Washington in his will states the tract was taken up "for and on account of a bituminous spring which it contains, of so inflammable a nature as to burn as freely as spirits, and is nearly as difficult to extinguish."

Actually there were three such springs, one near the edge of the river and the other two a few hundred feet away. They were not true springs but simply holes in the ground, which filled with rainwater and through which issued a jet of natural gas, giving the water the appearance of boiling. When lighted they burned with a bright flame until extinguished by high wind. During summer they were entirely dry at times.

In 1841, William Tompkins, in drilling a salt well a short distance above the Burning Springs, struck a large flow of gas at nearly 1,000 feet. This gas was subsequently employed in lifting the saltwater to the furnaces, illuminating the works at night, and in boiling the brine. Tompkins was credited with being the first person in America to use natural gas for manufacturing. Other saltmakers soon followed.

Today no trace remains of these springs, and the exact location is unknown. There is another Burning Springs in Wirt County, associated with the early oil industry.

Gerald S. Ratliff
Charleston

Roy Bird Cook, "The Burning Springs Land," *Washington's Western Lands*, 1930.

Burning Springs Oil Field

The oil and gas industry in West Virginia originated at Burning Springs, located in Wirt County on the Little Kanawha River upstream from Elizabeth. The community's name was derived from two springs from which natural gas escaped and sometimes burned. William Palmer Rathbone began purchasing land here in 1840, eventually gaining more than 10,000 acres. The following year he arrived in Burning Springs with his sons. The Rathbones collected oil from the surface of the river and sold it as an elixir known as "rock oil." They also began drilling for salt brine, but found the brine contaminated by oil.

After the first oil-producing well was drilled in Pennsylvania in 1859, Samuel D. Karnes leased the brine well from Cass Rathbone and began pumping seven barrels of oil from the ground daily. The Rathbones followed suit, drilling just below the mouth of Burning Springs Run. In July 1860, they struck oil and began producing 100 barrels a day. Their next two wells each produced more than 600 barrels daily. The discovery drew thousands of people to Burning Springs, turning it into "a Sodom of sin, anointed with oil." Lighting in the town was provided by the abundant natural gas from the wells. The oil was shipped to a refinery in Parkersburg constructed by Johnson Camden.

The Burning Springs field was one of two producing oil fields in the world at the outset of the Civil War. In May 1863, Gen. William E. Jones raided Burning Springs and set fire to the oil field. An estimated 150,000 barrels of oil was burned, turning the Little Kanawha into a "sheet of fire." Production resumed a year later, and after the war hundreds of wells were drilled in the area. The oil industry declined rapidly in the Burning Springs area in the latter part of the century. A park was opened at Burning Springs in 2004. Oil is occasionally pumped from the Rathbone well for souvenirs.

See also Natural Gas and Petroleum, Rathbone Wells

Joe Geiger
Huntington

Howard B. Lee, *The Burning Springs and Other Tales of the Little Kanawha,* 1968; Louis Reed, "Conflict and Error in the History of Oil," *West Virginia History,* October 1963.

Burning Springs Raid

In April and May 1863, Confederate Generals William E. Jones and John D. Imboden conducted an extensive raid into West Virginia. Their plan called for destruction of all railroad bridges and trestles of the Baltimore & Ohio Railroad between Oakland, Maryland, and Grafton. They also hoped to recruit men for their army and possibly influence the May elections. Following skirmishes at Beverly, Buckhannon, Oakland, Morgantown, and Fairmont, the raiders arrived on May 9 at Burning Springs, Wirt County. There they set fire to 150,000 barrels of oil, oil tanks, engines for pumping, engine houses, wagons, and oil-laden boats. The boats exploded, sending burning oil down the Little Kanawha River until the stream became a sheet of flame with massive clouds of dense, jet-black smoke filling the air. This fiery sight was described by General Jones as a "scene of magnificence that might well carry joy to every patriotic heart."

The Confederate raiders returned to their camp in Rockingham County, Virginia, having largely accomplished their mission. Their combined forces lost 12 killed, 45 wounded, and 26 captured. Federal casualties were estimated at 25 killed, 75 wounded, and 700 taken prisoner.

See also Jones-Imboden Raid

Tim McKinney
Fayetteville

Burnsville

Burnsville is located at the confluence of the Little Kanawha River with Salt Lick Creek and Oil Creek, in Braxton County. Originally called Lumberport, the town was founded in 1830 because of the readily available river transport and abundant timber resources in the surrounding area. Capt. John M. Burns established a sawmill there shortly after the end of the Civil War, in 1866. Later industries included the manufacture of wagons by a group including Fidler, Bodkins, and others, and a veneer mill.

The town prospered until the relocation of the lumber mill to Wirt County in 1899. The West Virginia & Pittsburgh Railroad came through in 1892. It was intersected by the Coal & Coke Railroad in 1906, making Burnsville a railroad junction town. Paddlewheel riverboats traveled the Little Kanawha River to Burnsville until 1931. At the turn of the century, oil and natural gas production became the dominant economic activity, and two gas compressing stations were built. Burnsville, although long established as a community, was not incorporated until 1902.

From 1891 to 1905, the Burnsville Academy operated in the town, a private "normal" or teacher-training school offering a classical education. Burnsville had a combined grade school and high school from 1920 until the last class graduated from Burnsville High School in 1969. Today loyal high school alumni meet in this old facility, now housing only a grade school, for an annual reunion.

Burnsville is located at the junction of Interstate 79 and State Route 5, just west of Burnsville Lake. The town flooded many times before the completion of the dam in 1978.

Harry V. Wiant Jr.
Morgantown

Burnsville Dam

Burnsville Dam is located on the Little Kanawha River about three miles upstream from the Braxton County town of Burnsville, and 124 miles above the river's confluence with the Ohio River at Parkersburg. The earthen and concrete dam is 90 feet high and 1,400 feet across the top. It was placed in operation in December 1978. It controls a drainage area of 165 square miles, and creates a lake of 968 surface acres at summer pool stage. The average depth of the lake is 20 to 25 feet.

As with most large U.S. Army Corps of Engineers reservoirs, Burnsville's purposes are flood control, flow augmentation, and recreation. A minimum flow of 20 cubic feet per second is maintained from the dam's five sluice gates and three low-flow gates.

Burnsville Lake is drawn down only 13 feet in wintertime, compared to 27 to 30 feet at neighboring Sutton Lake, which controls a larger drainage area. Burnsville has never exceeded 52 percent of its storage capacity. That figure was reached during the largest flood on record, on August 1, 1996.

The pastoral setting at Burnsville Dam and Lake leads to high recreational use. Campgrounds include Riffle Run near the dam, and Bulltown on the upper end of the lake. There are five boat-launch ramps at the lake. The Bulltown Historic Area, which is part of the reservoir complex, includes structures dating back to the mid- to late-1800s, a Civil War battlefield, and a visitors center. A cooperative study by the Corps of Engineers and the West Virginia University School of Forestry is mapping a plan for future operation and management of the historic area. The 12,256-acre Burnsville Lake Wildlife Management Area provides excellent hunting. The area includes a large network of popular hiking trails.

Skip Johnson
Sutton

Burr Conspiracy

The Burr Conspiracy, possibly a secessionist scheme, brought the nation's attention to the Western Virginia frontier early in the 19th century. The episode was fueled by Ohio Valley settlers' anger at being denied navigational access to the Mississippi River and by the frustrations of an ambitious politician. Col. Aaron Burr, vice president (1801–05) of the United States, had killed Alexander Hamilton in a duel in 1804 and fallen into disgrace. In 1805, Burr attempted to resuscitate his career by parlaying western sectional discontent into a military expedition into the Southwest. He traveled through the Ohio and Mississippi valleys to formulate his plans. During the trip, he met Harman Blennerhassett, a wealthy Irish expatriate living on an Ohio River island near present Parkersburg. Blennerhassett became one of Burr's financial backers and allowed his estate to serve as a base of operation.

Burr's plans unraveled in 1807 with his arrest while leading followers down the Mississippi. Despite the fact that his subsequent treason trial ended in acquittal, historians have remained divided as to the conspiracy's objectives. Was it a treasonous attempt to separate the West from the United States, a private military expedition against the Spanish-ruled Southwest, or, as Burr's defenders claimed, a peaceable attempt to settle western lands? The truth, obscured by the destruction of Burr's papers, probably will never be known.

The Burr conspiracy's enduring legal legacy was its clarification of the definition of treason in American law. President Jefferson, perhaps partly motivated by personal animosity, relentlessly prosecuted Burr. Chief Justice John Marshall's ruling in the Fourth Circuit federal court case, *U.S. v. Burr*, found that treason required overt action, rather than mere intention or even conspiracy, and that Burr had not crossed that line. The impact on the Blennerhassetts was ruinous, forcing them to flee their island home and ending a romantic episode of Ohio Valley history.

See also Harman Blennerhassett, Blennerhassett Island

Ray Swick
Blennerhassett Island State Park

Milton Lomask, *Aaron Burr—The Conspiracy and Years of Exile 1805–1836,* 1982.; Jean Edward Smith, *John Marshall: Definer of a Nation,* 1996.

Peter Burr House

The Peter Burr House near Bardane in Jefferson County is an eight-room, two-story log, beam, and board building. This National Register of Historic Places site is one of fewer than a dozen structures in Jefferson County that survive from before 1760. It was constructed by Peter Burr, a prosperous Connecticut farmer, and occupied by his son, Peter II. Father and son were members of the prominent family that included Aaron Burr.

Constructed about 1751, the house is an extremely rare example of a very early family homestead and is considered to be the oldest standing wood frame structure in West Virginia. The methods used in the construction of the house are typical of those used in small family homes of this period, particularly in Burr's native New England. These methods have their origins in yeoman home construction of the Elizabethan period in England.

The exterior of the Peter Burr House is of hand-riven clapboard. It uses heavy log uprights and beams, and the exposed parts are neatly finished. The outside walls are lined between the log beams with brick and mortar and then plastered. The chairboard, which is joined together with wooden pins, has a hand-trimmed beading around the edge. The flooring consists of smooth, wide boards, and these are nailed with wrought iron nails, as are the clapboard weatherboards.

William D. Theriault
Bakerton

Bushwhackers

In West Virginia, some took advantage of the Civil War to settle personal grievances or pursue personal gain or other non-military ends. They were called bushwhackers from their habit of ambushing or "bushwhacking" their adversaries from under cover. Usually they claimed to be attached to one side in the struggle, often the South. Early in the war, the Confederate Congress authorized the formation of partisan ranger companies, and the state of West Virginia formed Unionist militia companies. These groups, while technically authorized by the appropriate civil government, frequently operated independently of any formal military command. The Partisan Ranger Law passed by the Confederate Congress was later repealed when regular officers including Robert E. Lee complained that they siphoned off men and that they failed to carry out strategic military plans in favor of seeking loot and glory. On one occasion, Lee described the partisans as "a band of thieves, stealing, pillaging, plundering and doing every manner of mischief and crime."

For example, the Moccasin Rangers terrorized residents in Calhoun County. Boyd Stutler, West Virginia's Civil War historian, wrote that the Rangers "had a certain nuisance value . . . but generally were not a credit to the Confederate cause. It was a great time to pay off old scores, and many of the acts of the Rangers were more personal than political." In Roane County, opposing bands of Northern and Southern sympathizers committed atrocities that resulted in a feud that continued into the 1880s. These so-called Roane County Land Wars or Bruen Land Wars were carried over from murders and attacks perpetrated during the war.

The worst partisan actions seemed to have been in areas where sympathies were divided rather than in those where either the Northern or Southern views predominated. At least one group in southern West Virginia appears to have escaped being cast in the same mold as their disrespectable comrades elsewhere. Capt. W. D. Thurmond organized a company of partisan rangers in Monroe County. The company served throughout the war, occasionally attaching itself to larger Confederate units for service in the New River Gorge and in the Greenbrier Valley. On the other hand, Anderson Hatfield's "Wildcats" in Logan County engaged in acts that some historians attribute to fostering hatreds leading to the Hatfield-McCoy feud.

See also Bruen Lands Feud, Hatfield-McCoy Feud, Moccasin Rangers, Thurmond's Rangers

Kenneth R. Bailey
WVU Institute of Technology

Butterflies

Butterflies, belonging to the second-largest insect order Lepidoptera, are brightly colored, diurnal insects with four scaled wings, two clubbed antennae, and three pairs of legs. Of the nearly 15,000 species of butterflies occurring worldwide, 130 species are represented in West Virginia. Because of its physiography and geographic position in the eastern United States, West Virginia hosts a rich diversity of plant life including many southern and northern species that reach the limits of their range here. Since most butterflies prefer habitats that produce an abundance of their host plants, the diverse flora of West Virginia supports butterflies typical of both northern and southern regions. In addition to being restricted to the immediate area of their host plants, many butterflies are also limited to specific habitat types and microclimates.

Within the order Lepidoptera, butterflies are divided into two superfamilies: the true butterflies (Papilionoidea) and the skippers (Hesperioidea). The less brightly colored skippers are distinguished from the true butterflies by their smaller size, large heads, stout bodies, and rapid flight. Of the ten families of true butterflies, five occur in West Virginia. These include the swallowtails (Papilionidae); whites and sulphurs (Pieridae); harvester, coppers, hairstreaks, and blues (Lycaenidae); metalmarks (Riodinidae); and the brushfoots (Nymphalidae). Hesperidae, one of the two families of skippers, also occurs in the state. Each family is further divided into a number of subfamilies, genera, and species.

Butterflies go through four stages of development: egg, caterpillar, chrysalis, and adult. Most butterflies will reach the adult stage from the egg in about four weeks unless the process is broken by hibernation or diapause. Females deposit the small, hard-shelled eggs on or close to the host plant. Most caterpillars hatch within a few days, chewing their way out of the egg. Feeding on the leaves, buds, or fruit of their host plants, caterpillars molt periodically over a period of approximately four weeks until growth is completed. With the last molt the caterpillar is enclosed in a hard-shelled chrysalis. The chrysalis is a transition stage, with some species remaining enclosed for almost a year while others emerge as adults within several days. Depending upon the species, adult butterflies may

The Monarch, West Virginia's state butterfly.

live from only a few days to almost a year, feeding, seeking mates, and reproducing. The longer-lived butterflies usually hibernate or migrate. The well-known Monarch, West Virginia's state butterfly, follows an annual migration route from the Mountain State to Central Mexico.

Abundant almost everywhere, and feeding as a group on an enormous variety of plants, Lepidoptera can be of great ecological and economic importance. Their larvae transform millions of tons of plant matter into animal matter and wastes that can be eaten by other animals or eventually recycled back into plant nutrients. Unlike such other members of Lepidoptera as the gypsy moth, butterflies are usually small in number and do not impose serious impacts on the flora of the state. They serve an important role as food sources for other invertebrates, birds, and other animals, and flower-visiting adults are second only to bees in the cross-pollination of many flowering plants.

See also Insects

Thomas J. Allen
Division of Natural Resources
Thomas J. Allen, *The Butterflies of West Virginia and their Caterpillars*, 1997.

Betsy Byars

Author Betsy Byars, Newbery Medal winner and author of more than 50 books for children and youth, was born August 7, 1928, in Charlotte, North Carolina. She graduated from Queens College in Charlotte, 1950, and currently lives in South Carolina. Much of her most productive work was done in West Virginia.

Byars's first book, *Clementine* (1962), and 15 others were written while she lived in Morgantown, from 1960 to 1980. Her husband, Edward Byars, was chairman of the mechanical engineering department at West Virginia University. Byars has received numerous distinguished awards for books set in West Virginia, including the Newbery Medal, 1971, for *The Summer of the Swans*; the New York Times Outstanding Book of the Year, 1979, for *Goodbye, Chicken Little*; and the American Library Association Notable Book award for *After the Goatman*, 1974. *The House of Wings*, for which she received the 1974 ALA Notable Book award, is set in Ohio.

Sharon Diaz
Harrison County Schools

Harry F. Byrd

U.S. Senator Harry Flood Byrd, the pivotal figure of 20th-century Virginia politics, was born in West Virginia, at his mother's ancestral home in Martinsburg, June 10, 1887. His brother was polar explorer Richard E. Byrd.

Byrd's mother, Eleanor Bolling Flood, was the great-granddaughter of Gen. Elisha Boyd, who built the Martinsburg mansion known as Boydsville in 1812. Her maternal grandfather, Boyd's son-in-law and Byrd's great-grandfather, Charles James Faulkner of Martinsburg, was U.S. ambassador to France and later an aide to Stonewall Jackson. Byrd was descended on his father's side from the William Byrd family, who were among Virginia's early aristocrats.

Harry Byrd, who grew up in Winchester, Virginia, and later lived in nearby Berryville, made a fortune as an orchardman and newspaper publisher. He owned newspapers in Winchester and Harrisonburg, Virginia, and in 1907 established the Martinsburg *Evening Journal*. Having served as governor of Virginia (1925–29), he was appointed to a U.S. Senate vacancy in 1933 and reelected each term thereafter until his retirement in 1965. The "Byrd Machine" ran Virginia politics throughout these years. The conservative Byrd opposed President Roosevelt's New Deal.

Senator Harry F. Byrd died October 20, 1966.

See also Charles James Faulkner

Robert C. Byrd

Robert Carlyle Byrd, the longest-serving United States senator from West Virginia, was born November 20, 1917, in North Wilkesboro, North Carolina. His name was originally Cornelius Calvin Sale Jr. His mother died in 1918, and he was sent to live with his aunt and uncle, Vlurma and Titus Dalton Byrd, in West Virginia. They raised him as their own child.

Titus Byrd was a coal miner and the family lived in several company towns, in houses with no running water or electricity. Robert Byrd's education began in a two-room schoolhouse. He was the valedictorian of the class of 1934 in Mark Twain High School in Stotesbury, Raleigh County. He married his high school sweetheart, Erma Ora James, in 1937. Byrd worked in a gas station and a grocery store. He learned the trade of meatcutting and by the late 1930s was working as a butcher for $85 a week. He worked in the shipyards in Baltimore and Tampa in World War II, then returned to West Virginia and opened a grocery store in Sophia, Raleigh County, and taught an

Robert C. Byrd, (1917–) as a young fiddler.

adult Bible class. In 1946, he began a political career that would last for more than half a century when he was elected to the House of Delegates. At about that time he briefly joined the Ku Klux Klan, an act he later regretted.

Byrd was reelected to the West Virginia House of Delegates in 1948 and was elected to the state Senate in 1950. He won a seat in the U.S. House of Representatives in 1952 and was reelected in 1954 and 1956. In 1958, he ran for the U.S. Senate, though he was initially opposed by both the coal companies and John L. Lewis, the president of the United Mine Workers. He won the Democratic primary and the general election by solid margins, and has been reelected by wide margins ever since; he is the first senator to have carried all of the state's 55 counties in a contested general election.

The coal miner's son took the oath of office in the Senate chamber in the presence of three future presidents, Senators John Kennedy and Lyndon Johnson and Vice President Richard Nixon. With the help of Johnson, then the majority leader, Byrd obtained a seat on the Appropriations Committee with the intention of securing funding for projects in West Virginia. In return he supported Johnson's candidate, Hubert Humphrey, in his unsuccessful campaign in the 1960 West Virginia presidential primary. In the 1950s and 1960s, he had a conservative voting record. While serving in Congress, Byrd, who never graduated from college, attended American University Law School at night for ten years. When he received his law degree in June 1963, President Kennedy, at his request, gave the commencement speech. Byrd was awarded a B.A. by Marshall University in Hunt-

ington in 1994, which he had attended briefly many years before.

Byrd took care to master the rules of the Senate. He was elected secretary of the Democratic Caucus in 1967 and used the office to meet the everyday needs of colleagues. His assiduous hard work enabled him to conduct an unannounced campaign for the position of majority whip, held by Edward Kennedy, and in January 1971, with the deathbed proxy of Sen. Richard Russell, he was elected to that position by the Democratic Caucus. Byrd's mastery of the rules and attention to the needs of fellow senators helped him to defeat Humphrey in the race to succeed Sen. Mike Mansfield as majority leader after Mansfield declined to run in the 1976 election.

By that time Byrd's voting record was less conservative and closer to that of most Senate Democrats, but as majority leader from 1977 to 1981 and as minority leader from 1981 to 1987 he did not seek to set party policy. The powers of any leader are limited in a body such as the Senate where the conduct of business often requires unanimous consent. In 1987, when he became majority leader again, he established some legislative priorities and then announced he would leave the position after the 1988 elections.

In January 1989, Robert Byrd obtained the position he had been aiming for all along, the chairmanship of the Senate Appropriations Committee. "I want to be West Virginia's billion-dollar industry," he said in 1990, and in succeeding years as chairman and, from January 1995 to May 2001, ranking minority member of the committee he brought much more than that into the state. Notable projects include the FBI Fingerprinting Identification Center in Clarksburg, IRS offices in Parkersburg, the Fish and Wildlife Training Center in Harpers Ferry, a Bureau of Alcohol, Tobacco and Firearms office in Martinsburg, a NASA research center in Wheeling, the National White Collar Crime Center in Fairmont and Morgantown, and the National Energy Technology Laboratory in Morgantown. This son of a miner looked after the interests of the coalfields, as well: Byrd obtained funds for miners displaced by the Clean Air Act of 1990; he co-sponsored the unanimously adopted resolution in 1997 opposing the Kyoto Protocol so long as it exempted developing countries; and he sought to reverse legislatively an October 1999 court decision against mountaintop mining.

But Byrd has not concentrated entirely on local issues. During his years in the Senate, he systematically read through the great books of the classical and modern eras and refers to them often in speeches. With the assistance of Senate historian Richard Baker, he wrote a two-volume history, *The Senate 1789–1989*, which he first delivered as speeches on the Senate floor. He has responded strongly when he feels that the prerogatives of the Senate, the Appropriations committees, or Congress generally have been flouted. He was one of five members of Congress to bring a lawsuit challenging the constitutionality of the line-item veto enacted in 1996; in June 1998, the Supreme Court ruled it unconstitutional. In 2002, he made a determined, if unsuccessful, stand against the Bush administration's call for a resolution authorizing war on Iraq, arguing that the requested authority was unconstitutionally broad.

Byrd was elected to his eighth term in the Senate in 2000 by a 78 percent to 20 percent margin, his greatest ever; he carried all 55 counties for the third time. He has served in the Senate longer than anyone except Strom Thurmond of South Carolina, who did not seek reelection in 2002. He served as president pro tempore of the Senate, fourth in line to succeed to the presidency, from January 1989 to January 1995 and again from May 2001 to January 2003. In May 2001, he was named by Governor Wise and the legislature as the West Virginian of the 20th Century. Senator Byrd published his long-awaited autobiography in 2005.

Michael Barone
The Almanac of American Politics

W.E.R. Byrne

A prominent attorney from a prominent family, writer William Easton Randolph "Bill" Byrne is best remembered as "the fishing lawyer" and author of *Tale of the Elk*. He was born October 26, 1862, in Fort Defiance, Virginia. After the Civil War, during which his father served as a Confederate officer, the family moved to West Virginia. Byrne attended school in Wheeling and Charleston, worked as a civil engineer, and studied law with his uncle, Supreme Court Justice Homer A. Holt. Byrne was admitted to the bar in 1884, began practicing law in Sutton, and was elected prosecuting attorney of Braxton County in 1892. He was an ardent Democrat but well-liked by everyone who knew him, regardless of party affiliation.

Byrne was said to practice law when he had to and to fish when he could. His love affair with the Elk River led to a lifetime study of the river and its environs. Byrne enjoyed sitting around the campfire telling stories with his numerous friends, who included prominent figures of the day. Eventually Byrne's stories and tales, first published as magazine articles, were compiled into the West Virginia classic, *Tale of the Elk*. Stricken with pneumonia at his Elk River camp, Byrne died December 11, 1937, at the age of 75.

See also Tale of the Elk

Bill Clements
West Virginia Book Company

Cabell County

Named for William H. Cabell, governor of Virginia (1805–08), Cabell County was created by an act of the Virginia General Assembly on January 2, 1809, from part of Kanawha County. Cabell County lies along the Ohio River in southwestern West Virginia, encompassing an area of 285.7 square miles and a population of 96,784 according to the 2000 census. The county seat is Huntington, which is part of a metropolitan statistical area including nearby communities in Ohio and Kentucky. The city of Milton, the village of Barboursville, and other incorporated towns lie generally east of Huntington, which abuts the Ohio River.

The area was once populated by the ancient Adena people. In the early 1700s, the Shawnees, Mingos, and Senecas used present Cabell County for hunting grounds. La Salle, who navigated the Ohio River in 1669, is thought to have been the first European to set foot in the area. Thomas Hannon, who came probably in the early 1790s, is regarded as the first permanent English settler.

In 1749, the French explorer Celoron de Blainville may have landed in what is now Cabell County during his exploration of the Ohio River. Mary Ingles, who was captured and held by Shawnees in 1755 until her escape after four months, is said to have been the first white woman to pass through present Cabell County. During the French and Indian War (1754–63), the Shawnees and Mingos sided with the French. During the American Revolution (1776–83), they allied themselves with the British, clashing again with settlers and discouraging further white settlement of the Ohio Valley until the end of the war.

Cabell County's location along the Ohio River made it a resting point in the 1800s for settlers migrating westward. Prior to the Civil War, settlers heading west used Indian trails, including trails through the present county. On the advice of George Washington, one of these trails was upgraded to the James River & Kanawha Turnpike (modern U.S. 60), which was extended to Barboursville in 1814.

During the Civil War era, residents of Cabell County were divided in their loyalties. After the election of President Lincoln in 1860, some citizens organized the Border Rangers, a militia loyal to the South. The first engagement in Cabell County was the Battle of Barboursville on Fortification Hill in 1861, in which the 2nd Kentucky regiment of Union volunteers dispersed the local militia. Later during the war, the pro-Southern town of Guyandotte, called "the worst secession nest in that whole country" by the *Wheeling Intelligencer*, was set ablaze and destroyed.

Despite the damage from the war, the economy of Cabell County recovered quickly. Railroad magnate Collis P. Huntington located the western terminus of the Chesapeake & Ohio Railroad just west of Guyandotte in present Huntington in 1870. The county seat was moved to Huntington by a county referendum in 1887, after being switched several times between Guyandotte and Barboursville.

By the early 1900s, industry in Cabell County included glassmaking, a flour mill, and furniture manufacturers. In 1921, the International Nickel Company plant opened. Blenko Glass, which established itself in Milton in 1921, manufactures vases and other glassware and sells stained glass throughout the world. In 1923, the Huntington area became the site of West Virginia's first commercial radio station still broadcasting today (WRVC, formerly WSAZ, which began transmitting from Pomeroy, Ohio, and moved its facilities to Huntington in 1927). In 1949, WSAZ-TV, the state's first television station, went on the air from Huntington. The completion of Interstate 64 in the 1960s, generally following the same east-west route as U.S. 60, strengthened development, though bypassing Huntington. Major sectors of the economy now include commerce, manufacturing, transportation, government, and education.

Marshall University was founded in 1837 as the Marshall Academy. It was named for the late U.S. Chief Justice John Marshall at the recommendation of his friend, Huntington lawyer John Laidley. In 1867, the new state of West Virginia created the State Normal School of Marshall College, giving Marshall a teacher-training mission. Marshall became a university in 1961.

Other major employers include CSX Huntington Division, the Cabell County Board of Education, St. Mary's Hospital, INCO Alloys (now Special Metals), Cabell Huntington Hospital, and the U.S. Army Corps of Engineers. Additional economic resources include dairy and poultry farms, livestock, corn, oil wells, and coal and natural gas. Huntington is a principal trading center and shipping port for the coalfields of southern West Virginia and eastern Kentucky.

Other than the Ohio River, Cabell County's major streams are the Guyandotte River and the Mud River, which flows into the Guyandotte at Barboursville. The Mud, whose banks have periodically overflowed with serious flooding of the lowlands, once was crossed by a covered bridge at Milton. This bridge, the only example of a Howe truss in West Virginia, has been moved to a pond at Pumpkin Park. The county's rivers and streams are used for boating, fishing, and swimming. Barboursville Lake north of U.S. 60 and Underwood Lake off State Route 2 are popular trout fishing sites.

The Huntington Museum of Art is a leading art gallery of the Appalachian region. Parks in the county include 70-acre Ritter Park in Huntington, Kiwanivista Park along U.S. 60 between Barboursville and Milton, and Memorial Park, dedicated to World War I veterans. Camden Park, an old fashioned amusement park, remains popular. Appropriate to the county's history as a railroad center, the annual New River Train excursion to the New River Gorge originates in Huntington and takes railroad buffs and autumn foliage observers across the state to Hinton each fall. County elected officials include three county commissioners, a county clerk, a sheriff, a prosecuting attorney, an assessor, and a circuit clerk.

FAST FACTS ABOUT CABELL COUNTY

Founded: 1809
Land in square miles: 285.7
Population: 96,784
Percentage minorities: 6.6%
Percentage rural: 23.0%
Median age: 37.5
Percentage 65 and older: 16.0%
Birth rate per 1,000 population: 12.3
Median household income: $28,479
High school graduate or higher: 80.0%
Bachelor's degree or higher: 20.9%
Home ownership: 64.6%
Median home value: $76,200

This information is from the 2000 U.S. Census. In 2000, West Virginia as a whole had 5 percent minorities, a median age of 38.9, median household income of $29,696, and a 75.2 percent home ownership rate.

The Cabell County Courthouse, Huntington.

The present Cabell County courthouse was constructed on land purchased in 1895 for $24,757 and was completed December 4, 1901. An extensive remodeling and expansion were completed in 1940. Notable figures from Cabell County include the late Carter G. Woodson, known as the father of black history; entertainer Soupy Sales; basketball star Hal Greer; Grammy Award winning gospel singer Michael W. Smith; and Dwight Morrow, a U.S. senator (1931) from New Jersey and ambassador to Mexico.

See also Huntington

Larry Sonis
Arlington, Texas

Robert J. Dilger, *Cabell County History*, 2000; George Selden Wallace, *Cabell County Annals and Families,* 1935; *Cabell County Heritage 1809–1996*, 1996.

Cabell Huntington Hospital

Cabell Huntington Hospital, the second-largest hospital in the state's second-largest city, is located on Hal Greer Boulevard in Huntington. It has 293 beds and 63 bassinets and is named after the county and city that financed its initial construction with taxpayers' money.

Community leaders in Huntington and Cabell County decided in 1945 that there was a critical need for a new acute care hospital and convinced the state legislature to approve a bill to authorize a city-county hospital. Voters in both the city and the county approved a $3 million bond issue in 1952, and construction soon began on the site of a former brickyard. The facility first opened for business in 1956. Community response was so great that a three-phase expansion program was begun soon afterward. Cabell Huntington was originally a 236-bed hospital, but the first phase of the expansion increased the size to 280 beds and 48 bassi-

nets in 1963, followed by a second expansion in 1976 that added more beds as well as expanded emergency room space, laboratory facilities, the cafeteria and business offices. A third phase of expansion was initiated after approval of a $9 million bond issue that included a 26-bed critical care floor that opened in August of 1981. The region's only birthing room and a high-risk labor room were part of the expansion in 1981 and 1982. The hospital has the only burn unit in the state, treating electrical and chemical burns as well as those caused by fire.

In 1989, construction began on a $12 million surgery suite addition, and in 1998 the new partnership with the Marshall University School of Medicine produced the most significant expansion of the physical plant. This new MU Medical Center, connected to the existing hospital, brings all of the School of Medicine physicians, faculty, and students together in one location.

The hospital is governed by a board of directors, representing a wide range of community interests, including labor and business. The board appoints the medical and dental staff, composed of approximately 325 physicians and dentists in the community. In 1985, the hospital began converting from a public nonprofit corporation to a private nonprofit corporation. In early 1988, this conversion was completed and Cabell Huntington Hospital, Inc., became the new corporation governing and overseeing Cabell Huntington Hospital.

Plans to merge operations with St. Mary's Hospital of Huntington and Pleasant Valley Hospital in Point Pleasant were completed in 1998 when the West Virginia Health Care Authority approved a certificate of need for the creation of the new Genesis Health Care Services, Inc. The short-lived combination lasted until late 2001, when Genesis was dissolved. Cabell Huntington now operates independently.

Tom Miller
Huntington

James E. Casto, *Huntington, An Illustrated History,* 1997; Kathy M. Cosco, "Cabell Huntington Hospital—Historical Progress," Report to the Community, 1997.

William H. Cabell

Virginia Governor William H. Cabell was a major Cabell County landowner and the man for whom the county was named. He was born in Cumberland County, Virginia, December 16, 1772. The son of Nicholas Cabell and grandson of Dr. William Cabell, a surgeon in the British Navy who settled in Virginia in 1724, Cabell attended Hampden-Sydney College (1785–89) and then entered the College of William and Mary, receiving a law degree in 1793. He served in the General Assembly from Amherst County from 1796 to 1799

and from 1802 to 1805, when he was elected governor of Virginia by the state legislature. He was elected to two more annual terms, serving until 1808.

Cabell was governor at the time of the Aaron Burr conspiracy, critical events of which took place at Blennerhassett Island near Parkersburg, and during Burr's arrest and trial for treason. Upon completion of his service as governor, Cabell became a Virginia State Supreme Court justice and later died at his residence in Richmond, January 12, 1853. He is buried at Shockoe Hill Cemetery in Richmond.

Kanawha County was divided in January 1809, soon after Cabell's service as governor, and Cabell County was formed. William Cabell later came to own more than 4,400 acres of land in the county, at Greenbottom, on the Ohio River north of present Huntington, including eight miles of riverfront. He bought the land about 1819 at a trustee's sale in Richmond, apparently sight unseen, and he never lived in Cabell County.

See also Cabell County

Emmitt Maxwell Furner II
Coolville, Ohio

Cabin Creek Quilts

Cabin Creek Quilts began in the spring of 1970 as a self-help quilting cooperative. The project was organized by volunteers from VISTA (Volunteers In Service To America), a Poverty War agency. They worked with coal miners' wives and widows in the Cabin Creek area of Kanawha County. Quilts and other products made of patchwork in traditional designs quickly made their way from the hills and hollows of West Virginia to shops on New York's fashionable Fifth Avenue, the White House, and Beverly Hills.

As many as 300 home patchwork makers and quilters worked for Cabin Creek Quilts, which was governed by its members and operated by a paid staff. The co-op organized skilled quilters into an efficient cottage industry, choosing attractive designs, buying fabric and supplies, and providing marketing and distribution. Quilters worked in their own homes and were paid on a piecework basis. By the late 1980s, imported Chinese quilts began cutting into the cooperative's market. The cooperative won cases concerning trade name infringements in the 1990s against Wal-Mart and the Orvis company. A fire, flood, repeated thefts, and vandals never stopped the group.

Cabin Creek Quilts was first located in Chelyan, at the mouth of Cabin Creek. The cooperative moved across the Kanawha River to the village of Malden in 1991 and restored two 19th-century houses which now serve as its operations headquarters and training and community buildings. Leading the way in the reconstruction of Booker T. Washington's boyhood home and the Women's Park in Malden, Cabin Creek Quilts continues to practice community service. More than 2,000 West Virginians have produced $7 million in sales through the co-op since 1970.

See also Crafts Movement, Quiltmaking

James Thibeault
Charleston

Cable-Stayed Bridges

Traditional suspension bridges use catenary or hanging cables, attached to towers at both ends and with cable or rod suspenders hanging vertically from the catenary cables to support the bridge deck below. By contrast, in cable-stayed bridges the individual support cables run from the tower directly to the bridge deck, radiating outward in a dramatic fan configuration. There are two elegant cable-stayed bridges on the Ohio River in West Virginia, one at Huntington and another at Weirton.

Within a total bridge length of 3,787 feet, the cable-stayed spans of the East Huntington bridge total 1,508 feet in two spans of 900 and 608 feet. The deck of the cable-stayed spans is supported by 31 pairs of steel cables, which are in turn supported by a single tower rising 280 feet above the deck. Completed in 1985, the cable-stayed spans were built to a design by Arvid Grant and Associates. The beautiful bridge connecting Huntington and Proctorville, Ohio, won the 1986 Federal Highway Administration's award for design excellence.

In 1990, the other cable-stayed bridge opened for traffic across the Ohio, connecting Weirton and Steubenville, Ohio. Including the girder span, the total bridge length is 1,971 feet, 9⅝ inches. Like the East Huntington bridge, the two main, cable-supported spans are unequal, being 820 feet and 687 feet, 11 inches. The most striking feature of this bridge is the 365-foot-high concrete tower in an inverted "Y" shape, which supports the cable stays. One of the legs of the tower has an elevator, while the other has a ladder. The cables consist of 26 pairs with 13 cables on the upstream and 13 cables on the downstream side of the deck. The cable system is symmetrical on each span. The piers and abutments were constructed by the Dravo Corporation in 1985 and the superstructure erected by S. J. Groves.

The bridges at East Huntington and Weirton are instantly recognizable landmarks, and the striking silhouette of a cable-stayed bridge is featured in the logo of the West Virginia Division of Highways.

Emory L. Kemp
WVU Institute for the History of Technology

Cable Television

West Virginians, living where rugged terrain prevented good rooftop-antenna reception in many places, were pioneers in the development of cable television. An entrepreneur, often a local television dealer, erected an antenna on a hilltop with good reception, amplified the incoming signal, and then brought it by wire down the hill into the homes below. Countless single-home systems were installed as well, as were many co-ops serving a few houses. The state's first commercial cable installations, at Piedmont, Mineral County, and Cameron, Marshall County, began operating in late 1949 and early 1950. The early unshielded wire systems, fragile in construction and subject to interference, were succeeded by shielded coaxial cable, already in use by hotels and apartment houses in larger American cities. The first coaxial cable systems in West Virginia began operating at Welch on July 1, 1951, and shortly after at Richwood, both receiving WSAZ-TV, Huntington.

Equipment was primitive in the early 1950s, and the first cable systems could carry no more than three channels, if that many were receivable at the antenna site, often not the case. Improved amplifiers made it possible to offer as many as five channels by the end of 1954, when there were rapidly growing cable systems in more than two dozen communities ranging in size from Webster Springs to Wheeling. Due to its rugged terrain, West Virginia had the highest number of cable subscribers per capita in the country. The state's early importance in cable television made its operators especially influential in steering the business nationally. For many years, more West Virginians served as officers and directors of the industry's trade association than was the case for any other state.

As early as 1955, the legislature considered declaring TV cable companies to be public utilities subject to regulation by the Public Service Commission. However, system owners succeeded in staving off governmental oversight several times, and it was not until 1988 that cable TV was brought under limited regulation. Meanwhile, the Federal Communications Commission had reserved to itself the authority to regulate rates for cable service.

Beginning nationally in the 1970s, major broadcasting companies, movie studios, other entertainment and media entities, and phone companies began acquiring cable systems and creating nationwide operations. In time, most West Virginia owners sold out to the conglomerates; by the year 2000, there were few independent operators still in business. The new owners rebuilt the old systems, employing fiber-optic cables and other newly developed equipment that vastly increased the numbers of channels available. Close to 90 percent of West Virginia's urban homes were connected by the end of the 20th century.

M. William Adler
Weston

Cabwaylingo State Forest

Located on Twelvepole Creek in Wayne County, 25 miles south of Wayne, Cabwaylingo State Forest takes its name from four neighboring counties, Cabell, Wayne, Lincoln, and Mingo. The state bought the forest's 8,123 acres in 1935.

Cabwaylingo's early history is intertwined with the Civilian Conservation Corps (CCC). A New Deal agency created by President Franklin D. Roosevelt, the CCC employed youth between the ages of 18 to 25 to work on construction projects throughout the nation. In West Virginia, the CCC worked on reforestation and construction projects in areas that later became state forests and parks.

From July 4, 1935, to October 20, 1938, CCC Company 3532 occupied Camp Anthony Wayne at what is now Cabwaylingo State Forest. In 1938, Company 1558V, made up of World War I veterans, moved in and stayed until April 11, 1939. The CCC surveyed timber and game, fought forest fires, cut weeds and brush, cleared trails, and constructed log cabins, which are still used.

Cabwaylingo offers hunting, fishing, and hiking. Facilities include a swimming pool, picnic areas, 13 log cabins, and 20 camping sites. The McClintic group camp, formerly the CCC barracks, includes a dining hall and two rustic buildings that can each sleep 50 people. Near the campgrounds stands one of the state's few remaining fire towers, Tick Ridge, which was built in 1935.

See also Civilian Conservation Corps, State Forests

Nancy Ray Adams
Pine Mountain Settlement School

John H. Woods, "CCC Days in West Virginia," *Wonderful West Virginia,* March 1988.

Cacapon River

The Cacapon (pronounced kuh-KAY-pon) River flows north-northeasterly for 112 miles through Hardy, Hampshire, and Morgan counties. Its long, narrow watershed drains 680 square miles of the Eastern Panhandle. The Cacapon is a major tributary of the Potomac River.

The Lost and Cacapon are the same river. During dry spells, the Lost River is lost from sight when it flows under Sandy Ridge at "the Sinks." It emerges as the Cacapon a few miles downstream, just upriver of Wardensville. North River, a major tributary, joins the Cacapon at the Forks of Cacapon.

The Cacapon River and its corridor are biologically rich. Its banks are clothed by a diverse forest that includes silver maple, river birch, and sycamore in the canopy. Paw paw, black willow, and spicebush crowd the understory, and wildflowers, ferns, and grasses cover the ground. About 79 percent of the basin is forested, 19 percent is used as farmland, while the rest is towns and water.

In the spring, common riverside songsters include red-eyed vireo, song sparrow, indigo bunting, scarlet tanager, and eastern phoebe. The river also supports wood ducks, Canada geese, belted kingfishers, ospreys, and an occasional bald eagle. A globally rare plant, harperella, occurs in patches along the lower Cacapon, while rare animals include the wood turtle, red-bellied turtle, and several mussel species. Beaver and white-tailed deer are common.

In addition to Lost River's sink, other natural landmarks include the bicarbonate spring at Lost River State Park near Mathias; Caudy's Castle, a sandstone promontory on which, according to legend, a homesteader held off a group of Indians, near Bloomery; and Eades Fort, a large cliff along the lower Cacapon near Largent, where folklore holds that Indians captured a family of cave-dwelling settlers.

Thomas Lord Fairfax conveyed many of the original land plots to the watershed's homesteaders from 1748 to 1761, and George Washington surveyed many of these from 1749 to 1751. The first fort in the chain of defenses on the frontier was constructed by Washington's troops during the winter of 1756 at Great Cacapon, located at the Cacapon's mouth.

The Cacapon River has been the subject of several studies. Its remote, narrow valleys led the National Park Service to score the lower 80 miles of the Lost and Cacapon rivers as eligible for the federal Wild and Scenic Rivers System, but lack of local support prevented the section from being added to the system. Former U.S. Labor Secretary Willard Wirtz chronicled the basin's colorful people, such as Caudy Davis, and its quirky history, in his 1990 *Capon Valley Sampler*. The Cacapon is the first river in the nation for which a comprehensive ecological headwaters-to-mouth baseline has been assembled.

The Cacapon is a popular recreational stream. The main stem of the river supports a warm-water fishery of smallmouth bass and rock bass. Some tributaries support reproducing brook trout populations, while other reaches are stocked seasonally with rainbow trout. On average, May offers the best paddling because the weather is warm and the water level is adequate. Taking most of a day, the most popular float is the eight-mile stretch from Capon Bridge to Bloomery. Six summer camps, including the nationally renowned Camp Rim Rock for girls, challenge children with the river's boating and swimming.

The Cacapon River watershed lies in a narrow band of land west of the eastern megalopolis and east of the coalfields, a serendipitous siting that has contributed to the river's generally good health. Principal land uses include farming for poultry, cattle, and field crops, timber harvesting, and second homes of absentee landowners.

See also Lost River, North River, Potomac River

George Constantz
Canaan Valley Institute

G. Constantz and J. Matheson, "Science, Grass Roots, and the Cacapon River," *Wonderful West Virginia,* October 1989; G. Constantz, N. Ailes, and D. Malakoff, *Portrait of a River: the Ecological Baseline of the Cacapon River,* 1993; W. Wirtz, *Capon Valley Sampler,* 1990.

Cacapon State Park

Cacapon State Park occupies a long, 6,000-acre strip of land stretching from just south of the Potomac River, which is the border between West Virginia and Maryland, southward to the Virginia state line. The entrance to the park is about 15 miles south of Berkeley Springs, the county seat of Morgan County. The park is bordered on the west by Cacapon Mountain, most of which lies within its borders.

Cacapon State Park came into being in the 1930s when the Civilian Conservation Corps constructed an 11-room log inn in the wide glen at the east side of the mountain. The CCC workers also built a dam and lake, and park facilities soon included a bathhouse, beach, picnic sites, and rental cabins. The park grew in following decades with the construction of new cabins, a maintenance building, and two new residences. A 50-room lodge, complete with a restaurant and banquet hall, was finished in 1956. The lodge was expanded in 1999. The new lodge has eclipsed the original inn, which has nonetheless been carefully maintained and is still rented out for gatherings. In 1973, the park matured into a full-fledged resort with the construction of an 18-hole golf course, designed by Robert Trent Jones Jr.

Today, Cacapon State Park's hiking, family recreation areas, horse trails, and beach draw both vacationers and local people. There are 31 rental cabins. The park's name, taken from the mountain and nearby river, is said to be a derivation of the Shawnee word for "medicine."

Stephanie Earls
Yakima, Washington

Calhoun County

Calhoun County, located in west-central West Virginia, has a size of 280.2 square miles and a 2000 population of 7,582. Grantsville is the county seat. Calhoun County is served by U.S. Route 33-119, State Routes 5 and 16, and other roads. Calhoun County is in one of the more remote parts of West Virginia and as a consequence was settled late. The area was favored by hunters and trappers in early times, and nowadays it is one of the places where traditional culture remains strongest.

The Little Kanawha River bisects Calhoun County in the north. The river has played an important role in the region since prehistoric times. Indians followed the river from the Ohio Valley to the rich hunting grounds in central West Virginia. Numerous native artifacts, as well as a few low mounds, have been found in Calhoun County.

White pioneers also traveled the Little Kanawha and its tributaries. The first recorded permanent settler in the county, Phillip Starcher, arrived in 1810 and built a cabin near present Arnoldsburg. More families trickled in during the early 1800s, including several Revolutionary War veterans. Although the area remained rural, population grew steadily. In 1856, Calhoun County was created from neighboring Gilmer County.

A fierce competition for the location of the courthouse began immediately. The county seat was moved four times in two years, and the Civil War began before matters could be settled. After the war, the courthouse was relocated one last time, to a farm on the Little Kanawha River. The town that grew up around it was named Grantsville in honor of Gen. Ulysses S. Grant.

The naming of the county seat for the Northern general represented the triumph of a new political faction since the naming of the county for John C. Calhoun, himself a strong proponent of the Southern, states-rights philosophy. Occupying a border county in a border state, Calhoun County residents were divided in their allegiances during the Civil War. They suffered greatly during the wartime chaos. County government ceased to function and citizens lived in confusion and fear. Calhoun's Moccasin Rangers, a notorious Confederate guerrilla band, controlled much of west-central West Virginia in 1861 and 1862.

The post-war years were marked by slow, steady growth. Timbering became an important economic activity as numerous rafts of logs were floated down the Little Kanawha to Parkersburg. Beginning in the late 1800s, Calhoun County became a major oil and gas producer, with a resulting increase in employment and population. One of the most prominent early entrepreneurs was Godfrey L. Cabot, who built the world's largest carbon black factory near Grantsville in 1901 and who founded Cabot Gas.

In the absence of railroads and all-weather roads, the river was used to ship merchandise and supplies in and out of the county. At the turn of the century, an important development in river transportation was made by a Calhoun resident, Capt. Norman Williams. His narrow, shallow-draft, gasoline-powered sternwheelers made navigation possible on the upper reaches of the Little Kanawha and its tributaries. Everything from

FAST FACTS ABOUT CALHOUN COUNTY

Founded: 1856
Land in square miles: 280.2
Population: 7,582
Percentage minorities: 1.1%
Percentage rural: 100%
Median age: 41.3
Percentage 65 and older: 16.7%
Birth rate per 1,000 population: 10.7
Median household income: $21,578
High school graduate or higher: 62.4%
Bachelor's degree or higher: 9.3%
Home ownership: 78.9%
Median home value: $46,000

This information is from the 2000 U.S. Census. In 2000, West Virginia as a whole had 5 percent minorities, a median age of 38.9, median household income of $29,696, and a 75.2 percent home ownership rate.

people to mail to oil field equipment traveled on these boats and their barges.

Calhoun Countians have made contributions in various fields. Probably the most prominent native son is the former Congressman, Robert H. Mollohan. Nourished by the rich traditions of their isolated area, Calhoun Countians including Phoeba Parsons and Noah Cottrell contributed to West Virginia's 20th century folk music revival.

Calhoun County's recovery from the Great Depression was slow, and the county suffered from the same out-migration that affected most of the state after World War II. The number of Calhoun Countians peaked at 12,455 in 1940 and declined thereafter. The county's economy in the late 20th century was based on livestock grazing, light manufacturing, and the oil and gas and pipeline construction industries. Reforestation has led to a resurgence of timbering and has made the county ideal for hunting and fishing.

See also Grantsville, Little Kanawha River, Moccasin Rangers

Robert G. Bonar
Grantsville

John Cuthbert, "Riverboat Days on the Little Kanawha River," *Wonderful West Virginia,* January 1996; Calhoun County Historical & Genealogical Society, *History of Calhoun County,* 1990.

James Morton Callahan

One of the first professional historians of West Virginia, James Morton Callahan was born at Bedford, Indiana, November 4, 1864. He was educated at Southern Indiana Normal School, Indiana University, and Johns Hopkins University. He was awarded a Ph.D. by Johns Hopkins in 1897, where he studied under Herbert Baxter Adams, one of the nation's most renowned historians. From 1898 to 1902, Callahan was lecturer in history at Johns Hopkins and served concurrently as director of the Bureau of Historical Research in Washington.

In 1902, he was appointed chairman of the Department of History and Political Science at West Virginia University at a time when those disciplines were gaining new attention and invigoration. In 1916, Callahan became dean of the WVU College of Arts and Sciences, a position he held until 1929.

Callahan continued to pursue his interests in international relations, a field in which he was a pioneer. Among his numerous published works were *American Foreign Policy in Mexican Relations, American Foreign Policy in Canadian Relations,* and *American Relations in the Pacific Far East.* In 1913, when West Virginia celebrated a half-century of statehood, Callahan wrote the popular *Semi-Centennial History of West Virginia.* Later he was the author of a three-volume *History of West Virginia, Old and New,* a work in the traditional mode of one volume of history and two volumes of biographies. His wife, Maude Fulcher Callahan, was also interested in state and local history and assisted her husband in the preparation of *History of the Making of Morgantown: A Type Study in Trans-Appalachian Local History.*

Long after he had retired, Callahan remained a familiar figure on the Morgantown campus. With his white hair, white suit, and white shoes, he was for many students a commanding figure even as he was nearing his 90s. He died March 16, 1956. In 1963–64, West Virginia University established the Callahan Lectures as a tribute to his services to the university and the state.

Otis K. Rice
WVU Institute of Technology

Calvin W. Price State Forest

Located in the southern part of Pocahontas County, with a small portion in Greenbrier County, Calvin W. Price State Forest is the newest of West Virginia's nine state forests. Covering 10,800 acres on the east

side of the Greenbrier River, the forest is named in honor of one of Pocahontas County's best-known residents, Calvin W. Price (1880–1957). Price was active in promoting conservation work during his many years as editor of the *Pocahontas Times,* a Marlinton newspaper.

The area of the forest was logged of its virgin timber between 1880 and 1920. The white pine was cut first and floated to a mill at Ronceverte before 1900. In the early 1900s, a large tract of timber was harvested by the Maryland Lumber Company. After the cut-over land was sold by the company in 1922, it was divided into two sections and resold. The section north of Laurel Run became part of Watoga State Park. The southern tract was purchased by the New River Company and sold to the state in 1953. It was dedicated as Calvin W. Price State Forest on May 15, 1954. At the dedication ceremony, Price said he was "sinfully proud" of the honor.

The management plan for the Calvin W. Price State Forest emphasizes timber, wildlife, and watershed protection with hunting, fishing, hiking, and camping the major recreational activities.

See also Calvin Wells Price, State Forests

William P. McNeel
Marlinton

Camden-Clark Memorial Hospital

The 370-bed Camden-Clark Memorial Hospital in Parkersburg is an acute care facility that serves Wood County and the surrounding Mid-Ohio Valley region. Camden-Clark offers specialty care in internal medicine, surgery, oncology, anesthesia, family practice, pediatrics, obstetrics and gynecology, emergency services, pathology, radiology, and radiation therapy. The hospital employs 1,500 people, including 200 physicians.

The forerunner to Camden-Clark was City Hospital, a 40-bed facility that opened in 1898 on Wells Avenue, now 13th Street. The hospital also operated a school of nursing. In 1920, City Hospital moved to the Camden mansion on Garfield Avenue, which had been home to the U.S. senator and industrialist, Johnson Newlon Camden (1828–1908) and his wife, Anne. After Anne's death in 1918, the Camden heirs decided to honor her by donating the mansion to the city to use as a hospital. With a donation and a subsequent bequest from Dr. Andrew Clark, the city altered the mansion and added a wing for a new hospital. In recognition of the Camden and Clark gifts, the hospital was dedicated as Camden-Clark Memorial Hospital on April 16, 1920.

Since then, the hospital has added new facilities and programs. In 1973, a new kitchen and mechanical wing opened. Two years later, the completion of North Wing Tower added patient rooms as well as a radiology department, coronary care unit, emergency department, laboratory, and pharmacy. Subsequent additions created the surgery suite in 1979, the Camden-Clark Memorial Hospital Medical Office in 1992, the Outpatient Physical Therapy Building on Dudley Avenue in 1999, and the cardiac catheterization laboratory in 2000. Outreach services include diabetes education workshops, television forums, CPR and first aid classes, cancer seminars, and cardiac rehabilitation education.

Although Camden-Clark closed its nursing school in 1969, it still serves as a learning site for students majoring in medical fields from West Virginia University at Parkersburg and area technical schools.

See also Johnson Newlon Camden, Parkersburg

Johnson Newlon Camden

U.S. Senator and industrialist Johnson Newlon Camden was born March 6, 1828, in Lewis County. He opened one of the first oil wells in West Virginia in January 1861 and later helped John D. Rockefeller establish Standard Oil's national monopoly of the oil business. Camden was appointed to the U.S. Military Academy at West Point as a young man but resigned after two years to study law. Before going into the oil business, he was a lawyer, ran a store and worked in a bank, was elected to local political offices, and speculated on land and oil production.

Camden's first oil well stood along Burning Springs Run in Wirt County on property that he leased from W. P. and J. C. Rathbone. He entered the refining business at Parkersburg in 1869. In 1875, Camden and his partners quietly sold out to Rockefeller's Standard Oil, while continuing to operate as the Camden Consolidated Oil Company. Running the company as a secret subsidiary for Rockefeller, Camden bought competitors and sometimes shut them down. He bought surplus oil to keep it from going to market, and starved independent Pittsburgh-area refineries of barrel staves to help establish Standard Oil's control of the industry. Standard Oil later sent him to Washington as an "observer" and lobbyist.

Camden's business interests linked him to Northern Republicans during and after the Civil War, but he was a member of the Democratic Party, which was filled with ex-Confederates in the post-war years. The West Virginia legislature elected Camden to the U.S. Senate in 1881. He exploited his Senate position for personal and business advantage. Senator Camden speculated financially on attempts to settle West Virginia's pre-statehood portion of the Virginia state debt. He also helped Standard Oil get into markets in Turkey and Japan, and worked to repeal laws unwanted by the oil industry.

U.S. Senator Johnson Newlon Camden (1828–1908).

From oil, Camden turned to building railroads to connect the Baltimore & Ohio in the northern part of the state to the Chesapeake & Ohio in the south and to provide streetcar service in Huntington and neighboring areas. The new rail lines opened up coal mines and timbering in new areas. Historian John Alexander Williams describes Camden as one of the first of West Virginia's political leaders to use his public position to serve his industry, a prototype of some who followed.

Camden died April 25, 1908.

See also Burning Springs Oil Field, Natural Gas and Petroleum

Dawn Miller
Charleston

Festus P. Summers, *Johnson Newlon Camden: A Study in Individualism,* 1937; John Alexander Williams, *West Virginia and the Captains of Industry,* 1976.

Camden Park

Camden Park, "Home of the Happy Clown," is located just west of Huntington in Wayne County. Once one of many streetcar parks designed to boost trolley passenger traffic on weekends and holidays, today it is West Virginia's only amusement park. Camden Park was established in 1903 as a picnic grove of the Camden Interstate Railway, both named for principal owner Sen. Johnson N. Camden of Parkersburg. Col. E. G. Via became park manager in 1903, bought the park in 1916, and ran it until his death in 1946.

An Indian mound, the third largest in West Virginia, is located within the park's boundaries. The top of the mound was used as a bandstand in the early part of the 20th century. At various times during its history, Camden Park operated a swimming pool, a zoo, scores of different

rides, and many other attractions, including a vintage carousel.

The streetcar line eventually gave way to a modern four-lane highway, U.S. 60, that goes past the park entrance. The 1937 Ohio River flood and then World War II caused major setbacks. In 1946, Camden Park was sold to Huntington furniture dealer James P. Boylin and brought back from the brink of extinction to become a popular, family-oriented park. Present Camden Park includes 22 acres. The carousel is still in operation, though the original hand-carved horses were sold. The park has two roller coasters, a penny arcade, cafeteria, and an overhead tram ride.

Camden Park celebrated its centennial in 2003.

See also Johnson Newlon Camden

Joseph Platania
Huntington

Camp Ashford

Built in 1943 by the U.S. War Department, Camp Ashford at White Sulphur Springs was one of two camps in West Virginia that housed prisoners of war during World War II. Camp Ashford prisoners worked on local farms and at nearby Ashford General Hospital, a 2,000-bed facility operated by the U.S. Army in what previously had been the Greenbrier hotel. The camp and hospital were named for Col. Bailey K. Ashford, an army doctor.

The 165-acre POW camp could accommodate up to 1,000 prisoners in former Civilian Conservation Corps buildings located on the property. Italian prisoners occupied the camp first; they were moved on October 23, 1943, when German prisoners arrived. The German prisoners stayed at Camp Ashford until after the war's end.

See also Ashford General Hospital, Camp Dawson, Italian Prisoners of War

Louis E Keefer, "The West Virginia WWII Home Front: Ashford General Hospital," *Goldenseal,* Spring 1993.

Camp Brock

In 1935, the state Department of Public Welfare established Camp Brock on the campus of West Virginia State College at Institute. Camp Brock was part of a system of camps intended to rescue children of families affected most severely by the Great Depression. The camps were segregated by race. Named for George D. Brock, a professor at the college who pioneered in health education for African-Americans, Camp Brock's purpose was to feed and strengthen more than 400 children from black families hardest hit by the Great Depression. The department proposed to build a permanent camp for African-American children in Fayette County similar to Camp Fairchance for white children. In 1937, the legislature approved a permanent facility, later

German prisoners of war at Camp Ashford.

named Camp Washington-Carver, but it was to be a 4-H camp, rather than a child welfare camp, and it was to be administered by West Virginia State College.

See also Camp Fairchance, Camp Washington-Carver, Great Depression, Kamp Kump

Jerry Bruce Thomas
Shepherd University

Jerry Bruce Thomas, *An Appalachian New Deal: West Virginia in the Great Depression,* 1998; Dolly Withrow, *From the Grove to the Stars: West Virginia State College 1891–1991,* 1991.

Camp Caesar

Camp Caesar, located on State Route 20 between Webster Springs and Cowen, is Webster County's 4-H camp. The camp began in 1922, when J. N. Berthy Sr. and C. D. Howard of Cowen donated five and a half acres of land. From that beginning, Camp Caesar has expanded to more than 300 acres with accommodations for more than 400 campers and extensive recreation facilities.

Valued for the beauty of its surroundings and the isolation of its remote location, Camp Caesar has been the site of important state encampments for many decades. It has hosted the annual West Virginia state conservation camp for more than 50 years. Since 1960, Camp Caesar has also been the site of Camp Lincoln, the annual youth camp of the West Virginia Republican Party. Camp Caesar is also used by many religious groups for their summer camps and is the home of the Webster County Fair, which is held the first week in September.

The 4-H camp got its unusual name because "Caesar" was the nickname given to Judd Wolfram, Webster County's first agricultural agent, by early campers. During the Franklin Roosevelt administration, Camp Caesar leased land to the federal government for the establish-

ment of a National Youth Administration facility for the training of unemployed young men.

E. Lynn Miller
Gilbert, Arizona

Camp Carlile

Camp Carlile was a military training camp on Wheeling Island from 1861 to 1865. Soon after the beginning of the Civil War, enlistment centers opened in Wheeling, causing great numbers to travel to the city to join the Union Army. The Ohio River, the National Road, and the B&O Railroad made Wheeling a transportation hub and a natural center for recruitment and training. Most loyal West Virginia military units were mustered into service at Camp Carlile, and many also mustered out there.

Some of the first troop movements of the Civil War originated at Camp Carlile in the early summer of 1861, when Col. Benjamin F. Kelley moved his forces out to engage the rebels of Philippi. Francis Pierpont received a military salute at the camp on the day of his election as governor of the Reorganized (Unionist) Government of Virginia, June 20, 1861.

The Wheeling camp had several names. The first was simply City Camp, and the second was Camp Logan. Eventually it was named Camp Carlile for John S. Carlile, an early leader in the movement to create West Virginia and a U.S. senator representing Reorganized Virginia. After Senator Carlile fell in popularity the camp was renamed again, this time as Camp Willey, for the U.S. senator and state founder, Waitman Willey.

The camp provided training for different branches of the army. Cavalry, artillery, and infantry were all present at Carlile at various times. Training lasted two to four weeks depending on the specialty of the troops being trained. Cav-

alry and artillery training lasted three to four weeks.

See also John S. Carlile, Civil War

Diane Davis Darnley
Wheeling

Camp Creek State Park

Located in Mercer County, Camp Creek State Park entered the West Virginia state park system in 1987. Named for the creek that meanders through it and the contiguous Camp Creek State Forest, the park's 500-plus acres offer a waterfall, campgrounds both rustic and developed, and hiking trails. The name of Mash Fork, one of the park's streams, suggests a moonshining past not uncommon in the region.

A handicapped trail with a railed boardwalk and benches winds through the forest to a stream. Another path, Farley Branch Trail, leads up a mountain from a series of ledges that look like stone steps. The stocked streams provide good fishing. The park also offers volleyball, badminton, and basketball courts. There are swings, a softball field, and shuffleboard.

A rugged, splashing waterfall on Mash Fork, surrounded by shady, moss-covered rocks, is a favorite spot for visitors in all seasons, though it diminishes to a trickle during summer droughts. White and pink rhododendron are a showy attraction in the hot months. The park, with its fine picnic facilities, is popular for family reunions, class picnics, and church gettogethers. Unlike most West Virginia state parks, Camp Creek is located quite close to an interstate highway (I-77, the West Virginia Turnpike), making the park easily accessible to travelers passing through the state.

See also State Parks

Maureen F. Crockett
St. Albans

Camp Dawson

Camp Dawson, named for Governor Dawson (1905–09), is the West Virginia Army National Guard's primary training site in West Virginia. In 1908, the legislature authorized the purchase of land to serve as a training base for the Guard. Camp Dawson came into being in 1909 when almost 200 acres were acquired along the Cheat River, just south of Kingwood in Preston County. The camp fell into disuse from the beginning of World War I until 1929 when Carleton C. Pierce became adjutant general. Pierce, who was from nearby Kingwood, was appointed to his post by another resident of Preston County, Governor Conley (1929–33).

During World War II, the U.S. government leased the camp to house prisoners of war, and it became one of two POW camps in West Virginia. Some 175 Italian POWs were sent to Camp Dawson where they were assigned tasks such as building and repairing roads. The prisoners were visited on a regular basis by Italian-Americans who had settled in northern West Virginia and enjoyed picnics and holiday entertainment with them.

Camp Dawson has continued to grow and now totals more than 4,177 acres. It is now used for training a number of units including the 201st Field Artillery, 19th Special Forces Group (Airborne), and the 229th Engineering Detachment.

See also Camp Ashford, Italian Prisoners of War, West Virginia National Guard

Kenneth R. Bailey
WVU Institute of Technology

Louis E. Keefer, "The West Virginia WWII Home Front: POW: The Italian Prisoners at Camp Dawson," *Goldenseal*, Spring 1993.

Camp Fairchance

In 1934, the state Department of Public Welfare established Camp Fairchance (originally called Camp Boone), at Low Gap, Boone County, at the site of a former Civilian Conservation Corps camp. Camp Fairchance was part of a system of camps established to rescue children from families especially hard hit by the Great Depression. The camps were segregated by race. Camp Fairchance provided nourishment and recreation for white children from relief families judged by public health nurses to be at risk for tuberculosis or other diseases.

The children at Camp Fairchance attended a camp school staffed by unemployed teachers working for the Works Progress Administration, a federal program. Campers could join a Boy Scout troop, a 4-H club, a drum and bugle corps, and other organizations. Children remained at Fairchance up to three months, and then they returned to their families, or to foster homes.

See also Camp Brock, Great Depression, Kamp Kump

Jerry Bruce Thomas
Shepherd University

Jerry Bruce Thomas, *An Appalachian New Deal: West Virginia in the Great Depression*, 1998.

Camp Good Luck

Camp Good Luck, believed to be the world's first 4-H club encampment, was held at Elkwater in southern Randolph County in July 1915. The camp was organized by Randolph County's agricultural extension agent, J. Versus Shipman. About 20 boys and girls camped for three days, sleeping in Jackson Crouch's barn and cooking outside over an open fire. Each camper brought a tin plate and cup, silverware, an empty mattress tick and blankets, toiletries, potatoes, vegetables, bacon, and a live chicken for the pot. Local farmers provided milk. Highlights included killing a big rattlesnake upon arrival, fishing and swimming in the nearby Tygart Valley River, playing games, telling stories and singing around the campfire, and learning about agriculture and home economics. A monument on U.S. 219 south of Huttonsville marks the site of Camp Good Luck.

See also 4-H

Bruce Betler
Elkins

Camp Horseshoe

Camp Horseshoe, located 11 miles northeast of Parsons on County Route 7 in the Monongahela National Forest in Tucker County, offers summer youth camping experiences. Special programs include Hi-Y Leadership Camp, Hemophilia Camp, Cancer Camp, and the Horseshoe Adventure Camp for low-income children. Camp Horseshoe is also available as a year-round conference center for adult groups of 20 to 200 people, featuring a ropes course and leadership center. The adjoining Horseshoe Recreation Area offers tent and trailer camping. The camp is operated by Ohio-West Virginia YMCA.

Camp Horseshoe was constructed in 1938–39 by the Civilian Conservation Corps for the U.S. Forest Service, and many of the original buildings are in use today. The Ohio-West Virginia YMCA has leased Horseshoe from the Forest Service since 1940. The heated dining hall, resident cabins, and meeting lodge have the original rustic look of the old CCC.

Heather Roberts Biola
Elkins

Camp Piatt

Camp Piatt was one of many U.S. military camps situated in West Virginia during the Civil War. The camp was located in Belle, at Malones Landing about 15 miles south of Charleston. The camp was strategically situated on the Kanawha River, where it served as a major hub for the steamboats which carried soldiers as well as supplies for the Union cause.

The camp was named after Col. Abraham Piatt, commander of the 34th Ohio Regiment Zouaves. Rebel sympathizers in the Kanawha Valley detested the soldiers of the 34th Ohio, who would sometimes loot and burn property of known Confederate backers in the area. Another regiment, the 23rd Ohio, moved into Camp Piatt following the battle of Carnifex Ferry. In this regiment were two future U.S. presidents, Rutherford B. Hayes and William McKinley, who were commissioned first lieutenants at Camp Piatt in 1863. Hayes was fond of Camp Piatt and the surrounding area. "This is a beautiful valley from Camp Piatt down. Make West Virginia a free state, and Charleston ought to be a sort of Pittsburgh," he wrote.

Scott M. Kozelnik
Little Egg Harbor, New Jersey

Belle Woman's Club, *Bicentennial Belle, West Virginia: 1776–1976*, 1976; Otis K. Rice, *Charleston and the Kanawha Valley: an Illustrated History*, 1981.

Camp Richwood

See Camp Woodbine.

Camp Washington-Carver

Named for Booker T. Washington and George Washington Carver, Camp Washington-Carver is located at Clifftop, Fayette County. It has the distinction of having been the first 4-H camp for African-Americans in the country, and its great chestnut lodge is the largest log structure in West Virginia. The camp was constructed under two New Deal work programs, the Works Progress Administration and the Civilian Conservation Corps. In 1940, the first building was completed, a two-room guest cottage. Also in that year, the water tank and pond were finished. In 1942, the log lodge, two frame dormitories, the swimming pool, and a bathhouse were constructed. The com-

The Great Chestnut Lodge at Camp Washington-Carver.

plex was dedicated and opened to the public on July 26, 1942.

From 1942 to 1979, Camp Washington-Carver served as an off-campus learning center for West Virginia State College. During the years of racial segregation, hundreds of black West Virginians participated in summer 4-H camps, Boys State and Girls State, Boy Scouts and Girl Scouts, mining encampments, home economics encampments, church camps, private camps, and other programs at Camp Washington-Carver. The dining hall, spacious grounds, and swimming pool were also rented for social gatherings such as picnics, weddings, and reunions throughout the year.

In 1979, the camp was transferred to the West Virginia Department (now Division) of Culture and History to become a rural cultural arts center. In 1980, Camp Washington-Carver was placed on the National Register of Historic Places. After extensive rehabilitation, the facility was reopened in 1984. On June 9, 1989, a permanent exhibit depicting the camp's history was installed in the great chestnut lodge. Camp Washington-Carver now occupies 83 acres of land owned by the Public Land Corporation.

The Division of Culture and History offers an annual summer schedule of activities at Camp Washington-Carver which include the African-American Heritage Arts Camp, a family theater series, and (until 2001) the annual Doo-Wop Saturday Night. The Appalachian String Band Music Festival, one of the most popular traditional music festivals in the East, attracts thousands of participants for a week-long celebration each August. Camp Washington-Carver continues to be a favorite spot for reunions.

Norman Jordan
Ansted

Camp Woodbine

Camp Woodbine, known today as Camp Richwood because of its location along the south side of the Cranberry River five miles north of Richwood, was occupied by Civilian Conservation Corps Company 521 on November 20, 1933. The CCC company was under the supervision of the U.S. Forest Service and assigned work duties in the Monongahela National Forest. Camp Woodbine was made up mostly of West Virginia CCC enrollees, with a few from Ohio. At one time, there were 13 black enrollees in camp. The camp was abandoned on October 23, 1935.

Work projects included the construction of fire trails and road building, fire fighting, traffic surveys on State Routes 39, 44, and 94 to determine if a new Richwood to Marlinton road was needed, timber stand improvement, and Woodland Park, now known as Woodbine Picnic Area. Members of Camp Woodbine oper-

ated a side camp, known as Camp Woodroe, near Marlinton.

The site of the camp is now used for annual reunions of former West Virginia CCC members.

Larry N. Sypolt
West Virginia University

Alexander Campbell

A founder of the Christian Church (Disciples of Christ), Alexander Campbell was a preacher, philosopher, author, scholar, publisher, orator, statesman, college founder, and sheep farmer. Throughout his adult life, he worked to bring about religious, political, educational, and social reforms.

The son of Thomas and Jane (Corneigle) Campbell, he was born September 12, 1788, in the county of Antrim, Ireland. He migrated to America in 1809 and in 1811 settled in Buffaloe [sic], Brooke County, now Bethany, where he farmed and produced fine wool. Campbell married Margaret Brown of Buffaloe, and after her death in 1827 he married Selina Huntington Bakewell of nearby Wellsburg. He had eight children by his first wife and six by his second, and was the uncle of state founder Archibald W. Campbell.

Campbell, a pacifist, grew to maturity in Ireland during an era of sectarianism and political violence. His father, Thomas Campbell, a teacher and Presbyterian clergyman, migrated in 1807 to Washington, Pennsylvania, a few miles east of present Bethany. Alexander Campbell attended the University of Glasgow (1808–09), after which the family reunited in America.

Having severed Presbyterian ties, Thomas Campbell drafted *The Declaration and Address of the Christian Association of Washington* (1809), a charter for religious reformation based on Christian unity and liberty. This led to formation of one of the largest indigenous religious bodies in America, the Christian Church (Disciples of Christ), the founders of which were Alexander Campbell, Barton Warren Stone, Thomas Campbell, and Walter Scott.

Alexander Campbell conducted Buffaloe Seminary in his home (1818–22). He operated one of the most influential religious presses on the frontier, editing and publishing *The Christian Baptist* (1823–30) and *The Millennial Harbinger* (1830–70). When Bethany became a post-town, Campbell served as the first postmaster (1827–65). As delegate from Brooke County to the Virginia Constitutional Convention in 1829, he argued for a public system of education and an end to slavery. Campbell's views on the latter subject were complex, and he was sometimes accused of being pro-slavery; while personally opposed to slavery, he felt that it had to be tolerated wherever it was legal, and that laws must not be broken in

seeking its end. As the main speaker at the historic educational convention in Clarksburg (1841), he argued again for public education.

He founded Bethany College (March 2, 1840), the oldest degree-granting institution in West Virginia, serving as president and professor until his death. Campbell was elected president of the first general convention of the Christian Church (Disciples of Christ) and at the same time was elected president of the newly established American Christian Missionary Society (1849), positions he held until his death.

Alexander Campbell died March 4, 1866, and is buried near the historic Campbell mansion at Bethany. The mansion is now a National Historic Landmark, one of only 15 in West Virginia.

See also Bethany College, Archibald W. Campbell, Christian Church (Disciples of Christ)

Rosemary Jeanne Cobb
Bethany College

Archibald W. Campbell

Newspaperman Archibald W. Campbell was a leader in the West Virginia statehood movement, editor and part owner of the Wheeling *Daily Intelligencer* newspaper, and a prominent member of the Republican Party. He was the nephew of Alexander Campbell, who was the founder and first president of Bethany College and a founder of the Christian Church (Disciples of Christ). Archibald Campbell was born in Steubenville, Ohio, April 4, 1833. He spent most of his childhood in Bethany and attended Bethany College, graduating in 1852. Campbell then attended Hamilton College Law School in Clinton, New York, graduating in 1855. He moved to Wheeling in spring 1856 to take a job at the *Daily Intelligencer.* In the fall of that year, he and John F. McDermot purchased the paper and Campbell became editor.

Campbell was a member of the fledgling Republican Party, and editorials in his paper favored Republican causes, especially the abolition of slavery and preservation of the Union. The *Intelligencer* was the only Republican daily paper in Virginia and the only paper in the state to endorse Abraham Lincoln for the presidency in 1860. Campbell strongly opposed Virginia's secession from the United States. He supported the creation of the Reorganized Government of Virginia, and he worked hard, through his editorials and behind the scenes, for the formation of the new state of West Virginia. President Lincoln appointed Campbell postmaster of the Wheeling Post Office in 1861. It was Campbell, according to his daughter, Jessie Campbell Nave, who wrote the text of the telegram (sent by Governor Pierpont) that reputedly convinced President Lincoln to sign the West Virginia statehood bill.

In his later years Campbell retired from the newspaper and traveled extensively. He died of a stroke at the home of a sister in Webster Groves, Missouri, February 13, 1899.

See also Alexander Campbell, Reorganized Government of Virginia, Wheeling Intelligencer

Gerry Reilly
West Virginia Independence Hall
Elizabeth Cometti and Festus P. Summers, *The Thirty-Fifth State,* 1966.

Canaan Valley

Canaan Valley, located in the northeast section of Tucker County, is an oval-shaped valley 14 miles long and two to four miles wide. The elevation ranges from 3,200 to 4,300 feet, giving Canaan Valley a cold climate similar to places in Canada. Freezing temperatures can occur throughout the year.

Canaan Valley is noted for its wetlands, about 6,740 acres, or nine percent of all West Virginia wetlands. The Canaan wetlands are home to plants such as the rare glade spurge, and other plants adapted to chilly, wet areas. Other unique wetland habitats at Canaan include balsam fir and red spruce boreal forest, high-elevation bogs, and wetland shrub communities with such dominant bushes as pipestem. The wetlands are also home to many kinds of wildlife, including mammals such as beaver and mink, and waterfowl, including herons, ducks, and geese. More than 170 species of birds have been reported in the valley, including migratory and resident songbirds. The damp, cold conditions of the valley are inhospitable to many herptiles, but amphibians such as mountain dusky and northern red salamanders and pickerel frogs, and reptiles such as the snapping turtle and water snake, are present.

The cold climate combined with tundra-like wetlands makes Canaan Valley a biologically rich and diverse area with more than 520 plant species, some 25 of which are rare in West Virginia, and more than 285 mammal, bird, amphibian, reptile, and fish species.

The northern part of Canaan Valley includes the Canaan Valley National Wildlife Refuge, managed for the protection of wetland plant and animal communities, including suitable woodcock nesting sites. In the southern part of the valley, the state owns about 6,000 acres, where Canaan Valley State Park is located. A boardwalk near the nature center at the park offers visitors a chance to walk through wetland habitats, seeing yellow birch, red spruce trees, and mountain bog plants. This is one of West Virginia's full-service resort state parks, a popular ski area that has helped to spawn the valley's booming second-home industry.

Canaan comes back

"Canaan Valley had a tragic history, and its comeback has been a slow one. A hundred years ago valley and surrounding ridges were covered by red spruce forest of a density that is hard to imagine today. . . . The lumberman came, ultimately, and if total and permanent destruction of the entire area had been an aim it could scarcely have been more fully realized. An official of the company boasted that in 100,000 acres they had not left one stick of timber that would make a two-by-four. . . .

"With all cover removed, organic material at ground level began to dry out; soon it was high-grade fuel, and the inevitable fires got started. There followed such a ground fire as this state has never seen before or since. For months this humus layer smoldered, and neither rains nor snows could stop the fire's slow advance. The village of Davis was saved by a series of deep trenches around it, these kept filled with water carried from the Blackwater River. When the destruction was complete, all vegetable material that wasn't soaked had burned, and with it all insects, worms, salamanders, mice, and other burrowing forms of life. Bare rocks remained, and thin mineral soil, this often several feet lower than ground level in the original forest. Canaan and its environs had become a desert. . . .

"Slowly at first, then more rapidly, the processes of ecological succession began to come into play. . . . Then nature received an assist; the Civilian Conservation Corps went into operation, and one of its projects was the reforestation of Canaan Mountain. In places there was no soil at all to work with, so trucks ran from the valley night and day, bringing dark muck soil to the mountaintop. One bushel, sometimes two had to be used for each tree, but the roots of spruce seedlings were packed in. They lived and they grew. Twenty-five years later there is a beautiful young spruce forest overlooking Canaan Valley."

—Maurice Brooks *The Appalachians* (1965)

Legend holds that an early fur trader compared the valley to the biblical promised land, giving the place its name. At some point it came to be pronounced "kuh-NANE," with the accent on the second syllable, in preference to the usual pronunciation. Early accounts of the valley do not depict a land of milk and honey, describing travel as treacherous, and the land as festooned with rocks, cavities, and impenetrable rhododendron thickets. Logging began in the 1880s and continued until the 1920s, taking all the virgin timber, mostly red spruce. Logging and subsequent fires sapped the rich organic soil, to the detriment of latter agricultural attempts in the valley.

Canaan Valley, today a popular tourist area for hiking, biking, skiing, canoeing, riding, and nature study, is close to other scenic and recreational sites, including Blackwater Falls, the 10,000-acre Dolly Sods Wilderness area, Cathedral State Park, and the spectacular rock cliffs of Seneca Rocks.

See also Canaan Valley State Park
Norma Jean Kennedy-Venable
Morgantown
Pictorial Histories Publishing Company, *Where People and Nature Meet: A History of West Virginia State Parks,* 1988; Norma Jean Venable, *Canaan Valley,* 1989.

Canaan Valley National Wildlife Refuge

Established with assistance from the Conservation Fund on August 11, 1994, the Canaan Valley National Wildlife Refuge, one of the largest and most diverse freshwater wetland areas in central and southern Appalachia, became the 500th refuge in the National Wildlife Refuge system. The refuge is located north of Canaan Valley State Park in Tucker County. National wildlife refuges, federal lands managed by the U.S. Fish and Wildlife Service, are intended to maintain the ecological diversity of an area for future generations. More than 580 plant species and at least 290 species of vertebrates are known to exist in the Canaan area, including the endangered Virginia northern flying squirrel and the Cheat Mountain salamander.

The refuge's goal is to preserve 24,000 acres of fragile wetlands and unique habitats. In 2002, through an agreement reached with the assistance of Sen. Robert C. Byrd and Congressman Alan B. Mollohan, the Conservation Fund, and the U.S. Fish and Wildlife Service, Allegheny Energy Company transferred 12,000 acres to the Canaan Valley National Wildlife Refuge. This augmented the 3,245 acres previously acquired, bringing total acreage in the refuge to 15,245.

See also Canaan Valley
Debra K. Sullivan
Charleston Catholic High School

Canaan Valley State Park

Canaan Valley State Park, located in Tucker County, five miles south of Davis, is a major ski resort and one of West Virginia's biggest state parks. In 1957, S. Maude Kaemmerling, a member of one of the early logging families in the area, willed 3,135 acres of remote Canaan (pronounced kuh-NANE) Valley to the state of West Virginia for recreational use.

Through President John F. Kennedy's Economic Development Administration, grant and loan funds became available to develop the proposed state park. An additional 2,879 acres of private land was acquired by the state, which brought the park to its present size of 6,014 acres. Canaan Valley State Park opened to the public in 1963.

Along with the typical cabins, lodges, campgrounds, hiking trails, swimming pools, and tennis courts, the Canaan plan also included skiing as a major source of outdoor recreation and revenue. In fact, the park became West Virginia's first ski resort, sparking a new industry in the state. Skiing had been done at Canaan Valley as early as 1953, when the Washington Ski Club installed a rope tow on Cabin Mountain. The state park ski slopes were built on the 4,420 foot Weiss Knob, the first major ski development with snowmaking equipment in West Virginia, and opened in December 1971. In the mid-1970s the state began leasing the huge facility to a private operator, though the state park system still provides certain services.

See also Canaan Valley

Connie K. Colvin
Mineral Wells
Pictorial Histories Publishing Company, *Where People and Nature Meet: A History of West Virginia State Parks*, 1988.

Cancer Valley

The nickname "Cancer Valley" was apparently first applied to the Kanawha Valley by *Mother Jones* magazine. The term expressed the belief that cancer rates in the middle and upper valley were abnormally high, presumably due to the concentration of industry, including chemical plants, in the area of Charleston, South Charleston, and neighboring cities. "Cancer Valley" was an apparent word play on the name "Chemical Valley," once promoted by regional industry and local municipalities and reflecting the Kanawha Valley's world leadership in the mid-20th century chemical industry.

Those believing that the "Cancer Valley" reputation was justified cited a State Health Department study showing cancer deaths in the Charleston neighborhood nearest to the chemical plants to have been much higher than average, as well as an estimate by the National Cancer Institute that 80 percent of cancer deaths had environmental causes. Skeptics countered that environmental causes include lifestyle factors, especially diet and smoking, which together account for a large majority of cancers. The unfortunate nickname had fallen largely out of use by the turn of the 21st century.

Cannel Coal

Cannel coal is a smoky, easily ignited bituminous usually found adjacent to other coal seams. The word "cannel" is derived from the Old English pronunciation of "candle coal," since the coal kindled easily and produced a steady, bright flame. Composed partly of ancient seed spores, formed in pools, cannel coal contained a high percentage of hydrogen and other volatile matter.

In the mid-19th century, the demand for illumination stimulated technological innovation. It was discovered that cannel, a non-coking coal, could yield about two gallons of crude oil from one bushel of coal. A boom in demand for cannel coal swept the U.S. in the 1850s, and the extensive cannel coal deposits located near the Elk, Coal, and Kanawha rivers in West Virginia became the basis for coal-oil plants that thrived from 1855 to 1860. Leading the field were Aaron Stockton, who produced coal oil at Cannelton by 1850, William M. Peyton, who led the effort to mine cannel coal at Peytona and ship it to market via the Coal River, and Sutton Matthews, who mined cannel on Falling Rock Creek near the Elk River. No less than 46 companies obtained charters to mine coal along the three rivers between 1847 and 1861, and by 1860 almost every county in West Virginia had a coal-oil plant within its boundaries.

The onset of the Civil War deflated the boom although in January 1862 the Richmond *Enquirer* reported that the Kanawha area produced 5,000 gallons of crude coal oil daily. The death knell for cannel coal oil sounded as the petroleum industry grew with the successful drilling of the Pennsylvania Drake Well in 1859 and the subsequent drilling of wells on the Little Kanawha River and elsewhere in West Virginia. Kerosene quickly became the illuminating oil of choice. Cannel mines, notably at Cannelton, continued producing into the 20th century, but cannel was then far less significant than other bituminous coals to the West Virginia economy.

See also Coal

Lou Athey
Franklin & Marshall College
Otis K. Rice, "Coal Mining in the Kanawha Valley to 1861: A View of Industrialization in the Old South," *Journal of Southern History,* November 1965.

Cap, Andy, and Flip

The country music trio of Cap, Andy, and Flip delighted Mountain State radio audiences during the 1930s. Composed of West Virginian Warren Caplinger (1889–1957), Tennessean Andrew Patterson (1893–1950), and Alabaman William "Flip" Strickland (1908–88), the group formed in Akron, Ohio, in 1930. Cap provided leadership, played guitar, and sang bass; Andy sang lead and played guitar and fiddle; and Flip sang tenor and played mandolin and tenor banjo.

At various times Cap, Andy, and Flip based their act at WWVA, Wheeling; WMMN, Fairmont; and WCHS, Charleston. As time passed, their repertoire increasingly consisted of sacred songs. They recorded but sparingly, on their own Fireside Melodies label. Flip left the team late in 1940, being replaced by Andy's son, Milton Patterson (b. 1924). Cap, Andy, and Milt remained together at WCHS until 1949 when the group dissolved. After Andy's death, Cap did DJ work on other Charleston stations. Flip resided in Indianapolis for many years before retiring to Alabama. Milt lives in Harriman, Tennessee.

Ivan M. Tribe
University of Rio Grande
Ivan M. Tribe, *Mountaineer Jamboree: Country Music in West Virginia,* 1984.

Allen Taylor Caperton

Senator Allen Taylor Caperton, born at Elmwood, the family estate in Monroe County, November 21, 1810, was the son of Hugh and Jane (Erskine) Caperton. After attending a school in Huntsville, Alabama, and the University of Virginia, he graduated from Yale College. For a time he studied law in a Staunton, Virginia, law office and engaged in a brief practice in that town. In 1832, he married Harriet Echols, whose brother, John H. Echols, later a noted Confederate general, married Caperton's sister.

A Whig prior to the Civil War, he represented Monroe County in the Virginia House of Delegates in 1841–42 and 1857–58 and served in the state Senate in 1844–48 and 1859–60. As a member of the Virginia constitutional convention of 1850, Caperton supported the western position in arguing for legislative representation on the basis of white population with no allowance for the number of slaves. Although he opposed secession, Caperton voted for it in the Virginia convention of 1861 in the belief that it might preserve peace. After Virginia entered the Confederacy, its state Senate elected him to the Confederate Senate, a position he held throughout the Civil War.

After the war, Caperton, by then a Democrat, returned to Monroe County. When Democrats gained control of West Virginia's government in 1871, Caperton resumed an active political life. The state Senate elected him to the U.S. Senate, where he served in 1875–76, succeeding Arthur I. Boreman. Caperton died in Washington, July 26, 1876, and was buried at Union, Monroe County.

Caperton belonged to a well-established family. His father was an early congressman, and later generations produced business leaders and a governor.

Otis K. Rice
WVU Institute of Technology
Oren F. Morton, *A History of Monroe County, West Virginia*, 1916; Jon L. Wakelyn, *Biographical Dictionary of the Confederacy,* 1977.

William Gaston Caperton III

Governor William Gaston Caperton III (1940–).

The 31st governor of West Virginia, William Gaston Caperton III, was born in Charleston, February 21, 1940, the only son of two children born to William Gaston Caperton Jr. and Eliza Ambler. He is a descendant of the frontier families who settled in Western Virginia prior to the Revolutionary War.

Caperton attended public school in Charleston and then attended Episcopal High School in Alexandria, Virginia. He graduated from the University of North Carolina in 1963 with a degree in business administration. Afterward, Caperton went to work at his father's insurance company, McDonough-Caperton-Shepherd, of which he was elected president in 1976. By the late 1980s, the McDonough-Caperton Insurance Group, as it was then known, had become one of the largest privately owned insurance companies in the nation.

Throughout his business career, Caperton flirted with politics by serving in several prominent campaigns, including those of U.S. Sen. Robert C. Byrd and Gov. and later U.S. Sen. John D. Rockefeller IV. In 1987, Caperton ran for governor against incumbent Republican Gov. Arch A. Moore Jr.

Caperton outpaced a crowded Democratic primary field and then won convincingly against Moore, in part due to the economic recession that had plagued the state for more than a decade and the state's mounting inability to pay its bills. Following his election victory, Caperton assembled a bipartisan team of financial experts to review the state's situation. The financial task force indicated that West Virginia faced liabilities that would equal as much as $367 million within the first year Caperton was in office, with additional debts whose total at that time could not be determined. In addition,

West Virginia had unfunded liabilities approaching what some estimated to be $4 billion in its teachers pension and workers' compensation systems.

When Caperton took his oath of office on January 16, 1989, he immediately called the legislature into special session. He asked lawmakers to address the financial crisis, to pass groundbreaking ethics legislation for public officials, and to enact a major reorganization of state government. The result of that special session was the desired ethics legislation, a major reorganization that instituted a cabinet form of government in the executive branch, and the largest tax increase in state history. The novice governor's popularity plummeted, but West Virginia's economic plight and the financial condition of state government improved throughout Caperton's two terms.

A year after Caperton took office, state teachers walked out of their classrooms in the first-ever West Virginia teachers' strike. The 11-day strike ended when Caperton and the legislature agreed to hold a special session on education to address salaries and other issues. The resulting Education Reform Act provided a large raise for teachers, while establishing faculty senates in individual schools and a state Center for Professional Development. "Most observers agree that 1990 brought both the high point and the low point of the first Caperton administration," wrote Caperton press aide Bob Brunner, who believed the act provided wide-ranging reforms and was a triumph for the governor.

Those early events set the tone for the remainder of Caperton's administration; perhaps most significantly, they established an unusually close working relationship with the legislature. Caperton met often with the legislative leadership to discuss problems and issues, solicited members' suggestions, and worked hard to build a consensus. These efforts were aided by a Democrat-controlled legislature and the relative stability of the leadership in the House of Delegates and Senate. By his second term, from 1993 to 1997, Caperton was winning passage of nearly all of his proposals.

Central to his administration was education; Caperton launched a three-pronged approach that pushed West Virginia to the forefront in the use of education technology. At his behest, West Virginia was the first to initiate a statewide effort to put computers in every classroom, beginning with kindergarten and continuing through elementary grades. The program included statewide training for teachers in the use of computers in education.

The third element of Caperton's education initiative was to establish the School Building Authority, a board that would distribute state funds to counties to build and modernize schools. It was a quasi-independent agency that could allocate money based on the merit of individual building and renovation proposals and encourage school consolidation. Caperton encouraged the building of new schools. As he said in 1993 when the School Building Authority's funding was challenged, "How can we expect our children to value schooling when it's obvious we don't value our schools?"

He established a Council for Community and Economic Development, a public-private body combining business leaders with government officials to chart the state's economic course. It served two purposes: business leaders were actively involved in the state's business recruitment efforts, and decisions central to the state's future were made with input from the private as well as the public sector. Similar oversight and policy councils were established in other key areas, such as workers' compensation, tourism, and pension programs.

Caperton was able to win major improvements to education, economic development, workers' compensation, infrastructure, and environmental regulation. West Virginia was among the top 10 states in economic activity at times during his administration. A concerted effort to focus health education on primary care and rural health services also began under Caperton.

Caperton and his wife of 23 years, Ella Dee Kessel Caperton, divorced while he was in office. Caperton had two sons from that marriage, William Gaston Caperton IV and John Ambler Caperton. In May 1990, Caperton was married to Rachael Worby, conductor and music director of the Wheeling Symphony Orchestra. Later Caperton and Worby divorced, and Caperton remarried in 2003.

At the end of Caperton's term in January 1997, several newspapers gave him high marks in education and economic development. "West Virginia will benefit from his work for years to come," the *Charleston Daily Mail* editorialized. *The Charleston Gazette* named him the 1996 West Virginian of the Year.

Caperton served on the National Governors' Association executive committee and was the 1996 chairman of the Democratic Governors' Association. In 1999, he was chosen president of the College Board, the non-profit organization that administers the SAT examinations and other educational programs.

Elizabeth Jill Wilson
Cottageville

Bob Brunner, *The Caperton Years: 1989–1993*, 1997; Otis K. Rice and Stephen W. Brown, *The Mountain State: An Introduction to West Virginia*, 1997; Elizabeth Jill Wilson, *The Caperton Years: 1993–1997*, 2 vols., 2005.

Capital Punishment

Until 1899, the death penalty in West Virginia was carried out by county governments. Following a public hanging in Ripley in 1897—a spectacle that attracted about 5,000 onlookers as well as the national press—legislation was introduced to transfer that responsibility to the state. Delegate John Darst, a Jackson County Republican, sponsored a bill calling for executions to be done only in Moundsville, "within the walls of the West Virginia Penitentiary . . . within an enclosure to be prepared for that purpose . . . so constructed as to exclude public view . . . ." Governor Atkinson signed the bill into law on February 18, 1899.

By this time, six other states had already abolished the death penalty. Opposition to capital punishment took root in West Virginia in the 1910s. Moundsville lawyer J. Howard Holt published *Crime and Punishment* in 1918, a pamphlet arguing that reform should be the only goal of punishment. He distributed copies of the tract to judges and legislators, but was discouraged that it had "apparently no good result."

Charges that capital punishment was too cruel eventually had some effect: In 1949, West Virginia abandoned hanging in favor of the electric chair, following a national trend toward more humane executions. The chair, constructed by an inmate who was an electrician, was first used in 1951 when Harry Atlee Burdette and Fred Clifford Painter were put to death for the murder of Edward C. O'Brien.

The international attention given to human rights in the wake of World War II led many western nations to reconsider capital punishment. Much of western Europe discontinued the practice, and opposition to the death penalty gained momentum in the United States. In West Virginia, bills calling for its abolition were introduced in the House of Delegates in 1955, 1957, 1959, and 1963. Finally, in 1965, Democrats Jesse Barker of Kanawha County and Robert Holliday of Fayette County successfully ushered HB 517 through the House. Despite opposition in both the House and Senate, this bill to repeal the death penalty was signed into law by Governor Smith.

Between 1899 and 1959, the state put 94 men to death. (Two women were sentenced to death, but both sentences were commuted to life in prison.) The majority of those executed had been convicted of murder, eight had been convicted of rape, and three had been convicted of kidnaping. During these 60 years, West Virginia reflected another national trend: It executed a disproportionately high percentage of African-Americans. Forty African-Americans were put to death— 42.5 percent of all executions. Census figures for 1900 to 1960 show that the state's total black population averaged about 5.7 percent.

Despite arguments that the death penalty deters crime, West Virginia enjoyed very low crime rates in the decades following abolition of the death penalty. From 1971 to 1998, the state had the lowest crime rate in the country, according to the FBI. According to State Police statistics for 1998, West Virginia ranked 49th in the nation with a reported crime rate of 25.47 per 1,000 residents. (New Hampshire, a death penalty state, had a slightly lower rate of 24.2.) The national crime rate was reported to be 46.15.

Though regular attempts have been made in the legislature to reinstate capital punishment, West Virginia remains one of 12 states that does not impose death sentences.

See also Crime

Christine M. Kreiser
Clarksburg

Stan Bumgardner and Christine Kreiser, "'Thy Brother's Blood': Capital Punishment in West Virginia," *West Virginia Historical Society Quarterly,* March 1996.

Shelley Moore Capito

Congresswoman Shelley Wellons Moore Capito was born November 26, 1953, in Glen Dale, Marshall County, the daughter of the best-known politician to come out of that community, Arch Moore Jr. Her father served six terms in the House of Representatives and three terms as governor of West Virginia.

Capito began her political career by getting elected to the House of Delegates from Kanawha County in 1996 and 1998. In 2000, when Bob Wise decided to run for governor instead of for reelection to the congressional seat he had held for 18 years, Capito won the Second District seat and became the first Republican in the House of Representatives from West Virginia since the early 1980s. She is only the second woman to represent West Virginia in Congress.

In the November 2000 election, she won by a narrow margin of about 5,600 votes in a district that covered 20 counties, stretching from the Ohio to the Potomac. Capito defeated former state Sen. Jim Humphreys, a Democrat and successful attorney who spent $6.4 million in his losing cause. Capito had only $1.4 million in campaign funds, but received help from spending by the Republican Congressional Campaign Committee and the U.S. Chamber of Commerce.

In 2002, when redistricting reduced the district to 18 counties, she faced a rematch with Humphreys. He spent even more heavily: more than $8 million, including about $2.5 million in the Democratic primary. Capito spent about $2.5 million and defeated him in the general election by a much bigger margin than in 2000. In her reelection bid in 2004, Cap-ito spent only a fraction as much in defeating Democrat Eric Wells.

Capito benefited from beginning her Congressional career at a time when fellow Republicans held a majority in the House and wanted to make sure they retained seats such as hers. Consequently, she received favorable committee assignments and more attention than is accorded to most newcomers. Being a swing vote on several key bills also drew attention to Capito, and she already had wide name recognition in West Virginia.

Her Congressional assignments have included the Banking and Financial Services Committee, the Transportation and Infrastructure Committee, and the Small Business Committee. In 2003, colleagues selected Capito to be co-chairwoman of the Congressional Women's Caucus. Also that year, she was appointed vice-chairwoman of the House Prescription Drug Task Force. She was one of the sponsors of the Medicare Prescription Drug Benefit, signed into law in December 2003.

Before entering politics, Capito worked as a career counselor at West Virginia State College (now University) and as director of the West Virginia Board of Regents Educational Information Center. She earned a bachelor of science degree in zoology from Duke University in 1975 and a master of education degree from the University of Virginia in 1976. She and her family live in Charleston.

See also Arch Moore

Jim Wallace
Charleston

The Capitol

Within days of the fire that consumed the picturesque downtown Charleston state capitol, political leaders began to plan for a new and grander structure. On January 21, 1921, the legislature adopted a joint resolution to raise a commission composed of the Board of Public Works, five members each from the House and the Senate, the Senate president and House speaker, and the governor. In July of 1921, they selected architect Cass Gilbert, whose achievements included some of the most famous buildings in the nation.

Site selection was not so clear cut, with many Charleston residents advocating the capitol be rebuilt at the downtown location while others favored the less congested east end of the city. Architect Gilbert and the commission's engineer, M. W. Venable, preferred another site near the current Charleston Area Medical Center on the Kanawha City side of the Kanawha River. The commission selected the site in the city's east end, however, reasoning the location would be less costly to develop.

The three units of the capitol complex were let as separate contracts, each financed, constructed, and inspected before the next was begun. Each unit was

The state capitol.

built for less than the legislative appropriation, first the west wing at a cost of $1,218,171.32; then the east wing at $1,361,425.00; and last the main unit and connecting wings for $4,482,623.21. Counting the costs of land acquisition and beautification, West Virginia invested a gross sum of $9,491,180.03 for one of the nation's most beautiful and functional capitols. "While not extravagant or elaborate in detail or material," the architect said, "nevertheless it can properly take its place as among the best buildings in the United States."

Groundbreaking for the west wing was in January 1924, and this first phase was completed in March 1925; the east wing was built between July 1926 and December 1927; and work on the main building and connecting wings commenced in March 1930, was completed in February 1932, and officially dedicated on West Virginia Day, June 20, 1932.

The wings measure 300 feet by 60 feet,

each including four stories and a basement; the exterior walls are constructed of Indiana select buff limestone; and the interior walls and floors are Tennessee marble. The main unit is 558 feet by 120 feet, with three stories and a basement; and the connecting wings are one story with connecting basement passages. These exterior walls are of the same limestone, but the interior walls and floors combine Imperial Danby Vermont marble and Italian Travertine marble. The combined floor space is 535,000 square feet; 4,640 tons of steel and more than 300,000 cubic yards of limestone were used in the construction. The dome rises 292 feet, is 75 feet in diameter, and is made of lead, coated with copper, and covered in gold leaf trimmed in blue. A 4,000-pound chandelier hangs about 180 feet above the ground floor in the dome's interior. The dome is taller but not as broad as the dome on our nation's capitol. Marble from France and Belgium as well

as decorative materials from other countries adorn the capitol's principal foyers and legislative chambers.

The capitol is as much a museum as an office complex, and this is evident at every turn in its corridors, from the Czechoslovakian crystal chandeliers to the quartered oak doors and black walnut desks, from the mythological heads carved at the entrances to the interior artistry of marble, bronze, and plaster. The hands of thousands of skilled craftsmen and artisans erected a grand monument, but also forged a substantial testament to a state's dedication and commitment, securely mooring the state's capitol on the banks of the Kanawha River.

See also Capitols of West Virginia

Bob Damron
Charleston

Bob Damron, "Building the Capitol," *Goldenseal,* Summer 1982; "Building the State Capitol: The Official Construction Photographs from the West Virginia State Archives," *Goldenseal,* Summer 1982.

Capitols of West Virginia

The first West Virginia state capitol was the 1859 Linsly Institute building in Wheeling, serving from June 20, 1863, to April 1, 1870. The building, still a Wheeling landmark, combines the Greek Revival and Italianate architectural styles. In 1870, the state capital was moved to Charleston. One of Charleston's most prominent citizens, Dr. John P. Hale, was given the contract for construction of a suitable building and ended up paying most of the cost himself. The 1870 capitol was built in the Italianate style, with Romanesque details. The legislature approved the return of the capital to Wheeling and on December 4, 1876, the city presented the state with a new structure. The 1876 capitol was a handsome blend of Greek Revival and Romanesque architectural styles, each facade dominated by a full-height pedimented porch.

The 1877 legislature decided to put the question of the capital location to a vote of the people. The election pitted the three cities of Charleston, Clarksburg, and Martinsburg against each other. Charleston won the vote, and the governor proclaimed that after eight years the city would be the state government's permanent capital.

The state's fourth capitol building, the second one in Charleston, was erected, incorporating the 1870 capitol into the new structure. The 85 rooms of the new building, which housed all the departments of state government, were completely occupied in 1887. The so-called Victorian capitol was built in the Second Empire style, with a mansard roof, gabled wall dormers, and towers. In 1903, an annex was built across the street. The annex was torn down in 1967.

On January 3, 1921, the Victorian capitol was destroyed by a fire of unknown origin. A temporary wood-frame building, located on the future site of the Daniel Boone Hotel, was erected in just 42 days and became known as the "pasteboard capitol." This 166-room building experienced the same fate as its predecessor when on March 2, 1927, it was completely destroyed by fire.

After the 1921 fire, a State Capitol Commission was created to find a permanent location for a complex of buildings that would serve the needs of the state government for a long time. A site in the east end of Charleston was selected, and noted architect Cass Gilbert was selected to design the capitol building. Gilbert designed three interconnecting units—the west wing was completed in 1925, the east wing in 1927, and the main domed unit in 1932.

See also The Capitol

Stan Cohen
Pictorial Histories

Capon Springs Resort

Capon Springs Resort, and associated farms, is a 5,000-acre retreat near the community of Capon Springs in Hampshire County. Managed by the same family since 1932, the resort is "one of the best-preserved 19th-century spring resorts in the state," according to research nominating it to the National Register of Historic Places.

Word spread about the reputed healing powers of the mineral waters of Capon Springs as early as the 1700s. In 1849, Baltimore investors bought several hundred acres and built the 500-room Mountain House at Capon Springs. After the Civil War, former Confederate Capt. William H. Sale took over and began a major expansion. He oversaw construction of several large guest houses, including the Annex, now the resort's main house.

After Sale died in 1900, the resort began to stagnate. A 1911 fire destroyed the Mountain House, along with several nearby buildings. The 320-acre retreat was auctioned in 1932 and purchased by Lou Austin, a devout and visionary Philadelphia entrepreneur who foresaw a prosperous industry in bottling Capon Springs water. Lou's wife, Virginia, threw herself into managing the floundering resort. The bottling business was abandoned after 1959, when Lou retired, although the water remains available free of charge at fountains and faucets.

A loan from the Romney banker and former West Virginia governor, John Cornwell, allowed the Austins to extend plumbing and electricity throughout the resort by 1938. Local workers were hired to build a new kitchen and dining room, where family-style meals are still served, and to renovate other buildings. A nine-hole golf course, fish pond, swimming pool, and additional guest cottages were also added. During World War II, dignitaries and military officials vacationed from nearby Washington, contributing to the resort's biggest boom. By the 1950s, Lou Austin had added several thousand acres of farm and grazing land to the estate to provide food for the roughly 200 guests the facility could now house.

As the Austins aged, their three oldest children gradually took over. Lou Austin died in 1976; Virginia followed him six years later. The third generation took charge in 1988, still holding to their grandfather's ideals of simplicity, informality, respect, and religion. Doors have no locks at Capon Springs, as guests follow the "Capon Way," an unspoken agreement of mutual trust.

Stephanie Earls
Yakima, Washington

Captain Bull

Captain Bull, an Indian leader, was born in the Northeast, possibly eastern Pennsylvania, and later settled in present West Virginia His father, the noted Delaware chief Teedyuscung, was killed during Pontiac's Rebellion, in which Bull himself took an active role.

In response to the uprising, the British superintendent of Indian affairs, Sir William Johnson, had Bull and his party captured at their village in New York. Released in 1768 on condition they never return, they chose the Western Virginia wilderness, not only for the abundant game and nearby salt springs, but also for the absence of other tribes. Settling in present Braxton County, Captain Bull's community lived peacefully, trading salt with the settlers.

In the following decade, however, tensions increased between the ever-advancing pioneer population and Indians of the Ohio River watershed, each side exacting retribution for past atrocities. The 1772 murder of Adam Stroud's family provided an excuse for a party from Buckhannon, including Jesse Hughes and others, to massacre Captain Bull's village. In fact, the Strouds had been killed by raiding Shawnees. In later years, as participants in the killing of Bull's people reflected on their deeds, details of the incident revealed its injustice.

What happened to Captain Bull himself remains uncertain. He does not seem to have been killed in the 1772 raid on his village. Some evidence suggests that he resettled somewhere in Missouri along the Mississippi River, where he may have died a peaceful death in the 1790s. Other reports indicate that he may have stayed in the Alleghenies and participated in the border warfare between Indians and colonials during the American Revolution. McWhorter's *Border Settlers of Northwestern Virginia* claims Captain Bull was killed in 1781 in the Tygart Valley area, and his body identified.

See also Bulltown, Jesse Hughes, Pontiac's Rebellion

Jaime Simmons
State Archives

Lucullus McWhorter, *The Border Settlers of Northwestern Virginia from 1768–1795,* 1975; Alexander Scott Withers, *Chronicles of Border Warfare,* 1994.

Cardinal

The northern cardinal, once known to most West Virginians as simply "red bird," became our state bird in 1949. It was chosen for the male's brilliant red coloration and crest and the lovely, although more subtle colors of the female, its statewide distribution, the beautiful, cheery song heard from early spring into summer, and its propensity to live near our dwellings and visit backyard bird feeders.

Spring courtship rituals often begin with the male offering the female a tidbit of food. The nest is made of twigs, vines, leaves, and small roots, lined with hair and fine grass. It is usually built close to the ground, in shrubs, or small trees. The female lays two to five eggs which are buff-white with dark marks. She sits on the eggs for 12 to 13 days and the young leave 10 to 11 days after hatching. There may be two, three, even four broods a season; the male cares for the existing brood while the female incubates the eggs of the next.

Cardinals eat 51 species of insects, 33 kinds of wild fruits, and 39 different weed seeds. To attract them to a feeder offer black oil sunflower or safflower seed.

Kathleen Carothers Leo
Division of Natural Resources

The Cardinal

The Cardinal is one of two Amtrak passenger trains with routes in West Virginia. The Cardinal begins its 921-mile, 23-hour trip in Washington and ends in Chicago, traversing southern West Virginia en route. Another Amtrak train, the Capitol Limited, travels across the state's Eastern Panhandle.

The Cardinal was born shortly after Amtrak, the National Railroad Passenger Corporation, began service in 1971. The train passes through the states of Virginia, West Virginia, Ohio, Indiana, and Illinois. It takes its name from the cardinal, the state bird of all five states.

The Cardinal follows the historic route of the old Chesapeake & Ohio main line through West Virginia. From the east, the train enters the state near White Sulphur Springs, proceeds to Hinton, passes through the New River Gorge towns of Prince and Thurmond, and continues to Montgomery, Charleston, and Huntington. Separate eastbound and westbound versions of the Cardinal travel through

West Virginia on Wednesday, Friday, and Sunday.

Because of its relatively low ridership, the Cardinal often has been the target of federal budget cuts. West Virginia's congressional delegation has fought to keep the Cardinal. In particular, Sen. Robert C. Byrd has worked with Amtrak officials to keep the Cardinal operating, touting the train's importance to the state's tourism industry.

See also Amtrak

John S. Carlile

U.S. Senator John Snyder Carlile, who played a controversial role in the creation of West Virginia, was born in Winchester, Virginia, December 16, 1817, in modest circumstances. Carlile did not attend school, but was educated by his mother. He started out clerking in a store. He began studying law and was admitted to the bar in 1840. Setting up his practice in Beverly, which was then the county seat of Randolph County, he later moved to Philippi, then to Clarksburg. In 1847, he was elected to the Virginia Senate, beginning an eventful political career. He served also in the Virginia constitutional convention of 1850–51, and in Congress from 1855 to 1857 and from March until July 1861. In early 1861, he was a delegate to the secession convention in Richmond, where he and other delegates from the western counties bitterly opposed Virginia's secession from the United States.

When the convention nonetheless approved secession, Carlile returned home to Clarksburg to lead the movement toward a separate state. Immediately following his return from Richmond, Carlile organized the Clarksburg Convention, which called for a meeting in Wheeling the following month. He helped organize the resulting First Wheeling Convention in May 1861, which favored statehood but adopted a "wait and see" attitude toward Virginia's secession referendum. After Virginia voters approved secession in the subsequent statewide referendum, the Second Wheeling Convention in June established the "restored"state of Virginia which would maintain a pro-Union government for Virginia throughout the Civil War. It was Carlile's "Declaration of the People of Virginia," adopted by the convention, that called for the creation of this government. Carlile and Waitman T. Willey were elected as Virginia members of the U.S. Senate by the new Unionist state legislature.

In the summer of 1862, when the Senate began considering admission of West Virginia to the union, Carlile's actions took a controversial turn. He insisted upon a referendum among the people of the proposed new state before statehood could be approved. Given the Confederate sympathies in several southern and eastern counties, this might have derailed statehood. Eventually, a substitute bill written by Senator Willey was passed, which required only the approval by a constitutional convention. Many of Carlile's former friends now angrily viewed him as a traitor to the cause of statehood, and there were calls to have him impeached. However, he continued to serve in the U.S. Senate until March 3, 1865.

Carlile's political career was effectively ended. President Grant later nominated him as ambassador to Sweden, but the U.S. Senate refused to confirm him. Carlile died October 24, 1878, in Clarksburg and is buried in the Oddfellows Cemetery.

See also Formation of West Virginia, Waitman Thomas Willey

Jim Barnes
Morgantown

Charles H. Ambler, *Waitman Thomas Willey,* 1954; George Ellis Moore, *A Banner in the Hills,* 1963.

Carnegie Hall

Industrialist Andrew Carnegie (1835–1919) built thousands of libraries, including libraries in Hinton, Huntington, and Parkersburg, but only four Carnegie Hall performing arts centers, in Lewisburg, New York, Pittsburgh, and Scotland. In 1902, Carnegie donated $33,000 to the Lewisburg Female Institute to build the local Carnegie Hall. The Louisville, Kentucky, architectural firm of Barrett & Thompson built the Greek Revival structure. Carnegie Hall provided classroom and stage space for the Institute, which was eventually renamed Greenbrier College for Women.

When the college closed in 1972, the state used the building as a facility for the mentally and emotionally disadvantaged. In the early 1980s, rumors began circulating that Carnegie Hall was about to be condemned and razed. A group of citizens formed Carnegie Hall, Inc., as a non-profit organization with the goal of restoring the building.

Today, Carnegie Hall is a regional center for arts and education. In addition to a year-round performance series, Carnegie Hall offers classes and workshops, children's programs, rotating museum exhibits, and juried art shows. Carnegie Hall sends regional artists and visiting performers to area schools, giving children the experience of creating art.

Carnegie Libraries

From 1886 to 1919, Andrew Carnegie and the Carnegie Corporation provided slightly more than $41 million for the construction of public and academic libraries in the United States. Eight Carnegie grants totaling $241,500 were eventually approved for communities in West Virginia: Wheeling—$75,000 (August 12, 1899), Huntington—$35,000 (December 30, 1901), Parkersburg—$34,000 (December 29, 1903), Bethany College—$20,000 (March 1905), Hinton -$12,500 (April 8, 1907), Bluefield—$10,000 (April 8, 1911), Williamson -$10,000 (February 13, 1913), and Charleston—$45,000 (March 14, 1913). Ultimately, however, only four grants totaling $101,500 were accepted. An academic library was built at Bethany College, and public libraries were completed in Hinton, Huntington, and Parkersburg.

The communities rejecting Carnegie grants generally did so because they could not raise the 10 percent annual maintenance fee required by Carnegie or could not secure suitable building sites. This was the situation with both Bluefield and Williamson. However, Charleston community leaders believed the city "should have a more commodious library than $45,000 would erect." A subsequent bond proposal in 1915 to raise more dollars failed after Carnegie refused to modify the award.

The most acrid refusal of an approved Carnegie grant came from Wheeling, where labor leaders led the defeat of a municipal bond levy stating that Wheeling was "one place on this great green planet where Andrew Carnegie can't get a monument with his money." Their opposition stemmed from steelworkers' deaths during the 1892 strike at Carnegie's Homestead, Pennsylvania, mill.

All the Carnegie library buildings in West Virginia remain intact, but none currently serves as a library.

Charles A. Julian
Wheeling Jesuit University

Carnifex Ferry, Battle of

In July 1861, Union forces pushed the Confederates out of the Kanawha Valley and occupied the strategic Gauley Bridge area. In August the Confederates launched a counterattack to regain control of the Kanawha Valley and disrupt the attempts to separate Western Virginia from Virginia. Confederate troops under the command of Gen. John Floyd crossed the Gauley River and defeated a small Union force at Keslers Cross Lanes. Floyd then retreated to an encampment along the steep western cliffs of the Gauley River at Carnifex Ferry. Union Gen. William Rosecrans assembled a force of 7,000 to drive the 2,000 Confederates away. Marching south from Summersville, Rosecrans's force made contact with Floyd on September 10, 1861. Instead of concentrating his force for an overwhelming assault, Rosecrans spent the day sending in his brigades one at a time as they arrived at the battlefield, allowing the outnumbered Confederates to repulse the piecemeal attacks. During the night, the Confederates decided to re-

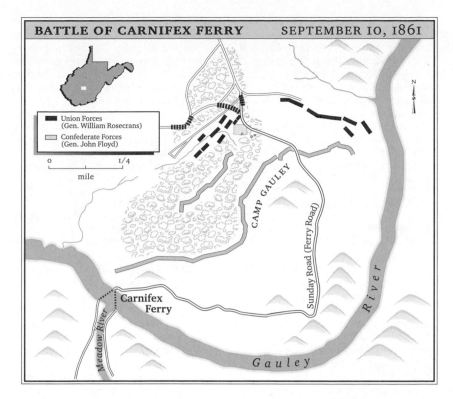

BATTLE OF CARNIFEX FERRY   SEPTEMBER 10, 1861

Union Forces
(Gen. William Rosecrans)

Confederate Forces
(Gen. John Floyd)

0   1/4
mile

CAMP GAULEY

Sunday Road (Ferry Road)

Carnifex
Ferry

Meadow River

River

Gauley

treat before they could be defeated in the morning. Floyd managed to get away before Rosecrans knew he was gone.

Casualties were light on both sides, but the battle had an important political effect. Beginning in May 1861, meetings had been held to organize a loyal Unionist government for Virginia to be headquartered at Wheeling. In October, just after the Battle of Carnifex Ferry, there was a vote in areas controlled by federal forces to decide whether to create a new state. The favorable vote was a key step in the formation of West Virginia. A loss at Carnifex Ferry and Confederate occupation of the Kanawha Valley might have changed that vote.

See also Civil War

David Bard
Concord University

David Bard, *Civil War: The New River Valley: Three One-Day Driving Tours,* 2004; Terry Lowry, *September Blood: The Battle of Carnifex Ferry,* 1985.

Carnifex Ferry Battlefield State Park

Located opposite the mouth of Meadow River, 12 miles south of Summersville in southern Nicholas County, this 156-acre park encompasses the Carnifex Ferry Civil War battlefield. Here, on September 10, 1861, Union forces led by Gen. William S. Rosecrans defeated Gen. John B. Floyd's Confederate troops, who were camped on a farm owned by Henry Patteson.

The state legislature, noting interest in the annual reunion of Carnifex Ferry battle veterans, passed a bill on March 14,

1931 to create the Carnifex Ferry Battlefield Park Commission. In 1935, the legislature appropriated funds to buy the Patteson farm. In 1950, during the administration of Governor Patteson, grandson of Henry Patteson, additional state funds were used to improve the park.

Historical attractions include the restored Patteson house and interpretative museum, and the annual Carnifex Ferry battle reenactment. Recreation areas fea-

ture hiking trails, picnic facilities, and a playground.

See also Battle of Carnifex Ferry

Carpenter Family

Members of the Carpenter family were among the first white people to settle in what is now central West Virginia, and their descendants populate a wide area today. Family stories recount the arrival in the late 1700s of brothers Benjamin and Jeremiah, who, along with their mother, were the first settlers on the upper waters of the Elk River. With a few belongings, including a fiddle, tied to the backs of oxen, they followed creeks and Indian paths through the wilderness until they reached the mouth of Laurel Fork, later called Centralia (near the Braxton-Webster county line). They established homes there. Legend holds that the Elk River was named for an elk killed by Jeremiah Carpenter.

The Carpenters have produced some of West Virginia's most distinguished fiddlers, their repertoire often reflecting the family experience. When Benjamin was killed in an Indian raid in the early 1790s, Jeremiah fled with his pregnant wife (an Indian, according to family lore) and waded about two miles up Laurel Creek to a huge, overhanging rock to hide until the threat had passed. His son, Solomon (in later years also known as "Old Solly"), was born under that ledge, and the tune "Shelvin' Rock," which commemorates the struggles of the pioneer period, was added to the family fiddling tradition. Its authorship is generally credited to Jeremiah.

"Camp Chase" is probably the most fa-

Shelt Carpenter, Elk Valley outdoorsman.

mous of the Carpenter tunes, partly due to the tale that goes with it. It seems that another Solomon Carpenter, known as "Devil Sol," was a prisoner during the Civil War at Camp Chase, Ohio, and fiddled his way to freedom playing this tune in a prisoners' fiddle contest. Apparently all the fiddlers played the same tune and Sol won by adding some unusual notes according to his fancy. Devil Sol's grandson, French Carpenter, carried his music into the mid-20th century.

Another fiddler, William "Squirrelly Bill" Carpenter, learned the family tunes, which he passed on to his son, Shelt, and grandson, Ernie. Ernie Carpenter's repertoire spanned five generations of fiddling Carpenters, and he won the attention of many contemporary fiddlers. Ernie, a recipient of the Vandalia Award in 1988, died in 1997. The Carpenter family home at the mouth of Laurel Fork was inundated by the Sutton Dam, completed in 1955 by the U.S. Army Corps of Engineers. Ernie Carpenter never got over his sense of loss of the old place, which was his fondest connection with the past.

See also French Carpenter, "Squirrelly Bill" Carpenter, Fiddle Tradition

Michael Kline
St. Mary's City, Maryland

Gerald Milnes, *Play of a Fiddle,* 1999; Gerald Milnes and Michael Kline, "Ernie Carpenter: Tales of the Elk River Country," *Goldenseal,* Summer 1986.

French Carpenter

Fiddler David Frank "French" Carpenter was a notable member of a famous musical family. He was born in Clay County, June 7, 1905, and learned most of his music directly from his father, Tom, who was known as a fiddling preacher. Tom learned from French's grandfather, the legendary Solly "Devil Sol" Carpenter, possibly the most influential fiddler in his part of West Virginia during the past 100 years.

Many played the Carpenter music after Sol, but French seemed to play it best. His playing was intricate and interestingly embellished. His timing was elusive and requires considerable attention to be appreciated. He used, to good advantage, the old West Virginia technique of lingering on a note, extending its duration for emphasis. His bowing was particularly fine, smooth, and subtle.

Carpenter's music was also influenced by Webster County fiddler Lewis Johnson "Uncle Jack" McElwain. Some of Carpenter's tunes were preserved on a recording released under two different titles: *Elzic's Farewell* (Kanawha 301, about 1976) and *Old-Time Songs and Tunes from Clay County, West Virginia* (Folk Promotions, 1964). It features Carpenter's music along with that of Jenes Cottrell, another well-known West Virginia musician. The Carpenter music continued to be played by Clay County fiddler Wilson Douglas,

who died in 1999. He devoted years to learning French Carpenter's music and probably knew more about Carpenter than anyone else alive at the time.

French Carpenter died May 22, 1965, several years before the old-time fiddling revival was in full swing. He was the nephew of Elk River outdoorsman "Squirrelly Bill" Carpenter and a first cousin, once-removed of fiddler Ernie Carpenter.

See also Carpenter Family, Fiddle Tradition

Michael Kline
St. Mary's City, Maryland

Squirrelly Bill Carpenter

Outdoorsman William "Squirrelly Bill" Carpenter was born on the Elk River, April 17, 1827, near the mouth of Laurel Creek on a homestead later lost in the building of Sutton Lake. Grandson of the Braxton County pioneer and legendary fiddle player Jeremiah Carpenter and his first wife, reportedly an Indian, Squirrelly Bill was himself grandfather to another fiddler of renown, Ernie Carpenter (1907–97).

Carpenter built dugout canoes, which he sold by length for a dollar per foot. He also occupied himself fishing, hunting, freighting, scouting, fiddling, and guiding prominent West Virginians, including Governor MacCorkle, through the wonders of the Elk Valley. Charleston attorney W.E.R. Byrne, in his classic book *Tale of the Elk,* tells of his adventures with Squirrelly Bill and his sons. Carpenter was said to have enjoyed an uncanny knowledge and understanding of nature and its signs. "He no doubt has caught more fish and killed more game than any other man that ever lived in this section," according to Carpenter's obituary in the *Braxton Central* newspaper.

According to grandson Ernie Carpenter, Squirrelly Bill never wore shoes but kept to moccasins until the end. He prac-

ticed other old ways as well. His son, Shelt, was fond of saying of his father, that, "In the old days we did everything by hand-power and awkwardness." Squirrelly Bill Carpenter died February 21, 1921, and is buried in Braxton County.

See also Carpenter Family

Peter Silitch
Strange Creek

W.E.R. Byrne, *Tale of the Elk,* 1995; Gerald Milnes and Michael Kline, "Ernie Carpenter," *Goldenseal,* Summer 1986; Gerald Milnes, *Play of a Fiddle,* 1999.

Carr China Company

The pottery factory that was to become Carr China Company was established in 1913 as the Consolidated Manufactories Company by the Merchants Association of Grafton. Begun as a community economic development project, the company built the brick, seven-kiln, 108,000-square-foot pottery plant to employ 250 people. The original company operated the pottery for two years but was declared bankrupt on January 1, 1916.

In June 1916, members of the Speidel, Bachmann, and Carr families brought Thomas Carr, the president of the Warwick Pottery Company in Wheeling, to take over the Grafton pottery. The new operation was called Carr China Company. After Thomas Carr's retirement in 1923, Carr China successfully competed in the hotel ware market for 30 more years.

Carr China made all types of dishware to prepare and serve food and beverages. They also made smoking accessories and special ware for hospitals. Their salesmen sold to many of the nation's restaurants, resorts, hotels, and hospitals. They also provided ware for West Virginia's state parks and the Jackson's Mill 4-H Center.

Their designs included Blue Willow, Dolly Varden, Dresden, Empire, Glo-tan, Rho-dendra, Roanoke, and many others. The names are on many pieces of ware.

Squirrelly Bill, Elk River fisherman

"From the mouth of Wolf Creek up to Stony Creek was long the favorite haunt of 'Squirley [sic] Bill' Carpenter, who, by the way, was a son of Solomon Carpenter, the chap who was born under the rock, as already recounted. 'Squirley' was an all-round fisherman, a canoe builder and operator, flatboat builder, and steersman, raftsman and general water-dog and fisherman; he was the most inveterate, persistent and uncompromising fisherman ever known in the valley of Elk. Spring, summer, autumn and winter made up the fishing season for him. The river frozen over with ice a foot thick didn't daunt him in the least. He would go up to the deep hole at Breech Clout, cut a hole in the ice, sit down on the rock—Breech Clout is the name of a huge rock jutting out from the north bank of the Elk, about one mile above Wolf Creek—and catch all kinds of fish, when it was so cold that any other living man would have frozen to death. His usual method of fishing when the weather was warm, was to roll up his trousers above the knees and wade out as far as he could into the edge of a deep hole and stand there all day, or until he had as many fish as he wanted. He was a bait and pawpaw pole fisherman, pure and simple, and despised the new-fangled fishing frumpery of rod, reel, flies or artificial lures, of any kind or character."

—W.E.R. Byrne *Tale of the Elk* (1940)

As World War II approached, Carr built extra warehouses to stockpile necessary English clay. They supplied chinaware to the armed forces, and their handleless mugs became well known to servicemen. After the war, competition with plastics and recovering foreign factories forced the Carr China Company out of business in 1953.

See also Pottery Industry

James R. Mitchell
State Museum

Taylor County Historical and Genealogical Society, *A History of Taylor County, West Virginia,* 1986.

Fannie Cobb Carter

Educator Fannie Cobb Carter (1872–1973).

African-American educator Fannie Cobb was born in Charleston, September 30, 1872, in the same year a new state constitution prohibited black children and white children from attending school together. Cobb early learned the value of education and dedicated her life to providing future generations with the tools they needed to move on in the world.

Cobb earned her teaching degree from Storer College in Harpers Ferry in 1891 and returned home to teach in Kanawha County's public schools. She continued her education by attending summer institutes at Oberlin College, the University of Chicago, and Columbia University, among others.

In 1908, Cobb organized the teacher-training department at West Virginia Colored Institute, now West Virginia State University, where she remained for 12 years. After her husband, Emory Carter, a Charleston lawyer, died in 1925, she was named superintendent of the State Industrial Home for Colored Girls in Huntington. However, Carter refused to accept her appointment until state officials removed the bars from the home's windows.

In 1935, Carter was named director of adult education for Kanawha County schools. She retired after two years, but her career was not yet finished. In 1945, Carter became dean of women at the National Trade and Professional School for Women and Girls in Washington, and at age 89 served as the school's acting president.

Fannie Cobb Carter returned to Charleston in 1962 and remained active in the African-American community until her death March 29, 1973, six months after her 100th birthday.

Christine M. Kreiser
Clarksburg

"Fannie Cobb Carter (1872–1973)," *Missing Chapters: West Virginia Women in History,* 1983.

George L. Carter

Industrialist George Lafayette Carter was born January 10, 1857, in Hillsville, Virginia. He made a fortune in the coal boom and founded the Carolina, Clinchfield & Ohio Railroad, better known as the Clinchfield, a major shipper of coal in southwest Virginia and neighboring West Virginia and Kentucky. Carter developed extensive iron and coal operations in Virginia before turning his attention to southern West Virginia.

Carter moved to his company town of Coalwood, McDowell County, in 1916. Starting in the 1910s and through the 1930s, Coalwood and neighboring Caretta, both Carter company towns, were cleaner and employees better paid than in many other coal towns of the time. Coalwood was later made famous in *Rocket Boys,* a 1998 memoir by native Homer Hickam, and the resulting movie, *October Sky.* Carter owed his success partly to his practice of vertical integration, controlling the product from the mine through the railroad to the wharves and docks of the major ports including Norfolk, Boston, and Bridgeport, Connecticut. Carter was eccentric in not hiring women or ever learning to drive a car. He died December 30, 1936, in Washington. He is buried in Hillsville. His son, James, continued at Coalwood for several years after Carter's death. Carter Coal Company was sold to Youngstown Sheet & Tube in 1947.

See also Rocket Boys

Charles F. Moore
East Tennessee State University

Cass

The lumber town of Cass, located on the Greenbrier River in east-central Pocahontas County, was founded in 1900 by the West Virginia Pulp & Paper Company, now MeadWestvaco. The town was named for Joseph K. Cass, a Pennsylvania paper manufacturer who was vice president of the company.

West Virginia Pulp & Paper, owned largely by the Luke family of New York, built a paper mill at Luke, Maryland, in 1892, and another at Covington, Virginia, in 1900. Both mills used red spruce as a source of fiber for paper pulp. During the late 1800s, John G. Luke began buying large tracts of timberland in the Cheat Mountain area in Randolph and Pocahontas counties. These lands included thousands of acres of old-growth red spruce and hardwood timber.

While the Covington mill processed smaller trees into pulp for paper manufacturing, the Cass sawmill was designed to cut the company's larger trees into lumber. In 1899, West Virginia Pulp & Paper purchased land along the Greenbrier River at the mouth of Leatherbark Creek. Here they built a band sawmill and the town of Cass to house workers at the mill. Cass prospered and by 1920 had a population of more than 2,000. By that time the original forests had largely been cut and, having no other industry, the town began a slow decline.

In 1943, the sawmill was sold to the Mower Lumber Company of Charleston, which cut second-growth timber and continued operating until July 1, 1960. Like most sawmill towns in the state, Cass seemed destined for abandonment. However, in 1962, the state of West Virginia purchased 11 miles of the logging railroad and established the Cass Scenic Railroad State Park. Later, additional miles of railroad, additional steam locomotives and railroad cars, and the town itself were purchased by the state. Company houses were renovated as park cabins. Today, Cass is one of the most popular parks in the state, drawing thousands of visitors each year to ride the special viewing cars drawn by antique steam engines up the steep grades formerly used by the log trains.

See also Cass Scenic Railroad, Sawmills, Timbering and Logging

Roy B. Clarkson
West Virginia University

Roy B. Clarkson, *On Beyond Leatherbark: The Cass Saga,* 1990.

Cass Scenic Railroad

The Cass Scenic Railroad, the major attraction at the Cass Scenic Railroad State Park in Pocahontas County, offers excursion rides on a historic logging railroad line. The railroad is the last segment of the once vast railroad network built, beginning in 1900, to harvest the red spruce on Cheat and Back Allegheny mountains to supply a pulp mill in Covington, Virginia, and the lumber mill in Cass. Today, restored logging locomotives, Shay and Heisler engines built between 1905 and 1945, pull and push the renovated logging flatcars full of tourists up the steep grades.

The logging railroad was abandoned when the mill closed in 1960. The property, including 11 miles of track, the shop, and other equipment and facilities, was purchased by the state in 1962 to create the new park. The first passenger trip was June 15, 1963, during the Centennial celebration.

The steep ascent is made possible by the specially geared locomotives and two switchbacks in the line. The first stop is at Whitaker Station, where the Mountain State Railroading and Logging Historical Association has re-created a 1940s logging camp and equipment display. At 4,842 feet, Bald Knob, 2,300 feet above Cass, provides tourists with an unobstructed view east across the Greenbrier Valley into Virginia. The railroad and park have been expanded to include the town of Cass, additional locomotives, gift and craft shops, museums, and a new depot and engine shop. Cass Scenic Railroad State Park includes 1,089 acres and offers lodging in historic company houses.

See also Cass

Louise Burner Flegel
Pine Knoll Shore, North Carolina
Roy B. Clarkson, *On Beyond Leatherbark: The Cass Saga*, 1990.

Ted Cassidy

Actor Theodore Crawford "Ted" Cassidy, known best for his role as Lurch in *The Addams Family* television program, remains one of Barbour County's most-remembered citizens. He was born in Pittsburgh, July 31, 1932, and raised in Philippi. Cassidy was six feet, one inch tall by the age of 11, eventually growing to six feet, nine inches. After high school, he attended but did not graduate from West Virginia Wesleyan College, then left West Virginia for a career in radio. Working as a staff announcer for WFAA radio in Dallas, he was part of the station's coverage of John F. Kennedy's assassination and was among the first to interview eyewitnesses. Within a year, Cassidy moved to California to pursue an acting career.

In 1964, Cassidy secured the television role that would make him famous. His unusual height and deep voice made him a natural fit for Lurch, the hulking butler of the comically ghoulish Addams family. Although the show was canceled in 1965, Cassidy continued to play small television roles well into the 1970s. His appearances include *I Dream of Jeannie, Star Trek, Bonanza*, and *The Six Million Dollar Man*. Cassidy also provided voices for animated cartoons such as *Space Ghost, The Super Friends*, and *Scooby Doo*.

Ted Cassidy died January 16, 1979, from complications following heart surgery. His remains were cremated and then buried in the backyard of his Woodland Hills, California, home.

C. Belmont Keeney
West Virginia Humanities Council

Castle Rock

Castle Rock in Pineville is a perpendicular formation over 130 feet in height, carved from Pineville Sandstone of the New River Series by the Guyandotte River, which flows by the rock's base, and Rockcastle Creek. The stratified layers of stone suggested to the early explorers the walls of an ancient castle. One of the earliest reports of the formation, in 1780, used the name "Castle Rock." It has attracted rock climbers, and at one time had a ladder to provide access to the small bit of level surface about two-thirds of the way to the top. Today stairs provide a way to this terrace. The community around the rock, which began in 1840, was first known as the Castlerock settlement and later became Pineville, the county seat of Wyoming County. The term "Rock Castle" was also used for the early post office.

See also Pineville

Raymond Thomas Hill
Athens

The Casto Hole

The Casto Hole is a cave hidden by the woods, located near Limber's Ridge on the waters of Straight Run, a branch of the Tug Fork of Mill Creek in Jackson County. It was a Unionist refuge during the Civil War and achieved notoriety in the scurrilous contemporary ballad, "The Casto Hole," by Elihugh Powers. It has since become a part of local historical lore.

Jackson and adjacent counties were mostly loyal to the Union, and a Tug Fork Home Guard militia was established to protect the local citizens and their homes from Confederate scouts and raiding parties. The Home Guard held meetings in the Casto Hole. At times of threat Unionists would go there for safety, and it has been said that runaway slaves could find refuge there. Nicholas Casto was elected captain of the local Home Guards.

Elihugh Powers, a prominent resident, was a Southern sympathizer. This prompted Nicholas Casto to write a poem, now lost to time, critical of the rebellious Southern states and censuring Powers for his belief in their cause. Powers responded with enthusiasm when he penned "The Casto Hole." Originally 27 verses, over time it was reduced to 19. It ridiculed the people and activities at the Casto Hole and stirred strong emotions in the county. High-tempered Casto youths wanted to tar and feather Powers, but calmer counsel prevailed. As time passed, the song came to be taken with more humor than hostility and some members of the Casto family were even said to laughingly recite some of the verses.

E. DeWitt Williams
Ripley
Hoyt O. Powers, "The Casto Hole," *Jackson County History and Folklore*, 1983; Fred Wolfe, "The Casto Hole," *West Virginia Heritage Encyclopedia*, 1976.

Cathedral State Park

Cathedral State Park is located in Preston County, near Aurora, on U.S. 50. The 133-acre park, at an elevation of 2,600 feet, has the only stand of virgin hemlock remaining in West Virginia. Cathedral State Park is considered the finest example of mixed hemlock and hardwood forest, including black cherry and yellow birch, in the state. The oldest hemlock in the park is about 500 years old, 123 feet tall, and 20 feet in circumference at the base. The stately hemlocks with their tall columnar trunks and fragrant shade imbue the forest with a cathedral-like atmosphere, hence the park's name.

In 1880, the Brookside Resort, offering recreational opportunities to visitors from Washington and Baltimore, was built on the present park site. Resort cottages and the barn still remain. In 1922, Brandon Hass, Brookside caretaker, purchased the forest. He sold the property to the state in 1942, with the stipulation the old forest never be cut down. In 1966, the park was entered in the National Registry of Natural Landmarks. Cathedral State Park is a day-use facility, with no lodging or camping accommodations.

Norma Jean Kennedy-Venable
Morgantown

Gale Catlett

Gale Catlett, West Virginia University basketball player and coach, was born December 31, 1940, in Hedgesville, Jefferson County. He was an outstanding high school athlete and a starter for the WVU basketball team in 1962 and 1963 when he was considered the team's best defensive player.

Catlett apprenticed under some of college basketball's best coaches: Lou Mills at Richmond; Ted Owens at Kansas; Lefty Driesell, then at Davidson; and Adolph Rupp at Kentucky. His first head coaching job was at Cincinnati, where he coached six years. He took over at WVU in 1978. The 1981–82 team finished 27-4 and posted the nation's longest winning streak, 23 games. The next year, WVU won 23 games and won the Atlantic Ten conference tournament. The 1989 Mountaineers (26-5) put together a 22-game streak, and won the Atlantic Ten regular season title. In 1998, the Mountaineers made it to the Sweet 16 of the National Collegiate Athletic Association Tournament for the first time since 1959, losing to Utah 65-62.

A 30-year WVU tradition of turning out an All-American or All-American candidate each year stopped under Coach Catlett. A fundamentalist who stressed defense, rebounding, and team play, he said, "My job is not to produce pro players. It is to recruit the best student athletes I can."

Catlett coached WVU to 13 20-win sea-

Cathedral State Park.

sons before he retired in 2002. His teams twice averaged more than 10,000 fans per game in the Coliseum. Catlett was named Coach of the Year in 1989 by *Eastern Basketball* magazine and finished as one of 10 finalists for the Associated Press National Coach of the Year award. He is among the elite 45 NCAA Division I coaches who have won 500 or more games, with 400 of his wins at WVU. In 30 years of coaching, Gale Catlett had only three losing seasons, all at WVU.

Norman Julian
Dominion Post

Norman Julian, *Legends: Profiles in West Virginia University Basketball,* 1998; *West Virginia University Basketball Media Guide,* 1998–99.

Catlette v. United States

In Richwood on June 29, 1940, Deputy Sheriff Martin Catlette and Police Chief Bert Stewart detained seven Jehovah's Witnesses, whose patriotism was doubted by members of the local American Legion. After legionnaires forced four of the Jehovah's Witnesses to drink doses of castor oil, they marched all seven through a jeering mob to the post office, where the Witnesses refused to salute the flag. Within several weeks this incident attracted the attention of the newly created Civil Rights Section of the U.S. Department of Justice. On June 3, 1942, the U.S. District Court in Charleston convicted Catlette and Stewart of violating the Witnesses' civil rights. Catlette's conviction was upheld by the Fourth Circuit of the U.S. Court of Appeals, in the case known as *Catlette v. United States*.

The legal action that followed the attack conferred it with historical significance. The incident provided the only federal conviction in the hundreds of brutal assaults on Jehovah's Witnesses that swept America that year. It was the Civil Rights Section's first successful prosecution of public officials who used their office to abridge citizens' civil rights. Finally, the Court of Appeals ruled that the statute applied to public officials who acted in violation of the laws prescribing their powers and duties. That understanding broadened the interpretation of the civil rights statute and was later adopted by the U.S. Supreme Court. This case expanded legal protection for religious liberties in the United States.

See also Barnette Case, Jehovah's Witnesses v. Pittsburgh Plate Glass Company

Chuck Smith
West Virginia State University

Chuck Smith, "Jehovah's Witnesses and the Castor Oil Patriots: A West Virginia Contribution to Religious Liberty," *West Virginia History,* 1998.

Caudy's Castle

Also known as Castle Rock, Caudy's Castle is a geologic formation located near the Forks of Cacapon, west of Bloomery in Hampshire County. Towering 400 feet above the forested valley and the Cacapon River, the fine white Oriskany Sandstone formation has been colored a tan hue by time and iron deposits. A trail ascending the landmark cliff begins near the west face and winds northeast to the jagged peak. The prominence provides a spectacular view of the surrounding mountains and valley.

The cone-shaped megalith gained its name during the French and Indian War when pioneer settlers, led by frontiersman James Caudy, purportedly took refuge in its craggy recesses. The constricted rock ledges allowed only single-file passage, and one by one, the Indians pursuing the fleeing settlers were pushed to their deaths by Caudy. Safely cloistered in a rocky recess, he prodded them with his long rifle as they negotiated the narrow passes.

Robert B. Wolford
Points

Hu Maxwell and H. L. Swisher, *The History of Hampshire County,* 1897; I. C. White, West Virginia Geological Survey, *Hampshire and Hardy Counties,* 1927.

Caves

Natural caves are found throughout eastern and southeastern West Virginia. Most West Virginia caves are formed by the dissolving of soluble rocks (primarily limestone and dolomite) by ground water. West Virginia caves typically have a year-round temperature of about 52 degrees and a relative humidity close to 100 percent. Caves have been extensively studied as part of geologic, biologic, and hydrologic investigations. They are an important recreational resource.

The first full report on West Virginia caves was by William E. Davies and was published in 1949 by the West Virginia

A spelunker in Friars Hole.

Geological and Economic Survey. Organ Cave was described as early as 1837. The private West Virginia Speleological Survey currently maintains records on West Virginia caves. "New" caves are discovered as cavers search the limestone areas of the state, so the number of known caves continues to grow.

The total number of caves reported in West Virginia as of 2004 was 4,241. Many of these are quite small; the number of caves with lengths or depths of 33 feet or more was 1,810. Only 106 caves have more than one mile of surveyed passage. The five longest caves in West Virginia are Friars Hole (Greenbrier and Pocahontas counties), 44 miles; Organ Cave (Greenbrier), 40 miles; The Hole (Greenbrier), 23 miles; Scott Hollow (Monroe), 22 miles; and Culverson Creek Cave (Greenbrier), 21 miles. The neighboring counties of Greenbrier, Pocahontas, Pendleton, Randolph, and Monroe have by far the greatest number of reported caves. Together they account for 2,977 caves, more than three-fourths of all West Virginia caves.

Cave soils are high in nitrates and were used by early settlers in the home manufacture of black powder. Soils from some West Virginia caves were mined as early as 1776. Organ Cave was apparently mined during the War of 1812 and during the Civil War. The Confederacy was desperate for gunpowder and established elaborate mining and extraction efforts to recover nitrates in numerous caves during the Civil War. At least 22 West Virginia caves were mined for saltpeter (potassium nitrate) during the Civil War. The best preserved saltpeter mining operation in West Virginia is in Organ Cave. Caves were considered to be natural bomb shelters during the Cold War, and civil defense signs were placed near numerous caves. Supplies were cached in a few, but they quickly deteriorated under the damp conditions typical of most West Virginia caves.

Caves represent an important natural resource. Many unique animals specifically adapted to life in the total darkness of caves are found throughout the limestone areas of the state. A single cave may represent the only known location for an organism, and several West Virginia caves are protected by the Nature Conservancy to provide a safe habitat for a variety of animals. Common cave animals from West Virginia include bats, salamanders, cave crickets, beetles, and a variety of cave-adapted invertebrates such as amphipods and isopods. No snakes are known to live in West Virginia caves.

Scientific research on West Virginia caves has been conducted by students and professors from many different colleges and universities. The Karst Waters Institute, a research group with an interest in "karst" regions worldwide (those areas where caves are prevalent), is headquartered in Charles Town. Several cave clubs or "grottos" of the National Speleological Society are located in West Virginia. Caves are a fragile environment protected by state law. No collecting of rock or mineral samples or animals is permitted. Most West Virginia caves are located on private property and should be entered only with permission of the landowner. Cave exploring can be a dangerous sport and should be learned in the company of experienced cavers with the proper equipment. Several caves are open to the public for guided tours, including Lost World (Greenbrier), Organ Cave (Greenbrier), Smoke Hole Caverns (Grant), and Seneca Caverns (Pendleton).

See also Friars Hole, Organ Cave, Seneca Caverns, Smoke Hole Caverns

William K. Jones
Charles Town

W. E. Davies, *Caverns of West Virginia,* West Virginia Geological and Economic Survey, 1965; W. K. Jones, *Karst Hydrology Atlas of West Virginia,* 1997.

Cedar Creek State Park

Cedar Creek State Park lies in Gilmer County. Located in the center of West Virginia, this park joined the state park system in 1955. Cedar Creek's 2,443 acres has a watershed that includes Sugar Camp Run, Big Two Run, and Little Two Run.

The park office and nature center is unique, a log cabin that formerly served as a home, then a gas station. Another attraction is the furnished one-room schoolhouse with a tin roof, where eight grades once studied together. Built in 1910, Pine Run School was moved to the park from neighboring Lewis County in 1989. Inside are a pot-bellied stove and a bucket of coal in the center of the room, 30 desks, a blackboard, a paddle, filled bookcases, a teacher's desk, a water jug with one tin cup, and a memorial to one-room-school teachers. In front is a 30-foot flagpole, made from a black locust trunk.

Visitors to Cedar Creek enjoy miniature golf, a swimming pool, campground, and playground. Picnic sites, one near a stream rippling over flat rocks, are popular. Fishermen come to fish the park's stocked ponds, and others come for tennis and game courts.

Maureen F. Crockett
St. Albans

Cedar Lakes Conference Center

The Cedar Lakes Conference Center in Jackson County originated in a 1949 act of the state legislature authorizing the development of a leadership training facility for students. The legislation was the result of a cooperative effort by the state associations of the Future Farmers of America and Future Homemakers of America with the vocational division of the State Board of Education.

Many sites were proposed, studied, and visited before the Jackson County site was approved. On March 15, 1950, 231 acres of land known as the Easter Farm was deeded to the State Board of Education by Oliver Kessel, a prominent Ripley citizen, and work began. The camp officially opened January 7, 1955, but was not named until 1957. The name Cedar Lakes was chosen from more than 100 names, due to the site's predominant physical features, two beautiful lakes and an abundance of native cedar trees.

Cedar Lakes has grown into an impressive facility with 30 buildings on 450 acres, cottages, classrooms, a crafts center, cafeteria, chapel, superintendent's house, and a modern motel-style lodge. Softball, swimming, tennis, fishing, hiking, miniature golf, and canoeing are also offered. An estimated 500,000 people visit Cedar Lakes each year. Since 1963,

Cedar Lakes has been home to the Mountain State Art & Craft Fair, West Virginia's largest outdoor craft event. The conference center continues to be operated by the West Virginia Department of Education and promotes the training of FFA-FHA youth leaders.

See also Mountain State Art & Craft Fair
Deborah J. Sonis
West Virginia Humanities Council
Debby Sonis Jackson, "Building Cedar Lakes," *Goldenseal,* Fall 1990.

Celoron de Blainville

In the mid-1700s, France and Great Britain stood on the brink of war for control of the Ohio Valley, including most of present West Virginia. French claims on the region were based on expeditions by the explorer La Salle in 1669. In 1749, the governor of Canada, Marquis de la Galissonnière, dispatched Pierre-Joseph Celoron de Blainville (1693–1759) down the Allegheny and Ohio rivers to strengthen France's position. In August, Celoron led 230 Canadian militia and Indian guides to the mouth of Wheeling Creek. His party buried a leaden plate at the junction of Wheeling Creek and the Ohio River, claiming all territory drained by the streams in the name of Louis XV, king of France.

Celoron's party traveled down the Ohio to the mouth of the Kanawha River at the present site of Point Pleasant and buried another plate. In all, he buried four plates along the Ohio, but the effort was fruitless. Great Britain's victory in the ensuing French and Indian War (1754–63) forced the French from the region, and France surrendered all claims on the Ohio Valley as part of the Treaty of Paris. The Point Pleasant plate, by then a historical curiosity, was found by a boy playing on the riverbank in 1846.

See also French and Indian War
Stan Bumgardner
Division of Culture & History

Celoron claims the Ohio Valley for Louis XV.

Elizabeth Cometti and Festus P. Summers, eds., "Expedition of Celoron," *The Thirty-Fifth State: A Documentary History of West Virginia,* 1966; West Virginia Writers' Project, *West Virginia: A Guide to the Mountain State,* 1941.

Cemeteries

Customs change with the passage of time. As early settlers spread into sparsely populated remote regions and away from established cemeteries, small family graveyards became common in Western Virginia. Churchyard cemeteries remained common in settled villages and towns. Today, depending on locality, West Virginians are still buried in family graveyards and in churchyards, but more often in large commercial cemeteries. Some are buried in cemeteries maintained for veterans or for members of fraternal organizations, and others in municipal cemeteries. Cremation, although increasing, remains less popular here than in the country as a whole.

Elements of our culture are on display in West Virginia's cemeteries. Gravestones commonly face east, the direction from which Christians believe the resurrection will come. Cemeteries often contain a yew or a cedar tree, evergreens that symbolize eternal life. Family graveyards are most commonly located on a hill or other high point, a cultural preference for reasons not entirely clear. Perhaps it was to put the departed above the fray of everyday affairs and nearer to heaven, or, as the poet Louise McNeill mischievously suggested, to use marginal land fit only for raising a crop of graves.

Formal cemeteries are often laid out according to impressive plans prepared by landscape architects. There was a movement in 19th-century America to establish park-like public cemeteries, with extensive grounds and impressive monuments. Charleston's Spring Hill and Wheeling's Greenwood are fine examples of such garden cemeteries in West Vir-

A tree trunk gravestone in Spring Hill Cemetery, Charleston.

ginia. Churchyard burial grounds are organized less formally than these great Victorian cities of the dead, while family graveyards just seem to grow. In the latter, the graves of succeeding generations often gather around those of the founding patriarchs and matriarchs. It is a naturally pleasing arrangement, replicating in death the family circle that prevailed during the lifetimes of those now gone. Topography also plays a role in family graveyards, which usually follow the lay of the (often rugged) land.

Gravestones characterize cemeteries of every sort and convey much cultural information. Many of the oldest grave markers were fashioned by local semi-skilled artisans from fieldstone. These markers may still be observed today, but the degree of weathering varies with the geology of the locale and the durability of available stones. By the early to mid-19th century, skilled regional stonecutters were at work providing markers. Gravestones from this period demonstrate individual artistic mastery as well as regional, cultural, ethnic, and personal values displayed in symbolic ways.

By the end of the 19th century, gravestone production became less regional and more commercial. Transportation allowed hard, durable marble and granite to be delivered to tombstone manufacturers from far away. As a commercial business, the after-life process from death to interment to permanent recognition through a grave marker became increasingly depersonalized. Today, with perpetual-care facilities being yet another option, after bereavement and mourning little further attention need be given by surviving family members. In contrast, the graves and graveyards of earlier days were kept up by family and friends, whose attention might be intensely personal and even a source of anxiety to those approaching death. An old traditional song titled "See that My Grave is Kept Clean" reflected this anxiety. No one wants to lie in a lonely, forgotten grave.

Even after the commercialization of burying, much traditional symbolism may be observed in grave markers. The religiously symbolic praying hands, a small lamb (for a child), an anchor, a weeping willow, or a broken chain demonstrate typical parting emotions evoked in three dimensional form. Around the turn of the 20th century, full-sized stone tree trunks, some carved in West Virginia, found favor with woodsmen and others. These often feature certain plants growing at their bases, such as ferns and ivy, to symbolize everlasting life.

With the increased interest in genealogy, old cemeteries are now getting more attention and renewed respect. Cemetery surveys have been done for many counties, locating cemeteries and mapping them to identify occupants. Community volunteers and local historical societies often perform this work. Some ancestors are honored with newly made markers to replace rough fieldstones or weathered headstones. When all is said and done, the most lasting artifacts to survive into the future to represent a common person's life on earth are the grave markers placed to mark their final resting place in cemeteries.

See also Burial Customs

Gerald Milnes
Augusta Heritage Center
James K. Crissman, *Death and Dying in Central Appalachia*, 1994.

The Centennial
The hills and valleys of the Mountain State came alive in 1963 as West Virginia celebrated 100 years of statehood. Musical events, drama, traveling exhibits, and festivities in each of the 55 counties highlighted the celebration. It began on West Virginia Day, June 20, 1962, with the appearance of former President Harry S. Truman at the state capitol in Charleston. One year later, on the state's 100th birthday, President John F. Kennedy delivered the featured address at the state capitol. It was a rainy day, and the president took note. "The sun does not always shine in West Virginia, but the people do," Kennedy said.

A nine-car Centennial exhibits train crisscrossed the state, making 58 stops in 95 days. Opening in Washington on May 31 and ending in South Charleston on September 2, the traveling exhibits focused on a message of pride in the past and confidence in the future. Attracting 319,000 visitors, the train was easily the most popular event during the anniversary year.

A Centennial showboat, the *Rhododendron*, carried the celebration to West Virginia waterways. The melodrama *East Lynne*, written in 1863, was presented on stage, along with other popular variety shows and local acts at the boat's 21 stops in West Virginia and Pennsylvania. The *Rhododendron* had a 264-seat theater and a river museum.

Many events marked the celebration, including a special ceremonial session of the West Virginia legislature held on April 20, 1963, in Wheeling, the state's first capital. It was on April 20, 1863, that President Lincoln issued a proclamation that in 60 days West Virginia would become a state. The legislature met in Wheeling's old U.S. Custom House, later known as West Virginia Independence Hall, the birthplace of West Virginia.

The Forum of the Future, conducted in Charleston on April 25, 1963, established an editorial tone for the Centennial. The forum, highlighted by a panel including Vice President Lyndon B. Johnson, focused on a state aware of its problems with a determination to work toward solutions.

A Centennial sports banquet, attended by 1,500 at the Charleston Civic Center on April 6, 1963, recognized the contribution of sports to West Virginia's heritage. Numerous sporting events, from fishing to football, were declared a part of the Centennial Games. In 1891, the West Virginia University Mountaineers had traveled up the Monongahela River by steamboat to play the first football game with the University of Pittsburgh. The *Rhododendron* carried the Pitt Panthers into Morgantown in October 1963 to play the Mountaineers at old Mountaineer Stadium before 32,000 and a national TV audience.

One of the most celebrated programs of the Centennial—the National Youth Science Camp—has continued every year since its beginning in 1963. Initiated to attract national recognition of scientific achievements and opportunities in West Virginia, the camp honored 100 scientifically talented senior high school students—two from each state—who spent two weeks at the camp in Pocahontas County. The huge Mountain State Art & Craft Fair held each July at Cedar Lakes in Jackson County is another Centennial event that has continued to the present.

Planning for the big celebration got under way early, when the legislature created a 15-member West Virginia Centennial Commission. The commission was reaffirmed in legislation of 1959, which also provided funding. Additional appropriations were voted in 1961 and 1963. Executive Director Carl R. Sullivan joined the staff in late 1961. When the Centennial year closed on December 31, 1963, virtually all elements of the program had been completed successfully,

and a modest surplus remained of the $1.1 million budget.

Lloyd P. Calvert
Belle

Centennial Golden Trout
The West Virginia Centennial Golden Trout received its first widespread stocking in 1963, the state's 100th anniversary year. The fish is a color mutation of the common rainbow trout, discovered by chance and then bred for the characteristic.

Petersburg fish hatchery manager Vincent Evans noticed a yellow-mottled fingerling among the hatchery's rainbow trout in 1955, giving it the name "Little Camouflage." When Evans transferred to Spring Run hatchery later that fall, the new Petersburg manager, Chester Mace, continued a careful watch over the little fish. In late fall of 1956, the "golden" was spawned with a regular rainbow trout. Because of limited facilities, the eggs of this match were mixed with all of the other rainbow eggs.

Late in 1956 and early 1957, fingerlings were transferred from Petersburg to Spring Run hatchery. Within a few weeks nearly 300 fingerlings had developed a true golden color.

During subsequent years, Evans and Mace supervised the selection and spawning of brood stock, with good color quality as their primary objective. By the spring of 1963, a sufficient number of golden trout were available for stocking in West Virginia waters. They continue to be a popular part of the Division of Natural Resources trout-stocking program. Goldens have a greater tendency to seek shaded waters than normal colored rainbow and are sometimes less active. Some fishermen say they are more difficult to catch and consider them a prize, while others object to the fish as non-native and unnatural.

Mike Shingleton
Division of Natural Resources

Central City
Central City is the historical name of the West 14th Street neighborhood of Huntington. It was a separate city from 1893 to 1909, when it was annexed by Huntington. After beginning as several farms, Central City grew into a manufacturing center due to the availability of raw materials, transportation facilities, and low-cost fuel. Manufacturers included a bung or stopper factory, a chain factory, and the Art Glass Company. Central City was known for its glass, bricks, and the Fesenmeier Brewery. Today, Central City is a popular historical district with its antique shops, a farmer's market, museums, specialty shops, and houses dating back to the 19th century. An annual Old Central City Days held in July since 1991 has featured a marble tournament, flea market,

parade, historical tours, and fireworks. West 14th Street, the heart of the district, was the main business street in Central City.

See also Huntington

Larry Sonis
Arlington, Texas

Ceredo

Ceredo is located on U.S. 60 in Wayne County, in the westernmost part of West Virginia. Reformer Eli Thayer established the town in 1857. Initially a "Free Soil" politician and later a Republican congressman from Massachusetts, Thayer believed that slavery could eventually be eliminated by limiting its spread to new territories. When Thayer turned his attention toward establishing a model free-labor community in the South, he acquired the property of Thomas Jordan, a slave holder who owned land between the mouths of Twelvepole Creek and the Big Sandy River. Abolitionists under the auspices of Thayer's Emigrant Aid Company moved there and founded Ceredo. The new town, on the banks of the Ohio River, was poised on the boundary between slave territory and free.

According to a 1917 newspaper article, early Ceredo had 500 settlers and several industries, including a shoe factory, match plant, iron foundry, grist mill, and woolen mill. Named for Ceres, the goddess of agriculture, the town was an experiment, meant to demonstrate that industry and free labor could prosper in the South. In 1861, when the Civil War erupted, Ceredo became a Union stronghold with recruitment camps and the headquarters of the 5th (West) Virginia Infantry under Col. John Ziegler.

Unfortunately, the war brought hard times to Ceredo. Only a handful of the original New England anti-slavery settlers stayed, and the majority of the industries failed. The population dropped to 125. Thayer experienced financial difficulties that forced him in 1868 to sell his interest in Ceredo to his mortgage holder, Charles B. Hoard. In the 1890s, the Norfolk & Western Railroad moved its western terminus to neighboring Kenova. Ceredo is the location of the historic Ramsdell House, and was the location of the Pilgrim Glass Company until 2002. Ceredo had 1,675 residents in 2000.

See also Abolitionism, Civil War, Wayne County

Don Chafin

Sheriff Don Chafin, born June 26, 1887, in Logan County, was educated in Logan public schools, at Marshall College (now Marshall University), and at the Mountain State Business College in Parkersburg. His career included service as a teacher, a store clerk, and store owner and operator, but he is best known as a politician and controversial lawman.

Chafin was elected assessor of Logan County at age 21 and sheriff at 25. After a term as county clerk, he was re-elected as sheriff in 1920. Chafin was a bitter foe of union organizers and, with financial support from coal companies, used his many deputies to keep labor organizers out of Logan County. United Mine Workers of America members hated Don Chafin so much that he was shot on sight and wounded when entering UMWA District 17 headquarters in 1919. During the Miners' March in 1921, he was a key figure in organizing forces to defend Logan County and arranged for airplanes to drop homemade bombs on the miners during the Battle of Blair Mountain.

Later in the 1920s, Chafin served prison time in a federal penitentiary after being convicted of violating Prohibition statutes. He moved to Huntington in 1929 where he purchased a ten-story building, renamed it the Chafin Building, and operated the Chafin Coal Company as well as many other business interests. In his later years, he was a noted philanthropist, giving money freely to many charities. Chafin died in Huntington, August 9, 1954.

See also Battle of Blair Mountain, Mine Wars, Miners' March

Kenneth R. Bailey
WVU Institute of Technology

Jim Comstock, *The West Virginia Heritage Encyclopedia*, 1976; Howard B. Lee, *Bloodletting in Appalachia*, 1969.

Chair Making

Traditional chair making involves the simple post-and-rung construction techniques that have been in use for centuries in the western world. While these chair types were once widely found in this country, only small regional areas within the nation have held to and depended on this chair design into the 21st century. The Appalachian area of the upland South, including West Virginia, is the most notable region. Chairs of this design are still commonly found on the porches and in the kitchens of Mountain State homes.

Whether lathe-turned (originally on treadle lathes and now on machine tools) or shaped with hand tools (drawknife, spoke shave), chairs that use the post-and-rung design formula are still made by country craftsmen in West Virginia. Names for these chairs vary widely according to materials or region and particular design, with some names being "ladderback," "slat back," "mule ear," "bent back," "Shaker," "post and rung," and "split bottom."

Traditional chair joinery entails working with natural drying characteristics of hardwoods, whereby the unseasoned "green" wood of the posts shrinks onto the dry and seasoned horizontal rungs for superior strength and endurance. The result is an exceptionally tight joint, made without glue or fasteners. This is an important aspect of traditional chair construction. While common in the work of independent chair makers, it cannot be duplicated in "factory made" chairs because of the logistics involved with the timing and handling of the larger amounts of materials needed for such production.

Rocking chairs, with widely differing styles, share many of the same aspects of design and construction found on standard split bottom chairs. They vary more widely in appearance, however, because of the arms and varied, sometimes woven, backs they sport, as well as the slats of common design.

A surprising number of native hardwood species are used in the makeup of traditional chairs. Oak, maple, ash, cherry, and walnut are favorites for the posts and back slats, while hickory is used almost exclusively for rungs because of its superior strength. The inner fiber of hickory bark is normally used for seating material, but white oak splits are also common. The long strips of seating material are often woven in a herringbone pattern by West Virginia chair makers.

Gerald Milnes
Augusta Heritage Center

Chamber of Commerce

The West Virginia Chamber of Commerce was established during the Great Depression. Phil Conley, editor of *The West Virginia Review*, is credited with organizing the state chamber. At his urging, in May 1935 a group of business leaders met at the Greenbrier Hotel in White Sulphur Springs. Additional meetings followed, culminating in the adoption of a constitution and bylaws in Parkersburg in January 1936. Richard Harte of Parkersburg was elected the first president of the state Chamber of Commerce.

The first Chamber of Commerce in America was the Chamber of Commerce of the State of New York, which traces its origins to 1768, in the colonial period. The U.S. Chamber of Commerce was founded in 1912. The national membership now includes about three million companies, nearly 3,000 state and local chapters, about 83 associations, and roughly 90 American Chambers of Commerce abroad.

Prior to the formation of the West Virginia Chamber of Commerce, various cities had their own chambers of commerce, including Huntington, whose chamber was established in 1895; Charleston, whose chamber was established in 1899; and Wheeling, whose chamber was established in 1918. Among the early objectives of the state chamber were to lobby the state legislature and Congress on matters of interest to West Virginia business; to seek favorable changes in taxation; to provide a bulletin to inform members of activity in Charleston; and to advertise the state.

The Chamber's goals are similar today. The West Virginia Chamber of Commerce had more than 1,400 member companies in 2003.

Robert C. Chambers

Judge Robert Charles "Chuck" Chambers served 10 years as the 53rd speaker of the House of Delegates (1987–96), the longest tenure in that office in state history. Nominated by President Bill Clinton as a federal judge for the southern district of West Virginia in June of 1997, Chambers was sworn in October 17, 1997, at the age of 45. He replaced Judge Elizabeth Hallanan who had moved to senior status the previous year.

Born August 27, 1952, in Matewan, a son of James E. and Geraldine Kiser Chambers, Judge Chambers lives in Huntington. He received a bachelor's degree in political science from Marshall University in 1974 and a law degree from West Virginia University in 1978. He served as legal counsel to the West Virginia Senate in 1978. He was first elected to the House of Delegates in 1978 from Cabell County and reelected to eight successive two-year terms until he retired from the legislature in 1996. He served two years as chairman of the House judiciary committee (1985–86), and the following year became the youngest speaker of the House of Delegates in West Virginia history. Chambers began private law practice in Huntington with his father in 1978 and was in law practice with Guy Bucci in Charleston when he received his lifetime appointment as a federal judge. He served as co-chairman of the state Democratic Party briefly before resigning in 1996 when he was recommended for the federal judiciary.

Tom D. Miller
Huntington

Champe Rocks

The Champe Rocks are two sandstone masses that rise on the east side of the North Fork of the South Branch of the Potomac River, six miles north of Seneca Rocks on State Route 28-55 in Pendleton County. They stand some 900 feet above the valley floor and overlook the narrow river plain near the site where John Champe, a Revolutionary War soldier, possibly lived for a short period of time.

John Champe was sent by Gen. George Washington in October 1780 to kidnap the traitor Benedict Arnold. Champe pretended to be an American deserter and joined the British, but he was unable to kidnap Arnold. He was forced to serve with the British Army until he escaped to rejoin the American forces. Washington, believing that the British would show

no mercy if Champe were to be captured by them, discharged Champe and encouraged him to establish his home on Abram's Creek in Grant County, between present Scherr and Mount Storm. After residing there for two years, Champe and his family relocated elsewhere before eventually settling in Craig County, Virginia, where he died.

The Champe Rocks are an outcropping of Tuscarora sandstone, the same hard stone which makes up Seneca Rocks.

See also Tuscarora Sandstone

Donald L. Rice
Elkins

E. L. Judy, *History of Grant and Hardy Counties, West Virginia*, 1951; Oren F. Morton, *A History of Pendleton County West Virginia*, 1910.

Louis Watson Chappell

A leading figure in the study and preservation of West Virginia folk music, Louis Watson Chappell was born October 29, 1890, at Belvidere, North Carolina. Educated at Wake Forest (B.A. 1917) and the University of Virginia (M.A. 1920), he received an appointment to the English Department faculty at West Virginia University in 1921. In the ensuing years he developed a keen interest in regional folk song study, stimulated in part by the work of his WVU colleague, John Harrington Cox.

Chappell's initial scholarship focused upon the ballad "John Henry." Whereas previous folk song scholars, including Cox, had considered the ballad to be a variant of "John Hardy," Chappell disagreed and spent several years methodically uncovering the distinctions, and regional origins, of the two folk songs. The results of his research were published in 1933 in his book *John Henry: A Folk-Lore Study* which set a new standard of thoroughness in ballad scholarship.

In 1937, Chappell purchased one of only a few portable disk recording machines in existence at the time. During the next decade, he employed this equipment in recording more than 2,000 songs and instrumental tunes throughout West Virginia. This collection, which is now preserved at the WVU Libraries, is considered to be among the most significant primary resources for the study of regional folk music history. Chappell died December 22, 1981, in Belvidere.

See also John Harrington Cox, John Henry

John A. Cuthbert
WVU Libraries

John A. Cuthbert, *West Virginia Folk Music*, 1982.

Charles Town

Established in 1786 by Charles Washington, brother of George Washington, Charles Town became the county seat when Jefferson County was formed from Berkeley in 1801. After the Civil War, county government was moved briefly to

Shepherdstown, returning to its original location in 1871. Charles Town's *Spirit of Jefferson—Farmer's Advocate* is now the oldest continuously published newspaper in the state.

Two treason trials were held in the courthouse at Charles Town. The first trial was of abolitionist John Brown and the raiders who survived his 1859 raid on Harpers Ferry; Brown was convicted and hanged in Charles Town. A second series of treason trials was held at the same site in 1922, during the West Virginia Mine Wars. The defendants, including union leader Bill Blizzard, were not convicted of treason.

Martin Robison Delany, born in Charles Town, worked with John Brown before the raid in the framing of Brown's provisional constitution. During the Civil War, Delany became the first African-American field officer in the U.S. military. Charles Town is also the birthplace of poet, critic, and novelist John Peale Bishop (1892–1944), who used it as the location for a series of short stories dealing with the effects of the Civil War on the town and vicinity. Bishop's novel, *Act of Darkness*, incurred the wrath of his neighbors for its transparent use of local residents. Charles Town was the home of Postmaster General William L. Wilson, who in 1896, established the first rural free delivery service in America, with the route running between Charles Town and nearby Uvilla and Halltown.

Charles Town is home to Charles Town Races, a popular horse racing track.

The town's population was 2,907 at the time of the 2000 census.

See also John Brown, Martin Robison Delany, Jefferson County

William D. Theriault
Bakerton

Charles Town Opera House

What is today known as the Old Opera House on George Street in Charles Town is actually two buildings, the first dating back to the 1890s. Then in 1910, Annie G. Packette raised $50,000 to construct a 500-seat theater. Its opening on February 11, 1911, ushered in an era of entertainment and service lasting for more than 30 years. The older building was retained as a secondary structure.

There were countless vaudeville performers, town meetings, silent and "talkie" movies, church services, political conventions, and other activities before the Opera House closed in 1948. It was condemned in 1956 but remained undisturbed until the 1970s, when community leaders restored the building as a performing arts center.

The main theater has 272 seats downstairs and 60 seats in a curved balcony at the rear. An orchestra pit is in front of the stage with the original curved rail around it. The theater lobby still includes a section of high tin ceiling and brass railing. The downstairs of the main building has been converted to an art gallery featuring regional artists. The secondary building, which has been used as apartments and as a tavern with two bowling lanes, now includes a dance studio, dressing rooms, offices, and other rooms.

The exterior is red brick with white trim in the federalist style, with prominent concrete keystones above windows. Three sets of double doors lead to the main lobby. The Old Opera House was entered in the National Register of Historic Places in 1978.

Michael Ridderbusch
WVU Libraries

Charles Town Races

The Charles Town Race Track opened on December 2, 1933, shortly after West Virginia legalized racing and parimutuel betting. The first track in the state, the Jefferson County complex contained 22 buildings and included 12 stables, a clubhouse, 44 betting windows, a 3,000-seat, steam-heated grandstand, and a 200-seat restaurant.

The 1933 and 1934 racing seasons were financial failures, and the new track went into receivership. Then Albert J. Boyle took over, putting up new money and convincing the creditors that he could make a go of it by pulling bettors from Washington and Baltimore and by promoting racing during the winter season. Boyle succeeded, and for more than 20 years he was a dominant figure in West Virginia racing.

By 1959, Shenandoah Downs, a competing race track, had opened nearby. One of the first tracks on the East Coast to be built for night racing, Shenandoah Downs competed for racing days, and profits, with the older Charles Town Race Track, whose facility could support only daylight meets. The owners of Maryland's Pimlico Race Course bought the Charles Town Race Track in 1959 and began extensive renovations. By 1964, they had installed lighting that enabled them to compete with the newer track.

Shenandoah Downs closed in 1976, with Charles Town picking up its racing days and doubling receipts. The Kenton Corporation bought both tracks in 1978. Sunday racing was approved in a 1979 referendum. In 1983, the Charles Town Race Track was sold to the Rapid America Corporation, a group of 15 businessmen that included 11 local investors.

With the future of the operation in doubt, Penn National Gaming agreed to purchase Charles Town Races if Jefferson County approved the installation of video lottery machines. The vote passed on November 5, 1996, and two months later, Penn National bought the racetrack, refurbishing the thoroughbred racing facilities. On September 10, 1997, the new owners opened a gambling center with 220 operating video lottery machines. A multi-million dollar simulcast center was added in January 1998. Like other West Virginia race facilities, Charles Town now relies extensively on non-racing income. The video lottery portion of the operation had been expanded to 3,500 video slots in 2003. The complex is now called Charles Town Racing and Slots.

William D. Theriault
Bakerton

William D. Theriault, "For Love and Money: Jefferson County Horse Racing," *Goldenseal,* Spring 1989.

Charleston

Charleston, the capital of West Virginia and the state's biggest city, is situated on the Kanawha River at the mouth of Elk River, at 600 feet elevation. It is the county seat of Kanawha County.

In 1771, hunters John Yeager, George Strader, and 16-year-old Simon Kenton set up camp near the mouth of the Elk. They trapped in the area until 1773, when they were attacked by Indians. Kenton and Strader escaped, but Yeager was killed. In 1775, Thomas Bullitt surveyed a 1,030-acre tract that encompassed much of present downtown Charleston. Bullitt was awarded the land for service in the French and Indian War.

The first settlers arrived in April 1788 and built Fort Lee by the Kanawha River near the present downtown. Their leader was George Clendenin. In December 1794, the Virginia General Assembly designated a 40-acre tract of George Clendenin's land a town. Originally known as Charlestown for Clendenin's father, Charles, the name later was shortened to Charleston. Daniel Boone was among the early residents, serving as a Kanawha County delegate in the Virginia General Assembly in 1791.

The local salt industry helped to build Charleston's early economy. Elisha Brooks is credited with building the first salt furnace in 1797. Eventually, salt works dotted the south side of the river in what is now Charleston's Kanawha City neighborhood, and upstream on both sides of the river. Other industries grew to serve the salt business, including the construction of flatboats and the making of barrels.

Local families enriched by the salt industry include such prominent names as the Ruffners, Noyeses, Brookses, Donnallys, and others, for whom Charleston's city streets are named.

The salt furnaces were labor intensive. The saltmakers employed many slaves, making Kanawha County an exception to the fact that Western Virginia had relatively few slaves. In 1850, there were as many as 1,500 slaves at the salt works, owned by the salt barons or leased from other owners.

The first steamboat arrived in 1820. Those elegant river queens opened up the sleepy little village to the sophisticated society of big cities along the Ohio River. The James River & Kanawha Turnpike, linking Charleston with Tidewater Virginia along the route of present U.S. 60, was completed in the 1820s.

When the Civil War erupted in 1861, the ease of river access to Ohio and the difficulty of traveling overland to Old Virginia doomed Confederate attempts to secure the Kanawha Valley. After the brief Battle of Scary Creek, west of Charleston, the Yankees occupied the valley. On September 13, 1862, the last real attempt to return Charleston to the South resulted in a hard-fought battle and hasty retreat by the federal troops. But the Confederates could not hold the town and fell back on October 29, never to return. At the beginning of the war, Charleston was a Virginia town with much sentiment for the

Rounding the corner at Charles Town Races.

Choosing the capital city

"During the year that I spent in Washington, and for some little time before this there had been considerable agitation in the state of West Virginia over the question of moving the capital of the state from Wheeling to some other . . . point. As a result of this, the Legislature designated three cities to be voted upon by the citizens of the state as the permanent seat of government. Among these cities was Charleston, only five miles from Malden, my home. At the close of my school year in Washington I was very pleasantly surprised to receive, from a committee of white people in Charleston, an invitation to canvass the state in the interests of that city. This invitation I accepted, and spent nearly three months in speaking in various parts of the state. Charleston was successful in winning the prize, and is now the permanent seat of government."

—Booker T. Washington *Up From Slavery* (1901)

Southern cause. The city produced Col. George S. Patton and the Kanawha Riflemen, who were among the best soldiers in the Confederate Army. (Patton was the grandfather of Gen. George S. Patton of World War II.) The Civil War in Charleston led to bitter divisions as many clung to Virginia while others took the Union side.

After the Civil War, a group of influential Democratic politicians, many of them ex-Confederates, was successful in having the capital of the new state of West Virginia moved from Wheeling to Charleston on March 28, 1870. In 1875, political rivalry between Charleston and Wheeling resulted in moving the capital back to Wheeling. The government was returned to Charleston after a statewide referendum, and in 1885 it was here to stay. A beautiful Victorian capitol, located in the city's downtown, went up in flames in January 1921. Government leaders engaged architect Cass Gilbert to design the present Italian Renaissance-style building. Dedicated in 1932, it remains Charleston's great landmark.

The arrival of the Chesapeake & Ohio Railway in 1873 on the south side of the Kanawha River, and the 1884 completion of the Kanawha & Ohio (later Kanawha & Michigan) on the north side, linked Charleston with the growing national rail network. The first bridge across the Kanawha was built in Charleston in 1891. An era of growth and wealth ensued, as numerous industries located near the resources and transportation. In the first half of the 20th century, the city served as a mercantile and banking center for the rich coalfields of the southern part of the state. By the end of World War II, Charleston was a powerhouse of industrial might, with local firms including Union Carbide, DuPont, Libbey-Owens-Ford, True Temper, and others.

Completed in the 1970s, Interstates 64, 77, and 79 intersect in Charleston. Kanawha Airport (now Yeager Airport) opened in 1947, adjacent to Coonskin Park, a 1,000-acre recreation area. The Charleston Area Medical Center, created in 1972 by consolidating the community's major hospitals, provides a full range of hospital care for southern West Virginia.

Charleston undertook an urban renewal program in the last decades of the 20th century. Criticized by some for the displacement of minority neighborhoods and occasional insensitivity to historic areas, the plan nonetheless preserved a viable downtown at a time when many municipalities were losing their inner cities. Town Center Mall, which opened in 1983, kept the retail tax base within city limits, and the old Capitol Street shopping district was later renovated for offices and restaurants.

The nearby Municipal Auditorium, a landmark art moderne structure built in 1939, continues as a cornerstone of the city's culture and entertainment community. The huge Civic Center brings sports events as well as the circus and other large shows to town, while the magnifi-

Charleston, as seen from historic Fort Hill.

cent Clay Center for the Arts & Sciences opened in 2003. The center, home to the West Virginia Symphony, features an art museum as well as science exhibits and a planetarium. Across town, the Robert C. Byrd Federal Courthouse added another architectural monument to the city in 1999.

Like the rest of West Virginia, Charleston has lost population in recent decades. The number of Charlestonians peaked at 85,796 in 1962 and had fallen to 53,421 by 2000. Nonetheless, Charleston remains West Virginia's center of government and business, whose people see it as a beautiful, vibrant city with a future.

See also Kanawha County

Richard A. Andre
Charleston

Charleston Area Medical Center

Charleston Area Medical Center (CAMC) is a large and complex health care center, originally formed by combining seven predecessor hospitals.

The first of the seven predecessors, Sheltering Arms Hospital, was opened at Hansford by the Episcopal Diocese in 1888. The economics of coal production in southern West Virginia changed radically with the defeat of the miners union in the Mine Wars and a general downturn in the industry, and Sheltering Arms was bankrupt by 1923.

In 1899, the city of Charleston began a new hospital on Cemetery Hill, but ran out of funds. Dr. Frederick Thomas offered to finish the facility, hire nurses and staff, and guaranteed to allow Charleston residents to pay $1 a day for hospital care. In 1904, the name was changed from Thomas Hospital to Charleston General Hospital. Sheltering Arms patients and nursing school were transferred to Charleston General with the closing of Sheltering Arms.

The Barber Sanatorium was constructed by Dr. Timothy L. Barber Sr. in 1904 on a lot in the front yard of his home on Virginia Street. In 1959, it became the Kanawha Valley Memorial Hospital. In 1982, Kanawha Valley Memorial moved to a new complex across Elk River. The hospital was sold to CAMC in 1986 to become the Women and Children's Division.

In 1907, Dr. William A. McMillan developed his hospital in a frame house at the corner of Elmwood Avenue and Morris Street. McMillan Hospital was soon moved two blocks south into a modern structure. In 1971, McMillan became a part of Charleston General Hospital, and its buildings were demolished in 1976. Drs. Romie and W. F. Walker purchased a stately home on Virginia Street. In 1921, it became the Mountain State Hospital, which was merged into Charleston Memorial Hospital in 1969.

Dr. E. Bennett Henson purchased and renovated an unused school building in Marmet to be an acute and chronic care hospital for polio patients. Widespread use of the new polio vaccines hastened the closing of the Marmet Hospital, which became a part of General Hospital in 1967.

As late as 1941, nearly every hospital in Charleston was proprietary. Dr. Daniel Barber wrote a seminal letter to the two newspapers stressing the need for a community owned institution open to all. In 1944, Mr. and Mrs. William Ziebold Sr. held a meeting in their home, and a community board was formed. It raised $2 million from 16,000 persons. From this effort Charleston Memorial Hospital was built, and dedicated in 1951 with 129 beds. By 1974, the original plan of 440 beds and 58 bassinets had been completed on the site of a former golf course in the Kanawha City neighborhood of Charleston.

Consolidation of the two rivals, Charleston General and Charleston Memorial, began with the urging of Dr. John Chambers and other staff members. On January 1, 1972, Charleston Area Medical Center was born. By November 1972, a letter of agreement was signed by CAMC and West Virginia University, to locate a branch of the WVU School of Medicine in Charleston. With financial, political, and advisory help from William J. Maier Jr., the WVU Educational Building was dedicated in the fall of 1977 on the grounds of CAMC Memorial Division. Two decades later, a third of all third and fourth year WVU medical students spend full time in Charleston for clinical training. CAMC and WVU jointly were responsible in 1998 for the education and training of 138 resident physicians and psychologists, and 245 students from health sciences and related disciplines.

At the end of the 20th century, CAMC was the largest hospital in the state, with 813 licensed beds, 50 nursery beds, a medical staff of 676, a nursing staff of 1,120 full-time equivalents, and a total of 4,200 employees. The Transplant Service performs many kidney transplants and transplants other body tissues as well. The Center for Reproductive Medicine provides a broad array of solutions for genetic and fertility problems. The cardiology and cardiovascular surgery sections care for more patients than any other hospital in the state, and are high on all national lists in numbers and safety. CAMC is the largest portion of a holding company, Camcare, along with CAMC Foundation, Carelink managed care, mobile laboratory services, and other components.

Warren Point
Charleston

Stan Cohen, *Birth of a Medical Center*, 1988; Dolores Fleming, *The Southern Pylons*, 1997.

Charleston Ballet

Conceived by Belgium native Andre Van Damme, the Charleston Ballet's 30-member company debuted at the city's Municipal Auditorium in April 1956. The company was an outgrowth of Van Damme's American Academy of Ballet, a school he established in Charleston after immigrating from Europe in the late 1940s. Van Damme's dream was to build a company that would offer an outlet for talented dancers from the Charleston area, and feature guest performances by professionals.

The Charleston Ballet was designated the official West Virginia State Ballet in 1972. Van Damme, who had been principal dancer with the ballet company of the Royal Opera of Brussels, choreographed more than 100 original ballets for the Charleston Ballet and routinely danced male lead roles during the early years. Prior to forming the company, he and his principal dancer, Julianne Kemp, had toured Belgium.

At Van Damme's death on February 3, 1989, Kemp, who was assistant director, kept the company going until a successor to Van Damme could be named. Eventually, Kim Pauley, his protégé and the company's principal ballerina, agreed to take the job of director. In 2003, Pauley continued dancing lead roles, while handling the business end of operating a dance company. She routinely imports professional dancers to handle major roles and work as her partner in the company's performances.

In recent years, the Charleston Ballet has offered two to three concert series each year, as well as a holiday season production of "The Nutcracker" and abbreviated programs for school children.

See also Andre Van Damme

Kay Michael
Charleston

Charleston Daily Mail

Charleston's evening newspaper, the *Charleston Daily Mail*, traces its origins to the late 19th century. The first newspaper with a similar name appeared in 1893, when F. R. Swann began publishing the *Evening Mail*. The *Evening Mail* became a morning paper in 1894 after George Warren sold his interest to John B. Floyd and John W. Jarrett, who changed the name to the *Charleston Mail*.

The "Mail" name disappeared in 1896 because of a purchase and consolidation. It reappeared in 1899 when Moses Donnally, the owner of the *Charleston Gazette*, purchased the *Star Tribune* and renamed it the *Charleston Mail*. Donnally published the *Charleston Mail* as a morning newspaper and the *Gazette* as an afternoon paper. In 1900, he sold the *Gazette*, and a year later he moved the *Mail* to afternoon publication. It appeared consistently until 1910, when it was sold to coal operator Samuel Dixon of Fayette County. The paper was eventually combined with another and called the *News Mail*.

In April 1914, the *News Mail* was purchased by Walter Eli Clark, who had been a teacher, reporter, Washington correspondent, gold prospector, and governor of Alaska. Clark reclaimed the *Charleston Mail* name and gave the paper stable ownership, established its identity as an independent Republican newspaper, and brought it into the modern era. On April 4, 1920, the *Charleston Mail* started a Sunday edition and itself became the *Charleston Daily Mail*. By 1927, the *Daily Mail* was doing well enough that it moved across Virginia Street from its old quarters to a new building at 1001 Virginia Street East, an address it now shares with the rival *Charleston Gazette*.

On January 1, 1958, the *Daily Mail* entered into a joint operating agreement with the *Gazette*. Under the agreement, the newspapers merged their business, advertising, circulation, and production departments into a single corporation. The *Daily Mail* and the *Gazette* retained separate news and editorial identities but merged their Sunday newspapers into the *Sunday Gazette-Mail*.

In 1935, Clark named Frederick M. Staunton publisher, and Clark continued to serve as president. Clark died in 1950. When Staunton retired in 1968, Lyell B. Clay, Clark's stepson, became publisher. In 1987, Clay sold the *Daily Mail* to Thomson Newspapers. Brothers Lyell and Buckner Clay, with part of the proceeds from the sale, established the Clay Foundation, a private charitable foundation.

With the sale of the newspaper, John F. McGee was named publisher, serving until 1990. Subsequent publishers included Terry Horne, who served from 1990 to 1995, and David Greenfield, who served from 1995 to 1997. Sam Hindman was named to the position in 1997 and succeeded by Nanya Friend in 2004. Thomson sold the *Daily Mail* to Media News Group in 1998. The newspaper's circulation was about 25,000 in 2005.

Daily Mail Editor J. D. Maurice, who retired in 1978, won the Pulitzer Prize in 1975, the only West Virginia journalist ever to do so.

See also Charleston Gazette, Clay Foundation, Newspapers

Judie Smith
West Virginia Humanities Council

Charleston Gazette

The state's largest-circulation newspaper since 1981, the *Charleston Gazette* has been owned by the Chilton family for nearly a century. Its history began in 1873, when Charles B. Webb started the weekly *Kanawha Chronicle* in Charleston. From the outset, the *Chronicle's* self-described editorial leanings were "Demo-cratic, liberal and progressive," an apt description of the present-day *Gazette*.

In February 1877, the *Chronicle* was sold to James B. Pemberton, who later served as Charleston mayor, and John W. Jarrett, a printer, who renamed it the *Kanawha Gazette*. Moses W. Donnally of Charleston, a publisher and oil developer, bought an interest in the *Kanawha Gazette* in 1884 and later bought Pemberton's share. In 1888, the *Kanawha Gazette* began regular daily publication; two years later, the name was changed to the *Daily Gazette*. In 1897, the Donnally Publishing Company sold the paper to the Gazette Company, headed by Col. O'Brien Moore. The *Gazette* published a daily and a weekly edition in the late 1890s and early 1900s. For two years, from 1905 to 1907, the Charleston Publishing Company took over the *Gazette*.

In 1907, the Chilton family acquired an interest in the newspaper and renamed it the *Charleston Gazette*. The Daily Gazette Company's incorporators included C.A. Ashcraft, T. S. Clark, Joseph E. Chilton, Sam B. Chilton, and William A. Mac-Corkle, the former governor and long-time Chilton associate. After W. E. Chilton of Charleston completed his term in the U.S. Senate in 1917, he became publisher of the *Gazette*, borrowing money to keep the shaky paper afloat. After a fire in 1918 destroyed the newspaper's plant at the South Side Bridge, the *Gazette* built new offices on Hale Street, where it remained for 42 years.

In 1922, William E. "Ned" Chilton Jr., son of the senator, became president of the Daily Gazette Co. and was later named managing editor. As an editorial writer, he helped to establish the newspaper's reputation as a voice for the powerless. His son, W. E. "Ned" Chilton III carried on the newspaper's crusading tradition from 1961, when he was named publisher, until his death in 1987.

In the late 1920s, the *Gazette's* financial condition improved and circulation increased, due in part to Robert L. Smith Sr., who oversaw the circulation, advertising, and business departments before being named general manager, stockholder, and board member. Smith was *Gazette* publisher from 1950 to 1961. By 1937, circulation exceeded 50,000, with high readership in the traditionally Democratic southern coalfields. Statewide circulation peaked at 86,000 in 1953. Within a decade, circulation began to decrease, primarily due to mining industry layoffs and the resulting migration from the state's coalfields. The *Gazette's* 2005 daily circulation was 50,737.

Beginning in the 1950s, the *Gazette* promoted several community events, including the annual North-South football game, soap box derby, Kanawha River boat races, and the city tennis tournament. In June 1950, the *Gazette* led a two-day community effort to build Coonskin Park on Charleston's outskirts.

On January 1, 1958, the *Gazette* entered into a joint operating agreement with the *Charleston Daily Mail*. Under the agreement, the newspapers merged their business, advertising, circulation, and production departments into a single corporation. The *Gazette* and *Mail* retained separate news and editorial identities, but merged their Sunday newspapers into the *Sunday Gazette-Mail*, produced by the *Gazette* staff. In September 1960, the *Gazette* moved its offices to the *Daily Mail* building on Virginia Street.

The *Gazette* has won many national awards, particularly for reporting on educational and environmental issues. After Ned Chilton's death in 1987, Robert L. Smith Jr. was named Daily Gazette Co. president and *Gazette* publisher. Upon Smith's retirement in 1992, Chilton's wife, Elizabeth, was named president, later becoming publisher as well.

See also Ned Chilton, William Edwin Chilton, Newspapers

Nancy Ray Adams
Pine Mountain Settlement School
John G. Morgan, "Gazette Gains First Century Milestone," *Charleston Gazette*, April 30, 1973.

Charleston National Bank

Charleston National Bank, now Bank One, was founded in 1884 as a national bank. Reflecting the growth of southern West Virginia's coalfields, the bank grew steadily, increasing assets to $500,000 by 1903. It originally occupied a structure on Kanawha Street, now Kanawha Boulevard, then moved to Capitol Street in 1906. The 1906 facility was impressive, standing seven stories tall. Other businesses occupied parts of the new building, which stood at Capitol and Quarrier, for many years a prime commercial intersection.

The bank continued to grow through the 1920s in spite of poor business conditions. By 1929, Charleston National had consolidated or merged with five other banks, making it the largest national bank in the state. By 1935 two banks, Charleston National and First Huntington National, together controlled a full 25 percent of the financial resources of all national banks in West Virginia. Charleston National was the biggest bank in the state, and remained so for many years.

In the early 1960s, Charleston National officials decided to build a new facility. Originally, Quarrier Street had stopped at the intersection with Capitol. As traffic was opened through the block, the 1906 bank building projected into the street, creating a "dog leg" in busy downtown traffic. The city was pleased to see the obstruction removed, and after the old bank building came down east-west Quarrier Street expanded to full width.

In 1969, the bank moved to its new facility, Charleston National Plaza, occupying an entire city block at Capitol and Virginia streets. The new location served as both a headquarters for the bank and a location for many other businesses that leased office space there. Construction of the Charleston National Plaza ushered in a new era of modern high-rise banks in Charleston.

After West Virginia liberalized its banking laws, Charleston National formed a bank holding company, Centurion Bancorp in 1981. Centurion in turn merged with Key Bancshares, the holding company of the First Huntington National Bank, in 1985 to form Key Centurion Bancshares. The "mega-merger" created the state's first billion-dollar bank holding company. In 1992, Key Centurion Bancshares was purchased by Bank One, a Chicago firm and one of the nation's largest bank holding companies. By 2002, Bank One was West Virginia's fourth-largest banking institution, doing business in 29 locations throughout the state. In 2004, Bank One was purchased by JP Morgan Chase.

See also Banking

Carrie Stollings
Charleston

Otis K. Rice and Stephen W. Brown, *A Centennial of Strength: West Virginia Banks,* 1991.

Charleston Ordnance Center

The Charleston Ordnance Center, formerly the U.S. Navy Ordnance Plant and now South Charleston Industrial Park, primarily consists of several large buildings and associated shops and rail lines. It is located between U.S. 60 and Interstate 64 in South Charleston. Construction began before World War I, with much expansion in World War II. The major operations involved fabrication of armor plate for naval vessels and the "pickling" (final finishing and acid treatment to remove oxide scale and other debris) of large battleship guns. The scale of the place is huge, with the largest building enclosing more than 900,000 square feet.

Completed too late to be of use in World War I, the Ordnance Center was closed in 1922. It reopened in 1939 and saw major service in World War II. It was a vital center of wartime production, employing 7,400 workers by 1944, half of them women. Among other munitions, they produced air-to-ground rockets, torpedo flasks, and more than 130,000 gun barrels for the large guns of battleships. The plant received the coveted Army-Navy "E" production award in 1942.

After the war, the plant was sold to the Parks Corporation, which still owns it. It was initially leased to FMC to build aluminum armored combat tanks for the post-World War II army. Many armored vehicles were built at the Ordnance Center for use in the Vietnam War. The complex was later leased to the American Motors Corporation as an automobile body parts stamping operation. About 1979, the lease was taken over by Volkswagen to stamp body parts for its popular Rabbit model. In 1988, Volkswagen closed its operation, and some of its employees formed the South Charleston Stamping and Manufacturing Company (SCSM), also stamping body parts for automobiles.

In 1997, SCSM was purchased by Mayflower Vehicle Systems. Of the two longest buildings, Mayflower occupied the south building and part of the north building. The remainder of the north building was home for several small and medium-sized enterprises. Mayflower employed a large workforce, stamping out body parts for Mercedes, General Motors, and Freightliner, among others. Mayflower was purchased by Union Stamping and Assembly in 2004.

Robert C. Hieronymos
Charleston

Charleston Town Center

When it opened in November 1983, the three-level Charleston Town Center was one of the largest indoor malls east of the Mississippi River. The mall, bounded by Civic Center Drive, and Quarrier, Lee, and Court streets, covers 26 acres and occupies an entire city block. It lies two blocks west of Charleston's Capitol Street, the traditional heart of the central downtown shopping district, and within sight of Interstates 64, 77, and 79. The mall shares interconnecting parking garages with the 352-room Charleston Marriott Hotel.

The center was the dream of Charleston Mayor John Hutchinson, who thought that a shopping mall in town would help the city remain the retail hub for southern West Virginia. The 931,000 square-foot structure was designed by the architectural firm RTKL of Baltimore, Maryland. Forest City Enterprises of Cleveland, Ohio, and Cafaro Co. of Youngstown, Ohio, built the $100 million regional shopping attraction, which was financed primarily by the developers. Federal grants totaling $14 million paid for the center's two parking garages and the parking garage at the nearby Marriott. The city of Charleston obtained a federal Urban Mass Transit Authority grant to pay for a walkway from downtown Capitol Street to the new shopping center.

Inside the mall, three clay brick-tiled passageways lead past 130 specialty stores and three department stores, six restaurants, and a food court. From the mall's opening until 2005, a three-story waterfall flowed over dark granite steps into a courtyard garden. Skylights let in natural light. Annual revenues from the mall were $200 million at the end of the century. Facing increased competition from outlying shopping areas, Charleston Town Center underwent a $3 million renovation in 2003.

Cheat Lake

The Cheat River dam was built as a privately owned hydroelectric facility in 1924–26. The resulting Cheat Lake covers 1,730 surface acres, stretching from the Mason-Dixon Line across the northeastern corner of Monongalia County. The lake is 13 miles long and from one to three miles wide.

The scenic qualities of the lake have spawned a major resort named Lakeview and several upscale suburban communities that serve Morgantown and West Virginia University. About 10,000 people live within a few miles of the lake. Interstate 68, a major east-west highway in the northern part of the state, crosses Cheat Lake. Coopers Rock State Forest overlooks the lake.

The lake partially covers land where an iron industry thrived during the 19th century, at and around Ices Ferry. That industry and the coal mining which followed in the 20th century degraded the Cheat River. By the 1950s, few fish were left. Conservation efforts that got under way in earnest in the 1990s cleansed the river and its tributaries. Cheat Lake was originally called Lake Lynn, for Albert M. Lynn, president of West Penn Company. The Lake Lynn Power Plant continues to make electricity, owned today by Allegheny Power Company.

See also Cheat River, Ices Ferry Ironworks

Norman Julian
Dominion Post

Earl L. Core, *The Monongalia Story,* 1974–84.

Cheat Mountain

Cheat Mountain extends from the Tucker-Randolph county line near Kerens southward approximately 48 miles to Thorny Flat at the headwaters of Shavers Fork in Pocahontas County. The northern portion consists of sharply folded sedimentary rock with steep slopes and narrow ridges. The main bulk of Cheat Mountain is a southward extension of Backbone Mountain and McGowan Mountain and is separated from them by the gaps of Dry Fork River above Parsons and Shavers Fork below Bowden. Southward, Cheat Mountain forms the dividing ridge between Tygart Valley River and Shavers Fork.

The summits of Cheat Mountain are formed by escarpments of hard conglomerates. The summits are uniformly high with many peaks, ranging from 4,000 feet at Pond Lick Mountain at the northern end, to an unnamed summit southeast of Mace, Pocahontas County, which is 4,840 feet. On the west slope, toward Tygart Valley River, the slopes are generally steep and abrupt. On the east, the descent is more sloping to form a high plateau extending to Shavers Fork, which is 2,218 feet at Bowden rising to 4,660 feet at Thorny Flat. East of Shavers Fork, the plateau extends to the summits of Back Allegheny and Shavers mountains. This entire plateau is often referred to as Cheat Mountain. The high elevation and abundant rainfall on these summits and on the plateau gave rise to an almost unbroken red spruce forest.

Cheat Mountain was a formidable barrier to the westward movement of early settlers. The Staunton-Parkersburg Turnpike, now U.S. 250, eventually crossed the mountain at Cheat Bridge at an elevation of 3,557 feet. During the Civil War, Union troops set up a camp near Cheat Bridge, known as Fort Milroy, to protect this crossing. Remains of this encampment and graves of Union soldiers who died there are still visible. These soldiers cut the first timber in the Cheat Mountain area with a small steam-powered circular sawmill.

After the Civil War, the magnificent red spruce timber attracted the attention of lumbermen. W. S. Dewing and Sons made extensive purchases and commenced cutting timber with the intention of floating it down Shavers Fork and Cheat River to their mill at Point Marion, Pennsylvania. Dewing introduced the first logging locomotive in this area, a small Shay engine hauled in by wagon. This endeavor proved unsuccessful, and in 1899 he sold his holdings to the newly formed West Virginia Pulp & Paper Company, now MeadWestvaco. They built a large band sawmill at the present location of Cass, Pocahontas County, and built the town to house the workers. Decades later in 1974, the southern portion of Cheat Mountain attracted another venture, now known as Snowshoe Mountain Resort with premier skiing, golf, condominiums, lodges, and restaurants.

Cheat Mountain and the associated Shavers Fork plateau form a high ecosystem that is unique in the eastern United States. The region is host to more than 50 rare northern species such as the Cheat Mountain salamander, the West Virginia northern flying squirrel, snowshoe hare, goshawk, Bartrams serviceberry, balsam fir, and Canada honeysuckle.

Roy B. Clarkson
West Virginia University

Cheat Mountain, Battle of

The Battle of Cheat Mountain was a Civil War battle fought near the Randolph-Pocahontas County line on September 12, 1861. It was an important loss to the Confederacy, with Gen. Robert E. Lee coming into Western Virginia to give support to Gen. William W. Loring, commander of the Army of Northwestern Virginia. The

large concern was for the safety of the Virginia Central and the Virginia & Tennessee railroads. Brig. Gen. Joseph J. Reynolds was in command of U.S. forces, with headquarters at Elkwater, and a strongly fortified post on top of Cheat Mountain in Randolph County. Confederate forces were gathered at Valley Mountain.

To begin the Confederate assault, Gen. H. R. Jackson was to create a diversion along the Staunton-Parkersburg Turnpike in front of the Cheat Mountain fortification, while Col. Albert Rust and his troops took a back route up the mountain. Gen. S. R. Anderson was to lead a detachment along a trail discovered by Lee. The sound of Rust's gunfire was supposed to announce the start of the assault, but continued rainfall and the discovery of his troops by enemy pickets led to the abandonment of the initial plan of attack. Lee then ordered an advance against Elkwater. Col. John A. Washington, Lee's aide-de-camp and the last owner of Mount Vernon, was killed while scouting for Lee at Elkwater. General Reynolds's troops easily repelled the Confederates, described as being "too wet and too hungry to fight." Lee finally attempted a flanking movement around the federal right, but this, too, ended in defeat.

See also Cheat Mountain, Civil War, Staunton-Parkersburg Turnpike

R. F. Hendricks
Marietta, Georgia

Stan Cohen, *The Civil War in West Virginia,* 1979; George Ellis Moore, *A Banner In the Hills,* 1963.

Cheat Mountain Club

The Cheat Mountain Club, located on 188 acres eight miles north of Durbin, was built in 1887 by the Cheat Mountain Sportsmen's Association as a private hunting and fishing lodge. This Randolph County lodge, surrounded by the Monongahela National Forest, once provided a mountain getaway for Thomas Edison, Henry Ford, and Harvey Firestone early in the 20th century. The club was built on railroad property with a 60-year lease, and at the end of that term, in 1947, the Western Maryland Railroad took possession. The Mower Lumber Company purchased the property in 1963 as a private hunting lodge and retreat. In 1987, four families bought the Cheat Mountain Club and opened the lodge and its environs to the public. Today the old lodge operates as a rustic inn, available to groups by special arrangement.

The three-story lodge has rooms with private baths and other rooms with shared baths. Narrow, steep steps lead to other sleeping quarters in the third floor loft. A giant fieldstone fireplace dominates the living room, which is filled with sofas and chairs. The decor shows the club's origin as a hunting lodge. Deer

antlers, a boar's head, and other trophies adorn the walls. When Ford, Edison, and Firestone visited in August 1918, the walls were covered with paper outlines of trophy trout caught in the nearby stream. Rock-strewn Shavers Fork runs behind the building, with cut stone steps leading down into the pool created by a low dam.

Maureen F. Crockett
St. Albans

Cheat Mountain Salamander

The Cheat Mountain salamander.

The Cheat Mountain salamander is found in West Virginia and nowhere else on Earth. It is a relatively small salamander, reaching a maximum length of four inches. Its back is black to dark brown and is usually marked with brassy flecks; the underside is a uniform dark gray. Its tail is shorter than the combined length of its head and body, a feature that helps to distinguish it from similar-appearing species. Because of its limited range and potential habitat loss, this species was placed on the federal threatened species list in 1989.

The Cheat Mountain salamander lives in cool forests in the higher elevations of five counties: Grant, Pendleton, Pocahontas, Randolph, and Tucker. During the day, these salamanders hide under logs or rocks, inside rotten logs, or underground. At night, they come out to hunt for their prey—small invertebrates such as mites and insects. Females lay small clusters of eggs in cavities found under rocks or in rotten logs; the eggs are suspended from the ceiling of the cavity by a short stalk. Like all members of the group known as woodland salamanders, the Cheat Mountain salamander has no lungs and must breathe through its skin. For this reason, the skin of these animals must remain moist. These salamanders may remain underground for extended periods during dry weather.

Craig W. Stihler
Division of Natural Resources

Cheat River

The Cheat River drains about 1,420 square miles in northern West Virginia. It flows free, untamed, and without dams from its headwaters to Cheat Lake, a few miles above the river's mouth. From its sources in the Allegheny Mountains of Pocahontas and Randolph counties, it runs about 156 miles. It drops from 4,600 feet at the beginnings of Shavers Forks to 780 feet just across the Mason-Dixon Line at Point Marion in Pennsylvania. There the Cheat joins the Monongahela River as its principal tributary. The five forks—the Blackwater River and Dry, Laurel, Glady, and Shavers forks—are arranged like a human hand with its wrist at Parsons, where the main Cheat officially begins.

George Washington visited in 1784 and wrote: "Cheat at the Mouth is about 125 yards wide—the Monongahela near dble that—the colour of the two waters is very differt [sic], that of Cheat is dark, the other is clear." Roots of laurel and hardwood leaves tint the water, hiding sharp rocks and treacherous currents. This led to drownings which some say caused settlers who began to live along its banks before the American Revolution to say the river "cheated" people of their lives. Others think it was named for the cheat grass that sprang up in newly cleared lands, or for an early French settler, or from a word of Indian origins.

The earliest white settlement was made in 1772 near Kingwood by a religious group, the Dunkards. Forks of Cheat Baptist Church was organized at Stewartstown in 1775, near the river's mouth. In the early 19th century, an iron industry along the lower reaches of the river supported 3,000 people at Cheat Neck and Ices Ferry, near Morgantown. Nearby iron ore beds fed crude furnaces made of sandstone. Wooden barges and flatboats were used to float the iron down the ten navigable miles of the Cheat, then to the Monongahela and the Ohio. The industry was crucial to American success in the War of 1812. Cannonballs made along the Cheat were used in the Battle of New Orleans.

George Washington projected the Cheat and Potomac rivers as links, along with canals, in a water route across the Alleghenies to connect the Atlantic Seaboard with the Ohio River. Over 30 years, he made five trips to the "western waters." In 1870, the Cheat River was declared a public highway, although by then the Baltimore & Ohio Railroad had replaced waterways as the main means of transportation through the region.

Coal and timber were extracted from the watershed, polluting the river and setting the stage for record flooding. A private dam to generate electricity, completed in 1926 near the state line, created a lake and suburban community for Morgantown. By the 1950s, fish had all but disappeared in lower Cheat. By the mid-1990s, the Cheat was considered the eighth most endangered river in the United States. Preservationists began to treat it more kindly. By century's end, fish had returned. Whitewater rafting has be-

come a chief industry, ironically making the Cheat's wild and raucous character into one of its greatest attractions.

See also Cheat Lake, Forks of Cheat, Forks-of-Cheat Baptist Church

Norman Julian
Dominion Post

Maurice Brooks, *The Appalachians*, 1965; Jim Comstock, *The West Virginia Heritage Encyclopedia*, 1976; Earl L. Core, *The Monongalia Story*, 1974–84.

Chemical Industry

The modern West Virginia chemical industry began in the Kanawha Valley in the 1920s and peaked shortly after World War II. Its roots are in the salt industry of the early 1800s. In the early 1900s, chemical manufacturers were attracted to the Kanawha Valley by the presence of salt brine, coal, oil, and gas; rail and water transportation; and skilled people from the salt industry. The Belle Alkali Company started a plant near Belle in 1915 to produce chlorine, caustic, and hydrogen by electrolysis of the brine. In South Charleston, the Rollin Chemical Company built a unit to recover barium peroxide and other barium salts. E. C. Klipstein & Sons started producing sulfur dyes, tear gas, and anthraquinone in 1915. Both these companies were eventually purchased by Union Carbide.

The Warner-Klipstein Chemical Company also started up in 1915, to produce chlorine, caustic, carbon disulfide, and carbon tetrachloride. In the 1920s, it became the Westvaco Chemical Corporation, and by 1930 it was the largest chlorine producing plant in the world, using brine from 17 wells on the site. During World War II, it produced barium nitrate for incendiaries, hexachloroethane for smoke screens, and catalyst for synthetic rubber. In 1948, it became part of FMC. In 1957, FMC developed a new source of brine at Bens Run in Tyler County on the Ohio River. The highly concentrated brine was shipped by barge to South Charleston, keeping the South Charleston plant competitive until the 1990s.

Farther down the Kanawha River, in 1917, the U.S. government hired the DuPont Company to build a new nitrocellulose plant to meet the demands of World War I. The Explosives Plant "C," including the entire new town of Nitro, was built in just 11 months using a work force of up to 19,000. The plant operated for one week and then was shut down when the war ended in 1918. The property was organized as an industrial park and was sold to private companies. At least 17 different companies have located at the site over the years. The Viscose Company established a plant in 1921 to make cotton linters, a gunpowder ingredient. Viscose became American Viscose, which built a new rayon fiber unit in 1937 that became the largest staple rayon plant in the world

by 1945. The plant later became Avtex Fibers, which operated until 1980. Other early companies locating in Nitro included Ohio Apex Chemical, Monsanto, Elko Chemical, the Nitro Pencil Company, the Nitro Soap Factory, and later, Fike Chemical.

In 1920, the Union Carbide Company bought a small refinery near Clendenin to experiment with promising research from the Mellon Institute in Pittsburgh. In 1925, they moved to the Rollin Chemical site in South Charleston to produce ethylene glycol antifreeze from natural gas constituents that were normally burned or discarded, creating the well-known Prestone brand. During the next 30 years, Union Carbide developed or commercialized more than 150 chemicals, including polymers such as vinyl chloride. The company also built units in Institute and created the Tech Center in South Charleston, which became its worldwide research and development center. "Carbide" as it was locally known, ushered in the age of petrochemistry at these West Virginia plants.

The 1920s also saw the startup in 1926 of the new DuPont plant at Belle, to make ammonia from coal using high-pressure synthesis. In 1927, the plant also began making synthetic wood alcohol, eventually supplying more than 40 percent of the market. The DuPont plant went on to make a number of important chemicals for the first time, including crystal urea, methyl methacrylate plastic or Lucite, nylon salt, Hypalon synthetic rubber, and Delrin acetal resin, making the site a pioneer in the new era of polymers.

World War II brought another major increase in the production of chemicals in the Kanawha Valley. In 1941, the government started a synthetic rubber program at the Institute site. The Carbide and Carbon Chemicals Corporation along with the U.S. Rubber Corporation built plants to make Buna S synthetic rubber. The first rubber was made in March 1943, at the site that later became Union Carbide's Institute plant. Nearby, the Monsanto Company was making chemicals for the new rubber industry also, and later became the world leader in rubber chemicals. All the companies ran at capacity to support the war effort. The Kanawha Valley became known as the chemical center of the world, and South Charleston was nicknamed Chemical City.

After World War II, the local industry reached its peak employment by 1950 and then started slowly declining. The chemical industry outgrew the Kanawha Valley. Many of the chemicals produced during the war became commodity chemicals, with demand for production volumes larger than the Kanawha Valley could support. Soon the major corporations were building larger facilities on the Gulf coast and in Texas, where oil and space were plentiful. The Kanawha Valley plants changed to smaller-volume specialty chemicals, plastics, and agricultural chemicals.

Some of the expansion took place within West Virginia. In the 1950s and 1960s, several new plants were built along the Ohio from Huntington to the Northern Panhandle. In 1947, American Cyanamid built a plant near Willow Island on the Ohio River to produce pigments and dyes. In 1954, Monsanto and Bayer built a polyurethane foam plant in New Martinsville. The venture, named Mobay, was later bought out by Bayer. GE and DuPont built new plastics plants in Parkersburg. In the 1960s, Union Carbide built a silicones unit near Sistersville.

As the 20th century ended, the increasingly competitive and globalized chemical industry caused many old companies to shut down or become part of new companies. A Goodyear plant, built in 1959 near Apple Grove to make rubber chemicals, is now called M&G Polymers and makes polyester resins used in beverage and food containers. The Monsanto plant at Nitro became Flexsys, a joint venture of Akzo-Nobel and Solutia. Flexsys closed the plant in 2004, citing foreign competition. Most of the Union Carbide Institute site was sold to a French company, Rhone-Poulenc, in 1986. In 1999, it was sold to Aventis, another European chemical company. Other parts of Carbide's South Charleston and Institute plants were sold to Arco and Lyondell. The Olin Chemical Company in South Charleston became part of Clearon Corporation. The Sistersville silicones plant was bought by an investment group named Crompton. And finally, in 2001, the Dow Chemical Company purchased the entire Union Carbide Company.

As companies merged and old plants were shut down, the number of chemical workers in West Virginia continued to shrink. Advances in technology and computerization also reduced the number of workers required. By 2001, only about 14,000 people were employed statewide in the chemical industry in about 40 plants. However, the industry is still a substantial part of West Virginia's economy, contributing 35 percent of the value of the state's manufacturing output, or about $5 billion per year, with about $1 billion in exports. The chemical industry continues to employ about 25 percent of West Virginia's manufacturing workers.

See also DuPont Belle Works, Nitro, South Charleston, Union Carbide Corporation

Charles J. Denham
E. I. DuPont Company

Lemuel Chenoweth

Bridge builder Lemuel Chenoweth was born June 25, 1811, near Beverly, Randolph County. On June 23, 1836, he mar-

Inside Lemuel Chenoweth's Barrackville covered bridge.

ried Nancy Ann Hart, the great-granddaughter of John Hart, a signer of the Declaration of Independence.

Chenoweth built churches, houses, sideboards, poster beds, buggies, wagons, a model of a reverse-cutting sawmill, and even dominoes. The Huttonsville Presbyterian Church built by him celebrated its 100th anniversary in 1983. Chenoweth obtained his greatest recognition for building covered bridges in Western Virginia. When bids were being received in the 1840s for the Staunton-Parkersburg Turnpike bridges, Chenoweth constructed a model of a covered bridge. Legend has it that the backcountry carpenter arrived at the state capital in Richmond with his bridge model packed in his saddlebags. His plain design attracted little attention until he placed his model between two chairs, stood on it, and challenged the other bidders to put their models to the same test. The story has been disputed, but the contract was awarded to Chenoweth to build all the main river crossings for the center section of the new turnpike.

In 1850, after Chenoweth had completed many bridges on the Staunton-Parkersburg Turnpike, bids were taken for bridges on the Beverly-Fairmont Turnpike which had been authorized in 1848. One of two bridges was to cross the Tygart Valley River at Philippi and the other to cross the West Fork River at Hunsaker's Ferry near Fairmont. He received the contracts for these bridges.

His many bridges also included the earliest covered bridge at Beverly (1846–47), the famous Philippi covered bridge (1852), and the Barrackville covered bridge on the Fairmont-Wheeling Turn-

pike (1853). His Beverly bridge was badly damaged by burning by Confederate General Rosser's forces on January 11, 1865, and rebuilt by Chenoweth in 1872–73. Chenoweth's major bridges all employed the Burr arch-truss structural design. This framing system, developed by Theodore Burr, improved bridge strength dramatically. Simple truss framing used triangular bracing to stiffen the structure. Burr's design integrated an arch into the truss framework, increasing strength and rigidity for longer spans.

Chenoweth died at his home in Beverly, August 26, 1887, and is buried in the Beverly cemetery.

See also Covered Bridges, Philippi Covered Bridge, Staunton-Parkersburg Turnpike

Donald L. Rice
Elkins

Virginia Yokum Downey, "Lemuel Chenoweth—Bridge Builder," in Eva Margaret Carnes, ed., *Centennial History of the Philippi Covered Bridge, 1852–1952,* 1952; Debby Sonis Jackson, "Lemuel Chenoweth,"*Goldenseal,* Summer 1988.

Cherokees

Before the European invasion of North America, the Cherokees were probably the largest indigenous society in the region that became the U.S. Southeast. Numbering around 20,000, they lived comfortably in the southern Appalachian Mountains, drawing on the wildlife and food resources of the diverse forest surrounding their villages and the rich soils they cultivated in sheltered mountain coves and river bottoms. Even after European diseases and warfare reduced their numbers by as much as 75 percent, the

Cherokee remained a potent force in warfare and diplomacy. Their geographic location in the western Carolinas, north Georgia, and eastern Tennessee allowed them to play off rival European powers against each other and to command a lucrative share of the trade in pelts and deerskins bound for ports in Virginia and South Carolina. Despite lost wars in 1760–62 and again during the American Revolution, they retained their independence and much of their landed patrimony. It was not until the U.S. government forcibly removed most of the Cherokee from their homeland that this society ceased to play a major role in the history of the American south.

Although the Cherokee claimed land south of the Great Kanawha River in present West Virginia, they did not depend on it for hunting and relinquished this claim in the Treaty of Hard Labor (1768). They used the Great Appalachian Valley corridor to fight and trade with their fellow Iroquoian language speakers in New York and Pennsylvania, and on at least one occasion engaged in a great battle with these enemies at a place near modern Shepherdstown. Cherokees also briefly played a role as allies of Western Virginia frontiersmen in the ill-fated Sandy Creek Expedition of 1756. Otherwise they did not threaten the Ohio Valley except in the upper New River area of present southwest Virginia. Young men responded to the entreaties of Mingo and Shawnee warriors to join in their assaults during the Indian wars that accompanied and followed the Revolution, but these were the actions of individuals, not of the Cherokee leadership.

Cherokees who were active in West Virginia were almost always members of the Overhill towns, one of five clusters of villages among which their people were distributed. The Overhill Cherokees lived along the Little Tennessee River in East Tennessee. The Middle and Valley towns were located south of the Great Smoky Mountains in what is now western North Carolina. The other clusters were located east of the mountains, in the foothills of the South Carolina and Georgia Blue Ridge.

Given the limited role that Cherokees played in West Virginia history, it is curious that a claim of Cherokee ancestry developed among many families in the Mountain State. This may be because after their 19th century "renaissance," the Cherokees were better known and more widely admired than the other Indian societies—such as Shawnee or Delaware—who are more likely to have participated in genetic exchanges on the Western Virginia frontier. Demographically, it is more probable that claims of Indian blood actually masked African-American ancestry. A third possible explanation comes from the migration of young Cherokee men from their North Carolina reservation during the late 19th and early 20th centuries. Other southerners, white and black, migrated north to West Virginia lumber and coal camps during this period, and it is possible that Cherokee migrants chose the same paths.

John Alexander Williams
Appalachian State University

Gregory Evans Dowd, *A Spirited Resistance: The North American Indian Struggle for Unity, 1745–1815*, 1992; William G. McLoughlin, *Cherokee Renascence in the New Republic*, 1986; Theda Perdue, *Cherokee Women: Gender and Culture Change 1700–1835*, 1998.

Cherry River Navy

The Cherry River Navy, organized in 1937, is headquartered in landlocked Richwood. The informal honorary society was established by John L. "Bugs" Teets, along with A. B. Campbell and Lee Reese, to draw attention to the need for the completion of State Route 39 from Richwood to Marlinton. The tongue-in-cheek logic apparently was that a road should be built since the Cherry River itself was unnavigable. Teets was the editor of a local newspaper, the *Nicholas Republican*.

In the 1930s, Richwood was a major population center and a thriving community with many timber-based industries that included a lumber mill, a tannery, and the world's largest clothespin factory. What the town did not have was a paved road connecting it to the east. The Cherry River Navy was successful in its mission. The extension of Route 39 linking Richwood to Marlinton was started in the fall of 1937. The road was finished in 1945.

In the Cherry River Navy, all members are admirals. The membership list has included presidents, governors, senators, astronauts, and local businessmen. Among past and present members are Jennings Randolph, Herbert Hoover, Harry Truman, Dwight Eisenhower, Hubert Humphrey, Robert Byrd, Arch Moore, Jim Comstock, Jay Rockefeller, Jon McBride, and Babe Ruth. The navy has maneuvered in Richwood since 1937 except for a break during and after World War II and another break following the death of founder Teets in 1984. Nowadays the Cherry River Navy sails in August every year in the Cherry River Festival Parade on a wheeled boat down Main Street.

See also Richwood

Amy Donaldson Arnold
Ivydale

Chesapeake & Ohio Railway

The Chesapeake & Ohio was a major force in opening the coalfields of southern West Virginia in the years after the Civil War. The railroad provided the impetus for the growth of Huntington in the west, White Sulphur Springs in the east,

Engineer William E. Bailey boards his C&O locomotive.

and towns in between such as Hinton and Thurmond. Many West Virginians can name members of their families who were, or still are, employees of the C&O and its successors.

The Chesapeake & Ohio Railroad was created in 1868 by the merger of the Virginia Central Railroad and the Covington & Ohio Railroad. At the beginning of the Civil War, the Virginia Central extended from Richmond to Waynesboro and was the second largest railroad in the state. While the Covington & Ohio had been chartered in 1853 to build from the western terminus of the Virginia Central to the Ohio River, no construction had taken place at the outbreak of the Civil War. The Virginia Central, located where the fighting raged, suffered significant damage during the war. When the war ended, Gen. William C. Wickham, a Confederate cavalry officer, became president of the railroad and restored the entire line to operation early in 1866.

In July 1867, the Virginia Central reached Covington, near the boundary between Virginia and the new state of West Virginia. Wickham also became president of the Chesapeake & Ohio after the 1868 merger and immediately began seeking funds to extend the railroad to the Ohio River.

The C&O soon attracted the support of Collis P. Huntington, one of the greatest railroad entrepreneurs in American history. Huntington had recently been the major figure in the completion of the first transcontinental railroad, the Union Pacific-Central Pacific. He saw the C&O as the eastern section of a true transcontinental railroad. His contacts with New York financiers were desperately needed by the C&O. To benefit from these contacts, however, the board and the stockholders of the railroad were forced to reorganize the company, turning operations over to Huntington and his friends.

Once in control, Huntington expanded the railroad rapidly. Construction started west from Covington and east from the newly developed town of Huntington on the banks of the Ohio. Using more than 7,000 men (including the legendary John Henry, the "steel driving man"), and well over the projected construction cost of $15 million, the line was completed on January 29, 1873. Construction was expensive and difficult because of the mountains between Covington and Hinton. West of Hinton the line followed the New River for a considerable distance, the narrow valley also a challenge to construction workers. Many fatalities and injuries resulted.

The difficult construction and the rapid expansion of the C&O, in addition to the national depression of 1873, forced the company into default. In 1878, the Chesapeake & Ohio Railroad was sold at foreclosure, reorganized, and renamed the Chesapeake & Ohio Railway. Financial conditions gradually improved as coal mines were opened along the route. A major step forward took place in 1882 when a 75-mile line was constructed from Richmond to Tidewater at Newport News, connecting the railroad with ocean shipping.

In the 1880s, the C&O pushed west to Cincinnati and smaller railroads were absorbed at a rate too rapid to sustain. Consequently, the line was forced into receivership again in 1887. A foreclosure sale was averted when J. P. Morgan interests purchased control of the company and instituted a successful financial recovery. In the process Huntington's role with the C&O ended, and his place was taken by Melville E. Ingalls.

The Ingalls era (1888–1900) began with the entry of the C&O into Cincinnati. Ingalls's leadership provided stability and with financial support from Morgan the company continued to expand. By 1900, the C&O had more than doubled the mileage it operated, new locomotives and rolling stock had been purchased, the line had been ballasted and re-laid with heavier rails, and the company paid a dollar per share annual dividend.

In the first decade of the new century, the Pennsylvania Railroad and the New York Central purchased large amounts of C&O stock in an effort to control rates for shipping coal. To further this end, the C&O purchased some of the small coal-hauling railroads in West Virginia that connected with the C&O, such as the Coal River & Western Railroad and the Guyandot Valley Railroad. Branches to Big Creek, Buffalo Creek, Rum Creek, Piney Creek, Cabin Creek, and Dingess Run, for example, were also constructed. The 98-mile Greenbrier Railway Company, purchased by the C&O in 1907, ran up the Greenbrier Valley to Bartow. Completed in 1904, it was built to provide access to timber for the large sawmills at Ronceverte. Eventually known as the Durbin Branch, it connected with what is now the Cass Scenic Railroad at Cass.

In Ohio the C&O gradually absorbed the Hocking Valley Railroad after 1905, giving connections to Columbus and Toledo. Other expansion in the Midwest gave the C&O access to Chicago and the Great Lakes. After World War I, the C&O went through several leadership changes before ending up under the direction of brothers Oris P. and Mantis J. Van Sweringen, colorful real estate developers in Cleveland. The Van Sweringens attempted to combine their railroads—the C&O, the Erie, the Pere Marquette, and the Nickel Plate—into one major system. While the Interstate Commerce Commission refused to allow the merger and the Van Sweringen empire was eventually disbanded, one result was the C&O's acquisition of the Pere Marquette Railroad, operating primarily in Michigan.

Because of its coal traffic the C&O survived the Great Depression better than most railroads. From 1937 to 1954, under the direction of Robert R. Young, the railroad grew to a 5,100-mile system with 35,000 employees and an annual revenue of $319 million. In 1962, with Walter J. Tuohy as president, the C&O acquired the faltering Baltimore & Ohio, in a contest with the New York Central which had earlier wanted to merge with the C&O. In 1972, the C&O, B&O, and Western Maryland were merged into the Chessie System. In 1980, the current CSX corporation was created, merging the Chessie System and the Seaboard Coast Line. Today, as one of the major rail systems in the United States, CSX has acquired significant parts of Conrail, thus reducing the major railroad systems of West Virginia to two: CSX and Norfolk Southern.

See also Chessie System, CSX, Railroads

Robert L. Frey
Miamisburg, Ohio
Charles W. Turner, et al., *Chessie's Road*, 1986.

Chesapeake & Potomac Telephone Company
See Verizon.

Chessie Kitten
Chessie, the C&O railroad kitten trademark, was a familiar face to West Virginia railway passengers during the golden age of train transportation. Chessie was born in early 1933 from the mind of Lionel Probert, assistant to Chesapeake & Ohio Railway President J. J. Bernet.

Two new passenger trains had recently been inaugurated, the Sportsman and the George Washington. An advertising campaign promoting the new trains was under way and Probert was about to settle on the slogan, "Sleep Like A Top." By chance he saw a reproduction of a paint-

Chessie, dozing on the C&O.

ing of a small kitten tucked between the sheets, a paw gently hugging the pillow and one eye partly open, the creation of Viennese artist Guido Gruenewald. Probert switched to the slogan "Sleep Like A Kitten," and Chessie became one of the most famous corporate logos in the history of advertising.

See also Chesapeake & Ohio Railway

Roy C. Long
Hinton

Chessie System
The Chessie System was a holding company developed by the Chesapeake & Ohio Railway to hold the stock of railroads it acquired. The C&O gradually merged these railroads into a system known today as CSX, which remains a major force in West Virginia's economy and transportation network.

In the years after World War II, the C&O attempted to acquire a number of railroads with only modest success. The Norfolk & Western, a major rival, was more successful, as it acquired the Virginian, the Nickel Plate, and the Wabash railroads in the late 1950s. In an effort to keep up, the C&O acquired the Baltimore & Ohio in 1960 and the closely aligned Western Maryland in 1964.

The merger of the C&O, the B&O, and the Western Maryland proceeded slowly. In 1972, the new president of the C&O-B&O, Hays T. Watkins Jr., announced the creation of the Chessie System (incorporated in 1973), which included the three railroads. Although operated as one, the three maintained separate corporate identities until 1976.

The Chessie System's logo was an outline of a sleeping cat, named Chessie, embedded in a blue circle. For many years Chessie had been the mascot of the C&O and had appeared on calendars, timetables, and advertisements produced by the railroad. This logo helped to maintain the image of the C&O within the merged system.

See also Baltimore & Ohio, Chesapeake & Ohio, CSX, Railroads

Robert L. Frey
Miamisburg, Ohio
Charles W. Turner, et al., *Chessie's Road*, 1986.

Chester Teapot

The red-and-white landmark known locally as "The World's Largest Teapot" stands in Chester, at the top of the Northern Panhandle. The teapot is a symbol of the local potteries that flourished in Chester, nearby Newell, and across the Ohio River in East Liverpool, Ohio. To historic preservationists it is a piece of commercial archeology, a representative of a type of figurative roadside architecture rapidly vanishing from our landscape.

The whimsical teapot first appeared on Chester's Carolina Avenue, State Route 2, in 1938. It was erected by William "Babe" Devon. Originally a huge wooden barrel for Hire's Root Beer, a spout and handle were added and the structure was covered with tin to form the shape of a teapot. The knob on the "lid" was a large glass ball. Inside, Devon sold postcards, ice cream, hot dogs, and soda pop through the 1930s and '40s. Later sold to several different owners, the teapot continued to sell seasonal gifts, china, and novelty pieces from its shelves until the late 1970s.

The land and buildings were purchased by C&P Telephone in 1984, and the teapot was moved in 1990 to a location next to the Jennings Randolph Bridge ramp. The smaller "creamer" was also restored and placed nearby. The "World's Largest Teapot" once again stands proudly by the roadside.

See also Pottery Industry

Katherine M. Jourdan
Indianapolis, Indiana

Chestnut Blight

The American chestnut, once the most prominent tree in West Virginia's forest, was felled in the early 20th century by a blight fungus imported from the Orient. Spores from the chestnut blight fungus float through the air or are carried by birds and animals to wounds in the bark of chestnut trees. The fungus grows through the bark until the tree is girdled. The resulting bark canker with orange blisters blocks sap flow to the leaves, causing the tree above the canker to die.

Loss of the American chestnut was hard felt in West Virginia, the only state completely within the tree's natural range. One fourth of the trees in West Virginia were once American chestnuts, but by 1929 live chestnuts were becoming rare because of the blight. American chestnut trees provided West Virginia with 118 million board feet of lumber in 1919, not counting the vast quantity of timber cut for telephone poles, railroad cross ties, tan bark, wood pulp, and fuel. The nuts were a valuable crop, providing feed for wildlife and domestic swine. They provided a tasty treat for humans, as well as an income and the joy of chestnuting for many rural families. As many

as 155,092 pounds of nuts were shipped from one railroad station in West Virginia in the fall of 1911.

There is hope for recovering at least part of our lost heritage. The American Chestnut Cooperators' Foundation distributes seedlings that have a potential for blight resistance. These all-American intercrosses are produced from large, surviving American chestnut trees that have shown heritable blight resistance. The most resistant intercrosses are available for grafting onto American chestnut rootstocks in their natural environment in the forest. Another group, the American Chestnut Foundation, hybridizes American chestnuts with blight-resistant Chinese chestnuts and backcrosses them with American chestnuts to winnow out unwanted traits from Chinese chestnut while retaining blight resistance. Both foundations support research on the dissemination of a virus that debilitates the blight fungus.

See also Forests

John Rush Elkins
Concord University

Lucille Griffin, "Battling the Blight: A Second Chance for the American Chestnut," *Goldenseal*, Winter 1995; Martha K. Roane, Gary J. Griffin, and John Rush Elkins, *Chestnut Blight, Other Endothia Diseases, and the Genus Endothia*, 1986.

Chief Logan State Park

Chief Logan State Park has served southern West Virginia since 1960. In that year, the land that was to become the park was purchased by the Logan County Civic Association for $90,000 and deeded to the State Conservation Commission (predecessor to the Division of Natural Resources) for $40,000. Originally designated as a recreation area, it gained state park status in 1968. The park, about four miles north of the town of Logan, consists of 3,303 acres in the Little Buffalo Creek watershed.

Using labor from the State Temporary Employment Program, early park improvements included creek channelization, development of hiking trails, and the establishment of picnic areas. A Kanawha 2700 Class locomotive was donated to the park by the C&O Railroad in September 1961, in remembrance of the days of giant steam engines. It remains on display today. The swimming pool was opened in 1964 with subsequent improvements. By 1976, picnic shelters, restrooms, a large restaurant, and an amphitheater were added. The amphitheater is the site of the yearly "Aracoma Story" production, a drama of the legend of the Indian Princess Aracoma, the daughter of Chief Cornstalk.

More recently, the park opened a wildlife exhibit, and the West Virginia Division of Culture & History opened a history museum at Chief Logan in 2003. The 1996 legislature added $5 million to

Chief Logan State Park for improvements to the park. The Earl Ray Tomblin Conference Center was dedicated in 2003.

See also State Parks

Robert Beanblossom
Division of Natural Resources

Children's Home Society of West Virginia

The Children's Home Society of West Virginia is West Virginia's largest child-service organization. Its mission is to ensure the physical and emotional safety of children and their families, improve family relationships, and preserve family and community ties. The society was formed by Charleston ministers at the city's YMCA on May 4, 1896. Their goal was to place orphaned and neglected children with caring families rather than crowd them into county poorhouses. For much of its history, the society's most identifiable institution was Charleston's Davis Child Shelter, an orphanage established in 1900 with financing from former U.S. Sen. Henry Gassaway Davis. The orphanage closed in 1961 as part of a national movement to remove children from institutions and place them in foster homes.

During the 1960s and 1970s, the Charleston society branched statewide, opening offices in Sistersville and Morgantown. In 1978, a new Davis Child Shelter was established in South Charleston through a state government contract to care for neglected, dependent, and abused children. In 1995, the Davis Child Shelter moved to a new facility near Yeager Airport in Charleston. Similar shelters were added in Northfork, Romney, Martinsburg, Daniels, Huntington, Parkersburg, and Fairlea in the 1980s and 1990s. Other statewide programs sponsored by the society include programs to reduce child abuse and neglect and community-and home-based protective services.

Stan Bumgardner
Division of Culture & History

Stan Bumgardner, *The Children's Home Society of West Virginia: Children—Yesterday, Today, Tomorrow*, 1996.

Ned Chilton

Newspaper publisher William Edwin "Ned" Chilton III was born in Kingston, New York, of an old Charleston family, November 26, 1921. A World War II veteran and a graduate of Yale, he became publisher of West Virginia's largest newspaper in 1961. The *Charleston Gazette* had been in his family since 1907, and in Ned Chilton's hands it became a major force for reform. A liberal Democrat, Chilton served four terms in the state House of Delegates in the 1950s but abandoned elective politics when he took over operation of the *Gazette*. He was a delegate to the Democratic National Convention in 1960 and 1964.

Publisher Ned Chilton (1921–87).

Almost immediately, Chilton began to use his paper to crusade for change. He opposed racial segregation, censorship, and the death penalty. Chilton came down hard on drunken drivers, pushing for tougher laws, and he held public officials to high standards. His most vocal outrage was aimed at Governor Moore, his contemporary. For decades, Chilton tried to convince readers that Moore, a popular Republican in a heavily Democratic era, was unsuitable to hold office.

Colleagues in publishing were not spared, as Chilton chastised what he called "the insipid press." During a 1983 speech to the Southern Newspaper Publishers Association, he said most papers published mere "spurts of indignation," then went on to something else. "The hallmark of crusading journalism is sustained outrage," Chilton told the publishers.

Chilton's editorial page was credited with ending the commissioner of accounts system of probate, which the *Gazette* castigated as the "ghoul system" for allowing politically connected lawyers to be appointed as commissioners and claim a percentage of every dead person's estate that passed before them. Chilton demanded that government operate publicly, and filed a suit forcing the State Bar and the West Virginia Board of Medicine to reveal complaints against lawyers and doctors. Another Chilton campaign resulted in an end to secret government meetings.

Ned Chilton died unexpectedly February 7, 1987, while in Washington to compete in a national squash match.

See also Charleston Gazette

Kay Michael
Charleston

Sam Chilton

Lawyer and raconteur Samuel Blackwell Chilton was born in St. Albans, Kanawha County, August 26, 1885, the nephew of U.S. Sen. W. E. Chilton. He attended Swarthmore College and Washington and Lee University, as well as West Virginia University, from which he received a law degree. He was a football player and baseball pitcher and Charleston High School's first football coach.

Chilton entered the family law firm but apparently never practiced seriously. He was an avid baseball fan and an authority on horse racing. He lobbied the legislature for the passage of the bill permitting horse racing in West Virginia, and was recalled in his obituary as the father of the state's racing industry. He was a renowned storyteller and humorist. His cousin, storyteller Riley Wilson, specialized in humorous monologues, but Chilton's stories were short with a funny punch line.

Chilton knew many important political figures. He once told presidential candidate George McGovern, campaigning in Charleston, that McGovern was his second choice. McGovern inquired of his first choice and Chilton replied, "Anyone else who runs." He quickly told McGovern that was an old political joke and then charmed the candidate for the rest of the evening. Chilton himself ran for West Virginia secretary of state eight times, all unsuccessfully. "The secretary of state does nothing and I do nothing, so I figure I would be eminently qualified for the job," he explained.

Sam Chilton was welcomed throughout his hometown. When a prominent downtown Charleston bar changed ownership, it was done on the condition that the storyteller's drinks would be free as long as he lived. He died October 4, 1977.

See also Riley Wilson

George Daugherty
Elkview

William Edwin Chilton

U.S. Senator William Edwin Chilton was one of the leaders of West Virginia's Democratic Party. He was a politician, lawyer, and businessman. His enduring legacy was to establish Chilton family ownership of the *Charleston Gazette*, a major force in West Virginia politics throughout the 20th century.

Chilton was born March 17, 1858, in Coalsmouth, now St. Albans. After attending local schools, he became a teacher and principal while studying law. He passed the bar in 1880 and was appointed to fill an unexpired term as Kanawha County prosecutor in 1883, but was defeated in the following year's election. Chilton ran unsuccessfully for state Senate in 1886, then worked behind the scenes in politics for several years. He became chairman of the state Democratic Party in 1892 and helped engineer the election of his friend, William A. MacCorkle, as governor. MacCorkle then appointed Chilton secretary of state (1893–97).

After their terms in office were over, the two men formed the law firm Chilton, MacCorkle, and Chilton with Chilton's brother in 1897. Chilton continued as a leader of the so-called Kanawha Ring, which fought industrialist and agrarian elements in the Democratic Party for control of the state party.

In 1911, Chilton was elected as a U.S. senator by the state legislature. While in the Senate, he chaired the five-man subcommittee considering the confirmation of Louis Brandeis to the U.S. Supreme Court. Brandeis faced opposition because he was Jewish and because he supported controls on big business. Senator Chilton also supported the League of Nations, and championed a bill that would have allowed West Virginia to sue Virginia for a share of the millions of dollars that had been realized from the sale of land to the new federal government in 1784. He lost the 1917 election to Republican Howard Sutherland, the first election after the constitution was changed so that U.S. senators were directly elected by voters. He also lost Senate elections in 1924 and 1934.

Besides law and politics, Chilton tried his hand at several businesses. He and others bought Charleston's electric streetcar system in 1905 and expanded the service throughout Kanawha County. In 1907, the Chilton family bought the *Daily Gazette*, and the name was changed to the *Charleston Gazette*. After his election defeat in 1917, he became publisher and assumed editorial control of the *Gazette*. Chilton's son took over the paper in the early 1920s. The elder Chilton kept the titles of associate editor and company vice president until his death on November 7, 1939, in Charleston.

See also Charleston Gazette

Greg Moore
Charleston Gazette

Charles Henry Ambler and Festus P. Summers, *West Virginia: The Mountain State,* 1958; Stan Cohen, *Kanawha County Images,* 1987; William Alexander MacCorkle, *The Recollections of Fifty Years of West Virginia,* 1928.

Chinaware

See Pottery.

Oliver Perry Chitwood

Historian Oliver Perry Chitwood, born in Franklin County, Virginia, November 28, 1874, earned an A.B. degree at William and Mary College and was librarian there from 1898 to 1899. In 1902–03, he was headmaster of Richmond Academy, and in 1904–05, he was a fellow in history at Johns Hopkins University. After completing a Ph.D. at Johns Hopkins in 1905, Chitwood briefly was professor of history and economics at Mercer University in Macon, Georgia. In 1907, he became professor of history at West Virginia University.

During nearly 40 years at WVU, Chitwood established his reputation as an authority on American colonial history. His *History of Colonial America* (1931) was for years a leading college textbook in that field. With co-authors, Chitwood wrote *A Short History of the American People*, a two-volume textbook (1945, 1948, and later) in American history. Among his other works was *John Tyler, Champion of the Old South* (1939), a biography of the Virginian who served as president of the United States from 1841 to 1845. Publication of this book was sponsored by the American Historical Association.

The long-lived Chitwood stated during the election of 1960 that he had voted in 16 presidential elections and expected to do so again. He playfully explained that when he was in the voting booth with no one else but God, his conscience required him to vote for the Democratic candidates. Oliver Perry Chitwood died February 3, 1971.

Otis K. Rice
WVU Institute of Technology

Christian Church (Disciples of Christ)

Of more than 220 Protestant religious bodies in the United States, one of the largest to have originated in America is the Christian Church (Disciples of Christ). The denomination traces its roots to the union in 1832 of the Christians, a movement that emerged in Kentucky in 1804 under the guidance of Barton Warren Stone, and the Disciples of Christ. The tenets of the Disciples were based on Thomas Campbell's *Declaration and Address of the Christian Association of Washington*, published in Washington, Pennsylvania, in 1809. The dominant unifying force was Thomas Campbell's son, Alexander Campbell of Bethany, (West) Virginia, a college founder, scholar, and author, and the editor and publisher of a powerful religious press. Adherents were sometimes called Campbellites, and Bethany became the unofficial headquarters of the movement.

The denomination adopted the name Christian Church (Disciples of Christ) in 1968. Their historic mission has been the unification of all Christians based on a belief in Christ and in the teachings of the New Testament as the central source of authority. Disciples are ecumenical in spirit and affirm diversity of individual understandings of faith. Baptism is usually by immersion, and discipleship is affirmed through the invitation of all believers to join in communion. Disciples membership increased from 22,000 to almost 200,000 members between 1832 and 1860. The need to cooperate beyond the local congregation resulted in the first national convention in 1849. In 1968, they set in place a structure that provides for operation under a representative government on local, regional, and national

levels. There are currently more than one million Disciples in the United States and Canada, approximately 11,000 being West Virginians.

See also Bethany College, Alexander Campbell, Religion

Rosemary Jeanne Cobb
Bethany College

Lester G. McAllister and William Edward Tucker, *Journey in Faith. A History of the Christian Church (Disciples of Christ)*, 1975; Winfred Ernest Garrison and Alfred T. DeGroot, *The Disciples of Christ. A History*, 1948.

Christian Panoply

The first book printed in what is now West Virginia, *Christian Panoply; Containing an Apology for the Bible in a Series of Letters Addressed to Thomas Paine*, was written by Richard Watson, D.D., Lord Bishop of Llandaff, England, in 1796. The book was published first in England and then republished many times there and in America. Issued in 1797 in Shepherdstown, by publishers P. Rootes and C. Blagrove, the 332-page calfskin-bound volume also contained *An Apology for Christianity* (1776), written in response to Edward Gibbon's *Decline and Fall of the Roman Empire*.

Rootes and Blagrove also published for a short time the *Impartial Examiner*, the second newspaper to be published in present West Virginia. Watson (1737–1816) was educated at Trinity College, Cambridge, taught chemistry there, became chairperson of the divinity department, and was named Bishop of Llandaff in 1782. Watson was known for his strong views as a supporter of the American Revolution, a defender of religious tolerance, and an advocate of fairer distribution of church revenues. His *Christian Panoply* was a rebuttal of Thomas Paine's *An Age of Reason*, which expounded antibiblical views.

Debra K. Sullivan
Charleston Catholic High School

Christmas Tree Farming

For many years, most of the commercial Christmas trees sold in West Virginia came from Maine or Canada, but that changed following World War II when the Christmas tree industry began shifting southward. Since then, West Virginia Christmas tree growers, retailers, and brokers have turned tree farming into a sizable business. More than 300 Christmas tree farms operated in the Mountain State in the 1990s with yearly sales approaching $2.5 million. According to the 2002 U.S. Department of Agriculture census, by 1997 the number of tree farms had dropped to 239 and tree sales totaled $2.2 million.

The Christmas tree season begins early in the year when thousands of seedlings go into the ground. It can take up to 10 years to grow a harvestable tree, six to nine feet tall. Insect control, weeding,

and mowing are year-round activities. The summer months are set aside for shearing and shaping the trees, and in early fall some trees receive artificial coloring to make them more appealing to the eye. Many Christmas tree farmers bring their trees to retail sales lots or farmers markets in towns and cities during the holidays, or sell their trees to retailers, but "choose and cut" farms also represent a sizable part of the Christmas tree industry.

Scotch pine and white pine are the most popular trees, but farmers also grow more expensive varieties such as Norway and blue spruces and Fraser and Douglas firs. In recent years, a Canaan balsam fir has been added to West Virginia tree farms. The seed, originally collected as a wild specimen in Canaan Valley, can be grown in a wide range of sites. Tree farmers are banded together in the West Virginia Christmas Tree Growers Association.

Deborah J. Sonis
West Virginia Humanities Council

Chronicles of Border Warfare

Written by Alexander Scott Withers of Clarksburg and published in 1831 by Joseph Israel, a Clarksburg printer, *Chronicles of Border Warfare* is a West Virginia classic. The book is a significant representative of the early 19th-century historical genre that featured 18th-century Indian wars and border heroes of the trans-Appalachian region. Like similar works of the time, it rested heavily upon recollections of participants and upon oral traditions rather than contemporary documents. Such works were very popular. Historian Lyman C. Draper declared that copies of the original edition of *Chronicles* were read by firesides until they were worn out and scarcely legible.

Chronicles received its impetus from the writings of Hugh Paul Taylor, a Covington, Virginia, antiquarian, who gathered stories of settlement and Indian warfare from pioneers still living, with the intention of publishing them in a local newspaper under the signature "Son of Cornstalk." Withers drew upon Taylor and also upon materials amassed by Judge Edwin S. Duncan of Peeltree, in present Barbour County. Withers also used materials and stories provided by Noah Zane of Wheeling, John Hacker of the Hackers Creek settlements, and others. Useful and colorful though it is, *Chronicles*, like similar works, suffers somewhat from the fallibility of human perceptions and recollections. Fortunately, the Reuben Gold Thwaites edition of 1895, with notes by Thwaites and Lyman C. Draper, provides corrections to some errors of fact or interpretation and a broader milieu for local events treated by Withers.

Otis K. Rice
WVU Institute of Technology

Roy Bird Cook, *Alexander Scott Withers, Author of Chronicles of Border Warfare: A Sketch,* 1921; David Scott Turk, "Hugh Paul Taylor, Historian and Mapmaker," *West Virginia History,* 1997.

Cicadas

Periodical cicadas belong to a group of plant-sucking insects known as homopterans. Although they are often referred to as 17-year locusts, this is not an accurate name for these insects because locusts are a type of grasshopper and cicadas are in a different insect group.

The 17-year life cycle starts when the female cicada lays eggs in the twigs of trees in early summer. These eggs hatch six weeks later and the young cicada nymphs burrow into the soil. The nymphs feed on small plant roots for 17 years, when they emerge from the ground and molt into adults. During the four-to six-week adult stage, the cicadas will mate and the females will lay eggs, starting the cycle over again. The cicadas are well known for the droning noise the males emit to attract mates. When a large number of cicadas emerge in an area, the droning of the males has been described as deafening.

There are seven broods of cicadas in West Virginia, on different 17-year schedules. These broods occupy different areas of the state, although with some overlap. The largest is Brood V, which is due to emerge in 2016 in many northern and central counties. Periodical cicadas do not bite or sting, but the female can cause damage to trees as she punctures twigs to make pockets to deposit her eggs. Typically, dead leaves occur on the injured twigs, causing a prominent "flagging" for the remainder of the season. Young fruit and shade trees are especially susceptible to damage.

Periodical cicadas are dark with orange markings and red eyes and legs. This distinguishes them from other cicadas found in the state such as the dog-day cicadas, or jarflies. These dog-day cicadas emerge every year and are larger with green markings and black eyes. They are not considered agricultural pests.

Amy Donaldson Arnold
Ivydale

Scott Shalaway, "Periodical Cicadas," *Wonderful West Virginia,* June 1999; West Virginia Department of Agriculture, "The Periodical Cicada in West Virginia," Pamphlet, 1999.

Circuit Courts

The 55 circuit courts form the bedrock of the West Virginia judicial system. They are state trial courts that handle felony cases and major civil litigation. They are courts of general jurisdiction, meaning that they hear all types of cases originating in the circuit, including appeals from special jurisdiction courts, such as the family court or the magistrate court. All cases, civil or criminal, that have been tried in the magistrate courts may be appealed to the circuit courts. In certain instances, the circuit courts have concurrent jurisdiction with the magistrate court over misdemeanors and small civil claims.

In some other states, including Ohio and Pennsylvania, these courts are called "common pleas" courts. The reason that they are called circuit courts in West Virginia is that from early days in Virginia judges at all levels would "ride circuit" between their various duty stations. For the circuit judges, these were the county seats.

At the beginning of the 21st century, West Virginia is divided into 31 judicial circuits, presided over by 62 judges. There are single-county circuits and multi-county circuits. The circuits vary from seven judges in one county (Kanawha) to a single judge each in two separate three-county circuits. These allocations are made by the legislature and in part reflect political power as well as a rational distribution of resources.

For most litigants, the circuit court provides the only justice they will receive.

There is no appeal of right to the state Supreme Court of Appeals, which reviews only those cases it chooses, so in more than 90 percent of civil and criminal cases the decision of the circuit court is final and binding on the litigants. The circuit courts are administered by the Supreme Court, as are all other parts of the state judiciary.

H. John Rogers
New Martinsville

Circuit Riders

Circuit riders were clergymen, usually of the Wesleyan tradition, who rode from one group of believers to another for the conduct of worship and religious instruction. They faced great hardships and rode many miles to carry out their ministry. The result of their work was the creation of strong churches throughout the early American republic, including present West Virginia.

The origins of the circuit rider can be traced to the organizational structure developed by John Wesley, the founder of Methodism. Wesley advocated the creation of "classes" of believers who would meet regularly for worship, Bible study, and to support each other in the faith. John Wesley appointed two superintendents in the United States—Francis Asbury being the best known—to ordain clergy and to lead the churches and classes already formed. Usually these ordained clergymen were assigned a number of classes located geographically in a circuit. Depending on the size of the circuit the preacher might visit a class only once or twice a year. Even today in small towns and rural areas it is not unusual for a United Methodist minister to have a circuit of four or five small churches.

Circuit riders were important in the formation of the Methodist and United Brethren traditions in West Virginia. Asbury himself traveled across the state several times and was responsible for founding a number of congregations. Circuit riders came into what is now West Virginia from two directions. The first circuit rider was John Smith from the Holston Conference in Tennessee. He was responsible in 1787 for creating Rehoboth Chapel, the first Methodist church west of the Alleghenies, near Union in Monroe County. Other riders, including Henry Bascom and Asa Shinn, came south from the Redstone Conference in Pennsylvania. These men created congregations in the northern part of the state, in cities such as Parkersburg, Clarksburg, and Grafton, and in smaller towns and rural areas.

By the early 1800s, the expansion of the two conferences began to overlap in central West Virginia. When Methodists split before the Civil War into northern and southern branches, generally the churches created by the Holston Conference became Southern Methodist and those created by the Redstone Conference remained Methodist Episcopal or Northern Methodist, although there were many exceptions. The result, for example, was the existence of Southern Methodist St. Mark's in Charleston, several blocks away from Christ Church M.E. This situation was repeated in many cities and towns in West Virginia and was perpetuated until the reunification of both branches of Methodism in 1939.

See also Methodists

Robert L. Frey
Miamisburg, Ohio

City National Bank

City National Bank was organized in Charleston in 1956 and opened its doors under President Donald Shonk in 1957. The new bank advertised that Muzak would be playing continuously for bank lobby patrons. In 1969, as another marketing innovation, City National introduced employee uniforms featuring bright green jackets, a practice which has since been discontinued.

As the bank prospered, a former bakery at the corner of 36th Street and MacCorkle Avenue in Charleston's Kanawha City neighborhood was purchased and extensively remodeled as bank headquarters. While the City National headquarters has since moved to suburban Cross Lanes, the Kanawha City facility remains the bank's main branch.

The bank's growth was reflected in its rapid rise in assets, $37.4 million by 1975 and over $81 million in 1982. In March 1984, after liberalization of West Virginia banking law, City Holding Company was created to facilitate the bank's expansion. Over the next decade, City Holding acquired a number of other banks throughout West Virginia and radically diversified its business by buying Jarrett-Aim Communications (a printing company), as well as an insurance company and an Internet service, Citynet. This diversification strategy failed, and by late 2000 bank stock had fallen to a fraction of its former price. In that year, the top management was changed and the federal Office of the Comptroller of the Currency intervened to require changes in bank policy. New management decided to close some branches and divested the bank of a number of assets, including the printing and Internet businesses. By 2003, the bank was no longer under direct federal supervision and the stock value had largely recovered. In 2005, City National was the fifth-largest bank in West Virginia, with deposits of $1.7 billion.

See also Banking

Carrie Stollings
Charleston

Civil Rights

The second conference of the Niagara Movement, led by W.E.B. DuBois, met at Storer College in Harpers Ferry in 1906. It was a significant gathering in the history of Civil Rights in America. The Niagara Movement, which had first met in 1905 at Niagara Falls, New York, resulted in the founding of the National Association for the Advancement of Colored People (NAACP) in New York in 1910. The Harpers Ferry meeting commemorated the 1859 raid by John Brown and his band on the federal arsenal there for arms in an attempt to free the slaves.

West Virginia was spared the worst of the lynching era, which cost the lives of thousands of African-Americans in the late 19th and early 20th centuries. President Woodrow Wilson finally spoke out against lynchings, but Congress never enacted anti-lynching legislation. In contrast, the West Virginia legislature enacted anti-lynching legislation in 1921. A decade later, a mob in Greenbrier County hanged two black men, Tom Jackson and George Banks, on a telephone pole after a shootout left two white constables dead. Under the law, Greenbrier County was forced to pay $5,000 to each estate of the lynched victims. Governor Conley deplored the lynchings. "Such matters must not be tolerated in West Virginia," he said. Up to that time, the state had had six lynchings, three blacks and three whites. Jackson and Banks added two more to the sobering total.

The anti-lynching bill was co-sponsored by Delegate Harry Capehart, of McDowell County, a black Republican from a region of the coalfields known as "the Free State of McDowell." The presence of Capehart and other African-Americans in the legislature indicated that voting was never a major problem for West Virginia black citizens, although they faced the other indignities and discriminations of the Jim Crow era. Segregation prevailed in schools, restaurants and hotels, places of entertainment, and other public facilities.

Another black legislator, Delegate T. G. Nutter, a Kanawha County Republican, was an NAACP lawyer. He represented the Huntington African-American couple Lewis and Cora White in a successful lawsuit against restrictive real estate covenants in the late 1920s. The couple sued H. B. White in the landmark case of *White v. White*. In this ruling, the West Virginia Supreme Court outlawed racial and religious discrimination in the sale of property.

In 1928, the high court desegregated the Charleston library in a lawsuit that Nutter represented for A. H. Brown, E. L. Powell, and W. W. Sanders. The city of Charleston had previously maintained a separate library for African-American citizens. The court said that taxpayers' money could not be used for a main library and exclude black taxpayers.

Willard L. Brown, the son of A. H. Brown, was the lead lawyer for the West Virginia NAACP in the historic U.S. Supreme Court school desegregation ruling in 1954. Generally known as *Brown v. Board of Education*, the far-reaching case included West Virginia and 16 other states, and the District of Columbia. West Virginian John W. Davis, the 1924 Democratic candidate for president and later a powerful New York lawyer, took the other side of the case, arguing in behalf of the state of South Carolina for the continuation of segregation. Governor Marland accepted the ensuing high court decision as the law of the land, and school integration proceeded in the state with a minimum of disturbance.

The desegregation of public places was a different story. They became targets of protest demonstrations, mainly by the Congress of Racial Equality (CORE) and ad hoc student groups. In Huntington, Marshall University students organized the Civic Interest Progressives, with leaders Pat Austin and Phil Carter. Protest demonstrations focused on the White Pantry Restaurant among holdout establishments. Charleston CORE leaders Elizabeth Gilmore and Cynthia Burks conducted sit-in demonstrations at the lunch counter of the Diamond, then the premier department store in the Kanawha Valley. In Bluefield, CORE members sat in at downtown places and picketed the YW-YMCA. They were organized by Othella Jefferson, a professor of education at Bluefield State College. Federal Judge Ben Moore ruled against racial discrimination at the Sky Chief Restaurant at Kanawha (now Yeager) Airport in 1955.

A. H. Brown filed the lawsuit against Sky Chief, through his son, Willard Brown.

Most public places had opened their doors to all by the time Congress passed the 1964 Civil Rights Act. In that year, Howard W. McKinney, executive director of the West Virginia Human Rights Commission, reported that all major hotels were desegregated, except the Shenandoah Hotel in Martinsburg, which accepted African-Americans for lodging rooms but not in the dining area.

In the 21st century, unfinished civil rights work remains in education and civil justice, said West Virginia NAACP President James Tolbert at the 2002 State Capitol observance of the Martin Luther King Jr. holiday.

Edward Peeks
Charleston

Edward Peeks, *The Long Struggle for Black Power*, 1971; Thomas E. Posey, *The Negro Citizen of West Virginia*, 1934; James D. Randall and Anna Evans Gilmer, *Black Past*, 1989.

Civil War

The causes of the American Civil War were varied and complex. Most of the issues at the heart of the sectional conflict, however, can be attributed to the institution of slavery, particularly matters pertaining to the extension of slavery into the western territories of the United States. Events such as John Brown's raid on the U.S. Arsenal at Harpers Ferry in 1859 made a precarious political situation much worse. The Republican Party had taken a stand on the slavery issue and made the non-extension of slavery one of the planks in its platform during the presidential election of 1860. When Republican Abraham Lincoln won the election, the states of the Deep South began the process of holding secession conventions.

By the time of Lincoln's inauguration in March 1861, the states of South Carolina, Mississippi, Florida, Alabama, Georgia, Louisiana, and Texas had left the Union. The states of the Upper South had so far either rejected secession or refused to call conventions. Virginia initially rejected secession, but kept its convention in session to see what Lincoln would do. When Fort Sumter surrendered to Confederate forces in April, Lincoln called upon the states to supply 75,000 militiamen for three months' service, including troops from the Upper South slave states that had not yet seceded. Lincoln's request for volunteers was the catalyst that caused these states, Virginia included, to join the Confederate States of America.

West Virginia has the unique distinction of attaining its statehood directly because of the Civil War. This region possessed geographic, economic, and settlement patterns that set it apart from eastern Virginia. Issues involving political apportionment, public spending on inter-

The Battle of Rich Mountain, July 1861.

nal improvements, and slavery exacerbated these differences in the decades preceding the conflict. When the Commonwealth of Virginia seceded from the Union on April 17, 1861, leaders primarily from the northwestern region of the state began the political process that eventually led to the creation of the new state of West Virginia on June 20, 1863.

Though no great battles approaching the magnitude of Gettysburg or Chickamauga were fought on West Virginia soil, the area that became the state of West Virginia nonetheless saw a great deal of military activity during the four years of conflict. Several small but strategically significant early battles, including Philippi and Rich Mountain, were part of Maj. Gen. George B. McClellan's campaign in June–July 1861 to secure the Baltimore & Ohio Railroad and gain control of the western part of Virginia for the Union.

Meanwhile, the process of recruiting men to fill the ranks of Union regiments from (West) Virginia had begun in earnest. By the end of the war, more than 32,000 soldiers had served in West Virginia regiments and other military organizations, although many of these men, probably a third at least, were natives of the nearby states of Pennsylvania and Ohio. The greatest Union sentiment was found in the 24 northwestern counties bordering Pennsylvania, the Ohio River, and along the lines of the Baltimore & Ohio Railroad. Like Maryland, Kentucky, Missouri, and the other border states, the allegiances of West Virginia's citizens were split. The number of Confederate soldiers who came from West Virginia counties numbered in the neighborhood of 18,000. Devotion to different causes resulted in much irregular warfare, with bushwhacking, raids by "partisan rangers," and guerrilla attacks common occurrences throughout the conflict. Towns such as Romney endured repeated occupation by both sides, as citizens witnessed firsthand the cruelties of civil war.

Soldiers from West Virginia fought in most of the large battles of the war. Confederate regiments from what is now the Eastern Panhandle of West Virginia brigaded together with other units from the Shenandoah Valley at First Manassas on July 21, 1861, under command of another native son, Thomas J. Jackson. There, on Henry House Hill, Jackson and his brigade earned the nickname "Stonewall" for their tenacious combat abilities. At Second Manassas in late August 1862, Confederate (West) Virginians in the Stonewall Brigade held their position against overwhelming odds behind the bed of an unfinished railroad. At Antietam, the 7th West Virginia Infantry (U.S.) sustained its highest number of casualties of the war during an attack on a sunken road that forever after was called "Bloody Lane." At Gettysburg, Union troopers in the 1st West Virginia Cavalry took part in a fruitless cavalry charge against Confederate infantrymen on July 3, 1863, during the waning moments of that great battle. That same day (West) Virginia Confederate soldiers in Gen. George Pickett's Division assaulted the center of the Union line on Cemetery Ridge, while artillerymen in Battery C, 1st West Virginia Light Artillery did their best to stop them. Hundreds of miles to the southwest of Gettysburg, seven soldiers of the 4th West Virginia Infantry were awarded the Medal of Honor for heroism in a Union assault on the Vicksburg defenses.

The largest military engagements fought within the present-day borders of West Virginia were at Harpers Ferry and Shepherdstown in September 1862, Droop Mountain in 1863, and Summit Point in 1864. Numerous smaller actions also were fought at places such as Scary Creek, Cheat Mountain, and Carnifex Ferry (1861); Lewisburg (1862); Bulltown (1863); and Charles Town (1864). Many of these smaller actions were fought between Union and Confederate soldiers who were West Virginia natives.

Large numbers of soldiers from West Virginia fought opposite each other, especially during the Shenandoah Valley campaigns of 1862 and 1864. For example, at the Battle of New Market on May 15, 1864, Union soldiers of the 1st and 12th West Virginia Infantry, supported by the cannons of batteries D and G, 1st West Virginia Light Artillery, encountered Confederates from the 22nd Virginia Infantry Regiment, recruited in the Kanawha Valley and commanded by Col. George S. Patton of Charleston. Several other Confederate units that fought at New Market were composed of West Virginians, and some of the cadets serving in the Virginia Military Institute battalion came from West Virginia.

When the Confederate armies surrendered in the spring of 1865, West Virginians of both the Blue and the Gray returned to their new state. Years later, when West Virginia Union veterans became eligible for federal pensions and Confederate veterans received pensions from their state governments, the West Virginia ex-Confederates again were on the losing side: West Virginia would not recognize their service, and the Commonwealth of Virginia would provide pensions only to its own residents. Today, the fratricide of the Civil War is symbolized on the grounds of the West Virginia state capitol, where a statue honoring West Virginia's Union soldiers stands in silent counterpoint to a statue of Stonewall Jackson, with Abraham Lincoln brooding between the two.

See also Battle of Carnifex Ferry, Battle of Cheat Mountain, Battle of Droop Mountain, Formation of West Virginia, Harpers Ferry Civil War Campaign, Stonewall Jackson

Mark A. Snell
Shepherd University

Richard Orr Curry, *A House Divided: Statehood Politics & the Copperhead Movement in West Virginia*, 1964; James McPherson, *Battle Cry of Freedom: The Civil War Era*, 1988; Richard A. Sauers, *The Devastating Hand of War: Romney, West Virginia During the Civil War*, 2000.

Civil Works Administration

A New Deal agency established in the late fall of 1933, the Civil Works Administration sought to provide emergency work relief for the many still unemployed as the country faced another winter during the Great Depression. Paying higher wages than the meager subsistence rates previously prevailing in local work relief, the CWA quickly put some 80,000 West Virginians to work on projects ranging from road work and the building of 35,400 fly-proof sanitary privies to making mattresses. Although the subject of intense political conflict, the agency provided much-needed relief to West Virginians before President Franklin D. Roosevelt, alarmed at the cost, ordered it to cease operations in the spring of 1934.

See also Great Depression, New Deal

Jerry Bruce Thomas
Shepherd University

Civilian Conservation Corps

The Civilian Conservation Corps (CCC) was the first of the New Deal agencies created by President Franklin D. Roosevelt after his inauguration in 1933, to address the problems of the Great Depression. West Virginia made up the Charleston District, Fifth Corps Area, of the CCC. The Fifth Corps also included Kentucky, Indiana, and Ohio.

The CCC was designed to put the nation's unemployed youth to work on reforestation and similar projects throughout the country. Members, called enrollees and commonly known as "CCC boys," had to be males between the ages of 18 and 25, unmarried, and employable. They were selected on the basis of family need and were paid $30 per month for their work, with $25 of each pay sent home to the enrollee's family. The enrollees were provided with food, clothing, shelter, medical needs, and work training.

Each enrollee spent two weeks at conditioning camp at Fort Knox, Kentucky, before being sent to a CCC camp, made up of a company of 200 men. The camps were administered by military and naval officers, with forest or park project supervisors teaching the enrollees forest and land conservation skills.

West Virginia boasted 65 CCC camps and two summer camps housing 55 different companies. Most of the camps were located in the Allegheny and George Washington national forests. These companies worked on reforestation and conservation projects; fought forest fires; built shelters, fire towers, fire stations, roads, and trails; strung electric and telephone lines; and planted thousands of trees.

The West Virginia state park system owes much to the CCC. Many of the early state parks were built by the CCC boys. The buildings, pavilions, and scenic overlook at Coopers Rock State Park were built by enrollees, for example, as were the administration building, stone cabins, swimming pool, stone culverts, and bridges at Watoga State Park. Cabins, trails, and other recreational facilities were constructed using rustic architecture by the CCC at Babcock, Lost River, and Cacapon state parks, as well as Oglebay Park. The reservoir area for Bluestone dam was cleared with CCC labor.

Educational activities also played a major role in the enrollee's daily routine. Camps were furnished with libraries, and classes were held to teach enrollees vocational skills and provide basic educational needs. They were also permitted to take high school and college classes. More than 55,000 youth participated in the Civilian Conservation Corps in West Virginia between 1933 and 1942. Their built-to-last construction techniques in our parks and forests will last as a testimony to their era for generations to enjoy.

See also Great Depression, New Deal, State Parks

Larry N. Sypolt
West Virginia University
Stan Cohen, *The Tree Army: A Pictorial History of the Civilian Conservation Corps, 1933–1942,* 1980; Milton Harr, *The C.C.C. Camps in West Virginia 1933–1942,* 1992.

Matthew Wesley Clair Sr.

Bishop Matthew Wesley Clair Sr., one of the first African-Americans elected bishop in the predominantly white Methodist Episcopal Church, was born October 21, 1865, in Union, Monroe County. His family moved to Charleston where, at age 15, Clair became a member of Simpson Methodist Episcopal Church. In 1889, he graduated from Morgan College in Baltimore, was licensed to preach, and was admitted on a trial basis into the Washington Conference of the Methodist Episcopal Church, an administrative district serving African-American church members in the Baltimore-Washington area.

Clair served a church in Harpers Ferry from 1889 to 1893. From 1897 to 1902, he was presiding elder of the Washington District. He earned his Ph.D. in 1901 from Bennett College in Greensboro, North Carolina. Resuming a pastor's position, Clair returned to Washington to pastor the Asbury Church from 1902 to 1919. While there, he edited the *Banner,* the conference paper, and spearheaded the construction of an 1,800-seat sanctuary for Asbury Church.

After serving as district superintendent of Washington, Clair was elected bishop in 1920 and assigned to the church's flourishing mission in Monrovia, Liberia. He stayed there for eight years, returning to Washington for a visit in 1924 where he was invited to offer the prayer at President Calvin Coolidge's dedication of a statue honoring Methodist Bishop Francis Asbury. Clair became a member of the Board of Education of the Republic of Liberia and of the American Advisory Commission on the Booker Washington Agricultural and Industrial Institute of Liberia.

Reassigned as bishop of the Covington, Kentucky, Episcopal Area in 1928, Clair served the black conferences in the Midwest for eight years, retiring in 1936. The only Methodist Episcopal bishop to have a son who also became a bishop, Bishop Clair died June 28, 1943, in Covington, Kentucky.

Debra K. Sullivan
Charleston Catholic High School

Elsie Clapp

Educator Elsie Ripley Clapp (1879–1965) in 1934 was named director of the community school in Arthurdale, Preston County, an experimental federal resettlement community established for victims of the Great Depression. She was a proponent of John Dewey's doctrine of progressive education, which held that a school is an integral part of its community and must help that community adjust to change. A basic tenet of the Arthurdale school was that the homesteaders—primarily native-born whites who had been relocated from the Scotts Run coal camps in neighboring Monongalia County—could use their own experiences and rural heritage to better their lives.

Under Clapp, the school stressed education for real-life situations. Arithmetic, for example, might be taught by showing children how lumber was measured to build a house. An effort to revive traditional music encouraged students to strengthen their reading and writing skills by making up calls for community square dances. Fiddles and guitars were built in shop classes.

Ultimately, however, this emphasis on self-reliance and traditional culture served to isolate Arthurdale residents. The school was refused accreditation because its curriculum did not meet state standards, and many thought Arthurdale attempted to recapture an agrarian ideal that was irrelevant in an urban and industrial world. Some also have speculated that residents resented the community school because it was run by outsiders. Elsie Clapp left Arthurdale in 1936, and the school became part of the Preston County public school system. Clapp authored the book, *Community Schools in Action,* in 1939.

See also Arthurdale

Christine M. Kreiser
Clarksburg

Clarksburg

Clarksburg, in north-central West Virginia, is the county seat of Harrison County and one of the state's oldest cities. Clarksburg is located at the junction of U.S. 50 and U.S. 19, two miles west of the junction of U.S. 50 with Interstate 79. The city lies at an elevation of 1,007 feet at the junction of Elk Creek and the West Fork of the Monongahela River. The 2000 population was 16,743.

Two miles south of town on U.S. 19 are two Indian mounds. The first European to claim land in the area was a trapper named John Simpson, in 1764. The first permanent settler was Daniel Davisson, who about 1773 acquired 400 acres of land where Clarksburg is now located. Clarksburg became the county seat when Harrison County was formed in 1784. Named for the Revolutionary War hero, George Rogers Clark, the town was chartered in 1785.

Clarksburg's early economy centered around such small industries as a gristmill, tannery, pottery, and saltworks, as well as the county government. Construction of the first courthouse began in 1787. That building was followed by four increasingly larger courthouses, the most recent one completed in 1932.

In 1787, the Virginia General Assembly established the Randolph Academy at Clarksburg, the first such educational institution west of the Alleghenies. In 1819, Clarksburg was chosen as the site of the first federal court west of the Alleghenies. The new court's first judge was John George Jackson, uncle of Confederate Gen. Thomas J. "Stonewall" Jackson.

Poor transportation slowed development until the 1830s, when the Northwestern Turnpike was built from Winchester to Parkersburg via Romney and Clarksburg. The arrival of the B&O Railroad in the mid-1850s opened the county to development. During the Civil War, the B&O line made Clarksburg an important Union supply base.

The availability of natural resources, coupled with easy access to railroad facilities, attracted industry and manufacturing to Clarksburg, including chemical plants, brickworks, potteries, foundries and machine shops, hardwood and casket companies, glass factories (including the Akro-Agate marble company), and the Jackson (later Phillips) Sheet and Tin Plate Company, the forerunner of Weirton Steel. Economic development brought successive waves of immigrants in the 19th and early 20th centuries, including Irish, Italians, Greeks, French, Belgians, and Spanish.

Telephone service, the first in the state, began in Clarksburg in the mid-1880s. In 1887, the city laid its first six miles of water lines; downtown streets were lit by electricity in 1889. In 1900, the first sewer lines were installed, Main and Pike streets were paved with brick, and the city's first trolley tracks were laid. Early 20th-century Clarksburg boasted eight banks, three hospitals, and several fine hotels, including the elegant seven-story Waldo, which opened in 1909. The seven-story Empire Bank building went up in 1907,

the nine-story Goff Building in 1911, and the ten-story Union Bank in 1912.

By 1929, Clarksburg had reached its peak population of 35,115. During the Depression the city lost industry and population, but during World War II the railroad again made it a central clearinghouse. New development came with the construction in the 1970s of Interstate 79 and the new four-lane U.S. 50 Appalachian Corridor D connecting I-79 to I-77, but plant closings in the 1980s had a negative impact. New expansion in the government and technology sectors began in the 1990s, including the relocation of the FBI Criminal Justice Information Services Center to Clarksburg and construction of a new federal building and a new building to house Fairmont State University's Clarksburg branch.

The city has a daily newspaper, three local television stations, and six radio stations. Air transportation is provided by nearby Benedum Airport at Bridgeport. The West Virginia Italian Heritage Festival, held each Labor Day weekend, has drawn thousands of visitors to Clarksburg each year since 1979.

Clarksburg was the birthplace of a number of prominent West Virginians, among them Stonewall Jackson; John W. Davis, U.S. solicitor general, ambassador to Great Britain, and Democratic nominee for president in 1924; and Cyrus Vance, secretary of state under President Jimmy Carter. It was the longtime home of the state's 17th governor, Howard M. Gore, and of Louis Johnson, assistant secretary of war under President Franklin D. Roosevelt and President Harry Truman's secretary of defense. Clarksburg is the burial site of Mary Payne Jackson and Mary Coles Payne, respectively the sister and mother of Dolley Payne Madison, wife of President James Madison.

See also Harrison County

Margo Stafford
Clarksburg

Dorothy Davis, *History of Harrison County, West Virginia*, 1970; James M. Pool, ed, *Clarksburg: A Bicentennial Album, 1785–1985*, 1986; "Clarksburg," *West Virginia Heritage Encyclopedia*, 1976.

Clarksburg Education Convention

The original Virginia Constitution did not provide for free schools, and the mother state was slow to address the problem. In 1829, the General Assembly authorized each county to establish district school systems and offered limited state aid for the building of schoolhouses. Monroe County opened a free school under this plan, at Sinks Grove in 1829, but discontinued the system in 1836.

Education reformers were spurred to action by the 1840 census, which demonstrated Virginia's extensive illiteracy. A series of conventions were held throughout the state. The first, held in Clarksburg

on September 8–9, 1841, was one of the most important meetings ever convened in West Virginia on the subject of education. The assembled Western Virginia educators, including Alexander Campbell and Henry Ruffner, demanded free schools. The convention highlighted east-west differences in Virginia, criticizing the state's educational system as top heavy with a fine university at Charlottesville for the wealthy but no provisions to educate the middle class. Ruffner called upon the General Assembly to create public schools that were "good enough for the rich . . . [and] fit for the poor." In 1846, the legislature revised the district plan, allowing citizens to petition counties to establish free schools. The state still refused to appropriate funding, placing the burden of school taxation on the counties. The only counties in present West Virginia to adopt this plan were Kanawha, Jefferson, and Ohio.

In 1863, one of the first acts passed by the West Virginia legislature established a system of free schools.

See also Alexander Campbell, Education, Henry Ruffner

Stan Bumgardner
Division of Culture & History

Otis K. Rice and Stephen W. Brown, *West Virginia: A History*, 1993.

Clarksburg *Exponent Telegram*

Clarksburg's *Exponent* and *Telegram* newspapers were owned by separate companies until 1927. After that year they were owned by Clarksburg Publishing Company, sharing staff and facilities but published separately. In 2002, they were combined into a single newspaper, the *Exponent Telegram*.

The *Telegram* was the older paper, originating as the *National Telegraph* in the Civil War era. It was founded December 27, 1861, by U.S. Sen. John S. Carlile and Robert Saunders Northcott. Both were staunch Unionists, and Carlile was an early leader of the West Virginia statehood movement. When Northcott departed for war service Carlile renamed the newspaper *Patriot*. Northcott, captured by Confederates and exchanged after nine months in Libby Prison, returned to buy the paper from Carlile, naming it *Clarksburg Telegram*.

In 1891, a group of prominent Clarksburg investors, including Republican leader Nathan Goff Jr., acquired the *Telegram*. Cecil B. Highland became a stockholder in 1902, beginning his family's century-long association with the newspaper, which became a daily that same year. A Sunday edition was added in 1914.

Meanwhile, an opposition paper was started in 1910 by men active in the Democratic Party, including future presidential candidate John W. Davis. Originally published as the *Culpeper Exponent*, the same name as an associated newspaper in Culpeper County, Virginia, the new newspaper became the *Exponent-American* in 1915. It became the *Clarksburg Exponent* two years later. Guy Tetrick, whose extensive genealogy collection is now housed at West Virginia University, was involved with the *Exponent* from the beginning and served as its manager from 1915 until the 1930s.

On August 27, 1927, the Telegram Company purchased Clarksburg Publishing Company and moved from the Empire Building on Fourth Street to Hewes Avenue, its present location. Retaining the name Clarksburg Publishing Company, the merged operation now owned both of Clarksburg's papers. A used Goss Staightline press purchased in 1928 printed both newspapers in an old-fashioned wide format for the next seven decades. It was believed to be the oldest press in daily operation in the United States when it was replaced in January 1998 by a Goss Urbanite that allowed full color capability and reduced the newspapers' width to modern standards.

Today, Clarksburg's newspaper is published seven days a week as the *Exponent Telegram*. With a daily circulation of about 19,000, the *Exponent Telegram* serves Clarksburg, Harrison County, and several surrounding counties. General Manager Cecil B. Highland Jr., who was involved with Clarksburg Publishing Company from 1957 until his death, January 13, 2002, was the only West Virginian ever elected president of the Southern Newspaper Publishers Association.

Gerald D. Swick
Nashville, Tennessee

Roy B. Clarkson

Professor Roy B. Clarkson is the historian of West Virginia's timber industry and one of the state's most prominent botanists. Clarkson was born October 25, 1926, and raised in Cass, Pocahontas County, still a major lumber boom town at that time. After service in the U.S. Army near the end of World War II, he began his college education at Davis and Elkins College, from which he graduated with a degree in mathematics and biology. Clarkson soon narrowed his concentration to biological studies and earned a Ph.D. in botany from West Virginia University. He joined the Department of Biology faculty there in 1956 and retired as professor emeritus in 1992.

Clarkson authored *Tumult on the Mountains: Lumbering in West Virginia, 1770–1920* (1964) and *On Beyond Leatherbark: the Cass Saga* (1990), both of which detail the history of the timber industry. He has co-authored four books on botanical subjects, has authored numerous articles, and has been the recipient of several research grants. His honors include election to membership in Sigma Xi and Gamma Sigma Delta; receipt of the Elizabeth Ann Bartholomew Award from the Southern Appalachian Botanical Society; and election to the West Virginia Agriculture and Forestry Hall of Fame.

Kenneth R. Bailey
WVU Institute of Technology

Claude Worthington Benedum Foundation

Established in 1944 by Michael and Sarah Benedum, the Claude Worthington Benedum Foundation is the largest philanthropic foundation contributing primarily to West Virginia organizations. The independent foundation operates two grants programs, one for West Virginia organizations and the other for Pittsburgh region institutions. Michael Benedum, a native of Bridgeport, amassed a fortune in the gas and oil industry. He and Sarah, a native of Monongalia County, married in 1896 and settled in Cameron in Harrison County.

The foundation is named for the Benedums' only child, Claude Worthington Benedum, who died at age 20 in the 1918 flu epidemic. After Michael Benedum's first major oil discovery, he moved his business headquarters and home in 1907 to Pittsburgh, where he lived for more than 50 years. Benedum died in 1959, and left his fortune to the foundation. By 1969, the foundation's assets had grown to more than $66 million. Through 2001, the foundation has awarded more than 6,100 grants totaling more than $242 million. The market value of its assets at that time was $325 million.

Approximately two-thirds of the Benedum Foundation's grant funds are awarded within West Virginia with the remaining third going to the Pittsburgh region. The West Virginia grants program focuses on initiatives that "help people help themselves." In the fifth codicil to his will, Michael wrote, "We know not where seed may sprout . . . . It is our duty to sow and to nurture, leaving it to others to harvest the fruits of our efforts." The Pittsburgh region grants program funds educational, health, and arts institutions.

See also Michael L. Benedum, Natural Gas and Petroleum

Sam Mallison, *The Great Wildcatter*, 1953.

Clay

The town of Clay, with a 2000 population of 593, is the county seat of Clay County. Clay is located about 41 miles northeast of Charleston on State Route 16, which doubles as Main Street in Clay. The town is situated on the banks of the Elk River near the center of Clay County, at an elevation of 708 feet. The Elk cuts a fairly deep gorge as it traverses this particular section of the county and does not provide much bottomland for the town, making growth difficult.

After Clay County was created in 1858 by the Virginia General Assembly, the first county court met at the McOlgin farm, the present site of Clay. As the community grew it was first called Marshall, and apparently Henry for a short while, before becoming Clay Court House and then Clay. Both the county and the town were named for Senator Henry Clay of Kentucky, a leading statesman of the era. Elk River was the prime means of transportation in the early years, with Governor MacCorkle noting in his memoirs that until 1880 it was impossible to drive a horse-drawn vehicle to the town from Charleston. Clay was incorporated in 1895. The Coal & Coke Railway reached Clay in 1905.

The town of Clay includes a satellite area known locally as Two Run, which contains some of the newer business establishments.

See also Clay County

Mack Samples
Duck

Clay Center

The Clay Center for the Arts & Sciences in downtown Charleston is the first of its kind in the state, combining a modern performing arts center with a visual arts museum and an interactive science center.

Private contributions from the Clay Foundation and the Clay family of Charleston, and a $22.5 million grant in 1996 from the state of West Virginia, launched the 234,000-square-foot Arts & Sciences Center. Individuals, foundations, and corporations from across West Virginia completed funding for the center, which is the product of a decade of planning and four years of fund-raising. The Clay Center was part of a major project conceived by the Charleston Renaissance Corporation to revive the downtown and a historic residential area while serving as a cultural and educational resource for students and citizens statewide. Construction began in 1999. The Clay Center opened to the public in 2003.

The Clark Performance Place contains the 1,883-seat Maier Foundation Hall that was constructed with double concrete walls and ceiling to insulate it from outside noise. The proscenium opening is 55 feet by 45 feet, and the main stage is 100 feet wide and 50 feet deep. The stage can be extended 30 feet by raising the double orchestra pit lift. The hall is the home of the West Virginia Symphony Orchestra. The Clark Performance Place also contains the Walker Studio Theater, which is suitable for smaller performances, receptions, and community activities.

The former Sunrise Museum of Charleston is housed in the Clay Center as the Avampato Discovery Museum, which includes the art museum and science center. The Juliet Museum of Art can accommo-

The Clay Center for the Arts & Sciences.

date a permanent art collection as well as traveling exhibits. Other features include a conservation vault and an art library. The Greater Kanawha Valley Science Center has as its central focus science education with interactive exhibits about earth science, health science, and physics. The domed theater offers laser shows, large-format films, and star shows.

Elizabeth Jill Wilson
Cottageville

Clay County

Clay County is located in central West Virginia, northeast of Charleston. It occupies 346.6 square miles. The Elk River bisects the county from east to west, entering at Duck and leaving at King Shoals. Rugged, laurel-covered hollows dart back from the narrow river valley, and level land is at a premium. Early settlers did not find the area particularly inviting, so the population was sparse during the 18th and 19th centuries. Yet the soil was rich, and some beautiful hillside farms developed during the days when Western Virginia was being settled and later, after West Virginia had become a state.

The first known white man to occupy the area was Sinnett Triplett, who came about 1812. He had a camp on what is now called Sinnett Branch, a tributary of Lilly Fork of Buffalo Creek, a few miles south of the present town of Clay. Triplett was followed by David McOlgin, who settled on the north side of Elk River near where the town of Clay would be located. McOlgin is considered the first permanent settler. By 1839, 28 families lived in what is now Clay County. The early settlers survived by farming, hunting, and later by logging. It was common to run log rafts down the Elk River, sell the logs in Charleston, then walk home.

Clay County was formed in 1858 from parts of Nicholas and Braxton counties and named for Henry Clay, the great U.S. senator from Kentucky. Clay was popular among the residents of Western Virginia because he often supported their causes. Two years after its formation, the 1860 census showed 1,787 people living in the county. By 1890 the figure had increased to 4,659.

There was internal strife in Clay County during the Civil War. Several Southern sympathizers were carted off to the military prison at Camp Chase, Ohio, during the conflict. It is believed that county resident Sol Carpenter was murdered because of his Southern leanings. Other Clay County men joined the Union Army.

The coming of the railroads during the 1890s brought substantial increases in both population and prosperity. The county had an abundance of coal and timber, and large corporations began operat-

ing in the area. Coal mining started out small, with Clay County producing only 2,860 tons in 1904, but eventually became a major industry. Much of the coal production was centered in Widen in the northeast corner of the county, a thriving private town controlled by industrialist Joseph G. Bradley. Known locally as "J. G.," Bradley was for many years the major power in Clay County. By 1960, the county was producing 900,000 tons of coal per year. Clay County's deep mine production dwindled to nearly nothing by 2001, but the county produced more than four million tons of surface-mined coal.

At one time Clay County was served by the Buffalo Creek & Gauley Railroad, which connected the coalfields at Widen to the Baltimore & Ohio Railroad at Dundon, near the town of Clay. The B&O then carried Clay County coal to the national market. Currently, there is no regular rail service.

The Interstate highway system, constructed during the last half of the 20th century, nearly missed Clay County. I-79 barely notches the northern tier of the county as it makes its way from Morgantown to Charleston. The county is served by State Route 4 which, for the most part, follows the Elk River to Charleston; State Route 16 from Gauley Bridge to Big Otter; and State Route 36, which intersects State Route 4 near Maysel and leads the traveler to I-79. Modern highway connections have made Charleston more accessible, and many Clay Countians have found employment in the Kanawha Valley.

Clay is one of West Virginia's poorest counties, with a fourth of its people living in poverty at the turn of the 21st century. Yet the county has an excellent system of public schools. Clay County is served by one high school, one middle school, and five elementary schools. Both Clay County High School and Clay Mid-

FAST FACTS ABOUT CLAY COUNTY

Founded: 1858
Land in square miles: 346.6
Population: 10,330
Percentage minorities: 1.8%
Percentage rural: 100%
Median age: 36.8
Percentage 65 and older: 13.7%
Birth rate per 1,000 population: 11.1
Median household income: $22,120
High school graduate or higher: 63.7%
Bachelor's degree or higher: 7.3%
Home ownership: 79.2%
Median home value: $55,600

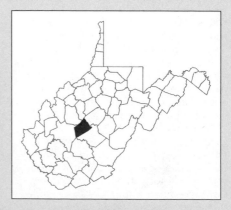

This information is from the 2000 U.S. Census. In 2000, West Virginia as a whole had 5 percent minorities, a median age of 38.9, median household income of $29,696, and a 75.2 percent home ownership rate.

dle School have been named National Schools of Excellence in recent years. A recent graduate, Carolyn Conner, distinguished herself at West Virginia University and went on to become a Rhodes Scholar.

The population of Clay County peaked in 1940 at 15,206, but the loss of mining jobs during the 1950s and '60s caused that number to drop to 9,330 by 1970. Widen was the scene of a fatal labor confrontation in 1952, and the company sold its mining operation in 1959. The once-thriving town all but disappeared during the 1960s. There have been slight ups and downs in the county population since 1970, with the 2000 census counting 10,330 people in Clay County.

Clay County has always been proud of its mountain music. Many of its old-time musicians have distinguished themselves at state and national festivals. French Carpenter, Doc White, Ira Mullins, Lee Triplett, Wilson Douglas, and Jenes Cottrell were all well known in their time as traditional mountain musicians. That tradition continues as John Morris of Ivydale and others have become staple performers at West Virginia music festivals.

The rugged hills of Clay County have produced some distinguished Americans. Lloyd H. Elliott left Clay County, attended Glenville State College, and went on to become president of both the University of Maine and George Washington University, and later, president of the National Geographic Society. Another Clay Countian, Neil Boggs, became a nationally known news commentator. Clay County made a contribution to world horticulture when the Golden Delicious apple was discovered on the Mullens farm near the head of Porter Creek in 1914.

See also J. G. Bradley, Clay

Mack Samples
Duck

Clay County Wild Man

The eccentric Orval Elijah Brown was born February 19, 1908, near Lizemores, in Clay County. Brown, a free-spirited individual, gained notoriety as the "Clay County Wild Man" during the Great Depression for his untamed physical appearance that included a flowing beard and the wearing of little more than a self-made loincloth. Despite his unkempt look, Brown claimed to live a disciplined life free of sex, drugs, and alcohol, and he continually worked to maintain his physical health.

Brown spent his early life on his family's farm in the Big Sycamore section of Clay County. He attended school through the eighth grade, was an avid reader, enjoyed various outdoor pastimes, and demonstrated an aversion to clothing. By the age of 20, Brown's behavior helped to make him a local folk hero. Hearing of a Tarzan-like man who lived in a cave, visi-

tors flocked to the Brown homestead to have their picture taken with the "Wild Man" for the price of 25 cents. Brown also traveled to local carnivals and fairs to sell his photos.

Brown's posing career was interrupted by service in the U.S. Army from 1930 to 1933, where he played football and took up boxing. He also served in the navy from 1941 to 1943. Upon his honorable discharge from the navy, he returned to Clay County. In September 1950, Brown was arrested and charged in the killing of his first cousin, Wilford Reedy. Accounts vary, but Brown said the act was in self-defense. However, he pleaded insanity and spent nearly 18 years at the state mental hospital at Weston. He was released in 1968 and moved to Carl, in Nicholas County, to live with his sister until 1995.

In 1995, Brown's health forced him to a veterans' hospital in Beckley. Brown then moved to a retirement home in Roane County. The Clay County Wild Man died March 20, 2005.

Brad Martin
Arthurdale

Art Department of Clay County High School, *Hickory and Lady Slippers, Life and Legend of Clay County People: Mullins Family History and Other Stories,* 1985.

Clay Foundation

The Clay Foundation, established in 1986, is a private charitable foundation in Charleston. Brothers Buckner W. Clay and Lyell B. Clay funded the foundation with part of the proceeds of the sale of Clay Communications to Thomson Newspapers in 1987. Clay Communications had owned the *Charleston Daily Mail,* the *Register-Herald* of Beckley, and radio and television stations and newspapers in Virginia and North Carolina.

Since its founding, the Clay Foundation has become one of the largest private grant sources for West Virginia nonprofit organizations. In 2000, the foundation had assets of approximately $67 million. The Clay Foundation's philanthropy emphasizes capital investments in buildings and community fund-raising campaigns.

The Clay Foundation's investment and guidance were instrumental in the establishment of one of the state's largest independent cultural institutions, the Clay Center for the Arts & Sciences of West Virginia in Charleston. The Clay Foundation and Clay family members together gave nearly $40 million to help build and endow the Clay Center, which includes an 1,883-seat concert hall and fine art and science museums. Previously, the Clay Foundation gave $5.2 million to build the seven-story Clay Tower at the University of Charleston and $2 million to construct Buckner Clay Hall at the University of Virginia School of Law, named for the late father of the Clay brothers.

In its first 15 years, the foundation was regularly one of the largest private contributors to the United Way of the Kanawha Valley, the Fund for the Arts, and the *Charleston Daily Mail*'s annual appeal for charitable giving to the poor. Charles M. Avampato, a former vice president of Clay Communications, has led the foundation since its beginning.

The Clay Foundation is separate from the Lyell B. and Patricia K. Clay Foundation of Charleston, Lyell B. Clay's private charitable foundation that supports college and other music education programs throughout the state.

Mark A. Sadd
Charleston

Clay Mining

For more than 140 years, clay mining was a major industry in West Virginia. Bricks for buildings and streets, tiles and pottery were manufactured from clay mined from residual clays developed by the weathering of limestone and shale and from transported clays deposited in rivers and swamps during the marine geologic age. These clay deposits are widely dispersed in West Virginia and were used by many individuals to make clay products, such as bricks for their own homes during the 19th century. In addition, many counties had large scale clay mining that spawned clay product industries. For instance, clay was mined in Berkeley County by the United Clay Products and Continental Clay Products; in Cabell County by the Barboursville Clay Manufacturing Company; in Kanawha County by the West Virginia Brick Company and the Charleston Vitreous Clay Products Company; in Lewis County by the Weston Brick and Coal Company and the Jane Lew Brick and Drain Tile Company; and in Marion County by the Colfax Brick Company and the Hammond Fire Brick Company.

While seams of clay are found throughout West Virginia, the clay in the Northern Panhandle historically was not only plentiful but also of exceptional quality because of the fineness (smallness) of its particles. Hancock County clay is of sedimentary origin, which means it is usually associated with coal and shale. In the early days of clay mining in Hancock County, the three-foot-thick seam of coal on top of the clay was ignored by miners more intent on reaching the high-quality clay for brick and pottery making.

Nowhere in the state did clay mining reach the scale it did in Hancock County, which for a number of years, was the brick and tile capital of the United States. Clay was first mined in Hancock County about 1830. Eventually more than a dozen companies were manufacturing bricks, sewer pipe, pottery, and speciality items such as chimney tops, terra cotta vases, and furnace linings from local clay and shale. A thriving pottery industry began in the same period and continues to manufacture dishes and tableware today. In the mid-19th century, the same workers who mined clay by hand in the winter made bricks or other clay products in the summer. They pulled clay out of the mine in carts over wooden stringers and dumped it into piles. When used for bricks, the clay was pushed through rollers several times to grind it to sufficient fineness, mixed with water in the "wet pan" and poured into brick molds to dry in the sun before being fired by wood in beehive kilns.

The process of extracting clay, which was mined in strip mines as well as in underground mines, was modernized from 1895 to 1915. Under the new mining methods, clay was hauled from the mines by locomotives to giant crushers and moved on conveyors to local manufacturing plants or to barges on the Ohio River or, later, to the railroad for transporting to other parts of the country where it was in great demand. The demand declined precipitously after World War I as shipping costs increased and synthetic materials began to replace clay products in roads and buildings. Clay is no longer mined in West Virginia, despite an estimate in the 1980s by the West Virginia Geologic Survey that 1.5 billion tons of high-quality clay was still available in Hancock County alone.

See also Brick Industry, Pottery Industry

Jeanne Grimm
Morgantown

Claymont Court

A painted yellow brick Federal-style mansion above the banks of Bullskin Run near Rippon, Claymont Court is the largest of the seven antebellum Washington family homes in Jefferson County. It is now a conference center for the Claymont Society, an organization established in 1974 to develop organic farming and other activities to promote the establishment of sustainable communities.

Bushrod Corbin Washington, one of George Washington's grand-nephews, built Claymont Court in 1820 on land once owned by Washington. Bushrod's brother, John Augustine Washington, built the smaller Blakeley south of Claymont and across the Bullskin. Claymont burned to the brick walls in 1838, and Bushrod, then a Virginia state legislator, promptly rebuilt the interior. Records show that the entire Washington clan lived at Claymont during the Civil War. In 1870, Bushrod Corbin Washington's grandson advertised the mansion for sale, and that branch of the Washington family moved away.

Subsequent owners enlarged the structure with upper floors on the east and west wings, and added a conservatory off the dining room. In 1901, novelist Frank R. Stockton purchased the mansion, where he lived for three years. Elsie Bogardus Murphy amplified the terraced eastern formal gardens in the 1920s, and industrialist R. J. Funkhouser restored the interior in the 1940s. After Funkhouser, the mansion stood vacant at times, including as recently as 1970–74. Claymont Court was added to the National Register of Historic Places in 1973. It was purchased by the Claymont Society in 1974.

The largest dwelling in Jefferson County, the mansion is 250 feet long, has 16 columns, 59 rooms, and 25 fireplaces, a south-facing two-story veranda, and cottage dependencies at either end. It sits on 300 acres of land, and has a 450-foot cattle barn converted into a conference center, and a number of other outbuildings. Claymont Court, called "Ruddiemont," is the setting for John Peale Bishop's novel, *Act of Darkness*.

See also Architects and Architecture, Blakeley, Washington Family

Georgia Caldwell DuBose
Harpers Ferry

Charlotte J. Fairbairn, *The Washington Homes of Jefferson County, West Virginia,* 1946; Millard K. Bushong, *History of Jefferson County, West Virginia,* 1941.

Franklin D. Cleckley

Justice Franklin D. Cleckley (1940–).

Justice Franklin Dorrah Cleckley, born August 1, 1940, in Huntington, was the first African-American to serve on the West Virginia Supreme Court of Appeals. He earned an LL.M. from Harvard (1969), a J.D. from Indiana University (1965), and a B.A. from Anderson College (1962). Cleckley served during the Vietnam War era in the U.S. Navy Judge Advocate General Corps.

The author of *Evidence Handbook for West Virginia Lawyers* and *West Virginia Criminal Procedure Handbook,* Cleckley in 1972 became the first black appointed a full professor at West Virginia University, whose law faculty he had joined in 1969. Cleckley in 1987 received the W. Robert Ming Advocacy Award from the National Association for the Advancement of Colored People for his championship of civil rights. In 1990, he formed the Franklin D. Cleckley Foundation, a nonprofit organization devoted to assisting former convicts with educational and employment opportunities. In 1994, Cleckley was appointed to an unexpired term on the West Virginia Supreme Court by Governor Caperton. He declined to run for reelection in 1996 and returned to WVU to teach law.

In celebration of Black History Month in 2001, the West Virginia Supreme Court referred to Cleckley's handbooks on evidence and criminal procedure as "the bible for West Virginia's judges and attorneys."

Larry Sonis
Arlington, Texas

Claymont Court, a Washington family home.

Clendenin Family

The Clendenins, prominent early settlers of the Greenbrier, Kanawha, and Ohio rivers, came to the region from central Virginia. They were among the founders of Charleston and of Kanawha and Mason counties, and the Kanawha County town of Clendenin is named for them. Archibald and Charles Clendenin (Clendinen), possibly brothers, were the progenitors of the family in America.

Archibald lived on the Cowpasture River in what is now Bath County, Virginia, and never came to present West Virginia. He died in 1749, leaving a wife, daughter, and sons Archibald and John. John, the younger son, lived in present Monroe County before moving to Tennessee. Archibald Jr. was among the earliest settlers of present Greenbrier County. At his homestead, about two miles west of present Lewisburg, on July 15, 1763, he was among a number of settlers killed by a party of Shawnee led by Cornstalk. Wife Ann soon escaped the Indians and daughter Jane was released many years later, but two young children were killed during or after the raid.

Charles Clendenin, born in Scotland about 1715, had emigrated to Augusta County by 1743. Charles settled with members of his family in the Greenbrier Valley in present Pocahontas County about 1771. Several of Charles's sons, including George Clendenin, were in the army of Col. Andrew Lewis during Dunmore's War of 1774. On their march from Lewisburg to the Battle of Point Pleasant the army camped for several days at the Mouth of Elk (present Charleston) to build canoes. It was at this time that the Clendenins first became acquainted with the fertile bottom land along the Elk and Kanawha rivers.

In December 1787, Col. George Clendenin purchased from Judge Cuthbert Bullitt 1,030 acres lying in the vicinity of the Mouth of Elk, the present site of Charleston. He, a company of 30 rangers commanded by Capt. William Clendenin, and other members of the family departed the Greenbrier Valley in 1788. They established Charleston, named in honor of father Charles Clendenin, who died there in 1790. George sold 507 acres of this land to his brothers, William and Alexander.

William Clendenin served as one of the first justices of the Kanawha County court, as well as sheriff, town trustee, and a representative to the Virginia General Assembly. In 1797, he moved his family to present Mason County, which he helped to found in 1804. He was appointed as one of the new county's justices and elected as its first representative to the General Assembly. William Clendenin held a commission as major during the War of 1812. He died September 15, 1828.

Alexander Clendenin, born in 1754 in Augusta County, came to Kanawha in 1788 and was an ensign in Capt. John Morris's company of militia. He later settled near Eightmile Island in Mason County, where he died in 1829. Charles Clendenin's son, Robert, was wounded at the age of 16 in his right hand and arm during a 1763 battle with the Shawnee in present Alleghany County, Virginia. He came to Kanawha in 1788 and was one of the justices of the county. He shortly moved to Kentucky and later to Ohio, where he died in 1808.

Mary Ellen, a daughter of Charles Clendenin, married George Stephenson. They settled at an early date along the Ohio River near Eightmile Island.

See also George Clendenin

Gerald S. Ratliff
Charleston

George Clendenin

Pioneer George Clendenin, born in Augusta County, Virginia, in 1746, was one of the first settlers in the Kanawha Valley and the founder of Charleston. His family settled in the Greenbrier Valley in 1771, and George first saw the Kanawha Valley when he accompanied Andrew Lewis on his march to Point Pleasant in 1774. Clendenin purchased a 1,030-acre tract on the north side of the Kanawha above the Elk, in the heart of present Charleston, from Judge Cuthbert Bullitt of Prince William County, Virginia, in 1787. Commissioned by Virginia Gov. Edmund Randolph, the Clendenin family, led by George, left Camp Union with 30 Greenbrier County Rangers on April 1, 1788, and arrived in the Kanawha Valley a month later.

As frontier defense was a major concern for western settlement the group set about constructing a stockade, a two-story fort, and sturdy cabins for protection against Indian attacks. This "fort at the mouth of the Elk" or "Clendenin's Station" later became known as Fort Lee. Through Clendenin's influence the Virginia Assembly authorized the formation of Kanawha County from parts of Greenbrier and Montgomery counties in 1789. On December 19, 1794, a 40-acre tract of Clendenin's land was selected and named Charlestown in memory of Clendenin's father, Charles. It was later renamed Charleston. By 1795, George became disappointed and embittered with the government in Richmond and sold his Charleston land holdings and moved to the mouth of the Kanawha on the Ohio. He died in Marietta, Ohio, in 1797 while visiting his daughter.

See also Clendenin Family

Cathy Hershberger Miller
State Archives

Julius A. DeGruyter, *The Kanawha Spectator,* 1953; John G. Morgan and Robert J. Byers, *Charleston 200,* 1994; Otis K. Rice, *Charleston and the Kanawha Valley: An Illustrated History,* 1981.

Paula Clendenin

Artist Paula Clendenin was born June 22, 1949, in Cedar Grove, Kanawha County. She has earned national acclaim for her paintings, richly colored, textured shapes that merge West Virginia's mountain landscape with mystical and spiritual symbols.

Clendenin attended West Virginia University, where she received a bachelor's degree and M.F.A. During her final semester of undergraduate school, she was inspired by a printmaking class to pursue art. She continued to make prints, but also began to paint on canvas. By the mid-1980s, Clendenin had developed a distinctive painting style, characterized by multilayered surfaces and mountain shapes. Her preferred medium is oil stick and paper.

Clendenin's work has been featured in more than a dozen solo exhibitions and in numerous exhibitions with other artists, including "The Spirit Within, Four West Virginia Artists," sponsored by the West Virginia Committee of the National Museum of Women in the Arts in Washington. More than 25 corporate, private, and public collections display her paintings. Clendenin's paintings also appear in collections at the Library of Congress, Dallas Library Commission in Texas, and Fleet-Boston, formerly the Bank of Boston.

Clendenin has won several honors including the Governor's Award three times in the West Virginia Juried Exhibition, and the Award of Excellence at Huntington Museum of Art's "Exhibition 280." Clendenin lives in Charleston and teaches at West Virginia State University. She has taught at several institutions, including the University of Houston, Marshall University, West Virginia Wesleyan College, and the Governor's School for the Arts.

See also Art and Artists

J. R. Clifford

Attorney John Robert "J. R." Clifford, the son of Isaac Clifford and Saltipa Kent Clifford, was born September 13, 1848, in present Grant County. During the Civil War he served as a corporal in the U.S. Colored Troops. Between 1875 and 1885, Clifford was a teacher and later principal at the Sumner School in Martinsburg. In 1882, he founded, edited, and published the *Pioneer Press*, West Virginia's first African-American newspaper.

In 1887, Clifford became the first African-American admitted to practice law before the West Virginia Supreme Court of Appeals. He was one of the first lawyers in the nation to challenge segregated schools. In *Carrie Williams v. The Board of Education Fairfax District*, he successfully argued that "discrimination against people because of color alone as to privileges, immunities and equal protection of the law is unconstitutional."

The case originated in Fairfax District of Tucker County.

In 1897, Clifford was elected as a charter member of the American Negro Academy. He served a term as vice president of the organization. He was chairman of the committee on arrangement of the 1906 meeting of the Niagara Movement, which was held in Harpers Ferry. This meeting laid the foundation for the founding of the NAACP and the 20th-century civil rights movement.

On October 6, 1933, J. R. Clifford died of a cerebral hemorrhage. Still practicing law until his death, at age 85, he was the most senior lawyer active in West Virginia. Clifford was buried at the Mount Hope Cemetery in Berkeley County. In 1954, the Civil War veteran's remains were re-interred at Arlington National Cemetery.

See also Niagara Movement

Joseph Bundy
Bluefield

Cliftonville Mine Battle

Although the Mine Wars of southern West Virginia are better known, a Brooke County gun battle was among the state's deadliest labor-management encounters. The battle took place at the Richland Coal Company's Clifton mine, east of Wellsburg near the Pennsylvania line, on the morning of July 17, 1922. Official reports put the dead at nine although there were rumors of more. Sheriff Harding H. Duval was among those killed. Duval had been disarmed and appeared to have been beaten as well as shot.

The events began Sunday night, July 16, as a crowd of striking miners gathered at the union hall in nearby Avella, Pennsylvania. With the goal of getting the non-union miners out of the mine, the union men marched four miles in the darkness to take up positions surrounding the mine. The heavily armed crowd was estimated at between 300 and 500 men.

Having received word of the planned assault, Sheriff Duval and about 20 deputies joined the company guards at the mine. As the Wabash Railroad 5:15 a.m. train sounded its whistle, the non-union miners appeared for work. At that point, the strikers attacked the mine, which was defended by the sheriff's forces. The strikers captured and set fire to the tipple, which later was dynamited by company men.

Except for the sheriff, all those killed at Cliftonville were union men. In the aftermath, 216 men were indicted, 78 of them for murder. Many charges were reduced or dropped as the trials went forward, with 30 men sentenced to three or more years in prison and others to lesser sentences.

See also Mine Wars

J. W. George Wallace
Brooke County Review

Mary Zwierzchowski, "The Cliftonville Riot: A Forgotten Panhandle Mine War," *Goldenseal*, Summer 1994.

Climate

Located in the mid-latitudes of the northern hemisphere, West Virginia has four distinct seasons. The annual average temperature ranges from near 45 degrees over the high mountains to around 55 degrees in the southwestern lowlands and the extreme Eastern Panhandle.

Annual precipitation is usually well distributed across the months, although July is frequently the wettest and October often the driest. Widespread rains and snows fall from late autumn into early spring. During the summer, more intense, but briefer, showers and thunderstorms provide the majority of precipitation. Occasionally, the remnants of a tropical storm affect the state. Annual precipitation includes both the rain and melted snow. The least amounts are usually in the "shadow" east of the Allegheny Front, where the high mountains block the neighboring lowlands from moisture-bearing winds from the west. Here, in the drainage of the South Branch of the Potomac, yearly amounts of 30 to 35 inches are typical. In contrast, some elevations above 2,500 feet on the western slopes of the central mountains average around 65 inches of precipitation. A yearly average of 40 to 45 inches encompasses much of the state. The extremes in annual precipitation range from 89 inches from Bayard, Grant County, in 1926 to only 9.5 inches in Upper Tract, Pendleton County, during 1930.

During January, daily high temperatures are usually from the mid-30s over the mountains to the lower 40s in the lowlands. Overnight low temperatures average from 15 degrees in the mountains to around 24 degrees in the southwestern lowlands. Average snowfall varies widely. It ranges from near 20 inches in the river valleys of the southwestern lowlands to over 125 inches in elevations above 2,500 feet in the northern and central mountains. Winter often brings prolonged periods of cloudiness to the mountains and western slopes.

During July, daily high temperatures average from the lower 70s above 3,000 feet in the mountains, to the upper 80s in both the southwestern lowlands and Eastern Panhandle. Overnight low readings normally range from the mid-50s in the mountains to mid-60s in the southwestern lowlands and extreme Eastern Panhandle. Adding to the discomfort level, weather patterns can become stagnant during the summer, resulting in an accumulation of haze and humidity. Unless the summer is dry, early morning fog is common from July through September.

See also Weather

Kenneth T. Batty
National Weather Service

Climax Locomotives

The Climax was the second most popular of the geared engines designed for use on logging railroads, after the Shays. Climax Manufacturing Company of Corry, Pennsylvania, built an inexpensive "Type A" that looked like a boiler and engine on a flat car, but larger locomotives had inclined cylinders that drove a cross shaft geared to a flexible shaft beneath the machine, which was in turn geared to each axle. Climax had a reputation for great flexibility on rough track.

As early as 1891, Climaxes were built for West Virginia. Several companies, including W. M. Ritter Lumber Company, bought as many as six small locomotives each for use on narrow gauge track. When Climax Manufacturing went out of business in 1928, more than 140 Climax engines had been used in West Virginia. Some companies that preferred Climax were Sewell Lumber at Landisburg (five narrow-gauge engines), Elk River Coal & Lumber at Swandale (four, one of which was the last Climax in service in the United States), and Moore-Keppel at Ellamore (six).

One of Moore-Keppel's Climaxes is being restored at the Cass Scenic Railroad, and another is in service on the Durbin and Greenbrier Valley, both in Pocahontas County. Of a mere dozen Climaxes left in America today, five were used in West Virginia.

George Deike
Cass

Curly Ray Cline

Musician "Curly" Ray Cline was born January 10, 1923, in Baisden, Logan County. He was one of the most significant bluegrass fiddlers from West Virginia from 1938 until his retirement in 1993. Cline was a member of the Lonesome Pine Fiddlers until 1966 and thereafter played with Ralph Stanley's Clinch Mountain Boys, one of the most important bands playing old-style bluegrass music. Besides recording with these bands, he cut 13 fiddle albums, seven of them for Rebel Records. Cline died August 19, 1997.

See also Lonesome Pine Fiddlers

Ivan M. Tribe
University of Rio Grande

Clover Archeological Site

The Clover archeological site is located on a high terrace on the Ohio River in the Green Bottom Wildlife Management Area, 20 miles north of Huntington. The site was listed on the National Register of Historic Places in 1992. It is also a National Historic Landmark, one of only 15 in West Virginia.

Clover was a large village dating to A.D. 1550 to 1600, the Protohistoric period on the verge of European contact. It is best known as being the original site for the Protohistoric Clover Phase described by James B. Griffin in his book, *The Fort Ancient Aspect,* in 1943. The site was extensively collected by John Adams and other amateur archeologists after 1920. Professional excavations were conducted by Nicholas Freidin and his Marshall University archeological field school from 1984 to 1988.

Excavations and surface collections at the site have yielded thousands of shell-tempered ceramics, stone tools, and bone tools and ornaments. Bone fish hooks and beads were recovered in all stages of manufacture. European brass and copper ornaments and glass trade beads help to date the village. Marine shell gorgets associated with the Southern Cult, pottery effigy bowls, and figurines suggest that the Clover Site and other Clover Phase villages had strong political and cultural ties with villages in what is now eastern Tennessee.

The John Adams collection of artifacts from Clover and other sites is curated at the Huntington Museum of Art.

Robert F. Maslowski
Milton

Coal awaits shipment in the Williamson rail yard, early 20th century.

Coal

West Virginia has coal deposits that range in age from the Late Devonian through the Mississippian to the Late Pennsylvanian geologic periods. The state's oldest known coal is found in several impure beds of the Upper Devonian Hampshire Formation, along the western edge of the mountains from Pocahontas County northward into Maryland. These coal beds are generally only a few centimeters thick and have not been mined except for a short-lived operation near Harmon.

Mississippian Period coal beds occur in the Price, Maccrady, and Mauch Chunk formations, but these beds rarely reach minable thickness or purity. Coal found in the Lower Mississippian Price Formation reaches minable thickness locally in the Sleepy Creek area of Hampshire and Berkeley counties. Several thin, impure coal deposits occur in the Lower Mississippian Maccrady Formation in the southeastern part of the state. Thin, laterally discontinuous coal beds occur in the Lower Mississippian Bluefield, Hinton, and Bluestone formations in southern West Virginia.

All of West Virginia's commercial coal production comes from Pennsylvanian Period coal beds, assigned to seven formations or groups. From the oldest to youngest, these are the Pocahontas, New River, Kanawha, Allegheny, Conemaugh, Monongahela, and Dunkard. They are divided into a southern, low-sulfur coalfield and a northern, high-sulfur coalfield. Coal beds of the southern coalfield are generally older (Lower and Middle Pennsylvanian), higher in rank, lower in sulfur content and ash yield, and generally of better quality than those of the

younger (Middle and Upper Pennsylvanian) northern coalfield. Generally, southern West Virginia mines produce clean-burning "compliance" steam coal for power generation, and much also is used for coke production for steel making; northern coal is also used for power generation, although these mines rarely produce compliance coal. There is more minable coal in the south.

The geologic distribution of coal was mainly determined by conditions during long-ago periods of peat accumulation, including the climate and the state of evolution of terrestrial plants at the time. Plants remained small until the Late Devonian, more than 350 million years ago, when large trees evolved and widespread forests first appeared. Once plants with woody tissues capable of being preserved appeared, peat accumulation was possible.

An abundant, year-round supply of fresh water was very important to the accumulation of the peat deposits that were to become the state's coal beds. Peat forms where plant debris accumulates faster than herbivores and decay destroy it. Peat bodies are like sponges, composed mainly of the woody parts of the plants. During the Pennsylvanian Period, more than 290 million years ago, the location of the continents was different. Present West Virginia was within a few degrees of the equator, and the state's numerous coal beds formed in tropical rain forests on a low-lying coastal plain. It rained frequently, without long dry spells. Rainwater low in dissolved minerals fell onto the surface of the peat bodies, soaked in, and percolated downward and out-

ward. The constant influx and movement through the porous peat of fresh rainwater excluded mineral-bearing ground and surface waters, keeping mineral content low and the pH of the water low. A cleaner coal resulted. The high growth rates of tropical rain forests allowed the peat to accumulate rapidly.

During the Pennsylvanian Period, present West Virginia was located in a slowly subsiding basin, a necessary condition for the preservation and burial of peat. As the basin subsided, sediments were continually deposited. Temperature and pressure rose as burial depth increased, slowly converting the peat into coal.

Coal rank is a measure of the amount of coalification, or transformation a coal bed has undergone in the progression from peat through coal. Increasing amounts of heat and pressure applied over geologic time progressively alter the original plant material through peat; lignite; subbituminous; high-, medium-, and low-volatile bituminous; anthracite; meta-anthracite; and graphite.

West Virginia's coal is bituminous in rank. Coal beds of the southern coalfields range in rank from low-volatile bituminous in the southeast and decrease progressively northwestward and stratigraphically upward to high-volatile bituminous in the area of the Kanawha Valley near Charleston. The higher rank of the older coal beds indicates increased coalification from deeper burial, and the southeastward increase in rank resulted from increased heat and pressure due to proximity to the mountain-building events known as the Appalachian Orogeny. With the exception of the Eastern Panhandle, coal beds of the northern coalfield are generally high-volatile bituminous. Coals of the Eastern Panhandle are highly variable in rank even over short distances. The lower rank of the state's northern coalfield is the result of less depth of burial, less time for coalification, and greater distance from the Appalachian Orogeny.

Not all coal beds are economically minable. Early in the 20th century, the West Virginia Geological and Economic Survey estimated that the state had an original resource base of more than 116 billion tons of coal, counting only seams greater than 12 inches thick. As of 2001, more than 21 billion tons had been mined or lost in mining, according to records kept by the West Virginia Office of Miners' Health, Safety, and Training. Allowing for the coal that cannot be mined for various reasons, it is estimated that more than 50 billion tons of recoverable resources remain, theoretically enough to mine at present rates for hundreds of years.

In practice, however, many constraints operate to radically reduce the amount of coal that is actually minable. Factors affecting the minability of a coal bed include thickness, quality, roof type, distance to the transportation network, overburden thickness and type, depth below valley bottoms, and various cultural factors. As a result, the minable reserve is significantly smaller than the overall coal resource base and tends to vary over time with changes in demand, in coal production and utilization technology, and in the physical infrastructure of the state.

West Virginia's coal is distributed unequally, both geographically and stratigraphically. There are vastly more coal resources in the southern coalfield than the northern coalfield, due to a progressive drying of the climate throughout the Pennsylvanian Period. The six coal seams with the highest original resources are (in billions of tons) the Pittsburgh coal (13.3); the Lower Kittanning/No. 5 Block coal (10.3); No. 2 Gas (8.0); Sewell coal (6.3); Stockton (4.7); and Cedar Grove (4.3). The five counties with the highest original resources are (in billions of tons), Logan (8.1); Boone (8.1); Mingo (6.3); Webster (6.3); and Nicholas (6.2).

See also Coal Industry, Geology

Bascombe M. Blake Jr.
Geological & Economic Survey

Coal & Coke Railway

The Coal & Coke Railway Company was incorporated May 14, 1902, by former U.S. Senator Henry Gassaway Davis and associates, to connect Charleston with the West Virginia Central & Pittsburg [*sic*] Railway in the vicinity of Elkins.

Davis had acquired extensive landholdings in the Roaring Creek area of Randolph County and other coal properties in Upshur, Braxton, and Gilmer counties. The construction of a railroad was necessary for the development of these properties. After selling the West Virginia Central & Pittsburg in the fall of 1902, Davis acquired 25 miles of track owned by the Roaring Creek & Charleston Railroad and the Roaring Creek & Belington Railroad, both serving his coal properties in Randolph and Barbour counties. He soon acquired 64 more miles of track, which had been constructed by the Charleston, Clendenin & Sutton Railroad, extending from Charleston toward Sutton.

With these acquisitions, only 107 miles of new track from Roaring Creek to Sutton had to be built to provide through traffic from Elkins to Charleston. Construction on the new segment of the Coal & Coke Railway began in the spring of 1903. It was completed on December 2, 1905, when the last spike was driven at Walkersville in Lewis County. Twelve tunnels totaling two miles of underground trackage and 30 steel bridges had been constructed to penetrate the mountainous terrain on the route from Roaring Creek (now Norton) in Randolph County to the new town of Gassaway on the Elk River in Braxton County.

When the Coal & Coke Railway was completed, it provided a much needed north-south route through the heart of West Virginia. The Coal & Coke connected with the Western Maryland Railroad at Elkins and with the Kanawha & Michigan at Charleston. The Coal & Coke Railway provided a way for West Virginia coal to get to outlets on the Great Lakes, as well as an alternate route to Atlantic Ocean ports. The first coal originating on the new line was shipped from Charleston to the Midwest on December 3, 1905. The first passenger train ran from Elkins to Charleston on January 21, 1906. For more than a decade, passengers and large quantities of coal, coke, timber, and other products were moved over the Coal & Coke.

After Davis's death in 1916, the Baltimore & Ohio Railroad purchased the controlling interest of the Coal & Coke, which became identified as the Charleston branch of the B&O.

See also Henry Gassaway Davis, Railroads

Donald L. Rice
Elkins

James M. Callahan, *History of West Virginia, Old and New,* 1923; Charles M. Pepper, *Life and Times of Henry Gassaway Davis,* 1920; Thomas R. Ross, *Henry Gassaway Davis, An Old Fashioned Biography,* 1994.

Coal Industry

Coal was known to exist in Western Virginia from colonial times, but not until the early 19th century was it exploited as a commercial fuel. Development came first along the Kanawha River near Charleston and the Ohio River near Wheeling, both areas of early settlement and industry.

The erection of salt furnaces in Kanawha County beginning in 1797 provided the initial stimulus to coal mining. By 1840, 90 furnaces produced a million bushels of salt annually and consumed 200,000 tons of coal. More than 900 salt workers, many of them slaves, mined coal to fire the salt evaporation furnaces. Although the salt industry began to decline after mid-century, the demand for coal continued for other uses, including the production of coal oil for lighting. Steamboats consumed great quantities of coal and also transported coal to the new and growing towns along the Ohio River and its tributaries. By 1860, 25 independent coal companies had been organized which employed more than 1,000 workers.

The Civil War retarded the industry's growth, but the explorations of future promoters, such as the Confederates Jedediah Hotchkiss and John D. and George W. Imboden, during the war and in the years following, laid the groundwork for rapid development as these men turned to peace-time industrial careers. Growth was especially dramatic in southern West Virginia, where the Chesapeake & Ohio Railroad wended its way through the New and Kanawha coalfields and connected Richmond and the new city of Huntington in 1873. The Pocahontas and Flat Top coalfields were linked to the national markets by the Norfolk & Western Railroad in the 1880s, when the line was completed from the port of Norfolk, reaching the Ohio River near Huntington in 1892.

The C&O did not attempt to control the land along its tracks, so the mineral lands in the New and Kanawha valleys were taken up by independent speculators or mining companies during the 1870s and 1880s. Pioneer operators in the New River field, therefore, tended to be independent investors who hired experienced mine managers. On the other hand, the N&W and its land company purchased hundreds of thousands of acres in the Pocahontas and Flat Top fields, which it leased to the actual operators. Pioneer operators in this field tended to be experienced practical coal miners, who had relatively little capital but a willingness to undertake hard physical labor and high levels of risk. Coal operators John Freeman and Jenkin Jones, later wealthy, reportedly arrived in Mercer County with little more than a pick and a shovel.

The northern West Virginia coalfields had their own pioneers. James Otis Watson, sometimes regarded as the father of the West Virginia coal industry, must be considered as the leader. Born in 1815 to parents who were among the first settlers in the Fairmont area, Watson learned all he could about mining coal and in 1852 organized the Montana Mining Company. He was the first operator in West

Virginia to ship coal by rail, in this case the Baltimore & Ohio Railroad, which linked Baltimore and Wheeling in 1852. Like the N&W and the C&O in southern West Virginia, the B&O sparked a boom in the northern West Virginia coalfields.

Under the direction of Watson's son, Clarence Wayland Watson, one of the major coal corporations in America took form. Clarence, later a U.S. senator, convinced his brothers to join him in founding the Briar Hill Coal Company in 1893. The Watsons soon merged their coal mining interests with those of U.S. Sen. Johnson Newlon Camden Sr. A trusted lieutenant of oil mogul John D. Rockefeller Sr., Camden brought political power and deep financial resources to the new Fairmont Coal Company. Clarence Watson's brother-in-law, Aretas Brooks Fleming, a Fairmont lawyer and governor of West Virginia (1890–93), also joined the company. In 1902, the Watson-Fleming-Camden syndicate, or the "Fairmont Ring" as some unaffectionately called them, acquired the Somerset Coal Company in Pennsylvania, and the following year purchased the B&O's holdings in the Consolidation Coal Company, a Maryland company. With the blessing of Rockefeller in 1909 the entire syndicate reorganized as the Consolidation Coal Company. "Consol" was controlled by Clarence Watson for the next 20 years, and it remains today a major producer of West Virginia coal.

The massive capital investment poured into the West Virginia coal industry produced a social and economic transformation of the region. Railroads carried away coal but also connected the state to the national markets. Finding few of the supporting services required to sustain a work force in this mountain vastness, investors rebuilt the region to fit their needs. In many locations, the resident farm population was too small to satisfy the demand for labor, so companies recruited workers from outside the region. Along with the coal mines that sprang up along the railroad lines were company towns, built by the operators to provide the necessary services for a rapidly expanding labor force. Economic pressures created by the industrial transition, such as rising property taxes, demand for farm products, and imported manufactured goods, started the older subsistence farming system down the road to extinction.

The explosive growth of production suggests the scale of the coal boom: In 1867, only 490,000 tons of coal were produced in West Virginia, but by 1887 that figure had grown to 4.9 million tons, and by 1917 it had rocketed to 89.4 million tons. The number of mine employees kept pace with production, growing from 3,701 in 1880 to nearly 90,000 in 1917.

With the burgeoning population of miners, many of them recruited from outside the state, came an ethnic and racial mixture previously unheard of in West Virginia. In some southern counties, the foreign-born and African-American populations combined to outnumber native-born whites. Social services that previously had been either unavailable or scarce in most rural areas of the state, such as electric power, public schools, public libraries, and a variety of stores, as well as doctors and dentists, became widespread in the coalfields.

The amenities came with a price, however. Prior to the Great Depression of the 1930s, more than 90 percent of the miners in southern West Virginia lived in company-owned towns without benefit of civic institutions. Combined with numerous work-related grievances standard among miners during the pre-union era, labor-capital relations in the coalfields were frequently strained. Generally, the pivotal issue was recognition of the United Mine Workers of America as bargaining agent for the miners. Some of the most famous strike episodes in the history of the American coal industry occurred in West Virginia between 1910 and 1933, including the Paint Creek-Cabin Creek strike of 1913–14; the Mine War of 1920–21, which included the March on Logan, Battle of Blair Mountain, and the Matewan Massacre; and the Monongalia-Fairmont coalfield wars, which occurred between 1927 and 1931.

The economic underpinnings of these conflicts were rooted in the larger economy. In addition to being philosophically opposed to unions, as most industrialists were, coal operators attempted to control labor costs within an environment of notoriously fickle markets. In these disputes, they resorted to every means at their disposal, legal and otherwise, to break the strikes and prevent unionization. Generally, the government sided with the companies. This period came to an end with the Great Depression, as the coal industry buckled in the general collapse of the American economy. Added to economic pressures was passage of the National Labor Relations Act in 1932, particularly Section 7(a) of the act, which granted workers the right to organize unions and provided further impetus for companies to abandon costly and unpopular paternalistic policies. Hence, they sold off the miners' houses and ceased to provide community services, such as education, police, and fire protection, and abandoned the now depressed mine settlements.

During the Depression and World War II, the coal industry laid the groundwork for a new era characterized by the accelerated introduction of labor-saving machinery. Mechanization had begun in the late 19th century with the introduction of the undercutting machine. In the early 1900s, underground coal haulage was improved with the gradual replacement of mules by electric locomotives, and by the 1920s underground work was revolutionized by the mobile loading machine, which organized formerly independent miners into supervised crews.

Miners resisted mechanization, but this was overcome when the union negotiated an agreement with the operators accepting a reduction in the number of workers but ensuring that the increased productivity would result in higher pay and shorter working hours for the miners who remained. By the early 1950s, a machine known as the continuous miner consolidated all of the basic steps in the mining process into one machine operation, radically reducing the labor force required. By the 1970s, mining was revolutionized again by the introduction of computerized longwall mining which sheared coal off sections hundreds of feet long onto conveyor belts. Mechanization underground had its equivalent in strip mining as companies sought to increase productivity and reduce costs. By the end of the 20th century, ever larger earth-moving machines decapitated entire mountains to remove the coal seams.

As the capital requirements increased, hundreds of coal companies either disappeared or were consolidated into fewer, much larger corporations. By the end of the 20th century, a handful of major multinational corporations dominated the industry. Production grew under these conditions. In 1997, West Virginia reached a peak coal production of more than 180 million tons. About 25 percent of coal mined is shipped to foreign markets and used mainly in steel manufacturing. Another 15 percent is used by the domestic steel industry. The rest of the coal mined in West Virginia is used to generate electric power.

Absentee ownership continued to be a political issue for most of the century, and the social costs of longwall mining, mountaintop removal, and the moving of coal on overloaded trucks also generated serious political controversy toward the end of the century. However, the decline in the number of workers required by the increasingly automated coal industry had the most direct effect on West Virginia families. In 1950, there were 127,000 coal miners, but by the end of the 20th century that number had plummeted to under 18,000 even though coal production reached record highs. Correspondingly, the high unemployment during this period produced a great out-migration as redundant miners and their families were forced to leave the state to search for employment elsewhere.

See also Coal, Coal Mine Disasters, Coal Mine Mechanization, Labor History,

Mine Wars, Mining Methods in the Hand
Loading Era

Ronald L. Lewis
West Virginia University

Kenneth R. Bailey, "A Judicious Mixture: Negroes
and Immigrants in the West Virginia Mines,
1880–1917," *West Virginia History,* January 1973;
Keith Dix, *What's a Coal Miner to Do? The
Mechanization of Coal Mining,* 1988; Ronald D.
Eller, *Miners, Millhands, and Mountaineers:
Industrialization of the Appalachian South, 1880–
1930,* 1982.

Coal Mine Disasters

Since 1883, when fatality records began to be kept, more than 21,000 miners have lost their lives in West Virginia coal mines. Most of these deaths were single fatalities, many of which were not investigated in the early years. In 1883, when 20 miners lost their lives, the legislature established the West Virginia Department of Mines, with Oscar Veasey appointed as the first mine inspector. Just three years later, West Virginia's first mining disaster occurred at the Mountain Brook shaft mine in the Preston County town of Newburg. A methane gas explosion there killed 39, making this the first in a long line. (An accident is classified as a "disaster" when three or more lose their lives; before 1961, the number was five.)

Coal production in the state increased from slightly more than two million tons in 1883 to more than 11 million tons by 1894. The next disaster occurred near Colliers, Brooke County, on November 20, 1894. Eight men lost their lives when coal was blasted using a dangerous method called "shooting from the solid," meaning that they blasted the coal loose without first undercutting it. Just two years earlier, three men had been killed there in the same manner.

By 1900, coal production had doubled, to more than 22 million tons. The boom ushered in a period of great carnage. Just three months into the 20th century, a miner's open light ignited methane gas at the Red Ash mine in Fayette County. The resulting explosion was instantly fatal to 46, many of whom were descendants of slaves, lured from the South by the promise of good jobs.

The recruiting of unskilled workers, including immigrants as well as black and white natives who were new to the mines, was a trend that would have disastrous results. The newcomers made up a majority of the victims in some disasters. For example, in 1907 at the Stuart shaft mine in Fayette County, an explosion, also caused by disregard of safety rules, killed 85 men, most of whom were waiting for the elevator at the bottom of the shaft. Only 37 were listed as "Americans," meaning white natives since black miners were identified as Negroes. After the explosion, the New River Company (which also owned the nearby Parral mine, home to an explosion that killed 23 in 1906) renamed the mines to make it easier to attract new workers, with Stuart becoming Lochgelly and Parral becoming Summerlee.

On December 6, 1907, the Fairmont Coal Company's interconnected Nos. 6 and 8 mines at Monongah exploded, killing at least 361 miners, the worst in U.S. history. Of those killed, only 74 were classified as "Americans." The resulting public outcry brought Congressional action, culminating in the creation of the U.S. Bureau of Mines in 1910. Of the 4,260 miners killed in West Virginia between 1910 and 1920, 579 would die in massive explosions and fires. Some of the more notable disasters during that time were at Jed (now Havaco), McDowell County, with 83 killed; Eccles, Raleigh County, where 183 died; and Layland, Fayette County, where 47 men survived five days trapped underground after an explosion killed 119 of their fellow workers.

As the 1920s rolled on, new state and federal regulations, along with insistence for improved safety from the United Mine Workers, began to create a safer environment for miners. But disasters still happened, some of them with large losses of life. In 1924, the Benwood mine in Marshall County exploded, killing 119. Three years later, the Federal No. 3 mine at Everettville, Monongalia County, blew up, killing 97.

Several smaller disasters occurred in the 1930s, with the worst being in Logan County's McBeth mine, where 18 died. On January 11, 1940, 91 died in a methane explosion at the Pond Creek No. 1 mine at Bartley, McDowell County, shattering any illusion that major mine disasters had become a thing of the past. During the war years, there were several disasters, including explosions at Osage and Pursglove No. 2 in Monongalia County, killing 56 and 20, and an underground fire at the nearby Pursglove No. 15 mine, which suffocated 13.

In the 1950s, ten disasters were added to the awful total. Notable among these were two explosions in the same mine in the McDowell County town of Bishop in 1956 and 1957, killing a total of 59 miners. An explosion in 1954 at Farmington, Marion County, killed 16 men at the Jamison No. 9 mine.

In the early 1960s, fires, roof falls, and flooding took their toll, but in nowhere near the numbers in previous years. Any resulting complacency was shattered on November 20, 1968, when the huge Consol No. 9 (formerly the Jamison No. 9) mine at Farmington exploded, killing 78. It was apparent that major changes still needed to be made. One year later, Congress passed the Federal Coal Mine Health and Safety Act of 1969. During this time, West Virginia also tightened its rules and regulations. These sweeping changes at the state and federal levels finally made a major change in coal mine safety and greatly reduced mine disasters.

However, they still happen. The worst disaster since the passing of the act was in 1972, at the Blacksville No. 1 mine in Monongalia County. On July 22, a fire occurred while a continuous mining machine was being moved to a new working section. Nine men, who were working deep in the mine, perished as a result of smoke and fumes that were carried through the mine's ventilation system.

Blacksville No. 1 was the site of another disaster 20 years later. By 1992, No. 1 had reached the end of its useful life and was being sealed. On March 19, while drainage pipes were being welded together and placed into the production shaft, a spark fell into the shaft, igniting methane gas that had accumulated there. Four miners were killed, making it apparent that as long as men work underground disaster will always be near.

The worst mine disaster in decades occurred on January 2, 2006, when an explosion killed 12 miners at the Sago mine in Upshur County. Days later, two men died in a Logan County mine fire.

As of January 2006, there have been 118 disasters at 104 different mines in West Virginia. The Glen Rogers mine in Wyoming County had four disasters. The Barrackville and Farmington mines in Marion County, and the Yukon mine near War in McDowell County each had at least three disasters.

See also Coal Industry, Coal Mine Health and Safety Legislation, Farmington Mine Disaster, Mine Safety, Monongah Mine Disaster

Rick Jarrett
Mine Research Group

Stan Cohen, *King Coal,* 1984; Lacy A. Dillon, *They
Died For King Coal,* 1985; Dillon, *They Died In The
Darkness,* 1976.

Coal Mine Health and Safety Legislation

Following major mine disasters, a flurry of legislative activity occurred as federal and state legislators tried to improve conditions in the coal mines. The greatest loss of life occurred at Monongah in 1907, when at least 361 miners were killed. Congress then created the U.S. Bureau of Mines, but that developed into a production-oriented agency.

Effective lobbying by coal operators seriously weakened each effort by Congress and the state legislature to provide meaningful protection. Following a 1951 disaster in West Frankfort, Illinois, which killed 119 miners, Congress struggled to pass a loophole-ridden bill that President Harry Truman reluctantly signed, while denouncing its shortcomings.

The Federal Coal Mine Health and

Safety Act of 1969 for the first time in history provided health protection and strict safety measures that have nearly eliminated the grim series of mine disasters. By limiting coal dust, the 1969 act enabled miners to work in a healthier environment, and compensated those suffering from pneumoconiosis or black lung. Also, West Virginia state legislation in 1969 for the first time provided that black lung was compensable. These actions followed the disastrous mine explosions at Farmington, Marion County.

Over the objections of coal operators, who contended that stricter regulations would make the industry uncompetitive, Congress empowered federal authorities to close unsafe mines. Inspection forces were beefed up and required to make unannounced inspections. Miners who reported unsafe conditions had their job security protected. Stiff fines were imposed for violations. Non-sparking electrical equipment was required. Other provisions improved ventilation, roof support and methane detection.

President Richard Nixon reluctantly signed the 1969 act, criticizing the black lung features and proceeding through his appointees to weaken its enforcement. In 1994, under President Clinton, West Virginian J. Davitt McAteer was appointed head of the Mine Safety and Health Administration, and enforcement improved noticeably.

Unlike prior legislation, the 1969 act succeeded for a number of reasons. Television reports during and following the Farmington disaster of November 20, 1968, which killed 78 miners, brought the plight of coal miners into everyone's living room. The Farmington widows and hundreds of coal miners were brought to the nation's capitol at the expense of Congressman Ken Hechler. Drs. I. E. Buff, Donald Rasmussen, and Hawey Wells held rallies throughout the coalfields and delivered telling testimony to Congressional committees. In defiance of their union leaders, 40,000 West Virginia coal miners staged a wildcat strike in the spring of 1969, demanding effective health and safety laws. David Finnegan in Congressman Hechler's office and Gary Sellers in the office of health care advocate Ralph Nader helped draft and lobby for the strongest possible law, and their efforts were materially assisted by San Francisco Congressman Phillip Burton.

See also Coal Industry, Farmington Mine Disaster

Ken Hechler
Charleston

Joseph E. Finley, *The Corrupt Kingdom*, 1972; Brit Hume, *Death and the Mines*, 1971; Duane Lockard, *Coal*, 1998.

Coal Mine Mechanization

Mechanization of West Virginia's coal mines took place gradually throughout

A continuous miner machine at work in a Nicholas County mine, 1999.

the first half of the 20th century. Traditionally, coal mining involved the distinct steps of undercutting the seam, then drilling and blasting the undercut coal into manageable pieces, and finally loading and hauling the coal to the surface. The complexity of these tasks and the tight spaces encountered underground, especially in low-coal seams, presented difficult challenges for inventors of mine machinery. Consequently, mechanization first influenced surface activities such as pumping the water from the mines, as well as hoisting and ventilation, and these advances enabled operators to drastically increase the physical scope of their underground operations. The appropriate power source proved critical to underground mechanization, and by the turn of the 20th century the versatility of electricity made it more attractive than steam or compressed air.

Underground mechanization first centered on haulage and undercutting. By the early 1900s, trolley-operated locomotives (often called "motors" by miners) replaced animal power for main-line haulage. Mules remained important for transport of mine cars to and from the working face to the main line until the 1920s, when cable-reel locomotives displaced them. By 1900, several types of undercutting machines eliminated the time-consuming task of undercutting by pick. However, miners continued to drill, blast, and load manually, and control of these critical skills enabled them to maintain much of their independence at the working face. Unfortunately, the large amount of coal dust, created by the new cutting machines and distributed throughout the

mine by mechanized ventilation, increased the probability of explosions.

In the 1920s, the mechanized carloading conveyor increased the hand loaders' efficiency by lowering the height for shoveling and streamlining the transport of coal. Their versatility in difficult mining conditions made hand-loaded conveyors popular in West Virginia, and some large operations relied on them into the 1950s. However, the innovation that would replace conveyors and bring an end to the hand-loading era also made its appearance in the 1920s: the mobile coal-loading machine.

Miners tended to resist mechanization, but United Mine Workers President John L. Lewis saw it as a means of increasing tonnage per worker and, subsequently, individual pay. Unionism in turn raised labor costs and encouraged operators to embrace full mechanization. By the late 1940s, mobile loading machines, particularly the Joy loader, combined with power drills, cutting machines, and conveyors or shuttle cars to drastically alter the traditional mining process. Much of the miners' traditional independence in the workplace dissolved as they ceased to be skilled workers and instead became hourly workers assembled into teams of machine operators led by a foreman. This mechanization of the working face dramatically increased tonnage per worker and displaced thousands of miners.

By the 1950s, the roof-bolter, or pinner, replaced the timbering system, clearing passageways and eliminating obstacles to the movement of machinery. The continuous-mining machine—which finally synthesized all the steps of hand mining into one phase—and continuous-belting for coal transport further reduced labor requirements, expanding the exodus of former miners to northern industrial centers.

Producing ten times the coal with half the workers, longwall-mining machinery increased in popularity in the 1970s. Eliminating the need for driving rooms and pillaring, longwall "plows" or "shears" dislodged coal from the face of an entire panel into an automatically advancing conveyor system. With longwall and other modern methods, West Virginia at the opening of the 21st century produces the most coal in its history, but with fewer miners than ever.

See also Joy Loading Machine, John L. Lewis, Mining Methods in the Hand Loading Era

Paul H. Rakes
WVU Institute of Technology
Keith Dix, *What's a Coal Miner to Do? The Mechanization of Coal Mining,* 1988.

Coal River

The Coal River, which joins the Kanawha River at St. Albans, forks into two large tributaries 19 miles above its mouth. The main or east branch, the Big Coal River, itself forks about 40 miles farther upstream into its major tributaries, Marsh and Clear forks. The river's west branch, known as the Little Coal, extends southward for about 20 miles to Madison, where it splits into its main tributaries, Spruce and Pond forks. Well-named, the Coal River system drains a large section of the southern coalfields.

Most likely, the Coal River was discovered by John Peter Salling in 1742, and named by him for the coal outcroppings he saw in the area. Alternatively, the river may have been named for himself by Samuel Cole, one of a group returning from Andrew Lewis's ill-fated Big Sandy expedition in 1756.

The triangular-shaped Coal River basin covers about 900 square miles, including almost all of Boone County and parts of Kanawha, Raleigh, Lincoln, Logan, and Putnam counties. The watershed is roughly 20 miles wide at its broadest and about 50 miles long at its longest. From St. Albans, about 13 miles west of Charleston, the Coal and its tributaries extend southeast to the Beckley area and south toward Logan. The Coal River basin was richly endowed with natural resources, especially coal and timber. In the 1850s, the Coal River Navigation Company built eight locks and dams on the Coal as far as Peytona, to ship bargeloads of high-quality cannel coal, which was used to make coal oil. Millions of bushels of cannel coal were removed from 1867 to 1881. Later, the river was used to float logs to St. Albans sawmills, and in 1889 cribs and booms were strategically located to direct the logs into the river's main channel. By

1905, the railroad had taken over the removal of timber from the Coal River region. As the woods were timbered out and logging declined, bituminous coal mining quickly replaced it. Today, railroads extend to the tributaries of both branches, and coal production from the area remains high.

In the early 20th century the Coal River was used extensively for recreation. Two river beaches, one at Upper Falls and one at Lower Falls, remained popular for much of the century. However, coal mine pollution increasingly interfered with enjoyment of the river by bathers. As coalfield streams were cleaned up late in the century, the Coal became popular with canoeists and fishermen.

See also Boone County, Coal River Navigation Company

William H. Dean
WVU Institute of Technology
William H. Dean, "Steamboat Whistles on the Coal," *West Virginia History,* July 1971.

Coal River Navigation Company

In the mid 1840s, William Madison Peyton and others organized companies to mine cannel coal at Peytona on Big Coal River and at Manningsville on its major tributary, the Little Coal. It had been discovered that the oily mineral could be refined into coal oil, which was used for illumination. In 1849, the Virginia General Assembly authorized the development of plans for slackwater improvements to make the Coal River more navigable. Peyton, Henry DuBois, and other mine owners with assistance from the state established the Coal River Navigation Company and hired the future Civil War general, William S. Rosecrans, as project engineer. Construction began in 1855 with eight locks and dams eventually being built on the Coal River, creating slackwater navigation for 35 miles upstream to Peytona, Boone County. A single lock and dam was built on the Little Coal River.

Construction of the stone-filled timber-crib dams and 125-by-24-foot timber-crib locks was completed by 1859. During the first year of operation, 400,000 bushels of cannel coal was barged out of the river. In 1860, that amount was doubled. With the start of the Civil War, navigation on the river and maintenance of the locks and dams were limited. In September 1861, one of the greatest floods ever in the Kanawha River watershed caused great damage to the structures.

After the war the new state of West Virginia reorganized the Coal River Navigation Company, and repairs were made on the locks and dams. However, the market for coal oil for illumination was sharply reduced with the discovery of petroleum and the making of kerosene. By 1882, the Coal River locks and dams had been

abandoned, and by 1900 little evidence of their existence remained.

See also Cannel Coal, Coal River

Gerald W. Sutphin
Huntington
Leland R. Johnson, *Men, Mountains and Rivers, An Illustrated History of the Huntington District,* U.S. Army Corps of Engineers, 1977.

Coalfield Baseball

Baseball was a vibrant force in industrial towns throughout West Virginia during the first half of the 20th century, especially in the coalfields. Coal companies looked for good players, usually rewarding them with easier jobs, shorter working hours, and time off. Coal companies financed teams to help unify their work forces in towns from Fairmont to Gary, and from Helen, Tams, Fireco, and Switchback to Eccles. There were company leagues, Negro leagues, and United Mine Workers leagues.

Class D minor league professional teams brought people such as Stan Musial to Williamson early in his career, before he became a St. Louis Cardinals star. But the team pay, even at the major league level, was so low that most men earned much more money digging coal than playing ball. Harry Perkowski from Raleigh County played for the Cincinnati Reds in the 1950s. He later recalled that he earned $100 a month playing major league baseball, and that the mines paid better. Fred "Sheriff" Blake, also from Raleigh County, pitched for the Chicago Cubs from 1925 to 1931. When he retired and lived in two rooms at the Beckley Hotel, Blake said his 10 years with major league teams never paid him any pension benefits at all.

Black players could not make the majors during the heyday of coalfields ball, since professional baseball remained segregated until Jackie Robinson broke the color barrier in 1947. In the meantime, the black professional teams offered a challenging alternative. Miner Angus Evans once played centerfield for the New York Black Yankees, and Grover Lewis played third for the legendary Homestead Grays. Born in 1903 into an Alabama mining family, Lewis had played outfield for all-black coalfield teams in Alabama and in Fairmont, on his way up to Homestead near Pittsburgh. When a broken ankle cut his professional career short, he returned to West Virginia to work in the mines, and to play for and manage the Raleigh Clippers.

Coalfield baseball teams withered away as company towns, company stores, and company houses and churches began disappearing after World War II. Mining machines slashed the coal work force statewide. From a high of 141,000 miners in 1947, there were only 45,000 miners in West Virginia in 1969 and just 16,000 in 2002. Coal towns where 3,000 people had lived in the early 1940s dropped to 400 or 500 people by the early 1960s, most of them retired. Broader social forces were at work, as well. Blake believed that the automobile and television spelled the destruction of coal town baseball. The once vibrant Raleigh County League was gone by the mid-1950s.

John McGraw mined coal and played ball with his brothers Gene and Willard in Lillybrook. In the 1980s, after he retired, John McGraw was sad. "These coalfields are gone, these coal camps. Nobody lives here much now. I wish they still had it around. I always liked baseball, crazy about it." McGraw believed miners were special. "Whenever they played, they played hard. Whenever they worked, they worked hard. A funny breed, that coal miner."

See also Baseball

Paul J. Nyden
Charleston Gazette

Coalfield Blues

During the booming 1920s, musicians from the southern West Virginia coalfields recorded some of the first solo guitar recordings ever made. They evolved a distinctive guitar style that reflected the diverse musical culture of the coalfields. Frank Hutchison, a white guitarist from Logan, blended white and African-American musical influences in the late 1920s. He recorded 35 songs and tunes for the OKeh Record Company between 1926 and 1929, and OKeh issued 28 of these. According to Sherman Lawson, a Logan County fiddler, Hutchison apparently learned much of his guitar style from a black guitarist and singer named William Hunt. Unfortunately, record companies did not record Hunt or many other black musicians in the West Virginia coalfields during the 1920s. From Hunt, Hutchison learned to play guitar with a closed pocket knife, by sliding it on the strings to produce a lonesome, crying sound. Hutchison played slide with his left hand while sometimes strumming and sometimes finger-picking with his right hand.

Dick Justice, also from Logan County, recorded blues, ragtime, British and American ballads, as well as old-time string-band tunes. Justice used both finger-picking and strumming, and he occasionally played with Frank Hutchison at informal get-togethers.

The duo Roy Harvey and Leonard Copeland, who lived around Beckley, recorded six guitar duets for Columbia Records in 1930. Their repertoire reflects the influences of parlor guitar, ragtime, blues, and popular music. Harvey and Copeland used both strumming and finger-picking. Roy Harvey was a railroad engineer. After losing his job for participating in a strike, he turned to music to make a living, recording numerous train songs. In addition to

Copeland, Harvey recorded with such notable musicians as Charlie Poole and the North Carolina Ramblers. Jess Johnson, a native of Raleigh County, played slide guitar with Harvey on the recording of "The Guitar Rag."

Some guitarists have carried the coalfields guitar tradition into the 21st century. One was the late Carl Rutherford, from Warriormine in McDowell County, who learned guitar from his family, particularly his uncle, Will Muncy, who owned reissued records of Frank Hutchison. In 1942, Rutherford learned to play in the same tunings that Hutchison, Leonard Copeland, and Jess Johnson used. Muncy showed Rutherford how to play guitar with a closed Case knife, just as Hutchison had done.

Rutherford's kinfolk who played banjo also influenced his finger-picking guitar style. He said the thumb-and-finger banjo picking of his mother and his Uncle Will gave him the idea of picking the guitar with his thumb and forefinger. In Rutherford's guitar picking, the thumb played an alternating bass rhythm while the first finger played melody. Thus both recordings and oral tradition have spurred the creative development of mountain guitar styles.

One of the outstanding performers of blues in the African-American tradition is Nat Reese of Princeton. Reese, a guitarist and vocalist, is a winner of the John Henry Award and of the 1995 Vandalia Award.

See also Frank Hutchison, Nat Reese
Jim McGee
Louisville, Kentucky

Coalfield Doctors

Coal company doctors once provided a large part of the primary medical care West Virginians received, especially in the state's southern coalfields. As the

Children's Bureau of the U.S. Department of Labor noted in a 1923 report, most mining communities were too small to support a regular medical practice. Thus, the coal companies had to bring in their own physicians. The companies devised a system whereby they assessed their miners so much per month, deducting the amount from their pay checks. In the 1923 survey, the bureau found that single miners paid $0.75 to $1.25 a month, while married miners paid $1.50 to $2. The fees covered all medical care except for birthing babies and surgical procedures.

Some companies gave the doctor the entire checkoff collected, while others held back 10 percent to 20 percent as reimbursement for collecting the fees. Many doctors covered more than one coal camp, but the camps were almost always no more than several miles apart. None of the doctors in the 1923 survey provided care for more than 150 to 200 families. However, the total travel involved in making house calls in even a compact territory might be considerable. One doctor listed in his records that during some years he traveled as much as 20,000 miles, averaging well over 1,000 miles a month.

The early coalfield physician was educated differently than his colleagues today. Although requirements increased as time passed, a person could obtain a medical degree in 1880 by spending two years in a preparatory academy followed by two years at a medical school. Once educated, the doctor's career was shaped by the isolation and the poor transportation on the narrow roads of the coalfields. These doctors had to be strong and self-reliant, and they had to be ready to travel in all kinds of weather, often for hours to get to the sick or injured. The

The medical situation is primitive

"Coal Mountain, West Virginia: The medical situation down here is so primitive I can't believe it. Almost no sterile technique possible for anything, including OB. I get an ulcer thinking about it. I had to buy a bottle of Lysol to use as an antiseptic for the present and salve my conscience a little. I haven't had a delivery yet, but there's one woman who should have crashed through ten days ago, so I expect a call from her any minute. My stomach churns whenever I think of it, and I toss for hours at night trying to figure out how to do a delivery here safely.

"That [first] afternoon . . . I damned near panicked. I didn't know what was in the office, who any of the people were, or anything about their medical problems. [My predecessor] had given me a quick tour of the office, what there is of it. He just waved his hand airily toward the shelves of drugs in the little lab—all proprietary names that meant not a thing to me after using the USP terms . . . . It seems the doctor here runs a regular drug store and is supposed to dispense all medications except vitamins and what comes out of a needle without charging anything extra . . . . He didn't have much in the line of patient records—a few cards in a box. I asked him about sterilizing equipment, and he said he bought all his bandages sterile, and not to bother with anything except boiling up needles and syringes in the little electric sterilizer. For deliveries I should just use the cleanest gloves in the OB bag and things would work out all right!"

—Bonta Hiscoe, M.D. from a letter (1949)

kitchen table in the patient's home often became a surgical or birthing table. The ability of the company doctor to improvise was an important characteristic, for he was usually completely on his own. He did not have a nearby hospital or colleague to turn to for help. Sometimes a relative or friend of the sick would give assistance.

Claude A. Frazier
Asheville, North Carolina
Claude A. Frazier and F. K. Brown, *Miners and Medicine: West Virginia Memories*, 1992.

Cockfighting

While illegal, cockfighting is practiced in some parts of West Virginia. It is an ancient blood sport, similar to bullfighting and dogfighting in that it brings serious injury and often death to the animals involved. Cockfighting has roots in many parts of the world, including the British Isles and northwestern Europe. Western Virginia's early settlers descended from these areas, and they brought knowledge of the sport with them. Soon cockfighting established itself in our mountains, as it did throughout North and South America and the Caribbean. It continues today.

Motorists driving through rural West Virginia, especially in the south, sometimes see gamefowl being raised within plain sight of the highway. Typically, the colorful roosters are tethered individually to their own small shelters, often horizontal barrels or A-frame coops, too aggressive to allow within reach of each other. Breeders make the distinction between raising the birds, which is legal, and fighting them, which is not.

Nonetheless, cockfighting takes place on an organized basis in West Virginia and in neighboring counties of Kentucky and Virginia. The existence of the sport sometimes seems to be well-known locally, and the intensity of law enforcement varies. Newspaper accounts report occasional arrests, including a May 2003 raid in McDowell County in which dozens of people were charged. Witnesses report cockfighting arenas in nearby Pike County, Kentucky, as well, with West Virginians among the participants.

Game cocks are specially bred, with breeders often keeping careful genetic records and sometimes developing special blood lines of their own. The cocks are smaller than roosters of most domestic food breeds and often exhibit brilliant plumage inherited from their jungle fowl ancestors. Bred and trained for aggressiveness and naturally equipped with dangerous spurs, fighting cocks often have metal knives or gaffs attached to their legs in preparation to fight. The birds attack by flying into each other, slashing or gouging until one is killed or unable to continue. A majority of the losers die as a result of injuries sustained.

Cockpits may be elaborate arenas, modified barns, or even portable set-ups. The actual fighting pit, above-ground and enclosed to contain the combatants, is surrounded by bleacher-style seats. Birds are said to have been "pitted" once they are placed there to fight. The most common type of cockfight in West Virginia is the derby, where several birds are entered and fight in pairs until one triumphs over all the others. The bouts are closely organized, with competing cocks weighed and carefully matched. If a bout drags on inconclusively, the weakening birds may be rotated to a secondary pit while a fresh pair are started in the main cockpit. Owners pay to enter their birds in a derby, with the winner typically taking the entire pot. Gambling is pervasive among owners and spectators, often for sizable amounts.

Ken Sullivan
West Virginia Humanities Council

Bernard L. Coffindaffer

Preacher Bernard Coffindaffer (1925–1993).

Mysterious crosses appeared along the highways of West Virginia and much of the Southeast in the 1980s and 1990s, in clusters of three, 20 feet tall, the centermost yellow and the others light blue. They are the legacy of the Reverend Bernard L. Coffindaffer of Nicholas County.

Coffindaffer, born January 27, 1925, was a Marine in World War II, serving in the Pacific and wounded on Iwo Jima. He became a successful businessman after the war, but his personal life was not successful. In 1966, his troubled marriage ended in divorce. The next year he underwent a profound religious conversion. Despite finding personal salvation, in 1970 he suffered a mental and physical breakdown and found himself hospitalized in the care of psychiatrists. In 1976, he married June Woodrum, a psychiatric nurse. In 1982, Coffindaffer underwent open-heart surgery.

While napping in 1984, he received what he described as a vision of the spirit of God, telling him to erect crosses, first in West Virginia, then in all 50 states. He promptly sold his extensive business interests and founded Cast Thy Bread, Inc., a nonprofit organization whose mission was to erect prefabricated crosses over the countryside. At their peak, almost 1,900 of the cross clusters were found in West Virginia, other states, and abroad.

Further heart troubles in the early 1990s slowed—but didn't stop—his efforts. However, the millions of dollars he poured into Cast Thy Bread were depleted, forcing an end to cross raising. Coffindaffer died unexpectedly of a heart attack, October 8, 1993, and is buried in Nicholas County, just across the highway from a set of crosses.

Frank P. Herrera
Martinsburg

Arden Cogar Sr.

Woodchopper Arden Cogar Sr., born July 2, 1934, in Webster County, is the winner of many woodchopping competitions. He won nine championships at the highly regarded festival in Hayward, Wisconsin, in 1955. He also competed in Canada and Australia, and in 1965 exhibited his prowess at the New York World's Fair. Cogar's woodchopping skills have garnered several world records that still stand, including a 1978 record in underhand competition for chopping a 12-inch block of yellow poplar in 15.15 seconds. He achieved another world record in 1976, in standing competition, for chopping a 10-inch square of yellow poplar in 16.20 seconds. Events requiring contestants to chop an upright log are his specialty, but Cogar also has won many awards in the underhand event, in which the log rests in a cradle made for that purpose. Cogar, as well as Arden Cogar Jr., participated in the first international team competition in 2001 in Webster County, where he has been a long-time supporter of the annual Woodchopping Festival, held each Memorial Day weekend.

Jaime Simmons
State Archives

Coke Making

Coke is a residue of coal obtained through a process known as destructive distillation. Special ovens are used to burn off the volatile matter—tar, oils and gases—in the coal, leaving mainly fixed carbon. Coke is used primarily in blast furnaces to make pig iron. It serves both as fuel to heat the iron ore and limestone and, by replacing the oxygen in the ore with carbon, as an ingredient in the steel. For centuries, charcoal was used in ironmaking, but a shortage of wood in Great Britain led ironmaster Abraham Darby to distill the world's first coke in 1711. With more plentiful wood, American ironmakers relied on charcoal until the 1840s, when unprocessed anthracite coal was widely adopted for furnace fuel. Coke made from bituminous coal displaced anthracite as the leading blast furnace fuel in America in 1869.

The first coke made in West Virginia was produced in Monongalia County on the banks of the Cheat River in 1843 for use in the Cheat Mountain iron industry. Coke making did not become an important industry in the state until the late-1880s. Coke production increased dramatically during the next 20 years, hitting an all-time high of 4,217,381 tons in 1910. McDowell, Fayette, Marion, and Preston were the leading coke-producing counties. Coke was made near the mines in beehive ovens—brick and stone enclosures with domed tops shaped like beehives. The ovens were loaded or "charged" with coal and sealed with firebricks to restrict the amount of air. The heat stored in the oven from the previous charge ignited the fresh coal. Coal gases escaped through the crown of the oven as noxious smoke. After 72 hours, the coking was complete, and the coke was quenched with a stream of water. During the 1910s, beehive ovens were displaced by more efficient byproduct ovens, which captured the escaping volatile matter for use in making chemicals. West Virginia had few byproduct plants, so the state's coke industry declined; beehive production dwindled to 836,738 tons in 1921. Beehive coke continued to be produced in the state, however, until 1981, when the ovens at Bretz in Preston County were shut down.

Michael Edward Workman
WVU Institute for the History of Technology
Michael E. Workman, *Northern West Virginia Coal Fields: Historical Context*, 1994.

College of Graduate Studies
See Marshall University Graduate College.

College of West Virginia
See Mountain State University.

Justus Collins
Coal operator Justus Collins was born in Clayton, Alabama, December 14, 1857. He began his coal career in his native South, reportedly supervising convict mine labor. About 1887, he resigned as secretary-treasurer of Woodward Iron Company, an Alabama mining firm, to move to the new "smokeless coalfields" of southern West Virginia.

In Mercer County, Collins organized Louisville Coal & Coke Company about 1887, one of the first mines to ship coal on the Norfolk & Western Railroad. In 1893 he opened Collins Colliery in Glen Jean, Fayette County, opened Greenbrier Coal & Coke at about the same time, and later the Whipple mine near Mount Hope. He built identical octagonal company stores at Collins and Whipple, and the Whipple store survives today as a local landmark. In 1906, both the Collins and Whipple mines were sold to the New River Company, and Collins organized Superior Pocahontas Coal. He opened Winding

Gulf mine in 1910, becoming a pioneer in the Winding Gulf Coalfield; his earlier mines were located in the neighboring New River and Pocahontas fields. In 1929, Collins consolidated his mining properties into the Winding Gulf Collieries Company.

Collins's comment that mine managers should strive for a "judicious mixture" of races and nationality groups, on the theory that diversity hampered unionization, is often quoted. Miners resented his labor policies, and he was avidly disliked by rival coal operators, including W. P. Tams and Samuel Dixon. Justus Collins left the coalfields as his business interests expanded, moving his family first to Charleston and then to Cincinnati. He died October 18, 1934.

See also Coal Industry

Ken Sullivan
West Virginia Humanities Council

Colonial Dames of America
Formally known as the National Society of the Colonial Dames of America in the State of West Virginia, the Colonial Dames have a statewide membership of slightly more than 200 women. The West Virginia chapter was organized in 1900, less than a decade after the founding of the national organization. Membership in the Dames is limited to women whose ancestry in America dates to the colonial era.

The organization exists to collect and preserve bygone traditions, and to educate citizens about the past. To that end, the West Virginia society maintains as its headquarters the historic Craik-Patton House, constructed in downtown Charleston in 1834 and moved to its present site at Daniel Boone Park by the Dames in 1973. The house, restored to its original period and opened to the public in 1985, was built by the Reverend James Craik for his bride. Upon the Craiks' departure from Charleston, the house became the property of Col. George Smith Patton in 1855. Following the colonel's demise at Winchester during the Civil War, his widow returned to California. The Patton line later included Gen. George Patton of World War II fame.

Carolanne Griffith Roberts
Southern Living

Columbia Energy Group
The Columbia Gas companies trace their roots to 19th century Ohio. In 1837, the Cincinnati Gas and Electric Company was formed by an act of the Ohio General Assembly to provide manufactured gas to nearly 52,000 customers. In 1883, the company expanded by acquiring the assets in surrounding communities owned by the Ohio Fuel Supply Company. Demand for natural gas service increased dramatically, and the Columbia Corporation was formed in 1906 to construct a

high pressure pipeline across the mountains from the gas fields in West Virginia, a distance of 185 miles. Two months later, the combined company was renamed the Columbia Gas & Electric Company.

During the next 25 years, the utilities industry expanded rapidly, and Columbia grew throughout the mid-Atlantic states by both building and acquiring companies. Congress responded to the growth of utility holding companies and their monopoly power by passing the Wheeler-Rayburn Bill, becoming known as the Public Utility Holding Company Act of 1935. Enforcement of the act resulted in the spin-off of several Columbia subsidiaries, including all those servicing electric customers. The remaining company was the largest natural gas utility in the eastern U.S.

Columbia continued its expansion throughout the rest of the century, building production and gas gathering pipeline systems in the Gulf of Mexico and in Appalachia. The two production regions were connected to storage and retail distribution companies located in seven northeastern states by high pressure gas transmission lines. All aspects of operations in West Virginia were integrated in a company named The United Fuel Gas Company.

In 1972, the company restructured itself along functional lines, with all subsidiaries taking the Columbia name. Management of the transmission pipeline system was headquartered in Charleston, under the name Columbia Gas Transmission Corporation. Appalachian production operations extending across nine states and two Canadian provinces were also headquartered in Charleston, and eventually known as Columbia Natural Resources. Retail distribution operations, known as Columbia Gas of West Virginia, were sold in 1983 to become the Mountaineer Gas Company.

Columbia was forced into bankruptcy in 1991, but emerged after reforming its gas supply contracts in 1995. The company grew dramatically to close the century as the second largest integrated gas utility in the nation. In 2000, a Merrillville, Indiana, utility known as NiSource acquired the common stock of Columbia. NiSource and Columbia were merged to form one of the largest utilities in the country. In 2003, NiSource sold Columbia Natural Resources to a group led by former CNR executives. Columbia Natural Resources was sold to Chesapeake Energy Corporation in 2005.

Columbia Natural Resources and Columbia Gas Transmission are contributors to *The West Virginia Encyclopedia*.

See also Natural Gas and Petroleum

W. Henry Harmon
Triana Energy
Albert F. Dawson, *Columbia System: A History*, 1938.

Company Stores

The company store proliferated in coal-mining, lumber, and textile company towns as the South industrialized in the late 19th and early 20th centuries. In the industrial village it was the central, often the only, retail store available to residents. It was owned by the company, as were the houses, saloons, and other buildings. Modeled in part on the earlier British "truck system," where laborers exchanged their labor for food, fuel, and clothing, company stores in the United States initially were justified as necessities since companies had to provision workers in the remote towns. Yet companies maintained and defended their control of stores well after an efficient transportation network had emerged.

In West Virginia the company store served as a commercial center, a community center, and a formative influence on coal town culture. In 1922, almost 80 percent of West Virginia miners lived in company houses and shopped in company stores, while only 10 percent of miners in Illinois did so. The company store was centrally located in the town, and the store building usually also included the post office and the payroll office. It served as a community center, and its architectural design, while functional, often revealed the cultural origins of its owner. The purpose of the store was profit and support of company policy. Although there is an ongoing debate over the exploitative policies of the company store, companies seldom closed stores even in economic slumps, and the store's use of the private currency called scrip promoted the financial health and stability of the company.

Going to the store was a daily ritual in the life of company town dwellers. Residents converged on the store shortly before the arrival of the mail to chat about work, train schedules, daily events, or family matters. After work, miners often congregated on the store porch after "drawing scrip," to review the day's work or talk of company affairs. Men and women dreamed of acquiring material abundance as they daily viewed the store products while their children stared in wonder at the candy, toys, and sundry items on display in the glass cases.

As coal companies consolidated into larger and larger organizations by the 1920s, store policy became less coercive and more subtle and persuasive in trying to hold onto the business of coal town residents. Since companies could no longer prevent the delivery of goods from independent stores to company houses, company stores began to cater to the consumer desires of residents. Corporations reorganized their stores as separate corporations in order to take advantage of economies of scale and undercut competitors. This technical separation also permitted large companies to circumvent state laws regulating company stores. The company store declined after midcentury with the spread of automobile ownership and the mass marketing of consumer goods through mail order catalogs and chain stores.

See also Company Towns, Scrip

Lou Athey
Franklin & Marshall College

Louis L. Athey, "The Company Store in Coal Town Culture," *Labor's Heritage*, January 1990.

Company Towns

Before 1880, much of West Virginia's rural landscape was made up of dispersed farms and small settlements along valley floors and coves. Country life was simple, quiet, and devoted chiefly to agricultural pursuits. During the decade of the 1880s, however, a transformation in settlement patterns began to take place with the development of industry, particularly coal mining. As railroads penetrated the coal-bearing landscape of West Virginia, mining entrepreneurs leased land, opened mines, and built whole communities. Almost overnight peaceful agricultural valleys changed to energetic company towns.

In coal country, a company town consisted of an agglomeration of dwellings and other buildings situated around the mine. The coal company bought or leased land on which the structures were built, typically including at least a company store, a tipple, dwellings, a church, a school, and a post office. Company towns were not incorporated places, and they had no institutions of government.

In most West Virginia company towns, houses were distributed in an orderly manner reflecting the economic and social hierarchy. The administrators occupied the better houses, either on slopes overlooking the settlement or in the center of the town. Lower-quality housing, often situated on the edge of the community, was occupied by white miners. Blacks and immigrants were located apart, often farther out in less desirable areas near the mine entrances or along hillsides. The mine superintendent usually lived in a mansion having from ten to 20 rooms and located on a large lot with trees and well-kept grounds. Superintendents sometimes attempted to surpass each other by building larger and more elaborate houses for themselves.

The miners' houses were much simpler. For economic reasons, there was a tendency toward uniformity in construction of simple three-or four-room dwellings monotonously similar in style. Houses were often painted the same color throughout the town, and some colors were associated with particular companies or towns. Company towns, even substantial ones, were often referred to as "coal camps."

There was a wide range in the quality of West Virginia company towns. Some were better than comparable independent communities, while others were filthy and decrepit. Some were harshly repressive, and others largely free. In West Virginia, company towns existed almost entirely within the coal industry. Timber companies operated rough logging camps of temporary duration and often portable. Cass and a few other large sawmill towns approached the company town model, though they rarely were entirely owned and governed by the mill company.

The life span of the company town usually was 50 to 75 years, or as long as the coal seams were productive. Company towns were especially plentiful in

A Marion County coal company store, about 1940.

Slab Fork, a Raleigh County company town, early in the 20th century.

southern West Virginia. In 1930, there were an estimated 465 coal company towns in West Virginia, with the majority in the southern counties of Raleigh, Fayette, McDowell, Logan, and Mingo. There are no company-owned towns today, although remnants of many survive as privately owned communities.

See also Coal Industry, Company Stores

Mack H. Gillenwater
Marshall University

Ronald D. Eller, *Miners, Millhands, and Mountaineers: Industrialization of the Appalachian South, 1880–1930,* 1982; Mack H. Gillenwater, "Cultural and Historical Geography of Mining Settlements in the Pocahontas Coal Field of Southern West Virginia, 1880–1930," Ph.D. dissertation, University of Tennessee, 1972.

Jim Comstock

Jim Comstock, country editor (1911–96).

Newspaperman James Franklin "Jim" Comstock was born February 25, 1911, in Richwood, the son of Harry Clinton Comstock and Myrtle Blanche Cunningham

Comstock. He received his B.A. from Marshall College in 1934.

He was a teacher at Richwood High School from 1938 until 1942 and also wrote for the *Clarksburg Telegram* during that period. Later he worked for a defense plant before serving in the U.S. Navy, 1944–46. Back in Richwood, he founded the *Richwood News Leader* in 1946 and served as its editor. In 1957, he founded the *West Virginia Hillbilly*, a weekly ("weakly," according to its masthead) newspaper that circulated both inside and outside the state. The paper was characterized by Comstock's wry humor and conservative politics.

In addition to his newspaper writing, Comstock's publications include the books *Pa and Ma and Mr. Kennedy* and *Best of Hillbilly*, and a 50-volume *West Virginia Heritage Encyclopedia*. Comstock operated a bookstore adjacent to the offices of the *Hillbilly,* and he started the Mountain State Press to publish books of West Virginia interest. Comstock ran as a Republican for Congress in 1963, losing to incumbent John M. Slack Jr. He also founded the University of Hard Knocks to recognize the accomplishments of successful individuals who never attended college. Alderson-Broaddus College in Philippi hosted the "university's" annual commencement ceremony on its campus.

Among Comstock's best-known practical jokes was once including pungent ramp juice in the ink used to print the *West Virginia Hillbilly.* The odor when he mailed that week's papers was so offensive that he received a reprimand from the postmaster general. On another occasion he perpetuated an elaborate hoax involving the use of a captive mountain lion, to convince editor Calvin Price of neighboring Pocahontas County that mountain lions still existed in West Virginia.

A popular speaker and the best-known newspaperman of his generation, Jim Comstock was Mr. West Virginia in the hearts of many Mountaineers. He spear-

headed the purchase and preservation of Nobel-Prize-winning author Pearl Buck's birthplace at Hillsboro, helped pay for the rescue of the historic Cass Scenic Railroad, and frequently conducted quizzes on West Virginia history for students. He sold the *Hillbilly* to Sandy McCauley in 1992. Comstock died May 22, 1996, at St. Mary's Hospital in Huntington and was buried in Mountain View Cemetery at the top of a hill overlooking his native Richwood.

See also Richwood, West Virginia Hillbilly

Tom D. Miller
Huntington

Concord University

Having lost the county seat to Princeton, the disappointed people of Concord lobbied for a state school, and on February 28, 1872, the West Virginia legislature passed the necessary legislation to establish a "branch state normal school" in the Mercer County community. The act required that certain land and a building be conveyed to the state, but the owner died before title was transferred.

The act was amended in 1873 and stipulated that the school would be transferred to Princeton if arrangements for land and a building were not completed within one year. Land was donated, $2,000 raised, a primitive building constructed, and, lacking a bell, a cow's horn trumpet called 70 students to begin classes on May 10, 1875. Capt. James Harvey French was the first principal and headed the school until his death in 1891, a 16-year tenure equaled by President Joseph Franklin Marsh Sr., (1929–45) and exceeded by current president, Jerry Lynn Beasley (1985–).

In 1895, $20,000 was appropriated for a new academic building to replace a small, brick structure built with state funds in the 1880s. With a fine school building, Concord became an institution of major importance in West Virginia. In 1896, "Athens," for the ancient Greek city

A 48-bell carillon crowns Marsh Hall at Concord University.

of learning and culture, was selected as the new name for the post office and village. The school's relatively isolated location was promoted in its catalogs as being "far removed from all those sources of vice and dissipation so numerous in the vicinity of many institutions of learning."

A fire destroyed the 1895 building the night of November 22, 1910, but by 8:00 a.m. community leaders arranged for teaching the 300 students in rooms throughout the town. The legislature directed that $14,000 from insurance plus $36,000 in appropriations be used for another new building to be located on 26.4 acres of donated land, and the campus was moved from the center of town to its present site on the outskirts when the building opened for students in September 1912. This building, now enlarged and completely renovated, is the core of Concord's campus, and in 1997 was crowned with West Virginia's only true carillon, a 20-ton musical instrument of 48 tuned, bronze bells cast in France.

Most unusual for the early 1900s, a woman, Frances Isabel Davenport, served for one year (1906–07) as principal. The title was changed from principal to president when the "branch normal schools" were separated from Marshall College (now Marshall University) in 1919, and the Athens institution became independent as Concord State Normal School. In 1923, the first baccalaureate degrees were awarded to three graduates, but the number of two-year "standard normal" diplomas exceeded baccalaureate degrees through 1936, when the program was abolished.

During the presidency of J. F. Marsh Sr., the college gained full accreditation in 1931. Reflecting an expanding curriculum, the institution's name was changed to Concord State Teachers College in 1931 and to Concord College in 1943. Enrollment averaged 657 during the Great Depression, and Marsh added 13 major buildings. During World War II, he secured an Army Air Force cadet training unit that increased enrollment to 950. Following the war and the loss of a military unit, returning veterans, subsidized by the GI Bill, kept enrollment around 1,000 through 1950, and the "Baby Boomers" increased enrollment to 2,019 by 1971.

While French, Marsh Sr., and Beasley hold the records of longest tenures of 16 or more years as head of the institution, two presidents have served for 14 years: Virgil Harvey Stewart (1945–59) and Joseph Franklin Marsh Jr. (1959–73). With post-war growth during the Stewart years, a Science Hall, housing units for married students, and a new athletic field were built.

Marsh Jr., son of a former president, was 34 when he entered office. He continued the expansion of the curriculum, emphasized quality and high academic standards, recruited a cosmopolitan faculty, and added major buildings to the campus. Almost all of Concord's current physical plant was built during the administrations of Marsh Sr. and Jr.

In the 1970s the Board of Regents proposed merging Concord with Bluefield State College, which was vigorously opposed by all constituencies of Concord. Although legislation failed, the Regents proceeded with an "administrative merger." After two years, the Regents announced that a return to separate administrations would occur in 1976. Enrollment, which had dropped from 2,019 in 1971 to 1,675 in 1976, increased, reaching 2,356 at the beginning of Beasley's presidency in 1985.

The college has prospered under President Beasley's leadership, and the main academic buildings have been expanded and renovated. A privately funded endowment exceeds $22 million. The legislature approved university status for Concord effective July 1, 2004. Concord University has an outstanding faculty, with 85 percent holding terminal degrees; modern facilities and residence halls (17 major buildings) in a 123-acre picturesque setting; a reputation for superior instruction and high standards; and, 13 nationally accredited bachelor's and master's degrees in more than 80 majors, minors and special programs. In 2005, *U.S. News & World Report* ranked Concord among the top three comprehensive, bachelor's, public colleges in the south, and the university enrolled approximately 3,000 undergraduate and graduate students.

Concord University is a contributor to *The West Virginia Encyclopedia*.

Joseph F. Marsh Jr.
Concord University

Confederate Soldiers in West Virginia

West Virginia is the only state born out of the Civil War, and its allegiances were severely divided by the conflict. Many residents served the Confederate cause, a majority of them joining the Virginia forces mobilized by Gov. John Letcher. Many saw their duty as the defense of their homes and soil from a Northern invasion.

Analysis of service records shows that the typical West Virginia Confederate volunteer was a farmer in his early 20s, about five feet, ten inches tall. Half the soldiers were married when they entered service. As with the Confederate forces from other states, the majority served in the infantry, with the cavalry being the second most popular branch of service. Fewer than 1,000 served in the artillery and a few hundred served in other capacities, such as medical, navy, or marines.

Confederate units composed principally of West Virginians included the 22nd, 31st, 36th, and 62nd Virginia infantry regiments; the 26th, 30th, and 45th battalions of Virginia infantry; the 8th, 16th, 17th, 18th, 19th, and 20th Virginia cavalry regiments; and Bryan's, Chapman's, and Lowry's artillery batteries. West Virginia Confederate soldiers fought in most of the battles east of the Mississippi, including Gettysburg, first and second Manassas, Antietam, and countless lesser skirmishes.

It is difficult to determine the number of Confederate soldiers from West Virginia. Records were destroyed when the Confederate capitol at Richmond burned, and regimental rosters were captured or destroyed in battle. For decades the most often quoted number of West Virginia Confederates was 7,000. More recent research, using sources such as the Compiled Service Records, shows that 16,000 to 18,000 men from West Virginia fought for the Confederacy.

If we accept the generally quoted figure that 32,000 men from West Virginia fought for the Union, the significance of 18,000 Confederates is that the true ratio of Union to Confederate soldiers from West Virginia counties is not five or six to one as historians held for many years. This ratio of 32,000 to 18,000 shows that loyalties of the West Virginia counties were not as unbalanced in favor of the Union as was once thought.

See also Civil War

Jack L. Dickinson
Huntington

Jack L. Dickinson, *Tattered Uniforms and Bright Bayonets: West Virginia's Confederate Soldiers*, 1995.

Congressional Medal of Honor

Fifty-three West Virginians have received the Medal of Honor since its creation by act of Congress on July 12, 1862, during the Civil War. Seventeen of the awards were made posthumously, to men who died while performing the deed for which they were cited, including the only conscientious objector to win the medal. The Medal of Honor is awarded for bravery above and beyond the call of duty to members of its military and naval forces. It is the highest award for heroism bestowed by the United States.

Medals of Honor were awarded to 23 West Virginians for deeds of heroism performed during the Civil War, at battles in places such as Vicksburg, Mississippi, and Petersburg and Sailors Creek, Virginia. Benjamin C. Criswell won his medal at the Little Big Horn River, Montana, with Custer's 7th Cavalry in 1876.

The record of Mountain State valor continued through the Philippine, Mexican, and Santo Domingo campaigns, with a total of seven recipients. Brothers Antoine (Tony) and Julien Gaujot won

their medals during the Phillipine Insurrection and America's 1914 invasion of Vera Cruz, Mexico, respectively. Hugh Frazer and Henry Nickerson also won their medals at Vera Cruz. Robert Cox and Claude Jones won their medals for noncombatant heroism aboard U.S. Navy vessels in efforts to save them from sinking. No West Virginian was awarded the Medal of Honor during World War I.

Ten West Virginians won Medals of Honor in World War II, including two in Germany (Clinton Hedrick and Jonah Kelley) and one each on Bougainville (Herbert Thomas) and Iwo Jima (Hershel Williams). During the Korean Conflict, West Virginians Darwin Kyle, Cornelius Charlton, and Ralph Pomeroy were awarded the Medal of Honor.

The Vietnam War was America's longest war. Nine West Virginians were awarded the Medal of Honor, but only one lived to receive his medal. These men paid the supreme sacrifice to earn the nation's top military honor. Thomas Bennett was the first conscientious objector to receive the Medal of Honor. He refused to carry a weapon but served in the army as a medic, and was killed by gunfire while rescuing a wounded soldier.

See also Tom Bennett

Larry N. Sypolt
West Virginia University

United States Congress, Senate Committee on Veterans Affairs, *Medal of Honor Recipients, 1863–1978: In the Name of the Congress of the United States*, 1979.

Congressional Representation

The first congressional delegation from the new state of West Virginia was seated when the 38th Congress convened in the middle of the Civil War on December 7, 1863. Peter G. Van Winkle from Parkersburg and Waitman T. Willey from Morgantown had been elected by the West Virginia legislature to be the first U.S. senators. Jacob B. Blair of Parkersburg (First District), William G. Brown of Kingwood (Second District), and Kellian V. Whaley of Point Pleasant (Third District) were elected by popular vote as the first three representatives.

The U.S. Constitution directs that each state have two senators regardless of population size. The full term of a senator is six years. To stagger the election of senators, the Constitution divides the Senate into three even-numbered groups or classes. The first West Virginia senators, Van Winkle and Willey, drew lots to determine in which class or election cycle each would participate, Van Winkle winning a full six-year term, to expire in 1869, and Willey a term to expire in 1865, after only two years. Willey was subsequently elected for a full six-year term and served until 1871.

Thirty men have served West Virginia as U.S. senators. One senator, Matthew

M. Neely, resigned his seat, which he did in January 1941 after being elected governor. Five senators died in office, and four of these seats were filled temporarily by appointment from the governor until an election could be held. None of the appointed senators was subsequently elected. The state legislature elected U.S. senators until the 1912 passage of the 17th Amendment to the Constitution, which required popular elections of states. The first popularly elected senator was Howard Sutherland, elected in 1916 with 50.1 percent of the vote.

The vast majority of the elected senators have served either six or 12 years. Three have served 18 years or more, Stephen B. Elkins (1895–1913), Harley M. Kilgore (1941–59), and Jay Rockefeller (1984–). The two longest-serving senators were elected and reelected in the latter half of the 20th century when the Democratic Party became dominant in the state. Jennings Randolph served more than 26 years (1958–85). Robert C. Byrd is the longest-serving senator in West Virginia history and one of the longest-serving in American history. He was first elected in 1958 and was reelected for an eighth consecutive term in 2000, the only person to reach this electoral landmark. If Senator Byrd serves his full term, which expires in 2007, he will have served 48 years as a U.S. senator.

The Constitution directs that each state have a number of members in the House of Representatives based upon its population size. The Constitution further directs that a census be held every 10 years to count the population, and this count is used to allocate the number of representatives for each state. The term of each representative is two years, and the entire House is elected every two years.

The West Virginia population rose steadily from the 1870 census, the first after creation of the state, until reaching its peak in the 1950 census. The size of the West Virginia delegation in the House likewise rose, from the original three to a maximum of six from the 1910s through the 1950s. In the latter half of the 20th century, the population declined in some decades and in others showed only slow growth compared with the rest of the nation. The number of West Virginia representatives consequently declined during the period from six to three, reaching the latter number after the 1990 census.

As of 2002, 96 men and two women have served West Virginia in the House of Representatives. As in the U.S. Senate, those elected late in the 20th century generally have served the longest, including Nick Joe Rahall of the Third District (1977–). Harley O. Staggers Sr. of the old Second District served longest of all, from 1949–1980.

Throughout West Virginia history, congressional representatives have been elected from single-member districts. However, in two elections, 1912 and 1914, one additional at-large representative was elected statewide until a new redistricting law could be passed increasing the districts from five to six in accordance with the 1910 census. States draw their own congressional districts. To pass a congressional redistricting law, the West Virginia House of Delegates, Senate, and governor must all approve, as is the case in all state statutes. If the governor and the two chambers of the legislature are all controlled by the same political party, then this party can draw districts to favor itself. Historically, West Virginia redrew its congressional districts only when a change in the number of representatives was required. However, since the U.S. Supreme Court ruling in the 1960s mandating districts of roughly equal population, West Virginia has passed a congressional redistricting law after every census to adjust district boundaries even if the number of districts did not change.

West Virginia's congressional politics reflects the state's history and location. For the first 100 years, West Virginia was a border state, between a solid Republican North and a solid Democratic South. West Virginia politics was born at the time of the Civil War. The northern Ohio Valley cities had been influenced greatly by the emerging anti-slavery Republican Party in the late 1850s and early 1860s. But its Virginia roots also influenced the new state. In fact, Western Virginia had sent almost all Democrats to the U.S. House of Representatives from the mid-1840s to the Civil War. In the early years after the creation of West Virginia, the best identification for the new state's senators and representatives was Unionists or Unconditional Unionists, a mixture of anti-secession and pro-Union Democrats, Republicans, and those sympathetic to the Republican Party. After the Civil War, most of West Virginia's national representation slowly identified with the Republican Party.

By the mid-1870s, the Democrats had gained supremacy in West Virginia, electing both senators and all three representatives. This Democratic supremacy lasted until the 1894 elections, following the financial Panic of 1893. This economic depression occurred when the Democrats were in control nationally, and in retribution the North, West, and the border states shifted to the Republicans for almost 40 years. For the most part, this was the case in West Virginia.

The next political party switch came with the Great Depression of the 1930s. The October 1929 stock market crash occurred while the Republicans were in control. By 1932, voting patterns had re-aligned again in the urban North, the West, and the border states, this time from Republican to Democrat. Once more, West Virginia was affected by the national trend. Although nationally the Republican Party dominated presidential elections at the end of the 20th century and the Republicans gained control of the U.S. House and the Senate in the historic elections of 1994, West Virginia remains staunchly in the Democratic column. Statewide, the Republicans have not won a U.S. Senate election since Chapman Revercomb in 1956, and the Democrats also dominate House elections in West Virginia. This congressional party domination is also reflected in most gubernatorial elections and the overwhelming Democratic control of the state legislature. In 2000, however, West Virginia surprised the nation by voting for Republican George W. Bush for president, and elected a Republican in the second congressional district.

Kenneth C. Martis
West Virginia University
Kenneth C. Martis, *The Historical Atlas of Political Parties in the United States Congress: 1789–1989*, 1989; Kenneth C. Martis and Gregory Elmes, *The Historical Atlas of State Power in Congress: 1790–1990*, 1993.

Phil Conley

Author, editor, and publisher Philip Mallory "Phil" Conley was born in Charleston, November 30, 1887. After graduating from West Virginia University in 1914, he taught one term at Glenville State Normal School. From 1914 to 1918, he served as superintendent of schools in Lincoln District in Marion County. He was superintendent of schools in Jenkins, Kentucky, from 1919 to 1921. During World War I, Conley served as a second lieutenant in the U.S. Army and was decorated with the Chevalier Legion of Honor of France.

From 1921 to 1923, Conley was managing director of the American Constitutional Association, a conservative organization formed by concerned businessmen in the wake of the West Virginia Mine Wars. He was publisher of the *West Virginia Review*, a popular magazine, from 1923 to 1946. In 1923, Conley founded the West Virginia Publishing Company and served as president until 1950. He was founder of the Charleston Printing Company, serving as president from 1936 to 1948 and chairman of its board of directors from 1948 to 1979. Meanwhile, in 1950 he established the West Virginia Education Foundation, which he served as president. This nonprofit organization later became the West Virginia Historical Education Foundation.

Conley was editor-in-chief of the *West Virginia Encyclopedia,* published in 1929. *West Virginia: Yesterday and Today*, one of his best-known books, was for many years a popular public school textbook and with various co-authors has passed through several editions. He presented numerous radio programs on West Virginia (one of which ran for ten years) and originated the Golden Horseshoe Contest.

Conley married Pearl Scott on August 5, 1914. They had one adopted daughter, Phyllis C. Warren. Phil Conley died in Charleston, August 1, 1979.

Marshall Buckalew
Charleston

William Gustavus Conley

Governor William G. Conley (1866–1940).

William Gustavus Conley was the 18th governor of West Virginia, serving from 1929 to 1933. Born January 8, 1866, near Kingwood in Preston County, Conley attended district schools and as a young man worked on the family farm, drove mules on railroad gangs, dug coal, and worked in quarries and sawmills to help support his sisters and widowed mother. He taught school from 1886 to 1891 and served as superintendent of Preston County schools from 1891 to 1893.

He earned a law degree from West Virginia University in 1893 and began practicing law in Parsons, Tucker County. While there Conley founded the *Parsons Advocate* newspaper in 1896 and acted as editor until 1903. A Republican, he became active in local politics as prosecuting attorney for Tucker County, a member of the Parsons city council from 1897 to 1899, and as mayor from 1901 to 1903. Returning to Kingwood, Conley continued his political involvement as city council member and mayor of that town from 1906 to 1908. Governor Dawson appointed Conley to an unexpired term as West Virginia attorney general in the spring of 1908, and in November he was elected to that office. He was narrowly defeated in the congressional race in West Virginia's second district in 1912, after which he practiced law in Charleston, representing corporate clients such as the Baltimore & Ohio and Pennsylvania railroads. Conley remained involved in Republican politics and pursued an interest in the coal industry as president of the West Virginia Eagle Coal Company and the Coalfield Fuel Company.

Conley defeated Democrat Alfred Taylor in the 1928 gubernatorial race by nearly 50,000 votes. His tenure as governor coincided with the darkest days of the Great Depression. More than 30,000 West Virginia coal jobs disappeared between 1929 and 1932, 100 banks failed, and farmers were devastated by severe droughts and the collapse of farm prices. Equal disasters plagued manufacturing in the state. Faced with these crises, Conley diverged from his intrinsic suspicion of what he referred to as government paternalism and promoted state fiscal initiatives and direct federal relief to combat the effects of the Depression.

Democratic victories in state elections in 1930, resulting in the first Democratic legislative majority in West Virginia since 1923, made the 64-year-old Conley a virtual lame duck halfway through his term. Realizing that he had no political future after the governorship and disturbed at the specter of unemployed West Virginia veterans marching on Washington in the summer of 1932, Conley altered his ideological aversion to what he called the "government nursing bottle" and carried out a moderately activist relief agenda. He shifted some county road funds into direct relief for the hungry and unemployed and issued state bonds for road construction in order to stimulate employment. He also advocated "sin" and luxury taxes to fund expanded state unemployment relief. Many of Conley's relief proposals, however, failed to win support from the Democratic majority.

Republicans and Democrats alike sought credit for implementation of the most important legislation of Conley's term, the Tax Limitation Amendment, which emerged from a special session called by the governor in the summer of 1932. Voters in the 1932 election approved the popular measure designed to provide universal property tax relief, and it took effect after Conley left office. The populist appeal of the amendment proved illusory, as low property tax ceilings forced the state to assume school financing and road maintenance services that previously had been the responsibility of the counties. Subsequent conservative Democratic administrations addressed revenue shortfalls created by the amendment with regressive taxation on such items as food and medicines.

After his term ended, Conley returned to private law practice in Charleston. He was head of the firm of Conley, Thompson, and Neff when he died at age 74, October 21, 1940.

See also Great Depression

John Hennen
Morehead State University

Jerry Bruce Thomas, *An Appalachian New Deal: West Virginia in the Great Depression*, 1998; John G. Morgan, *West Virginia Governors*, 1980; John Alexander Williams, *West Virginia: A History*, 1984.

Conrail

The Consolidated Rail Corporation (Conrail) was created in 1976 to operate the bankrupt Penn Central Railroad. It was a for-profit corporation with credit guaranteed by the U.S. government.

In West Virginia, Conrail operated the old New York Central (later Penn Central) line from Point Pleasant through Charleston to a connection with the former Virginian (now Norfolk Southern) Railroad east of Charleston. By 1976, this line was of limited significance to the economy of West Virginia, thus the creation of Conrail had little effect on the state. Any hope for effective competition with the Chessie System was not realized because Norfolk Southern routed only small amounts of traffic over the former Virginian line.

For the first five years, Conrail appeared to do no better than Penn Central. Freight traffic suffered with industrial decline in the service region, and equipment and rail maintenance languished. New management after 1980 and liberalized operating rules allowed after passage of the Northeast Rail Reorganization Act of 1981 brought a turnaround. Conrail posted its first profitable quarter in 1981 and from then until 1999 yielded a profit annually.

The Northeast Rail Reorganization Act had identified 1984 as the year to make Conrail totally private, and plans were made to sell the system to Norfolk Southern. So much opposition developed that Norfolk Southern withdrew its bid. Eventually, Norfolk Southern and CSX (formerly Chessie) developed a plan to divide Conrail between themselves. This plan included Norfolk Southern acquisition of the former Conrail line in West Virginia. In 1999, Conrail ceased to exist as a separate entity.

Robert L. Frey
Miamisburg, Ohio

Conservation Movement

The vast original forests in what is now West Virginia had some of the greatest stands of hardwood timber to be found anywhere. These forests were intensely exploited between 1870 and 1920 and eventually timbered out. Because of the considerable amount of slash left behind, fires followed the timber cutting, setting back natural forest regeneration and exposing soils to erosion. With the headwaters of the Monongahela River denuded of vegetation and no longer able to regulate the flow of water, devastating flooding occurred in March 1907. This flooding seriously affected agricultural lands and cities in the Monongahela basin, including Pittsburgh, causing about $100 million in damages.

Actions by Congress in 1908 and by the West Virginia legislature in 1909 prepared the way for the establishment of a National Forest Reserve in the Monongahela watershed. The Weeks Bill, passed by Congress in 1911, enabled cooperation between the states and federal government for the protection of watersheds of navigable streams including the acquisition of lands. The first land in West Virginia was acquired in 1915, becoming the Monongahela National Forest on April 28, 1920. Protection of the newly acquired woodlands was the early focus, with fire prevention in the cut-over woods being a major concern. The passage of the Clarke-McNary Act by Congress in 1924 broadened the purpose of the national forests to include the production of timber.

The Shenandoah (now George Washington) National Forest was created in 1917, with its bulk in Virginia but including parts of Pendleton, Hardy, and Hampshire counties. The Jefferson National Forest, including a small part of Monroe County, was created in 1936.

In 1933, during the Great Depression, President Franklin D. Roosevelt established the Civilian Conservation Corps, designed to put unemployed youth to work and to apply conservation measures to lands newly acquired by the federal government and to similar state lands. Camps were soon established throughout the country. The Monongahela National Forest had 12 such camps operating at one time. The "CCC boys," many just out of major cities, accomplished great things. They planted trees; fought forest fires; built roads, trails, fire towers, telephone lines, and structures; conducted fish and wildlife habitat and monitoring work; and made watershed improvements. Their labor provided valuable park and forest facilities still in use in the 21st century.

Early settlement, later timbering, and the general exploitation of the land, its flora and fauna, all had taken a serious toll on the state's wildlife. Deer, turkey, and bear populations were seriously diminished. Local scarcities of deer were noted as early as 1841, and by 1900 only remnant deer and turkey populations were left, concentrated in remote areas of the high mountains. Black bears were reduced to about 500 animals. The beaver, once common throughout the state, was extirpated by 1923 because of its valuable fur.

A deer restocking program was initiated in 1933 by the state and sportsmen's groups and continued until 1957. Deer are now common throughout the state, and in some counties there are too many. Wild turkeys benefited from farm abandonment, hunting restrictions, and forest maturation. Turkey restoration was accomplished by trapping birds and transplanting them to new habitats. Today the wild turkey is abundant in all 55 counties. The black bear became the state animal in 1955. With carefully designed hunting regulations and a greater public acceptance, bears now exist in a large portion of the state and number about 10,000 animals. Beavers, which contribute greatly to the development of wetlands, were reintroduced in the state's high elevations from 1933 to 1940. This largest rodent is now distributed statewide.

Wildlife conservation started as early as 1869, when the state legislature passed the first game law, protecting game species between February 14 and September 15 and protecting all species of nongame birds except a few considered injurious. The legislature of 1877 created a Fish Commission, and the first game and fish warden was appointed. Forest fires caused mammoth destruction in 1908 and were largely responsible for legislation of 1909 authorizing the governor to appoint a Forest, Game and Fish Warden. The Game and Fish Commission was created by the legislature in 1921. Through many subsequent legislative and executive actions these early efforts evolved toward the modern Division of Natural Resources, its work now complemented by the Division of Forestry and other agencies. In the 1930s, Governor Kump, himself deeply interested in the outdoors, put the state's first comprehensive conservation bureaucracy in place, with sections for forestry, law enforcement, game management, fish management, state parks, and education.

Early wildlife management efforts mostly consisted of establishing refuges and small game propagation and stocking. The legislature of 1915 gave authority to the state's Forest, Game and Fish warden to establish refuges for protection of wild game and birds. Such early efforts generally failed to accomplish objectives. Therefore, the present approach to wildlife management is that of habitat restoration and development. Federal funding, authorized by passage of the Pittman-Robertson and Dingell-Johnson acts, has greatly benefited fish and wildlife conservation efforts in West Virginia and throughout the country.

As the 20th century progressed toward its conclusion, environmental organizations joined the traditional hunting and fishing constituency in adding impetus to the conservation effort. The wise use of the natural environment became an issue of concern to the travel and tourism industry, whose success in West Virginia was increasingly based on outdoor recreation and the state's scenic beauty. Sometimes the groups differed in philosophy and goals but all agreed on the importance of conserving West Virginia's great outdoors.

See also Civilian Conservation Corps, Division of Natural Resources, George Washington National Forest, Jefferson National Forest, Monongahela National Forest

Walter A. Lesser
Elkins

Kenneth L. Carvell and William R. Maxey, *Protectors of the Forest Resources, A History of the West Virginia Division of Forestry, 1909–1998,* 1998; Roy B. Clarkson, *Tumult on the Mountains,* 1964; Steven L. Stephenson, ed., *Upland Forests of West Virginia,* 1993.

Consolidated Bus Lines

Consolidated Bus Lines, with offices in Bluefield, West Virginia, served southern West Virginia, eastern Kentucky, and southwestern Virginia during the middle part of the 20th century. Consolidated provided an essential service to the busy coalfields, and later became part of a national bus line. Its 1,200-mile system extended from Huntington to Roanoke, Virginia, and provided service to cities and towns such as Charleston, Logan, Welch (its busiest hub), Mullens, Princeton, Williamson, East Rainelle, Beckley, and Pineville; as well as Grundy and Richlands, Virginia, and Pikeville, Kentucky. By 1953, Consolidated Bus Lines employed 337 individuals and operated about 100 buses. In 1952 alone, these buses traveled 5,873,468 miles and carried an estimated 7,881,663 passengers.

The company was founded by James Elliott "Jack" Craft, a native of Breathitt County, Kentucky. Largely uneducated, Craft migrated to the coalfields of West Virginia to find work in the mines. After working long enough to repay the coal company his transportation expenses, he worked at different locations throughout the southern coalfields. It was in McDowell County that he fell in love with the great invention of that time, the automobile. Capitalizing on that interest, he started by driving coal company executives on their rounds and in 1921 established a Welch taxi service with a single Model-T Ford. After this proved profitable, he expanded into providing bus service to various coalfield towns. As his business grew Craft acquired other small bus lines, establishing Consolidated in January 1934. On August 1, 1956, Craft sold his business to Virginia Stage Lines, a Trailways affiliate. Bus service was discontinued in most of southern West Virginia by the early 1970s.

Robert Beanblossom
Division of Natural Resources
James Elliott Craft, *Wheels on the Mountain,* 1969.

Consolidation Coal Company

The Consolidation Coal Company, a major mine operator in West Virginia and neighboring areas throughout the 20th century, was a vehicle of wealth and power for an important political family.

Consolidation Coal Company was organized in Maryland in April 1864 and soon took control of a number of mines in Maryland's George's Creek coalfield. The company was well-named, building itself by the consolidation of smaller operations. During the 1880s and 1890s, because of the low cost of beginning mining operations and a high protective tariff, coal flooded from America's mines. As supply exceeded demand, falling prices hurt producers. The consolidation of mines, by those with the capital to do it, was an opportunity to eliminate competition. "Consol," as it was often called, expanded into West Virginia and Pennsylvania by this method. In early 1903, the company purchased a majority interest in the Fairmont Coal Company, which itself had consolidated most of the mines in the Fairmont field. With financial backing from the Baltimore & Ohio Railroad, Consol also purchased Clarksburg Fuel Company in West Virginia and the Somerset Coal Company in Pennsylvania.

The Fleming-Watson family, principal owners of Fairmont Coal Company, found a solid foothold in the acquiring company. In 1906, the family strengthened its position and paid $5 million for 53 percent of the stock of the Consolidation Coal, Fairmont Coal, and Somerset Coal companies. This way, the influential family took control. In 1909, with the collaboration of their partner, U.S. Sen. Johnson N. Camden, and the blessing of Camden associate John D. Rockefeller, the three companies were combined into Consolidation Coal Company. Former Governor Fleming served as chief counsel and on the board of directors, while his brother-in-law, U.S. Sen. Clarence W. Watson, remained as either chairman of the board or president of the corporation until 1928.

Continued expansion in West Virginia, Pennsylvania, and Kentucky during the first two decades of the 20th century made it increasingly difficult for independent companies to compete with the growing company. When the economy went bad, as it did in 1929, the weaker coal companies collapsed and Consolidation Coal Company itself went into receivership. The company survived and continued to consolidate its holdings, but the Fleming-Watson group lost control at this time. Today, Consol remains the nation's largest bituminous coal producer, with most of its mines in northern West Virginia and neighboring areas of Pennsylvania. The company, now named CONSOL Energy, is controlled by Rheinbraun, a German firm.

See also Johnson Newlon Camden, Coal Industry, Aretas Brooks Fleming, Clarence W. Watson, James O. Watson

Jeffrey B. Cook
North Greenville College

Jeffrey B. Cook, "The Ambassador of Development: Aretas Brooks Fleming, West Virginia's Political Entrepreneur, 1839–1923," Ph.D. dissertation, West Virginia University, 1998; John Alexander Williams, *West Virginia and the Captains of Industry,* 1976.

Constitution of 1830

As Virginia's western population grew, it became apparent that the state's original constitution of 1776 was in need of reform. In 1816, at Staunton, representatives from 38 counties called for a constitutional convention. Westerners wanted a greater share of government as their portion of the population grew. Representation in the House of Delegates was the principal issue, because it was not based on population. Eastern conservatives, fearing loss of power to the growing West, opposed changing representation to a population basis.

In 1824, a second meeting in Staunton again called for a constitutional convention. Finally, during the 1827–28 session, the legislature agreed to submit the matter to a vote of the freeholders or property owners. By a vote of 21,896 to 16,646, the voters approved the calling of a convention. By and large, easterners opposed the call, and westerners favored it. In the spring of 1829 the voters elected convention delegates. Of the 96 delegates, 36 were from the west.

In October 1829, the delegates assembled at Richmond. It was the last great gathering of the greatest generation of Virginians. Among the delegates were two former presidents, James Madison and James Monroe, U.S. Chief Justice John Marshall, both U.S. senators, and 11 of Virginia's congressmen. James Monroe was chosen president of the convention.

The westerners gained only slight concessions. Representation in the legislature was equally divided into four sections—Tidewater, Piedmont, Shenandoah Valley, and Trans-Allegheny. The right to vote was slightly extended, but not to all white male taxpayers as the west preferred. Popular election of the governor was defeated, though his term was extended from one to three years. Efforts to reform the method of appointing judges and local officials failed.

Adopted by the convention on January 15, 1830, by a vote of 55 to 40, the new constitution was submitted to the voters. Only the freeholders, householders, and leaseholders could vote, and they did so, 26,055 for and 15,563 against. Lacking any provision for amendments, the new constitution could not be changed but only replaced, as was done in 1851 with the adoption of still another constitution.

See also Constitution of 1851

Louis H. Manarin
Richmond, Virginia

Merrill D. Peterson, ed., *Democracy, Liberty, and Property: The State Constitutional Conventions of the 1820's,* 1966.

Constitution of 1851

By the time the census of 1840 was taken, the white population of Western Virginia exceeded that of the rest of the state. Westerners quickly pointed out that they had only 56 of the 134 delegates and 10 of the 29 senators in the Virginia General Assembly. Conventions met in Clarksburg and Lewisburg in 1842 and demanded a constitutional convention to remedy matters. Between 1842 and 1849 several constitutional convention bills were introduced in the legislature but went nowhere due to the opposition of easterners. Finally on December 3, 1849, Gov. John B. Floyd called for a constitutional convention. After long debate a bill calling for a referendum passed the legislature on March 4, 1850. In April voters went to the polls and overwhelmingly approved the measure. In August the voters elected delegates to the constitutional convention.

When the delegates convened in Richmond on October 14, 1850, the convention was called to order by Joseph Johnson of Harrison County. Following the appointment of standing committees, the convention recessed on November 4. When the convention reconvened on January 6, 1851, it began crafting a new constitution for Virginia, one making significant concessions to the West. It was agreed that the seats in the House of Delegates would be apportioned based on the white population recorded in the 1850 census. This meant that the Trans-Allegheny counties would have 83 of the 152 seats. In the Senate the East received 30 of the 50 seats, but a provision was included calling for the General Assembly to reapportion representation in both houses in 1865 and every ten years thereafter. Property qualifications were abolished as a requirement for voting, meaning that every white male citizen who was 21 or older could vote if a resident of the state for two years and of his county, city, or town for one year. Efforts to abolish voice voting and to institute voting by secret ballot failed to pass. Those voters who owned property in more than one county were limited to voting in only one.

Provision was made for the popular election of the governor for a four-year term. The office of lieutenant governor was created, also to be elected by popular vote. The governor's powerful advisory council, which had been controlled by the legislature, was abolished. The appointment powers of the governor were curtailed, and all judges and local officials and members of the Board of Public Works were to be chosen by popular vote. This meant the local selection of local officials, which the western delegates had fought for unsuccessfully in the 1829–30 Convention.

Several changes were made to the legislature. Annual meetings were discontinued and biennial sessions instituted. Delegates were elected for two years and senators for four. More power was given to the Senate by allowing senators to introduce legislation and allowing the Senate to amend the budget bill, which by law originated in the House. The delegates to the convention agreed that one half of a capitation tax paid by every voter was to be used to promote schools and education. To appease Eastern slaveholders, the property tax rate on slaves was set lower than on land and livestock.

Westerners could consider the final document a victory, and it became known as the Reform Constitution. Approved by the convention by a vote of 75 to 33, the new constitution was submitted to the voters for ratification or rejection between October 23 and 25, 1851. The voters cast 75,748 votes for and 11,060 against ratification. The Constitution of 1851 made satisfying progress toward addressing longstanding sectional differences within the Commonwealth of Virginia—though not, as it proved, progress enough to withstand the coming crisis of the Civil War.

See also Constitution of 1830

Louis H. Manarin
Richmond, Virginia

David L. Pulliam, *The Constitutional Conventions of Virginia from the Foundation of the Commonwealth to the Present Time,* 1901; William J. Van Schreeven, *The Conventions and Constitutions of Virginia 1776–1966,* 1967.

The Constitution of West Virginia

West Virginia has had two constitutions, one ratified in 1863 and a second in 1872. The 1863 constitution was drafted at a convention held in Wheeling between November 26, 1861, and February 18, 1862.

The writing of a constitution was an essential step toward the creation of the new state. Voters in Western Virginia had authorized the convention and elected the delegates following Virginia's decision to secede from the United States. The delegates relied heavily on the Virginia constitution of 1851, but made several significant reforms to address inequities that had long provoked Western Virginians. The new constitution provided for equal apportionment based on population; included no property qualifications for voting; required that all property be taxed equally at face value; required the legislature to establish a system of public schools "as soon as practicable;" and barred the state and local governments from borrowing money. The framers also adopted the New England township concept for local governments, thus eliminating the county court system that many had found to be so corrupt and inefficient under Virginia.

Voters approved the convention's draft, which was then submitted to Congress along with the petition for statehood. After some debate, Congress assented to the petition on the condition that a provision on slaves and "person[s] of color" in the proposed constitution be changed. A referendum on March 26, 1863, accepted the condition, thus enabling West Virginia to become the 35th state later that year.

After the Civil War ended in April 1865, the West Virginia legislature adopted an array of "loyalty" requirements and other provisions severely limiting the ability of former Confederates to vote, hold office, and use the courts. These measures created widespread and bitter dissent and quickly led to the demise of the 1863 constitution. In 1871, the voters approved both a constitutional amendment eliminating the loyalty requirement for voting and a call for a new constitutional convention. That convention began in Charleston in January 1872, amid much rhetoric from former Confederates. Despite the swagger, the delegates did not really change all that much. They scrapped the township system. The new constitution also had express bans on the use of political or religious test oaths and on boards or courts of voter registration. (The latter ban was effectively reversed by a 1902 amendment.) It continued to require equal apportionment, equal taxation, and public education.

Since then, West Virginians have passed more than 50 substantive amendments to the 1872 constitution. The pace of amendments has accelerated over time, there being only three in the 19th century. There have been periodic pushes for a new constitution. In 1964, the legislature enacted a law that authorized the election of delegates to a constitutional convention. The movement stalled, however, after the state Supreme Court invalidated the law because it improperly apportioned delegate selection and after major amendments in the late '60s and early '70s significantly modernized state government. Most notable among them were the Modern Budget Amendment of 1968, the Legislative Improvement Amendment in 1970, and the Judicial Reorganization Amendment in 1974.

The West Virginia constitution has 14 articles. The first two include general provisions about the state and its relation to the federal government. Article III, the state's bill of rights, includes the basic freedoms of speech, press, religion, petition, and assembly; guarantees to due process and (by implication) equal protection of the law; and an array of procedures designed to ensure fair treatment of the criminally accused.

Articles IV through VIII describe the relationship between, and the powers of, each of the three branches of the state government. Article IV defines the qualifications of voters and officers and sets forth the means and grounds for removal of the latter. Article V provides for separation of the branches of government. Article VI creates a legislature that consists of a Senate and a House of Delegates. Either house may initiate bills; the Senate has the power to advise and consent on gubernatorial appointments; the House has the power to impeach and the Senate the power to convict. Article VI also prescribes that the legislature shall meet for 60 days near the beginning of each year, although extended and special sessions may also be held.

Article VII lists the constitutional executives: governor, attorney general, secretary of state, treasurer, auditor, and commissioner of agriculture. Each is elected by the people and serves a four-year term. The governor has the powers to (among other things) make appointments, remove officers, and veto legislation. A veto, except of the budget, can be overridden by a simple majority of the legislature.

Article VI, Section 51 describes the budget process in detail. The governor submits his budget at the start of the legislative session; that budget must include the unaltered totals submitted to the governor by the legislative and judicial branches for the operations of their respective branches, meaning that each branch independently sets its own operating budget. Although the legislature may alter the governor's figures, it must use the form of the executive budget. To the extent that it seeks to create its own fiscal policies, the legislature must use the supplementary appropriations process. It cannot create a deficit. After the legislature passes the budget bill, it is submitted to the governor, who may approve or veto it in whole or in part. That is, the governor has a line-item veto power. No budget veto may be overridden except by a two-thirds vote of each house.

The judiciary created by Article VIII consists of the Supreme Court of Appeals, circuit courts, and small claims and misdemeanor "magistrate courts." The legislature also has the as-yet-unexercised power to create an intermediate court of appeals. The Supreme Court consists of five justices elected to 12-year terms, and they decide the rules for selection of a chief justice. Article VIII also provides for the election of circuit court clerks, who serve six-year terms.

Article IX establishes the offices and the form of government at the local level. Counties are governed by a county commission of three members, each from a different area of the county, who are elected to staggered six-year terms. (Counties may, however, alter the form of their government if they follow specified procedures.) The county commission exercises legislative and executive powers within the county as authorized by the legislature. They also retain very limited judicial powers including probating wills. Other county offices created by Article IX include prosecuting attorney, sheriff, county clerk, assessor, and surveyor, each of whom is elected and serves a four-year term.

Article X, Section 1 imposes low ceilings on the level of taxation that can be applied to various classes of property. The legislature may raise the ceilings by 50 percent for a period of three years but only if 60 percent of the voters approve. Simple majorities may also approve extra local levies for up to twice the ceiling and up to five years. Taxes within each class of property must be equal and uniform. Sections 4 and 6 prohibit, respectively, the state and local governments from incurring an indebtedness, except in narrow circumstances.

The requirement in Article XII, Section 1 that the legislature shall provide for a "thorough and efficient system of free schools" has been interpreted to mean that children in West Virginia have a fundamental right to attend a public school free of charge. Thus, the legislature has an obligation to equalize, as much as practicable, educational opportunities across the state. By virtue of Section 2, the educational system is supervised by a state board of education and a state superintendent of schools, who is appointed by the board. Article XII also provides for boards of education to be elected at the local level and authorizes the legislature to create county superintendent positions.

Article XIII, now largely repealed, deals with land titles.

Article XIV establishes two methods for amending the constitution. The first uses a constitutional convention; it has not been invoked since 1872, except in the aborted 1964 effort. Under the frequently engaged second method, amendments must pass each house of the legislature by at least a two-thirds vote and must then be approved by a vote of the people. The Article sets forth additional procedures for both methods.

Robert M. Bastress
WVU College of Law

Robert M. Bastress, *The West Virginia State Constitution: A Reference Guide*, 1995; Otis K. Rice and Stephen W. Brown, *West Virginia: A History*, 1993; *Debates and Proceedings of the First Constitutional Convention of West Virginia*, 1939.

Constitutional Convention of 1861–63

The Constitutional Convention of 1861–63 was West Virginia's first constitutional convention and provided the foundation for state government in preparation for statehood. It convened on November 26, 1861, upon the authorization of the voters the previous month. Fifty-three delegates were in attendance, and John Hall of Mason County was chosen president. While nearly half of the delegates were farmers, lawyers and ministers also were numerous at the convention and wielded great influence. Methodist ministers in particular were influential.

The convention tackled the subject of statehood and, after considerable debate over the name, chose West Virginia at the suggestion of Waitman T. Willey of Monongalia County. It also addressed the question of the boundaries for the proposed state, with some conservatives attempting to derail the statehood movement by adding counties in southwestern Virginia and the Shenandoah Valley. In the end, the convention added Greenbrier, Mercer, McDowell, Monroe, and Pocahontas to the 39 counties originally planned for the new state. Partly as a result of the desire to keep the entire Virginia route of the B&O Railroad in Union territory, the counties of Hampshire, Hardy, Pendleton, Berkeley, Frederick, and Jefferson were given the option of joining the new state, if decided by their voters.

A controversial issue at the convention was slavery. Delegates ranged from slave owners to abolitionists. Gordon Battelle, a Methodist minister from Ohio County, called for a ban on importation of slaves into the state and for gradual emancipation. A compromise provided that no African-Americans, slave or free, could enter the new state.

The constitutional convention created a structure for the state government. Legislative elections were to be held annually. Governors were to be elected for two-year terms with no restrictions on the number of terms. County courts were abolished in favor of boards of supervisors with no judicial powers. Townships were established on the local level. A free school system was set up. An important proviso was the assumption of a proportionate share of Virginia's antebellum debt by West Virginia and creation of a sinking fund to pay off this obligation.

The constitutional convention approved the constitution on February 18, 1862, and adjourned, subject to recall. It reconvened on February 12, 1863, with Abraham D. Soper as president and with representation from every county but Webster and Monroe. The convention met to approve constitutional provisions on slavery which Congress had insisted upon as a condition of admission of West Virginia to the Union.

Slave children born after July 4, 1863, were to be freed. Slave minors were to be freed upon their 21st birthdays. A spirited debate took place over a resolution calling for compensation to slave owners for emancipated slaves, and in the end, the matter was tabled. The revised constitution was approved on February 17, and the convention adjourned. On March 26, West Virginia's first constitution was overwhelmingly ratified by the voters, by a majority of 28,321 to 572.

See also Constitution of West Virginia, Constitutional Convention of 1872

Randall S. Gooden
New Middletown, Ohio

Charles H. Ambler, Frances Haney Atwood, and William B. Mathews, eds., *Debates and Proceedings of the First Constitutional Convention of West Virginia*, 1939; Charles H. Ambler and Festus P. Summers. *West Virginia: The Mountain State*, 1958; Otis K. Rice and Stephen W. Brown, *West Virginia: A History*, 1993.

Constitutional Convention of 1872

In the bitter aftermath of the Civil War, ex-Confederates were initially denied key political rights, including the right to vote and to hold political office. They and their sympathizers, and even moderate opponents who thought that political penalization of former Rebels had become excessive, joined in 1870 in electing a Democratic-Conservative legislature and governor of West Virginia. This first non-Republican regime since statehood immediately set out to undo the "Yankee" constitution of 1863. The legislature on February 23, 1871, called for a referendum on a proposal to hold a new constitutional convention.

Generally opposed to anything that Republican Unionists had achieved, the advocates of change enunciated several specific objections to the Constitution of 1863. They attacked the lack of protection from political proscription such as the former Confederates suffered, the free public school system, the township system of government, a judicial scheme that strayed from familiar Virginia roots, the secret ballot, the role of ministers in public office, and the alleged high cost of government.

The close results of the convention referendum and the later ratification of the new constitution reflected the acrimonious split that characterized state politics at the time. In August 1871, the convention proposal carried by 2,562 votes, 30,220 to 27,658. The result of the delegate election on October 26, 1871, was more extreme, as 66 of the 78 delegates were Democrats. The minority of 11 Republicans and one Unionist Democrat became known as the Twelve Apostles, whose hard task was to maintain the statemakers' faith against heavy odds.

Meeting in a converted Methodist

church in Charleston on January 16, 1872, the convention lasted for 84 days before pointedly adjourning on April 9, 1872, the anniversary of Gen. Robert E. Lee's surrender. It selected former Confederates to all convention offices, including the president, Samuel Price of Greenbrier County, the former lieutenant governor of secessionist Virginia. Price, in turn, appointed former Confederates to most standing committee chairmanships.

Despite the rhetoric, convention measures did not reach the revolutionary extremes some expected. Former Confederates often vented their anger in nasty debate about whether to place the U.S. flag in the hall, Bill of Rights content, African-American voting and office-holding, and the free public school system. The influence of moderate former Confederates, the desire for northern investment, and the fear of operation of the 14th and 15th amendments to the U.S. Constitution tempered results. In the end, the right of blacks to vote and to seek public office remained. The free public school system survived intact and segregated. A fortress bill of rights maintained the supremacy of individual civil rights in peace and war. Oral voting was an option to the ballot. The convention resurrected the county court, created a new judicial system, returned to limited biennial legislative sessions, lengthened executive terms, and maintained a weak governorship.

On August 22, 1872, the electorate ratified the new constitution by a vote of 42,344 to 37,777. At the same election, the voters rejected a separate controversial convention proposition that would have restricted office-holding to whites.

See also Constitution of West Virginia, Constitutional Convention of 1861–63

John Edmund Stealey III
Shepherd University

Robert M. Bastress, *The West Virginia State Constitution: A Reference Guide*, 1995; *Journal of Constitutional Convention, Assembled at Charleston, West Virginia, January 16, 1872*, 1872.

Constitutional Officers

The governor, secretary of state, auditor, treasurer, commissioner of agriculture, and attorney general make up the executive department of state government. These are the so-called constitutional officers, mandated by Article VII, Section I, of the West Virginia constitution.

An unusual feature of West Virginia state government is that all the executive officers are elected individually, and not appointed by the governor. Governor Caperton attempted unsuccessfully in 1989 to amend the constitution to make these offices appointed. His Better Government Amendment was defeated at the polls by a vote of 220,700 against and 28,634 for, one of the worst defeats of a proposed constitutional amendment in the history of the state.

All the constitutional officers are elected statewide to four-year terms, which begin on the first Monday after the second Wednesday of January following their election. A governor may serve any number of terms, but not more than two terms in succession. The remaining constitutional officers may succeed themselves as many times as they are elected. The governor could not serve consecutive terms prior to ratification of the Governor's Succession Amendment in 1970. Republican Arch A. Moore Jr., of Marshall County in 1972 became the first governor to succeed himself under the amendment.

The governor must have attained the age of 30 and the attorney general the age of 25 at the beginning of their respective terms. The remaining constitutional officers must be of legal voting age, and all must meet residency requirements.

See also Constitution of West Virginia, Executive Branch

Karl C. Lilly III
State Senate

Contemporary American Theater Festival

The Contemporary American Theater Festival, a four-week summer theater festival located on the campus of Shepherd University in Shepherdstown, annually produces four new American plays in rotating repertory in the festival's two theaters. The festival was founded in 1990 in partnership with Shepherd by Ed Herendeen and college president Michael Riccards. It has since grown to be the largest fully professional theater in West Virginia and has won praise for its productions from playwrights such as Joyce Carol Oates, Jon Klein, and Jeffrey Hatcher.

The festival is a member of the Theatre Communications Group, the leading organization of nonprofit theaters in the nation, and has a League Of Regional Theaters 'D' contract, allowing the festival to bring in a company of Equity actors and other theater professionals from around the country. The Contemporary American Theater Festival has seen more than a dozen world premieres, and many of its plays have moved to other regional theaters and to off-Broadway in New York City. In 1999, the festival received the Governor's Award for Outstanding Cultural Organization for the commissioning and production of Cherylene Lee's *Carry the Tiger to the Mountain*.

In addition to annually producing four plays, the Contemporary American Theater Festival has featured professional puppetry, dance, and music groups as well as a late-night comedy club.

See also Shepherd University

James McNeel
Washington

Contentment

Standing contentedly at the western edge of Ansted, a mile east of Hawks Nest State Park, this one-story house, fronted by a wide, comfortable porch, recalls cottage rows at many antebellum springs resorts. The resemblance is not coincidental. Built about 1830, the house stood close to the James River & Kanawha Turnpike (now U.S. 60), which also passed by White Sulphur Springs. Due to the slope of the land, rear rooms are at a slightly higher level than those in front, and are reached by several steps in the hall, an early instance of a "split level" arrangement.

In 1874, Col. George Imboden, who had traversed the area earlier as a Confederate officer, bought the house, added two rooms on the western end, and lengthened the porch. Imboden and David T. Ansted, an English geologist, were instrumental in opening coal mines in Fayette County, and when the settlement near the house was incorporated as a town in 1891 it was named for Ansted, with Imboden the first mayor. Imboden's second wife gave their home the name Contentment.

The Fayette County Historical Society maintains the house, which is furnished in period antiques, as the centerpiece of a museum complex open in summer months. Contentment was added to the National Register of Historic Places in 1974.

See also George W. Imboden

S. Allen Chambers Jr.
Society of Architectural Historians

Roy Bird Cook

Pharmacist and historian Roy Bird Cook was born April 1, 1886, at Roanoke, Lewis County. He was the son of David Bird Cook, a farmer and newspaper reporter, and Dora Conrad Cook. In 1898, David Cook moved his family to Weston, where he became the manager for the *Weston Independent*.

By the time of his graduation from high school in 1904, Roy Bird Cook had completed a home study course in pharmacy. At the age of 19, Cook was the youngest person to be licensed in pharmacy in West Virginia. He first practiced in Weston, later joining the Keller-Cook Company in Huntington and the Krieg, Wallace & McQuaide Company in Charleston. In 1935, Cook became the president of the Cook Drug Company. He held this position until shortly before his death.

After his first wife's death in 1930, Cook married Eleanor Poling, who became director of the state Department of Archives and History. The couple were active in the West Virginia Historical Society, which Cook helped found. He also served as the editor of the Society's quarterly, *West Virginia History*, from 1939 to 1941. Cook wrote several books on the history of Lewis County and biographies of Stonewall Jackson and Alexander Scott Withers. He contributed articles to the *West Virginia Review* and other publications. Cook served as a trustee of the Kanawha County Public Library and received the Award of Merit from the West Virginia Library Association in 1957.

Cook collected Civil War and early West Virginia documents and memorabilia, including correspondence from Stonewall Jackson, Robert E. Lee, and

Scene from a production at the Contemporary American Theater Festival.

William McKinley among others. His collection is housed at West Virginia University and is in high demand by writers and scholars. Roy Bird Cook died November 21, 1961.

Christy Venham
WVU Libraries

Coon Hunting

The image of the mountaineer in coonskin cap is rooted in history and tradition, and raccoon hunting has been a part of our culture since the first settlers moved into what is now West Virginia. Although the number of coon hunters has decreased, the lure of the chase is still strong in many parts of the state, particularly in the southern counties. Ironically, the coon hunting tradition runs deepest in the coal producing counties south of Charleston, a region that historically has had a smaller raccoon population than other areas, especially the central and northern counties.

The rangy, rawboned coonhounds are believed to be mostly descendants of the foxhounds that were brought across the Atlantic from England in the 1600s. The principal coonhound breeds are Black and Tan, Walker, Plott, English, Bluetick, and Redbone. Coons are hunted at night. An important part of coon hunting, as in mountain fox chasing, is listening to the dogs bark on trail, although some hunters prefer a silent dog, often a cur, that can ambush a raccoon, forcing it to tree sooner. Either way, the dog is expected to bark when the coon is finally treed, to call the hunter to the site. Then the coon is spotlighted and often shot from the tree, usually with a pistol, though many hunters do not kill coons. For them, the sport is simply in the chase and the treeing.

Coons are hunted in fall and winter, with a season running from early October through February. Declining fur prices have resulted in fewer coon hunters in West Virginia, but our number of hunters remains high compared to many states. Popular adjuncts to coon hunting are field trial and night hunt competitions. There are about 40 coon hunting clubs in the state whose members participate in these activities.

See also Hunting, Hunting Dogs
Skip Johnson
Sutton

Stephen Coonts

Author Stephen Paul Coonts, born July 19, 1946, in Morgantown, became a best-selling action and adventure novelist with the 1986 publication of *Flight of the Intruder*, introducing the fictional naval aviator, Jake Grafton.

Coonts grew up in Buckhannon and earned a B.A. in political science from West Virginia University in 1968. He was commissioned an ensign in the navy upon graduating, and made two combat cruises aboard the aircraft carrier USS *Enterprise* during the Vietnam War. He left active duty in 1977 and moved to Colorado, where after a brief time as a taxi driver and police officer he earned a law degree from the University of Colorado in 1979. Coonts then returned to Buckhannon, where he briefly practiced law at the firm of Hymes and Coonts. From 1981 until 1986, he was in-house counsel for Petro-Lewis Corporation, a Denver oil and gas company.

A full-time writer since 1986, Coonts was inducted into the WVU Academy of Distinguished Alumni in 1992. From 1990 to 1998, he was a trustee of West Virginia Wesleyan College. Coonts's Jake Grafton books also include *Final Flight* (1988), *The Minotaur* (1989), *Under Siege* (1990), *The Red Horseman* (1993), *The Intruders* (1994), *Cuba* (1999), *Hong Kong* (2000), *America* (2001), and *Liberty* (2003). Three of his other works are *War in the Air* (1996), *Fortunes of War* (1998), and *Saucer* (2002). Coonts's novels have been translated and republished in at least 20 other countries. He and his wife, Deborah, reside in Las Vegas. They also have a farm in Pocahontas County.

Larry Sonis
Arlington, Texas

Samuel Cooper

Rabbi Samuel Cooper, born November 14, 1908, in Toronto, Canada, came to Charleston in 1932 to lead the High Holiday services for the B'nai Jacob Congregation. A recent graduate of Yeshiva University seminary in New York City, the young man so impressed congregation members that on his return journey home, he was followed by a delegation that caught up with him in Baltimore and offered him the permanent position of rabbi. Cooper agreed, and embarked on nearly a half-century in the B'nai Jacob pulpit.

Cooper's achievements included overseeing B'nai Jacob's move from a small former church building to a newly constructed synagogue and community center on Virginia Street in 1949, which remains the congregation's home. As B'nai Jacob's first native North American rabbi, he guided the congregation from old-style Orthodox Judaism to a more modern Orthodox (traditional) orientation. He played an active role in Charleston civic life, serving on numerous boards and commissions. In 1967, Cooper was named West Virginian of the Year by the Charleston *Sunday Gazette-Mail*, and he received a Human Rights Commission Award in 1971. He was also an active and early supporter of the state of Israel, attending the World Zionist Congress in Basle, Switzerland, in 1946.

Rabbi Cooper married Lillian Bass of New York City, and the couple had three sons. He retired from B'nai Jacob in 1981. He and his wife moved to Florida where he died January 2, 2006.

See also Jews

Deborah R. Weiner
Jewish Museum of Maryland

Wilma Lee and Stoney Cooper

Wilma Lee and Stoney Cooper were among West Virginia's best known husband-wife country music teams. Natives of Randolph County, Wilma Leigh Leary (b. February 7, 1921) married Dale Troy Cooper (b. October 16, 1918) in 1941. Known for their strong acoustical sound and distinct mountain style, their band, the Clinch Mountain Clan, usually consisted of mandolin, Dobro guitar, bass, and sometimes a banjo or second fiddle. Stoney played a fine fiddle, and Wilma Lee could accompany herself on either guitar or banjo.

They worked for a time at radio station WMMN Fairmont and at various locales outside the state. However, the highpoint of their radio careers was a decade (1947–57) at WWVA Wheeling, followed by 20 years at the *Grand Ole Opry* at WSM Nashville. Their biggest hits, recorded for Columbia and Hickory, included "Come Walk With Me," "Each Season Changes You," "Big Midnight Special," and "There's a Big Wheel," as well as memorable sacred songs typified by "Thirty Pieces of Silver," "Legend of the Dogwood Tree," and "Walking My Lord Up Calvary Hill."

After Stoney Cooper's death on March 22, 1977, Wilma Lee continued performing with the Clinch Mountain Clan on the *Opry* and became a favorite at bluegrass festivals. She recorded for both Rounder Records and Rebel Records. Daughter Carol Lee Cooper forged her own musical career as leader of the Carol Lee Singers, long known for their harmony vocal support at the *Opry*.

Ivan M. Tribe
University of Rio Grande

Ivan M. Tribe, *Mountaineer Jamboree: Country Music in West Virginia*, 1984.

Coopers Rock State Forest

Coopers Rock State Forest is located 13 miles east of Morgantown on the Monongalia-Preston county line. The forest is named for Coopers Rock, a series of cliffs capping the mountain above Cheat River Gorge. These landmark cliffs are formed of hard sandstone of the Pottsville series, overlying softer sandstone below.

The forest has 12,713 acres, used for recreation, timber management, and watershed and wildlife protection. Forest land on the north side of Interstate 68, known as the West Virginia University Forest, is leased by WVU for forestry research, teaching, and demonstration. The recreational area south of I-68 includes camping sites, a concession stand,

and the spectacular main overlook which offers a panoramic view of the gorge and surrounding mountains.

The state forest was established in 1936. During the Great Depression, the Civilian Conservation Corps made numerous improvements, building the overlook with its stone steps, the rustic picnic shelters, and other structures. In 1996, Governor Caperton capped a seven-year campaign by local and national preservation groups to bring 2,000 more acres into the forest. The view on the "other side" of the mile-wide gorge was thus protected from development. Trails around the top of the gorge and extending into the forest offer hikers excellent views of blossoming rhododendron and mountain laurel in June and fall foliage in autumn. Wildlife is abundant and includes wilderness birds such as ravens, as well as hawks, owls, and songbirds. Foxes, chipmunks, and squirrels can be seen throughout the forest. No-hunting zones surround recreational facilities. One of the earliest enterprises along the Cheat River was the smelting and forging of iron, which was produced at what is now Coopers Rock. The impressive Henry Clay Furnace, a cold blast iron furnace, was built about 1836 and still stands as a monument to the early iron industry. It was fired by charcoal, produced from the abundance of nearby forest trees. Remains of charcoal pits can still be seen in the forest.

Norma Jean Kennedy-Venable
Morgantown

Judith Rodd, *A Guide to Coopers Rock State Forest*, 1994.

Copperhead Movement

In the colorful jargon of the Civil War, the "Copperheads" were Northern Democrats who supported the war, but with some reservations. They opposed what they considered to be unconstitutional attacks on states' rights, including the outright abolition of slavery, and the suspension of the writ of habeas corpus by President Lincoln.

Historian Richard O. Curry, an authority on the creation of West Virginia, points out that the Copperhead movement had strong adherents in the state, including John S. Carlile, an early proponent of statehood who later reversed course. While historians once puzzled over Carlile's vote against the creation of West Virginia, Curry finds that it makes sense if his Copperhead philosophy, expressed in numerous speeches and articles, is examined. For example, as U.S. senator from loyalist Reorganized Virginia, Carlile criticized the Emancipation Proclamation. Curry points out that Carlile's opposition to the Willey Amendment, the U.S. Senate action that cleared the way for admission of West Virginia to the Union by providing for the abolition of slavery in the new state, was based not on opposition to the creation of the new state but on his view that Congress could not impose its will on the states, particularly dictating the terms of ending slavery.

Carlile was not alone in his views. Other conservative unionists of Western Virginia grew concerned as the Civil War developed into a crusade against slavery. Among them were John J. Davis, Andrew Wilson, John C. Vance, Sherrard Clemens, William W. Brumfield, and John S. Burdett. Daniel Lamb was among those who opposed statehood if it meant giving in to "abolitionist fanaticism." While the Copperhead movement largely failed to win any major concessions during the Civil War, Curry concludes that an alliance between ex-Confederates and Copperheads in the late 1860s helped speed the end of Reconstruction in West Virginia. This resulted in the creation of a new state constitution in 1872 and a shift of power from Republicans to Democrats.

See also John S. Carlile, Reconstruction

Kenneth R. Bailey
WVU Institute of Technology

Richard O. Curry, *A House Divided: A Study of Statehood Politics and the Copperhead Movement in West Virginia*, 1964.

Core Arboretum

The Core Arboretum, devoted to the study and appreciation of trees, plants, and nature, is named for its founder, the distinguished botanist Earl Core. The 91-acre arboretum in Morgantown is managed by West Virginia University's Department of Biology. Primarily known for native West Virginia plants, the arboretum also contains exotic trees and shrubs of special interest.

The arboretum is mostly steep hillside and Monongahela River floodplain. A 3.5-mile trail network provides access to old-growth forest with a rich herbaceous flora. Planted trees and shrubs occupy small lawn areas. The arboretum has more than 300 kinds of woody plants and more than 300 species of herbaceous plants, including spectacular spring wildflowers. Observers have identified 180 species of birds there.

Professor Charles Frederick Millspaugh first suggested the need for an arboretum at the university in 1890. In 1948, President Irvin Stewart approved biology department chairman Earl Core's proposal to found an arboretum on part of farmland acquired for campus expansion. The university established official boundaries and an endowment for the arboretum in 1998. Generations of students have used the arboretum for outdoor lab work. Research performed there has led to many advanced degrees and to journal articles. However, most visitors appreciate the area primarily as an oasis of nature in a busy urban area.

See also Earl Core

Jon Weems
West Virginia University

Earl Core

Naturalist Earl Lemley Core was born January 20, 1902, in Monongalia County. He was educated at West Virginia University and Columbia University, where he received a Ph.D. in 1936. Core joined the WVU biology faculty in 1926 and served until 1972. He was chairman of the biology department from 1948 to 1967, and curator of the herbarium for many years beginning in 1934.

As an undergraduate, Core participated in P. D. Strausbaugh's early botanical expeditions and went on to collect thousands of specimens for the WVU herbarium. On his first expedition, Core discovered a new species, at the time considered the rarest plant in the world. In 1936, he organized the Southern Appalachian Botanical Club and served as the founding editor of the club's journal, *Castanea*.

Core collaborated with his mentor, Strausbaugh, to write the classic *Flora of West Virginia*, which was originally published in four volumes from 1952 to 1964. Core's other book credits include *Vegetation of West Virginia*, *Woody Plants in Winter*, and *The Wondrous Year: West Virginia Through the Seasons*. His most popular book, *Spring Wild Flowers of West Virginia*, has been in print since 1948.

In 1948, Core persuaded WVU administrators to set aside nearly 100 acres of steep, wooded hillside and floodplain as an arboretum. Today the Core Arboretum stands as a living tribute to Core's contributions to teaching and research. It serves as an outdoor classroom and botanical laboratory and as a quiet place for the public to enjoy and appreciate nature. Core died December 8, 1984, in Morgantown.

See also Core Arboretum, Flora of West Virginia, P. D. Strausbaugh

Scott Shalaway
Cameron

Corncribs

Corncribs, a common feature of the West Virginia landscape since early times, provide rodent-proof storage for field corn. Traditionally, corn was left to dry in tall shocks in the field until November, then hauled to the corncrib. Husking bees brought neighbors together to get the corn crop ready for storage. The best ears were put aside for corn meal or saved for seed.

The first cribs in Western Virginia date to the mid-1700s, soon after settlers arrived. Early cribs were simple log structures with either a shed roof or gabled roof. An overhang on one end of the gable to shelter the doorway was common in present southern West Virginia. Log cribs in the north and in the present Eastern Panhandle were often constructed in a V-shaped design, with the side walls slanting inward so that the floor area was smaller than the area under roof.

The floor of the corncrib was elevated above ground on stone pillars to discourage rodents and to facilitate air circulation. Spacing between the logs provided interior ventilation. During the 19th century, sawed lumber replaced logs in the construction of cribs, which were sided with slats with regularly spaced gaps between. Early crib roofs were usually made of split-wood shingles, later replaced by tin roofing or asphalt shingles.

A common design featured dual cribs under a single roof, with a passage through the center that allowed a wagon sheltered access to the cribs on both sides. Other cribs were attached to barns as a lean-to addition. Often the Appalachian corncrib shared space with a granary. Corncrib designs by the early 20th century included a thinner and taller rectangular structure that enabled the corn to dry more quickly.

Traditional farmers raising cattle and hogs depended on the well-built corncrib. Dairy and beef cattle remain an important part of the state's agriculture, and most producers now use cylindrical, steel-mesh corncribs with a conical roof. Among small farmers in West Virginia many wooden corncribs are still in use.

Scot E. Long
Hebron, Ohio

Cornstalk

Cornstalk, a Shawnee leader who lived in what is today southeastern Ohio, commanded Indian forces at the Battle of Point Pleasant. He may have been born in Pennsylvania about 1720, although nothing is known of his earliest years. He took part in the French and Indian War, and is known to have led raiders who in 1759 killed 10 members of a Virginia family. In 1763, during Pontiac's War, Cornstalk raided the Greenbrier settlements in present West Virginia.

Like these episodes, the Battle of Point Pleasant, which took place in October 1774 during Dunmore's War, reflected the strenuous resistance of Indians along the trans-Allegheny frontier to English encroachments upon their territory. Western tribes residing north and west of the Ohio River would form military confederations under different leaders at different times from the 1760s through the conclusion of the War of 1812. Cornstalk was one such leader. His and his people's efforts fit into this continuum of Indian opposition.

Cornstalk's tribesmen and other Indian allies lost at Point Pleasant, and Cornstalk helped to negotiate the Treaty of Camp Charlotte at the peace conference that followed the battle. His sister, the Shawnee leader Nonhelema, also known as the Grenadier Squaw, was also present at the negotiations. The fragile peace was soon shattered by the onset of the American Revolution. Great Britain invited the Shawnee to join them as allies against the American rebels. Cornstalk journeyed back to Point Pleasant in 1777, evidently troubled by the likelihood of a military struggle that he believed the Shawnee would lose, to warn white settlers of the resumption of hostilities. Suspicious of their old enemy, local authorities detained him as a hostage at Fort Randolph. Cornstalk, his son Elinipsico, and the subchief Red Hawk, were murdered in captivity on November 10, 1777, by enraged whites who blamed them for the recent killing of two white men. Cornstalk is said to have been the father of Aracoma, who settled with her white renegade husband, Boling Baker, at present Logan during the Revolutionary War period.

See also Aracoma, Battle of Point Pleasant, Grenadier Squaw, Indian Wars

Richard P. Lizza
West Liberty State College

Fredrick Webb Hodge, ed., *Handbook of American Indians North of Mexico*, Part 1, 1959; Louise Phelps Kellogg, "Cornstalk," *Dictionary of American Biography;* Otis K. Rice, *The Allegheny Frontier: West Virginia Beginnings, 1730–1830,* 1970.

John Jacob Cornwell

John Jacob Cornwell was the 15th governor of West Virginia, serving from 1917 to 1921 and leading the state during World War I. Born on a farm in the community of Mole Hill (later Mountain) in Ritchie County, July 11, 1867, Cornwell as a child moved with his family to Hampshire County. He was educated in Hampshire County public schools, at Shepherd College, and at West Virginia University, which he attended in 1889–90. Formerly a teacher at Romney, he read for the law there, became president of the local bank, invested in railroads and apple orchards, and edited the *Hampshire Review*, a newspaper that he purchased with his brother in 1890. After passing the bar examination in 1894, he handled cases for the Baltimore & Ohio Railroad, beginning a lifelong relationship with the corporation.

A conservative Democrat, Cornwell was a state senator from 1899 to 1905 and the Democratic nominee for governor in 1904, losing to William M. O. Dawson. He was elected governor in 1916, defeating progressive Republican Ira Robinson, a state supreme court justice, by less than 3,000 votes. Cornwell took the oath as governor only 33 days before the United States declared war against Germany, the beginning of American involvement in World War I. He called the state legisla-

Governor John Jacob Cornwell (1867–1953).

ture into emergency session, aware of the critical role West Virginia would play in supplying industrial and agricultural resources for the war mobilization. The lawmakers approved Cornwell's plan for a West Virginia Council of Defense, an ad hoc body with extensive powers to regulate wartime production. He supported and got a compulsory work law requiring all able-bodied males (there were some exemptions) 16 to 60 to work at least 36 hours weekly for the duration of the war.

To foster wartime unity, Cornwell sought to paper over his party's poor relationship with black West Virginians even as he assaulted their power base. He held no political loyalties to West Virginia's African-American voters, and his Republican opponent had swept most black precincts. West Virginia blacks had capitalized on their political enfranchisement in the state to resist systematic bigotry, using their political leverage to considerable effect under Republican administrations dating back to 1897. Cornwell embarked on a silent purge of black Republican appointees to the state's bureaucracy and cut state appropriations to black institutions. To create the appearance of patriotic solidarity, however, he appointed prominent African-Americans to an advisory committee of the State Defense Council. Cornwell thrived in the wartime climate of emergency, using the state and local defense council network to urge West Virginians to maximize production and be on guard for possible disloyal neighbors.

With the Armistice, the governor turned much of his energy to suspected new threats to American security, emerging as a national spokesman against organized labor's attempts to extend wartime gains into the postwar era. Although Cornwell had courted and won the support of Socialist voters in 1916, by 1919 his rhetoric incorporated socialism, Bolshevism, and organized labor into one vast conspiracy. Cornwell's inflammatory pronouncements during national coal and steel strikes in 1919 and during the West Virginia Mine War of 1919–21 reflect some of the more divisive tactics of that volatile period. His fevered rhetoric against such relatively mild reform proposals as public oversight of railroads, combined with the transparently antilabor thrust of his promotion in 1919 of Red Flag legislation and Constabulary legislation (creating the State Police), militated against labor-management reconciliation in the troubled postwar Red Scare years. His presidency (while still in office as governor) of a statewide open-shop propaganda organization, the American Constitutional Association, punctuated Cornwell's increasing intolerance for alternatives to corporate rule in the state and nation.

Cornwell's position on organized labor did not stem from any denial that injustices in American industry needed mediation. He supported mine safety and child labor legislation, the eight-hour day, and workers' compensation. But to Cornwell such advances should be bestowed by enlightened industrial leaders and not the product of collective militancy by workers' organizations. His logic dictated that industrial unions, which he interpreted as impediments to the natural growth of business, were unpatriotic. He therefore felt justified in carrying the fervent language of the wartime crusades into the arena of labor-management conflict. Convinced that attempts by the United Mine Workers of America to organize southern West Virginia miners represented incipient industrial revolution, Cornwell suspected that his highly visible stand against the union marked him for assassination by UMWA leaders.

No assassination attempt materialized, but the explosiveness of labor-management conflict during Cornwell's term (including the bloody Matewan Massacre), following the ideological excesses of the wartime mobilization, loom large in Cornwell's legacy. They overshadow such accomplishments as a good roads amendment, the rationalization of the state budget process, and progress toward resolution of the Virginia debt controversy.

When he left the governor's office, Cornwell became a director and general counsel of the B&O and remained highly influential in the conservative wing of the West Virginia Democratic Party. He maintained residences in Baltimore and Romney, dying in Cumberland, Maryland, September 8, 1953, at the age of 86.

See also Mine Wars

John Hennen
Morehead State University

Lucy Lee Fisher, "John J. Cornwell, Governor of West Virginia, 1917–1921," *West Virginia History,* April 1963 and July 1963; John Hennen, *The Americanization of West Virginia: Creating a Modern Industrial State, 1916–1925,* 1996; John G. Morgan, *West Virginia Governors,* 1980.

Corricks Ford, Battle of

The Battle of Corricks Ford saw the first general officer killed in the Civil War, Confederate Gen. Robert S. Garnett. Cut off by the Rich Mountain defeat of Col. John Pegram on July 11, 1861, General Garnett first withdrew to the Staunton-Parkersburg Turnpike at Leadsville (now Elkins). There Garnett was mistakenly informed that the town of Beverly, just ahead, was held by Union forces and turned his troops northeast to avoid them.

Union Brig. Gen. Thomas A. Morris, on July 12, directed pursuit of Garnett's troops into Tucker County, down Pleasant Run to Shavers Fork. The Southerners were overtaken the following morning, bivouacked at Kalers Ford. A running battle down Shavers Fork to First and Second Corricks Ford ensued. The Confederates' wagons bogged down in mud and sand at the second crossing. From a bluff overlooking First Corricks Ford, skirmishers tried to hold off the Union soldiers. At the second crossing, General Garnett was shot and killed. General Morris captured a large number of Confederate soldiers and their baggage train, then saw to it that his former West Point classmate's body was transported to his family in eastern Virginia. The remnants of Garnett's Southern troops, reorganized at Parsons Ford, eventually found their way to Monterey, Virginia.

See also Civil War, Tucker County

R. F. Hendricks
Marietta, Georgia

George E. Moore, *A Banner In the Hills,* 1963; Stan Cohen, *The Civil War in West Virginia,* 1979.

Cotiga Mound

Cotiga Mound, a National Register of Historic Places site, was a prehistoric burial mound located near the Tug Fork in Mingo County. An exploratory excavation by the West Virginia Geological and Economic Survey in the late 1970s confirmed that it was a man-made feature. The mound was excavated in its entirety in 1991–92 by GAI Consultants and the sub-mound was excavated by Robert D. Wall. The mound, which was 11 feet high and 90 feet in diameter at the time of excavation, was lost to the construction of Appalachian Corridor G, U.S. 119.

Based on structural evidence and radiocarbon dates, Cotiga Mound was built in several distinct episodes between 205 B.C. and A.D. 75, with much of its construction and use occurring around 102 B.C. It was roughly contemporaneous with other Early to Middle Woodland mounds in West

Virginia and Kentucky identified as Adena, including the mounds at Moundsville and South Charleston.

The Cotiga Mound contained the remains of between seven and 18 cremated individuals ranging from infants to older adults. Grave goods and associated artifacts included modified animal bone, stone tools, mica, and three copper bracelets. The remains of at least two circular paired-post structures were identified beneath the mound. Evidence suggests they were built a short time before the mound construction, and were probably used for mortuary rituals and ceremonies, rather than as houses.

In accordance with an agreement between the West Virginia Department of Transportation and the West Virginia Committee on Native North American Archaeological and Burial Policies, all of the human remains and directly associated grave goods from Cotiga Mound were reburied. A lawsuit filed by the Council for West Virginia Archaeology and other interested parties challenging the agreement was not successful. This was the first time in West Virginia that Native American remains recovered from a state and federally funded project were reburied.

See also Archeology

C. Michael Anslinger
Cultural Resource Analysts

Jenes Cottrell

Traditional musician and craftsman Jenes Cottrell, born September 14, 1901, was descended from the earliest settlers of Clay County. Known for their farming and trading, the Cottrells also worked with wood. During the arts and crafts revival beginning in the 1960s, Jenes Cottrell became one of the best-known practitioners of the old ways. He made toys, rolling pins, chairs, and canes, and he put in chair bottoms of woven wood splits. He had a fine, foot-powered, spring-pole lathe which he used to demonstrate his skill at festivals throughout West Virginia and beyond. He drew people as flies swarm to sugar. Somewhere along the way Cottrell had begun to make banjo heads using aluminum torque converter rings from 1956 Buick transmissions. He quickly became known for making and playing banjos. Murray Smith, a Clay County banker, began treks with Cottrell all over the country to carry him to meet the public.

Cottrell was born, lived, and died on Deadfall Run, the home of his ancestors. He lived there with a sister, Sylvia O'Brien, also a musician and an exemplar of the old ways. There was never any electricity, gas, or running water in Cottrell's home. The house had never been painted. He never owned a car or a telephone. Jenes Cottrell was a quiet man with simple wants and a simple life who was proud of his heritage. He died December 7, 1980, and is buried on the farm.

See also Sylvia O'Brien

Jane Taylor Cox George Walton

Tom Screven, "Remembering Jenes Cottrell," *Goldenseal,* April–June 1981.

Council of Churches

One of the state's oldest organizations, the West Virginia Council of Churches is a Christian organization made up of 18 denominations and branches of denominations reflecting a membership of 600,000 people.

The Council arose from pioneering Sunday school work. In 1827, the churches of Berkeley and Jefferson counties organized an ecumenical Sabbath School Union. Fifty years later, the first convention of State Sabbath Schools was held in Wheeling. In 1880, an ecumenical effort growing out of the International Sunday School Association was organized in West Virginia. That organization, the West Virginia Sunday School Association, directed its efforts toward youth education and leadership training. In the 1920s, under the leadership of the Reverend Z. B. Edworthy, the association promoted weekday and vacation church schools, high school Bible study, and social action through county councils.

In 1924, the association changed its name to the West Virginia Council of Churches and Christian Education. In 1950, the name was shortened to West Virginia Council of Churches. The Council formally incorporated in 1924.

In the 1970s, the Council added two major programs. Ministry with the Aging enlisted older people to contribute their skills and knowledge to the Council's programs. The second program, Disaster Response, began after the Buffalo Creek Disaster of 1972 in Logan County. A third program, begun in 1980, was designed to help people who had been in prison readjust to community life and to address matters concerning the criminal justice system. The Council continues these programs today, as well as others directed toward faith and order, family, governmental relations, interfaith relations, and peace and justice.

Members of the Council are major Protestant denominations, including the African Methodist Episcopal Church and the African Methodist Episcopal Zion Church, as well as Antiochian and Greek Orthodox Churches, the Roman Catholic Diocese of Wheeling-Charleston, and the Salvation Army. The West Virginia Council of Churches is not affiliated with either the National or World Council of Churches.

See also Religion

Nancy Ray Adams
Pine Mountain Settlement School

Counties

West Virginia has 55 counties, created from 1754 to 1895. Randolph County is the largest, at 1,040 square miles, and Ohio the smallest, at 107 square miles. Kanawha County has the most people, with 200,023 residents in 2000, and Wirt has the fewest, 5,873.

West Virginia inherited the county system of local government from Virginia, and 50 of West Virginia's counties were created before the two states separated. Virginia counties, in turn, were patterned after those of England, where counties date back more than a thousand years. West Virginia experimented with a modified township system in its original 1863 constitution, but the constitution adopted in 1872 and still in force today reverted to the Virginia model. All West Virginia counties descend from two counties of Virginia, Frederick and Augusta, created in 1743 and 1745, respectively, and named for the prince and princess of Wales.

The great majority of West Virginia counties were created between the late 18th and the late 19th centuries. The early exception was Hampshire, West Virginia's oldest county, created in 1754 and celebrating its 250th anniversary in 2004. Berkeley, West Virginia's other colonial-era county, was created in 1772. Ohio and Monongalia counties were cre-

ated in a single act of legislation in 1776, the first year of American independence, along with Yohogania, a phantom county whose territory was later lost to Pennsylvania in a boundary resolution. A total of 13 counties were established in the 18th century.

The most fruitful period of county formation was the quarter-century preceding the Civil War, when nearly half of West Virginia counties appeared. These years saw the filling out of the settlement pattern, with nearly all parts of the present state fully occupied by 1861. New counties were established to provide convenient access to government, the ideal said to have been no more than a day's ride by horseback from any citizen's home to the county courthouse.

The status of two counties, Jefferson and Berkeley, remained uncertain when West Virginia was formed in 1863. Their inclusion in the new state was confirmed by the U.S. Congress in 1866. Very early maps of West Virginia omit these easternmost counties, with the Eastern Panhandle ending abruptly at Morgan County. Only one county, Frederick, voted not to become part of West Virginia when offered the opportunity. It remains within the boundaries of Virginia.

Five counties were created after West Virginia became a state, four of them within a decade of the end of the Civil War. Two of the new counties, Lincoln

Counties, founding dates, and county seats

Barbour, 1843, Philippi	Mineral, 1866, Keyser
Berkeley, 1772, Martinsburg	Mingo, 1895, Williamson
Boone, 1847, Madison	Monongalia, 1776, Morgantown
Braxton, 1836, Sutton	Monroe, 1799, Union
Brooke, 1797, Wellsburg	Morgan, 1820, Berkeley Springs
Cabell, 1809, Huntington	Nicholas, 1818, Summersville
Calhoun, 1856, Grantsville	Ohio, 1776, Wheeling
Clay, 1858, Clay	Pendleton, 1788, Franklin
Doddridge , 1845, West Union	Pleasants, 1851, St. Marys
Fayette, 1831, Fayetteville	Pocahontas, 1821, Marlinton
Gilmer, 1845, Glenville	Preston, 1818, Kingwood
Grant, 1866, Petersburg	Putnam, 1848, Winfield
Greenbrier, 1778, Lewisburg	Raleigh, 1850, Beckley
Hampshire, 1754, Romney	Randolph, 1787, Elkins
Hancock, 1848, New Cumberland	Ritchie, 1843, Harrisville
Hardy, 1786, Moorefield	Roane, 1856, Spencer
Harrison, 1784, Clarksburg	Summers, 1871, Hinton
Jackson, 1831, Ripley	Taylor, 1844, Grafton
Jefferson, 1801, Charles Town	Tucker, 1856, Parsons
Kanawha, 1788, Charleston	Tyler, 1814, Middlebourne
Lewis, 1816, Weston	Upshur, 1851, Buckhannon
Lincoln, 1867, Hamlin	Wayne, 1842, Wayne
Logan, 1824, Logan	Webster, 1860, Webster Springs
Marion, 1842, Fairmont	Wetzel, 1846, New Martinsville
Marshall, 1835, Moundsville	Wirt, 1848, Elizabeth
Mason, 1804, Point Pleasant	Wood, 1798, Parkersburg
McDowell, 1858, Welch	Wyoming, 1850, Pineville
Mercer, 1837, Princeton	

See individual counties for further information.

and Grant, were named for heroes of the war. A third, Mineral, was created in part due to wartime differences in mother Hampshire County, the people in the mountainous western territory that became the new county having favored the Union to a greater extent than did the residents of the eastern river valleys who remained Hampshire Countians.

Mingo, the youngest West Virginia county, was carved from Logan County in 1895, and named for Chief Logan's people, the Mingo tribe.

As in other parts of rural America, in West Virginia the county is the unit of government to which many citizens feel most closely attached. Candidates contend vigorously to be sheriff or county commissioners, and occasional "courthouse wars" have broken out over the location of the county seat. The county seat of Jefferson traveled from Charles Town to Shepherdstown and back again in the bitter aftermath of the Civil War, for example, and in 1893 the Tucker County records were stolen away from St. George before the legal transfer of the county seat to Parsons. Every West Virginia county has a colorful story, many of which have been recorded in excellent books of county history.

See also County Government

Country Doctors

In West Virginia most physicians until the 20th century were country doctors, often beloved figures practicing from their offices in small towns or the countryside. There were few physicians and some covered a large area. For practical reasons, the physician carried tools and a large supply of medications with him. Horseback was the original means of transportation. Then came the horse and buggy, more comfortable and easily able to transport supplies and a sick patient. In the 20th century, the Model T and the Model A Fords took the place of horses for the most part.

One of the first physicians known to have lived and practiced in Western Virginia was Dr. Jesse Bennet, known as a thorough anatomist and an excellent surgeon, born near Philadelphia in 1769. He and his family moved to a small community six miles above Point Pleasant on the Ohio River in 1797. A few years before coming to present West Virginia, Bennet, at age 25 and under emergency conditions, had performed a cesarean section on his wife and also removed both ovaries. Both mother and child did well.

Dr. Henry Harvey was born in Fincastle, Virginia, in 1788 and graduated from the University of Pennsylvania in 1808. He began practice in Buffalo, Putnam County, and practiced there until his death in 1837.

Dr. Richard Ellis Putney about 1815 set up practice in Malden. He was said to

have been the third "regularly educated physician" in the Kanawha Valley, having a degree from Jefferson Medical College in Philadelphia. His son, Dr. James Putney, was born in Malden in 1816. After attending Washington College (now Washington & Lee University), James "read medicine" under his father's supervision and later attended Cincinnati Medical College. When the Civil War broke out James Putney joined the Union side as a surgeon and was sent into battle in the Valley of Virginia. He developed a neurological disorder, but despite pain and an increasing inability to walk he continued his practice until he died in 1876.

Dr. Sydenham Herford graduated from Jefferson Medical College in 1833 and four years later moved to Buffalo, where he died in 1884. Dr. Eli Herdman Moore was born in Brooke County in 1814. He entered Washington College in Pennsylvania, but illness forced him to return to Wellsburg within a few months of graduation. He read medicine with Dr. John C. Campbell of Wheeling, and was able to graduate from Jefferson College in 1840. Returning to Wellsburg, he died not long afterward.

Dr. James Dye of Chloe in Calhoun County was born in 1867. His brother, Dr. W.T.W. Dye, had a large rural practice. James attended Starling Medical College in Cincinnati, graduated in 1891, and took over his brother's country practice. W.T.W. then settled in the county seat, Grantsville, where he practiced until his death in 1941. Constant work and little rest exhausted James as it had his brother. He bought a farm near Parkersburg and quit medicine for a period. Years later, Dr. James Dye returned to Chloe and took up again his busy rural practice. James was active until he died at age 86. By then he had delivered more than 5,000 babies and tended to the medical and surgical needs of countless patients.

In 1898, Phoebia G. Moore became the first woman to enter and remain in West Virginia University Medical School. After two years at WVU, she entered Bennett Medical College in Chicago and then returned home to Mannington to a busy rural practice. She traveled the muddy and rutted roads by horseback, later by horse and buggy, and finally she wore out five Model A Fords. It is said that Dr. Moore once gave her shoes to a poor patient and returned to town in stocking feet. By the time of her death in 1953, she had delivered hundreds of babies, many of whom had been named for her.

See also Medicine

Warren Point
Charleston

"Country Roads"

"Take Me Home, Country Roads," which branded West Virginia "almost heaven,"

has been one of the most popular songs about the state since its release in 1971 by singer John Denver. The song was completed on the night after Christmas in 1970 by Denver and his friends Bill Danoff and Taffy Nivert of the Fat City Band, and was first performed by its writers as an encore at a Washington club the next evening. First released as a single, "Take Me Home, Country Roads" climbed the charts, eventually reaching number two and remaining in the top 40 for 14 weeks. The song was included on Denver's "Poems, Prayers, and Promises" album, and before the year's end both the single and the album had gone gold.

Denver performed "Country Roads" in West Virginia on several occasions, notably for the opening of the new Mountaineer Stadium in Morgantown in 1980 and on a telethon broadcast statewide from the Cultural Center in Charleston to benefit the victims of the disastrous 1985 floods. A popular arrangement of "Country Roads" by Dr. James Miltenberger is regularly performed by the West Virginia University Mountaineer Marching Band as part of its pre-game activities. In 1999, the state secured the rights to use "Country Roads" to promote tourism in West Virginia. Like other songs about West Virginia, "Take Me Home, Country Roads" emphasizes love of homeplace and is proudly sung throughout the state.

H. G. Young III
WVU Parkersburg

Country Store

The country store in the 19th and early 20th century was the focal point for the community, frequently serving a radius of three or four miles. Lighting was by kerosene or gas lights. The store had a coal stove with benches around it. The post office was usually in a corner of the store, so the residents came each day to get their mail, buy their stamps or money orders, and send orders to Montgomery Ward or Sears, Roebuck.

The store carried the staples country people were unable to produce for themselves. Salt, sugar, rice, beans, and hominy were stored in barrels and weighed out by the grocer to the amounts requested by the purchaser. Tea, cheese, prunes, and dried peaches were also bought in bulk. Twenty-five-pound bags of flour and ten-pound bags of cornmeal were always available. The store had spices, coffee, tea, candy, chewing gum, cornflakes, cream of wheat, rolled oats, smoking and chewing tobacco, cigarettes, and snuff. Fresh meat was not stocked before refrigeration became available.

The housewife could buy cotton cloth by the yard, as well as thread, pins, and needles. A cabinet with a locked door held patent medicines: castor oil, camphor, turpentine, Vicks Salve, and Raymond's Red Oil were available. Feed for the farm animals was stored in a side room, along with horse collars and collar pads, horseshoes, nails, staples, wire fencing, and farm tools. Any item the farmer needed could usually be found, including shoes, boots, overalls, work jackets, socks, stockings, and underwear. Shelves held writing tablets, pencils, crayons, pens, and ink. A glass case held eye glasses and gift items. One small room contained a barrel of kerosene to be sold by the gallon for lamps.

The country store performed a valuable function by providing a center of trade in a cash-short economy. Butter or eggs were bartered for groceries. If eggs were scarce, the chickens were traded and kept live in a building outside the store. In the winter black walnuts were cracked and sold to the storekeeper. Field-dressed rabbits were also bought by the storekeeper and shipped to New York, their fur to be used in the garment industry. Stores commonly bought ginseng and other herbs, and other items of country produce.

On summer evenings the store was a neighborhood gathering place for the men for a game of horseshoes or for baseball practice. In the winter or bad weather they gathered inside by the stove for dominoes, checkers, or a card game.

Eileen Cain Stanley
Kenna

County Fairs

West Virginia has a rich heritage of fairs and festivals that grew out of early agricultural exhibitions, at community, county, and multi-county levels. These early exhibitions were intended to spread knowledge of farming methods and the selection of superior animals or crops, and to foster pride in agricultural achievements. Today's county fairs serve the same purposes and many others.

The exhibition of animals and animal and plant products in competition remains a central theme. Thus fairs draw entries of products from apples and black walnuts to yams and zucchini, and of canned and baked goods, as well as numerous breeds and species of domestic animals, ranging in size from rabbits to draft horses. Organizations charged with rural development take advantage of these opportunities to showcase new ideas. Fairs provide a venue for youth in 4-H and Future Farmers of America clubs to exhibit the products of their projects in friendly competition. These events are meant to instill a respect for animals and to promote ethical practices in raising and showing animals and plant products.

Contests of skill, or just for fun, from attempts to catch greased pigs to horse or tractor pulling contests, and from animal showmanship to sheep shearing, became prominent events as fairs developed. Country music shows in the evening, food booths (many with specialties prepared on site), and carnival rides and booths have been added over the years. Fairs are important social and entertainment events, looked forward to throughout the year. Many a farm-raised child remembers the thrill of a first Ferris wheel ride, and many a "town kid" was awed to learn where milk comes from, by the size of a bull, or by the cuddliness of a lamb or bunny in a close encounter at the county fair.

Exhibits and demonstrations of farm machinery and products for farm use have become staple events at West Virginia county fairs. Parades began in early years as animals were paraded to open the fair. They have evolved to parades through the local town, featuring a fair queen and her court, floats from many organizations, bands, fire trucks, horses and buggies, and marching units ranging from dance schools to riding clubs. Craft demonstrations, shows, and sales, and raffles of cars, guns, or equipment have become common events at rural fairs.

County fairs take place throughout the state. In 2003, the West Virginia Association of Fairs and Festivals had 132 member events statewide, including county fairs as well as craft festivals and similar events. These fairs and festivals occur in 49 of the 55 counties.

Keith Inskeep
West Virginia University

County Government

West Virginia is one of the most rural states, and West Virginians think of their counties as home in the way urban Americans think of their cities or neighborhoods. County government provides the basic level of government service for most of us. Three-member elected county commissions govern 54 of the 55 counties, while an elected five-member commission governs Jefferson County. England, from which America got the foundation for its governmental structure, at an early date developed shires (now called counties) as administrative subdivisions to govern its rural areas. Virginia adopted the English county system from its early colonial period. West Virginia, after briefly experimenting with the New England township system under the original 1863 state constitution, reaffirmed the Virginia model in the constitution of 1872, which is still in force.

West Virginia county commissions combine administrative, legislative, and minor judicial functions in the one body, so the principle of separation of powers does not prevail. The major functions served by county commissions are to provide general governmental services, such as police and fire protection, health and welfare services, culture and recreation, social services, and education. The main revenue source is the real property tax. Others are the personal property tax, natural resource severance taxes, user fees, and the hotel occupancy tax.

Until November 5, 1974, West Virginia counties were governed by so-called county courts. On that date, voters ratified the Judicial Reorganization Amendment. This amendment to the state constitution moved sections pertaining to county commissions from the part of the constitution dealing with the judiciary to another article dealing with counties. The amendment changed the name "county court" to "county commission" because the governing bodies of

Picnickers celebrate the 1904 Lewis County Fair.

counties were not courts, but rather administrative governing bodies. By force of habit, many West Virginians still refer to their county government as the county court.

In addition to the county commissioners, each county has a number of other elected officials. The sheriff is the chief law enforcement officer and also responsible for collecting taxes levied by the county. The prosecuting attorney is the chief legal officer of the county and prosecutes both civil and criminal cases on behalf of the public, is responsible for providing legal advice to county agencies, and represents the state in certain legal matters. The clerk of the circuit court carries out administrative functions for the circuit court system, including maintaining records and various duties with regard to juries, and serves as an election officer to prepare ballots for elections and conduct absentee voting. The county clerk is the chief record keeper for the county commission, maintains vital statistics, records land transactions and wills, and serves as the chief voter registration official for the county. The assessor sets values for real and personal property for purposes of taxation and maintains records pertaining to those values.

See also Counties

Donald R. Andrews
University of Charleston

County Poor Farms

Before the welfare reforms of the New Deal, county farms, also known as county infirmaries or poor farms, played a major role in the care of people who because of poverty, infirmity, or old age were unable to care for themselves. Early West Virginia law followed Virginia precedent, making counties responsible for care of the poor. At first, county governments appointed overseers of the poor, who were to see that the indigent received adequate care. Most counties found that the overseer system worked haphazardly and turned to the establishment of a county farm, where any person in need might live in the county's care. The farms were operated by caretakers appointed by the county courts, usually on the basis of bids. Although the overseers continued to have general responsibility for the poor, the county farms provided the chief means of public support.

In the 1920s, county welfare boards replaced the overseers of the poor, and the state began to play a greater role in indigent care, establishing agencies to see to the welfare of children and veterans. Private agencies such as the Salvation Army, Red Cross, and Community Chest also helped. As unemployment grew with the coming of the Great Depression, however, both public and private agencies were swamped with the rising demand

for assistance, and county farms designed to care for a few became crowded with many victims of the hard times. At the Kanawha County farm, for example, nearly 300 adults and children crowded into a building built in the 19th century to house 75 people.

As families disintegrated during the Depression, hundreds of children ended up in the crowded county poor farms, where they often had to share sleeping quarters with aged and mentally infirm adults. In 1933, shocked by press revelations of the desperate conditions, Maj. Francis Wheeler Turner, director of the state department of public welfare, set up temporary camps to rescue children from the poor farms and proposed to replace the county farms with regional farms operated by the state. Turner's plan proved abortive as welfare reform moved in other directions. The federal Works Progress Administration helped Mercer County to experiment with a new kind of county farm that used family cabins rather than a single common dormitory. Other New Deal reforms, however, especially Social Security, led to the creation of a social welfare system that made the institutional housing of the poor a thing of the past. Most county farms soon closed, although some continued until the last residents died or moved out in the 1960s.

See also New Deal, Poverty

Jerry Bruce Thomas
Shepherd University

Richard Brammer, "A Home for the Homeless: Remembering the Pleasants County Poor Farm," *Goldenseal*, Fall 1994; Joe Cosco, "Cabell County Poor Farm, 1853–1929," *Goldenseal*, April–June 1979; Jerry Bruce Thomas, *An Appalachian New Deal: West Virginia in the Great Depression*, 1998.

County Unit Plan

The county unit plan for school systems, adopted in 1933, was among the most sweeping education reforms in West Virginia's history. Previously, schools had been run by city and magisterial district boards, a system that provided local autonomy but was often marred by inefficiency, corruption, and nepotism. The Great Depression forced changes. The reduction in property tax provided by the Tax Limitation Amendment, approved in 1932, diminished the amount of money available to local districts, which had previously provided nearly 95 percent of the cost of education. The state had to assume greater responsibility for public education.

Various plans were proposed, but the county unit plan supported by Governor-elect Herman Guy Kump was chosen, becoming effective May 22, 1933. The plan was a compromise between local autonomy and state control. It abolished 398 local school districts, including 54 independent ones, replacing them with 55

county districts, one for each county of the state. Each district was governed by a five-member county school board, elected by popular ballot. For the first time, all school superintendents were required to have a college education.

In its first year, the plan cut the number of teachers from 16,282 to 15,340, saving $4,564,710. School bus transportation across former district lines allowed smaller schools to consolidate. The county districts still struggled, but they managed to pay their teachers and continue nine-month school terms. In many other states, teachers' salaries fell millions of dollars in arrears and terms were cut to six months during the Depression. Some West Virginia counties had to reduce term length in 1933 and again in 1937–39, but for the most part, the state maintained its commitment to a nine-month term.

The county unit plan did not please everyone. Several lawsuits were brought against it. Seeking more funds for teachers and education, Superintendent of Schools W. W. Trent was frequently at odds with Kump and his successor, Governor Holt. Money for school construction and building maintenance was virtually nonexistent. The average salary for teachers and principals dropped 12 percent. Governor Kump called for further reductions in teachers' salaries but was rebuffed by the legislature. The loss of local schools through consolidation was often emotionally painful for small communities, but overall the county unit system was praised around the nation for what it achieved.

See also Education, W. W. Trent

Gerald D. Swick
Nashville, Tennessee

Charles H. Ambler, *A History of Education in West Virginia: From Early Colonial Times to 1949*, 1951; Jerry Bruce Thomas, *An Appalachian New Deal: West Virginia in the Great Depression*, 1998.

The Courts

West Virginia, like all the states, has separate state and federal court systems. State courts process more than 98 percent of all litigation. The matters decided by state courts interpret and develop the laws that address the daily concerns of citizens.

The West Virginia Supreme Court of Appeals is the state's only appellate court; it makes the final judicial determination in all questions of state law. The five justices on the court serve 12-year terms; each year, they elect one of their number to be chief justice. Like all state judges in West Virginia, the Supreme Court justices are chosen in partisan elections.

The state system has two types of trial courts: circuit courts, which are general jurisdiction trial courts; and magistrate courts, which are limited jurisdiction trial courts. Most important cases of law begin and end in circuit court. The legislature determines the number of judicial circuits and the number of judges in each circuit. There are 31 circuits; some circuits include several counties, but 16 circuits encompass only one county. The number of judges in a circuit ranges from one to seven. Circuit judges have eight-year terms.

Family law masters conduct hearings in cases involving divorce and child custody, visitation, and support. Mental hygiene commissioners preside over hearings on involuntary hospitalization, guardianship, and conservatorship. These officials then recommend how the court should dispose of such cases. A magistrate court is located in each county to litigate minor civil cases and misdemeanor criminal cases. Based on its population, a county may have from two to 10 magistrate judges. They serve four-year terms and may be non-lawyers. Decisions in magistrate court may be appealed to circuit court, where an entirely new trial is conducted. Cities and towns may establish municipal courts. They are administered locally and are limited to the enforcement of city ordinances. The 122 municipal judges are chosen in elections or by appointment.

Every state has at least one U.S. District Court within its boundaries, and West Virginia has two. The Southern District is centered in Charleston and also holds court in Beckley, Bluefield, Huntington, Parkersburg, and Lewisburg. The Northern District, centered in Elkins, also holds court in Clarksburg, Martinsburg, and Wheeling. These courts address questions of federal law and federal crimes arising in West Virginia. They may also hear state civil cases arising in West Virginia between a citizen of West Virginia and a citizen of another state. Appeals of decisions of the U.S. District Courts in West Virginia are made to the fourth circuit of the U.S. Court of Appeals, which sits in Richmond. Federal district judges serve life terms. The president appoints them with the advice and consent of the U.S. Senate. These judges are West Virginians, who were suggested to the president by the state's U.S. senators and governor. Each district court also has a bankruptcy court attached to it.

See also Judicial Branch, Law, Supreme Court of Appeals

Chuck Smith
West Virginia State University
Richard A. Brisbin Jr. "The West Virginia Judiciary," in Christopher Z. Mooney, Robert Jay Dilger, and Richard A. Brisbin, Jr., *West Virginia's State Government: The Legislative, Executive, and Judicial Branches,* WVU Institute for Public Affairs, 1993.

Rose Agnes Rolls Cousins

Aviator Rose Agnes Rolls Cousins, the first black woman to become a solo pilot

Aviator Rose Agnes Cousins (1920–).

in the Civilian Pilot Training Program at West Virginia State College, was born March 26, 1920. Rose was interested in "boy" things and while growing up competed with her brother. Entering college at West Virginia State at 16, she majored in business administration, but association with the pilot's program rekindled a childhood desire to fly. In 1940, she learned to fly, reportedly telling the instructor, "I'll just put my hair up and you can pretend I'm a man." In an open cockpit, Rose learned to put the plane into a spin, fly upside down, and land with the engine off. In order to qualify for a license, she completed a cross-country flight alone, guided only by sight and a compass.

In 1941, she went to Tuskegee Institute with the first group of ten male students from West Virginia State College to try out for the Air Force training program for black combat pilots. She was rejected because of her gender. Returning to West Virginia she was employed for a time at West Virginia State College.

Rose eventually returned to Fairmont to care for her parents and spent the majority of her working life at Fairmont Clinic where she became manager of medical records. She now lives with her daughter in Washington. Though she found little opportunity to use her flying skills, Rose Cousins is remembered for her courage and tenacity in choosing to become a pilot.

Ancella R. Bickley
Charleston
Mary Rodd Furbee, "'I was Never Afraid of Anything': Pilot Rose Rolls Cousins," *Goldenseal,* Summer 1997; Dolly Withrow, *From the Grove to the Stars: West Virginia State College 1891–1991,* 1991.

Covered Bridges

The covered bridge was a central European invention adopted and perfected in North America. It has been estimated that more than 10,000 were built across the United States between 1805 and 1900. The total number of covered bridges built in Western Virginia is unknown. Harrison County alone once had more than 50. In 1959, a census of America's covered bridges listed 47 still in existence in the Mountain State. That number had fallen to 17 in 2002.

The remaining covered bridges can be found at Philippi and Carrollton, Barbour County; Center Point, Doddridge County; Herns Mill and Hokes Mill, Greenbrier County; Fletcher and Simpson Creek, Harrison County; Staats Mill and Sarvis Fork, Jackson County; Locust Creek, Pocahontas County; Walkersville, Lewis County; Barrackville, Marion County; Indian Creek and Laurel Creek, Monroe County; Dents Run, Monongalia County; and Fish Creek, Wetzel County. The Mud River Covered Bridge at Milton, Cabell County, was moved from its original location and recently rebuilt at Pumpkin Park.

Turnpikes sanctioned by the commonwealth of Virginia made it necessary to build many of the region's bridges, which were covered to protect the timber framing from the weather. The bridge building fell to an eclectic group of entrepreneurs, who began with timber and one basic design element, the triangular truss, and changed American bridge design for the next 100 years.

Most bridge builders were local self-taught master carpenters with extraordinary skills. Among the best-known were Lemuel Chenoweth and James Moore. Chenoweth built most of the bridges

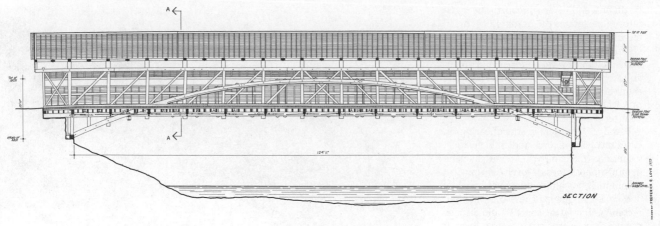

A Burr arch truss supports Barrackville covered bridge.

in the central portion of the Staunton-Parkersburg Turnpike, including the ones at Philippi and Barrackville. Moore supervised the major crossings of the Gauley and Greenbrier rivers along the James River & Kanawha Turnpike.

The craftsmanship displayed in the construction of these spans is represented in the painstaking mortising, fitting, and pegging. The intricate truss patterns were named for the clever men who designed them. Theodore Burr, famous for the Burr arch truss, patented his system in 1817. The Barrackville and Carrollton covered bridges are examples of the Burr design, which integrated an arch into the truss framework. Several West Virginia bridges used the Long truss, a system of boxed X's patented by Col. Stephen H. Long in 1830. These bridges include Staats Mill and Sarvis Fork, with Center Point, Hokes Mill, and Indian Creek representing modifications of the Long truss. The Philippi bridge, one of only six remaining two-lane covered bridges in the U.S., is unusual in that the builder employed the Long design in conjunction with a double arch system.

The Warren double-intersection truss was patented in Britain by James Warren and T. W. Morzani in 1838. The Locust Creek covered bridge is the only remaining example of this design in West Virginia. William Howe was granted a patent in 1840 for substituting vertical rods in place of some wooden tension members. The Mud River covered bridge is the last remaining example of a Howe truss on a covered bridge in West Virginia.

Other truss designs, including kingpost, multiple kingpost, and queenpost, are also represented in the state's surviving covered bridges. The kingpost is the oldest and simplest design, consisting of a simple triangular truss dating back to the Middle Ages. The Dents Run and Fish Creek covered bridges both use the kingpost truss. A version of the kingpost, known as the queenpost, was modified by the addition of a horizontal cross-supporting member to allow for greater

spans. The Walkersville, Laurel Creek, and Herns Mill covered bridges all use the queenpost truss. Another modified version of the kingpost is the multiple kingpost. This design allowed even greater spans by adding more triangular sectional units to the trussing system, as shown in the Fletcher and Simpson Creek covered bridges.

The covered bridges that remain possess intrinsic beauty and charm, a testimony to the craftsmanship of their builders. Their practical straightforward design created long-lasting structures, which have survived the gales of war, floods, ice, and even grievous fires over the past century and a half.

See also Bridges, Lemuel Chenoweth, Philippi Covered Bridge, Turnpikes

Todd A. Hanson
Given

Stan Cohen, *West Virginia's Covered Bridges: A Pictorial Heritage*, 1992.

A. W. Cox

Businessman Artemus Ward Cox, named for a well-known American humorist, was born on a farm at Red Knob, Roane County, August 18, 1885. He completed his eighth-grade education in a one-room country school. At age 17 he operated a sawmill owned by his schoolteacher father. After a few years, "A. W.," as he was known, passed the state teacher's examination and began a brief teaching career in Mingo County and later in Clendenin, Kanawha County.

While working part-time in a Clendenin store, A. W. resolved to make retailing his life's work. He went into business with C. M. Morrison. In 1914, Cox moved to Charleston and bought the George Ort Department Store on Capitol Street. That store became the first in a chain of 21 A. W. Cox stores in West Virginia, Virginia, Ohio, and Kentucky. With Wehrle B. Geary, he founded The Diamond, which became one of West Virginia's finest department stores, and the nearby Daniel Boone Hotel, the city's foremost hostelry. Both ventures were

important in the development of downtown Charleston, and the buildings remain city landmarks today.

A member of several civic organizations, Cox was a generous contributor to numerous small churches and to individuals in need. Two special beneficiaries were St. Mark's Methodist Church, of which he was a member, and Morris Harvey College. Cox served on the college board of trustees for 24 years and as president of the board from 1943 until his death on September 4, 1964.

Marshall Buckalew
Charleston

Billy Cox

Musician William Jennings "Billy" Cox, also known as the "Dixie Songbird," ranked as one of West Virginia's premier country music vocalists and songwriters during the 1930s. Born August 4, 1897, near Charleston, Cox learned to play guitar and harmonica in his youth and started performing on WOBU (later WCHS) radio in 1928. He recorded for Gennett, 1929–31, and from 1933 to 1940 for American Record Corporation, which later became Columbia. From 1936, Cliff Hobbs (1916–61) of Cedar Grove sang harmony on Cox's records, to provide the popular country duet sound. Among his 150 recordings "Sparkling Brown Eyes" and "Filipino Baby" became country music standards. Several songs celebrating the New Deal have attracted scholarly attention, and Cox recorded versions of traditional British ballads, as well. A reckless lifestyle prevented Cox from realizing much benefit from his skills. He died in poverty, December 10, 1968.

Ivan M. Tribe
University of Rio Grande

Ivan M. Tribe, *Mountaineer Jamboree: Country Music in West Virginia*, 1984.

John Harrington Cox

One of the pioneers in the field of American folk song scholarship, John Harrington Cox was born in Madison County, Illinois, May 27, 1863. Educated at Brown and Harvard (Ph.D. 1923) universities, he received an appointment on the English Department faculty at West Virginia University in 1903. His early efforts at the university were devoted to the study of Old and Middle English, and Medieval literature, in which fields he achieved distinction as an educator, author, and editor.

Cox collected his first folk song in 1913. Two years later, on July 15, 1915, he presided over the founding of the West Virginia Folklore Society, serving as its first president, archivist, and editor. Though the society met formally only twice, it established a network of field collectors across the state that continued to function loosely under Cox's direction for many years.

During the early 1920s, Cox organized and edited an extensive body of the folk songs collected under the Society's auspices as the basis of his Ph.D. dissertation. Produced under the direction of the noted Harvard scholar, George Lyman Kittredge, the dissertation was published as *Folk-Songs of the South* by the Harvard University Press in 1925. The first major collection of American folk songs by an American editor to appear in print, the volume became a model in both its scholarship and format for many subsequent American folk song publications. Despite the title it consisted almost entirely of West Virginia songs.

In the years that followed, Cox prepared an extensive body of additional folk songs for publication. These materials remained in manuscript until they were published in 1939 by the National Service Bureau in two mimeographed volumes: *Traditional Ballads Mainly From West Virginia*, and *Folk-Songs Mainly From West Virginia*. Cox died in Morgantown, November 21, 1945.

John A. Cuthbert
WVU Libraries

Cozy Records

Cozy Records, located in Davis, Tucker County, was probably the most successful and long-lasting recording company ever in West Virginia. Started by John Bava (1913–97), a coal miner who sang and wrote songs, Cozy turned out vinyl records in the 78 rpm and 45 rpm formats, as well as long-play albums, for three decades. The music ranged from country string bands to rock 'n' roll to polkas.

Musicians, including radio personalities such as Dusty Shaver and Hank the Cowhand, came from all over the region to record at Bava's studio. When a Bava recording became an area hit in the 1950s, the song was sometimes released on Coral Records, a major record label with which Cozy had a relationship; this is how such West Virginia groups as the Lonesome Pine Fiddlers and Rex and Eleanor Parker reached national audiences.

Collectors especially seek out "The Ambridge Boogie," a 1958 rockabilly tune by Dale Brooks (1933–), a disc jockey in Berkeley Springs and later in Spencer. Brooks also wrote "I'd Like To Hear My Name," a gospel song recorded by more than one Cozy artist and published by John Bava's Music, which printed many songbooks through the years.

Increasingly, Bava's interest turned to religion. With a family band including his wife, Lucy, and daughters, Janet and Juanita, he embarked on a musical ministry on radio and TV and at his Gorman Church of God in Gormania.

See also Lonesome Pine Fiddlers, Rex and Eleanor Parker

John Douglas
Berkeley Springs

Crafts Movement

West Virginia's handicrafts revival originated in the late 1950s and early 1960s, due to a fortunate confluence of native skills, government attention, and the state's centennial celebration. Among the first to take action were the Future Homemakers and Future Farmers clubs, which raised funds in the mid-1950s to construct the Craft House at the Cedar Lakes Conference Center near Ripley. A variety of weekend classes began at the Craft House in 1959.

During the 1960s War on Poverty, the U.S. Economic Development Administration funded a technical assistance grant to the West Virginia Department of Commerce for a program to encourage the marketing of handcrafts. Carl Little, Don Page, and Jane Cox George of the Commerce staff worked throughout the state to stimulate interest among craftspeople, solve individual problems, and encourage crafts education. This continued through the late 1970s.

The first Mountain State Art & Craft Fair took place in July 1963 at Cedar Lakes as part of the state centennial. The fair was a joint project of the Commerce Department, the Department of Education, Department of Agriculture, and the Department of Natural Resources. During the '70s and early '80s, the Art & Craft Fair was recognized as the most important vehicle for West Virginia craftspeople to reach the buying public. While crafts marketing has evolved, the fair remains important today. Its success helped to encourage the establishment of other fairs and festivals. The West Virginia Artist's and Craftsman's Guild arose from the first Art & Craft Fair and continues to the present.

West Virginia crafts development profited from the back-to-the-land movement of the late 1960s and early 1970s. In those years, numerous bright, talented young people left the nation's mainstream in search of roots, inexpensive land, and independence. Many found these things

The handiwork and tools of a Webster County craftsman.

in West Virginia, and some established themselves as serious craftspeople working at home.

Self-help cooperatives also played a part. In 1968, Florette Angel of the Commerce Department helped to organize Mountain Artisans, a quilt cooperative. With the design talents of Dorothy Dembosky Weatherford and a series of poverty warriors from the Volunteers in Service to America (VISTA) program, skilled quilters from several rural counties were taught new designs using brightly colored fabrics to produce quilts, skirts, jackets, and vests. One of West Virginia's newest residents, Sharon Rockefeller, promoted the co-op's products in national markets.

Several additional cooperatives began through the efforts of the federal Community Action program, including Appalachian Craftsmen, who made learning toys and apparel. The Rural Arts and Crafts Cooperative of the Parkersburg area became known for patchwork toys. VISTA worker James Thibeault began Cabin Creek Quilts, which focused on home furnishings. As government and foundation support decreased, only Cabin Creek Quilts survived into the 21st century.

In 1975, Tim Pyles was hired by the Bureau of Vocational Education to revitalize the crafts education program at the Cedar Lakes Crafts Center. Weekend and weeklong workshops were begun, with the focus on technique, design, workmanship, and marketability. The Appalachian Blacksmiths Association, the Mountaineer Woodturners, and several regional quilting groups were outgrowths of the Crafts Center experience.

With the opening in 1976 of the Cultural Center at the state capitol, a new crafts shop developed under the guidance of Rebecca Stelling of the Department of Culture and History. For many years, this shop was the most important place to buy West Virginia crafts. The Culture and History marketing program nurtured crafts development and encouraged the marketing of crafts throughout the state and beyond.

The 1980s and 1990s witnessed the maturing of the crafts movement. Producers discovered out-of-state markets. The stronger craft fairs survived. Government agencies continued to foster the crafts, both as economic development and to hone the state's image with tourists. The Little Kanawha Craft House in Parkersburg is the marketing center for an eight-county development project. The Art Company of Davis caters to skiers and other Tucker County tourists. The Wheeling Artisan Center was founded as a part of a center city redevelopment project. Poplar Forest, the marketing arm of another crafts cooperative, is located in an outlet center at Flatwoods. The largest project so far has been Tamarack, operated by the West Virginia Parkways Authority at Beckley. Marketing work of more than 2,000 crafts and food producers to nearly a half-million visitors, Tamarack had sales of $7.6 million in 2004. The new century ushered in MountainMade.com, serving the craftspeople of northern West Virginia, with funding from the federal Small Business Administration. Their new gallery in Thomas and a web site on the Internet may be the signal for a new chapter for crafts marketing in West Virginia.

See also Back-to-the-Land Movement, Cabin Creek Quilts, Handcrafts, Mountain State Art & Craft Fair

Tim Pyles
Tamarack
Don Page
Beckley

Cranberry Glades

Located in southwestern Pocahontas County in the Monongahela National Forest, the Cranberry Glades are an island of northern muskeg in the Southern Appalachians. Several northern plants, animals, and birds reach their southernmost limit here. There are other glade areas in West Virginia, such as Cranesville Swamp, parts of Canaan Valley, and Droop Mountain Bog, but Cranberry is best known due to its large size.

The glades include 1,000 acres and occupy a high valley hemmed in by Cranberry Mountain on the east and south, Kennison Mountain on the west, and Black Mountain to the north. Cranberry River passes through the glades and exits through a narrow water gap between Kennison and Black mountains. Here it passes over erosion-resistant sandstone, which has not allowed the river to cut a deep channel, thus slowing the rate of flow. This accounts for the poor drainage and unique environment of the glades.

The Brooks family of French Creek, Fred, A. B., and later Maurice, were the first naturalists to study this area. Their annual trips, beginning in 1898, usually included a week or two of tenting, long days of collecting plants, birding, and trapping rodents, followed by evenings sorting and identifying specimens by lantern. They published numerous papers on the Glades in scientific journals, which attracted other naturalists to visit.

The glades lie at 3,300 to 3,400 feet above sea level. They consist of open spaces, alder thickets, and bog forests. Dense thickets of speckled alder separate the five openings or glades, which collectively occupy about 100 acres. Around the edges are bog forests made up of red spruce and various hardwoods.

The ten-acre Flag Glade is most accessible. A boardwalk allows visitors to see a cross section of the different ecological conditions and many of the unique plants, birds, and small animals. The largest is Big Glade (59 acres) where two rare plants, bog rosemary and buckbean, occur. Round and Long glades are both ten acres in size. The smallest open area is Little Glade (one acre).

Much of the glades is covered by sphagnum moss, bird-wheat moss, and reindeer moss. These form hummocks up to three feet high. Growing over these are prostrate cranberry vines. Several species of orchids and insectivorous plants occur. Birds reaching their southern breeding range limit here are Swainson's and hermit thrushes, Nashville and mourning warblers, and purple finches.

The glades have been designated as the Cranberry Glades Botanical Area.

See also Bogs, Cranberry River

Kenneth L. Carvell
Morgantown

Maurice G. Brooks, *The Appalachians*, 1965; Earl L. Core, *Vegetation of West Virginia*, 1974.

Cranberry River

The Cranberry River flows through the heart of the remote Cranberry backcountry of Greenbrier, Webster, and Pocahontas counties. The river rises on Cranberry Mountain just above the Cranberry Glades Botanical Area at an elevation of 4,600 feet. It meanders sluggishly through the glades and beyond for about seven miles before tumbling through the mountains for another 25 miles to join the Gauley River at an elevation of 1,920 feet. Cranberry River drains 74 square miles inhabited by wildlife and covered with maturing second-growth stands of northern hardwoods, including black cherry, sugar maple, tulip poplar, hemlock, basswood, birch, and various species of oak. Red spruce grows at the highest elevations of the watershed.

The Cranberry region was difficult to get into and not desirable for homesteading. The land was still in pristine condition when the Cherry River Boom & Lumber Company acquired 200,000 acres at the turn of the 20th century. By 1930, the area that is now Cranberry Wilderness was completely logged, and the valuable timber had been hauled to Richwood. Wildfires burned over much of the region following the logging operations. The Civilian Conservation Corps converted some of the old logging railroad grades to U.S. Forest Service roads.

The river is popular with fishermen from throughout the eastern United States. In the spring, kayaks run the section from the Cranberry campground to the river's mouth. The Forest Service maintains seven camping shelters along the Cranberry River and about 75 miles of hiking trails throughout the back country. The Cranberry River and surrounding landscape lie within the Gauley Ranger District of the Monongahela National Forest. The opportunities for wilderness hiking, backpacking, horseback riding, hunting, fishing, cross-country skiing, bicycling, camping, and wildlife viewing are excellent.

See also Cranberry Glades

Emily Grafton
Morgantown

Cranesville Swamp

Cranesville Swamp is located in Preston County, nine miles north of Terra Alta. The swamp totals about 600 acres, of which a part is in Maryland. A high mountain bog formed thousands of years ago, the swamp is a unique ecological area. Many plants and animals common to more boreal and northern areas such as Canada, live at Cranesville as survivors from the Ice Age. Special physiographic conditions at the swamp help maintain these relict populations.

The area, named for local "cranes" (actually great blue herons), was described by the mountain man and hunter Meshach Browning, who stated that the swamp area in the 1850s was full of panthers, wolves, bobcats, black bears, trout, and other wildlife. Today, the Nature Conservancy owns more than 300 acres of Cranesville Swamp. Visitors to the sanctuary may tour the swamp by a boardwalk leading into the bog. There they can see eastern larch, a northern deciduous swamp conifer, and other bog plants including cottongrass, cranberry, and the carnivorous sundew.

See also Meshach Browing

Norma Jean Kennedy-Venable
Morgantown

Bruce Crawford

Journalist Bruce Crawford was born December 5, 1893, in Norton, Virginia. He spent his boyhood in Fayette County, before his family moved back to Norton for his high school years. After a brief stay at West Virginia University and service in the army during World War I, he became owner and editor of a Norton newspaper, *Crawford's Weekly*.

In 1931, Crawford traveled to Harlan County, Kentucky, with a committee of celebrities including authors Theodore Dreiser and John Dos Passos, to investigate the bloody miners' strike there. He received a gunshot wound and returned home to write editorials sympathetic to the striking miners. This earned him a reputation as a radical among the business leaders in Norton upon whose advertising his newspaper depended. Forced to sell his weekly because of declining revenues, he returned to West Virginia to edit the *Bluefield Sunset News* for several years.

From 1938 to 1941, Crawford directed the West Virginia Writers Project, a Works Progress Administration program that provided work for unemployed writers. The project's most enduring work was the classic book, *West Virginia: A Guide to the Mountain State*, initially blocked as too radical by Governor Holt and published only after Holt left office in 1941.

Crawford later served as secretary of the West Virginia Publicity Commission, directed the Highway Safety Bureau of the West Virginia State Police, and in about 1946 founded the West Virginia Advertising Company, which, until his retirement in 1961 handled campaign publicity for many state Democratic candidates.

Crawford died in St. Petersburg, Florida, August 15, 1993.

See also West Virginia: A Guide to the Mountain State

Jerry Bruce Thomas
Shepherd University
Arthur C. Pritchard, "'In West Virginia I Had More Freedom': Bruce Crawford's Story," *Goldenseal*, Spring 1984; Jerry B. Thomas, "'The Nearly Perfect State': Governor Homer Adams Holt, the WPA Writers' Project and the Making of *West Virginia: A Guide to the Mountain State*," *West Virginia History*, 1993.

William Crawford

Frontiersman William Crawford was born September 2, 1722, in present Jefferson County. He was a farmer, soldier, and surveyor, and the land agent of George Washington.

Crawford first saw the upper Ohio Valley during the French and Indian War, as a militia soldier under Gen. Edward Braddock in 1755 and with Gen. John Forbes during the capture of Fort Duquesne in 1758. After the French and Indian War, Crawford fought during Pontiac's Rebellion and served as a major in Virginia Governor Dunmore's army during Dunmore's War; in the summer of 1774 he directed the construction of Fort

Fincastle (later Fort Henry) at Wheeling. He was commissioned colonel in 1776, and served under Washington during the Revolution at the battles of Long Island, Trenton, Princeton, Brandywine, and Germantown.

Washington had known Crawford since his youth, and often employed him as his chief surveyor. Crawford had accompanied Washington and Dr. James Craik, later surgeon-general of the Continental Army, on their canoe journey down the Ohio River in October 1770 in search of valuable bottomlands. The next year, Crawford surveyed thousands of acres in present West Virginia, including 2,314 acres in Wood County, known as Washington Bottom, and 10,000 acres at the confluence of the Ohio and Kanawha rivers in Mason County. These tracts were registered by Crawford for Washington in 1772.

Colonel Crawford's death was tragic. He led a force of 500 militia against the Wyandot Indians at their village at Sandusky, Ohio, in June 1782. His force was defeated and retreated in panic. Crawford was captured by the Delaware, who mistakenly blamed him for the treacherous murder of about 100 Moravian Christian Indians at Gnadenhutten the previous February. He was tortured and burned at the stake on June 11, 1782.

See also George Washington

Philip Sturm
Ohio Valley University
Allan W. Eckert, *That Dark and Bloody River*, 1995; Allen W. Scholl, *The Brothers Crawford: Colonel William, 1722–1782, and Valentine Jr., 1724–1777*, 1995.

Porte Crayon

See David Hunter Strother.

Michael Cresap

Frontiersman Michael Cresap was born June 29, 1742, at Oldtown, Maryland. His father, an Indian trader, was the first settler at that site along the Potomac River, across from present Hampshire County. Cresap was married to Mary Whitehead in 1764 at Philadelphia. The following year, Cresap and his wife occupied a new stone house in Oldtown which he had built, a structure that now houses the Michael Cresap Museum.

In the early 1770s, Cresap led Virginia frontiersmen in their opposition to Pennsylvania's assertion of authority in the area south and west of the Monongahela River. This action established him as a leader in the region. In 1774, hostilities were renewed between whites and Indians in the upper Ohio Valley. Cresap had begun to clear land near Wheeling, where he was chosen by frightened settlers to lead an armed band to the Shawnee villages in Ohio to take revenge for several attacks and murders of whites. The result was a series of Indian skir-

mishes, known as Cresap's War. The most despicable act of this engagement was the murder on April 30 of several Indians at Yellow Creek, including a brother and sister of the Mingo Chief Logan by a group of settlers led by Daniel Greathouse. Logan and others, including Thomas Jefferson in his *Notes on Virginia*, blamed Cresap for the murders, though Cresap was not present at the killings and later condemned them. Logan's campaign of revenge helped to bring on Dunmore's War, which culminated in the October 1774 Battle of Point Pleasant.

In June 1775, Cresap was elected captain of the First Company, Maryland Rifles, which endured a forced march to join the siege of Boston. He became seriously ill during the march and ensuing battle and started home to recuperate. Cresap died, though, at New York City, October 18, 1775.

See also Chief Logan, Daniel Greathouse, Greathouse Party Massacre

Philip Sturm
Ohio Valley University

Crime

As early as 1971, West Virginia's crime rate was the lowest in the nation, at 1,401.4 crimes per 100,000 people. Although the national crime rate peaked in 1980 and has since fallen substantially, West Virginia still had the lowest rate in the nation until 1998. That year, the West Virginia crime rate reached 2,547.2 crimes per 100,000 people, second-lowest in the nation. In 2004, the state's crime rate was seventh-lowest, standing at 2,777.4, compared to the national rate of 3,982.6.

West Virginia's low crime rate is generally attributed to the rural nature of the state. Thirty-two percent of West Virginians live in a rural jurisdiction, as compared to 10.3 percent of the population nationwide. Other elements, including population density, age demographics, the mobility of the population, the jurisdiction's infrastructure, economic conditions, cultural factors, and the degree of support for law enforcement also contribute to the absence or presence of crime in a community. Certainly, West Virginia's high average age and low population density are among the factors contributing to the low crime rate in the state.

Nearly 90 percent of West Virginia crimes are nonviolent, a portion that hasn't changed much since 1961, although the number of both violent and nonviolent crimes has increased. The most common crime in the state is larceny-theft, accounting for more than 60 percent of offenses in 2004. Murder and non-negligent manslaughter, the least frequent crime in West Virginia, was committed at a rate of 3.7 per 100,000 in 2004, down from a peak 7.4 in 1975. Eighty percent of crimes in West Virginia occur in urban jurisdictions. Drug offenses are low in West Virginia, compared to other places. In the late 1990s, West Virginia's crime rate remained fairly stable, leaving West Virginia by 1999 with the fourth-lowest crime rate in the nation, remaining at fourth in 2000 and 2001. Since then West Virginia's crime rate has steadily increased, though still low by national standards.

In addition to its low crime rate, West Virginia also has one of the lowest incarceration rates in the nation. In 2001, West Virginia had the 11th-lowest incarceration rate, with 277 prisoners with a sentence of more than one year per 100,000 residents. West Virginia also had one of the lowest prisoner populations in the nation, with 5,026 prisoners incarcerated for a sentence of one year or more. However, the state's prison population has more than doubled in the past decade. West Virginia prisoner population had the sixth-highest growth rate in 2004, with a 6.6 percent increase. Criminal justice professionals and policy makers are examining the state's sentencing practices as they analyze this troubling increase in incarcerations.

Although the state crime rate has gradually risen against the backdrop of sharply falling national rates, West Virginia at the beginning of the 21st century has among the lowest crime rates, lowest incarceration rates, and lowest prisoner populations in the country. All things considered, our state remains among the very safest places to live and raise a family.

Brad Douglas
Division of Corrections

Croatian Cultural Club

The Croatian Cultural Club was founded in Benwood, Marshall County, in 1955 by Mike Perkovic, an immigrant Croatian coal miner who worked for decades to preserve and present Croatian culture around the state. Perkovic's children had been playing tambouritzan music since the 1930s and had a regular Sunday Slavic music hour on WWVA in Wheeling. Until World War II, Croatian and other Slavic languages could be heard in the streets and markets of Benwood and nearby mining communities such as Boggs Run. But by the mid-1950s, these traditions had begun to wane. Established in the abandoned Benwood School on Eoff Street, the Croatian Cultural Club was embraced by the community as a means of fostering traditional cultural and social customs of all ethnic groups. Traditional music, dance, culinary arts, and after school Croatian recitation classes were emphasized by Mike Perkovic until his death in 1969. Fraternal lodge meetings and other local events were regularly held at the club.

Today the club with its homey atmosphere is managed by Mike's son, John Perkovic, and still serves an important so-

cial function in the neighborhood. The club offers a full menu of ethnic foods, music, and cultural events by appointment and is available for parties and retirement dinners.

Michael Kline
St. Mary's City, Maryland
Michael Kline, "The Music Made Everything Okay: Michael Kline Interviews the Perkovic Family of Boggs Run," *Goldenseal,* Summer 1982.

Claudius Crozet

Born in France, January 1, 1790, engineer Claudius "Claude" Crozet was destined for a military career. Following his education at the École Polytechnique (1804–07) he entered the military academy at Metz (1807–09) and was commissioned a sub-lieutenant of artillery.

Appointed to Napoleon's headquarters, Crozet served in Germany and Holland beginning in 1809 until Napoleon's defeat at Waterloo in 1815. The following year he immigrated to the United States and was appointed an assistant professor at the U.S. Military Academy. From 1817 to 1823, he served as professor of engineering at West Point, before being appointed state engineer of Virginia in 1823. He served until 1832 and was reappointed again in 1837. As state engineer, he was in charge of the Board of Public Works of Virginia, involved in numerous turnpike projects including the layout of the Northwestern Turnpike from Winchester to Parkersburg.

Claude Crozet

He engineered a course through
  Russian snow
And staked a road beyond the torpid
  Nile,
Around the Alps and to the river Po,
Mapped out an army's passage mile by
  mile.
His emperor who conquered half the
  earth
Holds last dominion under English
  sand -
And Claude Crozet, who found an
  exile's berth,
Surveys a turnpike through the Gauley
  land.
He takes his compass from a leather
  sack,
Sets up a tripod, lets his line fall
  plumb,
And shadowing the short-cut bison
  track
Lays out a broader road for days to
  come.
Now troops may march by Gauley
  shore
And booted captains ride,
And great wheels roll the freight of war
Up Gauley's flint-ribbed side.
      —Louise McNeill

Later, Crozet was involved in railway construction, most notably the Blue Ridge Tunnel, which at 4,273 feet was at the time the longest of its kind in North America.

Crozet was a founding member of the Virginia Military Institute faculty, where he introduced the study of descriptive geometry in the curriculum. He taught at VMI from 1837 to 1845. He later served under Gen. Montgomery C. Meigs in the building of the Washington Aqueduct (1857–59). He became principal of the Richmond Academy in 1859 and served until his death, January 29, 1864.

Crozet made a significant contribution to the road network in Western Virginia during his tenure with the Board of Public Works. He was one of the outstanding civil engineers of America in the first half of the 19th century.

Emory L. Kemp
WVU Institute for the History of Technology
William Couper, *Claudius Crozet: Soldier—Sailor—Educator—Engineer (1789–1864),* 1936; Robert F. Hunter and Edwin L. Dooley Jr., *Claudius Crozet,* 1989.

George Crumb

Composer George Crumb was born in Charleston, October 24, 1929. His *Poem for Orchestra* was given its premiere performance by the Charleston Symphony Orchestra, with his father playing clarinet and his mother playing in the cello section, when he was only 17 years old. After graduating from Charleston High School, he earned a bachelor of music degree from Mason College of Music (later absorbed into Morris Harvey College, now the University of Charleston), master of music degree from the University of Illinois, and doctor of musical arts degree from the University of Michigan, where he studied with Ross Lee Finney. From 1965 to 1997, he served as professor of music at the University of Pennsylvania.

In 1968, Crumb was awarded the Pulitzer Prize for *Echoes of Time and the River: Four Processionals for Orchestra,* commissioned by the University of Chicago for its 75th anniversary and premiered by the Chicago Symphony Orchestra. Among the unusual sonic devices used in this piece is the rhythmic intoning of the West Virginia motto "Montani semper liberi." Crumb's many settings of poetry by Federico Garcia Lorca include *Ancient Voices of Children,* which won the Koussevitzky and UNESCO International Rostrum of Composers awards in 1971. His *Star Child* received a 2001 Grammy Award for best classical contemporary composition. He also wrote several volumes of keyboard music published as *Makrokosmos.*

Although Crumb's music abounds in its use of exotic sounds and instruments, such as Tibetan prayer stones, African mbira, and Japanese temple bells, his

Composer George Crumb (1929–).

West Virginia roots are evident in his frequent use of the mandolin, sometimes with bottle-neck technique, as well as musical saw, banjo, and hammered dulcimer. Crumb's imaginative musical scores are characterized by meticulous notation, incongruous juxtapositions, new performance techniques, and highly refined timbral nuances.

The Charleston *Sunday Gazette-Mail* named George Crumb West Virginian of the Year in 1968, with soprano Phyllis Curtin. He lives in a suburb of Philadelphia.

H. G. Young III
WVU Parkersburg

George Crumb, *Echoes of Time and the River: Four Processionals for Orchestra*, 1967; Don Gillespie, ed., *George Crumb: Profile of a Composer*, 1986.

CSX

CSX is the successor corporation to the Chessie System, created as a result of the merger of other railroads with the Chessie System in 1980.

In the 1970s, it was evident the Norfolk & Western and the Southern Railway System were progressing toward a merger. To remain competitive the Chessie System sought a partner for itself. The other railroad system in the South most affected by the pending N&W-Southern merger was the Family Lines, a loose affiliation of the Seaboard Coast Line and the Louisville & Nashville railroads and their predecessor lines. On November 1, 1980, the Chessie System and the Family Lines merged into the CSX Corporation. The merger was complex as the two systems retained separate identities for some time, and the L&N did not merge into the Seaboard Coast Line corporation until 1982.

In 1999, CSX and Norfolk Southern absorbed Conrail, the major railroad in the northeast, and divided its lines between themselves. Thus CSX and Norfolk Southern dominated rail transportation in the eastern United States at the beginning of the 21st century.

See also Chesapeake & Ohio Railway, Chessie System

Robert L. Frey
Miamisburg, Ohio

The Cultural Center

One week after the United States celebrated its bicentennial, Governor Moore dedicated the West Virginia Science and Culture Center on July 11, 1976. Located just west of the state capitol and behind the Governor's Mansion, the $14-million structure, designed by C. E. Silling of Charleston, was constructed to showcase the Mountain State's artistic, cultural, and historic heritage. The center became the home of the new West Virginia Division of Culture and History, including its arts and historic preservation units, and the State Archives, State Theater, and State Museum. The West Virginia Library Commission shares the building, with its offices and a major library there.

The center's great hall, with its white Alabama marble walls accented by West Virginia oak, a red Tennessee marble floor, gold and wood coffered ceiling, and two large dodecahedron-shaped bronze and crystal chandeliers, welcomes visitors. The 468-seat theater, behind the great hall, hosts West Virginia's performing artists, dance, theater, jazz, and film festivals, affairs of state, and performance broadcasts of West Virginia Public Broadcasting's "Mountain Stage." The Library Commission's reference room is at the left of the great hall and the Archives library is to the right.

The State Museum, closed for renovation in 2006, previously displayed artifacts and exhibits profiling West Virginia's land and people, paleontology, minerals, frontier life, industries, and wartime history. Changing exhibitions showcased items from the museum's extensive collections, as well as traveling exhibits and winners of the biennial West Virginia Juried Exhibition. The building's non-public upper levels house book and manuscript collections of the State Archives and the closed stacks of the Library Commission. The Cultural Center is the site of the annual Vandalia Gathering folk festival each Memorial Day weekend, and hosts other events throughout the year.

H. G. Young III
WVU Parkersburg

Carolanne Griffith, "For a Tour of West Virginia's New Science and Culture Center," *Wonderful West Virginia*, December 1976.

The Cultural Landscape

People who settle new areas create cultural landscapes, and usually do so without realizing the lasting impact they will have. Cultural landscapes include all the changes humans make to natural landscapes. People modify the shape of the land's surface, remove or alter its vegetation, and place structures on the land. Through the simple act of living in a place, people leave an imprint of their way of life, or culture, on the landscape that surrounds them.

Structures on the land include not only actual buildings, but also such things as fences, gates, and bridges, and even changes in the kinds of plants or trees found in an area. Some structures, like land division systems used to separate neighboring landholdings, may seem less obvious but still leave lasting imprints on the landscape, especially when viewed from a mountaintop or airplane where patterns in the shape of agricultural fields or woodlots become apparent. The "metes and bounds" survey system brought from England is used in West Virginia, and it creates irregularly shaped land parcels because it relies on natural landmarks such as rivers or ridge tops.

Cultural landscapes mirror the prevailing culture. What we see in the landscape is an unconscious reflection of all the ideas, values, and beliefs that people have about how to use the land, and what styles, building materials, or even land survey systems, make the most sense to them. When Scotch Irish, English, and German immigrants settled West Virginia's land, they relied on their native folk cultures when constructing houses and barns. Many had been farmers in Europe, so they built isolated farmsteads in this region because that form of settlement was more familiar to them than living in towns. The abundant forests provided logs for their houses and numerous outbuildings.

Early farmsteads typically included a one-room cabin, perhaps with a loft, or a two-room cabin with the rooms connected by an open breezeway, all covered by a single roof with gabled ends. People who study material culture call these structures single or double pens, respectively, and log barns were often built in the same styles. Some scholars identify the specific cultural origins of log buildings by the way the logs are joined, especially at the corners. Two-story log cabins with chimneys at both ends are known as I houses. They typically signified a wealthier family. Farmsteads included outbuildings such as springhouses, smokehouses, barns, corncribs, and other structures.

Today, people's tastes are more influenced by popular culture, reflecting commercial trends and fashions. Few people built log cabins from local timber during the past 50 years, but plenty of ranch-style or split-level houses were constructed. Many remnants of the earlier material folk culture still can be found in the landscape.

All buildings, not just houses and farm structures, are part of the cultural landscape. The appearances of factories, offices, and stores change over time, contributing to the evolving look of our landscapes. People used to come into town to do their shopping, but today many head for a shopping center or a mall developed along one of the major roads on the outskirts of cities. Strip development along highways now offers shoppers clusters of nearly everything they might desire, including car dealers, grocery stores, fast food restaurants, and seemingly ubiquitous Wal-Mart stores.

Cultural landscapes may be "read" by those who care to do so. Landscapes are full of clues about the people who create and inhabit them. Signs on businesses or even town names often tell us about the ethnic background of the people who created them. A name like McCready's Hardware Store suggests that, at least initially, the store belonged to someone of Scottish descent. West Virginia place names like Glasgow or Glengary also hint at the important role of Scots in settling this region of the country. Likewise, names painted on mailboxes or inscribed on stone markers in cemeteries reveal ethnic information about residents in the area. Religious preferences of early settlers persist today in the denominations of churches found in communities around the state, providing further hints about ethnicity in the cultural landscape.

Factories and other places of employment offer clues about how people earn a living, and which natural resources are plentiful. A coal preparation plant in southern West Virginia suggests the presence of coal mining nearby. The state's abundant coal reserves contributed to the establishment of steel mills in the Northern Panhandle and the neighboring Pittsburgh area. Such things have great consequences for the landscape. Think about how different Weirton looks compared to Lewisburg. Weirton's steel mills would look out of place in the broad agricultural valley of Greenbrier County, and the opposite is true, as well.

Cultural landscapes are found not only in rural places or small towns. Cities also have their own distinctive cultural landscapes. Very large cities can display astonishingly different styles of land use, each providing information about what socioeconomic groups live in a particular area and which economic activities are important there. The capitol complex in Charleston, for example, clearly demonstrates the important role of state government functions in our capital city. The downtowns of large cities also display a much greater concentration of professional architecture. Small town and rural landscapes tend to be dominated by "vernacular" architecture, structures built in locally popular styles and not designed by professional architects. The cultural landscapes of residential areas can be very interesting because many homeowners try to express their personalities in the way they paint or decorate their houses and by what they display in their yards.

People make decisions individually about their own property every day, and collectively these decisions have a profound effect on how the landscape looks.

The style of house they build, the kind of flowers or crops they plant, or the types of churches or businesses that are constructed at first may not seem linked together. But, over time, all these decisions add up to create the cultural landscapes that we see in the world around us. When armed with some basic information and a lot of curiosity, anyone with a keen eye can make better sense of a walk down main street or a drive in the country simply by reading the cultural landscape.

See also Folklore, Material Culture

Lizbeth Pyle
Morgantown

Henry Glassie, *Pattern in the Material Folk Culture of the Eastern United States*, 1968; John Fraser Hart, *The Rural Landscape*, 1998; John Brinkerhoff Jackson, *Discovering the Vernacular Landscape*, 1984.

Dan Cunningham

Lawman Daniel Webster "Dan" Cunningham was born in Jackson County, January 16, 1850. His remarkable career involved him in the Hatfield-McCoy Feud, the West Virginia Mine Wars, bloody land disputes, political skullduggery, and the destruction of moonshine stills. Cunningham first taught school, then was hired as a deputy U.S. marshal by Marshal (later Governor) George W. Atkinson. He continued to serve through the terms of Marshals H. S. White, Frank Tyree, and Frank Thompson.

Cunningham was charged with murder in connection with the Bruen lands feud, a late-19th century vendetta stemming from the resentment of outside ownership and long-simmering hatred of opposing Civil War factions in Jackson and Roane counties. Cunningham's brother, Nathan, served as a deputy U.S. marshal and land agent for the absentee Bruen land company and evicted squatters from their land. Nathan Cunningham was murdered during the feud, and Dan Cunningham was alleged to be part of a group that exacted vengeance in 1887 by murdering Rev. Tom Ryan, a member of the opposing faction. Arrested in Roane County, Cunningham was tried and acquitted in Jackson County.

Cunningham was involved in arresting both Hatfields and McCoys during the decade-long feud violence on the border of Kentucky and West Virginia. Frequently in danger, and once captured by hostile McCoys in Kentucky, Cunningham nevertheless overpowered several armed men and brought them to justice. On another occasion the Hatfields caught him in West Virginia and humiliated him by taking him to the Logan county seat as their prisoner.

When Judge B. F. Keller issued sweeping injunctions against union organizing efforts in the New River coalfields in 1902, Cunningham was responsible for serving warrants and arresting violators.

In performing his duties, he was involved in several spectacular gun battles with striking miners, including one in which miner John Harless was killed by Cunningham's deputies and the Battle of Stanaford, in which six union sympathizers were killed. He was recalled in the autobiography of labor organizer Mother Jones as that "big elephant, Dan Cunningham."

After retiring from the U.S. Marshal Service, Cunningham served as a city detective in Charleston, as a special police officer for the Kanawha & Michigan Railroad, and as a deputy game warden for the West Virginia Game, Fish and Forestry Commission. He was a member of the Kanawha County Board of Examiners for teachers for eight years. Cunningham died February 5, 1942, at age 92.

See also Battle of Stanaford, Bruen Lands Feud

Kenneth R. Bailey
WVU Institute of Technology

Kenneth R. Bailey, "The Murder of John Harless, or Federal Justice, Southern West Virginia Style," *New River Symposium Proceedings*, 1991; Ludwell H. Johnson III, ed., "'The Horrible Butcheries of West Virginia,' Dan Cunningham on the Hatfield-McCoy Feud," *West Virginia History*, 1985–86; James P. Mylott, *A Measure of Prosperity, A History of Roane County*, 1984.

Richard Currey

Writer Richard Currey was born October 19, 1949, in Parkersburg. He served as a navy medical corpsman during the Vietnam War, and studied at West Virginia University and Howard University.

Currey's first poem was published in 1974. In 1980, his collection of poetry, *Crossing Over: A Vietnam Journal,* was published, and he became the D. H. Lawrence Fellow in Literature and writer in residence at the University of New Mexico. He was awarded a National Endowment for the Arts fellowship and had his first short story published in 1981. In 1987, he received his second NEA fellowship, and his first novel, the semi-autobiographical *Fatal Light*, about a West Virginia soldier in Vietnam, was published. *The Wars of Heaven*, a collection of his short stories, followed in 1990. The title story from the book is included in the 1998 O. Henry Award prize story collection. His novel, *Lost Highway*, about a West Virginia country-western singer, was published in 1997.

Currey bases his fiction on his own experiences, often drawing from his own family and life in the hills of his native West Virginia. He won the Bravo Award for Literary Excellence in New Mexico and the Charles H. Daugherty Humanities Award in West Virginia in 1998. Richard Currey founded the Santa Fe Writers Project.

James Slack
Charleston

Phyllis Curtin

Operatic soprano Phyllis (Smith) Curtin was born in Clarksburg, December 3, 1921, graduated from Wellesley College, and in 1946 appeared at famed Tanglewood Music Center under Leonard Bernstein and with the New England Opera under Boris Goldovsky. She made her debut with the New York City Opera in 1953, where she sang both classical and modern repertoire, including all major Mozart heroines and many new works. *Life* magazine devoted three pages of photos to her seductive "dance of the seven veils" in Richard Strauss's *Salome* in 1954. The following year she premiered the title role in Carlisle Floyd's *Susannah*, which she later sang at the Brussels World's Fair in 1958, followed by leading roles in premieres of Floyd's *Wuthering Heights* and *The Passion of Jonathan Wade*. More than 50 new works were written expressly for her, including operas by Darius Milhaud and Alberto Ginastera and a song cycle by Ned Rorem. She also sang with the NBC Opera Company on television and on tour. Curtin made her Metropolitan Opera debut in 1961 and developed an international reputation with performances at the Teatro Colón in Buenos Aires, La Scala in Milan, and the Vienna Staatoper.

In 1976, President Gerald Ford invited her to sing for a White House dinner honoring West German Chancellor Helmut Schmidt. Curtin taught at the Berkshire Music Center and Yale University before she retired from public singing in 1984 and served as dean of the Boston University School of the Arts from 1983 to 1991. In her native state, Phyllis Curtin sang with the Charleston Symphony Orchestra in 1958 and 1968, at the 1963 meeting of the Music Educators National Conference in Charleston, was named West Virginian of the Year with composer George Crumb in 1968 by the Charleston *Sunday Gazette-Mail*, and received a Lifetime Achievement Award at the 1999 Governor's Awards for Culture, History and the Arts.

H. G. Young III
WVU Parkersburg

Dagmar

A striking, statuesque actress famous for her dumb-blond act, Dagmar was born Virginia Ruth Egnor in Logan County, November 29, 1921. She grew up in Huntington, where she attended Huntington High School and Huntington Business College.

During World War II, she and her husband, Angelo Lewis, moved to New York City. In New York, she modeled sweaters and began her acting career on Broadway in *Laughing Room Only*, a show featuring the comedy team of Olsen and Johnson. As Jennie Lewis, she appeared in comedy skits on early television variety shows.

In 1950, her acting career took off when she was hired to be on NBC's *Broadway Open House*, the network's first late-night television show. The show's host, comedian Jerry Lester, changed her name to Dagmar for one skit and the name stuck. Dagmar's deadpan delivery of punch lines and clever misuse of words made her instantly popular. She appeared on stage with Milton Berle and Frank Sinatra, and on Edward R. Murrow's *Person to Person* television show. Her picture, taken by photographer Alfred Eisenstaedt, appeared on the July 16, 1951, cover of *Life* magazine. In the early '50s, at the height of her popularity, she received 2,000 fan letters a week.

By 1952, *Broadway Open House* was off the air and Dagmar had her own variety show, *Dagmar's Canteen*, which had a short run. After the 1950s, Dagmar curtailed her schedule, but continued to perform in nightclubs and in summer theater productions. Dagmar lived in Con-

necticut until 1996, when she moved to Ceredo, Wayne County. She died October 9, 2001.

Danske Dandridge

Poet Danske Dandridge was born in Copenhagen, November 19, 1854, while her father, Henry Bedinger, was serving as ambassador to Denmark. She was christened Caroline Dane Bedinger, her father giving her the nickname Danske ("Little Dane"). She lived her life from age 19 in Shepherdstown. She lived for a brief time at the Bower, the historic Dandridge family home near Leetown, following her marriage to A. B. Dandridge in 1877. The family then moved to Poplar Grove, near Shepherdstown, which she inherited from the Bedingers and renamed Rosebrake. She was educated at Mary Baldwin College in Staunton, Virginia.

Although mostly unknown today, Dandridge's work appeared in *Harper's* and *The Century*, two of the most respected periodicals of her time. Her books, now out of print, include *Joy and Other Poems* (1888), *George Michael Bedinger, a Kentucky Pioneer* (1909), *Historic Shepherdstown* (1910), and *American Prisoners of the Revolution* (1911).

Dandridge's poetry, which registers an emotional attachment to nature, family, and religion, is often self-consciously literary in its use of language and subject matter. Occasionally, it contains unmistakable homoerotic overtones. Lush descriptions, careful attention to poetic form, and original voice characterize Dandridge's writing. Danske Dandridge committed suicide June 3, 1914, at age 59, after a long struggle with depression. The Bower and Rosebrake are Jefferson County landmarks, both listed in the National Register of Historic Places.

Cheryl B. Torsney
West Virginia University

Daniel Boone Hotel

One of West Virginia's premier hotels, the Daniel Boone of Charleston, was built on the site of the state's first governor's mansion and the temporary "pasteboard capitol" which had been quickly erected in 1921 after the nearby capitol building was destroyed by fire. The hotel, on the corner of Capitol and Washington streets, was built in 1929 by a group of Charleston citizens known as the Community Hotel Corporation to provide an elegant center for hosting politicians and visiting dignitaries in the bustling capital city. The building is significant as an example of a Classical Revival high rise in downtown Charleston, and its brick and terra cotta walls, lobby, mezzanine, and dining room areas are expressive examples of first-class hotel architecture of the 1920s and 1930s.

The capitol soon moved to Charleston's

east end, but the new hotel nevertheless became for many years the unofficial headquarters of West Virginia state government. The Daniel Boone served as a base for most state legislators during the 60-day legislative sessions. Many laws were conceived, discussed, or modified in the smoke-filled rooms of the hotel, and most of Charleston's major meetings, banquets, and conventions were held there. Many prominent Americans stayed at the Daniel Boone, including Eleanor Roosevelt, Adm. Richard Byrd, Presidents Herbert Hoover and Harry Truman, Victor Borge, Gene Autry, Bob Hope, Debbie Reynolds, Wendell Willkie, Jack Dempsey, Guy Lombardo, the Lawrence Welk Orchestra, Vice President Lyndon Johnson, and Sen. and Mrs. John F. Kennedy. When Elvis Presley visited Charleston in 1975, his entourage occupied 63 rooms including the penthouse suite.

In 1981, the Daniel Boone Hotel closed. After renovation and remodeling the building was reopened in 1984 as 405 Capitol Street, an office building with fountains, a spacious atrium, and a 30-foot indoor waterfall. The building is listed on the National Register of Historic Places.

Stan Cohen
Pictorial Histories

Daughters of the American Revolution

The National Society of the Daughters of the American Revolution was organized in Washington in 1890. Membership in the patriotic organization is open to any woman at least 18 years old who is descended from a person who provided military or other service to the cause of American independence. The West Virginia State Society of the DAR was organized in 1899. There have been a total of 69 chapters throughout the state; in 2000 there were 44 chapters in the state society, with a membership of some 2,200 women.

The state society of the DAR provides a college nursing scholarship as well as awards to American history essay contest winners in the elementary and middle schools. It also maintains a visitors' cottage at Tamassee DAR School in South Carolina. The society presents awards to outstanding Reserve Officers Training Corps cadets, to high school good citizens, and to volunteers who work with veteran patients. Notable among its efforts in historic preservation was the successful project to restore the Taylor County home of Anna Jarvis, the founder of Mother's Day. In 1979, the house was listed on the National Register of Historic Places.

Cora P. Teel
Marshall University

Dagmar (1921–2001) was a well-paid star in 1951.

Davis & Elkins College

Davis & Elkins College was founded in Elkins in 1904 by Southern Presbyterians, in cooperation with former senators Henry Gassaway Davis and Stephen B. Elkins, who gave land and financial support. The aim of the founders was to establish a Presbyterian college in West Virginia "which shall do for the people of that state what Hampden-Sydney, Washington and Lee, and Davidson colleges have done for Virginia and North Carolina." Ultimately, the college came to be supported by the reunited Presbyterian Church (U.S.A.).

First located in one building south of Elkins, the college initially included an academy or secondary school served by the same four-man faculty. In 1926, a new campus was developed on land surrounding Senator Elkins's mansion, Halliehurst, overlooking the town from the north. The academy was discontinued. Subsequently, the Davis mansion, Graceland, and land adjacent to the Elkins farm were added to the campus. By 1998, the campus consisted of 170 acres and 20 major buildings, six of them listed on the National Register of Historic Places. Halliehurst served as the office for the president and other administrators, and Graceland had been painstakingly rehabilitated as a fine inn and conference center.

From the beginning, D&E served students from the local area and from other states and nations. Enrollment grew slowly, never exceeding 250 prior to World War II. There were three presidents in the first six years. During the presidency of James E. Allen (1910–35), efforts to attract students led to modification of the classical curriculum to include all of the liberal arts and the addition of business administration, teacher education, and engineering. D&E gained recognition for its championship football and basketball teams, the "Scarlet Hurricanes," coached by Cam Henderson and enthusiastically promoted by Jennings Randolph, the college's director of publicity and later a U.S. senator. In the Allen era, Charles Albert, Harry Whetsell, Raymond Purdum (each later serving as president), and Virgie Harris, Harry Shelton, and Benton Talbot (later dean) joined the faculty, all remaining several decades.

The college barely survived the 1930s. There were three presidents in seven years. World War II and its aftermath marked a critical turning point during the administrations of Presidents Raymond R. Purdum (1943–54) and David K. Allen (1954–64). Purdum's success in getting three military training units based on the campus enabled Davis & Elkins to prosper through the war years. Then an influx of veterans subsidized by the GI Bill boosted enrollment to more than

900, which necessitated additions to faculty and facilities. Full accreditation, achieved in 1946, was of vital significance. The establishment of an Air Force ROTC program in 1951 helped stabilize enrollment during the Korean and Vietnam conflicts. During the Purdum presidency, national honorary and social fraternities established chapters at D&E, and Memorial Gymnasium was erected.

President David Allen's administration reorganized the college's business and accounting procedures, created the development and chaplain's offices, the counseling and placement centers, and erected five new buildings. Soccer replaced football, and soon Coach Greg Myers fielded NAIA championship soccer teams. Under the leadership of Dean Thomas R. Ross, the faculty developed a strong liberal arts core curriculum, tenure, sabbatical leave, and retirement systems; added cooperative programs in forestry and engineering; and secured admission to the Washington Semester program.

In the period after 1964, the administrations of Gordon E. Hermanson (1964–82) and Dorothy I. MacConkey (1985–98) were especially significant. Both succeeded in increasing the participation of the trustees and in attracting interest in the college on the part of the current Elkins and Davis families.

Enrollment and endowment increased somewhat during the Hermanson years. A new campus plan gave impetus to the building of a chapel, science center, the Hermanson Center-Auditorium, the Boiler House Theater, and three residence halls. Majors in computer science, environmental science, and recreation management and tourism were added and independent study programs expanded. Under the leadership of Dean Margaret Purdum Goddin, honors and nursing programs were developed. The Augusta Heritage Center for the Traditional Arts was established, bringing students from throughout the United States and many foreign countries to popular summer workshops.

Notable achievements of President MacConkey's administration include extension of computer use for all administrative, library, and many academic functions; introduction of a hospitality and tourism management program; renovation of Halliehurst, Graceland, Jennings Randolph Hall, and the Gate House; and construction of the splendid Booth Library, Gates Tower, and Robert C. Byrd Conference Center. She greatly increased endowment, including initial funding for endowed chairs. The first faculty member to be appointed to an endowed chair was Gloria Payne, who served the college for 53 years. In the last year of her presidency, MacConkey launched a $17 million campaign for funding an athletic complex and to increase endowment.

G. Thomas Mann became the 12th president of Davis & Elkins College in 1998. The college enrollment was 603 in fall 2003, in full-time equivalents.

See also Augusta Heritage Center, Henry Gassaway Davis, Stephen B. Elkins

Thomas Richard Ross
Davis & Elkins College

Thomas Richard Ross, *Davis & Elkins College: The Diamond Jubilee History,* 1980.

Henry Gassaway Davis

Politician and industrialist Henry Gassaway Davis, known in the early 20th century as West Virginia's "Grand Old Man," was born November 16, 1823, in Baltimore, Maryland. His formal education did not extend beyond elementary school.

Starting as a farmhand, young Davis became a brakeman for the Baltimore & Ohio Railroad in 1842, later serving as conductor and station agent. Traveling the route from Washington to Cumberland, he noted the potential wealth of forestlands in areas that soon became part of West Virginia. He invested his savings and his wife's inheritance in thousands of acres of undeveloped land in the region, often paying only a dollar per acre. He left the B&O in 1858 to focus on his personal interests.

Davis, realizing the relationship of political power to business, won election to the House of Delegates in 1865 and the West Virginia Senate in 1868. He sponsored bills to create Mineral and Grant counties and to obtain for himself a charter for a corporation having vast powers to build a railroad and exploit the natural resources in north-central West Virginia.

U.S. Senator Henry Gassaway Davis, (1823–1916), about 1904.

In 1870, Davis helped lead the Democratic Party to victory, which began the party's quarter-century control of West Virginia. The next year, the legislature elected him West Virginia's first Democratic U.S. senator. He served from 1871 to 1883, becoming in time chairman of the Appropriations Committee. He opposed the Republican Radical Reconstruction program, denounced corruption in Grant's administration, and urged creation of the U.S. Department of Agriculture. Davis was a delegate to nine Democratic National Conventions and a dominant force in the state party for three decades. He was the Democratic nominee for vice president in 1904.

Tariff protection was more important than party affiliation to businessman Davis. Thus, he tacitly supported Republican Benjamin Harrison for president in 1888. Subsequently, Davis helped his son-in-law, Republican Stephen B. Elkins, win a U.S. Senate seat, where he influenced tariff legislation beneficial to the Davis-Elkins business interests.

Using the charter he had obtained in 1866, Davis built the West Virginia Central & Pittsburg [sic] Railway and its branch lines two decades later, thus enabling him to transport his coal and lumber to eastern markets. Later, he constructed a railroad connecting Charleston and Elkins. Profits from these enterprises and from banking and real estate brought him an immense fortune. He founded Elkins and other towns along his railroad routes.

His philanthropic legacies include Davis & Elkins College, Davis Memorial Hospital, and Davis Memorial Presbyterian Church in Elkins, several YMCAs, and Charleston's Davis Child Shelter. Fine equestrian statues of Henry Gassaway Davis stand in downtown Charleston and at the college gates in Elkins.

Davis received appointments from three presidents to successive Pan-American Conferences (1889–1902) and served as chairman of the Pan-American Railway Committee for several years. His last public service was in 1913 as chairman of the Semi-Centennial Commission which planned West Virginia's "Golden Jubilee," celebrating 50 years of statehood.

Henry Gassaway Davis died in Washington, March 11, 1916.

See also Davis & Elkins College, Stephen B. Elkins

Thomas Richard Ross
Davis & Elkins College

Thomas Richard Ross, *Henry Gassaway Davis: An Old Fashioned Biography*, 1994; John Alexander Williams, *West Virginia and the Captains of Industry*, 1976.

John W. Davis

Lawyer, diplomat, and presidential candidate John William Davis was born in Clarksburg, April 13, 1873. He was edu-
cated at Washington and Lee, graduating from the university in 1892 and from the law school in 1895. He taught law at W & L from 1896 to 1897. Davis practiced law in Clarksburg, 1897–1913, and was president of the West Virginia Bar Association in 1906.

Davis began his political career in the state House of Delegates in 1899 and was elected to Congress in 1911. As a congressman, Davis concentrated on drafting legislation, most notably the provisions in the 1914 Clayton Anti-Trust Act that banned the use of injunctions against labor unions. In that, he noted that "the labor of a human being is not a commodity or article of commerce." He resigned during his second term to become solicitor general of the United States, a position he held from 1913 to 1918. Davis was ambassador to England, from 1918 to 1921, and a member of the American delegation to the 1918 Geneva conference on the treatment and exchange of prisoners of war. He began practice in New York (1921) and was president of the American Bar Association (1922). Most widely known as the 1924 Democratic candidate for president, Davis lost overwhelmingly to Republican Calvin Coolidge and failed to carry either West Virginia or his native Clarksburg.

After the election, Davis returned to New York to his law firm, Davis Polk Wardwell Gardiner & Reed, where he practiced until his death. A staunch supporter of economic, property, and states' rights, Davis was fiercely anti-New Deal. In spite of his differences with President Roosevelt and many party leaders, he continued to support the Democratic Party. His first marriage to Julia McDonald produced a daughter, Julia Davis, author of *The Shenandoah* and other books. Widowed, he later married Ellen G. "Nell" Bassell.

One of the most accomplished lawyers of his time, Davis argued 141 cases before the U.S. Supreme Court. His last case was one of the most controversial, when he argued in 1952 for the continuation of racial segregation in South Carolina. The case *Briggs v. Elliot* was one of four cases comprising the landmark 1954 *Brown v. Board of Education*. Davis's name was often mentioned as a potential U.S. Supreme Court justice.

John W. Davis died March 24, 1955, in Charleston, South Carolina.

See also Julia Davis

Gretchen Krantz-Evans
Davis Polk & Wardwell, Germany

William H. Harbaugh, *Lawyer's Lawyer: The Life of John W. Davis*, 1990.

John Warren Davis

Educator John Warren Davis was born February 11, 1888. He was president of West Virginia State College from 1919 to 1953 and molded it into one of the strongest black colleges in the country.

John Warren Davis (1888–1980).

Born in Milledgeville, Georgia, Davis held degrees from Morehouse College, studied at the University of Chicago, and was awarded honorary degrees from a number of institutions including Harvard University and the University of Liberia. From 1914 to 1917, Davis served as registrar and faculty member at Morehouse, and from 1917 to 1919, he was the executive secretary of the 12th Street Branch of the Young Men's Christian Association in Washington.

Upon his 1919 arrival at what was then called West Virginia Collegiate Institute, Davis found that only 12 of the 28 faculty members had college degrees and only 27 of the 297 students were in college courses. He immediately set about strengthening both faculty and curriculum, and in 1927, the North Central Association fully accredited the institution. This made it one of four black colleges in the United States to be accredited and the first public college in West Virginia to be accredited. In 1929, it became West Virginia State College.

A part of the genius of Davis's presidency was that he placed West Virginia State College on the national scene. He enrolled it as a member of national organizations and was personally active in national educational circles, particularly in associations such as the Conference of Presidents of Land Grant Colleges for Negroes, the American Teachers' Association, and the North Central Association.

Under Davis's leadership, the college acquired and managed Washington-Carver 4-H Camp in Fayette County, established a field artillery ROTC program, and operated a Civilian Pilot Training Program which trained black fliers, several of whom became Tuskegee Airmen in World War II. West Virginia State College developed a record for excellence which attracted faculty and students from across the country. The institution's facilities expanded through the construction of 12 new buildings and enrollment more than tripled.

As he aged, Davis emerged as one of the nation's foremost spokesmen in matters of black higher education. He became an adviser to presidents and in 1952 accepted a U.S. government appointment in Liberia. Retiring from West Virginia State College in 1953, Davis continued his government service until 1954 after which he accepted an appointment with the NAACP Legal Defense Fund.

John Warren Davis died in Englewood, New Jersey, July 12, 1980.

See also West Virginia State University
Ancella R. Bickley
Charleston

John C. Harlan, *History of West Virginia State College*, 1968.

Julia Davis

Author Julia Davis, the daughter of distinguished lawyer and statesman John W. Davis and Julia Leavell McDonald Davis, was born July 23, 1900, in Clarksburg. Educated at Wellesley and Barnard colleges (B.A. 1922), she married William McMillan Adams in 1923 and began writing books for young readers. Her first, *The Swords of the Vikings* (1928), was followed by a biography of Stonewall Jackson, *Stonewall* (1931), a narrative of the Lewis and Clark expedition, *No Other White Men* (1937), and others. Davis also achieved success with her adult fiction, historical and biographical writings, and drama—more than two dozen books in all, including the Shenandoah volume for the landmark Rivers of America series.

Two later marriages, to Paul West and Charles P. Healy, brought stepchildren and other children who needed homes into her care, and Davis also was active in charitable organizations in New York. *The Sun Climbs Slow* (1942) is based on her experiences with two Spanish children who came to stay with her as a result of upheavals during the Spanish Civil War. In 1974, she and William Adams remarried. After his death in 1986, Julia Davis lived and continued to write in Jefferson County, near Media Farm, the McDonald family farm and the scene of the happy childhood summers described in *Legacy of Love* (1961).

Julia Davis died January 30, 1993, in Charles Town.

See also John W. Davis, Literature
Barbara Wilkie Tedford
Glenville State College

Julia Davis, *The Embassy Girls,* 1992; Davis, *The Shenandoah,* 1945.

Rebecca Harding Davis

Author Rebecca Harding Davis, born in Washington, Pennsylvania, June 24, 1831, as Rebecca Blaine Harding, moved with her parents, Richard and Rachel Wilson Harding, to Wheeling about 1836. She later attended the Washington (Pennsylvania) Female Seminary, where she graduated as valedictorian in 1848. She then returned to Wheeling and honed her literary skills as a writer for the *Intelligencer*. Ignored by literary critics for much of the past century, she is now recognized for her role in the development of realistic fiction. During the 1860s, she published a number of stories and serialized novels in the *Atlantic Monthly* and benefited from the encouragement of its editor, James Fields. Her best-known story, "Life in the Iron Mills: A Story of Today," published in the *Atlantic Monthly* in 1861, is a powerful depiction of the plight of mill workers in a town based on Wheeling, the author's home for most of the first half of her life. Her first two novels, both published in 1862, echo the social realism of "Life in the Iron Mills." *Margret Howth* again focuses on the exploitation of workers, while *David Gaunt* probes moral and political conflicts raised by the Civil War.

The publication of "Life in the Iron Mills" led to the author's correspondence with a young Philadelphia journalist and law student, Lemuel Clarke Davis. They met in 1862, and when they married the following year she moved to Philadelphia. Between 1864 and 1872, Rebecca Davis gave birth to three children and built a career as a writer for newspapers and magazines. Many of her later works of fiction dealt with conflicts she faced as she tried to combine her personal and professional lives.

Public issues, however, remained at the forefront of her concerns. In one of her best novels, *John Andross* (1874), she attacked the political corruption of Boss Tweed's New York. She wrote for the *New York Tribune* for 20 years, breaking her ties only when advertisers pressured the paper to end her series exposing industrial problems. She continued as a regular columnist on economic and political topics for another newspaper, the *Independent*, well into her 70s. Davis's last book was an autobiography, *Bits of Gossip* (1904). She died on September 29, 1910, in Mount Kisko, New York, at the home of her son, Richard Harding Davis, a popular journalist who was by then far better known than his mother.

Elizabeth Johnston Lipscomb
Randolph-Macon Woman's College

Sharon M. Harris, *Rebecca Harding Davis and American Realism,* 1991.

William M.O. Dawson

The 12th governor of West Virginia, William Mercer Owens Dawson, was born May 21, 1853, in Bloomington, Maryland, just across the Potomac River from what is now the Eastern Panhandle of West Virginia. Dawson was the son of Francis Ravenscraft Dawson and Leah (Knight) Dawson, and after his mother's death

Governor William M.O. Dawson (1853–1916).

moved as a child with his father to Western Virginia. Dawson was educated in the public schools and was the last governor not to have a college education. He taught school briefly and in 1873 moved to Kingwood, where he became editor and then owner of the weekly *Preston County Journal*.

Dawson's first elected political position was as chairman of the Preston County Republican committee in 1874. Six years later he was elected to the state senate and reelected in 1884. He advocated railroad rate regulation and served on the Banks and Corporations, the Finance, and the Mines and Mining committees, and on a special subcommittee to investigate tax laws. In 1891, Dawson became chairman of the Republican state committee and served until 1904. Governor MacCorkle, a Democrat and a contemporary, considered Dawson an outstanding political organizer, saying he was second only to U.S. Sen. Stephen B. Elkins in that regard. Historian Otis Rice credited Dawson with providing a modern organization to the state Republican Party, with connections to every county. Dawson was a key factor in bringing the Republicans back to power in the 1890s, after a long line of Democratic governors.

Dawson served as West Virginia's secretary of state from 1897 until his election as governor in 1904. He was not an impressive public speaker, but his years of political experience and his contacts helped him secure a victory over conservative Democrat John J. Cornwell, 121,520 to 112,457, even though Dawson ran behind the rest of the Republican slate. Conservatives in the Republican Party had attempted to prevent Dawson's nomination, concerned about his anti-corporate tendencies. During his tenure as secretary of state he had drafted legislation, popularly known as the "Dawson corporation law," which significantly increased state revenue.

A progressive Republican, Dawson campaigned in favor of the tax reforms proposed by the tax commission appointed by his predecessor, Governor White, and in favor of railroad regulation, including increased taxation, an anti-pass law, establishment of a railroad commission, and safety legislation. As governor, Dawson also called for an anti-lobbying law and for a comprehensive primary election law requiring parties to hold state-funded primary elections for all state and national party candidates. He recommended other progressive measures, including a pure food and drug act, the establishment of a legislative reference library to assist in drafting bills, mine safety legislation, and a public service commission.

Dawson called the legislature into extra sessions to address these issues, but his reforms were opposed by business elements in both parties. He was largely unsuccessful in implementing his progressive agenda. After leaving office, he remained politically active, supporting Congressman and former chairman of the tax commission William Hubbard against Republican incumbent Nathan B. Scott for U.S. Senate. In 1912, he embraced Theodore Roosevelt's Bull Moose presidential candidacy. Dawson later served as a member of the Public Service Commission established under Governor Hatfield.

Dawson fought poor health for many years and eventually succumbed to tuberculosis. He had a son by his first wife, Luda Neff, and after her death he married Maude Brown in 1899 and had a daughter and son. Dawson died in Charleston at age 62, March 12, 1916.

Nicholas Burckel
Marquette University
Nicholas C. Burckel, "Publicizing Progressivism: William M. O. Dawson," *West Virginia History,* Spring–Summer 1981; John G. Morgan, *West Virginia Governors,* 1980; Otis K. Rice and Stephen W. Brown, *West Virginia: A History,* 1993.

Mack Day

Lawman Malcolm Malachi "Mack" Day was born in Virginia, July 29, 1873. His father, Joshua, abandoned the family, and his mother, Narcissa, later remarried and adopted stern religious beliefs that became the core of her son's life.

Day left Virginia as a young man to become a miner in McDowell County. He educated himself among much younger students at Bottom Creek Grade School, and began contracting to deliver timber. His position in the county was solidified when on Christmas Day, 1898, he married Charlotte June Milam, from one of the region's first families. Going on to sire 12 children, Day became a pillar of McDowell County. He was saved and bap-

tized, and later ordained a minister; built a 14-room house on top of Belcher Mountain; joined the Odd Fellows and the Knights of Pythias; and finally became sheriff of the county. He joined the Ku Klux Klan during the brief 20th-century revival of the Klan in West Virginia.

Claiming that God had called him to enforce Prohibition, Day attempted to dry out one of the state's wettest regions, even arresting an uncle and his own son. Legend has it that Day performed one man's wedding, later shot him, and went on to preach his funeral. Though his shootist reputation is considerable, Day is known to have killed on only three occasions. In 1925, Mack Day himself was shot and killed by a bootlegger at Pageton. He died February 14, 1925. The Klan and other organizations marched through Kimball to the cemetery on Belcher Mountain, where he is buried.

Jean Battlo
Kimball
Jean Battlo, "Booger Man: Recalling Revenuer Mack Day," *Goldenseal,* Summer 1996.

Alston G. Dayton

Judge Alston Gordon Dayton, once notorious among union miners for his labor law rulings, was born in Philippi, October 18, 1857. He graduated from West Virginia University in 1878 and apprenticed in law with his father, Spencer Dayton. He married Columbia May Sinsel on November 26, 1884, and had one son, Arthur Spencer Dayton, who became an attorney in Barbour County.

Dayton was prosecuting attorney in Upshur and Barbour counties before being elected to Congress. He served in the House of Representatives from 1895 to 1905, when he was appointed judge of the U.S. District Court for the Northern District of West Virginia. His appointment to the bench resulted from the friendship of U.S. Sen. Stephen B. Elkins, the most prominent West Virginia Republican of that era.

Judge Dayton became a bitter enemy to the United Mine Workers with his rulings in *Hitchman Coal & Coke v. John Mitchell.* In 1907, he issued a sweeping temporary injunction against the UMW to prevent organizing, claiming that the union violated Hitchman's individual employment contracts, the so-called "yellow-dog contracts" which forbade employees to join a union. He further ruled that the union was an unlawful organization because it was a monopoly in violation of the Sherman Antitrust Act. Litigation on the temporary injunction lasted until 1913, when he made the injunction permanent. While this case was being litigated, Dayton issued a number of other injunctions effectively neutralizing the UMW in West Virginia's northern coalfields. In 1917, the U.S. Supreme Court supported Dayton's ruling on the

employment contract based on the historical view of the sanctity of contracts, but rejected his argument that the United Mine Workers was an illegal organization. Dayton served on the bench until he died on July 30, 1920, while visiting Battle Creek, Michigan.

See also Hitchman Coal & Coke v. Mitchell, Yellow-Dog Contract

Kenneth R. Bailey
WVU Institute of Technology
Richard D. Lunt, *Law and Order vs. the Miners, West Virginia, 1907–1933,* 1992; John Alexander Williams, *West Virginia and the Captains of Industry,* 1976.

Wills De Hass

Antiquarian Wills De Hass was born at West Alexander, Pennsylvania, July 4, 1817. Educated at Western University (now University of Pittsburgh) and Washington and Jefferson College, he practiced medicine in Wellsburg and Wheeling, and in Kentucky and Washington. His early interest in historical and scientific studies led to extensive investigations into regional history and to archeological digging in the Upper Ohio Valley. He was an active member of several scientific and historical societies. While living at Moundsville, De Hass became involved in the excavation of the Grave Creek Mound. When the Grave Creek Mound museum was abandoned about 1844, he acquired possession of the Grave Creek tablet and skull, transferring them to the Smithsonian in 1850. Throughout the latter half of the 19th century, De Hass conducted archeological investigations relating to mound builders for the Smithsonian Institution's Bureau of American Ethnology.

A writer and lecturer on archeological subjects, De Hass turned to frontier history for his best-known work, *History of the Early Settlement and Indian Wars of Western Virginia,* which was first published in Wheeling in 1851. This book contains historical accounts of the settlement of the Ohio Valley and northwestern Virginia, the British expulsion of the French from the region, warfare between settlers and Indians prior to 1795, and biographical sketches of well-known frontiersmen. An ardent Unionist, De Hass recruited the 77th Ohio Regiment from border counties of Virginia and Ohio as the Civil War commenced, and he supported the formation of the state of West Virginia. He died January 24, 1910.

Harold Malcolm Forbes
WVU Libraries
Wills De Hass, *History of the Early Settlement and Indian Wars of Western Virginia; Embracing an Account of the Various Expeditions in the West, Previous to 1795,* 1851; Delf Norona, "Skeletal Material from the Grave Creek Mounds," *West Virginia Archeologist,* February 1953; *Who's Who in America, 1901–1902,* 1901.

Levi Johnson Dean

Architect Levi Johnson Dean was born in Frametown, Braxton County, January 9, 1878. He studied architecture by correspondence course and commenced his practice in Charleston. He relocated to Huntington and by 1910 was practicing for himself. In 1921, he was the 19th architect licensed under the new West Virginia licensing law. By 1947, Dean had a list of 139 commissions, including 47 schools, 20 churches, 22 residences, and 16 apartment buildings. His sons, S. Brooks and E. Keith Dean, joined the firm and continued after his death.

Many of Dean's buildings are located in Huntington, eastern Kentucky, and southern West Virginia. He concentrated on public buildings, including schools, city halls, and churches. His public buildings include the Jackson County Courthouse; Gassaway City Building; the B'nai Israel Synagogue, Second Presbyterian Church, and United Woolen Mills in Huntington; Nicholas County Courthouse addition in Summersville; the Richwood City Hall; and Matewan Missionary Baptist Church. Residential commissions include houses in Huntington, Williamson, and elsewhere. His largest residential commission is the 1925 Ricketts house in Huntington.

Dean was expert at many architectural styles popular at the time. His use of styles was appropriate to each of the commissions. These included Gothic Revival, Art Deco, Commercial Style, and Renaissance Revival, as well as more fanciful revivals. The Ricketts house has Tudor and Prairie School influences, and Dean's office in downtown Huntington (1927) contains Moorish Revival elements.

Levi Johnson Dean died September 22, 1951.

Michael Gioulis
Sutton

Eugene Victor Debs

Labor organizer and four-time Socialist Party candidate for president, Eugene Victor Debs (1855–1926) played a controversial role in the West Virginia coal strike of 1912–13, which spanned the terms of Governors Glasscock and Hatfield. The strike caused unprecedented violence between Baldwin-Felts mine guards and miners from Cabin and Paint creeks, near Charleston. Hatfield's suppression of the press in early May of 1913 and his predecessor's detention of scores of miners and their sympathizers, including Mother Jones, prompted a ten-day visit by a special committee of the Socialist Party of America led by Debs. Debs's meeting with Hatfield caused a furor among the more radical socialist labor factions who accused Debs of "selling out." Yet Debs helped bring the U.S. Senate to investigate the injustices of the West Virginia coalfields, later explaining his diplomacy in West Virginia as the only chance for the United Mine Workers of America to survive there.

In April 1919, Debs returned to West Virginia as an inmate of the West Virginia State Penitentiary at Moundsville, where he served the first few months of a ten-year sentence for opposing U.S. involvement in World War I and protesting President Wilson's treatment of conscientious objectors. Among his visitors in prison was his close friend William Blenko of Milton, founder of Blenko Glass.

Thomas Douglass
East Carolina University

David A. Corbin, "Betrayal in the West Virginia Coal Fields: Eugene V. Debs and the Socialist Party of America, 1912–1914," *Journal of American History* 64, 1978; Roger Fagge, "Eugene Debs in West Virginia, 1913: A Reappraisal," *West Virginia History*, 1993.

Declaration of Rights of the People of Virginia

One of the most important steps on the road to West Virginia statehood was the vote, 88 to 55, of the Virginia secession convention on April 17, 1861, to take Virginia out of the Union. Of the 47 delegates to the convention from Western Virginia, only 15 voted for secession. Most of the western delegates hastened home, and John S. Carlile of Clarksburg took the lead in arousing resistance to secession. The Clarksburg Convention, promoted by Carlile, and numerous mass meetings led to the First and Second Wheeling Conventions in May and June, respectively.

At the first session of the Second Wheeling Convention (June 11–25, 1861), Convention President Arthur I. Boreman appointed a committee of 13 to prepare an agenda for the meeting. The committee presented a Declaration of Rights of the People of Virginia, which drew upon principles that were in the Virginia bill of rights of 1776 and reiterated in the Virginia constitutions of 1830 and 1851. The committee report branded the calling of the secession convention by the General Assembly "a usurpation of the rights of the people" and charged the convention and the governor with an attempt to separate the people of Virginia from the United States and force them into "an illegal confederacy of rebellious states." The Declaration of Rights, signed by 86 of the 100-plus delegates, provided a rationale for legitimizing a reorganization of the Virginia government on the basis of loyalty to the Union, a crucial step in the process by which West Virginia achieved statehood two years later.

See also Formation of West Virginia

Otis K. Rice
WVU Institute of Technology

Charles Henry Ambler and Festus P. Summers, *West Virginia: The Mountain State*, 1958; Granville Davisson Hall, *The Rending of Virginia: A History*, 1902; Virgil A. Lewis, *How West Virginia Was Made*, 1909.

Deer

The white-tailed deer is the deer of West Virginia. It is primarily a browsing animal, usually feeding on trees and shrubs, but often seen grazing in fields during winter and spring. Although deer see only in black and white, they have good eyesight. They have an acute sense of smell and excellent hearing.

The white-tailed deer possesses four sets of external glands. Those located in the face are used for rubbing scent on trees and shrubs. The glands on the legs and between the toes secrete a strong, penetrating odor used to communicate between individuals and groups of deer, thus allowing deer to identify and follow one another by the scent left on the ground. Urination on the glands inside the hind legs increases the penetrating odors, especially during the breeding season.

In males new antler growth begins in April and continues until September. Once the antlers become fully grown in September the blood vessels feeding them recede and the antlers harden. The velvet covering is then rubbed off and the antlers are polished on trees. The number of branches or "points" on the antlers is greatly affected by nutrition, and there is usually an increasing number with age.

Fall marks the whitetail breeding or rutting season, triggered by shorter days and a peak in hormone levels. The rutting season begins in October and extends into January with the peak of breeding occurring during the latter part of November. The gestation period averages 201 days. Between May and July does give birth usually to two spotted fawns, occasionally triplets. Newborns weigh between four and eight pounds. Within a few hours after birth, fawns are able to walk or run with surprising agility. Although young deer eat grasses and other plants by the time they are a month old, they rely on their mother's milk for about four months. Fawns grow rapidly and by the end of September are able to survive by themselves if necessary.

During the big timber cutting years in West Virginia, from 1880 to 1910, deer became scarce. This was also the period of the professional hunter, who (with no restrictions on the use of dogs, bag limits, or seasons) killed deer for market. By 1910, the whitetail in West Virginia had reached its lowest level, with an estimated population of only 1,000 animals. The recovery from this slaughter was slow. In 1910, the first hunting season was established, and only bucks were legal. Since that time, restocking, hunting restrictions, law enforcement, and careful management have enabled whitetails to spread into all counties of the state.

Deer population in the southern counties remains low in many areas, but in many other parts of the state deer are so numerous as to be of concern. Farm crop damages continued to increase in the 1990s, and hunting regulations were adjusted to reduce deer populations in many of the counties where damage was prevalent.

Thomas J. Allen
Division of Natural Resources

Deer Season

The hunting of white-tailed deer in West Virginia is a cultural, social, and economic phenomenon that transcends all other types of hunting in the state. Approximately half of the state's 55 counties close their schools during the entire first week of the traditional buck season. The closure is officially called "Thanksgiving break," but unofficially the reason is the lure of deer hunting. Many West Virginians take time off from work.

West Virginia holds a variety of deer seasons, including archery, antlerless, muzzleloader, and bucks only, with the last the centerpiece. Our deer hunters have a long tradition of being primarily buck hunters, often to the dismay of wildlife officials, who would prefer a more balanced reduction of deer populations. Typically, about one in seven West Virginians buys a license to deer hunt, and a majority of those buy that license specifically for buck season. Approximately 350,000 hunters, including non-residents, take part in buck season. Deer hunting is predominantly a man's sport.

Surveys have shown that deer hunting in West Virginia generates approximately $150 million in retail sales, with 50 percent of that amount spent in buck season. The economic impact of deer hunting is especially important in rural areas, where 65 percent of our population lives. Also, 78 percent of our deer hunters come from the rural areas of the state.

The social aspect of buck season is significant. Family members gather for the hunt, much as they would for a traditional holiday, and friends and associates make buck season the occasion for a yearly gathering. The old-time mountain deer camp of lore and legend is largely gone, however, because hunting opportunities have spread throughout the state. The custom now is "backyard hunting," that is, staying at home to hunt. The increase in the deer population in West Virginia, as elsewhere, is startling. Our deer numbers have rebounded from a low of approximately 1,000 in 1910 to current estimates of more than 800,000.

See also Deer

Skip Johnson
Sutton

Tom J. Allen and Jack Cromer, "White-tailed Deer in West Virginia," Bulletin, 1977.

Deforestation

Two-thirds of West Virginia was still covered by ancient growth forest in 1880 on the eve of the industrial transition, but during the next 40 years the state was almost completely denuded.

One of America's first industries, water-powered sawmills, multiplied with the population along colonial waterways and expanded with the westward movement into the receding frontier. Steam-powered circular sawmills replaced water-powered mills during the 19th century, and at the turn of the 20th century huge steam and electric-powered band mills, each capable of cutting thousands of acres per year, were built by the larger companies. Railroads greatly facilitated the removal of the virgin forest by providing the transportation for hauling heavy equipment into the woods and by shipping lumber in volume to the national markets.

In West Virginia as elsewhere, the lumbermen's philosophy of "cut out and get out" ensured the rapid depletion of the forest. Large capital investment resulted in heavy debt which in turn demanded maximum and constant production if lumber companies were to remain solvent. The wealth of the virgin forest invited overexpansion, and lumbermen borrowed capital which had to be repaid. Often it was cheaper for big mills to continue cutting timber even at a loss than to stop production when prices inevitably declined from overdevelopment and cutthroat competition. Economic conditions, improved milling technology, and the absence of an American ethic of conservation all conspired to hasten the deforestation of West Virginia.

From the beginning, farmers depended on the forest to supply building materials and the logs they floated to downstream mills to sell for cash. Expansion of the logging industry came slowly during the 19th century, but then accelerated to a crescendo between 1880 and 1920. During this period even the state's most remote mountain counties were integrated into the national markets by the 4,000 miles of railroad track that had been laid.

Cutting the timber resulted in major changes not just to the landscape but to all aspects of life. Towns sprouted up like wildflowers, new legislation and case law buttressed industrial expansion, and agriculture began its long decline. Many farmers thought that the country would be opened for farming once the timber was cut, but the soil was generally too poor for commercial farming, and farmers were unable to compete with their Midwestern counterparts in the markets to which they were now connected by the railroads.

The decline in agriculture was accelerated by the environmental disaster that deforestation left in its wake. Forest fires repeatedly swept over the land, 710 of them burning 1.7 million acres in 1908 alone. The streams became polluted and devoid of life, while floods ravaged the valleys below, and erosion washed away topsoil into the streams, silting up navigable watercourses. To save the inland waterways, the federal government embarked on a plan to protect the Ohio and Potomac watersheds by establishing the Monongahela National Forest in 1920. By then entire ecological systems had been destroyed.

Once the mountains had been skinned of their forest, the lumber companies closed their operations and moved on to greener country in the South and West. Without lumber the railroads soon pulled up their tracks and withdrew from the mountains as well, leaving a displaced people and a degraded land to confront the Great Depression.

See also Forests, Timbering and Logging

Ronald L. Lewis
West Virginia University

Ronald D. Eller, *Miners, Millhands, and Mountaineers: Industrialization of the Appalachian South, 1880–1930*, 1982.

Julius DeGruyter

Historian and illustrator Julius Allan De-Gruyter was born October 19, 1894, in Charleston. His grandfather served as the city's wharf master, and his father was mayor from 1885 to 1889. Before De-Gruyter began to document his city's history, he sold life insurance, was city councilman for four years, and served in the West Virginia House of Delegates from 1931 to 1933 and from 1945 to 1947. It was his last job, as city clerk, that sparked an interest in pulling facts together into a readable volume. DeGruyter's first work, *The Kanawha Spectator: History of the Kanawha Valley* (1953) was followed, in time for the 1963 state Centennial celebration, by *A Brief History of Kanawha County and the Kanawha Region*.

A self-taught painter and illustrator, DeGruyter's art appeared in numerous exhibits, and is represented in the collections of the former Sunrise Museum and the State Museum. The artwork includes scenes of early Charleston. DeGruyter wrote of local city government in *Charleston, West Virginia: Its Charters and Municipal Affairs* (1950) and brought out a second volume of *The Kanawha Spectator* in 1976. In a change of subject, he drew on the pioneer era as background for a fictional love story, *Drum Beats on the Sandusky* (1969). Julius DeGruyter died February 12, 1980, in Huntington.

Carolanne Griffith Roberts
Southern Living

Martin Robison Delany

Activist and physician Martin Robison Delany, an African-American, was born free in Charles Town, May 6, 1812. In 1822, the Delany family was forced to flee for violating a Virginia law forbidding the education of blacks. The family settled in Chambersburg, Pennsylvania.

In 1831, Delany moved to Pittsburgh. He studied medicine as an apprentice under Dr. Andrew N. McDowell and became his medical assistant. From 1843 to 1847, Martin Delany founded, edited, and published the *Mystery*, an abolitionist newspaper. He shut down the *Mystery* to become co-editor of Frederick Douglass's newspaper, the *North Star*. After attending Harvard Medical College in 1850, Delany returned to Pittsburgh and opened a medical practice.

The 1850 Fugitive Slave Act inspired Delany to publish *The Condition, Elevation, Emigration, And Destiny of the Colored People of the United States*, in 1852. Working with the Underground Railroad, he moved to Chatham, Canada. In 1858, he aided John Brown in convening the Chatham Convention. Afterward, he explored the Niger Valley region of Africa as a possible site for African-American emigration.

In 1861, Delany published *Blake: or, The Huts of America*, a fictional work detailing the horrors of slavery. In February 1865, he was commissioned as a major in the U.S. Colored Troops. He was the only African-American Civil War officer to be given a field command. He died in Wilberforce, Ohio, January 4, 1885.

Joseph Bundy
Bluefield

Delta Tau Delta

The national collegiate fraternity Delta Tau Delta was founded at Bethany College in 1858, arising from indignation about a rigged vote in a literary contest. At the time, Bethany College had three literary societies, one of which was the Neotrophian Literary Society. The societies provided a forum for students to compete in poetry, public speaking, and essay writing. Within the Neotrophian, a group of students was trying to control who won the oratory prize. Eight students in the Neotrophian, angered by this move, formed Delta Tau Delta, whose purpose was to return integrity to the literary society.

Delta Tau Delta did not set out to be a national fraternity, but in its early years, it granted charters to nearby West Liberty Academy (later West Liberty State College), West Virginia University, and Jefferson College in Canonsburg, Pennsylvania. By 1861, Bethany's Delta Tau Delta founding members had graduated or left to serve in the armed forces. Because the original chapter dissolved, the Jefferson College chapter assumed control of the fraternity. In 1867, Delta Tau Delta revived its Bethany Chapter, which remained active until 1895. Seventy years later, 13 students at Bethany formed a new local fraternity and petitioned to become a chapter of Delta Tau Delta. Meanwhile, new chapters of the fraternity had organized at colleges and universities throughout the country.

By 2001, Delta Tau Delta had initiated 139,492 men. The fraternity has 5,850 undergraduate members in 119 chapters and colonies, and 27 alumni chapters. In 1978, the fraternity renovated its original house on Bethany's campus. A year later, the Delta Tau Delta Founders House was placed on the National Register of Historic Places.

Democratic Party

Except for the decade after statehood and the generation after 1896, the Democratic Party has dominated the political history of West Virginia. At the end of the 20th century West Virginia ranked as one of the most Democratic states in the nation as measured by voter registration (2-1), control of the legislature (majorities in both houses since 1930), and elected statewide positions. Only two Republicans have served as governor since 1930. This record of party supremacy is ironic, since West Virginia traces its statehood to the support of the national Republican Party and the strength of the party's Union effort.

The Democratic Party in newborn West Virginia started as a coalition of pro-Union Democrats, pro-Confederate Democrats, and former Whigs. It gained political supremacy in 1872 after voting restrictions against former Confederates were removed from the state constitution.

During the subsequent period of party dominance (1872–96) the state elected a series of mostly conservative Democratic governors who, as historian Richard Brisban points out, "were small-government in their philosophies, pro-Confederate in their sentiments, pro-business in their initiatives." With the exception of Emanuel Willis "Windy" Wilson, who advocated an activist agenda, these governors resembled their conservative counterparts in other states.

The Democratic Party slipped into minority status with the election of 1896. That year West Virginia followed the tide as Republicans gained majority status in every section of the nation except the South. In the next generation, West Virginia Democrats elected only one governor (John Cornwell 1917–21) and controlled the House of Delegates only three times. The standing of the party was so poor that in 1924 Democratic presidential candidate John W. Davis, a West Virginia native, did not carry his home state.

The Great Depression and the New Deal activism of President Franklin Roosevelt ushered in a new era of Democratic dominance in West Virginia, beginning in 1932 and continuing to the present. Economic hardship favored the Democrats' call for an activist government. Democrats also benefited by the decline of their Republican opposition and their party's continued regional strength in the southern counties. In Logan County, Democrats enjoyed an advantage in voter registration of 16-1 in 1996.

The decentralized nature of the state's politics and the disorganization of the political opposition enabled the Democratic Party in West Virginia to weather several internal crises. In the late 1930s Democrats faced an ideological split when Governor Holt's conservative policies alienated labor unions. In a turning point in the party's history, M. M. Neely resigned his U.S. Senate seat and with the support of the unions successfully ran for governor. His victory validated labor's role in the party, but increasingly the Democratic machine he controlled until his death in 1958 appeared to be motivated more by patronage than ideology.

In the 1950s the party survived the controversy surrounding Governor Marland's attempt to initiate a major tax revision on the coal industry. And in the 1960s it overcame the corruption scandal of Governor Barron's administration.

In recent years the Democratic Party in the state, according to scholar John Fenton, has reflected a three-way division, with one faction headed by labor, another controlled by rural conservatives, and a third, statehouse, faction. This encouraged candidates to court support from a particular faction while reflecting a common political profile which characterized most rank-and-file Democrats—socially conservative in values, economically liberal in attitude, and pro-business in action. The result was to encourage moderate candidates and positions.

The successful candidacies of party outsiders Jay Rockefeller and Gaston Caperton in the last third of the 20th century suggest the declining influence of traditional party factions. Both men promoted a more progressive image of the party and recruited across faction lines. The nomination of Charlotte Pritt for governor in 1996 further demonstrated the increasing fluidity of the party as it faced a growing Republican challenge at the end of the century.

Despite setbacks in the 1996 gubernatorial contest and the 2000 and 2004 presidential elections, West Virginia Democrats nonetheless started the 21st century in a dominant position, holding the edge in registration and retaining control of the legislature and all the statewide executive offices. Whether the coalition of often varied interests will continue united remains the question for coming decades.

Robert Rupp
West Virginia Wesleyan College

Richard A. Brisbin Jr., et al., *West Virginia Politics and Government*, 1987; John F. Fenton, *Politics in the Border States*, 1957; Neil R. Peirce, *The Border South States: People, Politics, and Power in the Five States of the Border South*, 1975.

Demography

By the mid-18th century, Europeans and Americans of European descent had begun to settle in the territory that eventually became West Virginia, most numerously in the Eastern Panhandle and Potomac Highlands regions. These settlers were primarily of German and Scotch-Irish origins, although there were significant numbers of English and other nationalities as well. They found no significant native population, although the Shawnee and other Indian groups traveled and hunted throughout present West Virginia.

Slave-holding was not common in most parts of Western Virginia, as the rugged landscape discouraged plantation agriculture. There were local exceptions in the major river valleys, including the Greenbrier, Kanawha, and Ohio valleys, and in the Eastern Panhandle. Extensive industrial slavery was practiced at the saltworks of Kanawha County. After the Civil War, the coal industry began to grow quickly and attracted many African-Americans to the new state and a variety of European immigrants, especially from southern and eastern Europe. Many African-Americans worked in the coal mines in the southern part of the state, including those in McDowell, Fayette, and Mercer counties.

West Virginia's present racial mix is not diverse. Most West Virginians reported a single-race background in the 2000 census, with just 0.9 percent of the state's residents reporting more than one race. Further, 95 percent of the residents of the state in 2000 reported their race as white. Only 3.2 percent of residents reported their race as African-American (57,232 residents), and 0.5 percent reported their race as Asian (9,434 residents). Nationally, residents reporting their race as African-American and Asian accounted for 12.3 percent and 3.6 percent of the population, respectively.

The state's population has grown older during the last 100 years. West Virginia had the highest median age of any state in the nation, at 38.9 years, according to the 2000 census. Florida had the next highest median age, at 38.7 years, while the national median was 35.3 years. West Virginia has not always had the nation's oldest population. Indeed, West Virginia's median age was below the national average in 1950 at 26.3 years (compared to the national median of 30.2 years) and in 1900 at 20.3 years (compared to the national median of 22.9 years). The state's current high age arose in large part from a massive out-migration of relatively young residents during the economic downturn of the 1980s.

Even though the state has the highest median age in the nation, West Virginia does not have the largest percent of population age 65 and older; Florida does. West Virginia gets its high median age from a population bulge in the 45–64 age group, with relatively small shares in the younger groups and a relatively high (but not the highest) share in the 65-and-older age group.

Age varies in different regions of the state, with the Northern Panhandle and the southeastern part of the state registering the highest median ages in 2000. The counties in the Eastern Panhandle and the southwestern part of the state recorded the lowest median ages in 2000. The exception was Monongalia County, with its high student population and the state's lowest median age, 30.4 years. Summers County had the oldest median age, at 43.4. Monongalia was the only county in West Virginia falling below the U.S. average median age.

The state's age structure affects the rate of natural increase, which is a major component of population growth. Natural increase is the annual difference between births and deaths. During the last half of the 1990s, births roughly equaled deaths in West Virginia. This is unusual, and indeed, the state has lately posted the lowest rates of natural increase of any state in the nation. The low natural increase has arisen because of low birth rates combined with high death rates. Both rates are attributable in part to the state's high median age, since an older population naturally has fewer births and more deaths. However, it turns out that even if we adjust for age, West Virginia's residents still have low birth rates (especially for women after their mid-20s) and high death rates.

West Virginia's demographic composition does not favor population growth. The state's residents are primarily white (whites have lower birth rates than blacks and Hispanics, the other most numerous elements in the U.S. population) and tend to be near the end of their child-bearing years. These characteristics produce low rates of natural increase. This, in turn, makes the state dependent on net migration (the annual difference between those moving into the state and those leaving) for overall population gains. Success in generating more in-migrants than out-migrants often requires strong economic performance, which has proven difficult for West Virginia in recent decades.

See also Population

George W. Hammond
Bureau of Business & Economic Research,
West Virginia University

Brian Lego, "West Virginia: A 20th Century Perspective on Population Change," ms., 1999; Otis K. Rice and Stephen W. Brown, *West Virginia: A History*, 1993.

Denmar Hospital

The Legislature established the West Virginia State Colored Tuberculosis Sanitarium in 1917 for the care of black TB patients. Denmar, on the Greenbrier River in Pocahontas County, was selected as the location. Denmar was the town and mill site for the Maryland Lumber Company, which was then completing its lumbering operations.

Virtually the entire town was converted to use for the sanitarium. The boarding house became the main hospital and administration building. Some houses were converted into living quar-

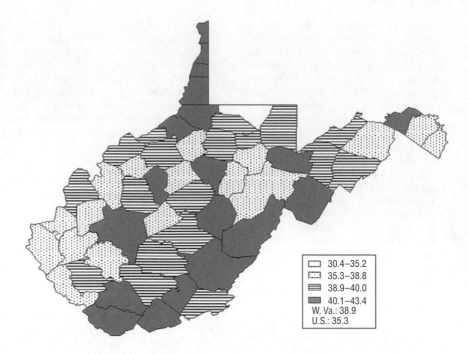

Median age by county, 2000.

30.4–35.2
35.3–38.8
38.9–40.0
40.1–43.4
W. Va.: 38.9
U.S.: 35.3

Worse in Morgantown

"A candidate for governor of West Virginia was in a heated campaign and he got a frantic call from one of his supporters in the northern part of the state. 'You better get up here,' the supporter said.

" 'I can't,' said the candidate. 'I have to stay here. They're telling lies about me in Charleston.'

" 'You think that's bad?' said the supporter. 'It's worse here. They're tellin' the truth about you in Morgantown.' "

—James F. Dent
The Dog with the Cold Nose
(1981)

ters for patients, with separate facilities for men, women, and children. Other houses became living quarters for employees. The mill structure and railroad shop building were used by the hospital farm and dairy. Access to the new hospital was provided by the Chesapeake & Ohio Railway's Greenbrier Division.

Dr. B. A. Crichlow was named superintendent and the sanitarium received its first patients on January 31, 1919. At this time, tuberculosis was often fatal, and many patients died while at Denmar. More than 300 are known to have been buried in a cemetery on the hospital grounds. Also buried at Denmar is the institution's second superintendent, Dr. Samuel J. Bampfield, who died February 22, 1940.

In January 1938, ground was broken for a three-story building to replace the deteriorating lumber company structures. Patients were moved into the new facility in January 1939. A wing to the building was completed in 1952. With advances in the treatment of tuberculosis, by the 1950s the need for tuberculosis hospitals was ending. In March 1957, Denmar was converted to a state hospital for the chronically ill.

Denmar Hospital was closed in July 1990. The facility reopened in November 1993 as the Denmar Correctional Center, housing medium-security prisoners. A birthing center for prisoners in the federal prison system occupies the former nurses' quarters at Denmar.

William P. McNeel
Marlinton

James F. Dent

Humorist and political cartoonist James Frederick Dent was born in Charleston, December 29, 1928. His talent for turning daily events into delightful anecdotes gained him national fame. *Reader's Digest* reprinted 194 items from his columns, and radio commentator Paul Harvey often used his work.

Dent was educated at Charleston's Stonewall Jackson High School and at West Virginia University. While at WVU, he worked during the summers as a copy boy at the *Charleston Gazette*. In 1952, after graduation, he went to work there as a reporter. He eventually became the *Gazette's* movie and book reviewer and political cartoonist. Under the byline Jay Fredericks, he wrote the *Sunday Gazette-Mail's* television column. *Gazette* publisher W. E. Chilton once joked that if he could also get the versatile Dent to sweep up, he could dismiss the entire news department and janitorial staff. Dent began writing the newspaper's "Gazetteer" column in 1962 and continued it until his death. His columns appear in two books, *The Dog With the Cold Nose* and *Jim Dent Strikes Back*. Dent's cartoons usually took a liberal slant on events in the news, as did the *Gazette*. West Virginia State Archives is now the repository for 5,700 of his political cartoons. James Dent died July 17, 1992.

Marmaduke Dent

Justice Marmaduke Herbert Dent was born April 18, 1849, and his childhood was framed by the tumultuous years of conflict over slavery, secession, and the Civil War. His father, Marshall Mortimer Dent, edited the Morgantown *Virginia Weekly Star*, 1856–62, a newspaper that favored compromise to save the Union. As a delegate to the Virginia secession convention, the elder Dent voted against secession.

In 1867, Dent enrolled in the first class at West Virginia University and later received the first B.A. (1870) and first M.A. (1873) degrees granted by the university. Afterward, he became a teacher, and moved to Taylor County where he served as deputy clerk and notary public. He also read the law, was admitted to the bar in 1875, and opened an office in Grafton.

Dent served on the city council, as town clerk, and on the county school board. In 1892, Dent won election to the West Virginia Supreme Court of Appeals on the Democratic-People's Party (Populist) fusion ticket, and served from 1893 to 1905.

Justice Dent declared war on the railroads by trying to restrain their open abuse of the special privileges granted to them by state charters. Dent generally constituted a minority of one on the court. He adhered to the theory that a judge must take "justice" into consideration when deciding a case, for example, by balancing the weakness of the poor victim against the power of the wealthy corporation. He reasoned that the state had created the corporations for public purposes and, therefore, should limit corporate powers when their actions were harmful to the public. Hence, Dent was much more likely to hold the railroads to a higher standard of behavior, and award damages to plaintiffs, than the pro-industry majority on the court.

Duke failed in his bid for reelection to the court in 1904, retired to his home in Grafton, and died September 11, 1909.

See also Supreme Court of Appeals

Ronald L. Lewis
West Virginia University

John Phillip Reid, *An American Judge: Marmaduke Dent of West Virginia*, 1968.

The Department of West Virginia

The Department of West Virginia was created June 28, 1863, during a military reorganization of Union forces in the Civil War. It included all Union forces from the new state of West Virginia and that part of Maryland west of the Alleghenies, and was 23,000 men strong. The department disbanded in June 1865 when most of its men were discharged at the close of the Civil War. The Depart-

Contrary to the law of the land

"Discrimination against the colored people, because of color alone, as to privileges, immunities, and equal legal protection, is contrary to public policy and the law of the land. If any discrimination as to education should be made, it should be favorable to, and not against, the colored people. Held in the bondage of slavery, and continued in a low moral and intellectual condition, for a long period of years, and then clothed at once, without preparation, with full citizenship, in this great republic, and the power to control and guide its destinies, the future welfare, prosperity, and peace of our people demand that this benighted race should be elevated by education, both morally and intellectually, that they may become exemplary citizens; otherwise the perpetuity of our free institutions may be greatly endangered."

—Justice Marmaduke Dent
Williams v. Board of Education
(1898)

ment of West Virginia should not be confused with the Army of West Virginia, commanded by Brevet Maj. Gen. George Crook during Gen. Philip H. Sheridan's 1864–65 Shenandoah Valley campaign. Today, the state organization of the American Legion is called the Department of West Virginia.

See also Civil War

Joy Gregoire Gilchrist-Stalnaker
Horner

DeSales Heights

On July 25, 1864, a colony of eight Catholic nuns set out for Parkersburg from Washington, D.C., and Frederick, Maryland. Led by Mother Superior Mary Appolonia Diggs, the Sisters of the Visitation of Holy Mary, a teaching order, did not arrive at their destination until August 6. The turbulent Civil War delayed their railroad journey three times.

In 1867, the sisters established a benevolent school for poor children within the city. On July 16, 1900, they took possession of a new home and school located on the outskirts of Parkersburg on Garfield Avenue. They named the red and brick monastery DeSales Heights, in honor of St. Francis DeSales.

For 75 years, the sisters ran a boarding school for young women at DeSales Heights until they closed the academy and opened the first Montessori school in West Virginia. During this time, the teaching mission of the order required the sisters to work in the secular world daily, but live in cloistered quarters in the Catholic tradition. After the Second Vatican Council

Catholic nuns at DeSales Heights, 1948.

(1962–65) liberalized church rules, the sisters could choose between the cloistered or uncloistered life. Talk of closing DeSales Heights began in the early 1990s mainly because it was too big and expensive to be maintained by the declining number of able-bodied sisters. In 1993, DeSales Heights was closed and the building was put up for sale. After vandalism and a fire, the building was demolished in 2002.

Jacqueline G. Goodwin
Pennsylvania State Education Association

Dialect

Everyone speaks a dialect who speaks at all, and the major languages occur in countless variations around the world. West Virginians participate in many dialects, with some variant of what is often called Appalachian English being heard in much of the state. While it is not spoken in all places nor by all West Virginians, this is what people think of when they think of a West Virginia dialect.

Dialect refers to the spoken language, and involves matters of pronunciation, accent, vocabulary, and grammar. Dialect may color one's writing, as regards the choice of words and form of expression, but often individuals exhibiting a rich spoken dialect express themselves in writing in the form known as Standard English. This has to do with the already substantial differences in written and spoken language, and the fact that written language is learned within the formal environment of schools while speech is absorbed within the intimacy of family and community.

As with other matters of culture, dialect differs in different parts of West Virginia. As a general rule, our language changes from south to north, in a fan-shaped progression from the southern coalfields to the two panhandles. Appalachian English is strongest in the southern part of the state and the rural interior counties, while many northern West Virginians exhibit speech patterns common in the Northern states.

Thus, parts of West Virginia share the language of surrounding areas outside the state's boundaries. The dialect of the southernmost counties of McDowell and Mingo, for example, is essentially the same as that spoken in the neighboring Central Appalachian counties of southwest Virginia and eastern Kentucky. Many West Virginians of the Potomac Highlands and Eastern Panhandle speak a dialect influenced by the nearby Shenandoah Valley and, increasingly, the Washington metropolitan area. The Northern Panhandle and north-central counties share speech characteristics of the neighboring Pittsburgh area.

While Appalachian English is heard in much of West Virginia, it is not universal. Many West Virginians were born outside the state and others outside the country. These citizens may speak other dialects of English, or indeed other languages. Some West Virginians have lost their native dialect intentionally or through acculturation. Those living in the state's cities and suburbs may exhibit no regional dialect at all. Speech varies with educational levels, and some individuals slip in and out of dialect at will. Scholars note, however, that educated speakers tend to observe standard grammar even while drawing vocabulary from the dialect. Accent may change with educational attainment but is unlikely to change completely.

Language differences persist over long periods, and West Virginia's spoken language continues to be influenced by early settlement patterns. Research suggests that the grammar of Appalachian English derives most directly from Scotland and Northern Ireland, while its pronunciation relates to that of southern England. The Scotch-Irish predominated in the settlement of much of Western Virginia, and certain elements characteristic of Scotch-Irish speech persist to the present: A-prefixing is common among the Scotch-Irish, for example, as in "a-hunting" or "a-going," and also common among speakers of Appalachian English. The speech of other areas of the state was influenced by other ethnic groups, including Germans in the Eastern Panhandle and Potomac Highlands.

African-Americans were also among Western Virginia's early settlers, and their numbers increased with later industrialization. They contributed to the language by their direct vocal presence and through their indirect influence in the Southern dialect which in turn influences the language of much of West Virginia. Both black and white speakers of Appalachian and Southern English give a single-vowel sound to such words as *mine*, *mile*, and *hide*, for example, while Northern pronunciation of such words tends to have a two-vowel sound: mine (my-een), mile (my-el), and hide (hy-eed).

Also contributing were the immigrants who came to West Virginia's mines and factories in the 19th and early 20th centuries. These included large numbers of Italians and other newcomers from southern and eastern Europe. The process continues today as foreigners emigrate to West Virginia and other migrants arrive from other places in America. It is likely that this process happens less rapidly here than in some parts of the country, however, given the slow rate of growth and the relative homogeneity of the state population. Generally speaking, research suggests relatively few contributions to the traditional speech of the mountain South from languages other than English.

Although dialects persist, one must not think of language as static. For example, the once-common notion that Elizabethan English or other archaic versions of the language survived in Appalachia is incorrect. Even had the region been settled in the Elizabethan era, which it was not, and had it remained perfectly isolated, the language would have evolved over the centuries even within the insular region. In fact, language changes both within groups and as outside influences come into play.

Speech is an intimately identifying characteristic, deeply personal and at the same time necessarily public. It is a marker that sets one apart, and like such markers as skin color or religious practice it may be subject to hurtful attention. Mountain people are sometimes negatively stereotyped as regards their dialect and other real or ascribed cultural characteristics. Other regions suffer similar aspersions, including the Deep South, the "Down East" section of Maine, and certain boroughs of New York City. Individuals respond differently, some reacting defensively with others finding a source of pride in the comforting language of home.

Wylene P. Dial, "Language," in B. B. Maurer, ed., *Mountain Heritage*, 1974; Cratis D. Williams, *Southern Mountain Speech*, 1992.

Diamond Department Store

Built in 1927 on the site where the old state capitol had burned in 1921, Charleston's grand Diamond department store was among West Virginia's flagship retail establishments. Designed by architect Charles Haviland, the original building was a state-of-the-art store. Its five floors featured daylight lighting, arcade display windows, modern ventilation, three fast elevators, and a pneumatic tube system to convey cash and receipts between sales stations and the central office. The 1927 building was improved and expanded in later years.

Merchants Wehrle B. Geary and A. W. Cox had merged their resources in 1926 to launch the elegant new store at the edge of Charleston's business district, on Capitol Street near its intersection with Washington. The name originated with Geary. He had opened the Diamond Shoe Store in 1906. This became the Diamond Shoe and Garment Co. in 1912 and reached full department store status in 1917, moving farther up Capitol Street each time. In the meantime, Cox was assembling his chain of retail stores.

Successful even during the Depression, the partners expanded to the corner in 1941 when an extension was added to the original building featuring two air-conditioned floors and a basement. In 1948 five floors were added to the 1941 addition, bringing this part of the store to a full seven stories. Ten escalators, West Virginia's first, were installed.

Renowned for personal service, the Diamond in its heyday offered portraits by photographers as well as an on-site artist; a discreet wig booth within its beauty salon for patrons with thinning hair; a book store with author signings and luncheons; and store-to-church bridal assistance. Hungry shoppers flocked to the luncheonette on the first floor and the large cafeteria on the fifth. Mechanized toylands, trains, and nativity scenes drew crowds to its street corner window during the holidays. Peak December days brought as many as 80,000 shoppers into the glamorously decorated emporium.

Associated Dry Goods bought the Diamond in 1956, built a $1 million addition eastward in 1965, and prospered until the completion of the Town Center Mall in 1983. The Diamond inventory was liquidated and the business closed in that year. The building, still a Charleston landmark, has been refurbished for use as state government offices.

Pat Hendricks
Charleston

Hazel Dickens

Musician Hazel Dickens was born in Mercer County, June 1, 1935, the eighth of 11 children. She is a pioneering old-time and bluegrass musician, known for preserving the traditional vocal styles of West Virginia. Dickens has influenced a generation of women musicians and actively supports working people in West Virginia and throughout Appalachia.

At 16, with her older siblings, Dickens moved to Baltimore to work. They took with them their mountain music, sharing it with other transplanted Appalachians and urban folk revivalists, including Alice Gerrard, with whom Dickens recorded her first albums. Songs such as "West Virginia, My Home" and "Mama's Hand" draw from Dickens's life in West Virginia. Other songs, such as "Black Lung," "Mannington Mines," and "They'll Never Keep Us Down," underscore her commitment to coal miners and labor unions. Her many albums include *Hard Hitting Songs for Hard Hit People* (1981), *By the Sweat of My Brow* (1984), and *It's Hard to Tell the Singer from the Song* (1986).

Dickens has been featured in a number of films, including *Songcatcher*; *Matewan*, about the West Virginia mine wars; and the Oscar-winning *Harlan County, U.S.A.*, for which she wrote original music. She was herself the subject of a documentary, *Hazel Dickens: It's Hard to Tell the Singer from the Song* (2001). She received an honorary doctorate of humanities in 1998 from Shepherd College. In 2001, Dickens won the National Endowment for the Arts' National Heritage Fellow-

> ## "West Virginia, My Home"
>
> West Virginia
> Oh my home
> West Virginia's
> Where I belong
> In the dead of the night
> In the still and the quiet
> I slip away
> Like a bird in flight
> Back to those hills
> The place that I call home
>
> It's been years now
> Since I left there
> And this city life's
> About got the best of me
> I can't remember why
> I left so free
> What I wanted to do
> What I wanted to see
> But I can sure remember
> Where I come from
>
> Chorus
>
> Well I paid the price for the leaving
> And this life I have's not one I thought
>   I'd find
> Well let me live, love, let me cry
> When I go, just let me die
> Among the friends who'll remember
> When I'm gone
>
> Chorus
>
> Home, home, home
> Oh I can see it so clear in my mind
> Home, home, home
> I can almost smell the honeysuckle vines
> In the dead of the night
> In the still and the quiet
> I slip away like a bird in flight
> Back to those hills that I call home
> Home
>
> —Hazel Dickens
> Happy Valley Music (1976)

ship, the highest honor given to folk artists in the United States. In 2002, she received the Lifetime Achievement Award from the North American Folk Music and Dance Alliance.

Hazel Dickens lives in Washington.

Linda Tate
Shepherd University
Neil Rosenberg, Alice Gerrard, and Hazel Dickens, *Hazel Dickens and Alice Gerrard: Pioneering Women of Bluegrass*, liner notes, 1996; Richard Straw, *Interviewing Appalachia*, 1994; Charles Wolfe, *Hazel and Alice*, liner notes, 1995.

Little Jimmy Dickens

Musician James Cecil "Little Jimmy" Dickens, born December 19, 1920, became one of West Virginia's most successful country music stars. Born in Raleigh County, Dickens gained early radio experience at WJLS Beckley and WMMN Fairmont. His entertainment career took him to several radio stations until 1949 when he joined the *Grand Ole Opry* at WSM in Nashville, Tennessee. He left the *Opry* in 1957, but rejoined in 1975. In 1948, Dickens signed with Columbia Records and had several hits, most notably "Take An Old Cold Tater And Wait," "Sleeping At The Foot Of The Bed," and "May The Bird Of Paradise Fly Up Your Nose." Although equally adept at "heart" songs, Dickens remains best known for humorous numbers, which the four-foot 11-inch performer renders on stage with considerable gusto. In 1983, Little Jimmy Dickens became the first and only Mountain State native elected to the Country Music Hall of Fame.

Abby Gail Goodnite
University of Rio Grande
Ivan Tribe, *Mountaineer Jamboree: Country Music in West Virginia*, 1984.

Dickinson Family

Colonel John Dickinson, a veteran of the Battle of Point Pleasant and resident of Bath County, Virginia, had two tracts of land along the Kanawha River surveyed in November 1784. A tract of 502 acres at Campbells Creek included the famous salt spring; Joseph Ruffner purchased this property in 1796. A tract of 704 acres lay in the area of present Belle. In 1796, about three years before his death, Dickinson conveyed this tract to his sons-in-laws, Samuel and John Shrewsbury. They settled there about 1798. The brothers began to acquire additional land, establish farms, and operate a salt business. They encouraged brother Joel Shrewsbury and his business partner and brother-in-law, William Dickinson Sr., to come from Bedford County, Virginia.

Joel Shrewsbury and William Dickinson Sr. purchased property, rented a salt furnace, and moved their business to the Kanawha Salines (now Malden) in 1814. Dickinson and Shrewsbury along with John Dickinson Lewis and Lewis Ruffner were dubbed the "Salt Kings of Kanawha." Lewis was a grandson of Col. John Dickinson. He first married Sallie, a daughter of Joel Shrewsbury. His second wife, Anne, was the daughter of the other partner, William Dickinson Sr. Two of Lewis's daughters married the two sons of William Dickinson Jr.

The firm of Dickinson and Shrewsbury was consistently the largest user of slave labor in the county, employing the slaves at their salt works and at the mines that supplied fuel for saltmaking. The John Q. Dickinson salt furnace at Malden, established by Dickinson and Shrewsbury in 1832, was operated for more than 100 years by the Dickinson family. It was for many years the area's last remaining salt operation.

William Dickinson Jr. (1798–1881) was born and reared in Bedford County, where he practiced law. He came to Kanawha in 1861 to handle the legal matters in the dissolution of the Dickinson-Shrewsbury partnership, which the courts finalized in 1866, after both partners had died. With his share of his father's estate, in 1867 William Jr. largely founded the Kanawha Valley Bank, later One Valley Bank and now part of BB&T. Son John Q. was president from 1882 until 1925 and grandson John L. from 1925 until 1949. Henry Clay Dickinson, another son of William Dickinson Jr., was the mayor of Charleston when he died in 1871. Dickinson family descendants have figured prominently in the affairs of the bank and the community down to the present.

See also Kanawha Valley Bank, Salt Industry

Gerald S. Ratliff
Charleston
Bill Drennen, *One Kanawha Valley Bank: A History*, 2001.

John Quincy Dickinson

Banker and saltmaker John Quincy Dickinson was born November 20, 1831, in Bedford County, Virginia. During the Civil War he enlisted in Company A of the Second Virginia Cavalry, commanded by his brother, Capt. Henry Clay Dickinson. In 1864, he was captured near Greene Court House, Virginia, and kept prisoner at Fort Delaware until the end of the war.

In 1865, Dickinson came to the Kanawha Valley and began repairing the family's salt works, which had been established by his grandfather, William Dickinson Sr., in 1832. They had been rendered inoperable due to damage caused by the great flood of 1861 and by the Union Army. Dickinson, with his father, William Dickinson Jr., brother Henry Clay Dickinson, and others, established the Kanawha Valley Bank in 1867. He succeeded his father as the bank's president in 1882, serving until 1925. Under his leadership the bank became the largest financial institution in Charleston. At about the time the bank was established he moved to the farm at present Quincy. He lived there and in Malden until 1893, when he moved to Charleston.

Dickinson acquired extensive holdings of coal, gas, and oil properties in Boone, Kanawha, Fayette, and Raleigh counties. He was directly interested in enterprises in 28 states, Cuba, and the Philippines. He was the first director of the West Virginia Bankers Association (1894) and the Kanawha Coal Operators Association (1904).

John Quincy Dickinson died November 26, 1925, at his Charleston home.

See also Dickinson Family, Kanawha Valley Bank

Gerald S. Ratliff
Charleston
Bill Drennen, *One Kanawha Valley Bank, A History*, 2001.

Dingess Tunnel

The Dingess Tunnel is a 3,327-foot tunnel in northwestern Mingo County, built for the original Twelvepole Creek route of the Norfolk & Western (now Norfolk Southern) Railroad in 1892. That route was the N&W main line between 1892 and 1904, when a new rail line opened on better grades along the Big Sandy River. The Twelvepole Creek route later was abandoned. The town of Dingess was a busy place while the Twelvepole line was in use, because goods shipped on the N&W were unloaded there and hauled to other towns in the area by wagonloads. In June 1905, two trains collided in the tunnel and three people were killed. When the N&W changed its route, the Dingess Tunnel fell into disuse. Since 1913, the Dingess Tunnel has been used as a highway tunnel. The tunnel has been the subject of tales about Mingo County's violent past. Writer Huey Perry described it as a notorious ambush site in his 1972 memoir of the Poverty War, *They'll Cut Off Your Project*.

Robert Y. Spence
Logan

Diocese of Wheeling-Charleston

The Roman Catholic Diocese of Wheeling-Charleston includes the entire state of West Virginia and is made up of close to 100,000 members. At its founding in 1850, the diocese had a different name and different borders. Catholics, in what was then Western Virginia, were under the spiritual care of the Diocese of Richmond, which at that time included all of Virginia. The vastness of the territory and the growing number of Catholics in the western part of the state convinced the second bishop of Richmond, Richard V. Whelan (1809–74), that the diocese needed to be divided. On July 19, 1850, Pope Pius IX established the Diocese of Wheeling, naming Whelan as its first bishop.

The Allegheny Mountains set the initial diocesan boundaries, including almost all of present West Virginia plus 17 counties (and part of another) in present southwest Virginia. Eight counties of the current Eastern Panhandle were left with the Diocese of Richmond. After the creation of the new state of West Virginia in 1863, the diocesan and state boundaries were different for more than 100 years. It was not until 1974, under a decree issued by Pope Paul VI, that the diocesan borders were realigned to agree with those of the state. The Virginia counties that had initially been part of the Diocese of Wheeling were transferred to the Diocese of Richmond, and the eight counties of the Eastern Panhandle were incorporated into the Diocese of Wheeling. The name of the diocese was also changed at that time to the Diocese of Wheeling-Charleston, with a co-cathedral at Sacred Heart Parish in Charleston.

See also Roman Catholics

Tricia Pyne
St. Mary's Seminary & University, Maryland

Joseph H. Diss Debar

The designer of the Great Seal of West Virginia and the state's first commissioner of immigration, Joseph Hubert Diss Debar was born near Strasbourg, France, March 6, 1820. Educated in the classics and the sciences, he was fluent in several languages and a talented artist. Diss Debar came to the United States in 1842. He moved to Parkersburg in 1846 as a land agent for John Dumas, who represented the claims of French veterans of the American Revolution in regard to land bonuses. Diss Debar resided in present West Virginia for the next 29 years, during which time he created numerous sketches of people and places of the era. He lived in Parkersburg and at St. Clara, a Doddridge County German-Swiss immigrant colony which he founded and named for his first wife, Clara Levassor, who had died in childbirth.

A supporter of the movement to create West Virginia, Diss Debar was commissioned in 1863 to design the Great Seal. Seeing the assignment in part as an opportunity to promote the new state's natural resources and economic potential, he created a two-sided medallion whose front depicts a farmer, a miner, the state motto, and other symbols. In 1864, he was appointed commissioner of immigration and worked in this capacity to recruit labor and landowners from abroad until 1871. Diss Debar involved the state in the 1867 Paris Exposition, winning a prize for the petroleum exhibit from the West Virginia oil fields. As immigration commissioner he produced *The West Virginia Hand-Book and Immigrant's Guide* in 1870. The Swiss colony at Helvetia was founded during his tenure, though it

is uncertain whether he had any role in the project.

Diss Debar served in the legislature from Doddridge County in 1864, and in 1872 he supported the Liberal Republicans in their bid to come to terms with ex-Confederates in ending Radical Reconstruction in West Virginia. He died in Philadelphia, January 13, 1905.

See also State Seal, Swan Lands

Bernard L. Allen
Conway, South Carolina

Sam Dixon

Coal operator Samuel L. Dixon was born in Scarborough, England, November 14, 1856. Educated in the English public schools, he emigrated to Fayette County in 1877, first working for an uncle in the coal business. In 1893, he and a partner organized the MacDonald mine in Fayette County. Other Dixon mines soon followed in the New River coalfield, including operations at Scarbro, Carlisle, Oakwood, Stuart, Parral, and Wingrove.

In 1905–06, with the financial backing of Boston coal dealer P. W. Sprague, and other New Englanders and Pennsylvanians, Dixon founded the New River Company. It included the original Dixon mining properties, and others at Price Hill, Sprague, Cranberry, Prosperity, Harvey, and elsewhere. The New River Company was the giant of the New River coalfield and is important as an early example of mine industry consolidation. Dixon was purged from the company during growing pains exacerbated by the recession of 1907–08, his Northern backers in 1912 bringing in professional management from outside the coal industry to replace him.

Dixon also owned the White Oak and the Piney River & Paint Creek railroads, and newspapers in Charleston, Fayetteville, and Beckley. He used these papers to involve himself in politics and ruled for

many years as the Republican boss of Fayette County. The colorful "King Samuel" was the most important and likely the most controversial operator in the New River field. He died July 6, 1934, in Price Hill, Raleigh County.

Ken Sullivan
West Virginia Humanities Council

Doddridge County

Doddridge County was formed February 4, 1845, from parts of Harrison, Lewis, Ritchie, and Tyler counties. It was named for Philip Doddridge, a Western Virginia congressman, state legislator, and member of the Virginia Constitutional Convention of 1829–30.

Located in the hills of north-central West Virginia, the area was first settled by European Americans about 1800. Indian trails, including the Monongahela-Scioto and the Middle Island trails, village sites, and burial mounds are evidence of an earlier native presence. The land that eventually became the county seat of West Union was part of 20,000 acres patented by James Caldwell in 1787 and settled by brothers Nathan, William, and Joseph Davis in 1808. The county encompasses 321.6 square miles.

The Northwest Turnpike, completed in 1838, connected Winchester and Parkersburg and resulted in the growth of many Western Virginia communities, including West Union. Likewise, the Northwestern Virginia Railroad, a subsidiary of the Baltimore & Ohio that ran from Grafton to Parkersburg, brought increased economic opportunity to Doddridge and surrounding counties when it was completed in the 1850s. Lumber became a leading enterprise in Doddridge County, supplying the burgeoning rail industry with crossties.

The Civil War interrupted the development of the county. Doddridge's sentiments were with the North. It sent

---

FAST FACTS ABOUT DODDRIDGE COUNTY

Founded: 1845

Land in square miles: 321.6

Population: 7,403

Percentage minorities: 1.7%

Percentage rural: 100%

Median age: 38.7

Percentage 65 and older: 14.8%

Birth rate per 1,000 population: 9.3

Median household income: $26,744

High school graduate or higher: 69.4%

Bachelor's degree or higher: 10.2%

Home ownership: 81.2%

Median home value: $57,000

This information is from the 2000 U.S. Census. In 2000, West Virginia as a whole had 5 percent minorities, a median age of 38.9, median household income of $29,696, and a 75.2 percent home ownership rate.

The Doddridge County Courthouse was built in 1899.

for growing grain. Doddridge is well-drained by a number of streams and creeks, the most important being Middle Island Creek, which flows northwestward for more than 75 miles to the Ohio River.

The significance of both industry and agriculture in West Virginia is depicted in the state seal, which was designed by Joseph Diss Debar, a French immigrant who settled in West Virginia in 1846. In the early 1850s, Diss Debar founded the Doddridge County community of St. Clara, named for his first wife, Clara Levassor. As a Doddridge County delegate to the legislature, he helped create a state office of immigration and was named the first West Virginia commissioner of immigration in 1864.

Doddridge County is the birthplace of the only West Virginian ever to be elected a member of the U.S. House of Representatives, the U.S. Senate, and the state's governor. Matthew Mansfield Neely was born near Grove, November 9, 1874. Neely began his political career as mayor of Fairmont. Until his death from cancer in 1958, Neely was a dynamic and controversial figure in state and national Democratic politics.

Doddridge County is divided into eight magisterial districts: Central, Cove, Grant, Greenbrier, McClellan, New Milton, Southwest, and West Union. The county is served by four elementary schools and one middle school. Doddridge County High School, now the county's only secondary school, was created in 1933 when the newly instituted county school system consolidated Carr High School and West Union High School.

As in much of West Virginia in the early 20th century, poor roads made travel through Doddridge difficult. The county's first roads were paved in 1914, and during the Depression many secondary roads were paved by the federal Works Progress Administration. In 1964, work began at Parkersburg to make U.S. 50 a four-lane highway, and the Doddridge section of the highway was completed between 1964 and 1972. Today, U.S. 50, which is Corridor D in the Appalachian Development Highway System, is the main transportation artery through the county.

In 2000, the population of Doddridge County was 7,403, slightly more than half what it was in 1900 (13,689). Population dropped sharply between 1940 and 1960, from 10,923 to 6,970, as West Virginia suffered a period of sustained out-migration, a reflection of shifting national economics. Doddridge made solid gains between 1970 and 1980, from 6,389 to 7,433, when West Virginia became a destination of the back-to-the-land movement; lost population in the 1980s; and has since rebounded.

See also Joseph H. Diss Debar, Philip Doddridge, West Union

representatives to the first and second Wheeling conventions, which reestablished a loyal government of Virginia and provided for the creation of West Virginia. Four Union units were raised in the county: Company H, 4th West Virginia Cavalry; Company C and Company M, 6th West Virginia Volunteer Infantry; and Company A, 14th West Virginia Volunteer Infantry. Before the war, a tavern and stagecoach stop about one mile from West Union was reputed to have been part of the Underground Railroad. Proprietor Luke Jaco opened the establishment about 1845 and may have used a nearby cave to harbor runaway slaves on their way to the Ohio River.

As the end of the 19th century approached, timber was supplanted in the local economy by oil and gas. The Center Point oil pool was opened by the South Penn Oil Company in 1892; between 1900 and 1929, many Doddridge wells commonly produced 50 to 100 barrels of petroleum per day. In addition to South Penn, major companies included Carter Oil, the Philadelphia Company, Carnegie Gas, and Hope Natural Gas. Numerous local independent drillers also worked the oil and gas fields.

Oil and gas spawned other industries in the county. These included carbon manufacturing, which used natural gas as a raw material, and glass making, which used gas as a cheap fuel. In the early 1900s, Ideal Glass and Doddridge County Window Glass operated in West Union; Acme Carbon, Castle Brook Carbon, Mountain State, and Southern Carbon companies were located in and around Smithburg.

Oil and gas production dropped off during the Great Depression, but new drilling began during World War II. Doddridge experienced a second drilling boom in the 1960s. A well at the mouth of Doe Run was found to contain 10 million cubic feet of gas and flowed 200 barrels of oil a day. Today, oil and gas production remains the county's most important industry.

Although the terrain is quite hilly, farming is important in Doddridge. Livestock, particularly cattle and sheep, and poultry are the county's leading agricultural products. Doddridge is part of the "Bluegrass Belt" that stretches from Tennessee north into West Virginia and southern Pennsylvania, providing rich pastures. The county's red, white, and yellow clay soil (with some limestone deposits) is also suitable

Christine M. Kreiser
Clarksburg

Doddridge County Historical Society, *The History of Doddridge County, West Virginia*, 1979; *Hardesty's West Virginia Counties: Doddridge, Marion, Upshur, Wetzel*, 1973.

Joseph Doddridge

Historian and clergyman Joseph Doddridge, the brother of Philip Doddridge, was born near Bedford, Pennsylvania, October 14, 1769. At age four, his family moved to the frontier, settling in Washington County, Pennsylvania. Doddridge received a strict religious education at home and attended school in Maryland until age 18. He then spent several years as an itinerant preacher in the Wesleyan Society, traveling for a time with the great Methodist bishop, Francis Asbury. In 1792, Doddridge was ordained a priest and became the first minister of the Protestant Episcopal Church in trans-Allegheny Virginia. There he established churches in Brooke and Ohio counties as well as in Pennsylvania and Ohio. After being married, he studied medicine to supplement his income as a minister, and thereafter he treated both the souls and bodies of his parishioners in his frontier travels.

While noted in his day as a minister, Doddridge is remembered now for his writings, ranging from a *Treatise on the Culture of Bees* to poetry, songs, and prose dealing with Indian life, including *Logan, the Last of the Race of Shikellemus, Chief of the Cayauga Nation*. His most important work was *Notes on the Settlement and Indian Wars of the Western Parts of Virginia and Pennsylvania from 1763 to 1783, Inclusive*. Theodore Roosevelt called this book, commonly known as Doddridge's Notes, "the most valuable book we have on old-time frontier ways and customs."

As frontier minister, physician, scholar, and author, Joseph Doddridge was an important contributor to the development of Western Virginia whose significance is in leaving a record of the history of that time and place. He died at his home in Brooke County, November 9, 1826.

See also Philip Doddridge

Dan B. Fleming
Blacksburg, Virginia

Charles H. Ambler, *West Virginia: The Mountain State*, 1940; Ambler, *West Virginia: Stories and Biographies*, 1937.

Philip Doddridge

Lawyer and sectional leader Philip Doddridge was born near Bedford, Pennsylvania, May 17, 1773. As an infant he moved with his family, including older brother Joseph Doddridge, to Washington County, Pennsylvania. At age 17 he moved again with his family to nearby Wellsburg, Virginia, and there read for the law. He became successful as a circuit lawyer and his reputation grew throughout the region. He was known as a great public speaker.

In 1815–16, Doddridge represented Brooke County in the Virginia legislature and soon took up the causes of the people living in the western part of the state. He fought to repeal the law that qualified only landholders to vote and became a leader for public education. In 1829, he was one of four selected to represent the northern district of Western Virginia at the Virginia Constitutional Convention of 1829–30. Other delegates included James Madison, James Monroe, John Marshall, and John Tyler. The convention attempted unsuccessfully to address the growing east-west sectionalism in Virginia. Doddridge was a major spokesman for the trans-Allegheny region. He failed at the convention, but his arguments against the East were influential in creating sentiment for the subsequent separation of West Virginia from Virginia.

In 1828, Doddridge was elected to Congress and reelected in 1830. Daniel Webster said of him, "He was the only man I ever feared to meet in debate." Philip Doddridge died in Washington, November 19, 1832. Doddridge County was named in his honor in 1845.

See also Constitutional Convention of 1830, Joseph Doddridge

Dan B. Fleming
Blacksburg, Virginia

Dogwood

Flowering dogwood is a small flowering tree with a short trunk and a spreading crown. Before the leaves appear, four showy white "petals" (actually leaf-like bracts) form a cross-shaped flower that is notched at the tips with red stains. This gives rise to the folklore that Jesus was crucified on a cross of dogwood, so distressing the tree that it never again grew big enough for a cross while blood-stained flowers would always remind people of the crucifixion. Other characteristics are opposite leaves, bright red berries in early autumn, and brilliant red and orange fall foliage. The clusters of berries are a tasty treat for birds, squirrels, and other wildlife.

Long profuse in West Virginia forests, dogwoods were devastated in the 1980s and 1990s by an anthracnose fungus. The fungus causes large brownish leaf spots, then spreads to twigs and stems, and eventually kills the tree. At century's end, the survival of the dogwood was in question.

In addition to the flowering dogwood, seven shrubby dogwood species grow in West Virginia. The dwarf cornel grows to only one foot height but also has four showy white petals and clusters of red berries, and creates an excellent landscape ground cover. Other dogwood shrubs have whitish flower clusters and are important for landscaping and wildlife.

Indians chewed dogwood twigs and used the bristle tip as a toothbrush. They also smoked the bark of shrubby dogwoods in their pipes, as part of a smoking mixture called kinnikinnick. Pioneers used the dense wood for shuttles on looms. Today, flowering dogwood is valued primarily as an ornamental and for carving durable sculptures and crafts.

William N. Grafton
WVU Extension Service

Dolly Sods

Dolly Sods is situated on a part of the Allegheny Plateau and features flat, windswept plains and striking topography. The elevation ranges from 2,600 feet to over 4,000 feet. The high-elevation grass balds, or sods, take their name from the Dahle (pronounced "dolly") family who grazed livestock on these sods at the turn of the 19th century. The Dolly Sods Wil-

Dolly Sods.

derness and Scenic Area, designated by Congress in 1975, is within the boundaries of the Monongahela National Forest in Tucker and Randolph counties. Its 10,215 acres contain an extensive system of hiking trails. To the northeast, the 2,400 acre Dolly Sods Scenic Area borders the wilderness. The picturesque Bear Rocks, located at the northern end of the scenic area, are managed by the Nature Conservancy.

The boulder-strewn plains of Dolly Sods were once covered with a majestic red spruce forest where trees grew to 90 feet tall and more than four feet in diameter. This original forest was logged in the 1800s, and the underlying thick, fertile soil was destroyed. The area is now primarily heath barrens where azalea, mountain laurel, rhododendron, and blueberries abound. Cranberries and the carnivorous sundew plant are found in upland bogs characterized by sphagnum moss. The climate of Dolly Sods is harsh, with frost and freezing temperatures possible all year. Almost constant prevailing winds from the west create "flagged" spruce, stunted trees with branches only on the eastern side, away from the wind. Managed by the U.S. Forest Service, Dolly Sods is used for backpacking, camping, and picnicking.

From October 14, 1943, to July 1, 1944, the army transformed parts of Dolly Sods into an artillery range for training of military troops bound for duty during World War II. In 1997, most trails and designated campsites were cleared of munitions left behind.

See also Bogs

Patricia Hissom
Davis

Norma Jean Venable, *Dolly Sods*, 2001.

Donaghho Pottery

Potter and businessman Alexander Polk Donaghho was born in Washington County, Pennsylvania, July 2, 1829, and he died in Parkersburg in 1899. It is thought that he learned his trade in the Monongahela Valley in Pennsylvania, at a pottery owned by an uncle. He came to Parkersburg in 1870 and began a pottery operation there in 1874. Donaghho crocks and other items of pottery are avidly collected today.

Probably working with a few employees, Donaghho made pottery by hand, "throwing" it on a potter's wheel just as it had been for hundreds of years. The majority of his ware had a generally cylindrical shape with slightly bulging sides. Virtually all of the crocks or wide-mouth pots featured a bold top molding and two ear handles on the shoulder below the rim. Jugs had a small top opening for a plug and a one-ring handle. Pottery canning jars usually had no handles but had a deep groove in the rim for the wax seal.

The ware was dried in a steam-heated room, after which it was stenciled with cobalt oxide. The pots were marked "A. P.

Donaghho," or "Excelsior Pottery" on big pieces, and "Parkersburg." Many were decorated with advertisements for retail establishments. When thoroughly dry, the ware was placed in a bottle kiln to be fired.

Donaghho pottery was salt-glazed, with damp salt reacting in the hot kiln to produce a sodium aluminum silicate glaze.

James R. Mitchell
State Museum

Stanley W. Baker, "Crocks and Churns: A. P. Donaghho and Parkersburg Stoneware," *Goldenseal*, Summer 1985.

Shirley Donnelly

Baptist preacher and amateur historian Clarence Shirley Donnelly was born in Rock Castle, Jackson County, February 2, 1895. He wrote a daily column for the *Beckley Post-Herald* for 27 years and authored more than 20 religious and historical publications.

Donnelly moved with his family from Rock Castle to Charleston when he was 14. He graduated from Charleston High School, where he edited the school's publication, *The Book Strap*. After graduation from Union Theological Seminary in Richmond, Virginia, he was ordained as a Baptist minister.

Donnelly began his ministry in 1919 at Main Street Baptist Church in Petersburg. In 1922, he accepted the pastorate at Oak Hill Baptist Church, where he stayed for 21 years. During World War II, he served in the U.S. Army as a chaplain. He was awarded several honors, including the Bronze Star, the Legion of Merit Award, and the American Defense Medal. After active duty, he was a chaplain for the West Virginia National Guard and the Veterans Administration Hospital in Beckley.

From 1946 to 1971, Donnelly was pastor of Crab Orchard Baptist Church near Beckley. As a minister he officiated in 2,349 civilian funerals and performed 1,355 weddings.

Donnelly's interest in history was evident in his newspaper columns, which highlighted local lore. The *Beckley Post-Herald* collected his columns in three volumes, *Yesterday and Today: A Keepsake, A Keepsake II,* and *A Keepsake III*. He also established the Fayette County Historical Society, and served as president of the Fayette, Oak Hill, and West Virginia historical societies. Donnelly died August 31, 1982.

Morris Purdy Shawkey, *West Virginia: In History, Life, Literature and Industry*, 1928; Fayette County Chamber of Commerce, *History of Fayette County, West Virginia*, 1993.

Douglass High School

Frederick Douglass Junior and Senior High School served for many years as a major academic, social, and cultural re-

source for black Huntington. Erected in 1924, on 10th Avenue at the corner of Bruce Street, the school was actually the second one in Huntington to bear the Douglass name. The first Douglass School, a building on 16th Street and Eighth Avenue, had grades one through 12 and graduated its first high school class in 1893. Both were named for the abolitionist Frederick Douglass.

The 1924 three-story brick building was constructed because of the changing educational needs at the secondary level and an increased black enrollment. When Douglass's name was transferred, the old school was renamed Barnett in honor of one of Huntington's pioneer African-American ministers.

Appointed principal of the new school in 1925, Henry Davis Hazelwood served until his retirement in 1949. His successors were Henry Smith Jones, 1950–51; Leonard H. Glover, 1952–55; and Joseph A. Slash, 1955–61. During the Hazelwood administration, Douglass emerged as a first-class high school, gaining accreditation from the North Central Association of Schools and Colleges in 1927. The school also fielded a band and varsity athletic teams, developed choirs and dramatic activities, and brought speakers and performers to the community.

Douglass High School closed in 1961 after the integration of public schools in West Virginia. In its two locations the school existed for 70 years, 33 years as a combined elementary-secondary institution, and 37 years as a junior and senior high school. During those decades, Douglass touched the lives of most of Huntington's black families and educated nearly four generations of their children. In 1985, the Douglass Junior and Senior High School building was listed on the National Register of Historic Places.

Ancella R. Bickley
Charleston

Ancella R. Bickley, "Douglass High School, 1892–1961," *Douglass High School Centennial Reunion Book*, 1993.

Dow Chemical Company

Started in 1897 in Midland, Michigan, Dow Chemical Company is one of the world's largest chemical, plastics, and agricultural products companies. In 2001, Dow merged with Union Carbide Corporation, acquiring Union Carbide's South Charleston Technical Center and its plants in South Charleston and Institute.

Herbert Dow, a Midland chemist, pioneered the use of electrolysis to extract bromine and chlorine. He also developed new processes for creating chemical compounds, including chloroform; carbon tetrachloride, an essential ingredient in fire extinguishers, cleaning fluids, and industrial solvents; and lead arsenate, which was used widely as a pesticide in the early 20th century.

Demand for chemicals increased during the two world wars. During World War I, Dow produced aspirin, synthetic indigo dye, Epsom salts, chemicals for explosives, insecticides, and solvents used in airplane fabrics. During World War II, Dow produced most of the nation's magnesium, which was essential for the production of aircraft parts, weapons, and aluminum alloys.

After World War II, Dow concentrated on products for everyday needs, including Styrofoam, Saran Wrap, and Ziploc bags; industrial and agricultural chemicals; paints and protective coatings; and plastics used in wall tiles, dishes, toys, pipes, car parts, and wiring. In 2003, Dow had annual sales of $33 billion and employed 46,000 people. The company became a major producer in the West Virginia chemical industry with the Union Carbide acquisition.

See also Union Carbide Corporation

Dolores I. Dowling

Nurse Dolores Imogene Dowling was born in South Point, Ohio, May 30, 1914, and died April 8, 1996, in Huntington. She graduated from Huntington's St. Mary's Hospital School of Nursing in 1934 and worked in Huntington as a registered nurse and medical secretary from 1935 to 1942.

Dowling joined the Army Nurse Corps on July 1, 1942, and left the service as a first lieutenant in 1946. A combat surgical nurse with the first Mobile Army Surgical Hospital, Dowling served with the 11th Field Hospital in North Africa and Sicily. She was one of the first American nurses to land during the 1943 invasion of Sicily at Gela. Dowling received four Battle Stars, a Bronze Assault Arrowhead, a Meritorious Service Award, and two Presidential Unit Citations. Injured in the line of duty, she later served as a nurse procurement officer for the surgeon general's office.

Dowling returned to civilian life as an office manager for the Greater Huntington Radio Corporation and WHTN-TV and radio, later working for the Greater Huntington Theatre Corporation. In 1963, she became secretary and administrative assistant at the Veterans Administration Regional Office in Huntington.

Russ Barbour
Huntington

Draft Animals

Draft animals are those used for pulling or drawing things. Horses, mules, and oxen were widely used as draft animals in West Virginia through the 19th and early 20th centuries in agriculture, transportation, logging, and mining. Draft animals are still bred by enthusiasts today and still employed in useful work.

Larry Shear with Belgian mares on a Wirt County farm.

Draft animals were common on farms well into the 1940s, with mules more often found in southern West Virginia. Oxen, which are castrated bull cattle, were mostly used in earlier times. Although oxen worked more slowly than horses, they usually did not need shoes, ate about half as much, and required only a homemade yoke instead of an expensive harness set. They worked better than horses in rough, muddy, and steep terrain.

Oxen of the American milking Devon breed, medium-sized, red cattle, were used for fieldwork and hauling on farms as settlers began moving into the region. As the name implies, Devon cattle could also be milked and provided beef for the pioneering family. Other oxen breeds used in West Virginia included beef and dairy types such as Aberdeen Angus, Hereford, Shorthorn, Ayrshire, and Holstein.

By the 1870s, the larger draft horses were employed in farming throughout the state, although seldom as purebreds. The influx of Percheron and Belgian stock increased the size of working horses used in the fields. Mules were also popular among West Virginians for working garden crops, cultivating potatoes, and plowing.

Freight-hauling teamsters traveled the early roads with horse-drawn wagons. Such wagons served as the main land transportation in the region until railroads were built in the latter half of the 19th century. Stagecoach lines operated along the Midland Trail and other turnpikes, including a Lewisburg-to-Charleston line whose coaches were pulled by four to six horses.

After the Civil War, as railroads replaced turnpikes in West Virginia, draft animals supplied the muscle for conveying cargo to and from the railroad terminals. Draft horses were used extensively to distribute goods in towns and cities during the 19th and early 20th centuries, with breweries, meat packers, and dairies often using fancy delivery wagons. In West Virginia cities during the 1880s, there were several horse-drawn streetcar lines whose cars were later replaced by electric trolley cars.

Draft animals, especially oxen and horses, were important in early logging. Before the mechanization of woods work draft animals were the only practical means of getting logs out of the deep hollows. Loggers used heavy chain and a variety of hooks, grabs, and couplers to fasten logs to the horse's harness and to each other. During the 1990s, Daniel Richmond used oxen for selectively logging his land in Raleigh County, finding that oxen have a minimal impact on the land compared to industrial logging.

Early coal mining used several types of draft animals. Mules bred from large draft horses were known as "mammoth mules" and worked in high coal seams or pulled heavy loads on track outside the mine. Oxen and Belgian horses also worked in the higher seams. Smaller mules were used in the lower seams. They sometimes worked at a crawl and did not panic when their ears touched a low ceiling. Miners also used Shetland ponies in the low seams to pull carts loaded with coal. Animals lived underground in some mines and were blind upon returning to the surface.

The oil and gas boom of the 1890s in northern West Virginia employed teams from livery stables and local farms to haul drills, pumps, and pipe. A compressor base hauled from Macfarlan to Smithville, Ritchie County, in 1914 required two dozen heavy horses. Horses also hauled large timbers to field sites for construction of wooden oil derricks.

By the 1950s it was considered backwards by many in West Virginia to own horses for farm work. In many cases, owning draft horses could keep a farmer from qualifying for a farm loan. However, there was a renewed interest in draft animals around the state during the 1960s and 1970s. The West Virginia Draft Horse and Mule Association was formed in 1984, with ownership of draft animals experiencing a revival that has continued into the new century. Kept as a hobby by many, the animals are also in practical everyday work by those sensitive to the impact of heavy machinery in logging and farming.

Scot E. Long
Hebron, Ohio

Jacqueline Goodwin, "Gentle Giants: The Draft Horse Revival," *Goldenseal*, Summer 1986; Lisa Gray Millimet, "'All They Knew was to Pull and Get It': Daniel Richmond about Then and Now," *Goldenseal*, Summer 1997.

Draper Collection

One of the richest stores of source materials relating to the trans-Appalachian frontier from the mid-18th century until after the War of 1812 is the Draper Collection in the State Historical Society of Wisconsin Library. The collection was amassed by Lyman Copeland Draper (1815–91), who devoted his life to gathering records of border heroes and their descendants. In his quest he traveled more than 60,000 miles, many of them on foot or bicycle. The manuscripts deal with the frontiers of New York, Pennsylvania, Maryland, Virginia, West Virginia, Tennessee, and the Carolinas. Those dealing with West Virginia matters are especially useful for the French and Indian War, Dunmore's War, and the Revolutionary War, as well as persons such as George Rogers Clark, Daniel Boone, Simon Kenton, Samuel Brady, and others.

Draper's hopes of writing biographies of Clark, Boone, Brady, and others were never realized. Nor did he accomplish his dream of using the Draper materials to annotate and produce a new edition of Joseph Doddridge's famous *Notes on the Settlement and Indian Wars of the Western Parts of Virginia and Pennsylvania*. Nevertheless, Reuben Gold Thwaites and Louise Phelps Kellogg of the Historical Society drew upon the papers to publish five volumes of valuable documents, one on Dunmore's War and four on the Revolutionary War. Thwaites used the collection for a new edition of Alexander Scott Withers's *Chronicles of Border Warfare*, another classic of West Virginia history. The Draper Collection also enabled Virgil A. Lewis to complete his *History of the Battle of Point Pleasant*, in which he corrected the mistaken view, which he himself had once held, that the battle was the first engagement of the American Revolution.

As the value of the Draper Collection became better known, some people in areas from which Draper had obtained materials regretted that they had allowed such useful records to be moved to Wisconsin. Librarian John Trotwood Moore of Tennessee tried in vain to persuade the Wisconsin legislature to order the State Historical Society to return to Tennessee 90 volumes of records from that state. In the 20th century, however, the advent of microfilm resolved difficulties faced by distant scholars desiring to use the Draper Collection, and the Draper records became readily available to researchers everywhere.

See also Chronicles of Border Warfare, Joseph Doddridge, Virgil A. Lewis

Otis K. Rice
WVU Institute of Technology

Dreamland

Opened as a private business in 1925 and operated by the city of Kenova each summer since 1974, Dreamland pool has been attracting fun-seekers for more than 75 years.

Grocer J. D. Booth of Kenova also had an ice business and had water wells for his ice house. Thinking about businesses that used water, he came up with the idea of a swimming pool. Built on the edge of the Big Sandy River where U.S. 60 crosses into Kentucky, Dreamland was an immediate success, partly because it was convenient to both Huntington and Ashland, Kentucky.

The pool was constructed on an imposing scale—125 feet by 250 feet—and graduated from only a few inches at its shallow end to a depth of nine feet at the other. A dance pavilion, added to the roof of the main building in the 1930s, was the scene of dances featuring touring big bands such as those of Glenn Miller, Benny Goodman, and Louis Armstrong, as well as local musical groups.

In 1949, the Booth family sold Dreamland to a group of Huntington businessmen, including Fred Salem, who later became sole owner. In 1973, as Salem was negotiating to sell the pool to the city of Kenova, a fire destroyed the three-story building topped by the dance pavilion. The purchase was completed nevertheless, and the pool opened in May of 1974 for its first season under municipal ownership.

James E. Casto
Herald-Dispatch

Muriel Miller Dressler

Poet Muriel Miller Dressler was born July 4, 1918, in Kanawha County. Both sides of her family go back several generations in the Kanawha Valley. She married Lester Dressler (whose family was from Cabin Creek) in 1936.

Dressler did not complete high school. Her love for literature came, as she was fond of saying, "at the heels of my mother as we planted or hoed the garden." She could quote long passages of Shakespeare and Chaucer before she learned to read the texts and could not remember when she first began to write poetry. Her first published poem, "Appalachia" (1970), quickly became her signature piece.

Dressler published two collections of poetry. The first, *Appalachia, My Land*, was published in 1973, and the second, *Appalachia*, in 1977. Both books gained popularity quickly, and she was invited to read her work at universities throughout the region and beyond, including Harvard, where she was in residence for several days in 1977. In 1975, she met Earl Hamner, creator of the television series *The Waltons*. He used one of her poems, "Elegy for Jody," as the centerpiece for a television special, "Morning Star, Evening Star," in 1986.

Short, curvy, vain, and hyperactive, Dressler remained a popular speaker on the college circuit until the mid-1980s when she suffered a massive heart attack. Afterward she spent much of her life away from the public spotlight, and by the late 1990s Muriel and Lester resided in a Kanawha Valley nursing home. Muriel Miller Dressler died February 27, 2000.

William Plumley
St. Pete Beach, Florida

Elizabeth Simpson Drewry

Legislator Elizabeth Simpson Drewry, the oldest of 10 children, was born September 22, 1893, in Motley, Virginia. The family moved to Elkhorn, McDowell County, where father Grant Simpson owned and operated a barber shop, when Elizabeth was still a young girl.

Drewry was educated in the McDowell County public schools. After attending Bluefield Colored Institute (now Bluefield State College), she went on to Wilberforce University. From there she entered the University of Cincinnati and finally graduated from what, by then, had become Bluefield Collegiate Institute.

Through her work, as a member of the Delta Sigma Theta Sorority and the National Association of Colored Women and her church, Drewry put forward community programs to aid needy children and adults. She spoke out on issues related to the status of blacks in American society and stressed the importance of education as a means of racial uplift. Drewry won her first political victory in 1950, becoming the first African-American woman elected to the West Virginia state legislature (though Minnie Buckingham Harper was the first to serve). Drewry was featured in *Ebony* magazine as one of 10 "top elected Negro women in the United States."

During her first term, Drewry helped to expose a scandal involving attempted bribery of legislators by coal operators. During her 13 years in the legislature, she helped to introduce legislation resulting in the 1956 constitutional amendment allowing women to serve on juries in West Virginia. She introduced and spoke out for other legislation that helped to initiate health care reform and to benefit women, teachers, and wage workers.

Although a stroke forced her to relinquish her seat in the House of Delegates during her eighth term, Drewry continued to be active in her church and her sorority. Drewry died in Welch, September 24, 1979.

See also Minnie Buckingham Harper
M. Lois Lucas
West Virginia State University

Droop Mountain

Droop Mountain, located in Pocahontas and Greenbrier counties, peaks at 3,136 feet. Due to its crouched appearance as seen from the levels of the Greenbrier

Valley and Hillsboro, it was originally called "Drooping Mountain." The first known reference to the current name was in 1775, when Charles Kennison was excused from Botetourt Court due to the distance from his residence beyond "Droop Mountain."

On November 6, 1863, Droop Mountain was the site of one of the most important Civil War battles fought on West Virginia soil. Confederate troops led by Brig. Gen. John Echols were defeated by a larger federal force led by Brig. Gen. William W. Averell. West Virginia dedicated Droop Mountain Battlefield State Park, now 287 acres, on July 4, 1928. In 1935, the Civilian Conservation Corps established Camp Price on the mountain. The CCC constructed footpaths throughout the property designed to highlight battle graves, breastworks, and battlefield monuments. Features of the park include picnic shelters, overnight cabins, a small Civil War museum, and an observation tower with a spectacular view of the surrounding countryside.

Droop Mountain's forests underwent considerable change in the early part of the 20th century. The magnificent American chestnut trees, which had made up as much as 25 percent of the forest in the area, were ravaged by a blight introduced to America from Asia in 1904. In addition, the effects of early logging practices and the severe drought of the 1930s combined to make conditions ripe for major forest fires. Following the fires, a sawmill was set up to salvage usable timber. As logs were processed at this mill, minié balls from the Civil War were frequently found embedded in the wood. Many of the original structures at Watoga and Babcock state parks are constructed of this salvaged timber. Today, the reforested mountain is thick with mature native hardwoods and evergreens. A distinctive feature of the area is the cranberry bog, an acidic wetland more commonly found in the northern United States and Canada.

U.S. 219 crosses Droop Mountain on the way from Lewisburg to Marlinton.

See also Battle of Droop Mountain

Hallie Chillag Dunlap
St. Albans

Droop Mountain, Battle of

Droop Mountain, located three miles south of Hillsboro in Pocahontas County, was the site of one of the most important Civil War battles in West Virginia, as well as the last large-scale engagement fought on our soil. The decisive Union victory ended Confederate efforts to control the new state.

Between August and December 1863, Gen. William W. Averell led his Union soldiers in three daring raids through the mountains and valleys of southeastern West Virginia and southwest Virginia, in

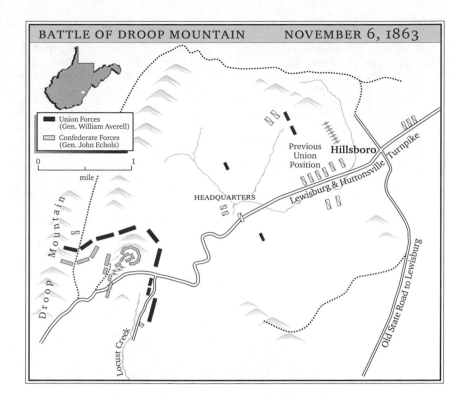

BATTLE OF DROOP MOUNTAIN   NOVEMBER 6, 1863

Union Forces (Gen. William Averell)
Confederate Forces (Gen. John Echols)

0   1
mile

Previous Union Position   Hillsboro

HEADQUARTERS   Lewisburg & Huttonsville Turnpike

Droop Mountain

Locust Creek

Old State Road to Lewisburg

an attempt to break or disrupt the vital Virginia & Tennessee Railroad in the vicinity of Dublin, Virginia.

Averell's second raid resulted in the Battle of Droop Mountain, fought November 6, 1863. Averell, based at Beverly, launched a pincer movement in conjunction with Gen. Alfred N. Duffie, at Charleston, moving to entrap the Confederate forces in the vicinity of Lewisburg. Although the plan failed, Averell's 5,000-man force of cavalry, infantry, and artillery, clashed with some 1,700 Confederates under Gen. John Echols on the crest of Droop Mountain.

Following nearly six hours of continual artillery fire, musketry, and hand-to-hand combat, Averell's infantry broke the Confederate left flank at "the Bloody Angle." The resulting Confederate retreat became a complete rout. Although Echols managed to escape and avoid Duffie, casualties were high on both sides. Averell and Duffie called off pursuit south of Lewisburg and returned to their respective base camps.

Although Averell had won a minor victory he failed to obtain his main objective, and within 10 days the Confederates reoccupied their previous positions. The battle site is preserved today as Droop Mountain Battlefield State Park.

See also Civil War, Droop Mountain, John Echols

Terry Lowry
State Archives

Terry Lowry, *Last Sleep: The Battle of Droop Mountain, November 6, 1863,* 1996.

Drovers and Livestock Drives

The emergence of market-based agriculture in the United States during the early 19th century created new opportunities for farmers and merchants. Driving livestock from rural farms to urban markets required passable roads and people to herd cattle, sheep, hogs, and even fowl. Before the advent of mass livestock shipments via rail in the 1850s, animals bound for urban slaughterhouses were driven on the hoof from farms, to feedlots, and then to the eastern cities. The people who drove the animals were both livestock raisers and professional drovers. In Western Virginia, large-scale animal drives persisted into the latter part of the 19th century because of delays in opening rail routes through the mountains.

Although animals were driven from farms throughout the state in all periods of its history, the present Eastern Panhandle counties played an early part in the improvement of American cattle raising and became a significant link in the food chain between vast Midwestern prairies and Eastern markets. As early as the 1750s, the farms along the South Branch of the Potomac River were well known for their cattle and the families, such as the Pattons, who raised and sold them. As large cattle operations moved west into Ohio and Illinois in the mid-19th century, West Virginia's roads became livestock highways. Drove yards and inns sprouted at regular intervals to serve the drovers and to pasture and water the stock. Brooke County's Drover's Inn, a local landmark now on the National Register of Historic Places, survives from this era. The National Road, which cut through the state's Northern and Eastern panhandles, became a leading 19th-century cattle trail. Farmers in West Virginia's more mountainous areas relied upon back roads that were little more than trails to drive cattle to such cities as Elkins and Pittsburgh, Pennsylvania.

During the 20th century, trucks replaced trails and rails as the prime movers of West Virginia livestock, and the long drive from farm and pasture to market was replaced by the short drive to town or the pickup by modern-era diesel-powered drovers.

David S. Rotenstein
Silver Spring, Maryland
Paul C. Henlein, *Cattle Kingdom in the Ohio Valley 1783–1860*, 1959; Richard K. MacMaster, "The Cattle Trade in Virginia, 1760–1830," in *Appalachian Frontiers: Settlement, Society, and Development in the Preindustrial Era*, 1991; Robert Whitcomb and Judith Whitcomb, "Mountain Cattle Drives," *Goldenseal*, Summer 1998.

Drover's Inn

The historic Drover's Inn, a Brooke County landmark located east of Wellsburg, represents an era when livestock, including cattle and swine and even geese and turkeys, was driven overland on foot to eastern markets. The drovers and their flocks and herds were served by inns and stockyards along the way. Drover's Inn, standing on a high point on the old Wellsburg to Washington, Pennsylvania, turnpike (now Washington Pike, State Route 27), was one such place.

The inn, built in 1848–51 by John Fowler and originally called Fowler's Inn, has also been known as the Inn at Fowlerstown. The handsome Greek Revival main structure, two and a half stories tall, was built of bricks fired on the property. Related buildings, including a log house and a frame house older than the inn itself, stand nearby. In its heyday, the Drover's Inn complex included a post office and general store, as well as extensive stockyards.

The stock drives ended after the arrival of the railroad, which happened in the 1850s in the Northern Panhandle, but the Drover's Inn survived to the present and is in public use today. The inn now offers a historic restaurant, tavern, and gift shop, as well as overnight lodging. The Drover's Inn was added to the National Register of Historic Places in 1992.

See also Drovers and Livestock Drives, Livestock

Joanne Dru

Movie and television actress Joanne Dru was born Joan Letitia Lacock, January 31, 1922, in Logan. Her father was a pharmacist. When she was a child, her family moved to Wheeling. She attended Wheeling High School but moved to New York before she graduated.

In New York, she had jobs as a magazine cover girl and was a John Powers model. While she was dancing in a show at the Paramount Theater, she met singer and actor Dick Haymes. They were married in 1941, and she began her movie career after they moved to Hollywood. After her first film, *Abie's Irish Rose* (1946), Dru appeared in the classic Westerns *Red River* (1948) and *She Wore a Yellow Ribbon* (1949), both starring John Wayne, and in *Wagon Master* (1950). Her movie career included more than 40 films. In 1961, she was featured in the television series *Guestward Ho!* and appeared on *Playhouse 90* and other television shows.

Dru was married to Haymes, 1941–49; to film actor and director, John Ireland, 1949–56; and to C. V. Wood from 1972 until his death in 1993. Joanne Dru died in Los Angeles, September 10, 1996.

Jill Thompson Decker
Vienna, Virginia

Anne S. Dudley

Abolitionist and teacher Anne S. Dudley, later Anne S. Dudley Bates, was born in Maine, January 5, 1833. She militantly opposed slavery before the Civil War and was one of 25 Free Will Baptist missionary school teachers who taught newly freed slaves in the Shenandoah Valley of West Virginia at the end of the war. Arriving in 1865, she taught in Charles Town and Harpers Ferry. Vilified by many of her fellow whites and excoriated in the local newspapers, she was supported by the African-American community. Archilles and Ellen Dixon, literate blacks of Charles Town, provided a log cabin for her first school. Shortly after, she moved to Harpers Ferry to help establish Storer College under the direction of Nathan Brackett, a Free Will Baptist minister assigned to the Shenandoah Valley.

In 1872, Dudley toured New England with Storer College student singers known as the Harpers Ferry Singers to raise funds for construction of Myrtle Hall, the women's dormitory. She relied on her motto, "All for Jesus," to give her courage, delivering her appeal for support from the pulpits of prominent Congregationalist preachers, including that of Henry Ward Beecher. She visited with abolitionist Gerrit Smith and won $2,000 in donations from him.

In 1879, Anne Dudley moved to New York to marry the Rev. L. E. Bates but continued to serve as a Storer trustee for the rest of her life. She died on July 28, 1923, in Fabius, New York.

See also Nathan Cook Brackett, Storer College

Barbara Rasmussen
Fairmont State University
Barbara Rasmussen, "Sixty-Four Edited Letters of the Founders of Storer College," M.A. thesis, West Virginia University, 1986.

Irvin Dugan

Cartoonist Irvin Dugan, born February 8, 1892, in Huntington, worked as a Huntington newspaper artist from 1927 until his retirement in 1957. For many years, his "Adam" cartoon character was a feature on the editorial pages of the *Herald-Dispatch* and the *Sunday Herald-Advertiser*.

Adam, a little old man with a handlebar mustache and a corncob pipe, was created during World War II to promote the sale of war bonds. In his first appearance, he was shown with a dinner pail under his arm and a newly purchased war bond in his hand. The caption read, "Here's mine. Where's yours?" The U.S. Treasury Department distributed the cartoon nationwide, and it was widely reprinted. After the war, Adam crusaded for various civic improvements and causes. Dugan said he named his creation Adam because, like the character of that name in Shakespeare's "As You Like It," he was "short of stature and long on wisdom."

Many well-known individuals, including coal mine labor leader John L. Lewis and Presidents Franklin D. Roosevelt and Harry Truman, wrote Dugan asking for originals of his cartoons. In 1974, Dugan donated a collection of such letters and 500 Adam originals to Marshall University. After retirement, Dugan moved to Phoenix, Arizona, where he died March 17, 1982.

James E. Casto
Herald-Dispatch

Dulcimer

This stringed folk instrument was developed somewhere in the Appalachian mountains before 1800, and was widely built and played throughout the region by the late 1800s. Because the dulcimer was largely unknown outside the mountains until recently, it remains the most recognizably Appalachian of instruments.

The dulcimer consists of three metal strings stretched across a slender wooden box about three feet long, with a fingerboard fretted to produce a major scale. The dulcimer was probably adapted from a Pennsylvania German folk zither, but differs significantly in appearance and use. The instrument is not difficult to build, and artisans of varying ability produced dulcimers with a variety of shapes, dimensions, materials, and construction details.

In the older style of playing, the musician sat with the instrument face up across the knees, and strummed with a flexible pick in the right hand. The left hand fretted one string to produce a melody, while the other two strings droned. Little is known of how the dulcimer was used socially, but its quiet tone makes it more suitable for playing melodies or for vocal accompaniment than for leading a dance.

Unable to compete with more assertive instruments such as the fiddle, banjo, and guitar, the dulcimer largely disappeared from public as the string band tradition developed in the early 20th century. The instrument was revived after

Dugan supported the war effort in this 1943 cartoon.

mid-century through the deliberate practice of folklorists such as Patrick Gainer and folk performers such as Basil Blake of Gilmer County. Since about the same time, the dulcimer has spread beyond Appalachia. Modern instruments are sometimes built with four or more strings, and musicians have developed techniques for playing a wide range of music. Today the dulcimer is often called the "Appalachian dulcimer" to distinguish it from the unrelated "hammered dulcimer," a many-stringed trapezoidal instrument played with small hand-held mallets.

Danny Williams
Morgantown

L. Allen Smith, *A Catalogue of Pre-Revival Appalachian Dulcimers*, 1983.

Dun Glen Hotel

The Dun Glen Hotel was located in Fayette County on the New River across from the railroad town of Thurmond. Local landowner Thomas G. McKell built the hotel in the Southside community in 1901, three years prior to his death. Although Thurmond was a small town, it accounted, as a shipping and collecting point for coal and other freight, for almost 20 percent of all the revenue generated in the Chesapeake & Ohio Railway system in 1910.

The prosperity of the Dun Glen Hotel mirrored that of Thurmond. The hotel was adjacent to the Dunloup Branch railroad, which ran to Glen Jean and the mines on the plateau. Opening night was a gala affair with an orchestra from Cincinnati providing the music. The well-patronized hotel was four and a half stories high and had 100 rooms. Alcohol was prohibited in Thurmond proper but flowed freely across the river at the Dun Glen Hotel. That increased business at the hotel and added to its lore and popularity. One story tells of a poker game at the Dun Glen that lasted 14 years. The famous landmark was burned by arsonists on July 22, 1930.

See also Thurmond

W. Eugene Cox
National Park Service

Dunbar

Dunbar is located on Interstate 64 in Kanawha County west of Charleston. It stands on the banks of the Kanawha River in a rich river bottom previously valued for truck gardening and other agricultural purposes, at an elevation of 603 feet above sea level. The original tract, surveyed by Samuel Lewis in 1774, was once part of George Washington's extensive land holdings in Western Virginia. The burial mound at nearby Shawnee Park suggests a rich prehistory.

Commercial wine production was undertaken within present Dunbar in the 19th century. The picturesque ruins, now part of Wine Cellar Park, were acquired by the city in 1974. The wine cellars were added to the National Register of Historic Places in 1978.

The present city was born during the rapid economic development of the Kanawha Valley during the early 20th century. Dunbar was laid out in 1919 by the Dunbar Development Company and incorporated in 1921. It was named for Dunbar Baines, a Charleston banker and lawyer. The Dunbar-South Charleston bridge, an important connection to the south side of the Kanawha River, opened as a toll bridge in 1953.

Dunbar is a suburb of Charleston. Early industries included Gravely Tractor, Dunbar Flint Glass, and Fletcher Enamel, a producer of metal kitchenware. Today, Dunbar is primarily a residential and commercial community. Its people work in Charleston, at West Virginia State University in neighboring Institute, and in the chemical and other industries in this heavily industrialized area. Dunbar had a 2000 population of 8,154.

Donald F. Duncan

Entrepreneur Donald Franklin Duncan, founder of the Duncan Yo-Yo Company and the Duncan Parking Meter Corporation, was born in Rome, Ohio, June 8, 1893. Duncan spent his childhood in Huntington. His formal schooling ended after eighth grade, and he left Huntington in his mid-teens. During World War I, he was a successful salesman for the Brock Candy Company in Chicago.

While in San Francisco in the late 1920s, Duncan saw his first yo-yo, a spinning top on a string. A common Filipino toy, yo-yo means "come-come" in the Tagalog language. Duncan bought the toy's manufacturer, modified the top and substituted a slip-string of Egyptian fiber. After successful marketing, the yo-yo gained widespread popularity. In 1962, its peak sales year, the Duncan company sold 18 million yo-yos and spinning tops.

With profits from his yo-yo company, Duncan founded the Duncan Parking Meter Corporation. When he sold the parking meter company in 1959, it made 80 percent of all meters sold in the world. In 1957, Duncan's sons took over the Duncan Yo-Yo Company and later sold it to the Flambeau Products Company. Donald Duncan died on May 15, 1971, in Los Angeles.

Ellis Dungan

Wheeling filmmaker Ellis Dungan was born May 11, 1909, in nearby Barton, Ohio. After high school he took to the road, hitchhiking across the United States several times and later traveling abroad. In Paris he studied photography for two years while working at the American Library.

Dungan enrolled in the film school at the University of Southern California in 1932 and took his first job as a director in a film studio in Madras, India. He spent the next 15 years as cameraman, editor, director, and production person in the prolific Indian film industry, working on feature films, documentaries, and World War II training films for the British government. He returned to Hollywood in 1950, then traveled back and forth to film action scenes in India for *The Jungle* with Marie Windsor and Cesar Romero; *Harry Black and the Tiger,* starring Stewart Granger and Barbara Rush; and *Tarzan Goes to India* with Jock Mahoney. Also in India, he shot the action scenes for 52 jungle adventure television programs for Frank Ferrin's *Andy's Gang*.

Dungan came home to the Ohio Valley in 1958, settling in Wheeling. During the next 30 years his Ellis Dungan Productions shot documentary films for Hollywood producer Duke Goldstone and produced many films for the state and region, including *Wheels to Progress* (1959) and *For Liberty and Union* (1977), about the creation of the state of West Virginia. Ellis married Elaine Runner in 1964. His last film, *Josiah Fox—Architect of the United States' First Navy,* was released in 1987, a tribute to his great-great-grandfather, who helped design the USS *Constitution,* "Old Ironsides."

Ellis Dungan was honored with a Lifetime Achievement Award by the West Virginia International Film Festival in 1989 and inducted into the Wheeling Hall of Fame in 1994. He died December 1, 2001, in neighboring Bellaire, Ohio.

Bill Drennen
Shepherdstown

Barbara Smik and Ellis Dungan, *A Guide to Adventure: An Autobiography,* 2002.

Filmmaker Ellis Dungan at work in 1962.

Dunkards

See German Dunkards.

Lord Dunmore

John Murray, fourth Earl of Dunmore and the last colonial governor of Virginia, is recalled in West Virginia history for the frontier conflict known as Dunmore's War. He also held the titles of Viscount Fincastle and Baron of Blair, and both Fort Fincastle at Wheeling (later Fort Henry) and Fort Blair at Point Pleasant (later Fort Randolph) were named for him. Dunmore was born in 1732.

In 1770, he was appointed governor of New York, and the following year was named governor of Virginia. In 1772, the Virginia House of Burgesses named two counties in his honor, Dunmore and Fincastle. Concerned about the safety of the forward settlements in the upper Ohio Valley and attracted by the possibilities of land speculation, he visited the Forks of the Ohio (Pittsburgh) and authorized the rebuilding of a stockade there, Fort Dunmore.

With renewed hostilities on the frontier in the spring of 1774, Dunmore mustered two armies to travel to the Ohio country and make war against the Shawnee. The northern army, under his own command, proceeded to Fort Dunmore, then down the Ohio River to the Hocking River, southwest of present Parkersburg. The southern army, under Col. Andrew Lewis, advanced to the mouth of the Kanawha River, there defeating the Shawnee under Cornstalk at the Battle of Point Pleasant.

On June 1, 1775, as Revolutionary fervor surged in Virginia, Governor Dunmore took refuge with his family on a British warship, and in 1776 he returned to England. He served as governor of the Bahamas, 1787–96, and died at Ramsgate, England, March 5, 1809.

Dunmore was one of the most unpopular figures of his day, accused of deliberately delaying his troops while the Indians attacked Lewis at Point Pleasant and despised for emptying the powder magazine at Williamsburg at the start of the Revolution. Every place in Virginia named in his honor was later renamed.

See also Dunmore's War, Battle of Point Pleasant

Philip Sturm
Ohio Valley University

Dunmore's War

Dunmore's War is the name given to the conflict in the Ohio Valley in the spring of 1774, culminating with the victory of Col. Andrew Lewis's militia over the Shawnee at the Battle of Point Pleasant, October 10, 1774. This was the last military engagement of the colonial period on the western waters. It was significant in that it pacified the Indians in the Ohio Valley during the first two critical years of the

Revolutionary War. The war was named for Lord Dunmore, the last colonial governor of Virginia.

The immediate cause of Dunmore's War was the appearance of several parties of surveyors along the Ohio River, who answered the call of Col. William Preston, surveyor of Fincastle County, Virginia, to meet his deputies at the mouth of the Kanawha River on April 14 and begin establishing the location of military bounty claims in Kentucky. Several skirmishes followed, highlighted by the treacherous murder on April 30 of relatives of the Mingo Chief Logan, who had previously followed a peaceful course. The Ohio tribes declared open warfare as a result of this unfortunate incident.

Governor Dunmore then assembled two armies to proceed from different directions, advance up the Hocking River in present Ohio, and attack the Shawnee villages on the Pickaway Plains. The northern army, made up of militia from Berkeley, Hampshire, and Frederick counties and commanded by the governor himself, proceeded to Fort Dunmore (Pittsburgh), then down the Ohio River, where he planned to meet the other army at the mouth of the Hocking. The southern army, led by Colonel Lewis, was composed of militia from Augusta, Botetourt, and Fincastle counties. It assembled at Camp Union (Lewisburg) in the Greenbrier Valley and journeyed down the Kanawha River to its mouth at Point Pleasant, arriving there on October 6. Each army was composed of approximately 1,000 men.

The Shawnee under Cornstalk attacked Lewis's force on October 10 at Point Pleasant, but by early afternoon the Indians were defeated. Cornstalk ordered a retreat and his men returned across the Ohio to their villages. In the meantime Governor Dunmore, unaware of the battle, ascended the Hocking River and made camp near the Shawnee towns. There he quickly negotiated the Treaty of Camp Charlotte with the Shawnee, guaranteeing the return of prisoners, horses, and property, and an end to hunting by Indians south of the Ohio. The settlement was formalized at Pittsburgh in 1775 by representatives of all the major Ohio tribes. The Indians were thus subdued until the murder of Cornstalk at Fort Randolph in October 1777, gaining valuable time for frontier patriots during the early years of the Revolutionary War.

See also Cornstalk, Lord Dunmore, Andrew Lewis, Battle of Point Pleasant, Treaty of Camp Charlotte

Philip Sturm
Ohio Valley University

Virgil A. Lewis, *History of the Battle of Point Pleasant,* 1909; Otis K. Rice and Stephen W. Brown, *West Virginia: A History,* 1993; Reuben Gold Thwaites and Louise Phelps Kellogg, *Documentary History of Dunmore's War, 1774,* 1905.

DuPont Belle Works

The DuPont Belle Works, a mainstay in the economy of the upper Kanawha Valley for more than 75 years, pioneered a new industry, commercial chemical synthesis at hyper pressures. Rootstock chemicals for the entire world supply of nylon came from the Belle Works from 1937 to 1946, and the plant remained important in the production of nylon until 1968. Located at Belle, on the Kanawha River 11 miles east of Charleston, this plant of the E. I. DuPont Company employed more than 5,000 people at its peak in the early 1950s.

The story began in the mid-1920s, when DuPont decided to commence the manufacture of ammonia using technology developed by Germany during World War I. The process used giant mechanical compressors called "hypers" to achieve pressures up to 15,000 pounds per square inch. Under these conditions, hydrogen made from coke gas would react with nitrogen from the air to make ammonia. DuPont built the Belle plant in 1925. Since coal (made into coke) was the primary ingredient it was natural for the plant to be built in the heart of coal country.

On April 1, 1926, the first high-pressure-process ammonia in North America was produced at Belle. This achievement provided the raw materials to manufacture a myriad of chemical products. The first commercial synthetic wood alcohol, or methanol, was made at Belle in 1927. The ability to make chemicals by combining coal gas and other chemicals at high pressures was an important technological breakthrough. It led to the creation of many new polymers, including nylon. Ammonia was also used to make the fertilizer known as urea that led to the so-called Green Revolution and helped to feed the burgeoning global population.

All of the nylon used by the U.S. armed forces during World War II came from chemicals produced by the Belle Works. Nylon was used for war needs such as parachutes and shoe laces. A new clear plastic called Lucite, made at Belle beginning in 1937, was used for the canopies of Allied warplanes. Other chemicals made at Belle such as Zerex antifreeze and hydraulic fluids also found wartime uses.

After World War II, the plant reached its peak employment as the peacetime uses of nylon, Lucite, Zerex, and urea exploded. As demand grew, the old processes were improved to use cleaner, more economical oil and natural gas as raw materials. The Belle Works switched from coke to natural gas in 1959. Other changes were made as large new plants were built in other locations where oil and natural gas were readily available. In 1978, the plant stopped producing ammonia, and in 1998 the last of the giant hyper compressors were cut up into scrap. Today, the plant still produces specialty chemicals but with automation and new technology the work force has fallen below 700. The hypers and the smoking coke ovens with their gleaming fires showing through the night are gone forever, but the contributions of the Belle plant to 20th-century American life are historic.

See also Chemical Industry, Nylon

Richard A. Andre
Charleston

Charles J. Denham, ed., *Sentimental Journey: The DuPont Belle Works: A 75-Year History 1926–2001,* 2001.

E

Eagle Rock

Eagle Rock is a natural landmark in the Smoke Hole canyon of the South Branch of the Potomac River, located near County Route 2 in Pendleton County a few miles north of Upper Tract. The nearly vertical geologic formation stands at the mouth of Cave Mountain Gap, where the South Branch sweeps into the isolated Smoke Hole region.

Eagle Rock, sometimes also called Eagle Rocks, is one of several dramatic rock formations along this stretch of the South Branch. They include Seneca Rocks, Judy Rocks, and others. Situated at riverside, Eagle Rock rises abruptly 300 feet into the air, a spectacular sight even in an area known for rugged scenery.

Eagle Rock is named for Revolutionary War veteran William Eagle, who is buried just across the South Branch from the striking landmark. Eagle, who is believed to have been present at both Valley Forge and Yorktown, is identified in some sources as a colonel although he entered the Revolutionary service as a teenager. He settled in the area as a farmer in the late 1700s, after the war, and died in 1848. According to folklore, Eagle once battled an actual eagle at the rock, and lost; the bird had been raiding his poultry from its home in the cliffs. William Eagle's grave site was discovered in 1927 and is now well-marked.

See also Smoke Hole

East Huntington Bridge

See Cable-Stayed Bridges.

East Lynn Lake

East Lynn Lake is located in Wayne County, 10 miles south of the city of Wayne on State Route 37. It is created by an earthen dam on the East Fork of Twelvepole Creek. The lake is 12 miles long, has a surface area of 1,005 acres of water at the summer maximum, and 44 miles of shoreline. Although constructed primarily for flood control, East Lynn has many recreational facilities including a campground, picnic areas, and hiking. Most of these areas are handicapped accessible. Boating is popular, and three launch sites are available for public use at the project. Boat and boat slip rentals are provided by a private marina. East Lynn Lake is one of the best places in West Virginia for catching muskie, crappie, hybrid striped bass, largemouth bass, and channel catfish.

East Lynn Lake is managed by the U.S. Army Corps of Engineers, which built the dam in 1969. An additional 22,928 acres of land is managed by the state as the East Lynn Lake Wildlife Management Area.

Leslie Birdwell
Huntington

East River

The East River, a New River tributary, begins at the rail yards in Bluefield. Despite its name, the East is more of a creek than a river, with a moderate rate of flow, falling 1,040 feet from its head to its mouth. East River follows a direct course 23 miles northeastward, from Bluefield to its juncture with the New River at Glen Lynn, Virginia. Originating in the valley between Stony Ridge to the northwest and East River Mountain to the southeast, the river is contained entirely in Mercer County, except for its last half-mile in Giles County, Virginia. A gristmill, no longer in use but still standing near Ingleside, was powered by the stream.

The East River Valley is an important transportation corridor, as traffic which has come through the mountain gap which the New River makes at Narrows, Virginia, finds in the narrow valley of the East an unimpeded route westward. The former Virginian and Norfolk & Western railroads both followed the East River, as does Norfolk Southern, their modern successor. State Route 112 follows the river, as do County Route 30 and busy U.S. 460.

East River Mountain

East River Mountain extends from near Tazewell, Virginia, northeastward for 35 miles to the water gap cut by the New River at the Narrows. In between, the mountain is unbroken by any deep gaps, because of the resistant Tuscarora Sandstone that forms the crest. This rock, a very hard and durable stone with a high silica content, is not easily eroded. There is a minor wind gap where State Route 598 crosses the mountain, the historic route of crooked old U.S. 52. East River Mountain forms the border of Mercer County, West Virginia, with Tazewell and Giles counties, Virginia. The big mountain posed a formidable obstacle to travel until the construction of the East River Mountain Tunnel in 1974, which now carries Interstate 77 and U.S. 52 southward to Virginia. The highest elevation along the Mercer County line is at Buckhorn Knob, 4,069 feet.

The geological structure of East River Mountain is anticlinal, that is, an upward arching of the strata. It is one of the anticlines that mark the westward edge of the Ridge and Valley Physiographic Province. Standing on the crest of East River Mountain, one may observe the parallel folds of the long, high mountains and wide valleys of the Ridge and Valley Province in Virginia to the southeast, a contrast to the Allegheny Plateau in West Virginia to the northwest, with broad, flat summits and winding streams. The base of East River Mountain in Mercer County has limestone formations, with sinkholes and caves. There are traces of minerals such as iron ore reported for locations on the mountain, but these deposits have no apparent economic value.

The East River parallels East River Mountain to the north, flowing from Bluefield across Mercer County to join the New River at Glen Lyn, Virginia.

Raymond Thomas Hill
Athens

Fog pours over East River Mountain onto Bluefield.

Eastern Panhandle

The Eastern Panhandle extends for about 110 miles from the Fairfax Stone to Harpers Ferry, and is joined to the rest of West Virginia by a neck of land less than 50 miles across. Along the Morgan-Hampshire county line, the width of the state is constricted to seven miles. The panhandle includes eight counties, 3,490 square miles, and 212,483 people. Thus, the panhandle accounts for about 15 percent of the land area of West Virginia and about 12 percent of the people.

While part of Virginia, the present Eastern Panhandle was mostly included in the colonial lands of Lord Fairfax. The Fairfax Lands were confiscated by Virginia soon after the American Revolution, and the land titles of various tenants and purchasers remained in dispute for many years.

The panhandle took shape when West Virginia was created. Hardy, Hampshire, and Morgan counties were included in the new state to control the Baltimore & Ohio Railroad for the Union during the Civil War. Provisions were made to include Berkeley and Jefferson counties as well, but their status was not finally settled until after the Civil War. Two new counties were created within the panhandle in 1866 when Mineral and Grant split from Hampshire and Hardy counties. The panhandle also includes Pendleton County.

Except for a small wedge of territory west of the Allegheny Front, the Eastern Panhandle lies within the Ridge and Valley physiographic region. The maximum elevation is 4,861 feet, at Spruce Knob, and the minimum elevation is 247 feet near Harpers Ferry; these are the highest and lowest points in West Virginia. Mountains and ridges are frequently topped with high residual sandstone hills known as knobs, and valleys are floored with limestone and shale.

The region is drained into the Potomac River by such streams as Patterson Creek, the South Branch of the Potomac, the Cacapon River, and the Shenandoah. Each is fed by lesser streams referred to as runs, branches, and creeks. Streams have frequently cut gaps through the northeast-southwest-trending ridges and flow through canyons or gorges such as the Trough of the South Branch, on the Hardy-Hampshire line. Before joining the Potomac, the South Branch and Cacapon rivers follow meandering courses.

The climate is characterized by cold winters and warm summers. The frost-free period is mid-April to mid-October. The prevailing winds from the west release much of their moisture as they move over the Alleghenies, and the annual rainfall is about ten inches less than the state average. Occasional storms from the Atlantic sweep across the region and cause severe flood damage, as in

Rural scene in the Eastern Panhandle, Pendleton County.

1985 when 3,200 homes were destroyed and many lives lost.

Before settlement and lumbering depleted the virgin forest, oak and chestnut dominated the western and northern slopes, and pine was abundant on the hard shale soils on the southern and eastern slopes. The present forest is mixed hardwoods with a scattering of pine.

The earliest inhabitants were nomadic hunting and gathering groups. Later, Indians engaged in cultivation. When whites crossed the Blue Ridge they encountered a few Tuscarora Indians living along the Potomac River and widely dispersed lesser groups. Their legacy includes a settlement site at Old Fields, tribal battlegrounds at Packhorse Ford and Hanging Rocks, the Seneca Trail and Warrior Path, and place names such as Potomac, Cacapon, and Opequon.

John Lederer is credited as the first white person to visit the panhandle, at a point near Harpers Ferry in 1670. Settlement began in earnest after Virginia interpreted the Treaty of Albany, signed in 1722 with the Iroquois Indians, as allowing whites to settle south of the Potomac and between the Alleghenies and the Blue Ridge. Based on tradition, the first settlement was near Bunker Hill, Berkeley County, in 1726, followed by Mecklenburg (now Shepherdstown) in 1727, Hampshire County in 1735, and Hardy County in 1744. The colonial settlers were divided among the English, German, and Scotch-Irish.

The rich limestone soils of the valleys were attractive for farming, which remains a mainstay activity. The 1997 Census of Agriculture noted 2,759 farms in the panhandle, with 92 percent of the crop acreage devoted to hay, corn, and

soybeans. However, 70 percent of farm sales are in poultry, and two-thirds of all poultry sales are in Hardy County. The Eastern Panhandle is also the state's major apple producing region.

In addition to a full range of retail and service activities, others industries include food and poultry processing, and the manufacturing of clothing, machinery, chemicals, and wood products. Mineral production includes coal and gas in Grant and Mineral counties, limestone in Jefferson and Berkeley counties, and sandstone in Morgan County.

Twenty-two percent of the population of the panhandle live in 23 incorporated places, including Martinsburg (14,972), Ranson (2,951), Charles Town (2,907), Keyser (5,303), and others. Martinsburg is an industrial and commercial center located along Interstate 81 in Berkeley County. Petersburg (2,423) is located in a basin where the South Branch River has cut Petersburg Gap through the surrounding mountains. Moorefield (2,375), located in the fertile South Branch Valley, is a processing center for poultry raised in Hardy, Grant, Hampshire, and Mineral counties. More than half of the population is rural nonfarm. The expansion of Washington and Baltimore has made Berkeley and Jefferson counties the fastest-growing region of the state.

The Eastern Panhandle is arguably West Virginia's most historic region. Two events that overshadow all others are John Brown's raid on the arsenal at Harpers Ferry and the ensuing Civil War. Federal and Confederate armies repeatedly invaded the region during the war. Romney changed hands 56 times, Keyser 14 times, and Harpers Ferry (a National Historic Park since 1944) eight times.

Howard G. Adkins
Ona

Otis K. Rice and Stephen W. Brown, *West Virginia: A History*, 1993.

Eastern West Virginia Community and Technical College

Eastern West Virginia Community and Technical College serves six counties of the Potomac Highlands and Eastern Panhandle from its headquarters located in Moorefield, Hardy County. "Eastern," as it is often called, was founded in 1999. It is a coeducational, state-supported, public college, and one of West Virginia's youngest institutions of higher learning.

Operating under its "Education That Works" motto, Eastern offers workforce education and a variety of educational certificate programs, as well as two-year associate degrees. The college also provides career education and continuing education. Eastern offers classroom education as well as distance learning courses, providing access centers at high schools and other locations throughout its service area.

Eastern has recently been among the fastest growing community colleges in West Virginia. It serves mostly non-traditional students, with a majority of the approximately 700 students enrolled at Eastern in 2005 attending part-time. Initially accredited as a branch of Southern West Virginia Community and Technical College, Eastern was seeking independent accreditation in 2005–06. Plans were under way to begin the college's first classroom-laboratory building in the summer of 2006.

John Bertram Easton

Labor leader John Bertram Easton was born September 26, 1880, in Allegheny County, Pennsylvania. He came to Williamstown, Wood County, in 1907 as a glassworker for Fenton Art Glass Company. Easton was a member of the Flint Glass Workers and represented that union in the Parkersburg Trades and Labor Assembly, where he was president for several years.

In 1921, Easton became a vice president of the West Virginia State Federation of Labor, and three years later he was elected president. In 1937, Easton led the State Federation out of the American Federation of Labor over the issue of industrial unionism versus the skilled trades, which the AFL had traditionally represented.

Long a believer in the importance of union members participating directly in the law-making process, Easton served in the state legislature from 1926 to 1928 as a delegate from Wood County. He ran unsuccessfully as a Republican for Congress from the Fourth Congressional District in 1928 and 1930. John Easton died December 20, 1961, in Williamstown.

Fred A. Barkey
Marshall University Graduate College

Easton Roller Mill

Easton Roller Mill, a landmark industrial site, is located at Easton, near Morgantown. Maryland entrepreneur Henry Koontz bought a 600-acre farm there in 1859. Construction of the mill began in 1864, during the Civil War, and the mill was in operation by 1867. Koontz milled flour and meal from wheat, corn, and other grains, and also ground feed for farm animals.

When Koontz died in 1876, the mill was taken over by the Anderson family. William Anderson and his brother, Tom, ran the mill until 1884. Later Eldridge Weaver owned the mill briefly, then Isaac Morris ran it until 1910.

From the 1870s to the 1890s, grain at the Easton mill was ground between large millstones. In the 1890s, more advanced milling technologies were introduced. Corn was still ground using millstones, while wheat was ground using large iron rollers. Roller mills produced a higher quality flour, more in demand. The milling machinery, including both the roller mills and the millstones, was powered by a Lane and Bodley 40-horsepower steam engine dating to the 1870s.

William C. Ley, prominent in the Cheat River iron industry, purchased the mill from Morris in 1910. He cut back operations in 1930, during the Great Depression. The mill was closed in 1940. It was willed to the Monongalia Historical Society in 1970, upon the death of Ley's daughter, Estella Ley Pickenpaugh.

In 1975, the mill was surveyed by the Historic American Engineering Record, and in 1978 it was placed on the National Register of Historic Places.

Norma Jean Kennedy-Venable
Morgantown
Norma Jean Venable, *Easton Roller Mill*, 1994.

Eccles Mine Explosions

On April 28, 1914, a miner in Eccles No. 5 mine in Raleigh County blew a hole through a barrier of coal in an effort to shorten the distance between his assigned working areas, effectively short-cutting the mine's ventilation and allowing methane to accumulate. Another miner's open-flame light ignited the gas, setting off a violent explosion killing all 174 men in No. 5. The mine connected with Eccles No. 6, operating in another coal seam, and nine men in No. 6 died of injuries and of afterdamp, the deadly gas left after a mine explosion.

It took four days to reach the first casualty. The massive recovery effort required a temporary morgue to deal with body identification, and a frantic attempt to locate enough coffins. Government mine officials were joined by local volunteers, and Governor Hatfield traveled underground with some of the exploration parties. This explosion remains West Virginia's second-worst mine disaster.

On March 8, 1926, another explosion killed 19 miners at Eccles, then operated by a subsidiary of the Stonega Coal Company. Around 6:55 p.m., a cutting-machine operator in No. 5 mine failed to test the face for methane, and an electric arc ignited the gas. Fine coal particles, present in the air because of a failure to rock-dust the mines, contributed to the explosion.

Again, both of the interconnected mines were involved. Thirty-five workers in No. 6 were rescued, but wreckage in No. 5 hindered progress. The following evening, rescuers discovered a chalked sign to come to a particular section. R. M. Lambie, the state's chief mine inspector, led the effort and was himself hospitalized after collapsing from exposure to afterdamp. Around 9:30 p.m. on March 9, rescuers reached ten men who had saved themselves by barricading.

See also Coal Mine Disasters

Paul H. Rakes
WVU Institute of Technology
Lacy A. Dillon, *They Died in the Darkness*, 1976.

John Echols

Confederate General John Echols was born at Lynchburg, Virginia, March 20, 1823. A graduate of Washington College (now Washington and Lee University) and Harvard, he became a lawyer in 1843 and was later commonwealth's attorney and a Virginia state legislator. He moved to Union, Monroe County, in 1843 to practice law and remained there until the outbreak of the Civil War.

Echols represented Monroe County at the Virginia Secession Convention and voted for secession. He organized a military company of which he was captain and was commissioned lieutenant-colonel in the Confederate Army in 1861. Later brigadier general, Echols participated in the battles of First Manassas and Kernstown, where he was wounded. He served in the Kanawha Valley in 1862 and commanded Confederate forces at their defeat at the Battle of Droop Mountain in November 1863. In May 1864, he commanded the Confederate right wing at the battle of New Market, and he was with Lee at Cold Harbor. He was assigned to command of the District of Southwest Virginia in August 1864 and later replaced Jubal Early as commander of the Department of Western Virginia. Reluctant to surrender after Appomattox, Echols decided to join with the forces of General Johnston in North Carolina. He accompanied Confederate President Jefferson Davis in his flight to Georgia and was briefly in command there.

After the war, Echols became a founding director of the Chesapeake & Ohio Railway. He was vice president and general manager of the railroad when the line was completed through the New River Gorge and on to Huntington. He left West Virginia and moved to Staunton to practice law following the war. He was twice married, first to the sister of Sen. Allen T. Caperton, of West Virginia. Echols died at Staunton, Virginia, May 24, 1896.

See also Battle of Droop Mountain, Civil War

Tim McKinney
Fayetteville
Tim McKinney, *Civil War in Fayette County, West Virginia*, 1988; Ezra Warner, *Generals in Gray*, 1959.

The Economy

West Virginia has a population of 1.8 million, including a civilian labor force of more than 800,000. Its abundant natural resources include coal, gas, timber, stone, cement, salt, and oil. Of approximately 764,000 persons employed in non-farm jobs at the end of 2000, the services sector accounted for 226,000, followed by wholesale and retail trade, 164,000; government (federal, state, and local), 140,000; manufacturing, 81,000; transportation and public utilities, 38,000; construction, 34,000; finance, insurance, and real estate, 30,000; and mining, 21,000. About 47,800 residents were unemployed in January 2004, a rate of 6.1 percent, compared with the national rate of 5.7 percent.

With a gross state product (the market value of all goods and services produced) of $40.2 billion in 2002, West Virginia ranked 39th among the 50 states and the District of Columbia. Per capita income was $21,274 in 2002. The unionized labor force was estimated at 14.2 percent of the work force in 2004. The state's 10 largest private employers as of 2000 were (in order of number of employees): Wal-Mart, Weirton Steel, Charleston Area Medical Center, Kroger, DuPont, CSX, Hospital Corporation of America, Verizon, Union Carbide, and American Electric Power.

Job training and education are conducted by colleges and universities, vocational-technical centers, employers themselves, and private consultants. The state has 22 public colleges and universities, led by West Virginia University in Morgantown and Marshall University in Huntington. Additionally, more than 200,000 students are enrolled in secondary and adult technical education programs. Secondary and primary education are administered through approximately 775 public elementary and secondary schools and more than 160 private schools.

With only one metropolitan statistical area (MSA) contained entirely within the state (Charleston, in 2000 ranked 167th out of 318 MSAs and primary metropolitan statistical areas in the nation), West Virginia is predominantly rural. However, it is not a major farming state. Agriculture is largely confined to river bottomlands, a few small plateaus, and fertile valleys in the Eastern Panhandle. The principal crops are hay, apples, peaches, and corn. Also produced are broiler chickens, cattle, and dairy products.

Some of the state's border counties lie within interstate metropolitan statistical areas and the Washington primary metropolitan statistical area. These include the Huntington-Ashland, Kentucky MSA; the Parkersburg-Marietta, Ohio MSA; the Wheeling MSA; the Weirton-Steubenville, Ohio MSA; and the Cumberland, Maryland MSA.

After more than a century of intensive exploitation, West Virginia still has abundant natural resources. They include an estimated 55 billion tons of recoverable coal reserves, 2.6 trillion cubic feet of natural gas, 11.7 million acres of timberland, and 27 million barrels of crude oil reserves.

Major glass, chemical, and advanced-technology industries are concentrated in the Ohio and Kanawha river valleys, with centers at Charleston, Huntington, and Parkersburg. Steel mills and manufacturing facilities extend from Pennsylvania into the northern part of the state, including Wheeling and the surrounding Northern Panhandle. Forests cover more than two-thirds of the land, much of it hardwoods suitable for the lumber industry.

West Virginia is located within 500 miles of 60 percent of the U.S. population and 33 percent of the Canadian population, giving the state's businesses relatively close access to markets via truck, rail, air, and river barge. More than 34,000 miles of public roadway include six interstate routes. Nine of the state's 32 public airports have regularly scheduled commercial airline service. Two main line freight carriers (CSX and Norfolk Southern) as well as Amtrak operate on more than 2,600 miles of railroad track. With 419 miles of navigable waterway, the state is developing its river terminals and public ports to accommodate the needs of shippers. West Virginia's navigable rivers feed into the Ohio River, providing access to the Midwest and the Gulf of Mexico.

West Virginia has made significant progress in developing its telecommunications infrastructure. There are more than 100,000 miles of fiber optic cable, and public and private sector strategies for future economic growth envision a continued emphasis on digital communications, including the Internet. The dominant telecommunications company is Verizon, which provides telephone and related services to more than 80 percent of the state's population.

The health care industry includes nearly 3,000 businesses and accounts for more than 13 percent of total personal income in West Virginia. It directly employs approximately 76,000 people and creates about $2 billion in revenues for other businesses.

Tourism is a growing industry, featuring ski resorts, state parks, whitewater rafting, and other attractions. The state's picturesque scenery, low crime rate, and other lifestyle factors are economic assets for tourism and for the retirement-home industry.

As an incentive for economic development, the state offers tax credits for business investment and job expansion, corporate headquarters relocation, small businesses, and capital companies, among other favorable tax provisions. The two primary business taxes are the corporate net income tax and the business franchise tax. Generators of electricity are charged an annual business and occupation tax; natural resource extractors pay severance taxes; and the state has a telecommunications tax. Employers also contribute to the state's unemployment compensation and workers' compensation funds. Direct consumer taxes include a personal income tax and a state sales tax.

West Virginia's modern economy has its roots in the rapid development of railroads, mining, and industry following the Civil War. The economic expansion attracted African-Americans from the South as well as immigrant workers from southern and eastern Europe, who joined the descendants of Germans, English, and Scotch-Irish who previously had settled in what is now the state. By the turn of the century, West Virginia had emerged as a significant contributor to the nation's industrialization and expansion, although it remained somewhat disadvantaged compared to neighboring states due to its rugged terrain.

Historically, coal has had a mixed impact on the West Virginia economy. West Virginians have gained jobs and income from providing a key fuel to domestic and overseas customers, and the success of the coal industry has produced secondary benefits among other segments of the economy. At the same time, dependence on coal has produced recurring boom-bust business cycles in various regions of the state. The coalfields are among the least diversified parts of West Virginia.

During the first half of the 20th century, the coalfields were unionized, and wages and living standards improved. However, during the 1950s and 1960s, increasing mine mechanization and weakened labor demand triggered an out-migration from the coalfields and an overall decline in state population. During the 1960 presidential election and afterward, the state received adverse national attention as a symbol of Appalachian poverty. (West Virginia's official poverty rate in 2000 was 17.9 percent, compared with the national average of 12.4 percent.)

The 1970s saw a resurgence of coal as an energy resource. During this period, the chemical, steel, and glass industries were modernized, and newer advanced-technology industries began to appear. Migration within the state from agricultural and mining regions to more urbanized areas reflected a desire on the part of many West Virginians to seek better educational and employment opportunities.

During the 1980s, as coal demand weakened again, new local regions of poverty appeared in the coalfields, and employment declined in the chemical and manufacturing industries. In response, the public and private sectors put renewed emphasis on cooperating to diversify the economic base, to improve education and job training, and to upgrade the state's infrastructure.

West Virginia's economy is expected to follow national trends projected through 2006. According to the state Bureau of Employment, these trends will include slow labor force growth; increased diversity and aging of the labor force; concentrated growth in the service industries; declines in manufacturing and mining; and overall job growth restricted by high job replacement needs. The fastest growing occupations are expected to be in health care and computer technology. Of 25 occupations with the largest and fastest employment growth, 18 will require at least a bachelor's degree.

The state's leadership in recent years has emphasized economic diversification, as well as improvements in education and infrastructure as critical to West Virginia's future. An emphasis on economic diversification and education and infrastructure improvements is intended to overcome factors that historically have hampered West Virginia's economy, including inadequate infrastructure, low educational achievement, outdated job skills, rugged topography, low population density, and lack of airport and port facilities.

The Bureau of Business and Economic Research at WVU noted in December of 2003 that, while a national and state economic recovery were under way, West Virginia probably would have sluggish growth averaging 0.8 percent a year through 2008. Part of the reason for the state's weak labor market performance was the loss of 7,900 manufacturing jobs from March of 2001 to June 2003. In addition, the steel industry was under increased domestic and international competitive pressure, and there were job declines in construction, trade, transportation, utilities, and information. Continued employment gains in financial services, business and professional services, health care, education, and leisure and hospitality were not enough to offset these losses.

Larry Sonis
Arlington, Texas

EcoTheater

See Maryat Lee.

Edgewood Country Club

Located in Charleston, Edgewood Country Club, chartered on April 4, 1898, as Glenwood Athletic Club, is the oldest private country club in West Virginia. The first clubhouse and golf course were situated on land extending from the Kanawha River north to Central Avenue and east to Delaware Avenue on the city's west side. When this acreage was subdivided in 1906, the club moved to its present location in the Edgewood section of Charleston. On June 21,1906, a new charter was issued to Edgewood Country Club. The membership consisted of Charleston's prominent families.

In 1907, under the leadership of its first president, Angus W. MacDonald, the membership constructed a clubhouse and tennis courts on three acres of land. With the purchase of an additional 100 acres, a golf course was added. For dances a special streetcar proceeded about the city to pick up members and transport them to the club. By 1934, a paved road, private cars, and bus service replaced the streetcar.

On Christmas night, 1935, a fire of unknown origin destroyed the clubhouse and its facilities except the squash courts. In 1936, the present clubhouse was built on the same acreage with other recreational areas erected in the following years. After selling its neighboring nine-hole golf course to the city of Charleston, the club in 1969 developed 600 acres for a new 18-hole championship golf course on Derrick Creek near Pocatalico, and in 1977 built a small clubhouse there. With gala dances and sport tournaments, Edgewood celebrated its centenary in 1998.

Elizabeth Lawton Beury
Charleston

Education

The first schools in Western Virginia emerged in the Eastern Panhandle, Greenbrier Valley, and the South Branch region. A 1748 survey team, with young George Washington as a member, mentioned "the School House" in the Moorefield area, suggesting the site of one of our state's earliest schools. Records of 1753 reveal schoolmasters employed in Romney and in a Greenbrier settlement. Shepherdstown had both German and English schools in 1762. Most early schools were staffed by itinerant schoolmasters who varied in their effectiveness and training. Known as "private subscription schools" since parents paid tuition, these schools—located in private homes, barns, and other available spaces—still left large expanses of present West Virginia without schools of any kind.

With the demise of the established church after the Revolution, the state of Virginia assumed responsibility for educating poor farmers' children. An alderman system, authorized in 1796, provided for the dividing of counties into districts, with schools to be established in each district.

In the northwestern region, children of the wealthiest families attended secondary private academies. Many of these academies offered upper-level courses in classical languages, theology, philosophy, science, grammar, and declamation, preparing graduates for college. In 1778, Brooke Academy opened, making it the earliest institution of its kind in trans-Allegheny Virginia. Randolph Academy in Clarksburg, the earliest regularly incorporated secondary school, counted among its first trustees Edmund Randolph, George Mason, and Patrick Henry. Other early academies included the Potomac Academy in Romney, Northwestern Academy at Clarksburg, and Lewisburg Academy. Marshall Academy, later Marshall College and now Marshall University, was established in present Huntington in 1837. Linsly Institute in Wheeling, which continues as a private school today, was founded in 1814 under a bequest from Noah Linsly.

Virginia established a "Literary Fund" for the support of education in 1810, but funds were not reliably available to meet educational needs. In 1818, money was earmarked to pay tuition for poor white children to attend schools. Since parents were reluctant to be labeled as paupers, these funds were often left unused.

Governor Thomas Jefferson had proposed to the state legislature in 1779 a statewide system of free public schools, but eastern and western sections disagreed on the plan's implementation. Most of the eastern upper class believed it necessary to train an intellectual elite for leadership and therefore favored higher education, while western leaders, placing a premium on practical skills, supported a program of free elementary education. The east prevailed. Virginia established a fine university in 1819 but provided little for schools at the primary and secondary level.

One-room school, Marion County, about 1900.

The 1840 Census revealed that illiteracy among Virginians was increasing regardless of place of residence. Aroused by Governor Campbell, conferences met statewide to examine educational issues. The first of these, held at Clarksburg in September 1841, was a pivotal event. Henry Ruffner proposed the establishment of free schools "good enough for the rich . . . [and] fit for the poor." Contentiousness between eastern and western counties grew, with westerners critical of the University of Virginia, which they believed to be populated by sons of wealthy landowners at the expense of other citizens. Few Western Virginia residents attended college at all, and those who did typically enrolled in institutions in Pennsylvania, Ohio, and Kentucky. The education of western leaders outside Virginia weakened allegiances and contributed to the eventual division of the state.

Legislation in 1846 authorized school commissioners to use local taxes to supplement state aid for the poor. Under this system schools arose in Kanawha, Ohio, and Jefferson counties, the only counties in present West Virginia providing free public schooling before the Civil War. Marshall and Mason counties, while approving the plan, did not have functioning schools until after the war. Funds continued to support the poor attending "old field" schools where the academic emphasis was basic—reading, writing, and arithmetic. By 1850, Western Virginia had 1,300 primary schools.

By 1860, Western Virginia had only one institution of higher learning, Bethany College, founded by Alexander Campbell and chartered in 1840. Baptist-affiliated Rector College had opened in 1839 but was destroyed by fire in 1855. Weston College, chartered in 1858, was sold at public auction in 1859. Allegheny College at Blue Sulphur Springs opened in 1860 but suspended operation later that year, and its buildings were burned by Union troops in 1864. Marshall College was established from Marshall Academy in 1858 but achieved true collegiate status only after its reorganization in 1867.

In 1863, the first constitution of West Virginia established a public free school system. Counties were to be subdivided into townships and townships into subdistricts where school affairs were to be handled in mass meetings. Locally controlled one-room schoolhouses soon dotted the state.

Rev. William Ryland White, a Methodist minister and principal of Fairmont Male and Female Seminary, became the first state superintendent of schools (1864–65). The legislature authorized a state levy for schools and required townships having more than 30 eligible Negro children to educate them in buildings separate from white children. A private

school for black children, opened in Parkersburg in 1862, was converted to a public school in 1866, and a year later one opened in Clarksburg. The U.S. Freedmen's Bureau established over a dozen private schools, most of which later became public schools. Storer College was founded in Harpers Ferry in 1867 by Freewill Baptists from the North. Its purpose was to educate former slaves.

The average school term, 2.7 months in 1865–66, increased to 4.1 months in 1869–70. In 1870, 2,405 teachers (including 641 women) staffed 2,257 schools. Two hundred sixty of the 495 new school buildings constructed in 1869–70 were log structures.

The constitution of 1872 expanded support of public education while continuing the segregation of white and black students. The state superintendent was named a member of the executive branch of government, making the office political. Even during the earliest years of statehood, inequalities in taxable wealth caused great variations in educational opportunities among the counties.

By 1910, West Virginia schools had fallen behind national averages. That year, the average school term in West Virginia was 125 days, compared to 150.3 days nationally, and the average teacher's monthly salary in the state was $36.70, versus $47.08 in the United States.

Progress was evident in some areas, however. Alexander L. Wade, superintendent of Monongalia County, devised a graduating system with set criteria of grades, promotions, and graduation. The system was used as a model nationally and made compulsory statewide in West Virginia in 1891. Teachers' associations, institutes, and journals became important in training teachers.

A normal school, whose purpose was to train school teachers, was established in 1867 at Marshall College, renamed the State Normal School, and in 1869 the Fairmont State Regency Normal was renamed the Fairmont Branch Normal (now Fairmont State University). Normal schools soon opened in West Liberty, Athens, Glenville, and Shepherdstown. Provisions were made for the training of African-American teachers with the opening of West Virginia Colored Institute (now West Virginia State University) in 1892, and Bluefield Colored Institute (now Bluefield State College) in 1895.

Changes were also made in teacher preparation and certification. The 1893 legislature provided for two levels of teacher certificates. The legislature enacted a uniform teachers' examination law in 1903, ending corruption in the granting of certificates by local boards.

School finance and geographic inequity continued to be a problem. When the state property levy was eliminated in 1907, the minimum district levy rates

were reduced with a local option to increase their levy. West Virginia adopted a minimum salary law for teachers in 1882, believed to be the first in the country. Unequal school terms and pay scales existed across the state, however, with discrepancies even within counties.

High schools gained importance during this time. With only 12 fully accredited high schools in 1910, State Superintendent Morris P. Shawkey created a high school division in the state Department of Education, highlighting the need for improved secondary education and increasing curriculum requirements. By 1925, the number of high schools burgeoned to 233, and the old academies had all but ceased to function. The number of junior high schools also increased dramatically.

Not surprisingly, public education suffered during the Depression. Schools closed, school terms were cut, and teachers sometimes went unpaid. A 1932 constitutional amendment cut tax rates on real property, reducing local school funding. Legislation approved in 1933 created the county unit plan, replacing 398 local school districts with 55 county systems, each administered by a five-member board. State aid increased substantially. By 1939, all counties had a nine-month term.

The 1940s and 1950s brought free textbooks for elementary students and the non-partisan election of school boards. The legislature created a nine-member non-partisan state Board of Education in 1947, vesting it with control over public schools and state colleges, with the exception of West Virginia University and its branch, Potomac State School (now Potomac State College). The state superintendent of schools became a state Board of Education appointee in 1958, retaining membership on the budget-making state entity, the Board of Public Works.

The U.S. Supreme Court's 1954 desegregation decision in Brown v. Board of Education brought changes to West Virginia as elsewhere. Governor Marland ordered full compliance, and the integration of West Virginia schools soon began. Twelve counties integrated their schools during the 1954–55 school year, 13 partially integrated, 18 waited for more instructions, 11 had no black students, and one rescinded an integration order when residents protested it.

As the state's population dropped after 1950, so did school enrollment. Between 1950 and 1970, there was a 22 percent decline in elementary school enrollment. Public kindergartens, mandated in 1973, helped balance the overall loss, as did lower drop-out rates in high schools.

Federal programs and shifting educational philosophies dramatically affected schools in the 1960s and 1970s. Important federal programs included Head Start, for preschool children from low-income families; Upward Bound, a college-type summer experience for economically disadvantaged youth; remedial reading and math programs; Title IX, banning sexual discrimination in schools; and the placement of teacher aides in classrooms. Ungraded primary school classrooms, open classrooms, and more freedom and responsibility for high school students all contributed to the changing character of schools.

In 1969 the legislature created two governing bodies for education. The Board of Education continued as the governing body for elementary and secondary schools, and the Board of Regents was established to govern the state's colleges and universities. The state superintendent was an ex officio member of the Board of Regents, and the Board of Regents chancellor was an ex officio member of the state Board of Education.

As schools changed, public support varied. The 1974 Kanawha County textbook controversy, at times violent, called attention to citizens' clashing viewpoints. Reform efforts in West Virginia, spurred by a back to the basics movement and the publication of "A Nation at Risk," a federal report criticizing the nation's schools, triggered increased graduation standards, testing programs for teachers, and more comprehensive student testing. Church-related and nondenominational private schools, some founded before the state itself, continued to grow in size and numbers. School consolidation, with roots in the 1930s, continued into the 21st century. The 4,551 one-room schools in 1930–31 decreased to one, located in Auburn, Ritchie County, by 1978–79. The School Building Authority, created in 1989 by Governor Caperton, provided a strong impetus to consolidation with policies favoring the creation of large schools. In 2004 Governor Wise indicated that the state would reconsider consolidation.

The West Virginia Education Association, founded in 1865 at the behest of the state superintendent, evolved into a forceful union, winning large gains in the strike of 1990. Politicians opposed to WVEA proposals were targeted for defeat, often successfully. The West Virginia Federation of Teachers, a rival group, gained a solid foothold.

Judge Arthur M. Recht handed down a major decision in 1982 attempting to narrow the financial gap among school districts. The results were mixed and after more than 20 years, the court ended its oversight of the public school system. Statistics for the 2003–04 school year reveal that 280,561 preschool through grade 12 students attend West Virginia's approximately 775 public schools and are taught by slightly over 20,000 teachers. Nearly 15,000 additional children attend 162 private schools served by 1,350 teachers.

See also County Unit Plan, Department of Education, Kanawha County Textbook Controversy, Recht Decision

Debra K. Sullivan
Charleston Catholic High School
Charles H. Ambler, *A History of Education in West Virginia: From Early Colonial Times to 1949*; Ambler and Festus P. Summers, *West Virginia: The Mountain State*, 1958; Otis K. Rice and Stephen W. Brown, *West Virginia: A History*, 1993.

Education, Board of

The West Virginia Board of Education consists of 11 members, including the state superintendent of schools and the chancellor of higher education. Both the latter are ex officio members, not entitled to vote. The other nine members, who must be citizens of the state, are appointed by the governor with the advice and consent of the state Senate, for overlapping terms of nine years. No more than five of the appointed members may belong to the same political party, and none may hold any other public office or public employment.

The Board of Education sets policy for elementary and secondary schools, selects the state superintendent of schools, and makes rules for carrying into effect laws and policies relating to education. The state superintendent of schools manages the West Virginia Department of Education in compliance with the policies of the Board of Education. Additionally, the board oversees the West Virginia Schools for the Deaf and Blind, located at Romney. Prior to 1969, the Board of Education also governed West Virginia's public colleges and universities except West Virginia University, which had its own board of governors.

For more than 30 years, the West Virginia superintendent of schools operated independently and without professional assistance. In 1905, the legislature created a four-member Board of Examiners, appointed by the superintendent, to hold examinations and issue teacher certificates. In 1908, the legislature replaced the Board of Examiners with a state Board of Education.

The first Board of Education was appointed by the state superintendent and was composed of the superintendent and five persons engaged in educational work. This board not only examined teachers but also prescribed courses of study. In 1919, the legislature abolished that board and created a new seven-member Board of Education. A later amendment to the constitution changed the membership of the board to nine members, appointed by the governor.

Significantly, a 1958 amendment to the constitution gave the state board the responsibility for general supervision of free schools, transferring that responsibility from the state superintendent. Also, the state superintendent was changed

from an elective position to an appointment by the board, substantially reducing the power and independence of the office.

In 1989, Governor Caperton proposed a constitutional amendment that would have removed the state Board of Education from the state constitution, placing public education under the new Department of Education and the Arts. This would have given the governor and legislators more control over the Board of Education, a virtually autonomous branch of government. The amendment was defeated in a special election in September 1989.

The first woman to serve on the state Board of Education was Lenna Lowe Yost of Morgantown, appointed by Governor Morgan in 1921. Except for 1957 through 1960, at least one woman has been on the board since Yost was selected. The Board of Education meets monthly.

See also Department of Education

Judie Smith
West Virginia Humanities Council

Education, Department of

The Department of Education, part of the executive branch of West Virginia state government, is responsible for carrying out the policies and programs of the state Board of Education. The department is overseen by the superintendent of schools, who is accountable to the board. Over the years the superintendent's staff and resources have increased tremendously, while his political independence has been curtailed. The department has been transformed into a modern professional bureaucracy, working to provide West Virginia children a good public education in the primary and secondary schools of the state.

The present department evolved slowly and in many steps. The first state superintendent of free schools, William Ryland White, was named in 1864. In 1908, the legislature created the state Board of Education, initially appointed by the state superintendent. It was the board's responsibility to supervise the free schools of the state and (after 1958) to select the state superintendent. Before 1958 the superintendent was elected.

Until 1910 the state superintendent, then Morris P. Shawkey, had only a small staff. In that year, his department increased to five divisions: High Schools, Rural Schools, Examinations, Publications, and Institutes. With the increase in secondary schools, a legislative act in 1919 provided that the state superintendent of schools maintain a Department of Public Schools and employ an assistant and other staff. The act of 1919 also abolished the Board of Regents, the Board of Education, and the School Book Commission, replacing them with a seven-member Board of Education serving both public schools and higher education. The state superintendent served as an ex-officio member of the Board of Education, with the remaining members appointed by the governor.

In 1946 a proposed amendment to the state constitution would have made the Board of Education a constitutional body. The amendment was supported by the West Virginia State Education Association but powerfully opposed by State Superintendent W. W. Trent, whose job would have changed from an elected to an appointive position. The amendment failed. In 1958, after Trent had left office, a successful amendment did change the structure of the now nine-member board, made it a constitutional body, and made the superintendent's job appointive. The appointment, rather than election, of the superintendent was meant to ensure that future superintendents would be professionally qualified and insulated from political pressures. It also deprived the superintendent of a political base, as Trent had foreseen.

Currently, the Department of Education consists of the office of the state superintendent, with a deputy superintendent and three divisions supervised by assistant superintendents: Administrative Services; Instructional and Student Services; and Technical and Adult Education Services. Changes in programs and staffing through the years have resulted from federal and state legislation which have mandated various services and programs. Major changes came at the end of the 20th century, when the department undertook the direct management of troubled county school systems. Schools in Logan, Mingo, Lincoln, and McDowell counties were managed by the department at various times. The Logan and Mingo boards of education regained control over their schools after a restructuring program.

Each of the three divisions consists of professional educators who coordinate, provide, and perform services for county boards of education, county schools, classroom teachers, correctional institutions, and the multicounty Regional Education Service Agencies. The department also has a legal staff that serves the state board and the state superintendent of schools. The department also employs 34 teachers and administrators at the correctional institutions. Since 1969, the Department of Education has had no responsibility for the state's colleges and universities.

James F. Snyder
Charleston

Edwards Moonlight

In 1922, Capt. Annis Boggs commissioned Ward Engineering of Charleston to build a floating dance hall, a double-deck excursion barge with a dance floor. In honor of Boggs's son, Edward, it was christened the *Edwards Moonlight*. The *Moonlight,* originally measuring 101 by 26 feet, was towed by steamboats, usually the *Shamrock No. 2.* It was docked near the north end of Charleston's South Side Bridge, in the city's downtown. The *Moonlight* traveled from there on dance cruises up and down the Kanawha River.

When Vice President Charles Curtis came on September 27, 1932, to dedicate the new Marmet Locks, he rode the *Edwards Moonlight* from Marmet back to Charleston. The *Moonlight,* towed on this occasion by the steamboat *F. M. Staunton,* carried more than 200 people to the dedication.

Armco Steel bought the *Moonlight* in the mid-1930s and used it as an office and landing barge in Huntington. It was re-hulled in 1948, increasing the dimensions to 112 by 30 feet. From 1955 to 1983, Amherst Industries leased the *Moonlight* as a dispatch barge located in Huntington, then sold it to Arch Minerals. This company owned the barge from 1983 to 1988. In 1988, Ken Joseph of Ashland, Kentucky, bought it with the hopes to renovate it as a restaurant. The *Edwards Moonlight* was brought home to the Kanawha River in 1999 and operated until 2003 as the General Seafood restaurant in South Charleston.

Jean Simpson
Charleston

William Henry Edwards

Businessman and entomologist William Henry Edwards was born in Greene County, New York, March 15, 1822. He graduated from Williams College in 1842 and was admitted to the New York bar in 1847.

Edwards came to the Kanawha Valley to inspect lands his family had purchased sight-unseen from promoters. A very early pioneer in the southern West Virginia coalfields, he opened the first coal mines on Paint Creek in 1852, erected the first cannel coal oil works in 1856, and opened mines at Coalburg in 1863. After the Civil War, Edwards had a steam towboat built in Wheeling at a cost of $30,000. The towboat, used to transport coal from Cannelton to Cincinnati, was capable of handling 12 barges, each one carrying 10,000 bushels of coal.

In addition to developing large business interests and building a sizable fortune, Edwards immersed himself in the study of natural history. Building on his experiences during a trip on the Amazon River as a young man in 1846 and the travel book he wrote about this adventure (*A Voyage on the River Amazon,* 1847) Edwards spent increasing amounts of time studying butterflies. Through collecting, personal experience, and correspondence, he obtained eggs and caterpillars of at least 165 species. As the specimens

William Henry Edwards (1822–1909).

developed, he wrote detailed descriptions and sketched the butterflies in their many stages. The culmination of this effort is found in his three-volume work, *The Butterflies of North America,* published in 1879, 1884, and 1897, which remains a standard. In addition, Edwards wrote papers on entomology for scientific journals, including 160 separate articles on Lepidoptera for the *Canadian Entomologist.*

Edwards gave up butterflies at the age of 75 and turned to the study of Shakespeare. He produced a book on the question of the authorship of Shakespeare's plays in 1900, and in 1903 produced a book of Edwards family genealogy. William Henry Edwards died April 4, 1909, at his home in Coalburg, Kanawha County.

Debra K. Sullivan
Charleston Catholic High School

Eleanor

Now a Putnam County residential community, Eleanor began as a government attempt to help victims of the Great Depression. During the 1930s, the U.S. Resettlement Administration offered subsistence homesteads in several communities nationally, including three in West Virginia, to provide houses and land at easy credit. The first such project was Arthurdale in Preston County, which began in 1933. Eleanor soon followed.

The site was a tract of flat land on the north side of the Kanawha River, often referred to as Red House. Potential homesteaders were evaluated on need and ability to work, although many were eliminated because of racial and ethnic discrimination. The men lived in barracks while they worked, building roads and houses and digging water and sewer lines. The houses were built to last, from locally made cinder blocks and chestnut wood.

Serious work began in 1934. The design included a community farm and barn, public gas and water works, workshops, a school, greenhouse, canning plant, market, gas station, restaurant, garage, and pool room. The community had its own newspaper, the *Melting Pot*, and home economists, a doctor, and public nurses. By 1935, families began moving into their new homes.

The town took its name from Eleanor Roosevelt, who visited several times. The experiment proved to be a success. As the economy improved, Eleanor made the transition from government to private ownership and was subsequently incorporated. Nearly all the original houses are still standing.

See also Arthurdale, Tygart Valley Homesteads

Rick Wilson
American Friends Service Committee

Election Day

West Virginians take a lively interest in politics. In times past, politicking continued through election day, even at the polls, a colorful scene as the party faithful and the candidates themselves handed out literature and buttonholed incoming voters. Election day had many of the aspects of a festive holiday, especially in rural areas where the polls provided a gathering place. The reforms of recent years have made elections quieter affairs, but the day remains special for many West Virginians.

West Virginia's first election was conducted in 1863, following creation of the state. Elections were conducted annually until a new constitution adopted in 1872 changed elections to the current two-year cycle. Primary elections are now conducted in May of even-numbered years, with the general election following on the first Tuesday after the first Monday in November of the same year. The purpose of the primary election is for each party to select its candidates for the November general election. Names may also be added to the ballot by petition rather than through a party primary, although this process is difficult. Given the strength of the Democratic Party in most of the 20th century, victory in the party primary was often tantamount to election.

The poll workers who coordinate the election on the precinct level are selected by the county commissions from names provided by the Democratic and Republican county executive committees. Generally, polling places have five workers for each precinct. In order to serve as a poll worker, one must meet the qualifications to vote. The workers are required to attend training prior to election day and are paid for their work.

Election day starts early, with the polls opening at 6:30 a.m. Before opening, the poll workers must prepare the polling place and get ready for their first voter. Throughout the day they check to determine if individuals are registered to vote and deal with all the details of the election. The secretary of state monitors elections from Charleston from before the polls open on election day until all the issues are resolved after midnight. Ballots are counted at the polling place in the case of paper ballots, and taken to the county clerks's office for counting when punch card ballots are used. Later, the county commission formally certifies the local election results to the secretary of state.

A final ritual begins when polls close and the unofficial election returns start to come in, as West Virginians gather at county courthouses and candidate headquarters to await the people's decision.

West Virginia has about 2,000 polling places in its 55 counties. With a minimum of five workers per precinct, there is an election day workforce of about 13,000 people. Election day is a big administrative task. Elections are further complicated because different counties use different voting methods. Efforts are under way that will result in one system of tabulating votes for all of West Virginia with the centralizing of voter registration records in the secretary of state's office. Since 1986, electioneering has been prohibited within 300 feet of the polls.

Bill Harrington
Charleston

Elizabeth

Elizabeth is the county seat of Wirt County. William Beauchamp settled there in 1796. Beauchamp farmed 1,400 acres at Tucker's Riffle on the Little Kanawha River. He had been a sailor in the American Revolution and was a lay preacher in the Methodist Church. In 1817, the town, which earlier had been known as Beauchamp's Mills, was renamed for Elizabeth Woodland Beauchamp, the wife of William's son, David. The town was chartered in 1822. Around 1835–40, David and Elizabeth's son, Alfred Beauchamp, built a brick house which came to be known as the "Old Red Brick." The first county and circuit courts met in this house when Wirt County was formed in 1848. Now known as the Beauchamp-Newman House, it is on the National Register of Historic Places.

William Beauchamp and sons Manlove and David developed grain mills and sawmills, and lumbering is still an important part of the local economy. Elizabeth and Wirt County were beneficiaries of an oil boom when the nearby Burning Springs oil field opened in 1860. Burning Springs was the second oil field in the United States. In 1863, the Confederate Army precipitated the end of the Burning Springs oil boom by destroying the town of Burning Springs and its oil wells.

Located on the Little Kanawha at the junction of State Routes 14, 53, and 5, Elizabeth is the commercial center for a rural region dependent on agriculture, oil, and gas for its economy. Wirt County has the smallest population of the 55 West Virginia counties, and Elizabeth's population was 994 in 2000.

See also Wirt County

Gordon L. Swartz III
Cameron

Elk River

The Elk River meanders 177 miles from its headwaters in Pocahontas County westerly to its confluence with the Kanawha River at Charleston. The river flows through some of West Virginia's most rugged and remote terrain, before finally reaching the state's major center of population. The important tributaries include Holly River, Birch River, Buffalo Creek, and Big Sandy Creek. Other tributaries that drain areas of 50 square miles or more are Little Sandy, Blue, and Laurel creeks, and Back Fork. The Elk River watershed of 1,532 square miles accounts for about 6.5 percent of the territory of West Virginia.

The water quality of the Elk River basin is excellent, and the Elk provides drinking water for the city of Charleston and other communities. West Virginia American Water Company has plants on the Elk at Webster Springs, Gassaway, and Charleston, the latter serving customers in Kanawha County and parts of Putnam, Boone, and Lincoln counties. Public service districts in Braxton and Clay counties obtain their water from Elk, as do the towns of Clay and Clendenin.

Upper Elk is a geological marvel: A subterranean network of caves, streams, and waterfalls, including a six-mile stretch in Randolph County where, in dry weather, the river sinks underground. According to legend, underground Elk was formed in 1896 when a hole opened in the stream bed and simply swallowed the river. Spelunkers frequently explore this dark side of Elk, but do so at their own risk because the headwaters are prone to sudden rises from storms that can fill the caverns.

The Elk watershed occupies the central portion of West Virginia. Eighty percent of the land in this basin of the Elk main stream is contained in Braxton, Clay, Kanawha, and Webster counties. Other counties within the basin are Nicholas, Pocahontas, Randolph, and Roane. Elk River begins as a trout stream, but for most of its length is a warm-water fishery, particularly noted for large muskellunge.

From its headwaters near Snowshoe Mountain Resort in west-central Pocahontas County, the Elk flows in a general northwest direction. At the Sutton-

Elk River.

Gassaway area it bends to the southwest and continues this general direction to its confluence with the Kanawha River at Charleston. In 1961, the U.S. Army Corps of Engineers completed a multi-purpose water resource dam on Elk at Sutton, 71 miles below the river's origin, creating Sutton Lake and taming the floods that had beset middle and lower Elk Valley residents for decades.

The elevation of the Elk at its source in Pocahontas County is approximately 4,000 feet. At Charleston the elevation of the river is 565 feet, making a total drop of 3,435 feet. Its average fall over the 177 mile course is 19 feet per mile.

The climate of the Elk River basin is humid continental, with generous, evenly distributed precipitation and a large yearly temperature range. Topographical features considerably modify the climate and result in large variations between the headwaters and the mouth of the Elk River, which are at about the same latitude.

Timbering, oil and gas drilling, and coal mining have been conducted in the basin for many years. The majority of the forest in the Elk River basin is composed of northern hardwoods. Agriculture within the basin is made up of numerous small farms.

The Elk River traverses the central heartland of West Virginia, covering regions little changed by industrialization and urbanization. Traditions survive here, the watershed harboring authentic mountain musicians, dancers, and craftspeople. Elk River was celebrated in a classic 1940 book, *Tale of the Elk,* written by W.E.R. Byrne, a lawyer, sportsman, and raconteur who fished and camped along the river's length in the company of such colorfully named characters as "Bearskin Bill" Hamrick and "Squirrelly Bill" Carpenter. According to historian Roy Bird

Cook in his preface to *Tale of the Elk,* the rivers's name derives from the Shawnee designation as "river of plenty fat elk."

See also W.E.R. Byrne, Tale of the Elk

Jerry D. Stover
Clay

W.E.R. Byrne, *Tale of the Elk,* 1940.

Elkins

Elkins, the county seat of Randolph County, is located on the upper Tygart Valley River, where the river flows to the northwest through a break between Rich and Laurel mountains. Elkins, elevation 1,930 feet, serves as a gateway to the Allegheny Mountains that lie to the east. The 2000 census listed the population as 7,032.

Elkins was founded in 1889, following the extension of the West Virginia Central & Pittsburg [*sic*] Railroad into Randolph County. Businessman Henry Gassaway Davis and his son-in-law, Stephen B. Elkins, purchased property near the village of Leadsville for the location of their headquarters and new railroad shops. Elkins served as a railroad center for more than 75 years with the movement of coal and lumber by the West Virginia Central & Pittsburg, the Coal & Coke, the Western Maryland, the B&O, and later the Chessie System.

Elkins is a mecca for sportsmen and outdoor enthusiasts who visit the streams and forests in the area. Offices of the Monongahela National Forest, the U.S. Fish and Wildlife Service, and the West Virginia Division of Natural Resources are located at Elkins.

Davis & Elkins College, founded in Elkins in 1904, accommodates students from many states and foreign countries in a strong liberal arts program. The Augusta Heritage Center, with offices at the college, offers popular annual workshops in folk music and the traditional arts. The Mountain State Forest Festival has been

held in Elkins since its inception in 1930. Elkins, a major lumber center, has various lumber mills, brokers, lumber equipment operations, and wood processing plants.

Elkins is a historic crossroads. U.S. 33, which connects to Interstate 79 at Weston, intersects U.S. 219-250 in Elkins. U.S. 219 connects Elkins to Parsons in the north and Marlinton in the south. From Elkins, via Huttonsville, U.S. 250 crosses the mountain ranges to the southeast through Pocahontas County and Monterey, Virginia. U.S. 33, now a modern four-lane highway west of Elkins, crosses five mountains on its way eastward from Elkins by way of Harman into Pendleton County.

See also Davis & Elkins College, Henry Gassaway Davis, Stephen B. Elkins, Randolph County

Donald L. Rice
Elkins

Hallie Davis Elkins

Hallie Davis Elkins was the daughter, wife, and mother of U.S. senators from West Virginia. She was born Mary Louise Davis on December 9, 1854, the eldest child of Henry Gassaway Davis. Her early years were spent in Frederick, Maryland, and Piedmont, (West) Virginia, where her father was station agent and superintendent for the B&O Railroad. She was educated in the Frederick schools and later at Mrs. Casey's School in Baltimore.

In 1871, her father was elected U.S. senator, as a Democrat. In Washington, Hallie at age 20 met the new delegate from the New Mexico Territory, Stephen Benton Elkins, a Republican. On April 14, 1875, they were married in Baltimore. When Elkins's term as delegate ended in 1877, he opened a law office in Washington, then a year later relocated to New York City where he devoted himself to the development of business interests in partnership with his father-in-law.

The Davis and Elkins partnership prospered, expanding into a business empire based on coal, timber, rail, and related enterprises. Since much of it was located in West Virginia, the Elkinses began construction in 1890 of a new home in the new town of Elkins, a sprawling mansion called Halliehurst. In 1895, Elkins was elected as a Republican to the first of three terms as U.S. senator from West Virginia.

Senator and Mrs. Elkins were the parents of four sons and one daughter. Following Elkins's death in 1911, their eldest son, Davis, was appointed to fulfill his father's unexpired term in the Senate. In 1918, Davis Elkins was elected to the U.S. Senate in his own right, also as a Republican.

In 1926, Hallie Davis Elkins made a gift of Halliehurst, including the house, a 60-acre tract of land, and $25,000 for an endowment to Davis & Elkins College. She died on March 1, 1933.

See also Davis & Elkins College, Henry Gassaway Davis, Stephen B. Elkins, Halliehurst

Margo Stafford
Clarksburg

Oscar Doane Lambert, *Stephen Benton Elkins,* 1955; Thomas Richard Ross, *Henry Gassaway Davis: An Old-Fashioned Biography,* 1994.

Elkins *Inter-Mountain*

The Elkins *Inter-Mountain* was established as a Republican newspaper in 1892. The weekly newspaper's first editor was N. G. Keim, who came to Elkins as a private tutor to Sen. Stephen B. Elkins's family. Keim remained as editor for two years and then was succeeded by a series of other editors until 1898, when Herman Johnson took over the *Inter-Mountain.* Johnson bought the newspaper from the Inter-Mountain Publishing Company.

The office of the newspaper suffered a fire in March 1897, but the *Inter-Mountain* continued to publish. It became a daily newspaper in October 1907. Eldora Marie Bolyard Nuzum, who was the first female editor of a daily newspaper in West Virginia as editor of the *Grafton Sentinel* during the late 1940s, later served 32 years as editor of the Elkins *Inter-Mountain.*

In August 1974, the *Inter-Mountain* suffered another disastrous fire, destroying the newspaper building and all equipment in the printing plant. Again, the newspaper continued to publish, with staff members taking the contents to Parkersburg to be printed. Nine days after the fire a new press arrived, and the *Inter-Mountain* was once again in publication in Elkins. By December it had moved into a new building.

The *Inter-Mountain,* now owned by Ogden Newspapers of Wheeling, is the only daily newspaper in Randolph and seven surrounding counties. The editor is Linda Howell Skidmore. Published Monday through Saturday afternoons with no Sunday edition, the 2005 circulation of the *Inter-Mountain* was 10,483.

Stephen B. Elkins

Senator Stephen Benton Elkins was born September 26, 1841, in Perry County, Ohio, and died at Halliehurst, his home in Elkins, January 4, 1911. His father, originally from Virginia, moved the family from Ohio to Missouri when Stephen was small. Young Elkins attended Masonic School at Lexington, Missouri, and graduated at the head of his class at the University of Missouri in 1860. After graduation he taught school at Harrisonville, Missouri. During this time Elkins taught Cole Younger, later a notorious outlaw, and Younger once saved Elkins from Confederate guerrillas during the Civil War.

Elkins, whose father and brothers were in the Confederate army, served two years in the Union army as a captain. He left the army in 1863. He attended law school at least briefly and was admitted to the Missouri bar in 1864. He moved west the same year, settling in Mesilla, New Mexico. He served as New Mexico's attorney general in 1867 and as its U.S. district attorney, 1867–70. In 1872, he was elected to represent the New Mexico Territory in Congress. Before his election his wife died, leaving him with two small daughters, Elizabeth and Sallie.

In Washington Elkins met Hallie Davis, daughter of Sen. Henry Gassaway Davis of West Virginia. Miss Davis, only 20, and Elkins were married in Baltimore in 1875. Recognizing the potential of the oil, coal, and timber industries, Senator Davis invited Elkins to become a partner in developing lands in West Virginia in 1877. In 1878, Elkins became a citizen of West Virginia. He and Davis joined with Davis's two brothers and R. C. Kerens and formed the West Virginia Central and Pittsburg [*sic*] Railway which opened a vast wilderness to development. Elkins was also associated with his father-in-law in Davis Coal & Coke and other enterprises.

In 1890, the Elkinses chose to build their castle-like home, Halliehurst, in Randolph County near the Tygart Valley River. Nearby was Graceland, home of Senator Davis, and the town of Elkins sprang up in the valley below.

In 1884, Elkins was elected executive chairman of the National Republican Committee, and he became a force in Republican politics nationally and in West Virginia. President Harrison appointed him secretary of war in 1891. The West Virginia legislature elected Elkins to the U.S. Senate in 1895, and he served until his death. Elkins is credited with helping to engineer the long ascendency of the Republican Party in West Virginia, lasting from the 1890s to the Great Depression. For many years he operated a formidable machine within the party.

The town of Elkins and Davis & Elkins College are named for Stephen Benton Elkins.

See also Henry Gassaway Davis, Halliehurst, Republican Party

J. E. Spears
Elkins

Elkinsia Polymorpha

Elkinsia Polymorpha, a plant fossil found in Randolph County, provided important information on the evolution of seed-bearing plants. In plant evolution, the development of seed for reproduction was an essential step that allowed plants to colonize areas and environments that had previously been unsuitable. Lower, simpler forms of plant life today continue to reproduce by means of spores, as did their very early ancestors of the Paleozoic

Era of geologic time. Those simpler forms include algae, fungi, mosses, and ferns.

By the time of the Mississippian and Pennsylvanian periods of geologic time, 345 million to 280 million years ago, terrestrial seed-bearing plants spread as great forests across much of the earth's landscape. Because of that great diversity of seed-bearing plants, scientists suspected that the origin had come earlier, but had no actual confirmation through the fossil record.

A fern-like fossilized plant found at a few locations along U.S. 33 a few miles east of Elkins has provided that "missing link" and is now recognized as the oldest seed-bearing plant in North America. This plant fossil, named *Elkinsia polymorpha,* occurs with several other types of plant fossils in Late Devonian-age stone known as the Hampshire Formation. The rocks in which these fossils are found are sedimentary mudstones and thin, impure coal beds that were deposited in swampy areas on an ancient coastal plain. *Elkinsia* was found by Joseph F. Schwietering of the West Virginia Geological and Economic Survey in the late 1970s.

Ron Mullennex
Bluefield

End of the World

Northeast of Charleston, on Elk River between Clay and Clendenin, is a spot known as the "End of the World." There the river runs along sheer cliffs for about a mile, making such a sharp turn that it appears to come to a dead end against the hillside. It was at this spot in 1904 that Jay Legg is said to have had a troubling vision of himself while floating a log raft down Elk River. Thinking his trouble lay ahead, Legg decided to return early to his home in Harden's Lumber Camp in Clay County, where he was shot to death that night by his wife, Sarah. His troubles are memorialized in a well-known local ballad.

The End of the World was a favorite spot of W.E.R. Byrne, author of the classic book, *Tale of the Elk,* and the river's most famous chronicler. Byrne, who contracted his final illness at his camp there, dedicated these lines to the End of the World:

"When former delights have relinquished their charm and the spirit turns backward its flow; When the order shall come to give over the fight, and the flag of life's battle is furled, Let me sleep—let me dream—by the murmuring stream, In my camp at the End of the World."

See also W.E.R. Byrne, Jay Legg

Christine D. Fenn
Westover

Endangered Species

The federal Endangered Species Act of 1973 protects species in danger of extinction. Two classes are recognized: An

The bald eagle, endangered until 1995.

endangered species is one in danger of extinction throughout all or a significant portion of its range; a threatened species is one at risk of becoming endangered if measures are not taken to improve its status. In West Virginia, 11 animals and five plants are listed as endangered; four animals and two plants are considered threatened.

The West Virginia northern flying squirrel, which occurs in the higher elevations of West Virginia, is endangered. This squirrel, associated with red spruce and northern hardwood forests, is slightly larger than the more common and widespread southern flying squirrel.

Several bats are endangered, including Indiana bats, gray bats, and Virginia big eared bats. Indiana bats hibernate in the caves of West Virginia during the winter, but no summer maternity colonies have been found. Most Virginia big-eared bats, which both hibernate and raise their young in caves, live in West Virginia. Only two gray bats have been observed here, hibernating in a Pendleton County cave.

Six species of freshwater mussels are listed as endangered: pink mucket pearly mussel, tuberculed-blossom pearly mussel, clubshell, northern riffleshell, fanshell, and the James spinymussel. Because these stream-bottom dwellers cannot tolerate poor water quality, threats include siltation, pollution, and increased water acidity. Another threatened aquatic species is the Madison Cave isopod, a small invertebrate that occurs only in the Shenandoah Valley.

The eastern cougar has not been seen in the state since the 19th century.

Once thought to be extinct, running buffalo clover was rediscovered in West Virginia in 1983. This plant has white blooms and spreads by runners. Shale barren rockcress is adapted to hot, dry, south-facing shale slopes; its small white flowers are borne on a tall, branching inflorescence. The northeastern bulrush, a rare wetland plant, is found in a few small ponds in Berkeley and Hardy coun-

ties. Another endangered aquatic plant, harperella, is found along three rivers in the Eastern Panhandle. A member of the carrot family, it has small white flowers.

Because bald eagle populations have increased recently, this eagle's status was upgraded from endangered to threatened in 1995. The first bald eagle nest in West Virginia was discovered in 1981, and by 2004, 14 nests produced 25 eaglets; bad weather reduced nesting success in 2005.

The Cheat Mountain salamander is found in only five mountainous counties of the state. The flat-spired three-toothed land snail, discovered in 1933, is also found only in West Virginia. It lives in a small area within the Cheat River Gorge.

Virginia spiraea, a four-foot high shrub with clusters of white flowers, grows along the banks of high-energy streams, with the world's largest population found along the Gauley River. The small-whorled pogonia, a rare orchid with greenish-yellow flowers, is found in West Virginia at one site in Greenbrier County.

Until August 1999, the peregrine falcon was among West Virginia's endangered species. Increasing populations in the East led to the removal of this bird from the list of endangered species. Peregrine populations, once flourishing across North America, declined rapidly after widespread pesticide use caused females to lay eggs with unusually thin shells. After use of DDT and related pesticides was restricted in the early 1970s, peregrine falcons were reintroduced. Between 1989 and 1990, 53 young falcons were released in West Virginia. Nesting pairs were observed in 1991, 1992, 1999, 2000, and 2002.

Craig W. Stihler
Division of Natural Resources

Thomas Dunn English

Poet Thomas Dunn English, also a physician and lawyer, was born June 29, 1819, in Pennsylvania. He lived in Logan County from 1852 to 1856. He is best known for his 1843 ballad "Ben Bolt." His West Virginia poems include "The Logan Grazier," "Guy-

andotte Musings," "The Boone Wagoner," "Gauley River," and "Rafting on the Guyandotte." Before moving to Lawnsville, now named Logan, the Philadelphia native worked in New York, where he edited a political newspaper, a comic journal, and a magazine of reviews, politics, and literature. Known for his temper, English quarreled with Edgar Allan Poe and faced libel suits from others.

News of the region's large coal reserves and virgin timber may have prompted English and his wife to move to Western Virginia. By 1853, English had bought 27 coal leases and incorporated two coal companies with holdings in Logan and Wayne counties. While he was buying coal leases, English also got involved in local governance. Lawnsville, where English lived, had never been legally incorporated. He and others petitioned the General Assembly of Virginia to incorporate the town as Aracoma, the name of Shawnee Chief Cornstalk's legendary daughter. English served as the town's postmaster, and was elected mayor. He practiced medicine infrequently.

In 1856, when English's coal schemes didn't succeed, he moved from Logan County to Tazewell, Virginia, to pursue a livelihood in journalism. He later settled in Bergen County, New Jersey. In 1862, he was elected to one term in the New Jersey legislature, and later served two terms in Congress. English died in New Jersey, April 1, 1902.

See also Logan

Bob Spence, "The Poet of Lawnsville," *Goldenseal,* July–September 1979.

The Environment

Western Virginia was a pristine region of virgin forests and clear streams during the 1700s. There was great diversity of plant and animal life. The forests included numerous groves of giant hardwoods, pines, and spruce, interspersed with smaller trees in openings where wildfires, windstorms, ice, insects, and disease had thinned the mature trees.

American Indians used the abundant

King Coal (from "The Three Kings")

King Coal dwells ever underground, surrounded by
    his gnomes,
Who carve him chambers in the earth, and scoop out
    rocky domes.
Ever they work by torch-light there—the clear sun
    never shines
To glad the heart of the pygmies toiling, moiling in
    the mines,
But still they burrow like patient moles, they work
    and gayly sing,
Their voices ringing through the vaults in praise of
    their grimy king.

—Thomas Dunn English
American Ballads (1879)

flora and fauna for food, shelter, and clothing. They made salt in the Kanawha Valley for their own use and to trade. There was little or no permanent native population in what is now West Virginia at the time of European settlement. Indians often traveled the region, however, and there is plentiful archeological evidence of earlier habitation. They left their mark on the environment through the use of fire in hunting and for clearing the forest and through the trapping of fur-bearing animals as the trade with Europeans expanded.

The first whites were explorers, hunters, and trappers. They soon depleted the large animals, such as woods bison, elk, and deer, as well as the fur-bearing beaver, river otter, fisher, and wolf. As the Indian threat from neighboring Ohio and Kentucky diminished, settlers cleared the widest and richest valleys and floodplains.

By the time of the Civil War, the railroad had crossed the northern mountains to Parkersburg and Wheeling. Iron furnaces belched smoke as pig iron was smelted, using charcoal made from the abundant hardwoods. The exploitation of high-quality timber, coal, oil, and gas continued through the 20th century. Lumber production peaked in 1907, with nearly 1.5 billion board feet sawed. There was a peak of 146 million tons of coal mined in 1927, another of 174 million tons in 1947, and even higher tonnages late in the century. Oil production peaked in 1901 at 16 million barrels, and natural gas peaked at 309 billion cubic feet in 1917.

By the middle of the 20th century West Virginians struggled with unreclaimed strip mines, acid drainage from deep mines, fire-scarred forests, and leaking oil and gas wells and pipelines. Sound environmental practices were slow in coming. Cutover forests suffered wildfires, which led to erosion and flooding. State and national forests and state parks were created to protect damaged watersheds. Fires in southern West Virginia had eliminated most wildlife and changed the forest to fire-resistant brush, oaks, and hickories. Farming had declined statewide, and abandoned fields gave way to brush and briers, then to young forests of maple and yellow poplar.

Huge dams at Bluestone, Tygart, and Sutton were built to reduce flooding of cities along the Kanawha, Monongahela, and Ohio rivers. These lakes, as well as the locks and dams on the navigable rivers, changed free-flowing rivers to slow-moving pools. This led to several freshwater mussels becoming endangered species and major changes in fish, bird, and aquatic plant populations. Additional large dams built more recently have continued to change the environment and landscape.

Deep mining of coal decreased relative to surface mining. Huge mountaintop removal mines later supplanted smaller strip mines and some deep mines. New environmental issues arose with the reclamation of mine sites with exotic plant species; the filling of valleys with rock and dirt; the weathering of exposed rocks and soils; increased erosion; and subsidence.

The forests faced another round of logging in the late 20th century. New technology permitted low-grade trees to be chipped, shaved, and veneered, before being glued together as beams, four-by-eight construction sheets, and other building materials. These engineered wood products were hailed by the industry as a profitable way to remove low-value wood from the forests while allowing the practice of long-term sustainable forestry. But environmentalists worried about overcutting, clear cutting, increased erosion from more log roads and larger machinery, opening the forest to exotic plants and animals, and the replacement of mixed woodlands with a few fast-growing tree species.

Other changes have occurred as four-lane highways supplanted two-lane secondary roads and earlier railroads. Fragmentation of the landscape by roads, suburban development, and second homes is common in the Eastern Panhandle, Greenbrier Valley, and around most cities. Sprawl put stresses on natural resources and the environment, with greater demands for energy, water, sewage treatment, and transportation. As much as one million acres in West Virginia have been permanently converted to housing, transportation, commerce, and similar uses from the time of early settlement to the present.

Demands by hunters have created high deer and turkey populations that cause vehicle accidents, and damage farm crops, forest trees, horticultural and fruit crops, and gardens.

There is a long history of air pollution from forest fires, burning coal refuse, burning underground coal seams, and burning natural gas and oil. Smoke from wildfires remains a major problem during droughts. Air pollution from coal-fired power plants, chemical and steel manufacturing, and other sources threatens human health. Pollution from vehicles and the burning of petroleum and methane fuels are also environmental issues. Increased demands for energy led to new technology of pressurizing and fracturing old oil and gas wells to recover more of the valuable resources. However, the disposal of salt brine, surface pipelines, and the need to access pipeline rights of way on private property continue to be of concern.

Water quality is of great concern. Erosion from highway construction and mining operations are major pollutant sources. Erosion from timbering, agriculture, natural gas roads, and building construction are additional sources of sediment. Coliform and chemical fertilizers and pesticides degrade water quality. Runoff from poultry litter is a controversial issue in the Potomac watershed. Sulfur, iron, and aluminum compounds frequently pollute waters escaping from old deep mines, surface mines, gob piles, and coal-cleaning facilities.

The landscape is under siege from human litter, aggravated by the proliferation of fast food restaurants and a shift to plastic shopping bags. A recent environmental improvement is the elimination of open trash dumps and the requirement that solid waste be disposed of in landfills or by other appropriate means. Communication towers, giant billboards, and other signs clutter West Virginia roadsides.

Federal and state laws began to address environmental concerns after mid-century. The mine waste dumps known as gob piles were reclaimed, with available coal recovered and the sites restored to a natural state. By the 1970s, laws and policies addressed water and air quality, soil sediment, toxic wastes, endangered species, wetlands, and land use.

Environmental conditions in West Virginia have generally improved over the past 50 years. Federal and state legislation have caused water from sewage plants, manufacturing, chemicals, and coal washing to be returned to streams in a better quality. The switch from cultivated crops to grassland farming has improved water quality from farms. The best of the nonrenewable natural resources are gone, but new technologies permit the profitable recovery and more efficient use of remaining resources. The renewable resources of timber and soil should continue indefinitely with good stewardship, and the windpower of northern ridgetops is only now being developed. The majority of our forests are still productive and of good quality, as are the better farms. Most streams are swimmable, drinkable, and fishable.

William N. Grafton
WVU Extension Service

Episcopal Church

The first Episcopal Church in what is now West Virginia was built about 1740 at Bunker Hill in Berkeley County. It is still in use today as an unorganized mission, where an annual service is conducted each September. Its successor is Zion Church in Charles Town.

Several other congregations began in the 1700s, and still others in the 1800s. In the Charleston area, St. John's Episcopal Church can trace its roots back to 1837, and parishioners there moved out to create All Saints Church in South Charleston and the Church of the Good Shepherd in Kanawha City. Trinity Church in Huntington held its first services at the Cabell County Courthouse in Barboursville in 1869 but soon moved to Huntington. In the 20th century, its membership fanned out to create three other parishes in the region.

Like the state itself, the Episcopal Church split from Virginia. At the national convention in Boston on October 9, 1877, a resolution passed creating the new Diocese of West Virginia. The initial convention of the new diocese met at St. John's in Charleston, with 14 clergy and 16 lay delegates. Their first choice as bishop, the Reverend J. H. Eccleston of New Jersey, turned down the appointment. At a subsequent meeting, delegates took 11 ballots before they chose George William Peterkin, a native of Maryland. On May 30, 1878, he was consecrated a bishop at St. Matthew's Church, Wheeling, the largest in the new diocese with 220 communicants. Bishop Peterkin established the diocesan office in Parkersburg and built the Church of the Good Shepherd there in 1891.

The second bishop was the Reverend William Loyall Gravatt, who had been born in Virginia and was rector at Zion Church, Charles Town, when he was elected bishop coadjutor on July 26, 1899. When Bishop Peterkin died in 1916, Gravatt became bishop and moved the diocesan headquarters to Charleston. The third bishop, the Right Reverend Robert Edward Lee Strider, was a native West Virginian, born April 9, 1887, in Leetown, Jefferson County. He was rector at St. Matthew's, Wheeling, when he was consecrated bishop coadjutor there in 1923. He became bishop in 1939 and moved the diocesan office to Wheeling.

In 1944, a committee began searching for a church camp site to honor the first bishop and his wife. Diocesan trustees eventually purchased land from the Hampshire Club on the South Branch of the Potomac River near Romney. Today the Peterkin Camp and Conference Center honors all three of the first bishops with the main lodge named Gravatt Hall and the chapel named for Bishop Strider.

Sandscrest Farms near Oglebay Park at Wheeling came to the diocese in the early 1950s, through the will of Mr. and Mrs. Harry S. Sands, members of St. Luke's on the Island, Wheeling. Planned as a retirement home for Episcopalians, it is used instead as a retreat for small conferences, and the Diocesan Council conducts three of its four quarterly meetings there each year. Reynolds Memorial Hospital in Glen Dale was owned by the diocese until 1973, when it was given to the community. The first official Diocesan Center was established in October of 1964 when Helen Ruffner Ritz gave a house and land on Virginia Street in Charleston in mem-

ory of her late husband, Judge Harold A. Ritz. The diocesan office is now permanently located there.

Bishop Strider had announced in 1949 that he intended to retire April 9, 1955, on his 68th birthday. William Camrock Campbell became the fourth bishop of the diocese on May 10, 1955, with more than 2,500 people attending the services at the Charleston Municipal Auditorium. The fifth bishop was Robert Poland Atkinson, elected bishop coadjutor on February 17, 1973. He became bishop when Bishop Campbell retired January 1, 1976. He ordained the first women priests in 1977 and took semi-retirement in 1989, when Bishop John H. Smith was elected.

Bishop Smith came from Vermont. At the time of Bishop Smith's retirement in 1999, there were 78 parishes and mission churches in West Virginia. During his ten years, the emphasis was on cluster ministry, which combined smaller churches with a ministry team to avoid each parish paying the full cost of clergy. More than half of the congregations are now part of one of the 11 clusters established in the diocese, including two that include a church in a neighboring state and diocese.

In 2001, the Reverend Mike Klusmeyer of Wheaton, Illinois, was elected Episcopal bishop of West Virginia. There were 10,800 baptized Episcopalians in West Virginia at the time.

See also Religion

Tom D. Miller
Huntington

Eleanor Meyer Hamilton, *The Flair & the Fire: The Story of the Episcopal Church in West Virginia, 1877–1977*, 1977.

Etam Earth Station

Located at Etam, Preston County, the Etam Earth Station is one of the major sites in the country for receiving transmissions from orbiting communications satellites. Four large dish antennas pick up signals at the station, which is operated by AT&T.

Etam lies just north of the 13,000-square-mile National Radio Quiet Zone. The zone spans a section of West Virginia and Virginia, established in 1958 by the Federal Communications Commission to reduce interference to the National Radio Astronomy Observatory at Green Bank in Pocahontas County. The radio quiet zone includes Sugar Grove in Pendleton County, nearly 100 miles southeast of Etam, where eight dish antennas also pick up electronic transmissions. Sugar Grove is home to the U.S. Navy Radio Station.

Etam and Sugar Grove stations are said to be part of a worldwide intelligence-gathering network named Echelon. According to press reports, the network includes the National Security Agency in the United States, and similar agencies in

Canada, Australia, New Zealand, and the United Kingdom. The network is widely reported to be able to tap into all types of electronically transmitted communications, including phone calls, e-mails, and faxes.

See also National Radio Astronomy Observatory

Ethnic Life

Immigrants from Europe flowed into what is now West Virginia from the early 18th century onward. These settlers were largely from the British Isles and Germany, with minority representation from many other places, and that population mix prevailed for more than a century.

In the latter decades of the 19th century and especially the first two decades of the 20th, West Virginia experienced another major wave of immigration. The newcomers came from different places than the early settlers. From 1880 through 1920, tens of thousands of individuals came from all parts of Europe, but especially the south and east, to work in the state's burgeoning industries, including railroads, timber, coal, steel, and glass. Among them were immigrants from Hungary, Slovakia, Poland, Italy, and Greece.

People migrated to West Virginia for various reasons. Many were recruited. Companies sent representatives to Europe and the American South to find workers. For many years the state employed a commissioner of immigration to encourage workers to come to West Virginia. Others came to avoid religious persecution or military conscription. Many came for economic reasons, especially toward the latter part of the 19th century when many European countries suffered hard times.

Once here, immigrants often joined with their compatriots to form tight-knit communities where they maintained native customs, food, music, language, and religious practices, even as they assimilated into America. Social groups sprang up to sponsor activities dedicated to preserving customs from the old country.

Today, immigrants continue to come to West Virginia, and for largely the same reasons as did their counterparts in times past. Again they come from different places than their predecessors. The vast majority of the new immigrants come from the Middle East, the Indian subcontinent, and parts of Asia and the Pacific Islands. They come for economic opportunity, and as before, many are recruited, though now for professional skills rather than as laborers. Many are doctors, others engineers. Once in West Virginia, they often send for relatives and colleagues.

And as before, they often form associations to continue the ethnic and cultural traditions of their native lands. For example, in the Charleston area Asian Indians number more than 2,200. This group formed the India Association and built a handsome India Center. Filipinos likewise form a close community in the capital city, and a son of a prominent Filipino family is one of Kanawha County's most popular state legislators. A thriving mosque on the outskirts of the city serves southern West Virginia Muslims.

But West Virginia now attracts relatively few immigrants, both as compared to its earlier history and to other parts of America today. The 2000 census shows that West Virginia had 1,808,350 people. There were 57,232 African-Americans. Of the ethnic groups listed, Asians number 9,334. Indians were the largest group among the Asians, at 2,856. Among other Asian groups were the Chinese and Filipinos, numbering 1,878 and 1,495 respectively. Hispanics in the state totaled 12,279, coming from Mexico, Puerto Rico, and Cuba. More than 96 percent of the state's population was native-born white, now including the descendants of last century's immigrants.

Located throughout the state, often clustered according to the original industry that drew them here, ethnic communities still flourish. Some have dispersed as industry ebbed and flowed, but other such communities still exist, and are joined by other, newer, ethnic groups to contribute to the culture of West Virginia.

See also Demography, Population

Cathy Pleska
Scott Depot

George Bird Evans

Sportsman George Bird Evans, author, illustrator, and dog breeder, was born in Uniontown, Pennsylvania, December 26, 1906. Educated at Pittsburgh's Carnegie Tech and the Chicago Art Institute, Evans earned pocket money playing jazz saxophone. Having married Kay Harris of Wheeling in January 1931, he moved to New York City where he freelanced as an illustrator for *Cosmopolitan* and other publications.

In 1939, Evans bought a historic farm near Brandonville in Preston County, where he developed the Old Hemlock line of grouse-hunting setters. Commissioned Lt. (j.g.) by the U.S. Navy, he spent World War II in Washington doing perspective drawings to illustrate repairs to damaged planes and ships.

Evans wrote 27 upland shooting books based on his shooting journals begun in 1934, and 115 magazine stories and reviews, as well as book introductions and other short pieces. He published many of his own books, many of them limited editions. He wrote of the beauty of bird-dog grouse hunting, not always accompanied by a kill. Living an eccentric and reclusive life, George and Kay jointly wrote five mystery books from 1950 to 1960 using the pen name Brandon Bird. One, *Hawk Watch*, was set in Berkeley Springs.

Exciting his readers with descriptions of his hunting experiences and life at Old Hemlock, Evans developed a loyal following. He often castigated state hunting authorities for the state's overlong grouse season which, he said, was responsible for the birds' depleted population. Evans died in Morgantown, May 5, 1998.

Peggy Ross
Reedsville

Catherine A. Harper, *George Bird Evans: Life of a Shooting Gentleman*, 1999.

Pete Everest

General Frank Kendall "Pete" Everest Jr., who earned the nickname "the fastest man alive," was a military aviator and a pioneer in U.S. rocket plane flying. He test-piloted 122 different models and makes of aircraft and logged more than 10,000 hours in about 170 aircraft types.

Everest was born in Fairmont, August 10, 1920. After graduating from high school, he attended Fairmont State College for a short time and later studied engineering at West Virginia University. He graduated from the Armed Forces Staff College in 1956. In July 1942, Everest completed the Aviation Cadet program and was commissioned as a second lieu-

tenant with the U.S. Army Air Force. He was sent to North Africa and flew 94 combat missions in Africa, Sicily, and Italy. In 1944, he was assigned to the China-Burma-India region. He completed 67 combat missions and destroyed four Japanese aircraft before his plane was shot down by ground fire in May 1945. He was captured and remained a Japanese prisoner of war until the end of hostilities.

Everest piloted both the Bell X-1 and X-2 rocket planes. He set the X-1 altitude record of 73,000 feet in 1949, and, in 1953, the world speed record of the F-100A at more than 750 mph. In 1956, he flew the X-2 at Mach 3, exceeding 1,900 miles per hour and breaking the record of Chuck Yeager, his rival and close contemporary.

Everest became a brigadier general in 1965. General Everest, with more than 20 military awards, and other honors, retired from the Air Force in 1973. He lives in Arizona.

Judie Smith
West Virginia Humanities Council

Everettville Mine Disaster

On April 30, 1927, an explosion roared through the Federal No. 3 mine owned by New England Fuel and Transportation Company of Everettville, Monongalia County. The explosion, the subsequent fire, and gas in the mine killed 97 men.

Flames and debris blown out of the mine by the force of the blast destroyed a nearby tipple, killing six workers and injuring several others. Only nine of the 100 men working in the mine at the time of the incident were able to escape. One miner made his way to safety and returned, with a rescue team and equipment, to help save eight of his coworkers. No others in the mine were saved, although messages later found by the rescue teams near the bodies of entombed miners indicated that some men had survived several hours after the blast.

When news of the tragedy spread, thousands of sightseers converged on the area, joining the trapped miners' families and friends who were keeping vigil by the mine. State police were called in to help rope off the area and assist with crowd control. Rescue efforts were hampered by the risk of another explosion and by the fire that continued to rage in the mine. Rescue teams worked in relays around the clock, but it was two weeks before the fires were fully contained and the last bodies were removed.

See also Coal Mine Disasters

Eleanor Spohr
Huntington

Lacy A. Dillon, *They Died in the Darkness*, 1976.

The Executive Branch

The executive branch of West Virginia state government is headed by the governor as chief executive and includes five other elected officers. The original con-

---

"Be worthy of your game"

"If I could shoot a game bird and still not hurt it, the way I can take a trout on a fly and release it, I doubt if I would kill another one. This is a strange statement coming from a man whose life is dedicated to shooting and gun dogs. For me, there is almost no moment more sublime than when I pull the trigger and see a grouse fall. Yet, as the bird is retrieved I feel a sense of remorse for taking a courageous life. About the time I passed fifty I noticed this conflict becoming more pronounced....

"How then, can you love a bird and kill it and still feel decent? I think the answer is, to be worthy of your game. Which boils down to a gentleman's agreement between you and the bird, never forgetting that it is the bird that has everything to lose. It consists of things you feel and do, not because someone is looking or because the law says you may or must not, but because you feel that this is the honorable way to do it."

—George Bird Evans
The Upland Shooting Life
(1971)

stitution of 1863 stated that the "executive department shall consist of a governor, secretary of state, superintendent of free schools, auditor, treasurer and attorney general." But there have been several constitutional changes. The secretary of state was an appointed office from 1872 until 1902, when voters amended the constitution and made it an elective office once more. The office of agriculture commissioner, an elective position, was created in 1911. The next change to the executive branch was approved by voters at the 1934 general election, adding the agriculture commissioner to the list. In 1958, voters removed the superintendent of schools as an elected state officer.

For more than 100 years, from 1863 to 1968, West Virginia was run by a weak governor, from the standpoint of powers granted by the constitution. Under both the constitutions of 1863 and 1872, the governor had to share his power with the other executives. He and they made up the Board of Public Works, which he chaired. The board was supposed to be interested primarily in works of internal improvement, including public lands and toll roads, but it evolved into the budget-making agency and became the most powerful executive agency in state government. Individual members would bargain with key legislators on appropriations for various agencies before final passage of the budget.

All that was changed in 1968 when voters ratified the Modern Budget Amendment. This shifted the budget-making power to the governor, making his office much stronger. Starting in 1969, the other members of the Board of Public Works had no voice in the preparation of the budget. The governor as chief executive decided how much tax revenue to put in the fiscal year estimate and then recommended how it was to be spent. The legislature could disagree on the expenditures but could not alter the estimates of revenue made by the governor.

Two years later, the voters ratified another amendment that allowed the governor to run for a second four year term. Previously, each governor had been limited to one term, and had to sit out four years before being eligible to run again, although the other executive officers can serve as many successive terms as the voters will allow. Dr. David G. Temple, professor of political science at West Virginia University, measured the extent of the changes resulting from those two amendments and concluded that West Virginia had jumped from 45th in the nation in terms of relative strength of the governor to a position where no state was ahead of this one in veto or budgetary powers. Republican Arch A. Moore Jr., elected in 1968 as the state's 28th governor, was the first beneficiary of both

the increased budgetary controls and the two-term provision. He became the state's first two-term governor by winning reelection in 1972 and later became the only person to serve three terms when he was elected as the state's 30th governor in 1984.

By century's end, two other governors had served eight years in succession. Democrat John D. "Jay" Rockefeller IV was chief executive from 1977 to 1984, and Gaston Caperton, also a Democrat, was elected to two terms, in 1988 and 1992. In 1996, Republican Gov. Cecil Underwood was elected to his second term, 40 years after his first. Underwood was elected the state's 25th governor in 1956 at the age of 34, the youngest in state history, and then became the oldest governor at age 74.

In contrast, some other state executive officers have served as long as 28 successive years. Edgar B. Sims of Harrison County was first elected state auditor in 1932 and was still serving at his death on June 20, 1960. More recently, Glen B. Gainer Jr. of Parkersburg served 16 years, and then his son, Glen B. Gainer III, was elected in 1992 and again in 1996, 2000, and 2004. Two men have been secretary of state for 16 years each, William Smith O'Brien of Upshur County from 1933 to 1949 and Ken Hechler of Cabell County, a former congressman, who served from 1985 to 2001. The longest tenure for a state treasurer has been 18 years, when Richard E. Talbott of Barbour County served from 1932 until his death December 17, 1949. The longest stint as attorney general began in 1969 when Chauncey Browning Jr. of Logan County was elected to the first of four successive four-year terms. But the record for time in the executive branch belongs to Commissioner of Agriculture Gus Douglass of Mason County, who was first elected to a four-year term in 1964 and continued to serve in 2005. The only break is the four years from 1988 to 1992 when Douglass made an unsuccessful bid for the Democratic nomination for governor.

There has been at least one attempt to create the office of lieutenant-governor, but voters rejected that proposed amendment to the constitution in 1930 by a 4-1 majority. The president of the state senate succeeds any governor who vacates the office by death, resignation, or other cause under the present constitution. More recently, there have been efforts to change the auditor, treasurer, and commissioner of agriculture to appointive rather than elective office, further consolidating the governor's power over the executive branch. Those amendments, proposed by Governor Caperton, were also rejected.

Tom D. Miller
Huntington
John G. Morgan, *West Virginia Governors,* 1980.

Exploration

The exploration of Virginia and present West Virginia gained momentum after the restoration of the Stuart monarchs in England in 1660 and the ensuing return of Sir William Berkeley, an ardent expansionist, as Virginia governor. Hoping to locate the South Sea (Pacific Ocean) and to promote trade with frontier Indians, Berkeley sent out in 1669–70 three expeditions under John Lederer, a young German then in the colony. On one of these trips, Lederer scaled the Blue Ridge Mountains and gazed down upon the Shenandoah Valley.

In 1671, Abraham Wood dispatched from Fort Henry, at the falls of the Appomattox River (present Petersburg, Virginia), the most important exploring expedition of the time. Known for Thomas Batts, its leader, and Robert Fallam, who kept a journal, the party crossed the Blue Ridge to the New River. Historians once believed that Batts and Fallam continued downstream to Kanawha Falls, a few miles below the juncture of the New and Gauley rivers in present Fayette County. In 1912, however, Clarence W. Alvord and Lee Bidgood, making use of Fallam's journal, concluded that the little band traveled only to Peters Falls, near the present Virginia-West Virginia border. In 1987, Alan Briceland, a geographer, set forth the view that Batts and Fallam turned southwestward from the New River to East River Mountain and then followed the East River, Guyandotte River, and Tug Fork to what is now Matewan, Mingo County.

Whatever their route and destination, Batts and Fallam had penetrated well into the Ohio River watershed, and the expedition became one basis for England's claim to the entire Ohio Valley. Meanwhile, with claims emanating from an alleged visit to the Ohio River by the great explorer La Salle in 1669, France had reason to challenge England's position.

By the beginning of the 18th century, western exploration in Virginia began to center around land acquisition schemes. In 1703, Louis Michel, a resident of Bern, Switzerland, who was associated with Swiss settlement promoters, enlisted the support of Baron Christopher de Graffenreid. In 1706, in the company of three French traders, Michel examined lands around the junction of the Potomac and Shenandoah rivers although the Swiss eventually accepted a more attractive offer from North Carolina. In 1716, Gov. Alexander Spotswood of Virginia, with 50 mounted gentlemen, along with their servants and Indian guides, crossed the Blue Ridge. On the banks of the Shenandoah River, he ceremoniously took possession of the Shenandoah Valley for England.

Explorations of Western Virginia again became important in the 1740s. Settlement promoters or speculators vied with each other in the search for desirable lands. Christopher Gist covered much of the Ohio Valley lowlands for the Ohio Company; Thomas Walker discovered the Cumberland Gap and viewed much of eastern Kentucky for the Loyal Company; Walker and others observed moves by the Greenbrier Company in southeastern parts of West Virginia; and John Howard and John Peter Salley explored the Coal River area, where, at present Peytona, they discovered fine coal seams. French authorities in Canada countered Virginia's moves by sending Celoron de Blainville down the Ohio to bury at strategic locations, including Wheeling and Point Pleasant, lead plates asserting French rights to the Ohio Valley.

See also Batts and Fallam Expedition, Celoron de Blainville, Frontier, John Lederer, Alexander Spotswood, Abraham Wood

Otis K. Rice
WVU Institute of Technology

Clarence W. Alvord and Lee Bidgood, *The First Explorations of the Trans-Allegheny Region by the Virginians, 1650–1674*, 1912; Alan Vance Briceland, *Westward from Virginia: The Exploration of the Virginia-Carolina Frontier, 1650–1710*, 1987; William P. Cumming, *The Discoveries of John Lederer*, 1958.

Extension Homemaker Clubs

In 1913, the West Virginia legislature met the long-recognized need for educational programs for farm families with the passage of an act that provided for the employment of agents to disseminate practical information relating to agriculture and domestic science. That same year, Nell M. Barnett was hired by West Virginia University to take charge of extension home economics.

Four-day extension schools began to be held in West Virginia communities, taught by local home economics teachers. In addition, correspondence courses in the domestic sciences were started, as were classes for women at the popular farmers' institutes held at Jackson's Mill and elsewhere. In 1914, extension home economics agents were placed in certain counties to further these efforts, with the organization of farm women into groups primarily to assist with the girls' tomato and canning clubs. By 1915, there were 16 registered groups made up of these women.

The outbreak of World War I accelerated the promotion of home food production and preservation. The homemakers clubs participated in Red Cross drives and the sale of Liberty Bonds. This intensified wartime effort was repeated during World War II, with particular emphasis on food preservation and participation in a nationwide mattress-making project, designed to provide decent bedding for low-income families. By this time extension home economic agents had been provided for almost all of the counties and the Farm Women's clubs, as they were now called, had increased accordingly.

As the population became less agricultural, extension programs were broadened to include home furnishings, health and nutrition, money management, and leadership development. With the change of emphasis the names of the clubs also changed: from Farm Women's clubs to Home Demonstration clubs in 1954, to Extension Homemaker clubs in 1968, and Community and Educational Outreach Service clubs in 1999.

During the segregation period, a separate system of African-American extension homemaker clubs was organized by agents employed by West Virginia State College. In 1954, West Virginia State's land grant status was transferred to West Virginia University, and in 1965 the black State Farm and Homemakers Council voted to join the West Virginia Homemakers Council.

The guiding hand during most of these years of homemaker education and service was that of Gertrude Humphreys. Her entire professional career was spent in West Virginia University extension work, from 1919 to 1965, including 35 years as state leader.

Margaret Meador
Princeton

Gertrude Humphreys, *Adventures in Good Living*, 1972.

F

4-H

4-H is a youth educational program conducted by the federal Cooperative Extension Service, in conjunction with state and local partners. The U.S. Department of Agriculture, state land-grant universities, and county governments cooperatively fund 4-H, and federal, state, and local extension staff and volunteer leaders develop and carry out its programs. In West Virginia, 4-H is conducted under the direction of the West Virginia University Extension Service.

The 4-H movement in West Virginia began in Monroe County in 1908 with the organization of clubs for farm boys and girls to teach them better farming and homemaking methods. These corn clubs and canning clubs were patterned on educational youth groups that had been developed in 1902 in Ohio and Illinois. The Monroe County clubs proved to be successful and were soon introduced into other counties.

In 1914, Congress passed the Smith-Lever Act, which made federal funding available for each state to develop its agricultural extension program. The youth extension movement was promoted and overseen by extension agents who recruited and trained local adult volunteer leaders to work with the boys and girls clubs. The first agriculture extension clubs for black youth in West Virginia were established in Seebert, Pocahontas County, in 1915 under the direction of educator J. E. Banks.

The 4-H name and four-leaf clover logo were being used to represent boys and girls clubs in West Virginia by 1918. The design, a four-leaf clover with an H on each leaf, had been introduced in other states by 1909, and the term "4-H club" first appeared in a federal document in 1918. The four H's represented fourfold development of the Head, Heart, Health, and Hands.

West Virginia was an early leader in the development and promotion of summer camps for rural boys and girls. The first organized camp for rural youth in the United States was held in Randolph County in 1915. The camp, sponsored by the West Virginia University Extension Service, was under the direction of J. Versus Shipman with the assistance of his wife, Bess, and William H. "Teepi" Kendrick. Kendrick would go on to establish and direct the first state 4-H camp in the United States at Jackson's Mill in 1921. Camp Washington-Carver, the country's first African-American state 4-H camp, was established in Fayette County in 1942. Today Jackson's Mill is a nationally

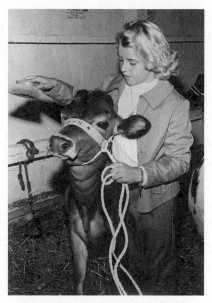

A young West Virginian grooms her 4-H calf.

recognized camp and conference center, and many of West Virginia's counties have permanent 4-H camps that host year-round learning and recreational experiences.

Originally targeted for rural boys and girls between the ages of nine and 19, 4-H has expanded over time to provide educational programs for urban and underprivileged youth. The original agricultural education programs have expanded to cover a wide variety of topics, to meet the varied and changing educational needs of the state's young people, while continuing to promote the 4-H motto to "Make the best better."

See also Camp Good Luck, Camp Washington-Carver, West Virginia University Extension Service

Michael M. Meador
Abingdon, Virginia

Guy H. Stewart, *A Touch of Charisma: A History of the 4-H Club Program in West Virginia,* 1969; Thomas Wessel and Marilyn Wessel, *4-H: An American Idea 1900–1980, A History of 4-H,* 1982.

Ferdinando Fairfax

Ferdinando Fairfax, a Jefferson County planter, was born in Virginia in 1774. He would have been second in line to become Lord Fairfax, if his father, Bryan Fairfax, had not declined the title in 1789 to become a minister in the Episcopal Church. Bryan was a cousin of the bachelor Lord Thomas Fairfax whose family had received vast lands in Virginia and present West Virginia from King Charles II in the 17th century. Ferdinando's godparents were George and Martha Washington.

Ferdinando Fairfax was wealthy and influential, even without the title or estate. In 1795, he became a founding trustee of the Charles Town Academy, which survived until 1905. Fairfax was one of the first 14 justices of the peace

when Jefferson County was created from part of Berkeley County in 1801. He owned more slaves than anyone else in the county, paying taxes on 62. He purchased from George Hite a tract of land on Liberty Street in Charles Town and established an inn. His plantation, Shannon Hill, near Kabletown, was sold by his daughter in 1825 to G. W. Hammond, who demolished the original house and built the present dwelling in 1840. Ferdinando Fairfax died September 26, 1820, in Jefferson County.

See also Fairfax Lands, Lord Thomas Fairfax

Barbara Rasmussen
Fairmont State University

T. K. Cartmell, *Shenandoah Valley Pioneers and Their Descendants: A History of Frederick County, Virginia,* 1963; Jefferson County Historical Society, *Between the Shenandoah and the Potomac: Historic Homes of Jefferson County, West Virginia,* 1990.

George William Fairfax

George William Fairfax, the manager of lands once including most of the Eastern Panhandle and himself a major landowner in present Jefferson County, was born in the Bahamas in 1724. He was the oldest son of William Fairfax, who was the cousin and agent of Lord Thomas Fairfax. Educated in England, George returned to America in 1746, to succeed his father as agent for Lord Fairfax, the proprietor of the largest land patent in Virginia and present West Virginia. George William Fairfax was the close friend and a relative by marriage of George Washington.

George William Fairfax accompanied the 1746 survey party that established the Fairfax Line and placed the original Fairfax Stone at the corner of present Preston, Grant, and Tucker counties. By 1748, he was operating from Belvoir, his father William's beloved estate on the lower Potomac, where Lord Fairfax had set up his proprietor's office. George inherited Belvoir at his father's death in 1757. He also owned Shannondale, 19,170 acres straddling the Blue Ridge south of Harpers Ferry in present Jefferson County, granted him by his father.

George William Fairfax worked intermittently as Lord Fairfax's agent until 1773, when he and his wife, Sarah, left permanently for England due to ill health. He died there April 3, 1787.

See also Fairfax Lands, Lord Thomas Fairfax

Peter Silitch
Strange Creek

Fairfax Lands

The Fairfax Lands originated in a 1649 grant by King Charles II to seven loyal supporters, of all of the land in the colony of Virginia between the Rappahannock and Potomac rivers from their headwaters to the Chesapeake Bay. By 1719, through purchases and inheritance, Lord Thomas Fairfax became sole proprietor. His domain included most of the Eastern Panhandle and Potomac Highlands of present West Virginia.

Under the royal grant, the proprietor was given governing rights. There was some dissatisfaction between the colony and Fairfax, and in 1733 the Virginia General Assembly attacked the proprietorship and its boundaries. In 1736, to establish the bounds of the grant, surveyors for Fairfax and Virginia followed the North Branch of the Potomac River to what they determined to be the Potomac's source, a small spring between Backbone Mountain and Dobbin Ridge in present Tucker County. In 1746, a second surveying party established the Fairfax Line from the headwaters of the Rappahannock in the Blue Ridge Mountains to this spring, where they placed a stone marker known thereafter as the Fairfax Stone. The vast region between the rivers was called the Northern Neck, although in modern times the name applies only to the section between the lower Potomac and Rappahannock, in Tidewater Virginia.

The Fairfax Line completed the boundaries of the royal grant. In England, Fairfax successfully defended the boundaries established by these surveys, and the British Board of Trade confirmed that he was entitled to the quitrents or taxes from the holdings. In 1747, Fairfax moved permanently to Virginia, and in 1752 established his residence, Greenway Court, near Winchester. George Washington had profitable associations at Greenway Court, in both his professional capacity as a surveyor and in the social context of the day, which included deer hunting and fox hunting with Fairfax.

Settling the boundary lines brought greater growth to established communities, including Alexandria, and the establishment of new communities in the Piedmont and the lower Shenandoah Valley, including Leesburg, Fairfax, Woodstock, Strasburg, Romney, and Mecklenburg (now Shepherdstown). The bounds of the proprietary encompassed a tremendous tract of five million acres. The Fairfax Lands included present Jefferson, Berkeley, Morgan, Hardy, Hampshire, and Mineral counties, and parts of Grant and Taylor.

Residents on the Fairfax Lands were required to pay an annual fee, or quitrent, to hold their land. This amounted to the paying of taxes to the lord of the manor, a feudal custom offensive to Revolutionary Americans. In 1776, Virginia abolished quitrents but nonetheless excepted Fairfax's proprietary. In 1779, during the Revolutionary War, Virginia seized property belonging to British subjects in the state but again excluded Fairfax; he was not classed as a British subject and did not take an active part for or against the Revolution. Fairfax died in 1781, and the Virginia Assembly, concerned that British subjects might inherit the holdings, abolished the proprietary in 1785.

See also Fairfax Stone, Lord Thomas Fairfax

Gilbert Gude
Bethesda, Maryland
Stuart E. Brown Jr., *Virginia Baron: The Story of Thomas 6th Lord Fairfax,* 1965; Charles Morrison, *The Fairfax Line,* 1970.

Lord Thomas Fairfax

Thomas, Sixth Lord Fairfax, was born October 22, 1693, at Leeds Castle, in Kent, England, the son of Thomas, Fifth Lord Fairfax, and Lady Catherine Culpeper Fairfax. It was through his mother that he inherited five million acres in Virginia. The land included much of the present Eastern Panhandle of West Virginia.

Fairfax was a student at Oxford University when his mother died in 1719. He took control of his land holdings in 1732 at the death of his agent, Robert "King" Carter. Fairfax first visited his land in Virginia in 1735, and in 1748 hired a surveying party that included the teenage George Washington to mark its boundaries. A boundary dispute with the Virginia government caused Lord Fairfax to return to England in 1737 to argue his case. The dispute was settled in his favor in London in 1745.

In 1747, Lord Fairfax took up permanent residence in the Virginia colony to supervise his land holdings. In 1752, he built Greenway Court, at the village of White Post, near Winchester, and became active in civil, local military, and religious affairs. Fairfax steered a careful path politically, and neither he nor his property was molested during the Revolutionary War by either Americans or British. He died at Greenway Court, December 9, 1781, and is buried at Christ Church in Winchester.

Lord Thomas Fairfax never married. His brother, Robert Fairfax, became the Seventh Lord Fairfax, and the line continues today in London with Nicholas, 14th Lord Fairfax, Baron of Cameron.

See also Fairfax Lands

Jill Thompson Decker
Vienna, Virginia

Fairfax Stone

The Fairfax Stone, which originally marked the western extent of the Fairfax estate, is an important West Virginia landmark. The estate, one of Virginia's largest colonial land grants, included most of the present Eastern Panhandle. The Fairfax lands extended to the headwaters of the Potomac River, and the setting of the stone in 1746 at the source of the Potomac North Branch helped to establish the North Branch as the river's main stem. The Fairfax Stone also marked the boundary between Maryland and Virginia, now West Virginia, at the westernmost end of Maryland.

The marker was significant in property disputes until 1912, when the U.S. Supreme Court confirmed the North Branch as the Potomac main stream, and a new concrete marker was placed. The current Fairfax Stone, the fifth, was dedicated as a state historic monument and became part of the West Virginia State Park system in 1957 when the Western Maryland Railroad gave four acres of land surrounding the stone to the state. The Fairfax Stone stands at the junction of Tucker, Grant, and Preston counties.

See also Fairfax Lands

Patricia Hissom
Davis

William Fairfax

William Fairfax, born in 1691 in England, a cousin of Lord Thomas Fairfax, and doubly related by marriage to George Washington, was second only to Lord Fairfax as the major early landowner in present West Virginia. William purchased Lord Fairfax's manors of Shannondale, South Branch Creek, and Patterson Creek, now in the Eastern Panhandle, to support his Belvoir plantation on the lower Potomac. At Belvoir, William Fairfax entertained the Washingtons, including his son-in-law, Lawrence Washington, George Washington's older brother and guardian.

William had served from India to New England, where he was collector of customs at Boston until 1732, when Lord Fairfax chose him as agent for his Virginia estate (more than five million acres, including most of the present Eastern Panhandle). Experienced, active, and honest, William was invaluable to Lord Fairfax in the colony, regarding relations with the Virginia government, land speculators, and settlers. At his urging the Fairfax estate was finally officially surveyed and its limits ascertained, as witnessed by the Fairfax Line of 1746.

In 1748, William launched 16-year-old George Washington on his career as surveyor, sending him to accompany his son, George William Fairfax, to Patterson Creek, to set boundaries for German-speaking settlers there. In 1754, William was commanding the Alexandria volunteers against the French and Indians in the Shenandoah Valley when he was incapacitated by illness.

William Fairfax died September 3, 1757, and was buried at Belvoir. His son, Bryan, became the Eighth Lord Fairfax.

See also George William Fairfax

Peter Silitch
Strange Creek
Stuart E. Brown Jr., *Virginia Baron: The Story of Thomas 6th Lord Fairfax,* 1965.

Fairmont

Fairmont is located in north-central West Virginia, where the West Fork and Tygart Valley rivers join to form the Monongahela. Fairmont was established by the Virginia legislature on January 19, 1820, on the farm of Boaz Fleming. It became the county seat when Marion County was created in 1842. The original name of Middletown was changed to Fairmont in 1843.

Neighboring Palatine was surveyed in 1838 and incorporated in 1867. A number of industries developed in Palatine, and it once outranked Fairmont in size and importance. Late in the 19th century, the Fairmont Development Company began developing the area southwest of Fairmont. The area was leveled and utilities and paved streets installed. Businesses and residences were constructed quickly, and on December 15, 1892, West Fairmont was incorporated. The present city was born February 18, 1899, when a new charter was granted by which Fairmont, Palatine, and West Fairmont were incorporated as the city of Fairmont.

Early in the 20th century, Fairmont developed a major glass industry, based on the availability of glass sand and abundant natural gas. Experienced glass workers were brought in to operate the plants and train new workers. Many came directly from Belgium, France, and Italy, while others, who had earlier immigrated to work at Pennsylvania or Ohio glass plants, were persuaded to transfer to Fairmont.

Local coal mines and other industries also developed a pressing need for labor. African-Americans from the American South and immigrants from southern and eastern Europe came to the region. The immigrants included Italians, Poles, Hungarians, Germans, and Austrians, and some from Turkey, Greece, and elsewhere. Experienced miners from England and Wales were brought over to teach proper methods to the new miners. Each group brought its skills and knowledge, or simply its muscle power, to the growing local economy. All contributed to the enrichment of what is today a diverse ethnic culture.

Businesses flourished in Fairmont, with Monongah Glass, Owens Illinois Glass, and Westinghouse Electric prominent among them. The town was headquarters for Fairmont Coal Company and later for Mountaineer Coal Division of Consolidation Coal Company. Today, it is the home of Fairmont State University and two high schools. Cook Hospital was formed here, and eventually became Fairmont General.

As in many cities, Fairmont suffered with the loss of industry and as retail business moved to outlying shopping centers. The population peaked at 29,346 in 1950, and was 19,097 in 2000. Re-

The Marion County Courthouse is a Fairmont landmark.

cently, efforts have been made to revive the downtown, including the restoration of the historic high-level bridge and the beautiful Marion County courthouse. Major investments have been made on the city's outskirts, particularly the Fairmont Technology Park. Fairmont benefits as well from the huge FBI fingerprint center on I-79 south, and from other developments on the emerging Morgantown-Clarksburg technology corridor.

Fairmont is the home of Congressman Alan Mollohan. Francis Harrison Pierpont, governor of the Reorganized Government of Virginia during the Civil War, came from Fairmont, as did four governors of West Virginia, Aretas Brooks Fleming, Ephraim F. Morgan, Matthew M. Neely, and Joe Manchin. Fairmont was the home of James O. Watson and his son, U.S. Sen. Clarence W. Watson, and son-in-law, Gov. Aretas Brooks Fleming; for many years these men controlled Consolidation Coal Company.

These industrialists and others built great mansions on Fairmont Avenue. Most of the grand houses have succumbed to time but interesting examples remain, including James Edwin Watson's palatial High Gate. Novelist John Knowles, a Fairmont native best known for the novel, *A Separate Peace,* dealt with this period of local history in the 1978 book, *A Vein of Riches.* Knowles used the original name of Middletown in fictionalizing Fairmont.

See also Marion County

Thomas J. Koon
Marion County Historical Society
Thomas J. Koon and Oce Smith, *Marion County, West Virginia: A Pictorial History,* 1995; Marion County Historical Society, *A History of Marion County, West Virginia,* 1985.

Fairmont High Level Bridge

Open for traffic in 1921, the High Level Bridge carries Jefferson Street 90 feet above the Monongahela River into the

heart of Fairmont. With three 250-foot spans, this reinforced concrete arch bridge is significant not only for its immense size, but also for its elegant proportions and noteworthy architectural details. The monumental structure was under construction from 1918 to 1921, at a cost of nearly $860,000. The bridge was designed by the Concrete Steel Engineering Company of New York and constructed by the John F. Casey Company of Pittsburgh. With a total length of 1,266 feet, it remains the largest reinforced concrete bridge in West Virginia.

Concrete as a building material is of ancient origin but was transformed into a powerful modern structural material with the advent of concrete reinforced with steel bars. At the beginning of the 20th century, reinforced concrete reached a mature stage with structural forms that could be executed only in this new material. A new age of very large concrete arch bridges was ushered in in 1915 by a pioneer in the use of reinforced concrete, C.A.P. Turner. An impressive number of such arch bridges were constructed during the next several decades. The Fairmont High Level Bridge ranks with this new generation of monumental bridges erected from coast to coast. It remains the sole representative of this genre in West Virginia and provides Fairmont a striking gateway unmatched by any other city in the state.

The High Level Bridge, reopened to traffic in 2000 after a $23.5 million restoration, is listed on the National Register of Historic Places.

See also Bridges, Fairmont

Emory L. Kemp
WVU Institute for the History of Technology
Carl W. Condit, *American Building Art: the 19th Century,* 1960.

Fairmont State University

Fairmont State University is situated on 90 acres a mile from downtown Fairmont. The college was formed in 1865, as West Virginia's first private normal (or teacher-training) school. The state purchased the school in 1868, after providing $5,000 to assist in building construction the previous year.

The school was known variously as the Fairmont Branch Normal School, the Branch of the West Virginia Normal School at Fairmont, the Fairmont State Normal School, and the Fairmont Normal School. The cornerstone for its first building was laid August 15, 1867, at the corner of Adams and Quincy streets in the heart of town. The first class of students, consisting of 17 females and 13 males, occupied the new building in April 1869. In 1871, Hyre D. Clark of Buckhannon was the first graduate.

That same year, James G. Blair became the principal, the fifth person to head the school in six years. (The title was not changed from principal to president until Charles J. C. Bennett occupied the position, 1907–10.) Blair successfully urged the state to include secondary school classes in the curriculum of normal schools, because most students arrived insufficiently prepared for professional training. Blair continued as principal until his death December 23, 1878. His successor, M. Lizzie Dickey, was one of the first women to hold a high post in education in West Virginia. She continued as acting principal until 1882. Another woman, Nancy R. Cameron (Morrow), was acting principal, 1889–90.

By 1880, Fairmont had more students than any other normal school. On March 23, 1893, it moved to new quarters between Fairmont and Gaston avenues and Second and Third streets in South Fairmont. When enrollment outgrew that facility, the school procured 18.5 acres southwest of town, its present location, and moved there in January 1917. Soon after, America's entry into World War I dropped the number of students to fewer than 400, but enrollment soared throughout the 1920s to a high of 1,856 by 1930–31. The student population never dropped below 1,200 during the Depression years.

The school shifted toward a college curriculum in 1912. In 1923, it was authorized to offer a four-year program but was to confine itself to training teachers. Renamed Fairmont State Teachers College in 1931, it became Fairmont State College in 1943 and a university in 2004.

World War II and its aftermath forced significant changes. Enrollment plunged as young men left for war. Eleven professors, a quarter of the faculty, joined them. By January 1944, only nine males registered for full-time study, out of 776 students in the 1944–45 academic year. Thirty-five Fairmont State College students and alumni died in military service. The GI Bill helped increase student population to 1,648 in 1946–47.

For three decades, Joseph Rosier (1915–45) presided over the college, the longest tenure of any president or principal. He guided Fairmont State through its move to Locust Avenue and the challenges of two world wars, a depression, and the enrollment boom of the 1920s. In 1945, Rosier passed the position to George W. Hand (1945–52). Hand's successor, John W. Pence (1952–59) oversaw long-desired construction projects. With federal loans, Fairmont State was finally able to build a men's dormitory, later named Pence Hall. Two wings were added to the women's dorm, Morrow Hall, which had been in use since 1922. The cafeteria was expanded, a student center erected, and the administration building partially remodeled.

Construction continued in the 1960s under President Eaton K. Feaster. A new women's dorm named North Hall was completed in 1964, and a fine arts building and a dining hall were finished in 1967. The football stadium, built by the Works Progress Administration during the 1930s and named in honor of President Rosier, was upgraded. Two private-sector projects, built just off campus in the 1960s, provided additional housing at a time when the student population doubled in five years.

After peaking at 1,798 in 1949–50, enrollment declined. Desegregation opened the campus to black students for the first time in 1954. Controversy came to the campus during the Red Scare of the 1950s, when art instructor Luella Raab Mundell's contract was not renewed. Mundell sued State Board of Education member Thelma Brand Loudin for slander, claiming Loudin had accused her of being a communist and an atheist. Mundell lost in an emotional trial that divided the community and drew national attention. President Hand, who had refused to fire Mundell, lost his position in 1952.

In 1925, Alpha Psi Omega, an international collegiate honor society for drama students, was founded at Fairmont State College. The success of Alpha Psi Omega led to the founding of Thespians, a similar society for high school drama students.

Fairmont State Community and Technical College was established as part of Fairmont State in 1974. Counting this community college division, Fairmont State offers more than 130 degree programs, including four-year and graduate degrees, as well as various degrees and certificates representing other educational accomplishments. The institution had its largest enrollment ever in 2002–03, with 3,442 at the college and 2,056 at the community college, as measured in full-time equivalents. The community and technical college and the university are partners within Fairmont State.

Gerald D. Swick
Nashville, Tennessee

Jo Ann Lough, "Fairmont State College Occasional Papers Number 5, A Legacy: Cause and Effect," 1994; William P. Turner, *A Centennial History of Fairmont State College*, 1970.

Fairmont *Times West Virginian*

The *Times West Virginian* is Fairmont's daily newspaper. It traces its roots to 1866 when J. N. Boyd's *Vedette* began publication in Fairmont. In 1868, the name of the *Vedette* was changed to the *West Virginian* when it was sold to the Reverend Josiah Dillon. After various changes in ownership the *West Virginian* became a daily in 1904.

The competing *Fairmont Times* was first published as an evening paper in 1900 by Gen. C. L. Smith and O. S. McKinney. Its first Sunday morning edition was published in 1918. The *Fairmont Times* moved into the building where the *West Virginian* was located in 1926. The two papers maintained separate identities, although both were published by the Fairmont Newspaper Publishing Co.

In 1931, the Sunday paper became the *Times West Virginian*, combining the names of the two papers with the editorial staff of the *West Virginian* responsible for its publication. In 1934, Ogden Newspapers of Wheeling purchased the morning *Fairmont Times*, the evening *West Virginian*, and the Sunday *Times West Virginian*. In 1963, Thomson Newspapers of Canada purchased these papers. In 1975, the two daily newspapers made the first move toward one paper with essentially two editions, with only two pages made over for the afternoon *West Virginian*. In 1976, the *West Virginian* suspended publication and only a seven-day-a-week *Times West Virginian* was published.

In 1999, the Fairmont *Times West Virginian* was purchased by Community Newspaper Holdings. The 2005 circulation was 12,500.

Fairy Diddle

In West Virginia the term fairy diddle refers to a near-mythic creature, and may be used for various woodland rodents, including tree squirrels, flying squirrels, ground squirrels, and even baby groundhogs. Most observers agree, however, that whatever the fairy diddle is, it is fast, smaller than the average tree squirrel, and makes a lot of noise if disturbed. This accurately describes the American red squirrel, also called the pine squirrel or chickaree. Thus in West Virginia fairy diddles are most often red squirrels. Half the size of the gray squirrel, the red squirrel is omnivorous and will attack and eat other small mammals. This behavior may have given rise to the myth, common in West Virginia, that fairy diddles raid the nests of other squirrels and castrate their young, creating so-called steer squirrels. Other West Virginians identify the fairy diddle itself as such a steer squirrel. Naturalists disallow both of these assertions.

Fairy diddle as a term is most often used in northern West Virginia. It may be spelled alternately fairydiddle, ferrydiddle, and ferrididdle. In the southern region, "mountain boomer" is used synonymously. Because of its association with rapid movement the term is often used descriptively, as in "quick as a fairy diddle."

Fall Foliage

The leaves of the deciduous trees of the hardwood forest drop each autumn. Just before falling, they suddenly glow with color. This annual pageant has tremendous visual appeal and is the main attraction of the state's fall tourism season. The eastern United States is the best place in the world to see colorful foliage.

Changing day length determines the onset of fall color. As summer ages, the days become shorter. When the appropriate day length is reached, a hormone begins to form in the leaves of hardwood trees. This chemical diffuses downward in the outer ring of the leaf stem cells, causing an abscission layer where the leaf stem is attached to the twig. The abscission layer begins near the outer edge of the leaf stem and grows inwardly, slowly decreasing the flow of water into the leaf. Chlorophyll, which provides the leaf's green color, can exist only in the presence of water. As the leaf is strangled, the chlorophyll breaks down and other pigments, which have been masked by the green, begin to show through. Carotenoids and xanthophylls provide the yellow and brownish colors of the fall foliage display. The reds are from anthocyanin, a pigment created by the conversion of sugar that can no longer move out of the leaf.

Trees have their own distinct colors. By early September sumac is a bright red. Birch turns golden; aspen greenish-gold; sugar maple reddish-orange to gold; soft maple ruby red; black gum deep red; hickories bright yellow; white ash and sourwood bluish to purplish; sassafras reddish becoming yellow; American beech yellowish to brown; flowering dogwood deep red; sycamore brown; yellow poplar bright yellow; and oaks leathery brown, although white oak is occasionally a deep burgundy and scarlet oak is named for its bright red color.

The leaves first color and then fall, a process essentially complete by Halloween. Leaf color usually peaks in the higher mountains and northern counties of West Virginia by late September and in the southern counties by mid-October. By November, nearly all of the colorful leaves have dropped, except on white oaks and American beech, which often hold some leaves until spring.

William H. Gillespie
Charleston

Fallen Timbers, Battle of

The Battle of Fallen Timbers, fought near present Toledo, Ohio, on August 20, 1794, ended the frontier era for Western Virginia and a long period of Indian warfare.

The Ohio Valley region had been a contested battleground, or "middle ground," from the 1750s through the American Revolution, and Indians continued raids into Western Virginia throughout the 1780s. In the late 1780s, relative peace encouraged the settlement of approximately 18,000 people in the six Virginia counties established in or west of the Appalachians in what would become West Virginia. The movement of settlers into the disputed territory west of the Ohio River and the failure of negotiations between the United States and the Native Americans, led to confrontation and war. Two disastrous defeats of the national army by the natives in 1790 and 1791 made Virginia settlers fear renewed raids.

In 1792, the United States raised a small army, appointed Gen. "Mad Anthony" Wayne as its commander, and continued its effort to negotiate a peace treaty. When these efforts failed, Wayne and his army advanced into the Maumee Valley of Ohio during the summer of 1794. They destroyed Indian villages and gardens, and decisively defeated a tribal coalition led by Little Turtle, Blue Jacket, and others at Fallen Timbers. The natives—defeated in action, starving, and realizing that the British would not assist them—finally conceded to the Americans in the 1795 Treaty of Greenville, which granted most of Ohio to the United States.

Van Beck Hall
Pittsburgh, Pennsylvania

Family Life

West Virginia families represent different cultures, work in different occupations, and live in different environments. Early settlers found themselves in an area where mountains and rivers created natural barriers and a sense of protection and isolation that contributed to family attachment. West Virginia families are still close, and in a state much more rural than the national average they still have space available for many outdoor activities.

A large majority of Mountain State families own their own homes. The 75.2 percent home ownership rate in 2000 was higher than the national average of 67.4 percent, and among the very highest in the country. Mostly, the houses are not luxurious. Many families live in houses that are more than 50 years old, and many with newer houses live in mobile homes or other manufactured housing. West Virginia families are emotionally attached to their homes regardless of the age or state of repair.

Family size has decreased, the number of older citizens has increased, and the number of children has decreased in modern times. In 2000, people 65 and over represented 15.3 percent of the population of West Virginia, while the national average was 12.4 percent. Youths under 18 years of age represented 22.3 percent of the population, with the national average being 25.7 percent. During the last two decades of the 20th century, the teen birth rate moved from substantially higher than the national rate to somewhat lower. The average household at the time of the 2000 census was 2.40 persons while the national average was 2.57 persons. Single-parent families are becoming more common.

The number of families in the state increased from the time of early settlement until the middle of the 20th century. At mid-century, families began to move away from West Virginia to seek employment. Many who have found it necessary to relocate for employment yearn to return to their extended family and their mountain home. Near the end of the century, some areas began again to show an increase in the number of families.

Family income in West Virginia lags behind the nation; therefore the amount of money available to spend on family support is limited. The median household income in 2004 was $32,589 while the national figure was $44,473.

The extended family remains important in West Virginia. Many families that have been in the state for more than one generation have family members clustered near their parents and siblings. Living in a home with a grandparent present is not uncommon. Cousins, grandparents, uncles, and aunts form influential kinship groups that have tremendous hold upon the group members and offer both emotional and material support.

Gender roles remain distinct in many West Virginia homes. Families include those who are responsible for making the living, traditionally men, and those who make the home, traditionally women. Two-paycheck families are increasingly common, but West Virginia has the lowest rate of women in the work force in the country. Women made up 45 percent of the West Virginia work force in 2000.

Child rearing frequently involves the whole family. Child care for working parents is often provided by grandparents or other relatives. Older children, neighbors, and relatives cherish the opportunity to hold, care for, and play with small children. Children often are indulged, perhaps beyond what might seem wise in other cultures. In the best cases they grow up surrounded by many loving, supportive adults in a variety of kinship connections.

Ora Beth Drake
WVU Extension Service, Retired

Farm Bureau

The West Virginia Farm Bureau Federation, the largest farm organization in the state, was created in 1918. Predecessor associations, known by various names including farm bureau, farm club, agricultural club, and farm cooperative, had been organized about 10 years earlier. The American Farm Bureau was organized in 1919, with West Virginia one of the states urging organization of the national group.

The West Virginia Farm Bureau directed its first efforts toward supporting agricultural programs and lobbying the legislature for better roads and favorable taxation of farm land. It helped to get a cooperative marketing law passed in 1923 and organized the West Virginia Farm Bureau Service Company under this law in 1925. The service company, which operated co-op farm supply stores, flourished until it was sold to Southern States Cooperative in 1941.

In 1928, the Farm Bureau created the insurance division to offer insurance to its membership. The insurance program continues today and represents an important function of the Farm Bureau. The Farm Bureau continues to lobby the legislature, as well, on issues of land use, property rights, and regulatory actions affecting agriculture. The West Virginia Farm Bureau has a membership of approximately 14,000 families.

See also Agriculture

Charles Sperow
Morgantown

Farm Security Administration

Established in 1937 as part of Franklin Roosevelt's New Deal, the Farm Security Administration sought to help the neediest farmers through loans, management advice, community equipment purchases, and, on a limited scale, medical insurance. One of its goals was to reduce farm tenancy, which prevailed on 25 percent of all West Virginia farms by 1939, and a few tenants received favorable mortgages, enabling them to purchase farms. Also, FSA photographers helped call attention to rural poverty, with Walker Evans, John Collier, Arthur Rothstein, Marion Post Wolcott, and Ben Shahn among those active in West Virginia. One of the most promising of New Deal efforts to address rural poverty and to keep farmers on the land, the agency never obtained the funding to achieve its statutory goals or to fully assess the causes of rural poverty. The FSA came to an end in 1942 because of the exigencies of war and waning congressional support for New Deal reformism.

See also New Deal

Jerry Bruce Thomas
Shepherd University

Farmington Mine Disaster

It was on a damp, cold morning on November 20, 1968, when a gas and dust explosion occurred in Consolidation Coal Company's No. 9 mine in the great Pittsburgh coal seam near Farmington and Mannington. There had been deadly explosions in the mine in 1901 and 1954, but this was far worse. A large cloud of black smoke and red flames spewed from the pit opening, and rock and debris were catapulted from the mine.

Twenty-one miners managed to scramble to safety, but another 78 men were not as fortunate. Attempts at rescue were delayed until the fires could be extinguished. For days afterward rescuers from across the coalfields worked amidst the debris, some of it dangerously unstable, looking to find and dig out survivors. Finally, after nine days, the mine was ordered sealed, a step that had been delayed out of consideration of the relatives of men inside. The mine was reopened a year later and most of the bodies removed, although 19 corpses were never recovered.

The legal and political consequences were profound. Shocked by the Farmington carnage, a mine safety conference was convened in Washington to discuss working conditions in the nation's coal mines. As a result of the disaster, national attention was brought to the issue of mine safety in late 1968 and early 1969. Congress and the Nixon administration responded with the passage of the 1969 federal Coal Mine Health and Safety Act. The federal law enacted strict prohibitions against miners working under unsupported roof, imposed tougher ventilation provisions, and gave federal mine inspectors the power to close any unsafe coal operation. The disaster also contributed to the eventual unseating of the corrupt United Mine Workers president,

Farmington mine disaster, November 1968.

Tony Boyle, who angered many by defending Consolidation Coal after the explosion.

See also Tony Boyle, Coal Mine Disasters, Coal Mine Health and Safety Legislation

Jeffrey B. Cook
North Greenville College

John Braithwaite, *To Punish or Persuade: Enforcement of Coal Mine Safety*, 1985; Brit Hume, *Death and the Mines, Rebellion and Murder in the UMW*, 1971.

Daniel D. T. Farnsworth

Governor and state founder Daniel Duane Tompkins Farnsworth was West Virginia's second chief executive and the one to serve the shortest term (February 26 to March 4, 1869).

Born on Staten Island, New York, December 23, 1819, Farnsworth came to what is now Upshur County in June 1821 with his parents and grandparents. His grandfather, also named Daniel, contracted Joel Westfall to build the first house in Buckhannon, a two-story, hewn-log structure on lot no. 27. When he was 15, the future governor went to Clarksburg to learn the tailor's trade, a profession he followed for 13 years. He then carried on a mercantile business in Buckhannon for another 13 years before he turned to farming. Farnsworth owned stock in several ventures, including a large flour mill on the island in Buckhannon, a railroad that ran from Clarksburg to Buckhannon, and the Buckhannon bank.

Farnsworth was one of the early magistrates of the new county of Upshur (1851) and, in later life, was an advocate of equal rights and the protection of labor. In 1860, he was elected to an abortive term in the House of Delegates of the Virginia General Assembly. As Virginia moved to secede from the Union, Farnsworth chose to serve during the summer of 1861 in the Second Wheeling Convention and there helped to create the loyal Reorganized Government of Virginia and later the new state of West Virginia. As an elected member of the General Assembly, he was seated as an ex-officio member at Wheeling. During the August session of the Second Wheeling Convention, Farnsworth served on a committee to establish the boundaries of the new state. The committee made its proposal on August 20, and the convention adopted the recommendations with a vote of 50 to 28.

Farnsworth was a fiery Unionist. Once, while speaking in Philippi, he defied the rebel soldiers who threatened to shoot him if he persisted. He declared that he would never be silent while he could speak for his country and its flag. Farnsworth was elected to the first House of Delegates of the new state of West Virginia, and later to the state senate. As state senate president, Farnsworth suc-

Governor Daniel D. T. Farnsworth (1819–92).

ceeded Governor Boreman, who resigned in the last days of his term after being elected as a U.S. senator by the state legislature. Farnsworth served seven days, until March 4, 1869, when William E. Stevenson, the third governor, began the term to which he had been elected the previous fall. Farnsworth was 49 at the time. Upon completion of his short term, Farnsworth, a Republican, returned to his state senate seat, where he served a total of seven years. Farnsworth also participated in the Constitutional Convention of 1872, during which he helped debar railroad company officers from serving in the state legislature. Farnsworth feared that if the railroad companies grew too powerful, it would be detrimental for the development of the state.

Farnsworth was twice married, first to Ann M. Gibson (1824–52) of Harrison County, and then to Mary J. Ireland (1830–1923). Six children were born of the first marriage and 10 of the second.

Farnsworth was in his 73rd year when he died December 5, 1892, at his home on Main Avenue, Buckhannon. He was interred in the Heavener Cemetery. Numerous progeny reside in the central West Virginia area, including his great-great-grandson, Daniel D. T. Farnsworth IV, a Weston optometrist. The governor's home has been restored and is operated as a bed and breakfast.

Joy Gregoire Gilchrist-Stalnaker
Horner

Guy F. Bailey, *The Farnsworth Family*, unpublished manuscript, Horner: Central West Virginia Genealogy and History Library; John G. Morgan, *West Virginia Governors*, 1980; *West Virginia Heritage Encyclopedia*, 1976.

Fasnacht

Fasnacht is the last wild splurge before Lent, the ancient Christian period of fasting, self reflection, penance, and abstinence from meat beginning on Ash Wednesday and lasting 40 days until Easter.

Corresponding to Mardi Gras, Carnival, and similar celebrations, the Fasnacht was brought to Randolph County from Switzerland by the settlers of Helvetia. They combined this traditionally Catholic celebration with the Protestant Winterfest of Zurich, wherein Old Man Winter is burned in effigy to hasten the advent of spring.

Helvetians prepare for Fasnacht by deep-frying donuts, rosettes, and hosenblatt pastries in lard, a meat by-product foregone during Lent. They decorate the community hall in colorful Swiss lampions (paper lanterns with candles), ribbons, and a gruesome Old Man Winter hanging by the neck in the middle of the dance floor. And they create elaborate masks.

At dark on the Saturday night before Ash Wednesday, the villagers and guests don their masks, congregate at the local restaurant, light lampions, then proceed up the road to the community hall where they parade around the dance floor as their masks are judged. They dance schotisches, waltzes, polkas, and squares until midnight, when the fiddler announces the hour to burn Old Man Winter. The prettiest maiden then mounts the shoulders of the tallest man and cuts down the ghoul. He is dragged out into the snow, roughed up and cursed, then thrown onto the bonfire amid applause.

See also Helvetia

Bruce Betler
Elkins

David Sutton, *One's Own Hearth is Like Gold: A History of Helvetia*, 1990.

Charles James Faulkner

Statesman Charles James Faulkner, the son of an Irish immigrant, was born July 6, 1806, in Martinsburg. Faulkner attended Georgetown College (now Georgetown University) in Washington and studied law in Winchester, Virginia. He entered the Virginia General Assembly at age 22 in 1829, his first political race. In 1833, Faulkner married Mary W. Boyd, the youngest daughter of Gen. Elisha Boyd, and through her acquired the plantation of Boydville and other properties. Faulkner served also in the West Virginia legislature, U.S. Congress (1851–59), and as U.S. minister to France.

In 1832, Faulkner spoke publicly for the gradual elimination of slavery. He advocated Western Virginia interests, such as voting rights for all white males regardless of property, when Virginia rewrote its constitution in 1850–51.

Faulkner was U.S. minister to France for 14 months before the Civil War. In 1861, he delivered his last report to Secretary of State William Seward. As Faulkner headed home to Martinsburg, Seward had him arrested as a suspected Southern sympathizer. He was never formally charged. Seward offered to release

Faulkner if he would swear an oath of allegiance. Faulkner refused and was eventually traded for another prisoner. During the Civil War, Faulkner served on Stonewall Jackson's staff.

After the war and the creation of West Virginia, Faulkner again refused an oath of allegiance to the United States and recovered his law license only with difficulty. Nonetheless, when Virginia sued to regain the counties of Berkeley and Jefferson, West Virginia called on Faulkner to represent the new state's interests at the U.S. Supreme Court. He was a voice of restraint as a delegate to West Virginia's Constitutional Convention of 1872, in which ex-Confederates set out to undo much of the 1863 Constitution, which they considered too Northern.

Faulkner died on November 1, 1884, in Martinsburg. Son Charles James Faulkner Jr., served West Virginia as a U.S. senator (1887–99), while his great-grandson, U.S. Senator Harry F. Byrd, ruled Virginia politics for many years in the 20th century. Boydville, the Boyd-Faulkner home, a Martinsburg landmark, is on the National Register of Historic Places.

See also Harry F. Byrd

Dawn Miller
Charleston

Donald Rusk McVeigh, "Charles James Faulkner: Reluctant Rebel," Ph.D. dissertation, West Virginia University, 1954.

Fauna

The fauna of West Virginia include all those animals typically identified as wild. Those animals that have been domesticated and kept in captivity, such as dogs, cats, horses, cattle, sheep, goats, and pigs are usually not included.

There are two basic groups, vertebrates and invertebrates. The vertebrates have a backbone, a bony internal skeleton, and limbs (legs or wings or fins) that are supported by several specialized bones. Vertebrates include mammals such as bear, deer, squirrels, rabbits, and bats; birds such as ducks, geese, grouse, turkey, hawks, eagles, robins, and hummingbirds; reptiles such as lizards, snakes, and turtles; amphibians such as salamanders, frogs, and toads; and fish such as bass, trout, catfish, carp, shiners, and bluegill.

In contrast, the invertebrates do not have a bony internal skeleton. Some have a hard outer skeleton (an exoskeleton) that supports their body shape, but have no bony structures within their bodies. Butterflies, bees, grasshoppers, crayfish, clams, snails, and spiders are some of the common invertebrate fauna with an exoskeleton. Other invertebrate fauna, such as earthworms, flatworms, and tapeworms, lack both an internal skeleton and an outer exoskeleton.

There are six major faunal groups present in West Virginia: (1) flatworms (planaria, flukes, and flatworms); (2) roundworms (hookworms and heartworms); (3) annelids (earthworms); (4) arthropods (insects, centipedes, millipedes, spiders, ticks, mites, and crayfish); (5) mollusks (snails, slugs, clams, and mussels); and (6) vertebrates (mammals, birds, reptiles, amphibians, and fish).

Biologists have reliable estimates of the numbers of different kinds of vertebrates that live in West Virginia: 63 species of mammals, 321 birds, 39 reptiles, 48 amphibians, and 178 fish. Invertebrates have not been nearly so well studied. Surveys indicate there are 16 species of mosquitoes, 18 species of crayfish, 68 species of horse flies and deer flies, 106 species of stoneflies, 120 species of mayflies, 130 species of butterflies, 176 species of caddisflies, 58 species of mussels (clams), 200 species of damselflies and dragonflies, more than 500 species of spiders, and more than 700 species of macromoths in West Virginia. Due to the small size, secretive behavior, and difficulties of identification of many other invertebrate groups, biologists have not been able to estimate their numbers. Certainly, the numbers of species of invertebrates greatly exceed the numbers of species of vertebrates. Likewise, the total number of individual invertebrates greatly exceeds the total number of individual vertebrates. The total number of species of West Virginia fauna probably exceeds 10,000.

West Virginia animals are quite diversified, due to the variety of habitats. Climate, geology, soils, and topography have combined in West Virginia to produce distinct plant communities. This diversity of plant communities is directly responsible for the diversity of the state's fauna. Every county and every habitat support a wide variety of animals.

West Virginia animals range in size from more than 500 pounds for the black bear to the countless microscopic invertebrate forms. They occur in the soil, in the water, in grass, and in trees. They run, jump, swim, crawl, burrow, and fly. Some have more than one mode of travel. Most are dependent on specific plant communities to provide their food, water, and shelter. Others are parasites and live on the inside or outside of other fauna. While some are nocturnal, others are diurnal.

Certain animals are specialists and occur only in specific habitats in specific regions of West Virginia. Several species (such as fish) are restricted to water. Cool mountain streams suffice for brook trout, while the slow-moving, warm rivers are ideal habitat for carp and catfish. Cave species are among the most specialized of all West Virginia fauna. Such groups as the cave crickets, cave crayfish, and cave salamanders spend their entire lives in darkness. Some beetles, such as the cobblestone tiger beetle, exist only on the gravel bars along islands in the Ohio River. The West Virginia northern flying squirrel and the Cheat Mountain salamander are restricted to the red spruce forests above 3,000 feet, while the northern water shrew is restricted to swiftly flowing, rocky-bedded streams at higher elevations.

Many other faunal species are generalists and live in almost every habitat in every county of West Virginia. Examples are the white-tailed deer, gray squirrel, cottontail rabbit, blue jay, cardinal, robin, spring peeper, American toad, box turtle, largemouth bass, bluegill, black bullhead, eastern tiger swallowtail, and silver-spotted skipper.

A few of the fauna are endemic to West Virginia, meaning they are found nowhere else. The best-known examples are the Cheat Mountain salamander and the West Virginia spring salamander.

Most West Virginia animals are resident species, spending their entire lifetime within our state's boundaries. All fish, amphibians, and reptiles, and most mammals (with the possible exception of a few bats), are year-round residents. All invertebrates, with the exception of a few species of butterflies such as the Monarch, are also year-round residents. Other animals are seasonal visitors, spending part of the year in West Virginia and migrating to some other area for the remainder of the year. Birds are the most obvious seasonal visitors. Some, such as the warblers, nest in West Virginia during summer months but migrate to Central America for the winter. Others, including waterfowl, pass through West Virginia while migrating between wintering grounds in southern coastal states and nesting grounds in Canada. A rare few, such as the rough-legged hawk that nests in Canada, are present in West Virginia only during winter months.

The last great change to affect West Virginia fauna was the Ice Age of Pleistocene times, approximately 10,000 B.C. Although glaciers never reached the region that is now West Virginia, there was permanent snow cover over much of the present state during most of the year. Tundra vegetation, and later northern boreal vegetation, dominated this region, with such species as balsam fir and red spruce covering much of the area, extending from mountaintops to river bottoms. Many northern species of animals occupied West Virginia during that long period of continual winter. But, as the climate warmed and the great ice sheets melted and receded northward, a retreat of northern plants and animals took place. The climate in the river valleys and other lowlands was too warm for northern species, and only those at the highest elevations, 4,000 to 5,000 feet, survived.

At these heights, the climate remained suitable for northern species such as the northern flying squirrel, snowshoe hare, and Cheat Mountain salamander. These are some of the northern fauna that today are considered to be relicts of the Ice Age.

The West Virginia fauna are again faced with a changing environment, this time due to humans, not to natural climate changes. Land-use practices during the past 200 years resulted in many changes to our state's fauna. Some species disappeared from West Virginia, while new species appeared. The clearing of lands by early settlers to create farms had both negative and positive impacts on our native animals. The passenger pigeon, timber wolf, bison, and elk disappeared. The mountain lion, beaver, river otter, and golden eagle were greatly reduced. In contrast, the bobwhite quail, barn owl, and opossum quickly adapted to these new habitats, and their numbers increased.

At the same time that some of the native fauna were being reduced, new animals became established in the Mountain State. Some were introduced intentionally and others accidentally. Some of the exotic fauna that are present throughout much of the state today include the English sparrow, European starling, carp, brown trout, rainbow trout, gypsy moth, honey bee, and zebra mussel.

Many developments impacted our fauna during the past 100 years, including logging, pesticides, acid precipitation, and the chestnut blight. One of the most significant was the damming of rivers. West Virginia has no natural lakes, apart from one small pond, thus those fauna that required deep lake waters typically did not exist here. As dams were constructed on the Ohio River and on the Bluestone, Cheat, Elk, Gauley, Guyandotte, Little Kanawha, Tygart, and West Fork rivers, vast acreages of new habitat were created. Birds, such as bald eagles, Canada geese, and cormorants, are the most obvious fauna that have been attracted to this new habitat.

The West Virginia fauna of today are a mix of four distinct groups: (1) native species that are similar to those that occupied the mountains before white settlement; (2) exotic species that were accidentally or intentionally introduced by humans; (3) species that have naturally invaded from the south and occupy the lower southern river bottoms, and (4) relict species from the last Ice Age that occupy the higher elevations.

Edwin D. Michael
Morgantown

Fayette County

Fayette County is located in south-central West Virginia, north of Beckley. Its land area is 666.5 square miles, and its 2000 population was 47,579. Named for the

The Fayette County countryside.

Marquis de Lafayette, Fayette County was formed by the General Assembly of Virginia in 1831. Its territory was carved from Kanawha, Nicholas, Greenbrier, and Logan counties. Parts of Fayette were taken to create Raleigh County in 1850 and Summers in 1871.

The county consists of a high plateau bordered on the east by Sewell Mountain and on the west by the Kanawha Valley. Flowing from southeast to northwest, the New River segments the county with its deep gorge, joining the Gauley to form the Kanawha River at Gauley Bridge.

The remains of prehistoric settlement have been located, notably between Armstrong and Loup creeks. Indian trails and campsites along New River and its tributaries yield information about movement of the natives. The Paint Creek valley was a thoroughfare for Shawnee raiders traveling to and from the eastern settlements, and it was along this stream that Mary Draper Ingles was carried from Virginia into captivity in Ohio in 1755. European settlement came in the late 18th century, largely along the rivers.

The county seat was first set in New Haven on the north side of New River, but was moved to the southside town of Vandalia (later Fayetteville) in 1837. In its first census, Fayette County in 1840 had 3,924 residents. On the eve of the Civil War, the county had 5,997 residents in 1860, 271 of whom were slaves. Residents divided on the issues severing the state and nation, and the ensuing warfare caused great destruction in the county. Robert E. Lee commanded in Fayette County in the fall of 1861. Strategically located Gauley Bridge saw repeated action, and the locally decisive Battle of Fayetteville was fought in fall 1862. The Confederate Thurmond's Rangers were among the local units operating in the area.

The building of the Chesapeake & Ohio Railway through the New River Gorge,

completed on January 29, 1873, opened the rich New River coalfield and a new industrial era. Many mining towns were built in the gorge and on the plateau, bringing boom times. The population jumped from 6,647 in 1870 to 60,377 by 1920, but Fayette remained rural with no town exceeding 2,500 people. Fayette was the leading coal producing county in West Virginia from 1888 through 1903, when it yielded to McDowell County.

Building the railroads and working the mines intensified demand for labor. Southern and eastern Europeans and African-Americans from the southern states migrated into the county. Their cultural influence on the county remains. Christopher Payne of Montgomery was the first African-American elected to the state legislature, in 1896, followed in 1902 by James M. Ellis of Oak Hill. In 1942, Camp Washington-Carver opened as a state 4-H camp for African-Americans, the first of its kind in the nation.

Accompanying the rapid industrialization were disastrous mine explosions such as those at Red Ash (1900), Rush Run (1905), and Parral (1906), and protracted labor strikes in 1902 and 1912–13. The most devastating industrial disaster, one of the worst in the nation's history, occurred during the building (1930–35) of the tunnel to harness the hydroelectric power of New River at Hawks Nest. More than 700 men, the majority of whom were black migrants, died of silicosis.

The development of towns depended upon geography and the economy. The mountainous eastern section of the county had no large towns; Fayetteville was the town center of the plateau south of New River until the growth of Oak Hill and Mount Hope in the 20th century. Towns in the western section of the county developed as Gauley Bridge and Montgomery grew on the banks of the Kanawha River. The northside plateau town of

FAST FACTS ABOUT FAYETTE COUNTY

Founded: 1831

Land in square miles: 666.5

Population: 47,579

Percentage minorities: 7.3%

Percentage rural: 60.4%

Median age: 39.6

Percentage 65 and older: 16.4%

Birth rate per 1,000 population: 12.0

Median household income: $24,788

High school graduate or higher: 68.6%

Bachelor's degree or higher: 10.7%

Home ownership: 77.2%

Median home value: $50,800

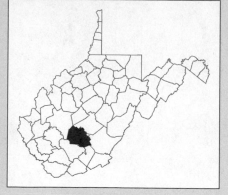

This information is from the 2000 U.S. Census. In 2000, West Virginia as a whole had 5 percent minorities, a median age of 38.9, median household income of $29,696, and a 75.2 percent home ownership rate.

Ansted, incorporated in 1891, became prominent in the industrial period.

The C&O's New River main line provided the county's economic lifeline. Inhabitants of New River Gorge, now almost empty of residents, outnumbered those living on the plateau during the coal heyday. Thurmond, a town in the gorge, boomed as a coal-shipping rail center, and Sewell was once offered as a new site for the county seat. The unique town of Kaymoor sprang up, with Kaymoor Bottom located on the gorge floor and Kaymoor Top on the rim of the gorge. The Kaymoor mine was located on the mountainside in between.

With coal in decline after mid-century, towns disappeared and the population fell from its 1950 peak of 82,443. Road construction helped to move Fayette County away from the gorge and the railroad located there. Although the earlier James River & Kanawha Turnpike (1825), the Giles, Fayette & Kanawha Turnpike (1848), and later secondary roads served the county well, late 20th-century arteries linked Fayette to the expanding interstate highway system. The West Virginia Turnpike (Interstate 64-77) traverses western Fayette County. Busy U.S. 19 (Appalachian Corridor L) runs northeasterly through the county, crossing the spectacular New River Gorge bridge, the county's chief landmark.

Fayette County's rushing streams and rugged terrain, which once hindered development, are major assets in the tourist industry. Whitewater rafting on the New and Gauley rivers offers excitement to both beginning and experienced rafters. Rock climbing, mountain biking, hiking, and fishing attract visitors, while the National Park Service expanded its operations at the New River Gorge National River. Older state parks such as Babcock and Hawks Nest remain popular.

Fayette County has had its share of colorful, powerful, and notable people. The Civil War years pitted Confederate William D. Thurmond against Unionist James C. Montgomery, and brought forth the financier, philanthropist, and county sheriff, Morris Harvey. Leaders in the industrial era included such powerful figures as Joseph L. Beury, John Nuttall, "King" Samuel Dixon, William H. McKell, George W. Imboden, William Nelson Page, and others. "Pistol" Nell Walker of Sewell, the longest serving female legislator (1940–62), gained fame by disarming a bank robber in the Winona National Bank. Mount Hope resident and double amputee Okey L. Patteson served as governor of West Virginia.

In addition to Fayetteville, the county's leading towns are Montgomery, Oak Hill, Ansted, Mount Hope, and Gauley Bridge. The West Virginia University Institute of Technology, a state-supported school established in 1895, is located at Montgomery.

See also Fayetteville, Hawks Nest Tunnel Disaster, New River Gorge Bridge, Thurmond

Lou Athey
Franklin & Marshall College

Tim McKinney, *The Civil War in Fayette County, West Virginia,* 1988; J. T. Peters and H. B. Carden, *History of Fayette County, West Virginia,* 1926; Fayette County Chamber of Commerce, *History of Fayette County, West Virginia,* 1993.

Fayetteville

The county seat of Fayette County, Fayetteville sits on the plateau south of New River. Originally called Vandalia because of its location on Abraham Vandal's farm, it became county seat in 1837. The name was later changed to Fayetteville.

Located on the Giles, Fayette & Kanawha Turnpike, the town remained small until after the Civil War. Fortified and attacked by both sides during the war, the town was devastated and its courthouse destroyed. The completion of the Chesapeake & Ohio Railway through the New River Gorge in 1873 accelerated population growth in the county, but the town was handicapped since it was located a few miles away from the nearest point on the railroad and much of that distance was precipitous mountainside. Two attempts in the early 20th century to fund construction of an electric trolley from Fayetteville to the railroad failed, but building a road connecting the town to the railroad solved the problem. Widespread automobile use and new highway construction assured that Fayetteville, incorporated under that name in 1883, would remain the county seat.

Fayetteville prospered as the county became a leading coal producer after 1880, and it declined after 1950. The New River Gorge bridge, completed in 1976, and an emerging tourism-based economy spurred economic activity among motels, bed-and-breakfasts, restaurants, and other businesses related to whitewater rafting and other outdoor activities. In the 2000 census Fayetteville's population reached 2,754, a gain of 26 percent over the census of 1990.

A distinct historic courthouse, built in 1895 in the town center, is the centerpiece of Fayetteville. Prominent citizens have included financier-philanthropist Morris Harvey, and two governors of West Virginia, Okey L. Patteson and Homer A. Holt. The proud heritage of its citizens is celebrated in the New River Gorge Heritage Festival held each year in Fayetteville on July 4.

See also Fayette County

Lou Athey
Franklin & Marshall College

J. T. Peters and H. B. Carden, *History of Fayette County, West Virginia,* 1926; Fayette County Chamber of Commerce, *History of Fayette County, West Virginia,* 1993.

FBI Center

In July 1995, the Federal Bureau of Investigation completed construction on its Criminal Justice Information Services Division complex in Clarksburg. The $200 million complex, located on 986 acres, is the national repository for the FBI's law enforcement records.

The division provides information on individuals, stolen property, criminal organizations, and activities to the FBI and other law enforcement, academic, employment, and licensing agencies. The division administers five programs: Fingerprint Identification, National Crime Information Center, National Instant Criminal Background Check System, Uniform Crime Reporting, and Law Enforcement Online.

The fingerprint program receives nearly 41,000 submissions per day. The FBI processes electronically submitted fingerprints and reports the findings within two hours in criminal cases and within 24 hours in civil cases.

The crime information program maintains a computerized index that can search for names, mug shots, fingerprints, and law enforcement records. A nationwide service, the database is available to law enforcement agencies 24 hours a day, 365 days a year.

The background check system identifies people who are prohibited from buying firearms. The crime reporting program compiles, analyzes, and publishes crime data.

The FBI's on-line information is available to law enforcement agencies to help them coordinate efforts to counter violent crimes, money laundering, organized crime, and terrorism, and to protect the country's infrastructure against attack.

The six-building complex includes a 500,000-square-foot main building which has a 600-seat cafeteria, 500-seat auditorium, and a 100,000-square foot computer center. More than 2,700 employees work at the complex.

Fences

The construction of fences around agricultural fields has been a tradition in West Virginia since the beginning of European settlement. As with other practices, the early settlers brought with them the fence-building methods of their forebears.

Fences were generally used only for the crop fields directly adjacent to the house and associated outbuildings. There was insufficient labor to fence off pastureland, and it was common practice to let livestock run freely until time for slaughter. To distinguish the ownership of livestock, ears were cropped in distinctive patterns.

Early fences were primarily wooden, made from the abundant timber. Some dry-laid and mortared rock fences were constructed in areas where limestone was plentiful, particularly the Eastern Panhandle. Most wooden fences were built in the worm style, consisting of split rails laid horizontally in a zigzag pattern. This style of fence originated in Scandinavia and was easy to construct. Worm fences took up an excessive amount of land, however, with the area within the zigzags on both sides of the fence impossible to plow. Post-and-rail fences, built by suspending rails between posts set into the ground, solved this problem since the posts ran in a direct line. Such fences used considerably less land and timber but were labor intensive. Once sawmills appeared board fences replaced earlier worm or post-and-rail fences.

The immediate house yard and kitchen garden were often enclosed with a picket or paling fence. The upright palings, pointed to discourage poultry from land-

Split-rail fences

"The split-rail fences bound in the pastures, with now and then a gate or a bar of poles.
"For the most part the chestnut timber was felled and split.
"There was art or what the natives called a 'sleight' in this, as there was art in laying the worm for the fence—the first line of rails, each corner on a stone, upon which the structure of the fence was to be erected; after which it was finished with a stake and rider. The great pastures running to the crest of the mountains were all enclosed with this fence. The haystacks standing in the meadows had a foundation of these rails for a base. They were enclosed by a like fence with a high rider to hold out the bullock, until the heavy snows came."

—Melville Davisson Post
"The Mystery at Hillhouse"
(1928)

ing, were nailed to horizontal crosspieces that were themselves attached to the fence posts. The palings were split like shingles with a froe, or made of sawed wood in later times. A well-made paling fence provided a tight, attractive enclosure.

The invention of barbed wire in the latter part of the 19th century made possible the fencing of large expanses of land that could never have been enclosed using traditional wood or rock fence techniques. Barbed wire had a profound impact upon farmers in West Virginia and throughout the United States. The open range could be enclosed. No longer was stock allowed to roam freely. Animals that had previously foraged at large now had to be provided with feed or pastured on land that the farmer owned.

More expensive woven wire fencing was also used to enclose fields, and in more recent times electric fences and high-tension wire. In recent years West Virginians have also tried by a variety of means to fence out deer, usually unsuccessfully.

Gates varied as well as fences. Simple hinged gates were most common, especially in board fences and wire fences. Gates, even large stock gates, were sometimes ingeniously weighted to close themselves. Zigzag fences and post-and-rail fences might be closed by replacing removable rails at the fence opening. Stone fences often had stiles, allowing one to cross by climbing up one side and down the other on rudimentary steps.

Whether wood, stone, or wire, fences helped to transform the countryside from a wilderness to an ordered agrarian landscape. With industrialization, practices continued to change. Laws that had governed the earlier agricultural society were rewritten during the late 19th and early 20th centuries. When West Virginia became a state in 1863, it inherited Virginia law and legal traditions that upheld the strict liability standard in cases involving the rights of farmers to use their property without interference from industry. In Virginia, agriculture continued

to enjoy legislative and judicial preference during the late 19th century, but the West Virginia Supreme Court increasingly gave priority to industry.

For example, the coming of the railroad brought the legal question of who was responsible for keeping the livestock off the railroad tracks, the farmer or the railroad. In Virginia, railroads were required to enclose their tracks, but in West Virginia the law dictated that farmers enclose their livestock. Farmers could sue the railroads for negligence if livestock were killed on the tracks, but the court placed the burden squarely on the farmers to prove that the engineer had been negligent in the operation of his locomotive, a practical impossibility. The logical progression of this legal reasoning culminated in 1919 when West Virginia enacted legislation that made it unlawful for livestock to be on the railroad right of way at all, with a penalty if this trespass resulted in an injury to the railroad.

Ronald L. Lewis
West Virginia University
John E. Adkins
Wilbur Smith Associates

Ronald L. Lewis, *Transforming the Appalachian Countryside: Railroads, Deforestation, and Social Change in West Virginia, 1880–1920*, 1998.

Fenton Art Glass Company

Fenton Art Glass Company opened in Martins Ferry, Ohio, in 1905 as a decorating firm, painting and embellishing glass made by others. Shortly thereafter the company saw the need for creating its own glass, and a factory was built at Williamstown, West Virginia, in 1906.

Fenton was the leader in producing iridescent pressed glass in imitation of Tiffany's expensive iridescent art glass. Collectors, decades later, named this "carnival glass," in the belief that it was given away at carnivals and fairs. It was predominantly sold as gifts and tableware in five-and-dime stores, which often bought Fenton glass in wooden barrel assortments. Fenton survived beyond a golden era of glass production that ended around 1910 by continually adding good-selling shapes, designs, and colors. When the second wave of closings swept the industry in the late 1970s and '80s, Fenton again survived because it continued to create new objects, colors, and decorative treatments.

Fenton produces glass by hand, often using a hand press to form the glass in metal molds. It has frequently experimented with art glass and high-end designer creations. Staples over the decades have included carnival glass, reintroduced in the late 1960s. Opal or "milk glass" sold well for decades, and in many forms the hobnail pattern was an exceptional sales line. Fenton, a family controlled company, created an on-site Ohio Valley glass museum and offers top-notch factory tours at its Williamstown plant.

See also Glass Industry

Dean Six
West Virginia Museum of American Glass
William Heacock, *Fenton Glass: The First 25 Years,* 1978.

Fernow Experimental Forest

The area that is now Fernow Experimental Forest, located on Elk Lick Run in the Monongahela National Forest, was recognized in 1934 as a typical example of West Virginia timberlands, based on plant and animal diversity, topography, timbering history, and climate. The forested watershed was set aside by the U.S. Forest Service for research use and named in memory of Bernhard E. Fernow, a pioneer in American forestry research. The experimental forest now totals 4,700 acres and concentrates on sustainable management and the impact of human activity on managed forestland.

Early research under the direction of George R. Trimble Jr. dealt with establishing and growing quality hardwoods. K. G. Reinhart simultaneously directed watershed research relating to floods and water yield. During the 1980s, Clay Smith directed research of various harvesting methods on the oaks, maples, beech, yellow poplar, and other trees common at Fernow. James H. Patric and Jim Kochenderfer continued leadership in water research with special emphasis on logging roads.

The headquarters for the Fernow Experimental Forest is the Timber and Watershed Lab located in Parsons. This lab was severely damaged by the November 1985 flood, but was renovated and continues to be a critical research unit for the U.S. Forest Service.

See also Monongahela National Forest
William N. Grafton
WVU Extension Service

Ferns

West Virginia's 87 species of ferns occupy many natural habitats throughout the state. Ferns play an important role in the

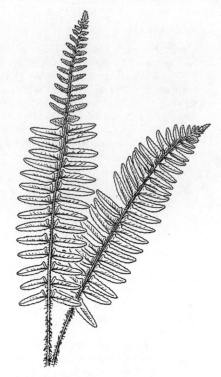

Christmas fern.

understory of both coniferous and deciduous woods. Though more prominently residents of moist-shady forests, ferns inhabit environments as divergent as peat bogs and the exposed faces of cliffs. Their delicate forms and textures add grace and beauty wherever they grow.

Most of our ferns are perennial, herbaceous plants. A few species are evergreen, such as Christmas fern. Christmas fern is found abundantly throughout West Virginia in the understory of various forest types. Its evergreen leaves have been used since Colonial times as an indoor decoration during the Christmas holidays.

Unlike flowering plants, ferns reproduce by producing microscopic spores on the undersides of their leaves, or, in the case of a few species, on separate spore-bearing stalks. Circular clusters of the elegant, six-to-seven-foot wands of cinnamon fern splay like fountains across wetland areas or on the periphery of lakes and streams. The spores are produced on large, cinnamon-colored stalks which usually grow within the center of the clustered leaves.

Each spring, new fern leaves emerge from the ground in a coiled spiral called a fiddle-head. Fern leaves unfurl gradually both laterally and vertically as they grow. The young fiddle-heads of several species of ferns are edible. They may be eaten raw, tossed into salads, or cooked in a little water and butter. The flavor is similar to that of asparagus.

Some of the more unusual types of ferns include climbing fern, filmy fern, rusty woodsia, Goldie's shield fern, and

adder's tongue fern. Climbing fern sends its wiry, three-to-four-foot stem across vegetation in glade-like habitats. Each little leaf is shaped somewhat like the palm of a hand. Rusty woodsia is found as far north as the Arctic. The delicate little filmy fern has close relatives in the tropics.

Emily Grafton
Morgantown

Harrison H. Ferrell

Dean Harrison Herbert Ferrell Jr. served West Virginia State College for 42 years. He was professor and chairman of German, 1928–66, and served the historically black college as dean and in other capacities from 1930 until 1970. Among West Virginia State's most distinguished leaders, he was known as simply "the Dean" to generations of college students.

Ferrell was born in Chicago, August 28, 1900. Stricken with polio in 1919, he learned to walk again but used a cane and leg braces for the rest of his life. He completed three degrees at Northwestern University, graduating with a Ph.D. in German philology in 1928. A musician of distinction, Ferrell played and taught the violin. In honor of his father, he founded the Ferrell Symphony Orchestra in Chicago before coming to West Virginia, the first all-black symphony orchestra in the United States.

Ferrell married Emily Miriam Grazia Bell on September 15, 1929. He died November 18, 1977. The Harrison H. Ferrell Administration Building was dedicated in his honor at West Virginia State College in 1980.

See also West Virginia State University
Ancella R. Bickley
Charleston
Grazia B. Ferrell, *The Dean: Harrison H. Ferrell,* 1981.

Ferries

Ferryboats have operated on the rivers of West Virginia since the days of early settlement. Ferries were well established by the end of the 18th century. By 1803, ferries operated across both the Ohio and Little Kanawha rivers at Parkersburg, across the Guyandotte and the Kanawha, and elsewhere. The types of ferries used were as varied as the streams they operated on, and they changed and improved over time.

The earliest and simplest ferries were canoes, skiffs, and rowboats, which transported only foot passengers. These were followed by larger boats capable of carrying livestock and horse-drawn vehicles and pulled across the river on a continuous cable loop attached to pulleys on each side of the stream. This cable-pulley system could be lowered to the bottom when other boats were traveling up or down the river, so as not to obstruct river traffic. The pulling of the ferry flatboat across the stream required a lot of manpower, although ingenious harnesses were sometimes contrived to allow the current to propel the ferry across the stream in both directions.

Animal-powered ferryboats or teamboats were used before the middle of the 19th century. Teamboats were outfitted with paddlewheels that were turned by animal power, usually by horses walking on a treadmill. A horse-powered ferry was advertised in the *Kanawha Register* in 1830, operating as the Charleston Middle Ferry at Charleston. With the coming of steam as a source of power, ferryboats were outfitted with steam engines and side wheels or sternwheels.

In the absence of bridges, ferries were an absolute necessity for any town located on a stream that wished to grow and prosper. Although operated privately, they were licensed by government as an important public service. Many ferry landings became identified by their operator's names and some, such as Harpers Ferry on the Potomac, gave their names to entire communities.

Where ferries were located was of great importance to the operator as well as the area he served. It was not unusual for town maps to include the location of all ferries. An 1850 map of Charleston shows Davidson's Ferry near the mouth of the Elk River and Goshorn's Ferry crossing the Kanawha River at Court Street. The 90-mile section of the New River area between the Narrows and Kanawha Falls exemplifies the importance of ferries along streams in West Virginia. Between 1761 and the 1940s, 27 ferries operated along this stretch of the New River.

Ferryboats were gradually replaced by bridges. In 2000, there were only four ferries still operating on the Ohio River, one of them from Sistersville, West Virginia, to Fly, Ohio. The Sistersville ferry has been running at the same location since 1817 and has been operated by the same family for four generations.

Gerald W. Sutphin
Huntington

Fesenmeier Brewery

Huntington's Fesenmeier Brewery was opened in 1899 when the Fesenmeier family arrived from Cumberland, Maryland, where they had been brewing beer since shortly after the Civil War. They purchased a defunct brewery located in what was then known as Central City. It had been built in 1891 by the American Brewing Company but failed to prosper and soon was closed. The Fesenmeiers were able to make the venture a success, and as Huntington grew—it annexed Central City in 1909—their brewery did a brisk business.

In 1914, when West Virginia voted for state prohibition, the brewery was con-verted into a meat-packing plant and, later, a cold-storage warehouse. In 1934, with the repeal of prohibition, it was reopened by the Fesenmeier company. Once again the brewery produced Fesenmeier and West Virginia brand beer, selling the latter under the slogan, "West Virginia, That'll Win Ya."

In the post–World War II era, however, small brewers such as Fesenmeier were unable to compete with the national brands and their multimillion-dollar advertising budgets. In 1968, the Fesenmeiers sold the faltering brewery and the new owner re-christened it the Little Switzerland Brewing Company. The handsome old brewery closed in 1971, and the next year was leveled to make way for a shopping center.

James E. Casto
Herald-Dispatch

Feuds

Feuds are a form of private warfare, organized along family lines and pitting one kinship group against another. These groups may include a single family and its kin on each side of the conflict, or an alliance of several families on each side; in either case, several surnames may be represented, as relatives, friends, and political or business associates are drawn into the struggle. Feuds typically occur in places where the formal institutions of government and law enforcement are absent or weak, leaving tribes or clans to enforce a rough justice according to their own notions. Feuding has deep roots in Europe, including areas of the British Isles that contributed heavily to the settlement of West Virginia.

The most notorious American feud was that between the West Virginia Hatfields and the Kentucky McCoys, fought in the Tug Valley largely in the 1880s. This was one of several vendettas occurring in central Appalachia, mainly Eastern Kentucky and its environs, during the late 19th century. The Turner-Howard feud, the French-Eversole feud, and the Tolliver-Martin feud are among the best known of the Kentucky feuds. The so-called Clay County War, involving the Bakers, Whites, and others, disrupted one Kentucky county for decades.

Apart from the single major exception of the Hatfields and McCoys, family feuds are uncommon in West Virginia's history. There have been periods of private warfare sometimes referred to as feuds but lacking the kinship factor. For example, a private war for control of the Bruen Lands was fought in Jackson and Roane counties in the 1870s and 1880s, between squatters on corporate lands and agents for the absentee land owners, including the colorful lawman Dan Cunningham. Vigilantism has occasionally occurred, as when the "Lincoln County Crew" took it upon itself to apprehend and execute two men suspected of ambushing storekeeper Allen Brumfield in 1889. Organized outlawry was more common, in events surrounding the Casto Hole in Jackson County, the Booger Hole in Clay County, the Black Hand among Italian immigrants, and in other instances. In none of these did combatants battle each other principally because of membership in opposing families, however.

The feuds came during an exceptional period of social strain and elevated violence within the mountain region, preceded by the bloody bushwhacker era during and after the Civil War and closely followed by the Mine Wars of the early 20th century. Violence became to some degree routinized during this period, sometimes involving otherwise respectable families for many years. The Hatfields, for example, took part in the guerrilla warfare of the Civil War era, then as feudists, and still later as active participants on both sides of the industrial violence that troubled their region. At the same time, the family was engaged in the full range of legitimate social and civic affairs, producing a governor of West Virginia soon after the feud and many local leaders, businessmen, and professionals.

Nonetheless, the cultural implications of feuding have been profound. The private wars fought by the Hatfields, McCoys, and others contributed to the creation of the hillbilly stereotype and to a regional reputation for violence, enduring parts of a folklore that West Virginia shares with the rest of Appalachia.

See also Bruen Lands Feud, Bushwhackers, Hatfield-McCoy Feud, Lincoln County Feud

Ken Sullivan
West Virginia Humanities Council
John Ed Pearce, *Days of Darkness: The Feuds of Eastern Kentucky*, 1994; Otis K. Rice, *The Hatfields and the McCoys*, 1982; David Hackett Fischer, *Albion's Seed: Four British Folkways in America*, 1989.

Fiddle Tradition

The tradition of playing the fiddle in all probability came to our mountains with settlers from the British Isles. Since then, West Virginia has produced some of the finest fiddlers in the nation, and continues to do so.

The overwhelming majority of fiddlers in West Virginia are unknown to the public stage. They play for their own enjoyment or for the entertainment of family and friends. It was not until recent times, with the birth and growth of traditional music festivals, that some fiddlers became widely known. For many years the West Virginia State Folk Festival in Glenville was about the only place that provided a venue for true mountain fiddlers. It was there that the Carpenters from Clay and Braxton counties were discovered. French Carpenter, who surfaced at

Fiddlers at the Pocahontas County Fair, August 1926.

Glenville in the late 1950s, became nationally known in traditional music circles.

West Virginia's best and most famous fiddler, Clark Kessinger, enjoyed a professional career in his youth, and was rediscovered in the late 1960s when he won the contest at the huge Union Grove festival in North Carolina. Braxton County's Melvin Wine enjoyed a national reputation for most of the last half of the 20th century, winning the prestigious National Heritage Fellowship of the National Endowment for the Arts.

Fiddle contests are probably older than West Virginia, but there is not much documented history on the subject. There is evidence that many county fairs featured such contests at one time, and there is oral evidence that they were common at rural social events.

During the last half of the 20th century, they became a staple at festivals in many rural West Virginia communities, as well as at the state's larger festivals. Many times the contests are divided into age categories, to allow for the declining dexterity of aging fiddlers. And while the junior divisions often provide the audience with some outstanding fiddling, it is the senior divisions that are more competitive and colorful.

One of the most intensive and competitive fiddle contests in our state has always been at the Glenville festival, even though the only prize is a blue ribbon. Clay County's Lee Triplett and Ira Mullins carried on a lifetime rivalry at Glenville, to the delight of the festival audience.

Many people still confuse commercial or Nashville-type fiddling with the lesser-known traditional fiddling. But once a listener is exposed to Clay County's Wilson Douglas playing "Yew Piney Mountain" or "Shelvin' Rock," or hears the music of the Hammons family from Pocahontas County, the difference becomes very ob-

vious. And when it comes to the hard-driving fiddle needed for traditional square dancing, West Virginia fiddlers are unequaled.

The old mountain fiddlers did not always tune the fiddle to the violin tuning of E, A, D, G. They would often cross-tune to E,A, E,A, or D,G, D,G, or several other varieties. Such tuning gave the fiddle a different sound and allowed for a 'drone' lick or a bagpipe sound. They would also often vary from the traditional 16 counts to a section and add a couple of drag licks on the end of the line. While the Nashville or modern fiddler is predictable, the old mountain fiddler was not. His fiddling did not have to fit into any particular pattern and usually didn't.

For years music scholars have argued that traditional fiddling would die as the old fiddlers passed from the scene. But the tradition goes on. A fine crop of middle-aged fiddlers was on the scene as the 20th century came to a close. Competition for the blue ribbons at the annual Vandalia Gathering in Charleston and the West Virginia State Folk Festival is as keen as ever.

See also French Carpenter, Hammons Family, Clark Kessinger, Melvin Wine, West Virginia State Folk Festival

Mack Samples
Duck

Gerald Milnes, *Play of a Fiddle*, 1999.

Fiestaware

West Virginia's most famous collectible was introduced to the marketplace in 1936. The first Genuine Fiesta, a cheap, attractive dinnerware, included four colors and 54 individual items all designed in the streamlined Art Deco style. Produced in Newell, Hancock County, by the Homer Laughlin China Company, Fiesta was originally designed by one of the premier ceramics designers in the world,

Frederick Hurten Rhead. As its popularity grew (during the 1940s, 2,500 workers produced 30 million pieces a year) new colors and serving items were introduced, as was Fiesta Kitchen Kraft, a food preparation, storage, and refrigerator-to-oven tableware.

History set the stage for Fiesta's success. The Great Depression was over, as was World War I. The United States economy was starting to boom, the Homer Laughlin factory had modernized production, and company leaders were focusing on artistic development. For the first time in history, colored glazes were available.

Fiesta colors have included: red, yellow, cobalt blue, green, and old ivory (all 1936), turquoise (1937), forest green, rose, chartreuse, and grey (1951), medium green (1959), antique gold, turf green (avocado), and mango red, a reproduction of the original red (1969). Production ceased from 1973 until 1986 when white, pink (rose), black, cobalt blue, and apricot were introduced. Since then yellow, turquoise, periwinkle blue, sea mist green, lilac, persimmon, sapphire blue, chartreuse, pearl gray, juniper, cinnabar, sunflower, plum, shamrock, tangerine, scarlet and peacock have been produced.

Throughout its history, Fiesta has set standards for technology, tableware trends, and pop appeal. Andy Warhol collected it, major restaurant chains use it, television commercials feature it, and collector newsletters track it. Certain older pieces have sold for as much as $2,000. New sets purchased through mail order catalogs and department stores sell for $20 a five-piece place setting.

See also Homer Laughlin China Company

Mack Miles
Charleston

Bob and Sharon Huxford, *The Collector's Encyclopedia of Fiesta*, 1992.

Fiestaware is a West Virginia collectible.

Filmmaking

Some of the earliest filmakers in West Virginia were amateurs. Jerry Galyean, Sam Moore, and "Gus" Capito of Charleston made interesting home movies. Otis Rymer Snodgrass made a travelogue along U.S. Route 60, *West Virginia the State Beautiful* (1929). The Myers brothers of Barbour County filmed *One Room Schoolhouses* about 1935. There was a series of commercial films made around the state called *See Yourself in the Movies* including Blundon Wills's *Charleston, the Beautiful on the Kanawha* (1932).

Several television stations produced documentary features. Public television was especially active after its inception in the 1960s. Among its products was *Even the Heavens Weep,* a 1983 Mine Wars documentary produced at WPBY by Beth Nogay. WNPB in Morgantown attracted a talented group of filmmakers. Its *Vandalia Sampler* series featured crafts and craftspeople. The *Different Drummer* series looked at unusual West Virginians and included films such as *Dancing Outlaw* (1991), *Point Man for God* (1987), and *Hammer on the Slammer* (1987), all by Jacob Young. *The Mountaineer* (1995) by John Nakashima focused on Appalachian stereotypes. Mark Samels's *Forks of Cheat* (1989) explored the Cheat River region. WNPB also made short fictional films based on screenplays by native writers.

West Virginia: A Film History was an especially ambitious production. A collaboration of the West Virginia Division of Culture and History, the West Virginia Humanities Council, and West Virginia public television, the six-and-a-half hour documentary was directed by Mark Samels. The film was first broadcast on West Virginia public television in February 1995 and later broadcast nationally.

Robert Gates of Charleston, an independent filmmaker, produced a strong anti-strip-mining film called *In Memory of the Land and People* (1978). Gates also collaborated with Bob Webb to produce a 90-minute documentary about Kanawha County cello maker Harold Hayslett (1996).

Among the state's independent feature filmmakers, Daniel Boyd, a professor at West Virginia State University, has been the most prolific. Boyd has made three feature-length dramatic films—*Chillers* (1988), *Space Preachers* (1990), and *Paradise Park* (1992)—using West Virginia locations and talent from within the state. He established the Paradise Film Institute to provide on-the-job training for would-be filmmakers and developed exchange programs with foreign schools.

Diana Sole and Dan Shreve of Motion Masters have produced such award-winning films as *A Principled Man* (2000) about civil rights leader Leon Sullivan. Motion Masters later undertook a film bi-

ography of Sen. Robert C. Byrd, titled *Soul of the Senate*, in collaboration with the West Virginia Humanities Council. Cambridge Educational, founded by Ty Gardner in the late 1970s, developed an impressive array of educational films produced by Charlotte Angel and Greg Harpold. Cambridge was later sold to Prime Media and moved away.

Other filmmakers include Bob Campbell of Elkins; Bill Drennen of Shepherdstown; Bill Hogan, Gary Simmons, and Larry Burdette of Charleston; Tom Nicholson, Ross Watne, and Chip Hitchcock of Morgantown; and Dan Richardson of Parkersburg. The West Virginia Filmmakers Guild, the West Virginia International Film Festival, and the West Virginia Film Office, all in Charleston, work to encourage filmmaking in the state.

Noted filmmakers of an earlier generation include Clarksburg native Leonard MacTaggert "Pare" Lorentz and Wheeling cinematographer Ellis Dungan. Known as "FDR's filmmaker," Lorentz conceived, edited, and published *The Roosevelt Year, 1933*, a review of FDR's first year in the White House. Lorentz later created two great New Deal documentaries, *The Plow that Broke the Plains* and *The River*. Dungan, an Ohio native who settled in Wheeling in 1958, shot films for Hollywood producer Duke Goldstone, and Ellis Dungan Productions later made many films for the state and region, including *For Liberty and Union* (1977), a film about the creation of West Virginia.

Recently the first known Hollywood film made inside the state was discovered. Caroline Gentry, born in Logan County, returned to Charleston and Logan to assist in *The Key to Power* (1920) that she co-wrote. *Stage Struck* (1925) starring Gloria Swanson was filmed in New Martinsville. In 1955, *Night of the Hunter* was partly filmed along the Ohio River near Moundsville. The movie was based on the suspense novel by Moundsville author Davis Grubb and starred actor Robert Mitchum. In 1971, James Stewart starred in his last Hollywood movie, *Fools' Parade*, filmed entirely in Moundsville and also based on a Grubb novel.

Francis Ford Coppola filmed one scene for *The Rain People* (1969) at a Grafton drive-in movie. In 1978, parts of *The Deer Hunter* were filmed in the Northern Panhandle. *Reckless* (1980) was filmed entirely in Weirton. *Pudden' head Wilson*, based on Mark Twain's novel, was filmed in Harpers Ferry in 1985. Martinsburg was the location for most of *Sweet Dreams* (1985), a film biography of Patsy Cline who grew up in nearby Winchester, Virginia. In 1987, John Sayles directed *Matewan* in Thurmond, Fayette County, which substituted for the actual Mingo County town of Matewan. Clyde Ware, who wrote for the TV series *Gunsmoke, Raw-*

hide, and *Bonanza*, returned to his native state to film two features: *No Drums, No Bugles* (1971), filmed in Braxton County, and *When the Line Goes Through* (1973), both starring Martin Sheen. Writer and director Lawrence Kasdan, whose credits include *Return of the Jedi* and other major hits, grew up mostly in West Virginia.

In 1992, L. A. Puopolo directed Gillian Anderson in *The Turning*, which was filmed on the state line at Bluefield. The film was screened at the West Virginia International Film Festival in 1998 with Puopolo in attendance. *The Silence of the Lambs* (1990), which stars Jodie Foster as Clarice Starling, a central character and a native of West Virginia, was filmed around Pittsburgh. One scene in the film takes place on the Elk River in Clay County though it was not filmed there. In 2000, *October Sky,* about novelist Homer Hickam's native McDowell County, was filmed outside the state. In 2001, *The Mothman Prophecies,* featuring the legendary Point Pleasant Mothman, was filmed in Pennsylvania. Much of *Gods and Generals*, a Civil War movie including a cameo appearance by Senator Byrd, was filmed in Harpers Ferry in 2002. Scenes for *Win a Date with Tad Hamilton* (2004), a story set in Fraziers Bottom, Putnam County, were shot in the Fayetteville area.

See also Ellis Dungan, Fools' Parade, Pare Lorentz, Night of the Hunter

Bill Drennen
Shepherdstown
Stephen Lee Fesenmaier
West Virginia Library Commission

Fire Towers

After decades of service West Virginia's forest fire towers were closed in 1990. At one time approximately 100 towers operated by federal and state forestry agencies dotted the state. Less than a dozen remain standing today, and none is in service.

The development of the fire tower network was a result of disastrous forest fires that swept the Mountain State following the cutting of the original virgin forest. The first fire towers were erected in 1916. These wooden structures had two floors. The first floor was the living quarters for the observer, and the second floor served as an observation room. With the advent of taller steel towers separate living quarters were provided, usually a small cinder block or log building adjacent to the tower. The first steel tower was built on Backbone Mountain near Parsons by Emory N. "Pop" Wriston in 1922.

During the spring and fall months, when fire danger was most severe, observers scanned the area around them for the first sign of fire. When a tell-tale plume of smoke appeared above the hori-

The Blair Mountain fire tower, January 1987.

zon, the observer relayed the information to a nearby district forestry office. Each tower contained a circular map of the surrounding area. By sighting along an alidade or fire finder, an observer could quickly take a bearing on the smoke. By comparing the readings from two or more towers one could pinpoint the location of the fire where the readings intersected on the map. This method is known as triangulation. Fire fighting crews were then dispatched to the scene to suppress the fire.

Today, most wildfires are reported by citizens or by observers in aircraft employed by the Division of Forestry.

Robert Beanblossom
Division of Natural Resources

Fish

West Virginia waters harbor a diverse assemblage of fishes. There are 154 native species in our lakes, streams, and rivers, but due to many accidental or intentional introductions, the total number present actually stands at 179. These species are distributed among 24 different families, with about 75 percent found in just five families. These five families are the carps and minnows (60 species), perches (31), suckers (18), basses and sunfishes (14), and catfishes (12).

The mountains that bisect the state have played a critical role in the kinds of fishes found here. Our western flowing waters (including the Monongahela, Little Kanawha, Kanawha, Guyandotte, and Big Sandy rivers and their tributaries) drain to the Ohio River, while our Atlan-

tic slope streams (the Potomac River and its tributaries and some tributaries of the James) flow eastward to the Chesapeake Bay. Although many of the same species can be found on both sides of the mountains, there are approximately 130 native species known from the Ohio River waters, but less than 50 from the Atlantic slope drainages. This lopsided difference is partially explained by the fact that the majority of fishes in North America originated during millions of years from river valleys found in the present central United States.

Of particular interest are the special fishes found in the New River of the upper Kanawha River drainage. The New, a remnant of the ancient Teays River system, is generally considered by geologists to be the second-oldest river in the world and the oldest in North America. Biological evidence supports the uniqueness of this drainage, which starts in North Carolina and continues on through the Virginias. Extremely special to these waters are seven fishes that are found nowhere else in the world. These are the New River shiner, bigmouth chub, Kanawha minnow, Bluestone sculpin, candy darter, Appalachian darter, and the Kanawha darter. It is thought that the barrier created by Kanawha Falls and the harsh environment of the New and Gauley river gorges contributed to the isolation and evolution of these endemic fishes, and to the fact that there are far fewer species above the falls than below.

Species typical to our large rivers are walleye, sauger, freshwater drum, bluegill, longear sunfish, smallmouth bass, largemouth bass, flathead and channel catfish, black and white crappie, gizzard shad, skipjack herring, mooneye, longnose gar, redhorse suckers (five species), buffalo suckers (three species), carpsuckers (three species), emerald shiners, channel shiner, logperch, banded darter, blackside darter, and variegate darter. Small-stream fishes include trout, mottled sculpin, blacknose dace, longnose dace, creek chubs, rosyface shiner, striped shiner, stoneroller minnow, fantail darter, greenside darter, johnny darter, white sucker, hog sucker, and mottled sculpin.

Lakes are artificial environments in West Virginia. (Trout pond, a two-acre lake in the Eastern Panhandle, is exceptional as our only natural lake.) Species in our large man-made lakes include smallmouth and largemouth bass, walleye, channel catfish, black and white crappie, bluegill, and emerald shiners.

The most common fishes in the state are smallmouth and largemouth bass, bluegill, green sunfish, rock bass, channel catfish, northern hogsuckers, white suckers, striped shiner, silver shiner, mimic shiner, rosyface shiner, spotfin shiner, silverjaw minnow, golden red-

horse, white sucker, hog sucker, fantail darter, and greenside darter.

West Virginia fishes have some odd habits, often to do with reproduction. Our official state fish, the brook trout, is the only native trout and the only native fish that spawns in the fall; its eggs incubate all winter until spring. Most of our fish species mate in spring or early summer and hatch within a couple of weeks. Then there is the incomparable behavior of the American eel, which becomes sexually mature after several years, migrates from our eastern streams to the Atlantic Ocean, mates, and their hatched young float back to the mainland in ribbon-like larval stage, transform into a transparent 'glass eel,' and then change into the typical dark-bodied juvenile. The Mound-building fishes, such as chubs and fallfish, carry stones by mouth to construct these piles as their nests, while depression nesters, such as the stoneroller minnow, may actually roll debris away. Many fishes may undergo drastic transformations before they find their mates. Some grow "horns," others including the darters get extremely colorful, and some have body parts that change shape and size.

Some fish have intriguing food habits. For example, the jawless lampreys are often parasitic on other fish. Our six-foot-long paddlefish eats only microscopic plants and animals. The stomachless minnows and suckers have teeth in their throats instead of their mouths, and suckers have a telescoping mouth designed for "sucking" food off the bottom.

Whatever their ways, West Virginia's fishes are a rich resource, an endless source of fascination, and a vital part of our state's fauna.

See also Fishing

Dan Cincotta
Division of Natural Resources

L. M. Page and B. M. Burr, *A Field Guide to Freshwater Fishes of North America North of Mexico,* 1991; J. R. Stauffer Jr., J. M. Boltz, and L. R. White, *The Fishes of West Virginia,* 1995.

Fish Hatcheries

The West Virginia Division of Natural Resources operates seven coldwater fish hatcheries to raise catchable-sized trout for its statewide stocking program. Rainbow, golden rainbow, brook, and brown trout are raised. The hatcheries are located primarily in the mountains of east-central West Virginia to take advantage of the many springs in that region of the state. The hatcheries hatch, raise, and stock fish.

Petersburg Hatchery, built in the early 1930s, is located near Petersburg in Grant County. It produces catchable-sized fish and provides rainbow and golden rainbow eggs and fingerlings to other hatcheries. Ridge Hatchery, located in Morgan County near Berkeley Springs, was also built in the early 1930s. It stocks trout in many of the streams and small impoundments in the Eastern Panhandle. Edray Hatchery, near Marlinton in Pocahontas County, was built in the 1930s and expanded in the 1940s. The hatchery also operates a series of leased ponds located downstream on Stony Creek.

Spring Run Hatchery is located near Dorcas in Grant County. This hatchery was constructed in the early 1950s at one of West Virginia's largest springs, which supplies about 3,000 gallons per minute. Spring Run is one of the largest hatcheries operated by the Division of Natural Resources, and supplies trout for stocking by the smaller hatcheries. Bowden Hatchery, another large hatchery, is located near Elkins in Randolph County. It was constructed by the U.S. Fish and Wildlife Service in the early 1960s and transferred to the state in 1997. Bowden's annual trout production is similar to Spring Run.

Reeds Creek Hatchery, located west of Ruddle in Pendleton County, was completed in 1979. Unique among West Virginia's trout hatcheries, Reeds Creek filters and re-uses 80 percent of its water. Reeds Creek, like Spring Run, provides trout to the smaller hatcheries that have low summer flows, and also transfers catchable-sized trout in the spring for stocking by other hatcheries.

Tate Lohr Hatchery is located near Oakvale in Mercer County and was also completed in 1979. It stocks much of southern West Virginia. This hatchery is a small rearing facility, and the majority of its trout are hauled in by Reeds Creek and Spring Run hatcheries during the spring.

The seven hatcheries annually produce and stock approximately 750,000 pounds of trout in 200 streams and small impoundments scattered across the Mountain State.

Mike Shingleton
Division of Natural Resources

Susanne Fisher

Soprano Susanne Fisher was born August 25, 1903, in Braxton County. Her rise to fame began when she sang the role of Cio-Cio-San in *Madame Butterfly* at the Metropolitan Opera on December 26, 1935. Fisher was the first West Virginian to sing at the Met.

She earned an artist's diploma in music at the Cincinnati Conservatory and, on a graduate fellowship, pursued vocal studies at the Juilliard School of Music. She then studied in France and Germany. Beginning in 1931, Fisher sang small parts at the Berlin State Opera, attended many rehearsals, and learned diverse roles. When the breakthrough opportunity came in *Madame Butterfly*, she knew every note and needed no rehearsals.

Fisher remained in Berlin for three seasons but in the fall of 1934 began a two-year stint in America at the Worcester festival. In 1935 and 1936, in addition to the Met, she sang with the New York Philharmonic Symphony Orchestra and the Cleveland Symphony Orchestra. During those summers she was the leading soprano at the Paris Comic Opera. She sang at Franklin Roosevelt's second inauguration in 1937.

Fisher married concert singer Clifford Menz, with whom she performed in operatic recitals. She died in Panama City, Florida, February 15, 1990.

Mary Lucille DeBerry
Morgantown

Fishing

With only 101 square miles of natural inland water surface, West Virginia does not possess the abundance of angling opportunities of many other states. But the quality of our fishing is excellent, particularly in size of fish. We grow large muskellunge; we boast a walleye fishery that produces fish comparable in size to those of the prime waters of North America; and three of our smallmouth bass streams are renowned for yielding trophy catches.

The designated state fish is the native brook trout, one of four cold water sportfish available in West Virginia, the others being rainbow, brown, and golden rainbow trout. The latter is a mutation of a normal-colored rainbow, discovered in 1955 at Petersburg trout hatchery in Grant County. It was first stocked in 1963 during West Virginia's Centennial celebration.

Native "brookies," colorful fish with yellow and red spots and pink-red fins, were once abundant in the eastern highlands, but their range has diminished because of land use changes. Our remaining native brook trout streams, mostly tiny mountain tributaries, are state treasures. West Virginia's most storied trout stream is Cranberry River, whose former grandeur has been restored with the building of two limestone treatment facilities to counteract acidity. A limestone station has also restored trout fishing in Blackwater River.

A notable trout fishing development of recent decades has been the addition of several new brown trout fisheries in West Virginia through a cooperative effort by Trout Unlimited and the Division of Natural Resources. The fishing organization and the state agency stocked fingerling-size browns in streams that previously had no trout, and in many cases the stockings have been successful.

The most prized of West Virginia's large game fish is the muskellunge, once confined to our rivers but which now also inhabits several large impoundments through stocking. West Virginia muskies in the 40-inch class are not uncommon, and a few have topped 50 inches. Muskie

Fly fishing in Bluestone River.

fishing in Elk River is legendary. The catch and release of muskies, including very large ones, has become common and has enhanced the quality of the state's muskie fishing. A mini-industry has grown up around the manufacture of muskie lures by several of our fishermen.

Lester Hayes Jr. of Nitro caught a 52.5-inch, 43-pound muskie in Elk River in 1955. In 1997, Anna Marsh of Buckhannon, fishing from the shoreline at Stonecoal Lake, topped the previous record weight by more than six pounds. Then in 2003, Glenn Boyd of Weston broke the length record with a muskie of 52.7 inches, also from Stonecoal.

Our walleye fishery does not produce large numbers of this tasty game fish, but 10- to 15-pounders are caught each year. Summersville Lake, Elk River, and Kanawha Falls are favorite walleye waters. Buckhannon fisherman Odie Cutlip has probably caught more trophy walleyes than any other state angler.

West Virginia's premier warm water fish, due to its relative abundance, is the smallmouth bass, a tenacious fighter whose surface acrobatics are a delight. New River, Greenbrier River, and the South Branch are all excellent smallmouth streams. In 1971, David Lindsay, 16, of Wiley Ford, Mineral County, bought a fishing license en route to the South Branch, and caught a nine-pound, 12-ounce smallmouth that remains the heaviest ever caught in the state.

The greatest abundance of warm water fish exists in the Ohio and Kanawha rivers, primarily below the navigation locks and dams.

The Division of Natural Resources awards trophy citations for 26 species of fish. In addition to those already named, other notables include largemouth bass, channel catfish, and flathead catfish. The latter is our heavyweight champion, occasionally exceeding 50 or even 60 pounds.

But big isn't necessarily better with

Mountain State anglers. Two of our most popular species are also two of the smallest: crappie and bluegill. The large Army Corps of Engineers and power company lakes boast excellent fishing for these two panfish, as well as for other species. These impoundments have added 18,395 surface acres of fishing in West Virginia. The DNR also owns or manages more than 100 other lakes ranging in size from under 10 acres to more than 300 acres.

Because of his book, *Tale of the Elk*, which is still popular with readers after 70 years, lawyer W. E. R. Byrne is one of West Virginia's best-known fishermen. So too is Eli "Rimfire" Hamrick, the Webster County mountaineer who would, according to legend, hang a "Gone Fishin'" sign on the door of his Webster Springs jewelry store. Chuck Yeager, the legendary pilot, caught his first trout on Cranberry River after returning from World War II.

See also Brook Trout, Fish

Skip Johnson
Sutton

Ann Kathryn Flagg

Playwright, teacher, and actress Ann Kathryn Flagg was born in Charleston, April 29, 1924. She graduated from Garnet High School in 1941 and West Virginia State College in 1945. She became a teacher of high school drama in Virginia and then toured with the American Negro Repertory Players. Later, she taught at Dunbar High School in Fairmont.

In 1952, Flagg resigned her teaching position to become director of the Children's Theater at Karamu House in Cleveland, Ohio. While in Cleveland, she won acclaim for her title-role performances in Sophocles' *Antigone* and Aristophanes' *Lysistrata*. She moved to Chicago in 1961 to obtain a master's degree at Northwestern University. While in Chicago, Flagg wrote *Great Gettin' Up Mornin'*. The play won first place in the National Collegiate Playwriting Contest and was broadcast by CBS-TV. Flagg's other plays include *Blueboy to Holiday—Over*, *A Significant Statistic*, and *Unto the Least of These*.

Flagg returned to teaching in 1963 for the Evanston Consolidated School District and Southern Illinois University. She died in Illinois in 1970.

Flat Top Lake

Flat Top Lake, like other lakes in West Virginia, is an artificial lake, formed by damming Glade Creek on Flat Top Mountain in southern Raleigh County. It was first developed in the early 1950s as a fishing reservoir. In the early days, the fishermen camped, but better roads including the nearby West Virginia Turnpike put the lake in commuting distance of Beckley. Originally there were mostly summer homes at Flat Top, but eventually the community became home to year-round residents when permanent housing was built and the Flat Top Lake Association was formed. The association owns 2,200 acres of land adjacent to the 230-acre lake. In addition to fishing, other water sports are popular. It is a gated community.

Raymond Thomas Hill
Athens

Flat Top Mountain

Flat Top Mountain, located along the contiguous boundaries of Mercer, Raleigh, Summers, Wyoming, and McDowell counties, is a part of the Allegheny Front located on the southern edge of the dissected Allegheny Plateau. There are two other Flat Top Mountains, one each in Hardy and Monroe counties.

Flat Top Mountain extends over about 400 square miles between the Bluestone River; White Oak, Talley, and Guyandotte mountains; and Micajah, Indian, and Stone ridges. Within the region are tributaries of the Bluestone and New rivers and headwaters of the Guyandotte River, Elkhorn Creek, and Tug Fork.

The summit of Flat Top is a tableland of about 40 square miles above 3,000 feet, surrounded by a serrated escarpment of steep walled gorges that rises from 2,400–2,500 feet above sea level. The maximum elevation is 3,560 feet at Huff Knob near the community of Flat Top. Other elevations include Bluff Mountain (3,476), Indian Grave Mountain (3,440), Bald Knob (3,400), Rich Knob (3,400), and Pilot Knob (3,480).

Tough Guyandotte sandstone has preserved the surface of Flat Top. Much of the region is underlain by rich deposits of Pocahontas coal. Underground mining began in the 1880s when the Norfolk & Western Railroad and branch lines made shipping possible. Near the turn of the 20th century there were more than 3,000 coke ovens and 150 mines operating in the region. In recent years much of the coal has been surface-mined at about 2,800 feet above sea level.

Flat Top is forested with regrowth hardwoods. Most farm land is devoted to livestock, and also to Christmas tree farming and other uses. Other economic activities are primarily recreational, with the Winterplace ski resort, Glade Springs Resort, Flat Top Lake, and Camp Creek State Park and State Forest among the region's attractions.

Although opened in recent years by modern highways, Flat Top was historically a rural and sparsely populated region of limited access. In 1911, the population of postal communities on the summit totaled 300, or about seven people per square mile. A branch of the Buffalo Trail extended along the mountain, and in the Civil War Union and Confederate lines extended across the Alleghenies from Flat Top to Sewell to Cheat mountains. The West Virginia Turnpike (Interstate 77) and U.S. 19 cross Flat Top Mountain, with the turnpike offering spectacular views from the southern slopes of the mountain.

Howard G. Adkins
Ona

Flatfoot Dancing

Flatfoot dancing is hard to define. "The music just goes in your ear, down through your soul, and comes out through your feet," an elderly West Virginia flatfoot dancer of note once said. So perhaps we can say that flatfoot dancing is the mountain artistic reaction to hard-driving fiddle music.

The term is often used interchangeably with clogging, but it should not be. Clogging is more structured and has certain universally accepted steps. Cloggers often raise their feet high off the floor, some kicking higher than their head. They often keep a steady shuffle with one foot, freeing the other foot and leg to do some fancy moving. And clogging is often done in teams. Flatfoot dancers, on the other hand, dance solo and tend to keep both feet close to the floor. The steps are not quite so fancy, and there are no standard steps. Among the old-time flatfoot dancers, the movement was often backward. Hence, many of them referred to it as "backstep dancing." Two of West Virginia's better known traditional musicians, Phoeba Parsons and her brother, Noah Cottrell, always referred to it as "backstepping."

Close observation of a good West Virginia flatfoot dancer will reveal a combination of several different kinds of dancing. There is a little of the Irish step-dance in it, sometimes a little polka shuffle can be observed, and perhaps a step or two has been borrowed from what Southern blacks called tap dancing. But the best part of it all is that every flatfoot dancer tends to do it a little different. It is the expression of how that particular dancer feels about the music that he or she is hearing. Good flatfoot dancers feel the hard drive of a fiddle deep in their spine. They put their soul on display and proudly demonstrate with the movement of their feet all of the good things about living in West Virginia.

Mack Samples
Duck

Flatwoods Monster

The legend of the Braxton County or Flatwoods Monster arose near dusk on September 12, 1952, when a group of local youths were startled from a game of football by a fireball streaking across the sky. The fireball fell to earth just beyond a hillside at Flatwoods. Joined by Kathleen May, a local beautician, the boys went to investigate. The group consisted of Mrs. May, Eugene Lemon, Teddy May, Ronald

Shaver, Neal Nunley, Teddy Neal, and Tommy Hyer.

The group of seven approached the top of the hill where the fireball had landed. Beyond the hill, they reported seeing a pulsating light. Then suddenly, to their left, two powerful light beams pierced the darkness. Turning their own flashlight in that direction, they saw a large man-like creature nearly 12 feet tall and about four feet wide. Making no sound, it floated toward them. The creature had a red face and bright green clothing, which hung in folds below the waist. Its head was shaped like the ace of spades and there was an almost sickening metallic odor emanating from its body. The witnesses quickly fled the scene. A later investigation found only a lingering odor, two large skid marks, and trampled grass.

Although the Monster has never reappeared, Flatwoods celebrated its 50th anniversary with a community festival in 2002. Over the years the Flatwoods Monster has developed a sizable following, taking its place alongside Mothman, Batboy, and other West Virginia legends of the bizarre.

Buddy Griffin
Glenville State College
Gray Barker, *They Knew Too Much About Flying Saucers*, 1956; James G. Jones, *Appalachian Ghost Stories And Other Tales*, 1975.

Aretas Brooks Fleming

Governor Aretas Brooks Fleming, businessman and Democratic Party boss, was born October 15, 1839, in Fairmont. He came from a prominent family with political connections throughout the region. Fleming studied law at the University of Virginia and began his practice in Fairmont during the Civil War. He was not rich, but he was well-born and able. He followed the Virginia tradition of marrying well when he joined himself to Carrie M. Watson in 1865. Her father was the industrialist James O. Watson, and her brother, Clarence W. Watson, was later U.S. senator.

Fleming's family ties and dedication to the Democratic Party brought political and business success. He won election to the House of Delegates in 1872, where he served until 1875. In 1878, he was appointed as judge of the second judicial circuit. He remained a state judge until he ran for governor. Fleming's basic interest in politics, however, derived from his primary interest in business. He invested in railroads, land, timber, oil, and coal. After 1886, Fleming's fortunes were joined with those of U.S. Sen. Johnson Newlon Camden, a Rockefeller business associate. Fleming gained the support and the backing of Camden, and the two men devoted their considerable talents to developing the Upper Monongahela coalfield.

Governor Aretas Brooks Fleming (1839–1923).

In 1888, with Camden's support, Fleming won the Democratic nomination for governor and then won West Virginia's most controversial gubernatorial election. Nathan Goff, Fleming's opponent, showed a 106-vote majority in the initial count, but Fleming challenged the residency of many black voters in Mercer and McDowell counties. Both Goff and Fleming were sworn in on inauguration day, but incumbent Governor Wilson refused to leave office. The state Supreme Court upheld Wilson, and the issue was finally settled in Fleming's favor in a party-line vote in the legislature in January 1890, more than a year after the election. As governor, he moved decisively to establish a business-friendly environment by adhering to the policies of limited constitutional government and low taxes. The state's reluctance to interfere in the economy made West Virginia a sanctuary for entrepreneurial energy. Commerce and industry grew steadily, creating new sources of wealth and further integrating West Virginia into the mainstream economy.

Questions were raised as to Fleming's character and whether he personally profited from his term in office. The evidence is strong that Fleming engaged in business and indeed expanded his multifaceted financial activities while in office. He operated within a regional culture that was captivated by the spirit of progress, and the governor, whether a Democrat or Republican, was expected to use the office to spur the state's economy and lure investors into West Virginia. Governor Fleming built an economic program that he expected to benefit both himself and the state.

Fleming returned to the practice of law after leaving office in 1893, aggressively pursuing his business interests. He and his brother-in-law, Clarence W. Watson, formed a number of coal companies prior to merging them into the Fairmont Coal Company in 1901. Efforts to eliminate competition reached their peak in 1903 when the Fairmont Coal Company was absorbed into the larger Consolidation Coal Company of Maryland.

The Fleming-Watson group controlled Consolidation Coal for the next 25 years. Operating in a time of great industrial expansion, they were successful in capturing most of the mines in the Fairmont field. Their success was marred by the deaths of 361 men and boys at Fairmont Coal's interconnecting Monongah mines in 1907. After the Monongah disaster, Fleming recognized that good business required the owners to operate a safe work place. Fleming wielded considerable influence among West Virginia coal operators, and he led the movement to establish the U.S. Bureau of Mines in 1910. His vision included an industrial transformation that was directed and controlled for the benefit of the home state. The Fleming-Watson family built a number of Fairmont businesses, and they retained controlling interest in Fairmont Coal and Consolidation Coal Company well into the 1920s.

Aretas Brooks Fleming died in Fairmont, October 13, 1923, and is buried there.

See also Consolidation Coal Company, Clarence W. Watson, James O. Watson

Jeffrey B. Cook
North Greenville College
Jeffery B. Cook, "The Ambassador of Development: Aretas Brooks Fleming, West Virginia's Political Entrepreneur, 1839–1923," Ph.D. dissertation, West Virginia University, 1998; John Alexander Williams, *West Virginia and the Captains of Industry*, 1976; Michael E. Workman, "Political Culture and the Coal Economy in the Upper Monongahela Region: 1774–1933," Ph.D. dissertation, West Virginia University, 1995.

Jack Fleming

Broadcast announcer Jack Fleming, the long-time "Voice of the Mountaineers," was born February 3, 1923, in Morgantown and was educated there through college. Six times he was chosen State Sportscaster of the Year. A navigator on a World War II bomber, Fleming later attended West Virginia University on the GI Bill. He began announcing WVU sports as an undergraduate in 1947, and, except for a few years when he worked away as a broadcaster in pro basketball and football, he anchored sports radio at the state's flagship university through 1997.

From 1960 to 1970, Fleming was general manager of WAJR Radio in Morgantown, and he was sports director of WTAE-TV in Pittsburgh, 1970–73. He was the announcer for the Pittsburgh Steelers from 1958 through 1993, broadcasting four Super Bowls. His 1972 call of the "immaculate reception," considered the greatest play in National Football League history, still airs perennially through NFL

Films. Fleming announced for the Chicago Bulls of the National Basketball Association, 1970–73.

Fleming's career included briefer stints as announcer for the Pittsburgh Rens of the old American Basketball League and for the Pittsburgh Pirates baseball team. For four decades, beginning in the 1950s, he co-anchored and co-produced broadcasts of the West Virginia State Scholastic Basketball Tournament. Jack Fleming died January 3, 2001.

Norman Julian
Dominion Post

Flick Amendment

Following the Civil War, former Confederates were barred from voting in West Virginia and the voting rights of African-Americans were not assured. The divergent issues were brought together in the Flick Amendment. It happened as the control of Radical Republicans eroded in the newly formed state. As a result of the October 1869 elections, several Liberal Republicans (also known as Let Ups) were elected to the legislature. Hoping to offset the growth of Democrats, they offered a constitutional amendment that would empower both blacks and former rebels. Named for William H.H. Flick, a newly elected Liberal Republican from Pendleton County, the proposed amendment was submitted to the voters in the election of April 17, 1871.

Passing with a vote of 23,546 for and 6,323 against, the Flick Amendment turned out to be of no consequence for African-Americans since the 15th Amendment to the U.S. Constitution, which granted the right to vote regardless of color or previous condition of servitude, had been ratified in 1870. What remained, ironically, was the re-enfranchisement of former Confederates. The provisions of the Flick Amendment were incorporated into the new Constitution of 1872. Liberal Republicans had hoped the amendment would eliminate some of the divisions within the Republican Party. However, the opposite occurred. The amendment split the party further while enfranchising many Democrats. This, in turn, led to a quarter-century of Democratic dominance in state politics.

See also Reconstruction

I. D. "Duke" Talbott
Glenville State College

Flood Control

By the late 19th century, the farmer's plow and woodman's ax had removed much of West Virginia's rich soil and lush forests, increasing the risk of heavy rains causing floods in creeks and rivers downstream in the watershed. In 1884, the Ohio River was the scene of a major flood that swept away countless homes. In 1913, the Ohio again flooded, and this time the high water brought with it a corresponding flood of public protest. Former president Theodore Roosevelt complained that millions of dollars were going to flood aid, but not one penny had been spent on flood control. President Woodrow Wilson appointed a special commission that recommended the erection of levees and the construction of flood-reducing reservoirs. However, action was limited until the 1930s.

In that decade, the federal government began building massive flood-control projects in West Virginia. The work continued for the next half-century. The first project completed was the dam on Tygart Valley River, designed for flood control and other purposes and finished in 1938. Bluestone Dam, on the New River above Hinton, was built by the U.S. Army Corps of Engineers in the 1940s. Several other Corps of Engineers flood-control dams followed, including Summersville, Sutton, and East Lynn in the 1960s, and Burnsville and Beech Fork in the 1970s. R. D. Bailey Dam was completed in 1980 and Stonewall Jackson, the last of the big flood-control dams, in 1988.

Floodwalls were also built, including the wall that protects Huntington from the Ohio and Guyandotte rivers. Because Huntington was home to so many essential defense plants, work was allowed to continue during World War II. Begun in 1938, the floodwall was completed in 1943. Floodwalls similar to that at Huntington were completed in Parkersburg in 1950 and Point Pleasant in 1951.

Today the Corps of Engineers has 37 flood-control projects in the state, including levees and floodwalls as well as dams and lakes. Although built primarily with flood control in mind, the man-made lakes have become recreational meccas, enjoyed by many thousands of people each year. In contrast, the locks and dams on the Ohio and Kanawha rivers, also built by the Corps of Engineers, have no flood-control function. These dams were built solely for navigation purposes, to provide a steady, dependable stream depth so that the rivers remain navigable year-round.

Flood-control dams operate on a simple storage principle, applied on a massive scale. Typically the water level is lowered in the fall to allow the dams to catch the run-off from the heavy rains of spring. Thus the lake waters rise to summer levels, complementing the recreational needs of boaters and fishermen. In addition to these cyclical changes, each dam is designed with a large reserve area to impound the waters of extreme floods. These reservations are rarely if ever under water.

Despite flood-control efforts, West Virginia remains prone to damaging floods. An April 1977 flood along the Tug Fork of the Big Sandy River saw 11 counties declared major disaster areas. In November 1985, record flooding in central and eastern West Virginia, especially in the headstream areas of the Greenbrier, Potomac, Monongahela and Little Kanawha rivers, resulted in 47 deaths and hundreds of millions of dollars in property damage. Occasionally, floods strike even in watersheds protected by dams, as was the case in the Little Kanawha Valley downstream of the Burnsville Dam in 1985 and 1994. In 2002, floods in southern West Virginia breathed new life into a long-standing controversy about the role of timbering and coal mining—especially mountaintop removal mining—in producing floods.

See also Floods

James E. Casto
Herald-Dispatch

Leland R. Johnson, *Men, Mountains, and Rivers*, 1977.

Flood of 1985

During the last week of October 1985, weak winds over the United States, south of 40 degrees latitude, allowed a late-season tropical storm named Juan to meander along the Gulf of Mexico coast. On Thursday, October 31, the weakening Juan moved north, leaving abundant moisture over the Southeast.

On Sunday, November 3, another storm formed in southeastern Georgia. This new storm was now in position to tap the moisture left in the atmosphere by Juan. Occasional rain fell over West Virginia on November 3. By the predawn on Monday, November 4, a large area of rain began to form from western North Carolina north to southern West Virginia. This rain continued to strengthen while shifting northeast toward Elkins and Petersburg by late morning. The storm center moved slowly north, reaching the Lynchburg, Virginia, vicinity by nightfall. The circulation around the storm pulled additional moisture from the Atlantic coast, and the winds blowing up the eastern slopes of the Appalachians augmented rain totals. These factors kept the heavy rains falling into Monday night. Rainfall rates of three to six inches in 12 hours were observed over the headwaters of the Potomac, Greenbrier, and Little Kanawha rivers. These same rainfall rates affected an even larger percentage of the Cheat, Tygart Valley, and West Fork river basins.

In response to the rain, many headwater rivers rose rapidly with the onset of darkness that Monday evening. Severe flooding took place overnight. After midnight, the rain became lighter, but by then, fatal flooding was under way. The 24-hour rainfall amounts, ending near dawn on Tuesday, November 5, were four to eight inches from the Covington and Roanoke area of Virginia northward, to include the area from Clarksburg to Petersburg in West Virginia. The low

Downtown Philippi in the flood of 1985.

clouds and light rain that fell during the day on November 5 did not affect river crest heights, but did hamper rescue operations from the air.

The Cheat and Greenbrier rivers crested at record levels. Record water heights were also seen on portions of the Tygart Valley, Little Kanawha, and West Fork rivers, and on the North and South Branches of the Potomac. At Parsons, the Cheat River crested 10 feet above flood stage and four feet higher than the previous record from July 1888. At Glenville, the Little Kanawha River crested 13 feet above flood stage and about two feet higher than the March 1967 flood. At Philippi, the Tygart Valley River crested nearly 15 feet above flood stage and around four feet higher than the previous record stage. At Moorefield, the South Branch of the Potomac River crested about 10 feet above flood stage and nearly four feet higher than June 1949, the previous record.

In West Virginia, 47 people were killed in the flood of 1985. Pendleton and Grant counties had the most fatalities. Towns such as Parsons, Rowlesburg, Philippi, Marlinton, Glenville, Petersburg, and Moorefield were severely damaged. The upper James and Roanoke rivers in neighboring Virginia also had fatal record flooding. In the aftermath of this flood, cleanup and recovery efforts were greatly aided by an unusually mild November.

See also Floods

Kenneth T. Batty
National Weather Service

Floods

Floods develop when the volume of water supplied to a stream exceeds the capacity of the stream's channel. In natural settings, rainfall runoff from hill slopes and mountainsides supplies most floodwater, with direct precipitation into streams and groundwater flow contribut-ing minor amounts. Melting snow may contribute to West Virginia floods from late autumn to early spring.

Flooding begins when flow reaches the top of a stream's banks and spreads over the nearby floodplain. Most large streams have broad low-lying floodplains that provide temporary storage of floodwater and reduce the flow. In contrast, floodplains may be small or missing altogether along steep mountain streams or on large streams flowing through narrow gorges. These streams are characterized by "flash floods," with little or no warning and extremely fast flows that may exceed 10 miles per hour.

Floods are natural events. They produce commonly overlooked benefits, including the bottomlands that make up most of the flat terrain in many parts of the Mountain State. The decrease in velocity when floodwaters leave their channels and spread onto bottomlands causes sand and silt to settle out and create rich alluvial soils. Floods also create the basic ecological structure of streams and bottomlands. Indeed, to understand the nature of any stream, one must first study the nature of its formative flood events.

Unfortunately, human intervention frequently leads to disastrous consequences. People often overlook the fact that floodplains are parts of rivers and are unprepared for the inevitable occasions when rivers exert their authority over their entire domain. It is human nature to blame the stream for causing damage, when in fact the real culprit may be decades of unwise floodplain development.

Floods are triggered by a complex variety of events. Dam or levee failures represent the most dangerous source. The Mountain State's most deadly flood, caused by the failure of poorly designed coal-refuse dams on Buffalo Creek in Logan County in February 1972, reached approximately 50,000 cubic feet per second near Saunders. The Buffalo Creek flood left 125 dead and 4,000 homeless.

There is a strong relationship between the size of the drainage basin and the type of precipitation that yields flooding. Small-stream floods commonly are triggered by short-lived local rainfall, such as intense late-spring or summer thunderstorms. Many of the record flows on small streams in West Virginia were isolated events, occurring when no other streams flooded.

Prolonged precipitation or melting snow provides water at much slower rates and seldom floods small streams. However, the cumulative effect of several days of such weather may lead to extreme flooding on large rivers, such as the Ohio or Potomac. The greatest historic flow of water in the Mountain State was caused by the repeated passage of frontal systems through the region during January 1937. Although most small streams stayed within their banks, they contributed to a discharge measured at approximately 690,000 cubic feet per second (446 billion gallons per day) in Ashland, Kentucky, on the Ohio River just downstream from West Virginia. The contributing watershed was 60,750 square miles. Similar patterns of recurring frontal storms produced record floods in March 1913 along the Ohio between Parkersburg and Point Pleasant, and in March 1936 on the Ohio above Parkersburg and the Potomac downstream from Paw Paw.

The remnants of hurricanes have caused some significant floods, probably including the great Kanawha River flood in September 1861. Hurricanes have greatest impact in the New and Potomac drainage basins but tend to be less effective west of the Allegheny Mountains.

The November 4–5, 1985, flood was the state's most damaging flood, with approximately $1.2 billion damage, 47 deaths in West Virginia, and 24 additional deaths in nearby states. This flood has been frequently and erroneously ascribed to Hurricane Juan but actually was triggered by the passing of two low pressure cells that originated in the Gulf of Mexico. In fact, the hurricane passed well west of the areas ravaged by the flood and totally disappeared from the weather map more than 24 hours before flooding began in earnest. The rainfall total right before and during the flood was nowhere near as exceptional as the flooding it produced, but this flooding was enhanced by an unusually wet October and the seasonal shutdown of water uptake by plants. While the 1985 flood set records for 47 stream-gauging stations in West Virginia, it was truly exceptional only in the South Branch Potomac and Cheat River basins.

The frequency of flooding varies, but a typical floodplain is inundated once every year or two. Most floods barely exceed the banks and fade from memory after flood watches are canceled. Much more rarely, cataclysmic floods with deep turbulent flow obliterate virtually everything on the floodplain. Floodplains immediately downstream from narrow water gaps are the most vulnerable during extreme floods.

Flood risk is usually expressed in terms of recurrence interval, the average return period for a flood equaling or exceeding a given discharge. The so-called "100-year flood," a typical design standard in floodplain management, is equaled or exceeded only once in an average 100-year span. Unfortunately, many people incorrectly construe this term to imply a guaranteed time interval between events. The law of averages can be fickle, and a 100-year flood may more aptly be expressed as one with one chance in a hundred of occurring in a given year. Two or more 100-year floods can occur on a river in a short span of time.

Two profound uncertainties cloud flood risk assessment. The first stems from the fact that most stream-gauge records are less than 30 years long, insufficient for predicting rare events. The data may be adequate for accurate predictions of smaller, more frequent floods, but late 20th-century events in West Virginia streams repeatedly showed that historic stream-gauge data may significantly under-predict the actual flood hazard. Existing flood insurance maps should be used with caution, because most were drawn prior to recent recalculation of flood frequencies for West Virginia.

The second uncertainty centers on the assumption that past floods are relevant predictors of future floods. An increase in rainfall intensity and resulting floods have been proposed as one of the most significant hazards caused by "global warming" of the last century. If this proposition is valid, it will be very difficult to anticipate the severity of future West Virginia floods.

J. Steven Kite
West Virginia University

Flora

West Virginia's original 1,700 plant species blanketed the entire state. Native forests still cover nearly 80 percent of the land or nearly 12 million acres. However, almost 30 percent of our plant species are aliens. The original species provided food, shelter, medicine, and beauty to Indians and the flood of Europeans who immigrated here. The new Americans brought nearly 900 alien plants of value and many weeds.

The native vegetation developed over millions of years as the mighty Appalachian Mountains slowly eroded to their present configuration. The earth's crust was subjected to earthquakes, continental shifts, and other cataclysmic forces that created a very diverse landscape. The present altitude ranges from 247 feet at Harpers Ferry to 4,861 feet at Spruce Knob. Rock layers vary from acid sandstones to shales conglomerates and alkaline limestones. Some rocks are high in iron, sulfur, calcium, aluminum, manganese, and silica. Coal and shale outcrops are common. Deep deposits of rich alluvial soils cover many river floodplains.

Climate, topography, man's activities, and animals have also shaped the plant life. Rainfall in West Virginia ranges from 66 inches at Pickens to 31 inches at Wardensville. The growing season varies from 92 days in Canaan Valley to 193 days in Williamson. The topography varies from extremely steep in the eastern mountains and southern coalfields to relatively flat along the Ohio River and on mountaintops. Mankind has introduced weeds, landscape plants, grasses, and crops. Timbermen cut valuable black walnut, red spruce, chestnut, white oak, and red oak, while leaving an abundance of low-value trees such as hickories, black locust, elms, black gum, beech, and scrub pine. Red spruce forests were reduced from a half million acres in the late 1800s to only 50,000 acres today by over cutting and damaging wildfires.

West Virginia has many migrating plants. Prairie plants have crossed the Ohio River and flourish along many rivers and larger streams. Along these waterways are found prairie cordgrass, switch grass, big bluestem, little bluestem, and Indian grass. Prairie species also persist in the Eastern Panhandle from previous geological eras. Botanists have recently located prairie ragwort, Cooper milkvetch, redroot, prairie-clover, and stiff goldenrod on Cave Mountain and nearby areas. All of these species are typical of midwestern and western prairies.

Boreal plants migrated southward during the ice ages, and many such as balsam fir and bog rosemary reach their southern limits in West Virginia. Atlantic coastal plain species are frequently found in the Potomac River and New-Kanawha drainages, where they have migrated westward. From the south, several plants have migrated northward along the New River and across the Cumberland Plateau. Crossvine, southern loosestrife, recurved fetterbush, spreading pogonia, and Carolina lily have their northernmost locations in West Virginia.

Another way to view West Virginia's vegetation is through plant communities. The very highest peaks are covered with red spruce forests. Below this occur northern hardwoods in the higher mountains. Below the northern hardwoods the western two-thirds of West Virginia is covered with cove and mixed mesophytic hardwoods. East of the high mountains, in the Potomac drainage, the forests are mostly oak-hickory-pine.

The highly variable topography, climate, and geology have created many small pockets of unusual vegetation, such as bogs, swamps, grass balds, heath barrens, riverbanks, cliffs, and shale barrens. These are the niches searched for by botanists and naturalists seeking unusual and rare plants.

Red spruce grows above 3,500 feet elevation and covers about 50,000 acres. Original red spruce forests covered nearly 500,000 acres, but heavy timbering followed by damaging wildfires destroyed 90 percent of the spruce. Spruce forests are dense, and the wet air and heavy shade allow ferns, mosses, bryophytes, and fungi to flourish, while most shrubs, grasses, and wildflowers are scarce. Common shrubs that tolerate the spruce forests are mountain holly, southern mountain cranberry, rhododendron, and mountain laurel. Common wildflowers are Canada mayflower, white wood sorrel, painted trillium, sweet white violet, fireweed, and yellow clintonia. Ferns and lycopodiums that flourish under the spruce are spinulose and intermediate wood ferns, long beech fern, New York fern, mountain wood fern, and stiff and common clubmosses.

Northern hardwood forests cover many higher mountains and northeast facing slopes from 2,500 feet elevation up to the red spruce belt. These forests extend from Preston, Tucker, and Grant counties on the Maryland border southward to Raleigh, Mercer, and Monroe counties on the Virginia border. Common shrubs and vines include smooth serviceberry, mountain holly, rhododendron, mountain laurel, striped maple, hobblebush, and Dutchman's pipevine. Common wildflowers of the northern hardwoods are Canada mayflower, yellow fawn lily, painted trillium, hellebore, ramps, spring beauties, white wood sorrel, Canada violet, sweet white violet, dwarf ginseng, and Oswego tea. Fern patches are common and include common polypody, cinnamon and interrupted ferns, and stiff and common clubmosses. Rare species are Canada yew, long-stalked holly, Appalachian blue violet, Fraser's sedge, white monkshood, star-violet, and goldthread.

The western hills of the Alleghenies from 2,500 feet elevation down to the Ohio River are blanketed by rich cove and mixed mesophytic hardwood forests. Dry upper slopes are frequently oak-hickory-pine. Narrow bands of elms, river birch, box elder, sycamore, black willow, silver maple, and cottonwood line most rivers and streams. These riparian zones are extremely important for water quality, erosion control, and wildlife habitat. Small trees and shrubs such as bluebeech, kinnikinnik, silky willow, riverbank grape, and brookside alder are common along these waterways.

Common shrubs of the cove and mixed mesophytic forests are spicebush, witch hazel, flowering dogwood, redbud, pawpaw, rhododendron, and summer grape. Common spring wildflowers are wake robin, cutleaf and two-leaved toothworts, twinleaf, yellow fawn lily, large-flowered trillium, wild blue phlox, bloodroot, dwarf larkspur, spring beauties, blue cohosh, squirrel corn, Dutchman's breeches, foamflower, Indian cucumber root, Solomon's seal, white, blue, and yellow violets, Michania, and wood nettle. Common ferns are silvery spleenwort, New York, Maginal shield, intermediate wood, and broad beech. Rare plants include butternut, mandarin, netted chainfern, southern loosestrife, blue ash, false rue-anemone, running buffalo clover, Shumard oak, Carey's saxifrage, and Guyandotte beauty.

East of the Alleghenies on the Potomac and Greenbrier drainages the forest is oak-hickory-pine except for the higher mountaintops. This was the oak-chestnut forest before chestnut blight killed all the chestnut during the 1930s and 1940s. Root sprouts of chestnut can still be occasionally found. The understory and shrubs consist of scrub oak, mountain laurel, flame azalea, redbud, deerberry, greenbrier, sweetfern, and beaked hazelnut. Common spring wildflowers include mountain lily-of-the-valley, mountain bellwort, spring iris, trailing arbutus, teaberry, pipsissewa, bedstraws, violets, and hairy forked chickweed. These forests are also open enough for New Jersey tea, bottlebrush grass, sticktights, mountain-mints, dittany, rattlesnake orchids, goldenrods, asters, and sunflowers to flourish as summer and fall flowers. Rare plants are downy arrowwood, box huckleberry, roundleaf dogwood, nodding wild onion, smokehole bergamot, smooth sunflower, bunchflower, and swordleaf phlox.

Grass balds and heath barrens occur at high altitudes between 3,800 and 4,800 feet. Most grass balds occur in a narrow belt running northeast from Spruce Knob to the Maryland border. These mountaintop sites have thin, acid soils and are exposed to constant winds and high rainfall and snowfall. Noteworthy grass balds and heath barrens include Dolly Sods, Dobbin Slashing, Roaring Plains, and Spruce Knob. These areas occurred naturally in the mid-1700s. Heavy timbering and the ensuing wildfires of the late 1800s and early 1900s greatly expanded the size of these habitats. Grasses of grass balds are hairgrass, redtop, Allegheny fly-back, and several sedges. Common associated plants are strawberry, cinquefoil, sheep sorrel, goldenrods, bracken and hay-scented ferns, and several clubmosses.

Heath barrens are dominated by low shrubs of black huckleberry, blueberries, chokeberries, Allegheny Menziesia, mountain laurel, rhododendron, mountain rosebay, smooth serviceberry, mountain ash, mountain holly, and aspens. Common wildflowers include trailing arbutus, bleeding heart, gaywings, fireweed, and pearly everlasting. Rare plants are wild holly, three-toothed cinquefoil, oceanorus, goldthread, wood lily, dwarf cornel, and woolly Hudsonia.

Open glades and swampy forests occur infrequently in flatter terrain above 2,500 feet. These ecosystems are open, wet acid soils covered by sedges, beakrushes, and sphagnum mosses that grade into shrubs and trees. They normally form on top of flat sandstones that are very resistant to erosion. Examples of these habitats are Cranberry Glades, Droop Mountain Bog, Canaan Valley, Big Run Bog, Blister Swamp, and Cranesville Swamp. In addition to sedges, beakrushes, and sphagnum mosses, open glades include cottongrass, large and small cranberries, purple-stem aster, purple fringed orchid, manna grasses, bog goldenrod, skunk cabbage, bog clubmoss, and marsh fern. Common shrubs are rhododendron, wild holly, speckled alder, winterberry, red and black chokeberries, and smooth arrowwood. Common swamp forest trees are hemlock, red spruce, white pine, yellow birch, red maple, and black ash. Rare plants of these habitats are Canada yew, rose pogonia, grasspink, twayblades, golden club, sundew, pitcher plants, bog rosemary, Jacob's ladder, balsam fir, buckbean, purple avens, glad spurge, and early coralroot.

Fast-flowing mountain streams flood frequently and carry lots of rocks, silt, logs, limbs, and ice that create difficult growing conditions for riverbank plants. However, some plants survive and even thrive in the narrow foot strips of boulders, roots, and sand along streams. Common riverbank trees are river birch, sycamore, silver maple, and box elder. Common shrubs are silky cornel, ninebark, brookside alder, willows, shrubby yellowroot, smooth azalea, poison ivy, and riverbank grape. Common herbs and grasses are monkeyflowers, great blue lobelia, cardinal-flower, tasselrue, stiff aster, and fringed loosestrife. Rare plants of riverbanks are Barbara's buttons, balsam squaw-weed, riverbank goldenrod, star tickseed, McDowell sunflower, sand cherry, smooth rose, and Virginia spiraea.

Cliffs, outcrops, and large boulders are common in steep West Virginia terrain. Lichens and mosses grow on most exposed rocks. Overhangs support ferns, heuchera, and the rare round-leaved catchfly which is found in the southwestern counties. These habitats may originate from sandstone (acid) or limestone (alkaline). Common plants on sandstone rocks include hairy lip fern, spleenworts, purple stonecrop, wild columbine, and purple laurel. Common plants on limestone rocks include red cedar, rocktwist, walking fern, and purple cliffbrake. Rare plants of these habitats are silvery nailwort and famiflower on sandstone and arborvitae, Canby's Mountain-lover, and crested coralroot on limestone.

Shale barrens are West Virginia's most unique plant habitat. They occur on steep south- and west-facing slopes on Devonian shales that are usually undercut by roads or streams in eastern West Virginia. The following 14 plants are known as endemics to southern Pennsylvania, western Maryland, western Virginia, and eastern West Virginia: nodding wild onion, shale barren rockcress, whitehaired leatherflower, Kates Mountain clover, yellow buckwheat, shale barren evening-primrose, mountain pimpernel, swordleaf phlox, shale skullcap, shale bindweed, shale barren goldenrod, shale barren aster, shale barren pussytoes, and pussytoes ragwort. Scrubby scattered trees growing on shale barrens include Virginia pine; red mockernut and pignut hickories; chestnut, post, and yellow oaks; red cedar; and dwarf hackberry. A few shrubs such as downy arrowwood, scrub oak, and dwarf hawthorn grow on shale barrens. Showy wildflowers are wild pink, bird-foot violet, goat's rue, mosspink, prickly pear cactus, gray beardtongue, smooth sunflower, and panicled bellflower.

West Virginia has five plants on the federal endangered or threatened list: harperella, northeastern bulrush, Virginia spiraea, shale barren rockcress, and running buffalo clover. The most valuable and best-known herbaceous plant is ginseng. It is not extremely rare but is regulated by digging permits to ensure its sustainability as a plant and part in our mountaineer heritage.

See also Forests, Trees

William N. Grafton
WVU Extension Service

E. L. Core, *Vegetation of West Virginia*, 1966; C. S. Keener, "Distribution and Biohistory of the Endemic Flora of the Mid-Appalachian Shale Barrens," *Botanical Review*, 1983; P. D. Strausbaugh and Earl L. Core, *Flora of West Virginia*, 1964.

Flora of West Virginia

Flora of West Virginia is a comprehensive guidebook to the approximately 2,200 wild plants found in the state. The 1,079-page book represents decades of research and study by botanists and West Virginia University professors P. D. Strausbaugh and Earl L. Core, their associates, and successors. In compiling the classic book, the authors drew upon resources at the WVU herbarium, library studies, and field work.

Flora describes the general features of West Virginia's vegetation, from types of forests to grass balds and heath barrens, shale barrens, aquatic plants, farm and garden weeds, artificial prairies, and plant migrations. The flora are presented by family, genera, and species. Each is described by physical characteristics, blooming season, habitat, and locations in the state. Line drawings, many of them by artist William A. Lunk, accompany the entries. Other contributing artists include A. S. Margolin, William F. Strunk, Nelle Ammons, Dorothy Megowen, Richard L. Brown, Jane W. Roller, Anthony J. Hyde, and Marguerite Givens.

Flora of West Virginia was originally published in four parts, beginning with part one in 1952 and ending with part four in 1964. The first one-volume edition was published in 1965 and reissued by Seneca Books of Morgantown in 1993. A group of six botanists from West Virginia, Maryland, and North Carolina is updating the book for future publication in a new edition.

See also Earl Core, Flora, P. D. Strausbaugh

John B. Floyd

Virginia Governor and Confederate General John Buchanan Floyd, the son of Virginia Gov. John Floyd, was born at Smithfield, Virginia, near present Blacksburg, June 1, 1806. He graduated from South Carolina College in 1829. A lawyer, Floyd was elected to the Virginia House of Delegates in 1847 and as governor in 1848. He was appointed U.S. secretary of war in 1857, and resigned that post on December 29, 1860. He was later accused of misusing the office by transferring arms from northern to southern arsenals in anticipation of secession.

When the Civil War began, Floyd quickly raised a brigade for Confederate service, and on May 23, 1861, he was appointed brigadier general. In August 1861, General Floyd was assigned to command the Army of the Kanawha, with the expectation that he could retain that region for the Confederacy. On September 10, 1861, his forces fought the Battle of Carnifex Ferry, Nicholas County. Forced to withdraw the following day, Floyd participated in the Sewell Mountain campaign with General Lee and with Floyd's political rival, Gen. Henry A. Wise, also a former governor of Virginia. On May 17, 1862, Floyd was put in command of the Virginia State Line, an independent force that included among its ranks many men from at least 22 West Virginia counties. Floyd died near Abingdon, Virginia, August 26, 1863, of natural causes.

Floyd's nephew, also John B. Floyd, was a Logan County state senator and close associate of the Hatfield family.

See also Battle of Carnifex Ferry, Civil War

Tim McKinney
Fayetteville

Russ Fluharty

Musician and folk personality Everett Russell "Russ" Fluharty, one of the most active figures in the folk arts revival, was born December 13, 1906. He energetically promoted West Virginia music and culture, especially the music of the hammered dulcimer.

A lifelong resident of the Mannington area, Fluharty learned to sing and play several instruments from his large extended family. In 1928, an uncle gave him an antique hammered dulcimer. (An ancient instrument, the hammered dulcimer consists of many strings stretched across a box and played with small beaters. It is not related to the Appalachian dulcimer.) The instrument was nearly unknown locally, so Fluharty developed a unique playing style as he taught himself to play his favorite hymns, patriotic tunes, and familiar old songs.

Fluharty began seeking opportunities to play and to tell others about the instrument. He was a naturally charming man, and audiences responded to his sincere, quaint manner. As interest in folk music grew during the 1960s and '70s, Fluharty was much in demand at schools, churches, and public events. He became known as "the dulcimer man." Fluharty also appeared at several national events, and the state Commerce Department sent him to travel shows in other states as an "ambassador of goodwill." He founded the Mountaineer Dulcimer Club, which remains active. Russ Fluharty died March 29, 1989.

Danny Williams
Morgantown

Ken Sullivan, "Russell Fluharty, the Dulcimer Man," *Goldenseal,* Winter 1986.

Fokker Aircraft Plant

Anthony H. G. Fokker (1890–1939), the famous Dutch aircraft designer whose fighter planes were the scourge of Allied airmen throughout World War I, during the 1920s also designed and built a series of successful civilian airliners. One of his two American assembly plants was established in 1928 in Glen Dale, Marshall County. An adjacent grass landing strip, now named Fokker Field and still used for local sports flying, was the busy site of Fokker test flights. At its peak, the Fokker plant employed 500 people from Glen Dale, Moundsville, and from the nearby Wheeling area. Fokker's best-known airliner, used by airlines throughout the world, was the high-wing Trimotor F-10A manufactured at Glen Dale.

The hope that the Northern Panhandle might become a major aviation hub was dashed by two events: the advent of the Great Depression, which virtually halted all growth in the aviation industry, and the March 31, 1931, crash of an F-10A that killed everyone aboard, including legendary Notre Dame football coach Knute Rockne. The crash was blamed on the plane's design, and Fokker sales plummeted. Fokker closed its Glen Dale operations, and in 1934 the building was sold to the Louis Marx Toy Company. A faint "Fokker Aircraft" is still visible on the outside of the main building.

See also Aviation

Louis E. Keefer
Reston, Virginia

Louis E. Keefer, "Wings Over Glen Dale: When Fokker Trimotors Flew Over West Virginia," *Goldenseal,* Winter 1991.

Folk Arts Revival

Beginning about 1950, interest in American folklore and folk arts blossomed nationally. Prominent musicians and painters included folk material and folk themes in their work, scholars and promoters sought out traditional performers and artisans, and state and local organizations developed programs to showcase folk heritage.

In West Virginia, serious efforts to identify and promote folklore began in the early 1960s, and the folk arts had a major place in the celebration of the state Centennial in 1963. Governor Barron created the Commerce Department in 1961, and appointed Hulett Smith the first commissioner. Smith hired David Callaghan, who worked throughout the four-year term in a variety of crafts-related positions. By 1963, Smith had created an Arts and Crafts Section within Commerce, and hired workers including Donald Page, Jane Cox (later Jane George), John Harper Jr., and K. Carl Little Jr. Early activities included identification and encouragement of traditional artisans, technical support to craftspeople wishing to increase production, and development of markets for handmade goods. In 1963, the department led the effort to organize a crafts fair at Cedar Lakes and in 1964 included a strong selection of native arts and crafts in the West Virginia pavilion at the New York World's Fair.

Smith succeeded Barron as governor in 1965 and continued vigorously to support folk arts. New workers in the crafts division included Norman Fagan, photographer Arnout Hyde Jr., and Florette Angel. Like most of those hired earlier, these three promoted traditional folklore in various capacities throughout their careers. *Goldenseal* magazine, the state's folklife quarterly, was founded in 1975 and remains popular in the 21st century. In 1976, a sales shop was established at the Cultural Center in Charleston, continuing for many years as the state's main outlet for quality handicrafts and an important retailer for craftspeople.

These and other efforts combined with the national folklore revival to produce a lively folk-arts scene in the state. The Mountain State Art & Craft Fair at Cedar Lakes, planned as a one-time statehood

Centennial event, remains a thriving annual event. The State Folk Festival at Glenville State College grew from a classroom exercise in Appalachian lore into a legendary showcase of genuine mountain music. By the end of the 1960s, there were at least four annual craft fairs in the state, several existing events had begun to include native folk music, a few small shops were offering local handcrafts, and at least three LP recordings of West Virginia folk music were available. By 1980, festivals, recordings, and craft outlets all numbered in the dozens, and awareness of our folk heritage had become firmly established.

See also Folk Music, Handcrafts

Danny Williams
Morgantown

Folk Dance

Folk dance, like other folk practices, is handed down by demonstration and imitation, passing over time from the original settlers to the present generation. Many ethnic groups participated in the populating of West Virginia, including northern and western Europeans in early times and southern and eastern Europeans in the great emigration accompanying the later industrialization of the state. African-Americans took part in both periods of settlement. Each group brought dance styles and other customs, and some shared dance traditions before arriving here.

Square dance is prominent among the many forms of folk dance in West Virginia. The square dance was once said to have come from Britain and to have survived in the rural areas of America such as West Virginia. This romantic idea, promoted by the legendary folk collector Cecil Sharp, has been challenged. Most scholars now attribute the square dance

to a general European tradition shared by early settlers in the region.

Another form of dance, the play-party, was common in areas where dancing was thought to be sinful, fiddle music the sound of the devil, and paired dancing too intimate. Play-party dances involve hand swings and skipping, and players move in a form reminiscent of the square dance. Participants form into rounds rather than squares and move to the song instructions sung by the dancers themselves and not usually to instrumental music or at the directions of a single caller. Although they had their origins in children's games, play-parties were for adults. As prohibitions against couples dancing diminished, the play-party died as a genre. Except in folk dance revival groups, the play-party is nearly completely forgotten now.

Other forms of folk dancing have persisted in West Virginia or have been brought here by enthusiasts. Clogging, flatfoot, and buck dancing can be seen at folk dance clubs and at the state's folk festivals. Cloggers are often organized into formal groups, and dance in teams, while flatfoot dancers do it solo. Clogging groups provide both instruction and public performances. More formal and extensive instruction may be obtained at the Augusta Heritage Center in Elkins. Groups such as the Friends of Old Time Music and Dance (Footmad) organize concerts and dances and encourage participation. Among the festivals often featuring traditional dancing are the Forest Festival in Elkins and the Vandalia Gathering in Charleston.

The deliberate teaching of folk dance was part of the folk revival of the 1960s and later. Teachers including Jane George and others taught dance styles indigenous to West Virginia while emphasizing the

formal folk dances of the British Isles, including Morris dance and other styles. Meanwhile, rural West Virginians kept up the old-time dance traditions unselfconsciously, gathering for regular weekly or monthly dances at fire halls, community centers, and schoolhouses. One such dance was held at New Creek, Mineral County, with others throughout the state.

See also Flatfoot Dancing, Folk Music

Barry Ward
West Virginia University

Robert G. Dalsemer, *West Virginia Square Dances,* 1982; Mike Seeger and Ruth Pershing, *Talking Feet: Buck, Flatfoot and Tap: Solo Southern Dance of the Appalachian, Piedmont and Blue Ridge Mountain Regions,* 1992.

Folk Medicine

In traditional folk medicine, the beliefs, techniques, sayings, and practices leading to cures and the reduction of pain are passed along by word of mouth and through observation. The transmission of medical knowledge usually takes place within the whole community and in some cases among special folk medicine practitioners. Serious ailments without known cures, such as cancer, and less dangerous but painful or annoying problems such as hiccups, warts, and earaches, are typical candidates for traditional medical cures.

Folk medical practices are usually grouped into three categories, and examples of each are found in abundance in Appalachia and West Virginia. A common, familiar category is that of household medicine. Kitchen staples such as salt and honey ease scratchy throats and hacking coughs. Turpentine mixed with sugar reduces stomach pains, an application of moist tobacco alleviates the pain of insect bites, and tobacco smoke helps with earaches, as does boiled human urine.

A second group of remedies uses plants and herbs found in the garden and in the wild. Ginseng harvested in West Virginia and made into a medicinal tea strengthens digestion and reduces fatigue. Practitioners as illustrious as George Washington and as far away as the residents of China have used American ginseng for strength and sexual potency. Foxglove is prepared as a heart tonic, sassafras is used as a blood thinner, and pokeberries aid recovery from intestinal difficulties. C. F. "Catfish" Gray of Mason County was a well-known herb doctor in the second half of the 20th century. Knowledge of herbs had been in his family for generations.

A third group of medical practices relies on magic. Ancient beliefs in the magical relationship between similar objects (homeopathic magic) on the one hand, and the magical connection between objects that have been in physical contact (contagious magic) on the other, provide the rationale for this category. Hence,

West Virginians dance at the 1998 Vandalia Gathering.

Singing was part of their lives

"Singing was part of the daily lives of the people, and they sang as they went about their work. Mother and grandmother sang as they worked at the spinning wheel or loom or as they went about the many chores of the household. Father and grandfather sang as they fed the stock, sharpened an axe, or as they sat before the fireplace. They sang not to entertain anyone but because it made them feel good to sing. Sometimes on the long winter evenings the children were entertained by songs and stories told by parents and grandparents.

"There were songs to express all kinds of feelings and sentiments. There were old ballads that told stories of knights and ladies, of love and adventure, thus enabling the singer to escape for the moment to another land far from his own environment. There were ballads that told how persons were motivated by evil emotions and driven to a tragic end by wrong doing. There were songs that expressed religious feeling or told stories from the Bible. There were funny songs that brought a good laugh to the singer and the listeners. There were songs to amuse the children especially at those fireside family gatherings on long winter evenings. Even the lullaby which the mother sang to her baby was probably a folk song which she had learned from her mother."

—Patrick Gainer
Mountain Heritage (1974)

warts may be transferred to a potato or to a dishcloth by touch. Pain can be "cut" by drawing a knife across a diseased limb.

While some were learned from the Indians, a great many of the folk cures found in West Virginia came over with the early immigrants from Europe. The use of household products, herbs, and magical beliefs readily crossed the Atlantic and served both the frontiersman and the aristocrat. In early times, folk treatments and those administered by trained physicians were often virtually the same.

As academic medicine advanced, traditional cures were supplanted. However, they were never abandoned, and sometimes supplemented the treatments and prescriptions of trained doctors. In rural areas including much of West Virginia, a scarcity of medical doctors and hospital facilities led to a widespread continuance of traditional practices which persists even today. This is also due in part to the high costs of conventional medical treatment and prescription drugs as well as the spiraling charges for medical insurance. It should also be noted that many traditional remedies remain in use because they work, and that herbal remedies are finding renewed respect among professionals.

See also Medicine

Barry Ward
West Virginia University

Folk Music

Folk music in West Virginia covers a wide range of styles and instrumentation. At West Virginia University's West Virginia and Regional History Collection, field recordings show that folk musicians played accordion, banjo, drum, fiddle, fife, guitar, hammered dulcimer, dulcimer, harmonica, jew's harp, mandolin, organ, piano, and saxophone.

There was also a rich oral ballad tradi-

tion. Cecil Sharp came to the southern mountains, including southeastern West Virginia, between 1916 and 1918. He was looking for traces of his native England's fading folkways. What he found was a trove of old songs, sung unaccompanied, that had been passed on from the first Scotch-Irish settlers and could be traced back to the British Isles.

Variants of the ancient ballad "Lord Lovell," for example, were found by later collectors in Upshur, Clay, Nicholas, Gilmer, Calhoun, and Marion counties. Other songs were descended from poems or popular songs that passed into oral tradition. Also, there were original songs of murder and tragedy, based on real events, that came from the hearts and imaginations of anonymous singers. Folklorist Patrick Gainer believed that most of West Virginia's traditional music came down as a cappella singing, sung by practically everyone as part of everyday life and with no instrumental accompaniment.

Although the influence of the British Isles predominated, the music had other roots, as well. Germans migrated from Pennsylvania into present West Virginia in the 18th and 19th centuries. While they have been long assimilated into the larger culture, they left a mark on certain tunes in fiddle repertoires in the state and on parts of West Virginia's dulcimer heritage.

African-Americans were brought as slaves to work in salt factories and on farms. Later they worked as miners and railroad workers. The black railroad experience has brought us a wealth of songs, and a genuine West Virginia folk hero, John Henry. Henry was a steel-driving man, swinging his hammer to drive long steel bits into rock to make holes for explosives. He met his death in a race with a steam drill at the Big

Bend Tunnel on the C&O Railroad in Summers County. Another song, "John Hardy," now a bluegrass banjo standard, commemorates the rowdier side of labor. The real John Hardy, also an African-American, killed a man in a card game in a McDowell County coal camp. He was hanged for it at Welch in 1894. Twenty years later, the influence of black blues musicians could be heard in 78 rpm recordings of a white country guitar player from Logan County named Frank Hutchinson.

The exploitation of West Virginia's abundant natural resources brought other nationalities from Southern and Eastern Europe. The land itself drew the Swiss to Helvetia in the late 1800s. There the Swiss farm families listened to marches, Old World favorites, and popular American tunes played by the community brass band. Waltzes competed for floor time with square dances called to Randolph County fiddle tunes.

In Marshall County, the Perkovic family preserved their Croatian heritage of Tambouritzan music on native instruments. They performed on radio station WWVA and toured the coalfields on a semi-professional basis. Some years later, Doc Williams became a mainstay of the *Wheeling Jamboree* weekly radio program on WWVA. Williams, whose roots also were in Eastern Europe, blended polkas and accordion music into his successful country music career.

Religion has sometimes been at odds with the wild and wooly aspects of West Virginia music, but religion provided its own powerful contribution. A frontier preacher would "line out" how a song went, saying the words for the congregation to repeat in song. This changed in most churches in the 19th century, when singing schools developed. Traveling teachers taught the "shape-note" method to local congregations. Gospel singing, black and white, has been an important part of West Virginia worship ever since. For years, Mount Nebo in Nicholas County has been the site of several large gospel singing conventions each summer.

Community music is still thriving. Square dancing is alive and well in West Virginia, and community centers and private clubs across the state present bluegrass and old-time music. Charleston, the capital city, is home to a community brass band.

The folk revival of the late 1950s and '60s, followed by the back-to-the-land movement of the '60s and '70s, brought renewed interest in West Virginia culture and local music. Gatherings such as the West Virginia Folk Festival at Glenville mushroomed as young people from the North and East flocked to hear authentic fiddling and see flatfoot dancing. Other festivals were established, including the

Stonewall Jackson Jubilee at Jackson's Mill and the Vandalia Gathering at the Capitol Complex in Charleston.

West Virginia music and musicians began to reach a larger audience. Small record labels recorded the music of heretofore obscure local fiddlers and singers. A film, *The Morris Brothers Old-time Music Festival*, captures part of this exciting time.

One such project was undertaken with the cooperation of the Hammons family in Pocahontas County by folklorists from the Library of Congress. This work provided the full context of West Virginia folk music, including stories and family and local history, a record of the joy, sorrow, and hard work of everyday lives.

See also Fiddle Tradition, Folk Arts Revival, Stonewall Jackson Jubilee, Vandalia Gathering, West Virginia State Folk Festival

Paul Gartner
Sod

John Harrington Cox, *Folk-Songs of the South*, 1925; Patrick W. Gainer, *Folk Songs from the West Virginia Hills*, 1975; Gerald Milnes, *Play of a Fiddle*, 1999.

Folklore

There are many categories of folklore, including oral folklore and the material culture. Oral folklore includes legends, proverbs, and dialect, as well as folk songs. Material culture encompasses such things as baskets, architecture, and corn-husking pegs, among many others. Celebrations are a part of folklore, including the traditions we observe at Christmas, Halloween, weddings, and birthdays. Every group, be they coal miners, computer programmers, or residents of a particular mountain valley, has its own folklore, and that lore has hundreds of aspects.

Numerous West Virginia local histories and travelers' accounts provide a glimpse of regional folklore as reflected in social mannerisms and beliefs as they existed from the pioneer era through the 19th century. *Marion County in the Making*, a 1917 book, was an early attempt to document folklore. It was a project by school teacher Dora Lee Newman and the Fairmont High School class of 1916. The book includes chapters on manners and customs, homes and homelife, remedies and superstitions, and songs and legends, as well as local history.

In 1915, C. Alphonso Smith at West Virginia University fomented interest in founding a folklore society in West Virginia. A society was soon formed and resulted, in 1925, in the important book *Folk-Songs of the South*. John Harrington Cox (also of WVU) edited the book, which, despite its title, consists almost entirely of West Virginia songs. This book went far to bring traditional regional folklore and folk music to the attention of

the general public, as well as scholars. The collecting work of 22 folklore society correspondents is reflected in the volume. Cox's 1939 publication, *Traditional Ballads, Mainly from West Virginia*, built on the earlier book.

During the New Deal of the 1930s, West Virginia was on the northern fringe of a major collecting effort to document cultural aspects of regional life in the South through the Federal Writers Project. The results are housed at the Library of Congress in the Archive of Folk Culture. Dozens of folklore collecting efforts followed throughout the 20th century. In 1932 another WVU professor, Louis Watson Chappell, published *John Henry: A Folklore Study*, which was widely admired. The John Henry story, known throughout the world and West Virginia's best-known folktale, was also taken up by Guy B. Johnson, whose *John Henry: Tracking Down a Negro Legend* appeared in 1929.

Between 1937 and 1947, Chappell pioneered field recording in West Virginia in a concerted effort to collect folksongs and fiddle music throughout the state. Acquired by WVU in the early 1970s, this remarkable collection of 647 aluminum disks joined other significant field recordings at the university's West Virginia and Regional History Collection. In addition to this Morgantown archive, the state archives in Charleston is another major research library holding folkloric materials. The Augusta Collection at Davis & Elkins College houses a sound and photo archive that documents West Virginia folklore.

The federal resettlement project at Arthurdale, in the 1930s, brought about an early effort to present folklife through festivals. Recordings of these events, which were encouraged and attended by Eleanor Roosevelt, are at the Archive of Folk Culture at the Library of Congress. Patrick Gainer was present at the Arthurdale events, and in 1950 he organized the West Virginia State Folk Festival at Glenville. Gainer had singers perform folksongs while they worked at a spinning wheel or in other contextual situations. Ghost stories, tales, spelling bees, and various folklife demonstrations and other expressions of folklore were integrated into the music presentations.

Also in the early 1950s, the West Virginia Folklore Society was revived under the leadership of Walter Barnes and Ruth Ann Musick of Fairmont State College and Gainer at WVU. Barnes and Musick started the *West Virginia Folklore Journal* as a quarterly publication of the society, and Musick was its editor until 1967.

West Virginia officially supported the celebration of folklore beginning with the administration of Governor Barron in the early 1960s. The 1963 Centennial celebration included publication of the book

Mountain Heritage and the first Mountain State Art & Craft Fair at Cedar Lakes. The popular fair has been held every July since that year. Hulett Smith, then head of the state Commerce Department and later governor, helped to create official programs in the folk arts.

In 1963, Gainer published *The West Virginia Centennial Song Book of 100 Songs,* and, after retiring from WVU, *Witches, Ghosts and Signs* (1975) and *Folk Songs from the West Virginia Hills* (1975). Marie Boette published *Singa Hipsy Doodle and Other Folk Songs of West Virginia* in 1971. Ruth Ann Musick added to the non-musical genre of published lore with *The Telltale Lilac Bush* (1965), *Green Hills of Magic* (1970), and *Coffin Hollow* (1976). Musick's books are the first studies to include a considerable amount of narrative folklore outside the Anglo-Celtic tradition, including material of continental European origin brought to West Virginia by immigrant coal miners. A booklet and set of recordings, *The Hammons Family*, published by the Library of Congress in 1973, was squarely within the earlier tradition. It was edited by Alan Jabbour and Carl Fleischhauer. A book, *Play of a Fiddle* (1999), by Gerald Milnes, documents folk music, dance, and folklore. *Goldenseal,* West Virginia's quarterly magazine of traditional life, has publicized numerous aspects of West Virginia folk culture since its inception in 1975.

The West Virginia State Folk Festival at Glenville is the state's longest continual folklife festival and one of the most authentic. The Augusta Heritage Center annually sponsors seven weeks of music and craft workshop programming and three annual festivals at Davis & Elkins College, beginning in 1972. Since 1976, the Vandalia Gathering has been held on the state capitol grounds, and continues as a major traditional music, story, and craft event on Memorial Day weekend. The Footmad Festival and Allegheny Echoes, more recent venues, provide participatory music and dance. The annual Appalachian Stringband Music Festival, sponsored by the Division of Culture and History at Camp Washington-Carver, is a major regional event.

The Mountain State Art & Craft Fair at Cedar Lakes promotes apprenticeship learning. The West Virginia folk arts apprenticeship program, supported by Culture and History, was initiated by the Augusta Heritage Center in 1989. The West Virginia Folklife Center at Fairmont State University, established under the leadership of Judy Byers in 1998, provides a folklore curriculum and teacher training seminar. The center preserves the archives of the Folklore Society and collections of Ruth Ann Musick, among other holdings.

In the last decades of the 20th century, major studies of cultural resources were undertaken in the Wheeling Heritage Area and by the American Folklife Center in the New River Gorge and the Coal River basin. Other heritage projects, such as the National Coal Heritage Area in the southern counties and a portion of the Staunton-Parkersburg Turnpike Alliance, are researching and interpreting local history and culture to encourage tourism. Almost every West Virginia county has a festival of some kind, and most celebrate a local tradition, occupation, local agricultural product, community homecoming, or other activity of interest.

See also Louis Watson Chappell, John Harrington Cox, Pat Gainer, John Henry, Mountain State Art & Craft Fair, Ruth Ann Musick, West Virginia Folklore Society, West Virginia State Folk Festival

Gerald Milnes
Augusta Heritage Center

Follansbee

Follansbee lies in Brooke County in the Northern Panhandle, six miles south of Weirton and four miles north of Wellsburg. State Route 2 is the town's Main Street.

The Mingo Indians once controlled the site, called Old Mingo Bottom by early white settlers. Isaac Cox built a log house there in 1772. In 1774, Cox transferred his land to John Decker, and Alexander Wells received a Virginia land grant for the same property. Decker sued, but Wells won. Wells passed the land to his son, who sold it to William Mahan.

The Mahans farmed the land until 1902, when they sold to the Follansbee brothers of Pittsburgh. The Follansbees erected a steel mill, using 40 acres for the mill and allotting the rest for town lots, naming the town for themselves. In 1906, Follansbee became a city, and immigrants from Great Britain, Wales, and Italy came to fill the jobs in the steel mill. The 1930s saw many projects, including a community house and a swimming pool. Follansbee saw its greatest growth in the 1920s, rising to 4,841 residents by 1930.

Follansbee prospered through World War II with metal and steel fabrication companies thriving. In 1954, the Follansbee mill was sold to the Louis Berkman Company. Rolling and annealing facilitiess were sold to Wheeling Steel (later Wheeling-Pittsburgh Steel) in 1958. Follansbee Steel still operates today. The city population has slowly declined since 1940, to 3,115 in the 2000 census.

Jane Kraina
Weirton

Nancy Caldwell, *A History of Brooke County,* 1975; Eura Cox Ulrich McIntosh, ed., *Diamond History of Follansbee, West Virginia,* 1984.

Food Preservation

People living in the area of present West Virginia have been preserving food since early times, and continue to do so today.

Leather britches, sulphured apples, and smokehouse ham are among the traditional foods that have been preserved by West Virginians. In addition, frozen blueberries, canned green beans, and sauerkraut are popular.

Food preservation methods include salting, smoking, pickling, and drying, all popular among settlers during the 18th and 19th centuries and to some extent still in use today. Canning, packaging, and freezing are of more recent origins.

These techniques were used to preserve the abundance produced by summer gardens, fall hunting, and winter hog killing, in a day when people stocked their own larders. Hams were smoked or dry-cured in salt, and salt also was used to make brines for pickling. Cucumbers, cabbage, corn, and mixed green vegetables were pickled by placing them in a solution of salt, water, and seasonings. Left in this brine at room temperature, raw cabbage will bubble and foam for two or three weeks. When this stops, the chopped cabbage has become sauerkraut, and it is ready to be rinsed, canned, and served.

Various meats and fish were smoked with apple or hickory wood. The drying of meats, fruits, and vegetables was common. Two popular dried foods are dried green beans, also called shucky beans or leather britches, and sulphured or bleached apples. To make bleached apples, fresh apples are sliced and peeled, and then placed in barrels with the gases from burned sulfur. Sulfur preserves moisture and color, but on most farms apples were preserved by drying without sulfur, often simply by spreading sliced apples in the sun. The beans are strung on long strings and hung up to dry, perhaps in a stove corner or hot summer attic. Rehydrated by long, slow simmering in water with salt and a little pork fat, they made a savory dish indeed.

For over 100 years West Virginians have canned food, by sealing pickled or boiled foods in glass jars at home and occasionally in tin cans at a community canning plant. With canning it is not necessary to use quantities of salt and sugar, except for fruit jams, jellies, and preserves, where large amounts of sugar are used. Home canning was encouraged in the early 20th century by the homemakers extension service.

Corn and potatoes were important staples, preserved in different ways. Potatoes were simply dug, cleaned, and stored in a cool, dry, frost-free place, often an underground cellar. Sometimes potatoes were simply buried in the ground, as were cabbages. Corn was preserved in many ways, including as grits, hominy, cornmeal, distilled spirits, whole kernel sweet corn, and dry shelled corn. Ears of homegrown popcorn were kept as a special treat. These

products and many others were stored in wood or metal bins, cloth bags, or sealed glass containers.

Prior to the electrification of West Virginia during the early and mid-20th century, few families relied on cold storage. Some used block ice and ice houses, but with the availability of electricity, freezing became widespread. Among the popular frozen foods in West Virginia were sweet corn, blueberries, beef and pork, and wild game.

See also Foodways

Mark F. Sohn
Pikeville College

Food Stamps

On May 29, 1961, Elderson Muncie of Bradshaw, McDowell County, an unemployed miner and father of 15 children, received the first food stamps in the nation. The purpose of the new federal program was to provide supplemental income for welfare recipients and families below certain levels of income. Prior to 1961, surplus commodities were distributed to the needy. Because of its high unemployment and poverty rates, West Virginia always has been a major focus of this program. The stamps originally used were later replaced by coupon books.

In his campaign for the presidential nomination in 1960, Sen. John F. Kennedy paid several visits to West Virginia and was moved by the malnutrition and poverty he observed. As president, Kennedy directed the government to establish a pilot food stamp program, with low-income families to be issued food stamps, which could then be exchanged at grocery stores. West Virginia was the first of eight states to issue food stamps. The Food Stamp Act of 1964 made the program permanent. West Virginia became the first state to implement the program statewide.

The bulk of the funding for the food stamp program comes from the U.S. Department of Agriculture, which also sets the guidelines and audits the state-administered programs. In West Virginia, public assistance agencies administer the program. In 2001, the West Virginia Department of Health and Human Resources assumed this responsibility.

The number of recipients of food stamps per capita always has been the highest in West Virginia of any of the 50 states. During the fiscal year 1999, an average of 247,249 individuals received food stamps in West Virginia, 13.7 percent of the population. During the same year, the nationwide average was 6.7 percent.

For several years prior to 2001, the West Virginia program was sanctioned by the federal government for its high error rate. Following steps to correct deficiencies, the federal sanction against West Virginia was lifted, and in May 2001 the

Dinnertime at a mountain home

"There was usually a large hearth with an enormous stone chimney. The large stone forming the hearth was generally broken by the heat from the fire. There was also the familiar crane with its two or three pots whose fragrant odors pervaded the whole house; a blazing fire; whole logs in the fireplace; a Dutch oven with bread cooking on the coals and another one with cornbread baking, and last but not least, the housewife herself busily placing the coals on top and under the ovens. There was a smell oftentimes of delicious salt-rising bread from a huge Dutch oven, and always a pot of salt-rising in the corner of the fireplace. A sweet fragrance of bacon and frying ham filled the air, while the hot corncakes cooked on the long-handled griddle and the cornbread was taken out of the oven with a knife under it to separate it from the bottom. In the corner of the fireplace stood a long shovel and a long-handled pair of tongs with a big bar of iron with which to put back the logs, and with a round broom made from the broom cane grown on the place. The frying pan, fragrant with the homemade sausage or the hot corn cakes, made the mouth of the tired man hungry as he looked on it. It was a scene of busy, happy work for the housewife and her daughters, and of waiting contentment for the men . . . ."

—Gov. William A. MacCorkle
The Recollections of Fifty Years of West Virginia (1928)

Department of Agriculture awarded the state extra funding of $1.9 million for its outstanding performance.

Ken Hechler
Charleston

Foodways

Moonshine, beets, and black walnuts. Biscuits and gravy. Meat loaf, mashed potatoes, and green beans. The foods of West Virginia are a combination of fast, slow, old, new, from-the-land, and ethnic. West Virginia food habits arose from the state's land forms, climate, settlers, and, since the Industrial Revolution, from a blending of transportation, communication, and appliances.

Long before peanut butter and microwave ovens found a place in the kitchens of West Virginians, Native Americans living in the area of West Virginia hunted black bear, buffalo, and white-tailed deer. They gathered hickory nuts, walnuts, chestnuts, persimmons, and cherries, and they raised corn, pumpkin, squash, and beans.

When the first white settlers arrived, Iroquois, Cherokees, and Shawnees taught them to gather and preserve foods. These settlers were probably Welsh, Scotch-Irish, and German, and they had no choice but to hunt and gather if they wanted to survive. Among their favorite wild food plants were ramps, poke, lambs quarters, creasy or cress, and dock. In addition to large game, they hunted rabbit, raccoon, squirrel, fox, opossum, wild turkey, ruffed grouse, and water fowl. The mountains of West Virginia were rich with game while the streams yielded trout, muskellunge, bass, and walleyed pike.

By the mid-19th century, most people living in the area of Virginia that was to become West Virginia worked small farms and did not keep slaves. Different ways led to a division in Virginia and the eventual formation of the new state. Identification with the North during the Civil War is reflected in West Virginia's food preferences. From areas to the north they adapted scrapple, Swiss cheese, wine, and kraut. They prepared rhubarb pie, buckwheat cakes, light potato rolls, salt-rising bread, and meatballs. As in the South, corn, grits, and country hams were also popular. West Virginia's food traditions became a mixture of North, South, and Mountain State.

As the state moved from an agrarian to an industrial economy, many families continued to gather herbs, rob wild honey, raise gardens, milk cows, and keep hogs. Company towns in the state's coalfields commonly provided space for gardening, and often even for the keeping of stock. Some West Virginians processed corn into moonshine and fresh pork into country ham. Beef consumption did not become popular until after the arrival of electricity, which in some rural parts of the state did not occur until the 1950s.

Today, many West Virginians continue to hunt, gather, garden, and farm, carrying on traditions that predate European settlement. Often served at dinner-on-the-grounds, homecomings, family reunions, and Christmas and Thanksgiving celebrations, some favorite Mountain State foods include fried apple pies, pan-fried chicken, country-fried steak, chicken and dumplings, macaroni and cheese, cheese grits, spoon bread, baked sweet potatoes, chow chow, corn relish, coleslaw and sauerkraut, leaf lettuce wilted in hot bacon grease, "dryland fish" or fried morels, pork sausage, wild berry pie, cherry cobbler, and black walnut fudge. A common winter favorite is soup beans cooked with salt pork or ham hock and served with skillet-baked corn bread, onions, and perhaps a glass of buttermilk. The special gravies of West Virginia include chicken, sausage, potato, ham, and tomato, and the gravy biscuit was popular here long before it was taken up by fast-food restaurants. At community suppers and festivals civic groups prepare ramps in season, dandelion greens, apple butter, wild grapes, and dried apple stack cakes.

When it comes to food, change is often the only constant. Already, two generations of West Virginia children have begged for McDonald's hamburgers and Kentucky Fried Chicken. Since the early 1980s, microwave ovens have speeded the pace of preparation, and supermarkets have added great choice, but even today the old-time apples, ramps, honey, and wild game of West Virginia have a place when we gather to eat.

See also Beans and Cornbread, Bee Hunting, Hog Butchering, Moonshine, Ramps

Mark F. Sohn
Pikeville College

Mark F. Sohn, *Hearty Country Cooking: Savory Southern Favorites,* 1998; Sohn, *Mountain Country Cooking: A Gathering of the Best Recipes from the Smokies to the Blue Ridge,* 1996.

Fools' Parade

Davis Grubb's 1969 novel *Fools' Parade* and the subsequent movie tell the story of three released convicts trying to make a new start with $25,452.36 from prison savings, if they could only cash the check. There are a host of murderous bad guys lined up to prevent them from doing that, in a yarn where the lines between good and evil are crystal clear. What follows is a heroic tall-tale chase on rail, on river, and by car down Grubb's native Ohio Valley, complete with multiple dynamite explosions.

The novel was adapted for the screen by James Lee Barrett, author of the screenplay for *Shenandoah,* and directed by Andrew V. McLaglen for Columbia Pictures. The 1971 film starred Jimmy Stewart as the legendary coal-shooter Mattie Appleyard (a character modeled after West Virginia storyteller Riley Wilson and the convict Holly Griffith), George Kennedy as the evil prison guard Doc Council, Strother Martin as Billy Lee Cottrill, and Kurt Russell as Johnny Jesus. Anne Baxter, William Windom, and Wheeling native Morgan Paull also played in the film, which was shot on location in Moundsville. Not much had to be changed for the 1935 setting: the West Virginia Penitentiary served as "Glory Prison," and the Marshall County Courthouse and the vacant Marshall County Bank building also served as realistic sets.

Filming began September 21, 1970, and concluded one month later when Davis Grubb himself came to Moundsville for the "Glory Days Dinner" accompanied by his Lhasa Apso dog Rowdy Charlie, making the $750 round trip from New York

The stars came to Moundsville to film Fools' Parade.

City in a Yellow Cab. In June 1971, the film premiered at the Court Theater in Wheeling.

See also Davis Grubb

Thomas Douglass
East Carolina University

Camilla Bunting, "When Hollywood Came to Moundsville: Filming Davis Grubb's *Fools' Parade*," *Goldenseal*, Summer 1995; Jack Welch, "Davis Grubb: a Vision of Appalachia," Ph.D. dissertation, Carnegie Mellon University, Pittsburgh, 1980.

Foreman Massacre

The latter half of 1777 was a time of bloody conflict between settlers and Indians in the Ohio Valley. On August 31, about 350 Indian warriors aligned themselves with the British in attacking Fort Henry, near Wheeling. Subsequently, a call for troops was made on the frontier, and among those to respond were Capt. William Foreman and a company of men from the South Branch Valley in the present Eastern Panhandle. When further reports of Indian raids came in, Colonel Shepherd, the commander at Fort Henry, sent Captain Foreman, Captain Ogle, and scout John Lynn on an expedition with 43 other men. They discovered that Fort Tomlinson, near the mouth of Grave Creek at present Moundsville, had been attacked and abandoned.

On September 27, 12 miles down the Ohio River from Wheeling, at the upper end of McMechen's Narrows, Foreman directed his party to set up camp. Lynn warned Foreman to move his men off the river trail and to travel along the hilltops. The next morning, however, Foreman kept his men on the trail, while Lynn moved his to a higher elevation.

Foreman's party halted to examine some Indian trinkets scattered along the trail. As their curiosity brought them into a single group, an ambush was launched

and 21 men killed, including Foreman and two of his sons. Another man was captured, and many more injured. During the attack, Lynn's men suddenly rushed down the hillside, firing rifles and yelling so loud that they tricked the Indians into running, but it was too late. The next day, Colonel Zane led a small party from Wheeling to bury the slain in a common grave near the scene of the ambush. In 1875, the remains were transferred to Mount Rose cemetery, and the Wheeling Chapter of the Daughters of the American Revolution has since erected a monument on the spot of the massacre.

Greg Leatherman
Fairmont

Forest Fires

Forest fires are among West Virginia's major environmental problems, damaging thousands of acres of timber each year and causing soil erosion and air and water pollution. There are disproportionately more fires in the southern coalfields, the counties south of the Kanawha River and west of the Bluestone. Absentee land ownership is highest in that region, and arson is a more frequent cause of forest fires there than in other parts of the state.

In addition to arson or incendiary fires, forest fires also start from a variety of accidental causes, including debris burning, campfires, railroads, equipment use, and fallen power lines. Fires in a miscellaneous category may start from hunters illegally attempting to smoke game from den trees, from burning underground coal seams, and from other causes. Lightning, a common cause of fire in western states, starts very few of West Virginia's forest fires.

West Virginia has statutory fire seasons in the spring (March, April, and May) and fall (October, November, and December). These are the periods when

fires are most likely to occur. With the leaves off the trees, the sun rapidly dries the forest floor, creating conditions that make it easy for fires to start. During the two fire seasons, outdoor burning is permitted only from 4:00 p.m. to 7:00 a.m.

West Virginia works with the federal government and private land owners in its fire program. Congress passed the Weeks Act in 1911, authorizing the federal government to purchase forestlands and to cooperate with the states in forest fire prevention. West Virginia appropriated fire protection funds in 1913 and contracted with the federal government to acquire additional funds for the purpose. Subsequent federal and state legislation in the 1910s and 1920s expanded forest fire protection efforts.

The West Virginia Game, Fish and Forestry Commission began an aggressive fire prevention campaign, putting together a traveling show to preach the gospel of forest protection. This consisted of a Model-A Ford truck equipped with a power plant and a portable screen, lantern slides, motion pictures, and projectors. There were also living accommodations including a tent. Emory N. "Pop" Wriston and a helper operated this rig for three years. They would set up on the courthouse lawn or some other central point and present programs to groups of all ages on forest protection, conservation, and forest fire prevention. Smokey Bear was introduced in 1944 by the Wartime Advertising Council and remains one of the nation's best-known advertising symbols to this day.

In recent times, about 1,100 forest fires burned an average of 38,000 acres annually in West Virginia. In a few exceptional years more than 100,000 acres burned. The dry years of 1987 and 1991 were especially bad, when 429,000 acres and 346,000 acres burned, respectively. After the establishment of organized forest protection the worst year was 1952, when 586,000 acres of forestland burned during the fall fire season and a total 638,000 acres during the year as a whole.

Although just as damaging in the long run, West Virginia's forest fires normally do not approach the intensity of those in the West. Our fires are mostly surface fires, burning forest litter and small trees and bushes. They "crown," or reach the tops of mature trees, during extremely severe fire weather. Hot fires kill large trees outright. More often, fires scorch the bark at the base of the tree, which may later fall off. Insects and diseases may then enter the tree, killing it or making it hollow and worthless for timber. Forest fires also kill wildlife; destroy habitat; and contribute to stream sedimentation, flooding and air pollution.

See also Fire Towers, Forestry

Robert Beanblossom
Division of Natural Resources

A mature coniferous forest.

Forestry

Forestry is the practice of managing forests. It is concerned with the growing of forest trees for lumber, pulp, and veneer production; trees and shrubs for ornamental purposes; forest-growing herbaceous plants for food and medicine; wildlife (including fish) for hunting, trapping, catching, and viewing; tree flowers for honey production; and nuts and soft fruits for wildlife and human food.

The early settlers felled trees for fuel and for building, and especially to clear the land, but timber as a major industry did not begin in West Virginia until the 19th century. By 1845, there were three dozen primitive sawmills, and by 1911, 83 band mills and approximately 900 circular mills were in operation. By the late 1920s, the original forests were nearly depleted. As the 20th century progressed, there was a strong offsetting trend at work as agricultural land was abandoned and allowed to revert to forest.

In 1935, a School of Forestry was established at West Virginia University. The first class graduated in 1939 and became the nucleus for professional forestry on privately owned lands in West Virginia. In 1968, a two-year associate degree in forestry was developed at Glenville State College. The first consulting forester in West Virginia, in Boone County, began work in 1946. Today, the number of professionally trained foresters in the state exceeds 400. About a third of them work for industry, a third work independently, and the remainder work for the government.

By the late 1980s, the forestlands of West Virginia had increased from a little more than 60 percent of the state's area in 1949 to 78 percent in 1988 and 2000. The logging industry grew as well, now cutting second-growth forests. New records were set by 1993, the first time that estimated lumber production exceeded 1.5 billion board feet since 1909.

The West Virginia Division of Forestry regulates logging in West Virginia. Loggers must have licenses, which they receive after having passed first aid, safety, and environmental tests. The law provides that the Division of Forestry must be notified of timbering operations as they begin and that loggers must manage erosion on the skid and haul roads and log landings. Critics call for stricter regulations, citing environmental concerns.

The Division of Forestry also works to control forest fires, tree diseases, and forest insects; collects and distributes statistics on the forest industry; regulates the digging of ginseng; manages state-owned forests for multiple purposes; and conducts various training programs for employees of forest product companies.

The entire Monongahela National Forest and parts of the George Washington and Jefferson national forests are in West Virginia. These, plus the several Army Corps of Engineers lakes and surrounding forests and other federal installations, several state forests, wildlife management areas, and municipal and county owned forest lands compose 15 percent of West Virginia's commercial forest land. Very large landholdings predominate in the state's private woodlands, with West Virginia forests owned by major national corporations, coal companies, railroads, utilities, and other concerns. Numerous West Virginians hold tracts of much smaller size, with the average acreage owned by individuals currently less than 20 acres. Surveys indicate that a majority of these small owners are interested only in the fringe benefits of forestry and not in harvesting timber.

See also Forests, Timbering and Logging, Trees

William H. Gillespie
Charleston

Division of Forestry

The Division of Forestry, an agency of state government, manages state forests and tree nurseries and assists timberland owners in managing their lands. In cooperation with the federal government, the division conducts periodic forest inventories on the 11.4 million acres of forested area in the state, and works to protect West Virginia forests from fire, insects such as the gypsy moth, and tree diseases such as oak wilt. Other duties include the conduct of forestry regulatory programs, such as the Logging Sediment Control Act; administering forest fire agreements with other states; attracting new forest product industries; and providing municipalities with educational programs to help them in maintaining ornamental and shade trees.

The first mention of forestry in West Virginia state government was in 1909, when the office of Forest, Game, and Fish Warden replaced the Fish and Game Warden office, itself created in 1897 to replace the 1877 Board of Fish Commissioners. Among other things, the 1909 act called for forest protection and research and provided fines and imprisonment for individual and industrial owners for intentionally or carelessly setting forest fires.

In 1933, the legislature established a Conservation Commission to assist with natural resource projects. It was created to enable the U.S. Civilian Conservation Corps to work in partnership with the state. The law also established the position of state forester. By bringing in professional foresters to assist with managing the camps, developing wild land recreation, planting trees, and fighting fire, the CCC demonstrated the first successful use of scientific forestry techniques in West Virginia. In 1961, new legislation reorganized the Conservation Commission as the Department of Natural Resources, with a Division of Forestry. In 1985, the Division of Forestry became a part of the Department of Agriculture and in 1990 a freestanding agency under the Department of Commerce.

In 1950, the federal Cooperative Forest Management Act provided for cooperation between the U.S. Forest Service and state forestry agencies to expand service to private nonindustrial forestland owners. This program has grown into the current cooperative forest utilization, forest inventory, forest protection, forest management, forest safety, and urban forestry programs.

Professional forestland managers in the Division of Forestry write management plans and oversee their implementation. They plan for the protection of sensitive habitat areas, for the preservation of rare and endangered species, for clean water, wildlife, and recreation, as well as for timber production. The complexity of forest ecosystems and the many years it takes to grow trees make the forest planning carried out by the Division far more difficult than most other types of land use planning.

See also Forests, Forestry

William H. Gillespie
Charleston

Ralph R. Widner, *Forests and Forestry in the American States: A Reference Anthology,* 1968.

Forests

West Virginia is the third most forested state. Forests cover approximately four of every five acres in West Virginia, supplying 2.5 percent of America's total timberland. West Virginia forests are important to the state's economy and a determining element in its ecology.

West Virginia woodlands are exceptionally diverse, with about 90 species of forest trees. There are at least a dozen other species of small trees, including redbud, dogwood, hawthorn, and sumac, and another dozen or so shrub species, including rhododendron, witch hazel, and others.

Several factors account for this rich diversity. These factors include the wide range in elevation, from 247 feet at Harpers Ferry to 4,861 feet at the top of Spruce Knob; the variation in annual precipitation, from 25 inches or less at Moorefield to nearly 70 inches at Pickens; the large difference in the average frost-free period, from 119 days at Bayard to 193 days at Logan; and the many ridges and coves that face different directions. The state's far-flung geography is also important. The tip of the Northern Panhandle stretches farther north than Philadelphia; the Eastern Panhandle reaches nearly to Washington; the state's western tip is 40 miles west of Cleveland; and West Virginia's southernmost point lies 60 miles farther south than Richmond. As a consequence of these many variations, trees with quite different requirements grow well in different parts of the state.

West Virginia's primarily hardwood forests can be divided into a western hills section, a high Allegheny Mountains section east of the western hills, and the ridge and valley area east of the Allegheny highlands. The trees in the western hills are similar to those found in the central hardwood forests of the Midwest; those in the high Alleghenies similar to those of the northern forests of New England; and those in the extreme eastern counties similar to those of the coastal states.

The 12 softwood tree species found in the original forest are all still present. Hemlock is probably the most common. Red spruce, once occupying nearly 469,000 acres mostly above 3,200 feet, and white pine, one of six pine species scattered in the state and once growing in nearly pure stands on approximately 300,000 acres, now grow on a greatly reduced acreage. Some, such as eastern larch or tamarack, balsam fir, and red pine reach their southernmost extent in West Virginia, but are not plentiful.

Since every tree in the forest supplies food and shelter for a varied and abundant assemblage of life, the total forest complex is wildlife habitat. The list of organisms present in the West Virginia woods is long, and includes bacteria, algae, fungi, worms and nematodes, insects and spiders, amphibians and reptiles, birds, mammals, ferns, and herbaceous and woody plants, among others.

The U.S. Census published the first statistical compilation on West Virginia forests in 1880. Naturalist A. B. Brooks compiled a report in 1910, and the U.S. Forest Service published reports in 1952, 1964, 1978, 1990, and 2003. The 2003 report shows that forests were distributed fairly uniformly throughout the state as of the year 2000. Only 10 counties had less than two-thirds of their land in forest and 26 counties were more than 80 percent forest. Webster County and McDowell County, both at 93 percent, were the most heavily forested; the least forested counties were Berkeley and Jefferson, at 44 percent. Only Maine and New Hampshire had more forest cover than West Virginia. In 1990, the West Virginia forest was described as 64 percent saw-timber, 26 percent pole-timber, and 10 percent still in the seedling stage.

The 1952 report stated that 64 percent of the state was forested. This changed to 74 percent in 1964, 75 percent in 1978, and 78 percent in both 1988 and 2000. This regrowing of the forests, one of the most important changes in West Virginia in the 20th century, resulted from the abandonment of agricultural lands. It is a remarkable rejuvenation, especially when one considers the thousands of acres irreversibly lost in recent decades to highways, utility rights of way, residential subdivisions, and urban sprawl.

The U.S. Forest Service reports also show a great expansion in overall volume of timber, from 8.7 billion board feet in 1945 to 17.5 billion in 1952, 29 billion in 1964, 33.6 billion in 1978, and approximately 70 billion in 1990. This is board feet in standing trees, or "stumpage." The forests overall are increasing at an annual rate of 2.3 percent.

Fire remains a threat to West Virginia forests and is especially prevalent in southern counties. Fires kill some trees outright, especially in the spring, and injure others. Decay-causing organisms move into the wounded trees, ruining them for lumber production. The over-browsing of deer is also a problem in our forests, resulting in the destruction of seedlings and damage to mature trees and shrubs.

See also Deforestation, Forestry, Division of Forestry, Reforestation, Trees

William H. Gillespie
Charleston

A. B. Brooks, *Forestry and Wood Industries,* 1910; Dawn M. DiGiovanni, *Forest Statistics for West Virginia: 1975 and 1989,* 1989; William H. Gillespie and Earl L. Core, *Forest Trees of West Virginia,* 1976.

Forks of Cheat

The area known as the Forks of Cheat lies between the Monongahela and Cheat rivers, including Stewartstown and the surrounding area in the northeast corner of Monongalia County and neighboring Pennsylvania. The name is confusing, in that it refers to the river fork created where the Cheat joins the Monongahela, rather than the place where the Cheat River itself forks into its tributaries. That is many miles upstream, at Parsons.

The Forks of Cheat has long been used as a regional name. An 1883 Monongalia County history says that the early settlers called all of the county's Union District west of Cheat River the Forks of Cheat. One of the earliest settlers was William Stewart, for whom Stewartstown was named. Irish-born, he came to the area in 1770. The Forks-of-Cheat Baptist Church has had four buildings on the same site and is believed to have the longest continuous history of any church in West Virginia. The church was established in 1775.

The Forks area was traversed by a major Indian trail, and early white settlers endured the frequent hazard of Indian raids. Settler John Evans, in a letter of April 18, 1778, reported recent attacks in which Indians had killed and captured ten people "above the mouth of the Cheat River," stolen horses, and burned a fort. A grandmother and three granddaughters were among those carried away. Stories such as this one were common.

Agriculture was the economic mainstay of the forks in the 19th century. The area also participated in the early iron industry of the region. Coal mining and natural gas were important in the 20th century. The construction of the Cheat Lake dam and hydroelectric station provided work in the 1920s, and recreational activities associated with the lake help shape the character of the area today.

U.S. 119 bisects Forks of Cheat on its way from Morgantown to Point Marion, Pennsylvania. The Mason-Dixon Line crosses the Forks of Cheat, separating West Virginia from Pennsylvania.

See also Cheat River

Hallie Chillag Dunlap
St. Albans

Forks-of-Cheat Baptist Church

The historic Forks-of-Cheat Baptist Church (1775) is located about six miles north of Morgantown, off U.S. 119 near the village of Stewartstown. Located very near the Pennsylvania line in the area between the Cheat and Monongahela rivers known as Forks of Cheat, it is the oldest church with continuous records west of the Alleghenies in West Virginia.

The historic congregation was organized the night of Sunday, November 7, 1775, by Rev. John Corbly and 12 charter members. The small, hand-written, parchment minute book is the church's oldest existing artifact. Other antiques include a silver communion pitcher, an hourglass, and two 1840 communion cups. Supposedly the hourglass was to time long-winded preachers.

Unique features of this small but still lively congregation include Homecoming Sundays each July, with the flying of the British flag to mark the church's original Colonial status, the famous bear meat picnic, and the annual opening of the "whiskey tombstone," a hollow grave marker once used to buy and sell spirits, unbeknownst to the church members at the time.

Joseph C. Gluck
West Virginia University

Formation of West Virginia

The creation of West Virginia was an outcome of the Civil War. Statehood was preceded by decades of sectional conflict between leaders of eastern and western Virginia, but sectionalism was a staple of politics in many other states (and still is in many places, including modern West Virginia). But while other states saw occasional calls for "dismemberment," only one—Virginia—actually split. East Tennessee, Western North Carolina, and North Georgia remained geographical expressions. West Virginia became the name of a state.

The process of West Virginia's formation was shaped by both the war's political and military contexts. Politically, the election of Abraham Lincoln, followed by the secession of seven Deep South states to form a southern Confederacy, precipitated a crisis in Virginia. A special convention sitting in Richmond to consider the issue seemed at first to favor keeping Virginia in the Union, but when Confederates attacked Fort Sumter on April 12 and President Lincoln called on the states for volunteers to suppress the rebellion, the Richmond Convention approved secession by a vote of 88 to 55, with delegates from counties later included in West Virginia casting 28 of the negative votes. In theory secession would not take effect until voters had ratified it in the regular spring election on May 23, but Virginia authorities began acting as though the matter were settled. State officials called county militias into state service on May 1 and directed them to gather at key railroad junctions, such as Grafton. Most local authorities, even in Western Virginia, went along with these actions, though in effect they made Virginia the ally of a Confederacy that it had not yet formally joined. The exception was in the Wheeling area, where local government continued to function and young men left the state militia to form companies of Union volunteers.

Unionist leaders rallied in Clarksburg on April 22 and summoned their own convention to meet in Wheeling on May 13. Initially, they concentrated on defeating the Virginia secession ordinance at the polls. When this failed, they debated other options. Meanwhile, federal troops crossed the Ohio River and joined with Unionist Virginia volunteers to push Confederate forces back from Grafton and eventually, at the battle of Rich Mountain on July 11, from the entire northwest corner of the state. A parallel invasion in the Kanawha Valley shortly followed. The swift Union conquest gave pro-Union pol-

iticians a safe place to deliberate, in contrast to East Tennessee, where despite a large Unionist majority activists were by this time going underground or fleeing northward for their lives.

A Second Wheeling Convention met in June 1861 to consider Western Virginia's options. Some leaders wanted to proceed directly to the formation of a new state; others thought it unwise to take such a step during wartime. A third group led by Waitman T. Willey of Morgantown effected a compromise whereby the Unionist remnant of Virginia's government was reconstituted as a "loyal" or "restored" state government, complete with governor, legislature, and representation in Congress. Key members of the Lincoln administration indicated their approval of this strategy, but sent ambiguous signals about the notion of a new state.

Nevertheless, a majority led by Willey decided to follow the complicated procedures that the U.S. Constitution requires for the formation of a new state out of the territory of another. While the Unionist Reorganized Government of Virginia under Governor Francis H. Pierpont worked to raise troops and to restore local government, the Second Wheeling Convention approved a "dismemberment ordinance" in August. It provided for a new state called "Kanawha" consisting of 39 counties extending from the Kanawha Valley north and east to Randolph, Tucker and Preston counties.

In November a third convention assembled in Wheeling to write a constitution for the new state. This convention changed the name to West Virginia and added five more counties in December and another four in April 1862, even though some of the additions, which form the present border with Virginia, were still under Confederate control. In May the Reorganized Virginia legislature gave dismemberment its approval, as did the U.S. Congress after the Constitutional Convention took steps to abolish slavery within the borders of the state.

President Lincoln's cabinet divided evenly on the issue of West Virginia statehood, with Attorney General Edward Bates leading the opposition while Treasury Secretary Salmon P. Chase defended the process as both constitutional and politically wise. Finally, on December 31, 1862, Lincoln decided in favor of statehood.

Countering the argument that relatively few voters had participated in the referenda that punctuated various steps of the statehood process, Lincoln pointed out that it was customary everywhere "to give no legal consideration whatever to those who do not choose to vote," for whatever reason. "The division of a state is dreaded as a precedent," he added. "But a measure made expedient by a war, is no precedent for times of peace. It is

said the admission of West Virginia is secession, and tolerated only because it is our secession. Well, if we can call it by that name, there is still difference enough between secession against the Constitution, and secession in favor of the Constitution." Following the ratification of West Virginia's anti-slavery amendment, in April Lincoln proclaimed West Virginia ready to take its place in the Union, which it did on June 20, 1863. Two additional counties (Berkeley and Jefferson) were transferred to the new state later that year.

The new state was constructed from blocks of counties, preserving the established borders with Kentucky, Ohio, Pennsylvania, and Maryland and creating a new border with Virginia based on existing county lines. Thus, while sectional differences and mountain barriers were often cited to justify the dismemberment, in fact the new border cut diagonally across geographical features in many places and followed the dividing ridge between eastern and western rivers for only 75 miles out of 400. Nevertheless, this was the only permanent boundary change to result from the Civil War.

See also Civil War, History of West Virginia

John Alexander Williams
Appalachian State University

Charles H. Ambler, *Francis H. Pierpont, Union War Governor of Virginia and Father of West Virginia,* 1937; Daniel W. Crofts, *Reluctant Confederates: Upper South Unionists and the Secession Crisis,* 1989; John Alexander Williams, "The Birth of a State: West Virginia and the Civil War," in Altina Waller, ed., *True Stories from the American Past,* 1994.

Fort Ancient Culture

Fort Ancient is the name given to a late prehistoric culture whose people lived in present Indiana, Ohio, Kentucky, and southern West Virginia between A.D. 1000 and 1650. The name was taken from the Fort Ancient Earthworks in Ohio, which was originally thought to be from the late prehistoric period, but was later found to be an earlier, Woodland-era site.

In West Virginia, Fort Ancient territory begins south of Sistersville, on the Ohio River, and includes the lower reaches of the tributaries of the Ohio and Kanawha rivers. Archeologists now believe that Fort Ancient society developed from local Woodland peoples and probably represented different ethnic and linguistic groups who shared similar traits, such as maize horticulture, shell-tempered pottery, bow-and-arrow technology, and in many instances, circular, palisaded villages. At least one early Fort Ancient village, Roseberry Farm in Mason County, had a burial mound associated with it.

Fort Ancient people lived in permanent villages, where they grew corn, squash, beans, and sunflowers, and harvested a variety of wild fruits and nuts. They hunted white-tailed deer, elk, black bear, wild turkey, rabbit, beaver, ruffed grouse, quail, and turtle. They also ate a variety of fish, and fresh-water mussels from the shoals of the rivers. Mussel shells were used as spoons, hoes, and shell ornaments. Crushed shells were added as a "temper" to pottery, to prevent the clay from shrinking and cracking when the pottery was fired. Although there are numerous historic references to bison in West Virginia, no skeletal remains have been found at any Fort Ancient site east of the Ohio River. Dog skeletons have been found at several sites.

Development of the Fort Ancient culture took place over a period of several hundred years. Early Fort Ancient sites have been found at Mount Carbon and Shadle Farm on the Kanawha River, at Island Creek and Barker's Bottom on the New River, and at Man and Gue Farm on the Guyandotte River. There were also early Fort Ancient sites at Roseberry Farm and the Miller site on the Ohio River. Protohistoric Fort Ancient sites, those from the very earliest historic period, with European trade goods have been found at Marmet, Buffalo, and Southside on the Kanawha River and at Logan on the Guyandotte River. Protohistoric sites are also found on the Ohio River at Clover, Rolfe Lee, Orchard, and Neale's Landing. Some of these sites, such as Buffalo, appear to contain both early and late Fort Ancient occupations. Many of these sites have never been formally investigated.

Artifacts found at Fort Ancient villages indicate a significant level of interaction with other culture areas in North America. Most of these villages were located along a network of long-distance trails in use for hundreds of years, leading from the Southeast to the Great Lakes, the Northeast, and the Plains. Exotic artifacts such as engraved marine shell gorgets from eastern Tennessee, and European trade items, such as glass beads and metal objects found at later Fort Ancient villages (after A.D. 1550), indicate participation in trade and perhaps intermarriage with Indian groups in direct contact with Europeans.

Fort Ancient villages flourished along the river valleys in West Virginia and the Ohio River until sometime after A.D. 1650, when pressures from the Iroquois from the north forced them to move out of the area. By the time the first European settlers appeared, most of the upper Ohio Valley region, including present West Virginia, was largely abandoned.

See also Archeology, Buffalo Archeological Site, Prehistoric People

Darla S. Hoffman
Cultural Resource Analysts
James B. Griffin, *The Fort Ancient Aspect, Its Cultural and Chronological Position in Mississippi Valley Archaeology,* 1943; Edward V. McMichael, *Introduction to West Virginia Archeology,* 1968.

Fort Ashby

Fort Ashby was built on John Sellers's farm within the present hamlet of Fort Ashby, Mineral County, in the fall of 1755, during the French and Indian War. The fort site is located near Patterson Creek, on the north side of Dan's Run Road just east of the road's intersection with U.S. 28. An old log building at the site, currently operated as a part-time museum, was probably a barracks within the fort. Fort Ashby was listed on the National Register of Historic Places in 1970.

A large number of settlers were killed by Indians along Patterson Creek during the summer and fall of 1755. To dissuade the remaining settlers from fleeing to coastal cities and to protect them, George Washington ordered that Fort Ashby and Fort Cocke (farther south) be built. Both were to be built in a quadrangular shape with 90-foot-long walls, bastions in the corners, barracks, and a magazine. A Virginia Regiment company commanded by Capt. John Ashby built Fort Ashby during late October and early November, 1755.

During April 1756, a large party of Indians surrounded the fort and demanded its surrender. Captain Ashby refused and the Indians soon departed. On April 17, 1757, George Washington ordered Fort Ashby abandoned by the Virginia Regiment. Afterward, the fort was probably garrisoned by the local militia until the Indian troubles ended. Whatever the case, Fort Ashby disappeared from all official military correspondence and was not mentioned again in surviving records. George Washington did not mention the fort in his diary during a visit to the area in 1782, which suggests that the fort was no longer in service.

See also French and Indian War

Greg Adamson
Dayton, Virginia
W. Stephen McBride and Kim Arbogast McBride, *Frontier Forts in West Virginia,* 2003.

Fort Boreman

Fort Boreman was a Civil War fort. Originally called Fort Logan, the Union garrison overlooked the confluence of the Ohio and Little Kanawha rivers at Parkersburg. When West Virginia became a state, June 20, 1863, the fort was renamed for Arthur I. Boreman, the new governor and a citizen of Parkersburg.

Construction of the fort began in early 1863 to protect the Baltimore & Ohio Railroad terminal and the river facilities at Parkersburg. Built of logs placed two high and two abreast, one contemporary drawing shows the fort as triangular while another represents it as five-sided. A system of trenches partly encircled the fort. Though its cannon were never fired in battle, Fort Boreman and its troops probably deterred attacks from the rebel forces that operated in the area, especially in southern Wood County. Associated with Fort Boreman is the "hanging tree," from which three men were hanged in 1866.

Following the war, the fort site became a favorite overlook and picnic area. Eventually it was forgotten, as the trenches filled in and brush engulfed the former military post. In 1997, the plight of this important local history site was brought before the Wood County commission by local historians asking for support in creating a park there. Fort Boreman Historic Park planned to open in 2006. The Fort Boreman site was added to the National Register of Historic Places in 2003.

Bob Enoch
Fort Boreman Historic Park Commission
H. E. Matheny, *Wood County, W. Va., in Civil War Times,* 1987.

Fort Edwards, Battle of

The largest battle of the French and Indian War in Virginia occurred in Hampshire County on April 18, 1756. It was fought on the west bank of the Cacapon River, about two miles northeast of the intersection of U.S. 50 and County Route 15 in present Capon Bridge.

A dispatch from Lt. William Stark to George Washington on April 18 reveals how the battle unfolded. Three men left Fort Edwards at Capon Bridge late in the day, searching for horses, and encountered a party of Indians near the fort. Two of the men managed to escape and alerted the fort's garrison to the presence of the enemy. Shortly afterward, Capt. John Mercer left the fort with a detachment of 40 to 50 soldiers from the Virginia Regiment to search for the Indians.

Captain Mercer's detachment had just topped a hill about one and a half miles northeast of the fort when they were ambushed by Indians. The soldiers immediately returned fire, and a battle ensued that lasted about 30 minutes. Finding themselves nearly surrounded after another group of Indians joined the engagement, the soldiers retreated to the fort. Captain Mercer, Ens. Thomas Carter, and 15 soldiers were left dead on the battlefield.

The *Pennsylvania Gazette* on October 21, 1756, presented a report of the battle as provided by John Long, an escaped Indian captive. Long was in camp with his captors at Bear Camp in Pennsylvania when a second war party appeared. The second party was composed of 150 warriors headed for the Cacapon River area. Later, Long was in Fort Duquesne, the French stronghold at present Pittsburgh, when the war party returned with about 17 scalps. Long overheard the Indians say that eight warriors had been lost during the battle and that one had died from his wounds on the trip home. Shingas, a Delaware war chief, was treated at the fort for a wound sustained during the battle and spent time there recuperating. The Indians claimed that they had engaged 200 soldiers during the battle and had killed several officers. Captain Mercer had seven or eight officers' commissions in his pocket when he was killed, which the Indians presented to the French as proof that they had killed several English officers.

See also French and Indian War

Greg Adamson
Dayton, Virginia

W. Stephen McBride and Kim Arbogast McBride, *Frontier Forts in West Virginia*, 2003.

Fort Henry

Fort Henry, originally known as Fort Fincastle, was constructed in the summer of 1774 on the Ohio River near the mouth of Wheeling Creek, the present site of Wheeling. The fort, attacked by Indians twice during the Revolutionary War, was a major defensive outpost in the upper Ohio Valley through the Indian Wars of the 1790s, second only to Fort Pitt at present Pittsburgh. The fortification was built under the supervision of Maj. Angus MacDonald, an engineer of the British regulars, and Maj. William Crawford of the Virginia militia, having been approved by Governor Dunmore. A tradition that George Rogers Clark planned Fort Fincastle is untrue. The fort was originally named to honor Dunmore, one of whose titles was Viscount Fincastle. After the outbreak of the Revolutionary War, Dunmore had come to be despised by Virginia patriots, and the fort was renamed Fort Henry to recognize Patrick Henry, first governor of the Commonwealth of Virginia. It was enlarged in 1777 to enclose a half acre.

The first attack on Fort Henry came during the early morning hours of September 1, 1777. The fort was defended by two companies totaling about 60 men.

Nearly half the militia were lured outside the post and killed by the Indians. Then a force of 200 Indians, mostly Wyandots and Mingos, besieged Fort Henry, defended by only 33 men, for three days and nights. After burning cabins and outbuildings in the vicinity, they withdrew across the Ohio River.

The second siege of Fort Henry occurred on September 10, 1782, when a similar band of 200 Wyandots and Delawares attacked the settlement. It was during this siege that Betty Zane, sister of Col. Ebenezer Zane, reputedly ran from the fort to the Zane cabin to obtain gunpowder to replenish dwindling supplies. Though there is no contemporary record of this feat, the legend persists. Three days later, the Indians withdrew. This was the last major engagement between Indians and whites on the frontier before the close of the Revolutionary War.

Fort Henry was not dismantled until the second decade of the 19th century. There is an account that Capt. Henry Shreve constructed his steamboat *Washington* in 1816 from timbers taken from Fort Henry, though this is unsubstantiated.

Philip Sturm
Ohio Valley University

Fort Lee

In April 1788, Col. George Clendenin was ordered to proceed west from present Lewisburg to construct a military outpost near the confluence of the Kanawha and Elk rivers as a defense against the Indians. He arrived with a band of 30 rangers and established the first permanent settlement within the present boundaries of Charleston. A fort, named Clendenin's Fort or Fort Lee, in honor of Gen. Richard Henry "Light Horse Harry" Lee, was built on land Clendenin had purchased from Judge Cuthbert Bullitt of Prince William County, Virginia.

The site, at the present corner of

Brooks Street and Kanawha Boulevard near downtown Charleston, offered a good spot for a canoe landing and a vantage point above the river. Completed in May 1788, the fort structure was about 36 feet long and 18 feet wide, with a height of about 18 feet. A stockade, constructed of logs placed upright and set side by side in ditches, was about 250 by 175 feet.

The establishment of Fort Lee gave some protection to the settlers, but the Indian menace remained until 1794. A story grew through the years that the fort was besieged by Indians in 1790 and that a woman heroine, "Mad Anne" Bailey, brought ammunition to the fort from Lewisburg. No basis of fact could be found for this incident, however.

The Clendenins, George and his brothers, William and Alexander, sold the fort to Joseph Ruffner in 1796, and it subsequently fell into disrepair. The stockade lasted until 1815, and the blockhouse was used as a dwelling place for many years. John P. Hale purchased the original lot and blockhouse in 1872 and moved the building, which finally burned down in 1891. The first white child born in Charleston, Lewis Ruffner, entered the world at the fort on October 1, 1797. A monument was erected in 1915 at the site which marks the site of Charleston's beginnings.

See also "Mad Anne" Bailey, Charleston, Frontier Defense, Indian Wars

Stan Cohen
Pictorial Histories

Fort Maidstone

The northern cornerstone of a chain of forts built by Virginia to protect frontier settlers from Indian forays during the French and Indian War, Fort Maidstone was built on the south side of the Potomac River opposite present Williamsport, Maryland. The fort was built on the farm of Evan Watkins near his ferry, Maidstone, on the main road connecting central Virginia, Maryland, and Pennsylvania.

During the fall of 1755 and spring of 1756, Watkins's farm served as an outpost and depot for the Virginia Regiment. On May 8, 1756, George Washington directed Capt. Robert Stewart to fortify Maidstone as feasible with available tools. Later, on July 3, Stewart informed Washington that the fort consisted of entrenchments with adjacent high ground and a guardhouse. This fort was never directly assaulted by Indians but several settlers were killed nearby. Mason and Dixon stopped by on July 3, 1765, while surveying their famous line between Maryland and Pennsylvania and stated in their journal that the fort was composed of logs. This suggests that the original fort had been remodeled or completely replaced at some point between May 1756 and July 1765.

Fort Henry protected Wheeling during the frontier era.

See also French and Indian War, Frontier Defense

Greg Adamson
Dayton, Virginia

Fort Pleasant

Fort Pleasant was built during the French and Indian War on Henry Van Meter's farm at Old Fields, near Moorefield, to protect the local settlers from Indian raids. The fort was constructed in late winter and early spring of 1756 by a detachment of the Virginia Regiment commanded by Thomas Waggoner. George Washington instructed that the fort be built in a quadrangular shape with 90-foot-long walls, bastions in the corners, barracks, and a magazine.

Once completed, the fort served as the headquarters for the Virginia Regiment on the South Branch. The fort was never directly attacked by Indians but several raids occurred nearby. In April 1756, the Battle of the Trough occurred just northeast of Fort Pleasant on the opposite side of the river at the head of the canyon known as the Trough, between a large group of Indians and 16 to 18 militiamen from other forts. More than half of the militiamen were killed along with an unknown number of Indians. Captain Waggoner heard them engaged but was unable to send aid because of high water.

A drawing of Fort Pleasant signed by James Witt and dated May 1770 is on file at the Hardy County Library. The drawing shows blockhouses at the corners of the fort, suggesting that the fort was either remodeled or totally rebuilt sometime after the French and Indian War. During a visit to Abraham Hite at Old Fields on September 28, 1784, George Washington indicated in his diary that the old fort was still standing.

See also French and Indian War

Greg Adamson
Dayton, Virginia

Fort Randolph

Fort Randolph, one of the most important military outposts of the Trans-Allegheny frontier, was located on the north bank of the Kanawha River at its mouth, at Point Pleasant. The fort was constructed in 1776 under the direction of Capt. Matthew Arbuckle, the militia commander at the site, and garrisoned by a company of troops sent from Pittsburgh. It replaced Fort Blair, built in 1774 following the victory over Chief Cornstalk and the Shawnee at the Battle of Point Pleasant and torched by Indians in 1775. The stockade was named for Peyton Randolph of Williamsburg, president of the Second Continental Congress.

With the outbreak of the Revolutionary War, Cornstalk and other Ohio chiefs who had signed the Treaty of Pittsburgh in 1775 found it increasingly difficult to restrain their warriors from joining the British. When Cornstalk and Red Hawk came to Fort Randolph in November 1777 to warn Arbuckle of the disaffection of their people, they were detained by the commander. Shortly after the arrival of Cornstalk's son Elinipsico, who came in search of his father, two hunters, Hamilton and Gilmore, were attacked by Indians and Gilmore was killed and scalped. In retribution, the three Shawnees were murdered by militiamen at the fort. Gov. Patrick Henry, Col. William Fleming, and Col. William Preston sent their regrets to the Shawnee through Cornstalk's sister, Nonhelema, who was friendly to the whites and lived at the fort.

Perhaps unrelated to the murder of Cornstalk, about 300 Wyandot and Mingo Indians attacked the fort on May 16, 1778. Unable to take Fort Randolph, they proceeded up the Kanawha River toward the Greenbrier settlements. Two militia volunteers disguised at Indians, John Pryor and Philip Hammond, overtook the force and warned the settlers, who took refuge at Fort Donnally.

Fort Randolph continued to protect the frontier, and it was garrisoned continuously during the Indian Wars of the 1790s.

See also Matthew Arbuckle, Cornstalk, Frontier Defense

Philip Sturm
Ohio Valley University

James Morton Callahan, *History of West Virginia, Volume I,* 1923; Phil Conley and William T. Doherty, *West Virginia History,* 1974; Otis K. Rice and Stephen W. Brown, *West Virginia: A History,* 1993.

Fort Savannah

In 1751, surveyors Andrew Lewis and his father found a large spring at the present site of Lewisburg, which they named Lewis Spring. The spring attracted settlers, and cabins were built nearby. The early settlers were dispersed during the French and Indian War, with the area once again populated by the late 1760s. In 1774, Camp Union was located there as the rendezvous for Lewis's troops. Fort Savannah was built there by the mid-1770s. William Richmond stated that his regiment wintered at the "Savannah Fort" between October 1775 and the spring of 1776.

Fort Savannah was a large militia fort. Though fortified by the time of the Revolutionary War, there is no evidence of British attacks on Fort Savannah. However, Indians raided in the area, with many battles reported. In 1778, a company under Samuel Lewis left Fort Savannah to assist nearby Fort Donnally, which was under attack by Indians, and drove them from the area. Later, in 1790, it is reported that "Mad Anne" Bailey made a heroic 100-mile dash from the besieged Fort Lee at present Charleston to "Fort Union in Lewisburg" to obtain gunpowder.

In 1782, a 40-acre tract was decreed by the Virginia Assembly to create the town of Lewisburg near the site of the fort, which (along with Lewis Spring) was set aside as public land. The Fort Savannah Inn, across the road from the reserved land, is today's visible reminder of Fort Savannah.

See also Forting, Frontier Defense, Lewisburg

Martha J. Asbury
EcoTheater

Virgil A. Lewis, *Life and Times of Anne Bailey,* 1891; Otis Rice, *A History of Greenbrier County,* 1986.

Fort Seybert

Fort Seybert was constructed on a bluff just west of the Sweedlin Valley Road approximately six miles northwest of Brandywine, Pendleton County. The first fort there was built in 1756 as a defense against Indians for the settlers inhabiting the South Fork Valley. A second Fort Seybert was built in 1758.

In April 1758, during the French and Indian War, Delaware and Shawnee warriors led by the war chief Killbuck surrounded the fort after capturing a woman and boy and killing a hunter outside the walls. They demanded that those inside surrender. The settlers deliberated a short time and agreed. Just before the gate was opened, a gun was fired at Killbuck from inside the fort, but its aim was deflected by another settler. When the settlers exited the fort, Killbuck greeted Capt. Jacob Seybert, their leader, by knocking out most of his front teeth with the butt end of a tomahawk. This action prompted the already frightened settlers to flee. Six to eight women and children and one man escaped and took refuge in forts in the Shenandoah Valley to the east. Nonetheless, the Indians succeeded in capturing 41 of the settlers.

After looting and setting the fort on fire, the warriors began separating the prisoners into two groups. Seventeen older adults were killed, including all the men. A bedfast Hannah Hinkle perished in the flames of the fort. The remaining group of 24 women and children were forced to return with the Indians to their villages in the Ohio country. Eventually, most of the captives were able to return from Indian captivity. Two or more of the smaller children remained with the Indians and at least three others died in the Indian villages.

A fort was rebuilt at the site after the 1758 massacre, known as Blizzard's fort after the property was sold to the Blizzard family in 1768. This third fort may have remained in use through the Revolutionary War period.

See also French and Indian War, Killbuck

Greg Adamson
Dayton, Virginia

Fort Stanwix Treaties

Two different treaties with the Indians, of special significance to Western Virginia, were negotiated 16 years apart at Fort Stanwix, near the present site of Rome, New York. The first was in the fall of 1768, when Sir William Johnson, the British superintendent of Indian affairs for the northern district in North America, met with 3,500 Indians representing the Six Nations of the Iroquois, with representatives present from the governments of Virginia, Pennsylvania, and New Jersey. By this treaty, the Iroquois surrendered title to vast territories, including the part of Western Virginia between the Little Kanawha and Ohio rivers, but excluding the present Northern Panhandle, for money and goods amounting to 10,460 pounds, seven shillings, and three pence.

The second treaty at Fort Stanwix, this one generally referred to as the "Treaty of Fort Stanwix," was made October 22, 1784, negotiated with the Iroquois by three United States commissioners. It provided for the further cession of western lands held by the Iroquois.

Fort Stanwix, built 1756–58, was named for Gen. John Stanwix. In 1776, it was renamed Fort Schuyler for Gen. Philip Schuyler of Revolutionary War fame. In 1781, the fort was destroyed by flood and fire. Rebuilt, the fort was again named Fort Stanwix.

See also Frontier Defense, Iroquois

R. F. Hendricks
Marietta, Georgia

Virgil A. Lewis, *History and Government of West Virginia*, 1912; "Fort Stanwix," *The Encyclopedia Americana*, Volume 11, 1955.

Fort Upper Tract

The exact location of Fort Upper Tract is not known, but it was built during the French and Indian War within or near the present hamlet of Upper Tract, by the South Branch Potomac in present Pendleton County. According to letters among George Washington's papers, Fort Upper Tract was built between August 21 and November 9, 1756, by a Lieutenant Lomax and 20 soldiers probably aided by local settlers. Washington, who was in charge of frontier defenses, directed that the fort be constructed of wood in a quadrangular shape. The fort was to have walls 60 feet long and bastions in all four corners. Barracks, a powder magazine, and other necessary buildings were to be built inside. The actual form of the fort is unknown.

According to a register kept by William Preston, the fort was destroyed in an Indian attack on April 27, 1758. Eighteen militiamen were killed at the fort. The attackers possibly included one or more Frenchmen. A letter in the Augusta County court records, written right after the fort fell, indicates that some of the rangers killed at the fort had been sent to reinforce Fort Upper Tract from Hog's Fort in

Brock Gap, about 22 miles to the east. Captain Dunlap, himself killed in the battle, had requested help upon spotting Indians in the area. The reinforcements arrived just before the fort was attacked. Local settlers Ludwick Fulk and William Elliot, their wives, and one stranger died with the militiamen.

No one in the fort survived to tell how it was captured. Fort Upper Tract was apparently never rebuilt.

See also Forting, Frontier Defense

Greg Adamson
Dayton, Virginia

William H. Ansel, *Frontier Forts along the Potomac and its Tributaries*, 1984; Lyman Chalkley, *Chronicles of the Scotch-Irish Settlement in Virginia 1745–1800*, 1912.

Forting

Forting was a formative experience for frontier West Virginians. Pioneer families moved from their homesteads to the safety of a nearby refuge fort when threatened by Indian war parties. If time permitted, the families brought food, clothing, and valuables with them. "They leaped from corn shuck beds and grabbed / The things they treasured most," as poet Louise McNeill said in her poem, "Forting."

Usually, they remained at the fort only as long as necessary. Typical stays ranged from several days to several weeks. On occasion, families lived in a fort for months. When the Indians left the immediate area, the settlers returned home. Forting was a seasonal activity. The greatest need for the shelter of a fort occurred between the months of April and October every year, the period of Indian raiding. Difficult travel made winter warfare relatively rare.

Life in a refuge fort could become quite uncomfortable. Rarely were the forts actually besieged, and families moved about the vicinity during daylight hours. Nonetheless, overcrowding was a problem. A fort measuring 50 feet square might hold 200 people. Periodic outbreaks of smallpox and other diseases also made fort life difficult.

Refuge forts first came into general use in Western Virginia during the French and Indian War (1754–63), though it was during the Revolutionary War (1775–83) that the practice reached its zenith. Indians took a vigorous part in both these wars and in many smaller campaigns of the same era. Following the defeat of the Ohio Valley Indians at the Battle of Fallen Timbers in 1794, the forts fell into disuse.

See also Frontier Defense, Indian Wars

John M. Boback
Alderson-Broaddus College

Roy Bird Cook, "Virginia Frontier Defenses, 1719–1795," *West Virginia History 1*, 1940; Joseph Doddridge, *Notes on the Settlement and Indian Wars of the Western Parts of Virginia and Pennsylvania, 1763–1783*, 1912.

Fossils

Fossils include the remains or traces of prehistoric plants and animals preserved in rock or sediments of the earth's crust. Fossils provide a record of former life, information that is vital in interpreting ancient environments, and a means of dating the rock layers.

West Virginia has a rich fossil record. Fossils are found in coal mines and excavations, including road cuts. Plant fossils are commonly found in shales that overlie coal beds. These coal beds are often exposed along highways in the southern, northwestern, and north-central parts of the state, including Interstates 68, 79, and 77. Fossil seashells are more likely to be found in the eastern counties bordering Virginia and Maryland.

Virtually all the bedrock of the state is from the geologic period known as the Paleozoic Era (570 to 240 million years ago), created from sediment laid down in ancient seas. Invertebrate fossils are abundant in these marine rock strata. The more common types include brachiopods, bryozoans, crinoids, corals, and trilobites. Molluscan remains including snails, clams, and squid-like animals called cephalopods are also common in some marine shales and limestones.

Early Paleozoic rocks outcrop at the surface only in the Eastern Panhandle and along the Virginia border in Mercer and Monroe counties. The oldest known fossils occur in the Antietam Formation in Jefferson County. This sandstone formation is from the early Cambrian Period, early in the Paleozoic Era, and contains abundant vertical burrows and sparse trilobites, gastropods, and brachiopods. Aquatic plants (algae) were common in shallow seas and formed wavy, laminated, fine-grained limestone deposits called stromatolites. Marine invertebrates become increasingly more diverse in limestones and shales of the Ordovician Period, which followed the Cambrian. Brachiopods and bryozoans are especially common. Brachiopods superficially resembled clams. Bryozoans were tiny bottom-dwelling animals that built moss-like, twig-like, or fan-shaped colonies commonly several centimeters or more in length. These calcareous colonies were perforated with tiny pores less than one millimeter in diameter, each of which housed a filter-feeding bryozoan.

During the Silurian and Devonian periods, later in the Paleozoic Era, West Virginia was covered most of the time by the sea. The earliest known land plants from West Virginia occur as fossils in the eastern counties in Late Devonian strata. They include leaves from large trees and two-meter high plants called Rhacophyton.

The Mississippian Period followed the Devonian, still part of the Paleozoic Era. Mississippian rocks are mostly marine strata and include abundant remains of crinoids and blastoids. These animals resemble flowers and were attached to the sea floor by a flexible "stem" made up of disc-like plates that resemble lifesavers. Their flower-like heads contained slender ciliated appendages used for filtering suspended organic materials from the surrounding seawater. Strata of Mississippian age outcrop in the southeastern part of the state, and are extensive in Greenbrier County where they have been quarried for limestone.

The Pennsylvanian Period followed the Mississippian. Pennsylvanian shales associated with coal beds contain abundant plant fossils. They are represented by roots, trunks, branches, and leaves. Lycopod or spore-producing trees including sigillaria and lepidodendron were especially common and developed in close association with peat swamps. The diamond or spindle-shaped pattern of lepidodendron is sometimes mistaken for fossilized snake skins. Ferns are also prevalent in some strata. "Kettle bottoms" are petrified mud casts of a fossil tree trunk extending up into the roof of a coal seam, resembling the bottom of a kettle or pot when seen from below. Kettle bottoms may fall into the mine without warning, a dangerous hazard for miners.

Vertebrate remains from Late Paleozoic strata include fish, amphibians, and reptiles. Fossils include teeth, scales, spines, bones, and coprolites (fecal material). Of particular interest are xenacanths, which were freshwater sharks. Amphibians also are represented by trackways, traces of ancient passage preserved in time in the geologic records.

See also Geology

Ronald Martino
Marshall University

D. H. Cardwell, *Geologic History of West Virginia*, 1975; W. H. Gillespie, J. A. Clendening, and H. W. Pfefferkorn, *Plant Fossils of West Virginia*, 1978.

Ruel E. Foster

Scholar Ruel E. Foster, born November 30, 1916, in Springfield, Kentucky, chaired the English Department at West Virginia University and served as Benedum Distinguished Professor of American Literature. He joined the faculty in 1941.

A graduate of the University of Kentucky, Foster received his doctorate from Vanderbilt University. There he was influenced by the so-called "Fugitives," writers who advanced agrarian values in life and literature. He was a close friend of writers Donald Davidson, Jesse Stuart, and Robert Penn Warren. Foster's books include *William Faulkner: A Critical Appraisal* (1951), *Elizabeth Madox Roberts, American Novelist* (1956), *Jesse Stuart* (1965), and (with Bob Conner) *Buck: A Life Sketch of James H. Harless* (1992). His literary criticism often dealt with the Southern literary renaissance. He was widely published as a poet and critic.

Foster believed that "the greatest American writers had a strong sense of place, from Cooper to Thoreau to Twain, Wolfe, Faulkner, and Hemingway." Appalachian literature was a main interest. His reviews of the works of West Virginia writers regularly appeared in literary journals, as well as state newspapers. He encouraged native writers, wrote forewords to some of their books, and after his retirement in 1987 continued to lecture and counsel. Alumni voted him "most effective teacher" at WVU in 1996. He served as tennis coach for six years. Foster was awarded the university's highest honor, membership in the Order of Vandalia. Professor Foster died November 10, 1999.

See also Literature

Norman Julian
Dominion Post

Fostoria Glass

The Fostoria Glass Company began in Fostoria, Ohio, in 1887. By 1891, an inadequate natural gas supply had caused the company to relocate to Moundsville. Fostoria hired skilled Wheeling-area glass men there and met with early success.

Fostoria made more than three dozen pressed glass patterns, more than 80 etched patterns, and more than 100 cut-glass patterns, representing immense amounts of glass production for the American table during nearly a century of existence. In the late 1920s, Fostoria mainly produced colored full dinner services with etched or cut decorations. In the 1930s, crystal surpassed dinnerware in the expanding line of Fostoria glass. Milk glass was popular in the 1950s and 1960s.

By mid-century, Fostoria had become the leading choice for elegant handmade tableware in a booming post-war society. Employment reached a high of 950 in the late 1940s, and Fostoria manufactured 8 million pieces of glass in 1950. Millions of pieces of glass were shipped from the company's factory. Later, Fostoria fell into decline due to changing tastes, foreign competition, and the increased use of plastics. In 1983, Fostoria was sold to Lancaster Colony Corporation, and the Moundsville plant closed in 1986.

Fostoria manufactured the "American" pattern which is the longest produced glass pattern in U.S. history and one of the most diverse, with almost 400 shapes made in this single pattern. Designed and patented in 1915, American remains in production today, long after Fostoria closed. Now marketed as American Whitehall, it is made by machine, not hand, by the Lancaster Colony Corporation at its Indiana Glass Company subsidiary.

See also Glass Industry

Dean Six
West Virginia Museum of American Glass

Leslie Pina, *Fostoria: Serving the American Table 1887–1986*, 1995.

Fowler Maps

Born in Massachusetts, Thaddeus Mortimer Fowler (1842–1922) produced at least 411 panoramic urban maps from his travels to 20 states and three Canadian provinces between 1870 and 1922. Of the 324 Fowler prints housed in the Library of Congress, approximately 30 represent West Virginia towns and cities. They present remarkable bird's-eye views of those places.

Learning the technique from notable bird's-eye mapmakers of the time, Fowler struck out on his own in the early 1880s. Settling with his wife in Morrisville, Pennsylvania, he traveled widely, visiting West Virginia between 1896 and 1900 and again during 1905, 1910, and 1911. He averaged four maps each year in West Virginia, creating views of such towns as Harrisville, Philippi, Cairo, New Martinsville, Morgantown, Bayard, Buckhannon, Weston, and, in a rare journey into the southern coalfields in 1911, Keystone.

Bird's-eye maps gained popularity during the latter half of the 19th and the early years of the 20th centuries. This popular form of commercial art, not generally drawn to scale, provided a three-dimensional portrait of street layouts, transportation routes, individual buildings, and major physical features of the vicinity.

Fowler's implements were few: folding ruler, compass, magnifying glass, parallelogram, and yardstick. To achieve the bird's-eye view, Fowler and other mapmakers would climb to the highest appropriate spot, perhaps a tall building, steeple, mountainside, or water tower. There they got an overview of the general structures and landmarks and their relation to the rivers, mountains, and other physical features, making rough drawings of their views. Then they drew individual sketches of houses, businesses, churches, parks, trees, and other landmarks, finally combining their work into one detailed map.

Debra K. Sullivan
Charleston Catholic High School

Fox Hunting

Fox hunting or fox chasing is common throughout most of West Virginia. As a true sport, no hunting or actual killing of a fox takes place and the thrill of the chase is the desired end unto itself. The activity consists of training and running hounds in packs of up to 30 dogs in wooded areas. It is a nighttime activity, and listening on a nearby hill becomes a social setting for men to brag and boast about their hounds, while jeering those whose dogs are far from "taking the lead" or not "hot on the trail." In this way, the chasers live vicariously through their dogs. They can make out the events while listening at a distance, distinguish one dog from another by its voice, and often describe in detail the actual chase, or "race," as it develops. It is common for fox chases to last until morning light.

Thaddeus Mortimer Fowler's map of Philippi.

Mountain fox chasing is related to the better known "club" sport where men and women ride to the hounds on horseback, in daylight, and in less formidable terrain. While the clubs favor Maryland hounds, mountain state fox chasers prefer Walkers, a lineage developed in Kentucky, as well as some lesser-known breeds. Red foxes are preferred and are considered to have a more sporting attitude than gray foxes. Many in the state belong to the West Virginia Fox Chasers Association and attend annual meets where dogs are numbered and judged as to their trailing abilities. The season runs from mid-August through the end of April.

See also Hunting Dogs

Gerald Milnes
Augusta Heritage Center

Gerald C. Milnes, "Listen to that Beautiful Music: Fox Chasing in the Mountain State," *Goldenseal,* Summer 1996.

Franklin

Franklin, the county seat and only incorporated municipality of Pendleton County, is situated along the banks of the South Branch of the Potomac River at the junction of U.S. 33 and U.S. 220, elevation 1,739 feet. The town originated in 1788, when the first county court of Pendleton County selected land owned by Francis Evick as the location for the county courthouse. Shortly afterward, Evick divided 46.5 surrounding acres into lots for a town and settlement began. The town initially became known as Frankford, an ap-

parent abbreviation for "Frank's ford," as the river crossing was called.

The town was officially established by a legislative act of the Virginia General Assembly on December 19, 1794, and renamed Franklin for Benjamin Franklin. The town's population has grown slowly, from the few early settlers in the late 18th century to approximately 200 residents in 1910, 500 in 1929, and 914 in 1990, declining to 797 in 2000. A prominent event in the town's history was a fire that destroyed the entire business section, the courthouse, and 19 private residences on April 17, 1924.

Tourism is a major industry due to nearby recreational areas such as Spruce Knob, Seneca Rocks, Dolly Sods, and Smoke Hole. The town is also home to the international office of the Mountain Institute, an organization seeking to preserve mountain environments and advance mountain cultures, as well as to CMI Inc., a manufacturer of mountain climbing equipment.

See also Pendleton County

Mary Dunkle Voorhees
Afton, Virginia

Elsie B. Boggs, *A History of Franklin: The County Seat of Pendleton County, West Virginia,* 1960.

Edward Bates Franzheim

Edward Bates Franzheim was born July, 20, 1866. He was one of West Virginia's major architects and among the first to receive formal, academic training in his profession. Youngest son of a prominent Wheeling family, he attended classes at

Chauncy Hall, a preparatory school for the Massachusetts Institute of Technology, then apprenticed with Boston architect John H. Sturgis. He subsequently studied abroad before returning to Wheeling in 1890.

Vance Memorial Presbyterian Church (1896), one of West Virginia's most exuberant Richardsonian Romanesque buildings, reflects his Boston training and demonstrates his mastery of the style. By 1902, Franzheim was probably the most successful architect in the state. That year he designed the Board of Trade-Court Theatre, a multi-purpose commercial structure in downtown Wheeling, and began a second career. For five years he managed the theater, took leading roles in its productions, and authored plays. Architecture remained his first love, however, as evidenced by his lavish domestic designs, in many different styles, for Wheeling's business and professional leaders. Franzheim was responsible for major alterations to Oglebay Mansion and the Fort Henry Club, and designed houses for prominent oil magnates in Sistersville.

Known as a "bon vivant," Franzheim carried a yellow cane and gloves, wore spats in season, and habitually arrived at the office in morning clothes, but changed to a black jacket in the afternoon. Franzheim died May 11, 1942. His many surviving works testify to his talent.

See also Architecture, Wheeling

S. Allen Chambers Jr.
Society of Architectural Historians

Frederick County, Virginia

By Act of November 12, 1738, Frederick County, Virginia, was created from the western lands of Orange County. Extending west and northwest from the Blue Ridge Mountains, Frederick was bound on the north by the Potomac River and on the south by Augusta County. Frederick originally encompassed all the land that was to become the northern half of West Virginia. Among the Virginia counties eligible for inclusion in West Virginia, Frederick was the only one to vote not to join the new state.

The earliest recorded land grants were to John and Isaac Van Meter, who received 40,000 acres each on June 17, 1730. Receiving a concession of land from the Van Meters, Joist Hite led a party of some 16 families into the lower Shenandoah Valley in 1732. Settling a few miles south of Shawnee Springs, Hite's followers established a settlement known as Opequon. In 1743, when the county's government was established, James Wood laid out Frederick Town on the site of Opequon. In 1752, Frederick Town was renamed Winchester. It is the county seat of Frederick County.

Frederick was divided into two counties in 1753. The part west of the ridge of the Allegheny Mountains became Hampshire County, now West Virginia. Named for the English shire, Hampshire was to become the oldest county in the future state of West Virginia.

While in command at Fort Cumberland, George Washington was elected to the House of Burgesses from Frederick County for the 1758–61 and 1761–65 sessions. After the French and Indian War, people began moving west and Frederick County experienced an increase in population. In 1772, Frederick again divided, this time into three counties. The northern end became Berkeley County, now West Virginia, the central portion remained Frederick, and the southern end became Dunmore (renamed Shenandoah in 1778).

Frederick Countians were early in their assertion of American liberties. On June 8, 1774, the freeholders met and adopted the Frederick County Resolves. Declaring it the inherent right of British subjects to be governed and taxed by their elected representatives, these Frederick Countians considered those acts of Parliament affecting internal policies of the colonies an unconstitutional invasion of their rights. Appointing a committee of correspondence, the freeholders deemed it important to communicate with other such committees. When war came, Capt. Daniel Morgan's rifle company left Frederick for service in the Continental Line.

Following the Revolution there were no immediate changes in the boundaries of Frederick, but in 1836 Clarke and a portion of Warren counties were carved

from Frederick reducing it to its present size of 426 square miles. By 1860, Frederick had some 13,000 inhabitants. During the Civil War the county was the scene of numerous engagements. In 1863, Frederick County citizens voted not to become part of West Virginia, while neighboring Jefferson and Berkeley voted to join the new state.

See also Augusta County, Hampshire County

Louis H. Manarin
Richmond, Virginia

Thomas Kemp Cartmell, *Shenandoah Valley Pioneers and their Descendants: A History of Frederick County Virginia (illustrated) from its Formation in 1738 to 1908*, 1909; William Wood Glass, "An Outline of The History of Frederick County," *Virginia and the Virginia County*, March 1950; J. E. Norris, ed., *History of the Lower Shenandoah Valley Counties of Frederick, Berkeley, Jefferson and Clarke, their Early Settlement and Progress to the Present Time*, 1890.

Frederick Hotel

The Frederick Hotel, built in downtown Huntington in 1905–06 at a cost of $400,000, was touted during its heyday as the most elegant hotel between Pittsburgh and Cincinnati. In addition to its 125 sleeping rooms, 45 of which had private bathrooms, the hotel also had 11 private dining rooms plus the Colonade Restaurant and the Elephant Walk Club. The hotel had its own power generators in the basement and an elaborate stained glass window in the lobby. It rented space to many shops and businesses on its first floor, which fronted on Fourth Avenue and 10th Street in the heart of the town. The owners claimed they traveled to Chicago and spent $100,000 for the hotel furnishings.

The Frederick was built in the neoclassical style by James Stewart, Huntington's first important architect. The building's well-preserved facade is attributed to a special hardened brick used in its construction. It was called repressed brick and was made about 50 miles down the Ohio River in Portsmouth, Ohio. Hotel Manager William R. Ritter Jr. closed the hotel to transient trade July 30, 1973, because occupancy rates had been dropping each year. He converted the old hotel to units for residential occupants and businesses, which is how it continues to function today.

Tom D. Miller
Huntington

Freedmen's Bureau

The Bureau of Refugees, Freedmen, and Abandoned Lands, known as the Freedmen's Bureau, was the first social welfare agency created to address the problems of freedmen and refugees in the former Confederate states or anywhere the U.S. Army had operated during the Civil War. Headed nationally by Gen. Oliver Otis

Howard, the bureau operated in West Virginia from 1866 to autumn 1868. Its headquarters were at Harpers Ferry, and of the several agents who conducted its business Lt. Augustus Ferzard Higgs and Capt. Jacob Clement Brubaker were the most important. Most bureau activities centered in Jefferson and Berkeley counties, but after Agent Brubaker conducted tours to places in the state where African-Americans resided, the agency appointed a sub-agent in Charleston and aided school construction in several communities.

Although the bureau addressed an initial refugee problem at Harpers Ferry and continual civil rights violations in Jefferson County, most of its activities involved the education of freedmen and the building of schools. It worked closely with William Ryland White, West Virginia superintendent of free schools, local black leaders, and white Free Will Baptists in the Shenandoah Valley. The bureau succeeded in stimulating official interest in public education of African-Americans, aided in the construction of 16 schools, and supported financially and politically the formation of Storer College, the first and for more than two decades the only institution for education of blacks above primary level in the state.

See also Reconstruction Era, Storer College

John Edmund Stealey III
Shepherd University

French and Indian War

The French and Indian War was the North American phase of a worldwide conflict between Britain and France. In Europe the conflict was called the Seven Years' War (1756–1763), but its Ohio Valley phase cannot be dated with such precision. Although commonly dated to 1754, the war may be said to have begun as early as 1752, when the French destruction of a pro-British Miami village in western Ohio helped to bring the Shawnees, Delawares, and other Ohio Indians into the French orbit. In 1753, the governor of Virginia dispatched the young George Washington to the upper Ohio to warn the French away from the valley. In 1754, Washington returned with troops to seize the region's most strategic point, the Forks of the Ohio at modern Pittsburgh, defeated a French detachment, and was defeated in turn when the French and their Indian allies forced his surrender at Fort Necessity on July 3. Shortly thereafter an Indian attack wiped out the first attempted white settlement in Tygart Valley near the Monongahela headwaters.

The Indians confronted the oncoming conflict with fear and resentment. Now dependent upon European manufactured goods, they appreciated the lower prices and better quality they got from British traders but recognized that the

French posed less of a threat to their hunting grounds than the land-hungry Virginians and Pennsylvanians. The French thrust toward the Ohio, coupled with Virginia's land hunger and the official pacifism of Quaker Pennsylvania, left the Ohio Indians little choice but to join with the French.

British authorities dispatched Maj. Gen. Sir Edward Braddock and 1,400 regular troops to the Ohio frontier in 1755. Braddock accepted Virginia militia and supplies from Pennsylvania but arrogantly ignored colonial advice about how to fight in Indian country. He led his army into one of the worst defeats in frontier history when he blundered into a French and Indian ambush at the Battle of the Monongahela, near present Pittsburgh, on July 9. Braddock was killed, and other participants, such as Washington, Andrew Lewis, and a young teamster named Daniel Boone, barely managed to make their way back to the settlements. A general assault followed on the Virginia frontier by Shawnee, Delaware, and Mingo war parties. Settlers newly planted in the Greenbrier and upper New River valleys were killed, captured, or frightened back across the mountains, while the older settlements in the South Branch and Potomac valleys came under heavy assault. Here a minority of residents held their ground, backed by a chain of small forts that Washington organized in 1756.

Virginia's government responded to Braddock's defeat by raising an army of several hundred frontiersmen commanded by Andrew Lewis and joined by around 100 Cherokee warriors. Lewis's orders were to march toward the Ohio via "Sandy Creek" (the Big Sandy River) and destroy the Shawnee villages in southern Ohio. Disaster again followed. Ill-disciplined, poorly supplied, and unlucky in the weather and scarcity of game they encountered, this Sandy Creek Expedition struggled forward for nearly a month in February–March 1756 before turning back in a state of near-starvation and mutiny.

The Western Virginia frontier remained open to assault until British regulars under Gen. John Forbes drove the French away from the Forks of the Ohio, present Pittsburgh, and established Fort Pitt there in 1758. This brought the Ohio Indians back under British influence, though occasional Indian raids into Virginia continued in 1759 and 1760. When defeats in Europe, India, and the Caribbean led the French to accept a general settlement in 1763, they agreed to give up all their North American territory. The astonished Indians, who did not consider themselves to have been conquered in battles fought far away in Canada and overseas, then confronted victorious British officials who to them seemed to have combined the imperious attitude of the French with the greed of

the frontiersmen. The result was further native resistance, in an episode known to history as "Pontiac's Rebellion," when assaults again fell on the Greenbrier, Monongahela, and Potomac frontiers. Finally, in 1764, an uneasy peace settled over the Ohio Valley, though the basic issue of who would control the region remained unsettled.

See also Indian Wars, Pontiac's Rebellion, Sandy Creek Expedition

John Alexander Williams
Appalachian State University
R. Douglas Hurt, *The Ohio Frontier: Crucible of the Old Northwest, 1720–1830*, 1996; Otis K. Rice, *The Allegheny Frontier: West Virginia Beginnings, 1730–1830*, 1970.

Freshwater Institute

The Freshwater Institute, located in Shepherdstown, is a program of the Conservation Fund, a nonprofit organization whose mission is to create partnerships among industry, nonprofit organizations, and government agencies to advance land and water conservation in America. The fund has also developed activities focused on demonstrating the sustainable use of natural resources, including the Freshwater Institute.

The Freshwater Institute was launched in 1987 and is a national program, although the 13-state Appalachian region is the core operating area. It works to improve and protect water quality and conserve watersheds while promoting rural growth and development. The work of the institute has focused on aquaculture or fish farming research and development; rural economic development; entrepreneurial training and education; acid mine drainage remediation; and community assistance. The institute's facilities include research laboratories, classroom-workshop space, fish culture systems, greenhouses, constructed wetlands, and other conservation demonstration projects. Some specific projects include an inventory and development of new, cost-effective treatments for acid mine drainage that will help waters return to their healthy states; development of an aquaculture education curriculum and teacher training workshops; and the first integrated aquaculture-hydroponic system powered by free natural gas.

Kathleen Carothers Leo
Division of Natural Resources

Friars Hole Cave

The Friars Hole Cave is the longest cave in West Virginia, with eight entrances and 44 miles of surveyed passage. The cave is located on the western flank of Droop Mountain in Pocahontas and Greenbrier counties. The cave lies mostly in middle Greenbrier Group limestones (Mississippian Age). Saltpeter was mined in the cave near the Snedegar entrance during the Civil War. All of the entrances of this

non-commercial cave are privately owned and several are on lands that are part of the Friars Hole Cave Preserve, which was started by Gordon Mothes in 1976. A photograph by Huntley Ingalls of the vertical pit entrance called the Crookshank Hole appeared in the June 1964 issue of *National Geographic*. Throughout the 1960s, various cavers explored and surveyed from the different entrances, and it was ascertained in 1976 that Friars Hole Cave at the southern end connected with Snedegars Cave at the northern end. With nearly 45 miles mapped, Friars Hole Cave is the sixth-longest cave in the U.S. and the 17th-longest cave in the world. Water flowing through the cave includes part of the subterranean flow of Hills Creek. The cave should be entered only with permission of the various landowners and only by experienced and properly equipped cavers.

See also Caves

William K. Jones
Charles Town

Frog Gigging

Every year, from early June to late July, hundreds of West Virginians may be found stalking the shorelines of farm ponds, recreational lakes, and warmer streams, armed with five- to ten-foot poles tipped with two or three metal spikes. Depending on how the trident-like poles, known as gigs, are rigged, they can either impale targeted bullfrogs, or pin them to the ground. Frog giggers pursue their sport mainly at night, using flashlights to spot their prey. The sudden glare of light temporarily immobilizes the frogs, making them easier targets for gigging.

In West Virginia, frog-giggers can legally take 10 bullfrogs a day during the brief annual season. A fishing license is required. Frogs can also be taken using fishing rods and fly lures. The rear legs of bullfrogs are considered a delicacy.

Rick Steelhammer
Charleston Gazette

Lynette "Squeaky" Fromme

A follower of cult leader and mass murderer Charles Manson, Lynette "Squeaky" Fromme (1948–) was convicted of trying to kill President Gerald Ford on September 5, 1975, in Sacramento, California. While serving a life sentence at the Federal Penitentiary for Women in Alderson in Greenbrier County, she escaped on December 23, 1987. Authorities captured her two days later near the prison. Upon sentencing for her escape, Fromme was transferred to the Lexington Federal Correctional Institution in Kentucky.

The Frontier

For nearly a century and a half, settlement west of the Allegheny Mountains was retarded by the rugged terrain and fear of the unknown. It was the demand

On the border

"Their lands lay nearest to the mountains. The geographical position made for feudal customs and a certain independence of action. They were on the border, they were accustomed to say, and had to take care of themselves . . . .

"Their fathers had pushed the frontier of the dominion northward and westward and had held the land. They had fought the savage single-handed and desperately, by his own methods and with his own weapons. Ruthless and merciless, eye for eye and tooth for tooth, they returned what they were given.

"They did not send to Virginia for militia when the savage came; they fought him at their doors, and followed him through the forest, and took their toll of death. They were hardier than he was, and their hands were heavier and bloodier . . . .

"Certain historians have written severely of these men and their ruthless methods, and prattled of humane warfare; but they wrote nursing their soft spines in the security of a civilization which these men's hands had builded, and their words are hollow."

—Melville Davisson Post
"A Twilight Adventure"
(1914)

for furs in Europe and the promotion of trade with the Indians that led to the earliest attempts to explore the region, by John Lederer, Thomas Batts and Robert Fallam, and Gabriel Arthur in the 17th century. In the first half of the 18th century, the trans-Allegheny was viewed for the first time as a settlement region, as the English colonial administration planned a strategy to compete with the French for control of the Ohio Valley.

The first attempt at settlement in what is now West Virginia in 1706 in the Shenandoah Valley, led by Swiss promoters Louis Michel and Baron Christopher de Graffenreid, failed because of territorial disputes between Virginia, Maryland, and Pennsylvania. In 1716, Gov. Alexander Spotswood and his Knights of the Golden Horseshoe claimed the Shenandoah region for England, with an eye to future development. There is evidence from the records of the Philadelphia Synod of the Presbyterian Church that there was a small settlement at "Potomoke," perhaps near Shepherdstown, in 1717, though it is uncertain on which side of the Potomac River the settlement was located. The earliest recorded settlement was that of Morgan Morgan, a Welshman who lived on Mill Creek near Bunker Hill in Berkeley County, beginning in 1731.

The earliest colonists, like Morgan, came through Pennsylvania to Western Virginia down the Valley of Virginia, a narrow corridor between the Blue Ridge and Allegheny mountains that funneled settlers to locations from western Maryland to the Carolinas. This route was used by most of those who came to Western Virginia in the years before the French and Indian War. Several German families, followers of Joist Hite, inhabited an area along the South Branch in Hampshire County in the early 1730s. Three Dutch brothers, Isaac, John, and Henry Van Meter, settled in Hardy County in the 1740s. These colonists, who had settled in the Fairfax Proprietary, had to buy or lease lands from Lord Fairfax.

In 1751, Andrew Lewis, surveyor for the Greenbrier Company, found Jacob Marlin and Stephen Sewell living in Pocahontas County, where they had been for two years. By the outbreak of the French and Indian War, some 50 families had settled in the Greenbrier Valley, including members of the Lewis, Renick, and Clendenin families. In August 1755, Indians attacked the Greenbrier settlements, killing and capturing more than two dozen colonists. The rest fled to safety across the Allegheny Mountains. Settlers filtering into the New River Valley in this period were also rebuffed. The Robert Files and David Tygart families first colonized the future location of Beverly in Randolph County in 1753. The next year, three German brothers, Israel, Samuel, and Gabriel Eckerlin, came to Dunkard Bottom in Preston County.

Most of these early colonists settled, legally or illegally, on lands granted to speculative land companies, such as the Ohio, Greenbrier, and Loyal companies. Expansive grants to these companies in the hundreds of thousands of acres dated from 1745. Most early settlers were killed, captured, or driven out of the forward settlements when war commenced, though dozens of families returned to Western Virginia as early as 1758, when the French were defeated in the upper Ohio Valley.

The Treaties of Hard Labor and Fort Stanwix with the Cherokee and Iroquois nations in 1768 increased the safety and quiet along the trans-Allegheny frontier. A few hardy individuals pushed the settlement line farther west, along the Monongahela River and its tributaries. John Simpson settled on the West Fork River in Harrison County in 1764 and Colonel Zackquill Morgan in Monongalia County in 1768. Colonists began returning to the Greenbrier Valley in 1769, including the Stuarts, Clendenins, Renicks, Donnallys, Lewises, and Keeneys. The Tygart Valley region was resettled in 1772; conspicuous families who settled there included the Stalnakers, Westfalls, Haddens, and Wilsons, who suffered from a dearth of crops the following year, called the "starving season."

In the years after the French and Indian War, another route of settlement was opened up, the Ohio River, fed by its conjoining tributaries, the Allegheny and Monongahela. Beginning in 1769, families descended the rivers and settled in the fertile bottomlands of the Ohio and its tributaries, the so-called "western waters." Among the first was Col. Ebenezer Zane and the allied families that came with him from Shenandoah County and settled at Wheeling Creek. The Joseph Tomlinson family, from Wills Creek, Maryland, colonized the Grave Creek settlement, now Moundsville, at about the same time. These early settlers came to the Ohio Valley in kinship-neighbor groups that migrated cohesively and sequentially to the region over a period of several years, the typical settlement pattern of the trans-Allegheny. Land speculators came early to the frontier, such as Col. George Washington and Dr. James Craik, who claimed tens of thousands of acres along the Ohio and its tributaries during a canoe trip in 1770. Washington was surprised to learn that much of the favorable land had already been claimed.

In the years leading up to the Revolutionary War, many other settlers came to the Ohio Valley. Walter Kelly, William Morris, and Thomas Bullitt came to live in the Kanawha Valley in the early 1770s. Isaac Williams, a Tomlinson in-law, cleared land across the Ohio from the mouth of the Muskingum River in 1775, later the site of Williamstown, near present Parkersburg. But with the coming of the Revolutionary War and the deterioration of peace with the Indians, most colonists along the Ohio removed their families to more secure settlements farther east.

It was in the decade and a half after the close of the Revolutionary War that settlers came by the thousands to Western Virginia and to Kentucky. Typical of the groups that came was the Capt. James Neal group that settled at Parkersburg, Wood County, in 1785. From that part of Monongalia County that became part of Pennsylvania in 1784, more than 40 of these associated families came sequentially over a period of 15 years. By the first national census in 1790, there were some 20,000 colonists living in what is now West Virginia. Only the interior and southern portion of the future state were unsettled at the turn of the 19th century.

Philip Sturm
Ohio Valley University

John A. Caruso, *The Appalachian Frontier: America's First Surge Westward*, 1959; Otis K.

Rice, *The Allegheny Frontier: West Virginia Beginnings, 1730–1830*, 1970; Philip W. Sturm, *Kinship Migration to Northwestern Virginia: The Myth of the Southern Frontiersman, 1785–1815*, 2004.

Frontier Defense

Much of West Virginia's early settlement took place under a state of border warfare with the Indian groups, including the Shawnee, Delaware, and Mingo (Western Seneca), which claimed most of the present state. To colonize this contested territory, the settlers had to be protected. Frontier forts were a major part of their protection.

During the French and Indian War (1754–63), the Virginia Colonial government established an extensive frontier defensive system. Central to this system was a chain of forts, most constructed and manned by colonial troops (called the Virginia Regiment), where settlers could go for refuge. County militiamen sometimes garrisoned these forts, but by the 1750s the militia system had deteriorated to such a degree that regular colonial troops were required to protect the frontier.

Forts were constructed during the 1750s along the South Branch of the Potomac, the Cacapon River, Patterson Creek, Opequon Creek, and the main Potomac River itself, as well as along the Greenbrier River. Among the better-known forts of this period are Ashby, Edwards, Maidstone, Pleasant, and Seybert. In what is now the Eastern Panhandle, forts were constructed roughly every 15 miles, under the overall supervision of Col. George Washington, commander of the Virginia Regiment. Although detailed descriptions of French and Indian War forts are rare, members of the Virginia Regiment were instructed to build square stockades, 60 to 100 feet on a side, with two opposite corner bastions.

By the Dunmore's War-Revolutionary War era (1775–83), the frontier had moved westward, and defense had shifted to more local or county control. The defensive system of the 1770s to the 1790s consisted of three primary parts: militia, scouts, and forts. The better-known forts of this period include Arbuckle's, Donnally's, Prickett's, Savannah, and Westfall's.

After the French and Indian War, the Virginia militia system had been revived. The militia was a county organization in which nearly all adult males were required to serve. Each county had at least one regiment of militia, commanded by a colonel, and the regiment was further subdivided into companies of 20 to 80 men. Each company was commanded by a captain. The county militia was under the overall command of the county lieutenant, a civilian officer and member of the county government. The county lieutenant could order out militiamen for service within the county, but for operations outside the county he had to call for volunteers, a limitation that often frustrated offensive plans.

The primary duties of the militia during the frontier wars included garrisoning the forts, protecting farmers during planting and harvesting, and pursuing Indian raiding parties. Western Virginia militiamen also participated in a number of offensive campaigns during the late 18th century. The most notable of these was the Point Pleasant campaign in 1774, culminating in the Battle of Point Pleasant.

The forts often were the base for scouts, or spies, who were dispatched to roam circuits of 30 to 70 miles each, looking for evidence of Indian raiding parties. Scouts were generally roaming throughout the region when danger was anticipated, from spring until fall. Scouts were also posted at known passes and advance areas during times of particular danger.

Forts were both privately built and built by the militia. Fort building styles varied widely, from individual two-story blockhouses, to bastioned stockades with a limited number of cabins, to very large stockades with corner blockhouses and many interior cabins. Many of these forts were built across eastern and northern West Virginia during the 1770s and early 1780s and in central and western West Virginia during the late 1780s and 1790s. The privately built forts were more often blockhouses, or small stockades; militia-built forts were often larger.

The local frontier defensive system was aided at times by the colony, state, or nation through peace negotiations with Indians, the construction of larger forts on the Ohio River (forts Randolph and Henry) and infrequent offensive campaigns. For the most part, however, the settlers depended on their local forts, militia, and scouts. Since the frontier settlements of the 1770s and after survived and expanded, and few, if any, of the forts of that period fell, this defensive system should be viewed as a success. Permanent peace came to the Western Virginia frontier only with elimination of the Indian threat within the Ohio Valley, which is usually dated from Gen. Anthony Wayne's victory at the Battle of Fallen Timbers in 1794.

See also Dunmore's War, Forting, French and Indian War, Revolutionary War, George Washington in West Virginia, individual forts

Kim McBride
Kentucky Archeological Survey
Stephen McBride
McBride Preservation Services

W. Stephen McBride, Kim A. McBride, and J. David McBride, "Frontier Defense of the Greenbrier and Middle New River Country," 1996; Otis K. Rice, *The Allegheny Frontier, West Virginia Beginnings, 1730–1830*, 1970; James Titus, *The Old Dominion at War: Society, Politics, and Warfare in Late Colonial Virginia*, 1991.

Stella Fuller

Social reformer Stella Fuller was a familiar face in Huntington for more than 70 years. She was born Stella Lawrence Cremeans in Point Pleasant, December 4, 1883, and grew up in rural Mason County. At age 19 she went to Huntington, where she attended business school. After graduation she moved to Welch to work for a law firm. She returned to Huntington after marrying Elmer Fuller in 1907.

Attracted by the religious and charitable programs of the Salvation Army, Fuller began attending services and volunteering her skills. Eventually she was hired as a part-time secretary. As she became more devoted to her Salvation Army career, she and her son moved into an apartment in the Citadel building, where she lived for 20 years.

Fuller left the Salvation Army in January 1943 and opened her relief operation on Huntington's Washington Avenue. Eventually, the Stella Fuller Settlement expanded into the area's largest haven for the disadvantaged and homeless. Stella Fuller died at age 97 on March 2, 1981, but her settlement continues to operate.

Joseph Platania
Huntington

G

Pat Gainer

Folklorist Patrick Ward Gainer (1903–81).

Folklorist Patrick Ward Gainer, professor of English at West Virginia University from 1946 to 1972, was born August 25, 1903, in Parkersburg. He was a musician, educator, major collector of West Virginia folklore, long-time president of the West Virginia Folklore Society, and founder of the West Virginia State Folk Festival at Glenville.

Starting in 1924, Gainer searched the hills and hollows of West Virginia, recording the folk songs and lore of the state's people. His research uncovered convincing evidence that many musical traditions of the mountain settlers derived from their British Isle forebears. Of the 299 ballads recorded by Francis Child in the British Isles during the latter years of the 19th century, Gainer discovered that 55 were also played and passed on by Mountain State musicians.

He was raised in the village of Tanner, near Glenville, Gilmer County. Born during a time when communities still gathered for music schools and "literaries," Gainer was able to reach back to an earlier time when superstitions, shape-note singing, and working "bees" were commonplace. His cultural grounding gave him the opportunity and desire to spend his career collecting and preserving the country life of the West Virginia mountains. Armed with his dulcimer and a clear tenor voice, usually singing without accompaniment, Gainer held class all over the state to spellbound students who heard him perform the ancient ballads and stories. His WVU courses were among the most popular offered at the institution.

Known nationwide as a folklife authority, Pat Gainer remains a respected memory in the minds of his many students. His works include the books *West Virginia Centennial Book of 100 Songs, 1863–1963* (1963), *Witches, Ghosts and Signs* (1975), *Folk Songs from the West Virginia Hills* (1975), the "Music" chapter in B. B. Maurer's *Mountain Heritage* (1974), and a 1963 recording for Folk Heritage Recordings, *Folk Songs of the Allegheny Mountains*. Pat Gainer died February 22, 1981.

See also Dulcimer, Folklore, West Virginia State Folk Festival

John H. Randolph
Bristol

John S. Gallaher

Journalist and politician John S. Gallaher was born in Martinsburg, December 1, 1797. He was apprenticed to local newspaperman John Arbutis and then worked for *Niles' Register* in Baltimore and the *National Intelligencer* in Washington. Returning to Harpers Ferry in 1821, Gallaher established the *Harpers Ferry Free Press*. (In 1831 it became the *Virginia Free Press*.) Gallaher also published *The Ladies' Garland* (1824) from Harpers Ferry, one of the earliest literary magazines in the United States devoted to the interests of women.

Gallaher was elected to the Virginia House of Delegates in 1830, playing a prominent role in Whig politics at both the state and national level. He became a state senator in 1842 and also served additional terms in the house. During this period he owned or managed several Whig newspapers and was instrumental in establishing the free school system in Virginia. He played a prominent role in having early railroads routed through the Eastern Panhandle, one of the factors that eventually led to the area's incorporation into the state of West Virginia.

In 1849, President Zachary Taylor named Gallaher auditor for the U.S. Treasury, and he served in that capacity in the Millard Fillmore administration as well. He resigned when Franklin Pierce became president but obtained a position in the quartermaster general's office until shortly before his death, February 4, 1877.

William D. Theriault
Bakerton

Game Laws

The regulations governing hunting and fishing seasons, bag limits, and related matters have undergone many changes since West Virginia's first game laws were passed in 1869.

Those first laws made it illegal to kill game between February 14 and September 15, and certain species of birds at any time. The penalty for a violation was not less than $5, nor more than $10, plus costs, and the violator could be imprisoned in default of fine for no more than 10 days. A novel provision in the 1869 act was that half the fine was to go to the person who informed on the violator, an incentive that did not prove popular with the public and eventually was discarded. The other half was to go to the general school fund; today, all hunting and fishing fines go into the school fund. In any case, there was no means of enforcement, and the first laws had little impact.

In 1882, three additional statutes were enacted that still remain in force in one form or another. One prohibited the hunting, chasing, or wounding of deer between January 15 and September 1. This law was a historic first step in restoring the deer population in the state. Another 1882 statute prohibited hunting on enclosed lands without permission, and the third made it unlawful to catch and destroy fish by means of any device other than hook and line.

The 1897 legislature brought enforcement of game laws by passing legislation that provided for the appointment of a state game and fish warden. His salary came from fines collected from violators. The first hunting licenses came in 1899 when non-residents were required to buy a license, which was good only in the county that issued the license.

The first significant statute of the 20th century came in 1901, when the legislature decreed that the state game and fish warden's salary would be paid from the state treasury, and, more importantly, that he could appoint deputy wardens. They became the forerunners of today's conservation officers. A prohibition on Sunday hunting, passed in 1909, was largely repealed by the legislature in 2001, but voters in a majority of counties reinstated the prohibition in ballot referendums. The same 1909 act prohibited fishing on Sunday, but this was later overturned.

The forerunner of today's Natural Resources Commission came on the scene in 1921 with the creation of a game and fish commission composed of three citizens appointed by the governor. Of more far-reaching impact, the same legislative session produced a law requiring that everyone above the age of 15 must have a license to hunt and fish, which is still the law today. The commission, which has had seven members since 1961, advises the Division of Natural Resources and the governor on conservation matters and approves or rejects hunting and fishing regulations.

A significant step was taken in 1933, with the creation of the Conservation Commission, the forerunner of the Division of Natural Resources (DNR). The DNR was created by the 1961 Legislature with sweeping changes that formed the agency as it is presently constituted. The same act upgraded the DNR's law enforcement division, which in 2002 had about 120 officers.

See also Division of Natural Resources, Hunting

Skip Johnson
Sutton

Jennifer Garner

Actress Jennifer Anne Garner, born in Houston, Texas, April 17, 1972, grew up in Charleston. She showed an early interest in the arts, dancing as a child with the Appalachian Youth Jazz-Ballet Company and appearing in plays staged by the Children's Theatre of Charleston and the Charleston Light Opera Guild.

Graduating from Charleston's George Washington High School in 1990, Garner attended Denison University. In 1995, she moved to New York City, where she secured a part as an understudy in a Broadway production of *A Month in the Country*. She had a starring role in the television series *Bone Chillers* and guest roles on numerous television shows, including *Spin City* and *Law and Order*. She had a recurring guest spot on *Felicity*, where she met her future first husband, actor Scott Foley. They married in October 2000 and later divorced. Garner had minor roles in films including *Deconstructing Harry, In Harm's Way, Mr. Magoo, Pearl Harbor,* and *Dude, Where's My Car?*.

Garner was catapulted into stardom in 2001 with her lead role on the television series *Alias*, in which she plays a college graduate recruited by the CIA. Garner won a Golden Globe for her role in *Alias*. She appeared with Leonardo DiCaprio in *Catch Me if You Can* in 2002 and starred with Ben Affleck in *Daredevil* in 2003. She and Affleck married in 2005, soon having a daughter.

Garnet High School

Garnet High School, Charleston's historic African-American high school, was founded in 1900 when a class of 12 black pupils in Kanawha County passed entrance examinations for high school work. The school was named for Henry Highland Garnet, an ex-slave born in Maryland who became U.S. consul to Liberia. Charles Wesley Boyd was the school's first principal. From 1900 until Garnet closed in 1956, 2,438 students graduated from the school.

In 1927, Garnet High School moved from its original location in the 500 block of Jacob Street to the corner of Shrewsbury and Lewis streets in Charleston's old African-American neighborhood. The new building included an auditorium; gymnasium; study hall; library; cafeteria; rooms for sewing, mechanical drawing, domestic science, and printing; laboratories for chemistry, physics, and biology; and other classrooms. By 1937, Garnet was classified as a first-class high school, with a faculty of 20 and a gross student population of about 400.

Four principals served during the existence of the school: Boyd, J.F.J. Clark, Scott M. Brown, and Henry E. Dennis. Garnet graduates include the Reverend Leon Sullivan, class of 1939, originator of the Sullivan Principles which contributed to the ending of racial apartheid in South Africa. Tony Brown, class of 1951, is the host of nationally syndicated television programs.

After integration of the public school system, Garnet High School became Garnet Career Center, an adult training program. It remains in use today.

See also African-American Education

Hazel P. Wooster
Charleston

Uncle Dyke Garrett

Clergyman William Dyke "Uncle Dyke" Garrett, born December 10, 1841, was Logan County's most famous preacher for the Church of Christ. He was born on Big Creek, the son of John and Eliza Godby Garrett. He enlisted on the side of the Confederacy in the Logan Wildcats (Company D 36th Virginia Infantry) at the start of the Civil War but was made the company's informal chaplain when it was found he was deaf in one ear. He deplored the war, denouncing it as against God's will, having evidently come to that conclusion after witnessing the execution of Southern deserters. Previously unordained, Garrett began thinking seriously about Christianity after the war and was converted by Alexander M. Lunsford, who preached in Mingo and Logan counties. Garrett became a circuit rider, preaching throughout Logan County the rest of his life. He was the inspiration for the construction of the Crooked Creek Church of Christ and helped establish a sister church in Logan Courthouse, now Logan.

Garrett married Sallie Smith in 1867, and he and "Aunt Sallie" remained married for 71 years. He was a friend of feudist Anderson "Devil Anse" Hatfield from at least the late 1860s onward, and his greatest fame was for converting Hatfield and baptizing him in Main Island Creek in October 1911. Devil Anse and Dyke Garrett were members of Camp Straton United Confederate Veterans, the social organization that controlled Logan County politics between 1870 and 1915, with Garrett serving as the group's spiritual leader. Beloved as the "Good Shepherd of the Hills," Garrett was a fiddler who danced to his own music, and he had a fine tenor voice. He died May 29, 1938.

See also Devil Anse Hatfield

Robert Y. Spence
Logan

Memphis Tennessee Garrison

Teacher and civic activist Memphis Tennessee Carter was born in Hollins, Virginia, March 3, 1890. Her father was a former slave who became a coal miner, and she grew up in the southern West

Memphis Tennessee Garrison (1890–1988).

Virginia coalfields. She married William Melvin Garrison of Gary, McDowell County, an electrician and coal company foreman, on October 5, 1918.

Garrison graduated from Bluefield State College in 1939. She taught school in McDowell County and also served as a welfare worker for the U.S. Steel Company in Gary, its company town. In this latter capacity, she helped to settle racial disputes, provided counseling to black miners and their families, and developed cultural and recreational opportunities for residents of the area.

Garrison was active with the Republican Party and with the National Association for the Advancement of Colored People. She helped to develop and sustain chapters of the NAACP in southern West Virginia, and served as a national vice president and as a field secretary who undertook special organizing and membership activities. One of her most important achievements was the creation of the Christmas Seal Project which became an important fund-raising effort for the NAACP.

After retiring from the McDowell County school system, Garrison moved to Huntington where she served as a substitute teacher and continued her public activities. She died in Huntington, July 25, 1988.

See also Gary

Ancella R. Bickley
Charleston

Ancella R. Bickley and Lynda Ann Ewen, *Memphis Tennessee Garrison: The Remarkable Story of a Black Appalachian Woman,* 2001.

Gary

The United States Coal & Coke's sprawling McDowell County industrial complex known collectively as Gary was for half a century among West Virginia's most productive coal mines. The model company towns making up Gary Hollow employed thousands of miners and shipped more than 200 million tons of high-quality "smokeless" fuel in its 54 years of full operation.

The creation of Gary marked the entry of J. P. Morgan's U.S. Steel into southern West Virginia, when Bramwell banker I. T. Mann, with Morgan's backing, exercised an option on prime coal-bearing land owned by the Norfolk & Western Railway's Flat Top Land Association. Morgan's company ultimately claimed a lease for more than 50,000 acres along Sandlick Creek of the Tug Fork and began constructing the huge works in 1901, designed to provide abundant high-quality coal and coke to the national industrial conglomerate. Thus, U.S. Coal & Coke was an affiliate of U.S. Steel.

Fully built, Gary Hollow contained 12 separate company towns, linked by paved roads and N&W rail spurs to the main company offices at No. 3 Works. The work force was highly diverse; a 1915 West Virginia Bureau of Mines report listed 1,479 hand-loading miners employed at Gary, with 227 white Americans, 271 African-Americans, 360 Hungarians, 224 Rumanians, 135 Italians, 145 Poles, and 117 miners of Slavic descent.

The nearly 15,000 West Virginians who inhabited Gary by the 1940s were served by 27 churches, ten company stores and three independent stores, three restaurants, nine elementary and two high schools, a clubhouse and athletic fields, a bowling alley, barbershop, pool hall, country club, bakery, dairy, and movie theater. The 1923 U.S. Coal Commission report awarded Gary 90 out of a possible 100 points for its cleanliness, urban amenities, and safety considerations.

Gary's parent company eventually decided that the operation was no longer profitable and pulled out of Gary completely by the 1980s, after selling the homes to the remaining inhabitants and depositing its records in the Eastern Regional Coal Archives in the Craft Memorial Library in Bluefield.

C. Stuart McGehee
West Virginia State University
Stuart McGehee, "Gary: A First-Class Operation," *Goldenseal*, Fall 1988.

Patrick Gass

Frontiersman Patrick Gass was born of Scotch-Irish parentage, June 12, 1771, near present Chambersburg, Pennsylvania. At age 21 he was a ranger stationed at Yellow Creek, Ohio, and later across the Ohio River at Bennett's Fort on Wheeling Creek, Virginia, guarding the frontier against the Indians. By 1797, the Gass family had located in Brooke County. Patrick enlisted in the army in May 1799 and in the fall of 1802 was sent to Kaskaskia, Illinois Territory.

In the autumn of 1803, Capt. Meriwether Lewis arrived at Kaskaskia seeking volunteers for the Lewis and Clark expedition. Gass volunteered and was accepted. When Sgt. Charles Floyd died early in the trip, Gass was chosen by the men to replace him as one of three noncommissioned officers. Although limited in education, Sergeant Gass kept a daily account of the exploration. This journal, published in 1807, was the only complete published account of the expedition until 1814.

As a private in the War of 1812, Gass participated in the battle of Lundy's Lane and was present during the British assault on Fort Erie. In 1815, he returned home to Brooke County and spent the rest of his long life there. Although addicted to strong drink throughout much of his life he settled down and married at age 59 and thereafter sired seven children. Gass, the last survivor of the Lewis and Clark expedition, died at age 98 on April 30, 1870, and is buried at Wellsburg.

See also Lewis and Clark

Gerald S. Ratliff
Charleston
Carol Lynn MacGregor, *The Journals of Patrick Gass: Member of the Lewis and Clark Expedition*, 1997; Newman F. McGirr, "Patrick Gass and His Journal of the Lewis and Clark Expedition,"*West Virginia History*, Vol. 3, 1941–1942.

Anna Johnson Gates

Anna Johnson Gates, born January 25, 1889, was West Virginia's first woman state legislator. A native of East Bank, Kanawha County, she was elected to the House of Delegates in 1922 and served a single term.

Gates sponsored 13 pieces of legislation during the legislative session, and five of her bills were passed. Among her successes was "Mother's Pensions" legislation, a state welfare program to provide income to any woman with children whose husband was unable to support the family. State legislation of this type was being approved across the nation at the time. Gates was also successful in getting a bill passed that provided the Kanawha County Board of Education the authority to establish, support, and maintain a public library. She chaired the House Committee on Arts, Science and General Improvements.

Previously a suffrage worker, Gates was elected to the legislature just three years after women received the right to vote. She chaired the Kanawha County Women's Democratic Executive Committee and was a delegate to the 1932 Democratic National Convention, which nominated Franklin D. Roosevelt for president. Anna Johnson Gates died January 12, 1939, at age 49.

Henry Louis Gates Jr.

Scholar Henry Louis Gates Jr., born September 16, 1950, is one of the leading African-American intellectuals in the United States. He grew up in Piedmont, Mineral County. Gates began his undergraduate studies at Potomac State College and completed them at Yale University. He received a Ph.D. in English at Cambridge University. In 1981, he received the prestigious MacArthur Fellowship, the so-called genius award.

The author of *The Signifying Monkey: A Theory of Afro-American Literary Criticism* (1988), a landmark work that won the American Book Award and helped to define the emerging discipline of black studies, Gates has since written a number of books including *Colored People: A Memoir* (1994) which describes his experiences growing up in Mineral County. In 1999, Gates edited *Africana: The Encyclopedia of the African and the African-American Experience,* also issued in CD-ROM as *Encarta Africana.* He holds the W.E.B. DuBois Chair at Harvard University and is the head of Harvard's Afro-American Studies department, and has also taught at Yale, Cornell, and Duke. He has served as general editor for several groundbreaking projects, including the *Norton Anthology of African American Literature* and the Schomburg Library of Nineteenth-Century Black Women Writers. A cultural and political commentator, Gates writes for such publications as *The Village Voice, Harper's,* and *The New Yorker*.

Linda Tate
Shepherd University
Henry Louis Gates, *Colored People: A Memoir,* 1994.

Horatio Gates

General Horatio Gates, born in England about 1728, was a resident of what is now the Eastern Panhandle of West Virginia during the period of his service as an American officer in the Revolutionary War. Gates, who had served as a British officer in the French and Indian War, returned to America in 1772. He was commissioned a lieutenant colonel in the colonial forces soon after his arrival in Virginia. He purchased a 659-acre farm in Berkeley County (now Jefferson), and began building his home, Traveller's Rest, in 1773.

In June 1775, the Second Continental Congress appointed Gates brigadier general, and a year later he became major general. Under his command, American troops defeated General Burgoyne at Saratoga in October 1777. This turning point in the Revolution gained him well-deserved praise, but in 1780 Gates suffered a disastrous defeat from Cornwallis at Camden, South Carolina, and was relieved of his command. Throughout his military service, Gates found occasion to visit Traveller's Rest. He sold the property in 1790 and, before moving to New York state, assembled his slaves and announced that they were free. Horatio Gates died April 10, 1806.

See also Revolutionary War, Traveller's Rest

S. Allen Chambers Jr.
Society of Architectural Historians

Gathering

Gathering, the harvesting of wild plant foods and herbs for domestic and commercial use, is practiced all over West Virginia. Everywhere, one finds place names associated with gathering: Bee Knob, Walnut Gap, Grape Island, Seng Camp Run, Chestnut Flat, and the communities of Ramp and Paw Paw, among many others. The presence of the mixed hardwood forest throughout the state, with its rich canopy and understory, provides for a remarkable diversity of greens, roots, berries, mushrooms, nuts, and fruits. This diversity supports an annual round of foraging practices that together make up a considerable part of the state's folk culture.

Gathering takes place in a complex social context, which requires both ecological and historical knowledge to navigate. Practices of gathering are informed by a concept of the "commons" and a strong awareness of the history of land use. American Indians living in Ohio spent the summer months in the mountains gathering food for the winter. Deemed vital for the survival of warring factions, the mountains were shared in common, a place where animosities among hostile tribes were suspended. Privatizing spaces and resources vital to human existence was unthinkable to the natives.

Today, gathering thrives where communities in the mountains have managed to maintain common access to gatherable resources on lands that may be held by corporations, the government, or neighbors, but are nonetheless generally open to all. Echoes of Indian gathering practices persist in names for gatherables such as "puccoon" (for blood root or red root), Shawnee lettuce, and in rumors of places and species favored by Native Americans. "The Indians liked to gather the red mushrooms that come up in the fall," an elderly woman from Peachtree Creek in Raleigh County stated.

Access to wild gatherables helps communities to sustain themselves both materially and culturally. Commercially valuable roots such as goldenseal (also known as yellow root), mayapple, blood root, and, most valuable of all, ginseng, have long supplemented family incomes. Wild produce supplements mountain diets. This includes ramps, poke, creasies or wild cress, black raspberries, red mulberries, blackberries, fox grapes, huckleberries, black walnuts, white or butternut walnuts, hazelnuts, and pawpaws. Each season brings its share of wild edibles: the morel mushrooms known in various parts of the mountains as "moodgers," "muggins," and "molly moochers"; the wine berries that people say are too juicy to preserve; the beechnuts that old-timers will tell you they peeled, salted, and ate on the spot as children.

Culturally, gathering fosters the sort of talk that promotes a sense of participation and continuity. Practitioners locate themselves not only in a contemporary community of like-minded people but also within a chain that spans the generations. People associate the land with those who have taught it to them. An 84-year-old woman from Boone County recalled that when she was a little girl her grandmother took her out to look for mushrooms and spring greens. Her grandmother would point out trees where Indians summering in the mountains would hang their meat to dry and the charred rocks where Indians baked their cornbread.

The practice of gathering involves people in a system of knowledge of historical, social, and ecological relationships. Morel fans insist that old apple orchards are the best places to go molly mooching.

Red mulberry trees, now scarce, may be found by those who can remember where farmers penned their hogs. Don't bother looking for wild cress in undisturbed ground, because, as one woman put it, "Creasies won't grow unless you cultivate the soil." Nut trees, not deemed worth much by loggers, become vital parts of the system. "We were taught never to cut down a nut tree," said one man, "because they are good for the animals." In this view, groves of pawpaws, hickories, persimmons, and patches of ramps, goldenseal, and ginseng planted near homes and throughout the mountains bear the trace of centuries of the practice of the commons.

See also Folklore, Foodways

Mary Hufford
University of Pennsylvania

Frank Gatski

Athlete Frank "Gunner" Gatski was born in Farmington, March 18, 1922. He grew up in No. 9 coal camp and played football at Farmington High School. He later played under Coach Cam Henderson at Marshall College (1940–42) and at Auburn University (1945). But it was in the pros that Gatski really emerged as a star, anchoring a powerful Cleveland Browns offensive line from his center position after beginning his career as a linebacker.

Gatski played 11 years for the Browns (1946–56) and one for Detroit (1957). He played in 10 championship games, eight on the winning side. He earned All-Pro honors in 1951, 1952, 1953, and 1955. He was named to the Professional Football Hall of Fame in 1985. Gatski has the unusual distinction of never having missed a game because of injury throughout his high school, college, and professional career.

In later years he was employed at the Pruntytown Industrial School for Boys and coached football there. Frank Gatski died in Morgantown, November 22, 2005.

John C. Veasey
Times West Virginian

Donald R. Gaudineer

Forester Donald R. Gaudineer was district ranger of the Greenbrier Ranger District of the Monongahela National Forest at Bartow from 1926 to 1934, and ranger of the Cheat Ranger District at Parsons from 1934 until his untimely death. Gaudineer was well-liked, and his six-foot seven-inch frame commanded much respect. He was a native of New York City and a 1922 graduate of the New York State Ranger College. He had served the U.S. Forest Service in Maine and New Hampshire before coming to West Virginia. His accomplishments at the Monongahela National Forest included new roads and trails, reforestation, and the construction of the original Middle Mountain Cabin, which stood until 2002.

Poke greens

"The tradition of gathering poke and other greens continues to this day. It is no uncommon sight in the spring to see women walking along the roadside picking a 'mess of greens.'

2 quarts tender young poke
12 young green onions, chopped
4 slices bacon
2 hard-cooked eggs, chopped
1 teaspoon salt

"Select tender young poke greens. Clean thoroughly. Bring to boil twice, discarding water each time. Cover with water in large kettle and cook until greens are tender, drain. Fry bacon until crisp, remove from drippings and set aside. Add poke greens, salt and chopped onions to the grease. Cook over low heat for 20 minutes, sprinkle with crumbled bacon and chopped hard-cooked eggs, and serve."

—Delmer Robinson
Appalachian Hill Country Cook Book (1980)

Gaudineer met tragedy on April 28, 1936, when he lost his life attempting to rescue his children from their burning home. Ranger Gaudineer's wife was the only survivor. On July 5, 1937, a new fire tower on the Randolph-Pocahontas county line on Cheat Mountain was dedicated in his memory. The tower was abandoned in the early 1970s, but Gaudineer Knob and Gaudineer Scenic Area still bear his name. Gaudineer Scenic Area, established by the U.S. Forest Service on October 1, 1964, is dedicated to the preservation of a virgin red spruce stand, one of the last remnants of the Mountain State's original forest.

See also Gaudineer Knob

Robert Beanblossom
Division of Natural Resources

Gaudineer Knob

Gaudineer Knob and the Gaudineer Scenic Area are named for Donald Gaudineer, a forester who lost his life while trying to save his children in a house fire. Located on Cheat Mountain in Randolph and Pocahontas counties off U.S. 250 between Durbin and Cheat Bridge, it is an example of a high boreal island in the Allegheny Mountains with two forest types: northern evergreen (red spruce) and northern hardwoods (American beech, yellow birch, sugar maple).

Atop the knob, elevation 4,450 feet, the U.S. Forest Service maintains a scenic overlook and a picnic area. About a mile away is a tract of about 50 acres of virgin spruce and associated hardwoods, representing the original forest and including some trees more than three feet in diameter and 300 years old. Some of the flora and fauna are similar to that of northern New England and southern Canada.

The variety of birds found in summer, especially the wood warblers and four kinds of brown thrushes, attracts many visitors. Also found here is the rare and endemic Cheat Mountain salamander. It was discovered in 1935 on White Top Mountain, about three miles away. The endangered northern flying squirrel and the varying (snowshoe) hare also occur.

See also Donald R. Gaudineer

George H. Breiding
Morgantown

Kenneth L. Carvell, "Gaudineer Knob," *Wonderful West Virginia*, September 1999.

Gauley Bridge

Gauley Bridge, population 738, is located in Fayette County at the picturesque confluence of the Gauley and New rivers, where the two streams join to form the Kanawha River. The name Gauley Bridge dates from the early 1820s when a wooden covered bridge was built to carry the James River & Kanawha Turnpike across the Gauley River. Because it commanded entry into the Kanawha Valley, the village

that sprang up was of strategic significance during the Civil War. Possession of Gauley Bridge was hotly contested, and the town was the scene of heavy fighting early in the war. During 1861 and 1862, Gauley Bridge, originally Southern in sympathy, was taken and retaken three times, and the wooden bridge was burned, rebuilt, and burned again. The piers and abutments of the old bridge still stand near the modern highway bridge.

The town achieved notoriety during the 1930s with the nearby construction of the Hawks Nest dam and tunnel. It was during the Great Depression and hundreds of unemployed workers, many of them Southern blacks, swarmed into Gauley Bridge to take construction jobs. The tunnel was driven three miles through Gauley Mountain, and tunnel workers almost immediately began to sicken and die. The cause was silicosis, a disease well known in Europe but not in the United States at that time. The death toll has been estimated at more than 750, making the Hawks Nest disaster among the worst industrial accidents in U.S. history.

Despite its long history, Gauley Bridge became an incorporated municipality only in 1978.

See also Hawks Nest Tunnel Disaster

Lyle Blackwell
Kingsport, Tennessee

Gauley Mountain

Gauley Mountain in Pocahontas, Randolph, and Webster counties is part of the dissected Allegheny Plateau that was uplifted in the Pennsylvanian Period of the Paleozoic Era. The mountain is underlain primarily with sedimentary rock formations. It lies within the Monongahela National Forest. A formidable landmark, Gauley Mountain rises in just 2.4 miles from an elevation of about 2,300 feet at a bend in the Elk River near Whitaker Falls to an elevation of 4,520 feet at Sharp Knob among the spurs of the Allegheny Mountains.

Gauley Mountain generally resembles the shape of a number seven, with the Gauley Divide, running west to east, making up the shorter, top stem. The divide is margined by Red Oak Knob (3,623 feet) and Bill Knob (3,074 feet) in the north and Bee Knob (3,234 feet) and Pompeys Knob (3,120 feet) in the south. The upright stem of the seven, Gauley Mountain proper, runs on a north-south axis from Randolph into Pocahontas County just west of Slaty Fork.

The area was timbered in the early 1900s; consequently, the hardwoods on Gauley Mountain are now generally 70 to 90 years old. Maple, beech, birch, oak, hickory, spruce, and pine dominate, along with markedly dense thickets of rhododendron. The Gauley Mountain Trail, which runs via an old railroad grade from near Slatyfork to the Little Laurel overlook

on the Highland Scenic Highway, offers views of red spruce groves, hardwoods, wildlife, and wildflowers and ferns in season.

Louise McNeill, the late poet laureate of West Virginia, born in Pocahontas County, provides vivid descriptions of the region and its people in her acclaimed book of poems, *Gauley Mountain* (1939). For McNeill the development of the Gauley country stands for the whole history of West Virginia.

There is another, much smaller, Gauley Mountain located between the Gauley and New rivers, near Ansted in Fayette County. This mountain summits at 2,547 feet. It is crossed by the Midland Trail, U.S. 60. The highway's marked switchbacks offer a thrilling drive and views of unique rock formations, timber, and steep relief. The short story "Time and Again" (1977) by West Virginia author Breece D'J Pancake takes place on this part of Route 60, immortalizing the mountain road for many readers.

See also Louise McNeill, Breece D'J Pancake

Hallie Chillag Dunlap
St. Albans

Gauley Mountain

Gauley Mountain was the master work of West Virginia poet Louise McNeill. The collection of poetry was published by Harcourt, Brace and Company in 1939, accompanied by a lavish introduction by Stephen Vincent Benét. The book tells the history of West Virginia in verse form.

McNeill (1911–93), West Virginia poet laureate from 1977 to 1993, was born in Pocahontas County on Swago Farm, a place carved from the wilderness by her pioneer ancestors. She grew up hearing stories of the old times, which became a powerful influence on her writing.

Gauley Mountain is set in a semi-mythical region populated by Shawnee, pioneers, slaves, and historical figures. In *Gauley*, "Mad Anne" Bailey, Francis Asbury, and generations of families tell their stories in ballad-like rhythms and authentic language. They portray mountain life from 1750 to 1935 and draw into focus the Indian wars and Civil War, the coming of hard roads, railroads, and immigrant laborers, as well as the cutting of the forest. Through it all the old families persist, the pioneer names recurring in individual poems covering nearly two centuries. The land, too, endures.

In 1991, McNeill participated in a radio version of *Gauley Mountain* for West Virginia Day, later made into a compact disk recording by Pocahontas Communications Cooperative.

See also Louise McNeill

Phyllis Wilson Moore
Clarksburg

Louise McNeill, *Gauley Mountain*, 1939.

Gauley River

The Gauley River rises on Gauley Mountain in western Pocahontas County, and drops nearly 4,000 feet along the 104-mile journey to its juncture with the New River. It meanders southwesterly through Webster County and turns to a more westerly direction through Nicholas County and into Fayette County, where it combines with the New to form the Kanawha River at Gauley Bridge.

The Gauley drains nearly 1,350 square miles, including the watersheds of several large tributaries that flow into it from the south across a wide, fan-shaped region. These are the Cherry, Meadow, Cranberry, Birch, and Williams rivers. The steep-sided walls of the Gauley and its tributaries are lined with massive rock outcrops. The hillsides are intermittently covered with tangles of rhododendron thickets and maturing forests.

Historically, the watershed remained mostly uninhabited due to its difficult terrain. Native Americans hunted in the region, as did the early European explorers. The first settlement of non-native people was at Peters Creek in Nicholas County at the end of the 1700s. Only a few settlements appeared along Gauley River until the coal and timber barons brought workers in at the end of the 19th century to extract the rich resources.

A Civil War battle took place on the mountain above the juncture of the Meadow River with the Gauley, on September 10, 1861. On that day, Union troops routed a garrison of Confederate soldiers who held a position overlooking the rivers. This was a strategic victory for the Union Army as the ferry located at the tiny hamlet of Carnifex came under Northern control. Carnifex Ferry is now a state park and is listed on the National Register of Historic Places.

Summersville Lake and Dam are located 34 miles above the mouth of Gauley River. The dam was constructed between 1960 and 1966, at a cost of $48 million, to reduce flooding along the heavily populated sections of the Kanawha and Ohio rivers downstream. Though its primary function is flood control, the lake is maintained for intensive recreational use including fishing, motorized boating, skiing, picnicking, sightseeing, hiking, and wildlife enhancement. During the late spring and early summer months, Summersville Lake provides 2,790 acres of surface water for recreation. During the fall and early winter, the water surface is lowered to allow for storage of spring floodwaters.

A 24-mile section of the Gauley River from the Summersville Dam downstream to the tiny town of Swiss is one of the premier whitewater rafting stretches in the eastern United States. The sport is facilitated by the release of lake water during the months of September and October, when thousands of rafters and kayakers pass through the river's scenic gorge. Due to its scenic beauty and heavy recreation use, 25 miles of the Gauley River and six miles of Meadow River were added to the National Park System as the Gauley River National Recreation Area in 1988.

See also Battle of Carnifex Ferry, Summersville Lake, Whitewater Rafting

Emily Grafton
Morgantown

Geography

West Virginia became a state in 1863 with 48 counties. Berkeley and Jefferson were added in 1866, and five new counties were created between 1866 and 1895. The state's 24,282 square miles are enclosed by an irregular boundary of 1,170 miles. Fifty-two percent of the boundary follows rivers, 31 percent follows the crestlines of Allegheny mountain ranges, and 17 percent of the boundary is man-made straight lines. The geographic center of West Virginia is four miles west of Centralia in Braxton County.

West Virginia is bisected by the 39th degree north latitude and 80th degree west longitude. South and west of a line drawn from New Martinsville to Morgantown then southward along the eastern edge of the Allegheny Plateau the climate is one of mild winters and cool to hot summers. North and east of this line cold winters and hot to cool summers prevail. There are four seasons of near equal length. In mountain regions temperature and rainfall extremes are common; nevertheless, the mean annual temperature is between 50 and 55 degrees, and the average annual precipitation of about 45 inches is evenly distributed throughout the year. On average, Pickens, in southern Randolph County, receives about 70 inches, while Brandywine, 85 miles to the east, gets only about 30 inches of rainfall each year. Storm-produced floods have the most adverse effect on the state.

Physiographically, the state is located in the Appalachian Highlands. There are 40 peaks more than 4,000 feet above sea level. Spruce Knob in Pendleton County at 4,861 feet is the highest point in West Virginia, and Harpers Ferry at 247 feet is the lowest point. The average elevation is 1,500 feet. Topographically, the surface consists of long, narrow ranges, ridges, and hills interspersed with valleys whose sides rise steeply from narrow valley floors. About two-thirds of the land area has a slope greater than 20 percent, 18 percent is steeper than 40 percent, and about 11 percent is in slopes less than 10 percent.

Marking the eastern border of Jefferson County are the Blue Ridge Mountains, a high belt of igneous and metamorphic rock. West of the Blue Ridge is the Ridge and Valley Province, where long and narrow ridges capped with sandstone are separated by valleys cut 400 to 2,400 feet below the ridge tops into limestone and shale. Peaks of hard sandstone on the ridge tops are called knobs, such as Bald Knob (4,840 feet) and Panther Knob (4,508 feet). In the limestone are caves, underground streams such as Lost River in Hardy County, sinkholes, and mineral springs. The most notable of the springs is White Sulphur Springs in Greenbrier County.

The folded belt ends at the Allegheny Front, a bold southeast-facing escarpment that rises abruptly to over 4,000 feet. The Allegheny Front roughly marks the Eastern Continental Divide, diverting about 85 percent of the state's drainage west to the Ohio River and the Gulf of Mexico, and 15 percent east to the Potomac River and the Atlantic Ocean.

West of the front, from Monroe and Greenbrier counties to the Pennsylvania border, are the Allegheny Mountains, a wedge-like region of mildly folded rock that has given rise to topographic belts with valleys as much as 1,000 feet deep and broad, plateau-like ridge tops. The rock mostly has strong resistance to erosion and forms pinnacles or cliffs. With elevations exceeding 4,500 feet, the Allegheny Mountains have some of the state's most spectacular scenery.

The western two-thirds of West Virginia is part of the Allegheny Plateau. From the Allegheny Front the sedimentary rock slopes westward at about 20 feet per mile to an elevation of 1,000 feet along the Ohio River. Ridges, capped with sandstone, and valleys, carved into shale, are narrow, winding, and twisting. Gorges of 500 feet are not uncommon, and most spectacular is the 1,100-foot New River Gorge. The extreme dissection of the plateau has produced perhaps the most rugged human habitat region in America.

West Virginia is one of the best drained states in the nation. About half of the precipitation is removed by rapid stream runoff, and from the higher mountains and plateau as much as two-thirds becomes runoff. Most streams, with the possible exception of the Ohio River, are in a youthful stage of development. They have a V-shape profile, are downcutting, occupy most of their valley floor, have rapids and falls, and are prone to flooding.

Rivers have always been important in the state's domestic, industrial, and recreational development. Only three cities of more than 10,000 population, Beckley, Bluefield, and Martinsburg, are not located on a major stream. A system of 13 locks and dams provides 350 miles of navigation on the Ohio, Kanawha, and Monongahela rivers. The Coal, Little Kanawha, Guyandotte, Big Sandy, and Potomac rivers have been used for navigation. Other major rivers include the New, Gauley, Elk, Cheat, Greenbrier, and Bluestone.

About 80 percent of West Virginia is covered in regrowth forest, with the particular forest type influenced by altitude, prevailing wind, steepness of the slope, soil, north-south exposure to the sun, and wet-dry side of the mountain. In general, an oak-pine forest is dominant in the Eastern Panhandle, red spruce and northern hardwoods (sugar maple, beech, birch, and red oak) are dominant in the Allegheny Mountains, and the Allegheny Plateau is a region of mixed hardwoods—oaks, hickory, yellow poplar, black cherry, walnut, elm, and ash. Virginia pine is ubiquitous on old farmed areas. Dense stands of laurel and rhododendron are common undergrowth, and sycamore, dogwood, redbud, and locust are widespread.

All wildlife common to the Appalachian highlands are found in the state. Hunting and fishing are major outdoor activities.

Archeological findings show that substantial Indian populations were widespread in prehistoric times, but on the eve of European settlement there were few Indians residing in what is now West Virginia, probably due to disease, scarcity of game, and tribal warfare. Place names such as Kanawha, Logan, Mingo, and Ohio, and the Warrior Path and Seneca Trail, are remainders of the native presence.

The first colonials settled in Berkeley County in 1726. During the next 50 years the largest ethnic groups to settle were Germans, Scotch-Irish, and English. In the late 19th and early 20th centuries, coal mining attracted large numbers of immigrants to the state, especially African-Americans and East Europeans. West Virginia's population peaked at 2,005,552 in 1950, and stood at 1,808,350 in 2000. It is a homogenous population. European Americans account for 96 percent and African-Americans three percent. Eighty percent of West Virginians were born in the state.

Population densities of 120 to 480 per square mile occur in contiguous counties in the Teays-New River Valley, the two panhandles, and the Monongahela River Valley. Densities of less than 30 per square mile occur in the central Ridge and Valley counties, and in the Little Kanawha river basin counties. Thirty-six percent of the West Virginia population is urban. There are 277 incorporated places, ranging from fewer than 100 in Thurmond, Brandonville, and Auburn to more than 50,000 in Charleston and Huntington. The urbanized areas are concentrated along the Ohio, Kanawha, and Monongahela rivers.

Tourism is a major industry in West Virginia. It arises from a plethora of resources and attractions, including unique natural features, whitewater rafting, skiing, the cultural heritage of the southern coalfields and Northern Panhandle, hunting and fishing, mountain lodges and campgrounds, and outdoor dramas.

Soils and climate permit most mid-latitude agricultural practices, but rugged terrain is a severe limiting factor, especially in the Allegheny Plateau counties. The number of farms declined from 97,000 in 1910 to 20,800 in 2004, and land in farms declined from 10 million to 3.6 million acres.

Three-fourths of the market value of agricultural products sold in 1997 originated in Ridge and Valley counties, largely the Eastern Panhandle. One-half of all market value was generated by poultry and poultry products, of which Hardy and Pendleton counties accounted for 71 percent. Cattle and calves are the second-leading agricultural commodity, and livestock farming makes hay the most common crop, produced on 525,000 of the state's 1.3 million acres of cropland.

West Virginia's Allegheny Plateau is located in the heart of the Appalachian bituminous coalfield. The first reference to coal dates to an outcrop on the Coal River in 1742. Commercial coal mining began in 1818 to provide fuel for the salt evaporators in the Kanawha Valley. Since the 1870s, coal has been a centerpiece of the state's economy.

To mine coal in the rugged, sparsely populated, and nearly inaccessible regions required railroads, coal towns, company stores, and imported laborers. For example, McDowell, a long-time leading coal producing county, had a population of 1,952 in 1870, 94,400 in 1940, and with the downward spiral of employment and production shifts the population declined to 27,329 in 2000. Statewide, coal employment peaked at 127,000 in 1950 and has since declined to fewer than 13,000. Coal production reached unprecedented levels late in the 20th century, with nearly 400 deep mines and more than 200 surface mines producing a record 182 million tons in 1997. Eighty-two percent of the coal is marketed outside the state.

All major manufacturing groups are represented in West Virginia. Lumbering and printing are the most ubiquitous activities, but primary and fabricated metals, chemicals and allied products, machinery, petroleum related, and glass are major concentrations in the Ohio, Monongahela, and Kanawha river valleys. About 40 percent of the state's total manufacturing employment is located in Kanawha, Hancock, Wood, and Cabell counties.

Howard G. Adkins
Ona

Raymond T. Hill, "The Physical Regions of West Virginia," in Howard G. Adkins, et al., ed., *West Virginia and Appalachia: Selected Readings*, 1977; Chang Lee and Hill, "Land Slope in West Virginia," *West Virginia Agriculture and Forestry*, 1976.

Geology

An acquaintance with geology is necessary for a full appreciation of West Virginia's settlement history, past and present land use, and economic and cultural development. Different areas exhibit different economic activities and cultural styles. Historically, many of those differences have been influenced, directly or indirectly, by geology. While all of West Virginia lies within what is considered the Appalachian region, the state is diverse, having several distinct physiographic areas, each with its own characteristics.

With few exceptions, the consolidated bedrock lying at and near the surface throughout West Virginia is sedimentary rock initially deposited as soft sediments during the Paleozoic Era, a geologic period that lasted from more than 570 million to about 230 million to 240 million years ago. Throughout that unimaginably long time, present West Virginia (and indeed, the entire Appalachian area, from New York to Alabama) was covered by or lay close to a shallow sea. The mountains of Old Appalachia, ancestors to our present mountains, lay to the east, and erosion of those highlands brought sediment into the shallow sea. This sea floor or Appalachian geosyncline intermittently subsided, continuing to accept sediment over thousands of centuries.

Intermittent basin subsidence as well as uplift of the adjacent Old Appalachian Mountains were caused by collisions and separations of the North American continental plate with the European-African plate. Cycles of deposition and subsidence, along with periodic climate changes, resulted in a diversity of sediments which became limestones, shales, siltstones, sandstones, and coals. These rock types formed in such environments as shallow seas, beaches and deltas, and coastal plains with rivers, swamps, bays, and lagoons. The mineral resources associated with the rocks (coal, oil, gas, salt, limestone, glass sand) have been important to the state's economy, historically and at present, and vary from one part of the state to another.

The close of the Paleozoic Era was marked by continental plate collision which compressed flat-lying strata and pushed them from east to west into uplifted folds, a great mountain-building event known as the Appalachian Orogeny. The large sedimentary basin that had existed in varying forms for more than 330 million years ceased to exist. Since then, the area has been shaped and characterized by weathering and erosion. The mountains have been eroded down to a fairly level plain, uplifted again about 30 million to 50 million years ago, and then eroded again to form our present landscape.

A final phase of some sediment deposition occurred during the Great Ice Age, or Pleistocene Epoch. During that most recent period of glacier advances into the present United States, lasting from about 1,000,000 to about 10,000 years ago, the glaciers never extended quite as far south as present West Virginia, but they nevertheless exerted still-present influences on the state's geology, landscape, and flora and fauna. The valley of the prehistoric Teays River, represented today by a broad, flat valley extending essentially from Charleston to Huntington (and across southern Ohio), is filled with lake sediments resulting from damming of the ancient river by glaciers at a point near Chillicothe, Ohio. The Ohio River, which did not exist prior to the Great Ice Age, was created by blockage and diversion of the Monongahela and Allegheny rivers. Thus today's Ohio Valley along West Virginia's western boundary is a direct result of glacier impacts. Thick terraces of lake sediments still exist along the banks of the Monongahela River in the Morgantown-Fairmont area.

Unique plants and animals occur in high altitude muskeg bogs called glades by local residents, left over from the Ice Age climate. These areas, the largest of which include Cranberry Glades, Canaan Valley, and Cranesville Swamp, contain numerous plant and animal species not found elsewhere this far south.

The area composing West Virginia may be subdivided by its geologic and resultant physiographic characteristics into several different provinces. The easternmost of West Virginia's geologic provinces is the Blue Ridge Mountains Province, which barely enters the state's boundaries along the eastern margin of Jefferson County, near Harpers Ferry. The Blue Ridge Mountains are made of the oldest rocks exposed in West Virginia, which have, by and large, undergone chemical transformations due to intense heat and pressure associated with the upthrusting of the mountains. The degree of rock deformation is greatest near the source of the deforming force and diminishes away from that point. Thus, rock deformation is intensive in this easternmost part of the state, closer to the continental plate collision in the area of the present Atlantic Ocean, and is generally very mild in the western part.

The Ridge and Valley Province lies west of the Blue Ridge, and includes most of the Eastern Panhandle and adjoining areas to the southwest. Rock strata in this area, originally deposited as flat-lying beds of sediment, are strongly folded and sometimes broken by the compressional forces that came from the collision of continents. The steeply dipping orientation of the strata combined with differing susceptibility to erosion has produced the physiography of the Panhandle. Thick beds of erodible shales and limestones underlie broad valleys, separated by steep, sharp-crested, linear ridges held up by resistive sandstone layers. The Tuscarora Sandstone, a very hard, quartz-rich rock originally deposited as sand beaches along an ancient shoreline, is an especially prominent ridge former. Seneca Rocks and numerous other sheer rock cliff formations in the area are created by the erosion-resistant Tuscarora Sandstone.

Early settlers valued the agricultural promise of the broad valleys of the Ridge and Valley Province and moved into them in the mid-1700s. The prominent historic and current land use is agricultural, including livestock and poultry, grain crops, and orchards. Mineral resources include limestone, which is quarried for multiple purposes such as soil fertilization, construction aggregate, water treatment, coal mine dust suppression, and chemical uses.

West of the Ridge and Valley Province, the rock layers become relatively flat-lying, producing a very different terrain. Rather than the broad, linear valleys and parallel narrow ridges of the Ridge and Valley, topography to the west is generally less regular. However, there is a transitional area between the Ridge and Valley and Appalachian Plateau provinces that has been termed the High Plateau because it lies at generally higher elevations than the adjacent Ridge and Valley and Plateau areas. In the High Plateau, the rock strata are moderately folded and only rarely faulted (broken and moved), forming a transition between the intensely deformed strata to the east and the gently folded strata to the west. The eastern boundary of the High Plateau is very distinctly delineated from the Ridge and Valley Province by the escarpment of the Allegheny Front in the northeastern area of the state, and by the St. Clair Fault in the southeast.

The High Plateau encompasses the Potomac Highlands area, much of which lies within the Monongahela National Forest and is popular as a recreation area. Tourism and outdoor activities including hunting, fishing, canoeing, skiing, and cycling contribute to the economy. Historically, the High Plateau was timber country, and its culture incorporates a measure of colorful tradition from the timbering boom of the late 1800s and early 1900s. Timber continues to be an important product. There is also an important livestock raising tradition. Portions of the area are underlain by limestone which, combined with the relatively wetter and cooler climate of this part of the state, produces favorable conditions for grazing.

Most of West Virginia lies within the Plateau Province. Still, substantial differences in terrain, mineral resources, and land use occur within that area, and relate largely to differences in geology. The Plateau area contains mineral resources unmatched anywhere else in the eastern United States. West Virginia's economy historically was founded on the rich coal deposits, extending from the Virginia and Kentucky borders in the south to the Pennsylvania and Maryland borders in the north. The Pittsburgh coal bed, which lies throughout a broad area of southwestern Pennsylvania and northern West Virginia, has been called the world's single most valuable mineral deposit. It has been mined in West Virginia for well over 150 years, and continues to be a major producer today. The rugged southwestern coalfields contain numerous coal beds, including some of the highest quality anywhere in the world.

While the commercial coal deposits extend the length of the state from north to south, they disappear to the west, so that the westernmost counties have no coal production. Those areas are rich in natural gas and petroleum, however, and have a long history of development of those fuels. Natural salt brines contributed to the early economic development of parts of the state, most notably the Charleston-Kanawha Valley area, whose chemical industry originated from exploitation of the area's shallow salt brines, beginning in the early 1800s.

Ron Mullennex
Bluefield

Frank George

Fiddler William Franklin "Frank" George was born October 6, 1928, in Bluefield. He graduated from Concord College in 1957. As a child, George was exposed to traditional Appalachian music and learned to play the fiddle and banjo on instruments made for him by his father, Otie George.

While in the army in Europe, George traveled to Scotland, England, and Ireland to learn the traditional music of the British Isles, which he recognized as the forerunner of Appalachian music. After leaving the army, George returned to Bluefield and continued his study of traditional music. Since 1967, he has been featured on 14 recordings.

George met his wife, Jane Taylor Cox, at the Mountain State Art & Craft Fair at Cedar Lakes in 1966. Jane, a significant figure in the Appalachian handicrafts revival, was born November 11, 1922, in Roane County and graduated from West Virginia State College in 1967. She was involved with the first Art & Craft Fair, a Centennial event in 1963, and later worked in crafts development at the state Department of Commerce. By the late 1960s, she worked with the West Virginia University Extension Service to promote awareness of West Virginia's cultural heritage through the Mountain Heritage programs, which featured traditional music, dance, cooking, crafts, and storytelling. Frank George actively participated in these programs from their beginning. They married in Norton, Virginia, on December 6, 1969.

Together the couple has promoted the traditional culture of Southern Appalachia and the British Isles throughout the United States and Europe. Both have received the prestigious Division of Culture and History's Vandalia Award for their contributions to the preservation of traditional West Virginia culture. Jane and Frank George moved to Roane County in 1978. They remain active in folk culture programs in their community and at several state folklife festivals.

See also Folk Arts Revival

Michael M. Meador
Abingdon, Virginia

George Washington National Forest

The George Washington National Forest extends for 140 miles through the mountains of western Virginia and eastern West Virginia. It includes 1,060,000 acres of federal land, mostly in Virginia. About a tenth of the forest land is in Hampshire, Hardy, Monroe, and Pendleton counties, West Virginia. The national forest boundaries also include a large amount of private land, especially in the valleys.

In West Virginia, the George Washington National Forest occupies a region of long, parallel mountains that are separated by well-defined valleys. Much of the acreage in West Virginia is on Great North and Shenandoah mountains, the latter with several peaks higher than 4,000 feet. The highest, Reddish Knob at 4,397 feet, is well-known for its outstanding vistas of the Allegheny Mountains to the west and the Shenandoah Valley and Blue Ridge Mountains to the east.

Unlike the Monongahela National Forest, which is mostly in a region of high annual precipitation, the George Washington National Forest has relatively low annual precipitation. In addition, much of the area is underlain by acidic, nutrient-poor shales and sandstones. Consequently, much of the national forest supports dry forests of oaks, hickories, and pines. American chestnut was once abundant, but became scarce following the chestnut blight. Limestone areas support a diverse forest that includes yellow poplar, basswood, and maple, and are notably rich in spring wildflowers. In cool ravines and higher elevations can be found forests dominated by Canada hemlock and northern hardwoods, especially northern red oak. White pine was once prevalent in some areas, especially on Shenandoah Mountain, but insects, fires, and logging greatly reduced its extent.

Deer, turkey, black bear, bobcat, ruffed grouse, and other wildlife are common. Mountain streams often support populations of native brook trout. In the fall, the southward migrations of hawks and eagles follow the ridge tops. These migrations can be viewed from observation points at Reddish Knob in Pendleton County and the Big Schloss in Hardy County.

Many unusual and interesting plants and animals live within the George Washington National Forest. The Cow Knob salamander is found on Shenandoah Mountain and a handful of nearby ridges, but nowhere else on earth. Portions of the national forest are managed to protect the salamander. Box huckleberry, a rare evergreen shrub, is found in Hardy County. Turkeybeard and dwarf trillium, both members of the lily family, have been found in West Virginia only on Shenandoah Mountain, which is also one of the few places in the state where the mountain fetterbush can be found. The George Washington National Forest supports some of the largest, most diverse shale barrens known. Shale barrens are very dry, rocky habitats that support many unusual plants and animals, including some plants found only in shale barrens in the Central Appalachians. Important populations of the shale barren rockcress, an endangered species, occur on national forest lands in Pendleton County.

The national forest includes some of West Virginia's best-known natural and scenic areas. These include Trout Pond, the only natural lake in West Virginia, and the Lost River Sinks, where the flow of Lost River disappears under Sandy Ridge, and then reappears as the Cacapon River. In early spring, the crest of Shenandoah Mountain has spectacular displays of flowering shrubs in the heath family, including mountain laurel, several azaleas, and in early April, mountain fetterbush, which has clusters of white flowers.

The national forest is popular with birders, hikers, mountain bikers, campers, anglers, and hunters. The Tuscarora Trail, a long-distance hiking trail that runs from central Pennsylvania to Shenandoah National Park, passes through part of the forest. Campgrounds, picnic areas, and other recreational facilities are scattered throughout. Portions of the national forest are managed for timber production and harvesting. The West Virginia portion of the George Washington has no congressionally designated national wilderness areas.

See also National Forest

Rodney Bartgis
Nature Conservancy of West Virginia

German Dunkards

The Dunkards, sometimes called German Baptist Brethren and known as the Church of the Brethren since 1908, were formed in Schwarzenau, Germany, in 1708, and had spread to present West Virginia within a half-century. This sect of pacifist Protestant dissenters is similar to the Mennonite, Amish, and Moravian denominations and is the parent of the United Brethren (1767), Old German Baptist Brethren (1882), Dunkard Brethren (1926), Grace Brethren (1939), and related sects. The name "Dunkards" originates from the practice of dunking believers three times forward during baptism. Their primary beliefs include adult baptism, foot washing at communion, and a generally conservative lifestyle.

Today, there are about 80 active Brethren and Dunkard congregations in West Virginia, mostly in the Potomac Highlands region, with a few scattered churches across the rest of the state. Numerous towns in Grant, Hampshire, and Hardy counties are named for Brethren individuals or families, most of whom still have descendants in the area. The Arnold, Bane, Hinkle, Keyser, Kline, Landis, Leatherman, Martin, Moser, Peterson, Powers, Rotruck, and Teter families are among those prominent in the history of West Virginia Brethren.

Early members emigrated mainly from Germany and Switzerland due to intense persecution at the onset of the 1700s. First settling in Pennsylvania, they helped populate the entire Alleghenies, particularly along tributaries of the Potomac River. The first white settlers west of the Alleghenies were the Dunkard Eckerlin brothers. These three men had been leaders of a cloister at Ephrata, Pennsylvania, but left after complaints that they were stern taskmasters. Along with Alexander Mack Jr., they next settled on the New River at Pulaski, Virginia. In 1756, having sold their land at that site, the brothers traveled to the Monongahela River, settling along the Cheat River at present Camp Dawson, near Kingwood. This settlement was called Dunkard's Bottom.

Suspected by harried settlements along the South Branch of the Potomac of being in sympathy with French and Indian forces, Samuel Eckerlin was detained while on a supply trip to Fort Pleasant, near present Moorefield. It was decided that a small party should accompany him to the Dunkard settlement for investigation. Among these were Frederick Ice, who established Ices Ferry in 1759, and Thomas Decker, who settled at present Morgantown in 1757. They discovered that French and Indian forces had attacked the settlement, killing everyone except the two Eckerlin brothers, who were captured. Brother Israel died quickly in captivity, but Gabriel was sent by the French to Europe, where he died in a French monastery.

See also Religion

Greg Leatherman
Fairmont

Martin Brumbaugh, *A History of the German Baptist Brethren in Europe and America*, 1961;

Klaus Wust, *The Saint-Adventurers of the Virginia Frontier—Southern Outposts of Ephrata*, 1977.

Germans

Germans were among our very earliest settlers. They arrived in what is now West Virginia in the 1720s, along the Potomac River. They called their settlement Mecklenburg (now Shepherdstown), having come from Mecklenburg, Germany. The town was incorporated in 1762.

Soon other Germans came. Among them were Jacob Reger, John Minear, and Johann Dahle. Reger settled in Hampshire County, but he and his family later moved to what is today north-central West Virginia, eventually settling farms in the Tygart, West Fork, and Buckhannon river valleys. Some of them settled along a tributary of Hackers Creek in what in 1816 became Lewis County. The creek was named for the German immigrant John Hacker, and near its headwaters there was established a small community named Berlin. Minear settled in present Tucker County and erected the first sawmill west of the Alleghenies. Dahle, a Hessian deserter from the British army during the American Revolution, settled in Pendleton County in 1781, and some of his descendants settled in what is today known as Dolly (from Dahle) Sods.

By 1748, according to a Moravian missionary to the region of the South Branch Potomac and Patterson Creek, there were so many Germans along those streams "that in order to reach the people a minister should be fluent in both German and English." In 1762, about 30 percent of the population of Jefferson and Berkeley counties was German, and the centers of the German population were Shepherdstown and Martinsburg.

Simultaneous with these developments in the Eastern Panhandle, Dunkards established small settlements in the Monongahela Valley, and the John Wetzel family settled along Wheeling Creek in the Northern Panhandle in 1772. John's son, Lewis Wetzel, would become, next to Daniel Boone, the most famous frontiersman in Western Virginia.

Over the next century, the number of Germans steadily increased. The desire to escape persecution in the fatherland in the wake of the 1848 Revolution, and the beginning of the Franco-Prussian War in 1870, provided some of the incentive, as did the desire of some Germans already settled in eastern Virginia to make a new start west of the Alleghenies. Also important was the work of West Virginia's first commissioner of immigration, Joseph H. Diss Debar, before and after he assumed the official position of commissioner in 1864.

Diss Debar established a German-Swiss colony in Doddridge County in the early 1850s and named it St. Clara. Between 1848 and 1860, two German-language newspapers were established in Wheeling, and by 1860 there were more Germans living there than in any other community. A German settlement had also been founded at St. Joseph in Marshall County, and more German settlements had appeared in Lewis County. German settlements, including Lubeck, had been made in Wood County in the 1850s. In 1865, Diss Debar appointed an agent in southern Germany. Because of the oil boom near Parkersburg, that community's German population dramatically increased from 1860 to the eve of World War I. Both Parkersburg and Wheeling had Germania singing societies.

America's entry into World War I in 1917 and the resultant anti-German prejudices caused the study of German to be dropped in many schools, caused the Germania Society in Parkersburg to discontinue, and slowed German migration into West Virginia. After the war, some Germans living in Cumberland, Maryland, moved to West Virginia to work in glass plants in Weston in the 1920s, and after World War II some West Virginia GIs brought German war brides home. In recent years German-owned corporations, such as Schott Scientific Glass of Parkersburg and Bayer of New Martinsville and South Charleston, have established a presence. Germans living in West Virginia have been for the most part members of one of the following religious groups: Lutheran, Presbyterian, Roman Catholic, Evangelical United Brethren, and Jewish.

West Virginians of German descent who have gained distinction in the past century include members of the Bloch family of Wheeling, leaders in the tobacco industry; Walter P. Reuther of Wheeling, long-time president of the United Auto Workers of America; opera singer Eleanor Steber of Wheeling; Lewis L. Strauss of Charleston, chairman of the Atomic Energy Commission and president of RCA; comedian Don Knotts of Morgantown; folklorist Marie Boette of Parkersburg; air ace General Charles "Chuck" Yeager of Hamlin; film producer Pare Lorentz of Clarksburg; oil wildcatters Michael Benedum of Bridgeport and "Wig" Bickel of Parkersburg; and the Nobel Prize winning writer, Pearl Sydenstricker Buck, of Hillsboro.

The best demographic estimates indicate that about one-fifth to one-fourth of West Virginians are of German ancestry.

Bernard L. Allen
Conway, South Carolina

Germany Valley

A canoe-shaped upland valley 10 miles long and two miles wide in western Pendleton County, Germany Valley has been eroded into the massive Wills Mountain Anticline. Southeast-dipping Tuscarora Sandstone forms prominent cliffs along the crest of North Fork Mountain. The strata are vertical in the River Knobs, the northwestern limb of the anticline, where the erosion-resistant Tuscarora is exposed in water gaps as impressive crags such as Seneca, Riverton, Judy, and Nelson rocks. Through these gaps the valley drains into the North Fork of the South Branch of the Potomac River.

Germany Valley is the most highly developed karst landscape in the Potomac watershed. Karst, which forms on the valley's soluble limestones, is characterized by caves, sinkholes, and subterranean drainage. Judy Spring, the source of Mill Creek, is the main resurgence for an integrated network of underground streams. From the time of first settlement the fertile limestone soils supported a prosperous livestock husbandry.

German language, culture, and folklore have persisted well into the late 20th century in parts of Pendleton County. Germany Valley, despite its name and the German ancestry of many of its residents, generally is not considered one of those places. However, topographic features preserve the surnames of mostly German early settlers: Harman Hills, Bland Hills, and Dolly Ridge within the valley; Harper Gap, Hinkle Gap, and Judy Gap along the River Knobs. About 1760, John Justus Hinkle built a blockhouse and stockade known as Hinkle's Fort.

Seneca Caverns, one of three major caves within the valley, was opened to the public as a tourist attraction in 1930. The Greer Lime Company began production at Key near Judy Spring in 1960. The quarry has periodically expanded its operations in the New Market Limestone, nearly pure calcium carbonate.

See also Pendleton County

John Craft Taylor
Union College

H. M. Calhoun, *'Twixt North and South*, 1974; Kenneth L. Carvell, "Germany Valley," *Wonderful West Virginia*, September 2000.

Ghostlore

West Virginia is an ideal place for ghostly encounters. Its hills cast long shadows into deep hollows, and patchy valley fog rises from cooling waters to hang from green ridges and skitter through the forest. Suddenly, a breath of wind cuts the fog into will-o-wisps that spin off into the pale moonlight and settle on a lonely road or in a mine's dark portal or by an empty railroad track, waiting for someone.

Among our countless ghost tales, there are three major types:

The first type is that of the helpful spirit that aids mortals in distress. Most prevalent is the benevolent ghost that returns to save a loved one in distress, such as a sick mother or trapped miner. The West Virginia hills echo with accounts of helpful spirits.

A thirsty ghost

"Mr. Peck had beaten his son to death, because he drank up all his wine. The day of the son's funeral he told the people he'd fallen and killed himself, and nobody knew but what this was true.

"That night, after the funeral, Mr. Peck decided to go downtown and buy himself a drink or two. On his way home he could hear something beside him, but couldn't see anything. He went on a little farther and saw a jug, tipped up, walking beside him. It seemed as if someone were drinking out of it.

"Then a voice said, 'Thirsty, Pop?' and repeated this over and over.

"Frightened, Mr. Peck grabbed the jug and broke it against his chest. A piece of the glass cut his throat badly, and as he was getting very weak, the voice said, 'I'm still here, Pop.'

"Then Mr. Peck fell over and bled to death."
Told by Ethel Cunningham, Smithfield 1948

—Ruth Ann Musick
Telltale Lilac Bush & Other Ghost Tales
(1965)

The second type is that of the unrested spirit. Usually the ghost of a person who has died suddenly or tragically before his time, it drifts upon the earth, attaching itself to a familiar person or place. Thus, the haunted house, haunted person, or vanishing hitchhiker story is created. In the latter, a ghostly hitchhiker disappears en route, having been picked up by a kindly motorist. When the baffled driver makes inquiries, it is learned that just such a person as the mysterious passenger died on that stretch of road years ago, perhaps in a car wreck. The bluegrass song "Bringing Mary Home" popularized the vanishing hitchhiker story in recent years.

The third type is that of the vengeful ghost, the least common tale to be found in our hills. Sometimes such a ghost returns to see that justice is done or that the truth be known. The Greenbrier Ghost is the most famous of these in West Virginia, a young wife whose spirit returned in a dream to condemn her murderous spouse. He was convicted of the crime, once an examination of the victim's exhumed body corroborated details of the dream.

The late Ruth Ann Musick, regional folklorist, specialized in collecting and analyzing our state's ghostly legends. She believed that a combination of social and historical circumstances contributed to the abundance of ghostlore in West Virginia. Isolated hills and little-traveled roads were scenes of potential violence, robbery, and murder. Until the late 1700s, unprotected settlements were preyed upon by Indians or white renegades. The Civil War left many fatalities in the hills, not all of them attributable to lawful combat. Later, railroads, road building, and construction of tunnels and bridges took a heavy toll in lives. Coal mining, long our deadliest occupation, has been particularly haunted by ghostly encounters. Sometimes a mining accident would kill only one person, sometimes many. Each of the major groups making up West Virginia's mine work force—native white mountaineers, blacks from the American south, and immigrants from southern and eastern Europe—brought their own rich heritage to bear on the tragedies.

Musick's folktale collections include *The Telltale Lilac Bush and Other West Virginia Ghost Tales, Coffin Hollow and Other Ghost Tales,* and *Green Hills of Magic: West Virginia Folktales from Europe.* Other collections include Stephen Brown's Civil War spirits in *Haunted Houses of Harpers Ferry*; James Gay Jones's *Appalachian Ghost Stories and Other Tales*; and Indian haunts in William Price's *Tales and Lore of the Mountaineers.* Dennis Deitz's *Greenbrier Ghost and other Strange Stories,* Parts I and II, mainly display the supernatural in contemporary settings, often as guardian angels, ghostly messengers of mercy.

See also Folklore, Greenbrier Ghost, Ruth Ann Musick

Judy Prozzillo Byers
Fairmont State University

Denise Giardina

Writer Denise Giardina was born October 25, 1951, in Bluefield, West Virginia, and raised in neighboring McDowell County. She is best known as a novelist and also has a long history of community activism, including a run for governor of West Virginia in 2000.

Giardina received a B.A. from West Virginia Wesleyan in 1973 and an M. Div. in 1979 from the Virginia Theological Seminary. In her five novels to date, all historical fiction, Giardina depicts Henry V in pre-Renaissance England in *Good King Harry* (1984); Dietrich Bonhoeffer in 1930s–40s Nazi Germany in *Saints and Villains* (1998); and in *Fallam's Secret* (2003) she explores the subject of time travel. Her most successful novels, *Storming Heaven* (1987) and *The Unquiet Earth* (1992), feature the fictitious coal miners Rondal Lloyd and Dillon Freeman mak-ing their hard way in central Appalachia, circa 1890–1990. In all of her books, Giardina is interested in the complexities and ambiguities of the individual destined to answer the call of his or her particular moment.

As a political activist Giardina participated in and wrote about Appalachian labor-capital conflicts of her day, including the A. T. Massey (mid-1980s) and Pittston (1989–90) coal strikes. In the following years she was vocal in her critique of surface mining, particularly mountaintop removal. She highlighted such issues in her unsuccessful campaign for governor as the candidate of the Mountain Party in 2000.

Giardina's honors include the Weatherford Award for both *Storming Heaven* and *The Unquiet Earth;* the Lillian Smith Award and an American Book Award for *The Unquiet Earth;* the Fisk Fiction Prize for *Saints and Villains*; and the Lillie Chaffin Award for Appalachian Writing.

Stephen D. Mooney
Virginia Polytechnic Institute
The Iron Mountain Review, 1999; Sandra Ballard, "Political and Spiritual Dimensions of the Work of Denise Giardina," Carson-Newman Studies, Fall 1997.

Millard F. Giesey

Architect Millard F. Giesey, whose buildings are found in many parts of West Virginia, was born in Wheeling, September 9, 1856. He attended the local public schools, then studied architecture at home. After five years of local study and apprenticeship, Geisey opened his office in 1886. For several years he was located in the Reilly Building at the corner of 14th and Market streets in downtown Wheeling. Giesey practiced with Edward Bates Franzheim and sometimes Frederic F. Faris, a partnership which led the profession in West Virginia.

During the 1890s, Giesey designed the Pocahontas County Courthouse, the Towers School in Clarksburg, and Ladies Hall, which is now Agnes Howard Hall, at West Virginia Wesleyan College in Buckhannon. In July 1899, he formed his partnership with Faris, and they maintained offices in the Masonic Temple Building in Wheeling. One of the most famous designs by Giesey and Faris was the West Virginia Building, of Neoclassical Revival design, at the Louisiana Purchase Exposition in St. Louis in 1904.

Several of Giesey's buildings have been placed on the National Register of Historic Places, including the Pocahontas County Courthouse and Jail, the L. S. Good House in Wheeling, the War Memorial Building in Wetzel County, the Fayette County Courthouse, and the Warwood Fire Station.

Giesey died in Wheeling, December 22, 1931.

See also Architects and Architecture

Cass Gilbert

Architect Cass Gilbert designed the West Virginia state capitol, which was built from 1924 to 1932 on the Kanawha River in the east end of Charleston.

Born in Zanesville, Ohio, November 24, 1859, Gilbert attended the Massachusetts Institute of Technology for one year before working briefly as a draftsman for the noted New York architectural firm of McKim, Mead, and White. In 1882, he entered a partnership in St. Paul, Minnesota, where he later designed the Minnesota state capitol, built 1896–1903. After attracting national attention, Gilbert moved to New York City. There he built the U.S. Custom House (1899–1905), in a Renaissance style with Germanic detail, and the Woolworth Building, a 60-story skyscraper with lacy Gothic detail in terra cotta over a steel frame. It is regarded as a model of tall commercial building design.

In Washington, Gilbert built the U.S. Treasury Annex (1918–19) and the federal courthouse (completed 1936), as well as the Supreme Court Building. Gilbert is also responsible for the planning of the campuses of the universities of Minnesota (Minneapolis) and Texas (Austin). Pleased that the budget for the West Virginia project had stayed within the amounts appropriated, Gilbert wrote in 1932 that the "State Capitol has been erected with a view to the dignity of the State, without excessive expenditure of money." He died May 17, 1934, in New York.

See also The Capitol

Emmitt Maxwell Furner II
Coolville, Ohio

Giles, Fayette & Kanawha Turnpike

The Giles, Fayette & Kanawha Turnpike was constructed as Virginia worked during the first half of the 19th century to improve transportation facilities in the western portion of the state. On March 1, 1837, the Virginia General Assembly passed legislation for the formation of the Giles, Fayette & Kanawha Turnpike Company. The goal of the company was to build a turnpike with a roadway width of 15 feet, "suitable for the passage of wagons and other wheeled carriages," from Pearisburg to Gauley Bridge.

Begun in 1838, the Giles, Fayette & Kanawha Turnpike was completed in 1848. Starting at Pearisburg, in Giles County, Virginia, it ran through Red Sulphur Springs, Pack's Ferry (near present Hinton), Raleigh Court House (present Beckley), and Fayetteville. Then it crossed Cotton Hill and New River, joining the James River & Kanawha Turnpike (present U.S. 60) at Kanawha Falls near Gauley Bridge. At a point near Fayetteville a separate road, the "Old State Road," which ran from Lewisburg and crossed the New River at Sewell, joined the Giles, Fayette & Kanawha Turnpike and continued with it to the Kanawha Turnpike.

The turnpike was valuable as a trade route and important because of its strategic value during the Civil War. Traveled by both Union and Confederate troops during the war, the turnpike took on particular significance in September 1862. On September 1, Confederate Gen. William W. Loring, following the orders of Robert E. Lee, left Pearisburg and moved up the turnpike with 4,000 soldiers. On September 11, Loring attacked federal troops at Fayetteville under the command of Gen. Joseph Lightburn. Lightburn was routed by the Confederates and eventually retreated to Charleston.

Like many early turnpikes, the Giles, Fayette & Kanawha was overtaken by the railroads in the late 19th century, becoming less important as a freight-hauling route. Portions of the old turnpike route were reused when roads were upgraded for motorized traffic in the early 20th century. In Fayetteville, a portion of the old turnpike is present State Route 16, which runs north and south of U.S. 19.

See also James River & Kanawha Turnpike

Michael K. Wilson
Charleston
James Morton Callahan, *Semi-Centennial History of West Virginia*, 1913.

Gilmer County

Gilmer County, located in the heart of West Virginia, was established in 1845 from parts of Kanawha and Lewis counties. It was named for Thomas W. Gilmer, a governor of Virginia. Gilmer County has an area of 342.4 square miles and a 2000 population of 7,160, the second lowest county population in West Virginia.

Organization of the county government began at the home of Salathiel Stalnaker in DeKalb. Citizens voted to establish the county seat at a place known as "The Ford," now Glenville. A disagreement about which community to use until a courthouse was built resulted in furtive maneuvering that spawned wild stories. Both were on a road that had been an old Indian trail (now State Route 5) along the Little Kanawha River toward Parkersburg, but a turnpike (now U.S. 33-U.S. 119) from Point Pleasant to Weston crossed at The Ford, giving it an advantage over DeKalb. The town of Glenville was laid out there in 1845.

The Little Kanawha provided transportation for people and commerce, and the river and its tributaries provided power for mills. Farming was the chief local occupation until timber, coal, oil, and gas were developed. Raising sheep, cattle, and tobacco gradually declined, although Gilmer remains a farming county. Its population peaked in 1940 and has declined since that time.

Gilmer County had mixed allegiances during the Civil War and suffered from guerrilla warfare. Fort Moore, a Union stockade, overlooked the Little Kanawha River atop College Hill in Glenville. Built in the spring of 1864 for Capt. W. T. Wiant's home guards to protect the community, it was burned that December by a Confederate unit under Capt. Sida Campbell. The slavery issue caused a split in Pisgah Methodist Episcopal Church in the 1850s. The ensuing Job's Temple, now the oldest church building in Gilmer County, is listed on the National Register of Historic Places.

Our state song, "The West Virginia Hills," was created in the hills of Gilmer County. It was written by Ellen Ruddell King while visiting relatives in Glenville. Her poem was put to music by Henry Everett Engle in 1885, at Engle's farm near Tanner. Engle also added the chorus. "The West Virginia Hills" was first pub-

---

FAST FACTS ABOUT GILMER COUNTY

Founded: 1845
Land in square miles: 342.4
Population: 7,160
Percentage minorities: 2.7%
Percentage rural: 100%
Median age: 36.8
Percentage 65 and older: 15.3%
Birth rate per 1,000 population: 7.3
Median household income: $22,857
High school graduate or higher: 70.0%
Bachelor's degree or higher: 17.1%
Home ownership: 72.4%
Median home value: $63,900

This information is from the 2000 U.S. Census. In 2000, West Virginia as a whole had 5 percent minorities, a median age of 38.9, median household income of $29,696, and a 75.2 percent home ownership rate.

A scene on the Little Kanawha River in Gilmer County.

lished in the *Glenville Crescent* newspaper in September 1885.

Glenville State College began in 1872 as a branch of the State Normal School. The first session opened in January 1873 in the old Gilmer County courthouse, with T. Marcellus Marshall as acting principal. By 1939 there were 55 one-room schools in the county, and a few larger ones. Eventually there were five high schools. In 1968, they were consolidated into Gilmer County High School. The Calhoun-Gilmer Career Center is an important educational resource for both counties.

A medium security federal prison opened in 2003, replacing the college as the largest employer in the county. An industrial park was established at Stouts Mills to stimulate economic development. U.S. 33 and U.S. 119 run together through the county. State Routes 5, 47, and a short section of 74 also pass through. Scenic roads include Cedar Creek Road (County Route 17, a West Virginia scenic backway) and the Little Kanawha Parkway (Route 5, a scenic byway).

Although not navigable by modern standards, the Little Kanawha River remains important to Gilmer County and has a large place in local history. Rafts, flatboats and, later, gasoline-powered paddlewheel boats carried goods and passengers until decent roads were provided in the 1930s. Between 1890 and 1931, barges carrying as much as 30,000 pounds and boats carrying 50 to 100 passengers were a regular sight. Outgoing freight included the county's timber and coal. The Gainers were prominent rivermen, and two of the other boat companies were owned by John Shuman and Clyde Conrad. The boats hauled dry goods, supplies for the growing natural gas industry, and other products into the valley. Models of boats built in the county are on display at the Gilmer County Historical Society.

The river's importance to county history is underscored by the fact that three of Gilmer's Little Kanawha bridges are on the National Register of Historic Places. They are of three distinct structural types, including the camel-back truss bridge at Stouts Mills, the Pratt truss bridge at Glenville, and the cable suspension bridge at Trubada.

Flooding of the Little Kanawha River is a recurring problem. High water in November 1985 reached 13 feet above flood stage at Glenville, the highest on record, allowing boaters on Main Street to touch the traffic light. Permanent water marks may be seen on brick buildings in town. Until 1985, the big flood of March 1967 had been considered the flood of the century. There were rowboats on Main Street that year as well, and again in 1994. The river is a source of water for public utility plants. The Little Kanawha is used for fishing, with an occasional canoe or johnboat. Migrating waterfowl attract hunters in season.

Cedar Creek State Park offers camping, hiking trails, fishing, swimming, picnic pavilions, miniature golf, and a restored one-room schoolhouse. The annual West Virginia State Folk Festival, founded in 1950 by Dr. Patrick Ward Gainer, draws crowds to Glenville each June.

See also Glenville, Glenville State College, Little Kanawha River, West Virginia State Folk Festival

Frances Myers Schmetzer
Glenville
Gilmer County Historical Society, *History of Gilmer County, West Virginia, 1845–1989*, 1994.

Ginseng

American ginseng, a long-lived herbaceous perennial, is an important forest resource in West Virginia. It exists in all 55 counties but is most prevalent in cool, moist forests having well-drained loamy soils and a moderate to heavy tree canopy with a heavy understory of shrubs and herbs.

Ginseng grows from ten to 18 inches tall, with occasional specimens as tall as two feet. The plant has a distinctive olive green color which makes it stand out to the practiced eye. The compound leaves, each consisting of five parts, vary in number from one in very young specimens to as many as four in more mature plants. Ginseng diggers, often known as "sangers," describe ginseng or "sang" by the number of prongs or leaf stems. The older plants have larger roots and more prongs. A four-prong plant will always elicit excitement among sangers.

The Chinese use the root for a wide variety of ailments including fatigue and pulmonary and gastrointestinal disorders. It is also employed as an aphrodisiac. It is mostly used in making a tea, but it is also carried as a dried root to ward off disease and promote good health. Recent biomedical research has isolated active compounds called saponin ginsenosides, which increase the efficiency of the adrenal and pituitary glands. Other active chemicals include panaxin, which stimulates brain function and aids heart and blood vessels; panacene, which acts as a painkiller and tranquilizer; and ginsenin, an anti-diabetic substance.

Ginseng has been harvested as a cash crop in West Virginia for at least 200 years. West Virginia has a harvesting season beginning on August 15 and ending on November 30 of each year. The statute requires diggers to plant the ripe berries (seeds) from harvested plants at the digging site.

Only dealers registered with the state Division of Forestry may export ginseng

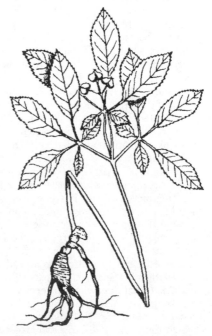

Ginseng.

root from West Virginia. Ginseng sales produce $5 million to $6 million each year, an important income supplement in the southern coalfields and rural communities. Recent ginseng prices have ranged from a low of $175 to more than $500 per pound of dried root. Division of Forestry records indicate an average annual root harvest of nearly 20,000 pounds, with the highest occurring in 1984 at more than 39,000 pounds and the lowest in 1987 at nearly 9,500 pounds. McDowell County, the southernmost West Virginia county, has averaged the greatest harvest with Wyoming, Logan, Mingo, Boone, Raleigh, Kanawha, Greenbrier, Fayette, and Randolph counties completing the top ten.

Robert D. Whipkey
Division of Forestry

Christopher Gist

Explorer Christopher Gist, one of the first white men to explore what is now West Virginia, was born about 1706 near Baltimore. He was an Indian trader, coroner, surveyor, and road builder, and considered an educated man for the time. He came from a prosperous family, but a fire destroyed his storehouse of furs in 1732 and left him penniless. Around 1745, he moved to near the Yadkin River in North Carolina.

In 1750, Gist was chosen by the Ohio Company to explore and survey the frontier west of the Alleghenies. He traveled much of Western Virginia, Ohio, Kentucky, and the Ohio Valley. He made a second expedition for the Ohio Company in 1751–52 through much of present West Virginia, and in 1753 he took residence in western Pennsylvania. In 1753, he guided young George Washington's unsuccessful mission to warn the French away from lands the English claimed in the west. In the French and Indian War, Gist was a guide for Braddock's disastrous military campaign against Fort Duquesne. In 1755, he joined the Virginia military commanded by Washington, serving as captain of scouts. In 1757, Gist was appointed an Indian agent and continued in this post until his death from smallpox in 1759.

He was known by the Indians as "Father Gist" because of his efforts in their behalf. The life of Christopher Gist covered much of the tumultuous colonial period of the 1700s. His three journals of his explorations made a valuable contribution to early knowledge of the region including what is now West Virginia. Gist did as much as anyone of his day to foster western experience, and biographer Kenneth P. Bailey felt that had historians chosen, Gist might have been recognized as "the outstanding frontiersman of colonial history."

See also Exploration, Ohio Company

Dan B. Fleming
Blacksburg, Virginia

Charles H. Ambler, *West Virginia: The Mountain State,* 1940; Kenneth P. Bailey, *Christopher Gist,* 1976.

Glaciation

Glaciers covered much of North America during the Pleistocene Epoch that began nearly two million years ago and lasted until about 10,000 years ago. Glaciers did not move over what is now West Virginia, but did dramatically affect the drainage pattern.

Prior to the Pleistocene the Monongahela River flowed northwestward by way of present Beaver and Grand rivers, in Pennsylvania and Ohio, to the preglacial St. Lawrence River, and the preglacial Teays River crossed central Appalachia via present New River to present Nitro and then followed the Teays Valley, exiting the state at present Huntington. When the Wisconsin Glacier became stationary along a line beginning in Ohio about 10 miles north of the top of the present Northern Panhandle of West Virginia and running southwestward to near Maysville, Kentucky, on the Ohio River, the preglacial routes of the Monongahela and New-Teays rivers were blocked by the ice front, forming ancient Lake Monongahela and Lake Tight (also known as Teays Lake). As the impounded water rose above divides leading to other basins, the modern Ohio River was pieced together in a continuous stream along the forward edge of the glacier, and the waters of the Monongahela and Ohio rivers were joined over the course between New Martinsville and St. Marys.

The Teays Valley between Nitro and Huntington is an interesting glacial relic. The lake of the Teays extended from Chillicothe, Ohio, to near Hawks Nest, and during its 25,000 years of existence was filled with lake clay and alluvial silt deposits. After the lake drained as a result of later changes, the Teays River was diverted probably through stream piracy by the Kanawha River to Point Pleasant where it joined the recently created Ohio River. The Teays Valley, currently drained by Hurricane Creek and Mud River, has in modern times become a major highway and rail transportation artery and a residential, commercial, and industrial region between Huntington and Charleston.

See also Geology, Lake Monongahela, Lake Tight, Teays River

Howard G. Adkins
Ona

Raymond E. Janssen, *Earth Science: A Handbook On The Geology of West Virginia,* 1973; West Virginia Writers' Project, *West Virginia: A Guide To The Mountain State,* 1941.

Glade Creek Mill

Glade Creek Mill, the focal point of Babcock State Park, is a much photographed landmark and the most familiar symbol

Glade Creek Mill, the focal point of Babcock State Park.

of old-time West Virginia. Ironically, it is but 30 years old in its present setting. The mill, actually a composite of two earlier mills, was brought to the banks of Glade Creek in the mid-1970s.

J. C. Boley, who had helped build Babcock State Park during his youthful days as a Civilian Conservation Corps (CCC) enrollee, served as the park's superintendent from 1944 to 1956. In his later role as assistant chief of the West Virginia state park system, Boley conceived the mill project to complement the original stone lodge and auxiliary structures at Babcock. He selected the mill site and chose Don Page of the Department of Commerce to design the project.

A two-year search identified two existing mills to provide building parts. However, both mills—Stony Creek Mill in Pocahontas County and Onego Mill in Pendleton County—had been operated by water-powered turbines. State engineers solved the problem of converting the new mill on Glade Creek to a more picturesque overshot water wheel. A Fitz water wheel, as well as enormous gears from the dismantled Meadow River Company lumber mill at Rainelle, were used in the work. A buried two-foot diameter water flume carries water from upstream to turn the wheel. Glade Creek Mill was dedicated in 1976.

See also Babcock State Park

Don Page
Beckley

Glass Industry

Although glass was made here much earlier, West Virginia became an important glass manufacturing state at the end of the 19th century. The emergence of a significant glass sand industry in the Eastern Panhandle and the growing availability of cheap fuels, especially natural gas, provided the natural resources critical to glassmaking. At the same time, railroads had improved transportation in

The bottle-making machine helped transform the glass industry.

the state, and local booster movements in numerous towns aggressively recruited manufacturing enterprises to build on the plentiful natural resources. Finally, neighboring states, especially Pennsylvania and Ohio, were home to an abundance of skilled craftsmen still essential to glass production at a time when technological changes had just begun to restructure the industry.

By the mid-19th century, factories, firms, and workers were increasingly specialized in the various branches of glassmaking: glass tableware, bottles and containers, and flat glass (plate and window glass). Each of these branches gave rise to different processes, new technologies, distinct companies, and even separate labor organizations to represent the workers. The skilled craftsmen who made glass tableware joined the American Flint Glass Workers Union; bottlemakers were members of the Glass Bottle Blowers Association; and window-glass craftsmen created a powerful union organization in the Knights of Labor Local Assembly 300. Likewise, the factory owners and entrepreneurs in the industry tended to be small, select groups with particular knowledge of their industry niche.

Expanding markets and technological change dramatically altered all segments of the glass industry in the 1890s. One significant change involved the development of tanks for melting the raw materials for glass. Tank technology relied heavily on natural gas as the fuel of choice, dispersing the industry to western Pennsylvania, Indiana, and eventually, West Virginia. The tanks replaced the clay pots previously used, and allowed a higher production. Thus, companies built larger factories after the turn of the 20th century.

Complementing the tank, which affected each branch of glassmaking differently, were specific market factors and production technologies. In glass tableware, the industry expanded to meet the growing demand from the hotel and restaurant trade. This coincided with the development of presses and molds that reduced the skill required for producing high-quality tumblers, bowls, and goblets. New firms such as the Fostoria Glass Company and the Fenton Art Glass Company could move to where fuel was cheapest. Both began operation in Ohio but soon moved to West Virginia, to Moundsville and Williamstown, respectively, taking advantage of offers of cheap land and gas by local developers. Fenton and Fostoria both developed molds and presses that made the companies market leaders while enabling them to employ less skilled and less expensive workers. Early in the 20th century, Fostoria's more than 900 workers made it the largest glass tableware factory in the country.

Technological change brought window-glass manufacturing to West Virginia in a different fashion. Seeking to preserve more traditional production processes in the face of the monopolizing efforts of the American Window Glass Company, many skilled workers opened cooperatives or small, family owned plants in places such as Clarksburg, South Charleston, and Salem. Typically, immigrants, especially from France or Belgium, were at the center of these enterprises. In the first two decades of the 20th century, French was commonly spoken in neighborhoods around these plants. Ultimately, however, further advances in technology would eliminate the older process. By the late 1920s, window glass had become a mass-production industry with a few large firms dominating the market. Fortunately for workers in West Virginia, the Pittsburgh Plate Glass Company located one of its plants in Clarksburg in 1916, and the Libbey-Owens-Ford Company established a plant in Charleston in 1916, sustaining the industry in the Mountain State into the 1970s.

In glass bottles and containers, West Virginia was at the center of technological change due to the influence of Michael Owens, a native of Point Pleasant. Owens, working for the Libbey Glass Works in Toledo, patented and perfected his fully automatic bottle-blowing machine in the first years of the 20th century. In partnership with Edward Libbey, his former employer, Owens began his own company in 1909 to manufacture bottles, establishing his first plants in Fairmont and Clarksburg. Within 10 years Owens also had plants in Charleston and Huntington, making small-mouth, milk, soda, and whiskey bottles. Although the Clarksburg plant closed in the 1920s, the other three Owens plants employed thousands of employees for decades longer, Charleston closing in 1963, Fairmont in 1982, and Huntington in 1993. But unlike glass tableware and window glass, both of which brought large numbers of skilled workers to West Virginia, glass bottles began in the state with a mass-production process relying on less skilled factory labor.

In several segments of the glass industry, West Virginia companies led the nation. In pressed glass tableware, West Virginia was home to about 15 percent of the plants operating in the United States between 1825 and 1980, and between 15 per

"It takes feeling for glass"

"Making glass isn't something that can be put down exactly in a textbook and executed right off according to the rules, by any bright young guy who can read the figures and work a slide rule.

"You can know everything about what goes into the batch and what should go into it, you can know about temperatures, about gas currents and the effect of ventilation in the top of the furnace house, but when that bright pond under the cap of the furnace begins to buck and stew, the situation seems to call for some veteran midwife of glass.

"The books are all right, but they just don't seem to be quite enough. It takes feeling for glass. . . . A lot of human temperament goes into the temper of glass."

—A. O. Barnette
Libbey-Owens-Ford glass worker

cent and 21 percent of the flat glass industry between 1947 and 1963. West Virginia accounted for an even larger share of the nation's production of glass bottles. Within the state, glass production ranked in the second tier of industries, far behind coal but close in importance to coke, chemicals, and steel in terms of number of employees and the value of its products. About 1910, glass factory employment totaled about 7,500 workers, making it the fourth-largest employer in the state.

In certain communities, glassmaking was far more important. Along the Ohio River, glass tableware was a significant employer in towns from Wellsburg to Williamstown; glass bottles and window glass plants shaped the landscapes of Clarksburg, Morgantown, Charleston, and South Charleston. In the early 20th century, the industry brought hundreds of migrants and immigrants to the state to fill the most skilled positions, while also recruiting thousands of native-born workers who entered the industrial world through glass manufacturing. By the 1930s, virtually all of these jobs were represented by unions, as the American Flint Glass Workers, the Glass Bottle Blowers Association, and the Federation of Flat Glass Workers adapted to meet the needs of mass-production workers.

Indeed, the glass industry produced important leaders for the state's labor movement; Rene Zabeau was a long-time officer in the West Virginia Federation of Labor from the 1940s to the 1960s, and Joseph Powell was president of the state AFL-CIO for more than two decades. Glassworkers also helped shape politics in their communities. After 1900, glass industry towns were noted for their tendency to vote for Socialist or Progressive candidates. Clarksburg, Salem, and South Charleston gave high percentages of their votes to Eugene Debs, and the small towns of Adamston, Harrison County, and Star City, Monongalia County, had Socialist mayors in the 1910s. In later years, many of these unionized glassworkers allied themselves with the liberal policies of the Democratic Party.

See also Fenton Art Glass Company, Fostoria Glass, Michael Joseph Owens

Ken Fones-Wolf
West Virginia University
Frederick Barkey, *Cinderheads in the Hills: The Belgian Window Glass Workers of West Virginia*, 1988; Ken Fones-Wolf, "Work, Culture and Politics in Industrializing West Virginia: The Glassworkers of Clarksburg and Moundsville, 1891–1919," *West Virginia History*, 1999–2000.

Glass Sand Mining

One of the highest quality deposits of silica sand in the United States is in Morgan County, giving rise to a sand-mining industry. Local mining started after the Civil War along the Oriskany sands formation, which runs from New York to southern Virginia. At first, men used sledge hammers and wedges to break large rocks into smaller ones, which were transported by mule-drawn carts to steam-powered crushers and mills. The stone was reduced to sand, then carried by rail to glass manufacturers. In 1893, Henry Harrison Hunter of Berkeley Springs won a blue ribbon at the World's Columbian Exposition in Chicago for the quality of sand that he had mined and processed.

By the early 1900s, many small companies had begun rudimentary mining operations along Warm Springs Ridge, just north of Berkeley Springs. One of these eventually developed into Berkeley Glass Sand Company, incorporated in 1911.

Meanwhile, Pennsylvania Glass Sand Company had, since 1894, been mining Oriskany sand in the same geological formation in Pennsylvania about 80 miles north of Morgan County. The growing business soon acquired the Hancock Works, which had been started by Noah Speer in 1872 along the Potomac River north of Berkeley Springs in West Virginia. The Pennsylvania investors opened a second plant on the east side of Warm Springs Ridge in 1904. In July 1927, the company was incorporated as Pennsylvania Glass Sand Corporation. Looking for larger silica reserves to support its investment in larger processing facilities, the company absorbed Berkeley Glass Sand and other companies, including the Hazel-Atlas Glass Sand Company near Great Cacapon.

The darkest day in Morgan County sand-mining history came June 7, 1926, before the companies were consolidated. As a Berkeley Glass Sand crew prepared an explosion, a spark prematurely set off what the company maintained was dynamite but others claimed was dangerous black powder. Six men were killed. Their deaths inspired John Unger, a local blind singer, to compose "The Miner's Doom," a ballad that was recorded in 1927 by early country music star Vernon Dalhart.

The modern era began in 1929 when Earle T. Andrews, a young engineer, was assigned by Pennsylvania Glass Sand Corporation to design and construct a new Berkeley Plant, the largest and most advanced silica facility of its time. The Berkeley Plant was still the core of the Morgan County sand-mining industry more than 70 years later. Andrews went on to become general manager of operations in 1941 and was president from 1963 to 1968, when the company was acquired by ITT. His son, Hale E. Andrews, then took over until his retirement in 1985. During these decades, a number of expansions and modernizations were made to supply markets in the glass, fiberglass, plastics, metallurgical, and chemical industries.

In 1985, U.S. Borax & Chemical Company, a subsidiary of the British RTZ Corporation, acquired Pennsylvania Glass Sand and the rest of ITT's sand-mining business. In February 1996, the company —now known as U.S. Silica—became affiliated with D. George Harris & Associates. As the 21st century began, the Berkeley Springs operation was part of a corporation with $250 million annual sales and facilities at 21 locations. About 200 people were employed at the mine, processing plant, laboratory, and corporate headquarters in Berkeley Springs.

See also Berkeley Springs, Oriskany Sandstone

John Douglas
Berkeley Springs

Jack Glasscock

Athlete John Wesley "Jack" Glasscock, one of 19th-century baseball's premier shortstops, was born in Wheeling, July 22, 1859. He was called "Pebbly Jack" because of his habit of "grounds keeping" at his position, picking up and tossing away pebbles, which some baseball historians claim were imaginary.

Glasscock, who played bare-handed, was one of the first to use a signal to inform his catcher which middle infielder would cover second on a steal and was one of the first shortstops to back up throws to the second baseman. Glasscock played in 1,736 games and had a batting average of .290 with 27 home runs and 752 RBIs. For five times in his career, he topped the .300 mark in his batting average.

Glasscock's debut occurred May 1, 1879, playing for the Cleveland Blues. In addition to Cleveland, he played for several other teams, including the Cincinnati Reds, the Indianapolis Hoosiers, the St. Louis Browns, and the New York Giants. While managing Indianapolis for part of 1889, Glasscock led the National League with 205 hits. In 1890, while playing with the Giants, he won the National League batting title, hitting .336.

In 1895, Glasscock returned to his hometown of Wheeling to manage and play first base for the Wheeling Base Ball Club. He died in Wheeling, February 24, 1947.

See also Baseball

William Ellsworth Glasscock

West Virginia's 13th governor, William Ellsworth Glasscock, is most remembered for his role in the Mine Wars. During his term (1909–13), the state also received national publicity for an affair involving the appointment of U.S. senators, and there were important governmental reforms.

Glasscock was born on a farm in Monongalia County, December 13, 1862, and

Governor William Ellsworth Glasscock (1862–1925).

educated in the public schools and at West Virginia University. He became a teacher and later a lawyer, being admitted to the bar in 1903. He became a superintendent of schools in 1887 and the clerk of the county circuit court in 1890. In 1905, at the recommendation of U.S. Sen. Stephen B. Elkins, President Theodore Roosevelt appointed Glasscock internal revenue collector for the District of West Virginia. Glasscock resigned to run for governor as a Republican in 1908. He was elected by a majority of 12,133 votes over Democrat Louis Bennett.

During Glasscock's administration, the legislature established an agency for road construction, a nonpartisan board to control public institutions, a Public Service Commission, a tuberculosis sanitarium, and the office of commissioner of agriculture. It enacted a workmen's compensation law and empowered the federal government to acquire state land for forest reserves. Medical examinations were required for pupils in public schools.

Two years after Glasscock took office, the Democrats gained control of the House of Delegates and a 15-15 split in the Senate. U.S. senators were appointed at that time by state legislatures. This gave Democrats the power to name the next U.S. senator, for the matter would be settled in a Democrat-controlled joint session even if a Republican were chosen by the evenly divided state Senate. Republican U.S. Sen. Nathan Goff's term would expire the following year. Then Elkins, the other Republican senator, died January 4, 1911, just after the legislature convened. Suddenly, the legislature was poised to name two Democratic senators.

To avoid those appointments, Republican state senators hid in Glasscock's office, preventing a quorum in the upper house. Without a vote, no U.S. senator

could be chosen. When the sergeant-at-arms sought to capture at least one Republican to force a vote, allies slipped them onto a train to Cincinnati, where they lodged in a hotel.

The national press publicized the standoff. The parties compromised: the Democrats chose two U.S. senators and the Republicans organized the West Virginia Senate, allowing them leadership of the upper house.

The Mine Wars erupted in April 1912, when miners struck over several key issues, including recognition of the union, abolition of the mine guard system, and the right to a checkweighman. Kanawha Valley coal companies refused to bargain. They armed their mine guards, many from the notorious Baldwin-Felts Detective Agency in Bluefield, with shotguns, rifles, and machine guns. The miners were scarcely less well-armed, and a bloody shooting war ensued.

Glasscock's response was denounced on constitutional grounds, but the West Virginia Supreme Court upheld his actions. When armed miners clashed with the companies' guards, he sent militia troops to preserve order. At one time the entire state force was on Paint Creek in the area of the Fayette-Kanawha border. In September, Glasscock declared the strike district under martial law; 1,200 state militia were rushed to the territory. Operators and strikers were ordered to surrender arms and ammunition. Congregating of miners was prohibited. A measure of peace was restored, but the conflict continued beyond Glasscock's term.

Speaking before the West Virginia capitol in August 1912, labor organizer Mary Harris "Mother" Jones denounced Governor Glasscock for the continued presence of armed mine guards. "I say that if the governor won't make them go then we will make them go," she declared. "We have come to the chief executive, we have asked him, and he couldn't do anything." Glasscock had left Charleston the day before the rally. Jones denounced him as a "dirty coward."

Disturbances quieted by mid-October. The governor lifted martial law. The militia withdrew. Hostilities resumed the following month, and Glasscock issued his second martial law proclamation. The militia withdrew again in January. Glasscock issued a third proclamation in February, near the end of his term, and troops were again rushed to the strike area. His successor, Governor Hatfield, dictated terms of peace, forced both sides to accept them, and brought the strike to an end in 1913.

The jailing of civilians including Mother Jones by military courts under the martial law proclamation was the most controversial act of Glasscock's administration. Glasscock was upheld by the West Virginia

Supreme Court of Appeals in the case *Mays and Nance v. Brown*, although state Attorney General Howard B. Lee later characterized the episode as a "rape of the constitution."

After his term as governor, Glasscock practiced law in Morgantown and took little part in public affairs. Friends said he never fully recovered from the strain of high office on his health. He died at his home, April 12, 1925, and was buried in Oak Grove Cemetery in Morgantown.

See also Henry D. Hatfield, Mother Jones, Mine Wars

Glade Little
St. Albans

Howard B. Lee, *Bloodletting in Appalachia*, 1969; John G. Morgan, *West Virginia Governors*, 1980; Otis Rice, *Charleston and the Kanawha Valley*, 1981.

Glen Ferris Inn

The Glen Ferris Inn at Glen Ferris is one of West Virginia's oldest. The original Federal-style vernacular building that still can be seen beneath a 1910 Classical Revival remodeling has hosted travelers since at least 1839, when it was a popular stagecoach stop on the James River & Kanawha Turnpike, now U.S. 60. During the Civil War, the building was a U.S. Army quartermaster depot from July through December, 1861. It was also headquarters of owner Aaron Stockton's several enterprises, including farming, timbering, and sawmills, flatboat building, and one of West Virginia's earliest commercial coal mining operations. The Glen Ferris Inn stands at the landmark falls of the Great Kanawha River, the point at which early navigation began.

Stockton, whose grandfather, Richard, was a signer of the Declaration of Independence, bought the property in 1817. A 1915 Fayette County newspaper account quotes a Stockton family member as saying the house was built by two Irishmen in 1815. Stockton first applied for a license to serve alcohol to guests in 1839. The inn prospered until 1874, when the recently completed C&O Railroad began delivering travelers to the new Kanawha Hotel on the other side of the river.

Known first as Stockton's Tavern, then informally as Hawkins Hotel, the inn remained in the Stockton family until 1920, when it was sold to a subsidiary of Union Carbide. It then became known as the Glen Ferris Inn. After 1981, it belonged to Elkem Corporation, which purchased Union Carbide's industrial operations in the area. The property was placed on the National Register of Historic Places in 1991. Guest accommodations include 15 rooms and two suites, the Old Stockton Dining Room, and a Riverside Dining Room.

See also Kanawha Falls

Rebecca Halstead Kimmons
Charleston

Glen Rogers Mine Disaster

A methane gas explosion November 6, 1923, inside the ill-fated Glen Rogers coal mine killed 27 men, the worst accident of any kind in Wyoming County history. Government officials blamed the inexperience of a crew constructing a ventilation passage, whose work diverted the airflow and allowed explosive gas to accumulate. Two of the victims were teenagers. Another five were among the many European immigrants who found work at the Raleigh-Wyoming Mining Company deep mine located in a sparsely populated part of southern West Virginia. Inspectors said a spark from an electric drill ignited a gas explosion and immediately killed four workers. Another 21 stationed nearby succumbed to the deadly gas. Two others drowned when they fell into a water-filled excavation ditch after nearly reaching the potential safety of the mine's air shaft.

The mine, opened in 1921, became one of the state's largest, with employment of nearly 1,000 men and annual production upward of one million tons during the 1930s and 1940s. Glen Rogers was the hometown of Governor Marland, whose father was a superintendent of the mine after the explosion.

Three other disasters occurred at Glen Rogers. Five miners died September 23, 1922, when equipment fell on them during construction of the facility's 720-foot deep shaft. A January 6, 1931, underground gas explosion claimed eight lives. Five workers died in a roof fall on December 9, 1957. A total of 160 fatalities occurred at the mine before it was closed in 1960 by its parent company, the Old Ben Coal Corporation of Chicago.

Karl C. Lilly III
State Senate

Lacy Dillon, *They Died in the Darkness*, 1976; U.S. Mine Safety and Health Administration, *Historical Summary of Mine Disasters in the United States*, 1998.

Little Sleepy Glenn

Marshall "Little Sleepy" Glenn, coach, star athlete, and medical doctor, was born in Elkins, April 22, 1908. He coached basketball at West Virginia University from 1934 to 1938, and football from 1937 to 1940. Some years he coached both basketball and football while also attending Rush Medical School in Chicago during the summer months.

Glenn was a quarterback and a basketball star at Elkins High School and excelled in both football and basketball at WVU from 1927 through 1930. He was WVU's best basketball player prior to World War II and captained both basketball and football. After graduation Glenn was head coach at Martinsburg High School before returning to coach at the university. The WVU teams Glenn coached in basketball posted a 61-46 record and in football

14-12-3. The 1938 team upset favored Texas Tech 7-6 in the Sun Bowl. Glenn introduced the T-formation to WVU football.

Glenn was a flight surgeon during World War II, serving with the navy in the Pacific. Following his sports career, Glenn practiced medicine in Charles Town until his death in an automobile accident October 12, 1983. He was inducted into the WVU Sports Hall of Fame in 1992.

"Little Sleepy" acquired his odd nickname because his big brother, also a star athlete at Elkins, was known as "Sleepy" Glenn.

Norman Julian
Dominion Post

Glenville

Located on the Little Kanawha River at the intersection of State Route 5 and U.S. 33-119, Glenville is the county seat of Gilmer County.

In the late 1700s and early 1800s, white pioneers began settling in the area they called "the Ford" because it was a place where travelers could cross the river. Later, the community was named Glenville because of its location in a glen. The first gristmill in Gilmer County was constructed there in 1812. The first courthouse was completed in 1850, the second in 1872, and the current courthouse in 1923. Glenville was incorporated in 1856.

As early as 1833, a high school was established in the Methodist Episcopal Church. After moving to the courthouse in 1850 and into a house in 1884, the school got its own building in 1913. Glenville High School was replaced by the consolidated Gilmer County High School in 1968. What is now Glenville State College was founded in 1872. In 1950, folklorist Patrick Gainer established the West Virginia State Folk Festival at the college.

Before the 1930s, the Little Kanawha River's commercial traffic dominated the town's economy. Road construction contributed to the demise of riverboating by the late 1930s. The natural gas and oil industry rose to prominence after oil was struck in 1875 at nearby Letter Gap. Glenville is now the headquarters of several oil and gas firms. The 1985 flood devastated the downtown, leading many businesses to move to the higher Hays City neighborhood at the main highway intersection.

The Little Kanawha Valley Bank was incorporated in 1901. Its small frame building, covered in pressed metal, is now on the National Register of Historic Places. By 1906, the First National Bank of Glenville and the Glenville Banking and Trust Company had also been created. Glenville is now served by United Bank and a branch of Calhoun Banks of Grantsville.

Early Methodist circuit riders and Baptist missionaries brought religion to Glenville early in the 19th century. The

Presbyterian Church was organized in 1847; the First Baptist Church, 1850; and Trinity United Methodist Church, 1896. Several other churches also serve the area today. Glenville has a golf club and recreation center, among several other facilities built at the old county poor farm.

In 1885 the *Glenville Crescent* first published Ellen King's poem, "The West Virginia Hills," which later became the official state song. While this newspaper didn't survive, the *Glenville Pathfinder* (1892) and the *Glenville Democrat* (1904) have.

David H. Corcoran
Glenville

Gilmer County Historical Society, *History of Gilmer County, 1845–1989*, 1994.

Glenville State College

Glenville State College, established in 1872, is located in Glenville, the county seat of Gilmer County. Originally founded as a teacher's college, Glenville State also emphasizes business, human services, music, and natural resources management.

The college began as the Glenville Branch of the State Normal School and was established by an act of the legislature on February 19, 1872. Local citizens Milton Norris and Nelson M. Bennett were leaders in acquiring an original tract of three acres with a two-story frame dwelling. This property was donated to the state and ready for use in the fall of 1873.

The first session of the college opened on January 14, 1873, in the old Gilmer County courthouse, with the colorful T. Marcellus Marshall as acting principal. Three months later, Louis Bennett of Weston was appointed principal. Bennett was later a candidate for governor and the father of World War I aviator Louis Bennett Jr. After two years he resigned, and Marshall was again chosen principal. In that capacity Marshall gave five years of devoted service.

Although the primary purpose in establishing Glenville Normal was to educate teachers, preparatory courses were also authorized to prepare students for college work. As high schools became more numerous, preparatory offerings were gradually reduced. During the 1920s, Glenville graduates were listed as completing the Short Normal, the Standard Normal, or the Junior College Course. Largely through the work of President Edward G. Rohrbough, in 1930 the school was authorized to begin granting four-year Bachelor of Arts degrees in education. The legislature changed the name to Glenville State Teachers College, making Glenville a college in name for the first time. Baccalaureate degrees were first granted in 1931 to a class of nine.

The 1930s and '40s were difficult times. The Depression, which hurt all levels of public education, meant tight budgets for the college. The regional economy began to improve during World War II, but enrollment fell in the years between 1942 and 1945 as young men left to serve in the military. Nonetheless, progress was made. In 1937 the college sought and received admission to the American Association of Colleges of Teacher Education. Construction during this period included the building of the Science Hall, which was completed in 1943.

In 1943, the legislature changed the name to Glenville State College. By the end of the 1940s, Glenville State College was offering both the B.A. and B.S. degrees in such academic fields as English, history, science, and music.

After World War II, Glenville State began 20 years of significant growth. In 1947, Harry B. Heflin became the third president of Glenville State College, and he served until 1964. During his tenure, the school began an accelerated building program to accommodate a growing student body. In May 1950, construction began on the Health and Physical Education Building. The building, which housed a gym, swimming pool, and infirmary, was dedicated in 1952. In 1956, the state Board of Education authorized the construction of the student center, known as the Pioneer Center for the name of the college sports teams, and work started that summer. In 1964 an addition was completed on the Pioneer Center, housing a ballroom, alumni offices, and recreation center. The enlarged building was named the Heflin Center in 1990 in honor of the former president.

In 1972, Glenville State College celebrated its centennial. William K. Simmons became president of Glenville State College in 1977. He stepped down in 1998 after a period of faculty discontent, having served longer than any other president except Rohrbough.

In the fall of 2002, there were 1,789 full-time equivalent (FTE) students enrolled at Glenville State College. The campus overlooks the town of Glenville from College Hill, once the site of a Civil War fort. The area is rich in Appalachian culture. Glenville is the site of the West Virginia State Folk Festival held each June in the town and on the college campus.

Nicole McDonald
Glenville State College

Joseph C. Gluck

Educator and clergyman Joseph C. Gluck was born January 31, 1915, in Auburn, Ritchie County, the son of Howard and Dora Zinn Gluck. He attended Harrisville High School and Bethany College. He earned a master's of divinity degree at Yale University and was ordained an American Baptist minister before enlisting as a navy chaplain in World War II.

Gluck was a mainstay on the campus of West Virginia University for more than a half-century after 1946, as dean of students, vice president for student affairs, and special counselor to students. He was a founder and early member of WVU's prestigious Order of Vandalia and received honorary doctorates from Alderson-Broaddus College and Bethany College.

From 1956 to 1984, Dean Gluck was pastor of the Forks-of-Cheat Baptist Church, established in 1775 at Stewartstown, north of Morgantown. He helped preserve history there and revived the tradition of eating bear at an annual church picnic. His wife, Margaret Hannah Gluck, of Cass, Pocahontas County, died February 18, 2002.

A gardener whose sweet peas are legendary, Gluck collected humorous stories. He shared widely both flowers and jokes. Dean Gluck died in Morgantown, February 18, 2004.

Mary Lucille DeBerry
Morgantown

Laura Spitznogle, "The Man of a Thousand Stories," *West Virginia University Alumni Magazine,* Fall 1998; Linda Hepler, "The Preacher and the Bear: A Monongalia Church Celebrates an Unusual Tradition," *Goldenseal,* Spring 1991.

Nathan Goff Jr.

U.S. Senator, Congressman, U.S. attorney, judge, and Republican Party leader Nathan Goff Jr., was born in Clarksburg of a prominent family, February 9, 1843. He was educated at Northwestern Academy in Clarksburg and at Georgetown College (now Georgetown University) in Washington. Goff left Georgetown in 1861 to join the Union service in the Civil War, enlisting as a private and rising to the rank of major and brevet brigadier general. He was captured at Moorefield in January 1864 and imprisoned in Richmond's notorious Libby Prison before being released in an exchange personally authorized by President Lincoln.

Goff began the practice of law in Clarksburg in March 1865. He served in the West Virginia House of Delegates in 1867 and 1868, and President Grant appointed him U.S. district attorney for West Virginia in 1868. In 1881, he briefly served as secretary of the navy under President Hayes. Goff was elected to the U.S. House of Representatives in 1882, serving from 1883 until 1889.

In 1888, Goff lost West Virginia's most controversial gubernatorial election to Aretas Brooks Fleming. Goff's initial 106-vote majority was challenged by Fleming, and both men were sworn in on inauguration day. The incumbent, E. W. Wilson, refused to vacate the office under the circumstances, and West Virginia found itself with three would-be governors. The issue was finally settled in Fleming's

favor in January 1890 by a party-line vote in the legislature.

In 1892, Goff was appointed a federal judge in the U.S. Fourth Circuit, which included Maryland, Virginia, West Virginia, and the Carolinas. Goff finished his political career with a term in the U.S. Senate, serving from 1913 until 1919.

His many high offices notwithstanding, Nathan Goff Jr. wielded his greatest power as party boss during the time the Republicans were building strength to recapture control of West Virginia politics. Goff controlled federal patronage in West Virginia during several Republican presidential administrations. He was succeeded as Republican leader by Stephen B. Elkins, the industrialist and U.S. senator who led the Grand Old Party into the 20th century.

Goff succeeded in business as in politics, inheriting wealth and multiplying it. With four others, he bought the *Clarksburg Telegram* in 1890. He invested in coal mining and profited extensively from the oil business. As a builder he added landmarks to the city, including the Waldo Hotel and his own lavish house, which was on the National Register of Historic Places at the time of its demolition in 1993.

Nathan Goff married Laura E. Despard in 1865 and Katherine Penney in 1919. He died at home in Clarksburg, April 23, 1920.

See also Clarksburg Exponent Telegram, Aretas Brooks Fleming

Marshall "Biggie" Goldberg

Athlete Marshall "Biggie" Goldberg was born in Elkins, October 25, 1918. At age 15, he became both an all-state football and all-state basketball player at Elkins High School. He also served as captain of the football, basketball, and baseball teams. After graduating, he went on to become a two-time All-American at the University of Pittsburgh, leading Pitt to the 1937 national football championship. As a senior, Goldberg asked to be moved from tailback to fullback. The famous Pitt coach, Jock Sutherland, told him it would be hard to repeat as an All-American at a new position, but Goldberg did it.

In 1939, he joined the National Football League's Chicago Cardinals. He missed the 1944 and 1945 seasons while serving in the military, then returned to lead the Cardinals to the NFL championship in 1947. Goldberg was a member of two famous backfields, at Pitt (with Harold Stebbins, Dick Cassiano, and John Chickerneo) and with the Cardinals (with Elmer Angsman, Paul Christman, and Pat Harder). He was elected to the NFL Hall of Fame in 1958, and to the West Virginia Sports Writers Hall of Fame. After his football days ended, he became a successful businessman in Elk Grove Village, Illinois, a suburb of Chicago. In 2002, he lived there in retirement.

Louis E. Keefer
Reston, Virginia
Donald L. Rice
Elkins

Golden Delicious

West Virginia is the native home of the Golden Delicious apple, the state's second major horticultural contribution to the commercial apple industry. The first was the Grimes Golden, discovered on the farm of Thomas Grimes near Wellsburg in the early 1800s.

The original Golden Delicious tree, described as a "chance seedling" and believed to be related to the Grimes Golden, was discovered in 1912 by Anderson Mullins on a hill near Porter Creek in Clay County. The tree was purchased by Stark Brothers Nursery, whose representatives built a cage around the tree and employed Bewel Mullins, Anderson's nephew, to maintain and keep written and photographic records of the tree for 30 years. The Golden Delicious, immediately acclaimed, soon became a leading cultivar in the United States and abroad.

The mother tree produced quality apples for nearly 50 years. The seedling had sprouted around the turn of the century, and the old tree had borne its last apple and died by the late 1950s. Today, the only evidence that the tree of gold grew up the hill from Porter Creek is a historical marker located on Route 1 nearby.

West Virginia has had the apple as its official state fruit since 1972, and specifically the Golden Delicious apple since 1995. Each fall, Clay County celebrates its famous apple with the annual Clay County Golden Delicious Festival.

See also Apples, Grimes Golden, Orchards

Golden Horseshoe, Knights of

See Alexander Spotswood.

Golden Horseshoe Test

The Golden Horseshoe contest started in 1929 when Phil M. Conley, president of West Virginia Education Foundation, proposed the idea to the state superintendent of schools. It recognizes students for their knowledge of West Virginia.

The top ten percent of eighth grade students are selected each April to take a written test prepared and scored by the state Department of Education on state government, history, geography, and politics. The winners are those receiving the highest score in each county (the number of winners per county being determined by enrollment), as well as one from the Schools for the Deaf and Blind at Romney. Each year 221 students participate in the one-day awards ceremony in Charleston.

The state superintendent of schools

The golden horseshoe pin.

presides over a knighting ceremony as the climax of Golden Horseshoe Day. Each student kneels and, with a tap on the shoulder by a sword, is dubbed a knight or lady of the Golden Horseshoe. Each receives a golden horseshoe pin, a certificate from the West Virginia Historical Education Foundation, a certificate from the state, a picture of the group with the governor, and a picture of his or her individual knighting.

Historically, the Golden Horseshoe originated in the colony of Virginia in 1716 when Lt. Gov. Alexander Spotswood organized a party of about 50 men to explore the region west of the Allegheny Mountains. Each member was presented a small golden horseshoe. The awarding of a golden horseshoe to the students currently honored is in recognition of their crossing the mountains of learning and knowledge, and is received as a high distinction.

See also Alexander Spotswood

Eileen Cain Stanley
Kenna

Goldenseal

Started in 1975, the state magazine *Goldenseal* documents traditional ways and lives of West Virginians through feature articles, oral histories, and old and new photographs.

Goldenseal was founded by Tom Screven, an Alabama native who moved to West Virginia in 1971 to work in the state Department of Commerce's Arts and Crafts Division. A folk arts authority, Screven feared that West Virginia's folklore was in danger of being lost as the state's oldest generation died. In 1973, he helped launch *Hearth and Fair*, a magazine about the state's crafts, lore, and life. In 1975, the Arts and Humanities Council, headed by Norman Fagan, committed funds to expand the magazine into an independent publication about West Virginia's traditional life. The new publication was named for goldenseal, a plant used for medicinal purposes by Native Americans and early settlers and commonly known as yellowroot.

In 1977, *Goldenseal* was placed under the new Division of Culture and History. In 1979, Ken Sullivan became editor, a position he held for nearly 18 years. During his tenure, Sullivan established a regular quarterly publication schedule, and the magazine's circulation grew from 8,000 to 33,000. Sullivan began the transition from free to paid circulation and put the magazine on a self-supporting basis.

The *Goldenseal Book of the West Virginia Mine Wars*, a collection of popular labor history articles was published in 1991 and later reprinted. *Mountains and Music*, a collection of *Goldenseal* music articles, was published by the University of Illinois Press in 1999.

In 1997, John Lilly succeeded Ken Sullivan as editor.

Nancy Ray Adams
Pine Mountain Settlement School

Ken Sullivan, "A Fond Farewell," *Goldenseal*, Spring 1997; "Our Founder," *Goldenseal*, Winter 1994.

Good Roads Movement

The good roads movement of the 1920s attacked one of West Virginia's perennial problems, the inadequacy of its roads. The first motor vehicles appeared at the beginning of the 20th century, but the rugged terrain and muddy roads slowed the advance of the automotive age. In 1919, under the slogan "Help Pull West Virginia Out of the Mud," the West Virginia Good Roads Federation campaigned for an amendment to the constitution that would empower the legislature to undertake road improvements.

Voters approved the good roads amendment in 1920 and another in 1928, and road building became a major activity of state government. The good roads amendments provided for the issuance of $85 million in state bonds to finance the construction and maintenance of a state road system that would at least connect the various county seats of the state. The legislature imposed gasoline taxes to pay interest and principal on the bonds. Some federal and county funds also went into road improvement.

The state road system grew rapidly. In 1921, the legislature expanded the state road commission to three members and classified all roads as state or county roads. At that time no two of the larger cities of the state were connected by an improved road of any kind, but by 1927 all of the larger cities were linked by hard-surface roads. By 1929, all but one of the 55 county seats had at least one hard-surfaced outlet to improved roads connecting with the rest of the state. Between 1921 and 1933, some $128 million was expended on the road system, and the spread of cars, trucks, and buses and related enterprises transformed the state's economy and society.

The good roads movement achieved important results, but haste in building meant that much of the work later had to be redesigned and rebuilt. Routes were sometimes determined by political log-rolling, and state road employment became a major item of political spoils. In the Depression, poor roads continued to plague West Virginia as the state assumed control of all roads but had inadequate funds to maintain or expand the system.

Jerry Bruce Thomas
Shepherd University

Charles H. Ambler and Festus P. Summers, *West Virginia: The Mountain State*, 1958; Jerry Bruce Thomas, *An Appalachian New Deal: West Virginia in the Great Depression*, 1998.

Howard Mason Gore

Howard Mason Gore, a farmer and businessman, was U.S. secretary of agriculture and 17th governor of West Virginia. He was born October 12, 1877, in Harrison County, the son of Solomon D. and Mariette P. Rogers Gore. He attended the local schools and graduated from Clarksburg High School prior to enrolling at West Virginia University, where he graduated in 1900 with a degree in agriculture.

Gore took charge of the family farm after the death of his father in 1907 and developed a reputation for his progressive methods of cultivation and the breeding of beef cattle. When World War I came he served as the assistant food administrator for West Virginia. In 1921, at the request of a national farm organization, he was hired by the U.S. Department of Agriculture to develop a plan for the government marketing of livestock and livestock products. Afterward, Gore was appointed chief of the Packers and Stockyards Administration when Congress adopted the plan as part of the Packers and Stockyards Act.

These activities brought Gore to the attention of President Coolidge, and the president appointed him as the assistant secretary of agriculture on September 17, 1923. Gore began to show interest in the fortunes of West Virginia's Republican Party, which led him to become more involved at the state level.

This set the stage for Gore's nomination and election to the governor's seat in 1924. He defeated Braxton County Democrat Judge Jake Fisher and Socialist candidate J. W. Bosworth in a spirited contest. The Republicans retained control of the West Virginia legislature, and the 32,000-vote margin Gore received was probably more a tribute to the victorious Republican presidential candidacy of Calvin Coolidge than to his own popularity.

In the interim between the November election and his inauguration as governor in March, Gore briefly served as U.S.

Governor Howard Mason Gore (1877–1947).

secretary of agriculture. He held the position until March 2, 1925, when he resigned. Two days later he was sworn in as the governor of West Virginia.

Like many other governors, Gore was committed to using the state government to modernize West Virginia. He continued the construction and improvement of West Virginia's newly created highway system. The farmer governor also had the satisfaction of seeing more state funds directed to the rural counties, and he legalized agricultural credit and cooperative associations.

In 1928, Governor Gore sought the Republican nomination for the U.S. Senate, but was defeated in the party primary by former Governor Hatfield. Gore did not retreat to private life. He served briefly as state agricultural commissioner in 1932, and in 1935 as director of the federal rural rehabilitation program for Harrison County. In 1941, Governor Neely appointed Gore to the state's three-man Public Service Commission, a position Gore held until his death, June 20, 1947.

Jeffrey B. Cook
North Greenville College

Charles H. Ambler and Festus P. Summers, *West Virginia: The Mountain State*, 1958; John G. Morgan, *West Virginia Governors*, 1980.

Goss-Ryan Heavyweight Fight

On June 1, 1880, the bare-knuckle prize fight for the championship of the world was held in the Brooke County town of Colliers, between defending champion Joe Goss and challenger Paddy Ryan.

Boxing was illegal in every state, and matches were often held in railroad villages to avoid big city police. Colliers was perfect—only 37 miles by railroad from Pittsburgh, across the state line but close enough to attract a crowd. Other spectators came from Ohio, which was even closer.

Four stakes were driven into a grass meadow, and rope was strung to form a crude boxing ring. Challenger Paddy Ryan was 28 years old, stood six feet one inch, and weighed 185 pounds. Joe Goss, the champion, was smaller at five feet eight inches, 178 pounds, and at age 44 was much older. But Goss was more experienced, having won 14 of 16 fights.

They fought by the popular bare-knuckles rules. Through the first 35 rounds, which took about 45 minutes, the fight was even, but by the 45th round Goss was tiring and Ryan, although badly pummeled, began to rally. By the 70th, Ryan had clearly taken charge. In the 80th round, he hit the now helpless Goss and knocked him to the ground. Goss's seconds revived him and stood him at the scratch line. He was promptly knocked down, and the process was repeated in each of the next seven rounds. Finally Goss was unable to come to scratch for the 87th round. The fight had lasted one hour and 27 minutes and boxing had a new champ.

C. Robert Barnett
Marshall University

The Government of West Virginia

The government of West Virginia was created as a result of the Civil War. The western counties of Virginia organized the new state with the adoption of its first constitution, and in 1863 West Virginia was accepted by the federal government as the 35th state of the United States. The new state suffered from instability until its present constitution was adopted in 1872, resolving disagreements between the formerly Confederate east and south and the Unionist north. The 1872 constitution, with later modernizing amendments, still serves as the basic law of the state.

Our state government is characterized by Southern-style rural county organizations with three-member boards of commissioners and powerful sheriffs, rather than the township-village format of New England and the Mid-Atlantic seaboard states. West Virginia's state government is fairly typical, with a large two-house legislature, a governor with moderate powers, and a unified court system.

The executive power is shared by the governor and five elected state officials (the secretary of state, auditor, treasurer, commissioner of agriculture, and attorney general) who serve four-year terms and are often reelected. The election of these officers is unusual since they are commonly appointed by governors in other states. The governor can succeed himself but is limited to two successive terms in office. Together with an office staff, the governor, aided by a department of administration, various other departments, and boards and commissions in the executive branch, oversees and guides the work of hundreds of appointed officials. A personnel division recruits and trains civil service workers using modern merit system principles.

West Virginia does not have a lieutenant governor, with the president of the state senate next in the line of succession after the governor. The governor may call special sessions of the legislature, exercise a line-item veto of appropriation bills, and veto bills in their entirety. He may "pocket veto" a bill simply by taking no action if the legislature adjourns within five days of the bill's passage. The governor has great influence in determining public policy through his annual State of the State messages, his preparation of the budget and submission of bills, and as head of his political party.

The legislature convenes at the beginning of the year in a 60-day session. The 100 delegates serve for two years each, and the 34 senators serve for four years each. Members of each house may be reelected to an unlimited number of terms. The legislature holds interim meetings of key members of the major standing committees for three days every month when not in official session. Since West Virginia is a small state with limited population, there are close relations and easy access between legislators and their constituents.

The size of West Virginia's congressional delegation fluctuated throughout the 20th century, as dictated by the U.S. Census, which is taken every 10 years. The state had six representatives from the 1910s through the 1950s. In the latter half of the 20th century, the population of the Mountain State either declined or showed only slow growth compared with the rest of the nation. Consequently, the number of representatives declined from six in the 1950s to three as a result of the 1990 and 2000 censuses.

West Virginia is a two-party state, although the Democratic Party now has a large majority of the voter registration and dominates both houses of the legislature. Occasionally, a Republican wins an elective executive office or the governorship; but in terms of public policy, the Republican Party is in the minority. Third-party organizations are weak and rarely obtain enough votes to be recognized as a legal political party and field candidates for office. West Virginia is a primary state, holding the primary election in May, late in the presidential campaign cycle.

There are 55 counties in West Virginia, mostly rural. The school systems are organized along county lines and run by county boards of education. Many counties are subdivided into public service districts to regulate water and sewer systems. Counties are legal entities for elections, property taxes, health and sanitation services, law enforcement, courts, and record keeping. Except for Jefferson County, counties are governed by a three-

The foyer in the Governor's Mansion.

member county commission with the county sheriff usually the strongest individual officer. Jefferson County has a five-member county commission. Counties are legal subdivisions of the state and are closely regulated by state law.

Most of the municipalities in West Virginia are small incorporated communities, with Charleston, Huntington, and Wheeling the largest cities. There is limited home rule authority. Unincorporated municipalities are governed by state law outlining the cities' structure, while cities with more than 2,000 inhabitants operate under charters spelling out their form of government (mayor-council, commission type, or council-manager) and their powers.

There are three major tiers of courts in West Virginia. The lowest are the magistrate courts, which exist in every county and process criminal misdemeanors and minor civil cases, and the municipal courts, which handle infractions of municipal law. At the next level, important litigation takes place in 31 circuit courts. These are the state's comprehensive general jurisdiction trial courts, with jurisdiction in all criminal, civil, and juvenile matters. The Supreme Court of Appeals is the highest state court, with five judges elected for staggered 12-year terms. Despite its name, the court hears original cases as well as appeals. It also possesses rule-making powers governing the operation of all state courts.

Consolidation, mergers, regional agencies, and cooperation among cities, counties, and even states have had a checkered history in West Virginia. In 1963, the legislature authorized counties to cooperate with other local governments and the federal government. One result has been the creation of regional development authorities to handle floods, fires,

and sewers. A second innovation was the creation of 11 regional councils to organize public service districts. There has been functional consolidation such as combined jails, bus transportation, and joint fire fighting arrangements.

Although West Virginia is a small state in size and population, it possesses a large number of local governments and organizations. With its 55 counties, many municipalities, magisterial districts, and other divisions, it is apparent that West Virginians have a strong local attachment and a strong loyalty to localities. The culture is traditional and conservative with strong historical ties. Government is highly personal, based on family and social connections, and is regarded as playing primarily a custodial role.

Evelyn L. Harris
Charleston

Governor's Mansion

The Governor's Mansion, facing the Kanawha River near the southwest corner of the State Capitol Complex, was built in 1924–25, during the term of Governor Morgan. Charleston architect Walter F. Martens consulted closely with Cass Gilbert, architect of the capitol, then under construction nearby.

The Georgian Colonial residence is constructed of red Harvard colonial brick laid in Flemish bond with black headers. It is fronted by a central, two-story portico with a bracketed pediment that is supported by four free-standing and two engaged fluted Corinthian columns. The arched entranceway, painted white to complement the brickwork as is all trim, frames a delicate fanlight above the door.

On either side of the structure, and extending about one-third of the depth, are porches surrounded by a low balustrade and rows of columns which rise to support a flat roof onto which several second-floor rooms open. These second-floor balconies also have low balustrades with distinctive designs in wood. The porch to the east is open, while the porch to the west is enclosed. A single story entranceway at the rear balances the central, front portico.

A bracketed cornice circles the mansion above the second floor, and third-floor dormers jut from the indented, slate-shingled mansard roof. The originally planned third floor was not added until 1946. Completing the grounds are the enclosed gardens and a garage over which the servant quarters were added in 1926.

Upon entry from the main portico, attention is immediately drawn to the checkered black Belgian and white Tennessee marble floor which is flanked by well-proportioned, dual Georgian staircases, a design inspired by architectural studies of the White House. The main floor also houses the elegantly designed and furnished drawing room, ballroom, state dining room, a sitting room, and the library. Eight bedrooms and four baths, including the governor's private quarters and family room, are located on the second floor, and the third floor contains two additional bedrooms.

From the time of Governor Morgan's occupancy, only the last week of his term of office, the mansion has welcomed thousands of daily tours and hosted hundreds of official, cultural and charitable activities. West Virginia's Executive Mansion remains the state's most visible symbol of elegance and hospitality.

See also Architects and Architecture, The Capitol, Walter F. Martens

Bob Damron
Charleston

Governor's Succession Amendment

The West Virginia Constitution of 1863 provided for the popular election of the state's governor, a provision that had been incorporated into the Virginia Constitution of 1851. The term of office was set at two years, with a provision that the governor might be elected for one or more successive terms. The Constitution of 1872, which remains in effect, set the term of office at four years, but prohibited a governor from succeeding himself. Arthur I. Boreman, the state's first governor, was elected to three consecutive two-year terms under the state's first constitution, and John J. Jacob, the fourth governor, was elected to a two-year term under the first constitution and a four-year term under the second. Then for more than 100 years no governor was elected to more than one term. The question of gubernatorial succession was from time to time a matter of discussion.

In 1970, during the first term of Governor Moore, citizens of the state ratified an amendment to the constitution that allows the governor to serve two consecutive terms. The Governor's Succession Amendment introduced a two-term pattern that prevailed for more than a quarter-century. Governors Moore, Rockefeller, and Caperton each succeeded themselves, and Moore won a third term following Rockefeller's intervening terms. Cecil Underwood, who was governor from 1957 to 1961, was again elected to the office in 1997 and became both the youngest and oldest of the state's governors at the times of his election. Underwood failed to be elected to a third term in 2000.

See also Constitution of West Virginia

Otis K. Rice
WVU Institute of Technology

Governors of West Virginia

From the birth of the state in 1863 through 2005, West Virginia has had 34 governors. All were male, white, and Christian, with European surnames. All but one were church members, and only one was not a Protestant. All were married, and all but one were fathers. Democrats outnumbered Republicans 19-15. Jacob was an Independent for four years after serving as a Democrat for two years. Among the church members were 12 Presbyterians, 11 Methodists, five Episcopalians, two Baptists, and one Catholic. Stevenson, the exception, never joined a church but was reared as a Calvinist.

Farnsworth, with 15 children by two wives, led the list of fathers. Collectively, he and the other governors fathered 107 children. Gore, the childless exception, became a widower about five months after his only marriage. Caperton became the state's first divorced governor during his first year in office. He remarried the following year and was again divorced and remarried after completing two terms.

With nine exceptions, the governors were born within the state or in the area of Virginia that was to become West Virginia. Boreman and Stevenson were born in Pennsylvania; Farnsworth and Rockefeller in New York; MacCorkle in Virginia; Dawson in Maryland; White in Ohio; Marland in Illinois; and Wise in Washington. Six governors were born south of Charleston in West Virginia, three in the Eastern Panhandle, and one in the Northern Panhandle. A majority were born north of Elkins.

Seven of the first 12 governors lacked college degrees. All others had a college or university education. Hatfield had two medical degrees. Twenty-one governors were lawyers.

The governors took office at an average age of about 47. Remarkably, Underwood was both the youngest and oldest. He began his first term in 1957 at age 34, and his second term 40 years later at age 74.

Moore served the longest time, 12 years, and Farnsworth the shortest, seven days.

As of 2005, there were six living former governors (Smith, Moore, Rockefeller, Caperton, Underwood, and Wise). Two of the 34 governors, Moore and Underwood, are officially counted twice because of intervening terms. Thus, Underwood served as the 25th governor and ultimately returned as the 32nd. Moore was the 28th and 30th.

Two former governors were found guilty of major crimes, Barron for bribing a juror and Moore for extortion, obstruction of justice, mail fraud, and tax evasion. Both served prison terms.

The 25 governors who died by 2002 reached an average age of about 73 years. Patteson was the oldest at 90 and Marland the youngest at 47. Pneumonia, with four victims, was the leading cause of death. Three or possibly four died of cancer and three of heart ailments. Other causes included tuberculosis, stroke, old age, Parkinson's disease, breakdown of health, persistent illness, and "total collapse of the energies."

See also Executive Branch

John G. Morgan
Charleston

Graceland

Graceland was once the summer residence of Henry Gassaway Davis, U.S. senator, industrialist, railroad builder, and 1904 candidate for vice president of the United States. The house is now a country inn, operated by Davis & Elkins College and located on the college's campus at Elkins.

The house is a notable example of Victorian architecture, primarily in the Queen Anne style. It was designed by the architectural firm of Baldwin and Pennington of Baltimore. Construction began in 1891 and was completed in 1893. The main house has two and a half stories with a large attic; the connected back building (service wing) has two stories with a smaller attic. The lower stories and chimneys are of native West Virginia sandstone, and the upper story is covered with wood shingles. The entire building is capped by a roof of red Vermont slate. The grand interior is elaborately and beautifully trimmed with West Virginia hardwoods, notably quarter-sawn oak, bird's-eye maple, cherry, and walnut. Other characteristic Victorian features include ornamental plaster moldings, richly carved mantels, balusters, column capitals, and beautiful stained glass.

From 1986 to 1996, Graceland underwent a major restoration during which the exterior and significant interior spaces were returned to original condition. The restoration was performed with the aid of many late 19th- and early 20th-century photographs submitted by Bruce Lee Kennedy, the daughter of Grace Davis Lee, for whom Graceland was named.

Part of the Davis and Elkins Historic District, which is a National Historic Landmark, Graceland has taken its place alongside America's architectural treasures. The mansion represents the best in late Victorian architecture.

See also Davis & Elkins College, Henry Gassaway Davis

Paul D. Marshall
Blufton, South Carolina

Grafton

Grafton, the county seat of Taylor County, is situated on hills rising from the Tygart Valley River at the intersection of U.S. 50 and U.S. 119. Chartered in 1856, Grafton is a child of the Baltimore & Ohio Railroad and was named for John Grafton, a prominent B&O engineer. Grafton has the distinction of being one of the nation's first railroad towns. It was the site of the first Mother's Day celebration, honoring Anna Reeves Jarvis, a Civil War nurse and a leader in the reconciliation movement after the war.

The railroad brought boom-town prosperity to Grafton, as the city became an important switching area for both freight and passengers. Coal and timber were major commodities hauled through Grafton. Passenger trains operated between Baltimore, Washington, Cincinnati, and St. Louis via Grafton, with links to New York and Chicago.

Grafton reached a peak population of 8,517 people in 1920. Today, though railroad operations are greatly reduced, the Chessie System (B&O's successor) still operates through Grafton. Glass and manufacturing industries, recreation and tourism, and the Grafton Hospital contribute to a more diversified economy. Grafton is home to the International Mother's Day Shrine and the Grafton National Cemetery, West Virginia's only national cemetery, established in 1865 to inter Civil War dead. The downtown historic district features architecture of the early 20th century and is listed on the National Register of Historic Places. Grafton's rich family, military, and railroad heritage has given it national recognition on the Civil War Discovery Trail and the American Discovery Trail. The 2000 population of Grafton was 5,489.

Ella Belling
Morgantown

Charles Brinkman, *A History of Taylor County*, 1989; Kenneth Carvell, "Grafton Then and Now," *Wonderful West Virginia*, October 2000; Wayne F. McDevitt, "Grafton and the B&O Railroad," *A History of Taylor County, West Virginia*, 1986.

Grafton National Cemetery

Grafton National Cemetery was authorized in 1865 when Congressman Swinton Burdett of Iowa introduced a bill creating a National Cemetery in northern West Vir-

Civil War dead rest at Grafton National Cemetery.

ginia. As commander-in-chief of the Grand Army of the Republic, a Union veterans organization, Burdett had toured Civil War battlegrounds of the area, and wished to establish a common cemetery for war dead. After Congress approved the bill, the War Department located a site accessible to railway lines, reasonably level, and in close proximity to battlegrounds, military hospitals, and other cemeteries.

Work began in 1867 on the 3.21-acre site purchased from the heirs of Alexander Yates. Within two years, 1,251 Union and Confederate troops, including 664 unknown soldiers, were reburied in the cemetery under the supervision of the U.S. Burial Corps. The original bodies interred at Grafton represented war dead from 32 West Virginia counties and 14 states. The first casualty of the Civil War, West Virginian Thornsberry Bailey Brown, is buried in the cemetery, his grave marked by a special monument.

The cemetery reached its capacity of 2,119 graves in 1961. In addition to Civil War casualties, veterans of the Spanish-American War, World Wars I and II, Korean War, and Vietnam War are buried on the cemetery's three terraces.

West Virginia National Cemetery, a separate cemetery five miles outside Grafton, was dedicated in 1987.

Debra K. Sullivan
Charleston Catholic High School

Grand Army of the Republic

The Grand Army of the Republic, national fraternal organization for Union veterans of the Civil War, was founded in 1866 in Illinois. All soldiers and sailors of the U.S. army, navy, and marine corps who served during the Civil War were eligible for membership, provided that they had an honorable discharge.

Although the Grand Army of the Republic (GAR) became the preeminent

veterans' organization arising from the Civil War, its membership grew slowly at first. However, membership rose rapidly during the 1880s and reached its peak in 1890, when 409,489 members were reported. Membership declined thereafter, and the last GAR member died in 1956. For many years, the organization was a powerful political force in its efforts to secure pension increases and other benefits for veterans and their dependents. The GAR also had auxiliary societies such as the Women's Relief Corps, the Ladies of the Grand Army of the Republic, and the Sons of Union Veterans of the Civil War.

Although attempts to organize a GAR department in West Virginia began as early as 1868, it was not until 1880 that Post No. 1 was organized at Martinsburg. A convention to form a permanent state department met in Clarksburg on February 20, 1883, with 11 local posts represented. An annual state encampment was held at different sites in West Virginia. At its peak in 1889, there were 3,161 members in 89 local posts throughout the state.

See also Civil War

Steve Cunningham
Charleston

Stuart McConnell, *Glorious Contentment: The Grand Army of the Republic, 1865–1900*, 1992.

Grandparents Day

Grandparents Day, observed on the first Sunday after Labor Day, was founded as a result of the efforts of a West Virginian, Marian Herndon McQuade. The first nationwide observance occurred in 1979.

McQuade, of Oak Hill, the mother of 15, began to advocate for the elderly in the 1950s. She met with President Dwight Eisenhower, and later with Presidents Richard Nixon and Gerald Ford, in her quest for a day set aside for grandparents. Governor Moore proclaimed West Virginia's first observance of Grandparents Day in 1973, the same year that Sen. Jennings Randolph introduced the U.S. Senate resolution for a national observance. In September 1978, President Jimmy Carter signed Public Law 96-62 designating the first Sunday after Labor Day as National Grandparents Day.

A Republican activist, McQuade served as sergeant-at-arms for the National Federation of Republican Women and ran for both the legislature and Congress. In 1971, she was elected vice-chairman of the West Virginia Committee on Aging and was appointed as a delegate to the White House Conference on Aging by Governor Moore.

Peggy Ross
Reedsville

Grandview Park

Grandview Park is located on State Route 9 east of Beckley. The name of the park refers to the panoramic view of the New River Gorge which can be seen from a huge rock atop a cliff overlooking the river far below.

In 1939, the West Virginia Conservation Commission purchased a 52-acre tract of land from the Admiralty Coal Company for development of a roadside park. Construction of facilities, such as parking areas, picnic shelters, benches, and hiking trails, began in 1940. The Civilian Conservation Corps provided the manpower. Later land purchases expanded the park to 892 acres. Grandview was a state park until 1990, when it became a part of the New River Gorge National River, managed by the National Park Service.

Cliffside Amphitheater was built in the park in 1961. A historical play commemorating the creation of West Virginia, "Honey in the Rock," written by Kermit Hunter, opened at the theater June 27, 1961. Another play, "Hatfields and McCoys" by Billy Edd Wheeler, opened in June 1970. Both plays, in addition to Broadway musicals, concerts, and other presentations are performed there each summer.

Blooming in late May, Catawba rhododendron shrubs provide a spectacular display around the main parking lot at Grandview. A small museum in the park offices displays mining memorabilia, natural history specimens, photographs, and maps. Books on local history are for sale. The park rangers conduct wildflower walks, bird walks, and tours.

See also New River Gorge National River

Leona Gwinn Brown
Daniels
Jim Wood, *Raleigh County, West Virginia,* 1994.

The Grange

A national society of farmers, the Grange established its first West Virginia lodge in the early 1870s at Summit Point in Jeffer-

FAST FACTS ABOUT GRANT COUNTY

Founded: 1866
Land in square miles: 478.0
Population: 11,299
Percentage minorities: 1.7%
Percentage rural: 77.1%
Median age: 39.3
Percentage 65 and older: 15.3%
Birth rate per 1,000 population: 13.2
Median household income: $28,916
High school graduate or higher: 70.8%
Bachelor's degree or higher: 11.4%
Home ownership: 80.9%
Median home value: $78,400

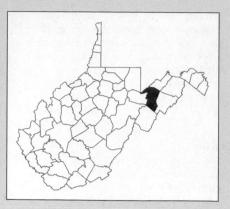

This information is from the 2000 U.S. Census. In 2000, West Virginia as a whole had 5 percent minorities, a median age of 38.9, median household income of $29,696, and a 75.2 percent home ownership rate.

son County. Formally known as the Patrons of Husbandry, the society set out to provide farmers with the most up-to-date agricultural information, to lobby against high railroad transportation costs and high tariffs on imported goods, and for rural mail delivery. The Grange's meetings also gave isolated farm families the opportunity to socialize.

The Grange, organized nationally in 1867, grew rapidly, becoming a powerful political force in the Midwest and other places. By 1875, the Grange had 20,000 lodges throughout the country and 800,000 members. In 1876, West Virginia had 378 lodges with a total of 10,700 members. The Grange was most popular in the north-central counties of Harrison, Lewis, Barbour, Doddridge, Marion, and Upshur. In West Virginia, the Grange worked to create a state board of agriculture, offer agricultural education to elementary and secondary school students, and lobby for laws to lower rail shipping costs.

Membership in the Grange declined in the 1880s because of continued rate discrimination by railroads against farmers, declining farm prices, and a lack of money. Farmers turned for help to another national organization, the Farmers' Alliance. Thomas Clark Atkeson, president of Morris Harvey College from 1896 to 1897, revived the state Grange and led the organization from 1897 to 1920. He was also dean of West Virginia University College of Agriculture 1897–1910 and a member of the State Board of Agriculture. During Atkeson's tenure, the Grange helped to create the Public Service Commission and pushed for tax reform.

In West Virginia, the Grange in 2001 had about 400 members in eight north-central and Northern Panhandle counties. In recent years, the Grange has lobbied in favor of personal property rights by opposing more stringent water quality

standards and the endangered species act, and called for a reduction in the deer population.

Charles H. Ambler and Festus P. Summers, *West Virginia: The Mountain State,* 1958; Edward Winslow Martin, *History of the Grange Movement,* 1969; Otis K. Rice and Stephen W. Brown, *West Virginia: A History,* 1993.

Grant County

Grant County is located at the western end of the Eastern Panhandle. It was created February 14, 1866, soon after the Civil War, and named for Gen. Ulysses S. Grant, who later became the nation's 18th president. Grant County was carved from the territory of Hardy County. Laurelton, near the center of the new county, was briefly the county seat. After that Maysville was county seat, until 1872, when a vote of the citizens brought the seat of government permanently to Petersburg.

The picturesque landscape ranges from the Allegheny Front and Dolly Sods in the north to the broad beautiful valley of the South Branch of the Potomac River. The historic Fairfax Stone marks a corner of Grant County, at the headwaters of the Potomac River. Early planters, many of them slaveholders, gained title to the fertile bottomland along the river valleys, especially the South Branch Valley in present Hardy County, but the hill farmers, often Unionist in sentiment during the Civil War, composed a major portion of the population. This fostered the creation of the new county in 1866.

Natural resources have long been the key to the economy of Grant County. Farming has been a basic occupation, especially livestock and poultry production. Coal mining in the Alleghenies and timber industries throughout the county brought prosperity at various times in the region's history. Huge logging projects in the late 19th and early 20th centuries

The mountains of Grant County.

provided much lumber for urban expansion along the eastern seaboard. Another key commodity of the forest was the bark of the chestnut oak, which drew the leather tanning industry to the area. Tanneries sprang up throughout the region, with especially large plants in Petersburg and Gormania. The Hoffman and Sons Tannery of Gormania was reputed to be the largest tannery in the world. Tanneries provided jobs in the plants, and much-needed seasonal income to the farmers who peeled bark from trees in their woodlands. Today forest industries remain important. Allegheny Wood Products is a leader in the industry, with a host of independent operators involved in timber production.

A key boost to the economy was the construction in 1965–66 of a huge mine-mouth generating plant by Virginia Electric Power near Mount Storm. It continues to provide power to Vepco's regional network under the management of Dominion Resources. Other key industries include Adell Polymers, which specializes in extruded plastics. Prior to its closing several years ago, Allied Egry, a division of SCM Corporation, supported a large work force engaged in the printing of business forms. Grant County Mulch is a large processor of forest by-products for the Mid-Atlantic market.

Petersburg has become a regional health provider with the expansion of Grant Memorial Hospital. Recently, a Veterans Administration clinic became part of the complex. The Grant County Nursing Home has also grown to serve the increasing number of elderly persons in the area.

Education has been a key to county development. Beginning with a large number of one-room schools to serve the widespread population of the county, the present system includes three elementary schools, at Dorcas, Maysville, and Petersburg; a high school at Petersburg; and a combined primary and sec-

ondary school complex at Mount Storm. South Branch Vocational Technical Center at Petersburg has served students and adults from Grant, Hardy, and Pendleton counties for many years. In recent years it has increased cooperation with Potomac State College at Keyser and the South Branch Center of Shepherd College in Petersburg. Shepherd's South Branch Center, an innovative satellite program, has enabled many area residents to pursue college education locally.

The county's history includes famous visitors such as George Washington, whose diaries recount early visits to the area while surveying for Lord Fairfax; Confederate Gen. Jubal A. Early, Union Gen. John C. Frémont, and Col. (later Gen.) James A. Mulligan were there during the Civil War. Mulligan, commander of the 23rd Illinois Regiment, was largely responsible for the construction of the fortifications overlooking Petersburg. The site, known locally as Fort Mulligan, is one of the best preserved fortifications in West Virginia. Recently, with the cooperation of local units of Sons of Confederate Veterans and Sons of Union Veterans, the Civil War Preservation Trust purchased the historic site for local management, making it a key attraction for visitors to the area. The group has also secured an easement for the development and publicizing of the site of the Battle of Greenland Gap, near Scherr.

Transportation has always been an issue in the opening and the development of the area. The earliest settlers followed streams, animal paths, and Indian trails. Nearly a century passed before the first great road project, the construction of the Northwestern Turnpike (modern U.S. 50), opened the northern section of the county on its way to the Ohio River. Road building continues to the present, with the long-anticipated Corridor H four-lane highway under construction. The railroad came to Grant County in 1910, as the Hampshire Southern Railway completed

construction to Petersburg. Today the local railroad is operated by the State Rail Authority as the South Branch Valley Railroad.

Petersburg also boasts the area's best airport, with a paved runway capable of accommodating corporate jets. The Petersburg Wave, a powerful updraft which is strongest in early spring, attracts glider pilots from all over the country each March.

No brief history of the land and people of Grant County would be complete without acknowledging both the beauty and the destructive power of the South Branch. Major floods brought devastation in 1924, 1936, and 1949. Worst of all was the great flood of 1985, which left 13 people dead in Grant County and much property damage. In normal times, the South Branch is a peaceful neighbor and an important recreation resource. The river, which makes its way into Grant County through rugged Smoke Hole canyon, is joined by the North Fork, a major tributary, just above Petersburg.

The population of Grant County in 2000 was 11,299, having risen steadily from 8,607 in 1970. The county's area is 478 square miles.

See also Fairfax Stone, Flood of 1985, Petersburg, Petersburg Wave

Harold D. Garber
Petersburg

Grantsville

Grantsville, the county seat of Calhoun County, is situated in a bend of the Little Kanawha River at the intersection of State Routes 5 and 16. Laid out in 1866 and named for Ulysses S. Grant in 1867, Grantsville was incorporated in 1896. It remains the only incorporated town in Calhoun County.

The courthouse, on the square in the center of town, was completed during World War II and is the fourth to occupy the site. The exterior is made of Arnoldsburg Formation sandstone, quarried locally. Grantsville has several other structures built from this same quality stone.

Grantsville benefited from the timber and oil and gas booms that began in the late 1800s. Consolidated Natural Gas, now Dominion, has maintained a district headquarters in Grantsville since the 1920s. In the early 20th century, Godfrey L. Cabot operated the world's largest carbon black factory two miles outside town, using natural gas as a raw material. More than 50 shallow-draft gasoline-powered sternwheelers were constructed in and around Grantsville for use on the Little Kanawha River.

The county's only newspaper, the *Calhoun Chronicle*, has been published in Grantsville since 1883. Calhoun General Hospital, constructed on a hill overlooking the town in the 1950s, now serves the citizens of Calhoun and surrounding counties as Minnie Hamilton Health Care Center. The Calhoun County Library is located in Grantsville, as is a town park featuring a swimming pool, picnic shelters, tennis and basketball courts, and a playground. Grantsville's modern water system supplies customers as far north as Ritchie County and south to Arnoldsburg.

Regular flooding, two disastrous downtown fires, and the relocation of Route 16 have changed the appearance of the town and destroyed many original buildings. Grantsville's current population, 565, is about half of what it was in the mid-1900s. In addition to Godfrey L. Cabot, other prominent residents have included antiquarian Boyd B. Stutler and Congressmen John M. Wolverton and Robert H. Mollohan.

See also Calhoun County

Robert G. Bonar
Grantsville

John Cuthbert, "Riverboat Days on the Little Kanawha River," *Wonderful West Virginia*, January 1996; *History of Calhoun County, West Virginia*, 1990.

Grave Creek Mound

Grave Creek Mound in Moundsville is the largest conical earthen mound in North America and a major West Virginia landmark. The mound currently is 62 feet high and 240 feet in diameter at the base and is estimated to contain 57,000 tons of earth. Archeologists speculate that three million basket-loads of earth were necessary to construct it.

Excavations conducted by the West Virginia Geological and Economic Survey in 1975 and 1976 identified a moat surrounding the mound, originally measuring 910 feet long, 40 feet wide, and four to five feet deep. At one time at least one passageway crossed the moat on the south side of the mound. Soil excavated from the moat was used in some stages of mound construction. Charcoal samples recovered from excavations yielded a radiocarbon date of 200 B.C., suggesting completion of moat construction at that time. It is believed that mound construction began sometime during the third century B.C. This is referred to as the Early Woodland period (1000–200 B.C.) by archeologists. The Grave Creek Mound is typical of many Adena (500 B.C.–A.D. 200) earthworks found throughout the Ohio Valley.

The first detailed description of the mound was written by Nicholas Cresswell in 1775. In March 1838, Abelard Tomlinson and his brother-in-law, Thomas Biggs, began digging at the mound. Tomlinson's excavations identified two burial vaults or tombs. The upper vault contained one individual surrounded by 1,700 bone and shell beads, five copper bracelets, a gorget, and several rectangular pieces of mica. The lower vault contained two individuals (male and female) surrounded by 650 shell beads. The male was buried with an atlatl (spear-thrower) weight.

The most controversial item rumored to have been found in the upper vault was a small inscribed tablet of sandstone, the infamous Grave Creek Tablet. At the time of discovery, many thought the inscriptions were covered in runes, or Norse writings, lending credence to the myth that the mounds were built by a lost tribe or civilization. Others believe that the tablet was a hoax. The matter has yet to be resolved.

Following Tomlinson's investigations, his excavation tunnels were vaulted with bricks and the mound became a tourist attraction. At various times throughout the remainder of the 19th century, the mound had a saloon and Civil War artillery on its summit, and horse races were often run around the base.

In 1909, the legislature appropriated funds to purchase the mound. The mound adjoined the state prison and was placed under the supervision of the prison warden. It was largely through the efforts of Delf Norona and the West Virginia Archeological Society that the original Mound Museum opened in 1952. The Grave Creek Mound was listed as a National Historic Landmark in 1966. In 1967, it became the Grave Creek Mound State Park, later becoming a historic site under the West Virginia Division of Culture and History. The Delf Norona Museum opened at the mound in 1978.

See also Delf Norona, Grave Creek Tablet, Moundsville

Patrick D. Trader
University of Kentucky

Delf Norona, *Moundsville's Mammoth Mound*, 1954.

Grave Creek Tablet

The Grave Creek Tablet is West Virginia's most controversial archeological relic. According to local legend, the tablet, an engraved piece of sandstone measuring approximately 1½ by 2 inches, was discovered in the spring of 1838 when Abelard Tomlinson and others first excavated Grave Creek Mound at Moundsville. Although accounts differ slightly, all agree that the tablet was found as laborers excavated near the mound's upper burial vault. Tomlinson, whose family owned the mound, claimed to have found the stone under the floor of the upper burial vault. Others who were present claimed to have found it themselves or said that it was pulled from a wheelbarrow of dirt taken from around the upper burial. At the time of its discovery, Tomlinson and the others did not attach any significance to the tablet, believing the characters carved into one side of the stone simply to be Indian hieroglyphs.

Soon after, however, Henry Rowe Schoolcraft, an eminent ethnographer, studied the tablet and became convinced that the characters were carved by Celts from ancient Spain or Britain, rather than early American Indians. With this pronouncement, the Grave Creek Tablet became the center of controversy. Different scholars concluded that the characters resembled those in a variety of ancient alphabets, including Tunisian, ancient Greek, Egyptian, Etruscan, and Phoenician, as well as those from Algiers, Libya, and the African interior. Other scholars, most notably archeologist Ephraim George Squier, denounced the stone as a fraud. Despite years of study and debate, the origin of Grave Creek Tablet was never conclusively resolved. The present location of the tablet is unknown, although the Smithsonian Institution has four casts of it.

See also Archeology, Grave Creek Mound

Lora Lamarre
State Historic Preservation

Terry A. Barnhart, "Curious Antiquity? The Grave Creek Controversy Revisited," *West Virginia History*, 1985–86; Delf Norona, *Moundsville's Mammoth Mound*, 1954.

Gravely Tractor

In 1911, Benjamin Franklin Gravely of South Charleston began tinkering with the design for a power-driven plow. Using a motorcycle engine and a push plow rigged to a single tractor wheel, Gravely constructed his first motor-driven plow. With the 2.5 horsepower engine and flywheel on one side and the gears on the other, the prototype was a crude version of the machine that would revolutionize garden cultivation. Gravely continued to refine the initial design, first in his kitchen and basement and later in a friend's machine shop.

On December 5, 1916, a patent was issued for the Gravely Motor Plow, and by 1922 Gravely had started his own business, the Gravely Motor Plow and Cultivator Company, located in Dunbar. The machine became so popular that often a year's worth of motor plows sold in just 90 days. The first Gravelys retailed for $150 to $175. Sales outlets were established in Florida and California, and there were European representatives in France, Switzerland, and Germany.

The early D-model Gravely had one wheel, was the size and height of a push plow, weighed 150 pounds, and was painted red. The Model L, introduced in 1937, had two wheels and increased power—from 2.5 to five horsepower. Mr. Gravely's passion for improvement resulted in frequent design changes within model lines, often delaying production. Gradually, the Gravely evolved into a powerful walk-behind garden tractor, capable of plowing, mowing, and a variety of other tasks. Eventually an optional sulky allowed the operator to ride rather than walk.

In 1937, Mr. Gravely retired from the day-to-day management of the company, and his business partner, D. Ray Hall, acquired control. Hall sold the company to Studebaker in 1960 for a reported $12.5 million. The last Gravely tractor rolled off the Dunbar assembly line in 1968, and production subsequently moved to Clemmons, North Carolina.

Jane Siers Winton
Charleston

John L. Marra, "Ben Gravely's Garden Tractor," *Goldenseal,* Summer 1997.

Catfish Gray

Herbalist and folk doctor Clarence Frederick "Catfish" Gray was known for his vast knowledge of traditional plant lore and for his quaint and engaging personality. Born in Jackson County, September 9, 1917, Gray worked a variety of jobs as he raised ten children.

After a work place accident in the early 1950s left him unable to perform physical labor, Gray gathered and sold wildflowers for money, turning to the great knowledge of woodland plants he had acquired from his family. Soon he was gathering herbs as well, and dispensing advice on using them to cure or prevent diseases. Gray gathered dozens of herbs, sorted, combined, and packaged them in a one-room building at his home near Glenwood, and mailed bags of his herbs and blends—usually for less than a dollar—to customers around the world. Gray dispensed his herbal cures along with advice about diet, religion, lifestyle, and the astrological aspects of illness. Gray also sold his herbs at craft fairs and other public gatherings, where his cheerful and sincere manner added to his reputation.

At the height of the folklore revival of the 1970s, Gray was a frequent newspaper and television interview subject. He was featured in the 1974 Appalshop documentary film, *Catfish: Man of the Woods,* and in a 1977 article in *Goldenseal* magazine. Catfish Gray died March 13, 2002, in Huntington.

See also Folk Medicine

Danny Williams
Morgantown

Ted Green and Allen Bennett, "Catfish: The Work and Ways of an Herb Doctor," *Goldenseal,* July–September, 1977.

Great Bend Tunnel

Great Bend Tunnel, also known as Big Bend Tunnel, is the place where John Henry defeated the steam drill, becoming one of the world's great folk heroes. It is located ten miles east of Hinton on the historic main line of the Chesapeake & Ohio Railway, now CSX. It is the longest tunnel on the C&O. The tunnel is straight, 6,450 feet long, and cuts off a seven-mile meander of the Greenbrier River around Big Bend Mountain.

Construction began in February 1870 at both ends of the tunnel and in two intermediate shafts, 365 and 170 feet deep, allowing work on six faces. About 800 men were employed during the three-year effort. This construction crew drilled the tunnel through hard red shale that tended to disintegrate when exposed to air, causing many rockfalls and landslides. A large but unknown number of men lost their lives. They included, by legend, mighty John Henry, the "steel-drivin' man."

The tunnel was completed on September 12, 1872. It was originally lined with timber, but frequent rockfalls required that the tunnel be completely lined with brick arching. This was finally completed in 1893. A second, parallel bore was completed in 1932, and the first tunnel was closed in 1974 after 102 years of service. Today, every train traveling this route still passes under Big Bend Mountain.

See also Chesapeake & Ohio Railway, John Henry

Ron Lane
Columbus, Indiana

The Great Depression

With unemployment figures exceeding 80 percent in some counties, West Virginia was one of the states hardest hit by the Great Depression of 1929–41. All sectors of the economy suffered, and the vicissitudes of hard times have had an enduring impact on life and labor in the state.

In politics, the Depression ended a long era of Republican domination as Democrats took over the legislature and the governor's office. Republican Governor Conley (1929–33) called for increased appropriations for relief and sought federal help but faced a growing financial crisis as state revenues faded. In 1932, West Virginia voters approved a tax-limitation amendment to the constitution and voted overwhelmingly for the Democratic ticket headed by Franklin D. Roosevelt for president and Herman Guy Kump (1933–37) for governor. Popular because it promised tax relief for farmers and homeowners, the amendment's unintentional consequences complicated the crisis. The limitations on property taxes denied to local governments their chief source of revenue and compelled the state to assume new powers over schools, roads, and indigent care. Kump and the legislature sought new sources of revenue through a mix of indirect taxes, including a consumer sales tax. In Washington, Congress quickly enacted Roosevelt's New Deal program.

Debates over policy and patronage split Democrats into two factions. The statehouse faction, headed by Governor Kump, controlled state patronage and tended to oppose New Deal programs, while the federal faction, headed by U.S. Sen. Matthew Mansfield Neely, supported the New Deal and reaped the benefits of federal patronage. Governor Holt, elected in 1936, was another statehouse-faction Democrat, and he generally continued the conservative fiscal policies of Kump. The statehouse Democrats boasted of their successes in paying off bonds and eliminating debt, but in the meantime the state provided meager support for education, roads, and other public services.

West Virginia's leading industry, coal, underwent wrenching changes. In the early stages of the Depression, the industry suffered from a virtual collapse as mining companies failed and unemployment grew, leaving once busy coal camps idle and stranding thousands of miners

Monongalia County miners suffered from the Great Depression.

and their families. New Deal legislation encouraged industrial cooperation on prices and wages and the development of collective bargaining, and under this impetus the United Mine Workers finally succeeded in unionizing the West Virginia coalfields. Many of the unemployed returned to the mines at higher wages, but the higher labor costs, competition from other energy sources, and falling prices of mining machinery eventually led to increased mechanization of the mines.

In the early days of the Depression, a return to the land led to an increase in the West Virginia farm population. But by the mid-1930s, many West Virginia farmers, finding it difficult to make a living on their mountain farms, began to abandon agriculture and to seek employment in towns and cities, often in other states. New Deal agricultural policies, plagued by ambivalence and inconsistency, provided support for soil conservation and land use planning but offered little to rescue the subsistence agriculture typical of West Virginia farmers.

At Eleanor, Arthurdale, and Tygart Valley, the New Deal experimented with planned communities which sought to combine agriculture and industrial work. Although the communities provided new homes and a better life for some, the results generally fell short of the hopes of their promoters.

Unemployed miners and farmers as well as other victims of the Depression found work in relief programs such as the Works Progress Administration and the Public Works Administration. These offered work to the unemployed and built needed facilities such as floodwalls in Huntington, the Kanawha Boulevard in Charleston, and airports, roads, bridges, schools, and health facilities throughout the state. Young people found help in the National Youth Administration, which provided job training and help to stay in school, and the Civilian Conservation Corps, which put young men to work on conservation projects in West Virginia and elsewhere. The state park system benefited greatly from CCC projects.

The pressure of federal policy also led to the reorganization of public welfare administration with the establishment of the Department of Public Welfare (later called the Department of Public Assistance) in 1932 and the closing of county poor farms after the establishment of social security in 1936. The new system required professionally trained social workers and led to the establishment of sociology and social work training programs at West Virginia University and the expansion of the social work profession in the state.

In 1940, Matthew M. Neely left his U.S. Senate seat to win the governorship for the federal-faction Democrats, opening the possibility of closer state-federal cooperation on New Deal matters, but the coming of World War II brought the New Deal to an end, leaving unresolved many of the problems of the Depression era.

See also William Gustavus Conley, Homer Adams Holt, Herman Guy Kump, Matthew Mansfield Neely

Jerry Bruce Thomas
Shepherd University
Paul Salstrom, *Appalachia's Path to Dependency: Rethinking A Region's Economic History, 1730–1940*, 1994; Jerry Bruce Thomas, *An Appalachian New Deal: West Virginia in the Great Depression*, 1998.

The Great Society

President Lyndon B. Johnson characterized his administration as an effort to create a "Great Society." He used the phrase as the theme of his domestic policy, as Franklin D. Roosevelt had used New Deal and John F. Kennedy used New Frontier.

Johnson's Great Society sought to redress matters of poverty and racial injustice, and its War on Poverty in particular quickly became important in West Virginia. Projects offered through the Office of Economic Opportunity, as well as other Great Society programs, brought measurable benefits. In 1965, per capita personal income in West Virginia was 76 percent of the national average, and in 1986 it had risen to 86 percent.

In 1965, Johnson traveled to Independence, Missouri, to sign the landmark Medicare legislation in the presence of former President Harry Truman, who had first advocated universal health care tied to the social security system as early as 1945.

Johnson peppered Congress with 113 major measures to implement other aspects of the Great Society, and before the 89th Congress finally adjourned on October 22, 1966, 97 bills had been passed to provide education for underprivileged children; immigration reform; expansion of research for cancer, stroke, and heart disease; aid for the arts and humanities; protection of air and water quality; creation of a "model cities" program; consumer protection and "truth-in-packaging" laws; fish and wildlife preservation; highway and tire safety; and major strides in civil rights.

One of the major measures benefiting West Virginia was the Appalachian Regional Development Act of 1965, funneling federal funds to support a new network of four-lane highways, health clinics, airport construction, water and sewer systems, libraries, and aid for colleges and universities. The Appalachian Regional Commission created under the act reflected what President Johnson labeled "creative federalism," involving shared decision-making by state governors and the federal co-chairman. This mechanism bypassed traditional pork barrel legislation to benefit the pet projects of congressmen, while unfortunately opening the pork barrel to governors.

America pulled back from Great Society activism during the conservative era of the 1980s and 1990s, with President Ronald Reagan and House Speaker Newt Gingrich both critical of Johnson's dream. But like the social security program initiated by FDR, Great Society programs such as Medicare, Head Start, Job Corps, and community action programs now operating throughout West Virginia, are alive, prospering, effective, and popular. Although the Vietnam War crippled budgetary support for Great Society programs, increased deficits, and fueled inflation, the programs themselves have survived and are widely supported.

See also Appalachian Regional Commission, War on Poverty

Ken Hechler
Charleston

Greater Kanawha Valley Foundation

The Greater Kanawha Valley Foundation is a charitable community trust organized in 1962 to accept contributions, create and administer funds, and make grants for the benefit of the people of the Kanawha Valley region. It is a collection of many separate funds, each with its own agreement, its own donors, and its own philanthropic purposes. It devotes special attention to programs in six distinct areas: arts and culture, education, health, human services, land use, and recreation.

The Greater Kanawha Valley Foundation began operations in 1962 with a single fund, the Frank A. Knight Memorial Fund. The Knight Fund was established with proceeds of the North-South Football Game, which was discontinued, and its assets, amounting to about $45,000, redirected by the circuit court of Kanawha County to the foundation for the benefit of the Children's Museum and Planetarium, later a part of Sunrise Museum. A general fund was created shortly after 1962, and in 1965 the foundation made its first discretionary grant of $1,000 to Morris Harvey College, now the University of Charleston.

Governance of the foundation is vested in an 11-member board of trustees, some of whom are appointed by civic and public organizations and some of whom are elected by the board itself. The distributions committee, upon consideration of requests, recommends grants for approval by the trustees. The scholarship committee, upon consideration of applications from students, recommends approval of scholarships to be awarded based upon criteria set forth in the agreements creating each scholarship fund.

By 2001, the Greater Kanawha Valley Foundation had assets exceeding $100 million, making it among the top 100 community foundations in the country.

The Greater Kanawha Valley Foundation is a contributor to *The West Virginia Encyclopedia*.

Becky Cain
Greater Kanawha Valley Foundation

Daniel Greathouse

Daniel Greathouse, born about 1750, is credited with masterminding the 1774 massacre of Mingo Chief Logan's family in what is now Hancock County. Daniel was the son of Harmon Greathouse, an early settler of the region and a renowned frontiersman. The massacre of Chief Logan's family is believed by some to have precipitated Dunmore's War, although historians such as Otis Rice have labeled the massacre as only one of a series of incidents leading to that conflict.

Daniel Greathouse apparently was an Indian hater who organized a group of men to attack the Indians at Yellow Creek, Ohio, across the Ohio River from the Northern Panhandle. On pretext of a friendly visit, Greathouse entered the Indians' camp but found them to be too well-established for an attack to succeed. When he discovered that several Indians had crossed the river and had gone to a tavern owned by Joshua Baker, at Baker's Bottom in present Hancock County, Greathouse prevailed upon Baker to allow the Indians to have too much alcohol. When the Indians were inebriated, some of Greathouse's group of men murdered them. Among those killed were Chief Logan's brother and sister. In retaliation, Logan led raids along the Virginia frontier that accounted for more than 13 deaths. Greathouse died sometime between 1776 and 1778 of measles.

See also Greathouse Party Massacre, Indian Wars, Chief Logan

Kenneth R. Bailey
WVU Institute of Technology
Audra Rickey Wayne and Barbara Ellen Wayne, *The Greathouse Family of West Virginia*, 1977; *History of the Upper Ohio Valley*, 1891.

Greathouse Party Massacre

On April 30, 1774, Daniel Greathouse led an ambush at Joshua Baker's Tavern, at Baker's Bottom in what is now Hancock County, against a party of Mingo Indians. This attack appears to have been motivated by the settlers' fears of an impending Indian attack, fears based upon rumors circulated in the upper Ohio Valley and the hostile actions between settlers and Indians. Greathouse assembled a party of frontiersmen, including his brother Jacob, Joseph Tomlinson, and others. The day before the attack they spied on the Mingo camp at the mouth of Yellow Creek, in present Ohio. They found that it was too strong to attack and recrossed the river to Baker's Tavern in present West Virginia.

On the night of the attack, a party of eight Mingos arrived at Baker's Tavern. Accounts of the ensuing events differ. The Greathouse party apparently plied the Indians with alcohol and then killed them in a premeditated act. None of the Indians who were in the tavern survived the attack. The Greathouse party also fired on two canoes of Indians who came to investigate the noise. After the ambush, Greathouse, his men, and some settlers retreated to nearby Washington, Pennsylvania. The massacre had dire consequences on the frontier. Among the dead were Chief Logan's brother and sister. The attack turned Logan against the settlers and led to several retaliatory raids during the summer of 1774. Logan, who mistakenly credited the attack to frontiersman Michael Cresap, spoke of his grief and ensuing anger in his famous speech.

See also Daniel Greathouse, Chief Logan

Thomas Swift Landon
Charleston

Greeks

Greeks entered West Virginia in significant numbers around the turn of the 20th century. The Turkish government had begun drafting Greeks living in areas under Turkish control into the Turkish Army to fight against their Greek countrymen. Many fled overseas, just at the time that West Virginia faced a labor shortage due to increased mining and manufacturing. The first Greeks to arrive were generally single men or married men who came alone. After getting settled, they would send for their families.

For example, in the first decade of the 20th century, around 300 Greeks settled in Harrison County to work at the Phillips Sheet and Tin Plate Company, known as the "Tin-plate" factory, owned by Weirton Steel. Greeks also worked in the iron and steel centers of Wheeling and Weirton and in many coal mines around the state. The 1910 census lists 787 foreign-born Greeks living in West Virginia. The 1920 census shows that the number of Greeks had grown to 3,186, with the majority in Harrison, Hancock, and Ohio counties. Though initially working in West Virginia's coal and manufacturing industries, many Greeks gravitated toward retail, such as restaurants, theaters, coffeehouses, and grocery stores. These were independent business people, doing the type of work they were accustomed to in Greece.

Greeks in West Virginia, as elsewhere, formed *kinotitoes*, governing bodies of local Greek communities, which would establish Orthodox churches and schools. Following a Greek custom, many immigrants opened *kaffeneions* (coffeehouses) in their homes, perpetuating Greek customs here. Greek holidays (particularly March 28, Greek Independence Day) were often celebrated with parades with many people dressed in the traditional clothing of Greece. After World War I, immigration from Europe declined and Greeks, as with many other ethnic groups, began to move away from their close-knit communities and into other West Virginia towns, working in diverse professions.

Cathy Pleska
Scott Depot
Dorothy Davis, *History of Harrison County*, 1970; Pamela Makricosta, "A Bundle of Treasures: Greeks in West Virginia," *Goldenseal*, Winter 1997; Margo Stafford, "All Greek and All Hard Workers," *Goldenseal*, Fall 1982.

Green Bottom

Green Bottom Plantation, located on the Ohio River in Cabell County, was the home of Albert G. Jenkins, a U.S. and Confederate congressman and Confederate general.

Joshua Fry received the Green Bottom lands for his participation in the French and Indian War. Wilson Cary Nicholas, governor of Virginia (1814–16), later purchased the land and established an overseer slave plantation on the site about 1812. In 1820, 53 slaves lived and worked at Green Bottom. Next, William H. Cabell, governor of Virginia (1805–08) and for whom Cabell County was named, purchased Green Bottom. In 1825, his agents sold Green Bottom and its slaves to Capt. William Jenkins, who moved there with his family in 1826. William Jenkins, the father of Gen. Albert G. Jenkins, built Green Bottom mansion in 1835. Albert Jenkins and two brothers inherited Green Bottom at the death of Captain Jenkins.

The General Albert Gallatin Jenkins house, a two-story brick home in the federal style, was placed on the National Register of Historic Places in 1978. Known today as the Jenkins Plantation Museum, it is operated by the West Virginia Division of Culture and History. Nearby lands make up the Green Bottom Wildlife Management Area. The Clover archeological site, located at Green Bottom, is a National Historic Landmark.

See also Clover Archeological Site, Albert Gallatin Jenkins

Karen N. Cartwright Nance
Barboursville

Greenbrier

The greenbrier is a tough climbing vine armed with spines or prickles and paired coiling tendrils. There are three species in West Virginia, the common greenbrier (or horsebrier), the saw brier, and the hispid (or bristly) greenbrier. The color of the stem, leaf shape, and prickles distinguish them. All have bluish-black berries in clusters. These persist in the winter long after more desirable fruits are gone and are eaten by black bear, raccoon, turkey, grouse, thrushes, catbirds, and mockingbirds. Greenbriers serve as important cover plants for wildlife, and many species of birds will nest among the vines. The young shoots are also heavily browsed by deer and rabbits. The roots have been used in making an amber-colored jelly and a drink like root beer. Greenbrier may be found in thickets, open woods, fields, fence rows, and along woodland borders throughout the state.

The often impenetrable thickets of greenbrier and their painful spines made an impression on early settlers. The Greenbrier River is named after these vines, as is the county and the world famous resort in White Sulphur Springs.

Kathleen Carothers Leo
Division of Natural Resources

Greenbrier College for Women

The Greenbrier College for Women, which once operated in Lewisburg, descended from the Lewisburg Academy. Dr. John McElhenney, who was the third pastor of Old Stone Presbyterian Church, came to Lewisburg in 1808. He and his wife organized a board of directors and succeeded in having a two-story brick building constructed to house the academy. McElhenney was president of this board from 1812 to 1860. A succession of principals and presidents followed, with Philander Custer and Alex Mathews being two of the most successful.

Having closed because of the Civil War, the academy was reopened in 1875 and its name changed to Lewisburg Female Institute. Across town the boys' division opened and by 1890 was known as the Greenbrier Military Academy, later Greenbrier Military School. Robert L. Telford was the last president to serve while the school was still known as Lewisburg Female Institute. Lewisburg Seminary was the third name, from 1911 to 1923. Then the school was named Greenbrier College for Women and continued as such until 1933.

Since its founding in 1812, the school had been associated with the Presbyterian Church, first the Synod and then the Presbytery, not faring well under either. On October 16, 1929, the college assets were transferred to an independent corporation, and it was chartered in 1933 as just Greenbrier College. French W. Thompson was president for the major part of this time, and the college prospered as a women's junior college. Greenbrier College closed in 1972, but its buildings remain Lewisburg landmarks. Its Greenbrier Hall, an impressive red brick structure, now serves as the Greenbrier Community College Center of Bluefield State College. Carnegie Hall and North House, once part of the campus, also remain an active part of community cultural life.

See also Greenbrier Military School, Lewisburg

Bettie S. Woodward
Lewisburg
Henry B. Graybill, *A Brief History of Greenbrier College*, 1949.

FAST FACTS ABOUT GREENBRIER COUNTY

Founded: 1778
Land in square miles: 1,022.8
Population: 34,453
Percentage minorities: 4.8%
Percentage rural: 71.7%
Median age: 41.6
Percentage 65 and older: 17.7
Birth rate per 1,000 population: 11.1
Median household income: $26,927
High school graduate or higher: 73.4%
Bachelor's degree or higher: 13.6%
Home ownership: 76.6%
Median home value: $71,300

This information is from the 2000 U.S. Census. In 2000, West Virginia as a whole had 5 percent minorities, a median age of 38.9, median household income of $29,696, and a 75.2 percent home ownership rate.

Greenbrier Company

The Greenbrier Company was one of several companies of speculators to which large land grants were given in return for settling the Virginia frontier. Land promoters were offered 1,000 acres of land for each family that actually established a homestead. Members of the company included Robert, John, William, and Charles Lewis as well as several prominent politicians of eastern Virginia.

The Greenbrier Company was granted 100,000 acres in the Greenbrier Valley in 1745. The company promoted the first settlements in the valley, largely based on surveys done in the region by Andrew Lewis, the son of John Lewis and later the commander at the Battle of Point Pleasant. Though settlers moved into the area in the 1750s, most were driven out by Indian attacks during the extended French and Indian War. Settlers returned to the Greenbrier Valley in the early 1760s.

The Greenbrier Company became embroiled in conflicting claims to its property as squatters moved into the region and established homesteads without regard to land title. In other cases land patents were granted, in lieu of payment for state service, in the region which had already been allocated to the company. West Virginia historian Otis K. Rice pointed out that the Greenbrier Company's powerful political connections made this company more adept than others at protecting its property and at profiting from the sale of disputed land to squatters and holders of conflicting patents.

Kenneth R. Bailey
WVU Institute of Technology
Otis K. Rice, *The Allegheny Frontier: West Virginia Beginnings, 1730–1830*, 1970.

Greenbrier County

Rich in history and natural resources, Greenbrier County is the fifth-oldest and second-largest county in West Virginia.

Formed during the Revolutionary War, March 1, 1778, from portions of Botetourt and Montgomery counties, Greenbrier County is named for the Greenbrier River. Now composed of 1,022.8 square miles in the southeastern portion of the state, its borders once stretched to the Ohio River, encompassing many other counties in present West Virginia. The county seat is Lewisburg.

The topography is rugged in the west with rolling valleys farther east. Greenbrier County is barricaded on its eastern border by a high range of the Allegheny Mountains, separating the county from neighboring Virginia. Grassy Knob in the northwest has the highest elevation, at 4,360 feet, and the lowest point is near Alderson, at 1,550 feet. This provides a surface relief within the county of nearly 3,000 feet and some of the finest scenery in the Mountain State. Greenbrier State Forest and a portion of Monongahela National Forest occupy parts of the county.

A vast system of limestone caves lies beneath the fertile soil. With 1,199 caves of all sizes, Greenbrier has far more caves than any other West Virginia county, including 412 caves over 33 feet in length. Organ Cave, near Ronceverte, is one of the oldest-known and most famous caves in West Virginia and was the center of a thriving saltpeter mining industry prior to the Civil War.

Agriculture is important in Greenbrier County, which has more than 184,000 acres of farmland. The West Virginia State Fair is permanently located at Fairlea, near Lewisburg.

Historically, lumber and coal are among Greenbrier's other important industries. The Meadow River Lumber Company, organized in 1910 in Rainelle, was once the site of the largest hardwood manufacturing plant in the world. Poplar, oak, and maple were among the native woods pro-

Greenbrier County farm country.

cessed at Meadow River. Coal mining boomed in parts of the county early in the 20th century. Mining continues today, although at a much lower level than for the state's major coal-producing counties.

Natural springs appear throughout the county, with several of them supporting thriving resorts in the 19th and early 20th century. Blue Sulphur Springs and White Sulphur Springs drew visitors from a wide region. The Blue, as it was called, was burned during the Civil War by Union troops and later suffered by not being on a rail route. The Old White at White Sulphur Springs fared much better and today is succeeded by the Greenbrier, a world-class resort that continues the tradition of grand hospitality.

The population of Greenbrier County in 1820 was 7,340 inhabitants. Families who settled here found rich land and abundant game, and fierce adversaries in the Indians who raided from the Ohio Valley. Although life was at first not easy, by 1820 Lewisburg and the Greenbrier Valley were an established gateway to the new western frontiers of Kentucky, Ohio, and Indiana. One writer of the period said that the James River & Kanawha Turnpike, now U.S. 60, was a "bustling parade of settlers moving west, tinkers, gypsies, and people just one step ahead of the sheriff."

During the Civil War, Greenbrier County was for the most part loyal to Virginia and the Confederacy. Strategically located on the James River & Kanawha Turnpike, Greenbrier suffered as armies clashed in battle as they moved through the region. During the May 1862 Battle of Lewisburg, Generals Hess and Cook fought in the streets of the town. Guests at the Star Hotel watched from the balcony as the battle unfolded below. In 1863, troops maneuvered in Greenbrier County for the decisive battle at Droop Mountain, just across the Pocahontas County line. The Battle of White Sulphur Springs took place in August 1863. Robert E. Lee found Traveler, his great war horse, in Greenbrier County.

The first school, Dr. John McElhenney's Lewisburg Academy, opened in 1812. Other early schools included the Williamsburg School, the Ronceverte School, the Bolling School, the Alderson Academy (a predecessor to Alderson-Broaddus College), and the Greenbrier Male Academy in Lewisburg.

Two schools became especially important. In 1875, the Lewisburg Female Institute took root in the old Lewisburg Academy building. It would become the Greenbrier College for Women. Across town, a school for young gentlemen opened its doors. It became known as the Greenbrier Military Academy (later Greenbrier Military School) in 1890 and closed in 1972. Today its campus is the home of the West Virginia School of Osteopathic Medicine.

Towns and cities within Greenbrier County include Lewisburg, White Sulphur Springs, Alderson, Ronceverte, Rupert, Rainelle, and Renick. The unincorporated communities include Caldwell, Smoot, Trout, Hart's Run, Asbury, Fort Spring, Frankford, and Williamsburg.

Greenbrier County had 34,453 people in 2000.

Lewisburg, the county seat, was established in 1782 and is among the oldest cities in West Virginia. Known first as "the Savannah" and later as "Camp Union," it was named Lewisburg in honor of Andrew Lewis and the Lewis family. Old Stone Presbyterian Church, the oldest church building in continuous use west of the Allegheny Mountains, is located in the Lewisburg National Historic District, which also includes the 1835 Courthouse, the North House Museum (once the Star Hotel and site of a speech by Henry Clay), Carnegie Hall, and the John Wesley Methodist Church, which still bears the scars of cannonballs from the Battle of Lewisburg.

Samuel Price of Greenbrier County, who voted against secession at the Virginia convention but nonetheless signed the ordinance of secession, was lieutenant governor of Confederate Virginia. Two Greenbrier Countians became governors of West Virginia, Henry Mason Mathews, 1877–81, and Homer Holt, 1937–41. Other notable Greenbrier County natives include World War I generals John Hines and Mason Mathews Patrick. General Hines later served as the U.S. Army chief of staff, from 1924 to 1926. General Patrick, the son of a Confederate surgeon, was chief of the Air Service of the American Expeditionary Force during World War I. He continued to serve as chief of the Army Air Service until 1927.

See also Greenbrier River, Lewisburg

Joyce Mott
North House Museum

Greenbrier Division

The Greenbrier Division, a branch line of the Chesapeake & Ohio Railway, served the Greenbrier Valley in Greenbrier and Pocahontas counties. Unlike most C&O branches in West Virginia, the Greenbrier Division was not a coal-hauling line, but served the valley's timber industry. Construction began in July 1899 and was completed to Cass in December 1900, to Durbin in 1902, and to Winterburn in 1905. The final length was 100.96 miles. At Durbin a junction was made in 1903 with the Coal & Iron Railroad, later part of the Western Maryland Railway.

The Greenbrier Division served the numerous sawmills and two tanneries that quickly located along the new railroad. This business, along with the existing communities and the agriculture of the valley, made the Greenbrier Division an important branch of the C&O for freight and passenger traffic.

By the early 1920s, the original timber had almost all been cut and motor vehicles were beginning to affect railroad traffic. However, this decade was one of the busiest for the Greenbrier Division, as the C&O began using the line as part of a freight route between eastern and western cities. The Depression of the 1930s led to the end of the through trains and the closing of almost all remaining industries on the division. World War II saw the last busy years. Through freight trains returned to the line and wartime rationing of gasoline and tires brought people back to the passenger trains.

Following the war, the decline in rail traffic resumed. Passenger service ended on January 8, 1958. In 1975, the C&O requested authority from the Interstate Commerce Commission to abandon the line. The authority was granted in 1978 and the last trains ran on December 27 and 28. The right of way was donated by the railroad to the state. The section between North Caldwell and Cass has become the Greenbrier River Trail.

See also Chesapeake & Ohio Railway
William P. McNeel
Marlinton

William P. McNeel, *The Durbin Route: The Greenbrier Division of the Chesapeake and Ohio Railway*, 1995.

Greenbrier Ghost

A state historic marker near the Sam Black Church exit of Interstate 64 commemorates the "only known case in which testimony from a ghost helped to convict a murderer." The victim lies about five miles away beneath a tombstone which reads "In memory of Zona Heaster Shue, Greenbrier Ghost, 1876–1897." About four miles from the historic marker, the log cabin where Zona Heaster Shue's body was found still stands.

The young woman died mysteriously two months after her marriage to Edward Shue. Her death was presumed natural until her spirit appeared in a dream to her mother, Mary, accusing her husband of murder. Mary Heaster said that her daughter appeared at her bedside (in the dress she died in) four times to tell her how Edward had come home from his work as a blacksmith and in a fit of rage had broken her neck with his hands. An examination of the exhumed body verified the ghost's tale. Edward Shue was found guilty of murder and sentenced to the state prison at Moundsville where he died eight years later.

The Greenbrier County Courthouse where Edward Shue was tried is there today, and the murder trial records carry the words of the Greenbrier Ghost as they were repeated in the trial testimony of her mother. This ghost story is one of the best-known in West Virginia, and at least two books on the Greenbrier Ghost have been written.

Dennis J. Deitz
South Charleston

Dennis J. Deitz, *The Greenbrier Ghost and other Strange Stories*, 1990.

Greenbrier Limestone

A limestone originating in the Mississippian geologic period, the Greenbrier Limestone is exposed primarily in the Greenbrier Valley and in the Potomac Highlands and neighboring areas. Throughout the rest of the state, it is buried deep beneath the Appalachian Plateau. It consists of a variety of limestone types. When the Greenbrier Limestone crops out, it forms rich valley bottoms ringed by mountains, most prominently the Greenbrier Valley and Canaan Valley. Because limestones are easily dissolved by migrating groundwater, many caves have developed in the Greenbrier Limestone; in fact it may be best-known for the large variety of caves (including Friars Hill Cave, the largest in West Virginia, as well as the Sinks of Gandy, Organ Cave, and others) that have formed within the limestone.

Limestone is a sedimentary rock, formed over very long periods by the settling of the shells of ancient sea creatures to the bottom of a body of water. The Greenbrier Limestone was deposited in a shallow ocean that flooded West Virginia in ancient times. It formed in a subsiding basin at a time when there was little mountain building activity to the east. The subsidence was greatest in southeastern West Virginia, where the Greenbrier Limestone exceeds 1,000 feet in thickness; it thins to less than 100 feet in the northwestern part of the state. The Greenbrier represents a hiatus in mountain building activity between the Devonian-Mississippian and the Pennsylvanian-Permian ages.

Deep beneath the Appalachian Plateau the Greenbrier Limestone is a source of natural gas. Some small oil fields have also been developed. The Greenbrier Limestone is an important source of crushed stone that is used in road building and in making concrete, and is quarried extensively near Elkins and Morgantown.

David Matchen
Geological & Economic Survey

Greenbrier Military School

The Greenbrier Military School, a private secondary school for boys, was located in Lewisburg. The history of the school can be traced to 1890 when the Greenbrier Military Academy was founded. The buildings of this school burned two years after it opened, and the school went through several changes in its name and ownership. In 1902, the school was bought by the Greenbrier Presbytery which renamed it the Greenbrier Presbyterial School. At that time, the school had ceased to be a military school.

In 1906, H. B. Moore was hired as the school's headmaster, and he shortly thereafter reintroduced the military curriculum. Moore brought two of his brothers to help him run the school. They purchased the institution in 1920 and reorganized it as the Greenbrier Military School. In 1925, a fire destroyed nearly all of the school's buildings. They were replaced with a classroom building and a dormitory that could house 250 boys. During World War II, the school had an enrollment of 345 students in grades seven to 12. Students were required to have four years of military training. The school closed in 1972, and the buildings were acquired for the newly formed West Virginia School of Osteopathic Medicine.

Michael M. Meador
Abingdon, Virginia

Otis K. Rice, *A History of Greenbrier County*, 1986.

Greenbrier River

The Greenbrier River rises in two forks in the high mountains at the northern end of Pocahontas County, at elevations exceeding 3,600 feet. The East and West forks join at Durbin, and from there the river flows in a generally southwesterly direction through Pocahontas and Greenbrier counties before joining the New River at Hinton in Summers County. From Durbin to Hinton, the Greenbrier flows 162 miles. The river's drainage area of 1,656 square miles includes most of Pocahontas and Greenbrier counties, and parts of Monroe and Summers. The major tributaries are Deer Creek, Knapps Creek, Spring Creek, Anthonys Creek, Howard Creek, Second Creek, and Muddy Creek.

The Greenbrier's relatively straight course through Pocahontas and most of Greenbrier County is due to its location along the boundary between the folded rock of the Ridge and Valley geologic province on the east and the flat-lying rock of the Appalachian Plateau to the west. The lower section of the river, below Ronceverte, swings to the west onto the Plateau and develops a more meandering course. The limestone soils of the Greenbrier Valley have made it a region of fine farms from the days of the first European settlers to the present.

Indians are believed not to have been permanent residents of the valley, but users of the area on a seasonal basis. European explorers, hunters, and trappers were in the valley by the late 1600s and early 1700s, and may have included both French and English. Land grants on the Greenbrier watershed were made in the 1740s and settlement was under way by the 1750s.

As they moved west, settlers followed the trails used by the natives. Several trails passed through the Greenbrier Valley, with the Seneca Trail perhaps the best known today. During the Civil War, the movement of troops brought the horrors of war to the valley. The 1863 Battle of Droop Mountain was fought within sight of the river.

The Chesapeake & Ohio Railway (now CSX), constructed after the Civil War, parallels the lower section of the river on its route from Virginia to the west. The railroad's former Greenbrier Division, now the Greenbrier River Trail, provided rail transportation to the upper part of the Greenbrier Valley.

The shallow river itself has been used as a means of transportation in only minor ways, except for three decades following the mid-1870s, when the white pine timber along the Greenbrier and its tributaries was floated to Ronceverte in annual log drives. Following the timber harvest, the valley benefited from the conservation movement. Much of the upper part of the Greenbrier watershed was included in the Monongahela National Forest, and reforestation efforts, accelerated by the Depression-era Civilian Conservation Corps, restored timber to the mountainsides.

This restoration of the beauty of the valley has helped make recreation, which had its beginnings with pre-Civil War resorts at the mineral springs, a major part of the area's economy at the beginning of the 21st century.

Like other streams, the Greenbrier River at times needs its floodplain to carry all its water. The earliest settlements, located away from the river, did not have a problem with high water such as the major flood of 1877. However, following railroad construction and the building of communities in the floodplain, people and their property have been in danger from flooding. Large floods in 1985 and 1996 caused major damage along the Greenbrier. Flood control has been a topic of study and controversy since the 1930s. No action had been taken as of 2004, leaving the Greenbrier

River the last major river in West Virginia to flow its entire length without manmade impediments.

William P. McNeel
Marlinton

Greenbrier River Trail

The Greenbrier River Trail is West Virginia's Millennium Legacy Trail, one of 50 such trails nationwide. It is perhaps the best-known and most used rail trail in the state and is managed by West Virginia's state park system. The 78-mile trail follows the old Greenbrier Division of the Chesapeake & Ohio Railway along the Greenbrier River, traveling from Cass in Pocahontas County to Caldwell, near Lewisburg, by way of Seneca State Forest, Marlinton, Watoga State Park, and Calvin Price State Forest. Many bicyclists begin their adventure at Cass and end in Caldwell, taking two or three days to complete the journey.

Built to haul the region's vast timber resources to market, the Greenbrier Division of the C&O was active from 1900 to 1978. Mark A. Hankins, of Lewisburg, whose grandfather and father had planned the Greenbrier Division as engineers, was instrumental in acquiring the right of way for the trail. With access from many points in Greenbrier and Pocahontas counties, the visitor doesn't have to ride or walk the entire trail to enjoy the scenery, wildflowers, and animals that share the river and trail. Trail maps showing the location of facilities and camping areas are available from visitor centers in Pocahontas and Greenbrier counties. The Greenbrier River Trail State Park, created in 1980, includes 950 acres.

Leslee McCarty
Hillsboro

Greenbrier State Forest

Greenbrier State Forest, created in 1938, straddles Kates Mountain near White Sulphur Springs in Greenbrier County. Like all state forests, it is dedicated to a multiple-use, sustained-yield program. The 5,130-acre forest is richly populated with wildlife. There are deer, racoons, wild turkeys, black bear, squirrels, chipmunks, and the unique Allegheny woodrat, sometimes called pack rat by local people. Greenbrier State Forest also includes the rare Kates Mountain clover and box huckleberry. Swordleaf phlox is equally rare and known in only two other counties in West Virginia. All of these rare plants can be seen in Greenbrier State Forest or within a few hundred yards of its boundaries.

There is a forest demonstration area along Harts Run between the cabins and the campground. This 20-acre demonstration forest is divided into separate plots, each displaying timbering practices. Another attraction is Kates Mountain road, which runs for miles along the

top of the ridge. The road begins at U.S. 60 in White Sulphur Springs, not far from the entrance to the Greenbrier resort, and ends at the forest headquarters building. The road was originally constructed as a scenic drive and for forest fire protection by the Civilian Conservation Corps in the 1930s. Recreational facilities at Greenbrier State Forest include a swimming pool, 13 vacation cabins, picnic facilities, hiking trails, and a campground.

Robert Beanblossom
Division of Natural Resources

The Greenbrier

The Greenbrier, situated on the eastern edge of Greenbrier County, traces its origins to the late 18th century and the health-restoring use of the mineral water from the White Sulphur Spring. The area remained remote, however, until made accessible in the 1820s by the James River & Kanawha Turnpike. In the ensuing antebellum years the resort's reputation was firmly established as the summer gathering place of wealthy and influential southerners. Henry Clay, Martin Van Buren, John Tyler, and many other political figures frequented White Sulphur. Closed during the Civil War, the resort's survival was ensured by the 1869 arrival of the Chesapeake & Ohio Railway. Its status as a southern mecca was incalculably enhanced by Robert E. Lee's visits after the war.

In 1910, the C&O purchased the resort and developed it into a major destination along its main line, building the central section of today's hotel and adding the first golf course. Both projects were completed in 1913, and the resort became a year-round operation. The name "Greenbrier" (after the county, river, and plant) became the preferred name over the 19th century's "White Sulphur Springs." The resort prospered in the 1920s both as a society rendezvous and as a meeting place for business owners and executives in the coal, rail, steel, insurance, banking, chemical, and automobile industries, as well as for members of the medical and legal professions.

In the early months of World War II, the U.S. State Department leased the Greenbrier and used it to intern Japanese, German, and Italian diplomats and their dependents who had been stranded in Washington. After seven months these "enemy alien diplomats" were exchanged for American diplomats interned overseas. In September 1942, the U.S. Army took over the resort, renamed it Ashford General Hospital, converted the hotel into a 2000-bed hospital, and used the recreational facilities for rehabilitation. The hospital specialized in vascular and neurosurgery; in four years 24,148 soldiers were admitted. General Eisenhower

The Greenbrier resort in springtime.

vacationed at the resort hospital upon returning from Europe in 1945.

After an extensive post-war refurbishing by New York decorator Dorothy Draper, the Greenbrier reopened in April 1948. In the 1950s, the resort was known as one of the favorite haunts of the Duke and Duchess of Windsor and as the home of golfing great Sam Snead. The U.S. government approached the C&O in 1956 with a proposal to build an "emergency relocation center" at the Greenbrier for the reassembly of Congress in case of nuclear war. Construction of the 112,000-square-foot underground facility was concealed by the simultaneous addition of a new hotel wing; both were complete by mid-1962. For 30 years the resort was one telephone call away from transformation into the site of the legislative branch of the federal government. A *Washington Post* article in May 1992 exposing the classified operation led to the closing of the government facility.

See also Ashford General Hospital, Camp Ashford

Robert S. Conte
The Greenbrier

Robert S. Conte, *The History of The Greenbrier, America's Resort*, 1998.

Greene Line

In 1890, 27-year-old Capt. Gordon C. Greene bought the steamboat *H.K. Bedford* and entered the Pittsburgh-Wheeling packet trade, carrying freight and passengers between the two cities. The same year he married his childhood sweetheart, Mary Becker, and they began life together on the *Bedford*. Within a few years Mary had learned the river and became one of the few women to become a licensed steamboat pilot.

The *H. K. Bedford* began Pittsburgh-Charleston service in 1896. Greene Line boats, headquartered in Cincinnati, operated on the Kanawha River from then until the end of the packet boat era in the 1930s. In 1903, Captain Greene built the side-wheel packet *Greenland*. The *Greenland* would be the largest side-wheeler ever to offer regular service on the Kanawha River. In 1904, the Greenes acquired the Cincinnati, Portsmouth, Big Sandy & Pomeroy Packet Co., adding four more packet boats to their fleet.

Capt. Gordon Greene died on January 27, 1927. Mary B. Greene, with sons Chris and Tom, continued to operate the company. Capt. Mary B. Greene, sometimes known as "Maw" Greene, became a legend on the rivers as both a pilot and master on her company's boats. She died in 1949.

Between 1890 and 1947, the Greene Line owned or operated 27 steamboats. The company acquired the famous *Delta Queen* in 1947, the last steamboat the Greene Line would own. In 1969, Overseas National Airway acquired the Greene Line and in 1973 changed the name to The Delta Queen Steamboat Co. The company now operates the *Delta Queen*, *Mississippi Queen,* and the *American Queen* on the Mississippi River system, as well as the *Columbia Queen* on the Columbia River in Oregon.

See also River Transportation

Gerald W. Sutphin
Huntington

Greenland Gap

Greenland Gap is a scenic 820-foot-deep pass through New Creek Mountain in Grant County. Both sides of the gap are framed by towering cliffs of Tuscarora sandstone. The North Fork of Patterson Creek, a trout stream, flows through the gap. Known for its natural beauty and virgin forests, Greenland Gap is the centerpiece of a 255-acre nature preserve owned by the Nature Conservancy. West Virginia has designated it a State Natural Landmark.

On April 25, 1863, about 1,500 Confederate soldiers under Gen. William "Grumble" Jones, advancing through Greenland Gap, encountered 87 Union soldiers who had taken positions in a church and cabins at the west end of the gap. The Union soldiers held off several assaults, refusing to surrender. After four hours of fighting, the church was set on fire and the Union forces surrendered. Union casualties were two killed, six wounded. The Confederates suffered seven soldiers killed, 35 wounded.

Rodney Bartgis
Nature Conservancy of West Virginia

Greenville Saltpeter Cave

The Greenville Saltpeter Cave is in Greenville, Monroe County. This is a noncommercial "wild" cave and is not open to the general public. The cave has four entrances and 3.8 miles of surveyed passages. The southern entrance is above the mill pond and is the place where Laurel Creek, which sinks about one mile north of Greenville, reemerges from the ground. The three northern entrances to the cave are in a small valley about a third of a mile north of the mill pond entrance. One of these, the northeastern entrance, is called the water entrance and is situated where a portion of the underground route of Laurel Creek is exposed to the surface.

The cave was owned by John Maddy in 1804 and then sold to Jacob and John Mann who manufactured saltpeter (potassium nitrate) at the site for several years. Saltpeter was used in the manufacture of gunpowder. The cave was again mined for saltpeter during the Civil War. Unfortunately, the saltpeter section of the cave has been heavily vandalized, and few traces of mining or the old leaching hoppers remain. The cave has several large rooms but few calcite formations. The passages intertwine and form a maze. All of the entrances are on private property. The cave is closed to visitors during the winter months to protect a large bat colony. The Greenville Saltpeter Cave occurs in the Union Limestone of the Greenbrier Group (Mississippian age).

See also Caves

William K. Jones
Charles Town

Greenwood Cemetery

Greenwood Cemetery, on the National Road (U.S. 40) in Wheeling, was incorporated in March 1866. Among the incorporators were Wheeling's Civil War mayor Andrew J. Sweeney, state founder Archibald W. Campbell, Dr. Eugene A. Hildreth, W. M. List, C. H. Berry, and other prominent citizens. The first interment was on July 22, 1866, for Caroline Morgan. Several bodies had been removed to Greenwood Cemetery prior to Morgan's burial.

James Gilchrist, a civil engineer, laid out the cemetery. Adorning the grounds with shrubbery, flowers, and trees, and enclosing the area with picket fences, he produced a park-like cemetery of the sort that became popular in the mid-19th century. Two cottages were built for the groundskeepers at the main entrance. Lots were sold, and Greenwood Cemetery went into business as a for-profit corporation. In 1919, Greenwood Cemetery became a nonprofit corporation and still maintains that status.

Greenwood Cemetery's grounds have been expanded from its original 37.5 acres and now include about 100 acres. The most recent addition to the cemetery is the 1983 Greenwood Chapel which was added to a 1909 receiving vault and is used for services during inclement weather. During the past century, numerous bodies have been re-interred at Greenwood when other cemeteries were taken by highways and other projects. More than 37,000 people are now buried in Greenwood Cemetery. Much of the story of Wheeling and the surrounding area can be gleaned from the gravestones.

The prominent citizens resting in Greenwood Cemetery include Campbell and Sweeney, as well as Mary Lovely Chapline Zane (1787–1858); the banker and cigarmaker Augustus Pollack (1830–1906); brewer Henry Schmulbach (1844–1915); Amelia Hay McElheran Sprigg (1785–1872); Stimpson H. Woodward (1812–1881); Capt. Samuel Sprigg Shriver (1843–1881); Tryphena Hornbrook (1821–1892); Dr. John Frissell (1810–1893); and department store founder Jacob C. Thomas (1822–1898).

See also Cemeteries

Gordon L. Swartz III
Cameron

Hal Greer

Athlete Harold Everett "Hal" Greer was born in Huntington, June 26, 1936. The six foot-two inch guard was a basketball star at Huntington's Frederick Douglass High School during the days of segregation. Recruited by legendary coach Cam Henderson, Greer was the first African-American athlete to play at Marshall College (now University) and one of the first to break the color barrier at a traditionally white college in the South. During his three-year college career, Greer scored 1,377 points, averaged 19.4 points per game, and set the Marshall record for field goals (.545).

Advancing to the National Basketball Association after his 1959 graduation, in 15 seasons with the Syracuse Nationals and Philadelphia 76ers Greer averaged 19.2 points per game and was a ten-time all-star. His 76ers team of 1966–67, considered one of the game's all-time greatest, ended the Boston Celtics' streak of eight consecutive championships. When Greer retired in 1973, he held the career record for most games played and ranked in the top ten in points scored, field goals attempted, and field goals made. After his retirement, the 76ers retired his number 15 jersey; he was inducted into the Naismith Basketball Hall of Fame; and he was named to the NBA's list of the 50 greatest players in league history. In 1978, the city of Huntington renamed 16th Street as Hal Greer Boulevard.

Greer, who has worked in business and real estate since leaving professional basketball, now lives in Arizona.

Stan Bumgardner
Division of Culture & History

Charles Hill Moffatt, *Marshall University: An Institution Comes of Age, 1837–1980*, 1981.

Grenadier Squaw

Nonhelema was the sister of Shawnee chief Cornstalk and, as the leader of a Shawnee village near the present Circleville, Ohio, a person of importance in her own right. Because of her unusual height and fine carriage the settlers identified her as the "Grenadier Squaw," in reference to the grenadiers, the finest and tallest soldiers in the British service. A Christian missionary had named her Katherine, and she was called Kate or Ketty.

She adopted the white settlers, serving as an interpreter, and in May 1776 was living at Fort Randolph, Point Pleasant, when Indians attacked. Although the Indians were driven off, Ketty learned that they intended to attack Fort Donnelly, near Lewisburg. She dressed heroic Philip Hammond and John Pryor Indian-style, and they managed to bypass the Indians and warn Fort Donnelly. The attack was beaten off until a relief force from Lewisburg, led by Col. Sam Lewis and Capt. Matthew Arbuckle, relieved the fort.

Nonhelema had a daughter, Fannie or Fawney. They were observed at the meeting between Lord Dunmore, Cornstalk, Col. Andrew Lewis and others at Camp Charlotte, riding fine horses with elegant saddles. Her 1785 petition to Congress for a grant of land near her Ohio home was never acted upon. She moved to a place near Pittsburgh. Another petition on her behalf was signed by 18 white settlers but, presumably, was ignored.

Her fate and that of her daughter are unknown.

See also Cornstalk, Indians

Joseph Crosby Jefferds Jr.
Charleston

Joseph C. Jefferds Jr., *Captain Matthew Arbuckle, A Documentary Biography*, 1981; Reuben Gold Thwaites and Louise Phelps Kellogg, eds., *Frontier Defense on the Upper Ohio, 1777–1778*, 1912.

Perry Epler Gresham

College president Perry Epler Gresham was born in Covina, California, December 19, 1907. He received an A.B. from Texas Christian University in 1931 and a bachelor of divinity degree from the same institution in 1933. He also studied at the University of Chicago, Columbia University, the Union Theological Seminary, Pacific School of Religion, and the University of Edinburgh.

Gresham was an ordained minister of the Christian Church (Disciples of Christ) and pastored congregations in Denver, Fort Worth, Seattle, and Detroit before moving to West Virginia to become president of Bethany College in 1953. He was president from 1953 to 1972 and later served four years as chairman of the college's board of trustees. During Gresham's presidency, Bethany launched a building program and hosted world leaders, speakers, and lecturers. Gresham implemented the Bethany Plan, a model liberal arts curriculum culminating in comprehensive examinations in the senior year.

Gresham was named to the Rhodes Scholar selection committee in West Virginia, and he received a Freedom Foundation Award for his service in education in 1963. He was a trustee of the West Virginia Foundation of Independent Colleges. His writing included *Disciples of the High Calling* (1953), *Sage of Bethany* (1959), *Campbell and the Colleges* (1972), *With Wings as Eagles* (1980), and other books. Gresham died in North Carolina, September 10, 1994.

See also Bethany College

Linda S. Comins
Wellsburg

James W. Carty Jr., *The Gresham Years*, 1970; Perry E. Gresham, *Growing Up in the Ranchland*, 1993.

Grimes Golden

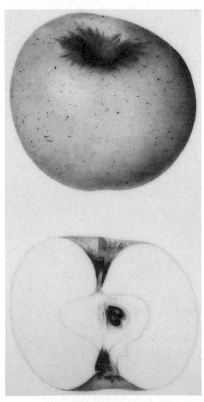

The Grimes Golden.

The Grimes Golden is one of two apple varieties originating in West Virginia, both of which are yellow apples. The first Grimes Golden was found in the early 1800s growing on the farm of Thomas Grimes near Wellsburg in Brooke County. Local legend claims that the tree grew from a seed planted by John Chapman, otherwise known as Johnny Appleseed.

Soon after the original tree was discovered, a large orchard was planted nearby using scions from the parent tree.

The Grimes Golden, popular for eating, cooking, and cider production for many years, made outstanding applesauce. The fruit was of medium size or larger, with tough yellow skin and firm, juicy flesh. Although the Grimes Golden is still around, it has largely been replaced in popularity by the Golden Delicious, the second apple variety to originate in West Virginia. The Grimes Golden is thought to be a parent of the Golden Delicious apple tree.

The original Grimes Golden tree bore fruit for more than 100 years and was carrying a crop of apples when it blew down in 1905. Wood from its trunk was used to make gavels for the West Virginia Agricultural Society, and part of the trunk was preserved at West Virginia University. A stone monument was erected at the site of the original Grimes Golden tree and is still standing today.

See also Apples, Golden Delicious

Amy Donaldson Arnold
Ivydale

Jim Comstock, *West Virginia Heritage Encyclopedia*, 1974; Creighton Lee Calhoun Jr., *Old Southern Apples*, 1995.

Gristmills

Gristmills grind grain into meal, flour, and animal feed. Among the world's oldest industrial enterprises, they were an indispensable part of agricultural economy and community life from colonial times until the middle of the 20th century. These mills commonly used rough circular revolving stones, called "buhrs" or "burrs," to grind grain, although a few crushed the grain with rollers or hammers. Most were erected on streams and used overshot water wheels. These are the picturesque side wheels of the sort seen on the well-known mill at Babcock State Park.

Records of the Virginia Company show a water-powered mill under construction in 1621, although the first American gristmill on record was built in New Amsterdam (New York) in 1634. Fearing Indian attacks, settlers in Western Virginia were slow to build gristmills despite abundant water power, relying on hand mills or mortar and pestle to grind grain. However, a few mills go back to the earliest days of settlement. The oldest working gristmill in West Virginia is Shepherd's Mill at Shepherdstown, built by Thomas Shepherd between 1734 and 1739. The Bunker Hill Mill in Berkeley County, the state's only remaining tandem-wheel water mill, was constructed in 1737 but was later rebuilt and is no longer operational.

The turbine, invented in 1827, made water-powered mills more efficient although less photogenic. Blaker's Mill, now at Jackson's Mill in Lewis County, is

turbine-powered. In the late 19th century, more modern sources of power began to be employed. The Easton Roller Mill in Monongalia County (1865) replaced its overshot water wheel and buhrs with steam power and rollers in 1894, milling up to a ton of flour a day. Howell's Gristmill in Wetzel County (1930) is powered by a 1912 gasoline engine, and French's Mill in Hampshire County (1911), a fully operational hammer mill, has converted to steam from electricity.

Gristmills have been a significant part of West Virginia's industrial and cultural history as well as notable features of its landscape for more than 250 years. In addition to providing meal and flour, they also served as meeting places where ideas and news could be exchanged. Although most of these mills are gone, some remain operational, and others, such as Reckart's Mill in Preston County (1865) and Cooper's Mill in Summers County (1869), are being restored.

See also Easton Roller Mill, Glade Creek Mill, Jackson's Mill

Jack Wills
Fairmont

Dave Gilbert, *Where Industry Failed: Water-Powered Mills at Harpers Ferry, West Virginia*, 1984; Michael Workman, "Low Tech: The Workings of a Water Mill," *Goldenseal*, Spring 1991.

Davis Grubb

Novelist Davis Alexander Grubb was born July 23, 1919, in Moundsville, in an area where both sides of his family had lived for generations. He came from prosperous forebears, his grandfather William Davis Alexander having been among the founders of Moundsville's Mercantile Bank, but the family fortunes were reduced by the Depression. Grubb's family was evicted from their home and the trauma, no doubt dramatized by Grubb, became in his writing a cry against the powerful and against capitalistic society. Grubb was likewise critical of organized religion.

Intending initially to be a graphic artist, Grubb studied design in Philadelphia after completing high school. In 1939, he went to New York City as a page for NBC and to write radio plays, alternating for the next decade between New York and Philadelphia, where he worked for an advertising agency. The brush, however, was never far from reach, and Grubb remained an artist all his life.

Grubb's first commercial writing was the script for a 1939 radio show aired by WBLK-Clarksburg. He also acted in the show. It was published, he said, in *Anthology of 100 Radio Plays*, and he received $5. He returned to Philadelphia and at night wrote stories. His first published story was "The Lollipop Tree" (*Good Housekeeping*, 1944). His renown came with his first novel, *Night of the Hunter* (1953), a gripping suspense story adapted to film in 1955 and for television in 1991.

Although *Night of the Hunter* is his most famous work, Grubb regarded his next novel, *A Dream of Kings* (1954), as his best. "I was very upset by the film version of *Night of the Hunter*, because it hadn't conformed exactly with what I had seen in my own mind," he said of the Robert Mitchum movie.

Grubb wrote *Shadow of My Brother* in 1956 (published in 1966), his only book not about Appalachia but about the lynching of a little black boy in Mississippi. *The Watchman* followed in 1958. The next work was *Voices of Glory* (1962), a book of 28 stories, or voices. One story evolved into another novel, *Fools' Parade* (1969), adapted to film in 1971. *The Barefoot Man* (1971) was next.

In 1977, Davis Grubb returned to West Virginia for a statewide speaking tour that lasted two years. Then he remained and worked on his last novel, until, near the end, he returned to New York, where he died of cancer July 24, 1980, at the age of 61. This novel, *Ancient Lights*, published posthumously in 1982, was his adventure into postmodernism, where characters and themes traverse time and space—a subject that fascinated him toward the end of his life. In all, Grubb published 11 books, four of them collections of short stories.

See also Fools' Parade, Night of the Hunter

William Plumley
St. Pete Beach, Florida

Camilla Bunting, "When Hollywood Came to Moundsville, Filming Davis Grubb's *Fools' Parade*," *Goldenseal*, Summer 1995.

Felix Grundy

U.S. Senator and Attorney General Felix Grundy was born in Berkeley County, September 11, 1777. At three he moved with his parents to Kentucky, where he attended school and later practiced law.

In 1806, Grundy was appointed to the Kentucky Supreme Court. He resigned in 1807 and moved to Nashville, Tennessee. In 1811, Grundy was elected to Congress and became a strong supporter of President Madison and the War of 1812. In 1814, Grundy resigned from Congress. Grundy also served in the Tennessee legislature, and in 1829 he was appointed to the U.S. Senate. He was appointed U.S. attorney general by President Van Buren in July 1838. In the famous case of the mutinied slave ship *Amistad*, Grundy advised that the recaptured Africans be returned to their Spanish masters, a position that proved unsuccessful in the U.S. Supreme Court.

Reelected to the Senate after one year as attorney general, Grundy died in Nashville, December 19, 1840. His Nashville home, Grundy Hill, was acquired by James K. Polk, who was elected president in 1844.

Linda Saylor-Marchant
Sommerville, South Carolina

Guineas

The Guineas are a group of apparently mixed racial origin located primarily in Barbour, Taylor, and Harrison counties, especially near Philippi and Grafton. Their numbers have been estimated as about 1,000 to 1,500, although the exact figure is hard to know for a group whose identity is partly imposed by others. The word "Guinea," widely used as a derogatory nickname for Italians and people of Mideastern descent, is sometimes resented by members of the West Virginia group. Many West Virginia Guineas historically have considered themselves to be of American Indian origins.

The Guineas are similar to other mixed-race groups of Appalachia, including the Melungeons of the mountains of Tennessee and Virginia, with whom they share some surnames. Most researchers consider these groups to represent a complex mix of African, Indian, and Caucasian (especially Iberian and Mediterranean) ancestry. Some argue that the intermingling took place very early in America's history, theorizing that such groups moved westward from the Atlantic coast, their ethnic identity already established. Eventually they settled in the mountain backcountry. However, research published in 1973 traced the origin of some West Virginia Guinea families to specific biracial and triracial unions that took place in the 18th and 19th centuries in other counties of present West Virginia.

Avery F. Gaskins, "An Introduction to the Guineas: West Virginia's Melungeons," *Appalachian Journal*, Autumn 1973; Barry J. Ward, "Going Yander: The West Virginia Guineas' View of Ohio," *Goldenseal*, April–June 1976.

Guyandotte

In 1810, the Virginia General Assembly recognized 20 acres of land owned by farmer and trader Thomas Buffington at the confluence of the Guyandotte and Ohio rivers as the new village of Guyandotte. A map showed six streets, three running east and west intersecting with three running north and south.

By the late 1830s, Guyandotte was a frequent port of call for steamboats traveling the Ohio River and a busy stagecoach stop on the James River & Kanawha Turnpike. The village boasted 40 homes, five stores, a non-denominational church, a primary school, and a gristmill said to be the largest between Cincinnati and Pittsburgh. In 1849, Guyandotte was officially incorporated and its boundaries enlarged.

The outbreak of the Civil War saw strong support for the South in Guyan-dotte, with many residents leaving to fight for the Confederacy. A Union post was established in the village, which on November 10, 1861, was attacked by a 700-man Confederate cavalry unit. The Confederates easily overcame the Union forces, most of whom were raw, untrained recruits, but they withdrew the next day when fresh Union troops arrived. Angered by the collaboration between the Confederates and the local residents, the Union troops burned the village.

With rail tycoon Collis P. Huntington's establishment of his new town on the Ohio just downstream from Guyandotte in 1871, the economic fortunes of Guyandotte began a steady decline. In 1911 the citizens voted (260 to 70) to become part of Huntington.

See also Battle of Guyandotte

James E. Casto
Herald-Dispatch

George S. Wallace, *Cabell County Annals and Families*, 1935.

Guyandotte, Battle of

On November 10, 1861, a Confederate cavalry force of more than 700 attacked a Union recruit camp for the Ninth (West) Virginia Infantry regiment at Guyandotte in Cabell County. Led by Col. John Clarkson, the Confederates quickly overcame the brief but spirited resistance of the federal recruits, who numbered slightly more than 100 men. The night was a joyful one for many of Guyandotte's citizens, a majority of whom had been outspoken advocates of secession. Ninety eight Union recruits and civilians from the town were captured and on the following day forced to begin a harrowing march to imprisonment in Richmond.

On the morning of November 11, as the Confederates were withdrawing from Guyandotte, a detachment of the Fifth (West) Virginia arrived from Ceredo on the steamer *S.S. Boston*. Accompanied by a number of Home Guards from Ohio, the Union troops burned a large portion of the town in response to accusations that the townspeople had aided the Confederates in planning and carrying out their attack. Probably a more important factor in the decision to burn the town, however, was Guyandotte's reputation as a hotbed of secession. Northern newspapers expressed outrage over the actions of the town's citizens and rejoiced at Guyandotte's destruction. Shortly after the raid, the *Wheeling Daily Intelligencer* wrote that due to the town's outspoken advocation of secession, Guyandotte "ought to have been burned two or three years ago."

See also Civil War, Guyandotte

Joe Geiger
Huntington

Joe Geiger, *Civil War in Cabell County, West Virginia 1861–1865*, 1991; Geiger, "Tragic Fate of Guyandotte," *West Virginia History*, 1995; Boyd Stutler, *West Virginia in the Civil War*, 1966.

Guyandotte River

The Guyandotte River is formed by the junction of Winding Gulf and Stonecoal creeks in Raleigh County and flows in a northwesterly direction to its confluence with the Ohio River at Huntington. Much of the land the Guyandotte flows through is extremely rugged, but as it nears the Ohio the slopes become more moderate and the ridges not as high. The Guyandotte has a total length of 167 miles and has five tributaries, the largest of these being the Mud River. The river's name is reputedly based on a Shawnee word, although some historians contend that it was named for a French trader, Henry Guyan.

In 1848, Virginia State Engineer Joseph H. Gill surveyed the Guyandotte from its mouth to Gilbert Creek, about 22 miles above Logan Court House (now Logan) and, describing the immense timber resources and coal deposits he saw there, recommended the state build a series of locks and dams to make the river navigable. Acting on his report, Virginia incorporated the Guyandotte Navigation Company and agreed to purchase three-fifths of the company's stock once private interests had purchased the other two-fifths.

Construction began, but the Guyandotte River dams were improperly placed and poorly built. Moreover, the company failed to secure clear title to some of the land it used, resulting in litigation. Construction was suspended, floods breached the dams, and the company went bankrupt. A successor company took over and briefly operated the system, but the poorly constructed dams required expensive repairs after every flood. A major flood in 1861 destroyed the project forever.

Nonetheless, with few roads through the rugged region, the Guyandotte remained an important transportation artery. Without locks and dams, large steamboats couldn't navigate the river. But the timber industry used it to float logs to market, and farmers used crude rafts to carry their produce downstream. Pushboats, along with a few small steamers, carried a steady stream of manufactured goods and other commodities upstream.

In the last quarter of the 19th century, logging was by far the principal industry along the Guyandotte. When a heavy rain caused the river to rise, intrepid raftsmen would set out on a wild downriver ride, guiding "fleets" of logs down to the mouth of the river at the village of Guyandotte. The rafters collected their pay, spent some (or maybe all) of it in Guyandotte, then walked back upriver to their homes.

When Congress ordered a survey of the Guyandotte in 1874, it found $400,000 worth of timber and farm produce moving downstream each year, matched by 300 tons of merchandise shipped upriver. In 1878, Congress provided money to have the remnants of the old dams cleared away, and for the next 20 years the river was regularly dredged. However, the coming of the railroad wrote an end to the era of Guyandotte River commerce. The rails reached Logan in 1904, and coal mining soon became the major business in the Guyandotte watershed.

The same kind of flooding that once signaled the beginning of wild log-raft rides down the river meant devastation for those who followed the railroad and settled in the valleys of the Guyandotte basin. Though usually of short duration, often lasting less than 24 hours, the floods generally happened quickly, with little or no warning.

Residents complained for years, until record floods in 1957 and 1963 finally prompted construction of a flood-control dam and reservoir near Justice. Dedicated in 1980, R. D. Bailey Lake was named for a circuit judge in Mingo and Wyoming counties who presided over a number of the criminal cases evolving from the bloody Mine Wars of the 1920s.

See also R. D. Bailey Lake

James E. Casto
Herald-Dispatch

Leland R. Johnson, *Men, Mountains, and Rivers,* 1977.

Gypsies

Though never present in great numbers, Gypsies have long been noted throughout West Virginia, part of the history and folklore of the state. The Gypsies fascinated the communities they camped near. Many myths surround them, and many places have tales of Gypsy travelers or Gypsy camps. The community of Gypsy, Harrison County, was named for the traveling nomads who once favored the bottomlands of the West Fork River as a camping spot.

A group of Gypsies settled permanently in Stumpy Bottom in Princeton, a small piece of lowland now overshadowed by U.S. 460. The original settlers came in caravans of covered wagons and set up tents in the mid-20th century. They initially traded horses and then fixed stoves. They ran a septic business and later established a paving business. Their community has endured some scandals, including a murder trial in 1995.

Gypsies are thought to have originated from India, later becoming nomads traveling through Europe. They appeared in Europe by the 15th century. Gypsies, especially in Europe, often call themselves Roma. Their language, called Romany, is still spoken by some Gypsies. Gypsies came to America among the early settlers, sometimes having been deported from European countries. However, most American gypsies came during the big migration from eastern Europe in the late 19th and early 20th centuries. They were organized into "kumpanias," similar to unions, each with an elder or chief to decide matters for the community.

Kumpania chiefs were often mistaken as Gypsy "Kings." In November 1931 Weirton was the site of the funeral of one such "king," Zeke Marks. More than 10,000 visitors came to the Schwerha funeral home. Marks lay unkempt in a bronze casket. A scarf sealed his mouth, and a rope bound his ankles. His hands were on his chest, and he held a $5 gold piece. Around him lay his possessions, including the paid bill for the funeral.

See also Ethnic Life

Jane Kraina
Weirton

Jane Kraina and Mary Zwierzchowski, "Death of a Gypsy King," *Goldenseal,* Winter 1998; Kraina and Zwierzchowski, "The World of the Gypsies," *Goldenseal,* Winter 1998.

Gypsy Moth

The gypsy moth is one of the major insect pests of hardwood trees in the East. The gypsy moth is not native to this country and was introduced into the United States in 1869 by a French scientist living in Massachusetts. The first major outbreak occurred in 1889 and since that time, gypsy moth populations have moved steadily from New England toward the southwest.

Gypsy moth caterpillars cause damage to the forest by defoliating and stressing trees. This provides an opportunity for secondary organisms to weaken the trees further and to cause mortality. When gypsy moth populations are dense, the caterpillars will feed continuously until the tree is completely stripped. Gypsy moths prefer hardwoods, but may feed on several hundred different species of trees and shrubs. In our region, the preferred food of the gypsy moth is oak.

The first reported defoliation by gypsy moths in West Virginia was in 1985 when slightly over 3,000 acres were defoliated in the Eastern Panhandle. The gypsy moth has subsequently spread down the ridges into Pendleton, Pocahontas, and Greenbrier counties, has crossed the higher mountains of Preston, Tucker, and Randolph counties, and is spreading southwest into Ritchie, Gilmer, Braxton, and Webster. As of 2003, over two million acres of hardwood forests in West Virginia have been defoliated.

In 1988, the state of West Virginia began to collaborate with private landowners in sharing the cost of aerially treating forestland with insecticides. West Virginia also participates in the national Slow the Spread program in cooperation with the U. S. Forest Service. These programs have succeeded in slowing the advance of the gypsy moth.

Amy H. Onken
U.S. Forest Service

Charles H. Haden

Judge Charles H. Haden II was born April 16, 1937, at Morgantown. He was educated in the Monongalia County schools, and at West Virginia University and the WVU College of Law. He married Priscilla Ann Miller on June 2, 1956.

Haden served in all three branches of West Virginia government. He was a member of the House of Delegates (1963–64) and state tax commissioner (1969–72). He was appointed as a state Supreme Court justice on June 21, 1972, and elected to that office as a Republican on November 7, 1972. He also served as a member of the Monongalia County Board of Education in 1967 and 1968. Haden practiced law in partnership with his father in the firm of Haden and Haden in Morgantown from 1961 to 1969. He was a member of the faculty of WVU College of Law in 1967 and 1968.

Haden was appointed U.S. district judge for the Northern and Southern Districts of West Virginia by President Gerald R. Ford, November 21, 1975. He became chief judge of the Southern District on May 13, 1982, and stepped down as chief judge, December 19, 2002. Among Haden's most noted actions as a federal judge were decisions in 1999 and 2002 restricting the practice of mountaintop removal mining. His original ruling was overturned by the fourth Circuit Court of Appeals in 2001, and his 2002 ruling was largely obviated by administrative changes by the Bush administration.

In May 2001, Judge Haden was inducted into the Order of Vandalia, the highest award given by West Virginia University. A professorship was established in his name at the WVU law school in 2004.

Judge Haden died March 20, 2004.

The Hale House

The Hale House hotel was built in Charleston in 1872 by its namesake, Dr. John P. Hale. Hale was the leader of the group responsible for having the capital moved to Charleston in 1870, and he and a group of local boosters built the first Charleston capitol building which was leased to the state.

Realizing that to accommodate the legislature the town would need a first-class hotel, Hale built the Hale House, a handsome four-story building with a mansard roof complete with dormers. One hundred feet square, it had 100 bedrooms and was billed as the finest in the state. The massive hotel was of eclectic architecture, with elements of the Italianate and Second Empire styles.

The Hale House was located in downtown Charleston, at the corner of Kanawha Street (now Kanawha Boulevard) and Hale Street (near the present South Side bridge). Dr. Hale's residence was across the street on the northeast corner. The Hale House burned in 1885 making way for a new and finer hotel, the Ruffner, which occupied the same corner until 1970.

See also John P. Hale, Ruffner Hotel

Richard A. Andre
Charleston

John P. Hale

Historian, physician, and businessman John Peter Hale was born May 1, 1824, at Ingles Ferry in the New River Valley of Virginia, the great-grandson of the legendary Mary Draper Ingles. Hale lived until 1840 at Ingles Ferry, then moved to the Kanawha Valley. In 1841–42, he attended Mercer Academy in Charleston. After studying medicine under Dr. Spicer Patrick, he attended the University of Pennsylvania School of Medicine, where he graduated in 1845.

Hale soon decided that medicine was not as interesting as the booming salt business. After consolidating various properties between Malden and Charleston by 1860, he became the owner of possibly the largest salt works in North America, supplying the thriving meat-packing center of Cincinnati. At the onset of the Civil War Hale organized an artillery battery for the Confederate Army, which fought at the Battle of Scary Creek. He served as a surgeon in the battles around Richmond in 1862.

After the salt business collapsed in the 1870s, Hale pursued other interests. Among his ventures were the first brick-making machinery in the valley, as well as the Bank of the West (organized 1863), and the first gas company in Charleston. In 1870, Hale started the first steam ferry at Charleston. At one time he owned all the ferries in the city.

Hale was a leader in having the state

John P. Hale (1824–1902).

capital moved to Charleston in 1870, and he led the group of private investors who built the first Charleston capitol building. In 1871, he became mayor. In 1872, he built his Hale House hotel, across from his residence at Kanawha and Hale streets. In the 1880s, the gray-bearded old gentleman engaged in the coal and timber business.

Perhaps the thrilling story of his great-grandmother's escape from the Shawnees in 1755 inspired Hale's lifelong devotion to history. In 1883, he published a pamphlet on Daniel Boone's years in the Kanawha Valley, and in 1886 he produced his classic book, *Trans-Allegheny Pioneers*. In 1891, he wrote his *History of the Great Kanawha Valley*. Hale helped found the West Virginia Historical and Antiquarian Society in 1890, the predecessor of the State Archives.

John P. Hale, a lifelong bachelor, died July 11, 1902. He is buried in a grave in Spring Hill Cemetery that was shaped on his orders to resemble a small mound, reflecting his interest in the ancient native cultures.

See also Charleston

Richard A. Andre
Charleston

Blind Ed Haley

James Edward "Blind Ed" Haley, born in 1883, was a legendary old-time country fiddler. His style influenced almost every musician who heard him, though he had to be heard on a street or courthouse square or other public place where he made his living. He never played on the radio or made any commercial records, but his influence on such musicians as Clark Kessinger and Georgia Slim Rutland has echoes today in modern contest fiddling.

For years, fiddle historians and tune collectors had been hearing about him throughout eastern Kentucky, southeastern Ohio, and West Virginia. Eventually, Mark Wilson and Gus Meade through fiddler J. P. Fraley and his wife, Annadeene, located Haley's son, Lawrence, in Ashland, Kentucky. Lawrence had extensive home recordings of his father. The Library of Congress was allowed to make copies and some were released on a Rounder Records album, *Parkersburg Landing*, and on two Rounder compact disk sets. Because he lived most of his life in the Ashland area he has been called a Kentucky fiddler, but Blind Ed Haley was from Harts Creek, Logan County. He died February 4, 1951.

John Hartford
Madison, Tennessee

Granville Davisson Hall

The chronicler, businessman, and state founder Granville Davisson Hall was born September 17, 1837, in Harrison County. Hall began his career as a school teacher in Harrison County when he was 17. In 1859, he left Harrison County to work in the printing office of the *Wheeling Intelligencer*. He remained in Wheeling only a few months, but in 1861 Hall returned to record the proceedings of the Wheeling Conventions. These conventions led to the separation of Virginia's northwestern counties and the creation of the state of West Virginia. Hall's notes, later published as *The Rending of Virginia*, became the main source of information on the formation of the state.

Hall served in several different positions in the new state government. He was elected the first clerk of the House of Delegates on June 20, 1863. In 1865, he was elected secretary of state and the same year also served as private secretary to West Virginia's first governor, Arthur I. Boreman. After the Civil War, Hall held several positions in the railroad industry and was eventually named president of the Louisville & Nashville Railroad.

Hall gained fame as a writer and journalist. He edited the *Wheeling Intelligencer*, and published numerous works of fiction and nonfiction. His nonfiction books included *Lee's Invasion of Northwest Virginia*, *Two Virginias*, and *The Rending of Virginia*. His fiction included *Daughter of the Elm* and *Old Gold*. Hall died June 24, 1934, at his home in Glencoe, Illinois, at the age of 96.

See also Formation of West Virginia

Christy Venham
WVU Libraries

K. K. Hall

Judge Kenneth Keller "K. K." Hall, born February 24, 1918, at Greenview, Boone County, spent 47 years on the state and federal benches.

Hall worked his way through New River State College (now WVU Institute of Technology) at Montgomery and later graduated from the West Virginia University Law School with the help of the GI Bill. During World War II he served on an aircraft carrier in the Pacific and earned 11 battle stars. He practiced law in Madison and was mayor of Madison from 1948 to 1952. By the age of 33, Hall was a circuit judge in West Virginia's 25th Judicial Circuit, serving from 1952 to 1969.

A Democrat, Hall was sworn in as a U.S. district judge for the Southern District of West Virginia on December 15, 1971, after being appointed by Republican President Richard M. Nixon. He was a controversial judge during his five years in that position, throwing out the state's outdated abortion laws and granting injunctions against a wildcat coal strike in 1976. He was appointed to the U.S. Court of Appeals for the Fourth Circuit, a 15-member tribunal that covers Maryland, North Carolina, South Carolina, Virginia, and West Virginia, in September 1976 by

President Gerald Ford. During his later years on the Fourth Circuit Court, Hall rejected the Citadel's attempt to ban women and in 1998 argued that the U.S. Food and Drug Administration should have the power to regulate tobacco.

Judge K. K. Hall died at his home in Charleston, July 8, 1999.

Tom D. Miller
Huntington

Elizabeth V. Hallanan

Judge Elizabeth Virginia Hallanan, West Virginia's first female federal court judge, was born January 10, 1925, in Charleston, the daughter of Walter Simms and Imogene Burns Hallanan. She received her A.B. degree from Morris Harvey College (now the University of Charleston) and her law degree from West Virginia University. She was a member of the State Board of Education from 1955 to 1957. Hallanan was elected to the House of Delegates in 1956 and appointed assistant commissioner of public institutions by Governor Underwood in 1957. She was also the first woman judge of a court of record in West Virginia when she became judge of the first full-time juvenile court in Kanawha County in 1959. She was a member and chairman of the Public Service Commission from 1961 to 1975.

Appointed by President Ronald Reagan in 1983 as a federal judge, she took the oath of office on November 30, 1983, and was best known for her eight-year jurisdiction of the case involving major problems in the state's child support program. Judge Hallanan was a member of the board of directors of Columbia Gas System, and of Charleston National Bank from 1975 until her resignation from both boards in 1983. She announced October 1, 1996 that she was taking senior status as a federal judge December 1, 1996.

Judge Hallanan died June 8, 2004.

Tom D. Miller
Huntington

Halliehurst

Halliehurst mansion was built in Elkins in 1890 on a 450-acre farm by Sen. Stephen B. Elkins, for whom the town is named. The house was named for his wife, Hallie Davis Elkins, who was the daughter, wife, and mother of U.S. senators.

Mrs. Elkins had admired a Rhineland castle she saw in Germany, and architect Charles T. Mott of New York City was commissioned to design Halliehurst based on the memory of his client. The house is made of wood with heavy timber framing throughout. Interior wall surfaces are plaster on wooden lath. The first floor exterior walls are covered with German drop siding, and upper stories are finished with wood shingles.

Halliehurst defies connection with any architectural style except possibly the Shingle Style. It certainly gives the im-

pression of a castle, when viewed as a whole, with its collection of towers of various diameters and heights. Its signature feature is the great south tower embraced by its two-story porch overlooking the south lawn, city of Elkins, and the mountain ridge beyond. Flanking the tower are columned wrap-around lower porches. All porches are accented with roof edge balustrades. The main roof was originally covered with slate.

First floor interior rooms are spacious, designed for the social events for which Hallie Elkins was well known. The parlor, dining room, library, and great hall are beautifully appointed with woodwork and trim of West Virginia hardwoods. Fireplaces are wide, and elegantly trimmed with tile, wood, and stone.

Once a happy family residence, and the site for political and business gatherings for one of the college founders, Halliehurst was the first building on the relocated Davis & Elkins College campus. Since restoration, it has served as a social center and college administration building, housing the office of the president and other officials of the college. Graceland, the Henry Gassaway Davis mansion, stands nearby.

See also Davis & Elkins College, Stephen B. Elkins, Graceland

Paul D. Marshall
Blufton, South Carolina

Hamlin

Hamlin, population 1,119, is the county seat of Lincoln County. Hamlin is located on the Mud River on State Route 3. The place was first settled by David Stephenson, who erected a cabin around 1802. The town was chartered by the Virginia General Assembly in 1853. It was named after the Hamlin Chapel, itself named for Methodist Bishop Leonidas Hamlin.

During the Civil War, Hamlin was occupied and traversed by troops from both armies. In late March 1863, Confederate Gen. Albert G. Jenkins occupied the town en route to Point Pleasant. After the war, in 1867, Hamlin was chosen as the county seat of newly created Lincoln County. A two-story, red brick courthouse was constructed around 1875, with a "substantial brick jail" built behind it after the original jail burned in 1886. By the mid-1880s, Hamlin was reported to be a prosperous town with five general merchandise stores, one grocery store, two millinery stores, two hotels, a grade school, a flour mill and a sawmill, a post office, one church, three doctors, six lawyers, and about 30 houses.

Hamlin's 20th-century history was marked by a disastrous courthouse fire in 1909, the construction of a new courthouse in 1911, and the construction of a modern courthouse in the 1960s. Carroll High School was lost to fire in 1949 and replaced by Hamlin High. A public library was built in the late 1990s.

See also Lincoln County

Brandon Ray Kirk
Ferrellsburg

Hammered Dulcimer

See Dulcimer.

Edden Hammons

Musician Edwin "Edden" Hammons, born February 28, 1875, in Pocahontas County, is remembered as one of the finest traditional fiddlers to have come from West Virginia. Hammons was a subsistence farmer and hunter, like many others at the time, who relied on his wits and music to earn a few dollars. Tales are told that he would rather fiddle than work.

Edden was a member of the extended Hammons family, known for its music and traditional ways, which had migrated into the Webster-Pocahontas area just before the Civil War. Edden and his wife, Betty Shaffer Hammons, raised seven children. Folklorist and West Virginia University professor Louis Chappell recorded Edden in a Richwood hotel room in 1947. The resulting 52 tunes document a frontier fiddling tradition with links to the Old World. Most of these tunes were released as record albums by West Virginia University Press.

Family recollections say the Hammons clan is descended from an Edwin Hammons who emigrated from Belfast, Northern Ireland, in the 18th century. Edden Hammons died September 7, 1955.

See also Hammons Family

Paul Gartner
Sod

Gerald Milnes, *Play of a Fiddle*, 1999; *The Edden Hammons Collection, Volume 1*, 1999 and *Volume 2*, 2000, compact disc recordings.

Hammons Family

The Hammons family of Pocahontas County is a family of traditionalists whose knowledge of music, storytelling, and woods lore have made them cultural guides and mentors since the late 19th century. A century-old account describes patriarch Jesse Hammons and his sons as expert woodsmen, and his son, Edden, as a talented fiddler. A short story in G. D. McNeill's 1940 book, *The Last Forest*, features a character inspired by Edden, and his fiddling was recorded by West Virginia University folklorist Louis Chappell in 1947.

A broader study of the family in the early 1970s focused on Jesse Hammons's grandchildren, Maggie Hammons Parker, Sherman Hammons, and Burl Hammons. The study led in 1973 to a Library of Congress double recording and a Rounder Records release. Both contain instrumental tunes, ballads, songs, stories, and lore; both accompanying booklets include early and modern photo-

graphs, and the Library of Congress booklet includes a family history constructed from documentary sources and the Hammonses' own narration.

The family's instrumental music includes a distinctive regional repertory of fiddle tunes forged on the early Appalachian frontier, as well as a banjo repertory (both picked and downstroked) of later vintage. Their singing tradition ranges from ancient British ballads through hundreds of American ballads and songs. All their music reflects a striking cultural synthesis, combining the artful irregularity and treble tension of the ancient British solo style with other Appalachian elements of Northern European, African-American, and possibly American Indian origin. Their storytelling is equally striking, featuring a distinctive rhetorical style and reflecting a fascination with the mysterious combined with skepticism about supernatural causes. Since the family subsisted on hunting, logging, trapping, and ginseng gathering for nearly two centuries, their woods lore was encyclopedic.

The fact that the Hammonses evoke the wilderness of the early Appalachian frontier fueled a growing interest in the family during the late 20th century. Thanks to documentary dissemination and a stream of visitors, they became symbols and resources for the next generation to tap. Their traditions have attracted many people from beyond their community and state, while influencing West Virginians such as Pocahontas County native Dwight Diller, who contributed to the Library of Congress publication, produced additional recordings, and learned and taught many Hammons family traditions. Many West Virginians feel an admiration for and connectedness to the Hammonses, perhaps because the family maintained in such full measure and with such grace cultural traditions that others have preserved but sketchily.

See also Folklore, Folk Music, Edden Hammons

Alan Jabbour
Library of Congress

John Cuthbert and Alan Jabbour, eds., *The Edden Hammons Collection: Historic Recordings of Traditional Fiddle Music from the Louis Watson Chappell Archive*, 1999; Carl Fleischhauer and Alan Jabbour, eds., *The Hammons Family: The Traditions of a West Virginia Family and Their Friends*, Rounder CD, 1998; Gerald Milnes, *Play of a Fiddle*, 1999.

Hampshire County

Hampshire, West Virginia's oldest county, is located in the Eastern Panhandle west of the Blue Ridge and Shenandoah River and east of the Allegheny Mountains, in the geological region known as the Ridge and Valley Province. Bordered to the north by the Potomac River (and the Potomac's North Branch), Hampshire County is crossed by the Potomac's South Branch and the Little Cacapon and Cacapon rivers, major Potomac tributaries. Another stream, the North River, flows across Hampshire before joining the Cacapon near the Morgan County line. All flow southwest to northeast, toward the main Potomac, which is born at the confluence of the North Branch and South Branch in Hampshire County's northwest corner.

Between these river valleys stand long ridges, the most prominent being South Branch Mountain and North River Mountain. The highest point in Hampshire County, on South Branch Mountain, is about 3,200 feet above sea level, while the county's lowest elevation, where the Cacapon River crosses into Morgan County, is 510 feet. Natural features include Capon Springs, a mineral spring and resort; Caudy's Castle, a spectacular rock formation overhanging the Cacapon River; and Ice Mountain, at the base of which ice can be found year-round some

FAST FACTS ABOUT HAMPSHIRE COUNTY

Founded: 1754
Land in square miles: 641.4
Population: 20,203
Percentage minorities: 2.0%
Percentage rural: 100%
Median age: 38.5
Percentage 65 and older: 14.6%
Birth rate per 1,000 population: 11.4
Median household income: $31,666
High school graduate or higher: 71.3%
Bachelor's degree or higher: 11.3%
Home ownership: 81.1%
Median home value: $78,300

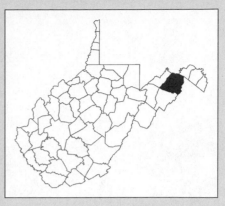

This information is from the 2000 U.S. Census. In 2000, West Virginia as a whole had 5 percent minorities, a median age of 38.9, median household income of $29,696, and a 75.2 percent home ownership rate.

A Hampshire County landscape.

years. Several protected natural areas lie within Hampshire County's boundaries, including Nathaniel Mountain and Short Mountain wildlife management areas. Other protected areas include Springfield, Edwards Run, Fort Mill Ridge, and a small portion of George Washington National Forest.

Present Hampshire County was first visited by Europeans about 1725, when explorers followed the Potomac River upstream from Harpers Ferry to the lower valley of the South Branch. Settlers were constructing homesteads by the mid-1730s. By 1748, approximately 200 people were living at Pearsall's Flats, the eventual site of Romney. In the early 1750s, Fort Pearsall was constructed nearby, protecting settlers from Indian attack and housing a school and a church.

At this time, the South Branch Valley was part of a larger estate claimed by

Thomas, Sixth Lord Fairfax. According to George Washington, who worked as a young man as a surveyor for Fairfax, many of the settlers were German. Settlers lived as Fairfax's tenants, though some refused to pay the annual fees known as quitrents. The settlers found no native inhabitants, as the area was then used by tribes as a seasonal hunting ground and not for permanent occupation. Earlier, prehistoric people had lived in what is now Hampshire County, a fact evident in the large mound in Romney's Indian Mound Cemetery, probably constructed by members of the Hopewell Culture between A.D. 500 and 1000.

Hampshire was created in 1754 through an act of the Virginia General Assembly. Fairfax gave the county its name, allegedly because he thought that the hogs produced there rivaled the fine hogs of Hampshire, England. Formed from parts of Au-

gusta and Frederick counties, Hampshire was the great mother county of the Eastern Panhandle, later providing the territory for all or part of five other West Virginia counties (Grant, Hardy, Mineral, Morgan, and Pendleton). Fairfax established the county seat of Romney, which shares credit with Shepherdstown as West Virginia's oldest incorporated town. (They were chartered the same day in 1762.) In 1777, Hampshire County encompassed approximately 2,800 square miles, on which could be found about 3,500 inhabitants. Fairfax's lands were confiscated by the state of Virginia after the Revolutionary War and redistributed to many small-tract landowners. Subsequently, the county's population increased rapidly.

The French and Indian War was the first of several conflicts to disrupt life in Hampshire County. In the mid-1750s, Indians (mostly Shawnee), encouraged by the French, attacked county settlements. Settlers either sought safety in nearby fortifications, including Fort Pearsall, Fort Cox (near the mouth of the Little Cacapon), Fort Capon (near Forks-of-Cacapon), and Fort Edwards (near present Capon Bridge), or fled eastward to the Shenandoah Valley. By the late 1750s, the colonial army had secured the county's settlement areas.

During the Revolutionary War, while most Hampshire residents supported the rebellion, some recent immigrants from England refused to raise arms against the king. A number of Tories living along the upper South Branch, including parts of present Hardy and Pendleton counties, banded together and threatened to join the British army. A nearby patriot militia quelled this uprising by overpowering the group and imprisoning its leaders.

Hampshire County figured significantly in the Civil War. While the county's westernmost section was largely pro-Union (in 1866 that section broke off and became Mineral County), most Hampshire Countians sided with the Confederacy. Divided loyalties, along with the presence of the Baltimore & Ohio Railroad at the county's northern border, rendered Hampshire a fiercely contested territory. The frequent presence of Union and Confederate troops led to continual clashing, including major skirmishes at Hanging Rocks and Blue's Gap. Romney, owing to its strategic location on the much-used Northwestern Turnpike (now U.S. 50), changed hands many times during the war, with the total number usually set at 56. In June 1866, Romney's Indian Mound Cemetery hosted one of the nation's first grave-decorating ceremonies honoring the Confederate dead. In September 1867, the same cemetery became the site of an early monument for fallen Confederate soldiers.

Romney is Hampshire's county seat and principal municipality. Points of interest include the Wilson-Woodrow-Mytinger House, built about 1770 and now the town's oldest surviving building; Literary Hall, the 1870 library and debate center for Romney's Literary Society, which was founded in 1819; and the West Virginia Schools for the Deaf and Blind (established in 1870).

Reduced in size by the creation of new counties during the 18th and 19th centuries, Hampshire County today incorporates 641.4 square miles. With a stable population of approximately 12,000 residents through the first seven decades of the 20th century, the county by 2000 claimed 20,203 residents, which reflects the recent trend of immigration and second-home ownership of people from the eastern megalopolis. Still largely rural, Hampshire County maintains an economy based largely upon agriculture (livestock, fruit, grain, and hay), logging and wood products, and tourism. The landscape still shows evidence of now-defunct industries, such as the iron ore furnace at Bloomery, in operation from 1833 to 1881.

Two West Virginia governors, John Jeremiah Jacob (1871–77) and Herman Guy Kump (1933–37), were Hampshire County natives. Governor John J. Cornwell (1917–21) grew up there from the age of two, and is buried in Indian Mound Cemetery.

See also Alexander Spotswood

Ted Olson
East Tennessee State University
Selden W. Brannon, *Historic Hampshire*, 1976; Hu Maxwell and H. L. Swisher, *History of Hampshire County, West Virginia, From Its Earliest Settlement to the Present*, 1972; West Virginia Writers' Project, *Historic Romney, 1762–1937*, 1937.

Hampshire Review

The *Hampshire Review* is the oldest business in the oldest county of West Virginia, and one of the oldest newspapers in the state. It is a weekly paper, started in 1884 by C. F. Poland. John J. and William Cornwell bought the *Review* in 1890. The two brothers absorbed a competitor, the *South Branch Intelligencer*, and added its founding date, 1829, to the *Review's* masthead.

John J. Cornwell was a state senator from 1899 to 1907, governor from 1917 to 1921, and chief counsel and a director of the B&O Railroad, while continuing to write editorials for the family paper. Upon his death in 1953, his grandson, John Ailes, became editor of the *Review*, and Ailes's wife became associate editor. Mrs. Ailes retired in 1988 and Mr. Ailes died in 1991, but the paper is still controlled by Cornwell descendants. The *Hampshire Review* is supposed to have hired the first three women in Hampshire County to work outside the household other than in domestic work. The newspaper is published on Wednesdays at Romney and focuses on local news. The circulation was 6,950 in 2004.

See also John Jacob Cornwell

Tanya Godfrey
Moorefield
Bill Moulden, "In The Family: A Hundred Years at the Hampshire Review," *Goldenseal*, Spring 1990.

Rimfire Hamrick

Eli C. "Rimfire" Hamrick, the Mountain State's prototypical mountaineer, was born in Bergoo, Webster County, March 28, 1868. He was one of the best woodsmen of his time and was friend and guide to the coal and lumber barons who used the mountains for hunting expeditions. Originally thought to be the model for the "Mountaineer" statue on the grounds of the state capitol, he later revealed that his younger brother, Ellis, had also posed.

In 1907, Hamrick was employed by the Webster Springs Hotel as a guide and handyman. One of his jobs was to kill and dress chickens for the hotel kitchen. According to legend, Rimfire came by his nickname when asked how he killed the chickens; he replied, "With a rimfire rifle, by God."

About 1910, Hamrick opened a jewelry, watch repair, and gunsmith shop in Webster Springs. In 1912, he was appointed county game and fish warden. Three years later he was appointed fire warden, eventually taking charge of the fire tower on Turkey Mountain, which he supervised for several years. In 1932, he ran for the legislature as a Republican in the 10th Senatorial District but lost to Albert G. Mathews.

Like many West Virginians, Rimfire Hamrick was never a man with only one trade. He worked at many things, but his greatest passion was hunting and roaming the woods. He died in his native Bergoo, April 1, 1945.

Jacqueline G. Goodwin
Pennsylvania State Education Association

Jim Comstock, ed., *West Virginia Heritage Encyclopedia*, 1976; Harry P. Sturm and H.G. Rhawn, *Rimfire: West Virginia's Typical Mountaineer*, 1967.

Hancock County

Hancock is the most northern and the smallest of West Virginia's counties. It encompasses only 88.6 square miles. The Ohio River marks Hancock's northern and western borders with the state of Ohio. Pennsylvania is to the east and Brooke County to the south. Elevations in Hancock County range from 666 feet to 1,337 feet. The Ohio serves as an important transportation artery. CSX is the major railroad line. U.S. 22 bisects the southern end of the county on an east-west axis and is the major roadway. U.S. 30, the old Lincoln Highway and the first transcontinental road for motor vehicles, crosses the northern tip of the county. The principal state road, State Route 2, parallels the Ohio River, connecting Hancock County to Wheeling and points south.

Hancock County's population was 32,667 in 2000, making it one of the state's most densely populated counties. Hancock ranks high in per capita income and the educational level of its citizens.

With 20,411 residents, Weirton is the largest city. Weirton is situated in the extreme southern part of the county, with a small portion of the city in neighboring Brooke County. Founded in 1909 by Weirton Steel, it became the nation's largest unincorporated city, a distinction it retained until 1947 when voters approved a city charter. Weirton is the only American city whose boundaries touch two other state borders, Pennsylvania on the east and Ohio on the west.

Chester is the second most populous town in Hancock County, with 2,592 people. Incorporated in 1907, Chester is located at the northern tip of the county. The county seat, New Cumberland, population 1,099, received its charter from

FAST FACTS ABOUT HANCOCK COUNTY

Founded: 1848
Land in square miles: 88.6
Population: 32,667
Percentage minorities: 3.6%
Percentage rural: 33.9%
Median age: 41.7
Percentage 65 and older: 18.4%
Birth rate per 1,000 population: 10.5
Median household income: $33,759
High school graduate or higher: 82.9%
Bachelor's degree or higher: 11.5%
Home ownership: 77.1%
Median home value: $70,500

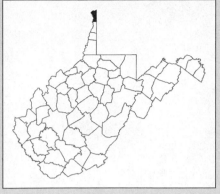

This information is from the 2000 U.S. Census. In 2000, West Virginia as a whole had 5 percent minorities, a median age of 38.9, median household income of $29,696, and a 75.2 percent home ownership rate.

Tomlinson Run State Park, Hancock County.

the state of Virginia in 1849. Hancock County has two sizable unincorporated communities, Newell and New Manchester. Newell has a population of 1,602 and is the home of the Homer Laughlin China Company, one of the county's largest employers. Tomlinson Run State Park is in Hancock County.

Hancock County has lost population since 1980. This trend reflects declining employment opportunities, particularly in industry. Earlier in the 20th century, the opposite was true. As manufacturing jobs proliferated, people moved to Hancock County, and the population grew at a steady, sometimes spectacular, rate. The county population peaked in 1980 at 40,418. Weirton, whose highest population was 28,201 in 1960, had lost more than a fourth of that total by 2000.

In the 18th century ownership of the upper Ohio Valley was contested among the European colonial powers of Great Britain and France, the colonies of Virginia and Pennsylvania, and the Indians of the surrounding region. The British eradicated French claims in the French and Indian War, which ended in 1763, but brutal fighting with the Indians continued into the 1790s. In the midst of this period, the first documented permanent settlements in what is today Hancock County were established. Harmon Greathouse arrived in 1771, and in 1776 John Holliday was operating a trading post at Hollidays Cove. The Virginia General Assembly created Brooke County from northern Ohio County in 1797; and on January 15, 1848, under the leadership of Joseph Bambrick, an Irish immigrant and member of the Virginia legislature, the northern half of Brooke became Hancock County. The county was named for John Hancock.

Though Virginia was a slave state, slavery scarcely existed in Hancock County.

The 1850 census listed three slaves, and in 1860 there were only two slaves in a county population of 4,445. Hancock voters overwhelmingly rejected the Virginia secession ordinance of 1861 (23–743) and later supported the creation of West Virginia by a tally of 263–67. More than 400 residents served in the Union army during the Civil War.

The county economy in the late 19th century remained very largely agricultural, with some transportation improvements and a few manufacturing and mining establishments. The first railroad received its charter in 1860. Abundant clay deposits led to the formation of firms producing bricks and pottery. An early natural gas well was drilled in 1862, and by 1864 natural gas was used to produce carbon black for printing ink. Intensive industrial development did not begin until the early 20th century, when two new enterprises transformed the county's economic base.

The Homer Laughlin China Company of East Liverpool, Ohio, purchased the Newell farm in 1902 across the Ohio River in Hancock County. At Newell, the company built the world's largest pottery, manufacturing dishes for household, hotel, and restaurant use. It began production of its popular "Fiesta" tableware in the 1930s. In 1909, Ernest T. Weir established Weirton Steel and the town of Weirton about one mile north of Hollidays Cove. Coincidentally, one of the first iron furnaces west of the Allegheny Mountains, the Peter Tarr Furnace, had operated in proximity to the site of the new mills from the 1790s until at least the second decade of the 19th century. Tarr produced iron cannonballs for Commodore Oliver Perry's successful campaign against the British on Lake Erie during the War of 1812.

By the 1950s, Weirton Steel had be-

come the state's largest employer and taxpayer, generating jobs for more than 13,000 and sending tens of millions in tax revenue to the state capital of Charleston. In 1984, Weirton Steel became the nation's largest employee-owned company with the establishment of an Employee Stock Ownership Plan. In 2004, International Steel Group purchased Weirton Steel, marking the end of worker ownership at the company.

Recreational tourism is Hancock County's growth industry in the early 21st century. Mountaineer Race Track, a greyhound racing facility, expanded into a major gambling complex in the 1990s. In 2003, Mountaineer was the county's second-largest employer.

See also Homer Laughlin China Company, Weirton, Weirton Steel Buyout

Richard P. Lizza
West Liberty State College
Peter Boyd, *History of Northern West Virginia Panhandle*, 1927; David T. Javersak, *History of Weirton, West Virginia*, 1999.

Handcrafts

The handcraft tradition in West Virginia, an integral part of the mountain culture, is rooted in history and necessity. The seeds of our state's arts and crafts tradition were sown when the Appalachian region was settled in the late 1700s and early 1800s, primarily by the English, Irish, Scotch, and Germans.

Many decorative arts, such as painting, drawing, and print-making, came to this country from Britain and other parts of Europe, but in the early days were practiced primarily by the upper classes who settled along the coast. The more practical craft skills brought over the mountains by Appalachia's immigrants flourished through necessity; knowing them meant survival. Practically everything the early settlers had, they made with their hands.Craftsmanship was a strong factor in the work of these early citizens of Western Virginia, but practicality was uppermost in the makers' minds. This is not to say that the early handcrafts were not beautiful, for they often were. Both elements, functionality and beauty, combined to make an object of pleasure and satisfaction for the maker and the user. Blacksmiths forged essential items, including tools and hardware, but they also formed decorative fireplace tools and wrought iron candlesticks. Tinsmiths fashioned kitchen utensils, including spoons, forks, and cups, as well as delicately pierced lanterns. Leathersmiths tanned hides and made carrying sacks, harnesses, saddle bags, belts, and even the blacksmiths' bellows; but they also used their talents to make beautiful vests and jackets.

Craftsmen turned natural materials found or grown in abundance into a wide variety of products. They cut timber to make furniture, fences, and log cabins and outbuildings. They whittled wood into bowls, cooking utensils of all types, musical instruments, gun stocks, and toys for their children. They split oak into thin strips, soaked them, and wove them into baskets. Brooms were made of straw or corn husks, gathered into a bundle and tied to a handle. Vegetables and nuts were boiled to make dyes. Carding wool, spinning the yarn, and weaving it into cloth were a part of the pioneer woman's work. Linen was made of the fibers of flax, whose seed was milled into linseed oil.

The needle skills brought to the mountains by the women settlers provided clothing, table linens, and blankets. Often made of scraps from worn-out clothes or left-over cloth, padded with worn-out blankets or cotton batting, and closely stitched together in layers, their quilts evolved into works of art, as decorative as they were practical. Today's most precious heirlooms are the woven coverlets and patchwork or applique quilts of that era.

Soap was made by boiling water, lye, and grease. The mixture was boiled until it dissolved and became smooth, then it was poured into a shallow pan, allowed to harden, and cut into cakes of soap. The lye itself was made from the drippings that result from pouring water over wood ashes. Candles were fashioned from tallow or beeswax and hardened in metal forms. Coopers bent wood into barrels for storage of grains and whiskey.

No doubt in some places handcrafts have been practiced without interruption since their arrival on our shores, but by 1890 many of the old ways were abandoned in much of America. However, in West Virginia, as in much of Appalachia, these skills persisted as part of daily life longer than in other areas because of the relative isolation of the region.

In the 1960s, another wave of immigrants to West Virginia, representing the counterculture back-to-the-land movement, inadvertently helped to rescue many endangered crafts and old ways of living. These were young people, often from middle-class backgrounds. At the time they came to West Virginia seeking cheap land and a simpler lifestyle, they thought they were joining the mountain people's lifestyle. Instead, by becoming students of the Appalachian culture, they helped to save much of its handcraft tradition from extinction.

In the late 1960s and early 1970s, handcraft cooperatives were formed across West Virginia as economic development projects during the War on Poverty. Often formed under the auspices of various state or federal agencies, the co-ops encouraged artisans to market their handcrafts collectively. The Mountain State Art & Craft Fair, started in 1963 as part of West Virginia's Centennial celebration, showcased the work of many of these craft cooperatives as well as that of individual artisans. The movement flourished with the encouragement of the state Commerce Department and later the Department of Culture and History. Today Tamarack, an arts and crafts showcase on the West Virginia Turnpike at Beckley, serves as a sales outlet for many artisans, as do MountainMade Foundation and other retailers. There is a robust handcrafts community in West Virginia, producing wares of excellent workmanship. These crafts sell at premium prices, often well above the cost of equivalent manufactured items, as yesterday's necessities ironically are transformed into the luxuries of today.

See also Back-to-the-Land Movement
Carter T. Seaton
Huntington

Allen H. Eaton, *Handicrafts of the Southern Highlands*, 1973; Rachel Nash Law and Cynthia W. Taylor, *Appalachian White Oak Basketmaking*, 1991.

Hanging Rock Observatory

One of West Virginia's best locations to view the annual migration of birds of prey is the Hanging Rock Raptor Migration Observatory in Jefferson National Forest on Peters Mountain in Monroe County. The observatory is a tower perched on the rocks at an elevation of 3,800 feet above sea level. The original tower was built in the 1930s by the Civilian Conservation Corps and was manned by forest fire spotters until the early 1970s. Vandals destroyed the old tower in 1996. Using the original construction plans, the Forest Service had the tower rebuilt. Peters Mountain, a prominent northeast-southwest ridge, intercepts a major migratory route. Migrating raptors follow the ridge past the tower each fall. The best time to visit will vary from year to year. The peak of the broad-winged hawk migration is usually September 16–21. The peak for sharp-shinned hawks is usually early October. Golden eagles and red-tailed hawks are best seen in mid-November.

Jim Phillips
Pipestem State Park

Nancy Hanks

Nancy Hanks (Lincoln), the mother of Abraham Lincoln, was probably born February 5, 1784. Though primary records relating to her early life do not exist, she is believed to have been born in Hampshire County, Virginia, on Mikes Run at the bottom of New Creek Mountain in what is now Mineral County, West Virginia. Around the time of her birth her grandfather, Joseph Hanks, acquired 108 acres of land and moved to that location. The Hanks family later moved via the Wilderness Trail into Kentucky. Nancy, apparently illegitimate, lived most of her life with her mother Lucy's family.

On June 12, 1806, Nancy Hanks married Thomas Lincoln in Kentucky. They had three children together, including Abraham. In 1816, the Lincolns moved to Spencer County, Indiana. There Nancy died from "milk sickness," an illness contracted by drinking milk from a cow that has grazed on snakeroot, October 5, 1818. She was 35 years old.

In 1929, Governor Conley appointed a committee to investigate the claim that Hanks had been born in West Virginia on Mikes Run. On September 21, 1929, the commission concluded that she had, based on the evidence of Lincoln biographer William E. Barton of Massachusetts. By 1933, the state had erected a replica cabin and stone memorial identifying the site as the birthplace of Nancy Hanks. In 1966, questions once again were raised about the site's authenticity and Governor Smith concluded there was no concrete evidence to determine with any certainty where Nancy Hanks was born.

Cathy Hershberger Miller
State Archives

Alberta Pierson Hannum

Writer Alberta Pierson Hannum was born August 3, 1906, in Condit, Ohio, and spent the greater part of her life in the Wheeling area. A graduate of Ohio State University (B.A., 1927) with graduate study at Columbia University in 1928, Hannum was the wife of Robert Fulton Hannum, the president of Fostoria Glass Company. Her works showed an early interest in life in the Appalachians, beginning with her first novel *Thursday April* (1931) and continuing through *Roseanna McCoy* (1947) and the memoir, *Look Back with Love: A Recollection of the Blue Ridge* (1969).

Hannum's other novels include *The Hills Step Lightly* (1934), *The Gods and One* (1941), *The Mountain People* (1943), and two books set outside the mountains, *Spin a Silver Dollar: The Story of a Desert Trading Post* (1945) and a novel about Navajos, *Paint the Wind* (1958). *Roseanna McCoy*, about the Hatfield-McCoy feud, was released by RKO General as a motion picture in 1949. *Spin a Silver Dollar* was released as a radio play in 1946 and published as *The Blue House* by the U.S. Information Agency in 1970. Known the world over through translation of her works into Italian, Korean, Laotian, Russian, and Yugoslavian, Hannum died on February 18, 1985, in Arlington, Virginia.

Debra K. Sullivan
Charleston Catholic High School

Happy Retreat

The house known as Happy Retreat is located in Charles Town, Jefferson County, a half-mile south of the intersection of U.S. 340 and State Route 9. A significant example of 18th-century and 19th-century Classical Revival architecture, it was built and occupied by Col. Charles Washington, the founder and namesake of Charles Town and brother of George Washington.

Charles Washington built Happy Retreat in 1780 as a house of two wings connected by a covered runway. He died before his plans were fulfilled, but the intended center structure was added when it was purchased by Judge Isaac R. Douglas in 1837. Douglas renamed the house Mordington, after his home in Scotland. The earlier name was restored in 1945.

The original stone kitchen and adjoining smokehouse may predate the original wings of the house. An octagonal white schoolhouse, similar to the one in the garden at Mount Vernon, still survives. The primary unit is joined to the flanking wings by five-foot-long brick connections, and is projected about eight feet in front of them. Both wings have north-south gables and a brick cornice to the extreme east and west.

George Washington visited Happy Retreat, and Revolutionary Gen. Daniel Morgan met there with Washington during one of the visits. In the west wing, Charles Washington laid out plans for Charles Town. Charles Washington died there in 1799 and is buried on the estate. Happy Retreat was added to the National Register of Historic Places in 1973.

See also Charles Washington, Washington Family

William D. Theriault
Bakerton

Della Brown Taylor Hardman

Artist Della Brown Taylor Hardman was born May 20, 1922, in Charleston. She was educated at Garnet High School, West Virginia State College, and Boston University. She served for 30 years as an art professor at West Virginia State College. Hardman traveled and studied widely, including at colleges in West Africa and Montreal. She finished her Ph.D. at the age of 72 at Kent State University. Her dissertation was about William Edward Scott, the second black artist to graduate from the Art Institute of Chicago.

Hardman worked in fabric and ceramics. Her work has been exhibited in galleries ranging from the Huntington Galleries (now Huntington Museum of Art) to a showing in West Africa. Hardman is considered one of the most influential female and African-American artists from West Virginia. She later moved to Massachusetts, and was awarded the first Humanitarian Award from the Martha's Vineyard NAACP for her community service. The Della Brown Taylor Art Gallery in the John W. Davis Fine Arts Building on the campus of West Virginia State University was named in her honor.

FAST FACTS ABOUT HARDY COUNTY

Founded: 1786
Land in square miles: 575.5
Population: 12,669
Percentage minorities: 3.1%
Percentage rural: 100%
Median age: 38.9
Percentage 65 and older: 14.9%
Birth rate per 1,000 population: 11.8
Median household income: $31,846
High school graduate or higher: 70.3%
Bachelor's degree or higher: 9.4%
Home ownership: 80.5%
Median home value: $74,700

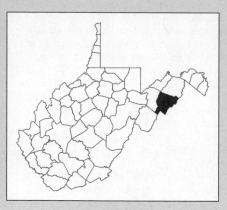

This information is from the 2000 U.S. Census. In 2000, West Virginia as a whole had 5 percent minorities, a median age of 38.9, median household income of $29,696, and a 75.2 percent home ownership rate.

Della Brown Taylor Hardman died December 13, 2005, at Martha's Vineyard.

D. B. Shawver
Charleston

Hardy County

With an area of 575.5 square miles, Hardy County is divided by South Branch Mountain. Four rivers penetrate its boundaries. On the west lies the South Branch of the Potomac, which is joined by the South Fork at Moorefield and flows north from there through the Trough and into neighboring Hampshire County. On the east is the Lost River, which disappears under Sandy Ridge and comes out as the Cacapon River. The rivers all flow north and eventually join the main Potomac River. Located in the Eastern Panhandle, Hardy County is bounded by Virginia on the east, Hampshire County on the north, Grant County on the west, and Pendleton County on the south.

Formed in 1786, Hardy County had been part of Hampshire County. The county was named for Samuel Hardy, a member of the Virginia state legislature, lieutenant governor, and a delegate to the Continental Congress. Eighty years later, Grant County broke away from Hardy in 1866. There are two incorporated towns: Moorefield, the county seat, formed in 1777, and Wardensville in the Capon Valley, chartered in 1832 and named for Jacob Warden. Hardy County had a population of 12,669 in 2000.

Hardy County was described as a borderland by historian Alvin E. Moore, who said the county was one of the last frontiers before settlers began crossing the Alleghenies, and then again during the conflict between North and South.

The Shawnees left cleared land in the Indian Old Fields. Early settlers were predominantly Scotch-Irish, German, English, and Dutch. They cleared land and built homes on disputed holdings of Virginia's so-called Northern Neck, those lands claimed by both Lord Fairfax and by the colony of Virginia. In 1748, Fairfax sent a survey party to the South Branch Manor. In that group was 16-year-old George Washington, who left an account of the Trough and other experiences of the trip in his journal.

The area saw bloodshed between the Indians and settlers, between the Tories and patriots of the Revolution, and during the Civil War. Besides providing men to fight, Hardy County was an important source of livestock and grain, helping to support the armies in all these conflicts.

Hardy County was divided in its allegiances during the Civil War, with those favoring the Union splitting off to form Grant County soon afterwards. Southern sympathizers joined McNeill's Rangers, a guerrilla band formed by Capt. John Hanson McNeill. Toward the end of the war, in their most daring raid, the Rangers, then led by McNeill's son, Jesse, captured two Union generals, George Crook and Benjamin Kelly, from among thousands of federal troops garrisoned in Cumberland, Maryland. They spirited the generals south to Richmond while being chased by embarrassed federal troops.

Hardy County has a portion of the George Washington National Forest within its boundaries, as well as Lost River State Park, which was constructed by the Civilian Conservation Corps in the late 1930s. The park is also the location of the Lee Sulphur Spring, one of the early spas, where the family of Robert E. Lee's father, Lighthorse Harry Lee, built a cabin and partook of the waters. The Lee cabin is still standing. Trout Pond, located in the National Forest, is West Virginia's only natural lake, although only two acres in size. An added attraction is Rock Cliff Lake, a 17-acre man-made lake in the same area. Canoe and kayak enthusiasts enjoy going through the Trough on the South Branch. This natural cut

Hardy County is farm country.

sues that must be understood as Hardy County moves into the new century.

Phoebe Heishman
Moorefield

Richard K. MacMaster, *The History of Hardy County 1786–1986*, 1986; Alvin E. Moore, *History of Hardy County of the Borderland*, 1963.

Hardy County Heritage Weekend

Hardy County Heritage Weekend began in 1953 when Mill Island, a private house built in 1840, was opened to the public and an offering was taken to raise money for the Hardy County Public Library. Initially a spring homes and gardens tour, the event moved to the last full weekend in September. Now the annual event encompasses the gracious antebellum houses of the area, traditional crafts, food, music, and Civil War reenactments.

Heritage Weekend is still one of the few occasions when tournament riding, or medieval-style jousting, is demonstrated. The Knights of the South Branch organized in 1957 to revive the sport, which had once been popular in the South. Jousters balance a nine-foot pointed lance while riding full tilt on horseback, attempting to capture three suspended rings which are as small as a half-inch in diameter.

As the event grew, money raised was distributed not just to the public library, but also toward historic preservation and restoration projects and educational programs in the county. Privately owned homes, some dating back to the late 18th century, are the highlight of the weekend. Hardy County has 19 houses and other buildings that have been named to the National Register of Historic Places. Many are open during Heritage Weekend. The National Register also recognizes the Moorefield Historic District, which can be seen on walking tours.

Phoebe Heishman
Moorefield

"John Hardy"

"John Hardy" is an anonymous murder ballad recounting actual events from the life of an African-American railroad worker who killed a man over money in a drunken gambling dispute at Shawnee Coal Camp (later called Eckman) near Keystone in McDowell County. Hardy was found guilty by a jury, sentenced, and hanged from a wooden gallows erected for the occasion in Welch on January 19, 1894. Earlier that day, Hardy was baptized and, before his execution, made a brief speech expressing sorrow for his misdeed and hope for an afterlife.

The ballad probably originated in McDowell County but moved quickly beyond the state's borders. Less than two decades after the hanging, published variants appeared in North Carolina and Kentucky as well as in West Virginia. As the song was transmitted, text changes occurred,

in the mountains is also home to bald eagles. The river offers trout and bass fishing. The South Branch Valley Railroad, a state-owned railroad, was purchased from the Baltimore & Ohio Railroad to supply the multi-million dollar poultry industry with grain, and is headquartered in Moorefield.

Hardy County is also home to Eastern West Virginia Community & Technical College.

Beginning in 1877, Hardy County, in particular, Moorefield, was hard hit by a series of floods. Record floods came in 1912, 1924, 1936, and 1949, the worst of these being the 1949 flood. A series of flood prevention dams were built on the South Fork starting in the 1960s, and

then on the Lost River watershed in the 1990s. The most devastating flood in the county's history hit in 1985, tearing away bridges, roads, railroads, homes, businesses, and people's lives. In the mid-1990s, work began on a levee around Moorefield. Before it was completed, two more floods hit in 1996.

The county's newest challenge is the construction of Corridor H, a four-lane road which will travel from east to west and eventually connect Hardy to the central part of the state on the west and to Virginia on the east. Planning and zoning regulations have never been a priority and now must be considered. At the same time, historic preservation, quality of life, and environmental concerns are is-

and the stories of Hardy and John Henry, the legendary African-American railroad worker who battled a steam drill in Summers County, became intermingled. A letter from former Governor MacCorkle to state archivist Henry S. Green in 1916 furthered the confusion. In his 1925 *Folk-Songs of the South*, West Virginia University professor John Harrington Cox documented nine versions of "John Hardy" where Henry and Hardy are assumed to be the same individual. Louis W. Chappell's 1932 *John Henry: A Folk-Lore Study* challenged the earlier documents and made clear distinctions between Henry, the heroic steel driving man, and Hardy, the outlaw and murderer.

"John Hardy" has been performed in folk, blues, country, bluegrass, jazz, and rock versions and recorded by Pete Seeger, the Carter Family, Earl Scruggs, Huddy Ledbetter (Leadbelly), and the Kingston Trio. Tunes have been notated in the collections of John and Alan Lomax, Cecil Sharp, Marie Boette, and Patrick Gainer.

See also John Henry

H. G. Young III
WVU Parkersburg

Louis W. Chappell, *John Henry: A Folk-Lore Study,* 1932; John Harrington Cox, ed., *Folk-Songs of the South,* 1925; Richard Ramella, "John Hardy: The Man and the Song," *Goldenseal,* Spring 1992.

Harewood

Harewood, whose name derives from an English term for the sycamore tree, is the oldest and most famous of Jefferson County's Washington estates and the only one that remains in family ownership. Standing some three miles west of Charles Town, on the southern side of State Route 51, Harewood now presides over 264 acres of field and pasture.

The stately limestone manor was built by Samuel Washington, whose brother, George, recorded in his diary on September 1, 1770, that "Samuel and his wife set out [from Mount Vernon] in my chariot for his house." This, the first known reference to Harewood, can be considered its date of completion.

Architecturally, Harewood is West Virginia's finest expression of formal 18th-century Georgian architecture. In all likelihood master builder John Ariss, who lived and worked in the area, was responsible for the five-part Palladian design. Although the northern wing and the section connecting it to the main block were not constructed until 1961–62, they match their original southern counterparts. The paneled drawing room is graced by a marble mantel, probably given by Lafayette to George Washington, and later installed at Harewood.

After Samuel Washington's death, Harewood became the home of his son, George Steptoe Washington, who was married to Lucy Payne. In 1794, her sister, Dolley Payne Todd, married James Madison in the house. Portraits of many Washingtons, including Samuel, look down from walls beautifully maintained by the present generation of their family.

See also Washington Family

S. Allen Chambers Jr.
Society of Architectural Historians

Roy Lee Harmon

Poet Roy Lee Harmon, founder of the West Virginia Poetry Society, served as the state's poet laureate under four governors for 38 years. He was born October 7, 1900, in Boone County, grew up in Danville, and graduated from Scott District School. He attended Morris Harvey College (now University of Charleston) before working as a reporter, eventually becoming the city editor for the *Raleigh Register*, a Beckley newspaper.

In 1937, Governor Holt named Harmon the poet laureate of West Virginia. James Lowell McPherson succeeded him in 1943, but Governor Meadows reappointed Harmon in 1946. He held the post until 1960, when Cabell County's Vera Andrews Harvey, who served only one year, replaced him. Governor Barron again named Harmon poet laureate in 1961. In 1979, Governor Rockefeller gave him emeritus status. Harmon's books are *Hillbilly Ballads* (1938), *Around the Mountains* (1941), *Up the Creek* (1948), *Unto the Hills* (1957), *Rhymes of a Mountaineer* (1968), and *Roses in December* (1978). He was elected to the House of Delegates in 1946 and served four intermittent terms. In addition to his writing and political career, Harmon was a television host in Oak Hill during the 1950s. He died on April 7, 1981.

James Slack
Charleston

Minnie Buckingham Harper

The first African-American woman to serve as a member of a state legislative body in the United States, Minnie Buckingham Harper was born in Winfield, Putnam County, May 15, 1886, later moving to the coalfields of McDowell County. She was appointed by Governor Gore on January 10, 1928, to fill the unexpired term of her husband, E. Howard Harper.

A Republican member of the House of Delegates from McDowell County, Mr. Harper died before completing his term. A homemaker and a resident of Keystone, Mrs. Harper had received the unanimous recommendation of the McDowell County Republican Executive Committee to fill her husband's position. Her appointment reflected both the growing role of women in American politics and the maturation of an African-American political coalition in southern West Virginia which by the 1920s had become an important part of the party structure of the state. Harper served less than a term in the House of Delegates, declining to run for the office in the next election. She later married John B. Patterson, a miner, and lived with him in Northfork until his 1956 death. She returned to Winfield, dying there February 10, 1978.

I. D. "Duke" Talbott
Charles M. Murphy
Glenville State College

Harpers Ferry

Harpers Ferry, located at the confluence of the Potomac and Shenandoah rivers, is the easternmost place in West Virginia and at 247 feet the lowest point in the state. Originally called Peter's Hole, Robert Harper had settled there by the 1740s and operated the ferry which gave the place its new name. Flooding was a common occurrence in this narrow gorge through South Mountain, while water power attracted people and made the town into a 19th-century industrial center. The U.S. Armory and Arsenal was established at Harpers Ferry in 1799. Inventor John H. Hall pioneered the first successful application of interchangeable firearms manufacture for his breech-loading rifle at nearby Hall's Rifle Works between 1820 and 1840. The Winchester & Potomac Railroad opened a line to Virginius Island at Harpers Ferry in 1836, one of the earliest railroads in the country, and the Baltimore & Ohio arrived in 1837.

John Brown, an abolitionist determined to free the slaves, decided to raid Harpers Ferry because of the arsenal, which could be used in arming the slaves. His attack was carried out on October 16, 1859, and all his men were killed or captured. Brown was tried at nearby Charles Town for treason and hanged on December 2, 1859. This trial focused the nation's attention on the moral issue of slavery and helped head the country toward war. Because of the town's strategic importance on the B&O at the northern end of the Shenandoah Valley, it changed hands many times during the Civil War. In September 1862, Stonewall Jackson accepted the surrender of more than 12,500 federal troops at Harpers Ferry, the largest surrender of U.S. forces until World War II.

After the war Freewill Baptist missionaries from New England acquired several buildings on Camp Hill and on October 2, 1867, started Storer College. The college was designed primarily to educate former slaves but was open to students of all races and both genders. It was one of the earliest integrated schools in the country. Storer College closed in 1955, and today the National Park Service uses part of the old campus as a training facility.

By the 20th century, Harpers Ferry was sliding into obscurity. It was saved by its history. In 1944, the lower town became a

Harpers Ferry nestles between two rivers.

unit of the National Park Service, which would eventually help put Harpers Ferry back on the national map. The site a gift of the state of West Virginia, Harpers Ferry National Historical Park by the 1960s began restoration of historic buildings. An economic boost was given to the town in 1970 when the National Park Service opened the Harpers Ferry Center, an interpretative services center serving Park Service units nationwide.

The community, the National Park Service, and others working together for historical preservation and heritage tourism have made Harpers Ferry a quality place to live and one of the nation's premier destinations for history-minded tourists. Harpers Ferry had a population of 307 in 2000.

See also John Brown

W. Eugene Cox
National Park Service

Harpers Ferry Armory and Arsenal

In 1792, Congress authorized the building of two national arsenals for the storage of arms and, in 1794, provided funds for the building of two armories for the manufacture of small arms.

Harpers Ferry, occupying the strategic location where the Potomac and Shenandoah rivers meet in a gap in the Blue Ridge and blessed with abundant water power, was chosen as the southern armory and arsenal. An industrial site was built from scratch in 1798. The first weapons were produced in 1799 and from then until the destruction of the armory in 1861, hundreds of thousands of muskets, rifles, and pistols were manufactured or assembled there. Spare parts were made at Harpers Ferry, as was ammunition. The U.S. Army and Navy carried these weapons into all of their military actions from the early 19th century to the Civil

War. The Lewis and Clark Expedition was outfitted in large part at Harpers Ferry.

The building of a government industrial site should have helped the local economy, but the early evidence shows that this may not have been the case. Instead of using the local iron ore, Pennsylvania ore was shipped to the armory. Corruption and favoritism in the letting of contracts and hiring of skilled labor plagued the armory until the coming of the Chesapeake & Ohio Canal in 1833 and the Baltimore & Ohio Railroad in 1837. These new transportation routes made the Harpers Ferry area a hub of industrial and agricultural activity and opened up new jobs and markets.

Along with the textile mills of New England, Harpers Ferry was an important site in the Industrial Revolution in America. Important advances toward modern industrial methods were made there, including the organizing of factory-style production. The use of interchangeable parts, a prerequisite for modern manufacturing, was perfected at Hall's Rifle Works at Harpers Ferry.

During the 1830s and 1840s, there were many changes in the production of the basic musket design at the armory. The development of more powerful gunpowder and the change from flintlock to percussion cap were the most important. By 1855, rifled muskets were being built at the armory by the thousands and marked with "HARPERS FERRY" on their lockplates.

With the raid by John Brown on the armory in October of 1859, the name Harpers Ferry became notorious across the United States. After the start of the Civil War, the armory, then controlled by the Virginia State Militia, was still producing arms, but for the Confederacy. When the Confederate army retreated

from Harpers Ferry in April of 1861, the retreating soldiers burned the arsenal buildings. The armory was never rebuilt.

See also Harpers Ferry

Greg Carroll
State Archives

Stuart E. Brown Jr., *The Guns of Harpers Ferry,* 1968; Dave Gilbert, *Where Industry Failed: Water-Powered Mills at Harpers Ferry, West Virginia,* 1984.

Harpers Ferry Civil War Campaign

In 1794, President George Washington received congressional approval to establish armories and arsenals throughout the young nation. The second site selected was Harpers Ferry. Located at the confluence of the Potomac and Shenandoah rivers, the village had abundant water power and was only 62 miles from the national capital at Washington. From 1800 to 1861, the arsenal produced 620,000 shoulder-arms and became the largest installation of its kind in the South.

Three times in the Civil War era Harpers Ferry was the scene of major national events. In 1859, abolitionist John Brown momentarily seized the arsenal in an unsuccessful attempt to start a slave insurrection. On April 18, 1861, the day following Virginia secession, several companies of state militia closed in on the 47 army regulars defending the arsenal. The Union soldiers set fire to the buildings and fled. The Virginians reacted quickly and saved most of the machinery. For a time, Harpers Ferry was the northernmost point of the Southern Confederacy.

The town changed hands eight times during the Civil War. The most spectacular of those campaigns occurred September 15, 1862, when Confederate Gen. Thomas J. "Stonewall" Jackson forced the surrender of a large Union garrison inside the town. The 12,500 prisoners taken by Jackson was the largest capitulation of federal troops in the war.

For most of the conflict, looters and guerrillas reduced Harpers Ferry to a no man's land, only a shadow of its former self. Artillery fire shattered homes and buildings; streets became avenues of accumulated trash; the vital railroad bridge across the Potomac was destroyed and rebuilt nine times. An 1865 visitor stated that "all about the town are rubbish, filth, and stench." However, like so many other communities, Harpers Ferry would rise from the ashes of war.

James I. Robertson Jr.
Virginia Polytechnic Institute

Chester G. Hearn, *Six Years of Hell,* 1996; Charles H. Moulton, *Fort Lyon to Harpers Ferry,* 1987.

Harpers Ferry National Historic Park

Harpers Ferry National Historic Park commemorates important events and issues of the Civil War era. Efforts to establish the park began in 1936 when Storer

College President Henry McDonald met with Congressman Jennings Randolph. At Randolph's recommendation, the Park Service conducted a survey of the Jefferson County site in 1937.

In 1944, President Franklin Roosevelt signed the bill establishing Harpers Ferry National Monument, including the authorization to accept 1,500 acres of donated land. The West Virginia legislature appropriated $350,000 to acquire 514 acres of land for the national monument in 1951, and 400 acres were added in 1953. John T. Willett became the first permanent commissioner of the park in 1954.

A major archeological and restoration effort followed, as well as modifications designed to facilitate parking and interpretation. The campus of Storer College was added to the park in 1960, followed by additional land on Maryland Heights in 1963. At that time the park's name was changed to Harpers Ferry National Historic Park. In 1974, Senators Randolph and Byrd initiated the legislation that expanded the park's boundary to 2,000 acres. By 1990, a 1,000-vehicle parking lot and visitor complex had been built two miles west of the lower town, with shuttle buses to the park.

As the boundaries have increased, the thematic emphasis has also expanded to include John Brown, the Civil War, African-American history, industry, transportation, and natural heritage. Harpers Ferry National Historic Park receives 500,000 visitors per year, making it West Virginia's most visited historic site.

See also Harpers Ferry, Storer College
William D. Theriault
Bakerton

Thomas Maley Harris

General Thomas Maley Harris was born June 17, 1813, at present Harrisville. He rose to prominence after the Civil War, when he served on the military commission that tried conspirators who acted with John Wilkes Booth in the assassination of President Abraham Lincoln.

His book, *Assassination of Lincoln: A History of the Great Conspiracy,* published in 1892, made Harris a target for critics of the verdict. The main complaint concerned the execution of Mary Surratt, a woman thought by many to have been innocent. However, historians later located a signed confession by George Atzerodt, who was executed July 7, 1865, along with Surratt and two other conspirators. The statement of Atzerodt clearly implicates Surratt in the conspiracy. Her hanging was said to have been the first time the federal government executed a woman.

In his youth, Harris took advantage of limited opportunities for education. As a young man, he began a teaching career at the Parkersburg Institute. He studied medicine at Louisville, where he gradu-

ated in 1843. When the Civil War began, Harris was practicing medicine in Gilmer County. He recruited the 10th West Virginia Infantry Regiment for service in the Union army and, on May 20, 1862, was made colonel of his regiment. Harris was commissioned brigadier general March 29, 1865. He was promoted to brevet major general April 2, 1865, for his part in the Union assault on Petersburg, Virginia.

Harris had always been against slavery. He gave an oration July 4, 1849, in which he attacked slavery on moral and economic grounds, for which he was criticized in the newspapers. Previously a Whig, he joined the new Republican Party about the time of the Civil War. He served in the House of Delegates in 1867, as state adjutant general (1869–71), and was mentioned as a possible candidate for governor.

Harris was once mayor of his hometown of Harrisville. He also served as U.S. pension agent 1871–76. Harrisville, the county seat of Ritchie County and previously known as Solus, was named for Harris in 1895. He died there September 30, 1906.

Sandra L. Moats-Burke
Harrisville

Harrison County

Harrison County lies in north-central West Virginia, at the juncture of Interstate 79 and U.S. 50. The county covers 417.9 square miles, with a 2000 population of 68,652. Clarksburg is the county seat. The rolling hills of Harrison County are drained by the West Fork River and its tributaries.

During the Indian wars of the early 1770s, forts were built along the rivers from the already established Fort Pitt to West's Fort at Jane Lew. Nutter's Fort, built in 1772 on Elk Creek, was one of the strongest. Two miles west of Nutter's Fort, where Elk Creek flows into the West

Fork River and on land Daniel Davisson claimed through settlement in 1773, a community of settlers by 1780 had built their adjoining houses in a rectangle to give some protection. At a meeting of citizens, Samuel Shinn suggested their settlement be named Clarksburg in honor of Revolutionary War hero George Rogers Clark. So many people had settled on the West Fork by the end of the Revolution that the Virginia General Assembly in 1784 formed the new county, to be named for Benjamin Harrison, governor of Virginia, 1781–84.

The first U.S. judicial district west of the Alleghenies was established at Clarksburg in 1819. John George Jackson, member of Congress (1803–11; 1813–17), brother-in-law of Dolley Madison, and federal judge, may have been the influence that made Clarksburg for many years the ideal place for ambitious young lawyers to set up practice. From among these lawyers came Joseph Johnson, the only governor of Virginia (1852–56) from west of the mountains; John S. Carlile, who led the first movement for the formation of West Virginia, at the Clarksburg Convention, April 22, 1861; and John W. Davis, Democratic nominee for president in 1924. John George Jackson's cousin and law partner, Jonathan Jackson, was the father of Gen. Thomas Jonathan "Stonewall" Jackson, born in Clarksburg in 1824.

The Virginia legislature chartered Randolph Academy in Clarksburg in 1787, which it was hoped would be a worthy western counterpart to William and Mary College. George Towers arrived from England in April 1796 to teach at the school. A dedicated scholar, Towers set a high standard. The Northwestern Academy, described as a "fine classical school," was established in 1841, and the Clarksburg Independent School District in 1867. Harrison eventually had ten public high schools, reduced through consolidation between

FAST FACTS ABOUT HARRISON COUNTY

Founded: 1784
Land in square miles: 417.9
Population: 68,652
Percentage minorities: 3.5%
Percentage rural: 43.4%
Median age: 39.2
Percentage 65 and older: 16.6%
Birth rate per 1,000 population: 11.4
Median household income: $30,562
High school graduate or higher: 78.4%
Bachelor's degree or higher: 16.3%
Home ownership: 74.8%
Median home value: $67,600

This information is from the 2000 U.S. Census. In 2000, West Virginia as a whole had 5 percent minorities, a median age of 38.9, median household income of $29,696, and a 75.2 percent home ownership rate.

Morning comes to Harrison County.

from the interior counties, helped swell the population from 27,690 in 1900 to 74,783 in 1920.

The abundance of energy sparked myriad industries. Glass factories fueled by natural gas made window glass, marbles, containers, and tableware. A steel mill was built as was a zinc smelting plant. Spur railroad lines made Clarksburg the distribution center for the central portion of the state. Later, the intersection of Interstate 79 with U.S. 50 reestablished the Clarksburg-Bridgeport area as an economic and distribution center.

Hope Gas Company established its central offices in Clarksburg early in the 20th century. In mid-century its parent company, Consolidated Natural Gas Transmission Corporation, chose Clarksburg for its corporate headquarters where it is known today as Dominion Hope. The National Carbon Company has operated a graphite plant in Anmore since 1904.

Veterans from a wide area of the state are served by the Veterans Administration Medical Center, built in 1950. Catholic and Protestant hospitals merged to occupy the United Hospital Center, erected in 1960.

Clarksburg's Benedum Airport is named for oil man Michael Benedum, a native philanthropist whose wealth returns to West Virginia through the Claude Worthington Benedum Foundation. The Mid-Atlantic Aerospace Complex at the airport consists of nine organizations including Northrup Grumman, Pratt & Whitney, and Lockheed Martin.

Seven golf clubs and numerous parks and athletic arenas provide recreation to Harrison Countians and their visitors.

Howard M. Gore, a Harrison County native, was governor of West Virginia 1925–29. Nathan Goff Jr. was U.S. senator, 1913–19; Jennings Randolph, born and reared in Salem, was U.S. senator, 1958–80. The writer Melville Davisson Post (1869–1930) was born at Lost Creek. Novelist Meredith Sue Willis (b. 1946) is a native of Shinnston.

See also Clarksburg

Dorothy U. Davis
Salem
Dorothy Davis, *History of Harrison County, West Virginia,* 1970.

Harrisville

Harrisville, the county seat of Ritchie County, is located at the junction of State Routes 31 and 16, five miles south of U.S. 50. The town was laid out in 1822 by Thomas Harris, who had moved his family there in 1807. The town was chartered in 1832, and the first post office opened in 1833, under the name Solus. The name changed several times until 1895, when the town was named Harrisville for Gen. Thomas M. Harris, nephew of the founder. Ritchie County was formed in 1843, and the first courthouse was built in 1844. It was replaced

1970 and 1997 to five. Salem College, founded in 1888 and bought by Japanese interests in 1989, became Salem-Teikyo University and is now Salem International University. Fairmont State University has a Clarksburg branch. Clarksburg has had a business school since the 1880s. The local Catholic school system is capped by St. Mary's High School in Clarksburg.

Harrison County was cattle country by the mid-19th century. The rich local soil produces a lush bluegrass which made Harrison beef a favorite in the East. With the opening of the Northwestern Turnpike in 1838, great herds were collected at Clarksburg and moved by drovers to Baltimore. After 1857, the railroad improved transportation, and by 1863 Harrison County was first in West Virginia in the production of beef cattle. In 1923,

Lost Creek was the largest cattle shipping point on the B&O system. The 19th-century mystery writer Melville Davisson Post made the Harrison County livestock country into a lush pastoral milieu for his upright rural detective, Uncle Abner.

As early as 1836, the Virginia Geological Report noted the county's rich coal deposits, and by 1903 Harrison County was fourth in the state in total tons of coal produced. Gushers sent petroleum into the sky at Salem and Shinnston at the turn of the 20th century. Funds from drilling on Hall's Run in the first decade of the century let Nathan Goff Jr. build in Clarksburg the Waldo Hotel, Goff Building, and the Oak Hall commercial building. Workers signed on in Italy to emigrate to Harrison County company towns to mine coal and, with native migrants by a brick structure in 1874. The present courthouse, a Harrisville landmark, was completed in late 1923.

The Pennsboro & Harrisville Railroad was built in 1875, operating between the two communities of its name. The broad-gauge Harrisville Southern Railroad ran to Cornwallis between about 1909 and 1929. A high school was established on the west end of town in 1894. That structure now houses the General Thomas M. Harris School Museum. A school built overlooking Harrisville in 1924 served students until 1994. Within the community are an elementary school, many businesses, two banks, a library, offices of the *Ritchie Gazette* and *The Pennsboro News,* a municipal park, and North Bend Golf Course. Harrisville is 870 feet above sea level, and the population in 2000 was 1,842. Municipal elections are held every two years.

General Harris, Harrisville's most distinguished citizen, died there in 1906. A medical doctor and Union officer, he served on the military commission that tried the conspirators responsible for the assassination of Abraham Lincoln. His son, John T. Harris, long-time clerk of the state Senate, founded the *West Virginia Blue Book* in 1916.

See also Ritchie County

D. J. Allen
Cairo

Minnie Kendall Lowther, *Ritchie County in History and Romance,* 1990; Ritchie County Historical Society, *The History of Ritchie County, West Virginia to 1980,* 1980.

Nancy Hart

Rebel spy Nancy Hart was probably born in July 1843, probably in Tazewell County, Virginia. By 1850, Nancy and her family were living in Boone County, according to the U.S. Census, and by 1860 they had moved to Roane County.

In the early days of the Civil War, Nancy Hart assisted Perry Conley and his Moccasin Rangers in their Confederate resistance to the Union efforts to control Western Virginia. Captured in Braxton County in the fall of 1861 while in her late teens or early 20s, Hart convinced the federal troops that she was innocent. When they released her, she returned to the Confederates with much information on the movements of federal troops and their Home Guard allies. She was again captured in the summer of 1862 and held in Summersville, where she talked her young guard into letting her hold his pistol. Hart then killed him, escaped, and returned with 200 Confederate troops to capture Summersville and several of the federal officers there.

After the war ended, her husband, Joshua Douglas, returned from Confederate service, and they settled in Greenbrier County. The 1900 census shows them living in Glade District of Webster County. Nancy Hart died in 1902 and was buried at Mannings Knob, in Greenbrier County near the Webster County line.

See also Civil War, Moccasin Rangers

Debra Basham
State Archives

Morris Harvey

Civic leader, financier, and philanthropist Morris Harvey helped transform Fayette County into a leading coal producer. He was born February 16, 1821, near Prosperity in Raleigh County, and grew up in Cannelton, Fayette County. Educated in the local schools, he worked in his uncle's store in Fayetteville where he learned county politics and land investing. Harvey served as county jailer in 1851; county sheriff from 1859 to June 1860; and sheriff again, 1865–69. He enlisted in Thurmond's Rangers, C.S.A., during the Civil War, but rarely talked of his war experience.

Land ownership became the basis for Harvey's wealth. In 1866, Harvey and his brother-in-law received a land grant from West Virginia of 1,000 acres on the west side of New River for $20. Boosting postwar industrialization, Harvey leased or sold his lands to rail or coal companies; the coal town named Harvey became part of the holdings of the New River Company. In 1900, he founded the Fayette National Bank.

Harvey became a devout member of the Methodist Church, South, after marrying Rosaltha Dickinson in 1871. He helped establish at least three churches in the county, and his gifts to the Barboursville Seminary led to its name being changed to Morris Harvey College in 1901. In 1978, the college became the University of Charleston. Morris Harvey died in Fayetteville, April 5, 1908.

See also University of Charleston

Lou Athey
Franklin & Marshall College

William "Coin" Harvey

Social reformer William Hope "Coin" Harvey, born in Buffalo, Putnam County, August 16, 1851, was one of the most remarkable personalities to emerge from West Virginia. He was a school teacher, lawyer, builder, silver miner, politician, land speculator, geologist, and best-selling author.

Harvey attended Buffalo Academy and Marshall College before leaving to read law. He was admitted to the bar at 19 and in 1874 was practicing law in Huntington. In 1883, Harvey went to Colorado and worked as a silver prospector and miner. It was then he became an advocate for "free silver," a populist cause and one of the great political issues of the day. After 10 years in the West, he relocated in Chicago and began writing and publishing books on the subject. One of his books, *Coin's Financial School,* sold more than a million copies and earned Harvey his nickname.

After the defeat of free silver presidential candidate William Jennings Bryan in 1896, Harvey propounded other reforms, including the abolition of imperialism, taxes, rent, interest, and profits. In 1900, he moved to Arkansas where he began building an extensive retreat and vacation resort. He also started construction of a huge pyramid to become a time capsule to perpetuate his theories and ideas. William "Coin" Harvey was nominated for president of the United States by the Liberty Party in 1932 and received more than 50,000 votes. He died at age 84, February 11, 1936.

Bill Wintz
St. Albans

Devil Anse Hatfield

Feudist Anderson "Devil Anse" Hatfield, patriarch of the Hatfield family and their leader during the Hatfield-McCoy feud, was born September 9, 1839, in present Mingo County. He married Levicy Chafin in 1861, and they had 13 children. Hatfield fought for the South in the Civil War, serving in the Logan Wildcats, an irregular group, and in the regular Virginia infantry. He deserted the infantry in 1863.

Hatfield was an imposing figure, six feet tall or taller. Military records describe him as having dark hair, dark eyes, and a dark complexion, and for most of his life he wore a full, dark beard. He was an outdoorsman and an avid bear hunter. His name is usually given as William Anderson Hatfield in the secondary sources, but he consistently used just Anderson. Various stories account for his colorful nickname, which distinguished him from cousin Anderson "Preacher Anse" Hatfield.

The Logan Wildcats were suspected in the 1865 murder of Kentuckian Harmon McCoy, a Union army veteran and brother of McCoy patriarch Randolph McCoy. Hatfield's uncle, Jim Vance, was a more likely

Anderson "Devil Anse" Hatfield (1839–1921).

culprit in this than Hatfield himself. Likewise, Hatfield had no personal involvement in a famous 1878 hog-stealing incident and trial. In 1880, he led the armed party rescuing son Johnse Hatfield from the brothers of Rose Anna McCoy. He took a decisive role in the bloody events of 1882, when brother Ellison Hatfield was mortally wounded in a drunken election-day brawl and three sons of Randolph McCoy were killed in retaliation. Hatfield was the leader in this decision and likely took part in the killings. Indicted in the crime, he was never tried.

Hatfield instigated but did not take part in the January 1, 1888, nighttime raid on the McCoy cabin. Calvin and Alifair, Randolph McCoy's grown children, were killed in the New Year's raid, and their mother, Sarah, bludgeoned. This atrocity brought matters to a head, putting the Hatfields on the defensive for the remainder of the conflict. Eventually four Hatfield sons and others were indicted for the cabin raid, and their cousin, Ellison Mounts, was hanged. This ended the family war.

Hatfield identified himself as a farmer to census takers and military recruiters, and he worked at farming and logging. In fact, he was a major property owner and increasingly a man of affairs as his many sons took up the physical work of the family. Troubled as the feud wore on, he interspersed attempts at peacemaking with continued aggression. He relished his growing celebrity, making himself available to the press and the public. Certain interviews of his, particularly with the *Wheeling Intelligencer* and with *New York World* reporter T. C. Crawford, helped to sensationalize the vendetta.

Devil Anse Hatfield lived many years after the feud. He was baptized by his old friend, preacher "Uncle Dyke" Garrett, in 1911. He died January 6, 1921, and is buried under a life-size statue of himself in Logan County.

See also An American Vendetta, Feuds, Hatfield Family, Hatfield-McCoy Feud
Coleman Hatfield and Robert Y. Spence, *The Tale of the Devil: The Biography of Devil Anse Hatfield,* 2003; Otis K. Rice, *The Hatfields & the McCoys,* 1982; Altina L Waller, *Feud: Hatfields, McCoys, and Social Change in Appalachia, 1860–1900,* 1988.

Hatfield Family

The Hatfields are West Virginia's most famous family, known worldwide for their bloody feud with the McCoys in the 1880s. The family had settled in the Tug Valley by 1800, when Ephraim and Anna Musick Hatfield moved their household from Russell County, Virginia, to the Kentucky side of Tug Fork. Hatfields eventually dispersed to both sides of the river, with the main branch of the family living in (West) Virginia by the time of the Civil War.

There are two founding events in Hatfield family history: A 1792 Shawnee raid in Russell County, which widowed Anna Musick and eventuated in her marriage to Ephraim, who was among the party that rescued her from the Indians. And in 1817, preacher Abner Vance fled a Russell County murder charge, finding refuge in Tug Valley. Vance later returned to Virginia and was hanged there, but not before establishing a family line on Tug Fork.

Hatfield and Vance blood united in the generation of Anderson "Devil Anse" Hatfield (1839–1921), whose mother was Nancy Vance. It was Devil Anse and his uncle, the fierce Jim Vance, who led the war against the McCoys, a neighboring Tug Valley family living largely in Kentucky. Hatfields generally bested their foes in the fighting and raids of the feud, but suffered more serious legal consequences in the ensuing trials. A Hatfield kinsman was convicted and hanged in Kentucky in February 1890, and another imprisoned.

Devil Anse Hatfield's nephew, Henry Drury Hatfield (1875–1962), was elected governor of West Virginia in 1912. Governor Hatfield was a medical doctor by training, who had helped to establish organized medicine in the southern coalfields. He was president of the state Senate before his term as governor, and later served as U.S. senator (1929–35). Hatfield was a progressive Democrat, best remembered for imposing the "Hatfield Settlement" which ended the bloody Paint Creek-Cabin Creek coal strike of 1912–13.

Attempting to abate the feud, Anse Hatfield in 1888 moved across the mountain from Tug Valley to Main Island Creek, south of Logan town, and in 1911 was baptized by his old comrade, the preacher "Uncle Dyke" Garrett. Anse died in 1921 and is buried with his immediate family under an imposing marble statue of himself at Sarah Ann. Today numerous Hatfields live throughout West Virginia's southwestern counties and in neighboring Kentucky. They are prominent in local politics, in business, and in medicine and other professions. The Hatfields break bread in occasional reunions with the McCoys, and in the summer of 2000 they were beaten and bathed by their old adversaries in a spirited Tug Fork tug-of-war.

See also Devil Anse Hatfield, Hatfield-McCoy Feud

Ken Sullivan
West Virginia Humanities Council
Elliott Hatfield, *The Hatfields, 1974;* Otis K. Rice, *The Hatfields & the McCoys,* 1982.

Henry D. Hatfield

The 14th governor of the state, Henry Drury Hatfield, was born September 15, 1875, on Mate Creek, near Matewan in what is today Mingo County. A nephew of feudist Anderson "Devil Anse" Hatfield, the young Hatfield attended a one-room

Governor Henry Drury Hatfield (1875–1962).

school in McDowell County. He entered medical school at the University of Louisville and graduated with a medical degree at the age of 21. After graduation he returned to the coalfields, becoming a coal-camp physician for the Pocahontas Coal Company in McDowell County. Appalled by the lack of medical facilities in the coal camps, he, along with state Sen. James Bevins, secured funding to establish three miners hospitals for the southern part of the state. At age 24, Hatfield was appointed to the board of directors for the hospital in Welch. For the next 13 years he served in that capacity.

In 1906, Hatfield, running on the Republican ticket, was elected to the McDowell County court, the local governing body which was the precursor to today's county commission, and served as its president for the next two years. In 1908, he took his seat in the West Virginia Senate. Although not successful in the passage of legislation, he introduced an array of measures to outlaw itinerant medicine salesmen, tighten dispensation of drugs, institute a board of examiners for nurses and physicians, and collect vital statistics on communicable diseases. "I have always believed, that the health of the citizens must be the first concern of the statesman," Hatfield remarked.

In the 1911 election the voters of West Virginia returned an evenly divided number of Republicans and Democrats to the senate. Both parties demanded the leadership. After protracted conflict during which Republican senators hid in Governor Glasscock's office and then fled to Cincinnati to deny a voting quorum, Hatfield's name was put forth by Democrats as an acceptable compromise candidate. He was elected president of the West Virginia Senate.

In 1912, Hatfield was elected governor, the state's youngest to that date. In that office he was able to secure passage of important legislation. Among the measures that passed while he was governor were a Public Service Commission, a workmen's compensation program, direct election of U.S. senators, woman's suffrage, a primary election bill, a corrupt practice act, a mine inspection bill, and restrictions on the mine guard system.

Among the measures that Hatfield secured none was more important to him than the workmen's compensation law. Hatfield had urged passage of this act while president of the state senate, and after that session adjourned he traveled to Germany to visit the Ruhr Valley coalfields. There he studied the compensation measure that Germany had passed, and he later modeled the West Virginia bill on that system. On February 21, 1913, workmen's compensation passed the West Virginia Legislature. The program provided a uniform system of compensation to injured workers, while relieving employers of liability in individual cases. Workmen's compensation paid funeral expenses of the deceased and a stipend to the widow and children; in case of partial or permanent disability the employee was paid a certain percentage of his salary. The system was financed by a tax on the employer and employee.

When Hatfield became governor the state was embroiled in a prolonged and violent strike in the coalfields of Paint and Cabin creeks. Martial law had been declared by his predecessor, and many miners had been tried and sentenced by military tribunals. On the day after his inaugural address, Dr. Hatfield left the governor's mansion and traveled to the strike region to spend the day treating wounded miners and the colorful Mary Harris "Mother" Jones. He granted a general pardon to Mother Jones and the miners who had been sentenced by military courts and appointed a board of arbitration to end the strike. He himself chaired the board. On April 28, 1913, both sides in the strike accepted the "Hatfield contract."

After his term as governor, Hatfield in 1917 entered the army medical corps as a captain and later major. He served as a chief surgeon during World War I. When the armistice was signed Hatfield returned to the private practice of medicine. In 1928, he again entered politics. He ran for the U.S. Senate against Matthew M. Neely. During his single term in the Senate, he was successful in establishing a veterans hospital in Huntington. Hatfield was defeated in 1934 by young Rush D. Holt. He returned to West Virginia and back to the practice of medicine. On October 23, 1962, at the age of 87, Henry Drury Hatfield died at his home in Huntington.

See also Medicine, Mine Wars, Paint Creek-Cabin Creek Strike

Carolyn M. Karr
Marshall University

Carolyn Karr, "A Political Biography of Henry Hatfield," *West Virginia History,* October 1966 and January 1967.

Hatfield Island

Hatfield Island lies in the Guyandotte River in the city of Logan. Named for Elias Hatfield in the early 1900s, it is often called Midelburg Island for Ferdinand Midelburg, a later owner. The 43-acre island, 2,000 feet long and 1,000 feet wide, was the site of the original settlement of Logan County by James and Joseph Workman in the 1790s. Purchased from Midelburg by the Logan Civic Association in the 1940s, the island later was bought jointly by the Logan County Board of Education and the Logan County Commission. Logan High School and its fieldhouse and athletic fields were constructed there in 1957. Logan Grade School was added in 1969 and Logan Middle School and Public Library in 1996–97. Today the island has two bridges, the east bridge joining Water Street in Logan and the west bridge connecting to State Route 10.

Robert Y. Spence
Logan

Sid Hatfield

Albert Sidney "Sid" Hatfield, controversial police chief of Matewan and martyred hero to union coal miners, was born May 15, 1893, near Matewan but on the Kentucky side of Tug Fork. He worked in area coal mines until Mayor C. C. Testerman named him Matewan's police chief in 1919.

In that position, Hatfield in early 1920 assisted a United Mine Workers campaign to organize Tug Fork miners. On May 19, when Baldwin-Felts detectives evicted several miners from their homes near Matewan because they had joined the union, Hatfield and a crowd of angry miners confronted the detectives. The "Matewan Massacre" resulted, a shoot-out in which seven detectives, two miners, and Mayor Testerman were killed. Hatfield survived unharmed and instantly became a miners' hero. Ten days later, he married Mayor Testerman's young widow.

In early 1921, a local jury acquitted Hatfield and 17 others of murder charges arising from the shoot-out. On August 1, 1921, Baldwin-Felts detectives shot Hatfield and his friend Ed Chambers to death in a hail of bullets as the two, with their wives on their arms, approached the McDowell County Courthouse in Welch. Miners considered it murder, and thousands of them rose in rebellion in late August and September in the celebrated March on Mingo.

See also Battle of Blair Mountain, Matewan Massacre, Mine Wars, Miners' March

Lon Savage
Salem, Virginia

Lon Savage, *Thunder in the Mountains: the West Virginia Mine War of 1920–21,* 1990.

The Hatfield-McCoy Feud

The Hatfield-McCoy Feud, a prolonged vendetta between neighboring families in the Tug Valley, was fought largely in the 1880s. The Hatfields lived mostly in Logan County (including present Mingo), and the McCoys lived mostly across the Tug Fork in adjacent Pike County, Kentucky. Their leaders were Anderson "Devil Anse" Hatfield and Randolph (Randall or "Ran'l") McCoy. Both families were deeply rooted in the region and extensively intermarried with other families and with each other; several surnames were represented in the struggle, and Hatfields and McCoys were involved on both sides. The affair was the most notorious of several feuds taking place in eastern Kentucky and neighboring areas at the time.

The earliest known violence between the families was the January 1865 murder in Pike County of Harmon McCoy, a Union army veteran and brother of Randolph McCoy. Harmon was believed to have been killed by the Logan Wildcats, a band of Confederate guerrillas usually led by Devil Anse Hatfield. While contributing to hard feelings which later found outlet in the feud, McCoy's murder was typical of bushwhacker violence throughout the border states during and after the Civil War.

In 1878, Randolph McCoy accused Floyd Hatfield of stealing a hog. Both were Pike Countians, and the resulting trial was held at the home of their neighbor, the magistrate Anderson "Deacon Anse" Hatfield. Floyd Hatfield prevailed when Bill Staton, though Randolph McCoy's nephew, testified in favor of Hatfield, and juror Selkirk McCoy, Randolph's cousin, provided the decisive vote for acquittal. Staton was harassed following the trial, then killed by brothers Sam and Paris McCoy, also nephews of Randolph.

Tensions increased at the spring 1880 elections at Blackberry Creek in Pike County. Devil Anse's son, Johnse Hatfield, visiting from Logan County, slipped away from the election grounds with Randolph McCoy's daughter, Rose Anna. Their off-and-on relationship, which may have produced an illegitimate child, galled both families for years to come.

Much worse trouble ensued at the Blackberry Creek election in 1882. Devil Anse's brother, Ellison Hatfield, was mortally wounded in a drunken brawl by three McCoy brothers, apparently in an argument over a small debt owed on a fiddle. Tolbert, Pharmer, and Randolph McCoy Jr., sons of Randolph, were captured by the Hatfields. Once Ellison died of his wounds, the three boys were tied to pawpaw bushes on the Kentucky side of the Tug and shot dead.

Following the killings of 1882, the feud simmered as McCoys attempted unsuc-

Murderland

"I have been away in Murderland for nearly ten days. No one, unless he has had the actual experience of a visit to the region made notorious by the Hatfield-McCoy feud would believe that there is in this country such a barbarous, uncivilized, and wholly savage region. There is nothing to be found equalling it in the history of the most lawless of our far Western border experience. The county of Logan, in West Virginia, where the powerful mountain family of Hatfield now lives, embraces a region wholly isolated from railroad or telegraphic communication. . . . There are no churches, and the school-houses supply very meagre means of educating the children of the mountain people who live in this isolated region.

"I visited this country for the purpose of getting at, if possible, the exact facts connected with the Hatfield-McCoy feud. . . . I found, after visiting this region, that there was much more to be considered here than the feud itself. The vendetta, so-called, which exists between the Hatfield-McCoy families is merely an incident in a series of cold-blooded murders which are almost without parallel in the history of the country. The story of the feud is a strange recital of family quarrels, of the usurpation of legal authority and of the downright violation of the law in every possible form."

—T. C. Crawford *An American Vendetta* (1889)

cessfully to have Hatfields arrested and tried in the courts. Perry Cline, a Pikeville lawyer who had previously disputed with Devil Anse over valuable timberlands, persuaded the governor of Kentucky to request extradition from Governor Wilson of West Virginia. Wilson refused, then and later, and at times it appeared that there might be armed conflict between the two states.

The McCoys suffered another great loss on the night of January 1, 1888, when Hatfields led by Devil Anse's uncle, Jim Vance, set fire to the family's Pike County cabin. Calvin and Alifair, Randolph McCoy's grown children, were killed, and their mother, Sarah, severely bludgeoned. This atrocity brought matters to a head, putting the Hatfields on the defensive for the duration of the conflict, hunted in their own West Virginia neighborhoods. Vance was soon killed by a posse of Kentuckians led by McCoy partisan Frank Phillips, and the two sides fought a pitched battle at Grapevine Creek, near present Matewan, on January 19. Eventually four Hatfield sons and others were indicted for the cabin raid, and their cousin, Ellison Mounts, was hanged in Pikeville, February 18, 1890. This ended the family war.

The Hatfield-McCoy Feud was exacerbated, especially in its later stages, by enterprising detectives, imperfectly deputized posses, sensationalizing newspaper men, and meddling lawyers. Historians, novelists, playwrights, and script writers have scarcely let it rest in the years since. Various explanations have been offered, including differences originating in the Civil War and strains caused by the rapid industrialization of the region. None adequately explains the depth of bitterness and the amount of blood shed between neighbors on the Tug Fork.

See also An American Vendetta, Feuds, Devil Anse Hatfield, Randolph McCoy

Ken Sullivan
West Virginia Humanities Council

Otis K. Rice, *The Hatfields & the McCoys*, 1982; Altina L. Waller, *Feud : Hatfields, McCoys, and Social Change in Appalachia, 1860–1900*, 1988.

Hatfield-McCoy Trail

The Hatfield-McCoy Trail, dedicated to all-terrain vehicles and a variety of other users, will traverse the counties of Wyoming, McDowell, Logan, Lincoln, Boone, Mingo, and Wayne. The plan is for 2,000 miles of recreational trails through the mountains of central Appalachia, starting in southern West Virginia and expanding into Kentucky and Virginia.

The Hatfield-McCoy Trail opened its first section in October 2000. As of 2005, five sections encompassing a total of more than 400 miles were open: two in Logan County, one in Mingo County, one in Boone County, and one in Wyoming County. The trails are open to off-road motorcycles, all-terrain vehicles, mountain bikers, and hikers. In 2005, 25,138 permits were issued to trail users.

The Hatfield-McCoy Regional Recreation Authority was created by the legislature to manage the trail system. The authority was the result of efforts by the Hatfield-McCoy Trail Coalition, which was formed in 1990. Construction was delayed while organizers negotiated with coal companies and other large land owners to allow access to the hundreds of miles of unpaved logging and mine access roads that crisscross the mountains. The Recreation Authority provides insurance to limit landowners' liability, controls and maintains the trails, and provides rangers to patrol them. The U.S. Bureau of Land Management provides consulting services to aid in the development of new trails and oversees quality control of existing trails.

The Hatfield-McCoy Trail is one of 16 trail systems in the United States designated as National Millennium Trails. It has received funding from the state and from the federal government. Most of the funding comes from legislative appropriations and revenue from the West Virginia Parkways Authority. Ultimately, the fees from trail users are expected to cover the costs of maintaining the Hatfield-McCoy Trail.

Hatfields and McCoys

In 1970, the play *Hatfields and McCoys* joined *Honey in the Rock* as part of the regular summer offering at the Grandview State Park amphitheater near Beckley. It was *Honey in the Rock* producer Norman L. Fagan's idea to produce a historical show about the famous feud between the West Virginia Hatfields and the Kentucky McCoys. When Ewel Cornett replaced Fagan as producer, Cornett put the idea into effect.

Cornett and songwriter Billy Edd Wheeler, a West Virginia native, began researching the project. Their research took them into the mountainous counties of southern West Virginia and eastern Kentucky. They talked to family members of the two clans, including members of the original Hatfield family and dozens of close descendants of both families.

Generally following Virgil Carrington Jones's book *The Hatfields and the McCoys* (University of North Carolina Press, 1948), and depending on their own personal research, Wheeler penned the play and lyrics and Cornett wrote the music. The show opened on June 20, 1970, West Virginia's birthday. On opening night, Willis Hatfield, a son of the Hatfield patriarch Devil Anse Hatfield, and a granddaughter of McCoy leader Rand'l McCoy embraced before a sold-out audience.

The feud musical then joined *Honey in the Rock,* and the historical plays still run in repertory at Grandview. The producing company, Theatre West Virginia, celebrated its 40th anniversary during the summer of 2000.

Ewel Cornett
Louisville, Kentucky

Hamilton Hatter

African-American educator Hamilton Hatter was born in Jefferson County about 1856. He completed the teacher training program at Storer College in Harpers Ferry in 1878 but remained for the next two years, working as a student assistant while he continued his education. He received a bachelor's degree from Bates College in Lewiston, Maine, in 1888. That year, Hatter joined the faculty at Storer College, where he taught a variety of subjects during the next eight years. From 1891 to 1906, he was a member of the college board of trustees.

Hatter was active in Republican Party politics in Jefferson County, where most party members were African-American in the years after the Civil War. When Republicans held their county convention in August 1892, African-Americans worked to have a black man placed on the ticket. As a result, Hamilton Hatter was nominated as the county's Republican candidate for the West Virginia House of Delegates. The selection of a black man attracted attention beyond county borders and was noted in several state newspapers. Although he lost the election to the incumbent Democrat, Hatter received 1,051 votes according to local newspapers.

In 1896, Hatter left Jefferson County to become the first principal of Bluefield Colored Institute (now Bluefield State College), which opened in December of that year. He was principal for ten years until he and much of the faculty were replaced in 1906. Hatter died in Bluefield, September 21, 1942.

Mary Johnson
State Archives

A. B. Caldwell, ed., *History of the American Negro, Volume 7: West Virginia Edition*, 1923.

Hawkshaw Hawkins

Hawkshaw Hawkins gained fame as one of West Virginia's best known country musicians. Born Harold Franklin Hawkins in Huntington, December 22, 1921, Hawkins got his start in music when he traded five trapped rabbits for his first guitar. He obtained his early entertainment experience with traveling shows and on radio at WSAZ Huntington and WCHS Charleston. During World War II, he appeared on WTUM Manila. He performed summer shows using trained horse acts and rope tricks.

From 1946 to 1954, "Hawk" worked on the *Wheeling Jamboree*, broadcast from WWVA. He then went to Nashville and the *Grand Ole Opry* for the rest of his life, except for a brief stint at the *Ozark Jubilee* in 1955. From 1946 to 1953, Hawkins recorded on King and hit the charts with five top-ten records. He then recorded for RCA Victor and Columbia. In 1962, he returned to King and recorded the hit "Lonesome 7-7203," but did not live to see it reach the top. On March 5, 1963, Hawkins, Patsy Cline, Cowboy Copas, and Randy Hughes died in a plane crash returning from a benefit concert.

See also Wheeling Jamboree

Abby Gail Goodnite
University of Rio Grande

Hawks Nest State Park

Famous for its scenic beauty since Chief Justice John Marshall visited the area in 1812, Hawks Nest State Park occupies cliffs, streams, and a lake formed by damming the New River in 1934. The park sits on both sides of U.S. 60, just west of Ansted, Fayette County.

The four-story lodge, designed by Walter Gropius's architectural firm, perches on a cliff 750 feet above the river. Most of the 31 guest rooms have balconies overlooking the gorge. The lodge has a meeting room, spacious lobby with a fireplace, gift shop, outdoor pool, and an elevator. The restaurant has a wide, two-story window wall facing the gorge. Nearby are tennis courts and a picnic pavilion.

Visitors may take an aerial tram from behind the lodge down to Hawks Nest Lake. At the river level are a snack shop, nature center, restrooms, boat ramps, and a boat rental shop. The park gets its name from ospreys, the fish hawks that ride the thermals between the high cliffs previously known as Marshall's Pillars.

The state bought the park lands in 1935, and the Civilian Conservation Corps made improvements including a picnic shelter, snack and souvenir shop, museum, and restrooms. The museum, which holds pioneer artifacts, features a glassed observation room offering a view of the gorge. A golf course was added to the park in 1999, when the state acquired previously private Hawks Nest Country Club.

The stone restroom, built by the CCC and shaped like a round tower, is unique. Near the lodge is the Lovers Leap overlook, and at the park's western edge lies a second overlook with easier access.

See also State Parks

Maureen F. Crockett
St. Albans

Hawks Nest Strike

The Hawks Nest Coal Company strike, January 1880, was the first of many strikes to place West Virginia miners in conflict with state officials as well as coal operators. The strike began when operators at Coal Valley (now Montgomery) told their union miners that they were being hurt by competition by the nearby Hawks Nest mines.

Miners from Coal Valley then stopped miners at Hawks Nest from working and threatened them with bodily harm if they returned to work. William Nelson Page, manager of the Hawks Nest mine, called on Fayette County Sheriff C. H. McClung. Fearing voter reprisals, McClung declined to intervene and instead called for Governor Mathews to send the militia. Mathews activated a militia company from Charleston, which quickly restored order. Several Coal Valley miners were charged in Fayette County civil court with intimidation and unlawful interference with Hawks Nest miners and placed under a peace bond.

This was the first coal strike in which the state used its troops to keep order, which was to be repeated in other strikes in 1894, 1902, and 1912. The strike featured several men who became prominent. Lawyer and future governor E. W. "Windy" Wilson defended the strikers in the Fayette County circuit court. Maj. John W. M. Appleton, the militia commander at Hawks Nest and previously a white officer in the 54th Massachusetts Regiment, the famous black regiment in the Civil War, later became West Virginia adjutant general. William Nelson Page, seeing the advantages of having a militia company to control strikers, formed Company C of the 2nd Regiment of the West Virginia National Guard and became its captain. He ended a 20-year career in the National Guard as a major.

Kenneth R. Bailey
WVU Institute of Technology

Kenneth R. Bailey, "Hawk's Nest Coal Company Strike," *West Virginia History*, 1969.

Hawks Nest Tunnel Disaster

Drilled through three miles of solid rock, the Hawks Nest Tunnel is a major hydroelectric water diversion tunnel and an engineering marvel. Largely constructed between 1930 and 1932, the project engaged almost 5,000 workers, consisting of local men and a majority of migrant workers, most of them southern blacks. The tunnel was part of a complex to generate power for Union Carbide's electrometallurgical plant in nearby Alloy. It was the largest construction project that had been licensed to that time in West Virginia, and it became the site of one of the worst industrial tragedies in the history of the United States.

In all, 2,982 men worked underground drilling and blasting. Only 40 percent of the underground work force worked more than two months and only 20 percent more than six months. Silicosis afflicted an astonishingly high proportion of this short-tenured work force. Silicosis, a progressive fibrosis of the lungs caused by inhaling pulverized silica dioxide, was a recognized hazard in hard rock mining and in granite sheds. Because the Hawks Nest Tunnel was licensed as a civil engineering project, even the modest forms of safety enforcement then available to miners did not apply. The combination of large work crews drilling and blasting in underground confined spaces, poor ventilation, lack of dust control and of personal breathing protection, and seams of exceptionally pure silica combined to create a manmade disaster. In less than two years after groundbreaking in April 1930, young men succumbed to acute silicosis. Hundreds would eventually die.

The circumstances cannot be considered accidental. Prior to groundbreaking, core samples made it clear that most of the tunnel would be drilled through high grade silica-bearing sandstone. Ultimately, a third of the tunnel was enlarged for the purpose of silica extraction.

Two great trials were held in 1933 and 1934 in Fayetteville and in Charleston to litigate claims against the contractor, Rinehart and Dennis of Charlottesville, Virginia, and the New Kanawha Power Company, a corporate entity created by Union Carbide. There would be 538 lawsuits filed against the two companies. In

The Hawks Nest Tunnel under construction.

the end, the out-of-court settlement was modest—$200,000—with individual awards ranging from $30 to $1,600. The largest trial ended with a hung jury, evidence of jury tampering, and generous compensation to the plaintiffs' attorneys.

The death toll cannot be stated with certainty. Hearings in the U.S. House of Representatives in 1936 attributed 476 deaths to work on the tunnel. A study published in 1986 indicates that as many as 764 men may have died from acute silicosis and related conditions. The Hawks Nest Tunnel became an important part of the labor culture of the 1930s, generating a novel and several short stories, as well as songs and several weeks of national news stories when the extent of the tragedy came to public light. The tunnel continues to operate and provide power to the Elkem Metals Corporation, the current owner of the Alloy plant.

Martin G. Cherniack
Clinton, Connecticut

Martin G. Cherniack, *The Hawks Nest Incident: America's Worst Industrial Disaster,* 1986; Jim Comstock , "476 Graves," *West Virginia Heritage Encyclopedia,* 1972.

Frank C. Haymond

Judge Frank Cruise Haymond was born in Marion County, April 13, 1887. He received his LL.B. degree from Harvard Law School. He practiced law in Fairmont and served for six years as judge of the Circuit Court of Marion County.

In July 1945, Haymond was appointed to fill a vacancy on the West Virginia Supreme Court of Appeals by Governor Meadows. Haymond was elected to the court in 1946 and was reelected to two more 12-year terms. At the time of his

death, June 10, 1972, Haymond had served longer on the high court than any past jurist.

Judge Haymond brought from Harvard a rigorous judicial philosophy that held that all related cases were to be systematically referenced and that the court must assiduously build on past decisions. There was to be no "legislating" from the bench. One hallmark of Haymond's opinions was the habitual citation of long lists of cases (from both state and federal courts) in support of his argument. Haymond was no legal innovator, and not one to impose his judgment on the situation. He believed that the courts should not go beyond what he called the plain meaning of a statute or decided case.

One of Haymond's last opinions reversed Judge George Triplett of Randolph County, who had declared incarceration at the aging Moundsville state penitentiary unconstitutional on the grounds that it violated the prohibition against cruel and unusual punishment. At the time, according to the *New York Times,* this prison had the highest per capita murder rate in the nation. Haymond's opinion excoriated Triplett at length for going beyond precedent and intruding upon the executive and legislative prerogatives. Ironically, less than a decade after Haymond's death the state Supreme Court unanimously declared imprisonment at the state prison unconstitutional on the grounds that the Haymond court had rejected, and mandated the building of a new penitentiary.

In 1970, Judge Haymond received the American Bar Association's prestigious ABA Medal, which is awarded to a lawyer

or judge who has "greatly advanced the cause of jurisprudence." No other West Virginian has ever been considered for this honor.

H. John Rogers
New Martinsville

Harold Hayslett

Instrument maker Harold M. Hayslett, born in Putnam County, December 26, 1917, established Hayslett Violins in 1954 in South Charleston. He had made 65 violins, 13 violas, 61 cellos, one double bass, and six bows as of 2003. At the international competition and exhibition sponsored by the Violin Society of America, Hayslett has received several certificates for tone and workmanship. He was awarded the prestigious gold medal for cello tone in 1980. Hayslett is listed in *The Violin Makers of the United States,* by Thomas James Wenberg, and he was included in the Governor's Arts and Letters Series in 1991.

Today Hayslett's instruments are cherished by collectors and players alike. He retired from Union Carbide as a pipe fitter in 1980, and was featured in the November 1982 *Union Carbide World* magazine in an article titled "Making Instruments of the Violin Family." His article "Shaping Blocks for Cello Sides" was published in 1990 in *The Journal of the Violin Society of America.* The video, *Building a Cello with Harold,* completed in 1996, was West Virginia filmmaker Robert Gates's in-depth look at Hayslett's life and work. Hayslett and his wife, Louise, live in South Charleston.

Bobby Taylor
State Archives

Hazel Atlas Glass Company

Hazel Atlas Glass Company, the glass-making giant in a state known for glass production, was created in 1902 by the merger of four earlier companies. The largest glass company in the United States from the 1930s until the 1950s, Hazel Atlas was a major producer of inexpensive "Depression Glass" table sets of pink, green, blue, colorless, and black glass. Hundreds of thousands of glass premiums given away in oats, coffee, and other products were made by Hazel Atlas.

Hazel Atlas glass plants in West Virginia included one along the Tygart River in Grafton (1916–60) that largely produced wide-mouth canning jars, and the world's largest tumbler factory in Clarksburg (1902–87). By 1920, the Clarksburg factory had 15 acres of floor space, employed 1,200 people, and shipped all over the world. The company's metal factories in Wheeling made lids and closures for glass containers.

By 1956, Hazel Atlas operated 12 plants across the U.S. and was contemplating a merger with Continental Can Corporation. Complex legal battles followed and anti-trust laws were used to prevent the

A Hazel Atlas canning jar.

merger. The result was that Continental Can acquired the Clarksburg tableware plant and Wheeling metal factory, with the other factories being sold to Brockway Glass Company. The handsome 1931 Hazel Atlas corporate headquarters at 15th and Jacob streets, a Wheeling landmark, was donated to West Liberty State College in 1964 and is now part of West Virginia Northern Community College.

Dean Six
West Virginia Museum of American Glass

He-Man Club

The Concord College He-Man Club began as a picnic in 1924 to honor retiring college president Christopher Columbus Rossey. Because those present enjoyed the event, the club became a permanent institution, its meeting an annual affair with as many as 600 attending. It was held near the college at Mercer Healing Springs for many years. Other sites were the Concord campus, Glenwood Park, Lake Shawnee, and the Elks Golf Club. The He-Man Club did not meet during the war years of 1943, 1944, and 1945.

Over time, the He-Man Club became a booster for Concord College (now University) athletics. The coaches present usually reported on their teams' prospects. The club also supported college scholarship funds. In its heyday, the club meeting was in part a political gathering, with governors, senators, congressmen, and candidates for various offices often present. The club was for many years for men only and was one of the few local men's groups without a ladies' auxiliary. In 1988, the first woman, Bessie Horn, was admitted. Although other women became members later, the name was not changed. The He-Man Club merged with Concord's Mountain Lion Club in 1996. The colorful name, taken humorously in later years, persists in the He-Man Golf Tournament, first held in 1998.

See also Concord University

Raymond Thomas Hill
Athens

Department of Health and Human Resources

The West Virginia Department of Health and Human Resources is a cabinet-level department of state government, responsible for the state's health and welfare programs and many social services. Upon its creation in 1989, the DHHR absorbed existing agencies with health and welfare functions, particularly the Department of Health and the Department of Human Services. These agencies date their origins through various predecessors to West Virginia's early days as a state.

The foundation for the Bureau of Children and Families, which now administers public assistance programs for the DHHR, was laid in 1863. That year, the first West Virginia legislature enacted a law giving counties the responsibility for poor relief and the operation of alms houses or poor farms. The Mother's Pension Law, authorizing counties to pay monthly pensions to mothers who had no property or resources and whose morals were above suspicion, was enacted in 1915. The Board of Children's Guardians, established in 1919, was replaced in 1931 by the Department of Public Assistance.

In 1936, the legislature authorized creation of county departments of public assistance within the Department of Public Assistance to administer at the local level all existing public welfare programs including those eligible for federal funding. The Department of Public Assistance later became the Department of Welfare. West Virginia piloted the U.S. Department of Agriculture's Food Stamp program in 1961 and was the first state to issue food stamps.

The health functions of the DHHR date back almost as far as its public assistance role. In 1881, the West Virginia Board of Health was established to regulate and license the practice of medicine and surgery; to conduct sanitary investigations; to maintain quarantine centers; and to establish county health boards with the consent of local governments. The Board of Health was abolished in 1915 and replaced by the Department of Health. In 1945, the Health Department assumed advisory medical supervision of state hospitals.

Major organizational restructuring took place in 1949, when the department shifted its emphasis from communicable diseases to chronic illnesses and other public health issues. The legislature created the Department of Mental Health in 1957. During the 1977 legislative session, a consolidated Department of Health was created, combining the old Department of Health, the Department of Mental Health, Commission on Mental Retardation, public institutions, and smaller boards and commissions.

The largest and most recent change came during the 1989–90 reorganization of state government, when the Department of Health and Department of Human Services merged to form the Department of Health and Human Resources. Also brought under the DHHR umbrella were the Human Rights Commission, the Women's Commission, and the Commission on the Hearing Impaired.

The DHHR is among the very largest agencies of state government. It has approximately 5,800 employees in five bureaus:

The Bureau for Public Health works with local health departments. The bureau administers programs that range in scope from regulating hospitals and nursing homes to working to reduce tobacco use.

The Bureau for Children and Families administers most of DHHR's major public assistance programs such as food stamps and Temporary Assistance for Needy Families, as well as Child Protective Services and Adult Protective Services. The "welfare agency" direction of the bureau changed in 1996 with the enactment of federal welfare reform during President Clinton's administration. These watershed reforms reduced welfare assistance by limiting the years of eligibility and encouraging welfare recipients to return to work.

The Bureau for Behavioral Health and Health Facilities runs state health facilities and regulates private providers of behavioral health services.

The Bureau for Child Support Enforcement establishes paternity, child support, and medical support and enforces support orders, including spousal support.

The Bureau for Medical Services is the state Medicaid office. Medicaid, a federal program of the Social Security Administration, pays for health care for women, children, and adults below a certain income level. At the beginning of the 21st century, Medicaid paid for more than half the births in West Virginia.

In addition to the five bureaus, the Office of Inspector General polices legal and ethical issues at the DHHR, provides an impartial hearing process to clients who feel they have been unfairly treated, and monitors the receipt and use of federal funds.

John D. Law
Department of Health and Human Resources

Danny Heater

Athlete Danny Heater, born in Braxton County, February 27, 1942, holds the national record for most points scored in a high school basketball game. He was a resident of Burnsville, and attended Burnsville High School. He scored 135 points in a varsity basketball game against Widen on January 26, 1960. Heater went on to receive an academic scholarship to attend the University of Richmond, where unfortunately he was never a starting player. Nevertheless, his record has stood for decades, and his feat is still a focus of community pride in the town of Burnsville. Heater lives in Germantown, Maryland.

Alan J. DeYoung
University of Kentucky

Ken Hechler

Congressman and historian Ken Hechler was born on Long Island, New York, September 20, 1914. He graduated from Swarthmore College, later earning M.A. and Ph.D. degrees at Columbia University. He taught at Columbia and Barnard College and helped Judge Samuel I. Rosenman edit the Franklin D. Roosevelt papers.

In 1942, Hechler was drafted as an infantry private, later graduating from officer candidate school and serving in Europe as a combat historian. He was awarded the bronze star and five battle stars, and after V-E Day interviewed Hermann Goering and other Nazi leaders. From 1947 to 1949, he taught at Princeton University and served on President Harry Truman's White House staff from 1949 to 1953. The American Political Science Association made him its associate director in 1953, and in 1956 he joined the campaign staff of presidential candidate Adlai E. Stevenson.

In 1957, Hechler moved to West Virginia to teach at Marshall College (now Marshall University) and the following year he defeated Republican Congressman Will E. Neal. He served 18 years in the House of Representatives, specializing in coal mine health and safety and protection of the environment. His leadership following the Farmington mine disaster enabled passage of the federal Coal Mine Health and Safety Act of 1969. Hechler crusaded for the abolition of strip mining and led the fight to preserve the New River. He actively supported Joseph "Jock" Yablonski's campaign to replace corrupt United Mine Workers President Tony Boyle. Hechler was the only member of Congress to march with Dr. Martin Luther King Jr. in 1965 in Selma, Alabama.

In 1976, Hechler ran unsuccessfully for governor. Later attempts to regain his seat in Congress failed, and he returned to teaching at Marshall and at the University of Charleston. In 1984, he was elected West Virginia's secretary of state and was re-elected in 1988, 1992, and 1996. He used the secretary of state's office as a pulpit for liberal reform. Hechler ran for Congress again in 2000, but was unsuccessful in the Democratic primary. In 2002, he received the Harry S. Truman Public Service Award in Independence, Missouri. In 2004, Hechler ran again for secretary of state and was defeated by Republican Betty Ireland.

See also Coal Mine Health and Safety Legislation

Dan B. Fleming
Blacksburg, Virginia

Heck's

Heck's Inc., a chain of discount department stores headquartered in Charleston, competed with K-Mart and Wal-Mart until it went bankrupt in the late 1980s.

In 1959, four Boone County businessmen opened the first Heck's department store in Charleston: Fred Haddad, Thomas Ellis, Lester Ellis, and Douglas Cook. Heck's offered a large inventory of clothing, home furnishings, hardware, health and beauty aids, jewelry, toys, small appliances, and sporting goods. It sold nationally advertised items and its own line of goods at low prices.

The company expanded greatly in the 1960s, '70s and '80s. It bought Woodrum Home Outfitting Company, West Virginia's largest furniture store, as well as several out-of-state discount chain competitors. It built a new headquarters on Kanawha Boulevard in Charleston and a distribution center in Nitro. At one point, Heck's was the only West Virginia company listed on the New York Stock Exchange. In 1980, Forbes Magazine ranked Heck's third nationally in profitability and growth, above K-Mart and below only Wal-Mart and one other chain.

At its peak in the mid-1980s, Heck's operated 127 stores in nine states, employed more than 8,000, and had assets of $300 million. But Heck's faced increased competition from Wal-Mart and others. Despite a redesign of its stores, profits fell. In 1987, the company filed for Chapter 11 bankruptcy. It continued to operate in a smaller capacity until 1990, when Jordache Enterprises purchased it by paying $1 and agreeing to assume its large debts. A year later, Jordache closed the remaining stores and liquidated their assets.

Scott Finn
Charleston Gazette

Heirloom Seeds

Heirloom vegetables are those kept going by seed-saving gardeners after most seed dealers and nurseries have dropped them. They taste better, or they have some special quality that the newer vegetables don't have. On the other hand, they usually lack a desirable quality, making them less attractive to commercial dealers. The Mortgage Lifter, the Zebra, and the Brandywine, heirloom tomatoes found in West Virginia gardens, take a week or 10 days longer to mature than the commercial Big Boy. The heirlooms are also less resistant to some tomato diseases.

Until the mid-20th century, the saving of agricultural seeds from year to year was a common practice among gardeners and farmers. Because of this, vegetables, fruits, and grains often evolved into regional strains that were adapted to local climate and soil conditions. With the advent of hybrid varieties, however, it was necessary to purchase seeds each year, as hybrid seeds are not true to the mother plant and in most cases generate only useless plants in the next generation.

Many traditional West Virginia gardeners cling to the older ways. They value the older, time-tested, non-hybrid fruits and vegetables, which have been saved, cared for, and planted. Some varieties are associated with certain families, communities, and even individuals and are exchanged by neighbors and relatives. Folkloric motifs and floating names are common, as well as oral history of a more substantial sort. The Wild Goose bean name, for instance, designates dozens of actual varieties in various localities in West Virginia. There is an associated story of a wild goose being shot with this bean found in its craw. According to most versions of the story, the seed was planted, propagated, and the result is this marvelously productive, tasty, and resourceful bean. Some seeds, as with the Mortgage Lifter, imply their worth through their name.

The free classified advertisements in the West Virginia Department of Agriculture's *Market Bulletin* have long provided a means for exchanging the heirloom varieties. Ruby Morris of Braxton County once told *Goldenseal*, the state's magazine of traditional life, that she grew nearly 30 different beans, including the Trout bean, the Grandpa bean, and the Red Cut Short bean. A Summersville woman offered Fat Man beans and Logan Giant pole beans in the *Bulletin*, as well as a brown-seeded half-runner, a contrast to the white-seeded half runner West Virginians have grown for generations.

An active market persists for Bloody Butcher corn, reputed to be the best for cornbread. Bloody Butcher's kernels come in colors from white to red—but never purple or black—and some of the kernels are variegated on the outside. The inside of the kernels is white. Bloody Butcher yields a cornmeal somewhere in taste between white corn meal and yellow corn meal.

Although not consciously based on science, the practice of seed saving ensures that heirloom varieties are subjected to continual review and scrutiny over generations of time. This selection process may pick only the hardiest, the earliest or latest, or the strongest seeds to be planted the following year. Ninety-nine percent of today's edible cultivated vegetables and grains were developed through this folk process, practiced worldwide through the millennia of agricultural history.

See also Vegetable Gardening

Gerald Milnes
Augusta Heritage Center
Bob Schwarz
Charleston Gazette

Hellhole Cavern

A large and spectacular cave in Germany Valley, Pendleton County, Hellhole occurs in middle Ordovician limestones along the axis of the Wills Mountain anticline. The entrance, consisting of three openings in a large sink, is a sheer drop of 160 feet into an enormous chamber with a floor expanse exceeding one acre. In November 1929, a team led by Arthur E. Krause, a Lutheran pastor and president of St. John's Academy in Petersburg, made the first recorded descent, which was accomplished by means of a windlass and steel cable. They explored several thousand feet of spacious passages, all that would be known for the next 40 years. By the 1940s, Hellhole and nearby Schoolhouse Cave were probably the most famous wild caves in the United States.

Since the early 1970s, National Speleological Society explorers have expanded the mapped passage length of Hellhole to 22.1 miles, with a maximum depth of 519 feet. Many of the cave's rooms and passages are quite large and often profusely decorated with stalactites, stalagmites, and other features. Presently the longest cave in the state north of the Pocahontas-Greenbrier line, Hellhole is still incompletely explored. Many cavers believe that its aggregate length may exceed 50 miles.

Hellhole is one of the most important bat caves in the East, containing a hibernating colony of more than 100,000 little brown bats as well as large numbers of endangered (and federally protected) Indiana and Virginia big-eared bats. In 1981, the U.S. Fish and Wildlife Service, with landowner cooperation, fenced the entrance sink to prohibit unauthorized entry. The cave remains closed to visitation.

See also Caves

John Craft Taylor
Union College

Helvetia

Helvetia, elevation 2,239 feet, is a small community in the rugged southwestern corner of Randolph County, settled in 1869 by German-speaking Swiss immigrants. It was named for their native Switzerland, officially known as the Confederation of Helvetic Republics. The village and its surroundings slowly grew

A Helvetia homestead, about 1900.

into a center of Swiss-German culture and mountain agriculture unique to the area. By 1900, its population reached about 500 people, but declined during the 20th century to fewer than 100 by the late 1990s.

Helvetia was founded on land owned in part by prominent lawyers and politicians—Jonathan M. Bennett, Gideon D. Camden, and John S. Hoffman. Their land agent, Carl E. Lutz, was a Swiss who promoted the settlement and later became commissioner of immigration for the state of West Virginia.

The Swiss settlers created a central village of skilled craftsmen with a constellation of farms in the surrounding mountains. They lived and worked in virtual isolation for more than 30 years, setting up familiar institutions and speaking their native Swiss-German dialects. About 1915, local timbering brought a narrow-gauge railroad and the beginning of social and economic change. From this time through the 1950s, Helvetians combined traditional farming and cheese making with timber and mill work to create a sustainable local economy. Their self-sufficient farms weathered the world wars and even the Depression without great hardship.

The Swiss-German language fell out of use as the 20th century progressed. After World War II, out-migration increased, and the timber and coal industries became more important than agriculture. By the 1970s, tourism began to add diversity to the local economy. During this time the village was placed on the National Register of Historic Places. Today residents find jobs with local businesses such as restaurants and inns, or with the postal service, school, library, health center, and general store. Due to its strong community and ethnic traditions, Hel-

vetia has maintained or revived numerous Swiss-American celebrations that are open to the public.

David Sutton
Webster, New Hampshire
David H. Sutton, *One's Own Hearth Is Like Gold: A History of Helvetia, West Virginia,* 1990.

Hemlock Woolly Adelgid

The hemlock woolly adelgid is a very small, aphid-like insect that threatens to decimate eastern and Carolina hemlock trees over most of their natural range, including West Virginia. A native of Asia, the hemlock adelgid was first reported in the western United States in 1924 and in the east in the mid-1950s. Lacking natural enemies in North America, this exotic pest now infests about half of the area where hemlock occurs in the eastern U.S. and is expected to reach the entire range of eastern hemlock within the next several decades. Infestations of eastern and Carolina hemlock are generally fatal, with tree death occurring from the sap-feeding adelgids within four to six years. Although horticultural oils and soaps can achieve control on small trees and ornamentals, there are currently no methods to control the adelgid in forest environments. Concerns for ecologically important hemlock habitat, in such areas as Cathedral and Blackwater Falls state parks, as well as the Monongahela National Forest, have prompted experimentation with the introduction of a biological control agent (a predatory beetle from Asia) and treatment of individual trees with injected and implanted pesticides. While early results of biological control methods in the northeast appear promising, more time is needed to assess the long-term effects of these efforts.

W. Russ McClain
Nature Conservancy of West Virginia

Cam Henderson

Coach Eli Camden "Cam" Henderson was born February 5, 1890, in Joetown, Marion County. He was an innovator in basketball and football. In basketball, he is widely credited with pioneering the zone defense as well as the modern fast break. In football, he reportedly helped originate the double-wing offense. He is a revered figure in Marshall University sports history.

Henderson grew up in Harrison County and attended Glenville State Normal College, where he played football, basketball, and baseball. Two years after graduation, Henderson was the principal of Bristol High School where he initiated the school's athletic program. Henderson's first college coaching position was at Muskingham College, Ohio. After three years, he returned to West Virginia to coach at Davis & Elkins College. In 12 seasons, he posted an 83-33-6 record in football and a 220-40 mark in basketball.

In 1935, he moved to Marshall College (now University) to coach football and basketball. The high point of his basketball coaching career came in 1947 when Marshall won the NAIB national tournament in Kansas City. Later that year, Henderson led the football team to a 9-2 regular season. The team was invited to play in the Tangerine Bowl on January 1, 1948, at the same time Marshall's basketball team was playing in the Los Angeles Invitational Tournament. Henderson traveled with the basketball team and sent assistant coach Roy Straight to handle football. The basketball team won its tournament, but the football team lost the bowl game 7-0.

Henderson resigned as the football coach following the 1949 season but continued to coach basketball through 1954–55. In 2004, Henderson remains Marshall's all-time winningest basketball coach (362-16), and his record in football (68-46-5) held until 2001. The college's basketball arena, the Cam Henderson Center, is named for him. Henderson died May 3, 1956.

See also Marshall University

Clark Haptonstall
Rice University

Sam Clagg, *The Cam Henderson Story: His Life and Times,* 1981; Fred R. Toothman, *Wild Wonderful Winners: Great Football Coaches of West Virginia,* 1991.

John Hendricks

Cable television pioneer John S. Hendricks was born March 29, 1952, in Matewan, Mingo County. He was introduced to early cable systems developed by relatives to improve television reception in the hilly terrain of southern West Virginia.

His family moved to Huntsville, Alabama, when Hendricks was six years old. He grew up in two places, attending school in Alabama while spending summers working in West Virginia. He earned a B.A. in history in 1973 from the University of Alabama, Huntsville, which presented him with an honorary doctorate in 1991.

Hendricks founded the Discovery Channel, the first cable network in the United States designed to provide high-quality documentary programming, which aired its first programming on June 17, 1985. Hendrick's company, Discovery Communications, later expanded operations to 160 countries with more than 1 billion subscribers. In 2004, company properties include the Learning Channel, Animal Planet, Travel Channel, Discovery Health Channel, and Discovery Kids networks. In 1999, Hendricks formed the short-lived Women's United Soccer Association.

Hendricks has earned several awards for his work in the communications field. He was honored with an Emmy award and the Academy of Television Arts & Sciences highest honor, the Governors Award, for conceiving the Learning Channel series *Great Books.* He was the first corporate leader to receive the National Education Association's Friend of Education award.

John Hendricks lives in Potomac, Maryland.

See also Cable Television

Henry Clay Furnace

The Henry Clay Furnace, the first steam-powered blast furnace in Western Virginia, was built on Clay Run in present Coopers Rock State Forest about 1836. Leonard Lamb erected the cut-stone furnace for Tassey, Morrison, and Company to supply pig iron to the nearby Jackson ironworks, an important regional ironworks.

After its completion, the furnace changed hands in rapid succession. The Ellicott brothers, Maryland ironmasters, purchased the Jackson ironworks and the Henry Clay Furnace property in 1839. The Ellicotts made extensive improvements to the ironworks, building a tram road that connected the furnace with the ironworks, which was located at Ices Ferry on the Cheat River. The brothers operated the furnace until about 1848, at which time the Ellicotts' business failed.

The furnace converted or smelted the iron ore to pig iron. The ore was mined along the hillsides surrounding the furnace. In operation, the furnace was "charged" or filled with alternating layers of charcoal, iron ore, and limestone until entirely full. At this point it was fired and brought up to temperature slowly. After about eight hours the furnace was ready to be tapped. First the slag, which was lighter and floated on top of the molten iron, was released, then the molten iron was cast. The molten iron was run into a series of voids made in a bed of sand in front of the furnace. The voids, where the actual ingots were cast, were all connected by channels, through which the molten iron flowed from the furnace. The resulting pattern of iron ingots in the sand resembled piglets suckling at a mother sow, hence the name.

Once in operation the furnace was operated week in and week out, generally from the spring thaw to the winter freeze. The pig iron was sent to Jackson ironworks for conversion into wrought iron for use to make cut nails, while some iron was used to make cast-iron stoves.

Because of the remote and rural nature of iron making, a small self-sufficient community of 50 to 75 workers arose around the furnace. Life was not easy, and most workers lived in rough log buildings. Still there was a school and church at the furnace and a few more substantial structures related to the furnace's operation. None of these structures remains. Henry Clay Furnace, however, still stands and is a popular hiking and biking forest destination. It was added to the National Register of Historic Places in 1970.

Lee R. Maddex
WVU Institute for the History of Technology

John Henry

John Henry was a legendary steel driving man, whose life is the basis for one of the world's best-known folk tales. His fame rests on a single epic moment when he raced the steam drill during the building of a West Virginia railroad tunnel. That moment has captured the imagination of balladeers and storytellers for the last century, and in their songs and tales they have woven for John Henry a whole life: an infant's prophecy, a woman he loves, a heroic test, and a martyr's victory.

Scholars cannot know the real contours of John Henry's life. He was probably born a slave and was perhaps a

The John Henry statue at Talcott.

convict after emancipation. He worked between 1870 and 1872 as a hammer man or steel driver during construction of the Big Bend (or Great Bend) Tunnel, on the Chesapeake & Ohio Railroad near the Greenbrier River in Summers County. These men used sledge hammers to drive long steel bits into treacherous red shale to bore the holes for the explosives that would open the tunnel.

In the ballad John Henry exhorts his "shaker," the working partner who clutched, rotated, and shook the dust from his drill:

"Shaker, you better pray.
If I miss this piece of steel,
Tomorrow be your buryin' day."

Their work was arduous, hazardous, and labor-intensive. Many died from bungled blasting, crashing rocks, and tunnel sickness or silicosis.

Scholars suspect that Capt. W. R. Johnson, contractor for Big Bend, hoped to import the Burleigh Steam Drill to replace human steel drivers. He may have organized a contest between the drill and his best human driver. Declaring, "A man ain't nothin' but a man," John Henry took up the challenge. He won the race, but overexerted himself and died, mourned by his woman, often called Polly Ann, and an infant son who appears destined to follow his father as "a steel-drivin' man." An anonymous musician, possibly a fellow worker, composed a song, which has since been performed in countless variations.

Drawing on this original ballad, many work songs, blues songs, and ballads commemorate John Henry, and he has inspired children's books, tall tales, folk art, sculpture, film, and theater. His statue stands near the entrance of Big Bend Tunnel. In popular culture he grew to represent an African-American hero of quiet, steadfast resistance, a labor hero who fought to protect the dignity of work and the value of humanity over machines, and a Southern hero withstanding slippery Yankee commodities.

The man behind the folkloric giant is elusive, and some doubt the existence of John Henry as a historic figure. In the early 20th century, scholars Guy Johnson and Louis Chappell tried to uncover biographical details. They interviewed tunnel workers and their descendants, and publicized their efforts to find the trail of John Henry, but neither fully succeeded. Building upon their research and expanding it through other historical records, one concludes that a man like John Henry in fact beat the steam drill, accomplishing the triumph that music accords him.

See also Chesapeake & Ohio Railway, "John Hardy"

Brett Williams
American University

Louis Chappell, *John Henry: A Folk-Lore Study*, 1968; Guy B. Johnson, *John Henry: Tracking Down a Negro Legend*, 1969; Brett Williams, *John Henry: A Bio-Bibliography*, 1983.

Herald-Dispatch

The *Herald-Dispatch*, the only daily newspaper in Huntington since 1979, is published each morning seven days a week. It began in 1909 with the merger of the *Herald* and the *Huntington Dispatch*, and descends from the city's early newspapers. The first of these was the *Independent*, moved from Winfield to Huntington by O. G. Chase in 1871, the same year rail tycoon Collis P. Huntington founded the city. The *Independent* soon merged with the *Cabell Press*, and the resulting publication was named the *Weekly Advertiser*. It became a daily publication as the *Advertiser* in 1889.

In 1893, Joseph Harvey Long, a young printer from Pennsylvania by way of Wheeling, arrived in Huntington to buy the *Herald*, which had begun publication in 1890. Eighteen months later he sold it and bought the *Advertiser*. The *Huntington Dispatch* began in 1904. When it and the *Herald* merged in 1909, a stock company owned the newspaper until Dave Gideon became sole owner in 1919. Then in 1924, Colonel Long bought the northwest corner of Fifth Avenue and Tenth Street to erect a building for his paper. The *Herald-Dispatch* built a new home just a few doors down.

After a brief rivalry, the two publishers announced a merger of the two organizations as the Huntington Publishing Co., with Long as chairman and Gideon as president. The mechanical and business operations were combined while the two news staffs operated independently. Both men were publishers until their deaths. Gideon died in 1950 and Long in 1958 at the age of 95. The publishing company also purchased radio station WSAZ during this time and in 1949 started one of the nation's first TV stations, WSAZ-TV, Channel 3. Both stations were later sold.

After Long's two sons, Edward and Walker died, and Gideon's nephew, William D. Birke, died in 1963, two widows took charge of Huntington newspaper publishing. Edward Long's widow, Hilda Long, became president and publisher of the *Advertiser* and Helen Birke became chairman and publisher of the *Herald-Dispatch*. Local ownership ended in January 1971, when the Huntington Publishing Co. was sold to the owners of the Honolulu *Star-Bulletin*. Eight months later, the Hawaiian company was purchased by Gannett Co., the current owner of the *Herald-Dispatch*. The *Advertiser* boasted a higher circulation than the *Herald-Dispatch* for many years, but as reading habits changed, afternoon newspaper circulation declined. In 1979, the *Advertiser* ceased publication and

merged into the *Herald-Dispatch*, with many of the reporters from the afternoon daily going to work on Huntington's lone remaining newspaper. The *Herald-Dispatch* had a circulation of 37,000 in 2005.

Tom D. Miller
Huntington

Frank Hereford

U.S. Senator Frank Hereford was born in Fauquier County, Virginia, July 4, 1825. He graduated from McKendree College, Lebanon, Illinois, in 1845 and in 1849 went to California, where he practiced law. He was Sacramento district attorney from 1855 to 1857.

Soon after the Civil War, Hereford returned east, establishing himself in Union, the county seat of Monroe County in the new state of West Virginia. He married Alice B. Caperton of the prominent Monroe County family. Hereford was among the Democrats who agitated successfully to restore the vote and other political privileges to West Virginia's ex-Confederates, and he was among those soon to benefit by this change. He served three terms in the U.S. House of Representatives from 1871 to 1877. In 1877, he was elected by the state legislature to fill the unexpired U.S. Senate term of his fellow townsman, cousin by marriage, and fellow Democrat, Allen T. Caperton, who had died in office. Hereford was defeated by industrialist Johnson N. Camden when he sought re-election to the Senate in 1881.

Hereford returned to practice law in Monroe County after leaving the Senate. He served as a presidential elector in 1888. Frank Hereford died in Union, December 21, 1891, and is buried in the local Green Hill Cemetery.

Charles H. Ambler and Festus P. Summers, *West Virginia: The Mountain State*, 1958; Festus P. Summers, *Johnson Newlon Camden: A Study in Individualism*, 1937.

Homer Hickam

Author Homer Hadley Hickam Jr. was born February 19, 1943, in Coalwood, McDowell County. He graduated from nearby Big Creek High School in 1960 and from Virginia Polytechnic Institute in 1964 with a B.S. in industrial engineering. Hickam served in the army in Vietnam, where he was awarded the Army Commendation and Bronze Star medals. He went to work for the National Aeronautics and Space Administration at Marshall Space Flight Center in 1981 as an aerospace engineer. He retired from NASA in 1998.

Hickam's first book was *Torpedo Junction*, a history of World War II submarine warfare off America's east coast, published in 1989. In 1998, Hickam's second book, *Rocket Boys: A Memoir*, the story of his life in the town of Coalwood, was published. A runaway best-seller, *Rocket Boys* was selected by the *New York Times* as one of its "Great Books of 1998" and nominated by the National Book Critics Circle as Best Biography of 1998. In February 1999, Universal Studios released the popular film *October Sky*, based on *Rocket Boys*.

Hickam's first novel, *Back to the Moon*, was published in 1999. *The Coalwood Way*, another memoir of Hickam's hometown, was published in 2000, and his third Coalwood book, *Sky of Stone: A Memoir*, was published in 2001. An inspirational book, *We Are Not Afraid: Strength and Courage from the Town That Inspired the #1 Bestseller and Award-Winning Movie October Sky*, was published in 2002. Hickam has started a series of novels featuring Coast Guard Lt. Josh Thurlow, beginning with *The Keeper's Son*, published in October 2003.

Hickam is married to Linda Terry Hickam, and they live in Huntsville, Alabama.

High Gate

High Gate mansion, located in Fairmont, was built in 1910 for James Edwin Watson, the son of coal pioneer James Otis Watson, brother of U.S. Sen. Clarence Watson and brother-in-law of Governor Fleming.

High Gate's architect was Horace Trumbauer of Philadelphia, whose commissions also included Boston's Ritz-Carlton Hotel, the Philadelphia Museum of Art, and the nucleus of Duke University. High Gate was designed in what has been referred to as "Jacobethan" Revival style, borrowing elements from the architecture of English manor houses of the Elizabethan and Jacobean periods, particularly the use of half-timbering. The style was popular along Philadelphia's Main Line and in the New York suburbs but is found infrequently in West Virginia. High Gate is perhaps the best example in the state.

The house's most distinctive feature is its size and massing, coupled with a strong use of horizontal and vertical elements. Basically rectangular, it has a large service wing on the southwest and a porte-cochere and four-story octagonal tower on the west front. Fine craftsmanship and detailing are apparent throughout. The principal ground floor rooms continue the Jacobethan theme, with oak-paneled walls, parquetry floors, and ornamental plaster ceilings. Other notable features are the marble vestibule, Corinthian pilasters in the foyer, leaded glass windows, an oak-paneled elevator, and even a German silver sink in what was the butler's pantry.

Following J. E. Watson's death in 1926, the house was sold to the Sisters of St. Joseph, who used it as a rest home and later a kindergarten. It then became a funeral home and the carriage house a nursing home. In 1993, the carriage house underwent rehabilitation by the nonprofit Friends of High Gate and later was transferred to the Vandalia Heritage Foundation which promotes historic preservation throughout northern West Virginia. High Gate was listed in the National Register of Historic Places in 1982.

Margo Stafford
Clarksburg

Highland Scenic Highway

Beginning at Richwood and extending to a point near Marlinton, the Highland Scenic Highway provides access to the high mountains at the headwaters of the Cranberry and Williams rivers. The first section of the road is along the North Fork of the Cherry River on State Route 39. After climbing to almost 4,000 feet on Kennison Mountain, the scenic highway leaves State Route 39 on Cranberry Mountain. It continues as State Route 150 along the top of Black Mountain, gaining an altitude of over 4,500 feet. Following a descent for the crossing of the Williams River, the highway climbs back to 4,300 feet on Tea Creek and Red Lick mountains before a junction with U.S. 219 on Elk Mountain.

Construction of the 22 miles of State Route 150, which was built specifically for the scenic highway, began in 1965 at the Cranberry Visitors Center and was completed in 1981. This section was dedicated on October 11, 1981. Today's Highland Scenic Highway is the completed portion of an originally envisioned scenic road extending from the southern end to the northern end of the Monongahela National Forest. Planned extensions to U.S. 250 in Randolph County and even to U.S. 50 in Grant County were never built. The Highland Scenic Highway was designated a National Scenic Byway in 1996.

William P. McNeel
Marlinton

Highway Development

The first overland routes in Western Virginia evolved from Indian and game trails that followed the prevailing ridges and valleys. Many of these trails formed the basis of an extensive system of turnpikes that spanned present West Virginia before the Civil War. In the late 19th century, new highway construction slowed and many established routes either devolved into local haul roads or were abandoned amid competition from the railroads.

A call to repair the state's highway system came in the 1890s, when dedicated bicyclists allied themselves with farmers who needed decent roads to carry their produce to market. At the time, responsibility for road construction fell to the counties, and local officials concentrated on building roads to their own county seat rather than from one county to another.

With the dawn of the automobile era came a statewide Good Roads Movement, which sought "to pull West Virginia out of the mud." Still, by 1909, 1,200 miles of paved highways connected only two county seats. Characterized by tight curves, high accident rates, and long driving times, many of these routes were rightly regarded as dangerous. Few travelers ventured beyond their own locality.

West Virginia launched a series of highway improvements beginning in 1917 with the creation of the State Road Commission, whose duties included building, maintaining, and classifying public roads, providing for a statewide system of connecting highways, and coordinating revenue-raising efforts. The agency also furnished information for the location, construction, and maintenance of

High Gate mansion, Fairmont.

inter-county or other main routes called Class A roads, which typically extended border to border within a county on an east-west or north-south orientation.

In 1920, a Good Roads Amendment consolidated 4,600 miles of country roads into a state highway system. In 1922, east-west routes were assigned odd numbers and north-south routes received even numbers. The first sequentially numbered routes (1 through 4) were intended to be the main statewide thoroughfares. Routes were marked on roadside utility poles, with the original road markers consisting of two red bands six inches wide, separated by a 12-inch white strip upon which the route number was stenciled in six-inch figures. The National Road through Ohio County (originally State Route 29, now U.S. 40) used the same red, white, and blue markers as it did in Pennsylvania and Ohio.

The Federal Highway Act of 1921 directed each state to recommend for federal designation a connected road system. Funds were now available for a Federal Aid highway system of primary and secondary roads which in West Virginia totaled nearly 2,000 miles. These "FA" routes received separate designation independent of state roads, although a number of state road miles were included and thus became eligible for federal funds. The highway act further encouraged states to build connector routes that were "interstate in character," a move that led to the establishment of a separate state road system controlled by the State Road Commission.

In late 1925, a federal board unveiled a national system of interstate routes and a uniform highway sign. Original federal routes in West Virginia included U.S. 11, U.S. 19 (replacing State Route 4), old U.S. 21, U.S. 40 (the National Road), U.S. 50 (replacing State Route 1, the old Northwestern Turnpike), and U.S. 60 (replacing portions of State Route 3, the Midland Trail). These roads still serve us today, with upgrading and some relocation of routes. U.S. highway numbers were erected on metal shield markers bearing the letters "W. Va." at the top, with "U.S." and the route number below in black letters and figures on white.

By the 1920s, interest in transcontinental highways brought about a number of "national trail" associations that incorporated historic turnpike alignments. Among those later included into the federal highway system were the National Old Trails Road that followed the National Road (U.S. 40), the George Washington Highway that shadowed the Northwestern Turnpike (U.S. 50), and the Midland Trail on the James River & Kanawha Turnpike alignment (U.S. 60).

The pace of highway development increased statewide in the 1930s and '40s. A 1933 legislative act brought every public road in West Virginia under direct state control. This law designated more than 4,400 miles of roads as primary state highways, and reclassified some 31,000 miles of county roads as secondary state highways. Next came the Federal-Aid Highway Act of 1944, which authorized designation of a "National System of Interstate Highways" that would connect principal metropolitan areas and industrial centers and serve the national defense. In 1947, the legislature appropriated funds for the West Virginia Turnpike, the state's modern, long-distance, multi-lane "superhighway." Completion of the 88-mile turnpike from Princeton to Charleston came in 1954 at a cost of $133 million, to be funded through the sale of bonds paid from tolls.

Highway development reached new levels with passage of the Federal-Aid Highway Act of 1956 that designated the 46,000-mile National System of Interstate and Defense Highways, also known as the Eisenhower Interstate System. These are the "interstates" we know today, modern high-speed, controlled-access highways of four lanes or more. Interstate highway construction in West Virginia proved costly and difficult and completion of the final sections did not occur until the late 1980s. Currently, the state has 549 miles of interstate highways; east-west routes include I-64, I-68, I-70, and I-470, while I-77, I-79, and I-81 run north to south.

In the 1960s, the Appalachian Regional Commission proposed more than 3,000 miles of modern roads in a system of 26 highway corridors to foster economic and social development throughout the 13-state Appalachian Region. By 1995, a quarter of all ARC highway funds had gone to West Virginia for six of the program's most expensive roads. Identified as Corridors D, E, G, H, L, and Q, these routes traverse some of the most rugged regions of the state. Most of West Virginia's corridor highways were complete by the 1990s, and only the controversial Corridor H remained unfinished by 2004.

In the last decades of the 20th century, the West Virginia Division of Highways supplanted the State Road Commission. With more than 5,000 employees, the DOH is responsible for the planning, engineering, construction, and maintenance of more than 34,000 miles of state highways, 549 miles of interstate highways, 1,736 miles of national highways, 6,343 bridges, and five national and 12 state scenic byways. Also, the DOH sponsors a variety of programs to improve the driving experience and beautify state roads, including the Adopt-a-Highway program and Operation Wildflower.

See also Appalachian Corridor Highways, Good Roads Movement, Interstate Highway System, West Virginia Turnpike

Billy Joe Peyton
West Virginia State University

Division of Highways

Largest of the West Virginia Department of Transportation's seven agencies, the Division of Highways has more than 5,000 employees in its capitol complex headquarters, ten district offices statewide, and 140 maintenance sites. The DOH is responsible for planning, engineering, right-of-way acquisition, construction, maintenance, regulating traffic, and administering funds for more than 6,300 bridges and more than 36,000 miles of state highways and other roads. It also participates in highway research and administers nontraditional transportation enhancement programs such as scenic byways, backways, and recreation trails.

The Division of Highways traces its roots to the early automotive age, as West Virginia worked to build a modern road system. The legislature in 1909 established the State Road Fund and the position of state commissioner of public roads, along with county road engineers, only to abolish the fund and state commissioner's position two years later. The 1913 legislature created the State Road Bureau. That was replaced with the State Road Commission by the 1917 legislature, which also agreed to match federal road funds and to maintain roads constructed with federal aid.

The 1920 Good Roads Amendment to the state constitution authorized the legislature to pass a law providing for designation, construction, and maintenance of a state road system and the appointment by the governor of a three-man State Road Commission to carry out the statute. Under its first chairman, Maj. C. P. Fortney, the State Road Commission designated, surveyed, and numbered a system of roads and adopted a uniform sign system. The 1932 legislature abolished the State Bridge Commission created by the 1929 legislature and transferred all responsibilities to the State Road Commission, now a four-man advisory board under a commissioner, Ernest L. Bailey. The number of districts was expanded from five to ten. The 1930s brought a "privilege tax" on vehicle sales, to be used to match federal aid funds, as well as the issuance of truck permits, use of weigh crews and automatic traffic recorders, listing of prequalified bidders, and the reassignment of buses and taxis to Public Service Commission jurisdiction.

State highway programs slowed by World War II received a boost in 1949 with the passage of a secondary road bond. A national study of transportation needs led to the creation in 1956 of both the interstate highway system and the federal Highway Trust Fund. In 1970, the State Road Commission was renamed the Department of Highways. It reached maximum employment of some 10,000 workers during that decade, as new road bonds and the leadership of Commissioner W. S. Ritchie Jr. spurred construction that resulted in the completion in 1988 of the state's original interstate system and significant progress on its 424-mile Appalachian Development Highway system.

Receiving its present name when the 1989 legislature created the Department of Transportation, the West Virginia Division of Highways is now a billion-dollar organization. The Division of Highways is headed by Commissioner Paul Mattox, who was appointed by governor Manchin in 2005. Mattox, an engineer, had worked for the agency early in his career.

See also Appalachian Corridor Highways, Good Roads Movement, Highway Development, Interstate Highway System

Carol Melling
Division of Highways

Hillbilly

Although it apparently did not appear in print until 1900 when it was used in a New York newspaper, the word "hillbilly" had been in use at least in the American backcountry for decades before that. The New York reporter said he heard the word in Alabama, but he could have heard it virtually anywhere across the rural South.

Certainly, the term goes back more than a century in West Virginia. A photograph taken in 1899, a year before the word's appearance in print in New York, shows a large group of white people with three black servants out for an elaborate picnic in a wooded setting in Greenbrier County. These prosperous people from Lewisburg most certainly knew the word hillbilly as a designation for social inferiors, yet someone of this group boldly hand-labeled the photograph "Camp Hillbilly," a voluntary association with a despised identity, a friendly jab at roughing it, and a sort of brag.

The word opens the cabinet of paradoxes about American social-class dynamics. Since the "billy" in hillbilly comes from Scots and means a companion, a comrade, and was generally used with affection and familiarity, it is possible that hillbilly first sprouted from the mouths of the very rural poor it was later used against. Like other pejoratives, in the context of social equals the word can be a friendly leveling device; but if offered belligerently or condescendingly or in contexts of unequal social status, it can start a fistfight.

The word hillbilly entered the urban American mainstream rather slowly. In 1915, it appeared in the title of a *Harper's Monthly* travel article ("Hobnobbing with Hillbillies") and also in a movie title, *Billie-The Hill Billy*, set in the Ozarks. But the application of the word to recorded commercial country music in 1923–24 greatly accelerated usage and added a non-threatening and even comic element to the meaning of hillbilly.

Hillbilly achieved a kind of chic in the economically destabilized 1930s when music promoter Glen Rice claimed to have found aboriginal country musicians in the wilds of the Santa Monica Mountains. He dubbed them "The Beverly Hillbillies," a radio musical group whose name preceded the popular 1960s television-series title. Hillbilly was becoming synonymous with "authentic" rural Americana isolated from the urban mainstream.

What seems laughable to the urban onlooker can also turn dangerous. The sinister threat in imaginary rural isolation came to fruition in the 1970 James Dickey novel and 1972 Hollywood movie, *Deliverance*, which featured the invasion of a rural stronghold by insensitive suburbanites. *Deliverance's* suggestion of the hillbilly's violent hostility against urbanites has successfully driven out earlier meanings. Since 1972, hillbilly often means warped by cultural isolation.

Whatever its connotations, it seems likely that the word will remain in wide circulation among West Virginians. In recent times, it has been applied to a much loved newspaper, the *West Virginia Hillbilly*, founded by Jim Comstock, and to the Man High School sports teams in Logan County.

J. W. Williamson
Appalachian State University

Hilltop House

The Hilltop House hotel is built on the hill above the historic town of Harpers Ferry. The hotel overlooks the spectacular landscape at the confluence of the Potomac and Shenandoah rivers. It was established by the African-American Lovett family in the late 19th century and has changed hands numerous times since then. The hotel now includes the main house and a separate annex building with conference areas and additional lodging rooms. The Hilltop House has changed over the years, resulting primarily from rebuilding after two fires.

The Lovetts came to Harpers Ferry after the Civil War. Storer College hired William and Sarah Lovett, and they enrolled their children there. The Lovetts owned another local hotel, the Lockwood House, from 1883 until around the turn of the century, and their son, Thomas, started hotel work as his parents' office clerk. Thomas Lovett built the Hilltop House, apparently just before 1890, and he and his family operated it for decades. The Lovetts turned the hotel over to Fred McGee in 1926, and in 1959 Baltimore lawyer Dixie Kilham bought the place. Kilham later sold to William Stanhagen.

The Hilltop House has entertained guests including Presidents Wilson and Clinton, Alexander Graham Bell, Mark Twain, members of Congress, and other

---

What is a hillbilly?

"A hillbilly is someone who can't look out his window without seeing the big hills, and feeling small and big at the same time because of them.

"He's somebody with a heritage of independence his hill-folk family gave him, because—cut off from other people by the mountains—*they* had to make it by themselves. Someone stubborn and tenacious because he's learned that, while faith can move a mountain, it might take a little time.

"He's friendly, because mountains teach that there are more important things to fight than people—and that if your closest friends are both sides of a mountain distant, they're better held onto than fought with. And he's industrious. Even living *lazy* in mountain country can work a man pretty hard.

"He's somebody who knows that only God can make a tree—and figures that if He troubled to make a whole state of forested mountains, that state must be specially blessed.

"A West Virginia hillbilly is a man with wealth underfoot, wealth towering over his head, and only the beauty all around him coming easy. He has his troubles—but plenty of toughness and faith to stick it out, sometimes looking poorer than he feels. . . .

"Why not give that stubborn, tenacious, independent hillbilly—the real backbone of all of us—credit for what he laid the foundation of? Let's hope we have the guts to live up to him, facing the wonderful, favorable odds his grit preserved for us. Take away his name and you take away the credit from him.

"Somebody asked George Washington what he'd do if it looked as if he were losing the war. He said, 'Give me but a banner to plant upon the mountains of West Augusta'—their name for this area in Washington's day—'and I will gather around me the men who will lift our bleeding country from the dust and set her free.'

"He knew his hillbillies."

—Jim Comstock

government officials over the years. It remains open for business.

Walton Danforth Stowell Jr.
Harpers Ferry

Hinton

Hinton, incorporated in 1880, is sited at the confluence of the Greenbrier and New rivers. It is the county seat of Summers County. Hinton was built on land purchased by the Chesapeake & Ohio Railroad in 1871 from the son of the first white settler, Isaac Ballengee, who had received a land grant for 210 acres from Virginia in 1777. Before the railroad, only six families lived in the area, but after the C&O arrived in the early 1870s the population grew rapidly. Hinton was laid out in 1874 and lots sold. Hotels, taverns, mercantile stores, an opera house, and boarding houses accommodated the railroad workers.

By 1892, the C&O had completed a roundhouse with 17 engine stalls and a car shop with a capacity of 40 cars in Hinton, providing employment for 540 men. For more than a half-century the town boomed as an important railroad center. In the 1950s, however, changes in coal mining methods, the working out of some older mines, the local abandonment of coke making, and the conversion of railroad locomotive power from steam to diesel drastically altered the economic life of Hinton. The C&O Railway laid off hundreds of workers, specialists in maintaining steam engines, and the town's population declined. Brick streets, elaborate municipal and commercial buildings, and two-story Victorian wood-frame houses with gingerbread trim and porches on both stories remain as testimony to the prosperity of the railroad era. The Hinton Historic District was added to the National Register of Historic Places in 1984.

The construction of Bluestone Dam on the New River, completed in 1949, provided employment for many local workers and created Bluestone Lake. The lake, now a popular recreation area, covers the site of several early farms and communities. Hinton hosts two major annual events, the Water Festival in August and Railroad Days in October. Strategically located as the gateway to New River Gorge, Hinton hopes for future growth as a recreational and retirement center.

See also Summers County

Stephen D. Trail
Hinton

Hinton News

The *Hinton News* was founded as the *Hinton Daily News* on May 5, 1902, by John W. Graham (1867–1941). Graham was previously the editor and publisher of the *Leader*, a struggling weekly. The *Daily News* was known for editorials that pulled no punches, and on one occasion an editor was jailed for his provocative re-

marks during a railroad strike. The *Daily News* grew into the most widely read paper in the area, its readership spreading into surrounding counties. It became the weekly *Hinton News* in 1978 and is the only local newspaper to serve Summers County.

On April 1, 1922, Graham sold the paper to H. C. Ogden, the Wheeling publisher, and continued in an advisory position until his death. The newspaper's present building was constructed by Ogden in 1926 and opened January 4, 1927. On April 23, 1947, John and Tom Faulconer of Hinton purchased the newspaper. They continued its operation until March 1, 1973, when they sold the *Hinton Daily News* to Charles D. Hylton, who named his son, Tony, editor and publisher. On June 2, 1978, the paper was sold to the *Welch Daily News* and because of declining local economic conditions became the weekly *Hinton News*, publishing each week on Tuesday. Today the *Hinton News* is owned by the Hinton Publishing Corporation. The newspaper's circulation was 4,200 in 2005.

Fred Long
Hinton

Historic Preservation

Historic preservationists identify, document, protect, and promote historic and prehistoric sites, structures, and objects. The first efforts in West Virginia were private initiatives by individuals or groups. Some focused on high-style private dwellings of prominent figures, while others attempted to preserve important prehistoric sites such as the Grave Creek Mound. Public preservation activities began in the 1880s when the Smithsonian Institution excavated several Adena mounds in the Kanawha Valley. In the absence of any federal or state preservation laws, these early efforts were haphazard at best.

Federal involvement in preservation came after passage of the 1906 Antiquities Act, the first legislation aimed at protecting federally owned sites. The Antiquities Act made the Department of the Interior the lead agency for national preservation activities. At its creation in 1916, the National Park Service assumed preservation responsibility for national parks, landmarks, and Civil War battlefields. With virtually no federal land in West Virginia at the time, these actions had little impact here. In the 1920s, the state began promoting historic sites in road maps and tourist publications. At the time, the state's aging Civil War veterans held reunions to commemorate their wartime experiences. From these unofficial pilgrimages sprang the first organized attempt to preserve West Virginia's Civil War heritage, culminating in the dedication of Droop Mountain Battlefield as our first state park on July 4, 1928.

An infant national preservation move-

ment materialized with the founding of the National Trust for Historic Preservation in 1949, but during the 1950s and 1960s federal urban renewal programs permanently altered the nation's architectural heritage through the wholesale demolition of historic buildings. These systematic losses led to passage of the National Historic Preservation Act of 1966, landmark legislation that established a national program to preserve, promote, and protect historic properties. Charleston's historic African-American neighborhood, the Triangle District, was lost during this period to urban renewal and highway construction, as were historic parts of the downtown. Parkersburg, Huntington, and other cities suffered similar losses.

A West Virginia preservation milestone came in 1944 when the National Park Service established Harpers Ferry National Historical Park, and in the 1950s launched extensive restoration efforts there. Another important step came in 1962, with the state's purchase and planned restoration of the former logging town of Cass. In 1965, the legislature created the West Virginia Antiquities Commission with the authority to identify historic sites, determine state preservation needs, and set priorities. The Antiquities Commission undertook surveys, listed sites to the National Register of Historic Places, and took an active role in preserving places such as West Virginia Independence Hall and Blennerhassett Island. More importantly, the commission imparted historic preservation ideals and created an atmosphere of public-private cooperation.

Spurred on by the nation's bicentennial, preservation activities accelerated in the 1970s. Legislation created the West Virginia Division of Culture and History in 1977, which absorbed the State Historic Preservation Office from the now-defunct Antiquities Commission. The Historic Preservation Office's mission includes preservation planning, public education, surveying and nominating historic properties to the National Register, and administering rehabilitation tax credits and grants according to standards established by the Department of the Interior.

A 1975 preservation conference in Wheeling launched plans for a grassroots organization dedicated to supporting and promoting historic preservation. With support from the National Trust, the Preservation Alliance of West Virginia came into existence in 1981. The Preservation Alliance is involved in advocacy, education, heritage tourism, and other initiatives. Another key preservation partner since its founding in 1988 is Main Street West Virginia, a state-run program that works with communities in revitalization efforts that capitalize on their history and architectural resources.

Since the 1990s, growing heritage tourism opportunities have raised awareness of our state's historical legacy and increased the level of public and private cooperation. Despite numerous successes, hundreds of significant historic sites and structures—especially those related to our rich industrial and ethnic heritage—remain under threat of being lost to urban sprawl, inadequate zoning, or neglect.

Billy Joe Peyton
West Virginia State University

Lora Lamarre, *Preserving Our Mountaineer Heritage: West Virginia Statewide Historic Preservation Plan*, 2002–2006, 2001.

History of West Virginia

Written records of West Virginia's history reach back only slightly more than 300 years, about half of which encompass the time when West Virginia was part of Virginia. Recorded history, however, is only a fragment of the West Virginia story and must be coupled with artifacts of preliterate people and other evidence which falls within the realms of geology, geography, and archeology.

Still evident after some 245 million years are the effects upon West Virginia of a great geological disturbance, a mountain-building era, known as the Appalachian Orogeny. At that time the floor of a portion of a great inland sea, which covered much of the interior of North America, was forced upward to create the Appalachian Mountains. In time the new land wore down to a large peneplain that tilts gently toward the Mississippi Valley. Natural forces, including erosion and the flow of streams, eventually produced a terrain marked by numerous valleys, rugged hills, and mountains that distinguish the state's landscape to this day. Immense deposits of coal, oil, natural gas, salt, limestone, and other resources laid down in long-past geological eras have been vital to the economic life of West Virginia in historic times. The huge glaciers of the Ice Age never reached present West Virginia, but they did much to determine the state's basic drainage patterns, especially with respect to the New, Ohio, and once-mighty Teays rivers.

The first inhabitants of West Virginia apparently descended from "Old Mongoloid" stock, or eastern Asians, who crossed the Bering Strait from Siberia to Alaska approximately 40,000 years ago. Over the centuries, Native Americans, or Indians, evolved through three major cultural stages, including Paleo-Indian, Archaic, and Woodland. Nomadic Paleo-Indian life centered upon the pursuit of large game animals and lasted until these animals became extinct about 6000 B.C. As early as 7000 B.C., Archaic Culture began to appear and continued over the next 6,000 years. A more reliable food supply that included small game, fish, roots, plants, and berries enabled the Ar-

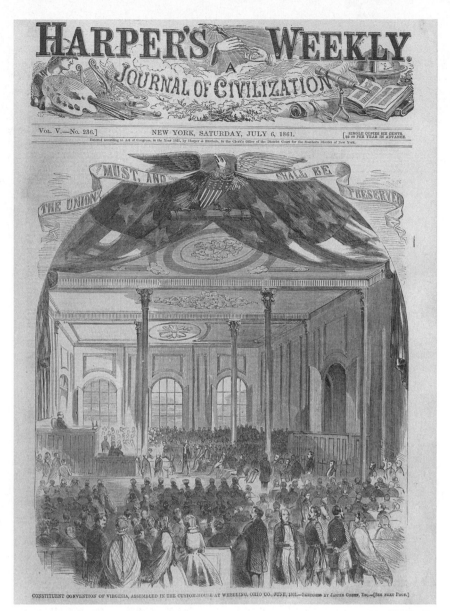

The Second Wheeling Convention, June 1861.

chaic people to live in camps, often for long periods of time. Woodland Cultures, including the Adena, Hopewell, and Mississippian, evolved between about 1000 B.C. and A.D. 1700 and were among the most advanced in prehistoric West Virginia. Woodland Indians cultivated such plants as corn, beans, and squash, made pottery, and practiced burial ceremonialism. They left hundreds of mounds and other structures scattered across West Virginia. Among the best known are the Grave Creek Mound at Moundsville, the South Charleston-Dunbar mounds, the Bens Run earthworks in Tyler County, and the Mount Carbon rock walls in Fayette County.

The first European explorers found only a few natives in present West Virginia. By then, the Indians had formed into tribes and warfare was common. Two of the most powerful groups in the eastern United States were the Iroquois

and Cherokee, both of which claimed parts of West Virginia. They probably forced weaker tribes, including the Shawnee, Mingo, and others, to abandon most of the state.

In 1606, King James I of England granted to the Virginia Company of London a vast expanse of land that included all of Virginia, present West Virginia, and Kentucky, as well as parts of North Carolina, Delaware, Pennsylvania, and even New York. The first English settlers arrived in Jamestown in 1607. During the 17th century, white settlers, as well as Africans, arrived in Virginia in ever-increasing numbers. As settlements pushed up the rivers of the Tidewater, native claimants to the land became more and more restless. In 1622 and 1644, clashes between English settlers and the Indians erupted into bloody wars with appalling losses and created conditions that made western exploration hazardous. Interest in advancing into frontier regions languished following the execution of Charles I and the establishment of the commonwealth under Oliver Cromwell, but it revived after the accession of Charles II to the throne in 1660.

Between 1669 and 1673, a surge of frontier exploration took place. Important explorers included John Lederer, who scaled the Blue Ridge Mountains northwest of present Charlottesville, Virginia; Batts and Fallam, who discovered the westward-flowing waters of the New River and laid the basis for English claims to the Ohio Valley; and Needham and Arthur, the latter the first person of European descent to visit the Kanawha Valley. After 1675, English expansion suffered setbacks partly due to troubles with the Susquehannock Indians, to Bacon's Rebellion in Virginia, and to the death in 1680 of Abraham Wood, a leading promoter.

Renewed interest in the Virginia frontier did not develop until after the beginning of the 18th century. By then, land suitable for settlement had become one of the most important reasons for exploration. The first known plans for a settlement in present West Virginia were made by Louis Michel, a resident of Bern, Switzerland, who in 1706 envisioned a settlement at present Harpers Ferry. A later attempt by Michel and Baron Christopher de Graffenreid was abandoned because of objections of the Conestoga Indians and the conflicting claims to the region by Virginia, Pennsylvania, and Maryland. In 1716, Gov. Alexander Spotswood of Virginia, with about 50 gentlemen later dubbed the "Knights of the Golden Horseshoe," their servants, and Indian guides, crossed the Blue Ridge Mountains by way of Swift Run Gap. Standing on the banks of the Shenandoah River, Spotswood claimed the land for England.

The location and date of the first settlement in West Virginia is uncertain. A settlement known as "Potomoke" in 1717 may have been at Shepherdstown. Morgan Morgan, a Welsh immigrant, however, has commonly been credited with making the first settlement in the state near Bunker Hill, Berkeley County, about 1731. It is now known that Morgan arrived about 1731 and that settlers were already in present West Virginia. Regardless of the location of the first settlement, it is clear that large numbers of immigrants did not arrive until after 1730, when Virginia enacted a land law that encouraged movement of people westward. Under that law speculators could acquire 1,000 acres for each family they recruited from outside the colony within a two-year period. This generous policy attracted large numbers of German and Scotch-Irish settlers, and by 1750 the population of the Valley of Virginia had reached a saturation point. In 1719, one of the largest land

grants in American history was acquired by Thomas, Sixth Lord Fairfax. The Fairfax estate included the Northern Neck of Virginia and present Jefferson, Berkeley, Morgan, Hampshire, Hardy, and Mineral counties, as well as parts of Grant and Tucker counties in West Virginia.

As settlers crossed the Allegheny Mountains, serious conflicts over the Ohio Valley developed between England and France. In order to press her claims to the region and to erect a buffer between the settlements and hostile Indians, Virginia made use of the same land policy that had proved effective in the Valley of Virginia. Speculators, however, were now allowed three years to settle the required number of families. The largest grants were made to the Greenbrier, Loyal, and Ohio companies. Meanwhile, France vigorously asserted her claims to the Ohio Valley. In 1749, Celoron de Blainville led an expedition down the Ohio River and at places along the way buried lead plates with inscriptions claiming the Ohio Valley for his country. During the years immediately following, the French built key forts in the disputed region. In the clash between English and French interests, Western Virginia was in the very center of the storm. In 1753, Gov. Robert Dinwiddie, determined to block French expansion into the Ohio Valley, sent 21-year-old George Washington with a message to the French commandant at Fort Le Boeuf near Lake Erie. Dinwiddie asserted that the French were intruding upon British soil and demanded that they withdraw. The French made it clear that they would remain. At that time the young Virginian perceived that possession of the Forks of the Ohio, present Pittsburgh, held the key to control of the Ohio Valley.

Acting upon Washington's advice, Dinwiddie dispatched a work party to erect a fort at that location. In April 1754, Washington with 150 militiamen set out to garrison the new fort. Meanwhile, a large French force had seized the Forks of the Ohio. In the skirmishes that followed, the French drove the Virginians from the region. In 1755, at the request of Governor Dinwiddie, Gen. Edward Braddock arrived in Virginia with two regiments of British troops. His coming transformed a frontier conflict into a war between two great empires. Unfamiliar with frontier modes of fighting, Braddock marched his army into an ambush, and his troops were defeated at the Battle of the Monongahela.

The clashes between the British and the French at the Forks of the Ohio were the initial hostilities in the conflict known in American history as the French and Indian War and in other parts of the world to which it spread as the Seven Years War. The war marked the beginning of a 40-year period in which the hunger for

land and a preoccupation with frontier defense set the tone for West Virginia affairs. The Ohio Valley remained one of the war's strategic theaters.

From the beginning, most Indians northwest of the Ohio River favored France, whose interests in the fur trade posed little threat to Indian land or ways of life. On the other hand, English settlements and agricultural pursuits were a danger that must be resisted. In Western Virginia hostile Indians destroyed the Greenbrier settlements and repeatedly attacked the upper Potomac settlers. The capture of the Forks of the Ohio by Gen. John Forbes in 1758 and the construction of Fort Pitt helped turn the tide of the war in favor of the English. By 1759, England controlled key positions in North America, and in 1763 the Treaty of Paris ended the fighting. France lost the Ohio Valley and the rest of her colonial possessions on the North American mainland. There was never then any doubt that English culture would be dominant in Western Virginia.

Western Indian tribes, fearful and embittered, joined together under Chief Pontiac and struck quickly at the English. The Greenbrier settlements were again destroyed, and settlers in the Monongahela Valley and other areas suffered heavy losses. In an attempt to appease the Indians, the British government issued the Proclamation of 1763, which forbade settlements west of the crests of the Allegheny Mountains. Later, by the treaties of Hard Labor, Fort Stanwix, and Lochaber, the Iroquois and Cherokee gave up their claims to lands in West Virginia. Beginning in 1769, waves of pioneers swept into the upper Ohio, Monongahela, Greenbrier, and Kanawha valleys.

The treaties, however, failed to consider the claims of such tribes as the Shawnee, Delaware, and Mingo. Once again, an influx of speculators and new settlers alarmed the western tribes and by the early 1770s provoked a new round of hostilities. The most serious was Dunmore's War. In its only battle, fought at Point Pleasant on October 10, 1774, the Virginians, led by Andrew Lewis, defeated the Indians under Shawnee Chief Cornstalk. The Treaty of Camp Charlotte restored peace. The Battle of Point Pleasant was a decisive factor in the neutrality of the Indians during the first two years of the American Revolution and allowed the continuation of settlements into Western Virginia and Kentucky.

Although Western Virginians participated in nearly every major battle of the Revolutionary War, for most families the war was a continuation of hostilities with the Indians, who now had British support. In 1777, the Indians broke their neutrality and attacked Fort Henry at Wheeling. Indian raids again became common in most of Western Virginia and continued even after the British surrendered at Yorktown in 1781. The last important Revolutionary War engagement in Western Virginia occurred in 1782 when about 200 Indians besieged Fort Henry. Clashes continued until 1794, when Gen. Anthony Wayne defeated the Indians in the Battle of Fallen Timbers and forced them to give up their claims to lands south of the Ohio River.

On the eve of the Revolution, avaricious speculators expanded their horizons. They proposed an ambitious scheme for a 14th American colony known as Vandalia, which included most of present West Virginia, southwestern Pennsylvania, and portions of Kentucky. The war prevented the establishment of the colony, and its promoters later attempted to gain approval for a 14th state known as Westsylvania. Congress, however, rejected the plan, and Western Virginia remained a part of Virginia.

In 1779, the Virginia general assembly passed a land law that had far-reaching effects upon West Virginia, even to the present. The law recognized the rights of original settlers. It also permitted the buying and selling of certificates that enabled speculators, many of whom were from outside West Virginia, to acquire hundreds of thousands of acres of land. Unfortunately, the law did not require land to be surveyed before its transfer. As a result, land claims were often imprecise and provided lawyers with a profitable business for decades in resolving disputes. Among the most baneful effects of the law on the state were the emergence of an enduring system of absentee land-ownership and arrested economic growth.

Until nearly the end of the 19th century, when large-scale industry became important, most West Virginians depended upon subsistence farming for their livelihood. Families continued to rely upon their fields and the forests for products commonly used in their foods, shelter, and clothing. Early industries, including grain milling and textile manufacturing, were often farm-related.

The War of 1812 stimulated industrial development, especially salt and iron. The Kanawha Salines at present Malden became by far the most important salt-producing center in the region. By 1815, 52 salt furnaces were operating along the Kanawha River for a distance of ten miles east of Charleston. Competition among saltmakers was so keen that in 1817 they organized the Kanawha Salt Company, sometimes regarded as the first trust in American history. Production in the Kanawha Valley peaked in 1846 when 3,224,786 bushels were produced. Salt stimulated the growth of timbering, flatboat construction, barrel making, and coal mining. The first iron furnace in Western Virginia was established by Thomas Mayberry at Bloomery near Harpers Ferry in

1742. The Peter Tarr Furnace on Kings Creek near Weirton, the first iron furnace west of the mountains, was erected in 1794. Later, the Wheeling area and the Monongahela Valley became the most important centers of iron manufacturing in West Virginia.

On the eve of the Civil War, Burning Springs in Wirt County emerged as one of the foremost oil fields in the United States. Natural gas, often found in the same locations as oil, had little importance before the war. During the 1840s, however, William Tompkins, a Kanawha Valley saltmaker, experimented with gas in the operation of his salt wells.

A growing population and expanding industries led to significant developments in transportation. The National Road, the first major highway in the region, was completed by the federal government from Cumberland, Maryland, to Wheeling in 1818. The highway helped to transform Wheeling into a major industrial and commercial center in the upper Ohio Valley. Three roads completed by Virginia before the Civil War included the James River & Kanawha Turnpike, the Northwestern Turnpike, and the Staunton-Parkersburg Turnpike. These highways stimulated economic development and promoted the growth of numerous new towns.

Although flatboats and keelboats were commonly used, the steamboat soon became the most important craft on Western Virginia's rivers. James Rumsey, a resident of Shepherdstown, was one of the pioneers in the development of the steamboat. Construction of steamboats for western rivers quickly became an important industry along the upper Ohio. The *George Washington*, launched by Capt. Henry M. Shreve at Wheeling in 1816, demonstrated that the steamboat had an important future on the inland waterways. Steamboats made river improvements imperative. In the 1850s, the Coal River Navigation Company, with funds provided by coal companies and the state, built nine locks and dams, the first such facilities in Western Virginia.

By the 1830s, interest in transportation in the United States began to shift to railroads. The first major line in Western Virginia, the Baltimore & Ohio, was completed from Harpers Ferry to Wheeling in 1853. The only other important line in Western Virginia before the Civil War was the Northwestern Virginia Railroad, opened in 1857 from Grafton to Parkersburg.

In the early 19th century, sectionalism began to appear in Virginia. The Blue Ridge and later the Allegheny Front marked a divide between eastern and western parts of the state. Differences between Virginians grew out of their cultural backgrounds, their divergent economic interests, and the overwhelming

political influence of Tidewater and Piedmont planters. Friction between the sections intensified over such political issues as expanding the vote, representation in the legislature, and popular election of state and county officials. Ironically, the Virginia constitution of 1776, crafted by leaders who proclaimed devotion to democracy, had a granite-like quality that assured the unassailability of eastern supremacy in state affairs.

Western dissatisfaction led to several attempts to reform the state constitution. The Staunton conventions of 1816 and 1825 and the Constitutional Convention of 1829–30 failed to meet western demands. Some western leaders favored separation from Virginia. The convention of 1850–51 made changes that addressed the political sources of western discontent. Under the new constitution a westerner, Joseph Johnson of Bridgeport, became the first popularly elected governor of Virginia. These successes, however, were overshadowed by economic inequities. The new constitution shifted the tax burden to the west by requiring that all property, except slaves, be taxed at its actual value, and it contained provisions that dealt severe blows to internal improvements favored by the west. Old rivalries between east and west were soon renewed.

In the three decades before the Civil War, slavery was increasingly an issue in the United States. Two prominent Western Virginians took a strong stand on slavery. Henry Ruffner, a Kanawha Countian who served as president of Washington College (now Washington and Lee University), published the *Ruffner Pamphlet* in which he attacked slavery as an evil that kept immigrants out of Virginia, slowed economic development, and hampered education. He urged gradual emancipation of all slaves west of the Blue Ridge Mountains. Alexander Campbell, a founder of the Disciples of Christ and president of Bethany College, contended, however, that the North should accept slavery in the South. He supported the Fugitive Slave Law of 1850 but believed that runaway slaves should be provided the necessities of food, shelter, and clothing. As tensions over slavery mounted, several churches divided over the issue. The Methodists, who split in 1844, included most of Western Virginia in their northern branch.

Some well-known abolitionists regarded Western Virginia as useful to their cause. In 1857, Eli Thayer of Massachusetts chose Ceredo for a settlement by 500 New England emigrants who were expected to demonstrate to Southerners that free labor was superior to slave labor. The Civil War led to the collapse of the experiment, and when the conflict ended only about 125 of the original settlers were left. Unlike Thayer's friendly invasion, abolitionist John Brown in 1859 led a bold raid on

Harpers Ferry so alarming to the South that some historians believe it made the Civil War inevitable.

The election of Abraham Lincoln as president in 1860 exacerbated feelings that led to the Civil War and ultimately to the formation of West Virginia. Following the fall of Fort Sumter and Lincoln's call for volunteers, Virginia held a convention in April 1861 to consider a course of action. The convention voted 88 to 55 to leave the Union. Of 47 delegates from present-day West Virginia, 32 voted against secession, 11 favored it, and four did not vote. John S. Carlile and other Unionist delegates hurried home and organized opposition to Virginia's decision. As a result of their efforts, 37 counties sent delegates to a meeting in May known as the First Wheeling Convention. There, Carlile urged immediate steps to establish a new state. Other leaders, including Waitman T. Willey, Francis H. Pierpont, and John J. Jackson, preferred to postpone action.

In June 1861, the Second Wheeling Convention established the Reorganized, or Restored, Government of Virginia at Wheeling. Francis H. Pierpont was chosen governor, and Willey and Carlile were named to the U.S. Senate to replace Virginia's senators who had cast their lot with the Confederacy. Throughout the Civil War, Virginia had two governments. The Wheeling government supported the Union, and the Richmond government the Confederacy. In August, the Second Wheeling Convention, in its Adjourned Session, took steps to establish a separate state. On October 24, 1861, the voters of 41 counties approved the formation of a new state, but less than 37 percent of those eligible to vote actually did so.

In order to become a state, West Virginia needed the approval of Virginia and a constitution acceptable to the Congress and the president. Since the Confederate government in Richmond would never agree to the dismemberment of Virginia, leaders of the proposed new state turned to the Reorganized Government. Governor Pierpont called a special session of the legislature that approved the request within a week. His role in establishing the state was so crucial that he is regarded as the "Father of West Virginia."

In the U.S. Senate, a petition that would allow West Virginia to enter the Union as a slave state was referred to the Committee on Territories, of which Carlile was a member. Unexpectedly, for reasons on which historians have disagreed, Carlile, who had previously favored creation of a new state, now included proposals that nearly destroyed the chances for statehood. At this critical moment, Willey offered a compromise to gradually abolish slavery in West Virginia. With the Willey Amendment to the state constitution, the statehood bill passed both

houses of Congress. The West Virginia Constitutional Convention reconvened in February 1863 and accepted the Willey Amendment. The amended constitution was approved by the electorate in a vote of 28,321 to 572. In accordance with a proclamation of President Abraham Lincoln, West Virginia entered the Union on June 20, 1863, as the 35th state.

When West Virginia became a state, the Civil War had already been raging within its borders for two years and had deepened the divisions among the state's people. Historians do not agree on exactly how many West Virginians served in Union and Confederate armies. Charles H. Ambler and Festus P. Summers estimated that from 25,000 to 45,000 West Virginians fought in the Civil War, about 80 percent for the Union and about 20 percent for the Confederacy. More recent estimates place the number of Union soldiers at no more than 60 percent and Confederates at about 40 percent. Boyd B. Stutler, in his *Civil War in West Virginia*, counted 632 actions, including battles, skirmishes, and other engagements in West Virginia.

The year 1861 was one of intense military activity. The Battle of Philippi on June 3 is sometimes regarded as the first land battle of the Civil War. Before the end of summer, Union forces controlled both the Monongahela and Kanawha valleys. A Union victory at Carnifex Ferry in September 1861 prevented the Confederates from driving a wedge between the two federal forces. Later, Gen. Robert E. Lee's efforts to regain lost territory ended in failure at the Battle of Cheat Mountain. By the winter of 1861–62, much of the military activity in West Virginia had degenerated into vicious guerrilla warfare involving such irregular bands as the Black Striped Company in Logan County and the Moccasin Rangers in Braxton, Nicholas, and other central counties. Some of the most notable military actions of 1862 and 1863 were in the form of daring Confederate raids into Union-held territory. They included the Jenkins Raid of 1862 and the Jones-Imboden Raid of 1863. The Battle of Droop Mountain on November 6, 1863, gave Union forces control over most of the territory of the new state of West Virginia.

The Reconstruction Era was hardly less traumatic than the Civil War. Divisions existed not only between Unionists and former Confederates, but also among the Unionists themselves. Unconditional Unionists, including Arthur I. Boreman, Archibald W. Campbell, and Waitman T. Willey, were willing to accept the emancipation of slaves and increased federal authority in order to maintain statehood. Conservative Unionists, however, adamantly opposed a government they considered dictatorial and abolitionist.

Fearful for the state's future, Governor

Boreman and Radical Republican leaders who dominated the legislature were determined to prevent former Confederates, most of whom were Democrats, from regaining political power. Repressive legislation provided for confiscation of the property of persons regarded as enemies of the state. The Radical-dominated legislature also enacted the Voters' Test Oaths of 1865 and the Voters' Registration Law of 1866. These measures restricted the right to vote and required state and local officials, as well as attorneys and school teachers, to take oaths of allegiance to West Virginia and the United States. Estimates of the number of disfranchised voters range from 15,000 to 25,000. By the end of the 1860s, the anomaly of these stern proscriptions at a time when the federal government was assiduously protecting the voting rights of African-Americans led to calls for change. In 1871, moderate Republicans joined with Democrats to pass the Flick Amendment to the state constitution, which ended political restrictions on ex-Confederates in West Virginia. Voters approved the amendment by a margin of more than three to one.

In 1870, the Democratic Party carried the West Virginia elections. The governorship of John J. Jacob initiated a period of Democratic control that lasted 26 years. Democrats immediately took steps to provide the state with a new frame of government. A convention assembled in Charleston and wrote the constitution of 1872, under which the state is still governed. The new constitution eliminated the township system and implemented a modified county court system. It extended the term of office of the governor from two to four years. From time to time voters have declined to authorize a new convention to modernize the state constitution. However, they have endeavored to retain the workability of a somewhat antiquated document by approving 70 of 118 proposed amendments.

One of the most sagacious and far-sighted provisions of the original constitution of 1863 was its mandate to the legislature to provide a "thorough and efficient" system of free public schools for all children in the state. The legislature created an administrative structure that included a state superintendent, county superintendents, and officials in townships, into which counties were divided for educational purposes. By 1870, the state had 2,270 schools, mostly with one room and one teacher. The constitution of 1872 retained the free school mandate. Some counties, nevertheless, faced lingering opposition to free schools largely because of objections to taxes needed for their support or to the free-school principle itself.

The development of West Virginia public schools in the last quarter of the 19th

West Virginia's Victorian-era capitol.

century and the early decades of the 20th century was similar to that of several southern and midwestern states. Important milestones were the designation of Marshall College as the state's normal training school for teachers in 1867 and the establishment of branch normals at Fairmont, Athens, Shepherdstown, Glenville, and West Liberty in the 1870s; the assignment of training for black teachers to the two "colored institutes"; the enactment of a compulsory attendance law in 1903; and the opening of 233 high schools by 1925 and 88 junior high schools by 1928. West Virginia pioneered the adoption of a graduating plan for public schools, formulated by Alexander L. Wade of Monongalia County. Beginning in the 1890s, it gradually became the pattern throughout the United States. With the adoption of the County Unit Plan of 1933, providing countywide rather than district school boards, West Virginia again led the nation in a major educational reform. During the 20th century, public schools were strongly influenced by the progressive education movement, whose leaders gained control of the educational administrative machinery at the state level and achieved power that lasted throughout the century.

As in other states, West Virginia education has been shaped to a considerable extent by federal policy and federal support. Under the terms of the Morrill Act, West Virginia University was founded in 1867 as the state's land-grant institution. The GI Bill of Rights of 1944 provided generous educational benefits to thousands of World War II veterans and improved the financial condition of nearly every college in the state. Segregation of West Virginia schools, mandated by the state constitution, was ended by the U.S. Supreme Court decision *Brown v. Board of Education of Topeka* (1954). Unlike several southern states, West Virginia achieved integration with little opposition. Ongoing federal programs launched in the 1960s, including Upward Bound and Headstart, have done much to provide equal educational opportunities for children throughout the state. Some major issues in education at the turn of the 21st century include the pros and cons of school consolidation, and the impact of the federal No Child Left Behind Act. At the same time, like other Americans, West Virginians have serious concerns regarding a decline of discipline and an increasing violence in the public schools.

In celebrating the 50 years of statehood in 1913, West Virginians looked back with pride upon an era of unprecedented industrial development. The achievement was largely in extractive industries and based upon coal, oil, natural gas, and timber resources, which had lain dormant for millennia. In the late 19th century, state government, whether in the hands of Democrats or Republicans, endeavored to extirpate the bitterness wrought by the Civil War and Reconstruction and to establish a climate favorable to industrial growth. By 1913, annual coal production exceeded 28 million tons. The state achieved first place in the nation in oil production in 1898 and in natural gas output in 1906. Timber production reached its peak in 1909.

Closely associated with such expansion was the building of hundreds of miles of railroads, including the Chesapeake & Ohio, Norfolk & Western, Coal & Coke, Western Maryland, Virginian, and Kanawha & Michigan lines. Railroad magnates such as Cornelius Vanderbilt, J. P. Morgan, Collis P. Huntington, and others acquired vast acreages of West Virginia land and mineral resources. By the end of the 20th century, major West Virginia railroads, after numerous mergers, were incorporated into such giants as CSX and Norfolk Southern, two of the largest landholders in the state. Also vital to industrial growth was the construction of locks and dams in the Ohio, Kanawha, Monongahela, Big Sandy, and Little Kanawha rivers, their upgrading in the 1930s, and further improvements as the 20th century drew to a close.

By 1900, West Virginia was clearly on the threshold of major economic and demographic changes. The state still had some 93,000 farms. Nevertheless, migration from rural areas to cities, one of the dominant trends in the nation, was also in progress in West Virginia. By 1994, farm acreage was less than 35 percent of that of 1900. Most were commercial rather than subsistence farms. Three-fourths of agricultural income came from livestock, including cattle and calves, poultry, and dairy products. Apples, peaches, and tobacco were important commercial crops.

By the late 1800s, rapidly expanding industries, especially coal, led to an acute need for labor, and both the state government and individual companies sent agents abroad to take advantage of the "New Immigration" from southern and eastern Europe. They recruited thousands of Italians, Poles, Hungarians, Austrians, and other nationalities, as well as African-Americans from the South. These ethnic groups added greater diversity to the state's population and culture.

West Virginia's rich resources and emerging extractive industries caught the attention of powerful business and financial interests outside the state. Many acquired large amounts of land for a small fraction of its real worth. State businessmen and politicians sometimes became allies of powerful non-resident interests whose activities left both benefits and problems. The new industrial age transformed much of the state from a society of small, independent farmers into one with a class-oriented social and economic structure of newly rich industrial barons at the apex and landless wage-earners at the bottom. Sizable amounts of West Virginia's wealth left the state, and the land from which it was drawn fell under the heavy cloud of a colonial economy.

As extractive industries, particularly coal, gained a prominent place in the West Virginia economy during the first half-century of statehood, capital investment in manufacturing increased fourfold between 1870 and 1900. The Northern Panhandle, Ohio Valley, and Kanawha Valley became major manufacturing areas. Wheeling was the leading industrial city in the state throughout the 19th century. Other prominent industrial centers included Charleston, Parkersburg, Newell, Wellsburg, Benwood, New Cumberland, and Huntington.

World War I was a major stimulus to industry, especially the manufacture of chemicals. The federal government laid the basis for the industry in the Kanawha Valley by constructing a mustard gas plant at Belle and a smokeless powder plant at Nitro, where a community of 25,000 people sprang up almost overnight. Chemical firms in the Kanawha Valley expanded rapidly in the decades after 1920 and manufactured a great variety of new products, including rubber, plastics, rayon, nylon, and automotive antifreezes. World War II further accelerated the making of chemicals in West Virginia. The Kanawha Valley became one of the chemical centers of the world. By 1970, every Ohio River county except Jackson had at least one chemical plant.

During the first half of the 20th century, textile, clay-product, glass, and electric power industries grew rapidly. Hancock County manufactured fine chinaware. The state was a pioneer in the development and use of modern glass-making machinery, but it was also known throughout the world for its Fostoria and hand-blown Blenko, Fenton, and Pilgrim glass products. After 1940, electric power production increased by about 2,000 percent.

By the mid-20th century, mechanization, foreign competition, and emergence of a global economy contributed to fundamental changes in West Virginia industry. Many traditional industries experienced decline. Increasingly, the state was confronted with technological unemployment. Thousands of miners and other workers lost their jobs and left. The population fell from 2,005,552 in 1950 to 1,860,421 in 1960. Further losses occurred in the 1960s and 1980s. Scores of once-thriving mining towns lost so many families that they became ghost towns. In the 1990s, however, the state's economy showed signs of improvement. Important growth areas included certain areas of manufacturing, such as the automobile and wood-based industries, as well as the service industries, and tourism and recreation. Investments by Japanese, Taiwanese, and British firms attested to an increasing globalization of the state economy. Service industries, including banking and insurance, real estate, and rapidly-expanding health care, made up 68 percent of the gross state product. By 1996, the state's improved economy seemed to be contributing to a reversal of nearly four decades of population losses. In 2000, the United States Census estimated the state's population at 1,808,350.

Industrialization in West Virginia produced conditions conducive to an organized labor movement. As early as the 1820s, Wheeling had a sizable wage-earning class and a labor newspaper. A strong labor movement, however, did not develop until after the Civil War. The first important union was the Knights of Labor, founded in 1869. The Knights established a local organization at Paden City in 1877, and within a few years 16 others were founded in the state. The great railroad strike of 1877, the first nationwide industrial strike, began at Martinsburg and ended only by federal intervention. In 1880, the Knights of Labor supported an unsuccessful strike by miners at Hawks Nest in Fayette County. Following these and other setbacks, the union gradually declined.

In 1881, the American Federation of Labor, made up of crafts of skilled workers, was organized. It advocated an eight-hour day, six-day work week, higher wages, and job safety and security. By 1914, the West Virginia Federation of Labor, which was affiliated with the national organization, included 152 local craft unions with 31,315 members. The union was especially strong among iron, steel, and tin workers; transportation employees; and glass workers. Wheeling had more than 40 percent of the union craft workers in the state. Wheeling, Fairmont, Clarksburg, Charleston, Hinton, Morgantown, and Parkersburg had central labor organizations made up of the craft unions.

The most powerful union in West Virginia has been the United Mine Workers of America. The union was formed in Indianapolis in 1890 and only gradually established itself in West Virginia. Only about half of state miners participated in a nationwide strike in 1894. Union membership declined in 1897 to a mere 206 workers. Between 1897 and 1902, the UMWA enlisted the support of well-known labor leaders from across the nation. They included Samuel Gompers, Eugene V. Debs, and Mary "Mother" Jones. Operators responded with court injunctions, yellow-dog contracts, blacklisting, and heavily armed mine guards. Nevertheless, in 1902 the union, with assistance from Jones, organized about 7,000 miners in the Kanawha Valley. For the next quarter-century, Mother Jones had a powerful influence with miners in West Virginia.

During the Mine Wars of the early 20th century, some of the most violent episodes in the state's labor history occurred in the coalfields. In 1912–13, troubles erupted on Paint and Cabin creeks, tributaries of the Kanawha River, when operators refused to renew contracts with the union. Sporadic violence occurred at Mucklow and Holly Grove and caused Governor Glasscock to impose martial law. The strike ultimately ended when Governor Hatfield helped arrange a settlement.

The great demand for coal and a shortage of labor during World War I produced conditions in which the industry flourished, wages rose, and union membership increased. Between 1919 and 1921, UMWA efforts to unionize the mines of southern West Virginia, particularly in Logan and Mingo counties, were marked by incidents of unusual violence, including the Matewan Massacre, Sharples Massacre, and the Battle of Blair Mountain. Labor suffered major setbacks. By 1924, the UMWA had lost half its members in West Virginia and was nearly bankrupt. Collective bargaining, one of the union's major goals, remained unachieved.

The Great Depression, beginning in 1929, proved a catalyst for fundamental political, economic, and social reforms in the United States. In 1932, Franklin D. Roosevelt, the Democratic candidate for president, promised a "New Deal" in handling the nation's extraordinary economic problems. The National Industrial Recovery Act of 1933 (NIRA) gave workers benefits for which they had long battled. It offered an eight-hour workday, an end to yellow-dog contracts, and the right to collective bargaining. After the U.S. Supreme Court ruled that NIRA was unconstitutional, many parts of the act relating to labor were included in the Wagner Act of 1935.

Under the leadership of John L. Lewis, coal miners made rapid gains in the more benign political environment. The Appalachian Agreements eventually ended unfavorable wage scales, and in 1946 a Miners' Welfare and Retirement Fund, one of the union's most important goals, was established. During the 1940s, the UMWA reached the zenith of its political influence in West Virginia when its leaders persuaded Matthew Neely to give up his U.S. Senate seat to run for governor. After 1950, mechanization and automation in coal mining drastically reduced the number of miners and began a long-term and eventually dramatic decline in UMWA membership and influence in the state.

Historically, mining has been one of the most dangerous industries. Most miners died in individual accidents killing one or a few miners at a time, but major mine disasters occurred at Monongah in 1907, Eccles in 1914, Benwood in 1924, and Farmington in 1968. Another disaster, at Buffalo Creek in 1972, was the result of the collapse of a coal company dam in which 125 people were killed and 17 communities destroyed. The dangers of underground work outside the coal

The new capitol takes shape, 1931.

industry appeared in 1932 during the construction of the Hawks Nest Tunnel, which diverted waters of the New River to a hydroelectric plant. Scores of men died of silicosis that might have been prevented had the company taken the proper precautions.

During the 1960s and 1970s, the actions of both federal and state governments led to improved safety and working conditions. In 1969, the federal government recognized pneumoconiosis, or black lung, as an occupational disease and set up a fund to support afflicted miners. A year later, the state established a Black Lung Fund.

One of the most distinctive events in the state's labor history occurred in the early 1980s when workers of the Weirton Steel Company purchased its properties and prevented the plant's closing. For a time, the new company was the largest employee-owned business in the nation, before suffering serious setbacks at the end of the 20th century. Employee ownership ended when Weirton Steel was sold to the International Steel Group early in the 21st century.

Political affairs since 1863 have reflected both changes and continuities in life in West Virginia. In the years immediately following statehood, the state was profoundly affected by the problems and tensions of Reconstruction. Partisan politics agitated discussions regarding the location of a permanent state capital. Republicans favored Wheeling, their center of influence. Democrats wanted the capital in southern West Virginia, where their party was strong. In 1877, the matter was submitted to the voters, who chose Charleston over Clarksburg and Martins-

burg as the permanent seat of government. The move was made in 1885.

In 1871, following the troubled eight years of Radical Reconstruction, the Democratic Party, augmented by disfranchised ex-Confederates and by Liberal Republicans, captured the governorship and the legislature. The so-called Bourbon Democrats often clung to the ideals of the rural South but promoted the development of industry, and their rule coincided with the beginnings of the industrial revolution in West Virginia.

Party labels in the late 19th and early 20th centuries are not always enlightening. Bourbon Democrats and conservative Republicans shared many of the same ideas and policies, and favored the development of the state's resources. The political and business relationships between Henry Gassaway Davis, who had enormous power in the Democratic Party, and his son-in-law, Stephen B. Elkins, who after 1894 had similar control over Republican affairs, illustrate the degree to which politics was tied to industrial welfare and influenced by great industrial tycoons. Four governors—George W. Atkinson, Albert B. White, William M. O. Dawson, and William E. Glasscock—are commonly known as "Elkins governors." Relations between West Virginia industrialists and those on the national scene often brought temporary prosperity and opportunities but in the long run helped move the state toward economic dependency.

Concerns over unbridled industrial exploitation of both natural and human resources, as well as government neglect of many vital services, helped set the stage for the Progressive Movement in West

Virginia. From 1900 to 1920, progressive ideals were at the center of state affairs. Although the movement transcended party lines, the greatest gains were made during the tenure of the Republican governors, particularly Henry D. Hatfield. One student of the period observed that at the end of the Hatfield administration West Virginia had as much progressive legislation as any state in the nation. Except for the Cornwell administration (1917–21), Republicans continued to control the governorship until 1933.

Like many other Americans, West Virginians were beguiled by the prosperity of the 1920s. In 1924, when John William Davis of Clarksburg received the Democratic nomination for president of the United States, West Virginia nonetheless gave its electoral votes to incumbent Republican Calvin Coolidge, whom they associated with the good times. Republican administrations in West Virginia during the 1920s were conservative, and the laissez-faire philosophy of government and economic affairs was the order of the day.

The Great Depression brought widescale unemployment, with thousands of people reduced to penury, and proved to be a watershed in American and West Virginia history. Laissez-faire doctrines fell before the activist philosophy of Roosevelt's New Deal, which projected an expanded role for government in economic, social, and cultural matters and allowed the Democratic Party to regain control over national and state affairs. The New Deal and the measures taken by Governor Kump and the legislature brought new hope to economically distressed West Virginians. Through such agencies as the National Industrial Recovery Administration, Works Progress Administration, Public Works Administration, Civilian Conservation Corps, National Youth Administration, and others, unemployment diminished and the economy improved. The easing of the Great Depression paved the way in West Virginia for a new Democratic era that continued into the 21st century. The period following World War II witnessed troubling new economic problems in West Virginia. The unsettled conditions, along with the popularity of Republican President Dwight D. Eisenhower, interrupted Democratic trends in the state and helped Republican Cecil H. Underwood capture the governorship in 1956.

While state politics have normally had little impact on the rest of the nation, the West Virginia primary of 1960 attracted national interest when it became a battleground between John F. Kennedy and Hubert H. Humphrey for the Democratic nomination for president. Kennedy's landslide victory in West Virginia proved to be a turning point in his campaign for the presidency.

During the 1960s, policies of the federal government exerted major impact upon conditions in West Virginia. President Kennedy's New Frontier and President Lyndon B. Johnson's War on Poverty pumped millions of federal dollars into the state. Among the most important new federal agencies was the Appalachian Regional Commission (ARC), established in 1965. Although it helped develop health-care centers, and supported vocational training, erosion control, and other projects, four-fifths of the ARC budget was devoted to construction of highways. At the close of the 20th century, more than 300 miles of Appalachian Corridor highways had been completed in the state.

Since the 1960s, one of the most significant changes in West Virginia government has been the emergence of a strong chief executive. The Modern Budget Amendment of 1968 made the governor responsible for preparation of the state budget. In 1970, the Governor's Succession Amendment permitted a governor to serve two consecutive terms. These amendments have led to a sharp increase in the influence and prestige of the governorship. Unlike other branches of state government, which have been dominated by Democrats, the governor's office since 1968 has alternated between Republicans and Democrats.

Leaders in both parties were deeply concerned about the condition of the state's economy. Economic improvements were sometimes made at high costs to the environment, and government officials sought ways to balance economic gains against environmental concerns. One controversial issue was strip mining, which liberals maintained must either be abolished or strictly regulated. Young John D. Rockefeller IV, who came to rural Kanawha County as a social worker in the 1960s, endeared himself to liberals by boldly advocating the abolition of strip mining. Following the energy crisis of 1973 and his election to the governorship, Rockefeller became a proponent of regulation rather than abolition. By the early 1990s, continued complaints over the destructive practices of coal operators led to threats by the federal government to take over regulation of surface mining in West Virginia. The actions of Governor Caperton and the legislature, which appropriated more funding for the employment of additional state inspectors, averted federal actions. By the late 1990s, mountaintop removal, the most profitable and arguably the most damaging form of surface mining, had become common and led to sharp public debate.

Public demands for greater access to education, health care, and other services produced rapid growth in both the size and costs of state government. In an effort to streamline administration, Governor Caperton reorganized the executive branch under seven "super secretaries," each responsible for several formerly separate agencies. His action, however, aroused criticism that another layer of expensive bureaucracy had been established.

In recent decades the state's governors, congressional representation, and other officials have made concerted efforts to promote economic development, including foreign investments. Sen. Robert C. Byrd, known nationally as an authority on Senate history and the U.S. Constitution, won federal appropriations in excess of $1 billion and brought numerous federal projects and facilities to West Virginia. By the mid-1990s, the state's economy bore signs of improvement although some ground was later lost in the recession that followed the national boom of the late 1990s. Between 1988 and 1997, the state budget more than doubled, rising from about $3.3 billion to approximately $7 billion.

As the 20th century slipped away, West Virginians could reflect upon the great changes that it had brought. The automobile, radio, motion pictures, television, computers, and other inventions had opened vistas little dreamed of when the century began. It had brought new opportunities for education and self-fulfillment, recognition of human rights for all people, and ever-increasing prospects for more people to share in the blessings the state had to offer. As always, however, problems remained. West Virginians had deep apprehensions about the future. Their concerns included the quality of education; the availability of health care, especially for children and the elderly; environmental matters; threats to cherished traditional values; and fears that the nation might not have in the future the prescience or the strength to manage the responsibilities of world power.

Otis K. Rice
Stephen W. Brown
WVU Institute of Technology

Hitchman Coal and Coke v. Mitchell et al.

The case of *Hitchman Coal and Coke v. Mitchell* grew from a critical issue in West Virginia history and became a landmark decision in U.S. constitutional law. Beginning in 1906, the Hitchman Coal and Coke Company, located in the Northern Panhandle near Benwood, notified each man who sought work there that he could be employed only if he agreed not to join the United Mine Workers of America. This kind of agreement, called a yellow-dog contract, was already common practice in much of the West Virginia coal industry.

The UMWA, which had working agreements with coal operators in northern states, was under pressure from those operators to organize the increasingly competitive and largely non-union West Virginia mines. In 1907, a federal district court issued an injunction prohibiting the union from seeking to influence the Hitchman workers to break their yellow-dog contracts. In 1917, the U.S. Supreme Court sustained the lower court ruling, thereby endorsing the combining of two powerful weapons against trade unionism, the injunction and the yellow-dog contract.

In the 1920s, the Hitchman doctrine helped to create a legal atmosphere extremely adverse to unions. Coal operators and other employers in West Virginia and across the country quickly took advantage of the judicially approved means of resisting labor organizations. The UMWA and other unions faced possible extinction until New Deal legislation and judicial decisions of the 1930s brought about a more favorable environment for unionism.

See also Yellow-Dog Contract

Jerry Bruce Thomas
Shepherd University

Irving Bernstein, *The Lean Years: A History of the American Worker, 1920–1933*, 1960; Richard D. Lunt, *Law and Order vs the Miners: West Virginia, 1907–1933*, 1992.

Joist Hite

Pioneer and land speculator Joist Hite, originally Hans Jöst Heydt, emigrated from Germany about 1710. Heydt traveled on his own ship and is said to have been a wealthy nobleman. He led 16 German and Dutch families to America, settling first in New York and later Pennsylvania. By 1731, Hite had moved to the Shenandoah Valley, where he had obtained a 100,000-acre grant from Virginia. Hite is credited with having started the first settlement on Opequon Creek in Berkeley County, in exchange for the grant. Later, the king confirmed Lord Fairfax's title to local lands, calling into question surveys and land sales Hite had made. After decades of legal battles Hite's side won, but not before both he and Fairfax were dead. Well respected by both Germans and Virginians, Joist Hite died in 1760.

See also Fairfax Lands

Jaime Simmons
State Archives

Warren R. Hofstra, "Land, Ethnicity, and Community at the Opequon Settlement, Virginia, 1730–1800," *Virginia Magazine of History and Biography*, July 1990.

Charles Hodel

Newspaperman Charles Hodel, a son of immigrant Swiss parents, was born January 13, 1889, in Ohio. He learned the printing trade and established himself in Beckley in 1912 as editor and general manager of the *Raleigh Register*, which became a daily in 1928. In 1929, Hodel and associates acquired control of the *Register's* competitor, the *Post-Herald*, a daily since 1924. It became the morning paper and the *Register* the afternoon and Sunday paper.

Hodel's two newspapers promoted many public projects and causes. Hodel was a leader in introducing the Beckley Area Rural Development Council. An early West Virginia conservationist, Hodel began an editorial campaign for conservation in the timbered-out hardwood forests of West Virginia. He also fought irresponsible strip mining.

He helped to found the local chamber of commerce and served a term as its president. As chairman of the chamber's airport committee, he was instrumental in developing the Beckley-Mount Hope Airport in 1933. Later, Hodel bought the land for the present Raleigh County Memorial Airport and held it until Raleigh County was able to buy it from him. Built in the early 1950s, the new airport attracted commercial airline service to the county.

Hodel helped to establish the West Virginia Historical Drama Association, now Theatre West Virginia, producer of the outdoor dramas "Honey in the Rock" and "Hatfields and McCoys" at nearby Grandview. He also campaigned for the development of New River Park in Beckley and worked to bring non-mining industry to the county. Hodel waged a long and bitter editorial battle with the United Mine Workers of America, and his campaign against illegal liquor sales and slot machines in private clubs was not popular with some.

Charles Hodel was the *Charleston Gazette's* "man of the year" in 1961, and was named in 1963 to the West Virginia Press Association's Hall of Fame. He died June 16, 1973, and his newspapers were sold to Clay Communications of Charleston in 1976.

Jim Wood
Beckley

Joseph Howard Hodges

Roman Catholic Bishop Joseph Howard Hodges was born in Harpers Ferry, October 8, 1911. He received his education at St. Charles College, in Maryland, and at the North American College, Rome, Italy. Hodges was ordained to the priesthood in 1935 for the Diocese of Richmond. He was engaged in pastoral work for the diocese, then served as director of the Diocesan Mission Band, 1945–52.

Hodges was made an auxiliary bishop of the Diocese of Richmond in 1952. He held this position until he was appointed coadjutor bishop with the right of succession to Archbishop John J. Swint (1879–1962) of the Diocese of Wheeling in 1961. He succeeded Swint as the fifth bishop of the diocese in 1962.

Hodges attended the Second Vatican Council and dedicated himself to implementing the liberalizing reforms to come out of the council. He was a leader in the state's ecumenical movement and in 1975 was recognized for distinguished service in the ecumenical cause by the West Virginia Council of Churches. An outspoken advocate for social justice for all West Virginians, he was a driving force behind the 1975 pastoral letter issued jointly by the Roman Catholic Bishops of Appalachia, "This Land is Home To Me," which addressed the issues of economic and political powerlessness.

Hodges sought and received approval from the Holy See for the redrawing of the diocese's boundaries in 1974, so that they would correspond with the state's boundaries. He also recommended the renaming of the diocese from Wheeling to Wheeling-Charleston that same year. Bishop Hodges died in Wheeling, January 27, 1985, at the age of 73.

Tricia Pyne
St. Mary's Seminary & University, Maryland

William Hoffman

Novelist Henry William Hoffman was born in Charleston, May 16, 1925. After his father left the family in the early 1930s, William and his only sibling, Janet, were raised primarily by a domineering but much loved grandmother. A staunch Presbyterian, Hoffman's fiction is influenced by his religious upbringing and his education at Hampden-Sydney College.

His first novel, *The Trumpet Unblown* (1955), is based on Hoffman's experiences as a medic in World War II. Two other novels, *Days in the Yellow Leaf* (1959) and *Yancey's War* (1966), also give dramatic testimony to the war's effects. Christian themes of spiritual quest after disillusionment, reconciliation, and ultimate redemption are found in *A Place For My Head* (1962), *The Dark Mountains* (1969), *A Walk to the River* (1972), *A Death of Dreams* (1975), *The Land That Drank the Rain* (1982), and *Godfires* (1985).

Another influence, nature, appears in Hoffman's feel for the land and his lifelong love of horses, the hunt, and the allure of the sea. His short stories—collected in *Virginia Reels* (1978), *By Land By Sea* (1988), *Follow Me Home* (1994), and *Doors* (1999)—have brought him an O. Henry Award and inclusion in *Best American Short Stories*. Hoffman's most recent novels are *Tidewater Blood* (1998), *Blood and Guile* (2000), *Wild Thorn* (2002), and *Lies* (2005). He won the 1999 Dashiell Hammett Prize for *Tidewater Blood*.

Hoffman has lived since 1964 on a farm at Charlotte Court House, Virginia.

William L. Frank
Longwood College
Henry W. Battle
Charleston

Hog Butchering

The farmer's winter food included a good supply of pork, and the butchering of hogs was an important annual ritual in the West Virginia countryside. Fat hogs were butchered as soon as the cooler weather permitted, usually around Thanksgiving. Butchering day started before daylight with heating the water in iron kettles over an outside fire. Soon the neighbor men arrived to help. When the water was boiling hot, the best sharpshooter in the group shot the first hog between the eyes. The hog was quickly bled, then lowered into a large barrel filled with hot water. After scalding, it was laid on a platform (usually the farmer's sled). Each man took a sharp butcher knife and scraped the loosened hair from the hog. The hog was then hung by the hind legs, using a rope and pulley attached to a frame or a stout tree limb. It was split and the heart, lungs, liver, and intestines removed. The carcass was then pulled up out of the way and left to cool. Working quickly, the men could have three hogs hung by noon.

The women prepared a noon-time meal for the butchers. The meal usually included fresh liver with onions. After eating and resting, the men cut the hogs into hams, shoulders, ribs, and so forth. By dark the meat for sausage and lard was cut into strips. Sausage grinding was a social event as neighbors gathered at night to help hand-grind all the fat for lard and the meat for sausage. Salt and spices were added to prepare the sausage for canning. All parts of the hog were used except the snout and the hoofs. The head was used for souse, head cheese, or mincemeat, and the entrails were cleaned by many families, the inner lining being used for sausage casing or chitlins. Even the bladder was washed, filled with air like a balloon and dried to make a ball for the children.

Eileen Cain Stanley
Kenna

Holidays and Celebrations

By and large, West Virginians observe the same holidays as other Americans and celebrate them in similar fashion. These include Independence Day, usually celebrated with fireworks and picnics, and the other patriotic holidays; the common religious and folk holidays; as well as Mother's Day and Father's Day, Memorial Day, Labor Day, Halloween, Thanksgiving, and New Year's Day.

In an overwhelmingly Christian state, Christmas and Easter are the main religious holidays. Christmas, observed in a secular or religious manner, depending on family inclination, was once celebrated in the mountains with fireworks. Some older people are still mindful of Old Christmas, its January 6 date an artifact of the 18th-century change from the Julian to the Gregorian calendar.

The Jewish holidays, including Rosh Hashanah, Yom Kippur, Passover, and Hanukkah, are observed by the small Jewish population, while Muslim West Virginians honor Ramadan and other Islamic holidays. Some African-Americans observe Kwanzaa instead of or in addition to Christmas.

Labor Day carries a special meaning in a hard working and once heavily unionized state. Unions observe Labor Day locally throughout West Virginia, and the day is welcomed by all as the final holiday of summer. The state's largest Labor Day event is the annual United Mine Workers picnic at Racine, Boone County, a carnival-like occasion which traditionally draws a large crowd and politicians of both parties.

Halloween, once a rowdy spree, has been domesticated in recent years. Municipalities set strict trick-or-treat hours, often a day or two before October 31, and sometimes try to divert children from the streets and into supervised parties. Middle-aged and older West Virginians remember a wilder holiday, especially in the rural countryside, with the blocking of roads and other serious mischief, including occasional, usually minor, destruction of property.

Ethnic holidays include Fasnacht, a German pre-Lenten observance corresponding roughly to the French Mardi Gras. Fasnacht is celebrated chiefly in the German Swiss community of Helvetia, Randolph County, with costumed feast and frolicking and the burning in effigy of Old Man Winter. Belsnickling is done among German-descended West Virginians, while the costumed Shanghai parade, of indeterminate origin, marks the New Year in Lewisburg.

West Virginia is among the few states to observe its own birthday as an official holiday, with citizens statewide pausing to honor June 20 as the day when, in 1863, Mountaineers became truly free. West Virginia Day celebrations typically take place in the capital city of Charleston, at West Virginia's birthplace in Wheeling, and elsewhere.

The first day of deer hunting season, the Monday before Thanksgiving, has semiofficial status as a West Virginia holiday, with public schools and some workplaces closing for the day or week. West Virginians likewise observe Groundhog Day, falling on the same date as the religious feast of Candlemas, as a popular folk holiday.

Mother's Day began in West Virginia, at Grafton, through the efforts of Anna Jar-

vis in honor of her mother, Anna Maria Reeves Jarvis. The less popular Grandparents Day originated through the efforts of Marian McQuade of Oak Hill.

Ken Sullivan
West Virginia Humanities Council

Hollidays Cove

Since 1947 a part of Weirton, Hollidays Cove traces its origins to the 1770s, when Harmon Greathouse settled the area near Harmon Creek in southern Hancock County. The town's namesake, John Holliday, built a fort in the valley near Greathouse's home in 1776.

When the British and their Indian allies besieged Fort Henry, downriver in Wheeling, in September 1777, a relief party from Hollidays Cove canoed down the Ohio, arriving after the siege ended. For the rest of the 18th century, Hollidays Cove served as a frontier outpost.

During the 19th century, Hollidays Cove remained an unimportant hamlet tucked away in Virginia's and later West Virginia's northernmost reaches. As late as 1880, only 250 people lived in Hollidays Cove. The village did not have a wharf on the Ohio River, but it did serve the agricultural interests of sheep raisers and orchardists in southern Hancock and northern Brooke counties.

Just after the turn of the 20th century, Hollidays Cove experienced an oil boom. Shortly thereafter, E. T. Weir built his steel mill and steel town just north of Hollidays Cove, changing the village history forever. In 1912, Hollidays Cove incorporated and for the next 35 years co-existed with Weirton, but was always overshadowed by the neighboring city's wealth and population. In 1947, voters in Weirton, Hollidays Cove, Marland Heights, and Weirton Heights voted to consolidate. On July 1, the city of Weirton incorporated and Hollidays Cove ceased its separate existence.

See also Weirton

David T. Javersak
West Liberty State College

Mary Shakley Ferguson, *The History of Hollidays Cove*, 1976; David T. Javersak, *History of Weirton, West Virginia*, 1999.

Holly Grove

Holly Grove is the oldest house in the city of Charleston. It was built in 1815 by Daniel Ruffner, fifth son of pioneer saltmaker Joseph Ruffner, who had arrived in the Kanawha Valley in 1796. Today the house is part of the state capitol complex in Charleston and is used for state offices.

Holly Grove was originally the centerpiece of a plantation encompassing all of the present East End of Charleston and much of downtown. Daniel Ruffner advertised Holly Grove as an inn because of its size and its proximity to the James River & Kanawha Turnpike. Famous guests included Henry Clay, Sam-

uel Houston in his younger days, John J. Audubon, and in October 1832, President Andrew Jackson.

In its original form Holly Grove was a two-story rectangular brick building with a small entry portico facing the Kanawha River. The walls were 18 inches thick, and there was a dining ell at the northwest end extending north. A fire in 1832 destroyed most of the original interior wood trim but enough remains to identify its grandeur and style. James H. Nash bought the house in 1902 and subsequently made significant changes. His renovation, including a grand half-circle portico with great columns, and extension of the attic to create a third-story space, are what we see today.

Holly Grove was added to the National Register of Historic Places in 1974.

See also Ruffner Family

Paul D. Marshall
Blufton, South Carolina

Holly River

Holly River begins as two separate forks in the rugged mountains of Webster and Randolph counties. These forks flow westward, coming together in Braxton County to form the Holly River mainstream just before the river enters Sutton Lake. The two forks and the main river drain an area of 148 square miles, the largest watershed of any of Elk River's tributaries.

The Left Fork of Holly, 25.1 miles long, is a popular trout stream. It originates in Randolph County two miles southwest of Pickens and flows through a corner of Holly River State Park. A well-known feature of the Left Fork is "Shupe's Chute," a curving, natural water slide carved into the rock on Fall Run, where the run enters the Left Fork. It was named for Walt Shupe, who was superintendent of the state park from 1966 to 1984.

The Right Fork of Holly is 23.9 miles long. It begins one mile northeast of the Back Fork of Elk River near Webster Springs and near the long-gone logging town of Skelt, at an elevation of 3,450 feet. It drops to an elevation of 950 feet at the junction of the two forks.

Main Holly River is the shortest river in West Virginia. It is only slightly more than three miles from where the two forks meet to the river's entrance into Sutton Lake at Holly Point, the bluff that overlooks the lake at the mouth of Holly. Formerly the Holly entered Elk River at this place.

The Palmer Lumber Company built a large band mill at the mouth of Holly in the 1890s and brought logs there from its extensive timber holdings in the Holly watershed. The company extended the West Virginia & Pittsburg [sic] Railroad from Holly Junction, just below the mouth of the river, to the sawmill, and from there up main Holly and the Left

Mollohan's Mill on the Left Fork of Holly River.

Fork. Later, John T. McGraw, a railroad tycoon at the start of the 20th century, bought the Palmer holdings, renamed the railroad the West Virginia Midland, and extended it up the Right Fork, where it meandered over Elk Mountain to Webster Springs.

Holly River State Park is located on the headwaters of the Left Fork of Holly River.

Skip Johnson
Sutton

Holly River State Park

Holly River State Park, located in the northeastern corner of Webster County, originated as an effort by the federal government to reclaim land ravaged by timbering in the late 19th and early 20th centuries. The park, its present heavy woodlands a sharp contrast to the early 1900s, offers extensive fishing, camping, hiking, and other recreational opportunities.

Immigrants from Switzerland settled the region about 1870, clearing and farming the eastern portion of the present park, which adjoins the Swiss-settled section of Randolph County. The area was severely affected by timbering, and it became progressively poorer with the timber gone, the game diminished, and most of the fish destroyed by silt and runoff.

The U.S. Department of Agriculture, under the direction of the Farm Security Administration, in 1937 began purchasing property to reforest the land and reclaim streams. For the next five years, the federal government continued the effort, purchasing additional land and building recreational facilities. Holly River State Park was created in 1938, under the management of the State Conservation Commission. The state took full control in 1954 when the federal government transferred the deed.

Additional land purchases in the 1970s and early 1980s brought the state park to its current size, including the 104-acre Potato Knob-Falls Run tract, purchased with help from the Nature Conservancy. In 1981, an experimental liming device was installed on Laurel Run to neutralize the stream's acidity, which had caused fish kills. It was one of the first liming devices created to combat acid rain's effects on West Virginia trout streams.

Holly River State Park, which includes more than 8,000 acres, has vacation cabins, campsites, a restaurant, and other attractions.

See also Holly River

Elizabeth Jill Wilson
Cottageville

Ella Lively Holroyd

Music teacher Ella Lively Holroyd was born in Mercer County, October 17, 1885. She was the oldest daughter among nine children. Her parents were James French Holroyd, who was a teacher at the Concord State Normal School (now Concord University) for 40 years, and Bettie Lively. Ella Holroyd spent about 75 years in teaching and music.

Holroyd entered the Cincinnati Conservatory in 1905 but left after two years so her younger sister could attend West Virginia University. For about four years, Holroyd taught at the Russell Creek Academy in Campbellsville, Kentucky, but she returned to the conservatory to complete her degree in piano and voice. Graduating with honors in 1914, she returned to Mercer County to teach in the public schools. For 18 years she combined teaching with post graduate work at Juilliard School of Music in New York, the Royal Conservatory in Milan, Italy, Chicago Musical College, Cornell, and Columbia. She received an M.A. from Columbia in 1948.

In 1932, Holroyd was asked by the president of Concord College to create a music department, and six years later Concord began awarding teaching certificates, awarding the first degree in music education in 1948. Holroyd retired in 1951 but continued to work with music students. She was awarded an Honorary Doctorate of Music by Concord College in 1964.

She died in Princeton, April 3, 1981.

Homer Adams Holt

Homer Adams Holt, born March 1, 1898, in Lewisburg, became West Virginia's 20th governor on January 18, 1937. After defeating his Republican opponent by a vote of 492,333 to 383,503, he was the

Governor Homer Holt (1898–1976).

first governor sworn into office after the beginning of the term was changed from March to January.

Holt was reared in Lewisburg and schooled at the forerunner of the Greenbrier Military Academy and at Washington and Lee University; he graduated from W&L in 1918 after serving as president of the student body. The 20-year-old mathematics major soon enlisted in the U.S. Army, where he served as second lieutenant but did not go overseas during World War I. After his discharge in May 1919 and a stint working in a Greenbrier County lumber mill, Holt returned to W&L as an instructor in the math department and a student in the law school. He received his law degree in 1923.

The young lawyer, by this time dubbed "Rocky," married Isabel Wood of Charlottesville, Virginia, in 1924, and became the father of three children. He opened a law practice in Fayetteville, becoming an expert trial attorney and also Fayette County Democratic chairman as well as an active participant in civic affairs.

In the pivotal election of 1932, when Republicans lost their long-standing domination of West Virginia, Holt was elected state attorney general at age 34. He worked with Governor Kump to shore up the state's ruinous finances following the stock market crash of 1929. It was Holt who argued many of the Supreme Court cases arising from the Tax Limitation Amendment. The amendment, added to the state constitution in the election of 1932, precipitated an immediate and disastrous shortfall in general revenue for state and local governments by setting limits on property levies.

Holt followed Kump into the governor's mansion with his thumping victory over Judge Summers H. Sharp in November 1936. As governor he took a conservative approach, paying only marginal allegiance to the New Deal policies

of President Franklin D. Roosevelt. From the beginning of his term, Holt made financial stability a mainstay of his administration, and he supported continuation of the consumer sales tax to offset restrictions on state revenues imposed by the Tax Limitation Amendment.

Holt was firmly mistrustful of labor union leadership. When 2,500 miners walked off the job in Fayette, Raleigh, Mercer, and McDowell counties during 1939, he sent them a letter promising the support of his office if they returned to work without a union contract. State union officials became so irate that they turned to U.S. Sen. Matthew M. Neely as their choice for governor in the next election, in opposition to Holt's candidate, R. Carl Andrews. Akin to his position on coal strikes was Holt's philosophical stance on the New Deal policies of the national Democratic Party. He aligned himself with the "statehouse faction" among West Virginia Democrats, as opposed to a liberal New Deal element in the party headed by Neely and several union leaders.

While Governor Holt labored to maintain the state's financial integrity, he disagreed with education leaders that special legislation was needed to raise additional funds for the public schools. Yet he supported a move to provide free textbooks for students. In 1938 he was an ardent supporter of the Short Ballot Amendment to the state constitution. The amendment, which called for election of only three statewide offices (governor, attorney general, and auditor, with the others being appointed by the governor) was rejected by the voters in 1938.

When M. M. Neely won the Democratic nomination for governor in 1940, while still serving in the U.S. Senate, Democratic factionalism again expressed itself in the fray over the appointment of a replacement for Neely in Washington. As outgoing governor, Holt appointed attorney Clarence E. Martin of Martinsburg, while Neely as incoming governor appointed Joseph Rosier, president of Fairmont State College. The governor makes such appointments, so the issue hinged on the exact moment Neely ceased being senator and became governor. The split between conservative and liberal Democrats in West Virginia widened further when the U.S. Senate finally seated Rosier after a lengthy deliberation. Fifteen years later, Holt bolted the party and supported a young Republican named Cecil H. Underwood in his 1956 race for the governorship.

Holt practiced law in Charleston upon leaving office in 1941 until 1947, when he became general counsel for the Union Carbide company in New York City. After becoming vice president and a director of the chemical giant he returned to private

practice in Charleston until his death January 16, 1976. He is buried in Rosewood Cemetery, Lewisburg.

Paul D. Casdorph
Charleston

John G. Morgan, *West Virginia Governors,* 1980; Otis K. Rice, *West Virginia: A History,* 1985.

Rush Holt

Senator Rush Dew Holt was born in Weston, June 19, 1905. Holt was educated at West Virginia University and Salem College (now Salem International University), where he graduated in 1924. He taught high school and at Salem and Glenville colleges, and served in the House of Delegates, 1931–35.

Originally an avid New Deal Democrat, Holt burst onto the statewide political scene in the senatorial campaign of 1934, defeating former governor and incumbent U.S. Sen. Henry Hatfield. At 29, Holt was the youngest person ever elected to the U.S. Senate, earning him the nickname "Boy Senator." Since the Constitution sets 30 as the minimum age for senators, Holt had to wait until his birthday in June 1935 to take his seat, nearly six months into the 74th Congress.

During the campaign, Holt was backed heavily by the United Mine Workers of America. Once in office, however, Holt voted against several important pro-labor bills, alienating the UMW and Matthew Neely, West Virginia's other U.S. senator and the unofficial leader of the state Democratic Party. Despite this public break with the union, Holt occasionally took on big industry. He was one of the first to demand a congressional investigation after news reports revealed that hundreds of workmen had died of silicosis while digging the Hawks Nest Tunnel in Fayette County.

In the 1940 Democratic primary, with the support of the UMW, Harley Kilgore, virtually unknown outside his own Raleigh County, trounced Holt and former Governor Kump in the primary and easily won the general election. Although embittered by his feud with the UMW and Neely, Holt remained in politics, returning to the House of Delegates for several terms, 1943–49. He unsuccessfully sought the Democratic nomination for governor in 1944 and for U.S. Senate in 1948, then changed his party affiliation to Republican in 1949. In 1952, he again attempted a comeback, running as a Republican for governor against Attorney General William Marland. He was defeated and again quit politics. Rush Holt died of cancer, February 8, 1955, at the age of 49. His son, Rush Holt, followed in his father's footsteps in 1998 when he was elected to Congress as a New Jersey Democrat.

Stan Bumgardner
Division of Culture and History

Home Rule

Governmental power in West Virginia is constitutionally located in the state, with counties and municipalities having no inherent right of self-government. In the interest of efficiency, however, some responsibilities have been delegated to local units of government. This delegation of governing authority from the state to local units of government is referred to as home rule.

Counties and municipalities are the most important units of local government. They exist side by side, but with little legal relations with each other, except for cooperation on state-authorized common projects. Over the years, the legislature has gradually bestowed broader powers on local governments, although their ability to tax remains greatly restricted. Generally, the legislature has conferred more powers on counties than on municipal governments. For example, counties and county school boards control property tax assessments. Still, West Virginia's home rule provisions are very restrictive. Local governments are not allowed to expand the limited taxing powers they have been given, nor are creative attempts to control crime or undertake environmental plans allowed.

Large municipalities are incorporated entities whose charters outline their governmental structure and available powers. All municipalities can own and control property, appropriate funds, and protect the health and welfare of their citizens according to their charter. The 1936 Home Rule Amendment to the state constitution provided that municipalities may adopt their own charters, consistent with state law. Prior to that only the legislature could enact such charters. In 1969, the legislature enacted a new Municipal Code that modernized regulation of cities and towns.

Evelyn L. Harris
Charleston

Homeplace

The homeplace is the home of the heart for many West Virginians. The term usually does not refer to one's actual present home, but rather to the place where one grew up or to the original home of one's extended family. In some cases a relative may still live at the homeplace, while other families work together to keep up the old family home, as a joint family camp or vacation home. Some West Virginians have held onto their homeplace for generations, while other families have lost theirs altogether. But many have such a place, at least in memory, which they cherish as the true home of themselves and their kin.

The use of the term is widespread, but more prevalent in the central and southern counties and perhaps the Eastern Panhandle. It is a term of country people and of country people who have moved away to cities and towns in West Virginia and elsewhere. A yearning for the homeplace helps keep native West Virginians attached to the state, and some retire to the homeplace after spending their working lives out of state.

The term homeplace usually does not refer merely to a house, but rather to the house and its environs, at least the immediate grounds and associated outbuildings. In this sense, the term is similar in meaning to homestead, although it carries more emotional weight. Often a homeplace will comprise an entire farm, perhaps reduced over time from a working spread to a few acres kept for recreation or sentiment.

West Virginians share the word and the idea of the homeplace with other residents of the Appalachian region and the Upper South. The multi-volume *Dictionary of American Regional English*, a comprehensive survey of American regionalisms, finds "homeplace" in use as far west as the Missouri Ozarks. The meaning is similar wherever the term is used, although the *Dictionary* specifies an additional, related meaning: that of the homeplace as one's place of residence when one also has other properties or places. Thus a farmer might speak of the house and farm where he lives as the homeplace, in contrast to outlying tracts. This is not the sense in which West Virginians commonly use the word.

In 1985, songwriter Kate Long of Charleston wrote "Who'll Watch the Homeplace," incorporating the feelings of many West Virginians. Recorded by Laurie Lewis, the song won the 1994 Song of the Year award by the International Bluegrass Music Association.

Ken Sullivan
West Virginia Humanities Council

Homer Laughlin China Company

In the 1920s, West Virginia was the third-largest producer of pottery or chinaware. The Homer Laughlin China Company in Newell, West Virginia, and neighboring East Liverpool, Ohio, was by far the largest manufacturer.

Homer Laughlin and his brother, Shakespeare, arrived in East Liverpool following the Civil War. After an unsuccessful stoneware-making venture with Nathaniel Simms, they began to wholesale yellow ware and Rockingham ware, both crude, cheap types of tableware. Hoping to upgrade the local industry in 1873, the city of East Liverpool raised $5,000 for the Laughlins to start a pottery to make white ware, a finer product. Their Ohio Valley Pottery made ironstone china until 1877 when Shakespeare Laughlin left. In the 1890s, Homer added a line of semi-vitreous porcelain, and in 1896 he incorporated as Homer Laughlin and Company. In 1898, he retired and moved to California.

W. E. Wells, Marcus Aaron, and other Pittsburgh investors took over the operation, retaining the Homer Laughlin name. They expanded at the turn of the century, built a second plant with 15 kilns and then a third. In 1903, they traded factories with the National China Company, ending up with three factories with 36 kilns. They expanded across the Ohio River into West Virginia beginning in 1902. On land purchased in Newell they built two more factories, and the town grew up around them. In 1914, they made semi-vitreous and white granite dinner, hotel, and toilet wares. In 1929, the Homer Laughlin China Company suspended operations in East Liverpool and concentrated in Newell, where they had five factories.

In the 1930s, Homer Laughlin China expanded its product lines, crowning the expansion with the famous Fiestaware, designed by Frederick Hurten Rhead in 1936. Fiesta shapes were streamlined with a semireflecting surface. The stylish dishes were made in a brilliant orange-red and in complementary colors: a fairly deep blue, a green that fit precisely between the red and the blue, and the brightest yellow that would go with the red and the blue. Fiesta soon added a more subdued color, ivory vellum, and in mid-1937, a sixth color, turquoise. The original Fiesta was discontinued in 1973 and is now avidly collected.

The Homer Laughlin China Company revived Fiesta in 1986, which helped the company to remain competitive in the tough home dinnerware market. Today, the Newell factory remains one of the largest potteries in the world. The company's business peaked in the years following World War II, then suffered as imported dinnerware began to make deep inroads into the business of American manufacturers. To compensate for the loss of retail sales, Homer Laughlin began producing restaurant china in 1959, which now accounts for two-thirds of its business. Flip the plate the next time you eat out anywhere in the United States, and chances are you will see the Homer Laughlin fleur-de-lis or another of the company's trademarks.

See also Fiestaware, Frederick Hurten Rhead

James R. Mitchell
State Museum

Jo Cunningham, *Homer Laughlin: A Giant Among Dishes 1873–1939,* 1998; William C. Gates and Dana E. Ormerod, "The East Liverpool, Ohio, Pottery District," in Ronald E. Michael, ed., *Historical Archaeology,* 1982; Bob Page, Dale Frederiksen and Dean Six, *Homer Laughlin: Decades of Dinnerware,* 2003.

Homestead Exemption

Since the Great Depression the West Virginia constitution and tax laws have been amended several times to provide expanding property tax relief to homeowners. These changes included the Homestead Tax Exemption Amendment, which the legislature placed before the voters in November 1973. The constitutional amendment, which was approved, exempted from property taxation up to the first $5,000 of taxable assessed value of an owner-occupied residential property when the owner was 65 or older. In 1980, the so-called homestead exemption was increased to $10,000, and it was expanded to include owners who are permanently and totally disabled and to apply the exemption to personal property in the form of mobile homes. The Property Tax Limitation and Homestead Exemption Amendment was approved by the voters in November 1982. This amendment increased the amount of the exemption to the present level of up to the first $20,000 of assessed value.

In 2001, the legislature approved an initiative allowing for a low-income person, who is entitled to a $20,000 homestead exemption, to claim an additional $10,000 credit on the personal income tax. The change is effective for property tax years that begin on or after January 1, 2003.

Jerry A. Knight
Department of Tax and Revenue

Hominy Falls Mine Disaster

At approximately 10 a.m. May 6, 1968, a continuous miner machine at the Gauley Coal & Coke Saxsewell No. 8 mine cut into an unmapped adjacent mine, which was filled with water. The resulting inundation drowned four miners and trapped 21 others. The trapped miners were in areas of the mine with high elevations, placing them above the water.

There were two groups of surviving miners. One group of 15 was nearer to the surface and in constant contact with rescuers. A second group of six miners was much deeper into the mine, close to the mine face. After five days of rescue efforts, the group of 15 miners was brought to the surface. There had been no contact with the other six miners and they were presumed to have died. Early on the morning of May 16, recovery crews found the final six survivors and brought them to the surface. Their saga became known as the "Miracle at Hominy Falls." Immediately following this disaster, laws were passed regulating the preservation of mine maps.

See also Coal Mine Disasters
David J. Kessler
Miners' Health Safety and Training

Honey in the Rock

Created as an annual event to celebrate West Virginia's birth and generate tourism in the Beckley area, the outdoor drama *Honey in the Rock* has been presented at Grandview for more than 40 years. Upon hearing a presentation by the play's author, Kermit Hunter, in 1954, the Woman's Club of Beckley agreed to endorse the project. Later, the West Virginia Historical Drama Association was incorporated to produce the outdoor drama.

Association board members included many Beckley business, professional, and government leaders, among them a former governor, Okey Patteson, and a future governor, Hulett Smith, and newspaper publisher Charles Hodel. The board began fundraising and with assistance from the state constructed Cliffside Amphitheater at Grandview. *Honey in the Rock* opened in 1961. In 1970, the play *Hatfields and McCoys* was added, and in the mid-70s the association became Theatre West Virginia, a repertory company, which performs at Grandview each summer and tours the schools and rural communities of West Virginia and surrounding states in the off season.

Honey in the Rock is about the birth of the state of West Virginia. Told through the experiences of the fictitious Morgan family, the play recounts the settling and development of the land and the political maneuvering in Wheeling to break away from Virginia. It includes famous historical figures such as Stonewall Jackson, soon-to-be president Andrew Johnson, and the state's first governor, Arthur I. Boreman.

The play's alumni include Academy Award nominee Chris Sarandon; actor, director, and playwright David Selby; actor David Schramm; and many theater professionals. *Honey* has stood the test of time because it is fine theater. As *New York Times* drama critic Milton Esterow said in his review of the play, "In a time when America is busy reliving its past and looking toward the future, *Honey in the Rock*, in a setting of breathtaking grandeur, perpetuates the magic of the theatre and the majesty of the land."

See also Hatfields and McCoys, Theatre West Virginia

Norman L. Fagan
Red House

Hoopie

"Hoopie" is a derogatory but usually good-natured name given to rural West Virginians (and sometimes Ohioans) who came north to work in the potteries of Chester and Newell, West Virginia, or East Liverpool, Ohio. The term is derived from the belief that many of these migrants or their ancestors had found employment making hoops in the cooper shops that supplied the potteries with barrels for packing chinaware. Today, it may refer to anyone from West Virginia and is used in a similar manner to "hill-billy" or "redneck." As with those names, hoopie is now sometimes appropriated by members of the target group, who refer to themselves as hoopies.

"Hoopie" may also mean an area of West Virginia. For example, northern West Virginians may speak of going to "Hoopie," anywhere south of the Northern Panhandle, to visit relatives. The word "hoopie" seems to be largely limited to the upper Ohio Valley and the surrounding region. Jokes abound, including the often-told one that contends that many Hoopies got off the boat in Newell because they thought the H.L.C. on the stacks of Homer Laughlin China Company stood for "Hoopies' Last Chance."

Susan M. Weaver
Kent State University

Hope Gas

John D. Rockefeller entered the natural gas business in West Virginia in 1898 when his Standard Oil formed Hope Natural Gas Company, the predecessor of Dominion Transmission Corporation and Hope Gas, which today do business as Dominion Hope. In that same year, Standard Oil also formed the East Ohio Gas Company. Hope produced gas in West Virginia and piped it to the Ohio border, while East Ohio piped it from there and sold it in Canton and Akron.

Facing action by the Securities and Exchange Commission in 1943, Standard Oil combined its gas subsidiaries, including Hope, under a new, independent gas company, Consolidated Natural Gas. In 1965, Hope Natural Gas Company and New York State Natural Gas Corporation merged to form Consolidated Gas Supply Corporation. The company centralized its distribution operations in West Virginia and retained the Hope Natural Gas Company name for that division.

After another reorganization in 1984, the distribution operations became a separate company, Hope Gas, and the interstate gas transmission operations became Consolidated Natural Gas Transmission Corporation. Both companies were part of the Pittsburgh-based Consolidated Natural Gas system companies. Then, in February 2000, CNG and Dominion Resources, a Richmond, Virginia, company, merged to form Dominion.

In 2004, Dominion Hope provided natural gas service to 439 communities in West Virginia in 32 of West Virginia's 55 counties. In that year Dominion Hope operated 3,000 miles of pipeline and one compressor station and employed 284 workers in West Virginia. Headquartered in Clarksburg, Dominion Hope's major service areas include the communities of Morgantown, Fairmont, Clarksburg, Weston, Summersville, Richwood, Parkersburg, St. Marys, Sistersville, and Paden City.

Gary Nicholas
Jane Lew

Hopemont Sanitarium

Hopemont, West Virginia's first tuberculosis sanitarium, met a pressing public health need, because in the early 20th century 1,000 West Virginians died annually from the disease. Getting tuberculosis was practically a death sentence. Nurses and physicians were brave to treat TB patients, often contracting the dread disease themselves.

The Anti-Tuberculosis League of West Virginia lobbied a bill through the legislature in 1911 to build a sanitarium. In those times, physicians believed such hospitals should be in high, cold places, and the site chosen was a farm near Terra Alta in Preston County. Hopemont started with a receiving building with offices, kitchen, dining room, and apartments. Two patients' cottages followed, one for each sex. As decades passed, larger hospitals were built on the spacious grounds. A separate institution for black patients was established at Denmar, Pocahontas County, in 1917. The living quarters at Hopemont had long porches, exposed to the weather. The theory was that patients benefited from fresh air year-round, though superintendent E. E. Clovis said it was "difficult to keep the patients from the bright and cheerful fire" in winter.

Patients were not forced into sanitariums. Rather, they came to Hopemont by choice, often after infecting their families. In good times, TB sufferers avoided the hospital so they could work and provide for their families, but in economically depressed years, staff had a hard time getting cured patients to leave.

As years passed, fear of tuberculosis lessened as medical research, early detection, and thoracic surgery brought people back to health. In 1965, Hopemont became a personal care center. Many of its numerous buildings have been razed or left empty.

Maureen F. Crockett
St. Albans

Maureen Crockett, "Hopemont: Curing Tuberculosis in Preston County," *Goldenseal*, Spring 1986.

Bill Hopen

Sculptor Bill Hopen of Sutton was born April 13, 1951, in New York City. His works appear in government buildings, museums, churches, and hospitals across West Virginia, elsewhere in the country, and abroad.

Hopen studied painting at Lehman College, a branch of the City University of New York, and is largely self-taught as a sculptor. In the mid-1970s, he moved from Manhattan to Sutton. West Virginia hardwoods and stone were the materials that he first used for carving. Later in his career he devoted himself largely to sculpture cast in lead crystal, bronze, and other metals.

Sculptor Bill Hopen at work.

In 1982, Hopen completed his first public sculpture commission, a marble Mother's Day memorial in Grafton. Hopen's commissions include two works at the state capitol, a 10-foot-tall bronze statue of Sen. Robert C. Byrd and "Fallen Partner," a statue honoring state law enforcement officers who died in the line of duty; a bronze of St. Francis of Assisi at St. Francis Hospital in Charleston; "Immigrants," a large exterior concrete installation at the Harrison County Courthouse in Clarksburg; bronzes of St. Joseph and Jesus at St. Joseph Hospital in Parkersburg; and "Mortality," a bronze memorial to Hawks Nest Tunnel Disaster victims at Tamarack in Beckley.

Other public commissions appear in Baton Rouge, New York, Wichita, and elsewhere, and Hopen's works are included in many private and corporate collections. Hopen married sculptor Ai Qiu Chen in 2001, and the couple maintains studio facilities near Shanghai as well as Sutton.

Hopewell Culture

See Prehistoric People.

Jeff Hostetler

Quarterback William Jeffrey "Jeff" Hostetler was born April 22, 1961, at Hollsopple, Pennsylvania. He starred in four sports in high school, earning All-American honors as a linebacker, all-league honors in basketball, and all-state honors in baseball. In 1981, he transferred from Penn State where he was a linebacker to West Virginia University to play quarterback. After sitting out that season, he led the Mountaineers to 9-3 records in 1982 and 1983 and to back-to-back bowl games, becoming one of the greatest quarterbacks in WVU history.

Hostetler joined the New York Giants in 1984 and became an instant hero in 1991 when, filling in for the injured Phil Simms, he led the Giants to the Super Bowl title. He played with the Oakland Raiders from 1993 to 1995 and was with the Washington Redskins in 1998. Hostetler married the daughter of WVU coach Don Nehlen and now lives in Morgantown where he owns a restaurant.

John C. Veasey
Times West Virginian

Jedediah Hotchkiss

Confederate cartographer and industrial promoter Jedediah Hotchkiss was born November 3, 1828, in Windsor, New York. He was educated at local schools and through self-study, and in 1853 he married Sara Comfort of Pennsylvania.

After a short period teaching in Pennsylvania and a walking tour in Virginia, Hotchkiss settled in Mossy Creek, Virginia, near Staunton, as a family tutor. During the 14 years before the Civil War he founded and taught in schools in Augusta County. There he indulged his interest in geology, acquired a detailed

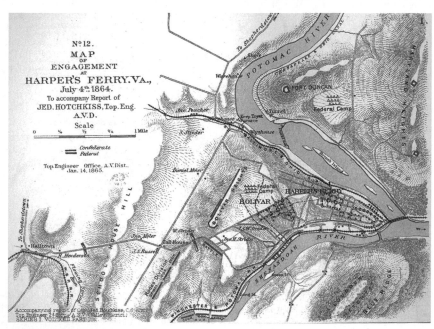

Jed Hotchkiss's map of Harpers Ferry.

knowledge of the Shenandoah Valley, and developed his skill as a surveyor.

It was in this capacity that he offered his services to the Confederate forces and became the foremost topographical engineer in the Army of Northern Virginia.

Hotchkiss served on Stonewall Jackson's staff, and his careful mapwork made an important contribution to Jackson's success. His journals and diaries are the largest single source of information on Jackson.

After the war Hotchkiss devoted most of his time to furthering the development of the natural resources of the two Virginias, in particular the coal-bearing areas of West Virginia. In 1871, he explored the newly extended Chesapeake & Ohio Railroad and described the now accessible resources in two illustrated articles in *Scribner's Monthly*. The year 1876 saw the publication for Virginia's legislature of Hotchkiss's *Virginia: A Geographical and Political Summary*, which included the first printed map of William Barton Rogers's 1835–41 geological survey of Virginia. From 1880 to 1885, he published the monthly magazine *The Virginias: a Mining, Industrial and Scientific Journal Devoted to the Development of Virginia and West Virginia*. Hotchkiss was closely associated with Frederick J. Kimball and Edward C. Clark in the evolution of the Norfolk & Western Railroad and the exploitation of the Flat Top coalfield. In the course of this work he surveyed hundreds of thousands of acres in the mountains of West Virginia.

Hotchkiss was concerned that the moral and religious condition of the mining communities should not be neglected. Thus, he ensured the building of a church at the new town of Dunlow, and was secretary of a committee appointed by the Lexington Presbytery to establish a school at Elkins. Although not immediately successful, this project was revived after his death and led to the founding of Davis & Elkins College in 1903. Hotchkiss died January 17, 1899, in Staunton.

Peter W. Roper
Loughborough, United Kingdom
Peter W. Roper, *Jedediah Hotchkiss: Rebel Mapmaker and Virginia Businessman*, 1992.

House of Delegates

The House of Delegates is the lower chamber of the West Virginia legislature and the larger of the two legislative bodies. To be eligible for election to the House, a person must be of voting age and a resident of the district for at least one year by the day of the election.

Delegates served one-year terms under the state's original 1863 constitution. Their terms have been set at two years since the adoption of the 1872 constitution, which is still in force. In the beginning the House had only 47 members, but by 1873 it had 65. It grew to 86 delegates by 1903, 94 by 1917, and finally to its current size of 100 members in 1953.

West Virginia is divided into 56 House districts. These districts sometimes follow county lines, but most districts include parts of more than one county. Unlike the Senate, which has two members for each of its 17 districts, the number of delegates per House district varies from one to several. For example, after the redistricting of 2001, Kanawha County had seven delegates in the 30th District, one in the 31st District, and three in the 32nd District. Although Kanawha County has long had the largest population and therefore the largest legislative delegation, that wasn't always the case. The 1872 constitution initially allocated the largest number of delegates, four, to Ohio County. Kanawha County was second with three delegates, while Berkeley, Harrison, Jefferson, Marion, Marshall, Mason, Monongalia, and Preston counties had two each. Others had just one each.

The House is equal to the Senate in the process of passing resolutions and bills, including the state budget. However, unlike the Senate, the House has no role in the confirmation or rejection of appointments made by the governor. Because the House chamber has more seats than the Senate chamber, it is the location for joint sessions of the legislature, such as when the governor delivers the annual State of the State address.

Only the House can impeach state officials. Impeached officials then face trial in the Senate. The House has impeached three officials, two state treasurers and a state auditor. In 1875, the House impeached Treasurer John Burdett, who was removed from office after trial in the Senate in 1876. In 1926, the House impeached Auditor John C. Bond, but he resigned before facing trial in the Senate. In 1989, the House impeached Treasurer A. James Manchin, who also resigned from office before facing trial in the Senate.

The House's presiding officer is the speaker, who is elected from among the members. The speaker of the House is second in line, behind the Senate president, to fill a vacancy in the governor's office. The longest-serving speaker was Robert C. "Chuck" Chambers, who presided for 10 years from 1987 through 1996. A close second was William Flannery, who became speaker in 1949 and died in office in 1958.

Another speaker, Ivor Boiarsky, died of an apparent heart ailment at age 51 in the waning days of the 1971 legislative session. He had been considered an especially effective leader. When he was House finance chairman, Boiarsky initiated the process that led to the 1968 ratification of the Modern Budget Amendment, which updated the state budget process. In his first year as speaker in 1969, he helped to pass a reorganization of the higher education system, which included the creation of the Board of Regents. Delegates chose Lew McManus on March 13, 1971, to succeed Boiarsky and re-elected him twice as speaker. In 2004 the speaker was Robert "Bob" Kiss of Raleigh County.

See also Legislature, Senate

Jim Wallace
Charleston
John Unger
Martinsburg
George W. Atkinson, "Legislative History of West Virginia," in James Morton Callahan, ed., *Semi-Centennial History of West Virginia*, 1913.

House Trailers
See Manufactured Housing.

Harold Houston
Labor lawyer Harold W. Houston was born at Freedom, Ohio, March 10, 1872. When he was very young, his parents moved to West Virginia and located in Jackson County and later in Charleston. He graduated from Charleston High School in 1889.

Houston earned a law degree from West Virginia University and began his legal practice in 1901 in Parkersburg. By 1912, he had returned to Charleston. During the next few years, he became the chief attorney and counsel for most of the major labor organizations in West Virginia, including militant District 17 of the United Mine Workers of America. Houston represented the miners during the famous Paint Creek-Cabin Creek strike of 1912–13 and, along with T. C. Townsend, successfully defended those UMWA leaders accused of treason against the state of West Virginia after the 1921 Battle of Blair Mountain.

Houston was a dedicated Socialist who ran for local, state, and federal office on that party's ticket. He helped to direct the Socialist involvement in the Paint Creek-Cabin Creek strike. After the treason trial, John L. Lewis fired Houston as union counsel and also dismissed the radical leaders of District 17. In 1931, Houston aided C. Frank Keeney with the organization of the West Virginia Mine Workers Union and the West Virginia Labor Party. Both organizations collapsed in 1933.

Houston married Sally Chambers, the widow of Ed Chambers, who was assassinated with Sid Hatfield at the McDowell County Courthouse in 1921. In his later years, Houston was involved in a number of business endeavors, including an automobile dealership and a real estate addition in the Spring Hill section of South Charleston that bears his name. Eventually, he retired to Lake Worth, Florida. He died January 17, 1947.

See also Blizzard Treason Trial, Mine Wars, T. C. Townsend

Fred A. Barkey
Marshall University Graduate College

Fred Barkey, "The West Virginia Socialist Party, 1898–1920," Ph.d. dissertation, University of Pittsburgh, 1971; Howard B. Lee, *Bloodletting In Appalachia,* 1969.

William Cooper Howells

Publisher and diplomat William Cooper Howells was born in Wales, May 15, 1807, and brought to the Wheeling area as a child. He was the father of novelist William Dean Howells.

At 21, Howells began work as an apprentice typesetter at the *Virginia Statesman,* a Wheeling newspaper. Before starting two Wheeling newspapers of his own, the *Gleaner* (1828) and the *Eclectic Observer* (1829), he worked for Alexander Campbell, founder of the Disciples of Christ and Bethany College, at Campbell's religious printing shop at present Bethany. Howells helped set type for the printed text of Campbell's historic debate with Robert Owen, the British utopian socialist and communalist. In 1828, Howells was financially ruined producing the book, *The Rise, Progress and Downfall of Aristocracy,* by Wheeling eccentric William Mathers, who failed to pay for printing. Howells then worked at various newspapers in nearby Ohio before again launching papers of his own, in which he supported the abolition of slavery and equality for African-Americans.

Howells left Wheeling in 1834 and became active in Ohio politics. His early advocacy of the young James A. Garfield led to Howells being named U.S. consul at Quebec City and later Toronto. He retired from diplomacy in 1883. His memoir, *Recollections of Life in Ohio from 1813–1840,* a wonderful evocation of politics and ideas in the upper Ohio Valley during that period, appeared posthumously.

Howells died August 28, 1894, in Jefferson, Ohio. Son William Dean Howells said that he was "not a very good printer, not a very good editor . . . but he was the very best man I have ever known."

George Fetherling
Vancouver, British Columbia

Chuck Howley

Athlete Charles Louis "Chuck" Howley was born in Wheeling, June 28, 1936. He attended Warwood High School, where he starred in football and basketball, and in 1954 he enrolled at West Virginia University. There he lettered in an unprecedented total of five sports. Between 1955 and 1957, Howley played football and was named to the All Southern Conference team three times. He was also a sprinter, a heavyweight wrestler, a trampolinist, and a diver. He was the Southern Conference Athlete of the Year in 1956. He was inducted into the WVU Sports Hall of Fame in 1991.

In 1958, Howley was drafted by the Chicago Bears of the National Football League but left the team with a knee injury the next year. Howley returned to Wheeling and spent 1960 working at a gas station. A Chicago teammate suggested Howley to coach Tom Landry, who was starting the Dallas Cowboys team. Howley played linebacker for 12 seasons for Dallas, 1961–73. He was named All-Pro six times and named to six Pro Bowls. With teammate Bob Lilly, he anchored the so-called Doomsday Defense and served as the foundation for one of the most successful teams in NFL history. He played for Dallas in the 1967 "Ice Bowl," losing to the Green Bay Packers in sub-zero weather.

In 1971, although Dallas lost Super Bowl V to the Baltimore Colts, Howley was named the Most Valuable Player, the only player on a losing team ever to win this award. The next year, Dallas won its first Super Bowl championship, beating Miami. Chuck Howley retired after the 1973 season and entered business in Dallas.

Tom Haas
Charlotte, North Carolina

Chester Hubbard

Congressman, businessman, and state founder Chester Dorman Hubbard was born in Connecticut, November 14, 1814, with New England roots dating back to 1621. He moved to Wheeling with his father's family as a child. He was educated in the Wheeling schools and at Wesleyan University of Connecticut, graduating as valedictorian of the class of 1840. He married Sarah Pallister in 1842.

After college Chester Hubbard entered his father's lumber mill business and later helped develop Wheeling as an iron and steel manufacturing center. He was president of the German Bank of Wheeling, of the Pittsburgh, Wheeling & Kentucky Railroad, and of C. D. Hubbard and Company, with other enterprises in iron, tin, nails, and other businesses.

Hubbard served in the Virginia legislature (1851–52), and in 1861 vigorously opposed secession as a delegate to Virginia's secession convention. His intention was "to show those traitors at Richmond . . . that we are not to be transferred like the cattle on the hills or the slaves on their plantations, without our knowledge or consent," Hubbard wrote at the time. He was elected a colonel of volunteers upon his return to Wheeling. Hubbard was a member of the First and Second Wheeling Conventions, which established the loyal Reorganized Government of Virginia and opened the way to West Virginia statehood. He was a member of the first state Senate (1863–64) and later served two terms (1865–69) in the U.S. House of Representatives. As a young man, he served on Wheeling's city council.

Chester Hubbard died August 23, 1891, in Wheeling, and is buried in Greenwood Cemetery.

See also Formation of West Virginia

Sam Huff

Athlete and sportsman Robert Lee "Sam" Huff, born near Morgantown, October 4, 1934, was recruited as a football star from

---

Not ready to change flags

Wheeling April 30, 1861
W. T. Willey, Esq.
Dr. Sir:

I was glad to learn from Dr. Logan this evening that you are again safe among your friends. The people of this county as well as those of your own are determined to remain in the Union at all hazards and will dare any thing and every thing for its accomplishment. We lack[,]however[,]wise and prudent counselors and are without recognized leaders.

How are we to accomplish what we have undertaken? Will you not point out the way? Many of us have looked to you for counsel and direction in the past and are almost doubtful as to the propriety of our position, unless we recognize you in the movement.

I believe the people of the North West are ready for any thing rather than Jeff Davis and the Southern Confederacy and I should like to show those traitors at Richmond that . . . we are not to be transferred like the cattle on the hills or the slaves on their plantations without our knowledge or consent.

We are to hold a public meeting in this city on the 4th. . . . Will you not come down and consult with us? The people will give you a hearty welcome. . . . I am no speechmaker and I turn to you or Pierpont or both of you imploringly to come and help us out.

The people here are ready and determined, and while they would not act rashly, will act resolutely.

They have taken their stand under the "stars and stripes" and have no disposition to change the old flag for the new.

Once more let me say come and help us lobby.

Yrs. Truly,
C. D. Hubbard

—Chester Hubbard to Waitman Willey

Farmington High School by West Virginia University head coach Art "Pappy" Lewis. Huff and Bruce Bosley bolstered a fearsome defense that led WVU to a 38-7 record between 1952 and 1955, including three consecutive wins over rival Penn State.

In the National Football League, Huff's New York Giants played in six championship games in eight years but won only one (1956). From 1964 to 1967, Huff played for the Washington Redskins, then owned by West Virginia native George Preston Marshall. After a one-year retirement, Huff returned as a player-coach for the Redskins in 1969 under coach Vince Lombardi. After one last season, his 13th in the league, Huff retired again. He returned to Farmington and ran for Congress in 1970 but lost the Democratic primary to incumbent Robert Mollohan. The three-time All-NFL linebacker was elected to the Pro Football Hall of Fame in 1982.

In 1987, Huff and his partner, Carol Holden, founded the West Virginia Breeders Classic at Charles Town. The annual horse racing event, which began with five races and a purse total of $200,000, has grown significantly. In 2001, there were eight races with a purse total of $1 million. In addition, the event is televised nationally. Huff and Holden own Sam Huff-Sporting Life Stable in Middleburg, Virginia, near Charles Town Races, where the West Virginia Breeders Classic is held each October.

Huff works as a broadcaster and lives on his farm in Middleburg.

Stan Bumgardner
Division of Culture and History

Jesse Hughes

Jesse Hughes, frontiersman and Indian fighter, was born near the Potomac South Branch in 1750. In 1771, he married Grace Tanner, settled on Hackers Creek in present Lewis County, and began a large family. Most of the time he scouted and hunted for the settlers. About five feet nine inches tall, he was a lean, strong, fast man of delicate frame and iron constitution. Described as irritable, vindictive, and suspicious, Hughes seems to have had a pathological hatred of Indians, especially after Indians killed his father in 1778.

Though not as well known as Simon Kenton or Lewis Wetzel, Hughes was their equal when it came to tracking and killing his foe. To pioneers, he was a protector and friend. In the clash between Indians and the land-acquisitive whites, he was invaluable in helping the settlers to prevail. His vengeful streak found terrible outlets in atrocities against the natives, but he saved many lives at great personal risk and experienced many harrowing escapades. Hughes probably participated in the Battle of Point Pleasant

with his younger brothers, Thomas and Elias. His service as a ranger was apparently with volunteer companies but never in command, possibly because of his unstable temperament.

When the Ohio Valley frontier wars ended in the 1790s, Jesse Hughes was left with no occupation, still ready to fight but with no enemies to pursue. He moved to Vincennes, Indiana, then to eastern Kentucky. By 1800, he had returned to Western Virginia, settling on Turkey Run just above Ravenswood. After some years he moved to Sand Creek to farm and hunt but was later legally dispossessed of his land at the age of 79. Homeless, he moved his family back to Turkey Run to live with a daughter where he died a lonely anachronism in the fall of 1829. Legend has it that the Hughes River was named for Jesse Hughes and brother Elias, though there were others of that name in the area at the time.

See also Hughes River

William H. Dean
WVU Institute of Technology
Lucullus Virgil McWhorter, *The Border Settlers of Northwestern Virginia from 1768 to 1795,* 1974.

Hughes River

While exploring the Little Kanawha River Valley in 1772, frontiersman Jesse Hughes discovered a major tributary and named it in honor of himself. He had previously dubbed a creek in Lewis County Jesse Run. In 1789, Hughes's detractors attempted to have Hughes River renamed "Junius River," in honor of an 18th-century British writer, but their effort failed.

The Hughes River drains Ritchie County and part of Wirt. It empties into the Little Kanawha River at the Wood-Wirt county line, 18 miles east of Parkersburg. At this convergence, Hughes River is 600 feet above sea level. About 12 miles upstream from its mouth, Hughes River divides into the North and South forks near the town of Cisco in Ritchie County. Harrisville, the county seat of Ritchie County, is located on the North Fork of Hughes.

The North Fork of Hughes River has its headwaters at the Ritchie-Tyler county line, near the community of Mountain, and it is 57 miles long. The South Fork is 54 miles long. It rises in southwestern Doddridge County, near the community of Porto Rico, and flows through southern Ritchie County to join the North Fork. Hughes River's chief tributary is 28-mile-long Goose Creek, which forms a part of the border between Wood and Ritchie counties. Goose Creek flows into Hughes River at the town of Freeport in Wirt County.

Geologically, the forks of the Hughes have eroded deep channels into the massive strata of the Waynesburg Sandstone, creating a rough topography, with steep sandstone cliffs and narrow valleys. Hughes River contains a variety of fish,

including muskie; spotted, small mouth and rock bass; flathead and channel catfish; and several species of sunfish. The Hughes River Wildlife Management Area, a popular hunting area, straddles the river northeast of Elizabeth.

Larry Bartlett
Parkersburg

Milton W. Humphreys

Born in Greenbrier County, September 13, 1844, the soldier and scholar Milton Wiley Humphreys was educated at Mercer Academy and Washington College, now Washington and Lee University. During the Civil War, on March 27, 1862, he enlisted in the Confederate service as a sergeant in Bryan's Battery, Virginia Artillery. At the battle of Fayetteville, May 19, 1862, Sergeant Humphreys fired his cannon at Union artillery from behind an intervening forest. This demonstration set a precedent for modern warfare by the use of indirect fire. He served throughout the war and was paroled at Charleston, June 12, 1865. After the war he became noted as an authority on gunnery and ballistics.

As a professor of Greek and ancient languages Humphreys taught at Washington and Lee University, Vanderbilt University, the University of Texas, and finally the University of Virginia. Professor Humphreys was a commissioner to the World's Fair at Vienna, and in 1882 was elected president of the American Philological Association. In 1926, he published a memoir of his Civil War service titled *Military Operations 1861–1863 at Fayetteville, West Virginia.* He died at Charlottesville, Virginia, November 20, 1928, at the age of 84. He is buried in the chapel at the University of Virginia.

See also Civil War

Tim McKinney
Fayetteville

Hot Rod Hundley

Athlete Rodney Clark "Hot Rod" Hundley was born in Charleston, October 26, 1934. Many who watched him play for West Virginia University in the 1950s considered him the greatest natural basketball talent the state ever produced. Hundley was a flashy standout at Charleston High School before enrolling at WVU. The six foot-four guard-forward averaged 34.1 points per game for WVU's freshman team in 1954 and, under coach Fred Schaus, led the varsity squad to a 72-16 record and three straight Southern Conference titles. Hundley earned first team All-American recognition his senior year and averaged 24.5 points per game and scored 2,180 points over his college career, ranking second in WVU history.

Despite Hundley's dazzling talent, he is best remembered as the "clown prince of college basketball." He was a master of trick shots and the behind-the-back dribble. Other antics included spinning the ball on his finger during games and humorously mocking opponents on the court. Hundley played six years in the NBA for the Minneapolis-Los Angeles Lakers and was named an all-star twice. Hundley has been a radio announcer for the NBA's Utah Jazz since 1974.

Stan Bumgardner
Division of Culture and History

Norman Julian, "Hundley Credits His Success to Start at WVU," *Dominion Post*, January 28, 1996.

Hungarians

Attracted by jobs in the burgeoning mining and manufacturing industries, Hungarians came to West Virginia in considerable number after 1900. Many were recruited by agents of coal and manufacturing companies in their own country or when they entered the United States at Ellis Island, New York. Companies sometimes guaranteed travel costs, to be worked off after arriving in America. These immigrants were said to have come "on transportation" and began their new lives in debt to their employers. Many planned to work awhile, save money, and then return to their old country. Some did return, but a greater number stayed, either due to assimilation or the inability to raise enough money for the return trip. Typically, single men or married men without their families arrived first, later sending for their loved ones to join them.

In 1890, there were 236 native Hungarians in West Virginia. By 1900, there were 1,062 Hungarians in the state, with about half of them split evenly between McDowell and Marion counties. Most were coal miners. The 1910 census lists a total of 5,939 Hungarians in West Virginia, although the influx slowed as indicated by the 1920 census listing 6,260, with Logan and McDowell counties with the greatest number. Hungarians were the second most numerous immigrant group in West Virginia mines after the turn of the 20th century, with Italians being first.

Hungarians were particularly conscious of retaining their customs and language, often requiring their American-born children to first speak Hungarian, and then learn English when they began public school. Some even formed Hungarian language schools. In this way, Hungarian traditions, foods, and religion were maintained in West Virginia. After World War I, immigration numbers fell, although some Hungarians did continue to enter West Virginia. Today, the close-knit Hungarian communities have dispersed, as other ethnic groups have done in the state through the last 60 years.

Cathy Pleska
Scott Depot

Kenneth R. Bailey, "A Judicious Mixture: Negroes and Immigrants in the West Virginia Mines, 1880–1917," *West Virginia History*, January 1973; Fredrick A. Barkey, "Immigration and Ethnicity in

West Virginia: A Review of the Literature," in Ronald L. Lewis and John C. Hennen Jr., eds., *West Virginia History: Critical Essays on the Literature,* 1993.

Hunting

Since before the time Europeans settled in these mountains, hunting has been a tradition in West Virginia. The image of the mountaineer in buckskin clothing and coonskin cap, and carrying a flintlock rifle, has endured. While dress and weaponry have changed, West Virginians' passion for hunting remains strong, and modern wildlife management has maintained viable populations of virtually all game species.

In fact, there are many more whitetail deer and wild turkeys now than there were 100 years ago, when both had been reduced to near extinction by habitat destruction and unregulated hunting. The black bear, our state animal, similarly threatened as late as the 1970s, has also made a remarkable comeback. These three species, which played such important roles in the survival of early settlers, constitute the centerpiece of Mountain State hunting.

West Virginia's first game laws were passed in 1869, although it was not until well into the 20th century that additional statutes gradually reversed the decline in game animals. Game laws have been refined over the years, as has enforcement, starting with the 1933 act that replaced game protectors with conservation officers.

All West Virginia hunting seasons are held in the fall, with the exception of spring gobbler season, which was begun in 1968 and has become immensely popular. All game species are native animals except for European wild boars, which were introduced into three counties in southern West Virginia through stocking. Boar hunting was begun in 1979 and continues as the most challenging of our big game seasons, due to the rugged terrain the hogs inhabit and their innate craftiness.

Although deer, bear, and turkey command the most attention, the gray squirrel and the cottontail rabbit lure thousands of hunters to the woods and fields annually. Historically, young hunters first hone their skills in the squirrel woods. Rabbit hunting is equally traditional, although rabbit numbers have declined because of changing habitat with the loss of fields and increasing forestation. The numbers of ruffed grouse, a bird that epitomizes the wild places of West Virginia, have dropped for the same reason. The trapping of fur-bearing animals, including mink, raccoon, foxes, and beaver, rounds out the West Virginia hunting scene, if on a reduced scale compared to decades ago.

October and November are the tradi-

tional hunting months, when most of the seasons merge, and early morning and late evening are prime times for hunters, with wild game on the move. Serious hunters adapt their strategy to the habits of the game they are seeking, and to the availability of food supplies in the woods. The most striking changes have come in bowhunting, with tree stands, elaborate camouflage, and high-tech bows in vogue now. In another respect, technology in weaponry has taken a step backward with the advent of a muzzleloader rifle season for deer.

Prior to the enactment of the first hunting laws in West Virginia in 1869, subsistence hunting took place throughout the year. But even then, autumn was the favored time because animals had grown to maturity and fattened on the plentiful foods of summer. Also, with colder weather the meat was easier to preserve. Present hunting laws recognize these factors, as well as the need to protect animals during the time of raising their young.

Early, unregulated hunting was done mostly for food and clothing. Like the Indians before them, the early settlers depended on animals, especially whitetail deer, for food, clothing, and even soap made from the tallow. Market hunting of deer played a part in that animal being reduced to near-extinction by the early 1900s, and at one time large numbers of cottontail rabbits were shipped from West Virginia to eastern markets.

The emergence of hunting clubs began in the early 1900s. Historian Roy Bird Cook, in his preface to sportsman W.E.R. Byrne's classic book, *Tale of the Elk*, mentions attending a meeting of the West Virginia Fish and Game Protective Association at Clarksburg in 1907. Today, more than 100 outdoor organizations exist in the state, most of them affiliated with the West Virginia Wildlife Federation.

Every county of the state has its legendary hunters. Topping the list is the fabled frontiersman Daniel Boone, who lived in Kanawha County for about 10 years. Powell Mountain in Nicholas County was named for William Powell, an early hunter in that region. Eli "Rimfire" Hamrick of Webster Springs, the renowned mountaineer, reputedly gained his colorful nickname due to his skill with a rifle firing rimfire cartridges. Perhaps the late Ed Buck was the last of the mountain men in West Virginia. A biology teacher at Richwood High School, he hunted and trapped for more than 40 years in the remote Cranberry Backcountry.

West Virginia has 1.5 million acres of public hunting land, about 10 percent of the state's total acreage.

See also Game Laws

Skip Johnson
Sutton

Hunting Dogs

Since the human nose is virtually worthless when compared to a hound's, hunters rely on dogs to trail, tree, spot, hold, point, find, and retrieve game. In West Virginia, dogs are used to pursue nearly every species of wildlife, from squirrel, cottontail, wild turkey, ruffed grouse, woodcock, opossum, and raccoon, up to black bear. (It is illegal to hunt deer with dogs.) The variety of hunting dogs used by Mountain State hunters is extensive. Breeds number in the dozens.

Bear hunters prefer hounds bred in the mountains, where the animals are raised to have no fear of bears. Breeds such as the Plott, Redbone, black and tan, Treeing Walker, and blue-tick are all used as bear dogs. A bear hunter's strike dog has the best nose in a pack. Strike dogs are experienced and used to determine if a trail is hot. If the strike dog is confident in the scent, other hounds are turned loose. One Webster County hunter said after the 2000 hunting season that a pack of his hounds held a Kanawha County bear treed for more than five hours while hunters tried to find their way to the remote scene. When the hunters finally arrived, the hounds were still barking, and the treed bear, which weighed more than 300 pounds, was shot.

Raccoon hunters use similar dog breeds. There are two types of trailing raccoon hounds, silent trailers and those with good voices. A silent trailer pushes its quarry quickly and brings it to tree faster than hounds baying on a track. During an era of high hide prices in the 1970s, when a prime raccoon pelt could bring $75, silent trailers were preferred because many raccoons could be taken quickly.

Hunting cottontail rabbits with beagles almost became a lost tradition during the 1980s as cottontail numbers plummeted throughout the East. Today, hunting rabbits with beagles is a pastime enjoyed by only a limited number of West Virginians.

Bird hunters frequently have friendly arguments over which breeds make the best bird dogs. A consensus among veteran hunters, however, shows the English setter as the best grouse hunting breed used in West Virginia. A setter's long hair protects it from heavy brush and thorns. The dog's intelligence and receptivity to extensive training make it an ideal choice for West Virginia's steep terrain.

Squirrel hunting with a hound is something few West Virginians get the opportunity to do, since quality squirrel dogs are not commonly available. Breeds that make good squirrel dogs include the Norwegian elkhound and Australian shepherd, along with several smaller breeds of terrier. On a typical squirrel hunt with a hound, the dog forces the squirrel to take quickly to a tree. While the dog barks below, the squirrel hides in place, allowing the hunter to circle the tree and

A coon dog of the Treeing Walker breed.

eventually find and shoot the squirrel.

Serious waterfowl hunters use Chesapeake Bay and Labrador retrievers for their sport. And of all the breeds of hunting dog, these are often considered to be the most trainable and intelligent. Retrievers also can be used as field flushing dogs on quail and pheasants. Autumn turkey hunters also occasionally use dogs, which do the work of finding flocks of wild turkeys. The dog runs into the flock and chases the birds, barking and scattering them in several directions. Afterward, the hunter sits down, camouflages his dog (which is trained to sit quietly), and begins to call the wild turkeys back to the gun. Dogs used for hunting wild turkeys during the fall season are probably the least available of all hunting dog breeds. Small terriers are often the dogs of choice for this duty, although setters and other breeds are occasionally used.

See also Hunting

Andy Hansroth
Charleston Gazette

Huntington

Located on the Ohio River near where West Virginia, Kentucky, and Ohio meet, the city of Huntington was founded in 1871 by railroad mogul Collis P. Huntington as the western terminus of his Chesapeake & Ohio Railway. Seeking a convenient spot to transfer cargo and passengers between the C&O and the Ohio's riverboats, he selected Holderby's Landing, a stretch of farmland just downstream from the mouth of the Guyandotte River.

Huntington directed his brother-in-law, Col. Delos W. Emmons, to purchase 21 farms totaling 5,000 acres. Rufus Cook, a Boston civil engineer, was hired to design a town plan featuring a geometric gridwork of intersecting avenues and streets, consecutively numbered so that any address would be easy to find. On February 27, 1871, the West Virginia legislature approved an act incorporating the new city, named for its founder. On December 31 of that year, Peter Cline Buffington was elected Huntington's first mayor. The community grew rapidly and by the early 1890s had a population of more than 10,000. In 1887, after considerable controversy, the seat of Cabell County was moved from Barboursville to Huntington.

In selecting a site for his new city, Collis P. Huntington chose well. The community prospered as a gateway to the coalfields of southern West Virginia. Coal flowed to market via Huntington, and manufactured goods traveled the other direction, a two-way traffic that spawned thousands of jobs in the river city. In addition to its role as a transportation hub and a center of retail and wholesale trade, Huntington also attracted manufacturers who produced a broad array of products, including railcars, steel, glass, china, brick, stoves, furniture, and even church pews.

Organized in June of 1872, the First Congregational Church is said to be the city's oldest church. Huntington today is home to more than 130 congregations, representing virtually every faith. That includes seven congregations located in a six-block stretch of downtown Fifth Avenue. In addition to its many churches, Huntington is known for its broad, tree-lined streets; for Ritter Park, fashioned in 1913 from land originally intended for use as a city incinerator; for the grand Keith-Albee Theater, which has welcomed moviegoers since 1928; for the handsome Cabell County Courthouse, dedicated in 1901; and for Heritage Village, with its many historic buildings.

Huntington is home to Marshall University. Older than the city itself, Marshall was established in a log church at its present location in 1837. Marshall has grown steadily over the years, especially since it became a university in 1961. Today, it boasts more than 15,000 undergraduate and graduate students, enrolled in a broad range of academic programs. Marshall's sports teams are a source of community-wide pride. And the Marshall School of Medicine, which admitted its first class in 1978, has helped make the city a regional health care center.

In the wake of the disastrous 1937 flood, when the Ohio inundated much of Huntington, the U.S. Army Corp of Engineers constructed an 11-mile floodwall to protect the city from future floods. Unfortunately, the wall also prompted the city to forget its historic ties with the river. That was corrected in 1984, with the

The Huntington skyline.

opening of the David W. Harris Riverfront Park.

The 1950s were years of remarkable growth and achievement for Huntington, the city's zenith, some would argue. The decade saw construction of Tri-State Airport, the Huntington Museum of Art, Cabell Huntington Hospital, and Veterans Memorial Field House. In the decades following, Huntington saw many factories close, businesses slump, and jobs disappear. Part of the decline stemmed from sweeping cutbacks in coal mine employment as automation took hold in the surrounding coalfields, part was attributable to the same "rust belt" phenomenon experienced by so many of the nation's other cities. Some felt the 1950s decision to route Interstate 64 outside Huntington was a mistake, and the later building of Huntington Mall far to the east clearly hurt downtown business. The city's economic woes were reflected in a dramatic population decline. Huntington lost nearly 35,000 residents from 1950 to 2000, leaving a population of 51,475. Some simply moved to growing suburban areas outside the city, but many left the region, seeking better opportunities elsewhere.

In 1993, more than 600 employees lost their jobs when the Owens-Brockway glass container plant, a fixture in the city for 80 years, closed. Stung by that closing, nearly 1,000 concerned residents braved a snowstorm to attend a public forum focusing on the city's future. From that meeting was born a new public-private partnership, dubbed Our Jobs, Our Children, Our Future. As part of that economic development effort, the closed Owens-Brockway plant was purchased and turned into an industrial park. And the same public-private partnership attracted more than 2,000 jobs in information services, establishing telemarketing

and market research as important elements in the Huntington economy.

See also Cabell County, Collis P. Huntington, Marshall University

> *James E. Casto*
> *Herald-Dispatch*

James E. Casto, *Huntington: An Illustrated History,* 1985; Doris C. Miller, *A Centennial History of Huntington,* 1971.

Collis P. Huntington

Railroad mogul and founder of the city of Huntington, Collis Potter Huntington was born October 22, 1821, at Harwinton, Connecticut. Raised in poverty, he left school at age 14 and became a Yankee peddler, traveling through the South to sell watches and other merchandise. Later he opened a general store at Oneonta, New York. When gold was discovered in California in 1848, Huntington went west and became a rich man, not from mining but by selling supplies to the miners.

Starting with an investment of $1,500, Huntington and partners Mark Hopkins, Leland Stanford, and Charles Crocker (collectively known to rail historians as the "Big Four") built two giant rail systems, first the Central Pacific and later the Southern Pacific. In 1862, Huntington persuaded Congress to designate the Central Pacific as the western half of the long-dreamed-of transcontinental railroad. It was successfully linked with the rival Union Pacific with the driving of a golden spike at Promontory Point, Utah, on May 10, 1869.

That same year, Huntington (without his partners) purchased the nearly bankrupt Chesapeake & Ohio Railway and set about extending its tracks from Richmond across southern West Virginia to the Ohio River. There, in 1871, at a site just downstream from the mouth of the Guyandotte River, he established a new

city bearing his name. Remembered as one of the great "robber barons" of his era, Huntington also founded the city of Newport News, Virginia, and the Newport News Shipyard. He died August 13, 1900.

See also Chesapeake & Ohio Railway, Huntington

> *James E. Casto*
> *Herald-Dispatch*

Cerinda W. Evans, *Collis Potter Huntington,* 1954; David Lavender, *The Great Persuader,* 1970.

Collis P. Huntington Statue

The statue of Collis Potter Huntington which stands at the restored C&O depot in Huntington, is the work of artist Gutzon Borglum, who is best-known for his sculpture of the heads of the four presidents carved in the face of Mount Rushmore in South Dakota. Huntington, who was born October 22, 1821 and died August 13, 1900, built the Chesapeake & Ohio Railway and founded the city of Huntington at its western terminus. The statue originally stood atop its granite base in front of the Chesapeake & Ohio's mid-town station.

On October 23, 1924, while a huge crowd looked on, the eight-foot bronze statue was unveiled and presented to the city and to the C&O at the request of Mr. and Mrs. Henry E. Huntington (Henry was Collis's nephew, and Mrs. Huntington was Collis's second wife, who had married Henry after Collis's death in 1900). Mrs. Huntington died just six weeks before the dedication.

The statue depicts Collis P. Huntington as a robust figure with a bald head, full beard, and moustache. He wears a buttoned, knee-length overcoat, and his right hand clasps the handle of a cane. The statue stood in front of the C&O depot until May 1977, when it was moved to Heritage Village in downtown Huntington. There it remained until the spring of 2000, when it was returned to its original site in front of a restored C&O depot that now is a CSX office building.

See also Collis P. Huntington

> *Joseph Platania*
> *Huntington*

Huntington Museum of Art

The Huntington Museum of Art, West Virginia's largest art museum, opened November 9, 1952, as the Huntington Galleries. By 1987, when the name was changed to the Huntington Museum of Art, the museum's art collection had grown to more than 10,000 objects.

The museum is located on more than 50 acres on McCoy Road in the Park Hills section of Huntington, with two nature trails and a subtropical plant conservatory. With close to 70,000 square feet of space, it hosts traveling exhibitions and has permanent galleries of British silver and portraits, antique firearms, Near East objects, and an Ohio Valley glass collection of more than 3,000 pieces. The museum's Daywood Collection features such artists as Childe Hassam and Andrew Wyeth and contains fine examples of late 19th-century and early 20th-century American and European artwork.

The museum's James D. Francis Art Research Library houses more than 11,000 volumes, and its Grace Rardin Doherty Auditorium seats close to 300. Five art studios are housed in two separate buildings on the museum grounds. The museum features visiting artists and occasionally hosts artists-in-residence. Studios 1, 2, and 3 are named for renowned architect Walter Gropius. The studios and Doherty addition of the museum are the only realized museum design by Gropius in the United States, and they were the last project of the aging architect.

To meet its education mission, the museum maintains an outreach program teaching more than 20,000 children about art each year.

John Gillispie
Huntington Museum of Art

Huntington State Hospital

Huntington State Hospital, today known as the Mildred Mitchell-Bateman Hospital, was established by the legislature as an insane asylum in 1897 and called the Home for Incurables. At the time of its inception, the public viewed such hospitals as places where the mentally ill were placed to remove them from society for custodial care. The tall wire fence and iron gates gave the Huntington facility the appearance of a penal institution rather than a hospital. The gates were taken away in 1950, and the gate house at the hospital entrance was removed in 1961.

The site, consisting of 30 acres of land, was donated to the state by the Chamber of Commerce of the city of Huntington. On the eastern edge of Huntington, the hospital fronts on Norway Avenue. In 1901, the name was changed to West Virginia Asylum, and the patient census was 150. The peak patient population was about 1,460 in 1956. In 1916, the name was changed to Huntington State Hospital.

Tragedy struck the hospital November 26, 1952. A fire on the evening before Thanksgiving killed 14 patients, with three more patients later dying of injuries.

In July 1958, the vocational rehabilitation center was established at Huntington State Hospital, the first in the nation to be located on the same grounds with a state hospital. The center offered vocational, social, psychological, medical, and related services necessary to enable the patient to prepare for a return to community living.

In 1995, the legislature again changed the facility's name, renaming it Hunting-ton Hospital. During the October 1999 celebration of the hospital's centennial, Governor Underwood announced the renaming of Huntington Hospital as the Mildred Mitchell-Bateman Hospital, a tribute to Dr. Mitchell-Bateman's lifetime career of helping the mentally ill. The 90-bed psychiatric hospital is administered by the Department of Health and Human Resources. Twelve buildings are located on the site.

See also Mildred Mitchell-Bateman

Hurricane

The city of Hurricane is located in Putnam County, on Interstate 64 midway between Huntington and Charleston. The population was 5,222 in 2000. The city was named for Hurricane Creek, and the most generally accepted version of how the creek received its name is that in about 1774 surveyors discovered the effects of a storm that had laid low giant trees. The place was located at the mouth of a large creek, and the creek was shown on early maps as Hurricane Creek.

Among the earliest settlers, James Conner of eastern Virginia made extensive exploration of the area in 1777, receiving acreages of land through grants from the governor of Virginia. His land holdings may have included 4,000 to 5,000 acres. About 1815, a small settlement began to form near the present eastern corporate limits of Hurricane. The settlement was named Hurricane Creek Bridge and was a stop on the James River & Kanawha Turnpike. When the Chesapeake & Ohio Railway arrived in the 1870s, the community was called Hurricane Station. When the town was formally incorporated in 1888, the name was shortened to Hurricane. The town became a city when the population reached 3,000 in the 1970s.

Hurricane has one high school, one middle school, and four elementary schools, as well as Hurricane City Park and Valley Park. The population has increased in recent years as Hurricane has become a center of Putnam County's growing suburban community.

Frank Hutchison

Musician Frank Hutchison, born March 20, 1897, was an early country musician whose songs and style reflected African-American blues influence. Born in Raleigh County, the white Hutchison moved to Logan County in childhood and later worked around the mines. He developed a slide guitar sound akin to the "bottleneck" style and also played harmonica to augment his singing. Hutchison made his living in the coalfields in the 1920s but left for Ohio in 1932, during the Great Depression.

Between 1926 and 1929, Hutchison recorded some 32 numbers for the OKeh Record Company, a few of them featuring fiddling by Sherman Lawson. In 1927, playing with Arnold and Irving Williamson, he made one of the earliest recorded versions of "John Henry," under the title, "Gonna Die with my Hammer in my Hand." Hutchison's best-known numbers included "Worried Blues," "The Train that Carried My Girl from Town," and "Coney Isle." Readapted as "Alabam," the latter became a major country hit for Cowboy Copas in 1960. Hutchison helped to instill a blues strain in modern country music, and was influential among coalfield musicians. His Logan County musical circle included banjoist Virginia Myrtle "Aunt Jennie" Wilson, who recalled that he and she were once engaged to marry. Eventually nearly all of his recordings were reissued on vinyl album and compact disk. Frank Hutchison, who died in Dayton, Ohio, November 9, 1945, did not live to see the revival of interest in his music.

Ivan M. Tribe
University of Rio Grande
Ivan M. Tribe, *Mountaineer Jamboree: Country Music in West Virginia*, 1984.

Huttonsville Correctional Center

The Huttonsville Correctional Center is a medium-security state prison. It is located near the town of Huttonsville, south of Elkins in Randolph County, on farmland once owned by descendants of some of the earliest settlers of the upper Tygart Valley. The center was founded in 1937 as part of the West Virginia penitentiary system. Established to relieve crowding at the state penitentiary at Moundsville, it became a separate institution in 1947.

Huttonsville inmates, varying in number from 240 to almost 900, have been for many years employed in general farm work. The prison is located on 68 acres, with almost 5,000 adjoining acres cultivated or used for grazing land under the ownership of the West Virginia Department of Agriculture and supervised by the West Virginia Farm Commission. Prison labor produces corn, potatoes, hogs, and beef cattle for distribution to other institutions under state control. Inmates also build furniture and operate a Braille publishing service that transcribes textbooks into Braille for distribution throughout the United States.

The prison now serves as a diagnostic and classification center for pre-sentence evaluation for placing the prisoners at the state prison at Mount Olive in Fayette County or for retention at Huttonsville. Huttonsville inmates take part in educational and vocational programs, leading to GED certificates and college credit.

Donald L. Rice
Elkins

Arnout "Sonny" Hyde Jr.

Photographer Arnout "Sonny" Hyde Jr., born September 7, 1937, in Bluefield, was best known for his long association with *Wonderful West Virginia* magazine. His images of nature and people have appeared in magazines, books, and calendars throughout the U.S. and Europe. More than 500 of his photographs have been featured in national magazines, including *Life, National Geographic, Readers Digest, Southern Living,* and *National Wildlife.*

Hyde became interested in photography while he was a student at West Virginia University. In the early 1960s, upon entering the U.S. Army, he studied photography and served for three years as an Army photographer. His photographs appeared in the Army newspaper *Stars and Stripes.* After his Army stint, Hyde went to work for the West Virginia Department of Commerce, in the photography lab. In 1968, he transferred to the state Department of Natural Resources, where he worked on the magazine *Outdoor West Virginia,* which was renamed *Wonderful West Virginia* in 1970. Hyde edited *Wonderful West Virginia* from 1982 until his retirement from state government in 1988. In 1997, under a private contract, he resumed editorship of the magazine.

Hyde published five books: *West Virginia; A Portrait of West Virginia; New River—A Photographic Essay; The Potomac—A Nation's River,* with text by Ken Sullivan; and *West Virginia: The Land and its People,* with text by his daughter Lucia K. Hyde. Arnout Hyde died August 9, 2005.

Hydroelectricity

West Virginia's streams have been harnessed for their energy since the days of early settlement. Countless gristmills and sawmills once crowded the banks of our creeks and rivers, many of them remaining in operation into the 20th century, and during the 19th century flowing water powered large factories on the Potomac and Shenandoah rivers at Harpers Ferry. By about 1900, water power was being used for the production of electricity in West Virginia. Although coal remains by far the most important fuel for electric generation in West Virginia, accounting for more than 98 percent of production in 2002, the production of hydroelectricity has slowly increased over the past century.

Hydroelectricity is produced by the capture of the energy of flowing water. Stream water is impounded by a dam to increase its "fall," and thus its gravity power, then diverted to an electric generator. There, the rushing water spins the blades of a turbine to produce electric power.

Unlike the huge dams and power plants in the western United States, hydroelectric plants in West Virginia are smaller and usually situated on existing dams. These dams were built primarily

The Hawks Nest Dam on New River, 1930s.

for flood control and navigation, and sometimes refitted after many years for the production of electricity. Constructed in 1924–26, Cheat Lake is one of the few lakes in West Virginia created primarily for the production of electricity. The dam and power plant at Cheat Lake are located across the state line in Pennsylvania.

The Ohio, Cheat, Kanawha, Gauley, Potomac, Shenandoah, and New rivers have all been used in the production of electricity. Perhaps the best-known hydroelectric facility in the state, the 102-megawatt Hawks Nest-Gauley Bridge hydropower complex on the New River, is also associated with one of the nation's worst industrial disasters. A tunnel was opened through Gauley Mountain to increase the fall of the water captured upstream at the dam. Construction of the three-mile tunnel began during the early years of the Great Depression, and hundreds of workers died from silicosis as the work progressed. The picturesque dam and lake are visible from Hawks Nest State Park, and the associated power plant is still in use after three-fourths of a century. The same company operated the nearby Glen Ferris dam and power plant, located at Kanawha Falls. Glen Ferris, the state's oldest hydro complex, ceased generating electricity in 2002 with an expectation to reopen later.

The production of hydroelectricity in West Virginia entered the 21st century in 2001, when the 80-megawatt power station on the Summersville Dam on Gauley River went into use. The plant is operated by the Gauley River Power Partners, which includes the city of Summersville.

Other recent hydropower plants include the 42-megawatt facility on the Ohio River at Belleville, which began producing electricity in 1999 and is operated by American Municipal Power-Ohio. A similar partnership produces power on the Hannibal locks and dam on the Ohio River near New Martinsville, and another is in the planning stage for Bluestone Dam in Summers County. These public-private partnerships were made possible by the federal Public Utility Regulatory Policy Act, passed in 1978.

After a century of production, hydro plants provide only a small fraction of all electricity generated in West Virginia. In 2002, hydroelectric accounted for 1,065,736 of the 94,761,752 megawatt hours of electricity produced, or 1.1 percent. Over the decade 1993–2002, the production of hydroelectricity fell at an annual rate of 0.5 percent, at a time when the state's overall production of electricity was increasing at an annual rate of 2.7 percent. Less than a fourth of the hydroelectricity produced in West Virginia is produced by the electric utilities, the remainder being generated by independent producers. These independent producers include projects such as those on the Ohio River at New Martinsville and Belleville, which produce electricity primarily for sale, as well as industrial producers which themselves consume the power they generate. The electricity generated at Gauley Bridge, for example, is used by the parent company's nearby ferrometals plant.

Hydroelectric plants now dot the major rivers of West Virginia, with installations at London, Marmet, Winfield, Gauley

Bridge, New Martinsville, Summersville, and elsewhere. These plants are owned by the major electric utilities, as well as industrial and independent producers, but they are much smaller than the huge coal-fired electric plants. In 2002, for example, American Electric Power's giant John E. Amos plant in Kanawha County could produce 2,900 megawatts, more than ten times as much electricity as all hydroelectric plants in West Virginia combined. The Hawks Nest-Gauley Bridge complex, at 102 megawatts, is the largest producer of hydroelectricity in West Virginia.

See also Hawks Nest Tunnel Disaster, Kanawha Falls, Lakes

Ice Mountain

Ice Mountain, along the North River near North River Mills, Hampshire County, has an extensive area of boulders and rock debris within which water freezes in the winter. The protective layer of rocks allows the ice to melt slowly through the spring and early summer. At the base of the slope, cool air emits from small vents among the rocks. In the past, the ice was reported to persist in some years until September, was used to make homemade ice cream, and was even used to cool a dairy for the summer storage of milk. Now, ice can generally be found only into June, although the cool air persists through most of the summer.

The cool conditions allow many northern plants, snails, and insects to live at Ice Mountain, despite a relatively low elevation. Among these plants are bunchberry, purple clematis, skunk currant, and nannyberry, which are typically found in West Virginia at elevations above 3,000 feet. Bristly rose and twinflower, plants of the far north, and the rare Appalachian oak fern also occur here. Away from the ice vents, the vegetation is typical for the region. The Nature Conservancy owns and manages Ice Mountain as a nature preserve. The elevation of Ice Mountain is 1,429 feet.

Rodney Bartgis
Nature Conservancy of West Virginia

Ices Ferry Ironworks

Jackson's Ironworks at Ices Ferry was northern West Virginia's most significant antebellum ironworks and an important nail production center until its closing in the late 1850s. Located on the east side of the Cheat River at Ices Ferry in Monongalia County, the ironworks was established by Samuel Jackson about 1809 for the manufacture of hand-wrought nails. The works used local ore, limestone, and fuel, and over the next 40 years the operation was expanded into an extensive ironworks complex. Local tradition holds that during the War of 1812 the ironworks supplied iron for shot used in the Battle of New Orleans and shipped nails and plates to Lake Erie for Admiral Perry's Lake Erie squadron.

By 1812, the first Western Virginia rolling mill was in operation at the ironworks, and in 1822 the region's first cut-nail machinery was installed there. About 1836, the Henry Clay Furnace (now part of Coopers Rock State Forest) was built to supply pig iron to the works; it was the first steam-powered furnace in Western Virginia. The Ellicott brothers, important Maryland ironmasters, purchased the property in the late 1830s and made a number of improvements, including the addition of puddling furnaces, the construction of a new rolling mill, and the integration of the outlying furnaces with the Ices Ferry site by means of animal-powered tram roads. Despite their innovations, the Ellicotts failed at Ices Ferry, and in later years, the ironworks changed hands frequently. By 1860, the ironworks closed for the last time. The lack of adequate transportation and the depletion of iron ore and fuel resources forced its closure. The once extensive ironworks now lies beneath the waters of Cheat Lake.

See also Henry Clay Furnace, Ironmaking

Lee R. Maddex
WVU Institute for the History of Technology
James R. Moreland, *The Early Cheat Mountain Iron Works*, 1992.

George W. Imboden

Born in Augusta County, Virginia, on June 25, 1836, George William Imboden became a distinguished attorney, Confederate soldier, and a leading citizen of Ansted. After attending Staunton Academy, he studied law and was admitted to the bar in 1858. In 1859, he married Mary Frances Tyree, daughter of an Ansted innkeeper. Imboden enlisted in the Southern service on April 17, 1861. He rose to the rank of colonel by December 1862, when he took command of the 18th Virginia Calvary which fought at Chancellorsville and in many other battles. He was seriously wounded at Gordonsville, Virginia.

Moving to Fayette County in 1870, Imboden actively promoted industrialization of the two Virginias. His older brother and business partner, Gen. John D. Imboden, had already established himself politically in Virginia. George acted as attorney and served as a director of the Gauley Mountain Coal Company, the Loup Creek Colliery, and the Deepwater Railway.

Imboden served Ansted and Fayette County from 1870 to 1922, holding office in the House of Delegates (1876), as president of the Fayette County Commission (1881–85), first mayor of Ansted (1891–92), and town recorder (1891–1907). A tall, slender man with piercing eyes and a no-nonsense military demeanor, he married Angia M. Dickinson, daughter of a Fayette County pioneer in 1869, after the death of his first wife. George W. Imboden died at home on January 8, 1922, and was buried in Confederate gray in Westlake Cemetery. His home in Ansted, known as Contentment, is a National Register property that now serves as a Fayette County museum.

See also Contentment, John D. Imboden

Lou Athey
Franklin & Marshall College

John D. Imboden

Soldier and industrialist John D. Imboden (1823–95).

General John David Imboden was born near Staunton, Virginia, February 16, 1823. He enrolled at Washington College (later Washington and Lee University) at age 16. A school teacher and attorney with a law office in Staunton, he served two terms in the Virginia Legislature.

At the outbreak of the Civil War he entered Confederate service as captain of the Staunton Artillery, a light battery which he formed and subsequently commanded at the initial capture of Harpers Ferry in 1861. Captain Imboden fought in the battle of First Manassas in July 1861, and in 1862 he organized the 1st Virginia Partisan Rangers, later known as the 62nd Virginia Mounted Infantry. He participated in the battles of Cross Keys and Port Republic, Virginia, under Stonewall Jackson, and in January 1863 was appointed brigadier general. In the spring of 1863, he led one contingent of the famous Jones-Imboden Raid through present West Virginia, during which he cut the Baltimore & Ohio Railroad line and captured large numbers of cattle. Imboden guarded the Confederate left flank in the advance on Gettysburg and performed with distinction in covering Lee's retreat. He later served at New Market, Fisher's Hill, Cedar Creek, and other battles. In the autumn of 1864, he contracted typhoid fever and was relieved of command.

After the war Imboden resumed his law practice and was active in the development of mining resources in his area. He was the business partner and older brother of George W. Imboden, a Fayette County coal operator. John D. Imboden died at Damascus, Virginia, August 15, 1895.

See also Civil War, George W. Imboden, Jones-Imboden Raid

Tim McKinney
Fayetteville

Immigration Commissioner

West Virginia's first immigration commissioner was authorized by the legislature in 1864. Joseph H. Diss Debar, himself an immigrant, was appointed to the position and charged with attracting other newcomers to the young state. After Diss Debar, apparently at least two other immigration commissioners served during the 19th century, and the job may have remained vacant at times for lack of funds or lack of interest.

Diss Debar and his early successors were especially interested in attracting farmers, and helped to settle immigrant agricultural communities at St. Clara and Helvetia. Official interest in the position revived at about the turn of the 20th century due to the need for labor for West Virginia's burgeoning industries, especially coal mining. The legislature reactivated the position in 1897. Funding was not provided, however, and no one was appointed until 1907 when John Nugent became the state's immigration commissioner.

John Nugent was a controversial figure who had been president of United Mine Workers of America District 17 and of the West Virginia Federation of Labor. No public funds were available for the immigration commissioner, and Nugent's salary and expenses were underwritten by coal companies from 1907 to 1913. Nugent visited England, Scotland, and Wales in 1907 to recruit miners. His activities became an issue in the 1913 U.S. Senate investigation of the Paint Creek-Cabin Creek mine strike. Nugent was alleged to have recruited immigrants to work in the Paint Creek mines even though he was aware that there was a strike in progress.

Following World War I, federal laws greatly restricted the influx of immigrants to the United States. The West Virginia immigration commissioner's position was left vacant for several years and dropped from the state's laws by 1931.

See also Joseph H. Diss Debar, John Nugent

Kenneth R. Bailey
WVU Institute of Technology

Indian Mound Cemetery

Indian Mound Cemetery is located at the western end of Romney on the north side of U.S. 50. It is on the east side of the South Branch Potomac, on a high terrace overlooking the river. The cemetery, which covers at least two acres of ground, was started shortly before the Civil War. It is named for a large Indian mound near its southeast corner. The mound is approximately 35 by 40 feet and about five feet high. The mound has not

been fully investigated archeologically so its exact age is not known. However, it is believed to have been built sometime between 550 B.C. and A.D. 1400. Two governors of West Virginia are buried at Indian Mound Cemetery, John Jeremiah Jacob (died 1893) and John Jacob Cornwell (died 1953).

See also Romney

Greg Adamson
Dayton, Virginia

Indian Trails

When the first Europeans came to North America, they soon became aware of a network of pathways extending from the Gulf Coast to the Great Lakes and everywhere in between. These pathways, or Indian trails, served as a means of interaction between Native American groups in various cultural regions. The remnants of trails that once crossed what is now West Virginia are links along these major Indian thoroughfares.

There was a long-distance trade network in place throughout North America for thousands of years. Marine shell and native copper were traded between the Great Lakes region and the Gulf Coast as early as 6000 B.C. In the Ohio Valley, copper ornaments and marine shell beads have been found at Adena mounds dating from 400 to 200 B.C. Many of the routes used by these early groups were still in use when the first European settlers arrived, and frequently these same routes became major highways. Some are still in use today.

In the 1920s, William E. Myer, working for the Bureau of American Ethnology, began a study of colonial period Indian trails in the Southeast. Myer died before his work was published, but his efforts produced a map illustrating regional interaction pathways, several of which span West Virginia. Most of the regional trails also have local names.

The Great Indian Warpath was one of the most important north-south trails in eastern North America. The route originated in the Southeast, in Creek territory, and extended north through eastern Tennessee, where it split into the Ohio Branch and the Chesapeake Branch. The Ohio Branch continued through southwestern Virginia, to the New River, then along the Kanawha River to the Ohio River, where it met other important trails and continued north to Lake Erie. The portion of the trail that followed the Kanawha River is also called the Kanawha or Buffalo Trail. The Midland Trail, U.S. 60, part of which was also the Kanawha Trail, follows the course of another old Indian trail from the Kanawha Valley to Virginia.

The Chesapeake Branch of the Great Indian Warpath proceeded north through the Valley of Virginia. This route, also called the Warrior Path, passed through present West Virginia for only a short dis-

tance in the Eastern Panhandle, where it paralleled modern Interstate 81 and U.S. 11.

There were numerous other Indian trails throughout Western Virginia. Many followed the river valleys, including the Paint Creek Trail, the Big Sandy Trail, the Guyandotte Trail, the Coal River Trail, and the Little Kanawha Trail. The Scioto-Monongahela Trail connected Lower Shawnee Town, in Ohio, to the Monongahela Valley and proceeded north into Pennsylvania. U.S. 50 now parallels its approximate course. The Seneca Trail was another important north-south route that began in Seneca territory in New York and stretched south through Pennsylvania into Western Virginia, through the Tygart and Greenbrier valleys, to the New River. U.S. 219 parallels the main branch of the Seneca Trail in West Virginia.

See also Indians, Midland Trail, Seneca Trail

Darla S. Hoffman
Cultural Resource Analysts

Indian Wars

Violent native resistance to Euro-American occupation of the Ohio Valley characterized the settlement period of West Virginia history, from the 1750s to the 1790s. When European or colonial governments were directly engaged, specific conflicts acquired formal names, such as the French and Indian War (1754–63), Pontiac's Rebellion (1763), and Lord Dunmore's War (1774). But notwithstanding the large-scale engagements and formal treaties that marked the named episodes, raids and counter-raids by small groups of fighters were typical of the period, and hostilities constantly occurred outside of the boundaries implied by the European system of naming and dating. "Border warfare," the term used by Alexander Scott Withers in his classic account of the period, is a more apt description of what actually took place.

The border in question was the territory drained by the Ohio River from its forks (modern Pittsburgh) to its falls (modern Louisville.) Contested between Britain and France until the French withdrew from North America in 1763, the Ohio then became both a boundary between white and Indian territory as well as the principal route of Euro-American advance and also of peaceful contacts among the two peoples. Ambushes and pursuits along the banks of the river were frequently reported, even after whites began to move north across the old border into the Indians' Ohio lands in the late 1780s. More than a thousand people on both sides were killed along the river during the decade that followed the American Revolution.

Indian raids usually struck at the western edge of white settlement, which meant that the fighting shifted from east to west: from the Greenbrier, upper New River, and upper Potomac valleys during the 1750s into the 1770s, to the Monongahela country (which then included the present Northern Panhandle) during the 1770s and 1780s, to the Kanawha and middle Ohio valleys, including Kentucky, during the 1780s and 1790s. But no part of the frontier was entirely safe until Indians began withdrawing from their Ohio homelands after the Treaty of Greenville in 1795.

Cultural contact and exchange were as common as conflict. This included genetic exchanges, trade in firearms and alcohol, armed encounters while hunting, and numerous other occasions where intercultural friction might lead to bloodshed.

Pitched battles such as occurred at the Monongahela (1755), Point Pleasant (1774), and Fort Henry (Wheeling; 1777, 1782) were the exceptions rather than the rule in border warfare. Generally the conflict exhibited the classic forms of guerrilla war: raids, ambushes, sneak attacks, massacres, and atrocities on both sides.

Euro-American authorities frequently engaged native leaders in negotiations, seeking to head off problems short of warfare (as well as to advance white interests regarding trade and land). However, leaders on both sides admitted difficulty in restraining their "foolish young men," as the Indians usually put it. Another defensive strategy was the building of frontier forts, which were of two types: garrisons established at key points near the western edge of settlement, such as Fort Pitt (at present Pittsburgh, established in 1758), Fort Fincastle (later Fort Henry, Wheeling; 1774), Fort Randolph (Point Pleasant; 1776), Fort Harmar (Marietta, Ohio; 1784), and Fort Lee (Charleston; 1788); and neighborhood forts in which settlers could seek shelter in times of Indian alarm. "Forting" became a formative frontier experience for generations of settlers.

When whites went on the offensive it was usually in direct immediate response to an Indian raid that had resulted in captives, or it was a larger military expedition that sought to find and destroy the Indian villages in Ohio from which the native raiders came. As often as not, these large-scale expeditions were unsuccessful, as in Braddock's Campaign and the Sandy Creek Expedition of the 1750s or the disastrous forays into the Ohio country led by Col. William Crawford (1782) and Gen. Arthur St. Clair (1791). Andrew Lewis's campaign of 1774 culminating in the Battle of Point Pleasant and Gen. Anthony Wayne's invasion of Ohio that led to victory at Fallen Timbers (1794) were successful examples of this "search and destroy" strategy.

Both sides furnished examples of warrior-heroes. Among the Indians were the Seneca Cornplanter (1737?–1835) and the Shawnee Cornstalk (d. 1777), both of whom were celebrated warriors who later became political leaders. White Indian fighters associated with West Virginia include Daniel Boone (1734–1820), Samuel Brady (1758–1796), Jesse Hughes (1750–1829), and especially Lewis Wetzel (1763–1808), "the Boone of northwestern Virginia." According to his modern biographer, Daniel Boone killed only three Indians during an entire lifetime on the frontier, thanks to his Quaker values and good-natured respect for the natives. Wetzel, on the other hand, was a classic frontier Indian hater, who is known to have hunted Indians for sport as well as defense.

The accounts of these and other heroes that Joseph Doddridge, Withers, and others made available to 19th-century readers were full of stalwart action and thrilling escapades, combined with frightening tales of Indian savagery and cruelty. However, an examination of treaty documents and reminiscences such as those collected by Lyman Draper shows that frequently white captives came to prefer life among the natives. This was especially true of younger men and older women, who seem to have valued the relative equality of Indian life over the patriarchal order of Euro-American culture. Sometimes such people were forcibly repatriated as a result of treaties; more often their experience of cultural conflict played out in private lives. Draper collected the story of William Renick, who spent a lifetime tracking down a younger brother taken captive by Shawnees in 1761, only to have the younger man reject the comforts of a prosperous Greenbrier Valley home when at last Renick located him. Instead, after a short stay with his brother, the former captive slipped away to his Indian home in Ohio one night, leaving his European clothing neatly folded on a chair. The descendants of Mary Draper Ingles, whose captivity and perilous escape across southern West Virginia in 1755 was a prelude to the Sandy Creek Expedition, reported that in her old age she sat in melancholy silence next to the fireplace, keeping to herself whatever memories lingered of her personal experience of border war.

John Alexander Williams
Appalachian State University
George Carroll, "Lewis Wetzel: Warfare Tactics on the Frontier," *West Virginia History*, 1991; Joseph Doddridge, *Notes on the Settlement and the Indian Wars*, 1912; Gregory Evans Dowd, *A Spirited Resistance: The North American Indian Struggle for Unity, 1745–1815*, 1992.

Indians

The first people known to occupy the territory of present West Virginia were the Paleo-Indians, who were here by 10,500 B.C. After that, the region was continuously occupied by native people until the 17th century. At that time, just before the encroachment of Americans of European descent, the native population disappeared from the area now comprising West Virginia. The first white visitors found the region empty of settled population. The reasons are unclear, but probably included tribal conflict and the European diseases traveling ahead of white settlers.

By the time the first settlers arrived, the native villages on the Ohio, Kanawha, and Monongahela rivers were abandoned. Archeologists have not been able to relate these villages to tribes known from the historic period. (The historic period is the period for which written records are available, beginning with the appearance of white explorers.) The historic tribes most closely associated with Western Virginia are the Shawnee, Delaware, and Cherokee, as well as Iroquoian-speaking groups including the Seneca, Tuscarawas, Susquehannock, and Mingo. Non-resident Indians were present on a frequent but intermittent basis during the early historic period, using the region for hunting and travel and fiercely resisting its settlement by whites. At various times this region was within the spheres of influence of the powerful Iroquois Confederation to the north, the Shawnees to the west, and the Cherokees to the south. Their impact on our history was profound.

With no resident native population at the time of white settlement, West Virginia now has no federally recognized American Indian tribes or tribal lands. Indians present here today originated elsewhere or descend from people who did, as do all other West Virginians. As a consequence, the state's small Indian population is richly diverse, from many tribal backgrounds. The 1990 census listed 2,458 Indians (officially "American Indians and Alaska Natives") living in West Virginia, while the 2000 census listed 3,606. For the first time in 2000 the Census Bureau also allowed for the reporting of mixed ancestry, resulting in an additional 7,038 people of American Indian ancestry in combination with other races. The total figure of Indians plus this mixed category was 10,644, or 0.6 percent of the state's population, in 2000.

Many West Virginians claiming partial Native American or Indian ancestry claim it through the Cherokee, often a maternal ancestor. There are important reasons for this. Identification with the Cherokee over other Indian tribes is in many cases probably due to the greater familiarity with the Cherokee. They were one of the largest and most powerful tribes in the Southeast and a factor in Western Virginia throughout the frontier era. As for gender, it was culturally easier for Indian women to marry white men than for Indian men to marry white women. Further, most tribes in Appalachia were matrilineal, with descent and inheritance traced through the mother rather than the father.

There are also several tri-racial groups in West Virginia, apparently combining Caucasian, African-American, and Indian ancestry. These groups include the so-called Guineas (sometimes considered to be an offensive term), the Melungeons, and descendants of the Buffalo Ridge Cherokee. The Allegheny Indian Council and Cultural Center, located in Phillipi, was founded about 1979. This group includes members sometimes referred to as Guineas, although some members prefer to assert an Indian identity. The organization has been successful in receiving education grants through the Indian Manpower Program operated by the Three Rivers Indian Center in Pittsburgh.

While most common in the mountains of Virginia and Tennessee, Melungeons were reported living in the upper reaches of Bluestone Reservoir before the land was purchased by the federal government. Surnames often held by Melungeons are common throughout southern West Virginia. The United Cherokee Indian Tribe of West Virginia is a tri-racial group that has members of Cherokee and Eastern Siouan descent. It is a branch of the Buffalo Ridge Cherokee, a tri-racial band in Amherst County, Virginia, whose members can trace their Eastern Siouan ancestry back to the late 1600s.

Many of the Native Americans now living in West Virginia are from tribes outside Appalachia, and have come here for the same myriad of reasons that people of other ethnic groups have. Indian mobility increased in the mid-20th century. The Bureau of Indian Affairs began its relocation program in 1954, and more Indians began moving off reservations to other areas. While large concentrations of American Indians remain on the major reservations, especially in the West, others live throughout the country and relocate for employment, retirement, and other reasons. In West Virginia the number of Indians increased dramatically in the last half-century, from 160 in 1950 to the 3,606 present here in 2000, according to the U.S. Census.

West Virginia Indians are organized into several groups. The largest, the Appalachian American Indians of West Virginia, has approximately 2,500 members, representing 43 different tribes or blood lines. These include tribes as diverse as the Lakota, Blackfoot, Apache, Navaho, Choctaw, Cree, and Aztec. The group is also known as the Appalachian Nation of Indians. It holds regional meetings across the state and promotes public awareness, education and outreach, social activities, and festivals.

Other native organizations include the West Virginia Native American Coalition; the People of the Earth Organization, of South Charleston; the Native American Indian Federation, of Huntington; the Native American History Council; and the Organization for Native American Interests, at West Virginia University.

West Virginians participate in cultural practices now common to Indians throughout the country. In the 20th century the term powwow became commonly used to designate Native American music and dance events. A powwow circuit was organized and today includes powwows sponsored by Indian organizations in West Virginia. These powwows are modeled after Plains Indian celebrations and include dancing, singing, native crafts, and foods such as fry bread, buffalo, venison, and other wild game. Traditional dances such as the Grass Dance, Hoop Dance, and Eagle Dance are performed, depending on the skills and status of the principal dancers. Indians participate as well in the annual Vandalia Gathering at the state capitol complex and at other events.

Robert F. Maslowski
Milton

The Influenza Epidemic of 1918

The Spanish Influenza epidemic of 1918, one of the world's deadliest and swiftest pandemics, swept over West Virginia during October of that year.

In 1918, the United States was involved in World War I, and thousands of young men had been inducted into the military. The first reported cases of Spanish Influenza did not occur in Spain but rather are thought to have occurred amongst soldiers at Fort Riley, Kansas, in March 1918. Troops being sent to Europe carried the disease with them and soldiers and civilians alike quickly succumbed. By summer of that year the epidemic had spread worldwide and thousands were dying from it.

The disease moved rapidly. Victims of the virulent virus would seem healthy one minute and then within a matter of hours be so debilitated as to be unable to walk. Those afflicted experienced severe weakness, generalized body aches, sore throats, and high fevers, often accompanied by delirium. Pneumonia was a common and deadly complication, as there were no antibiotics to fight viral or bacterial infections. One peculiar and frightening aspect of the epidemic was that those killed were mostly young healthy persons rather than the debilitated and elderly as with other diseases.

On October 5, 1918, the West Virginia superintendent of health sent a letter to county health officers ordering that all cases of the disease be reported, all affected persons be quarantined, and all public places be closed. Many people wore facemasks when they went out in public and while caring for the sick.

Despite these measures, 71,079 West Virginians were reported as having contracted influenza between October 15 and November 15, and 2,818 were reported as having died. The majority of deaths were aged five to 39. In that year, 25 percent of all reported deaths in West Virginia were due to influenza and its complications. It should be noted that the exact number of the state's influenza victims is unknown. Physicians and nurses were overwhelmed and accurate records were not kept. Many health care providers were not able to file reports and others inaccurately estimated the numbers of cases in their area.

During the height of the epidemic in West Virginia, entire communities were without medical aid. There were severe shortages of doctors, nurses, medical supplies, and caskets. Often doctors and nurses succumbed to the disease. Most victims were cared for at home as there were few hospitals.

The epidemic left West Virginia and most of the United States as quickly and mysteriously as it arrived. It was reported as having subsided in the state by the end of October 1918, having left a deadly path of destruction.

Michael M. Meador
Abingdon, Virginia

Mary Draper Ingles

To escape her Shawnee Indian captors, Mary Draper Ingles of southwestern Virginia traversed 800 miles of wilderness, including West Virginia's rugged New River Gorge. Mary was born in Philadelphia in 1731 to Scotch-Irish immigrants. Until she was 13, her family homesteaded in Lancaster, Pennsylvania. In 1744, the Drapers migrated southwest to found Draper's Meadow (now Blacksburg, Virginia). In 1750, Mary Draper married her neighbor, William Ingles.

Frontier war erupted between the French and British in 1755. A war party of French-allied Shawnee attacked Draper's Meadow and captured Mary Ingles, her two sons, and her sister-in-law. The Shawnee took the captives to a village along the Scioto River, where it joins with the Ohio. Ingles emerged as the captives' courageous leader and earned the Shawnees' respect.

Indian families adopted Mary Ingles's children and sister-in-law. Mary was put to work sewing shirts for two French traders living with the Shawnee. When the traders took Ingles down the Ohio River to a salt-making camp in Kentucky, she escaped with another captive. Ingles traveled up the Ohio and Kanawha rivers and on through the New River Gorge, scaling rock cliffs, eating tree bark, and sleeping in hollow logs. She suffered starvation, frostbite, and delirium. Once home, she continued living on the New River and had several more children. Son Thomas Ingles wrote of his mother's daring escape and journey home several years after her death. Since then, her story has been the topic of novels, plays, and movies, including the popular *Follow the River* by James Alexander Thom.

See also French and Indian War

Mary Rodd Furbee
Morgantown

Insects

Insects are small, six-legged animals with no internal skeletons. Of the approximately 1.5 million named species of animals, about 1 million are insects. In North America alone, there are about 100,000 species of insects. Although there are no official counts of West Virginia insect species, estimates place the number at 20,000 or higher.

One reason for the success of insects is that they can live in a wide range of habitats. West Virginia's mountain topography creates a diversity of habitat types, which has resulted in a wide variety of flora and fauna. This can be seen in a group of beetles known as the snail-hunting ground beetles. The mountainous region of the eastern United States is the world center of diversity for this insect, with much of the diversity localized in the mountains of West Virginia.

Many plants and animals exist in West Virginia at the northern or southern limits of their range. Much of this is due to the fact that, as a result of ancient glacial events, high-altitude regions of the southern Appalachian Mountains in West Virginia resemble northern boreal forests. Insects that live in these areas are normally found only in much more northern latitudes. The Atlantis fritillary and pink-edged sulphur butterflies can be found associated with blueberry plants (their host) in parts of the state such as Dolly Sods. These two butterfly species are much more common in northern parts of the continent. A number of other relict insect species have been described in West Virginia.

Although harmful insects make up less than 1 percent of the classified species, insects widely are recognized for the negative roles they play in the environment. Some insects carry diseases that may affect humans, other animals, and plants. Mosquitoes and some other insects inflict irritating bites, even when no disease is transmitted. Still others are quick to sting. Many insects are agricultural pests, such as the eastern tent caterpillar. This caterpillar is just one of several native moth species that can be especially destructive to fruit trees. Another agricultural pest, the periodical cicada or 17-year locust, emerges every 17 years to reproduce, causing potentially extensive damage to valuable timber trees.

The honeybee is the state insect.

Many of the most harmful agricultural pests are insects that have been introduced to the state. Among these is the gypsy moth, which was intentionally introduced to the U.S. by a private citizen in Massachusetts in 1869 for experiments in silk production. The gypsy moth has made its way into West Virginia. Both state and federal programs now work to slow the spread and minimize the effects of this pest, which can destroy trees, especially valuable hardwoods.

Despite the harmful roles some species can play in human endeavors, insects are major and important parts of the ecosystem in West Virginia, as they are everywhere. Insects are a necessary component of the food chains of a number of bird, fish, and other animal species. Fishermen exploit this, their "flies" mimicking different life stages of various insect species.

Many of the state's agricultural crops depend on insects, such as the honeybee, for pollination. The honeybees in turn provide a valuable product in their honey, now averaging about 1.2 million pounds a year. In 2002, the legislature made the honeybee the official state insect of West Virginia.

Amy Donaldson Arnold
Ivydale

Thomas J. Allen, *The Butterflies of West Virginia and their Caterpillars*, 1997; George Constantz, *Hollows, Peepers, and Highlanders*, 1994; Steven L. Stephenson, *Upland Forests of West Virginia*, 1993.

Instant Libraries

During the last quarter of the 20th century, the West Virginia countryside was dotted with small public libraries of an unusual, playful shape. The building program began in 1973, when the West Virginia Library Commission expanded its ambitious library construction project, which was launched in 1965, by adding the "instant" library program. The program placed small library buildings in communities that had never had library service and in communities that received mobile library services only once every

three or four weeks. Some city libraries used the instant libraries as a dynamic and inexpensive method of expanding branch services.

Under the guidance of Frederic J. Glazer, secretary of the West Virginia Library Commission from 1972 to 1996, an eight-sided building was designed. The distinctive shape gave instant identification to the library, provided 1,200 square feet of usable space, and suggested the fun of a carousel.

Supported with state and federal construction funds, the Library Commission encouraged communities to organize library boards, obtain site approval, and agree to provide annual funding for library operations. The Library Commission matched local initiatives by providing the building, furnishings, library materials, professional assistance, and state funds to help support operations.

In 1973, the Buffalo Creek Memorial Library in Logan County received the first instant library and, thanks to the donation of a second unit by the AFL-CIO, demonstrated how two modular units could be linked. By 1976, 26 instant libraries were serving the residents of West Virginia, not including the demonstration model that was installed in the Cultural Center at the Library Commission offices. A survey conducted in 1996 listed 39 instant libraries in West Virginia. There were also 34 "outpost" libraries, smaller and less architecturally exciting modular facilities.

See also Libraries

Karen Goff
West Virginia Library Commission

Integration

West Virginia's history of race relations is an unusual one. Born in the Civil War, the state had abolished slavery in its 1863 constitution as a condition of admission into the Union. Unlike states farther south, in West Virginia African-Americans never lost the right to vote during the repressive "Jim Crow" days following Reconstruction, and the state was largely spared the wave of lynchings that swept much of the country in the 19th and early 20th centuries. In some places, especially the southern West Virginia coalfields, blacks attained political clout by the end of the 19th century, electing members of the legislature and holding many local offices. Nonetheless, in public education and in key areas of public accommodation West Virginians were segregated by race during most of the state's history.

This was the situation on May 17, 1954, when the Supreme Court of the United States ruled in *Brown v. Board of Education* that segregated schools were unconstitutional. This landmark ruling overturned an earlier case, *Plessy v. Ferguson* (1896), in which the court had declared that "separate but equal" facilities did not violate the 14th Amendment.

Seventeen states, including West Virginia, had dual schools systems in 1954. Following the Brown ruling, Governor Marland pledged to obey the edict and foresaw no serious difficulty in integrating West Virginia schools. State Superintendent of Schools W. W. Trent saw the adjustment as largely administrative. State Negro Schools Supervisor J. W. Robinson expressed agreement with the ruling, believing that the decision would increase opportunities for black teachers. At the time of the decision there were 420,000 white and 26,000 African-American students attending school in West Virginia.

Four other states and the District of Columbia also announced that they would promptly comply with the court ruling. The *Brown v. Board* ruling was not accompanied by a plan or recommendation for implementation. This led to many states interpreting the decision so as to delay integration. Some, including Georgia and South Carolina, vigorously resisted.

While the response to *Brown v. Board* was generally positive in West Virginia, there were concerns and delays in some areas. Those counties closer to the Virginia border, including the Eastern Panhandle and the southern region of the state, were slower in accepting the ruling.

For example, Greenbrier County took an approach that delayed integration. On September 16, 1954, the *Greenbrier Independent* newspaper announced at the beginning of the school year that segregation was to continue. The Greenbrier board of education had decided to return to segregated schools after a week's trial at integration. Three hundred students from White Sulphur Springs High School had protested integration by refusing to attend school. The board ordered black students to return to the schools they had attended during the 1953–54 school year.

In Boone County, 11 students complained about the integration of Scott High School in the county seat of Madison. Some parents in Barbour County protested and called for a gradual approach. Taylor County suggested a "right of choice" plan, while Mercer, Berkeley, and Mineral wanted to wait until the Supreme Court devised a plan for implementation. A small protest took place in Marion County when mothers picketed the Annabelle School near Fairmont. The protest was curtailed when a local judge threatened to issue an injunction. Monongalia County, like most counties in West Virginia, responded to the decision favorably. The school board stated on July 7, 1954, that "all Negro pupils will be admitted and integrated this school year in the school located within their respective residential areas."

On October 15, 1954, the West Virginia Association of Teachers (white) and the West Virginia State Teachers Association (black) merged to form the West Virginia Education Association. West Virginia Boys State also changed its policy to include all representatives from the 55 counties regardless of race, creed, or color.

By the end of the 1956–57 school year, 20 of 55 counties in West Virginia were considered fully desegregated and 21 partially, with the Eastern Panhandle counties of Berkeley, Hampshire, and Jefferson still segregated. Eleven counties reported having no black students. At the beginning of that school year an anti-integration demonstration was held in Mercer County, but the board refused to yield and the demonstrations eventually ceased. The following year the attempted integration of Little Rock High School in Arkansas captured the national headlines. McDowell County experienced a protest at Welch High School with some protesters carrying "We Support Little Rock" signs. Another demonstration took place in Mercer County, but by mid-October schools in both Mercer and McDowell were operating without incident.

The 1958–59 school year was interrupted by a school bombing at Osage, near Morgantown. Bomb threats took place in Oak Hill, Point Pleasant, Charleston, and Beckley. The legislature acted quickly, making bomb threats a felony and requiring schools to make up lost days due to bomb threats.

As the public schools were integrated, West Virginia colleges moved in the same direction. State Attorney General John G. Fox ruled that the federal mandate should be applied to higher education. Soon after his ruling, the state Board of Education, which also governed higher education at the time, adopted a policy of non-segregation, allowing the admission of any qualified student to any state college or university. By the 1955–56 school year, with the exception of Glenville State, all institutions of higher learning in West Virginia had enrolled African-American students. Ironically, some of the greatest changes came at the traditionally black institutions, West Virginia State College and Bluefield State. Both grew with the admission of white students and eventually had white majorities. An unfortunate consequence of the *Brown* decision was the closing of Storer College in Harpers Ferry, a private institution and the state's oldest black college, due to budget concerns and the integration of other colleges.

The *Brown* decision not only influenced public schools and higher education, but also housing, employment, voting, and public accommodations. African Americans were concerned about discrimination in hiring practices, hous-

ing, and public accommodations. Groups such as the Charleston United Church Women and later the West Virginia Human Rights Commission fought to open doors previously closed. One of the first demonstrations against segregated seating practices took place in March 1960 when a group of Bluefield State College students picketed two movie theaters in Bluefield. They also attacked segregated lunch counters at Kresge and Woolworth stores with limited success.

A significant force in the move toward equality of access and opportunity was the creation of the West Virginia Human Rights Commission in 1961. The Commission established 35 local community relations commissions to share information and discuss issues related to equality and racism. At the time of its creation many hospitals, restaurants, hotels, and pools refused to admit African-Americans. By 1966, the commission reported that such "blatant racial discrimination" was over. Unlike other Southern states, West Virginia had moved to integrate school and public facilities prior to the signing of the 1964 Civil Rights Act. The schools in West Virginia were considered fully desegregated by 1964.

The struggle for equality of opportunity in West Virginia was not perfect and not without negative consequences. The closing of local African-American schools resulted in a loss of community identity in many black communities. Some black teachers lost their jobs and others were placed in predominantly white schools.

See also African-American Education, African-American Heritage

Sam Stack
West Virginia University

Paul Johnson, "Integration in West Virginia Since 1954," M.A. thesis, West Virginia University, 1959; Douglas Smith, "In Quest of Equality: The West Virginia Experience," *West Virginia History*, April 1978.

Interstate Highway System

West Virginia's interstate highway system originally consisted of six separate federal expressways totaling 515 miles and constructed over 31 years. Begun in 1957, the network was completed in 1988 at a cost of nearly $2.8 billion. It was expanded in 1991 to include Interstate 68 from a junction with Interstate 79 near Morgantown eastward through Preston County, a total of 32.2 miles to the Maryland border, and from there on to I-70 at Hancock. This seventh interstate was formerly designated Corridor E (U.S. 48), which had been completed in 1976 as part of the Appalachian Development Highway system.

The longest interstate highway in West Virginia is I-77, which enters the state from Virginia via a tunnel under East River Mountain near Bluefield and travels north 187.21 miles to exit via a bridge

Interstate 79 in central West Virginia.

River Gorge Bridge on U.S. 19 near Fayetteville. The Glade Creek bridge, east of Beckley, towers approximately 700 feet above a gorge even more rugged and inaccessible than that of New River, a 2,179-foot span which cost nearly $29 million to build. With piers and abutments founded on 36-inch diameter caissons into solid, unweathered rock, the bridge required 1,347,417 pounds of structural steel. Continued traffic growth in the area between Charleston and Huntington brought about a number of six-lane widening projects on the other end of I-64. By 2004, more than seven miles between Nitro and Dunbar had been upgraded, and plans were under way for additional mileage including a paired bridge from Dunbar to South Charleston.

Interstate 79 begins at its junction with I-77 two miles north of Charleston and continues northward to the Pennsylvania border north of Morgantown. The 160.52-mile expressway through Kanawha, Clay, Braxton, Gilmer, Lewis, Harrison, Marion, and Monongalia counties cost $447.9 million to build and was a late addition to the interstate system. In October 1961, Federal Highway Administrator Rex Whitten signed a memo authorizing the extension of I-79 into West Virginia from what had previously been exclusively a Pennsylvania highway. The entire 310-mile highway now stretches from Charleston to Erie, Pennsylvania, and connects with I-68 just south of Morgantown. Traffic volumes generated by Clarksburg-area development such as the FBI center resulted in a number of projects to widen I-79 to six or eight lanes. More than four miles of this upgrading has been completed, with additional work continuing in 2004 to widen two bridges on the route near Bridgeport to eight lanes.

One of the state's most heavily traveled interstates is the 26-mile segment of I-81 that crosses the Eastern Panhandle from Virginia to Maryland. It is a small portion of a 900-mile expressway from Knoxville to the Canadian border north of Watertown, New York. Crossing the moderate terrain of Berkeley County, the West Virginia section of I-81 cost less than $1 million per mile to build, the cheapest of the state's interstates. To meet the demands of traffic that has tripled since the road was built, West Virginia plans to widen all of I-81 to six lanes. By 2004, six projects on the route were complete, with others still under way to widen bridges over the route in anticipation of additional widening.

In the Northern Panhandle 14.45 miles of Interstate 70 cross through Ohio County from Ohio to Pennsylvania. It includes a tunnel just east of the Ohio River in downtown Wheeling and is part of a 2,000-mile national superhighway that begins in Baltimore and ends near Salina, Utah. Interstate 470 is a 3.95-mile bypass

across the Ohio River north of Parkersburg. It was also the most expensive to build, costing more than $1 billion, and took the longest time to complete. Interstate 77 includes the 88-mile West Virginia Turnpike, built prior to passage of the federal Interstate Highway Act of 1956. The turnpike was constructed in 1952–54 at a cost of $133 million and was a mostly two-lane limited-access highway from Princeton to Charleston for 20 years before a special act of Congress authorized the state Department of Highways to upgrade it as a portion of I-77 at a cost of $618.6 million. The upgrading of the turnpike was completed in 1987.

The second-longest interstate is I-64, which enters the state at the Kentucky border east of Huntington, passing through Wayne, Cabell, Putnam, and Kanawha

counties, where it joins I-77 south to a point near Beckley and then resumes its separate easterly route through Raleigh, Summers, and Greenbrier counties to the Virginia border near White Sulphur Springs. Interstate 64 travels 123 miles as a separate highway, and shares 50 miles with I-77. Even though the first interstate construction contract in the state was awarded on I-64 in 1957 for a $131,900 bridge across a secondary road in Cabell County near the Putnam County border at Culloden, I-64 was the last interstate completed. The final 35.82 miles of I-64, between Sam Black Church in Greenbrier County and the West Virginia Turnpike (I-77), were opened to traffic on July 15, 1988.

This final segment of I-64 contains a bridge that rivals the state's famed New of downtown Wheeling that begins in nearby Ohio and terminates with I-70 east of Wheeling.

Interstate exits or interchanges are numbered in miles from the point at which the route enters the state, west to east on even-numbered interstates and south to north on those with odd numbers. Thus, Exit 58B for the Civic Center in Charleston is approximately 58 miles from the Kentucky border west of Huntington, while I-77 Exit 173 for Camden Avenue in Parkersburg is approximately 173 miles from the Virginia border near Bluefield.

The state's share of the cost of the interstate system was ten percent, and much of the money came from a trio of constitutional amendments ratified by voters that authorized the issuance of general obligation bonds to finance highway construction. The Better Roads Amendment of 1964, which was voted on in the 1964 general election, was approved by a vote of 455,294 to 116,438 and provided $200 million for the "building and construction of state roads and highways." Four years later, voters ratified the Roads Development Amendment of 1968 by a vote of 366,958 to 159,971, providing another $350 million. In a special election in November 1973, voters again approved a Better Highways Amendment for $500 million in highway funding, by a vote of 172,187 to 61,308.

As the 21st century began, the improvement and maintenance of the 549-mile interstate system represented an ongoing commitment by state highway officials. By 2004 road-widening projects, usually from four lanes to six, were underway or completed on I-64 between Charleston and Huntington, on I-79 around Clarksburg, and I-81 in the Eastern Panhandle. Other projects will be undertaken as traffic demands and funds allow.

See also Highway Development, West Virginia Turnpike

Tom D. Miller
Huntington

Interwoven Mills

Interwoven Mills, a maker of men's hosiery, was Martinsburg's largest employer for several decades. It had its start in 1890–91, when entrepreneurs from Philadelphia and New Brunswick, New Jersey, invested the money to build the country's first electric-powered mill. The company went through a number of name changes, beginning as Middlesex Knitting Company, then becoming Kilbourn Knitting Mill and later Interwoven Hosiery, among other names. Local people most often referred to it as the Kilbourn Mill.

By the 19th century's end, Interwoven had outgrown its original building and moved to a permanent site on the Baltimore & Ohio Railroad. By the end of 1906, the company had 2,000 domestic accounts which included some of the country's largest retail businesses, and was shipping goods overseas; salesmen also sold Interwoven products door-to-door. By 1921, Interwoven had opened branch plants in Hagerstown, Maryland; Chambersburg, Pennsylvania; and Berkeley Springs.

Interwoven prospered until the 1929 stock market crash and ensuing Depression. Like many factories around the country, Interwoven was confronted by organized labor during the 1930s and 1940s. Interwoven workers took part in the Textile Workers of America's nationwide strike in 1934. Approximately 80 percent of the employees walked out, forcing the company to operate with a skeleton crew. Despite the fact that the Interwoven strikers remained out beyond the end of the general strike, they did not settle any of their grievances. These unresolved issues contributed to a 1941 strike.

During World War II, Interwoven manufactured socks for army and navy personnel. Beginning in the 1950s, the company suffered from international and local competition. Employment dropped from more than 3,000 in the early 1950s to 900 in 1960. Ownership changed in 1962. Interwoven decided to move most of its operation to North Carolina, and Kayser-Roth, Inc., purchased the Martinsburg operation. Kayser-Roth closed the Martinsburg complex in February 1976, bringing an important chapter in the city's industrial history to an end.

See also Martinsburg, Textile Industry

Jerra Jenrette
Edinboro University

Invertebrates

Invertebrates, as animals without backbones are called, include the major part of the animal kingdom, an estimated two million kinds of multicellular organisms. Invertebrates include a spectrum of forms varying from simple sponges to the fascinating, complicated, and versatile insects and spiders. By a very large margin they account for most species of animals in West Virginia and most individual animals as well.

Many invertebrates are found in saltwater environments. Others inhabit freshwater, including the freshwater sponges of West Virginia. A freshwater jellyfish can be found in the Ohio River and in ponds, reservoirs, and other still waters. The umbrella shaped sexual forms, nearly an inch long, are seen sporadically in great numbers on sunny late summer days. Tiny fat, hydra-like polyps, the asexual forms, are found on submerged objects year-round.

Among the flatworms, our common aquatic planarian is flattened and spindle shaped, 5–20 mm long, a carnivore and scavenger. A bit of raw liver on a string may attract planaria in a spring or stream.

Roundworms are parasites or predators of other organisms. A few grams of rich soil or pond mud may contain tens of thousands of individuals and dozens of species of these microscopic, spindle-shaped animals. Nematode diseases were once common in humans but are rare now in West Virginia. Heartworm in dogs, a debilitating and deadly disease of the heart and lungs, is caused by a kind of nematode.

A nematode relative, the horsehair worm (10–70 cm) develops within a grasshopper or spider, gradually devouring the internal organs while the host still lives. Popular (and untrue) regional folklore holds that an actual horsehair placed in water will transform into a horsehair worm. In fact, the parasite remains with the host until they encounter water, which the worm enters to find a mate, leaving the depleted host to die.

Segmented worms, which are known as annelids, include the earthworms that are vital to soil formation, organic matter transformation, nutrient cycling, and as fish bait. Earthworms travel in mucus they secrete which protects their flexible skin and lubricates their passage through soil. Most common species have been introduced from the old world. While native annelids survive, especially in freshwater, they are mostly uncommon or overlooked and their identification is difficult.

Leeches are reputed as thirsty bloodsuckers, but relatively few of the 40 to 50 species in North America will feed upon mammals and birds. All are aquatic parasites or predators of reptiles, amphibians, and fishes. A few kinds will not refuse human blood if offered during a swim in a farm pond.

Two classes of mollusks occur in West Virginia, snails and clams. Snails glide by muscular action of their foot over self-secreted mucus paths. Freshwater and most terrestrial snails carry a spiraled calcareous shell, as their dwelling and refuge. The head at the front of the foot has retractable, eye-bearing tentacles above the mouth. Aquatic snails feed largely on surface films of algae, diatoms, and debris. Some are predators of other mollusks and corals. Land snails and their shell-free cousins, the slugs, subsist on the tender parts of plants. The flat-spired three-toothed snail, classified as a threatened species, inhabits Coopers Rock State Forest, where its sole small territory is crossed by a footpath.

Mussels, which are freshwater clams, have paired calcareous shells hinged together by an elastic ligament. The body is a headless, eyeless, hatchet-shaped foot which plows through sediments or anchors the animal in place. The foot is enclosed by a double curtain of gills and an all enveloping mantle, a cloak-like organ that secretes and maintains the shell. Food is gathered by moving currents of water over the gills through ciliary motion, trapping and holding plankton and organic debris in mucus.

Mussels, long prized for their mother of pearl shells, have been dredged nearly to extinction from the Ohio River and its tributaries. One of West Virginia's freshwater mussels is classified as an endangered species and five as threatened species. Rules prohibit their capture and restrict the taking of other mussel species, but pollution, disturbance from river traffic, and competition from the introduced zebra mussel exert heavy pressure on the whole group.

Arthropods, a second and enormous group of segmented invertebrates, are distinguished by an external skeleton joined by flexible membranes armoring the body and its appendages. Branches of the arthropod family include insects, arachnids, and crabs. Other arthropods, the millipedes, centipedes, most crustaceans, and some primitive and immature insects retain the repeated segmental form and laddered nervous system of annelids. Arthropods are characterized by diversity and abundance. West Virginia is home to thousands of arthropod species: scores of families of insects, nine families of centipedes, 20 families of millipedes, 38 families of spiders, many crustaceans, and many rare arthropods in those and other groups.

See also Insects, Mussels

James Arnold
West Virginia Entomological Society

Irish

The Irish were present among the early settlers in Western Virginia and came in particularly large numbers after the turn of the 19th century. They helped to build the early transportation network, beginning with the National Road, which arrived in Wheeling in 1818. An old Catholic cemetery in Triadelphia, Ohio County, has several tombstones dated 1819 from these early Irish.

With the National Road completed to Wheeling, great numbers of immigrants, including the Irish, found their way west to heavily industrialized Wheeling. The Irish also helped to build the Chesapeake & Ohio Canal along the Maryland side of the Potomac River from Washington to Cumberland, Maryland, beginning in 1828. Cholera produced mass graves along the canal route. The old Catholic cemetery at Shepherdstown holds some of these unnamed workers. The canal's great Paw Paw Tunnel, in Maryland across the river from Paw Paw, West Virginia, was dug by the Irish with picks, shovels, and bare hands. The tunnel opened in 1850 and finally completed the canal.

As the canal was being built, so too were the turnpikes, with the Irish heavily represented among the laborers. In the 1820s, the James River & Kanawha Turnpike ran from Lewisburg to Charleston. The Northwestern Turnpike was constructed in the 1830s from Winchester, Virginia, to Parkersburg. And in 1841, serious work commenced on the Staunton-Parkersburg Turnpike, which linked the Valley of Virginia to the Ohio River at its completion in 1847.

Overtaking the canal and turnpikes were the railroads. The first to come into Western Virginia was the Baltimore & Ohio, begun in Baltimore in 1828 and reaching Wheeling in January 1853. This 380-mile project employed thousands of men, many of them Irish. For three years Irish laborers built the tunnel at Tunnelton, reputedly the longest in the world, while living in the B&O labor camp at Greigsville outside Fairmont. In 1857, an auxiliary branch, the Northwestern Virginia Railroad, was finished from Grafton to Parkersburg. Later railroad lines using Irish labor included the Chesapeake & Ohio in the 1870s and the Norfolk & Western in the 1880s.

The large number of Irish workers in Western Virginia can be tied to the great out-migration of the Irish famine, 1845–50, when 1.2 million people left their homeland. The Irish workers could be an unruly bunch, often finding relief from their hard labors in saloons and continuing their homeland fights in the hills of Western Virginia.

Lewis County attracted a large Irish population. In the 1840s, a land company recruited Irish settlers from the nearby turnpike and B&O crews. Many Irish moved into the Sand Fork, Loveberry, and Leading Creek districts. In 1848, a Catholic Church was established at Sand Fork, and St. Patrick's Church at Weston was built. The Lewis County Irish, as so many others, were fervent Union supporters during the Civil War, and a great portion of Company B, 15th Virginia Infantry, under Michael Egan, were Irish recruits. One of the more revered Irish figures in Lewis County was Monsignor Thomas Quirk (died 1937), who ministered to the people for 50 years, often on horseback.

The Catholic Church was closely tied to the Irish of West Virginia. The first Catholic Church in West Virginia was established in Wheeling in 1822, composed largely of German and Irish parishioners. American Catholicism had a pronounced Irish look by the 1850s, and by the 1890s the hierarchy was almost entirely Irish. Thus the first bishop of the Diocese of Wheeling in 1850 was Richard V. Whelan. In Wheeling in 1853 when nativists adhering to the Know Nothing party threatened a papal diplomat visiting Wheeling, the bishop and his guest were protected by hundreds of armed Irish. Many of the clergy in the state had roots in Ireland, often recruited from All Hallows Missionary College in Dublin, and the backbone of the orders of religious women were German and Irish.

Many local names reflect the Irish presence in West Virginia, including Irish Ridge in Marshall County and St. Colman's Catholic Church on Sullivan's Knob at Irish Mountain in Summers County. The building of the C&O Railroad brought many Irish into the latter area, giving Hinton, the Summers county seat, a strong Irish presence and a St. Patrick's Church, one of six in the state. In Kanawha County at Coalburg stands a large Celtic cross, erected in 1912 by William S. Edwards to honor the Irish workers in his mines. Other Celtic crosses in cemeteries in Greenbrier County and elsewhere attest to an Irish presence.

The American Ancient Order of Hibernians, an Irish fraternal order founded in New York City in 1863, had two divisions in Wheeling in 1875 and one in Benwood. By 1884, the AOH had groups in Rowlesburg, Clarksburg, Parkersburg, Coal Valley, and Charleston. At its height in 1894, there were 647 men in 12 Hibernian divisions in West Virginia.

By the end of the 19th century, the Irish came to occupy positions of authority in West Virginia. Thomas O'Brien, a Wheeling citizen and Irish native, was elected state treasurer in 1880. Thomas Riley, whose father was Irish-born, was elected attorney general in 1892. The industrialist Michael J. Owens, born the son of Irish immigrants in Parkersburg, invented the bottle-making machine and was a founder of Libbey-Owens-Ford. U.S. Sen. John Kenna, one of two West Virginians whose statues are in the U.S. Capitol, had an Irish immigrant father. Bernard McDonough built a business empire from a Parkersburg base and later founded one of West Virginia's largest philanthropic foundations.

See also Roman Catholics

Margaret Brennan
Wheeling Area Historical Society
James M. Callahan, *History of West Virginia*, Volume I, 1923; Tricia T. Pyne, *Faith in the Mountains: A History of the Diocese of Wheeling—Charleston, 1850–2000*, 2000.

Irish Mountain

Irish Mountain, located above the New River in Raleigh County at elevation 2,691 feet, was named for the Irish immigrants who settled, farmed, and populated it. The first arrival was Maurice Sullivan from County Kerry, who purchased 435 acres from John Gwinn in 1855. The next year, John Quinlan from County Clare also bought land from Gwinn. During the 1860s, McCarthys, Nees, Dillons,

St. Colman's Chapel on Irish Mountain.

Carsons, and Simon O'Connor settled on the mountain.

In 1876, Maurice Sullivan sold for one dollar an acre of land atop the mountain to J. J. Kane, bishop of Wheeling, for a church and cemetery. By 1878, the Irish had cleared the land and built a small log church, 18 by 30 feet, with three windows on either side and a double-door entry with a cross above. They made the family pews, altar, and other furnishings which are still there today. The church, named for St. Colman, a popular saint in western Ireland, was the first Roman Catholic church in Raleigh County. It was a mission church of St. Patrick's in Hinton, whose pastors held monthly Sunday services at St. Colman.

The 1880 census listed eight Irish families of 43 persons occupying the mountain. In 1910, there were 17 families and 82 persons listed. After that, the exodus off the mountain began, but the population in the cemetery grew. In 2002, few, if any, descendants of the settlers lived on the mountain, though some retained their ancestral lands. The cemetery and church, its original logs covered with boards and painted white, are still maintained. St. Colman Church and cemetery were placed on the National Register of Historic Places in 1984.

There is another Irish Mountain, elevation 3,320 feet, associated with the Irish Tract settlement in Greenbrier, Summers, and Fayette counties.

See also Irish, Irish Tract

Lois C. McLean
Beckley

Leona G. Brown, "Recalling an Irish Mountain Family," *Goldenseal,* Spring 1991; Lois C. McLean, "Irish Mountain," *Goldenseal,* Spring 1991; Jim Wood, *Raleigh County, West Virginia,* 1994.

The Irish Tract

Beginning in the early 1870s, following their construction jobs on the Chesapeake & Ohio Railway, seven Irish immigrants and their spouses purchased contiguous acreage, mostly mountainous, in Fayette and Greenbrier counties north of Green Sulphur Springs. This area became known as the Irish Tract. Part of the Greenbrier land became Summers County in 1871, so the tract is now divided among three counties. The purchasers were Richard Twohig, Terence Foley, Florence Donahue, Thomas Hurley, Cornelius Coughlin, Michael Goheen, and Michael Relihan. A log Catholic church was erected in 1879, and the present Sacred Heart Church of Spring Dale was built in 1899.

By 1900, there were 18 farms of the settlers and their children and later Irish arrivals on more than 3,000 acres within a common boundary. Nearby were the farms of Michael Powers and Cornelius McGillicuddy. Irish immigrants to the surrounding area prior to 1870 included Daniel Griffin, John Donahue, and James Hurley, all of them church members.

The highest elevation within the tract, at over 3,300 feet, was named Irish Mountain, not to be confused with the better-known Irish Mountain in nearby Raleigh County. Farming on the extensively cleared areas continued until the 1940s. The last cultivation within the original tract ceased in 1983. More than 200 people have resided within the tract boundaries. Only one descendant of the founders lives there today, although many people bearing the old names live in the general area. The cemetery has 175 graves.

See also Irish, Irish Mountain

Basil Hurley
Temperance, Michigan

Basil Hurley, "Tales from the Irish Tract," *Goldenseal,* Spring 1998.

Ironmaking

With an abundance of iron ore, timber for charcoal, limestone for flux, and waterpower, it is not surprising that ironmaking was one of Western Virginia's earliest industries. Ironmaking began in present Jefferson County in 1742, when the Quaker William Vestal erected Vestal's Bloomery near the Shenandoah River. Bloomeries such as his served an important role on the frontier, producing small batches of wrought iron, a commodity needed for the manufacture of nails, tools, and agricultural implements. Other bloomeries were subsequently established, including one at Bloomery, Hampshire County, in the early 1760s. Several bloomeries were likely constructed along the tributaries of the South Branch of the Potomac near Moorefield in the early 1790s.

Gradually, blast furnaces and forges appeared. Furnaces and forges had a much greater output than the bloomeries and enabled the local manufacture of skillets, pots, salt pans and kettles, and other cast-iron goods, as well as bar iron, nails, and other wrought-iron products. John Semple, a Bladensburg, Maryland, entrepreneur, constructed West Virginia's first blast furnace, the Keep Tryst Furnace, along the Potomac River in present Jefferson County in 1763. Keep Tryst initiated a new era, but the American Revolution interrupted the westward expansion of the iron industry, and several decades passed before it crossed the mountains. The completion of the short-lived Peter Tarr Furnace, about 1794 in present Hancock County, signaled the start of post-Revolution iron production in northwestern Virginia.

Another ironmaking region emerged in present north-central West Virginia, where about 1798 Samuel Hanway established the Rock Forge on Deckers Creek near Morgantown. Samuel Jackson, a Pennsylvania Quaker, established Jackson's Ironworks about 1809 at Ices Ferry on the Cheat River in Monongalia County. It grew in succeeding decades to become one of the state's leading antebellum ironworks. The local iron industry (also called Cheat Mountain iron industry) continued to mature, reaching its peak in the late 1850s. Still another ironmaking region developed in Hardy and Hampshire counties (including present Grant and Mineral counties), where the earliest furnaces were put in operation about 1800. This region's most significant and enduring ironmaking concern was the Capon Iron Works, built by James Sterrett about 1832. Located near Wardensville, this ironworks operated into the 1880s.

By 1860, 28 charcoal iron furnaces had been constructed in 11 Western Virginia counties. These counties formed a crescent from Jefferson County to Hancock County, with Monroe being the single outlying exception. By the Civil War, the majority of Western Virginia's ironmakers had ceased production. This was primarily due to the general lack of transportation improvements in Western Virginia, which prohibited iron products getting to the larger markets, and to a lesser extent to the competition of inexpensive anthracite iron from eastern Pennsylvania. Following the Civil War, newly created West Virginia's charcoal iron industry experienced a short-lived rebirth. But this technology was now virtually obsolete with the industry's adoption of coke fuel, and these furnaces ceased production by the early 1880s.

West Virginia's modern ironmaking era began in the New River Gorge at Quinnimont. There in 1874, investors hoping to create the "Pittsburgh of the South" erected a coke-fueled blast furnace along the recently completed Chesapeake & Ohio Railway. The furnace used coke made from New River coal and iron ore from Alleghany County, Virginia. Transporting iron ore a great distance was an unusual practice, and it caused the furnace to fail repeatedly, ultimately closing for good in 1884.

During this same period, the Northern Panhandle emerged as the modern center of coke-based iron and steelmaking in West Virginia. Wheeling's first ironworks, Top Mill, was established about 1834 by Pittsburgh ironmasters. By 1860, there were at least four Wheeling ironworks that produced cut nails, a very important 19th-century commodity. In the early 1870s, Wheeling nailmakers integrated their manufacturing operations, first constructing modern coke-fueled blast furnaces and then in the early 1880s added steelmaking facilities. Wheeling nailmakers survived the decline of the cut nail industry by diversifying the product line to include welded-steel pipe (a Wheeling first in 1882), sheet steel, steel slabs, and other semi-finished steel products. In 1920, the last three independent Wheeling steelmakers, the La Belle Iron Works, the Wheeling Steel & Iron Company, and the Whitaker-Glessner Company, merged to form the Wheeling Steel Corporation, which became the Wheeling-Pittsburgh Steel Corporation in 1968. The old La Belle mill continues to produce cut nails today.

The manufacture of tin plate, needed for tin cans, resulted in the formation of West Virginia's other major iron and steel producer, the Weirton Steel Corporation. In 1890, Congress enacted the McKinley Tariff to stimulate the domestic production of tin plate, and subsequently tin plate mills were established at Wheeling, Morgantown, Chester, and Clarksburg. In 1905, Earnest T. Weir purchased the Jackson Iron & Tin Company tin mill located at Clarksburg, and by 1909, had relocated his mill to Holiday Cove in Hancock County. The company thrived, resulting in the formation of the Weirton Steel Corporation in 1918. After a decade, Weirton Steel in 1929 merged with Michigan Steel of Detroit and M. A. Hanna Steel of Cleveland to form National Steel Corporation. In 1982, under an Employee Stock Ownership Plan (ESOP), the Weirton workers purchased the plant from National Steel Corporation. After a period of bankruptcy Weirton Steel ceased to be an employee-owned company in 2004, when it was sold to International Steel Group of Ohio.

Today, Wheeling-Pittsburgh Steel and Weirton Steel form the backbone of West Virginia's 21st-century iron and steel industry.

See also Ices Ferry Ironworks, Peter Tarr Furnace, Weirton Steel Buyout, Wheeling Steel

Lee R. Maddex
WVU Institute for the History of Technology

Iroquois

The League of the Iroquois was a French term for a confederacy of native peoples speaking related languages and living in contiguous territory during colonial times in what is now upstate New York. The confederates themselves called their league "the longhouse," metaphorically invoking the typical communal dwelling of their culture. Dutch and English colonists called the league "the Five Nations," for the Mohawk, Oneida, Onondaga, Cayuga, and Seneca. After 1722, this became the Six Nations as the league admitted the Tuscaroras.

Legend attributes the origin of the league to two founders, the supernatural Deganawidah and the mortal Hiawatha. Apparently the confederacy was in existence a generation or two before Iroquoian-speakers first encountered European explorers in 1534. After an initial period of disadvantage when European diseases devastated Iroquois longhouses and the league was cut off by rivals from the earliest beachheads of European trade, the geographical location of the league proved to be advantageous. Through trade and diplomacy, the Iroquois were able to play off Europeans in Canada—successively the French and the British—against those in the Middle Atlantic regions—successively the Dutch, English, and Americans. As a result, the confederacy retained its independence and influence from the mid-17th to the late 18th centuries.

The Iroquois also claimed dominion over other native societies, first by conquest during the Indian wars of the mid-17th century and later by establishing a sort of protectorate over non-Iroquoian peoples such as the Lenape (Delaware). Iroquois conquest is thought to be one explanation—along with European diseases—for the depopulation of native peoples in what is now West Virginia during the 17th century. It was also the basis of the confederacy's territorial claim to the upper Ohio Valley, a claim that colonial negotiators found convenient to accept, since alliance with the Iroquois allowed the British to assert ownership of interior territories that had been explored mainly by their rival claimants, the French. The French accepted this claim in the Treaty of Utrecht in 1713 but continued to compete for trade and influence in Iroquoia until they finally gave up all their North American territories at the end of the French and Indian War (1763).

Except for brief sojourns by Tuscaroras en route to their new home in New York, Iroquois did not live in Western Virginia during the 18th century, although they continued to hunt here, especially the Senecas. Thus Virginia negotiators were able to buy their claim to the land between the "back mountains of Virginia" and the Ohio River at the Treaty of Lan-

caster in 1744. (Or so the Virginians asserted; Iroquois leaders denied making such an extensive grant and sold it again at the Treaty of Fort Stanwix in 1768.) The Lancaster treaty stimulated an influx of speculators and settlers into lands west of the Alleghenies, beginning in the Greenbrier, New River, and Monongahela watersheds. This in turn set in motion 50 years of intermittent border warfare, as non-Iroquoian peoples such as the Shawnees and Delawares who had not been consulted at Lancaster disputed the Virginian advance into their traditional hunting grounds. At times the Iroquois "uncles" of these peoples sought to restrain them; at other times, Iroquois warriors, especially Senecas, joined in the fighting.

After the American Revolution, the Shawnees denounced the Six Nations' failure to protect their dependents and allies from the relentless Euro-American advance and set about organizing a rival western confederacy. Thereafter the Iroquois could speak only for themselves, and their role in the Ohio Valley dwindled to the maintenance of a small Seneca reservation on the region's northern edge.

John Alexander Williams
Appalachian State University
Daniel K. Richter, *The Ordeal of the Longhouse: The Peoples of the Iroquois League in the Era of European Colonization*, 1992.

Island Creek Coal Company

The predecessor to Island Creek Coal Company was founded by Huntington lawyer Z. T. Vinson and other investors as a West Virginia enterprise. They sold their firm to U.S. Coal & Oil Company, backed by Northern capital and managed by William H. Coolidge and Albert F. Holden. In 1902, Holden and Coolidge spent their summer in Logan County, inspecting a 30,000-acre land tract owned by the heirs of James Andrew Nighbert on Copperas Fork of Island Creek. The company bought that tract for $600,000 in cash and stock in their company. They built a railroad line from the city of Logan, where the Chesapeake & Ohio Railroad had completed its Guyan Valley Extension, and Island Creek shipped its first trainload of coal in December 1904. During the same years, the company built the town of Holden as a model coal town, four miles from Logan.

The firm grew quickly, opening ten mines within three years and employing thousands of immigrant miners. U.S. Coal & Oil was soon renamed Island Creek Coal Company and, working three of Logan County's six coal seams, became a leader in the industry. Soon it expanded into Mingo, Wyoming, McDowell, and Fayette counties. In following years, it also bought other firms and opened mines in other states in the eastern U.S. The first company president was Holden, who died young. He was followed by Thomas B. Davis, James Draper Francis, Raymond Salvati, and Stonie Barker. In 1969, Island Creek lost its independent identity as it was sold to Armand Hammer of Occidental Petroleum Company. A few years later, some of Island Creek's assets were sold to a new firm, Ioxy. The company moved its headquarters from Holden, and much of that town was purchased by the West Virginia Department of Highways to make room for four-lane U.S. 119, Appalachian Corridor G.

Robert Y. Spence
Logan

Italian Heritage Festival

The first West Virginia Italian Heritage Festival was held in downtown Clarksburg in 1979. The idea was proposed by the librarian at the Clarksburg-Harrison Public Library, and a board of directors was formed, consisting mostly of prominent citizens of Italian descent. A parade, street concerts, authentic Italian food, cultural events (including art shows and opera), crafts, sports (bocce, morra, and golf), and the crowning of a festival queen were all part of the first Italian Heritage Festival and continued in later festivals.

Italians were the most numerous ethnic group to come to West Virginia during the massive immigration that accompanied the industrialization of the state. Clarksburg remains one of the centers of Italian-American population in West Virginia. The festival was designed to celebrate the state's Italian-American culture and highlight the contributions of the early immigrants. Each year the festival honors surviving immigrants by having them participate in a special parade. Prominent Italian-American entertainers

and sports figures have been a part of the festival program, with past festivals having included Jerry Vale, Frankie Avalon, Joe DiMaggio, and Rocky Graziano. Recognition is given to the outstanding Italian-American man and woman of the year, who must be a native or resident West Virginian, and also to "honorary Italians." The West Virginia Italian Heritage Festival is held each Labor Day weekend beginning on Friday and concluding on Sunday.

See also Clarksburg, Ethnic Life
Merle Moore
Webster Springs

Italian Prisoners of War

During World War II, more than 45,000 Italian prisoners of war were held in the United States. Two separate groups, totaling some 500 men, spent part of their 1942–45 captivity in West Virginia. The first and largest contingent arrived in the summer of 1942 to build Camp Ashford, a standard U.S. Army double-barbed wire compound near White Sulphur Springs. While so engaged, many also helped Greenbrier Valley farmers to make hay and harvest the year's crops. The Italians moved on in October, replaced by the German POWs who worked at Ashford General Hospital. Ashford General was operated by the military at what was formerly (and later) the Greenbrier resort.

The second and smaller group of some 175 Italian POWs was assigned to Camp Dawson, Preston County, the long-time (and still) home of the West Virginia National Guard. Their main task, under U.S. Army direction, was to build and repair roads. During their stay they became well-known to the many Italian-American families in northern West Virginia, who visited the prisoners on Sundays at Camp Dawson for picnics and entertain-

ment. The Italians were glad to be safely out of the war, and after their repatriation in 1945, many returned to build new lives in America.

See also Ashford General Hospital
Louis E. Keefer
Reston, Virginia

Louis E. Keefer, "POW: The Italian Prisoners at Camp Dawson," *Goldenseal*, Spring 1993; Keefer, *Italian Prisoners of War in America 1942–1946: Captives or Allies?*, 1992.

Italians

Individuals of Italian extraction constitute one of the most important ethnic groups in West Virginia's population. Most of these Italian-Americans date their connection with the state to ancestors who were recruited during the early years of the 20th century to serve the labor needs of West Virginia's rapidly developing industrial economy. With more than 17,000 Italian immigrants in the state by 1910, they made up 30 percent of West Virginia's foreign-born population. In fact, so many Italians had entered the state that for over a decade before the First World War, the Italian government maintained a consular office in northern West Virginia to look after them.

The influx produced important enclaves of Italian immigrants throughout much of West Virginia. Most of these population concentrations were located in six counties in the northern part of the state, with Marion County leading the way, followed by Harrison, Tucker, Randolph, Preston, and Monongalia. At the same time, significant clusters of Italians were also drawn to southern West Virginia. McDowell County, with 2,300, could boast the most Italian immigrants in the state in 1910, although the Fayette County communities of Boomer, Harewood, Longacre, and Smithers constituted the greatest single concentration of Italians in the state.

While immigrants were attracted to West Virginia from all over the Italian peninsula, the majority came from that country's southern regions of Campania, Calabria, and Sicily. Many of the Sicilian immigrants came from the center of that island and were fleeing the depressed conditions in the sulfur mining industry. The region of Calabria, at the "foot" and "ankle" of the Italian boot, produced even more emigrants. So many Calabrians came from such communities as San Giovanni in Fiore, Cacurri, and Caulonia that they constituted the core of the Italian population in both the northern and southern sections of the Mountain State.

The great majority of Italian immigrants were employed in the coal industry as pick-and-shovel miners. West Virginia mines were among the most mechanized in this country, but miners born in

Italian Heritage Festival in downtown Clarksburg.

America or northern Europe generally operated the new machines and usually earned better money, while their counterparts from less favored regions did the handwork. Despite this disparity and the fact that many such immigrants were kept hopelessly in debt by unscrupulous coal companies, West Virginia Italians were able to significantly improve their financial position.

In part, the Italians achieved real economic progress and acceptance by the sheer dint of hard labor. The records for coal production by hand tools are all apparently held by Italians. For instance, in 1924, Carmine Pelligrino of Rosemont in Marion County mined 66 tons of coal in one 24-hour period and earned the nickname "Sixty-six" (later shortened to "Sixty"). Eleven years later, Dominic Fish (formerly Pesca) of Boomer mined by hand 48 tons of coal in one day and 52 tons the next at the Union Carbide mines at nearby Alloy.

Italian miners in West Virginia also improved their economic position by self-sacrifice and frugality. Raising livestock and tending gardens kept down expenses and helped to produce some prodigious savings relative to their income. The U.S. Department of Labor reckoned that such Italian miners sent more money back to their home country than any other comparable group of immigrants.

Although large numbers were involved in digging coal, West Virginia's Italians were an occupationally diverse group. Even in the coal camps, they often held a variety of jobs such as teamsters, carpenters, blacksmiths, shoemakers, stonemasons, and laborers. In many places, Italians were a vital part of the business community. The occupational diversity of Italians was especially notable in the northern part of the state where urban industrial settings were more common. For instance, historian William Klaus has shown that Italians in Marion County were not just miners, but also worked in glass and other manufacturing establishments, on railroads, in skilled trades, on farms, and in their own small businesses. The same could be said for the substantial groups of Italians who labored in the mines and mills of Wheeling, Weirton, and other Ohio River valley industrial centers.

While many Italian immigrants eventually left West Virginia, many others stayed and made a long lasting impact on the state and its institutions. Italian union members and organizers such as Tony Stafford and Armando Folio helped to make the Mountain State one of the most union-oriented states in the nation. West Virginia Catholicism and its ancillary institutions have been strengthened considerably by the infusion of Italian parishioners. The continuing influence of Italians in West Virginia is symbolized by the growth of the yearly Italian festivals held in the state at Clarksburg and Wheeling in the north and Bluefield and Princeton in the southern part of the state. As late as 1970, Italians with at least one parent born in the old country constituted West Virginia's second-largest ethnic group.

By the third generation, Italians had moved into the center of political life in many parts of the state. In 2005, Joe Manchin became West Virginia's first governor of Italian descent. His uncle A. James Manchin, secretary of state and treasurer, had preceded him as one of the state's most popular politicians.

Fred A. Barkey
Marshall University Graduate College

Fred Barkey, "Here Come the Boomer 'Talys: Italian Immigrants and Industrial Conflict in the Upper Kanawha Valley: 1903–1917," in Ken Fones-Wolf and Ronald L. Lewis, eds., *Transnational West Virginia*, 2002; Kenneth Bailey, "A Judicious Mixture: Negroes and Immigrants in the West Virginia Mines, 1880–1917," *West Virginia History*, 1973.

Itmann Company Store

The huge Pocahontas Fuel Company store at Itmann displays perhaps West Virginia's most spectacular surviving coalfields architecture. Named for West Virginia financier Isaac T. Mann, president of the Bank of Bramwell and an officer and principal shareholder in Pocahontas Fuel, the company town of Itmann was built in 1916 and began mining the Pocahontas No. 3 seam along the Guyandotte River in Wyoming County in 1917. Served by the Virginian Railroad, the Itmann operation was highly productive, shipping two million tons of high-quality "smokeless" coal each year during the 1950s, and employing 1,800 West Virginians.

At the center of the company town, which also had a theater, school, and recreation hall, was the massive stone store, built between 1923 and 1925. Housing the post office, doctor's office, freight station, payroll office, and other management functions, as well as the store itself, the cut-stone Classical Revival structure was built by Italian immigrant stonemasons. Its distinctive architecture, including an interior courtyard, has been variously ascribed to an English castle or an Italian prison.

The mine and company store closed in the 1980s, and the landmark building was listed on the National Register of Historic Places in 1990. The imposing structure, often mentioned as a likely site for heritage tourism along the Coal Heritage Trail national scenic byway, is in private

The Itmann company store.

ownership and has served as a homeless shelter and a veteran's hall. The Itmann company store was designed by Bluefield architect Alexander Mahood.

See also Alexander Blount Mahood, I. T. Mann

C. Stuart McGehee
West Virginia State University

It's Wheeling Steel

A half-hour musical variety radio program, *It's Wheeling Steel* debuted over WWVA in Wheeling on November 8, 1936. Conceived and produced by the Wheeling Steel Corporation's advertising director, John L. Grimes, the program's purpose was to promote public relations and serve as a vehicle for advertising the corporation's products.

The program's content consisted of light classics, popular songs, and show tunes, performed by an orchestra of local musicians, as well as an assortment of amateur "headliner" performers, all of whom were drawn from the corporation's extended family of employees. The program was an instant success with local audiences. When it was picked up by the Mutual Broadcasting System in January 1939, its appeal proved to be nationwide. In 1941, *It's Wheeling Steel* jumped to the NBC Blue Network, where it rose to fifth place in listener ratings.

The program was at the height of its popularity when it was discontinued in 1944, primarily due to Grimes's declining health. The show's arranger, Lew Davies, later assisted Lawrence Welk in developing a musical variety show for television that was a reflection of *It's Wheeling Steel's* format and character.

See also Wheeling Steel, WWVA

John A. Cuthbert
WVU Libraries

J

Jackson County

Jackson County is located in the Appalachian foothills on the Ohio River between Parkersburg and Point Pleasant. It has 472 square miles of rolling, hilly land, with large flat bottoms on the Ohio River, Big Mill Creek, and Big Sandy Creek. Jackson was created from parts of Wood, Mason, and Kanawha counties by an act of the Virginia legislature, March 1, 1831. The county was named in honor of Andrew Jackson, the hero of the Battle of New Orleans and seventh president of the United States.

The first white person to visit the area of Jackson County was probably Gabriel Arthur, a Virginian who with a party of Cherokees visited a large village of Indians that he called Monetons, now thought to have been Shawnees, in 1674. La Salle and a party of French explorers are supposed to have visited the Ohio River in the summer of 1669, but the claim cannot be substantiated. French traders were here by 1696 and their English rivals by 1703. In 1749, a party led by Celoron de Blainville and including about 200 French and Indians came down the Ohio to bury lead plates and claim the lands for France. Christopher Gist, the noted explorer, visited in 1750.

Col. George Washington, Dr. James Craik, and their party passed on their way down the Ohio River in 1770. In 1771, Capt. William Crawford made a survey of 2,448 acres for Washington in present Jackson County. The first permanent settlement was made by three Revolutionary War veterans, William Hannaman,

A Jackson County swinging bridge.

FAST FACTS ABOUT JACKSON COUNTY

Founded: 1831
Land in square miles: 472
Population: 28,000
Percentage minorities: 1.3%
Percentage rural: 73.6%
Median age: 38.8
Percentage 65 and older: 15.3%
Birth rate per 1,000 population: 13.1
Median household income $32,434
High school graduate or higher: 77.4%
Bachelor's degree or higher: 12.4%
Home ownership: 79.6%
Median home value: $78,500

This information is from the 2000 U.S. Census. In 2000, West Virginia as a whole had 5 percent minorities, a median age of 38.9, median household income of $29,696, and a 75.2 percent home ownership rate.

Benjamin Cox, and James McDade in May 1796, when they built cabins in the western part of the present county. Other early settlers were Capt. William Parsons and Samuel Tanner in 1797. Jackson was settled during the early decades of the 19th century. The first schoolhouse was erected in 1806 and the first church in 1840.

The Battle of Buffington Island, fought in Jackson County and neighboring Ohio in July 1863, ended Confederate Gen. John Hunt Morgan's daring raid north of the river. The battle on and around the island near Ravenswood involved Union gunboats and was the only naval action ever fought within West Virginia. Jackson Countians had mixed allegiances during the Civil War, provoking bitter antagonisms that persisted for many years. A period of feud-like violence in the 1870s and 1880s, known as the Bruen land wars, was traceable in part to divisions arising in the Civil War.

Jackson County's population, 4,890 in 1840, rose to more than 19,000 in 1900. The county boomed in the late 1800s, due to timbering and the oil and gas industries. Population dropped over the course of the 20th century until the 1950s, when the Kaiser Aluminum and Chemical Corporation built a large aluminum plant near Ravenswood in 1954. Unlike most of West Virginia, Jackson County's population grew each decade after 1950. It is still growing, ranking 11th in population growth among West Virginia counties during the 1990s, with an increase to 28,000 by 2000.

Throughout the changes, Jackson County remained farm country. It had the second-highest number of farms among West Virginia counties in 1997, and only six counties had more farmland. Jackson County farmers drew relatively little income from their farms, however, suggesting that most were part-time farmers or hobby farmers. The county includes a siz-

able contingent of rural gentry, some of them influential in the affairs of the state.

The Kaiser Aluminum plant, an integrated facility that included the smelting and processing of aluminum, was sold to Ravenswood Aluminum Corporation in 1988 and became part of Century Aluminum in 1995. The community was divided by a bitter strike at Ravenswood Aluminum in the early 1990s. In 1999, Century Aluminum divided and sold part of the operation to Pechiney Rolled Products. In 2004, the Alcan company of Montreal was negotiating to buy Pechiney, including the Ravenswood facilities. The aluminum plant remains the county's largest employer.

Jackson County is served by Interstate 77 and U.S. 33, CSX Railroad, Jackson County Airport, and barge traffic on the Ohio River. The two biggest towns are Ripley and Ravenswood.

Ripley, the county seat, was laid out in 1831 by Jacob Starcher and received its charter December 19, 1832. The town was named in honor of Harry Ripley, a minister who drowned in Big Mill Creek. Ripley's role as the county seat was challenged by a referendum in 1886 which proposed that Ravenswood was a better choice with its larger population and its location on the Ohio River. The referendum was defeated, ending a 54-year dispute between large landowners on the river and small inland landowners.

Ripley was the site of West Virginia's last public hanging in 1897. In 2000, Ripley's population stood at 3,263. Ravenswood, Jackson County's largest town with a 2000 population of 4,031, was laid out in 1836 on land previously owned by George Washington.

The Cedar Lakes Conference Center, a 450-acre complex near Ripley, was established as a state FFA-FHA camp in 1950. Each summer it hosts the Mountain State Art & Craft Fair, founded as part of West Virginia's 1963 Centennial and now one of the state's largest festivals. West Virginia's American Baptist Conference Center is located just south of Ripley, on a 1,334-acre complex in Parchment Valley. In addition to serving around 700 churches, the center also serves as the archives for the West Virginia Baptist Historical Society. The Jackson County Maritime and Industrial Center, a 159-acre complex located along the Ohio River, includes a 25-acre barge loading-unloading facility. The county also has Jackson General Hospital, a fine school system, a public library with facilities in Ripley and Ravenswood, an estimated 135 churches, and local chapters of most civic and fraternal organizations.

Notable residents have included Jesse Hughes (1770–1829), a scout, frontier settler, and Indian fighter who lived and was buried here; Andrew D. Hopkins (1847–1940), an eminent horticulturist; Frederick Poe Graham (1907–82), an aviation editor, war correspondent for the *New York Times,* and author of books on aviation; Edythe L. Rowley (1900–74), social secretary for the White House under five presidents; and O. J. Morrison (1869–1952), founder of O. J. Morrison Department Stores.

See also Buffington Island, Bruen Lands Feud, Dan Cunningham, Ravenswood Aluminum Strike

E. DeWitt Williams
Ripley

Dean W. Moore, *Washington's Woods,* 1971; Jackson County History Book Committee, Jackson County Historical Society, *Jackson County, West Virginia, Past and Present,* 1990.

Jackson Family

In government, politics, business, industry, and military affairs, few West Virginia families have produced more persons of distinction than the Jacksons. The family was descended from John (1716–1801) and Elizabeth Cummins Jackson (1720–1825), of Scotch-Irish stock. John was described as a "diminutive man" and his wife as "a stately blonde," who was well educated and the person from whom "the Jacksons got all their brains." In the early 1760s, the couple settled in the Tygart Valley, where John became a farmer and land speculator. Three thousand acres, including the site of Buckhannon, were patented to Elizabeth.

Of their ten children, George and Edward were the most prominent. Their sons and grandsons became important political and business leaders. George (1757–1831) was a three-term congressman. Edward (1759–1828), the grandfather of Confederate Gen. Thomas "Stonewall" Jackson, founded Jackson's Mill in Lewis County. During the 1820s, his son, David E. Jackson (1788–1837), after whom Wyoming's Jackson River and Jackson Hole were named, was a prominent explorer and fur trader in the West. In 1827, Jackson, William Sublette, and Jedediah Smith be-

came partners in the Rocky Mountain Fur Company and engaged in a profitable fur trade along the upper Missouri River.

The Jackson family produced an unusual number of state legislators and congressmen. They included George Jackson, John George Jackson (1777–1825), Edward Brake Jackson (1793–1826), William Lowther Jackson (1825–90), John J. Jackson Sr. (1800–77), James Monroe Jackson (1825–1901), all of West Virginia; and William Thomas Bland (1861–1928) of Missouri, a grandson of John George Jackson. Jacob Beeson Jackson served as governor of West Virginia from 1881 to 1885. The family also produced a long line of prominent judges, local, state, and national, from the late 18th century to the 20th century. They included George Jackson, John George Jackson, John J. Jackson Jr. (1824–1907), William Lowther Jackson, and James Monroe Jackson. John J. Allen (1797–1871), a justice of the Virginia Supreme Court of Appeals, was a son-in-law of John George Jackson.

For generations, the Jackson men were active in military affairs. The most prominent were Thomas J. "Stonewall" Jackson (1824–63) and his cousin William Lowther Jackson, humorously known by comparison as "Mudwall" Jackson. Others included George Jackson, John George Jackson, and John Jay Jackson Sr. Several family members developed important business interests, including ventures in railroads, engineering, banking, mining, timbering, and retailing. They included Andrew Gardner Jackson (1856–1942), James Madison Jackson (1818–71), and Thomas Moore Jackson (1852–1912).

Stephen W. Brown
WVU Institute of Technology

Roy Bird Cook, *Family and Early Life of Stonewall Jackson,* 1963; Dorothy Davis, *History of Harrison County, West Virginia,* 1970.

Jacob Beeson Jackson

Jacob Beeson Jackson, West Virginia's sixth governor, was born April 16, 1829, in Parkersburg. He was a member of one of the region's most distinguished families. His father was John Jay Jackson Sr., and his grandfather was former Virginia Congressman John George Jackson of Clarksburg, a leader in what historian John Alexander Williams describes as Western Virginia's pre-Civil War oligarchy. By the time of Jacob's birth, John Jay Jackson was fast establishing himself as one of Virginia's most prominent attorneys, and he would become a prominent judge.

Unlike his two older brothers, John Jay Jr. and James Monroe Jackson, Jacob did not attend college. After studying at the Reverend Festus Hanks's school in Parkersburg, he taught school before deciding to become a lawyer. He was taught

Governor Jacob Beeson Jackson (1829–93).

the law by his father and was admitted to the bar in 1852. He began his legal career in St. Marys, the county seat of Pleasants County. Jackson served as Pleasants County's prosecuting attorney for nine years. His work took him from time to time to Wheeling, where during the Civil War he was arrested for making pro-Confederate remarks. In 1864, he returned to his native Parkersburg, where he was known for his eloquent speaking ability, and became active in the Democratic Party. He was known by the nickname "Jake."

In 1870, Jackson became Wood County's prosecuting attorney. Five years later he was elected to the House of Delegates and served one term. In 1879, he was elected mayor of Parkersburg. By this time, his father had been dead for two years. Brother John Jay Jackson Jr. had been a federal judge for 18 years, having been appointed by President Lincoln in August 1861.

In November 1880, Jacob Jackson was elected governor of West Virginia and took up residence in the capital city of Wheeling. Jackson had been a Copperhead during the Civil War, as the Southern-sympathizing Northern Democrats were called, and his election as governor confirmed the emergence of formerly pro-Confederate Democrats as the ruling power in West Virginia. Jackson defeated Republican George C. Sturgiss of Monongalia County, a man of opposite views who had opposed the reenfranchisement of former Confederates in the previous decade.

Governor Jackson worked for, in his words, "the intelligent majority." He called the legislature into a special session in 1882 to re-codify the state's laws, but he is remembered for his attempts at tax reform. He ordered a thorough assessment of personal property for taxation. During the 1873–78 economic depression, the legislature had exempted certain businesses from taxes, but following the depression the West Virginia Supreme Court of Appeals ruled that all property not specifically exempted by the state constitution had to be assessed. Jackson's assessment order represented an important step forward, but met with limited success due to the foot dragging of local assessors and the opposition of railroads and other taxpayers. While he was governor, his only child, William Wirt Jackson, served as Jackson's personal secretary.

After Jacob Jackson left the governorship on March 3, 1885, he returned to the private practice of law in Parkersburg. He was president of the Citizens National Bank at the time of his death, December 11, 1893, in his home at the corner of Seventh and Avery streets in the city of his birth.

See also Jackson Family, John Jay Jackson Sr.

Bernard L. Allen
Conway, South Carolina
Charles H. Ambler and Festus P. Summers, *West Virginia: The Mountain State*, 1958; John G. Morgan, *West Virginia Governors*, 1980; Thomas C. Miller and Hu Maxwell, *West Virginia and Its People*, Volume 3, 1913.

John George Jackson

John George Jackson, legislator, congressman, federal judge, industrial entrepreneur, and land speculator, was born September 22, 1777, near Buckhannon, the son of George and Elizabeth Brake Jackson. With little formal education, he became well versed in the classics, with a proficiency in Latin and Greek, the law, and such practical subjects as surveying. In 1798–1801 and 1811–12, Jackson represented Harrison County in the Virginia House of Delegates, where he pressed for constitutional reforms in voting and legislative representation. He was one of the chief promoters of the Staunton Convention of 1816, which debated Virginia's sectionalism and changes to the state constitution.

As the representative of the First District of Virginia in Congress in 1803–10 and 1813–17, Jackson was a staunch Jeffersonian Republican and states' rights advocate. He was regarded as a spokesman for his brother-in-law, President James Madison, and engaged in fiery debates with opponents of the administration. In 1809, one encounter produced a duel with North Carolina Congressman Joseph Pierson. Although the legislature appointed Jackson a brigadier general in the Virginia militia during the War of 1812, he resigned his post due to disagreements with regular army officers. Upon returning to Congress in 1813, he supported nationalistic policies, including a protective tariff and a national bank.

President James Monroe appointed Jackson a federal judge in 1819 for the newly established District of Virginia West of the Allegheny Mountains, a position he held until his death.

Along with extensive land holdings in West Virginia and Ohio and a successful law practice, Jackson emerged by 1812 as one of the foremost businessmen of the upper Monongahela Valley. Near his Clarksburg residence, he developed an industrial community known as Miles End that included gristmills, a woolen and cotton factory, ironworks, and salt works. He helped organize the Virginia Saline Bank at Clarksburg and in 1817 became the president and chief stockholder of the Monongahela Navigation Company, which constructed locks and dams on the West Fork River.

In 1800, Jackson married Mary Payne, a sister of Dolley Madison. Two years after her death in 1808, Jackson married Mary Sophia Meigs, the daughter of U.S. postmaster-general Return Jonathan Meigs, Jr. Following a rapid decline in his health, Jackson died of an apparent stroke on March 28, 1825, and is buried beside both his wives in Clarksburg.

See also Jackson Family

Stephen W. Brown
WVU Institute of Technology
Stephen W. Brown, *Voice of the New West: John G. Jackson, His Life and Times*, 1985; Dorothy Davis, *John George Jackson*, 1976.

John Jay Jackson Jr.

Judge John Jay Jackson Jr. was born August 4, 1824, near Parkersburg. A year after his graduation from the College of New Jersey (now Princeton University) in 1845, he was admitted to the bar and joined his prominent father in the practice of law.

Jackson served as a prosecuting attorney of Wirt County (1848) and Ritchie County (1849) and as a Whig member of the General Assembly of Virginia (1851–55). In the political maneuvering over secession in the spring of 1861, he took a strong stand for the Union. In August 1861, Abraham Lincoln appointed Jackson a federal district judge, and his court became a symbol and agency of federal power in northwestern Virginia and later West Virginia. Some Republicans criticized him for his narrow interpretation of laws aimed at Southern sympathizers, thinking him too lenient, but he retained the confidence of President Lincoln. In 1870, Jackson's appointment of federal commissioners to supervise elections in West Virginia opened the vote to ex-Confederates and led to Democratic control of the state.

In later years, Jackson became notorious among those trying to organize labor unions in West Virginia. In August 1897, he issued an injunction against Eugene V. Debs and others that effectively ended a union campaign to organize West Virginia miners. Five years later, he blocked an effort by Mother Jones and other United Mine Workers leaders to organize the miners of northern West Virginia.

Jackson was a commanding figure both on the bench and off, and after age 80 continued his daily horseback rides across town to his court in Parkersburg. At the time of his retirement in 1905, he had served 44 years, longer than any other federal judge. Judge Jackson died September 2, 1907, in Atlantic City.

See also Jackson Family, John Jay Jackson Sr.

Edward M. Steel
West Virginia University
Jacob C. Baas Jr., "John Jay Jackson, Jr.: His Early Life and Public Career, 1824–1870," Ph. D. dissertation, West Virginia University, 1975.

John Jay Jackson Sr.

General John Jay Jackson, one of the founders of West Virginia, was born near Parkersburg, February 13, 1800. His grandfather, George Jackson, was a three-term congressman. John G. Jackson, the father of John Jay and son of George, took over George's seat in Congress and served five terms.

Educated at Washington College (now Washington & Jefferson College) in Pennsylvania and at West Point, John Jay Jackson served in the Seminole War as a member of Gen. Andrew Jackson's staff. In 1823, he resigned his commission and returned to Parkersburg to practice law. After two brief terms as a prosecuting attorney he was elected to the General Assembly of Virginia, where he served six terms. He commanded a brigade in the Virginia militia from 1842 to 1861.

In April 1861, Jackson served in the convention in Richmond that voted for Virginia to secede from the United States. Jackson himself voted against secession and before leaving Richmond presided over the Powhatan Hotel conference of Western Virginians who resolved to try to keep Virginia loyal to the union. At the first Wheeling Convention the following month, he and other conservatives delayed an attempt to create a new state. By 1863, he supported the move for the creation of a separate state, but opposed the final step in that process because he was pro-slavery and the Willey Amendment which cleared the way for West Virginia to become a state provided for an end to slavery.

Although active in West Virginia politics, Jackson did not seek elective office. He capped his public service as a member (1871) of the commission to ascertain West Virginia's share of the Virginia debt, an intractable problem that was not finally settled until 1919.

Jackson was the father of Gov. Jacob

Beeson Jackson and Judge John Jay Jackson Jr. He died January 1, 1877.

See also Jackson Family, Jacob Beeson Jackson, John Jay Jackson Jr.

Edward M. Steel
West Virginia University
Jacob C. Baas Jr., "John Jay Jackson, Jr.: His Early Life and Public Career, 1824–1870," Ph.D. dissertation, West Virginia University, 1975; Stephen W. Brown, *Voice of the New West: John G. Jackson, His Life and Times*, 1985.

Lily Irene Jackson

Artist Lily Irene Jackson was born in Parkersburg, September 17, 1848. She was the daughter of attorney John Jay Jackson Jr., who was a member of the prominent Jackson family and later an important federal judge. During the Civil War, Lily at the age of 12 assisted federal troops in Parkersburg by guiding them to land belonging to her grandfather Jackson, where they were to bivouac.

Jackson was best-known as a painter of animal portraits and floral arrangements, and as an advocate for the arts. On February 21, 1887, she organized the Parkersburg Art Society and was elected its president. In 1892, she called upon West Virginia women to contribute to the state's exhibit at the 1893 Chicago World's Fair. She herself exhibited two large oil paintings at the fair. One depicted two of her dogs and was titled *Watching and Waiting*. The other, titled *Anticipation*, was of two St. Bernard dogs. Jackson was at the fair for the opening of the West Virginia exhibit, June 20, 1893.

Today, some of Jackson's paintings are owned by the Daughters of American Pioneers, an organization which she helped found in 1899, and are housed in the Cooper Cabin in Parkersburg's City Park. Other paintings are owned by the state of West Virginia and are to be found in the Blennerhassett Museum of Regional History in Parkersburg and in the State Museum in Charleston.

Upon her father's death in 1907, Jackson inherited the family estate. She died December 9, 1928, in Parkersburg, and was buried in a shroud of her own making.

See also John Jay Jackson Jr., Jackson Family

Bernard L. Allen
Conway, South Carolina
Cuthbert, John A., *Early Art and Artists in West Virginia, An Introduction and Biographical Directory*, 2000.

Mudwall Jackson

Confederate General William Lowther "Mudwall" Jackson was born in Clarksburg, February 3, 1825. At age 23 he served as a judge in Ritchie County. His antebellum career also included service as lieutenant governor of Virginia and a term as president of the Virginia state senate. At the outbreak of the Civil War, he was serving as a circuit judge in Parkersburg.

Jackson was a Southern loyalist. With the coming of war he sought to control the Wood County militia and to seize its three cannons for the Confederacy. During Parkersburg's Jail House Riots in 1861, Jackson engaged the militia's colonel in a fist-fight. Days later, when Judge Jackson dismissed charges against three Southern guerrillas who had been arrested for bridge burning, pistols were drawn in the courtroom and Jackson was forced to leave Parkersburg.

He joined the Confederate Army as a private. After helping to organize an infantry unit, he was promoted to colonel. He served on the staff of his cousin, Gen. Thomas J. "Stonewall" Jackson, and was jokingly nicknamed "Mudwall." In 1863, Jackson led troops against his former Ritchie County neighbor, Union Gen. Thomas Harris. He served under Gen. W. E. "Grumble" Jones during the Jones-Imboden Raid into the Little Kanawha Valley. Jackson was promoted to brigadier general in 1864 and commanded forces at the Battle of Droop Mountain.

After the war Jackson returned to Parkersburg but found the atmosphere hostile. He moved to Louisville, where he served as a circuit judge until his death, March 24, 1890.

See also Jackson Family, Jones-Imboden Raid

Larry Bartlett
Parkersburg
Minnie Kendall Lowther, *Ritchie County In History and Romance*, 1990; Herman E. Matheny, *Wood County W. Va. in Civil War Times*, 1987.

Stonewall Jackson

West Virginia's most famous soldier never quite overcame the lonely childhood of an orphan. Thomas Jonathan Jackson was born near midnight on January 20–21, 1824, in Clarksburg. The death of his father and the destitution of his mother led to the boy being raised by a bullish uncle on the ancestral Jackson estate near the village of Weston. A lack of familial love molded Jackson into a shy, reticent, independent, and determined adult.

In 1842, the poorly prepared, rough-hewn teenager entered the U.S. Military Academy at West Point. He firmly believed that "you may be whatever you will resolve to be." Such resolution enabled him to graduate a surprising 17th in a class of 59 cadets. Jackson was assigned to the artillery, which was always his favorite branch of service.

Three promotions for gallantry came in the Mexican War. In 1851, Jackson left the army and spent the next ten years at the Virginia Military Institute in Lexington as a professor of natural and experimental philosophy and instructor in artillery. He was not a stimulating teacher. That, combined with a number of odd mannerisms, made him the campus character. Yet during those years Jackson allied himself with the Presbyterian faith, dedicated his whole life to God, and became one of the most actively pious men of his day.

When Virginia left the Union in 1861, Jackson dutifully went with his native state. He commanded the strategically important post at Harpers Ferry until being appointed a brigadier general of infantry. In the opening battle at Manassas on July 21, 1861, he and his brigade won the name "Stonewall" for steadfastness at the critical point in the engagement.

Unusually tall (six feet) and heavy-set (175 pounds), Jackson had brown hair, huge hands and feet, plus pale blue eyes that seemed to penetrate whoever faced him. He was so unpretentious that for the first year of the Civil War, Jackson wore the blue uniform of a VMI faculty member. His favorite mount was a small, unimpressive-looking horse affectionately called Little Sorrel.

Jackson repeatedly sought permission to lead a force into northwest Virginia to save his home area from being kept in the Union by federal invaders. Meanwhile, his successful 1862 campaign in the Shenandoah Valley electrified North as well as South. For 11 months thereafter, in a near-model partnership with Gen. Robert E. Lee, Jackson was instrumental in victories at Cedar Mountain, Second Manassas, and Fredericksburg. By the end of 1862, the lonely orphan from the mountains was regarded by many as the most accomplished soldier in the world.

The brilliant career ended in May 1863, at Chancellorsville. Having used his favorite tools—secrecy, swift marching, a sudden and heavy attack where least expected—Jackson was accidentally shot by his own troops in the chaos of battle. The amputation of his left arm led to pneumonia. On May 10, 1863, Stonewall Jackson died after uttering the words: "Let us cross over the river and rest under the shade of the trees."

He is buried in the Stonewall Jackson Cemetery in Lexington, Virginia.

See also Civil War, Jackson's Mill

James I. Robertson Jr.
Virginia Polytechnic Institute
James I. Robertson Jr., *Stonewall Jackson: The Man, The Soldier, The Legend*, 1997.

Jackson's Mill

Jackson's Mill, located near Weston in Lewis County, was Confederate Gen. Thomas J. "Stonewall" Jackson's boyhood home and since 1921 has been the location of West Virginia's state 4-H Camp.

The site was first settled by Thomas Jackson's grandfather, Edward, around

1800. He constructed a house, gristmill, and sawmill on the property. Thomas's father, Jonathan Jackson, was raised there but moved with his new bride, Julia Neale, to nearby Clarksburg in 1818 to practice law. Thomas was born in Clarksburg in January 1824. Following the death of his father in 1826 and his mother in 1831, Thomas and his sister, Laura, were brought to live at Jackson's Mill. The property at that time, which consisted of 1,500 acres, was owned by Jackson's bachelor uncle, Cummins Jackson, who farmed the West Fork River bottoms with the assistance of several slaves. Thomas lived there until 1842, when he left to enter the U.S. Military Academy at West Point, New York. In 1919, a large stone monument was erected at Jackson's Mill in his memory.

Cummins Jackson left Jackson's Mill in 1847 to search for gold in California and died there in 1849. His property at Jackson's Mill was held in heirship until 1868 when it was purchased by his sister, Catherine Jackson White. Upon her death in 1876, the farm was sold outside the Jackson family. In 1915, a five-acre tract of the original property, which included the old gristmill and the site of Cummins Jackson's house, was purchased by the Monongahela Power Company. In 1924, the property was donated to the state of West Virginia as a statewide meeting place for youth enrolled in the 4-H program. The first 4-H camp at Jackson's Mill had been held in 1921.

Since that time the facility, which has 500 acres of land, has been extensively developed. Major features include a large dining hall patterned after Mount Vernon, an assembly hall, 14 cottages donated by various West Virginia counties and named for them, and the building that housed West Virginia's exhibit at the 1933 Chicago World's Fair. Other features include a small airport, the McWhorter cabin, constructed in the 1790s near neighboring Jane Lew and moved to the site in 1929, numerous gardens, and the Jackson Lodge for small conferences. Blaker's Mill, a water powered gristmill constructed in 1794 near Alderson in Greenbrier County, was relocated to Jackson's Mill in the 1980s. Sites associated with the Jackson family include a gristmill constructed around 1841 and now maintained as a museum, the family spring, the Stonewall Jackson monument, and the Jackson family cemetery where his paternal grandparents and other relatives are buried.

Jackson's Mill is operated by the West Virginia University Extension Service as a multipurpose year-round conference center for adults and youth.

See also 4-H, Jackson Family, Stonewall Jackson

Michael M. Meador
Abingdon, Virginia

Roy Bird Cook, *Family and Early Life of Stonewall Jackson*, 1948; Michael M. Meador, *Historic Jackson's Mill: A Walking Tour*, 1991; Guy H. Stewart, *A Touch of Charisma: A History of the 4-H Club Program in West Virginia*, 1969.

John Jeremiah Jacob

West Virginia's fourth governor, John Jeremiah Jacob, was born December 9, 1829, in Hampshire County. He was the first governor born within the area that became West Virginia and the first Democratic governor of the state. His father, John J. Jacob, was a captain in the Revolutionary War, a Methodist minister, and sheriff of Hampshire County. After his father's death in 1839, Jacob's mother, Susan McDavitt Jacob, moved the family to Romney, where Jacob attended the Romney Classical Institute. In 1849, he attained a B.A. at Dickinson College in Carlisle, Pennsylvania. Returning to Romney to teach, he also began studying law.

Jacob married Jane Baird, of Washington, Pennsylvania, in 1853, and they were the parents of three children. In 1853, he was appointed professor of political economy at the University of Missouri, where he continued until 1860, resigning to pursue the study and practice of law in Columbia, Missouri. Jacob returned to Romney in the summer of 1865 and established a law partnership with Col. Robert White.

Jacob was elected to the 1869 session of the House of Delegates as a Democrat. He soon was nominated for governor and defeated Republican incumbent William E. Stevenson in the election of 1870. His two-year term began March 4, 1871. Jacob came to the governorship as a conservative when circumstances, including economically difficult times and the adoption of a new constitution, prevented many of his proposals from being implemented.

A constitutional convention, called by popular referendum in 1871, met in 1872. The Democrats, who had won the governorship and gained a majority in both houses of the legislature in the 1870 election, controlled the convention and were responsible for the fundamentally different laws instituted by the new constitution. The new constitution removed restrictions on the political rights of West Virginians who had served the South during the Civil War. The new constitution changed the gubernatorial term from two years to four, and eliminated the right of a governor to succeed himself. However, Jacob's first term ended before the new constitution and the one-term limit went into effect.

Although Jacob won his first term as a Democrat, in his second term he became the only governor to be elected as an independent. At the constitutional convention, a group of Democratic leaders decided to support wealthy industrialist

Governor John J. Jacob (1829–93).

Johnson Newlon Camden for governor. At the Democratic state convention a few weeks later, they were successful in nominating Camden, but were viewed as having acted with impropriety. Jacob's supporters joined with the Republicans and encouraged Jacob to run against Camden as an independent. No Republican candidate was nominated. After a heated and bitter campaign, Jacob's integrity and reputation for protecting the state's interests were preferred to Camden's wealth and connections to big business. Jacob was elected for a second term which began March 4, 1873.

The 1872–73 legislature faced the task of modifying laws to conform to the newly adopted constitution, which became effective January 1, 1873. The governor and the legislature were in frequent conflict over the limits of his appointing powers. Jacob's administration was further disrupted by the 1875 removal of the capital from Charleston to Wheeling, just five years after the seat of government had been moved from Wheeling to Charleston. In addition to the expenses incurred in financially difficult times, the move disrupted and disturbed government operations.

At the conclusion of his second gubernatorial term on March 4, 1877, Jacob decided to remain in Wheeling and practice law. He was elected to represent Ohio County in the House of Delegates for the 1879 legislative session. In 1881, he was appointed Ohio County circuit judge to fill a vacancy. Jacob was then elected to the same office a year later and served as judge until 1888, when he returned to his law practice.

Jacob died in Wheeling, November 24, 1893, two weeks short of his 64th birthday, and was buried in a family cemetery at Romney.

See also Constitution of West Virginia

Harold Malcolm Forbes
WVU Libraries

Encyclopedia of Contemporary Biography of West Virginia, 1894; John G. Morgan, *West Virginia Governors*, 1980; "West Virginia's Fourth Governor," *West Virginia Review*, April 1945.

Elmer Forrest Jacobs

Architect Elmer Forrest Jacobs was born June 11, 1866, in Preston County. He attended West Virginia University and Carnegie Institute of Technology in Pittsburgh before he began designing fire-resistant factories in Pittsburgh. In 1894, Jacobs set up his practice in Morgantown.

Jacobs designed homes, factories, banks and other commercial enterprises, mills, churches, post offices, and schools in northern West Virginia and in Pennsylvania. He also was responsible for adaptive reuse and sensitive additions to existing buildings. His work is seen particularly in downtown Morgantown, in residential South Park, and on or near the West Virginia University campus, where Jacobs added the two wings to Woodburn Hall. Although he did not design the original 1896 Seneca Glass Company building still standing on Beechurst Avenue, he did design a major portion of it that had to be rebuilt after a fire in 1902. He also designed the Union Stopper Company building nearby, later known as Beaumont Glass, which was recently demolished.

Jacobs's career coincided with the growth of Morgantown from 1894 to 1915, when the city increased from 2,000 to 10,000 people and the demand for domestic, educational, commercial, and industrial housing was critical. Most of his extant buildings in Morgantown are now on the National Register of Historic Places. Jacobs died in Morgantown, October 9, 1945.

Dolores Atchison Fleming
Morgantown

Dolores Fleming, "Architect Elmer Jacobs: The People's Choice," *Dominion Post: Panorama*, May 8, 1988.

T. D. Jakes

Charismatic preacher and self-described spiritual physician, Bishop T. D. Jakes is senior pastor of the 30,000-member, non-denominational Potter's House church in Dallas, Texas. Jakes's message about the healing power of God's word reaches national and international audiences through television programs, conferences, audio and videotapes, and books.

Thomas Dexter Jakes was born June 9, 1957, in South Charleston. As a boy, he preached to imaginary congregations and carried a Bible to school, which earned him the nickname "Bible Boy." He attended West Virginia State College, later completing his undergraduate and master's degrees and a doctorate of ministry through correspondence courses.

In 1980, he started his first church, Greater Emmanuel Temple of Faith, with 10 members in a storefront in Montgom-

ery. Two years later, the Union Carbide plant where Jakes worked closed and he turned to full-time ministry. As word spread about Jakes's uplifting sermons, the congregation grew and moved, first to a refurbished theater in Smithers, Fayette County, and then to South Charleston. By 1993, the church's membership had increased so rapidly that Jakes moved to a larger building in nearby Cross Lanes. In 1996, the congregation numbered close to 1,000. That year, Jakes relocated his ministry to Dallas, where he founded the Potter's House, located on 28 acres. Church services include ministries to homeless people, prisoners, prostitutes, and people with AIDS, as well as treatment for drug and alcohol abusers, and adult education.

T. D. Jakes Ministries, the non-profit company that sells Jakes's videos and audiotapes, grossed $19 million in 2000. Jakes has written 22 books, including *Woman, Thou Art Loosed!*, which has sold more than one million copies, and *Maximize the Moment*, a *New York Times* business bestseller.

James Gang

On Monday, September 6, 1875, four armed men walked to the entrance of the Bank of Huntington. It was early afternoon and the bank's president had gone to lunch. The cashier was alone. While two men stayed outside, the two others entered with revolvers drawn and robbed the bank of $20,000.

The bank president returned from lunch in time to witness the getaway. The robbers mounted their horses, fired their pistols in the air, and rode into the hills south of town, heading toward Wayne County. The Cabell County sheriff organized a posse and started after the robbers. Some of the posse chased the desperadoes into Kentucky. Eventually, one of the robbers was captured in Tennessee with some of the stolen loot on him. He was returned to Huntington for trial, found guilty, and sentenced to the West Virginia Penitentiary. Another of the gang was wounded by two Kentucky farmers and later died of his injuries. The two others, supposed to be Frank James and Cole Younger, escaped with most of the money.

This event spawned a host of legends, including stories of Frank James hiding in Wayne County. According to local folklore, James tended a farm, made well-crafted furniture, and lived peaceably under the alias of Frank Morris near Cove Gap, a community close to the Lincoln County line, for several years. Furniture credited to him has been handed down through Wayne County families.

Another persistent West Virginia legend identified the U.S. senator and industrialist Stephen B. Elkins as the outlaw Jesse James. Elkins and James were con-

temporaries. Both men grew up in Missouri, and Elkins arrived in the East from New Mexico territory near enough to the time of James's death to fuel the rumor. In fact, Elkins had taught Cole Younger in school, and Younger had befriended him during the Civil War. There was at least some contact between Elkins and Younger in later life.

Joseph Platania
Huntington

James Produce Company

The C. H. James family founded the James Produce Company and built it into one of the state's most successful minority businesses. The business began in 1883 when Charles H. James and his brothers started as backpack peddlers serving the coalfields of southern West Virginia. Their father was Francis James, a free black from Ohio, who established the family in West Virginia at the end of the Civil War. The business prospered, wagons were purchased, and warehouses in Charleston were acquired. Cash was scarce, so much business was done through barter, with customers trading eggs, chickens, or produce for merchandise.

When E. L. James, Charles's son, took over, he converted the operation from retail to wholesale. The 1929 stock market crash forced the company into bankruptcy, and it was E. L. who built a new business. After his death in 1967, his son, Charles II, worked to modernize the business with computers and refrigerated trucks. In 1973, he secured financing that allowed the company to double its storage capacity.

Charles James III joined the business in 1985 and within three years had bought the company from his father. He arranged certification as a minority contractor to the federal government, adding millions to gross sales. At its peak, C. H. James & Co. generated approximately $30 million in annual sales. In 1992, Charles III moved the business to California, and in 1999 he sold it to pursue other business ventures in the food service area.

Betty L. MacQueen
Chesapeake, Virginia

James River & Kanawha Canal

The James River Company was formed by the state of Virginia in 1785 to develop a water route from Richmond over the Allegheny Mountains to the Ohio River. Encouraged by George Washington after his 1784 exploratory trip into the Ohio Valley and up the Kanawha River, the original plans included improvements to allow navigation past the falls of the James at Richmond; a turnpike across the mountains from the upper James to the Kanawha Valley; and improvements to the Kanawha River to its junction with the Ohio. Eventually, it was planned to build a continuous canal across the mountains, linking the two great rivers.

The project was started in 1820 with canal work on the lower James. The state-owned James River Company was reorganized as a stock company in 1835 and named the James River & Kanawha Company. A road, the James River & Kanawha Turnpike, was constructed from Covington to the falls of the Kanawha near Gauley Bridge and then on to the mouth of the Big Sandy River at the Ohio. Construction of the canal on the James River was completed by 1840 between Richmond and Lynchburg and by 1851 had been extended to the town of Buchanan, northeast of present Roanoke.

While the work was being done on the James, the Kanawha River was improved by clearing channels, dredging, and building wing dams. Although the Civil War brought the project to a halt, work resumed as soon as the conflict was over.

The James River & Kanawha Canal later became the focal point of a grand proposed waterway that would link the Tidewater regions of Virginia with the foothills of the Rocky Mountains. This route, proposed to Congress by West Virginia founder Waitman T. Willey and an Ohio colleague in 1870 and known as the Central Water Line, would follow the James River & Kanawha Canal to the Ohio River, then down the Ohio to the Mississippi River, up the Mississippi to the Missouri River, and finally up the Missouri to the Kansas River to the Rocky Mountains. This route never materialized because of the improving railroad and road systems following the Civil War.

The James River & Kanawha Company continued to operate the Virginia portion of the canal while competing with the developing railroad systems. In November 1877, a severe flood hit the James River Valley doing great damage to the canal system. On March 5, 1880, the James River & Kanawha Company ceased operations and went out of business.

See also Midland Trail, James River & Kanawha Turnpike

Gerald W. Sutphin
Huntington

Leland R. Johnson, *Men, Mountains and Rivers*, 1977; Emory Kemp, *Great Kanawha Navigation*, 1998.

James River & Kanawha Turnpike

The historic James River & Kanawha Turnpike, now the route of U.S. 60 and parts of Interstate 64, began as a meandering game trail. Native Americans used the trail for centuries to reach the Kanawha salt licks, and later it was an important passage for European immigration through the Appalachians. Col. Andrew Lewis's army traveled over it to the Battle of Point Pleasant in 1774. By 1785, the state of Virginia authorized construction of the Old State Road, along the path of

the Lewis trail. In 1791, the road was improved to the head of navigable water on the Kanawha River at Kellys Creek (present Cedar Grove), where westward travelers secured bateaux or flatboats made at "the Boatyards" for their downstream journey.

Opened to the Ohio River by 1800, the Old State Road underwent major repairs in 1803 and received legislative authorization to collect tolls for maintenance in 1809. However, the growing importance of Kanawha salt necessitated a more reliable all-weather road. Pursuant to an 1820 legislative act, Virginia authorized the James River Company "to make a convenient road by the most practicable route from the James to the Great Falls of the Kanawha," near present Gauley Bridge, as an overland connector in the company's James River & Kanawha Canal project. Company surveyors located the road through Greenbrier and Fayette counties on the north side of the New and Kanawha rivers because it required fewer bridges and furnished better grades at lower cost. Covered bridges over the Greenbrier and Gauley rivers opened in 1822, and by 1824 the road ran from Lewisburg to Montgomery's Ferry, 25 miles above Charleston.

In 1829, the Virginia legislature authorized extending the road to the mouth of the Big Sandy River on the Ohio. Completed in 1832, this road crossed the Kanawha at Charleston, followed an existing route along the south side of the river to Coalsmouth (present St. Albans), then followed Teays Valley to the Mud River. It crossed the Guyandotte River at Barboursville and terminated at present Kenova on the Ohio. A branch road extended to the town of Guyandotte. Following the so-called "central line," this turnpike was a significant east-west passage until the Civil War.

Completion of the Chesapeake & Ohio Railroad to Huntington in 1873 ushered in a period of decline for the turnpike that lasted until the automobile era. By World War I, the Kanawha route experienced a rebirth as part of the Midland Trail, a transcontinental highway that in 1926 became U.S. 60. It remained the primary east-west route through southern West Virginia until the completion of I-64 in 1988, when it became a secondary route for local traffic. In response, business owners and elected officials in Greenbrier, Fayette, and Kanawha counties formed the Midland Trail Scenic Highway Association to promote scenic, historic, and recreational opportunities along the old route. In 1989, Governor Moore designated U.S. 60 from White Sulphur Springs to Charleston as the Midland Trail Scenic Byway. This original 119-mile segment became a National Scenic Byway in 2000, and in 2001 the remaining West Virginia portion of U.S. 60 from

Charleston to Kenova became a State Scenic Byway.

See also James River & Kanawha Canal, Midland Trail

Billy Joe Peyton
West Virginia State University

Anna Jarvis

Social activist Anna Maria Reeves was born in Culpeper County, Virginia, September 30, 1832. Her family moved to Philippi, Barbour County, in 1845. In 1852, Reeves married Granville E. Jarvis and two years later they moved to Taylor County. The Jarvis family grew quickly, but it was not a happy one. Only four of the couple's 12 children survived to adulthood.

From the depths of her loss came Jarvis's commitment to eradicating the unsanitary living conditions that often spread deadly diseases. She organized Mothers' Day Work Clubs which raised money to buy medicine for needy families and cared for families stricken by tuberculosis. Club members worked with local physicians to obtain clean water supplies and safe sewage disposal.

During the Civil War, Jarvis believed the work clubs to be neutral havens in the deeply divided north-central counties. Club members nursed both Union and Confederate soldiers. After the war, Jarvis planned a Mothers' Friendship Day to bring together veterans from both sides, and her clubs have been credited with helping their communities survive postwar enmities.

Anna Maria Reeves Jarvis died in Philadelphia, May 9, 1905. Her daughter, Anna, campaigned diligently for a day to commemorate the spirit of her mother's work. In 1914, President Woodrow Wilson signed a congressional resolution recognizing the second Sunday in May as Mother's Day.

See also Mother's Day

Christine M. Kreiser
Clarksburg

Jazz

West Virginia music is more than mountain fiddlers and ballad singers. The state has produced topnotch jazz musicians as well. Typically, they learned their music here but went on to build their professional careers on the national music scene.

Bandleader Don Redman (born Piedmont, Mineral County, 1900) was writing band arrangements while still in high school. After attending Storer College in Harpers Ferry, Redman went to New York to play saxophone with various outfits in the 1920s. Soon he was writing for Fletcher Henderson's pioneer big band, where he met young Louis Armstrong, with whom he recorded. He joined McKinney's Cotton Pickers in 1927 and made it an influential band. Redman's compositions included "Gee, Baby, Ain't I Good to You?" and "Chant of the Weed." He continued to lead groups and write for radio and television until his death in 1964.

Nearly as celebrated was Leon "Chu" Berry (born Wheeling, 1910). Noted for his strong tenor saxophone on up-tempo numbers, Berry worked with jazz greats Benny Carter, Roy Eldridge, and Lionel Hampton before fronting a combo with "Hot Lips" Page in 1940. Touring with Cab Calloway in October 1941, Berry was killed in a car accident in Ohio.

Garland Wilson and Teddy Weatherford were acclaimed pianists. Wilson (born Martinsburg, 1909) was first recorded by producer John Hammond in the 1930s. Like some other black musicians, Wilson became an expatriate and was living in Paris when he died in 1954. Weatherford (born Bluefield, 1903) made a flash in the 1920s and spent his last years in Asia.

Others who shone in the Swing Era included Tommy Benford, Hubert "Bumps" Myers, Billy Moore, Frankie Masters, and William "Keg" Purnell. Benford (born Charleston, 1905) was a drummer with Jelly Roll Morton, Fats Waller, and Duke Ellington. Myers (born Clarksburg, 1912) was a saxophonist with Jimmie Lunceford, Carter, and Hampton. Moore (born Parkersburg, 1917) was a pianist-arranger for Charlie Barnet and Tommy Dorsey. Masters (born Pleasants County, 1904), led a popular dance band for years. Purnell (born Charleston, 1915) was a drummer with Carter and Eddie Heywood.

Many jazz groups of the early 20th century played "Them There Eyes," "Sweet Georgia Brown," and other tunes written by Maceo Pinkard (born Bluefield, 1897).

More recently, Ernest Farrow (born Huntington, 1928) played bass for Stan Getz and Yusef Lateef. Musa Kaleem (born Orlando Wright, Wheeling, 1921) played sax with James Moody and Erroll Garner. Ray Wetzel (born Parkersburg, 1924) was a promising trumpeter with Woody Herman and Stan Kenton when he died in a car accident in 1951. Butch Miles grew up in Charleston and went on to play drums with Count Basie, Mel Torme, and Dave Brubeck. Winston Walls, another Charleston native, made a reputation playing Hammond organ.

Singer Ann Baker (1915–99), who lived for many years in Charleston, replaced Sarah Vaughan with Billy Eckstine's band in the 1940s and had a long solo career. Singers Iris Bell (born Charleston, 1934) and Jennie Smith (born 1938) of Fayette County toured with the likes of Lionel Hampton.

The last quarter century saw new faces in contemporary jazz. Bob Thompson, who has spent much of his life in Charleston, made more than a dozen albums and is known to many as the pianist on the "Mountain Stage" radio show produced by West Virginia Public Radio and distributed nationally by Public Radio International. One of his recordings, *Brother's Keeper,* was with John Blake, a fine violinist who attended West Virginia University. Soprano Saxophonist Marion Meadows, originally from Beckley, made a national mark with his albums for RCA.

There are many amateur and college jazz groups in West Virginia. The Shenandoah Jazz Band of Shepherd College, a group of professors and friends, plays Dixieland and swing at local festivals. The Gary Marvel big band played swing-style music throughout the Eastern Panhandle for a number of years in the 1980s and '90s. New River Jazz is a group of volunteer musicians from Raleigh, Fayette, and Nicholas counties that plays swing music. The Manhattan Jazz Quartet, a Lewisburg group, plays regularly at the Greenbrier resort.

Any discussion of Mountain State jazz must mention Hugh McPherson, who grew up during the 1920s, led a regional swing band and, from the 1940s into the 1980s, was the state's major, sometimes solitary, jazz disc jockey.

John Douglas
Berkeley Springs

Jefferson County

Located in the Eastern Panhandle, Jefferson County is the easternmost county of West Virginia, bounded by the Potomac River and Maryland on the north; the Blue Ridge Mountains and Loudoun County, Virginia, on the east; Clarke County, Virginia, on the south; and Berkeley County on the west. It occupies 212.4 square miles. Its municipalities include Charles Town, the county seat (established in 1786 by George Washington's brother, Charles); Ranson (1910); Harpers Ferry (1851); Bolivar (1825); and Shepherdstown (1762). Jefferson County was established from a portion of Berkeley County by the Virginia General Assembly on October 26, 1801. It was named for Thomas Jefferson.

The earliest permanent white settlement probably occurred in the second decade of the 18th century. Land speculators Joist Hite and John and Abraham Van Meter acquired large tracts in the Northern Neck of Virginia, which included present Jefferson County. Land was sold to German and English immigrants, many of them arriving from Pennsylvania, New Jersey, and Delaware. Shortly thereafter, other settlers arrived from the Tidewater area of Virginia. Many of the later arrivals received land from Thomas Lord Fairfax. As Hite's settlers and those holding grants from Fairfax began to lay claim to the same property, Fairfax and Hite engaged in a lawsuit in 1749. The suit was not settled until 1786, leaving local land titles in dispute for many years.

Historic Jefferson County Courthouse, Charles Town.

During the 1740s and 1750s, George Washington surveyed several plats in the Jefferson County area for Fairfax. Using his surveying fees, he purchased his first piece of land, from Robert Rutherford on Bullskin Run. Washington's brothers also acquired land in present Jefferson County, and the family flourished there until the Civil War. More Washington family descendants are buried in Jefferson County than in any other place. Several homes built by family members still grace the countryside.

The arrival from the north and east by Germans, English, and Scotch-Irish, and from the south of Virginia planters, created a cultural mix that persisted for much of the county's history. Shepherdstown and Harpers Ferry looked northward, developing strong economic ties with Baltimore and Hagerstown, Maryland, and Philadelphia, as well as nearby Martinsburg. Charles Town and Smithfield maintained ties with Winchester and the South. During the 1700s, the slave population was not large and was concentrated mostly on a few plantations, but by 1850 slaves numbered 3,960, or 27 percent of the total population.

For most of its history, Jefferson County's economy has been primarily agricultural, producing grain and other crops in the 18th and 19th centuries and orchard fruit in the late 19th and early 20th centuries. Limestone quarrying has also been important. Deposits of iron ore spurred the development of an iron industry along the Shenandoah River as early as 1742, and at Friend's Orebank along the Potomac east of Bakerton in the 1760s. Friend's Orebank operated for a century and a half, until World War I.

Two important events that shaped the future of Jefferson County were the

FAST FACTS ABOUT JEFFERSON COUNTY

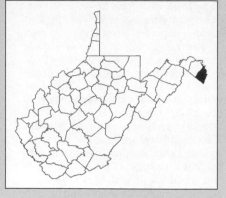

Founded: 1801

Land in square miles: 212.4

Population: 42,190

Percentage minorities: 9.0%

Percentage rural: 68.1%

Median age: 36.8

Percentage 65 and older: 11.2%

Birth rate per 1,000 population: 13.9

Median household income: $44,374

High school graduate or higher: 79.0%

Bachelor's degree or higher: 21.6%

Home ownership: 75.8%

Median home value: $116,700

This information is from the 2000 U.S. Census. In 2000, West Virginia as a whole had 5 percent minorities, a median age of 38.9, median household income of $29,696, and a 75.2 percent home ownership rate.

establishment of the federal armory at Harpers Ferry in 1799 and the arrival of the Baltimore & Ohio Railroad in 1834. John Brown's raid on Harpers Ferry was prompted by the presence of the armory, the town's proximity to defensible positions in the mountains, and the belief that the surrounding slave population would rise up and support the insurgents. Martin Robison Delany, born in Charles Town, was among 34 blacks who had met with Brown in Canada prior to the 1859 raid to develop a provisional constitution for the liberated slaves. During the Civil War, Delany became the first African-American field officer in the U.S. Army.

The presence of the B&O influenced the decision in 1863 to include Jefferson County in the new state of West Virginia, although most residents had sided with Virginia when the mother state seceded from the Union. Disenfranchised after the war because of their support of the Confederacy, they were unable to prevent the transfer of the courthouse from Charles Town to Shepherdstown in 1865. The county seat was returned to Charles Town in 1871, and relations between the two towns remained cool for decades.

Two treason trials were held in the Jefferson County courthouse. The first trial was of John Brown and the raiders who survived the 1859 raid. Brown was found guilty and hanged. A second series of treason trials was held at the same site in 1922. Defendants included Bill Blizzard, who allegedly led coal miners in the armed march culminating in the Battle of Blair Mountain. No one was convicted of treason in 1922.

Jefferson County's economy, particularly its growing industrial base, was hurt by the Civil War. The Harpers Ferry armory was not reopened after the war, and part of its facilities were used to establish an educational institution for African-Americans, Storer College, in 1869. Shepherd Normal School, established in Shep-

herdstown in 1871, later became Shepherd College (now University).

Jefferson County's population grew slowly from the end of the Civil War until World War II, to nearly 16,000. Agriculture remained the major source of revenue, with corn and wheat being the major crops. The orchard industry was introduced in the 1880s, and many dairy farms were established in the 1920s and 1930s. During the 1980s and 1990s, the number of farms declined, partly because of the decreased profitability of farming and partly because of the pressure exerted by residential development. By the year 2000, raising beef cattle and horse breeding were the most promising areas for agricultural growth. With the opening of the Charles Town Racetrack in 1933, Jefferson County became the first track in the state to offer parimutuel betting. The racetrack is still one of the major employers in the area.

In 1944, Congressman Jennings Randolph introduced legislation authorizing the purchase of land in Harpers Ferry for establishment of a national park. Harpers Ferry National Historical Park grew out of this effort. The facilities of Storer College were absorbed into the park when the college closed in 1960. The National Park Service also maintains design and interpretive centers at Harpers Ferry, which serve Park Service units nationwide. Since 1997, the U.S. Fish and Wildlife Service has operated its National Conservation Training Center at Shepherdstown. Recreational and historic tourism account for an increasing number of visitors to Jefferson County as well as growing revenues.

Like much of the neighboring area, Jefferson County began to grow more rapidly in the 1970s. Between 1970 and 2000, the number of residents increased from 21,280 to 42,190. During this period, the county experienced much residential growth without a proportionate

increase in its business and industrial base, as the majority of its people commuted outside of the county to work. The county is part of the metropolitan Washington area.

As it enters the 21st century, Jefferson County faces the challenge of balancing population growth with the need to preserve the environmental and historic resources that attract people to the area.

See also John Brown, Fairfax Lands, Harpers Ferry

William D. Theriault
Bakerton

Millard K. Bushong, *A History of Jefferson County, West Virginia*, 1941; Magazine of the Jefferson County Historical Society, 1935 to present.

Jefferson National Forest

The Jefferson National Forest, primarily located in southwest Virginia and southeast West Virginia, was established by President Roosevelt on April 21, 1936. The Jefferson is about 720,000 acres in size and is situated in the Ridge and Valley Physiographic Province including the Allegheny and Blue Ridge mountains. Jefferson National Forest lands stretch from Rockbridge County, Virginia, west into Letcher and Pike counties, Kentucky, and from Washington and Grayson counties, Virginia, north to Monroe County. The West Virginia portion of this forest contains 18,530 acres in Monroe County and is part of the New River Valley and New Castle Ranger Districts, accessible by State Routes 15, 17, and 20. Oak-pine forests cover the mountainous West Virginia forestlands, which range in elevation from 2,000 to 3,600 feet.

The Jefferson, along with all other national forests, is administered by the Forest Service, U.S. Department of Agriculture. The forest supervisor, located in Roanoke, Virginia, administers both the Jefferson and George Washington national forests. The early management focus was primarily aimed toward protection, with fire prevention in the slash-filled cut-over woods as a major concern. Forestlands have recovered since that time, and present policy is to manage for multiple resources including wood, water, wildlife, recreation, and livestock forage. A portion of the congressionally designated Mountain Lake Wilderness is situated in Monroe County, including parts of Potts and Little mountains.

See also National Forests

Walter A. Lesser
Elkins

Jefferson Rock

Jefferson Rock, a prominent outcropping of the sedimentary stone known as Harpers shale, is on the southern hillside of Harpers Ferry, just above St. Peter's Church. From it may be seen a prime view of the confluence of the Potomac and

Shenandoah rivers in the gap between the Maryland and Virginia heights.

The rock was named for Thomas Jefferson, who wrote in his 1785 book, *Notes on the State of Virginia*, that the view was "worth a voyage across the Atlantic." Other people would visit the rock afterward, and compare their impression with that of Jefferson. Some, including John Quincy Adams, made critical comparisons. "There is not much of the sublime in the scene, and those who first see it after reading Mr. Jefferson's description are usually disappointed," Adams wrote in 1834.

The uppermost slab of Jefferson Rock originally rested on a natural stone foundation that was reduced to unsafe dimensions by erosion and souvenir seekers. Four short stone piers were placed under the slab between 1855 and 1860 to stabilize and further distinguish the rock, making it seem to some as a "steam ferryboat" immortalized in stone.

Walton Danforth Stowell Jr.
Harpers Ferry

Jehovah's Witnesses

The religious movement eventually known as Jehovah's Witnesses originated in the late 1870s in Pittsburgh, and soon spread to West Virginia. Between 1882 and 1884, this group, then called Bible Students, mailed more than a million copies of the booklet *Food for the Thinking Christian* (1881). One of these reached James McClung, postmaster, justice of the peace, and pastor of Mt. Pleasant Baptist Church in Mt. Lookout, Nicholas County. McClung accepted the booklet's teachings and announced to his church that he understood the Bible in a "new light." Eight families accepted this new teaching. Contention arose over who would use the church building, McClung's followers or those preferring the traditional teachings of the congregation. For a period of time the first group to reach the Mt. Pleasant building had its use, but in 1890 the Bible Students built the New Light Church. Jehovah's Witnesses recognize Mt. Lookout as the first place their movement owned a building.

In the late 1920s, Jehovah's Witnesses from Mt. Lookout established congregations throughout central West Virginia. Congregations were founded in the northern part of the state by Witnesses from Pittsburgh. By the end of the 20th century there were more than 90 Jehovah's Witness congregations throughout West Virginia.

In the mid-1930s, Jehovah's Witnesses became the object of persecution across the United States, initially for their zeal in proselytizing and later for their refusal to salute the flag and what was seen as unpatriotic behavior as World War II approached. In the 1940s, they were violently attacked, often with the complicity of government officials, in Bluefield, Clarksburg,

Follansbee, Huttonsville, Keyser, Martinsburg, Morgantown, New Martinsville, Philippi, Richwood, St. Marys, Wellsburg, and Williamson. Throughout the state Jehovah's Witnesses' children were expelled from school for refusing to salute the flag. In response the Witnesses established several "Kingdom Schools" around the state, the first in September 1941, in Clarksburg. Three Kanawha County families filed court challenges to the expulsions and won a landmark U.S. Supreme Court decision in *West Virginia State Board of Education v. Barnette* (1943).

See also Barnette Case, Jehovah's Witnesses v. Pittsburgh Plate Glass Company, Catlette v. United States

Chuck Smith
West Virginia State University

Jehovah's Witnesses v. Pittsburgh Plate Glass Company

The December 1941 firing of seven Jehovah's Witnesses from the Pittsburgh Plate Glass plant in Clarksburg resulted in an extremely rare use of administrative law to expand legal protections of religious liberty. The case is also an example of the tenacity of Jehovah's Witnesses in using the legal system to advance religious freedom. The seven refused to participate in union-sponsored, flag-salute ceremonies at the plant. That resulted in their firing, when union truckers refused to accept glass the seven Jehovah's Witnesses produced.

Paul Schmidt, one of the seven, requested assistance from Eleanor Roosevelt, who referred his letter to the President's Committee on Fair Employment Practices. In April 1942, a committee investigator visited West Virginia to investigate the charges. In August, Schmidt traveled to Washington and entreated the committee to take action. On November 24, in the case identified as "In the matter of seven Jehovah's Witnesses v. Pittsburgh Plate Glass Company" the committee ruled in the workers' favor but suspended the ruling pending the glass company's response. On December 24, the committee ordered that the workers be reinstated with full seniority. They finally returned to work on March 2, 1943, after the committee had obtained assurances from the unions to prevent their harassment on the job.

See also Barnette Case, Catlette v. United States, Jehovah's Witnesses

Chuck Smith
West Virginia State University

Chuck Smith, "War Fever and Religious Fervor: The Firing of Jehovah's Witnesses Glassworkers in West Virginia and Administrative Protection of Religious Liberty," *American Journal of Legal History*, 1999; Smith, "Paul Schmidt: A Workingman's Tenacious Pursuit of Religious Liberty," *Journal of Law and Religion*, 1999–2000.

Albert Gallatin Jenkins

Congressman and Confederate General Albert Gallatin Jenkins was born November 10, 1830, at Green Bottom, Cabell County. He was educated at Marshall Academy (now Marshall University), Jefferson College, and Harvard Law School. Jenkins practiced law in Western Virginia and served in the U.S. Congress from 1857 to 1861.

At the start of the Civil War he enlisted recruits for a Virginia unit called the Border Rangers and was elected their captain. In July 1861, at Scary Creek in Putnam County, Jenkins's leadership was instrumental in defeating the Union force. In August he formed the 8th Virginia Cavalry (CSA) and became its colonel. In November Jenkins with other cavalry units staged a surprise raid on a Union camp at Guyandotte.

In early 1862, Jenkins was elected to the First Confederate Congress. In August he was appointed brigadier general. He went on to command a battalion of cavalry at the Battle of Gettysburg. Jenkins was recognized as a fearless cavalry raider.

In May 1864, Jenkins was wounded at Cloyd's Mountain, Virginia, and died on May 21. He now rests in the Confederate plot in Spring Hill Cemetery in Huntington. Jenkins's Green Bottom plantation house, maintained as an historic site by the West Virginia Division of Culture and History, was listed on the National Register of Historic Places in 1978.

See also Civil War, Battle of Scary Creek, Green Bottom

Jack L. Dickinson
Huntington

Jack L. Dickinson, *Jenkins of Greenbottom: A Civil War Saga*, 1988; Joe Geiger Jr., *Civil War in Cabell County, West Virginia 1861–1865*, 1991.

Jenkins Raid

On August 11, 1862, the federal government directed that 5,000 soldiers stationed in and near Charleston be brought to Washington, to be used in the more active eastern theater of war. This reduction of federal strength in the Kanawha Valley did not pass unnoticed. On August 18, Confederate Gen. William Wing Loring began planning an attack into the region. Loring sent his cavalry on an extensive sweep through the area north of the Kanawha Valley. Gen. Albert G. Jenkins, a Cabell County native, led the raiding party. He started from Salt Sulphur Springs in Monroe County on August 22, with 550 men.

Jenkins's troopers rode first into the Tygart Valley, skirmishing briefly with U.S. forces near Huttonsville. On August 30, the raiders attacked and occupied Buckhannon, where they captured 20 prisoners, 5,000 stands of small arms, and a vast supply of ordnance, stores and clothing. The following day Jenkins's men occupied Weston. They paroled a few prisoners, destroyed the telegraph office, and rode for Glenville. Remaining briefly at Glenville, the raiders arrived at Spencer on September 2. There they surprised and captured several companies of the 11th West Virginia Infantry. Arriving at Ripley, on September 3, the Confederates found no enemy force and captured the federal paymaster, relieving him of $5,525.

On September 4, Jenkins and his men crossed the Ohio River and became the first to raise the Confederate flag on Ohio soil. The following day they attacked federal forces at and near the Mason County courthouse, then moved into Buffalo, Putnam County. On September 8, Jenkins's raiders rode into Barboursville, skirmished with the enemy, remained there for two days, then rode into Wayne, Logan, and Raleigh counties. The Jenkins raid proved that Union defenses in the Kanawha Valley were inadequate and on September 12, 1862, a larger Confederate force captured Charleston, remaining there until mid-October.

See also Civil War, Albert Gallatin Jenkins

Tim McKinney
Fayetteville
Jack Dickinson, *The 8th Virginia Cavalry*, 1985; Tim McKinney, *The Civil War in Fayette County*, 1988.

Jennings Randolph Lake and Dam

Jennings Randolph Lake and Dam is located on the North Branch of the Potomac River, five miles north of Elk Garden, Mineral County. Originally named Bloomington Lake for nearby Bloomington, Maryland, the project was renamed in honor of U.S. Sen. Jennings Randolph. Completed in 1981 at a cost of $175 million, the dam is 296 feet high with a top length of 2,130 feet. It is one of the largest rock-filled, rolled-earth dams east of the Mississippi. Its reservoir has a capacity of 31 billion gallons.

Built to improve the water quality, the lake acts as a pollution trap. It has a control tower with five pairs of intakes located at different depths. Since the acid drainage from abandoned coal mines in the reservoir's watershed stratifies at different levels, regulating the outflow through the several intakes controls the acid content of the water released from the lake. This has resulted in improved water quality downstream, with the return of aquatic life and the establishment of a successful trout fishery at the base of the dam. The dam also helps to control flooding along the North Branch. Releases of water for whitewater rafters, kayakers, and canoeists are made from the reservoir on selected spring weekends. There are boat launches, scenic overlooks, a campground, and a picnic area at the lake. The lake is a handsome body of water and since its establishment has attracted nesting bald eagles and ospreys.

Gilbert Gude
Bethesda, Maryland

Jenny Lind House

The term "Jenny Lind," often applied generically in West Virginia to any building of simple construction, refers to a type of construction, not a building style.

A Jenny Lind house was built on a foundation of piers made from stone, block, brick, or wooden posts. The piers were aligned around the perimeter of the building, and across the center if the floor plan was large enough to require a central girder. Framing for the floor was formed by nailing together four planks set at right angles to each other, as if the builder were constructing the sides of a shallow box. This box sill sat on top of the piers and was supported by them. Floor joists spanned the inner space of the box, and plank flooring was nailed on top of the sill and joists.

The construction of the walls is a defining feature of the Jenny Lind style. The walls had no studs or internal framing. The vertical planks were attached directly to the outside of the box sill at the bottom and nailed at the top to a horizontal two-by-four ribbon board running around the entire perimeter of the house. These vertical plank walls were structural elements, supporting the roof. Some Jenny Lind houses had double-thick walls with vertical planks nailed on the inside as well as the outside. This was especially important if the house had two stories. Cracks opened between these planks as the wood cured, so three- or four-inch battens, also called weather stripping, were nailed over the cracks, resulting in another uniquely Jenny Lind characteristic, the board-and-batten pattern.

Roof construction was usually of conventional design, with joists and rafters. Once a popular technique for building inexpensive but durable houses, Jenny Lind construction is rarely seen today.

Ken Sullivan, "'Cheap, Quick and Drafty' The Jenny Lind House," *Goldenseal*, Spring 1990.

Jews

Jews have lived in West Virginia since long before the creation of the state. From the state's largest cities to some of its most rural hamlets, Jewish West Virginians have worked, raised families, and participated in local civic and social life, while forming their own religious congregations and adapting their cultural traditions to the West Virginia milieu.

Jewish migration to Western Virginia mirrored the broader migration of Jews to the United States: first came the Ger-

David Scott, a Jewish merchant of McDowell County.

mans, then the East Europeans. From 1840 to 1880, adverse economic conditions and governmental repression in Germany caused Jews to move to the United States in the hundreds of thousands. Many gravitated to small cities and towns in the nation's interior, where they could resume their traditional "old country" occupations as peddlers and merchants.

Jewish immigrants settled on the (West) Virginia side of the Ohio River as early as the 1770s. The first Jewish community in Western Virginia formed in Wheeling by the mid-1840s, establishing a religious congregation in 1849. German Jews came to Charleston in the 1850s and formed a congregation in 1873. Some family names descending from these German Jews are familiar to Charlestonians today and include May, Loewenstein, Frankenberger, Hess, Peyser, Jelenko, Loeb, Baer, Kleeman, Mayer, and Schwabe. By 1880, Jews lived in most of the developed areas of the state, including Clarksburg, Huntington, and Parkersburg. Others traveled the mountains with packs on their backs, bringing the goods of the town into the countryside, much as Jews had done in Europe.

After 1880, the state's German Jews were joined by a much larger East European contingent. Between 1880 and 1920, social and economic upheaval in Russia, Poland, and Austria-Hungary caused two million Jews to emigrate to America. The vast majority settled in major cities. However, their arrival coincided with the explosive growth of West Virginia's coal industry, and some Jewish immigrants in Baltimore and New York, hearing of the potential the state's growing economy offered to small business-people, found their way to the coalfields. By the 1920s, they had significantly increased the Jewish populations of older settled areas such as Charleston and had also established Jewish communities in developing coal and steel towns such as Beckley, Logan, Welch, Weirton, and Williamson. Meanwhile, smaller towns from Monongah in the north to Anawalt in the south to Sutton in the agricultural heartland became home to tiny clusters of Jews.

In all these places, Jews settled into the occupation they knew best: retailing. They were often the developers and mainstays of downtown business districts. Some became involved in local politics, many others in civic organizations and social clubs. Notable Jewish political figures have included Congressman Ben Rosenbloom of Wheeling, West Virginia Supreme Court Justice Fred Caplan, and mayors of Huntington, Glen Jean, Keystone, Northfork, and Romney.

Anxious to preserve their religion and heritage, Jews have formed their own organizations and participated in local, national, and international Jewish causes. Their religious life has centered around local synagogues, where they attend services, celebrate Jewish holidays, and provide a religious education for their children. All three branches of Judaism—Reform, Conservative, and Orthodox—have been represented in the state.

Jews have always been a tiny minority in West Virginia. At its height in the early 1950s, the Jewish population of the state probably reached no more than about 7,000. The decline of the state's economy caused the out-migration of West Virginians of all backgrounds, including Jews. The number of Jews in smaller towns dwindled, in many cases, to none. Congregations that once existed in towns such as Fairmont, Keystone, Kimball, Logan, Weirton, and Welch are gone. Today, West Virginia's Jews, numbering about 2,500, are concentrated in the largest cities: Charleston, Huntington, and Wheeling. Small congregations also exist in Beckley, Bluefield, Clarksburg, Martinsburg, Morgantown, Parkersburg, and Williamson.

Deborah R. Weiner
Jewish Museum of Maryland

Job's Temple

Job's Temple, a church nestled on a hillside near the confluence of Job's Run and the Little Kanawha River in Gilmer County, had its origins in the differences leading up to the Civil War. The church was an offshoot of an earlier congregation, Pisgah Methodist Episcopal Church, located two miles to the east. Differences of opinion in the community brought

about the need for separate places of worship. Job's Temple was established as a Methodist Episcopal Church, South.

The log structure was constructed about 1861–65. Built of hand-hewn yellow poplar logs, it is 30 feet by 24 feet. The interior is finished with hand-planed poplar boards. Regular services were suspended about 1912, and the church was neglected until the 1930s when a campaign was launched to preserve it. Extensive efforts were made in the 1950s to further restore the historic building. The Job's Temple Association was incorporated in 1978. The following year the log church was placed on the National Register of Historic Places. The historic cemetery includes 141 graves.

The tradition of annual homecomings initiated in 1936 has continued to the present, with the exception of three years during World War II when gasoline was rationed. Each year on the second Sunday of August more than a hundred descendants and friends gather from several states to worship at Job's Temple.

Doris M. Radabaugh
Parkersburg

Fanny Kemble Johnson

Author Fanny Kemble Johnson, born May 22, 1868, in Rockbridge County, Virginia, wrote short stories and poetry. She began her writing career shortly after moving to West Virginia in 1897. Johnson married Vincent Costello two years later. They moved from Charleston to Wheeling in 1907, and back to Charleston in 1917. Her only published novel, *The Beloved Son* (1916), is set in the Natural Bridge area of Virginia, where she was raised.

Johnson's work can be found in such diverse places as Ella Mae Turner's 1923 compilation, *Stories and Verse of West Virginia,* and in *Weird Tales*, the pulp magazine in which her story, "The Dinner Set," was published in 1935. Her short stories appeared in some of the early 20th century's leading literary magazines, including the *Atlantic Monthly, Harper's,* and *Century*. Her story "The Strange Looking Man" was included in a best short stories collection of 1917, and her "They Both Needed It" was among the best short stories of 1918. In 2000, "The Strange Looking Man" was included in the Oxford University Press anthology *Women's Writing on the First World War*. Johnson died February 15, 1950, in Charleston.

Christine M. Kreiser
Clarksburg

Kitty Frazier, *West Virginia Women Writers, 1822–1979,* 1979; "West Virginia Women and the Arts," WVU Public History Program, 1990.

Johnnie Johnson

Rock 'n' roll pioneer Johnnie Johnson was born July 8, 1924, in Fairmont. He began playing the piano at the age of five.

The son of a coal miner, Johnson grew up listening to "hillbilly" and big band music. He left West Virginia in 1941, during World War II, to work in a Detroit defense plant. He entered the Marines in 1943 as one of the first 1,500 African-Americans admitted to the Corps, and became a member of the Special Service Band.

Johnson performed in Chicago from 1946 to 1952, before moving to St. Louis. It was there that he formed his own band—the Johnnie Johnson Trio—and on New Year's Eve 1952 he hired rock 'n' roll pioneer Chuck Berry. Johnson soon became Berry's piano player and collaborated with Berry on songs that form the foundation of rock 'n' roll, including "Maybellene," "Sweet Little Sixteen," "School Days," and "Roll Over, Beethoven." Berry's hit "Johnny B. Goode" was written as a tribute to Johnson.

Johnson played at both of Bill Clinton's presidential inaugurations and at the Kennedy Center in Washington. In September 1999, the U.S. Congressional Black Caucus awarded him a congressional citation. In 2000, Johnson was inducted into the Rock 'n' Roll Hall of Fame in the sidemen category.

Johnnie Johnson died April 13, 2005.

Shirley L. Stewart
West Virginia University

Travis Fitzpatrick, *Father of Rock & Roll: The Story of Johnnie "B. Goode" Johnson,* 1999.

Joseph Johnson

Virginia Governor Joseph Johnson, born in Orange County, New York, December 19, 1785, later lived in New Jersey and traveled with his mother and younger brother to Winchester, Virginia, in 1800. Leaving Winchester in the spring of 1801, they journeyed west and settled in Harrison County.

There Johnson began working for Ephraim Smith as his farm manager. Shortly after Smith's death, Johnson married Sarah (Sally), one of Smith's daughters, on May 16, 1804, and settled on the Smith farm. There they lived and raised 13 children. In 1807, Joseph acquired additional acreage on Simpson Creek, where four years later he built a water-powered mill that he owned and operated until January 18, 1854. He continued to manage the farm and mill and became a land speculator.

Early in his political career Johnson allied himself with the party of Thomas Jefferson, then known as Republicans and later as Democrats. In 1811, he was appointed a constable, and during the War of 1812 he became captain of the Harrison Riflemen and marched his company to Norfolk in 1814. In 1815, Johnson successfully ran for the House of Delegates and secured the passage of an act establishing the town of Bridgeport on 15 acres of his land at Simpsons Creek Bridge. Between 1815 and 1821, he served five terms in the Virginia House of Delegates.

Johnson was elected to the U.S. House of Representatives in 1822. Between 1823 and 1847 he served 13 years in Congress. Interested as many westerners were in internal improvements, he served on the Committee on the Cumberland Road and supported road, canal, railroad, and navigation bills. On the tariff issue Johnson frequently voted to protect domestic industries. Closer to home, he fought to extend postal routes into the western counties and opposed proposals to close post offices in his district.

In 1847, he again ran for the House of Delegates and represented Harrison and Doddridge counties for one term. In August 1850, Johnson was one of four delegates elected to represent the six counties in his district in the Virginia Constitutional Convention of 1850–51. As the oldest member, he called the convention to order on October 15, 1850. Johnson chaired the suffrage committee, which recommended universal white adult male suffrage with residency requirements. He vigorously defended the report against all efforts to add payment of a tax as a requirement to vote. Western Virginia won important reforms at the convention.

In March 1851, Johnson was elected governor of Virginia by the General Assembly, to take office January 1, 1852. Meanwhile, the new constitution, which called for the popular election of the governor, was under consideration by Virginia voters. The popular election rule would prevail if the constitution was ratified. After the convention adjourned on August 1, 1851, the Democratic convention met in Staunton, and Johnson was nominated to run for governor by his party.

The new constitution was adopted, and Johnson won the election and became the first popularly elected governor in Virginia history. He assumed the governor's office on January 1, 1852, by right of his election by the General Assembly. On January 15, 1852, he was declared the winner of the popular election and accepted the office on that basis on January 16. Johnson spent his four-year term implementing the new constitution, promoting internal improvements, and encouraging development of Virginia's natural resources, and manufacturing and agricultural interests through a statewide railroad system. Although a states-rights, slave-owning Democrat, Johnson vigorously condemned the fugitive slave laws and championed the right of blacks to receive equal protection under Virginia's laws.

After leaving office on January 1, 1856, Johnson returned to Bridgeport. In 1860, he served as a member of the electoral college. While opposing secession generally he nonetheless supported Virginia's decision to secede, espoused the Confederate cause, and then served as a presidential elector for Jefferson Davis. When Union forces occupied the Bridgeport area, he left and spent the war years near Staunton. Returning to Bridgeport and the new state of West Virginia after the war, Johnson spent his remaining years there. A Baptist by faith, he was baptized into Simpson Creek Baptist Church on June 2, 1866. He died in Bridgeport, February 27, 1877, and was buried in the old Brick Church Cemetery next to his wife, who had died in 1853.

Louis H. Manarin
Richmond, Virginia

George W. Atkinson and Alvaro F. Gibbens, *Prominent Men of West Virginia*, 1890; Catherine Johnson Patton Clark, "Governor Joseph Johnson," *Southern Magazine*, 1936; Bart Earl Kester, "Joseph Johnson, Governor of Virginia," M. A. thesis, West Virginia University, 1939.

Louis A. Johnson

Attorney Louis A. Johnson was born January 10, 1891, in Roanoke, Virginia, although he spent most of his life in Clarksburg. He was the boxing and wrestling champion at the University of Virginia, where he received his law degree. Following overseas service in World War I, he rose to become national commander of the American Legion. He was admitted to the bar in Clarksburg in 1913. He soon joined the firm of Steptoe and Pixley, which later became Steptoe and Johnson, an influential firm with offices in Clarksburg, Charleston, and Washington.

From 1937 to 1940, Johnson served in the Franklin Roosevelt administration as assistant secretary of war. He then resumed the practice of law at Steptoe and Johnson. In the election of 1948, Johnson chaired President Truman's finance committee which helped engineer Truman's surprise upset victory over Thomas E. Dewey. On March 28, 1949, Johnson was appointed U.S. secretary of defense to succeed the ailing James V. Forrestal. He feuded with other cabinet members and infuriated Truman by openly trying to undermine Secretary of State Dean Acheson, leading Truman to fire Johnson on September 19, 1950. Johnson spent most of his remaining years in Washington. He died there April 24, 1966.

Ken Hechler
Charleston

Frances Benjamin Johnston

Photographer Frances Benjamin Johnston was born in Grafton, January 15, 1864, but spent much of her youth in Rochester, New York, and in Washington. She began studying art at Notre Dame Convent in Govanston, Maryland, as an adolescent. From 1883 to 1885, she studied at the Académie Julian in Paris. She later continued her education at the Art Students League in New York.

Johnston began her professional life as an artist-reporter. Sensing a changing trend in journalistic illustration while working as the Washington correspondent for a New York newspaper, she turned to photography, studying under Thomas William Smillie, then head of the Division of Photography at the Smithsonian Institution. She soon achieved national renown as the first woman press photographer. She went on to enjoy a long and remarkable career as one of the leading documentary, portrait, and artistic photographers in the District of Columbia and the nation. She received employment from the Benjamin Harrison and William Taft presidential administrations.

Among Johnston's most significant achievements was a photographic survey of early American architecture of the South, conducted from 1933 to 1941 with the support of the Carnegie Corporation. Her work is represented in many museums, including the Museum of Modern Art in New York, the Baltimore Museum of Art, and the Library of Congress. Johnston died in Washington, March 16, 1952.

John A. Cuthbert
WVU Libraries

Pete Daniel and Ray Smock, *A Talent for Detail: The Photographs of Miss Frances Benjamin Johnston*, 1974.

Jones Diamond

Happenstance and a game of horseshoes led to the finding of the Jones Diamond. The diamond, also called the Horseshoe Diamond, was found on Rich Creek, near Peterstown in Monroe County, on Annie and Grover Jones's property. The Jones family had 17 children, the first 16 of whom were boys, a record for consecutive male births that landed the Joneses in Ripley's *Believe It or Not*.

In 1928, while pitching horseshoes, Grover and his oldest son, William "Punch" Jones, found a shiny stone. Punch carried it home, placed it in a box in the tool shed, and forgot about it. During World War II, Punch worked at an ammunition plant, using carbons to make gunpowder. Knowing that diamonds are a crystalline form of carbon, he wondered about the shiny stone he had picked up years earlier. His hunch was confirmed when a geologist at Virginia Polytechnic Institute pronounced the stone an alluvial diamond.

The blue-white gem weighed 34.46 carats and measured 5/8 inch in diameter. One of a few diamonds found in America, it is uncertain how the stone came to Rich Creek. From 1944 to 1968, the Jones Diamond was on display at the Smithsonian Institution. Upon return to West Virginia, it was exhibited at the State Fair. The Joneses owned the diamond until the early 1980s, when it was sold by Sotheby's for an undisclosed amount.

Nancy Clark,"Horseshoe Pitchers Discover Huge Diamond in the Rough," *Wonderful West Virginia*, 1981; Arnout Hyde Jr., *New River: A Photographic Essay*, 1991; Charles B. Motley, *Gleanings of Monroe County*, 1973.

Harriet B. Jones

Physician Harriet B. Jones was born June 3, 1856, in Ebensburg, Pennsylvania, but she grew up in Terra Alta, Preston County. She attended the Wheeling Female College and graduated from the Women's Medical College of Baltimore in 1875. Specializing in gynecology and abdominal surgery, Jones opened a private practice in Wheeling in 1886, becoming the first woman licensed to practice medicine in West Virginia.

Jones served as the assistant superintendent of the state hospital in Weston from 1888 to 1892, when she returned to Wheeling to open a women's hospital. A public health crusader, Jones was secretary of the West Virginia Anti-Tuberculosis League, which sponsored educational programs in every county. She campaigned vigorously for the establishment of Hopemont Sanitarium, which opened near Terra Alta in 1913. She also supported the creation of the West Virginia Children's Home and the West Virginia Industrial Home for Girls.

Jones was active in the West Virginia Federation of Women's Clubs and the Women's Christian Temperance Union. As a staunch advocate of women's rights, Jones was an officer in the West Virginia Equal Suffrage Association. After women won the vote in 1920, she was elected as a Republican from Marshall County to a term in the state House of Delegates in 1924. Jones died June 28, 1943.

Christine M. Kreiser
Clarksburg

Jim Comstock, ed., *West Virginia Women*, 1974; Barbara J. Howe, "West Virginia Women's Organizations, 1880s–1930 or 'Unsexed Termagants . . . Help the World Along,'" *West Virginia History*, 1990.

Mother Jones

The agitator Mary Harris "Mother" Jones, a leader in the American labor movement from the 1890s until her death in 1930, made a profound impression on West Virginia.

An Irish immigrant, Mary Harris was born in probably 1837. Her family arrived at Boston in 1850, then followed her father's work as a railroad construction laborer into Canada. She attended Toronto Normal School, leaving in 1859 to teach in a convent school in Michigan. She later taught in Memphis, where her husband, George, and four children died during a yellow fever epidemic in 1867. Returning north, Jones operated a dressmaking business in Chicago until 1871 when the

Mary Harris "Mother" Jones (1837–1930).

Great Fire burned up the business and her possessions.

Then she turned to the cause of labor, becoming a surrogate mother to the nation's workers. In 1897, she joined Eugene Debs's Social Democracy and the United Mine Workers of America national strike in the Pittsburgh district, the first UMWA victory. Jones joined the UMWA's organizing drive in the Pennsylvania anthracite region, and was commissioned a national organizer. Sent to survey the West Virginia coalfields in December 1900, she reported that "conditions there were worse than those in Czarist Russia."

Jones returned to West Virginia the next May and many times afterward. Short and sturdy, silver-haired with glasses, she dressed in conventional black but wore boots on her feet. After a year in the New River coalfield, Jones was sent to the Fairmont field. Two weeks after a strike was called in June 1902, she was arrested and taken to Parkersburg for violating Judge John J. Jackson's injunction. When freed, she returned to New River, where the strike continued until the bloody Battle of Stanaford in February 1903.

After seeing UMWA locals established in the Kanawha Valley and the reorganization of the West Virginia Federation of Labor, Mother Jones answered a call from striking textile workers in Philadelphia. She returned to West Virginia in 1912 to aid union miners on Paint Creek and Cabin Creek. During this violent conflict, Jones was arrested in Charleston. Taken to Pratt she was court-martialed and held under house arrest from February to May, 1913, when she precipitated a congressional investigation.

After testifying before another congressional committee in 1915, and forsaking

the Socialists, Mother Jones returned to West Virginia in 1917 where she held meetings and gained union recognition in the Fairmont and Winding Gulf coalfields. She joined the steelworkers' organizing drive in Pittsburgh in 1919, then traveled back to the hills of West Virginia and on to Mexico City. She returned to West Virginia by 1921 when the miners rebuffed her attempt to block their 1921 March on Logan. She then went to Washington, sick in mind and body. She recovered enough to write her autobiography and in 1924 to call on Governor Morgan, seeking pardons for miners imprisoned after the Logan March. Despite failing health, she tried to stop John L. Lewis's takeover of the UMWA.

On May 1, 1930, Mother Jones celebrated her birthday in Maryland. One hundred years old, by her count, she made her debut before newsreel cameras, condemning the Prohibition Act "as a curse upon the nation" that violated her right to have a beer instead of water.

Mother Jones died November 30, 1930, and is buried in Mount Olive, Illinois.

See also Mine Wars

Lois C. McLean
Beckley

Dale Featherling, *Mother Jones, the Miners' Angel*, 1974; Elliott J. Gorn, *Mother Jones: The Most Dangerous Woman In America*, 2001; Mary Jones, *The Autobiography of Mother Jones*, 1925.

S. L. Jones

Folk artist Shields Landon Jones was widely recognized for his hand-carved, painted wood sculptures. Jones was born October 17, 1901, and grew up on a farm in western Monroe County, one of 11 children. Remarking on his childhood, Jones said, "I wasn't a very good student because I spent too much time drawing pictures." He spent his adult life in Summers County, working 46 years in railroad construction. Jones, a Primitive Baptist, began his artistic career following retirement.

Discovered in 1972 at Pipestem State Park by the nationally renowned folk art collector, Herbert Wade Hemphill Jr., Jones moved from small whittled animals to the human figure, beginning with portrait-size heads. His sculpture is smoothly contoured, complemented by flat colors applied to facial features, hair, and clothing. Jones attached carved accents, notably crisp bow ties for men and hemispheric breasts for women, with some of his figures carrying musical instruments, tools, or other objects.

When declining health forced Jones to cease carving, he concentrated on drawing and painting, which has been collected as "Outsider" or non-academic art. His artwork is in the permanent collections of the National Museum of American Art, the Museum of American Art, the Museum of American Folk Art, and

Folk carvings by S. L. Jones.

West Virginia coal mining, said in his report that the raiders covered 700 miles, fought two battles and several skirmishes, and captured nearly 700 prisoners, 1,000 cattle, and 1,200 horses. In addition to the oil, they burned 16 railroad bridges and a tunnel, two trains of cars and several boats. However, the damages were short-lived, and the Confederates never seriously threatened the area again.

See also Burning Springs, Civil War, George W. Imboden, John D. Imboden, William Lyne Wilson

Gerald D. Swick
Nashville, Tennessee

Stan Cohen, *The Civil War in West Virginia: A Pictorial History*, 1976; Boyd B. Stutler, *West Virginia in the Civil War*, 1966.

Joy Loading Machine

By replacing the labor-intensive job of hand-loading coal, the Joy loading machine helped revolutionize mining in the 20th century. When it was introduced in the 1920s, the Joy loader was one of several coal-loading machines on the market. The Joy displaced the others because it required less maintenance, could be moved easily, and was more adaptable to various coal seams and different mining conditions. A simple machine, the Joy loader featured two arms attached to the front of a short conveyor belt. The arms moved in a wide sweep, gathering loose coal and scooping it onto the conveyor belt, which then deposited the load into a shuttle car.

Inventor Joseph Francis Joy was born in Cumberland, Maryland, September 13,

the West Virginia State Museum. Jones's creations were sold in art galleries from New York to Texas. S. L. Jones died December 15, 1997.

Fawn Valentine
Alderson

Jones-Imboden Raid

Between April 24 and May 22, 1863, Confederate cavalry under Generals William E. "Grumble" Jones and John D. Imboden carried the Civil War into north-central West Virginia. Their goals were to disrupt the Baltimore & Ohio Railroad at Oakland, Maryland, and at Grafton, cut telegraph communication, and weaken federal control in the area.

The Confederates made a two-prong attack, with Imboden riding from Staunton through Beverly to Buckhannon with 3,365 men. Jones led 2,100 men through Petersburg and Moorefield, skirmished at Greenland Gap in Hardy County, then was repulsed at Rowlesburg. He fell upon Morgantown, April 28, capturing supplies and many horses, including those of curiosity-seekers who came to town to learn what the excitement was. One of the Confederate raiders, future Postmaster General William Lyne Wilson, later returned to Morgantown as president of West Virginia University.

On April 29, at Fairmont, Jones waged the largest battle ever fought in that part of the state against a force of 500 regulars, home guards, and volunteers. There was some civilian involvement on both sides of the fight. The Confederates prevailed, burning the personal library of Francis H. Pierpont, governor of the Restored Government of Virginia, and exploding an iron railroad bridge across

the Monongahela River. Jones linked up with Imboden at Buckhannon, skirmishing along the way, and together they moved to Weston. Jones continued west to Burning Springs, where he set fire to an estimated 150,000 barrels of oil and the producing wells, sending a sheet of flame floating down the Little Kanawha River.

Imboden, later associated with his brother, George, in the development of

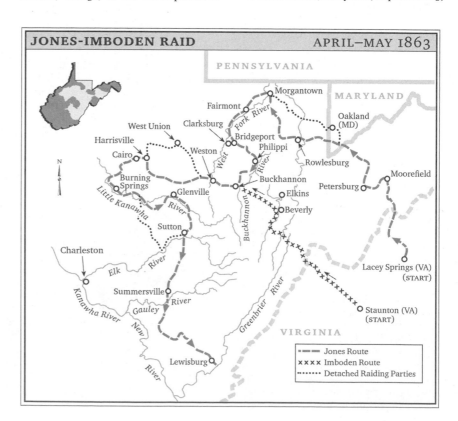

JONES-IMBODEN RAID   APRIL–MAY 1863

PENNSYLVANIA

MARYLAND

Morgantown

Fairmont

Oakland (MD)

West Union   Clarksburg

Harrisville

Cairo   Weston   Bridgeport   Philippi

Rowlesburg

Moorefield

Burning Springs

Glenville   Buckhannon   Petersburg

Elkins

Beverly

Sutton

Charleston

Little Kanawha River

West Fork River

Buckhannon River

Lacey Springs (VA) (START)

Summersville

Staunton (VA) (START)

Elk River

Gauley River

Kanawha River

New River

Greenbrier River

VIRGINIA

Lewisburg

- – - Jones Route
- xxxx Imboden Route
- ····· Detached Raiding Parties

1883. He was introduced to coal mining at a young age, and himself had loaded coal in the old way. In 1919, he won a patent for his design of a mechanical loader, which became the Joy loading machine and in its various models dominated the market for coal-loading equipment for decades. Some of the first Joy loaders were shipped to Logan County and installed in a mine owned by Harry S. Gay.

The Joy loader's use was at its peak in the mid- to late-1950s, and at that time there were models for coal seams of different heights. By 1954, the Joy Manufacturing Company said that 72 percent of all coal loaded mechanically was loaded by Joy loaders. In many areas the Joy name was synonymous with coal loading, and the job of Joy operator was a coveted position on a mine crew. The continuous miner, a machine that extracted coal and loaded it as well, eventually replaced loading machines.

At the turn of the 21st century, Joy loaders were still being used in three Consol Energy mines and one Eastern-Peabody mine in northern West Virginia. However, they were not being used independently but in conjunction with continuous miners. Joseph Joy died in February 1957, in Fort Pierce, Florida.

Keith Dix, *What's a Coal Miner to Do?: The Mechanization of Coal Mining,* 1988.

Judicial Branch

The constitution of West Virginia mandates a government divided into the legislative, executive, and judicial departments (Article V). The constitution vests the state's judicial power in a Supreme Court of Appeals and circuit courts and in the intermediate appellate courts and magistrate courts that the legislature might establish (Article VIII).

When West Virginia separated from Virginia, its court system mirrored that of the mother state. The Constitution of 1863 established the Supreme Court of Appeals, with three justices, and 11 circuit courts, and it provided several justices of the peace for every county. The justice of the peace courts were substantially the same as those established by Virginia in 1662. These courts decided minor civil controversies and acted as conservators of the peace until they were replaced by the magistrate courts in 1974. Besides the court structure, West Virginia also retained much of Virginia's system of laws. In fact, the Constitution of 1863 adopted Virginia common law and statutes as the law of West Virginia until such time as they were changed or repealed by the legislature. Some common law decisions made by Virginia courts are still part of the laws of the Mountain State.

The Constitution of 1872, now in force, increased the number of Supreme Court justices to four (now five) and strength-ened the justices of the peace. The county commissioners, who replaced the township system of local government, had some judicial powers and commonly were referred to as the county court.

The most important modern event in the development of the West Virginia judiciary was the people's ratification of the Judicial Reorganization Amendment on November 5, 1974. It reorganized a court structure that had remained virtually the same since the attainment of statehood. The catalyst for judicial reform was in the decision *State ex rel. Reece v. Giles, J. P.* (1973), wherein the Supreme Court of Appeals held that the system of funding justice of the peace courts from fines was unconstitutional.

The amendment that followed replaced the justice of the peace courts with a system of magistrate courts, and gave the legislature the authority to establish a court of appeals between the circuit courts and the Supreme Court. Most importantly, the Judicial Reorganization Amendment created a modern unified court system, a simple, integrated hierarchy of courts. At its base is a magistrate court in each county; these courts process criminal misdemeanors and minor civil cases. Important litigation takes place in 31 circuit courts, which are the state's comprehensive general jurisdiction trial courts. These courts have jurisdiction in all criminal, civil, and juvenile matters. The legislature has not yet created the intermediate appellate court allowed by the 1974 amendment. West Virginia is the most populated of the 11 states without such a court.

At the pinnacle of the system is the Supreme Court of Appeals, the court of last resort which must dispose of all petitions for appeal and decide those it chooses to hear. The court also serves as the administrative authority over the unified court system. In this capacity, it establishes procedural rules, determines policies for fiscal and staff management, supervises the caseload of the courts, and oversees the ethics for the bench and bar.

The Supreme Court accomplishes these responsibilities with the assistance of the administrative office of the courts. The director of the office is appointed by the court and serves as the administrative officer of the court system. This office also coordinates the training of circuit judges and magistrates. It encourages judges to seek training in such programs as the National Judicial College. It also conducts judicial training conferences that provide information on changes in state law and federal decisions that affect procedures, and reviews current trends in law, criminal sentencing, and other timely subjects. Almost every magistrate is a non-lawyer. Magistrates must attend considerable classroom training and pass exams on law and procedure. West Virginia's train-ing program for magistrates exceeds the training for non-lawyer judges provided by most states.

The Judicial Reorganization Amendment empowered the Supreme Court to promulgate rules. These rules govern people's access to the courts, how courts operate, the cost of using the courts, and the evidence and procedures allowed in litigation. Compared to other states, West Virginia's Supreme Court exercises considerable management over the courts.

The unified court system allows for centralized financial and personnel management. The administrative office oversees some aspects of personnel policy for nonjudicial personnel. It keeps statistics on the operations of all state courts, purchases their supplies and equipment, and gives other administrative assistance. The office also prepares the budget for all state courts. The constitution (Article VI, section 51) prevents the state legislature from decreasing any item in the budget submitted by the judiciary. A 1978 legislative attempt to decrease the judicial budget resulted in a lawsuit that confirmed the court's inherent power over the judiciary's budget (*State ex rel. Bagley v. Blankenship,* 1978).

The Supreme Court of Appeals, as the state's only appellate court, has an enormous workload. The court has complete discretion over its docket; citizens have no constitutional or statutory right to have any case or controversy reviewed by the court. The court must, as a practical matter, respond to significant political, social, and legal questions. As the number of appeals increased after 1960, the court moved from two annual sessions to meeting nearly continuously. It is among the busiest appellate courts in America. In 2004, the court heard 2,449 cases and issued 159 opinions and 434 orders.

West Virginians choose their judges in partisan elections; between elections, vacant judgeships are filled by appointment. The state's judges tend to keep in touch with the people and are aware of the practical significance of their decisions. Judges are participants in the political process. Although they have constraints on them not shared by members of the legislative and executive branches of government, judges make decisions of important political, social, and economic consequence.

For a number of important issues, the Supreme Court of Appeals is a noteworthy entity in West Virginia policymaking. At times the court's decisions create new public policy or incrementally adjust existing policy. It is important to note, however, that in most of its cases the court engages in straightforward application of West Virginia statutes and common law. Innovations and changes made in public policy by the court play an important role in policymaking, but are a small proportion of the court's decisions.

The court has made many important innovations in West Virginia law. For example, the court narrowed the immunity of employers from suits by injured workers (*Mandolidis v. Elkins Industries*, 1978), holding that workers' compensation coverage did not bar suit against intentional employer negligence. In *Pauley v. Kelly* (1979), the court ruled that unequal per-pupil funding among West Virginia counties violated the state constitution's mandate for a "thorough and efficient" school system. A complete restructuring of the prison system was required by the decision in *Crain v. Bordenkircher* (1986).

See also Courts, Judicial Reorganization Amendment, Supreme Court of Appeals

Chuck Smith
West Virginia State University

John Patrick Hagan, "Political Activism in the West Virginia Supreme Court of Appeals, 1930–1985," *West Virginia Law Review*, 1986; John C. Kilwein, "The West Virginia Judicial System at the Crossroads of Change," *The West Virginia Public Affairs Reporter*, 1999; John W. Mason, "The Origin and Development of the Judicial System of West Virginia," in Callahan, ed., *Semi-Centennial History of West Virginia*, 1913.

Judicial Reorganization Amendment

The Judicial Reorganization Amendment was the most significant modern restructuring of the West Virginia judiciary. It was one of several amendments to the West Virginia constitution that took effect during the first two terms of Governor Moore and together reorganized state government. Ratified by state voters on November 5, 1974, by a vote of 217,732 for and 127,393 against, the amendment brought major changes to West Virginia's courts and county governments.

Prior to the amendment, counties were governed by administrative bodies that were referred to as "county courts." Proponents of the amendment argued that the name was misleading because the so-called county courts were actually executive administrators of county government, with only minor judicial functions. The Judicial Reorganization Amendment designated county courts with a more fitting title, county commissions.

The other major changes all dealt with the internal structure of West Virginia's judicial system. Under the amendment, the judges of the West Virginia Supreme Court of Appeals were renamed as justices, and the president of the Supreme Court was designated its chief justice.

More significantly, the amendment eliminated the longstanding justice of the peace system and replaced it with a modern magistrate court system. Magistrate courts were established in each county, responsible for adjudicating criminal misdemeanors as well as civil cases where the amount in controversy was no greater than $1,500. County magistrates were to be elected by the voters of each county. The amendment provided that all magistrate court verdicts were subject to review by the state's circuit courts.

Circuit courts, in addition to having appellate review over all magistrate court decisions, were provided with original jurisdiction over felony criminal cases, civil cases where the amount totaled more than $1,500, and cases involving a juvenile. Circuit court verdicts were placed under the appellate control of the West Virginia Supreme Court of Appeals. The Judicial Reorganization Amendment also gave the state legislature the opportunity to create an intermediate court of appeals between the state's circuit courts and the Supreme Court, to alleviate the Supreme Court's large appellate case load; however the legislature has never exercised this option.

See also Constitution of West Virginia

Benjamin Sullivan
Charleston

Judy Gap

Judy Gap, located in western Pendleton County at an elevation of 2,180 feet, is an erosional notch in standing beds of the hard Tuscarora Sandstone, a major ridge-forming stratum. The standing beds at this location are the west limb of the Wills Mountain anticline. The vertical wall of Tuscarora Sandstone parallels the North Fork of the South Branch Potomac for miles, forming an alignment of low ridges called the River Knobs, through which many water gaps, such as Judy Gap, have been eroded. Judy Run passes through the gap on its way to the North Fork.

Trails near Judy Gap, which was named for one of the early German-Swiss families who migrated into the area, offer scenic views of Germany Valley, Spruce Mountain (the state's highest), Seneca Rocks, the Fore Knobs, and the Dolly Sods. The Judy Rocks outcrop massively at the gap, and continue as a stony fin through Germany Valley. Judy Gap is a familiar point of reference for hikers, campers, tourists, and others who visit the mountains. The North Fork Mountain Trail in the Monongahela National Forest stretches from Judy Gap to Smoke Hole Caverns. Judy Gap lies south of Riverton and Seneca Rocks, at the intersection of State Route 28 and U.S. 33, which passes through the gap on its way to Franklin, the Pendleton County seat. There is also a community named Judy Gap, as well as the geologic formation.

Larry Sonis
Arlington, Texas

Jug of Middle Island Creek

The Jug is located southeast of Middlebourne, Tyler County, on Middle Island Creek, the longest stream in West Virginia not to bear the designation of river. Here the meanders of the creek encompasses a peninsula of land by flowing southward for three and a half miles before reversing direction and returning to within 100 feet of itself. This big loop is shaped something like the handle of a jug.

Recognizing the potential for water power, George Gregg, an early settler of the area, had a raceway cut across the narrow neck of the peninsula where the drop between the two stretches of the creek was about 13 feet. Here Gregg had constructed, sometime before 1800, a gristmill and sawmill. In early days it was the custom of farmers living along the loop to float their grain to mill in a johnboat in the morning, then while waiting for the milling, have their craft hoisted by windlass across the narrow neck and then drift downstream with the grist to their homes in the afternoon.

Gregg's mill did a thriving business until being washed off by a flood on April 6, 1852. Later mills at this location were destroyed by floods in 1858, 1873, 1875, and 1884. Floods enlarged the mill raceway to the point that the creek, during normal flow, was diverted almost entirely through this cut. Thus by the end of the 19th century the Jug had became an island. The West Virginia Conservation Commission constructed a dam and bridge across the raceway in 1947, thereby restoring the flow of water in the original channel. Today the Division of Natural Resources owns and operates the vast majority of property within the Jug as a wildlife management area.

Gerald S. Ratliff
Charleston

Gladys Gregg, "The Jug," *History of Tyler County, West Virginia*, 1984; "Tyler County," Jim Comstock, ed., *Hardesty's West Virginia Counties*, 1973.

Justice of the Peace

From the founding of the state until January 1, 1977, justices of the peace functioned as the lowest rung of the West Virginia judiciary. The office had its origins in England and was transplanted to Virginia in the 17th century. In West Virginia, "JPs" were given jurisdiction over misdemeanor offenses and small civil claims. The justices of the peace would also set initial bail in felony cases and conduct preliminary hearings.

Justices of the peace received no salaries but were compensated by the costs assessed against the losing party in civil cases and against criminal defendants who were convicted. Thus, it was long part of the legal folklore of West Virginia that "JP" stood for "judgment for plaintiff," that is, the person who brought the suit. If a defendant was acquitted in a criminal case, the justice was not compensated. In the early 1970s, in two separate cases, the West Virginia Supreme Court of Appeals ruled the fee system unconstitutional.

In 1974 the voters approved the Judicial Reform Amendment, which established the county magistrate system as a part of a general restructuring of the judicial branch. The magistrates, like the JPs, were elected, but they are now paid a salary and are subject to the discipline of the Supreme Court. A broad-based coalition, including business, labor, and civic leaders led the successful fight for the passage of the amendment. The only political figure of any standing to oppose passage was newly elected Supreme Court Justice Richard Neely.

The name of the new magistrate courts was taken from the federal model. In other states these courts are called district courts or occasionally municipal courts. West Virginia's municipal courts, left unchanged by the 1974 amendment, continue to handle misdemeanor cases within the boundaries of municipalities.

H. John Rogers
New Martinsville

Juvenile Courts

The juvenile courts operate as parallel institutions within the West Virginia legal system. Circuit judges preside over the juvenile courts, and only the largest counties have full-time assistant prosecutors who specialize in juvenile cases.

In 1967, the U.S. Supreme Court mandated major change in the juvenile courts throughout the nation. In the ruling known as *In re Gault*, the court held that children charged with juvenile delinquency (a juvenile cannot be charged with a "crime," only with "delinquency") were entitled to basically the same procedural rights as an adult. Thereafter a juvenile came to have the advantages of a system inclined to offer a second chance combined with, at the juvenile's election, all of the procedural rights of an adult. If the alleged offense is particularly heinous, the prosecutor may petition to have the juvenile tried as an adult, thereby subjecting the child to adult punishment.

Generally, the juvenile court's jurisdiction depends upon the age of the offender. The critical fact is the age of the youth at the time the alleged crime was committed. If the youth was under 18 at that point, then he or she is tried in juvenile court (subject to procedures allowing removal for trial as an adult); if over 18, then the prosecution is conducted through the regular circuit court procedures. Once a youth reaches 18 he or she becomes an adult for purposes of the criminal justice system and would be tried as an adult, not a juvenile. A juvenile court that sentences a juvenile can retain jurisdiction over the youth until he or she reaches 21, however, and a youth correction center can house sentenced delinquents until the age of 23.

Over the years, public opinion as regards young offenders has swung back and forth between a paternalistic philosophy and one of punishment. In 1963, the West Virginia Supreme Court of Appeals in *State ex rel. Slatton v. Boles* ruled that the state policy is to "protect and reclaim juveniles" and that these children should be treated as delinquents rather than as criminals.

H. John Rogers
New Martinsville

John Joseph Kain

Roman Catholic Bishop John Joseph Kain was born near Martinsburg, May 31, 1841, the son of Jeremiah and Ellen Murphy Kain. He received his education at St. Charles College, Ellicott City, Maryland, and St. Mary's Seminary, Baltimore, where he attained highest honors. He was ordained to the priesthood in 1866 for the Diocese of Richmond. His first pastoral assignment was to his home parish of St. Joseph's in Martinsburg, with missions from Leesburg, Virginia, to Harpers Ferry. He dedicated the seven years he spent as pastor there to rebuilding the communities after the Civil War.

In May 1875, Kain succeeded the Right Reverend Richard V. Whelan (1809–74) as the second bishop of the Diocese of Wheeling. As bishop he worked to meet the needs of the newly arrived immigrants who came to labor in West Virginia's mines and factories, continuing his predecessor's efforts to build the churches and schools required to serve them. When he left the diocese in 1893, 15 new parishes had been established and six schools founded. Respected for his intellect, Kain was frequently consulted for his positions on the issues of the day, including labor unions and education.

Kain remained in Wheeling until his appointment as Archbishop of St. Louis in 1893. He died at the age of 62, October 13, 1903, and is buried in St. Louis.

See also Diocese of Wheeling-Charleston, Roman Catholics

Tricia Pyne
St. Mary's Seminary & University, Maryland

Kamp Kump

In the summer of 1934 the state Department of Public Welfare established Kamp Kump, named for Gov. Herman Guy Kump and located near Winfield in Putnam County. Part of a system of camps intended to rescue the children of families especially hard-hit by the Great Depression, Kamp Kump served as a temporary emergency receiving center for nearly 200 children removed from county poorhouses. Thus the camp provided a first step in the rehabilitation of children who had lived under debilitating conditions as county wards, in some cases for many years. After improving the nutrition and physical condition of the poorhouse children at Kamp Kump, welfare officials placed them in foster homes, or with relatives or their parents.

See also Camp Brock, Camp Fairchance, Great Depression

Jerry Bruce Thomas
Shepherd University
Jerry Bruce Thomas, *An Appalachian New Deal: West Virginia in the Great Depression*, 1998.

Kanawha County

Kanawha County, named for the Kanawha River which flows through it, was created November 14, 1788. Initially ten times its present size, the county remains West Virginia's fourth largest, at 913.4 square miles. Its population, the state's largest, was 200,073 in 2000, down from its 1960 peak of 252,925. The terrain ranges from the rolling hills of Teays Valley in the west to the 2,600-foot mountains on its southern border. Charleston, the capital of West Virginia and the state's largest city, is the county seat of Kanawha County.

Kanawha County has a rich prehistory going back to 10,500 B.C. More than 500 archeological sites have been recorded, including St. Albans, one of the most significant Early Archaic sites in the eastern United States. People of the Adena and Hopewell cultures occupied the region at the time of ancient Rome and left behind numerous structures, including the second-largest mound in the state at South Charleston. No Indians seem to have lived in the county in the historic era, but they often passed through.

The earliest European to visit the area was probably Gabriel Arthur, as a captive of the Indians in 1674. Then came John Peter Salling and John Howard, Coal River explorers in 1742, and the captive Mary Draper Ingles in 1755. By 1771, Simon Kenton was hunting and trapping in the valley; Walter Kelly, though killed within a year, is credited with the first settlement in 1773, at Cedar Grove at the mouth of Kellys Creek. William Morris and others followed in 1774 and later, especially after Dunmore's War temporarily reduced native opposition. Charleston was settled in 1788 by George Clendenin.

The salt industry stimulated early economic development. Beginning with Elisha Brooks's 1797 furnace on land leased from Joseph Ruffner at the mouth of Campbells Creek, near present Malden, the industry blossomed to 52 furnaces producing 3,000 bushels of Kanawha "red salt" per day by 1815, and three times that by the late 1840s. Coal was mined to fuel the salt works by 1817, and cannel coal production boomed in the late 1840s at locations as diverse as Coal River, Mill Creek, and Cannelton. Further, sluice dams and dredging in the 1820s which allowed steamboat traffic, the 1829 authorization to complete the James River & Kanawha Turnpike to the Ohio River, and the long-awaited 1832 chartering of a Bank of Virginia branch stimulated growth. Malden was the early industrial center, but by 1830 Charleston emerged as a respectable town of 750 people as salt magnates moved away from Malden's grime. The combination of salt workers, household servants, and laborers in Charleston, and agricultural laborers on plantations that lined the flood plain, gave the Kanawha Valley a high concentration of black workers, mostly slaves.

Given its commercial bent, the county generally supported Whig political candidates, such as Lewis Summers and George W. Summers, for their economic development views, and found itself in opposition to the Democrats who dominated Virginia east of the mountains. A number of prominent Kanawha Countians, including George Summers, Spicer Patrick, and James H. Brown, opposed Virginia secession. Nevertheless, the county was split by the Civil War. A number of Confederate companies, most no-

FAST FACTS ABOUT KANAWHA COUNTY

Founded: 1788
Land in square miles: 913.4
Population: 200,073
Percentage minorities: 9.5%
Percentage rural: 24.7%
Median age: 40.2
Percentage 65 and older: 16.5%
Birth rate per 1,000 population: 12.0
Median household income: $33,766
High school graduate or higher: 80.0%
Bachelor's degree or higher: 20.6%
Home ownership: 70.3%
Median home value: $80,700

This information is from the 2000 U.S. Census. In 2000, West Virginia as a whole had 5 percent minorities, a median age of 38.9, median household income of $29,696, and a 75.2 percent home ownership rate.

tably George S. Patton's Kanawha Riflemen, were mustered in the valley. Union troops from Ohio and Kentucky under Brig. Gen. Jacob Cox occupied the valley in July 1861 only to be driven out for six weeks in the fall of 1862 by a Confederate advance led by Brig. Gen. William W. Loring. Thereafter, Charleston and the valley remained in Union hands for the duration of the war. Nevertheless, much damage had been inflicted by retreating armies and by the valley's worst flood on September 29, 1861.

After the Civil War, Kanawha County participated fully in West Virginia's transformation from a traditional economy to extractive industry and then to industrial production. Timber and particularly coal production were stimulated by the railroads. The Chesapeake & Ohio arrived in 1873, following the south side of the Kanawha River. Charleston passengers had to take a ferry trip to the depot until the first South Side Bridge was erected in 1891. The north side of the river became the province of the Kanawha & Michigan Railroad in the 1880s and 1890s. Traffic north along the Elk River was consolidated into the Coal & Coke Railroad by 1906. Between 1875 and 1898, ten locks and dams provided year-round navigation on the Kanawha. Several branch railroads opened numerous coal camps and made the county the state's second-largest coal producer by 1888.

Another stimulus for county development came from state government. The capital was moved from Wheeling to Charleston in 1870, back to Wheeling in 1875, then permanently to Charleston in 1885. The famous fire of 1921 caused the capitol building to be relocated from downtown to its present east end site by 1932.

World War I initiated the modern transformation of the county. Attracted by abundant water, salt brines, coal, gas, and petroleum, the government built the explosives plant at Nitro and ordnance facilities in South Charleston, while small chemical firms located in the valley. From these beginnings, further stimulated by World War II, large chemical complexes were developed by DuPont at Belle, FMC in South Charleston, Monsanto in Nitro, and Union Carbide, first in Clendenin, then at its large production and research facilities in South Charleston and Institute. Kelly Axe had brought additional diversity to the valley in 1904, while small glass producers paved the way for Libbey-Owens-Ford to build its large plate glass plant in Kanawha City in 1916. New locks updated river transportation in the 1930s, and air travel, initiated at Wertz Field in Institute, received modern facilities at Kanawha (now Yeager) Airport in 1947.

Kanawha County has been the center of some of West Virginia's most turbulent events. Bloody coal strikes at Cabin Creek and Paint Creek focused national attention on the mining industry in 1912–13, and the county served as a staging area for the 1920–21 union organizing confrontations at Matewan and Blair Mountain. More recently, controversy flared over school textbooks in 1974, and numerous groups have converged on state government with their concerns.

In addition, Charleston has become the state's banking center on foundations laid by Kanawha Valley Bank, 1867, Charleston National Bank, 1884, and several others by 1910. Lawyers, particularly the so-called Kanawha Ring at the turn of the century, have wielded much power, and most West Virginia lawyers practice here. The 1972 merger of five hospitals into Charleston Area Medical Center created a premier medical center. Higher education stretches back to the West Virginia Colored Institute (now West Virginia State University), 1892, and the Montgomery Preparatory School (now West Virginia University Institute of Technology), 1895. Morris Harvey College (now University of Charleston) moved from Barboursville to Charleston in 1935. Finally, with its French and Belgian glassworkers, Italian and Irish stone masons, Welsh, Polish, Hungarian, and African-American miners, Jewish, Greek, German, and Lebanese merchants, Asian chemists and doctors, Kanawha County has contributed to the ethnic diversity of the state.

Notable individuals who have resided in the county include frontiersman Daniel Boone; educators Henry Ruffner and Booker T. Washington; Civil War Gen. William S. Rosecrans; naturalist William H. Edwards; presidential assassin Leon Czolgosz and attempted assassin Sara Jane Moore; entrepreneurs Alex Schoenbaum and Fred Haddad; union presidents Arnold Miller and Cecil Roberts; League of Women Voters president Becky Cain; civil rights activist Leon Sullivan; journalist Tony Brown; composer George Crumb; writers Denise Giardina, Mary Lee Settle, and Eugenia Price; and athletes Jerry West, Rod Hundley, and Randy Moss. Kanawha County has produced 13 members of the U.S. Congress, four members of the U.S. Senate, and six governors of West Virginia.

R. Eugene Harper
University of Charleston

Stan Cohen, *Kanawha County Images*, 1987; W. S. Laidley, *History of Charleston and Kanawha County*, 1911; Otis K. Rice, *Charleston and the Kanawha Valley*, 1981.

Kanawha County Textbook Controversy

In 1974, Kanawha County was polarized by disagreement over the selection of textbooks for the 46,000 students attending the county's 124 public schools. It be-

The Rev. Marvin Horan speaks against proposed textbooks.

gan in April, when the five-member Kanawha County Board of Education voted unanimously to adopt 325 recommended texts and supplementary books in language arts. The books had previously been available for public review.

At the board meeting the following month, board member Alice Moore challenged the philosophy and content of some of the books. The wife of a fundamentalist minister, Moore had been elected to the school board in 1970 as a strong opponent of sex education. Purchase of the books was delayed until a consensus could be reached, and Moore, joined by several ministers, began a campaign against the books.

Despite petitions bearing 12,000 signatures and public condemnation of the books by 27 ministers and others on the grounds of immorality and indecency, the board voted 3-2 at the June meeting to accept most of the books. During July and August anti-text sentiment mounted, especially in the rural eastern end of the county, as the books and excerpts from them were circulated.

Opponents called for a boycott and attendance was down 20 percent at the opening of school on September 3. Picketing at schools quickly spread to businesses, industrial plants, and coal mines, with 3,500 miners staging a wildcat sympathy strike. On September 6, the Board of Education was granted an injunction by the Kanawha Circuit Court prohibiting protesters from interfering with the operation of the schools. A board compromise to remove the disputed books pending review by an 18-member board-appointed citizen committee was rejected and protest escalated. Shots were fired, cars and homes firebombed, schools dynamited and vandalized, and 11 protesters arrested. Schools were closed on September 12 for four days.

Throughout October and November,

sporadic violence continued as protesters demanded the resignation of pro-text board members and the superintendent of schools. Protesters rejected the board proposal to place the disputed texts in school libraries with access by parental permission. Another compromise was proposed which accepted a modified version of Moore's text guidelines that barred texts that pry into home life, teach racial hatred, undermine religious, ethnic, or racial groups, encourage sedition, insult patriotism, teach that an alien form of government is acceptable, use the name of God in vain, or use offensive language.

In December, the board reached tentative agreement on a set of policies under which several committees were established with parents involved in textbook selection and adoption. An inquiry by the National Education Association was held in Charleston.

Protest continued into 1975, fueled by the involvement of extremist groups such as the John Birch Society and the Ku Klux Klan. The trial and sentencing of Rev. Marvin Horan for plotting the bombing of schools brought an unsettled end to the violence, but protesting continued intermittently through 1977.

Shirley A. Smith
Charleston

James Moffett, *Storm in the Mountains: A Case Study of Censorship, Conflict, and Consciousness*, 1989.

Kanawha Falls

Kanawha Falls, the largest waterfall in West Virginia, is an important natural landmark. The falls are located on U.S. 60 in Fayette County, just downstream from Gauley Bridge, where the New and Gauley rivers converge to create the Kanawha River. The community of Kanawha Falls is downstream from the falls on the east bank, with Glen Ferris located at the falls on the west bank.

Water drops more than 20 feet at the falls, which cross the Kanawha River in an irregular line. This forms a formidable natural barrier, establishing the boundary between the New River and Kanawha River ecological systems. The falls prevent the upstream movement of fish, with many fewer species in the multistate river basin above the falls.

The falls were a popular stopping place on the James River & Kanawha Turnpike. Aaron Stockton settled there about 1812, and by the 1830s had opened an inn to accommodate this trade. His inn, now called Glen Ferris Inn and still open for business, is listed on the National Register of Historic Places.

Since about 1900 the falls have been augmented by a low dam along the crest. Hydroelectric power has been generated there for more than a century by the Union Carbide company and its predeces-

sors and successors, the electricity used mainly in the production of metal alloys at nearby company facilities. A thriving community developed around these industrial activities in the early decades of the 20th century. The shallow lake created by the dam and falls extends upstream to Gauley Bridge, combining with the mountain setting to create one of the most picturesque views in West Virginia.

See also Fish, Glen Ferris Inn

Kanawha Madonna

The mysterious Kanawha Madonna artifact.

The Kanawha Madonna is a mystery from West Virginia's prehistoric past. This rough wooden statue of a person cradling a small four-legged animal across its chest is housed in the West Virginia State Museum.

The statue, carved from a single tree trunk, stands nearly four feet high. The base is eight inches high with an outside diameter of about 13 inches and a hole, as if for mounting a pole, of about four inches in diameter in its center. The features and hands of the person have weathered away, but there apparently was once a human face. The left ear is intact. The animal is 14 inches long.

The statue was discovered by four teenage boys in an almost inaccessible cave in a cliff overlooking the Kanawha River near Chelyan. It was lying on its back under a four-inch-thick flat stone. It was later obtained by Dr. John P. Hale, distinguished local citizen and president of the West Virginia Historical and Antiquarian Society. Hale visited the cave and in 1897 presented a paper on the statue and its finding to the society. The origin of the name, Kanawha Madonna, is unknown.

The age of the statue is a matter of some disagreement. A radiocarbon date in 1964 estimated the statue to be around

350 years old. Recent testing dated the wood (though not necessarily the statue) to A.D. 1440 to 1600, and identified the wood as honey locust. A similar figure was found in 1869 in a cave near Pineville, Kentucky, and housed for many years in the Museum of the American Indian in New York. Somewhat similar figures have been unearthed at Etowah, Georgia, in Florida, and in the Spiro mounds of Oklahoma.

See also Archeology

Joseph Crosby Jefferds Jr.
Charleston

Kanawha Records

Kanawha Records, an outgrowth of Folk Promotions, was probably the first independent company to record authentic indigenous mountain music as performed by contemporary West Virginia musicians. The company, active from about 1963 through 1970, was created by Ken Davidson, who found, recorded, and promoted players of old-time music. He revived the career of fiddler Clark Kessinger, a popular national recording artist in the late 1920s and early '30s. With the issue of three albums by Kessinger, a new audience of folk enthusiasts was introduced to his music. Davidson recorded fiddlers W. Franklin George and French Carpenter, banjoist Jenes Cottrell, and issued an album of the revivalist Hollow Rock String Band playing never-before recorded tunes of fiddler Henry Reed. Several of Davidson's most important early recordings were acquired by County Records of Floyd, Virginia.

See also Folk Music

Rebecca Halstead Kimmons
Charleston

Kanawha Riflemen

Lawyer George Smith Patton, a Richmond native and 1852 graduate of Virginia Military Institute, organized the Kanawha Riflemen, a Virginia militia company, after moving to Charleston in 1856.

As the Civil War approached, the group and its comrades were unabashedly pro-Southern. In 1861, the worst fears of the Kanawha Riflemen were realized as federal troops headed up the Kanawha River for Charleston. Led by Patton, their 24-year-old major, the Riflemen met the Yankees at Scary Creek, a tributary of the Kanawha, on July 17, 1861. During the brief but bloody skirmish which also involved other Confederate units, the federals lost 15 killed, 11 wounded, and seven captured.

The Kanawha Riflemen were soon incorporated into the regular army of the Confederacy as Company H of the 22nd Virginia Volunteer Infantry, where they left a heroic record. Patton suffered a severe shoulder wound at Scary Creek but went on to lead the 22nd Virginia Regiment until his death in the Battle of Winchester, September 25, 1864. He was the great-grandfather of Gen. George S. Patton of World War II.

The 1861 Kanawha Riflemen had a strength of from 75 to 100, of whom 20 were lawyers. The unit comprised the manhood of many of Charleston's wealthy families. Many of the Kanawha Riflemen rest in Charleston's Spring Hill Cemetery.

See also Civil War, Kanawha County, Battle of Scary Creek

Richard A. Andre
Charleston

Kanawha River

Soon after Jamestown was founded in 1607, the settlers learned from the Indians about a river beyond mountains to the west. The natives called it the Conoy and said it was named for a small tribe that once dwelt along its upper reaches. They told the settlers that it flowed up from the south, turned northwest where it ran through a pass in the western mountains, and continued on to "the South Seas."

The river was variously called the Conoy, Conoise, Cohnawa, and finally the Kanawha. Eventually merging with the Ohio and Mississippi, the Kanawha forms one continuous stream that does indeed continue to the southern sea. The name New River applies to the waterway from where it rises in the mountains of North Carolina until it reaches its confluence with the Gauley River at Gauley Bridge. From there on it becomes the Kanawha or Great Kanawha River and continues northwest on a meandering course of 97 miles to the Ohio at Point Pleasant. The Kanawha has a fall of 108 feet over its entire length, including a drop of more than 20 feet at Kanawha Falls, only a mile below its head.

The river to the pioneers was like a westward highway. Early travelers from the east first reached the Kanawha at the mouth of Kellys Creek, where Cedar Grove is now located. They had come over a roundabout pack horse trail in order to miss the New River gorge. By 1775, the Morris family was located there and had established a boat yard. They provided settlers going west with flatboats, rafts, and dugout canoes. By floating down the Kanawha and Ohio, travelers could reach the Mississippi at present Cairo, Illinois, if they made it through without being ambushed by Indians or river pirates.

Before the first lock system was completed in 1898, the river had ten separate rapids or shoals between Charleston and Point Pleasant. They were all well-known to rivermen but still caused numerous wrecks, often resulting in the loss of lives and cargoes. Johnson Shoals at Scary Creek and Red House Shoals between

The Kanawha River is a working waterway.

present Red House and Winfield were the most treacherous.

Before 1820, steamboats were not reliable enough to negotiate the shoals in the Kanawha. For about 15 years keel boats regularly traveled to Charleston with limited cargoes and passengers. The standard keel boat was some 40 feet long and about eight feet wide, and bringing one upstream required a crew of about ten rugged men. These boatmen owned the river, and most settlers avoided them.

The colorful era of steamboats on the Kanawha is well recorded. The boats were the economic backbone of the valley, and they contributed to the social and cultural life of the area. The plush packet boats, showboats, and excursion boats provided an outlet from the rough conditions associated with the salt works and coalfields.

The navigational improvement of the river has been ongoing since the first steamboat tried to get up over Red House Shoals in 1819. That year the Virginia legislature passed an act for navigation improvements which included cutting chutes through the river's shoals, building wing dams, and removing snags. It was not until 1898 that dependable steamboat schedules could be maintained. Ten locks and dams had been constructed by then, which provided a six-foot depth the length of the river. In 1936, three new locks and roller-type dams replaced the old system. They raised the water stage to nine feet, and they were high enough to stop most of the floods caused by backwater when the Ohio River flooded. Finally after a series of dams were installed on the tributaries, high water on the river ceased to be a problem. The Great Kanawha had been tamed, the dams providing deeper water where

that was needed for navigation while also preventing disastrous rises.

Pollution has been one of the most serious problems to deal with concerning the Kanawha River. Industrial and municipal waste had been dumped into the river since salt was manufactured at Malden. As industry increased and communities became larger, pollution of the river became a major problem. Finally with public support and education, followed by legislation and law enforcement, the river is no longer a health hazard and can once again be used for recreational purposes. The Kanawha River remains the lifeblood of the valley as it has been since the time of the Indians.

See also Locks and Dams

Bill Wintz
St. Albans

Leland Johnson, *Men, Mountains and Rivers*, 1977; Gerald W. Sutphin and Richard A. Andre, *Sternwheelers on the Great Kanawha River*, 1991; William D. Wintz, *Annals of the Great Kanawha*, 1993.

Kanawha Salines

The Kanawha Salines salt-producing district stretched approximately ten miles along both sides of the Kanawha River, from Witcher Creek downstream to the present Kanawha City neighborhood of Charleston. After Joseph and David Ruffner successfully drilled for brine and erected the first furnaces in 1808, the Salines rapidly became the largest salt-making area in the United States, a position it held until the 1830s. As time passed, the most productive part of the Salines field was around Malden, where brine waters were of greater salinity. The salt was used for meat preservation in the Ohio Valley. After the 1830s, New York salt and foreign importation affected Kanawha sales, but the area retained its primacy until the 1850s when agricultural production shifted westward from the Ohio Basin and other salt fields developed.

Kanawha Salines was also the name of the post office in the community known as Terra Salis, east of Georges Creek on the north side of the Kanawha. In 1831, Terra Salis became Malden when David Ruffner laid out lots, streets, and alleys.

Dozens of salt furnaces and salt well rigs crowded the riverbank, and tramways brought coal from mines in the nearby hills. Up to 1,500 slaves, several hundred white laborers, and a few dozen owners, overseers, and managers manned the works. Dozens of coopers, boat-builders, well-drillers, teamsters, carpenters, and masons supported the industry. Transient rivermen from steamboats and flatboats combined with these residents to earn the Salines a notorious and raucous reputation. Travelers often commented on the continuous noise of steam engines and machinery, the almost constant presence of coal smoke, ash particles, and cinders, and the dismal appearance.

See also Malden, Salt Industry

John Edmund Stealey III
Shepherd University

John E. Stealey III, *The Antebellum Kanawha Salt Business and Western Markets*, 1993.

Kanawha Salt Company

The Kanawha Valley salt industry overexpanded during the boom years surrounding the War of 1812. As a result, salt prices fell below manufacturing and distribution costs, causing salt companies to fail.

Dominant producers, including Andrew Donnally and the four Steele brothers, reacted to the overproduction and cutthroat competition by buying up distressed competitors, but ultimately they lacked the capital to control more than half of Kanawha Valley salt production. Unable to monopolize production, they sought another form of combination to satisfy other manufacturers by sharing profit and risk through output restrictions and centralized marketing. On November 10, 1817, Donnally and the Steeles with 16 other producers created the Kanawha Salt Company to control production and marketing for all involved. The idea was to raise prices by limiting production. The agreement limited total salt production to a maximum of 450,000 bushels and set production quotas for participating producers. The company could purchase or lease other salt furnaces to control their production. Dividends were paid according to participating producers' share of the total output.

The Kanawha Salt Company began operation on January 1, 1818, and was to continue until December 31, 1822. But the company never included all manufacturers as at least five never entered the agreement. This first attempt by a majority of Kanawha manufacturers to combine for common ends did not survive the year as the devastating Panic of 1819 crushed all western commerce.

The Kanawha Salt Company is sometimes mistakenly said to have been the first "trust" in the United States. Actually, the company was an output pool and central sales agency. It is the earliest known output pool in the United States. This abortive agreement served as the precursor of six different antebellum salt arrangements to control salt production and marketing. What Kanawha saltmakers attempted became common business practice in the post-Civil War United States as arrangements for concert and combination spread to other industries.

See also Salt Industry

John Edmund Stealey III
Shepherd University

John E. Stealey III, *The Antebellum Kanawha Salt Business and Western Markets*, 1993; Stealey, ed., *Kanawhan Prelude to Nineteenth-Century Monopoly in the United States: The Virginia Salt Combinations*, 2000.

Kanawha State Forest

Kanawha State Forest is located in Kanawha County, on the headwaters of Davis Creek and middle fork of Davis Creek seven miles south of downtown Charleston. Before its acquisition by the state, the site was extensively logged and mined. The West Virginia Conservation Commission acquired 6,705 acres on September 21, 1937, for $30,525. On April 6, 1938, Camp Kanawha of the Civilian Conservation Corps was established at the mouth of Shrewsbury Hollow to begin development of the area.

The CCC removed all of the abandoned houses, coal tipples, and other structures no longer in use, and constructed roads, the forest superintendent's residence, office, maintenance building, and picnic shelters. The superintendent's residence and picnic shelters were built using native chestnut logs that had been felled by the recent chestnut blight. The CCC also built a dam across Davis Creek to create a small lake. Camp Kanawha closed June 30, 1942, with the onset of World War II. In 1973, an additional 2,500 acres were acquired for Kanawha State Forest to make a total of 9,205 acres.

Kanawha State Forest is a wildflower haven. According to a 1966 report, the area holds 574 species from 292 genera representing 93 families. About 65 tree species grow in the forest. Recreational facilities include numerous hiking trails, swimming pool, stables, picnic sites, nine picnic shelters, several playgrounds, shooting range, and a 45-site campground. Hunting is permitted in season. Kanawha State Forest is managed by the West Virginia Division of Natural Resources.

Robert Beanblossom
Division of Natural Resources

Kanawha Trail

The Kanawha or Buffalo Trail followed the Kanawha River from the Ohio River to Cedar Grove, then overland to Ansted. From there it followed the Meadow River and the Midland Trail (now U.S. 60) to Virginia. An alternate of this trail ran through Teays Valley from the Ohio River to the Kanawha River, near St. Albans. Another variation crossed the New River above the mouth of the Bluestone, passed through present Beckley, and followed Paint Creek north to the Kanawha River. This trail was used by the party of Shawnees who took Mary Ingles captive in 1755, during the raid on Drapers Meadows.

The Kanawha Trail also followed a portion of the route called the Ohio Branch of the Great Indian Warpath by William E. Myer in *Indian Trails of the Southeast* (1928). The Ohio Branch extended from Creek territory in Georgia and Alabama, up through eastern Tennessee and southwestern Virginia to the New and Kanawha rivers. At the mouth of the Kanawha several trails met. The main trail continued in a northwesterly direction through Ohio to Lake Erie.

There were numerous Indian villages along the Kanawha Trail until the middle 1600s. Exotic artifacts such as engraved marine shell gorgets from the eastern Tennessee region, as well as European copper and brass ornaments, and glass trade beads have been found at Pratt and Marmet, Kanawha County, and Buffalo, Putnam County, indicating movement along this route.

See also Indian Trails

Darla S. Hoffman
Cultural Resource Analysts

Kanawha Valley Bank

In April 1867, William Dickinson Jr., his sons, and others associated with the Kanawha Valley salt industry founded the Kanawha Valley Bank. In 1869, the group built a two-story bank at the present intersection of Kanawha Boulevard and Capitol Street in downtown Charleston. In 1870, Henry Clay Dickinson was chosen president of Kanawha Valley Bank and also elected mayor of the city. He died in May 1871, to be succeeded by a brother-in-law and then by father William Dickinson, the bank founder. Upon William's death in 1882, son John Quincy Dickinson became president for the next 43 years.

Of the three banks opened in Charleston immediately after the Civil War, Kanawha Valley Bank was the only one to survive the financial panic of 1873. From initial capitalization of $30,000 the bank grew to more than $600,000 in assets by

The 1929 Kanawha Valley Bank building.

1882. In 1893, John Q. Dickinson chose to invest in a substantial new building, five floors on Front Street (now Kanawha Boulevard) with an elaborate stone and brick facade and turret. The move was a statement of confidence to the business community and to the swarm of speculators coming to West Virginia with the boom in timber, coal, and oil and gas.

In 1894, John L. Dickinson became cashier of the bank, a position he retained until he was elevated to the presidency following the death of father John Q. Dickinson in 1925. A month before the stock market crash of 1929, John L. Dickinson moved his bank into new quarters on the former site of the capitol of West Virginia. The 20-story building, the tallest and most prestigious business address in the state for many years, remains a Charleston landmark.

John L. Dickinson was succeeded as president of Kanawha Valley Bank in 1949 by Hayes Picklesimer, who had first come to work at the bank in 1918. In 1967, Hugh Curry became president and set in motion the process that eventually modernized West Virginia banking regulations by legislative action to allow branch banking. He hired Robert F. Baronner from Pennsylvania, whose experience in branch banking was critical. Baronner was in charge of developing a new high-rise bank building, One Valley Square, into which the bank moved in 1976. Becoming president in 1975, Baronner oversaw the change to a national bank charter, the establishment of the bank holding company, and the acquisitions and expansions that made the renamed One Valley Bank the largest bank and bank holding company in the state.

J. Holmes Morrison rose to the presidency of One Valley Bancorp of West Virginia in 1991, the same year Phyllis Arnold became president of the bank itself. In 2000, One Valley Bank was acquired by BB&T Bank Corporation of North Carolina. In 2005, BB&T was West Virginia's largest banking institution.

See also Banking, Dickinson Family

Bill Drennen
Shepherdstown

Bill Drennen, *One Kanawha Valley Bank: A History,* 2001.

Kanawha Valley Hospital

The Barber Sanatorium in Charleston, forerunner of Kanawha Valley Hospital, was built in 1904 by Dr. Timothy L. Barber, Charleston's public health officer and Kanawha County's smallpox doctor.

In 1909, Dr. Hugh G. Nicholson leased the 20-bed sanatorium and added a nursing school. In 1912, when Dr. George A. MacQueen took over the lease, the name was changed to Barber Sanatorium and Hospital. Two years later, it merged with nearby Grace Hospital and incorporated as Kanawha Valley Hospital and Sanatorium. In 1925, a new corporation, Kanawha Valley Hospital, bought the facility. By that time, the hospital had an operating room, laboratory, and obstetrical department. During the next 25 years, it continued to expand its facilities and services. In the early 1950s, the hospital and the school of nursing received full accreditation. In 1957, the hospital's income began to decline. Two years later, the stockholders and directors sold out to Kanawha Valley Memorial Hospital, a nonprofit corporation. In 1961, the hospital closed its school of nursing.

Kanawha Valley Memorial Hospital operated at its original Virginia Street site until 1982, when it moved to a new 170-bed facility on Pennsylvania Avenue, near the Elk River. The hospital merged with Charleston Area Medical Center in 1986. After renovations, it reopened in June 1988 as CAMC's Women and Children's Hospital.

See also Charleston Area Medical Center

Karst

Many of the most scenic areas of West Virginia are found in the eastern and southeastern parts of the state where carbonate rocks (limestone and dolomite) are exposed to the surface. The landscape formed by the slow chemical dissolution of soluble rocks is called "karst" by geologists. The results of chemical weathering of rocks are expressed by the formation of sinkholes (dolines), sinking streams ("lost rivers"), large springs, and caves.

The most characteristic feature of a karst landscape is the lack of surface streams; most of the water in these areas is flowing in underground channels through caves. The sinking streams and drainage through the bottoms of the numerous sinkholes divert most of the rainfall to underground routes where the water may travel for several miles before returning to the surface at large springs. Although the karst aquifers of West Virginia are some of the most productive in the state, the very localized occurrence of ground water in cave conduits and the lack of surface drainage sometimes make the karst areas seem water-poor. The ground water in karst areas is also especially susceptible to contamination because of the fast flow rates (sometimes greater than one mile per day) and little opportunity for filtering of the water. Many of the springs in limestone regions contain high bacteria counts and should not be used as a drinking water source without treatment.

Several large West Virginia creeks sink and run underground for part of their course. The Lost River near Wardensville sinks completely during low conditions and reemerges as the Cacapon River. Hills Creek in Pocahontas County sinks completely into a large cave, and the water splits. Some of the flow goes under Droop Mountain to Locust Creek and some goes underground about 11 miles south to Spring Creek in Greenbrier County. Milligan Creek in Greenbrier County rises and sinks at least four times before its resurgence at Davis Spring at Fort Spring. Davis Spring drains an area of 72 square miles and with an average flow of about 110 cubic feet per second is the largest spring in West Virginia. Culverson Creek sinks at the base of a limestone cliff west of Frankford and resurges four miles to the east in a series of springs along Spring Creek.

The most extensive karst features in West Virginia may be found in the Greenbrier valley of Greenbrier, Monroe, and Pocahontas counties. The towns of Union and Lewisburg are situated on karst sinkhole plains, and Lewisburg lies mostly within a compound sinkhole. The scenic course of U.S. 219 from the Virginia state line in Monroe County north through Greenbrier County traverses a mature sinkhole plain. The sink of the Lost River in Hardy County is just upstream of the State Route 55 bridge, and the river reemerges a mile downstream as the Cacapon River. The karst relief of Berkeley and Jefferson counties is more subtle, but numerous "ribbons" of exposed carbonate rocks called karren are evident in the fields and pastures of the area.

See also Caves, Geology, Lost River

William K. Jones
Charles Town

William K. Jones, *Karst Hydrology Atlas of West Virginia,* 1997; J. S. McColloch, *Springs of West Virginia,* 1986; W. B. White, *Geomorphology and Hydrology of Karst Terrains,* 1988.

Kates Mountain

Located directly across from the entrance to the Greenbrier Resort in White Sulphur Springs and included in the 5,000-acre Greenbrier State Forest, 3,240-foot Kates Mountain is a familiar landmark in eastern Greenbrier County. The name derives from Kate Carpenter who, along with her husband, Nicholas, was among the first white settlers in the Greenbrier region. In 1756, Nicholas was killed in an Indian attack, but Kate managed to escape with their infant daughter, Frances. Because Kate Carpenter was able to conceal herself and her child, they avoided capture and for that heroic act the ridge has ever since been known as Kates Mountain.

Kates Mountain is known for many species of unusual flora, particularly for its rare Kates Mountain clover and box huckleberry. John K. Small first discovered the clover in 1892. Its large white blossoms, twice the size of ordinary white clover, flower in April and May. It thrives only on true shale barrens. The box huckleberry was first discovered in the late 18th century and then largely forgotten until it was rediscovered in the 1920s in small patches in Virginia, Maryland, Tennessee, and Kentucky. It grows as a ground cover under rhododendrons and white pines and is the only kind of huckleberry in this region with evergreen leaves.

Scenic Kates Mountain road begins at White Sulphur Springs and travels the ridge before ending at the state forest headquarters.

See also Greenbrier State Forest

Robert S. Conte
The Greenbrier

James Kay

Businessman James Kay, born March 20, 1849, in Lanark, Scotland, migrated to America in 1869. By 1870, he had arrived in Charleston, doing stone work for the advancing Chesapeake & Ohio Railway. As an independent contractor he built major arch culverts through the New River gorge, also taking contracts in Ohio and Canada. In 1875, Kay married Scottish immigrant Julia Ballintyne and purchased a farm in Talbot County, Maryland. He returned to Quinnimont in 1879 to construct the coke ovens at Hawks Nest. He acquired coal lands in the New River area before being called to New York.

In 1884, Kay returned to West Virginia. As president of the Royal Coal and Coke Company in Prince, he installed a clever cable car system to carry coal across the New River to the railroad. In 1899, the Low Moor Iron Company employed him to open the Kaymoor mines near Fayetteville. He arranged for an elaborate tramway system to move miners and coal up and down the west face of the gorge. The remnant of this pioneering mining complex is now part of the New River Gorge National River.

Kay also acquired and developed Cabin Creek coal lands. In 1909, he opened mines on Campbells Creek, and a year later became postmaster for Coal Fork. In Charleston, he established the Elk Milling and Produce Company, the Empire Savings & Loan Co., and the Palmer Shoe Co.

In his later years he incorporated his assets into the Kay Company, and this family concern continued to produce coal from the Kayford area of Cabin Creek into the 21st century. James Kay died April 9, 1934, in Charleston and is buried in Spring Hill Cemetery.

Henry W. Battle
Charleston
Tad Randolph
Grayling, Michigan

Kaymoor

Located on the south side of the New River Gorge in Fayette County, the company town of Kaymoor evolved from a mining camp in 1899 into an industrial village. Named after James Kay, its first superintendent, Kaymoor originated as a "captive" mine of the Low Moor Iron Company on lands that had been purchased during the Reconstruction era by A. A. Low, a wealthy New York merchant and financier of the C&O Railroad. Production from Kaymoor was destined for the company's iron furnaces in Low Moor, Virginia.

Rugged terrain dictated the layout of the mines and villages of Kaymoor. Horizontal or drift mine entrances were cut into the cliffside two miles apart and 560 feet above New River. Villages, known as Kaymoor One and Two, arose near the railroad that was down the mountain at river level, and on the rim of the gorge. Thus two distinct living areas developed, one in the river bottom and the other far above. The mines were located on the canyon wall between the two. The layout of the operation required a steep inclined tramway, remembered as the "haulage" by former residents.

Kaymoor was sold on March 1, 1925, to the New River Pocahontas Coal Company. The new owner, a huge international company, shipped Kaymoor coal to the Virginia coast to fuel naval and merchant marine vessels.

Life in Kaymoor resembled that of other coal towns. Miners were recruited from near and far, bringing diverse ethnic and racial groups together. The United Mine Workers slowly gained strength, and a coal town culture emerged that sustained the residents in the smoky industrial village during periods of boom and bust. Its coal seam worked out by 1961, Kaymoor closed in 1962. Now a part of the New River Gorge National River park, Kaymoor's ruins remain a monument of the industrial era.

Lou Athey
Franklin & Marshall College
Lou Athey, *Kaymoor: A New River Community*, 1986.

Elizabeth Kee

Congresswoman Elizabeth Kee took her place in the House of Representatives in 1951. West Virginia's first congresswoman was part of a political dynasty that began with her husband, John, and continued with her son, James.

Elizabeth Kee was born Maude Etta Simpkins in Radford, Virginia, June 7, 1899. She changed her given name to Elizabeth at a young age. In the early 1920s, she married John Kee, a state senator and lawyer from Bluefield, who was first elected to Congress in 1932. A New Deal Democrat, John Kee chaired the House Foreign Affairs Committee. Elizabeth was his secretary, often working directly with her husband's Fifth District constituents. She was elected to his seat upon John's death in 1951.

Her candidacy in the special election was not taken seriously until she won the support of United Mine Workers districts 17 and 29. With labor and other Democratic power brokers behind her, Kee narrowly defeated Republican Cyrus Gadd. She was elected to a full term in 1952 and was seldom opposed in future races.

Kee dedicated herself to unemployment and veterans' issues. She argued that imported oil led to massive unemployment in the coalfields, and she helped implement the Kennedy administration's Accelerated Public Works Act to provide unemployment relief. A member of the House Veterans Affairs Committee, Kee lobbied for improved care at veterans' hospitals, higher pay for personnel, and the construction of new facilities.

The congresswoman retired in 1964 and was succeeded in Congress by her son, James. She returned to Bluefield. Elizabeth Kee died February 15, 1975.

Christine M. Kreiser
Clarksburg
William H. Hardin, "Elizabeth Kee, 1899–1975," *Missing Chapters II: West Virginia Women in History*, 1986.

Frank Keeney

Unionist Frank Keeney was born March 15, 1882, on Cabin Creek, Kanawha County. He first entered the mines as a boy. He emerged as a rank-and-file leader during the Paint Creek-Cabin Creek strike of 1912–13, when he led the opposition to efforts by United Mine Workers officials and Governor Hatfield to end the dispute with a compromise settlement.

Keeney became president of UMW District 17 in 1917. Within three months,

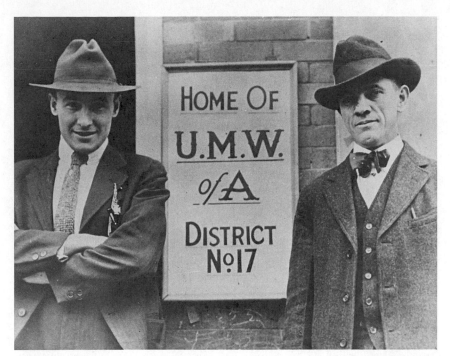
Fred Mooney and Frank Keeney (right).

2,000 new members were enrolled, 12 new locals organized, and District 17 had the largest membership in its history. In 1919, he announced his intention to organize the remainder of southern West Virginia, including the bastions of anti-unionism, Logan and Mingo counties. The coal operators were equally determined to keep the union out. Consequently, Keeney's tenure as district president was marked by the years of bitter, bloody, industrial warfare known as the West Virginia Mine Wars. Keeney and 550 of his fellow miners were indicted for murder and treason resulting from the 1921 Miners' March on Logan. Keeney was acquitted.

In 1922, realizing that the coal companies were unable to continue paying the war-inflated union wage rates, Keeney agreed to temporary wage cuts. The UMW's national leadership disagreed. Asserting the union's position of "no backward step," UMWA President John L. Lewis dismissed Keeney and withdrew the autonomy of District 17.

By March 1931, the UMWA membership in southern West Virginia had dwindled to less than 600 members. Keeney formed an independent union, the West Virginia Mine Workers Union, and within a few weeks had organized an estimated 20,000 miners. The independent union lasted for two years until it collapsed due to lack of finances. Keeney continued his labor activities with the Progressive Miners of America. After the collapse of the Progressive Miners of America, Keeney left the labor movement. He owned and operated a nightclub in Charleston, and later worked as a parking lot attendant. He died May 22, 1970, at age 88.

See also Mine Wars, Miners' March, West Virginia Mine Workers Union

David A. Corbin
Office of Senator Robert C. Byrd

Keith-Albee Theatre

Huntington's Keith-Albee Theatre was one of the most lavish motion picture houses ever built and, with 3,000 seats, was said to be second in size only to New York City's Roxy. The "$2 million temple of amusement," as a contemporary newspaper account called it, was built by Huntington businessmen A. B. and S. J. Hyman in the 900 block of Fourth Avenue, on land that had been occupied by the Zenner-Bradshaw Department Store and the offices of the *Huntington Advertiser* newspaper. The Keith-Albee was designed by New York architect Thomas W. Lamb, working with the local firm of Meanor and Handloser. The theater was affiliated with the Keith-Albee vaudeville circuit, which booked the entertainers for its big stage.

The Keith-Albee's May 7, 1928, opening program featured screen star Reginald Denny in a comedy called "Good Morning, Judge," a newsreel, and five stage acts. But the theater itself, with its elaborate interior, giant golden stage curtain, ceiling studded with stars and clouds, 19 uniformed ushers, eight-piece orchestra, and a mighty Wurlitzer organ, clearly was the star of the evening.

The theater was designed for live entertainment as well as motion pictures, and continues to offer both. In recent decades, the Keith-Albee has not only attracted film fans but also has been home to the Marshall Artists' Series, which each year presents touring Broadway shows, dance companies, and musical groups. In 1975, the huge theater was divided so three different movies could be shown simultaneously. Heirs of the Hyman brothers continued to operate the Keith-Albee until 2006.

James E. Casto
Herald-Dispatch

Benjamin F. Kelley

General Benjamin Franklin Kelley, born in New Hampshire, April 10, 1807, moved to Wheeling in 1836. For more than two decades, Kelley was a merchant, and in 1851 he became freight agent for the newly arrived Baltimore & Ohio Railroad. When the Civil War began, Kelley formed the 1st (West) Virginia Infantry, and was named its colonel on May 22, 1861. Severely wounded in action at Philippi on June 3, 1861, he was promoted to brigadier general. Kelley's principal duty throughout the war was to guard the vital B&O line in Maryland and West Virginia. His command frequently defended the railroad and depots from Confederate raiding parties, especially those led by Capt. John H. McNeill of the famed McNeill's Rangers. The Rangers operated out of the Moorefield area.

During the Jones-Imboden raid through central West Virginia in late April and early May 1863, part of Kelley's forces, especially the 5th Brigade, destroyed bridges and otherwise attempted to delay and disrupt the Confederate raid. Following the battle of Gettysburg in July 1863, General Kelley participated in the pursuit of General Lee's Army of Northern Virginia.

In August 1863, federal authorities acting on Kelley's orders arrested the wife and four-year-old son of Captain McNeill. Seeking revenge, a detachment of McNeill's Rangers slipped into Cumberland, Maryland, Kelley's headquarters, during the night of February 21, 1865. Kelley and his superior, Gen. George Crook, were captured.

After the war Kelley was a political appointee in numerous posts until his death at Oakland, Maryland, July 16, 1891. He is buried in Arlington National Cemetery.

See also Civil War, Jones-Imboden Raid

Tim McKinney
Fayetteville

Kelly Axe and Tool Company

The Kelly Axe and Tool Company, at one time the largest ax manufacturer in the world, operated in Charleston for nearly 80 years. Founder William C. Kelly (1849–1933) began making axes in Kentucky in 1874 and later moved operations to Indiana. Drawn to Charleston by the area's transportation facilities and abundant natural gas, Kelly Axe acquired a 53-acre site extending west from Patrick Street on June 30, 1904, and constructed a factory complex that eventually included about 50 buildings. The manufacture of scythes began in January 1905, and ax production started shortly thereafter. The company later added other edged tools.

Kelly Axe was one of the first large industries in the Kanawha Valley and for many years provided jobs for several hundred men and women. The company used some immigrant labor; in 1910, for example, most of the company's ax grinders were natives of Poland or Russia. Kelly Axe became part of American Fork and Hoe Company in July 1930. In 1949, the company changed its name to True Temper, the brand name long used for its products. Despite name changes, Charlestonians continued to refer to the large operation as Kelly Axe. True Temper's Kelly works declined after the mid 1960s and closed on May 28, 1982.

Mary Johnson
State Archives

Elizabeth J. Goodall, "The Charleston Industrial Area: Development, 1797–1937," *West Virginia History,* October 1968.

Teepi Kendrick

William H. "Teepi" Kendrick, one of the pioneers of the West Virginia 4-H program, was born in Selma, Alabama, May 7, 1882. In 1899, he moved to Morgantown to attend West Virginia University. He married Olive Garrison of Morgantown in 1901.

West Virginia University established corn clubs for boys and canning clubs for girls in the decade before World War I, as a way to teach modern agricultural practices to rural youth. In 1913, Kendrick became the state club agent in charge of these groups, and it was under his leadership that the name 4-H was adopted in West Virginia. Also under his guidance, the educational emphasis of the program was broadened to emphasize youth development rather than merely agriculture.

Kendrick was primarily responsible for the location of the state 4-H camp at Jackson's Mill and for its development as the first state 4-H camp in the United States. He was also one of the co-founders of the West Virginia 4-H All Stars, an organization founded in 1919 as a way to recognize outstanding 4-H leaders, members, and other people who have made significant contributions to the 4-H program. Kendrick died May 25, 1937, and was buried in Morgantown.

See also 4-H, Jackson's Mill

Michael M. Meador
Abingdon, Virginia

John E. Kenna

U.S. Senator John Edward Kenna was born in Kanawha County, April 10, 1848, the son of Irish immigrant Edward Kenna and Margery Lewis, who was the great-granddaughter of Andrew Lewis.

Edward Kenna was killed by his Lewis brothers-in-law in a scandalous public shooting at Charleston's fashionable Ka-

nawha House hotel in June 1856. In 1858, his widow moved her family, including young John, to Missouri, where a brother lived, remaining until the outbreak of the Civil War. The family lived there in relative poverty, and John Kenna later recalled working as a boy on the Missouri farm. He joined the Confederate army at age 16, served for the remainder of the war, and was wounded. In August 1865, he returned to Kanawha County, where his mother had reestablished the family. Kenna studied at St. Vincents Academy in Wheeling until 1868, then studied law at a law office in Charleston. He was admitted to the bar in 1870.

Elected Kanawha County prosecuting attorney in 1872 at age 24, Kenna rose rapidly as a politician. He was elected circuit judge in 1875 and to the U.S. House of Representatives in 1876. He was reelected to Congress in 1878, 1880, and 1882. Along with Governor MacCorkle, future Sen. W. E. Chilton, and others, Kenna was a member of the so-called "Kanawha Ring" of the Democratic Party. Assisted by his powerful connections, Kenna built his popularity in the Kanawha Valley by working for improvements to the Kanawha River navigation system and by his efforts to have the state capital moved permanently back to Charleston. In 1883, the state legislature elected him to the U.S. Senate, unseating the powerful Henry Gassaway Davis, a leader of a rival faction within the party. Kenna was returned to the Senate for a second term in 1889. He died in Washington at age 45, January 11, 1893, of an illness described as pleurisy complicated by heart trouble.

Remembered by W.E.R. Byrne, author of the West Virginia nature classic, *Tale of the Elk,* as a "great lover of the outdoors," John Kenna was a hunter, fisherman, and accomplished photographer. A noted orator, he appeared with a traveling circus in his campaign to move the state capital to Charleston, working in that effort with

a popular circus clown. He was unusual as a Roman Catholic in high office in the West Virginia of his day. Kenna is one of two West Virginians memorialized by a statue in the U.S. Capitol. The Jackson County community of Kenna is named in his honor.

John F. Kennedy

On June 20, 1963, the 100th birthday of West Virginia, President John F. Kennedy made his last appearance in the Mountain State. Speaking in Charleston, he declared: "I would not be where I am now, I would not have some of the responsibilities which I now bear, if it had not been for the people of West Virginia." He referred to the 1960 West Virginia primary, when he triumphed over Hubert H. Humphrey.

The success of Senator Kennedy in winning the Democratic primary on May 10, 1960, eliminated the religious barrier to Catholics to run for president. It was also an early example of the very expensive media campaigns that have since become common. The campaign also began televised campaign debates between Kennedy and Senator Humphrey, preceding the famous debates held in the fall between Kennedy and Nixon.

Although Kennedy narrowly defeated Richard Nixon nationally in 1960, he won by the comfortable margin of 46,000 votes in West Virginia. However, he ran far behind other statewide Democratic candidates and this poor showing has been attributed to an anti-Catholic vote. Former Governor Smith, the Democratic state chairman in 1960, said, "I suspect every voter in West Virginia was besieged with different types of hate literature" and attributed Kennedy's loss of some counties to the anti-Catholic effort.

What was the Kennedy legacy in the Mountain State? In his first act as president, Kennedy doubled the surplus food allotment for the poor in West Virginia.

Last visit to Senator Kenna

"There was a great deal of pathos in our last visit to him. He was then in his second term in the Senate and he had been mortally ill for quite a long time. Joe and Will Chilton and I had gone together to Washington to see him. We thought it was the last time we would see him alive. Throughout the whole conversation there was not one allusion to his illness. He knew he was not going to get well and we knew it also, but with all, it was a pleasant conversation, dealing with the facts of the day, the politics of the state, and the news from home. It was nearly train time and we got up to leave. We had all been diverting our minds from the one thing we knew was imminent. As I say it had been a very pleasant party. When we got up we stood by the bedside. He said 'don't go, stay a little while longer.' We told him it was train time; and then the thought that was in each man's heart came to the sick man also. He reached over and caught Joe Chilton's arm and we all stood there—for just then it seemed to strike all of us and him, that this would be the last time he would see us or we would see him alive, and he dropped his hand from Joe's arm and in a voice which I can hear today, said 'boys, stay a little longer.' There was a silence. After a moment his hand dropped from Joe's arm and we walked out."

—Gov. William A. MacCorkle *The Recollections of Fifty Years of West Virginia* (1928)

President Kennedy and Governor Barron, June 20, 1963.

He also extended welfare benefits for the needy, initiated the national food stamp program in West Virginia, and in a few months drastically increased the amount of federal aid sent to the state. In three years he boosted West Virginia's rank in defense contracts from 50th to 25th and helped the state to obtain new buildings and to improve the park system. Perhaps the greatest boon was the inclusion of a north-south highway as part of the federal interstate highway system. Kennedy's election gave the people of the state an uplift of spirit and a sense of pride for the major role they had played in his becoming president.

The words from his last visit to the state were: "The sun does not always shine in West Virginia but the people always do." Kennedy found a special place in the hearts of West Virginians, his photograph going in many homes that previously had displayed pictures of the beloved Franklin Roosevelt or union leader John L. Lewis.

See also Kennedy-Humphrey Primary

Dan B. Fleming
Blacksburg, Virginia

Dan B. Fleming Jr., *Kennedy vs. Humphrey, West Virginia, 1960,* 1992.

Kennedy-Humphrey Primary

The May 1960 West Virginia primary election stands as a landmark. It dispelled the widely held belief that being a Roman Catholic was a crippling handicap for a presidential candidate. In this overwhelmingly Protestant state, Catholic Sen. John F. Kennedy of Massachusetts soundly defeated Protestant Sen. Hubert H. Humphrey of Minnesota, winning in 50 of the 55 counties.

In the month preceding the West Virginia voting, Kennedy had defeated Humphrey in the Wisconsin primary. Kennedy's winning percentage there was a comfortable 56-44 but not enough to make Humphrey give up as a candidate. The religious issue had surfaced conspicuously in Wisconsin when an ad in weekly newspapers throughout the state urged Protestants to vote for Humphrey.

Apart from religion, all the advantages seemed to be on Kennedy's side as their contest moved into West Virginia. He had plenty of money for advertising, staff salaries, and other campaign expenses. He enjoyed a reputation as a World War II hero. Humphrey had not served in the war. Humphrey also had emerged from Wisconsin heavily in debt, forcing him to campaign as cheaply as possible in West Virginia. Franklin D. Roosevelt Jr., son of a president immensely popular in West Virginia, came to the state to campaign for Kennedy.

Despite Kennedy's seeming advantages, a Lou Harris poll three days before the election showed Humphrey with a 45-42 edge. Kennedy devoted most of a TV appearance the Sunday evening before the election to trying to defuse the religious issue. Theodore H. White in *The Making of the President 1960* called it "the finest TV broadcast I have ever heard any political candidate make." Concluding the telecast, Kennedy said when a president swears on the Bible in his oath of office he is swearing to support separation of church and state. "And if he breaks his oath, he is not only committing a crime against the Constitution, for which the Congress can impeach him—and should impeach him—but he is committing a sin against God."

After that Sunday evening telecast, Lou Harris conducted another poll. The result gave Kennedy a slight edge. His edge was anything but slight in the voting two days later. The statewide totals: Kennedy 236,510; Humphrey 152,187. Once the outcome was clear, Humphrey announced he was no longer a presidential candidate, and Kennedy said, "I think we have now buried the religious issue once and for all."

See also John F. Kennedy

Herb Little
Charleston

Dan B. Fleming Jr., *Kennedy vs. Humphrey: West Virginia, 1960,* 1992; Theodore H. White, *The Making of the President, 1960,* 1961.

Kenova

Kenova lies at the westernmost point of West Virginia, in Wayne County at the juncture of U.S. 60 and U.S. 52 and the confluence of the Ohio and Big Sandy rivers. L. T. Peck, the founder, chose the site just west of Ceredo because it was the place where the Norfolk & Western Railroad proposed to build the first bridge across the Ohio River above Cincinnati. Peck organized the Kenova Association, purchased 900 acres of bottomland, and started his town in 1889. The site was named Kenova from the abbreviations of the three adjoining states: "Ken" for Kentucky, "O" for Ohio, and "Va" for (West) Virginia.

In 1890, the original line of the Norfolk & Western running from Kenova down to Mingo County was completed. There was an influx of engineers, firemen, conductors, brakemen, and other railroad personnel. In 1892, the N&W Ohio River bridge was completed. That year the Baltimore & Ohio Railroad also entered the community. Kenova was incorporated as a town in 1894. From its founding into the early 1900s, Kenova was predominantly a railroad town and served as a terminal for the N&W, C&O, and B&O lines.

Kenova experienced two disastrous floods, in 1913 and 1937, but residents recovered from these calamities and the town grew. During the 1920s, Kenova received its charter as a city. Although Kenova's population has declined from a peak of nearly 5,000 in 1970 to 3,485 in 2000, it remains the largest city in Wayne County.

Joseph Platania
Huntington

Simon Kenton

Frontier scout and "long hunter" Simon Kenton was born April 3, 1755, in Fauquier County, Virginia. He left home at 16 after a fight in which he erroneously thought he had killed a neighbor, who had married the girl Kenton fancied. During his travels Kenton met and befriended Daniel Boone, George Rogers Clark, and Simon Girty, as well as the famous Shawnee Chief Logan.

Upon leaving home, Kenton first traveled north through present West Virginia to Pittsburgh and then explored, hunted, and trapped through much of the Ohio Valley. He spent several winters in the 1770s trapping game along the Ohio River between the Big Sandy and Kanawha rivers. The cane fields of Kentucky were where Kenton made a name for himself as a scout and woodsman.

In 1774, Kenton served as a frontier scout in the Muskingum War and later that same year in Lord Dunmore's War. During the Revolution he served as a scout under George Rogers Clark. When he was not actively serving as a scout, early settlers grew to depend on Kenton as a guide, surveyor, and reliable hunter. Kenton saved the life of Boone and prevented the destruction of Boonesborough during an Indian attack in 1777.

Kenton later founded his own station in what is now Mason County, Kentucky. After losing his wife to a fire in 1797 he moved to Ohio the following year. Kenton had spent more than a year in 1820–21 imprisoned for bad debts in Kentucky until being released upon the revocation of Kentucky's debtor's law. He died in Ohio, April 29, 1836, at the age of 81.

See also Daniel Boone, Dunmore's War
John E. Adkins
Wilbur Smith Associates

Samuel Kercheval

Historian Samuel Kercheval was born in 1767 in Frederick County, Virginia. He married Susan Chinn of Lancaster County, Virginia, on September 23, 1787, and they had 12 children. Kercheval interviewed longtime residents of the lower Shenandoah, the Potomac, and the South Branch valleys, collecting numerous accounts of the events and customs of frontier life during the Indian wars and the Revolution. He vividly recounted these oral histories in *A History of the Valley of Virginia*, published in Winchester in 1833. Kercheval focused on the history and the natural features of the region from the Potomac River to the Fairfax Line. His work effectively preserved the early oral traditions of the Eastern Panhandle and

South Branch Valley. He acknowledged the important contributions of some contemporary chroniclers by including in his book extended quotes from Joseph Doddridge's 1824 *Notes on the Settlement and Indian Wars* concerning frontier warfare and the daily life of the pioneers; John Jeremiah Jacob's 1826 account of Dunmore's War; and Charles James Faulkner's 1832 account of the boundary dispute between Maryland and Virginia. Kercheval continued collecting historical materials and had prepared an enlarged second edition of his book, when he died in Middletown, Virginia, November 14, 1845. The new edition was published posthumously in 1850 and was reprinted in 1902. A 1925 edition, incorporating editorial notes, was reprinted numerous times.

Harold Malcolm Forbes
WVU Libraries

Samuel Kercheval, *A History of the Valley of Virginia*, 1833.

Clark Kessinger

Clark Kessinger was among the most prolific and influential fiddlers of the 20th century, and one of West Virginia's most important traditional musicians. He was born July 27, 1896, near Charleston. Kessinger made his initial mark as a recording artist between 1928 and 1930, when he recorded more than 60 instrumentals with his nephew, guitarist Luches Kessinger. Clark and Luches recorded as the Kessinger Brothers for the Brunswick label. The most popular of these 78 rpm releases was "Wednesday Night Waltz," though lively dance tunes such as "Hell Among the Yearlings" and "Turkey in the Straw" also sold well.

The Kessinger Brothers started performing on radio station WOBU (later WCHS) when the Charleston station began broadcasting in 1927. Clark Kessinger remained in the Kanawha Valley and performed locally for the next 30 years, leading up to his rediscovery during the folk music revival of the 1960s. During the next decade, he recorded extensively, played music across the country, and won numerous fiddling contests. In 1966, he was a guest artist on the *Grand Ole Opry* radio program, on NBC-TV's *Today Show*, and at the prestigious Newport Folk Festival in Rhode Island. Three new albums of his music were released by Kanawha Records.

An energetic and creative musician, Clark Kessinger was recognized for his highly developed technical ability and irrepressible showmanship. He died in St. Albans, June 4, 1975.

See also Fiddle Tradition

John Lilly
Goldenseal

Charles Wolfe, "Clark Kessinger: Pure Fiddling," *Goldenseal*, Fall 1997.

Keslers Cross Lanes, Battle of

On the night of August 21, 1861, the Confederate army of Gen. John B. Floyd, some 2,100 strong, crossed the Gauley River at Carnifex Ferry, Nicholas County, and began to entrench their position. During the afternoon of Sunday, August 25, the 7th Regiment Ohio Volunteer Infantry, Union forces commanded by Col. Erastus B. Tyler and numbering approximately 850 men, advanced from near Gauley Bridge to Keslers Cross Lanes, less than three miles from General Floyd's camp. Tyler failed to scout the area properly or post sufficient pickets. During breakfast the next morning his regiment was caught in a surprise attack by Floyd's army. Initially overwhelmed, men of the 7th Ohio fled for their lives until several companies formed a line of defense on a nearby hill. The ensuing battle lasted only 30 to 45 minutes. At its conclusion the 7th Ohio had been entirely routed from their position, with a loss of two killed, 29 wounded, and 110 missing. The Confederates lost one regimental flag and had several men killed and wounded. This Confederate victory temporarily severed the Union army's lines of communication between the Kanawha Valley and Union headquarters in Wheeling.

See also Civil War

Tim McKinney
Fayetteville

Terry Lowry, *September Blood: The Battle of Carnifex Ferry*, 1985; Tim McKinney, *The Civil War in Fayette County West Virginia*, 1988.

Kettle Bottom

The term kettle bottom, in miners' jargon, refers to a dangerous geologic formation found in the roofs of underground coal mines. Kettle bottoms increase the risk of mine roof falls.

Kettle bottoms were generated in ages long past when an underground mineral deposit formed inside of slate, or when the root mass of an ancient tree petrified. The kettle bottom creates a single compact mass which can shift or even dislodge itself from the surrounding slate and fall. Kettle bottoms pose a deadly danger because they are difficult to detect and usually fall without warning from the mine roof. Any disturbance to nearby rock strata, such as drilling or even striking the mine roof with a hammer to determine stability, causes vibrations and increases the risk of the mass falling. Early miners described the empty space left after a kettle bottom fell as looking like the interior of an inverted kettle.

The risk associated with the kettle bottom itself falling, or the instability caused in the surrounding roof after a fall, creates mine safety problems. Roof bolting can be particularly dangerous in areas where kettle bottoms are present. Heavy timbers are generally used to brace kettle bottoms while permanent roof supports are installed.

Shae Davidson
The Plains, Ohio

Keyser

Keyser, the county seat of Mineral County, is located on the North Branch of the Potomac River in the Eastern Panhandle. The place was first called Paddy Town, supposedly for Patrick McCarty, an early landowner who operated a nearby iron furnace. Later the community was called New Creek, for the creek that joins the North Branch at this location.

The first white men to pass through present Keyser are believed to have been William Mayo and George Savage, sent by Lord Fairfax in 1736 to seek out the source of the Potomac River. The first local land grant was issued by Fairfax to Christopher Beelor on March 20, 1752. Early industry included an iron furnace and foundry, a salt well, and a salt-making plant. The town received an economic boost with the arrival of the Baltimore & Ohio Railroad in 1852, and was renamed for B&O official William Keyser. Mineral County was created in 1866, with Keyser as its county seat.

The Civil War came to Keyser in 1861. Fort Fuller was built on the present site of Potomac State College of West Virginia University. Keyser changed hands 14 times during the war due to the importance of the railroad.

Keyser, elevation 809 feet, was incorporated in 1913. In 2000, its population was 5,303. State Route 46 intersects with U.S. 220 at Keyser, with the latter road then crossing the Potomac into Maryland.

See also Mineral County

Deborah Cruse
WVU Potomac State College

Keystone

Keystone, once notorious because of Cinder Bottom, its widely known red-light district, is located beside Elkhorn Creek on the main line of the Norfolk & Western Railway in McDowell County. The town was incorporated in 1909. Serving surrounding coal company towns, Keystone became a regional center for wholesale grocers, retail stores, saloons, and entertainment as the area underwent rapid population growth. It was named for Pennsylvania, the Keystone State, from which many coal officials came.

Keystone was known for its racial diversity. Boasting the state's first-ever African-American mayor, as well as M. T. Whittico's *McDowell Times*, the state's leading minority newspaper, Keystone was a center of McDowell County's "Free State" community of color. The fictional town of Annadel in Denise Giardina's novel, *Storming Heaven,* is based on Keystone.

Keystone had 2,500 residents by 1950, when the closing of some local mines and the mechanizing of others began to reduce the population. The saloons and brothels began to close as the population waned, as did the town's respectable businesses. Floods and fires threatened the community. Keystone received widespread attention in 1999 when the First National Bank of Keystone was closed by federal agencies, in one of the costliest bank failures in FDIC history. Several bank managers were tried and convicted on various charges. By 2000, Keystone's population had fallen to 453.

C. Stuart McGehee
West Virginia State University

Harley Kilgore

U.S. Senator Harley Martin Kilgore was born in rural Harrison County, January 11, 1893. He was the only son and the elder of two children of Quimby Hugh Kilgore, an oil well driller and contractor, and Laura Jo Kilgore. The family moved to Mannington when Harley was young, and he graduated from Mannington High School in 1910. In 1914, Kilgore earned his law degree from West Virginia University and was admitted to the bar. He taught school in 1914–15, and was a principal in Raleigh County for one term. He then turned to the practice of law. Kilgore joined the army during World War I, where he was commissioned a second lieutenant in 1917. Upon promotion to captain he served as a company commander.

On May 10, 1921, Kilgore married Lois Elaine Lilly in Huntington. Living in Beckley, he held a number of political positions, including city recorder and prosecuting attorney; in 1932, he was elected judge of the Criminal Court for Raleigh County. A merciful judge, he believed that criminals should be rehabilitated if possible.

In 1940, a struggle for control of the Democrat Party pulled Kilgore into the state's political spotlight. To ensure that the party ran a liberal for governor, Matthew M. Neely gave up his seat in the U.S. Senate to run for governor himself. Soon after Neely's announcement, Kilgore, also a liberal, announced that he would run for the state's other U.S. Senate seat, opposing fellow Democrats Rush D. Holt and Herman Guy Kump in the primary. With labor's support Kilgore won both the primary and general elections. In an unusual set of circumstances, he became the senior senator from West Virginia, due to a squabble over the seating of Neely's successor.

When he arrived in Washington, Kilgore made a friend of Sen. Harry Truman, who along with Kilgore was concerned with the inefficiency of the government procurement system. When the Truman Com-

Senator Harley M. Kilgore (1893–1956).

mittee examined World War II expenditures, Kilgore headed up a number of the investigations, which led to exposure of fraud and incompetence. As chairman of a military subcommittee on war mobilization, Kilgore led an investigation of the scientific and organizational weaknesses in the war effort. This led to the establishment of the Office of War Mobilization. Ultimately, Kilgore initiated a debate over the establishment of the National Science Foundation, which was created in 1950. Kilgore investigated international cartels and how foreign companies used their business relations, before, during, and after World War II to advance their cause to the detriment of the U.S. national interest. Despite attempts to link him to communism, Kilgore was easily re-elected in 1952, the first West Virginian elected to a third term in the U.S. Senate.

After the war, Kilgore supported Truman's Fair Deal and foreign policies, influenced the appointment of Clarksburg native Louis A. Johnson as secretary of defense, authored the liberalized Displaced Persons Act and Youth Corrections Act, and continued to examine the problem of monopolies. He died in office, February 28, 1956, of a cerebral hemorrhage and was buried in Arlington National Cemetery.

Robert Franklin Maddox
Marshall University
Robert Franklin Maddox, *The War Within World War II: The United States and International Cartels,* 2001; Maddox, *The Senatorial Career of Harley Martin Kilgore,* 1981.

June Kilgore

Artist June Kilgore, born in Huntington, September 29, 1927, is an abstract expressionist painter who spent 30 years as an art professor at Marshall University. She was one of the most influential West Virginia artists of the 20th century. Kilgore's work, although not figurative, holds a strong sense of the spiritual and a very emotional communication. She is known also for her eloquence in talking about art. Kilgore is cited as an influence in the development of several accomplished artists in West Virginia, Dolly Hartman and Sally Romayne among them.

Kilgore's work is part of prestigious collections, including those of Sen. John D. Rockefeller IV and the Federal University of Brazil. Hers was the first retrospective of a West Virginia artist's work done by the Cultural Center at the state capitol in Charleston. She has had one-person exhibitions at galleries in Charleston and elsewhere, including the Pratt Institute in New York. She was honored with the Distinguished West Virginian award in 1995 by Governor Caperton. In 1997, Kilgore won one of the three $5,000 Governor's Awards in the West Virginia Juried Exhibition. Her abstract acrylic painting, "Black Garden Stone for Meditation (With Guardians): Transcendence" also received the highest honor in the show, the D. Gene Jordon Memorial Award. June Kilgore lives in Huntington.

D. B. Shawver
Charleston

Killbuck

Killbuck is the English name of a prominent war chief, medicine man, and village councilman of the Delaware tribe. His Indian name may have been Bemineo. Killbuck achieved enduring fame by leading bloody raids against frontier settlements in present eastern West Virginia during the French and Indian War.

Killbuck apparently lived for short periods among the settlers in the South Branch Valley before the commencement of hostilities in 1755. He is credited with leading 60 to 70 warriors who surrounded and killed most of a group of 16 to 18 militiamen at the Battle of the Trough in late April 1756. The militiamen had been attempting to surprise Killbuck's band, which was camped at a spring at the head of the Trough, on the South Branch Potomac just northeast of Old Fields.

On April 28, 1758, Killbuck appeared at Fort Seybert with 40 to 50 Delaware and Shawnee warriors and intimidated the fort's garrison into surrendering. After the capitulation of the fort, 17 adults were executed, and 24 women and children were forced to return with the Indians to their villages in the Ohio country. The day before, Fort Upper Tract nine miles to the west had been captured and destroyed by Indians possibly aided by French soldiers. All of the fort's 23 occupants were killed. Killbuck either directed the capture of this fort or at least was instrumental in its downfall.

Kercheval in his *History of the Valley of Virginia* reports that Vincent Williams Jr. and Peter Casey Jr. visited and talked with Killbuck during the later Revolutionary War. The two men reported that Killbuck was blind at the time. Killbuck died at the Delaware village in present Coshocton, Ohio, in 1779. Numerous descendants of Killbuck are scattered across the United States.

See also The Trough, Fort Seybert

Greg Adamson
Dayton, Virginia

William H. Ansel, *Frontier Forts along the Potomac and its Tributaries*, 1984; Samuel Kercheval, *A History of The Valley of Virginia*, 1833.

Kimball War Memorial

The War Memorial in Kimball, McDowell County, was the first building in the country erected to honor African-Americans who fought in World War I. In the early years of the 20th century the southern West Virginia coalfields had a large black population. During World War I, McDowell County alone mustered 1,500 black soldiers. The War Memorial also became home to the country's first all-black American Legion Post, named for Luther Patterson, one of the first African-American casualties of the war.

Designed by architect Hassel T. Hicks of Welch, the memorial was dedicated in 1928. The two-story brick structure is Classical Revival in style, with a massive two-story Roman Doric portico on the front facade. A focal point of community life for many years, the building served as a social, recreational, and cultural center for black and white residents alike and hosted such well-known entertainers as Cab Calloway and his band.

As mining jobs disappeared and McDowell's population declined, the building fell into disrepair. After it was gutted by fire in 1991, a citizens group was organized to undertake the renovation and restoration of the building. The Kimball War Memorial was placed on the National Register of Historic Places in 1993.

Margo Stafford
Clarksburg

Kingwood

Kingwood, located on State Routes 7 and 26 in the northeastern corner of West Virginia, is the county seat of Preston County. Overlooking the Cheat River Valley at an elevation of 1,862 feet, Kingwood was settled in 1807 and chartered by the Virginia legislature in 1853. It was named for a grove of tall, stately trees. Kingwood had a 2000 population of 2,944, governed by a mayor and city council. Kingwood is the site of Preston County's hospital, chamber of commerce, sheriff's office and jail, a large volunteer fire department, library, civic groups, two radio stations, several churches, and various businesses.

Once a coal and timber town, Kingwood's current largest private industry is the Matthews International Corporation (formerly Sheidow Bronze), a foundry employing 260 people. Kingwood is the site of the annual Buckwheat Festival. The town has two newspapers, the *Preston County Journal* and the *Preston County News*. The 646th Quartermaster Company's Army Reserve Training Center is less than a mile southeast of Kingwood, and the National Guard's sprawling Camp Dawson, a year-round military training site, is just northeast. An 18-hole golf course adjoins the camp. Deer, bear, and turkey hunting and whitewater rafting attract visitors to the area.

See also Preston County

Peggy Ross
Reedsville

Kingwood Tunnel

The Kingwood Tunnel was constructed on the Baltimore & Ohio Railroad between 1849 and 1852 near Tunnelton, in Preston County. The tunnel was named for nearby Kingwood, and Tunnelton was named for the tunnel. The tunnel's completion allowed the completion of the B&O across Western Virginia to Wheeling. During the Civil War, the Confederates tried unsuccessfully to destroy the tunnel during the Jones-Imboden Raid of 1863.

The Kingwood Tunnel was one of many tunnels and bridges that engineers had to design to bring the B&O through Western Virginia's mountainous terrain. The tunnel was constructed by a work force composed primarily of Irish immigrants working with simple tools. The workers tunneled on each end, with three additional shafts being constructed from the top of the hill. Temporary railroad tracks were laid to transport supplies over the mountain during construction. The tunnel measured nearly 4,100 feet in length and required the movement of nearly 200,000 cubic yards of earth and rock. At the time it was reputedly the longest rail tunnel in the world.

A major problem with the Kingwood Tunnel was its design as a single-track tunnel, which made it a chronic bottleneck. A new double-track tunnel was completed in 1912 below the original tunnel to help alleviate train congestion in the area. The original tunnel was closed and sealed in 1962.

Brad Martin
Arthurdale

Mary Kinnan

Indian captive Mary Kinnan was born Mary Lewis, August 26, 1763, in New Jersey. In 1778, she married Joseph Kinnan. They moved to Randolph County in 1787, settling in the Tygart Valley.

In May 1791, three Shawnee raiders entered the Kinnan home. Joseph Kinnan was fatally shot by the Indians and a neighbor child was also killed. Among those who escaped was Jacob Lewis, Mary's brother. Mary fled the house with her young daughter, but a pursuing Indian seized and killed the child. Kinnan herself was captured and held prisoner. It is believed that she was taken by her captors to a point near the Buckhannon River, then down the Ohio by way of the Little Kanawha. She was then taken to a village near Fort Wayne on the Maumee River, an Ohio tributary. She was sold several times and eventually became the property of an Indian woman. They settled about 20 miles from Detroit.

Nearly two years passed before Kinnan could identify herself to an Indian trader, Robert Albert. She later gave him a note to send to her friends. In 1793, Kinnan's letter arrived in her old community in New Jersey and was read to a Presbyterian congregation. A collection was taken up and her brother, Jacob Lewis, was sent to rescue Kinnan. After almost a year he arrived in Detroit, visited the Indian encampment and saw his sister. In October 1794, Lewis rescued his sister. They eventually returned to New Jersey.

Kinnan never returned to her home in (West) Virginia, living the rest of her life in New Jersey. She died March 12, 1848.

McKinnie L. Phelps, *The Indian Captivity of Mary Kinnan, 1791–1794,* 1967.

John S. Knight

Newspaper publisher John S. Knight Sr. was born in Bluefield, October 26, 1894. His father, Charles Landon Knight, had come to southern West Virginia the previous year to practice law, but found legal work not to his liking. Instead, C. L. Knight developed a relationship with Hugh Ike Shott, founder of the *Bluefield Daily Telegraph.* The elder Knight supplemented his income by writing feature stories for the *Telegraph.*

After leaving southern West Virginia, the elder Knight tried a couple of professions before moving to northeastern Ohio and buying the Akron *Beacon Journal* on October 12, 1903. After serving in World War I, John S. Knight Sr., became a reporter with the *Beacon Journal* and took over as editor when his father died September 26, 1933. He built the Knight-Ridder Newspapers chain, which had 3.2 million readers at the time of his death, June 16, 1981, and owned some of the nation's most powerful newspapers including the *Miami Herald,* the *Philadelphia Inquirer* and the *Detroit Free Press.*

John S. Knight Sr. was a conservative Republican but was noted for his bitter opposition to the Vietnam War. Based in part on his long record of service and also for his columns expressing opposition to American involvement in Vietnam, he received the Pulitzer Prize on May 6, 1968.

William R. Archer
Bluefield

Knights of Labor

Formed in 1869, the Noble Order of the Knights of Labor was a secret fraternal organization that sought to include all workers regardless of ethnic origin or sex. The Knights offered membership to those in all trades, including professionals such as doctors, lawyers, and bankers in addition to craftsmen and laborers. The Knights of Labor began organizing in West Virginia in the late 1870s and by the mid-1880s had organized local assemblies that made up 16 district assemblies. The Knights had dropped their secrecy by the 1880s and actively and openly represented its members in labor disputes.

The 1890s saw the Knights in competition for membership with the newly organized United Mine Workers of America, and for a while, the Knights were able to keep their numbers strong. Even though the Knights eschewed strikes as a means of securing their goals, competition from the UMWA led the organization to take part in the 1897 coal strike. The UMWA, with vigorous organizing campaigns, strong stands against coal operators, and growing national influence, began to eat into the Knights' constituency. The competition was so intense that the UMWA accused the Knights of actually aligning with the operators and securing "scabs" to help break strikes of UMWA miners. By the early 1900s, only a few local assemblies continued to exist in the West Virginia coalfields and the Knights quickly disappeared.

Kenneth R. Bailey
WVU Institute of Technology
Evelyn Harris and Frank Krebs, *From Humble Beginnings: West Virginia State Federation of Labor, 1903–1957,* 1960; Maier B. Fox, *United We Stand: The United Mine Workers of America,* 1990.

Don Knotts

Comedic actor Don Knotts will be forever remembered as the nervous deputy Barney Fife on the *Andy Griffith Show* on television. Knotts, who was born in Morgantown, July 21, 1924, graduated from Morgantown High School and received a drama degree from West Virginia University. After appearing in Broadway and screen versions of *No Time for Sergeants* in the 1950s, he became a regular on the *Steve Allen Show.* Knotts received five Emmy Awards for his work on the *Andy Griffith Show* from 1960 to 1965. After leaving the show, he earned three additional Emmys for guest appearances and starred in a number of feature films. Knotts returned to television in the late 1970s, portraying a meddling landlord on *Three's Company,* which co-starred another West Virginia native, Joyce DeWitt. In the 1980s and 1990s, Knotts performed in a number of stage productions and appeared occasionally on Andy Griffith's show, *Matlock.*

Don Knotts died in Los Angeles, February 24, 2006.

Stan Bumgardner
Division of Culture and History
"From Mayberry to Charleston," *Charleston Gazette,* April 29, 1993.

John Knowles

Writer John Knowles, born in Fairmont, September 16, 1926, attained literary fame in 1959 with his first novel, *A Separate Peace.* The book was inspired by his war-years experience at a private school, Phillips Exeter Academy in New Hampshire. Knowles later attended Yale University.

A coming-of-age novel often compared to J. D. Salinger's *Catcher in the Rye,* Knowles's first book continues to be widely read and has achieved the status of a modern classic. *A Separate Peace* was nominated for the National Book Award and earned its author a Rosenthal Award and the William Faulkner Award for best first novel. Knowles's other published works include *Morning in Antibes* (1962), *Double Vision: American Thoughts Abroad* (1964), *Indian Summer* (1966), *Phineas: Six Stories* (1969), *Paragon* (1971), *Spreading Fires* (1974), *A Vein of Riches* (1978), *Peace Breaks Out* (1981), and *The Private Life of Axie Reed* (1986). *A Vein of Riches,* set in and around "Middletown," apparently a fictional Fairmont, was Knowles's notable use of a West Virginia coal country setting for his fiction.

John Knowles died November 29, 2001, in Florida.

See also Literature

Gordon Simmons
Division of Culture and History

Korean War

The Korean War began on June 25, 1950, when the armies of Communist North Korea pushed across the 38th parallel into South Korea. In late July, draft boards in West Virginia mailed draft notices to single men born in 1924 and 1925 who were not veterans of World War II. This draft call for West Virginia totaled 652 men, but inductions did not begin until late September.

Three West Virginia National Guard battalions and one Air National Guard squadron were ordered to federal service during the Korean campaign. Of the National Guard units, the 201st Armored Field Artillery Battalion and two companies of the 126th Transportation Truck Battalion were assigned to Germany. Members of the 167th Fighter Squadron of the West Virginia Air National Guard served in Europe and as combat replacements in Korea. Serving directly on the Korean front were four companies of the 1092nd Engineer Combat Battalion from Parkersburg and Salem, also National Guard. The West Virginia members of this battalion served two years in federal service during the Korean War, at one time fighting as infantrymen. They saw strenuous service in the first four of the seven major campaigns of the Korean War, from the first UN counteroffensive through the second Korean winter offensive, before returning to West Virginia in 1952. On July 27, 1953, a cease-fire agreement was signed at P'anmunjom.

The Korean War took the lives of four million people, including 37,000 Americans. More than 8,000 are still listed as missing in action. West Virginians totaling 112,000 men and women served in the Korean War. Of that number, 801 died, and 2,088 were wounded. Four West Virginians received the Congressional Medal of Honor during the Korean War. Army private Kenneth Shadrick of Wyoming County was the first U.S. serviceman killed in action in the Korean War, on July 5, 1950.

Larry Legge
Barboursville

George James Kossuth

Photographer George James Kossuth was born April 12, 1885, in Clifton, Mason County. His family moved to Wheeling during his infancy. As a teenager he apprenticed with Wheeling photographer Frank Giffen.

Kossuth opened his own studio in 1909, and quickly became the leading portrait photographer in the city. In the ensuing years he photographed nearly every celebrity who visited Wheeling. Kossuth's studio became famous as a gathering place for local and visiting artists and musicians. He played an active role in the city's cultural life, serving on the board of directors of the Wheeling Symphony and promoting the development and activities of many other organizations, including the Oglebay Institute Mansion Museum and the Stifel Fine Arts Center.

Kossuth eventually achieved broad fame for his insightful portraits of many of the world's celebrities, especially in the field of music. Richard Strauss, Fritz Reiner, Karl Muck, Jerome Hines, Fritz Kreisler, Jascha Heifetz, and John Philip Sousa were among the musical giants whom he photographed. Another was the conductor Leopold Stokowski, who employed Kossuth as his personal photographer for a period of six years. Among the dignitaries in other fields that he photographed were Clarence Darrow, Richard Nixon, Carl Sandburg, and Lowell Thomas. Also an art collector, connoisseur, and conservator, Kossuth is credited with rediscovering and preserving the work of the Wheeling artist Jeanie Caldwell Daugherty. Kossuth died in Wheeling, September 14, 1960.

John A. Cuthbert
WVU Libraries

Tom Kromer

Novelist and short story writer Thomas Michael Kromer was born in Huntington, October 20, 1906, to Grace Thornburg and Czech immigrant Albert Kromer, a coal miner and glass worker. The Kromers also lived at times in Fairmont, Kingwood, and Williamstown.

Best-known for his first novel, *Waiting for Nothing* (1935), Kromer chronicled the plight of the dispossessed of the Great Depression. His fiction attracted the attention of the literary left, including Lincoln Steffens, who published some of Kromer's short fiction in his magazine, *Pacific Weekly*, and Theodore Dreiser, who wrote an introduction for the British edition of *Waiting for Nothing*. Maxim Lieber, who had been Thomas Wolfe's literary agent, handled most of Kromer's published work, placing parts of Kromer's unfinished novel, *Michael Kohler*, in *American Spectator* magazine, which was edited by playwright Eugene O'Neill and others. *Michael Kohler* draws on firsthand accounts of coal mining, the glass industry, and, like *Waiting for Nothing*, the psychological tumult of the Depression.

Kromer attended Marshall College (now Marshall University) for brief periods between 1925 and 1929. He crisscrossed the country after 1929, often traveling by freight train. He married in 1936 and settled down in Albuquerque for a quarter-century. He gave up writing about 1940, becoming an invalid. He returned to Huntington in 1960, living there with family until his death January 10, 1969.

Thomas Douglass
East Carolina University
Tom Kromer, *Waiting for Nothing and Other Writings*, 1986.

Ku Klux Klan

The term Ku Klux Klan refers to a number of secret, racist societies that have existed at various times since 1865. The Klan originated in the South following the Civil War, seeking to reestablish and maintain white supremacy after the emancipation of the slaves. In West Virginia, Klan chapters organized in the late 1860s, after African-Americans acquired political rights and ex-Confederates were disenfranchised. Once voting privileges were restored to former Confederates in 1871, the KKK virtually disappeared in West Virginia for the next half-century.

The Klan reemerged nationally in the 20th century, with a significant revival in West Virginia in the late 1910s and early 1920s. National membership briefly totaled several million, and thousands of Klansmen rallied in Washington and elsewhere. An out-of-state Klan publication carried reports from several West Virginia locations in 1924, including Clarksburg, Parkersburg, Williamson, and McDowell County. The Klan of the 1920s

opposed Catholics, Jews, immigrants, and labor unions as well as blacks. Several Catholic public school teachers in West Virginia were fired at the Klan's insistence. The KKK also dabbled in politics and influenced the outcome of a number of local elections. Scandals weakened the organization, but several Klan chapters survived until 1944, when the secret order officially disbanded.

The years after World War II were bleak for Klan recruiters in West Virginia, and racial desegregation did not bring a large Klan revival in the 1950s and 1960s. There has been limited Klan activity in West Virginia since the mid-1970s, part of an attempted national resurgence. Many of the modern Klans are tied to neo-Nazi, Christian Identity, and other white supremacist groups. The contemporary Klans are not only xenophobic but also anti-government, and some of the groups advocate the overthrow of the federal government.

Teresa Statler-Keener
West Virginia University
David Chalmers, *Hooded Americanism: The History of the Ku Klux Klan*, 1987.

Kudzu

Kudzu is a fast-growing, weedy vine of the bean (legume) family. Characteristics of the vine are large three-part hairy leaves; showy, fragrant clusters of deep purple flowers, and fuzzy bean-like pods. It is native to Japan and China, where it has been used in foods and medications and for cattle forage for centuries. It was introduced into the United States in 1876 at a Philadelphia trade exposition, as an ornamental. Kudzu was later planted throughout the South for forage and erosion control.

Kudzu was likely introduced into West Virginia in the 1930s for the same reasons it was planted in the South. It now occurs in more than half of the counties in West Virginia. In southern West Virginia the vine is an aggressive weed that occasionally covers patches of five acres or more along stream banks, roadsides, and forest openings. Most patches in northern West Virginia cover less than one-tenth acre. The vines can grow up to a foot per day and easily overtop brush and trees in ghostly green mounds which smother the life from the underlying plants.

In the southern United States, kudzu covers more than seven million acres of farmland, forests, roadsides, and forest openings. Kudzu vine supposedly cannot withstand the cold winter temperatures of northern West Virginia or in the high mountains. Still, there are healthy populations near the Pennsylvania border in Morgantown and Reedsville. The large roots are a potential source of quality starch for cooking and contain daidzin, which suppresses alcohol addiction.

William N. Grafton
WVU Extension Service

Kumbrabow State Forest

Kumbrabow State Forest was created during the Great Depression, as were many of West Virginia's state parks and forests, in response to President Franklin D. Roosevelt's administration of the Civilian Conservation Corps Act of 1933. This legislation allowed for the development of state parks and forests at federal expense, if the state owned suitable land. The Allegheny highlands of southern Randolph County were widely recognized as suitable and were viewed as holding great promise as future public forest. Despite previous removal of magnificent stands of red spruce and hemlock, and subsequent wildfires, the high elevation (2,300–3,390 feet) and abundant rainfall of the area were expected to promote rapid forest regrowth. The land for Kumbrabow was purchased on December 29, 1934. The forest was named for a combination of elements of the names of Governor Kump, businessman Spates Brady, and attorney Hubert Bowers, all of whom were influential in the creation of the park.

Until 1941, Kumbrabow State Forest was home to two CCC camps whose duties included fire hazard reduction, forest stand improvement, and wildlife surveys. Corpsmen also built a picnic area with a pavilion and a camping area and five primitive cabins, which remain in use today. More recent additions include a sixth, handicapped accessible cabin and cross-country ski trails. Today, Kumbrabow is a successful example of a multiple-use public land, supporting demonstrations of modern timbering methods, forest management, and rare species conservation, as well as popular recreation activities including fishing, hunting, hiking, bird-watching, and camping.

W. Russ McClain
Nature Conservancy of West Virginia

Herman Guy Kump

Herman Guy Kump, the 19th governor of West Virginia, was born October 31, 1877, in Capon Springs, Hampshire County, the son of Margaret Rudolph and Benjamin Franklin Kump. He grew up on a 500-acre farm devoted to stock raising. Educated in local schools through the eighth grade, Kump then attended Shenandoah Normal School near Winchester, Virginia. As a young man, he taught two terms in his former school in Hampshire County, worked briefly as a deputy county clerk, and for more than two years served as a paymaster of the Consolidation Coal Company's Monongah mine.

From 1903 to 1905, Kump attended the University of Virginia law school, then opened a law practice in Elkins. A Democrat, he launched his political career by successfully running for prosecuting attorney in Randolph County in 1908. After two terms he was defeated in the 1916

Governor Herman Guy Kump (1877–1962).

primary. He served in the army during World War I, serving in Washington as a captain in ordnance. In 1921, he was elected mayor of Elkins, serving until 1923. He helped found the Citizens National Bank of Elkins, and was its president for many years. In 1928, he was elected judge of the 20th judicial circuit.

In 1932, as West Virginia faced the worst of the Great Depression, Kump ran for governor, defeating the labor-backed Republican T. C. Townsend in a sweeping Democratic victory that also saw Franklin D. Roosevelt defeat Herbert Hoover for the presidency. For the first time since 1894, Democrats controlled the governorship and both houses of the legislature in West Virginia.

As Kump prepared to take office, the banking system teetered on the verge of collapse, the state faced a severe fiscal crisis, and the unemployment rate was among the highest in the nation. Before his inauguration, Kump spent 10 days in Virginia, studying the Old Dominion's system of public finance and seeking advice from conservative Democrats Harry Flood Byrd and Gov. John Garland Pollard. He also turned to experts at West Virginia University headed by John Fairfield Sly, a political science professor. Sly and his colleagues, who came to be known as Kump's "little Brain Trust," in reference to Roosevelt's famous group of advisers, helped prepare a legislative program.

The 41st legislature met for 240 days, through a regular session and two extraordinary sessions, as the governor and lawmakers found themselves facing not only a severe economic crisis but also a constitutional quagmire caused by the tax limitation amendment to the constitution. Passed by voters in the 1932 election in the hope that it might serve as an economic panacea, the tax amendment severely reduced customary sources of revenue, leaving unfunded many ser-

vices and obligations of municipal and county governments, including for a time the wages and salaries of policemen, firemen, school teachers, and road workers. The state Supreme Court complicated matters by twice nullifying legislation to implement the amendment.

Faced with the need for $20 million in new revenues, Kump and his advisers devised legislation that generated new funds through sales taxes, an income tax, and a series of indirect taxes. Because the tax limitation amendment curtailed local revenue sources, Kump's program necessarily increased the state's power over roads, finance, and schools at the expense of local governments and school boards. Reform prompted by federal legislation such as the 1935 Social Security Act also led to a state system of unemployment compensation and increased state control over public welfare matters once left largely to counties.

Although he had heartily endorsed Roosevelt during the 1932 election, Kump soon found himself at odds with Roosevelt's New Deal. More attuned to the agenda of business than to labor and deriving more support from traditional Democrats than from liberal New Dealers, Kump led the conservative "Statehouse Democrats" in a bitter struggle against the pro-New Deal Democrats, headed by U.S. Sen. Matthew M. Neely. Kump feared that federal initiatives threatened state prerogatives, resented the growth of organized labor under favorable federal legislation, often warned of the harmful potential of government relief, and opposed revising state law to ease participation in federal programs requiring state matching funds. His program of fiscal conservatism restored the state treasury to a healthy condition and improved the state's bond ratings, but education, highways, charitable institutions, and other state services suffered from neglect.

Prohibited by law from seeking reelection, Kump left office on January 18, 1937, and returned to Elkins where he resumed his legal practice and banking activities. Although he unsuccessfully sought the Democratic nomination as U.S. Senator in 1940 and 1942, he never served in public office again.

Kump married Edna Scott on October 9, 1907, and they had six children. He died February 14, 1962, at his home in Elkins.

See also Matthew Mansfield Neely, New Deal, Tax Limitation Amendment

Jerry Bruce Thomas
Shepherd University

Albert Steven Gatrell, "Herman Guy Kump: A Political Profile," Ph.D. dissertation, West Virginia University, 1979; John G. Morgan, *West Virginia Governors*, 1980; Jerry Bruce Thomas, *An Appalachian New Deal: West Virginia in the Great Depression*, 1998.

Kyashuta

Kyashuta was a Seneca, born around 1725 on the Genesee River in New York. He died around 1794 in southwestern Pennsylvania. In 1753, Kyashuta accompanied George Washington on his mission to advise the French to withdraw from their newly constructed forts in the Ohio Valley. After Braddock's defeat in 1755, Kyashuta replaced Half-King as the primary representative of the Six Nations (Iroquois) in the Ohio River country until around 1778.

Kyashuta was a significant figure in affairs affecting Western Virginia. He directed war efforts against the settlers during the French and Indian War (1754–63) and Pontiac's Rebellion (1763). His command of combined Indian forces during these wars was responsible for the abandonment of the Greenbrier River and Monongahela River settlements. After a series of violent incidents against both Indian and white border dwellers, culminating in the murder of Logan's family in April 1774, Kyashuta urged his associates to refrain from war against the Virginians. While he had general agreement from the Delawares, his influence over the Mingoes and Shawnees was waning. Most of their warriors joined with Wyandotte warriors to resist the invading Virginia militia during Dunmore's War, which culminated in the October 1774 Battle of Point Pleasant.

During the subsequent American Revolution, Kyashuta assisted the Mohawk Joseph Brant in directing the Indian war effort against Virginia and other states. As he had done at the end of Pontiac's Rebellion, Kyashuta became a strong peace advocate after hostilities ceased.

In 1770, Kyashuta was engaged in his autumn hunt along the Ohio River when he chanced upon George Washington in present Wood County. Washington noted in his diary that he felt obliged to pay compliments to his old acquaintance, "As this person was one of the Six Nation Chiefs, & the head of them upon this River." Washington's diary records Kyashuta's intimate knowledge of the Kanawha Valley, including vegetation, soils, topography, transportation conditions, and distances between significant landmarks.

Douglas McClure Wood
Nitro

L

La Belle Ironworks

The Wheeling-La Belle Nail Company (formerly La Belle Ironworks) manufactures cut nails using 19th-century machines and technology. Located in south Wheeling, the La Belle Ironworks was founded in 1852, and takes its name from the French name for the Ohio River, La Belle Rivière, "the beautiful river." Making cut nails was an important 19th-century American manufacture, and nail production became a hallmark of Wheeling industry. By 1875, the city was known as the Nail City, and La Belle was Wheeling's leading nail producer. But as cut nail use declined in the late 1880s in favor of modern wire nails, La Belle diversified its product line, first through the manufacture of tin plate, and later with the production of steel plates, tubes, and sheets. In 1920, La Belle merged with Wheeling Iron and Steel and Whitaker-Glessner Company to form Wheeling Steel Corporation (now Wheeling-Pittsburgh Steel Corporation) and continued to produce cut nails, developing a specialized market in hardened nails for use in masonry. D-Mac Industries bought the nail plant in 1997, and operates it as Wheeling-La Belle Nail Company. It survives today as one of the two remaining cut nail factories in the United States.

See also Ironmaking, Wheeling

Lee R. Maddex
WVU Institute for the History of Technology
Earl Chapin May, *From Principio to Wheeling, 1715 to 1945: A Pageant of Iron and Steel*, 1945; Henry Dickerson Scott, *Iron & Steel in Wheeling*, 1929.

Division of Labor

The West Virginia Bureau of Labor, the predecessor to the modern Division of Labor, was created by the state legislature in 1889. The rapid increase in the number and variety of factories and the growth in industrial development had dictated a need for a state agency to monitor and report on issues affecting business and employment. Labor organizations strongly promoted the need for a state labor agency and pushed the appointment of Richard Robertson, editor of a Wheeling newspaper, as the first commissioner of labor. Governor Wilson instead chose Edward Robertson, twin brother to Richard and the superintendent of the penitentiary at Moundsville, for the post. Speculation was that Wilson, a Democrat, was displeased with the Republican views Richard Robertson expressed in his newspaper.

Though its duties were relatively minor at its creation, issues relating to safety, working hours and working conditions, the employment of children, reporting of statistical data relating to industrial production, and the regulation of weights and measures eventually fell under the purview of the Bureau of Labor. From 1889 to 1914, the Bureau of Labor maintained its offices in Wheeling, unlike other executive departments of government. While the official reason is not clear, Wheeling was the largest city in the state until well into the 1900s; it was the center of West Virginia's Upper Ohio Valley industrial region; and, until after the United Mine Workers successfully organized the Kanawha and New River coalfields, had the largest concentration of unionized workers in the state. By 1914, the state's economic focus had shifted to southern West Virginia and Commissioner of Labor Jack H. Nightingale established offices in the state capitol on June 1, 1914.

The Bureau of Labor became the Department of Labor in 1930. The chief official has been known as the commissioner of labor since the inception of the Bureau. In the first of Governor Caperton's two terms, the Department of Labor became the Division of Labor and was included in the newly created Bureau of Commerce. The current Division of Labor organization places its legislatively mandated responsibilities in section sub-groups: Weights and Measures, Wages and Hours, Manufactured Housing, Safety-Boiler Inspection and General Administration. In 2004, there were approximately 100 employees in the Division of Labor. The agency is headquartered at the capitol complex in Charleston.

Kenneth R. Bailey
WVU Institute of Technology

Labor History

The industrialization of West Virginia during the late 19th and early 20th centuries attracted enormous capital into the state's railroads, timber, coal, and other industries. Industrialization dramatically altered the size and composition of the population. West Virginia's southern coalfield population nearly quintupled between 1880 and 1920, from 93,000 to 446,000. In the new coal company towns, native whites, blacks, and some 25 different nationalities converged in a bewildering array of cultures. Nevertheless, the miners soon came to focus on their common economic interests, and to improve their bargaining position through union organizing.

The effort to establish the miners' union, and the operators' resistance, played a major role in shaping the history of West Virginia in the 20th century. The United Mine Workers of America made little progress during the first decade of the century, although the octogenarian labor organizer Mary Harris "Mother" Jones had sporadic success in the Ka-

nawha Valley. UMWA President John Mitchell came to Charleston in 1907 to launch a major union offensive, only to be defeated by injunctions and company guards.

For their magnitude and level of violence, several struggles for union recognition have entered the realm of legend: the Paint Creek-Cabin Creek mine war of 1912–13; the Mingo mine wars of 1919–21; and the March on Logan in 1921. The march involved at least 10,000 people and entailed episodes that have become infamous in their own right, including the Battle of Blair Mountain, the Matewan Massacre, the assassination of Matewan police chief Sid Hatfield by company agents, and the treason trials.

Although violent strikes in the coal industry are an important theme in the history of organized labor, other strikes in West Virginia achieved national prominence as well. One of the most important, the national railroad strike of 1877, began on the Baltimore & Ohio Railroad at Martinsburg and brought transportation to a standstill throughout most of the eastern United States.

When U.S. District Judge Alston G. Dayton decided with the Hitchman Coal and Coke Company in 1907 that union organizers were violating the federal anti-trust laws, and allowed an injunction to stop them, he handed companies a powerful weapon for their war against organized labor. With the government on their side, the companies crushed the union movement, and the period of the 1920s was the low point for organized labor in the Mountain State.

Although the early struggles failed, they nevertheless produced numerous indigenous leaders, some with national recognition, such as Frank Keeney, Fred Mooney, and Bill Blizzard. Much later, Arnold Miller, a miner from Cabin Creek who led the reformist Miners for Democracy, ousted Tony Boyle as president of the UMWA in 1972. Still later, in 1995, another miner from Cabin Creek, Cecil Roberts, became president of the UMWA. There were others too, such as Wheeling-born Victor and Walter Reuther, both of whom became officials of the United Autoworkers. Walter became president of the UAW and played an important role in the CIO and the civil rights movement.

Business and government repression during the 1920s prepared the ground for a triumphal return of organized labor with the election of President Franklin D. Roosevelt in 1932. The National Industrial Recovery Act in 1933, particularly Section 7a, which guaranteed workers the right to collective bargaining and outlawed yellow-dog contracts, was hailed as labor's Magna Carta. The act was declared unconstitutional in 1935, but by then most of the industrial workers in West Virginia had been unionized. Quick

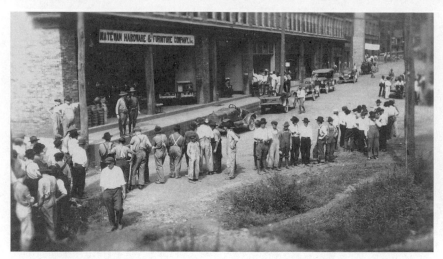
Miners line up for strike relief in Matewan, about 1921.

passage of the Wagner Act that same year preserved labor's right to collective bargaining.

Some unions had seemed to be headed for extinction, but Roosevelt's New Deal gave them new life. West Virginia's glassworkers are a case in point. By the 1930s, the tri-state upper Ohio River region had more than half of the glass factories in the nation. These factories specialized in bottles, window glass, or tableware. By the 1880s, glassworkers were organized into three strong craft unions based on these specializations. The glassworkers' unions were dominated by French, Belgian, and German immigrants who passed the craft on to their sons. Their tight control of production provided strong incentive for glass companies to mechanize their plants in the early 20th century. The unions fought bitter strikes but failed to deflect the introduction of technology by the 1920s. Legislation protecting the right to organize unions during the 1930s revived the glassworkers' organizations and boosted union membership among West Virginia's 13,000 glassworkers.

UMWA President John L. Lewis challenged the American Federation of Labor in 1935 by initiating a campaign to organize workers by industry rather than along craft lines. The resistance of the AFL resulted in the creation of a federation of industrial unions, the Congress of Industrial Organizations. When the West Virginia Federation of Labor refused to expel unions that also belonged to the CIO, the national AFL revoked the federation's charter. In 1937, the state labor federation was accepted into the CIO's new state organization. Later, most West Virginia unions participated in the merger of American unions into the AFL-CIO.

Although the newly formed Steel Workers Organizing Committee (United Steelworkers of America) successfully organized most of the American steel industry

in the late 1930s, the group failed in its protracted campaign to displace the Employees Security League, a company union at Weirton Steel. When the National Labor Relations Board recognized the Security League as the legitimate bargaining agent for Weirton employees in 1950, it became the largest independent union in the steel industry. It survives today as the Independent Steelworkers Union.

Chemical industry giants, such as Du-Pont, also attempted to retain the loyalty of their employees in West Virginia through employee representation plans. Chemical companies practiced "welfare capitalism," or company paternalism, to engender loyalty among employees and their families by organizing recreational leagues, publishing newsletters, hosting company picnics, and favoring the relatives of current workers when hiring new employees. Nevertheless, these efforts did not prevent the labor movement from trying to organize the chemical workers, and between the 1930s and 1960s, the United Mine Workers District 50, the International Association of Machinists, and the Oil, Chemical and Atomic Workers competed to unionize these plants. Since the 1960s, those chemical workers who were union members belonged to either the International Chemical Workers Union (AFL) or the Oil, Chemical and Atomic Workers Union (CIO).

Labor and capital relations became relatively stable during and after World War II. The restructuring of the post-war economy, however, posed a threat to organized labor that was most evident in the coal industry. Machinery began to replace miners during the late 1940s and continued unabated at the turn of the 21st century. The number of miners declined from 127,304 in 1950 to 59,098 in 1960, and by 1999 only about 20,000 miners remained in West Virginia. Similar processes were at work in the other basic industries. The net result has been

fewer jobs and an out-migration of West Virginians to other states. The dramatic decline of employment in the heavily unionized basic industries, and the rapid rise in the non-unionized service sector, have produced a sharp decline in organized labor in West Virginia.

See also Mine Wars, Railroad Strike of 1877, Yellow-Dog Contract

Ronald L. Lewis
West Virginia University

Charles H. Ambler and Festus P. Summers, *West Virginia: the Mountain State*, 1958; Charles P. Anson, "A History of the Labor Movement in West Virginia," Ph.D. dissertation, University of North Carolina, Chapel Hill, 1958; David A. Corbin, *Life, Work, and Rebellion in the Coal Fields: The Southern West Virginia Miners, 1880–1922*, 1981.

Lake Monongahela

During the Pleistocene Epoch, or Ice Age, mile-thick ice sheets repeatedly covered much of northern North America. Although not themselves reaching present West Virginia, the ice sheets affected the area by damming rivers, temporarily forming large lakes and creating new drainage patterns which persist to the present. Before this time, the ancestral Monongahela River, known to later geologists as the Pittsburgh River, drained what is now northern West Virginia, flowing northward past present Pittsburgh toward Lake Erie and the St. Lawrence River. Lake Monongahela formed when the advancing ice, and later glacial sediments, dammed this river near Pittsburgh.

Lake Monongahela waxed and waned in response to changes in ice volume, stretching as far south as present Weston at its largest but sometimes completely ceasing to exist when the glaciers shrank. It is estimated that Lake Monongahela filled to an elevation near 1,100 feet above sea level. Erosion eventually opened an outlet south of present New Martinsville, draining Lake Monongahela southward into the ancient Teays River watershed, eroding a deep channel and forming the present Ohio River.

The age of Lake Monongahela is based on studies of lake sediments and terrace deposits. The presence of a magnetic polarity switch within the oldest terrace deposits indicates that Lake Monongahela existed initially between 730,000 and 900,000 years ago, since the earth's polarity is known to have switched during that time. Other terrace deposits indicate much later periods of ponding as glacial sediment choked and dammed the Ohio River.

The oldest sediments are dominated by pollen indicative of a pine-spruce forest. This suggests severe climatic conditions, likely due to the proximity of the ice sheet to the north. Later sediments contain pollen and plant fossils of a hemlock-hardwoods association, suggesting a more moderate climate.

See also Lake Tight

Bascombe M. Blake Jr.
Geological & Economic Survey

Lake Tight

Although not themselves reaching present West Virginia, glaciers of the Ice Age affected the area by repeatedly damming the ancestral Kanawha River system northwest of present Chillicothe, temporarily forming large lakes and creating new drainage patterns which persist to the present. The ancestral Kanawha River, known as the Teays River, followed the course of today's New River from present North Carolina into West Virginia. It flowed westward from present Charleston into the present Ohio River at what is now Huntington. From there it followed the course of the present Ohio River to near Portsmouth, where it turned northwest and flowed diagonally northwestward across present Ohio into northern Indiana and central Illinois, eventually reaching the Mississippi Valley via the present Illinois River. The course of the modern Kanawha River formed when the Pocatalico River captured the Teays River at the present community of Scary, resulting in the abandonment of the Teays Valley.

Lake Tight was the lake formed when ice or glacial sediments blocked the Teays River system. The size of Lake Tight waxed and waned in response to changes in ice volume, and the lake completely ceased to exist at some times. Maximum lake size occurred during the first period of ponding with lake levels in excess of 900 feet above sea level. The impoundment near present Chillicothe backed the waters up across present southwestern Ohio to Huntington, then up the Teays Valley and the present Kanawha and New rivers as far as today's Hawks Nest State Park. Surviving lake sediments exceed 100 feet in some places.

The presence of a magnetic polarity switch within the oldest terrace deposits indicates that Lake Tight existed initially between 730,000 and 900,000 years ago. Three lower terrace deposits suggest periods of late Illinoian and Wisconsin ponding as glacial sediment choked and dammed the Ohio River.

See also Lake Monongahela, Teays River, Teays Valley

Bascombe M. Blake Jr.
Geological & Economic Survey

Lakes

In 2004, the West Virginia Department of Natural Resources listed 117 public fishing lakes and ponds in the state. Forty-nine of the state's 55 counties have at least one public lake, with some counties having as many as seven. Trout Pond, located in Hardy County, is the state's only natural lake and has a two-acre surface.

The largest lakes in the state are the ten created by impoundment dams built and operated by the U.S. Army Corps of Engineers. The primary purpose of these structures is flood control, with secondary purposes including recreation, river flow augmentation, fish and wildlife conservation, and water storage for municipal and industrial water supply. The oldest of these lakes is Tygart Lake on the Tygart Valley River, and the newest is the Stonewall Jackson Lake on the West Fork River. Bluestone Lake, built in 1949, is the largest lake in the state with a 2,040-acre surface. State parks have been developed around four of the Corps of Engineers lakes: Tygart, Stonewall Jackson, Bluestone, and Beech Fork. There are many small flood control lakes, as well. They include North Bend Lake in Ritchie County with a 305-acre surface, Elkford Lake in Jackson County with a 278-acre surface, and Dunkard Fork Lake in Marshall County with a 49-acre surface.

There are 13 navigational dams with locks built and operated by the Corps of Engineers. Seven of these high-lift gated structures are located on the Ohio River with an additional three each on the Kanawha and Monongahela rivers. These dams, with their movable gates, are not flood control structures but are operated to maintain a minimum nine-foot navigational depth throughout the length of the river on which they are located. The pools created by these navigational dams provide recreational opportunities, economic development potential and water supply for the communities along their banks.

The three largest non-government lakes in the state are Cheat Lake (Lake Lynn) on the Cheat River, Mount Storm Lake on the Stony River, and Stonecoal Lake on Stonecoal Creek. All three are operated by electric power companies. Cheat Lake is used to generate hydroelectricity, while Stonecoal and Mount Storm supply water for steam generation at coal-fired electric plants. A low dam at Kanawha Falls has been used in the generation of hydroelectricity for more than a century, creating a picturesque lake just downstream from Gauley Bridge. A dam on New River diverts water through Hawks Nest tunnel for the generation of electricity, creating the lake at Hawks Nest State Park.

There are numerous other impoundments throughout the state, such as farm ponds used for agricultural purposes and coal mining impoundments used to hold coal tailings from coal preparation plants. Some of the coal impoundment ponds are several surface acres in size.

Gerald W. Sutphin
Huntington

Lakin Hospital

Created by an act of the Legislature in 1919, Lakin State Hospital was established as an institution "for the care and cure of the mentally ill colored persons of this state." The hospital began operations on February 1, 1926, when 162 patients were transferred from Weston State Hospital. In 1954, the year the U.S. Supreme Court held that segregated public schools were unconstitutional, Lakin staff and patients were integrated. An act of the legislature in 1974 changed the name to Lakin Hospital.

Located on the Ohio River about eight miles from Point Pleasant in Mason County, Lakin for many years provided mental health services to adults and children. Its facilities included brick dormitories for adult patients, a center for emotionally disturbed children, and a rehabilitation center which provided job training and other services. By the end of the 1970s, Lakin's mission shifted. Adult psychiatric services were discontinued and care of the elderly and physically handicapped adults was expanded, while the children's program remained. Lakin in recent years has provided long-term, intermediate care services for geriatric patients. Its nursing care unit is certified for Medicaid reimbursement. Programs at Lakin are designed to assist its residents in becoming more independent and self-reliant while providing them with a better quality of life.

Larry Sonis
Arlington, Texas

Daniel Lamb

State founder Daniel Lamb was born January 22, 1810, in Connellsville, Pennsylvania, to Quaker parents. In 1823, Lamb's family moved to Wheeling, where Lamb received his education. In 1831, he was elected city clerk. Shortly after, he became treasurer of the Fire and Marine insurance company. In 1834, he became secretary and treasurer of the Wheeling Savings Institution, an early bank. He also began to study law with a distinguished Wheeling lawyer, Morgan Nelson, and was admitted to the bar in 1837. He practiced law until 1848, when he became the cashier of the Northwestern Bank of Virginia at Wheeling.

When the secession vote split Virginia, Lamb was one of those who took the lead in crafting the government and constitution that would lead to the creation of West Virginia. He was a member of the first constitutional convention for West Virginia and a member of its legislature from 1863 to 1867. After the Civil War, Lamb opposed the implementation of "test oaths" to prevent former Confederates from voting and advocated policies to integrate former Confederates into the political structure of West Virginia. Though he was suggested for nomination to several statewide offices, Lamb refused them and stood for election only for the U.S. Senate in 1871, when he was defeated by Democrat Henry Gassaway Davis. Lamb resumed his law practice after the Civil War and followed that career until his death.

The first codification of West Virginia's laws, known as the Lamb Code, was begun by Daniel Lamb and finished by James H. Ferguson. In *Prominent Men of West Virginia,* Daniel Lamb was characterized as "rather a dull, heavy speaker but a careful and sound reasoner." He died in Wheeling, June 28, 1876.

Kenneth R. Bailey
WVU Institute of Technology
George W. Atkinson and Alvaro F. Gibbens, *Prominent Men of West Virginia,* 1890; Atkinson, *Bench and Bar of West Virginia,* 1919.

Land Ownership

A large majority of West Virginia's privately held land is owned by relatively few individuals or firms, many of them from outside the state. The largest private landowners are coal, timber, natural gas companies and electric utilities, and railroads. Land ownership is most concentrated in the historic southern coalfields south of Charleston. About a fifth of West Virginia's 15.5 million acres is publicly owned, mostly by the state and national governments. These land-ownership patterns, deeply rooted in the past, have long influenced the politics, economic growth, and social development of our state.

Beginning in the 1730s, Virginia offered great conveyances of land to those who would explore the West and promote settlement there. A succession of expansionist governors continued the policy. By 1783, western land was being offered as pensions to Revolutionary War veterans. The land was not surveyed first, and estimates of the supply of land were incorrect. The transferrable grants enabled speculators to purchase veterans' land rights at deep discounts, often amassing large acreages. By 1805, some 250 individuals or interlocking entities each owned at least 10,000 acres of land. A few commanded great empires.

Records of these transactions were kept in the Virginia land office in the state capital, and were by law superior to claims registered in frontier courthouses. Deeds were equalized in 1831, but by then almost all of the land was claimed. At the same time, settlers moved west and established their own claims without regard to absentee owners. More land was conveyed than existed, so claims overlapped. Until the Civil War, the overlap was unrecognized or of little concern.

Industrialization changed the demand for land and revived interest in old claims. Timbering and mining required vast acreages, thus farmers and industrialists competed for control of the same economic resource. Politically weaker, the farmers suffered as state law and policies increasingly favored industry after 1880. When industrialization began in earnest in the mountains, speculators set about asserting long-quiet claims and displacing farmers. Forced sale, duplicity, adverse possession, ejectment, and compromise were commonly used to acquire land.

Land-ownership patterns continue to affect the state's economy. Critics argue that West Virginia property tax policies discourage improvements to land. Unimproved land is not taxed as heavily per acre as improved land is, making land speculation an attractive investment and sometimes keeping land inactive for decades.

In some counties as much as 70 percent of the land is unimproved and controlled by nonresidents, including the federal government. The Monongahela National Forest was established in the early 20th century on land purchased from former U.S. Senators Henry Gassaway Davis and J. N. Camden and others who previously had timbered and mined the region. The federal government alone owns about 1.4 million acres in West Virginia, and pays no property tax at all. Federal allocations compensate local governments for their revenue losses, but the sum is generally lower than what property taxes would generate. In the southern coalfields, land ownership is concentrated among corporations, with companies owning more than three-fourths of the surface acreage of McDowell County and two-thirds of neighboring Logan County.

State and regional historians generally accept the theory of concentrated and absentee land ownership, and the view was developed for a general readership in an extensive 1974 newspaper series by Tom Miller of the Huntington *Herald-Advertiser.* Proponents argue that inequitable land distribution has produced a "colonial" economy, operated by and largely for the benefit of people outside the state. Others have challenged these views, including Dale Colyer of West Virginia University College of Agriculture and Forestry in a 1981 report for Mountaineers for Rural Progress.

See also Bruen Lands Feud, Swan Lands, Taxation

Barbara Rasmussen
Fairmont State University
Barbara Rasmussen, *Absentee Landowning and Exploitation in West Virginia, 1760–1920,* 1994; Otis Rice, *The Allegheny Frontier: West Virginia Beginnings, 1730–1830,* 1970; John Alexander Williams, *West Virginia and the Captains of Industry,* 1976.

Last Public Hanging

John F. Morgan was the last man hanged publicly in West Virginia, on December 16, 1897, afer he was convicted of murdering Chloe Greene and two of her three children in the Grass Lick area of Jackson County. The execution drew more than 5,000 spectators, including a *New York Sun* special reporter assigned to cover the spectacle.

The chain of events that led to the hanging began less than six weeks earlier on November 3, 1897. Morgan, a local handyman and friend of the Greene family, hid in the pre-dawn darkness with a hatchet in hand. One by one he attacked his victims, delivering fatal blows to Mrs. Greene, Jimmy Greene and Matilda Pfost. Another daughter, Alice Pfost, was attacked but survived. It was she who alerted neighbors to the crime.

Morgan was arrested within hours and incarcerated in Ripley. He was indicted on November 4, tried and convicted the following day, and sentenced the day after that. Two weeks before the hanging, Morgan escaped. He was at large two days before he was finally captured. Excitement was aroused by Morgan's repeated oaths that he would never hang, at least on the scheduled date, but the execution happened as scheduled on December 16.

Shortly after the sensational event, the West Virginia state legislature passed a bill prohibiting public executions. It was among the first states to do so.

See also Capital Punishment

Jacqueline G. Goodwin
Pennsylvania State Education Association

George Robert Latham

George Robert Latham, congressman and U.S. consul to Australia, recruited and commanded the first Union troops in north-central West Virginia during the Civil War. Latham was born in Prince William County, Virginia, March 9, 1832, on what later became the Bull Run battlefield. He moved to Taylor County in 1849. He taught school in Taylor and Barbour counties while he studied law at night. He passed the bar in 1859 and opened his practice in Grafton in 1860.

At the onset of the Civil War, Latham transformed his new law office into a recruiting station. The troop he formed, Company B, 2nd Virginia Infantry, was ordered by Latham to remain in Grafton to vote against Virginia's 1861 Ordinance of Secession before leaving for battle. Later that year, the company participated in the Battle of Corrick's Ford, near Parsons. Latham served nearly to the end of the war and saw some of the fiercest fighting. He had three horses shot from under him at the second Battle of Bull Run. He was brevetted brigadier general in 1865.

At the close of the Civil War, Latham served as congressman for the Second District of West Virginia, 1865–67. From 1867 to 1870, he was U.S. consul to Australia. Upon his return from Australia,

Latham moved to Buckhannon and was elected superintendent of Upshur County schools. He was appointed as supervisor of the census for West Virginia's First District in 1880.

Latham remained in Buckhannon until his death December 16, 1917. His Buckhannon home, purchased in 1866, is still standing. Latham was the father of artist Annie Latham Bartlett.

See also Annie Latham Bartlett

Kim Howard
French Creek

Jean Lee Latham

Author Jean Lee Latham, born in Buckhannon, April 19, 1902, pursued a number of careers before beginning to write books for children and young adults. After graduating from West Virginia Wesleyan College in 1925, Latham taught English at Upshur County High School for three years. She then taught drama and education classes at the Ithaca (New York) Conservatory for one year, earning her M.A. in 1930 at nearby Cornell University.

Latham was editor-in-chief at Chicago's Dramatic Publishing Company from 1930 to 1936, writing adult plays and radio shows, while also launching her freelance writing career. During World War II, she trained Signal Corps inspectors for the War Department, receiving a Silver Wreath for this work in 1944.

It was her children's writing that brought acclaim. She wrote *The Story of Eli Whitney* in 1953. This biography was followed by others focusing on such diverse personalities as Samuel Morse, Cyrus W. Field, Sir Francis Drake, Sam Houston, and Rachel Carson. *Carry On, Mr. Bowditch* won the prestigious 1956 Newbery Award, and *Trail Blazer of the Seas* was awarded the Boys' Clubs of America Junior Book Award in 1957. In addition to her works of children's fiction and nonfiction, Latham also wrote juvenile plays and adapted children's classics such as *Aladdin* and *Jack and the Beanstalk*.

During her freelance years, Latham spent much of her time in Florida. She died there, June 13, 1995.

Debra K. Sullivan
Charleston Catholic High School

Laurel Lake

Situated in the 12,854-acre Laurel Lake Wildlife Management Area about 12 miles northeast of Lenore off State Route 65 in Mingo County, Laurel Lake has 29 acres of surface water for fishing, swimming, and boating. The lake and its surrounding terrain are managed by the West Virginia Division of Natural Resources on property owned by Island Creek Coal Company, Georgia Pacific Corporation, and the Cotiga Develop-

ment Corporation, which entered into the original lease to construct the lake in 1960.

Laurel Lake is surrounded by rugged topography with steep slopes and hills up to 1,700 feet above sea level. A mixed hardwood forest includes oak and hickory with an understory of dogwood, sassafras, sumac, blackberry, and grape. The lake is stocked with trout monthly from February through May. Other fish include channel catfish, largemouth bass, and bluegill. Minnow use is prohibited as bait. Game include deer (which may be hunted by bow only), turkey, raccoon, grouse, and squirrel. The lake has standard campsites with water, toilets, and showers. Other recreational facilities are game courts, a playground, hiking trails, boat rentals, a skeet range, and picnicking areas. Operating funds for Lake Laurel are derived from fishing, hunting and trapping license fees, supplemented with swimming and camping fees.

Larry Sonis
Arlington, Texas

The Law

Upon gaining statehood, West Virginia adopted the law of Virginia. Both the 1863 and the 1872 constitutions (especially the latter) were patterned after Virginia's Constitution of 1851, although the new state added important provisions guaranteeing equal apportionment, equal taxation, and public education.

Early issues arose out of the Civil War's after effects. "Test oaths"—oaths swearing that the taker had never engaged in rebellion against the United States—were used to bar ex-Confederates from, among other things, voting, filing lawsuits, and holding public office. The state Supreme Court upheld each oath that it considered. Resentment against the oaths and hostility to the government were intense. A federal court ruling in 1870 and the 1871 Flick Amendment to the state constitution restored voting rights for the ex-Confederates. They and their sympathizers then took control of West Virginia, and the following year saw a new constitution proposed and ratified. Although the 1872 Constitution eliminated the Northern-style local government system and re-adopted the local government model that had prevailed in Virginia before the war, it otherwise did not differ that much from its 1863 predecessor. It remains in effect today, much amended.

The remainder of the 19th century was a period of relative stability in West Virginia law. No constitutional changes of real significance occurred. Attention focused on the Supreme Court of Appeals in the aftermath of the extremely close gubernatorial election of 1888. Doubt about the count's integrity led the legislature to forego declaring a winner when it met the following January. On inaugu-

The West Virginia Supreme Court of Appeals.

ration day, both major party candidates, the president of the senate (as the successor in case of a vacancy), and the incumbent governor, claimed the executive office. Ruling in *Goff v. Wilson* and *Carr v. Wilson*, the Supreme Court agreed with the incumbent governor that he should remain in office until his successor was certified and sworn in. The legislature met the following January and finally certified the winner of the election.

No doubt the 1888 election, which was riddled with vote fraud, provided much of the impetus for the electoral reforms that soon followed, including the adoption of the "Australian" or standardized printed ballot in 1891. The effect was to give West Virginia voters, for the first time, a realistic opportunity to cast a secret ballot. A constitutional amendment of 1901 required voter registration in 1902.

The decades immediately before and after the turn of the century saw legal developments reflecting the strains of converting from an agrarian to an industrial society and the emergence of the extractive industries, timber, coal, oil, and gas. Much litigation was devoted to disputes over land titles, mineral and timber rights, workers' injuries, and labor disputes. A new era of social insurance began with the passage of the state's first workers' compensation law in 1913. So long as the employer paid his premiums into a state-run fund, or guaranteed self-insurance, injured workers could not sue but would be entitled to compensation without regard to who was at fault in the accident.

The 1932 Tax Limitation Amendment brought major changes to the state's tax and finance system, imposing stringent limits on the rates at which property could be taxed. The immediate effect was near chaos, as local governments suddenly found themselves without the means to deliver basic services. The Supreme Court nevertheless enforced the amendment against legislative efforts to allow local governments to circumvent the limits. The long-term effects have been to force local governments to adopt a variety of other revenue-raising strategies, and, most importantly, to shift primary responsibility for funding public education away from local property taxes and onto the state treasury.

Throughout their first century, West Virginia's law-making bodies were, for the most part, conservative institutions, often dominated by coal interests and having little interest in governmental or social change. The 1960s, however, introduced a reform era that persisted long enough to accomplish meaningful change. In 1968, the legislature proposed, and the people adopted, the Modern Budget Amendment, which streamlined and detailed the budget process while significantly increasing the governor's budgetary role and power. Two 1970 amendments allowed governors to succeed themselves and established a commission of private citizens to deal with legislative pay. The Judicial Reorganization Amendment of 1974 restructured the court system, enhanced the Supreme Court's powers to administer the system, and substituted a more equitable magistrate court system for the old justice of the peace courts. In 1982, responding quickly to a Supreme Court decision, the legislature proposed a constitutional amendment that equalized and modernized the procedures for property tax assessments across the state. The people ratified it that same year.

The 1960s and 1970s also saw the passage of various statutes reforming government and expanding governmental regulation over private industrial and commercial activity. The legislature enacted, for example, laws giving citizens a right to notice about and to attend most government meetings, creating a citizen's right of access to most governmental documents, and imposing ethical requirements on public officials and employees. Other laws passed during the reform period promoted environmental protection, mine safety, consumer protection, and equal treatment in the workplace and in public accommodations.

The trend toward reform and activism had a longer run in the Supreme Court than in the political branches. Beginning in the 1960s, accelerating in the 1970s, and continuing into the 1990s, decisions from the Court expanded judicial protection of individual rights, modernized tort law, rewrote governmental immunities doctrines, caused a major overhaul of the property tax system, and mandated reforms in major governmental institutions. The Court required state officials

and the legislature to overhaul (among other things) the juvenile justice system, the mental health system, the prison system, and the school finance system.

Through the years, Supreme Court decisions reshaped West Virginia law in important ways. A trilogy of heavily criticized cases—*State ex rel. Nance v. Mays, Ex parte Jones,* and *Hatfield v. Graham*—was decided during a 1913 labor rebellion and accorded vast power to the executive branch to use martial law and to preempt civilian courts. A later ruling, *Ex parte Lavinder* (1921), only moderately tempered that power. *West Virginia-Pittsburgh Coal Company v. Strong* (1947) significantly limited surface mining; it established that deeds severing and conveying mineral rights did not authorize the owner of the minerals to use methods of extraction that were more disruptive to the surface owner's rights than methods in use at the time of conveyance. In a case of both legal and political importance, *State ex rel. Smith v. Gore* (1964) required equal apportionment in the election of delegates to a constitutional convention and derailed a move to draft a new state constitution. *Pauley v. Kelly* (1979) recognized the fundamental right of every child in West Virginia to an equal and effective education and led to the so-called Recht Decision calling for a restructuring of the state's school finance system. *Pittsburgh Elevator Company v. West Virginia Board of Regents* (1983) permitted (in effect) the legislature to waive the state's sovereign immunity. Proclaiming the state's commitment to equality, *Allen v. West Virginia Human Rights Commission* (1984) ordered the Commission and other state officials to ensure prompt consideration of human rights complaints. Another long-standing civil action, *Crain v. Bordenkircher* (1986–95) ultimately resulted in a finding that the conditions at the state penitentiary failed to meet constitutional standards and led to the construction of a new facility. Many cases, recently including *State ex rel. Barker v. Manchin* (1980), *Frymier-Halloran v. Paige* (1996), and *West Virginia Citizens Action Group v. West Virginia Economic Development Grants Committee* (2003), have set forth basic principles governing separation of powers among the branches of government.

Many individuals have been instrumental in shaping the law in West Virginia. The two Supreme Court justices with the longest tenures on the court, Frank Haymond (1945–72) and Henry Brannon (1889–1912), both exerted a persuasive force on their colleagues, as did George Poffenbarger (1901–22). Three recent justices enjoyed both a long tenure and widespread respect for their work. Richard Neely (1973–95) wrote with an eloquent and erudite flair in both his opinions and in substantial off-the-court books and articles. The opinions

of Thomas Miller (1977–94) were known for their careful research and craftsmanship and those of Thomas McHugh for their solid reasoning. Two justices from the 1970s, Charles H. Haden Jr. (1972–75) and James Sprouse (1973–75), performed admirably on the court and went on to give distinguished service on the federal bench, Haden as a district judge and Sprouse with the court of appeals. Haden was the only Republican since 1928 to have won election to the Supreme Court. In 1988, the voters elected Margaret Workman, the first woman to sit on the high court. She remained there with high marks for her work until resigning in 1999.

Franklin D. Cleckley has contributed in multiple ways. As a lawyer, he gained fame as a highly skilled trial and appellate advocate in civil rights cases from 1970 through the 1990s. His treatises on criminal procedure and evidence have dominated those fields in the state since their publication, and as a professor at the state's law school he has exerted a profound influence on many members of the bar. In 1994, he became the state's first African-American justice on the Supreme Court, where he served until 1996. During that time, he wrote many scholarly opinions that left a legal legacy far exceeding the brevity of his tenure. Another individual who has achieved prominence at various levels is Arthur Recht, who was highly regarded as a lawyer and then as a trial judge. In the latter role, he was assigned and decided critical aspects in cases involving the constitutionality of the West Virginia school finance system and its penitentiary. He served with distinction on the Supreme Court from 1994 to 1996.

The work of attorney Dan Hedges did much to shape the reforms of the 1970s and 1980s. Working primarily as a lawyer for legal services programs, Hedges won major cases across a spectrum of issues that included public education, welfare, juvenile justice, consumer law, mine safety, the environment, civil rights, mental health institutions and procedures, and prisoners' rights.

In 1878, the 11-year-old West Virginia University created a "chair of law and equity," thus establishing what would become the College of Law. Throughout its existence, it has been West Virginia's only law school, and most of the state's lawyers have graduated from it.

To practice law in West Virginia, a lawyer must gain admission to and maintain membership in the West Virginia State Bar, which is an administrative agency of the Supreme Court. Discipline and regulation of lawyers are administered through the Office of Disciplinary Counsel, another agency of the Supreme Court.

Various private groups with a legal focus have also formed. The oldest is the

West Virginia Bar Association, whose membership has primarily comprised attorneys representing business and commercial interests. The West Virginia Trial Lawyers Association focuses on the concerns and interests of lawyers representing plaintiffs in tort litigation, divorce clients, and criminal defendants. The Mountain State Bar organized to deal with issues particular to racial and ethnic minorities. Other lawyer groups have formed around various practice specialties.

Robert M. Bastress
WVU College of Law

Charles Henry Laws

Physician and civic leader Charles Henry Laws was born in Phoebus, Virginia, June 23, 1883. After graduating from Leonard Medical College in North Carolina in 1911, Laws began medical practice in Elkins. With the outbreak of World War I he volunteered for military service and was commissioned 1st lieutenant, becoming the first African-American physician in the U.S. Army Medical Corps, the 372nd Infantry. He served a year overseas in a combat zone, nine months within the sound and range of German guns.

After the war Laws returned to his medical practice in Elkins, and in 1922 he relocated to Hinton to replace a local doctor who had died. This was an era of virulent, organized racism in southern West Virginia and across the country, with the Ku Klux Klan marching through Hinton in 1924. Nonetheless, when a new city council was seated in 1927, following the merger of Hinton with nearby Avis and Bellepoint, Laws was among those elected to office. He was the first of his race to give public service to the newly incorporated Hinton, serving on its first city council, and was reelected for four consecutive terms.

Charles Henry Laws died at Beckley Memorial Hospital, March 7, 1962, and was buried at Hinton.

Fred Long
Hinton

Layland Mine Explosion

In 1915, the New River & Pocahontas Consolidated Coal Company operated a series of drift mines at Layland, Fayette County, eight railroad miles north of Quinnimont. At 8:30 a.m. March 2, a blast swept through Layland No. 3 mine, killing 114 men. The explosion blew out the drift mouth and struck dead a grocery delivery man walking nearby.

Seven survivors exited the mine shortly after the explosion, giving hope to gathering crowds that others might be alive. Rescuers recovered several bodies during the next three days, and on March 6 five more survivors escaped the mine. These men had barricaded themselves from the afterdamp and rescuers learned from

William Derenge wrote this will while trapped in the Layland mine, but was later rescued.

them that 41 men had done the same deeper in the mine. They hurriedly entered the mine and located a famished group of survivors. Fearing the worst, some of these miners had scribbled short notes to their loved ones.

Controversy surrounded the Layland disaster. When the secretary of the interior suggested gold medals for federal rescuers, state officials and local volunteers questioned the contribution of the federal team, and some individuals insisted that the trapped miners had been saved by their own wisdom. Federal representatives, using the latest methods, determined that the disaster resulted from the ignition of methane propagated by coal dust, but state officials insisted that careless blasting of a coal face produced the explosion.

See also Coal Mine Disasters

Paul H. Rakes
WVU Institute of Technology

H. B. Humphrey, *Historical Summary of Coal-Mine Explosions In The United States, 1810–1958,* 1960; *Annual Report of the West Virginia Department of Mines,* 1915.

Blanche Lazzell

Born in Maidsville, Monongalia County, October 10, 1878, Blanche Lazzell was one of West Virginia's most notable artists and is recognized as one of America's leading abstract painters and print makers. She received a diploma from West Virginia Conference Seminary in 1898 and an art degree in 1905 from West Virginia University. She traveled to New York City in the fall of 1907, where she studied at the Art Students League with Kenyon Cox and William Merritt Chase.

Unusually independent for a woman of her time, Lazzell traveled twice to Paris, where she absorbed the principles of Cubism and studied with such early modernists as Charles Guerin, Fernand Léger, and Albert Gleizes. She is most known as one of the founding members of the Provincetown Printers, a Provincetown, Massachusetts, group that favored the single block color print. From 1916 on, Lazzell worked in this method of printing and in other media including watercolor and oil.

During the Depression, she was commissioned by the Works Progress Administration to create several color wood-block prints of scenes in and around Morgantown and a mural for the courthouse titled "Justice over Monongalia County." By 1937, Lazzell returned to Provincetown to study with Hans Hofmann. She continued to work prolifically in her studio on the wharf in Provincetown until her death on June 1, 1956. She was buried in Bethel Cemetery in Maidsville.

Throughout her lifetime, Blanche Lazzell exhibited in many prestigious exhibitions including the Salon d'Automne in Paris and the International Print Makers Exhibit in Los Angeles. Her work is represented today in major museums and galleries, including the Smithsonian Institution, and in the permanent collections of West Virginia Wesleyan College and WVU.

Mary Louise Soldo Schultz
West Virginia University

League of Women Voters

The League of Women Voters, a grassroots nonpartisan organization seeking to increase participation in government, is organized at all three levels of government—local, state, and national. Each level of the league has its own board of directors and its own agenda for political action. In West Virginia, there are local leagues, as well as a state league. The first meeting of the West Virginia league was held in 1944, and the group was recognized by the national office in 1947.

The league advocates for governmental reforms, educates the public about the governmental process, and provides nonpartisan information about those running for office. While the league never takes positions on candidates, it does take positions on issues. It has positions on issues pertaining to government, the environment, human services, and international relations. Members study issues before reaching a consensus, and then advocate for issues at the appropriate level of government.

The League of Women Voters was founded on February 14, 1920, in Chicago, during the victory convention of the National American Woman's Suffrage Association. The women had gathered to celebrate their success in winning the right to vote. During their convention they decided to carry on with the task of educating women about the political process and the use of the vote. To founder Carrie Chapman Catt winning the vote was only the first step; the next was to learn how to use it. So the Suffrage Convention created the League of Women Voters. While it was founded primarily to educate women about the vote, its mission included all citizens and its membership has included men since 1974.

Becky Cain
Greater Kanawha Valley Foundation

Lebanese and Syrians

The flow of immigrants from modern-day Lebanon and Syria to West Virginia began in the 1880s and peaked in the 1920s. They came as refugees from increasingly rigid Ottoman rule, which after centuries of relative acceptance had grown hostile to Arab Christian enclaves and their special economic and cultural relationships with the empire's rivals of France and Great Britain. They settled principally in the cities, especially Charleston, Wheeling, Huntington, and Parkersburg.

Lebanese and Syrians almost never worked on West Virginia's farms or in the mines and factories. They single-mindedly continued their mercantile traditions, which date to Biblical times, and assumed a leading role in state commerce. Pack peddlers, both men and women, carried notions, fabrics, apparel, and household goods on foot throughout the remote, developing mineral lands of West Virginia. As they prospered, Lebanese and Syrian merchant families helped introduce retail competition into regions previously monopolized by coal and timber company stores. By the 1930s, key towns included Lebanese and Syrian-owned clothing, hardware, and department stores. In the cities, where general merchandisers already were well established, Lebanese and Syrian families tended to own fruit stands and green groceries.

Fred Haddad of Madison founded the discount department store chain, Heck's, Inc., a national pioneer in volume purchasing, distribution, and merchandising and the first West Virginia-based corporation listed on the New York Stock Exchange. Other retailers of humble origins grew into multi-store chains such as Gabriel Brothers, Ammar Brothers, and Aide's.

As soon as they were able, the Lebanese and Syrians established religious communities in West Virginia's largest cities. Adherents of Orthodoxy, governed by the Patriarch of Antioch, Turkey, constitute the largest denomination represented in West Virginia, with parishes in Charleston, Beckley, and Huntington. In 1905, St. George Orthodox Church of Charleston was established and became one of the largest Antiochene parishes in the United States. The church's iconostasis—a large screen of icons depicting the apostles of the early church—is considered one of the most significant works of religious art in West Virginia. In 2000, the liturgies at St. George still were chanted largely in Arabic.

Founded in 1906, Our Lady of Lebanon Church in Wheeling is home to Maronites, Eastern Rite Catholics who accept the leadership of the Roman Catholic pope. Our Lady of Lebanon Church, one of the oldest Maronite parishes in the United States, was the scene of an alleged miracle when a life-sized icon of Mary depicted as Our Lady of Lebanon survived an all-consuming fire. The icon hangs inside the rebuilt church.

In addition to Orthodox and Maronites, a small group of Syrian Melkites, also Eastern Rite Catholics, settled in Parkersburg. Representatives of the Druse, an Islamic sect, settled in Charleston, Princeton, and Bluefield. After World War II, as the flow of Christian Lebanese and Syrians to West Virginia slowed to a trickle, the majority of the Arab influx to the state was Moslem. In the 1980s, Syrian Moslems helped found the Islamic Center of West Virginia.

The cultural life of the Lebanese and Syrians, perhaps because of its exoticism, remains guarded and little known to most West Virginians, with a few exceptions. Each August, Wheeling is host to the *Mahrajan,* a homecoming for Leba-

The Skaffs, a Lebanese merchant's family in Charleston.

nese families from that area. Each fall, St. George Orthodox Church holds a popular dinner in which food of the homeland is served.

Nick Joe Rahall of Beckley is one of a few people of Lebanese descent who has served in the United States House of Representatives. Rahall, a Democrat, has served the Third Congressional District of West Virginia since 1976.

Mark A. Sadd
Charleston

John Lederer

Explorer John Lederer, a German physician interested in trading with the Indians, was the first European to journey into the mountains of Virginia. Commissioned by Gov. William Berkeley to find a way through the Appalachian barrier, Lederer made three expeditions in 1670. On the first and third expeditions, he reached the summit of the Blue Ridge and saw the Shenandoah Valley. However, discouraged by the sight of more mountain ranges to the west and his inability to locate a passage through, he turned back. His second journey proceeded southwesterly through Virginia and North Carolina, probably reaching the present South Carolina border, but also failed to locate a passage through the mountains.

Lederer's discoveries helped open up trade with Indians. His map and journal, translated from Latin and published in London in 1672, have encouraged historians to provide varying interpretations of Lederer's observations on the geography, fauna, and Indians of the region he explored.

Harold Malcolm Forbes
WVU Libraries

Lyman Carrier, "The Veracity of John Lederer," *William and Mary Quarterly*, 1939; Dieter Cunz, "John Lederer, Significance and Evaluation," *William and Mary Quarterly*, 1942; John Lederer, *The Discoveries of John Lederer*, 1958.

Charles Lee

General Charles Lee, the third-ranking American general in the Revolutionary War, lived in Berkeley County late in his life. He was born in Cheshire, England, February 6, 1732, and died in Philadelphia, October 2, 1782. Commissioned a lieutenant, Lee served in America with Braddock's expedition during the French and Indian War and was later wounded in New York. He subsequently fought under Burgoyne in Portugal (1762) and as a major general in the Polish army during the Russo-Turkish War (1769–70).

Lee returned to America in 1773, settling in Berkeley County in 1778. A vigorous advocate of the American cause, he resigned his British commission and was appointed major general in the Continental Army. After acquitting himself well at the siege of Boston and in defense

of Charleston, South Carolina, he was captured by the British during Washington's retreat through New Jersey. Whatever his motives, Lee supplied the British with a plan to defeat the Americans before being exchanged. His later performance at the July 1778 Battle of Monmouth provoked verbal rebukes from Washington and led to a court martial in which he was found guilty of disrespect and suspended from command for one year. Insulting letters to Congress after the suspension led to Lee's dismissal from the army in 1780.

Lee occupied his Berkeley County home, Prato Rio, until shortly before his death.

See also Prato Rio

Jack Wills
Fairmont

John Richard Alden, *General Charles Lee: Traitor or Patriot?*, 1951; George Athan Billias, *George Washington's Generals*, 1964; Theodore Thayer, *The Making of a Scapegoat: Washington and Lee at Monmouth*, 1976.

Howard B. Lee

Attorney General Howard Burton Lee, born in Wirt County, October 27, 1879, was a teacher, lawyer, politician, and author. Graduating from Marshall College (now University) in 1905, he became a teacher in Putnam County before winning a scholarship to Washington and Lee University in Lexington, Virginia.

While still a student at W&L, Lee was elected as a Republican member of the West Virginia legislature, representing Putnam County. Lee began his law practice in Bluefield in 1909 and served as Mercer County prosecuting attorney from 1916 to 1924. Elected state attorney general in 1924, he served in that post for eight challenging, eventful years. His term saw the impeachment of a state auditor for embezzlement, the lawlessness and violence of Prohibition, and continued labor troubles in the southern coalfields. Lee later practiced law in Charleston until he retired in 1943. After his retirement, he lived much of the time in Stuart, Florida.

Beginning with *The Story of the Constitution* in 1932, Lee wrote a dozen books, both on legal subjects and regional history. His *Bloodletting In Appalachia* (1969) is perhaps the best known. In it, he drew on his personal experience to help detail the history of the state's Mine Wars. "It's the most horrifying story you've ever read," Lee said in a 1978 interview. "Unfortunately, every word of it is true."

In 1982, Marshall University presented Lee, then 102 and believed to be the school's oldest living graduate, with an honorary Doctor of Humane Letters degree. He died May 24, 1985, at age 105.

James E. Casto
Herald-Dispatch

Howard B. Lee, *Bloodletting In Appalachia*, 1969.

Maryat Lee

Playwright Maryat Lee, born Mary Attaway Lee at Covington, Kentucky, May 26, 1923, founded EcoTheater in Hinton in 1973 and moved it to Lewisburg in 1984. Lee graduated from Wellesley College in 1945 in religious studies, then studied at Columbia University and Union Theological Seminary.

In 1951, she wrote and produced the street play *Dope!*, which drew on her research into the religious origins of theater and her interest in persuading untrained people to act. She believed that the kind of acting she taught would bring out the hidden person underneath the roles and masks that society imposes. Named among the best plays of 1952–53, *Dope!* played in a vacant lot in East Harlem to crowds of 2,000 for five nights. It was widely published. Later, the social and cultural disruptions of the 1960s spawned street theater in New York, and Lee became one of its leaders, founding SALT (the Soul and Latin Theater) in East Harlem, using local people as actors. She wrote and published several plays during this period.

In 1970, seeking Appalachian roots, Lee moved to Powley Creek, near Hinton in Summers County. Here she established EcoTheater as an indigenous mountain theater, using Summers County people as actors. She developed an innovative way of composing plays, by gathering oral histories and turning them into drama. She published *Four Men and a Monster* (Samuel French, 1969) and wrote other plays, including *John Henry* (1979) and *The Hinton Play* (1980). In 1984, Lee moved to Lewisburg and worked on developing EcoTheater into a national organization. She died of a heart attack in Lewisburg, September 18, 1989.

William W. French
West Virginia University

Sally Fitzgerald, ed., *The Habit of Being: The Correspondence of Flannery O'Connor*, 1979; William W. French, *Maryat Lee's EcoTheater: A Theater for the Twenty-First Century*, 1998; Maryat Lee, "To Will One Thing," *Drama Review* 27-4, 1983.

Robert E. Lee

Born at Stratford in Westmoreland County, Virginia, January 19, 1807, Robert Edward Lee was the fifth child of Henry "Light-Horse Harry" Lee of Revolutionary War fame. Entering West Point in 1825, Lee graduated second in his class in 1829 and was commissioned second lieutenant in the U.S. Army Corps of Engineers. In 1831, he married Mary Custis, the great-granddaughter of Martha Washington and heiress of several estates. By 1838, Lee had risen to the rank of captain, and during the Mexican War he was assigned to the staff of Gen. Winfield Scott. From 1852 to 1855, he served as superintendent of West Point, where he revitalized the curriculum.

In 1859, Lee was called upon to lead a force of marines to put an end to John Brown's Harpers Ferry raid. With the outbreak of the Civil War Lee resigned his commission in the U.S. Army and was given the rank of general in the Confederate forces. Placed in command of the Department of Northwestern Virginia, General Lee attempted to retain military control of West Virginia for the Confederacy. Unprecedented rainfall, bickering subordinates, inexperienced officers, and rampant disease all contributed to failed campaigns at Cheat Mountain, Randolph County, and Sewell Mountain, Fayette County. On October 29, 1861, General Lee departed West Virginia en route to Richmond. By the time of his surrender on April 9, 1865, Lee had overcome his West Virginia defeats and placed himself firmly in the ranks of the greatest field commanders in world history. He died at Lexington, Virginia, October 12, 1870.

Lee first saw his great war horse, Traveller, during the Sewell Mountain campaign. He later purchased the horse, which was bred and born in Greenbrier County.

See also Battle of Cheat Mountain, Civil War, Sewell Mountain, Traveller

Tim McKinney
Fayetteville

Tim McKinney, *Robert E. Lee at Sewell Mountain: The West Virginia Campaign,* 1990; Ezra Warner, *Generals in Gray,* 1959.

Jay Legg

On February 10, 1904, Sarah Ann Legg shot and killed her husband, Jay, in their home at Harden's lumber camp in Clay County. Jay worked on the Elk River, driving logs downstream to Charleston. For some reason he returned home early on February 10 and was fatally shot by his own rifle. His wife was the only suspect.

At her trial in 1905, Sarah changed her story of the shooting from suicide by Jay to an accidental shooting, and finally to self-defense. Allegations of infidelity on Sarah's part were presented at her trial and no doubt helped convict her of murder. Although she spent some time in jail, Sarah appealed her case, was retried, and finally acquitted in 1910, leaving Susan Legg, Jay's mother, a bitter old woman who believed justice had not been served.

Jay and Sarah's four-year-old son was believed to have witnessed the shooting and to have told his grandmother that his mother had killed his father. This was reported in "The Murder of Jay Legg," one of several versions of a folk ballad that preserves the Legg story. A recording by Laurie Boggs Drake of Ivydale includes the following stanza:

His little child held up his head
As his life blood ebbed away;

And to his mother he did say,
"What made you kill poor Jay?"

Christine D. Fenn
Westover

Legislative Improvement Amendment

The Legislative Improvement Amendment was one of several amendments to the West Virginia constitution that took effect during the first two terms of Governor Moore. These amendments, which also included the Modern Budget Amendment and the Judicial Reorganization Amendment, collectively restructured state government.

The Legislative Improvement Amendment made changes to the operation of the state legislature, rewriting several sections of Article 6 of the West Virginia constitution. Among other things the amendment provided for a regular 60-day session each year and established a seven-member citizens' commission to approve pay raises to state legislators. The amendment also provided that the legislature would convene as usual on the second Wednesday in January, in 1973 and every fourth year thereafter, then adjourn until the second Wednesday in February to allow the newly elected or reelected governor time to get settled and to prepare his state budget proposal. In other years, the legislature would continue its session uninterrupted from the second Wednesday in January onward. The amendment also set dates for the submission to the legislature of the governor's proposed budget.

The Legislative Improvement Amendment was proposed by a joint resolution of the state legislature in 1970 and approved by the voters in the regular fall election that year. The vote was 208,032 for and 141,970 against.

See also Constitution of West Virginia

Legislature

The legislature is an equal branch of the West Virginia government along with the executive and judicial departments, under the state constitution's separation of powers provision. The Senate's 34 members serve four-year terms and represent 17 two-member districts. The terms are staggered, with one senator from each district elected every two years. The 100 members of the House of Delegates serve two-year terms in 56 districts, with the entire membership elected at once. Districts in each chamber are realigned following every federal census.

West Virginia's Legislature originally had only 65 members, 18 senators and 47 delegates. The total grew to 89 in 1872 when the Senate membership was set at 24 and terms were increased from two to four years, and the House was fixed at 65 delegates and their terms expanded from one to two years. The current number of members was established for the House in 1952 and for the Senate in 1964.

Republicans held a decided numerical edge, particularly in the House, through the first six decades of the legislature's existence. In 1921, 99 of the 124 members were Republicans. Ten years later, Democrats had an 81-43 advantage, and when the party took control of the Senate 24-6 in 1933, it never lost the majority in either chamber through the remainder of the century. The most Republicans reelected from 1932 on totaled 43 in the House in 1972 and 12 in the Senate in 1968. In 1991, Donna Jean Boley of Pleasants County was the lone Republican among 34 senators. As few as nine Republicans were delegates following the 1964 and 1976 elections, reaching a maximum number of 43 in 1972.

The Senate had 15 members from each party after the 1910 and 1912 elections and the first such tie led to one of the most unusual events in legislative history. At the time, U.S. senators were appointed by the legislature. During the 1911 legislative session when the two parties deadlocked, Republican senators absented themselves from the state. They rode a train to Cincinnati where they stayed in a hotel and prevented the Senate from being able to meet in Charleston because of the lack of a quorum of 16 members. The tie was never broken, but a compromise was worked out whereby Republicans elected the Senate president and Democrats chose the U.S. senators. Much of the credit for the compromise is given to the clerk of the Senate at the time, John T. Harris of Parkersburg.

The legislature, required to convene at the seat of government, met in Wheeling from 1863–70, in Charleston the following five years, and again in Wheeling from 1875 until the capital was permanently moved back to Charleston in 1885. Members first convened in the present statehouse in 1932. The legislature met biennially between 1875 and the ratification in 1954 of a constitutional amendment providing for full two-month sessions one year, followed by a 30-day budget session the next year. Annual 60-day sessions were established by the Legislative Improvement Amendment, ratified in 1970.

Men have dominated the makeup of the legislature. Democrat Anna Johnson Gates became the first woman member when she won one of Kanawha County's six House seats in 1920. Republican Minnie Buckingham Harper of McDowell County became the first African-American woman to serve in a legislature in the United States when she was appointed in 1928 to the House seat left vacant by the death of her husband. Democrat Hazel Hyre of Jackson County became the first female senator in 1934 upon appointment to fill the unexpired term of her dead husband.

The West Virginia Senate chamber.

In 1966, Betty H. Baker, Hardy County Democrat, was the first woman elected to the Senate. Marshall University professor Marie E. Redd in 1998 became not only just the 18th female, but also the first African-American of either gender to be elected to the West Virginia Senate. There was a high total of 27 women legislators in 1989–90.

By 1995, legislators were paid $15,000 annually, up from the $500 salary set by a constitutional amendment ratified in 1920 and the $1,500 approved by state voters in 1954. After proposed pay raises were rejected in the 1962 and 1966 statewide general elections, the constitution was amended in 1970 to provide for the creation of a citizens legislative compensation commission whose members were appointed by the governor. Lawmakers then could reduce but not increase levels of compensation and travel and expense reimbursement recommended by the seven-member commission.

Regular legislative sessions start on the second Wednesday of January of each year except every fourth year, when the session begins a month later to allow the incoming governor to prepare a state budget. Sessions may be extended by a concurrent resolution adopted by a two-thirds vote of the members elected to each house, or by proclamation of the governor for consideration of the budget only. Concurrent resolution by two-thirds may extend a session for budgetary as well as other legislative matters. The governor may call extraordinary sessions, and only items listed in the chief executive's proclamation may be considered. The legislature also has the authority to call itself into special session by a three-fifths petition, but since the agenda would be plenary or open-ended, the power has been rarely exercised.

Two annual sessions comprise a legislature, which begins in odd-number years following legislative elections the previous fall. Every legislature elects its officers to serve for the coming two sessions. The parties caucus beforehand, and majority-party nominees are virtually assured election by the full bodies during the opening organizational proceedings. The Senate elects a president and the House a speaker. The presiding officers each appoint floor leaders, committee chairs, and vice chairs and a pro tempore president and speaker, respectively. Each house also elects a clerk, sergeant-at-arms, and a doorkeeper, who are not members of the legislature.

Significantly, the Senate president and the House speaker are next in line to succeed as governor should that office become vacant during the chief executive's term. The two officers also possess broad legislative powers besides presiding during floor sessions. They may refer bills and resolutions to committee; control the corridors, passageways, and rooms assigned to each house; appoint committee members; sign acts of the legislature; designate office space; appoint members of conference committees on session matters of disagreement between the two houses and chair their respective rules committees. The two co-chair the legislature's Joint Committee on Government and Finance, which controls most legislative-related business, especially during interim meetings. The joint committee, with seven members from each house, was created in 1965 to study and survey matters of government, finance, and claims against the state and make recommendations to the full legislature. Its agencies include the commission on special investigations, court of claims, legislative auditor, rule-making review committee and divisions responsible for bill drafting, duplicating, tech-

William Robinson Leigh

Artist William Robinson Leigh, a leading 20th-century painter and illustrator of the Old West, was born September 23, 1866, in Berkeley County. Leigh studied at the Maryland Institute under Hugh Newell from 1880 to 1883, and at the Royal Academy in Munich, Germany, from about 1883 to 1892. Like David Hunter Strother, he sent letters home to West Virginia detailing his experiences abroad, which were published in the Martinsburg newspaper.

On returning to the United States, Leigh established a studio in New York, where he worked as an illustrator for *Scribners Magazine*. He spent the summer months during this period in Martinsburg, where he painted numerous landscapes and genre paintings, including *West Virginia Woodchopper, Fishing in the Mill Pond, West Virginia Forest,* and *Loitering.* He was also active locally as a portrait painter during this period. His life-size canvas of *Sophie H. Colston* (1896), now in the National Museum of American Art, is considered to be one of the masterpieces of late 19th-century American portraiture.

In 1906, influenced by Thomas Moran, Leigh took a train excursion with the artist Albert Groll to New Mexico. Enamored with the region and its inhabitants, he dedicated the bulk of his career to de-

William Robinson Leigh's portrait of Sophie Hunter Colston, Hampshire County, 1896.

picting the Old West on canvas. His idealism and photorealistic style were severely criticized by Eastern art critics at first, but Leigh eventually achieved broad national acclaim as one of the nation's finest realist painters.

During the 1920s and 1930s, Leigh visited Africa with scientific safaris, organized by the American Museum of Natural History. He subsequently organized exhibits and painted backdrops for the Museum's African Hall. Leigh was also an author of short stories. Several months before his death in New York, March 11, 1955, he was elected to membership in the National Academy of Design.

John A. Cuthbert
WVU Libraries

Lewis and Clark Expedition

In 1803, President Thomas Jefferson asked Congress to appropriate funds for an exploration of the part of the continent bordering on the Missouri and Columbia rivers. Jefferson chose Meriwether Lewis, an experienced army officer and frontiersman, to head the expedition. Captain Lewis then chose William Clark, a fellow frontier officer, to join him.

Lewis proceeded first to the U.S. Army's arsenal at Harpers Ferry, where he acquired weapons and other supplies manufactured there. The supplies were transported overland to Pittsburgh, where the party set out down the Ohio River on September 1, 1803. It took Lewis and Clark a little more than two years to reach the Pacific.

The hundred miles from Pittsburgh to Wheeling were extremely difficult because of low water and an abundance of driftwood on the Ohio River. When he finally arrived at Wheeling, Captain Lewis described it as "a pretty considerable Village of fifty houses." The party rested for two days during which time Lewis met Dr. William Patterson, the owner of the largest collection of medicines west of the mountains. As he set out from Wheeling, Lewis found the Ohio broader and deeper and lined on both banks with hardwoods. Just below Wheeling, he stopped at an Indian earth mound (Grave Creek Mound in Moundsville) and described it in great detail in his journal.

The trip down the Ohio was a practice run for the rest of the trip. To determine whether the Missouri country to which they were headed could sustain a population comparable to the Ohio River country, Lewis took notes on rainfall, temperature, kinds of timber and vegetation, and farming techniques as he descended the river. When he reached the army outposts on the lower Ohio (beyond the border of present West Virginia), Captain Lewis was authorized to enlist 12 men to join the expedition. Among them was Sergeant Patrick Gass, a West Virginian

whom Lewis later praised for his faithful service, diligence, and integrity. Gass's journal, which his captain instructed him to keep, became the first published account of the expedition.

See also Patrick Gass

Susan E. Lewis
Morgantown

Stephen E. Ambrose, *Undaunted Courage: Meriwether Lewis, Thomas Jefferson, and the Opening of the American West*, 1996; Gary Moulton, ed., *The Journals of the Lewis & Clark Expedition*, 1989.

Andrew Lewis

General Andrew Lewis was born in County Donegal, Ireland, in 1720. The Lewis family emigrated to America and settled in the Shenandoah Valley around 1732. Father John Lewis procured a land grant west of the Blue Ridge contingent on finding settlers for his holdings.

John Lewis taught Andrew fort building and surveying. In 1751, they surveyed the Greenbrier Valley and named the river for the vexatious greenbriers that abounded in the region, then as now. Later, Andrew surveyed Western Virginia tracts with his friend, fellow surveyor, and comrade-in-arms, George Washington. Lewis served as captain in the Virginia militia and commanded his county's militia. During the French and Indian War he was with Washington in 1754 at Fort Necessity, and he accompanied Braddock's disastrous expedition to Fort Duquesne in 1755. He was wounded each time. Captured at Duquesne, Lewis was interned at Montreal. In 1756, Major Lewis led the unsuccessful Sandy Creek Expedition across present southern West Virginia, meant to stop Shawnee depredations on American settlements. Lewis was a member of the Virginia House of Burgesses and helped negotiate the Treaty of Fort Stanwix (concluded 1768), which ceded to England all of the Iroquois claims to lands east of the Ohio River.

Indian troubles persisted in Western Virginia, and in September 1774 Lewis marched a frontier army from Camp Union, now Lewisburg, westward to the Ohio River. At the Battle of Point Pleasant, October 10, 1774, Lewis's 1,100 Virginia militiamen defeated a confederation of tribes led by Cornstalk. Lewis's brother, Charles, died in the day-long battle. Historian John P. Hale called the Battle of Point Pleasant a "military academy" which educated future military heroes. It was the last great Indian battle east of the Ohio River, and the Virginians' victory encouraged westward pioneer movement throughout Western Virginia.

Although he never lived in present West Virginia, Andrew Lewis had a profound effect on our state's history. He died September 26, 1781, in Bedford County, Virginia.

See also Lewisburg, Battle of Point Pleasant

Garrett C. Jeter
Charleston

Lewis County

Lewis County, located in north-central West Virginia at the crossroads of Interstate 79 and U.S. 33, was created from part of Harrison County in 1816. Named for Col. Charles Lewis, killed in the Battle of Point Pleasant, it was a huge territory from which were later formed all or part of six other counties. Modern Lewis County has an area of 391.4 square miles. The 2000 population was 16,919.

White people first settled in present Lewis County in 1769. Mostly of Scotch-Irish, German, and English lineage, they included John Hacker and Indian fighter Jesse Hughes. The first courts were conducted in 1816 in the hamlet of Westfield on the new county's northern edge. To establish a more central seat of government, one year later the county purchased the farm of pioneer settler Henry Flesher, at the confluence of the West

FAST FACTS ABOUT LEWIS COUNTY

Founded: 1816
Land in square miles: 391.4
Population: 16,919
Percentage minorities: 1.4%
Percentage rural: 70.6%
Median age: 40.1
Percentage 65 and older: 16.4%
Birth rate per 1,000 population: 11.3
Median household income: $27,066
High school graduate or higher: 73.7%
Bachelor's degree or higher: 11.2%
Home ownership: 73.0%
Median home value: $63,400

This information is from the 2000 U.S. Census. In 2000, West Virginia as a whole had 5 percent minorities, a median age of 38.9, median household income of $29,696, and a 75.2 percent home ownership rate.

Stonewall Jackson Lake in Lewis County.

Fork River and Stonecoal Creek. The new county seat was initially called Preston, then briefly renamed Fleshersville, and finally, in 1819, Weston.

In its first 30 years, Lewis County's economy was based largely on a self-sustaining agriculture. The primitive roads limited trade with distant points. The building of turnpikes through the county in the mid-1840s improved business and made Lewis County an important commercial and political center. The town of Jane Lew was established. Weston's first church building was erected in 1844; the first newspaper began publishing in 1846; the first bank opened its doors in 1852; and the first school was built in 1855.

The county's representatives in the Virginia legislature were able to secure the state's first major investment of money west of the mountains, with the locating at Weston of Virginia's third asylum for the insane. Construction of Weston Hospital began in 1859 but was halted by the outbreak of the Civil War. In June 1861, federal troops seized the gold deposited by Virginia in a Weston bank for the construction project. The gold was taken to Wheeling for the use of the loyalist Reorganized Government of Virginia.

Lewis Countians were divided in their loyalties during the Civil War. Thomas J. "Stonewall" Jackson had grown up at Jackson's Mill. His service to the South gave heart to the small local elite, the doctors, lawyers, and a good number of the merchants, many of whom had roots in Tidewater Virginia. The greater number of people, the less affluent, were loyal to the Union. They had as their hero U.S. Gen. J.A.J. Lightburn, who had grown up near Weston. The war years passed in alternate occupations by loyal and rebel forces; arguments and violent clashes between neighbors and within families; ar-rests and internments; and a few bush-whackings.

After West Virginia's creation in 1863, the new state government resumed the asylum project and completed it in 1880. For 50 years, until the beginning of World War I, the mental hospital was the largest single item in the state budget. It made Lewis one of West Virginia's most prosperous counties.

Commerce generated by the hospital made feasible the building of a branch railroad, a narrow-gauge connecting Weston with the Baltimore & Ohio at Clarksburg, in 1879. Farmers could then ship their produce to the most distant markets at reasonable costs. Local livestock found a market as far away as Europe. One of the state's earliest telephone systems was installed in 1885. By 1890, municipal water and sewer systems were under construction; electric lights and paved streets followed. At the same time, the branch railroad, now called the West Virginia & Pittsburgh, was being converted to standard gauge and extended south to Sutton and Richwood. Weston was its headquarters and also headquarters for several companies engaged in central West Virginia's timber industry. Lewis County is heavily forested with valuable hardwoods.

Weston's first public school building was erected in 1872. Ten years later, a smaller structure was built for African-American children. Lewis County's first high school was established in 1895 at Weston. Other high schools were built, in 1912 at Jane Lew and at Walkersville in 1920. In 1914, the county's Catholic population built a school in Weston. Most recently a new junior high school was erected in Weston, a new county high school at Bendale, and a new elementary school at McGuire Park.

About 1900, oil and natural gas in fab-ulous quantities were found deep under Lewis County, creating an overnight boom. Cheap gas attracted several glass manufacturers to the county, the earliest ones making window glass, the later ones beverage glassware. Weston and Jane Lew continue to be centers of natural gas production, storage, and transportation, and glass manufacturing.

Lewis County lies between the major northern and southern coalfields of West Virginia. However, some coal of lesser quality began to be mined near Walkersville as early as 1907, and strip mining of coal occurred in all parts of the county following World War II and continuing for 30 years.

In 1913, Weston became the southern terminus of regional electric trolley car service, connecting it and Jane Lew on an hourly schedule with Clarksburg and Fairmont. The first paved roads were built in the mid-1920s. Weston's Main Avenue remained a thriving commercial center until the development of malls and superstores in other counties, and more recently in the county but outside the city. The development of modern highways made the railroad less important, and the rails linking Weston with Clarksburg and Buckhannon were taken up. A branch line continues to operate across the southern part of the county, hauling coal from Braxton, Webster, and Nicholas counties to the CSX main line at Grafton.

Weston State Hospital closed in 1994. Lewis County remains a center for medical care, with the completion in 1972 of the Stonewall Jackson Memorial Hospital and the opening in 1994 of a new hospital for the mentally ill. Medical care for central West Virginians is today one of the county's chief sources of employment and income.

The county potential for tourism is only beginning to be realized, with I-79 and Corridor H (U.S. 33 east) placing it within a day's drive of half of America's population. New motels and restaurants now operate on those highways. The development of Stonewall Jackson Lake and Dam brought major change to southeastern Lewis County in the late 20th century. The dam, originally opposed by local residents facing displacement, was completed in 1988. The new Stonewall Jackson Lake State Park, West Virginia's premier state resort park, opened in 2002.

See also Weston

Joy Gregoire Gilchrist-Stalnaker
Horner

John L. Lewis

Unionist John Llewellyn Lewis, president of the United Mine Workers of America from 1920 until his retirement in 1960, was born February 12, 1880, in Lucas, Iowa, the son of an immigrant Welsh coal miner.

Lewis began his mining career at age 17. In his early 20s, he left the Lucas mines for a five-year sojourn through the West. After his travels he returned to mining and quickly became a union leader. As a delegate to the UMWA conventions, Lewis attracted the attention of American Federation of Labor President Samuel Gompers, who chose him to be a field representative for the AFL. Lewis used his growing prominence in the AFL to develop a base of support in his home union. He held various positions in the UMWA before becoming president in 1920.

The 1920s were difficult years for the mine workers' organization. Coal companies, using sympathetic governmental and court systems, were particularly successful in preventing union activity in West Virginia and Alabama. In West Virginia, frustrated miners fought back with their 1921 march on Logan County, resulting in the Battle of Blair Mountain. By the end of the decade, the UMW dwindled to fewer than 1,000 dues-paying members in West Virginia. Relief came with the election of Franklin Roosevelt as president. In 1933, the progressive Roosevelt administration secured passage of the National Industrial Recovery Act. Protecting the right of workers to organize and bargain collectively, the NIRA resulted in huge growth in America's unions, including the UMWA. In the late 1930s, Lewis led the drive to establish an organization of industrial unions, the Congress of Industrial Organizations (CIO), for those whom he felt were being neglected by the AFL.

During World War II, Lewis incurred the enmity of President Roosevelt and many Americans by authorizing work stoppages designed to win benefits for miners. Following the war, he secured the first health and retirement plan for UMWA members in return for tacit acceptance of increased mechanization in union coal mines. Through his long career, Lewis received both scorn and admiration for his efforts on behalf of coal miners. His iron control over union organization led to dissension in the union and resulted in the Miners for Democracy movement, which eventually deposed Lewis's successor, Tony Boyle.

John L. Lewis is remembered as an exceptional orator, a tireless worker for his union members, and an effective advocate for all organized labor. He retired as president of the UMWA in 1960 and died at Washington, June 11, 1969.

Kenneth R. Bailey
WVU Institute of Technology
Saul D. Alinsky, *John L. Lewis,* 1970; Maier B. Fox, *United We Stand,* 1990.

Virgil A. Lewis

Historian Virgil Anson Lewis was born July 6, 1848, in Mason County, the son of George W. and Lucie Edwards Lewis.

Though he would be remembered for his work in education and history, Lewis's ancestors were noted for their military service on the frontier. His great-grandfather, Benjamin Lewis, was wounded in the Battle of Point Pleasant and, in 1792 after the end of the Revolution and Indian conflict on the Virginia frontier, settled in what became Mason County.

Lewis was educated in the "old field" schools of Mason County. He taught for several years in Mason County and then in 1878 became the principal of the Buffalo Academy in Putnam County. He decided to read law and was admitted to the bar in 1879. He was not happy with the law as a career and soon returned to Mason County and to teaching.

History was Lewis's great passion. He was one of the organizers of the West Virginia Historical and Antiquarian Society in 1890, and he was awarded an M.A. in history from West Virginia University in 1893. In the early 1890s, he became noted for his educational and historical writing. Between 1890 and 1910, he wrote *Manual and Graded Course of Study for County and Village Schools of West Virginia; General History of West Virginia; History and Government of West Virginia; Life and Times of Ann Bailey; The Story of the Louisiana Purchase; Hand Book of West Virginia; How West Virginia Was Made;* and three biennial reports of the State Department of Archives and History.

He was elected as the state superintendent of schools in 1892. In 1905, Governor Dawson appointed Lewis as the first director of the State Department of Archives and History, a post which he held at the time of his death, December 5, 1912. Lewis's contribution to West Virginia's heritage lives on in the West Virginia Historical Society's Virgil A. Lewis Award.

Kenneth R. Bailey
WVU Institute of Technology

Lewisburg

Lewisburg, the county seat of Greenbrier County, was established as a town by the Virginia General Assembly in 1782. Previously, the area had been known as Fort Savannah, Camp Union, and Big Levels. Lewisburg is at the crossroads of the Seneca and Midland trails, now U.S. 219 and U.S. 60, and modern Interstate 64.

Pioneer John Lewis and his sons, Thomas and Andrew, camped in what is now Lewisburg while surveying the area in 1751. In 1774, Gen. Andrew Lewis assembled more than 1,000 men there for the 160-mile march to Point Pleasant, where the frontier militia narrowly defeated Indians led by Cornstalk.

Lewisburg's birth can be credited, in large measure, to the presence of the Lewis Springs, but its growth from settlement to town also benefited from the mustering of the militia there. Other cir-

cumstances that contributed to Lewisburg's growth were the construction of forts west of the Greenbrier, and its role as the county seat of Greenbrier County. After 1831, an annual session of the Virginia Supreme Court met at Lewisburg, and a state law library was established there.

Lewisburg was the site of a battle during the Civil War on May 23, 1862. Union troops under the command of George Crook defeated the Southern forces, led by Henry Heth. At the Confederate Cemetery on McElhenney Road, a cross-shaped mass grave holds the remains of 95 Confederate casualties of the battle. Union Maj. Rutherford B. Hayes, later president, served at Lewisburg.

A devastating blow occurred August 3, 1897, when fire destroyed much of downtown. Lewisburg rebuilt and evolved in the next century into the hub of one of the state's major farming areas and a center for education and the arts. The West Virginia School of Osteopathic Medicine was established in 1974 at the former Greenbrier Military School. The Greenbrier Valley branch of the New River Community and Technical College, and Carnegie Hall, a regional cultural center, are housed on the former campus of Greenbrier College.

Today, the largest local employer is ABB, a global technology company. Another major employer, combining technology and agriculture, is British United Turkeys of America, which produces turkey breeding stock. The Robert C. Byrd Clinic, which opened in 1997 at the School of Osteopathic Medicine, provides family health care to a six-county area. Tourism is a growing industry.

This city of about 4,000 residents lives its history. Homes, churches, art galleries, antique shops, restaurants, professional offices, and other businesses occupy many of the 18th- and 19th-century structures designated in 1978 as an historic district on the National Register of Historic Places. The Old Stone Presbyterian Church is said to be the oldest church building in continuous use west of the Alleghenies. Lewisburg celebrates New Year's Day with the Shanghai parade, a costume parade. The annual West Virginia State Fair takes place at neighboring Fairlea.

See also Battle of Lewisburg, Greenbrier County

Belinda Anderson
Asbury

Lewisburg, Battle of

The Battle of Lewisburg, a Union victory, occurred as U.S. troops maneuvered from Western Virginia toward Tennessee in the spring of 1862. Gen. John C. Frémont, commander of the Mountain Department for the U.S. Army, planned to concentrate his forces in Monterey, Vir-

Washington Street (U.S. 60) in Lewisburg.

Big Bill Lias

Gangster William George "Big Bill" Lias, the flamboyant Wheeling bootlegger, leader of organized crime, and professional gambler, was born July 14, 1900, either in Wheeling or Greece, and christened William George Liakakos. By 1920, he had left the family grocery business for a career in the illegal sale and distribution of liquor during Prohibition.

A short sentence in the Atlanta federal penitentiary prepared Lias for a new life in illegal gambling once Prohibition was repealed. When operation of the numbers racket was made a felony in 1939, he opened a string of casino-nightclubs along Market Street in Wheeling, where he was also prominent in prostitution and politics. In 1945, he purchased Wheeling Downs racetrack on Wheeling Island. In 1948, the federal government charged Lias with income tax evasion; his track and other assets were seized in 1952, the year before Washington failed in an attempt to deport him. By then he was a national figure whose control over "wide-open Wheeling" had made the city a magnet for free-spending adherents to the sporting life. He had criminal ties to Detroit and Cleveland.

Lias's rise was accompanied by violence, including gang wars and the mysterious death of his first wife in 1934. Yet Big Bill was lionized as well as feared by ordinary citizens as much as he was despised (and feared once again) by the local establishment and press. He survived more than one assassination attempt and lived out his life in obvious but never ostentatious comfort, alternating between homes in Wheeling and the Detroit area. In the 1950s, *Life* magazine estimated Lias's weight at 368 pounds. His acts of public charity during the Depression and later meant that he would be known for his largess as well as his largeness. Big Bill Lias died June 1, 1970, in Wheeling.

See also Wheeling

George Fetherling
Vancouver, British Columbia

Libertarian Party

In 1972, a year after the national Libertarian Party was founded, a small group of West Virginians headed by Harold Harvey of Beckley began work to promote a state Libertarian Party. The party's basic tenet is that individuals should be free to choose how to live, with minimum government assistance or interference. Government's role, according to Libertarians, should be to protect citizens and their property, and essentially only that.

In 1980, the Libertarian Party fielded its first candidate for statewide office when Jack K. Kelley of Parkersburg ran for governor. In 1994, after years of inactivity, the party regrouped around five Libertarians, led by John K. Brown of

ginia, and then move southwest until he reached the Virginia & Tennessee Railroad near Christiansburg. There, Frémont was to connect with troops under the command of Gen. Jacob D. Cox.

Cox, unaware that Frémont's command had been detained by fighting in the Shenandoah Valley, advanced as planned. While three of his four brigades occupied Princeton, a town that had been lost to Confederate forces earlier in May 1862, his fourth brigade, under the command of Col. George Crook, moved to Lewisburg. From his position Crook and his 1,600 men were within supporting distance of the troops located in Princeton, but also unknowingly vulnerable to attack from Confederate Brig. Gen. Henry Heth.

On the morning of May 23, 1862, 2,200 men under the command of General Heth attacked Crook's position. Despite facing superior numbers, Crook and his men repelled the advance, killing 38, wounding 66, and reportedly capturing nearly 100 prisoners, while losing only 13 under his command. Although the victory was widely reported and a boost to waning Union morale, its importance was overshadowed by federal losses in the Shenandoah Valley on the same day.

See also Civil War, Lewisburg

Donald C. Simmons Jr.
South Dakota Humanities Council

E. B. Long, *The Civil War Day by Day: An Almanac, 1861–1865*, 1971; Frank J. Welcher, *The Union Army, 1861–1865: Organization and Operations*, 1989.

Hurricane. Two years later, Libertarians collected the required number of signatures to get candidates on the 1996 general election ballot. The party's gubernatorial candidate, Wallace Johnson of Beckley, received more than one percent of the total votes cast that fall, guaranteeing automatic ballot access for the 1998 and 2000 elections. This was the first time since 1924 that a third party in West Virginia had gained official political party status.

In 1998, the first Libertarian was elected to office in West Virginia when William W. Clem ran unopposed in the Jefferson County surveyor's race. He was reelected in 2002. Statewide in 2000, the Libertarian candidate for governor, Bob Myers of Huntington, failed to gain one percent of the votes cast in that race, and the party lost its ballot status. That meant that the Libertarians would again have to petition to get on the ballot by collecting the required number of signatures set by state law.

In the 2000 general election, out of 1,067,822 registered voters, 956 were registered as Libertarians. Registered Libertarians were recorded in 52 of the state's 55 counties. Simon McClure of Bridgeport ran as the Libertarian candidate for governor in 2004.

Libraries

Early libraries in Western Virginia were subscription libraries supported by their members. Among the first subscription libraries was the Buffalo Creek Farmer's Library of Monongalia County (1813), with others established at about the same time in Wheeling and Morgantown. Romney, Harpers Ferry, Lewisburg, and Martinsburg had libraries by 1826, with others established in Pendleton and Jefferson counties in the 1850s. In 1859, a library company in Wheeling was chartered by the state of Virginia. This became the Wheeling Public Library in 1883, under the control of the Board of Education. It was the only real public library in the state before 1900.

Early in the 20th century, libraries were built in West Virginia with funds provided by philanthropist Andrew Carnegie, who built libraries nationwide. The Carnegie libraries were at Huntington (1903), Parkersburg (1905), and Hinton (1924). In 1915, the legislature passed a bill "to empower cities and towns to levy taxes for the purpose of establishing and maintaining public libraries and reading rooms." The West Virginia Library Association, organized in 1914, campaigned for this legislation. Fourteen public libraries were established between 1917 and 1930. In 1929, the legislature created the West Virginia Library Commission, but did not provide funding. In 1935, Governor Kump, in a message to the state legislature, said "I should like to see a beginning made in the direction of placing library service within easy reach of every citizen."

Conditions improved very little until the State Federation of Women's Clubs hired consultants Paul A. T. Noon and Mildred W. Sandoe to study the situation. Their report, completed in 1938, showed that 88 percent of West Virginians were without library services and recommended substantial funding by the state legislature; in 1941 the first funds were allocated. The Library Commission was then located in Morgantown on the campus of West Virginia University. The first executive secretary, Gordon L. Bennett, served in 1942; Clara Johnson in 1943–44; and Dora Ruth Parks from 1945 to 1971. Library service was improved in 1952 with the creation of regional library systems, enabling a small professional staff to serve a large population. In 1953, the Library Commission moved to Charleston.

The passage of the Library Services Act by Congress in 1956 enabled the Library Commission to acquire federal funding for public libraries in West Virginia. The commission hired consultant Ralph Blasingame to make recommendations for improving library service. This report was completed in 1965. By the autumn of 1966, the commission adopted a plan for implementing the Blasingame proposals. These included development of service center libraries and a system of direct service via bookmobiles. The bookmobiles, named Read-O-Rama and the Flying Book Express, provided service in rural counties primarily in southern West Virginia.

In 1964 and 1965, the federal Library Services Act was amended to provide funds for library education and library construction. Between 1965 and 1976, 53 public libraries were constructed with federal, state, and local funds exceeding $17 million. In 1969, state legislation was passed to allow the Library Commission to make direct grants for operating expenses to libraries complying with its administrative rules. When Dora Ruth Parks retired in 1971, great improvements had been made. By 1972, 80 percent of the state's population had some sort of library service, and 92 public libraries owned a total of 1,644,419 books.

With increased state support and the advent of federal aid, the Library Commission was ready for the new executive secretary hired in 1972, Frederic J. Glazer. Coming from a background of both public relations and public library administration, Glazer set out on a whirlwind of promotional programs for public libraries in West Virginia. State per-capita funding had stood at less then ten cents, and Glazer succeeded in increasing it to almost four dollars by 1996.

With the organization of legislative appreciation dinners sponsored by the State Library Association and the selling of everything from candy jars to neckties, public libraries impressed the state legislature with the job they were doing. Most persuasive was the increased use of public libraries. According to the West Virginia Library Commission Statistical Reports, circulation per capita increased from 3.39 in 1979 to 8.15 in 1990 to 9.42 in 1996. Building programs, including small "instant" and "outpost" libraries, brought the number of public libraries to 178 by 1996.

In 1973, a program was established between the Library Commission and Marshall University to train library personnel in small and remote libraries. This program provided basic training for clerical and support staff and has continued to the present. Other training in library skills was presented by the Library Development section of the Library Commission. Another ambitious program was developed with the University of South Carolina, for granting a master's degree in library science through distance learning. More than 69 people completed their professional degrees between 1993 and 1995.

In the 1980s the Library Commission contracted with Virginia Polytechnic Institute to provide a statewide automation network. The "VTLS" system gradually replaced card catalogs and allowed users to check online for books in the collection of all participating libraries. It has grown and developed and is still in use in most public libraries in the state.

Controversy followed the Library Commission's decision in 1996 to remove Glazer as executive secretary. Dave Childers of the commission staff became acting secretary. In 1997, David Price was hired as the fifth executive secretary for the Library Commission. Price resigned in 2001, and J. D. Waggoner was hired from within the agency to fill the top job in 2002. The executive secretary answers to the Library Commission, whose nine members are appointed to staggered four-year terms by the governor.

In 2003, the public library system in West Virginia consists of 97 library systems serving citizens from 175 facilities and seven bookmobiles. There is at least one public library facility in each of the 55 counties. Every public library has access to the Internet through the Statewide Library Network developed and maintained by the West Virginia Library Commission. In 2002, public libraries in West Virginia owned 5,002,976 books, 143,499 audios, 143,392 videos, and maintained 7,567 periodical and newspaper subscriptions. The libraries circulated 7.5 million items, answered 1.2 million reference questions and saw 6.1 million West Virginians cross their thresholds.

Merle Moore
Webster Springs

"Life in the Iron Mills"

"Life in the Iron Mills" is a classic short story set in the factory world of 19th-century Wheeling. The first published work of Rebecca Harding Davis, it appeared anonymously in April 1861 in the *Atlantic Monthly* and caused a literary sensation with its powerful naturalism that anticipated the work of Theodore Dreiser and Emile Zola. Davis's story is emphatically on the side of the exploited industrial workers, who are presented as physically stunted and mentally dulled but fully human.

The story's protagonist is Hugh Wolfe, a "puddler" who stirs molten metal in a vast foundry beside the Ohio River. On his breaks, he carves korl, a waste product of iron smelting described by Davis as "a light, porous substance, of a delicate waxen, flesh-colored tinge." Hugh's statue of a woman is noticed by some bourgeois visitors. They discuss the work condescendingly and awaken Hugh's sense of natural rights. They raise his hopes but offer no concrete help, and Hugh makes a series of bad decisions that lead to tragedy. Meanwhile, the korl woman is kept by the narrator as a reminder of Hugh, his aspirations, and his achievements.

"Life in the Iron Mills" was reprinted in the early 1970s and has continued to be an important text for those who study labor and women's issues.

See also Rebecca Harding Davis

Meredith Sue Willis
South Orange, New Jersey

Rebecca Harding Davis, "Life in the Iron Mills," in *Life in the Iron Mills: With a Biographical Interpretation by Tillie Olson,* 1972.

Joseph A. J. Lightburn

General Joseph Andrew Jackson Lightburn was born at Webster, Pennsylvania, September 21, 1824. He moved with his family to Lewis County in 1840. As a young man he was a friend and neighbor of Thomas Jackson, who became Gen. "Stonewall" Jackson during the Civil War. In 1842, Lightburn sought admission to West Point, but Jackson received the appointment. Enlisting in the army as a private in 1846, Lightburn served five years, leaving the army in 1851 with the rank of sergeant. Between that time and the outbreak of the Civil War he operated the family's mill and farm in Lewis County.

A Union man, Lightburn went to Wheeling in 1861 and later became colonel of the 4th West Virginia Infantry. In the spring of 1862, he was ordered to Charleston, and was subsequently placed in command of U.S. forces in the Kanawha Valley, with headquarters at Gauley Bridge. In September 1862, Confederate forces won temporary control of the Kanawha Valley and Lightburn's army was forced out. Later, he was ordered to Mississippi, where he was promoted to brigadier general and participated in the battle of Vicksburg. He also took part in the battles of Jackson, Mississippi, and Chickamauga, Tennessee. Wounded in action during Sherman's advance on Atlanta, he returned to duty in 1865, serving in the Shenandoah Valley until resigning on June 22, 1865.

Lightburn became a Baptist preacher in 1867 and that same year was elected to the West Virginia legislature. He died in Lewis County, May 17, 1901. In 1915, a monument to General Lightburn was placed at Vicksburg National Battlefield Park.

See also Civil War

Tim McKinney
Fayetteville

Lilly Brothers

The Lilly Brothers were an early West Virginia bluegrass band. Mitchell Burt "Bea" (1921–2005) and Charles Everett Lilly (1924–) were born at Clear Creek, Raleigh County. In their mid-teens they developed a mandolin-guitar harmony duet and worked occasionally on radio at WCHS Charleston and WHIS Bluefield, and especially at WJLS Beckley from April 1939. They also worked at WNOX Knoxville with Molly O'Day and Lynn Davis. In 1948, the Lilly Brothers moved to WWVA Wheeling where they worked with Red Belcher for two years. Everett also served two stints as mandolinist with Lester Flatt and Earl Scruggs.

Between 1952 and 1970, the Lilly Brothers, along with West Virginia banjoist Don Stover (1928–96), made their biggest impact in Boston, where they introduced bluegrass to New England audiences. In this period they recorded for the Event, Folkways, Prestige, and County record labels. In 1970, Everett's son, Jiles, died in an auto crash, and the distraught father decided to return to Raleigh County. Since then the Lilly Brothers have played together infrequently, mostly at bluegrass festivals and on a 1973 tour of Japan. Everett has remained active with his sons and others in bands known as Clear Creek Crossing and the Lilly Mountaineers. In 2002, the Lilly Brothers and Don Stover were inducted into the International Bluegrass Music Association's Hall of Honor.

Ivan M. Tribe
University of Rio Grande

Ivan M. Tribe, *Mountaineer Jamboree: Country Music in West Virginia,* 1984.

Cousin Abe Lilly

Attorney General Armistead Abraham "Cousin Abe" Lilly was born March 25, 1878, at Jumping Branch, Summers County, the son of Robert G. and Virginia Lilly. He was raised in Raleigh County, attended Concord College, and graduated from the Southern Normal University in Tennessee, from which he received his law degree in 1900. That same year he entered into the practice of law in Beckley and was elected to the West Virginia legislature. He was elected prosecuting attorney of Raleigh County in 1904 at the age of 26. Lilly, a Republican, was elected to statewide office as attorney general in 1912. After election as attorney general, he moved to Charleston where he lived for the rest of his life.

During his tenure as attorney general, Lilly and Governor Hatfield decided to appeal the Virginia Debt Suit to the U.S. Supreme Court. In becoming a state West Virginia had willingly assumed a part of the Virginia state debt that existed prior to the division of the mother state. The amount was at issue, however, and Virginia eventually sued. The suit dragged out over the remainder of the 1800s and into the 1900s before being resolved. In settling the debt, which was paid in following years through the sale of bonds, it is estimated that Lilly and Hatfield saved the state a large sum of money. Lilly ran for governor in the 1916 primary, losing the Republican nomination to Ira E. Robinson. In 1922 he sought, but failed to obtain, nomination for U.S. senator.

Cousin Abe was the scion of one of southern West Virginia's largest families. He organized the Lilly Reunion Association in 1929 and served as its president until his death. Lilly died June 21, 1956, in his penthouse on top of Charleston's Ruffner Hotel, of which he was principal owner.

See also Lilly Family, Virginia Debt Question

Kenneth R. Bailey
WVU Institute of Technology

Lilly Family

The Lilly family is one of the largest families in the state, playing a prominent part in the history of the southern counties. Each year thousands of Lillys and their friends and relatives gather for the Lilly Reunion at Flat Top, Mercer County, one of the biggest family reunions in West Virginia.

The Lillys trace their origins to France. The first of their ancestors in America was a John Lilly, who was among those emigrating with Lord Calvert to found Maryland in 1633. John's great-grandson Robert Lilly, who lived to age 114 and is buried at Flat Top, founded the family in West Virginia.

Robert Lilly and the Reverend Josiah Meadows crossed the Alleghenies together and settled in present Summers County, establishing the village of Lilly at the juncture of the Little Bluestone and Bluestone rivers, south of present Hinton. The village existed from the late 1700s until 1946, when it was razed due to the construction of the Bluestone

Dam. Two or three oak trees planted by John H. Lilly in 1885 are still standing where the school used to be and some of the foundation rocks for the schoolhouse are still in place.

The early Lillys seem to have taken very seriously the Biblical injunction to be fruitful and multiply. Ten to 12 children in each family was common. There were so many Lillys with the same names, they were given nicknames to distinguish them. These nicknames, usually reflecting some identifying characteristic, included Bear Wallow Bob, Miller Bob, and Shooting Bob, as well as Squire Bob, a justice of the peace. Sockhead Andy Lilly wore a stocking cap, and Jerusalem Jim was a preacher in the Primitive Baptist church, to which most early Lillys belonged.

The Lillys have produced teachers, farmers, attorneys, doctors and lawyers. Among the most distinguished was the Honorable Abraham A. "Cousin Abe" Lilly, who served as attorney general for West Virginia and was one of the organizers of the Lilly Reunion Association. After his term as attorney general, he practiced for many years in Charleston, living at the old Ruffner Hotel. His son, Goff P. Lilly, was also a noted attorney.

See also Cousin Abe Lilly

Barbara Singer Lawrence
Josephine Lilly Singer
Milton

Limestone Glades

Limestone glades are sparsely vegetated areas of limestone bedrock that occur in the Potomac Highlands. They are found in Grant, Hardy, and Pendleton counties, with a good example at Cave Mountain on the Pendleton-Grant line. They typically occur on dry, exposed upper hill slopes, on limestone of the Tonoloway and Helderberg formations. The glades are interspersed with more densely vegetated grasslands and woodlands. The limestone glades have some of West Virginia's most unusual vegetation types and harbor many specially adapted and rare plants.

The occurrence of natural forest openings on limestone substrates is probably due to extreme temperature fluctuations and lack of water in the shallow soils, but may also be related to natural fire cycles and avalanches. Limestone glades may be considered early successional communities which eventually will progress to full forest, but succession is very slow due to harsh soil conditions. Woodlands and grasslands adjacent to the glades have developed on less exposed places with deeper soils and less surface rock.

Although the glades have sparse vegetation, the plants that survive there are distinctive and include rare species such as yellow or Virginia nailwort and the en-

demic Smoke Hole bergamot. Scattered grasses and stunted trees typical of the surrounding communities also grow in the glades. The associated grasslands, also called limestone barrens, are dominated by side-oats grama, bottle-brush grass, and little bluestem. The associated woodlands are dominated by red cedar, chinquapin oak, and redbud.

Jim Vanderhorst
Division of Natural Resources

Lincoln County

Lincoln County is one of the five counties created after West Virginia became a state. It is a southwestern county, bounded by Cabell, Putnam, Wayne, Logan, Boone, and Kanawha counties. The Guyandotte River flows through the western part of Lincoln County, while the Mud River flows in the north. Hamlin is the county seat. State Route 10 and State Route 3 are the main roads, although four-lane Corridor G (U.S. 119) touches Lincoln County in the east. Lincoln County has an area of 437.3 square miles and a population of 22,108 in 2000.

Prehistoric people lived in a village near present West Hamlin. Later Indians, primarily the Shawnee, used present Lincoln County for hunting or as a buffer from the white settlers farther east. Throughout the 1780s and 1790s, fragments of several Indian tribes formed the Mingo tribe and had a strong presence in the area. Indian caves, graves, and mounds are common.

Lincoln County was first populated by whites when the McComas family settled on the Guyandotte near present West Hamlin in 1799. The Hatfields followed about 1800, settling on the river just above the McComases. Other early settlers included William W. Brumfield, at the mouth of Big Ugly Creek about 1801; John Tackett, at Trace Fork in 1801; and David Stephenson, at present Hamlin in 1802. In the next few decades, the region was quietly settled, with much economic

activity centering on "the Falls of Guyan," near present West Hamlin. Hamlin, originally Hamline, was a key site on the Mud River. It was established by the Virginia Assembly in 1853 and named for a nearby Methodist church, which took its name from Bishop Leonidas Hamline. Another important town in that vicinity was Griffithsville, established about 1854 and named after an early settler, Alexander Griffith.

In the late 1840s, locks and dams were constructed on the Guyandotte River to carry coal and timber from the valley. Throughout the 1850s, steamboats including the *Major Adrian* and the *R. H. Lindsey* made trips up and down the Guyan, as the Guyandotte River is often called. An 1861 flood destroyed the locks and dams, and they were never rebuilt.

The people were about equally divided during the Civil War. There were several military engagements in what is now Lincoln County, but no large battles. Soon after the war, on February 23, 1867, Lincoln County was formed from Boone, Cabell, Kanawha, and Putnam counties, and named for the assassinated president. In 1868, Lincoln's boundaries were drastically changed: Putnam's territory was given back; more land was taken from Boone, Cabell, and Kanawha; and new land was incorporated from Logan and Wayne counties. There was yet another boundary shift in 1869, in which Lincoln took in all of the Harts area and most of the headwaters of Mud River. In the same year, Hamlin was made the permanent county seat.

For the next several decades, timbering was big business in Lincoln County. Men made their living by cutting timber and rafting it downriver to the town of Guyandotte, on the Ohio River. For a brief period, steamboats returned to the Guyan, including the *Jennie George*, *Guyan Valley*, *Favorite*, and others.

FAST FACTS ABOUT LINCOLN COUNTY

Founded: 1867
Land in square miles: 437.3
Population: 22,108
Percentage minorities: 1.0%
Percentage rural: 100%
Median age: 37.4
Percentage 65 and older: 13.1%
Birth rate per 1,000 population: 12.3
Median household income: $22,662
High school graduate or higher: 62.7%
Bachelor's degree or higher: 5.9%
Home ownership: 79.1%
Median home value: $60,000

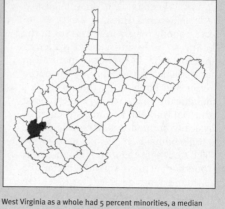

This information is from the 2000 U.S. Census. In 2000, West Virginia as a whole had 5 percent minorities, a median age of 38.9, median household income of $29,696, and a 75.2 percent home ownership rate.

A Lincoln County farmstead.

The river culture passed away with the construction of the Chesapeake & Ohio Railroad along the Guyandotte River in 1902–04, built to develop the coalfields in Logan County. In 1905, the oil and gas business began in Griffithsville, while the timber industry boomed on Big Ugly Creek in the 1910s. Industrialization turned nasty with the burning of the courthouse on November 19, 1909, suspected to have been done to destroy land records and confuse titles.

In the early 20th century, discoveries in oil and gas brought employment and a surge in the county population. From 1900 to 1910, the number of Lincoln Countians jumped from 15,434 to 20,491. After that time, the county's population remained virtually unchanged throughout the remainder of the 20th century. During the Great Depression, conditions in Lincoln County were especially bad. By 1935, 89 percent of all families regularly accepted government relief, although county officials had initially resisted the relief efforts of the Roosevelt administration.

In the 20th century, Lincoln County's education advancements were marked by the construction of four high schools: Duval High School in Griffithsville (1914), Hamlin High School in Hamlin (1922), Guyan Valley High School in Pleasant View (1927), and Harts High School in Harts (1954). In later years concerns arose as to the education provided to Lincoln County young people. The 1982 ruling by Judge Arthur Recht of the Ohio County Circuit Court that the state legislature had failed to provide an efficient educational system for all children of the state arose from a court case originating in Lincoln County. The state board of education took control of Lincoln County schools in 2000, arguing that local administrators were doing an unacceptable job. Many Lincoln Countians disagreed. They vigorously resisted the take-over and related attempts to consolidate their schools. Nonetheless, the state board voted in 2003 to replace Lincoln County's four high schools with one consolidated high school.

Lincoln County is the birthplace of Gen. Charles "Chuck" Yeager, the first man to fly faster than sound. John S. Witcher of Hamlin was a Union general during the Civil War, member of the House of Delegates, secretary of state, congressman, collector of internal revenue, and paymaster for the army. Clark W. May of Griffithsville was speaker of the House of Delegates, state Senate president, and state attorney general, before his premature death in 1908. Gubernatorial candidate Lloyd Jackson, of Hamlin, had a long career in the state Senate and served as its president.

Brandon Ray Kirk
Ferrellsburg

Lincoln County Feud

The Lincoln County Feud occurred on Harts Creek in Lincoln and Logan counties in 1889–90. It was primarily caused by competition between country merchants, with alliances based on family grudges. It has been called the Lincoln County War, the Brumfield-McCoy Feud, and the Brumfield-McCoy-Adams-Hall War. A song written about the trouble was titled "The Lincoln County Crew."

The feud began when Paris Brumfield killed Boney Lucas at the West Fork of Harts Creek around 1884. Paris thereafter feuded with Lucas's father-in-law, Cain Adkins (a preacher, doctor, constable, and schoolteacher), as well as Cain's son-in-law, Green McCoy, a fiddler from Pike County, Kentucky. Meanwhile, Paris's oldest son, Al Brumfield, was making enemies over his prosperous operation of a whiskey boat and log boom in Harts. His rivals were Deputy Sheriff John W. Runyon, a timber boss, storekeeper, and saloon operator originally from Kentucky, and Ben Adams, Al Brumfield's uncle by marriage, who accused him of log theft. They reportedly hired Green McCoy and Milt Haley to kill Brumfield. Haley, a fiddler and first cousin to Runyon, had married into the Adams-Mullins family on Trace Fork.

On September 22, 1889, McCoy and Haley ambushed Al Brumfield as he and his wife rode a single horse past Thompson Branch. Brumfield was shot in the arm while his wife was shot in the jaw. Both Haley and McCoy disappeared into Kentucky but were jailed in Martin County in late October. Brumfield and a posse brought them to Hugh Dingess's home on Smoke House Fork in Logan County, where about 100 men gathered for protection against an Adams-Adkins-Runyon mob organized nearby. While there, McCoy made a confession and, at some point, he or Haley played the fiddle, either "Brownlow's Dream" or "Hell Up Coal Hollow." They were then taken to Green Shoal and—by varying accounts— cut, shot, hanged, or hit over the head with the butt end of an axe. Sometime later, local preacher Ben Walker headed a burial party which interred Milt and Green in a single grave on West Fork.

The feud ended sometime during the winter of 1890. Cain Adkins escaped by horseback to his childhood home in Wayne County, leaving his family to make their way out on a rented boat. John Runyon sold out to Al Brumfield, who became Harts' chief businessman during the 1890s. Paris Brumfield was murdered by his son Charley in 1891.

John Hartford
Madison, Tennessee
Brandon Ray Kirk
Ferrellsburg

Linger Chair Factory

The Linger chair factory, located in Upshur County near Rock Cave, made the sturdy ladder-back chairs known to generations of 4-H campers at Jackson's Mill. Waitman T. Linger started making chairs in 1887 at Beans Mill, Upshur County. After a disastrous fire, his small family-run business relocated to several places over the years, including Alton, Sago, Indian Camp, and then French Creek in 1928. During this period Linger ran a successful cant hook handle manufacturing business in addition to making chairs.

The factory was moved to Rock Cave in 1950, after being sold to James G. Linger, Waitman T.'s grandson. After operating successfully for almost 20 years, he sold the business in 1969 to the Upshur County Chair and Craft Cooperative, which was formed with the help of a federal grant. By 1971, ownership had returned to James G. Linger. The factory was sold in 1973 to Richard Virship, who operated it until 1981, when he stopped making chairs and put the business up for sale.

After remaining idle for 17 years, the chair factory was purchased by Lonnie Bender in 1998. Repairs and restoration began on the century-old machines, which include a 1902 nine-foot back-knife pattern lathe, a boring machine, and a mortise machine. Bender learned chair making during an apprenticeship with Tom Lynch, a former apprentice at the factory, and with guidance from James G. Linger. Bender expected to put the chair factory back into full production, crafting stools and the chair known locally as the Linger ladder back. This chair is constructed from West Virginia hardwoods using greenwood mortise-and-tenon interlocking joints, a traditional technique that ensures strength and longevity.

Most of the chairs made at the chair factory over the years were sold locally, many to the Jackson's Mill 4-H Camp to use in the seat-weaving classes and in the dining hall. Many remain in use today.

See also Chair Making

Tom Lynch
Rock Cave

Linsly School

Linsly School, an independent, co-educational, college preparatory boarding school located in Wheeling, is the oldest private academy west of the Allegheny Mountains. Incorporated in 1814, the school is named for Noah Linsly, a prominent Wheeling lawyer whose will provided funds for a so-called Lancastrian academy, based on a system using trained older students to tutor younger ones.

Originally located on Chapline Street and open to boys and girls, Linsly soon became an all-boys institution. In 1859, Linsly Institute, as it was then called, erected a new three-story structure, still standing at 1413 Eoff Street. With West Virginia statehood in 1863, government officials leased the building and it served as the first state capitol until 1870. Following the Civil War, the school faced serious financial difficulties, but under the leadership of John Birch, principal from 1874 through most of the late 19th century, the school survived and flourished. In 1877, a cadet battalion was formed, and in 1942 the school became known as Linsly Military Institute. A new building at Thedah Place was erected in 1925, as well as an imposing statue, "The Aviator." In 1968, the school relocated to the new Banes Hall on Knox Lane. The military program was discontinued in 1979, and in 1988 girls were again admitted.

Today Linsly educates 427 students in grades five through 12, with one-fourth boarding students and three-fourths day students. The school expanded under the long-serving headmasters, Guy Holden and Basil Lockhart, who collectively served from 1916 to 1972. The present headmaster, Reno DiOrio, appointed in 1979, builds on this tradition.

Margaret Brennan
Wheeling Area Historical Society
Philip Ross, *Forward and No Retreat: The Linsly Story*, 1994; *Wheeling Intelligencer*, September 1, 1859.

Literacy

West Virginians rank a little above the national average as regards the ability to read and write at acceptable levels. A 1998 report from the National Institute for Literacy indicated that 20 percent of West Virginians over age 16 function at "Level 1" literacy, the lowest category, as opposed to 22 percent nationally. Level 1 literacy includes those adults who have difficulty reading and comprehending a short newspaper article, reading a street map, or calculating costs on an order form. In a separate report, the U.S. Department of Education estimated that 17 percent of West Virginia adults have significant difficulty with literacy tasks relating to everyday life and work.

Such people may be able to read or write in a rudimentary fashion, and are thus not illiterate in the traditional sense, but they lack the literacy skills necessary to manage a successful, fulfilling life. The completely illiterate, those unable to read or write at all, comprise a much smaller part of the population, now estimated at two percent to four percent. This number has decreased significantly over time, from a fifth or more of the population in West Virginia's early years as a state.

Literacy is unevenly distributed across the state, generally improving from south to north and reflecting the education levels and relative affluence of West Virginia counties. Eight of the 11 counties with Level 1 literacy rates of 25 percent or higher lie south of the Kanawha River in the southern coalfields. Statewide, individual counties range from Monongalia and Putnam (the best, at 14 percent Level 1 literacy) to McDowell (37 percent).

The group known as Literacy West Virginia is the main non-governmental organization working to improve literacy skills in West Virginia. Literacy West Virginia resulted from a 2004 merger of the West Virginia chapters of the two main national literacy groups, Literacy Volunteers of America and Lauback Literacy Action. More than 1,000 volunteer tutors provide reading instruction to adult students throughout the state. Most volunteer programs are affiliated with Literacy West Virginia and based in libraries, churches, and community centers.

The West Virginia Adult Basic Education program of the state Department of Education has official responsibility for literacy training. The Governor's Council on Literacy, created in 1991, assists in coordinating and expanding literacy efforts in West Virginia. The council, composed of 25 individuals representing libraries, education, business, labor, government, higher education, and others, sponsors an annual scholarship program for GED graduates, distributes literacy mini-grants, coordinates family literacy services, conducts public awareness and outreach efforts, and facilitates linkages with business and industry.

See also Education

Literature

The origins of West Virginia's literary heritage predate statehood. While numerous published writers made Western Virginia their home, there are a select few whose influence and importance stand out. Novelist, journalist, and travel writer Anne Royall (1769–1854), who spent her early adult years at Sweet Springs in Monroe County, was one of the earliest. Aside from her uncommon independence for a woman of her day, Royall's outspokenness toward prominent figures and issues anticipates by decades the muckraking tradition that was eventually to characterize American journalism. In addition to her novel, *The Tennessean* (1827), she is noted for *Letters from Alabama* (1830) and *Sketches of History, Life, and Manners in the United States* (1826).

The African-American essayist and Civil War officer, Martin Delany (1812–85), was born at Charles Town and is best-known for his anti-racist writings, most particularly *Blake: or, the Huts of America*, originally serialized in 1859–62. David Hunter Strother (1816–88), born at Martinsburg, established himself as an illustrator and travel writer under the pen name Porte Crayon and went on to greater fame as a Civil War correspondent and military officer. Yet another literary pioneer is Rebecca Harding Davis of Wheeling (1831–1910), author of one of the earliest and most enduring examples of social realism, the short story "Life in the Iron Mills" (1861).

Western Virginians produced a rich historical literature, particularly from the region's dramatic frontier period. The best-known accounts are *Notes on the Settlement and Indian Wars of the Western Parts of Virginia and Pennsylvania from 1763 to 1783* (1824) by Joseph Doddridge (1769–1826); *Chronicles of Border Warfare* (1831) by Alexander Scott Withers (1792–1865); and *History of the Early Settlement and Indian Wars of Western Virginia* (1851) by Wills De Hass (1817–1910). *Trans-Allegheny Pioneers* by John P. Hale (1824–1902) was published in 1886. Supplementing these is the extensive collection of interviews, letters, and documents compiled by Lyman Draper (1815–91) from 1840 to 1891.

Two of West Virginia's governors were

accomplished men of letters. George Wesley Atkinson (1845–1925) authored *The History of Kanawha County* (1876), and William Alexander MacCorkle (1857–1930) is noted for *The White Sulphur Springs* (1916), *Some Southern Questions* (1908), and for his memoir, *The Recollections of Fifty Years of West Virginia* (1928).

The emergence of West Virginia writers of national prominence begins in the late 19th century. Harrison County's Melville Davisson Post (1869–1930), author of the Uncle Abner detective stories, is widely regarded as influential in the development of the modern mystery genre. The poet Anne Spencer (1882–1975), who grew up in Bramwell, Mercer County, was a noted participant in the Harlem Renaissance. Poet and essayist John Peale Bishop (1892–1944) was born at Charles Town and shared the international literary spotlight with the likes of Faulkner and Gertrude Stein.

Pocahontas County poet Louise McNeill (1911–93) came into prominence with her collection titled *Gauley Mountain* (1939), and served as West Virginia's poet laureate from 1979 until her death. Also notable in the early 20th century was Julia Davis (1900–93) of Clarksburg, author of *The Shenandoah* (1945) in the Rivers of America series, among other works. Bridging the period of the Second World War were writers such as Webster Springs native Hubert Skidmore (1909–46), whose social realist fiction often dealt with class and cultural conflict in West Virginia. His novel, *Hawks Nest* (1941), was a fictionalized account of the death toll in building the Hawks Nest Tunnel. His twin brother, Hobert (1909–69), was also an author, whose works included a fictional treatment of twin brothers, *The Years Are Even* (1952).

It was the post-war period, however, that occasioned the first full flowering of West Virginia literature. There are the notable literary contributions of Moundsville's Davis Grubb (1919–80), whose suspense novel, *Night of the Hunter* (1954), was a National Book Award finalist. Fairmont native John Knowles (1926–2001) rose to enduring prominence for *A Separate Peace* (1960); he also wrote *A Vein of Riches* (1978), a novel based on his hometown's rich industrial heritage. A less-acknowledged but much accomplished writer, William Hoffman, who was born in Charleston, began what has become a long literary career in this same period.

It is also in this period that we find the towering achievement of Mary Lee Settle's *Beulah Quintet*. These five novels—*Prisons, O Beulah Land, Know Nothing, The Scapegoat,* and *The Killing Ground*—published between 1956 and 1982, can be regarded as a literary reckoning with the West Virginia experience. Collectively they constitute not only an impressive aesthetic accomplishment but also a

Novelist Davis Grubb (1919–80).

near-definitive coming to terms with regional social history in a narrative, fictional form. Settle, born in Charleston in 1918, wrote many other novels, including several about West Virginia. The magnitude of her work exceeds any literary precedents.

It would be another generation before anyone would undertake anything approaching Settle's project. This time Wheeling served as the historical backdrop for the novels of Keith Maillard—*Light in the Company of Women* (1993), *Gloria* (1999), *Clarinet Polka* (2003), *Alex Driving South* (1980), and *Hazard Zones* (1995).

Also prominent among this next generation was short-story writer Breece D'J Pancake (1952–79) who grew up in Milton, Cabell County. Though mindful of earlier work, particularly Tom Kromer's (1906–69) *Waiting for Nothing* (1935), Pancake exhibited a vision of common local experience, teaching Appalachian writers that regional everyday life could provide a landscape for new and original work.

There have followed several highly regarded literary figures from West Virginia, each with a sense of place as integral to their fiction, yet each distinctive in voice. Jayne Anne Phillips (*Fast Lanes*, 1984; *Shelter*, 1994), Richard Currey (*Wars of Heaven*, 1990), Pinckney Benedict (*Wrecking Yard*, 1992; *Dogs of God*, 1994), Lisa Koger (*Farlanburg Stories*, 1990), Meredith Sue Willis (*Oradell at Sea*, 2002), and Gretchen Laska (*The Midwife's Tale*, 2003) have all created imaginative landscapes that are identifiably West Virginian and yet avoid the conventions of local color writing so prevalent in regional literature since the late 19th century. The latter half of the 20th century saw the coming of age of West Virginia

literature; never before have so many written so well. But, as with so many West Virginians in the 20th century, most of the authors have left to find their careers elsewhere though they still write about West Virginia. Of this generation, Denise Giardina, author of acclaimed coalfields novels *Storming Heaven* (1987) and *The Unquiet Earth* (1992), and other novels, continues to reside in the state.

Coming of age as a literary theme also finds voice in this critical period of West Virginia writing. Chuck Kinder's *Snakehunter* (1973) and Lee Maynard's *Crum* (1988) put small town and rural experiences of growing up on the state's literary map.

Not surprisingly, nonfictional memoir also flourishes in our state's literature. Notable instances include Louise McNeill (*Milkweed Ladies*, 1988), Cynthia Rylant (*But I'll Be Back Again*, 1989), Henry Louis Gates (*Colored People*, 1994), Mary Lee Settle (*Addie*, 1998), and John O'Brien (*At Home in the Heart of Appalachia*, 2001). *Red, White, Black & Blue: A Dual Memoir of Race & Class in Appalachia* (2004) by William Drennen and Kojo Jones, edited with analysis by Dolores Johnson, is an unusual collaborative memoir. Homer Hickam's *Rocket Boys* (1998) was the most popular of these books, becoming a best-selling book and successful movie. In these memoirs, the same features so prominent in literary fiction are in evidence: West Virginia as both shared landscape and a uniquely lived experience, providing a setting for themes both particular and universal. Clearly, there are numerous forms of nonfiction, such as Strother's travel writings, that transcend ordinary journalism. A more recent candidate would be Jedediah Purdy's evocation of West Virginia as a tonic to the prevailing culture of cynical commercialism, *For Common Things* (1999).

Other areas of West Virginia literature have demonstrated growth in quality and number in the postwar era. In the case of poetry, this trend is evident in the anthology assembled by Barbara Smith and Kirk Judd: *Wild Sweet Notes: Fifty Years of West Virginia Poetry, 1950–1999* (2000). More than 130 contributors were included, ranging from traditionalists such as Louise McNeill and Kanawha County's Muriel Miller Dressler (1918–2000)—the book's title is taken from a line in Dressler's signature poem "Appalachia"—to current poets, such as Maggie Anderson, Irene McKinney, and Marc Harshman.

Children's literature underwent a parallel development in the last decades of the 20th century. From a modest number of authors, notably Jean Lee Latham (1902–95) and Alvena Seckar, an explosion in juvenile literature has followed the publication of Rylant's *When I Was Young in the*

When I Was Young in the Mountains

When I was young in the mountains,
Grandfather came home in the evening
covered with the black dust of a coal
mine. Only his lips were clean, and he
used them to kiss the top of my head.

When I was young in the mountains,
Grandmother spread the table with hot
corn bread, pinto beans and fried okra.

Later, in the middle of the night,
she walked through the grass with me
to the johnny-house and held my hand
in the dark. I promised never to eat
more than one serving of okra again.

When I was young in the mountains,
we walked across the cow pasture and
through the woods, carrying our
towels. The swimming hole was dark
and muddy, and we sometimes saw
    snakes,
but we jumped in anyway.

On our way home, we stopped at
Mr. Crawford's for a mound of white
butter. Mr. Crawford and Mrs. Crawford
looked alike and always smelled of
sweet milk.

When I was young in the mountains,
we pumped pails of water from the well
at the bottom of the hill, and heated
the water to fill round tin tubs for
our baths.

Afterward we stood in front of the old
black stove, shivering and giggling,
while Grandmother heated cocoa
    on top.

When I was young in the
    mountains,
we went to church in the
    schoolhouse
on Sundays, and sometimes
    walked with
the congregation through
    the cow
pasture to the dark
    swimming hole,
for baptisms.

My cousin Peter was
    laid back into the
water, and his white
    shirt stuck to him,
and my Grandmother
    cried.

When I was young in the mountains,
we listened to frogs sing at dusk and
awoke to cowbells outside our windows.
Sometimes a black snake came in the
yard, and my Grandmother would
    threaten it with a hoe.

If it did not leave, she used the hoe
to kill it. Four of us once draped a
very long snake, dead of course, across
our necks for a photograph.

When I was young in the mountains,
we sat on the porch swing in the
evenings, and Grandfather sharpened
my pencils with his pocketknife.
Grandmother sometimes shelled beans
and sometimes braided my hair. The
dogs lay around us, and the stars
sparkled in the sky. A bobwhite
whistled in the forest.
Bob-bob-bobwhite!

When I was young in the mountains,
I never wanted to go to the ocean,
and I never wanted to go to the desert.
I never wanted to go anywhere else in
the world, for I was in the mountains.
And that was always enough.

—Cynthia Rylant © 1982

Mountains (1982). While Rylant has gone on to publish more than 60 books for children, she has been joined by several other writers, including Marc Harshman, Anna Egan Smucker, Cheryl Ware, Cheryl Ryan, Robyn Eversole, Joseph Slate, and Brenda Seabrooke. Three West Virginia children's authors have received the prestigious Newbery Award: Latham (1956), Betsy Byars (1971), and Rylant (1993). In addition to these, the Newbery Award-winning author, Phyllis R. Naylor, set her *Shiloh* novels (1991, 1996, and 1997) and the boys versus girls series (1993–2003) in actual West Virginia locales.

The one kind of genre fiction that has fared well in West Virginia is mystery, something that might have gratified Melville Davisson Post. Aside from writers of literary thrillers such as Benedict and Hoffman, traditional mystery novels and stories have been plentiful from John Suter (1914–96), Dave Pedneau (1947–90), John Douglas, Carlene Thompson, and John Billheimer.

The inability to either evade or completely erase demeaning prejudice has perhaps proven to be the sort of creative tension that can provoke and sustain a rich and diverse literary countertradition. In the opening lines of Richard Currey's novel *Lost Highway* (1997) the protagonist, returning home to West Virginia, recalls his initial sense of shame regarding the place of his origin. When he first left the state, he had passed himself off as a Virginian, but eventually abandoned the pretense. This is but one instance of a prevalent feature in West Virginia literature: a dual consciousness of shame and pride in response to popular conceptions and stereotypes. West Virginia writing has undeniably turned out to be an effective personal and cultural response to a generally negative image, capable of subverting that image in equally imaginative ways and turning it to purposes the larger culture could hardly have anticipated or intended.

Gordon Simmons
Division of Culture and History

Little Beaver State Park

Established in 1972, the 562-acre Little Beaver State Park is a day-use park in Beaver, a few miles southeast of Beckley. Development there began in the late 1930s with Civilian Conservation Corps workers clearing land, cutting stone, and building roads. Originally a 4-H camp, the park's main attraction now is the 18-acre lake, with its dock, rowboats, and paddle boats. A sandy beach bounded by white pines offers one of the loveliest swimming areas in the state. The lake was created in 1941, with the damming of Little Beaver Creek by the WPA.

Fishermen catch bass, channel catfish, crappies, bluegill, and especially the stocked trout at Little Beaver State Park.

There is the paved Lake Front Trail suitable for handicapped use, and also a pier for handicapped people. Local people have filled the park's museum with their collections of antique bottles and farm implements. There are covered picnic shelters near the museum and near the lake. Youngsters enjoy the recreation building, game room, and playground.

Hiking trails lace through the rhododendron bushes and hemlock trees in the hills around the lake or follow the shore. Visitors can use picnic tables and shelters, some at the water's edge, others back in the woods. Little Beaver State Park is a popular place for family reunions, with many scheduled there each summer.

Maureen F. Crockett
St. Albans

Little Bluestone River

With headwaters on Flat Top Mountain in eastern Summers County, the Little Bluestone River flows in a northeasterly, then a southeasterly direction until it joins the Bluestone River at the site of the former village of Lilly. Lying entirely in Jumping Branch District at a mean elevation of 1,500 feet, the Little Bluestone is a small river, only nine-and-a-half miles long. It has a cumulative tributary drainage of 34.86 square miles. The principal tributaries are Spicelick Creek, Parker Creek, and Suck Creek. Its most prominent physical feature is a waterfall at a point known as Fall Rock, the site of the last remaining gristmill in the county.

Lilly, razed but never submerged by the builders of Bluestone Dam, was named for Robert and Mary Frances Moody Lilly, the progenitors of the vast Lilly family in southern West Virginia, who settled near the mouth of the river in the late 1700s. Their son-in-law, Josiah Meador, a sergeant-major in the colonial army and Battle of Yorktown veteran, founded the Bluestone Baptist Church, one of the oldest Baptist churches west of the Allegheny Mountains, at the village.

The Little Bluestone has supported farming, timbering, and milling operations, and its lower reaches have been part of the Bluestone Dam Conservation Project since the 1940s.

Jack Wills
Fairmont

Jack Lilly, "The Lost Village of Lilly," *Goldenseal,* Summer 1998; M. V. Mathes, et al., *Drainage Areas of the Kanawha River Basin*, 1982; William Sanders, *A New River Heritage*, 1992.

Little Kanawha River

The Little Kanawha River enters the Ohio River at Parkersburg, 169 miles from its beginning near Craddock, Upshur County. As it flows westward through Braxton, Gilmer, Calhoun, Wirt, and Wood counties, the Little Kanawha gathers water from numerous creeks and streams. Its largest tributary is the Hughes River.

Riverboat on the Little Kanawha, Grantsville, early 1900s.

Indians had left the Little Kanawha before the time of white exploration, but a small band under Chief Bull settled there in 1765, just as white settlers were entering the area. They lived near the salt licks at the community now called Bulltown. Many of them were massacred by white men in 1772 and their bodies thrown into the river. The upper watershed was explored by John Hacker in 1770. The pioneering Carpenter family settled in the region shortly thereafter. The Bulltown area was settled by white men in the 1770s, with settlement at Parkersburg soon following. Eventually, the communities of Burnsville, Gilmer Station, Glenville, Elizabeth, Grantsville, and Creston would also be established along the Little Kanawha.

In 1838, Claudius Crozet, the director of the Virginia Board of Public Works, recommended that 10 locks and dams be constructed to permit navigation on the Little Kanawha from Parkersburg to Bulltown salt works. The Little Kanawha Navigation Company began selling stock in 1847, and the reorganized company finally let contracts for the first four locks and dams in 1867. By 1874, boats could travel from Parkersburg upriver past Palestine, Wirt County. These were private locks owned by the company. In 1891, the "government lock" was built near Burning Springs. The remaining locks recommended by Crozet were never built, but these five were sufficient to enable shallow-draft riverboats access all the way to Burnsville.

From the mid-1800s and into the 1930s, boats powered by steam and later by gasoline carried people, mail, and freight up and down the river. The boats that plied the Little Kanawha were much smaller than the big paddle wheelers that churned the Ohio River. A windowed cabin, sometimes two decks tall, protected passengers and freight from the weather. Divided into rooms and a galley, the cabin was home to the crew, which sometimes included the family of the captain. A wheelhouse perched atop the

whole. Commercial navigation came to an end as roadways connecting the towns along the river's banks improved.

The West Virginia oil and gas industry developed within the Little Kanawha watershed. The state's first oil well and one of the very earliest in the world was drilled at Burning Springs in 1860. The Burning Springs oil field was fired by Confederate raiders in 1863, creating an inferno so intense that oil burned on the surface of the river.

Burnsville Dam was built on the upper reaches of Little Kanawha in 1978, providing flood control and recreation.

See also Bulltown, Burnsville Dam
Joy Gregoire Gilchrist-Stalnaker
Horner

Joy Gregoire Gilchrist, "It was Crowded Up There," *Goldenseal,* Summer 1994; Larry N. Sypolt, "Some Historical Background: Navigation on the Little Kanawha," *Goldenseal,* Summer 1994.

C. E. Lively

Labor spy Charlie Everett Lively was a coal company agent who befriended Matewan Police Chief Sid Hatfield, then turned against him in the Matewan Massacre trial and later participated in Hatfield's assassination. Born March 6, 1887, Lively came to Matewan in early 1920 as the union drive to organize Tug River miners began. He joined the union and, after the Matewan Massacre in May 1920, engaged the miners in long discussions of the event, while secretly reporting to the Baldwin-Felts Detective Agency. Lively revealed his true identity and testified against Hatfield and the miners in their trial in early 1921; nevertheless, all the defendants were acquitted.

The following August 1, Hatfield was ordered to stand trial in the McDowell County Courthouse in Welch on charges of leading a shooting raid on the McDowell County town of Mohawk. As he and his friend Ed Chambers climbed the courthouse steps, unarmed and with their wives by their sides, Lively and a half dozen other Baldwin-Felts detectives killed both Hatfield and Chambers in a fusillade of bullets fired from the top of the steps. The shooting helped incite the miners' armed march on Mingo County in the ensuing weeks. In December 1922, Lively was acquitted of murder in the deaths.

C. E. Lively died in Huntington, May 28, 1962.

See also Baldwin-Felts Detective Agency, Sid Hatfield, Matewan Massacre

Lon Savage
Salem, Virginia
Lon Savage, *Thunder in the Mountains*, 1984.

Livestock

Early Western Virginians farmed for themselves and for the market, producing a variety of field and garden crops as well as livestock. Nearly every farm had a few milk cows, a flock of hens and of sheep, a number of mules or horses (perhaps work oxen, as well), and a drove of free-ranging hogs. These were used for the family's own subsistence and for the work of the farm. Livestock was also produced commercially from early times, bred as draft animals and for meat production. The selling of surplus livestock at local markets or to drovers allowed farmers to acquire goods that could not be grown or made on the farm.

Pre-industrial livestock production, particularly for the period from 1760 to 1830, was a major enterprise in what is today the Eastern Panhandle. The counties of Hampshire, Hardy, and (present day) Pendleton were well-known for raising and driving cattle in large numbers as early as the late 1750s. Historian Richard K. MacMaster suggests that cattle owners and herdsmen in the valley of the Potomac's South Branch were essentially the landed aristocracy of Western Virginia, much like large plantation owners of the lowlands. Hardy County produced more cattle than any other Virginia county by 1786, and was one of the leading cattle producers in the country. It was common for Hardy County cattlemen to own more than 50 head of cattle, with many owning more than 100. By the 1820s, cattle drives of 5,000 head were not uncommon in the Potomac Valley.

Between 1865 and 1920, West Virginia's agricultural economy underwent a profound transformation, caused in part by the related events of the coming of the railroads and the cutting of the forest. The railroads provided the means by which livestock could be transported to external markets, replacing the stock drives that had sent livestock to market in earlier times. Railroads also provided transportation for the logging industry, and by 1910 West Virginia's seemingly endless supply of timber had been nearly exhausted. Newly cleared forests opened vast tracts of land for the production of livestock, further commercializing West Virginia agriculture.

Historian Ronald L. Lewis, in his book, *Transforming the Appalachian Countryside*, provides a detailed account of the impact that railroad development and deforestation had on livestock production. Between 1870 and 1920, for example, cattle production in heavily timbered Randolph County increased from 8,228 to 14,684, sheep production from 8,523 to 18,214, and the number of swine from 2,834 to 5,128. Such increases were a direct result of increased rangeland due to deforestation and the expansion of external markets due to rail transportation. As the 1900s progressed, however, commercial livestock production waned as people and agricultural production shifted westward. West Virginia found it difficult to compete with the Midwest where farming conditions are superior.

Statewide hog production dropped by 80 percent from 1964 to 1997, while the number of dairy cows plunged by an even greater percentage; the number of beef cattle increased slightly over this period. The overall downward trend has been most pronounced in the fertile valley bottoms of the Potomac and Shenandoah valleys in the Eastern Panhandle. Many farmers in these counties have virtually eliminated commercial livestock production and replaced it with poultry production. The growing of turkeys and chickens, especially broilers, has shown a dramatic increase in recent years and represents the continued transformation of West Virginia's agriculture. Cattle remains most important among West Virginia livestock, both in dollar value and number of head, but at the beginning of the 21st century the value of the cattle herd has been far surpassed by the value of West Virginia's burgeoning poultry flock.

See also Agriculture, Draft Animals, Poultry

J. Todd Nesbitt
Lock Haven University of Pennsylvania
Ronald L. Lewis, *Transforming the Appalachian Countryside: Railroads, Deforestation, and Social Change in West Virginia, 1880–1920*, 1998; Richard K. MacMaster, "The Great Cattle Trade in Western Virginia," in Robert Mitchell, ed., *Appalachian Frontiers: Settlement, Society, and Development in the Preindustrial Era*, 1991.

Locks and Dams

West Virginia, "The Mountain State," could just as easily have been called "The River State." With 11 of its rivers equipped with locks and dams at some point in the state's history, West Virginia holds the distinction of having had more locks and dams than any other state in the nation.

The rivers and streams of eight Eastern Panhandle counties flow into the Potomac River, which marks the border between West Virginia and Maryland. The rivers and streams of the remaining 47 counties find their way into the Ohio River as it flows along the state's western boundary for 277 miles, more than a fourth of the river's total length. The Ohio River for these 277 miles is included within the territory of West Virginia, with the state line running along the opposite shore.

Since early in the nation's history the Ohio has been improved for navigation. These improvements include dikes, dredging, and clearing, and the construction of two systems of locks and dams. Twenty-one of the original system's 53 locks and dams were located along the West Virginia section of the Ohio River. These wicket dams and single-lock structures were built by the federal government and operated for more than 40 years before being replaced by new high-lift dams with dual lock chambers. Since 1824, Congress has assigned the U.S. Army Corps of Engineers the responsibility of maintaining year-round navigation on America's inland rivers. The Corps established nine feet as the depth to maintain for year-round navigation. Locks and dams, dredging, and the removal of obstacles to navigation ensure year-round nine-foot navigation depth, but do not provide flood protection.

West Virginia's second greatest river is the Kanawha or Great Kanawha. Located completely within the boundaries of the state, the Kanawha flows 97 miles in a northwesterly direction from Gauley Bridge past the state capitol at Charleston to join the Ohio at Point Pleasant. Between 1875 and 1898, ten low-lift wicket dams with single-lock chambers were built on the river by the federal government. The first two units of this system were the first movable wicket dams completed in the United States, and when the system was completed, the Kanawha was the nation's first river to be completely canalized with wicket dams. During the 1930s, three high-lift gated dams with dual lock chambers replaced the Kanawha's first system of locks and dams.

The Elk River had a single lock and dam, built approximately two miles above its junction with the Kanawha in 1848. This structure was removed in 1881. Beginning in 1855, eight locks and dams were built on the Coal River, another Kanawha tributary, and a single lock and dam was built on the Little Coal River. More than a half-million tons of cannel coal was shipped on the Coal River before and shortly after the Civil War. The system was abandoned in 1882.

In 1847, citizens of Parkersburg, Elizabeth, and Glenville organized the Little Kanawha Navigation Company with few improvements being accomplished until the Burning Springs oil boom began in 1860. After the Civil War, the company built four locks and dams on the Little Kanawha, providing a four-foot navigation depth from Parkersburg to Burning

Springs. In 1891, the federal government built a fifth lock and dam near Burning Springs, providing slackwater navigation to Creston, 48 miles above the Ohio River. In 1905, the entire system was acquired by the federal government, which operated it until 1951 when it was turned over to the state of West Virginia.

The Guyandotte Navigation Company was incorporated by the state of Virginia in 1849 after a state engineer surveyed the valley and described its vast resources of timber and coal. Five locks and dams were built on the Guyandotte, providing slackwater navigation 31 miles upriver from the town of Guyandotte and the Ohio River. Two additional locks and dams were built in 1853, extending navigation to Branchland. This system of poorly built stone-filled crib structures was abandoned after the Civil War.

The Big Sandy River marks the border between West Virginia and Kentucky from Fort Gay to the Ohio River. In 1874, the U.S. Congress authorized a survey of the Big Sandy, and its Tug and Levisa forks to determine the feasibility of building locks and dams. The result of the survey was that three locks and dams were built on the Big Sandy and one each on the Tug and Levisa. In 1947, operations at all the projects except Lock and Dam No. 1 on the Big Sandy were discontinued. Lock No. 1 was closed in 1952. Today the Big Sandy River is navigable for a distance of approximately nine miles. The backup pool of Greenup Locks and Dam located 24 miles downstream on the Ohio River creates this nine miles of navigable water.

The Monongahela River is formed a mile south of Fairmont, where the West Fork and the Tygart Valley River merge. From here the river flows in a northeasterly direction for 128 miles until its junction with the Allegheny, forming the Ohio River at Pittsburgh. The West Fork was the first river west of the Allegheny Mountains to have navigation passes built into dams for the passage of boats. The West Fork had six dams built on it, but these structures were seriously damaged by floodwaters in 1824 and abandoned shortly thereafter.

In 1838, the Monongahela Navigation Company of Pennsylvania built a series of seven locks and dams from Pittsburgh to the West Virginia border. The success of these structures led the neighboring citizens of Virginia to request their state to improve the upper Monongahela with locks and dams to stimulate economic growth. After the Civil War, the federal government acquired the navigation system on the Monongahela and built Lock and Dam Nos. 8 through 15, extending year-round navigation from Pittsburgh to three miles up the Tygart Valley River. During the 1950s and 1960s, seven old locks and dams were replaced with three high-lift gated dams with dual lock chambers on the river.

There are other rivers in West Virginia that have been rivers of commerce but have not been improved by locks and dams. Among these are the Cheat River, Buckhannon River, New River, Greenbrier River, and Gauley River.

See also Big Sandy River, Coal River, Guyandotte River, Kanawha River, Little Kanawha River, Monongahela River, Ohio River

Gerald W. Sutphin
Huntington

Leland R. Johnson, *Men, Mountains, and Rivers,* 1977; Johnson, *The Headwaters District,* 1979; Gerald W. Sutphin and Richard A. Andre, *Sternwheelers On The Great Kanawha River,* 1991.

Log Construction

The prevailing theory about the origins of log construction throughout the southern Appalachian region, and West Virginia in particular, is that this building method arrived with early settlers from Pennsylvania. The two dominant ethnic groups to settle Western Virginia, the Scotch-Irish and the Pennsylvania Germans, were influenced by Finnish and Swedish log building and construction techniques in Pennsylvania. The Finns and Swedes were well situated there by the time the Scotch-Irish and Germans arrived in the New World beginning in the late 17th century.

In part through necessity, hewn logs were the material of choice for home and farmstead buildings of the pioneers. However, after sawn boards became widely available by the mid-19th century, many in the Mountain State continued the log form of construction. Logs were generally free to landowners, and for reasons of both economy and tradition, numerous log buildings were constructed well into the 20th century. Older log buildings today are most prevalent in the eastern counties where the "rain shadow" of the state's highest ridges means limited rainfall, helping to preserve the structures.

The most widely found log-notching technique in West Virginia is the half dovetail. The V notch is also common, while full dovetail and square notching are rare. Some more crudely constructed outbuildings and barns feature round logs (instead of being hewn flat on the sides) with rough saddle-notched joinery. Today many older houses are sealed both inside and out with boards, hiding the carefully hewn logs that form the strength of the construction. Likewise, "puncheon" floors, formed through laying hewn logs together to form a flat-surfaced floor, are rarely seen as they have been covered over with smoother boards.

Given that trees used for logs are by nature limited in length, types of building construction were therefore similarly limited. Early buildings were raised by manpower, thus providing another limiting factor to their size. Larger buildings could be constructed through the use of the log "crib," a square section of logs ranging from 12 to 30 feet on a side. Two cribs, placed from eight to 20 feet apart, are joined by one roof in both house and barn design and became a distinct architectural form, the dog trot or breezeway style. This traditional style, especially in barns, remained a popular style that is widely duplicated in more recent lumber-framed buildings, even though the limiting factor of log length no longer applies.

Upon close inspection, most logs in older buildings may be seen to consist of the more durable species of Appalachian hardwoods. In the limited high altitude growing area of the eastern mountains, red spruce was the species of choice. However one can also find chestnut, oak, and yellow poplar (tulip poplar in a large, mature stage) throughout the state, and many older houses and barns contain more than one variety of tree. Pine is often used today in the log "kit homes," or mass produced log houses that are delivered to home sites and assembled.

See also Architects and Architecture, Material Culture

Gerald Milnes
Augusta Heritage Center

Gerald Milnes, "The Barns of Pendleton County," *Goldenseal,* Spring 1998; Lynwood Montell and Michael Lynn Morse, *Kentucky Folk Architecture,* 1976.

Log Driving and Rafting

The most colorful era of the lumber industry in West Virginia occurred in the days when loggers floated their timber downstream to the mills. During the summer and fall, woodsmen labored from daylight until dark, six days a week, felling, trimming, and skidding timber. Cutting and skidding continued during the winter when ice facilitated the quick passage of logs down the mountain to the river landing below. "Arks" from 70 to 100 feet long and 18 feet wide were built. The bunkhouse ark contained double-decked bunks and a large stove to keep the men warm; the cooking and dining hall occupied a second ark.

The main drive down the river began with the first sign of spring when the ice began to break up. The logs were then rolled into the swollen stream and carried along by the current, with the arks following behind. Log driving was demanding, dangerous work, much of it performed in icy water. Many West Virginia rivers could not be successfully driven because they were too rapid, narrow, or filled with obstructions, but others were ideally suited for driving. The Greenbrier became the most famous of the driving rivers, its reputation mythologized in the popular novels of W. E. Blackhurst and the poetry of Louise Mc-Neill.

Loggers who worked along navigable streams preferred to construct log rafts to float their timber downstream, rather than driving loose logs. The average log rafts consisted of about 70 logs. The earliest rafts generally were assembled by fastening the logs together with poles running across the timbers and held together with wooden pins. Nails and chain dogs, two wedges joined by a chain, made the raft strong and gave it flexibility and yet allowed it to be constructed and dismantled quickly. To the rear of the raft were attached oars from 20 to 50 feet long which permitted raftsmen to steer.

The history of rafting is as varied as the rivers themselves. At Rowlesburg, Preston County, a lumber depot built at the junction of the Baltimore & Ohio Railroad and the Cheat River served as a destination of many rafts steered down the Cheat River. The Kanawha River was, of course, the drainage stem of several important interior rivers, and large sawmills along its banks were the destination of innumerable rafts in the 19th century. Log driving and rafting peaked prior to 1900 when railroads replaced streams as the chief means of transporting logs to the milling centers.

See also Timbering and Logging

Ronald L. Lewis
West Virginia University

W. E. Blackhurst, *Riders of the Flood*, 1954; Roy B. Clarkson, *Tumult on the Mountains: Lumbering in West Virginia, 1770–1920*, 1964; Ronald L. Lewis, *Transforming the Appalachian Countryside: Railroads, Deforestation, and Social Change in West Virginia, 1880–1920*, 1998.

Logan

The city of Logan is located on the Guyandotte River just off U.S. 119 (Appalachian Corridor G), at the junction of State Routes 10 and 44. The population of Logan was 1,630 in 2000. It is the county seat of Logan County. Logan was first known by explorers of the 1780s as "Islands of the Guyandot." In 1827, it was named Lawnsville after Anthony Lawson built a trading post at the confluence of the Guyandotte River and Main Island Creek. The first mayor was the poet Thomas Dunn English, who had the village chartered as the town of Aracoma by Virginia's General Assembly in 1853. The U.S. Post Office established the first mail route, and the town was known as Logan Courthouse until 1907, when Mayor Scott Justice and the town council renamed it the city of Logan. For many years it has been a hub of the eastern coal industry.

The city's greatest period of growth was between 1889, when a newspaper was established, and 1929, which marked the end of the expansion of the local coal industry. At its height during World War II, many businesses operated in Logan, including clothing stores, groceries, furniture stores, hotels, banks, automobile dealerships, public buildings, schools, and doctor and lawyer offices. Logan's population peaked at 5,166 in 1940. After World War II, the city began to decline as mine mechanization cut the population of Logan County.

Among the famed residents of Logan was Dr. Henry D. Hatfield, who served as governor of West Virginia between 1913 and 1916. Logan is the home of Southern West Virginia Community and Technical College and of Logan Regional Medical Center. Logan High School, Grade School, and Middle School and the Public Library occupy Midelburg (or Hatfield) Island, adjacent to the historic downtown.

See also Logan County

Robert Y. Spence
Logan

Logan Banner

The *Logan Banner*, Logan County's only daily newspaper, was founded in 1888, first published by Henry Clay Ragland. The newspaper is Logan County's oldest commercial business still in existence in the county.

Ragland edited the *Logan Banner* as a weekly publication until his death in 1911. It was a Democratic newspaper under his ownership. The Brazie brothers, Charles and William, published the newspaper after Ragland, but changed its political affiliation to Republican. The *Banner* continued to represent the GOP through the ownership by Clarence Frey, who came to Logan County in 1921. When Frey took over, the newspaper was saddled with debts, but it began a steady growth from then on. The weekly *Logan Banner* became an afternoon daily in 1935, publishing five days a week until 1981 when the present schedule was adopted, Monday through Friday afternoons and Sunday morning.

Frey was publisher of the *Logan Banner* from 1921 until his death in 1960. With the help of Frey's partner, Robert O. Greever, Frey's widow continued the newspaper under her ownership until 1965, when the *Logan Banner* was sold to a publishing company located in Tennessee. The new company sent publisher Jim Muscia to Logan. He later purchased the paper and operated it for several years before selling it to the Smith Newspapers in 1975 with Tom George as publisher. For a few years Tom Schmitt was publisher after George. Richard Osborne was promoted to the position of publisher in 1988 and continues today.

The *Logan Banner* serves Logan, Boone, Mingo, Lincoln, and Wyoming counties. The 2005 circulation was 9,000.

Chief Logan

Chief Logan, born about 1725 in Pennsylvania's Susquehanna Valley, was the son of an Oneida chief, Shikellamy, whom the Moravians had converted to Christianity. Named Tah-gah-jute, or Talgayeeta, at birth, Logan was renamed in recognition of his father's friendship with James Logan, a Pennsylvania statesman and Indian negotiator.

After his father's death in 1748, Logan became chief of the Cayuga tribe, one of the Six Nations. He maintained good relations with European colonists while protecting tribal rights. About 1770, Logan moved his family to the Ohio River Valley, eventually settling at Yellow Creek, Ohio, 40 miles above Wheeling and near present Hancock County, to join the Mingoes, a multi-tribal confederation allied to the Six Nations. As chief, he consistently acted to maintain peace, several times averting retaliatory raids, while trying to protect the land north of the Ohio from white settlement.

When a band of frontiersmen led by Daniel Greathouse slaughtered a group including members of Logan's family near Yellow Creek in 1774, Logan abandoned peaceful ways and vowed vengeance. He led raids throughout the upper Ohio Valley and into the Mononga-

Logan's speech

"I appeal to any white man to say, if ever he entered Logan's cabin hungry, and he gave him not meat; if ever he came cold and naked, and he clothed him not. During the course of the last long and bloody war, Logan remained idle in his cabin, an advocate for peace. Such was my love for the whites, that my countrymen pointed as they passed, and said, 'Logan is the friend of white men.' I had even thought to have lived with you, but for the injuries of one man. Col. Cresap, the last spring, in cold blood, and unprovoked, murdered all the relations of Logan, not sparing even my women and children. There runs not a drop of my blood in the veins of any living creature. This called on me for revenge. I have sought it: I have killed many: I have fully glutted my vengeance. For my country, I rejoice at the beams of peace. But do not harbour a thought that mine is the joy of fear. Logan never felt fear. He will not turn on his heel to save his life. Who is there to mourn for Logan?—Not one."

—Chief Logan from Thomas Jefferson's *Notes on the State of Virginia* (1781)

FAST FACTS ABOUT LOGAN COUNTY

Founded: 1824
Land in square miles: 455.8
Population: 37,710
Percentage minorities: 3.7%
Percentage rural: 77.2%
Median age: 39.3
Percentage 65 and older: 14.5%
Birth rate per 1,000 population: 13.4
Median household income: $24,603
High school graduate or higher: 63.1%
Bachelor's degree or higher: 8.8%
Home ownership: 76.8%
Median home value: $62,500

This information is from the 2000 U.S. Census. In 2000, West Virginia as a whole had 5 percent minorities, a median age of 38.9, median household income of $29,696, and a 75.2 percent home ownership rate.

hela Valley. Soon after, the Shawnee and Delaware tribes of Ohio began attacking settlements across the Ohio River.

In response to increasing frontier warfare, Virginia Governor Lord Dunmore raised an army and instructed Andrew Lewis to form another to march against the Ohio tribes. At the Battle of Point Pleasant, the Shawnee and allied tribes led by Cornstalk were defeated by Lewis's army on October 10, 1774. Logan avoided the peace negotiations that followed, but delivered to John Gibson the famous speech later quoted by Thomas Jefferson that eloquently voiced Logan's grief and erroneously accused Michael Cresap of his relatives' murders. He resumed his conciliatory political efforts but developed a deep melancholy over the warfare that continued. Logan was involved in a heated family conflict when he was killed, allegedly by a nephew, in 1780.

Logan County, the town of Logan, and Chief Logan State Park are named for Logan, as, indirectly, is Mingo County.

See also Greathouse Party Massacre, Indians

Harold Malcolm Forbes
WVU Libraries
John Jeremiah Jacob, *A Biographical Sketch of the Life of the Late Captain Michael Cresap,* 1971; Franklin B. Sawvel, *Logan the Mingo,* 1921.

Logan County

Logan County was created by the Virginia General Assembly, May 7, 1824, from parts of Giles, Tazewell, Cabell, and Kanawha counties. The county lies south of Charleston in the heart of the southern West Virginia coalfields. Logan County, with an area of 455.8 square miles, is bisected by the Guyandotte River. The county seat, first named Lawnsville, was laid out in 1827. The town government was reorganized by the poet Thomas Dunn English in 1853–54, and the town was renamed Aracoma. It became the city of Logan in 1907, under Mayor Scott Justice.

Logan County was settled between 1792 and 1824 by pioneer families from Washington and Montgomery counties, Virginia, and Pike County, Kentucky. Through the 19th century the population lived mostly on family farms, though many men cut timber in the winter months to float to Catlettsburg and Guyandotte, on the Ohio River at the mouths of the Big Sandy and Guyandotte rivers, respectively.

Logan County experienced unsettled conditions during the Civil War. The county seat was occupied, then burned, by Union forces under Col. Edward Siber in 1862. After Reconstruction, Democrats regained control of the county under "Major" John William Straton. The courthouse was rebuilt. The town served as a gathering spot for farmers and timbermen during court days, which were held every three months.

In 1874, a great change began when the Confederate veteran, lawyer, and journalist Henry Clay Ragland arrived in Logan. Allied with Straton and Straton's son-in-law, James Andrew Nighbert, Ragland worked to build a coal and railroad economy. Nighbert, Ragland, and their allies created the first successful newspaper, the *Logan County Banner,* to argue for industrialization. Success was assured when the Chesapeake & Ohio Railroad constructed its line from Huntington to the city of Logan in 1904. In the meantime the Norfolk & Western Railroad had built its main line in 1893 on the "Sandy side," the nickname for the part of Logan County lying within the Big Sandy River valley. Rapid development following the arrival of the railroad led in 1895 to the creation of Mingo County from that section of Logan.

Between 1904 and 1929, the Logan coalfields boomed. Holden, Omar, and many other coal company towns were created. The older towns of Man and Chapmanville adapted to the new economy. The darker side of Logan County's coal economy also developed during those years. By the time of World War I, many miners believed they were exploited by the coal companies. That resentment added to tensions during the 1919–21 mine strike in Mingo County. Coal power was represented politically by Logan Sheriff Don Chafin. In 1919 and in August and September 1921, miners from the Kanawha Valley and the surrounding region launched two armed marches on Logan County to bring the United Mine Workers of America to the local mines. The marchers fought a three-day battle with Chafin's forces at Blair Mountain in September 1921, and were turned back only through the intervention of the U.S. Army.

The Great Depression and World War II brought further changes. Federal labor legislation passed during Roosevelt's New Deal finally made possible the establishment of the miners union, which changed the political complexion of the community and ensured the success of the Democratic Party. During and after the war, coal companies mechanized to increase production and reduce the number of miners. Many left to find employment elsewhere. From a high of approximately 11,000 miners in 1940, the number fell to 1,146 by 2001. Logan County population fell by half, from a peak of 77,391 in 1950 to 37,710 in 2000.

The county suffered industrial tragedy with the fire at Holden 22 Mine in March 1960 and the Buffalo Creek disaster in February 1972. Eighteen lives were lost at Holden 22, while another 125 lives were

All-terrain vehicles on the Hatfield-McCoy Trail, Logan County.

lost when a coal waste dam owned by the Pittston Corporation collapsed and destroyed a dozen communities on Buffalo Creek.

One of the most significant events in Logan County history was the Hatfield-McCoy Feud, which began in 1882 and ended in 1890. A subject of films, television programs, records, and many books, the feud pitted the family of West Virginian Anderson "Devil Anse" Hatfield against the family of Randolph "Randal" McCoy of Kentucky. Thirteen persons were killed.

Logan County's cultural contributions include its folk music, represented best by the Harts Creek tradition in fiddle-playing, the clawhammer banjo playing of Virginia "Aunt Jennie" Ellis Wilson, and the original songs of Frank Hutchison, Jerrel Stanley, and Archie Conway. Since 1975, the county has presented an annual Arts and Crafts Fair. Since 1976, it also has presented an original drama, *The Aracoma Story*, based on the legend of a daughter of Shawnee war leader Cornstalk.

Logan County received national political attention in the spring of 1960, when Sen. John F. Kennedy campaigned for the presidential nomination in the county. Many in Logan County believed that the War on Poverty of his successor, Lyndon B. Johnson, had been suggested by President Kennedy. The War on Poverty, however, did little to change the dynamics of Logan County's history, and the continuing decline of coal employment has eroded the county's economic base during the last 30 years. More recent concerns have included the debate over strip mining and whether or not the coal industry should be regulated more strictly by state and federal officials.

See also Battle of Blair Mountain, Buffalo Creek Flood, Hatfield-McCoy Feud, Logan, Mingo County

Robert Y. Spence
Logan

Robert Y. Spence, *Land of the Guyandot*, 1976.

Logan Wildcats

The Logan Wildcats was the unofficial name of Company D 36th Virginia Infantry of the Confederate Army during the Civil War. The company was created at Logan Courthouse on June 3, 1861, and consisted of about 85 men led by officers Henry M. Beckley, Astynax McDonald, Mont Lawson, James Nighbert, Dick Ferrell, and James Dingess.

Mustered into the Southern army under Lt. Col. John McCausland in Charleston, the company saw its first action in the Battle of Scary Creek in Putnam County. It was then reorganized and joined Gen. John B. Floyd near Little Sewell Mountain in August 1861. The company was in the battle of Carnifex Ferry on September 10, 1861. Then the

unit was sent west and was present at the Union siege of Fort Donelson, Tennessee. During the campaigns of 1862 through 1865, Company D was used as a rear guard unit during several campaigns. The Wildcats were present at the Battle of Cloyd's Mountain, where Gen. A. G. Jenkins was wounded, later dying. The company was active in the May 1864 action around Christiansburg. It also was active in the Shenandoah Valley campaigns of late 1864 and early 1865. The 36th Virginia Infantry disbanded on April 12, 1865.

Another unit termed the Logan Wildcats was a band of armed irregulars led by Anderson "Devil Anse" Hatfield that was active in Logan and Wyoming County late in the war. In recent times the sports teams of Logan High School have been called the Logan Wildcats.

Robert Y. Spence
Logan

Lonesome Pine Fiddlers

The Lonesome Pine Fiddlers were West Virginia's pioneer bluegrass band, based for many years beginning in 1938 at WHIS radio in Bluefield. Bass player Ezra Cline (1907–84) led the group, while fiddler Curly Ray Cline (1923–97) was their key musical figure. Other significant members included Charlie Cline (b. 1931), Ned Cline (1921–44), Melvin Goins (b. 1933), Ray Goins (b. 1936) and Paul Williams (b. ca. 1934). Ezra was a cousin to brothers Curly Ray, Charlie, and Ned Cline, and all were from Baisden in Logan County. The Fiddlers had an old-time string band sound until Larry Richardson and Bob Osborne joined them in 1949 on banjo and mandolin, recording for Cozy Records in 1950. After that, the Fiddlers had a bluegrass sound. They recorded 22 sides for RCA Victor from 1952 through 1954, including "Dirty Dishes Blues" and "Windy Mountain."

The band left West Virginia in 1953, going first to WJR Detroit and then to WSLI Pikeville, Kentucky. In the early 1960s, they recorded albums for Starday and did television at WCYB Bristol, but slowly became less active. In 1966, Curly Ray Cline joined the Stanley Brothers and subsequently fiddled for Ralph Stanley until retiring in 1995. As the colorful cornerstone of Stanley's Clinch Mountain Boys, Curly Ray was a figure in the bluegrass revival and influential in the traditional side of the music. Charlie Cline remained musically active in Alabama, but the Goins Brothers band—led by two Bramwell natives—have remained more faithful to the original Lonesome Pine Fiddlers bluegrass sound.

Ivan M. Tribe
University of Rio Grande

Ivan M. Tribe, *Mountaineer Jamboree: Country Music in West Virginia*, 1984.

Joseph Harvey Long

Newspaperman Joseph Harvey Long, once considered the dean of West Virginia newspaper publishers, was born near Jonestown, Pennsylvania, May 21, 1863, the descendant of German immigrants. Long moved to Wheeling in 1881 to become a printer at the *Wheeling Sun Leader*. In 1890 he and a partner founded the *Wheeling News*. Moving to Huntington in 1893, he purchased the *Herald*, which he sold in 1895 when he acquired the *Advertiser*. Long built this small daily paper into the Huntington Publishing Company, which published the *Herald-Dispatch* as well as the *Advertiser*. He was chairman of the board when he died.

Long was active in many fields, although his passion was the newspaper publishing business. Governor Glasscock gave him the title colonel in 1911. From 1916 until 1921, he was the postmaster of Huntington. A five-term president of the Huntington Chamber of Commerce, 1936 to 1941, Long also served on the board of directors of the Ohio Valley Bus Company, First Huntington National Bank, Huntington-Ohio Bridge Company, Huntington Symphony Orchestra Association, and Morris Memorial Hospital. He was a leader in establishing the city's flood wall system and several schools. He also actively supported the Democratic Party. Long died December 28, 1958.

See also Herald-Dispatch

Carter T. Seaton
Huntington

Pare Lorentz

Leonard MacTaggart "Pare" Lorentz, "FDR's filmmaker," was born in Clarksburg, December 11, 1905. The family moved to Upshur County, where Leonard went one year to Wesleyan College in Buckhannon. He then transferred to West Virginia University, there honing his skills as a storyteller for *West Virginia Moonshine* magazine. In 1925, he left for New York. Within seven years he had been a movie critic and contributor to many top magazines, including *Scribner's, Vanity Fair, McCall's* and *Town and Country*.

In 1933, Pare Lorentz conceived, edited, and published *The Roosevelt Year, 1933*, a pictorial review of FDR's first year in the White House. In 1935, he was contracted by the U.S. Resettlement Administration to create a motion picture about the New Deal. The result was a classic, *The Plow That Broke the Plains*, a 30-minute documentary that ran in movie theaters across the country. In 1937, he shot and edited *The River*, once again creating an emotional representation of environmental problems and what the administration was doing about them.

Roosevelt appointed Lorentz head of the short-lived U.S. Film Service in 1938. Lorentz joined the Army Air Corps and made hundreds of training films for World War II pilots flying previously uncharted routes around the world. His last film, *Nuremberg,* was assembled from millions of feet of captured Nazi film and news footage to educate Germans about the rise of the Nazi Party.

Pare Lorentz lived in Armonk, New York, until his death, March 4, 1992. His ashes were interred to the sound of bagpipes at the family cemetery in Upshur County. Lorentz was awarded the Legion of Merit in 1946 and the first Lifetime Achievement Award by the West Virginia Division of Culture and History in 1990. In 1997, the International Documentary Association created the Pare Lorentz Award to honor the best documentary film of the year.

See also Filmmaking

Bill Drennen
Shepherdstown

Pare Lorentz, *FDR's Moviemaker,* 1992; Bess Lorentz Wade, *Lest We Forget,* 1968.

Loring Raid

Within a few months after the beginning of the Civil War, federal forces had occupied the strategic Kanawha Valley from Gauley Bridge at the headwaters of the Great Kanawha River to Point Pleasant where the Kanawha flowed into the Ohio. So it remained until September 1862, when events in Maryland set in motion the circumstances that led to Gen. William W. Loring's raid on Kanawha Valley. Robert E. Lee, seeking to bring the war to a decisive end, took his army into Maryland, where he eventually would meet the enemy at Antietam. As the Union army under Gen. George McClellan maneuvered to stop Lee, about 5,000 federal occupation troops in the Kanawha Valley, half of the force, were called away. That seriously weakened the Union position.

Richmond learned of the federal move and ordered General Loring to begin an attack on the Kanawha Valley from the Confederate stronghold around Pearisburg, Virginia. Loring's command consisted of nine regiments of infantry and artillery batteries. Serious fighting began on September 10 at Fayetteville, resulting in a federal retreat by Gen. Joseph Lightburn that did not end until his troops fled across the Ohio River at Ravenswood.

On September 13 an attempt was made by the Union forces to halt the rout at Charleston, but Southern artillery gained the heights on Fort Hill and smashed the federals who were lining the west bank of the Elk River after cutting the suspension bridge at what is now Washington Street. The Confederate victory, joyously received by many Charlestonians with sons fighting in the Southern army, was short lived. After about a month, the return of the Union soldiers from Maryland made the Confederate position untenable. The boys in gray left the valley never to return

as soldiers but instead as defeated men to a new state called West Virginia.

See also Civil War

Richard A. Andre
Charleston

Lost River

The Lost River and the Cacapon River are actually the same. The stream is known as the Lost River from where it originates in several springs near Brock's Gap, south of Mathias, to where it disappears about four miles southwest of Wardensville. It flows in a northeasterly direction through the rich but narrow Lost River Valley, which includes Lost River State Park, before passing through the gap at McCauley. All of the Lost River is located in Hardy County.

The river is "lost" at Sandy Ridge, between Baker and Wardensville, where, when the water level is low, the main flow sinks under some large rocks into a subterranean passage. It remains underground for a little more than two miles. If it has rained recently, the surface streambed may still have some water in it, but the major flow remains underground. In flood times, the above-ground river becomes a roaring stream and passes through the chasm it has cut at Sandy Ridge. When the river emerges, it is called the Cacapon River. The Cacapon continues to follow a northeasterly course across the eastern portion of Hampshire County and the west-central part of Morgan County to the Potomac River. The total distance of the Lost River is 33 miles from its source to where it emerges. The Cacapon and Lost River channel distance from source to mouth is 110.9 miles. The Lost River and Cacapon drain 692.25 acres.

See also Cacapon River

Mary Dunkle Voorhees
Afton, Virginia

P. Conley, *The West Virginia Encyclopedia,* 1929; N. Powell, *What to See and Do in the Lost River and South Branch Valleys,* 1997; J. L. Tilton, W. F. Prouty, R. C. Tucker, P. H. Price, and I. C. White, West Virginia Geological Survey, *Hampshire and Hardy Counties,* 1927.

Lost River State Park

West Virginia acquired the land for Lost River State Park in 1933, and the park, with its 3,712 acres in the mountains of Hardy County, opened in 1937. The park is located on tributaries of Lost River, which flows across the county to the Wardensville area. There the Lost River sinks into a mountain; when it returns to the surface on the other side it becomes the Cacapon River.

A park landmark is the Lee Cabin, built in 1804 by Henry "Lighthorse Harry" Lee, a Revolutionary War general and the father of Robert E. Lee. The wealthy Virginia family built the two-story log building as a summer retreat from the heat of their eastern Virginia home. The original foundation has stone blocks so true they look as if they were cut by machine. Antique tools and furniture fill the rooms today. Across the creek lies Lee Sulphur Spring. With its strong taste and smell of sulfur, 19th-century visitors thought the spring water cured many ailments.

Cranny Crow, a rocky escarpment atop Big Ridge Mountain, is the most prominent lookout in the park, popular with hikers and photographers. Hiking trails, both easy and strenuous, wind through the park. The Staghorn and Howards Lick trails provide easy walking on well-marked paths. Lost River State Park was built by the Civilian Conservation Corps, whose Camp Hardy was located near the present entrance to the park. Starting in 1934, CCC boys built cabins at Lost River, with porches and fieldstone fireplaces.

Cranny Crow overlook at Lost River State Park.

The park also has a restaurant, a riding stable, a swimming pool, and other attractions.

Maureen F. Crockett
St. Albans

Lost World Caverns

The cave known as Lost World Caverns is located about two miles north of Lewisburg. It is one of the largest caverns in West Virginia and a popular tourist attraction. The cave has about 6,000 feet of surveyed passages, and about 600 feet can be seen on the normal lighted tour. Tours to the unlighted wild part of the cave can be arranged.

The cave was discovered in 1942 and was called Grapevine Cave. It was originally entered by means of a 115-foot vertical shaft rigged with a rope or rope ladder. The present entrance was dug through the hill in 1968 and improved in the early 1980s to provide a more accessible walk-in entrance. The highlight of the tour is a large room about 300 feet long, 50 feet wide and 50 feet high, displaying many calcite formations. The unusual columns, stalagmites, and stalactites make this one of the most spectacular caves in West Virginia.

Bob Addis, who was manager of the cave, set a Guinness World Record for "stalagmite sitting" in 1971 by staying on top of the "war club" stalagmite for 15 days, 23 hours, and 22 minutes. Geologically, Lost World Caverns is in the Greenbrier Group limestones of the middle Mississippian Age.

William K. Jones
Charles Town

Lottery

The West Virginia Lottery originated in November 1984, when voters passed a lottery amendment to the state constitution. The first instant "scratch" tickets were sold on January 9, 1986. A televised wheel spin show was introduced, providing a jackpot to promote instant game sales. It was followed by the introduction of the on-line games, "Lotto 6/36" in November 1986 and "Daily 3" and "Daily 4" in February 1987. The televised wheel spin was discontinued in 1988. In its place, a variety of instant games were introduced, offering prize pay-outs of 60 percent or more. Within eight years instant ticket sales had increased by 336 percent.

In 1988, West Virginia became a charter member of the Multi-State Lottery Association's "Lotto America" game, the forerunner of today's "Powerball." Numerous large jackpots have been won by West Virginians, including the world-record $314.9 million jackpot won by Jack Whittaker in 2002.

Lottery profits were initially transferred to the state's general fund. In 1989,

lawmakers dedicated lottery profits to programs benefiting education, senior citizens, and tourism. Millions of dollars have since been provided for elementary, secondary, and higher education, including PROMISE scholarships. Matching funds for Medicaid as well as the costs of in-home health care and senior support services are also funded from lottery revenue. In addition, lottery funds support the state's toll-free tourist information number and the cooperative tourism advertising grants.

The scope of the lottery was broadened in 1994, when West Virginia lawmakers passed legislation allowing slot-machine style video lottery terminals at racetracks, pending voter approval in the tracks' respective counties. "Travel Keno," an on-line game, was legalized for certain locations licensed for the sale of alcohol. Jefferson County voters approved video lottery at Charles Town Racetrack for the fall of 1997. The number of video lottery terminals at West Virginia's four racetracks totaled 10,632 by June of 2004.

In 2001, the legislature outlawed the "gray machines," private video poker machines that previously had operated on the fringe of the law in bars and convenience stores. Nine-thousand video lottery terminals were authorized in their place, licensed by the lottery and limited to five per commercial location and ten per fraternal organization. By the end of 2004, video lottery sales represented more than 70 percent of the lottery's total revenue.

The seven-member West Virginia Lottery Commission was created in 1985 to assist and advise the director of the lottery. Members are appointed by the governor with the approval of the state Senate. The lottery contracts with private vendors to provide the instant and on-line central computer systems for all traditional games. The vendor also supplies field support for sales, including terminal repairs. The video lottery is operated by Lottery Commission staff.

By its 18th anniversary in 2004, the West Virginia Lottery had generated $5.7 billion in sales and nearly $2 billion in profits.

Nancy Bulla
Charleston

Louie Glass Company

The Louie Glass Company was established in Weston in 1926 to produce quality, hand-formed, mouth-blown stemware and glass articles. Founded by Austrian native Louie Wohinc and fellow immigrant glass workers, the firm was one of several related Weston-area glass companies. Louie Glass manufactured colorless and colored stemware, tumblers, vases, pitchers, and many other products

which were sold by the hundreds of thousands to glass jobbers and decorators.

Louie Wohinc died in 1950. Daughter Margaret Wohinc managed the company as president from 1950 until it was sold in 1972, during a time when women were uncommon in the glass industry and rare in top management positions. The new owners, Princess House, had long been a major buyer of Louie Glass for its home party sales plan. In 1978, Louie Glass became a subsidiary of Colgate-Palmolive. In 1986, Louie shipped $24 million worth of glass and employed 525 people. The company changed ownership several times, but kept the Louie Glass name alive until the late 1990s. At that time, the name was changed to Princess House which sold the facility to Glassworks West Virginia in 2000. Glassworks continued to create quality hand-crafted glass at Weston until July 2003 when the 77-year-old business closed, citing dwindling markets and overseas competition.

Dean Six
West Virginia Museum of American Glass

Minnie Kendall Lowther

Historian and journalist Minnie Kendall Lowther was born March 17, 1869, near Fonzo, Ritchie County, the descendant of a prominent pioneer family. A horse-riding accident in the early 1890s confined her to a wheelchair for several years, ending her early career as a teacher.

During her recovery Lowther began to write historical articles and a column of social news for the *Ritchie Standard*. In 1911, she published her book, *The History of Ritchie County*. Lowther later became the editor of several newspapers, among the first West Virginia women to hold such positions. She successively was editor of the *Pennsboro News*, the *Wetzel Republican*, the *West Union Record*, the *Glenville Democrat*, and the *Methodist Protestant Church Record*. Her most significant editorial post was as editor and part owner of the *Upshur Record* of Buckhannon, for several years prior to 1920.

About 1920, Lowther moved to Washington. Here she gave tours at Mount Vernon; was active in the Daughters of the American Revolution; and resumed her career as a historian with the book *Mount Vernon, Arlington and Woodlawn* (1922). Later books include *Marshall Hall* (1925); *Friendship Hill, Home of Albert Gallatin* (1928); *Mount Vernon, Its Children, Its Romances, Its Allied Families and Mansions* (1930); and *Blennerhassett Island in Romance and Tragedy* (1936).

Lowther worked as a newspaper columnist in Washington, and spent her last years as a newspaper writer in Parkersburg. She died in Harrisville, in her native Ritchie County, September 18, 1947.

Ray Swick
Blennerhassett Island State Park

Loyal Company

Formed in 1749 by Dr. Thomas Walker and John Lewis, the Loyal Company was established to promote settlement by colonists in the trans-Allegheny sections of Virginia. The Loyal Company, as well as the Greenbrier Company, was colonial Virginia's response to England's interference in the distribution of Virginia land. England asserted that the crown could award title to Virginia land by royal grant. On the other hand, colonists maintained that the Virginia Charter gave them control over the land of Virginia and to land extending far into the continental west.

On July 12, 1749, the Loyal Company was granted 800,000 acres by Virginia, having received support at the highest levels of Virginia government. On March 6, 1750, Thomas Walker and five others went on an expedition to search out lands for the company. They went into central Kentucky and returned by way of present southern West Virginia. By 1754, the Loyal Company had settled about 200 families on its lands, including some along the New and Bluestone rivers in present West Virginia. Indian warfare destroyed most of the settlements of the Loyal Company during the French and Indian War.

After the war, Britain attempted to control violence on the frontier by prohibiting settlement west of the Alleghenies. This move upset settlers and land speculators alike. The Loyal Company, along with the Greenbrier and Ohio companies, helped push through the 1770 Treaty of Lochaber to give them western territory to expand. Signed with the Cherokee, this treaty added approximately 9,000 square miles to the territory of Virginia. The desire to expand westward brought Virginia, as well as other colonies, into conflict with British policy and advanced the journey toward independence.

Stephen G. Smith
Old Fields

Daniel Bedinger Lucas

Daniel Bedinger Lucas, lawyer, soldier, author, and member of the West Virginia House of Delegates and a Supreme Court justice, was born in Charles Town, March 16, 1836. After receiving his early education in several private academies, he attended the University of Virginia, graduating in 1856. He studied under Judge John W. Brockenbrough at Lexington, Virginia, and was admitted to the practice of law in 1859.

Lucas moved to Richmond before the Civil War. When the war began, he served with Confederate Gen. Henry A. Wise in the Kanawha Valley campaign in 1861. In January 1865, he escaped from Virginia through the Union blockade and went to Canada where he tried to assist in the defense of Capt. John Y. Beall, a Confederate who had been accused of spying and guerrilla warfare in the North. Beall was convicted and executed on Governor's Island, New York, in February 1865. Lucas remained in Canada until after the war ended. Shortly after Lee's surrender at Appomattox, he wrote "The Land Where We Were Dreaming," a poem that was among the earliest works to romanticize the lost cause of the Confederacy.

When Lucas returned to West Virginia, he married Lena T. Brooke, with whom he had one child, a daughter. He resumed the practice of law and was elected to the House of Delegates in 1884 and 1886. As a legislator, he was noted for his attacks on the favors given to railroads and worked for their regulation. He was nominated as U.S. senator by Governor Wilson in 1887. However, Lucas, a man who has been described by historian John Alexander Williams as "one of the few politicians of his day who was genuinely incorruptible," lost to Charles J. Faulkner in a bitter legislative battle. Lucas later served as a justice of the West Virginia Supreme Court of Appeals from 1889 to 1893.

Lucas wrote several books, including *Memoir of John Yates Beall; The Wreath of Eglantine; The Maid of Northumberland; Ballads and Madrigals*; and *The Land Where We Were Dreaming and Other Poems of Daniel Bedinger Lucas*. He died July 24, 1909.

Kenneth R. Bailey
WVU Institute of Technology

Lumberjack Contests

Although crosscut saws were invented earlier, it was not until about 1870 that they replaced the ax as the preferred instrument for felling trees. Competitive chopping and sawing soon became a part of logging camp life as restless timber cutters known as woodhicks spent their Sundays matching skills. As the log camps were phased out, fairs and festivals began holding competitions. The current champions are well-trained professional athletes. Some work in the woods, but most do not.

The third-oldest lumberjack contest in North America is held annually at the Mountain State Forest Festival in Elkins. The 2004 event was the 69th. In the beginning, the show was dominated by a burly logger from Webster County named Howard Paul Criss Jr., who by the 1930s was affectionately called Paul Bunyan Criss. He was the first acknowledged world champion.

As his fame spread, the Kelly Axe Company of Charleston hired Criss to advertise its products. He gave chopping exhibitions across the country, performed in Radio City Music Hall, shaved bearded men with his five-pound ax, and split apples held between his wife's thumb and forefinger on a block of wood that was also split with the same powerful blow of the ax. He and his sawing partner, Upton Sears, also of Webster County, used a specially made crosscut saw to cut the famous Mingo Oak after it died in 1938.

Arden Cogar Sr., of Webster Springs, started the Webster County Woodchopping Competition, now the Southeastern U.S. World Championships, in 1960. Cogar became the first American, and one of only three or four ever, to win a championship in Australia, where woodcutting contests are also popular. He has since won 56 other world titles plus dozens of regional titles and hundreds of contests.

Some record times set at major competitions include Arden Cogar Jr. of Charleston, chopping through a 13-inch horizontal white pine log in 14.02 seconds in 2001 and a 13-inch vertical white pine log in 15.01 seconds in 1996. Arden Cogar Sr. cut a 12-inch yellow poplar horizontal log in 15.15 seconds in 1978, an eight-by-eight-inch horizontal yellow poplar in 7.05 seconds in 1975, and a 10-by-10 vertical white pine in 14.45 seconds in 1972. Melvin Lentz is credited with chopping a 13-inch horizontal yellow poplar in 18.85 seconds and a 12-inch yellow poplar vertical block in 15.97 seconds, both in 1995. Melvin Lentz and Paul Cogar, using a crosscut saw, in 1999 cut two times through an eight-by-eight yellow poplar log in 5.08 seconds, and Lentz, using a one-person crosscut saw, cut through a 20-inch ponderosa pine in 19.76 seconds in 1990. Lentz, using a modified chain saw, cut through a 34-inch ponderosa pine log in 4.85 seconds in 1993.

William H. Gillespie
Charleston

Luna Park

Located on Charleston's West Side, Luna Park was built by J. B. Crowley in 1912 on the north bank of the Kanawha River. The amusement park occupied seven acres on what had been a three-hole golf course. At present, the park's site is bordered by the river, Park and Glenwood avenues, Park Drive, and Grant Street.

At the main entrance on Park Avenue stood a large wooden fence with two flag-topped spires. Behind the fence, a footbridge led to level ground where park goers could ride the Royal Giant Dips Coaster, a merry-go-round, and a Ferris wheel; play games of chance and skill on the midway; and picnic under shade trees. Other park attractions were a zoo, skating rink, boxing ring, and dance pavilion. Special entertainment included free outdoor movies, hot air balloons, and trapeze artists. People walked to the park or rode streetcars. Excursion boats from Gallipolis and Point Pleasant stopped to let off passengers.

On May 5, 1923, a fire started by welders working on a new swimming pool destroyed most of the park. Although Luna's owners announced that they would rebuild, the park never reopened. The walkways were eventually paved and houses constructed on the site.

Louise Bing, "Remembering Luna Park," *Goldenseal,* Fall 1982.

Luten Concrete Bridge
See Frank Duff McEnteer.

Lutherans
Lutheranism traces directly from the Reformation work of Martin Luther and its doctrinal statements, the Augsburg Confession (1530) and the Book of Concord. Having spread across northern Europe, Lutheranism came to America in waves of immigration over two centuries. This resulted in a sometimes confusing multiplicity of church synods, as early immigrants changed and acculturated while newer ones held to the familiar traditions from their home countries.

Lutherans entered Western Virginia in the 1730s, as Pennsylvania Germans migrated down the Shenandoah Valley. Mecklenburg (now Shepherdstown) was chartered in 1762, and German craftsmen populated the town's German Street. St. Peter's Lutheran Church was established in 1765, and others followed. When the Roush family moved west to present Mason County and called the Reverend Paul Henkel, a prominent early mission developer, to visit in 1806, Lutheranism reached the Ohio River. By 1809, the Lutheran churches of Virginia, under the parent Ministerium of Pennsylvania, numbered 48. Twelve of them were within the present territory of West Virginia, from Martinsburg to Lewisburg, plus Mason County in the west.

A second cluster of "mountaintop" churches developed along northern transportation routes. St. Paul's in Aurora, Preston County (1787), and St. John's in Red House, in neighboring Garrett County, Maryland (1790), began a community of congregations serving mountain farming communities. The National Road and then the Baltimore & Ohio Railroad spread congregations to locations such as Wheeling, Grafton, Elkins, and Davis. By the end of the 19th century, industrial Wheeling held the largest concentration of Lutherans in West Virginia. Lutherans from Ohio spread up the Kanawha River, bringing the first congregation, St. Paul's, to Charleston in 1892.

Often isolated and individualistic, West Virginia Lutherans nevertheless developed a distinctive family feeling of mutual support. As controversies over doctrinal statements and the use of English subsided in the 20th century, national mergers have brought most Lutherans together. Most West Virginia Lutheran congregations are affiliated with the Evangelical Lutheran Church in America, with a few other congregations belonging to the Missouri Synod. Significant 20th-century leaders of the church in West Virginia include Dr. Donald D. Anderson, Dr. W. P. Cline, Dr. W. Roy Hashinger, Dr. Beryl B. Maurer and the Reverend George C. Weirick. By 2002, the West Virginia-Western Maryland Synod of the Evangelical Lutheran Church in America claimed 15,488 baptized members in 62 congregations.

See also Religion

R. Eugene Harper
University of Charleston

Beryl B. Maurer, "Unto the Hills," *Proceedings: Twelfth Annual Assembly West Virginia-Western Maryland Synod,* 1999; Maurer and Mary Miller Strauss, *Lutherans on the Mountaintop in West Virginia and Western Maryland,* 1992; *The West Virginia Synod: An Interpretation,* 1962.

Jessica Lynch
Private Jessica Lynch of Palestine, Wirt County, became a widely applauded celebrity following her rescue during the Iraq War. Lynch, a 19-year-old supply clerk with the Army's 507th Maintenance Company, was captured by Iraqi forces after her group was ambushed on March 23, 2003. Lynch was riding in a Humvee that crashed, severely injuring her.

On April 1, a team of Navy SEALS, Marine commandos, and Army Rangers launched a night-time raid on an Iraqi hospital and rescued Lynch. The bodies of 11 U.S. soldiers were also recovered. Lynch was taken to a hospital in Germany and later sent to Walter Reed Army Medical Center in Washington. Before she was released from the hospital, she was awarded the Bronze Star, the Purple Heart, and the Prisoner of War medal.

She returned to her hometown in July 2003 and left the army later that year. Lynch, who was born April 26, 1983, was selected as the 2003 West Virginian of the Year by Charleston's *Sunday Gazette-Mail.* Accounts of the events between Lynch's capture and rescue were incomplete and contradictory, and Lynch herself had no recollection of the period. The official version of the Lynch rescue was cast into doubt by reports that Iraqi doctors had attempted to hand over Lynch and by charges that the Pentagon staged the hospital raid for its publicity value. Lynch herself expressed no misgivings about the official portrayal of her experience. *I Am a Soldier, Too: The Jessica Lynch Story,* an authorized biography by Rick Bragg, was published in 2003.

William Alexander MacCorkle

Governor William Alexander MacCorkle was born May 7, 1857, in Rockbridge County, Virginia, on his father's plantation in a rose brick house called Sunrise. West Virginia's ninth governor, he was the last of six Democrats who held the office for a total of 26 consecutive years, the longest period of domination of the governorship by one party in our state's history.

MacCorkle, the son of a Confederate major, promoted the development of the resources of West Virginia while worrying about the consequences of industrialization. He predicted in his inaugural address on March 4, 1893, that "the state is rapidly passing under the control of large foreign and non-resident landowners." He asserted that "the men who are today purchasing the immense acres of the most valuable lands in the state are not citizens and have only purchased in order that they may carry to their distant homes in the North the usufruct of the lands of West Virginia." He cautioned that the state shortly might be in a condition of vassalage to the North and East comparable to Ireland's relationship to England.

MacCorkle was descended from the Scottish Highlands clan of Torquil or MacTorquil, which was modernized as MacCorkle. His father, also named William, had been a manager of the James River & Kanawha Canal. Both parents were of Scotch-Irish descent.

"It was by pure luck that I came to West Virginia," he wrote in his *Recollections of Fifty Years of West Virginia.* A traveler from Pocahontas County was passing the MacCorkle home in Virginia when his wagon broke down. Invited in for dinner, the West Virginian mentioned that he needed someone to teach school in the district of which he was a trustee. MacCorkle, then 19, went back to Pocahontas County with him. He spent about a year at Little Levels, which he later described as "one of the most beautiful sections of the earth." He subsequently studied law at Washington and Lee University, graduating in 1879. He returned to West Virginia to practice law in Charleston. Initially, he taught school in the mornings and practiced law later in the day.

Later a rich man, MacCorkle lived modestly during his early years as a lawyer. "During the winter I slept on a bare table in a cold room," he wrote, "with the thorough understanding with myself that I would some day surely sleep on a good bed in a warm room." For awhile MacCorkle roomed with William E. Chil-

Governor William A. MacCorkle (1857–1930).

ton, who became his long-time law partner and political associate. In 1881, he married Belle Goshorn, the daughter of an established Charleston family. There were two children, William G. and Isabelle. Elected Kanawha County prosecuting attorney in 1880, MacCorkle served until 1889.

MacCorkle was the Democratic Party nominee for governor in 1892. He defeated Republican Thomas E. Davis of Ritchie County by less than 4,000 votes. His election as governor represented the triumph of the so-called Kanawha Ring, led by MacCorkle, Chilton, and U.S. Sen. John Kenna. Unable to enact his own party's programs after the election of a Republican legislature in 1894, MacCorkle cooperated with the opposition in efforts to raise the standards of state institutions and to free those agencies from the influences of politics.

Like many other West Virginia governors, MacCorkle was concerned about highways. He foresaw the need for consolidating the county road systems under a state agency. During his administration, MacCorkle borrowed money on his personal credit to complete the copying of land titles recorded in the Virginia Land Office in Richmond. He urged that the West Virginia Board of Health control the examination of physicians wanting to practice medicine in the state; proposed that banks be required to keep on hand at least 15 percent of deposits; and recommended investigation of insurance companies desiring to do business in West Virginia.

MacCorkle was the last of the so-called Bourbon governors, Southern-leaning Democrats who clung to traditions of the agrarian past while entering into uneasy compromise with the emerging industrial order. The Republicans who followed were whole-heartedly committed to the new age. Republicans took control of the legislature midway through Mac-

Corkle's term, and his collaboration with them marked a transition from one political era to the next.

At the end of his term as governor, MacCorkle resumed the practice of law in Charleston. Many of his efforts were devoted to the industrial development of the Kanawha Valley. The period saw the building of railways, interurban rail lines, coal operations, and manufacturing enterprises. The Kanawha Land Company, formed under his leadership, attracted two glass companies. The South Charleston Crusher Company, formed by MacCorkle and others, produced about 500 tons of stone ballast a day for the Chesapeake & Ohio Railway. MacCorkle later served a term in the state senate. He was elected to that position in 1910.

He was an organizer of the Citizens National Bank, absorbed in 1929 by the Charleston National Bank, which he served as chairman. In World War I, MacCorkle was state chairman of the Liberty Loan campaigns. He was the author of *Some Southern Questions, The Personal Genesis of the Monroe Doctrine,* and *The Book of the White Sulphur,* as well as the autobiographical *Recollections of Fifty Years of West Virginia.* He lived in the South Hills section, overlooking the Kanawha River and midtown Charleston. His handsome mansion, later a museum, was named Sunrise for his ancestral Virginia home. It remains a Charleston landmark.

Gov. William A. MacCorkle died of pneumonia September 24, 1930. He was cremated. The ashes were sealed in a bronze urn and placed in a shrine on the estate.

Glade Little
St. Albans

William Alexander MacCorkle, *The Recollections of Fifty Years of West Virginia,* 1928; John G. Morgan, *West Virginia Governors,* 1980.

Madison

Madison is located on the headwaters of Coal River, where Spruce and Pond forks come together to form the Little Coal River. State Routes 85 and 17 converge at Madison, which lies at an elevation of 716 feet just east of U.S. 119 (Appalachian Corridor G).

Madison is the county seat of Boone County. Originally called Boone Court House, the town was renamed about 1865, presumably for James Madison, the fourth president of the United States. Other theories hold that it was named for lawyer James Madison Laidley or for Madison Peyton, the coal operator for whom Peytona on Big Coal River was named. Madison was incorporated in 1906.

The first courthouse at Madison, a log structure, was burned by Union troops early in the Civil War. The second courthouse, made of local brick, served until 1913, and a frame building was used by county officials for the next several years.

The present courthouse, occupied in 1921, is on the National Register of Historic Places.

Located on a principal route through the southern coalfields, Madison occupied a strategic place during the Mine Wars. Miners twice rallied at the town ballpark in August 1921 to consider whether to continue their march to neighboring Logan and Mingo counties. Thousands of armed marchers passed through the town and surrounding region on their way to and from the fighting at Blair Mountain, which is located up Spruce Fork from Madison.

The population of Madison was 2,677 in 2000. Residents work in retail business, for county government and the county schools, and in natural resources, including timber and coal and related industries.

See also Boone County

Magistrate Courts

West Virginia's magistrate courts decide small claims, misdemeanors, and other minor matters. The courts were created by the Judicial Reorganization Amendment of 1974 and replaced the justice of the peace system.

As amended, Article VIII, Sections 1 and 10 of the West Virginia Constitution direct the creation of magistrate courts, and Section 10 sets forth their basic framework. The section provides for magistrates to be elected by the voters of an entire county and to serve four-year terms. The legislature sets the qualifications for magistrates, except that Section 10 prohibits both the legislature and the court system from ever requiring that magistrates must be lawyers. The section also authorizes the legislature to provide for magistrates' jurisdiction, except that it may not include felonies, civil cases involving more than an amount set by law, or any determination of title to real estate. Each magistrate has countywide jurisdiction, and in counties with more than one magistrate business between them must be allocated according to a method prescribed by the circuit's judge or chief judge. Section 10 concludes by setting magistrate court juries at six persons and barring magistrates from receiving any pay for their services other than their legislatively-set salaries. Under the justice of the peace system, the justices were paid a fee for each case they handled; that practice is now expressly prohibited.

Magistrates must be at least 21 years of age, have a high school education or its equivalent, and be free of any felony or serious misdemeanor convictions. Magistrates must also complete basic instruction in law and procedures before and after taking office.

State law currently sets the maximum amount in controversy for magistrate court civil jurisdiction at $5,000 and provides for magistrate court resolution of most landlord-tenant matters. The legislature has specifically barred magistrates from dealing with suits in equity, eminent domain cases, certain real estate matters, and specified tort actions, regardless of the amount in controversy.

Magistrates' criminal jurisdiction extends to all misdemeanors, preliminary examinations on warrants involving felonies, arrest warrants in all criminal matters, search and seizure warrants, and some probation matters. Magistrate courts also serve as the point of entry for criminal cases which are themselves outside the magistrate's jurisdiction. An arrested person is entitled to a speedy probable cause hearing and a determination on bail. These matters are routinely handled in magistrate court.

Both civil and criminal appeals from magistrate court are made to the circuit court.

See also Courts, Judicial Branch, Justice of the Peace

Robert M. Bastress
WVU College of Law

Alex Mahood

Architect Alexander Blount "Alex" Mahood was born in Lynchburg, Virginia, March 7, 1888, and completed his professional training at the École des Beaux Arts in Paris. Mahood arrived in Bluefield in February 1912 to supervise construction of the Law and Commerce Building, the first modern office building in southern West Virginia. He established his architectural firm on the penthouse floor of the new building just as the southern West Virginia coalfields exploded in population, wealth, power, and influence.

Mahood designed and built some of the most characteristic and stately structures in the Mountain State. His neoclassical work may be found from Morgantown, where he designed the circular Performing Arts Center at West Virginia University, to Bluefield, where his West Virginian Hotel still stands at 12 stories as the tallest building in the state south of Charleston. Mahood was adaptable and prolific, designing the Mercer and Raleigh county courthouses, numerous schools, colleges, and office buildings, fraternal and social halls, as well as hundreds of spacious and elegant homes. He was a shrewd businessman as well, serving as president and chairman of the board of the Commercial Bank in Bluefield.

Mahood and his wife, the former Kathleen Sparrow, had three children, Belva, John, and Alex Jr., who continued in architectural practice in southern West Virginia after the elder Mahood's death at the age of 82 on Christmas Day, 1970. Mahood's drawings, plans, photographs, and the records of his extensive practice are located in the Eastern Regional Coal Archives in the Craft Memorial Library in Bluefield.

See also Architects and Architecture
C. Stuart McGehee
West Virginia State University
Alex Mahood Jr., "The Mahood Family History," *Mercer County History 1984,* 1985.

Mail Pouch Barns

Long a part of American culture, the Mail Pouch Chewing Tobacco signs on barns, bridges, and buildings are among the early examples of outdoor advertising. The signs first appeared in the late 19th century, when Bloch Brothers Tobacco Company of Wheeling began to use painted signs to promote their tobacco. By 1910, signs bearing the slogan, "Chew Mail Pouch Tobacco, Treat Yourself to the Best," were appearing in what became trademark yellow and white letters on a black background.

Bloch Brothers concentrated its advertising in rural areas where chewing

A Mail Pouch barn in Jackson County.

tobacco was popular. Most of the signs were in nine states: West Virginia, Pennsylvania, Ohio, Kentucky, Illinois, Indiana, New York, southern Michigan, and western Maryland. There are also some signs along the west coast in California, Oregon, and Washington.

The company employed "space men" who would find barns and buildings that could easily be seen by passersby and negotiate a lease for sign space with the farmer or owner. Contract workers were paid by the square foot to paint the signs. As many as 4,000 Mail Pouch signs may have appeared on outdoor buildings. The average life of a sign was 30 to 40 years.

By the 1960s, Bloch Brothers began cutting back on its sign-painting campaign, for several reasons. The rural population was declining as people moved to urban areas, television and radio were taking over the advertising market, new regulations governed tobacco advertising, and federal highways legislation barred outdoor advertising within 660 feet of a federally funded road. In 1969, the company stopped painting new barn signs. Within a few years, however, the company began repainting some signs. In 1974, Congress designated Mail Pouch signs as National Historic Landmarks. Harley Warrick, the last of the barn painters, painted a Mail Pouch sign on a clapboard wall inside the State Museum in Charleston in 1976.

The company, now owned by Swisher International, stopped painting signs in 1992. At that time, West Virginia had more than 200 Mail Pouch signs, mostly in the northern part of the state.

See also Bloch Brothers Tobacco Company

Tom Harvey, "Treat Yourself to the Best," *Goldenseal*, October–December 1976; Tom Screven, "An Interview: Harley E. Warrick Visits New Museum," *Goldenseal*, October–December 1976.

Malden

Malden, east of Charleston, was the commercial center of Western Virginia's richest and most industrialized region in the early 19th century. This part of the Kanawha Valley was first known as Terra Salis and then Kanawha Salines, names taken from the underground brine deposits that were developed into a salt industry from 1810 until after the Civil War. Daniel Boone and others produced salt there in the 1790s. America's first deep well was drilled for salt brine in 1808 by the Ruffner family.

Malden was created as a New England-style village called Saltborough in the 1830s, when the Ruffners subdivided and sold lots east of their saltworks at today's Port Amherst. In 1840, the landmark Kanawha Salines Presbyterian Church was constructed by a congregation that had been organized in 1819 by Dr. Henry

Ruffner. By 1850, Malden had several hotels, a bank, and many saloons. There were fine houses for the saltmakers and many small houses for the white and black workers in their saltworks. In the 1880s, the town was incorporated as Malden. The origin of the name is not known.

African-American families, well before the Civil War, organized a Baptist congregation in 1852. Gen. Lewis Ruffner helped finance construction of their African Zion Baptist Church in 1872, where Booker T. Washington was church secretary and a lifelong member. In 1865, Washington, at age nine and released from slavery, had come with his family to work in the salt industry and local coal mines. Race relations in the Kanawha saltworks were remarkable for any state south of the Mason-Dixon Line. Workers were paid based on the work produced without regard to race. They were not segregated at work or in the housing provided near the saltworks.

Today, the African Zion Baptist Church, with a model of Washington's Freedom Cabin constructed nearby, and the saltmakers' fine Kanawha Salines Presbyterian Church stand as landmarks to diversity and hard work among the many historic structures in Malden. In 1980 much of the community was listed as a historic district in the National Register of Historic Places.

See also African Zion Baptist Church, Kanawha Salines, Kanawha Salt Company, Ruffner Family, Booker T. Washington

Larry L. Rowe
Malden

Sam Mallison

Publicist Sam Thomas Mallison, born September 9, 1894, had a long career as a journalist, politician, and corporate executive. Born and educated in North Carolina, Mallison worked on several small newspapers there before becoming city editor of the *Clarksburg Telegram* in 1916. He later became the paper's political correspondent, covering the state legislature. As editor, Mallison gave young Jennings Randolph a job as sports writer, while Randolph was a student at nearby Salem College.

While in Clarksburg, Mallison became friends with Howard M. Gore and went to Washington as Gore's private secretary when Gore became assistant secretary of agriculture in 1924. After becoming governor, Gore appointed Mallison state auditor (1927–29). Mallison later served as capital correspondent for the Ogden newspapers.

In 1937, Mallison was hired as head of public relations for the Benedum-Trees Company, Michael Benedum's worldwide collection of oil, pipeline, and refining companies. He worked for the company for 28 years. While there, Mallison

wrote *The Great Wildcatter*, an uncritical but highly readable biography of Benedum, a Bridgeport native and successful oil man. A skilled raconteur, Mallison in 1961 published *Let's Set a Spell*, a collection of personal anecdotes covering a range of subjects from the governor's office to death row at the West Virginia Penitentiary.

Sam Mallison died in San Angelo, Texas, January 30, 1979.

H. John Rogers
New Martinsville

Sam T. Mallison, *The Great Wildcatter*, 1953; Mallison, *Let's Set a Spell*, 1961.

Mammals

The 63 species of native wild mammals in West Virginia represent seven of the 10 orders of mammals found in North America. Most West Virginia species have a nearly statewide distribution, and are survivors from wildlife common to the wide area of the eastern deciduous forests present when the settlers arrived. A few other species—the northern water shrew, northern flying squirrel, snowshoe hare, Appalachian cottontail, rock vole, red-backed vole, and woodland deer mouse—are boreal or northern relicts, left behind when the northern forest retreated to isolated high elevations following the Ice Age. Except for the red-backed vole and deer mouse, all boreals are uncommon and occur only in the high Allegheny mountains of eastern West Virginia. Three other uncommon species, the spotted skunk, Rafinesque's big-eared bat, and golden mouse, are part of a southern fauna and reach their northern limits in southern West Virginia. The prairie vole, our only small mammal of Midwestern origin, has spread eastward across the Ohio River into the state. Several native species present in the early days were eliminated, including the mountain lion, porcupine, bison, elk, gray wolf, and coyote.

Three non-native or exotic species have become established. These are the Norway rat and the house mouse, which probably arrived with the earliest European settlers, and the European wild boar, released by the Department of Natural Resources in 1971 as a game species for reclaimed surface mines. Boar populations now exist in Boone, Logan, Raleigh, and Wyoming counties. Rats and mice are abundant throughout the state, frequently inhabiting fields and streamside habitats distant from dwellings. The roof rat or black rat, the first exotic rodent to reach West Virginia, has been replaced by the more aggressive Norway rat and is considered extinct in our region.

West Virginia is home to three mammals protected by the federal Endangered Species Act. They are the Virginia big-eared bat, the Indiana bat, and the

This eight-point buck is a magnificent West Virginia mammal.

northern flying squirrel. Both bats live in the eastern counties, where they form large hibernation colonies in the many limestone caves of that area. The northern flying squirrel lives in the northern hardwood and spruce forests at elevations of more than 3,000 feet. Other rare mammals, listed as "species of special concern," include the northern water shrew, star-nosed mole, rock vole, meadow jumping mouse, and Appalachian cottontail.

Among the rabbits and hares, the eastern cottontail is the common species below 3,000 feet. The boreal Appalachian cottontail, a secretive, uncommon cottontail, is at home in dense heath thickets among spruce and other conifers at the high elevations of the Alleghenies. A relatively good population exists in Dolly Sods. Declining numbers of the Appalachian cottontail are attributed to habitat destruction and fragmentation and invasions of the more adaptable and competitive eastern cottontail. The spectacular snowshoe hare is restricted to the high elevations in the eastern counties.

Rodents make up a significant proportion of the state's small mammals, both in numbers of individuals and numbers of species. Our only native rat, the Allegheny woodrat, lives in caves and rock crevices of the deciduous woodlands and is relatively common throughout much of the state. The abundant white-footed mouse is found statewide and is easily recognized by the golden wash of its fur. A relative, the deer mouse, has large ears and eyes and inhabits woodlands of the eastern mountains. A related but distinctly different kind of deer mouse is the

smaller, small-eared, and short-tailed prairie deer mouse. Its habitat is fields in counties bordering the Ohio River. A very small brown mouse, the harvest mouse, is a seed-eater that nests above the ground in tall grass and is near the northern limits of its range in West Virginia.

Among the voles, another group of small rodents, the meadow vole is the herbivorous, common "field mouse" statewide. Its rare relative, the rock vole, was first discovered by scientists in Cranberry Glades during early explorations of the mountains. Populations of the rock vole are declining as the more aggressive meadow vole invades the higher elevations, and as its cool, moss-covered rock and woodland glades habitat dries from global warming. The red-backed vole, although a boreal species, has adapted to become the most common vole in the mountain forests, occupying the cool forests and extending southward along the north sides of the mountains into Fayette, Raleigh, and Mercer counties. The prairie vole, found in drier fields of counties along the Ohio River, is relatively common even though at the eastern edge of its range.

The eight species of shrews found in West Virginia, together with their relatives the moles, play a big role in keeping forest and agricultural pests under control. These small predators are poorly known, even though their total number is enormous. The shrews' high metabolic rate drives their round-the-clock search for grubs, insect larvae, worms, spiders, and other soil invertebrates. The short-

tailed shrew is ubiquitous and probably our most abundant mammal. This shrew, often mistaken for a mole, is known to prey on baby mice, voles, and smaller shrews as well. Its relative, the least shrew, a very small brownish short-tailed shrew of old field habitat, is rare. Even smaller shrews include the masked, the smoky, and the tiny pygmy shrew. The pygmy shrew, unknown in the state until reported in 1986 from Canaan Valley, was later found to be widespread. The southeastern and northern water shrews are quite rare.

The beaver, our largest rodent, was exterminated soon after first settlement but reintroduced in the 1930s. They now occur throughout most of the state wherever there are small streams near deciduous woodlands, and in some areas have become a nuisance. Mammals helped by the wetland conditions created by beaver dams include raccoons, muskrats, and mink.

Among the carnivores, two native species, the fisher and the river otter, were exterminated and subsequently reintroduced as game species. In the mid-1800s, the fisher, a large weasel often referred to as "black fox," was fairly common in the spruce forests, but populations declined rapidly, first from trapping, then by habitat destruction. Reintroduced in the 1960s with 23 individuals from New Hampshire, the species has made a modest comeback with reforestation and a decline in trapping for fur. The river otter was abundant in most streams in 1925 but exterminated by the 1930s. Transplants of river otters from southern states into the Little Kanawha and West Fork rivers in the 1980s have shown modest success.

Large predators form the most notable gap among West Virginia wildlife. Bounties were paid for gray wolves until about 1822, and the species was exterminated by 1900. Mountain lions steadily declined in numbers and were declared extinct in 1924. Logging operations accompanied by road building and settlements steadily reduced the habitat for this large solitary cat. Predation on livestock and the decrease in deer population ensured its demise. Unconfirmed reports of this native predator are common, but there is no evidence to verify the continued presence of mountain lions in West Virginia. On the other hand, the shy and seldom seen bobcat, which subsists on smaller game, is relatively common in large wooded tracts in the state.

Today's largest mammalian predator is the coyote, a recent newcomer. This native species was quickly extirpated by the early European settlers but returned in recent years. Following the demise of large predators and over-population of managed game species, the coyote moved in to fill the vacant large predator niche. The species appears to have invaded primarily from the Midwest through Ohio and Kentucky. The coyote depends for food mostly upon medium and small prey—young turkeys, cottontails, and voles. Deer carrion from highway roadkills or field dressing also is an important source of food. Coyotes sometimes hybridize with dogs producing "coy dogs." The abundance of feral dogs in the state, along with coyotes and hybrids, is a growing problem to suburbanites and farmers.

Black bear populations declined as timbering reduced habitat and poaching was uncontrolled. Management of the bear as a game species and regrowth of the forests have led to today's relative abundance of bears.

At the time of settlement of the area that was to become West Virginia, mammals were abundant and provided meat for the table and fur to use and sell. Clearing land for farming and the extensive timbering of the forests greatly reduced habitats for many species. Native deer, elk, bear, bison, mountain lion, fisher, otter, and rabbit populations were reduced dramatically, and all but bear, deer, and rabbit were extirpated. All except the elk, bison, and mountain lion have been reintroduced, and elks apparently have entered the state from neighboring Kentucky. Continuing human endeavors such as surface mining, filling, draining, and redirecting streams, development of farm lands into subdivisions occupied by growing numbers of people and their pets, and proliferation of roads, power lines, and shopping malls, have changed forever the distribution, habitats, and populations of the mammals of the state.

Mary Etta Hight
Marshall University

Man Trip

In coal mining, a *trip* refers to a train of mine cars used to haul coal, supplies, or miners into or out of a mine. A man trip is a trip primarily transporting miners. Additionally, the elevators in vertical shaft mines are also known as man trips. In the early years of mining, ponies or mules would power a man trip. Large mines would have underground stables and barns to house the animals. As mining modernized in the early 20th century, electric locomotives replaced animal power. Today most West Virginia mines use battery-powered vehicles to convey their workers.

David J. Kessler
Miners' Health Safety and Training

A. James Manchin

Politician Antonio James Manchin, born April 7, 1927, in the United Mine Workers barracks at Farmington, was the fifth child of an Italian immigrant family. In 1948 at age 21, he was elected as a Democrat to the House of Delegates.

In more than a half century as a public

official, Manchin would be chided as a flamboyant opportunist and hailed as a champion of the people. As a first-term delegate, he championed civil rights causes. That may have cost him re-election in 1950. He left office to become a schoolteacher. In the 1960s, President Kennedy named Manchin director of the state Farmer's Home Administration. Later he was special assistant to the national director of FmHA.

Manchin often showed independence. He befriended many Republicans, including Governor Moore. After Manchin lost in his first run to be secretary of state in 1972, Moore in 1973 named him head of REAP, the Rehabilitation Environmental Action Program. As a highly visible "junk czar," Manchin removed with great fanfare thousands of cars, appliances, and old tires from the countryside. His grassroots style carried him to many schools, fire halls, and VFW posts in the state.

He was elected secretary of state in 1976. In 1980, he was easily reelected. In 1984, he was looked to as a possible gubernatorial candidate. He chose to run for state treasurer instead of opposing his friend Moore, with whom he later split. Manchin led the Democrat ticket in votes, but fell into trouble once elected. With a stock market turndown in 1987, Manchin bore much of the blame when the state lost nearly $300 million in investments for which he was responsible. He was impeached and resigned in 1988.

Manchin's political career was resurrected in 1998 when he ran for his old seat from Marion County for the House of Delegates and won. He was reelected in 2000 and 2002. Manchin died November 3, 2003, in Fairmont.

Norman Julian
Dominion Post

Joe Manchin

Joseph "Joe" Manchin III, who was elected in 2004 to be the 34th governor of West Virginia, was born August 24, 1947, in Fairmont. He grew up in the Marion County town of Farmington, where he worked in his grandfather's store, Manchin Grocery, and his father's furniture store.

After graduation from Farmington High School in 1965, Joe Manchin went to West Virginia University on a football scholarship but a knee injury ended his playing days. In 1968, the furniture store burned down, and Manchin took one semester off to help his family rebuild it as Manchin's Carpet Center. He graduated in 1970 with a bachelor's degree in business administration. After that, he returned to Marion County to operate the carpet store. Later, he became the owner of Enersystems, Inc., an energy-brokering company.

Manchin met his wife, the former Gayle

Governor Joseph Manchin III (1947–).

Conelly of Beckley, at WVU. They married August 5, 1967, while still in college. They later became parents to three children: Heather, Joseph IV, and Brooke.

Joe Manchin entered politics in 1982, when he won election to the House of Delegates, where he served one term. In 1986, he was elected to the West Virginia Senate. He won reelection to the Senate in 1988 and 1992. During his Senate years, Manchin promoted reforms in welfare, health care, and Medicaid.

As both a lawmaker and a candidate for higher office, Joe Manchin consistently supported anti-abortion legislation, which put him at odds with official abortion rights positions of the Democratic Party. He also supported legislation that drew opposition from consumer advocates, such as a bill that would have required the use of manufacturers' parts in auto repairs rather than less expensive "aftermarket" parts. Despite Manchin's generally conservative credentials, he sometimes opposed attempts to reduce the size of state government. For example, he opposed a plan in 1990 to sell off state-owned liquor stores. In 1994, he threatened a filibuster to block a proposal to sell seven state-owned hospitals, including one in his Senate district. As early as the mid-1980s, there was talk that Manchin might run for governor someday. He decided that the time was right in 1996, when Gaston Caperton was finishing his second term and was constitutionally prohibited from running for a third consecutive term as governor.

Manchin faced a bitter battle for the 1996 Democratic nomination from Charlotte Pritt, who had served with him in the Senate. Manchin was the conservative candidate, backed by business groups as well as the National Rifle Association and West Virginians for Life. Pritt was the liberal candidate, backed by labor. Pritt won. Manchin declined to support her in the November election, which she lost to Republican Cecil Underwood, who picked up many of Manchin's supporters.

In 2000, Manchin stepped aside to allow fellow Democrat Bob Wise to run for governor. Manchin instead ran for secretary of state and won. In the Democratic primary, he defeated Pritt, who was a late entry in the race, as well as Sen. Mike Oliverio and former Sen. Bobby Nelson. As secretary, he emphasized customer service and attempted to reverse a trend of voter apathy.

But in 2003, even before Governor Wise decided not to seek reelection in the wake of admitting he had been unfaithful in his marriage, Manchin announced his candidacy for the Democratic nomination for governor in 2004. In the two months after Wise announced he would not run, Manchin raised almost $1.2 million in donations, which gave him a campaign war chest his opponents could not match when they later entered the race. In the May 2004 primary, he received 52 percent of the vote in defeating former Sen. Lloyd Jackson and lawyer Jim Lees.

Despite having been seen as the business candidate with many labor organizations against him in 1996, Manchin received key labor endorsements in 2004, including those of the AFL-CIO, the United Mine Workers of America, and the West Virginia Education Association. That allowed him to claim that he could pull business, labor, and government together to bring good jobs to West Virginia. Manchin also campaigned on promises to improve the efficiency of government and to avoid raising taxes. He went on to win the election that November over Republican Monty Warner.

Joe Manchin was the first Roman Catholic to be elected governor of West Virginia and the first of Italian descent. He was the scion of a large and energetic Marion County family, active in business, the professions, and politics. For many years his uncle, A. James Manchin, was among the state's best-known politicians, serving as secretary of state and state treasurer and himself once considered gubernatorial material.

See also A. James Manchin

Jim Wallace
Charleston

Mandolidis Case

The *Mandolidis* case was named for an official misspelling of the surname of James Manolidis, an Elkins Industries sawmill worker injured when his hand came into contact with a ten-inch table saw that didn't have a safety guard. Manolidis was the lead plaintiff in *James Mandolidis, et al. v. Elkins Industries, Inc.,* an appeal from Randolph County Circuit Court that the West Virginia Supreme Court of Appeals decided June 27, 1978.

Mandolidis is a landmark case because

it greatly expanded a worker's right to sue an employer, even if the worker was covered by the workers compensation program. In the decision, Justice Darrell V. McGraw Jr. said the court recognized "a distinction between negligence, including gross negligence, and willful, wanton and reckless misconduct." Such misconduct was interpreted as a deliberate intention on the part of the employer. This intention need not involve an actual desire to injure the worker, but rather an awareness of exposing the worker to a risk entailing a high probability of physical injury. In such cases, damages might be sought beyond the compensation provided by the workers compensation program. Such redress was allowed under the original 1913 workers compensation statute but had been restricted in recent decades under a 1936 court decision.

The *Mandolidis* ruling came after three new justices were seated on the five-member court as a result of the 1976 general election. All three—Darrell V. McGraw, Thomas E. Miller, and the late Sam Harshbarger—were perceived as favorable to workers. The president of the state Chamber of Commerce and other business leaders criticized the ruling and asked the legislature to pass a law to lessen its impact. Governor Rockefeller asked the 1982 legislature to consider a change in the law, but the legislature decided to appoint a study commission which made its recommendation in 1983. That year the Mandolidis bill (HB1201) was enacted, modifying the seven-year-old decision. The new law softened the impact of the court decision but provided more rights to workers than prior to *Mandolidis*.

Tom D. Miller
Huntington

I. T. Mann

Financier and industrialist Isaac Thomas Mann was born in Greenbrier County, July 23, 1863. After an apprenticeship at his father's Greenbrier Valley Bank in 1889, Mann helped organize the Bank of Bramwell, which became a financial pillar of the southern coalfields.

Mann visited financier J. P. Morgan in New York in 1901 and in a famous seven-minute interview received backing for an ambitious scheme to acquire coal-bearing lands in McDowell County from the Philadelphia-based Flat Top Land Association, a Norfolk & Western Railway affiliate. Mann became suddenly wealthy, powerful, and prominent.

As president of the Bank of Bramwell and president of the Pocahontas Fuel Company for three decades, "Ike" Mann held vast holdings in coal, timber, and especially financial institutions, with investments scattered from Chicago to Mexico City. Mann served as a delegate to the 1908 Republican national conven-

tion, and was a serious candidate for the U.S. Senate in 1912. His main residence was a magnificent mansion in Bramwell, where he also built a stone Presbyterian church, but he spent much of his later years at his home in Washington. He also maintained vacation homes in Maine and Florida.

Mann's overextended business empire virtually collapsed in 1929 at the onset of the Depression, and he died at the age of 68 on May 18, 1932, in Washington. Aggressive, competitive, and ambitious, I. T. Mann was one of the few native-born West Virginians to make a fortune in the southern West Virginia coalfields. The Wyoming County town of Itmann is named for him.

See also Bramwell

C. Stuart McGehee
West Virginia State University

Joseph T. Lambie, *From Mine to Market: The History of Coal Transportation on the Norfolk &Western Railway,* 1954; W. P. Tams, *The Smokeless Coal Fields of West Virginia: A Brief History,* 1963.

Ellie Mannette

Musician Elliot Anthony "Ellie" Mannette, a principal innovator and designer of the steel drum as a musical instrument, was born in the village of San Souci, Trinidad, November 5, 1927.

As teenagers in the 1940s, Mannette and his friend Winston "Spree" Simon originated the modern steel drum band sound. Discarded barrels were abundant in oil-rich Trinidad, and Mannette experimented with hammering bumps in the steel bottom or "pan" of an upside-down 55-gallon oil drum. Each raised section resounded with a clear note when struck, and by 1947 Mannette had perfected a drum with two octaves of a diatonic scale. Today, steel drums continue to be made mostly by hand, using many of Mannette's original techniques.

In 1951, the Trinidad All Steel Percussion Orchestra, of which Mannette was a member, appeared at Britain's Festival of the Arts and introduced orchestrated steelpan music to the world. Mannette migrated to the United States in 1967. Building and tuning pans, he promoted the art of playing the instrument and began conducting lectures and workshops. The director of West Virginia University's Creative Arts Center saw Mannette performing at a workshop in North Carolina and persuaded him to come to the Mountain State.

Mannette arrived in Morgantown in 1992 and became an artist-in-residence and coordinator of the steel drum program at WVU. He started training students in aspects of the art form with the University Tuning Project, in which a student could learn how to construct his own steel drum. In 2000, Mannette founded Mannette Steel Drums, Ltd., whose drums are distributed worldwide.

In 1999, Mannette received the highest U.S. honor in the arts, a National Heritage Fellowship from the National Endowment for the Arts. In 2000, he returned to his homeland to receive the Trinidad and Tobago Chaconia Silver Medal from the minister of culture. He also was awarded an honorary doctorate from the University of the West Indies at St. Augustine.

Mannette lives in Morgantown.

Mannington

Mannington is located on U.S. 250 west of Fairmont, at the juncture of Pyles Fork and Buffalo Creek. First called Forks of Buffalo and later Koon Town, Mannington was named for Charles F. Manning, a Baltimore & Ohio Railway civil engineer, in 1854. The arrival in 1852 of the B&O main line, building across Western Virginia from Baltimore to Wheeling, gave Mannington a long-standing economic advantage. Mannington was chartered as a town by the Virginia legislature in 1856 and by West Virginia in 1871. It was incorporated as a city in 1921.

Like the surrounding region, Mannington supported the Union during the Civil War, although a minority of local men served with the Confederacy. The presence of the strategically important B&O brought military attention early in the war, with a Union regiment establishing Camp Buffalo a few miles away in May 1861. Confederates raided nearby Fairmont during the 1863 Jones-Imboden raids, but did not visit Mannington. Many Union veterans are buried in local cemeteries.

Mannington is located in the midst of rich oil and gas and coal fields. The town participated fully in the oil and gas boom of the late 19th and early 20th centuries, serving the industry as a services and distribution center. At about the same time, Mannington developed into a regional pottery center, building what was believed to be the largest toilet ware plant in the world. The town was wired for electricity in 1898, and electric streetcar service arrived by 1905. Soon it was possible to travel by streetcar to Fairmont, Clarksburg, and many smaller communities. Transportation developments later in the century passed Mannington by, as Interstate 79 was built in the eastern part of the county.

Mannington is the site of the annual Mannington District Fair and was home to the late folk musician, Russell Fluharty, winner of the Vandalia Award. The 2000 population was 2,124.

Manufactured Housing

Modern manufactured housing originated with the advent of homemade travel trailers in the 1920s. Factory-built trailers soon appeared, and by the late 1940s manufacturers were producing trailers up to 30 feet long, complete with bathrooms. Many would be used as permanent housing, and in the post-war era house trailers soon sheltered millions of Americans. They included large numbers of West Virginians.

While the U.S. Census Bureau has no official definition of manufactured housing, the category generally includes residential dwellings not built on their permanent foundations. These include manufactured and modular homes as well as double-wide and single-wide trailers. By this definition there were 142,728 manufactured homes in West Virginia in 2000, 16.9 percent of all housing units. This was up from 128,168 in 1990. Only South Carolina and New Mexico have higher percentages of manufactured housing. The popularity of factory-built homes increased dramatically in West Virginia during the last decades of the 20th century. According to the West Virginia Manufactured Housing Association, 63 percent of all new housing located in the state in the 40 years after 1961 was manufactured or factory-built housing.

Most of the factory-built homes in West Virginia are manufactured in Pennsylvania, North Carolina, Georgia, Alabama, and northern Indiana. In 2002, Excel Homes built a factory at Ghent, Raleigh County, with plans to build more than 1,000 modular homes annually.

The distribution of factory-built housing in West Virginia is widespread but uneven, with the southern coalfields and several rural counties in the state's midsection having much higher numbers of manufactured homes as a percentage of all housing units. Of the dozen counties with 25 percent or more manufactured housing in 2000, all were south of Parkersburg and half were south of Charleston. In 2000, Ohio County had the lowest ratio, 4.6 percent, with Lincoln and Boone counties having the highest percentage, at 33 percent and 32.8 percent respectively. The counties with the lowest ratio of factory-built homes are the more urbanized counties, due in part to zoning restrictions.

Manufactured housing may be partly responsible for the fact that West Virginia, despite below-average income and relatively high levels of poverty, had the third-highest home-ownership rates in the United States in 2000. The West Virginia Housing Development Fund maintains that the popularity of factory-built homes is a contributing factor to this strong socioeconomic indicator. Because older mobile homes are available for as little as several thousand dollars, individuals with lower incomes have the opportunity to purchase these used units. The average price of new units is also much lower than the average prices of new and existing site-built houses. The majority of the factory-built homes in the state are owner-occupied, with only 23 percent being rented quarters. More than three-fourths of West Virginia's manufactured houses are sited on their own real estate.

Michael Tod Ralstin
Chesterfield, Virginia

Maple Syrup

Maple syrup is made from the sap of several species of maple, but primarily sugar maple. The production of maple syrup in West Virginia is largely limited to the northern high country where sugar maples thrive. Maple sap production occurs on warm days following freezing nights. During the late winter harvest, sugar camps and sugarhouses are the focal points of production. The West Virginia Department of Agriculture lists four commercial maple syrup producers in the state. Others make syrup on a smaller scale, and some farmers lease out their trees or sell sap to larger syrup producers. In 2002, 57 farms produced maple sap in West Virginia, and 2,857 gallons of syrup was produced.

The sugar water harvest lasts about six weeks, usually in February and March, and as the season progresses the sap becomes darker in color and stronger in flavor. When the sap is rising, it flows freely when the trunk is tapped. The favored method is to drill holes into which spiles are inserted. Spiles are spouts that conduct sap. Once buckets were hung under the spiles and collected manually, but nowadays commercial producers connect the spiles to plastic tubes that run in elaborate networks to collecting tanks. Once gathered, water is removed from the sap by reverse osmosis at the commercial operations, followed by evaporation. Reverse osmosis is a technical process, while evaporation is done the old-fashioned way, by boiling. Forty to 50 gallons of sap is required to make one gallon of syrup. If boiling continues long enough, the syrup turns to maple sugar. Once the syrup is ready, producers grade, date, bottle, and ship the product.

The basic process of making maple syrup from sugar trees has not changed in centuries. Indians once chipped gashes in maple trees and inserted reeds to catch the sap, which they boiled down over a fire. Today, hobby syrup makers drill holes, hammer spiles, hang buckets, collect sap, and evaporate water over an outdoor fire or in the kitchen.

Mark F. Sohn
Pikeville College

Maps, Atlases, and Gazetteers

Numerous maps of West Virginia and its constituent parts were produced both before and after statehood was achieved. The principal maps of Virginia that include some or all of present West Virginia are the Fry-Jefferson map that appeared in 1752 and the heavily revised versions of 1755 and 1757; Bishop James Madison's maps of 1807 and 1818; and many of the series of more than 500 maps produced for the Virginia Board of Public Works between 1815 and the Civil War. That series includes the excellent maps of Virginia counties produced by Boye and Wood during the 1820s as well as several maps by Claudius Crozet, who supervised construction of improvements in the state's transportation system, in both eastern and western Virginia, at various times from the 1820s into the 1850s.

According to the author Delf Norona, the Richardson's map of 1864, now apparently lost, seems to have been the first map of the new state of West Virginia that did not include the mother state as well. Throughout the remainder of the 19th century, general maps of West Virginia appeared primarily in popular atlases such as those produced by Cram, Mitchell, and Northrup. A comparison of the maps of West Virginia in various editions of those atlases reveals much about the rapid development of new towns, roads, and railroads during the latter decades of the 19th century. All of these maps, however, were superseded by Rand McNally's new map of West Virginia produced around 1899. Rand McNally's cartographic technology was very advanced, and the map was so detailed that earlier maps were made obsolete.

Special purpose maps featuring West Virginia began to appear during the late 19th century, and the variety of such maps has expanded considerably since then. These maps focus on some specific natural or cultural feature such as topography, natural resources, transportation, political boundaries, public utilities, and numerous others.

Two important types of special purpose maps, in terms of what they tell us about the development of many West Virginia towns, are panoramic and fire insurance maps. Panoramic or bird's-eye maps are three-dimensional. They portray urban areas as if viewed from above and show street patterns and buildings as they once existed. Panoramic maps of at least two dozen West Virginia towns were produced between 1896 and 1911. Fire insurance maps, particularly those produced by the Sanborn Company, are an unrivaled source of information about the evolution of many West Virginia municipalities between 1878 and 1990. Among other things they show the size and shape of all structures, property boundaries, street names and widths, building use, and house and block numbers.

Road and railroad maps from different periods also reflect important changes. The earliest known road map produced by a state agency appeared in 1911. Gaso-

line companies and the American Automobile Association, as well as the state, continued to publish them during the years that followed. Eventually road maps became more than an aid to motorists and began to feature information about scenic and recreational activities in an attempt to boost tourism.

Many of the rail companies that have operated in West Virginia, particularly the larger ones, periodically issued maps of their lines. The initial map of this type was published by the Baltimore & Ohio in 1867. CSX and the Norfolk Southern, the major railroads currently operating in the state, continue to issue maps.

The best topographical maps of West Virginia are produced by the U.S. Geological Survey and the West Virginia Geological and Economic Survey. The Geological and Economic Survey has also published numerous maps related to the state's natural resources.

Apparently there were no Virginia atlases before the Civil War. The first West Virginia atlas (White's) appeared in 1873. Three more, by Ice, Hixson, and Hevenor, were published during the 1930s. All of these early atlases were devoted primarily to maps of counties, shown individually or in groups, and supplemented by a substantial amount of information about each county.

Clagg and Britton's 1956 atlas differed from the earlier ones by emphasizing historical factors and statewide economic data rather than county maps and information about each county. The governor's office periodically produced economic atlases containing similar information during the 1960s and 1970s. More recent state atlases by Puetz (1988), DeLorme (1997), and Long (1998) are similar in design to those appearing before 1956.

Joseph Martin's 1836 gazetteer of Virginia seems to be the only such publication prior to the division of the state. The first multistate gazetteer to include West Virginia, along with Maryland and Delaware, appeared in 1884. Gannett's gazetteer (1904) was the first to be devoted exclusively to West Virginia place names and locations. The most comprehensive state gazetteers were published by the U.S. Geological Survey (1981), the West Virginia Geological and Economic Survey (1987), and DeLorme (1997).

Frank S. Riddel
Marshall University

Marble King

Marble King, located in Paden City, manufactures more than a million marbles each day. The company operates seven days a week, 365 days a year. Berry Pink and Sellers Peltier founded the company in 1949. Marble King was originally located in St. Marys. In January 1958, a fire destroyed the factory. Roger Howdyshell,

who managed the Marble King facility, moved the company to Paden City. Howdyshell led Marble King to the forefront when he manufactured the first American-made "cat's eye" marbles, the playground favorites featuring a swirl of colored glass in a clear marble.

In 1983, Howdyshell bought Marble King. He continued to operate the facility until his death in 1991, and the company is still owned by the Howdyshell family. Marble King marbles are found in games, decorative vases, industrial applications, and in spray paint cans. The company's marbles have been featured in movies such as *Goonies, Hook,* and *Home Alone.* Marble King continues to be the leader in marble production, shipping its marbles worldwide. Each year, Marble King sponsors the National Marbles Tournament.

See also Marbles

Beri Fox
Paden City

Marbles

West Virginia is a world center of glass marble manufacturing, with all but one North American manufacturer located within the state. Play marbles account for only a small portion of production, with most marbles sold to industry for use as aerosol can agitators, in filtering applications, and for other uses. Marble factories also make "gems," clear glass disks used in aquariums and to anchor flower arrangements.

The advent of marble-making machinery in the early 20th century helped bring the industry to West Virginia, which already had a robust glass industry. By the late 1930s, there were several marble manufacturing plants in the state, including the Akro Agate Company in Clarksburg. Akro Agate was founded in Ohio in 1910 and moved to Clarksburg in 1914. Like other glass producers, the company was attracted to West Virginia because of the abundance of glass sand and natural gas. Akro Agate was among the nation's most productive marble makers, remaining in business until 1951.

Other early marble companies include Master Marble in Anmoore and Bridgeport, which exhibited millions of marbles at the 1933 World's Fair in Chicago; Heaton Agate of Cairo; and Ravenswood Novelty Works of Ravenswood, known for its "Buddy" brand. Champion Glass of Pennsboro and Mid-Atlantic of West Virginia in Ellensboro are still in business, although each produces a limited supply of play marbles. Alley Agate, which was located at different times in Paden City, Sistersville, Pennsboro, and St. Marys, is the parent company to Marble King, which continues to produce marbles in Paden City.

Vitro Agate in Vienna and Parkersburg operated from 1932 to 1987 and was later bought out by Jabo Inc. of Ohio. Jabo-

Vitro established a second marble plant in Williamstown, and is among the four remaining machine-made glass marble operations in North America. Jabo's Marietta, Ohio, plant is the only American marble manufacturer located outside West Virginia. Dave McCullough, Ritchie County native and president of Jabo-Vitro, learned marble making from Don Michels of Champion Glass and Louis Moore of Vitro Agate. Although the main products at Jabo-Vitro are industrial marbles and gems, McCullough began in 1991 to create several color designs of play marbles for a limited run each spring and fall. Known as "Classics," these are sought by collectors.

Before Martin Christensen invented the marble-making machine in 1905, all glass marbles were handmade. A resurgence of the handcraft came about in the late 20th century, largely due to an increased interest among collectors in contemporary art-glass marbles. One of the leading artists is Jim Davis of Pennsboro, who learned to make handmade marbles at the encouragement of Louis Moore. His signature pieces include the balloon, peacock, and snakeskin patterns. The work of Davis and his sons is sold at Davis Handmade Marbles in Pennsboro. Jim's brother, Andy Davis, also mastered skills in contemporary art-glass marbles, working in antique style with solid core, dichronic, and mica-flake designs since 1995.

Eddie Sesse of Belmont, who works at Fenton Art Glass in Williamstown, is a relatively young artist in handmade marbles. By age 28, Sesse had produced many innovative designs, including the cyclone swirl, as well as traditional patterns.

Scot E. Long
Hebron, Ohio

Marco

During the 1930s, the Huntington *Herald-Dispatch* started running drawings of an unidentified human-like buffalo in its sports section. By 1954, Marshall College had named the buffalo "Marco." He was the brainchild of Jack and Vause Carlsen who were the editors of Marshall's yearbook, *The Chief Justice*, that year.

The actual Marco mascot, a student dressed up in a buffalo costume that is often seen at Marshall events, first showed up in 1965. Also that year the students, faculty, and administration voted to change Marshall's nickname from the "Big Green" to the "Thundering Herd." Marshall had used both nicknames for decades. The first mention of the "Thundering Herd" nickname came from former *Herald-Dispatch* sports editor Duke Ridgley, when he referred to the Marshall football team as the Thundering Herd after it defeated Glenville State Teachers College, 26-0, in the opening game of the 1925 season. That was the same year that

The Thundering Herd, based on a novel by Zane Grey, was showing in the movie theaters.

Marco the buffalo has embodied the Herd for generations of Marshall fans. The mascot's outfit has changed several times throughout the years. His current look was introduced in the fall of 1985, and six years later Marshall student Allen Young won the national championship of college mascots.

See also Herald-Dispatch, Marshall University

Clark Haptonstall
Rice University

Jacob Rader Marcus

Jacob Rader Marcus, the "dean of American Jewish historians," spent his childhood in West Virginia before moving on to a distinguished career as rabbi and historian. Born near Connellsville, Pennsylvania, March 3, 1896, Marcus came with his family to Wheeling as a young boy, where his father, merchant Aaron Marcus, was a founder and first president of the Orthodox congregation, Ohev Shalom. In 1915, the family relocated to Farmington, Marion County.

Marcus attained his rabbinical ordination in 1920 from the seminary for Reform Judaism, Hebrew Union College in Cincinnati. After receiving his Ph.D. from the University of Berlin in 1925, he devoted the next 70 years to advancing the field of American Jewish history from his post on the Hebrew Union College faculty. He taught the first university course in American Jewish history and published numerous books, including the four-volume *United States Jewry, 1776–1984*. In 1947, recognizing the need to preserve congregational records and documents of American Jewish communal life, he established the American Jewish Archives, one of the world's largest repositories for materials on the Jewish American experience. As author, editor, archives director, and teacher of generations of rabbis and historians, Marcus had a profound influence on American Jewish studies. He continued to perform these duties almost until his death at the age of 99, November 14, 1995.

See also Jews

Deborah R. Weiner
Jewish Museum of Maryland

Marijuana Cultivation

The production, use, possession, and sale of marijuana are illegal in West Virginia as in other parts of the country. Nonetheless, demand for the drug remains strong, and West Virginia is reputedly among the places inside the United States where marijuana is cultivated in significant quantities. Precise production figures are impossible to come by, but West Virginia has been among the top ten states as regards

marijuana plant eradication each year since 1985.

Legally, marijuana is the plant *cannabis sativa*. The active ingredient is a group of chemicals known collectively as tetrahydrocannabinols (THC). Enforcement of the state and federal laws concerning marijuana cultivation is part of a larger effort known as the War on Drugs, involving multiple and overlapping jurisdictions. Within the state, the state police, county sheriff departments, and city police are involved, as well as the Department of Natural Resources, Civil Air Patrol, and National Guard. At the federal level, the Drug Enforcement Administration is the principal agency.

The Appalachian High Intensity Drug Trafficking Area (AHIDTA), which includes sections of West Virginia, Kentucky, and Tennessee, combines the resources of state, local, and federal agencies toward the eradication of marijuana and other drugs. The primary focus of the AHIDTA is marijuana cultivation and distribution. In West Virginia, the AHIDTA includes Boone, Braxton, Cabell, Gilmer, Kanawha, Lewis, Lincoln, Logan, Mason, McDowell, Mingo, and Wayne counties.

The economic data on marijuana cultivation represents projections based on documented eradication, arrests, and related factors. Such projections suggest that marijuana is a major cash crop in West Virginia. The National Organization for the Reform of Marijuana Laws estimates the value of marijuana production in West Virginia to be $300 million, three times the value of all legal agricultural crops grown in the state. Some police authorities question the magnitude of this estimate. Others point out that the comparison is misleading, in that the value of West Virginia agricultural production lies heavily in livestock and poultry rather than crop production.

The number of marijuana plants destroyed in West Virginia ranged from 40,149 in 1998 to 73,345 in 2003, according to the DEA. The marijuana is found in hundreds of outdoor plots, averaging a few dozen plants each, with a small fraction of the total found growing indoors. Using DEA estimates of the value of a mature plant at from $500 to $700, the value of the 73,345 plants destroyed in West Virginia in 2003 may be calculated at from $37 million to $51 million.

There are two other issues closely related to illegal marijuana cultivation, industrial hemp and medical marijuana. Hemp is a variety of *cannabis* that has less that one percent THC. The fibers and other parts of the hemp plant can be used for making textiles, rope, paper, paint, clothing, plastics, cosmetics, foodstuffs, insulation, animal feed, and other products. Historically, hemp was a valuable and legal crop in the United States, including present West Virginia.

The West Virginia legislature in 2002 legalized the cultivation of hemp under tightly controlled circumstances. This legislation also established licensing procedures to allow local farmers to plant, grow, harvest, possess, process, and sell hemp commercially. No funds were provided for the program, however, and as of 2004 the state Department of Agriculture had promulgated no regulations. The department expects to take no action in the absence of guidance or a more permissive attitude by federal authorities.

While nationally there is a movement toward decriminalizing the use of marijuana for medical purposes, West Virginia has no such program.

Tom Haas
Charlotte, North Carolina

Marion County

Marion County lies in north-central West Virginia. The area was once part of the original vast Augusta County, Virginia, and was later split between Monongalia and Harrison counties. Interstate 79, U.S. 250, and U.S. 19 intersect in Marion County, at Fairmont, the county seat. The county has an area of 313.6 square miles and a 2000 population of 56,598. The Monongahela River is born in Marion County, with the convergence of the West Fork and Tygart Valley River at Fairmont.

Early settlers began to move into present Marion County after the end of the French and Indian War. Prominent among them were Capt. James Booth, Jacob Prickett, and David Morgan. The Indian threat created the need for frontier forts and several were erected. Pricketts Fort was the most important of these forts and has been reconstructed in recent years as a tourist attraction and state park.

In 1787, Boaz Fleming led a party of

Pricketts Fort is a Marion County attraction.

FAST FACTS ABOUT MARION COUNTY

Founded: 1842
Land in square miles: 313.6
Population: 56,598
Percentage minorities: 4.9%
Percentage rural: 41.8%
Median age: 39.9
Percentage 65 and older: 17.8%
Birth rate per 1,000 population: 10.5
Median household income: $28,626
High school graduate or higher: 79.5%
Bachelor's degree or higher: 16.0%
Home ownership: 74.8%
Median home value: $63,600

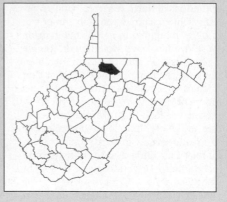

This information is from the 2000 U.S. Census. In 2000, West Virginia as a whole had 5 percent minorities, a median age of 38.9, median household income of $29,696, and a 75.2 percent home ownership rate.

relatives and friends from Milford, Delaware, across the mountains to the area of present Fairmont. The group settled there and later found that some of them resided in Monongalia County and the others in Harrison County. Fleming started a petition to have a new county created. Failing in his first attempt, he tried again in the early 1820s after he had founded Middletown (present Fairmont) to be the county seat of the proposed county. His second attempt also failed, and Boaz Fleming died without seeing his desired county established.

Finally in 1842, William S. Morgan, a delegate from Monongalia County, introduced a bill in the Virginia House of Delegates to create a new county from parts of Monongalia and Harrison counties. It was named after Revolutionary War hero Francis Marion. Middletown was chosen as the county seat of Marion County, and its name was changed to Fairmont the following year.

Marion County supplied important leaders in the West Virginia statehood movement. Francis H. Pierpont helped to establish the Reorganized Government of Virginia in Wheeling and served as its governor until the close of the Civil War and the reestablishment of a loyal Virginia government in Richmond. Pierpont practiced law in Fairmont and is buried there. Farmington native Waitman T. Willey served as senator for the Reorganized Government of Virginia and was the first U.S. senator from West Virginia. Four West Virginia governors were Marion County natives: Aretas Brooks Fleming, Ephraim F. Morgan, Matthew M. Neely, and Joseph Manchin. Robert Mollohan represented the district in the U.S. House of Representatives, and his son, Alan, continues to do the same.

The main line of the Baltimore & Ohio Railway traversed Marion County in the early 1850s. The arrival of the railroad

transformed the region, making it a place of strategic importance during the Civil War and preparing the way for the exploitation of the county's natural resources in the post-war period. Great fortunes were made in coal and oil and gas during the late 19th and early 20th centuries, and the remnants of this wealth may be seen today in the grand houses on Fairmont's Fairmont Avenue. Prominent among the new generation of business leaders were the intermarried Flemings and Watsons, who founded Consolidation Coal Company and produced a West Virginia governor and U.S. senator, the Hutchinsons, and others. James E. Watson's palatial High Gate mansion and other structures associated with Marion County's industrial elite are now on the National Register of Historic Places.

Unfortunately, industrialization exacted a high cost. West Virginia's two most notorious coal mine disasters happened a few miles apart in Marion County, at Monongah in 1907 and Farmington in 1968. Farmington claimed 78 lives and Monongah a staggering 361. Both disasters were followed by significant new federal legislation intended to improve mine safety.

Marion County boomed during the early decades of the 20th century, with the population doubling between 1900 and 1930. The county's industrial economy peaked about the time of World War II. Like many other parts of West Virginia, the county has lost population since 1950, declining from a high that year of 71,521 to 56,598 in 2000. There were signs that the population had stabilized by the turn of the new century, with only a slight loss in the 1990s. Large investments in the high technology office park outside Fairmont have brought jobs and a modern focus to the local economy.

Coach Camden Eli "Cam" Henderson (1890–1956), and football heroes Robert

L. "Sam" Huff and Frank "Gunner" Gatski were Marion Countians. Fairmont native Mary Lou Retton thrilled the nation when she became an Olympic gold medalist in gymnastics in 1984, and today a city street is named for her. Writer John Knowles, best known for the novel *A Separate Peace*, was a native Marion Countian. His 1978 novel, *A Vein of Riches*, is set in a fictionalized Fairmont.

See also Fairmont

Thomas J. Koon
Fairmont

Walter L. Balderson, *Fort Prickett Frontier and Marion County*, 1977; Thomas J. Koon and Oce Smith, *Marion County, West Virginia: A Pictorial History*, 1995; Glenn D. Lough, *Now And Long Ago: A History of the Marion County Area*, 1969.

The *Market Bulletin*

The *Market Bulletin*, a newsletter for farmers and those interested in farming, is published by the West Virginia Department of Agriculture. The *Bulletin* was begun in 1916 when James H. Stewart was agriculture commissioner. The 2001 circulation was 58,900, including the 900 out-of-state subscribers who must pay $5 a year to receive it. The publication is sent free to West Virginians who request it and is also available on line.

The newsletter covers the latest developments in farming techniques, recipes, veterinary and apiary topics; suggests solutions to problems; carries a letter from the commissioner; and runs pages of free classifieds. The most popular part of the *Bulletin*, these ads cover what farmers want to buy or sell, including equipment, cattle, farms, goats, help, hogs, horses, plants, poultry, and sheep, as well as jobs. The *Bulletin* was an important information source for back-to-the-land homesteaders of the 1960s and 1970s, and is read by farmers and would-be farmers. The *Bulletin* also lists miscellaneous sales and carries notifications of farm-related meetings, as well as information on current stock prices and a sales calendar and locator.

Since its inception, the size of the *Bulletin* has been changed more than once. It first had an oversized format similar to an old *Life* or *Look* magazine. It was cut to compact booklet dimensions in an attempt to keep mailing costs down, and then increased again to its current 8½ by 11 format. Today's *Bulletin* runs about 12 pages.

Peggy Ross
Reedsville

William Casey Marland

Thirty-four-year-old William Casey Marland was elected governor of West Virginia in 1952, at the height of a meteoric career. Only five years earlier he had been a law student at West Virginia University.

Born in Illinois, March 26, 1918, Mar-

Governor William C. Marland (1918–65).

land moved at age seven with his family to Glen Rogers, Wyoming County. His father was mine superintendent there. Marland was educated at the University of Alabama and WVU Law School, with time out for service in the navy in World War II. He received his law degree in June 1947, and the following August was named law clerk for Judge Ben Moore of the U.S. District Court for Southern West Virginia, a position traditionally offered to the top law student each year at WVU. In August 1948, Marland was made assistant attorney general by Attorney General Ira J. Partlow. This was followed by Marland's appointment in late December 1949 by Governor Patteson to the position of attorney general (vacated by Partlow), which resulted in his subsequent election to that office in 1950.

In late 1951, Kanawha County Democratic boss Homer Hanna Sr. and Governor Patteson decided that the much maligned Democratic "statehouse machine" needed a new face to offer the electorate as their next governor. They turned to their young attorney general, Marland.

Although the Democrats had placed five consecutive candidates in the governor's mansion since 1932, there were bitter divisions within the party. A long-festering schism between pro-labor FDR liberals led by M. M. Neely and pro-industry, anti-FDR conservatives led by Homer "Rocky" Holt (and later complicated by a third group of "anti-corruption" independents), made Marland's nomination in the 1952 Democratic primary difficult. This same internal division, combined with Republican charges of statehouse corruption, made Marland's general election race against Republican Rush D. Holt a real cliffhanger. Even with the help of Senator Neely and United Mine Workers President John L. Lewis, Marland posted only a narrow 26,000-vote victory. The Democratic Party's hold on the governorship would end in 1956 with the election of another 34-year-old, Republican Cecil Underwood.

Marland quickly exhibited his maverick nature when he introduced a ten cents per ton severance tax on the state's natural resources, principally coal. The legislature, dominated by the coal industry and the Chamber of Commerce, repeatedly beat back attempts by the governor to upgrade the state's highways and schools via the proposed severance tax. The measure was defeated by Marland's own party during his first three months in office, which signaled the beginning of four frustrating years for the young governor.

Governor Marland often took decisive action when faced with big decisions, such as the severance tax. His personal campaign for industrial development saw him barnstorming from coast to coast in an effort to lure industry to West Virginia. He is best remembered for his no-nonsense implementation of public school desegregation following the 1954 U.S. Supreme Court decision, *Brown v. Board of Education*. On the other hand, Marland was guilty of perpetuating the infamous statehouse spoils system by giving both his father and brother high-salaried jobs. This unpopular behavior

---

Governor William C. Marland proposes the severance tax

"For the past fifty years, we have seen our natural resources exploited, in many cases extravagantly and wastefully, by outside capital. We should welcome the orderly development of our resources, but it seems to me only just that those things should be asked to furnish a substantial part of our revenue. West Virginia has been endowed with great wealth in natural resources, and, in my opinion, some of that wealth should be invested in our two major problems of state government; namely roads and schools. We can build West Virginia by building our educational facilities as investments in our children, who, after all, are our greatest resource for the future. Building our highway system is an investment that will induce into our State industries to take the place of our depleting resources, and promote the growth of those we now have.

"I speak, of course, of turning to the natural resources of West Virginia for a severance tax to carry out this program."

—Governor Marland
January 22, 1953

combined with his abrupt manner and an increasing use of alcohol created serious political and personal problems.

U.S. Sen. Harley Kilgore died in early 1956. Barred by law from seeking a second term as governor, Marland made a strong bid for Kilgore's seat, only to lose to Republican Chapman Revercomb and the Eisenhower landslide. In 1958, the death of Senator Neely gave Marland another chance at high office. This attempt fell short when he was defeated in the August primary by Jennings Randolph.

Marland struggled financially between the two senatorial contests, and in January 1960, he left West Virginia for a sales job in Chicago. From then on, the former governor's drinking problem advanced into total alcoholism, causing him to lose the job and his health. After several periods of hospitalization, he joined Alcoholics Anonymous. In the summer of 1962, he took a job as a taxidriver to "compose his character," as he put it. Three years later with his alcoholism arrested, a chance remark to a passenger prompted his discovery by a Chicago *Daily News* reporter. His subsequent reentry into the mainstream of society drew national attention. Sadly, his new life ended eight months later on November 26, 1965, when he died of cancer at the age of 47.

In some respects a tragic figure, Bill Marland nonetheless was a politician ahead of his time. Since his death, most of his ideas have been implemented, including the coal severance tax, economic diversification, a state income tax, an expanded state park system, and improved public education and transportation systems.

Paul F. Lutz
Marshall University
Paul F. Lutz, *From Governor to Cabby*, 1995.

Marlin and Sewell

Jacob Marlin and Stephen Sewell, the first white residents of the Greenbrier Valley, had established themselves by 1749 at the mouth of Knapps Creek, the present site of Marlinton, Pocahontas County. They were discovered living there by surveyors John Lewis and his son, Andrew, in 1751. Marlin and Sewell had built a cabin together but later argued over religion and separated. By the time the Lewises found them, Sewell had moved from the cabin to a nearby hollow sycamore tree as the best way to avoid further dispute and preserve his friendship with Marlin.

The two men may have been land scouts rather than actual settlers, and soon afterward Sewell was among a group of 18 who received a large land grant north of the Greenbrier River. He and Marlin permanently parted ways some time after the Lewises came upon them at Knapps Creek. Sewell later built a cabin on the eastern side of Sewell Mountain on what is now known as Sewell Creek near present Rainelle. He was killed by Indians, apparently at the cabin site and probably in 1756 during the French and Indian War. Marlin, who returned to the East, survived the Indian wars.

Marlin and Sewell were among the very first English colonials to establish themselves on the "western waters," those streams flowing westward to the Gulf of Mexico rather than eastward to the Atlantic. Their remarkable story soon became part of regional folklore and history. They left their names on the map of the area, including most notably the town of Marlinton and Sewell Mountain, but also a dozen more streams, mountains, and other places.

See also Marlinton

Marlinton

Marlinton, the county seat of Pocahontas County, is located on the Greenbrier River at the mouth of Knapps Creek. The 2000 population was 1,204.

Marlinton is generally considered to be the location of the first white settlement in the Greenbrier Valley. Jacob Marlin and Stephen Sewell arrived about 1749, but left after a few years. By the early 1800s, two turnpikes, one coming west from Warm Springs and the other connecting Greenbrier and Randolph counties, made a junction at Marlin's Bottom (as it was first known). A covered bridge was built across the river in 1854.

The name was changed to Marlinton in 1886, but the site remained as farmland until the 1890s, with only a Presbyterian church and a hotel. Land developers promoted the movement of the county seat from Huntersville to Marlinton, and voters approved the change in December 1891. When the Chesapeake & Ohio Railway constructed its line up the Greenbrier River about 1900, the town quickly developed. On April 2, 1900, Marlinton was incorporated. By 1910, Marlinton had a tannery, two banks, two newspapers, about 20 stores, a hospital, opera house, volunteer fire department, school, water system, electric power, and a population of 1,086.

As with many rural communities, recent years have posed special challenges to Marlinton. The tannery closed in 1970, the railroad line in 1978, and improved roads make it easy for shoppers to travel to larger communities. Major floods in November 1985 and January 1996 caused great damage. But Marlinton remains the seat of government for the county, and its businesses are orienting towards the growing tourism industry. The town is expanding its public services and is beginning to use its heritage as a base for the future.

See also Marlin and Sewell, Pocahontas County

William P. McNeel
Marlinton

Marlinton Opera House

The Marlinton Opera House was built by J. C. Tilton in 1910. The structure is 50 feet by 116 feet, and its 25-foot-high walls were constructed entirely of concrete. Light railroad rails were used as reinforcement, making this among the first buildings in West Virginia to use reinforced concrete. Seating was provided on the main floor and a balcony.

The opera house was in use by 1911. In addition to providing a site for traveling shows and Chautauqua presentations, it was used for local dramatic productions, basketball games, high school graduations, church services, a skating rink, and a newspaper office.

The property was sold in 1914 due to default on deeds of trust. Although the Opera House was back in Tilton family ownership by 1916, it did not remain a performance center for long. For most of its existence the building was a car dealership and then a warehouse for a building supply store. The future of the Opera House was in doubt when the property was acquired in 1991 by the Pocahontas County Landmarks Commission to be restored, and it has been returned to use as a performance facility. The Marlinton Opera House was listed on the National Register of Historic Places in March 2000.

William P. McNeel
Marlinton

Dan Maroney

Labor leader Daniel Vincent Maroney was born on Cabin Creek, Kanawha County, June 10, 1921. With ties to the network of Irish Catholic miners concentrated in the Kanawha Valley communities of East Bank, Coalburg, North Coalburg, and Shrewsbury, Maroney served as the international president of the 150,000 member Amalgamated Transit Union from 1973 to 1981.

Maroney graduated from East Bank High School and served in the army during World War II. After the war, Maroney attended Beckley College (now Mountain State University) and Morris Harvey College (now University of Charleston) and in 1947 became a bus driver for the Charleston Transit Company and soon afterward for Atlantic Greyhound. His early work experience was interrupted when his army reserve unit was activated to serve in the Korean War. Upon returning to civilian life, he helped to unionize bus drivers at Greyhound and Charleston Transit. By the late 1950s, Maroney had become president of Greyhound Local Union 1493. He soon became chairman of the Southern and then the National Council of Local Greyhound Unions. During the 1960 presidential primary, Maroney assisted John F. Kennedy in his West Virginia campaign. As a result, he remained among the contacts frequently used by the Kennedy family, especially Sen. Ted Kennedy.

In 1965, Maroney was elected a vice president in the Amalgamated Transit Union. Eight years later, he was elected president. He also served as a vice president of the national AFL-CIO and on the board of directors of the Union Labor Life Insurance Co. He died in Charleston, April 29, 1999.

Fred A. Barkey
Marshall University Graduate College

Maronite Christians

Our Lady of Lebanon, at 2216 Eoff Street in Wheeling, is the only Maronite church in West Virginia and one of only 54 Maronite parishes in the country. It is the spiritual and cultural center for many citizens in the Northern Panhandle of Lebanese descent. The Maronites observe their own special rite, adhering to the eastern branch of the Roman Catholic Church. The patriarch of Antioch is head of the church, under the pope.

Maronites claim descent from the first Christians who received their faith directly from the Apostle Peter, founder of the church at Antioch. Followers of St. Maron, a fourth-century Syrian monk, these early Christians remained separate from both Rome and the Eastern Orthodox Church, retaining the Syriac culture as well as Aramaic, the language spoken by Jesus. This sect remained culturally isolated for so long that members believe it most closely resembles the liturgy and theology of the early Christians.

The first Lebanese immigrant to settle in Wheeling was Roger Saad, about 1888, although an immigrant named Bechalani may have lived in Wheeling for a time about 1854. The southern Lebanese Christians began emigrating at this time, and into the 20th century, because of persecution and political upheaval at the hands of ruling Muslims. During a revolution against Turkish rule in 1860, thousands were killed. Nearly half of the remaining population of Maronites perished during Turkish rule during World War I.

The number of southern Lebanese Christians in Wheeling at that time was about 300. In 1906, Father Paul K. Abraham offered the first liturgy for the new congregation. By 1922 a second, larger church was built on its present site. On December 19, 1932, a tragic fire destroyed the 1922 church building, yet it also provided the occasion for a perceived miracle. According to a report in the *Wheeling News-Register,* "While the rest of the church was engulfed in a raging inferno, the firemen recalled, the life-sized por- trait of Our Lady of Lebanon, which was then hanging above a side altar, remained untouched by flames. When firemen attempted to spray water on the portrait, the stream of water parted and did not touch the work of art."

Cheryl Ryan Harshman
West Liberty State College

Marsh Wheeling Stogies

The stogie became popular in 1827, when Wheeling tobacconist George W. Black first sold the distinctive cigars to wagon drivers on the National Road. Stogies, longer and thinner than the traditional cigar, were named for the Conestoga wagon that many of the wagoneers drove. Making them was a cottage industry in Wheeling until well after the Civil War. One of the cigar makers was Mifflin Marsh, who in 1840 at age 22 was selling stogies to steamboat crews and passengers, as well as Conestoga drivers, at the price of four for a penny.

Wheeling is a union town, and in 1869 the stogie makers were among the first trades in the city to unionize. That same year Marsh went into business with his son, William, and formed M. Marsh and Son. Mifflin Marsh was president of the company until his death in 1901. William, who succeeded his father, served as president until 1920.

Stogies traditionally were rolled by hand, and a good roller could produce 1,000 stogies a day. As cigar-making was mechanized, M. Marsh and Son rented more than 40 machines in 1931, each producing 5,000 stogies a day. Women were hired as machine operators, especially during World War II. Marsh employed 600 workers, its peak number, at this time. With a general decline in the market after the war, Marsh soon became the only large stogie manufacturer still in business. Today, the Marsh Wheeling stogie remains a good cheap smoke, with the Mountaineer, Virginian, and Deluxe labels. The dark, slender cigars sell in the five-pack for less than $2. The Wheeling plant closed in 2001, and Marsh Wheeling cigars are now made in Indiana.

Katherine M. Jourdan
Indianapolis, Indiana

Catherine Marshall

Author Catherine Marshall (Catherine Sarah Wood Marshall LeSourd) was born September 27, 1914, in Johnson City, Tennessee, to Presbyterian minister John Ambrose Wood and his missionary wife, Lenora Whitaker Wood. The family moved to West Virginia and lived in Keyser during the late 1920s and the 1930s. Catherine completed Keyser High School in 1932, and enrolled at Agnes Scott College in Decatur, Georgia.

During her junior year in college Catherine met the popular Rev. Peter Marshall; they married in 1936 in Keyser. Af- ter their son's birth in 1940, Catherine was homebound with tuberculosis for nearly three years. In 1949, she faced another crisis when her 46-year-old husband, then chaplain of the U.S. Senate, died of a heart attack. She edited 16 of his sermons and prayers for the book, *Mr. Jones, Meet The Master* (1950), and completed his biography, *A Man Called Peter* (1951).

In 1959, Marshall married editor Leonard E. LeSourd, and they collaborated as book publishers. Her best-loved novel, *Christy* (1967), based on her mother's girlhood in the southern mountains, spawned a CBS television series, youth book series, television movie, and a musical. Her inspirational autobiography, *Meeting God at Every Turn,* was published in 1980.

Catherine Marshall died in Florida, March 18, 1983. Her second novel, *Julie*, was published posthumously in 1984.

Phyllis Wilson Moore
Clarksburg

Catherine Marshall, *Light in My Darkest Night,* 1989; Marshall, *Meeting God at Every Turn,* 1980.

Marshall County

Marshall County is situated at the base of the Northern Panhandle, bordered by Ohio County to the north, Wetzel County to the south, Pennsylvania to the east, and the Ohio River to the west. The county seat is Moundsville. Marshall was created from part of Ohio County on March 12, 1835. The county was named for John Marshall, chief justice of the U.S. Supreme Court (1801–35).

The early settlers were astonished by the imposing size of the Grave Creek Mound, at 62 feet high and 240 feet in diameter the largest of the conical mounds built by the prehistoric Adena people. In 1771, Joseph Tomlinson, the original European owner of the mound, established the first settlement on the site that became Moundsville. Following the mound's excavation in 1838, its first museum opened in 1839. The state acquired the mound in 1909 and opened a museum in 1952, which was replaced by the Delf Norona Museum in 1978.

Christopher Gist was the first European to record a visit to present Marshall County, while exploring for the Ohio Company in 1751. The first white settlers were John Wetzel and his family in 1769 or 1770. They were soon followed by the Zanes and others. Settlers depended upon Fort Henry, erected at Wheeling in 1774, for protection against the Indians and their British allies.

The *Western Virginian and People's Press*, established in Elizabethtown in 1831, was the first of at least 26 newspapers. The *Moundsville Daily Echo*, established as a weekly in 1891 and expanded to daily publication in 1896, is the only newspaper currently published in Marshall County.

FAST FACTS ABOUT MARSHALL COUNTY

Founded: 1835

Land in square miles: 315.3

Population: 35,519

Percentage minorities: 1.6%

Percentage rural: 49.6%

Median age: 40.4

Percentage 65 and older: 16.3%

Birth rate per 1,000 population: 10.3

Median household income: $30,989

High school graduate or higher: 79.7%

Bachelor's degree or higher: 10.7%

Home ownership: 77.6%

Median home value: $62,600

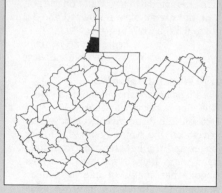

This information is from the 2000 U.S. Census. In 2000, West Virginia as a whole had 5 percent minorities, a median age of 38.9, median household income of $29,696, and a 75.2 percent home ownership rate.

The Ohio River was the chief transportation route until the completion of the Baltimore & Ohio Railroad from Baltimore to Wheeling at Rosby's Rock near Moundsville, December 24, 1852. In the 1890s, Benwood, McMechen, and Moundsville were connected by an electric railway that provided trolley cars until replaced by buses in 1941. State Route 2 became an important north-south highway with its completion in 1936. U.S. 250, State Routes 86 and 88, and numerous county routes have long provided a network of roads for Marshall County.

The State Penitentiary was established in Moundsville in 1866. Both men and women were inmates until a women's prison opened in Summers County in 1948. Eighty-five men were hanged and 19 electrocuted at Moundsville between 1899 and the abolition of capital punishment in 1965. The penitentiary was closed in 1995 and has been transformed into a tourist attraction.

Marshall County's economy was agricultural through most of the 19th century, and agriculture remains important today. Industrial activity began in Benwood with ironmaking in the 1850s. Steelmaking surpassed iron, and the Benwood works grew into large steel mills by 1900. The production of lumber, coal, coke, limestone, and clay developed into important Benwood-area industries. Moundsville's early industries included brooms, buggy whips, bricks, building supplies, and glassware. The Fostoria Glass Company opened in Moundsville in 1892 and produced high-quality tableware. The United States Stamping Company, producers of enameled cooking ware, began operations in 1901.

In the early 20th century, industrial activity expanded into paper box manufacturing, pottery, well-drilling tools, women's clothing, guns, and various building materials. Wheeling Metal and Manufac-turing Company opened in Glen Dale in 1904 to produce metal ceilings, metal roofs, gutters, and downspouts. The Leadclad Wire Company was established in 1922 by Wheeling Metal to produce rustproof fencing. The United Zinc Smelting Corporation operated from 1918 to 1945. In the late 1920s, the arrival of the Fokker Aircraft Corporation, the Triangle Conduit Company, and the Judelson Dryer Company created hundreds of new jobs. An explosion on April 28, 1924, at Benwood's Wheeling Steel coal mine killed an entire shift of 119 men. Louis Marx & Company opened the world's largest toy plant in 1934 at the former Fokker Aircraft plant in Glen Dale, employing 800 workers in the 1970s. The toy factory closed in 1980.

The chemical industry gained importance during World War II with the opening of major plants, including Allied Chemical, Pittsburgh Plate Glass, and Mobay. Industrial expansion in the 1950s and 1960s included coal mining, electric power generation, carbon, glass, tools, primary metals, and bronze casting. In the last decades of the 20th century, industry declined. Fostoria Glass closed in 1986. Coal mining remained important. Marshall County's two underground mines, employing 756, produced 10,338,000 tons in 2000. McElroy Mine led the entire state with 6,763,573 tons of coal mined, and Shoemaker Mine was tenth in total production.

The primary churches in the 19th century were Methodist, Presbyterian, and Episcopal, and many Protestant and Catholic churches are represented in the county today. Reynolds Memorial Hospital, founded by B. M. Spurr in 1899 to care for discharged convicts and the unfortunate, opened a new facility in Glen Dale in 1963. The Hare Krishna community of New Vrindaban constructed the Palace of Gold beginning in 1973, and it became an important tourist attraction.

Marshall County's incorporated communities are Benwood, Cameron, Glen Dale, McMechen, and Moundsville. Marshall County's population was 35,519 in 2000, a decrease of 4.9 percent from 1990. The county has an area of 315.3 square miles.

Notables from Marshall County include Delf Norona, archeologist, historian, and philatelist; Davis Grubb, novelist and short-story writer; Harriet B. Jones, the first female doctor in West Virginia; Arch A. Moore, twice governor of West Virginia; Edwin Holt Hughes, Methodist bishop who was instrumental in uniting the three branches of Methodism in 1939; and C. B. Allman, the biographer of Lewis Wetzel, an early county resident and Indian fighter.

See also Moundsville

Harold Malcolm Forbes
WVU Libraries

Marshall County Historical Society, *History of Marshall County, West Virginia,* 1984; Scott Powell, *History of Marshall County, From Forest to Field: A Story of Early Settlement and Development of Marshall County, W. Va., with Incidents of Early Life and Roster of Soldiers of the Several Wars,* 1925.

John Marshall

John Marshall, the chief justice of the United States (1801–35) who helped to shape the American nation, was an early explorer of West Virginia and left his name on a major educational institution.

Born at the foot of the Blue Ridge Mountains, September 24, 1755, Marshall grew up on the Virginia frontier. At the age of 20, he joined the Continental Army to fight for American independence. He later entered the practice of law in Richmond, and by 1790 had become the leading appellate lawyer in Virginia. Marshall served in the House of Delegates, the state executive council, and as a delegate to the Virginia convention that ratified the U.S. Constitution. In 1797, President John Adams induced Marshall to go to Paris as American emissary, and he returned to a hero's welcome. He was elected to Congress in 1799, and appointed secretary of state in 1800. The following year, Adams named him chief justice.

Marshall's great decisions established the basis of American constitutional law and established the authority of the Supreme Court. They include *Marbury v. Madison, McCulloch v. Maryland,* and *Gibbons v. Ogden.*

In 1812, Chief Justice Marshall led a 20-man survey party mapping the route across Western Virginia between the James River and the Ohio. The Marshall group traveled down the New River Gorge in wooden boats, and the cliffs at Hawks Nest were known for many years as Marshall's Pillars. The path he laid out became the route of the James River & Kanawha Turnpike, the C&O Railroad, and Interstate 64.

Marshall's most enduring link to West Virginia resulted from the Virginia Constitutional Convention of 1829–1830. Marshall, then 75, made an extraordinary impression. John Laidley, a delegate from Cabell County, returned home and founded a small institution that he called Marshall Academy in honor of the great chief justice. Over the years Marshall Academy became Marshall University. John Marshall died July 6, 1835. The Liberty Bell cracked tolling his death.

See also Marshall University

Jean Edward Smith
Marshall University

Jean Edward Smith, *John Marshall: Definer of a Nation*, 1996.

Paul Marshall

Architect Paul D. Marshall was born July 19, 1930, in Charleston. His work comprises 122 preservation and restoration projects on prominent public buildings and structures, including the State Capitol; Old Main at Marshall University; Woodburn Hall at West Virginia University; Graceland, former home of Sen. Henry G. Davis in Elkins; bridges in Barrackville and Philippi; and other projects.

Marshall graduated from Stonewall Jackson High School in 1948. A fourth-generation glasscutter, he worked at Libbey-Owens-Ford in Kanawha City until 1965. He learned architecture while working as a draftsman for two Charleston firms, Martens & Son and Zando, Martin and Milstead. In 1970, he became a registered architect in West Virginia. Two years later he started his own architectural firm in Charleston, which was incorporated in 1977 as Paul D. Marshall & Associates.

Marshall published studies of historic buildings and sites, including the 1980 New River Gorge National River cultural resources study. In Charleston, Marshall's projects include the Glenwood and Breezemont mansions, First Presbyterian Church, and Capitol Theater. Outside Charleston, Marshall worked on Dutch Hollow Wine Cellars in Dunbar; Blaker's Mill at Jackson's Mill; buildings at Bulltown historic area; High Gate Carriage House in Fairmont; and the James C. McGrew House in Kingwood.

Marshall retired in 1998 and moved to South Carolina. A member and officer in several national, state, and local professional organizations, he remains active in the American Institute of Architects.

Marshall Plane Crash

On November 14, 1970, a chartered DC-9 airliner owned by Southern Airways slammed into a hillside just short of Huntington's Tri-State Airport near Ceredo, killing all 75 of the passengers and crew.

The victims included nearly the entire Marshall University football team, all but one of their coaches, and several fans. The team was returning from a game against Eastern Carolina University which had been played that afternoon in Greenville, North Carolina. It was the first time the team had flown to a game the entire season.

The victims included head coach Rick Tolley, athletic director Charles Kautz, 37 players, and 38 other fans, coaches and crew members. Among the fans were Huntington City Councilman Murrill Ralsten and Michael Prestera, just elected to the House of Delegates from Cabell County in the previous week's election.

At the National Transportation Safety Board hearings, conducted in Huntington a month later, the findings listed the probable cause of the crash as "either failure of the pilots to properly read their altimeters or an altimeter error." The NTSB said it could not be specific as to what caused the crash but equipment installed at the airport a few months after the crash might have prevented the accident, according to later published reports.

The tragedy was a traumatic event, and still remains a part of the collective memory of Marshall University. A campus memorial near the Marshall Student Center, a bronze-and-copper fountain with 75 separate jets of water in memory of the 75 who died, is the scene of annual ceremonies to remember the Marshall University plane crash victims.

See also Marshall University

Tom D. Miller
Huntington

Marshall University

Marshall University traces its origins to a subscription school conducted for the children of local farmers in a small log church on the knoll where Old Main now stands. The school was founded in 1837. Trustees petitioned the General Assembly of Virginia to establish an academy, which was incorporated March 30, 1838, and named for Chief Justice John Marshall, who had recently died. After purchase of the site, the trustees erected a two-story, four-room brick building, funded through private subscriptions. State assistance came from the Virginia Literary Fund, marking the beginning of chronic underfunding from state government. Private donations supplemented teachers' salaries.

By 1850, both the financial support and quality of instruction had declined to the point that the trustees offered the institution to the Western Virginia Conference of the Methodist Episcopal Church, South. The conference accepted the offer, with local trustees in control until the Virginia Assembly amended the act of incorporation in 1858. The amended charter also granted college status to Marshall. For two years the school operated with an improved curriculum and faculty until the beginning of the Civil War, when Marshall College closed its doors.

From 1861 until 1867, the buildings were put to various uses, including a residence for John W. Hite, a trustee and a creditor of the property. In 1863, the property was sold at public auction to Hite's daughter, Salina Hite Mason. At the end of the Civil War, the new state of West Virginia turned its attention to higher education and the training of competent teachers. After legislative conflicts over the location of proposed normal schools, the West Virginia State Normal School was established at Marshall College on February 27, 1867. Mason sold the property for $3,600, and on August 1, 1867, state regents took over the college.

The first term began June 15, 1868, with 25 students enrolled in three departments: the normal, the academic, and the primary. The normal department trained teachers for public schools; the academic department prepared students for business or for further education. The primary department served students aged six to 14 and provided normal-school students the opportunity to observe teaching methods. The first class, consisting of one female and three male normal-school students, graduated in June 1870. During these first years, a new brick addition was built at the west end of the existing building. Completed in 1870, this building was incorporated into subsequent additions and, in 2002, was the oldest section of Old Main still standing.

The surroundings of Marshall College underwent a dramatic change in the 1870s with the establishment of the new city of Huntington. The years 1886–96 under Principal Thomas E. Hodges marked an expansion of the academic as well as the normal curriculum and the music department. Annual legislative appropriations averaged about $3,800, and $25,000 was earmarked for a new building. In Hodges's last year, 1895–96, enrollment finally surpassed 200, and a business college was established. Growth continued under the leadership of Principal Lawrence J. Corbly (1896–1915).

In 1907, Corbly's title was changed from principal to president, in keeping with the expanded curriculum. During Corbly's administration, intercollegiate athletics was established, and the student newspaper, the *Parthenon*, and *Mirabilia*, the student yearbook, began publication. Old Main acquired the western addition so familiar to generations of alumni, and College Hall, a dormitory for women, was established in the easternmost portion of Old Main. Course offerings were organized into 18 departments, and higher standards of schoolwork resulted in better placement of graduates. It should be

Old Main symbolizes Marshall University for many people.

noted that at this point in its history, Marshall was in effect a secondary school. In 1909, Marshall graduates were finally admitted to the freshman class of universities. By 1913, course work was added to include the equivalent of freshman and sophomore years of college. Legislative appropriations increased from $20,336 in 1897 (including $12,000 for new construction) to $158,000 in 1915, $45,000 of which went for a new science building and a gymnasium.

The years between 1915 and 1946 marked a steady growth in appropriations, expansion of the physical plant, growing enrollments, and improvement of the curriculum. Marshall was elevated to a four-year college in 1920 and awarded its first baccalaureate degrees to four men in 1921. Under President Morris Shawkey (1923–35), departments were divided between two colleges; Marshall received its first accreditation from a regional accrediting agency; more faculty possessed terminal degrees; student government became active; and Marshall athletics acquired a nickname, the Thundering Herd. In spite of Depression-era lapses in funding, a music building, student union, library, and president's home were added to the campus.

In 1935 a new era began, when James Allen of Davis & Elkins College took over as president of Marshall, accompanied by D&E's successful coach, Eli "Cam" Henderson. The centennial celebration in 1937 brought descendants of John Marshall to the campus for the unveiling of a bust of the great chief justice. Two dormitories were built, providing the first campus housing for men, and the Albert Gallatin Jenkins Laboratory School was constructed as a model school for the College of Education. President Allen retired at the beginning of World War II, after inaugurating graduate courses

leading to the master's degree, first awarded in 1940. Coach Cam Henderson remained until 1955, building legendary football and basketball teams that competed on the national level and sent players into the professional ranks.

The war years under President John D. Williams (1942–46) saw a change in the student population. The U.S. Army Air Force selected Marshall for one of its Cadet Training Detachment centers, preparing inductees for flight school. From a post–World War I low of 191 students, enrollment had risen steadily until it peaked in 1939 with 2,177 students. By 1944, however, enrollment had dropped to 720—660 women and 60 men. The end of the war brought an influx of veterans, armed with the GI Bill. Enrollment mushroomed to 2,005 students in 1946.

Marshall entered a period of stability and growth under the 22-year administration of Stewart H. Smith (1946–68). Beginning in 1948 with the appointment of a separate dean for the graduate school, campus programs and building projects flourished. Construction of a dining hall (1946), a new science building (1950), dormitories (1958, 1962, 1967), gymnasium (1961), library remodeling and addition (1967), and an academic building (1968), kept pace with an enrollment that reached 8,177 by 1968. The greatest change in Marshall's fortunes came in 1961, when the school was granted university status.

Smith's retirement ushered in a period of administrative turbulence that echoed national events. Between 1968 and 1974, two presidents (Roland Nelson, 1968–70; John Barker, 1971–74) and one acting president (Donald Dedmon, 1970–71) presided over campus unrest and athletic disaster. Following expulsion from the Mid-American Conference for recruiting irregularities, Marshall barely had begun

rebuilding the athletic program when tragedy struck November 14, 1970, with the crash at the Tri-State Airport of the plane carrying the football team, coaches, and fans, killing all 75 persons aboard.

In 1974, Marshall began an era of unprecedented growth. Under President Robert B. Hayes (1974–83), federal legislation authorized the establishment of a school of medicine in partnership with the Veterans Administration. The Joan C. Edwards School of Medicine, the only medical school in America named solely for a woman, specializes in rural health care delivery. The physical plant increased with the addition of two new classroom buildings, a basketball arena, and a major addition to the Science Building.

The administration of Dale F. Nitzschke (1984–90) brought a performing arts center, a new football stadium, and expansion of campus technology. Nitzschke also established the Society of Yeager Scholars, an accelerated academic program. Needs of students with learning disabilities were addressed in the innovative H.E.L.P. program, developed by College of Education professor Barbara Guyer.

President J. Wade Gilley (1991–99) oversaw the development of the technologically advanced John Deaver Drinko Library and dedication of the Jomie Jazz Center. A major new component was added in 1997, when the West Virginia Graduate College in South Charleston merged with Marshall. The M.D., the Ph.D. in Biomedical Science, and the Ed.D. attest to the quality of the academic program. A doctorate of psychology was added in 2002, under the presidency of Dan Angel (2000–04). Stephen Kopp became Marshall's 39th president in 2005.

Athletic fortunes also changed between 1974 and 2000. The football team recovered from its tragic loss and gradually built a program that has garnered two national NCAA I-AA championships, seven conference championships, and seven bowl appearances since 1988.

In the 1990s more than $231 million was invested in the physical plant. Advances in technology have resulted in state-of-the-art teleconferencing facilities, online courses, and academic programs in Internet certification. In 2005, enrollments exceeded 16,000, and public and private revenues totaled more than $200 million.

Marshall Community and Technical College, an autonomous partner of the university, is based on the main Huntington campus.

Cora P. Teel
Marshall University

Charles Hill Moffat, *Marshall University: An Institution Comes of Age 1837–1980,* 1981; Robert Chase Toole, "A History of Marshall College, 1837 to 1915," M.A. thesis, Marshall College, 1951.

Marshall University Graduate College

Marshall University Graduate College originated in the late 1950s as the Kanawha Valley Graduate Center of West Virginia University. Before that, the Kanawha Valley had had no institution offering advanced degrees. In 1958, the need for local graduate education was articulated by officials at Union Carbide Corporation and other Kanawha Valley chemical concerns. Representatives from these industries formed the Kanawha Valley Graduate Center Committee to establish a graduate center in the Charleston area.

Initially, WVU provided a small number of graduate courses, paid for by student tuition and company subsidies. The cost was high, and the offerings were limited to chemistry and engineering subjects. It was soon obvious that the Kanawha Valley needed a graduate institution of broader scope. Prince Woodard, the first chancellor of the West Virginia Board of Regents, began a campaign in the late 1960s to make the Graduate Center a free-standing institution of higher learning, receiving state appropriations.

During the 1967 legislative session, $350,000 was appropriated to the center and tuition was lowered to a reasonable rate. From seven or eight courses in 1958, the center could now offer 35 courses. The new courses included business as well as education and behavioral studies. Enrollment figures soared from 67 students in 1958 to 461 in 1967.

In 1972, the Board of Regents suggested that legislation be enacted to create a new, independent graduate college designed primarily to serve part-time, commuting students. The new college would have its own administrative offices but use the classroom facilities of other institutions, and attune its schedule to the needs of working students. The legislature approved the Board of Regents recommendation, and the West Virginia College of Graduate Studies emerged on July 1, 1972. Enrollment for the fall semester was 1,499. COGS, as it was known, served a large territory including all of southern West Virginia except those counties traditionally served by Marshall University. Circuit-riding professors taught evening classes in 16 counties, most often in high school classrooms.

In 1989, as part of a restructuring of the governance system of higher education, the college officially became the University of West Virginia College of Graduate Studies. In part because of an in-depth study of the state's higher education system by the Carnegie Foundation, legislation was passed creating dual systems. The college joined the university system which also included WVU, Marshall University, the West Virginia School of Osteopathic Medicine, Potomac State College, and WVU's community college at Parkersburg. The Carnegie Report praised the College of Graduate Studies for its efforts to deliver graduate education to remote areas and recommended that COGS offer courses wherever needed, regardless of location. Thereafter, the college became a statewide institution.

After the retirement of long-time president James Rowley in December 1991, Dennis P. Prisk became the fourth president of the college. On July 1, 1992, the name was changed to the West Virginia Graduate College. The administrative offices, which had been located on the campus of West Virginia State College since 1980, moved to a new $4 million building in South Charleston. A second structure was added in 1997. The handsome two-story building features advanced technology and 12 additional classrooms.

In 1997, the West Virginia Graduate College became Marshall University College of Graduate Studies. About half of the classes are taught at the South Charleston campus, with the rest taught at other locations or by Internet and distance learning technology.

Kathleen M. Jacobs
Charleston

Marshall's Pillars

The prominent cliffs capping the New River Gorge near Ansted, now known as Hawks Nest, were originally named Marshall's Pillars in honor of then Chief Justice John Marshall's surveying expedition in 1812. These cliffs are formed from the Nuttall Sandstone, dating from the Early Pennsylvanian Epoch.

The Nuttall Sandstone is a silica-cemented quartz arenite. The erosion-resistant Nuttall stone forms the lip of the New River Gorge for many miles upriver from Hawks Nest and forms the large plateau from Oak Hill northward to Summersville. The cliffs around Summersville Lake and along the Meadow River canyon are also formed from the Nuttall Sandstone, as are the rock ledges forming Kanawha Falls.

As at many promontories, there is a legend at Hawks Nest of Indian lovers plunging to their death when forbidden to marry by their hostile tribes. In 1873, the eastern and western sections of the Chesapeake & Ohio main line were joined near Hawks Nest. Today the cliffs are the namesake for Hawks Nest State Park, overlooking a small lake on New River.

See also Hawks Nest State Park
Bascombe M. Blake Jr.
Geological & Economic Survey

Marshes

Marshes are wetlands dominated by emergent herbaceous vegetation and are often found in association with other wetland types, such as forested swamps and bogs. Marshes are habitat for a large variety of plants, fish, salamanders, frogs, turtles, mammals, and birds, and are especially important for many species considered rare in West Virginia.

In West Virginia, marshes are typically found in natural depressions, around artificial impoundments, and where water flows are impeded by drainage obstructions in low-lying areas, such as an old beaver dam. Because of the rugged topography, marshes cover only about 14,000 acres of West Virginia, a relatively small proportion compared to other states.

Marshes occur throughout the state, with large marsh areas in Canaan Valley and along the Meadow River in Greenbrier County. Other marshes occur at Green Bottom Swamp in Cabell County, Short Mountain Wetlands in Hampshire County, Altona-Piedmont Marsh in Jefferson County, and Cranesville Swamp in Preston County.

Construction that impeded natural drainage and deforestation of swamps has increased marsh acreage in parts of West Virginia. However, marshes have been destroyed by many human activities, including draining, ditching, filling, and impounding. For example, marshes on marl deposits in Berkeley and Jefferson counties, which support many rare species, have been reduced from about 2,700 acres in 1750 to fewer than 300 acres at present. Conservationists have been working to protect marshes by setting them aside as nature preserves, restoring areas impacted by drainage attempts, and increasing public awareness of their importance to wildlife.

Rodney Bartgis
Nature Conservancy of West Virginia

Walter Martens

Architect Walter Frederic Martens was born on March 15, 1890, in Danville, Illinois. His early training was in the office of architect L. F. W. Stuebe of Danville, where he worked as a draftsman from 1913 to 1918 and as a junior member from 1919 to 1921. Martens moved to West Virginia in 1921 and opened his practice in Charleston.

Just two years later, Martens won the competition for a coveted commission to design the West Virginia executive mansion, official residence of the governor. Martens's Georgian revival design for the governor's mansion was approved with praise by Cass Gilbert, architect of the nearby state capitol. The mansion's completion in 1925 opened the door for many new commissions in Charleston and elsewhere in the state. In 1929, Martens completed the work for Homeland, a skillfully designed Colonial-revival residence in Lewisburg. Martens designed several distinctive Charleston homes in revival styles using stone, including the house of Mrs. Cyrus W. Hall at Ruffner and Kanawha Boulevard and Torquilstone for the son of Governor MacCorkle. Martens's mastery of revival styles was demonstrated throughout the 1920s in designs for many of West Virginia's churches and residences, and also in the Science and Liberal Arts Halls of Davis & Elkins College (1924) and in the French Chateauesque style of the Charleston Women's Club.

The 1930s practice of Walter Martens is characterized by a shift to the contemporary styles of Art Deco and Moderne. Deco-style designs by Martens include the 1935 Cavalier and Belvedere Apartments, both in Charleston. With the ambitious Kanawha Boulevard still under construction, Martens completed a larger Deco-style project at Riverview Terrace apartments in 1937. He formed a new partnership with his son, Robert, beginning in 1941. In the 1940s and later, Martens and Son designed several modern buildings including Ripley High School and the Charleston Civic Center.

Walter Martens served on the state Board of Architects, and in 1944–45 he was the West Virginia chapter president of the American Institute of Architects. In 1952, he was bestowed with the distinctive honor of fellowship in the AIA.

Martens died in Charleston, July 8, 1969.

See also Architects and Architecture, Governor's Mansion, United Carbon Building.

Carl Agsten Jr.
Charleston

Alexander Martin

Educator and clergyman Alexander Martin was the first president of West Virginia University. Born in Scotland, January 24, 1822, he moved with his parents in 1836 to Jefferson County, Ohio, adjoining the Northern Panhandle. He graduated from Allegheny College, Pennsylvania, in 1847.

Martin served as principal of Kingwood Academy in Preston County in 1846, and after college he taught at Northwestern Academy in Clarksburg. He then served as a Methodist pastor in Charleston before returning as principal of Northwestern Academy. He later served as a pastor in Moundsville, then as professor of Greek at Allegheny College. He returned to (West) Virginia as pastor of the Fourth Street Church in Wheeling. During the Civil War Martin was West Virginia president of the Christian Commission, a social services agency working to relieve the hardships of war.

Martin was a guiding influence in the passage of public schools legislation by the new West Virginia legislature in December 1863. At the request of Gordon Battelle, who chaired the education committee at the constitutional convention, Martin had drafted "An Outline of a System of General Education for the New State." In it, he argued that education should be "as free as the air . . . and the light of Heaven."

In 1867, Martin became the first president of the Agricultural College of West Virginia, which was renamed West Virginia University at his recommendation in 1868. The core of the historic downtown campus took shape during the Martin years, including University Hall (now Martin Hall) and initial construction on New Hall (now Woodburn).

Martin left WVU in 1875 in a dispute regarding direction of the university; later historians characterized him as uncompromising and tactless in support of high standards, discipline, and coeducation at the institution. He became president of Indiana Asbury University, developing it into present DePauw University and serving as DePauw president until 1889. He died at Greencastle, Indiana, December 16, 1893. Alexander Martin was one of a group of "Northern Methodists" who helped to found West Virginia and to establish the young state's institutions.

See also Education, West Virginia University

Ken Sullivan
West Virginia Humanities Council

Martin v. Hunter's Lessee

The 1816 U.S. Supreme Court decision originally called *Fairfax's Devisee v. Hunter's Lessee* had lasting implications for West Virginia. After the death of Lord Fairfax in 1781, Virginia confiscated his lands, including much of what is now the Eastern Panhandle of West Virginia. Lands thus confiscated were resold.

David Hunter's purchase of 739 acres of the former Fairfax lands was challenged by Denny Martin, Fairfax's heir, who sold his interest in the lands to Chief Justice John Marshall and his brother, James. In 1810, the Virginia Court of Appeals upheld Hunter's claim. Martin's claim, then in the hands of James Marshall, was appealed to the U.S. Supreme Court. John Marshall recused himself from the case, and in 1812 Justice Joseph Story delivered the decision of the court. The decision reversed the Virginia court and gave the 739 acres to Fairfax's heir, and thus to the Marshall brothers.

This did not end the matter. The Virginia court of appeals refused to recognize the decision, challenging the constitutionality of the Judiciary Act of 1789, which gave the Supreme Court the right to overrule state courts. With the Supreme Court's appellate authority under question, Justice Story delivered a second decision on the case, then renamed *Martin v. Hunter's Lessee*. This decision, handed down on March 20, 1816, again gave the lands to Fairfax's heir and reasserted the constitutionality of the Judiciary Act of 1789.

C. Belmont Keeney
West Virginia Humanities Council
Stuart E. Brown Jr., *Virginia Baron: The Story of Thomas 6th Lord Fairfax*, 1965; Jean Edward Smith, *John Marshall: Definer of a Nation*, 1996.

Martinsburg

Martinsburg, county seat of Berkeley County, was laid out in 1773 by Gen. Adam Stephen. The tract of land along Tuscarora Creek had been settled in the 1740s by Joseph Morgan and his brother, John Morgan, from Pennsylvania. Adam Stephen established both gristmills and flaxseed-oil mills along the banks of Tuscarora Creek. Stephen built his house of native limestone on lot 104. The house has been restored by the General Adam Stephen Association.

Berkeley County was established in 1772, and Stephen succeeded in getting Martinsburg declared the county seat over Jacob Hite's proposed Hitetown (now Leetown). Martinsburg was named for Thomas Bryan Martin, a nephew of Lord Fairfax. The county jail, once joining the courthouse, was completed in 1774, but the courthouse was not completed until 1779. Martinsburg was incorporated by the General Assembly of Virginia in 1778.

The Baltimore & Ohio Railroad came to Martinsburg in 1842, and a roundhouse and machine shops were established. Many of the early railroad workers were Irish, and soon the area east of Tuscarora Creek was called Irish Hill. During the Civil War, the B&O suffered great loss, particularly in Martinsburg, where all of the buildings belonging to the railroad were destroyed. Martinsburg was quick to recover after the war, with a new roundhouse being completed in 1866. The great railroad strike of 1877, the first nationwide industrial strike, originated among B&O workers at Martinsburg. Henry Hannis purchased the old Nadenbousch distillery in 1867 and rebuilt it into a nationally known distillery. A city waterworks was established in 1873, and natural gas was put in many of the downtown buildings by 1873.

A second railroad, the Martinsburg & Potomac, came to Martinsburg from the Williamsport, Maryland, area in 1873. By 1888, this railroad was extended to neighboring Frederick County, Virginia. By the time of the city centennial in 1878, Martinsburg was booming. Several three-story buildings had been built in the main downtown section. The B&O had restored and added to the old 1849 National Hotel, which had become the train station after the Civil War. The new Berkeley Hotel opened in 1876. In 1890, electricity came to Martinsburg.

The Middlesex Knitting Company was

established in 1890. The Martinsburg Mining, Manufacturing, and Improvement Company bought several hundred acres on the south side of Martinsburg, laid out lots, and recruited textile firms. Within a few years the Shenandoah Pants Company, the Crawford Woolen Company, the Interwoven Mill, and Southern Merchant Tailoring Company opened plants, making Martinsburg a leading textile city.

By 1940, Martinsburg had four movie houses and was the main business section of Berkeley County. After World War II, change came to the city. Shopping malls developed. Americans ceased to travel by train, and the railroad shifted from steam power to diesel. The interstate highway was built across the county. By 1990, the B&O shop had closed.

In the latter part of the 20th century, much was done to help preserve many of Martinsburg's historical buildings. Seven large historic districts were listed in the National Register of Historic Places. In December 1980, the home of Belle Boyd, the colorful Confederate spy, had become a museum and archive center. Currently, the complex of B&O roundhouse and shop buildings, now a National Historic Landmark, is being restored. The 1890 Federal building in the Richardsonian Romanesque architecture style is being turned into an art museum. The 1912 Apollo Theater has been restored.

Martinsburg lies on Interstate 81, at the heart of West Virginia's bustling Eastern Panhandle. The city population decreased from 15,621 to 14,972 from 1950 to 2000, while Berkeley County grew from 30,359 to 75,905.

Don C. Wood
Berkeley County Historical Society

Martinsburg *Journal*

The *Journal*, the daily newspaper serving Martinsburg and surrounding areas, was established in 1907 as the *Evening Journal* by 19-year-old Harry F. Byrd, future U.S. senator and governor of Virginia and that state's political boss for much of the 20th century. Byrd sold the paper to associate Max von Schlegell in 1912. Von Schlegell sold the newspaper to H. C. Ogden in 1923. The *Journal* remains part of the powerful Ogden Newspapers of Wheeling to the present.

Published as the *Evening Journal* until 1913, the title was changed to the *Martinsburg West Va. Evening Journal*. In 1920, the name was again changed, to the *Martinsburg Journal*. That title remained until 1978, when the newspaper became known as the *Evening Journal* again. In 1990, the newspaper switched from an afternoon to a morning newspaper and added a Sunday edition, becoming the *Morning Journal*. The title was changed in 1993 to the present name, the *Journal*.

In 1953, a fire damaged the Martinsburg *Journal* building, but the newspaper was able to publish a four-page issue and maintained a regular schedule. Operating from another location for several days, the *Journal* never missed a day of publication, and the building was renovated. G. Ogden Nutting, the present publisher of Ogden Newspapers, started his newspaper career in 1956 as a reporter and news editor for the *Journal*.

The *Journal* is published mornings seven days a week. The 2005 daily circulation was 21,500.

Martinsburg Roundhouse

The Baltimore & Ohio Railroad reached Martinsburg in 1842 and built a major shop complex there. Its first shops were burned by Stonewall Jackson's troops during the Civil War.

A new shop complex was built in 1866. The beautiful domed locomotive roundhouse and two rectangular shops were masterpieces of structural engineering and railroad architecture. The brick roundhouse was especially significant. It was designed by German immigrant Albert Fink, a renowned 19th-century civil engineer and railroad economist. The roundhouse is a completely circular, domed structure with its soaring roof supported by an internal cast-iron framework. This conical, skeletal framework provides more than 20,000 square feet of open floor space, allowing ample working space and light around the central 50 foot turntable and between the 16 locomotive bays. The cathedral-like iron framework is an ancestor of the modern skyscraper's steel framing system.

The great railroad strike of 1877, one of the most widespread and violent labor uprisings in American history, began at the Martinsburg B&O shops. For days, the Martinsburg railroad complex was awash in strikers and troops, but it escaped the destruction wrought upon other railroad facilities across the nation. After the great strike, the buildings remained in use as a locomotive service facility until about 1899.

In the early 20th century, the roundhouse and shops were converted to other railroad uses such as bridge fabrication, switch fabrication and repairs, car repairs, and so forth. In the late 1980s, CSX Railroad (the modern owner of the B&O lines) abandoned the complex and eventually sold the roundhouse and shops to a local non-profit corporation. The structures and surrounding property are being restored. The roundhouse, a National Historic Civil Engineering Landmark and also a National Historic Landmark, is the oldest remaining domed roundhouse in the United States and possibly the world.

Michael Caplinger
WVU Institute for the History of Technology

Louis Marx & Company

The popular Big Wheel was made at Louis Marx & Company.

Louis Marx, a leader of the 20th century toy industry, began working for toy manufacturer Ferdinand Strauss in 1912. Marx (1896–1982) established Louis Marx & Company in 1919, paying manufacturers to produce toys for him until he acquired manufacturing facilities in 1921. The early success of his toys was highlighted by the introduction of the yoyo in 1928. Marx designed and manufactured a wide variety of toys, and the company copied toys made by other manufacturers, improved them, and sold them at lower prices. Millions of durable Marx toys were sold through stores and mail-order catalogs.

In the early 1930s, Marx acquired manufacturing plants at Erie and Girard, Pennsylvania, and Glen Dale, West Virginia, near Wheeling. In Glen Dale, he purchased the recently closed, quarter-mile-long Fokker Aircraft plant for the manufacture of heavy-gauge metal vehicles and large non-mechanical toys. In 1948–49, an addition was built for the production of plastic toys. The huge Glen Dale factory manufactured more toys than any other Marx plant, helping Marx become the largest toy maker in the world in the 1940s and 1950s.

Large toys produced at Glen Dale included dollhouses, trucks, service stations, airports, the popular Big Wheel tricycle and numerous other riding toys, and toy replicas of the White House and U.S. Capitol. The factory also made play sets with plastic miniature figures, including Johnny West, Fort Apache, Roy Rogers, Flintstones, knights, vikings, cowboys, Indians, soldiers, astronauts, the presidents, and the Sindy Doll.

Four unions were active at Glen Dale, and employment exceeded 2,000 in the early 1960s, but decline began after Louis Marx sold the company to the Quaker Oats Company in April 1972. Losing money, Quaker sold to Dunbee-Combex Ltd in April 1976. Glen Dale's 800 workers were laid off in January 1980, and the renamed Dunbee-Combex-Marx soon filed for bankruptcy. The stock of toys was sold through auction to collectors and museums. The tools, trade names, and production rights for the toys manufactured at Glen Dale were sold to various companies. Toys manufactured by Marx are now sought after by collectors. The Official Marx Toy Museum opened in Moundsville in 2001.

Harold Malcolm Forbes
WVU Libraries

Maxine A. Pinsky, *Greenberg's Guide to Marx Toys, 1923–1950*, 1988–90; Michelle Smith, *Marx Toys Sampler: A History & Price Guide*, 2000.

Mason College of Music and Fine Arts

The Mason College of Music and Fine Arts in Charleston was founded in 1906 by Dr. William Sandheger "Sandy" Mason, an accomplished violinist and the founder of the Mason Quartet, as well as a city symphony and civic chorus in Charleston.

Mason (1873–1941) was born in Charleston. A talented musician, he studied in Cincinnati, New York, Munich, and Paris before returning to Cincinnati to be first violinist in the city's symphony orchestra. He conducted choirs in Houston and Columbus. In 1904, he moved back to Charleston and started the Mason School of Music and Fine Arts.

In 1936, a new charter changed the name to Mason College of Music and Fine Arts. It offered preparatory classes for children, college classes for undergraduates, training for public school teachers, and arts classes for adults. The school attracted talented teachers from Charleston and abroad, including some who were fleeing Nazi persecution. These teachers drew promising students. Pulitzer Prize-winning composer George Henry Crumb of Charleston received his undergraduate degree from Mason.

After the death of Mason in 1941, his sister-in-law, Matilda Mason, was the college's president for 14 years. Grace Martin Taylor, head of the school's art department for two decades, succeeded her as president. In 1956, Mason College of Music and Fine Arts merged with Morris Harvey College, now University of Charleston.

See also George Crumb, Grace Martin Taylor, University of Charleston

Mason County

Mason County, formed in 1804 from part of Kanawha County, is named for the statesman George Mason. The Ohio River forms the western boundary, and the Kanawha River divides the northern and southern parts of the county. Mason has long been a leading agricultural county, producing milk and livestock, corn, hay, tobacco, and orchard fruit.

The size of the county is 445.8 square miles. Low-lying land is regularly visited by floods, which were disastrous in 1913 and 1937. The interior of Mason County is hilly and forested with oak, maple, hickory, and Virginia pine. The highest point is about 1,300 feet. The population in the 2000 census was 25,957. The biggest

McClintic Wildlife Management Area in Mason County.

town is historic Point Pleasant, the county seat, which lies at the confluence of the Kanawha and Ohio rivers.

A Shawnee village existed at Old Town creek until about 1765. John Peter Salling's party descended the Kanawha River and reached the Ohio on May 6, 1742. French explorer Celoron de Blainville buried a lead plate at the mouth of the Kanawha in 1749. Christopher Gist surveyed the Ohio Valley as far as the Kanawha in 1751.

In the autumn of 1770, George Washington surveyed some 52,000 acres of Ohio River bottomland from Point Pleasant to Letart, which would later be divided among fellow officers as bounty land for service in the French and Indian War. Washington's companions, Andrew Lewis, George Muse, Peter Hogg, Andrew Stephens, Andrew Waggener, John Polson, John West, Charles Thurston, Dr. Craik, and Hugh Mercer would be among the first settlers of the county. Washington also surveyed a tract of 10,900 acres for himself on the south side of the Kanawha. In 1774, Washington sent agents to clear and build on the land, but this plantation was abandoned during the Revolutionary War, along with plans for a colony named Vandalia which was to have its capital at Point Pleasant.

On October 10, 1774, a force of 1,100 Virginians under Gen. Andrew Lewis was attacked at Point Pleasant by Shawnee Indians led by Chief Cornstalk. In the battle, Col. Charles Lewis, brother of Andrew, was killed, along with 150 other whites and an unknown number of Indians, before Cornstalk withdrew his warriors across the Ohio. The Battle of Point Pleasant was the only engagement of Lord Dunmore's War.

Shortly afterward, Fort Blair was built near the battle site, succeeded by Fort Randolph, but permanent settlement of Mason County did not begin until after the Revolution. The town of Point Pleasant was chartered by the Virginia Assembly on December 19, 1794, on land belonging to Thomas Lewis. Daniel Boone was a resident during the 1790s. Other early residents included Anne Bailey, frontier scout. German families from the Shenandoah Valley settled in the Graham Tract, in the northern part of the county, purchased by John Roush, an early sheriff. Mason County was formed in 1804. In 1820, the population of the county was 4,868.

During the Civil War, military action was limited, but included a Confederate cavalry raid at Point Pleasant on March 30, 1863. Mason County's most famous Civil War figure is Confederate Gen. John McCausland, who grew up in the Kanawha Valley and returned to a farm near Pliny after the war.

Mason County was well represented in the West Virginia statehood movement. Charles B. Waggener was one of three secretaries of the First Wheeling Convention on May 13, 1861. In the Second Wheeling Convention, Daniel Polsley of Mason County was selected lieutenant governor of the Reorganized Government of Virginia. John Hall was president of the West Virginia constitutional convention, and John M. Phelps was elected president of the senate in the first West Virginia legislature, which met in Wheeling on June 20, 1863.

The economy of Mason County was diverse and flourishing by the mid-19th century. Abundant timber supported a boat yard at Letart and a later shipbuilding industry at Mason and Point Pleasant. Sand and gravel quarries, oil and natural gas wells, and coal mines were developed. Mining began in West Columbia (where George Washington had seen a "coal hill on fire") in 1847 and

FAST FACTS ABOUT MASON COUNTY

Founded: 1804
Land in square miles: 445.8
Population: 25,957
Percentage minorities: 1.6%
Percentage rural: 71.4%
Median age: 39.7
Percentage 65 and older: 15.2%
Birth rate per 1,000 population: 11.9
Median household income: $27,134
High school graduate or higher: 72.4%
Bachelor's degree or higher: 8.8%
Home ownership: 81.0%
Median home value: $65,100

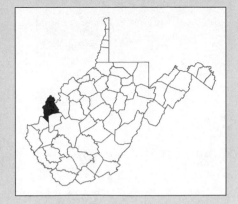

This information is from the 2000 U.S. Census. In 2000, West Virginia as a whole had 5 percent minorities, a median age of 38.9, median household income of $29,696, and a 75.2 percent home ownership rate.

neighboring Clifton in 1853. Mining continued until the 1960s. In the 1850s and late 1860s, entrepreneurs from Connecticut founded the towns of New Haven and Hartford in the Pomeroy Bend area. The city of Mason was incorporated in 1856. These three towns became centers of a booming new industry based on salt brine. At Mason, Dr. H. Stieren of St. Louis established a bromine factory in 1868 which became the largest producer of bromine in the world. A Mason County native, Michael J. Owens (1859–1923), invented a bottle-making machine and became a key figure in the American glass industry. The State Hospital for the Colored Insane and the State Industrial School for Colored Boys were established at Lakin in 1923.

Industry continued to develop through the 20th century, the products including polyester resins, plastic film, TNT, synthetic hydraulic lubricants, metal alloys, malleable iron casting, furniture, dresses, and ceramic insulators. Marietta Manufacturing Company began an operation at Point Pleasant in 1915 and produced small ocean-going craft during World War II. The electric power industry became a major employer after World War II with the construction of the Philip Sporn plant at Graham Station and the Mountaineer plant at New Haven.

River commerce has been important throughout the county's history. The Gallipolis Locks and Dam was constructed in 1933–37. One of the largest such facilities in the world when built, it has since been replaced by the Robert C. Byrd Locks and Dam.

On December 15, 1967, the Silver Bridge at Point Pleasant collapsed into the Ohio River, plunging some 50 vehicles into the water and killing 46 people. In the early 1990s, a major controversy made statewide headlines. When plans were announced to construct a pulp mill at Apple Grove, strong opposition by environmentalists contributed to the demise of the project. Sightings of "Mothman," a monstrous flying creature, were reported around Point Pleasant late in the 20th century.

Mason County contributed to West Virginia its first official state historian, Virgil A. Lewis (1848–1912). Lewis, who lived in Mason City, also served as the first state superintendent of schools. The Mansion House museum at the Point Pleasant Battlefield Monument State Park is devoted to early county history. The West Virginia State Farm Museum exhibits antique farm tools and machinery, a one-room schoolhouse, and a replica of a pioneer Lutheran church. There are two state public hunting and fishing areas in Mason County: the McClintic Wildlife Management Area and the Chief Cornstalk Wildlife Management Area.

See also Mothman, Point Pleasant, Battle of Point Pleasant, Silver Bridge Collapse

Arline R. Thorn
St. Albans

Jim Comstock, ed., *Hardesty's West Virginia Counties*, 1973; Phil Conley, *West Virginia Encyclopedia*, 1929; John Alexander Williams, *West Virginia: A Bicentennial History*, 1976.

Mason-Dixon Line

In 1761, the proprietors of the colonies of Pennsylvania and Maryland, to settle a long dispute, asked the Royal Astronomer at Greenwich to recommend surveyors to fix their common boundary. In 1763, Charles Mason and Jeremiah Dixon arrived from England at an agreed spot, south of Philadelphia, to begin their work using the latest equipment. After meticulous preliminaries, they began the east-west line separating Pennsylvania from Maryland and (West) Virginia in 1765. By 1767, Mason and Dixon had marked about 233 miles when hostile Indians halted their work in present Monongalia County. What they marked was the first scientifically accurate boundary in the colonies, ratified in 1769.

About 15 years later, astronomer David Rittenhouse of Philadelphia and surveyor Andrew Ellicott of Maryland extended Mason and Dixon's line to the southwest corner of Pennsylvania. Later, they extended this boundary due north from that corner to a stake on the north side of the Ohio River, just west of the mouth of Little Beaver Creek. In 1786, this stake provided the starting point for dividing the western United States into rectangular townships.

The work of Mason, Dixon, Rittenhouse, and Ellicott provides the northern border of West Virginia along Preston, Monongalia, and Wetzel counties, and the eastern border of the Northern Panhandle. The Mason-Dixon Line, originally marking the northern boundary of the southern states of Virginia and Maryland, soon entered the popular consciousness as the dividing line between North and South, and it remains so today.

Peter Silitch
Strange Creek

Samuel T. Wiley, *History of Monongalia County, West Virginia, from its First Settlements to the Present Time*, 1883; John Noble Wilford, *The Mapmakers*, 1981.

Mast

Mast is the fruit, nuts, and seeds of trees and shrubs that falls directly to the ground and is not scattered by the wind. Hard mast has a hard exterior, such as beechnuts, walnuts, and acorns. Soft mast has a fleshy exterior and includes black cherry, sassafras, grapes, apples, and blackberries. Mast production varies widely by species, location, and year, and especially by weather. Mast was an important factor in agricultural production in West Virginia in earlier times, when mountain farmers allowed their hogs to forage in the forest. Mountaineers also depended on the game fed by mast, and consumed mast directly as nuts, wild fruits, and berries.

Because a greater percentage of West Virginia is forested than surrounding states, our wildlife species are more dependent upon mast for food. The most important mast species for wildlife are the oaks, which may produce more than 700 pounds of acorns per acre in good seed years. Acorns comprise about 70 percent of the fox squirrel's diet, 37 percent for turkeys, 54 percent for deer, and anywhere from 10 percent to 50 percent for ruffed grouse, blue jays, black bear, raccoon, wood ducks, and nuthatches. Wildlife biologists annually rate mast abundance which they use to predict wildlife abundance and subsequent game harvests.

It is believed that the devastation of

the American chestnut by the chestnut blight severely affected wildlife populations in the state. In many areas of West Virginia chestnut was the dominant species and was a substantial component of the diet of wildlife. Current mast production is thought to be significantly less without the American chestnut as oaks typically have sporadic seed years.

Kathleen Carothers Leo
Division of Natural Resources

Material Culture

Material culture refers to the material products of a society, those things that can be touched, as well as the knowledge, traditions, expertise, and infrastructure that allow the production of those things. The material culture includes the built landscape, the houses, barns, bridges, fences, and so forth, as well as the tools and the knowledge that make possible the creation of these things and the furnishings and other equipment that allow their use and enjoyment.

West Virginia's material culture varies in different parts of the state, but in most places agriculture, centered around the family farm, dominated the cultural landscape until the late 1800s and in some cases much later. This lifestyle served as the focal point for the development and diffusion of West Virginia's material folk culture. To a greater or lesser degree the pre-industrial family farm was a largely self-sufficient economic unit, especially in the more mountainous parts of the state. Patterns of self-subsistence were less common in less rugged areas, where commercial agriculture was able to establish itself from an early date.

Typically, a mountain farm used no more than ten to 15 acres to produce crops to feed its people and animals. Additional forested acreage was used for sustenance as well but was not farmed intensively; hogs were allowed to forage there, and families hunted wild game and collected items such as nuts, greens, sassafras, goldenseal, and witch-hazel. The family might own the forestlands or share them in common with others.

In early days, clothes were produced directly from the wool harvested from sheep. The production of woolen cloth was a multi-step process. Before the wool was spun children and grandmothers would use steel brushes known as "cards" to card or comb the wool so that its fibers would be straighter and easier to spin. After the wool was carded it was spun into yarn on a spinning wheel. Women would typically get together to do spinning, making the work a social occasion similar to a quilting party, where women gathered to socialize while making quilts. Spun yarn was then woven by using a loom constructed from local timber. Within nearly every Western

Dovetail notching from an 1820s Mason County corncrib.

Virginia log home one could find a spinning wheel and loom. Both were part of the material culture, as were the fabrics they produced.

Cooperative labor was commonly used to erect cabins, barns, and fences. Extended families and close kinship networks provided the bulk of collective labor for such activities. With most hollows being settled by just a few families, all directly dependent upon the land for survival, the development of work-swapping relationships was critically important. Shared-labor events were commonly referred to as "workings" and included the heavier tasks of farming as well as building.

Log houses and barns are some of the best early representations of our material folk culture as they are more permanent than other creations. The log cabin was primarily Scotch-Irish in form and German in construction technique. Traditional log houses in West Virginia are a combination of two types: the Appalachian log house (also referred to as the Scotch-Irish log house) and the Pennsylvania German log house.

Pennsylvania German log houses were rectangular, typically having three rooms, with a chimney in the center of the house. Pennsylvania Germans used three corner-notching techniques: dovetailing, V- notching, and saddle notching. The horizontally cut dovetail joint was preferred as it was more effective at carrying rainwater away from the notch. The Scotch-Irish log house, in contrast, was square and had only one large room. The chimney was at the end of the house rather than the center.

In all, the Scotch-Irish house was faster and simpler to build. As Germans moved

south and east into Western Virginia from Pennsylvania, they retained the aforementioned corner-notching techniques while adopting the simpler square house design used by the Scotch-Irish. The limited availability of flat land influenced the size of dwellings. It was more practical to construct smaller log houses, often located along hillsides.

Thus, most log houses built in Western Virginia represented the Scotch-Irish square form and the German corner-notching techniques. The synthesis of these two log house types represents a unique form of material culture that extends throughout the southern Appalachians. A similar integration of German and Scotch-Irish building techniques and construction types may be seen in many West Virginia barns.

Once the log house and barn were built, it was necessary to fence in or fence out livestock. The wooden split-rail fence was most common, with chestnut being the preferred wood due to its durability. Three types were commonly used: the post and rail, the snake, and the buck. A paling fence, tight enough to exclude poultry and small wildlife, often enclosed the house, yard, and kitchen garden.

Tools were necessary for any sort of building. The ax, of which there were three common types, the felling ax, the broad ax, and the foot adz, was probably the most important and versatile tool on the family farm. Axes were used for chopping, shaping, and splitting the wood necessary for every type of construction and for firewood. More precise splitting was often done with a froe and mallet. These were used to split fence palings and clapboards as well as the roof shingles for log houses and barns. Another important tool was the drawknife, which was useful in making furniture as well as handles for axes, plows, and rakes.

Material folk culture was dominant within West Virginia until the industrialization of the state precipitated a change from subsistence farming to industrial capitalism. As railroad, timber, and coal companies transformed West Virginia, people gradually made the transition from farming to the selling of their labor for a wage in coal mines and factories. As West Virginians became proletarianized, losing access to their productive natural resources, the demise of many aspects of the folk culture followed. For many West Virginians this transition to modernity has been incomplete, as many aspects of folk culture are practiced throughout the hills and hollows of the Mountain State.

See also Architects and Architecture, Barns, Fences, Outbuildings

J. Todd Nesbitt
Lock Haven University of Pennsylvania
Ronald D. Eller, *Miners, Millhands, and Mountaineers: Industrialization of the Appalachian South, 1880–1930,* 1982; Henry H. Glassie,

Pattern in the Material Folk Culture of the Eastern United States, 1969; Warren E. Roberts, "Folk Craft," in Richard M. Dorson, ed., Folklore and Folklife, 1972.

Matewan

In 1983 novelist, screen writer, and independent film director John Sayles and his producer, Maggie Renzie, came to West Virginia to produce a film about the Matewan Massacre. The "Massacre" was a real event that took place in 1920 in Matewan, on the Tug Fork in Mingo County, during the West Virginia Mine Wars. There was a shoot-out between police chief Sid Hatfield and his allies on the union side and Baldwin-Felts Detective Agency guards hired by the coal mine owners.

Sayles first wrote about the incident in his novel, Union Dues (1977). For four years he reworked his screenplay, directed another film, Brother From Another Planet, and finally came to Thurmond, Fayette County, to shoot the film about Matewan. He hired cinematographer Haskell Wexler to shoot his depiction of the class war between the local workers and coal mine owners. The plot remains largely faithful to historic fact, told through the fictional characters of labor organizer Joe Kenehan (Chris Cooper) and the boy preacher Danny Radnor (Will Oldham). The black miner "Few Clothes" Johnson (James Earl Jones) is based on a historic figure of the same name active in an earlier phase of the West Virginia Mine Wars.

Matewan was nominated for an Oscar for best cinematography. The film has been shown all over the world, and has won many awards. The story line loosely resembles that of the great 19th-century novel by Emile Zola, Germinal. Sayles wrote a book about making the movie, Thinking in Pictures: The Making of the Movie Matewan, published in 1987.

Stephen Lee Fesenmaier
West Virginia Library Commission

Matewan Massacre

In January 1920, the United Mine Workers of America launched a major campaign to organize the non-union coalfields of southern West Virginia. Along the West Virginia-Kentucky line, some 3,000 miners responded by joining the union and, under coal company policies forbidding employment of union miners, were discharged from their jobs. Hundreds also were forced to vacate their company-owned homes, and many who refused were forcibly evicted by hated Baldwin-Felts detectives.

On May 19, 1920, 13 Baldwin-Felts detectives, including Al and Lee Felts, brothers of one of the agency founders, arrived in the Mingo County town of Matewan on the Tug River to evict striking miners and their families from company houses. The detectives, under an intermittent drizzle, forced several families, including women and children, from their homes at gunpoint and dumped their belongings out on the road. Word of the evictions enraged area miners, who began arming themselves.

Matewan's police chief, Sid Hatfield, 27, a strike supporter, tried to stop the evictions as being unauthorized by law. At 4:00 p.m., as the detectives prepared to leave, Hatfield, accompanied by Matewan Mayor Cable C. Testerman and a host of angry miners, confronted Al Felts near the Matewan railroad station and tried to arrest him. Felts, in turn, tried to arrest Hatfield. As the men argued, shooting started.

Hatfield admitted he fired but said Al Felts shot first. A number of the miners and several detectives joined in. When it ended a minute or two later, ten persons—seven Baldwin-Felts detectives (including both Felts brothers), two miners, and Mayor Testerman—had been fatally shot.

Hatfield and 17 strikers were tried for murder in early 1921 and were all acquitted; such was the hatred of the detective agency. The "Matewan Massacre" is often cited as the opening of the West Virginia Mine War of 1920–21, which escalated into an armed conflict involving thousands after Hatfield's murder at Welch later in 1921.

See also Baldwin-Felts Detective Agency, Sid Hatfield, Mine Wars

Lon Savage
Salem, Virginia

Lon Savage, Thunder in the Mountains: The West Virginia Mine War of 1920–21, 1990.

John Frederick Matheus

Writer and scholar John Frederick Matheus was born in Keyser, September 10, 1887. When he was a youth, his family moved to Steubenville, Ohio, and some of the settings of Matheus's short stories are in the West Virginia-Ohio-Pennsylvania area. Other works are based on folktales learned about during his travels in Europe, Africa, and the Caribbean.

Matheus graduated from Western Reserve University (now Case Western Reserve) in Cleveland, Ohio, in 1910 and received an A.M. degree from Columbia in 1921. He later studied at the Sorbonne in Paris and the University of Chicago. From 1922 until his retirement in 1958, Matheus taught foreign languages at West Virginia State College. While at the school, he served for a brief period on a U.S-League of Nations commission investigating slavery in Liberia.

Matheus was active during the period of the Harlem Renaissance, a flowering of African-American arts and literature in the 1920s. He wrote poetry, plays, and short stories that focused on themes and characters of importance to African-Americans. His plays in particular dealt with the hardships and exploitation characteristic of the black race in that era. Matheus also was a writer for newspapers in Charleston and Cleveland.

Although Matheus was more interested in playwriting, his short stories garnered greater literary success. His short story "Fog" won first place in the Opportunity magazine short story contest in 1925, and "Swamp Moccasin" received first prize in the Crisis magazine short story contest in 1926.

The opera Ouanga! was written and composed by Matheus and black composer-violinist Clarence Cameron White, who was named director of music at West Virginia State College in 1924. The opera is an account of the life of Jean-Jacques Dessalines, the slave who led a revolution in Haiti and became its leader in the early 19th century. Ouanga! was performed at the Metropolitan Opera House and Carnegie Hall.

Matheus died in Florida, February 19, 1983.

Judie Smith
West Virginia Humanities Council

Henry Mason Mathews

Henry Mason Mathews, the fifth governor of West Virginia, was born at Frankford, Greenbrier County, March 29, 1834. His father, Mason Mathews, was a merchant who served as a member of the Virginia House of Delegates. The younger Mathews attended Lewisburg Academy in preparation for study at the University of Virginia, where he received A.B. and A.M. degrees. Following graduation in 1856, he studied for a year at Judge John W. Brockenbrough's law school in Lexington, Virginia, receiving a B.L. degree with honors.

Between 1857 and the outbreak of the Civil War, Mathews practiced law in Lewisburg, where he and his young wife, the former Lucy Clayton Fry, established a residence. To supplement his income, Mathews taught history, literature, and modern languages at Allegheny College, a local school for boys. The couple had five children. When the Civil War erupted, Mathews enlisted as a private in the Confederate Army, eventually rising through the ranks to major of artillery prior to the surrender.

A popular young man with great ambition, Mathews was overwhelmingly elected to the new West Virginia Senate in 1865. He was not allowed to serve, however, due to laws that barred former Confederates from election to public office. After passage of the Flick Amendment restored the political right of ex-Confederates, Mathews was elected attorney general of West Virginia in 1872, and served from 1873 to 1877 as one of the most popular attorneys general in the history of the state. He served as a member of the 1872 West Virginia Constitutional

Governor Henry M. Mathews (1834–84).

Convention, which returned the rights of former Confederates. Mathews used his popularity as attorney general to propel himself to the governor's mansion in 1876. As the Democratic nominee he easily defeated Republican Nathan Goff Jr. of Harrison County. Mathews was the first Confederate veteran to be elected governor, and he represented the pro-Southern, "Redeemer" faction of the Democratic Party. He was the first of the so-called Bourbon governors.

Governor Mathews served during difficult times. There were strikes and riots during much of his administration, including the national railroad strike of 1877 which began at Martinsburg. In his inaugural address Mathews called for peaceful resolutions of disputes and for harmony, but his call for peace was largely ignored. He had to ask President Rutherford B. Hayes for federal troops to help stop the railway strike at Martinsburg, because the state militia sympathized with the strikers. State troops had to be called out three years later to halt the Ansted mine strike in Fayette County. The Virginia Debt question, the troublesome matter of West Virginia's contribution toward paying off the Virginia state debt at the time West Virginia left the mother state, remained an issue throughout Mathew's term. His administration was unusual for the period, however, as he appointed representatives of both parties to important positions within his administration.

Mathews returned to Lewisburg in 1881, at the completion of his term as governor, where he practiced law and served as president of the White Sulphur Springs Company. He died unexpectedly on April 28, 1884, at the age of 50, and is buried at the Old Stone Church Cemetery in Lewisburg.

Donna Addkison-Simmons
Brookings, South Dakota

Dumas Malone, ed., *Dictionary of American Biography*, 1933; John G. Morgan, *West Virginia Governors*, 1980; Robert Sobel and John Raimo, eds., *Biographical Directory of the Governors of the United States, 1789–1978*, 1978.

Kathy Mattea

Musician Kathleen Alice "Kathy" Mattea is one of West Virginia's principal contemporary country singers, with 27 Top 40 songs to her credit. Mattea was born in Cross Lanes, Kanawha County, June 21, 1959. In junior high school she learned to play the guitar, and in high school she practiced her vocal skills singing classical music in choir class.

In 1976, Mattea entered West Virginia University and joined a band called Pennsboro. Two years later, she relocated to Nashville, working as a tour guide among other jobs. Eventually, she began singing "demo" recordings of other songwriters' material for music publishing companies. This led to a contract with Mercury Records in 1983 and her debut album the following year. In 1986, "Walk the Way the Wind Blows" became her first major hit, and she also recorded the autobiographical "Leaving West Virginia." Subsequent top hits have included "Goin' Gone," "Love at the Five & Dime," "Eighteen Wheels and a Dozen Roses," "Come from the Heart," and "Burnin' Old Memories."

In 1988, Kathy Mattea married Jon Vezner, who had written several of her hit songs. She was named the Country Music Association's Female Vocalist of the Year in 1989 and 1990. Soon afterward, Mattea became the first Nashville star to speak openly about AIDS and participate in programs to benefit AIDS research.

Abby Gail Goodnite
University of Rio Grande

Ivan M. Tribe, *Mountaineer Jamboree: Country Music in West Virginia*, 1984.

Jack Maurice

Newspaperman John Daniell "Jack" Maurice was the only West Virginia journalist to win a Pulitzer Prize. Maurice was born in Vivian, McDowell County, October 23, 1913. He grew up in the West Virginia and Kentucky coalfields. After Huntington High School, he moved on to Marshall College (now University) and graduated magna cum laude in 1935. Immediately upon graduation from Marshall, Maurice began his newspaper career as a reporter with the Huntington *Herald-Dispatch*.

In 1938, he joined the staff of the *Charleston Daily Mail* as a reporter. World War II interrupted his career in 1943, and he served three years in the U.S. Navy Reserve, where he attained the rank of lieutenant. Maurice returned to the *Daily Mail* in 1946 as the newspaper's chief editorial writer. In 1950, he was named editor, and in 1969 he became editor-in-

chief. In 1979, he became a contributing editor and columnist, retiring in 1984.

In 1958, Maurice won the Sigma Delta Chi award for editorial writing. His most notable accomplishment came in 1975, when he won journalism's highest honor, the Pulitzer Prize, for a series of editorials he wrote the year before amid a battle over textbooks in Kanawha County.

Jack Maurice died in Charleston, December 20, 1999.

Hu Maxwell

The prolific historian and forester Hu Maxwell was born in St. George, Tucker County, September 22, 1860. Until he turned 15, Maxwell was educated at home by his mother, Sarah Bonnifield Maxwell. He later graduated from Weston Academy (1880) and won an appointment to the U.S. Naval Academy in Annapolis, but poor health forced his resignation.

Maxwell returned to West Virginia, where he taught school and learned the timbering business. He became editor and part owner of the *Tucker County Pioneer* newspaper and devoted much of the rest of his life to writing and publishing.

Maxwell wrote histories of Barbour (1899), Hampshire (1897), Randolph (1898), and Tucker (1884) counties and contributed two short articles to *History of the Mingo Indians* (1921). With Richard E. Fast, he wrote *The History and Government of West Virginia* (1906), and he co-authored the three-volume classic, *West Virginia and Its People* (1913), with Thomas Condit Miller.

Maxwell combined his knowledge of timbering with his passion for study and traveled throughout the country conducting surveys for the U.S. Forest Service. In addition to government bulletins, he wrote *Idyls of the Golden Shore* (1889), a collection of poems about California. He also published *A Tree History of the United States* (1923).

Hu Maxwell died August 20, 1927.

Christine M. Kreiser
Clarksburg

Jim Comstock, ed., *The West Virginia Heritage Encyclopedia*, 1976; Ella May Turner, *Stories and Verse of West Virginia*, 1925.

May Moore Mound

The May Moore Mound is a prehistoric Adena mound located on private property in Mason County, on the Ohio River south of Point Pleasant. The mound is mentioned in the *Report on the Mound Explorations of the Bureau of Ethnology* by Cyrus Thomas, describing the extensive explorations of mounds and earthworks conducted throughout North America between 1882 and 1886 by the Smithsonian Institution. Thomas described the mound as being located on the farm of Judge Moore and the largest in the area. The report fails to mention any excavation of the mound.

In 1962, West Virginia Archeological Society members Delf Norona, Oscar Mairs, and Bob White visited the May Moore Mound, which Norona described as possibly the third largest in West Virginia. Although the mound appeared to have been cut into several times previously, it seemed to be intact enough to retain much valuable information. At the present time, the mound is one of the few remaining Adena mounds that is relatively undisturbed.

See also Adena, Archeology, Mound Builders, Prehistoric People

Darla S. Hoffman
Cultural Resource Analysts
Edward V. McMichael, *Introduction to West Virginia Archeology,* 1968; Cyrus Thomas, *Report on the Mound Explorations of the Bureau of Ethnology,* 1894.

Jon McBride

Astronaut Jon Andrew McBride was born August 14, 1943, in Charleston. He grew up in Beckley. McBride graduated from Woodrow Wilson High School in Beckley, attended West Virginia University, and received a bachelor's degree in aeronautical engineering from the U.S. Naval Postgraduate School.

McBride says that from the day a U.S. Navy recruiter took him for a flight while he was attending WVU, flying has been at the center of his life. Joining the navy, he earned his wings as a naval aviator and flew 64 combat missions in Vietnam. McBride became an astronaut in 1979, piloted the space shuttle Challenger on an eight-day mission in 1984, and was scheduled to pilot another shuttle mission that was grounded in the wake of the Challenger accident in January 1986. He was assigned to NASA headquarters in 1987 as assistant administrator for congressional relations. He retired from NASA and the navy in 1989 to pursue a business career.

In 1996, McBride made an unsuccessful bid for the Republican nomination for governor of West Virginia. He lives today in Lewisburg, and in Arizona and Florida.

James E. Casto
Herald-Dispatch

Joseph E. McCarthy's Wheeling Speech

U.S. Sen. Joseph E. McCarthy's speech to a group of Wheeling Republicans on February 9, 1950, launched the 1950s red scare, giving McCarthy a national platform that he would not relinquish for four years. The speech at Wheeling's McLure Hotel was part of the Lincoln Day celebration, an annual Republican political holiday. McCarthy had a speech on housing that he could have given. Former U.S. Sen. Francis Love, who met him at the airport, suggested he give one on the perils of communism instead.

McCarthy, a Wisconsin Republican, claimed in his speech to have a list of 205 communists who worked in the U.S. State Department with the knowledge of Secretary of State Dean Acheson. McCarthy had no such list, and whether he actually said the 205 number isn't clear. The next day's *Wheeling Intelligencer* said he did, but the reporter later told Congress he wrote his story from McCarthy's prepared remarks, not the actual speech.

The allegation "did not cause a ripple in the room," said one Wheeling lawyer who attended the speech. Nevertheless, the senator's charges were national headlines in a couple of days. McCarthy made the same charges several times during the next few days, often changing the numbers. He never produced his list, and a congressional inquiry found there was no substance to his charges.

None of it mattered. Republicans rode to a huge victory in the 1950 elections, and McCarthy was reelected to the Senate in 1952. He held various anti-communist hearings until 1954, when he recklessly challenged the U.S. Army, whose integrity was beyond impugning. McCarthy's efforts never uncovered a single communist in the U.S. government. His name has become synonymous with witch-hunts and baseless allegations.

Greg Moore
Charleston Gazette
Greg Moore, "Wheeling Speech Set McCarthy On His Path," *Sunday Gazette-Mail,* February 6, 2000; Thomas C. Reeves, *The Life and Times of Joe McCarthy,* 1982; Richard H. Rovere, *Senator Joe McCarthy,* 1959.

John McCausland

Confederate General John McCausland was born in St. Louis, September 13, 1836. When his parents died in 1843, he came to live with relatives in Henderson, (West) Virginia, near Point Pleasant. He later attended Virginia Military Institute and graduated first in his class in 1857. He returned a year later as an assistant professor of mathematics, serving on the VMI faculty as a colleague of Thomas J. Jackson, later known as Stonewall.

When Virginia seceded in 1861, McCausland organized and took command of the 36th Virginia Infantry. After the Battle of Cloyd's Mountain in May 1864, he assumed command of a cavalry brigade and was soon commissioned as a brigadier.

In July 1864, he was ordered to conduct a raid into Pennsylvania in retaliation for federal depredations in the Shenandoah Valley. His forces occupied Chambersburg and demanded $100,000 in gold from the citizens. When they refused, McCausland, following orders, evacuated the town and burned the business district. A pursuing federal force surprised his brigade while camping near Moorefield, and defeated it. McCausland and a portion of his men managed to escape.

After the fall of the Confederacy, Mc-

Causland fled the country, fearing that he might be tried for his actions at Chambersburg. He returned in 1867 and spent the remainder of his life on his large farm in Mason County. He remained an unrepentant rebel to the end, bitter about the failure of the "Lost Cause." He died January 22, 1927, the next-to-last Confederate general to succumb. He is buried at Henderson.

See also Civil War

Jim Barnes
Morgantown
Michael J. Pauley, *Unreconstructed Rebel: The Life of General John McCausland CSA,* 1993; James I. Robertson, "John McCausland," in Patricia L. Faust, ed., *Historical Times Illustrated Encyclopedia of the Civil War,* 1986; Boyd B. Stutler, *West Virginia in the Civil War,* 1966.

McClain Printing Company

McClain Printing Company of Parsons, Tucker County, has printed many books of West Virginia history and lore. The company was incorporated in 1958 as an outgrowth of the weekly newspaper, the *Parsons Advocate,* which was then 62 years old. Ken and Faith Reynolds McClain had bought the newspaper in 1943. McClain was approached about 1957 by West Virginia University professors who feared that early West Virginia histories would be lost if they were not reprinted. The newspaper reprinted Alexander Scott Withers's classic history, *Chronicles of Border Warfare,* as its first venture in book publishing, about 1958.

When Ken McClain retired in the early 1970s, his son-in-law and daughter, George and Mariwyn Smith, moved to Parsons. He took over the printing company and she the newspaper. When George Smith retired in 1997, son Kenneth E. Smith became the third generation to run the printing company.

In the first 35 years, McClain Printing Company produced comprehensive county histories of more than 35 West Virginia counties, as well as thousands of other titles. They include bestsellers such as Roy B. Clarkson's *Tumult on the Mountains* and Howard B. Lee's *Bloodletting in Appalachia*; the works of West Virginia poet laureate Louise McNeill and folklorists Ruth Ann Musick and James Gay Jones; and reprints of classic histories by Wills DeHass, W. C. Dodrill, and others.

Mariwyn McClain Smith
Parsons

McColloch's Leap

Samuel McColloch, one of four brothers who emigrated from the South Branch of the Potomac to Wheeling in 1770, is remembered as the courageous horseman who leaped with his horse from Wheeling Hill, 300 feet to the bottom, to escape Indians.

Early on the morning of September 1, 1777, Indians appeared at the crest of

A dramatic depiction of McColloch's Leap.

Wheeling Hill. Believing that the enemy force consisted of only a few warriors, the militia of Fort Henry pursued, under the command of Capt. Samuel Mason. After following the Indian trail down to Wheeling Creek, they were suddenly ambushed by a large Indian war party and most of the militia were killed. A few survivors hastened to the neighboring forts with the news of the assault upon Fort Henry.

One of those forts was Van Meter's, located on Short Creek several miles to the north, and commanded by Maj. Samuel McColloch. He hastily assembled two or three men and rode to the relief of Fort Henry, but upon his approach he was cut off by a small party of warriors. Turning his horse, and closely pursued by the Indians, he managed to gain the crest of Wheeling Hill, only to be cut off once more. McColloch spurred his horse to the edge of the precipice and leaped to the waters of Wheeling Creek far below.

Surprisingly, McColloch survived the leap with nothing more than a few scratches and bruises, and his horse survived as well. McColloch returned to Van Meter's and gathered together a force of about 40 militia. On the following day they rode to the relief of Fort Henry, only to find that the Indians had lifted their siege a few hours earlier.

McColloch later lost his left arm in a hunting accident and was killed in another Indian ambush in 1782. Today a granite monument on U.S. 40 marks the site of the heroic leap of Samuel McColloch.

See also Fort Henry

William Hintzen
Freetown, Indiana

J. H. Newton, G. G. Nichols, and A. G. Sprankle, *History of the Pan-Handle,* 1879.

Kyle McCormick

Newspaperman Kenneth Kyle McCormick, West Virginia state archivist, newspaper editor and historian, was born June 13, 1891, in Union, Monroe County.

He graduated from the University of Virginia, married Lucy Cargill, and served in the military during World War I. For a time he was employed as the principal of Point Pleasant High School. In the mid-1920s, he moved to Princeton, Mercer County, and published the *Princeton Observer* from 1927 to 1957. In 1957, he was appointed by Governor Underwood as the state historian and archivist and served in that capacity until 1961. McCormick authored two histories, *The Story of Mercer County* (1957) and *The New-Kanawha River and the Mine War of West Virginia* (1959). He served on the West Virginia Library Commission and was president of the West Virginia Newspaper Council. McCormick died on November 1, 1971, in Princeton and was buried there.

Michael M. Meador
Abingdon, Virginia

Charlie McCoy

Musician Charles Ray McCoy may be the most significant harmonica player in country music history. Born in Oak Hill, March 28, 1941, McCoy moved to Florida as a child but retained close ties to his home community. He came to Nashville in 1959, and from the mid-'60s was heard on numerous recording sessions as well as on many of his own albums—mostly instrumental—for the Monument and Step One record labels. His best-known numbers include "Today I Started Loving You Again" and "Orange Blossom Special."

While primarily a country musician, McCoy also performed with a rock 'n' roll band. He may be heard on albums by Roy Orbison and Bob Dylan. In addition to harmonica, he also plays drums, trumpet, and bass. McCoy served as musical director for the long-running television program *Hee Haw.*

Ivan M. Tribe
University of Rio Grande

Ivan M. Tribe, *Mountaineer Jamboree: Country Music in West Virginia,* 1984.

Randolph McCoy

Feudist Randolph McCoy, often called Randell or "Old Ranel," was the McCoy family patriarch during the Hatfield-McCoy feud. He was born in Logan County, October 30, 1825, one of 13 children of Daniel and Margaret McCoy, neighbors of the Hatfields. In 1849, McCoy married his cousin, Sarah McCoy, whose father gave the young couple a small farm on Blackberry Fork of Pond Creek in Pike County, Kentucky. There, they raised 13 children.

In 1878, McCoy accused Floyd Hatfield, a cousin of Anderson "Devil Anse" Hatfield, of stealing a hog. It was the first episode of the Hatfield-McCoy Feud. The case was settled in Floyd Hatfield's favor when one of McCoy's own relatives testified against him. From then on McCoy agitated against the Hatfields, going so far as to reject his own daughter, Rose Anna, after she fell in love with Devil Anse's son, Johnse Hatfield. In 1882, three of McCoy's sons killed Ellison Hatfield, Devil Anse's brother, in a drunken brawl at a Pike County election. The Hatfields took revenge by ritually executing the three McCoys. McCoy kept up steady pressure on local and state authorities, finally succeeding in 1887 when his relative, Perry Cline, persuaded the governor of Kentucky to prosecute the Hatfields. In retaliation the Hatfields, on New Year's morning 1888, attacked and burned the McCoy home, killing two of McCoy's children and severely beating his wife.

Defeated, McCoy moved to Pikeville. From then on, Cline was the effective leader of the McCoy forces in the feud and Ranel McCoy became an embittered old man, running a ferry in Pikeville and talking to anyone who would listen about his sufferings at the hands of the Hatfields. He died while tending a cook fire on March 28, 1914, at the age of 88. He and Sarah McCoy are buried in the Dils Cemetery in Pikeville.

Altina L. Waller
University of Connecticut

McCoy's Mill

McCoy's Mill, located along U.S. 220 three miles south of Franklin, is one of West Virginia's oldest landmarks. Framed by the rugged mountains of Pendleton County, the mill employed generations of millers, drawing its water power from Thorn Creek just before the creek empties into the South Branch Potomac.

The first mill on this site was built about the time of the French and Indian War by Ulrich Conrad Sr., who came as a pioneer settler from Switzerland in 1753. According to Elsie Byrd Boggs's *History of Franklin,* Conrad supplied the soldiers in Lord Dunmore's War with flour and meal in 1774.

Conrad's son inherited from his father in 1777, and Gen. William McCoy, a

Franklin merchant, later acquired the property. General McCoy died in 1835, and the mill was acquired by his nephew, William McCoy. This McCoy found the business so lucrative that he decided to replace the old mill with a modern one. Construction of the new mill began in 1845.

The 1845 mill is the present four-story mill building, its large hand-hewn beams supported by a thick stone foundation. This new mill originally had the familiar overshot mill wheel, but this was replaced by a more efficient underwater turbine in the early 20th century. Grain was milled here until the mid-1900s, and the mill and connecting residence were adapted late in the century as a furniture workshop and bed and breakfast inn. McCoy's Mill was listed on the National Register of Historic Places in 1986.

Kathleen M. Jacobs
Charleston

Bernard P. McDonough

Industrialist and philanthropist Bernard Patrick McDonough Jr. was born May 25, 1903, in Texas, to an Irish railroading family. His immigrant grandfather had previously settled the family in Clarksburg and later in Belpre, Ohio, near Parkersburg. Young Bernard and his sisters returned to their grandmother in Belpre after the death of their mother. He was educated there and at Notre Dame and Georgetown universities.

Leaving Georgetown University in 1925, McDonough tried various sales jobs before entering the construction business. By 1929, he specialized in building gas stations in Parkersburg and the surrounding area. McDonough continued in construction in the 1930s. He expanded operations during World War II, building railroads and entering the marine barge business in New Orleans. In 1945, he began a concrete business in Houston.

McDonough's businesses coalesced and grew in the 1950s and later. He turned from the founding of companies to acquisitions, with key early purchases being Kanawha Sand & Gravel (1948) and the O. Ames Company (1955), a Parkersburg tool manufacturer where he had worked as a young man for 15 cents an hour. He turned to other interests as well, renewing family ties with ancestral Ireland. Eventually he had extensive investments there, including hotels and Dromoland Castle. The McDonough Company reached its full maturity as a Fortune 500 company in the 1970s, with major operations in footwear (Endicott Johnson Shoes), hand tools, and building materials. The Marmac Company continued in the barge business.

McDonough turned to philanthropy as his businesses succeeded. He made major gifts to Georgetown University, Wheeling College (now Wheeling Jesuit University), and other institutions. The Bernard P. McDonough Foundation, his principal philanthropic vehicle, remains one of the largest private foundations in West Virginia. The foundation is a contributor to *The West Virginia Encyclopedia*.

Bernard McDonough died October 12, 1985.

McDowell County

McDowell County, the southernmost county in West Virginia, was formed in 1858 from part of Tazewell County, Virginia. The new county was named after James McDowell, a governor of Virginia (1843–45). It consists of 538.4 square miles of rugged mountain land, on the headwaters of the Tug Fork. McDowell County is served by U.S. 52, several state and county routes, and the Norfolk Southern Railroad. The county seat is Welch.

After the Revolutionary War, the federal government granted vast tracts of unoccupied land to military veterans and others. Many of these grants passed into the hands of speculators. In 1795, the original owners of all the land now included in McDowell County, Wilson Nicholas and Jacob Kenney, sold their grant to Robert Morris, a Philadelphia financier and a signer of the Declaration of Independence. Morris could not effectively control such a large acreage. Settlers began moving in, and Morris lost control of his lands as the newcomers asserted squatters' rights. By the 1830s, much acreage had fallen back into public ownership in tax forfeitures. On the eve of the Civil War, the state of Virginia owned two-thirds of the land in McDowell County.

The first white residents of present McDowell County were Mathias and Lydia Harman, who settled in a cabin along the Dry Fork about 1802. In 1829, William Fletcher received 20 acres of land at the site of present Welch. Settlement was slow, due to the rugged terrain. In 1860, there was a population of only 1,535 in the new county.

Apart from sporadic guerrilla warfare, the Civil War largely passed by McDowell County. Nonetheless, McDowell had been founded on the eve of war, and the unsettled conditions hindered the orderly commencement of county affairs. The notion of the "free State of McDowell," later a motto expressing the county's independent ways, originated during this free-wheeling period.

For years, citizens battled over the site of the county seat. Between 1858 and 1872, the county court met at various places. In 1872, the county seat was located at Peeryville (now English), the largest town at that time. Two decades later, the county seat controversy arose again. The population around Welch had increased significantly with the arrival of the Norfolk & Western Railway in the early 1890s, and the town was incorporated in 1894. McDowell Countians voted to move the county seat to Welch in 1892, amid allegations of fraud. Violence seemed imminent, but James A. Strother and Trigg Tabor secretly moved the county records to Welch, where the county seat has remained to this day.

Until the late 19th century, the county's vast coal deposits remained largely untouched. By the 1870s, investors began purchasing much of McDowell County in anticipation of the arrival of the railroad, which would make it possible to ship coal and timber to market. By 1892, the Norfolk & Western Railway had spanned the county and within the next decade constructed spurs into most of the coal mining areas.

The native population was not large enough to supply the labor needs of the new mines. As coal companies recruited immigrants from southern and eastern

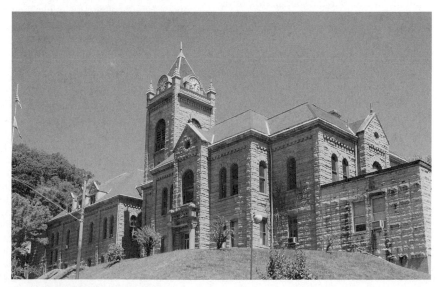

The McDowell County courthouse in Welch.

FAST FACTS ABOUT MCDOWELL COUNTY

Founded: 1858

Land in square miles: 538.4

Population: 27,329

Percentage minorities: 12.9%

Percentage rural: 88.5%

Median age: 40.5

Percentage 65 and older: 16.1%

Birth rate per 1,000 population: 11.6

Median household income: $16,931

High school graduate or higher: 50.0%

Bachelor's degree or higher: 5.6%

Home ownership: 80.1%

Median home value: $22,600

This information is from the 2000 U.S. Census. In 2000, West Virginia as a whole had 5 percent minorities, a median age of 38.9, median household income of $29,696, and a 75.2 percent home ownership rate.

Europe and blacks from the American South, McDowell became one of the most diverse counties in the state and remained so for many years.

McDowell, which had had no slave population and no free blacks after emancipation, became the state's center of African-American population in the industrial era. McDowell County blacks established a power base within the state and local Republican Party, governing communities such as Keystone in the early 20th century and regularly sending delegates to the state legislature. A fourth of the population was black in 1950. In 2000, African-Americans made up 11.9 percent of the county's population, the highest percentage in the state.

By the mid-20th century, McDowell was the leading coal producing county in the nation, until it was surpassed by neighboring Logan County in 1955. McDowell established itself as the third most populous county in the state in 1920, and its population peaked at 98,887 in 1950.

After 1950, mine mechanization led to widespread job losses and people left to seek work elsewhere. As of 2000, the population of McDowell County was 27,329. The loss of coal jobs and the lack of economic diversification brought hard times. By the end of the 20th century, McDowell was the poorest county in West Virginia. In 1999, 47.5 percent of McDowell County families with children lived in poverty. The primary employers include numerous small coal mines, the state of West Virginia, and the county school board.

McDowell has three public high schools, Mount View, Iaeger, and Big Creek. Mount View High School is also used as an off-campus site for Bluefield State College. In 2001, the state Board of Education took over administration of the McDowell County school system. In 2004, plans were

made to consolidate Iaeger and Big Creek high schools.

McDowell County has ten incorporated communities: Welch, Kimball, Keystone, Northfork, Gary, Anawalt, Davy, Iaeger, War, and Bradshaw. Most residents live outside these municipalities, however, usually in former coal company towns. There are two wildlife management areas, Berwind Lake and Anawalt, as well as Panther State Forest. The county's only golf course is at the Gary Country Club.

The primary river is the Tug Fork, a Big Sandy tributary which flows through the northern section of the county. The major tributaries of the Tug Fork in McDowell County are Elkhorn Creek and the Dry Fork. McDowell County suffered severe flooding in July 2001 and May 2002, destroying or damaging hundreds of homes and businesses. The 2002 floods and related weather killed four people.

The McDowell County coalfields gained national attention with the publication of Coalwood native Homer Hickam's 1998 book, *Rocket Boys,* and the subsequent film, *October Sky.* The first World War I memorial was built at Welch, and the nation's first World War I memorial for African-American veterans was located at Kimball. Fire gutted both buildings, with the Welch memorial being destroyed; extensive renovations of the Kimball memorial were under way in 2003. Welch is also the location of the first municipal parking building in the nation.

McDowell County has the distinction of having had the first female African-American state legislator in the United States, when Minnie Buckingham Harper was appointed to the House of Delegates by Governor Gore in 1928. Other important natives include Henry D. Hatfield, governor of West Virginia (1913–17) and U.S. senator (1929–35); state Attorney

General Edward P. Rucker (1897–1901); and state Attorney General Ira J. Partlow (1945–49).

See also Welch

Mark S. Myers
Morgantown

Jean Battlo, *McDowell County in West Virginia and American History,* 1998; David A. Corbin, *Life, Work, and Rebellion in the Coal Fields: The Southern West Virginia Miners, 1880–1922,* 1981.

Uncle Jack McElwain

Musician Lewis Johnson "Uncle Jack" McElwain was born January 3, 1856, and died April 30, 1938, having lived his entire life on Laurel Creek at Wainville, near the community of Erbacon in Webster County. He was the most respected fiddler in central West Virginia during his lifetime. He took part in many fiddle contests and no one can recall him ever being beaten. McElwain's fame and talent touched numerous fiddlers in his day, including members of the fiddling Carpenter, Hammons, and Wine families. The noted southern West Virginia fiddler, "Blind Ed" Haley, was known to have made trips to Webster County to visit McElwain and trade tunes. McElwain often traveled with another Webster fiddler, Tom Jack Woods, said to have been seven feet tall. McElwain's most notable contest win was at the Chicago World's Fair in 1893.

Although we have no recordings of McElwain's playing, oral history reveals much about his playing style and repertoire. He is said to have played in the "old West Fork style." This refers to the West Fork of the Little Kanawha, where the McElwain family lived before coming to Webster County in the 19th century. A former neighbor and old-time fiddler recalled that when Uncle Jack played "Old Sledge," his best tune, "you seemed to rise up three feet off the ground!" McElwain's legacy is firmly entrenched in the playing of numerous central West Virginia fiddlers of recent years who credit their tune sources to "Uncle Jack."

See also Fiddle Tradition, Blind Ed Haley

Gerald Milnes
Augusta Heritage Center

Gerald Milnes, *Play of a Fiddle,* 1999.

Frank Duff McEnteer

Engineer Frank Duff McEnteer, the builder of a thousand bridges, was born May 23, 1882, in Reynoldsville, Pennsylvania. He graduated from Harvard engineering school in 1905 and moved to Clarksburg in 1911 to superintend the construction of the Palace Furniture Company building. The concrete-frame building, still in use, is one of the earliest reinforced concrete buildings in West Virginia. It launched McEnteer upon a career in building reinforced concrete structures, then essentially a new engineering material and form.

In 1914, McEnteer was appointed to superintend the multi-span concrete arch bridge on Fourth Street in Clarksburg. In the same year, with P. M. Harrison, he incorporated the Concrete Steel Bridge Company. The company showed steady growth and by 1924 had 52 separate construction teams in the field. Branch offices were established in Pittsburgh, Harrisburg, Huntington, and Knoxville, with a subsidiary company in Florida.

Although the intention of the firm was to build short to medium span bridges, in its later years several large bridges were built, including the Alderson bridge across the Greenbrier River in 1915. On the eve of the Great Depression, in 1928–29, the company encountered unexpected difficulties with a Pennsylvania bridge project. The company was forced into bankruptcy and was liquidated in 1931.

Following the demise of the company, McEnteer joined the State Road Commission until World War II. He arrived in the Middle East in 1942 and in 1943 was made chief engineer of the construction division of the U.S. armed forces in the entire region.

Upon his return to Clarksburg following the war, he opened a consulting firm which he headed until his death on September 4, 1957. Frank Duff McEnteer's handiwork is evident throughout West Virginia and surrounding states, with many of his bridges still in service.

Emory L. Kemp
WVU Institute for the History of Technology

Darrell McGraw

Attorney General Darrell Vivian McGraw Jr, born November 8, 1936, in Wyoming County, served previously as a justice of the West Virginia Supreme Court of Appeals. He was educated in local public schools and at Pineville High School and at Berea Academy, Kentucky, with bachelor's, master's, and legal degrees from West Virginia University. McGraw served in the U.S. Army from age 17 to 20. He was student body president at WVU in 1959.

After law school, McGraw was admitted to the state bar, serving in private practice and as counsel to Governor Smith. He served also as counsel to the legislature. A Democrat, he was elected to the Supreme Court in 1976, one of three liberals elected to the court that year. He quickly established himself as an outspoken jurist and was a lightning rod for conservative critics. Landmark actions of the court during his time included the 1978 Mandolidis decision, which significantly expanded the rights of injured workers to sue and was opposed by many employers.

McGraw, who served as chief justice in 1987, failed in 1988 to gain reelection to a second term on the court. He was elected state attorney general in 1992 and reelected in 1996, 2000, and 2004. He has emphasized consumer protection as attorney general. In 2000, he won an important settlement against Ohio direct mail operator Benjamin Suarez. Attorney General McGraw involved West Virginia in a multi-state suit against the tobacco industry, producing a 1997 settlement expected to net the state a total of $1.5 billion over 25 years.

Darrell McGraw comes from a politically active family. Warren R. McGraw, previously state Senate president, in 2004 was a justice of the Supreme Court. The brothers often served simultaneously among the state's highest officials, and Warren R. McGraw II, Warren's son and Darrell's nephew, served in the House of Delegates from 1993 to 2002. Darrell McGraw lives in Charleston with his wife, educator Jorea Marple.

John T. McGraw

Businessman and Democratic Party activist John T. McGraw was born January 12, 1856, at Grafton. His Irish immigrant father worked as a laborer to build the Baltimore & Ohio Railroad and was among the first residents of Grafton. Young McGraw was educated in the Catholic schools of Grafton, at St. Vincent Academy in Wheeling, and at Yale University, where he received a law degree in 1876.

McGraw entered the practice of law and in 1880 was elected prosecuting attorney of Taylor County, beginning a long career as a leader in the Democratic Party. He served as prosecuting attorney until 1885, and in 1886 was appointed by President Cleveland as collector of internal revenue for West Virginia. McGraw was a member of the Democratic National Committee (1896–1916 and 1918–20), chaired the state party (1904–08), and was a delegate to the Democratic National Convention in 1912 and 1916.

In his rise to fortune and influence, McGraw cultivated the grand old men of the West Virginia Democratic Party, Henry Gassaway Davis and Johnson Newlon Camden, both U.S. senators and both major industrialists. Like them, he speculated in timber lands in the Pocahontas County area in the 1880s, and he tried unsuccessfully to induce Davis to extend a railroad into the region. McGraw was among the founders of the Pocahontas Development Corporation which built the town of Marlinton and succeeded in having the county seat moved there in 1891. He worked with leaders of the Chesapeake & Ohio Railroad to bring the C&O's Greenbrier Division to the upper Greenbrier Valley. It arrived in Marlinton in 1900.

John T. McGraw suffered financial reversals in his later years. His Bank of Grafton failed in 1912, and he reportedly withdrew to Baltimore to live for a period with his sister's family. McGraw died April 29, 1920, in Baltimore and is buried in Grafton.

Kermit McKeever

Kermit McKeever, father of the modern West Virginia state park system, was born at what he called "the mountain place" near Renick, Greenbrier County, March 10, 1910. A graduate of Glenville State College in education and West Virginia University in forestry, McKeever began his career in 1942 as superintendent of Lost River State Park.

McKeever believed that if the park system was to grow and prosper, its managers must pay attention to West Virginia politics. McKeever paid attention. He became superintendent of Watoga State Park in 1944 and four years later he had the job of running the entire park system. During Governor Marland's term (1953–57), McKeever planned Blackwater Falls and Holly River state parks, while Grandview State Park came to fruition during Governor Underwood's first term in office during the late 1950s. Hawks Nest and the modern resort parks—Pipestem, Canaan, Cacapon, and Twin Falls—came along during Governor Barron's term in the early 1960s.

McKeever firmly opposed entrance fees to the parks. He disagreed with the perennial criticism that the parks don't pay for themselves, pointing out the indirect returns. "Canaan . . . opened the door to millions of dollars in businesses, taxes, and employment. The parks have many times paid for themselves."

Kermit McKeever retired in 1978 and died in Charleston, September 8, 1995. During his tenure as parks chief the number of state parks grew from 14 to 35, with a new one opening about every 16 months. McKeever Lodge at Pipestem was named for him.

See also State Parks
Maureen F. Crockett
St. Albans

Bill McKell

Coal operator William "Bill" McKell was born in Chillicothe, Ohio, March 1, 1871, son of Thomas Gaylord McKell (1845–1904) who had built the Fayette County community of Glen Jean and named it for his wife. T. G. McKell owned valuable Sewell and Fire Creek seams of high quality "smokeless" coal in the New River Coalfield.

Young Bill, after graduating from Yale, settled and built his home at Glen Jean in 1893. Upon his father's death he managed the family inheritance with his brother, John. He constructed a fine two-story building of native stone for his Bank of Glen Jean. The bank closed in January of 1939. After a disagreement and court battle with the Chesapeake & Ohio Railway, McKell built his own branch railroad to connect with the C&O's competitor, the Virginian Railway, at Pax. Completed in 1913, this 15-mile railway was a short line with a long name—Kanawha, Glen Jean, & Eastern. A lifelong bachelor, Bill McKell took an active interest in sports and Fayette County Republican politics. He developed a slow-pitch softball game called "Let-em-hit-it" that became a favorite local pastime.

By the mid-1930s McKell was facing competition from other coal operations, such as the New River Company, and the organizing efforts of union miners. Failing health forced McKell to return to Ohio where a cousin cared for him. As his empire began to collapse, William McKell died in August of 1939. His holdings were sold to the New River Company of Mount Hope.

W. Eugene Cox
National Park Service

McKendree Hospital

The completion of the Chesapeake & Ohio Railroad in 1873 opened the New River Gorge to the coal and timber industry. By the turn of the century numerous coal mines were in operation, and many accidents were occurring in this hazardous occupation. The medical system was overwhelmed with the sudden population increase created by the mining and lumber industry boom, and improvements were urgently required. In recognition of this need the West Virginia legislature passed an act on February 24, 1899, providing for the construction of three hospitals, Miners Hospitals 1, 2, and 3. Later, all three would be known for the towns in which they were located. Named for its small community nestled on the east side of the deep New River Gorge, Miners Hospital No. 2 became known as McKendree Number 2. Miners Hospital No. 1 was located at Welch, with No. 3 in Fairmont.

McKendree Hospital started providing medical care in November 1901. An interesting feature of the legislation that created these hospitals was that those engaged in hazardous occupations were to be treated free of charge. In 1903 about 63 percent of McKendree's patients were miners. Patients other than coal miners were charged $1.59 per day in 1902. A two-year nurses' training school opened at McKendree on March 1, 1910. McKendree was converted to a home for elderly African-American patients in the early 1940s. The hospital that had served the New River communities so faithfully was abandoned a decade later and was subsequently torn down.

W. Eugene Cox
National Park Service

William E. Cox, "McKendree No. 2: The Story of West Virginia's Miners Hospitals," *Goldenseal*, Fall 1981; Paul Nyden, "Mabel Gwinn, New River Nurse," *Goldenseal*, Fall 1981.

McKinley's Palace

One of West Virginia's most famous and elegant mansions is Willow Glen, known in the Wheeling area as McKinley's Palace. Requiring six years to build (1914–20), the mansion was the gift of Johnson Camden McKinley to his new bride, Agra Bennett McKinley.

Born in Parkersburg, McKinley came to Wheeling in 1893, and by 1908 had become a millionaire coal operator. He was named for his uncle, the industrialist and U.S. senator, Johnson Newlon Camden. His young wife, a member of Weston's distinguished Bennett family, had on her 18th birthday been presented at the court of King George V and Queen Mary of England.

Built of locally quarried sandstone, Willow Glen featured a grand salon where more than 300 guests danced to the music of Fred Waring at the mansion's completion in 1920. In addition to the ballroom, Willow Glen had 11 bedrooms, eight baths, a formal dining room, a library, a billiards room, and, in the basement, a mine that provided coal for the furnace. The mansion was furnished with treasures from the McKinleys' extensive travels, each room containing some unique objet d'art or item of furniture, such as a bed once owned by Benjamin Franklin. Many of the stained-glass windows and other interior features, such as lighting and metal fixtures, were especially designed for the home by Tiffany Studios.

Designed by Pennsylvania architect Fred Dempwolf, the house was added to the National Register of Historic Places in 1983. Willow Glen is still privately owned and occupied, with its 1920s grandeur intact.

Louis E. Keefer
Reston, Virginia
Olive Watson
Wheeling

Irene McKinney

Poet Laureate Irene McKinney was born April 20, 1939, in Belington, Barbour County. She received her bachelor's degree from West Virginia Wesleyan College in 1968, her master's from West Virginia University in 1970, and her Ph.D. from the University of Utah in 1980. Her first book of poems, *The Girl with the Stone in Her Lap*, was published in 1976. She is the director of creative writing at West Virginia Wesleyan College, having also taught at the University of California at Santa Cruz, the University of Utah, and Huttonsville Correctional Center.

In 1984, McKinney's collection of poetry, *The Wasps at the Blue Hexagon*, was published. She won a poetry fellowship

from the National Endowment for the Arts in 1985. She has also won the Utah Arts Council Prize Award in Fiction, the Breadloaf Scholarship, the Cincinnati Review Annual Poetry Prize, the Kentucky Foundation for Women Award, and the Appalachian Mellon Fellowship. Governor Caperton appointed her state poet laureate in 1993. McKinney has served as poet-in-residence for the West Virginia Commission on the Arts and is the co-founder of *Trellis*, a West Virginia poetry journal. Her other collections of poetry are *Quick Fire and Slow Fire* (1988) and *Six O'clock Mine Report* (1989).

Irene McKinney lives in Buckhannon.

James Slack
Charleston

J. Kemp McLaughlin

Aviator James Kemp McLaughlin was born in Braxton County, December 7, 1918. He began his military career in September 1941 as a cadet in the Army Air Corps. Early in 1942, Lieutenant McLaughlin was assigned to the 92nd heavy bombardment group of the Eighth Air Force. The 92nd was among the first American units to see combat.

In October 1943, Captain McLaughlin piloted the lead bomber in a mission against the ball-bearing works of Schweinfurt, Germany. Two-hundred-sixty B17 bombers participated in the raid which is considered the biggest aerial battle in history. Referred to as "Black Thursday," 25 percent of the American force was lost but an estimated 70 percent of the German ball-bearing production facilities was destroyed, seriously weakening the Nazi war effort. In November 1943, McLaughlin participated in bombing facilities in Norway which were crucial in the German attempts to develop an atomic bomb. His B17 returned to base with an engine on fire after pursuit by Luftwaffe fighters.

A lieutenant colonel at war's end, McLaughlin had flown 39 combat missions and was awarded the Distinguished Flying Cross with three clusters, the U.S. Army Air Corps Air Medal with eight clusters, the French Croix de Guerre, and a Presidential Unit Citation. After the war McLaughlin founded the West Virginia Air National Guard, of which he was the first commander. In 1951, he led the squadron on active duty in the Korean War. Following service in Korea he was promoted to full colonel, and in 1962 he was appointed assistant adjutant general with promotion to brigadier general.

Retired in 1977 from the military, he served as Kanawha County commissioner from 1962 to 1968.

See also Air National Guard

Richard A. Andre
Charleston

J. Kemp McLaughlin, *The Mighty Eighth in WWII: A Memoir*, 2000.

McLure Hotel

The grand McLure Hotel opened on the corner of Market and Monroe (now 12th) streets in downtown Wheeling on March 4, 1852, shortly before the Baltimore & Ohio Railroad reached the city. John McLure had relocated from Pennsylvania in 1806 and became a prominent merchant and boat builder. He named his hostelry the McLure House, and it stayed in the family through four generations. The original hotel had 165 rooms and an open court with a watering trough and hitching posts. The McLure was one of the largest and best hotels in the region, and during the Civil War hosted Generals Frémont, Rosecrans, Sherman, and Grant. The founders of West Virginia often gathered there after debating issues of the day at the nearby U.S. Custom House, now known as West Virginia Independence Hall.

The hotel was remodeled in 1899 and grew to 225 rooms. Many famous persons have visited the McLure, among them Jenny Lind, Sara Bernhardt, and John D. Rockefeller. E. M. Statler, the founder of the Statler hotel chain and most famous hotelier of his day, started in the hotel business as a bellboy at the McLure and later became its manager. At least 11 presidents have been guests, including Eisenhower, Kennedy, and Nixon. On February 9, 1950, at the McLure, Sen. Joseph McCarthy delivered the famous speech that began the McCarthy era.

The original building was demolished and an extensive renovation of the hotel was completed in 1985. In 1998, the McLure was purchased by Pelican International Properties and in November 1999 its name was changed to the Ramada Plaza City Center Hotel.

Margaret Brennan
Wheeling Area Historical Society

Louise McNeill

Poet Laureate Louise McNeill was widely praised both early and late in her poetic career. As a poet she also accomplished many of the tasks normally reserved for historian, biographer, and folklorist. There are, as well, a legion of West Virginians who warmly recall Louise McNeill as their professor of history or English.

She was born January 9, 1911, on the family farm in Pocahontas County and died June 19, 1993, near Charleston. Her father, G. D. McNeill, was also an author, having written a still valuable account of the decline of wilderness along the Cranberry and Williams rivers. His book, *The Last Forest,* contained rich anecdotal and narrative material.

Louise McNeill is best remembered as the author of *Gauley Mountain,* her first full-length collection of poems, published by Harcourt Brace (1939) with a foreword by Stephen Vincent Benét. Much is rightly made of its vivid portrayal of character and

Poet Louise McNeill in her prime.

folkways. Although reminiscent of Edgar Lee Masters's *Spoon River Anthology,* her portrayals show a greater depth and poignancy. Additionally, *Gauley Mountain* reveals McNeill as a poet with great technical skill, able to create a masterful range of imagery and rhythm. In all of her work, not only *Gauley Mountain,* she created a wide range of characters, especially rich with the details of life lived in rural Appalachia. McNeill was often hailed for her unflinching acceptance of local speech and dialect into the overall construction of her rhythmic poetry.

McNeill continued publishing poetry throughout her life but did not publish another major collection until 1972. She was appointed poet laureate by Governor Rockefeller in 1979, holding that title until her death. Her later years saw a rebirth of public interest in her work and several important publications, including her prose memoir, *The Milkweed Ladies* (1988). The humble yet rich environment that shaped her psyche and eventually her poems is clearly revealed in this book. The exceptional concluding chapter, "Night at the Commodore," shows how, rooted in family and history, McNeill can see not only for herself, not only for her native West Virginians, but also for the entire nation, the true and ominous magnitude of the unleashing of the atomic bomb.

Also published later in her life was *Hill Daughter: New and Selected Poems* (1991), a compilation underscoring the strength and vitality of the entire body of her work. This book is also important for the revealing biographical introduction written by Maggie Anderson, one of a generation of younger poets influenced by McNeill.

McNeill married Roger Pease in 1939, and was known by his surname as well as her own. She taught history and English at West Virginia University, Potomac State College, Concord College and Fairmont State. In Louise McNeill we had not only a supremely gifted poet and dedicated chronicler of family and folk tradition, we had a writer who could still say: "Until I was sixteen years old, until

the roads came, the farm was about all I knew."

See also Gauley Mountain

Marc Harshman
Wheeling

Louise McNeill, *Gauley Mountain,* 1939; McNeill, *Hill Daughter: New and Selected Poems,* 1991; McNeill, *The Milkweed Ladies,* 1988.

McNeill's Rangers

McNeill's Rangers, a Confederate guerrilla force consisting of Company E of the 18th Virginia Cavalry and the First Virginia Partisan Rangers, began operations in September 1862 under the leadership of Capt. John H. "Hanse" McNeill. Operating out of the Moorefield area, the Rangers attacked Union troops, camps, and property of the vital Baltimore & Ohio Railroad.

While most of their operations were independent, the Rangers would on occasion join up with other partisan groups or Confederate regulars in operations against Union forces. In May 1863, they took part in the wide-ranging Jones-Imboden Raid through much of north-central West Virginia.

Captain McNeill was mortally wounded on October 3, 1864, at a raid on Union forces at Mount Jackson, Virginia. His son, Jesse, took command of the Rangers and led them until the end of the war. On February 21, 1865, they were successful in kidnaping Union generals George Crook and Benjamin Kelley from their hotels in Cumberland, Maryland, and delivered them to Gen. Jubal Early at Staunton, Virginia.

At the end of the war, Jesse McNeill and 30 men surrendered to Union troops on April 24, 1865, at New Creek (now Keyser), thus ending the exploits of the partisan band. Probably never numbering more than 100 men at any time, they managed to do damage to Union operations and tie down troops to a degree far out of proportion to their number.

Jim Barnes
Morgantown

John Blue, *Hanging Rock Rebel,* 1994; Virgil Carrington Jones, *Gray Ghosts and Rebel Raiders,* 1956; John E. Stanchak, "McNeil's Rangers," in Patricia L. Faust, ed., *Historical Times Illustrated Encyclopedia of the Civil War,* 1986.

John Camillus McWhorter

Judge and author John Camillus McWhorter was born July 5, 1866, in Upshur County. His father was a medical doctor, and his grandfather was a Revolutionary War veteran and early settler. McWhorter was educated in the local public schools and at Fairmont State Normal School (now Fairmont State University). He received a law degree from West Virginia University law school in 1894 and entered the practice of law.

McWhorter served as judge of West Virginia's 12th judicial circuit from 1904 to 1913. He was also an active prohibitionist, serving in 1912 as the chairman of the West Virginia Ratification Federation which succeeded that year in passing a prohibition amendment to the West Virginia constitution. McWhorter later drafted the 1913 Yost Law, providing for enforcement of state prohibition, which became effective in 1914.

McWhorter is best remembered for writing *The Scout of the Buckongehanon*. The 1927 novel helped to popularize the legend of Buckongehanon (or Buckongahelas) as the Indian namesake of the Buckhannon River and the town of Buckhannon. McWhorter wove the story of the Pringle brothers and their famous tree of refuge and other regional lore into his historical novel. He also wrote and spoke on the subject of local history and published numerous short stories.

John Camillus McWhorter died March 25, 1937.

See also Buckongahelas

Meadow River

The Meadow River is a major tributary of Gauley River. It has its headwaters along the Greenbrier-Summers county line, in the high mountains northwest of Alderson. From there the Meadow River flows in a northwestward direction to join the Gauley just downstream from Summersville Lake and near Carnifex Ferry Battlefield State Park.

Meadow River rises at an elevation of 3,945 feet and enters the Gauley River at 1,182 feet, for a total descent of 2,763 feet. The lower section of Meadow River, much of which is located within the Gauley River National Recreation Area, is a rocky, turbulent stream. The Meadow is 52.6 miles long, with a watershed of 371.3 square miles. From near Rainelle to its mouth, the Meadow River forms the boundary between Fayette and Greenbrier and Fayette and Nicholas counties.

The rich hardwood timberlands of the Meadow River watershed were harvested in the late 19th and early 20th centuries. The logging of the region had awaited the arrival of railroad transportation, just after 1900, since the rocky river was unsuitable for log drives. The Meadow River Lumber Company operated one of the biggest sawmills in West Virginia at Rainelle until 1970.

Rainelle and Rupert are located in the Meadow River Valley, as are many smaller communities. The major tributaries of Meadow River are Anglins, Brackens, Glade, Meadow, Sewell and Little Sewell, and Big Clear and Little Clear creeks. The Meadow River is followed for several miles in Greenbrier County by U.S. 60, the historic route of the James River & Kanawha Turnpike, and the river is paralleled for most of its length by a railroad. Interstate 64 intercepts the headwaters of Meadow River at Dawson, Greenbrier County.

Meadow River Lumber Company

During the first decade of the 1900s, brothers Thomas and John Raine incorporated the Meadow River Lumber Company and purchased 32,000 acres of timber in western Greenbrier County. There they built a large sawmill, the town of Rainelle, and a 20-mile railroad. Thomas Raine was president of the company until 1912, when John became president until 1938. Later, Howard Gray was president until 1961, and his son was president until the company was sold to Georgia-Pacific in 1970.

The original 1910 sawmill burned in August 1924 and was rebuilt by March 1925 with three nine-foot band saws. At its peak, the Rainelle mill cut an average of 110,000 board feet per day and was the world's largest hardwood sawmill. From the early 1930s until the 1960s, the mill sawed an average of 20 million board feet per year. In 1928, a record 31.6 million board feet was sawed.

Meadow River Lumber Company operated a system of portable lumber camps built on railroad cars that could be moved to new timber supplies. The company eventually owned 75,000 acres and also bought timber from nearby coal and land companies. Teams of horses skidded the logs to the railroad until 1930, when the company switched to overhead cable skidders mounted on railroad cars. These skidders could move logs within a three-quarter-mile circle to a central point for transport to the sawmill.

Boards were air dried in 40-foot stacks and then in one of 14 dry kilns before being sold or processed into products. The company operated a furniture plant until World War II and a planing mill which manufactured such items as stair treads, baseboards, and molding. A flooring plant averaged one million feet per month, and a shoe heel plant produced four million to six million wooden heels per year.

Rainelle was a model company town with public water, electricity, and nice houses with yards and garden plots. Georgia-Pacific tore down the outdated mill in 1975 and rebuilt at a new location. The original mill site is now a shopping center.

See also Rainelle

William N. Grafton
WVU Extension Service

Clarence Watson Meadows

Clarence Watson Meadows, the 22nd governor of West Virginia (1945–49), was born in Beckley, February 11, 1904. His mother hoped he would become a Baptist minister, but he ultimately followed his father's bent and entered politics. While growing up, Clarence often appeared in

Governor Clarence W. Meadows (1904–61).

minstrel shows, comedies, and dramas in his community. His penchant for acting carried over to his undergraduate years at Washington and Lee University and into his adult career when he established Beckley's Little Theater and men's chorus. As for his mother's wishes, Governor Meadows explained that he never quite felt he had received "the call," although he did serve as a Sunday school teacher and Baptist deacon.

Following his graduation from college, Meadows entered law school at the University of Alabama, where he received his degree in 1927. After working a year in a Birmingham law firm, he returned to Beckley and set up his own practice. In 1930, the Raleigh County Democrat was elected to the West Virginia House of Delegates. Two years later he left the legislature and won election as prosecuting attorney in his home county. In 1934, Meadows married Nancy Massie of Clifton Forge, Virginia, a marriage that produced four daughters. Not content with county office, the energetic politician captured the post of state attorney general in 1936 and was reelected in 1940. In May 1942, Governor Neely appointed Meadows to fill the vacant Tenth Circuit judgeship, to which he won election to a full term in 1943.

The popular and congenial Meadows jumped into the 1944 Democratic gubernatorial primary, winning 52 of the 55 counties. He went on to a 64,000-vote victory over Republican D. Boone Dawson of Charleston in the November general election. His election was well received. Even the opposition had good things to say about the governor-elect, as evidenced in a Republican newspaper editorial that described Meadows as a "conscientious, honest and trustworthy public official."

On inauguration day, Meadows appointed Okey L. Patteson of Mount Hope to the newly created position of executive assistant. Four years later, Patteson would succeed Meadows as governor. Meadows was vitally interested in improving the public schools and quickly introduced legislation calling for a $30 per month pay raise for teachers with additional increments promised. In addition he commissioned Dr. George D. Strayer of Columbus, Ohio, to undertake a broad study of the state's school system. Two years later, the Strayer Report was released, calling for increased funding of education via a more equitable statewide assessment of the property taxes that supplied the bulk of education funds.

Meadows also realized the importance of improving transportation. In November 1947, he dedicated Charleston's Kanawha Airport (now Yeager Airport). "Today, the very heart of West Virginia has been opened to the people of the world," he observed at the airport dedication. The following year, he proposed a $50 million "farm-to-market" road bond issue, which was overwhelmingly approved by voters.

Among Meadows's last acts as governor was his call for the construction of a state office building to replace scattered rental space that cost the state perhaps $100,000 annually. This building, designed by Cass Gilbert Jr., the son of the original capitol architect, is second in architectural significance only to the nearby capitol building. Moreover, he recommended a pay raise for all state employees to encourage them not to leave for higher-paying jobs in the private sector.

After leaving office in 1949, Meadows opened a law office in Charleston and also dabbled in oil and gas ventures. Six years later, he moved to Fort Lauderdale, Florida, where he continued to practice law while engaging in real estate development. In August 1961, while visiting his wife's family in Clifton Forge, he became ill and was hospitalized. A few weeks later, on September 12, 1961, he died at age 57 due to a combination of heart and kidney problems. Meadows was buried in Clifton Forge but, a year later, the body was reinterred in Beckley's Wildwood Cemetery.

See also Strayer Report

Paul F. Lutz
Marshall University

Mechanization Agreement

The National Bituminous Coal Wage Agreement of 1950 between the United Mine Workers of America and the Bituminous Coal Operators Association is referred to as the Mechanization Agreement since it authorized extensive mechanization in union coal mines.

Mechanization had been increasing in the mines since the 1920s, but it was in the late 1940s that the United Mine Workers decided to actively encourage mechanization as a way to reorganize the indus-

try. The decision had many ramifications. Mechanization would increase productivity and reduce costs, while forcing the marginal mines to close. Mechanization would strengthen the larger companies and the larger mines, since they had the resources to invest in machinery and the capacity and reserves to use the machinery efficiently.

Mining jobs were lost with the increased use of machines and the closing of inefficient mines. The strategy of the UMWA was that higher wages and better working conditions could occur only through mine mechanization and the employment trade-off was worth that price. Thus, faced with a declining market for coal from increased use of oil, UMWA President John L. Lewis decided in the late 1940s that the union would use its economic power to reorganize the industry and encourage mechanization. The result would be fewer miners working for higher wages.

Immediately prior to the 1950 agreement, major coal companies representing the steel companies and northern operators came together and formed the BCOA. The UMWA and BCOA then negotiated the 1950 and future contracts based on the understanding that the union would not resist mechanization in exchange for being entitled to a share of the proceeds.

See also Coal Mine Mechanization

John David
WVU Institute of Technology

Medicine

The practice of medicine in West Virginia is both specialized and generalized, urban and rural. Qualified physicians work in solo and group private practices, rural clinics, large and small hospitals, university health science centers, free clinics, health departments, nursing homes, corporations, and HMOs, and some make house calls.

The practitioners include both medical doctors and doctors of osteopathy. In 2003, there were 3,575 MDs and 507 DOs practicing in West Virginia. The overall physician-to-population ratio is 180 doctors per 100,000 people, compared with 198 per 100,000 nationally, ranking the state 29th in the nation. West Virginia has 125 specialists and 54 primary care physicians per 100,000 population, compared with national figures of 139 and 59, respectively. The overwhelming majority of physicians have office-based practices, with 90 percent engaged in direct patient care.

Thirty-six percent of active physicians are graduates of foreign medical schools, one-third came from in-state medical schools and residency programs, and 31 percent trained elsewhere in the United States. Sixty-eight percent of physicians are between 35 and 64 years old, similar to national figures. The average age is 46.

Three-fourths of physicians are white. Asians and Pacific Islanders are the second largest group (20 percent), with African-Americans at one percent and Hispanics at three percent. Female physicians were 18.9 percent of the total in 2001, nearly one-fifth. The number of doctors in West Virginia is growing, although at a slower rate than nationally.

West Virginia's physicians serve a population of approximately 1.8 million, 35th in the nation. West Virginia is the second most rural state. Its population is also the oldest, with the highest median age, 38.9 years in 2000. The uninsured population is 17 percent higher than the national average. Lack of access to a primary health care provider (30 percent) is higher than the U.S. figure (17 percent). The percentage of people living below 200 percent of the poverty level is 43 percent, contrasted to 31 percent nationally. Of the 55 counties, the federal government has designated 95 percent as medically under-served or as having a health provider shortage.

West Virginia physicians are trained at three state-supported medical schools. West Virginia University School of Medicine was founded in 1902 and is in Morgantown. It has a clinical campus in Charleston affiliated with Charleston Area Medical Center, and another regional campus in Martinsburg. The West Virginia School of Osteopathic Medicine, located in Lewisburg, was established in 1972. It prepares family physicians for West Virginia and surrounding Appalachian states. Marshall University School of Medicine, located in Huntington, was established in 1977. Its mission is to prepare rural primary care physicians through undergraduate and residency training.

All three schools train medical students along with other health science students through the state-funded Rural Health Education Partnerships. In 2004, there were 184 medical school graduates in West Virginia, including 72 graduates of the School of Osteopathic Medicine, with females making up 40 percent of all West Virginia medical school graduates. Students at West Virginia medical schools were 92 percent white, six percent Asian and Pacific Islander, and two percent African-American.

The origins of our state's medical practice may be traced to the latter part of the 18th century. The Appalachian Mountains posed a major obstacle to the practice of medicine, due to travel difficulties west of the Shenandoah Valley. One of the earliest physicians in present West Virginia was Dr. Jesse Bennet, who set up a practice near Point Pleasant on the Ohio River in the 1790s. Other doctors followed, establishing practices near navigable waterways such as the Kanawha, Ohio, and Monongahela rivers. The advent of railways and better roads contributed to the expansion of medical practice in the 19th century.

The scarcity of medical practitioners in West Virginia has fostered a tradition of folk medicine. This is due to the wide availability of herbal cures in the rural countryside, plus the independent, self-reliant nature of the Appalachian people. While untrained "granny" midwives and self-taught folk doctors are largely a thing of the past, West Virginians have participated in the recent revival of herbal remedies. Nurse-midwives historically have provided many in-home deliveries, and the tradition continues in modern birthing centers. Several prominent leaders in public health and community medicine have worked in the Mountain State.

The medical profession became organized in 1867 when Dr. James Edmund Reeves and 32 of his colleagues established the West Virginia State Medical Association. The West Virginia Society of Osteopathic Medicine was established in 1902.

Starting in the late 19th and into the early 20th century, the genesis of the modern system of rural primary care delivery was found in the West Virginia coalfields. There "coal camp doctors" provided needed care to coal miners and their families through pre-paid, per capita financing, a precursor to the modern health-maintenance organization. Since mid-century, the United Mine Workers union and small communities built upon this innovation by providing country doctors through rural medical centers. With help from the Appalachian Regional Commission, private and religious foundations, and state and federal resources, there are today more than 80 rural primary care centers throughout the state.

Major challenges confront the practice of medicine in West Virginia in the 21st century. They include a sluggish economy, large numbers of uninsured patients, inadequate reimbursement, and rising costs of malpractice insurance. Exacerbating the situation, West Virginia manifests numerous unhealthy statistics. For example, deaths (before age 65) due to injuries, sudden infant death, congenital anomalies, diabetes, heart disease, suicide, cancer, and lung disease exceed national rates significantly. Risk factors—smokeless tobacco use, physical inactivity, obesity, hypertension, and cigarette smoking—contribute to excessive rates of premature mortality. Costs are enormous and measured in human, social, and economic terms.

Regardless of obstacles, the medical practice in West Virginia remains healthy. A new generation of medical practitioners is being prepared to advance the cause of patient care while improving the health of the public into the 21st century.

See also Country Doctors, Public Health

Lamont D. Nottingham
WVU School of Medicine

Memorial Arch

The Memorial Arch, the only structure of its kind in West Virginia, stands at the intersection of 11th Avenue and Memorial Boulevard in Huntington. The clean lines of this impressive arch reflect the solemn nature of its purpose as a tribute to Cabell County soldiers who fought in World War I.

The arch was designed by Huntington architect Jerry DeYoung, and it is patterned after the Arc de Triomphe in Paris. The arch is 42 feet tall, 34 feet wide, and nine feet thick. The exterior is made of Indiana limestone.

In the early 1920s, the Cabell County War Memorial Association was formed. This group drafted plans for a boulevard and a suitable memorial, and it was responsible for the erection of the Memorial Arch. On November 11, 1924, Armistice Day, the cornerstone was laid.

The arch cost $40,000 to build. It took the association almost ten years to raise the money, and much of the labor and materials were donated. After eight years of intermittent construction, in the fall of 1929 work on the monument was completed. The ceremony of dedication of the Memorial Arch was held on November 11, 1929.

Joseph Platania
Huntington

Memorial Day

The Memorial Day tradition originated during and soon after the Civil War when women, perhaps first in the South, began to gather to decorate the graves of fallen soldiers. At the war's end the practice was adopted by the Grand Army of the Republic, a Union veterans organization, which in 1868 established May 30 as Decoration Day. Memorial Day was first established as an official state holiday, May 30, by New York in 1873. Now Memorial Day is a holiday throughout the United States, observed on the last Monday in May since 1968.

Memorial Day is observed in West Virginia in the same way as in other parts of the country. West Virginia National Cemetery at Grafton observes the holiday on Sunday of Memorial Day weekend, while the old Grafton National Cemetery has a larger celebration on the following Monday. The holiday is observed in countless other public and private services statewide, and the long weekend signals the beginning of summer.

The observance of Memorial Day in West Virginia arises from other, unofficial roots as well. It was common here and in other parts of Appalachia to bury the dead without funeral services during the hard winter months when travel was difficult. Then in the spring a memorial service was held for those people who had died during the winter, often in May when abundant flowers were available. The graveyard was cleaned and graves decorated, either on the day of the service or in preparation for it, and families gathered together to attend to these important duties.

This practice continued as an annual memorial service in church cemeteries and family graveyards even after transportation improved and it was no longer necessary to delay winter funerals. Often the service lasted much of the day, with "dinner on the ground" at noon. These services, primarily religious and sentimental rather than patriotic in nature and which may be celebrated on Memorial Day or at some other time of the congregation's choosing, survive in some rural areas today.

See also Holidays and Celebrations

James K. Crissman, *Death and Dying in Central Appalachia*, 1994.

Mennonites

The first Mennonites in present West Virginia settled near Lewisburg in 1788 when preacher Isaac Kauffman (Coffman), his wife, and eight children moved from Page County, Virginia. While no congregation was established, the Greenbrier Mennonites likely held religious meetings in their homes, a common practice among Virginia Mennonites of that time.

The roots of the Mennonite Church lay in the Anabaptist movement arising in Zurich, Switzerland, in the 16th century. Anabaptists believed in baptizing only adults old enough to decide religious matters for themselves; that church and state should be separate; and that individuals should be free to live and worship according to conscience. Stressing literal obedience to Christ's commandments, Anabaptists refused to swear oaths or go to war. In 1536, a former Catholic priest by the name of Menno Simons joined the movement. Due to his influential leadership, Anabaptists were commonly called Menists or Mennonists, and later, Mennonites.

Persecution and economic hardship in Europe spurred immigration to North America. Mennonites first came to Pennsylvania in 1683, gradually spreading south into the Shenandoah Valley of Virginia.

In the late 1850s, two Mennonite ministers from the Shenandoah Valley made preaching forays across the mountain to the west. During the Civil War, Potter John Heatwole lived in the Seneca Rocks area. He was one of several Mennonites who took refuge in the mountains to avoid being forced to fight in the war. After the Civil War, Mennonite circuit riders expanded their preaching trips into Pendleton, Randolph, Tucker, and Hardy counties.

Around 1884, Mennonites erected their first meetinghouse in West Virginia in Pendleton County near Seneca Rocks. In 1913, the building was moved to Roaring Creek and reassembled. It still stands and is known as the Roaring Mennonite Church. About 1890, a meetinghouse was built near Lost River in Hardy County. In the late 1800s and early 1900s, additional congregations were established in the areas covered by the circuit riders. Resident leaders replaced the circuit riders.

As the 20th century progressed, the Mennonite mosaic in West Virginia became quite diverse. New congregations started in Pocahontas (1959), Monroe (1976), Barbour (1982), Hampshire (2000), and Greenbrier (2003) counties. Congregations are affiliated with various branches of the Mennonite Church, including Beachy Amish Mennonite Church, Mennonite Christian Fellowship, the Allegheny and Virginia conferences of the Mennonite Church USA, Mountain Valley Mennonite Churches, and Southeastern Mennonite Conference. In 2000, there were 13 Mennonite congregations in West Virginia with a total of 568 adherents.

Some Mennonites continue to practice plain ways of dressing, living, and worship while others have adapted to the general surrounding culture. Probably most in West Virginia are of the more traditional type as regards dress but are fairly modern in the use of technology. Few if any forego the use of automobiles and electricity.

See also Religion

John R. Swartz
Petersburg

Harry A. Brunk, *History of the Mennonites in Virginia 1900–1960,* 1972.

Mercer County

Mercer County is among the most diverse and complex of West Virginia's 55 counties. Its 423.9 square miles range from the rolling farmland of the New River Valley on the east, to the craggy promontory of Pinnacle Rock State Park to the west, and the coalfields beyond. Mercer County's history is as varied as its geography.

Drained by the New, Bluestone, and East rivers, Mercer County has the highest mean elevation of any of the state's counties. Its most prominent topographic features are the towering edifice of East River Mountain to the south and the Bluestone Gorge to the northeast. Mercer lies on the Virginia state line, surrounded by Summers, Raleigh, Wyoming, and McDowell counties in West Virginia, and the Virginia counties of Giles, Bland, and Tazewell. Substantial evidence attests to the prehistoric habitation of the region, including palisaded Mississippian culture corn-farming villages at Crump's Bottom and Clover Bottom.

Fog-shrouded Bluestone Gorge in Mercer County.

White settlers migrated into the region before 1800, and established settlements at Beaver Pond, Lake Shawnee, Oakvale, and Flat Top. There was no resident native population at the time of white settlement, but the region participated in the bloody conflict with Indian raiders that characterized the late 18th century. Additional settlers, including Primitive Baptist dissenters at Camp Creek, brought the population to 2,000 by 1837, when Mercer County was created from parts of Giles and Tazewell counties. The county was named for Revolutionary War Gen. Hugh Mercer. Princeton, the new county seat, was named for the 1777 Battle of Princeton, New Jersey, at which General Mercer fell. Most of the people were farmers, growing corn, oats, and wheat, and in their isolation they created a self-sustaining local economy including a saltworks, tannery, gristmill, and foundry.

The sectional tensions that brought on the Civil War found Mercer County decidedly southern in its sentiments. There were several hundred slaves among the 6,000 inhabitants of 1860. Remoteness and rugged terrain kept Mercer County from playing a significant role in the conflict, yet incursions by both sides resulted in skirmishes in the New River Valley and especially at Princeton, where the May 1862 Battle of Pigeon's Roost resulted in the burning of the county seat. Several companies of Confederate troops were recruited from the eastern portion of the county along the New River.

Reconstruction brought turmoil to Mercer County, as the state-making Republican Unionists created Summers County in 1871, stripping some 128 square miles from Mercer. Moreover, state authorities in Wheeling tried to move the county seat from secessionist Princeton to Athens, but West Virginia's "redemption" by the Democrats in 1872 returned

county government and the all-important land records to Princeton.

The most significant events in the county's history occurred after the Civil War, as railroads and coal mining rapidly industrialized southern West Virginia. Large areas of Mercer County in its northwestern portion are underlain with massive deposits of the famed "smokeless" Pocahontas No. 3 coal seam, which became a target of aggressive northern capitalists. Mining began soon after the Norfolk & Western Railway arrived in 1883. The first mine opened on Mill Creek at Coopers in 1884, and soon coal operators from Pennsylvania began opening mines along the Bluestone River, at Buckeye, Duhring, Goodwill, and Freeman.

Coal mining was labor intensive, and the population of Mercer County grew dramatically, rising from 7,500 in 1880 to 16,000 in 1890, 23,000 in 1900, and 50,000 in 1920. The increasingly diverse population included large numbers of African-Americans and southern and eastern European immigrants. Large mining operations opened at McComas, Turkey Gap, and Coopers, and the "Millionaires' Town" of Bramwell grew up suddenly. In 1942, Mercer County's 3,500 miners produced 3,500,000 tons of coal. A huge DuPont plant produced gunpowder at Nemours.

Even more significantly, the N&W had chosen an open meadow at the headwaters of the Bluestone and East rivers for its Pocahontas Division headquarters. Naming the new community Bluefield for the azure chicory growing along neighboring Stony Ridge, the railroad attracted utilities, banks, and wholesale and retail warehouses to the new town. Soon Bluefield was the largest community in the county, and one of West Virginia's major cities. Huge stone buildings such as the 12-story West Virginian Hotel

FAST FACTS ABOUT MERCER COUNTY

Founded: 1837

Land in square miles: 423.9

Population: 62,980

Percentage minorities: 7.4%

Percentage rural: 46.9%

Median age: 40.2

Percentage 65 and older: 17.4%

Birth rate per 1,000 population: 12.5

Median household income: $26,628

High school graduate or higher: 72.1%

Bachelor's degree or higher: 13.8%

Home ownership: 76.8%

Median home value: $63,900

This information is from the 2000 U.S. Census. In 2000, West Virginia as a whole had 5 percent minorities, a median age of 38.9, median household income of $29,696, and a 75.2 percent home ownership rate.

symbolized both the power of the coal industry and the rapid transformation which had occurred.

As the new industrial city grew, another courthouse struggle ensued in 1906. This time Democratic Princeton barely defeated Republican Bluefield in the battle for the county seat. When the rival Virginian Railroad chose Princeton for its regional headquarters, the county seat, too, began to share the growth produced by the coal industry.

Mercer County's population continued to grow robustly until 1950, when its 75,000 residents began to feel the effects of mechanization of the mining industry. Thereafter the number of Mercer Countians declined, to 62,980 by 2000. Transportation connections wrought yet another series of changes, as the intersection of four-lane U.S. 460 and Interstate 77 near Princeton again reshaped county population and settlement patterns. The 1974 completion of East River Mountain Tunnel on I-77 eliminated a long-standing barrier to north-south traffic across the state line. The railroads, now all part of Norfolk Southern Corporation, remain important in the Mercer County economy.

No Mercer Countian has served as West Virginia governor, although Bluefield's powerful Democratic Kee family held the Fifth District seat in the U.S. House of Representatives from 1932 to 1972. Elizabeth Kee became the Mountain State's first woman in Congress. Prominent Mercer Countians include Bluefield's Hugh Ike Shott, politician and editor of the influential *Bluefield Daily Telegraph*. Howard B. Lee served as attorney general of the state from 1925 to 1933. Bluefield was home to the feared Baldwin-Felts Detective Agency, pioneer radio station WHIS, and Nobel Prize winner John Forbes Nash. W. M. Ritter's timber operation began at Oakvale. Mercer County is home to

Bluefield State College and Concord University, both institutions of the West Virginia higher education system. Hank Williams was last seen alive in Bluefield, and Cal Ripken Jr. played minor league baseball for the Bluefield Orioles. Mercer County has 16 sites listed on the National Register of Historic Places.

See also Bluefield, Princeton

C. Stuart McGehee
West Virginia State University

David E. Johnston, *A History of Middle New River Settlements and Contiguous Territory*, 1906; Kyle McCormick, *The Story of Mercer County*, 1957; Mercer County Historical Society, *Mercer County History*, 1984, 1985.

Mercer Healing Springs

Mercer Healing Springs, located between Princeton and Athens in central Mercer County, was the site of a successful health and recreational resort in the early years of the 20th century. The spring itself, discovered sometime between 1870 and 1880, was reputed to have medicinal properties but was not commercially developed until around 1900 when the Mercer Healing Springs Corporation was formed. The original buildings included a springhouse, bathhouse, stables, and cottages for guests.

Sometime prior to 1908, the company was bought out by original member Rufus G. Meador. In 1911, Meador reportedly invested $60,000 in constructing a new four-story 65-room hotel, which featured full-length front and back porches, a ballroom, and special rooms for music, reading, and games. Mercer Healing Springs was popular with area residents for summer activities until 1922, when a disastrous fire completely destroyed the hotel and effectively put an end to the resort as a business concern. Today the property is privately owned.

See also Mineral Springs

Michael M. Meador
Abingdon, Virginia

Stan Cohen, *Historic Springs of the Virginias: A Pictorial History*, 1983; Michael M. Meador, "Taking the Waters: The Mercer Healing Springs Resort," *Goldenseal*, Fall 1982.

Methodists

By the time West Virginia was established in 1863, the Methodist Church claimed the largest number of congregations in the new state. Challenged only by the Baptists, Methodism had been successful in meeting the needs of people scattered in sparsely populated settlements throughout the mountains.

Several reasons account for the success of Methodism in West Virginia. First, the organizational structure of the church allowed a small number of people to create a "class" led by a local lay leader. These classes were linked by ordained clergymen who visited regularly to lead worship services and to administer the sacraments. The geographical area over which these clergymen rode was called a circuit, and the clergymen were called circuit riders. The classes in a circuit were bound together in a quarterly conference, and several circuits were grouped together into an annual conference. Conferences met for worship and instruction, and the annual conference assigned pastors to the circuits.

The second reason for the success of Methodism was the inspiring commitment of the leadership of the early church and their circuit riders. Bishop Francis Asbury, the best-known early American Methodist, visited West Virginia more than 30 times. Bishop Asbury's enthusiasm and dedication were replicated by circuit riders Robert Ayres, Asa Shinn, Henry Bascom, Thomas Ware, John Smith, and many others who rode circuits in West Virginia in the late 18th and early 19th centuries.

The third reason for the success of Methodism was the democratic theology of its message. Unlike the Congregational and Presbyterian denominations, in which salvation was reserved for a few, the message of Methodism was that salvation was attainable by all. While the organization of Methodism was authoritarian, the theology of founder John Wesley and his followers treated all people as equals—a popular view in frontier America.

Two Methodist circuits were established in the area of West Virginia in the 1780s. The Redstone Circuit included southwestern Pennsylvania and northern West Virginia. It was eventually subdivided into the Ohio Circuit to the north and the Clarksburg Circuit to the south, the latter located primarily in West Virginia. The second was the Greenbrier Circuit in southeastern West Virginia. Perhaps the earliest class on the Greenbrier Circuit was formed a few miles from Union, Monroe County, in 1780. By 1786, the class had erected Rehoboth Church, claimed to be the first church built west of the Allegheny Mountains. Bishop Asbury visited Rehoboth several times, holding sessions of the Greenbrier Conference there in 1792, 1793, and 1796. From here Methodism continued to move west into the Kanawha Valley, where the Little Kanawha Circuit was formed in 1799.

The early part of the 19th century saw a tremendous increase in religious zeal, sparked in part by the Second Great Awakening. Methodism participated extensively in this movement, and as congregations grew they encountered differences that eventually led to schisms, two of which were felt keenly in West Virginia. The Methodist Protestant Church (1830) grew out of differences over the authority of the bishop and the role of the laity. The Methodist Episcopal Church, South (1844), a more divisive rift, was created primarily by differences over slavery. A "Plan of Separation" was drafted in an effort to seek an amicable dissolution, but this was a failure from the outset and intense competition erupted to claim congregations for the Northern Methodists or the Southern Methodists. West Virginia was a major battleground in this struggle, and Northern Methodist clergy were a major force in the movement for statehood.

Before the century ended, controversy over the holiness movement and creationism led to further division. The Church of the Nazarene, the Pilgrim Holiness movement, and several other denominations or movements resulted from these controversies. Each established congregations in West Virginia, further fragmenting the Methodist movement.

But Methodism was not all discord. Congregations in the three branches of Methodism ministered effectively to their communities, contributed to missionary outreach, and established or participated in church-sponsored education. The Northern Methodists established West Virginia Wesleyan College, and the Southern Methodists established Morris Harvey College (now the University of Charleston).

During the early 20th century, all three branches of Methodism became more structured and more urbanized. Members of the clergy were increasingly better educated, and the church assumed a more aggressive social mission. While this growth often created tension between the church leadership and the rank-and-file, membership grew rapidly throughout the state. Unlike the previous century, the 20th century became one of reconciliation and reunification. After more than 25 years of negotiations, the three major branches of Methodism, the Methodist Episcopal Church, the Methodist Episcopal Church, South, and the Methodist Protestant Church, merged in 1939 into a single Methodist Church.

In 1968, the Methodist Church merged with the Evangelical United Brethren Church, itself the result of a merger of the United Brethren in Christ (UB) and the Evangelical Association (EV) in 1946, to create the United Methodist Church. The UB and EV denominations had developed primarily among the German-speaking populations of Pennsylvania, Maryland, and Virginia. The UB church was a significant force in West Virginia from the 1820s, but the Evangelical Association had only a handful of congregations in the state.

Today United Methodism is faced with interesting challenges. The episcopal and educational leaders of the denomination move toward a vision of a global church, but many local congregations, particularly in small towns and rural areas, remain wary of such views. Membership, while increasing in other countries, is now declining in the United States and West Virginia. There are 125,336 members of 1,341 United Methodist churches in West Virginia, according to a 2000 church survey.

See also Francis Asbury, Religion, United Brethren

Robert L. Frey
Miamisburg, Ohio
B. B. Maurer and Keith A. Muhleman, *Mission in the Mountain State,* 1981; Frederick A. Norwood, *The Story of American Methodism,* 1974.

Metropolitan Theater

The Metropolitan Theater in downtown Morgantown was billed as "West Virginia's most beautiful playhouse" when it opened in 1924. Architect C. W. Bates was commissioned to build the theater by the Comuntzis brothers, Greek immigrant businessmen. The finished building cost more than $500,000 and was one of the state's finest examples of neoclassical revival architecture, a scaled-down version of New York's famous Metropolitan Opera House. Opening night featured a vaudeville program. The theater stopped featuring such acts in September 1928, and booked its first talking motion picture six months later.

The Metropolitan was the only one of Morgantown's four theaters left open by 1931. It was known as "The House of the Pipe Organ" because of the large organ that accompanied performances. Some of the era's biggest stars performed at the theater, including Bing Crosby, Bob Hope, Helen Hayes, and Jack Benny. After World War II, the theater began to show mostly movies. Later, West Virginia University used it for classes and local dance companies for recitals. It was placed on the National Register of Historic Places in 1984, but closed just three years later.

Efforts to renovate the theater began in the early 1990s. The Metropolitan Theater opened again in the fall of 2003.

Greg Moore
Charleston Gazette

M. Blane Michael

Federal Judge M. Blane Michael was born February 17, 1943, in Charleston, South Carolina. He grew up in Grant County, graduating from West Virginia University in 1965 and New York University School of Law in 1968. He worked at the Wall Street law firm Sullivan & Cromwell from 1968 to 1971. He served as assistant U.S. attorney, Southern District of New York, from 1971 to 1972.

Michael returned to West Virginia in 1972 to care for his ailing father. He was appointed special U.S. assistant attorney, Northern District of West Virginia, in 1972. He operated a solo law practice in Petersburg from 1973 to 1975, then became a law clerk to Judge Robert Maxwell in the U.S. District Court for the Northern District of West Virginia in 1975–76.

After his father's death, Michael moved to Charleston and served as special counsel to Governor Rockefeller from 1977 to 1980. Remaining active in Democratic politics, Michael ran political campaigns for Rockefeller and U.S. Sen. Robert C. Byrd. He joined the Charleston law firm Jackson & Kelly in 1981 and was a partner in the firm until 1993.

On October 1, 1993, Michael was confirmed as a judge for the Fourth U.S. Circuit Court of Appeals in Richmond. He replaced James Sprouse of Williamson on the federal court, which is the only level of appeal before the U.S. Supreme Court. When Michael was nominated by President Bill Clinton for the lifetime judicial appointment in 1993, he was among the first nominees by a Democratic president in more than a decade. He is one of eight West Virginians to have served on the Fourth Circuit and is recognized as a liberal on the generally conservative court.

Michael maintains an office in the Robert C. Byrd U.S. Courthouse in Charleston, traveling to Richmond for court sessions several times a year. States included in the Fourth District are Virginia, West Virginia, Maryland, North Carolina, and South Carolina.

Judie Smith
West Virginia Humanities Council

Louis Michel

The explorer and land speculator Louis Michel of Bern, Switzerland, was among the earliest advocates of Swiss settlement in Western Virginia. In 1703, he wrote from Pennsylvania of his plans to visit the western mountains. He associated himself with Bern druggist George Ritter, who proposed to settle several hundred Swiss merchants, traders, artisans, and farmers in America. However, nothing came of the Ritter plan.

In 1706, Michel and other explorers visited present Harpers Ferry and established at least a temporary settlement there. As a result of this trip, Michel produced and later published the first map of the region. His map clearly shows the forks of the river at Harpers Ferry, where the Shenandoah River enters the Potomac. It depicts the Shenandoah upstream from Harpers Ferry with considerable accuracy, but demonstrates no sound knowledge of the upper Potomac or the present Eastern Panhandle.

Returning to Switzerland, Michel joined with Baron Christopher de Graffenreid in another plan to establish a Swiss colony in Western Virginia. The desired land at Harpers Ferry was caught up in conflicting claims, and Indians warned against settling there. When North Carolina made the Swiss promoters a better offer, the plans were shifted southward. New Bern, North Carolina, was settled about 1710 but soon uprooted by Indians.

Middlebourne

Middlebourne, the county seat of Tyler County, lies on Middle Island Creek, 12 miles southeast of Sistersville on State Route 18. In 2000, Middlebourne's population was 870. Many residents work in the chemical and manufacturing plants along the Ohio River.

Robert Gorrell came to the area in 1798. He purchased all the land that is now Middlebourne and built a cabin. About 1812, he laid out town lots, and on January 27, 1813, Middlebourne was officially founded and named. In 1816, it became the county seat of recently created Tyler County. Middlebourne was incorporated on February 3, 1871. The town had a tannery and other businesses, and in the 1890s the area experienced an oil boom. A hotel was constructed to house visitors. In 1905, Jim Sellers and J. W. Grimm bought a brick-making machine. Their brickyard provided bricks for many of the buildings in town.

Today, Middlebourne is home to small businesses and several churches, plus county government buildings. The county historical society is located in the old Tyler County High School building, a handsome brick structure built in the Neoclassical style in 1907. The Middlebourne Historic District, added to the National Register of Historic Places in 1993, includes the school, the courthouse, and many commercial and residential properties.

Jane Kraina
Weirton

Midelburg Island

See Hatfield Island.

Midland Trail

The Midland Trail is the national east-west automobile route constructed in the 1930s, designated as U.S. 60 and crossing the center of America from the Chesapeake Bay to the Pacific Ocean. In West Virginia, the Midland Trail was the first state-maintained highway. In 1988, the section from White Sulphur Springs to the state capitol was designated as West Virginia's first state scenic highway. In 2000 this eastern portion of West Virginia's Midland Trail was designated a national scenic byway, and the state designation as a scenic byway was extended from the state capitol to the Kentucky border at Kenova.

This route has an ancient beginning as a buffalo trail and was later used by Indians. In 1774, Gen. Andrew Lewis used it to march his 1,000-man army from today's Lewisburg to Point Pleasant, where he defeated Chief Cornstalk. In 1824, a private Virginia company upgraded the route into the James River & Kanawha Turnpike.

After 1873, the turnpike fell into disrepair because the Chesapeake & Ohio Railway had been completed from the Chesapeake Bay to the Ohio River. The Midland Trail carried only local traffic during the era of fast and comfortable railway travel. In the 1930s, it was paved and reborn as a national highway after the American Automobile Association asked federal authorities to develop a national highway system. Today the Midland Trail is promoted as a tourist destination and historic travel route representing the "Golden Age of the American Automobile."

See also James River & Kanawha Turnpike

Larry L. Rowe
Malden

Midwifery

Lay-midwives in West Virginia, sometimes known as granny women, delivered many babies up until the middle of the 20th century. In the 1930s and 1940s, hospital births became more common and home births began to decline. By 1983, there were no known granny-midwives practicing in the state. However, a new movement of young lay-midwives began in the 1970s, providing for the few women who were choosing home birth at that time. They have an organization, founded in 1976, called the Midwives Alliance of West Virginia, with 11 members in 2002.

Traditionally, lay-midwives learned their skills from experience, and from older midwives and doctors. They could go to the local health department for classes and a license. A few were registered nurses. Most lay-midwives were associated with a doctor who supported them in their work. Granny women relied on many home remedies such as herbal teas and salves. Their childbirth kit might include castor oil, camphor, Lysol, homemade pads of folded newspaper and cloth to protect the bed, and scissors and string for cutting and tying the umbilical cord. Those who were licensed carried silver nitrate to put in the baby's eyes to prevent infection. All used boiling water for sterilizing equipment in the home.

Minnie Hammonds of Huttonsville began midwifery at age 16, apprenticed to her mother. She delivered her first baby alone at age 17, and at 18 she delivered her own child alone. Annie Brake of Valley Head began midwifery in 1921; her physician told her how to do it, and she did. Hazel Libert in the Buckhannon-Elkins area had no instruction, but she lived on a farm and had aided the farm animals on many occasions. These three delivered more than 500 babies with no maternal deaths and only one infant death.

Certified nurse-midwives have existed in the United States for 75 years, but have gained significantly in numbers and popularity in the last 25 years. They are registered nurses who have graduated

---

"More than a thousand babies"

"Mama always said that most of being a good midwife was in knowing the family history. Not just the birthing story of any given woman—although that was a good thing to keep in mind—but the whole history. The Teller family, for instance, runs to twins, though this may skip a generation or two, like it did for Shirley Teller Meroe, who had twins after her mother and grandmother going without. Her twin girls went on to have twins of their own.

"Mama called this 'the history of the body,' as there were a lot of folks, family and otherwise, who had gone before this person, and remembering those people was nearly as important to a midwife as anything we might do with our hands. Mama knew I would understand, seeing as how I was to be a midwife, too. I come from a long line of midwives, from my Great-granny Denniker to Granny Whitely to Mama to me. This is our own story—a history intertwined with more than a thousand babies we've brought into these hills of West Virginia."

—Gretchen Moran Laskas *The Midwife's Tale* (2003)

from one of the advanced programs approved by the American College of Nurse-Midwives and passed the certification test. A nurse-midwife cares for a woman throughout her pregnancy, delivery, and post-partum period. Often she becomes the woman's primary caregiver during her childbearing years. Nurse-midwives deliver babies in West Virginia hospitals and birthing centers, with an obstetrician who will help if the delivery becomes complicated. They can write prescriptions and do minor surgical procedures in the office. Care for the whole woman—emotional, spiritual, and physical—is a primary concern of nurse-midwives. There were 53 certified nurse-midwives licensed in West Virginia in 2002.

Mary Alice S. Milnes
Elkins

I. Lynn Beckman, "Home Delivery: Amy Mildred Sharpless, Mountaintop Midwife," *Goldenseal,* Winter 1993; Ruth Belanger, "Midwives' Tales," *Goldenseal,* October–December 1979; Ancella Bickley, "Midwifery in West Virginia," *West Virginia History,* 1990.

Migration

Migration was a persistent feature of life in West Virginia during the 20th century. Since the second decade of the century, when high birth rates led to continued growth of the overall state population, West Virginia suffered a net loss through migration—that is, more people left the state than moved in. After 1950, the birth rate declined and the pace of migration accelerated, leading to dramatic population losses at a time when the nation at large was growing rapidly. Though the 1970s saw a modest surge of return migration due to the national energy crisis and resulting coalfield prosperity, the outflow of people resumed in the 1980s and continued at a slow rate through the century's end.

Although migration itself was persistent, the sources and direction varied considerably at different times. During the first decades of the century, while coalfield and urban counties grew, rural counties that lacked extractive industries lost people. For example, a cluster of five Little Kanawha Valley counties lost four percent of its population between 1900 and 1910, followed the next decade by an eight percent loss. As the timber industry declined during the 1930s and 1940s, rural counties along the Virginia border suffered similar declines. Then in the 1950s and 1960s came the great flood of coalfield migrants, which, after a brief halt in the 1970s, continued through the end of the century. During the 1980s, deindustrialization affected the Ohio and Kanawha valleys, with the result that urban people for the first time joined the migrant stream.

Military recruiters and the draft during World War II and the Cold War un-intentionally but effectively stimulated migration by introducing West Virginia soldiers to employment opportunities and diversions in all parts of the nation. Otherwise, migrant streams tended to flow along established paths. Thus during the early years of the century, farm youth from western West Virginia made their way north to Ohio cities such as Akron and Cleveland, while in the northern and eastern parts of the state the B&O Railroad led many migrants to Baltimore or Washington. Wartime recruiters sent special trains to central West Virginia to procure workers for shipyards, defense plants, and government offices in Virginia and Maryland, while the "hill-billy highways" of the 1950s and 1960s led to industrial cities in the Midwest. Southbound 1980s migrants from southern West Virginia clustered sharply in North Carolina counties adjacent to Interstate 77. Clustering was less pronounced at greater distances, however. Census data for 1990, for example, cannot distinguish the residential patterns of West Virginia migrants to Florida from those of migrants from other states.

Migrants were typically young people in their prime working years. Their leave-taking was usually a rational decision, though often emotional and painful. One national study shows that within a generation, white migrants from West Virginia and other upper south states were as prosperous as other white residents of midwestern and western states. Black West Virginians, who migrated in larger proportions than did whites, did not fare as well, due to racial barriers that persisted nationally. Anecdotal evidence suggests that women adjusted to the stresses of migration more readily than

men, and that many of the classic patterns observed among foreign immigrants also prevailed among Appalachian migrants—chain migration, for example, the process by which migrants from a single family or locality established beachheads in a distant location and then clustered there as more and more members of the chain left home. However, except for aggregate population and economic studies, the phenomenon of migration as it affected individuals and localities has not been examined closely. Thus, until the social, cultural, and individual impact of migration at both the point of origin and destination is studied more intensively, we cannot be certain how well anecdotal evidence reflects the general migration experience.

See also Population

John Alexander Williams
Appalachian State University

Robert C. Coles, *The South Goes North: Volume III of Children of Crisis,* 1971; Carl E. Feather, *Mountain People in a Flat Land: A Popular History of Appalachian Migration to Northeast Ohio, 1940–1965,* 1998; James N. Gregory, "The Southern Diaspora and the Urban Dispossessed: Demonstrating the Census Public Use Samples," *Journal of American History,* June 1995.

Mill Point Prison Camp

The federal prison camp at Mill Point, Pocahontas County, opened in 1938. The inmates came initially to build State Route 39, now part of the Highland Scenic Highway. Those first inmates lived in tents, and later moved to permanent quarters. Once completed, the camp had a dining hall, dormitories, warehouse, boiler plant, school, administration building, infirmary, sawmill, and craft shop. Near the prison were houses for essential employ-

Mill Point Federal Prison Camp closed in 1959.

ees, including the warden, electrician, captain of the guards, cook, plumber, and parole officer. Thirty employees ran the prison for 300 inmates.

Sentences ran from six to 18 months at Mill Point Federal Prison Camp. The minimum-security prison on top of Kennison Mountain had no locks or fences, and minimal supervision. Inmates stayed inside the white posts spaced every 40 feet around the perimeter. Escape was as easy as strolling into the nearby woods, but the staff took a head count every few hours. During the years it was open, the prison had only 20 escapes. The inmates included moonshiners and World War II conscientious objectors. It was a curious mix. The well-educated war objectors taught those moonshiners who couldn't read or write.

The prison closed in 1959. The valley is now a center point for trailheads into the Cranberry Back Country.

Maureen F. Crockett
St. Albans

Maureen Crockett, "Doing Time on Kennison Mountain: Pocahontas County's Forgotten Prison," *Goldenseal,* Spring 1985.

Arnold Miller

Unionist Arnold Ray Miller, who brought democratic reform to the United Mine Workers of America, was born the son and grandson of miners on April 25, 1923, at Leewood on Cabin Creek in Kanawha County. He quit school in his mid-teens to become a coal miner.

In 1942, Miller joined the army. As an infantryman during the D-Day invasion, he received severe facial wounds from machine-gun fire and lost most of his left ear. Over the next two years, he underwent 19 operations in military hospitals in England. Returning home in 1946, he worked at an auto repair shop for several years until he found a mining job. In 1970, black lung disease and arthritis forced him to retire from the mines.

While working as a miner, Miller was president of his union local and one of the founders of the Black Lung Association. In February 1969, he helped the Black Lung Association lead a three-week coal strike and a march on the state capitol that led to the passage of West Virginia's first black lung compensation law. In May 1972, the Miners for Democracy organization chose Miller in a meeting at Wheeling College (now Wheeling Jesuit University) to challenge UMW President Tony Boyle. A federal judge had ordered a special election because of irregularities in Boyle's victory over Jock Yablonski in the union's 1969 election. Boyle later went to prison for arranging the murders of Yablonski, his wife, and daughter.

After defeating Boyle in December 1972, Miller immediately issued orders to let rank-and-file members elect their regional leaders instead of having them chosen by the president. During his presidency, Miller had the union's constitution rewritten to allow members to approve or reject new contracts. In 1974, he negotiated the national coal contract with an improved health care plan.

Despite early successes, turmoil marked Miller's presidency. He won reelection in 1977 but received less than half the vote in a three-man race. Soon, he faced an industry-wide wildcat strike from miners upset over cuts in health benefits. An attempt to recall him was ultimately defeated on grounds that it violated the union's constitution.

After a series of health problems, Miller resigned as president in 1979. He died July 12, 1985, in Charleston.

See also Miners for Democracy, United Mine Workers of America

Jim Wallace
Charleston

James H. Miller

Judge James Henry Miller, best remembered today for his extensive history of Summers County, was an important leader in West Virginia law, politics, education, and business from 1879 until 1929. Miller was born February 9, 1859, in what would later be Summers County. He attended local public schools and graduated from Concord Normal School (now Concord University) in 1879. He taught school for a few years in Summers County and then studied law in Hinton and at the University of Virginia.

Miller served as superintendent of Summers County schools from 1882 to 1884 and as Summers County prosecuting attorney from 1884 to 1900. As a Democrat, he was active in West Virginia politics. He served as a delegate to the 1896 Democratic National Convention and as chairman of the State Democratic Committee, and ran unsuccessfully for state auditor in 1900 and for secretary of state in 1920. In 1904, he was elected as judge of the Circuit Court of the Ninth West Virginia Circuit and served in that office until 1920.

In 1882, Miller married Jane Tompkins Miller of Gauley Bridge. His *History of Summers County*, published in 1908, was a monumental work covering the history, geography, and genealogy of southern West Virginia. Judge Miller died in Hinton on his birthday, February 9, 1929.

Michael M. Meador
Abingdon, Virginia

Jim Comstock, ed., *The West Virginia Heritage Encyclopedia,* 1976; James H. Miller, *History of Summers County: From the Earliest Settlement to the Present Time,* 1908.

Mrs. Alex. McVeigh Miller

Novelist Mittie Frances Clarke Point, born April 30, 1850, wrote as Mrs. Alex. McVeigh Miller, the name of her second husband. The author of 80 dime novels published from 1881 to 1915, she was one of the best-known romance writers of her age. Her fiction brought her wealth and fame.

A native of Doswell, Virginia, she was educated at home and at the Richmond Female Institute, from which she graduated on June 30, 1868. After graduation, she married Thomas Jefferson Davis and gave birth to a daughter. Both her husband and child died within two years, leaving her alone in Washington. Grief-stricken, she returned to her family in Richmond, where she wrote stories for the *Old Dominion* and *Temperance Advocate* magazines.

In May 1878, she abandoned her writing when she married Alexander McVeigh Miller and moved to Fayette County. She soon began writing again, hoping to augment her husband's meager earnings as a schoolteacher. Her first success came in 1883 with the sensational romance titled *The Bride of the Tomb*. Numerous lucrative publications followed, enabling Miller to build a mansion called The Cedars in Alderson, and to finance her husband's political career, helping him win a seat in the West Virginia Senate from 1901 to 1909.

Miller earned more than $100,000 from her romance novels. In 1908, after discovering her husband's infidelities, she divorced him and moved to Boston with her daughter, Irene. Facing poverty again after years of plenty, Miller eventually settled in Florida, where she died December 26, 1937, at the age of 87.

Miller's Alderson house later became the home of Congresswoman Ruth Bryan Owen Rhode, the daughter of William Jennings Bryan. The Cedars was placed on the National Register of Historic places in 1978.

Kathleen Kennedy
Point Marion, Pennsylvania

Thomas Burk Miller

Justice Thomas Burk Miller was born in Buffalo, New York, April 1, 1929. He graduated from the University of Virginia in 1950 and served in the U.S. Navy for three years during the Korean War. He later attended the West Virginia University College of Law, graduating in 1956. Miller served as a justice with the West Virginia Supreme Court of Appeals from 1977 to 1994, running as a Democrat. Before and after his judicial stint, he practiced with what is now Schrader, Byrd & Companion in Wheeling.

The accession of Justices Miller, Sam Harshbarger, and Darrell V. McGraw Jr. to the Supreme Court in 1977 constituted a liberal revolution. The revolution ended the next time they faced the electorate. Justice Miller was easily reelected, but William Brotherton replaced Harshbarger in 1984 and McGraw was defeated by Margaret Workman in 1988. Miller resigned from the court in 1994 and returned to his law firm in Wheeling.

The cases the former justice considered his most significant include *Morningstar v. Black and Decker* (1979), which held that the court had the ability to create (rather than "find") common law; *Bradley v. Appalachian Power Co.* (1979), where the court abolished the comparative negligence rule; and *La Rue v. La Rue* (1983), which created out of whole cloth the concept of equitable distribution of marital assets. The court also said that homemakers in divorce cases were entitled to have a monetary value placed on their services. Justice Miller was disappointed with the court's decision in *Hinerman v. Daily Gazette Co.* (1992), a libel suit brought by a Weirton attorney. In his dissent, Miller wrote "the majority essentially changed our libel law by misstating the facts and misinterpreting Supreme Court cases."

Miller, who had not evidenced any previous interest in politics, led the ticket in both the primary and general elections in his 1976 Supreme Court race, unusual for a candidate from the Northern Panhandle. He repeated the feat in his 1988 campaign. Miller lives today in Wheeling.

See also Supreme Court of Appeals

H. John Rogers
New Martinsville

Okey Mills

Sheriff Okey Austin Mills was born March 7, 1915, near Sweeneyburg, Raleigh County, and attended schools in Pemberton, Stotesbury, and Beckley. At age 20, he succeeded his father to become the youngest Raleigh County jailer. Mills was an avid amateur athlete, playing on and managing baseball teams throughout the area. He acquired a reputation on the baseball field as batter, pitcher, and fielder in American Legion and coalfield leagues, playing until age 60.

Recovering from a mining accident, Mills enlisted in the army in 1942 as a paratrooper with the famous 82nd Airborne Division. He was wounded in the invasions of Normandy and Holland, surviving the Battle of the Bulge, Ardennes, and other battles.

In 1948, Mills campaigned for Raleigh County sheriff after serving as a deputy and won. He was the youngest sheriff in county history and went on to become the only man to hold that office five times, and the first to serve consecutive terms. Sheriff Mills served intermittently from 1949 to 1981. He married Nettie Mae Neely in 1951. Between terms and after retirement, Mills was active in numerous political, veterans, and civic organizations. Okey A. Mills died January 5, 2001, in Beckley.

Lois C. McLean
Beckley

C. F. Millspaugh

Naturalist Charles Frederick Millspaugh was born in Ithaca, New York, June 20, 1854. He attended Cornell University and went on to receive a medical degree in 1881 from the New York Homeopathic Medical College.

Millspaugh played a significant role in establishing botany as an important field of study at West Virginia University, although he was on the faculty for only three years. He was the first botanist to begin a systematic inventory of the flora of West Virginia. He made several lengthy field surveys across the state, collecting and identifying plants. Through the results of this work, in 1896 he published *Flora of West Virginia* with Lawrence William Nuttall; the book should not be confused with the 20th century classic of the same name.

Prior to his work at WVU, Millspaugh practiced medicine for nine years. Much of his practice included the use of herbal medicines to treat illness. The knowledge he accumulated through his medical practice and his love of botany led him to publish a reference on native medicinal plants called *American Medicinal Plants*. The work was published in sections from 1884 to 1887. It has 180 full-page color plates and includes recommendations on how to use each species.

As a botanist with the State Experiment Station, Millspaugh also experimented with plants that had potential economic use. One such project was to attempt to grow an imported willow, the Austrian basket osier, in the hopes of developing a West Virginia willow-ware industry. The climate did not prove to be suitable for the plant to thrive.

Millspaugh was at WVU from 1891 to 1893. He left to become curator of botany at the Field Museum of Natural History in Chicago. He held this post until his death, September 15, 1923.

See also Botany, Lawrence William Nuttall

Emily Grafton
Morgantown

Milton

Milton, in Cabell County, is situated in a level basin of the Mud River, 31 miles west of Charleston and 18 miles east of Huntington. The town's 2000 population was 2,206.

In the 1780s, cheap land, wild game, and good soil drew settlers to the region. Some of the first comers were John Morris, Edmund Morris, John Jordan, Andrew Jordan, Charles Venable, James Beckett, Joseph Rece, Abia Rece, John Everett, Nathan Everett, and Thomas Harmon.

The first semblance of a town or village at Milton occurred in relation to the James River & Kanawha Turnpike, which was built in the early 1830s. The Mud River covered bridge, which has been restored and moved to the fairgrounds, was a vital link for the turnpike. By 1869, the C&O Railway had begun construction in the vicinity, and a train station was subsequently built. The depot attracted numerous small interests, and in 1872 a town was laid out and lots were sold. On September 16, 1876, the town of Milton was incorporated and named in honor of Milton Rece, a large landowner at the time.

In the early 1900s, gas and oil were discovered in the area. The abundance of these important natural resources attracted such industries as Blenko Glass, which was established in 1922 and today employs about 60 workers. Farms historically have dotted the region, and tobacco has been an important cash crop. Timbering also was an important early industry, with the logs floated down the Mud River to the sawmill.

Milton saw significant growth with the completion of Interstate 64, and many residents who live there now commute to Charleston or Huntington. Milton is home to the Pumpkin Festival, which is held during the first full weekend in October. The Union Baptist Church, a Milton landmark, was founded in 1809. The church has been restored, but bayonet marks and bullet holes from the Civil War may still be seen. Writer Breece D'J Pancake (1952–79) was a Milton native.

Mine Safety

In the late 1800s and early 1900s, West Virginia became one of the country's major coal-producing states. As coal production increased, so did the number of explosions and deaths. Mining accidents claimed thousands of lives annually throughout the nation. Most coal operations neglected basic safety precautions. The prevailing sentiment, especially among those in power, was that miner carelessness was at the core of mine accidents, and that casualties were an inevitable price of rapid industrialization. West Virginia had one of the worst records for safety and health protection in the nation, and the state's mining law, passed in 1887, was regarded by many as the nation's weakest.

In 1905, the West Virginia Department of Mines was created. Following a series of small mining disasters, sentiment slowly began to change. West Virginia's chief mine inspector called for more and better-trained inspectors who would have greater authority to shut down mines operating outside the law.

Governor Dawson appointed a commission of miners and mine operators to review current industry conditions and draft a bill that would address key safety issues. In February 1907, a substantial revision of West Virginia's mine safety laws was passed. This new law charged mine foremen with instructing inexperienced miners and conducting frequent mine examinations, but still was less stringent than in some other states.

Meanwhile, mine disasters continued unabated. In December 1907, a massive explosion ripped through the Fairmont Coal Company's No. 6 and 8 mines in Monongah, killing at least 361 people in the single worst mining disaster in U.S. history.

Congress faced pressure to study mining conditions and create uniformity among states with regard to setting higher standards for mining conditions. Some believed that federal regulation was driven not by concern for miners but by a desire to fend off state-by-state legislation that might jeopardize local competitiveness. In West Virginia, the legislature rejected every mine safety law proposed in 1908 and passed no major safety legislation for the next seven years. By 1915, legislation brought some substantial improvements, calling for provisions for preventing underground mine fires and requiring foremen and fire bosses to pass state examinations and receive state certification.

Nationally, mine safety came under closer scrutiny. In 1908, President Theodore Roosevelt advocated the formation of a federal agency to investigate mine accidents, teach accident prevention, and conduct mine safety research. Two years later, the U.S. Bureau of Mines was formed.

Although mine deaths decreased dramatically during the next several decades, too many miners continued to die needlessly in mining accidents. The next turning point came in 1968, when 78 miners died in a fire at a Farmington coal mine. This event jolted the mining community and helped trigger the passage of sweeping federal legislation. Miners rallied together, marching on the West Virginia state capitol and on Washington, demanding that Congress take action. On December 30, 1969, the Coal Mine Health and Safety Act was signed into law. Eight years later, the law was strengthened and extended to cover metal and nonmetal mines.

Mines are safer today than in times past. Our state experienced only three mine fatalities in 2005, the lowest number in history. Tragically, that record was followed, only two days into 2006, by the explosion at Sago Mine in Upshur County. Claiming 12 miners, Sago was West Virginia's worst mine disaster in four decades. It was soon followed by other fatalities in Logan and Boone counties.

Today, the West Virginia Office of Miners' Health Safety and Training oversees the health and safety of all persons employed at West Virginia mines. Its duties include regular inspections and the certification and training of mine workers. Its federal counterpart, the U.S. Department of Labor's Mine Safety and Health Administration, enforces safety and health laws at mines throughout the nation. Together, these agencies have played a significant role in the dramatic decrease of mine fires, explosions, and fatalities. Technological advances in mining equipment and mining methods, effective miner training, a heightened awareness of an effective safety program's importance, and a more cooperative relationship among mining companies, labor, and government in dealing with safety issues have all been important factors.

See also Coal Industry, Coal Mine Disasters

J. Davitt McAteer
Shepherdstown

William Graebner, *Coal-Mining Safety in the Progressive Period*, 1976; Glenn F. Massay, "Legislators, Lobbyists and Loopholes: Coal Mining Legislation in West Virginia 1875–1901," *West Virginia History*, April 1971.

The Mine Wars

The Mine Wars, which took place in the southern West Virginia coalfields from 1912 to 1922, included the Paint Creek-Cabin Creek Strike (1912–13), the Battle of Matewan (May 1920), the Battle of the Tug (May 1921), and the Miners' March on Logan (August 1921) and the ensuing Battle of Blair Mountain. Combatants included, on the miners' side, the legendary labor organizer Mary Harris "Mother" Jones; local United Mine Workers leaders Frank Keeney, Fred Mooney, and Bill Blizzard; Matewan Police Chief Sid Hatfield; and others. On the other side were Albert Felts, the head of the Baldwin-Felts Detective Agency; Don Chafin, the high sheriff of Logan County; and others.

By 1912, southern West Virginia miners were placing their hopes for the future in their union, the United Mine Workers of America. There had been early attempts to organize the region's miners, most importantly during the national strikes of 1897 and 1902. They had only limited success, but the union did gain an important foothold in eastern Kanawha County.

In April 1912, miners along Paint Creek and Cabin Creek in Kanawha County walked off their jobs, and the great Mine Wars began. Their basic demand, employer recognition of the union, seemed simple enough, but they and the coal operators alike knew that this would mean the end of company housing, company stores, company schools, company guards, and company churches, as well as better pay for the miners and control over their own lives and work.

The Paint Creek-Cabin Creek strike lasted a year and a half. Miners were beaten, ambushed, and killed by mine guards, machine-gunned by an armor-plated train called the Bull Moose Special, illegally court-martialed, and deported from the state. The miners responded in bloody ambushes of their own, including the Battle of Mucklow, which left 16 men dead. Two labor newspapers were suppressed and their editors incarcerated. Governor Hatfield, working with local UMWA officials and coal officials to abort the strike, dictated settlement terms to the miners. Led by the newly emerged rank-and-file leadership of Frank Keeney and Fred Mooney, the miners renewed their struggle and remained on strike until the coal companies agreed to their original demands.

In 1919, Keeney, then president of UMWA District 17, launched a drive to unionize the rest of southern West Virginia. Gunfights, explosions, and other forms of conflict occurred in numerous coal towns, including Roderfield, Willis Branch, Glen White, Mohawk, War Eagle, Borderland, Noland, Freeburn, and Merrimac. In these battles miners fought the newly established state police as well as mine guards and strikebreakers.

In May 1920, the Battle of the Tug erupted in Mingo County, three days of unabated violence on a 10-mile front along the Tug Fork. Determined to stop coal production, miners fought pitched battles with mine guards, deputy sheriffs, and state police in the towns of Blackberry City, Alden, Sprigg, New Howard, and Rawl.

On May 19, 11 Baldwin-Felts agents, after evicting striking miners in Red Jacket, tried to board a train in nearby Matewan to return home. They were confronted by the mayor of Matewan and the chief of police, Sid Hatfield, a former UMWA miner. When the shooting stopped, three townspeople, including the mayor, and seven of the Baldwin-Felts detectives were dead. Mingo County became known to the nation as "Bloody Mingo," and Hatfield became a regional folk hero. On August 1, 1921, Baldwin-Felts detectives had their revenge when they shot to death Hatfield and his deputy, Ed Chambers, both unarmed, on the steps of the McDowell County courthouse in Welch.

There followed the famous Miners' March on Logan. In probably the largest armed labor uprising in American history, perhaps as many as 20,000 miners marched 90 miles and engaged in a two-week battle with more than 5,000 Logan County deputy sheriffs, mine guards, and state police. The Battle of Blair Mountain ended when President Warren G. Harding placed the region under martial law, and ordered 2,500 federal soldiers and a bombing squadron into the state.

The Miners' March ended the Mine Wars. Keeney fell into dispute with the national president of the UMWA, John L. Lewis, who dismissed him and withdrew the autonomy of District 17, precipitating a collapse of the UMWA in southern West Virginia. As a result, the coal industry's control of the region would not be challenged again until the New Deal of the 1930s.

See also Battle of Blair Mountain, Coal Industry, Matewan Massacre, Miners' March, Paint Creek-Cabin Creek Strike, United Mine Workers of America

David A. Corbin
Office of Senator Robert C. Byrd

David A. Corbin, *Life, Work, and Rebellion in the Coal Fields: The Southern West Virginia Miners, 1880–1922*, 1981; Richard D. Lunt, *Law and Order vs. The Miners: West Virginia, 1907–1933*, 1979; Lon Savage, *Thunder in the Mountains: The West Virginia Mine War 1920–21*, 1990.

Mineral County

From its verdant low valleys to the towering backbone of the Allegheny Front, 3,000 feet above the North Branch of the Potomac River, Mineral County lies a stone's throw from Maryland and just a three-hour drive from Washington. Home of Potomac State College and named for its vast mineral resources, Mineral County was a railroad and coal center at the beginning of the 1900s. The county has an area of 330 square miles and a 2000 population of 27,078. Keyser is the county seat.

Located in the Eastern Panhandle, Mineral County was part of Hampshire before the Civil War. Local residents were more pro-Union than those living in the eastern part of Hampshire County. Following the war, in 1866, the new county was created. West Virginia had become a state just three years earlier.

There were skirmishes during the Civil War, and towns changed hands several times, usually only briefly. The village of New Creek, just south of Keyser, was a training camp for Union soldiers from Pennsylvania, Ohio, Indiana, and Illinois. Mineral County's Y-junction, where the Northwest Turnpike intersected the New

FAST FACTS ABOUT MINERAL COUNTY

Founded: 1866
Land in square miles: 330.0
Population: 27,078
Percentage minorities: 3.8%
Percentage rural: 61.8%
Median age: 39.1
Percentage 65 and older: 15.1%
Birth rate per 1,000 population: 11.4
Median household income: $31,149
High school graduate or higher: 80.3%
Bachelor's degree or higher: 11.7%
Home ownership: 78.0%
Median home value: $73,500

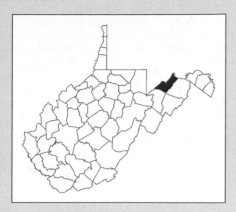

This information is from the 2000 U.S. Census. In 2000, West Virginia as a whole had 5 percent minorities, a median age of 38.9, median household income of $29,696, and a 75.2 percent home ownership rate.

Creek road (now U.S. 50 and U.S. 220), was strategic for troop and supply movements into the Shenandoah Valley.

The present Eastern Panhandle of West Virginia was well-known to George Washington. He had crisscrossed the region as a young surveyor and commanded frontier defense during the French and Indian War. In 1755, he ordered a stockade and fort erected in present Mineral County as a defense against incursions by Delaware and Catawba Indians. The original log blockhouse still stands at Fort Ashby.

Many immigrants in the 19th century worked their way across the coalfields of Pennsylvania, down through Maryland, and settled in Mineral County. The area's population reflects a diverse mixture of Mennonites, German Swiss, English, Scots, Italians (mostly from southern Italy), and Jews. Even Chinese found their way to Keyser in the early 1900s. Elk Garden became home for many Irish, including Flanigans and Faheys, McIntires and McDonoughs, Kilroys and Keegans, Conlons, Kenneys, and Joyces.

Perhaps the most prominent historic figure was the industrialist Henry Gassaway Davis, who began as a brakeman for the Baltimore & Ohio Railroad at age 20 and later associated with U.S. presidents. He lived in Piedmont early in his life, as a storekeeper and railroad agent. Davis later was elected to the U.S. Senate and ran for vice president in 1904, when he and Democratic presidential candidate Alston Parker lost to Teddy Roosevelt. Davis founded Elkins and owned his own railroad.

Davis's purchase of the famous "Big Vein" of coal atop the Allegheny Front at Elk Garden led to a local industrial boom from the 1880s into the early 20th century. From 1881 to 1923, 315 acres of coal was mined and 2,000 miners worked at Elk Garden. The era was marred in 1911 by the explosion at No. 20 mine, killing 23

miners, fathers and sons among them. High-quality semibituminous coal from Davis's Big Vein was displayed at the St. Louis World's Fair in 1893 and powered Admiral Dewey's fleet at the Battle of Manila Bay.

The arrival of the B&O Railroad, which reached the northern part of present Mineral County in 1842 and arrived at a point across the North Branch from Piedmont a decade later, had a major impact. The railroad increased the population in northern Hampshire County, and contributed to the political differences within the county that led to the creation of Mineral County in 1866. Keyser, named for a vice president of the B&O, was a key railroad point from which coal and produce were shipped. Keyser was selected as the county seat as a compromise between Elk Garden and Piedmont. Keyser earlier had been known as Paddytown, named for Patrick McCarty of County Tyrone, Ireland, who had settled there in the mid-1700s.

Keyser today is the region's hub. Once home to a B&O roundhouse, its citizens now work in education, agriculture, retail, vocational training, the arts, health care, and at small industrial parks. Major employers include MeadWestvaco at nearby Luke, Maryland, and Allegheny Ballistics Laboratory at Rocket Center. The opening of Jennings Randolph Lake on the North Branch holds potential for attracting tourists from nearby Baltimore and Washington.

Potomac State College, beautifully situated atop a small hill that once had a fort, is a two-year branch of West Virginia University. Most of the approximately 1,200 students complete their last two years at WVU in Morgantown. Once Keyser Preparatory School, the school was tuition-free in the early 1900s.

Several other Mineral County towns have rich histories. Piedmont, closely as-

The Mineral County courthouse.

sociated with the nearby Maryland communities of Westernport and Luke, is the hometown of Henry Louis Gates Jr., of Harvard, a prominent African-American scholar. Piedmont once had a roundhouse and machine shops of the B&O, and its people are closely tied to Mead-Westvaco at Luke.

Ridgeley was a stockade and fort; Fort Ashby, a frontier post; and Doll's Gap is said to be the birthplace of Nancy Hanks, mother of Abraham Lincoln. Other Mineral County villages and towns include Burlington, Blaine, Antioch, Beryl, Sulphur, Cross, Fountain, Ridgeville, Short Gap, and Wiley Ford.

See also Keyser

Jack Canfield
Charleston
Jack Canfield, *A Penny for Coming Back*, 1995; Gilbert Gude, *Where the Potomac Begins: A History of the North Branch Valley*, 1984; Mineral County Heritage Society, *Mineral County, West Virginia*, 1980.

Mineral Springs

The mountains between Virginia and West Virginia once had many spring resorts that catered to the medical and recreational needs of people who lived in the lowlands along the Atlantic coast. Some were established as early as the mid-1700s, and a few remain today. The springs range southwestward from Berkeley Springs in the Eastern Panhandle to Mercer Healing Springs near Princeton, with White Sulphur Springs and (in Virginia) Warm Springs being the most prominent.

The resorts were built around mineral or thermal springs. The mineral springs contained various dissolved salts; the thermal springs had temperatures varying from 62 to 106 degrees Fahrenheit. Most of the springs in the Blue Ridge region and along the Allegheny Front issue from Oriskany sandstone and Helderberg limestone (both of the Devonian geologic age). Rainwater enters a permeable formation along an outcrop at a high elevation and permeates down to an outcrop at a lower elevation. The temperature of the water is normally the same as the earth's temperature. Thermal spring water comes from deep in the earth, where temperatures are higher.

The classification of the waters may be broken down into six categories. Saline waters have dissolved salts of calcium, magnesium, and sodium. Sulfur waters contain hydrogen sulfide and have a "rotten egg" smell. Chalybeate waters contain iron. There are also some alkaline, calcic (lime), and thermal waters.

At a time when medical science could do little for patients, it was believed that the spring waters could cure common diseases. Lured by advertising, patients came to drink the water, to bathe in it, or to rub themselves with it. The therapeutic effect of the water may be questioned, but the overall experience may well have been healthful. Certainly the elevation of the mountain resorts and the clean air helped many, and the diseases common to low-lying areas were not found in the mountains.

A number of factors contributed to the demise of the spring resorts. The destruction that occurred during the Civil War and the changing social system in the South after the war were contributing factors, as were better medical treatment and newly discovered cures for diseases. The coming of the automobile in the early 1900s changed the fabric of American life, including travel and recreation habits. Many resorts suffered disastrous fires. Some never reopened after the hotel or main buildings burned down, and many never regained their former glory. It appears that arson was the cause of some fires, perhaps reflecting fragile financial health.

The old resorts have found various uses. Examples include Minnehaha Springs in Pocahontas County, now a boys' summer camp; Sweet Springs in Monroe County, until recently a state home for the aged; Salt Sulphur Springs in Monroe County, now a private residence. Barger Springs in Summers County is a community of private summer homes or camps, and Mercer Healing Springs is a private farm. Little remains at Red Sulphur Springs in Monroe County and Blue Sulphur Springs in Greenbrier.

Today only a few of the resorts are still in business. The most famous of these is the world-renowned Greenbrier at White Sulphur Springs, in Greenbrier County. The others are the Capon Springs Resort in Hampshire County, the Berkeley Springs State Park in Morgan County, and Pence Springs in Summers County. Lee Sulphur Spring in Hardy County remains open to the public at Lost River State Park.

Stan Cohen
Pictorial Histories
Stan Cohen, *Historic Springs of the Virginias: A Pictorial History*, 1981.

Minerals

The rocks of West Virginia are overwhelmingly sedimentary in origin and generally lack eye-catching mineral specimens or large deposits of metallic ores. However, many sedimentary rocks are important to our modern industrial society, and mining these deposits adds to the state's economy by providing construction materials, chemical feedstocks, and jobs. The main limiting factor affecting the marketability of industrial minerals is transportation costs. These materials tend to be heavy and bulky and largely limited to a local market.

Limestone and dolomite are sedimentary rocks formed in warm, shallow seas. Known as carbonates, they are mined for construction aggregate and for use in road building, agricultural lime, coal mine safety dust, in coal-fired power plant scrubbers, acid mine drainage neutralizers, and for other uses. Highway construction and increasing needs for pollution controls associated with coal mining and utilities should result in an increased demand for carbonate products.

Most of the state's limestone production comes from the eastern counties, where the major carbonate formations are exposed and accessible. Geologically, these limestones come from groups laid down in the Paleozoic Era, mostly from the Mississippian Period (ending 310 million years ago) and earlier. Some come from as early as the Cambrian Period, which ended 500 million years ago. In the central and western parts of the state, these rock strata are too far beneath the surface to be mined. West Virginia has sandstone formations suitable for many purposes. Currently, most sandstone is produced from Pennsylvanian Period units, geologically younger than most of the limestone quarried in West Virginia. The sandstone is quarried from parts of the state distant from carbonate supplies, replacing limestone as a construction aggregate. An exception is the Oriskany sandstone, a high-purity quartz arenite, mined near Berkeley Springs. The Oriskany product can be used for a wide variety of applications, including making glass, stoneware, and abrasives. In the past, sandstones have been quarried for building stones, cobble and curb stones, and millstones. There is little market for these products today.

Most of West Virginia's economic sand and gravel deposits occur in alluvial and terrace deposits and along the Ohio River, formed as outwash deposits during melting of Pleistocene glaciers. The material is dredged from the river channel or excavated from the adjacent terraces. Deposits of limited extent and quality occur along streams in other parts of the state, but production there is generally small and intermittent. Demand for sand and gravel is dependent on the number and location of major construction projects.

West Virginia has enormous reserves of clays and shales that are suitable for the manufacture of brick, cement, and clay dummies used in blasting. The brick and cement manufacturers use shales of the Ordovician-age Martinsburg Formation, and the clay dummies are produced from the Pennsylvanian-age Bolivar Fire Clay. Many Pennsylvanian-aged clay deposits were once mined for making bricks, especially for paving roads. Additionally, there are large deposits that can be used for producing lightweight (expanded) aggregate, refractories, and similar products. Limited demand and high transportation costs currently restrict exploitation of these resources.

Salt was a necessary and scarce commodity during frontier times and was recovered from various natural seeps known as "licks." Salt was produced commercially at natural seeps and very shallow wells where the Kanawha River crosses the Warfield Anticline slightly upstream of the mouth of Campbells Creek, near Charleston. The anticline brings the sandstones of the New River Formation, which are known as the "salt sands" by drillers due to the presence of saltwater or brines, closer to the surface. Salt was recovered from the salt brine by evaporative boiling in large kettles and pans. Lesser amounts were similarly produced below the falls of the Little Kanawha River. It is interesting to note that petroleum was an unwanted byproduct of salt production.

Modern brine production is from deep wells drilled into the Silurian Salina Formation. These salt deposits, formed by the evaporation of ancient seawater, are more than 50 feet thick in much of the Northern Panhandle and north-central portion of the state. These deposits lie between 5,000 and 9,000 feet below the surface. Fresh water is pumped through an injection well drilled into the salt zone, dissolving the salt. The resulting saline solution is pumped to the surface through a nearby production well. It is used as a feedstock for the manufacture of chlorine, caustic soda, and derivatives for a variety of chemical processes.

Iron was as essential to pioneer life as was salt, and needed for a variety of agricultural and household purposes. Since transporting heavy iron implements was difficult in the days of horse and wagons, local iron industries developed at an early stage in West Virginia's history wherever ore could be found. Small, workable deposits of iron minerals occur in many areas of the state, and small furnaces were located in these areas to smelt the ore and produce raw bar iron for the pioneer blacksmiths.

Iron ores found in West Virginia occur in thin, isolated deposits within sedimentary rocks. The ore minerals are generally hematite (Fe_2O_3) and siderite ($FeCO_2$) and are generally mixed with many impurities. Improved transportation methods and the richer iron ore beds discovered around Lake Superior lowered costs, resulting in the inability of the local iron ores to compete economically.

See also Geology

Bascombe M. Blake Jr.
Geological & Economic Survey

Miners for Democracy

The Miners for Democracy, a dissident movement within the United Mine Workers of America, successfully challenged the corrupt administration of the union in the early 1970s. The Miners for Democ-

racy, or MFD as it was often called, was organized in Clarksville, Pennsylvania, in April 1970, a few months after the assassination there of Joseph "Jock" Yablonski, a rebel leader within the miners' union. Although it was several years before UMWA President Tony Boyle was imprisoned in the murder-for-hire scheme that left Yablonski, his wife, and daughter dead in their beds on New Year's Eve, the assumption was widespread in the coalfields that union leaders were responsible for the killings. The organization of the MFD reflected this assumption and the growing determination of rank-and-file miners to clean up their union.

From the beginning the Miners for Democracy had strong northern and southern factions, led respectively by Mike Trbovich of Pennsylvania and Arnold Miller of West Virginia. When the 1969 election of Tony Boyle as UMWA president was overthrown by a federal judge in 1972 on grounds of vote fraud, the Miners for Democracy attempted to compromise factional differences in order to produce a winning slate. At a conference at Wheeling College (now Wheeling Jesuit University) they chose to run Miller for union president and Trbovich for vice president. The MFD candidates won control of the UMWA in a special December 1972 union election.

The Miners for Democracy proved more effective in opposition than in office. Turmoil soon characterized the Miller administration, compounded by the original distrust of MFD coalition factions, a lack of administrative experience by the newly elected officers, and a general unrest in the coalfields during the energy crisis of the 1970s. Although important reforms in union procedures were made and a favorable coal industry contract was negotiated in 1974, President Arnold Miller managed to get reelected only by a plurality of votes in 1977. Miller survived an attempted recall on technical grounds but resigned his office in 1979 in a face-saving arrangement that made him the union's president emeritus.

See also Tony Boyle, Arnold Miller, United Mine Workers of America

Miners Health Plan

In 1946, the United Mine Workers of America Health and Retirement Funds were created in a contract between the UMWA and the federal government. President Truman and his interior secretary, Julius Krug, negotiated the Funds' creation to end a national strike by the UMWA.

Before the Funds, the health care system in the coalfields was poor. An official medical survey of the coal industry, authorized by the 1946 agreement and directed by Rear Admiral Joel T. Boone, revealed that retired and disabled coal

miners were living in conditions of inadequate housing and considerable poverty. Moreover, coal miner families experienced rates of tuberculosis and infant mortality considerably higher than national averages. The United Mine Workers took the position that the conditions described in the Boone Report were the natural consequence of working in the mines. The union called for alleviation of the unhealthy conditions and for assurance that future employment in the industry would not result in destitution in old age.

When the war ended in 1945, the UMWA had proposed a royalty of 10 cents per ton of coal to be paid to the union to provide medical services in the coalfields. The coal operators rejected the idea. But when negotiations began toward a new national contract in 1946, creation of a health and welfare fund for the miners was the union's top priority. Operators again rejected the idea, and the miners walked off the job on April 1, 1946.

Faced with the prospect of a long strike that could hamper post-war economic recovery, Truman ordered Krug to seize control of the mines and force the miners back to work. The miners refused; after a week Krug negotiated an agreement and the strike was ended. The deal created a welfare and retirement fund to make payments to miners and their dependents and survivors. Three trustees would manage the system, which would be financed by a levy of five cents on each ton of coal produced. The Krug agreement, worked out with UMWA President John L. Lewis, also created a separate medical fund to be managed by trustees appointed by the union. This fund was to provide cradle-to-grave health care for miners and their families.

The Funds eventually built 10 hospitals in West Virginia, Kentucky, and Virginia, greatly improving health care in the coalfields. By the 1980s, however, medical benefits for retired miners became a sticking point between the UMWA and coal industry management. Some companies operating in West Virginia and neighboring areas, such as A.T. Massey Coal and Pittston Coal, tried to avoid paying for retiree health care benefits. After the UMWA waged a lengthy strike against Pittston in 1989, Labor Secretary Elizabeth Dole appointed a commission to investigate the retiree health care issue.

The Dole Commission's work led Congress in 1992 to approve the Coal Act, authored by Sen. Jay Rockefeller. Under this law, all coal companies were required to pay for the cost of their retirees' health care. So-called orphan retirees, those whose last employer went out of business, would be funded out of coal industry taxes that otherwise support the Abandoned Mine Land Reclamation Fund.

Throughout the 1990s and into 2002, coal companies continued court challenges to the Coal Act. Congressman Nick Rahall of southern West Virginia sought legislation that would make the transfer of money from the Abandoned Mine Land fund to the miners health plan easier. The Funds continue to finance health care for more than 50,000 retirees and dependents.

See also Appalachian Regional Hospitals

Ken Ward
Charleston Gazette

Maier B. Fox, *United We Stand: A History of the United Mine Workers,* 1990; Curtis Seltzer, *Fire in the Hole: Miners and Managers in the Coal Industry,* 1985.

Miners Hospitals

The industrialization of West Virginia in the late 19th century brought dangerous new occupations to the Mountain State. Coal mining was particularly hazardous, in an era when hundreds of West Virginia miners were injured or killed annually and when a single accident might bring scores of casualties. In February 1899, the state legislature passed a law requiring the building of state hospitals for those engaged in dangerous occupations. Three hospitals were built in different sections of the state. While not restricted to miners, they were known as Miners Hospitals One, Two, and Three and in fact drew a majority of their patients from the surrounding coal mines.

Miners Hospital No. One opened at Welch on January 28, 1902. Young Dr. Henry D. Hatfield, the nephew of feudist "Devil Anse" Hatfield and later governor of West Virginia, was made hospital president. Miners Hospital No. Two, located at remote McKendree in the New River Gorge, opened for patients in December 1901, while No. Three in Fairmont had opened the previous October. The McKendree and Welch hospitals both opened affiliated nursing schools by 1910.

As intended, the hospitals dealt largely in industrial medicine and the treatment of victims of trauma and other injuries. Burns provided the largest category of injuries at McKendree during its first year of operation, followed by crushing. That year the hospital also treated 30 gunshot wounds, from which eight people died, a reflection of troubled times in the coalfields. Miners accounted for two-thirds of the McKendree patients the first year, with a sizable minority also coming from the nearby railroad. Each hospital served a large region, and they were heavily used. Welch No. One had to lodge patients in aisles and corridors, according to an early report.

The Miners Hospitals offered a valuable backup to the "company doctor" system prevalent in the coalfields, providing care for patients whose needs exceeded the ability of the local doctor's office or coal company clinic. The hospitals served for several critical decades, until improved transportation and additional medical facilities made modern health care more readily available. McKendree was the first to go, closing as a hospital in the 1940s although it served for several additional years as a home for elderly black patients. Fairmont No. Three closed in 1980. Miners Hospital No. One survived longest, being replaced by Welch Emergency Hospital and continuing today as Welch Community Hospital.

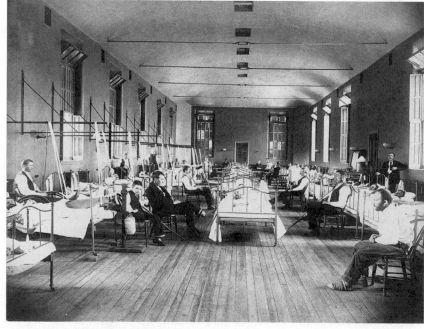

A crowded ward in the Welch miners hospital.

See also Henry D. Hatfield, McKendree Hospital, Welch Community Hospital

The Miners' March

The 1921 Miners' March on Logan, probably the largest armed uprising in American labor history, involved more than 15,000 coal miners opposed by more than 5,000 mine guards, deputy sheriffs, and state police, 2,500 U.S. soldiers, and 14 bombing planes.

On August 1, Sid Hatfield, chief of police of Matewan and a hero among the miners for his role in the 1920 Battle of Matewan, was shot to death by Baldwin-Felts detectives as he approached the McDowell County courthouse in Welch. A week later, on August 7, 1921, 5,000 miners met in Charleston to present demands to Governor Morgan. Encouraged by United Mine Workers district president Frank Keeney and others, miners began to assemble later that night at Lens Creek near Charleston to prepare to march south. They intended to overthrow the governor's proclamation of martial law in Mingo County and to wipe out the anti-union mine guard and deputy sheriff systems in Logan and Mingo counties.

Union leader Bill Blizzard served as field commander. World War I veterans among the miners helped to organize the marchers along military lines. They used sentries, patrols, codes, and passwords, and had their own doctors, nurses, and medical and sanitary facilities, commissaries, and food tents.

On August 24, the march began. President Harding sent Brig. Gen. Henry Bandholtz to evaluate the situation and issued an ultimatum telling the miners to end the march. The miners continued. On August 25, they began arriving at Blair Mountain in northern Logan County. Sheriff Don Chafin, a hated symbol of anti-unionism in southern West Virginia, met them there with a combined force of deputies, mine guards, civilian volunteers, and others. Chafin's men had fortified their position on top of the ridge and were armed with machine guns and explosives.

By September 1, the miners had captured half of the 25-mile mountain ridge and were ready to descend upon Logan. President Harding, however, placed the strike zone under martial law, and ordered federal troops and a bombing squadron into the state. Unwilling to resist U.S. soldiers, the miners agreed to lay down their guns.

Keeney, Blizzard, union leader Fred Mooney, and more than 550 marchers were indicted on charges ranging from murder to treason against the state of West Virginia. All the union officials were acquitted, mostly for lack of evidence. One marcher, Walter Allen, was found guilty of treason; he jumped bail and disappeared

"A rebellious and treasonous enterprise"

"In West Virginia, men have taken up arms against the state and the nation. The head of the national government, who is the commander-in-chief of the army and navy, commanded them to disperse. They defied this constitutional authority. So they are engaged in rebellion—a defiance of the government of the state and the nation with arms.

"The cause or causes do not matter. Whatever the cause or the causes, get this fact and get it straight: the men of this state who are bearing arms against the government are in rebellion against all the people of the United States, engaged in a rebellious and treasonable enterprise; and those who lend them aid and comfort are engaged in the same business. . . .

"Today, less than three years after world freedom was gained, the people of our own state of West Virginia are threatened by a greater danger than the hateful German power threatened in 1918. This greater danger is right here at our door. The enemy is right here, not thousands of miles away. The enemy not only dares to shed the blood of peaceful citizens, but he would shatter our government. He would make . . . us subservient to the will of a small class of our citizenship, which has now become a violent, murderous, and treasonable mob. The lives of peaceful citizens are precious enough: but there is a thing more precious, and the enemy would destroy it. That more precious thing is our free government."

—Charleston Daily Mail September 1, 1921

while the case was pending in the state Supreme Court. Another, lay preacher John Wilburn, was convicted of murder and sentenced to ten years. Governor Morgan pardoned him in 1925.

See also Bill Blizzard, Don Chafin, Mine Wars, John Wilburn Trial

David A. Corbin
Office of Senator Robert C. Byrd

Miners' Vacation

Traditional coal miners' vacation became formalized after 1950 with the establishment of the Bituminous Coal Operators Association to conduct collective bargaining with unionized mine workers. West Virginia's coal miners overwhelmingly belonged to the United Mine Workers of America, and the union's national contracts recognized the last week of June and first week of July as the mandated period for the annual miners' vacation. With coal mining the dominant economic activity in the northern and southern regions of the state, the coming of miners' vacation in those areas took on the atmosphere of a major holiday.

Vacation money combined with regular wages swelled the pay envelopes of miners. The time off and increased pocket money created a festive mood throughout coalfield communities. Spending increased dramatically as miners purchased items for home repairs or made preparations for vacation travel, fishing trips, or other excursions. Although many made use of the break to tackle large personal projects, ever-increasing numbers headed for summer vacation spots. Myrtle Beach, South Carolina, became an overwhelmingly popular destination for Appalachian miners during this period. Some vacationing families visited relatives who had moved away to find work.

Coal companies had readily agreed to the mandated sabbatical because the industry needed at least one week for renovations and repairs, and miners' vacation remained an integral component of West Virginia's coal subculture well into the 1980s. By the close of that decade some major coal corporations had withdrawn from the BCOA and hoped to establish contracts with a more modern flexible work schedule. Accordingly, companies such as Pittston implemented a graduated leave policy, staggering vacations and allowing off only 10 percent of the work force at a time. The number of non-union mines also increased, lessening the influence of centralized bargaining on vacation periods. Modern mechanized operations often demanded that annual furlough be taken in conjunction with the intricate and time-consuming moves of longwall mining machinery. Some of today's West Virginia coal mines continue with the traditional vacation period.

See also Coal Industry, Holidays and Celebrations

Paul H. Rakes
WVU Institute of Technology

Department of Mines

Renamed the West Virginia Office of Miners' Health, Safety and Training in 1991, the Department of Mines was created early in the 20th century to strengthen enforcement of the state's mine safety laws. Its duties today are to inspect all mining-related sites, train and certify mine employees, investigate all serious accidents, and maintain health and safety data related to mining. In addition to the main Charleston office, there are regional offices in Fairmont, Oak Hill, Danville, and Welch.

Although commercial coal mining had existed in present West Virginia since the first half of the 19th century, the first state mine safety laws were not enacted until 1883. That year, the legislature required the appointment of a state mine inspector, whose job was to see that mines were properly drained and ventilated. A bill providing for better ventilation in the mines had been first introduced in the legislature in 1875. State laws were strengthened in 1887, the year following the Mountain Brook mine disaster that claimed 39 lives in Preston County. The 1887 legislation created a position of chief mine inspector and set up four inspection districts. Mining laws were also printed in book form for the first time.

The Department of Mines was created in 1905. In 1919, the legislature provided for the establishment of mine rescue stations to train personnel in rescue and first-aid work. By 1929, the department had 25 inspectors and three inspectors at large, with an annual budget of $191,040, not including the salary of the chief of the department. In 1985, the department was merged into a new Department of Energy, later renamed the Division of Energy. The current Office of Miners' Health, Safety and Training was established as part of a reorganization of the Division of Energy.

The policies and procedures of the mine agency have been updated through the years to keep pace with changes in the coal industry, including advances in technology and mining practices. Current mining statutes are set forth in Chapter 22A of the West Virginia Code. The agency in 2004 had 110 employees, including 74 inspectors.

See also Coal Industry, Mine Safety

Larry Sonis
Arlington, Texas

Mingo

Menkwa or Minqua, a word of Algonquin origin used to refer to speakers of Iroquoian languages, came to refer in the late colonial period to members of the Six Nations who lived outside of the Iroquois homeland in upstate New York. Euro-Americans adopted the term and eventually standardized the spelling as Mingo.

Thus Shikellamy, whom the Six Nations stationed at the Forks of the Susquehanna River to keep watch over the subject Indian peoples living on land the Iroquois claimed in Pennsylvania, was an Oneida. His youngest son, Tahgahjute or James Logan (Chief Logan), whose English name had been chosen to honor a colonial official, lived most of his life in Pennsylvania and Ohio and was known as a Mingo. Similarly in western Pennsylvania in the mid-18th century, Tanacharison or Half-King, a Seneca, presided over a Mingo village as well as several nearby villages with mixed populations of Mingos, Delawares, Shawnees, and other native origins. Most of the Mingo warriors who were actively engaged in attacks on West Virginia settlements came from this vicinity or from villages farther west in Ohio.

Mingos were not a "tribe" in the sense that this biblical term is usually applied to native societies. There was no Mingo language or culture, for example, apart from languages and cultural forms that Mingos shared with other Eastern woodland peoples. From the Euro-American standpoints, however, Mingo actions in warfare and trade were what mattered, and so whites included Mingo in their list of enemies in the long struggle for the Ohio Valley frontier. Thanks primarily to Logan—more specifically to his four raids on white settlements during the summer of 1774 and the famous speech in which he justified his actions—Mingos figured prominently in white annals of frontier warfare.

Following the collapse of native resistance in the 1790s, most Mingos went west with their Delaware and Shawnee neighbors. Though far from their Iroquois origins, they nevertheless gradually reverted to their former ethnic identities. Their descendants in modern Oklahoma are known as Seneca-Cayugas.

See also Indian Wars, Indians, Chief Logan

John Alexander Williams
Appalachian State University

Mingo County

Mingo County, created in 1895 from the southern part of Logan County, is the youngest county in West Virginia. It lies on the Tug Fork between McDowell and Wayne counties, with a territory of 423.5 square miles. It is also bordered by Wyoming, Logan, and Lincoln counties, and by Pike County, Kentucky, and Buchanan County, Virginia. Mingo County lies in the heart of Appalachia. It is named for the Mingo Indians, for whose best-known chief, Logan, the mother county was named.

Mingo County was created after the population of the Tug Valley boomed with the construction of the Norfolk & Western Railway through the region. Williamson is the county seat. Other principal towns include Delbarton, Matewan, and Gilbert. Mingo County is drained by the Tug Fork and the Guyandotte River and their tributaries, and the headwaters of Twelvepole Creek. The county is served by U.S. 119 (Appalachian Corridor G), U.S. 52, and several state and county routes, and by the Norfolk Southern Railroad, the successor to the N&W.

The first white settlers were farmers who entered the Tug Valley about 1800. They were largely of English, Scotch-Irish, and German origins. They were followed much later by those who came to

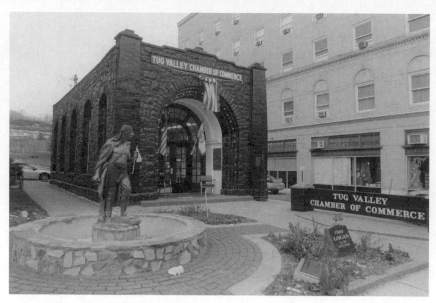

The Tug Valley Chamber of Commerce building is made of Mingo County coal.

mine the coal and build the railroads of the industrial era. These newcomers, arriving in the late 19th and early 20th centuries, brought a wide ethnic diversity to the new county. They included Italians, Russians, Poles, Czechoslovakians, and African-Americans, as well as Jews, Greeks, Lebanese, and others.

Mingo County has vast coal deposits. Commercial mining began with the arrival in 1890 of the N&W, which established a major rail yard at Williamson. The early mines were underground mines. Deep mining continues, but in recent decades there has been a shift toward surface mining in Mingo County, including mountaintop removal mining. Mountaintop removal has been controversial due to the altering of the terrain and the filling in of streams and valleys after the extraction of the coal. Some say that the practice has aggravated recent flooding of the region. Its defenders point out that this mining method has created flat land which is being used for economic development such as an industrial park and a prison.

Loggers, who had floated timber down the Tug in earlier years, also increased their efforts with the arrival of the N&W, building branch lines into the woods and soon harvesting the county's virgin forests.

Mingo County was still part of Logan County when the infamous Hatfield-McCoy Feud occurred. Most of the Hatfields resided in what became Mingo County, where they farmed and timbered and were politically active, and many of the feud's key events took place within the present county. The main part of the feud began in 1882. A total of 13 people were killed as the conflict continued into the 1890s. Several Hatfield partisans were jailed, and one, Ellison "Cottontop" Mounts, was hanged in Kentucky. The

vendetta died down after that. It became notorious due to the sensational publicity given it by the regional and national press.

Mingo County participated violently in the Mine Wars of the early 20th century. Matters came to a head in Matewan in May 1920, when police chief Sid Hatfield confronted agents of the Baldwin-Felts Detective Agency who had been evicting striking miners from local company-owned houses. A gun battle ensued, leaving ten people dead, mostly detectives. This shootout, which came to be known as the Matewan Massacre, was part of a chain of events leading up to the Battle of Blair Mountain in Logan County the next year, the largest armed uprising in America since the Civil War.

Despite the strains of change, Mingo prospered with industrialization. Matewan had opened a hospital in 1905, and Williamson Memorial Hospital was founded in 1918. County population increased from 11,359 in 1900 to 19,431 in 1910, peaking at 47,409 in 1950. Then the population fell, due to the mechanization of coal mines and other causes, including regional job losses due to the shift of the N&W from coal-fired steam locomotives to diesel. There were 28,253 Mingo Countians at the time of the 2000 census.

The Tug and Guyandotte rivers flood occasionally, sometimes doing great damage to Mingo County. The most devastating recent floods occurred in 1977 and 1984, causing the loss of many homes and the demise of many businesses in the riverside communities of Williamson, Matewan, Kermit, and Gilbert. The R. D. Bailey Dam was completed on the Guyandotte in 1980 as a flood-control project, and floodwalls were built at Williamson (1991) and Matewan (1996) to protect those towns from the Tug.

The local school system is operated by an elected county board of education.

FAST FACTS ABOUT MINGO COUNTY

Founded: 1895
Land in square miles: 423.5
Population: 28,253
Percentage minorities: 3.6%
Percentage rural: 89.0%
Median age: 37.2
Percentage 65 and older: 12.4%
Birth rate per 1,000 population: 12.8
Median household income: $21,347
High school graduate or higher: 59.6%
Bachelor's degree or higher: 7.3%
Home ownership: 77.7%
Median home value: $61,100

This information is from the 2000 U.S. Census. In 2000, West Virginia as a whole had 5 percent minorities, a median age of 38.9, median household income of $29,696, and a 75.2 percent home ownership rate.

Williamson has a campus of Southern West Virginia Community and Technical College. Southern began as a branch of Marshall University in 1969, becoming a community college when the state established the community college system. It offers associate degrees and provides education and training programs for local companies.

Prominent among Mingo County's recent citizens has been industrialist James H. "Buck" Harless of Gilbert, who parlayed small truck mines and sawmills into multimillion-dollar companies. The Discovery Channel and the Learning Channel were founded by John Hendricks, who was born in Matewan. The Dingess area produced Baltimore stripper Blaze Starr. Gen. Robert "Doc" Foglesong is chief of U.S. Air Force operations in Europe. Don Blankenship is the chief executive officer of Massey Energy, a leading producer of coal. Elliott Maynard is a justice of the West Virginia Supreme Court of Appeals.

Mingo County is still dependent on coal and its related industries; however, the tourism industry is emerging. Important developments include the Hatfield-McCoy Trail and the Williamson Area Railroad Museum. Additional tourism projects include the annual Hatfield-McCoy Reunion and Marathon, the King Coal Festival, and the preservation of Matewan as a national historic district. The completion of four-lane Appalachian Corridor G (U.S. 119) has opened the county to visitors from north and south.

See also Hatfield-McCoy Feud, Matewan Massacre, Williamson

Linda Van Meter
Williamson

Nancy Sue Smith, *History of Logan and Mingo Counties,* 1960; Altina Waller, *Feud: Hatfields, McCoys, and Social Change in Appalachia, 1860–1900,* 1988.

Mingo Oak

The Mingo Oak stood near the head of Trace Fork of Pigeon Creek near the Logan-Mingo county line. A monarch of the mountains, the tree was reported to be the largest white oak in the world. For the last 100 years it lived, the Mingo Oak was one of the best-known shrines in West Virginia. Residents referred to it as "the church in the wildwoods" because early settlers erected a pulpit surrounded by rustic benches beside its massive trunk. Almost every Sabbath day during the summer and early fall, rural ministers gathered their followers to conduct religious services underneath the canopy of green. It has been estimated that more than 500 sermons were preached there.

The Mingo Oak was cut in the fall of 1938 after succumbing to the fumes of a burning coal refuse pile. It was cut by a special crew imported for the purpose from Webster County. The tree was felled by two loggers, Paul Criss and Upton "Uppie" Sears, with the help of Civilian Conservation Corps enrollees. At the time its age was calculated at 577 years, having sprouted in the year 1361. It stood 145 feet tall, just over eight feet in diameter at breast height, and had a limb spread of 96 feet. The trunk scaled at 15,000 board feet, and was calculated to weigh 55 tons. A movie was taken during the cutting, and sections of the Mingo Oak were preserved for the West Virginia State Museum and the Smithsonian Institution. Judge R. D. Bailey of Wyoming County had a gavel made from the wood of the tree. Approximately 2,000 people gathered to watch the fall of this West Virginia giant.

Robert Beanblossom
Division of Natural Resources

Mining Methods in the Hand-Loading Era

Most early mines were of the drift entry type, which located an outcrop of coal on a hillside and tunneled directly and horizontally into the seam. Drift mines presented fewer logistical problems than vertical shaft mines and required minimal capital to open.

Most operations used the room-and-pillar method. Miners drove parallel main tunnels called entries from the entry point toward the mine's other side. Mining then proceeded in reverse fashion, from the farthest point back toward the front. Breakthroughs connected main tunnels at specified intervals. The "mains" were generally named according to their direction, such as North Main or Southwest Main. Miners advanced side entries at right angles to the mains, with designations such as 1st Left, 2nd Left, or 3rd Right depending on their relationship to the mine opening and main entries. The rectangular block of coal outlined by the side entries and the mains—perhaps 500 by 2,000 feet—created a panel. Miners then opened rooms with connecting breakthroughs through this panel. Smaller blocks of coal—for instance 75 by 80 feet—between breakthroughs and adjacent rooms, known as pillars, were left in place to support the roof. Miners extracted or "pulled" the pillars as a last step in mining an area, getting the last of the coal while retreating toward the side entries and permitting the roof or top to fall behind them. It was the most dangerous part of the work.

Ventilating the myriad of tunnels was complicated. A few early mines relied on natural ventilation or used large furnaces to create a draft. By 1900, steam and electric fans made larger mines possible. Trap doors at strategic points and the construction of masonry or wooden stoppings in breakthroughs established a path for air to follow. Many operations continued the dangerous practice of circulating the same air from one working section to another until late in the 20th century. As a result, liberated gasses, dust, and powder smoke permeated the atmosphere of the last working section in the air cycle.

In a room or entry, the solid coal to the miner's front was the face, the pillar walls to the sides the ribs, and any discarded refuse the gob. One or two miners worked a place, depending on the room or entry width. The miners loaded coal by hand. Hand loaders owned their own implements, but paid tool maintenance fees for the operation's blacksmiths and purchased blasting powder from the company.

Hand mining required skill, and young miners usually served an apprenticeship under a relative. Lying on their sides, miners first used a pick to undercut the

A pick and shovel miner at work, about 1940.

coal three to four feet deep. Undercutting required two to three hours each shift, and standing water often made the task particularly unpleasant. Based on his knowledge of the coal seam, the miner then chose the appropriate places to manually drill the coal face and tamp the holes with explosives. Well placed, the subsequent blast dislodged the coal as far back as the undercut. Poorly placed, the shot broke away little or no coal, and dropped the material in a solid block. This was known as a hung shot. Careless or unskilled blasting preparations could produce a blown-out shot that suspended and ignited the coal dust. After shooting, miners loaded the coal into a mine car, set timber roof props, and extended the track for the next cycle. Throughout the process, skilled miners read the geological signs and sounds for danger.

Mule drivers gathered the loaded mine cars from the various rooms and delivered empties. They took strings or trips of the loaded cars to the main entries for transfer to the outside. Although by 1900 many mines used compressed-air, steam, or electric mine locomotives for mainline haulage, mules remained a significant part of the process into the 1920s. Boys as young as nine served as trappers, opening and closing ventilation trap doors to permit the passage of these trips.

Because of the skill required and their freedom from direct supervision at the working face, hand loaders developed a strong sense of pride and independence. Machines took over the undercutting step early in the century, but the basic routine of manual drilling, blasting, and loading remained prevalent through the 1930s.

Paul H. Rakes
WVU Institute of Technology

Keith Dix, *What's a Coal Miner to Do? The Mechanization of Coal Mining*, 1988; W.P. Tams, *The Smokeless Coal Fields of West Virginia, A Brief History*, 1963.

Minnehaha Springs

Minnehaha Springs is located at the junction of Knapps Creek and Douthat Creek, about nine miles east of Marlinton in Pocahontas County. During the Civil War the Confederate Army had a camp, Camp Northwest, located to the east of Minnehaha Springs. In 1890, a post office was established and given the name Driscol, from lumberman John Driscol.

In the early 1900s, residents began to look at the spring, with its large flow, constant temperature, and alleged medicinal properties, as the future of their community. The completion of the Chesapeake & Ohio Railway's Greenbrier Division to Marlinton in 1900 put the spring within reach of travelers. The spring, named for the Indian maiden of Longfellow's poem, is a thermal spring with traces of many minerals. In 1912, the Minnehaha Springs Improvement Company was formed, and a bathing pool opened to the public. A post office with the name Minnehaha Springs was established, which closed in 1989.

A two-story hotel building, on the hill above the spring, was completed in 1914. It had several owners and was open only sporadically over the years. The hotel was destroyed by fire February 4, 1945.

Although not successful, this hotel was the first facility in Pocahontas County built and operated strictly for the tourist business and a forerunner of today's much more lucrative local tourism economy. A more successful use of the property has been as a summer youth camp, beginning in 1944 and continuing to the present. The camp, now named Twin Creeks, was for boys before becoming coed in 2001.

Minnehaha Springs also was the location of another early effort to capitalize on the recreational potential of Pocahontas County, the Allegheny Lodge.

See also Allegheny Lodge, Mineral Springs

William P. McNeel
Marlinton

Minter Homes

The Minter Homes Corporation, a manufacturer of ready-to-build housing, was established in Huntington in 1913 as a division of Huntington Lumber & Supply Company. Founded in 1912 by William E. Minter, the lumber company was well situated to capitalize on the logging in southern West Virginia. It was located near three major logging streams, Twelvepole Creek, and the Guyandotte and Big Sandy rivers, while the Chesapeake & Ohio, Baltimore & Ohio, and Norfolk & Western railway lines converged at Huntington and nearby Kenova.

The Sears, Roebuck Company and Montgomery Ward already had established a market for pre-cut houses. Minter Homes emulated these better-known competitors by issuing a catalog of house plans and supplying the specifications and all materials needed for construction. Customers could choose anything from three-room cottages to elaborate, columned mansions.

In addition to supplying custom millwork, doors, windows, interior trim, mantels, and other building supplies, the corporation shipped individual house packages and entire mill or industrial villages throughout the South and East. Notable among these villages was the town of Nitro, established in 1917 by the U.S. War Department for the manufacture of munitions for World War I. Minter Homes supplied the plans and materials for 1,724 houses, which were built at Nitro between February and July, 1918. The company did not limit itself to supplying individual cottages and bungalows. In addition to school buildings and churches, the catalog also listed bunkhouses, boarding houses, and multi-family dwellings, all suitable for construction in mining or lumber camps.

At the peak of its operations, the company employed 125 people in the mill in addition to 10 traveling salesmen and had an annual business of $3 million. By 1954, Minter Homes had gone out of the ready-cut home business, concentrating its work on custom millwork, finished lumber, windows, doors, and other items for building contractors. With only six employees in 1982–83, the company finally closed its doors.

See also Nitro

Cora P. Teel
Marshall University

Billy Mitchell

Brigadier General William L. "Billy" Mitchell (1879–1936), pioneer aviator, was chief of the Army Air Service in 1921. He eagerly expanded the role of airplanes in the military. The decision to commit U.S. Army troops to end the 1921 Miners' March on Logan afforded him an opportunity to demonstrate that the planes could provide tactical information in rugged, mountainous terrain and be useful in quelling civil disturbances. Arriving in Charleston on August 26, Mitchell ordered the 88th Squadron, part of the 1st Provisional Air Brigade, to southern West Virginia to take part in ending the fighting then going on between miners and operators on the border of Logan County. The planes, which have remained a controversial part of the story of the West Virginia Mine Wars, were used for reconnaissance and did not exercise force against the combatants.

See also Battle of Blair Mountain

Kenneth R. Bailey
WVU Institute of Technology

Maurer, Maurer, and Calvin F. Senning, "Billy Mitchell, the Air Service and the Mingo War," *West Virginia History,* October 1968.

Mildred Mitchell-Bateman

Physician Mildred Mitchell-Bateman was born in Georgia, March 22, 1922. She became the first black woman in West Virginia to hold a high-level state administrative position when, in 1962, Governor Barron appointed her as the director of the Department of Mental Health. She served in that post for 15 years.

Mitchell-Bateman holds a bachelor's degree from Johnson C. Smith University in North Carolina and a medical degree from the Women's College of Pennsylvania. She married William L. Bateman in 1947.

Her career in West Virginia began in 1947 with her acceptance of a position as staff physician at Lakin State Hospital, which served black mental patients. Leaving Lakin to establish her own practice, Mitchell-Bateman went on to study at the Meninger School of Psychiatry in Topeka. Invited to return to Lakin in 1955, she became superintendent of the hospital in 1958, and two years later assumed a position as supervisor of professional services for the West Virginia Department of Mental Health. Subsequently, she was appointed director of the department.

Mitchell-Bateman became the vice president of the American Psychiatric Associa-

tion in 1973 and a member of the Presidential Commission on Mental Health which developed the Mental Health Systems Act of 1980. After leaving public service, she chaired the Department of Psychiatry at the Marshall University Medical School and was later the clinical director of Huntington State Hospital. The state hospital was renamed in her honor in 1999.

Ancella R. Bickley
Charleston

West Virginia Women's Commission, *American Sampler: West Virginia's African-American Women of Distinction, Volume I,* 2002.

Moccasin Rangers

The Moccasin Rangers were a Confederate guerrilla company that operated around the headwaters of the Little Kanawha River during the first two years of the Civil War. The Moccasins, led by Perry Conley, drew most of their members from Calhoun County, but at various times included men from Webster and Braxton counties. Other leaders were George Downs, Daniel Duskey, and Peter Saurburn. Conley's name has been linked to Confederate spy Nancy Hart, from whom he received intelligence on Union forces.

The Moccasins were regarded as bushwhackers by many. According to West Virginia Civil War historian Boyd Stutler, they were responsible for atrocities on the civilian population in the region and only rarely participated in actual combat with federal troops. A group of Moccasin Rangers captured Ripley in 1861 and looted the town. The group, led by Duskey, was later captured and the men were treated as common criminals rather than prisoners of war. Indicted, tried, and sentenced to prison for robbery, they appealed to the Confederate government to intervene. The Confederates finally secured their release by trading two Union officers for them. The Confederate government tried to legitimize the Rangers by enlisting them as Company A of the 19th Regiment of Virginia Cavalry. The Rangers were neutralized only after the Union Army occupied the area in force. Some members of the Moccasin Rangers continued their service in regular Confederate units, including the 19th Regiment, until the end of the war.

See also Bushwhackers, Civil War

Kenneth R. Bailey
WVU Institute of Technology

Calhoun County Historical and Genealogical Society, *History of Calhoun County,* 1990; Boyd B. Stutler, *West Virginia in the Civil War,* 1966.

Modern Budget Amendment

In November 1968, West Virginians ratified the Modern Budget Amendment. The vote was 323,560 for and 159,255 against, a majority of 164,305. This amendment to the state constitution greatly strengthened the power of the governor of West Virginia,

particularly as regards the state's budget and finances.

Until ratification of the amendment, West Virginia had had a very weak governor, among the weakest in the United States. Previously, West Virginia had been one of only five states not having a chief executive budget system, one where the governor of the state was solely responsible for formulating, presenting, and executing the state's budget. Instead, from 1863 until 1968 West Virginia had a powerful Board of Public Works, composed of the elected members of the executive branch, including the treasurer, attorney general, secretary of state, auditor, and agricultural commissioner, as well as the governor. This board collectively controlled the state's finances and budget covering most areas of fiscal control, greatly diluting the power of the governor.

The budget-making powers granted the chief executive in the 1968 amendment were so sweeping that West Virginia's governor now ranks among the strongest in the United States. In addition, the Modern Budget Amendment gave the governor the power to veto the entire budget bill, any supplementary appropriation bill, or any line item in them, and to reduce any items in the bills. Governor Moore was the first to benefit from the change. The Modern Budget Amendment was one of several amendments passed during Moore's first two terms that together restructured West Virginia state government.

See also Constitution of West Virginia

Donald R. Andrews
University of Charleston

Alan Mollohan

Congressman Alan Bowlby Mollohan, who was born in Fairmont, May 14, 1943, is a congressman's son who has served longer than his father in the U.S. House of Representatives. For six years, beginning in seventh grade, he attended Greenbrier Military School in Lewisburg. Mollohan went on to graduate from the College of William and Mary and West Virginia University's College of Law before beginning a legal career with a Fairmont law firm in 1970. First elected to the House in 1982, he has been reelected every two years since then.

Alan Mollohan's father, Robert Mollohan (1909–99) was elected to the House in 1952 and 1954 before running as the Democratic nominee for governor in 1956, when Republican Cecil Underwood was elected. Robert Mollohan lost an attempt to return to Congress in 1966, but he reclaimed the seat in 1968. He was reelected every two years after that until he retired in 1982.

In replacing his father in 1982, Alan Mollohan defeated not only Democratic primary opponents but also Republican

John McCuskey. In 1984, Republican Jim Altmeyer waged a strong but unsuccessful campaign against Mollohan. After that, Mollohan usually did not face strong opponents in his reelection bids. The notable exception was in 1992, when he was pitted against another incumbent congressman, Harley Staggers Jr., also the son of a congressman, in the Democratic primary. Because of West Virginia's loss of about 8 percent of its population during the 1980s, when most other states gained population, the size of the state's House delegation dropped from four to three members. Unfortunately for Staggers, in re-drawing the boundaries the state legislature cut him off from most of his former district in eastern West Virginia and put him into a northern district mostly made up of Mollohan's old district. Mollohan won 13 of the 19 counties in the new First District and received 65 percent of the vote.

In 1986, Mollohan was appointed to the powerful House Appropriations Committee. That put him in a position to direct more federal funding to West Virginia, often working in cooperation with Robert Byrd, the senior Democrat on the Senate Appropriations Committee. Over the years, he became the top Democrat on the Appropriations subcommittee that funds the Department of Veterans Affairs and the Department of Housing and Urban Development, as well as several independent agencies, including the National Aeronautics and Space Administration, the Environmental Protection Agency, and the National Science Foundation.

Since the beginning of his career in Congress, Mollohan has been a member of the Congressional Steel Caucus and opponent of many international trade treaties. As a strong opponent of abortion, he has also been a member and co-chairman of the Pro-Life Caucus. Mollohan was instrumental in the creation of the West Virginia High Technology Consortium Foundation, the Institute for Scientific Research, the Mid-Atlantic Aerospace Complex, and the Canaan Valley Institute.

In 1976, Mollohan married Barbara Whiting, who was a speech therapist in the Ohio County schools although she is originally from Glenville. They are the parents of four sons and one daughter.

Jim Wallace
Charleston

Moncove Lake

Moncove Lake, like other lakes in West Virginia, is a man-made impoundment. It was created by the damming in 1959 of Devil Creek in eastern Monroe County. The name was coined from "Mon," the first three letters of the county name, and "cove," referring to a small valley.

The lake was built as a part of the Moncove Public Hunting and Fishing area,

Moncove Lake is beautiful any time of year.

purchased in 1958 by the West Virginia Conservation Commission, now the Division of Natural Resources. Originally, the area consisted of 270 acres, including the 144-acre lake. In 1997, an additional 626 acres was added to provide more hunting lands.

Moncove Lake State Park was created in 1991 by the West Virginia legislature. The diversity of habitat, including old fields, forest, and wetlands, attracts many kinds of game and song birds, and animals such as rabbits, squirrels, and deer. Moncove Lake State Park has 48 campsites, a swimming pool, and two bathhouses. Fishing, boating, picnicking, and nearby hunting draw a variety of users.

Moncove Lake is located six miles northeast of Gap Mills.

Raymond Thomas Hill
Athens

Monongah Mine Disaster

On December 6, 1907, a massive explosion ripped through the Fairmont Coal Company's No. 6 and 8 mines in Monongah, Marion County. The powerful blast, which shook the earth and was heard several miles away, killed at least 361 men, making it the worst mine disaster in U.S. history. Although investigators never definitively pinpointed the cause, they concluded that an underground train wreck, a blasting operation gone awry, or an open flame lamp had created an ignition and stirred accumulations of dust and gas, thereby triggering the massive explosion.

Many of the men employed at the two mines were recent immigrants, with especially high concentrations from Italy, Hungary, and Russia. Because there were no trained rescue workers at the time, miners from Pennsylvania, Maryland, and Ohio—many of them fellow immigrants—hastened to Monongah to help

with rescue efforts. Putting ethnic rivalries aside, these rescue crews inched through 700 acres of underground workings, battling fires, cave-ins, and deadly, explosive gases with little more than picks and shovels. Eventually, the mutilated bodies of men and boys—some as young as eight—were pulled from the carnage. The actual number of deaths has been estimated as substantially higher because the miner identification system was destroyed in the explosion.

In the weeks following the explosion at Monongah, three other major mine disasters occurred, prompting the last month of 1907 to be nicknamed "Black December." In the final tally, 3,241 American miners were killed on the job that year, the largest number killed in a single year in this country's history. In spite of such horrific accidents, many mining operations, including Monongah, continued to ignore recognized safety precautions, using open candles instead of shielded lamps, employing cheap dynamite instead of controllable explosives, and skipping tests that would detect methane gas. Such practices were already being followed in Europe.

As a result of the national outcry following Monongah and the other mining disasters, Congress initiated fundamental reforms. In 1908, President Theodore Roosevelt advocated the formation of a federal agency to investigate mine accidents, teach accident prevention, and conduct mine safety research. Two years later, the Bureau of Mines was formed.

J. Davitt McAteer
Shepherdstown

William Graebner, *Coal-Mining Safety in the Progressive Period*, 1976.

Monongahela Culture

The ancient Monongahela people lived in what is now northern West Virginia and adjacent areas of Ohio, Pennsylvania, and Maryland in the late prehistoric and near-historic (or protohistoric) periods (A.D. 1200–1690). The Monongahela were contemporaries of the Fort Ancient people living farther south, but culturally distinct. They built circular houses and lived in small, circular, stockaded villages. These were located along the Ohio River and its major tributaries, north of the vicinity of present Moundsville, and along the Monongahela River, north of present Fairmont. Because of the smaller floodplains in the northern Ohio River drainage, the Monongahela people also occupied numerous upland villages along major Indian trails located along drainage divides.

The Monongahela practiced intensive corn horticulture, made shell-tempered pottery, and hunted deer, elk, bear, and turkey with the bow and arrow. Excavated villages from the late prehistoric period include Britt Bottom and the Saddle Site in Marshall County, the Duvall Site in Ohio County, and Belldina's Bottoms in Monongalia County. Villages with later occupations, where European trade goods have been recovered, include the Hughes Farm Site in Ohio County and the LaPoe Site near Morgantown.

Archeologists have failed to connect West Virginia's prehistoric people to specific Indian tribes of the historic period. Based on early 17th-century cartographic, historic, and ethnohistoric documentation, however, the later Monongahela people of the protohistoric period may have been Iroquoian speakers belonging to the Massawomeck (Black Minqua) and the Atiouandaron groups. The Black Minqua wore a black badge on their breasts, and some archeologists believe these are the cannel coal pendants that are common at Monongahela sites. The Monongahela supplied furs to Iroquoian tribes in the lower Great Lakes and acted as middlemen in the marine shell trade which originated in the Chesapeake Bay area. By 1635, they were dispersed by the Seneca, and those remaining joined the Susquehannocks (White Minqua) in eastern Pennsylvania.

See also Archeology, Fort Ancient Culture, Prehistoric People

Robert F. Maslowski
Milton

Monongahela National Forest

The Monongahela National Forest is the only national forest that is completely within the boundaries of West Virginia. The first land was purchased in 1915, and in 1920, by presidential proclamation, it became the Monongahela National Forest.

In the late 19th and early 20th century, logging and timber operations had removed much of the hardwood stands of the Allegheny Mountains, causing serious ecological damage to these mountains and erosion along the streams. In March 1907, the land along the banks of the Monongahela River was devastated by flooding. As a result of this damage and damage to woodlands and streams in other areas of the United States, Congress enacted the Weeks Law in 1911 which authorized the federal government to cooperate with the various states to purchase land for the protection of the watersheds of navigable streams. Through other federal legislation, the purposes of the national forests were extended to include reforestation and timber production, wildlife management, and outdoor recreation.

The Monongahela National Forest is managed by the U.S. Forest Service, with the supervisor's office in Elkins and district offices in Parsons, Richwood, Bartow, Marlinton, Petersburg, and White Sulphur Springs. Tourist centers are maintained near Cranberry Glades and at Seneca Rocks. The forest now includes almost 920,000 acres in 10 counties, extending from Preston in the north to Greenbrier in the south. The forest also includes extensive land in Grant, Tucker, Pendleton, Randolph, Pocahontas, Webster, and Nicholas counties, along with 11 acres in Barbour County. The forest is the largest geographic entity in West Virginia, covering almost six percent of the total area of the state. Three state parks, Canaan Valley Resort, Watoga, and Blackwater Falls, as well as two state forests, Seneca and Calvin Price, are inside the national forest. Timber, grazing, land uses, and minerals continue to provide revenue to the state and federal governments.

The Civilian Conservation Corps was active within the Monongahela National Forest from the creation of the Corps in 1933 until its termination in 1942. There were 21 CCC camps in the forest. Their projects included the construction of roads and trails, forest management, fire protection, and other conservation efforts. The roads and trails built by the CCC still provide the public with access to remote wilderness areas.

There are five federally designated wilderness areas in the forest, at Otter Creek, Dolly Sods, Laurel Fork North, Laurel Fork South, and Cranberry, as well as one National Recreation Area, Spruce Knob-Seneca Rocks. There are caves at Smoke Hole and Seneca Caverns, a tract of virgin timber at Gaudineer Knob, botanical gardens at Cranberry Glades, and wilderness trails at Dolly Sods. The forest also contains the Fernow Experimental Forest in Tucker County, maintained by the Forest Service to study hardwood forests management.

The Monongahela National Forest encompasses the high mountain country of West Virginia, including Spruce Knob, at 4,861 feet the state's highest point. Many major rivers find their headwaters within the forest, including the Elk, Gauley, Greenbrier, Potomac, Cheat, and the Monongahela itself. Seneca Rocks, one of West Virginia's best-known landmarks, is among the scenic wonders of this great upland empire.

Tom Haas
Charlotte, North Carolina
Stan Cohen, *The Tree Army*, 1980; Allen De Hart and Bruce Sundquist, *Monongahela National Forest Hiking Guide*, 1999; United States Forest Service, "USDA Forest Service Interim Strategic Outreach Plan," 2000.

Monongahela Power Company

Monongahela Power Company, doing business under the name Allegheny Power as a subsidiary of Allegheny Energy, of Hagerstown, Maryland, has its roots in Fairmont. In the summer of 1890, Fairmont Electric Light and Power began operating a 30-kilowatt plant on the Monongahela River, providing the city with electric lights. By 1900, the Schmulbach brewing interests of Wheeling acquired control of Fairmont Electric and built Fairmont's first electric streetcar line. A second plant with a capacity of 210 kilowatts was built. In 1903, local businessmen bought the company back and incorporated it as the Fairmont and Clarksburg Traction Company.

As demand for lighting and other purposes supplanted electric streetcars as the major market for electricity, the company name and corporate strategy continued to evolve. In 1921, the company changed its name to Monongahela Power and Railway Company. Two years later, it was renamed Monongahela West Penn Public Service Company. The company continued to grow through acquisition and expansion, serving an increasing number of customers as the demand for electricity rose. By 1944, the company was completely out of the streetcar business, and in 1945 the corporate name was changed to Monongahela Power Company.

As a subsidiary of Allegheny Energy, Monongahela Power (Allegheny Power) in 2001 served about 358,000 electric customers and 24,000 natural gas customers in a service area of about 13,000 square miles including parts of West Virginia and Ohio. The holding company, Allegheny Energy, operates three other subsidiaries: Potomac Edison Company (serving parts of Maryland, Virginia, and West Virginia); West Penn Power Company (serving portions of Pennsylvania); and Mountaineer Gas Company of West Virginia. Allegheny Power delivers electricity, primarily coal-generated, and natural gas to about 1.7 million residential, business, and industrial customers in an area of approximately 31,000 square miles. In April 2001, Allegheny Energy was put on the *Fortune* 500 list and ranked 417th based on its revenues.

Larry Sonis
Arlington, Texas

The Monongahela River

The Monongahela River is formed at Fairmont, by the merging of the West Fork and Tygart Valley River. The "Mon," as it is often called by people of the region, terminates 128 miles away at Pittsburgh, where it joins the larger Allegheny to form the Ohio River. Navigable for its entire length due to a system of locks and dams, the river drains a basin of 7,340 square miles. An ancient predecessor river was once blocked by glacier ice north of Pittsburgh to form the prehistoric Lake Monongahela, which occupied portions of present Ohio, Pennsylvania, and West Virginia.

The Monongahela watershed includes much of north-central West Virginia, southwestern Pennsylvania, and western Maryland. The Cheat River joins the Monongahela in Pennsylvania just north of Morgantown, and another major tributary, the Youghiogheny River, enters near Pittsburgh. Fairmont and Morgantown are the major cities on the Monongahela, apart from Pittsburgh at the river's mouth.

Early downstream commerce was by flatboats built at Morgantown and other points along the river. Too heavy and cumbersome to travel back upstream, they were floated downstream and sold for lumber at the end of the journey. Later, keelboats operated in both directions. These graceful craft, with a central keel from which ribs curved upward to create a cargo box, had a narrow deck on each side along which men walked, pushing poles against the river's bottom and banks.

One of the early and very famous products of commerce transported on the river was Monongahela rye, a whiskey sold and respected as far downstream as New Orleans. On March 3, 1791, Congress placed a tax on distilled spirits. This enraged the makers, and the short-lived Whiskey Rebellion of 1794 resulted.

On March 17, 1811, the first steamboat on a western river, the *New Orleans,* was launched on the Monongahela at Pittsburgh. It wasn't until April 1826 that a steamboat traveled as far upstream as Morgantown. In 1837, the Monongahela Navigation Company was formed to improve the river for navigation. By 1844, four dams had been built upstream from Pittsburgh. Two additional dams were built in 1854 and 1865. In 1871, the federal government conducted a survey of the river and as a result eventually built another nine dams, finishing with No. 15 in 1904. This made the Monongahela the first river in the United States to be totally controlled for navigation. The modern system of nine locks and dams was built 1904–64, with six dams in Pennsylvania and three in West Virginia. As late as 1930, a major drought lowered the Mon's water level so much that it was possible in places to walk across the river bottom.

Despite the navigation dams, the lower Monongahela flooded heavily in 1907, causing more than $100 million of damage along the river and in the city of Pittsburgh. An aroused public supposedly pointed to the timbered and burned-over watersheds of the Monongahela tributaries—the Cheat, Buckhannon, West Fork, and Tygart Valley rivers—as the cause. Congress passed the Weeks Law in 1911, providing for the establishment of national forests as a way of reforesting lands to prevent subsequent floods. West Virginia was one of the first two southern states to pass enabling legislation, and the first steps to establish the Monongahela National Forest were taken in 1915.

William H. Gillespie
Charleston

Earl L. Core, *The Monongalia Story,* 1974–1984.

Monongahela Silt Loam

Monongahela silt loam is the state soil of West Virginia. It is widespread through the state, occurring on more than 100,000 acres in 45 counties. Described by the U.S. Department of Agriculture as a very deep, moderately well-drained soil, Monongahela silt loam is a prime agricultural soil. It is well suited to the production of cultivated crops as well as hay, pasture, and timber.

Actually a series or family of soils sharing related characteristics, Monohgahela silt loam was first identified in Greene County, Pennsylvania, in 1921. It was named for the Monongahela River, which drains Greene County and much of north-central West Virginia. Monongahela silt loam also occurs in a large region outside the Monongahela River watershed, in parts of several states. The soil derives largely from sandstone and shale, sedimentary rocks formed millennia ago by the siltation of streams. It occurs particularly on terraces but is also present on slopes of as much as 25 percent grade. The soil is slightly acidic.

Monongahela silt loam was designated the official soil of West Virginia by the state legislature in April 1997. Governor Underwood honored the soil and its advocates by the issuance of a colorful poster in a ceremony in his office in November of the same year.

Monongalia County

In July 1775, Virginia formed the District of West Augusta on the western frontier. In October 1776, West Augusta was subdivided into three large counties, Monongalia, Yohogania, and Ohio. Since that time many counties in Pennsylvania and present West Virginia have been formed from the original Monongalia County. The county's present size is 368.8 square miles.

The first white settlement in what is now Monongalia County was made in April 1758 by Tobias Decker with a party of 50 people. They built cabins where Deckers Creek enters the Monongahela River, the present site of Morgantown. Delaware Indians raided this settlement in October 1759, and the survivors scattered, finding safety in other settlements nearby. During the 1760s, several permanent settlers established homesteads. In 1766, Zackquill Morgan registered a land claim. In 1783–84, he had surveyor Maj. William Haymond divide this land into building lots and streets, and in 1785 legislation establishing Morgan's Town was enacted. Indian raids continued until 1791, and at an early date Kerns Fort was constructed on the east side of Deckers Creek.

In November 1814, Monongalia Academy was established, and in 1831 the trustees also formed Morgantown Female Collegiate Institute. Both schools flourished, and Morgantown became known as an educational center. In 1858, Presbyterians established a second school for females, Woodburn Female Seminary. When West Virginia was formed, June 20, 1863, the legislature made plans to establish a federal land grant college under the terms of the Morrill Act. Several towns expressed interest in having the college, but Morgantown officials backed up their request by pledging the buildings and resources of Monongalia Academy and Woodburn Female Seminary to the new college. Thus on February 7, 1867, West Virginia Agricultural College was established. In 1868, the name was changed to West Virginia University.

In the 1790s, iron ore was discovered on Chestnut Ridge, and by 1798 the Davis furnace was in operation, producing a ton of iron daily. An iron community sprang up on the Cheat River at Ices Ferry, which at its peak in the 1840s had a population of 2,500. There were three other furnaces, the Woodgrove, Henry Clay, and Anna. Ices Ferry had a foundry, rolling mill, and nail factory. This industry prospered until 1848 and then operated intermittently until 1868.

During the Civil War, Monongalia County staunchly supported the Union, supplying many more men for the northern armies than for the Confederacy. On April 28, 1863, several hundred Confederate soldiers under the command of Gen. William "Grumble" Jones raided Morgantown to steal horses, cattle, and supplies, and to try to capture Waitman T. Willey, U.S. senator for the Reorganized State of Virginia. Fortunately, Willey had left for Washington earlier that morning. Troops remained in the Morgantown area for two days, looting stores and

FAST FACTS ABOUT MONONGALIA COUNTY

Founded: 1776
Land in square miles: 368.8
Population: 81,866
Percentage minorities: 7.8%
Percentage rural: 31.6%
Median age: 30.4
Percentage 65 and older: 10.7%
Birth rate per 1,000 population: 10.5
Median household income: $28,625
High school graduate or higher: 83.6%
Bachelor's degree or higher: 32.4%
Home ownership: 61.0%
Median home value: $95,500

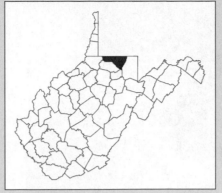

This information is from the 2000 U.S. Census. In 2000, West Virginia as a whole had 5 percent minorities, a median age of 38.9, median household income of $29,696, and a 75.2 percent home ownership rate.

rounding up horses, and then left in the direction of Fairmont.

The first railroad reached Morgantown in 1886. This was a branch of the Baltimore & Ohio, which had extended north along the east side of the Monongahela River from Fairmont. This line was completed to Connellsville, Pennsylvania, by 1894, providing through service to Pittsburgh. By 1906, the Morgantown & Kingwood Railroad was running regular trains to Kingwood, continuing on to the main line of the B&O at Rowlesburg. By 1912, the Monongahela Railroad had been completed to Pittsburgh, opening up the rich coal reserves on the western side of the river.

In 1889, the first oil was discovered in Monongalia County. Under the advice of I. C. White, professor and state geologist, an oil well was drilled on Doll's Run near Core. This well was so productive that within three months there were 20 other wells nearby, and natural gas found with the oil was being diverted for commercial use. The oil and gas industry expanded farther and farther into western Monongalia County, and many boomtowns sprang up and flourished until their wells gave out. By 1890, the rapid expansion of the oil and gas industry resulted in establishing a vast tank field southeast of Morgantown which at its peak could store more than a million barrels of oil.

The excellent transportation, large supply of cheap natural gas, and deposits of glass sand found along Deckers Creek persuaded the Seneca Glass Company to move from Ohio to Morgantown in 1896. Other glassmakers soon followed, some making fine lead glass, known for its sparkle, brilliance, and good etching character. Others produced soda-lime glass for tumblers, tableware, windshields, canning jars, glass stoppers, and other utilitarian products. The industry thrived for nearly a century, until foreign imports reduced demand. Morgantown glass was known worldwide for its beauty and workmanship.

Efforts to build navigation locks on the Monongahela started in the 1840s near Pittsburgh, and continued slowly toward the headwaters. By 1889, navigable slack water had been extended to the Morgantown area, and regular riverboat service to Pittsburgh was established. Passenger service continued for many years, but competition from railroads made river travel less attractive. Today only freight moves on the Monongahela, including coal and limestone.

By 1890, a coal mine had opened at Beechwood, along the B&O Railroad near the Marion County line, and extensive coal mining was later stimulated by the demands of World War I. Completion of the Monongahela Railroad and discovery of the thick, accessible Pittsburgh coal seam on Scotts Run attracted many large mines and thousands of workers. Monongalia was a leading coal producer for half a century, adding greatly to the economic development of the area, and major production continues today in mines in western Monongalia County.

From the first, the university expanded, but the most spectacular development occurred after World War II, when enrollment doubled and large scale expansion programs became a reality. The purchase of land for the Evansdale and Medical campuses in the late 1940s and the continuous stream of new buildings have made Morgantown a leader in many fields of higher education. A unique feature of the university is the PRT, or Personal Rapid Transit System, which connects the three campuses. Running on elevated tracks, these modern, rubber-tired cars operate on their own to help meet university transportation needs.

Although much significant research is carried on throughout the university, the medical center, with its teaching and research facilities and hospitals, has gained particular fame. Among their facilities are the Mary Babb Randolph Cancer Center and the John Michael Moore Trauma Center, which are known for their facilities and significant contributions to state-of-the-art medical techniques and knowledge. Mylan Pharmaceuticals, one of the country's major drug makers, operates from modern facilities near the university campus.

Monongalia County, with a 2000 population of 81,866, is one of West Virginia's most prosperous counties. Interstates 79 and 68 converge at Morgantown, providing high-speed highway travel to the north, south, and east.

See also Morgantown, West Virginia University

Kenneth L. Carvell
Morgantown

James M. Callahan, *History of the Making of Morgantown, West Virginia*, 1926; Earl L. Core, *The Monongalia Story: A Bicentennial History*, 1974–1984; West Virginia University Public History Option, *Morgantown: A Bicentennial History*, 1985.

Monroe County

Monroe County encompasses 473.8 square miles of the southeastern portion of West Virginia, the Virginia border being its eastern and southern boundary. The New River separates Monroe County from Mercer County. The western end of Monroe County became part of Summers County in 1871. Greenbrier County is to the north. The Great Eastern Divide runs through Monroe County, separating the watersheds of the Atlantic and the Gulf of Mexico.

Monroe was segmented from Greenbrier County against the objections of the mother county. Nevertheless, the Virginia General Assembly passed the bill to establish the new county on January 15, 1799. It was named for James Monroe, the newly inaugurated governor of Virginia and later president of the United States. In the future, 15 counties across the nation shared the name Monroe, but this was the first one and the only one that James Monroe himself signed into being.

The selection of a county seat was a problem. There were no towns, but James Alexander's farm along the heavily traveled north-south Indian trading path was well placed for one. Alexander entered into a bond to convey one acre for a courthouse and an adjacent ten acres for a town. Despite objections that the site was not centrally located, a courthouse and a jail were constructed, and the town of Union came into existence. The name, which became an ironic one when Monroe County preferred the Confederacy in the Civil War, is said to have been chosen

A Monroe County pastoral scene.

because it was the point of union or mustering place for the militia.

The presence of small mounds scattered about the southern end of the county suggests Monroe County's prehistory. It is generally accepted that this area was a hunting ground for various Indian tribes at the time of the arrival of the first white settlers. These first Europeans were Scotch-Irish and Germans from the Shenandoah Valley. Many had received land grants for service during the French and Indian War. Others had been enticed by the efforts of various land-holding companies.

The new county prospered with the young nation. Water power meant mills, and there was no shortage of water power in Monroe County. At one time Second Creek had a mill for each of its 18 miles. Indian, Laurel, Turkey, Rich, and Wolf creeks also contributed their power. Gristmills, sawmills, and woolen mills thrived. The limestone country produced fine spring water, abundant grass for grazing, and sweet soil for growing crops. Within the caves beneath the land was saltpeter (potassium nitrate) for the manufacture of gunpowder, a very early industry that supplied powder for the Revolutionary War and later the Confederate Army.

During the Civil War, Monroe County favored the South. Ninety-five percent of men eligible for military service were in one of the 12 locally formed units that served the Confederate States. As a result of its Southern allegiance Monroe County was occupied by Union forces for three years after the war.

The early settlers established Presbyterian, Baptist, and Methodist churches. Rehoboth Methodist Church (1784) still stands as the oldest church building west of the Alleghenies. Education came with the first settlers, and a schoolmaster was among the victims of the 1755 massacre at Baughman's Fort on the Greenbrier River. The Literary Fund established by the Virginia Assembly in 1809 was the beginning of public education. The Union Academy, established in 1820 to teach a classical education, existed until 1861. Attempts to revive the school after the Civil War were unsuccessful.

Spas and resorts developed around Monroe's mineral springs, most notably Sweet Springs, Salt Sulphur Springs, and Red Sulphur Springs. They catered to a clientele from the eastern and southern states. While each of the resorts advertised its water for specific ailments, many of the visitors sought to escape the malaria and yellow fever that plagued the coastal cities or simply the heat and humidity of the lower country. After the Civil War the springs never regained their antebellum grandeur. The elegant Jeffersonian architecture of the Old Sweet Springs and the formidable stone buildings of Salt Sulphur Springs remain as monuments to past glory. In the late 20th century, spring water regained a place in the economy of Monroe County through the bottled water industry, drawn mostly from the seemingly limitless aquifer beneath Peters Mountain. The Sweet Springs Water Company has won the gold medal several times at the international water tasting festival held annually at Berkeley Springs.

Two U.S. senators were among notable Monroe Countians. Allen Taylor Caperton first served as a senator to the Confederate States from 1861 to 1865. After amnesty was granted he was elected to the U.S. Senate, where he died in office in 1876. Frank Hereford of Union succeeded him. Anne Royall, one of the first women journalists in America, lived much of her early life at Sweet Springs. Col. Andrew Summers Rowan, famous for carrying the "Message to Garcia" in the Spanish-American War, was from Monroe.

Modern Monroe County is a farming county with a population of 14,583 in 2000. Monroe Countians formed the first Corn Club in West Virginia in 1907, the beginning of the 4-H clubs in the state. Cattle, dairy, and sheep farming keep pace with the crop farming of hay, corn, oats, wheat, and tobacco. Timber is also a major contributor to the economy. In recent years large natural gas deposits have been found.

The Goodrich Corporation rubber fabrication plant in Union is the major employer within the county. The Greenbrier resort at White Sulphur Springs, the Celenese plant at Narrows, Virginia, and Westvaco at Covington, Virginia, employ Monroe County commuters. Creekside Resort on Indian Creek, High Meadow Lodge at Wolf Creek, and the cottages at Salt Sulphur attract visitors to the county. An 18-hole golf course has been developed at Lindside, south of Union.

FAST FACTS ABOUT MONROE COUNTY

Founded: 1799
Land in square miles: 473.8
Population: 14,583
Percentage minorities: 7.3%
Percentage rural: 89.4%
Median age: 39.7
Percentage 65 and older: 15.4%
Birth rate per 1,000 population: 9.1
Median household income: $27,575
High school graduate or higher: 73.7%
Bachelor's degree or higher: 8.2%
Home ownership: 84.5%
Median home value: $64,700

This information is from the 2000 U.S. Census. In 2000, West Virginia as a whole had 5 percent minorities, a median age of 38.9, median household income of $29,696, and a 75.2 percent home ownership rate.

Tranquility has always been the password to Monroe County. For one recent period the county had the lowest crime rate in the state, and the second-lowest crime rate of any county in the United States. Recent population growth suggests that the county's attractions are no longer a secret.

See also Bottled Water, Allen T. Caperton, Andrew S. Rowan, Salt Sulphur Springs, Sweet Springs

Jay Banks
Union

James W. Banks, *200 Years from Good Hope*, 1983; Oren Morton, *History of Monroe County, West Virginia*, 1916.

Margaret Prescott Montague

Writer Margaret Prescott Montague was born at Oakhurst estate at White Sulphur Springs, November 29, 1878. Her father, a graduate of Harvard who had studied law in London, had moved to West Virginia for health reasons.

Montague's books were set primarily in the southern mountains. *The Poet, Miss Kate, and I*, published in 1905, was a loosely written story including character sketches, descriptions of nature, and philosophical ramblings. *The Sowing of Alderson Cree*, her 1907 novel that later was made into a movie, was set in West Virginia and revolved around a feud. *In Culvert's Valley* (1908), *Linda* (1912), and *Deep Channel* (1923) provided character studies of mountain people. Her brother was superintendent of the state school for the deaf and blind in Romney, and Montague's interest in the students there inspired her *Closed Doors* (1915). She struggled with visual problems herself, including night blindness, tunnel vision, and later cataracts.

Montague wrote two stories in 1923, "Up Eel River" and "The Today Tomorrow," both featuring the mythic lumberman, Tony Beaver. Her Tony Beaver tales were collected into the book, *Up Eel River*, in 1928. Tony was a sort of West Virginia Paul Bunyan. In the book he and his crew cut timber and ride logs, raise a garden of monstrous-sized vegetables, make moonshine powerful enough to make a rabbit spit in a bulldog's eye, and receive a visit from Miss Preserved Green. Miss Preserved is a soul-saving missionary woman from Maine or Spain, they can't remember which, and they send her home an enlightened woman. Tony's exploits capture the spirit of early West Virginia logging camps. According to Montague, Eel River and its inhabitants were the products of the fertile imaginations of West Virginia woodsmen, although it is possible that the tales and Tony himself were invented by Montague.

Montague departed from mountain themes when she wrote "England to America" about World War I. This story, which won the O. Henry Award in 1919,

was praised by President Woodrow Wilson and considered to be a plea for a league of nations.

Montague died September 26, 1955, in Richmond, Virginia.

See also Tony Beaver, Oakhurst Links

Debra K. Sullivan
Charleston Catholic High School

Montani Semper Liberi

The Latin term, "Montani Semper Liberi," which translates in English as "Mountaineers are always free," is the West Virginia state motto. The first West Virginia legislature adopted the motto on September 26, 1863. The joint committee on the state seal incorporated the motto on the front or obverse side of the new state seal, below the image of rock, miner, and farmer. This committee employed Joseph H. Diss Debar, of Doddridge County, to make drawings in compliance with their instructions for a state seal. According to a 1906 report by State Archivist Virgil A. Lewis, the motto was suggested by Diss Debar. He was a Swiss-speaking immigrant, and the Latin phrase had been long used by Swiss mountaineers to express their independence of spirit. It is believed that Diss Debar also influenced the state officials to place another Latin phrase, "Libertas E Fidelitate," meaning "freedom and loyalty," on the reverse of the state seal.

See also Joseph H. Diss Debar, State Seal

Rachelle Bott Beckner
Charleston

Fred Mooney

Unionist Fred Mooney, secretary-treasurer of United Mine Workers of America District 17 from 1917 to 1924, was a radical leader in the West Virginia Mine Wars. He was born in a log cabin on Davis Creek, Kanawha County, January 23, 1888. He began work in the local mines at the age of 13, as a trapper boy operating the trap doors which controlled underground ventilation, but managed to attend school until he was 18.

Mooney was among the miners' leaders during the most active period of the Mine Wars, a time including the 1921 armed march on Logan and Mingo counties and the Battle of Blair Mountain. His name is often linked with that of Frank Keeney, president of District 17 during Mooney's term as secretary-treasurer.

Perhaps his most lasting contribution is his book *Struggle in the Coal Fields: The Autobiography of Fred Mooney*. Here he gives firsthand accounts of key events of the Mine Wars, including the trials following the armed march, when more than 500 miners were indicted for treason and murder. Almost all, including Mooney and Keeney, were acquitted. Mooney struggled alongside such notable figures as Mother Jones and Bill Bliz-

zard, as well as Keeney, and the characters in his book and his life read like a directory of West Virginia labor history. Fred Mooney committed suicide in Fairmont, February 24, 1952.

See also Frank Keeney, Mine Wars

Gordon L. Swartz III
Cameron

David A. Corbin, *Life, Work, and Rebellion in the Coal Fields: The Southern West Virginia Miners 1880–1922*, 1981; Fred Mooney, *Struggle in the Coal Fields: The Autobiography of Fred Mooney*, 1967.

Moonshine

The making of illegal or moonshine whiskey has a long history in West Virginia and elsewhere. The word entered the English language about 1785 when white brandy was smuggled on the southeast England coast of Kent and Sussex. Those who made or transported the beverage worked under moonlight to escape the law. Moonshine is illegal because producers do not abide by state or federal laws regarding the licensure, manufacture, sale, and taxation of distilled spirits.

In West Virginia, field corn, soft creek water, and industrious farmers came together to make moonshine, sometimes also called mountain dew or white lightning. Moonshine is typically 100-proof whiskey, aged little or none, and was an important cash crop. So long as revenue agents did not cause trouble, making moonshine was an efficient and profitable way to market corn. With a good still, one-and-a-half bushels of corn was reduced to a gallon of whiskey which was worth more than the grain itself and less bulky to transport.

From the mid-18th century, settlers from Scotland, Ireland, Wales, and England came to the mountains with distilling equipment and the necessary know-how. They quickly adapted their Old World recipes to include American field corn. Whiskey was drunk in far greater quantities than today and used to barter for salt, nails, and taxes. Some used it to buy property, and a good copper still and the condensing coil or "worm" had considerable value themselves.

On March 3, 1791, soon after the colonies became a nation, Congress imposed the first taxes on stills and whiskey. Such laws caused the 1794 Whiskey Rebellion, an uprising in western Pennsylvania and parts of present West Virginia. The settlers, mainly Scotch-Irish, saw the tax as unfair. President Washington himself led troops to stop the rioting, and the federal government kept the tax in force for 11 years. Whiskey remained untaxed from then until 1862, except for three years following the War of 1812.

About 1910, states began to enact state prohibition laws in anticipation of the great national drought soon to follow. West Virginia prohibition took effect in

1914. Then, from 1920 until 1933 the U.S. government enforced nationwide prohibition, causing a dramatic increase in moonshining. Even when national prohibition ended, parts of the South remained dry. In any case, some imbibers remained partial to clear mountain whiskey, and illegal distilling continued. After 1950, as local prohibition laws were voted out and economic conditions improved, the demand for illegal whiskey fell and production of moonshine declined.

Mountaineers traditionally used corn in making moonshine. The first step is to sprout the corn, then crush the sprouted grain and mix with water. This mixture, called mash, is fermented in open barrels. If moonshiners have yeast and use it, the fermentation takes up to four days; if they don't have yeast and if the weather is cool, fermentation takes longer, maybe two weeks. When fermentation is complete, the mildly alcoholic liquid, now called beer, is ready to distill or "run off." The beer is heated in the still's pot or copper kettle to the temperature, well below boiling, when alcoholic vapors rise from the liquid. These vapors are condensed back to liquid in the worm, a coil of copper tubing which passes through a cooling water bath. Each batch was typically run off two or more times to get the maximum whiskey from the fixings.

Illegal whiskey is still made and readily available to those who know where to look for it. Homemade corn liquor is just about a thing of the past, however, since sugar is now usually substituted for most of the grain.

See also Whiskey Rebellion

Mark F. Sohn
Pikeville College

Joseph Earl Dabney, *Mountain Spirits: A Chronicle of Corn Whiskey from King James' Ulster Plantation to America's Appalachians and the Moonshine Life*, 1974.

Arch Moore

Arch Alfred Moore Jr., a Republican from the Northern Panhandle, became the first West Virginia governor in 100 years to serve a second term, and he returned later for a third. He was the state's 28th governor and also the first West Virginia governor to serve as chairman of the National Governors Conference. Moore was one of our strongest chief executives and among the most popular, and he became one of the most controversial. He served as governor from 1969 to 1977 and from 1985 to 1989. In 1990, he was imprisoned on federal charges.

Moore was a strong, aggressive leader who benefited from a constellation of factors that served to amplify his leadership. The Modern Budget Amendment, passed in 1968, made him the first West Virginia governor with full budget-making authority, and the Governor's Succession Amendment (1970) made him the first in

Governor Arch A. Moore Jr. (1923–).

modern times who was able to succeed himself in office. Likewise, Moore benefited from abundant federal funds, especially for road building, and was fully able to exploit them thanks to the bonding authority provided by the 1968 Roads Development Amendment.

Moore was born April 16, 1923, at Moundsville into a Republican family. His grandfather, F. T. Moore, was a ten-term member and a minority leader in the House of Delegates. Arch attended Lafayette College in Pennsylvania and later West Virginia University. From 1943 to 1946, he served as an army infantryman and earned the rank of combat sergeant. He was severely wounded when a bullet struck the right side of his face and had to learn to talk again during his long hospital recovery. Moore later opened a law practice in Moundsville and was elected to the House of Delegates from Marshall County in 1952. He served only one term before trying for higher office.

In 1954, he made his first run at Congress, and was defeated by Rep. Robert Mollohan, a Democrat. Moore ran again in 1956, defeating Lee Spillers for the seat that Mollohan had abandoned to run for governor. Thereafter Moore won each time he tried, serving six terms in Congress from 1957 through 1969. He was elected governor in 1968.

Moore made a considerable amount of news in his first term as governor, mostly by his use of executive authority. For example, he abruptly fired 2,627 striking highway workers. He became a key figure in the settlement of a national coal strike. His hand in the settlement benefited about 39,000 West Virginia coal miners who were out on strike.

During his tenure as governor, monthly welfare payments increased for about 20,000 families with dependent children. Meanwhile, other welfare payments were started for 13,000 blind, aged, and dis-

abled West Virginians. And a $30 state clothing allowance reached about 44,000 welfare children in 1971 and 1972. Moore played an important role in getting hospital insurance for 61,000 public employees, including both state and county workers. He also led the fight to get pay raises of $1,500 for 17,000 public school teachers and somewhat smaller pay increases for other public school employees. He had legislation introduced to start public kindergartens for 30,000 five-year-old children. He pressured lawmakers to increase workers compensation benefits by as much as 75 percent.

There were six special legislative sessions during Moore's first term, then a record. He often used special sessions to focus on legislation he really wanted.

The Roads Development Amendment, a $350 million bond amendment, was approved by the people in 1968 and gave Moore the money to match federal funds for highway construction. This was in addition to the money remaining from a $200 million bond issue, the Better Roads Amendment, approved in 1964. Thus, ample money was available for one of the state's largest highway expansion programs.

Meanwhile, voters passed another constitutional change in 1970 that opened the way for Moore to become the first West Virginia governor to succeed himself since 1872. The Governor's Succession Amendment was ratified with a vote of 213,758 for and 157,597 against. In the heavily publicized 1972 election, he won a second consecutive term as governor despite an almost two-to-one Democratic majority throughout the state. He gained national attention by defeating John D. Rockefeller IV, a bright new hope in the Democratic Party.

Moore won an unprecedented third term as governor in 1984, despite a stronger than expected challenge from former House Speaker Clyde See, a Hardy County Democrat. Moore got 53 percent of the vote. The victory marked his return to political office after a failed attempt to unseat U.S. Sen. Jennings Randolph in 1978 and a loss against incumbent Jay Rockefeller in a race for governor in 1980.

While Moore remained a popular figure and usually succeeded at the polls, his integrity came seriously into question in 1986. He faced repeated attacks, which he called "vicious and ugly." Moore's critics took him to task for not releasing his income tax returns and for dodging questions about alleged unethical behavior during his earlier terms as governor. In 1975, he had been indicted along with an aide on charges of extorting $25,000 from a company seeking a bank charter. He flatly denied the charge, and he and his aide were acquitted the following year.

Moore was criticized for a last-minute

settlement of a $100 million lawsuit against the Pittston Coal Company for $1 million in cleanup charges for the Buffalo Creek disaster of 1972, a coal dam collapse that killed 125 people and left thousands homeless in Logan County. The state was left with an eventual debt of $9.5 million for the cleanup work when Moore made the $1 million settlement just prior to leaving office in 1977.

During his final campaign, Moore refused to discuss these issues with the news media, and his opponent attacked him for it. But Moore still defeated See. He launched his third term as governor in 1985 by cutting workers compensation premiums by 30 percent, a pro-industry move that ultimately would contribute to a huge deficit in the program. In 1986, he helped end a deadly prison riot at the old state penitentiary in Moundsville by personally negotiating for the release of 43 hostages. As his term approached an end, he and Democratic leaders in the legislature deadlocked over the deteriorating state budget.

Worse was yet to come. Additional corruption charges were filed as Moore neared the end of his third term. In 1990, Moore was found guilty on federal charges of mail fraud, tax fraud, extortion, and obstruction of justice. He was fined $3.2 million and agreed to pay $750,000 in the settlement. Moore was released from prison in 1993 after serving three years of a five-year, 10-month sentence. Upon serving his time and getting out of prison, Moore did not return to politics but, at age 75, attempted to get his law license back so he could once again practice law.

Richard S. Grimes
Charleston

Sara Jane Moore

The criminal Sara Jane Moore, born in Charleston, February 15, 1930, attempted to assassinate President Gerald R. Ford on Sept. 22, 1975, in San Francisco. Moore, whose maiden name was Sara Jane Kahn, graduated from Charleston's Stonewall Jackson High School in 1947. She later moved to California, where she joined left-wing groups and became an FBI informant.

Three weeks before Moore attempted to shoot President Ford, Charles Manson associate Lynette "Squeaky" Fromme had also tried to assassinate the president. Like Fromme, Moore received a life sentence and was taken to the Federal Penitentiary for Women at Alderson in Greenbrier County. Moore's assassination attempt has not been linked to the earlier attempt by Fromme. In February 1979, Moore escaped from Alderson but was captured three hours later. She was sentenced to an additional three years on the escape charge. Later, she was transferred to a federal prison in Dublin, California.

Moorefield

Chartered in October 1777 by the General Assembly of Virginia, Moorefield, the county seat of Hardy County, is the fourth-oldest town in West Virginia. Located at the confluence of the South Fork of the South Branch with the main South Branch of the Potomac, Moorefield was laid out on 62 acres of land belonging to Conrad Moore. The town was named for Moore, and his home, the Old Stone Tavern, still stands on Main Street. Early property owners included families with the names of Van Meter, Harness, McNeill, Renick, Hite, Cunningham, Williams, Inskeep, Fisher and Hutton.

Moorefield has always been an agricultural community. The early settlers began farming the rich bottomland that surrounded the town, raising cattle, along with corn and hay for feed. From the 1930s, the poultry industry has been a significant economic factor, and Moorefield became known as the Poultry Capital of West Virginia.

Although Southern in sympathy, the town housed whichever troops were in local control during the Civil War. The Confederate McNeill's Rangers operated in the area.

In 1985, floodwaters devastated Moorefield taking homes, businesses, and lives. Fifteen years later the economy was booming and local unemployment was among the lowest in the state. Hester Industries, WLR Foods, and American Woodmark had all expanded. Hester was part of ConAgra and WLR was part of Pilgrim's Pride, both part of the expanding poultry industry.

Moorefield is the home of the annual West Virginia Poultry Festival and Hardy County Heritage Weekend. As the 21st century began, Moorefield was looking at a potential explosion in population and growth. Construction on the controversial and long-delayed four-lane Corridor H, which will traverse the county, began in 2000. Local officials are faced with the desire to protect the historic district and traditions of the community while still planning for future growth and expansion.

See also Hardy County

Phoebe Heishman
Moorefield

Moorefield, Battle of

After burning Chambersburg, Pennsylvania, Confederate cavalry under Gens. John McCausland and Bradley Johnson camped on August 6–7, 1864, in the fertile South Branch Valley at Old Fields, about three miles north of Moorefield, Hardy County. The generals ignored scout reports of union troops nearby and warnings from the local McNeill's Rangers, Confederate partisans, that their position was exposed.

At dawn on August 7, Union troops under Gen. William W. Averell moved south from Keyser along the route of present Route 220. They attacked Johnson's headquarters at the Willow Wall mansion owned by Daniel McNeill. The Confederates were routed and fled south into the town; the Union captured 500 men and 400 horses. "This affair had a very damaging effect upon my cavalry for the rest of the campaign," commanding Confederate Gen. Jubal Early later wrote. The weakened Early would be repeatedly defeated by Sheridan and expelled from the Shenandoah Valley of Virginia, a Union victory which helped ensure Lincoln's re-election that fall.

In a local skirmish north of Moorefield on November 28, 1864, Rosser's Confederate cavalry and McNeill's Rangers rebuffed Union Col. R. E. Fleming's raid and spared the South Branch Valley from destruction. The battlefields are part of the Middle South Branch Valley rural historic district determined eligible for the National Register of Historic Places in 1998 although not added to the National Register. The district includes 15 major farms and plantations, laid out in "long lots" by Lord Fairfax or early settlers to include mountain land, hills, and river bottomland.

See also Averell's Raid, Civil War, John McCausland

Bonni V. McKeown
Capon Springs
Stephen G. Smith, *The First Battle of Moorefield: Early's Cavalry is Routed*, 1998.

Moorefield Examiner

The *Moorefield Examiner*, a Hardy County weekly newspaper, and its predecessors date their origins to 1845. In 2002, the same family had published the *Examiner* for a full century. In 1902, Samuel Alexander McCoy and G. W. McCauley bought the *Hardy County News* from Capt. J. J. Chipley. By the end of the year, "Mr. Sam" was the sole owner and the paper was called the *Weekly Examiner*. Following McCoy's death, his daughter, Katherine, and her husband, Ralph E. Fisher, took over the paper's management in 1936. R. E. Fisher's death in 1968 brought in the third generation, Phoebe Fisher Heishman and her husband, David.

The editorial page of the *Examiner* has always promoted county growth and supported historic preservation, among other causes. From countywide telephone service to the building of four-lane Corridor H, editors have pushed for what they believed would be best for Hardy County. Like other country weeklies, the *Examiner* serves the home county and those who left home and moved to other places; recently the paper had subscribers in more than 40 states. The *Examiner* has survived floods, economic woes, and angry subscribers. In 2005 it serviced a circulation of 4,600.

Phoebe Heishman
Moorefield

Morel

When the blue violets bloom and the dandelions go to seed, morels, an edible spring mushroom, are in season. A warm rain spurs their growth. In parts of West Virginia morels are known as "molly moochers" and "dry-land fish." Other common names include hickory chickens, pine cones, and honey combs, and indeed the mushroom top is shaped like a pine cone and textured like honey comb. Both yellow and black morels grow in West Virginia, as do other varieties inferior in taste. Morels differ from many other mushrooms in that they are hollow and their stem and cap are a single joined piece. Yellow morels range in height from an inch or two to a foot, and the cap is about half of the total.

The common name, dry-land fish, comes from the fact that West Virginians traditionally batter the mushrooms and fry them like fish or chicken or even fried green tomatoes. But morels are as popular in the rest of the United States and in Europe as they are in West Virginia. Writing in 1903 the famous French chef, Auguste Escoffier, offered six morel recipes.

Even though morels are widely collected, the novice must be careful. The morel has a poisonous look-alike, the wrinkled thimble cap. Morels themselves are poisonous if eaten uncooked. However, when morels are purchased in markets or collected by experts and properly prepared, they are as safe as any other food. They enjoy a fine reputation for woodsy flavor and robust mushroom texture.

See also Foodways

Mark F. Sohn
Pikeville College

David W. Fisher and Alan E. Bessette, *Edible Wild Mushrooms of North America*, 1992; Marilyn Kluger, *The Wild Flavor*, 1973.

Morgan County

Extending south from the Potomac River in the Eastern Panhandle, Morgan County is 231.3 square miles of mostly parallel north-south ridges. It lies within the foothills of the Appalachian mountain chain. The wild and scenic Cacapon River snakes north through the county, emptying into the Potomac at the unincorporated hamlet of Great Cacapon. There is archeological evidence of prehistoric people in Great Cacapon and other locales along the Potomac and Cacapon rivers.

The Cacapon Mountains divide Morgan County into the sparsely settled, forested, and mountainous western segment and the more populous east, which includes the county seat of Berkeley Springs. Panorama Overlook marks the northern end of the Cacapon Mountains. The view from the pull-over on State Route 9 includes Great Cacapon and the confluence of the Cacapon and Potomac

FAST FACTS ABOUT MORGAN COUNTY

Founded: 1820
Land in square miles: 231.3
Population: 14,943
Percentage minorities: 1.7%
Percentage rural: 100%
Median age: 40.7
Percentage 65 and older: 16.6%
Birth rate per 1,000 population: 9.8
Median household income: $35,016
High school graduate or higher: 75.8%
Bachelor's degree or higher: 11.2%
Home ownership: 83.3%
Median home value: $89,200

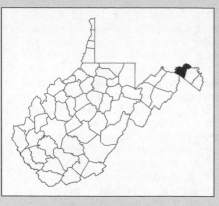

This information is from the 2000 U.S. Census. In 2000, West Virginia as a whole had 5 percent minorities, a median age of 38.9, median household income of $29,696, and a 75.2 percent home ownership rate.

rivers amid the jumble of the western mountains.

When 16-year-old George Washington arrived in March 1748 on his first surveying trip of Lord Fairfax's huge land grant, he camped at the "fam'd warm springs," according to his diaries. Maps named them Medicinal Springs and hundreds of hardy health seekers were already visiting in summer, drawn by stories passed on by the Indians. They have since become known as Berkeley Springs, the centerpiece of the historic county seat town.

The source of the thermal springs is unknown, but they flow constantly at about 1,000 gallons per minute with an unchanging mineral content. Described since colonial times as clear, sparkling and tasteless, the waters emerge at the base of Warm Springs Ridge from five major and numerous minor springs. Their temperature is 74 degrees Fahrenheit regardless of season. The springs have been used as the town water supply since 1892. Today, two commercial water companies bottle the spring water and market it throughout the East.

Washington returned nearly a dozen times to "take the waters," and first met steamboat inventor James Rumsey at the springs. On December 6, 1776, the Virginia House of Burgesses established a town there for the purpose of providing lodging for those coming to cure their ills. The town was called Bath, still its official name although the post office name of Berkeley Springs is commonly used. Lots were purchased by the colonial elite who chose to make Bath the country's first spa. Morgan County was created from parts of Hampshire and Berkeley counties in 1820. It was named for Daniel Morgan, a Revolutionary War hero who was said to have taken the waters for gout.

In spite of periodic ups and downs, the care and feeding of visitors has been a major industry in Berkeley Springs for more than two centuries. Hotels have come and gone, bathhouses have been built and razed. Repeated fires and the Civil War took their toll. One of America's earliest travel writers and a first-rate sketch artist, David Hunter Strother (Porte Crayon) lived at, and later owned, his family's hotel in Berkeley Springs. There are buildings still in use from various periods in Berkeley Springs' spa history, including the 1815 Roman Bath House and Berkeley Castle, built as a summer cottage in 1885.

The Baltimore & Ohio Railroad has been a major force in Morgan County since before the Civil War, making its way parallel to the Potomac River. The railroad, now CSX, still traverses Morgan County, though the trains seldom stop. Nearly all the railroad stops disappeared as population centers by the 1930s, and today only Paw Paw remains along with a spur in Berkeley Springs to serve the U.S. Silica sand mining operation.

Paw Paw, on the Potomac River on the westernmost edge of the county, is Morgan County's other incorporated town. Once-vast apple orchards have disappeared from the area, but Paw Paw remains active with a high school, library, and health clinic. The paw paw fruit that grows wild on trees along the riverbanks gave its name to both the town and the largest man-made structure on the C&O Canal—a tunnel dug more than half a mile through Sorrel Ridge, just across the river in Maryland.

Two of the county's most notable industries trace their beginnings back to the 1890s. High-grade white silica sand was initially mined by several small, local companies. Today the sand, used to make glass, is mined and sold nationally by U.S. Silica. The county's other major industrial employer is Seely Pine Furniture, a custom-order furniture maker owned since 1996 by former Governor Caperton's family. U.S. Silica maintains the private Potomac Airpark, sized for corporate jets.

Agriculture had a golden age in the early part of this century. Thousands of acres of tomatoes were cultivated, and more than two dozen canneries kept a large portion of the population engaged during the fall. From 1937 to 1941, the Tomato Festival provided a break for the workers in early September and brought thousands of visitors to Berkeley Springs.

Morgan County has two state parks, both vital to its tourism industry. The village green surrounding the warm springs in the center of town was set aside as public land by Lord Fairfax and designated Bath Square by the town's colonial founders. In 1929, it became Berkeley Springs State Park, complete with historic bathhouses. It is West Virginia's smallest state park, at five acres, and the only one at which visitors can get a mineral bath and massage. Since 1974, the annual Apple Butter Festival has filled its lawns on Columbus Day weekend.

Cacapon State Park was built as a Civilian Conservation Corps project in 1933 and has grown into one of the most popular resorts in the state park system. In the 1960s, the state added a Robert Trent Jones 18-hole golf course to the park's 6,000 acres. More than 22,000 acres is available for public use in Sleepy Creek Hunting and Fishing Grounds on Morgan County's eastern boundary.

With a 2000 population of 14,943, Morgan County is one of the fastest-growing counties in the state. It is a popular haven for retirees and artists from the nearby Washington-Baltimore metropolitan area. The significant second-home population and locally owned tourism industry recall historic periods when colonial elite and Victorian industrialists made Berkeley Springs their preferred destination.

See also Berkeley Springs

Jeanne Mozier
Berkeley Springs

Frederick T. Newbraugh, *Warm Springs Echoes: About Berkeley Springs and Morgan County*, 1967.

Ephraim Franklin Morgan

Ephraim Franklin Morgan, West Virginia's 16th governor, was born on a farm near Forksburg, Marion County, January 16, 1869. He earned a law degree from West Virginia University in 1897 and served with the First West Virginia Regiment during the Spanish-American War. He was city solicitor in Fairmont, 1900–01, and a judge of the Marion County Intermediate Court, 1907–13. Appointed by Governor Hatfield to the Public Service Commission in 1915, Morgan resigned in late 1919 to run as a Republican for governor.

Elected with a plurality of the popular vote in a four-candidate race in 1920,

Governor Ephraim F. Morgan (1869–1950).

Governor Morgan, like his Democratic predecessor John J. Cornwell, was compelled to dedicate much of his energy to the bitterly divisive West Virginia Mine Wars. Although Morgan displayed personal courtesy to some labor leaders, notably the famous Mary Harris "Mother" Jones, he left little doubt that he believed the governorship enabled him to promote the interests of the state's coal operators. So loyal were Morgan and most of the West Virginia political elite to the coal industry that a U.S. Senate Committee on Education and Labor declared in June 1921 that the state was in effect "an industrial autocracy."

In the fractious 1920 election, Morgan had defeated Democrat Arthur B. Koontz by less than 60,000 votes. He had also faced a pro-labor non-partisan candidate, Samuel B. Montgomery, and West Virginia's most prominent Socialist, Matthew S. Holt. The fact that he earned fewer votes than the combined total of these more liberal, pro-labor opponents suggested that Morgan's anti-union politics, which carried considerable weight with powerful industrial leaders, was not particularly appealing to rank-and-file West Virginia voters. Nonetheless, he persisted. In the mainstream of a nationwide business campaign to portray organized labor as un-American, Morgan annually endorsed America First Day, sponsored by one of the state's premier anti-union organizations, the American Constitutional Association. A persistent critic of anything he defined as not "One Hundred Percent American," Morgan was a staunch opponent of the League of Nations. He warned West Virginia schoolteachers that they stood on the front lines in a war against the "Bolshevistic doctrines that are being disseminated throughout the country."

Morgan's suspicion of organized labor

crested in his handling of the tumultuous Mine Wars, which he inherited from Cornwell. Morgan repeatedly petitioned President Warren G. Harding to dispatch federal forces to break the United Mine Workers of America organizing campaign in Mingo and Logan counties in the spring of 1921, which had been marked by escalating labor-management violence. When Harding resisted, Morgan declared martial law in the southern coalfields, relying on the new West Virginia State Police and an anti-union "vigilance committee" of private citizens for enforcement. In the aftermath of the assassination of union hero Sid Hatfield in August 1921, thousands of miners embarked on the famous Miners' March through Logan County. According to historian Clayton Laurie, Harding at this stage felt compelled to send federal troops, concluding that Morgan and county officials were themselves part of the problem.

This federal intervention halted the march, and ensuing strike-related trials bankrupted the UMWA in southern West Virginia. Morgan served as governor for more than three more years. A major accomplishment of his administration was the building of a new state capitol to replace the fine Victorian capitol which burned two months before he took office. The west wing of the current capitol was completed in March 1925, the last month of Morgan's term. The Governor's Mansion was built during the same period, and Morgan moved his family into the house a few days before leaving office.

In 1940, after working for the U.S. Department of Commerce and then re-entering the private sector, Morgan ran for the U.S. Senate as a virulent critic of Franklin Roosevelt's New Deal. Republican power brokers and party voters reviewed the accomplishments of the Morgan years, and apparently concluded they were inadequate. By this time, due partly to the labor law reforms of the New Deal, organized labor had mobilized politically within the Democratic Party and the political calculus in West Virginia had changed. Morgan ran third in the Republican primary, his own party not willing to risk having the former governor on the ticket.

After accepting his position with the Department of Commerce, Morgan spent much of his time in Washington, living the last years of his life there. He died at the Navy hospital in Bethesda, Maryland, January 15, 1950.

See also Battle of Blair Mountain, New Deal, Mine Wars

John Hennen
Morehead State University

John Hennen, *The Americanization of West Virginia: Creating a Modern Industrial State, 1916–1925*, 1996; Clayton D. Laurie, "The United States Army and the Return to Normalcy in Labor Dispute Interventions: The Case of the West

Virginia Coal Mine Wars, 1920–1921," *West Virginia History*, 1991; John G. Morgan, *West Virginia Governors*, 1980.

Morgan Morgan

Morgan Morgan, traditionally considered the first white settler of West Virginia, was born in Wales, November 1, 1688, and emigrated to Delaware about 1712. About 1714, Morgan met and married Catherine Garretson, with whom he had nine children. He was a merchant tailor and coroner and achieved enough standing in the Delaware colony to be one of the executors of the will of its lieutenant governor, John Evans. Morgan, Catherine, and five of their children moved to Virginia about 1729.

Morgan received an original land patent for 1,000 acres in the Bunker Hill area of present Berkeley County in 1735, land that he had settled about 1731. By 1740, there were enough others in the area that Morgan helped to establish Christ Episcopal Church in what is now Bunker Hill, along with fellow early settlers Joist Hite and Dr. John Briscoe. Morgan built a log house that still remains. The building was restored by the Berkeley County Historical Society in 1976.

Modern historians have established that Morgan Morgan was not actually West Virginia's first settler, but rather among the very early arrivals. His children were also influential pioneers. Morgan's son, David, was a renowned Indian fighter in the Monongahela Valley; his son, Zackquill, was the founder of Morgantown, and Morgan Morgan II was a prominent minister. Morgan Morgan died November 17, 1766, near Bunker Hill.

See also Zackquill Morgan

Georgia Caldwell DuBose
Harpers Ferry

Zackquill Morgan

Morgantown founder Zackquill Morgan was born in Berkeley County in 1735. He was the seventh of eight children of Catherine Garretson Morgan and Col. Morgan Morgan, traditionally considered the first white settler of West Virginia. Zackquill and his brother, David, fought during the French and Indian War in Braddock's Expedition of 1755 and Forbes's Expedition of 1758. He moved to Monongalia County about 1771, where he claimed by tomahawk right land along the Monongahela River and Deckers Creek.

Early in the Revolution, Zackquill Morgan was appointed county lieutenant with the title of colonel. He fought with General Gates at the Battle of Saratoga in 1777 and served with distinction throughout the war. Colonel Morgan's 1771 claim was surveyed and deeded to him on April 29, 1781. On 50 acres of this land, Maj. William Haymond surveyed streets and lots during 1783 and 1784, and Morgan

began selling parcels. In 1783, Morgan became the proprietor of an "ordinary" (a tavern or inn), and the Virginia General Assembly designated his home the Monongalia County courthouse until one could be built. He discussed possible locations of roads with George Washington, who visited in 1784. Morgan's Town was established by the General Assembly on October 17, 1785.

Morgan and his first wife, Nancy Paxton, had three children. He and his second wife, Drusilla Springer, were the parents of 11 children. After his death January 1, 1795, Morgan was buried in the cemetery at Prickett's Fort. Following a failed attempt in 1925 by Morgantown citizens to remove his remains to his hometown, a granite monument marking Morgan's grave was erected in 1927.

See also Morgan Morgan, Morgantown

Harold Malcolm Forbes
WVU Libraries

French Morgan, *A History and Genealogy of the Family of Col. Morgan Morgan, the First White Settler of the State of West Virginia*, 1950; West Virginia University Public History Option for the Morgantown Bicentennial Commission, *Morgantown: A Bicentennial History*, 1985.

Morgan's Raid

In the summer of 1863, Confederate Gen. John Hunt Morgan led 2,460 cavalry men on a long raid across Kentucky, Indiana, and Ohio, before remnants of his force escaped southward through West Virginia. This raid was the only time a large Southern force entered Indiana or Ohio. The raiders led the local militias and growing numbers of regular Union troops on a wild chase across three states.

In planning his ambitious 1863 raid, Morgan sought to carry the war to the North. Crossing into Indiana on July 9, 1863, he proceeded to push his cavalry to Cincinnati by the 14th. Though his units spread destruction and havoc across southern Ohio they lost men and horses quickly. The northern forces closed in on Morgan at Buffington Island, Ohio, across the river from Ravenswood, West Virginia. On the morning of July 19th, a battle was fought here that sealed Morgan's fate. The 13th West Virginia Infantry was part of the blocking force. The Union men were aided by several gunboats guarding the fords.

The defeated Confederates began to swim the river to the West Virginia side in small groups. Many drowned, but those that did make it were helped back to Southern lines by West Virginia Confederate supporters who hid them and gave them food and guidance. Several hundred Confederates, often aided by local Confederate partisan rangers, eventually filtered through West Virginia to rejoin the Confederate army. Morgan had fled farther north along the river and was

captured a week later near East Liverpool, Ohio.

See also Buffington Island

Greg Carroll
State Archives

Morgantown

Morgantown, the county seat of Monongalia County, is a regional financial, educational, commercial, and medical center. Col. Zackquill Morgan settled on the Monongahela River about 1771 and had a town surveyed on his land in 1783. In 1785, the Virginia General Assembly officially established Morgan's Town. The original town consisted of today's downtown area, with small water-powered industries located along Deckers Creek and the river. The General Assembly granted Morgantown its first charter in 1838, when the town had 650 residents.

From 1796 to 1818, when the National Road opened as a competing route, Morgantown was a jumping-off point, as boat builders supplied migrants heading north via the Monongahela to the Ohio River. The first steamboat arrived in 1826 although it was many years before regular service was established.

Residents established the first school in 1803. By 1860, the Monongalia Academy, Morgantown Female Academy, and Woodburn Female Seminary educated white students. In 1867, West Virginia's legislature established the West Virginia Agricultural College in Morgantown, and in 1868 the school's name was changed to West Virginia University. The legislature created two public school districts in Morgantown in 1868, one for whites and one for blacks. Schools stayed segregated until 1954.

A branch line of the Baltimore & Ohio Railroad arrived in 1886, from Fairmont, but did not continue northward from Morgantown until 1894. The arrival of the railroad and the discovery of oil, gas, and coal in the surrounding county soon spurred substantial growth. Between 1890 and 1920, while industry expanded statewide, Morgantown developed major industrial valleys along Beechurst Avenue and in Sabraton. The glass industry attracted skilled itinerant and European (Belgian, French, and German) glassworkers, many of whom lived in the Seneca, Sunnyside, and Wiles Hill neighborhoods. The American Sheet and Tin Plate Company drew immigrants from Greece, Hungary, and Italy to live in the Sabraton area; Welsh immigrants lived in Greenmont.

Morgantown did not grow much beyond its original 1785 boundaries until the mid-1890s. In 1901, the city annexed Greenmont, Seneca, and South Morgantown, and population jumped from 1,895 in 1900 to 9,150 in 1910. South Park developed as an exclusive neighborhood in the early 1900s. Morgantown annexed

Morgantown is the county seat of Monongalia County.

part of Evansdale in 1947 and Suncrest and Sabraton in 1949. In most neighborhoods, deed restrictions banned blacks from owning property. In Suncrest, deeds sometimes banned immigrants and Jews from owning property.

WVU's expansion in the 1960s and 1970s led to further development in Evansdale and Suncrest, neighborhoods originally established in the 1910s and 1920s. Retail shopping areas developed in Suncrest and Sabraton; the Mountaineer Mall opened in 1974.

During the early 1780s, Michael Kern built a church for all denominations, Morgantown's first church. Gradually, residents established congregations that often reflected their ethnic and racial backgrounds. By 2000, the Methodists, Greek Orthodox, African-Methodist Episcopal, Christian Missionary Alliance, Quakers, Roman Catholics, and Jews, among others, had places of worship in the city.

At the end of the 20th century, Morgantown was an award-winning community. Main Street Morgantown, organized in 1983, led the downtown revitalization efforts. The Greenspace Coalition coordinated community conservation efforts, and a variety of community and governmental agencies cooperated to establish the Caperton Rail Trail along the Monongahela River. Mountaineer Field, with 65,000 plus fans, is more populous than any city in the state on game days. Ruby Memorial Hospital cares for patients from throughout West Virginia. WVU's many international students, faculty, and staff made the city very cosmopolitan for its size. The 2000 population of Morgantown was 26,809.

Barbara J. Howe
West Virginia University
Earl L. Core, *The Monongalia Story,* 1974–1984; Connie Park Rice, *Our Monongalia: A History of African Americans in Monongalia County, West Virginia,* 1999.

The *Morgantown Weekly Post*

The *Morgantown Weekly Post* was established by Henry M. Morgan and Nimrod Nelson Hoffman in 1864. A daily edition, the *Morgantown Evening Post,* was published from 1899 to 1904. The *Morgantown Chronicle,* founded in 1904 and edited by Hu Maxwell, published daily and weekly editions. The *Post* and the *Chronicle* merged in 1908.

The resulting *Morgantown Post-Chronicle,* a Republican newspaper, was renamed the *Morgantown Post* in 1918. Herbert Chester Greer (1878–1948) became publisher in 1923, and his family still controls the Morgantown paper. His wife, Agnes Reeves Greer (1880–1972), was publisher after Greer's death. John Brooks Cottle (1897–1967) was editor from 1929 until his death.

Meanwhile, the *New Dominion* was established as a Democratic weekly by Julian Fleming and William Jacobs in 1876. It was named in counterpoint to Virginia's nickname, the Old Dominion. The *Morgantown News,* published 1900–05, merged with the *New Dominion* to form the *New Dominion-News* in 1906. The *Morgantown Republican* merged with the *New Dominion-News* in 1909. The name was changed to the *Weekly New Dominion* in 1911. The weekly ceased publication about 1918.

The *New Dominion's* daily edition was Morgantown's first daily newspaper. Edited by Justin M. Kunkle, the *Daily New Dominion* appeared September 7, 1897. The name was shortened to the *New Dominion* in 1906. In 1930, the *New Dominion* and the *Morgantown Post* began sharing plant facilities but retained separate editorial offices. The name of the *New Dominion* was changed to the *Dominion-News* in 1930. Walter L. "Bill" Hart (1902–72) became editor in 1935. Hart retired in

1966 but continued to write a column until shortly before his death.

The initial issue of Morgantown's first Sunday newspaper, the *Sunday Dominion-Post,* with Brooks Cottle as the first editor, appeared on October 31, 1965. The *Morgantown Post* and the *Dominion-News* moved into the newly constructed Greer Building in March 1968. During a 1973 strike of the Newspaper Guild, a combined edition was published daily. The two papers were then merged into the *Dominion Post,* with morning, afternoon, and Sunday editions.

When a rival morning newspaper appeared in 1976, the *Dominion Post* began publishing only once a day. When the rival ceased publication in 1978, the *Dominion Post* continued daily publication. Herbert and Agnes Greer's grandson, David A. Raese, became publisher in 1987. The circulation in 2004 was 20,454 on weekdays and 24,192 on Sundays.

See also Newspapers

Harold Malcolm Forbes
WVU Libraries

Morgantown Glass Works

Morgantown Glass Works began production in 1900 adjacent to the already successful Seneca Glass in Morgantown. By 1903, the company had grown to employ more than 400 and had developed significant glass exporting. The same year financial restructuring changed the corporate name to Economy Tumbler. After several other name changes the company emerged in 1939 as Morgantown Glassware Guild and operated under that name until it closed in 1971. It was purchased by Fostoria Glass in 1965, but the change in ownership did not result in a name change.

Production included colorful stem ware, artistic vases in an Italian freehand style, practical pitchers and tumblers, and stylish etched tableware. Elaborate hand-colored encrustations and brilliant glass colors were hallmarks of this successful firm. The company drew national attention when Jacqueline Kennedy selected a colorless, simple, and elegant line of stemware made by Morgantown Glassware for use in the White House in 1961 after the Kennedy election. This line was then marketed as President's House stemware.

See also Glass Industry

Dean Six
West Virginia Museum of American Glass

Morgantown & Kingwood Railroad

In the late 1800s, the Fairmont, Morgantown & Pittsburgh Railroad was constructed, linking the Grafton-Wheeling line of the Baltimore & Ohio Railroad at Fairmont with the Cumberland, Maryland-Pittsburgh line of the B&O at Connellsville, Pennsylvania. A few years later, businessmen in the Morgantown area chartered the Morgantown & Kingwood Railroad to build southeast from Morgantown to tap coal mines in the area, but the line progressed only a few miles before financial support gave out.

Stephen B. Elkins, U.S. senator and industrialist, purchased the railroad a few years later and extended it to the B&O main line at M&K Junction near Rowlesburg. The line was completed in 1907 and until the late 1940s served about 15 coal mines. It also operated as a secondary through route between M&K Junction and the Fairmont, Morgantown & Pittsburgh Railroad at Morgantown.

The B&O leased the Morgantown & Kingwood in 1920 and totally absorbed the line in 1922. After the B&O takeover it was known as the M&K branch. In the early 1970s, the line was severed between Kingwood and Reedsville. Then trains out of M&K Junction or Morgantown had to serve the two disconnected segments of the branch railroad. Two coal mines continued to ship coal until 2000.

See also Baltimore & Ohio Railroad, Railroads

Robert L. Frey
Miamisburg, Ohio

Mormons

In 1830, Joseph Smith organized the Church of Jesus Christ of Latter-day Saints in upstate New York. The church is commonly known as the Mormon Church, because of the Book of Mormon, which its members consider to be another testament of Jesus Christ. Mormons affirm that the church is the restoration of biblical Christianity and feel obligated to carry this message throughout the world. The first Mormon missionaries entered Cabell County in 1832 and by year's end more than 40 individuals had been baptized in the county. However, during most of the 1800s church leaders counseled Mormon converts to gather to the headquarters of the church in Utah, which left few if any Mormons in West Virginia during those years. A permanent Mormon presence in the state began in 1886 with the creation of the West Virginia Conference, which brought about a small but steady increase in converts. Unfortunately, such success often produced distrust and hostility toward Mormons in West Virginia and elsewhere. Missionaries were beaten and shot at; meetings were disturbed by angry mobs; and members were ridiculed and harassed. Such persecution hastened the Mormon converts' emigration to Utah. This animosity lasted until the early 20th century, when it subsided.

After the turn of the century, church leaders began asking members to stay and built up local congregations By 1930, there were nearly 2,500 Mormons in the state, organized mainly into three congregations at Huntington, Charleston, and Fairmont. Each passing decade saw the growth of the church, and on August

23, 1970, the first "stake" (congregations administered within a specific geographical region) was organized at Charleston with a membership of nearly 4,000. For the Mormon Church the organization of stakes represents the maturation of the church in a region. In 1979, a second stake was organized at Fairmont and a third one followed in Huntington in 1982. At the beginning of the 21st century there are some 13,000 Latter-day Saints in the state, organized into three stakes with more than 30 congregations.

Over the years the Mormon Church has provided its Mountaineer members with many programs designed to build individual spirituality and to strengthen families. Missionaries continue to take a message of the restored gospel throughout the state. The church has also been active in humanitarian efforts throughout West Virginia, responding to emergency situations, such as floods, as well as supplying tens of thousands of pounds of food and clothing to underprivileged families during the 1990s.

See also Religion

Lisle G. Brown
Marshall University

Diane Hill Zimmerman, *"Almost Heaven": A History of the Church of Jesus Christ of Latter-Day Saints in West Virginia*, 1998; *Deseret News 2004 Church Almanac*, 2003.

Morris Harvey College

See University of Charleston.

Dwight Whitney Morrow

The financier, diplomat, and U.S. Senator Dwight W. Morrow was born January 11, 1873, in Huntington. His father, James Elmore Morrow, served as principal of Marshall College, now Marshall University. The family moved to Pittsburgh in 1875, when Dwight was a young child.

After earning his law degree in 1899 from Columbia University, Morrow entered law practice in New York City. In 1914, he joined the banking firm of J. P. Morgan and Company. Morrow's experience in negotiating international loans and his expertise in international shipping proved useful during World War I, when he facilitated shipments of supplies and munitions. A friend of Calvin Coolidge since college, Morrow resigned from the Morgan company in 1927 to accept the ambassadorship to Mexico. He resigned as ambassador in 1930 to run successfully for U.S. senator from New Jersey. He had barely begun his term when he died at his home in Englewood, New Jersey, October 5, 1931.

Morrow Library at Marshall University, named for James E. Morrow, was founded in part by Dwight Morrow. Dwight Morrow's daughter, Anne, married Charles Lindbergh.

Cora P. Teel
Marshall University

Randy Moss

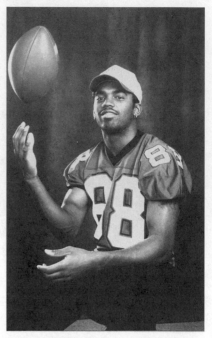

Randy Moss at Marshall University.

Athlete Randy Gene Moss, wide receiver for the Oakland Raiders football team, was born in Rand, Kanawha County, February 13, 1977. At DuPont High School, he won all-state honors for football, was chosen West Virginia high school player of the year (1995), and twice was named state basketball player of the year.

Charges following a racially mixed fight in high school cost Moss a Notre Dame scholarship. A probation violation cost him a scholarship to Florida State University. He played football for two seasons at Marshall University (1996–97), where he set virtually every school and conference season record and was a first-team All-American both years.

In 1997, *The Sporting News* named Moss college football's top receiver, *Street & Smith* called him "the number one reason to watch college football," and *USA Today* and *Sports Illustrated* named him best college receiver. In 1998, the Minnesota Vikings picked him in the first round of the National Football League draft. Nearly a dozen sports publications and organizations named him rookie of the year. Setting numerous receiving records during his first three seasons, he earned Pro Bowl appearances all three years, twice earning Most Valuable Player titles. In 1998 and 2000, Moss led the NFL in touchdown catches. In 2000, he signed a $75 million contract extension with a record-setting $18 million signing bonus, making him the highest-paid non-quarterback in the NFL.

Moss moved to the Oakland Raiders in 2005. His daughter, Sydney, and son,

Thaddeus, live with their mother in West Virginia.

Sandy Wells
Charleston Gazette

Mosses

More than 400 species of moss are found in West Virginia. Some can be identified by eye or with a hand lens, but most must be examined with a microscope. Mosses occur abundantly on exposed and compact soil, decaying organic matter, rotting logs, old burns, rocks, and on the bark of trees. Mosses are bryophytes, which also include liverworts and hornworts. Since mosses are larger and more conspicuous, more is known about these plants.

In West Virginia, sphagnum mosses are among the best-known mosses. These occur in boggy areas. They are used as soil additives and to pack roots of plants, since sphagnums have large hollow cells which retain water, thus staying moist for long periods. Sphagnums are the source of peat reserves.

Haircap moss occurs on a wide range of sites from swampy areas to dry fields. These erect mosses form a dark green, rug-like cover. The tall wiry stems with their spore-bearing capsules are present throughout the year. Another common moss in West Virginia is cushion moss. The light green clumps form cushions and are common on the forest floor of open woodlands.

Carpet moss forms dense mats over fallen logs and rocks. The individual plants resemble coarse ferns. The moss plants form intertwined layers that can be lifted up in large mats without disturbing individual plants. A similar moss is fern moss, which forms carpets over rocks and decaying wood. The plants of fern moss are fern-shaped but have a much more delicate form. Carpet mosses and other "sheet mosses" are harvested in the wild and sold for use in the florist and nursery industries.

Mosses are often the first plants to invade denuded areas, thus stabilizing soil and restricting erosion. Moss carpets facilitate invasion of other plants, preparing the way to a cover of woody plants. Some plants, such as rhododendrons, always seed-in on a moss cover, where moisture conditions are ideal for seeds to germinate.

Mosses absorb large amounts of water and restrict surface runoff, thus reducing erosion. Studies of stem flow on trees show that after light rains, little moisture reaches the forest floor since the dense moss layer near the tree base absorbs most of this water. Moss plants are very sensitive to water and atmospheric pollution and can be used as an early indicator of pollution or environmental stress. No moss species are restricted exclusively to West Virginia, although certain rare species have been found here.

Kenneth L. Carvell
Morgantown

Mother's Day

Mother's Day is observed annually on the second Sunday in May. The first official observance was held May 10, 1908, at Andrews Methodist Episcopal Church in Grafton and simultaneously in Philadelphia. The holiday resulted from a vigorous campaign by Anna Jarvis, born near Grafton. Her birthplace and Andrews M. E. Church have been preserved. Her home was headquarters for Union Gen. George B. McClellan in 1861.

A day honoring mothers had been the dream of Jarvis's mother, Anna Maria Reeves Jarvis, who formed Mothers' Day Work Clubs to combat child mortality. She insisted that every mother in Taylor County belong to one. The clubs bought medicine, inspected milk and water supplies, and learned about health and sanitation from physicians. Members had to swear not to allow political divisions within their organizations during the Civil War. In 1868, Anna Maria Jarvis organized Mothers' Friendship Day celebrations to squelch festering resentments from the war years.

A bill to establish a national Mother's Day was introduced in the U.S. Senate May 9, 1908, but failed to pass. Ministers, temperance groups, and women's suffragists soon convinced 45 states to establish the holiday, and President Woodrow Wilson proclaimed the first national Mother's Day on May 10, 1914. Jarvis deplored the commercialization of the holiday that quickly followed.

Gerald D. Swick
Nashville, Tennessee

Taylor County Historical and Genealogical Society, *A History of Taylor County, West Virginia*, 1986; Howard H. Wolfe, *Mother's Day and the Mother's Day Church*, 1962.

Mothman

Mothman is one of several legendary West Virginia monsters, along with Bat Boy and the Flatwoods Monster. Persistent sightings began in November, 1966, and totaled 26 over a one-year span. The reports of a large, winged creature with glowing red eyes were centered in the Point Pleasant area, usually in or near a vast, abandoned munitions facility known as the TNT plant. Skeptics offered various explanations, some arguing that the creature was a stray sandhill crane.

As sightings increased, so did reports of other strange phenomena. Disruption of electronic devices such as telephones, police dispatch radios, and televisions, as well as automobiles, were rumored, and there were numerous reports of UFO appearances. New York writer John Keel, one of the paranormal investigators drawn to Point Pleasant, connected the stories of strange occurrences to the Mothman. Keel additionally included anecdotes regarding the presence of mysterious "men in black" and the tragic December 15, 1967, collapse of the Silver Bridge that spanned the Ohio River at Point Pleasant. His account, first published in 1975 as *The Mothman Prophecies*, became the basis of a 2002 feature film starring Richard Gere.

In one popular theory, the Mothman's advent and the subsequent Silver Bridge disaster were linked to a 200-year-old curse attributed to Shawnee Chief Cornstalk who led the Indians at the Battle Point of Pleasant and who later was murdered there. Sightings of the Mothman diminished after the Silver Bridge collapse.

The legend has had a literary impact. In Pinckney Benedict's 1994 novel *The Dogs of God*, the Mothman makes a brief though dramatic appearance. Chuck Kinder's 2004 memoir *The Last Mountain Dancer* also makes prominent mention of the Mothman. Young Breece D'J Pancake, before he became celebrated as a short story writer, published a 1966 letter in the *Huntington Herald Dispatch* arguing that Mothman was in fact a California condor.

In September 2003, an original life-sized sculpture of the mysterious winged creature was installed in downtown Point Pleasant.

See also Batboy, Flatwoods Monster, Silver Bridge Collapse

Gordon Simmons
Division of Culture and History

John Keel, *The Mothman Prophecies*, 1975; Donnie Sergent Jr. and Jeff Wamsley, *Mothman: The Facts Behind the Legend*, 2001.

Motor Racing

One of the first accounts of auto racing in West Virginia is from the July 4, 1923, holiday. The race took place at Shattuck Park, on a half-mile horse track at the old West Virginia Fairgrounds in South Parkersburg. There was also some early 1920s racing in the Welch area.

The Dunbar Fairgrounds track, originally built for horse racing, was used before World War I by early motorcyclists. In the 1940s, a quarter-mile clay track was built there, incorporating the grandstand straightaway of the original half-mile track. Located in the populous Kanawha Valley, Dunbar was the scene of various motor racing events through the first half of the 20th century.

The early racers were full-sized, Indianapolis-type cars. Then in the late 1930s and early '40s, "midget" race cars were introduced to the area. These four-cylinder cars were scaled-down versions of Indy racers, open-wheel, open-cockpit, short-wheelbase cars that provided lots of excitement.

Racing was suspended during World War II, due to the rationing of fuel and tires. In the spring of 1946, midget car races began again. By the late 1940s, the midgets raced on Sunday afternoon in several locations, including Dunbar and St. Albans, at Scott Field and Gihon Park in Parkersburg, and at Glenville, Pennsboro, and Williamson. One of the premier tracks for the small cars was located in Evans at the former Jackson County Fairgrounds. It became the first racetrack in West Virginia to put up lights for nighttime racing in the summer of 1947. In the late 1940s, the Thomas Speedway was built in Shinnston for the midgets, perhaps the first track in West Virginia built especially for car racing.

By the early 1950s, open-wheel stock cars took over. These were 1930s-era coupes without fenders and fitted with high-powered V-8 engines. They were easy to get and considered much safer than the open-cockpit midgets. Fords were popular because parts were readily available and modifications could be made cheaply. One of the best drivers, Owen Spradling of South Charleston, had great success with a 1934 Ford powered by a 1956 Mercury motor. Frequent crashes were an exciting part of stock car racing, and fans enjoyed the rough-and-tumble style.

The pre-war coupes raced throughout the 1950s. By the middle 1960s, the open-wheel sprint cars and the full-fendered late-1950s stock cars were most popular. The biggest boost to this type racing may have been the reopening of the Pennsboro track in 1964 and the opening of Elkins Speedway around the same time. In 1958, Ohio Valley Speedway was built. In the early 1960s, the Ona track opened. It remains the only paved oval track in West Virginia. The West Virginia Motor Speedway was built at Mineral Wells in 1985, presenting late-model dirt track racing. U.S. Auto Club, All Star, and other events were also presented there.

Before the late 1950s, most auto races were regulated by small, regional groups. In West Virginia, such groups as the Vienna Racing Association and the Central West Virginia Racing Association established equipment and safety rules. Ona was a NASCAR-sanctioned track, presenting four Grand National races in 1964 and 1970, along with USAC sprint car races and other races. The Elkins track held a Grand National race in 1954. Elkins also ran NASCAR-sanctioned modified or Sportsman (pre-war coupes) racing during 1954 and was part of the national point system of NASCAR.

During NASCAR's early years several West Virginia drivers raced at some of the big tracks in the South, including Floyd "Budd" Chaddock, Arden Mounts and Budd Harless from the Gilbert area, and Johnny Patterson and Jimmy Thompson

from the Huntington area. In the middle 1960s, Junior Spencer spent two or three years running the NASCAR tracks with success. Some of NASCAR's early stars, including Lee Petty, Monty Ward, and Junior Johnson raced in West Virginia during this period.

Other West Virginians also made their mark on motorsports. Billy Cassella from Weirton was a USAC national dirt track champion. Dave Mader Jr., who was from Clarksburg and moved south in the mid-1950s, soon became a member of the Darlington Hall of Fame 100 mile-per-hour club. NASCAR racer Larry Frank was from the Wheeling area, and Parkersburg's Paul Goldsmith raced both Indianapolis and NASCAR events. Ravenswood native "Billy Denver" (William Corum) was killed at Indianapolis practicing for the Indy 500 around 1933.

West Virginia's dirt track pioneers included Dave Kurtz (Weston), Keith Hammer (Elkins), and Jerrold King (Dunbar). Others included Claude "Cowboy" Frazier, M. R. "Slim" Rutherford, Gene Tallman, and Max Britton. Midget racers include "Speedy" Estep, killed racing a stock car in 1953 in Columbus, Ohio; O. B. Cottrell; Charlie Stewart, an early West Virginia midget racing champion; Red Langham; Smokey Stoker; and Keith Bristle, a deaf racer. Doc Folded, who was also a motorcycle racer, was killed in an airplane crash coming into Kanawha Airport in the early 1950s. The East Street Garage in Charleston was the headquarters for the midget racing gang.

West Virginians are among the most loyal motor racing fans, traveling by the thousands to races throughout a wide region on NASCAR weekends. Efforts have been made to build a major track in the state. The West Virginia Motorsports Council was established by Governor Wise in 2001. The Council worked with industry promoters to establish major NASCAR tracks at Flatwoods and Quincy, thus far without success.

Eric Denemark
West Virginia Motorsports Council
Tom Adamich
Cuyahoga Falls, Ohio

Mound Builders

There are 424 recorded prehistoric mounds in West Virginia, left by ancient people who once occupied the region. Most are constructed of earth or stone or a combination of both. The majority of mounds in the state are concentrated along the major river valleys, including the Kanawha, Ohio, and Potomac. Major mound groups cluster near South Charleston, Moundsville, and Moorefield. A significant number of rock mounds are found along ridgetops in Nicholas County. The largest earthen, conical mound in North America is the Grave Creek Mound, located in Moundsville.

Archeologists divide prehistory in the eastern United States into several cultural periods. The majority of mounds identified in West Virginia were constructed during the Early Woodland Period (1000–200 B.C.), primarily in the period referred to as Adena (500 B.C.–A.D. 200). Because much archeological data in Appalachia is still elusive, little is known of everyday Adena life. What we know comes largely from the mounds and earthworks they left behind. The Adena were hunters and gatherers. They built mounds over the remains of chiefs, shamans, or other people of high social standing. The remains of the common folk were burned and buried in small log tombs. Skeletons of Adena people reveal that they were unusually tall and powerfully built. Women over six feet tall and men seven feet tall have been discovered. The Adena lived in circular houses made of wickerwork and bark.

Adena mounds were generally constructed in stages. Excavations conducted at Cotiga Mound in Mingo County identified at least six stages of mound construction. Circular, paired-post structures are often found underneath mounds. Some archeologists believe that these sub-mound structures were charnel houses used in burial rituals; others suggest that they were roofless ritual enclosures not necessarily used for mortuary activities. Grave goods from Adena Period mounds include hematite celts and cones, copper beads and bracelets, tubular pipes, inscribed tablets, and shell beads.

During the 19th century, the Myth of the Moundbuilders was a popular notion. It was thought that a lost race or civilization, such as the Lost Tribes of Israel, had built mounds in North America. Many people believed that American Indians were savage and primitive, and would have been incapable of constructing large earthworks.

Some of the earliest studies conducted in North American archeology centered on mounds. In 1846, Ephraim Squier and Edwin Davis conducted a survey of mounds found in the Mississippi and Ohio River valleys, including Western Virginia. Their work culminated in the 1848 publication, *Ancient Monuments of the Mississippi Valley*. While their study was a landmark, it supported and perpetuated the Moundbuilders Myth.

In 1882, the Smithsonian Institution established the Division of Mound Studies. Cyrus Thomas, appointed to direct the division, sent teams of archeologists to explore and excavate mounds in the Ohio and Mississippi River valleys. One was the South Charleston Mound in Kanawha County. Excavations identified a skeleton in a log tomb 24 feet below the mound summit, laid on sheets of copper and surrounded by 10 other burials. In 1894, Thomas published the *Report on the Mound Explorations of the Bureau of Ethnology*. This report, supported with scientific evidence, concluded that the mounds were built by the ancestors of Native Americans, finally putting the Myth of the Moundbuilders to rest.

See also Archeology

Patrick D. Trader
University of Kentucky

Edward V. McMichael, *Introduction to West Virginia Archeology*, 1968; Delf Norona, *Moundsville's Mammoth Mound*, 1954, reissued 1998.

Moundsville

Moundsville, the county seat of Marshall County, is located on the Ohio River at the mouth of Grave Creek. Joseph, Samuel, and James Tomlinson built the first cabin on the flats of Grave Creek in 1771. In 1798, Joseph Tomlinson laid out lots in a tract named Elizabethtown, in honor of his wife, Elizabeth Harkness Tomlinson. In 1832, neighboring Moundsville was established on land owned by Simeon Purdy. Elizabethtown, incorporated in 1830, was named county seat when Marshall County was formed in 1835. The first courthouse was used from 1836 until 1875; the second, and current, courthouse opened in 1876.

Moundsville was named for Grave Creek Mound, built by Adena Indians between 250 B.C. and 150 B.C. The largest earthen, conical burial mound in North America, Grave Creek Mound is 240 feet in diameter and 62 feet high. It is maintained by the state of West Virginia as part of the Grave Creek Mound Historic Site, which includes the adjacent Delf Norona Museum.

In 1866, Elizabethtown and Moundsville were consolidated under the name of Moundsville. The first recorded school was established in the community in 1799; school sessions were held regularly by 1826. Free schools were established in Moundsville in 1866. The first public building was a jail completed in 1836. In July 1866, work began on the West Virginia Penitentiary; the maximum-security prison remained in operation in Moundsville until 1995. After the prison was closed, the Northern Regional Jail and Correctional Facility was constructed in Moundsville.

Early industries included iron works, factories, tanneries, mills, and coal mining. In the 20th century, Fostoria Glass Company produced art glass dinnerware and U.S. Stamping made enamelware at Moundsville. Novelist Davis Grubb (1919–80) was born in Moundsville and often featured the community in his writing, usually as the fictitious Glory, West Virginia. Two of his novels were adapted as major motion pictures, *Night of the Hunter* (1955) and *Fools' Parade* (1971), both filmed in Moundsville.

Moundsville had a population of 9,978 in 2000.

See also Grave Creek Mound, Davis Grubb, Marshall County, Moundsville Penitentiary

Linda S. Comins
Wellsburg

Moundsville Penitentiary

When West Virginia became a state in 1863, it had no state prison. Prisoners were held in county jails. To alleviate crowding, Governor Boreman in 1864 ordered convicted felons from throughout the state be imprisoned in the Ohio County Jail and asked the legislature for funds to construct a state penitentiary. The legislature appropriated $50,000 in 1866, and five acres (later expanded to ten) were acquired in Moundsville for construction of the main prison. The Gothic style West Virginia Penitentiary opened in 1867 with 840 cells for men and 32 for women. Legend has it that Moundsville was given the choice between the penitentiary and the new state university and chose the prison as the more promising institution.

It is believed that Joseph Fairfax was the prison's original architect, although several others have worked on later additions. The massive stone walls, buttressed and crenelated, form an intimidating facade stretching for three city blocks opposite Moundsville's prehistoric mound. The prison was built on the 19th-century "Auburn Plan," with barred cells stacked in tiers inside the enclosing stone walls.

Prisoners manufactured brooms, whips, and men's clothing for state use until the 1930s, when production changed to soap, paint, men's clothing, and tobacco. The production of license plates, signs, and printing became the main products in the 1950s, and a vocational and educational program was established.

Overcrowding became a problem in the 20th century. In 1947, women prisoners were transferred to the new state women's penitentiary in Pence Springs. The size of the Moundsville prison doubled in 1959 with the completion of a section that had been under construction for 30 years. Overcrowding persisted, however, and tension increased with the number of prisoners. Deadly riots in 1973 and 1979 prompted Ohio County Circuit Judge Arthur Recht to place the facility under judicial control. Despite efforts to improve conditions, another riot on New Year's Day 1986 led the state Supreme Court to order the penitentiary's closing. The last prisoners were transferred to the new Mount Olive Correctional Complex in Fayette County in 1995.

The Moundsville Penitentiary is on the National Register of Historic Places.

See also Crime, Moundsville, Mount Olive Prison

Stan Bumgardner
Division of Culture and History

Mount Carbon Prehistoric Site

Early white settlers observed extensive rock walls on the high ridge between Armstrong and Loop creeks, 1,500 feet above the Kanawha River in Fayette County. These were documented by Col. P. W. Norris for the Smithsonian Institution's Bureau of American Ethnology in 1891, and by Dr. John P. Hale, reporting to the West Virginia Historical and Antiquarian Society in 1898. Dr. James H. Kellar, professor of anthropology and an expert on Georgia's rock walls, spent a week there in June 1958.

The origin of the walls remains a mystery. No pottery, which often accompanies a social organization, has been found. The numerous projectile points are too diverse to suggest a chronology. The best guess seems to be that they were constructed during the Archaic Period. The "walls" were like windrows, long piles of large, usually flat, undressed rocks, reported in about 1820 to be six or seven feet high. More recent visitors estimated heights up to about three feet and saw much scattered rock. An early observer, George W. Atkinson, estimated a continuous wall, three and a half miles long, with numerous openings. Later observations suggest up to four widely separated horseshoe-shaped walls with the base of the "shoes" going across the ridge and the arms extending along the precipitous slopes. The walls do not appear to have been for defensive purposes or for use as animal pens.

There was an outcropping of Kanawha black flint below the ridge with evidence of a flint industry. Numerous granite hammer stones have been found (and there is no granite in this area). Such stones were used by historic as well as prehistoric peoples.

Surface mining has now destroyed these evidences of an early culture.

See also Archeology, Prehistoric People

Joseph Crosby Jefferds Jr.
Charleston

Mount de Chantal Visitation Academy

Mount de Chantal Visitation Academy in Wheeling, founded in 1848, is a college preparatory school for girls and boys from Montessori through the fourth grade and girls only through the 12th. It is the only remaining all-female secondary school in the state. The institution was established by Richard V. Whelan, first bishop of the Roman Catholic Diocese of Wheeling, who invited eight Visitation Sisters from Baltimore to open a school for girls, the Wheeling Female Academy. The school was first located at 14th and Eoff streets but in 1865 moved to a new building on the former Steenrod farm three miles outside the city. It was named Mount de Chantal after Saint Jane de Chantal, co-founder of the Visitation

Order. Architecturally, the Mount de Chantal building is a good example of eclecticism with "Mission" style features. It was placed on the National Register of Historic Places in 1978. A boarding school until 1982, the Mount, with approximately 200 students today, has traditionally been known for its strong academic and fine arts programs.

Margaret Brennan
Wheeling Area Historical Society

Mount Nebo Gospel Sings

The West Virginia State Gospel Singing Convention, at Mount Nebo in Nicholas County, draws groups and soloists from West Virginia and nearby states during four annual summer events.

The nonprofit West Virginia Mountain State Gospel Singers Corporation, chartered in 1956, organizes the gospel sings. The June singing convention is on the second weekend; the annual state convention is the last full week in July; the Labor Day convention spans the holiday weekend; and the special sing, featuring invited groups, is the second Saturday in September. The June, July, and Labor Day sings are open to all groups and soloists.

The conventions grew from the homecoming sing at the Nazarene Church Camp, two miles west of Mount Nebo. In 1949, organizers invited groups from neighboring Greenbrier and Fayette counties to participate in the Nicholas County homecoming. Because of its success, the three-county event grew into an annual statewide singing convention. The convention outgrew the church camp and moved to Camp Caesar in Webster County. Convention leaders, recognizing the need for a large permanent home, bought 40 acres of land near Mount Nebo and set up parking and camping facilities.

In 1982, *Goldenseal* magazine reported that the annual July convention drew 15,000 people. In 2000, attendance at the annual convention was an estimated 6,000 to 7,000.

James Samsell, "Singing on the Mountain," *Goldenseal,* Summer 1982.

Mount Olive Prison

The Mount Olive Correctional Complex, which opened in February 1995, replaced the 129-year-old West Virginia State Penitentiary in Moundsville. Located in Fayette County, about six miles from Montgomery, Mount Olive houses only maximum security prisoners. The prison is administered by the Division of Criminal Justice Services, a branch of the West Virginia Department of Military Affairs and Public Safety.

Planning, design, and construction of the $61.8 million complex took 11 years. The facility was designed to house up to 802 male prisoners, more than any other prison in the state. By 1999, Mount Olive

Mount Olive prison is a maximum security penitentiary.

was operating above capacity, prompting the addition of bunk beds to some housing units.

The 120-acre complex comprises 16 buildings, which include eight housing units, a post office, power plant, warehouse, fuel depot, maintenance garage, hospital and medical clinic, classrooms, gymnasium and chapel, library, and laundry. The state's diagnostic unit, which conducts court-ordered evaluations of inmates, is located at Mount Olive.

Industries at the facility include the tag plant, where license plates are made, the sign shop, validation sticker shop, and the soap factory. The prison's education department offers classes in adult basic education, social skills, graphic arts, carpentry, automotive repair, and welding. Public tours of the facility are available.

The state operates nine correctional centers and two work release centers, including Mount Olive. Denmar Correctional Center houses only medium-security prisoners. The state has four minimum security facilities—Anthony Correctional Center, Beckley Correctional Center, and work release centers in Charleston and Huntington. Huttonsville Correctional Center is a medium- and maximum-security facility. The correctional centers at Pruntytown and Saint Marys hold minimum- and medium-security prisoners.

See also Crime, Moundsville Penitentiary

Mount St. George

Mount St. George, located east of Wellsburg, Brooke County, was one of the grandest private estates built in West Virginia during the 20th century. Originally the home and working farm of James B. Vandergrift, a Pittsburgh steel heir, the property was first called Vancroft. The sprawling mansion, completed in 1904,

features low roof lines, a stone turret, stone chimneys, and a recessed balcony and porch at the gabled entry. The house is approached by a grand colonnaded arbor, or pergola, the largest such structure in the state. The estate includes an oval race track, a clubhouse with a pit for cockfights, a fieldstone grotto, and several other residences.

In 1922, the property was acquired by the Catholic Knights of St. George, turned into a home for aging clergy and friends, and renamed Mount St. George. Through the years several additions expanded the property. The Knights of St. George merged with the William Penn Association, which closed the facility in 1992. In 1998, the Catholic Knights of America, a fraternal benefits company, purchased the property, reopening an assisted living facility "for Catholics and their Christian friends."

At the time of the purchase by the Catholic Knights of America, the property consisted of the mansion and much of the original furniture and furnishings, additions built in 1926 and 1975, three private residences, a farm shed, retreat house, storage building, barn, lodge building, and private cemetery. Mount St. George was added to the National Register of Historic Places in 1986.

J. W. George Wallace
Brooke County Review

Mount Storm Lake

Mount Storm Lake, a 1,200-acre impoundment, is located in Grant County on the Stony River, a tributary of the North Branch of the Potomac River. The lake was named for the nearby community of Mount Storm. Built in 1965 to supply water for steam generation at a coal-fired power plant, Mount Storm Lake continues to be used for that purpose.

Dominion Power's 1,600-megawatt

electric generating plant dominates the shoreline of Mount Storm Lake. The water used to make steam is warm when returned to the lake, raising the temperature of the lake. Located in an area known for cold weather and at an elevation of 3,244 feet, Mount Storm remains largely ice-free in winter. The warm lake water often produces heavy fog during cold weather.

Fisherman frequent the warm lake year-round, fishing through the winter. Mount Storm Lake is popular with boaters as well, and it is a favorite with scuba divers from a wide area. The divers enjoy the warm water and lake depths of as much as 132 feet. Recreational aspects of Mount Storm Lake are managed by the West Virginia Department of Natural Resources in conjunction with Dominion Power.

Mount Storm Lake is one of two impoundments on Stony River. The smaller Stony River Reservoir, located upstream, was built in 1913 by Westvaco (now Mead-Westvaco) to augment dry weather flows of the North Branch to ensure adequate water for paper-making at the company's Luke, Maryland, mill. Releases from Mount Storm Lake and Jennings Randolph Lake on the North Branch itself now serve to augment the flow of the North Branch. Mount Storm Lake is not used for flood control.

Mountain Artisans

Founded in 1968, Mountain Artisans was organized as a cooperative quilting business, owned and operated by the women who made the patchwork creations. Based in Charleston, the nonprofit cooperative was formed by a group of idealistic young women, including Sharon Percy Rockefeller and Florette Angel, and their successful designer, Dorothy Weatherford.

A renewed interest in traditional crafts and the back-to-the-land movement of the 1960s provided fertile ground as Mountain Artisans helped to generate a renaissance in quiltmaking. Their marketing efforts garnered national recognition, including the prestigious Coty American Fashion Critics' Award. In their 1972 Coty Award citation, Mountain Artisans was recognized as helping to spur the American crafts movement.

Their quilted fabrics were used by distinguished interior designers such as Parish-Hadley, the firm that had assisted Mrs. John F. Kennedy in redecorating the White House. Fashion designer Oscar de la Renta used Mountain Artisans fabrics in his fashions, and upscale department stores across the country sold their work, from Saks Fifth Avenue to Neiman Marcus.

The *Mountain Artisans Quilting Book,* published by Macmillan Publishing in 1973, documented the cooperative's history and featured how-to instructions on making their quilts and patchwork items.

Dissolved in 1978, the Mountain Artisans name has been revived under private ownership.

See also Folk Arts Revival

Rebecca Stelling
Mountain Artisans

Mountain Boy

The steamboat *Mountain Boy* was one of six steamboats that moved West Virginia's capital between 1870 and 1885. The boat was built on the Monongahela River at Brownsville, Pennsylvania, in 1868 on a hull 135 feet long, 26 feet wide, and four feet deep. It was built for J. W. Oakes, president of the Kanawha and Gallipolis Packet Co. The *Mountain Boy* was running regularly on the Kanawha and Ohio rivers when chartered to move the state capital from Wheeling to Charleston in 1870. There was no charge. When asked to perform this work, Captain James Newton agreed enthusiastically: "I will go with cannon, music and floating flags and will consider the honor sufficient pay."

On March 28, 1870, state officials with state records and property boarded the *Mountain Boy* for the trip south. They traveled from Wheeling down the Ohio to Point Pleasant, and then up the Kanawha River. As the *Mountain Boy* approached Charleston, the steamer *Kanawha Belle* with a brass band and reception committee welcomed the state capital to Charleston. In 1875, the state legislature voted to move the capital back to Wheeling after the citizens of that city offered to build the state a new and better capitol than the one being used in Charleston. Only in 1885 did the capital return permanently to Charleston, this time aboard the *Chesapeake* and the *Belle Prince.*

Meanwhile, the *Mountain Boy* had been destroyed by river ice at Cincinnati in December 1873.

See also Capitols of West Virginia

Gerald W. Sutphin
Huntington
Gerald W. Sutphin and Richard A. Andre, *Sternwheelers on the Great Kanawha River,* 1991.

Mountain Cove Spiritualist Community

Founded in 1851 by trance medium James L. Scott and jointly led by renowned Christian mystic Thomas Lake Harris after 1852, the spiritualist colony was located on Osborne Creek in Fayette County's Mountain Cove district. Receiving a "call to the mountain," where a spiritualist utopia could become a "new Eden," Scott led some 100 members from a spiritualist circle in Auburn, New York, to the property on the James River & Kanawha Turnpike. Among the migrants were families with the names of Hunt, Hopping, Dwight, Nichols, Norton, Sheridan, Cottrell, and Piggot.

Industrious and resourceful, community members established a church, a mill, two stores, and a school for their children. Members lived in their own private homes, while sharing common spiritualist beliefs and communitarian values. They published the first newspaper in Fayette County, the *Mountain Cove Journal and Spiritual Harbinger,* a vehicle for disseminating spiritualist views as well as promoting economic development.

Spiritualism is the belief that life continues after death and that the living can communicate, usually by means of a medium, with spirits of the deceased. Scott and Harris taught reliance upon the leader as being the only means for members to communicate with the spirits. This charismatic authoritarianism was soon challenged by believers who wanted to seek contact with the spirits directly, an idea appealing to women as well as men. Soon, Nancy P. Hunt could hear "rapping" and feel "a tingling of her feet," which meant to her that a spirit was trying to contact her.

Conflict erupted within the community when Scott demanded adherence to "mutualism" which required all private property be subject to divine direction that was available only through him. Controversy over leadership and spiritualist beliefs raged within the community during 1852–53. Scott and Harris departed, and community property was dissolved. The Mountain Cove communitarian experiment, inspired by the Second Great Awakening, soon melted into the diverse fabric of West Virginia history.

See also Fayette County

Lou Athey
Franklin & Marshall College
Bret E. Carroll, "Spiritualism and Community in Antebellum America: The Mountain Cove Episode," *Communal Societies,* 1992; J. T. Peters and H. B. Carden, *History of Fayette County, West Virginia,* 1926.

Mountain Institute

The Mountain Institute, a nonprofit conservation group, was founded in West Virginia in 1972 as the Woodlands Institute. The current name was adopted in 1995 to reflect more accurately the organization's interests. The institute, founded by Daniel Taylor-Ide and King Seeger, is now headquartered in Washington. The main goal of the Mountain Institute is to preserve mountain cultures and environments worldwide. The institute has programs in three mountain ranges: the Andes of South America, the Himalayas of Asia, and the Appalachians of North America. Programs vary in the different regions, but the underlying focus is to help local people determine and carry out conservation programs appropriate for their communities.

The Appalachian program is centered in West Virginia at a 400-acre teaching campus and natural botanical area located on the upper slopes of Spruce Knob. The Spruce Knob Center is used for educational programs, conferences, and ecological research. One program for high-school students is the month-long West Virginia Scholars Academy. Each summer, 14 to 18 rising high-school seniors are selected to participate in the intense program, which includes college-level studies as well as diverse educational, environmental, and research opportunities.

Amy Donaldson Arnold
Ivydale

Mountain Lion

Mountain lions were fairly common in the Mountain State when early settlers moved into the area, and these cats were most abundant in the Allegheny Mountains. Mountain lions are known by many names, including cougar, catamount, painter, panther, and puma. The numerous Panther Knobs and Panther Runs found across the state provide evidence of this animal's wide presence and its influence on the minds of early Mountaineers.

The eastern cougar, which occurred in West Virginia, is one of 15 subspecies found in North America. Cougars vary in color from yellow brown to almost gray, but no black cougars have been found in North America. There is little biological data on eastern cougars, but western animals reach a length of eight feet and weigh up to 160 pounds. Males are usually larger than females.

As Europeans settled the wilderness, mountains lions were viewed as a threat to both humans and their livestock. Bounties were offered for dead mountain lions in many areas. In Randolph County, for example, bounties were paid on 73 panthers between 1852 and 1859. Persecution and the loss of habitat effectively extinguished the big cats in West Virginia. According to naturalist A. B. Brooks, "The last record of a killing of a panther was in 1887 when Col. Cecil Clay and Francis McCoy shot one on Tea Creek, Pocahontas County." In 1936, tracks in the vicinity of Kennison Mountain, Pocahontas County, were reported by workers from the National Museum of Natural History.

Although there are still sightings of mountain lions in the Mountain State, the source of these animals is difficult to determine. Two cougars captured in Pocahontas County in 1976 were western cougars that had been transported there and released. Do any real eastern cougars still exist in West Virginia? We may never know, but if they do, they are considered endangered and protected.

Craig W. Stihler
Division of Natural Resources

Mountain Party

West Virginia politics has never been hospitable to third parties, and in 1999 the legislature made things harder when it doubled the number of petition signatures needed to get on the ballot. So there was some surprise in 2000 when activists launched the Mountain Party and gathered 13,000 signatures to gain ballot status. Denise Giardina, a noted author with no political experience, agreed to run as the Mountain Party candidate for governor.

Every new party needs a cause, some issue which raises public attention and is ignored by both major parties. For the Mountain Party it was the opposition to strip mining. But the underlying cause for the party's appearance in 2000 was frustration with what supporters perceived as an entrenched Democratic Party and an unresponsive political system. The new party's name was suggestive of its "green" image, and the Mountain Party combined its environmentalism with a populist agenda of saving small schools and small businesses. Giardina aggressively took on King Coal in a state identified with and, many argued, dominated by the coal industry.

Although she attracted media attention with her quixotic campaign, Giardina garnered only 10, 000 votes or 1.6 percent of the total votes cast. That number, however, was more than the one percent required to qualify the Mountain Party for an automatic place on the next election ballot.

In 2004 the Mountain Party nominated as its gubernatorial candidate Jesse Johnson, a Charleston actor and filmmaker. Johnson received 18,113 votes or two percent of the vote in the general election which was enough to keep his party's slot on the ballot in the next election. The low totals reflect the continuing challenge facing any third party effort in West Virginia. Whether the Mountain Party survives depends on future elections, but, as with many third parties, its existence indicated tensions within the state's political system.

See also Denise Giardina

Robert Rupp
West Virginia Wesleyan College

Mountain Stage

West Virginia Public Broadcasting's *Mountain Stage* began in 1983 as a radio show, originally hosted by Larry Groce and George Daugherty. One of the longest running contemporary music programs on radio, *Mountain Stage* is a performance program recorded before a theater audience. It has grown from a once-a-month statewide broadcast to a weekly two-hour syndicated show reaching a global audience with 26 original shows a year.

The radio program's first national broadcast was in 1985, live from the Piccolo Spoleto Festival in Charleston, S.C. Regular national broadcasts began in 1986 on National Public Radio, and in 1989 Public Radio International took over distribution. Since 1990, *Mountain Stage* has consistently been aired on at least 100 radio stations and in 1999 began airing worldwide on *Voice of America*. Since 2001, *Mountain Stage* has also been broadcast on public television.

Mountain Stage is the largest presenter of musical performances in West Virginia, bringing in more than 100 different performers each year. More than 10,000 people attend the show annually. Usually taped at the Cultural Center in Charleston, *Mountain Stage* has often gone on the road nationwide and to several places in West Virginia. Among the musicians to perform on *Mountain Stage* have been Mary Chapin Carpenter, Lyle Lovett, Alison Krauss, Bill Monroe, Ricky Skaggs, Kathy Mattea, and others.

Mountain Stage was created by executive producer Andy Ridenour and recording engineer Francis Fisher, who originally wanted to produce a program featuring West Virginia musicians. They approached Groce with the idea, but he persuaded them to shift the show's focus to give it a national appeal while still staying grounded in the Mountain State. More than 200 West Virginia artists have performed on the show, including traditional, bluegrass, folk, contemporary and country musicians, singers, and songwriters.

Greg Proctor
Charleston

Mountain State Art & Craft Fair

The Mountain State Art & Craft Fair, held annually during the Fourth of July weekend at the Cedar Lakes Conference Center near Ripley, began in 1963 as part of West Virginia's Centennial celebration. Representatives of the departments of Agriculture, Commerce, and Education met with Cedar Lakes personnel to plan the state's first fair exclusively for the arts and crafts.

Fifty-four artists and craftsmen participated in the first fair. The event had grown to include about 200 by 2004. Sponsoring agencies now include the Department of Agriculture, Department of Education, Division of Tourism, WVU Extension Service, Division of Natural Resources, Tamarack, and the West Virginia Art and Craft Guild. Attendance at the 1963 event was 6,575, with fair-goers growing in numbers in subsequent years. In 2003, the attendance was 23,112.

Artists and craftsmen who exhibit at the fair are selected by a jury of craft experts. The number of out-of-state exhibitors is limited to 25 percent. The fair is open to craftsmen over the age of 18 who work in either traditional or contemporary arts and crafts, and on-site demonstrations are among the event's main attractions. Categories for exhibits and demonstrations range from baskets to wood furniture. Traditional dance and music are also part of the fair, and foods such as buckwheat pancakes, brown beans and cornbread, and homemade ice cream are available.

The Mountain State Art & Craft Fair is one of the leading arts and crafts fairs in the nation. The event has been named among the top five traditional crafts shows in *Sunshine Artist* magazine and has been featured in the travel guide *Best Festivals Mid-Atlantic*.

See also Folk Arts Revival, Handcrafts

Mountain State Forest Festival

The Mountain State Forest Festival was first held on October 30–31 and November 1, 1930, in Elkins. Except for an eight-year lapse from 1941 to 1949, the festival has been held annually ever since, though the time has been moved to the first week in October. Elkins is the county seat of Randolph County, a heavily forested area noted for its hardwood trees and colorful fall foliage. George Dornblazer, generally considered the father of the Forest Festival, was director general of the first festival. His directors and officers included 80 civic leaders.

The event has now expanded to nine days and is put on by 250 volunteer workers. While centered on the campus of Davis & Elkins College, the Forest Festival involves almost every business and organization in Elkins. Events now include performances by the Wheeling Symphony, appearances by nationally known country musicians, craft and art shows, wood chopping and other timbering contests, old English knight tournaments, dances, parades, and a carnival. Major attractions include a highly competitive fiddle contest and a fire-engine parade which draws fire departments from throughout West Virginia. The coronation of Queen Silvia by the governor of West Virginia is a highlight of the Forest Festival. Although the two maids of honor and the minor court come from Elkins, the queen must come from another county and the 40 princesses from all over the state, making the festival truly statewide.

A magnet for West Virginia politicians, the festival has also attracted national attention. Presidents Franklin Roosevelt, Truman, Nixon, Ford, and Carter visited the event. Other national figures who have taken part in the festival are Eddie Rickenbacker, Eleanor Roosevelt, Adlai Stevenson, Chuck Yeager, Sam Rayburn, Hubert Humphrey, and Neil Armstrong. The Forest Festival consistently attracts between 125,000 and 150,000 visitors, and newspapers have estimated crowds at more then 200,000 when a U.S. president takes part.

See also Elkins

J. E. Spears
Elkins

Mountain State Press

The Mountain State Press was founded by Jim Comstock, the colorful publisher of the *West Virginia Hillbilly* weekly newspaper. Comstock recruited a young Marshall University graduate, Peter Wallace, to help with this new venture, and in February 1978 Comstock and Wallace became the incorporators of Mountain State Press. The articles of incorporation stated that the purposes of the press were to promote and publish books by West Virginians and books "which support and reinforce the values, priorities, and culture of West Virginia." Approximately 400 people became contributing members, paying dues to support the press and receiving books and discounts in return.

The press is managed by a board of directors. Professor William Plumley of the University of Charleston served as the first president of the press. The first book published was *As I Remember It*, reminiscences by Stanley Eskew. A reprint of W.E.R. Byrne's classic, *Tale of the Elk*, soon followed. Mountain State Press has published more than 50 books. Authors represent all areas of the state and a wide range of subject matter. Since shortly after its inception, Mountain State Press has been located at the University of Charleston.

See also Jim Comstock

Betty L. MacQueen
Chesapeake, Virginia

Mountain State University

Mountain State University, originally Beckley College and later the College of West Virginia, was founded in 1933. The school was chartered as a private, nonprofit junior college. Classes began in September 1933 in rented rooms in Beckley's First United Methodist Church. Ninety-seven students were enrolled the first year.

G. E. Hartman, D. K. Shroyer, J. Lewis Bumgardner, Joe L. Smith Sr., and Beckley Mayor Grover C. Hedrick served as the first board of trustees of Beckley College. The first president was Bumgardner, who was succeeded by Hedrick. Shroyer became president in 1960, retiring in 1968. John W. Saunders served from 1968 until his death in 1988. George Balsama was then appointed, serving until 1989. Vice President Robert G. Lilly served as interim president until July 1990. Charles Polk is now president of Mountain State University.

The college began to establish its present campus along South Kanawha Street in the mid-1930s. Hedrick Hall was built in 1936, to house classrooms and offices. Bumgardner Hall was built in 1940, and Hartman Hall in 1964. In 1985, a grant from the Benedum Foundation provided funds for major renovations to all three buildings, which now constitute Benedum Center, the administrative complex

for Mountain State University. In 1968, the student union building and Shroyer Hall were built. O'Dell Hall was built in 1972 as a girls' dormitory, but has since been remodeled for other uses.

The college bought several existing buildings during the 1980s. The United Methodist Temple building, now the John W. Eye Conference Center, was acquired in 1989 and remodeled for use for classroom space and convocations. Many neighboring residences became part of the campus, and one now serves as the office of the president. The Erikson Alumni Center, the English Language Institute, and administrative services occupy other old houses along South Kanawha Street. In 1998, the college purchased the former Beckley Junior High School campus. The main school building, renamed Carter Hall in recognition of donations made by the Carter Family Foundation, now houses the School of Business. This purchase also included Van Meter Gymnasium and a building now used as the health services building.

The Lewin Family Bell Tower near the center of the campus is an impressive landmark. Beckley businessman Max Lewin funded this tower as a memorial to nine of his family members and others who perished in the Holocaust. Near the bell tower, the Robert C. Byrd Learning Resource Center, built in 1997, houses the library, a media center, a television production studio, an audio studio, computer laboratories, and offices. A full-time dining facility, the Cougar Den, occupies the lowest floor of this building.

Beckley College changed its name to the College of West Virginia in September 1991, after gaining approval from the North Central Association of Colleges and Schools to offer baccalaureate degrees in general business, accounting, computer information systems, computer science, nursing, and health care administration. The College of West Virginia became Mountain State University in August 2001.

Mountain State University is accredited by the North Central Association of Colleges and Schools. It offers associate, baccalaureate, and master's degrees in many fields, as well as special programs in adult education, independent study, online learning, and distance learning. The fall 2002 enrollment (full-time equivalents) was 2,619. An active athletic program provides competition in basketball, softball, and volleyball. In 2004, the Mountain State University Cougars basketball team won the NAIA Division I national championship.

Leona Gwinn Brown
Daniels

Mountaineer Field

On autumn Saturdays, Mountaineer Field is where fans from throughout the state

Mountaineer Field was packed when WVU played Purdue in 1995.

gather for West Virginia University football action. The stadium on the Evansdale Campus in Morgantown is a first-class facility. It was not always that way after WVU football began in 1891. Various fields were used in the early years, including pastures and fields used for other sports such as baseball.

The first Mountaineer Field opened in 1924 and was completed in 1925. The 34,000-seat football field was located at the Falling Run site between Sunnyside and the original, downtown campus. Fans cherish the memory of games there. The top stadium crowd was 38,681 on November 10, 1979, the last home game at Old Mountaineer Field.

As expansion became necessary, many wanted simply to upgrade and add seats to the existing field. In 1977, Governor Rockefeller and others decided West Virginia needed a facility that would show the state moving forward and create pride among its people. A major college football stadium opened in Morgantown on September 6, 1980, with a 41-27 win over Cincinnati. It was the first game of new coach Don Nehlen, who would become the most successful coach in Mountaineer history. The stadium opened with seating for 50,000, but expansions increased the seating to 63,500. Every seat was needed for its largest crowd of 70,222 on November 20, 1993, when West Virginia in the midst of an undefeated season beat Miami of Florida 17-14, to win the university's first title in the Big East Conference.

Today, Mountaineer Field is a modern sports complex. In 1994, luxury skyboxes were added, providing great views of the field. In 1998, the Caperton Indoor Facility was completed, allowing practice to take place regardless of weather. The plush Puskar Center houses office and lounge space, as well as team trophies, tributes to past Mountaineers, and a weight room. The most recent additions include a state-of-the-art video screen in the South bowl and a new lighting system for televised night games. In 2003, WVU announced that the stadium had been renamed Milan Puskar Stadium, home of Mountaineer Field, in recognition of benefactor Milan Puskar.

See also West Virginia University

Charles W. Morris III
State Museum

Mountaineer Race Track

Mountaineer Race Track & Gaming Resort, located in the Northern Panhandle town of Chester, was called Waterford Park when it opened as a thoroughbred horse racing track in 1951. The complex has since grown to include a 360-room hotel, restaurants, an 18-hole golf course, a fitness center, and a 5,100-seat theater and events center, in addition to the racetrack and the 3,168 slot machines present in 2004.

In the 1970s and 1980s, the track was floundering, and in 1981 the state legislature passed and county residents endorsed Sunday racing in an effort to keep the facility operating. Nevertheless, Waterford closed in 1983, reopening in 1984 after the legislature granted tax concessions. In 1990, as a Lottery Commission pilot project, the first 165 video lottery machines were installed at the track. MTR Gaming Group purchased the track, then known as Mountaineer Park, in 1992. The track's fortunes began to improve with the passage of the Racetrack Video Lottery Act of 1994. By the year 2000, more than $1 billion was being wagered at Mountaineer's video slot machines annually, more than 50 times as much as was taken from live horseracing.

The resort is a major employer in Hancock County. Out-of-state gamblers account for the majority of visitors. In 2003, about 65 percent of the resort's patrons came from Ohio and 30 percent from Pennsylvania.

Mountaineer hosts the West Virginia Derby, a nationally recognized race for three-year-olds and the centerpiece of the track's year-round thoroughbred racing program. The race is broadcast on ESPN and has attracted Triple Crown participants.

The Mountaineer

For several decades, the West Virginia University Mountaineer mascot has symbolized the rich heritage and cultural pride of the Mountain State and its people. In addition to sporting events, the mascot attends community functions and schools as a goodwill ambassador for the university. The costume of the Mountaineer is an idealized version of the clothes of the frontier settler of Western Virginia, a full buckskin suit and coonskin cap. To rally fans' spirits at university sporting events, he roams the sidelines, greets fans, and fires an authentic, muzzle-loading rifle.

In the 1920s, the first, unofficial Mountaineers appeared spontaneously at WVU sporting events. Early volunteers—Burton "Irish" Crow, Lawson Hill, William "Buckwheat" Jackson, and others—garbed themselves in flannel shirts, bearskin capes and coonskin caps. In 1936, the Mountain honorary society selected the first official buckskin-clad Mountaineer from among the WVU student body, Boyd Harrison "Slim" Arnold. In 1990, Natalie Tennant made history by becoming the first female Mountaineer.

The Mountain honorary society continues to screen student applicants for the post. Finalists are chosen for their outstanding character and their enthusiasm. At a WVU basketball game, the finalists compete in a traditional "cheer off." The winning mascot receives a tuition waiver or scholarship.

The Mountaineer mascot figure was

first used in commerce in 1972 and registered as a U.S. trademark in 1985. Mountaineer memorabilia, including retired rifles and costumes, are housed in a glass case in the Vandalia lounge of the Mountainlair student union on the downtown campus. A bronze statue of the Mountaineer graces the Mountainlair front lawn.

See also West Virginia University

Mary Rodd Furbee
Morgantown

Mountaintop Removal Mining

Opponents of strip mining won passage of the federal Surface Mining Control and Reclamation Act in 1977. It regulated but did not outlaw surface mining, which was often more economical than deep mining. The act specifically allowed mountaintop removal, but only as an exception when the resulting flat land would be used for development.

Mountaintop removal mining, which had begun in West Virginia in 1967 at Cannelton, became more feasible as huge earth-moving machines were introduced into the rugged Appalachian terrain by the early 1980s. The "Big John" dragline, capable of moving 65 to 75 cubic yards at a scoop, came to the Hobet 21 mine in Boone and Lincoln counties in 1983. Today the largest machinery moves more than 100 cubic yards at a time.

By the mid-1990s, the 1990 Clean Air Act amendments had spurred demand for the low-sulfur, high-Btu coal of West Virginia's southern coalfields. More than 500 feet was being shaved off the tops of mountains and dumped as valley fills. At least 500 miles of streams had been filled, and more than 300 square miles of West Virginia had been surface-mined in some way by 2000. Residents complained that blasting shook homes, and dust from mining and preparation plants covered houses and cars. Runoff from valley fills flooded streams and homes. Some communities were nearly eliminated when mines bought out residents who complained.

In 1998, attorney Joe Lovett of Mountain State Justice in Charleston filed a case in federal district court charging that state and federal laws prohibited dumping the tops of mountains into streams. He also argued that there had been complete disregard for the original congressional intent of using the flattened mountains for commercial development. Patricia Bragg of Pie in Mingo County was the lead plaintiff in the case, known as *Bragg v. Robertson*. Lovett was joined by co-counsel Patrick McGinley and Suzanne Weise of Morgantown, and James Hecker of Trial Lawyers for Public Justice.

They won a major victory in October 1999 when Chief U.S. District Judge Charles H. Haden II ruled that a 100-foot buffer zone prevented waste placement in streams that ran at least part of the year. However, Governor Underwood, coal companies, and the United Mine Workers of America protested. Haden stayed the decision. In April 2001, the Fourth U.S. Circuit Court of Appeals overturned the decision, stating that the case should be tried in state court.

Though the U.S. Supreme Court declined the *Bragg v. Robertson* case, attorney Lovett persisted and in early May 2002 won another dramatic decision from Judge Haden. In the new case, *Kentuckians for the Commonwealth v. Rivenburgh*, Haden ruled that the Army Corps of Engineers could not, under Section 404 of the Clean Water Act, allow valley fills in perennial and intermittent streams. He agreed with Lovett's interpretation that fills are waste material and therefore prohibited by Section 404, which only allows waste in streams for development, such as shopping centers. Valley fills are only allowed, Haden ruled, when land flattened by the mountaintop mine will be used for housing or commercial development, as the Surface Mining Control and Reclamation Act intended.

This ruling was overturned on appeal. Yet the battle over valley fills continued. The industry won one round when the Bush administration changed Section 404 in May 2002, making valley fills legal. But opponents halted fills again with a July 2004 victory in federal court. Judge Joseph R. Goodwin, who took over after Judge Haden's death in March 2004, ruled that the Corps of Engineers must stop the routine, seemingly automatic approval of valley fills under Nationwide Permit 21. Now the Corps must thoroughly examine the environmental impact of large fills, perhaps denying some. Yet, despite the stalemate on fills, coalfield observers sensed a shift toward more productive use of mined-over flat lands, closer to the spirit of the 1977 legislation. These observers cited the use of mined land for golf courses, industry, and housing, especially in Mingo County.

See also Coal Industry, Charles H. Haden

Penny Loeb
Great Falls, Virginia

Mud River

The 45-mile-long Mud River, which empties into the Guyandotte River at Barboursville in Cabell County, has its headwaters near the hamlet of Mud in Lincoln County, an unincorporated community said to have been founded in 1872. From there, the Mud River, never bigger than a big creek except during times of flood, flows through the communities of Spurlockville, Palermo, Sias, and Myra before reaching Hamlin, the county seat of Lincoln County. Crossing the county line into Cabell County, the Mud continues north to Ball's Gap, then on to Milton. From Milton, the river turns west, heading for Barboursville and its confluence with the Guyandotte.

In the 19th century, trees were felled on nearby hillsides and rafted down the Mud River. Gristmills, sawmills, tanneries, and brick kilns were located along the river's banks. Sturdy covered bridges, swinging foot bridges, flatbed ferries, and willow-shaded fords carried traffic over the river. Today, some Mud Valley residents continue to farm, with tobacco and corn the chief crops.

In 1938, Congress approved construction of a flood-control reservoir on the Mud River, but there seemed to be little public interest in the project and it was never built. A flood-control dam was built on the upper Mud River in the mid-1990s, creating a 306-acre lake near Spurlockville.

James E. Casto
Herald-Dispatch

P. Joseph Mullins

Sculptor P. Joseph Mullins was born March 15, 1941, in Charleston. He graduated from Stonewall Jackson High School and served two years in the army infantry. He earned a bachelor's degree in art from Morris Harvey College (now University of Charleston) and a master of fine arts degree from Ohio University.

In the late 1960s, Mullins worked as an urban planner for the Governor's Office of Federal and State Relations. He later served as executive director of Mountain Artisans Inc. From 1977 to 1984, he was executive director of the Parkersburg Arts Center.

In 1987, Mullins's entry won the West Virginia Veterans' Memorial design competition. Work on the $3.8 million project was completed in 1999. Mullins conducted extensive research for the memorial project. He interviewed combat veterans, read war books, traveled to Vietnam twice, and consulted with museum curators, uniform supply houses, and others. The memorial at the state capitol features four bronze figures—a World War I infantryman, a World War II sailor, a Korean airman, and a Vietnam War marine. The memorial's black granite walls bear the names of more than 10,300 West Virginians who died in the four U.S. wars of the 20th century.

Mullins's work also includes commissions for the University of Charleston, churches, and individuals.

Multiflora Rose

Multiflora rose, a major agricultural nuisance, is a thorny non-native spreading shrub with high arching stems, reaching ten or more feet in height and often forming impenetrable thickets. Profuse clusters of single, one-inch white flowers appear in June, followed by quarter-inch red fruits in August.

Introduced to the eastern U.S. in 1866 as rootstock for ornamental roses, the multiflora rose was later promoted in the 1930s by the U.S. Soil Conservation Service for use in erosion control and as living fences. Multiflora rose was also encouraged as a source of food and cover for wildlife by state conservation departments as late as the 1960s, including the West Virginia Division of Natural Resources.

The shrub is extremely prolific and invades pastures and other unplowed lands, crowding out native vegetation. It is currently considered a noxious weed in several states, including West Virginia. Multiflora rose spreads aggressively, its large numbers of fruits eaten and dispersed by birds. Dense thickets of multiflora rose exclude most native shrubs and herbs from establishing and may reduce available nesting habitat for native birds.

Current efforts to control multiflora rose include frequent repeated cutting or mowing, pulling of young plants, use of herbicide, and in severe infestations, heavy equipment such as bulldozers. There are also two naturally occurring biological controls that affect multiflora rose to some extent: a native fungal pathogen (rose-rosette disease), spread by a tiny native mite, and a non-native seed-infesting wasp, the European rose chalcid. To date, rose-rosette disease shows the most promise for control of the invasive shrub, with more than 90 percent of many populations killed by the disease. Rose-rosette disease is spreading naturally through the East and Midwest.

W. Russ McClain
Nature Conservancy of West Virginia

Museums

There are about 200 museums in West Virginia. Most are dedicated to one subject, usually some aspect of history, but there are many that take more than one or two subjects as their mission. Some museums display traveling exhibits on various subjects. Some have diverse permanent collections.

There are 12 museums operated by the state or national government in West Virginia. The West Virginia State Museum in the Cultural Center in Charleston is the oldest museum in the state, founded in 1905, and has the largest collection, 56,000 objects of history, art, technology, and natural science. There are 13 historical state parks. Cass Scenic Railroad State Park's collection of geared, steam, mountain-logging locomotives is unique in the nation.

There are six county historical museums and nine city museums. There are about 60 historic house museums. One of the finest is the Oglebay Mansion Museum in Wheeling. It is one of the four

largest museums in West Virginia. There are also many historic courthouses. The historic federal building where the statehood debates took place in Wheeling is today a museum, West Virginia Independence Hall.

There are three restored mills. The Easton Roller Mill teaches about a more modern method of flour production than the older grindstone-operated mills at Jackson's Mill and Babcock State Park.

There are 11 forts, military museums, and battlefield parks. Pricketts Fort is a reconstructed stockade with cabins, where the 18th-century frontier is interpreted. Adjacent to the stockade is the restored early 19th-century Job Prickett House.

There are seven glass museums. Oglebay Glass Museum has a superlative collection from five 19th-century glass factories in Wheeling. The Fenton Glass Company has a room with a large selection of the many types of glass that the company made throughout the 20th century. There are two glass factory museums.

There are three police museums. For example, the Fayette County Jail and Law Enforcement Museum is in an old jail and tells about penology and law enforcement.

There are nine transportation museums, most related to railroads. The Baltimore & Ohio Railroad Museum is located in the 1905 Beaux Arts-style station in Wheeling, now West Virginia Northern Community College. There is a firefighting museum in Huntington.

There are seven restored schools and education museums. For example, the Nicholas County Historical Society has restored the Irish Corner one-room school and located it in Memorial Park in Summersville. There are two farm museums, including the West Virginia State Farm Museum at the Mason County Fairgrounds near Point Pleasant.

There are 23 art museums. Eight are associated with colleges, but the most prominent is the privately administered Huntington Museum of Art housed in the Bauhaus-style building designed by architect Walter Gropius. There, the museum shows its important permanent collection and a regular program of changing exhibitions. It is one of the four largest museums.

There are two children's museums, including the Youth Museum of Southern West Virginia in Beckley. The Youth Museum presents changing exhibitions. In 2000, it received a prestigious national award from the National Endowment for the Arts. The Buckskin Area Council Boy Scout Museum in Charleston is the largest such museum, although there are good scout exhibits in other museums.

There are 12 science museums and nature centers. The Museum of Radio and

Technology in Huntington shows the development of electronic technology in the 20th century. The Core Arboretum at West Virginia University is one of three arboretums. The Good Children's Zoo in Oglebay Park and the West Virginia Wildlife Center in French Creek are the two zoos in the state.

Sunrise Museum, previously located in Sunrise Mansion in Charleston and one of the four largest museums, changed its name to the Avampato Discovery Center and moved to a new home in the Clay Center for the Arts & Sciences in 2003. The Cook-Hayman Pharmacy Museum at West Virginia University is the only pharmacy museum. There are two coal institutions. The Exhibition Coal Mine and Coal Camp in Beckley exhibits methods of mining and mining artifacts.

There are six African-American museums. The Zion A.M.E. Church and the Freedom Cabin show what life was like when Booker T. Washington was a child in Malden.

There are four religious sites. Among them is Old Rehoboth Church Museum in Union, Monroe County, one of three 18th-century log buildings in the state.

The West Virginia Association of Museums was organized in 1990 to strengthen the state's museums individually and as a group. Every year an annual conference is held, and workshops are presented on a variety of specialized subjects including conservation of objects, basic museum operations, cataloging, disaster preparedness, and interpretation.

James R. Mitchell
State Museum

Ruth Ann Musick

Folklorist Ruth Ann Musick was born September 17, 1897, in Kirksville, Missouri. She earned a B.S. in education from the Kirksville State Teacher's College and an M.S. from the State University of Iowa. After teaching school, she earned a Ph.D. in English from the State University of Iowa in 1943. While there, folklorist Edwin Ford Piper first interested her in folklore.

Musick brought this interest to West Virginia. She came to teach mathematics and English at Fairmont State College (now Fairmont State University) in 1946 and remained until her retirement in 1967. She started a folk literature class at the college and in 1950 helped to revive the West Virginia Folklore Society, with Walter Barnes of Fairmont State and Patrick Gainer of West Virginia University. In 1951, she founded the *West Virginia Folklore Journal* and served as editor until 1967.

Musick became West Virginia's folklore ambassador, promoting folklore through education, public speaking, radio, and television. She published four major folktale collections: *Ballads, Folk Songs, and Folk Tales From West Virginia; The Telltale*

Lilac Bush and Other West Virginia Ghost Tales; Green Hills of Magic, West Virginia Folktales From Europe; and *Coffin Hollow and Other Ghost Tales.* She wrote two popular folklore columns for West Virginia newspapers, "The Old Folks Say" and "Sassafras Tea." Musick died in Fairmont, July 2, 1974. She bequeathed to Fairmont State her unpublished folklore estate, now archived in the West Virginia Folklife Center at the university. In 1980, the university library was renamed the Ruth Ann Musick Library.

See also Folklore

Judy Prozzillo Byers
Fairmont State University

Muslims

A Muslim is a follower of the religion of Islam. Islam belongs to the family of Western monotheistic religions, those who worship one God, which also include Judaism and Christianity. The Muslim communities of West Virginia are of relatively recent origin. Prior to the 1960s, there were scattered Muslim families in West Virginia, primarily of Middle Eastern extraction. They arrived with other immigrants from that part of the world in the early 1900s. These were mostly from merchant classes and engaged in various businesses. They were too few and too scattered to establish a community of Muslims in any organized fashion. However, they were successful in their own life and integrated themselves well into their communities. Many continued to observe Islam individually.

The major influx of Muslim families into West Virginia occurred in the 1960s and 1970s when the expanding U.S. economy encouraged the immigration of qualified professionals and other technical personnel. The government initiated an examination for medical doctors from foreign countries which would make them eligible for graduate training in the United States. This opened the doors for qualified foreign doctors to enter this country. At the same time American schools started aggressively enrolling foreign students for graduate education. In that era most of the immigrants from these countries were professionals, primarily doctors, engineers, pharmacists, veterinarians, teachers, and so forth. West Virginia received its share.

Muslims remain a small minority among 1.8 million West Virginians, numbering a few thousand. However, they have settled in well-defined communities in major cities and around educational institutions. Charleston, Huntington, Beckley, Morgantown, and Princeton boast a significant Muslim presence, with second-generation Muslim West Virginians now growing up in their parents' adopted homeland. Montgomery, Logan, Parkersburg, and other smaller cities have a few Muslim families and students who participate in community activities of the Islamic Center in Charleston. Muslims in West Virginia represent countries of South Asia, Southeast Asia, Middle East, Africa, Eastern Europe, and North America.

The first religious and cultural center, the Islamic Center of West Virginia, was built and opened in Charleston in 1988. Mosques, or Muslim worship houses, opened in Princeton, Beckley, Morgantown, and Huntington rapidly thereafter. All of these are managed and supported by community members on a voluntary basis since Islam has neither an organized church nor ordained clergy. However, Charleston now has a full-time Imam, a prayer leader and teacher, who is also responsible for overseeing the Islamic Center and for community liaison.

Imam Mohammad Jamal Daoudi
Islamic Association of West Virginia

Mussels

Freshwater mussels are members of the mollusk family Unionidae. They have a hard outer covering consisting of two halves, or valves, and a soft inner body. They are not true mussels and are more appropriately called bivalves. Native bivalves possess a large muscular "foot" that is used for locomotion.

There are 60 species of Unionids native to West Virginia, occurring in all parts of the state. They live a fairly sedentary life buried in the stream bottom, where they feed by filtering algae and other organic debris from the water. As a result, they also filter pollutants, and their health provides a sensitive environmental indicator.

Freshwater mussels are probably the most endangered group of animals in North America. In West Virginia, the Monongahela River watershed, except for a few tributaries, is almost devoid of native bivalves due to acid mine drainage. These bivalves require a fish host for completion of their life cycle, and fish carry them into new areas or to areas previously occupied. Construction of dams eliminates valuable riffle habitat and also inhibits fish movements. Native Americans used these animals for food and the shells for ornamentation and tools. More recently shells were used for the making of buttons, but by the 1940s shell was replaced by plastic. Today shells are used to produce nuclei for the cultured pearl industry. West Virginia does not allow the commercial harvest of freshwater mussels.

Though no true mussels are native to West Virginia, zebra mussels were introduced from Europe into the Great Lakes by commercial barge traffic about 1986. Currently they are found in the navigable portions of the Ohio, Kanawha, and Monongahela rivers in West Virginia. Zebra mussels can cause great economic losses since they clog water intake pipes, and they rep-resent a serious competitor and threat to native species. Major losses of native mussel species have been reported in areas such as the Mississippi River, lower Ohio River, and the Great Lakes watershed. West Virginia naturalists expected the worst as zebra mussels spread rapidly through the state's waters in the decade of the 1990s. In 2000, West Virginia experienced high losses of native mussels in the Ohio River due to the competition of zebra mussels. Since then, zebra mussel populations have fluctuated widely in the Ohio River, giving hope that the native mussel populations will survive.

Janet L. Clayton
Division of Natural Resources

Hunter John Myers

Outdoorsman John "Hunter John" Myers, born about 1765, became a legendary figure in Western Virginia in the early 19th century. In 1798, John Myers married Catherine Everhart, the daughter of Revolutionary War Gen. George Everhart. In the early 1800s, he began accumulating land and built a comfortable log home in the Meadow Branch valley between Martinsburg and Berkeley Springs.

Myers earned his nickname by making his living as a hunter and trapper on Sleepy Creek Mountain. The countryside around him grew more settled and filled with people, but Myers continued to typify the frontier mountaineer. His clinging to the old ways inspired author John Esten Cooke's first novel, *Leather Stocking and Silk; or, Hunter John Myers and His Times,* published in 1854. Cooke's novel is an average adventure romance in the James Fenimore Cooper mold, but the vivid portrait of Myers, his home, and family give the book what zest and appeal it has.

Myers also loomed large in the imagination of writer-artist David Hunter Strother (Porte Crayon). Strother was taken by Hunter John's life in the wild and, in 1837, painted a portrait of him from memory. Myers is believed to have died in 1835, but his descendants remained in the Meadow Branch area until about 1915. Some still live in the Eastern Panhandle. The Myers property is now part of Sleepy Creek Public Hunting and Fishing Area.

John Douglas
Berkeley Springs

Karl Dewey Myers

Poet Laureate Karl Dewey Myers was born February 12, 1899, in Tucker County, with defects so severe that he was not expected to survive the day of his birth. Although he lived, he never weighed more than 60 pounds, never walked, and never attended school. He educated himself through persistent self-study.

Myers first attempted poetry when he was 16. Operating an Oliver typewriter that he was unable to lift and inspired chiefly by Elizabethan poets and Edgar Allan Poe, he began to write. Although his initial efforts were met with rejection, he eventually found publication in small magazines and local newspapers. Governor Gore appointed Myers as the state's first poet laureate on June 9, 1927. He held this title until March 10, 1937, when Beckley sportswriter Roy Lee Harmon replaced him. Myers's poems were compiled in two collections, *The Quick Years* (1926) and *Cross and Crown* (1951).

Myers died December 4, 1951, after spending his final years in and out of nursing homes. He was buried in an unmarked grave in the Odd Fellows Cemetery in Elkins. Admirers later erected a monument at the site believed to be his grave.

James Slack
Charleston

Walter Dean Myers

Author Walter Dean Myers, regarded as one of the most influential African-American writers of juvenile fiction, was born Walter Milton Myers, August 12, 1937, in Martinsburg. At the death of his mother when he was three years old, Myers moved to New York City's Harlem district to be raised by foster parents Florence and Herbert Dean. He graduated from Empire State College in 1984.

Myers has published more than 65 books of fiction, nonfiction, and poetry dealing with the concerns of minority children. He has received numerous literary awards which include Newbery Honor Book, 1989, for *Scorpions. Harlem*, which was illustrated by his son, Christopher, received the Caldecott Honor Book, 1998, Coretta Scott King Award, 1998, and Boston Globe Horn Book Honor Book, 1997. He received the Coretta Scott King Award for his books in 1980, 1985, 1989, 1991, and 1997. In 2000, Myers received the first ever Printz Award for *Monster*. Myers now lives in New Jersey.

Sharon Diaz
Harrison County Schools

Rudine Sims Bishop, *Presenting Walter Dean Myers*, 1991; Thomas McMahon, ed. "Walter Dean Myers," *Authors & Artists for Young Adults*, 1998.

Mylan Pharmaceuticals

Mylan Pharmaceuticals, a division of Mylan Laboratories, is the nation's largest maker of generic drugs. The company has West Virginia roots and a major manufacturing facility in Morgantown.

In 1961, Milan Puskar started the company in a former skating rink in White Sulphur Springs. It began as a distribution company, but started making vitamins and antibiotics when it moved to Morgantown in 1965. Mylan began manufacturing its generic version of penicillin G in 1966, which launched its success. In

1970, the company incorporated in Pennsylvania as Mylan Laboratories. Puskar left the company in 1972, but returned four years later at the urging of its board. The company boomed in the 1980s, when Congress made it easier to receive Food and Drug Administration approval for generic drugs.

Mylan now makes generic versions of drugs to treat diseases such as arthritis, depression, diabetes, Parkinson's disease, and schizophrenia. In the United States, more than 200 million Mylan prescriptions were filled in 2003, which ranks the company third nationally. In 2001, the company settled a lawsuit with the Federal Trade Commission for $100 million without admitting any wrongdoing. The FTC said the company had cornered the market and raised prices up to 3,000 percent on two drugs.

Mylan Laboratories announced plans to acquire non-generic drug maker King Pharmaceuticals in 2004, in a $4 billion stock swap. Mylan headquarters are in Canonsburg, Pennsylvania, with manufacturing facilities in Morgantown and Puerto Rico. The Morgantown facility employed more than 1,500 people in 2003.

Scott Finn
Charleston Gazette

Myrtle Beach

Myrtle Beach, the booming South Carolina beach town favored by generations of West Virginia vacationers, remained a virtually untouched stretch of sand dunes and wax myrtle until the early 20th century.

First inhabited by Waccamaw and Winyah Indians, the area was explored in the 1520s by Spaniard Lucas Vasquez de Allyon. In the 18th century, the area was visited by such legendary buccaneers as Captain Kidd and Blackbeard, but it remained a little-visited backwater until the 20th century. A developer began selling oceanfront lots for $25 in about 1900, with buyers receiving an extra lot free if they spent more than $500 on their homes or vacation cottages.

Originally called New Town, Myrtle Beach was incorporated in 1938. As Myrtle Beach began to carve out a niche as a coastal vacation destination in the 1960s, West Virginians responded, drawn by the informal atmosphere, relatively low prices, and comparatively short driving distances—less than 500 miles from much of the Mountain State. By the 1970s, nearly any West Virginia discussion of the beach meant Myrtle Beach.

In 1985, a section of Myrtle Beach became the Mountain State's unofficial shoreline, during a ceremony in which flamboyant State Treasurer A. James Manchin came ashore in a boat, waving a West Virginia flag, to cheers from a crowd of vacationing West Virginians.

Manchin declared a 225-foot section of coastline in front of a condominium complex developed by a West Virginia company to be the state's "only access to the sea." He then stuck a flagstaff in the sand, declaring it to be West Virginia soil.

The development of such year-round attractions as more than 100 golf courses and 11 entertainment theaters featuring everything from country music to ice skating helped make tourism in Myrtle Beach a $2.6 billion a year business by the late 1990s. In 1998, Myrtle Beach was rated the nation's second-fastest growing city by American Demographics, and in 1999 American Automobile Association statistics showed it to be the country's second-most-visited summer destination. While only about 1,500 people lived year-round in Myrtle Beach proper in the late 1960s, more than 30,000 were living in the city by the late 1990s. The town's population routinely swells during peak holiday periods to more than 300,000, many of them West Virginians.

Rick Steelhammer
Charleston Gazette

The Mystery Hole

The Mystery Hole, an old-fashioned roadside attraction.

A Fayette County roadside attraction since 1972, the Mystery Hole was the brainchild of Donald Wilson, a Union Carbide retiree and navy veteran. The Mystery Hole has been an eye-catching sight on a bend in U.S. 60 near Hawks Nest, a Quonset hut with a statue of a gorilla on the roof and a Volkswagen Beetle that appeared to have crashed into its side.

Souvenirs, trinkets, and old posters awaited inside, but the main attraction was Wilson himself. He always provided a friendly greeting and offered a tour through the Hole, a mindbending walk beneath the building to a realm where the laws of gravity and Newtonian physics seemed to have found no foothold. The cost was $1 for those who had it and nothing for those who didn't.

Wilson was a deeply religious man who delighted in bringing laughter and amazement to his visitors. He was fond of quoting Proverbs 17:22: "A merry heart doeth good like a medicine," and gently interwove evangelical themes with his discourse about the mysteries of the Hole. Visitors frequently returned, often bringing new initiates. The Mystery Hole garnered a great deal of press and was the subject of a song by Ann Magnuson and a painting by artist David Riffle.

Donald Wilson died February 21, 1998, and the Mystery Hole closed. In 1999, Sandy and Will Morrison bought the roadside attraction and reopened it.

Rick Wilson
American Friends Service Committee

John Forbes Nash Jr.

Nobel Prize mathematician John Forbes Nash Jr. was born in Bluefield, June 13, 1928. Nash excelled in mathematics at Carnegie Tech (now Carnegie Mellon University) before entering the doctoral program at Princeton University in 1948. Inspired by professor John von Neumann, who contributed to the development of the computer and the hydrogen bomb, Nash focused on game theory, a theoretical approach to rivalries. His doctoral thesis greatly impacted economics in that it demonstrated how game theory could be applied to business competition. "It wasn't until Nash that game theory came alive for economists," Robert Solow, Nobel laureate in economics from MIT, said.

After a brief stint as a consultant with the Rand Corporation, Nash became a professor at the Massachusetts Institute of Technology. In 1959, Nash was hospitalized for schizophrenia, abruptly ending his teaching career. He isolated himself for more than 20 years, unable to teach or do mathematics, until the effects of the disease abated in the 1980s. Colleagues rallied to revive Nash's reputation and lobbied the Nobel Prize Committee to recognize him as one of the fathers of new mathematics. In 1994, Nash was honored with the Nobel Prize in Economics for his 1950 doctoral dissertation. In 1998, Nash was the subject of a best-selling biography, *A Beautiful Mind*, which was later made into a movie.

Stan Bumgardner
Division of Culture and History
Sylvia Nasar, *A Beautiful Mind*, 1998.

National Bank of Commerce

The National Bank of Commerce (now Huntington Banks) was founded in 1918 in Nitro, near Charleston, as the Citizens Bank of Nitro. In 1920, the bank moved to Charleston and was renamed the State Street Bank. Two years later, the name was changed to the Bank of Commerce, and in 1930 it became a national bank, the National Bank of Commerce. In 1964, the bank purchased the old Kanawha County library property and in 1968 built the 17-story building then known as Commerce Square. This now houses Huntington Banks at the corner of Lee and Dickinson streets.

John E. McDavid of the National Bank of Commerce was among the leaders of the Independent Bankers Association, which had been formed in the 1970s to oppose branch banking, mergers, and bank holding companies. This effort was unsuccessful, but nonetheless the National Bank of Commerce prospered un-

der the new banking rules. By 1990, West Virginia had 69 bank holding companies and 134 subsidiaries. The National Banc of Commerce Company was among the state's largest bank holding companies. In 1991, the bank changed its name to Commerce Bank. At that time, it operated 27 full-service offices in ten West Virginia counties, including offices in many Kroger grocery stores.

Commerce Bank became Huntington Banks when purchased by Huntington Bancshares in 1993. Huntington Banks also purchased CB&T Financial Corporation of Fairmont. Huntington Banks first entered West Virginia in 1989 when it acquired First National Bank of Morgantown. It later purchased Peoples Bank of Martinsburg. With the mergers complete, Huntington became the third-largest bank holding company in West Virginia, with 27 offices in 2004. Huntington Banks was not named for the city of Huntington and did not originate there. It opened in 1866 in Columbus, Ohio, as W. Huntington & Company. In 1905, it was incorporated as the Huntington National Bank of Columbus.

The National Bank of Commerce recently operating in West Virginia had no connection to the earlier bank of the same name. The National Commerce Bancorp of Memphis, entered West Virginia in 1999. At first known as First Market Bank, the West Virginia locations adopted the name National Bank of Commerce in 2000 and became SunTrust in 2004.

National Coal Heritage Area

In 1996, Congress designated an 11-county area in southern West Virginia as the National Coal Heritage Area. These counties are Boone, Cabell, Fayette, Logan, McDowell, Mercer, Mingo, Raleigh, Summers, Wayne, and Wyoming. The legislation authorized the National Park Service to enter into a cooperative agreement with the state of West Virginia to provide support for developing partnerships and conserving resources throughout the region. Congressman Nick J. Rahall, of West Virginia's Third District, led the effort to establish the heritage area.

The 1996 congressional vote implemented the Omnibus Parks and Public Lands Management Act. The act allowed the National Park Service to develop resource protection initiatives for areas of national importance through the use of partnerships and private ownership rather than the traditional methods of federally owned parklands.

For more than 80 years, southern West Virginia enjoyed economic growth and development based on coal mining. However, during the second half of the 20th century, coal industry employment declined and many southern counties suffered from unemployment and out-migration of people. The primary mission

of the heritage area is to preserve, protect, and interpret lands, structures, and communities associated with West Virginia's coal mining heritage and to stimulate tourism and economic development.

The National Coal Heritage Area operated initially as a loose partnership of tourism and history agencies of West Virginia state government with the National Park Service, under the direction of a steering committee. In 2002, the West Virginia legislature established an independent National Coal Heritage Area Authority to manage the heritage area.

See also Coal Industry

Mack H. Gillenwater
Marshall University

National Conservation Training Center

Completed in 1997, the National Conservation Training Center north of Shepherdstown in Jefferson County is part of the U.S. Fish and Wildlife Service. As the nation's only full-service training complex for fish and wildlife professionals, the center offers more than 250 courses on topics ranging from habitat conservation and wildlife refuge management, and laboratory and field sciences, to public outreach and environmental negotiation.

The campus, about 75 miles northwest of Washington, is set on 538 acres amid hardwood forests and meadows on the Potomac River. The center, which cost $143 million, includes two classroom buildings, a biology laboratory, a multimedia studio, a fitness center, dining hall, and three residential lodges. The buildings' pitched roofs and weathered look are designed to blend with local farm structures.

The 120-person staff is made up of federal employees from the Fish and Wildlife Service, National Park Service, Bureau of Land Management, and National Forest Service, as well as private contractors. The staff design and teach classes, schedule meetings at the center, and serve as liaisons between the center and the agencies they represent. Half the center's courses are taught on site. Others are offered at other places outside Shepherdstown and by satellite and computer.

The National Conservation Training Center is used primarily by the U.S. Fish and Wildlife Service's 8,000 employees. It also serves as a conference site where government wildlife specialists and land management employees, and representatives from environmental groups and private industry can discuss issues relating to commerce and conservation. In January 2000, the center was the site of peace talks between Israel and Syria.

National Forests

National forest lands compose almost seven percent of West Virginia's surface area, more than 1,613 square miles in 14

Early logging in Monongahela National Forest.

counties of the eastern and southeastern mountains. The Monongahela National Forest lies entirely within West Virginia, encompassing parts of 10 counties from Preston and Tucker southwestward to Nicholas, Greenbrier, and Pocahontas. The George Washington and Jefferson national forests, headquartered in Roanoke, Virginia, extend into four West Virginia counties along the state line.

These federally owned lands were established following passage of the 1911 Weeks Act. The act authorized the purchase of forestland for the long-term protection of watersheds of navigable streams, following the massive cutting of eastern forests in the late 1800s and early 1900s. The first land to be acquired for national forest (originally known as forest reserves) purposes in West Virginia was in 1915, when the 7,200-acre Arnold Tract in Tucker County was purchased by the federal government following authorization by the state legislature. This land became part of the Monongahela National Forest, which was created on April 28, 1920. The George Washington National Forest was established in 1917 as the Shenandoah National Forest and renamed in 1932, and the Jefferson National Forest was established in 1936. The passage of the Clarke-McNary law by Congress in 1924 authorized the purchase of forested, cut-over, or denuded lands for the production of timber in ad-

dition to the flow regulation of navigable streams. The authorization to purchase land for timber production made possible the acquisition of land that could not have been bought under the original 1911 Weeks Act.

Subsequent laws were passed enabling national forestland to be managed for all natural resources, including wildlife, recreation, and livestock forage, in addition to water and timber management provided by the early legislation. National forests are operated by the Forest Service, U.S. Department of Agriculture.

See also George Washington National Forest, Jefferson National Forest, Monongahela National Forest

Walter A. Lesser
Elkins

C. R. McKim, *50 Year History of the Monongahela National Forest,* 1970.

National Hillbilly News

The *National Hillbilly News* was an early country music fan magazine published in Huntington. Orville and Jenny Via operated the Poster Print Company, which often printed posters and handbills for the personal appearances of local WSAZ radio musicians. They founded the *National Hillbilly News* as an outgrowth of their business. The first issue of the bimonthly publication appeared in mid-1945, and it remained in business for about five years. Although the maga-

zine's coverage was national, it emphasized news concerning artists who played on West Virginia stations such as WWVA, WSAZ, WMMN, and WCHS. Columnists for the *News* included Norma Winton (Barthel) of Moffett, Oklahoma, who spent four decades as president of the Ernest Tubb Fan Club. In 1950, the *National Hillbilly News* switched to a smaller format, but apparently did not make it through the year. The surviving issues—along with other early journals of this type such as the short-lived *Musical Echoes* of Davis, Tucker County—today provide useful sources on the social significance of country music radio in the pre-television era.

Ivan M. Tribe
University of Rio Grande

Ivan M. Tribe, *Mountaineer Jamboree: Country Music in West Virginia,* 1984.

National Historic Landmarks

National Historic Landmarks, which are sites of national historic significance, are designated by the U.S. Secretary of the Interior. They represent a higher level of recognition than the National Register of Historic Places, whose sites may be merely of state or local significance. West Virginia has 16 National Historic Landmarks.

The National Historic Landmarks program was authorized in 1935, and most landmarks are identified through rigorous study by National Park Service personnel. The majority are buildings, but archeological sites, bridges, ships, astronomical installations, and even whole towns may be considered. Owners receive bronze plaques officially identifying their properties as National Historic Landmarks, and most display them proudly.

West Virginia's landmarks are wonderfully diverse. They include the Clover site, overlooking the Ohio River in Cabell County. There, archeologists have uncovered evidence of human occupation dating from 9,000 years ago and a well-preserved 16th-century townsite of the Fort Ancient culture. Moundsville's Grave Creek Mound, our other archeological National Historic Landmark, dating from about 250–150 B. C., is one of the largest mortuary mounds in the world.

Also included are the 1849 Wheeling Suspension Bridge, in its day the longest suspension span in the world and the first bridge across the Ohio River, and West Virginia Independence Hall, the birthplace of West Virginia, in downtown Wheeling. Bethany has two National Historic Landmarks. The Alexander Campbell Mansion illustrates the life of the founder of one of America's largest indigenous religious movements, the Disciples of Christ. Nearby Old Main is the prodigious architectural centerpiece of Bethany College, which Campbell founded. Morgantown also has a National Historic

Landmark associated with American education, the Alexander Wade House. As superintendent of Monongalia County schools during the 1870s, Wade inaugurated a system of graded classes that was later adopted nationwide.

In the northeastern corner of the state, Preston County's Elkins Coal & Coke Company Historic District at Bretz contains one of the nation's largest concentrations of beehive coke ovens. Far to the southwest, in Mingo County, the Matewan Historic District witnessed a nationally significant labor history event, the bloody 1920 Matewan Massacre.

The Greenbrier resort in White Sulphur Springs is also a National Historic Landmark. West Virginians can also be proud of Weston State Hospital, a gargantuan stone building designed to reflect the most advanced mid-19th century theories for treatment of the mentally ill. The Davis & Elkins Historic District in Elkins includes Halliehurst, home of Stephen B. Elkins, secretary of war under President Benjamin Harrison and U.S. senator from 1895 to 1911, and the adjacent Graceland, home of Henry Gassaway Davis, also a U.S. senator and father-in-law to Elkins. Traveller's Rest in Jefferson County was the home of Revolutionary War Gen. Horatio Gates.

Andrews Methodist Episcopal Church in Grafton was designated a National Historic Landmark because it was here that Anna Jarvis founded Mother's Day in 1908. Perhaps the most unusual National Historic Landmark in West Virginia is the Reber Radio Telescope at the National Radio Astronomy Observatory at Green Bank. The most recently designated National Historic Landmark in West Virginia is the Baltimore & Ohio Railroad Martinsburg Shops complex in Berkeley County.

National Historic Landmarks are afforded no special protection, a fact that one of West Virginia's former landmarks tragically illustrates. The boarding house prison where Mary Harris "Mother" Jones, the union organizer, was held in the Kanawha County town of Pratt was designated a National Historic Landmark in 1992 but demolished by its owners in 1996.

See also National Register of Historic Places

S. Allen Chambers
Society of Architectural Historians

National Mine Health and Safety Academy

The National Mine Health and Safety Academy opened August 17, 1976. The academy, located on an 80-acre campus at Beaver, near Beckley, is the world's largest educational institution devoted solely to safety and health in mining. The modern academy complex includes classrooms and laboratories accommodating 600 students, dormitory space for 320 people, as well as a cafeteria, library, auditorium, and recreation facilities. It is the central training facility for federal mine inspectors and mine safety professionals from various government agencies, the mining industry, labor organizations, and the international mining community. Its mission is to reduce accidents and to improve the health and safety of miners through education and training. The academy serves not only coal mines but also mines producing sand and gravel, gold, silver, copper, uranium, and other minerals.

Academy personnel, working with other mining professionals, design and develop instructional programs and training materials. These programs and materials cover topics such as mine safety and inspection procedures, accident prevention and investigation, industrial hygiene, emergency procedures, mining technology, and nontechnical subjects. The academy is operated by the Mine Safety and Health Administration of the U.S. Department of Labor. About 28,000 students attend annually, an average of 200 to 300 daily. The training courses usually last three days, but some are as long as eight days. Recently the academy library consolidated Department of Labor mine library collections from throughout the country at the Beckley facility.

The academy's services are not limited to the United States. In response to growing international concern about mine health and safety, the academy has expanded its efforts to improve the health and safety of miners worldwide. Cooperative programs give representatives and inspectors from other nations' mining industries the opportunity to participate in academy health and safety classes, training programs, and activities. International visitors to the National Mine Health and Safety Academy have included delegations from Russia, Ukraine, Poland, China, Thailand, South Africa, and other countries.

Melody Bragg
National Mine Health and Safety Academy

National Park Service in West Virginia

The National Park Service was created in 1916 as an agency of the Department of the Interior and charged by Congress to manage the nation's parks. It became the primary federal agency preserving and providing for the protection, interpretation, and public enjoyment of America's most significant natural and cultural properties. The nomenclature of the NPS includes 20 titles besides national park, including such designations as national seashore and national river.

West Virginia has five National Park Service areas. The first, Harpers Ferry National Historical Park, was authorized as a national monument on June 30, 1944, commemorating Harpers Ferry's importance in the Civil War and as the site of John Brown's 1859 raid, as well as its history as an early 19th-century industrial center. The Appalachian Trail, a National Scenic Trail, travels several miles through Monroe County and also dips into West Virginia at Harpers Ferry, where it crosses the Potomac River, as the trail winds through 14 states from Georgia to Maine. It was established in 1937 and entered the park system on October 2, 1968.

Bluestone National Scenic River in the southwestern part of the state preserves 11 miles of the lower Bluestone River. It was authorized on October 26, 1988. Gauley River National Recreation Area, authorized the same date as the Bluestone, includes 25 miles of the Gauley River and six miles of the Meadow River. The Gauley River contains several Class V rapids, making it one of the most adventurous whitewater boating rivers in the east. The New River Gorge National River was created by the National Parks and Recreation Act of 1978 (November 10). It is a rugged whitewater river flowing northward through deep canyons. The 53-mile section from Hinton to Fayetteville is abundant in natural, scenic, historic, and recreational features.

In addition to parks, the NPS manages the Stephen T. Mather Training Center at Harpers Ferry, on the site of the historic black Storer College. Interpretive park rangers from across the nation train at this center. Also at Harpers Ferry, the Harpers Ferry Center conserves curatorial artifacts and develops for parks nationwide planning documents, museum exhibits, outdoor wayside exhibits, publications, and films. West Virginia is part of the Northeast Region of the National Park Service, with Park Service units in West Virginia reporting to the regional director in Philadelphia.

W. Eugene Cox
National Park Service

U.S. Department of the Interior, *The National Parks: Index 1995*, 1995; U.S. Department of the Interior, *The National Parks: Shaping the System*, 1991.

National Radio Astronomy Observatory

The National Radio Astronomy Observatory, funded by the National Science Foundation and operated by Associated Universities, Inc., is located near Green Bank, Pocahontas County. Radio astronomy differs from visual astronomy in that the dish-shaped telescopes gather radio waves rather than light waves. The Green Bank site was chosen in 1955 for its surrounding mountains, which shield it from radio interference, and its low population and lack of industrial development. Construction began in 1958, and the first radio telescopes were in operation by fall 1959. Today the NRAO provides free access to its research equipment to scientists from all over the world.

Green Bank's 140-foot telescope, the world's largest equatorially mounted radio telescope, operates at short wavelengths. The Interferometer, a series of 85-foot telescopes, operated at Green Bank for the U.S. Naval Observatory from 1964 until 1996. A 300-foot meridian transit telescope began observations in October 1961 and operated until it collapsed in 1988. Its replacement, the Robert C. Byrd Green Bank Telescope, the world's largest fully steerable radio telescope, was dedicated on August 25, 2000. The 16-million-pound telescope's surface dimensions are 100 meters by 110 meters. It can be pointed with an accuracy of one arcsecond, equivalent to the width of a human hair seen from six feet away. The 2,004 panels that make up the telescope's surface are mounted at their corners on actuators, little motor-driven pistons, which make it easier to adjust the shape of the surface.

The NASA Search for Extraterrestrial Intelligence began at the NRAO in April 1960, when astronomer Frank Drake began Project Ozma, using the 85-foot Tatel telescope that is sensitive enough to detect routine radio signals such as we produce on Earth. The SETI project continued until it lost congressional support in 1993. In 1995, the search was revived in Project Phoenix, privately supported and based in Australia but also using the 140-foot telescope in Green Bank from September 1996 until April 1998, for the focus on northern stars with planets.

The Reber Radio Telescope was designated a National Historic Landmark in 1989. The Reber telescope is the original parabolic 31.4-foot antenna built by Grote Reber in 1937 and moved to Green Bank in 1959–60. It is on display there with a replica of the original Jansky antenna built by Karl G. Jansky, the originator of radio astronomy, and the Ewen-Purcell Horn Antenna.

Louise Burner Flegel
Pine Knoll Shore, North Carolina

National Recovery Administration

The National Recovery Administration (NRA), an important New Deal agency, was created with the passing of the National Industrial Recovery Act (NIRA) in 1933. The NRA was established by President Franklin Roosevelt to prepare and enforce codes of fair competition within key industries and ease antitrust restrictions on Depression-wracked businesses. In return, business accepted the famous Section 7a of the NIRA which gave employees the right to organize and bargain collectively. The effects on West Virginia's coal industry were profound, as

The Robert C. Byrd radio telescope.

the coalfields quickly went from non-union to union.

Gen. Hugh S. Johnson was the first head of the NRA and the creator of its symbol—a bold, blue eagle bearing the legend "We Do Our Part." Johnson saw the eagle as a powerful rallying point, and it quickly took hold in West Virginia and across the country. The Blue Eagles sports teams of New Martinsville's Magnolia High School were named for the famous symbol, and retain the name today.

In 1935, the Supreme Court ruled that the National Industrial Recovery Act was unconstitutional. The NRA fell with its parent act, though Section 7a survives today as part of the National Labor Relations Act.

See also Great Depression

Deborah J. Sonis
West Virginia Humanities Council

National Register of Historic Places

The National Register of Historic Places officially recognizes historic buildings, sites, structures, objects, and districts throughout America. The prestigious list was created under the National Historic Preservation Act of 1966 and is administered by the National Park Service for the U.S. Secretary of the Interior. In West Virginia the Archives and History Commission acts as the state review board for nominations to the National Register. The program is coordinated by the Historic Preservation Office, a part of the West Virginia Division of Culture and History.

The National Register of Historic Places is an active, popular program, and the

number of listed places increases from year to year. As of September 2004, there were 910 listings in West Virginia. Many of these listings included several structures or other contributing resources, and some were large historic districts. The total number of contributing resources was 17,248.

National Register properties are scattered throughout the state, although most numerous in the historic Eastern Panhandle and in Charleston, Wheeling, and other major cities. The listings include the Matewan Historic District in Mingo County (also a National Historic Landmark); the state capitol complex; the Pence Springs Resort in Summers County; West Virginia Independence Hall, our state's birthplace in Wheeling; Halltown Union Colored Sunday School in Jefferson County; and numerous other sites and structures.

Properties are approved for the National Register of Historic Places according to their significance in American history, architecture, archeology, engineering, or culture. The significance may derive from events or people associated with a property, its architecture, or the fact that it has provided or may provide important information in history or prehistory. Ordinarily, cemeteries, church structures, birthplaces or graves of historic figures, sites that are primarily commemorative in nature, or buildings that have been moved or reconstructed are not eligible for the National Register. There are exceptions in all of these categories, however. For example, a church might be listed for its architectural significance even though it remained a place of worship; Charleston's St. John's Episcopal Church falls into this category. Ordinarily, a property must be at least 50 years old to be considered for the National Register.

Properties may be nominated for their local, state, or national significance. Sites deemed to be of exceptional national significance may also be named National Historic Landmarks, a higher and much less common level of recognition. There are 16 National Historic Landmarks in West Virginia.

Most properties listed on the National Register of Historic Places are privately owned. Listing on the National Register conveys important benefits beyond official recognition. These benefits include eligibility for certain grants and tax credits. National Register status does not protect properties against alteration or even demolition, although local historic landmarks commissions or review boards may offer limited protection. A property may be removed from the National Register of Historic Places if it loses its historic integrity.

See also National Historic Landmarks
S. Allen Chambers, *Buildings of West Virginia*, 2004; West Virginia Division of Culture and History, *Historic West Virginia: The National Register of Historic Places*, 2000.

National Road

A lack of dependable all-weather transportation routes over the Appalachian Mountains was among the factors that kept colonists within 150 miles of the coastline throughout the colonial period in America. Despite a lack of reliable interior roads, settlers began to stream over the mountains in increasing numbers after the Revolution. With no state or private enterprise possessing the resources to develop the infrastructure to bind the nation, in 1802 the federal government proposed an all-weather road to connect eastern markets with the westward-flowing waters of the Ohio River. Congress authorized construction of the National Road from Cumberland, Maryland, to Wheeling in 1806.

President Jefferson appointed three commissioners who employed a six-member surveying team to locate a route for America's first interstate highway. Civilian contractors bid on the right to build it for the U.S. Treasury Department under the direction of its secretary, Albert Gallatin, and construction superintendent David Shriver. Road crews consisting primarily of Irish and English immigrants started in Maryland in 1811 and continued working westward through Pennsylvania and West Virginia in subsequent years. Mail service on the unfinished road began to Wheeling in 1818; workers completed construction on the original 131-mile route in 1821 at a cost of $1.7 million.

Officially designated as the Cumberland Road, the highway crossed the rugged mountains of western Maryland before leveling out and taking a general northwesterly course through the Pennsylvania countryside to Ohio County, (West) Virginia. Following the valley of Wheeling Creek, it passed Roney's Point, Triadelphia, and Elm Grove to its western terminus on the Ohio River. Wheeling's strategic position at the confluence of river and road led to its rapid growth as a major inland port for goods and passengers moving between the east and west. A river ferry connected Wheeling with Zane's Trace, an important post road across southern Ohio to Limestone (now Maysville), Kentucky. Part of the trace later became incorporated into the western extension of the National Road laid out and built in the 1820s–30s through Ohio and Indiana to Vandalia, Illinois.

Heavy freight wagons and livestock clogged the highway and rapidly destroyed the roadbed east of Wheeling. Project management passed to the U.S. Army Corps of Engineers in 1825 as federal interest in the highway lagged in light of decreasing appropriations and increasing competition from railroads and canals. As a result, the federal government agreed to overhaul the roadbed, construct a series of tollhouses, and give the road to the states for operation as a turnpike. In total, the government spent $6.8 million to build and repair the road from Cumberland to Vandalia. After the B&O Railroad reached Wheeling in the 1850s, the National Road entered a period of decline that lasted until the automobile era when it was incorporated into U.S. 40, a major transcontinental route from Atlantic City to San Francisco. Although modern Interstate 68 has superseded it, the National Road survives as a scenic byway that offers a slower-paced alternative for travelers who wish to experience the 200-year history of America's first federal highway.

Billy Joe Peyton
West Virginia State University
Karl Raitz, ed., *The National Road*, 1996; Thomas B. Searight, *The Old Pike: A History of the National Road*, 1894.

National Youth Science Camp

The National Youth Science Camp was founded in 1963, as part of the West Virginia Centennial celebration. Each year since then, two students from each state and the District of Columbia have been selected to attend this four-week camp in Pocahontas County in the summer following their graduation from high school. Students are chosen through a competitive process. The criteria for selection include academic achievement and an interest in science.

The goals of the sponsoring National Youth Science Foundation include promoting science leadership and encouraging excellence in science. The camp includes lectures from prominent scientists, hands-on science activities, and outdoor recreation. The National Youth Science Camp is located near Bartow, within the boundaries of the Monongahela National Forest. The camp's location allows for trips to the National Radio Astronomy Observatory in Green Bank, and to Spruce Knob, Seneca Rocks, Dolly Sods, and other natural areas. Campers also travel to Washington, where among many other activities they attend a luncheon where they meet with senators from their home states and hear from prominent political speakers.

The National Youth Science Camp is funded by the state of West Virginia and through corporate and private donations. An endowment is being established to support the camp in the future. To ensure that financial considerations do not keep deserving students from attending, all delegates attend the camp free of charge.

Amy Donaldson Arnold
Ivydale

Natural Gas and Petroleum

Among West Virginia's resources are abundant natural gas and petroleum, with gas being more common than petroleum. They were formed in a geologic process as organic-rich sedimentary rock was subjected to heat and pressure, transforming the organic material into natural gas and petroleum. Gas and petroleum migrate out of the source bed and move upward through the overlying rock until they reach the surface or accumulate in a reservoir under the ground. Reservoirs consist of permeable rock topped by an impermeable seal. If migrating natural gas or petroleum encounters a seal, it will fill the underlying reservoir, resulting in an accumulation.

In West Virginia, the most common source beds are the organic-rich Devonian Shales. They are located throughout the subsurface of the western part of the state, and they outcrop in parts of the Eastern Panhandle. Natural gas is much more commonly encountered than oil, and is found throughout the state west of the Allegheny Front. The most common reservoirs are the thin sandstones of the Upper Devonian and Lower Mississippian geologic periods. Other reservoirs include the Lower Devonian Oriskany Sandstone and the Mississippian Greenbrier Limestone. Oil is restricted to reservoirs located primarily in northern and central West Virginia.

First found in the Kanawha and the Little Kanawha river valleys in the 18th century, West Virginia's oil and gas have long been important economic resources.

Derricks invaded Sistersville during the oil boom.

Early in the 19th century, the Ruffner family found both oil and gas while drilling for salt brine near present Malden along the Kanawha River, and the Lemon and Creel families found oil and gas along the Hughes River, a tributary of the Little Kanawha. The extraction of oil was facilitated by tools first used by the Ruffners in salt-well drilling.

Oil was produced successfully near present Freeport, along the Hughes River in Wirt County by George Lemon, as early as 1819. Within a generation, builders of the Northwestern Virginia Railroad had discovered large quantities of natural lubricating oil along Oil Spring Run, and in 1857 they built a station where Oil Spring Run flows into Goose Creek, a Hughes tributary. They named the place Petroleum.

Two years later, Dr. R. W. Hazlett of Wheeling and his partners in the Virginia Petroleum Company successfully drilled along Oil Spring Run. Soon others commenced drilling operations in the Little Kanawha basin. Among them were Charles H. Shattuck, Gen. Samuel D. Karnes, and John C. "Cass" Rathbone. Karnes hit oil while drilling for it in an abandoned salt well owned by Rathbone's father, William P. Rathbone of Burning Springs. Cass Rathbone, understanding the significance of that discovery, drilled a 200-barrel well at 139 feet. With the Drake well in Pennsylvania, these were among the very first oil wells in the United States.

By the outbreak of the Civil War, fortunes were being made in the West Virginia oil fields. The boom persisted despite the fiery Confederate raid on Burning Springs in May 1863. The first of at least six refineries was built in Parkersburg in 1861, and by 1872 more were under construction. Some of the beneficiaries of the rush to Burning Springs (Peter Godwin Van Winkle, Arthur Ingraham Boreman, Jacob Beeson Blair, John Jay Jackson Jr., and the Rathbones) were among those working toward the creation of West Virginia on June 20, 1863.

After the Civil War, another person who profited from the rush to Burning Springs, Johnson Newlon Camden, helped develop another major oil field in the Little Kanawha basin. Named Volcano, it was situated near the headwaters of Oil Spring Run along the Wood-Ritchie county line. Camden, later a U.S. senator, joined John D. Rockefeller's Standard Oil Trust in 1875 and began actions that eventually led to the closure of all the Parkersburg refineries except the one founded by Camden in 1868.

In 1890, Michael L. Benedum, who would become the most famous "wildcat" or independent driller in the state's history, entered the industry as an employee of Standard Oil. In 1893, Sistersville became the nation's premier oil field boomtown. In 1898, West Virginia's oil production passed that of Pennsylvania. In 1906, the state's natural gas production exceeded that of any other state, a position it held for 18 years.

Success after 1889 was due in large part to the application of the anticlinal theory of oil and gas location, developed by geologist Israel C. White of West Virginia University. White's theory was first tested at Mannington in 1889, and when applied along Sand Fork of the Little Kanawha at the Copely well in 1900, it sparked the Lewis County boom. Thereafter the industry began to shift from western West Virginia toward the north-central area. The companies benefiting most from the shift were the South Penn Oil Company (now Pennzoil) and the Hope Natural Gas Company (now Dominion Hope), both controlled by Rockefeller's Standard Oil.

Nearly a century later, oil and gas are still major industries in the Mountain State. They were responsible in 1999 for the employment of more than 15,000 people and help to keep the state among the nation's major suppliers, storers, and transmitters of energy. Although Pennzoil, which was founded in 1889, significantly curtailed its West Virginia operations within a few years of celebrating its centennial, Hope continues to operate from its base in Clarksburg, as does another Dominion Resources company, Consolidated Natural Gas Transmission, an interstate pipeline and storage company.

Although Standard Oil closed its Parkersburg refinery in 1936, a major refinery built in 1913 at St. Marys by a Standard competitor was operated by Quaker State until the 1980s. The carbon black industry, which produces carbon by the incomplete combustion of natural gas, was pioneered in Calhoun and Wirt counties near the end of the 19th century by Godfrey Cabot and continues to have a significant presence in the state. Development of the oil and gas industry received a boost in 1911 when the Blue Creek field was discovered along a tributary of the Elk River. The Charleston-based United Fuel Gas Company, later Columbia Gas then Columbia Gas Transmission and the independent Columbia Natural Resources and its successor companies; the Elk Refining Company; Hope; and Pennzoil would become major developers of the field. Three years later, Pure Oil Company, founded by the Dawes family of Marietta, Ohio, would commence development of a major oil field in another part of the Kanawha Valley near Cabin Creek before being absorbed by a competitor.

As of 2002, West Virginia produced about 180 billion cubic feet of natural gas every year. Production occurs in just about every county west of the Allegheny Front. This volume has been maintained consistently through the last 20 years. Oil production declined steadily through the latter part of the 20th century and is generally between 1.5 million and 2 million barrels per year.

Active oil fields, where drilling is still being done, are limited to parts of Wetzel, Tyler, Ritchie, and Pleasants counties. Gas wells are being drilled in many parts of West Virginia. The oil and gas industry drills about 800 to 1,000 wells per year. Most of these are to shallow (less than 5,000 feet deep) targets in the Upper Devonian and Mississippian sections. Exploration for deeper targets (including the Oriskany) generally requires greater expense and higher technology. Most recently, new exploration in the central part of the state has brought in new gas production in the Ordovician section at depths exceeding 10,000 feet.

See also Appalachian Basin, Michael L. Benedum, Burning Springs Oil Field, Johnson Newlon Camden, Geology, Rathbone Wells, I. C. White

Bernard L. Allen
Conway, South Carolina
David Matchen
Geological & Economic Survey

David L. McKain and Bernard L. Allen, *Where It All Began: The Story of the People and Places Where The Oil and Gas Industry Began—West Virginia and Southeastern Ohio, Part One*, 1994; Eugene D. Thoenen, *History of the Oil and Gas Industry in West Virginia*, 1964.

Natural History

Natural history is the study of organisms and natural objects, and their origins and interactions with one another. The natural history of West Virginia is most influenced by the Appalachian Mountains, which are the oldest continuously vegetated land mass on Earth. The numerous geologic formations and varied topography also contribute to the state's diverse natural history. West Virginia's topographic regions include the Ridge and Valley section in the east, whose western boundary is the spectacular Allegheny Front, a mountain range running in a southwestward diagonal across Mineral, Grant, and Pendleton counties. West of the Alleghenies is the Appalachian Plateau, which includes two-thirds of the state. Elevations in the state vary from less than 300 feet to nearly 5,000, providing a multitude of ecological niches.

The high Alleghenies force prevailing east-moving cloud masses to deposit heavier rainfall westward and create a desert-like "rain shadow" east of the mountains in the drier Ridge and Valley. The effect is dramatic: The annual rainfall in Canaan Valley averages about 60 inches. In Petersburg, which is about 20 miles east, the rainfall drops to 30 inches annually. Likewise, the growing season varies widely, ranging from 193 days in Logan to 92 in Canaan Valley. The extreme differences have created a magnificent mosaic of habitats for plants and animals.

There are nearly 2,600 species of vascular plants in West Virginia. A third of these are non-native exotics, which have been introduced from elsewhere. The larger families are grasses, sedges, mint, rose, and composite. Forty-four species of orchids and nearly 1,000 species of mosses, bryophytes, and lichens grow in West Virginia. About 320 species of birds and 179 species of fish are the largest vertebrate groups. Eighty-seven amphibian and reptile species and 66 mammal species occur in West Virginia. Invertebrate species of insects, mites, and worms are numerous, but their number can only be estimated.

Plant communities and species are often adapted to very specific soils and climates. Barren rocks, thin soils, and bogs are often habitats for mosses, lichens, and fungi. There seem to be plants adapted to every niche in the landscape. Some ferns, grasses, and herbs thrive in dense shade, while others display vigor in full sunlight.

The wide diversity of plant life produces abundant food for wildlife all year long, and West Virginia wildlife include animals that are as specialized as plants. There are crossbills and red squirrels that eat pine cone seeds. Herons and ducks must have an aquatic environment, while mollusks strain their food from flowing waters of larger streams and rivers. Insects are the most numerous group, and many rely on only one or a few plant species for food. The monarch butterfly must have milkweeds, and the eastern tent caterpillar depends on cherry and apple trees. Black bear, opossum, and deer are generalists, eating a wide variety of foods that permit them to have wider territorial ranges and more easily survive food shortages.

People and natural causes have greatly influenced the diversity of life in the Mountain State. Indians used fire as a hunting tool and to maintain openings in the forest for villages, grazing animals, and food plots. Early European trappers rapidly eliminated most furbearers and larger food animals such as beaver, river otter, wolves, woods bison and elk, as well as the passenger pigeon. George Washington's journal and hunter Meshach Browning's book are among the sources that inform us on the flora and fauna of the late 1700s and early 1800s.

Pioneer farmers cleared the vast majority of rich, level valleys of the major streams and rivers by the 1870s and greatly reduced the plants and animals of valley habitats. During the mid-19th century, Philip Pendleton Kennedy fished and hunted the Blackwater River. His book, *The Blackwater Chronicle*, provides early glimpses into the Alleghenies' natural history.

Timber exploitation during the latter decades of the 19th century was followed by disastrous wildfires that turned forests into blackened, worthless landscapes. The Brooks family of naturalists described the negative impacts on animals and forests. Books by Maurice Brooks (*The Appalachians*) and A. B. Brooks (*Forestry and Wood Industries*) provide excellent descriptions of the timbering operations. Author G. D. McNeill of Pocahontas County gives a moving description of the loss of wilderness along the Cranberry and Williams rivers in his 1940 book, *The Last Forest*. Entomologist A. D. Hopkins described large areas of red spruce killed by bark beetles in the 1890s.

Coal mining and oil and gas development caused major pollution of water resources due to acid drainage and salt brine spills that killed fish and aquatic plants. The locks and dams on West Virginia waterways are invaluable for commerce and flood control but have devastated native fishes, freshwater mussels, and other aquatic species as free-flowing rivers became stagnant pools.

Contemporary threats to nature come from acid rain from burning fossil fuels, strip mining and mountaintop removal of coal, vacation homes on riverbanks and mountaintops, and fragmentation of habitat by urban sprawl and road building. The biggest threats to our unique natural forests, bogs, and shale barrens are exotic invasive plants and high deer populations. The conversion of wetlands, riverbanks, and other important wildlife habitats remains the major threat to animal life.

West Virginia's natural balance is being severely challenged by exotic plants and animals such as kudzu, multiflora rose, "Kentucky 31" fescue grass, starlings, house finches, wild boar, and rainbow trout, which have frequently flourished at the expense of native species. Chestnut blight became established in the 1920s and virtually eliminated this common and valuable forest tree. Beech bark disease, anthracnose of butternut and dogwood, woolly adelgids of hemlock and balsam fir, and gypsy moth are introduced diseases and insects wreaking havoc on our forest.

West Virginia's natural history is tied to its many headwater streams and rivers and the prized hardwood forests of oaks, maples, ash, hickories, and other trees. Virgin spruce once covered a half-million acres, and the remaining 50,000 acres of spruce still harbor many rare plants and animals, including the northern flying squirrel and Cheat Mountain salamander. Caves are treasures for unusual animals and insects.

West Virginia is blessed with a wide variety of common and rare flora and fauna, but this natural history has been and continues to be negatively impacted by human activities.

See also Environment, Fauna, Flora

William N. Grafton
WVU Extension Service

Natural Resources

West Virginia's natural resources may be broken down into several groups, including geological formations such as coal, oil, natural gas, and other such resources; the state's soils; its plants and animals; and its water. These resources were exploited only lightly by the Indians who preceded white settlers in the region. The natives hunted, fished, and collected roots, fruits, and other wild foods. Their most destructive practice was to set forest fires to maintain grassy openings to provide places for living and fields for growing maize and pumpkins. Indians also used fire in the hunting of buffalo, elk, and deer, which were killed for meat and skins.

It was said that prior to the arrival of Europeans a squirrel could have crossed the present state through the treetops and never touched the ground. The magnificent virgin forests were broken only by the Indian clearings and other openings made by natural fires, a few "bald" mountaintops, and bogs. White hunters and trappers of the late 1700s and early 1800s quickly depleted the buffalo, elk, wolf, mountain lion, and furbearers (beaver, river otter, and fisher). Indians also trapped extensively for furs as trade with Europeans increased. Next came the settlers, who built cabins and cleared the rich valleys for farms, then the loggers.

The forests of the Eastern Panhandle and the Ohio Valley were cut with ax and crosscut saw during the mid-1800s, and the high mountains of the interior of the state followed a few decades later. Simultaneously, industrialists began to mine coal and drill for oil and gas. Significant oil production began after the Civil War and peaked at about 16 million barrels in 1901. Serious natural gas production began in 1906 and remained strong through the 20th century. The oil and gas industry employed 15,000 West Virginians at the turn of the 21st century.

Salt, which was made within the boundaries of the present state by both the Indians and early settlers, was among the first minerals commercialized in Western Virginia. Salt was being produced from springs and wells in the upper Kanawha Valley by the early 19th century. This salt brine later became the basis for many of West Virginia's chemical plants. Early drilling for salt brine frequently produced oil that flowed away to pollute rivers, or natural gas that was burned off as a waste product. The development of new markets and new technologies soon made these resources valuable, as well. Wirt County's 1860 Rathbone well was second only to the Drake well of Pennsylvania among the nation's earliest oil wells. Western West Virginia is still dotted with hundreds of gas wells and associated iron and plastic distribution pipes.

Iron ore was discovered and made into pig iron at numerous furnaces in both panhandles and in present north-central West Virginia from the late 1700s until the mid-1800s. These furnaces used charcoal and limestone, as well as iron ore. Coke, which is made from coal, later replaced charcoal in the making of iron and steel. In the late 1800s, businessmen envisioned a major industrial center in the New River Valley using locally abundant coal and timber, limestone from the Greenbrier Valley, and iron ore from neighboring Virginia. The ruins of the iron furnace at Quinnimont, Fayette County, bear witness to this vision for

New River, while the mines at nearby Kaymoor once shipped coal and coke to iron furnaces at Low Moor, Virginia. Huge quantities of timber and coal were shipped from New River from the 1870s onward. The forests and the coal resources of southern West Virginia were being exploited by the late 1800s and early 1900s, when railroads fought for rights of way along the Coal, Guyandotte, Tug, and Big Sandy rivers.

Coal has remained king since the late 1870s. Generally, the coals from West Virginia's southern coalfields are low in sulfur and pollute less and are now in great demand because of air quality standards. Automated longwall mining machines and other modern equipment allow efficient recovery of coal underground. Modern explosives and huge machinery permit large surface mines, including mountaintop removal mines.

Cold, high-quality water from some deep mines in the southern coalfields is used to raise trout in aquaculture operations. Other old mines contribute only acid mine drainage, which promises to be a problem for a long time to come.

Sand and gravel are extracted from the islands and riverbed of the Ohio River, but in much less quantities than earlier. Limestone and sandstone quarries still mine large quantities of stone for road construction and for cement, glass, and other uses.

Geological formations are the basis of our soils and dictate the topography of our state. Massive layers of hard sandstones cap many ridges and break down to form a landscape of deep narrow valleys with steep slopes. Limestone soils are more common in the Greenbrier Valley, Monroe County, and the Eastern Panhandle, where they produce the lush grass supporting a long-standing livestock industry. Soils of the mid- and upper Ohio River Valley are derived from calcareous shales and clays.

West Virginia's water resources include the headwaters of the Potomac and Ohio rivers. Most of our streams and rivers are high-quality waterways that are fishable, swimmable, and drinkable. With water shortages in much of the nation, the protection of West Virginia's abundant water resources had become an item of public discussion by the turn of the 21st century. Pollution is evident from coal mining, highways, poultry and other agricultural operations, timbering, manufacturing, and home sewage. Twentieth-century changes brought hundreds of farm ponds, dozens of small flood-control and water-supply reservoirs, and more than a dozen large lakes, all affecting West Virginia's water resources. The Ohio, Kanawha, and Monongahela rivers were transformed from free-flowing streams to a series of locks

and dams creating one pool after another for the entire length of these streams.

Springs are a major water resource in West Virginia. Many of these, such as Berkeley Springs, White Sulphur Springs, Webster Springs, and Dunmore Springs, were once developed into resorts with bathing facilities to improve health. Today, our springs provide high-quality bottled water and aquaculture sites.

The best oil, gas, and coal have already been used. Greater effort and expense will be needed to retrieve the remaining reserves. However, renewable resources, such as soils, water, plants, and animals need wise use and stewardship to continue providing a high quality of life for West Virginians.

William N. Grafton
WVU Extension Service

Division of Natural Resources

The West Virginia Division of Natural Resources traces its origin to 1897 legislation calling for the appointment of a game and fish warden and prescribing his duties. Governor MacCorkle appointed Capt. E. F. Smith of Hinton as the first state game and fish warden.

The 1909 legislature changed the title to chief forest, game, and fish warden, while increasing the responsibilities of the position. In 1921, realizing the need for an expanded conservation program, the legislature created the Game and Fish Commission. The three commissioners were appointed by the governor, with G. O. Young of Buckhannon as the first chairman. The commissioners were given the authority to appoint the chief game protector and district deputies. A. B. Brooks was appointed as first chief game protector. However, the responsibilities of the forestry division were taken away from the Game and Fish Commission. In 1929, the legislature added forestry back to the agency, creating the West Virginia Game, Fish, and Forestry Commission.

Four years later in 1933, when Congress established the Civilian Conservation Corps, Governor Kump requested and the legislature passed legislation establishing the Conservation Commission of West Virginia. The governor was given the authority to appoint a director and six advisory commissioners. H. W. Shawhan was appointed as the first director of conservation.

In 1959, Warden M. Lane, director of conservation, outlined a proposal for reorganization of the Conservation Commission to correct an overlapping of duties. Two years later at the urging of Lane and with the blessing of Governor Barron, the state legislature established the Department of Natural Resources, with Lane as director, effective July 1, 1961. The Department of Natural Resources would consist of five divisions, including

Parks, Forestry, Game and Fish, Land Reclamation, and Water.

In 1985, the legislature transferred the Division of Forestry from the Department of Natural Resources to the Department of Agriculture. The Division of Parks was transferred from Natural Resources to a newly created Department of Commerce, which later became the Department of Commerce, Labor, and Environmental Resources. The state parks unit later became the Division of Tourism and Parks. Forestry later became a free-standing division under Commerce. On January 1, 1990, the Department of Natural Resources name was changed to the Division of Natural Resources under the Department of Commerce, Labor, and Environmental Resources. In 1995, Parks was returned to Natural Resources from the Division of Tourism. In 1999, further changes were made, with the Division of Natural Resources to be administered under the Bureau of Commerce.

The purposes of the Division of Natural Resources are to conserve and manage wildlife for intrinsic, recreational, and economic benefits; to promote conservation by preserving natural areas of exceptional scenic, scientific, cultural, archeological, or historic significance; to provide outdoor recreation; and to promote travel and tourism. The agency regulates hunting and fishing; manages wildlife diversity preservation and study; enforces wildlife and boating laws; operates state parks; oversees wildlife management and recreation areas; and holds title to public lands in the state and to the beds of rivers, creeks, and streams.

In 2005, Frank Jezioro was the director of the Division of Natural Resources. There are approximately 825 permanent employees, serving in the environmental resources, law enforcement, parks and recreation, public information, real estate management, and wildlife resources sections, plus executive administrative staff.

Jack I. Cromer
Beverly

Nature Conservancy

The Nature Conservancy is a private, non-profit conservation organization. Its mission is to preserve plants, animals, and natural communities by protecting the lands and waters they need to survive. The Conservancy relies upon scientific information to determine what rare plant and animal populations and ecosystems are the highest conservation priorities, how to conserve lands supporting these features, and how to restore natural areas that have been damaged by human activity. It often protects natural areas by buying land. It also achieves its mission by cooperatively working with private landowners, corporations, and government agencies.

Founded in 1951 by a group of scientists concerned about the loss of natural areas, the Conservancy currently has chapters in every state. The West Virginia Chapter was founded in 1963 by volunteers, many of whom were associated with West Virginia University. By 1999, the Nature Conservancy had grown to more than one million members, including more than 4,000 in West Virginia and had protected more than 11 million acres in the United States and Canada, including more than 40,000 acres in West Virginia. It has worked with partner organizations in Latin America, the Caribbean, the Pacific, and Asia to preserve 55 million acres internationally.

Nationwide, the Nature Conservancy owns 1,600 preserves, the largest private system of nature sanctuaries in the world. The Conservancy manages 20 West Virginia preserves, ranging in size from 1.5 acres to more than 2,000 acres. These include Cranesville Swamp, Greenland Gap, Ice Mountain, Brush Creek, Slaty Mountain, Panther Knob, and Pike Knob. The Conservancy has also helped government agencies acquire many natural areas, including Canaan Valley National Wildlife Refuge, Cathedral State Park, Dolly Sods Wilderness Area, the New River Gorge National River, the Ohio River Islands National Wildlife Refuge, and Shannondale Springs Wildlife Management Area.

Rodney Bartgis
Nature Conservancy of West Virginia

Phyllis Reynolds Naylor

Author Phyllis Reynolds Naylor, a Newbery Medal winner and the author of more than 100 books for children and youth, was born January 4, 1933, in Anderson, Indiana. She graduated from American University in 1963 and now lives in Bethesda, Maryland.

Her ties to West Virginia began May 26, 1960, when she married Rex V. Naylor and visited Grafton, Buckhannon, and Preston County, places where he and his

family had lived. Then in 1987, when awarded a grant from the National Endowment for the Arts, she spent the funds traveling throughout West Virginia, talking to people, reading *Goldenseal* magazine, and taking notes.

Naylor found a setting for her most successful books in the small towns and among the people of the Mountain State. *Shiloh* (Newbery Medal, 1992, West Virginia Children's Book Award, 1994, and film adaptation, 1997), *Shiloh Season,* and *Saving Shiloh,* are all set in and near the Tyler County town of Friendly; the beagle Shiloh is named for a nearby community. *Send No Blessings* is set in Hinton; *Josie's Troubles* is set in Webster Springs; *Boys Start the War* (West Virginia Children's Book Award, 1996) is the first in a 12-part boys versus girls series set in a fictional Buckhannon; and *Wrestle the Mountain* is based on the Farmington coal mine disaster.

The University of Charleston awarded Phyllis Reynolds Naylor the Appalachian Medallion in 1997.

Sharon Diaz
Harrison County Schools
Agnes Garrett and Helga P. McCue, eds., "Phyllis Reynolds Naylor," *Authors & Artists for Young Adults,* 1990; Phyllis Naylor, *How I Came to be a Writer,* 1978.

Church of the Nazarene

The Church of the Nazarene arose as an attempt to unite the scattered groups that identified with the American holiness movement, primarily through the work of the National Holiness Association and its camp meetings in the years from 1867 to the mid-1890s. The church was established as a national body in 1908. The denomination is an offshoot of American Methodism and a member of the World Methodist Council.

The lively and informal tone of the revival service is the customary norm for the Sunday morning worship service (except for celebrations of the Lord's Supper, which are more formal) and the

"The best place to live"

"We live high up in the hills above Friendly, but hardly anybody knows where that is. Friendly's near Sistersville, which is halfway between Wheeling and Parkersburg. Used to be, my daddy told me, Sistersville was one of the best places you could live in the whole state. You ask *me* the best place to live, I'd say right where we are, a little four-room house with hills on three sides.

"Afternoon is my second-best time to go up in the hills . . ., morning's the best, especially in summer. Early, *early* morning. On one morning I saw three kinds of animals, not counting cats, dogs, frogs, cows, and horses. Saw a groundhog, saw a doe with two fawns, and saw a gray fox with a reddish head. Bet his daddy was a gray fox and his ma was a red one.

"My favorite place to walk is just across this rattly bridge where the road curves by the old Shiloh schoolhouse and follows the river. River to one side, trees the other— sometimes a house or two."

—Phyllis Reynolds Naylor *Shiloh* (1991)

model for the conduct of the evening service. West Virginia Nazarenes, perhaps to a greater degree than Nazarenes elsewhere, have retained the style of revivalism. Most West Virginia Nazarene congregations have continued the custom of holding mid-week prayer and Bible study meetings, and two annual revival meetings (from four days to two weeks), usually with an itinerant evangelist or visiting pastor. They also have continued the tradition of an annual district camp meeting for at least a week each summer. The Nazarene camp and conference ground, established in 1947, at Summersville, has been important in nourishing this tradition.

Sunday school is important to Nazarenes, and until recent years Sunday School enrollment often exceeded church membership. Well into the 1930s, it was not uncommon for the Nazarenes to plant a new congregation by first planting a Sunday school.

The first congregation of the Church of the Nazarene in West Virginia seems to have appeared in 1909 in Martinsburg, where an independent holiness congregation became part of the fledgling denomination. Within a year or two, the Martinsburg congregation appears to have evaporated.

Soon afterwards, Howard Sloan, a dentist and preacher from East Liverpool, Ohio, who served as superintendent of the Pittsburgh District of the Pentecostal Church of the Nazarene, held a revival meeting in Newell, Hancock County. At its close in 1910, he organized the first enduring work of the denomination in West Virginia. Newell First Church began with 13 charter members, most of them skilled pottery workers.

In 1915, a member of the Newell congregation moved to Mannington to work in a pottery factory there and opened his home to a "cottage prayer meeting." The prayer meeting group sponsored a revival meeting, and out of the revival a congregation of 35 was established. The third-oldest surviving congregation in West Virginia is at Grafton. Howard Sloan organized this congregation in 1919, with 14 members.

The Church of the Nazarene came to the Eastern Panhandle in 1939, as a project of the Washington-Philadelphia (now Washington) District. The first congregation, with 21 members, was established in Berkeley Springs after a cottage prayer meeting and tent revival. But it was only in the 1950s that Nazarenes began to think seriously about evangelizing in the east. In short order, they established congregations in Martinsburg, Romney, and Wiley Ford. Both Martinsburg and Romney had experienced abortive attempts earlier, and the congregations there have remained small.

The area of greatest concentration of Nazarenes in West Virginia has been in the Charleston-Huntington corridor. Huntington First, established in 1923, is the oldest congregation in that area. Churches in South Charleston and Charleston, the next oldest, date from 1928; Davis Creek, reputedly the largest rural congregation of any denomination in West Virginia in the 1940s and 1950s, dates from 1930, as does Dunbar.

Women played an active role in the Nazarene ministry from an earlier time than in most other Protestant churches. The first two regular pastors at Davis Creek were Florence Walling (1934–45), who also served Dunbar in 1943, and Vola Vaughn (1945–1947). Alum Creek has had two female pastors, Allie Spencer (1944–47) and Gussie Thaxton (1952–59). A woman remained longest as the pastor in Newell, Lula Kell, from 1917 to 1926. About 20 women have held regular pastoral posts in West Virginia Nazarene churches.

In 2003, the West Virginia North and West Virginia South districts and the Nazarene congregations in the Eastern Panhandle reported a total of 121 congregations, 14,500 members, and a 9,800 weekly average in morning worship. There is at least one Nazarene congregation in all but seven of West Virginia's county seats.

See also Religion

Paul Bassett
Kansas City, Missouri

Greasy Neale

Alfred Earle "Greasy" Neale, born in Parkersburg, November 5, 1891, was one of West Virginia's greatest all-around athletes. In high school he was a star. He attended West Virginia Wesleyan College and excelled in football, basketball, and baseball. During the 1912–13 basketball season, Neale scored 139 field goals, an amazing number at that time. After graduation in 1915, he was named coach of the Wesleyan football team but continued to play for the team, a common practice in that era.

Neale was an early professional football star, playing with the Canton (Ohio) Bulldogs, 1915–17, on a team that included the great Jim Thorpe. In his playing days he stood six feet tall, weighed 170 pounds, and played offensive end and halfback as well as defensive end and back.

Neale was also an outstanding baseball player, playing for the Cincinnati Reds and Philadelphia Phillies from 1916 through 1924. He played 768 major league games as an outfielder with a .259 batting average. In the infamous World Series of 1919, he hit .357 for the Reds, in a series fixed by members of the opposing Chicago White Sox.

In addition to West Virginia Wesleyan, Neale coached at Marietta College, Washington & Jefferson University, Yale, and the University of Virginia. He also coached a minor league baseball team in Clarksburg as well as the Ironton (Ohio) Tanks, an independent football team. His greatest fame as a coach came from 1941 to 1950, when he coached the Philadelphia Eagles to two world championships in the National Football League.

Neale is credited with developing the "naked reverse," the five-man defensive line, and man-to-man pass defense. He was inducted into the National Football League Hall of Fame in 1969. He died in Lake Worth, Florida, November 2, 1973.

Robert L. Frey
Miamisburg, Ohio

Needham and Arthur Expedition

Abraham Wood of Fort Henry, Virginia, sent James Needham and Gabriel Arthur, the latter probably an indentured servant of Wood, with eight Indians to explore the southwest interior from Virginia. Needham and Arthur were provided with provisions for a three-month journey. They returned just over a month later, and Wood sent them out again and added four horses for their travel. They left on June 25, 1673. The only account we have of this exploration is by Wood, who was not on the trip. He wrote a letter about the exploration on August 22, 1674, to John Richards in England, where the letter remained for many years undiscovered.

Needham and Arthur traveled southwest from Fort Henry, the site of present Petersburg, Virginia, into North Carolina and Georgia. Needham was killed by one of the Indian guides in October. Gabriel Arthur would remain with the Indians, traveling to the present-day states of Alabama, Georgia, Kentucky, Tennessee, South and North Carolina, and Virginia. He may have seen or visited Florida and West Virginia. Arthur visited the Big Sandy River in Lawrence County, Kentucky, or Wayne County, West Virginia. In a remarkable feat of survival and an epic journey, Arthur would finally reach Wood's house on June 18, 1674, having been away for more than a year. This ended Abraham Wood's sponsoring explorations, and Virginia's age of exploration (1650–74) was ended.

See also Gabriel Arthur

W. Eugene Cox
National Park Service

Alan Vance Briceland, *Westward From Virginia: The Exploration of the Virginia-Carolina Frontier 1650–1710*, 1987.

Matthew Mansfield Neely

Matthew Mansfield Neely, the 21st governor of West Virginia (1941–45), was born November 9, 1874, near Grove, Doddridge County, the second of three children of Alfred and Mary (Morris) Neely. His father was a farmer and country doctor. His mother's side of the family

Governor Matthew M. Neely (1874–1958).

claimed a relationship to the poet Robert Burns.

Neely earned his teaching certificate at 18, and his first job was as a teacher across the state in Mineral County. He taught in Mineral County for two years, and in 1897 he enrolled at West Virginia University. A year later he volunteered for service in the Spanish-American War, enlisting as a private and serving more than seven months, mostly in Georgia and Tennessee, before returning to WVU. Neely was president of the senior class in 1901. He received his A. B. degree that year and his law degree a year later. He opened a Fairmont law office in 1902 and married Alberta C. Ramage of Fairmont on October 31, 1902. They had three children, Alfred R. Neely, John Champ Neely, and Corrine Neely.

His first attempt at politics was successful when he was elected mayor of Fairmont in 1908, serving two years before being elected clerk of the House of Delegates. After serving as House clerk from 1911 until 1913, Neely was elected as a Democrat to the U.S. House of Representatives on October 14, 1913, to fill an unexpired term. He was reelected three times before being elected to the U.S. Senate in 1922. Six years later he was defeated in the Hoover landslide of 1928. But he was again elected to the Senate in 1930 by a majority of more than 133,000, which was the greatest to that date for any candidate in the state. He topped that record when he was reelected to the Senate in 1936 by an even greater majority. He resigned from the Senate, January 12, 1941, to become governor.

Neely had decided to run for governor in 1940 after his list of prospective candidates was ignored by the Democratic faction headed by Governor Holt. When Holt's group decided to run R. Carl An-

drews, the Democratic state chairman, in the primary election, Neely filed as a candidate himself. The party was bitterly divided. Neely led the liberal, pro-labor wing, while the conservative statehouse faction was led by Holt and former Governor Kump. Neely won the Democratic primary in 1940 with 200,653 votes to 152,544 for Andrews. He then defeated Republican Daniel Boone Dawson, 496,028 to 383,698, in the general election.

Neely resigned from the Senate at the last minute, to keep the appointment of his successor away from outgoing Governor Holt. He resigned as senator and took the oath of office as governor almost at the same instant. Neely took four oaths of office—the first at 11:35 p.m. on January 12 "with the intention that it should become effective the instant I was completely divested of my office as U.S. Senator." The second was held at approximately 11:45 p.m., and the third just after midnight. The fourth and formal inauguration was held about noon on January 13. Neely appointed Joseph Rosier, also a Fairmont resident, to his vacancy in the Senate on his first day in office, but Holt had already appointed Clarence E. Martin. The U.S. Senate, after prolonged consideration, finally accepted Rosier on May 13, 1941. Neely himself attempted to return to the Senate in 1942, before completing his term as governor. He defeated Kump in the primary but lost in the general election to Republican Chapman Revercomb of Charleston.

Historian Jerry Bruce Thomas considers Neely a major figure in the state's political history and—along with United Mine Workers leader Van Bittner—the architect of the Democratic-labor alliance that dominated West Virginia politics for many years. He served as congressman, senator, and governor, as well as mayor of a major city, a record of service that is unequaled. He was both a friend of labor and a defender of the state's business interest in Congress and the Senate, championing major coal, humanitarian, and progressive legislation. As governor, he was not remarkably successful at getting his programs passed by the state legislature, because the New Deal was ebbing and because of his own combative personality.

Neely returned to the House of Representatives in 1945 after defeating Republican A. C. Schiffler of Wheeling by a narrow margin of 950 votes. He reentered Congress on January 16, 1945, the day after completing his four-year term as governor. But in 1946, Neely lost a bid for another term in the House of Representatives when Republican Francis J. Love of Wheeling defeated him, 45,691 to 40,370. In 1948, he won another term in the Senate by turning the tables on Revercomb. In 1954, he won again and

was halfway through that Senate term when he died January 18, 1958.

Tom D. Miller
Huntington

Charles Lively, ed., *West Virginia Blue Book, 1940, 1941*; John Morgan, *West Virginia Governors*, 1980.

The Negro Citizen of West Virginia

Thomas E. Posey's classic book, *The Negro Citizen of West Virginia*, published in 1934 in the midst of the Great Depression, documents the history of African-Americans in a state that practiced racial segregation but permitted blacks to participate in its political and economic affairs.

Posey, a professor of economics at West Virginia State College (1927–51), later headed the Labor and Industry Division of the U.S. Agency for International Employment. His book traces the historic role of black West Virginians, elaborating on their accomplishments individually and collectively within a segregated society. In addition, Posey discusses essential social legislation and litigation. The section titled "The Negro in the Courts of West Virginia," which outlines significant court cases that helped to establish equal rights for all citizens, is especially useful. Posey concludes that "there is no state in the Union with more constructive legislation pertaining exclusively to Negroes than the state of West Virginia." The book also has a section titled "The Education of the Negro in West Virginia." Posey discusses the evolution of separate educational and other facilities during the period of segregation in West Virginia and outlines how much of the social infrastructure for African-Americans was won through black political participation. This was especially true in the southern coalfields, where black politicians attained considerable power.

See also African-American Heritage
I. D. "Duke" Talbott
Glenville State College

Thomas E. Posey, *The Negro Citizen of West Virginia*, 1934.

Don Nehlen

Donald Eugene Nehlen, West Virginia University football coach, was born in Canton, Ohio, January 1, 1936. He played high school football and lost only three games as a starting quarterback at Bowling Green State University. He coached his alma mater to some of its best records before becoming an assistant at Michigan in 1977. From there, in 1980 he came to WVU, which had only one winning season in the previous six.

Nehlen inherited a just-opened new Mountaineer Field and finished his first campaign 6-6. The next year, he improved to 9-3 and upset Florida 26-6 in the Peach Bowl. In 1982, Nehlen's Mountaineers upset Oklahoma 41-27 at Norman for one of the school's greatest victories. That win catapulted WVU into the elite of college football. Jeff Hostetler, who would become Nehlen's son-in-law, quarterbacked the victory.

The 1988 team finished the regular season unbeaten for the first time in school history behind quarterback Major Harris, a contender for the Heisman Trophy. WVU won the Lambert Trophy, but lost 34-21 to Notre Dame at the Fiesta Bowl. In 1993, the Mountaineers again went undefeated, won the first Big East championship, and won the Lambert again. Third-ranked at the end of the regular season, WVU lost 41-7 to Florida, thereby also losing another shot at the national title.

Nehlen stressed fundamental football throughout his coaching career. Although he had the dubious distinction of losing more bowl games than any other coach, he led WVU football to unprecedented levels. In a state with, proportionately, few high school standouts, he elevated recruiting in nearby states and in Florida. He often attracted players without big names and turned them into All-Americans. Many played professionally. The most successful football coach in West Virginia University's first century, Nehlen is one of the 20 most winning coaches nationally. Nehlen retired from WVU football and coaching after the team's 49-38 victory over Mississippi in the December 2000 Music City Bowl.

Nehlen's overall coaching record was 202 wins, 128 losses and eight ties. His record at WVU was 149-93-4. Don Nehlen entered the College Football Hall of Fame in 2005.

Norman Julian
Dominion Post

New Cumberland

New Cumberland, on the Ohio River north of Weirton, is the county seat of Hancock County, West Virginia's northernmost county. The town was laid out in 1839 by John Cuppy on the site of Fort Chapman and received its charter in 1849. The original name was either Vernon or Cuppytown, but Cuppy changed it to New Cumberland to please those who purchased lots in the town, some of whom came from Cumberland, Maryland. John Chapman erected the first house in the spring of 1840, and other houses, businesses, a church, and a school quickly followed.

When Hancock County was formed in 1848, New Cumberland competed with New Manchester to become the county seat. A referendum resulted in New Cumberland being chosen, but the county government refused to comply. Additional elections were held until New Manchester won the popular vote. In 1884, another election finally resolved the matter, and New Cumberland be-

came the permanent county seat. In 1862, Company I, 12th Regiment, West Virginia Volunteer Infantry was organized in New Cumberland. In 1876, the *Independent*, New Cumberland's first newspaper, began publication.

New Cumberland has not seen rapid population or industrial growth in the 20th century. The 2000 population was 1,099. The city has not experienced the industrial growth that early leaders anticipated and serves now, in addition to being the county seat, as a residential community for larger cities such as Pittsburgh, Weirton, and Wheeling.

See also Hancock County

Kenneth R. Bailey
WVU Institute of Technology

New Deal

When the Great Depression came, West Virginia was one of the states hardest hit. In 1932, West Virginia Democrats, inspired by Franklin D. Roosevelt's call for a "New Deal" and led by gubernatorial candidate Herman Guy Kump, won political control of the state for the first time in 35 years. Though Governor Kump and his successor, Homer Holt, sometimes resisted the initiatives from Washington, the New Deal helped West Virginians deal with one of the highest unemployment rates of the Depression era.

Federal work relief agencies such as the Works Progress Administration organized public projects to provide income to the unemployed. The Civilian Conservation Corps and the National Youth Administration addressed the lack of opportunities for youth. The Public Works Administration provided work as well as needed public facilities through more capital-intensive projects, including the construction of several West Virginia courthouses. Thousands of West Virginians worked for these relief agencies, and almost everyone was affected by the Social Security law of 1935. Social Security enabled the state to move away from its antiquated and piecemeal system of poorhouses and local care of indigents, the elderly, and the disabled and to establish a modern system of unemployment relief and welfare. New Deal agencies also sponsored experimental cooperative communities at Tygart Valley (Dailey), Arthurdale, and Red House (Eleanor).

Though some work relief projects amounted to little more than leaf raking, others left an enduring legacy. At the beginning of the 21st century, many roads, bridges, parks, airports, government buildings, and public housing facilities built under New Deal programs continue in service. They include Kanawha Boulevard in Charleston and Richwood Avenue in Morgantown; Boreman Hall at West Virginia University; flood-control walls in Huntington; and state parks, including

Babcock, Cacapon, Holly River, Lost River, and Watoga.

The New Deal brought about a friendlier legal atmosphere for organized labor, enabling the United Mine Workers of America finally to organize West Virginia coal miners in 1933–34 and increasing the political power of the labor movement in the state. The unionization of coal and other basic industries and the popularity of Social Security and other social legislation associated with Roosevelt's New Deal assured that West Virginia would be solidly Democratic for decades to come. As U.S. senator, Matthew M. Neely championed the Roosevelt reforms that the more conservative "statehouse" Democrats led by Kump and Holt were sometimes reluctant to embrace. As governor after 1941, however, Neely found that a conservative legislature frustrated his efforts to make the state more liberal.

Though the New Deal helped make the Depression more tolerable and brought needed reforms to West Virginia, it failed to find a path toward enduring solutions to the state's basic economic dilemmas. The New Deal ended with the coming of World War II.

See also Great Depression

Jerry Bruce Thomas
Shepherd University

Stephen Edward Haid, "Arthurdale: An Experiment in Community Planning," Ph.D. dissertation, West Virginia University, 1975; Paul Salstrom, *Appalachia's Path to Dependency: Rethinking A Region's Economic History, 1730–1940*, 1994; Jerry Bruce Thomas, *An Appalachian New Deal: West Virginia in the Great Depression*, 1998.

New Martinsville

New Martinsville is located on the Ohio River at the junction of State Routes 2 and 20. Edward Dulin is believed to have been the first white settler in 1773. Dulin was killed by Indians, and his daughter sold some of his land to Presley Martin. In 1838, "Martinsville" was incorporated, and in 1846 became the county seat of newly formed Wetzel County. Long called "New" Martinsville to distinguish it from the other Martinsville, Virginia, the town was officially renamed in 1871.

New Martinsville has seen massive floods, which made the streets navigable only by boat. One of the worst floods hit on March 19, 1936, and the city was again flooded in September 2004.

New Martinsville is the meeting place of the former West Virginia Short Line, now part of CSX, and the Ohio River Division of the Baltimore & Ohio Railroad, now also CSX. In the early part of the 20th century, the town bustled with a tannery, planing mill, foundry, brick works, oil well supply, and the Viking Glass Company. Now, many residents commute to surrounding plants and mines. Others work at Wetzel County Hospital or New

Martinsville's branch of West Virginia Northern Community College.

New Martinsville is a partner in the Hannibal locks and dam hydroelectric facility. Located on the Ohio River at the north end of town, the hydro plant contributes substantially to the city budget. New Martinsville operates one of only two municipal electric systems in West Virginia and residents benefit by low electric rates.

In 1925, Gloria Swanson's film *Stage Struck* was filmed in and around New Martinsville. Hydroplane racers from around the world participate in the River Heritage Days Regatta each year. The 2000 population of New Martinsville was 5,984.

Christina Myer
Wheeling

New River

First bubbling from a small hillside spring in the high mountains of northwest North Carolina, the New River starts its 320-mile journey northward across Virginia and into West Virginia. There it joins with the Gauley River to form the Kanawha River at Gauley Bridge.

At the West Virginia border the tail waters of Bluestone Lake soon slow the New River to a wide expanse of lazy water. The dam, just above the railroad town of Hinton, was built primarily for flood control and completed in 1949. Below the dam, as the elevation drops and hills push against its banks, the river moves faster as it approaches its famous gorge. Below a long stretch of shoals and the beautiful Sandstone Falls, the New starts to show its most rugged characteristics, plunging through shoals and rocks, creating eddies and large pools, and intermittent rapids. The water is calm enough, however, with rapids here and there, to permit canoeing from Hinton to Thurmond with a portage around Sandstone Falls. McCreery is another favorite place to launch canoes and float to Thurmond. Below Thurmond the river becomes a wilder ride, with some whitewater of class VI difficulty.

A major geologic feature is located at Quinnimont where an incised meander, typical of older rivers, makes a huge turn in the river. Grandview Park occupies the heights above. A rough and winding road crosses over the next big bend downstream, on its way from Prince to Thurmond. It provides at the top a wonderful panoramic view of the gorge.

The New was discovered by European Americans in the 17th century, perhaps as early as 1654 or by the later Batts and Fallam expedition, sent out in the summer of 1671 by Abraham Wood. It was known for at least 80 years as the Woods River.

In the late 19th and early 20th centuries, coal was king in southern West Virginia. Numerous coal company towns lined the New River Gorge in Fayette and Raleigh counties. Thurmond, now an embarkation site for whitewater rafting, was then a railroad boom town, a major collecting and shipping point for coal trains from surrounding mines. Downstream is Sewell, named for explorer Stephen Sewell. A ferry once operated at Sewell, near present Babcock State Park. The last coke-making operation in the gorge closed in 1965 at Sewell.

The New River Gorge mines are now gone, but the mining history lives in the literature, surviving architecture, nearby museums, and in the memories of mine families. Fayette Station, a coal mining community that survives in name only, is the take-out point for many rafting trips. An 1889 iron truss bridge, rebuilt in 1998, carries vehicles across the New River here, in the shadow of the New River Gorge Bridge far above.

The coal and timber booms followed the Chesapeake & Ohio Railway, which built its main line through the New River Gorge in 1873. The river's potential had been known and studied from much earlier times. George Washington considered a canal for the lower New, and Chief Justice John Marshall boated the river in 1812 to assess its navigation potential. Captured in 1755 on the New River by Shawnees, Mary Draper Ingles was taken to the Ohio country where she made her heroic escape. She traveled along the New River in West Virginia on her return home.

The New River Gorge National River, a National Park Service unit in West Virginia, now conserves and protects 53 miles of the New River from Hinton to Ames.

See also Batts and Fallam Expedition, Thurmond, Whitewater Rafting

W. Eugene Cox
National Park Service

William E. Cox, *Life on the New River: A Pictorial History of the New River Gorge*, 1984.

New River Community and Technical College

The New River Community and Technical College serves the New River watershed and adjoining areas from campuses at Bluefield, Beckley, Lewisburg, and Summersville. It is one of West Virginia's youngest educational institutions.

The college was created early in the 21st century as part of changes intended to provide autonomy for the state's community colleges. Such colleges had traditionally been administered by host institutions, Bluefield State College in this case. Senate Bill 448, passed by the state legislature in 2004, made New River Community and Technical College essentially independent of Bluefield State.

New River absorbed the community college functions of Bluefield State College, as well as Glenville State College's community college campus at Summersville. The newly created college serves Fayette, Greenbrier, Mercer, Monroe, Nicholas, Pocahontas, Raleigh, Summers, and Webster counties from its four campuses. Initially accredited as a component of Bluefield State, New River worked toward its own accreditation.

New River Community and Technical College offers numerous associate degrees and several certificates. The college had 1,527 students enrolled in the fall 2004 semester, equal to 1,198 full-time equivalents.

See also Bluefield State College

New River Gorge Bridge

The New River Gorge Bridge in Fayette County is one of West Virginia's best-known landmarks. It is the second-highest bridge (876 feet above the riverbed) in the United States, after the Royal Gorge Bridge over the Arkansas River in Colorado, and until 2003 it had the world's longest single-arch steel span.

In June 1974, the first steel was positioned over the gorge by trolleys operating on 3,500-foot cables strung between 330-foot towers on each side of the gorge. The arch and deck of the bridge were constructed as a truss. The arch was designed to support most of the gravity load, and hanging beams connecting the deck to the arch below were built to carry lateral loads. Design work was done by the engineering firm of Michael Baker Jr., Inc., and the bridge was built by the American Bridge Division of U.S. Steel. Construction took more than three years and was finished October 22, 1977.

The $37 million project completed the last link of Appalachian Corridor L (U.S. 19), reducing to one minute the driving time across the New River Gorge, which previously had taken about 40 minutes, and providing a popular shortcut between Interstate 79 near Sutton and the West Virginia Turnpike north of Beckley. From 1979 to 1994, traffic along the shortened route nearly quadrupled to more than 10,000 cars and trucks daily, and was projected to double again to more than 20,000 vehicles daily by 2014.

The length of the New River Gorge Bridge is 3,030 feet, and the arch length is 1,700 feet. The width of the deck is 69 feet, four inches. The bridge weighs 88 million pounds (44,000 tons), including 44 million pounds of steel. The arch alone weighs more than 21 million pounds. A special steel, designed to rust to a durable, attractive finish, was used to avoid the need for repainting.

Annually, on the third Saturday of October since 1980, the bridge has been closed for "Bridge Day," West Virginia's largest one-day festival. Pedestrians are permitted on the bridge on Bridge Day, and rappellers and even parachutists from around the world come to test their

The New River Gorge Bridge.

skills. The National Park Service operates Canyon Rim Visitor Center just north of the bridge on U.S. 19, introducing tourists to the New River Gorge National River and offering a fine view of the soaring structure.

See also Bridge Day, New River Gorge National River

Larry Sonis
Arlington, Texas

New River Gorge National River

One of only three national rivers, the New River Gorge National River was established by Congress on November 10, 1978. A unit of the National Park System, the park was created for the purpose of conserving and interpreting outstanding natural, scenic, and historic values and objects. The first superintendent was James Carrico, who established temporary park headquarters on Main Street in Oak Hill. The first day of operation was May 7, 1983, when the first visitor center for the new park opened near Fayetteville.

There are now four visitor centers in the park to educate and inform visitors about the cultural, natural, and recreational opportunities along the national river. The park boundary starts in Hinton and runs 53 miles downriver to the New River Gorge Bridge.

The New River with its deep gorge and forested flanks is very scenic and offers water-related activities including whitewater rafting, kayaking, canoeing, and fishing. Some of the best warm-water fishing in the state of West Virginia is located on the New River, where mountain biking and hiking trails may also be enjoyed year round. Several abandoned mining communities and many coke ovens are located in the gorge, once the center of the New River Coalfield. Mining and railroading have left a rich industrial heritage, interpreted at Thurmond and other sites.

The National Park Service is directing its resources to maintaining the park in its natural state, preserving its cultural past for future generations, and presenting educational and interpretive programs to visitors, asking that they join in protecting this treasure of West Virginia and the nation.

See also National Park Service in West Virginia, New River, New River Gorge Bridge

W. Eugene Cox
National Park Service

New River State School

See West Virginia University Institute of Technology.

New Vrindaban

New Vrindaban, located off U.S. 250 east of Moundsville in rural Marshall County, began in 1968 as a project of the International Society for Krishna Consciousness. The society, a Hindu organization, was founded in New York in 1966 by Srila Prabhupada. In his native India in 1944, Prabhupada had founded *Back to Godhead*, an English-language magazine devoted to the Hindu god Krishna. In 1959, he took vows of renunciation and was named A. C. Bhaktivedanta Swami. He arrived in New York in 1965 at the age of 69. His International Society for Krishna Consciousness flourished in the American counterculture of the 1960s.

Prabhupada's disciple, Kirtanananda Swami Bhaktipada, whose birth name was Keith Gordon Ham, was the founder of New Vrindaban, following Prabhupada's guidelines. The name comes from Vrindavana, India, the place of Lord Krishna's childhood. The project began modestly. In 1968, there was no electricity, no running water, and no easy access to the only building, a battered shack. Now New Vrindaban has a temple, a guest lodge, restaurants, gift shops, a prize-winning rose garden, and various other enterprises, as well as its most impressive structure, Prabhupada's Palace of Gold, which was constructed by Krishna devotees.

New Vrindaban, which had become one of West Virginia's leading tourist attractions as well as an important religious site, underwent a crisis late in the 20th century. Its leader, Bhaktipada, was arrested in 1987, charged with racketeering and accused of ordering the murders of two society devotees. He was imprisoned from 1996 to 2004. New Vrindaban was expelled from membership in the International Society for Krishna Consciousness for several years, and the community fell into decline. The community has refocused on the teachings of Srila Prabhupada.

Gordon L. Swartz III
Cameron

John Hubner, *Monkey on a Stick: Murder, Madness and the Hare Krishnas,* 1988; New Vrindaban Community, *Prabhupada's Palace of Gold,* 1986.

New York Central

In the early 20th century, the New York Central System was one of the largest rail networks in the United States. The NYC entered West Virginia at Point Pleasant and followed the east bank of the Kanawha River through Nitro into Charleston. Its Charleston passenger station was near the present Capitol Market, and the market building was the old freight house. The New York Central's major rail yard was east of Charleston at Dickinson, near present Riverside High School. This yard was also used by Virginian Railroad trains. East of Dickinson the NYC main line was used by the Virginian to Gauley Bridge and passed through Cedar Grove, Cannelton, and Smithers. A branch ran beyond Gauley Bridge and terminated at Swiss, Nicholas County.

The earliest part of the New York Central System in West Virginia was the Kanawha & Michigan, originally known as the Kanawha & Ohio Railway Company. By 1888, it had completed a 58-mile line from Charleston to Point Pleasant, where it connected with the Toledo & Ohio Central. The K&M purchased the Charleston & Gauley Railway and extended its lines east to a connection with the C&O and later the Virginian. Between 1898 and 1903, lines were pushed farther east and north into the coalfields, and freight traffic increased significantly.

In 1900, the Toledo & Ohio Central gained control of the K&M and the Kanawha & West Virginia Railroad. The K&WV ran 34 miles from Charleston up the Elk River to Blue Creek and then east to Kellys Creek. For many years it carried a significant amount of timber and coal, and in 1916 six passenger trains a day operated from Charleston to Blakeley on Kellys Creek. In 1910, the New York Central gained control of the Toledo & Ohio Central, into which it merged the K&M, the K&WV, and several other railroads in 1938. The Toledo & Ohio Central was finally merged into the New York Central System in 1952.

In 1968, the New York Central System merged with the Pennsylvania Railroad to create the ill-fated Penn Central. Out of the failure of this merger came the Consolidated Rail Corporation, known as Conrail, in 1976. The old Kanawha & Michigan became part of Conrail. In 1999, Conrail was split between the Norfolk Southern and CSX. The former K&M trackage became part of the Norfolk Southern.

Throughout their life, the New York Central components Kanawha & Michigan Railway and Kanawha & West Virginia Railroad were dedicated to transporting coal from the West Virginia mines immediately north of the Kanawha River to the mills and factories of Ohio's cities. But passenger service was not neglected. In 1916, 12 passenger trains a day were scheduled into Charleston, with eight of them continuing to Gauley Bridge for a connection with the Virginian Railway. Four of the passenger trains ran from Charleston to Toledo with convenient connections to Chicago.

See also Railroads

Robert L. Frey
Miamisburg, Ohio

Newspapers

The Eastern Panhandle was the birthplace of newspaper publishing in West Virginia. Three newspapers were founded there before 1800: the *Potowmac Guardian and Berkeley Advertiser* in Shepherdstown in 1790; the *Impartial Observer* in 1797 in Shepherdstown; and the *Berkeley Intelligencer* in 1799 in Martinsburg.

In the early years of the 19th century, other regions produced their first newspapers. The *Monongalia Gazette* was founded at Morgantown in 1804; the *Wheeling Repository* was established in 1807; Clarksburg's *Bye-Stander* commenced in 1810; Wellsburg's *Charlestown Gazette* appeared in 1814 (Wellsburg was called Charles Town at the time); and Weston's *Western Star* began in 1820. The *Kenhawa Spectator* began publication in Charleston in 1820, and Lewisburg's *Palladium of Virginia and the Pacific Monitor* was founded in 1823. The *South Branch Intelligencer* was established in 1830 in Romney and published until 1896, when it merged with the *Hampshire Review*, which is still publishing. Charles Town's *Spirit of Jefferson* commenced in 1844, merged with the *Farmers' Advocate* in 1948, and continues publication today. By 1850, 21 weeklies and three dailies, published in both the English and German languages, were serving a population of approximately 300,000 in Western Virginia.

Before the creation of West Virginia in 1863, 43 towns had established at least one weekly newspaper, and larger towns supported several. The *Wheeling Intelligencer,* established in 1852, was the only daily newspaper before the Civil War. The proliferation of newspapers reflected the needs of rival political parties, demand for news of social and political controversy, the need for legal and official notices in recently created counties, and recent technological advances in printing. Although the earliest newspapers were primarily filled with national and foreign news, country editors soon learned that their efforts should be devoted to local and regional news. Throughout the early 19th century, religious and agricultural journals were popular, and many were published in Western Virginia. However,

the region's population was small and dispersed over a rugged terrain, illiteracy was widespread, and poor transportation hindered newspaper circulation. By 1863, approximately 250 newspapers had been established, with most failing within a short time. A notable exception was the *Point Pleasant Register;* founded as a weekly in 1862, it became a daily in 1916 and continues publication today.

The press of antebellum Western Virginia was generally Unionist and anti-slavery, but many areas also supported pro-Southern newspapers. Wheeling's *Intelligencer* was anti-slavery, pro-Union, and the strongest supporter of the statehood movement. Another newspaper opposed to slavery was the *Ceredo Crescent*, established in 1857 when Ceredo was founded as an anti-slavery community in a slave state. The Civil War was detrimental to many of the state's newspapers. The publishers of the *Fairmont True Virginian*, Harrisville's *Ritchie Democrat*, and Lewisburg's *Greenbrier Weekly Era* closed their papers to join the Confederate army. Pro-Southern presses of Charleston's *Kanawha Valley Star* and Martinsburg's *Virginia Republican* were seized by Union soldiers. Pro-secessionist newspapers in Philippi, Romney, and other towns in areas of strategic importance were destroyed by Union troops. Other pro-secessionist newspapers, such as the *Parkersburg News*, were destroyed by civilian mobs.

At least 15 Civil War camp newspapers were published on confiscated presses for army units on active duty in western Virginia. These regimental publications included *Yankee*, the *Knapsack*, the *Old Flag*, and the *Wandering Soldier*, all Union newspapers, and the *Guerilla*, the only Confederate military newspaper printed in what became West Virginia.

Following statehood in 1863, editors changed their mastheads to reflect the name of the new state, although some delayed the change for months. Notable developments after the Civil War made newspaper publishing more lucrative. News companies supplied preprinted sheets to local publishers who added their own copy and advertisements. The introduction of less expensive wood-pulp paper reduced costs. Legislative printing contracts sustained printers in the state capital, which moved from Wheeling to Charleston in 1870, back to Wheeling in 1875, and then permanently to Charleston in 1885.

In the late 19th and early 20th centuries, dramatic growth in the lumber, coal, oil, gas, iron, glass, and salt industries brought substantial increases in population and the establishment of new towns. Immigrants, many of whom were industrial workers, established newspapers in the German and Italian languages. African-American newspapers included Martinsburg's *Pioneer Press,*

Charleston's the *Advocate*, and Keystone's *McDowell Times*. The *Volcano Lubricator, Sistersville Oil Review, West Virginia Walking Beam* and the *Derrick Herald* served the oil fields. College newspapers were established at West Virginia University and Marshall College which continue publication to the present. Cheap paper, news distribution networks, and the invention of the linotype, the telephone, and the typewriter decreased production costs and encouraged the proliferation of newspapers. With at least 223 different newspapers (dailies, weeklies, semi-weeklies, and tri-weeklies) publishing concurrently in 1912, more papers were being issued within the state than at any other time. Unlike most of their predecessors, many newspapers founded from 1866 to 1915 have survived to the present.

The presence of so many newspapers in the early 20th century created fierce competition for readers and advertisers. World War I brought more expensive paper, rising wages, and higher postal rates, which forced many smaller papers to suspend publication or merge with competitors. Several newspapers closed when their owners departed for military duty. Although the number of daily newspapers remained fairly constant, the number of weeklies continued to decline after the war. West Virginia's slow population growth in the 1920s and 1930s and the widespread poverty of the Great Depression reduced the number of weeklies to 130. With the onset of World War II, labor shortages, paper shortages, and high costs again forced closures and mergers.

After 1950, the number of weekly newspapers began another decline as tens of thousands of West Virginians left the state. Mechanized mining produced rapidly declining employment in the coal industry while unemployment also increased in other areas of manufacturing. Although circulation remained relatively stable during the 1960s and early 1970s, population losses and an unfavorable economic climate triggered a gradual decline of newspapers through the 1970s.

Ironically, West Virginia's innovative publishers led the nation during this period in technological advances. The installation of the first offset presses in the early 1960s permitted the printing of several different newspapers per day, allowing the owners of such presses to contract to print nearby newspapers as well as their own. By 2002, only 25 presses printed all the newspapers operating in West Virginia as well as many from other states. The disastrous 1985 flood also dramatically changed the technology of newspaper production. The *Pocahontas Times* was the first West Virginia newspaper to use a desktop publishing system after the flood demolished its printing plant, instantly moving the paper into the computer age. Other flood-ravaged newspapers quickly adopted computerized production, and every one continued to publish. Today, all West Virginia newspapers rely on automated information processing and computerized typesetting systems.

After 1979, the number of dailies fluctuated slightly but remained at about 25 through the 1990s and into the new century. With ever-expanding competition for the support of readers and advertisers, the number of weeklies and other non-dailies gradually declined, with 62 publishing in 2004. In addition, two dailies and 17 weeklies served West Virginia colleges and universities. The *Charleston Gazette* had the largest circulation for a daily newspaper at 55,563, and the city's *Sunday Gazette-Mail* had the highest Sunday circulation at 94,325. Leading circulation among weeklies were the *Nicholas Chronicle* at 7,839 and the *Weston Democrat* at 6,729. Including free distribution newspapers, the total circulation of West Virginia newspapers was 781,753 in 2004.

Harold Malcolm Forbes
WVU Libraries

Harold M. Forbes, *West Virginia Newspapers, 1790–1990,* 1989; Delf Norona and Charles Shetler, *West Virginia Imprints, 1790–1863: A Checklist of Books, Newspapers, Periodicals and Broadsides,* 1958; Otis K. Rice, "West Virginia Printers and Their Work, 1790–1830," *West Virginia History,* July 1953.

Niagara Movement

The Niagara Movement, a short-lived but important activist organization founded by African-American intellectuals at Niagara Falls in 1905, had its first public meeting at Harpers Ferry the following year. Its origins lay in the growing differences between Booker T. Washington, then the most powerful black leader in the United States, and an increasingly vocal group of more radical intellectuals. While Washington counseled accommodation with whites and stressed economic advancement, his critics urged protest and demanded full civil rights.

When an attempt to bridge these differences in a conference in New York in January 1904 failed, Washington's critics concluded that an organization dedicated to militant action was necessary. William Monroe Trotter, W.E.B. DuBois, and 27 other black men met in Canada, near Niagara Falls, in July 1905, and formed the Niagara Movement. Niagarites adopted a Declaration of Principles denouncing unequal treatment in areas such as suffrage, education, and labor.

In August 1906, the Niagara Movement held its first public meeting at Storer College in Harpers Ferry. This meeting is noteworthy because of a daylong tribute to John Brown, which included a barefoot pilgrimage to John Brown's Fort and DuBois's "Address to the Country." Du-Bois claimed for blacks "every single right that belongs to a freeborn American" and rededicated conferees to "the final emancipation of the race which John Brown died to make free." The meeting's sometimes strident rhetoric dismayed Storer College officials, who, believing the African-American school had been hurt, apparently responded coolly when Niagarites considered returning in 1907.

At the height of its success, the Niagara Movement reported about 400 members and chapters in 34 states, but the organization struggled from its inception. Washington's opposition limited support, and organizational problems and internal feuding further weakened the movement. Annual meetings were held in Boston in 1907, Oberlin, Ohio, in 1908, and Sea Isle City, New Jersey, in 1909. The 1910 meeting never materialized, and the Niagara Movement finally dissolved in 1911 when DuBois suggested members join the recently formed, interracial National Association for the Advancement of Colored People.

See also Storer College, Booker T. Washington

Mary Johnson
State Archives

David Levering Lewis, *W.E.B. DuBois: Biography of a Race, 1868–1919,* 1993; Lewis, "Address to the Country," *W. E. B. DuBois: A Reader,* 1995; Elliott M. Rudwick, "The Niagara Movement," *Journal of Negro History,* July 1957.

Nicholas County

Named for Wilson Cary Nicholas (1761–1820), a Virginia governor and U.S. senator, Nicholas County was created by the Virginia legislature from parts of Greenbrier, Kanawha, and Randolph counties on January 30, 1818. Located in central West Virginia on the Allegheny Plateau, Nicholas County encompasses 656.8 square miles, with economic resources including bituminous coal, limestone quarries, timber, fruit farms, tobacco, and livestock. Its two largest cities are Summersville, the county seat, and Richwood. The county population was 26,562 in 2000.

In 1775, Maj. William Morris, accompanied by his slave, Peter Morris, claimed lands in present Nicholas County and offered them to his oldest son, William Jr., who sold them to his brother, Henry. Henry moved to the land in 1791 and built a cabin for his family along Peter Creek, named for his father's slave. Other settlers followed. In 1792, two of the Morris daughters were killed by the renegade Simon Girty, who had stayed with the family under false pretenses during the winter. On April 7, 1818, the first meeting of the Nicholas County court was held at the home near Keslers Cross Lanes of John Hamilton, who donated 30 acres to establish the county seat, named Summersville in 1820 and incorporated in 1860.

Nicholas County was bisected by the Weston & Gauley Bridge Turnpike, completed in 1859. This north-south thoroughfare, connecting Gauley Bridge and Weston via Summersville, contributed to the development of the county.

Nicholas County was the site of military encounters in 1861 that proved to be an early turning point in the Civil War. On August 26, Gen. John Floyd led his Confederate forces across the Gauley River to attack the Union's 7th Ohio Regiment at Keslers Cross Lanes. The assault took the Union forces by surprise, and they were routed. On September 10, additional Union forces advanced against Floyd at Carnifex Ferry, prompting the Confederates to retreat and keeping the strategic Kanawha Valley under Union control for the early part of the war. In October, Robert E. Lee, who had been assigned

Cranberry River flows through Nicholas County.

FAST FACTS ABOUT NICHOLAS COUNTY

Founded: 1818

Land in square miles: 656.8

Population: 26,562

Percentage minorities: 1.2%

Percentage rural: 77.9%

Median age: 39.4

Percentage 65 and older: 15.0%

Birth rate per 1,000 population: 10.7

Median household income: $26,974

High school graduate or higher: 70.0%

Bachelor's degree or higher: 9.8%

Home ownership: 82.8%

Median home value: $60,100

This information is from the 2000 U.S. Census. In 2000, West Virginia as a whole had 5 percent minorities, a median age of 38.9, median household income of $29,696, and a 75.2 percent home ownership rate.

to Western Virginia, decided not to attack Union forces under Gen. William S. Rosecrans.

In July 1861, Confederate spy Nancy Hart led an attack that burned most of Summersville to the ground. She was later captured and jailed but used her beauty to lure a guard into giving her his pistol, whereupon she shot him dead and escaped. After the war, she returned to neighboring Greenbrier County, married, and lived there until her death.

Around the turn of the 20th century, the railroad brought economic growth to Nicholas County. The lumber industry expanded rapidly, and the Cherry River Boom and Lumber Company built one of the world's largest sawmills at Richwood. Other industries followed, including a paper mill, handle and hub factories, a tannery, and what was then the world's largest clothespin factory. Later in the 20th century, coal led another economic surge, until the coal industry softened in the 1970s and early 1980s. More recently, Nicholas County has sought economic diversification. Along with Fayette, Raleigh, and Summers counties, Nicholas County is part of the 4C Economic Development Authority, which was created to foster regional economic growth. The completion of four-lane Appalachian Corridor L (U.S. 19) through Nicholas County in the 1990s brought heavy north-south traffic and prosperity to roadside businesses.

Nicholas Countians work in manufacturing, commerce, and for the service industries and government. Some work as miners and a few hundred on farms. The largest employers are the Nicholas County Board of Education, Summersville Memorial Hospital, Columbia West Virginia, Inc., and Wal-Mart. The county population peaked in 1980 at 28,126 residents, declined to 26,775 in 1990, and remained stable as of 2000.

Nicholas County has 19 schools with more than 5,000 students. County elected officials include three county commissioners, a county clerk, a sheriff, a prosecuting attorney, an assessor, and a circuit clerk. Summersville and Richwood have municipal police departments. The judiciary in the county includes two magistrates, a county court judge, a municipal police court judge (Summersville), and a state circuit court judge (28th circuit).

Summersville Lake, the largest impoundment lake in West Virginia, was dedicated by President Lyndon B. Johnson on September 3, 1966. Its 60 miles of shoreline and 2,800-acre surface offer recreational benefits in addition to the flood control and other purposes for which it was created. The lowering of the reservoir each fall turns the lower Gauley River into rushing whitewater, creating a popular rafting season.

Nicholas County has many other points of interest. The Carnifex Ferry Battlefield State Park is an important historic site. The county is known for its annual county fair, the big ramp festival at Richwood, and the potato festival at Summersville. Music in the Mountains, one of America's major bluegrass festivals, is held at Summersville each summer. Nicholas County campgrounds include the Battle Run Campground, Mountain Lake Campground, and the Summersville Lake Retreat. Visitors to the county, which is positioned at the southern end of the Monongahela National Forest, also may enjoy vacation rentals, hiking and biking, boat rentals, horseback riding, scuba diving, whitewater rafting, and visiting the local Kirkwood Winery, home of the Grape Stomping Wine Festival.

See also Summersville

Larry Sonis
Arlington, Texas

Night of the Hunter

Night of the Hunter, a classic suspense novel written by Davis Grubb in 1953, was made into a movie in 1955. The story, about a demonic preacher who menaces two young children in hopes of extracting the secret of their father's ill-gotten wealth, is set in and near Grubb's native Moundsville. It was the only movie directed by actor Charles Laughton, from a screenplay by Laughton and James Agee. The black-and-white film starred Robert Mitchum as a serial killer preacher, Shelley Winters as an unfortunate widow, and silent film star Lillian Gish. Most of the movie was shot on set in California, with locations filmed on the Ohio River in the Northern Panhandle. Mitchum gives what is often considered his best performance as the preacher. The film was included in the Library of Congress's list of 100 best American films. A made-for-television version of *Night of the Hunter* was produced in 1991.

See also Davis Grubb, Literature

Merle Moore
Webster Springs

Nitro

Named for the nitrocellulose used in smokeless powder, not nitroglycerin, the town of Nitro was built during World War I to manufacture munitions. DuPont Company, the premier explosives producer, had selected the Kanawha River site near Charleston, but did not build the plant. Because of political objections to any company receiving such a large contract, on January 17, 1918, the War Department hired a New York engineering firm to build the plant using DuPont's preliminary plans, then engaged Hercules Powder to operate it under the supervision of Daniel J. Jackling, a copper executive.

Within 11 months, some 110,000 workers, using 104 railroad cars of materials daily, built not only a powder plant with nitric and sulfuric acid facilities, drying towers, storage, and proving grounds, but also a complete town with a civic center, hospital, and executive housing in the hills. Rows and rows of prefabricated bungalows, up to 60 a day, were built and segregated by race and nationality.

The war ended before Nitro was finished. With the Armistice, construction and initial production stopped, the companies and Jackling were released from their contracts, and the army inventoried and sold off the Nitro plant beginning August 1, 1919. The Charleston Industrial Corporation bought the facility and gradually attracted chemical-related industries and a stable population. Nitro, with a 2000 population of 6,824, remains a major center of chemical production.

See also Chemical Industry, World War I

R. Eugene Harper
University of Charleston

R. Eugene Harper, "Wilson Progressives vs. DuPont: Controversy in Building the Nitro Plant," *West Virginia History*, 1989; William D. Wintz, *Nitro: The World War I Boom Town*, 1985.

Norfolk Southern Corporation

The Norfolk Southern Corporation is the holding company created in 1982 in the merger of two large railroad systems, the Norfolk & Western and the Southern. The Norfolk Southern holding company should not be confused with a railroad of the same name that ran from Norfolk, Virginia, to Charlotte, North Carolina. This railroad became part of the Southern System in 1974 and was renamed the Carolina & Northwestern in 1981.

The N&W was itself the product of the merger of several major railroads, including the Virginian, the Nickel Plate, the Wabash, and the Pittsburgh & West Virginia. The N&W served many coal mines in southern West Virginia as did the affiliated Virginian. The Southern Railway System was also a conglomeration of many smaller lines that were organized into the dominant system of the South in the late 19th century by the J. P. Morgan interests. The N&W was traditionally one of the most profitable railroads in the nation because of its heavy coal traffic. The Southern Railway was known for its efficient operations and its excellent safety record.

In 1999 Norfolk Southern and the CSX Corporation absorbed Conrail (the major railroad in the Northeast) and divided its lines between themselves. Thus Norfolk Southern and CSX dominate rail transportation in West Virginia and throughout the eastern United States at the beginning of the 21st century.

See also Norfolk & Western Railway, Railroads

Robert L. Frey
Miamisburg, Ohio

Norfolk & Western Railway

The Norfolk & Western Railway was a major force in opening the coalfields of southern West Virginia. The N&W was the result of an 1881 merger between the Atlantic, Mississippi & Ohio Railroad, running from Norfolk to Bristol, Virginia-Tennessee, and the Shenandoah Valley Railroad. Interested in the coal deposits in the Flat Top Mountain area on both sides of the Virginia-West Virginia state line, the new N&W constructed the 75-mile New River Extension northwest from Radford, Virginia, to Pocahontas, Virginia, just west of Bluefield. The Pocahontas name soon applied to an entire new coalfield, which lay mostly within West Virginia. On March 17, 1883, the first carload of Pocahontas coal arrived in Norfolk. From the earliest days, Bluefield was a major location on the N&W, first as the western terminal and then as a major division point.

Although West Virginia passed a law in 1895 preventing railroads from engaging in the business of buying and selling coal, efforts to break the linkage between railroads and mine owners were seldom effective. In order to develop the coalfields further, the Philadelphia bankers behind the N&W formed the Flat Top Coal Land Association, which acquired and developed many coal mines in the area. This association eventually became a subsidiary of the N&W known as the Pocahontas Coal & Coke Company.

While the N&W built spurs to newly opened mines, expansion westward from Bluefield toward the Ohio River had to wait until the completion of Elkhorn Tunnel through Flat Top Mountain in 1888. Then the N&W built across McDowell, Mingo, and Wayne counties, reaching the Ohio at Kenova, west of Huntington. During construction the N&W found itself in the middle of the Hatfield-McCoy Feud at the Hatfield Bend of Tug Fork, according to the correspondence of President Frederick J. Kimball. In 1890, the N&W acquired the Scioto Valley Railway, an isolated 126-mile line that ran from a small town near Columbus to Coal Grove, Ohio, located across the river from Kenova.

Rapid expansion across southern West Virginia and into Ohio and southwest Virginia, the development of coal loading docks in Norfolk, major improvements in equipment and facilities, and the assumption of a $6.5 million debt of the Shenandoah Valley Railroad were too much of a financial challenge. Like many other railroads, the Norfolk & Western in 1895–96 went through bankruptcy and reorganization. In 1900, as the N&W was beginning to recover from its financial difficulties, the Pennsylvania Railroad began purchasing its stock. Although never able to gain more than 39 percent of the stock, the Pennsy remained the major stockholder in the N&W for the next 60 years.

In 1901, the N&W acquired the Cincinnati, Portsmouth & Virginia, gaining access to Cincinnati. Shortly thereafter the N&W connected with the Pennsylvania in Columbus, and the basic Norfolk & Western system was complete, with the exception of improvements to the main line and several additional branch lines to tap coal resources. The most important of the main line improvements was the 59-mile Big Sandy Extension through Wayne and Mingo counties, which replaced the original, inefficient Twelvepole Creek route to the Ohio.

Through World War I, the Great Depression and World War II, the N&W remained one of the most successful railroads in the nation and a major factor in the economy of West Virginia. It remained primarily a coal-hauling railroad, and for most of its history relied on coal-powered trains. It developed a fleet of outstanding steam locomotives, many of them constructed in the company shops at Roanoke, Virginia. Many of them operated well into the 1950s. The N&W was the last major railroad to give up steam power.

About the time steam locomotives disappeared from the N&W tracks, the corporation began to expand by acquiring other railroads. In 1959, it acquired the Virginian, essentially a redundant system from the West Virginia coalfields to the Virginia docks. The Atlantic & Danville, running from Norfolk to Danville, Virginia, was purchased three years later. Challenged in part by the C&O acquisition of the B&O, in 1964 the N&W acquired the Nickel Plate in a merger that included the Wabash Railroad, the Akron, Canton & Youngstown, and the Pittsburgh & West Virginia. As a condition of this merger the N&W temporarily assumed control of the Erie Lackawanna, but that eventually became part of Conrail.

Finally, in 1982, two giants of the region merged as the N&W and the Southern Railway System became the Norfolk Southern Corporation. Today the NS is one of the major railroad systems in the nation with 15,000 route miles of track, 23,000 employees, and annual operating revenues in excess of $4 billion.

See also Norfolk Southern Corporation

Robert L. Frey
Miamisburg, Ohio

Joseph T. Lambie, *From Mine to Market*, 1954; E. F. Pat Striplin, *The Norfolk & Western: A History*, 1981.

Normal Schools

Several West Virginia colleges originated as normal schools, whose purpose was to train primary and secondary school teachers. The need for normal schools was recognized early in our history as a state. On February 3, 1865, the legislature asked the governor to appoint a commission to plan a state normal school system. On February 27, 1867, the legislature established the West Virginia State Normal School at Marshall to provide "instruction and practice for common school teachers in the science of education and the art of teaching." Soon five other normals were established, in Fairmont (1869), in West Liberty (1870), and in Glenville, Athens, and Shepherdstown (all 1872). Over time, the normal schools matured into Marshall University, Fairmont State University, West Liberty State College, Glenville State College, Concord University, and Shepherd University. A board of regents governed the system.

All the normals but Fairmont were essentially high schools in the early years. Their fate was entangled in state politics for decades, with meager appropriations and periodic attempts in the legislature to abolish the schools. In 1877, the normals established a three-year term beyond the elementary grades, with occasional curriculum revisions thereafter. There were 360 normal students statewide in 1879–80, and after 1900 women outnumbered men as students at most of the schools. There were 2,592 normal school students in 1908.

The first normal schools were for whites only. Then, on February 21, 1895, the legislature established Bluefield Colored Institute (now Bluefield State College) to provide a normal school course for blacks.

With the development of more high schools, the normal schools upgraded their offerings. They increasingly focused on teacher training courses, which were implemented in all the normals in 1905–07. By 1917, the regents began to abolish high school courses in the normal schools, and, in 1920, the state board of education authorized Marshall College to offer a bachelor's degree in education in addition to its normal diploma. The other normals soon followed. In 1931, the legislature renamed the remaining normal schools as state teachers colleges.

Barbara J. Howe
West Virginia University

Charles H. Ambler, *A History of Education in West Virginia From Early Colonial Times to 1949*, 1951; Otis K. Rice, "West Virginia Educational Historiography: Status and Needs," in Ronald L. Lewis and John C. Hennen Jr., eds., *West Virginia History: Critical Essays on the Literature*, 1993.

John C. Norman

Physician John Clavon Norman Jr., a noted thoracic and cardiovascular surgeon and researcher, was born in Charleston, May 11, 1930. His mother, Ruth Stephenson Norman, was a teacher, and father John Clavon Norman Sr., an architect and structural engineer, was West Virginia's second licensed African-American architect.

John Norman Jr. was the valedictorian of the graduating class of Garnet High School in 1946 and enrolled in Howard University. Transferring to Harvard, he graduated in 1950. In 1954, Norman received an M.D. from Harvard Medical School. After an internship and residency in New York, he served aboard the aircraft carrier *Saratoga* in 1957–58 before completing his surgical training at the University of Michigan.

Norman was an assistant professor of surgery at Harvard and joined the surgical team at Boston City Hospital in 1964. He became involved in medical research projects concerning organ transplants, in 1967 successfully transplanting the spleen of a healthy dog into a hemophiliac dog.

While in Boston, Norman began research into a left ventricular assist device, a battery-operated pump for cardiac patients. His efforts took him to the Texas Heart Institute in 1972. For the next several years, he worked on the development of the first abdominal left ventricular assist device, which could be transplanted temporarily in patients who suffered cardiac failure after open-heart surgery. Norman also researched potential power sources and materials for artificial hearts. He later worked as a surgeon at Newark Beth Israel Medical Center before returning to West Virginia in July 1986 to become chairman of the surgery department at the Marshall University School of Medicine. He served in that capacity until August 1989.

John C. Norman is the author of more than 500 scientific papers and eight books. He was named the Charleston *Sunday Gazette-Mail* West Virginian of the Year in 1971, and in 1985 he received the Congressional High Technology Award. He now lives in Cambridge, Massachusetts.

Judie Smith
West Virginia Humanities Council

Delf Norona

Amateur archeologist Delf Norona was born in Hong Kong, April 14, 1895, and died in Moundsville, April 12, 1974. Norona spent the majority of his early life in the Philippine Islands. A British subject, he emigrated to Canada as a young man and then moved to the United States, where he served in the U.S. Army during World War I. After leaving the service, Norona taught himself shorthand and served as a court reporter. In 1930, he moved to West Virginia.

Norona's greatest contribution was his intense interest in the Grave Creek Mound, archeology, and history. In 1949, he and others formed the West Virginia Archeological Society, and he served as an officer for many years. Instrumental in the development and construction of the Mound Museum in 1952, Norona served as its curator until the day of his death. In 1965, Norona became the first recipient of the Sigfus Olafson Award for his outstanding contributions to West Virginia archeology. He wrote numerous articles for *West Virginia History* and *West Virginia Archeologist*. He also served as the president of the West Virginia Historical Society and as secretary of the American Philatelic Society. The modern museum at the Grave Creek Mound was named the Delf Norona Museum in his honor.

See also Archeology, Grave Creek Mound

Patrick D. Trader
University of Kentucky

North Bend State Park

In 1951, the West Virginia legislature allotted $125,000 to buy land for North Bend State Park, located near Cairo in Ritchie County. Bonds Creek and the north branch of the Hughes River pass through the 2,005-acre park, which has tennis courts, miniature golf, picnic areas, a playground, and an outdoor theater. North Bend has many trails, including an interpretive trail with annual events especially for the handicapped.

North Bend is located in West Virginia's historic oil and gas fields, and about 50 wells dating from the 19th century were once active in the present park area. Visitors may still see a few of these old wells. The park area also included more than two miles of the Harrisville Southern Railroad. The North Bend superintendent's residence, built in 1866 by Christopher Douglas, is a white, Federal-style house situated down the hill from the park lodge. Andrew S. Core, a Union general in the Civil War, had a home at the site of the lodge.

North Bend State Park has several campgrounds, cabins, and a hilltop lodge for overnight guests. The lodge offers a gift shop, meeting room, and a restaurant with glass windows on three sides so diners can watch sunrises, sunsets, and deer. In 2001, the park added a 305-acre lake with 62 deluxe campsites. Since 1968, North Bend has been the site of the annual Nature Wonder Weekend, which involved nature foods promoter Euell Gibbons in its early years. Wild-food enthusiasts from across the nation gather for this weekend each September.

See also State Parks

Maureen F. Crockett
St. Albans

The North Branch

The North Branch of the Potomac River is one of two branches of the Potomac and usually thought of as the river's main stem. The historic spring at the Fairfax Stone is considered the head of the North Branch and of the Potomac itself, marking in colonial times the western extent of Lord Fairfax's lands. From the Fairfax Stone the North Branch flows to Green Spring, Hampshire County, where it joins the South Branch to become the Potomac proper. Throughout its length, the North Branch forms the boundary between West Virginia and Maryland.

The tributaries of the North Branch include the Stony River and Patterson Creek, in West Virginia, and Wills and Georges creeks and the Savage River, in Maryland. Cumberland, Maryland, is the largest city on the North Branch. Other communities include Keyser, the county seat of Mineral County, and Ridgeley, Wiley Ford, Piedmont, Gormania, and Bayard, West Virginia, and several towns on the Maryland side. The North Branch is dammed upstream from Piedmont, forming the Jennings Randolph Lake.

The Potomac headwaters form the western boundary of the Atlantic slope, interlacing in the high Alleghenies with the headwaters of the Ohio to define the eastern continental divide. This is historic country, representing for many years the limits of colonial American settlement. The frontier wars were fought in the North

Branch Valley and neighboring regions for much of the 18th century, with young George Washington in charge of Virginia's defense during the critical French and Indian War period. Washington had forts built at Fort Ashby, on Patterson Creek in Mineral County, and elsewhere in the North Branch watershed.

The Potomac Valley forms a natural transportation corridor, used heavily from early times to the 20th century. The Chesapeake & Ohio Canal, now a national park paralleling the river, was built as far west as Cumberland in 1850. The coming of the Baltimore & Ohio Railroad in the 1830s and 1840s further transformed the region. The B&O largely follows the Potomac and the North Branch from Harpers Ferry to Piedmont, and its completion opened rich coal and timber lands to development. West Virginian Henry Gassaway Davis, U.S. senator and major industrialist and once a resident of Piedmont, was among those to exploit the region.

Unlike the pastoral South Branch Valley, the North Branch for much of its history has made its living largely by industry and by natural resource extraction. Coal has been mined in the North Branch region from the 19th century to the present, and there are industrial sites at Piedmont, West Virginia-Luke, Maryland, and at many other points in the watershed. Pollution has been an issue, and steps were taken in the last half of the 20th century to rectify the problem. Millions of people in metropolitan Washington and other downstream areas depend on the water of the Potomac watershed.

All of Mineral County is drained by the North Branch and its tributaries, as are most of Grant and parts of Tucker and Hampshire counties. Much of western Maryland lies within the watershed, as well. The North Branch flows 75.8 miles from its head to its mouth, and is the major geographic feature tying together a diverse bi-state region.

See also Jennings Randolph Lake and Dam, Potomac River

Ken Sullivan
West Virginia Humanities Council

North Fork Mountain

A linear ridge running northeast to southwest in Grant and Pendleton counties, North Fork Mountain extends 34 miles from North Fork Gap to Snowy Mountain (Dry Run) Gap. The mountain runs parallel to the North Fork of the South Branch. It represents the southeast limb of the Wills Mountain Anticline, a large geologic structure that extends northward into central Pennsylvania. At North Fork Mountain southeast-dipping, Silurian-age Tuscarora sandstone forms prominent northwest-facing cliffs, some more than 100 feet high, along the mountain

crest. These cliffs offer some of the most spectacular scenery in West Virginia. Elevations increase southward, from about 3,120 feet at Chimney Top to about 4,500 feet at Kile and Panther knobs, near the Virginia border south of Circleville. The appearance of this mountain from the west, visible along its entire length from nearby State Route 28, is perhaps the most distinctive of any in the state. The North Fork Mountain Trail extends 24 miles northward from U.S. 33, offering majestic vistas of Germany Valley and North Fork Valley and the Allegheny Front. There are 360-degree views from Chimney Top.

By purchase and conservation easements, the Nature Conservancy has protected several thousand acres on the mountain's southern reaches. Several preserves harbor rare plant and animal communities. Pike Knob (4,280 feet elevation) features grass balds and a virgin red pine forest, this species' southernmost natural occurrence. On Panther Knob are a rare dwarf pitch pine woodland and a virgin red spruce forest. Many globally rare plants are present in these unique habitats, cold and dry, which result from high elevations, windswept sandstone cliffs, and the area's location in a "rain shadow" of low annual precipitation.

John Craft Taylor
Union College

J. Lawrence Smith, *The Potomac Naturalist: The Natural History of the Headwaters of the Historic Potomac*, 1968; Paul Trianosky, "Saving North Fork Mountain," *Wonderful West Virginia*, September 1997.

North House Museum

The North House Museum in Lewisburg features the Greenbrier Historical Society's collections, which represent the period from the Revolutionary War through World War II. The collections include Civil War artifacts and documents, an 18th-century Conestoga wagon, the first rural free delivery postal buggy, and the pack saddle used to break Robert E. Lee's horse, Traveller. The rooms showcase examples of early Virginia furnishings.

The brick house with ornate wood work was built in 1820 by court clerk John A. North. In 1830, North sold the house to James Frazier, who converted it into the Star Tavern. Later, the house once again served as a residence, the home for presidents of Greenbrier College for Women.

The museum was founded in 1938 when the city of Lewisburg created the Greenbrier County Museum Committee. The Greenbrier Historical Society, begun in 1859, disbanded during the Civil War and re-formed in 1963, later assumed the responsibility for the museum. The society moved the museum from the second floor of the city library to North House in 1976. The North House Mu-

North House Museum in Lewisburg.

seum is open daily except Sunday, and the society's archives and library are open for research on selected days. Documents relating to the history of the Greenbrier Valley include books, serial publications, manuscripts, maps, genealogical records, and pictures.

See also Lewisburg

Belinda Anderson
Asbury

North River

The North River begins on the forested slopes of South Branch Mountain in Hardy County. From there, it flows northeast for 47 miles through a sparsely settled countryside of forested hills and mostly agricultural bottomlands to its confluence with the Cacapon River at Forks of Cacapon. The North River is the Cacapon's largest tributary, with a drainage area of 204.71 square miles and 16 named tributaries of its own.

The North River flows past an old tannery in Rock Oak, then through a gap in Short Mountain into Hampshire County and the small town of Rio. The North then runs through a broad agricultural valley past the small communities of Delray and Hanging Rock, past historic North River Mills and Ice Mountain before entering the Cacapon River.

In colonial times, the Great Wagon Road crossed the North River at North River Mills, located between Sandy Ridge and Grape Ridge, on its way west from Winchester, Virginia. The area's fertile bottomlands, in addition to the system of land grants by Lord Fairfax, encouraged settlement, and place names remind us today of this region's colonial history. For example, George Washington's personal physician, Dr. James Craik, took advantage of the Lord Fairfax land grants and speculated on land in the North River Mills area; local residents use water from Craik's Spring to this day.

Like others in West Virginia, the people who settled the North River watershed made use of the natural resources they found. Tanneries in the headwaters community of Rock Oak prepared hides using tannins extracted from oaks and other local vegetation. Lime kilns, such as the one on Hiett's Run once operated by Perry Gess, converted the limestone found in parts of this watershed to lime for use in agriculture and construction. And the water itself drove mills, like two of the three mills that gave the once bustling community of North River Mills its name.

Neil Gillies
Cacapon Institute

The North-South Game

Every August, the finest football players from West Virginia's northern high schools (including those in the Eastern Panhandle) come to Charleston to compete with their counterparts from southern high schools in the North-South Game. Each squad of 33 players includes many who go on to successful college sports careers, and some who make it to the National Football League. Among game alumni who have played in the professional ranks are Mike Barber and Walter Easley (both San Francisco 49ers), Rich Braham (Cincinnati Bengals), Carl Lee (Minnesota Vikings), Curt Warner (Seattle Seahawks), and Robert Alexander (Los Angeles Rams).

The first North-South Game attracted only a small crowd on New Year's Day, 1934, and ended in a scoreless tie. *Charleston Gazette* sports writer Frank Knight, who during the classic's 1940s and 1950s heyday was its biggest booster, called that first game "one of the greatest defensive combats in the history of scholastic sports in West Virginia." After the games were rescheduled for summer, under the lights at Charleston's Laidley Field, attendance soared.

Through 2004 the overall series stands at 31 wins for the South and 17 wins for the North, with three ties. The game was suspended from 1956 through 1975 due to an NCAA ruling on summer all-star contests. Recent games have not been so well attended because of competing TV sport shows and other summer events, but West Virginia towns still have their high school football heroes, and the annual North-South classic remains a traditional and exciting showcase for them.

Since 1983, a North-South boys basketball game has been played each year in the Kanawha Valley, except 1993, when the game was played in Paden City. As of 2004, South dominated the series, 19-3.

Louis E. Keefer
Reston, Virginia

Northern Panhandle

The Northern Panhandle began to take shape in 1779 when Pennsylvania and Virginia agreed that their boundary would be the Mason-Dixon Line extended due west five degrees, and then straight north to the Ohio River. In 1784 Virginia ceded all its territory north and west of the Ohio to the United States, making the river Virginia's western boundary. Virginia retained control of the 585 square miles between the borders of Pennsylvania and the Ohio River. This long sliver of territory, extending 64 miles to an apex at Chester, became the northernmost part of West Virginia when our state was created in 1863. Near New Cumberland and Follansbee, the panhandle is only four miles wide.

The panhandle is a part of the Allegheny Plateau and slopes westward from a maximum elevation of about 1,400 feet down to the Ohio River. At Chester the river is about 660 feet above sea level, and about 620 feet at New Martinsville near the base of the panhandle. The plateau is drained to the Ohio by creeks that include Grave, Wheeling, Kings, Harmon, Buffalo, Fish, and Cross. The Ohio River and its flood plain are the most conspicuous physical features. Other interesting physical features include the Narrows, McColloch's Leap, and the river islands. The climate of the Northern Panhandle is humid, with cold winters and warm summers.

Before railroads the Ohio River was the major transportation artery. Flatboats, keelboats, and steamboats were built and launched along the river, especially at Wheeling. Ohio River navigation remains important and is maintained by a system of modern locks and dams, of which two are located at New Cumberland and Pike Island.

Humans were living in the Northern Panhandle region as early as 7000 B.C. and probably earlier. Grave Creek Mound at Moundsville, the largest of its kind in the country, is the panhandle's most important prehistoric feature. The mound was built in the Adena period, probably between 400 and 200 B.C. By the time of white colonization, the Indians who had followed their mound-building ancestors were sparse and mainly members of the Delaware tribe.

By 1769, the frontier had reached the upper Ohio. The Wetzels settled in present Marshall County, and the Zane brothers arrived at Wheeling. During the American Revolution, Fort Henry, near the mouth of Wheeling Creek at present Wheeling, withstood a two-day siege by 300 British and Indians in 1782. Eight decades later, much of the leadership in establishing the state of West Virginia came from the Northern Panhandle. Wheeling was the state capital from 1863 to 1870, and from 1875 to 1885.

The early settlers derived their livelihood from agriculture, but industry was the region's future. An abundant resource base included coal, iron ore, petroleum and natural gas, timber, clay, and glass sand, while the National Road, Ohio River, and the later railroad provided transportation.

The Northern Panhandle is an urban-industrial region important in the production of glass, pottery, iron and steel, chemicals, petroleum and natural gas, and coal. According to the 2000 census, 141,060 people live in the panhandle, at a regional density of 241 people per square mile, more than three times the state average. Forty-five percent of the panhandle's residents live in Wheeling, Weirton, and Moundsville.

Chester and Newell began as pottery towns using clay dug from nearby hills. New Cumberland, the county seat of Hancock County, was famous for brickyards and pottery works. The first iron furnace west of the Alleghenies was located at a site on Kings Creek in 1794, and in 1909 Weirton was founded when the Weirton Steel company began production at the site on the Ohio River. For two decades after 1984 Weirton Steel was the largest employee-owned steel firm in the United States.

Wellsburg, settled in 1772, is the county

An Oglebay Park golf course nestles into the rolling hills of the Northern Panhandle.

seat of Brooke County and was the site of the first glass plant (1814) in present West Virginia. The city continues to make hand-crafted glass. Bethany College at Bethany is the oldest degree-granting college in the state. Follansbee and Beech Bottom were steel towns on the Ohio River.

Wheeling, the county seat of Ohio County, is the regional hub and premier manufacturing city. Flour milling, tobacco, iron and steel, boat building, pottery and glass, and chemicals have been important in the economy of Wheeling. Other Ohio County towns include Bethlehem, Triadelphia, Clearview, and Valley Grove, as well as West Liberty, which is the location of West Liberty State College, chartered as a private academy in 1837.

Moundsville, named after the prehistoric burial mound at the mouth of Grave Creek, is the county seat of Marshall and site of the state prison from 1866 to 1995. Other Marshall County towns include Benwood, Cameron, Glen Dale, and McMechen.

In recent years the Northern Panhandle has become an attractive tourist region. The attractions include Oglebay Park, Palace of Gold, Winter Festival of Lights, Wheeling Suspension Bridge, the Grave Creek Mound, West Virginia Independence Hall, Wheeling Downs, Mountaineer Race Track, and glass making.

Howard G. Adkins
Ona

Northfork Basketball

Northfork High School, located deep within the southern coalfields in McDowell County, attracted national attention when its basketball team won a record-setting eight consecutive state championships. From 1974 through 1981, the Blue Demons marched through 47 Class AA tournament games without a single defeat.

Two events from the summer of 1966 marked the turning point in Northfork's basketball fortunes: Racial segregation ended in eastern McDowell County when Northfork-Elkhorn High absorbed historically black Elkhorn High, and Jennings Boyd was appointed head basketball coach at the integrated school, which shortened its name to Northfork High. Boyd, who coached Northfork to nine of its 10 state titles, compiled an incredible won-lost record of 90.9 percent in 15 years of tournament play. Boyd attributed Northfork's success to being "blessed with talent" and having "total cooperation and support" from both racial communities. Northfork High School was absorbed into Mount View High School in 1985.

See also Jennings Boyd

Tim L. Wyatt
Woodbridge, Virginia

Northwestern Virginia Railroad

As the Baltimore & Ohio Railroad was being completed to Wheeling, Parkersburg supporters continued to push for a connection to their city. In 1851, the Virginia legislature approved the charter for a railroad to run from the B&O main line near the mouth of Three Forks Creek in Taylor County to Parkersburg. This junction point generated the new town of Grafton. To protect the original main line the charter specified that the new line, the Northwestern Virginia Railroad, was not to be operated until one year after the completion of the original line to Wheeling.

The Northwestern Virginia Railroad was financed almost entirely by B&O interests. The B&O itself contributed at least $1 million, and the city of Baltimore added another $1.5 million. About $500,000 of stock was sold, primarily to citizens in northwestern Virginia. Benjamin Latrobe, a well-known early railroad civil engineer, was made chief engineer for the new railroad and quickly completed a survey of the route. Thomas Swann, who had retired as president of the B&O, returned from a European vacation and became president of the new line. Although the 104-mile route was less rugged than the original main line to Wheeling, construction was not rapid. The Northwestern Virginia Railroad did not begin operation until May 1, 1857.

In December 1856, the B&O leased the Northwestern Virginia Railroad for five years. Efforts by the State of Virginia to purchase control of the Northwestern Virginia were forestalled when the B&O purchased most of the bonds of the new railroad before Virginia could act. Many leaders in northwestern Virginia saw their economic future tied more clearly to Baltimore than to Richmond and Norfolk, later a factor in the creation of West Virginia.

Construction costs of the Northwestern Virginia Railroad were higher than anticipated, and the railroad was a financial disappointment until the Civil War. Since the line was a key link to Cincinnati and St. Louis, however, the B&O reorganized the Northwestern by assuming the first mortgage from the City of Baltimore and by rebuilding the railroad. As part of this reorganization the B&O absorbed the Northwestern Virginia Railroad, and after January 1, 1865 it became known as the Parkersburg Branch.

Robert L. Frey
Miamisburg, Ohio

Northwestern Virginia Turnpike

The Northwestern Virginia Turnpike was chartered by the General Assembly of Virginia in 1827, to connect Winchester to Parkersburg. Later known as U.S. 50, it soon became the most important east-west road in the state. Planned as the major rival to the National Road, this route linked a significant portion of northwestern Virginia to Baltimore, via Winchester, rather than to Richmond and the Tidewater, contributing to Western Virginia's Unionist tendencies in the Civil War. The Northwestern Turnpike, which ran generally parallel to the later Baltimore & Ohio and the Northwestern Virginia railroads, declined in importance from the mid-1850s.

From the beginning, the Northwestern Turnpike and the Staunton-Parkersburg Turnpike were rivals in a race to the Ohio River. Winchester and Staunton both pressured the General Assembly for favorable treatment of "their" routes. But the Northwestern Turnpike was better organized in that it was placed at the outset under control of a state board of directors including the governor. The last section was finished to Parkersburg in 1838, and all bridges were completed by 1840, a decade before the Staunton road was in continuous operation.

Col. Claudius Crozet, Virginia's chief engineer, surveyed the route from Winchester through Hampshire County by way of Capon Bridge to Romney and across the South Branch in Mineral County to Patterson's Creek. Then he proposed that the road cross eight miles of Maryland and reenter Virginia at Aurora in Preston County. Though he was criticized in Virginia for a plan that would traverse another state, Crozet maintained the viability of the survey, insisting that it would allow for a branch connecting to the National Road, perhaps diverting some traffic to Winchester. From Aurora, the turnpike crossed the Cheat River, then passed through Rowlesburg, Grafton, Pruntytown, and Bridgeport to Clarksburg on the West Fork River.

Crozet's successor, Charles B. Shaw, favored Parkersburg over Sistersville as the terminus on the Ohio River, since it was in a direct line to Cincinnati. Under his direction, the route continued from Clarksburg to Salem, West Union, Pennsboro, Ellenboro, and Murphytown to Parkersburg, completing the last mileage in 1838. As was the case with all the early turnpikes, the directors and engineers faced continuing problems with labor shortages, contractor incompetence, and right-of-way problems. Since the project was financed by the state, lack of funding was not a major drawback, as it was with the Staunton-Parkersburg Turnpike.

The Northwestern Turnpike, passing as it did through the more populous counties of Western Virginia, was immediately successful. Toll collections were adequate, and profits permitted the early macadamizing of much of the route. As early as 1841, Nathaniel Kuykendall, former superintendent of the eastern section, operated a stagecoach and mail delivery service. Nonetheless, problems typical of 19th-century roads plagued the turnpike. For example, the damage caused by rains and spring flooding required constant repair. In spite of increasing competition from the railroad, the turnpike operated at a small profit and was able to meet its financial obligations throughout the 1850s. The Civil War was unkind to the Northwestern Turnpike. The new state of West Virginia was slow to assume responsibility, and by the end of the war the road was nearly impassible. Inadequately maintained in the late 19th century, it finally became part of the U.S. highway system in the 20th century.

See also Claudius Crozet, Highway Development

Philip Sturm
Ohio Valley University

Norwalk Motor Car

The Norwalk motor car, made in Martinsburg from 1912 to 1922, was West Virginia's most successful attempt at automobile manufacturing. The car was named for Norwalk, Ohio, where production had begun in 1910. After financial difficulties in Ohio the operation was moved to Matinsburg, where local investors were recruited.

The flagship vehicle of the Norwalk Motor Car Company was the Norwalk Underslung Six, a huge car by modern standards. It featured a 500-cubic-inch, in-line six-cylinder, 8.6 liter engine; by comparison, a 350-cubic-inch, 5.7 liter V8 is considered a large engine early in the 21st century. The wheelbase of the Underslung Six was 136 inches, more than 20 inches longer than a full-sized 2004 Cadillac, and the big wheels stood 40 inches tall. The car, a convertible, came in different versions, including two-passenger and three-passenger roadsters and a six-passenger touring car. The touring car sold for $3,100, several times the price of a Ford Model T.

Financial difficulties continued to trouble the company, and few of the big Underslungs were built after 1915. Norwalk instead manufactured smaller four-cylinder cars as well as trucks. Two Norwalk fire trucks were put into use by Martinsburg firefighters. The company closed in 1922. The big factory, later used by Interwoven Mills, burned in 1989.

There were several other attempts to manufacture automobiles in West Virginia in the early 20th century, including the Remington of Charleston, the Jarvis-Huntington and the Enslow of Huntington, and others. None lasted as long or produced as many cars as the Norwalk Motor Car Company. Late in the century West Virginia developed a thriving business in the manufacture of auto parts and components, including the Toyota engine and transmission plant in Putnam County, NGK Sparkplugs of Kanawha County, a major stamping plant in South Charleston, and other operations. No automobiles have been assembled here in recent decades.

Daniel J. Friend, "The Norwalk: Martinsburg's Motor Car," *Goldenseal*, Summer 2003; Joseph Platania, "The Elusive Jarvis-Huntington: Early Automobiles of West Virginia, *Goldenseal*, Fall 1999.

John Nugent

John Nugent was born in Wales in 1862 of American parents and was educated in Perry County, Ohio, public schools. He came to West Virginia as a United Mine Workers of America organizer in 1902. He was elected president of UMWA District 17 in 1904 and, in 1905, as president of the state Federation of Labor, holding both offices simultaneously for two years. He was elected in 1907 for one term to the House of Delegates from Kanawha County.

While serving in the legislature, Nugent accepted the post of immigration commissioner for the state of West Virginia, a semi-public position created to attract foreign labor and financed by coal companies. Nugent resigned as president of District 17 and was forced out as president of the state Federation of Labor shortly after becoming immigration commissioner. In 1913, he was questioned by the U.S. Senate investigating committee about his alleged efforts to import strikebreakers to West Virginia during the Paint Creek-Cabin Creek Strike. Nugent left West Virginia in 1913 for Kentucky, where he became an official with the Consolidation Coal Company. He died in Letcher County, Kentucky, December 7, 1926.

See also Immigration Commissioner, Paint Creek-Cabin Creek Strike

Kenneth R. Bailey
WVU Institute of Technology

Evelyn K. Harris and Frank J. Krebs, *From Humble Beginnings, the West Virginia State Federation of Labor, 1903–1957*, 1960.

Lawrence William Nuttall

Amateur botanist Lawrence William Nuttall collected plant specimens, including fungi, during the late 1800s and early 1900s. He was born near Philipsburg, Pennsylvania, September 17, 1857. In 1878, after attending the Perryville (Pennsylvania) Academy, he moved to Nuttallburg in the New River Gorge in Fayette County to join his father, the pioneer coal operator John Nuttall. When he wasn't working he studied plants, and in just seven years collected about 1,000 species of flowering plants, many of which were named after him, and hundreds of fungi. At least 108 of the fungi species were new to science.

Many of Nuttall's specimens were sent to various authorities for identification, one of whom was botanist C. F. Millspaugh of West Virginia University. After collaborating for several years, they jointly published *Flora of West Virginia* in 1896, not to be confused with the later book by the same name. In succeeding years, Nuttall continued collecting in West Virginia and other areas of the nation, contributing to publications including *Flora of the Southeastern States, North American Uredinales,* and *Flora of Santa Catalina Island.*

In 1927, just before moving to San Diego, Nuttall donated his plant collection to the WVU Herbarium. This collection included thousands of seed plants and fern specimens, but was particularly valuable for the more than 1,400 species of fungi, most of which were first described from Fayette County.

Nuttall died in San Diego, October 16, 1933. In 1953, a trail in the WVU Arboretum was named in his honor.

See also Botany, C. F. Millspaugh, Nuttallburg

Kathleen Carothers Leo
Division of Natural Resources

Nuttallburg

Nuttallburg, a once-thriving New River Gorge coal town, was located at the mouth of Short Creek on the river's north side. Founder John Nuttall, born in England, traveled to America, established anthracite mines in Pennsylvania, and later pioneered the southern West Virginia coal industry. He bought coal lands on New River beginning in 1870 for $2 to $8 per acre. Nuttall worked hard to have his Nuttallburg Coal & Coke Company ready to ship coal when the C&O Railway was completed through the New River Gorge in 1873.

Nuttallburg's population peaked in the 1920s at 500 residents, served by two schools, two churches, a powerhouse, store, clubhouse or hotel, and public water system. John Nuttall built several rows of coke ovens to produce coke for steel manufacturers. His oldest son, Lawrence W. Nuttall, secretary-treasurer of the company, was an accomplished botanist.

John Nuttall expanded his land holdings and late in his life built a seven-mile railroad up the steep canyon to open additional mines on the Keeney's Creek headwaters. He died in Fayette County in 1897. By 1919, the Nuttallburg mine was sold to Henry Ford, the automobile millionaire. Ford mechanized the operation and built the world's largest incline tipple in 1923. Nuttallburg was a mined-out ghost town by the early 1960s.

Today, Nuttallburg's ruins provide a picturesque setting for the massive sandstone cliffs of Beauty Mountain called the "Endless Wall" by rock climbers. The turbulent whitewater below carries thousands of rafters annually past John Nuttall's old company town.

William N. Grafton
WVU Extension Service

Eldora Marie Bolyard Nuzum

Journalist Eldora Marie Bolyard Nuzum, born in Grafton, May 10, 1926, was the first female editor of a daily newspaper in West Virginia. She began her career as a young staff writer at the *Grafton Sentinel* and was made managing editor in 1946. She joined the *Elkins Inter-Mountain* in 1953, beginning a long association with the powerful Ogden newspaper chain. While at the *Grafton Sentinel*, she founded the weekly *Preston Independent* and was involved in reviving the *Mannington Times*.

Nuzum was named president of the Association of Newspaper Editors of West Virginia in 1967. She was invited to the White House three times and interviewed Harry S. Truman on a whistle-stop train tour through Grafton. In 1974, the Elkins newspaper building burned to the ground, but Nuzum and her staff never missed an issue. She retired from the *Inter-Mountain* in 1992 after 32 years as its editor.

Eldora Bolyard Nuzum was the wife of Jack Robert Nuzum, a Randolph County circuit judge who also represented Taylor and Randolph counties in the House of Delegates. She lived her last years as editor emeritus of the *Inter-Mountain,* dying at her Elkins home August 20, 2004.

Cassandra Bolyard Whyte
Charleston
Jennifer Whyte Onks
Charleston

Nylon

Nylon, invented in 1935 in a DuPont laboratory in Delaware, was brought into commercial production through intermediate materials supplied by the company's Kanawha Valley plant. Nylon was the first of a new family of wholly synthetic textile fibers, and although the name describes a generic class of polymers it has also become a synonym for ladies' stockings, its first commercial application. Today, a tenth of the world's textile and carpet fibers are made from nylon. It is also widely used as an engineering plastic in automobiles, machinery, and appliances.

The "nylon 66" polymer, so-called because each of the two reacting chemicals, hexamethylene diamine and adipic acid,

These hyper compressors were used in the making of nylon chemicals.

has six carbon atoms, was patented in September 1938. By that time, work had already begun on producing the necessary chemicals in commercial quantities at the DuPont Belle Works, near Charleston. The Belle Works had benzene and hydrogen, the two starting chemicals required to make the nylon 66 intermediates, both products of the coke-making process. The coke was produced at the Belle site from West Virginia coal. From 1937 until 1939, four pilot plants were built at Belle to develop the technology for producing hexamethylene diamine and adipic acid starting with benzene and hydrogen.

The diamine and the adipic acid were combined to form the raw polymer called "nylon salt." The nylon salt was shipped to the Seaford, Delaware, DuPont plant where it was forced through a die plate containing very small holes to form nylon fibers. The fibers were then sent to textile mills to be woven into products such as hosiery, parachutes, and rope.

The first nylon fiber was produced at Seaford on December 15, 1939. By 1941, a second spinning plant had been built at Martinsville, Virginia. Most of the early production was used by the government during World War II for materials critical to the war effort, such as parachutes (where it replaced silk) and cord for B-29 bomber tires. However in 1940, DuPont put four million pairs of stockings on sale nationally. The "nylons" sold out in four days.

From 1937 until 1946, every pair of nylon stockings, every nylon parachute in World War II, and every nylon-bristle brush came from Belle Works nylon salt, made from West Virginia air, water, and coal. Nylon salt continued to be produced at the Belle Works until 1968, although many other plants were built around the world after 1946 to meet the growing demand.

Charles J. Denham
E. I. DuPont Company

Charles J. Denham, ed., *Sentimental Journey: The DuPont Belle Works—A 75 Year History 1926–2001,* 2001; John F. McAllister, *The First Nylon Plant,* 1995.

Oak Hill

Oak Hill is located on the plateau south of New River in Fayette County, elevation 1,961 feet. Settlement in the area began as early as 1820, and population grew rapidly after the building of the Giles, Fayette & Kanawha Turnpike by 1848. The turnpike served as the main street of Oak Hill, which is now located on modern U.S. 19 (Appalachian Corridor L).

Surrounded by the best farmland in the county, Oak Hill developed as a trading center for local farmers before the coming of the railroad. Then the construction of the White Oak branch of the Chesapeake & Ohio Railway, the completion of the Virginian Railway, and the mining boom in nearby Minden, Scarbro, and Whipple transformed Oak Hill into an important banking and regional trading center. Incorporated in 1903, the town's population accelerated in the early 20th century, fluctuated with the coal industry's boom and bust cycles, and stabilized in the 1990s near 7,000 citizens with the building of new highways and the growth of tourism.

Oak Hill emerged as the leading urban center in Fayette County under the guidance of distinguished leaders such as businessman, banker, and coal operator Charles T. Jones, who with Albert G. Sevy advanced public education by establishing the town's first high school in 1902. In that year, James M. Ellis of Oak Hill became the second African-American elected to the West Virginia legislature. Now Oak Hill is the biggest town in Fayette County with a population of 7,589 in 2000, and a communications center, with a newspaper and radio and television stations.

See also Fayette County

Lou Athey
Franklin & Marshall College

Shirley Donnelly, *History of Oak Hill, West Virginia,* 1953; J. T. Peters and H. B. Carden, *History of Fayette County, West Virginia,* 1926.

Oak Hill Wrestling

The weekly wrestling show, *Saturday Night Wrestling,* was a live television program aired on WOAY-TV of Oak Hill, Fayette County. The show, popular through a wide region and remembered today as part of West Virginia's broadcasting folklore, lasted more than 20 years. It featured professional wrestlers and local talent in matches performed first in the station's studio and later in an arena adjacent to the television station. Hundreds of fans would fill the auditorium every Saturday night, and it was not unknown for spectators to jump into the ring. Wrestling bears were sometimes part of the program.

For 22 years, Oak Hill resident and WOAY announcer Shirley Love hosted the wrestling program. The show was first aired in 1954 and lasted until 1977. Wrestling fans traveled from Virginia, Kentucky, and Ohio to join West Virginians as spectators. Love, later a state senator, recalled that live interviews with the fans, broadcast between wrestling bouts, were among the show's most popular features.

World Professional Wrestling, an organization based in Logan that promotes the sport in West Virginia, Virginia, Ohio, and Kentucky, is an outgrowth of the Saturday night wrestling program.

Oak Park

Oak Park was an amusement park located along Deckers Creek in the Bretz community about one mile east of Masontown, Preston County. Oak Park was initially owned by the Elkins Coal & Coke Company, but ownership was later transferred to the Baltimore & Ohio Railroad and later to the Morgantown & Kingwood Railroad. The park was an easy train ride from Morgantown, and helped to fill up trains on weekends and holidays. Oak Park opened in 1908.

Oak Park's nearly 100 wooded acres offered day visitors a wide variety of recreational activities as well as food, with lodging for those who wished to stay overnight. Visitors from West Virginia as well as neighboring Pennsylvania and Maryland frequented the park throughout the summer months. Park attractions included a 65-foot wooden slide, two roller coasters, walking paths, picnic areas, a carousel, a Ferris wheel, a swimming hole, paddle boats, and carnival-style game stands. One of the main attractions was the baseball games played at the park between teams formed in surrounding towns and by mine companies.

The advent of the automobile, the steady decline of the rail and coal industries, and the onset of the Great Depression led to the park's eventual demise. In 1930, Oak Park closed its gates.

Brad Martin
Arthurdale

Peggy Ross, "Echoes of Things Past: Preston County's Oak Park," *Goldenseal,* Summer 1994; Charles A. Thomas, *Images of America: Preston County,* 1998.

Oakhurst Links

Oakhurst Links, near White Sulphur Springs, was the first organized golf club and course in America. It was founded in 1884 at Oakhurst, the estate of Russell Montague, who had moved from Boston to Greenbrier County in 1878. Montague was joined in founding the club by George Grant, a retired British army officer; Alexander and Roderick MacLeod from Scotland; and Lionel Torrin, who was the owner of a tea plantation in India, avid golfer, and regular summer visitor. Frazer Corron, a local carpenter, made golf clubs for the club members.

The nine-hole course was played for about 15 years by the club, but as members aged or moved, the course gradually fell into disuse. Nonetheless, Oakhurst helped to establish golf in America. It was the home of the first regularly played tournament in the U.S., with the 1888 Challenge Medal as trophy; Montague was the first winner. The original medal and one replica are now at Oakhurst, restored for play in 1994 by Lewis Keller Sr., who purchased the property from Cary Montague in 1959. Oakhurst Links is now a living museum course, open to the public. Visitors may play 1884-era golf with reproduction equipment.

Oakhurst estate was the home of writer Margaret Prescott Montague, the daughter of Russell Montague.

See also Margaret Prescott Montague

Martha J. Asbury
EcoTheater

Martha Asbury, "Oakhurst Links: A Romance with Golf," *Wonderful West Virginia,* January 1998; Tom Bedell, "Time Travel at Oakhurst Links," *Diversion,* March 2000.

Sylvia O'Brien

Banjo player Sylvia Cottrell O'Brien was born in Clay County, October 23, 1908, a descendent of the earliest white families in central West Virginia. She learned to play the banjo from her brother, Jenes Cottrell, when she was "just a tadpole," she recalled. She played in the old-time "clawhammer" style. Jenes, famous as a traditional craftsman and musician, overshadowed his sister during his lifetime.

Jenes and Sylvia lived together in a house built by them and their parents on Deadfall Mountain, near Big Otter, without electricity or running water. Sylvia continued this simple existence until her mid-80s, moving then to a nearby house trailer. "The Deadfall Mountains they are my home, where the wildcats holler and the wild deer roam," she proclaimed in a poem of her own writing. She recalled midnight suppers when musicians around Otter Creek and Ivydale got together for an evening of old-time music and home-cooked food.

Briefly married and soon widowed, O'Brien worked in a Baltimore boarding house during World War II. She returned home to West Virginia and became a regional celebrity during the folk culture revival beginning in the 1960s. In 1982, the British Broadcasting Corporation filmed O'Brien at her home. In 1989, she received the Vandalia Award, West Virginia's highest folklife honor. Her banjo repertoire included "Wildwood Flower," "John Brown's Body," and "Min-

Sylvia O'Brien (1908–2001) was a talented folk musician.

ner on a Hook." Sylvia O'Brien died in Clay County, December 26, 2001.

See also Jenes Cottrell

Susan A. Eacker
Morehead State University

Ken Sullivan, "'We Lived Good Back Then': Vandalia Award Winner Sylvia O'Brien," *Goldenseal*, Fall 1989.

Molly O'Day and Lynn Davis

Singer Molly O'Day was born Lois La Verne "Dixie Lee" Williamson in Pike County, Kentucky, July 9, 1923. Molly learned guitar and sang while brothers "Skeets" played fiddle and "Duke" played banjo. In 1939, when Skeets went to WCHS radio in Charleston, Dixie joined him briefly, then went to WBTH Williamson that fall. In the spring of 1940, they moved to WJLS Beckley. Relocating to WHIS Bluefield, she met the leader of the "Forty-Niners," Leonard "Lynn" Davis (1914–2000) and the two married in April 1941. They moved frequently during the next five years, with Dixie Lee adopting the name Molly O'Day while working at WHAS Louisville. Lynn and Molly performed duets, but Molly's solo numbers had the bigger impact, as she pioneered the position of solo female singer.

Country music pioneer Fred Rose signed Molly to a Columbia Records contract in 1946, wanting her to record Hank Williams compositions. Lynn and Molly had already learned "Tramp on the Street" from Williams, and Molly recorded that song and seven others in December 1946. During the next five years she cut 36 songs for Columbia including "Matthew Twenty-Four" and "Teardrops Falling in the Snow."

In early 1950, Molly and Lynn gave up show business to serve the Lord. They returned to Huntington just before their conversion, and were baptized in the Ohio River. Molly sang only in churches and Lynn became a minister. During the 1960s, they recorded albums for two record labels. In 1973, Molly and Lynn started a gospel record program at WEMM FM Huntington. Molly died December 5, 1987, and Lynn continued the show until his own death in 2000. He began each program with Molly's recording of "Living the Right Life Now."

Abby Gail Goodnite
University of Rio Grande

Abby Gail Goodnite and Ivan M. Tribe, "'Living the Right Life Now': Lynn Davis & Molly O'Day," *Goldenseal*, Spring 1998.

Herschel Coombs Ogden

Newspaperman Herschel Coombs Ogden, Wheeling newspaper publisher, civic leader, and philanthropist, was born January 12, 1869, near Fairmont in Marion County. In 1888, with a bachelor of arts degree from West Virginia University, he relocated to Wheeling and entered the newspaper business. Ogden founded the *Wheeling Daily News* in 1890, which in 1935 merged with the *Wheeling Register* to become the present *Wheeling News-Register*. He purchased the historic *Wheeling Intelligencer* in 1904 and began to build the largest and most influential newspaper chain in West Virginia, today's Ogden Newspapers, Inc.

Ogden was an influential citizen of Wheeling and West Virginia. He led the state's tax reform fight of 1932 and helped in the adoption of the Workmen's Compensation Act and the West Virginia Child Labor Law. H. C. Ogden encouraged Wheeling to establish its first public high school and a school for vocational education. He also led the movement to create Oglebay Park and Oglebay Institute.

H. C. Ogden married Mary Frances Moorehouse in 1890 and they had two daughters and five grandchildren. Grandson George Ogden Nutting now heads the family company, which owns newspapers in West Virginia and other states, as well as *Mother Earth News*, *Grit*, *Outdoor Times*, and other magazines. H. C. Ogden died March 31, 1943, and is buried at Greenwood Cemetery.

See also Wheeling Intelligencer

Margaret Brennan
Wheeling Area Historical Society

Ogden Newspapers

Ogden Newspapers is a media corporation that publishes 39 daily newspapers, several magazines, weekly newspapers, and shoppers. The company's headquarters is in Wheeling.

Herschel C. Ogden founded the *Wheeling Daily News* in 1890, which later merged with the *Wheeling Register* to become today's *Wheeling News-Register*. Ogden purchased the *Wheeling Intelligencer* in 1904 and began to build what has become the largest newspaper chain in West Virginia.

Ogden-owned newspapers in West Virginia, in addition to the *Intelligencer* and *Wheeling News-Register*, include the *Parkersburg News* and *Parkersburg Sentinel*, the *Journal* in Martinsburg, the *Inter-Mountain* in Elkins, the *Wetzel Chronicle*, the *Weirton Daily Times*, the *Tyler Star News* in Sistersville, and the *Shepherdstown Chronicle*. Additionally, Ogden owns newspapers in Florida, Hawaii, Iowa, Kansas, Michigan, Minnesota, North Dakota, New York, Ohio, and Pennsylvania. The company publishes several magazines, including *Mother Earth News* and *Grit*.

H. C. Ogden's grandson, G. Ogden Nutting, is the present publisher of Ogden Newspapers. He started his newspaper career in 1956 as a reporter and news editor for the *Martinsburg Journal*, which H. C. Ogden had bought in 1923. Robert Nutting is company president and chief executive officer.

See also Herschel Coombs Ogden

Earl Oglebay

Businessman Earl Williams Oglebay, was born March 4, 1849, in Bridgeport, Ohio, to a Wheeling businessman's family. He became one of West Virginia's most successful industrialists and a generous benefactor. At the age of 28, he became president of his father's bank, the National Bank of West Virginia, making him the youngest bank president in the nation. Business dealings led him to opportunities in iron ore speculation. In 1884, he started work as an associate in a Cleveland iron ore firm, and within six years, became a key partner. In 1890, John D. Rockefeller, Oglebay, and banker David Z. Norton formed a partnership, Oglebay Norton

Co., a Great Lakes ore shipping line. In 1901, Oglebay sold his iron ore interests to U.S. Steel.

In 1901, Oglebay bought a mid-19th-century mansion on a 25-acre ridgetop tract between Wheeling and Bethany which he began to restore as a summer home. Soon, Oglebay's Waddington Farm had grown to about 1,000 acres. Oglebay, concerned that West Virginia's farm economy was entering a decline, began a series of experiments to determine how best to raise alfalfa in the state's humid climate. He also assembled a demonstration herd of purebred Guernsey dairy cattle, and brought in experts in a variety of agricultural fields, including a poultry scientist from Cornell University, a dairyman from Wisconsin, a soil scientist from the Midwest, and a horse expert from England. He hired 75 workers to implement the recommendations of these experts and keep track of the results.

Oglebay set up the state's first agricultural education program at Waddington Farm. In recognition of his work, the College of Agriculture at West Virginia University named Oglebay Hall in his honor.

While Oglebay served on the state Board of Education for 15 years and was a generous contributor to his alma mater, Bethany College, his most enduring gift was the bequest of Waddington Farm to the city of Wheeling. Today known as Oglebay Park, it serves Wheeling and has become a vacation destination for millions of visitors from outside the region, with four golf courses, two pools, a lodge, and the Good Children's Zoo. Waddington Gardens, with its showy seasonal plantings, offers a glimpse of the park's earlier life as Waddington Farm, where Earl Oglebay oversaw the planting of 150,000 trees and shrubs.

Oglebay died June 22, 1926. His mansion is now a museum of late 19th-century life.

See also Oglebay Park

Rick Steelhammer
Charleston Gazette

Morris Purdy Shawkey, *West Virginia: In History, Life, Literature and Industry*, 1928.

Oglebay Park

Oglebay Park, near Wheeling in rural Ohio County, occupies land first claimed by Zachariah Sprigg in the late 1700s. When Sprigg died, the land was divided among his three daughters. One of his daughters married Wheeling doctor Hanson Chapline, and the Chaplines built the central portion of what is now Oglebay Park's Mansion Museum. The property was purchased by George W. Smith in 1856. Smith named the farm Waddington, after his family's ancestral English estate.

Waddington Farm was bought by Earl William Oglebay in 1901. A rich banker and industrialist who was fascinated by agriculture, Oglebay turned the place into an experimental farm and purchased about 1,000 additional acres surrounding the mansion and its original 25 acres. He willed Waddington Farm to the City of Wheeling upon his death, for use as a public park. In 1926, Wheeling accepted the $2 million farm and renamed it Oglebay Park.

Today, Oglebay Park, a 1,650-acre resort, is managed by the Wheeling Park Commission. It includes several golf courses, the Mansion Museum, a glass museum, many gardens, an amphitheater, Schenk Lake, Good Zoo, Schrader Environmental Education Center, and several guest cottages. Wilson Lodge has guest rooms and dining facilities and is a popular conference site.

Each winter, Oglebay Park hosts the Festival of Lights, a large holiday light display. The festival covers more than 300 acres on a six-mile drive through the park.

See also Earl Oglebay

Christina Myer
Wheeling

Ralph H. Weir, *The Story of Oglebay Park, Wheeling, West Virginia, and the History of Oglebay Institute and the Oglebay Family*, 1963.

Ohio Company

The Ohio Company was organized during the colonial period by a group of prominent Virginians, including Thomas Lee, Thomas Cresap, Augustine Washington, and George Fairfax. In 1747, the company petitioned the king for 500,000 acres to settle the frontier and for permission to trade with the Indians. The company was awarded 200,000 acres in Virginia's northwestern corner. These lands were in present West Virginia and southwestern Pennsylvania. If the Ohio Company was successful in settling 200 families within seven years and if a fort was built for protection of the settlers, it could secure an additional 300,000 acres adjacent to the original grant.

The Ohio Company immediately came into conflict with both hostile Indians and the claims of other land companies which had patents for at least some of the same land. The French had not given up claims to the Ohio Valley and used their influence with Indian tribes to keep up raids on frontier settlements and to interfere with trade, further complicating the Ohio Company's efforts to fulfill the terms of its contract. Nonetheless, the Ohio Company successfully maintained its existence through the French and Indian War and the American Revolution. However, conflicting claims from the Indiana and Vandalia companies, lengthy court battles, and the deaths of many of the company's principal supporters led to its demise by 1792.

Kenneth R. Bailey
WVU Institute of Technology

Kenneth P. Bailey, *The Ohio Company of Virginia and the Westward Movement*, 1939.

Ohio County

Ohio County, located in the Northern Panhandle, was created in 1776. It was one of the first counties in Virginia west of the Allegheny Mountains and, with Monongalia and Yohogania, one of the three counties formed from the District of West Augusta. Yohogania County was dissolved when the Virginia-Pennsylvania border dispute was settled in 1784, and thereafter Ohio County had all of the present Northern Panhandle and neighboring areas to the south. Other counties were later carved from its territory, including Brooke, Hancock, Marshall, Tyler, and Wetzel.

Once covering 1,432 square miles, today Ohio County covers 109 square miles. It is bordered by Brooke County to the north, Pennsylvania to the east, Marshall County to the south, and the Ohio River to the west. The river has long been crucial to the economy of the area. It is open year-round for navigation and provides transport for millions of tons of cargo through the Wheeling area.

Wheeling is by far the largest community (31,419) in Ohio County, followed by Bethlehem (2,651) and West Liberty (1,220). The county's 47,427 people are predominantly white, with black citizens comprising just three percent of the total and other minorities largely nonexistent. Nonetheless, Ohio County has a rich ethnic and religious diversity, the heritage of massive immigration in the late 19th and early 20th centuries.

The topography is generally hilly. Wheeling Creek, together with the smaller Short Creek and Little Wheeling Creek, all drain to the Ohio River. The Pittsburgh coal seam, which underlies Ohio County and a wide surrounding region, is the richest natural resource.

Ohio County was organized at a meeting of the landholders in December 1776, to elect the administrators and select a seat for the court. They chose Black's Cabin on Short Creek, the present site of West Liberty. One of the first orders of business was to lay out a road from Fort Henry (Wheeling) to present Elm Grove, six miles. Because of the unstable conditions brought on by the American Revolution and associated Indian warfare, the court did not meet from June 1777 until April 1778.

Early in the Revolutionary period Black's Cabin was renamed West Liberty to celebrate the love of liberty of those first pioneers. In 1779, a courthouse was completed at West Liberty. Construction was begun on a more substantial courthouse in 1796.

By this time Wheeling was growing as a transportation and commercial center and agitating for the relocation of the

The Ohio River sweeps past Wheeling in Ohio County.

county seat. Wheeling won out, and the court was moved to that city December 27, 1797. In June 1798, it was decided to erect a courthouse with a jail, stocks, and whipping post in the vicinity of present 10th Street. This small structure was used until a new building was authorized in 1836, to be constructed at the southeast corner of 12th and Chapline streets. This served as the courthouse until the former state capitol was acquired for use as a courthouse in 1885. The present seat of government is the City-County Building, dedicated in 1960 on the same site as the old state capitol.

The histories of Ohio County and Wheeling are closely interrelated. In 1749, the French expedition under Celoron de Blainville had landed at Wheeling Creek and claimed the site for their king, but the French and Indian War invalidated that claim. The first white men to settle in the area were the Zane brothers who visited the region in 1769 and brought their family and friends from the South Branch Valley of the Potomac River. Because of its strategic location, the community grew quickly. In 1774, the British constructed a fort at the site, Fort Fincastle, later changed to Fort Henry to honor Patrick Henry.

With peace restored in the 1780s, the county again flourished. In 1818 the National Road terminated at Wheeling; in 1849 the suspension bridge was completed over the Ohio; and in 1853 the Baltimore & Ohio Railroad reached the city. The grouping of railroad, national road, and river ensured Wheeling's growth and prosperity during the long Victorian era.

During the Civil War, Ohio County had divided loyalties. Some of the old families continued their allegiance to Virginia and sent their sons to the Confederate Army, while many others fought for the Union. In 1861, the loyal Reorganized Government of Virginia was founded at the Wheeling Custom House. While there was no fighting in the area, Camp Carlisle on Wheeling Island was a major army recruiting and training center from 1861 to 1865. Our state was born at the Custom House in Wheeling, later known as West Virginia Independence Hall, and in 1863 the first state capitol was located in the city.

Ohio County and especially Wheeling continued their industrial preeminence after the Civil War, manufacturing nails, calico, beer, and cigars, among other products. Coal mining expanded in the rural countryside. Steel established itself as the region's major industry at the turn of the 20th century, with Wheeling Steel (later Wheeling Pittsburgh Steel) founded in 1920.

Today, Ohio County is known for its outstanding public school system. The county is also home to a business college and a parochial school system, as well as Wheeling Country Day School and Mount de Chantal and Linsly schools. Four institutions of higher learning are located in the county: West Liberty State College, Bethany College, West Virginia Northern Community College, and Wheeling Jesuit University. The Ohio County Public Library has served its patrons since 1882.

Ohio County has two fine parks: Wheeling Park and Oglebay. The Oglebay winter Festival of Lights draws thousands to the area each year. The Oglebay Institute is the largest private arts organization in West Virginia and the oldest arts council in the nation. The Wheeling Symphony Orchestra is the oldest in the state.

Ohio County's industrial economy peaked in the first half of the 20th century. As in some other parts of West Virginia, the population declined in later decades, from a high of 73,115 in 1940 to 47,427 in the year 2000. Efforts have been made to diversify the local economy. Ohio County has acquired 471 acres called the Fort Henry Industrial and Business Centre. Cabela's, catering to the outdoor lifestyle, opened a huge store there in 2004 which attracts both customers and tourists. Plans are under way for future development.

Many important West Virginians have called Ohio County home, from baseball star Jesse Burkett to opera singer Eleanor Steber, writer Rebecca Harding Davis, and football player Chuck Howley.

Margaret Brennan
Wheeling Area Historical Society

Ohio River

The Ohio River begins at Pittsburgh, with the union of the Allegheny and Monongahela rivers. From there the Ohio travels 981 miles to Cairo, Illinois, where it joins the Mississippi. The Ohio drainage basin totals 204,000 square miles, including

FAST FACTS ABOUT OHIO COUNTY

Founded: 1776
Land in square miles: 109.0
Population: 47,427
Percentage minorities: 5.5%
Percentage rural: 20.3%
Median age: 40.6
Percentage 65 and older: 18.8%
Birth rate per 1,000 population: 10.1
Median household income: $30,836
High school graduate or higher: 83.0%
Bachelor's degree or higher: 23.1%
Home ownership: 68.6%
Median home value: $71,400

This information is from the 2000 U.S. Census. In 2000, West Virginia as a whole had 5 percent minorities, a median age of 38.9, median household income of $29,696, and a 75.2 percent home ownership rate.

most of West Virginia. For 277 miles the Ohio River forms the western border of our state.

Native Americans had a variety of names for the Ohio. The French called it La Belle Rivière, "the beautiful river." From the beginning of western expansion, the Ohio was a major route to the West, and it remains an important transportation corridor today. The Ohio Valley has much historical and archeological significance, having provided food, habitat, and transport for native people for 15,000 years before the arrival of settlers of European descent. As recently as 2,000 years ago, people of the Hopewell culture lived and traded in the Ohio watershed, and evidence of their complex society can be found in burial mounds throughout the area. When the French explorer La Salle traveled through the region in the late 1660s, it was home to tribes of Shawnee, Erie, Omaha, Miami, and Susquehannock. Indians fiercely resisted the settlement of the Ohio Valley in the late 18th century, and the threat was not resolved until the 1790s.

Operating from their stronghold in Canada, the French asserted rights to the Ohio watershed, basing their claims in large part on the exploration of LaSalle. Increasingly their presence was challenged by the westward expansion of British Americans. The French surrendered their North American territories, including the Ohio Valley, to the British in 1763, at the end of the French and Indian War. Two decades later, the British ceded the region to the United States as a result of the Revolutionary War. The Battle of Point Pleasant, between Virginia colonial militia and Ohio Valley Indians, was fought on the banks of the Ohio in present West Virginia in 1774, just prior to the Revolution. The Louisiana Purchase in 1803 put the entire Mississippi watershed in American hands, opening unrestricted access to the Gulf of Mexico and increasing the importance of the Ohio as a transportation route.

Early travel on the river was by keelboats and flatboats or by canoes of all sizes. Beginning in 1811 and continuing into the 1900s, steamboats traveled both ways along the river, and federal efforts were made to remove obstacles such as snags and sandbars. The problem of seasonal low water was more difficult. In dry seasons it was sometimes possible to wade across the Ohio River on foot and impossible to travel continuously by boat. The Lewis and Clark Expedition spent long days pulling and carrying boats through the low water of the upper Ohio in the fall of 1803, a common occurrence at the time.

The Ohio now varies in width from 1,000 to 1,600 feet, and the average depth ranges from 10 to 20 feet, with many deeper places. The depth and width have been increased by a series of 19 locks and dams, seven along West Virginia's border. These provide a minimum nine-foot navigation channel for the river's entire length. Large floods (especially those of 1847, 1884, 1913, and 1937) brought the construction of floodwalls and levees on the Ohio, and flood-control dams on the tributaries.

All of West Virginia except the Eastern Panhandle and a small part of Monroe County lies within the Ohio River watershed. The principal tributaries in West Virginia are the Little Kanawha, the Kanawha and its tributaries (including the Elk, Gauley, Greenbrier, and New rivers), the Guyandotte, and the Big Sandy River and the Tug Fork of Big Sandy. The principal West Virginia cities on the Ohio are Weirton, Wheeling, Moundsville, New Martinsville, Paden City, Sistersville, St. Marys, Parkersburg, Ravenswood, Point Pleasant, and Huntington.

As a transportation route, the Ohio has contributed to the growth and prosperity of the region. Fueled by the abundance of coal found in all the adjoining states, heavy industries such as steel and metal alloys found a home in the upper Ohio Valley. The production of electricity from coal is also a major industry. After World War II, growth along the river was a direct result of cheap and easy barge transportation for the industrial products manufactured in the river cities. Today, the primary shipping consists of bulk natural resources such as coal, sand and gravel, and petrochemical products.

Geologically, the Ohio River is quite young. Although the continental ice that covered much of northern Ohio and Pennsylvania more than 10,000 years ago never reached present West Virginia, the Ohio Valley was at the southern edge of the glaciation that lasted throughout the Pleistocene Epoch. Glacial ice blocked the ancient Teays River, which once continued the course of the present Kanawha River westward across southern West Virginia and Ohio, forcing the water of the Teays into a new channel, thus forming the Ohio River. The steep bluffs along stretches of the Ohio likely were carved by glacial meltwater.

Hardwood forests that sustained a rich flora formerly lined the river and created habitat for a large diversity of fauna. The Ohio River supported an abundance of fish and mussels before the onset of pollution that resulted from the numerous industrial plants along its shoreline and on its tributaries. During the mid-20th century, fishermen typically could catch only catfish and carp. Gamefish such as largemouth bass, striped bass, and sauger are once more abundant, however, as a result of pollution control and management by the West Virginia Department of Natural Resources and other agencies.

There are 32 islands in the Ohio River in West Virginia, many of them included in the Ohio River Islands National Wildlife Refuge. The Ohio River is a major migration corridor for many species of waterfowl, and the islands support an abundance of wildlife, including bald eagles, osprey, cormorants, beaver, muskrats, raccoons, and white-tailed deer.

See also Floods, Glaciation, Ohio River Islands National Wildlife Refuge, Teays River

Jane C. Michael
Morgantown

R. E. Banta, *The Ohio,* 1949.

Ohio River Islands National Wildlife Refuge

Established in 1990 by the U.S. Fish & Wildlife Service, the Ohio River Islands National Wildlife Refuge protects habitat for wildlife in one of America's busiest waterways. Scattered along 362 miles of the Ohio River in three states, 17 of the refuge's 21 islands lie within West Virginia, two in Pennsylvania, and two in Kentucky. Important wetland habitats along the main stem of the Ohio River are targeted for future refuge acquisition and protection.

The refuge is home to more than 40 species of freshwater mussels, including the federally endangered fanshell and pink mucket. Refuge islands provide vital feeding and resting habitat for many birds during spring and fall migration. Two hundred species of birds use the refuge during the year, including bald eagles, great blue herons, osprey, and prothonotary warblers. Other wildlife, from rare tiger beetles to common white-tailed deer, also inhabit this floodplain refuge.

As part of the national wildlife refuge system, the Ohio River islands are managed under a "wildlife first" mission, but visitors are welcome. Refuge properties are open daily from sunrise until sunset. Although most of the islands are accessible only by boat, Middle Island at St. Marys offers bridge access, with a self-guided auto tour, a wildlife viewing blind, and a nature trail on the island. The refuge encourages wildlife-dependent recreation including wildlife observation and photography, fishing, and hunting. Special events with an environmental education emphasis take place primarily during the summer months.

See also Ohio River

Janet Butler
Ohio River Islands National Wildlife Refuge

Ohio Valley University

Ohio Valley University at Parkersburg is a private liberal arts institution allied with the Church of Christ. In 1957, a group from West Virginia and Ohio purchased 132 acres between Parkersburg and Vienna for the purpose of establishing a college with an independent board of trustees composed of members of the church.

The institution was chartered February 28, 1958, and began operation as a junior college September 12, 1960. The first classes were held in temporary facilities in South Parkersburg. Beginning in 1963, new buildings were occupied on the permanent campus, where an administration and library building, the Ethel Merritt Erickson Theater, three dormitories, a dining hall, student union, and activity center are located. This area is now known as the South Campus.

Ohio Valley College expanded in 1994 by purchasing an adjacent property, the former St. Joseph's Seminary, creating a 250-acre campus. Two dormitories, a commons area, Stotts Administrative Center, Isom Academic Center, gymnasium, dining hall, a student center, and baseball and soccer fields occupy the North Campus.

The first president, Don Gardner, led the college from 1959 to 1964. He was succeeded by E. Lewis Case, 1965–66. Ohio Valley College was accredited by the state of West Virginia in 1965 and by the North Central Association of Colleges and Schools in 1978. A baccalaureate degree in Bible was added in 1981. In 1993, the North Central Association approved baccalaureate degrees in business administration, elementary education, liberal studies, and psychology. In 1998, additional business degrees in accounting, management, human resource management, and marketing were approved. Since 2000, the school has offered secondary education programs in English, mathematics, natural sciences, physical education, and social studies, as well as certification in special education.

The college operates the Institute for Adult Learning on the South Campus, from which adult learners may complete a B.S. degree in organization management and an associate degree in professional studies. There is an English as a second language program in the summertime to accommodate foreign students. The college manages Noah's Harbor Daycare Center for the children of faculty, staff, and students. Ohio Valley College prepares students for the Christian ministry, among other professions.

In 1993, Ohio Valley College was consolidated with Northeastern Christian Junior College of Villanova, Pennsylvania, which closed its campus. Faculty and trustees of Northeastern Christian also joined the Ohio Valley College. In 2005, Ohio Valley College changed its name to Ohio Valley University. The institution had an enrollment of more than 500 students.

President James Marvin Powell served the college from 1966 to 1969, succeeded by Justin B. Roberts, 1970–77. E. Keith Stotts, the longest serving president, led the college from 1977 to 1998. Robert W. Stephens Jr., an Ohio Valley College alumnus followed Stotts, and in 2005 James A. Johnson was president.

Philip Sturm
Ohio Valley University
Philip W. Sturm, *Dreams and Visions: The Silver Anniversary History of Ohio Valley College*, 1985.

Ohio Valley Medical Center

Ohio Valley Medical Center is a 200-bed hospital in downtown Wheeling. It began as City Hospital on January 1, 1890, following an initiative by Wheeling women's groups led by the women of St. Matthew's Episcopal Church. City Hospital took quarters in the former Wheeling Female Seminary and opened to patients in 1892. On January 14, 1914, the East Building of the present hospital complex was opened on the old seminary site, and the hospital officially became Ohio Valley General Hospital.

City Hospital Training School for Nurses opened in conjunction with the hospital in 1892 and was the first nursing school in West Virginia. The first two nurses trained there received their diplomas in 1894. In 1926, the Nurses Residence was built to house the large classes of nurses. The school of nursing closed in 1988.

On January 26, 1973, the hospital's board of trustees voted to change the name to Ohio Valley Medical Center to reflect the growing services, staff, and broader geographic focus of the facility. In April 1976, the hospital embarked on the most extensive building program of its history, a new eight-story patient tower designed to accommodate 200 replacement beds previously located in the East Building. On April 27, 1980, this new West Building opened.

Now one of the area's largest employers, Ohio Valley Medical Center offers an array of primary and tertiary care, from emergency and trauma services to rehabilitation and medical education of future physicians and other medical professionals. Ohio Valley Medical Center is part of the Ohio Valley Health Services and Education Corporation, parent company of OVMC and East Ohio Regional Hospital. It is also affiliated with Family Services-Upper Ohio Valley. Until 2004 the hospital operated Peterson Rehabilitation Hospital in the Woodsdale section of Wheeling.

Howard P. Gamble
Ohio Valley Medical Center

Ohio Valley Trades and Labor Assembly

The Ohio Valley Trades and Labor Assembly is West Virginia's and the nation's oldest central labor organization. It was founded in Aetnaville, Ohio, in 1882, and since 1885 its offices have been in Wheeling. At the peak of its influence, 1890–1920, the assembly consisted of more than 40 locals and almost 40 percent of the state's union members.

Throughout much of its history, the assembly sanctioned strikes and conducted boycotts and arbitrations. It fathered the state's first workers compensation bill (1913) and influenced Wheeling city leaders to construct the municipality's first water filtration plant. The assembly promoted equal pay for men and women, women's suffrage, the eight-hour workday, immigration restrictions, and social insurance.

Members supported cultural and educational improvements such as improved schools, transportation enhancements, and public libraries. In 1904, however, the assembly spearheaded a drive that defeated a proposal to erect a Carnegie Library in the city. Their opposition was in protest of Andrew Carnegie's ruthless suppression of Pennsylvania steel strikers a decade before.

For most of the 20th century, the assembly provided political support to candidates sympathetic to labor. One highlight was its support for Eugene V. Debs, the Socialist candidate for president in 1912. The West Virginia Socialist platform was written by a former assembly president, Valentine Reuther, the father of United Auto Workers founder Walter Reuther.

The assembly published its own paper, *Wheeling Majority* (1907–20) and the *Labor Journal Quarterly* (1944–56). It sponsored Wheeling's largest parade, the Labor Day parade, as well as providing a hospital fund and an educational fund for working-class boys to attend Linsly Military Institute in Wheeling. Since the 1950s, the influence of the assembly has waned considerably. Today, much of its efforts are directed to promotion of community services such as the United Way.

See also Labor History

David T. Javersak
West Liberty State College
David T. Javersak, "Response of the O.V.T.&L.A. to Industrialism," *The Journal of the West Virginia Historical Association*, Spring 1980; Javersak, "The Ohio Valley Trades and Labor Assembly: The Formative Years, 1882–1915," Ph.D. dissertation, West Virginia University, 1977.

Sigfus Olafson

Sigfus Olafson, archeologist, historian, and geologist, was born November 1, 1897, in northwestern Minnesota, the grandson of Icelandic immigrants. He attended public schools in Minnesota and as a young man worked with surveying crews and gained practical experience in the field of geology. After serving in World War I, Olafson went to work for the Yawkey-Freeman Corporation and was sent to West Virginia to help find and develop the company's coal and gas resources. In the mid-1920s, he settled in Madison, Boone County. Eventually Olafson was transferred to the Yawkey-Freeman New York office and became the corporation's president. After retirement he moved back to Boone County.

As a geologist, Olafson came in frequent contact with the artifacts of West Virginia's prehistoric inhabitants. Through his careful observations, research, and writings, he established himself as a competent amateur authority in the field of prehistoric archeology of the eastern United States. He was an early member of the West Virginia Archeology Society, served as the group's president for many years, and wrote articles for the society's journal. He also served as president of the Eastern States Archeological Federation. In retirement, Olafson helped to found the Boone County Genealogical Society and co-authored, with his daughter Jean, several books on Boone County genealogy. He died February 28, 1987, and was buried in Madison.

See also Archeology

Michael M. Meador
Abingdon, Virginia

Old Appalachia

Old Appalachia was an ancient, Paleozoic Era land mass of igneous and metamorphic rock located where the North American Atlantic sea coast and its borderlands now lie. About 600 million years ago, Old Appalachia began a geologic history of mountain building and reduction of which Appalachia's Blue Ridge and Piedmont physiographic regions are the modern remnants.

Throughout most of the Paleozoic, Old Appalachia was bordered on the west by an inland sea that extended across the present middle part of the United States to the modern Rocky Mountains. The deepest part of the inland sea was a geosyncline trough that filled with sediments washed down from the flanks of Old Appalachia. As the sediments accumulated in the trough the coast of the inland sea gradually sank but Old Appalachia's borderland was maintained by uplifts.

The igneous and metamorphic rock of Old Appalachia and the newer sedimentary formations in the geosyncline trough were uplifted during the later mountain-building period called the Appalachian Orogeny. After being eroded to a near featureless plain in the Mesozoic Era, the Appalachian land mass was again uplifted. Each time the land mass was re-elevated the rocks were warped, buckled, folded, and broken, and the rejuvenated streams resumed their erosive cutting power.

South of New England and the Adirondacks, the differences in deformation and resistance of the bedrock to erosion have resulted in the current Appalachian Highlands of four physiographic regions: On the eastward side of Old Appalachia is the non-mountainous Piedmont Region. The westward side of Old Appalachia is the mountainous Blue Ridge Region that

marks the boundary of West Virginia in eastern Jefferson County. The other two regions, the Plateau and the Ridge and Valley, make up the remainder of our state.

See also Appalachian Mountains, Appalachian Orogeny, Geology

Howard G. Adkins
Ona

The *Old Farm Hour*

The *Old Farm Hour* was the live Friday night jamboree program from WCHS radio in Charleston. Shows were held in the WCHS Auditorium, and during its period of peak popularity the *Old Farm Hour* regularly drew crowds of 2,000 people. Frank Welling (1898–1957), a musician, homespun philosopher, and radio announcer, played a key part in the program's success, usually in his comic role of "Uncle Si." Charleston-area musicians who appeared on the program included the legendary fiddler Clark Kessinger, singer-yodeler Billy Cox, and vocalist Buddy Starcher. During the program's zenith in the late 1930s and early 1940s, cast members included the Bailes Brothers, the Delmore Brothers, Cliff and Bill Carlisle, and the duo of Slim Clere and T. Texas Tyler. Local favorites affiliated with the *Old Farm Hour* at one time or another included Tommy Cantrell, tap dancer Orville Q. Miller, and the sacred vocal trio of Cap, Andy, and Flip (Warren Caplinger, Andy Patterson, and William Strickland).

During World War II, the shows were reduced to one per month. The program never regained its former popularity after the war, and the *Old Farm Hour* had passed into history by the late 1940s. Country music enjoyed something of a renaissance in Charleston on early morning WCHS-TV in the 1960–73 period as first Buddy Starcher and then Sleepy Jeffers had popular programs featuring Wick Craig, the Davis Twins, Herman Yarbrough, and Lori Lee Bowles in addition to themselves.

See also Clark Kessinger, Buddy Starcher, WCHS

Ivan M. Tribe
University of Rio Grande

Ivan M. Tribe, *Mountaineer Jamboree: Country Music in West Virginia*, 1984.

Old-Growth Forests

When European settlers first arrived, West Virginia's 15 million acres were almost entirely forested. As late as 1880, two-thirds of the state was still covered by original forests, but by 1920 virtually the entire state had been deforested. Old-growth forest was once abundant here, but few forests escaped the logging of the 19th and 20th centuries. By 2000, West Virginia had reforested and our state had more forestland than it has had for 100 years, but only small remnants of the grand pre-settlement forest remain. Indi-

Old-growth forest in Cathedral State Park.

vidual old trees are not uncommon, fortunately, since boundary trees were often left untouched, and many trees were spared because of their low timber value.

Old-growth forests have trees of many ages, and conditions favorable for trees to reach their natural longevity. The age of old-growth varies widely by species. White oak and hemlock can live for more than 500 years, while red spruce rarely exceeds 300 years.

Some of the best remaining old-growth stands are dominated by conifer and hardwood mixtures. Cathedral State Park in Preston County is a wonderful example of a cove forest, with hemlock, beech, sugar maple, red and white oak, and cucumber tree. The largest hemlock measures over 21 feet in circumference, and is probably more than 500 years old. Pierson Hollow in Carnifex Ferry Battlefield State Park has a similar mixture of hemlock, yellow poplar, and white oak. Nearby Koontz Bend in Fayette County also has old hemlock, along with black birch and red maple. A ten-acre stand along Anthony Creek in Greenbrier County contains white oak, pignut hickory, black gum, and white pine which all exceed 200 years of age.

Two of the state's better-known conifer stands occur on Pike Knob of North Fork Mountain in Pendleton County, and the virgin hemlock area in the West Virginia University forest in Preston County. Pike Knob has the southernmost station for red pine, many of which are 200 years old. These pines were used as a seed source for reforestation projects of the Civilian Conservation Corps in the 1930s. The hemlock stand along Little Laurel Run in the WVU forest survived because the logging concern went bankrupt just as its railroad tracks reached the area. Because of its streamside location, it also escaped the slash fires that ravaged the mountains. Gaudineer Knob in Pocahontas County is the state's best-known old-growth red spruce stand, a small remnant of the once vast red spruce forest of the highlands. This stand escaped logging in the 1920s because of a surveyor's error.

A fine example of an old-growth oak stand is the Murphy Tract in Ritchie County, managed by the West Virginia Nature Conservancy. This stand occupies a dry ridge with very thin soils, and has five species of oak, along with maple, beech, and hickory. Because of the infertile soils, towering trees with large trunks are absent here. Nevertheless, 400-year-old white oaks may be found, some no larger than 30 inches in diameter at breast height. Horner's Woods in Lewis County has 300-year-old white and chestnut oaks, along with black oak, sugar maple, and beech.

See also Forests

James Rentch
West Virginia University

Kenneth L. Carvell, "Virgin Timber Stands: Why Were They Spared?" *Wonderful West Virginia,* July 1996; Mary Byrd Davis, ed., *Eastern Old-growth Forests: Prospects for Rediscovery and Recovery,* 1996.

Old Stone Presbyterian Church

The Old Stone Presbyterian Church in Lewisburg is claimed to be the oldest church building in continuous use west of the Alleghenies. The sanctuary on Church Street was built in 1796 from native limestone, with walls 22 inches thick. Church history says the women worked with the men of the congregation, riding horseback to the Greenbrier River to fetch bags of sand for the mortar. Rev. Benjamin Grigsby dedicated the structure, originally named Lewisburg Presbyterian Church, with this verse: "Except the Lord build the house, they labor in vain that build it." (Psalm 127:1)

The establishment of the former Greenbrier College for Women and Greenbrier Military School followed the education effort begun in 1808 by Old Stone's Rev. John McElhenney, who served as pastor for more than six decades.

The church escaped damage during the Civil War, when it was used as a hospital and for billeting troops. Following the Battle of Lewisburg, May 23, 1862, Confederate dead lay in the sanctuary. The Union commander refused to allow services, in retaliation for sniper fire that killed one of his wounded soldiers. The Confederates were unceremoniously buried in a trench along the south wall of the church. After the war, 95 soldiers were reburied in a common grave mounded in the form of the cross, on a hill just beyond Old Stone.

Old Stone Presbyterian Church, placed on the National Register of Historic Places in 1972, remains in active use. Its churchyard cemetery has the graves of many local families.

See also Lewisburg

Belinda Anderson
Asbury

John F. Montgomery, *History of Old Stone Presbyterian Church,* 1983.

Old-time Music

Old-time music is music from the home and community. Much of this music predates recordings. It consists of traditional instrumental fiddle tunes from the Old World, such as "Soldier's Joy," and Old World ballads such as "Barbara Allen." It also includes original American ballads, based on real events, such as "John Henry," and popular music and poems that passed into oral tradition.

Folklorists, including John Harrington Cox, Louis W. Chappell, and Patrick Gainer, had been documenting and later recording West Virginia music since World War I, but many Mountain State musicians first came to widespread attention during the folk revival of the 1960s and 1970s. Through commercial recordings and increasingly popular festivals, they reached a broad audience. This group included, among others, the Roane County fiddler Frank George; Burl, Sherman, Maggie, and Edden Hammons of Pocahontas County; Putnam County banjo player Elmer Bird; Ernie Carpenter and Melvin Wine from Braxton County; fiddler Emery Bailey of Calhoun County; Wood County fiddler Glen Smith; Kanawha County fiddle legend Clark Kessinger; and Clay County musicians French Carpenter, Wilson Douglas, Doc White, Ira Mullins, Lee Triplett, John Morris, Jenes Cottrell, and Sylvia O'Brien. Most of them were gone by the year 2000, but they have left their music in the hands of a large generation of musicians who learned from them.

Old-time music is not the same as bluegrass, which is much younger. Whereas old-time music is generally limited to fiddle, guitar, and banjo, bluegrass often adds mandolin, bass, and dobro. Bluegrass is often played faster, and the various instruments take solo "breaks," whereas normally in old-time music all instruments play all the time. Much old-time music has a purpose other than just its sound. The fiddle tunes are for dancing. The ballads commemorate events. Bluegrass is performance music, developed from the first for a commercial audience, whereas old-time musicians often sat in a circle, playing to each other. Both genres are traditional, but old-time musicians seek to retain the traditional form, while bluegrass music continually evolves without such a strict commitment to established tradition. Bluegrass draws on blues, fiddle tunes, old-time country music, and gospel harmony. The fiddle is tuned differently, and the bowing is very different. There is more emphasis on tight vocal harmonies.

Traditionally, the old-time music lived in homes, farms, timber camps, or coal towns and was part of lives filled with hard work. Elmer Bird remembered his father playing music to relax after a day in the fields. In Braxton County, Smithy Wine's tunes lived into the 21st century in his great-grandson, Melvin, who caught them from his father, fiddler Bob Wine. They had been passed on from Bob's father, Nels, who sang the tunes as he learned them from Smithy. A regular every year at the West Virginia Folk Festival in Glenville before he died in 2003 at age 93, Melvin passed his tunes on to his son, Grafton, his friend Gerry Milnes, and others. And so the music has been carried on, from father to son, or grandfather to grandson, singer to singer, and fiddler to fiddler. It is a living tradition.

See also Bluegrass Music

Paul Gartner
Sod

Marie Boette, *Singa Hipsy Doodle and Other Folk Songs of West Virginia,* 1971; Cecelia Conway, *African Banjo Echoes in Appalachia: A Study of Folk Traditions,* 1995; Gerald Milnes, *Play of a Fiddle: Traditional Music, Dance and Folklore in West Virginia,* 1999.

John Hunt Oley

General John Hunt Oley, one of Huntington's first prominent citizens, was born in Utica, New York, September 24, 1830. At the outset of the Civil War, Oley served with the 7th Regiment of the New York National Guard. He was one of six New Yorkers sent to Western Virginia to drill troops following a request by Francis Pierpont, governor of Reorganized or Unionist Virginia. In the fall of 1861, Oley organized the 8th (West) Virginia Infantry, which would later become the 7th West Virginia Cavalry. He was promoted to colonel in 1863, and was made a brevet brigadier general in 1865.

After the war, Oley lived in Charleston and was appointed internal revenue collector for West Virginia. In 1871, he moved to the fledgling community of Huntington, where he was employed by railroad baron Collis P. Huntington as an agent for the Central Land Company. Oley also was elected recorder and treasurer of Huntington and was instrumental in the formation of Trinity Episcopal Church. Gen. John Hunt Oley died March 11, 1888, and was buried in Spring Hill Cemetery in Huntington. A monument marking his grave was paid for through contributions by the citizens of Huntington.

Joe Geiger
Huntington

Joe Geiger, *Civil War in Cabell County, West Virginia 1861–1865,* 1991; George Selden Wallace, *Cabell County Annals and Families,* 1935; *Wheeling Intelligencer,* March 1888.

The One-Room School

The picturesque names of West Virginia's one-room schools offer a county-by-county geography lesson, as evidenced by the likes of Hickory Grove, Lost Creek, Perry Ridge, Joel's Branch, Evergreen, Horse Creek, and Punkin Center. As one teacher put it, "it seemed like every hill and holler had one." That is an exaggeration, but nonetheless historian Otis K. Rice documented some 4,551 schoolhouses dotting the Mountain State during the 1930–31 school year. Their number declined with the adoption of the "county unit" school system in 1933 and as better roads allowed for easier automobile and school bus travel.

In their heyday, one-room schools were generally located within two or three miles of their students, who usually walked to school. The buildings tended to be cheaply constructed and featured rough-cut frames, lap siding, tin roofs, south-facing windows, and a potbelly stove. Outside there was a coal house, well, and, on the perimeter of the school grounds, outdoor toilets for each sex. Hundreds of the school buildings survive today, many of them recycled as barns, churches, and even homes.

Teaching in a rural one-room school could be a formidable task, beginning with simply getting to the school. Poor roads or lack of roads often forced teachers to board with students' families. Prior to World War II, teachers typically completed a two-year terminal degree program, receiving a Standard Normal Certificate. Many simply passed a state test after high school and began teaching while attending college during the summer. A one-room school teacher had to be the proverbial "jack-of-all-trades," serving as educator, principal, janitor, nurse, and guidance counselor.

In the early days, teachers relied on the *McGuffy Reader*, *Ray's Arithmetic*, the *Elson Reader*, and *Mitchell's Geography*, and later used the same sort of materials used in larger schools. Writing paper was expensive, so students spent much of the day at the blackboard or used small handheld slates at their desks. The typical school day began with everyone taking part in the Lord's Prayer, Pledge of Allegiance, and patriotic songs. The remainder of the day the teacher moved about the classroom instructing small groups of students representing grades one through eight in the Three R's. Older students often helped to teach the younger ones. Morning and afternoon recesses saw students playing such games as "Ante Over," which involved throwing a ball over the school's roof and back, "London Bridge," "Kick the Can," "Drop the Handkerchief," and "Go Sheepy, Go." A full hour was given over to lunch, prepared at home and often carried to school in a tin lard bucket.

Although most one-room schools closed by the mid-1950s, Auburn School in Ritchie County remained open until 1978. The era of the one-room school has been preserved in several places across the state, including the Marshall University One-Room School Museum in Huntington.

See also Education

Paul F. Lutz
Marshall University

One Valley Bank

See Kanawha Valley Bank.

Opossum

The opossum, known simply as "possum" to most West Virginians, is the only marsupial found in North America. An opossum's beady eyes, pointy snout, naked ears, and prehensile tail make it one of West Virginia's most recognizable mammals.

Marsupials are primitive mammals best known for carrying their young in pouches. After a late-winter pregnancy of just 13 days, newborn opossums the size of honeybees climb up their mother's abdomen and into her pouch. There they latch onto one of 13 nipples and continue to develop outside the womb for about eight weeks until weaned. Adults weigh four to 15 pounds, about the size of a large house cat.

As in states farther south, possums play a part in West Virginia's folklore and occasionally in its cuisine. They are known for their ability to feign death or "play possum" as a means of escaping dangerous situations. This amazing response to danger is involuntary and usually effective. Opossums are the ultimate generalists and opportunists. They live just about everywhere, including fields, farmland, towns, parks, marshes, and woods. And they eat almost anything—fruits, nuts, roots, insects, eggs, small rodents, and even carrion. Opossums do not hibernate, though they may stay in their dens for several days during winter storms. When they venture outside during bitter cold weather, their paper-thin ears and near-naked tails are subject to frostbite.

Scott Shalaway
Cameron

Orchards

The earliest development of a commercial fruit industry in West Virginia occurred in the Northern Panhandle and down the Ohio Valley. Legend has it that Johnny Appleseed (John Chapman, 1774–1845) and his brother floated down the Ohio River to what is now Wellsburg, where they planted several apple nurseries. Whatever their origin, apple trees from regional nurseries were distributed throughout the area. Apple production increased until there was a surplus beyond local needs, and the first commercial shipments down the Ohio occurred in the early 1800s. The Northern Panhandle apple industry appears to have prospered until the Civil War, when shipments came to a halt. This resulted in a marked decrease in local commercial production, but during this time and into the late 1800s apple trees and small orchards appeared on farms throughout the state.

Although it was largely responsible for the failure of commercial fruit growing in the Northern Panhandle, the Civil War resulted in the beginning of the industry in the Eastern Panhandle. William S. Mil-

Pleasant Green School, Pocahontas County, October 1921.

ler (considered by many to be the father of modern commercial orchard development in West Virginia) planted his first orchard of 16 acres near Gerrardstown, Berkeley County, in 1851. At the start of the Civil War, Miller had a large supply of orchard stock and no market. He solved this problem by expanding his own orchard and at the close of the war had nearly 4,000 peach trees and several hundred apple trees coming into production.

Fruit production rapidly expanded throughout the Eastern Panhandle counties of Jefferson, Berkeley, Hampshire, Morgan, and Mineral. By 1889, West Virginia apple production had reached about 4.5 million bushels. Production fluctuated from a low of less than two million bushels in 1921 to a peak of more than 12 million bushels in 1931. Annual production at the end of the 20th century averaged more than 3.5 million bushels. Peach production has varied from a low of approximately 200,000 bushels in 1934 to a high of more than 900,000 bushels in 1954. Average peach production was 279,000 bushels during the decade of the 1990s. West Virginia ranks ninth or tenth in apple production and 13th or 14th in peach production in the U.S., with a combined annual crop value averaging more than $17 million the past 10 years. There are currently about 7,000 bearing acres of apples and 1,200 bearing acres of peaches in the state. All but six to eight of the commercial orchards in the state are located in the Eastern Panhandle.

Where 40-foot-tall "standard" apple trees once were the norm, most commercial producers now grow semi-dwarf or dwarf apple trees. High-density planting requires fewer acres of land with many more trees per acre, perhaps 300 dwarf trees rather than 50 standard trees. Sometimes the small trees are supported on wire trellises, like grapevines in a vineyard. Thus, while the acres of land in orchard production have decreased, the total apple harvest has remained relatively constant.

In the past, most farms had a small orchard to provide for the family's needs, while today's commercial orchard producers are specialized, growing only tree fruit. There is one growing exception: more tree fruit producers are beginning to explore the addition of small fruits to their operations, including strawberries, red raspberries, blackberries, black raspberries, and blueberries.

There was a great change in the fruit industry with the decline of large-scale hard cider production as a result of the Temperance movement and other causes. Cider apples, chosen for tartness and juicing qualities and with little attention to appearance, fell out of favor. Modern dessert apples, chosen for their taste when eaten fresh, came to predominate.

The most common apples grown commercially in West Virginia today include Red Delicious, Golden Delicious, York Imperial, Rome Beauty, Stayman, and Gala. Other varieties grown here include Granny Smith, Braeburn, Fuji, Jona Gold, Pink Lady, Ginger Gold, and Cameo. There is an increasing interest in old apple varieties, and some growers are growing so-called "heritage" apples, including Wolf River, Black Limbertwig, Walker's Pippin, Virginia Beauty, and Baldwin. West Virginia is the native home of two commercial apple varieties, the Grimes Golden and the Golden Delicious.

In 1930, the West Virginia University Experiment Farm was established at Kearneysville, Jefferson County. Now known as the WVU Kearneysville Tree Fruit Research and Education Center, its faculty and staff continue the tradition of research and educational programs in support of the tree fruit industry.

See also Apples, Golden Delicious, Grimes Golden

Richard K. Zimmerman
Henry Hogmire
WVU Extension Service

Organ Cave

Organ Cave is located at the community of Organ Cave, about five miles southeast of Lewisburg in Greenbrier County. Organ Cave has 11 entrances and is the second-largest cave in West Virginia with about 40 miles of surveyed passages. The first recorded owner (1783) of the cave was John Gardner. By 1822, the cave was owned by John Rogers and was visited by guests staying at the various sulfur spring resorts in the area. Owner James H. Boone installed light bulbs in 1914 powered by a Delco generator with 72 storage batteries. The commercial tour uses the historic Organ entrance that is a large blind valley where a stream sinks at the base of a 100-foot limestone cliff. The tour covers about a half-mile of passage. Guided wild cave tours may also be arranged in the undeveloped parts of the cavern.

Organ Cave is named for a calcite drapery that resembles a pipe organ. The cave was mined for saltpeter to manufacture gunpowder during both the War of 1812 and the Civil War. Some of the wooden hoppers used to leach nitrates from the cave soils may be seen at the end of the tour. The cave has a rich diversity of aquatic invertebrate animals and has been studied for a number of years. The fossil bones of the Pleistocene sloth *Megalonyx jeffersonii* described by Thomas Jefferson in 1799 were reportedly found in Organ Cave. The cave is developed in the lower Greenbrier Group limestones of the Mississippian Era.

See also Caves

William K. Jones
Charles Town

Paul J. Stevens, "Caves of the Organ Cave Plateau," West Virginia Speleological Survey Bulletin, 1988.

Oriskany Sandstone

The Oriskany Sandstone is a prominent ridge-forming sandstone in eastern West Virginia and an important producer of natural gas across the state. Deposited early in the Devonian Period, 400 million to 345 million years ago, it forms a consistent blanket, 100 to 150 feet thick, throughout the region and thins only to the west.

The Oriskany is buried at the Allegheny Front and is not exposed in the western portions of West Virginia. It is a quartz-rich sandstone known as an arenite. Not as durable as the Tuscarora Sandstone, which forms Seneca Rocks, the Oriskany forms many smaller, subsidiary ridges in the Eastern Panhandle. Close observation of the Oriskany reveals layers of crossbedding, as well as thin interbedded layers of limestone. Its most recognizable feature may be thin layers containing fossil molds.

The sand grains of the Oriskany are often held only loosely together. This makes the Oriskany useful as a source of silica for glass making as well as a natural gas reservoir. It is mined for glass sand at Berkeley Springs and is a target for gas exploration in many parts of the state. Some of the largest gas fields in West Virginia, including Elk-Poca in Jackson County and South Burns Chapel in Monongalia and Preston counties, produce from this sandstone or related deposits. The most prominent natural landmark composed of Oriskany Sandstone is the Smoke Hole canyon of Grant and Pendleton counties. The Oriskany also holds up many of the subsidiary ridges in the region. In the Eastern Panhandle it forms many small gumdrop-shaped mountains.

See also Geology, Glass Sand Industry, Tuscarora Sandstone

David Matchen
Geological & Economic Survey

Orthodox Christianity

Orthodox Christianity includes independent, national apostolic churches that exist in communion with each other but not with the Roman Catholic Church. Although practices vary, Orthodox Christians have much in common with Roman Catholics, with the important difference that they do not accept the supremacy of the Pope. Orthodox churches with a formal presence in West Virginia are the Antiochian, the Carpatho-Russian, the Greek, and the Serbian, each with its distinct hierarchy in North America.

In 1768, Orthodox Christians first colonized what is now the United States with a church in Florida. As early as 1880, Orthodox Christians from Russia, Greece, and the Ottoman Empire began to settle in the coalfields of southern West Virginia. Later, they came to work in the mines and steel mills in the northern part of the state.

West Virginia's first Orthodox Christians held prayer services in private homes. Soon, they built churches and imported priests to conduct liturgies in their native languages and to serve their spiritual needs. St. Mary Carpatho-Russian Orthodox Church, first in Elkhorn, McDowell County, and now located in Bluefield, was founded in 1880 and developed into a formal community by 1895. In 1892, Syrian and Lebanese immigrants founded St. George Orthodox Church in Charleston, the oldest and largest Antiochian presence in West Virginia. Greeks founded six congregations that continued to exist in 2003.

Small Orthodox parishes were founded in Logan and McDowell counties in the early 1900s and withered away. Only West Virginia's largest cities were able to retain Orthodox churches of the various jurisdictions. In 2004, West Virginia had established Orthodox communities in Beckley, Bluefield, Charleston, Clarksburg, Huntington, Morgantown, Weirton, and Wheeling. Eleven individual churches were listed in a 2000 church survey, with an estimated 4,310 adherents.

In the late 1990s, nearly a dozen monks of the Russian Orthodox Church Outside of Russia founded the Holy Cross Skete or hermitage in Wayne County. The Russian Orthodox Church Outside of Russia broke away from the Russian Orthodox Church during the Bolshevik revolution and remains in schism with the Patriarch of Moscow.

See also Religion

Mark A. Sadd
Charleston

Osage and Pursglove Mine Disasters

By 1942, despite decades of production, the numerous coal operations of the Scotts Run district near Morgantown had never experienced a mining disaster. Then, with the mines in full production for World War II, three disasters within eight months killed 89 miners.

On May 12, 1942, a worker in Christopher No. 3 at Osage left a ventilation door open, and methane accumulated in a dusty area of the mine. At 2:25 p.m. an electric arc from machinery set off an explosion which coursed through three sections, killing 53 miners, destroying ventilation apparatus, and causing roof falls. Three others later suffocated in the noxious "afterdamp" gasses along the main haulageway. Several miners elsewhere in the mine managed to reach safety through a return airway.

On July 9, 1942, a roof fall in nearby Pursglove No. 2 Mine suspended a volume of coal dust into a methane-charged atmosphere and dislodged a trolley wire. An arc between the wire and track ignited the mixture and sent an explosion through two of the mine's sections, killing 20.

The misfortunes of Scotts Run continued when early on January 8, 1943, a haulage locomotive fire spread to the coal seam. Ventilation currents carried the heavy smoke into the working sections, and the midnight foreman perished in an attempt to open trap doors and cut off the air. Sixty-five miners made it to safety, but one mine crew and the motorman remained unaccounted for. All 12 miners perished. On January 24, officials decided to flood and seal the mine. Seals were removed on April 23, 1943, but dewatering the mine proved difficult and the body of the missing motorman was not located until May 20, 1944.

Paul H. Rakes
WVU Institute of Technology
Paul H. Rakes, "Casualties on the Homefront: Scotts Run Mining Disasters During World War II," *West Virginia History,* 1994.

Otter Creek Wilderness Area

The 20,000-acre Otter Creek Wilderness Area is located in the Monongahela National Forest in Tucker and Randolph counties. This area lies in a bowl formed by Shavers Mountain to the west and McGowan Mountain to the east. The elevation of the wilderness area ranges from 1,800 feet at the mouth of Otter Creek to 3,900 feet on McGowan Mountain.

The area was heavily logged by the Otter Creek Boom & Lumber Company from 1897 to 1914. The U.S. government acquired the majority of land in the Otter Creek area in 1917, for inclusion in the new Monongahela National Forest. Logging proceeded again from 1968 to 1972, when an effort began to have the area designated a wilderness area. Under the Eastern Wilderness Act passed by Congress in 1975, the area was given this designation. Otter Creek is one of five wilderness areas in West Virginia.

Otter Creek Wilderness Area provides recreation for hikers, campers, hunters, and cross-country skiers. The creek cascades over stones and around boulders, providing nature photographers numerous picturesque scenes. There are 45 miles of rugged, unblazed, unsigned trails. Most follow old railroad grades, logging, and farm roads where fallen trees are not removed. The longest trail and the main feature of the area is Otter Creek Trail, which is more than 11 miles long and crosses the creek three times. Numerous waterfalls, ranging from three to ten feet high, as well as swirling rapids can be found along the Green Mountain Trail. Hunting is permitted; mountain biking and motorized or mechanical equipment are not.

Otter Creek is home to a large population of black bear. Also abundant are wild turkey, white-tailed deer, snowshoe hare, cottontail rabbit, beaver, and grouse, along with a small number of brook trout and salamanders. Poisonous timber rattlesnakes are also found. Spruce trees dominate the higher elevations, with black cherry and yellow birch on the middle and lower slopes. A few apple trees remain, and Norway Spruce trees were once planted in an attempt to replace the harvested timber. The area receives more than 55 inches of precipitation each year, with heavy rains and deep snows not unusual. Frost may occur during any month of the year.

Christopher Marsh
Charleston

Outbuildings

Outbuildings are an essential part of any farm or rural homestead, providing storage, work areas, and housing for animals.

Otter Creek gives its name to the Wilderness Area.

The first settlers in West Virginia built most or all of the buildings on their farms out of logs, the prevalent building material during the clearing of the land. Later farmers used stone, sawn timber, and brick, and in recent times, manufactured materials. A farmstead consisted of a house, one or more barns, and outbuildings. The outbuildings included smokehouses, granaries, corn cribs, garages, privies, springhouses, chicken houses, and lesser buildings.

Historically, smokehouses served both to preserve and store food, although modern smokehouses tend to be smaller metal sheds used purely for smoking meat. Historically, the smokehouse was usually located close to the farm kitchen. Until the late 19th century, log construction was favored for building smokehouses. The tightly chinked logs would hold the smoke and heat but release moisture, which a brick or stone building would not do.

Storage cellars are still used in West Virginia. They commonly are dug into a hillside convenient to the house, rather than under the house, the earth providing insulation against heat and cold. Cellars are most commonly used to store root vegetables through the winter, but all sorts of food can be preserved in a storage cellar, including canned goods. A popular arrangement was to build a small above-ground room over a root cellar, with the upper room entered separately and perhaps used as a workshop. Some cellars are built over springs, which emerge from the hillside in that place; a pool fed by the spring can keep milk and other dairy products at a constant cool temperature year-round. Cellars of this sort often are referred to as dairies.

The icehouse was a common farm outbuilding in the days before electric refrigeration. An icehouse was usually a low building with a stone foundation, dug into the earth, often a hillside. Large blocks of ice were cut in winter from nearby ponds, lakes, and rivers and stored in the icehouse, packed with sawdust to insulate against summer heat.

Corn cribs are important structures on any farm for the storage and drying of corn. They are typically long, narrow buildings built of slats with ventilation spaces between or, historically, of logs left unchinked. The corn crib is usually constructed on high piers, either of wood or smooth stone, to keep rodents out and to keep the corn away from damp ground. Often, two corncribs are joined by a single peaked roof. The interior passageway between the cribs is kept clear to allow a wagon to load or unload grain out of the weather.

Chickens were common, and chicken houses provided shelter and a secure roost. Early chicken houses were sturdy, often tightly chinked, log structures built on continuous stone foundations to prevent predators from burrowing inside. On most small West Virginia farms, the chicken population would be low, enough to produce eggs and meat for the consumption of the farm family, perhaps with a surplus for sale or barter. However, modern chicken farming takes place in prefabricated metal barns with automated feeders, and a single barn often houses thousands of chickens.

See also Barns, Material Culture

Elizabeth Oliver Lee
Maidsville

Owens-Illinois Glass Company

The Owens-Illinois Glass Company, based in Toledo, Ohio, operated three glass factories in West Virginia. These factories were located in Fairmont, Huntington, and Kanawha City. All three based their manufacturing operations on the revolutionary Owens bottle-making machine. This machine was invented by West Virginia native Michael Owens in 1903, with the financial backing of glass manufacturer Edward Libbey. The success of this machine led to the establishment of the Owens Bottle Machine Company. As the company grew, the name was changed to the Owens Bottle Company in 1919. In 1929, the Owens Bottle Company merged with Illinois Glass Company to become Owens-Illinois.

Owens-Illinois Glass Company opened in Fairmont in November 1910 as the Owens Bottle Works. The factory was built on 40 acres on the east side of Fairmont. When production began, the plant ran 24 hours a day and employed about 200 workers. This plant had six furnaces as well as six of Michael Owens's bottle machines, producing a total of 180,000 bottles per day. Over the years production grew steadily at the Fairmont factory, and by the 1970s more than 1,000 people were employed there. But in 1978, Owens-Illinois began phasing out operations at the Fairmont plant. Nearly 700 people were laid off from their jobs by 1980. In March 1982, the plant closed.

In 1914, Charles Boldt started manufacturing glass in Huntington, in the southwest section of the city. The factory began with three furnaces and two of Michael Owens's bottle machines. In 1918, Owens-Illinois purchased the Huntington factory. The Huntington Division employed more than 1,100 people by 1947 and had expanded to five furnaces. The name of the plant was later changed to the Glass Container Division of Owens-Illinois. The operation had made billions of glass containers by 1971. However, during the 1980s glass production at the plant began to decline. When the Huntington factory closed in 1993, the last 650 workers were laid off.

In 1917, the Owens Bottle Company opened a plant at the upper end of Kanawha City, which is now part of Charleston. The bottling plant was built across the street from a related enterprise, the Libbey-Owens-Ford sheet glass plant which was constructed in 1916. The bottle factory produced fruit jars, jars for industrial products, and after the end of Prohibition, beer bottles. By the 1930s, the Kanawha City plant was the largest bottle-making factory in the world. However, production declined in the 1950s and the factory closed its doors in 1963. The former glass factory site is now part of a shopping center.

See also Glass Industry, Michael Owens

Christy Venham
WVU Libraries

Michael Owens

Businessman Michael Joseph Owens, America's foremost genius in the development of mechanical glass production, was born in Point Pleasant, January 1, 1859. The son of poor Irish immigrants, Owens went to work with his father in a Mason County coal mine before he was ten years old. When a slate fall injured young Owens, the family moved to Wheeling where he began a life-long career in glass production by tending a furnace at the Hobbes-Brockunier glass works.

By the age of 15, Mike Owens had become a skilled glassblower and was working with craftsmen two and three times his age. He rose rapidly in trade union ranks and became an officer in the American Flint Glass Workers national organization. His reputation as a diligent worker and a leader of men attracted the attention of Edward D. Libbey who hired Owens to manage his ailing factory in Toledo, Ohio.

Owens did more than rescue the Libbey operation. He also began experiments that placed the Libbey interests in the forefront of technological developments which would revolutionize the ancient hand methods of glass production. By 1895, Owens had perfected machinery for blowing tumblers, light bulbs, and lamp chimneys. A few years later, he had successfully automated the production of bottles. From 1912 to 1916, Owens turned his attention to perfecting the mechanical process for making window glass, which had been pioneered by Irving Colburn.

By 1917, Owens's life had come full circle. He returned to West Virginia in 1909 to establish a state-of-the-art bottle factory at Fairmont, and in 1916 he launched at Charleston a factory which would become the world's largest producer of window glass. Seven years later, December 27, 1923, Michael Owens died suddenly while working on a way to manufacture safer glass for automobiles.

See also Glass Industry, Owens-Illinois Glass Company

Fred A. Barkey
Marshall University Graduate College

Pack Peddlers

Pack peddlers played an important role in West Virginia rural life well into the 20th century. They brought consumer goods to areas with sparse population and few stores. They also followed late 19th-century rail lines into emerging coalfields and logging areas, where a growing work force created a new market.

Peddlers carried all kinds of portable goods, from clothing and accessories to rugs and bedding, kitchenware and household items, toys, and musical instruments. To rural residents, the peddler's arrival was an exciting occasion. A Greenbrier County woman reminisced that during her 1880s childhood, regular visits from a Jewish peddler "gave us something to look forward to. It was almost like having Santa Claus come. . . . We loved to see the big bundle opened up, for we seldom saw new things." A Ritchie County man recalled that in the 1910s, two Syrian brothers visited his family's farm twice a year. After spending the night, in the morning they would spread their wares on the floor for all to view. "What a sight for us kids," he commented.

Most peddlers were immigrants, and many barely spoke English, adding to the exotic nature of their visit. These young entrepreneurs—primarily Syrians, Lebanese, East European Jews, and Italians—viewed peddling as a stepping stone to store ownership. They often relied on their ethnic networks to get started, in-cluding wholesalers from Baltimore and Cincinnati who saw a growing market in West Virginia and sent their countrymen to peddle in the mountains, supplying people with goods on credit.

Peddlers faced numerous challenges. They trudged up steep mountains toting heavy packs on their backs, though the more successful acquired a horse and wagon. Traveling alone and carrying cash, they courted danger, and stories of the robbery and murder of peddlers abound. Some coal operators who saw them as competition to company stores tried to keep them out of the coalfields. But on the whole, rural inhabitants throughout the state gave a warm reception to these purveyors of products from far away, despite their strange accents and foreign ways.

Many peddlers remained in West Virginia, and some became prosperous merchants, contributing to the development of numerous towns. They formed the basis of the state's Syrian, Lebanese, and Jewish communities. Their descendants, such as Congressman Nick Rahall, continue to contribute to West Virginia today.

Deborah R. Weiner
Jewish Museum of Maryland

Irving Alexander, "Wilcoe: People of a Coal Town" and "Jewish Merchants in the Coalfields," *Goldenseal*, Spring 1990; Arthur C. Prichard, "Two Hundred Pounds or More: The Lebanese Community in Mannington," *Goldenseal*, April 1978.

Paden City

Paden City is a glass-making town. It is situated on the Ohio River on State Route 2, between New Martinsville and Sistersville, partly in Tyler County and partly in Wetzel County. Obadiah Paden first settled there in 1790. Two years later, the state of Virginia granted 685 acres to Robert Woods. The whole area was Ohio County at the time. Known originally as Paden Valley, Paden City remained largely agricultural through the 1800s, until Pittsburgh industrialist Thomas Watson began to develop the area around the turn of the 20th century.

Paden City was incorporated in 1916. Because of its location on the Ohio River and the Baltimore & Ohio Railroad, the town grew quickly. Early factories included the Paul Wissmach Glass Company, makers of cathedral glass; the Duquesne Bottle Factory; Slider Brothers Cement Block Company; Euclid Manufacturing Company, makers of stone laundry tubs; Monongahela Iron and Steel Company; and Brown Lumber Company.

A prominent business, Paden City Pottery, was established in 1911 by a Frenchman, John Lessel. Lessel was an award-winning potter and looked to Paden City for its clay deposits. He encountered business difficulties, and in 1916 the Paden Land Company took over the company. Paden City Pottery originally employed 50 people and then grew to more than 400 employees. The company came out with one of the first ovenproof dinnerware lines; later it made fine china. By the 1950s, the pottery could not compete with prices from Japanese potteries and was forced to close down.

Paden City is the home of the Marble King factory, which produces a million glass marbles a day. It opened first in St. Marys in 1949, and then moved to Paden City in 1958. The 2000 population of Paden City was 2,860.

Jane Kraina
Weirton

William Nelson Page

Mining engineer, coal operator, and railroad builder William Nelson Page was born in Campbell County, Virginia, January 6, 1854; he died in Washington, March 7, 1932. Private tutoring as a youth and occasional studies in engineering courses prepared him to learn his profession by practical experience.

He directed the Hawk's Nest Coal Company in Ansted (1878–85) and the Mt. Carbon Company (1885–89) in Powellton, and built the Victoria Iron Furnace in Goshen, Virginia (1881–85), as he worked toward linking West Virginia's New River coal to Virginia iron ore deposits. Page saw the Hawks Nest Coal Company through tumultuous times during the strike of 1880. From 1889 to 1917, he was president of Gauley Mountain Coal Company in Ansted and (1905–17) of the Loop Creek Colliery in Page. Secretly backed by capital from Standard Oil magnate Henry H. Rogers, Page directed the building of the Virginian Railway (1898–1909), a coal railroad running from Deep Water on the

These merchants who began as pack peddlers include the founders of prominent West Virginia families.

Kanawha River to Norfolk. Moving to Washington in 1917, he worked there to protect coal and steel interests.

Founder of the Ansted National Bank and incorporator of the Sheltering Arms Hospital in Hansford, Page belonged to the post-Civil War group of "New South" promoters who envisioned rapid growth and progress to be achieved by bringing English and New York capital into the Virginias for regional industrialization.

See also Hawks Nest Strike, Virginian Railway

Lou Athey
Franklin & Marshall College

Paint Creek-Cabin Creek Strike

The Paint Creek-Cabin Creek Strike of 1912–13 was one of the most dramatic and bloody conflicts in the early 20th-century labor struggles in southern West Virginia known as the Mine Wars. The strike began on April 18, 1912, when the coal operators on Paint Creek near Charleston rejected the demand of their unionized workers for a wage increase. As the strike spread to nearby Cabin Creek and other nonunion mining sections, the dispute focused increasingly on the larger issue of unionization. While economics remained important, more of the strikers' demands focused on recognition of the United Mine Workers of America as their bargaining agent and sought an end to the use of mine guards, black listing, and the denial of workers' rights to free speech and assembly.

Claiming that the UMWA was a tool of their competitors in the Midwest, the coal operators were determined to break the strike and drive the union out. The mine district quickly became an armed camp as the operators brought in hundreds of Baldwin-Felts detectives, built machine gun emplacements, evicted

strikers, and began importing nonunion workers. The miners secured weapons of their own. Inspired by labor activists such as the fiery Mother Jones and aided by the Socialist Party, they took the offensive. Guerrilla warfare and pitched battles at places such as Mucklow, Dry Branch, and Eskdale inflicted significant casualties to both sides by early 1913.

The strike's continuing bloodshed and the attempts by two West Virginia governors to curtail it brought national attention. In an unprecedented exercise of military rule during peace time, Governor Glasscock imposed martial law on the district three times. More than 200 miners and their allies, including the 86-year-old Jones, were arrested. And, in what the union maintained was a flagrant abuse of their rights to be tried in civil courts, a hundred or more of these civilians were court-martialed and sentenced to prison terms. Many thought that Glasscock's successor, Henry D. Hatfield, acted in a heavy-handed manner when he imposed a settlement on the strike. Although Governor Hatfield pardoned the majority of the court-martialed defendants, he kept the most radical strike supporters in jail without charges and sent the National Guard to close the Socialist newspapers in Charleston and Huntington. Hatfield's actions helped ensure an inquiry into the strike in 1913 by the U.S. Senate, the first investigation into the actions of a state government by a committee of Congress.

The Paint Creek-Cabin Creek Strike was also notable for producing a group of new leaders in District 17 who would influence labor relations in southern West Virginia for several decades. Fueled by continuing discontent with the Hatfield settlement, Cabin Creek miners led a re-

volt which resulted in the election in 1916 of rank and file activists, including Frank Keeney as president and Fred Mooney as secretary-treasurer. Keeney and Mooney led District 17 miners in the dramatic struggle of the early 1920s, culminating in the massive armed march on Logan and the Battle of Blair Mountain.

See also William Ellsworth Glasscock, Henry D. Hatfield, Mother Jones, Mine Wars

Fred A. Barkey
Marshall University Graduate College

Painted Trees

Some American Indians used a form of symbolic drawing called pictography. Information was conveyed using drawings of objects, humans, animals, tools, weapons, houses, canoes, and so forth, combined in a particular sequence. Various colors of paint and charcoal were used. The pictographs were often painted at face level on a section of tree trunk from which the rough outer bark had been removed to create a smooth surface. The pictograph usually told of war or hunting exploits. Pictographs were often encountered along trails in West Virginia during the 18th century by European settlers, explorers, and soldiers.

Pictographs were once abundant on West Virginia's Paint Creek. The creek, whose history was researched by the late Sigfus Olafson, runs parallel to the West Virginia Turnpike for many miles and empties into the Kanawha River at Pratt. Olafson discovered, through examining local land surveys and grants, and from a letter in the Draper Collection, that the Fayette County stream was named as early as 1774, for the many painted trees on its banks.

The Warriors Path ran alongside Paint Creek and led the New York Iroquois south to wage battle against the tribes of Virginia and North Carolina. Local 19th-century tradition held that the Indians danced around the trees after painting the trees to symbolize the enemy they had targeted for attack. This may have continued until dawn, with the warriors hurling tomahawks and spears into the trees as part of their exhausting ceremony.

Olafson concluded that there were two painted tree sites on Paint Creek. "One of these, sometimes called 'the Big Painted Trees,' was in a fair-sized bottom on the west side of Paint Creek immediately below the little village of Long Branch in Fayette County," he wrote in 1958. "This bottom is well suited for Indian encampment and is at the point where the Coal River path, a more direct but also a more difficult route to the Indian towns on the Scioto, joined the main path on Paint Creek." This site is north of Pax, near the present Turnpike toll plaza.

About three and a half miles farther up Paint Creek, at the mouth of Sandfork in

Munitions seized during the Paint Creek-Cabin Creek strike.

Raleigh County, was the second site, Upper Painted Trees. Olafson said that this site was apparently of less importance, and infrequently mentioned in surveys.

See also Draper Collection

Robert F. Maslowski
Milton

Sigfus Olafson, "The Painted Trees and the War Road, Paint Creek, Fayette County," *The West Virginia Archeologist*, September 1958.

Brad Paisley

Born October 28, 1972, in Glen Dale, Marshall County, country musician Brad Paisley began playing music as a child. Encouraged by his grandfather, Warren Jarvis, Paisley by age eight was studying guitar with local musician Clarence "Hank" Goddard. Two years later Paisley fronted the C-Notes, a band of older musicians including Goddard. At age 14 Paisley became the youngest-ever regular cast member of the *Jamboree USA* radio show on Wheeling station WWVA. Remaining with that show for the next eight years, he also opened local concerts for such visiting country music acts as Little Jimmy Dickens, George Jones, and the Judds.

By the mid-1990s, Paisley had moved to Nashville, signed a songwriting contract with EMI Music Publishing, and made several demo recordings. Signing with Avista Records, he recorded his debut album, *Who Needs Pictures* (1999), which featured several of his own songs. The title song rose to the Top Ten on the country chart and another song, "He Didn't Have to Be," rose to number one. Many fans of traditional country music viewed Paisley as the most promising newcomer in mainstream country music. In 2000, the Academy of Country Music named Paisley "Top New Male Vocalist" and the Country Music Association gave him the Horizon Award. He released his second album, *Part II*, in 2002, and his third, *Mud on the Tires*, in 2003. He released his *Time Well Wasted* album in 2005, including the hit song, "Alcohol." Brad Paisley joined the *Grand Ole Opry* in 2001.

Ted Olson
East Tennessee State University

Paleo-Indian

See Prehistoric People.

Breece D'J Pancake

Writer Breece Pancake, born June 29, 1952, grew up in Milton, Cabell County. He attended West Virginia Wesleyan College and graduated from Marshall University. From an early age, Pancake was interested in local history and culture and enjoyed listening to the older generation of storytellers in Milton.

Pancake viewed writing as his calling, but worked at a variety of jobs and taught for a time at two military schools in Virginia. In 1976, he entered the Creative Writing Program of the University of Virginia and studied with such authors as James Alan McPherson, Peter Taylor, and Mary Lee Settle. In the mid-1970s, he wrote human interest stories for a Milton newspaper and began serious work on short stories. Early stories were published in literary magazines at the University of Virginia in 1976. His first major breakthrough was the publication by *The Atlantic Monthly* of "Trilobites" in December 1977.

Many of Pancake's stories are set in Milton, fictionalized as "Rock Camp." Others are set in the southern coalfields, Huntington, the north-central mountains of the state, and along curvy mountain roads. The stories are starkly written, sometimes with ironic humor, and always without sentimentality. His characters are often poor, lost, or trapped by forces beyond their control or by their own past. They are not among the winners in life, but they grimly keep on plodding.

Pancake committed suicide on Palm Sunday, April 8, 1979. *The Stories of Breece D'J Pancake* was published by Atlantic Monthly Press/Little Brown in 1983. In 1984, Holt, Rinehart and Winston published a paperback edition. The book was published in Great Britain in 1993, in German in 1990, and in a Brazilian Portuguese edition in 1994.

Rick Wilson
American Friends Service Committee

Thomas E. Douglass, *A Room Forever: The Life, Work, and Letters of Breece D'J Pancake*, 1998.

Panther State Forest

Panther State Forest, located near Iaeger in McDowell County, is West Virginia's southernmost state forest. The forest derives its name from Panther Creek. In 1940, the state of West Virginia, to meet a need for public recreational facilities in the southern coalfields, decided to establish a state forest in the Panther Creek area. The *Welch Daily News* spearheaded a campaign to raise funds for the project. A "Pennies for Panther" drive collected small donations from school children, union locals, service clubs, and other organizations.

Panther State Forest is rich in plant life. Among its wildflowers are mayapple, fire pink, touch-me-nots, jack-in-the-pulpit, bishop's cap, and blood-root. Of particular interest is Japanese loosestrife, which has been found at only two other places on the North American continent. Small colonies of this rare plant have been discovered at Kanawha State Forest and in Louisiana. At Panther, however, Japanese loosestrife grows profusely, possibly brought to this country on oil and gas drilling equipment from Asia. The 7,810-acre forest offers hunting and fishing and has a swimming pool, a group camp, and a small campground, along with day-use facilities such as hiking trails, picnic areas, and game courts.

Robert Beanblossom
Division of Natural Resources

Robert Beanblossom, "Panther State Forest: Recreational Jewel of McDowell County," *Wonderful West Virginia*, August 1987.

Pardee & Curtin Lumber Company

The Pardee & Curtin Lumber Company, formed in 1873 when George W. Curtin and Barton Pardee erected a steam sawmill at Fetterman near Grafton, and incorporated in 1892, is the oldest continuously operating lumber company in West Virginia. In 1888, a disastrous flood destroyed the Fetterman mill, and in 1890 the company erected a band sawmill at Sutton. This mill operated until 1904. Their Palmer mill, which was purchased in 1901 and located on Elk River above Sutton, operated until 1907.

In 1898, Pardee & Curtin purchased a band sawmill at Elizabeth, Wirt County. They moved this mill to Curtin, Nicholas County, near the mouth of Cherry River, where they operated from 1900 to 1925. This was a double-band mill with dry kilns and a planing mill. The company expanded its Nicholas County operations by building a single-band sawmill on Cherry River at Coal Siding in 1905. This was followed by a double-band mill in 1909 at Hominy Falls, which operated until 1921 when it was moved to the mouth of Deer Creek, operating there until 1925. Collectively, these mills produced 720 million board feet of lumber between 1900 and 1925. Logs were brought to sawmills by Pardee & Curtin's narrow-gauge railroad, the Cherry & Hominy, which had 85 miles of track.

In 1926, the mill, shop, and Shay locomotives at Curtin, Nicholas County, were moved to Bergoo, Webster County. This sawmill operated at the new site from 1928 to 1945 and produced 220 million board feet of lumber. Pardee & Curtin also operated nine deep mines and seven coal tipples in Webster County between 1929 and 1959, producing 23 million tons of coal. At its peak the company employed 2,000 people in the Webster County area.

In 1955, Pardee & Curtin built the first all electric single-band sawmill in the state at Curtin, Webster County. This mill has been modified several times and currently operates three six-foot band mills and has the capacity to produce 25 million board feet per year. The company now leases the mill and functions primarily as a natural resource manager with more than 140,000 acres of timber, coal, oil, and gas properties.

See also Sawmills, Timbering and Logging

Roy B. Clarkson
West Virginia University

Rex and Eleanor Parker

Musicians Rex and Eleanor Parker, sometimes working with their daughters as the Parker Family, were musical fixtures on radio and television on several stations for more than a half century. Charles "Rex" Parker was born in Maplewood, September 21, 1921, and worked as a country musician on WCHS Charleston and WJLS Beckley with various musicians from the late 1930s. On August 31, 1941, he married Eleanora Niera, born February 28, 1922, the daughter of Spanish immigrants, and they began their career as a country music duo on WHIS Bluefield the next day. The Parkers also worked on WOAY Oak Hill and other stations, moving into television during the 1950s. They recorded sparingly for the Cozy and Coral labels, but did turn out two major original songs with "Build Your Treasures in Heaven" and "Moonlight on West Virginia."

In 1959, the Parkers had a conversion experience and thereafter performed only sacred music, recording several albums on King in the early 1960s. By this time, daughters Conizene and Rexana had joined them. Their *Songs for Salvation* program was a live, weekly feature through most of the 1960s and 1970s on WOAY-TV. In later years, their activity was confined largely to local churches and a Sunday morning radio program in Princeton and occasionally Beckley. After Rex's death on June 2, 1999, Eleanor has continued doing the program aided by Conizene and sometimes Rexana.

Ivan M. Tribe
University of Rio Grande

Parkersburg

Parkersburg is situated at the confluence of the Little Kanawha and Ohio rivers, with a 2000 population of 33,099. It was first known as Thorntonburg, after Robert Thornton of Pennsylvania, who had claimed 400 acres there in 1773. With the formation of Wood County from Harrison County in 1799, the settlement (by then known as Newport) was made the county seat. In 1800, the Virginia Assembly granted a charter for Newport, on the north side of the Little Kanawha, and for Monroe, on the south side. Ten years later, Newport was rechartered and renamed for Capt. Alexander Parker, of Carlisle, Pennsylvania, who had bought the property from Thornton in 1785.

In 1795, Harman and Margaret Blennerhassett purchased what had previously been called Backus Island, two miles below Parkersburg. Aaron Burr, gaining the Blennerhassetts' trust in 1804, made Blennerhassett Island a rendezvous for his disastrous proposed expedition to Spanish-held lands in the southwest. Today, the Blennerhassetts' island mansion, grandly replicated, is a major tourist attraction and centerpiece for a state historic park.

Riverboat transportation grew in importance during the first half of the 19th century. The completion of the Northwestern Turnpike into Parkersburg in 1838, the Staunton to Parkersburg Turnpike in 1847, and the Northwestern Virginia Railroad in 1857, brought important land links to the Ohio River at Parkersburg. New development followed.

During the Civil War, 3,000 Wood Countians, many from Parkersburg, served in the U.S. Army and approximately 500 in the Confederate. In 1861–62, Parkersburgers Dr. John W. Moss, Peter Godwin Van Winkle, Arthur Ingraham Boreman and Jacob Beeson Blair were among the founders of the unionist Reorganized Government of Virginia, which led to the creation of West Virginia. Boreman was the first governor of West Virginia and served three successive terms. Van Winkle was elected to the U.S. Senate three times. Joseph H. Diss Debar of Parkersburg was called upon to design the West Virginia state seal. By the end of the 20th century, Parkersburg had supplied three more governors: William Erskine Stevenson, Jacob Beeson Jackson and Albert Blakeslee White.

In 1861 and after, Parkersburg found itself the center of a booming oil industry, surrounded by major oil fields at Burning Springs, Wirt County; Volcano, Wood County; and elsewhere. Johnson Newlon Camden established one of the country's first oil refineries in Parkersburg in 1869, and later was three times elected a U.S. senator.

Parkersburg was the first city in West Virginia to establish a public high school for blacks, Sumner High School, in 1886. Mountain State Business College was founded in 1898; Ohio Valley College in 1960; and in 1961, the Parkersburg Branch of West Virginia University was located at nearby Cedar Grove.

The Parkersburg Rig and Reel Company, an oil field service company, was for 70 years one of the city's chief employers. The O. Ames Company, the world's largest manufacturer of shovels, arrived in 1910 from Massachusetts. The American Viscose Corporation started rayon production in South Parkersburg in 1927, closing in 1974. A major DuPont plant was built at Washington Bottom in 1949, followed by Marbon Chemical (G.E. Plastics today) in 1957.

See also Harman Blennerhassett, Margaret Agnew Blennerhassett, Arthur Ingraham Boreman, Northwestern Virginia Turnpike, Peter Godwin Van Winkle

R.F. Hendricks
Marietta, Georgia

Bernard L. Allen, *Parkersburg: A Bicentennial History,* 1985; Nancy Marsh and Mrs. Albert Moellendick, *The Story of Parkersburg,* 1953.

Parkersburg Community College

See WVU at Parkersburg.

Parkersburg News

The *Parkersburg News* serves Parkersburg and surrounding areas seven days a week.

The first *Parkersburg News* began publication before the Civil War. An early editor and proprietor, Charles Rhoads, was known as a secessionist and described by a Wheeling newspaper as a "disunionist." In May 1861, the office of the *News* was destroyed by a crowd of pro-Union men, and Rhoads was driven out of town. It was 36 years before a paper of the same name, with different ownership, began publication in February 1897. The new *Parkersburg News* was a morning paper.

In 1915, Wheeling publisher Herschel C. Ogden, an ancestor of the present owners of Ogden Newspapers, became the owner of the *Parkersburg News*. The purchase was among the first steps in establishing the now extensive Ogden newspaper chain.

Meanwhile, Ogden's company had acquired a rival newspaper, the *Parkersburg Daily Sentinel*, in 1912. The *Sentinel* was founded as the *Parkersburg Weekly Sentinel* by Robert Hornor in 1875. In 1899, Hornor's son, also named Robert, began the *Parkersburg Daily Sentinel.* The weekly edition continued, becoming a semi-weekly in the 1890s until it ceased publication in 1920. The *Daily Sentinel* was established as a voice of the Democratic Party and as competition for the Republican-oriented *Daily State Journal.*

The morning *Parkersburg News*, published seven days a week, had a weekday circulation of 20,700 in 2004. The circulation of the evening *Parkersburg Sentinel*, published Monday through Friday, was 5,414. Both newspapers are published by Ogden Newspapers.

See also Herschel Coombs Ogden

Parsons

Parsons, the county seat of Tucker County, is located at the head of Cheat River, at the intersection of U.S. 219 and State Route 72. Parsons became an incorporated town on June 12, 1893, and an incorporated city on February 18, 1907. It was built on the route of the West Virginia Central & Pittsburg [sic] Railway, which was constructed through Tucker County in the 1880s. Parsons became the county seat on August 7, 1893, although the county records had actually (and unlawfully) been moved from St. George to Parsons on the night of August 1, 1893. Parsons was named for Ward Parsons, not the first settler but the most prominent and the largest landholder. The Battle of Corricks Ford, a Confederate defeat, took place near present Parsons on July 13, 1861.

Parsons boomed early in the 20th century and peaked during the period from 1920 to 1940, according to Cleta M. Long's *History of Tucker County*. Census reports show Parsons with a population of 84 in 1890 and 2,077 in 1940. Changes in the natural resources economy caused the population to fall in the 1950s and 1960s. The flood of November 1985 was the major factor in a later and larger loss of population, from 1,937 in 1980 to 1,453 in 1990. The town's population stabilized after 1990, increasing slightly to 1,463 in the 2000 census.

The 1985 flood was hard on Parsons, with water cresting at 24.3 feet. More than 90 percent of businesses in the area, as well as hundreds of homes, were damaged or destroyed. About 40 houses located in the flood plain were later acquired and demolished by the federal government. Many of those whose homes were purchased after the flood chose to settle outside Parsons. A study completed in July 1999 by the *Parsons Advocate,* the county newspaper, showed that only 45 percent of the families relocated in Parsons; business licenses dropped 40 percent, and total receipts for city services dropped 24 percent while total expenditures increased 4 percent. Parsons entered the 21st century as a town in transition, building its way from an economy based on natural resources to one based on tourism, while recovering from the setback of a great natural disaster.

See also Tucker County

Mariwyn McClain Smith
Parsons

Phoeba Parsons

Traditional musician Phoeba Cottrell Parsons, born in Calhoun County, April 21, 1908, was a banjo player, ballad singer, storyteller, teller of riddles, and flatfoot dancer. She picked up her brother's homemade banjo at age ten, even though "he didn't want me to play because he was afraid I'd beat him." This brother, Noah Cottrell, was also a respected banjo picker, fiddler, and storyteller. He died in 1991.

After Phoeba married in 1928 she ceased playing music and didn't take up the banjo again until the 1960s. In 1975, she won the banjo contest at the West Virginia State Folk Festival at Glenville, which is generally regarded as the state's most authentic music festival. The following year she was one of a select group of musicians to represent the Mountain State at the Festival of American Folklife in Washington. In 1987, she received the Vandalia Award, West Virginia's highest folklife honor. Parsons's traditional clawhammer banjo style, unaccompanied ballad singing, riddles and storytelling, and mastery of the fiddlesticks have influenced countless numbers of younger musicians. As she noted in a 1987 interview with folklorist Michael Kline, "Nobody showed me nothing, [but] I learned a lot of people how to play."

Phoeba Parsons died July 4, 2001.

Susan A. Eacker
Morehead State University

Squire Parsons

Musician Squire Parsons Jr. has gained national renown in the field of gospel music as a singer and songwriter. Parsons was born April 4, 1948, in Newton, Roane County. He attended Spencer High School and is a 1970 graduate of West Virginia Institute of Technology, where he earned a degree in music. In 1975, he became the baritone singer for the Kingsmen Quartet, thus launching his public singing career. Parsons, no longer with the Kingsmen, is best known for his 1981 hit, "Sweet Beulah Land," which was voted favorite song of the year by *Singing News*, a gospel music publication. He has written numerous other modern classics, including "Master of the Sea," "The Broken Rose," "Oh, What a Moment," and "He Came to Me." All told, Parsons has written more than 600 gospel songs.

He has been voted Favorite Baritone two years, and Favorite Gospel Songwriter five years in the *Singing News* annual competition. Squire Parsons and his wife, Linda, live in Leicester, North Carolina. They have four children.

Skip Johnson
Sutton

Okey L. Patteson

Okey Leonidas Patteson, the "Great Persuader" from Mount Hope, tackled difficult decisions as West Virginia's 23rd governor from 1949 to 1953. His greatest legacy is the West Virginia University school of medicine, which today one enters via four-lane Patteson Drive. Patteson, according to John Morgan's book, *West Virginia Governors*, left office more popular than when elected. He was the first West Virginian to overcome a severe physical handicap and be elected governor.

Patteson was born September 14, 1898, at Dingess in Mingo County. His parents, originally from Nicholas County, moved the family to Mount Hope in Fayette County when Okey was a child.

Patteson's election as a Democratic governor coincided with the upset victory of President Harry S. Truman in 1948. During four years in office, Patteson wrestled with issues relating to the Korean Conflict, choosing the location for a state medical school, juggling bonuses for veterans of World War II, highway construction controversies, and a prison riot.

Following his education at West Virginia Wesleyan College and at Carnegie Tech (now Carnegie Mellon University) in Pittsburgh, Patteson launched a career in business and in 1923 married Lee Hawse from Romney. Tragedy struck in

Governor Okey L. Patteson (1898–1989).

1932 when the 34-year-old businessman was bird hunting with brother-in-law Karl Warden. Patteson had leaned his loaded 12-gauge Winchester shotgun against his car, thinking he had left the safety on. As he closed the left rear door after retrieving his gun case, the shotgun fell and discharged with a deafening roar, shooting Patteson's feet from under him. Doctors at Beckley amputated both legs below the knees. During his six-week hospital convalescence Patteson was fitted with artificial limbs. Within four months, he was walking again and driving his own car.

His determination to overcome obstacles found new outlets in real estate and politics. He ran for Fayette County Democratic committeeman and later for sheriff, winning every election he entered. In 1944, he managed the gubernatorial campaign of Clarence W. Meadows. When Meadows won, he named Patteson executive assistant, a newly created position. Given the assignment of handling tough problems, Patteson mastered the art of persuasion and four years later was endorsed by Meadows as his successor. Defeating the "crown prince" and "organized machine" labels that branded anyone supported by an incumbent governor in those times, Patteson won the primary with more votes than the combined votes of his opponents. In the general election, he defeated state Sen. Herbert S. Boreman, grand-nephew of West Virginia's first governor. An estimated 2,500 persons jammed the state capitol to hear Patteson's inaugural address.

Patteson is best remembered for the politically tough decision of where to locate the state's first medical school. The contest was between the metropolitan capital city of Charleston and the university community of Morgantown. After months of seeking advice, the governor opted for Morgantown as "the logical and best place for the location of the school," insisting the weight of evidence favored location on a university campus.

Other newsworthy events during Patteson's term included construction of the West Virginia Turnpike, although Patteson lost in federal court his argument that the turnpike should be four lanes instead of the original confusing two- and three-lane configuration favored by the Turnpike Commission. A veterans bonus was passed for West Virginia veterans of the two world wars. The penny-a-bottle "pop" tax was created to finance the medical school. A prison riot in 1951 was attributed to crowded conditions and idleness; no one was injured. An eight-story office building designed by capitol architect Cass Gilbert's son and now occupied by the Division of Motor Vehicles was built for $4 million.

Patteson endorsed Attorney General William C. Marland as his successor, but later broke with Marland, saying his "faith was misplaced," in that Patteson had considered Marland to be "strictly sober." (By this time, Marland's problems with alcoholism were a matter of public discussion.) Patteson's work after the governorship was largely in real estate and banking. He served as president of Raleigh County Bank and was an original member of the Board of Regents, which oversaw higher education. He remained a popular figure in Democratic circles. "Being governor was a wonderful opportunity. I wouldn't take anything for the experience. But I don't think I would be interested in even trying to go through the ordeal again," he said.

In 1961, more than six years after the death of his first wife, Patteson married Dorothy R. "Bebe" (Reuter) Warden, who had been a family friend for years. Patteson quietly visited others facing handicaps in hospitals, remembering long after 1932 a man with artificial limbs who had inspired him after his own hunting accident. He died July 3, 1989.

Jack Canfield
Charleston

John Morgan, *West Virginia Governors*, 1980.

Paulownia

Paulownia is a fast-growing exotic tree now widely naturalized in the lower elevations of West Virginia. Paulownia is also called "empress tree" or "princess tree" because its name honors a Russian-Dutch princess. The tree, native to China, has tiny, light seeds that served as packing material in the days before plastic foam. Seeds escaping from opened crates helped establish paulownia along rivers and railroads.

Paulownia has huge, velvety, heart-shaped leaves and distinctive, blue-purple flowers. Sprouts from stumps grow with astonishing speed, sometimes over 20 feet in a year. Premium logs of forest-grown paulownia sold for $10 per board foot in 1996, the highest price paid for any wood grown in West Virginia. The strong, very light wood seasons quickly with a minimum of distortion or cracking. Buyers ship most logs to Japan, where craftsmen fashion paulownia wood into stringed instruments, furniture, bowls, and decorative items.

Jon Weems
West Virginia University

Paw Paw

Strategically located on the Potomac River, the B&O Railroad and the C&O Canal, Paw Paw was named for the banana-like pawpaw fruit that grows in the area. It is the westernmost settlement in Morgan County, incorporated as a town on April 8, 1891. Paw Paw had 524 people in the year 2000.

Travelers heading west often crossed the gap in the mountains here, some settling to farm along the river. Gen. Edward Braddock's army camped on a hill just east of town during the French and Indian War. The site became Camp Chase, a federal camp during the Civil War where more than 16,000 Union soldiers were stationed to guard the railroad. Today, it is Camp Hill Cemetery.

In 1836, the C&O Canal Company began to carve a 3,118-foot tunnel through Sorrel Ridge about a half-mile north of town, across the Potomac in Maryland. The Paw Paw Tunnel was completed in 1850. At 24 feet high, it is the largest manmade structure on the C&O Canal. Mules and canal boats transported manufactured goods through it until 1924.

The Baltimore & Ohio Railroad arrived in 1838 and the Western Maryland Railroad in 1905. Once six trains per day stopped at Paw Paw. Passenger service ceased in 1961, and the railroads are no longer a major employer. Industry has come and gone, including tanneries, apple orchards, railroads, and canals. In 1982, Paw Paw was the site of the first branch bank in West Virginia.

Each year, Paw Paw celebrates homecoming with a parade and festivities on Memorial Day weekend. Paw Paw serves as the westernmost entry to the Washington Heritage Trail, a National Scenic Byway.

Jeanne Mozier
Berkeley Springs

Morgan County Historical Society, *Morgan County, West Virginia and Its People*, 1981.

Pawpaws

The pawpaw, North America's largest native edible fruit, is present throughout West Virginia. The only temperate member of the Annonaceae family, the pawpaw is a rich, nutritious fruit with a custard-like texture and sweet taste. The oval or kidney-shaped fruits vary from the size of a plum to that of a large potato. The skin is light green and the creamy flesh is yellow. Each fruit contains several large, dark brown seeds.

Pawpaw trees prefer slightly acidic, well-drained soil, and often are found along the banks of creeks and rivers. The leaves are about 12 inches long, glossy, distinctly veined, and droopy. Pawpaws tend to be small, understory trees, usually not more than 30 feet high. In spring, before the leaves appear, pawpaw trees produce bell-like blossoms, dark burgundy in color. The fruit ripens in early autumn and is ready to eat when fragrant and slightly soft.

Early European explorers in America recorded that the pawpaw was highly regarded by Native Americans, who ate the fruit and used the tree's bark for making baskets. Consumed fresh in season, pawpaws later found a place in the folk diet of rural West Virginians. Pawpaws are still known primarily as a wild food, although a few growers are now cultivating them.

Colleen Anderson
Charleston

Christopher H. Payne

Christopher Payne (1848–1925) was the first African-American to serve in the House of Delegates.

West Virginia's first black legislator, Christopher Harrison Payne, was born in Monroe County, September 7, 1848. Raised near Hinton, Payne worked as a farmhand. Although born free, he was compelled to serve as a body servant in the Confederate Army during the Civil War. He attended night school in Charleston after the war and taught school in Monroe, Mercer, and Summers counties. An ordained Baptist minister, Payne continued his education at Richmond Theological Institute and earned a Doctor of Divinity degree from State University in Louisville, Kentucky.

In 1888, Payne became the first African-American elected to represent West Virginia at a Republican national convention and later was elected to two more. Elected to the legislature from Fayette County in 1896, Payne became the first black to serve in the West Virginia House of Delegates.

In addition to his pastoral duties and political activities, Payne founded or edited three weekly newspapers. The first was the *West Virginia Enterprise,* established by Payne in 1885 and published in Charleston. His second and third papers were the *Pioneer* and the *Mountain Eagle,* both published in Montgomery.

Following his term in the legislature, Payne served as a minister in Huntington where he lived with his wife, Annie, and their daughter, Mollie. The Republican Party rewarded Payne for his loyalty with two federal patronage jobs. He served as deputy collector of internal revenue, and in 1903 President Theodore Roosevelt appointed Payne as consul general to the Danish West Indies. Following his appointment, the citizens of St. Thomas elected him judge advocate, and he remained in the islands until his death December 5, 1925.

See also Fayette County

Connie Park Rice
West Virginia University

Thomas E. Posey, *The Negro Citizen of West Virginia,* 1934.

Henry Payne

Cartoonist Henry Payne was born in Charleston, May 13, 1962. He graduated in 1984 from Princeton University. He began his career in editorial cartoons there, winning the College Media Advisers Cartoon Contest and the Tribune Company Syndicate's National College Cartoonist's Contest for his work at the *Daily Princetonian* and the *Nassau Weekly.*

After college, Payne began as staff artist and editorial cartoonist for the *Charleston Daily Mail,* where he previously had worked as an intern for two summers. Payne, a self-described conservative, left West Virginia in 1986 to join Scripps Howard News Service in Washington, where he also served as editor of a cartoon wire service. He began syndication in 1987 with United Feature Syndicate, which distributes his cartoons to more than 60 newspapers worldwide. Other publications that have carried his work include the *New York Times, USA Today,* and the *National Review.*

In 1989, Payne was the first editorial cartoonist in the country to make his work available via computer, and he cofounded a Scripps Howard Network to illustrate stories with computer graphics. In 1999, he joined the *Detroit News,* where he produces cartoons and columns. In addition to his artistic skills, Payne has written articles about economic, consumer, and environmental issues that have appeared in publications such as the *Wall Street Journal, National Review, Reason, Rocky Mountain News,* the *Pittsburgh Post-Gazette,* and the *Detroit News.* Payne was a runner-up for the Pulitzer Prize in 1986 and the Mencken Award in 1992. He published his first book, *Payne & Ink: The Cartoons and Commentary of Henry Payne, 2000–2001,* in 2002.

Elizabeth Jill Wilson
Cottageville

Pence Springs

Pence Springs, the name of a mineral spring and community, is located in Summers County, 12 miles east of Hinton on State Route 3. The spring's sulfurous water is noted for a distinctive "rotten egg" taste arising from the concentration of hydrogen sulfide. In early times the spring was frequented by herds of wild animals, particularly buffaloes, that drank the salty water. The site also was visited by Indians, probably attracted by the abundant game. The broad fields between the spring and the Greenbrier River contain prehistoric sites, which were studied in 1984 by scholars from the University of Kentucky.

During the 19th century, the water of the spring was believed to have medicinal properties, and many visitors were attracted to the site. The property was not developed commercially as a resort until 1872 when a wooden hotel was constructed. The number of visitors rapidly increased in the late 1870s after the Chesapeake & Ohio Railway Company built its main line down the Greenbrier River. The railroad constructed a passenger station across the river from the resort. In 1878, the property containing the spring was sold to Andrew S. Pence, who extensively developed the site and built up a thriving business by selling water bottled at the spring. In 1904, Pence Springs water was presented the highest award in its class and a silver medal at the St. Louis Exposition. At one time, a plant to manufacture and bottle ginger ale operated at the spring.

Eventually Pence Springs became so popular that several boarding houses and hotels operated in addition to the original hotel. About 1900, E. M. Carney of Kanawha County purchased property near that of Pence and erected a rival hotel. Pence filed a lawsuit against Carney in 1904, after Carney drilled into the seam that carried water to Pence's spring and began to sell the water in competition with Pence. The suit, which went to the West Virginia Supreme Court, was decided in favor of Carney.

In 1918, a large brick hotel was constructed by the Pence family on the hill overlooking the original spring. This hotel operated until the 1930s but closed due to lack of revenue. In 1947, the property, containing the original spring, brick hotel, and fields along the river, was purchased by the state of West Virginia for use as the state prison for women. The prison functioned until 1985, at which time the prisoners were transferred to the federal women's prison in nearby Alderson.

In 1986, the property was purchased by Ashby Berkley, who renovated the hotel and reopened it for guests. He and his sister, Rosa Lee Miller, sold the property in 2001. Berkley reclaimed it in 2003, again briefly operating it as an inn. The hotel was placed on the National Register of Historic Places in 1985.

Michael M. Meador
Abingdon, Virginia

Pendleton County

Formed in 1788 largely from Rockingham County, and smaller portions of Augusta and Hardy, Pendleton County was named for Virginia statesman Edmund Pendleton (1721–1803). Bounded on two sides by Virginia, it adjoins the Shenandoah Valley. Its surface area, 696.9 square miles, ranks fifth-largest in the state. Franklin is the county seat and only incorporated municipality.

FAST FACTS ABOUT PENDLETON COUNTY

Founded: 1788
Land in square miles: 696.9
Population: 8,196
Percentage minorities: 3.7%
Percentage rural: 100%
Median age: 41.1
Percentage 65 and older: 17.8%
Birth rate per 1,000 population: 9.3
Median household income: $30,429
High school graduate or higher: 72.0%
Bachelor's degree or higher: 10.8%
Home ownership: 79.4%
Median home value: $76,600

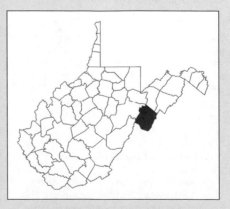

This information is from the 2000 U.S. Census. In 2000, West Virginia as a whole had 5 percent minorities, a median age of 38.9, median household income of $29,696, and a 75.2 percent home ownership rate.

Pendleton County is known for its fine mountain scenery.

Pendleton's three parallel valleys are drained by the Potomac's South Branch and its tributaries. Spruce Knob in the county's southwestern corner rises to 4,861 feet, the highest elevation in the state. Pendleton's total vertical relief of 3,708 feet, the distance from the highest to lowest points, is the greatest of West Virginia counties. The county has 295 known limestone caves, whose aggregate mapped length totals nearly 37 miles. Pendleton County is spectacularly beautiful, with scenic features including Seneca Rocks, Champe Rocks, Germany Valley, Seneca Caverns, and the Smoke Hole canyon.

The first known white settlement had occurred by 1740 near present Cherry Grove on the North Fork of the South Branch. By 1747, several families had acquired lands at Fort Seybert on the South Fork, and shortly thereafter at Upper Tract on the main South Branch. Germans were most numerous among the early settlers. German culture became concentrated especially in the vicinities of Sugar Grove and Thorn Creek, where a German-speaking tradition persisted among elderly residents into the late 20th century.

The area, then part of Augusta County, was exposed to Indian raids during the French and Indian War. In 1758, Shawnees led by Killbuck subdued Forts Seybert and Upper Tract, killing dozens of settlers and militia. Hinkle's Fort in Germany Valley escaped destruction and continued through the Revolution. Only one Indian raid, in 1781, occurred in Pendleton after 1764. During the American Revolution the people's sympathies were divided, with a significant Tory presence.

From 1790 to 1860, Pendleton's population increased from 2,452 to 6,164; there were 50 free blacks and 244 slaves in 1860. Franklin, formerly known as Frankford, was chartered in 1794. In 1821, territory was lost to Pocahontas County, and the northern half of Highland County, Virginia, was taken from Pendleton when that county was formed in 1847. Subsequently Pendleton's borders have remained unchanged. The niter and gunpowder industry, particularly at the Trout Rock caves, was important during the War of 1812. For nearly a century before 1860, Pendleton stockmen participated in the South Branch's prosperous cattle industry. Perhaps the most notable antebellum citizen was William McCoy, who served 22 years (1811–33) in the U.S. House of Representatives, part of this tenure as chairman of the House Ways and Means Committee. McCoy's Mill, whose predecessor mill was built at the mouth of Thorn Creek by Ulrich Conrad about the time of the French and Indian War, remains a local landmark today.

During the Civil War the county government and a majority of citizens supported the Confederacy. More than 700 Pendleton soldiers fought for the South. But Unionists in the Seneca and Brushy Run sections contributed several hundred men to Home Guard companies. The result of divided allegiance was vicious guerrilla warfare in the county. The most prominent leaders of the respective sides were brothers: Confederate James Boggs and Unionist John Boggs. The Confederate Niter and Mining Bureau operated the saltpeter works at Trout Rock, which were raided repeatedly by federal forces. After the war, William H. H. Flick, an Ohio carpetbagger and Union veteran who served as Pendleton's delegate to the West Virginia legislature, introduced the Flick Amendment which in 1870 restored the voting rights of ex-Confederates.

At least four railroad projects were proposed during the next 40 years, but none materialized. Pendleton never obtained a permanent railroad, although several temporary logging railroads penetrated the county in the early 20th century. In 1918 and 1920, the newly created Shenandoah and Monongahela national forests were extended into the county's eastern and western reaches. The Shenandoah National Forest was renamed for George Washington in 1932.

Several crises struck Pendleton between the two world wars. In April 1924, a catastrophic fire destroyed the business district of Franklin. In addition to economic depression and severe drought, the failure of all three county banks in 1931, and the absence of a bank until 1937, reduced many residents to barter. The county benefited from federal projects during Roosevelt's New Deal, including the building of 300 miles of improved roads, and increased state aid to schools. Ralph M. Hiner of Franklin served as speaker of the House of Delegates from 1933 to 1935. County population peaked at 10,884 in 1940. During World War II, army mountain troops trained on Seneca Rocks and other crags. The war spurred massive out-migration, which would continue to 1970, when the census recorded a population of 7,031.

Since 1970 the population has grown slowly, to 8,196 in 2000, of which 174 were African-American, 73 Hispanic, and 63 of mixed racial heritage. Franklin had 797 inhabitants in 2000, a decline from 914 in 1990. Agriculture has continued as the economic mainstay, especially livestock and poultry. In 1997, the average size of the county's 590 farms was 297 acres; these yielded agricultural products worth $67.65 million. Major employers have included Greer Lime Company (since 1960) in Germany Valley; Allegheny Wood Products (since 1973) at Riverton; and the Pendleton Nursing Home (since 1975) at the county seat. The 2000 median household income was $30,429, above the state average. The county's largest employer in the late 20th century, the Hanover Shoe plant, which had a peak work force of about 700 and about 360 in mid-1999, ceased operations in January 2000.

In 1965, Congress created the 100,000-acre Spruce Knob-Seneca Rocks National Recreation Area. The Treasure Mountain Festival, held at Franklin each September, was inaugurated in 1969. That same year the U.S. Navy began operating a major communications center at Sugar Grove. Not until 1977 did the North Fork area acquire modern dial telephone service, replacing vintage hand-crank telephones. The worst natural disaster in the county's history occurred in November 1985 when raging floodwaters killed 16 people and inflicted severe property damage. Except for neighboring Pocahontas

County, the population density of Pendleton County is the lowest in the state.

See also Franklin

John Craft Taylor
Union College

Elsie Byrd Boggs, *A History of Franklin: The County Seat of Pendleton County, West Virginia*, 1960; H. M. Calhoun, *'Twixt North and South*, 1974; Oren F. Morton, *A History of Pendleton County, West Virginia*, 1910.

Penn Central Railroad

In 1957, the business world was surprised with the announcement of plans to merge the Pennsylvania Railroad and the New York Central System, traditional rivals. The merger between these two giants raised much opposition and took more than a decade for the Interstate Commerce Commission to approve. On February 1, 1968, the Pennsylvania New York Central Transportation Company was created, commonly called the Penn Central. Its history was a short one. Whereas both predecessor railroads had been solvent, in 1970 the new corporation entered bankruptcy. From its ruins, Congress created Conrail through the Reorganization Act of 1973.

In West Virginia, the Penn Central absorbed the rail lines of both predecessor railroads. This included a few miles of the Pennsylvania Railroad's Pittsburgh-St. Louis main line, which crossed the Northern Panhandle south of Weirton with a connection to Wheeling.

Most of Penn Central's trackage in West Virginia came from the New York Central side of the merger. The main line ran from Point Pleasant through Nitro to Charleston. From Charleston it continued east to the big rail yard at Dickinson, near today's Riverside High School. This line continued to Gauley Bridge, then onward to Rainelle and points beyond. Another line ran from Charleston into northeastern Kanawha County. Designed to tap local coal mines, this branch was originally part of the Kanawha & West Virginia Railroad. Through a long and complicated history the branch from Gauley Bridge to Rainelle and beyond had been owned jointly by the New York Central and the C&O. As a result of the creation of the Penn Central these lines east of Dickinson were operated by the Chessie System.

The collapse of the Penn Central was the greatest business failure in the history of the United States to 1970. However, the railroad was never a major factor in West Virginia's economic history, as compared to the Baltimore & Ohio and Chesapeake & Ohio (now CSX), the Norfolk & Western (Norfolk Southern), the Western Maryland (also CSX), or the Virginian Railway.

See also Conrail, Railroads

Robert L. Frey
Miamisburg, Ohio

Pentecostalism

Pentcostalism is a relatively new religious movement, having its beginnings, most authorities say, in 1901, with the teachings of Midwestern preacher Charles Fox Parham. He taught that speaking in tongues, or glossolalia, would be the movement that would empower the Christian church for the "last days harvest" by serving to evangelize the world. Six years later, an intense outbreak of tongue speaking in Los Angeles, when an African-American disciple of Parham, William J. Seymour, led his church in a much larger and more influential exercise of the practice, essentially initiated the expansion that has made Pentecostalism the fastest-growing Protestant denomination in the world. Today this movement is the largest religious division to have originated in the United States, with churches in 385 of the 399 counties of Appalachia.

In West Virginia and Appalachia there has been a fusing of Pentecostal theology and the Holiness movement, the latter being a development from the early Wesleyan faith. John Wesley, who along with his brother, Charles, founded the Methodist church, contended that simple conversion or initial redemption should not constitute the end-all of Christian development. Rather, the convert should continue throughout his or her spiritual life to climb toward perfection in sacred development, practicing a pietistic lifestyle that in its ultimate form would be called Sanctification.

In Appalachian Pentecostalism, this holiness state would become linked with the anointment of the Holy Spirit, a spiritual condition which was thought to permit the believer to engage in speaking in tongues, healing the sick, casting out demons, taking up serpents, and drinking deadly poisons (the five signs of a believer as pronounced in Mark 16:17–18). Consequently, in West Virginia and other areas of Central Appalachia we find many churches that are identified as Pentecostal Holiness or Holiness Pentecostal.

Perhaps the most interesting division between Pentecostal churches in West Virginia and in most states of Central Appalachia is the theological split that separates the "Trinitarian Pentecostals," who baptize in the name of the Father, the Son, and the Holy Spirit, and the "Oneness Pentecostals," who baptize only in the name of Jesus. In some cases the Oneness Pentecostals formally reject the Trinity, but in other cases they proclaim that they are Trinitarians and that their baptism only in the name of Jesus simply celebrates the importance John the Baptist placed on the role of Jesus in the original River Jordan baptisms.

Of the 55 West Virginia counties there are only three that have no Pentecostal churches at all, as of a 2000 church census. However, it must be noted that some Pentecostal denominations do not have "Pentecostal" in their formal title. This is true for the Assemblies of God; the Church of God Cleveland, Tennessee; the Church of God of Prophecy; the Church of God, Mountain Assembly; the Fire Baptized Holiness Association; the International Church of the Foursquare Gospel; the Open Bible Standard Churches; and the Original Church of God. Of these, Assemblies of God, the Church of God Cleveland, Tennessee, and the Church of God of Prophecy have numerous fellowships in West Virginia.

It is difficult to document the size of the Pentecostal movement because so many of the churches are totally independent, belonging to no organization above the local fellowship and frequently keeping no formal membership records even of their own congregation. Such church polling organizations as the Glenmary Research Center of Nashville frequently must depend on computer-generated models that produce only estimates of regional, state, or national counts.

See also Religion

Howard Dorgan
Appalachian State University

Deborah Vansau McCauley, *Appalachian Mountain Religion: A History*, 1995.

Pepperoni Rolls

The pepperoni roll, a West Virginia delicacy, is a roll baked with pepperoni inside. The grease from the pepperoni creates an orangeish-red spot on either end. While pizza crust hardens after baking, pepperoni rolls remain a soft treat that you eat right out of your hand.

Fairmont baker Giuseppe "Joseph" Argiro, founder of the Country Club Bakery, is credited with having invented the pepperoni roll in 1927. Argiro, a former miner, remembered his coworkers eating bread and pepperoni at work and combined the two. The innovative baker passed the recipe down to his son, Frank "Cheech" Argiro, who later owned Country Club Bakery. Other West Virginians picked up the pepperoni roll idea and developed their own versions. Filippo Colasessano, also a former miner, opened his own Fairmont lunch spot, and in 1957, Colasessano's son, "Spider," started selling pepperoni rolls there. Spider Colasessano experimented with the recipe, adding cheese, hot peppers, and even hot dog sauce.

Future production of pepperoni rolls was threatened in 1987, when the U.S. Department of Agriculture wanted to reclassify the roll bakeries as meat packers, forcing them to meet more stringent regulations. Sen. Jay Rockefeller addressed the issue with then-Secretary of Agriculture Richard Lyng. Rockefeller was concerned that the mostly family-operated bakeries would die, and along with them the cherished tradition of the pepperoni roll. Fortunately, the U.S.D.A. backed off.

While still most popular in the areas of heaviest Italian settlement, particularly in northern West Virginia, today pepperoni rolls may be found in most parts of the state. In fact, pepperoni rolls promise to spread far outside their traditional homeland in the 21st century, as a version of the popular snack is now included in the U.S. military's MRE's (Meals Ready to Eat). The war-going pepperoni rolls are produced by a North Carolina company.

Rachelle Bott Beckner
Charleston

Personal Rapid Transit System

The Personal Rapid Transit (PRT) commuter system connects Morgantown's downtown business district, the West Virginia University downtown campus, WVU Evansdale campus, the WVU Towers residence halls, and the WVU medical center. The first fully automated urban guideway transit system, it was conceived by the WVU College of Engineering during the 1960s in response to national discussions of traffic congestion. Phase I of the project was completed in 1975. Phase II, which expanded and improved the system, was completed in 1979.

The PRT consists of five passenger stations, 73 vehicles, 8.7 miles of guide-ways, maintenance facilities, and a central computer center. Passengers use turnstiles that take coins or a PRT card, and the cars are controlled at the computer center; there are no station or vehicle operators. Each vehicle can carry eight seated and 12 standing passengers and travel up to 30 miles per hour. The speedy blue-and-gold cars run on rubber wheels in a U-shaped concrete guide-way, with power and signal rails along the guide-way wall. At peak capacity, the system can transport 1,100 people in 20 minutes.

In addition to being a unique part of the WVU student experience, the PRT has had a lasting impact on public transportation. It is a valuable research tool, allowing fast data collection in five peak periods per day. It has proven itself on hilly terrain, and in weather ranging from sun to fog to snow and ice. The first transportation system to model itself after the PRT was the Kobe Rapid Transit System in Japan, and there are other automated commuter systems in Detroit, Jacksonville, Miami, and Irving, Texas.

See also West Virginia University

Elizabeth Ann H. McClain
Montrose
W. Russ McClain
Nature Conservancy of West Virginia

Peter Tarr Furnace

The first iron furnace west of the Allegheny Mountains was built in present Hancock County in the early 1790s by a Mr. Grant, and acquired in 1801 by Peter Tarr and James Rankin. Known to history by Peter Tarr's name, the furnace was located along Kings Creek, a tributary of the Ohio River, just north of Weirton. At its peak, the furnace produced two tons of iron per day. Initially, the molten iron was fashioned into skillets, kettles, and other household utensils. During the War of 1812, the Peter Tarr furnace produced cannonballs for the navy, supposedly including cannonballs used by Commodore Perry's victorious fleet during the Battle of Lake Erie.

Peter Tarr died in 1839. His furnace's foundation and oval-shaped salamander, where the iron ore was heated, are still intact below ground level. Partially restored by the Hancock County Historical Society in 1968, the Peter Tarr furnace is listed on the National Register of Historic Places.

See also Ironmaking

Pam Tarr
Daniel Hart
Charleston

Jack Welch, *History of Hancock County*, 1963.

George William Peterkin

Bishop George William Peterkin, born March 21, 1841, in Washington County, Maryland, attended the University of Virginia and was preparing to enter the Episcopal priesthood when the Civil War interrupted his studies. At the age of 20, he joined the Confederate 21st Virginia Infantry, June 28, 1861, and served under Robert E. Lee in present West Virginia. He was a lieutenant for the duration of the war and was present at Appomattox, as an aide to Gen. W. H. Pendleton, during the surrender ceremonies.

After the war, Peterkin graduated from the Theological Seminary of Virginia in 1868. After being ordained as an Episcopal priest in 1869, he served in churches in Virginia and Maryland until 1878. Following the creation of the Diocese of West Virginia in late 1877, Peterkin, then minister of Memorial Church in Baltimore, was elected bishop for West Virginia and consecrated at Wheeling, May 30, 1878.

Peterkin established his residence in Parkersburg. During his 24 years as bishop, 1878–1902, he visited every county in West Virginia, expanding the influence of the church throughout the state. He consecrated 37 new churches, conducted 49 ordinations of priests in West Virginia and four in Brazil, confirmed 5,078 communicants in West Virginia, and traveled to other states and foreign lands to preside over 1,376 confirmations. In 1887, he founded Sheltering Arms Hospital in Hansford, pioneering in the medical care of coal miners. In 1892, he published *Records of the Protestant Episcopal Church in West Virginia,* one of many church-related treatises prepared by him.

Peterkin helped erect a monument in 1901 on Valley Mountain to memorialize the deaths of the Confederate soldiers who had died there in 1861. He died in Parkersburg, September 28, 1916. The church's Peterkin Center retreat near Romney is named for Bishop Peterkin.

See also Episcopal Church

Donald L. Rice
Elkins

Eva M. Carnes, "George W. (Bishop) Peterkin at Valley Mountain," *Magazine of History and Biography*, 1961; George W. Peterkin, *A History and Record of the Protestant Episcopal Church in the Diocese of West Virginia*, 1902.

Peters Mountain

Peters Mountain, on the Virginia-West Virginia border south of Lewisburg, was probably named after Peter Wright, an early settler. About 50 miles long, it is a continuation of the same geological formation as East River Mountain; the two mountains are separated by the water gap cut by the New River at the Narrows. Throughout most of its length, the crest of Peters Mountain is formed by the same hard white Medina Sandstone that forms the crest of East River Mountain. The crest of Peters Mountain is the boundary between Monroe County and Giles and Craig counties in Virginia, except for 12 miles where the state line veers southeastward to include the Waiteville area, bringing that section within West Virginia. The last ten miles of Peters Mountain is wholly within Alleghany County, Virginia. The elevation varies from 3,000 to 4,000 feet, with the highest point, near Zenith, reaching 4,050 feet. Peters Mountain, long a barrier to transportation, is crossed only by State Route 311 and the old Salt Sulphur Turnpike. A few miles of the Appalachian Trail follows the crest of the mountain, and also a small part of the Allegheny Trail. Peters Mountain is the site of Hanging Rock Observatory, a bird watching station noted for the fall migration of raptors.

See also East River Mountain

Raymond Thomas Hill
Athens

Petersburg

Petersburg, the county seat of Grant County, is situated on the South Branch of the Potomac River near the Hardy County border, 30 miles from the Virginia line. The town is located at the junction of U.S. 220 and state routes 42 and 28. The 2000 population was 2,423.

Settled in 1745 as Lunice Creek, its name was changed to Petersburg, probably in honor of early merchant Jacob Peters, then to Grant Court House when it became the county seat in 1870, and finally back to Petersburg. The town has a hospital, city library, volunteer fire department, newspaper, high school and elementary school, nine churches, several restaurants and motels, a variety of retail stores, and a new city park. Winter weather is mild and summers warm but pleasant. Grant County Airport is nearby.

Widely known for its excellent trout fishing, Petersburg's proximity to the river, Smoke Hole Canyon, Spruce Knob, Seneca Rocks, and the North Fork Mountain attracts many visitors. Annual celebrations include the Spring Mountain Festival and the Tri-County Fair (shared with Hardy and Pendleton counties). The Petersburg Wave, a powerful seasonal updraft, makes Petersburg popular with glider pilots.

See also Grant County, Petersburg Wave

Peggy Ross
Reedsville

Petersburg Wave

A powerful natural updraft near Petersburg, Grant County, the Petersburg Wave attracts glider-plane pilots from around the world each March. When the prevailing westerly wind, having swept across a 4,000-foot plateau encompassing Dolly Sods and Roaring Plains, reaches the eastern rim of the plateau, it plummets down the steep Allegheny Front into the valley where the two forks of the South Branch of the Potomac River merge near Petersburg. After reaching the valley floor, the wind rises again in a powerful standing wave with enormous lift.

In March, when the wave action is strongest, the Grant County Airport in Petersburg hosts a wave camp to accommodate glider pilots. The Federal Aviation Administration gives the pilots exclusive use of a rectangle of airspace over Petersburg and the Allegheny Front during the wave camp. After being towed by plane to heights of 3,000 to 5,000 feet, the gliders, which have no engines, are cut loose. After riding the wave, the pilots land their gliders on the grass berm of the paved landing strip, or, if they run out of air, in one of the pastures or hayfields of the surrounding region. A typical glider flight lasts about two and a half hours.

Pins are awarded to camp participants for altitudes reached. Diamond pins are awarded for pilots who gain more than 5,000 meters, gold pins for those gaining more than 3,000 meters, and silver pins for those gaining at least 1,000 meters. Winning altitudes are verified through readings taken from on-board barographs. If the needle marks imprinted on a metal sheet attached to the barograph's drum indicate sufficient gain, the marks are sprayed with lacquer to preserve the readings, which are sent to the Soaring Society of America for confirmation.

Nearly all of the East Coast records for altitude have been set at the Petersburg Wave.

See also Petersburg

Judie Smith
West Virginia Humanities Council

Petroglyphs

Archeologists distinguish between two types of prehistoric rock art, petroglyphs, images pecked or carved on rock, and pictographs, images painted on rock. West Virginia has 27 recorded Indian petroglyphs and two pictographs. Common motifs include human figures, animals, animal tracks, and geometric designs. Notable sites include Salt Rock, Cabell County; Brown's Island, Hancock County; Hamilton Farm, Monongalia County; Table Rock, Timmons Farm, and Clifton Heights, Ohio County; and Ceredo and Wildcat Branch, Wayne County. The Harrison County Site is a rockshelter with a unique combination of petroglyphs and pictographs.

In 1964, Oscar Mairs and Hillis Youse recorded the Luther Elkins Site in Wyoming County. This simple Indian glyph with clusters, vertical linear and curvilinear designs, a sunburst pattern, a swastika-like pattern, and turkey tracks, became the state's most controversial petroglyph. Barry Fell, a Harvard biologist, interpreted the clusters of lines as a Christian message written by Irish monks in the sixth century Ogam language. Heated debates between archeologists and Fell supporters ensued, with Fell's interpretations discredited in the view of most professionals.

Most petroglyphs are assumed to date to the Late Prehistoric or Protohistoric Periods (A.D. 1200–1690). The only datable image is a six-foot shaman with weeping eye mask at Salt Rock, dated at approximately A.D. 1600. The mask motif is similar to shell masks found on protohistoric village sites. Professional archeologists believe several Ohio Valley petroglyphs were carved by Algonquians and some motifs represent the ideology and mythology of certain elements of the Ojibwa and other Algonquian tribes. The underwater panther, thunderers, serpents, tracks, and power lines are design elements common to Ojibwa mnemonic birch bark scrolls as well as West Virginia petroglyphs.

See also Archeology, Prehistoric People

Robert F. Maslowski
Milton

Dean Braley, *Shaman's Story: The West Virginia Petroglyphs*, 1993; Janet G. Brashler, "An Application of the Method of Multiple Working Hypotheses to Two West Virginia Petroglyph Sites," *West Virginia Archeologist*, Spring 1989.

Philippi

Philippi is located in north-central West Virginia on the Tygart Valley River. Chartered in 1844, it is the county seat of Barbour County. Both the city and the county were named for Philip Barbour, a Virginia congressman and delegate to the 1829–30 Virginia Constitutional Convention.

Philippi was the site of the first land battle of the Civil War, June 3, 1861, a skirmish afterward remembered as the "Philippi Races" for the hasty retreat of the Confederate forces. The town's famous covered bridge, constructed in 1852, served both northern and southern troops. For many years the only two-lane covered bridge serving a federal highway, its exterior was reconstructed in 1991 using the original plans of its designer, Lemuel Chenoweth. Civil War encounters in Philippi are reenacted every spring during the Blue and Gray Reunion. The Philippi Historical District was recently named to the National Civil War Discovery Trail.

The courthouse, constructed in 1903, replaced the original frame building. Another landmark is Alderson-Broaddus College, a liberal arts institution related to the American Baptist Churches U.S.A. Other major employers include the public school system. The economy is based on natural resources, particularly coal and wood. The 2000 population of Philippi was 2,870.

A residential community, Philippi is within approximately half an hour of Audra State Park and Tygart Lake State Park. Also easily accessible are Canaan Valley State Park, Blackwater Falls State Park, and Snowshoe Resort. Adaland, the 1868 Greek Revival home of Barbour County Sheriff Augustus Modisett, stands near Philippi.

See also Lemuel Chenoweth, Battle of Philippi, Philippi Covered Bridge

Barbara Smith
Philippi

Philippi, Battle of

With the beginning of the Civil War, both the North and South saw the mountains of Western Virginia as a strategically vital area. The region was seen as the source of thousands of tough recruits and of essential raw materials, an important staging area for attacks into the heartland of their opponents, and it was traversed by the Baltimore & Ohio Railroad, one of only two east-west railroads in the country at that time.

When Confederate troops threatened the B&O at Grafton, the federal government quickly moved troops into the area. Just before dawn on June 3, 1861, the first land battle of the Civil War involving organized troops took place at Philippi, about 15 miles south of Grafton. Some 3,000 federal troops under the general command of Maj. Gen. George B. McClellan and the immediate command of Col. Benjamin F. Kelley and Col. Ebenezer Dumont drove about 800 Confederates under Col. George A. Porterfield from the town. The outnumbered Rebels retreated so briskly that the battle was sometimes humorously referred to as the "Philippi Races." While no one was killed in the brief encounter, Kelley was severely wounded and two Confederates suffered leg wounds, necessitating the first amputations of the Civil War. One of the amputees was Virginia cavalryman James Hanger. He later founded Hanger Prosthetics, still a major manufacturer of artificial limbs.

The Northern victory stiffened Unionist resolve in Western Virginia. Within three weeks, the first Wheeling Convention voted to nullify the Virginia ordinance of secession, declared the offices of the state government at Richmond vacated, and named Francis H. Pierpont governor of the "restored" government of Virginia. The victory also secured the B&O for the Union and played an important part in General McClellan's meteoric rise to the command of the Army of the Potomac.

The federal strategy at Philippi included what was probably the first employment of the railroad to effect the convergence of divergent forces upon an enemy in world history.

See also Baltimore & Ohio Railroad, Civil War

James W. Daddysman
Alderson-Broaddus College

Philippi Covered Bridge

The covered bridge over the Tygart Valley River in Philippi was completed in 1852 by the noted bridge builder Lemuel Chenoweth. He was assisted by his brother, Eli, and stone mason Emmett J. O'Brien. The bridge is one of only six remaining two-lane covered bridges in the United States and the only such bridge carrying a federal highway, U.S. 250. It is a major West Virginia landmark.

Chenoweth chose the Stephen Long truss-arch configuration for his design of the Philippi bridge. Except for the loss of siding and roofing materials during the Civil War, the original design and shape of the bridge remained nearly intact until the late 1920s. Curves of the arched portals were squared at that time and knee braces changed to permit passage of large trucks. In a 1938 renovation the wooden deck was removed and replaced with a new concrete deck supported by steel girders and two new intermediate concrete piers.

Originally, the bridge was an important component of the Beverly and Fairmont road, a major connector to the Staunton-Parkersburg Turnpike. The turnpike was an important link between Western Virginia and Richmond and Norfolk. These transportation links became the focus of both sides during the Civil War. On June 2 and 3, 1861, there was a brief skirmish between Confederate forces under Col. George Porterfield and Union troops commanded by Col. Benjamin F. Kelley, considered to be the first land battle of the Civil War.

The bridge was seriously damaged by fire in the winter of 1989. Immediately after the fire, the governor issued a statement promising restoration. Soon after the declaration a public meeting was held in Philippi during which the people voted to restore the bridge to its 1861 appearance.

Because the bridge continues to carry modern heavy loads it was necessary to retain the steel girders and concrete deck. The approaches were completely redesigned. In addition to structural analysis there was a field study including measured drawings and recording of original details and features. Archival information included record drawings published in 1934, construction documents from the 1938 reconstruction, and the original specifications discovered in the archives of the Virginia Department of Public Works. All information both technical and archival led to a scholarly restoration of the Philippi Covered Bridge, completed in September 1991.

See also Lemuel Chenoweth, Battle of Philippi

Paul D. Marshall
Blufton, South Carolina

Stan Cohen, *West Virginia's Covered Bridges—A Pictorial Heritage*, 1992; Emory L. Kemp, *West Virginia's Historic Bridges*, 1984.

Philippi Mummies

Two mummies created in the late 19th century have become an unusual attraction at the Barbour County Historical Society Museum near the Philippi Covered Bridge. They are the work of Graham Hamrick, a Philippi store owner and part-time undertaker, who developed and patented a mummification process.

In 1888, after trials with vegetables and animals, Hamrick preserved two anonymous female corpses he had obtained from the West Virginia Hospital for the Insane in nearby Weston. Reportedly, Hamrick also mummified a hand, a human head, and a baby. The head and the baby have vanished; the hand was in the possession of a Charleston woman early in the 21st century. In 1892 Hamrick received patent no. 466,524 for an intricate preservation formula that included water, saltpeter, and sublimed sulfur set afire.

Sporadic viewings were reported through the years. Up until the mid-1960s, the mummies were a regular part of the Barbour County Fair where anyone older than 14 could pay to see them. *West Virginia Hillbilly* editor Jim Comstock visited Philippi in 1963 to write a story. He found the baby and two female mummies in a barn. Soon afterward, they again disappeared from public view. Frank Beyer purchased the mummies from a Hamrick family estate sale in 1970. Damaged in the flood of 1985, the mummies were treated by a local funeral home. They remain in the Beyer family's possession and are on loan to the history museum.

Jeanne Mozier
Berkeley Springs

Jayne Anne Phillips

Novelist Jayne Anne Phillips was born in Buckhannon, July 19, 1952. She attended West Virginia University, graduating magna cum laude in 1974. During the next two years, she traveled west, working and writing in California and Colorado. In 1976, she enrolled in the University of Iowa's Writers Workshop, receiving a master of fine arts degree in 1978. Phillips has published two short story collections, *Black Tickets* (1979) and *Fast Lanes* (1987), and three novels, *Machine Dreams* (1984), *Shelter* (1994), and *Motherkind* (2001). Her short stories have been widely anthologized, and her writing appears in *Esquire*, *Harper's*, *Granta*, and other magazines.

The Philippi Covered Bridge crosses the Tygart Valley River.

Phillips has received a Guggenheim Fellowship; the O. Henry Award; the Sue Kaufman Award for First Fiction for *Black Tickets;* and an American Library Association Notable Book citation and the *New York Times* Best Book citation for *Machine Dreams.* For the most part, Phillips sets her fiction in 20th-century West Virginia, tracing family histories and individual struggles for escape and redemption. Her stories often focus on the redemptive power of love, on family love or its absence, and on the forces of change that are at work in Appalachia.

Phillips now lives in Massachusetts.

Thomas Douglass
East Carolina University

Thomas Douglass, "Jayne Anne Phillips," *Appalachian Journal,* Winter 1994; Kenneth Shepherd and Jean W. Ross, "Jayne Anne Phillips," *Contemporary Authors: New Revision Series,* 1988.

Pickens Leper

George Rashid, known as the Pickens leper, migrated to the United States from Syria in 1902. He suffered from leprosy, now also called Hansen's disease, an ancient affliction characterized by loss of feeling and even of skin and flesh. The ominous first signs of the dreaded disease appeared while Rashid was working as a railroad section hand in Maine. He tried to keep his affliction secret by wearing gloves and long-sleeved shirts. When suspicious coworkers began asking questions he and his wife became wanderers, ending up in Elkins working for his brother, Charley. In July 1906, Charley Rashid alerted Dr. W. W. "Ben" Golden of George's medical condition.

Knowing that he had leprosy from having been exposed to it in Syria, George Rashid caught a pre-dawn eastbound coal train out of Elkins in a desperate attempt to return home, believing that if he could swim in the Jordan River he would be healed. Railroad officials apprehended him in Cumberland, Maryland. Since he was aboard a Baltimore & Ohio train, the company accepted responsibility for him and shipped him to Pickens, Randolph County, the most remote terminal on the line.

In Pickens, Dr. James L. Cunningham had quarters erected for Rashid and cared for him as best he could. While performing a physical examination, the doctor discovered that Rashid also had an untreatable heart condition known as mitral stenosis. In October 1906, caretaker James Thomas found him dead, not of leprosy but more likely from his heart condition. George Rashid now rests beside the abandoned railroad tracks a few feet from where he died.

L. Wayne Sheets
Charleston

L. Wayne Sheets, "The Pickens Leper," *Goldenseal,* Fall 1997.

Piedmont

The Mineral County town of Piedmont was named for its location at the foot of the Allegheny Mountains. Located on a bend of the North Branch of the Potomac River, Piedmont's elevation is 871 feet. The 2000 population was 1,014.

Originally in Hampshire County, Piedmont's history is closely intertwined with the development of the Baltimore & Ohio Railroad, which crosses the river into Maryland just west of town to begin its long ascent to the Eastern Continental Divide. The B&O, which extended its main line through Piedmont in 1852, gave the town its start as it became the site of machine shops for the railroad. Additionally, Piedmont is located in the heart of the local coalfield. The town grew in the mid-1800s, from about 1,200 in 1855 to 2,000 in 1869. Piedmont was chartered in 1856.

Notable residents of Piedmont include industrialist and U.S. Sen. Henry Gassaway Davis (1823–1916), who lived in Piedmont early in his life as a storekeeper and railroad agent. The scholar and author Henry Louis Gates Jr. (1950–), head of the Harvard University Afro-American Studies Department, grew up in Piedmont.

A major employer in the Piedmont area is the paper mill in nearby Luke, Maryland. The Luke mill was founded in 1888 as the Piedmont Pulp & Paper Company, later West Virginia Pulp & Paper and now MeadWestvaco.

William Pierce

White supremacist William Pierce, born September 11, 1933, in Portland, Oregon, established his headquarters at a rural compound near Hillsboro, Pocahontas County, in 1984.

Pierce, a former physics professor, was co-founder in 1974 of the National Alliance, at its peak the largest neo-Nazi organization in the United States. He is best remembered as the author of the racist novel, *The Turner Diaries*, published under a pseudonym in 1978. The novel, which features the violent overthrow of the U.S. government by white racists, includes a truck bombing of a federal building. It is believed to have been an inspiration to 1995 Oklahoma City bomber Timothy McVeigh and to have sparked other bloodshed as well.

Pierce's West Virginia compound was sited on 400 acres in southern Pocahontas County. He lived there with some of his followers, managing National Alliance political affairs and business operations. The group distributed hate literature and supremacist music from this headquarters, netting an estimated million dollars annually from worldwide sales. By the turn of the 21st century the National Alliance made extensive use of the Internet in its sales and propaganda operations.

William Pierce lived quietly at the National Alliance headquarters, occasionally appearing in local and statewide media reports. He became more famous after the Oklahoma City bombings. His activities were followed closely by the Southern Poverty Law Center, the Anti-Defamation League, and other groups that monitor extremist organizations. Pierce died in Pocahontas County, July 23, 2002.

Francis Harrison Pierpont

State founder Francis Harrison Pierpont, first and only governor of the Reorganized Government of Virginia, was born near Morgantown, January 25, 1814, and died at Pittsburgh, March 24, 1899. He was a great-grandson of Col. Zackquill Morgan, founder of Morgantown. He received his middle name in honor of Gen. William Henry Harrison, under whom his father was serving at the time of his birth. Often called "the Father of West Virginia," Pierpont's statue stands in Statuary Hall in the Capitol Building in Washington, one of two West Virginians so recognized.

While Francis was an infant, his family moved to a farm in Marion County and later, when he was 13, to Fairmont, where his father built and operated a tannery. Educated in a log schoolhouse near his home, Pierpont entered Allegheny College, Meadville, Pennsylvania, in 1835. Following graduation, he taught school in Harrison County but also studied law and was admitted to the bar at Fairmont on May 2, 1842. Among the friends of his youth and young manhood were Waitman T. Willey, Gordon Battelle, and John S. Carlile, all of whom played key roles in the West Virginia statehood movement.

In 1848, Pierpont began an association with the Baltimore & Ohio Railroad, serving as a right-of-way attorney in Marion and Taylor counties. He started a coal mine on family property in 1854 and entered into a partnership with coal pioneer James Otis Watson, whose family later controlled Consolidation Coal Company. On December 26, 1854, Pierpont married Julia Augusta Robertson of Wisconsin. Beginning in 1856, he helped to found Fairmont Male and Female Seminary, forerunner of Fairmont State College (now University).

In the opening days of the Civil War, Pierpont spoke frequently and forcefully for the Union and against secession. He was a representative to the First and Second Wheeling Conventions in 1861, where he worked with other conservatives such as Willey to delay the immediate declaration of a new state, which he believed to be unconstitutional. On June 20, 1861, Pierpont was unanimously elected as governor of the unionist Reorganized State of Virginia, which sat at Wheeling until West Virginia entered the Union two years later.

Pierpont worked assiduously to obtain funds for the loyal government, raise troops for the state militia, defend northwestern Virginia from guerrillas and keep as much of it as possible under federal control, and protect the B&O and Northwestern Virginia railroads. He worked hard for the recognition and admission of West Virginia. Following the establishment of the new state, he headed a loyal Virginia government at Alexandria. In May 1865, at the direction of President Andrew Johnson, he proceeded to Richmond, where he headed the civil government as reconstructed under the Lincoln-Johnson Plan. As a result of the creation of military government in Virginia under the Military Reconstruction Act of 1867, Pierpont was removed from office on April 4, 1868, by Gen. John Schofield, the military governor.

Following his return to West Virginia, Pierpont served a term in the West Virginia House of Delegates but lost his seat when the Democrats "redeemed" the government and took control of the young state. His partnership with Watson, a Democrat, was dissolved due to political tensions. In his retirement he helped to found the West Virginia Historical Society and served as president of the General Conference of the Methodist Protestant Church. Pierpont died at the home of his daughter in Pittsburgh and was buried with military rites at Woodlawn Cemetery, Fairmont.

See also Formation of West Virginia, Reorganized Government of Virginia

Philip Sturm
Ohio Valley University

Charles H. Ambler, *Francis H. Pierpont: Union War Governor and Father of West Virginia,* 1937.

Pigeon Roost, Battle of

The Battle of Pigeon Roost occurred in Princeton, Mercer County, May 17, 1862, during the Civil War. The battle culminated a month-long series of engagements, in which Union forces under the command of Gen. Jacob Cox attempted to destroy the Virginia & Tennessee Railway in southwest Virginia. Defending the railway and surrounding territory were three Confederate brigades under the command of Gen. Humphrey Marshall. Cox's force had two officers destined to become U.S. presidents, Lt. Col. Rutherford B. Hayes and Sgt. William McKinley.

Union forces left Fayetteville in mid-April 1862, passed through Beckley, and entered Mercer County by way of Flat Top Mountain. An advance guard was attacked on April 30 near Camp Creek, but their Confederate attackers were driven back toward Princeton after the main Union force arrived. Retreating Confederates burned Princeton on May 1.

Federal troops moved through the ruins of Princeton and advanced 25 miles before being stopped at Pearisburg, Virginia, on May 10. They retreated to Princeton where they skirmished with pursuing Confederates on May 16. As evening fell, the Confederates were able to reoccupy Princeton, spreading out on Pigeon Roost, a ridge south of town. By the next morning, Union forces had reentered Princeton and more soldiers continued to arrive throughout the day. The Confederates were also reinforced in their position on the ridge overlooking town.

The Battle of Pigeon Roost occurred on the morning of May 17 and consisted primarily of fighting between the 51st Virginia infantry and soldiers of the 37th Ohio. The Union men were noisily approaching Princeton from the southeast, unaware that the Confederates were lying in ambush. The attack left an estimated 18 federal troops killed and 38 wounded. No further fighting ensued even though both armies were drawn up for battle facing each other. On the evening of May 17, Union forces began to withdraw northward, ending the campaign to destroy the railroad at Dublin.

Michael M. Meador
Abingdon, Virginia

David Bard, *Civil War: The New River Valley,* 2004.

Pike Knob Preserve

Pike Knob Preserve is located on North Fork Mountain in Pendleton County and is owned by the Nature Conservancy. It includes 1,095 acres of majestic views and numerous rare plants and Pike Knob itself, which rises nearly 4,300 feet in elevation. The preserve was purchased from a timber company and from the Frank and Nelson families, to provide long-term protection for the unique natural area. The preserve is renowned for breathtaking vistas downward across the rolling fields and pastures of neighboring Germany Valley. To the east one can see Shenandoah Mountain and the Laurel Fork highlands on the Virginia border. Spruce Knob, Roaring Plains, and Dolly Sods dominate the western landscape as one stands on Nelson Sods and looks across the valley of the North Fork of the South Branch of the Potomac River.

The preserve is also the location of West Virginia's only virgin red pine forest and contains prime examples of grass bald and dwarf pine barren habitats. Rare plants occurring on the preserve are bristly rose (southernmost station), purple clematis, white alumroot, mountain harebell, Allegheny wild onion, Appalachian oak fern, and three-toothed cinquefoil.

The preserve is reached after a steep walk up the Old Circleville-Franklin Turnpike from a dead-end dirt road off U.S. 33.

See also North Fork Mountain

William N. Grafton
WVU Extension Service

Pilgrim Glass

The Pilgrim Glass Corporation was established in Huntington by Alfred Knobler. The factory was later located in nearby Ceredo, with its sales office in New Jersey.

Knobler, who had left Virginia Polytechnic Institute with a degree in ceramic engineering during the Great Depression, found work as a salesman for Trenton Potteries in New Jersey. One of his suppliers was Tri-State Glass Manufacturing Company in Huntington. Its owner, Walter Bailey, could not get enough natural gas in the winter so he wanted to sell the business. Knobler convinced Columbia Gas to extend a larger pipeline to the company, and in 1949 he created the Pilgrim Glass Corporation from Tri-State's modest facilities. He opened the new plant on Walker Branch Road in Ceredo in 1956.

During the early years, Pilgrim's main product was hand-blown crackle glass in a variety of colors. The onion-skin or crackle effect was achieved by immersing the hot piece in cold water and then reheating it. In the mid-1950s, two brothers from Italy, Alessandro and Roberto Moretti, came to work at Pilgrim. When Knobler saw their remarkable skill in making off-hand novelties, he added a series of glass animals to the Pilgrim line. Alessandro (Sandy) is now retired and Roberto has died, but brother-in-law Mario Sandon continued to create glass animals and other sculptures until the plant closed.

In 1968, plant manager Karel Konrad introduced cranberry glass, and the company became the largest producer of cranberry glass in the world. And after the mid-1980s, cameo glass was produced at Pilgrim under the supervision of Kelsey Murphy and Robert Bomkamp.

The Pilgrim Glass Company continued for more than 50 years, closing in 2002 when the aging Knobler was unable to find a purchaser.

See also Glass Industry

Tom D. Miller
Huntington

Pinch Reunion

The Pinch Reunion was established by Judge William W. Wertz and other Elk River residents in 1902. For three days in August the gathering is held at Rockwood Glen, in Pinch, northeast of Charleston in Kanawha County.

The first reunion was organized as a Fourth of July Sunday school picnic for students who had attended the old Pinch School (1865–1913). The old school, once used as a community building, now belongs to the Pinch Reunion Association. Programs, refreshments and entertainment have changed over the years. Earlier festivities were conducted more like an old-time camp meeting, complete with church on Sunday. Spelling bees and debating societies have been replaced with beauty pageants, car shows, all-terrain vehicle racing, golf tournaments, parades and musical entertainment. In the past gubernatorial candidates from both parties, beginning with Governor MacCorkle, were invited as guest speakers. This practice was abandoned in the 1970s, although politicians still frequent the event.

The U.S. Postal Service permits the Pinch post office the use of a one-day philatelic postmark. These canceled envelopes are valued by collectors. A state highway marker was erected in 1972 commemorating the Pinch Reunion.

Cathy Hershberger Miller
State Archives

Pineville

Pineville, the county seat of Wyoming County, is located on Rockcastle Creek at the place where the creek enters the Guyandotte River. The town lies at an elevation of 1,323 feet, at the intersection of State Routes 16, 10, and 97. The 2000 population of Pineville was 715.

Castle Rock, the towering sandstone formation for which Rockcastle Creek is named, is located at Pineville and is the major local landmark. The community was previously called Castlerock, and the post office there was once named Rock Castle. The town was renamed Pineville for the local pine forest and incorporated under that name in 1907.

The area of present Wyoming County was first settled about 1800, and by 1850 there was sufficient population to organize Wyoming from part of Logan County. Hiram Clay first settled near the site of present Pineville, in 1863. Pineville became county seat in 1907, replacing Oceana after a series of disputed elections. The Wyoming County courthouse, renovated in recent years by the county commission, was built in the Neoclassical Revival style in 1916 of locally quarried stone. It is on the National Register of Historic Places. A statue of preacher W.H.H. Cook, an early settler of the area and influential citizen, stands in front of the courthouse.

Judge R. D. Bailey (1883–1961) was a Pineville resident.

See also Castle Rock, Wyoming County

Maceo Pinkard

Musician Maceo Pinkard was born in Bluefield, June 27, 1897. Educated at Bluefield Colored Institute (now Bluefield State College), Pinkard became one of the most successful songwriters of the 1920s Jazz Era.

After graduation, he toured with his own band and ended up in Omaha, where he published his first song, "I'm Goin' Back Home," and founded a theatrical agency. He wrote his first hit, "Mammy o' Mine," in 1919 after moving to New York.

Three years later, he provided the music for *Liza*, a pioneering Broadway show with an all-black cast that introduced a new dance, the Charleston.

Pinkard wrote for show business, with numbers such as "Here Comes the Show Boat" for *Show Boat*, and for the jazz world, where songs such as "Them There Eyes," "I'll Be a Friend," and "Sugar" were recorded by Louis Armstrong, Bix Beiderbecke, and Billie Holiday, among others. He helped set up Duke Ellington's first recording session in 1923. Sometimes Pinkard wrote for the classic women blues singers, turning out the risque "You Can't Tell the Difference After Dark" for Alberta Hunter. In 1929, he enlisted blues diva Bessie Smith for *Pansy*, a black musical comedy that proved to be a Broadway fiasco despite his solid score.

Pinkard was so well-regarded that in 1939 he was one of the composers spotlighted in an all-black program at the New York World's Fair. His most famous song, "Sweet Georgia Brown," became the Harlem Globetrotters' theme and, in 1976, was heard again on Broadway in the score of *Bubbling Brown Sugar*.

Maceo Pinkard died July 21, 1962.

John Douglas
Berkeley Springs

Pinnacle Rock

Pinnacle Rock is located on the south side of U.S. 52 between Bluewell and Bramwell, in Mercer County. The impressive formation is on the steep northern flank of the Abbs Valley Anticline, formed millions of years ago during the mountain-building period known as the Appalachian Orogeny. Pinnacle Rock is a hogback formed of erosion-resistant rock known as Stoney Gap Sandstone. The Stoney Gap Sandstone was deposited by southwest-flowing streams during the Late Mississippian geologic period.

A prominent local landmark, Pinnacle Rock is part of Pinnacle Rock State Park, a seasonal, day-use facility that opened in 1938. The park includes nearly 400 acres and has a large, rustic picnic shelter and other picnic facilities, and wonderful vistas and overlooks. A two-mile hiking trail connects Pinnacle Rock with Jimmy Lewis Lake, a fishing lake within the park. Rock climbing is allowed with prior arrangement.

Bascombe M. Blake Jr.
Geological & Economic Survey

Pipestem Resort State Park

Pipestem Resort State Park is located on the Summers-Mercer county border on State Route 20 south of Hinton. The park, which is mostly in Summers County, was named for the native pipestem plant whose hollowed-out twigs were used by Indians and early pioneers as stems for tobacco pipes. The plant, also known as meadowsweet, is common to the vicinity of the park and in other parts of West Virginia. Before its development as a park the area was known as Pipestem community with its own post office and school.

Development of Pipestem State Park was begun in the 1960s after the purchase of 4,027 acres from 56 individual landowners, some of whom contested the terms of settlement. The park, which opened on Memorial Day 1970, is one of West Virginia's premier state parks. It is situated on the east rim of the scenic Bluestone River gorge. The elevation varies from 2,932 feet at its highest point on Pipestem Knob, to 1,550 feet at river level. Fine views of the park and its surroundings are available from the lookout tower on Pipestem Knob and from observation points scattered along the gorge's rim.

The McKeever Lodge with 112 rooms and suites is located on the rim of the gorge, and the 30-room Mountain Creek Lodge is located 1,000 feet below on the gorge floor. This lower lodge is accessible by a 3,600-foot-long aerial tramway that began operation in 1972. The park also has camping facilities and 26 rental cottages. The two lodges provide a variety of dining facilities. Pipestem State Park has both indoor and outdoor swimming pools, a nature center, gift and craft shops, horseback riding, biking, cross-country skiing, a lake, hiking trails, and an amphitheater. The park has two golf courses: an 18-hole course that opened in 1969 and a Par-3 nine-hole course, which opened in 1967. Pipestem hosts over a million visitors each year and is a major employer in the region.

Michael M. Meador
Abingdon, Virginia

W. Page Pitt

Journalism educator William Page Pitt, born November 19, 1900, in New York City, moved with his family to Shinnston, Harrison County, when he was 12. As a teenager, he worked summers in a coal mine. He graduated from Muskingum College, Ohio, in 1925 and taught for a year at Glendale College, Ohio. He later earned a master's degree at Columbia University in New York.

In 1926, when Pitt arrived in Huntington to join the faculty of what was then Marshall College, he found one journalism class with five students. In his 45-year career at Marshall, he built its journalism program into one with dozens of classes, hundreds of students, and a reputation for excellence. Today, Marshall University's W. Page Pitt School of Journalism and Mass Communications is named in his honor.

A legendary figure on the Marshall campus, Pitt often was referred to as the "Grand Old Man of Journalism," a title the West Virginia Senate made official in a proclamation issued when he retired in

1971. After the age of five, Pitt was sightless in one eye and had only three percent vision in the other. Nonetheless, he refused to let himself be handicapped by his vision problem. Not only a successful college educator, he was a prolific writer whose byline frequently appeared in national magazines and newspapers.

After his retirement, Pitt moved to Stuart, Florida, where he died September 13, 1980.

James E. Casto
Herald-Dispatch

Pittsburgh Coal Seam

The Pittsburgh coal seam underlies much of northern and north-central West Virginia and neighboring Pennsylvania, and is found as far south as Mason and Putnam counties. In geologic terms the Pittsburgh coal belongs to the Monongahela series. In West Virginia the seam covers an area of approximately 2,600 square miles. Pittsburgh coal is noted for its consistently high Btu content and its low ash, as well as an average thickness of between six and eight feet. A primary concern with the seam is its high sulfur content.

The high coking quality of this coal enabled the growth of the steel industry in the Pittsburgh area and the Northern Panhandle of West Virginia. Pittsburgh coal was mined in small amounts in the early 1800s. The first commercial shipment of Pittsburgh coal was sent to Baltimore in 1851 from a mine near Newburg, Preston County. Mining expanded as railroads penetrated the northern West Virginia coalfields. Today, Pittsburgh coal continues to be mined and accounts for higher production than any other seam in the state. Currently most Pittsburgh coal is mined from large deep shaft mines using longwall mining machines. Approximately 80 percent of the coal produced from the Pittsburgh seam goes to generate electricity while the remaining 20 percent goes to export and other markets.

David J. Kessler
Miners' Health Safety and Training

Pittston Strike

In 1987, the Pittston Coal Company withdrew from the Bituminous Coal Operators Association, which had traditionally negotiated union contracts for the coal industry. Pittston then implemented a number of work changes after the existing contract between it and union miners expired. On April 5, 1989, 500 West Virginia miners joined 1,200 miners in Virginia and Kentucky on strike, refusing to work after contract negotiations broke down between Pittston and the United Mine Workers of America.

Pittston responded by securing injunctions against the union and attempting to bring in nonunion miners. The strikers used picketing and sit-down demonstrations, and donned camouflage apparel to demonstrate their militancy and solidarity. Cecil Roberts, then UMWA vice president and a native of Kanawha County, was the central union figure in the strike zone. Tension between striking miners, company guards, and state police ran high. More than 500 miners were arrested during the strike.

Although the strike's decisive events happened out of state, West Virginia miners supported the effort in a number of ways. In Logan County, the UMWA set up a "Camp Solidarity" for the purpose of housing UMWA members and other labor activists sympathetic to the miners' cause. On June 6, 1989, around 60 miners embarked on a four-day march from Logan County to Charleston, retracing the path of the 1921 Armed March on Logan. On June 10, thousands rallied in the state capital and listened to speeches by UMWA President Richard Trumka, activist Jesse Jackson, and Governor Caperton, who called for cooperation between business and labor. Another rally was held on Labor Day in Welch. Around 4,000 miners and relatives heard speeches by Caperton and Sen. John D. Rockefeller.

The most dramatic turn of the strike came in September 1989 when union miners seized Pittston's central processing plant in Virginia, the Moss No. 3 plant. The seizure, organized by the UMWA leadership, was intended to halt coal production. The strikers occupied the plant from September 17 to September 20 without any serious incidents of violence.

The seizure of Moss No. 3 garnered the attention of the federal government. In October, Elizabeth Dole, U.S. Secretary of Labor, visited the strike zone. She met with both sides and appointed former labor secretary William J. Usery Jr. as a special mediator. After months of negotiations, a settlement was announced January 1, 1990.

See also Labor History

C. Belmont Keeney
West Virginia University
Richard A. Brisbin, *A Strike Like No Other Strike: Law and Resistance During the Pittston Coal Strike of 1989–1990*, 2002.

Place Names

The study of the names of West Virginia places involves geography, as well as history, folklore, religion, biology, and language. In many cases place names evolved naturally and informally, from common use through the folk process. When done formally, names were chosen or approved by government officials, including the post office; by private companies, such as railroads naming their stations or mining companies naming their company towns; and by others. Scholars often can find accurate information about the sources of names given formally, but folk names are often hard to trace.

Plants and animals, including birds, are common sources of names in West Virginia; for example, Buffalo, Bass, Thornwood, Pineville, Blue Jay, Bob White, and Crow. Hydrological features, landforms, and geological structures provided names for places such as Rock, named for a cliff on the Bluestone River, while the river itself was named after the blue-gray stone that predominates in the upper reaches of its watershed. The communities of Lost River and Birch River are named for rivers. The towns of Hurricane and Tornado were named for weather phenomena. Besides White Sulphur Springs, there are many other West Virginia communities named after springs.

Many names reflect cultural elements or contemporary events. Some arise from national historic figures, such as Calhoun, Clay, and Webster counties; others from battles, such as Princeton, named for an important battle at Princeton, New Jersey, during the Revolutionary War. (And Mercer County, which Princeton serves as county seat, was named for Gen. Hugh Mercer, who died at the Battle of Princeton.) Other names remember persons of local importance, such as Bramwell and Parkersburg. Women are not forgotten, providing the names for Eleanor (for Mrs. Roosevelt), Belva, Jane Lew, and Arista, among others. Religious associations provide many names: Mt. Nebo, St. Marys, Corinth, Medina, New Vrindaban, and of course, Bethlehem. Asbury was named for Bishop Francis Asbury, a founder of the Methodist Church in America. Indian words, as well as fanciful white notions about Indians, are the source of names such as Naugatuck, Matoaka, Kanawha, and Pocatalico. Names borrowed from other places are common also and include London, Berea, and New Martinsville. Classical names include Troy, Egeria, Sabine, and Pliny.

An interesting group of place names are those formed by the combination of other names. For example, Kenova was named because of its location on the border of Kentucky, Ohio, and Virginia. Ovapa was named after Ohio, Virginia, and Pennsylvania. Sometimes the initials and the last name of a person were used to form a name, as Itmann from I. T. Mann and Elgood from E. L. Good.

Odd was named because the people running it wanted an unusual or odd name. Another settlement made a request for a post office, and the sender supposedly added a postscript saying, "we need a post office, that's true." So postal officials named it True. Some names reflect spelling mistakes, such as Lerona instead of Lenora. Philippi was named after Philip Barbour, not the Biblical city. It is the county seat of Barbour County.

There is a historical succession in naming, representing changing times and changes in prevailing authority, which is to say that names change. Native names were supplanted by those of early white settlers, with many of those names themselves succeeded by names provided by later industrialists. A large part of the current place names of southern West Virginia were provided by the coal companies, including coal operator surnames such as Tams or Caperton and compound names such as Fireco or Ameagle. More recently, the tourism industry has brought its names with ski resorts naming mountain slopes and whitewater rafters renaming many features of the New River Gorge.

Raymond Thomas Hill
Athens

Hamill Kenny, *West Virginia Place Names: Their Origin and Meaning*, 1945; Quinith Janssen and William Fernbach, *West Virginia Place Names,* 1984.

Plant Lore

For ages, humans have used plants for a myriad of purposes. Plants have also been a nuisance or danger. Some grew in dense tangles that were barriers to travel, such as the thickets of rhododendron known as "laurel hells." Plants such as poison ivy, poison sumac, and stinging nettle were wisely avoided, while other plants were poisonous if eaten. Plant lore is the vast body of traditional knowledge about wild plants built up through long experience.

Wild plants provided food, medicine, fuel, and shelter for American Indians, early white pioneers, and those who followed. The first signs of spring once sent people to the fields for wild greens. Leaves of violets, dandelion, pokeberry, and spring cress (cressy or creasey greens) were cherished after a long winter. Young cattail sprouts tasted like tender cucumbers. Ramps provided a strong garlic taste and stronger odor that caused many schoolboys to have to sit outside their classrooms. Today, ramp dinners are popular social events. The tender fiddlehead stems of ferns were cooked as greens or canned for future use. Tasty roots of Indian cucumber and toothwort provided fresh tidbits.

Bulbs of Jack-in-the-pulpit (Indian turnip) were baked by Indians but eaten raw only when practical jokers could trick unwary people into doing so. Within minutes the victim's mouth, throat, and stomach burned with a pain that was only intensified by drinking water.

Other bulbs used for food included spring beauty, wild yam, and Jerusalem artichoke. Fruits and berries of mayapple, cherries, blackberries, pawpaw, persimmon, elderberries, blueberries, huckleberries, strawberries, and serviceberries were eaten fresh or canned as jellies, jams, and preserves for winter.

Walnuts, hickory nuts, beech nuts, and hazelnuts have always been favorite foods for humans and wildlife. Acorns were pounded or ground into flour for porridge or cakes. The sugar maple tree was an extremely valuable source of maple syrup and maple sugar. In its day, the American chestnut was unsurpassed in quality and quantity of nuts, readily gathered by the sack-full or bushel. Chestnut lumber, split rails, and poles for barns and cabins were highly valued. The loss, when American chestnut was virtually eliminated by chestnut blight in the 1920s and 1930s, was immense.

Nearly every community had a folk doctor who collected plants, leaves, fruits, seeds, and roots. The medicinal plants were learned from American Indians, European traditions, and by trial and error. Numerous plants with "snakeroot" names were tried as snakebite cures. Touch-me-not (jewelweed) contains slimy juice used as a cure for poison ivy, stinging nettle, and bee stings. People chewed the inner bark of the prickly ash or toothache tree to numb aching teeth, and willow bark, which contains salicin (from which aspirin was later derived), to cure aches and pains. Goldenseal (yellowroot), black and blue cohosh, and mayapple were frequently used medicinals and were collected for sale. Ginseng was the king of the wild medicinals in dollar value, and remains so today.

Roots of chicory and dandelion and wild coffee fruits provided a substitute for coffee. Leaves of several wild mints were used for teas and flavoring. The red fuzzy seeds of staghorn sumac were brewed into "Indian lemonade." Spring was not complete without sassafras tea, made from fresh sassafras roots to thin the blood and prepare the body for summer's hot temperatures. Spicebush, anise, and ginger provided spices and flavorings.

American Indians used bloodroot to dye leather, arrows, and baskets, and for war paint. Craftspeople still prefer its deep red color. Dyes from black walnut (yellow-brown), butternut or white walnut (reddish-brown), osage orange (olive drab), and goldenrods (yellow) were just a few of the natural dyes used by our ancestors.

Plants were valued for their beauty as well as for practical reasons. Dogwood, dwarf iris, azaleas, and rhododendrons are among the most beautiful flowering plants. The pure white serviceberry (service or sarvis) flowers were often collected for memorial services in early spring when circuit-riding preachers could finally travel the muddy roads after winter. A bouquet of pink lady's slipper was the special treat children often gave to their mothers in May.

Tales and uses of plants fill many books. Dense wood from persimmon was used for golf club heads, while the wood

Sourwood in bloom.

of dogwood was used as machine bearings. Dogwood twigs were chewed and used as a toothbrush. Recent research has found a high fluoride content in these twigs. Sourwood trunks grew straight except for abrupt bends caused by killing winter temperatures, making them perfect for sled runners. The tannin of chestnut oak, hemlock, and sumac barks was used to tan leather; sumac is still called "shoemake" by many country people. Sumac stems have a large soft pith that was easily hollowed out to make spouts to collect maple sap. The best red spruce boards were used to build airplanes and for piano sounding boards. And mountain boys knew that rhododendron forks made excellent sling shots, combined with rubber strips from an inner tube and maybe an old shoe tongue for the pouch.

Leaves of sourwood and teaberry, or black birch and sassafras twigs, were chewed for thirst. White oak, hickory, and white ash splints or strips still are the choice for making baskets and chair bottoms.

Evergreen plants of groundpine and princess pine were mixed with holly and Christmas fern for Christmas decorations. Mistletoe hung above the door during the same season. The dustlike spores of groundpine provided the original explosive light in flash photography.

Allegheny flyback grass of mountain pastures was virtually impossible to cut with a scythe, which merely bent the tough wiry stems, resulting in the stems' flying back upright. The canebrakes of the South reached our southern counties and gave Canebrake in McDowell its name.

Oil from anise plants was used to mask human smell on fish bait and was thought to put fish in a trance, making them easier to catch. Scouring rush stems, naturally encrusted with silicon, were used to clean pots and pans. Skunk cabbage flowers produce heat and can grow through the snow and ice of mountain bogs. Bears coming out of hibernation readily eat the plants which may be the laxative needed after three to four months of no food.

String and thread were made from bark of basswoods, leatherwood, and In-

An Ohio River sunset, from the Pleasants County shore.

dian hemp. Fleas were repelled by walnut leaves scattered in the yard and pennyroyal plants added to bedding for pets. Finally, who can forget swinging on a grapevine hanging from the top of a tall oak tree?

William N. Grafton
WVU Extension Service

Pleasants County

Pleasants County, named for James Pleasants, governor of Virginia (1822–24), is one of the smallest counties in West Virginia. It has 134.7 square miles and a 2000 population of 7,514. Pleasants County was created in 1851 from portions of Wood, Ritchie, and Tyler counties.

Pleasants County is located on the Ohio River northeast of Parkersburg. The main roadways are State Route 2 and State Route 16. Middle Island Creek, French Creek, Cow Creek, and Bull Creek are four major streams entering the Ohio River in Pleasants County. Five Ohio River islands are within the county boundaries. The mostly rural county is dotted with small communities such as Schultz, Horseneck, Calcutta, Arvilla, Hebron, Nine Mile, Mt. Carmel, Shawnee, and Henry Camp. St. Marys and Belmont are the only incorpo-

rated places in Pleasants County, with populations of 2,017 and 1,036 respectively. St. Marys is the county seat.

The earliest permanent settlers were Jacob and Isaac LaRue, in 1797. Soon Riggses, Reynoldses, Tripletts, Smiths, Baileys, and others settled in the area. The person who was most prominent in the creation of the county was Alexander H. Creel. In 1843, he established a river port village named Vaucluse at the mouth of Green Run just south of present St. Marys. He constructed a road linking Vaucluse with the Northwestern Turnpike 13 miles away at Pike. At its height Vaucluse rivaled Parkersburg as a major port on the Ohio, and many businesses built warehouses there. However, a massive fire and the flood of 1848 doomed Creel's village to an early death.

In 1849, Creel bought back land he had sold to Hugh Pickens and established the city of St. Marys. At the time there was talk of bringing a railroad down Middle Island Creek to the town site. When the county was created, the first county court was held in Creel's house. He donated the property on which the first Pleasants County courthouse was built, now the site of the second courthouse.

In early years, agriculture was the main source of income. The oil boom of the 1860s brought new opportunities. The first gusher was struck at Horseneck, near the Wood County border in the Hendershot oil field. Because oil had to be transported in wooden barrels, cooper shops, once numbering as many as 13, sprang up in St. Marys. Oil and gas have remained important to the Pleasants County economy to the present. The industry has boomed several times, including the 1890s and 1980s.

Important oil industry technologies were developed or improved in Pleasants County. In 1864, Bazel Childers developed a system for fracturing the oil-bearing rock to increase production by the use of explosives deep in the well. In the early 20th century, James Dinsmoor came into the area determined to prove that more oil could be retrieved from wells previously considered exhausted. His secondary recovery system was a big success and one of the reasons for the establishment of the Ohio Valley Refining Company at St. Marys in 1913. The refinery was an important employer for Pleasants County until it was closed in 1987.

Pleasants County history has been greatly influenced by its location on the Ohio River and its proximity to the railroad. In 1882, the Baltimore & Ohio Railroad decided to extend down the Ohio from Wheeling to Parkersburg. When completed, the rail line opened transportation and communication for the county regardless of weather or river conditions.

After World War II, large industries moved into the county. One of the most significant was American Cyanamid at Willow Island in 1946. Others soon followed, including the Cabot Corporation in the southern part of the county. Construction climaxed in the late 1970s with the building of the Pleasants Power (now Allegheny Energy) plant at Willow Island. This construction project brought the most tragic day in the history of Pleasants County. On April 27, 1978, 51 men fell to their deaths in the collapse of a cooling tower that was being built.

The county's economy has changed in recent years. Many retail businesses have been lost to competition from larger stores in the Parkersburg and Marietta area. The Colin Anderson Center, a state facility for the mentally retarded located three miles north of St. Marys, was closed and re-opened as a medium-security prison. The Dominion Hope gas company opened a gas-fired electricity generating plant at Bull Creek in 2002. This brings the number of power plants to three, counting the two of the Willow Island site, making Pleasants County one of West Virginia's leading electricity producers.

FAST FACTS ABOUT PLEASANTS COUNTY

Founded: 1851

Land in square miles: 134.7

Population: 7,514

Percentage minorities: 1.7%

Percentage rural: 58.1%

Median age: 38.9

Percentage 65 and older: 14.9%

Birth rate per 1,000 population: 10.8

Median household income: $32,736

High school graduate or higher: 79.4%

Bachelor's degree or higher: 9.7%

Home ownership: 80.4%

Median home value: $75,300

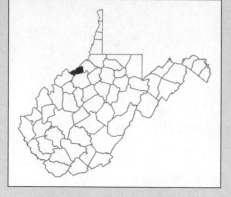

This information is from the 2000 U.S. Census. In 2000, West Virginia as a whole had 5 percent minorities, a median age of 38.9, median household income of $29,696, and a 75.2 percent home ownership rate.

Notable natives of Pleasants County include Hiram A. Carpenter, river man, farmer, and contractor; Brooks F. Ellis, educator and petroleum geologist; West Virginia historian Charles H. Ambler; Congressman Cleveland M. Bailey; and John Deaver Drinko, attorney and philanthropist.

Matthew Scott Bailey
St. Marys High School

Robert L. Pemberton, *A History of Pleasants County, West Virginia*, 1929; Pleasants County Historical Society, *History of Pleasants County, to 1980*, 1980.

Plum Orchard Lake

Plum Orchard Lake was constructed in 1962 by the STEP (State Temporary Employment Program), a public works program that put unemployed coal miners to work at $1 an hour on conservation projects. The lake impounds 202 acres, provides 6.5 miles of shoreline, and has a maximum depth of 40 feet. The lake is nestled between Packs and Haystack mountains on Plum Orchard Creek, near Oak Hill in Fayette County.

The surrounding Plum Orchard Lake Wildlife Management Area encompasses 3,201 acres. Purchased in 1960 by the West Virginia Conservation Commission, the area is now managed by the Wildlife Resources and Parks and Recreation sections of the Division of Natural Resources. Most of the area is forested in hickory and mature oaks. The wildlife management area is managed for forest game habitat, and deer, wild turkeys, raccoons, squirrels, and grouse are abundant. It is open to hunting.

The lake provides fishing for sunfish, large mouth bass, channel catfish, and crappie and was initially opened for fishing on June 12, 1963, the state's Centennial Year. Recreational facilities include two rustic campgrounds, a rifle range, picnic facilities, and hiking trails. Plum Orchard Lake is located on County Route 23 off the West Virginia Turnpike (Interstate 77).

Robert Beanblossom
Division of Natural Resources

Pneumoconiosis

See Black Lung Disease.

Pocahontas County

Pocahontas County is the third largest county in West Virginia, with 942.6 square miles, but among the least populous, with 9,131 residents in 2000. Eight rivers have their headwaters in the county. Elevations range from slightly under 2,000 feet to several points above 4,800 feet. Located mostly within the upper Greenbrier Valley, Pocahontas County is underlain by sandstone, shale, and limestone.

At the time of first European movement into the Greenbrier Valley, Indians did not have permanent settlements in the area. Generally accepted as the first white settlers are Jacob Marlin and Stephen Sewell, who located at present Marlinton about 1749 and remained till at least 1751. Settlement was under way by the early 1750s, but Indian attacks during the French and Indian War drove most settlers out of the valley. Settlement resumed in 1761, but attacks continued through the Revolutionary period and till at least the early 1790s.

The act creating Pocahontas County was passed by the Virginia General Assembly on December 21, 1821. The land came mainly from Bath County, plus small parts of Randolph and Pendleton. Huntersville was selected as the county seat. The 1830 census counted 2,542 residents.

In the years before the Civil War, road improvements helped to reduce isolation. Turnpikes from Warm Springs, between Lewisburg and Huttonsville, and from Staunton to Parkersburg made travel easier. In 1854–56, a bridge was constructed across the river at Marlins Bottom.

There are references to schools as early as the 1790s. A major improvement came in 1842 when the General Assembly chartered three academies for the preparation of students for the University of Virginia, at Green Bank, Hillsboro, and Huntersville. Today there are five schools in Pocahontas County.

The first church is believed to have been the White Pole Meeting House, built before the Revolutionary War. It continues today as the Wesley Chapel United Methodist Church in Hillsboro. A Presbyterian congregation was organized in the Hillsboro area between 1783 and 1788. Today the original Methodists, Presbyterians, and Episcopalians have been joined by adherents to many creeds and denominations.

Excellent grazing lands in the Little Levels and other areas supported the beginnings of the livestock industry that is still important today. Slaves were present from the earliest years but not in extensive numbers, as farms were not large.

Pocahontas County voters supported Virginia's secession from the Union by a 360 to 13 vote, but Pocahontas sent sons to both armies in the Civil War. In the late summer of 1861, the county suddenly became part of the front line. Local activity that fall and winter included a brief visit by Robert E. Lee; battles at Cheat Mountain, Bartow, and Top of Allegheny; and a miserable winter for the men of both armies stationed at the highest camps in elevation used during the war. Movements by a Union force in late 1863 resulted in the last significant Civil War battle in West Virginia, at Droop Mountain on November 6. The federal victory helped to assure Northern control and thus the survival of the new state.

The completion of the Chesapeake & Ohio Railway into neighboring Greenbrier County in 1869 brought a railroad near, and a timber boom ensued. By the late 1870s, Pocahontas County logs were being floated to Ronceverte. Until 1908, the drives were an annual event on the Greenbrier River. The Williams River and, less successfully, the Shavers Fork of Cheat were also used to move logs. Pocahontas County sawmill operators also floated rafts of lumber to the railroad.

In the early 1880s, investors began to buy up Pocahontas land and timber, including John T. McGraw and U.S. Senators Johnson N. Camden and Henry Gassaway Davis. These men and others worked to bring a railroad into the upper Greenbrier Valley. McGraw purchased the land at Marlinton in 1891, and on December 8, 1891, the voters approved Marlinton as the new county seat. The first newspaper in the county, the *Pocahontas Times*, was established in 1883.

The Greenbrier Division of the C&O

A Pocahontas County farm scene.

Italian, Austrian, German, and other national origin (few remained once the jobs were gone, however) as well as additional blacks. A group of Dutch immigrants arrived in 1847, and descendants of these settlers include the author Pearl S. Buck. English immigrants settled in the Linwood-Mingo area, beginning in 1883. In the 1960s and 1970s, a number of homesteaders belonging to the counterculture movement came to the county. The Greenbank Observatory and Snowshoe have brought other new residents.

Floods have been a major factor in the county's recent history. There were significant floods in 1908, 1913, 1933, 1936, and 1967. The flood of November 4–5, 1985, was the largest this century, and on January 19, 1996, a flood almost as big hit the county. Flood control has been a dominant concern of the county's citizens in recent years.

William P. McNeel
Marlinton

was completed to Marlinton and Cass in late 1900, to Durbin in 1902, and on to Winterburn in 1905. In 1903, the Coal & Coke Railroad (later part of the Western Maryland Railway) was completed from Elkins to Durbin, connecting with the C&O. Numerous sawmills were quickly put in operation along the new railroad lines, as well as tanneries at Frank and Marlinton. With the need of the lumber companies for farm products and the easier access to market provided by the railroads, agricultural output grew. There were 15,002 residents in 1920, the most ever recorded.

By the late 1920s, virtually the entire county had been timbered. Much land was damaged in the 1930s by severe forest fires that followed the logging. The Monongahela National Forest was created in 1920, and the first land for the forest in Pocahontas County was acquired in 1923. The Depression brought the Civilian Conservation Corps, which located ten camps within the county. In addition to reforestation and fire control, the CCC did the original development of Droop Mountain Battlefield and Watoga state parks, Seneca State Forest, and Edray Fish Hatchery.

Since World War II the tanneries and the largest lumber operation (Cass) have closed, both railroad lines into the county have been abandoned, and farming has declined. On balance, several new timber-related operations have opened, and the county remains a leader in cattle and sheep production. Tourism has grown from a minor part of the county's economy, based on hunting and fishing, into a major industry. After the Cass mill closed in 1960, the state acquired the remaining segment of logging railroad and created the Cass Scenic Railroad State Park. Calvin Price State Forest, Bear Town State Park, Handley Wildlife Management

Area, and the Greenbrier River Trail are also state-owned recreational facilities.

The Snowshoe ski area opened on Cheat Mountain in 1974. An adjoining ski area, Silver Creek, opened in 1983. Snowshoe Mountain Resort (now including Silver Creek) has become the largest ski area in the southeastern United States and the county's largest employer.

In 1955, the Deer Creek Valley near Green Bank was selected for the new National Radio Astronomy Observatory, with the first telescope completed in 1959. The newest telescope at Green Bank is the largest fully steerable radio telescope in the world. The observatory was a major factor for the location of the National Youth Science Camp in the county in 1963.

Post Civil War economic growth brought a broadening of the population mixture. Railroad construction and the lumber industry brought in workers of

Pocahontas Land Corporation

One hundred years old in 2001, the Pocahontas Land Corporation has roots in the 1880s rush to acquire land and coal resources in the Flat Top Coal Field in southern West Virginia. Frederick Kimball, president of the Norfolk & Western Railway, formed the Flat-top [sic] Coal Land Association, corporate ancestor of the Pocahontas Land Corporation, to oversee the purchasing and development of coal lands. With headquarters in Bramwell, the company eventually acquired more than 300,000 acres, mostly in McDowell and Mercer counties. In 1901, the Flat-top Coal Land Association was reorganized as the Pocahontas Coal & Coke Company. In 1925 the company moved to Bluefield, and in 1939 changed its name to Pocahontas Land Corporation.

In announcing its centennial, the company reported that 1.7 billion tons of coal

FAST FACTS ABOUT POCAHONTAS COUNTY

Founded: 1821

Land in square miles: 942.6

Population: 9,131

Percentage minorities: 1.6%

Percentage rural: 100%

Median age: 41.9

Percentage 65 and older: 17.3%

Birth rate per 1,000 population: 8.8

Median household income: $26,401

High school graduate or higher: 70.9%

Bachelor's degree or higher: 11.8%

Home ownership: 80.3%

Median home value: $64,000

This information is from the 2000 U.S. Census. In 2000, West Virginia as a whole had 5 percent minorities, a median age of 38.9, median household income of $29,696, and a 75.2 percent home ownership rate.

had been mined from Pocahontas lands since 1901 with another 1.7 billion in reserve. Holdings now extend far beyond southern West Virginia. By 2002, the corporation and its subsidiary, Pocahontas Development Corporation, had gained control of 1.05 million acres of natural resource properties in Alabama, Illinois, Kentucky, Tennessee, Virginia, and West Virginia. Pocahontas Land Corporation has donated property for public uses such as the Hatfield-McCoy Trail and the Twisted Gun Golf Course, the latter built on reclaimed surface mine property in Mingo County. The Pocahontas Land Corporation remains a subsidiary of the Norfolk Southern Corporation, which is the successor to Norfolk & Western.

See also Norfolk & Western Railway
Kenneth R. Bailey
WVU Institute of Technology
Charles Kenneth Sullivan, *Coal Men and Coal Towns, Development of the Smokeless Coalfields of Southern West Virginia, 1873–1923*, 1989.

Pocahontas No. 3 Coal Seam

Covering some 900 square miles in Mercer, Wyoming, and McDowell counties, and neighboring Tazewell County, Virginia, the rich Pocahontas No. 3 coal seam was first mined by Jordan Nelson, whose backyard coalbank eventually attracted serious interest from the Philadelphia founders of the Norfolk & Western Railway. The N&W completed its line to the Pocahontas, Virginia, location of Nelson's coalbank in March 1883 and began the rapid industrialization of the region.

Largely owned by the N&W's Pocahontas Land Corporation, which leased mining rights to independent coal companies, the Pocahontas Coalfield has been one of the most productive in the nation. The low-volatile, low-sulfur, "smokeless" coal originated during the Lower and Middle Pennsylvanian Period and is older and better than most coal found elsewhere in the world. It stood 11 feet thick at Pocahontas, was perfect for making coke for use in steelmaking, and was the chosen fuel of the U.S. Navy during the age of steam. Of the original three billion tons in the field, some 900 million remain.

The exploitation of the Pocahontas No. 3 seam transformed southern West Virginia, creating the cities of Bluefield, Bramwell, Keystone, Northfork, Kimball, Welch, and Gary, and numerous coal company towns. The huge demand for miners in the labor-intensive early years created great racial and ethnic diversity. The U.S. Coal Commission's 1923 survey showed that 20,000 of West Virginia's 92,000 miners worked in the Pocahontas region. Twenty percent were foreign-born immigrants, 33 percent African-American, and the remainder native-born whites. The Pocahontas coalfield saw little of the endemic violence of the West Virginia Mine Wars, although union hero Sid Hatfield was assassinated on the steps of the McDowell County courthouse in Welch.

See also Coal Industry, Pocahontas Land Corporation

C. Stuart McGehee
West Virginia State University
Joseph T. Lambie, *From Mine to Market: The History of Coal Transportation on the Norfolk and Western Railway*, 1954; Edward A. Rehbein, C. Douglas Henderson, and Ronald Mullennex, "No. 3 Pocahontas Coal in Southern West Virginia—Resources and Depositional Trends," *West Virginia Geological and Economic Survey Bulletin B-38*, 1981.

Pocahontas Times

The *Pocahontas Times* has been recording the life of Pocahontas County since its first issue of May 10, 1883. The *Times*, the county's first paper, was founded by James B. Canfield and Hezekiah B. Marshall and first located at Huntersville, which was then the county seat. Subsequent owners were C. Forrest Moore and Samuel B. Loury, 1888–89, and John E. Campbell, 1889–92. The paper was moved to Marlinton in May 1892, after that community became the site of county government.

In November 1892, the *Times* was acquired by the Reverend William T. Price and his family. For a number of years, the names of sons James, Andrew, Norman, and then Calvin appeared on the masthead, as editors, in various combinations. In 1906, Calvin Price became sole owner and editor, his brothers having moved on to other professions. At his death on June 14, 1957, his daughter, Jane Price Sharp, took over. In 1981, William Price McNeel, a grandson of Calvin Price, became editor, serving until 2005. By the 1990s, five generations of the Price family had worked on the paper.

The *Times* is unique among the state's weekly newspapers as it almost totally skipped the "hot metal" period in printing technology, having rejected a linotype metal-casting typesetting machine after a brief trial in 1901–02 to return to handset type. By the 1980s, the paper was one of the last papers in the country to still be using handset type as part of its production process, along with a phototypesetting machine. Then due to damage caused by the November 1985 flood, the *Times* became one of the first papers in West Virginia to switch completely to the use of computers.

In August 1901, the present building was completed and occupied. As it retained the characteristics of a weekly newspaper and printing office at the turn of the 20th century, the building was placed on the National Register of Historic Places. The paper, with a circulation of 5,900 in 2004, follows Pocahontas Countians to most states of the union.
William P. McNeel
Marlinton

Pocatalico River

The Pocatalico River, a tributary of the Kanawha River, has its mouth at Raymond City in Putnam County, near Poca, at an elevation of 582 feet. Pocatalico is supposed to have been an Indian name and is reported in various spellings from the time of early white settlement in the region. The towns of Poca and Pocatalico, and Pocatalico Creek, are in turn named for the river. In local usage the Pocatalico is often referred to as the Poca River, and one record from as early as 1808 identifies it as the "Poky."

Coal was discovered on the Pocatalico in 1798, and mines operated in the Raymond City area for several decades prior to World War II. Extensive timbering was done along the river, beginning about 1895.

From its headwaters near Looneyville, the Pocatalico River passes in a southwestward direction through Roane, Kanawha, and Putnam counties. Its watershed includes the southern corner of Jackson County, as well. The length of the Pocatalico is 67.7 miles, and its course is very crooked. The main tributaries are Manila, Heizer, Frog, Pocatalico, and Johnson creeks, and Rocky, Legg, Middle, and Flat forks.

The Pocatalico River sweeps in an arc north of Charleston. Its drainage area includes some of the capital city's outlying suburbs, although Pocatalico's people more commonly live in the rural countryside. The river's watershed lies across the historic road from Charleston to Ripley and Parkersburg, the same general route now followed by Interstate 77. Walton, Sissonville, Pocatalico, and Poca are located on or near the Pocatalico River, and there are numerous smaller communities.

Livia Simpson Poffenbarger

Livia Simpson Poffenbarger, newspaper publisher and Republican activist, is best remembered for her efforts to establish the Battle of Point Pleasant (1774) as the American Revolution's opening salvo.

Born in Pomeroy, Ohio, March 12, 1862, Livia Nye Simpson grew up in nearby Point Pleasant. The daughter of a well-known lawyer and influential Democrat, Simpson made a name for herself when she demanded the right to speak in support of a candidate at the 1888 state Democratic convention. Simpson later bought Point Pleasant's Republican newspaper, the *State Gazette*, and rescued it from financial ruin. Her commitment to Republican politics deepened with her 1894 marriage to George Poffenbarger, a lawyer and fellow party supporter.

Poffenbarger established a local chapter of the Daughters of the American Revolution in 1901 and quickly organized her Point Pleasant campaign. Despite arguments from historians that the battle was the last in the colonial frontier wars, Poffenbarger secured a congressional resolution naming Point Pleasant the first battle of the Revolution.

Poffenbarger sold the *State Gazette* in 1913 but continued her political and civic work. During World War I, she earned national acclaim for her efforts on behalf of Liberty Loans and was awarded an honorary law degree from West Virginia University. She served on a number of national Republican committees and directed the state women's suffrage campaign, although she apparently had little affinity for the cause. At the age of 70, Poffenbarger became involved in an anti-temperance group, the Women's Organization for National Prohibition Reform. She died in Charleston, January 27, 1937.

See also Battle of Point Pleasant

Christine M Kreiser
Clarksburg

Nancy Whear, "Livia Simpson Poffenbarger, 1862–1937," *Missing Chapters II: West Virginia Women in History*, 1986; "'Manufactured History': Re-Fighting the Battle of Point Pleasant," *West Virginia History*, 1997.

Point Pleasant

Point Pleasant, the county seat of Mason County, is located at the confluence of the Ohio and Kanawha rivers. Pierre-Joseph Celoron de Blainville marked the first recorded visit in 1749, when he left a lead tablet claiming the area for the French. Another significant visit was the 1770 survey party led by George Washington. Plans for a proposed 14th colony to be called Vandalia, with Point Pleasant as the capital, were thwarted by the Revolutionary War.

The Battle of Point Pleasant was fought on October 10, 1774, a victory for Virginia militia over Indians led by Cornstalk. Forts Blair and Randolph occupied the site from 1774; by 1781 settlers were established, and in 1794 the General Assembly of Virginia chartered the town as Point Pleasant. In 1796, Walter Newman erected a hewn-log house, which still stands. Jonas Smith recorded the first plat of the town in 1819, and Point Pleasant was incorporated in 1833.

River transportation and boat building dominated the economy of the town throughout the 19th century. The establishment of the Marietta Manufacturing Company, a boat construction company, in 1916 continued the tradition until it closed in 1967. In the same year, the Silver Bridge collapsed on December 15, killing 46 persons.

The community of 4,637 is served by four branch banks, Pleasant Valley Hospital, a hotel, a high school, middle school and three elementary schools, a daily newspaper, a mayor-council form of government, two city parks, and a public library. Two local chemical and plastics plants contribute to the Point Pleasant economy.

Notable residents include Daniel Polsley (1803–77), lieutenant governor of the Reorganized Government of Virginia, 1861–63, and member of Congress, 1867–69; George Poffenbarger (1861–1951), justice of the West Virginia Supreme Court, 1901–22; Bernard Bell (1911–71), recipient of the Congressional Medal of Honor; and Brereton Jones (b. 1939), governor of Kentucky, 1991–95.

Significant landmarks include the Point Pleasant Battlefield Monument State Park; the newly restored Lowe Hotel, dating from 1903; the Pioneer Cemetery, which includes the graves of several Revolutionary War soldiers; the West Virginia State Farm Museum; and Langston School (1848), one of the oldest black schools in West Virginia still standing, which now houses the offices of the county board of education.

See also Battle of Point Pleasant, Mason County, Silver Bridge Collapse

Cora P. Teel
Marshall University

Point Pleasant, Battle of

The Battle of Point Pleasant was fought in October 1774 between Virginians led by Andrew Lewis and Shawnee led by Cornstalk. It was the only major engagement of Dunmore's War and the most important battle ever fought in present West Virginia.

In response to hostilities along the Ohio River that spring, Lord Dunmore, the last colonial governor of Virginia, assembled two armies to attack the Shawnee villages in Ohio. The northern army,

The battlefield monument at Point Pleasant.

led by Dunmore himself and composed of militia from Berkeley, Hampshire, and Frederick counties, departed from Cumberland, Maryland, and proceeded to Fort Dunmore (present Pittsburgh). The second army, commanded by Col. Andrew Lewis, was made up of militia from Augusta, Bedford, Botetourt, Culpeper, and Fincastle counties. Lewis's force gathered at Camp Union (present Lewisburg) and journeyed down the Kanawha River to its mouth at Point Pleasant, arriving on October 6. The plan was for the two armies to meet at the mouth of the Hocking River, ascend that river, and attack the Indian towns together. Each army numbered about 1,000 men.

The Shawnee had reconnoitered both armies from the time of their departure. In an effort to prevent their meeting, Cornstalk decided to attack the southern army first. During the night of October 9–10, his 900 warriors crossed the Ohio River above the mouth of the Kanawha, hoping to attack before the soldiers awoke. However, two men, James Robinson and Valentine Sevier, left camp early the morning of the 10th to hunt, wandered into the Shawnee force, and sounded the alarm. Lewis then sent two columns of 150 men each, under his brother, Col. Charles Lewis, and Col. William Fleming, up the bottomland to meet the enemy. Musket fire mingled with fog obscured the battlefield, and the hand-to-hand fighting was fierce.

A flanking movement along Crooked Creek to the hill above the battlefield, led by Lt. Isaac Shelby, later the first governor of Kentucky, was mistaken by Cornstalk to be the arrival of militia reinforcements. The Shawnee retreated late in the afternoon, dumping the bodies of their dead in the river. Within a few days, Cornstalk signed an armistice with Governor Dunmore at Camp Charlotte, near the Shawnee towns. The treaty was formalized at Pittsburgh in 1775.

There is a tradition that the Battle of Point Pleasant was the first battle of the Revolutionary War. Most historians disagree, given the nature of the struggle and the lapse of time before hostilities began in New England. While many Virginians were upset with Dunmore's dissolution of the House of Burgesses in 1773, they still fought willingly under the British colonial governor in defense of their homesteads. There is no need to make lavish claims, since the Battle of Point Pleasant had its own singular results. Most importantly, it pacified the Ohio Valley for more than two years. Failure to defeat the Ohio tribes would have meant fighting a two-front war during the critical early stages of the Revolution before the Saratoga victory, October 17, 1777, and the resulting French alliance. Such a two-front war might have brought defeat to the infant independence movement.

See also Cornstalk, Dunmore's War, Andrew Lewis

Philip Sturm
Ohio Valley University
Virgil A. Lewis, *History of the Battle of Point Pleasant*, 1909; Reuben Gold Thwaites and Louise Phelps Kellogg, *Documentary History of Dunmore's War, 1774*, 1905.

Dick Pointer

On May 29, 1778, Dick Pointer, a black slave, helped to save about 60 settlers in the Greenbrier Valley. Warned that a band of Shawnee Indians had left the Ohio Valley with the intent of attacking the Greenbrier settlements, the settlers with Pointer among them decided to shelter at Fort Donnally near Lewisburg. The Indians attacked the fort the next day.

On the morning of the attack Pointer and a white man, William Hammond, were the first to hear the alarm, given by settler William Hughart as he rushed to close the fort door on the attacking Indians. The Indians began hacking at the door with tomahawks. Their effort failed due to the quick thinking of Pointer and Hammond, who rolled a hogshead of water behind the door. Pointer also managed to fire at the invaders, thus alerting the sleeping inhabitants.

The surprised settlers fought the Indians as they jumped from their beds. At dark, the Indians retreated and the attack was over. For his bravery Pointer was granted a life lease to a piece of land, where he lived until his death at about age 89 in 1827. In 1795, the thankful friends of Dick Pointer petitioned the Virginia Assembly for his freedom but were refused, although he was purchased and freed in 1801. In 1976, a stone was dedicated in Lewisburg to honor Dick Pointer's heroism. His musket is now in the State Museum in Charleston.

Cathy Hershberger Miller
State Archives

Poles

Polish immigrants were among the earliest and most numerous of the many ethnic groups that poured into West Virginia during the first two decades of the 20th century. Attracted to the job opportunities being created by the state's rapidly growing industrial sector, Poles and other Eastern and Southern Europeans were recruited by agents of state government and the private representatives of mines, mills, railroads, and factories.

By 1908, Poles were the third-largest immigrant group working in the West Virginia coal mines. At that time, apart from native whites and African-Americans, only Italians and Hungarians were represented in the mines in greater numbers. In several mining communities, such as Raleigh in Raleigh County, Scotts Run in Monongalia County, and Whipple and Carlisle in Fay-

ette County, Poles were the largest ethnic group. Polish immigrant miners were evenly distributed throughout the coalfields. Of the ten leading West Virginia counties with significant concentrations of Polish miners, five, led by Marion County, were in the northern part of the state and five, led by Fayette County, were in the south.

Polish labor also supplied a significant part of the work force in several areas of manufacturing. Poles were particularly important to the production of iron and steel products in Wheeling and Weirton in the Northern Panhandle. Moreover, Poles made up the largest part of the work force that made Charleston's Kelly Axe factory (later True Temper) at one time the largest producer of axes, hatchets, and related hand tools in the world.

Whether they were coal miners or factory laborers, Polish workers in West Virginia fit the classic pattern of the so-called "birds of passage" immigrants who were single males or married men without their wives who intended to return to the old country as soon as they made their fortune. However, as more Poles made the decision to stay and their numbers swelled to almost 15,000 by 1930, ethnic institutions sprang up to serve them. A Saint Ladislaus Catholic Church was established in Wheeling, while in Weirton the Sacred Heart of Mary served a large Polish and Italian community. In some places, outdoor grottos such as Our Lady of Grace in Wheeling were constructed for special services. Furthermore, Polish fraternal organizations, athletic clubs, musical aggregations, and especially polka societies dotted the landscape.

Like many immigrant groups who came to West Virginia, some Poles left the Mountain State for opportunities elsewhere or returned to their homelands. Nevertheless, still vibrant strains of Polish-American culture remain, especially in the northern-industrial sections of the state.

See also Ethnic Life

Fred A. Barkey
Marshall University Graduate College
Frederick A. Barkey, "Immigration and Ethnicity in West Virginia: A Review of the Literature," *West Virginia History: Critical Essays on the Literature*, 1993.

Political Corruption

In his best-selling book, *The Making of the President 1960*, Theodore White said that West Virginia was among the most politically corrupt places in the country. The basis for White's observation was the 1960 West Virginia Democratic primary election in which John F. Kennedy buried Hubert Humphrey by a mixture of state-of-the-art political techniques and old-style vote buying.

There is other evidence to justify White's harsh assessment. In the last third of the 20th century, West Virginia governors

THE WEST VIRGINIA PROBLEM.

This 1904 cartoon saw the free-flowing cash of Senators Davis and Elkins as a problem.

were charged with felonies four times in federal court, with two acquittals and two guilty pleas. Two state senate presidents were convicted and sent to prison, and numerous elected and appointed officials (plus a few associates) suffered a similar fate.

On February 14, 1968, the U.S. attorney announced the indictment of former Gov. W. W. Barron (1961–65) and several close associates on public corruption charges. Although Barron was acquitted, all of his co-defendants were convicted. Suspicions were kindled when, soon after the trial concluded, the jury foreman visited a Charleston car dealer and bought a new luxury vehicle, paying cash. The foreman had been paid $25,000 to "hang" the jury but was able to produce an acquittal. He and Barron both subsequently pleaded guilty to jury tampering and were sentenced to lengthy prison terms. Their wives, who exchanged the money, were given immunity.

Following Barron in the prisoners' dock was former Attorney General C. Donald Robertson. After pleading guilty in 1972 to charges involving kickbacks on federal housing assistance, Robertson served 14 months in prison.

Gov. Arch Moore was indicted for bribery in 1975, near the end of his second term. He testified in his own behalf and was acquitted. Moore was elected to a third term in 1984. His second encounter with the federal prosecutor came in

1990, after he was defeated in his bid for a fourth term. A Beckley businessman, John Kizer, claimed that Moore had exacted campaign contributions from him by promising favorable treatment with regard to his workers' compensation account. Kizer had been repeatedly threatened with prosecution before he agreed to testify against Moore.

John Leaberry, a Huntington lawyer who had been Moore's campaign director and later his workers' compensation commissioner, called Moore and made arrangements to meet him near Parkersburg. Leaberry had recently appeared before a federal grand jury that was investigating Moore, and in contacting Moore he offered to discuss that testimony. Unfortunately for Moore, Leaberry was "wired" with a hidden microphone and the meeting was monitored by federal agents. Shortly afterward, Moore waived indictment and pleaded guilty. He was sentenced to five years in prison.

In 1993, West Virginia Lottery director Elton "Butch" Bryan and Ed Rebrook, counsel for the lottery, were convicted of insider trading and sent to prison. The gist of this offense is using privileged information in financial transactions. Bribery cases involve the 1989 prosecutions of former State Senate President Dan Tonkovich and Larry Tucker, his successor in the office.

Some critics question whether West Virginia is any more corrupt than other

places, pointing out that federal prosecutors have considerable leeway in pursuing cases. This is especially true with regard to those highly discretionary corruption cases that could be prosecuted in either federal or state courts or ignored altogether. An indicted politician guarantees local headlines and accolades from the Justice Department in Washington.

Michael Carey, who as U.S. attorney in Charleston sent Moore, Tonkovich, and Tucker to prison, published a list of public official prosecutions for 1984 through 1991 in the 1992 *West Virginia Law Review*. Of the 77 separate public official prosecutions listed by Carey, only a little more than one-third of the defendants were sentenced to any substantial prison time (from one to 20 years). By comparison, the official report of William Kolibash, who served as U.S. attorney in the Northern District of West Virginia at roughly the same time, deals exclusively with major drug traffickers and organized crime figures, all of whom received substantial sentences upon conviction.

Nor should it be concluded that 20th-century politicians were necessarily more corrupt than their predecessors. West Virginia politicians participated enthusiastically in the excesses of the late 19th century, routinely mixing business and politics. U.S. Sen. Johnson Newlon Camden (1881–87, 1893–95) exploited public office for personal gain, and a cartoon labeled "The West Virginia Problem" showed U.S. Senators Davis (1871–83) and Elkins (1895–1911) leaning on the pork barrel, checkbooks in hand.

H. John Rogers
New Martinsville

Politics

West Virginia was born in political controversy. Abraham Lincoln's recognition of its statehood in 1863, under the unnatural conditions of the Civil War, prompted former Virginia Gov. Henry A. Wise to declare the new state the "bastard child of a political rape." While few West Virginians accept Wise's bitter judgment, probably most will agree that our political history has been especially partisan and sometimes unseemly.

A review of the state's history also reveals that politics in West Virginia was also parochial. Many political movements that swept across the nation had little permanent impact here. For example, the state avoided the harsh Reconstruction policies that prompted states farther south to stay committed to the Democratic Party during the national realignment of 1896. While those states experienced troop occupation after the Civil War and delayed readmission to the Union, West Virginia did not. Moreover, our state ended Confederate disenfranchisement by 1871, and it never denied the vote to African-Americans.

West Virginia also largely avoided the impact of both Populism, the "bottom-up" political rebellion which swept the South and West in the 1890s, and Progressivism, the "top-down" political reform which swept the North and Midwest in the early part of the 20th century. Such movements bypassed the state in part because of the political influence of conservative leaders in both major parties, including Senators Johnson N. Camden and Henry G. Davis in the Democratic Party and Davis's son-in-law, Stephen B. Elkins, among the Republicans. The closest the state came to mirroring either political reform movement was in the gubernatorial administrations of Democrat E. Willis Wilson (1885–89) and Republican Henry D. Hatfield (1913–17). Wilson mounted a populist campaign in 1884 that challenged monopolies and railroads, while Hatfield initiated such progressive reforms as primary elections and utility regulation.

Our state not only had few successful reform movements, but also few charismatic or powerful political leaders who could overcome what historian John Alexander Williams calls an "enduring and complex sectionalism." Only two politicians were able to dominate their time and set up a long-term control over state politics. The first was Republican U.S. Sen. Stephen B. Elkins, who from 1895 to his death in 1911 operated West Virginia's first political machine. The second was Democrat M. M. Neely, U.S. senator and governor, who in 1940 with the help of organized labor fashioned a political machine that impacted state politics for the next two decades.

Although West Virginia may have had two major parties since its creation, it rarely has had a competitive two-party system. Instead it has followed a pattern of cyclical competition, with infrequent shifts in power from one party to another. In such a situation the pivot of political power becomes the dominant party's primary rather than the November general election.

A review of the first 14 decades of our history reveals four distinct and uneven periods of partisan dominance. The first period witnessed Republican control from 1863 to 1871 as that party elected the state's first four governors. Republican electoral success, however, was based on restrictions that denied the vote to the many thousands who had served or supported the Confederate cause. When those restrictions were removed under the 1871 Flick Amendment to the state constitution, the stage was set for a Democratic takeover. During this second period, 1872–96, Democrats elected the next five governors and controlled the legislature. During the years of the so-called Bourbon Democrats (a label derived from the anti-reform French monarchy, kings who were said "never to have learned anything and never to have forgotten anything") the party reflected a conservative ideology, a rural orientation, and pro-Confederate sympathies.

Republicans regained control in the 1896 election and kept power until 1932, when the Great Depression and Franklin Roosevelt's New Deal altered the political landscape of West Virginia and the nation. During the 1896–1932 Republican period the party elected six of the seven governors and had a majority in 11 of the 14 legislative sessions. The GOP takeover in West Virginia was part of a national realignment which saw the party effectively champion policies of economic growth to attain a majority status in every region except the South.

The fourth and longest period of party dominance started in 1933 and continued through the rest of the 20th century. With two exceptions (Cecil Underwood and Arch Moore) all the governors during this period were Democrats. In 1940, organized labor became a major player in state politics when the United Mine Workers contributed to Neely's win in the gubernatorial primary. After that election unions remained important in state politics for many years.

Although Neely's victory was interpreted at the time as an ideological victory for organized labor and liberalism, his political machine during the next two decades appeared less interested in promoting a political agenda than in collecting political spoils. That perception increased the deep-seated voter cynicism which has a long tradition in West Virginia. Voter trust was further eroded in the 1960s and then again in the 1980s when two former governors, Democrat Wally Barron and Republican Arch Moore, were sent to prison for corruption.

In the last quarter of the 20th century two reformers from outside the political mainstream became governors, Jay Rockefeller in 1976 and Gaston Caperton in 1988. Each won re-election and Rockefeller went on to the U.S. Senate. Although both Rockefeller and Caperton adopted a more professional, moderate, and media-driven style of politics, at the end of the century West Virginia politics continued to be viewed as pervasive, partisan, and personal. Political observers still awaited the cyclical comeback of the Republican party, still predicted the replacement of a personal style of politics by media-driven politics, and still pondered the question of how politics can permeate a state, but leave so few permanent marks of change or reform.

See also Stephen B. Elkins, Flick Amendment, Matthew Mansfield Neely, Political Corruption

Robert Rupp
West Virginia Wesleyan College

Pontiac's Rebellion

Pontiac's Rebellion, an uprising against settlers in the Ohio Valley and Great Lakes region, followed the French and Indian War's conclusion in 1763. Western Virginians were among those to suffer.

Pontiac (about 1720–69) was a member of the Ottawa tribe and recognized as a leader within that group by the mid-1750s. Pontiac accepted the teaching of Neolin, a militant prophet of the Delaware tribe, who argued that whites and Indians originated from different creators and that Indians must align to expel whites, particularly the English, or suffer cultural disintegration. As allies of the French during their losing seven-year struggle with Great Britain, western tribes had engaged in extensive cooperation among themselves, a basis for further collaboration. When Pontiac realized that an English victory meant not only occupation of French trading centers but also waves of settlers dispossessing Indians of land, he quickly joined the message of the prophet with his own charismatic appeal to forge a military alliance among elements of the Ottawa, Delaware, Kickapoo, Miami, Potawatomi, Seneca, Shawnee, and Wyandotte.

Pontiac instructed Indians to feign friendship, gain entrance to all western British forts, kill the soldiers, and then slaughter helpless nearby settlers. Coordinated attacks commenced in the spring of 1763, eradicating most fortifications. The largest of those that survived were Detroit and Fort Pitt. In Western Virginia's Greenbrier region, the Shawnee chief Cornstalk led approximately 60 warriors who posed as friends to white residents they encountered and then murdered them. Dozens of whites died as a result of these tactics.

Pontiac himself directed the assault upon Detroit but an informer warned the garrison, forcing the Indians to mount a siege. The fort withstood the siege and British countermeasures ultimately forced Pontiac to negotiate peace in 1766 in Detroit after unsuccessfully attempting to convince tribes along portions of the Mississippi River to join the Indian alliance. While visiting near what is now Caholia, Illinois, Pontiac died when knifed by another Indian.

See also French and Indian War
Richard P. Lizza
West Liberty State College
Howard Henry Peckham, *Pontiac and the Indian Uprising*, 1947.

Population

In 1790, the year of the first U.S. Census, the population of the territory now comprising West Virginia was 55,873. The nation's population in that first census was 3,929,214. West Virginia's population grew from 1790 until the 1950s, peaking that year at 2,005,552. According to the

2000 Census, there were 1,808,350 West Virginia residents, compared to 281 million residents for the United States. West Virginia's share of the U.S. population has fallen from 1.4 percent in 1790 to 0.6 percent in 2000.

This implies that the state's population growth has fallen well short of national growth during the last 210 years. This was not always so. From 1900 to 1950, West Virginia's population growth exceeded national growth, as the expansion of mining and manufacturing boosted economic growth. However, the strong population gains registered during the first half of the century were not repeated during the last half.

After reaching a high of two million in 1950, the number of West Virginians has risen and fallen with the state's economy. With increasing mechanization in the coal mines and increased economic opportunity elsewhere, the population dropped by 261,000 residents from 1950 to 1970. The energy crises of the 1970s brought a resurgence in coal mining, which contributed to a rebound in the state's population to near the 1950 level by the end of the decade. Unfortunately, a global recession during the 1980s, coupled with economic restructuring in the state's major manufacturing and coal mining sectors, pushed the number of residents down to 1,793,477 by 1990. West Virginia added nearly 15,000 new residents during the 1990s, the second slowest growth rate posted by any state during the decade.

The reasons behind the slow population gains during the last decade are related to the state's demographic structure. Population change depends primarily on two factors, natural increase and net migration. Natural increase is the annual difference between births and deaths. Since the number of births during the 1990s was very close to the number of deaths, West Virginia's population got little boost from natural increase. This means that population growth in the state during the 1990s was dependent on net migration, which is the difference between the number of residents moving into the state and the number leaving the state. During the 1990s, West Virginia lost about as many residents as it attracted, primarily because the state's economic growth failed to match national gains and the gains posted by many states on the East Coast.

West Virginia's population levels have always differed significantly in the various counties. In 1900, Kanawha County, with the largest population in the state, had 54,696 residents, compared to Hancock County with 6,693 residents. However, during the last 100 years the population gap between larger and smaller counties has risen dramatically. The largest county in 2000 was again Kanawha County, with 200,073 residents, compared to Wirt County with 5,873 residents.

County population growth tends to follow regional economic performance. None of the major southern coal-producing counties, Boone, Logan, McDowell, Mingo, or Raleigh, ranked in the top ten in population size in 1900. With the expansion of the coal industry during the first half of the century, McDowell, Raleigh, and Logan counties all ranked in the top ten in population in 1950. But due to changes in the coal industry and the lack of diversification in these counties' economies, only Raleigh remained in the top ten in 2000. The experience of McDowell County is a good illustration. In 1900, the Census Bureau counted 18,747 residents in McDowell. By 1950 that number swelled to 98,887 residents, while the 2000 Census found just 27,329 residents.

Overall population growth during the post-World War II period has favored counties with larger cities and the "bedroom" counties from which cities draw commuters. By far the fastest growing regions of the state during the last 50 years were three counties in the Eastern Panhandle (Morgan, Berkeley, and Jefferson) and Putnam County. These four counties have benefited from the expansion of nearby metropolitan areas. Indeed Berkeley and Jefferson are now classified as part of the Washington Primary Metropolitan Statistical Area, while Putnam County is now part of the Charleston Metropolitan Statistical Area. Counties registering the largest population losses during the last 50 years were the coal-dependent counties, particularly in the southern part of the state, and the manufacturing counties in the Northern Panhandle.

Population change has also had an impact on West Virginia's cities. In 1900, the largest city in the state was Wheeling, with a population of 38,878, followed by Huntington, Parkersburg, Charleston, and Martinsburg. By 2000, the top five cities were Charleston, with 53,421 residents, Huntington, Parkersburg, Wheeling, and Morgantown. In addition, during the last ten years, West Virginia's incorporated places have lost population, in contrast to population gains registered by the state's unincorporated areas.

West Virginia remains a rural state with mostly small cities. In 1900, 86.9 percent of the state's residents lived in sparsely populated rural areas, compared to 60.4 percent nationally. West Virginia was not unusual in this respect at the beginning of the century, as ten other states registered larger shares of residents living in rural areas. By 1990 though, 63.9 percent of West Virginia's residents lived in rural areas, compared to 24.8 percent nationally. Only Vermont was more rural, with 67.8 percent of its residents living in rural areas in 1990. Most other states have seen their residents concentrate in urban areas during the 20th century. West Virginia has participated in this trend, but the state's rugged topography and dependence on resource extraction have meant that a large share of residents live in rural areas.

See also Demography

George W. Hammond
Bureau of Business & Economic Research
Brian Lego, "West Virginia: A 20th Century Perspective on Population Change," ms., 1999; Otis K. Rice and Stephen W. Brown, *West Virginia: A History*, 1993.

Port Amherst

Port Amherst, located five miles east of Charleston on the north bank of the Kanawha River near the mouth of Campbells Creek, is an important river port and one of the oldest communities in the Kanawha Valley. Mary Draper Ingles made salt there during her captivity by the Shawnees in 1755, and a settlement grew around the salt spring. It had several earlier names including Reed, Dana, and Tinkersville. It was named Port Amherst in 1956, although many residents still refer to the residential community as Reed.

The Campbell's Creek Coal Company from its beginning in 1865 shipped coal down the Kanawha River to western markets. The company and its successor, the Amherst Fuel Company, were unusual in that they operated their own coal mines and transported the coal on company-owned barges, having first brought the coal to the river on their own short-line railroad.

By the early 20th century, extensive marine facilities had been developed at the Reed terminal, now Port Amherst. This terminal featured a large rail yard, rail-to-barge loading facility, and shops capable of building rail and mine cars, barges, and steam-powered river vessels. Acquired by the Amherst Fuel Company in 1950, Port Amherst Ltd. and associated companies continue to provide a variety of services in the diverse field of marine and rail transportation, bulk material transfer, and shipment. Madison Coal and Supply, a Port Amherst subsidiary headquartered at Port Amherst, operates 18 towboats on the Ohio, Mississippi, Monongahela, Allegheny, and Kanawha rivers and provides a variety of towing services. This firm specializes in the transportation of bulk material and large equipment used for construction and dredging projects.

Todd A. Hanson
Given
Todd A. Hanson, *Campbell's Creek: A Portrait of a Coal Mining Community*, 1989.

Melville Davisson Post

Born in Harrison County, April 19, 1869, Melville Davisson Post became immensely popular as a writer starting with his 1896 short story collection, *The Strange Schemes*

Twilight in the hills

"There was a long twilight in these hills. The sun departs, but the day remains. A sort of weird, dim, elfin day, that dawns at sunset, and envelops and possesses the world. The land is full of light, but it is the light of no heavenly sun. It is a light equal everywhere, as though the earth strove to illumine itself, and succeeded with that labor.

"The stars are not yet out. Now and then a pale moon rides in the sky, but it has no power, and the light is not from it. The wind is usually gone; the air is soft, and the fragrance of the fields fills it like a perfume. The noises of the day and of the creatures that go about by day cease, and the noises of the night and of the creatures that haunt the night begin. The bat swoops and circles in the maddest action, but without a sound. The eye sees him, but the ear hears nothing. The whippoorwill begins his plaintive cry, and one hears, but does not see.

"It is a world that we do not understand, for we are creatures of the sun, and we are fearful lest we come upon things at work here, of which we have no experience, and that may be able to justify themselves against our reason. And so a man falls into silence when he travels in this twilight, and he looks and listens with his senses out on guard."

—Melville Davisson Post "A Twilight Adventure" (1914)

of *Randolph Mason* (Putnam). He continued to publish until his death. Much of his work is set in the 19th-century West Virginia countryside.

His best-known works are the Randolph Mason series, published in three volumes, and the more successful collection, *Uncle Abner: Master of Mysteries* (Appleton, 1918). Post wrote other short works, mostly detective fiction, including the Monsieur Jonquelle series and the Walker of the Secret Service series and many articles, essays, and treatises. Among Post's longer works are *Dwellers in the Hills* (Putnam, 1901), *The Mountain School-teacher* (Appleton, 1922), and *Revolt of the Birds* (Appleton, 1927), which are all underrated but indicative of Post's varied and huge talent. His total output was approximately 230 titles.

Post's love of the outdoors, the forests, and the weather shows through in all his major works. In "Woodford's Partner" in *Strange Schemes of Randolph Mason* (Putnam, 1896), Post takes six pages to describe the Valley of Virginia as if he were standing on a mountaintop delivering a lecture. It is a tribute to the farmers, the cattlemen, the traders, and businessmen who lived and died and prospered in the land between the frontier and the East Coast.

From a long line of Western Virginians, Post's forebears date back to 1773 when Daniel Davisson settled in the heart of future Clarksburg. With a law degree from WVU (1892) and the successful launching of a writing career with *Randolph Mason*, Post married Ann Bloomfield Gamble Schoolfield in 1903 and together they traveled the world and the East Coast before settling down at the "Chalet" in Harrison County. Their European adventures helped Post find settings for much of his other work. Their one child died shortly after birth, and Mrs. Post died of pneumonia in 1919. Still rising in skill and fame, Post loved to ride and

while riding in 1930, he fell. He died on June 23 of the injuries and was buried in Harrison County.

See also Uncle Abner

Charles F. Moore
East Tennessee State University
Jack Sandy Anderson, "Melville Davisson Post," *West Virginia History*, July 1967; Charles A. Norton, *Melville Davisson Post: Man of Many Mysteries*, 1973.

Potomac Highlands

The Potomac Highlands include Grant, Hampshire, Hardy, Mineral, and Pendleton counties, West Virginia, and neighboring areas of Maryland and Virginia. The West Virginia counties are the mountainous uplands of the Eastern Panhandle, drained by the Potomac headwaters. The western edges of Grant and Mineral counties lie west of the Allegheny Front and are a part of the Allegheny Mountains. All the other territory is east of the Allegheny Front and a part of the Ridge and Valley system.

Within West Virginia's Potomac Highlands, a region of 2,722 square miles, are many of our state's most spectacular mountain features. They include Spruce Knob (4,861 feet), the state's highest point. Other features of renown include Seneca Rocks, the Trough, Lost River, and the Smoke Hole. The dominant vegetation of the Potomac Highlands is forest, with regrowth northern hardwoods at the lower levels and spruce and pine at the higher elevations.

Elevation has a direct effect on temperature and precipitation. Cool to cold winters and warm summers are normal throughout the Potomac Highlands, but the precipitation varies greatly. Annual snowfalls of 60 to 100 inches occur in some mountain areas. Some mountain areas and western slopes receive an annual rainfall of as much as 70 inches, but many parts of the Potomac Highlands lie within the "rain shadow" east of the Alle-

ghenies. In the South Branch Valley rainfalls of 30 to 35 inches yearly are typical.

Archeological remains show that the Potomac Highlands region was inhabited in prehistoric times. The earliest known inhabitants occupied the Potomac Valley and subsisted on a livelihood of hunting and gathering. As their culture advanced, a more settled lifestyle based on agriculture evolved, but the native population was never very large in the Highlands. Their legacy remains in names, mounds, village sites, and trails.

Terrain conditions influenced the colonial and post-colonial settlement and occupancy of the Potomac Highlands. Hampshire was the first county of present West Virginia, formed in 1753, and in 1866 Grant and Mineral counties were the last organized. The population of the Highlands is 79,445 with a regional density of about 29 people per square mile. The people are mostly rural nonfarm residents, with Keyser (population 5,303 in 2000) the largest urban place in the region. Agriculture (especially poultry and livestock), tourism, forestry products, and manufacturing are the primary economic pursuits in the Potomac Highlands.

See also Eastern Panhandle, Geography
Howard G. Adkins
Ona

Potomac River

The Potomac River begins at a spring in the northeastern corner of Tucker County. The spring is the site of a small monolith, a replica of the first Fairfax Stone that once marked the boundary of the land grant to the sixth Lord Fairfax, which ran to the farthest headwaters of the Potomac. This is the North Branch of the Potomac, which flows 97 miles to its confluence with the South Branch. The Potomac forms the boundary between West Virginia and Maryland from the Fairfax Stone to Harpers Ferry, and from Harpers Ferry to the Chesapeake Bay it is the boundary between Maryland and Virginia. The river itself belongs to Maryland under a 1632 grant by Charles I, but Virginia (and consequently West Virginia) gained water rights under a 1785 compact. The total length from spring to bay is 287 miles.

The other main fork of the Potomac is the South Branch, which flows down from its highest headwaters in Highland County, Virginia, through Pendleton, Grant, Hardy, and Hampshire counties. The North and South branches, with the North and South forks of the South Branch and other Potomac tributaries and the main river itself, together drain all of the Eastern Panhandle and Potomac Highlands of West Virginia, and much of neighboring Virginia and Maryland. The Shenandoah River, a major tributary, enters the Potomac at Harpers Ferry.

The Potomac meets the Shenandoah just beyond these old bridge piers at Harpers Ferry.

The Potomac is rich in history and prehistory. Archeologists believe that humans were present as hunter-gatherers in the Potomac watershed before 10,000 B.C., and by the arrival of the early European traders and settlers Indian communities were commonplace on the lower Potomac. The Potomac Valley Indians were great traders. The name itself is derived from a 1608 map by Capt. John Smith that indicated the location of a tribe, Potowmeck, and was translated as the "landing place for goods" or "emporium."

Aiming to develop a transportation corridor into the Appalachians, George Washington and others formed the Potowmack Company in 1784, but the company's navigational improvements failed to make river commerce feasible for more than several months of the year. A successor, the Chesapeake & Ohio Canal Company, built a canal on the Maryland side of the river that parallels the Potomac between Cumberland, Maryland, and Washington. Today the Chesapeake & Ohio Canal National Historical Park preserves all 184.5 miles of the waterway, the most intact example of America's canal era.

George Washington also gave encouragement to James Rumsey, the inventor of a steamboat that Rumsey successfully demonstrated on the Potomac at Shepherdstown in 1787. In 1790, at the direction of Congress, Washington selected the site for the U. S. capital at the confluence of the Potomac and what is today the Anacostia River. President Washington had a national armory located at Harpers Ferry, where the Shenandoah joins the Potomac. In Civil War times the Potomac River served as the boundary between the Union and the Confederacy.

The Potomac is noted for its great beauty and its recreational value. The South Branch, with its North and South forks, runs down from West Virginia's highest mountains. Seneca Rocks, West Virginia's best-known natural landmark, stands on the bank of the North Fork in Pendleton County. Nearby Spruce Knob, elevation 4,861 feet, is the highest point in the state. The South Branch and its tributaries flow through both the Monongahela and George Washington national forests.

Generally, the North Branch valley is an old industrial area, rich in mining and manufacturing history. The North Branch is dammed above Piedmont, where the Jennings Randolph Lake helps to regulate water quality downstream. The valley provided a vital transportation route from as early as the French and Indian War, and still does today.

Although the Potomac is one of the cleanest rivers of the Atlantic Seaboard and is being further improved through efforts of federal, state, and local governments, it still has critical problems. Acid drainage from abandoned coal mines pollutes the North Branch, while sediment, herbicide, pesticide, and chemical fertilizer runoff from suburban development and farming operations enter the river system at many points. Agricultural runoff associated with the growing poultry industry in the upper Shenandoah Valley and the South Branch and hogs in western Maryland has been an issue in recent years. The lower river suffers from the urban runoff of oils and heavy metals from streets, parking lots, and abandoned industrial sites on the Anacostia River, which ranks high as one of America's dirtiest urban rivers.

See also Fairfax Stone, North Branch, South Branch

Gilbert Gude
Bethesda, Maryland

Arnout Hyde Jr. and Ken Sullivan, *The Potomac: A Nation's River*, 1993.

Potomac State College

Potomac State College of West Virginia University is located in Keyser, the county seat of Mineral County. The college was founded in 1901 when the West Virginia legislature created the Keyser Preparatory Branch of West Virginia University. Col. Thomas B. Davis, a local businessman, donated 17 acres of land for the school on Fort Hill, formerly the location of Fort Fuller. During the Civil War, this fort had played a critical role in maintaining Union control of the Baltimore & Ohio Railroad. Today the site, on high ground overlooking the town, provides a beautiful location for the college.

The institution essentially functioned as a secondary school for the first 20 years. It began operation in 1902 as the West Virginia Preparatory School, with a single building combining offices, classrooms, library, and gymnasium. Lloyd Friend was appointed as principal, with a faculty of four. In 1905, a commercial department was added, as well as music, elocution, and teacher training. Pre-engineering and agriculture programs were added in 1911.

A fire destroyed the school on May 3, 1917. A special session of the legislature appropriated $30,000 for a new building. The legislature established an agricultural, industrial, and vocational department to comply with the Smith-Hughes Act, which provided federal funds for vocational education. In 1919, 125 acres of land was purchased for the operation of the agriculture program. The new building also was completed during that year.

In 1921, the school became a junior college and began offering the first two years of the baccalaureate programs and certain vocational programs. The name was changed to Potomac State School. The first president was J. W. Lakin, who served for the next 15 years; previously the title had been principal. In 1926, Potomac State was accredited by the North Central Association of Colleges and Secondary Schools. Three years later, all secondary work and teacher training were eliminated and all course work was placed on the college level to coordinate with the lower division work offered at West Virginia University.

In 1935, the college was placed under the management of the Board of Governors of West Virginia University. The legislature changed the name to Potomac State School of West Virginia University. In 1951, the college assumed its current name, Potomac State College of West Virginia University. It began serving as a regional campus of the university and still does. All of the college's academic and administrative services are coordinated through the university in Morgantown, while the responsibility for budgetary support of programs and activities resides within the college. Potomac State offers 16 degree programs at the two-year associate level, including agriculture, business, criminal justice, and the arts and sciences. In fall 2004, the college had 1,305 students.

Among the distinguished individuals who attended Potomac State College are Henry Louis Gates Jr., noted intellectual and chair of the Afro-American Studies Department at Harvard; John Kruk, former professional baseball player, most notably affiliated with the Philadelphia Phillies; and Admiral Joseph Lopez, former commander-in-chief of the Allied Forces in Southern Europe and former commander-in-chief for the U.S. Naval forces in Europe.

Donna Hanna-Walker
Charleston

Charles Ambler, *A History of Education in West Virginia*, 1951; "Potomac State School," *The West Virginia Encyclopedia*, 1929.

Potomak Guardian

West Virginia's first newspaper, the *Potowmac Guardian, and Berkeley Advertiser*, was issued in Shepherdstown in November 1790 by Nathaniel Willis (1755–1831). The earliest known issue is dated June 27, 1791. Sometime after November 14, 1791, the date of the last known Shepherdstown issue, Willis moved to Martinsburg, resuming publication by April 3, 1792. He changed the name of the newspaper to the *Potomak Guardian, and Berkeley Advertiser* by the February 23, 1795 issue, then shortened it to the *Potomak Guardian* on February 1, 1798.

More than a printer, Willis was a journalist with strong interests in politics and current affairs. His views were staunchly Jeffersonian Republican, and his attacks on local Federalists resulted in ill feelings culminating in physical retaliation and vandalism. When his apprentice established a rival newspaper, the *Berkeley Intelligencer*, Willis decided to quit. Armstrong Charlton became publisher October 30, 1799, and continued the *Potomak Guardian* through at least January 8, 1800, the last issue known.

Harold Malcolm Forbes
WVU Libraries

Otis K. Rice, "West Virginia Printers and Their Work, 1790–1830," *West Virginia History*, July 1953.

Pottery Industry

The pottery industry, which produces dinnerware, food storage and food preparation containers, and other ceramic products, was a major industry in West Virginia in the 19th and early 20th centuries. It remains important today, particularly in the Northern Panhandle where Homer Laughlin China Company is a very large dinnerware producer. Artisan potters practice their craft throughout the state, producing fine ware in limited quanities for the arts and crafts trade.

Lead-glazed red pottery was known everywhere in early America, which was rich in iron-red clay. The ware was fragile and did not ship well. Thus a pottery was necessary in every locale, producing utilitarian lead-glazed red earthenware from the same native clay as bricks.

Six redware potteries are known to have existed in the late 18th and the 19th centuries in present West Virginia. Samuel Butters worked in Clarksburg from before 1809 until after 1820. R. Brown was in Wellsburg about 1841. Elisha and William Day potted in Wheeling from 1825 to 1899. The Foulke Pottery operated in Morgantown from 1784 to 1800, and John W. Thompson was there before 1854. Stephen Shepherd worked in Charleston before 1818 until after 1838.

There was some stoneware clay here, and more was imported where needed. Stoneware reached a stone-like hardness through high-temperature firing. Late 19th-century potters knew how to make saltglazed stoneware decorated in cobalt blue. Thirty-four stoneware potters made crocks, jars, jugs, water coolers, and wax-top canning jars. They worked in the Monongahela Valley at Bridgeport, Clarksburg, Morgantown, Pruntytown, Shinnston, and other places. In the Ohio Valley they potted at Wellsburg, Wheeling, Parkersburg, and elsewhere. A. P. Donaghho was a 19th-century Parkersburg potter whose stoneware is avidly collected today. In Monroe County stoneware was made at Lindside and in Mercer County at East River.

During the early 19th century American potters tried to improve their wares to compete with cheap imported English Staffordshire earthenwares. They made yellow ware and covered it with a mottled brown glaze, known as Rockingham or, mistakenly, Bennington ware. Between 1848 and 1857, the Larkin brothers' Virginia Pottery in Newell, Hancock County, made the first molded ware in present West Virginia using this glaze. Newell's location on the Ohio River permitted local potters to learn about advances made in the pottery center in neighboring East Liverpool, Ohio.

Porcelain was the most sophisticated ceramic ware. The Ohio Valley China Company in Wheeling made porcelain between 1890 and 1895, and Wheeling Pottery Company made it between 1879 and 1900.

By the turn of the 20th century, American potteries perfected good white earthenware, similar to the dinnerware most of us use today. In the Northern Panhandle, Homer Laughlin made a variety of wares from 1873 to the present, and other industrial potteries were active until the early 1980s. Trenle Blake China Company made dinnerware in Ravenswood in the 1920s. H. R. Wyllie China made dinnerware in Huntington in the 1920s. Carr China made hotel ware between 1916 and 1953 in Grafton. D. E. McNicol China made hotel ware in Clarksburg between 1914 and 1954. The Paden City Pottery Company made dinnerware between 1911 and 1957, selling the bulk of their production to restaurants, state parks, and hotels.

Before the advent of indoor plumbing, sanitary ware was also made in West Virginia, including pitchers, basins, chamber pots, slop jars, toothbrush holders, soap dishes, and shaving mugs. Later the production turned to sinks and flush toilets. La Belle Pottery and Riverside Potteries Company made this ware in Wheeling in the late 19th century, succeeded in 1903 by Wheeling Potteries Company. After 1905, Homewood Pottery in Mannington, followed by Bowers Pottery between 1923 and 1941, and then Kimm Products after 1950, made the heavy ware. Other sanitary potteries included Eljer Company in Cameron about 1923, Broadway Pottery Company between 1897 and 1940, Keyser Pottery Company after 1905, and Wheeling Sanitary Manufacturing Company, about 1923.

Wire porcelain insulators were made by many potteries, including John Boch between 1907 and 1937, and Boch-Metsch Porcelain Company between 1919 and 1922, both of Newell. Davidson Porcelain Company worked between 1921 and 1936, as did Davidson-Stevenson Porcelain Company between 1913 and 1921 in Chester. General Porcelain worked in Parkersburg about 1923.

James R. Mitchell
State Museum

Poultry

At the beginning of the 21st century, West Virginia's poultry industry includes some of the best-known names in the business: Pilgrim's Pride, Perdue, and, until recently, British United Turkeys of America (BUTA). From the fully integrated operation of Pilgrim's Pride, which bought out WLR Foods in 2001, to the turkey breeder operation of the Aviagen division which bought out BUTA, poultry production brings in more than $250 million a year. Broiler sales account for about two-thirds of that.

Poultry accounts for more than half of all cash receipts in agriculture in the state. In addition, nearly 3,000 people are employed in the various plant operations. About 270 million chick eggs are produced in West Virginia each year, mostly

Poultry was once a farmyard enterprise.

for hatching. Annually the growers raise about 90 million broilers and more than four million turkeys; the hatcheries set millions of eggs a week. The center of the state's poultry industry is in the South Branch Valley and the five counties of the Eastern Panhandle, where most of the 350 producers of broilers and turkeys are located.

Records were first kept on chicken production in 1924, although poultry research began at West Virginia University in 1897. In 1919, a poultry extension program was started, and in 1934 the first West Virginia State Poultry Association meeting was held in Morgantown. That annual event moved to Moorefield in 1953 and has been there ever since.

In January 1938, records indicated there were four million chickens on farms in West Virginia. Turkeys numbered 274,000. There was no reference to broiler chickens at that time, but two years later four million broilers were produced. During World War II, broiler meat production was emphasized to supply food for the war effort.

Beginning in 1950, great changes took place in the poultry industry. Poultry farming changed from the keeping of a flock of chickens as part of a diversified farm operation to the specialized production of broilers under contract to a major meat processor. Disease and parasite controls, feed-conversion enhancements, accelerated growth, and bigger housing were among the changes. As compared to early tar paper sheds with dirt floors, today 25,000 broilers are housed in 40-by-500-foot houses where heat, water, and feed are controlled by computers. A three-and-a-half pound broiler is raised for slaughter in six weeks and about 325,000 are processed each day at the plant in Moorefield.

In the 1980s, the West Virginia poultry industry escaped potential disaster after Avian influenza was detected in Virginia and also in Pennsylvania. The state's borders were closed to outside birds, while farmers tightened security and sanitation measures. The preventive measures worked, and the virus was kept outside the state.

In 1985, a disastrous flood hit West Virginia. Poultry houses, along with many thousands of birds, were lost; the processing plants were flooded; and the South Branch Valley Railroad, which brought in grain and other products for feed, was devastated. Growers whose flocks were not flooded received air-lifted feed until roads could be opened. The plants were back in business within two weeks as mud was hosed out, the machinery fixed or replaced, and potable water was restored.

The last decade of the 20th century saw many changes in the poultry industry. Wampler-Longacre bought out Rockingham Poultry Marketing Cooperative and became WLR Foods, Inc. Hester Industries, a family-owned processing operation, was sold to ConAgra, one of the nation's largest diversified food industries. Perdue established breeder flocks in Hardy and Pendleton counties and then purchased Advantage Foods, a processing operation in Petersburg, which it later closed. Pilgrim's Pride bought out ConAgra early in the new century, and Perdue acquired WLR.

An ongoing challenge of the poultry industry in West Virginia is to meet the opposition from environmental groups, which claim poultry is responsible for putting unwanted nutrients in the watershed in the form of massive amounts of chicken manure. A cooperative effort by the industry, the state, and various agencies has established composting, litter controls, and sale of litter out of the area.

See also Agriculture

Phoebe Heishman
Moorefield

H. M. Hyre and B. W. Moore, *The West Virginia Poultry Association: 1934–1984*, 1985.

Poverty

West Virginia consistently ranks among the poorest states in the nation. The 2000 Census found almost 316,000 people, or 17.9 percent of West Virginians, living below the federal poverty threshold of $16,895 a year for a family of four with two children. The national poverty rate was 12.4 percent.

The poverty rate in West Virginia is higher among families with children, and varies widely in different regions of the state. In McDowell, the poorest county, 47.5 percent of families with children were poor in 2000, compared with 21.4 percent statewide and 10.5 percent in Putnam, the least-poor county. The per-

centage of people, particularly children, living in poverty increased throughout the 1980s and then declined during the 1990s. The number and percentage of people living in poverty started to increase again in 2001.

Poverty activists believe that the situation is worse than the official numbers suggest, arguing that official poverty thresholds do not actually include enough money for today's families to meet minimum expenses. The thresholds were designed in the 1960s and have been adjusted for inflation but not, critics say, for changing social circumstances. At that time, for example, most families expected to live on one income. Wives stayed home with the children. Today, both parents are expected to work, meaning families may have child-care costs, perhaps two cars, and other job-related expenses.

Advocates for the poor compiled a "Self-Sufficiency Standard for West Virginia," estimating that two parents and two children in McDowell County, for example, need $34,780 a year, nearly twice the federal poverty threshold, to meet minimum expenses. Roughly three-fourths of McDowell households fall below this standard.

Another useful meter of family well-being is the rate at which children qualify for free or reduced-cost school lunch. About half the state's public school children received free or reduced-cost lunch in spring 2002. A family of four with an income of no more than $33,485 a year would qualify for reduced-cost meals. Again, regions differ. In Brooke, Putnam, and Hancock counties, a third of students qualify, the lowest rates in the state. In McDowell County, more than 80 percent qualify. At some individual schools in the state, nearly every child qualifies. In 1954, 6.7 percent of the state's school children were "on relief," as a different program was then described. Nationally, only 2.8 percent were. The state's high rate was attributed to the deaths and unemployment of wage earners in the coalfields.

West Virginia's poverty rate has fallen in recent decades, from 22.2 percent in 1970 to 17.9 percent in 2000. Progress has been uneven, with the rate falling to 15 percent in 1980, then rising to 19.7 percent in 1990 before falling again. The gap between national and state rates has narrowed over the period, from 8.5 percent in 1970 to 5.5 percent in 2000. Again, the progress has been uneven, with the gap shrinking to 2.6 percent in 1980 and widening to 6.6 percent in 1990.

Some residents bristle at references to poverty. By other measures, West Virginians count themselves wealthy. The 2000 Census found that 554,000 West Virginia families, or 76 percent, owned their homes, up from 72 percent in 1990, among the very highest rates in the country. Modest dwellings and mobile homes account for many of these residences.

West Virginia is the only state wholly within Appalachia, as defined by the federal government. Poverty has been one of the region's enduring characteristics. Periodically, outsiders "discovered" the region and its problems. Some were inspired to help. In 1932, a group called Save the Children began sending food and other necessities to children of miners in Kentucky, and then West Virginia.

In 1933, federal programs encouraged by Eleanor Roosevelt built communities to resettle stranded industrial workers. The government bought land and built houses and entire villages at Arthurdale, in the Tygart Valley, and in Putnam County. The Works Progress Administration and other programs of Franklin Roosevelt's New Deal administration brought work relief to thousands throughout the state. Old methods of caring for the poor gave way under the onslaught of the Great Depression. Many thousands were impoverished at least temporarily, and the county poor farm system was replaced by modern social welfare agencies.

John F. Kennedy campaigned extensively in West Virginia during the 1960 presidential primary election, again drawing national press attention to the area. Some West Virginians still wince at the February 6, 1960, *Saturday Evening Post* story that highlighted examples of debilitating poverty within a few steps of ostentatious wealth. Throughout Kennedy's administration and President Lyndon Johnson's War on Poverty, federal money flowed into West Virginia for early childhood education, job training, literacy programs, roads, and direct relief for families. Some programs started at that time continued to operate 40 years later.

Historians point out that West Virginians have not been able to share sufficiently in the wealth that they helped to create. For generations, raw materials have been shipped out and expensive finished goods shipped in. The very shape of the land contributed to the state's economic and cultural conditions. The mountains peak within West Virginia, so major rivers flow away from the center to the borders and into other political and economic regions. As early communications and trade followed water routes, much of the population accumulated near the borders. This feature has given the state little unity. Regions differ down to the contour of the earth and soil types, so that even the industries they support are different. In the Eastern Panhandle and the Ohio River Valley, for example, a significant agricultural economy survived into the 21st century, which offers little similarity to the long industrialized economies of the Northern Panhandle or the southern coalfields.

Once established, poverty can be self-perpetuating. Habits of dependency develop. Impoverished children are less likely to be healthy and ready for school when they arrive, and more likely to struggle or fail. School frustration or failure may be used to predict teen pregnancy, criminal behavior, idleness, and ultimately being poor. Poverty stresses parents and couples, contributing to domestic violence, mental and physical health problems, and drug and alcohol abuse.

Dawn Miller
Charleston

Joe Powell

Labor leader Joseph William "Joe" Powell was born in Morgantown, February 19, 1924. As president of the West Virginia Labor Federation, AFL-CIO, he represented approximately 90,000 workers in nearly 400 union locals. Throughout his 23-year tenure, Powell lobbied for legislation on issues important to workers. He and other union leaders won incremental increases in compensation benefits for injured workers. At times, he struggled to defend established rights. He also suffered defeats, including a 1995 workers' compensation reform bill that cut benefits to injured workers and a failure to get collective bargaining rights for public employees.

Powell attended Harrison County public schools. In 1941, at age 18, he began work as a glass cutter for Rolland Glass Company in Clarksburg. A year later, after the United States had entered World War II, he enrolled in a specialized military training program at Virginia Polytechnic Institute and served in the U.S. Army Air Corps. After completing his military service, Powell returned to Rolland and joined the Glasscutters League of America, AFL-CIO. In 1964, he became state director of the American Federation of State, County & Municipal Employees, AFL-CIO. In 1973, he directed the West Virginia AFL-CIO Committee on Political Education.

A year later, after the sudden death of West Virginia Labor Federation President Miles Stanley, the union's executive board appointed Powell interim president, and he served the remaining three years of Stanley's term. He was elected president in 1977, and held that post until he retired in 1997.

See also West Virginia State Federation of Labor

Harry Powers

In August 1931, Harry F. Powers, the "Bluebeard of Quiet Dell," was charged with killing Dorothy Lemke of Massachusetts and Asta Eicher and her three children of Illinois. The bodies were found at Powers's home in Quiet Dell, near Clarksburg. Personal effects of the victims were also found on the premises.

Powers had obtained information about these two wealthy widows from the American Friendship Society of Detroit, a match-making organization that specialized in introducing prosperous singles. Powers (using the alias Cornelius O. Pierson and describing himself as a civil engineer) had promised to marry each of the women, thus luring them to their destruction. He had been previously arrested on lesser charges as John Schroeder and as Herman Drenth, perhaps his real name.

Standing five feet four inches, weighing 175 pounds, and wearing thick glasses, Powers ran a small grocery store in Clarksburg's Broad Oaks neighborhood. The sensational story attracted so much attention that Powers's trial was held at the Moore Opera House in Clarksburg to accommodate the crowd of spectators. Powers was tried and convicted of Lemke's murder and sentenced to death by hanging. His wife, Luella, denied all knowledge of her husband's criminal activities and was never charged with any crime.

Powers was executed at the state penitentiary in Moundsville on March 18, 1932. The gruesome story inspired *Night of the Hunter*, a novel by West Virginia native Davis Grubb which was later made into a critically acclaimed motion picture.

See also Night of the Hunter

Christine M. Kreiser
Clarksburg

Stan Bumgardner and Christine Kreiser, "'Thy Brother's Blood': Capital Punishment in West Virginia," *West Virginia Historical Society Quarterly,* March 1996.

Prato Rio

Thanks to its most famous owner, the irascible Gen. Charles Lee, Prato Rio is one of West Virginia's most eccentric houses. Lee bought the original log house, now a portion of the rear wing of Prato Rio, in 1775 from pioneer settler Jacob Hite, and gave it a Spanish name that translates "stream through the meadow." Lee built a limestone addition, and gave it a unique arrangement. Instead of constructing partitions, he drew chalk lines on the floor to indicate various rooms. According to a visitor, the chimney "served in some degree to separate the cooking department from . . . bedroom, parlor, library, dog-kennel and all."

Lee, who was inordinately fond of his three hounds, named them Father, Son, and Holy Ghost, and avowed that "their breath was as sweet as man's." After his dismissal from the army, Lee lived the life of a hermit at Prato Rio. Upon learning that George Washington, hoping for a reconciliation, intended a visit, he pinned a note to the door: "No dinner cooked here to-day."

Later owners have made additions and alterations (including partitions), but the house and its setting remain much as they were in Lee's time. Prato Rio, on the western side of Jefferson County Route 1 in Leetown, is privately owned. The house was added to the National Register of Historic Places in 1973.

See also Charles Lee

S. Allen Chambers
Society of Architectural Historians

Prehistoric People

Our knowledge of prehistoric people is based on artifacts that have survived. Because of the loss of less durable artifacts to the deterioration caused by time and environment, our knowledge of the earliest people is based on stone tools, their distribution across the landscape, and comparisons with other areas in the United States. Late prehistoric and protohistoric populations are better understood because of the survival of a wider range of artifacts and the excavation of burial sites and living sites.

The first people in West Virginia were Paleo-Indians (10,500–9000 B.C.). They were big game hunters whose ancestors were Asian. The climate at this time was much colder, and species such as mastodon, mammoth, musk ox, and caribou were hunted. Settlements were widely scattered and temporary. The characteristic artifacts of this period are fluted projectile points, including those known as Clovis and Cumberland. Many were made of high-quality flints from Ohio and Pennsylvania. Eighty-one fluted points have been reported from West Virginia. Several were found at Blennerhassett Island and sites along the Ohio and Kanawha rivers.

The Terminal Paleo-Indian period (9000–8000 B.C.) is marked by the appearance of a variety of corner and side-notched projectile points such as Thebes and Dovetails. These points have heavy basal grinding and flaking patterns characteristic of Clovis, but differ in that the blades are broader and the bases are notched rather than fluted.

At the beginning of the Early Archaic period (8000–6000 B.C.) there was a shift toward a more temperate climate which aided in the extinction of mammoth and mastodon. There was also a shift from big game hunting to more varied or broad-spectrum hunting and gathering, which included the hunting of deer and small mammals as well as collecting nuts, berries, seeds, and other plant foods. From the Early Archaic to the Protohistoric, deer provided from 70 percent to 90 percent of the meat in the diet of West Virginia Indians. A significant site for Early Archaic is the St. Albans Site on the Kanawha River.

The Middle Archaic period (6000–3000 B.C.) is characterized by a continuation of the broad-spectrum hunting and gathering. Ground stone tools are now included in the artifact inventory. Artifacts made by pecking, grinding and polishing include adzes, axes, and bannerstones which were used as balance weights on spear throwers. Mortars and pestles and nutting stones indicate increased use of plant foods. Greater regionalization is noted in new projectile point styles. Archaic projectile points were used with the atlatl (spear thrower). The Glasgow Site on the Kanawha River is a stratified site that spans this period.

The Late Archaic period (3000–1000 B.C.) was a time of population increase with more complex social organization. Several wild plants were cultivated and some, including squash and lambs-quarters, were eventually domesticated. Several distinct cultural groups appear. In northern West Virginia the Globe Hill Shell Heap and East Steubenville represent the Panhandle Archaic. These are the earliest sites with evidence of bone tool technology and human burials. In southern West Virginia the Buffalo Archaic is found along the Kanawha River floodplain. In the northern Ohio Valley, upper Kanawha Valley, and the eastern mountains, transitional Broad Spear points are occasionally found which originate in the Atlantic coastal zones and the Carolina Piedmont. These point types, associated steatite and sandstone vessels and cultivated sunflower represent a Transitional Archaic period dating from 2000 to 1000 B.C. Similar associations are found at Hansford on the Kanawha River.

Intensive use of the Mid-Ohio Valley began during the Late Archaic Period about 5,000 years ago. A pollen profile from Mason County indicates local vegetation disturbances were caused by fire and led to an increase of weedy seed plants, many of which were subsequently domesticated. Historic references indicate that Indians across North America used controlled burning as a land management technique, and these practices were used in West Virginia during the Late Archaic.

The Early Woodland period (1000–200 B.C.) includes two major developments, the manufacture of pottery and the construction of burial mounds. While pottery appears to the north and south about 1000 B.C. the earliest pottery in West Virginia appears between 400 and 500 B.C. Most Adena burial mounds date between 400 and 200 B.C. Hundreds of mounds were constructed along the Ohio and Kanawha rivers. The largest Adena Burial Mound is the Grave Creek Mound in Moundsville. Other large mounds that have been preserved include Criel in South Charleston, May Moore, and Camden Park. During this period local Indians continued to experiment with plant domestication and additional plants such as sunflower, lambs-quarters, smartweed, and maygrass were domesticated. Woodland horticulture is also documented in the analysis of charcoal from Woodland pits, which have an increase in pine and other woods that are associated with land clearing.

The Middle Woodland Period (200 B.C.–A.D. 400) is poorly documented in West Virginia. In Central Ohio, the Hopewell flourished and built numerous large earthworks. In West Virginia, Middle Woodland phases included Armstrong in the south and Fairchance and Watson Farm in the north. Indians continued living in scattered hamlets and mound building was not as prominent, although Fairchance had a large burial mound associated with its settlement. Occasionally mica or prismatic bladelets made of Ohio Flint Ridge flint are found on these sites but no major Hopewell earthworks are documented in West Virginia.

The Late Woodland Period (A.D. 400–1200) was a period of transition characterized by population migrations and diffusion of major technological and social innovations. There was increasing dependence on domesticated plants, coupled with hunting and gathering. Most Late Woodland Indians continued to live in small hamlets and single-family farmsteads. One exception is the Childers Site, which is an intensively occupied Woodland village dating to A.D. 650. About A.D. 700 the bow and arrow was introduced into West Virginia and is identified by the presence of Jack's Reef and Levanna Triangular projectile points at Parkline Phase sites in Putnam County. Shortly thereafter corn is introduced at Woods Phase sites (A.D. 700 to 1200) in Mason County. During most of the period local populations continued living on farmsteads and in small hamlets.

The Late Prehistoric Period (A.D. 1200–1550) is marked by the advent of intensive corn cultivation and a more sedentary village life. Diagnostic artifacts include shell-tempered pottery, triangular arrow points, ceramic pipes, shell hoes, shell beads, bone beads, and bone fishhooks. Late Prehistoric villages were generally circular and ranged from two to five acres in size. There were three Late Prehistoric populations in West Virginia. The Monongahela were located in the northern and eastern panhandles. Villages making Page Cordmarked pottery were located at Tygart Lake and Seneca Rocks, with scattered temporary settlements in the eastern mountains. Fort Ancient villages were located in the southern half of the state along the Ohio, Kanawha, New, Bluestone, and Guyandotte rivers.

During the Protohistoric period (A.D. 1550–1690) Indian villages had access to European trade goods but no direct contact with Europeans. Buffalo, Clover, and Rolfe make up the Clover Complex. Buffalo and Clover are early protohistoric sites while Rolfe Lee, with the highest percentage of late trade goods, is the latest protohistoric site in West Virginia, dating to A.D. 1640. The Orchard Site appears to be an early protohistoric site related to the Madisonville Phase in the Cincinnati area. Other less well defined sites in southern West Virginia include Marmet and Logan, which have been largely destroyed by the expansion of those towns, and Snidow on the Bluestone River. A diagnostic artifact found on these sites is the shell gorget, which originates from village sites in middle Tennessee and indicates close political relationships between the two areas.

The question of who were the descendants of these protohistoric villagers still remains to be answered. These villages were abandoned by the mid-1600s because of Iroquois incursions. By the time white settlers entered the area in the 1700s, all of the villages were abandoned and West Virginia was used as a hunting ground by the Shawnee, Cherokee, and Iroquois tribes. While it has been suggested that Fort Ancient and the subsequent protohistoric villages may have been ancestral to the Shawnee, the burial practices at Buffalo and other protohistoric sites suggest that these villages were eastern Siouan, and may have been linguistically and culturally related to Siouan villages in Virginia and the Carolinas.

See also Archeology, Indians

Robert F. Maslowski
Milton

McMichael, Edward V. McMichael, *Introduction to West Virginia Archeology*, 1968; Robert F. Maslowski, "Protohistoric Villages in Southern West Virginia," *Upland Archeology in the East, Symposium* 2, 1984; William J. Mayer-Oakes, "Prehistory of the Upper Ohio Valley," *Annals of Carnegie Museum*, 1955.

Presbyterians

Presbyterian Scotch-Irish immigrants made up a large portion of the earliest settlers of European stock in what is now West Virginia, arriving in the back country in the early 18th century. They entered through the present Eastern Panhandle; through the northwest, by coming down the Ohio from Pittsburgh; and through the southeast, from the Valley of Virginia into Tygart Valley and portions of Monroe, Greenbrier, Kanawha, and Pocahontas counties.

Dispatched by the Synod of Philadelphia in 1720, Daniel McGill organized Presbyterians into a "church order" at "Potomoke," south of the Potomac River, perhaps at or near Shepherdstown. Other early Presbyterian churches were at Bullskin, Jefferson County, 1736; Tuscarora, Berkeley County, 1740; Back Creek, Hedgesville, 1741; Moorefield, 1741; and Falling Waters, Berkeley County, 1745. Other pre-Revolutionary churches were planted in Hampshire, Mineral, Jefferson, and Hardy counties, 1761–73. In the Revolutionary Era, churches took root in Huttonsville, Pickaway, Romney, Gerrardstown, Lewisburg, Union, Renick, Wheeling, Charles Town, Morgantown, West Liberty, Weirton Heights, Pughtown, Hillsboro, and Follansbee, 1781–98.

In 1789, the initial meeting of the Presbyterian General Assembly adopted a strategic policy to send missionaries to the American frontier settlements in order to form new congregations. It was the first denomination to regularly send missionaries to the West, according to church historian Ernest Trice Thompson. Many missionaries were unmarried young graduates of Hampden-Sydney College or Liberty Hall Academy, the precursor of Washington and Lee University.

John McCue was among the Presbyterian missionaries who followed the early settlers into the region west of the Alleghenies. McCue planted churches in Lewisburg, Union, and Spring Creek (Renick) in 1783, the historic "three cornerstones" which were indispensable to the future development of Presbyterianism westward to the Ohio River.

In 1808, the Committee on Missions of the Synod of Virginia sent John McElhenney as a Presbyterian evangelist in Greenbrier and Monroe counties. He was installed as pastor of churches in Lewisburg and Union the following summer. McElhenney served as pastor of the Union Presbyterian Church until 1834. He served the Old Stone Presbyterian Church of Lewisburg until his death in 1871. Soon after their arrival, John and Rebecca McElhenney founded the Lewisburg Academy, where John was principal and instructor for two decades. McElhenney and those trained by him organized congregations in the Greenbrier Valley, in Charleston, and in the Ohio Valley at Point Pleasant and Parkersburg.

Among the graduates of Lewisburg Academy and Washington College (now Washington and Lee) was Henry Ruffner, the son of Col. David Ruffner, a founder of the salt industry in the Kanawha Valley. Henry Ruffner became the first principal of Charleston's Mercer Academy. In 1819, he founded the Kanawha Church of Charleston and the Kanawha Salines Church at present Malden. Ruffner was appointed professor at Washington College in 1819 and served as president from 1836 to 1848. In 1841, he gathered with other western Virginians at a convention in Clarksburg and called for a system of free public schools. Ruffner's vision was carried forward in the next generation by his son, William Henry Ruffner, and significantly influenced the public education movements in Virginia and West Virginia.

Henry Ruffner was an opponent of slavery, an institution that helped split the Presbyterian denomination into northern and southern factions as the Civil War commenced. By the time of the creation of West Virginia in 1863, several Presbyterian congregations were divided. Some favored membership in the Northern Presbyterian denomination; others favored alignment with the Southern General Assembly. Charleston's Presbyterian congregation remained neutral during the war, but in 1872 split into the First Presbyterian Church (Southern) and the Kanawha Presbyterian Church (Northern).

With the birth of the First Presbyterian Church of Williamson in 1894, the denomination began a concerted movement into the developing coalfields south of Charleston. Southern West Virginia coal camps presented a fertile and challenging home mission. While many new ministers were called to the coalfields, city and town ministers also left their local parishes after Sunday morning services to teach and preach in coal communities along the railroads in the afternoon and the evening.

After World War II, the Presbyterian Church in West Virginia experienced dynamic growth, especially in Kanawha Presbytery under the leadership of Frank McCutchan Ryburn, who served as Evangelist and Superintendent of Home Missions, 1948–64. By 1950, Charleston and surrounding communities held one of the largest concentrations of Presbyterians, in proportion to population, in the country.

Despite losses in membership in West Virginia in recent decades, Presbyterians and their institutions have contributed greatly to the state's moral and social fabric. Many Presbyterians have served West Virginia as governor and in the U.S. Senate and House of Representatives. During and beyond the Civil Rights era of the 1950s and 1960s prophetic Presbyterians with West Virginia ties, such as Angie King, Robert B. McNeill, Dunbar H. Ogden, and William A. Benfield Jr., were courageous voices for racial justice and harmony.

Women have had a major impact on West Virginia Presbyterianism through historic societies, auxiliaries, and organizations which have stressed Bible study, prayer, global mission, hunger relief, peacemaking, and advocacy for justice and mercy. Since the reunion of the major northern and southern streams of American Presbyterianism in 1983, as the Presbyterian Church (U.S.A.), West Virginia women have occupied significant leadership positions. From 1985 to 1998, Dorothy I. MacConkey was president of Davis & Elkins College, a Presbyterian-related institution founded in 1904. Patricia L. Kennedy of the Montgomery Presbyterian Church served as chair of the General Assembly Council, Presbyterian Church (U.S.A.), 1990–91. Elder Gay Mothershed currently serves as Executive Presbyter of the Presbytery of West Virginia.

There are a total of 23,650 members of 202 Presbyterian U.S.A. churches in West Virginia, according to a 2000 church survey.

See also Religion, Henry Ruffner

Dean K. Thompson
Louisville Seminary

Dorsey D. Ellis, *Look Unto The Rock*, 1982; Ernest Trice Thompson, *Presbyterians In The South*, 3 volumes, 1963–73; *History of the Presbytery of Kanawha, 1895–1956*, 1956.

Preston County

The Virginia General Assembly established Preston County on January 19, 1818, taking the land from Monongalia County. The new county was named for James Patton Preston, then governor of Virginia. Already, the Indians had retreated, forts Morris and Butler were no longer in use, the American Revolution and the War of 1812 were past, and the settlers could devote themselves to improving the quality of their lives.

Preston County lies mainly within the Appalachian Plateau, with elevations varying from 873 feet to 3,216 feet. The Cheat River divides the county into two sections, the eastern being a little larger. Preston County borders Pennsylvania in the north and Maryland in the east, and the West Virginia counties of Monongalia, Taylor, Barbour, and Tucker in the west and south. The Mason-Dixon Line is its northern boundary. The county consists of 653.9 square miles in eight magisterial districts: Grant, Kingwood, Lyon, Pleasant, Portland, Reno, Union, and Valley. The population in 1818 was about 3,000, and in the year 2000 it was 29,334.

Kingwood, named for the majestic trees growing in the area at the time, is the county seat of Preston County. A stone courthouse replaced the log buildings previously used. One of the court-

Country roads serve most of Preston County.

houses that replaced the 1820s building was burned by an arsonist in 1869, destroying most of the county records for the years 1818–69.

In early days, the northern part of the county was served by the National Road (present U.S. 40), which ran through Pennsylvania just above Preston's border, linking the area to Cumberland, Baltimore, and Wheeling. Indian trails and packhorse routes were supplemented with the building of the Northwestern Turnpike (present U.S. 50 in southern Preston County), to connect Winchester and the Ohio River. Over these roads teamsters carried away agricultural products and brought back commercial goods.

In the 1850s, the coming of the Baltimore & Ohio Railroad provided the means to ship timber products, such as staves, and coal from Preston's vast resources. New towns grew up along the east-west railroad. The industrial age brought danger as well as prosperity. At Newburg, a thriving coal and railroad town, the explosion at Orrel Coal Company's shaft in January 1886 killed 39 men.

The earliest school was at German Settlement (now Aurora). Subscription schools preceded public or "free" schools. The first two academies for higher education were at Brandonville and Kingwood. In 1850, the two academies had three teachers and 70 pupils. The curriculum seems to have varied, possibly according to the specialities of available teachers. Terms were for about five months each. Courses included languages, surveying and the sciences, grammar, geography, and arithmetic with varying rates of tuition. Later, each magisterial district had a high school, except Pleasant District; Portland had two. By 2000, some of these high schools had been torn down, and those that survive are now middle schools. One new high school was built for all county students, Preston High at Kingwood.

Following the presidential election of 1860, there was great agitation as Virginia considered whether to join the South in seceding from the Union. Preston citizens gathered at Kingwood and agreed to stand by the Union. Their representatives to the secession convention in Richmond were William G. Brown and James McGrew. Both remained strong for the Union before and after the vote in which the Virginia majority decided to secede. Brown and McGrew escaped Richmond with their lives, returning to Preston to rally the people against secession. They and others were among those who organized the Union sympathizers into a new state. Many Preston men gave their lives in the Civil War, mostly on the side of the Union. Preston Countians in large numbers have answered the calls for service in World Wars I and II, the

FAST FACTS ABOUT PRESTON COUNTY

Founded: 1818

Land in square miles: 653.9

Population: 29,334

Percentage minorities: 1.2%

Percentage rural: 87.9%

Median age: 39.1

Percentage 65 and older: 15.0%

Birth rate per 1,000 population: 9.5

Median household income: $27,927

High school graduate or higher: 74.0%

Bachelor's degree or higher: 10.8%

Home ownership: 83.0%

Median home value: $63,100

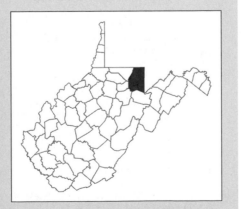

This information is from the 2000 U.S. Census. In 2000, West Virginia as a whole had 5 percent minorities, a median age of 38.9, median household income of $29,696, and a 75.2 percent home ownership rate.

Korean War, Vietnam, Desert Storm, Iraq and other duty posts.

The county has progressed in many areas. A hundred years after the coming of the railroad, construction of Interstate 68, crossing the northern part of the county, eased travel between Monongalia County and Maryland. Construction of roads and bridges has been expensive and challenging due to the rugged terrain. While agriculture, coal, and timber are still important parts of the economy, so are education, health care, technology, tourism, and historic preservation. The Communications Satellite Corporation's earth tracking station at Etam provides a link in a communications system of international importance.

Preston County is known throughout West Virginia for its robust winters. Sometimes cold weather strays into the other seasons as well. The great frost of June 4, 1859, killed crops in the fields. They were replanted with hardy buckwheat, which was successful. For decades buckwheat was a staple crop, and buckwheat pancakes have remained a Preston county favorite since that time. Thousands gather for several days every September in Kingwood to celebrate buckwheat with coronations, parades, and other events while they consume prodigious quantities of pancakes, local sausage, and maple syrup. This is also the occasion for some of the largest of many annual family reunions which bring people back to their Preston County homes.

See also Kingwood

Janice Cale Sisler
Bruceton Mills

S. T. Wiley, *History of Preston County, West Virginia*, 1882; Preston County Historical Society, *Preston County, West Virginia, History*, 1979; Terri L. Funk, Assessor of Preston County, "General Information," pamphlet, 2001.

Preston County Buckwheat Festival

Begun as a homecoming in 1938, Preston County's annual Buckwheat Festival occurs the last weekend of September in Kingwood. It is one of West Virginia's oldest local festivals. Held every year except for four years during World War II, the festival has flourished. Named for the crop which was once among the county's most important, the Buckwheat Festival brings in thousands of people for the four-day event. Historic Hazelton Mill operates only around festival time to grind and bag the flour, which is sold in the region year-round with that from other mills. The buckwheat itself, a hardy cereal once grown on local mountain farms, now comes from elsewhere.

Fair-like with its farm animals, food, blue-ribbon competitions, and carnival atmosphere, the Preston County Buckwheat Festival features three days of parades, the last having as many as 400 units. The crowning of Queen Ceres and

King Buckwheat highlights the festival, which is commemorated by an annual first-day postage cancellation. The festival is sponsored by Kingwood's Volunteer Fire Department, and every Preston County community is represented by participating volunteers. Hundreds of people staff the community building's kitchen to serve six tons of sausage made from locally raised and locally butchered pork in 20,000 plus buckwheat-cake meals.

Peggy Ross
Reedsville

Cal Price

Country editor Cal Price (1880–1957) enjoys a smoke.

Newspaperman Calvin Wells "Cal" Price, born November 22, 1880, was the longtime owner and editor of the *Pocahontas Times* in Marlinton. He was widely known as a journalist and for his civic involvement and conservation endeavors. Calvin W. Price State Forest was dedicated in his honor in 1954.

Price is best remembered as a country editor. He wrote in his newspaper often and knowledgeably about conservation, his reputation as a naturalist arising from his famous "Field Notes" column and his panther and bear stories. His father, William T. Price, had bought the *Times* in 1892 with sons James and Andrew. At age 16, youngest son Calvin began working with his brothers, and he became the sole owner in 1906. He was the publisher and editor for 51 years.

William T. Price was a Marlinton native

and the son of James A. Price, who came to Pocahontas County about 1828. The family has remained prominent in the county. After Calvin Price's death in 1957, daughter Jane Price Sharp edited the *Pocahontas Times* until 1981. She continued to work at the paper with her nephew William Price McNeel, Price's grandson and editor through 2005.

In 1939, Calvin Price was selected by the president of the National Editorial Association to appear on "We The People," a New York radio show. He received an honorary law degree from West Virginia University in 1942. Other honors included being president of the West Virginia Newspaper Association and membership in the West Virginia Journalism Hall of Fame. Price died in Marlinton, June 14, 1957.

See also Calvin W. Price State Forest, Pocahontas Times

Louise Burner Flegel
Pine Knoll Shore, North Carolina
Pocahontas County Historical Society, *History of Pocahontas County, West Virginia*, 1981.

Samuel Price

Senator Samuel Price, judge, legislator, and lieutenant governor of Confederate Virginia, was born in Fauquier County, Virginia, July 28, 1805. When he was about ten years old, his family moved to Preston County. They later moved to Kentucky, where Price studied law. Moving back to Western Virginia, he settled in Nicholas County and was admitted to the bar in 1828. By 1830, he served as a census taker and as commonwealth's attorney. He was clerk of the county court for Nicholas County from 1831 to 1834.

Price was elected to the House of Delegates in 1834 from Fayette and Nicholas counties and later reelected to a second term. He moved to Wheeling in 1836. That same year Price became prosecuting attorney for Braxton County, serving from 1836 to 1850. In 1837, he married Jane Stuart. They spent 39 years together and raised nine children.

In 1838, Price moved to Lewisburg. In 1847, he was again elected to the Virginia legislature, as a Whig from Greenbrier County. He was outspoken in favor of internal improvements, especially a rail link from the east to the Ohio River. The voters returned him to the House of Delegates again in 1848 and 1849. As a delegate to the Virginia Constitutional Convention of 1850–51, Price was one of four delegates who represented the district of Greenbrier, Pocahontas, Fayette, Raleigh, Nicholas, and Kanawha counties. When he returned to Greenbrier County, his constituents voted to send him back to the House of Delegates under the new constitution. The session began on January 12, 1852, and he resigned on April 27 and returned to his law practice.

Price next returned to Richmond as a

member of the Secession Convention of 1861. He sought reconciliation and voted against secession; however, he subsequently signed the Ordinance of Secession. In 1862, he was arrested by Col. (later Maj. Gen.) George Crook for refusing to take the oath of allegiance to the United States. While on parole, awaiting proper exchange, Price was rescued by Confederate forces. The next year, 1863, he was elected lieutenant governor of Confederate Virginia, which also made him president of the state senate. He served until forced to vacate the office by Union victory in May 1865.

Returning to Lewisburg, Price was appointed circuit judge later in 1865, but he declined the appointment because he would not take the "test oath" affirming loyalty to the United States. In 1866, he became a director of the Chesapeake & Ohio Railroad. In 1872, the voters of Greenbrier County elected him as their representative to the West Virginia constitutional convention. He was elected president of the convention that drafted a new constitution for West Virginia, restoring the rights of former Confederates and enabling pro-Southern forces to take control of the state.

Unsuccessful as a candidate for U.S. Senate in 1876, Price was appointed to fill the vacancy caused by the death of Sen. Allen T. Caperton, serving from August until the following January. In addition to his legal and political careers, Price was a faithful lifelong member of the Presbyterian Church. He served his church as Ruling Elder for more than a quarter of a century. He died at his home in Lewisburg, February 25, 1884, and is buried at nearby Stuart Manor.

Michael M. Meador
Abingdon, Virginia

Pricketts Fort

Pricketts Fort was built at the confluence of Pricketts Creek and the Monongahela River in 1774 by Capt. Jacob Prickett. It was not a military fort, but a civilian refuge fort designed to shelter local settlers from Indian attack. When the threat of Indian uprisings occurred, up to 80 families from the surrounding countryside would hurry to the fort. They would stay as long as the threat existed, from days to weeks. Life in the cramped quarters rapidly became unpleasant, and "forting up" was long remembered by those who endured it.

In 1974, a replica frontier fort was built as near as could be determined to the original site of Pricketts Fort. The fort officially opened as Pricketts Fort State Park during the 1976 Bicentennial. The rebuilt fort covers a 110-by-110-foot square, with 12-foot-high log walls and blockhouses at each corner. Lining the stockade walls are tiny sleeping cabins, with earthen floors. A meetinghouse and a storehouse occupy the common.

The Job Prickett house, a 19th-century brick residence, is located near the fort, as is the Prickett family cemetery. The historic graveyard is the burial place of fort builder Jacob Prickett and of Col. Zackquill Morgan, the founder of Morgantown. The fort site and its environs, listed on the National Register of Historic Places in 1972, are open for public tours from mid-April through October. Visitors enjoy seeing costumed artisans at work. These historical interpreters also serve as guides for tours, telling visitors about daily life on the frontier of Western Virginia. A visitor center includes a museum shop and an orientation exhibit.

The Pricketts Fort Memorial Foundation, under long-term contract with the State of West Virginia, manages the visitor center, the historical interpretation program, and special events.

See also Forting, Frontier Defense
Melissa May Dobbins
Pricketts Fort State Park

The Pride of West Virginia

The West Virginia University band program was founded in 1901 by Walter Mestrezat. It has grown into a diverse organization that includes a wind symphony, wind ensemble, concert band, varsity band (a pep band), and other ensembles.

The largest and most visible of the WVU bands is the Mountaineer Marching Band, the "Pride of West Virginia." Announcer Jack Fleming called it that during the 1972 Peach Bowl broadcast, and the name stuck. Don Wilcox had just been named director of bands, and he guided them to national prominence. In 1997, the Pride of West Virginia received the Sudler Trophy as the nation's No. 1 college marching band. At the end of that season, Wilcox turned the directorship of the marching band over to his assistant, John Hendricks.

The Pride has had ten directors. Mestrezat served 37 years and Wilcox 27. Both were known for their innovations. The Pride has grown from an all-male contingent of six members to an inclusive group of 330 members. The marching band became coed about the time Don Wilcox took charge, and during his tenure once included a blind member, Clara Pingley. The WVU bands perform about 50 times a year.

See also West Virginia University
Norman Julian
Dominion Post

Primitive Baptists

Beginning in the 1820s, Baptist churches in Appalachia and elsewhere split into those favoring and those opposing missionary work. Staunchly Calvinistic Baptists resisted the intense missionary efforts then under way in both foreign and domestic fields. They believed in predestination, that before the beginning of time God had chosen or "elected" those individuals who would receive salvation. The church's role was to identify and gather together these chosen ones, or the saints as they were known. Thus, it was not only impossible to save or convert sinners through evangelical or missionary work but also actually contrary to God's plan. Known initially as "Anti-Missionary Baptists," these churches slowly became identified as "Old School Baptists" or "Primitive Baptists," because they claimed to be modeled after the "primitive church" as established by St. Paul.

Today four Primitive Baptist divisions exist in West Virginia, differing according to their understanding of predestination and certain other matters. These are the Single and Double Predestination Primitives, the Progressive Primitives, and the Primitive Baptist Universalists.

Organized into five small associations of individual congregations, Primitive Baptist Universalists are found in only a handful of regions of northeast Tennessee, southwest Virginia, eastern Kentucky, and in McDowell and Greenbrier counties, West Virginia. There are also out-migrant fellowships in Ohio and Pennsylvania. Advocating a theology that pronounces a universal heaven for all after Resurrection, Primitive Baptist Universalists believe in hell only as a factor of the present world, a kind of emotional and psychological destitution generated by separation from God as a punishment for worldly sins. Known in the mountains of Central Appalachia by the pejorative misnomer, "No-Hellers," these unusual Primitives are Calvinistic at both ends of their theological perspective. They believe not only in the traditional concept of universal Adamic sin but also in the universality of Christ's atonement for that sin, meaning that at Resurrection the slate is wiped clean for all humankind so that the total human family is returned to communion with God in a kind of eternal Eden. Thus, redemption is every bit as inescapable as was original sin. The key scriptural passage for this movement is in I Cor. 15:22 "For as in Adam all die, even so in Christ all shall be made alive."

Because Primitives generally do not cooperate with state or national canvasses of denominational affiliations, it is almost impossible to report their numbers; nevertheless, the 2000 *Religious Congregations & Membership in the United States*, published by the Glenmary Research Center of Nashville, found 36 Primitive Baptist churches distributed over 15 counties of West Virginia.

Howard Dorgan
Appalachian State University

Princeton

The county seat of Mercer County was named for the Battle of Princeton, New Jersey, where the county's namesake,

Revolutionary Gen. Hugh Mercer, died. When the county was formed in 1837, William Smith donated 1.5 acres of land for a courthouse. The post office was opened in 1838. By 1860, Princeton had grown to about 40 houses and two hotels. During the Civil War, the town was briefly occupied by the Confederates under Col. Walter Jenifer. When Jenifer was forced to evacuate the town, he ordered it burned. Only a few structures escaped destruction.

Fortunately, county records had been removed to Concord Church, now Athens, and were later returned to Princeton. There were unsuccessful attempts to move the county seat to Concord Church or to Bluefield. Following the Civil War, Princeton grew, a bank was established there, and the town became a trading center. In 1905, the Virginian Railroad developed a shop and yards in Princeton. This contributed to the growth of the town, which was chartered as a city in 1909.

Two major highways, Interstate 77 and U.S. 460 intersect outside Princeton, and have contributed to its recent growth with the construction of motels and restaurants. Princeton is the southern terminus of the West Virginia Turnpike, which coincides with I-77 from there to Charleston. Several industries have also located in the city. Princeton had a small airport, which was used for flight training during World War II. The former airport is now the location of the city hall, a softball field, and Princeton Community Hospital. Recreational facilities include a minor league baseball team, as well as a city park. Princeton had a 2000 population of 6,347.

See also Mercer County

Raymond Thomas Hill
Athens

Mercer County Historical Society, *Mercer County History*, 1985.

Pringle Tree

From about 1764 to 1767, the brothers John and Samuel Pringle lived in the hollow cavity of a big sycamore tree near the confluence of Turkey Run and the Buckhannon River in present Upshur County. The hollow was supposed to have been so big that an eight-foot fence rail could be turned inside the tree. This was during the French and Indian War, and the Pringles had deserted from the British-American army at Fort Pitt. They found the wilderness of the Buckhannon Valley a perfect hide-out. Upon John Pringle's 1768 return from the trading post on the South Branch, where he had gone to buy ammunition, the brothers decided that they were no longer considered renegades and left their tree home. By 1769, they had led a small group of settlers back to the Buckhannon Valley to begin a permanent settlement there.

A highway historic marker on U.S. 119 north of Buckhannon marks the location of the Pringle Tree. The current sycamore is supposedly the third generation of the famous Pringle Tree, said to have grown from the roots of the original. Sycamores are the largest trees native to West Virginia, capable of growing to 100 feet or more. It was not uncommon for hunters and others to find temporary shelter in hollow sycamores, but the Pringles are the only ones known to have set up extended housekeeping.

Noel W. Tenney
Tallmansville

W. B. Cutright *The History of Upshur County, West Virginia*, 1907.

Charlotte Pritt

Gubernatorial candidate Charlotte Pritt (1949–).

Charlotte Jean Pritt, the first woman to seek to become governor of West Virginia as the candidate of a major political party, was born January 2, 1949, at Charleston's St. Francis Hospital. She was raised at Buzzard Rock, near Sissonville on the outskirts of the capital city. She graduated from Sissonville High School and received a B.A. and M.A. from Marshall University. She was a teacher in her early years.

In the 1980s, the Kanawha County Democrat was elected to the West Virginia House of Delegates, serving from 1985 to 1988. In 1988, she campaigned for state Senate and won. She remained in the Senate from 1989 to 1992.

Pritt left the Senate in 1992, saying she had been drafted to run for governor. She was defeated in the Democratic primary after a bitterly fought battle with Gaston Caperton, the incumbent governor. She went on to oppose Caperton as an independent candidate in the general election in November. Scars of that campaign were to follow her four years later, when she again sought the governor's seat.

This time she overwhelmed her primary opposition and faced Republican Cecil Underwood in the November 1996 general election.

She lost to Underwood by a vote of 324,518 to 287,870. She suffered from a divided party. Some Democrats, still remembering her independent race against the party incumbent in 1992, bolted to Underwood, who also benefited by the support of the coal industry and others alarmed by Pritt's liberal, pro-labor politics.

In 2000, Pritt ran for secretary of state, losing by a substantial margin in the Democratic primary to Joe Manchin, whom she had defeated in the 1996 gubernatorial primary. Pritt resumed her academic pursuits after the 2000 campaign, teaching seminars and pursuing a degree in nutrition.

Kay Michael
Charleston

Proclamation of 1763

Settlement west of the Allegheny Mountains was sparse in the mid-1700s due to the threat of attacks by Indians and disputes between the English and French over control of the region. The British secured their rights to the area by their victory in the French and Indian War. As settlers prepared to pour into the region following the end of the war in 1763, the English government feared additional conflicts with Indians, which could have disrupted their profitable fur trade in the Ohio Valley. On October 7, a proclamation by King George III prohibited all settlement west of the Alleghenies. The Proclamation Line ran along the divide between the eastern rivers and the Ohio watershed, leaving only the Eastern Panhandle of modern West Virginia open to settlement, plus a fraction of Monroe County.

Settlers, for the most part, abided by the proclamation, although speculators, such as George Washington, took advantage of the situation by claiming large tracts of land for themselves. The two British agents assigned to enforce the proclamation, Sir William Johnson and Col. John Stuart, negotiated two treaties in 1768 that reopened the region to settlement. The Treaty of Hard Labor with the Cherokee and the Treaty of Fort Stanwix with the Iroquois cleared the way for settlement in all but the extreme southern part of present West Virginia. As a result, in spring 1769, numerous communities sprang into existence virtually overnight.

See also French and Indian War, Fort Stanwix Treaties, Treaty of Hard Labor

Stan Bumgardner
Division of Culture and History

Progressive Miners of America

The Progressive Miners of America, a reformist union, was organized in 1932 by miners dissatisfied with the leadership of the United Mine Workers of America. The movement had its roots in March 1930 when disgruntled members of the UMWA, led by Alexander Howatt and John H. Walker, formed the Reorganized United Mine Workers of America. This organization attempted to overthrow what they called the dictatorship of UMWA President John L. Lewis, appealing to the Illinois court system to recognize them as the legitimate UMWA. While the Reorganized Mine Workers initially gained substantial support in Illinois and West Virginia, the Illinois courts ruled in favor of the old UMWA. Without legal standing the rebel group collapsed in 1931.

One year later, in September 1932, the leaders of the Reorganized Mine Workers reunited to form the Progressive Miners of America. With Joe Ozanic as its president, this new union promised to give more power to local unions and allow them to elect their own officials, rights not then available to members of the UMWA. With support from the American Federation of Labor, the Progressive Miners aggressively campaigned against John L. Lewis and the UMWA.

Frank Keeney and Thomas Haggerty led the Progressive Miners fight in West Virginia. Competition between the rival unions grew intense in southern West Virginia, particularly at the mining town of Ward, Kanawha County. In certain instances UMWA members physically attacked field organizers for the PMA and, as a result, many miners were afraid to join the new union.

The conflict continued until UMW District 17 President Van A. Bittner negotiated a union-shop agreement with the local coal operators in May 1939. This union-shop agreement required any miner working at a given mine to join the UMWA. Shortly thereafter, support for the PMA collapsed and the union disbanded.

See also Frank Keeney, United Mine Workers of America

C. Belmont Keeney
West Virginia Humanities Council

Evelyn L.K. Harris and Frank J. Krebs, *From Humble Beginnings: The West Virginia State Federation of Labor, 1903–1957,* 1960; John Brophy, *A Miner's Life,* 1964.

Prohibition

Prohibition began in West Virginia in 1914, years before it was a reality for the nation as a whole. Supporters had long tried to prohibit the sale of alcohol in the state. In 1883, a prohibition amendment passed the House of Delegates by a 49-14 vote but was defeated in the Senate, 15-11. In 1888, a prohibition amendment to the state constitution was defeated during the general election by 34,887 votes.

By 1910, 37 of the state's 55 counties were completely dry or allowed the pro-

hibition of the sale of liquor under local option laws. In 1911, the legislature approved the submission of another prohibition amendment to the people. This time it was ratified, in the general election of November 1912, by a majority vote of 92,342 votes. Statewide prohibition became law at midnight June 30, 1914.

The prohibition law, article 6, section 46, of the state constitution, rigidly controlled all products containing even small amounts of alcohol. The few exceptions were in the field of pharmaceuticals and in religious practices. State prohibition was enforced under the Yost Law, passed by the legislature in 1913 and creating the Department of Prohibition.

As prohibition spread among the states Congress adopted the Webb-Kenyon Act of 1913, which made it illegal to ship intoxicants via interstate commerce from wet states to dry states. In 1917, the Reed "bone-dry" amendment to the Post Office Appropriation Act forbade liquor shipment into states that prohibited manufacture and sale within the state but allowed importing.

The 18th Amendment to the U.S. constitution finally brought full national prohibition. On January 8, 1919, the West Virginia legislature ratified the 18th Amendment, by a Senate vote of 26-0 and a House vote of 81-3. West Virginia became the 21st state to ratify the prohibition amendment. National prohibition became effective under the Volstead Act on January 16, 1920.

In 1934, the prohibition law was repealed. West Virginia voters approved amendments to the state constitution bringing it in line with the U.S. constitution, once again allowing for the manufacture, sale, and transporting of alcoholic beverages within the state. Many locations remain partly dry today, however, including several towns, all of Calhoun County, and the rural areas of several other counties. In these places wine and liquor cannot be sold by the bottle but may be consumed in bars and restaurants. Beer is available throughout West Virginia.

Mary Merolle
Charleston

PROMISE Scholarships

PROMISE scholarships are awarded to high school graduates who complete school with at least a 3.0 grade point average in the core and overall coursework as well as a certain score on the ACT or SAT test. Championed by Governor Wise, the scholarships are modeled after similar programs in Georgia and elsewhere. PROMISE stands for Providing Real Opportunities for Maximizing Instate Student Excellence.

Approved by the legislature in 1999 but not funded until 2001, the scholarships were first awarded in 2002. The scholar-

ships provide full tuition for a student to attend a state college or university or an equivalent scholarship to attend an in-state private college. The maximum amount was $3,160 in 2004.

The scholarship is not based on family income, the college's resources, or any factors other than academic eligibility. In addition to a 3.0 grade point average, a student initially had to achieve a composite ACT score of at least 21 or a combined SAT score of 1,000. In 2003, a stipulation was added that required a minimum score of 19 in each subject area of the ACT, or at least a 470 on the verbal section and a 460 on the math section in the SAT. In 2004, the standards again rose. To retain the free tuition from year to year, students must maintain a 2.75 grade point average as college freshmen and 3.0 average as sophomores.

The scholarship program is funded by lottery and video lottery revenues and any other legislative appropriation. The cost increased from $5.5 million appropriated in the 2001 fiscal year to $39 million in 2005. In 2002, 3,843 students used the award. The number increased in 2003 to 4,392, and decreased in 2004 to about 4,025. Critics of the program expressed fears that costs would expand beyond control, suggesting that it might be necessary to cap the awards or continue to raise the standards. About 25 percent of high school students receive PROMISE scholarships.

Prospect Rock

Prospect Rock, 1,300 feet high, located on Cacapon Mountain in Morgan County west of Berkeley Springs, overlooks the juncture of the Potomac River and Cacapon River and the states of West Virginia, Pennsylvania, and Maryland. The well-known landmark was renowned for its fine view as early as the 18th century. George Washington was a frequent visitor, traveling there with his wife, Lord Fairfax, and others.

Prospect Rock, an Oriskany sandstone cape in an area known also as the Cacapon Rocks, is reached by hiking through Cacapon State Park. There is a nearby highway overlook on State Route 9. A roadside marker states that "*National Geographic* magazine rates this scene among America's outstanding beauty spots." The magazine published a photograph of the view in its August 1940 issue.

Tanya Godfrey
Moorefield

Pruntytown Correctional Center

Pruntytown Correctional Center, located at Pruntytown near Grafton, is a coed prison that houses females in all security classifications and males primarily in medium security. The capacity is 78 for females and 292 for males. Pruntytown Correctional Center was originally estab-

Pruntytown boys practice their shop work.

lished as the Industrial School for Boys in 1891 and served as a male juvenile facility until 1983. Females were housed at the Industrial Home for Girls in Salem.

For generations of West Virginia youth, the name Pruntytown was synonymous with reform school. A court could commit a boy to Pruntytown, or parents could commit a boy whom they felt was out of their control by getting a judge or magistrate to issue an order. Boys as young as six to eight years old were once housed in the facility. In 1914, the legislature established a minimum age of 10. Originally stressing a military-style discipline, a program evolved that emphasized education, training, and farm work. By 1917, eight years of education were offered, providing a full grade-school education. Previously, the institution had offered schooling up to the fourth grade.

As racial segregation became more prevalent, the State Industrial School for Colored Boys opened at Lakin, Mason County, in 1922, and all of the black boys from Pruntytown were moved there. The Lakin school also served to ease overcrowding at Pruntytown, where the population had increased to more than 400. In 1956, Pruntytown was reintegrated when Lakin closed. A forestry camp at Davis also opened, with boys from Lakin and Pruntytown.

The philosophy of youth incarceration began changing in the 1970s. In West Virginia, decisions by the Supreme Court and the legislature stopped the commitment of children who had not committed specific crimes. As a result, the population declined from 250 in the 1970s to 52 boys who were transferred to the Industrial Home for Youth in Salem when Pruntytown closed.

The facility reopened in 1985, housing minimum custody adult male inmates whose primary work function was to renovate the center. In 1988, the Division of Corrections transferred 32 adult female prisoners who had been incarcerated at the Federal Correctional Institution for Women at Alderson. Today, Pruntytown Correctional Center emphasizes work assignments and educational opportunities. Many of the inmates work off-grounds for other state and municipal agencies such as the Division of Highways and the city of Clarksburg.

Public Broadcasting

The West Virginia Educational Broadcasting Authority was established by the legislature in 1963 following a 1962 executive order. The Authority, which operates as West Virginia Public Broadcasting, holds the licenses for all West Virginia public radio and public television stations. Setting policies of West Virginia Public Broadcasting, the Authority is composed of 11 members, four from higher and public education as established by the legislation and seven appointed by the governor. Public radio and television from their inception have emphasized educational broadcasting. In addition to original programs, the stations carry national programs offered by the Public Broadcasting Service, National Public Radio, Public Radio International, and other broadcast services.

In West Virginia, public radio began in the 1960s. In 1961, WMUL, licensed to Marshall University, began broadcasting, becoming the first radio station in the state to receive a license designated as non-commercial. In 1966, WVBC, licensed to Bethany College, began broadcasting, and WVWC, licensed to West Virginia Wesleyan College, went on the air in 1968.

In 1969, public television stations began broadcasting, with WWVU-TV in Morgantown and WMUL-TV (later WPBY-TV) in Huntington. The first VHF non-commercial station in the state, WSWP-TV in Grandview, started in 1970. With the exception of WSWP, these early radio and television stations were all associated with colleges and universities.

Initially, because of the decentralized nature of the early educational broadcasting system, each station produced its own programming, which it might share with other stations. Most of the evening programs were syndicated national shows, with occasional local programming. As the system matured, in-state program production was largely centralized, first for radio and then for television. The next step was to coordinate the two, as far as possible. In the 1990s, a policy of cooperation was implemented between West Virginia Public Radio and West Virginia Public Television. There is now considerable overlap of radio and television personnel in the production of programming. Features that are aired on public television's *Outlook* are broadcast during radio's *Morning Edition*, and public radio's *Mountain Stage*, one of West Virginia's most successful public broadcasting ventures, has selected programs rebroadcast on public television.

Mountain Stage, a live variety show that started in 1985, began national distribution in 1986. Other significant radio programs have included *Inside Appalachia* and *Dateline West Virginia*. Television programs produced in West Virginia include *Outlook* and *The Law Works*. The state's public television stations broadcast nationally syndicated shows such as the *MacNeil/Lehrer News Hour*. Syndicated television programs directed at children include *Sesame Street, Mister Rogers' Neighborhood,* and *Reading Rainbow*.

In 2004 public radio broadcast from 14 locations in West Virginia, while public television broadcast from the original three stations and additional channels in seven other communities. Most original radio programming was produced at the public broadcasting headquarters facility in Charleston, and the daily radio broadcasts originated there. Charleston and Morgantown shared production of TV programming. An estimated 450,000 people in West Virginia and neighboring areas tuned in to West Virginia Broadcasting's radio and television programming each week in 2004.

Public Health

The State Board of Health was established by the legislature in 1881, with an annual budget of $1,000. By 1890, local health boards had been established with health officers instructed to place warning placards on residences to control smallpox, scarlet fever, measles, and diphtheria, the leading causes of death at that time. Early effects of the state board included the establishment of hospitals for the mentally ill at Spencer (1893) and Huntington (1897) and the construction of Miners Hospitals in Welch, Fairmont, and McKendree after 1899.

In 1908, responding to a worldwide epidemic, the Board of Health recommended that West Virginia make provision for the care and treatment of tuberculosis. The state's first tuberculosis sanitarium was founded in 1913 at Hopemont in Preston County; Denmar Sanitarium for black tubercular patients was established in Pocahontas County in 1917. Pinecrest, also a TB sanitarium, opened in Beckley in 1930. Significant advances in public health were made during the administration of Governor Hatfield (1913–17), himself a medical doctor. The State Department of Health was established in 1915, replacing the Board of Health.

Smallpox was among the world's worst diseases until well into the 20th century, highly contagious and often fatal. West Virginia was not spared. In 1906, 19 cases of smallpox were reported in Hampshire County within a radius of four miles. Quarantine had not been properly enforced due to a difference of opinion regarding the diagnosis. In 1903, the death rate from smallpox was reported as being from 12 to 20 percent of reported cases. The Board of Health recommended that authorities urge everyone to be vaccinated, and revaccinated at every remotely suspected exposure to the disease. In 1927, 1,099 cases of smallpox were reported. The last case of smallpox was reported in 1948.

The Division of Vital Statistics was established by the West Virginia Legislature in 1917. This was a first attempt to centralize the registration of births and deaths. It was done on a cooperative basis because the law did not require reporting of this information to the state until 1921. Prior to 1921, physicians, midwives, and undertakers were required to report births and deaths only to the clerk of the county courts of the county in which the event occurred.

The state received a federal grant for the control of venereal disease in 1919. Funding for maternal and child health began in 1921, along with the collection of vital statistics. The first nutrition campaign was discussed and the state's milk control program began, both in 1927.

Statewide distribution of Salk polio vaccine began in 1953 as a step toward the prevention of paralytic poliomyelitis following a year when 21,000 new cases were reported nationally. The Division of Disease Control with the assistance of a Federal Grant, began a statewide polio vaccination program in 1957. Salk vaccine was administered to persons up to 20 years of age and to expectant mothers. This proved to be a turning point in the fight against this crippling disease. The last case of polio in West Virginia was reported in 1968.

Today, local health departments protect environmental health from risks associated with drinking water, sewage and wastewater, and food and milk sanitation. They offer disease prevention and control, responding to epidemics, rabies, tuberculosis, and sexually transmitted diseases, including AIDS. They address community health problems like tobacco use and physical inactivity. Some health departments offer clinical services including prenatal, family planning, breast and cervical cancer, immunizations, pediatrics, nutrition, home health, and primary care.

The West Virginia Public Health Association, an affiliate of the American Public Health Association, was organized in 1924. Members include nurses, sanitarians, physicians, dentists, health educators, laboratory technicians, clerks, administrators, epidemiologists, biostatisticians, nutritionists, outreach workers, academics, and retirees. Public health practitioners are trained at West Virginia University through the Master of Public Health degree offered by the Department of Community Medicine. The accredited program is offered statewide via distance learning and the teaching of adjunct faculty.

Public health in West Virginia is overseen by the West Virginia Bureau for Public Health. Services are provided in all 55 counties and in larger cities through local health departments. The total budget is $150 million. The demand on these funds is substantial. Entering the 21st century, West Virginia is one of the least healthy states. The leading causes of death are heart disease, cancer, diabetes, stroke and lung disease. West Virginia exceeds national figures in smokeless tobacco use, physical inactivity, obesity, hypertension, and cigarette smoking.

See also Department of Health and Human Resources, Medicine

Lamont D. Nottingham
WVU School of Medicine

Public Service Commission

The West Virginia Public Service Commission regulates prices, services, and operations of motor carriers and public utilities such as gas, electricity, telecommunications, water, and sewer. The three commissioners are appointed to six-year terms by the governor and approved by the state senate, and no more than two commissioners may be from the same political party. The governor appoints one of the commissioners as chair, who serves at the will and pleasure of the governor. The PSC finances its operations by an assessment on the revenues and property of the utilities and carriers it regulates. The legislature appropriates amounts from these funds for the use of the PSC.

The PSC was created by the legislature in 1913. Prior to that time, regulation of railroads and public utilities had been handled by the Board of Public Works, the State Road Commission, and the legislature itself. The need for an independent regulatory body had been made evident by the West Virginia Supreme Court ruling in the case of *Coal & Coke Railway Company v. Conley and Avis* (1910), which struck down maximum railroad transportation rates previously established by the legislature. The Supreme Court upheld the delegation of legislative rate-making powers to the PSC in *United Fuel Gas Company v. PSC* (1914), and later ruled that the functions of the PSC are "quasi-judicial and quasi-legislative." In other words, the Commission functions like both a court and a legislature, establishing rules and interpreting and enforcing them.

The PSC originally had jurisdiction over the Workmen's Compensation Fund as well as public utilities, railroads, and ferries. In 1915, the legislature amended the PSC law to remove Workmen's Compensation, to reduce the number of commissioners from four to three, and to reduce their terms of office to six years.

The Commission's primary work centered on the regulation of railroads during its early years. In 1935, the law was amended to give the PSC more control over utility expansion, construction, and self-dealing. In 1937, the PSC was given jurisdiction over motor carriers of goods and passengers. Following the relative decline of railroads after World War II and the expansion of electric, gas, and telephone services throughout the state, the Commission's activities became more concerned with utility regulation. It no longer sets railroad rates. The advent of high energy prices and high inflation in the 1970s caused a tremendous increase in utility rate case activity.

Because of public outcry against ever-increasing utility rates and utility industry dissatisfaction with Commission procedures, in 1978 the legislature commissioned an independent study of the PSC's structure and operation. This report led to passage of major changes in the PSC's statute in 1979. The reorganization required by these amendments divided the technical and legal staff into advisory and advocacy functions and created a separate motor carrier division. Communications between advocacy staff and the decision-making sections of the PSC were discouraged. The reorganization also established the Consumer Advocate Division, with institutional safeguards to guarantee its independence. In 1986, a new division was created within the PSC to provide assistance to public water and wastewater providers.

In 2004, the PSC employed a total of 320 persons and had an annual budget of more than $23 million.

Billy Jack Gregg
Public Service Commission

Board of Public Works

West Virginia became a state in 1863. From then until the Modern Budget Amendment was ratified in 1968, a Board of Public Works exercised great collective executive authority. In 1918, it acquired constitutional status by ratification of an earlier amendment. The Board of Public Works continues today, with curtailed powers.

Historically the board consisted of seven elected executive officials: the governor, secretary of state, auditor, treasurer, attorney general, commissioner of agriculture, and state superintendent of schools. Ratification of a constitutional amendment in 1958 made the superintendent of schools an appointee of the West Virginia Board of Education, but he remains a member of the Board of Public Works.

Before 1968, the board enjoyed wide-ranging powers, which increased through the years. The board's most potent authority was control of the state's finances, including the areas of budgeting, expenditures, custody of public funds, assessment, taxation, and accounting. Having vast discretionary power, its approval was required for many steps in the administrative process. The system made it almost impossible to know whom to hold accountable for executive actions, particularly in budget and fiscal management. The governor's power was limited, as one member among seven and having no particular power over the budget.

In 1968, the voters approved a single, strong chief executive by ratifying the Modern Budget Amendment, giving the governor primary responsibility for the state's budget and fiscal management. The governor's power greatly increased. The powers of the Board of Public Works were accordingly reduced and today involve mainly the buying and selling of state property, the assessment of the property of public utilities, and other limited functions.

See also Modern Budget Amendment
Donald R. Andrews
University of Charleston

Daniel Boardman Purinton

Daniel Boardman Purinton was a faculty member and president of West Virginia University. He was born February 15, 1850, in Preston County. He received a B.A. degree from WVU in 1873, taught in WVU's Preparatory Department (1873–78), and earned his M.A. degree in 1876. He later received a doctorate from the University of Nashville. He married Florence A. Lyon in 1876.

A Republican and Baptist, Purinton taught logic (1878–80), mathematics (1880–84), metaphysics (1885–89), and vocal music (1873–89) at WVU. He became vice-president and acting president of WVU in 1881. Purinton was an early and strong supporter of co-education and made the motion, on June 17, 1889, that WVU should admit women as degree candidates. His sister-in-law, Harriet Lyon, was the first woman to graduate from the school.

Purinton left WVU in 1890 to become president of Denison College. He returned to become president of WVU in 1901. He served as both president and dean of the College of Arts and Sciences until July 31, 1911.

Purinton wrote about 40 songs and the book, *Christian Theism* (1889), and was president of the West Virginia Baptist General Assembly and Ohio Baptist Education Society. He died in Morgantown, November 27, 1933.

See also West Virginia University
Barbara J. Howe
West Virginia University

Earl L. Core, *The Monongalia Story*, 1974–1984; William T. Doherty Jr. and Festus P. Summers, *West Virginia University: Symbol of Unity in a Sectionalized State*, 1982.

Putnam County

On March 11, 1848, a bill was passed by the General Assembly of Virginia to form Putnam County from portions of Kanawha, Mason, and Cabell. The new county was named in honor of Gen. Israel Putnam, who commanded the Continental Army at Bunker Hill. It straddled the Kanawha River, midway between Charleston and Point Pleasant. The census of 1850 showed a population of 5,336, including 632 slaves. Putnam, with 350.6 square miles of river valleys and rolling hills, was entirely a farming county until the late 1800s.

The town of Winfield, named for Gen. Winfield Scott, was established as the county seat when the first county meeting was held. Winfield, a river town with no railroad or paved road leading to it until 1930, was slow to expand. A devastating fire in 1928 destroyed one of the main town blocks. After the Winfield navigation dam was completed in 1936 and the new Kanawha River bridge was opened in 1957, the town became a progressive, growing community.

When the Civil War cast its shadows on the Kanawha Valley, it was apparent that Putnam would be a divided county within a divided state. Friends, neighbors, and even family members separated over the issues of the day. Enlistments were equally divided, as about 400 Putnam citizens joined each side. There were four significant engagements in Putnam County, at Scary Creek, Red House, Hurricane Bridge, and Winfield, and Putnam men served on many battlefields far from home.

Coal was discovered on the Pocatalico River in 1798, but it was not mined commercially until the late 19th century. In the early 1900s, five mining companies were operating between Raymond City and Plymouth. By 1907, Putnam County mines employed 1,000 men and produced more than 400,000 tons of coal a year. Much has been written about the grim living conditions and labor struggles in the West Virginia coalfields, but Putnam seems to have been spared the worst of it. At the beginning of World War II, the county mines shut down. The younger miners went into the service, and the older men with families found war-time jobs at the Nitro plants and other locations.

Older residents will remember that the Kanawha River divided the county dur-

Suburban subdivisions characterize much of Putnam County.

FAST FACTS ABOUT PUTNAM COUNTY

Founded: 1848
Land in square miles: 350.6
Population: 51,589
Percentage minorities: 2.0%
Percentage rural: 40.5%
Median age: 37.7
Percentage 65 and older: 11.6%
Birth rate per 1,000 population: 11.3
Median household income: $41,892
High school graduate or higher: 83.8%
Bachelor's degree or higher: 19.7%
Home ownership: 84.0%
Median home value: $102,900

This information is from the 2000 U.S. Census. In 2000, West Virginia as a whole had 5 percent minorities, a median age of 38.9, median household income of $29,696, and a 75.2 percent home ownership rate.

ing the age of railroad and highway transportation and before the river bridges were built. The only way to cross the Kanawha was by the unpredictable Winfield ferry. But once the river had united Putnam County. While the steamboat trade flourished, the division of the county was not much of an issue. People rode the daily packet boats to and from Charleston, and some were even picked up at their own landings. This created a popular social culture as passengers visited with one another in the dining rooms and along the deck rails. Lasting friendships were established from both sides of the river.

With the coming of the railroads, river travel diminished. With coal mining on the north side of the river and farming on the south side, the county became divided politically, economically, and socially, as well as geographically. Public improvements usually benefited only one side, which kept most bond issues from passing and caused the county to fall behind.

Finally, with the completion of the Winfield Bridge and Interstate 64, Putnam County began to prosper. The county created a planning commission, and eventually roads were improved, utilities ex-

tended, and areas zoned for housing and commercial and industrial development.

Now Putnam has thriving communities on both sides of the Kanawha River. They include Red House which was named for a house-size red rock that can be seen high on the hill behind the town. The ferry to present Winfield was established in 1818. Nearby Eleanor was built in 1934 as a federal project to relocate displaced families to small homestead farms. By the end of World War II, the Eleanor families had bought out the federal government's interest and established their own municipal government.

Buffalo, on the north side of the Kanawha River near the Mason County line, was laid out and incorporated in 1833, making it the oldest established town in Putnam County. Buffalo was originally a farming community, but with the location of the Toyota plant there in the 1990s it has become a manufacturing and rural residential center.

Bancroft, settled in 1848 and first named Energetic, was located three miles below the mouth of Pocatalico River, or Poca River as it is commonly known. Many Plymouth mine employees lived at Bancroft. Nearby Poca was a trade and shipping center for Poca River farmers until after the Civil War. Many Raymond

City miners preferred to live in Poca. In 1895, a timber company began extensive operations on the waters of Pocatalico, which added to Poca's growth.

On the south side of Kanawha River, Hurricane lies in the middle of Teays Valley, halfway between Huntington and Charleston. It was established in 1874 as Hurricane Station after the Chesapeake & Ohio Railroad was completed. Surrounded today by growing suburbs, Hurricane is the center of one of the fastest-growing areas in West Virginia. Farther east in Teays Valley, Scott Depot includes the area that extends from Scary Creek Hill to State Route 34. Scott Depot was an early stop on the C&O, and construction workers were housed there during the building of the railroad.

Nitro, a World War I boom town, was completed in 11 months in 1918. The town on the Putnam-Kanawha county line had 25,000 people and the plant was producing 700,000 pounds of gunpowder per day when the war ended in the same year. The entire Nitro site was bought by a development company and its industrial facilities sold off, the beginning of a prosperous chemical industry in the Kanawha Valley.

By 1998, the 150th anniversary of Putnam County, all previous expectations for growth and development had been exceeded. The Toyota plant had been completed at Buffalo, a warehouse complex at Nitro was in operation, and the Rock Branch Industrial Park was at full capacity. There is a new Kanawha River bridge at Buffalo, and plans have been approved to upgrade busy U.S. Route 35 with a bypass to I-64. With a 2000 population of 51,589, Putnam County is one of the most prosperous and fastest growing counties in West Virginia. Putnam County population grew by more than 20 percent from 1990 to 2002, a rate exceeded only in the Eastern Panhandle.

See also Eleanor, Kanawha River, Winfield

Bill Wintz
St. Albans

Jim Comstock, ed., *Hardesty's West Virginia Counties,* 1973; William D. Wintz, *History of Putnam County, Volume 1,* 1999.

Quiltmaking

The practice of quiltmaking—stitching layers of fabric and fiber into a textile sandwich—developed in antiquity. It is usually identified as women's work and pleasure. In America, quiltmaking was influenced by both the mass culture and local folk ways. West Virginia quilts are in many ways the same as quilts made by women of similar circumstances throughout the nation, dictated by fashion and fabric supply. Quiltmaking styles are rarely confined to political boundaries such as state lines, for popular culture and taste are national and regional in character.

Thus, antique quilts from the Mountain State are similar to others made throughout the Southern highlands. For example, West Virginia quilts share a feature with quilts made in other areas settled primarily by Scotch-Irish: a quilting pattern made by stitching rows of concentric arcs across the surface of a quilt, known as "the fans." In areas of German settlement, quilts more often have distinctive borders and use a variety of quilting motifs to distinguish construction components.

Still, our quiltmaking has its distinctive features. West Virginia quiltmakers retain old ways of doing things by hemming a quilt (folding the lining to the front for edge finish) rather than binding it, and by using the earlier pattern name "Dutch Girl" for an applique figure known elsewhere as "Sunbonnet Sue." Some quilts carry material evidence of the diversified farmstead, such as the use of hand-carded batts of homegrown wool as the insulating inner material. Quiltmakers in southern West Virginia may join their blocks in a zigzag manner, a setting known as "Fence Rail," uncommon elsewhere and possibly Welsh in origin.

In early days, before American cotton textile mills came into operation, fabric for quiltmaking was an expensive, imported commodity. The considerable amount of time and materials required to construct a quilt limited the practice mostly to the well-off. During the decades before the Civil War, prosperous quiltmakers with cultivated taste cut and stitched luxury fabrics from England and France into decorative finery for the bed. Western Virginia quilts from this era are similar to ones made in Maryland, Pennsylvania, Ohio, and eastern Virginia. Floral applique and repeating pieced blocks on a white background with consistent fabrics (instead of an assortment of sewing scraps) are typical.

After the Civil War, industrial development brought affordable cotton cloth and thread, and sometimes sewing machines, into the homes of working-class women. The "scrap" quilt made its appearance, displaying the wide variety of printed cotton fabrics now available. Pieced block patterns were marketed through newspapers and other periodicals during the late 19th century and throughout the 20th.

By the turn of the century, a confluence of factors in West Virginia led to the development of a distinctive quilt style, the utility crazy quilt. Crazy quilts were a national fad in the 1880s and the Gay Nineties; their eclectic look suited Victorian taste. Crazy quilts may be constructed with odd and random pieces of fabric, rather than the precisely cut shapes required for other patchwork. The ease of preparation might have appealed to West Virginia women with little or no previous quiltmaking experience, such as wives of immigrant laborers and rural women who had previously lacked exposure to the craft. In West Virginia, the crazy quilt flourished long after fading from the national scene, stitched from pieces of recycled garments, printed feed sacks, and polyester double knits.

In West Virginia, quiltmaking is celebrated with annual quilt shows around the state. Women's groups not uncommonly turn to quiltmaking as a way to raise money. The federal War on Poverty engendered a number of cooperatives devoted to quiltmaking, notably Mountain Artisans and Cabin Creek Quilts. Family quilts are preserved and cherished.

Fawn Valentine
Alderson

Fawn Valentine, *West Virginia Quilts and Quiltmakers: Echoes from the Hills,* 2000.

A handmade West Virginia quilt in the lone star pattern.

R. D. Bailey Lake

R. D. Bailey Lake is located on the Guyandotte River near Justice, on the Wyoming-Mingo county line. Named in honor of the late Judge R. D. Bailey, the lake provides flood protection for the lower Guyandotte River basin, including the city of Huntington. The dam was the first rock-fill dam developed by the U.S. Army Corps of Engineers with a concrete face, a complex and difficult job. The 310-foot-high dam is the second-highest in West Virginia (Summersville Dam is highest at 390 feet), and measures 1,400 feet across. The intake structure, a 310-foot concrete tower, has gates at four intervals. Water can normally be released from any of the four levels to control water temperature and water quality downstream.

Construction was begun in June 1967, but floods and contractual difficulties caused delays. The entire project cost $180 million and was finally completed in 1980. R. D. Bailey Lake catches runoff from a 540-square-mile drainage area. Under maximum storage conditions, the seven-mile lake would extend to 22 miles and impound more than 66 billion gallons of water. The Corps of Engineers acquired 19,000 acres of land in conjunction with the development of the dam and lake, which is leased to the West Virginia Division of Natural Resources as a wildlife management area. Recreational facilities include a boat launching area and marina, picnic facilities, overlooks, and a camping area at the upper end of the lake. Clinging to the edge of a former strip-mine bench, 300 feet above the dam, the visitors' center includes exhibits relating to the historical, geological, and engineering aspects of the lake.

See also R. D. Bailey, Lakes

Robert Beanblossom
Division of Natural Resources

Radio

WHD at West Virginia University received the state's first radio station license on March 16, 1922. The year before, KDKA of Pittsburgh, since 1920 the nation's first commercially licensed station, had broadcast the first college football game on radio, featuring a contest between West Virginia University and the University of Pittsburgh. The oldest extant West Virginia radio station is WSAZ (now WRVC) in Huntington, originally licensed in October 1924. Other long-time stations include WWVA of Wheeling, which began broadcasting in December 1926, and WCHS of Charleston, which went on the air as WOBU in September 1927.

WHIS of Bluefield in 1931 foreshadowed later media issues when it broadcast the murder trial of Minnie Stull, accused of scalding her three-year-old stepchild to death. It was the first such direct broadcast outside of Russia, according to the station. In an appeal of her conviction and death sentence, Stull claimed that the broadcast had made a "circus" out of her trial. In a retrial in Greenbrier County, she received a life sentence, and served 20 years.

Until the mid-1940s, the number of commercial radio stations in the state grew steadily, from four in 1925 to six in 1928, nine in 1939, and 13 by 1945. During this period, commercial radio was expanding rapidly across America. Advertising revenue supported growth, and public demand for music and entertainment spurred a major increase in the number of radio receivers.

In 1946, the West Virginia Broadcasters Association was organized with a dozen member radio stations. Howard Chernoff of WCHS was the first president. The WVBA was created to represent the interests of the statewide broadcasting industry. In 1939, the West Virginia Network had been formed by WCHS, WSAZ, WPAR in Parkersburg, and WBLK in Clarksburg to pool efforts and broadcast special events such as sports to stations around the state.

By 1947, there were 39 stations in the state, including 11 FM licensees. The first FM station in the state was WCFC of Beckley, which began regular programming on August 15, 1946. As of 1952, West Virginia had 57 radio station licensees. The network affiliations of stations on the air at that time included Mutual (eight), CBS (six), ABC (five), NBC (four), and Mutual and ABC (two). By 1956, the most competitive radio station markets were Charleston and Wheeling, with six stations each, Parkersburg with four, Clarksburg and Huntington with three stations each, and Beckley, Bluefield, Morgantown, Logan, Welch, and Fairmont with two stations each.

As television emerged in the 1950s as the dominant household medium, radio survived through change. Before television, West Virginia radio stations offered network and local programs including musical performances, variety shows, comedies, dramas, and special events. Now entertainment yielded further to recorded musical selections as the backbone of program content. Continued emphasis was put on news, something radio still delivered with more immediacy than television could. Audiences were retained as radio became something people could enjoy while doing something else, whether they were driving, performing household chores, or doing school homework. Radio also continued to specialize, offering music formats and program content tailored to distinct audience segments. Some stations played only country music, for example, while others found other specialties.

The first non-commercial radio station in West Virginia was WMUL-FM at Marshall University, which began broadcasting November 1, 1961, a year before Governor Barron created the West Virginia Educational Broadcasting Authority. The legislature passed public broadcasting legislation in 1963, and Congress passed the Public Broadcasting Act in 1967. Today a statewide public radio system serves West Virginia from Charleston. WVMR, a non-affiliated public AM station, broadcasts from Marlinton, and there are several college stations as well.

The West Virginia Broadcasters Association in 2004 had 131 radio station members facing the same economic pressure and future uncertainty as does the industry nationally. Corporate consoli-

R. D. Bailey Lake nestles among the mountains.

dation continues as companies such as Clear Channel Communications and Infinity Broadcasting acquire local stations across the country. The convergence of media, particularly the rise of pure Internet stations, has led some analysts to predict a major restructuring of commercial radio. Cable music services are available in West Virginia, and satellite radio is also at hand, offering a signal whose strength does not vary from area to area as drivers travel the nation's highways.

Still, commercial radio thrives in West Virginia as it does elsewhere, reflecting the habits of a loyal audience spanning more than three quarters of a century.

See also Public Broadcasting

Larry Sonis
Arlington, Texas

Martha Jane Becker and Marilyn Fletcher, *Broadcasting in West Virginia: A History*, 1989.

Dyke Raese

Coach Richard Ambrey "Dyke" Raese directed West Virginia University to its only major sports national championship, winning the 1942 National Invitation Tournament in basketball. Raese was born July 27, 1909, in Davis, Tucker County, played all sports at Davis High School, and later coached the high school basketball team to a 110-42 record in six years. He was educated at West Virginia University and married Jane Greer.

The NIT was the major tournament when Raese coached at the university. His players all came from within 75 miles of Morgantown, and included Floyd "Scotty" Hamilton, a Grafton native who became WVU's first All-American basketball player. Last picked in a tournament field of eight, WVU upset three teams in 1942, including defending champion Long Island University, to take the title. Long Island was coached by Clair Bee, also from Grafton and a best-selling author of boys sports books.

Raese coached at WVU from 1938 to 1942, with a win-loss record of 55-29, before serving in World War II. After the war, he entered Greer Industries, which included radio stations, the Morgantown *Dominion Post* newspaper, and limestone and steel plants. The father of businessman and gubernatorial candidate John Raese, Dyke Raese was inducted into the WVU Hall of Fame in 1992. He died August 7, 2000.

See also Clair Bee

Norman Julian
Dominion Post

Norman Julian, *Legends: Profiles in West Virginia University Basketball*, 1998.

Henry Clay Ragland

Henry Clay Ragland was a Logan County newspaper publisher and lawyer who founded the *Logan County Banner* in 1888. Ragland was born May 7, 1844, in Goochland County, Virginia, the son of Hugh N. and Eliza Eades Ragland. He enlisted in Company B, 5th Virginia Cavalry, on his 17th birthday and served in the Confederate Army of Northern Virginia until captured by Union troops near Luray, Virginia, in 1864. He spent the remainder of the war in Point Lookout prison in Maryland.

Ragland worked as a teacher in Goochland County before moving to Wayne County, in 1870. He learned printing from H. K. Shumate and moved to Logan in 1874. He married Louisa Buskirk on January 9, 1878, and became friends with James Andrew Nighbert, the town's leading merchant, thus finding his place in the community. Ragland made his newspaper a voice for Logan County and the Democratic Party. He was a leading local booster and a proponent of industrialization. He argued for the creation of a coalmining and railroad economy, and that goal was achieved when the Chesapeake & Ohio Railroad and Island Creek Coal Company arrived in Logan County a few years before Ragland's death on May 1, 1911.

Robert Y. Spence
Logan

Nick Joe Rahall

Congressman Nick Joe Rahall II represents West Virginia's Third Congressional District. Born May 20, 1949, in Beckley, he first won election to the House of Representatives in 1976. When Rahall entered Congress in 1977, he was its youngest member. He had previously served as a staff assistant to U.S. Sen. Robert Byrd.

The opportunity for Rahall in 1976 opened when incumbent Congressman Ken Hechler decided to run in the primary for the Democratic nomination for governor, a bid he lost to Jay Rockefeller. Hechler then ran as a write-in candidate to retain his House seat, but Rahall spent more than $100,000 to defeat him in the November general election.

Hechler again tried to reclaim his seat two years later, opposing Rahall in the 1978 primary. But Rahall gathered important endorsements from such leading Democrats as Byrd and House Speaker Tip O'Neill and spent considerably more than Hechler. Rahall won with 56 percent of the vote. Hechler challenged Rahall once more in 1990, but Rahall again held on. He turned back a challenge in the fall from Republican Marianne Brewster, who came within four percentage points of defeating him. Since that time, Rahall has faced only weak opposition in his heavily Democratic district.

The main issues Rahall has concentrated on during his service in the House have been transportation, infrastructure, energy, and the environment. In 2005, he was the top Democrat on the Committee on Resources and second most-senior Democrat on the Committee on Transportation and Infrastructure. As one of the key architects of the Transportation Equity Act for the 21st Century, he established the Rahall Transportation Institute, located in the Third District at Marshall University.

Rahall has looked to tourism in attempts to diversify the district economy, which historically had depended heavily upon natural resource extraction. In 1978, he authored legislation establishing the New River Gorge National River as a unit of the National Park Service. A decade later he gained enactment of legislation creating the Gauley River National Recreation Area and the Bluestone National River. Rahall legislation also established the National Coal Heritage Area, comprising most of the counties of the Third District.

As the representative of a district with a long history of coal mining, Rahall has been a leader in Congress on mining issues, chairing the House Subcommittee on Mining and Natural Resources from 1985 until 1993. One of his pet causes has been a long struggle to reform the Mining Law of 1872. Rahall was the chief sponsor in the House of the 1992 Coal Act, working with Senators Rockefeller, Byrd, and others to secure the benefits of miners under union health care plans.

Congressman Rahall springs from the sizable Lebanese community in southern West Virginia. His immigrant grandfather established a prosperous business family, beginning as an itinerant coalfields peddler early in the 20th century. Rahall worked in family businesses before beginning his service in Congress. He is a graduate of Woodrow Wilson High School in Beckley and, in 1971, of Duke University. Rahall also did graduate work at George Washington University in 1972.

Congressman Rahall has three children, Nick Joe III, Rebecca, and Suzanne, from his first marriage. Rahall remarried in 2004, to Melinda Ross.

Jim Wallace
Charleston

Railroad Strike of 1877

The Panic of 1877, a national economic recession, had a disastrous effect on the earnings of the Baltimore & Ohio Railroad. In response, the railroad announced a ten percent pay cut for all employees. The pay cut exacerbated earlier wage cuts, and the railroad firemen's union called a strike which soon spread along the rails from Baltimore to Chicago.

The first violence occurred in West Virginia, when strikers in Martinsburg attempted to stop trains from running. Governor Mathews quickly mobilized the militia company in Martinsburg to control the strikers. The unit was commanded by Capt. Charles J. Faulkner Jr., and was made up largely of volunteers who were railroad workers themselves or related to railroad workers. Consequently, the militiamen were subjected to extreme pressure from relatives and fellow workers. The unit was assigned to guard a train that attempted to leave the railroad yard in Martinsburg. A striker fired upon the militiamen and was mortally wounded by return fire. The militia then withdrew and refused to take further action against the strikers.

Governor Mathews sent another militia unit from Wheeling to the scene, and when the Wheeling unit also proved unable to handle the strikers he called upon President Rutherford B. Hayes for federal troops to preserve order. Federal troops were successful in ending the violence at Martinsburg, and the strike ended later in the summer of 1877. The strike showed that West Virginia authorities were ill-prepared to handle unrest among laboring groups and led to calls, mostly unheeded, for development of a professional national guard to control labor disturbances.

See also Labor History

Kenneth R. Bailey
WVU Institute of Technology

Kenneth R. Bailey, *Mountaineers are Free: A History of the West Virginia National Guard*, 1978; Edward Hungerford, *The Story of the Baltimore and Ohio Railroad, 1827–1927*, 1928.

Railroads

The Baltimore & Ohio, America's first commercial railroad, extended its line into what is now West Virginia in the 1840s, entering the northern reaches of the state at Harpers Ferry, crossing to Cumberland, Maryland, and then back to Grafton and traveling on to the Ohio River at Wheeling by 1853. This line was important in the Civil War.

In the south, the Virginia Central (later Chesapeake & Ohio) had reached what is now Clifton Forge, Virginia, by 1856. To connect this line to the west, Virginia incorporated the Covington & Ohio, which did considerable work in what is now southern West Virginia before the war. After the war the Virginia Central and the Covington & Ohio were merged to form the Chesapeake & Ohio. In the period 1869–73, this line was built through the wild New River Gorge, reaching the Ohio in January 1873. Although the C&O was built as part of the great transcontinental scheme of its builder, Collis P. Huntington, local coal soon became a dominant commodity as mines opened along the new railway. Competing railroads soon invaded the southern coalfields, primarily the Norfolk & Western in the 1880s.

Meanwhile, to the north, the B&O continued to expand its lines in the northern West Virginia coalfields, sending its coal to the sea at Baltimore and westward to the Great Lakes.

By 1900, what became the Western Maryland Railroad had entered the coal trade and was building new lines in the Eastern Panhandle and adjacent areas. It ultimately became an important hauler of coal to the port of Baltimore. Short lines grew up, including the Coal & Coke Railway, which had been built to tap the coal and timberlands of central West Virginia

Most West Virginia coal moves by train.

and became part of the B&O in 1917. Likewise, the Kanawha & Michigan, which entered the state at Point Pleasant and terminated at Charleston, later became part of the huge New York Central System.

The last entry into West Virginia's coalfields was the Virginian Railway. Completed in 1909, it originated at Deep Water in Fayette County. The Virginian competed with both N&W and C&O for the eastern coal markets, but didn't have lines to the west and never competed for the even larger Midwest trade. Lacking a large merchandise or passenger trade, it became mostly a one-commodity line, virtually a coal conveyor from southern West Virginia to the sea at Hampton Roads, Virginia.

By contrast, the B&O's lines in West Virginia were part of its main line to Cincinnati and St. Louis, and carried a huge merchandise and passenger trade in addition to West Virginia coal. Likewise, the C&O developed an important passenger service between Washington and Cincinnati at an early date. The N&W had little through trade beyond coal, and its Cincinnati-Norfolk passenger service suffered from a lack of connections to the major cities of the Northeast.

West Virginia's huge lumbering industry was served by company-owned lumber railroads to bring the logs to the mills, using gear-driven Shay, Climax, and Heisler locomotives to master the steep grades. The sawed lumber was then shipped by the main line railways to the principal markets of the nation. Other short lines included the very early Winifrede Railroad, which carried its coal to barges on the Kanawha River before the region had rail connections to the outside world, and the Campbell's Creek Railroad, connecting with the New York Central east of Charleston.

West Virginia's railroads helped to develop the state's coal industry and fostered the establishment of great industrial centers, especially in the Kanawha Valley and Northern Panhandle. They also connected West Virginians with the world. News and correspondence could move at the speed of light by the telegraph lines that followed the railroads; mail and express arrived from every corner of the continent; and travel to far places was quick, easy, and comfortable. Most importantly, the state's raw materials could be transported cheaply and efficiently from sometimes remote locations, and finished goods could be distributed to people throughout the state. The coming of the railroads is the seminal economic event of the 19th century for West Virginia and the nation.

The steam locomotive was the power that allowed railroads to be created, just as steam powered the factories and mills served by those railroads. In the early 20th century, a movement to electrify railroads gained some momentum, and in the 1920s the Virginian and the Norfolk & Western electrified considerable territory within western Virginia and West Virginia. However, this technological change was eclipsed in the late 1930s by the introduction of very powerful diesel-electric locomotives. As coal haulers, the West Virginia railroads resisted the move from coal to diesel fuel. By the early 1950s, the C&O and B&O finally dieselized. The N&W held out as an all-steam railroad until 1956, and operated its last steam equipment in West Virginia in 1960. The diesels required less maintenance and fewer service stops. Shops were consolidated and closed and employment in these areas dropped. Railroad towns such as Grafton and Hinton suffered a loss of jobs.

In the 1960s, suffering from the competition of airlines, highways, and trucks, and from archaic government regulation, railroads began to merge. In 1960, the Chesapeake & Ohio and the Baltimore & Ohio began a gradual consolidation that eventually included the Western Maryland and culminated in the creation of the Chessie System in 1972. Chessie merged with the Seaboard System (itself an amalgam of five major southeastern lines) to form CSX Transportation, which today controls the lines remaining from the former C&O, B&O, and Western Maryland within the state. The Norfolk & Western, at about the same time, merged with the Southern Railway to form Norfolk Southern, which today controls the lines of the former N&W and Virginian within West Virginia. (The Virginian had merged into N&W in 1959.) In 2005, Norfolk Southern and CSX Transportation control railroading within the state. Both systems still rely on coal transportation as their main commodity from West Virginia.

West Virginia Congressman Harley Staggers pushed through laws that essentially deregulated railroads in the early 1980s. Today the remaining major systems haul more freight than ever before with a tiny fraction of the motive power and employees, and about one-third of the trackage that existed at the height of the railway age about 1920. Railroads remain important in West Virginia today, even though the number of lines has shrunk.

Thomas W. Dixon Jr.
Lynchburg, Virginia

Rainbow Gathering

In July 1980, the Rainbow Family held its annual reunion in Monongahela National Forest, at Three Forks of the Williams River in Webster County. News of the reunion provoked strong reactions.

The Rainbow Family, a loosely organized group whose main activity is its annual reunion, has been variously char-

acterized as hippies and drifters or as peaceful nature lovers and ecologists. The annual gatherings grew out of social, political, and cultural movements that had gained popularity in the 1960s and early 1970s. Included in these movements were back-to-the-landers, people who sought to return to a simpler, self-sustaining way of life; anti-war protesters; and hippies. In 1970, recognizing their common approach to life, they decided to stage a yearly event. The name "rainbow" was chosen to signify the diversity of people involved. The first gathering, in 1972, was near Aspen, Colorado, in the Roosevelt National Forest and on private land.

In the month before the West Virginia event, Secretary of State A. James Manchin and a group of Marlinton residents filed suit in federal court to bar the Rainbow Family from having its reunion in the Monongahela National Forest. At the time, Manchin was quoted in news reports as saying that West Virginia didn't need "this bunch of derelict misfits." Manchin also asked the U.S. Forest Service to withdraw the group's camping permit. The federal court suit was dropped before the reunion started.

An estimated 6,000 people attended West Virginia's Rainbow Gathering. For 20 years, the 1980 event continued to make news. On June 25, 1980, two women who were apparently hitchhiking to the reunion were murdered on Droop Mountain, in southern Pocahontas County. In 1993, Jacob Beard, a Pocahontas County native, was convicted of killing Nancy Santomero, 26, of Huntington, Long Island, New York, and Vicki Durian, 26, of Wellman, Iowa. Beard's conviction was overturned in 1993, and he was acquitted of the murders after his second trial in June 2000.

The Rainbow family returned to West Virginia for an uneventful gathering in the Monongahela National Forest in 2005.

Rainelle

Rainelle, once one of West Virginia's busiest sawmill towns, lies at the intersection of U.S. 60 and State Route 20 in Greenbrier County, near the Fayette County border. Rainelle was a company town, built by the Meadow River Lumber Company about 1910. It was named for Thomas and John Raine, the company founders.

Rainelle was a model lumber town. Its sturdy frame houses, built of the company's hardwoods, were white-painted and plastered. The houses were provided with running water, bathrooms, and electricity long before such amenities were common in the area. The United Methodist church and company offices were finished in various fine woods, showcasing the company's products. The

Pioneer Hotel welcomed visitors to the downtown, while the larger King Coal Hotel opened in nearby East Rainelle.

For many years, the Meadow River Lumber Company operated at Rainelle what was said to be the largest hardwood lumber plant in the world. The company produced flooring and lumber for many other uses at Rainelle, including millions of women's shoe heels annually in the 1930s.

Rainelle's fortunes paralleled those of its major employer, and the town slowly lost population in the last decades of the 20th century. The Georgia-Pacific Company bought Meadow River Lumber Company in 1970 and closed the mill in 1975. The 2000 population of Rainelle was 1,545.

Rainelle occupies historic country, at the base of Sewell Mountain and near the juncture of Sewell Creek and Meadow River. Early explorer Stephen Sewell was killed by Indians at his nearby cabin in 1776. U.S. 60 follows the route of the James River & Kanawha Turnpike, also known as the Midland Trail. The highway remained a major thoroughfare from the 1790s until Interstate 64 was completed in the 1980s.

See also James River & Kanawha Turnpike, Meadow River Lumber Company

Raleigh County

By the end of the 20th century, Raleigh County ranked fifth in population among West Virginia's 55 counties, with a 2000 population of 79,220. Beckley, the county seat, was the state's eighth-largest municipality with a 2000 population of 17,254. In land area, at 610.2 square miles, Raleigh is tenth.

Raleigh County was established in 1850 by an act of the Virginia General Assembly, with Beckley as its county seat. The county's founder, Alfred Beckley (1802–88), a West Point graduate, named the county after Sir Walter Raleigh, and the town after his father, John James Beckley, first clerk of the U.S. House of Representatives and first Librarian of Congress.

In 1742, John Peter Salling, a German from Orange County, Virginia, led an expedition down the New and Kanawha rivers, noting rich seams of coal along the way. He named Coal River, which has its headwaters in Raleigh County. Dr. Thomas Walker of Albemarle County, Virginia, while searching for lands for the Royal Company crossed through Raleigh, including the present site of Beckley. He too remarked on the coal deposits. Christopher Gist of North Carolina, heading an expedition financed by the London Company, visited the New and Bluestone rivers in 1750–51. By the late 1700s, speculators, including Alfred Beckley's father, were acquiring hundreds of thousands of acres in Raleigh and adjoining counties.

Glade Springs resort is among Raleigh County's recreational attractions.

Raleigh's first permanent white settler is not known, but William Richmond, a Revolutionary War veteran, is a good candidate. He acquired a ten-acre tract on New River at Sandstone Falls in 1799. In 1797–98, Francis Farley, an old Indian fighter, was employed by three Greenbrier County (now Monroe) merchants to hack a six-foot bridle path through Raleigh westward 115 miles to present Louisa, Kentucky, on the Big Sandy River. They wanted a path wide enough for the pack animals of trappers from whom they bought large quantities of beaver pelts.

They hoped eventually to widen the path, known as "Farley's Trace," into a wagon road. But a road through Raleigh was not realized until 1810–11, when the Virginia General Assembly, acting on a petition from farmers in Monroe and Giles counties, authorized a primitive state road through Raleigh and Fayette to the Kanawha River as a shortcut to the saltworks at Malden. It was this road that opened the interior of Raleigh to settlement, which followed shortly thereafter. In the 1840s, the Giles, Fayette & Kanawha Turnpike followed the same general route.

Alfred Beckley came to Raleigh after resigning his army commission, hoping to cash in on the 56,679 acres he had inherited from his father. He built his home, Wildwood, at Beckley, settling there with his family in 1837. The county's 1850 population was 1,765.

Since Raleigh was a turnpike crossroads, U.S. and Confederate armies repeatedly traversed the county, as they fought to control Western Virginia. Federal troops occupied the county in early 1862. Col. Rutherford B. Hayes and Sgt. William McKinley were stationed in Beckley for a time during this period. Although no major engagements were fought in Raleigh, skirmishes were frequent. Many homes were burned, and bushwhackers were common. In 1863, Beckley was bombarded by federal artillery.

Mostly Confederate in sentiment, Raleigh supplied two companies of troops to the Southern army. Numerous civilians were arrested by federal authorities and imprisoned at Camp Chase, Ohio, including Alfred Beckley, briefly a Virginia militia general. Others, arrested by the Confederates, were imprisoned at Richmond. Many civilians fled the county. For 35 months, from late autumn 1862 through early autumn 1865, Raleigh suffered a collapse of civil government. County records were sent to Pulaski County, Virginia, for safekeeping.

After the Chesapeake & Ohio Railroad opened its line through the New River Gorge in 1873, the timber industry flourished, mainly along the mountains bordering the river. The C&O had chosen the north side of the New River, the Fayette County side, meaning a delay in the birth of the Raleigh coal industry, except for the 1891 mine at Royal which was on the river. In 1901, the C&O built a branch line nearly to Beckley, and by 1910 the C&O and Virginian railroads had penetrated every section of the county. Mining boomed. Twenty-one coal companies operated in Raleigh in 1910, producing 2,873,448 tons of coal. The banner year was 1925, when production reached 17,598,224 tons.

FAST FACTS ABOUT RALEIGH COUNTY

Founded: 1850

Land in square miles: 610.2

Population: 79,220

Percentage minorities: 10.4%

Percentage rural: 40.8%

Median age: 39.5

Percentage 65 and older: 15.4%

Birth rate per 1,000 population: 11.1

Median household income: $28,181

High school graduate or higher: 72.0%

Bachelor's degree or higher: 12.7%

Home ownership: 76.5%

Median home value: $69,800

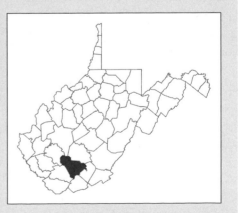

This information is from the 2000 U.S. Census. In 2000, West Virginia as a whole had 5 percent minorities, a median age of 38.9, median household income of $29,696, and a 75.2 percent home ownership rate.

Peak output came in 1943 during World War II when Raleigh mines produced 16,221,163 tons. From then on, production dropped, falling to a low of 5,191,534 in 1974, then leveling off and rising slightly over the following years. Peak mining employment was 14,226 in 1937, but that fell to 1,803 by 1991. Raleigh's coal production came at a high cost. Between 1897 and 1992, 2,121 Raleigh County workers died as the result of mining accidents. In 1914, 183 miners perished in the Eccles mine explosion, the worst in the county's history and second-worst in West Virginia.

County population peaked with the coal industry. There were 96,273 Raleigh Countians in 1950, falling to 76,819 by 1990.

Offsetting the decline in coal has been the development of Raleigh County as a major southern West Virginia trading, government, tourist, and medical center. Mountain State University, formerly Beckley College, is located in Beckley and the Appalachian Bible College at nearby Bradley. The development of the West Virginia Turnpike (I-77) and I-64 has given the county north-south and east-west interstate routes. The four-lane U.S. 19 (Appalachian Corridor L) connects with I-79 in Braxton County, giving northern travelers a shortcut to the southeast resort states via Beckley. The Beckley to Grundy, Virginia, four-lane Coalfields Expressway is under development.

Notable Raleigh Countians include U.S. Sen. Robert C. Byrd; musician Little Jimmy Dickens; former Congressman E. H. Hedrick; U.S. Sen. Harley M. Kilgore; Jon McBride, astronaut; Gov. Clarence W. Meadows; Congressman Nick Joe Rahall; Chris Sarandon, movie and television actor; former Congressman Joe L. Smith Sr.; Gov. Hulett C. Smith; and John Roscoe Turner, a president of West Virginia University. Raleigh County was especially well represented between 1945 and 1949, with Kilgore in the U.S. Senate, Hedrick in the U.S. House, and Meadows as governor of West Virginia, all at the same time.

Raleigh varies in elevation from 800 feet at Jarrolds Valley in Clear Fork District to 3,560 feet at the summit of Huff Knob on Flat Top Mountain in Shady Spring District. Beckley, at 2,360 feet, averages 55 inches of snowfall annually, exceeding all major cities except Elkins. It is also one of the coolest, with an average temperature of 50.9 degrees, again exceeded only by Elkins at 49.4 degrees. And it is among the wettest at 42.12 inches annually, topped by Elkins and Charleston. The Guyandotte and Coal rivers begin in Raleigh County.

There are three major parks—Grandview, home of two historical dramas, now part of New River Gorge National River; Little Beaver State Park; and Lake Stephens, a county park.

See also Beckley

Jim Wood
Beckley

Jim Wood, *Raleigh County, West Virginia*, 1994; Official County Court, Circuit Court, and Land Book records of Raleigh County; West Virginia Department of Mines annual reports.

Ramps

Ramps, a member of the lily family and a spring culinary treat, grow from New Brunswick and Minnesota south to Iowa, and in the mountains to North Carolina and Tennessee. In West Virginia, extensive beds of ramps are found in the rich mountain woodlands, particularly in the Monongahela National Forest which runs along the state's eastern boundary.

The broad, flat leaves resemble the lily-of-the-valley, and its thin stem and pearly white bulb are reminiscent of the wild onion. Ramps appear in the early spring, but the leaves wither and disappear before flowering time in June and July when delicate white flowers are seen.

This small, highly odoriferous plant was a favorite with early people in the Southern Appalachian mountains, whose winter diet lacked fresh fruit and vegetables. In the very early spring, often when snow still covered the glens, the deep green leaves of the ramp were sought as a welcome addition to the supper table, a taste treat and nutritional supplement. In cooking, the whole ramp, green and bulb, is used. Ramps are typically parboiled and eaten in quantity as a side dish. Many enjoy eating the bulbs raw or substituting the bulbs for onions in recipes.

Many devotees claim ramps possess healing powers, from the prevention of colds, which may be true due to their high content of Vitamin C, to the cleansing of the blood. The ramp's European cousin, the ramson, recently has been identified as having antibiotic properties. Ramp "feeds" abound in small communities throughout West Virginia in April. The granddaddy of them all, Richwood's "Feast of the Ramson," has been held annually since 1938.

See also Foodways

Barbara Beury McCallum
Charleston

Barbara Beury McCallum, *Mom & Ramps Forever*, 1983.

Z. D. Ramsdell

Soldier, postal official, manufacturer, and merchant Zophar D. Ramsdell learned the shoe trade in Massachusetts. Born November 21, 1816, he relocated to Ceredo in 1858 at the invitation of town founder Eli Thayer, who brought in about 500 settlers as part of an experiment to build an anti-slavery community in the slave state of Virginia. Ramsdell was a manufacturer and seller of boots and shoes, and he continued the business until the outbreak of the Civil War.

In 1861, he became a captain in the 5th Virginia Regiment, renamed the 5th West Virginia when the western counties gained statehood. After the war, President U. S. Grant appointed Ramsdell a postal inspector. He served in the West Virginia Senate in 1868 and 1869 and is said to have written the state's first school law. After his legislative stint, he again served the postal service for several years. He was a state-appointed trustee for the Virginia Central Railroad during its transformation into the Chesapeake & Ohio. Ramsdell was a delegate to the Republican national conventions that nominated Grant, Hayes, and Garfield for president.

Ramsdell died of consumption, December 9, 1886. The restored Z. D. Ramsdell House, a two-story Greek Revival brick building on Ceredo's B Street, serves as a museum. Ramsdell built the house, now on the National Register of Historic Places, in 1858. Tradition has it that Ramsdell aided runaways. His property was said to have contained a tunnel that could have accommodated escaping slaves.

See also Ceredo

Glade Little
St. Albans

Elizabeth Knight McClintic. "Ceredo: An Experiment in Colonization." M.A. thesis, Harvard-Radcliffe, 1937; Mose A. Napier, *Ceredo: Its Founders and Families*, 1989.

Randolph County

Randolph County, the largest county in the state with an area of 1,046.3 square miles, is located at the western edge of the Potomac Highlands in east-central West Virginia. Its high, forested mountains, many of which exceed 4,000 feet, lie at the headwaters of the Cheat, Tygart Valley, Elk, and Potomac rivers. The highest point in the county is in its extreme northeast corner on the Roaring Plains, a level area of land next to Dolly Sods, with an elevation of 4,782 feet. The lowest point is at 1,800 feet, at Laurel, where the Tygart Valley River leaves Randolph County for Barbour. Shavers Fork of Cheat River, which bisects Randolph County, enters the county at an elevation of 3,700 feet and leaves it at 1,765 feet.

The earliest settlements were those of the Robert Files (Foyles) and David Tygart families, who settled near present Beverly and Dailey in 1753–54. Most of the Files family were massacred by the Indians, and the Tygart family fled within a few months. By 1772, settlers had claimed most of the prime valley lands, but the continuing incursions of Indians deterred widespread settlement. A series of forts, including Wilson's, Roney's, Friend's, Hadden's, Currence's, and

The view from Rich Mountain is typical of Randolph County.

Westfall's, were built in the 1770s under the direction of frontiersman Benjamin Wilson. These forts offered some protection, but more than 100 settlers lost their lives in Indian raids during a period of 20 years.

Randolph County was formed from Harrison County in 1787 and was named for Edmund Randolph, governor of Virginia and later attorney general and secretary of state of the United States. The county seat was established at Edmundton in 1787. Edmundton was renamed Beverly and chartered in 1790. Beverly remained the county seat of Randolph County until the government was moved to Elkins in 1899, following a protracted and strongly contested legal battle for the location of the courthouse.

Farming was the principal livelihood for the settlers who had occupied the level terrain of the Leading Creek drainage and the broad bottomlands of the Tygart Valley River. These bottomlands extend 35 miles along the meandering river from Valley Head to Leadsville (Elkins). The coming of the early turnpikes brought some commercial activity, but the turmoil of the Civil War stunted development.

Most Randolph Countians preferred the Southern cause when the Civil War split the nation. The county voted in favor of secession when Virginia left the Union in 1861. Residents served on both sides during the bloody conflict, with most joining the Confederate forces. Some of the earliest action of the war took place in Randolph County. The Battle of Rich Mountain occurred five miles west of Beverly on July 11, 1861, when Gen. William S. Rosecrans routed the Confederate troops led by John Pegram. Other significant conflicts and fortifications were at Laurel Hill, Beverly, Huttonsville, Elkwater, Valley Mountain, and Cheat Mountain. Both Union Gen. George B. McClellan and Confederate Gen. Robert E. Lee received their early combat experience of the Civil War in Randolph County.

Since the turn of the 20th century, the county has been a major producer of hardwood lumber. There are extensive lumber and woodworking operations in Elkins, Beverly, Dailey, Mill Creek, Norton, and other areas. In 2005, Randolph County produced 61.3 million board feet of hardwood lumber and thousands of tons of pulpwood and rustic fencing. Some of this production came from the 202,000 acres of national forestland in the county.

Railroads played a vital role in the economic growth of Randolph County after industrialists Henry Gassaway Davis and his son-in-law, Stephen B. Elkins, extended the West Virginia Central & Pittsburg [*sic*] Railroad to Leadsville in 1889. They later constructed the Coal & Coke Railroad to Charleston. Within a decade, major railroad extensions provided the county with a direct connection with the main line of the Baltimore & Ohio Railroad. This offered a nationwide market for the county's abundant timber and coal. The Western Maryland Railway and the Chessie System continued to serve the county until the 1980s, when the CSX Railroad ended its service to the region. The West Virginia Railroad Authority now serves Randolph County.

With the coming of rail transportation, mining Randolph County's vast coal reserves became an important economic activity and remained so for many years. Coal production was 884,735 tons in 1920 and peaked at 1,237,000 tons in 1980, but had dwindled to practically nothing by 2004. In 2005, the county still had an estimated coal reserve of 2,416,000,000 tons.

The Elkins-Randolph County Airport, constructed in 1934–35, served as a terminal for major and commuter airlines for a half-century and is now the home port for many private and corporate aircraft. An automated flight service station operated by the U.S. government at the airport provides updates on weather and flight data for aircraft entering into the air space of West Virginia.

Davis & Elkins College, founded in Elkins in 1904, was named in honor of its two patrons, Henry Gassaway Davis and

FAST FACTS ABOUT RANDOLPH COUNTY

Founded: 1787

Land in square miles: 1,046.3

Population: 28,262

Percentage minorities: 2.3%

Percentage rural: 65.1%

Median age: 38.8

Percentage 65 and older: 15.1%

Birth rate per 1,000 population: 11.4

Median household income: $27,299

High school graduate or higher: 73.5%

Bachelor's degree or higher: 13.6%

Home ownership: 75.7%

Median home value: $71,800

This information is from the 2000 U.S. Census. In 2000, West Virginia as a whole had 5 percent minorities, a median age of 38.9, median household income of $29,696, and a 75.2 percent home ownership rate.

Stephen B. Elkins. The college is a four-year liberal arts institution affiliated with the Presbyterian Church. Other long-established institutions are the West Virginia Children's Home and the West Virginia Odd Fellows Home.

Agencies of federal and state governments maintain a strong presence in Randolph County. The Monongahela National Forest, with almost 909,000 acres in ten West Virginia counties, is headquartered in Elkins. The U.S. Fish and Wildlife Service and the West Virginia Division of Natural Resources administer and provide research in managing game and wildlife in the region. At Huttonsville, the state maintains the Huttonsville Correctional Center which houses an inmate population of about 900.

Randolph County became a haven for European families seeking land and opportunity in the United States in the 1880s. Several Irish families settled at Kingsville in 1845–60, and an English colony was established at Mingo Flats in 1883–95. Swiss immigrants were lured to the county in large numbers and established communities at Helvetia, Alpena, and Adolph during the period of 1869–81. The original settlers of the county included Germans and many Scotch-Irish.

Randolph County had 446 operating farms in 2002, with 101,108 of the county's 665,424 acres classified as farmland. There were 272 cattle farms, 33 hog farms, and 39 sheep farms sustained by more than 16,000 acres of corn and hay production. The population of the county was 27,803 in 1990, rising to 28,262 in 2000. Prominent Randolph Countians include Davis and Elkins, both U.S. senators as well as industrialists, and Senators Howard Sutherland and Jennings Randolph. Gov. Herman Guy Kump was a Randolph Countian, as was Gov. William W. Barron. Football player Marshall

"Biggie" Goldberg began his sports career at Elkins High School.

See also Elkins

Donald L. Rice
Elkins

Albert S. Bosworth, *History of Randolph County*, 1916; Anna D. Kek, ed., *Randolph County Profile-1976*, 1976; Donald L. Rice, *Randolph 200: A Bicentennial History of Randolph County, West Virginia*, 1987.

Jennings Randolph

Senator Jennings Randolph, who served in the U.S. Congress for 40 years, was born March 8, 1902, in Salem, Harrison County. His grandfather, Jesse Randolph, was the first mayor of Salem, a member of the state legislature, and the founder of Salem College (now Salem International University). His father, Ernest Randolph, was a lawyer and active in Democratic politics.

Jennings Randolph attended public school and Salem College Academy, from which he graduated in 1920. He then attended Salem College, where he was on the track, tennis, and basketball teams. In 1923, while still a student, he was elected to the college's board of trustees, on which he served for 50 years. He worked as a reporter and sports editor at the *Clarksburg Telegram* as a college student. After graduating from Salem in 1924, he worked in Charleston for the magazine, *West Virginia Review*. In 1926, Randolph became athletic director at Davis & Elkins College in Elkins. His football team won national fame for beating Navy 2-0 in 1926.

In 1930, the 28-year-old Randolph ran for Congress in the Second District, losing to three-term Republican incumbent Frank Bowman by only 1,111 votes. In 1932, Randolph ran again. This time he defeated Bowman by a 53 percent to 46 percent margin, part of the Franklin Roosevelt landslide. Randolph was present at

the Roosevelt inauguration, and when he retired from the Senate more than 50 years later he was the last member of Congress to have served during Roosevelt's first term. He was a solid supporter of Roosevelt's New Deal and something of a Roosevelt favorite. He worked with First Lady Eleanor Roosevelt on her project to create a model town at Arthurdale.

Randolph was reelected by solid margins in the next six elections, but in 1946, when Republicans won a big majority in the House, he was defeated. On leaving Congress, he became director of public relations at Capital Airlines, which later became part of United Airlines. An aviation enthusiast, in 1958 he flew from Morgantown to Washington on a plane fueled with gasoline made from West Virginia coal.

In January 1958, U.S. Sen. Matthew Neely died. Governor Underwood appointed Republican John Hoblitzell to fill the vacancy until a special election could be held in November. Randolph ran for the seat, beating former Governor Marland for the Democratic nomination. In the same primary, Congressman Robert Byrd was nominated to run against incumbent Republican Sen. Chapman Revercomb for a full term. There was a recession in 1958, which turned out to be a strong Democratic year. Both Byrd and Randolph were elected with 59 percent of the vote. Because he was elected to fill a vacancy, Randolph took office shortly after the election. Thus, he became West Virginia's senior senator, with a few week seniority over Byrd, who was sworn in at the regular inauguration in January 1959.

From 1965 to 1981, Randolph was chairman of the Senate's powerful Public Works Committee and from 1981 to 1985 the ranking minority member on the committee. Randolph supported the Interstate Highway program and massive

Senators Jennings Randolph (left) and Hubert Humphrey, November 22, 1959.

road-building efforts. He sponsored the 1965 Appalachian Regional Development Act, which created the Appalachian Regional Commission, and remained a primary supporter of the ARC throughout his service in the Senate. He sponsored legislation to aid the handicapped, to compensate victims of black lung disease, to ensure clean air and clean water, and to fund vocational and career education. On many cultural issues Randolph took conservative stands, but he supported the Civil Rights Act of 1964 and subsequent civil rights legislation. Eleven times he sponsored a constitutional amendment to allow 18-year-olds to vote, and in 1971 had the satisfaction of seeing it approved. He sponsored the creation of the National Academy of Peace.

Jennings Randolph was, in the tradition of his namesake William Jennings Bryan, an old-style orator. When he rose to announce that he had "a few words" to say, he could be counted on to contribute many more than a few. Yet his good nature and his self-evident good intentions ensured that he caused few resentments from colleagues, by whom, on both sides of the aisle, he was held in great affection.

In 1960, 1966, and 1972, Senator Randolph was reelected by wide margins. In 1978, at age 76, he was opposed by former (and future) Governor Moore, and for the first time conducted a modern campaign with pollsters and carefully calibrated television advertisements. He was reelected with just 50.5 percent of the vote. As this term approached its end, it was not clear whether he would run for reelection. Governor Rockefeller, who had worked hard for Randolph's reelection in 1978, was invited to Randolph's Capitol hideaway office. In his 1998 eulogy of Randolph, Rockefeller recalled, "He had a very nice breakfast there. He was very relaxed. Then he simply turned to me and he said, 'Jay, would you like to be the next senator from West Virginia?' "

To the public Randolph said, "It's been a happy road. I have no regrets . . . I believe the Bible says there is a season and a time for every purpose. It is time for me not to run for reelection." Jennings Randolph spent his final years in a nursing home and died May 8, 1998, at age 96.

Michael Barone
The Almanac of American Politics

Donald L. Rasmussen

Doctor Donald L. Rasmussen, black lung crusader, was born February 24, 1928, in Colorado. He came to West Virginia in 1962 as associate chief of internal medicine at Miners Memorial Hospital, in Beckley. Throughout the 1960s, he actively engaged in ground-breaking research in the chronic lung disease of coal miners.

Rasmussen advanced his conclusion that simple pneumoconiosis which fre-

quently did not show up on lung x-rays nevertheless caused the breathlessness among miners that might be apparent only through exercises on a treadmill accompanied by a blood-gas test. By the late 1960s, Rasmussen joined with doctors I. E. Buff and Hawey Wells to hold a series of rallies at which thousands of miners demanded state and federal action to protect against high levels of coal dust and to compensate those afflicted with black lung.

In dramatic testimony as well as articles in influential medical journals, Rasmussen was a driving force in the passage of state and federal black lung legislation. He was also an active participant in the United Mine Workers presidential campaigns of Jock Yablonski and Arnold Miller against W. A. "Tony" Boyle. In 1969, the American Public Health Association conferred its Presidential Award on Rasmussen for exceptional service in the fight against black lung. In 1995, he was named "Civil Libertarian of the Year" by the West Virginia Civil Liberties Union.

See also Black Lung Disease, I. E. Buff

Ken Hechler
Charleston

The Rathbone Well

The Rathbone Well, West Virginia's first major oil well, was drilled in 1860. William P. Rathbone, a New York City judge and alderman, and his sons, John Castelli "Cass" Rathbone and John Valleau "Val" Rathbone, had purchased 12,000 acres at Burning Springs Run in Wirt County in 1840. They laid out a small village, Burning Springs, later Rathbone, and operated a general store, gristmill, and boat yard. They also bottled and sold petroleum as a medicine, "Rathbone's Rock Oil, Nature's Wonder Cure."

In 1860, a Pennsylvania promoter, Samuel D. Karnes, leased an acre from the Rathbones and introduced derrick drilling techniques modeled after those of the pioneering Drake oil well at Titusville, Pennsylvania. Within a few weeks, Karnes was producing 30 barrels of oil a day. Following his lead, Cass Rathbone sank a well on his property to a depth of 140 feet, hitting a gusher that produced 100 barrels a day. News spread and others rushed to Burning Springs. Johnson Newlon Camden, later a U.S. senator and Standard Oil director, along with partners including John Jay Jackson Sr., brought in "The Eternal Center" well in January 1861, earning them $23,000 the first week of production. The Rathbones made a fortune leasing one-acre tracts to wildcatters.

On May 9, 1863, a Confederate raiding party under Gen. William E. Jones set fire to the Burning Springs oil field and to crude oil being stored in the area. Flames from the fire could be seen in Parkers-

burg, 40 miles away. Though Camden and the Rathbones repaired the damage and continued to drill, Burning Springs never rose to its pre-war production. The discovery of new fields elsewhere in Wirt and surrounding counties moved the center of the industry to other locations.

See also Burning Springs, Burning Springs Raid, Natural Gas and Petroleum, Wirt County

Philip Sturm
Ohio Valley University

Ravenswood

Named after Lord Ravenswood in Sir Walter Scott's novel, *The Bride of Lammermoor*, Ravenswood is located in Jackson County along the Ohio River at an elevation of 620 feet. It was incorporated as a town on March 10, 1852, by the Virginia legislature. With a 2000 population of 4,031, Ravenswood is the largest community in Jackson County.

George Washington surveyed the area in 1770 and later acquired 2,448 acres. Early settlers included Ezekiel McFarland (1799) on Big Sandy Creek, followed by Lawrence Lane and John Nesselroade. During the Civil War the Battle of Buffington Island was fought near Ravenswood in 1863, and the area was troubled by bushwhacking between Union and Confederate supporters. The economy grew rapidly due to agriculture, banks, canning, trading, and riverboat commerce. The Ravenswood, Spencer & Glenville Railroad was established in 1886.

Ravenswood citizens have worked in the aluminum industry since 1953, and in health services, schools, and local government; other employers include construction companies, trucking, plastics, train and river freight, and automotive supplies. The Ritchie Bridge across the Ohio River opened Ravenswood to Ohio. A small airport serves light planes.

In the early 1990s, a bitter labor dispute split Ravenswood. The old Kaiser Aluminum plant was operated by Ravenswood Aluminum Corporation at the time. The town was divided as the strikers fought to get their jobs back while others chose to work nonunion. The impasse was finally resolved in 1992 under the threat of a pending National Labor Relations Board ruling on unfair labor practices.

See also Ravenswood Strike

Dean Moore
Cincinnati, Ohio

Ravenswood Strike

When union contract negotiations broke down at the Ravenswood Aluminum Corporation, supervisors turned away workers reporting for the midnight shift on October 31, 1990. A bitter struggle ensued with members of Local 5668 of the United Steelworkers of America, lasting until

June 29, 1992, and becoming one of the most widely reported labor disputes of the late 20th century. While commonly perceived as a strike, the union considered the dispute a company lockout.

Ravenswood Aluminum, located at Ravenswood, Jackson County, began as a plant of Kaiser Aluminum as the giant metals company expanded in the aftermath of World War II. From its opening in 1954 until Kaiser sold its aluminum plants in 1988, Ravenswood workers had never been on strike. But with the globalization of the industry in the 1980s, manufacturers sought cost-cutting measures that workers said jeopardized their safety and health. Indeed, during the summer before the lockout, four workers had died on the job at Ravenswood.

Local 5668 made safety and health a prime bargaining issue when negotiations began in the fall. The union confronted new owners with different ideas; the plant had changed ownership several times between 1988 and 1990. The current owners had acquired the plant through a leveraged buyout with a determination to cut production costs. Management demanded concessions and refused to budge on safety issues.

The next 20 months nearly tore the town apart. The plant owners decided to operate with replacement workers, known as "scabs" to the strikers. The practice was illegal if the company had in fact locked out the workers, but the state's panel from the Department of Employment Security ruled that Ravenswood Aluminum had not engaged in a lockout. The union appealed to the National Labor Relations Board, where hearings and a decision would take months. Local 5668 worked to maintain morale through rallies, pickets, support groups, and a pooling of resources led by strikers and their families. Both the company and the union claimed that the other side engaged in violence and intimidation, and there were shootings, destruction of property, and other incidents in the community and around the plant and picket lines.

Meanwhile, the union began a "corporate campaign," charging illegal activities by the ownership group, which included the international fugitive Marc Rich. Union members found themselves in demonstrations at corporate headquarters and government meetings in such places as Switzerland and the Netherlands. This campaign attracted such attention that negotiations finally reopened in April 1992. With an NLRB decision imminent, negotiators reached an agreement that allowed all union members to return to the plant.

Ken Fones-Wolf
West Virginia University

Tom Juravich and Kate Bronfenbrenner, *Ravenswood: The Steelworkers' Victory and the Revival of American Labor,* 1999.

Rebel Records

Rebel Records, which operated in Asbury, Greenbrier County, from 1974 through 1979, developed into a major force in bluegrass music. The company had been founded in 1959 at Mt. Rainier, Maryland, by Bill Carroll and Richard Freeland, the latter soon becoming the sole owner. In its early years the firm recorded several country and bluegrass singles, primarily by artists in the Baltimore-Washington area, but by the 1970s concentrated on the bluegrass album market. The Country Gentleman, the Seldom Scene, and Ralph Stanley's Clinch Mountain Boys, among the largest names in the music, constituted Rebel's principal acts. In 1974, Freeland moved his operation to Asbury in Greenbrier County, where it remained until he sold the firm to David Freeman of Roanoke, Virginia, who already owned County Records. Freeman continues to operate both companies from Virginia. Expatriate West Virginians who have recorded for Rebel include fiddler Curly Ray Cline, the Goins Brothers, Cliff Waldron, and Wilma Lee Cooper. In 1992, Richard Freeland re-entered the business when he started Freeland Records, also in Asbury, which remains in operation today.

See also Bluegrass Music

Ivan M. Tribe
University of Rio Grande

Recht Decision

West Virginia education policy was shaped throughout the late 20th century by a court decision rendered by Judge Arthur Recht in a case challenging the equity of school policy. In 1975, Janet Pauley filed a class-action law suit against the Lincoln County school system, alleging the Pauley children and others attending schools in property-poor counties were not receiving educational opportunities equal to students in richer counties. She also alleged the quality of their education did not meet the "thorough and efficient" standard required by the state constitution. Pauley's attorney, Dan Hedges, argued this standard guaranteed all school children in the state an equal opportunity to a high quality, free public education. The case was dismissed from Circuit Court and appealed to the West Virginia Supreme Court of Appeals.

The Supreme Court, ruling in Pauley's favor, confirmed that education was "a fundamental, constitutional right." Public school children were entitled to an equal opportunity to public education statewide, and the Supreme Court ruled that the legislature has a constitutional mandate "to develop a high quality statewide education system." The case was remanded to Circuit Court to collect evidence to see if West Virginia's schools met these constitutional standards. Judge Recht of Ohio County presided over the trial.

For 17 months, testimony was presented by more than 30 education experts in an effort to establish the standards for a "high quality education" and to determine whether all West Virginia schools met those standards. On March 11, 1982, Judge Recht issued a voluminous opinion detailing the standards established by the expert testimony. He ruled that West Virginia schools fell short of meeting these standards and that the funding system caused unequal education opportunities from county to county.

This decision, generally referred to as the "Recht Decision," was controversial. Critics alleged the standards were set so high that they could never be achieved. Proponents argued the state's survival depended upon the education of its youth. The State Department of Education was charged with the duty to implement the decision. On December 12, 1984, in the case of *Pauley v. Bailey*, the West Virginia Supreme Court approved the Education Department's Master Plan for Public Education.

While no school in West Virginia has ever met all of the standards established by the Recht decision or the Master Plan, the litigation led to sweeping improvements in public education. Hundreds of millions of dollars was spent on new schools, upgraded facilities, and improved curriculum. The school aid formula was modified to provide a more equal distribution of state funds to counties. The Circuit Court retained jurisdiction in the case to monitor the schools' progress. In January 2003, Judge Recht ended the decades-long period of educational reform by closing the case and relinquishing jurisdiction.

See also Education

William McGinley
West Virginia Education Association

The Recollections of Fifty Years

The Recollections of Fifty Years of West Virginia, a West Virginia classic, was written by William Alexander MacCorkle, West Virginia's ninth governor (1893–97). Many of the 26 chapters detail the talents, quirks, and foibles of notable lawyers during a period of intense social, political, and industrial change. It was a time when basic issues of land ownership, land use, mineral rights, taxes, and transportation were carved out in the state's courtrooms, and MacCorkle knew the principal players.

MacCorkle came to West Virginia in 1876 to teach in Pocahontas County, later studied law at Washington and Lee University, then opened a law practice in Charleston. His reminiscences of fellow lawyers and the judges before whom they practiced fill most of the pages of his *Recollections.* He sketches in the state's history and his own early life and ancestry in the early chapters. A local color chapter describes the people and customs of the mountains. MacCorkle discusses his experience as governor in four chapters near the end of the book. *The Recollections of Fifty Years* was published by G. P. Putnam's Sons Publishing Company in 1928, two years before MacCorkle's death. There is a foreword by John W. Davis of Clarksburg, presidential candidate and U.S. ambassador to Great Britain.

See also William Alexander MacCorkle

Phyllis Wilson Moore
Clarksburg

William Alexander MacCorkle, *The Recollections of Fifty Years of West Virginia*, 1928.

Reconstruction

Reconstruction was the period after the Civil War, when the nation attempted to "reconstruct" the returning Southern states. West Virginia's Reconstruction experience was unique. As a former slave state it underwent some of the readjustments of other such states. But West Virginia had been created by the war, as a Union state in opposition to the secession of Virginia. Thus its Reconstruction most resembles the experience of the border slave states that did not secede, Kentucky, Missouri, and Maryland. While not subject to the harsh measures applied farther south, these states suffered a legacy of bitterness from the often violent competition between Union and Confederate loyalists during the post-war years.

As in all the former slave states, there was an attempt after the war by men who had been political outsiders to democratize and modernize the political system. In West Virginia, however, the outsiders were not "carpetbaggers" or freed slaves but local white politicians long held down by Virginia's laws of representation and taxation. West Virginia Unionists were sharply divided between traditional states' rights Democrats, who feared federal power and racial change, and unconditional Unionists, soon to be Republicans, who accepted federal dictates on emancipation in return for guarantees of statehood. The new state government's attempts to eliminate the old county court system of local government, to establish public education, and to reform property assessments and taxation were rooted in earlier, failed efforts to free the mountain sections of Virginia from slaveholder control. Much of what the new West Virginians wanted from Reconstruction was what they had for decades wanted from Virginia.

There was some fear that the young state would be lost, reabsorbed into Virginia after the war. These concerns were exacerbated by Virginia's recalcitrance and the decision of the statemakers to include within West Virginia a southern tier of counties that had supported secession and the Confederacy. There was also a lingering residue of guerrilla warfare.

So the new Unionists' treatment of Confederate sympathizers was linked not to freedmen's rights or to Republican economic programs as it was in the Deep South, but to the fate of the state itself.

The result was that oaths attesting to past Union loyalty, harshly enforced to eliminate the votes of former Confederates, stood at the heart of political Reconstruction in West Virginia. The conservative orientation of many statemakers meant the Republican majority created by these voting restrictions was not used to promote black freedom, however. The end to slavery, the grant of basic civil rights, and the black vote all came because of federal pressure, and never were allowed to threaten preexisting racial relations. While spared the worst of the Jim Crow period that followed, African-Americans emerged from the Civil War and Reconstruction as second-class citizens in West Virginia.

By 1870, when it was clear that the state's survival was assured, that anti-Confederate restrictions could not be maintained, and that common interests in industrial development could unite moderates of all factions, the test oaths were rescinded. An amendment to the state constitution, formalizing these changes, was passed by the voters in 1871. Their voting strength thus bolstered, Democrats took power. As in other "redeemed" states, Reconstruction changes were not completely swept away in West Virginia. Although the less-than-democratic county court system returned and support for black institutions waned, public schools remained, as did the secret ballot, and the young state moved toward an industrial, not agrarian, future.

See also Flick Amendment, Formation of West Virginia

Ralph Mann
University of Colorado

Red Ash, Rush Run Explosions

West Virginia's first major mine explosion of the 20th century occurred March 6, 1900, at Red Ash Mine on New River in Fayette County. On the night of March 5, a machine operator had left open a ventilating trap door, allowing methane to gather. The next morning, some workers, violating both custom and state law, traveled toward their working faces before the late-arriving fireboss had completed his gas checks. Probably, their open lights set off a methane ignition which instantly brought explosive coal dust into the air, adding to the intensity of the blast. Several kegs of blasting powder ignited as the explosion coursed through the mine, twisting rails, destroying mine cars, and hurling men, mules, and timbers against the ribs.

As usual in coal mine explosions, most of the 46 victims suffocated in the carbon monoxide atmosphere (afterdamp) fol-

lowing the blast, including the fireboss, who had held his vest to his face in a futile effort to filter the afterdamp. Recovery workers reached the last of the victims on March 10, and the mine resumed operation on March 26.

Five years later a second tragedy occurred at the Red Ash Mine, by then connected to the neighboring Rush Run Mine. Rush Run and Red Ash mines maintained, by the standards of the day, excellent ventilation. Yet, fine coal dust created by mining machinery abounded. On the evening of March 18, 1905, only 13 men remained underground in the two mines. In a freak occurrence, a mine car ran over some loose explosives. The resulting concussion and flame suspended and ignited coal dust, causing a massive explosion which coursed through both mines.

Carelessly, a rescue party, some carrying open-flame lights, entered the Red Ash portal. Either burning timbers or the rescuers' open lights set off another explosion. Although not as powerful as the first, this second explosion on March 19 killed all 11 members of the rescue party underground, shot flame out the drift mouth, and tossed people standing outside several feet down the hillside toward New River. It required ten days to restore ventilation and recover all 24 bodies.

See also Coal Mine Disasters

Paul H. Rakes
WVU Institute of Technology

Lacy Dillon, *They Died in Darkness*, 1976; Shirley Donnelly, *Notable Mine Disasters of Fayette County, West Virginia*, 1951.

Red House Shoal

The Red House Shoal is located on the Kanawha River near the town of Red House in Putnam County. A rock ledge in the river with nearly a three-foot drop, the shoal was a serious obstacle to navigation before the river was dammed and its depth increased. Beginning in 1829, the State of Virginia began blasting and excavating shoals in the Kanawha River including the Red House shoal. The blasting at Red House Shoal created a very swift chute for boats to navigate through. This chute became a famous challenge among rivermen. The *Robert Thompson*, the first steamboat to attempt to get to Charleston, failed because of its inability to pass the shoal in 1819. The *Thompson* spent two days trying to pass over it before returning to the Ohio River. Just over a year later, the *Andrew Donnally* would best the Red House Shoals and land at Charleston. Passage became easier when the chute was blasted, but because of a bend in the river just upstream and the swiftness of the current passing through the chute, Red House remained difficult until the high-lift locks and dams were built in the 1930s.

See also Kanawha River

Gerald W. Sutphin
Huntington

Leland R. Johnson, *Men, Mountains and Rivers,* 1977; Gerald W. Sutphin and Richard A. Andre, *Sternwheelers On The Great Kanawha River,* 1991.

Red Jacket Case

The 1927 federal court case *United Mine Workers of America v. Red Jacket Consolidated Coal and Coke Company,* affirming the use of injunctions against union organizing efforts, was a landmark event in West Virginia labor history. The litigation was an important element in massive employer resistance to unionization in West Virginia's southern coalfields. It symbolized for many the central role of the courts in accommodating the industry.

By 1920, the UMW had launched a vigorous campaign to unionize southern West Virginia. John L. Lewis announced the effort in a January speech in Bluefield soon after becoming president of the union. Coal operators were equally determined to stay nonunion, and a major conflict ensued.

One tactic the operators used was to require each of their employees to sign a so-called yellow-dog contract, in which the worker agreed not to join a union or to urge others to do so. Then, if the union attempted to recruit a company's miners, the company sued to enjoin the union from interfering with these individual employment contracts. The tactic spread throughout the region during the early 1920s. In all, 231 southern West Virginia coal companies filed federal court actions, and the requested injunctions were issued to each. The court orders barred union organizers from (among other things) holding meetings, distributing information, urging the companies' workers to join the union, paying court costs for fired workers evicted from their company houses, and giving aid to striking miners. State courts issued similar injunctions to 85 more companies. The union appealed the federal cases, which were consolidated in the Fourth Circuit Court of Appeals into the *Red Jacket* case.

That court sustained a previous judge's finding that the union had violated antitrust laws by conspiring to interfere with production and shipment of coal, and that the union had interfered with the company's employment contracts with its workers by asking miners working under the yellow-dog contract to join the union. Thus the injunctions were held to be proper. The UMW appealed to the U.S. Supreme Court, but it denied review.

The *Red Jacket* decision rendered southern West Virginia virtually off-limits to the UMW, a condition that persisted until federal legislation in the mid-'30s effectively overturned the holdings in the case.

See also Labor History, Yellow-Dog Contract

Robert M. Bastress
WVU College of Law

Red Robin Inn

A landmark tavern on old U.S. 119 at Borderland, a few miles north of Williamson, the Red Robin Inn was for many years owned and operated by Charlie Blevins, retired coal miner and memorable singer and banjo picker. Later obliterated by the construction of the Corridor G highway, the inn was a gathering place for local story swappers, and the scene of many great old-time music jam sessions. The Red Robin Inn doubled as a regional museum with implements related to coal mining and farming hanging on the wall above the bar and dozens of photographs of local characters, most notably the picture of a barefoot, 12-toed moonshiner taken at his trial in a local courtroom.

Charlie Blevins's tales recalled the earliest settlement of Mingo County. He said his pioneer ancestors walked to the area leading an old milk cow. When they got hungry or thirsty they just stopped and milked. He lamented that the construction of Corridor G would "wipe out our heritage." After the demise of the Red Robin Inn in March 1993, Charlie Blevins relocated across the Tug Fork River in Pike County, Kentucky, and opened a museum called the Red Robin Plateau.

Michael Kline
St. Mary's City, Maryland

Red Spruce Forests

Red spruce forests covered the higher slopes and mountaintops of the Alleghenies when Europeans ventured into the wilderness in the mid-1700s. Later

A red spruce forest at Gaudineer Knob.

naturalists, including A. B. Brooks, Charles Millspaugh, and A. D. Hopkins, estimated that the original red spruce covered 469,000 acres, mostly in present Pocahontas, Randolph and Tucker counties. Unwise practices of converting spruce forests to grazing land by the slash and burn practice of girdling trees and then burning the forest, destroyed large areas of the original spruce forest. Wildfires escaping from campfires of Civil War troops and "rings of fire" set by deer hunters added to the toll. The remaining red spruce was cut by timber barons, except for a 50-acre tract near Gaudineer Knob.

The red spruce, West Virginia's only native spruce, was a magnificent tree, reaching 70 to 100 feet in height and two to three feet in diameter. Many of the pure spruce forests produced 30,000 to 50,000 board feet per acre, while the better Canaan Valley stands averaged 80,000 to 100,000. By comparison, many good hardwood stands of today only average 15,000 to 20,000 board feet per acre.

Most of the spruce was sawed into lumber or converted to pulp for papermaking. High-quality boards were used as airplane frames and sounding boards for pianos. By 1920, most of the spruce forests had been intentionally or accidentally destroyed. Only 50,000 of the original 469,000 acres regenerated with red spruce. The rest became pasture or hardwoods that were often dominated by scrubby trees, shrubs, or waste areas.

Spruce forests are the stronghold for many warblers, snowshoe hare, Cheat Mountain salamander, northern flying squirrel, and northern fox squirrel. Dolly Sods and Spruce Knob are examples of spruce forest destruction, while Blackwater Falls State Park and Gaudineer Knob-Shavers Fork are examples of good spruce forests.

William N. Grafton
WVU Extension Service

Red Sulphur Springs

Red Sulphur Springs, located on State Route 12 in southern Monroe County, was the site of a popular mineral spring resort from the 1820s until World War I. The spring water emerges from the ground at 54 degrees F. and leaves a purplish-red sulfurous deposit which was used to treat skin conditions. The water was believed to be useful in the treatment of tuberculosis. Modern analysis shows the water to be high in bicarbonate, sulfate, and calcium.

The history of Red Sulphur Springs is uncertain before 1800, but it is thought that Indians made use of the spring. The site was acquired around 1800 by Nicholas Harvey. His sons were the first to develop the property in the 1820s by constructing cabins for the use of visitors.

In 1833, the property was purchased by Dr. William Burke who formed a corporation and embarked on an ambitious building campaign. A spring pavilion and several buildings for the accommodation and entertainment of 300 guests were constructed.

The golden age of the Red Sulphur resort came before 1861. During the Civil War soldiers from both armies occupied the buildings. Following the war the resort continued operation, and in the 1890s it was purchased by Levi Morton, U.S. vice-president under Benjamin Harrison. Morton upgraded the property and operated the resort successfully until around 1915, when he offered it to the state of West Virginia for use as a tuberculosis sanatorium. He sold the property after his offer was rejected by the state. Around 1920, the buildings were dismantled and the resort ceased operation.

See also Mineral Springs

Michael M. Meador
Abingdon, Virginia

Redeemers

The Redeemers, once a faction in the Democratic Party, helped to establish Democrat rule in West Virginia after the Civil War. Though Republicans were the Union party and had controlled West Virginia throughout the war, Democrats remained a force in state politics. The Democratic Party was composed of groups that historian John Alexander Williams labeled the "Redeemers, Regulars, Agrarians and the Kanawha Ring." The Redeemers, largely former Confederates whose philosophies reflected rural and antebellum values, were strongest in eastern and southern counties. The Redeemers were hampered by post-war laws restricting the right of ex-Confederates to vote and hold office. During this period Regulars such as Johnson Newlon Camden and Henry Gassaway Davis increased their political power at the expense of the ex-Confederates. Redeemers, representing the landed aristocracy, viewed industrialists such as Davis and Camden with suspicion.

The party eventually realized that ex-Confederates had to be brought back into the political arena. The solution was the 1871 Flick Amendment, which guaranteed the right to vote to all males over 21 and repealed the political restrictions on former Confederates. Redeemers then quickly became a force in Democratic politics, and several members of the group were elected to statewide office. Redeemers had great influence in the Constitutional Convention of 1872 and restored much of the pre-Civil War political organization at the state and county levels. In 1876, Henry Mason Mathews, a Redeemer and former Confederate officer, was elected the first of the so-called "Bourbon" governors. His election was the culmination of the redemption of the former Confederates. Gradually there was a melding of philosophies between the Regulars and Redeemers which would see Democratic governors seek, and support, industrial development of West Virginia.

See also Flick Amendment

Kenneth R. Bailey
WVU Institute of Technology

John Alexander Williams, "The New Dominion and the Old: Antebellum and Statehood Politics as the Background of West Virginia's 'Bourbon Democracy,'" *West Virginia History*, July 1972.

Blind Alfred Reed

Musician Blind Alfred Reed, a street singer and fiddler from Pipestem, Summers County, composed and recorded some of the most creative topical country songs on Victor Records between 1927 and 1929. Although born in Floyd County, Virginia, June 15, 1880, Reed lived most of his life in West Virginia.

In 1927, he wrote "The Wreck of the Virginian" and recorded it in Bristol, Tennessee, in July. Other Reed ballads also dwelled on local and regional tragedies, such as "The Fate of Chris Lively and Wife" and "Explosion in the Fairmont Mines." Still others of his songs included a lyric with an anti-flapper message, "Why Do You Bob Your Hair, Girls?," and a humorous view of domestic violence, "Black and Blue Blues." Some reflected a populist viewpoint such as "How Can a Poor Man Stand Such Times and Live?" and the sacred "There'll Be No Distinction There."

Deeply religious, Reed served as a Methodist lay preacher until his death January 17, 1956. He sometimes performed with his son, Arville, and a fiddler neighbor, Fred Pendleton, as the West Virginia Night Owls. His complete recordings appeared on compact disc on the Document label in 1998.

Ivan M. Tribe
University of Rio Grande

Henry Reed

Musician Henry Reed was a legendary West Virginia fiddler whose repertory contributed to the old-time music revival in the last half of the 20th century. Many of his tunes have gone back into circulation in fiddling circles, and one particular tune, "Over the Waterfall," is now widely known throughout the country.

Born James Henry Neel Reed, April 28, 1884, near Peterstown in Monroe County, he spent much of his adult life in nearby Glen Lyn, Virginia. He learned music in Monroe County, absorbing the tunes of many fiddlers of the older generation, including "Quince" Dillion, born in 1810 and a fifer in the Mexican War.

Reed was known as a fiddler, three-finger banjo picker, and harmonica player.

His music ranged from the older Virginia repertory of frontier days to late 19th-century rags, waltzes, and popular songs and 20th-century country songs and bluegrass tunes. He never recorded commercially, but Alan Jabbour, a graduate student at Duke University, recorded him frequently in 1966–67. Jabbour played Reed's tunes on fiddle with a Durham-Chapel Hill ensemble, the Hollow Rock String Band. Henry Reed's music quickly radiated throughout the country among young instrumental musicians drawn to old-time Appalachian music.

Henry Reed died June 16, 1968, in Glen Lyn. By the later 20th century, his tunes were a significant component in the general repertory of American old-time music, although few had heard him directly until the Library of Congress mounted all of his recordings on its Internet web site.

See also Fiddle Tradition

Alan Jabbour
Library of Congress

Ida L. Reed

Hymnist Ida Lilliard Reed, born into a Methodist family, November 30, 1865, on a hilltop farm near Philippi, wrote some 2,000 hymns and songs. The best-known of her hymns, "I Belong to the King," still commonly appears in Protestant hymnals. Reed also wrote poems and children's stories intended for Sunday schools and used throughout the world. She wrote several books, including her autobiography, *My Life Story*, published in 1912. Her book, *The Story of a Song: What It Means to Belong to the King,* was published in 1911. Her last book, published in 1940, was titled *Songs of the Hills*. Reed also wrote for a Christian journal titled *West Virginia Protestant.*

One of eight children, Reed experienced many illnesses and family deaths and constant poverty but persisted in believing and stating that God's love is available to all people and is expressed through nature and in the caring of people for each other. Self-educated, Ida Reed never earned royalties on her work, instead selling her pieces outright for a few dollars each. She never married, although her name is sometimes given as Smith. A marker on the Arden Road north of Philippi points the way to her birthplace and home. Ida Reed died July 8, 1951.

Barbara Smith
Philippi

Reedsville Experimental Community
See Arthurdale.

Nat Reese

Blues musician Nathaniel H. "Nat" Reese was born March 4, 1924, in Salem, Virginia. When he was four, Reese's family moved to Itmann, Wyoming County, where coal jobs were plentiful. In 1935, the family moved to Princeton where

Bluesman Nat Reese (1924–).

Reese heard a rich musical mix from big-name jazz musicians, local black musicians, and performers on such radio broadcasts as the *Grand Ole Opry*. He learned to play instruments, including guitar, piano, organ, bass, and string harp.

Reese worked in the coal mines after classes at Genoa High School. For two years, he played jazz and blues on Bill Farmer's Saturday night show on radio station WHIS Bluefield. He attended Bluefield State College for two years, then left to serve in the U.S. Army during World War II. During and after his college years, he was part of a dance band that played jazz, polkas, and blues throughout the southern coalfields.

In the early 1950s, Reese moved to Michigan and worked in construction, returning to West Virginia in 1959 to work for the State Road Commission. In 1962, he was hired as a photographic silk-screen printer at Rockwell International's aviation plant in Princeton, where he stayed for 13 years.

Reese, who lives in Princeton, plays and teaches at the annual Augusta Heritage Arts Workshops at Davis & Elkins College, and continues to perform regularly. His recordings include "Just a Dream" and "West Virginia Blues by the West Virginia Blues Man." Among his honors are the 1988 John Henry Award and the 1995 Vandalia Award.

Michael Kline, "Something to Give: Nat Reese's Early Life and Music," *Goldenseal*, Winter 1987.

Reforestation

In early times, forests were so common in present West Virginia that standing timber was an over-abundant commodity. Cleared land was worth more than land with trees. The clearing of land for agriculture was the dominant cause of forest reduction. Logging historian Roy B.

Clarkson, in his book *Tumult on the Mountains*, discusses the lack of value that timber had and the years of arduous labor necessary to clear fields. He concludes that the "very best timber" ever to grow in West Virginia was destroyed in the clearing of farmland.

According to census statistics, about 1.8 million acres, 12 percent of the total acreage of what is now West Virginia, was cleared for agriculture before 1850. In the decade of the 1850s, 600,000 more acres was cleared. This was followed by 400,000 acres in the 1860s; 1.3 million acres in the 1870s; 800,000 acres in the 1880s; 900,000 acres in the 1890s; and 200,000 acres between 1900 and 1909. By the latter decades, the land was being cleared for its timber as well as for farming. The forests had been largely removed from the counties bordering the Ohio River, and the valuable timber adjacent to principal streams had been removed in nearly every part of the state except the southern counties. Narrow gauge railroads soon made it possible to log in that area.

By 1900, 61 percent of the states's land was cleared. Then the process began to reverse itself. Hundreds of thousands of acres used to grow food for draft animals was released from production with the advent of automobiles and farm tractors. Hybrid seeds and mineral fertilizers increased crop yields and released additional acreage from production. In West Virginia, the abandonment of the steeper cropland accelerated. Soon seeds from trees on adjacent land were carried to the cleared tracts by the wind, gravity, or animals; and nature began its inexorable reclamation of cleared land. Old fields grew into briars and brush and eventually returned to forest.

A 1945 news release by the U.S. Forest Service listed 9.86 million acres of forestland in West Virginia. This is 64 percent of the state's total land area. A new inventory in 1961 showed a dramatic increase to 74 percent of the land area. By 1975, the forest area had increased to 11.6 million acres, or 75 percent of the land area. This increased by 1988 to 12.1 million acres, or 78 percent of the state. It remained the same in 2000. The net reforestation is remarkable considering the thousands of acres removed by the construction of interstate highways, oil and gas and utility rights-of-way, surface mining activities, the growth of urban areas, and the construction of thousands of new rural homes.

At the beginning of the 21st century, West Virginia is the third most densely forested state, ranking behind Maine and New Hampshire. Seven counties have less than 60 percent of their area in timberland, and 20 counties exceed 80 percent. Both Webster and McDowell counties have more than 93 percent of their area in forests. The reforestation of West Virginia is not yet complete, but it is well on its way.

See also Forests

William H. Gillespie
Charleston

Roy B. Clarkson, *Tumult on the Mountains: Lumbering in West Virginia—1770–1920,* 1964.

Regional Education Service Agencies

Prior to the 1970s, West Virginia school systems formed local consortiums in order to pool resources and effort. In 1972, West Virginia passed legislation authorizing the state Department of Education to create Regional Education Service Agencies (RESAs). County boards of education were grouped into eight regional units, or RESAs, to provide certain services on a regional basis.

Each RESA is governed by a board of directors. Each county superintendent, one representative from each county's board of education, and a member selected by the state Department of Education serve on the board of directors of each RESA. Related agencies or institutions may also have representatives if the RESA chooses to include them. Each RESA is administered by an executive director who is hired by its board of directors. The executive director and chairperson of the board of each RESA periodically meet with the state Board of Education.

A wide range of services and programs is provided through this regional arrangement. Schools share staff who provide direct student services, such as physical therapy, occupational therapy, and speech therapy. RESAs sponsor spelling bees, science fairs, and other academic competitions. They organize partnerships with outside institutions, such as the "Gear Up" program for college readiness. Professional training is offered on a wide variety of topics for staff and substitute teachers within the region. Recently, RESAs have begun to provide technical assistance to improve low-performing schools. Through RESAs, member schools attain greater equality of educational opportunities, delivery of services at a lower per-student cost, more effective use of funds, and more efficient administration.

Elizabeth Ann H. McClain
Montrose

Regionalism

West Virginia, born of irreparable regional differences in the mother state of Virginia, soon developed a strong regionalism of its own. West Virginia's regions are based ultimately in geography and geology. Areas having good soil and workable terrain, including much of the Eastern Panhandle and major river valleys, became agricultural areas and remain so today. The state's rich natural resource base determined the regional character of other areas, including the southern coalfields.

The layout of the state's rivers, providing early travel routes and bottomland for settlement, helped to establish regional distinctions. The Ohio River, while offering a broad valley suitable for both farms and cities, also furnished transportation to the South and Midwest. Not surprisingly, the valley and adjoining areas developed economic and political affinities away from eastern Virginia. The same combination of terrain and transportation later favored industrial development. The Ohio Valley became in the 20th century West Virginia's main industrial corridor, with chemical, steel, glass, manufacturing, and power-generation plants scattered from Hancock County to Wayne County. The Kanawha and Monongahela valleys developed as industrial centers as well, for similar reasons.

West Virginia has two broad physiological provinces, the Ridge and Valley, including most of the Eastern Panhandle and the string of counties to the southwest of the panhandle along the Virginia state line, and the Allegheny Plateau, which includes the rest of the state.

These broad regions interacted with people from the time of early settlement. The flat-floored valleys and limestone soils of the Ridge and Valley region were sought by German, Scotch-Irish, and English settlers for agricultural use, and these settlers developed trade centers to support their efforts. The valleys of the Eastern Panhandle and the adjoining Virginia-border counties continue to be the state's premier farm region. By contrast, a similar level of farming intensity did not develop on the meandering narrow valleys and steep ridges of the Allegheny Plateau. It was coal that had the decisive influence on the rugged plateau.

Coal underlies about two-thirds of West Virginia in distinct northern and southern coalfields, and is the state's most valuable natural resource. It is located almost entirely within the Allegheny Plateau, and is a broadly unifying factor in the plateau region. In the southern coalfields the coal companies attracted European immigrants and blacks from the American South to augment a rural and agrarian native white population that was too small to provide the necessary labor force for mining. Railroads were constructed into and across the region to haul coal, and coal company towns were built to house miners and provide the essentials of life. Everywhere in the southern counties one is aware of the influence coal has had on the region. Coal did not produce such pronounced regionalism in the northern coalfields, which had a larger pre-industrial population and well-established towns and cities.

The founders of West Virginia may have had some concern for geographical unity, but the state they created in 1863 had two panhandles and sprawled over more geographic area than its relatively modest acreage would suggest. The Eastern Panhandle retained strong social and economic ties with eastern Virginia, and in recent years has experienced the suburbanization of the Washington-Baltimore corridor. The affinities of the Northern Panhandle and the upper Monongahela Valley were related to the Midwest and Pittsburgh. In the corridors of the Upper Kanawha, Teays, and lower Ohio River valleys, the affinities were more intrinsically influenced by government services, chemicals, special metals, and transportation industries.

Howard G. Adkins
Ona

Rehoboth Church

Rehoboth Church in Monroe County is claimed to be the oldest church building west of the Allegheny Mountains. The church, listed on the National Register of Historic Places, lies two miles east of Union on State Route 3.

About 1786, Edward Keenan, who had converted to Methodism from Catholicism, deeded five acres for the church and burying grounds. The beginning of an independent American Methodist Church had occurred only a few years before. Tradition says that Francis Asbury preached the Rehoboth dedication sermon as he stood in the church's doorway because the crowd was too large for the small structure. Asbury also held sessions of the Greenbrier Conference at Rehoboth in 1792, 1793, and 1796.

Rehoboth Church is made of logs hewn on the inside only. The inside measures 21 feet by 30 feet, and the walls to the eaves are 13 logs high. The building's only door is 40 inches wide and only 65 inches high. The church has a window on the east end, located behind the pulpit to provide light for reading, and a larger window on the north side. A pulpit of rough-hewn walnut and poplar boards stands high against the east wall to give the preacher a good view of the worshipers in the balcony, and some of the backless puncheon benches used by Rehoboth's early congregations are still in place.

Rehoboth Church still stands where it was built. The Rehoboth Museum Center contains several artifacts from the region, including a communion table from the church.

See also Francis Asbury, Methodists

Religion

While certain religions predominate, West Virginia has a diversity of religious beliefs, practices, and expressions. In 2000, there were 4,139 churches, syna-

Trinity United Methodist Church in Pickaway, Monroe County.

gogues, mosques, and temples in the state. The number of adherents of all religious faiths was 650,016, which was 35.9 percent of the state's total population. This is a considerably lower rate of religious affiliation than for the nation as a whole, which had 50.2 percent religious adherence in 2000.

West Virginians professing a religion were overwhelmingly Christian and very largely Protestant. The largest denomination was United Methodist, which accounted for 8.3 percent of the total state population and 23.2 percent of religious adherents. There were 1,341 Methodist churches, with 150,985 adherents. American Baptist USA had 463 churches with 108,087 adherents, accounting for 6.0 percent of the population and 16.6 percent of all adherents. Roman Catholics accounted for 5.8 percent of the population and 16.2 percent of all adherents, with 149 churches and 105,363 adherents. There were 11 other Christian denominations counting 10,000 or more adherents each, including numerous holiness, pentecostal, and evangelical believers. There were also small Jewish and Muslim populations, and others adhering to non-Western religions.

West Virginia's religious makeup is a product of the state's history. As early settlers ventured into the western wilderness, religious beliefs and practices journeyed with them. These settlers included many Scotch-Irish, which suggests that Presbyterianism was the dominant form of Christianity in the early years. During the Second Great Awakening (1790–1830), however, the Baptists and Methodists gained thousands of converts, and have been the largest Christian denominations in West Virginia ever since.

Energetic Methodist missionary Francis Asbury had already begun his travels throughout the region in the late 18th century. Methodist circuit riding, in which itinerant preachers traveled by horseback from congregation to congregation, spread the message and helped Methodism to flourish. Baptist, Presbyterian, and Episcopal churches developed slowly in the late 18th century and expanded their mission in the 19th century. Unique to the Northern Panhandle was the development of a new denomination, the Disciples of Christ, and Roman Catholicism first flourished there, as well.

During and before the Civil War, several denominations split due to various positions on slavery and states' rights. Although West Virginia's statehood came about for mostly secular reasons, clergy and lay leaders were frequently present at statehood conventions. Particularly influential were members of the Methodist Episcopal Church, the "Northern" Methodists. They held considerable political power in the early years of the state, their numbers including Governor Boreman and early U.S. senators and congressmen.

Methodists were also prominent in the establishment of the education system, including the public schools. When West Virginia University's first president, Alexander Martin, a Methodist minister, was fired during a political purge, the Methodists boycotted the school for a time. West Virginia's Methodist Conference later founded its own educational institution, West Virginia Wesleyan College, in Buckhannon.

Other denominations have historical ties to institutions of higher education throughout the state, although the relationships have in some cases lapsed. These institutions include Bethany College (Disciples of Christ), Salem College, now Salem International University (Seventh-Day Baptist), Morris Harvey College, now University of Charleston (Methodist), Alderson-Broaddus College (American Baptist), Ohio Valley College (Church of Christ), Wheeling Jesuit University (Roman Catholic), and Davis & Elkins College (Presbyterian).

After the Civil War, West Virginia's previously agrarian economy became increasingly industrial. Wheeling, the Northern Panhandle, and the Monongahela Valley developed strong manufacturing bases, and extractive industry claimed much of the rest of the state. Both manufacturing and extractive industries needed more workers than were present in the native population, and growing numbers of newcomers were attracted to the state.

Many immigrants from southern and eastern Europe, often Catholics, settled in the mining and manufacturing regions. Bishop Patrick J. Donahue (1894–1922) oversaw the development of numerous churches and missions, as well as schools, hospitals and orphanages to serve a growing Catholic population. Catholic parishes flourished in the southern coalfields as well as the industrial north, and Catholic communities developed in other areas as well.

"A call to preach"

"In the earlier days of freedom almost every colored man who learned to read would receive 'a call to preach' within a few days after he began reading. At my home in West Virginia the process of being called to the ministry was a very interesting one. Usually the 'call' came when the individual was sitting in church. Without warning the one called would fall upon the floor as if struck by a bullet, and would lie there for hours, speechless and motionless. Then the news would spread all through the neighborhood that this individual had received a 'call.' If he were inclined to resist the summons, he would fall or be made to fall a second or third time. In the end he always yielded to the call. While I wanted an education badly, I confess that in my youth I had a fear that when I had learned to read and write well I would receive one of these 'calls'; but, for some reason, my call never came."

—Booker T. Washington *Up From Slavery* (1901)

Eastern European immigrants took jobs in manufacturing and mining, some of them establishing Eastern Orthodox congregations. Today there are active Orthodox congregations in Morgantown, Wheeling, Charleston, and elsewhere. Sizable numbers of Jews immigrated to West Virginia during the same period, and synagogues were established throughout the state. Muslims came as well, initially living quietly among mostly Christian neighbors. Their numbers increased in the 20th century, and mosques were established in South Charleston and elsewhere.

According to the late West Virginia University scholar Manfred Meitzen, the religious life of the newly created state was "characterized by biblical literalism, fundamentalistic morality, revivalism, and the preeminence of Protestantism." While allowing for diversity and exceptions, these characteristics still apply to a considerable extent. Many Appalachian scholars have noted the distinctly Protestant nature of the region, marked by a strongly Puritan code of ethics.

Christian faith in West Virginia has often focused on individualistic piety rather than a well-developed social gospel. Often this became manifest through non-denominational family chapels and community churches. Even among these unaffiliated congregations a strong Baptist polity often prevails, emphasizing localized control, unsupervised clergy, biblical literalism, and the power of the Holy Spirit. Fervent preaching focuses on otherworldly salvation and charismatic gifts. Salvation through Jesus Christ is rarely connected to social action. Bedrock fundamentalism takes exotic expression in some cases, including serpent handling and speaking in unknown tongues, while others profess very old beliefs such as predestinarianism.

While its overall contours remain Christian and Protestant, West Virginia's religious landscape continues to change. Groups once uncommon in the state made inroads in the 20th century, including Jehovah's Witnesses and, more recently, the Mormons. Once-dominant mainstream churches have lost membership, as elsewhere in the country, while large and often independent evangelical "megachurches" have grown. West Virginians continue to attend church at lower rates than other Americans, but it is likely that a majority of Mountaineers, churched and unchurched, still subscribe to the fundamentalist creed that Professor Meitzen said characterized that state at its creation.

Chett Pritchett
Wesley Theological Seminary, Washington
Manfred O. Meitzen, "West Virginia," *Religion in the Southern States*, 1983; Otis K. Rice and Stephen W. Brown, *West Virginia: A History*, 1993.

Religious Broadcasting

As they developed, the mass media of radio and television provided communication for religious as well as secular messages, partly displacing the itinerant preachers who once traveled the roads and trails to evangelize. The tradition continues today, featuring preaching, especially on Sundays, as well as live and recorded music and talk.

The main centers of religious broadcasting are in Charleston, Huntington, and the Beckley-Bluefield area. Charleston is home to Praise 101, WJYP AM Christian broadcasting, featuring praise, worship, and light gospel music. Stations WCAW, WMXE, WOKU, and WXAF also broadcast religious programs in Charleston in 2005.

Bishop T. D. Jakes, one of America's most successful broadcast preachers, got his start in the Charleston area. Jakes began his ministry in Montgomery and expanded into television on WCHS and WVAH in Charleston. In 1996 he relocated to Texas, where he heads a highly successful church and a national media ministry.

Chief among Huntington's religious stations is WEMM, with more than 30 years of commercial-free religious broadcasting with the same ownership, format, and dial position. Another major station is JOY Radio 1600 and 1420 AM. Huntington's most famous radio and television preacher is Pastor Darryl Huffman of the New Life Church; he is carried on INSP, a national religious network.

In Beckley, WJLS AM is a Southern gospel music radio station. Brother Carlos Lewis has a Saturday morning radio show, *Hour of Prayer*, that is one of the longest running religious radio shows in the United States. Beckley's WWNR AM has broadcast the Reverend Andrew Durgan's *Sweet Hour of Prayer* on Sunday mornings for more than 50 years. Durgan was the first black funeral director in the state. Fellow minister Helen Dobson is West Virginia's senior black woman preacher, having more than 50 years of radio ministry to her credit.

Another well-known Beckley radio minister is Sister Loretta Taylor, who is pastor of her own house of prayer. Family members including children and grandchildren accompany her to WJLS on a weekly basis. WAEY, WAMN, WGTH, WPIB, and WYRV also broadcast in the Beckley-Bluefield area. To the north in Fayette County is Oak Hill, home to WOAY AM, all religious programming.

The history of West Virginia religious broadcasting is deeply interwoven with gospel music. Molly O'Day, a national recording star at mid-century, began performing over Charleston's WCHS in the early 1940s. She and husband Lynn Davis carried on a radio ministry from Hun-

tington for many years after 1950. Rex and Eleanor Parker and their gospel group, the Merrymakers, aired live daily broadcasts out of WOAY Oak Hill and WHIS Bluefield following World War II. The broadcasts were carried simultaneously by stations in Princeton, Welch, and Pineville.

Like the Parkers, John Bava, a coal miner and preacher, remained dedicated to old-style gospel music played live in the studio. He was possibly the most significant performer and preacher to broadcast over WDNE Elkins; his gospel group, the Country Cousins, also taped many shows from WMMN Fairmont which were aired on other stations. Bava started his own magazine, *Musical Echoes,* a publishing company, and a recording company.

See also T. D. Jakes, Molly O'Day and Lynn Davis, Rex and Eleanor Parker, Religion

Rebecca Dean
Bethlehem, Pennsylvania
Howard Dorgan, *Airwaves of Zion: Radio and Religion in Appalachia,* 1993.

The Rending of Virginia

This classic book, originally published in Chicago by Mayer & Miller in 1902, was Granville Davisson Hall's most important non-fiction work. *The Rending of Virginia* is perhaps the most significant and insightful memoir and history of the West Virginia statehood movement by an observer. A fiercely partisan, pro-statehood view, the volume explains the causes of Virginia's rupture and justifies the accomplishments of Western Virginians and their allies.

Hall was a native Harrison Countian and Republican who learned stenography as a teenager, who had exposure to national issues, and who possessed a refined sense of history. He understood the importance of individual political history, family connections, and personal relationships when he appraised the drama of state-making as a reporter for the *Wheeling Daily Intelligencer* and when he recalled the period for his book. He forthrightly celebrated the heroes and exposed the villains of the statehood epoch.

Rejecting the fashionable "Lost Cause" myth that elevated the defense of Southern states-right dogma and deemed that slavery was not the cause of the Civil War, Hall in *The Rending of Virginia* sought to counter turn-of-the-century distortions of the secessionist record and the prevailing amnesia of what he saw as Virginia's treasonous past. Hall saw West Virginia's separation as arising simply from the long-standing political hypocrisy of Virginia's rulers. From the American Revolution, these leaders professed democratic and republican principles and consistently suppressed western political and economic aspirations in their attempts to maintain slavery at all costs. In Hall's view, the despotic Virginians' statecraft failed and caused the division of the state and the flowering of national patriotism in Western Virginia during the secession crisis.

See also Formation of West Virginia

John Edmund Stealey III
Shepherd University

John E. Stealey III, "Introduction," Granville Davisson Hall, *The Rending of Virginia*, 2000.

Jesse L. Reno

General Jesse Lee Reno was born in Wheeling, April 20, 1823. He graduated from the U.S. Military Academy at West Point in 1846, eighth in a class that also included George B. McClellan, George Pickett, and another cadet from (West) Virginia, Thomas J. Jackson, later known as Stonewall.

Reno served in a howitzer battery throughout the Mexican War of 1846–48. He twice was promoted for gallant and meritorious conduct, to first lieutenant at the Battle of Cerro Gordo and to captain at the Battle of Chapultepec, in which he was wounded.

At the outbreak of the Civil War, Reno was in command of a federal arsenal in Alabama when it was seized by state forces in January 1861. He later commanded the U.S. arsenal at Fort Leavenworth, Kansas, until called east in late 1861 to take command of a brigade, for which he was promoted to brevet brigadier general. Reno led his brigade in Gen. Ambrose Burnside's expedition to the coast of North Carolina, participating in the attack and capture of Roanoke Island and Newberne in 1862. Reno was soon elevated to division command, and then to brevet major general. His division participated in the Union debacle at Second Manassas, with Reno temporarily commanding Burnside's 9th Corps during part of the campaign.

On September 14, 1862, Reno was felled by enemy fire at Fox's Gap during the battles for South Mountain, Maryland, and died a few minutes later. In a last conversation with Brig. Gen. Samuel Sturgis, himself a member of the Class of 1846, Reno said, "Hello Sam, I'm dead." The city of Reno, Nevada, was named in General Reno's memory.

Mark A. Snell
Shepherd University

Reorganized Government of Virginia

When Virginia voters approved the Secession Ordinance in May 1861, those in Western Virginia who opposed leaving the Union had to decide whether to recreate a loyal Virginia government or to seek the creation of a new state. In practice, it proved necessary first to do the one and then the other. For those who preferred to create a new state, the crux of the problem was how to satisfy the constitutional process for creation of a state from the boundaries of an existing state. Leaders such as John S. Carlile and Francis H. Pierpont influenced the Second Wheeling Convention to form a "Reorganized Government of Virginia" which became effective on July 1, 1861, with headquarters in Wheeling. This government provided a loyal, unionist government for Virginia and eventually provided the necessary consent to the creation of West Virginia.

The Reorganized Government immediately set about the task of re-establishing government functions at the state, county, and local level. Virginia's secession had split local officials into Union and Confederate factions. These men fought one another for control of county and local governmental units, resulting in anarchy in much of Western Virginia. Francis H. Pierpont, elected governor of the Reorganized Government of Virginia on June 20, 1861, called on President Abraham Lincoln for military aid. Gen. George B. McClellan and his army brought security to Pierpont's government and legitimacy when McClellan recognized him as the governor of Virginia. Pierpont called the newly elected legislature into session on July 1. The general assembly immediately began the re-establishment of governmental functions, provided for the raising of military units for federal service, and elected new U.S. senators and representatives to represent Virginia in Washington.

The creation of a new state remained a central issue and the Reorganized Government authorized a constitutional convention, to which delegates were elected on October 24, 1861. A constitution for the proposed new state was written and was ratified in April 1862 by voters in those counties where federal troops were in control. Governor Pierpont then called on the legislature of the Reorganized Government to agree to the formation of West Virginia from the state of Virginia. Since there was another government of Virginia sitting in Richmond, it was not at all certain that the actions of the Reorganized Government would find approval in Congress or the courts. The issue then moved to Washington, where, after great debate and much soul searching by congressmen and President Lincoln, the creation of West Virginia was approved. A new legislature was chosen and Arthur I. Boreman was elected as the first governor, to take office on June 20, 1863.

Meanwhile, the governor of the Reorganized Government, Francis H. Pierpont, who had been reelected in November 1862, moved the Reorganized Government to Alexandria, Virginia, where it continued to govern those parts of Virginia under Union control. At the end of the war, Pierpont moved his capital to Richmond and continued to serve as governor of Virginia until 1868.

Kenneth R. Bailey
WVU Institute of Technology

Charles H. Ambler, *West Virginia: The Mountain State*, 1940; Richard O. Curry, *A House Divided*, 1964.

Republican Party

Although the birth of West Virginia is associated with the party of Lincoln, the state has witnessed only two periods of Republican Party dominance, one in the early years of statehood and the other at the end of the 19th century. To understand the uneven record of the GOP in the Mountain State one must understand how sectional differences during the war extended into politics after the war. While Republicans dominated areas of Unionist sentiment in the north and west, they were weak in the southern and eastern counties, areas of Confederate and subsequently Democratic support.

The first period of Republican dominance (1863–71) was underpinned by a proscriptive law that denied voting rights to former Confederate soldiers and sympathizers. When those voter restrictions were removed under the 1871 Flick Amendment to the state constitution, Democrats gained enough votes to take control of the young state. The Republican Party assumed minority status until the election of 1896. For a generation, the party that had founded West Virginia and elected the state's first four governors was unable to elect a governor or to control the state legislature, as a coalition of former Confederates, Peace Democrats, and conservative Unionists retained a political majority.

The second period of Republican supremacy (1896–1930) was ushered in by William McKinley's victory in the 1896 presidential contest. In West Virginia the GOP regained majority status as voters embraced the pro-business and moderate social policies championed by Republicans on the state and national levels. From 1896 until 1930, Republicans won every gubernatorial contest except one (1916) and controlled both houses of the legislature in all but three sessions. The dominant political leader, U.S. Sen. Stephen B. Elkins, exercised firm control over the party organization until his death in 1911.

Republican hegemony came to an end with the Great Depression, an economic seismic event that realigned politics in West Virginia and the nation. After 1932 an energized Democratic state party supported by an active federal government and a strong labor union movement kept the Republicans in a minority status. Throughout the rest of the 20th century the party never controlled the legislature, and only two Republicans were elected governor. In presidential contests

The Underwoods were among Republican families to occupy the Governor's Mansion.

the state voted Republican only three times, on each occasion when a Republican incumbent won a national landslide (1956, 1972, and 1984).

During this period the party suffered what political scientist V. O. Key has called the "atrophy of party organizations." As late as the 1990s, Republicans often did not nominate a full slate of candidates for the statewide offices or provide serious competition in many counties. This lack of competition exposed a lack of organization, unity, and leadership. Only two party figures emerged during the last half of the 20th century, and neither was able to rebuild party organization or increase Republican legislative strength. The charismatic Arch A. Moore, a former Republican congressman, won election three times as governor (1968, 1972, 1984), but ended his long career convicted of jury tampering. The other Republican leader, Cecil Underwood, had the distinction of being both the state's youngest governor (1956) and oldest governor (1996).

West Virginia ended the 20th century still a Democratic state, but Underwood's victory over a divided Democratic Party in 1996 signaled a possible renewal of Republican fortunes. A series of legislative gains coupled with George W. Bush's presidential victories in West Virginia in 2000 and 2004 suggested that the Re-

publicans could become competitive statewide. If their comeback to majority status occurs, it will not be due to proscriptive law as in the 1860s or to a dramatic national realignment as in 1896, but rather due to a gradual realignment within the state based on cultural issues.

See also Democratic Party, Stephen B. Elkins, Arch Moore, Politics, Cecil Underwood

Robert Rupp
West Virginia Wesleyan College

Mary Lou Retton

Gymnast Mary Lou Retton was born January 24, 1968, in Fairmont. She made history at the 1984 Olympic Games in Los Angeles when, at 16, she became the first American woman ever to win a gold medal in gymnastics and the first native West Virginia woman to win a gold medal in Olympic competition. Retton was raised in Fairmont, where she attended local schools before moving to Texas to train.

Her perfect 10 on the vault to win the gold in the all-around gymnastics competition was chosen by NBC as one of the "Greatest 100 Moments In Olympic History." Retton's five medals at the 1984 Olympics made her the single biggest American winner, prompting the Associated Press to name her Female Amateur Athlete of the Year and *Sports Illustrated* to select her as Sportswoman of the Year. She became the first woman to star in Wheaties commercials and was given movie roles in *Scrooged* and *Naked Gun 33⅓*. In 1985, she was inducted into the U.S. Olympic Committee Hall of Fame. Retton is married to Houston financial analyst Shannon Kelly and devotes her time to helping young people. A board member of the Children's Miracle Network, she remains in demand as a motivational speaker. Mary Lou Retton Drive in Fairmont is named for the Olympic star.

Larry Sonis
Arlington, Texas

Walter Phillips Reuther

Labor leader Walter Phillips Reuther, long-time president of the United Auto Workers and a founder of the modern labor movement, was born to German immigrant parents in Wheeling, September 1, 1907. Reuther's father, Valentine, was president of the Wheeling brewers union and a leader of the city's Socialist Party.

Walter began work as an apprentice tool and die maker at Wheeling Steel in 1924. By 1927, he moved to Detroit, where he became one of the highest-paid skilled workers at the Ford Motor Company. Fired by Ford for his union activities, he and his brother, Victor, bicycled through Europe and worked for more than a year at a Ford-built plant in the Soviet Union. Reuther returned to De-

troit just at the time when industrial unionism was becoming a major force. Seizing the moment, he organized and was elected president of what became one of the most important locals in the United Auto Workers.

Reuther's national reputation grew as he made significant contributions to the progress of the UAW. By 1937, he represented 30,000 workers in 76 shops and had helped to develop strategies, including the sit-down strike, that won union contracts from major automakers. In less than a decade, he moved up through union offices to become national UAW president. Over the next few years, Reuther achieved massive gains for his membership that included cost-of-living increases, productivity pay raises, and unemployment benefits. He was elected president of the Congress of Industrial Organizations in 1952. Three years later, he helped merge the CIO with the American Federation of Labor.

Reuther's detractors claim that as he grew in power, he became increasingly conservative, as exemplified by his political attacks on communists and other left wingers who had helped to build the UAW. It has also been argued that the prosperity Reuther obtained for auto workers came at the price of diminished rank-and-file control over union policy and an acquiescence in management's control over production decisions. But in the late 1960s, Reuther led his auto workers out of the AFL-CIO in protest to that giant labor alliance's failure to organize the growing service sector of the American economy.

Regardless of their differences, champions and detractors agree that Walter Reuther was arguably the most influential labor leader in post-World War II America. He died in a plane crash, May 9, 1970.

Fred A. Barkey
Marshall University Graduate College

Revenuer

The revenuer enforced the laws regulating the licensing and taxing of whiskey. He focused on destroying illegal stills and arresting illicit distillers, becoming in the process a colorful, often notorious, figure of history and folklore.

The federal government established its authority to tax alcohol early in the history of the country, forcefully suppressing the Whiskey Rebellion in the mountains of Pennsylvania and Western Virginia in the 1790s. However, the making of moonshine or untaxed whiskey continued in rural districts, including the territory that became West Virginia in 1863. Before the establishment of national prohibition, enforcement efforts were often directed by U.S. marshals and deputy marshals, with varying levels of support from local authorities. Among

A revenuer remembers a busy year

"In 1904, I had to arrest a woman, Ella Pittman, for the illegal sale of moonshine whiskey at a Baptist camp meeting. This was in Raleigh County, and I also found the still where it was being manufactured. She had a partner, S. T. Willis, and they were taken before United States Commissioner Rollinson at Falling Spring and after examination committed to jail to await prosecution. . . .

"Also in 1904, I had to arrest Postmaster McCormick at Shady Springs on a charge of selling liquor illegally. The accused was taken before United States Commissioner Hugh A. Dunn of Beckley and will answer to the federal grand jury at the next term of court in Charleston.

"The oldest moonshiner in the state of West Virginia, or perhaps in the Union, is Wiley Hall. He is now serving a sentence in the Raleigh County jail at Beckley. Judge Keller refused to send him to the penitentiary on account of his age. Next April, he will be 83 years old. He began making white lightning, as he calls it, in 1839 in Patrick County, Virginia. Hall came to West Virginia in 1870 and has run moonshine stills in Mercer, Raleigh, Wyoming and Summers counties. He has been a dangerous man in his time, but of late years has preferred to retire into the brush rather than face the revenue officers. . . .

"Hall is a confirmed blockader and will likely die in the business. . . . He has raised a large family and most all of them are moonshiners, as are many of his relatives, some of them pretending to be preachers."

—Deputy U.S. Marshal Dan Cunningham, 1904

West Virginia's best-known revenuers from this period was Daniel Webster Cunningham (1850–1942), a deputy marshal whose duties included liquor law enforcement among other responsibilities.

West Virginia began statewide prohibition in 1914, followed by national prohibition in 1920. Alcoholic beverages of all sorts were strictly prohibited, except for medical and religious purposes. With these landmark changes, the collection of liquor tax revenue was no longer the issue. All alcoholic beverages were now illegal, and complete suppression was the goal. Nonetheless, federal revenue agents continued to be involved in liquor law enforcement, and liquor agents of all sorts continued to be called revenuers. At the state level, revenuers reported to the West Virginia Department of Prohibition, led by a state commissioner appointed by the governor. The West Virginia State Police were involved in liquor law enforcement as well, after creation of the agency in 1919. The federal government added a prohibition department to the Internal Revenue Service, and its agents continued in prohibition enforcement into the early 1930s.

There was widespread resistence to prohibition, and revenuers were busy throughout the 1920s. A total of 683 stills were seized in West Virginia during 1923–24, the 14th-highest number in the country. In addition to locally made moonshine, revenuers sought also to destroy bootleg whiskey, which had been made legally in foreign jurisdictions and smuggled into the United States. McDowell County Sheriff Mack Day, killed by a bootlegger in 1925, was among West Virginia revenuers of the prohibition era. After the repeal of national prohibition in 1933 and state prohibition in 1934 the revenuer's work changed once more. The suppression of untaxed liquor was again the issue. Ironically, however, the scale of moonshining was greatly reduced by the widespread availability of quality legal whiskey at reasonable prices in state liquor stores. As the 20th century progressed, the number of stills seized in West Virginia was much lower than during prohibition, with a mere 32 seizures reported in 1968. Enforcement actions were uncommon by the turn of the 21st century, as moonshiner and revenuer alike slipped into the province of history and myth.

See also Dan Cunningham, Mack Day, Moonshine, Prohibition

William Chapman Revercomb

Senator William Chapman Revercomb was born July 20, 1895, in Covington, Virginia. He attended Washington and Lee University, and following army service during World War I, earned a law degree from the University of Virginia in 1919. In 1925, Revercomb married Sara Hughes of Ashland, Virginia. They had four children.

Revercomb practiced law in Covington until 1922, when he relocated to Charleston and continued to practice his profession. Over the following years he would serve as a member of the Republican State Committee and as chairman of the State Judicial Convention of 1936. In 1942, Revercomb defeated former senator and sitting governor Matthew M. Neely for West Virginia's open U.S. Senate seat. He quickly made a reputation as one of the Senate's more conservative members. Running for reelection in 1948, he was defeated by Neely.

Revercomb settled back into the practice of law. This, however, did not stop him from attempting to return to the Senate. After claiming the Republican nomination in 1952, he was defeated by incumbent Harley Kilgore. Revercomb's fortunes changed when Kilgore died before completing his term. In 1956, an election was held for the remaining two years of Kilgore's unexpired term. Revercomb defeated Governor Marland in the general election to return to the Senate. Revercomb served until 1958, when he was defeated by Congressman Robert C. Byrd. Revercomb was the last Republican to be elected to the U.S. Senate from West Virginia in the 20th century.

Chapman Revercomb's last attempt for elective office was a losing effort in the 1960 gubernatorial primary. He died October 6, 1979.

Michael K. Wilson
Charleston

Samuel Worth Price Jr., "A Stalwart Conservative in the Senate: William Chapman Revercomb," M.A. thesis, Marshall University, 1978; "William Chapman Revercomb, 1895–1979," *Biographical Directory of the United States Congress, 1774–Present*, 2002.

The Revolutionary War

The Revolution in Western Virginia featured none of the sprawling battles and large marching armies that characterized the war in the east. Nonetheless, westerners participated on both sides of the conflict and on battlefields throughout the country. Patriotic citizens answered at least ten troop calls, most famously including the riflemen who rushed from Martinsburg and Winchester to reinforce George Washington at Boston in the Bee Line March of 1775. Western Virginians supplied the materials of war, as well, including food, clothing, and wagons.

As in other areas, Western Virginians were divided on the question of American independence. Some vainly hoped to find a neutral position while others were Tories or Loyalists, preferring the British side in the struggle. There was considerable, usually nonviolent, resistance to Patriot authorities in the Potomac Highlands, and Col. Zackquill Morgan suppressed what he believed to be a serious Tory threat in the Monongahela Valley.

Militarily, the Revolution in present West Virginia was a continuation of the frontier wars, reminiscent of the earlier French and Indian War in that it typically involved Indian raids against the settlers in their homes and forts. The Indians were encouraged and supplied by British authorities in the west, especially General Hamilton at Detroit. Often Indian raiding parties, particularly the Shawnee, acted alone, picking off isolated families and attacking small forts. Larger attacks frequently included British or Tory elements, often leading or advising the native warriors.

The year 1777 was particularly violent. Fort Henry at Wheeling was attacked in late August and early September, and a few weeks later Indians ambushed and killed 20 militiamen at nearby McMechen. There were numerous smaller raids, particularly in the Monongahela and Greenbrier watersheds. It was brutal guerrilla warfare, catching up the innocent and helpless as well as armed combatants, and our ancestors long remembered the "year of the bloody sevens."

Events continued intermittently in the same vein for the remainder of the war. Point Pleasant's Fort Randolph was attacked in 1778, as was Fort Donnally in Greenbrier County. Fort Henry was attacked for the second time in 1782, very late in the war, and it was during this siege that Betty Zane made her legendary gunpowder run.

The frontier provided the new nation a valuable western buffer throughout the Revolution, allowing Patriots in the east to concentrate on the British armies confronting them. The line of settlements was pushed eastward by Indian pressure during the war, particularly in the New, Greenbrier, and Monongahela watersheds. But the Northern and Eastern panhandles held firm, and a generation of western leaders was honed by wartime experience. Western Virginians made gains against their Native American adversaries, although Indian warfare continued for several years after the end of the Revolution.

See also Bee Line March, Fort Henry, Fort Randolph, Zackquill Morgan, Tories, Betty Zane

Ken Sullivan
West Virginia Humanities Council

James Tyree Rexrode

Folk artist James Tyree Rexrode, who created a visual record of rural West Virginia life in the early 20th century, was born in Pendleton County, December 25, 1887. He began teaching when he was 17 and taught in several one-room schools in the area.

As a teacher, Rexrode began taking pictures. He photographed classes and school activities and occasions such as weddings and minstrel shows. He also drew cartoons for his students. After his wife's death in 1966, he turned to a new art form to occupy his time. Starting out sketching local buildings, churches, schoolhouses, and mills, Rexrode began painting on grey uncoated cardboard, working at an oilcloth-covered table in his kitchen.

At first painting from photographs, Rexrode then turned to remembered scenes from his youth. His early works were displayed at the Shenandoah Valley Folklore Society at the Harrisonburg Arts and Crafts Festival in neighboring Virginia in 1968. Later exhibits were held at the opening of the Virginia Military Institute Hall of Valor at the New Market Battlefield Park, the Maple Festival at Monterey, Virginia, and elsewhere.

Rexrode began offering his work for sale at an art and craft shop in Winchester, Virginia, and other shops in the area soon were selling his work. His work was also sold at the American Folk Art Shop in the Georgetown section of Washington, and other places.

Rexrode developed a category he called "old-timey subjects" that included butchering, one-room schools, old-time Christmas, barn raising, quilting, and harvesting, among others. In her 1976 book *Contemporary Folk Artists*, Elinor Horwitz called Rexrode "Grandpa Moses" because of the similarity of his work to that of Grandma Moses.

Rexrode died February 23, 1976, and was buried in Sugar Grove Cemetery, Pendleton County.

Reymann Memorial Farm

The Reymann Memorial Farm, located near Wardensville in the Cacapon Valley in Hardy County, is the largest of several experimental farms operated by West Virginia University. The property was donated as two separate farms in 1917 by members of the Reymann family, prominent Wheeling brewers and businessmen. It remains today as two separate tracts under joint management. The farm is operated by the Division of Animal and Veterinary Sciences at WVU's Davis College of Agriculture, Forestry, and Consumer Sciences.

The memorial farm established an excellent cattle herd early in its history, and continues the tradition of animal husbandry today. In 2004, there were more than 150 cattle on the 996-acre farm, as well as 75 sheep, more than 1,500 turkeys, and more than 2,000 chickens. Among other structures, the farm had a large cattle barn, large cattle performance barn, and a large poultry building. Although located at a distance from Morgantown, Reymann is used as a laboratory for several courses taught at the university's Division of Animal and Veterinary Sciences. The farm is used as well for faculty and graduate student research. In 2004, research was under way at Reymann in both animal and crop sciences, and in practical farm management.

West Virginia University has six other farm properties, located in Monongalia, Preston, Jefferson, and Monroe counties, and two experimental forests, in Monongalia-Preston and Randolph counties.

See also West Virginia University

Alexander Welch Reynolds

General Alexander Welch Reynolds, born April 26, 1816, in Lewisburg, served in the armies of the United States, the Confederate States, and in Egypt. He was a grandson of Frances Hunter Lawrence Arbuckle Welch (second wife of Captain Matthew Arbuckle, who served at the Battle of Point Pleasant) and Alexander Welch, pioneer surveyor.

A graduate of the U.S. Military Academy at West Point in 1838, Reynolds served as an officer in the army in the Seminole War, the Mexican War, and in the west. At the outbreak of the Civil War he entered the Confederate army as a colonel. With considerable combat experience, including command of the 50th Regiment of Virginia Infantry at the Battle of Carnifex Ferry (after which he was known as "Old Gauley" for the river on whose banks the battle was fought), he rose to the rank of brigadier general.

After the war, on the recommendation of fellow West Virginian and Confederate general, John P. McCausland, Reynolds accepted a commission as colonel in the forces of the khedive of Egypt, the ruler of Egypt under the Ottoman Empire. Reynolds served in Egypt in various posts, including adjutant general, from 1870 until his death on May 26, 1876. Although there is a memorial to him in the Old Stone Church cemetery in Lewisburg, General Reynolds was buried in Egypt.

Joseph Crosby Jefferds Jr.
Charleston

Weymouth T. Jordan Jr., John D. Chapla and Shan C. Sutton, *Soldier of Misfortune, Alexander Welch Reynolds of the U. S. Confederate and Egyptian Armies*, Greenbrier Historical Society, 2001.

Frederick Hurten Rhead

Ceramist Frederick Hurten Rhead designed the famous Fiestaware line of tableware while working at the Homer Laughlin China Company in Newell, Hancock County. Born in Staffordshire, England, August 29, 1880, he came to America in 1902.

Rhead held responsible positions from age 19 in the Wardle Pottery in England, and later worked at potteries across the United States. He received a Gold Medal at the 1915 San Diego Exposition for his design of mirror black, a recreation of the 17th-century Chinese K'ang Hsi glaze.

Rhead was at the top of his profession when he joined the Laughlin Company in 1927. He potted, taught, wrote, created glazes and shapes, and designed the Fiesta line in 1935. Rhead created other Laughlin tableware designs as well, including the popular Virginia Rose and Harlequin, a colorful successor to Fiesta. Rhead worked for the rest of his career at Homer Laughlin, moving to New York shortly before his death, November 2, 1942.

See also Fiestaware, Homer Laughlin China Company

James R. Mitchell
State Museum

Sharon Dale, *Frederick Hurten Rhead: An English Potter in America*, 1986; Bob and Sharon Huxford, *The Collector's Encyclopedia of Fiesta*, 1992.

Rhododendron

The *rhododendron maximum*, more commonly called great rhododendron or big laurel, was designated the official state flower of West Virginia, January 29, 1903, after being recommended by the governor and voted on by students in the public schools. The name comes from the Greek *rhodo*, meaning "rose" and *dendron*, meaning "tree."

Throughout the world there are more than 800 species of rhododendron, the most abundant being the purple or Catawba rhododendron and *rhododendron maximum*, also known as great laurel or rosebay. The rosebay alternates growth years with blooming years. The range of the rhododendron in the United States is in the eastern and midwestern states. It is common in much of West Virginia, the massed plants putting on a spectacular show when in full bloom.

The *rhododendron maximum*, from the family Ericaceae, is found in wet woods and swamps and is characterized by white, pink, or purple flowers, with orange or green spots and sticky flower stems. The rhododendrons are evergreens, with leaves that are leathery and smooth. The height of this plant can be from five to 40 feet, with flowering in June and July. The leaves are poisonous to cattle and deer.

The family Ericaceae includes heaths and heathers, and like them, the rhododendron requires moist, well-drained soil. If the plant has the right soil, moisture, and drainage, it requires little else. The rhododendron is efficient at extracting the nutrients it needs from acid soil. Rhododendrons are often used in landscaping and there are many hybrids. The hard wood of this plant is used for tool handles and is a favorite of craftspeople for making walking sticks and furniture. Its well-shaped forks make excellent slingshots.

Christine D. Fenn
Westover

The *Rhododendron*

The West Virginia Centennial showboat *Rhododendron* plied the Kanawha, Ohio, and Monongahela rivers in 1963 in celebration of the state's 100th birthday. The showboat was created from the sternwheeler *Omar*, originally launched by the Ohio River Company of Cincinnati in 1935, decommissioned after 24 years of service, and given to the state in 1961. The following year, it was remodeled, leaving the boiler room and machinery used to power the paddlewheel intact as part of a river museum, and adding a 264-seat theater.

The *Rhododendron* made visits to Charleston, Montgomery, St. Albans, Winfield, Point Pleasant, Kenova, Huntington, Ravenswood, Parkersburg, Williamstown, St. Marys, Sistersville, New Martinsville, Moundsville, Wheeling, Wellsburg, Weirton, Chester, Morgantown, Fairmont, and Pittsburgh. Summer performances of Mrs. Henry Woods's 1863 melodrama *East Lynne* were supplemented by local entertainment at each stop.

Because of low bridges in Pittsburgh, the showboat was unable to visit Morgantown until the fluted smokestacks were hinged and the pilothouse made adjustable. Then the *Rhododendron* triumphantly arrived in Morgantown on October 18, carrying the University of Pittsburgh football team to the annual "backyard brawl" for West Virginia University's homecoming. In November, the *Rhododendron* journeyed to Cincinnati for a nine-day run of *The Boyfriend*, performed by the University of Cincinnati's drama department. After the Centennial, the *Rhododendron* was sold to the town of Clinton, Iowa, where it became a river museum.

See also The Centennial, Showboats

H. G. Young III
WVU Parkersburg

Lloyd P. Calvert, "Here Comes the Showboat," *Travel West Virginia*, Summer 1963; John Marquis and Charles Jones, Final Report of the West Virginia Centennial Commission, 1963.

Red Ribble

Photographer Rufus E. "Red" Ribble was born in Blacksburg, Virginia, May 14, 1878. For nearly 40 years, he traveled Fayette, Raleigh, Kanawha, Wyoming, Boone, and Nicholas counties to photograph coal miners, coal towns, family reunions, club events, church congregations, and school groups.

Ribble produced large panoramic pictures by using a wide-format Cirkut camera. The Cirkut camera, designed for taking photographs of large groups or landscapes, revolves on a geared tripod while exposing the film, making it capable of taking a continuous photograph that can capture a full 360-degree view. Photographs were made by contact printing of the full-size negative, with no enlargement, producing a sharp, clear image. The finished photograph, as printed by Ribble, was eight inches high and up to four feet long.

By 1919, Ribble had moved to the small community of Prince on the New River in Fayette County. Relocating to Mount Hope by 1920, he continued to record images of southern West Virginia until late 1957. It is estimated that he produced more than 600 such photographs during his career. Even today these negatives, some of which are more than 75 years old, produce a clear view of the coalfields as they appeared to the eyes of the photographer. Red Ribble died December 27, 1967, in Oak Hill.

Melody Bragg
National Mine Health and Safety Academy

Otis Rice

Historian Otis Kermit Rice was born June 6, 1919, in Hugheston, Kanawha County. He earned undergraduate degrees at Morris Harvey College (now University of Charleston), an M.A. in education (West Virginia University, 1945), and a Ph.D. in history (University of Kentucky, 1960). After being a teacher and principal in Kanawha County schools, Rice taught at West Virginia Institute of Technology (1957–87), where he was chairman of the history department and dean of the School of Human Studies. He also taught at Marshall University, Morris Harvey College, and the West Virginia Graduate College.

Great Rhododendron, our state flower.

One of West Virginia's most published historians, Rice was the author of *The Allegheny Frontier*, which received an Award of Merit from the American Association for State and Local History; *Hatfields and McCoys*; *Frontier Kentucky*; *Charleston and the Kanawha Valley*; *History of Greenbrier County*; *Sheltering Arms Hospital*; and *West Virginia: The State and Its People*. He co-authored with Stephen W. Brown, *West Virginia: A History*, a college text; *The Mountain State*, a middle school text; as well as *A Centennial of Strength: A History of Banking in West Virginia*.

Rice served as president of the West Virginia Historical Society (1955–56) and the West Virginia Historical Association (1967–68); book review editor of *West Virginia History* (1976–79); member of the editorial board of *Filson Club Quarterly* (1985–87) and the board of advisers of the WVU Library (1988–95); vice chairman of the Kanawha County Bicentennial Commission (1986–90); and first vice president, West Virginia Historical Education Foundation (1992–2003). Among other awards, he received the first Virgil A. Lewis Award of the West Virginia Historical Society (1991) and the first Governor's Award for Outstanding Contributions to West Virginia History or Literature (1999). He received an honorary doctorate from West Virginia University in 2000. On July 22, 2003, Rice was named West Virginia's first Historian Laureate.

Otis Rice died September 22, 2003, in Charleston. He stands among the foremost historians of West Virginia and attained his broadest influence as a writer of secondary and college textbooks.

Stephen W. Brown
WVU Institute of Technology

Rich Mountain, Battle of

After the decisive defeat of Confederate forces on June 3, 1861, at Philippi, Brig. Gen. Robert S. Garnett, the new Confederate commander, established two defensive positions, at Laurel Hill and Rich Mountain, near present Elkins. Suspecting that the 20,000 Union troops under Gen. George B. McClellan would strike the naturally weaker Laurel Hill fortification, Garnett took 3,200 men there, leaving Col. John Pegram and 1,300 men to defend Rich Mountain.

In fact, McClellan did the opposite, sending a diversionary force to Laurel Hill while he marched with three brigades to Rich Mountain. While Brig. Gen. William S. Rosecrans, guided by local Unionist David Hart, made a wide flanking movement, McClellan took a position in front of the Confederate lines to complete a pincer movement. Pegram's Confederates resisted but were soon forced to give way, most of them eventually surrendering to the Yankees. Learning of Pe-

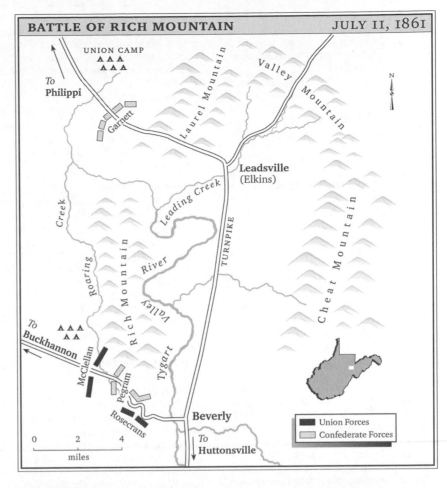

BATTLE OF RICH MOUNTAIN   JULY 11, 1861

UNION CAMP
To Philippi
Garnett
Laurel Mountain
Valley Mountain
Leadsville (Elkins)
Leading Creek
Roaring Creek
Rich Mountain
River
TURNPIKE
Cheat Mountain
To Buckhannon
McClellan
Pegram
Valley
Tygart
N
Rosecrans
Beverly
To Huttonsville
0 2 4
miles

■ Union Forces
□ Confederate Forces

gram's defeat at Rich Mountain, Garnett abandoned Laurel Hill. False information convinced him that his line of retreat along the Staunton-Parkersburg Turnpike was cut off, and he began an arduous and circuitous retreat toward Red House, Maryland. In a rear-guard action at Corricks Ford, Garnett was shot and killed, the first general to die in the Civil War.

The Battle of Rich Mountain was fought July 11, 1861. Despite the relatively small number of troops involved, the battle had two important results. First, the victor, General McClellan, would be given command of the Army of the Potomac for the next two years. More significantly for our state's history, trans-Allegheny Virginia was to all intents and purposes lost to the Southern cause, helping to clear the way for the formation of West Virginia on June 20, 1863.

See also Civil War, Battle of Corricks Ford, Battle of Philippi

Jack Wills
Fairmont

Richwood

Richwood is located at the confluence of the North Fork and South Fork of the Cherry River in Nicholas County, at 2,268 feet above sea level. Founded as a sawmill town by the Cherry River Boom and Lumber Company, Richwood was incor-

porated in 1901. The area originally was known as Cherry Tree Bottoms but was renamed Richwood to reflect the wealth of timber in the area.

By the 1930s, with a population of 7,000, Richwood was home to several factories, including the largest sole leather tannery and the largest clothespin factory in the world. Neither survives today. The 2000 population of Richwood was 2,477. The *West Virginia Hillbilly*, a colorful weekly newspaper with national circulation, was published in Richwood. Its editor, Jim Comstock, was one of the best-known West Virginians until his death in 1996.

Richwood remains notorious for the Feast of the Ramson, an annual ramp festival held in April. Richwood bills itself as the Ramp Capital of the World. Another annual event, the Cherry River Festival, is held in August.

In 1933, there were two Civilian Conservation Corps camps established near Richwood. Camp Woodbine was located north of Richwood on the Cranberry River at the current site of the Woodbine picnic area. Camp Cranberry was also located on the Cranberry River, near the current site of the Cranberry Recreation Center. These two camps, along with others operated by the U.S. Forest Service, were involved in forest management and protection. The annual CCC reunion in

Richwood, which began in 1978, takes place at the former site of Camp Woodbine. As many as 500 people attend this event, including alumni from CCC camps all over the country.

Amy Donaldson Arnold
Ivydale

Ridge and Valley Province

The Ridge and Valley physiographic province, a geographic region, is characterized by intermittent high ridges and deep valleys. It is located between the Blue Ridge and the Allegheny Front and extends for 1,200 miles from the St. Lawrence Valley to central Alabama. It is a part of the Appalachian Mountains, and covers about a fifth of our state, including all of five counties and parts of seven others in eastern West Virginia.

More than 200 million years ago, at the end of the Paleozoic Era, ancient igneous and metamorphic rock moved northwestward, creating linear folds in the younger sedimentary formations of the Ridge and Valley province. Narrow, steep, and sharp crested ridges developed, from 2,000 feet to 4,800 feet high. A typical example of the tight linear folds are the 12 mountain ranges encountered along a 38-mile straight line from Capon Springs, Hampshire County, to New Creek, Mineral County. Many of the ridges in the Eastern Panhandle, particularly in Pendleton County, are topped by peaks, known as knobs, that extend several hundred feet above the prevailing ridge tops. These include High Knob, 3,287 feet; Panther Knob, 4,508 feet; and Brushy Knob, 2,800 feet.

The valleys are eroded in many instances from 500 to 1,800 feet below the ridge tops, into the weaker limestone and shale formations. Caves, sinkholes, and underground streams such as Lost River in Hardy County are evidence of limestone. Springs are ubiquitous in the Ridge and Valley province, and none is more renowned than White Sulphur Springs in Greenbrier County. The most famous valley is the Shenandoah, located in part in Jefferson County, one of the world's longest mountain valleys and a great north-south natural highway from early times to the present.

Master streams such as the South Branch of the Potomac and the Cacapon, Shenandoah, Greenbrier, and Bluestone rivers have incised their meanders in the valleys. These and their tributaries cross ridges through water gaps, coming together at nearly right angles to produce a trellis-like drainage pattern. The valleys with their gently rolling surfaces and limestone soils have been devoted to farming since the first settlements, and counties of the Ridge and Valley Province currently generate three-fourths of the value of agricultural products of West Virginia. The ridges covered with re-growth forest of spruce, pine, and northern hardwood figure prominently in the state's forest industries. And the natural features are combined in such a way as to produce one of America's most scenic regions.

See also Geography

Howard G. Adkins
Ona

Delorme, *West Virginia Atlas and Gazetteer*, 1997; Nevin M. Fenneman, *Physiography of Eastern United States*, 1938.

Leonard Riggleman

College president Leonard Riggleman was born in a cabin in Randolph County, April 16, 1894. A mountain farm boy, educated in a one-room school, he passed the uniform teachers exam in 1913 and taught three years before leaving to study for the Methodist ministry at Morris Harvey College (now University of Charleston), then located at Barboursville, Cabell County.

There he earned his bachelor's degree in 1922, and met his wife, Pauline Steele of Huntington. After receiving a master's degree at Southern Methodist University, Riggleman accepted a pastorate in Milton (1924–28) and taught for the agricultural extension service and for Morris Harvey. He was elected vice president of the college in 1930 and president in 1931.

Saving, then building, Morris Harvey College became Riggleman's life's work. By various stratagems he kept the institution afloat, negotiated the difficult decisions to move the college to Charleston in 1935, and to break from the Methodist Church. War delayed his campaign for a permanent campus until September 1947. During the next 15 years, he built a campus centered around Riggleman Hall, the main classroom building, and led the college to accreditation in 1958.

Although Riggleman retired in 1964, he led the fight to prevent Morris Harvey College from being given to the state in 1974 but acquiesced in its becoming the University of Charleston in 1978. A noted speaker, active churchman, and Kiwanian, Riggleman served on state commissions, was a founding member of the Association of College and University Presidents, and was the *Charleston Gazette's* West Virginia Man of the Year in 1955. He died on May 19, 1983.

See also University of Charleston

R. Eugene Harper
University of Charleston

Mark Garrett, *Sincerely Yours: The Life and Work of Leonard Riggleman,* 1980; Frank J. Krebs, *Where There is Faith: The Morris Harvey College Story, 1888–1970,* 1974.

Ripley

Ripley, the county seat of Jackson County, is situated in a bend of Big Mill Creek 12 miles from Ravenswood. It is 616 feet above sea level. The town may have been named for Harry Ripley, a popular, circuit-riding Methodist minister who drowned in Mill Creek in 1830. The earliest settler in the area was Capt. William Parsons, who built the first road between Clarksburg and Point Pleasant in 1807.

The first of three courthouses, a one-story structure, was built on the town square in 1832. In 1858, the original was replaced with a two-story brick and sandstone structure. The third and present courthouse was built in 1920. An 1886 referendum confirmed Ripley as county seat, defeating rival Ravenswood. In 1897, when John Morgan was hanged in public on the edge of Ripley for the hatchet murders of three members of the Greene family, it created such a sensation that the state legislature passed a bill requiring that all future executions take place inside the state penitentiary.

By 1883, Ripley's population reached 614. The town had hotels, blacksmith shops, tailors, merchants, a gristmill, tanyard, woolen mill, planing mill, master carpenter, lumber companies, attorneys, and two physicians. The first free school had been opened after West Virginia became a state in 1863. The first high school was opened in 1913.

The town's first post office was opened in 1832. The first newspaper was the *Jackson Democrat*. It was established in 1864 and became the *Jackson Herald* in 1877. Ripley has been served by the Jackson County Library since the 1940s.

The first annual Jackson County Fair was held at Ripley in 1877. By 1989, fair attendance reached 30,000 with 2,000 exhibits. It is joined today by the nearby Mountain State Art & Craft Fair. No longer isolated, Ripley lies at the intersection of U.S. 33 and Interstate 77. The town is a center of commerce to a population of 3,263 with several restaurants, stores, motels, banks, churches, twin theaters, two newspapers, and several residential suburbs.

See also Jackson County, Last Public Hanging, Mountain State Art & Craft Fair

Carolyn Flesher Bolovan
Fremont, Indiana

Chuck Ripper

Painter Charles Lewis "Chuck" Ripper of Huntington is one of the country's best-known wildlife artists. His detailed paintings have appeared on nearly 100 magazine covers and 80 U.S. postage stamps, as well as in books and on greeting cards, jigsaw puzzles, playing cards, and even bank checks.

A native of the Pittsburgh area, Ripper was born in October 1929. His father was a blacksmith by trade but also an amateur landscape painter who spent hours in the woods, with his young son tagging along. His mother was an elementary art teacher. Both parents encouraged his interest in nature and art. While Ripper was a student at the Art Institute of Pittsburgh, he had his first bird painting published in *Nature* magazine. An author saw it and, not knowing Ripper was only 19 years old, invited him to illustrate his forthcoming book. The young artist completed the necessary 61 drawings and delivered them shortly before his 20th birthday.

In 1953, Ripper moved to Huntington to work as art director for the now-defunct Standard Printing & Publishing Co. At night and on weekends, he continued to draw and paint wildlife. In 1964, he quit his job to become a full-time freelance artist.

James E. Casto
Herald-Dispatch

Ritchie County

Ritchie County was carved out of portions of Wood, Lewis, and Harrison counties in 1843. Situated in northwest West Virginia, Ritchie County has an area of 455.3 square miles and is traversed by four-lane U.S. 50 and several secondary roads. The county is drained by two forks of the Hughes River and by numerous creeks, including 30-mile-long Goose Creek. There are many narrow but fertile valleys and gentle uplands suitable for livestock raising and the county's generally small farms.

Named for a Virginia journalist and politician, Thomas Ritchie, the county is known for its oil and gas production. Ritchie County was home for 50 years to George Lemon (1788–1866), a pioneer in the petroleum industry. The county seat is Harrisville.

In 1822, Thomas Harris, who had moved westward from Clarksburg in 1807, laid out the community which by 1833 was known by the post office name of Solus. The place experienced little growth before the 1843 birth of Ritchie County. Three years after that important

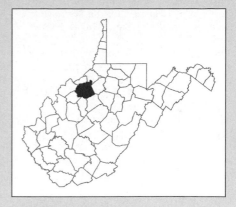

FAST FACTS ABOUT RITCHIE COUNTY

Founded: 1843
Land in square miles: 455.3
Population: 10,343
Percentage minorities: 1.3%
Percentage rural: 100%
Median age: 39.9
Percentage 65 and older: 15.2%
Birth rate per 1,000 population: 10.8
Median household income: $27,332
High school graduate or higher: 73.4%
Bachelor's degree or higher: 7.1%
Home ownership: 81.7%
Median home value: $51,100

This information is from the 2000 U.S. Census. In 2000, West Virginia as a whole had 5 percent minorities, a median age of 38.9, median household income of $29,696, and a 75.2 percent home ownership rate.

event, Solus was renamed Ritchie Court House. In 1895, the town's founder was honored, along with his nephew, Gen. Thomas M. Harris, by the new name, Harrisville.

The first white settler within the present boundaries of Ritchie County was John Bunnell, who built a cabin by 1800 at the present site of Pennsboro. Sometime before 1810, John Webster bought Bunnell's property and built the Old Stone House, a large structure which is now on the National Register of Historic Places. The town of Cairo (once known as Egypt, and also called the McKinney Settlement) was renamed Cairo when a Baltimore & Ohio Railroad station was located there in 1856. The village of Petroleum, important to the development of the oil industry, is a dozen miles west of Cairo, on Goose Creek.

One of the first residents in the northeastern section of the county was Daniel Haymond, who settled near the head of the North Fork of the Hughes River in 1817. A son of William Haymond of Harrison County, Daniel Haymond was twice elected a Virginia state senator. The Haymond settlement grew sufficiently to acquire the name of Federal Hill, and by 1850 there were 200 residents. Its name was later changed to Mole Hill. This name lasted until 1949, when the residents of Mole Hill agreed to let the name be changed once again, this time to Mountain. Making a Mountain out of Mole Hill was a publicity stunt encouraged by the Borden Milk Company and its New York advertising agency.

Ritchie County was well served by Virginia's 19th-century road network. In the late 1830s, the Northwestern Virginia Turnpike, originating in Winchester, was built through the county and on to Parkersburg. The county's population doubled by 1850, and had nearly doubled again 10 years later. The turnpike (now U.S. 50) for many years collected tolls at Tollgate, a village in eastern Ritchie County.

A few years later, the Staunton-Parkersburg Turnpike (called the Staunton Pike, now State Route 47) was built through the southern section of Ritchie County. It followed the South Fork of the Hughes River from Smithville to Cisco. Smithville was named after Barnes and Aaron Smith. When Smithville was planned, sometime around 1844, a street was named for the one-time engineer for Napoleon, Claudius Crozet, who served as the Virginia state engineer when the Staunton-Parkersburg Turnpike was built.

The Ritchie Mines, an unusual natural asphalt deposit, was discovered by Frederick Lemon, the son of George Lemon, in 1852, near Macfarlan. In 1859, Frederick Lemon sold the property, which was mined until the early 20th century.

The early oil and gas and timber indus-

The Ritchie County countryside near Harrisville.

tries led to the construction of railroads, including the Cairo & Kanawha (the C&K, also known as the Calico), the Pennsboro & Harrisville, the Harrisville Southern, and the Sand Hill & Laurel Fork.

Ritchie County today produces timber, with lumber products a chief industry. Simonton Windows near Ellenboro manufactures windows for houses, offices, and commercial buildings. Glassware, marbles, and clothing are also manufactured in the county. Oil and gas wells, some still producing after many years, punctuate the countryside, and from time to time new wells are drilled.

While Ritchie County lost a third of its residents in the first half of the 20th century, the county's population stabilized after 1960. The 2000 population was 10,343. The county is served by four banks and two newspapers. Its students attend the consolidated Ritchie County High School and several elementary schools. North Bend State Park, located on the North Fork of Hughes River near Cairo, features a 30-room lodge, eight cabins, and two riverside campgrounds.

See also Thomas Maley Harris, Northwestern Virginia Turnpike, Ritchie Mines, Staunton-Parkersburg Turnpike

R. F. Hendricks
Marietta, Georgia
Ritchie County Historical Society, *The History of Ritchie County, West Virginia, to 1980,* 1980.

Ritchie Mines

A rarity of nature was discovered in 1852 near Macfarlan Creek, Ritchie County, by pioneer oilman Frederick Lemon. Embedded in the hills was a vein of natural asphalt, or grahamite, which could be mined like coal. The crystallized petroleum melted easily and yielded about 150 gallons of oil per ton. A series of owners sought to mine asphalt at a profit at Ritchie Mines. The owners included J. L. and J. A. Graham, for whom the substance was named. In 1865, a narrow-gauge railroad was built to the mine. The line was later rebuilt, extended, and operated as the Cairo & Kanawha Railroad, affectionately known as the Calico Railroad.

Grahamite was first discovered in West Virginia and later found in the American West, as well as Cuba, Mexico, and South America. The Ritchie Mines was the only asphalt mine in West Virginia, although asphalt has been mined outside the state. At the Ritchie Mines, the asphalt was mined from a narrow fissure or slit in the ground, the asphalt lode ranging in width from less than a foot to nearly five feet. It was mined to a depth of 300 feet. Irish immigrants were recruited as laborers.

The operation had limited success. Although the asphalt was rich in petroleum, it was cheaper to pump oil from wells at nearby Burning Springs, Volcano, and Cairo. Efforts to sell the asphalt as a paving material were more fruitful. Asphalt from Ritchie County was used to pave streets in Washington and in London. The mine shipped several train cars daily at its peak, but during a half-century of operations it produced more woes than wealth. In 1865, the site was bought for an amount variously reported at from $500,000 to $3 million; 11 years later it is supposed to have sold for $2,000. An explosion caused the mines to be closed in 1873. A new owner resumed mining in 1885, but the mine was abandoned in 1909. Today the mine site is part of the Ritchie Mines Wildlife Management Area.

Larry Bartlett
Parkersburg
Minnie Kendall Lowther, *History of Ritchie County,* 1911; Ritchie County Historical Society, *A Photographic History of Ritchie County, West Virginia,* 1989.

Charles Lloyd Ritter

Lumberman Charles Lloyd Ritter was born in Muncy, Pennsylvania, October 6, 1865. In 1889, he came to West Virginia and entered the lumber business at Oakvale, Mercer County. Two years later he moved to Welch, where he organized the Tug River Lumber Company. Its offices later moved to Bluefield and then to Bristol, Virginia, before Ritter brought the company to Huntington in 1901.

Ritter settled permanently in Huntington, marrying Mabel McClintock, a Marshall College (now Marshall University) graduate, in 1902. He purchased many important commercial properties in the Huntington business district and invested in lumber, coal, gas, and mineral developments in West Virginia and nearby states. He was a director of the First National Bank of Huntington, president of the Ritter-Burns Lumber Company, the Ritter Hardwood Lumber Company, the C. L. Ritter Lumber Company, the Central Realty Company, the Huntington Land Company, the Rock Castle Lumber Company, the Turkey Foot Lumber Company, the Norfolk Land Company, the Empire Furniture Company, and others.

Ritter died in Huntington, December 22, 1945. He is remembered today in the name of Huntington's Ritter Park, to which he donated acreage.

Mary Lou Pratt
Huntington

Ritter Park

Ritter Park, a 75-acre municipal park located on the south side of Huntington, is nearly a century old. Most of the land, 55 acres, was originally purchased by the city in 1908 as the site for a proposed municipal incinerator. But nearby residents were so opposed to the incinerator plan that Mayor Rufus Switzer agreed to convert it to the city's first major public park. The park got its name when businessman C. L. Ritter donated an additional 20 acres.

Ritter Park was dedicated in 1913, but due to a change in administration at City Hall development of park facilities did not begin until the late 1920s and early 1930s. During the Great Depression, federal support from the Works Progress Administration contributed to constructing the roads and stonework around the park. More recent additions include a playground, indoor and outdoor tennis courts, and an open amphitheater. There is a historic log cabin maintained by the Daughters of the American Revolution, and a one-mile walking track around the park perimeter is a popular place for residents to jog, walk their dogs, or simply stroll for exercise.

See also Huntington, Charles Lloyd Ritter

Tom D. Miller
Huntington

W. M. Ritter Lumber Company

Incorporated in 1901 by William M. Ritter, the W. M. Ritter Lumber Company quickly became one of West Virginia's largest lumber and sawmill companies. The company had operations in several counties of West Virginia and in Virginia, Kentucky, Tennessee, and North and South Carolina. The company grew so quickly that Ritter organized it into four divisions to govern operations in the six states into which his business had spread.

With growth, the company headquarters was moved from Welch to Columbus, Ohio, and then to Roanoke, Virginia. Recognizing that the forests were being depleted, Ritter sought to diversify. In 1923, the company acquired the Red Jacket Consolidated Coal and Coke Company with stores and mines near Matewan and in Virginia. The company stores were sold in 1957 and the coal reserves were leased to the Island Creek Coal Company in 1957. In 1960, the entire Ritter company was sold to the Georgia-Pacific Corporation. In nearly 60 years of operation, the W. M. Ritter Lumber Company sold more than three billion board feet of lumber.

See also William M. Ritter

Kenneth R. Bailey
WVU Institute of Technology

William M. Ritter

William McClellan Ritter, born February 19, 1864, in Lycoming County, Pennsylvania, was one of West Virginia's most prominent lumbermen. Having learned the lumber business on his father's Pennsylvania farm, he began a logging operation in Mercer County in 1890. He was successful and, in addition to harvesting timber for others, soon set up his own mills. His operations included Mercer, McDowell, and Mingo counties, as well as Buchanan County, Virginia, and Pike County, Kentucky.

Ritter incorporated as the W. M. Ritter Lumber Company in 1901 and expanded his operations into Tennessee, North Carolina, and South Carolina. He first used circular-saw mills but changed to much larger band-saw mills, including a double band mill operation at Maben, Wyoming County. During World War I, Ritter moved his primary residence from Welch to Washington, where he served on the War Industries Board as an adviser to Chairman Bernard Baruch. In addition to his lumber interests, Ritter owned and operated coal companies and railroads in Virginia and West Virginia, including the Red Jacket Coal Company near Matewan in Mingo County. In 1907, the W. M. Ritter Lumber Company was indicted by a federal grand jury on a charge of peonage. Ritter, on behalf of his company, entered a guilty plea and paid a fine on the charges.

Ritter's later life was spent in Washington, from where he directed his many business interests. In 1924, he made national headlines by sharing $3,000,000 in Ritter company stock with his employees. Ritter was married twice. When he died May 21, 1952, as the result of complications from a stroke, he was survived by his wife, Anita Bell Ritter, and a foster son, Paul D. Ritter. He was buried in a family cemetery in Hughesville, Pennsylvania. William M. Ritter was a cousin of lumberman Charles L. Ritter of Huntington, for whom Ritter Park is named.

See also W. M. Ritter Lumber Company
Kenneth R. Bailey
WVU Institute of Technology

Kenneth R. Bailey, "A Temptation to Lawlessness, Peonage in West Virginia, 1903–1908," *West Virginia History*, 1991; Dennis E. Reedy, *The W. M. Ritter Lumber Company Family History Book,* privately printed; "Ritter, Pioneer Lumber, Coal Operator, Dies in Capital," *Charleston Daily Mail*, May 22, 1952.

River Transportation

Long before Europeans ventured across the Appalachian Mountains, Indians were plying the inland rivers in various types of boats, the most notable being the bark canoe. Made of birch, hickory, or elm bark, these ranged from small two-person canoes to much bigger boats capable of carrying more than a dozen men and heavy cargo. Other vessels used by the Indians were dugout canoes made of tree trunks that had been hollowed out by fire and ax. The bark canoe was easily transportable, readily repaired, and could be used as a shelter on land, if needed. The dugout canoe was heavy, awkward, and was not taken from the river.

Early settlers found these native boats useful, and both dugout and bark canoes were extensively adapted for trade and travel. A variety of other vessels were developed to carry heavier commerce. The most popular were the keelboat and flatboat.

Keelboats were usually 60 to 80 feet long and 15 to 20 feet wide. Constructed with a shaped bow and stern and a keel running the full length of the deep hull, they were used to transport passengers and freight both upstream and downstream. Going downstream the boat floated with the current, but moving upstream required six to 18 men setting pike poles in the bottom of the river and pushing against the pole while walking the length of the boat. Keelboats operated from the 1780s until about the beginning of the Civil War.

There were many varieties of boats referred to as flatboats, all more primitive than keelboats. These traveled only downstream and were torn apart when they reached their destination, to be used locally as building material. Known as flatboats, Kentucky boats, Orleans boats, or broadhorns, according to certain design differences, these boats were roughly built, box-like vessels ranging up to 90 feet or longer by 20 to 24 feet wide. Floating downstream, steered by heavy long paddles and a rudder, the flatboat came to be known as the "Ark of the Empire" because of the number of immigrant families and the amount of Ohio Valley products such boats moved to the west and to New Orleans. Flatboats were used to ship bulk products downstream until after the turn of the 20th century.

In 1811, the first steamboat on the inland rivers was launched on the Ohio River at Pittsburgh. Named the *New Orleans*, it was followed by thousands more. Significant improvements in steamboat design were made in the *Washington*, launched at Wheeling in 1816. Steamboats would be the major mode of river transportation until well into the 20th century. By the 1830s, there had been improvements in the design and construction of the sidewheel and sternwheel boats and their steam engines, and

A towboat and barges approach the East Huntington Bridge on the Ohio River.

450 boats operated on the Ohio River and its tributaries. Extensive navigation improvements to the rivers were begun during this period and continue to the present.

In West Virginia steamboats operated on the Big Sandy, the Kanawha and Little Kanawha, the Ohio, Monongahela, and even on a short stretch of the New River at Hinton. There were three major types of steamboats: the packetboat, carrying passengers and limited freight between cities and towns; ferryboats, carrying passengers and light vehicles across streams; and towboats that were used to push sometimes large fleets of barges loaded with bulk raw materials. There were several variations of these vessels, including excursion boats, showboats, and raftboats.

Steamboats were the major means of passenger transportation within the Mississippi River basin until after the Civil War and competed successfully with trains until the 1920s. Between the 1920s and 1930s, packetboats disappeared from inland rivers, while towboats were improved by being constructed of steel and powered with diesel engines and propellers. Larger barges made of steel replaced the old wooden barges.

Today's modern towboats equipped with radar, sonar, satellite communications systems, and licensed personnel provide the nation with the cheapest method of transportation available for the shipment of bulk commodities, including West Virginia coal. Rivers remain important for the movement of bulk goods. At present the Ohio, Monongahela, Big Sandy, and Kanawha are all used for river navigation. Hundreds of millions of tons of cargo are shipped on these streams each year. Coal and coke are the leading commodities moved by water in West Virginia, followed by petroleum, sand and gravel, and chemicals. Huntington is the country's largest inland port, based on tonnage shipped.

Passenger travel is a thing of the past on West Virginia waters, and excursion boats have had mixed success. The P. A. Denny which operated for many years on the Great Kanawha River, departed Charleston in 2004. The Blennerhassett Island fleet runs visitors from Parkersburg to the Island and back. There have been excursion boats at Huntington, Wheeling, and other towns, but none has been successful for more than a few years.

See also Locks and Dams, U.S. Army Corps of Engineers

Gerald W. Sutphin
Huntington

Archer Butler Hulbert, *Waterways Of Westward Expansion, The Ohio River And Its Tributaries*, 1903; Louis C. Hunter, *Steamboats On The Western Rivers*, 1949; Ethel C. Leahy, *Who's Who on the Ohio River*, 1931.

Roadside Historical Markers

Roadside markers throughout West Virginia mark the location of significant historical events, as well as prehistoric sites and many geological and natural features. The popular program was begun in 1934. Since then, nearly 1,000 markers have been installed on our state's roadsides.

The marker program was first managed by the Commission on Historic and Scenic Highway Markers, which initially identified 440 sites for marking. These markers were erected in 1937, with funding from the Federal Emergency Relief Administration, an agency of President Franklin Roosevelt's New Deal. The State Road Commission cooperated in installing the markers. The original basic design, 42 inches wide and 30 inches high, with a circular state seal at the top, is still in use today. The handsome monuments, mounted on round steel posts, have been made of cast aluminum for most of the program's history. The short historical message is repeated on both sides, although a few markers have a different text on the front and back.

While activity waned after the early years, the centennial of the Civil War and of West Virginia statehood revived interest in the marker program in the 1960s. Existing markers were inventoried, damaged and missing markers were replaced, and nearly 300 additional sites were marked. Since that time, new markers have been added yearly, as funds permit. Administrators point to the high cost of new markers, as well as vandalism, accidental damage, and inadequate funding as particular problems. In recent years, markers have been financed largely by private donations and by funds provided by West Virginia Celebration 2000 and administered by the West Virginia Humanities Council.

Today, the roadside markers program is operated by the Archives and History Section of the West Virginia Division of Culture and History, with the cooperation of the Division of Highways. New markers are approved by the Archives and History Commission. Guides to the texts and locations of roadside markers have been issued from time to time, most recently in 2002.

Marking Our Past: West Virginia's Historical Highway Markers, 2002.

Roane County

Roane County has an area of 486.2 square miles, its terrain hilly with narrow valleys. Ridges and hilltops rise to 1,000 feet, with some to 1,500 feet in the southeastern section. The principal streams are the Pocatalico River and Big Sandy Creek in the south, and several tributaries of the Little Kanawha River in the north. Wirt, Calhoun, Clay, Kanawha, and Jackson counties border Roane County.

U.S. 33 crosses Roane County east to west through Spencer; State Route 36 travels from Clay County north to Spencer; and State Route 14 goes north from Spencer to Wood County. U.S. 119 comes up from the south to intersect U.S. 33 at Spencer and then follows U.S. 33 eastward. Interstate 79 crosses the southern tip of the county.

Roane County was created by an act of the Virginia legislature on March 11, 1856, from parts of Kanawha, Jackson, and Gilmer counties. The new county was named for Judge Spencer Roane, a son-in-law of Patrick Henry. The citizens of the new county chose New California (later Spencer) as the county seat over Looneyville.

Jesse Hughes, the scout, hunter, and explorer, is reputed to have been the first person of European descent to enter the area, around 1770. He later settled in present Roane County, along with relatives such as the Gandees, Tanners, Bonnets, and Alkire-Holswades. Many residents of Roane County trace their ancestry to Hughes. The first settlers came in 1809. The families of John Kelly, Ware Long, and Francis Garner settled along Big Sandy Creek below the present community of Left Hand. Later John Ashley and his family arrived at the same site, thereafter known as Ashley's Settlement. Spencer was first settled by the Samuel Tanner and Jonathan Wolfe families in 1812, with the Runnions arriving in 1818. Those first settlers lived in isolation until the 1830s when families such as the Goffs, Greathouses, Vandals, and Carpenters settled in the Spring Creek area.

Spencer and the other villages served the surrounding countryside with gristmills, general stores, tanneries, and other services. Spencer developed as the chief town after the construction of the Gilmer, Ripley & Ohio Turnpike and other roads in the 1850s and the town's selection as the county seat. Reedy, the principal business center in the northern part of the county and the county's other municipality, was established at the crossroads of the Ravenswood-Reedy Turnpike and the Reedy-Spencer Road.

Walton, on the Pocatalico River, is the principal community in the southern part of the county. Charles Droddy came to the area in the 1820s to buy furs and game, met Sarah Gandee, and married her before the end of the decade. They bought a large tract of land and started a gristmill, general store, and a boarding house. This area at the crossroads of two important trails became known as Droddyville or Droddy's Mills. Meanwhile, the first post office in present Roane County, established around 1844, was located at a place named Walton, a few miles from present Walton. In 1856, the post office and the name were moved to Droddyville, which became Walton. Walton High

Civil War graves overlook Spencer, the county seat of Roane County.

School was established in 1923. It and Spencer High School were consolidated into a new Roane County High School in 1993.

Roane County depended on an agricultural economy centering on cattle and sheep. The number of farms rose from 834 in 1870 to 2,825 in 1900, while average farm size fell by two-thirds. During the same period the portion of the county's land used for crops or pastures rose from 67 percent to 87 percent. Roads leading to river ports on the Ohio, Little Kanawha, and Elk rivers served as the main arteries for mail service and the import and export of goods. Major road and bridge improvements came in the 1870s and 1880s. A branch of the Baltimore & Ohio Railroad gave a major boost to the economy, especially the cattle and timber industries. It operated from 1892 until the early 1960s. During this time, too, was the beginning of the oil and gas industry, with drilling beginning around 1868. Spencer became an oil town in the early 1900s. Spencer State Hospital, originally known as the Second Hospital for the Insane, opened July 18, 1893, and employed many area residents until its closing in 1989.

Roane County had a population of 15,446 in 2000 and was served by three banks and two weekly newspapers. Roane County Library has locations in Spencer, Walton, and Left Hand. There is one hospital, Roane General. The leading industries are petroleum, natural gas, and timber and its products. The chief agricultural products are hay and grain, livestock, dairying, and poultry. Residents of Roane County in 1999 had a per capita income of $13,195, compared to $16,477 for West Virginia as a whole.

Spring Heights Education Center, a 1,000-acre United Methodist outdoor religious center, is located north of Spen-

cer. Charles Fork Lake is the location of the annual Tour de Lake bike race, and during the second week of October Spencer hosts the Black Walnut Festival. Col. Ruby Bradley (1907–2002) decorated military nurse and war heroine, was among the notable Roane Countians.

See also Jesse Hughes, Spencer

David F. Matthews
Fairmont State University

Maxine Kee, "Roane County," in Jim Comstock, ed., *West Virginia Heritage Encyclopedia*, 1976; James P. Mylott, *A Measure of Prosperity: A History of Roane County, West Virginia*, 1984.

Robert C. Byrd U.S. Courthouse

Dedicated on May 28, 1998, the Robert C. Byrd United States Courthouse in downtown Charleston was the first courthouse to use federal design guidelines requiring separate and secure corridors for judges, prisoners, and the public. The 440,000-square-foot building, named for West Virginia's eight-term U.S. senator, incorporates Neoclassic, Egyptian, and Art Deco designs. The building replaced the former federal courthouse on Quarrier Street.

An $80.4 million federal appropriation paid for the land, architectural design, and construction. Architects Skidmore, Owings, and Merrill of New York designed the building. Original plans included 10 stories topped by a silver, perforated steel dome, which would have complemented the state capitol's gold dome across the city. After construction bids exceeded appropriation estimates, architects eliminated one story and the steel dome.

Bounded by Virginia, Quarrier, Truslow, and Goshorn streets, the courthouse occupies one city block. The main entrance on Virginia Street, a four-story portico leading to three doors, features three tall stained glass panels, 39 feet high by 10 feet wide, topped by a panel 33 feet high and 32 feet wide. David Wilson designed the panels, which include geometric motifs and colors found throughout the courthouse. Precast concrete slabs resembling limestone make up the building's exterior. An aluminum cornice tops the structure. The building has 11 levels, including two levels for underground garages, four floors for court-oriented federal offices, three levels for courtrooms, judges' chambers, and a law library, and two levels for mechanical and electrical equipment.

In 1999, the courthouse won design awards for architecture and art from the General Services Administration, and the government-public construction award from *Buildings* magazine.

Cecil Roberts

Labor leader Cecil Edward Roberts Jr. was born October 31, 1946, on Cabin Creek, Kanawha County. A sixth-generation coal

FAST FACTS ABOUT ROANE COUNTY

Founded: 1856
Land in square miles: 486.2
Population: 15,446
Percentage minorities: 1.4%
Percentage rural: 78.9%
Median age: 39.5
Percentage 65 and older: 14.8%
Birth rate per 1,000 population: 11.2
Median household income: $24,511
High school graduate or higher: 66.8%
Bachelor's degree or higher: 9.0%
Home ownership: 79.6%
Median home value: $56,600

This information is from the 2000 U.S. Census. In 2000, West Virginia as a whole had 5 percent minorities, a median age of 38.9, median household income of $29,696, and a 75.2 percent home ownership rate.

miner and a fiery orator, Roberts has served as president of the United Mine Workers of America since 1995. He succeeded Richard L. Trumka, who resigned as UMW president to become secretary-treasurer of the AFL-CIO.

Roberts graduated from West Virginia Institute of Technology in 1987. His great-uncle, Bill Blizzard, was a legendary union organizer during the Mine Wars of the early 20th century. Beginning in 1971, after military service in Vietnam, Roberts worked for six years at various underground mining jobs at Carbon Fuel's No. 31 mine in Winifrede. In the 1970s, he served on the mine, safety, and political action committees for Local Union 2236. He was also active in Miners for Democracy, the group of union members who ousted the union's corrupt leaders in 1972.

In 1977, Roberts was elected vice-president of UMWA District 17, which covered Boone, Logan, Mingo, Lincoln, Wayne, Kanawha, Clay, and parts of Raleigh and Wyoming counties. Five years later, running on a slate with Richard Trumka, he was elected UMWA vice-president. In 1989, Roberts played a key role in the union's successful 10-month strike against the Pittston Company. He led miners during daily demonstrations and negotiated to restore health benefits to retired miners. For his efforts, Roberts received the Martin Luther King award from the Rainbow Coalition.

Serving initially as Trumka's successor, Roberts was first elected UMW president in 1997. He has served continuously since that time.

See also Miners for Democracy, Pittston Strike, United Mine Workers of America

Spanky Roberts

Aviator George Spencer "Spanky" Roberts, the first African-American military pilot from West Virginia, was a member of the famous Tuskegee Airmen during World War II. He was born September 24, 1918, in London, Kanawha County, the son of Spencer and Estella Roberts. He graduated from Fairmont's Dunbar High School in 1934 and from West Virginia State College (now University) in 1938, with a B.S. in mechanical arts.

After receiving his pilot's license in the Civilian Pilot Training Program, Roberts entered aviation cadet training with the first class of Tuskegee Airmen, who trained at the Tuskegee Institute in Alabama. He completed his training on March 7, 1942, and was commissioned a 2nd lieutenant. He entered combat in North Africa in May 1943, eventually flying more than 100 missions against the enemy in Africa, Europe, and the Middle East.

Following the war Roberts became the senior Air Corps ROTC instructor at Tuskegee Institute. He also served in Korea and Okinawa. In 1963, Roberts was as-

signed to Griffis Air Force Base where he was responsible for all ground radar in the Air Force. During the Vietnam War he served as deputy for logistics for fighters in Vietnam. Roberts retired with the rank of colonel at McClellan Air Force Base in 1968. His decorations included the Air Force Commendation Medal with four oak clusters and two presidential citations. He died March 8, 1984, in Sacramento, California.

L. Wayne Sheets
Charleston

Ancella R. Bickley, "Dubie, Spanky, and Mr. Death: West Virginia's Pioneering Black Airmen," *Goldenseal*, Summer 1997.

C. Donald Robertson

Charles Donald Robertson, state attorney general for eight years and candidate for the Democratic nomination for governor, was born June 9, 1926, in Clarksburg. He received his undergraduate and law degrees at West Virginia University. He married Shirley Anne Stotler, and they had two children. He served as a member of the House of Delegates from Harrison County for four years (1956–60). Elected attorney general in 1960, he was re-elected in 1964. In 1968, he ran for governor in the Democratic primary and lost to James Sprouse.

After leaving public office, Robertson was indicted along with his brother, Dana Robertson, and former state Federal Housing Administration Director James F. Haught in 1971 on federal charges of taking kickbacks on FHA low-income housing assistance. He pleaded guilty to conspiracy and one count of using interstate communication facilities to further a racketeering scheme. He was sentenced in December of 1972 to five years in federal prison and fined $15,000. Robertson was believed by many to be one of the individuals who assisted federal investigators in their probe of former Governor Barron and members of his administration, leading to criminal indictments of Barron and three other state officials on charges of bid-rigging of state contracts and taking kickbacks.

C. Donald Robertson died on April 27, 1996, in Charleston.

Tom D. Miller
Huntington

Rock Climbing

Rock climbing is a growing sport in West Virginia. Popular sites include Seneca Rocks, the New River Gorge, and Summersville Lake.

Seneca Rocks in Pendleton County, an imposing sandstone fin, rises 1,000 feet to a knife-edge summit. It challenges climbers with more than 400 routes from easy to very difficult. According to legend, Indians made the earliest ascents of Seneca's vertical walls. Paul Bradt, Don Hubbard, and Sam Moore undertook the

first documented climb of Seneca Rocks in 1939, only to discover when they reached the summit the mysterious inscription: "D.B. Sept. 16, 1908." During World War II, the military used Seneca Rocks to train soldiers in climbing and other mountaineering skills. Since the early 1950s, Seneca has seen a steady increase of recreational climbers.

In the late 1970s, a small group of climbers began exploring the miles of sandstone cliffs that line the New River Gorge. By the mid-1980s, a few climbers visited the area regularly. Part of New River Gorge National River, the canyon now boasts more than 1,500 established routes and a wide variety of climbing, from gentle slabs to steep overhangs.

Twenty miles north of the New River Gorge, the cliffs surrounding Summersville Lake also provide hundreds of high-quality climbs. The sandstone conglomerate cliffs surrounding the lake offer vertical to steep, overhanging sport routes and a few traditional routes. During the late spring, summer, and early fall Summersville is popular with visiting climbers from Washington and surrounding areas. Summersville boasts safe, bolt-protected sport routes rating from easy to very difficult. Several famous overhanging routes such as "Mercy Seat" and "Apollo Reed" add to the fame of Summersville Lake. During the winter when the Army Corps of Engineers drains the lake, additional routes (reachable only by boat in the summer) become available for climbing.

Several rock climbing guide services now operate at Seneca Rocks and the New River Gorge.

Lucia K. Hyde
Charleston

Rock Lake Pool

Rock Lake Pool, located in South Charleston, was created in the 1930s from an abandoned limestone quarry. The 200-by-400-foot pool was one of the largest concrete-bottom pools in the United States. Water slides, spraying fountain, and trapeze swings helped make Rock Lake a popular recreation spot. As many as 4,000 people were known to visit on a hot summer day. WCHS-TV broadcast dance shows from the upstairs of Rock Lake's clubhouse.

In the 1960s, Rock Lake became a civil rights battleground. The pool remained racially segregated even after the 1964 Civil Rights Act outlawed discrimination in places of public accommodation. African-American clergymen Homer Davis and Paul Gilmer led those seeking to desegregate Rock Lake, the only public swimming pool of any size in the Charleston area. Protests included a march featuring a speech by the Reverend C. T. Vivian, an aide to Martin Luther King Jr., and a human blockade in front of the ticket window. Finally in 1967, Rock Lake allowed blacks to use the facility.

While Rock Lake survived the civil rights controversy, factors such as the building of government-subsidized swimming pools and rising insurance costs later contributed to the pool's demise. The owners closed Rock Lake in 1985 and sold the property in the early 1990s. In 1993, Putt-Putt Golf and Games Center opened there, featuring three miniature golf courses amid the 60-foot cliffs, as well as paddle-boats, picnic facilities, and arcade games. Later, a go-cart track was added as Rock Lake became a popular recreation facility once again.

Allison Smith
Charleston

Rock Springs Park

Rock Springs Park was an amusement park located in Chester, at the tip of the Northern Panhandle. While its lush valley of shade trees and cool springs attracted picnickers as early as the 1880s, Rock Springs was opened as a commercial park in May 1897. Like other such parks, its development was connected to the street car system. A new bridge over the Ohio River had opened a few months before, carrying a trolley line directly to the park's entrance. During the next decade developers J. E. McDonald and C. A. Smith made the park a showcase of the tri-state area. In its peak years, Rock Springs employed 350 workers and had daily attendances as high as 20,000. Popular rides were the Old Mill, Shoot the-Chutes, and the Scenic Railway. Pleasure seekers could also swim, boat, stroll the gardens, see a stage production, visit the zoo, or dance in the casino.

By the 1950s, the park had suffered a number of financial blows, including the rescinding of railroad excursion rates and the Depression. Reduced in size and grandeur, it continued to operate until 1970 when it was purchased by the Department of Highways. All structures were sold at public auction in 1974 to make way for the new road and Ohio River bridge. The Rock Springs carousel, a 1920s Dentzel model with 48 carved horses, found a home with the Freels Foundation in San Francisco. The spring "that flowed from a solid wall of rock" is now a trickle in the basin between the roads.

Susan M. Weaver
Kent State University

Jay Rockefeller

John Davison "Jay" Rockefeller IV became West Virginia's 29th governor in 1977. Rockefeller, whose great-grandfather was at one time considered the richest man in the world, was born in New York City, June 18, 1937. At the age of 12, he enrolled at Phillips Exeter Academy in New Hampshire, where he became inter-

Governor Jay Rockefeller (1937—) was later a U.S. Senator.

ested in Far Eastern studies. He later obtained a degree in Asian languages and history from Harvard, and spent from 1957 to 1960 at the International Christian University in Tokyo.

Rockefeller came to West Virginia in 1964 as a poverty volunteer with Action for Appalachian Youth, becoming a social worker in Emmons, Kanawha County. Fighting the carpetbagger label and adopting West Virginia as his home, he climbed to the governor's office in a dozen years after his arrival in the state. He raised his four children in West Virginia and acquired homes in Charleston and Pocahontas County.

Rockefeller entered politics in January 1966, changing his registration from Republican to Democrat and filing as a Kanawha County candidate for the House of Delegates. His break from the Rockefeller family's Republican affiliation attracted national attention. In the primary he received the most votes of about 60 candidates for 14 House seats, and in the November general election was the top vote getter.

In 1967, Rockefeller married Sharon Percy, the daughter U.S. Sen. Charles Percy of Illinois. Rockefeller announced his candidacy for secretary of state in 1968. In the primary for his first statewide campaign, he carried every county but Mingo. He defeated his Republican challenger by more than 155,000 votes in the general election.

The first indication that Rockefeller intended to run for governor came in 1970. He declared that "strip mining of coal must be prohibited by law, completely and forever," a landmark stand by a West Virginia politician. In January 1972, Rockefeller announced his candidacy for governor and overwhelmed his two opponents in the primary, setting up a fierce contest against popular incumbent Arch Moore. In the general election Moore de-

feated Rockefeller by 73,355 votes. Rockefeller believed his stand on strip mining influenced his poor showing in the coal counties in the southern part of the state, and later altered his position. Campaign spending drew attention, as Rockefeller reported spending more than $1.5 million, then a high for one candidate in a single election. Moore spent $696,029.

Rockefeller's four-year term as secretary of state ended January 15, 1973, and on March 1 he became president of West Virginia Wesleyan College. There he worked to bring a turnaround in declining enrollment and an improvement in the private college's financial situation. He submitted his resignation as president of Wesleyan in May 1975, and in October he announced another race for governor.

Easily outdistancing the other seven Democratic candidates in the primary, Rockefeller carried every county but Barbour and Monroe. The state Supreme Court had ruled Moore could not run for a third consecutive term, and former Gov. Cecil Underwood became the Republican nominee. Wealth once again became an issue. In the general election Rockefeller defeated Underwood by a vote of almost two to one, 495,659 to 253,423, the largest majority in state history. Records showed almost $2.8 million had been spent on Rockefeller's campaign.

The new governor had to deal with heavy snowfalls across the state, acute fuel shortages, rampaging floods, and a 111-day coal strike during his administration. On his recommendation, large segments of state government were reorganized, to include the state Department of Health, the Department of Culture and History, and the creation of a state Department of Economic and Community Development. Rockefeller's establishment of the position of special assistant to the governor for economic and community development was his attempt to fulfill a campaign promise to give priority to economic development. Among the achievements was the location of a $500 million coal liquefaction demonstration plant in Morgantown.

Governor Rockefeller moved into the national spotlight in 1978 by becoming chairman of the President's Commission on Coal. He insisted that coal be given a higher standing in the national energy policy and worked to expand coal markets in the U.S. and abroad. In 1979, during the third year of his term, Rockefeller carried out a campaign promise by persuading the legislature to gradually eliminate the three percent sales tax on food. The tax was returned and increased after his term as governor.

With the election of 1980, the incumbent Rockefeller again faced Arch Moore. This time Rockefeller prevailed, defeating Moore by about 64,500 votes. Rockefeller reported in a pre-election statement that he would spend $9.5 million in this campaign, but the final report after the election showed that he spent closer to $12 million. Moore spent about $1 million in his unsuccessful effort.

After his second term as governor, a time in which the state plunged into a deep recession, Rockefeller was elected to the U.S. Senate in 1984 and reelected in 1990, 1996, and 2002. As a senator, he has continued to emphasize economic development, and was successful in persuading Toyota to build a plant in Putnam County. He has taken a particular interest in the steel industry. He was among those aiding the employee buyout of Weirton Steel in 1984 and has worked to arrange aid and protection for American steelworkers. He was successful in passing legislation in 1992 to ensure continued funding of the United Mine Workers health insurance through a levy on coal production. Rockefeller has continued to advocate comprehensive health care reform. In 2005, he was vice chairman of the Senate Intelligence Committee.

In the 2004 presidential campaign there was speculation that Rockefeller might be selected as John Kerry's running mate, but he said at the time, "I have no interest in any other job than being the senator from West Virginia."

Richard S. Grimes
Charleston

Rocket Boys

In 1998, retired NASA engineer and McDowell County native Homer H. Hickam Jr. published his boyhood memoir, *Rocket Boys*. The book recalls the waning days of coal mining in the town of Coalwood, the dawn of space exploration in the late 1950s, and the lofty aspirations of a group of mountain boys. In 1999, Universal Studios released the film *October Sky*, based on Hickam's book. The best-selling book and popular movie brought national attention to Coalwood and Hickam's classmates.

Hickam was born February 19, 1943, in Coalwood, where his father was the mine superintendent. Hickam remembers his youth as two distinct time periods: before October 4, 1957, and after. On that day, the U.S.S.R. launched Sputnik, the first space satellite. Fascinated by the ensuing space race, Hickam and five of his Big Creek High School buddies—Roy Lee Cooke, Willie Rose, Jim O'Dell Carroll, Quentin Wilson, and Sherman Siers— began building rockets themselves.

With encouragement from their high school chemistry teacher, Freida Joy Riley, Hickam and his friends immersed themselves in advanced math and physics. They tested their rockets at an abandoned coal dump, which they named Cape Coalwood. The boys won the county science fair with their exhibit, "A Study of Amateur Rocketry Techniques," and went on to take top prize at the 1960 National Science Fair.

Hickam graduated from Virginia Tech, served in Vietnam, and worked for the U.S. Army Missile Command in Huntsville, Alabama. From 1981 until his retirement in 1998, he worked for NASA. Hickam's other books include *Torpedo Junction, Back to the Moon, The Coalwood Way,* and *Sky of Stone*, also a Coalwood memoir.

Rat Rodgers

Athlete Ira Errett "Rat" Rodgers was among the greatest Mountaineer football players, lettering in 1915–17 and 1919. He was born at Bethany, May 26, 1895, and started his athletic career as a high-school level prep student at Bethany College (1911–14) before moving to West Virginia University.

Rodgers was named to All-American teams in 1916, 1917, and 1919. He was the leading scorer in the nation in 1919, with 19 touchdowns and seven conversions for 147 points. Rodgers accounted for more touchdowns by running or passing (66) than any other player in WVU history. He ran for 42 touchdowns and passed for 24 others over his career. He was recognized as WVU's greatest all-time athlete, starring in basketball and baseball as well as football.

Rodgers, who died February 22, 1963, served the university for four decades as a professor and coach and is in WVU's athletic Hall of Fame. He was admitted to the College Football Hall of Fame in 1953.

John C. Veasey
Times West Virginian
Kent Kessler, *Hail West Virginians!*, 1959.

Ruth Bryan Owen Rohde

Congresswoman and diplomat Ruth Bryan Owen Rohde was the daughter of the great populist orator, William Jennings Bryan. She was born in Illinois, October 2, 1885. The first woman elected to Congress from the South and America's first woman ambassador, she represented Florida's Fourth District, 1929–33, and was U.S. Minister to Denmark, 1933–36. In Congress she sponsored legislation creating the Everglades National Park, and later she served on the drafting committee for the United Nations charter and as an alternate delegate to the U.N.

In 1939, Rohde came to the Alderson mansion known as the Cedars, owned by Borge Rohde, a Danish captain whom she met in Denmark and married in 1936. For the next several years she lived off and on at the Greenbrier County estate, which previously had been the home of Mrs. Alex. McVeigh Miller, a novelist. Rohde served on the advisory board of Alderson's Federal Reformatory for Women, 1938–54.

Rohde died July 26, 1954, on a trip to Denmark. She is buried in Copenhagen.

See also Mrs. Alex. McVeigh Miller

Jack Rollins

Songwriter Walter E. "Jack" Rollins, born September 15, 1906, in Keyser, wrote the lyrics to "Here Comes Peter Cottontail" and "Frosty the Snow Man," two of America's most popular songs. Rollins left his Mineral County home at 18, working first at a glass factory in Pittsburgh and later traveling with a carnival.

Rollins sold song lyrics as a freelancer before joining music publishers Hill and Range in New York in 1948. In 1949, he wrote the lyrics to "Peter Cottontail," with Steve Nelson writing the music. The song sold more than a million copies, with recordings by Guy Lombardo, Gene Autry, Dinah Shore, Roy Rogers, and others. In 1950, Rollins wrote "Frosty the Snow Man," with Nelson again supplying the tune. The song was popularized by Jimmy Durante and later recorded by many others. Rollins, who authored about 500 songs, also wrote "Smokey the Bear" in 1952.

Rollins spent nearly 30 years in Hollywood, moving to Cincinnati in 1965. He died January 1, 1973, and is buried in Keyser.

Roman Catholics

The first significant Catholic presence in Western Virginia came in the years immediately following the American Revolution, when Virginia repealed its anti-Catholic laws. Small Catholic communities soon formed in what is now the Eastern Panhandle and in Wheeling.

A turning point came with the arrival of the Baltimore & Ohio Railroad in the mid-1840s. The railroad employed many laborers, some of whom were Catholic Irish immigrants who would settle in the region. Up until that time, the Catholics of Western Virginia had been under the spiritual care of the Diocese of Richmond, which represented the entire state of Virginia. Encouraged by the increase in the number of Catholics in the west, the bishop of Richmond, Richard V. Whelan, petitioned Rome to create a new diocese. On July 19, 1850, Pope Pius IX established the Diocese of Wheeling, naming Whelan as its first bishop.

The Allegheny Mountains were used as the initial boundary of the new diocese. The outbreak of the Civil War and the creation of the new state of West Virginia in 1863 meant that diocesan and state boundaries would be distinct from one another for more than 100 years. It was not until 1974, under a decree issued by Pope Paul VI, that the diocesan borders were realigned to agree with those of the state. The name of the diocese was changed at that time to the Diocese of Wheeling-Charleston.

The most important period of growth in the Catholic population was in the second half of the 19th century, when West Virginia began to industrialize. Bishop

John J. Kain (1875–93), who succeeded Whelan, served during this period. Immigrant Catholics came to work in the mines and factories, the ethnic groups arriving in successive waves. In the first part of the 19th century, immigration was dominated by the Irish and Germans. By the end of the century, immigrants from southern, central, and eastern Europe began to make up a substantial percentage of the state's Catholic population.

Rt. Rev. Patrick J. Donahue (1894–1922) was bishop of the Diocese of Wheeling during a continuing period of tremendous growth. In the 28 years he served, the Catholic population more than tripled, from approximately 20,000 when he was appointed in 1894 to more than 62,000 at his death in 1922. Donahue approved the establishment of nearly 150 churches and missions during his years as bishop and encouraged the founding of schools, hospitals, and orphanages.

Bishop Donahue was succeeded by John J. Swint, who served from 1922 to 1962. Bishop Swint came to office during a period sometimes referred to as "bricks-and-mortar Catholicism." The great wave of immigration was past, and attention turned from meeting the immediate needs of arriving immigrants to establishing the institutions to serve them and their children. At his death, close to 100 churches, a new cathedral, one college, 43 elementary and high schools, and five hospitals had been established under Bishop Swint's leadership.

Bishop Joseph H. Hodges (1962–85) succeeded Swint as the fifth bishop of the diocese. Bishop Hodges represented the diocese at the Second Vatican Council (1962–65). He dedicated his years as bishop to implementing the modernizing reforms of the council.

The successor to Hodges was Bishop Francis B. Schulte, who had been auxiliary bishop of the Archdiocese of Philadelphia. Evangelization was an important priority for Bishop Schulte. Schulte was succeeded by Bernard W. Schmitt in 1989. As he attended to issues of spiritual vitality, religious education, and social issues, Bishop Schmitt also addressed the staffing of parishes and missions as the number of clergy declined. Schmitt was succeeded by Michael J. Bransfield in 2005.

After more than 100 years of growth, West Virginia's Roman Catholic population peaked in the mid-20th century and has declined somewhat since that time. While exact numbers are hard to find, it appears that there were something over 110,000 Catholics in 1960 and about 100,000 in 2000. Catholics account for over five percent of the state's population.

Today, the Diocese of Wheeling-Charleston, made up of 112 parishes, is the second-largest provider of social services in the state, operating programs that range from emergency relief to parenting classes. The Catholic school system, which includes Wheeling Jesuit University, 32 elementary and high schools, and preschool and day care programs, is the largest privately run school system in West Virginia. From Wheeling Hospital, in the Northern Panhandle, recognized as the first hospital founded in West Virginia, to the Children's Health Care Clinic in Pineville in the southern coalfields, the Catholic health care system has served the state's citizens for the past 150 years.

See also Diocese of Wheeling-Charleston, Religion

Tricia Pyne
St. Mary's Seminary & University, Maryland

Romney

The oldest incorporated town in West Virginia (along with Shepherdstown, chartered on the same day in 1762), Romney is the principal municipality in Hampshire County and the county seat. Romney is located in the lower valley of the Potomac River's South Branch. The earliest Europeans to reside there were Job and John Pearsall, who established homesteads before 1738. By the late 1740s, the town, then known as Pearsall's Flats, numbered approximately 200 settlers who had banded together for security during perilous times on the Appalachian frontier. With the outbreak of the French and Indian War in 1754, these settlers sought refuge in nearby Fort Pearsall, which was guarded by George Washington's troops.

By 1762, Thomas, Sixth Lord Fairfax, who owned much of what today is the Eastern Panhandle of West Virginia, persuaded Virginia's colonial governor to accept Pearsall's Flats as the county seat for Hampshire County, which had been created by the Virginia General Assembly in 1754. Fairfax renamed the place "Romney" after a town in his native England.

Owing to its strategic location on the Northwestern Turnpike, a 19th-century stage road following present U.S. 50, Romney changed hands during the Civil War at least 56 times. Most of the town's residents had sympathized with the South. Romney's Indian Mound Cemetery in June 1866 hosted one of the reunified nation's first Confederate grave decoration ceremonies, and in 1867 an early monument commemorating the Confederate dead was erected there. Historically important buildings in Romney include the Wilson-Woodrow-Mytinger House, the town's oldest surviving structure (about 1750); Literary Hall, built in 1870 by the Literary Society, West Virginia's first debating organization (founded 1819); and the West Virginia Schools for the Deaf and Blind (established 1870). Romney had 1,940 residents in 2000.

Ted Olson
East Tennessee State University

Rosbys Rock

Rosbys Rock is located in Marshall County about seven miles southeast of Moundsville on Big Grave Creek Road. It marks the spot near where on Christmas Eve, 1852, the last spike was driven to complete the Baltimore & Ohio Railroad from Baltimore to the Ohio River, the first rail line linking the Atlantic coast to the Ohio Valley.

Although there was no golden spike, there was a great celebration a few weeks later in Wheeling to commemorate the completion of the railroad and the arrival of the first train. To mark the spot where the final spike was driven the following words were carved upon the rock: *Rosbbys* [sic] *Rock Track Closed Christmas Eve 1852.* The stone itself is a huge sandstone rock of 900 cubic yards, about 64 feet long and 20 feet thick.

The nearby village, also called Rosbys Rock, greatly expanded with the advent of the railroad. Eight passenger and eight to 12 freight trains passed through every day at the height of service. The last passenger train made its final run through Rosbys Rock on October 26, 1957. After the final freight runs in 1972–73, the line was abandoned and removal of the tracks and bridges began in 1974.

With the railroad gone, Rosbys Rock returned to being a small town with only one general store and a few homes. Now even the store is gone. But the village and its great rock remain, reminders of a busier time.

See also Baltimore & Ohio Railroad
Sarah Harshman
Marc Harshman
Wheeling

Eleanor Roosevelt

Anna Eleanor Roosevelt, born October 11, 1884, in New York City, involved herself in important social reforms in West Virginia during the Great Depression. She became interested in social issues and politics while studying in England at the turn of the century.

In 1905, Eleanor's uncle, President Theodore Roosevelt, walked her down the aisle to marry her distant cousin, Franklin Delano Roosevelt. Mrs. Roosevelt returned to social activism and politics during World War I, after discovering that her husband was having an affair with her social secretary. She became a staunch women's activist, a skilled public speaker, and a writer for national publications.

While she was first lady, Mrs. Roosevelt visited the poverty-stricken multitudes across the country during the Great Depression and specifically sought relief for women and children. In 1933, she con-

Eleanor Roosevelt on a visit to Arthurdale.

vinced her husband to use Congressionally approved federal funds to establish the first national subsistence homestead community in Arthurdale, Preston County. She oversaw much of the project and visited Arthurdale several times. The federal government eventually established 99 subsistence homestead communities nationwide, including two more in West Virginia, at Dailey (Tygart Valley) and Red House. Red House was renamed Eleanor in her honor.

After her husband's death, Mrs. Roosevelt served as U.S. representative to the United Nations from 1945 to 1953 and 1961 to 1962. She also chaired the U.N. Human Rights Commission and the National Commission on the Status of Women. She died in New York City, November 7, 1962.

See also Arthurdale, Eleanor, Tygart Valley Homesteads

Amanda Griffith
Arthurdale Heritage

William Starke Rosecrans

General William Starke Rosecrans, the Union general who drove Confederate forces from Western Virginia in 1861, was born near Kingston, Ohio, September 6, 1819. He graduated fifth in his class from West Point, 1842, and served until 1854 as a lieutenant of engineers. As a civilian he worked in 1855–57 in Kanawha County as superintendent of a cannel coal company and president of the Coal River Navigation Company.

When the Civil War erupted, Rosecrans joined Gen. George McClellan's staff and was commissioned brigadier general, May 16, 1861. He commanded McClellan's right wing at the Battle of Rich Mountain (July 11), conceiving and executing the maneuver which won. Succeeding McClellan as regional commander on July 23, he suppressed rampant marauding by authorizing each town or district to elect a five-man committee of public safety. Meanwhile, Gen. Robert E. Lee left Richmond to coordinate the movements of quarreling Con-

federate generals William Loring, Henry Wise, and John Floyd. Ensuing operations from August to mid-November were plagued on both sides by sickness, rain, muddy roads which stalled supplies, numerous incompetent officers, and what Rosecrans characterized as "monstrously green" troops.

Rosecrans marched south from Clarksburg in early September to reinforce Gen. Jacob Cox at Gauley Bridge. Rosecrans encountered Floyd at the Battle of Carnifex Ferry, on September 10. Floyd retreated, as did Lee, who was thwarted at Cheat Mountain on September 12. The Confederates regrouped and concentrated at Big Sewell Mountain, but Rosecrans wisely drew off. Lee, seeing no prospect of breaking the stalemate, departed in late October. In operations around Gauley Bridge from October 29 to November 14, Floyd attempted to strike Rosecrans, but was outmaneuvered and forced to retreat. With Floyd's retreat to Peterstown, the Confederacy's most significant effort to recover West Virginia collapsed.

On March 11, 1862, Gen. John Frémont relieved Rosecrans, who finished the war in the West. He later served as minister to Mexico (1868–69) and in Congress from California (1881–85). He died at Redondo Beach, California, on March 11, 1898, and is buried in Arlington National Cemetery.

See also Battle of Carnifex Ferry, Battle of Cheat Mountain, Coal River Navigation Company, Robert E. Lee, Battle of Rich Mountain

David S. Newhall
Centre College

Benjamin L. Rosenbloom

Congressman Benjamin Louis Rosenbloom of Wheeling, representing the First Congressional District from 1921 to 1925, was the only Jewish congressman in West Virginia history. Rosenbloom was born in Braddock, Pennsylvania, June 3, 1880. He attended West Virginia University, playing on the 1901 and 1902 football teams. He later studied law at WVU and was admitted to the West Virginia bar in 1904. He practiced law in Wheeling until his retirement in 1951 and participated actively in the Ohio County Bar Association.

Rosenbloom served as state senator from Wheeling, 1915–19. A Republican, he was elected to Congress in 1920 and reelected in 1922. There he participated in early efforts to halt pollution of the nation's streams, and he was an outspoken opponent of Prohibition. He left Congress after his second term, unsuccessfully seeking the Republican nomination for U.S. Senate. He served as Wheeling's vice mayor from 1935 to 1939 and also sat on the city council.

Rosenbloom was a member of numerous Wheeling fraternal organizations, including the Moose, Elks, Odd Fellows, Knights of Pythias, and University Club. He was a contributing member of Wheeling's Jewish community and belonged to the Jewish fraternal organization B'nai B'rith. He died in Cleveland, Ohio, March 22, 1965.

Deborah R. Weiner
Jewish Museum of Maryland

Rotary

Rotary International, an organization of civic clubs and individuals, was founded by Paul P. Harris, in Chicago, in 1905. Based on the motto, "Service above Self," it has become not only a focus for local civic activities but also a force for international understanding, with clubs in most of the countries of the world. A well-known effort has been Rotary's "Polio Plus" campaign. Millions of children have been vaccinated and polio has been eliminated in much of the world.

The first Rotary club in West Virginia was established in Wheeling on March 10, 1915; followed by Huntington on July 1, 1915; and Charleston on December 1, 1915. Rotary now divides West Virginia into two districts, District 7550 (essentially south of the Kanawha River, including Charleston), having as of 2005, 1,500 members in 32 clubs; and District 7530, in the north, having 1,300 members in 31 clubs. Seven clubs in the Eastern Panhandle are part of another, multi-state district. Rotary clubs meet for a meal, usually lunch but in some cases dinner or breakfast, each week. Regular attendance is required. Local Rotary clubs typically include leading business and professional people. Rotary, once exclusively male, has successfully recruited women members since 1978. The Charleston club elected its first two women members in 1987. Rotary International made it universal in 1989.

Joseph Crosby Jefferds Jr.
Charleston

Andrew S. Rowan

Andrew Summers Rowan, famous for carrying a message from the American president to a Cuban rebel general, was born April 23, 1857, in Gap Mills, Monroe County. In 1898, when the U.S. faced war with Spain, President William McKinley needed to contact Cuban Gen. Calixto Garcia for military intelligence. Rowan, a lieutenant in the 19th U.S. Infantry, was chosen as the messenger.

From Jamaica, Rowan sailed in a small fishing boat across 100 miles of open sea to Cuba. His party then hacked its way through dense jungle to avoid Spanish patrols on the roads and trails. He delivered the message to Garcia. He left the same day to make the perilous trip back to the U.S. with some of Garcia's officers, crossing hostile waters in a boat with gunnysacks for sails. Later, Rowan was awarded a Distinguished Service Cross. Cuba's government gave him its highest honor, the Order of Carlos Manuel de Cespedes.

The incident became famous when Elbert Hubbard sold millions of copies of his 1899 pamphlet, *A Message to Garcia*. The pamphlet which lauded Rowan as an example to young men who needed "a stiffening of the vertebrae which will cause them to be loyal to a trust, to act promptly, concentrate their energies, do the thing—carry a message to Garcia." Rowan died January 10, 1943, and was buried with full military honors in Arlington National Cemetery.

Belinda Anderson
Asbury

Anne Newport Royall

Journalist Anne Newport was born June 11, 1769, and raised on the Pennsylvania and Virginia frontiers. At 17, she moved to Sweet Springs, Monroe County, with her widowed mother, who became Maj. William Royall's housekeeper. Royall encouraged Anne's use of his large library and tutored her in the history and politics of the Revolution and early Republic, an uncommon education for women of her era. She married Royall in 1797. Following his death in 1812, she moved to Charleston, (West) Virginia, then traveled throughout the South.

By 1824, Anne Royall had lost her inheritance to scheming relatives and was refused a pension as the widow of a Revolutionary War veteran. Needing an income, she resumed traveling and wrote, published, and marketed 11 volumes picturesquely describing people and places from New England to Western Virginia to the deep South. In 1831, she settled in Washington, where she began a weekly newspaper, *Paul Pry*, to "expose all and every species of political evil and religious fraud" and to "advocate the liberty of the press, the liberty of speech, and the liberty of conscience." When the growing unpopularity of her rancorous journalism forced discontinuation of *Paul Pry*, Royall quickly established *The Huntress*, published 1836–1854, which was less vitriolic and more entertaining.

Royall's writing about politics, religion, and social movements and her characterizations of the personalities and life of the nation's capital manifested her greatest hope, "that the union of these States may be eternal." She died October 1, 1854.

See also Literature

Harold Malcolm Forbes
WVU Libraries

Bessie Rowland James, *Anne Royall's U.S.A.*, 1972; Alice S. Maxwell and Marion B. Dunlevy, *Virago! The Story of Anne Newport Royall (1769–1854)*, 1985.

Ruffner Family

Joseph Ruffner (1739–1803) and his wife, Elizabeth, were the progenitors of the original Ruffner family of the Kanawha Valley. A native of the Luray area of the Shenandoah Valley of Virginia, Ruffner purchased in 1794 from John Dickinson 502 acres including the famous salt spring at the mouth of Campbells Creek. Arriving to inspect the lands in the spring of 1795, Ruffner was so impressed with the nearby Clendenin lands that within five years he was to own everything from the Elk River up the Kanawha to the "head of the bottom," except for a few town lots. This included all of present downtown Charleston plus the city's East End. He returned to the Kanawha Valley in the autumn with his wife, sons Joseph, Tobias, Samuel, Daniel, and Abraham, and daughter Eve. David Ruffner, the eldest son, remained behind until 1796 to close out the family business affairs in Old Virginia.

The Ruffners settled on the former Clendenin lands and leased the salt property to Elisha Brooks. Upon the death of Joseph in March 1803, his estate, including the salt property that was destined to become the most valuable land in the Kanawha Valley, descended to his sons.

Of all the Ruffners, Joseph's son David (1767–1843) most strongly influenced the development of the Kanawha Valley. He and brother Joseph devised methods and tools for drilling the first salt well into the Kanawha bedrock, pioneering the industry that would produce within the Kanawha Salines up to 3.2 million bushels of salt annually. David was the first to use coal in the manufacture of salt. In 1831, he laid out the present town of Malden on his land. He was a justice of the peace for 47 years, a colonel of militia, and served several terms in the legislature of Virginia.

Henry (1790–1861), the eldest son of David and Ann Brumbach Ruffner and the grandson of Joseph Sr., was a Presbyterian minister who in 1819 organized the first church of that denomination in Charleston. Henry Ruffner was the author of the anti-slavery "Ruffner Pamphlet" and other published works and was president of Washington College, now Washington and Lee University. His son, William Henry Ruffner, was a superintendent of public schools of Virginia.

Lewis (1797–1883), youngest son of David and Ann, was a saltmaker, state legislator, justice of the peace, and a delegate to the Wheeling Conventions of June and November 1861. In 1863, he was appointed a major general of militia for the new state of West Virginia. His second wife, Viola Knapp Ruffner, was credited with being the mentor of Booker T. Washington.

Daniel Ruffner, fifth son of Joseph Sr., was a saltmaker who in 1815 built Holly Grove mansion, which is located in the present state capitol complex and is the oldest house in Charleston. Opened in 1826 as a house of public entertainment, Holly Grove included such notables as Henry Clay, Sam Houston, Andrew Jackson, and John J. Audubon among its visitors.

See also Holly Grove, Henry Ruffner, Booker T. Washington

Gerald S. Ratliff
Charleston

Henry Ruffner

Henry Ruffner, educator and anti-slavery pamphleteer, was born in Luray, Virginia, January 16, 1790. He attended Lewisburg Academy (1809–12) and Washington College (1812–13), now Washington and Lee University. After licensure in 1815 with the Lexington Presbytery, Ruffner organized the Presbyterian denomination in Kanawha Valley, from which came the Kanawha Salines Presbyterian Church in Malden (1819). He taught ancient languages (1819–48) at Washington College and served as its sixth president (1836–48). Ruffner resigned in 1848 and participated in the emancipation movement in Louisville until 1850.

Ruffner is best known for his controversial anti-slavery treatise, *Address to the People of West Virginia* (1847), more popularly known as the "Ruffner Pamphlet." The *Address* argued for gradual emancipation not on moral grounds, but economic and social; slavery, Ruffner wrote, discouraged the growth of industry, agriculture, free labor, and education. He argued further that Eastern Virginia was able to unfairly deny funds for improvements in Western Virginia because enumerating slaves under Virginia's form of the three-fifths rule gave Easterners unjust political advantage. If necessary, he asserted, Western Virginia should consider separation from Virginia in order to rid itself of the practice.

As a participant in the 1841 Clarksburg Education Convention, Ruffner advocated a free, district-based public education system for Western Virginia and proposed funding this system with property taxes.

Henry Ruffner died in Malden, Kanawha County, December 17, 1861.

See also Ruffner Family

Garrett C. Jeter
Charleston

Ruffner Hotel

The venerable Ruffner Hotel succeeded the Hale House on the northwest corner of Hale and Kanawha streets in Charleston. The Ruffner was built in 1885 and owned and operated until about 1900 by A. L. and Meredith Ruffner and the Charleston Hotel Company.

The Ruffner was grand in every way, and it came on the scene in Charleston with the splendid new Victorian state capitol, also built in 1885. With 180 bedrooms, the Ruffner as originally built featured a spire on one corner and an elegant portico facing Kanawha Street. Except for the capitol, the red brick Ruffner was the biggest building in Charleston and its elegant profile was familiar to generations. The South Side Bridge, the first bridge across the Kanawha River, was built almost at the Ruffner's doorstep in 1891, allowing easy access to the C&O Railroad depot directly across the river.

As Charleston grew, other fine hotels were built, such as the Kanawha, the Holley, and finally in 1929, the Daniel Boone. But up until its demolition for a parking lot in 1970, the Ruffner never fell into ill repute. Its restaurant was noted for fine cuisine into the 1950s.

In January 1946, a historic fire destroyed nearby buildings and almost reached the eight-story Ruffner. After 1900, the Lilly family owned the hotel, and after 1941 Attorney General Abraham A. "Cousin Abe" Lilly resided in the elegant penthouse. A Lilly daughter recalled that Lilly raised flowers and even corn in the penthouse garden hothouse.

See also Cousin Abe Lilly

Richard A. Andre
Charleston

James Rumsey

James Rumsey, born in Cecil County, Maryland, in March 1743, invented a steam engine capable of propelling a boat by means of hydraulic jet propulsion. He first demonstrated the engine on the Potomac River near Shepherdstown on December 3, 1787. This was 20 years before Robert Fulton's boat, though the Fulton design was more practical, and it is Fulton who is honored today as the inventor of the steamboat.

Rumsey was a successful miller, mill mechanic and designer, canal builder, blacksmith, and rustic architect. He kept an inn at Berkeley Springs and built and designed the first bath houses there for people who sought the healthful waters. There, he met George Washington, for whom he designed a house and other buildings. That association bought credibility for his steamboat inventing, for he demonstrated the boat to Washington and received a certification from Washington that he had seen the boat function. Washington wrote in his diary, September 6, 1784, "The model & its operation upon the water . . . not only convinced me of what I before thought . . . quite impractical, but that it might be turned to the greatest possible utility in inland navigation."

People called Rumsey "crazy Rumsey" until the successful demonstration of his engine on the Potomac in a boat built by Joseph Barnes. Gen. Horatio Gates famously cried, "My God, she moves," as the boat achieved four knots traveling upstream. Washington and others urged Rumsey to seek further support for his invention, and he went first to Philadelphia, where he enlisted the aid of Benjamin Franklin. Franklin and other supporters founded the Rumseian Society to help advance Rumsey's steamboat and other inventions. While seeking a patent for his steamboat in England, Rumsey died there on December 20, 1792. Friends carried out a scheduled steamboat demonstration on the Thames shortly after his death.

Georgia Caldwell DuBose
Harpers Ferry

Darwin O. Curtis, "The Rumseian Experiment," 1987; Frederick T. Newbraugh, "My God, She Moves," *Valleys of History,* Summer 1970.

Rural Electrification

Electric service, when it came to rural West Virginia in the third and fourth decades of the 20th century, helped ease the drudgery of country living. Electricity reduced the labor of women, in particular. One of the first electrical appliances purchased in rural areas was the refrigerator, since block ice was not readily available in the country. Another important acquisition was the electric water pump, which eliminated the need to carry water. Washing machines took much of the work out of laundry day and produced better results, as did electronic irons. Farm Women's Clubs began promoting acceptance and safe usage of electricity with the support of the West Virginia University Agricultural Extension Service. Sponsored by power companies, a demonstration site for farm electrification was built in 1940 at the Jackson's Mill state 4-H camp.

Electricity generated from natural gas had brought streetlights to the citizens of Parkersburg in 1888, the first use of commercial electric power in the state. By soon after the turn of the 20th century many urban areas used electricity in businesses and residences, but there was less incentive for power companies to run electric lines to sparsely populated rural areas. When the Rural Electrification Administration was created in 1935 as part of President Franklin Roosevelt's New Deal, less than ten percent of farms in West Virginia had electricity. The REA offered long-term, self-liquidating loans to state and local governments, farmers' cooperatives, and nonprofit organizations to provide electric service to farmers and rural residents.

When a 1935 government survey of 50,000 rural West Virginians revealed a large market eager for electricity, the industry moved to meet the demand before nonprofit competitors could do so. Private power companies vigorously opposed the creation of REA cooperatives, and apparently only two such co-ops were successfully established in the state.

A utility truck places a power pole in Harrison County, 1937.

Co-op organizers believed their efforts, while often unsuccessful in themselves, were the catalyst for public utilities taking action to install rural electric lines.

In 1937, the Harrison Rural Electrification Association was established and within two years succeeded in gaining electrical service at reasonable rates for its 743 members. By 1940, the Hardy County Light and Power Association served 142 members, while the Craig-Botetourt Electric Cooperative served 119 Monroe Countians from its base in neighboring Virginia. The Harrison Rural Electrification Association, based in Clarksburg, had grown to 4,713 customers by 1989 with 724 miles of line in Harrison, Barbour, Upshur, Lewis, Doddridge, Marion, and Taylor counties.

Progress by a Monroe County farmers' electric co-op in the late 1930s was put on hold during World War II as the economy shifted to military production. After the war the Monroe co-op organizers tried again, but the power company began building the lines that finally brought rural electricity to the county.

Some parts of West Virginia are still served by electric co-ops. A portion of Monroe County is still served by the Craig-Botetourt Electric Cooperative. The Shenandoah Valley Electric Cooperative, which purchased Hardy County Power and Light in 1954, is also based in Virginia; it supplies electricity to some residents in the Eastern Panhandle. The Harrison Rural Electrification Association continues to serve north-central West Virginia, with about 5,500 customers in 2005.

The balance of West Virginia's residential electric needs is provided by two power companies, Appalachian Power Company, serving the southwestern part of the state and the Northern Panhandle, and Allegheny Power, which provides electric to central and eastern West Virginia. Coal remains by far the most important source of electric power generated in the state. The REA was abolished in 1994 and its functions were assumed under the Rural Utilities Service.

Scot E. Long
Hebron, Ohio

Helen Steele Ellison, "Electricity Comes to the Country," *Goldenseal*, Summer 1989; Debby Sonis Jackson, "Power for the People," *Goldenseal*, Summer 1989; Jerry Bruce Thomas, *An Appalachian New Deal: West Virginia in the Great Depression*, 1998.

Rural Free Delivery

Rural Free Delivery, the U.S. Post Office's program to provide direct delivery of mail to every household in the country, began on October 1, 1896, in West Virginia's Eastern Panhandle. Before this, there was no rural mail delivery, although more than half the country's 76,000,000 citizens lived in rural areas. Patrons had to visit their local post offices to send or receive mail. In 1891, Postmaster General John Wanamaker had conducted a limited experiment with rural free delivery which was greeted enthusiastically in the press.

In 1895, Congress finally appropriated sufficient funding to allow the Post Office to conduct a more comprehensive study of the service's potential. Wanamaker's successor, William Lyne Wilson, a native of Jefferson County, selected his home state for the inaugural effort. Wilson, a former attorney, had served briefly as president of West Virginia University before his election to Congress in 1882, where he served six terms. In later years he was president of Washington and Lee University and regent of the Smithsonian Institution.

On September 1, 1896, Wilson dispatched Col. Thomas B. Marche to Charles Town to oversee the operation. Harry C. Gibson, John W. Lucas, and Frank Young were hired as carriers out of Charles Town, serving under Postmaster Captain George H. Flagg. Melvin T. Strider was hired to carry the mail from nearby Uvilla, and I. Keyes Strider was chosen to operate out of Halltown. The new service debuted on October 1. This effort was so successful that 15 more routes were soon established in other states. By the end of 1897, a total of 82 routes were in operation. Within a few years free rural delivery of mail would be the norm across the country, and "R.F.D." entered the lingo of America.

See also William Lyne Wilson

Margo Stafford
Clarksburg

Jim Comstock, ed., "William Lyne Wilson," *West Virginia Encyclopedia*, 1976; Carl H. Scheele, *A Short History of the Mail Service*, 1970; Margo Stafford, "RFD: A West Virginia First," *Goldenseal*, Summer 1983.

Cynthia Rylant

Cynthia Rylant, author of more than 100 books for young people, was born June 6, 1954, in Hopewell, Virginia, and raised in southern West Virginia. The daughter of John T. and Leatrel Smith, Rylant uses her mother's maiden name as her pen name. She received a B.A. degree from Morris Harvey College (now University of Charleston), an M.A. from Marshall University, and an M.L.S. from Kent State University. She attributes her experiences growing up in West Virginia as the wellspring of her writing.

From ages four to eight, Rylant lived with her grandparents in rural Raleigh County, an experience celebrated in her Caldecott Honor-winning books *When I Was Young in the Mountains* (1982) and *The Relatives Came* (1985). Her first book of poetry, *Waiting to Waltz* (1984), draws upon the 10 years she spent living with her mother in the nearby town of Beaver. Rylant lives today in the state of Washington.

Her published works include picture books, short stories, poetry collections, nonfiction, and novels. Written in a style described as spare, lyrical, and honest, her work has won every major award in the field of children's literature. *A Fine White Dust* was named a Newbery Honor Book in 1987. *Appalachia: The Voices of Sleeping Birds* won the 1991 Boston Globe-Horn Book Award for nonfiction. *Missing May* was awarded the Boston Globe-Horn Book Award for children's fiction in 1992 and the John Newbery Medal in 1993.

Anna Egan Smucker
Bridgeport

Something About the Author, 1994.

S

Saddle Mountain

Saddle Mountain is the name applied to the section of New Creek Mountain that includes the distinctive notch or gap known as the Devil's Saddle. The proper name of the gap is Dolls Gap.

A striking natural landmark, the saddle notch is located in Mineral County just north of the Grant County line. It is visible from afar and often photographed from U.S. 50, which passes several miles to the west. Dolls Gap is a dry gap or wind gap, with no stream passing through. While it was cut by an ancient stream in ages past, subsequent geological uplifting has raised the gap well above the surrounding valley floors. Today it indeed resembles a giant saddle carved into the ridge. New Creek Mountain continues in an unbroken line beyond the gap in both directions, enhancing the dramatic impression.

Dolls Gap passes through Saddle or New Creek Mountain at an elevation of 2,000 feet. Nancy Hanks, the mother of Abraham Lincoln, is believed to have been born in the adjoining valley, just southeast of Dolls Gap.

See also Nancy Hanks, Mineral County

Sagebrush Roundup

The *Sagebrush Roundup* was Fairmont radio station WMMN's response to the growing popularity of live-audience country music jamborees in the pre-World War II years. Modeled after the WWVA's *Wheeling Jamboree*, Nashville's *Grand Ole Opry* and similar programs, the *Roundup* began in December 1938, originating from the National Guard Armory. Notable performers included Cowboy Loye Pack, Cherokee Sue and Little John Graham, Blaine Smith, Budge and Fudge Mayse, Jake Taylor, Buddy Starcher, and Grandpa Jones, the latter two of whom went on to attain national reputations. The *Roundup* remained popular for several years. During the war, performers such as Wilma Lee and Stoney Cooper and Lee and Juanita Moore made their base at WMMN.

In 1947, WPDX Clarksburg began seriously competing with WMMN for the country music market in northern West Virginia. By 1948, only Jake Taylor's Railsplitters and Hank the Cowhand (David Stanford) and his Foggy Mountain Gang remained on the *Roundup* roster. The last *Sagebrush Roundup* broadcast took place on October 2, 1948. However, the name remained in use into the early 1950s on daytime programs featuring Hank the Cowhand and Blaine Stewart. Since 1985, a revival of the fondly remembered program has been held at Bunner's Ridge near

Saddle Mountain is well named.

Fairmont, and has featured guest appearances by Wilma Lee Cooper, Little John Graham, and Buddy Starcher. The new *Sagebrush Roundup* consists of Saturday night concerts which are not broadcast.

See also Wheeling Jamboree

Ivan M. Tribe
University of Rio Grande

Ivan M. Tribe, *Mountaineer Jamboree: Country Music in West Virginia*, 1984.

St. Albans

The town at the mouth of Coal River was not named St. Albans until 1871, and by then it had already had three other names. As early as 1800, the settlement was called Coalsmouth. In 1829, Phillip R. Thompson, who owned a large tract of land within the present city limits, had it laid out as a town and named it "Phillipi." However, a post office was never established in that name. In 1868, John Cunningham acquired the old Thompson property and redeveloped it as a town which he had incorporated and named Kanawha City. According to differing accounts, St. Albans received its permanent name either for St. Albans, Vermont, or St. Albans, England.

The first settlers were brothers Lewis and Christopher Tackett, who settled at the mouth of Coal River and built a fort about 1786. Keziah Young, a daughter of Lewis Tackett, many years later recalled a fatal Indian attack on Fort Tackett. Early industries included two gristmills, a tan yard, various lumber mills, a boat yard, a brick yard, and a carriage maker. St. Al-

bans entrepreneurs established a lock and dam system on Coal River and promoted a branch railroad system there. The same group maintained a steamboat landing and wharf facilities on the Kanawha and in 1911 obtained a streetcar line extension from Charleston. Manufacturing plants attracted to St. Albans included several sawmills, two glass plants, a foundry, a rubber plant, a chemical plant, and a TNT plant.

St. Albans has always provided educational and cultural opportunities. There were early boarding schools for both girls and boys, and the former Shelton College offered courses in liberal and cultural arts. Today St. Albans has become a residential community for industrial plants at nearby Nitro, Institute, and South Charleston, with other citizens commuting to Charleston. St. Albans is located on the Kanawha River west of Charleston. Its population in 2000 was 11,567.

Bill Wintz
St. Albans

St. Albans Archeological Site

The St. Albans site, placed on the National Register of Historic Places in 1974, contained some of the most important archeological deposits yet discovered in the eastern United States. Identified in 1963 by Samuel D. Kessell, the site was recognized when artifacts were found on the eroded bank of the Kanawha River at St. Albans. Exploratory investigations indicated that cultural deposits extended to a depth of perhaps 35 feet below the surface. Extensive excavations were conducted by the West Virginia Geological and Economic Survey in 1964–66, and again in 1968. Archeologists from Marshall University, Cultural Resource Analysts, Inc., and colleges in Michigan and North Carolina conducted smaller-scale excavations in the 1990s.

The importance of the site was based on a sequence of stratified Archaic occupation periods, recognized primarily by projectile points, knives, scrapers, drills, and adzes made of flint, and larger implements including hammerstones and anvils made from river cobbles. Hearths and other types of thermal features were possibly used for processing food. The density and distribution of remains suggest the occupations represent seasonal camps of highly mobile hunter-gatherer bands.

Because the stratified occupations contained hearths with charcoal, it was possible to date them and their associated artifacts. Thus, for the first time archeologists were able to establish relatively precise ages for the Charleston Corner Notched, Kessell Side Notched, MacCorkle Stemmed, St. Albans Side Notched, LeCroy Bifurcated Base, and Kanawha Stemmed projectile point types, and obtain better information for the age of the poorly dated Kirk Corner Notched point type. The suite of radiocarbon dates available for the site indicates a period of Early Archaic occupation spanning from approximately 8000 to 6000 B.C. Earlier occupations might be present in more deeply buried deposits.

See also Archeology

C. Michael Anslinger
Cultural Resource Analysts

St. Francis Hospital

Charleston's St. Francis Hospital was founded in 1913 by Patrick J. Donahue, West Virginia's Roman Catholic bishop. The Laidley estate at 333 Laidley Street was purchased and renovations to create a hospital were overseen by Father Lewis Centner, pastor of Sacred Heart Church in Charleston. A group of Franciscan Sisters arrived from Williamsville, New York, on December 13, 1913, to manage the hospital, which opened January 15, 1914. St. Francis has remained at its original location throughout its history.

Within two years of the opening of St. Francis Hospital, it became necessary to construct a new facility to meet the growing demand. The new hospital opened January 24, 1917, with 71 beds, operating rooms, x-ray machines, laboratories, a chapel, and a chaplain's apartment. St. Francis Nursing School opened in January 1915 and graduated its first class in January 1917; the nursing school closed in 1961.

In 1921, the Franciscan Sisters were re-called to New York, and the Sisters of Saint Joseph of Wheeling took over the hospital. In 1924, money from the John B. Crowley estate paid for a new addition. New nursing school facilities were built in 1939 and were designed to be converted into hospital space if necessary. By 1950, St. Francis had 130 beds. A 1971 extended care facility increased the bed capacity to 187; this was quickly converted to an acute care facility which called attention to the drastic demand for more beds.

In 1975, the board of directors developed plans for a long-range construction project to meet the rapid changes of modern medicine and provide more space for patients. The plans called for the construction of a new patient tower, parking garage, medical office building, renovation of the 1971 building, removal of the 1917 brick hospital, and establishment of a garden entrance. Additional hospital services and clinics were added, and by 1990 St. Francis Hospital had been transformed to the modern medical complex familiar to Charlestonians today. In 1995, the Sisters of Saint Joseph of Wheeling sold St. Francis Hospital to Columbia HCA. In 2005, St. Francis was bought by LifePoint Hospitals of Tennessee.

See also Medicine, Roman Catholics

Tracey A Rasmer
Diocese of Wheeling-Charleston

St. George's Chapel

Called Norborne Church or Berkeley Church during its occupancy, St. George's Chapel in Jefferson County was part of the Norborne Parish. Constructed about 1771, of local limestone, the chapel was two stories high and had two tiers of windows on all sides. The pulpit was probably a gift of James Nourse of nearby Piedmont, who had it built and carved in London. Beginning with the disestablishment of the Anglican Church in America after Independence, revenues to support the chapel declined, and it probably suffered both neglect and vandalism. In 1803, the Anglican Church had lost all endowments and property, with most real estate being turned over to the Overseers of the Poor. The chapel was abandoned about this time, when a new church was built in Charles Town. The ruins, located approximately one mile west of Charles Town on State Route 51, have been the subject of numerous myths and legends and have been noted frequently in local literature. A sketch of the structure by David Hunter Strother was published in his "Personal Recollections of the War by a Virginian," in *Harper's New Monthly Magazine*, in July 1866.

William D. Theriault
Bakerton

"Old Norborne Parish," *Magazine of the Jefferson County Historical Society*, 1976 and 1979.

St. John's Chapel

St. John's Chapel, one of the oldest Roman Catholic churches in West Virginia, is located near the eastern boundary of Monroe County on State Route 3 adjacent to the historic Sweet Springs resort. It is near the remains of Lynnside Manor (built 1845, burned 1933), the traditional home of the Lewis family who were instrumental in the building of St. John's Chapel. It is in the Greek Revival style with a gabled roof and cupola.

The chapel was built perhaps as early as 1853 but definitely by 1859 at the behest of William Lynn Lewis and his wife, Letitia Preston Floyd Lewis. Letitia was the daughter of Virginia Gov. John Floyd, who is buried near the church. Her brother, John B. Floyd, was also a Virginia governor, the secretary of war on the eve of the Civil War, and a Confederate general. She converted to Catholicism in her late teens. William Lynn Lewis's grandfather founded the Sweet Springs resort and was the brother of Andrew Lewis, after whom Lewisburg is named.

The church was used by Irish immigrants working at the Sweet Springs resort and those who worked on the Chesapeake & Ohio Railroad; by wealthy Catholic landowners, primarily the Lewises and the Woodvilles; and by African-American workers on the Lynnside estate. The first record of baptism is November 13, 1853, and the number of baptisms peaked at 174 in 1860. By 1875, there were only 14 baptisms.

The Diocese of Wheeling-Charleston purchased the property in 1977. The chapel was restored, then rededicated by Bishop Joseph Hodges on April 17, 1983. It was added to the National Register of Historic Places as a part of the Lynnside Historic District in 1991.

See also John B. Floyd, Roman Catholics, Sweet Springs

Robert S. Conte
The Greenbrier

St. Joseph's Hospital

In 1900, Patrick J. Donahue, West Virginia's Roman Catholic bishop, founded St. Joseph's Hospital. It was originally located in the old Visitation Convent at Avery and Fifth streets in Parkersburg. The convent was renovated, and the hospital opened with 21 beds. Four Sisters of Saint Joseph of Wheeling and two assistant nurses were invited to Parkersburg to run the new hospital. Sister Immaculate Feeney was the first administrator; she had served at Wheeling Hospital during the Civil War. The hospital's nursing school opened in 1905 and operated until 1969. Many of the hospital's patients were charity cases.

The constant flow of patients necessitated the addition of a new wing in 1903, followed by a second wing in 1924. By

1929, St. Joseph's administrators decided to build a new hospital. A building committee of hospital doctors and prominent Parkersburg businessmen conducted a city-wide campaign to raise $300,000 for the new facility. The committee realized its goal within ten days, despite the recent stock market crash. The new hospital was built on the old McConahey estate at 19th Street and Murdoch Avenue, on an elevation overlooking the Ohio River. The new six-story brick structure was built for $600,000 in a Colonial design with three acres of landscaped grounds. St. Joseph's bed capacity rose from 100 to 170. The C. Z. Ruth Memorial Annex was built in 1962 to accommodate major services including inpatient and outpatient facilities.

In the late 1960s, St. Joseph's administrators developed a long-range plan for expanded hospital facilities. In 1977, the completion of a $20 million construction and remodeling program increased the number of hospital beds to 216, along with additional clinics and expanded hospital services. In 1996, the Sisters of Saint Joseph entered into a joint venture with Columbia HCA, and by 2001 their governance role in the hospital ended.

See also Medicine, Roman Catholics

Tracey A. Rasmer
Diocese of Wheeling-Charleston

St. Joseph Settlement

Nestled in the hills above the Ohio River on the Marshall-Wetzel county border are the pristine farms of the St. Joseph Settlement, also known as the German Settlement. The people who live here are members of the St. Joseph settlement and the proud descendants of German Catholic immigrants who came to America in the 1850s. They came from the southern German states of Bavaria and Hess, areas that opposed King Frederick William IV's absolute monarchy. Facing compulsory military conscription and high land prices at home, they looked for a fresh start in America.

The first tracts of land, small farms of 50 and 100 acres, were purchased from Isaac Hoge for $3 an acre. Eventually the settlers acquired a swath of land that is now 12 miles long and four miles wide. The earliest record of the community's religious organization was June 5, 1853. By September 9, 1853, Hoge and his wife, Rachel, agreed to deed two acres to Bishop Whelan of Wheeling to be held in trust for the use of the German Roman Catholic congregation. The church, schoolhouse (now a public library and parish museum), rectory, community building, and cemetery are still the heart of the St. Joseph community.

The first school was built of hewn logs in 1854 and served as both school and chapel until 1856, when the first church was built. Because the settlers emphasized education and religion, priests and nuns have been important throughout the community's history.

St. Joseph reached its heyday during the 19th-century oil and gas boom. Oil derricks dotted the landscape and small stores and support businesses thrived. Elements of the German culture lingered on for several generations. Students were taught German and English well into the 20th century, and German words and phrases remained in use until recently. Today the families who live in the settlement carry their ancestors' names and care for farms handed down through the generations.

Cheryl Ryan Harshman
West Liberty State College

St. Lawrence Boom and Manufacturing Company

One of the more interesting periods in the history of the Greenbrier River was its use to transport logs from the woods to the sawmill. Although some timber was moved on the Greenbrier before the Civil War, the major use of the river for this purpose was during the harvest of the white pine timber in Greenbrier and Pocahontas counties in the late 1800s and early 1900s.

The St. Lawrence Boom and Manufacturing Company was responsible for most of the white pine timbering. In 1870 Col. Cecil Clay of Philadelphia began timber purchases in the valley and the company was organized the next year. Clay also laid out a new town, Ronceverte, at the location selected for the company's sawmill. The name of the company came from an early name for the location of Ronceverte, St. Lawrence Ford.

By the mid-1870s, Greenbrier River log drives were becoming an annual occurrence. The normal pattern was to begin cutting the timber in the summer, with the loggers working from several logging camps. The logs were moved to the banks of streams and by late winter large piles of logs were ready for the high water to move them to the river and then on to Ronceverte. With sufficient water the logs could be in the booms at Ronceverte within a month of the drive getting under way, but usually it took several rises in the river to move all the logs to the mill.

The St. Lawrence company cut white pine timber along the river and on its major tributaries as far north as Deer Creek, near Cass, totaling 45,000 acres or more. The last log drive was in 1908, with the logs cut on Knapps Creek, which enters the river at Marlinton. Ironically, this last drive of the "white pine era" was made up of hemlock. The company continued in operation for a few years after the last drive in the river. In 1902, St. Lawrence began to receive logs from Anthonys Creek by rail and built a second mill near Neola in 1909. The mill at Ronceverte was closed that year or the next.

William P. McNeel
Marlinton

St. Mary's Medical Center

St. Mary's Hospital, now St. Mary's Medical Center, in Huntington was opened November 6, 1924, by eight Pallottine Missionary Sisters. The founding sisters

St. Joseph Church at the St. Joseph Settlement.

had left their home in Bremerhaven, Germany, and barely missed sailing on the doomed Titanic, coming eventually to New York state where they learned English from the Sisters of St. Francis. They came to West Virginia in August of 1912 to open Holy Family School in Richwood and then opened Sacred Heart Hospital in 1913. The next step was to open St. Joseph's Hospital in Buckhannon in 1921, and then the sisters came to Huntington to open St. Mary's, a 35-bed nonprofit facility.

The School of Nursing on the hospital grounds was added in 1929, and today the 440-bed hospital is the second-largest in the state. It is the largest private employer in Cabell County and is recognized as a regional leader in comprehensive cardiac care, with more than 550 open-heart surgeries annually. Its most recent addition is a $17 million, 75,000-square-foot outpatient center which opened July 28, 1997. The hospital opened its new radiation oncology center in 1999.

On November 4, 1997, St. Mary's announced it would join an alliance with Cabell-Huntington Hospital and Pleasant Valley Hospital in Point Pleasant to reduce operating costs and protect against the possibility of a buyout by a national hospital chain. The new group, Genesis Affiliated Health Services, Inc. was given $1.25 million by each of the three hospitals to cover start-up costs and administrative expenses. Dissatisfaction with the arrangement arose, and Genesis was dissolved in 2002.

Tom D. Miller
Huntington

St. Marys

St. Marys is the county seat of Pleasants County. Frenchmen Isaac and Jacob La-Rue, now buried on nearby Middle Island, settled here in 1790 on land granted to them for service in the Revolutionary War. The town was established in 1849 by Alexander H. Creel. According to legend, Creel had a vision of the Virgin Mary while passing the site in a boat. She directed him to look at the (West) Virginia shore, saying that a happy and prosperous city would be built there.

Nonetheless, the town saw little growth for its first several years. Then the regional oil boom beginning in the 1860s led to the opening of several cooper shops to make wooden barrels to transport the oil. St. Marys became a shipping port on the Ohio River, as freight was carried down the Ellenboro Pike (State Route 16) to the wharf. From 1910 until 1928, a factory making buttons from river mussel shells employed between 50 and 100 men. In 1914, the Ohio Valley Refining Company began operating and was a major employer until it closed in 1987. Two glass factories operated in St. Marys. Paramount Glass was located near the button

factory, and in 1919 St. Marys Glass opened near the refinery. In 1936, the Alley Agate Manufacturing Company began making glass marbles and dishes in the former St. Marys Glass building. Sadly, both glass factories were destroyed by fire.

St. Marys is located on the Ohio River at the intersection of State Routes 2 and 16, east of Parkersburg. The town population peaked at 2,442 in 1960, declining to 2,017 in 2000.

See also Pleasants County

Matthew Scott Bailey
St. Marys High School

Robert L. Pemberton, *A History of Pleasants County, West Virginia*, 1929; Pleasants County Historical Society, *History of Pleasants County to 1980*, 1980.

Salem International University

Located at Salem in Harrison County, Salem International University (formerly Salem College) was established in 1888 by local residents with the help of the Seventh-Day Baptist religious denomination. A key leader in the establishment of the school was Jesse Randolph, mayor of Salem, and grandfather of future U.S. Sen. Jennings Randolph. The first president was John L. Huffman.

Salem College began as an academy and maintained an academy or preparatory department until 1929, while adding college-level classes. It started with a

single building on Main Street. Around 1900, a drunken mob armed with torches was deterred from burning down the college by President Theodore Gardiner, who met the mob with gun in hand and threatened to shoot anyone who stepped on campus. The standoff occurred during a time of widespread arson caused by rivalry between citizens of the town and workers in the booming oil fields. Gradually, other buildings were built on the Main Street campus.

Salem College saw much development during the long presidencies of S. Orestes Bond (1919–51) and K. Duane Hurley (1951–73). Salem had long been accredited by the West Virginia State Department of Education, and under Hurley's leadership in 1963 gained full accreditation by the North Central Association of Secondary Schools and Colleges. A great increase in enrollment followed. For many years Salem had offered evening extension classes at public high schools in various locations. A Clarksburg campus was established in 1958 and expanded in 1964 when the former Waldo Hotel building was transformed into a downtown residence campus.

Dormitories and other buildings were built in Salem in the 1960s, and by the early 1970s a new campus was developed in the "Valley of Learning" near the front campus. This included Carlson Hall of Science (a large classroom building),

Salem International University was originally Salem College.

Randolph Campus Center, and the Benedum Learning Resources Center (a library). Later the T. Edward Davis Physical Education Building and the Brewster All-Faiths Chapel were added. Fort New Salem, designed to represent an early 19th-century Appalachian pioneer village, and the Barker Equestrian Center.

Presidents since 1973 include Dallas Bailey (1973–78), James Stam (1978–82), Ronald Ohl (1983–2001), Richard Ferrin (2002–05), and R. John Reynolds (2005–).

In 1989, Salem College affiliated with Teikyo University of Japan and changed its name to Salem-Teikyo University. Programs in English as a second language and Japanese Studies were added to the curriculum. A new academic calendar was developed, replacing traditional semesters with four-week modules, allowing undivided attention to one class. Academic departments were consolidated and a new mission statement was developed, emphasizing the development of world citizens with an international viewpoint. Many students came from Japan and other nations, especially in Asia. Students were offered the opportunity of a semester of European Studies at Teikyo campuses in Berlin and the Netherlands. A re-entry program in Japan was established for Salem-Teikyo's Japanese students to take their last four classes in Japan; Salem faculty members were given the opportunity to spend time in Japan to teach in that program.

Salem disaffiliated with Teikyo at the turn of the new century. In October 2000, the name was changed to Salem International University; in June 2001, a new partnership was established with Informatics, a Singapore institution emphasizing global on-line education. Salem underwent difficult times while these changes were under way. Layoffs were undertaken to ease the school's financial problems, along with a reduction in tuition and other changes. The college announced significant financial improvements in 2004, and in 2005 it was bought by the Palmer Group of Philadelphia.

Enrollment at Salem International University in 2005 was 725 students. The distinguished alumni include U.S. Senators Jennings Randolph, Rush Holt, and Joseph Rosier, as well as Gov. Cecil Underwood and Matthew M. Neely, who served as a congressman, U.S. senator, and governor.

See also Jennings Randolph, Seventh-Day Baptists

Robert B. Florian
Professor Emeritus of History
Orestes S. Bond, *The Light of the Hills*, 1960; Myron J. Smith, *100 Years of Opportunity: A Pictorial History of Salem College, 1888–1988*, 1988.

Soupy Sales

Comedian Soupy Sales (Milton Supman) was born January 8, 1926, in North Carolina and raised in Huntington. He achieved fame as a wacky, pie-throwing television personality. After graduating in 1943 from Huntington High School and then earning a B.A. in journalism from Marshall College, he started his career as a script writer and disc jockey at WHTN Radio in Huntington. At night, he played club dates in the Tri-State area.

In 1950, Sales left Huntington and broke into television, hosting children's shows in Cincinnati, Detroit, New York, and Los Angeles. ABC aired *Lunch with Soupy Sales* on Saturdays during the 1959–60 season, and brought the show back from December of 1960 to March of 1961. From January to March of 1962, Sales hosted an ABC mid-season nighttime replacement series from Hollywood. *The Soupy Sales Show*, a weekday morning show, debuted in 1964 from New York, and went into national syndication from 1965 to 1967. In 1976, Sales hosted ABC's one-season morning game show, *Junior Almost Anything Goes*. Another *Soupy Sales Show* was offered in syndication in 1978 and lasted a year. Sales also made appearances on prime-time television shows including *The Ed Sullivan Show*.

Sales published a memoir, *Soupy Sez* in 2003. His zany and witty slapstick style endeared him to generations of fans. He holds an honorary doctorate in humane letters from Marshall University and is honored by the Soupy Sales Plaza in front of the Huntington Civic Center. In 2004, Sales lived in New York City.

Larry Sonis
Arlington, Texas

John Peter Salling

John Peter Salling (or Salley) was among five Virginia explorers who departed March 16, 1742, from a few miles east of Natural Bridge, on a journey to the Mississippi River. The Governor's Council of Virginia had granted a commission for this trip to John Howard for the purpose of reinforcing British claims in the west.

The promised reward of 10,000 acres of land for a successful expedition encouraged Howard's son, Josiah, and Salling, John Poteet, and Charles Sinclair to accompany the elder Howard on the trip. At New River, they constructed a boat covered with buffalo hides and embarked as the first Englishmen to explore that region. They followed the New until the river became too dangerous to navigate, leaving at a major falls and traveling overland to the Coal River, then followed the Great Kanawha and Ohio rivers, and reached the Mississippi on June 7. The party descended the Mississippi to just below the mouth of the Arkansas River, where, on July 2, they were captured by a large company of Indians, blacks, and Frenchmen. Transported as captives to New Orleans, they were imprisoned as spies, in spite of Howard's claim that they were negotiating peace treaties with the Indians.

After two years' confinement, Salling escaped on October 25, 1744, eventually returning by a southern route to his home in Augusta County, Virginia, in May 1745. Salling's account provided Virginians with their first information about previously unknown regions, including present West Virginia, and he is credited with the discovery of coal on Coal River. In December 1744, Howard was being transported to France when the ship was intercepted by the English. He is known to have reported his adventures after landing in London, but his account has not survived.

Harold Malcolm Forbes
WVU Libraries
Richard Batman, "The Odyssey of John Peter Salley," *Virginia Cavalcade*, Summer 1981; Fairfax Harrison, "The Virginians on the Ohio and the Mississippi in 1742," *Virginia Magazine of History and Biography*, April 1922.

Salt Industry

From the colonial through early national periods, salt was a scarce domestic commodity that had to be imported. As settlers crossed the Allegheny Mountains, they found numerous salt licks, frequented by animals and native people, that naturally furnished small quantities of salt but not enough to meet the needs of an expanding settled society. As dependence on imported salt continued, the quest for commercial sources led to salt manufacturing at many licks. The first major enterprises in present West Virginia developed in 1797 under Elisha Brooks at the Great Buffalo Lick on the Kanawha River; in 1809 by John Haymond and Benjamin Wilson at Bull Town, Braxton County, on the Little Kanawha River; and around 1812 at John George Jackson's works on the West Fork, near Clarksburg. Only the Kanawha salt field had the brine density to attain more than local importance.

At the Great Buffalo Lick at Kanawha Salines or present Malden, the Ruffner brothers built the first commercial furnace in 1808. Within two years, they and other entrepreneurs had constructed 16 furnaces. During the War of 1812, salt production quadrupled on 52 furnaces to reach one million bushels. This enormous growth of capacity caused Kanawha manufacturers to produce more salt than their markets could consume and as early as 1814–15 stimulated the creation of innovative legal arrangements to control excess production, prices, and markets. These agreements of combination, which took several forms, are the earliest known in American industrial and legal history.

Salt production in the Kanawha Valley was a relatively simple process. Shallow wells reached the subterranean brine water. Steam engines pumped the salty water from one or more wells to an elevated tank. From that point, water ran as needed into the evaporator, a giant flat pan heated by steam. As the brine evaporated, its salt crystallized. Workers skimmed the salt onto drain boards. After a period, the salt was lifted and wheeled to a storage house where it was packed into barrels for shipment.

Kanawha saltmakers pioneered in technological adaptation and inventiveness. They adapted coal as furnace fuel when wood became scarce; invented various well-drilling tools later adapted for petroleum drilling; early and extensively harnessed steam engines for pumping; and modified their furnace construction by the 1840s to the Kanawha grainer evaporative system, a low-pressure method of evaporating salt that survived over 100 years. They also molded the institution of slavery to meet industrial needs.

The importance of the Kanawha Salines manufacturers plummeted when another West Virginia brine field was discovered in the 1850s. Three Kanawha saltmakers developed the West Columbia salt field in Mason County on the Ohio River. Soon furnaces emerged at Hartford City, Mason City, and across the river around Pomeroy, Ohio. The Mason field had the advantage of being closer to markets. Also, Ohio River salt manufacturing fit well with the primary local economic activity of mining coal. The evaporators burned the "slack" or fine coal that otherwise would have been discarded. With minimal fuel costs and the adoption of business arrangements and productive technology from the Kanawha field, the Ohio River field eventually marginalized the Kanawha salt producers.

In the 1850s, the Kanawha salt field reached its peak and began to decline. The western movement of meat packing, the growth of a national railroad system, and other discoveries of salt contributed to the Kanawha industry's demise and eventually adversely affected the Ohio River field as well. Salt production on one or two furnaces persisted in both fields until the mid-20th century. By that time Kanawha Valley salt making had been replaced by a booming chemical industry, which found other uses for the region's brine waters and industrial know-how.

See also Chemical Industry, Malden

John Edmund Stealey III
Shepherd University

John E. Stealey III, *The Antebellum Kanawha Salt Business and Western Markets*, 1993; Stealey, ed., *Kanawhan Prelude to Nineteenth-Century Monopoly in the United States: The Virginia Salt Combinations*, 2000.

"Salt Pork, West Virginia"

Jazz saxophonist Louis Jordan, leader of the Tympany Five, made a best-selling recording of the song "Salt Pork, West Virginia," in 1946. There are at least three versions by Jordan, the most recent recorded by Mercury records, October 29, 1956, in New York. All three versions feature a driving beat, reminiscent of the rhythmic thump associated with rail travel, and each ends with Jordan singing the names of a series of cities much like train conductors did. The cities include Philadelphia, Washington, Richmond, Birmingham, Atlanta, Savannah, Jacksonville, Tampa, Miami, Houston, Dallas, and Fort Worth. Finally, Jordan concludes, "I think I'll go on home now; Bluefield, my Salt Pork, West Virginia."

Jordan performed in southern West Virginia on several occasions. "Salt Pork" was composed in 1945 by Jordan associates Fleecie Moore and William Tennyson Jr., and memorializes a real-life encounter with a Bluefield justice of the peace, Wallace W. "Squire" McNeal. McNeal's niece, Nancy (McNeal) Byrd, recalled that McNeal told the family that Deputy J. Earl Bailey had arrested Jordan for speeding and suspicion of drunk driving, offenses that could have resulted in the impoundment of Jordan's car. During a hearing on the matter, McNeal, Mercer County Democratic Party leader and president of the local Billy Sunday Club, was charmed by Jordan's sense of humor. He released Jordan, and in return, the singer offered to buy the JP a meal at the city's finest restaurant. When McNeal declined the offer, Jordan and his sidemen immortalized the episode in song.

William R. Archer
Bluefield

Salt Sulphur Springs

The soothing waters of Salt Sulphur Springs, near Union in Monroe County, were discovered in 1805. A stone bathhouse, still standing, was built about 1820. At about the same time, a hotel, showing the Federal influence in its architectural appointments, was built at a cost of $30,000. The hotel is now a private residence with an adjacent guesthouse.

Isaac Caruthers and William Erskine turned the property into a popular resort at a time when mineral waters were considered a cure for headaches, neuralgia, and other health problems. Salt Sulphur waters were described by historian Oren F. Morton as "chalybeate and sweetly sulphurous and containing iodine." Modern analysis shows the principal minerals to be sulfate, calcium, bicarbonate, and sodium. A notable visitor in 1844 was U.S. Sen. John C. Calhoun, a South Carolinian who advocated the right of states to nullify federal legislation.

The resort closed following the Civil War, during which the property was used by both armies for headquarters and respite. In 1882, Col. J.W.M. Appleton revived Salt Sulphur, but the mineral springs vacation trade declined at the turn of the century, and the resort again closed at Appleton's death in 1913. The last effort to operate Salt Sulphur as a resort ended in 1936.

The old hotel, a striking stone building standing at a curve on U.S. 219, two miles south of Union, is part of a complex of buildings and spring sites, one of the largest groupings of antebellum native stone buildings in West Virginia. Sometimes called Old Salt Sulphur Springs or "Old Salt," the resort was added to the National Register of Historic Places in 1985.

See also John W. M. Appleton

Belinda Anderson
Asbury

Stan Cohen, *Historic Springs of the Virginias: A Pictorial History*, 1981; Oren F. Morton, *A History of Monroe County, West Virginia*, 1974.

Saltpeter Mining

Saltpeter or potassium nitrate (KNO_3) was of key importance to the survival of early settlers in what is now West Virginia. Saltpeter was used by settlers to salt meat and to make dyes, and it was a key ingredient in gunpowder, which was made by mixing small amounts of sulfur and charcoal with saltpeter.

The earliest explorers in the region brought a supply of gunpowder with them. Soon, it was discovered that naturally occurring saltpeter could be found in the many limestone caves and sandstone shelters. Noncommercial mining of saltpeter began prior to the American Revolution, and the caverns of Western Virginia were a major source of saltpeter for the colonial army. Commercial production continued through the War of 1812 and then fell off after the war ended.

During the Civil War, the Confederates made extensive use of these mines to make up for the loss of other saltpeter sources due to the Union blockade. Twenty-two caves in present West Virginia were mined between 1862 and 1865. Confederate miners often produced the saltpeter entirely underground to avoid detection, but many mines were discovered and the workers imprisoned. Schoolhouse Cave in Pendleton County is the only cave known to have been mined for saltpeter by Unionists during the Civil War. Following the war, saltpeter mining was discontinued as new technologies rendered the mines obsolete.

Saltpeter was produced by simple but effective methods. Earth was shoveled into wooden hoppers and water poured in to leach out the saltpeter. The water was then evaporated, leaving the valuable saltpeter. Many artifacts of the process have been found in West Virginia caves, including hoppers and tools. Such

SALT INDUSTRY / SALTPETER MINING 637

artifacts may be seen by visitors to Organ Cave in Greenbrier County.

See also Caves

John E. Adkins
University of Charleston
Peter Hauer, "Saltpeter Mining in West Virginia," *Goldenseal*, July–September 1975.

Salvation Army

William and Catherine Booth founded the Salvation Army in London in 1865 to serve the spiritual and physical needs of the lower and working classes. Based on John Wesley's theology of perfectionism and influenced by Phoebe Palmer's holiness doctrine, the Salvation Army brought its Christian mission to America in 1880. The Salvation Army opened its first West Virginia "corps" or church in Wheeling in 1883. As industrialization brought thousands of workers to the timber and mining industries between 1880 and 1920, the Army extended itself throughout the state. Early salvationists rode horses and trains and drove up riverbeds to take the gospel to the small towns and timber and coal camps. By 1906, there were six corps in the state. The number grew to 11 in 1916 and to 18 in 1926.

During this time, the Salvation Army expanded its evangelical mission to include social services and gained adherents among all classes through its charity work. In 1912, former governor William A. MacCorkle became active in the Salvation Army. When he died in 1930, MacCorkle left his Charleston mansion, Sunrise, to the Salvation Army. The Army gained worldwide attention during World War I when Salvation Army "lassies" served doughnuts and coffee and provided aid to soldiers serving in Europe. Following the war, "Doughnut Day" fundraisers were held in West Virginia to raise money for the Salvation Army.

The Army has provided emergency relief throughout West Virginia, particularly following mine disasters. Today, the Salvation Army continues to serve the spiritual and welfare needs of West Virginians, providing food and clothing to those in need.

Connie Park Rice
West Virginia University

Sampson Sanders

Plantation owner Sampson Sanders was born in 1786 to William and Martha Green Sanders of Loudoun County, Virginia. Sampson's parents moved the family across the frontier through North Carolina and Tennessee before settling in what is now Cabell County about 1800. The family name is sometimes given as "Saunders."

Following his father's death in 1802, and with the advice and guidance of his mother, Sampson Sanders built his inheritance into the largest land holding in Cabell County. He owned large acreages on the Guyandotte and Mud rivers east of Barboursville and the largest flour mill in Cabell County. At his death, Sanders owned at least 51 slave adults and children, one of the largest slave holdings in Western Virginia. By his will in 1849, all his slaves were freed regardless of age. They also were given cash, equipment, and legal assistance to start new lives. They migrated northward as a group, settling in Cass County, Michigan, where descendants live today. These families retained the Sanders name as their own.

Sampson Sanders died June 21, 1849, and is buried with his mother near Milton. Saunders Creek, a Mud River tributary, is named for the family.

Carrie Eldridge
Chesapeake, Ohio

Sandstone Falls

Sandstone Falls, the largest waterfall within the New River Gorge, spans the New River where it is 1,500 feet wide. Divided by a series of islands, the river drops 10 to 25 feet at this point. The ledge creating Sandstone Falls is made of Stony Gap sandstone of the Hinton Formation, deposited as sand during the Mississippian Period of geologic time. The falls were created as softer shale and conglomerate eroded beneath the harder sandstone, leaving the overlying stone to form a high ledge which breaks off in sections.

U.S. Chief Justice John Marshall, who was appointed by Virginia in 1812 to head a commission to investigate a water route through the mountains, observed the falls and found them to be the most serious obstacle to boat travel on New River. He wrote, "A . . . formidable obstruction is the falls at Richmond's mill. These are designated in the neighborhood by the name of the 'Great Falls' of New River." Marshall and his fellow explorers prudently took their boat out of water and let it down by skids. Mary Draper Ingles, who was captured by the Shawnees in 1755, passed Sandstone Falls after her escape.

Sandstone Falls is located eight and a half miles below Hinton. On the east side of the gorge, an overlook on State Route 20 offers a view of the falls from 600 feet above the river. The falls, one of the most photographed spots in West Virginia, is a popular tourist attraction. On the west side of the river, County Route 26 carries visitors to the falls access point. A boardwalk crosses two bridges leading to islands and observation decks below the falls. The area is a favorite fishing spot for smallmouth bass and catfish.

Arnout Hyde Jr.
Wonderful West Virginia

Sandy Creek Expedition

The Sandy Creek Expedition, with Maj. Andrew Lewis in command, was dispatched in February 1756 during the French and Indian War to attack the Shawnee villages in Ohio. At the time of the defeat of Gen. Edward Braddock's forces in July 1755, the Indians had rampaged through the forward settlements in the New, Greenbrier, and Tygart river valleys. Scores of settlers were killed, wounded, or captured, among whom were Mary Draper Ingles and Capt. Samuel Stalnaker, both of whom eventually escaped from the Shawnee villages. Many white families retreated across the Alleghenies or to the Shenandoah Valley.

Frontiersmen who remained behind demanded that Governor Robert Dinwiddie authorize a force of militia to punish the Shawnees. Several companies totaling more than 300 men, of whom nearly one-third were Cherokee Indians, left Fort Frederick on the New River near In-

Sandstone Falls, the biggest falls on New River.

gles Ferry on February 18. William Ingles, husband of Mary Draper Ingles, was among them.

The expedition was doomed almost from the beginning due to harsh weather, swollen streams and rivers, and lack of provisions. They reached the headwaters of the Big Sandy River on February 28, and within a few days flour rations were cut by half. Game was scarce, and the men refused to slaughter and eat their horses and pack animals. In spite of Major Lewis's appeals and threats, fewer than 30 officers and men volunteered during a March 13 council to continue. The force returned to Fort Frederick, and the House of Burgesses subsequently cleared Lewis of any fault in the expedition's failure. Among the few benefits of the campaign were closer ties between the Virginia colonial government and the Cherokee Nation.

See also Andrew Lewis

Philip Sturm
Ohio Valley University
Elizabeth Cometti and Festus P. Summers, "[Colonel William] Preston's Journal of the Sandy Creek Expedition," *The Thirty-Fifth State: A Documentary History of West Virginia*, 1966.

Chris Sarandon

Actor Chris Sarandon Jr. was born July 24, 1942, in Beckley. He graduated from Woodrow Wilson High School in Beckley in 1960. In 1964, he received a bachelor's degree in theater from West Virginia University. He later earned a master's degree from Catholic University in Washington, where he met and married Susan Tomalin, who later gained fame as the actress Susan Sarandon. In 1994, he married Joanna Hall Gleason, an actress who has appeared in plays and musicals.

Chris Sarandon has appeared on stage and screen, with films including *The Nightmare Before Christmas* (1993), *The Princess Bride* (1987), and *Fright Night* (1985). Sarandon was nominated in 1976 for a Best Supporting Actor Oscar and a Best Acting Debut Golden Globe Award for his performance in the motion picture *Dog Day Afternoon*, which starred Al Pacino. In 1980, Sarandon starred as Jesus Christ in the television movie *The Day Christ Died*. His television work has included appearances on such network shows as NBC's *Judging Amy, Felicity, and ER*.

In a magazine interview in 1998, Sarandon cited the influence in his life of WVU Professor Patrick Ward Gainer, who taught a folklore course, and Professor Emeritus Charles Neel, who suggested that Sarandon consider majoring in theater. "After a couple of productions, there was no turning back," Sarandon said. In 2005, Sarandon lived in Los Angeles.

Larry Sonis
Arlington, Texas

Abel Morgan Sarjent

Abel Morgan Sarjent founded a religious sect called the Halcyon Church in what is now Mason County on July 11, 1802. He was a former Universalist minister, born September 6, 1764, probably in Maryland.

Halcyon tenets proclaimed that the end of time was near, when the wicked would be destroyed while the purehearted would be saved. Sarjent decried fleshly appetites and advocated a temperate diet of vegetables and milk. He became one of Western Virginia's first prominent men to openly denounce slavery and aid the escape of runaway slaves. Women, another oppressed group that attracted his support, were allowed to become ministers in his church.

Sarjent's following grew rapidly as he traveled through Western Virginia, western Pennsylvania, Ohio, and Kentucky preaching, debating other ministers, and publishing a religious periodical and numerous tracts. By 1807, Halcyons, numbering in the thousands, extended from Louisville to Pittsburgh.

Dissension soon weakened the new religion. A few younger Halcyons broke from Sarjent's control. Accounts of extreme fasting and bizarre behavior, linked with stories labeling Sarjent a charlatan, damaged his credibility. So did the jealousy of other ministers, mainly Methodists and Baptists alarmed by his sudden fame and success. Peaking about 1807, the Halcyon Church slid into decline. Less than a decade later it was extinct. Many Halcyons became Universalists. The Mormons later incorporated some Halcyon principles into their faith.

Abel Sarjent died in Indiana, August 10, 1839, nearly forgotten by the people of the Ohio Valley.

Ray Swick
Blennerhassett Island State Park

Satellite Television

During the 1970s and 1980s, West Virginians erected thousands of satellite dishes to receive broadcast signals for residential television viewing. Early models measured several feet in diameter, quite large compared to today's small satellite dishes. As their popularity increased satellite dishes became a major landscape feature, prompting jokes that they had replaced the rhododendron as West Virginia's "state flower."

Satellite dishes became popular in rural places with rugged topography, like West Virginia, for good reasons. Roof-top antennas worked poorly because hilly terrain interfered with reception. Rural dwellers were faced with the unsatisfactory option of having to run lines to antennas on distant hilltops.

While cable TV flourished in cities, the low population densities characteristic of rural West Virginia made it uneconomical to run miles of cable to serve relatively few customers. Instead, rural residents looked to the sky. Consumers purchased their own satellite dishes from growing numbers of small businesses that sold and installed them. These dishes captured C-band transmissions, which were unencrypted at the time. Families rationalized the high costs of early dishes because they paid nothing for the programming they received.

After broadcasters began encrypting their satellite signals, the programming was available only through illegal decoding boxes. As technology and the law evolved, the old satellite dishes became useless and began to disappear from the landscape by the last years of the 20th century. The infrastructure of businesses selling and servicing satellite dishes disappeared, as well.

Modern satellite television works like any other utility service, with monthly payments required. Households subscribe to systems that include a satellite TV dish antenna, integrated receiver-decoder box, and remote control, for a fee comparable to cable service. The much smaller satellite dishes are permissible in cities and towns that once banned the large dishes, so satellite television is no longer just a rural phenomenon. Urban residents now choose between cable and satellite service. Satellite TV companies now also provide some local channels, a feature missing in the past. The new satellite dishes are tiny by comparison to their predecessors, pervasive but inconspicuous features of the rural countryside and city and suburban neighborhoods.

See also Cable Television

Lizbeth Pyle
Morgantown

Savage Grant

On December 15, 1772, Virginia Governor Dunmore, as agent for King George III, granted 28,627 acres along the Ohio River and the lower Guyandotte and Big Sandy rivers to John Savage and 59 others who had served under George Washington at the Battle of Great Meadows, Pennsylvania, in the French and Indian War. This grant extended from what is now Cattlettsburg, Kentucky, to about Nine Mile Creek in northern Cabell County, approximately 24 miles. It included all of the original site of Huntington and most of the land added to the city since its founding.

Although reportedly none of the old soldiers ever lived on their land, some of the grantees met on the land grant in 1775 for a partial division, and all of the tracts eventually were claimed by descendants or assignees of the 60 men. Cabell County historian George S. Wallace states that William Buffington, of Hampshire County in what now is eastern West Virginia, purchased Lot 42 from

John Savage himself and willed this parcel to his sons, Thomas and Jonathan. About 1796, Thomas and Jonathan Buffington came to the mouth of the Guyandotte River to take possession. Thomas built his home on the east side of the Guyandotte at the river's mouth, while Jonathan built on the west side.

Thomas Buffington was one of the earliest settlers of what was to become Cabell County. He was instrumental in the founding of the town of Guyandotte, the first county seat, in 1810.

See also Cabell County

Joseph Platania
Huntington

Sawmills

To supply their modest needs for lumber, early settlers used man-powered whip saws and water-powered sawmills. As the need grew, steam-powered circular sawmills were developed in the early 1800s. In 1835, there were 15 such mills in Western Virginia. With the coming of the first railroads shortly before the Civil War, the number of steam mills rapidly expanded, and by 1880 there were more than 400 of them in West Virginia. These mills were mostly small and portable, and had little effect on the vast timber reserves of the state. As late as 1870, two-thirds of West Virginia was still covered by old-growth forest.

It was not until the introduction of the band sawmill that lumber production dramatically increased. Rather than a toothed circular blade, the band saw was a long, thin, continuous band of steel, eight to 13 inches wide and with teeth on one edge. The band saw ran over wheels as large as eight feet in diameter. These wheels carried the saw at great speeds. The band saw cut lumber faster than circular saws, and it made a thinner cut, wasting less wood as sawdust.

Logs were brought to the mill on railroads built for the purpose. At the mill they were dumped into a pond. The logs were then carried up a ramp on a cleated chain into the mill, rolled onto the carriage, and carried past the saw where boards were cut. After trimming, the lumber was graded and moved to dry kilns for kiln drying or stacked in ventilated piles for air drying. Machinery in the mill, other than the carriage, was operated by belts running off a long main drive shaft which, in turn, was run by a belt from the steam engine. The carriage was powered by a steam cylinder. Unusable slabs, sawdust, and scrap wood were burned to provide heat for steam generation.

The first band mill to operate in West Virginia was in 1875. As railroads made the state more accessible, the number of band mills greatly increased. By 1909, the peak year of lumber production in West Virginia, there were 83 band mills and 1,441 other lumber mills. Almost 1.5 billion board feet of lumber was produced that year. Prior to 1920, more than 180 band mills had operated or were operating in the state. Approximately 30 billion board feet of lumber was cut in West Virginia from 1880 to 1920, estimated to be enough to build a boardwalk two inches thick and 13 feet wide from the earth to the moon.

The original forests were depleted during this period, and after that the lumber industry rapidly declined. By 1920, there were only 398 sawmills operating in the state, surviving by making a second cutting of trees. The day of the big bandsaw mills was over in West Virginia. Giant steam-powered mills gave way to smaller mills powered by diesel engines and electricity.

Nature has amazing powers of recuperation, however, and at the turn of the 21st century West Virginia is the third most forested state in the United States with 11.7 million acres of forest. These timber lands supported 161 commercial sawmills in 2004. Fifty-five of them were band mills, with several having two or more saws operating in the same building. The other 106 were circular mills, some of which have more than one saw. The lumber industry is again thriving, employing 30,000 workers and contributing $3.2 billion annually to the economy of West Virginia.

See also Timbering and Logging

Roy B. Clarkson
West Virginia University

A. B. Brooks, *Forestry and Wood Industries*, 1910; Roy B. Clarkson, *Tumult on the Mountains: Lumbering in West Virginia 1770–1920*, 1964.

Sawmill workers at Meadow River Lumber Company, about 1940.

Burl Sawyers

Burl Allan Sawyers served eight and a half years as state road commissioner, and later served prison time for corruption in the execution of his duties. He was born at Smoot in Greenbrier County, March 29, 1912, and educated as an engineer. He lived most of his life in Charleston, where he once ran unsuccessfully for sheriff of Kanawha County.

Sawyers was first appointed state road commissioner on July 1, 1955, by Governor Marland, after serving as an administrative assistant to Marland. He lost the job February 1, 1957, when Governor Underwood, a Republican, named a member of his own party to the post. Sawyers was reappointed four years later by Democrat Wally Barron. Sawyers resigned as commissioner in 1965 when Governor Smith suspended him because of federal indictments against Sawyers, Governor Barron, Deputy State Road Commissioner Vincent J. Johnkoski, Finance and Administration Commissioner Truman Gore, longtime Barron friend Bonn Brown of Elkins, and Clarksburg auto dealer Fred Schroath. All were charged with conspiracy to take kickbacks and rigging state contracts. Barron was acquitted but Sawyers entered a guilty plea on August 31, 1965, and was sentenced to two years in federal prison and fined $5,000. Sawyers died August 14, 2002, in Putnam County.

See also William Wallace Barron, Political Corruption

Tom D. Miller
Huntington

Scary Creek, Battle of

Located in Putnam County on the west side of the Kanawha River just opposite Nitro, Scary Creek was the site of one of the earliest battles of the Civil War and one of the first Confederate victories.

Fought July 17, 1861, the battle was the result of a movement by Gen. Jacob D. Cox of Ohio, under the direction of Gen. George B. McClellan, to clear the Kanawha Valley of the Confederate Army of Gen. Henry A. Wise of Virginia.

On July 11, 1861, Cox launched a three-pronged movement eastward from Point Pleasant with his infantry, cavalry, and artillery, an attempt to entrap Wise at Charleston. By July 16, following some insignificant skirmishing and a clash at Barboursville, the bulk of Cox's forces had consolidated at the mouth of the Pocatalico River, downstream and on the opposite side of the Kanawha. The following day, Cox's advance party crossed the Kanawha River and encountered Confederate pickets at the mouth of Little Scary Creek. He dispatched about 1,300 federal soldiers under field command of Col. John W. Lowe of the 12th Ohio Infantry to engage the approximate 900 Confederates at Scary Creek. The Confederates were led by Col. George S. Patton, great-grandfather of Gen. George S. Patton of World War II. A near five-hour battle of heavy musketry and artillery fire ensued, including a number of unsuccessful federal charges across the Scary Creek bridge. Patton was seriously wounded and Capt. Albert Gallatin Jenkins rallied the disorganized Confederates to victory.

Casualties were slight on both sides, and the southern victory was short-lived as Wise abandoned the Kanawha Valley by August 1 due to pressure by McClellan

on Confederate forces in northern West Virginia.

See also Civil War, Albert Gallatin Jenkins

Terry Lowry
State Archives
Terry Lowry, *The Battle of Scary Creek: Military Operations in the Kanawha Valley, April–July 1861*, 1982.

Scenic Highways

In 1991, Congress created the National Scenic Byways program to recognize national and state roads of special scenic value. The Federal Highway Administration funds the program. After a road is designated as a scenic byway, it is eligible for funds to protect, maintain, and improve the roads and adjacent areas.

West Virginia offers two scenic designations, byway and backway. To meet the minimum criteria for byway designation, a road must be accessible to the public and have at least one outstanding scenic, historic, cultural, natural, archeological, or recreation quality. A backway must meet additional criteria: provide a rural or "semi-primitive" experience; be unpaved or have only a few stretches of pavement; and offer nearby walking paths to areas with at least one outstanding quality.

As of 2005, West Virginia had one All American Road: Historic National Road (16 miles) follows U.S. 40 from the Ohio state line to the Pennsylvania state line. The state had four nationally designated byways: Midland Trail (117 miles) follows U.S. 60 from Charleston to the Virginia border; Highland Scenic Highway (43 miles) through the Monongahela National Forest; Coal Heritage Trail (98 miles) from Beckley via State Route 16 and U.S. 52 at Welch to Bluefield; and the Washington Heritage Trail (137 miles) through Jefferson, Berkeley, and Morgan counties in the Eastern Panhandle. There are 12 state-designated byways, located throughout West Virginia, and 12 backways.

Every four years, the state Division of Highways re-evaluates each byway and backway to determine if it still meets the program's standards.

See also Highland Scenic Highway, Midland Trail

Fred Schaus

Coach Frederick Appleton "Fred" Schaus, West Virginia University basketball All-American, coach, and athletic director, was born June 30, 1925, in Newark, Ohio. An all-stater there, after coming to WVU he set many individual records as a player and made All-American in 1949. Schaus passed up his senior year in college to play in the National Basketball Association, where he became an all-pro.

Schaus coached at WVU from 1954 to 1960, with a 146-37 record, the school's

best winning percentage. He guided WVU to a No. 1 national ranking at the end of the 1958 regular season. His 1959 team lost 71-70 to California in the National Collegiate Athletic Association tournament final. Schaus left WVU to return to the NBA as coach, vice president, and general manager of the Los Angeles Lakers. There he directed two of his WVU All-Americans, Jerry West and Rod Hundley. He came back to WVU as athletic director (1981–89). Winning teams, an expansion of facilities, and establishing the athletic department as a self-supporting entity were achievements during his years.

Fred Schaus was named to the WVU Hall of Fame in 1992. He lives in Morgantown.

Norman Julian
Dominion Post
Norman Julian, *Legends: Profiles in West Virginia University Basketball*, 1998.

Henry Schmulbach

Brewer and businessman Henry Schmulbach was born in Germany, November 12, 1844, and moved to Wheeling as a child. The Schmulbachs joined a thriving German immigrant community in the Northern Panhandle. Henry went to work with his uncle in the retail grocery business while still a teenager, later switching to the wholesale liquor trade.

In coming years Schmulbach established himself as a leader in Wheeling business and industry. He worked as a merchant until 1881, then purchased the Nail City Brewery in 1882, renaming it the Schmulbach Brewing Company and increasing capacity to 200,000 barrels annually. He was president of the German Bank, now WesBanco, president of the Wheeling Bridge Company, and president of local telephone and streetcar companies. He was the owner of steamboats and a stockholder in several iron and nail companies.

Like many in the streetcar business, Schmulbach established an amusement park to bolster ridership on weekends and holidays. His Mozart Park was built on top of a hill overlooking South Wheeling. Schmulbach built an impressive inclined railway to reach the hilltop park, opening it to riders in 1893. The incline itself soon became a major attraction, reportedly carrying as many as 1,200 passengers an hour.

In 1904–07, Schmulbach had the Schmulbach Building constructed, West Virginia's first high-rise office building. Still a Wheeling landmark, it is today the headquarters of Wheeling-Pittsburgh Steel. Schmulbach's Chapline Street house is one of a group of eight Victorian row houses added to the National Register of Historic Places in 1984. Many visitors find a humorous resemblance to a dollar mark in his intertwined initials on the doorway.

Henry Schmulbach died at home in Wheeling, August 12, 1915.

See also Germans, WesBanco, Wheeling

Alex Schoenbaum

Restaurateur Alex Schoenbaum, dwarfed by Big Boy.

Businessman Alex Schoenbaum, born August 8, 1915, in Richmond, founded Shoney's and made it into one of the nation's largest family restaurant chains. Schoenbaum was an All-American tackle at Ohio State University, where he graduated from the Fisher College of Business in 1939. He settled in Charleston in 1943.

In 1947, Schoenbaum opened the Parkette Drive-In and Bowling Alley on Charleston's west side. Four years later, he purchased Big Boy hamburger chain franchise rights for the southeastern states. The number of restaurants grew, and in 1953 they were named Shoney's when Schoenbaum's nickname was selected as the company name in an employee contest. In 1971, Schoenbaum and Ray Danner, a Shoney's Big Boy franchise holder in middle Tennessee and the founder of Captain D's restaurants, merged their companies to form Shoney's Big Boy Enterprises, Inc. In 2002, Shoney's had 935 locations in 28 states. By that time the company had suffered financial reverses and was operating under other ownership.

Schoenbaum's philanthropy and that of his wife, Betty, is honored in the naming of Schoenbaum Hall at Ohio State, Schoenbaum Library at the University of Charleston, and the Schoenbaum Family Enrichment Center and a Schoenbaum soccer facility in Charleston. Alex Schoenbaum, who lived his later years in Charleston and Florida, died December 6, 1996.

Larry Sonis
Arlington, Texas

School Consolidation

West Virginia had thousands of schools in the late 19th and early 20th centuries, and hundreds of self-taxing school districts. As late as the 1907–08 school year, according to one report, the state had 6,156 schools in 395 districts. There were 40 high schools and 262 multi-roomed "graded" schools that year, but the overwhelming majority, 5,854, were tiny, one-room schools. The consolidation of these many schools and districts into a much smaller number of larger units is a century-old process that remains a touchy issue today.

As early as the late 19th century small, community-run schools were being castigated as unsystematic, inefficient, and backward. They all but disappeared in the metropolitan areas during this era, but rural communities retained their schools. Country schools were almost always buildings of one room, occasionally two, educating the children of local families. Kinship and political connections were often more important than education or experience in getting a teaching job.

Rural schools suffered from seasonal attendance and lack of resources. Nonetheless, the one-room school and later the rural high school were centers of communication, socializing, and athletic participation, and they served as places to vote. They were the symbols of civilization itself in many communities.

School and school district consolidations accelerated during the Great Depression and after World War II. The county unit plan, an important education reform that went into effect in 1933, combined hundreds of small school districts into 55 county systems. By 1959–60, the number of schools in West Virginia had been cut to 2,843, less than half the number reported a half-century before. Meanwhile, the student population had nearly doubled, from 235,191 to 460,429, but this growth in the number of students soon reversed itself. The loss of mining and industrial jobs in the 1950s and 1960s reduced the school-age population of many counties, while undercutting school budgets. Efforts were made to consolidate the remaining small schools as their student numbers dwindled. Better highways and a growing fleet of school buses facilitated the closing of schools.

Later consolidation efforts were driven in part by the 1982 Recht Decision, a judicial ruling that called for equity in school funding and equal instruction for all children in West Virginia. This led many counties to close small, often older, schools where instructional costs were high and where it was sometimes hard to maintain standards. The state School Building Authority, established in 1989 at the urging of Governor Caperton, is recognized as a major force in school consolidation in recent decades. The authority has required consolidation in some cases and has been seen as giving higher priority to the construction and remodeling of schools where consolidation is a consideration.

The result of these changes was that during the 20th century thousands of schools and hundreds of school districts disappeared in West Virginia. The state became the primary governing entity for West Virginia schools, eclipsing communities and counties. By the end of the 20th century, fewer than 900 schools remained. There are occasional suggestions that 55 county school systems are too many, and that they should be further consolidated, also enabling school consolidations between counties.

While pervasive, school consolidation has been controversial. The controversy continued into the early 21st century, and there were indications that the policy was being re-evaluated at the upper levels of government. Proponents point to the modern school buildings created by consolidation throughout the state, noting that these schools are better equipped than their smaller predecessors. They note wider curricular and extra-curricular offerings than at smaller schools, and the presence of more faculty and staff. They also argue that larger schools allow the offering of a better education at a lower average cost per student.

Critics claim that school consolidation erodes rural locales by withdrawing children and fiscal resources from small communities, and makes it difficult for children to participate in school activities. Poor families are further disadvantaged if parents have difficulty coming long distances to meet with teachers or to support school activities. And critics argue that the children most likely to be harmed by district-wide consolidation are poorer, since consolidated schools are often built in or near towns where wealthier students and their families have easier access. They point out that consolidated schools rarely save as much money as expected. Some recent research questions the academic advantage of larger schools, as well.

See also County Unit Plan, Education, Recht Decision

Alan J. DeYoung
University of Kentucky

Schoolhouse Cave

Located in Germany Valley, Pendleton County, Schoolhouse Cave is found in middle Ordovician limestones along the crest of the Wills Mountain Anticline. Early accounts refer simply to "the large cave in the Harman Hills." The modern name was derived from the nearby one-room Cave School, which closed in 1945.

During the Indian and Revolutionary wars the occupants of Hinkle's Fort used the cave as a source of niter (or saltpeter), the primary ingredient in the manufacture of gunpowder. The most intensive niter mining operation probably occurred during the War of 1812. At some point the miners constructed scaffolding and a tramway across the entrance room to the high passage containing the niter-bearing cave earth. Schoolhouse is the only niter cave known to have been worked by Unionists during the Civil War.

Before November 1939, no explorer had penetrated beyond the "Jumping Off Place," about 600 feet into the cave, where the floor drops away into a deep pit. The final 1,000 feet, a series of formidable pits and traverses, was explored by rock climbers of the Potomac Appalachian Trail Club during numerous expeditions from February 1940 to March 1941. During 1942, the daunting task of surveying the cave was completed. Although more challenging caves would be discovered subsequently, into the 1950s Schoolhouse retained its reputation as "the toughest cave" in the nation. In 1999, the large entrance was gated, prohibiting entry to conserve colonies of endangered and federally protected Virginia big-eared bats. The massive cave gate is one of the largest in the country.

See also Caves, Saltpeter Mining

John Craft Taylor
Union College

Scotch-Irish

Sometimes referred to as "Scots-Irish" or "Ulster Scots," the Scotch-Irish were second only to the Germans in the settlement of the Eastern Panhandle. And they were the primary frontiersmen who trekked across the Alleghenies into much of the rest of West Virginia. The Scotch-Irish were also known for their pioneering in the Valley of Virginia, the Carolinas, Kentucky, Tennessee, and lands farther west.

The Scotch-Irish came to America from Ulster, or northern Ireland, which had been settled as a Protestant province primarily by Presbyterian Scots in the early 17th century. With each passing generation, these Ulster Scots took on their own culture and lifestyle. They were no longer Scottish Lowlanders, and certainly they were not Irish, their Catholic enemy. A hundred years after the Protestant settlement of Ulster, hard times and anti-Presbyterian laws would influence the emigration of more than 200,000 of these Scotch-Irish to America.

The great migration consisted of five different periods: 1717–18, 1725–29, 1740–41, 1754–55, and 1771–75. As many as half of these emigrants became inden-

---

A Scotch-Irishman speaks of his own

"These people were high-spirited, energetic, careful, loving principle as they loved life, pertinacious, thrifty, filled with the love of country, deeply imbued through centuries of oppression with the thought of civil and religious liberty. They . . . resolutely turned their faces to the rich interior of America and undertook the greater task of subduing the Indian, laying low the forest, tilling the land and raising the home, erecting the church and the school, all under equal rights to every man. . . .

"The homes of these people were homes of plenty, not wastefulness. Wherever I have seen them they were cultivated people, for wherever any community of them existed the school and the college rose next to the house of worship. There is not a large family holding the names of these people which has not sent one of its sons to some institution of learning. Their houses are filled with the substantial and beautiful things which adorn a house of plenty. In my . . . home the old clock which has rung the births, the deaths, the marriages, and has for one hundred and fifty years looked upon all of the changes of the day; the old candle stand; the book case; the corner cupboard; and the grandmother's chair; the high poster bed upon which I was born—all made by a Scotch-Irishman, and which adorned the house of my grandfather and his father and my father, are as exquisitely carved and beautifully formed, and evidence as much taste as anything known to me in any place or any country."

—Gov. William A. MacCorkle *The Recollections of Fifty Years of West Virginia* (1928)

---

tured servants in America, which delayed their movement onto the frontier. Others, who had paid their own passage across the ocean, searched for land soon after arriving in America. The Scotch-Irish normally came to Pennsylvania because of its accessible ports, particularly Philadelphia, and the colony's record of liberal land policies and religious tolerance. As available land diminished in Pennsylvania, the Scotch-Irish next moved south into the rich Valley of Virginia. Often the sons and daughters of these settlers moved farther south and west.

By the middle of the 18th century, the Scotch-Irish had spearheaded settlements across the Alleghenies into present West Virginia. Western lands were opened to white settlement only after the British-American victory in the French and Indian War; the defeat of Pontiac's Rebellion, a massive Indian attack all along the frontier in 1763; and a series of treaties with the Indians. The American Revolution would soon bring further bloodshed to settlements west of the mountains. However, with the American victory over the British and their Indian allies, by the end of the 18th century the Allegheny region was again open to settlement. The Scotch-Irish would reap the rewards of victory as they expanded the white frontier farther across the Alleghenies.

As pioneers the Scotch-Irish were noted for their restless nature; their hardiness as hunters and settlers; their spirit of adventure; their strong Protestant faith (and yet their passion for drinking and gambling); their quick temper; their contempt for nobility and titles; and their ferocity toward the Indians. They came from an uprooted people, and they showed little mercy in uprooting others. The German pioneers were often better farmers, and their lands

were usually superior. However, in time of war, or when quick action was demanded on the frontier, the Scotch-Irish were unmatched. No other ethnic group would be as significant in shaping the culture of West Virginia.

Ronald R. Alexander
WVU Institute of Technology

Billy Kennedy, *The Scots-Irish in the Shenandoah Valley*, 1996; James G. Leyburn, *The Scotch-Irish: A Social History*, 1978; Otis K. Rice, *The Allegheny Frontier: West Virginia Beginnings, 1730–1830*, 1970.

Nathan B. Scott

U.S. Senator Nathan Bay Scott was born December 18, 1842, in Guernsey County, Ohio, west of Wheeling. He worked in a general store as a boy and in 1859 traveled to Leavenworth, Kansas, then worked as an ox driver from Leavenworth to Denver. Returning to Ohio, he enlisted in the Union army about 1863.

From these modest beginnings Scott rose to become one of West Virginia's four "richest and most powerful men by 1900," according to historian John Alexander Williams. At the end of the Civil War, Scott entered the glass industry in Bellaire, Ohio, and he made his fortune in business and banking. He moved to neighboring Wheeling in 1875, becoming in 1876 the president of Central Glass Company. He later served as an officer in banks in Wheeling and Washington, and invested in coal and timber in Logan and Mingo counties in West Virginia's southern coalfields. Scott was a founder of the Dollar Savings & Trust Company, a predecessor of WesBanco.

Scott entered West Virginia politics when he was elected to the Wheeling City Council in 1880. Two years later, he was elected as a Republican to the state Senate, serving two terms, 1883–91. He became a member of the Republican National Committee in 1888, serving 24 years. In 1898, Scott was elected to the U.S. Senate and reelected in 1904, but he lost the Republican nomination in 1910 in a bitter inter-party rivalry.

In the U.S. Senate, Scott was a close ally of Sen. Stephen B. Elkins, the leader of West Virginia Republicans until his 1911 death. As it happened, Elkins died in office just as Scott's second term was expiring, in an era when U.S. senators were elected by the state legislature. The prospect of the Democratic legislature replacing two Republican U.S. senators at once led to one of the most notorious standoffs in West Virginia politics, as Republican state senators first hid in the governor's office and then fled the state to prevent a vote by denying a quorum.

After leaving the Senate, Scott lived the rest of his life as a banker in Washington. He died there, January 2, 1924.

See also Stephen B. Elkins, Senate

Scotts Run

During the 1930s, Scotts Run became a symbol of the Great Depression in the coalfields. During the coal boom sparked by World War I, this four-mile-long hollow near Morgantown went through a rapid transition from farmland to one of the most intensely developed coal districts in the state. In the mid-1920s, between 36 and 42 coal mines shipped more than two million tons of coal out of Scotts Run. The great demand for labor attracted a very diverse population of perhaps 4,000 people, 60 percent of them foreign-born and 10 percent to 20 percent African-Americans.

When the demand for coal subsided in the mid-1920s, the northern West Virginia coal operators abrogated the union contract and a series of violent strikes ensued. Because they had been on strike for several years, miners and their families were already destitute when the national economy collapsed in 1929. The inability to speak English, racism, and the lack of education or alternate skills only compounded their plight. Both local and national relief agencies, such as the Red Cross, the American Friends Service Committee, and Presbyterian and Methodist home missions, entered Scotts Run to provide assistance.

It was through the Friends that First Lady Eleanor Roosevelt learned about Scotts Run and decided to make an inspection of the area. Disturbed by the living conditions she found there, Mrs. Roosevelt gave her personal attention to the relief efforts. Largely through her initiative the federally planned community of Arthurdale, Preston County, was constructed as a pilot program to relocate "stranded" industrial workers in more favorable settings, and most of the

new residents of Arthurdale were from Scotts Run.

By World War II, people began to abandon the hollow for military service or better opportunities elsewhere, and little physical evidence remains of this once booming coalfield.

See also Arthurdale, Great Depression, New Deal

Ronald L. Lewis
West Virginia University

Scrip

Scrip, a private currency, was the medium of exchange in many West Virginia coal towns. Issued by coal companies in a bewildering variety of forms, scrip was made of metal or paper. Paper scrip lacked durability and was easily counterfeited, so companies largely replaced it with scrip coins, a trend promoted by the invention of cash registers which permitted accounting of large quantities of metal scrip.

Companies bought paper scrip from their printer, and some that owned a pantograph machine manufactured their own metal scrip. In the West Virginia coalfields, scrip usually was purchased from either the Osborne Register Company of Cincinnati or the Ingle-Schierloh Company of Dayton, Ohio.

Coal companies received significant advantages in using scrip. Scrip reduced the outflow of capital, strengthened company cash flow, and reduced payroll theft, thereby lowering the cost of security. It also assured the company store of payment since scrip was deducted from miners' wages on payday. Miners often received pay envelopes marked with a curling line across them, a symbol miners called the "bobtail check" or the "snake." It meant no wages due.

Initially a convenience to miners and companies in rural areas, scrip became a means to cycle the value of a miner's

labor back to the company. Companies allowed miners to "cut" or "draw" scrip daily. Scrip was good for full face value at the company store, but companies would not buy back their scrip for cash. Traders appeared who bought scrip at a discount of 25 percent and upwards, while independent stores located nearby often accepted scrip at a 10 percent to 30 percent discount.

In West Virginia a struggle to regulate scrip occurred between 1887 and 1925. Labor organizations, supported by independent merchants, lobbied for the 1891 scrip law. The new legislation brought reforms, but punishment provisions were negligible and enforcement non-existent. Companies were prohibited from issuing scrip except as a promise to pay the sum specified in legal money.

Thus, a company could not issue scrip in lieu of currency, but only for work already performed or as an advance on pay. This legalized the use of scrip for credit. A later scrip law of 1925, written by coal company lobbyists, made scrip non-transferable. This reduced the use of scrip by independent stores.

Coal companies continued to use scrip as credit for preferred employees or to provision new workers migrating to their locale via "transportation." The latter practice required a man to work off his debt and led to vicious incidents of debt peonage in the state prior to 1917. Coal operators maintained that scrip "educated miners to sound credit practices" and prevented miners from being fleeced by independent stores. Investigators in 1925 concluded, to the contrary, that prolonged scrip use encouraged poor budgeting practices and prevented development of "a sense of the value of money and savings."

Scrip use declined as automobiles and mail order sales broke the hold of com-

Coal company scrip was once common.

pany stores, credit became more widely available, and wider use of coin vending machines created opposition to metal scrip. Scrip disappeared with the collapse of the coal industry in the 1950s, but it retains a big place in the memory of West Virginians.

Lou Athey
Franklin & Marshall College

Second Homes

Second or vacation homes are increasingly common in parts of West Virginia. The presence of such homes represents a maturing of the regional tourism industry, as visitors find favorite vacation spots attractive enough to want to spend more time there and to make the major investment required to buy a house. Sometimes vacation homes become retirement homes, as well. Their often affluent occupants have a positive impact on the local economy, as does the construction employment and commercial activity involved in building and selling second homes.

Critics point out, however, that large numbers of second homes may strain local services for the benefit of part-time residents, while driving up property taxes and sometimes raising property values beyond the means of local people. Some question the cultural impact, as second-home developments bring in people with different values and habits. Others worry about the loss of wildlife habitat or farmland.

The number of second homes in West Virginia has grown substantially in recent years, with a statewide average increase of 71 percent from 1990 to 2000. For the decade, West Virginia had the fifth-highest growth in the country. Second homes are not equally distributed through the state, however; nor is the growth in second homes equally distributed. The easternmost counties of the Eastern Panhandle, for example, have relatively high numbers of second homes, but the number of new units is growing at a much lower rate there than in some other parts of the state. Presumably this is due to the relative scarcity of building land as the year-round population of the Panhandle counties increases. The number of second homes actually decreased in Jefferson County during the 1990s, as such dwellings were converted to full-time occupancy or replaced by full-time housing.

Pocahontas County, home of Snowshoe Mountain Resort, was identified in 2002 by the Northeast Regional Center for Rural Development as among the nation's top 50 counties for second homes. Pocahontas County leads West Virginia in the number of seasonal homes as reported by the 2000 census with 3,060, an increase of nearly 115 percent since 1990. Similar trends may be seen around Ca-

naan Valley, with the number of second homes in Tucker County growing 200 percent during the 1990s. Second homes at Snowshoe, Canaan, and other resorts are often maintained as vacation rentals, occasionally used by their owners but available for rent on a short-term basis.

The distribution of second homes in West Virginia suggests that fine mountain scenery and outdoor recreational opportunity are key considerations. The 12 counties having 1,000 or more second homes form a contiguous unit stretching along the Virginia border from Berkeley County to Monroe County. This area includes West Virginia's highest elevations and its two major skiing areas, and nearly all of the Monongahela National Forest. The distribution of these counties along the state's eastern border suggests that proximity to East Coast population centers is also an important consideration in the location of second homes. In this regard it is expected that the completion of four-lane Corridor H through the Eastern Panhandle to Virginia will lead to additional development. For the foreseeable future, West Virginia is likely to remain the region's home away from home.

Jason Siniscalchi
West Virginia University

Secondary School Activities Commission

The Secondary School Activities Commission, known as the SSAC, governs athletic competition among West Virginia secondary schools. The organization traces its origins to the early 20th century, when the West Virginia High School Athletic Association was organized at Charleston on June 17, 1916. The 11 charter members were Bluefield's Beaver High School, Charleston, Clarksburg's Washington Irving High School, Elkins, Fairmont, Grafton, Huntington, Parkersburg, St. Marys, Sistersville, and Wheeling. The name of the organization was changed to the West Virginia Secondary School Activities Commission in 1955. In 1967, the West Virginia legislature recognized the SSAC as a legal entity, an arm of the county school boards. It is authorized by law to make rules and regulations governing the interscholastic athletic and band activities of its members.

The original Athletic Association was organized to allow high schools to take a more active role in the control of athletic activities. Previously high school contests had been organized by club or other promoters with little attention to rules, regulations, or requirements such as eligibility to play. The new organization was a state association to be controlled by the schools. The officers, designated as the Board of Appeals, were to be selected from among the principals of the member schools. The organization grew

rapidly and the responsibilities of the officers (especially those of the secretary-treasurer) became burdensome. In 1946, a full-time executive secretary was appointed by the board.

The primary objectives of the SSAC include standardization of requirements and regulations governing eligibility; providing the means for settlement of disputes between schools; and promoting the ideals of sportsmanship for all participants. The SSAC sponsors state championships in 13 sports: basketball, track and field, baseball, football, wrestling, golf, tennis, cross-country, volleyball, softball, cheerleading, soccer, and swimming. The commission also conducts clinics for coaches and officials; sets requirements for the performance of officials; presides over regional band festivals; maintains sportsmanship ratings for its member schools; and administers a program of academic achievement awards and scholarships.

Tim L. Wyatt
Woodbridge, Virginia

Secretary of State

The secretary of state is one of the constitutional officers of West Virginia, who are elected statewide and whose positions are mandated in the state constitution. Elected every four years, the secretary of state serves with the governor and the four other constitutional officers on the Board of Public Works.

During its first session, the legislature provided that the secretary of state keep the state seal, preserve executive department records, and render such services "in the dispatch of the executive business" as the governor may require. The language of the code was taken directly from the Virginia general powers statute enacted in 1860.

Through the years, the legislature has given the secretary of state broader authority. Today, the office has two business divisions and four public divisions handling a variety of duties. Notably, the secretary of state is the state's chief elections officer, responsible for maintaining the integrity of the electoral process. The secretary of state also serves as repository for corporation filings; administrator of the notary public application process; registrar and regulator of charitable organizations; process server for certain legal parties such as some out-of-state defendants; keeper of Uniform Commercial Code filings; archivist and clearinghouse for state administrative rules and regulations; and a partner with the Department of Education in promoting civics education. Other licensing requirements administered by the secretary of state include those for athletic agents, private investigators, ministers authorized to perform marriages, and newspapers certified to accept legal advertising.

West Virginia's first secretary of state was Jacob Edgar Boyers, a Tyler County Republican. With three exceptions, the job has not been a stepping stone to higher office. William E. Chilton, secretary of state from 1893 to 1897, later served in the U.S. Senate; John D. Rockefeller IV held the post from 1969 to 1973 before his election as governor and later as U.S. senator; and Joe Manchin was elected governor in 2004 after serving one term as secretary of state. Two of West Virginia's secretaries of state, William Smith O'Brien (1933–48) and Ken Hechler (1985–2001), were elected to four terms. In 2004, Betty Ireland became the first woman ever elected as secretary of state.

Larry Sonis
Arlington, Texas

Sectionalism and the Virginias

Sectionalism in Virginia and later West Virginia evolved as a consequence of settlement patterns and other geographic, political, social, and economic factors. As Virginians pushed west, sectional differences emerged. The area east of the fall line, the point on the rivers where the first rapids or falls were encountered, became known as the Tidewater. The territory from the fall line west to the Blue Ridge was designated the Piedmont, literally meaning the foot of the mountains. Between the Blue Ridge and Allegheny mountains was the Shenandoah Valley. Beyond the valley was the Trans-Allegheny, today mostly West Virginia. As this section developed, the inhabitants experienced a feeling of alienation based in part on cultural and philosophical differences and the failure to legislate change to ensure equitable representation in the state capital in Richmond.

Early in the 18th century, Scotch-Irish and German settlers moved into the Shenandoah Valley from Pennsylvania and began traversing the passes through the Allegheny Mountains. These people represented different cultural backgrounds from eastern Virginians, who were largely English in origins, and they developed different economic interests. As the settlements in the Trans-Allegheny region increased, the inhabitants petitioned for the establishment of counties to provide local government and representation in the state legislature. The westerners looked to the state for the services necessary to develop their region.

Under the Virginia Constitution of 1776 each county elected two delegates to the House of Delegates. The eastern part of the state had more counties and therefore more representatives. The large, slave-holding eastern farmers opposed any tax increase to pay for internal improvements that might benefit western interests. When some Valley and Trans-Allegheny counties threatened to secede in 1816, the state senate was reapportioned to provide additional senators from the western counties. This was a hollow victory, since the senate could not initiate legislation.

Efforts to pass legislation calling for a constitutional convention were defeated in the House. Finally, a bill passed in 1828 and the Constitutional Convention of 1829–30 convened in Richmond. Efforts to address western grievances were defeated by the eastern delegates. Failure of the delegates to address suffrage, representation, and local government organization issues in the Constitution of 1830 left the residents of the Trans-Allegheny dissatisfied. They voted against adoption, but were defeated.

Efforts to provide transportation to and from the western region were hampered by eastern control of the legislature. The James River & Kanawha Canal was developed to provide a link, but when railroads became a viable option the eastern establishment continued to support the canal venture. The Baltimore & Ohio Railroad was restricted to the northwestern part of the state. Acts to incorporate various railroad companies were proposed, but the belief that they would be sold to the B&O quickly brought defeat. Inability to ship to eastern markets forced westerners to look to the west, shipping goods down the Ohio and Mississippi and not back through Virginia.

The two sections gradually grew apart on the issue of slavery. The general absence of slavery in the western and northwestern sectors, coupled with the eastern power base opposing many of the western issues, caused westerners to feel more kinship with northern and northwestern states. The majority of westerners did not espouse abolitionist views, but many favored gradual emancipation. Believing that slavery was a deterrent to economic growth, leaders in the Trans-Allegheny supported the view that natural resources and free workers would attract capital, industry, and people.

Throughout the first half of the 19th century, immigration into the Trans-Allegheny continued from the northern states. These people brought with them cultural and philosophical differences and no ties to Virginia's heritage and traditions. Many brought an allegiance to their native region. When the churches split north and south in the 1840s, those who aligned with the northern branches of various denominations received their literature from Pittsburgh, Philadelphia, and Baltimore. These churches served to indoctrinate the people on certain religious and social issues. Academically, westerners often continued their education in colleges in Ohio and Pennsylvania. Few traveled across the mountains to attend the University of Virginia.

When the census of 1840 provided numerical proof that the white population of the Trans-Allegheny exceeded the rest of the state, westerners demanded a referendum calling for a constitutional convention. It was not until the end of the decade that the Constitutional Convention of 1850–1851 met and produced the Constitution of 1851, which incorporated most of the reforms called for by the inhabitants of the Trans-Allegheny section.

By then, it was too late. When the Civil War came, westerners were sufficiently divided over the issues of states rights and slavery to allow outside forces to seize the opportunity to control the Trans-Allegheny section. The advance of Union forces into the area coupled with the inability of Confederate forces to establish a firm hold west of the Allegheny Mountains sealed the section's fate.

Louis H. Manarin
Richmond, Virginia

Charles Henry Ambler, *Sectionalism in Virginia from 1776 to 1861*, 1910; Ambler, "The Cleavage Between Eastern and Western Virginia," *American Historical Review* 15, 1909–1910.

David Selby

Actor David Lynn Selby, best known for his television portrayals of Quentin in *Dark Shadows* (1968–71) and Richard Channing in *Falcon Crest* (1982–90), was born in Morgantown, February 5, 1941. He earned bachelor's and master's degrees from West Virginia University (1963–64) and a doctorate in drama from Southern Illinois University (1970). He has received honors from both schools.

Selby has acted extensively on stage, including many Broadway performances. His West Virginia credits include the Beckley outdoor drama, *Honey in the Rock* (1961–62). He starred in the award-winning *Sticks and Stones* at the New York Public Theatre. In Los Angeles, he received awards for *Night of the Iguana* and *The Crucible*. Film appearances include *Rich and Famous, Up the Sandbox, Raise the Titanic,* and *Super Cops.*

In 1998, Selby received the first Life Achievement Award from WVU's Creative Arts College. He serves on the advisory board of the WVU Creative Arts Center. He belongs to the Cleveland Playhouse Hall of Fame and the Hartford Stage Company. He received the Shakespeare Theatre's 1999 Millennium Recognition Award. In 2003, Selby spoke at WVU's Commencement and received an honorary doctor of humane letters degree from WVU.

David Selby married Claudeis "Chip" Newman of Morgantown in 1963. They fund a Guest Artist Series at WVU. They live in Los Angeles and have three children.

Sandy Wells
Charleston Gazette

Senate

The Senate is the upper chamber of the West Virginia legislature. The state constitution requires that a senator be at least 25 years old, a resident of the district for at least one year prior to election, and a citizen of the state for at least five years.

Under West Virginia's original 1863 constitution, senators served two-year terms, but since a new constitution was adopted in 1872 senators have served four-year terms. The Senate has always had two members from each district, but the number of senatorial districts has increased over the years with a corresponding increase in the number of senators. In the beginning, there were nine districts and a total of 18 senators. In 1872, the numbers increased to 12 districts and 24 senators. By 1903, there were 15 districts and 30 senators. That remained unchanged until 1939, when the state was divided into 16 districts with 32 senators.

The most recent change in the size of the Senate occurred in 1964, when lawmakers decided to create a 17th district in Kanawha County by overlaying it onto the 8th District, which already covered the county. Since then, four senators from two geographically identical districts have represented Kanawha County residents, and the total number of senators has stood at 34. Senatorial terms are staggered so that one member from each district is elected every two years, with the entire Senate thus up for reelection in a four-year period.

The Senate has twice been evenly split between Republicans and Democrats, after the elections of 1910 and 1912, with 15 members of each party each time. That caused a notable deadlock in 1911, when the selection of members of the U.S. Senate was still in the hands of state legislators rather than the voters. Sen. Nathan Scott's term had expired and Sen. Stephen Elkins died in office that January, so the legislature had the rare opportunity to choose both of West Virginia's U.S. senators. The Democrats controlled the House of Delegates but a Republican, William Glasscock, was governor. In an attempt to prevent the state from sending two Democrats to the U.S. Senate to replace the Republicans Scott and Elkins, Republican state senators decided to deny the West Virginia Senate a quorum; Glasscock would be able to make the appointments if the legislature failed to do so. The Republican senators initially holed up in the governor's office, but to avoid the possibility that the Democrats would use state law to compel them to appear in the Senate chamber, they fled to Cincinnati. They eventually agreed to a compromise that allowed the Democrats to choose the new U.S. senators while Republican Henry Hatfield became state Senate president.

The Senate is equal to the House of Delegates as regards passing resolutions and bills, including the state budget. But the Senate has the sole authority to confirm or reject appointments made by the governor. In the impeachment process, it is the Senate's duty to hold a trial for a state official impeached by the House of Delegates. The one time when the Senate sat as a court of impeachment was when it removed Treasurer John Burdett from office on January 21, 1876. Two other officials were impeached by the House, in 1926 and 1989, but both chose to resign rather than face trial in the Senate.

The Senate president is first in line to fill a vacancy in the governor's office, because West Virginia has no lieutenant governor. D.D.T. Farnsworth, West Virginia's second governor, was the only Senate president to become governor by succession. He held office for a brief seven days in 1869 after Governor Boreman resigned to become U.S. senator. Senate President Robert Carr tried to assert the right to become governor after the disputed election of 1888. He failed when incumbent E. W. Wilson was allowed to remain in office until the dispute was resolved more than a year later.

Some of the darkest days of the Senate occurred in the 1980s, when the political careers of two successive presidents, Dan Tonkovich and Larry Tucker, and Senate Majority Leader Si Boettner were cut short by guilty pleas in a series of influence-peddling cases. Tonkovich and Tucker both pleaded guilty to extortion. Boettner pleaded guilty to tax evasion.

The longest-serving Senate president has been Earl Ray Tomblin, who was in his 12th year in that office in 2006.

See also House of Delegates, Legislature

Jim Wallace
Charleston
John Unger
State Senate

George W. Atkinson, "Legislative History of West Virginia," in James Morton Callahan, ed., *Semi-Centennial History of West Virginia*, 1913; Darrell E. Holmes, ed., *West Virginia Blue Book*, 2001.

Seneca

The name Seneca derives from a Dutch word meaning the ones who live farthest out, a reference to the tribe's westernmost geographic position within the Iroquois Confederacy or Six Nations. English colonists Latinized this word, giving them the name of a Roman philosopher. The Senecas called themselves the "people of the great hill," a reference to their largest fortified village in the Genesee Valley of western New York. But it is as Seneca that this people is memorialized on West Virginia maps.

The Senecas were the most populous of the Six Nations. This, plus their traditional position as "keepers of the Western door" of the metaphorical Iroquois Longhouse, gave them leadership of the Iroquois expansion in the 17th-century Beaver Wars, conquests that underpinned the confederacy's territorial claim on the Ohio Valley and its claim to be "Chief of all the Indians" in colonial warfare and diplomacy. The Senecas were especially pivotal in their relations with the French in Canada. Initially bitterly hostile, they began to change when they captured a soldier named Louis Joncaire. Impressed by his conduct under torture, they allowed him to live and adopted him. Through his influence, the Senecas welcomed French traders and, beginning in 1726, allowed the construction of a supply base that grew into a great stone fortress at Niagara. Fort Niagara became the base for a renewed French thrust southward into the Ohio Valley. Sent by Virginia authorities to warn the French away from the region in 1753, the young George Washington was so impressed with Joncaire's importance that he returned home with a plan for his assassination.

As allies of the French, Senecas participated in the defeat of Braddock's army at the Battle of the Monongahela (1755) and in the raids on the Virginia frontier that followed. After the British emerged victorious, Senecas fought on in the coordinated uprising known as Pontiac's Rebellion (1763–66). Another defeat led to the Treaty of Fort Stanwix (1768), whereby the Six Nations ceded all lands south and east of the Ohio River, which despite Shawnee repudiation of this treaty led to an inrush of settlers into Western Virginia. During the early years of the American Revolution, Seneca leaders worked to keep the Six Nations neutral, but when three of the Iroquois nations became British allies in 1777, the Seneca joined them, attacking American posts and settlements across a wide front, including the Monongahela Valley. Following the American victory, further land cessions reduced the Seneca to a tiny reservation along the Allegheny River headwaters.

Though individual Senecas and their Mingo cousins continued fighting after 1784 as allies of the Shawnees, the warrior-statesman Cornplanter became a spokesman for peace with the Americans and for Seneca adoption of Euro-American ways. A new religion preached by Cornplanter's brother, Handsome Lake, in the early 19th century provided the basis for cultural synthesis and a modest renaissance centered on the Allegheny reservation. In West Virginia, however, only a few place names remain to mark the respect and fear that Senecas once invoked on the Ohio Valley frontier.

See also French and Indian War, Indians, Iroquois

John Alexander Williams
Appalachian State University

Daniel K. Richter, *The Ordeal of the Longhouse: The Peoples of the Iroquois League in the Era of European Colonization*, 1992; Anthony F. C. Wallace, *The Death and Rebirth of the Seneca*, 1969.

Seneca Caverns

The cave known as Seneca Caverns is located off U.S. 33, three miles northeast of Riverton in Pendleton County, at an elevation of 2,200 feet. It was opened to the public in 1930 and is one of four commercial caves in West Virginia. The entrance to Seneca Caverns is in a shallow sink behind the gift shop.

Seneca Caverns is about 500 feet long, and the tour exits from a rear entrance almost due east from the start. It has calcite formations throughout the length of the tour including stalagmites, stalactites, cave coral, and flowstone mounds. Several of the formations are pure white in color. The cave is located in limestone of the Black River Group (Ordovician Age) along the crest of the Wills Mountain Anticline. Stratosphere Balloon Cave is also located on the Seneca Caverns property and was formerly open to the public. Stratosphere Balloon Cave was described by Bishop Francis Asbury in his journal for June 21, 1781, and is also known as Asbury Cave.

See also Caves

William K. Jones
Charles Town

Seneca Glass Company

In 1891, a group of glassworkers, largely neighbors from the Black Forest area of Germany, opened the Seneca Glass Company in Fostoria, Ohio, in a factory recently vacated by Fostoria Glass Company's relocation to Moundsville. In 1896, Seneca Glass followed Fostoria to West Virginia. Seneca selected Morgantown, becoming the first of more than 20 glass factories to operate there. By the next year Seneca employed 250 workers.

From the beginning Seneca created quality, hand-blown lead glass. Early price lists show tumblers, bar bottles, pitchers, decanters, covered candy jars, nappies, finger bowls, sugar and creamers, water sets, vases, and endless varieties of stemware. Seneca used nearly every decorating technique. Glass was sand-blasted, acid-etched, plate-etched, needle-etched, hand-cut, and in other ways embellished.

The company opened a second factory in nearby Star City in 1911. Following national trends, Seneca added colored lead glass in the 1920s and produced colored glass until closing in 1983. Seneca specialized in high-end, elegant cut glass. In the most elaborate patterns 14 hours could be spent in cutting a single goblet, resulting in an expensive piece.

Such elegant glass attracted clientele from around the globe. Many U.S. embassies ordered Seneca Glass; the president of Liberia chose Seneca, as did U.S. Vice-President Johnson. Seneca was the last elegantly cut American lead crystal sold by Tiffany's as the demand for expensive cut crystal faded. Today the factory along the Monongahela River houses a shopping complex while retaining the architecture and some artifacts from one of the world's finest glass houses.

Dean Six
West Virginia Museum of American Glass
Bob Page and Dale Frederiksen, *Seneca Glass Company 1891–1983*, 1995.

Seneca Rocks

Seneca Rocks is a formation of sheer towering whitish rocks located near the confluence of Seneca Creek and the North Fork of the South Branch of the Potomac. In the early morning mist the jagged outline of Seneca Rocks resembles the bony back of a giant dinosaur. This vast mountain of pale stone whose rocks rise 1,000 feet from the forest floor provides cliffs and lofty crags inviting exploration by birds, rock climbers, and agile visitors.

The name comes from the Seneca Indians, who once used this vast wilderness for hunting, fishing, and trade routes. Today the Seneca Rocks area is part of the Monongahela National Forest.

Seneca Rocks is composed of the Tuscarora Sandstone deposited during the Early Silurian Period approximately 425 million years ago, when the waters of an ancient sea covered what is now West Virginia. The Tuscarora Sandstone has been compacted by great pressures into an erosion-resistant rock called a quartz arenite. Now this rock, once seashore sediments, forms high mountains along the entire length of the Appalachians. Rocks near the Seneca Rocks Visitor Center are upended and rotated 90 degrees to form the west flank of the Wills Mountain Anticline, an upward fold formed more than 200 million years ago at the end of the Paleozoic Era.

A 1.3-mile trail provides access to the Seneca Rocks overlook, which has spectacular views. The trail ascends 960 feet. Signs along the trail explain geological aspects of the rocks.

Seneca Rocks is a popular wilderness recreation area offering rock climbing, hiking, swimming, and bird watching. The cliffs are home to nesting peregrine falcons, introduced in the 1980s by the West Virginia nongame wildlife program. There are many other bird species, including bluebird, several kinds of woodpeckers, orioles, and high-elevation warblers and thrushes. Wildlife includes chipmunk, white-tailed deer, cottontail rabbit, black snake, timber rattlesnake, and fence lizard. Spring wildflowers include ginger, blue cohosh, blue phlox, and azalea.

See also Geology, Tuscarora Sandstone
Norma Jean Kennedy-Venable
Morgantown

Seneca State Forest

Seneca State Forest is located in Pocahontas County, on the Greenbrier River. It includes 11,680 acres and is the oldest unit in the state park and forest system. Most of the land was acquired by the West Virginia Game and Fish Commission in January 1924 with the purchase of 10,847 acres from A. D. Neill.

At that time, the cutting of the virgin timber on the land was nearing completion. The Raine Lumber Company had timber rights when the state bought the property, and continued logging until 1929. The state built a fire tower in its new forest in 1924 and built the first public campground in West Virginia in 1928. Also in 1928, the first state tree nursery was established at Seneca. Civilian Conservation Corps Camp Seneca was established in June 1933, across from the

Seneca Rocks is West Virginia's best-known landmark.

present forest headquarters. By the time the CCC camp was closed in June 1938, access roads, trails, picnic areas, eight cabins, and a lake had been constructed. Reforestation, timber stand improvement, and game and fish management programs were also begun by the CCC enrollees.

The recreation facilities were opened to the public in the summer of 1937 and hunting was allowed the following year. The forest was named for the Seneca Trail, which passed through present Pocahontas County although not through the forest.

William P. McNeel
Marlinton

The Seneca Trail

The Seneca Trail was a major thoroughfare during the time the Iroquois Confederation was consolidating its power in eastern North America. The trail was named for the Senecas, one of the Six Nations making up the great Indian empire. The Seneca Trail traversed many counties of present West Virginia, generally in a north-south direction, with some of its most recognizable sections in Tucker, Randolph, and Pendleton counties.

This old path started in western New York near Niagara Falls and extended south through western Pennsylvania by way of the Allegheny and Youghiogheny rivers into western Maryland. From the area of current Oakland, Maryland, the trail entered present Tucker County by way of Horseshoe Run northeast of St. George, crossed the Shavers Fork of Cheat River, and continued south up the Left Fork of Clover Run. It then crossed Pheasant Mountain into Randolph County and followed Leading Creek south to the Tygart Valley River. After passing the vicinity of present Elkins, the trail followed the course of the Tygart Valley River to its headwaters and crossed into what is now Pocahontas County. It continued by way of Edray, Indian Draft Run, and Marlinton, winding its way through Pocahontas County in the vicinity of Hillsboro and Droop Mountain to the Greenbrier River near the Pocahontas-Greenbrier county line. The trail then followed Anthony's Creek to White Sulphur Springs and followed the Greenbrier River to the New River and Bluestone River, exiting West Virginia a few miles west of Bluefield, as it continued southward to the Carolinas and Georgia. The trail, in general, follows the route of present U.S. 219 through West Virginia.

Branches of the Seneca Trail radiated in many directions. One of the most important began near Elkins and crossed the four forks of Cheat River to Harman and, by way of Horsecamp Run, crested the mountain to descend by Seneca Creek to its mouth near Seneca Rocks.

Some historians refer to this branch as the Shawnee Trail, since that band of Indians used the trail when raiding settlements in the South Branch Valley from the west. Modern U.S. 33 follows much of this branch.

See also Iroquois, Seneca

Donald L. Rice
Elkins

Serpent Handling

Handling serpents as a form of Christian worship originated in Tennessee and dates back to the early 1900s. Historians recognize George Hensley, an illiterate Church of God evangelist, as the founder. Hensley lived with his family in Grasshopper Valley, Tennessee, near Chattanooga. His son, James, credited Amanda, George Hensley's wife, as being the spiritual leader of the family.

George, while pondering the passage in Mark 16:17–18 which says that believers shall take up serpents, climbed White Oak Mountain and prayed for a sign. It was there that he spotted a large rattlesnake, put the snake in a gunnysack and took it to a revival meeting. George stood up and cited the gospel text, handled the serpent himself, and then challenged the people to prove their faith by doing the same.

As serpent handlers headed north during the 1920s and 1930s, they found a ready reception among some miners in Kentucky and West Virginia. Few of the early serpent handlers in West Virginia ever met George Hensley. Their prophet was Kentuckian Raymond Hayes. Hayes made a trip to Fayette County in 1946 and visited with Elsie Preast, who began to handle serpents regularly at the Church of All Nations. Preast said he knew that serpent handling had been practiced 17 to 18 years earlier on Cabin Creek, near Charleston.

West Virginia is the only state that legally permits serpent handling. At the turn of the 21st century, the most active serpent handling church in West Virginia was located near Jolo, McDowell County, where Robert and Barbara Elkins, along with Dewey Chapin, her son, were the leaders. Other important leaders over the years in the serpent handling churches in West Virginia were Joe and Myrtle Turner and their family at Camp Creek, Boone County, and Brother Hammonds and his wife at Fraziers Bottom, Putnam County.

In a serpent handling church, one may observe not only preaching, praying aloud together on one's knees, dancing and singing but also serpent handling, fire dancing, speaking in tongues, the laying on of hands for healing, testimonies, and at times, poison drinking and foot washing. An observer may also witness "stigmata," the oozing of blood from the hands or feet in empathy with the death of Jesus.

Serpent handling functions sacramentally in the lives of these Christians. When they pick up a snake, constantly calling upon the name of Jesus, they celebrate the central truth of the Gospel, that "through faith in Jesus there is victory over death"; and they experience, in a most dramatic way, that not even a serpent bite can separate them from eternal life with Jesus.

Mary Lee Daugherty
University of Charleston

Serviceberry

Serviceberries are also called Juneberries or sarvis. There are five species in West Virginia, including three shrubs and two small trees. Serviceberries are found throughout the state, growing in fencerows, thickets, woods, and on rocky outcrops. Identifying characteristics include oval leaves about two inches long with small, sharp teeth on the margins and gray bark with darker lines spiraling up the stem. Graceful, drooping clusters of five-petaled white flowers give off a sweet fragrance before or as the leaves unfold in April and May. The sweet, juicy fruits turn from a bright red to purplish black as they ripen from June through August. The fruits are excellent to eat plain, and for pies, jellies, or jams. Birds, squirrels, and black bears eagerly seek the ripe fruits. Serviceberries are popular landscape plants because of their dense flower clusters, yellowish-red autumn leaves, and small size.

In New England, serviceberries are called shad bush because they bloom in early spring when the shad fish move upstream to spawn. In the southern Appalachians, serviceberry is the preferred name. In pioneer days, circuit-riding preachers would hold early spring funeral services for all people who had died when deep snows prevented travel. These funeral services occurred when the serviceberry was in full bloom.

William N. Grafton
WVU Extension Service

Mary Lee Settle

Novelist Mary Lee Settle was born in Charleston, July 29, 1918. Her father, a mining engineer, moved his young family frequently as he followed the boom and bust of what his daughter later referred to as the manic-depressive coal industry. When Mary Lee was 10 years old, the family finally settled down in Charleston where Mary lived until she was 18. After two years at Sweet Briar College in Virginia, she moved to New York, and then to England where she joined the Women's Auxiliary Air Force during World War II. *All the Brave Promises* (1966) is a moving account of her wartime experiences.

Novelist Mary Lee Settle (1918–2005).

Following the war Settle returned to the United States, worked as an editor, and later taught fiction writing at Bard College and then at the University of Virginia. Even though she spent most of her adult life outside West Virginia, and a number of years outside the country, living in London, Paris, Rome, and Turkey, Settle had deep roots in the Mountain State. Her great-grandfather came to the Kanawha River Valley after the War of 1812, and built a home in 1844 at what became known as Cedar Grove. After several years in Turkey (where she wrote *Blood Tie*, winner of the National Book Award for Fiction in 1978), Settle returned to her ancestral home at Cedar Grove and tried to write in its familiar surroundings. However, what she described as too much past and too much family made the attempt unsuccessful.

Although Mary Lee produced many novels as well as nonfiction during the past 50 years, her literary reputation rests on the *Beulah Quintet*, a sequence of five historical novels spanning four centuries. The *Quintet* took the author more than 25 years to research and write. It is the story of West Virginia from the appearance of the first white people in the 1750s to the present, the centuries linked together by a network of families and kinships. *O Beulah Land* (1956), the first and best known of the five books, focuses on the settlement of Canona (a fictional Charleston) in the years before the American Revolution. *Know Nothing* (1960) came next, picking up the descendants of *Beulah Land*'s characters some 60 years later and following them to the outbreak of the Civil War. *Prisons* (1973), the author's personal favorite, is out of chronological order since it fills in the period prior to *O Beulah Land*. *Prisons* was undertaken when Settle realized that she must go back to the 17th-century English civil war to re-

veal her prevailing theme, the struggle for freedom, as it was originally expressed by the soldiers in Oliver Cromwell's army. Returning to her West Virginia chronology and setting in *The Scapegoat* (1980), she presented a full treatment of the early 20th-century Mine Wars, casting Mother Jones as a principal character. *The Killing Ground* (1982), the story of modern Canona, completed the saga.

Settle's creative outpouring did not diminish with age. In 1998, she published *Addie,* a revealing autobiography which demonstrates the profound influence of family and place on her writing. In 2001, at the age of 83, the author published *I, Roger Williams*, a novel based on the life of the founder of Rhode Island.

Mary Lee Settle died September 27, 2005.

See also Literature

Susan E. Lewis
Morgantown

George P. Garrett, *Understanding Mary Lee Settle*, 1988; Brian Rosenberg, *Mary Lee Settle's Beulah Quintet: The Price of Freedom*, 1991; Mary Lee Settle, *Addie: A Memoir*, 1998.

Seventh-day Adventists

The Seventh-day Adventist denomination arose from the teaching of William Miller (1782–1849) and was formally organized in 1863. Adventists believe in the imminent second coming of Christ. Seventh-day Adventist teachings first appeared in West Virginia through published materials about 1879. By the end of the year several people at Rockport in Wood County were keeping Saturday as the seventh-day Sabbath, and upon their request evangelist Isaac Sanborn was sent from Virginia. During the next year Sanborn held meetings in Wood, Roane, and Kanawha counties. He concluded his work in the state in December 1880, and reported 40 adherents to the faith.

During the next three years the evangelistic work was continued by J.R.S. Mowrey and others. By the middle of 1883, two churches had been organized, one in Wood County and one in Kanawha. In 1885, the "West Virginia Mission" was organized under the watchful care of the Ohio Conference. Evangelistic meetings continued throughout the state during the late 1880s, and on September 15, 1887, the West Virginia Conference of Seventh-day Adventists was organized with W. J. Stone as its first president. Meanwhile, the first camp meeting had been held the week before with about 125 people attending.

The early decades of the 20th century were a period of aggressive evangelism in the young, struggling conference. In the 1940s, leading Adventist evangelists R. L. Boothby and L. R. Mansell conducted evangelistic campaigns in Charleston, Bluefield, and Huntington. By 1950, the conference consisted of more than 2,000

members. Churches and church schools were established throughout the state. On August 22, 1971, the conference was reorganized as the Mountain View Conference of Seventh-day Adventists with its main office in Parkersburg.

In 2002, there were 2,450 Seventh-day Adventists in the conference and 34 churches. At about the time of the 1971 reorganization the conference purchased more than 200 acres south of Huttonsville and developed it as a retreat area for adults and youths, a well-equipped campground called Valley Vista.

James W. Daddysman
Alderson-Broaddus College

Seventh Day Baptists

The Seventh Day Baptists are evangelical Protestants similar in nature and doctrine to other Calvinistic Baptists, but who observe the Sabbath on the seventh day, Saturday, rather than on Sunday. The denomination, which is organized as a conference of individual churches with no hierarchy, believes that the Saturday Sabbath was established by God's will and confirmed in the practices of Jesus.

The origins of the faith can be traced to the English separatist movements of the mid-1600s, when many reformers called for renewed emphasis on Scripture rather than on established church traditions. Arguing that preserving the seventh-day Sabbath was an indisputable requirement of Christianity as specified in the Bible, the first church was organized in 1650 in London. The first Seventh Day Baptist church in America was founded in Newport, Rhode Island, 21 years later. During the 18th and 19th centuries, the movement spread across America, reaching the Pacific coast by 1900. Seventh Day Baptists have historically been characterized by their missionary work, civic involvement, and educational endeavors.

Of the many schools established by the denomination's Educational Society, three became colleges, including Salem College (now Salem International University) in West Virginia. The Salem Seventh Day Baptist Church was founded in 1792, and together with other churches in the local region, Salem has been an important stronghold for the denomination within the state. Once established in West Virginia, Seventh Day Baptists through their missionary efforts or permanent relocation helped spread the faith in other states, including Georgia, Delaware, Maryland, New Jersey, Pennsylvania, South Carolina, and Virginia.

The denomination has about 5,000 members in the U.S. and Canada, with about 50,000 members worldwide. There were three Seventh Day Baptists churches in West Virginia with a total of 411 adherents according to a 1990 church survey, with the churches all located in Doddridge and Harrison counties. Perhaps the most notable practitioner from the state was U.S. Sen. Jennings Randolph.

See also Jennings Randolph, Salem International University

Barry Mowell
Fort Lauderdale, Florida

Corliss Fitz Randolph, *A History of Seventh Day Baptists in West Virginia, Including the Woodbridgetown and Salemville Churches in Pennsylvania and the Shrewsbury Church in New Jersey*, 1905.

Sewell Mountain

Sewell Mountain in Fayette and Greenbrier counties is a part of the dissected Allegheny Plateau that was uplifted from the sea during the mountain-building period known as the Appalachian Orogeny, millions of years ago. The rock formations are sedimentary. Shale is more abundant and sandstone the most important in landform development, but coal is the mineral of economic importance.

From an elevation above the New River Gorge at about 2,200 feet, Sewell Mountain increases eastward over the next 10 to 12 miles to 3,200 feet elevation. At this point Sewell Mountain appears as a ridge about three-quarters of a mile wide and eight miles long. It extends in a northeast to southwest direction, capped with sandstone knobs (Busters, Myles, Stevens, Ford, and others) that top out at 3,460 feet. From the top, the ridge descends rapidly to the valleys of Sewell Creek and Meadow River. Sewell Mountain is neighbored to the south, east, and north by Walnut Ridge (3,223 feet), Fork Mountain (3,309 feet), Sims Mountain (3,282 feet), Little Sewell Mountain (3,000 feet), and Laurel Creek Mountain (3,063 feet). Sewell Mountain is drained westward primarily by Glade Creek through Babcock State Park to the New River at the now defunct coal and coke town of Sewell.

In the Sewell Mountain Campaign in 1861, Gen. Robert E. Lee established his headquarters on the summit, and it was here that he first saw Traveller, the great war horse he later purchased for $200 in Confederate currency. Mining in the Sewell coal seam began in the 1870s as railroads penetrated the region. Underground shaft and drift mines 400 to 500 feet deep and surface contour stripping at about 2,800 feet were common mining methods during the next century. In 1910, the Raine brothers established the Meadow River Lumber Company and the town of Rainelle at the confluence of Sewell Creek and Meadow River. To supply the mill, which was capable of cutting 3,000 acres of virgin timber a year, they acquired more than 75,000 acres of timber, much of it in the Sewell Mountain region. The Meadow River Lumber Company logged Sewell Mountain until it closed in 1970.

In the mid-1700s, Stephen Sewell explored the region and his name was later given to a coal seam and a company town, and to Sewell Creek, Sewell Mountain, Big Sewell Mountain (3,212 feet) in Summers County, and Little Sewell Mountain. The early route over Sewell Mountain followed a meandering buffalo trail that became known as the Lewis Trail in 1774. In 1824, the route became a part of the James River & Kanawha Turnpike, and a section of the Midland Trail in 1924 when it was designated U.S. 60. Traffic was diverted from the Sewell Mountain region when I-64 was completed in 1988, and U.S. 60 has been designated as the Midland Trail Scenic Highway. Sewell Mountain remains a scenic delight, with active farming communities, verdant second-growth forest, and varied topography.

See also Geology

Howard G. Adkins
Ona

Roy B. Clarkson, *Tumult on the Mountains: Lumbering in West Virginia, 1770–1920*, 1964; U.S. Geologic Survey Maps, West Virginia 7.5 Minute Quadrangles: Corliss, Danese, Fayetteville, Meadow Bridge, Meadow Creek, Rainelle, Thurmond, and Winona.

Shale Barrens

Shale barrens are hot, dry, open areas of steep Devonian shale in eastern West Virginia, occurring from Mercer County in the south to Hampshire and Berkeley counties in the northeast. Shale barrens also occur in neighboring areas of Virginia, Maryland, and Pennsylvania.

Shale barrens occur on slopes facing south or west into the hottest sunlight and are often undercut by a stream or road. They lack true soil, moisture and humus are scarce, and the shale is slightly acid. These are harsh habitats, but shale barrens host lizards and snakes, and a few plants thrive on the extreme conditions. Fourteen plants are endemic to West Virginia's shale barrens, growing there and nowhere else.

Shale barren rockcress is a federally designated endangered species. Five others are rare enough to be monitored by federal botanists. These are nodding wild onion, yellow buckwheat, Kates Mountain clover, shale evening-primrose, and pussytoes ragwort. Other shale barren endemics are mountain pimpernel, shale bindweed, whitehaired leatherflower, swordleaf phlox, shale barren pussytoes, shale barren aster, shale barren goldenrod, and shale skullcap.

Slaty Mountain near Sweet Springs, Monroe County, is often cited as the best shale barren in West Virginia. Kates Mountain near White Sulphur Springs is important because several prominent botanists discovered the rare shale barren plants there while vacationing at nearby Greenbrier resort. White's Draft near Alvon and Meadow Creek near Neola are high-quality barrens in the Monongahela National Forest. Larenium is a Mineral County park with an excellent shale barren. Other quality shale barrens are on private land near White Sulphur Springs, Blue Bend, Headsville, Dorcas, Rig, and Wardensville.

William N. Grafton
WVU Extension Service

E. L. Core, *Vegetation of West Virginia*, 1966; C. S. Keener, "Distribution and Biohistory of the Endemic Flora of the Mid-Appalachian Shale Barrens," *Botanical Review* 49:6,1983.

Shanghai Parade

The Shanghai Parade, held each New Year's Day on Washington Street in Lewisburg, is a community celebration of uncertain origins. Originally a costume parade emphasizing the frightful, in modern times Shanghai has incorporated floats, music, horseback riders, antique cars, farm equipment, and other elements of conventional parades. Participation and attendance vary with the weather, with some years seeing several dozen entries and hundreds of spectators.

Once featuring revelers in scary disguise who went about with both candy and switches, Shanghai resembles other midwinter rituals, including mummers plays and parades, Mardi Gras, and the West Virginia traditions of belsnickling and Fasnacht. Apparently limited to Lewisburg at present, the Shanghai custom was once practiced in other places in the region, including Pendleton County. A Pocahontas County fiddle tune named "Shanghai" may be associated with the tradition. Some older residents of this part of the state recall that "shanghying" once went on for days, usually in the week before and the week after Christmas.

Scholar H. B. Graybill, who researched the Lewisburg Shanghai Parade in the 1930s, believed that it began in the late 19th century, though others think the popular celebration goes back further. While organized by committee nowadays, Shanghai was largely by consensus and informal invitation in times past. A 1930s Greenbrier County newspaper offered the following call to revelry:

"Let millionaire and pauper meet
And go marching down the street.
The lid is off, fun is rife
Let's have the best time of your life."

See also Belsnickling, Fasnacht, Holidays and Celebrations

Shannondale Springs

A former health spa at mineral springs on the Shenandoah River approximately five miles from Charles Town, Shannondale Springs resort opened in the summer of 1820. A hotel was constructed the same year.

The resort was incorporated in 1838 under a new group of investors who had strong economic and political ties to the Whig Party. Thereafter, the springs became a gathering place for the rich and influential, attracting the political elite and many members of the First Families of Virginia. During its heyday (1840–58) Shannondale Springs hosted jousting-at-rings tournaments, fancy dress balls, lavish fireworks displays, hot air balloon ascensions, horse races, and political rallies.

The hotel burned in March 1858, leaving most of the cottages and outbuildings intact. The resort continued to function at a reduced level after the Civil War, serving middle-class families, providing facilities for hunting, fishing, dances, and local church groups. A new hotel was constructed in 1890 on the site of the old one. Built to benefit from a financial boom that did not materialize, Shannondale Springs was sold in 1902 to H.C. Getzendanner, who extensively renovated the facilities. The hotel burned again in 1909 and was not rebuilt.

Shannondale Springs was visited by several presidents, including James Monroe, Millard Fillmore, Andrew Jackson, and Martin Van Buren.

See also Mineral Springs

William D. Theriault
Bakerton

William D. Theriault, "Shannondale," *West Virginia History,* 1998.

Shape-Note Singing

The shape-note method for teaching singing, once popular in West Virginia churches, first appeared in *The Easy Instructor: A New Method of Teaching Sacred Harmony,* published in Philadelphia in 1801. Sometimes called "fasola" singing, this system labels musical pitches using four syllables rather than letter names, assigns the syllables to the major scale (Fa-Sol-La-Fa-Sol-La-Mi-Fa), and notates the syllables with four different shapes: right triangle for Fa, circle for Sol, square for La, and diamond for Mi. Other shape-note books followed the 1801 hymnal, including the 1846 *Christian Minstrel* that introduced a second system using seven shapes, one for each degree of the diatonic scale.

Itinerant singing masters moved from community to community throughout the South, conducting singing schools and selling shape-note songbooks, particularly among Methodists, Baptists, Presbyterians, and Churches of Christ. Shape-note singing spread into West Virginia and continued throughout the 20th century, primarily in small, rural churches. William Este Fortney, one of many singing masters, conducted singing schools across the state for more than 40 years, while Ruth Boggs perpetuated the tradition among African-Americans as director of the New Era District Number Two Shape-Note Choir in Beckley. Shape-note collections have music, and many pieces sung at camp meetings by various populist, ecstatic religious movements.

H. G. Young III
WVU Parkersburg

Edward Cabbell, "Where Could I Go But to the Lord? Shape-note Singing Among Blacks in Southern West Virginia," *Goldenseal,* Winter 1981; Jack Welch and Alice Fortney Welch, "Shape-note Singing in Appalachia: An Ongoing Tradition," *Goldenseal,* April–September 1978.

Shavers Fork

Shavers Fork is a large tributary of the Cheat River. Its headwaters are in Pocahontas County. From there, it flows through Randolph and Tucker counties, joining the Black Fork near Parsons to form Cheat River. Shavers Fork is 88.5 miles long. It has 25 main tributaries in its 214-square-mile watershed, which is more than 97 percent forested. Most of the watershed lies within the Monongahela National Forest, and nearly two-thirds of it is public land. The Shavers Fork region was extensively logged early in the 20th century. The elevation ranges from 1,650 feet at the mouth of Shavers Fork to more than 4,500 feet at the headwaters.

Shavers Fork is one of West Virginia's best trout streams. Popular fishing spots include the Stuart National Recreation Area and the High Falls of Cheat, a 15-foot waterfall at the mouth of Falls Run. The Shavers Fork Coalition, a non-profit organization formed in 1997, is dedicated to the preservation of the Shavers Fork watershed.

On July 13, 1861, the Battle of Corricks Ford was fought at a crossing of Shavers Fork, near present Parsons. Confederate Gen. Robert S. Garnett was killed in the battle, which was a Northern victory.

See also Cheat River

Tanya Godfrey
Moorefield

Sam Shaw

Newspaperman Samuel Cockayne Shaw was the beloved and eccentric editor of the *Moundsville Daily Echo* from 1951 until his death in 1995. Born August 10, 1913, Sam succeeded his father, Samuel Craig Shaw, as editor (1917–51), who had succeeded his father, James David Shaw, as editor (1891–1917).

Shaw was a tinkerer, long-distance runner, hiker, musician, photographer, linguist, and bird watcher. During World War II, he served as a decoder in army radio intelligence. His letters home were printed in the *Echo* and won him the Ernie Pyle Award. Later his quirky "Jots" column served as a sounding board for community projects, including the Moundsville Ohio River bridge, for which he crusaded for 30 years.

A graduate of Washington and Jefferson College, Pennsylvania, with majors in physics and mathematics, Shaw designed the traffic light synchronization for Moundsville and installed the town's first direct-dial telephones and the first two-way radios in police cruisers and taxis. In the 1950s, the city installed an electric fire alarm system. At the unveiling ceremony, it failed to work. Shaw looked at the alarm unit, identified its need of a resistor, and asked for the toaster from the firehouse's kitchen. He then wired the toaster to the alarm system to complete a resistance circuit when the toaster's lever was depressed. The system worked for years with the toaster in place.

A firm believer in physical fitness, Shaw rode his black bike around town gathering the news. He entered hundreds of long-distance races, nearly always coming in last and earning the nickname Flying Turtle. One of his proudest achievements was finishing first for male runners between 75 and 79 years old in Pittsburgh's 1990 Great Race.

Sam Shaw died December 23, 1995.

Cheryl Ryan Harshman
West Liberty State College

Morris Purdy Shawkey

Morris Purdy Shawkey, remembered as the father of secondary education in West Virginia, was a great builder of public schools. He was born February 19, 1868, in Pennsylvania. He entered business college in 1885 and later received undergraduate and graduate degrees from Ohio Wesleyan University, including a doctorate of pedagogy. In 1895, Shawkey came to West Virginia as professor of education at West Virginia Wesleyan College. He served the public schools in West Virginia for the next 40 years.

Shawkey became superintendent of Kanawha County schools in 1906. In 1908, he was elected state superintendent of free schools. He served three terms from 1909 until 1921. It was during this period that he rendered his greatest service to West Virginia. Shawkey launched a program for building new high schools and new junior high schools, creating school libraries in each school, consolidating schools, busing students to schools, and upgrading teacher standards. Under his leadership between 1909 and 1921, 125 new high schools were built, the standardized course of study was established, and the number of first-class high schools increased from six in 1909 to 116 in 1920.

In 1921, Shawkey became superintendent of Beaver Pond School District of Bluefield. In July 1923, he was appointed president of Marshall College, where he served until July 1, 1935. During Shawkey's years, Marshall was accredited by the Southern Accreditation Association and by the North Central Association. Marshall's College of Arts and Sciences became a member of the American Association of Colleges and the Pre-Medical program met the standards set by the American Medical Association. The campus was expanded, the student body grew rapidly, and a new library, student union, and other buildings were constructed.

Shawkey died February 6, 1941.

Marshall Buckalew
Charleston

Shawnee

The Shawnees were the southernmost of the Algonquian-speaking peoples of the eastern woodlands; hence their name, which derives from "southerner" in these languages. Originally centered in the mid-Ohio Valley, they descended, according to some archeologists, from the pre-historic Fort Ancient culture whose remains have been found in the Kanawha Valley, among other places. But they left this homeland during the 17th century, presumably in response to Iroquois attacks during the Beaver Wars, and were recorded by Europeans in such widely separated locations as Kentucky, Alabama, South Carolina, and Pennsylvania. A Shawnee companion of the French explorer, Robert Cavelier de la Salle, even traveled to Paris. The Shawnees entered frontier annals on a regular basis after Quaker missionaries found some of them living on Pequa Creek near present Lancaster, Pennsylvania, in 1692.

It is possible that the 17th century record represents the separate wanderings of the Shawnee's principal divisions—Chalakaatha, Mequashake, Pekowi, Hathawikila, and Kishpoko—since the divisions traditionally lived in separate village clusters and were only loosely confederated. European transcriptions of these names in places such as Chillicothe and Piqua, Ohio, Sewickley, Pennsylvania, and Pickaway, West Virginia, testify to some of these wanderings. Thus it was the Pekowi who began the Shawnee return to the Ohio Valley when they moved from eastern to western Pennsylvania in 1728. By 1750, some 1,200 Shawnee were living in villages along the Ohio River, from which they launched attacks against the Virginia frontier during the French and Indian War and Pontiac's Rebellion. Later they moved their villages to the Scioto River in southern Ohio, and after their defeat in Lord Dunmore's War they moved again to the Miami River headwaters in southwest Ohio. They consistently claimed Virginia west of the Alleghenies to be their hunting lands, along with most of Kentucky. They also denied the right of the Iroquois to dispose of this territory, as the Iroquois did in land sales to colonial governments in 1744 and 1768.

Under the influence of a nativist religious revival first preached by the Delaware prophet Neolin, Shawnees took the lead in defending the Ohio country from the white advance across the Appalachians in Western Virginia and Kentucky and also sent emissaries to other tribes to preach the necessity of Indian unity. These efforts suffered a temporary setback with the Shawnee defeat in Dunmore's War, but they continued during the American Revolution. During 1775–76, the Mequashake Shawnees led by Cornstalk adopted a neutralist position between the British and the rebel colonists, but members of other Shawnee bands formed war parties on their own or in concert with Mingos and militant Delawares. When Cornstalk was imprisoned and then murdered at Fort Randolph in 1777, the Mequashake joined the other bands in general warfare all along the frontier. White settlements along the Ohio, in the Kanawha Valley, and in Kentucky bore the brunt of these attacks, which continued through 1782, culminating in the famous second siege of Fort Henry at Wheeling in September of that year.

The Shawnees, along with other Indians resident in Ohio, were outraged when the British accepted Virginia's claim to the territory between the Great Lakes and the Ohio and ceded this territory to the United States in the 1783 Treaty of Paris, following the Revolution. Disputing the validity of the British cession, Shawnee militants urged the other Ohio tribes and also the Cherokees to fight on. Assaults on the frontier and on white settlers traveling the Ohio River multiplied after 1786 and continued into the early 1790s. Though Euro-American beachheads were established in 1788 north of the Ohio at Marietta and Cincinnati, native resistance succeeded in defeating armies sent against their villages in 1790 and 1791. Only after a combined force of regular troops and militia commanded by Gen. Anthony Wayne defeated a Shawnee-led Indian force at the Battle of Fallen Timbers in northwest Ohio in 1794 did the militants agree to give up their Ohio lands.

The Treaty of Greenville in 1795 cleared the way for white settlement on both banks of the Ohio and ended the threat of raids in what is now West Virginia. Even then, however, the militant Shawnee spirit remained unconquered. In the early 19th century, a new revitalization movement spread under the leadership of the prophet Tenskwatawa and his warrior brother Tecumseh. This movement was centered in new Shawnee villages in what is now Indiana and did not directly affect West Virginia.

See also Battle of Fallen Timbers, Cornstalk, French and Indian War, Indians, Revolutionary War

John Alexander Williams
Appalachian State University

Jerry E. Clark, *The Shawnee*, 1993; Gregory Evans Dowd, *A Spirited Resistance: The North American Indian Struggle for Unity, 1745–1815*, 1992; James H. Howard, *Shawnee! The Ceremonialism of a Native Indian Tribe and its Cultural Background*, 1981.

Shay Locomotives

The Shay locomotive was a workhorse of the logging railroads of the mountains of West Virginia. It was one of three designs of gear-driven engines developed primarily for use on the steep, rough, temporary tracks of logging country. The boiler was off-center to the left, to balance the

A Shay locomotive at Cass.

cylinders, crank-shaft, flexible shaft, and gearing on the right side, which drove the wheels, all of which were powered. This was a flexible, powerful, but slow locomotive, able to climb mountain grades of 10 percent and more.

Between 1882 and 1927, about 219 new Shays, weighing from 10 tons to 150 tons, were shipped from Lima Locomotive Works in Lima, Ohio, to West Virginia, more than any other state except Washington. West Virginia Pulp & Paper Company at Cass purchased 10 new and three used Shays, including more large engines (two 100-ton and three 150-ton) than any other lumber company in the world. Pardee & Curtin Lumber Company bought 10 new Shays, mostly 36-ton machines for its operations at Curtin on the Cherry River, the largest narrow gauge logging line in the state. On the steep coal mine branches in the New River Gorge, the Chesapeake & Ohio Railway used 15 huge 150-ton Shays, the most any major railroad ever owned.

In the early 1960s, the last working Shays were at the Ely-Thomas mill in Fenwick and in occasional use at Meadow River Lumber's operation at Rainelle. Eight Shays survive at the Cass Scenic Railroad, five of them operable and used to pull tourist trains up Cheat Mountain. Several from West Virginia are on exhibit in other states.

Other geared locomotives, made by the Climax and Heisler manufacturing companies of Pennsylvania, were used on West Virginia mountains. Climax engines were second in popularity only to the Shays, with 140 working in West Virginia at one time or another. Thirteen Heislers were used in West Virginia, including one in service today at Cass. A 70-ton Climax is undergoing restoration there, and another is in service at Durbin.

See also Railroads, Timbering and Logging

George Deike
Cass

Sheltering Arms Hospital

The Sheltering Arms Hospital was established near Hansford after Episcopal Bishop George Peterkin became concerned about the social and medical needs of miners in the Kanawha and New River coalfields. In 1887, Peterkin formed a corporation to provide charitable and medical services in the coalfields. Sheltering Arms Hospital saw its first patient in 1889. The board of directors voted to establish a nursing school at the hospital in 1901.

Sheltering Arms was a pioneer in prepaid health care, as coal and rail companies agreed to charge workers a monthly rate for use of the hospital. However, some officials were wary of the plan, and many families were slow to welcome the program, still viewing hospitals as places

where people were sent to die. Gradually the new hospital's effectiveness wore away this opposition. By 1901, half of the companies in the area participated.

The hospital experienced personnel problems throughout its operation. Sheltering Arms suffered a high turnover in its administrative and nursing staff. Conflicts over the workload of student nurses also plagued the hospital.

Despite these problems the hospital grew rapidly from its creation until World War I. The war drew away many nurses and interns. The postwar coal slump and 1919 strike decreased the hospital's income. These factors, as well as competition from newer hospitals, forced Sheltering Arms to close. A merger agreement with Charleston General Hospital fell through in 1924, but the patients and nursing school were transferred to Charleston General. Sheltering Arms is considered one of the seven predecessor hospitals to the Charleston Area Medical Center.

See also Charleston Area Medical Center, Medicine, George William Peterkin

Shae Davidson
The Plains, Ohio

Shenandoah Bloomery

Shenandoah Bloomery, near Charles Town, also known as Vestal's Bloomery, was the first ironworks west of the Blue Ridge Mountains and the first in present West Virginia.

A bloomery was a cheaper, simpler way to produce iron than by using a blast furnace. Like contemporary blast furnaces, the bloomery used charcoal for fuel, but unlike the blast furnace the iron ore never reached a temperature high enough for it to melt. In the bloomery operation, charcoal and iron ore were ignited and air applied. A spongy iron developed. The spongy iron contained large amounts of impurities, mostly slag and dirt, and had to be hammered to eliminate these impurities. Bloomery production was limited, less than 100 pounds of iron per firing. A bloomery was most frequently used in frontier situations, meeting local needs until more established blast furnace and forge operations appeared.

William Vestal, John Traden, Richard Stevenson, and Daniel Burnet contracted Thomas Mayberry in 1742 to construct a "Bloomery for making Barr iron, upon the present plantation of William Vestal lying upon Shunandore [*sic*]." Mayberry agreed to erect a bloomery, raceways, water wheels, and dam. The completed bloomery was located in Jefferson County on the north bank of Evitts Creek, near its confluence with the Shenandoah River.

Vestal operated the bloomery until about 1760, when the property passed to the Fairfax family. George William Fairfax and his brother-in-law, John Carlyle,

planned to operate Bloomery Mills, but it is unlikely that the pair ever smelted any iron. Today, the town of Bloomery is the only tangible reminder of the pioneering ironworks.

Lee R. Maddex
WVU Institute for the History of Technology
"Iron Industry in Jefferson County," *Jefferson County Historical Society Magazine*, December 1964.

Shenandoah Downs

Shenandoah Downs, one of the first horse tracks in the eastern United States to be built for night racing, opened in Charles Town in 1959 in competition with the older Charles Town Race Track. In 1957, Shenandoah's owners had bought land north of Charles Town Race Track and applied for a permit for night harness racing. The corporation then asked to have the permit extended to include night thoroughbred racing. Turned down by the West Virginia Racing Commission, the owners of the new track took the case to the West Virginia Supreme Court and won, putting Shenandoah Downs in competition with Charles Town Race Track.

The two Jefferson County tracks competed for about two decades. Shenandoah Downs had the advantage of night racing, and led Charles Town in annual revenues. When the Charles Town Race Track installed lighting in 1965, the number of racing days at the two tracks became more equal, and the Charles Town track gradually gained the upper hand. In 1972, the Shenandoah Corporation, which then owned Shenandoah Downs, also bought the Charles Town Race Track. In 1976, Shenandoah Downs was closed.

The Kenton Corporation bought both tracks in 1978 and briefly reopened Shenandoah Downs. The track permanently closed later that year and became a training track.

See also Charles Town Races

Shenandoah River

The Shenandoah River and its main tributaries flow northeastward for almost 150 miles, chiefly through the Shenandoah Valley in Virginia between the Blue Ridge and the Allegheny mountains. The two forks of Shenandoah meet at Front Royal, Virginia, and from there the Shenandoah mainstream continues for 55 more miles, joining the Potomac River at Harpers Ferry. The final stretch of the Shenandoah flows through Jefferson County, West Virginia. The Shenandoah has a 3,000-square-mile drainage area, which includes a large portion of Virginia west of the Blue Ridge and much of Jefferson County.

The word "Shenandoah" is of Indian origin, and its meaning is a matter of dispute. The most popular interpretation is "Daughter of the Stars." Areas along the North and South forks of the river near

Front Royal have yielded the first evidence of inhabited structures in North America, dating to 9300 B.C. Native Americans began farming along the Shenandoah about A.D. 900.

The valley was explored by John Lederer, a German doctor, in 1669. Lederer crossed the Blue Ridge near Swift Run Gap in present Madison County, Virginia, and took detailed notes of the wildlife, terrain, and several Indian tribes he encountered. In the early 18th century, Lord Fairfax, an Englishman, inherited a large part of the northern valley. Young George Washington surveyed parts of Fairfax's estate, including lands now part of the Eastern Panhandle of West Virginia.

Called the breadbasket of the Confederacy, the Shenandoah Valley was an important military objective during the Civil War. Gen. Thomas "Stonewall" Jackson made his reputation defending the valley against federal troops early in the war.

In 1945, West Virginia author Julia Davis published *The Shenandoah*, part of the Rivers of America series. Davis told the history of the valley and the river, drawing on her own research and the experiences of ancestors who settled and lived in the area. Still in print more than a half-century later, her book provides a poetic vision of both the river and the valley. "More than history, the Valley is a way of life," Davis wrote. "It is the rich fields, and the mountains older than measured time. It is the stillness of the hot noon, or of moonlight, or of snow. It is the calm old houses, where the oak leaves and the doves have time to set up their music in the heart of a child."

William D. Theriault
Bakerton

Julia Davis, *The Shenandoah*, 1945.

Shenandoah Valley

The Shenandoah Valley lies largely within the state of Virginia, with only about 20 miles of the lower valley falling within the boundaries of West Virginia. The valley comprises one of America's historic landscapes, its gentle terrain providing an important thoroughfare since prehistoric times and the theater for some of the most dramatic battles of the Civil War.

The Shenandoah River and its north and south branches reach from the Shenandoah's confluence with the Potomac at Harpers Ferry far southwestward into the Virginia interior. There the headwaters interlace with tributaries of the James River, forming part of the extended Valley of Virginia that stretches from West Virginia to Tennessee. Roads down this great valley, including modern Interstate 81, have long provided passageway through the surrounding mountains.

In West Virginia the Shenandoah Valley lies entirely within Jefferson County, with the river flowing in great bends along a course parallel to the county's eastern border with the state of Virginia. The southern corner of Jefferson County is within the Shenandoah watershed, including the county seat at Charles Town.

The Shenandoah Valley includes some of the oldest settled territory in West Virginia, with a history dating back to the early decades of the 18th century. Its settlers included several members of George Washington's family, with the teen-aged Washington himself in 1750 buying land on the South Fork of Bullskin Creek, a Shenandoah tributary. Several Washington family homes survive in the area today. Vestal's Bloomery, an early ironmaking facility, was established at Bloomery in 1742, and nearby Shannondale Springs was developed as a popular spa during the 19th century. Crucial events of the Civil War period took place in Harpers Ferry, at the foot of the valley, including John Brown's 1859 raid and important fighting early in the war. Stonewall Jackson's triumphant Valley Campaign, a string of Confederate victories in 1862, took place farther up the valley and largely outside present West Virginia.

The Shenandoah Valley in West Virginia now shelters sizable residential communities. State Route 9 traverses the valley east of Charles Town, daily carrying numerous commuters to and from jobs in the Washington metropolitan area. The valley ends as the Shenandoah joins the Potomac at Harpers Ferry, amid scenery described by Thomas Jefferson as worth a trip across the Atlantic Ocean.

See also Harpers Ferry, Jefferson County, Washington Family

Heyward Shepherd

Heyward Shepherd was an African-American killed at Harpers Ferry on October 17, 1859, by John Brown's raiders. In life, Shepherd was a porter at the local railroad station and a property owner in nearby Winchester, Virginia. In death, as a free black man ironically killed by abolitionists during a raid to liberate slaves, he became a symbol to people who believed John Brown's mission had been wrong. Because he was shot while at his job, Shepherd also came to symbolize blacks loyal to the South.

In 1920, the United Daughters of the Confederacy and the Sons of Confederate Veterans decided to erect a memorial to Shepherd. Opponents were concerned over the intent of the monument, then called the Faithful Slave Memorial, and delayed its placement at Harpers Ferry for a decade. The Heyward Shepherd Memorial finally was sited near the scene of Shepherd's fatal wounding and dedicated on October 10, 1931. The event drew a sharp reaction from W.E.B. Du-Bois and the National Association for the Advancement of Colored People and proved divisive at black Storer College, whose administration participated in the dedication.

See also John Brown, Harpers Ferry, Storer College

Mary Johnson
State Archives

Mary Johnson, "An 'Ever Present Bone of Contention': The Heyward Shepherd Memorial," *West Virginia History*, 1997.

Lydia Boggs Shepherd

Society hostess Lydia Boggs Shepherd (Cruger) was born February 26, 1766, in present Berkeley County. She passed her childhood on the Virginia frontier, where father John Boggs served as a militia captain. The family settled near Wheeling in 1774, where they experienced the dangers of the period's recurring Indian wars.

About 1782, Lydia married Moses Shepherd. By 1800, the couple's business success, growing political influence, and enormous land holdings gave them great wealth. It was symbolized by Shepherd Hall, their stone mansion, which hosted some of the era's most famous political figures, including six U.S. presidents. The Shepherds' friendship with Sen. Henry Clay helped to secure the routing of the National Road from Wellsburg to Wheeling. After Moses's 1832 death, Lydia married Daniel Cruger, a former New York congressman. She died, eccentric and reclusive, at Shepherd Hall, September 26, 1867.

Lydia Boggs Shepherd Cruger sparked a controversy in 1849 by denying that Betty Zane made the famous gunpowder run to save Wheeling's Fort Henry during the 1782 siege. According to Cruger, the heroine actually was Molly Scott. The truth remains unclear. No contemporary documentation is known to exist proving who carried the powder or even if the incident occurred at all. Solid secondary evidence, however, some of it dating as early as 1802, substantiates the traditional account with Zane as its central figure. Shepherd Hall, also known as Monument Place, is listed on the National Register of Historic Places.

See also Betty Zane

Ray Swick
Blennerhassett Island State Park

Shepherd University

Shepherd University was founded in the Reconstruction era as a consequence of a dispute over the location of the Jefferson county seat. In 1865, as a wartime measure, Union authorities moved the county seat from Charles Town to Shepherdstown, where it was housed in a large Classical style building that Rezin Davis Shepherd had built in 1860 for the town's use. With shifting political fortunes in the new state of West Virginia, the county seat re-

McMurran Hall at Shepherd University.

turned to Charles Town in 1871. Eager to make use of the former courthouse, Shepherdstown residents secured a lease from Shepherd's heir, obtained a charter for "a classical and scientific institute," and opened the doors of Shepherd College in September 1871. In 1872, the legislature designated Shepherd as one of the six state normal schools whose main purpose was the education of teachers. The others were Marshall, West Liberty, Fairmont, Glenville, and Concord.

A coeducational institution from the beginning, by 1874 Shepherd had 160 students, making it the largest of the normals. Like the others, for more than a generation it was scarcely a high school, and meager state funding scattered among the six made it impossible for any of them to become a true normal school. Only the tuition fees, private contributions of local residents, and the dedication of principal Joseph McMurran (1871–82) and his faculty—who often worked without pay—kept Shepherd College alive during the lean years of the 1870s. Enrollment fell below 100 in 1878 and never reached the 1874 level again for more than a quarter-century.

Recognizing the inability of the state to adequately support the normals, legislators and governors at the turn of the century often threatened to close them altogether, particularly as locally funded high schools developed, but the regional popularity of the normals thwarted efforts to eliminate them. In the first decade of the 20th century, Shepherd turned in earnest to its original normal school mission, and under the administrations of John G. Knutti (1903–09) and Thomas C. Miller (1909–20) improved physical facilities, curriculum and faculty, laying the groundwork for the normal school to become a teachers college. Miller, like his predecessors, held the title of principal, but in 1919 he was officially designated president.

During the three long presidencies of W.H.S. White (1920–47), Oliver S. Ikenberry (1947–67), and James A. Butcher (1968–88), Shepherd gradually moved beyond its original mission to become an authentic college with regional and national standing. In White's era important changes included the elimination of the secondary grades, the addition of extension classes, and finally, in 1930, designation as a four-year teachers college with the authority to issue the bachelor of arts degree in both elementary and secondary education. In 1931, the legislature changed the name to Shepherd State Teachers College to reflect the new status. Gradually the school added more liberal arts degrees, and in 1943 the legislature authorized a return to the original name, Shepherd College.

Even after the attainment of four-year status, the coming of the Depression and World War II denied the college needed resources. During the war, the college's proximity to Washington helped to offset the wartime declines in enrollment as several training programs for the army and navy brought large numbers of servicemen to Shepherdstown. Like other colleges and universities, Shepherd benefited from the GI Bill, which brought a rush of veterans to the campus after the war.

President Ikenberry presided over this critical period as the college added majors and expanded its arts and sciences, humanities, and business programs while also strengthening its education degrees. Ikenberry also placed a strong emphasis on improvement of the college's physical plant and acquired land for future growth. These efforts brought accreditation from the North Central Association in 1950. In the summer of 1954, the college admitted African-American students for the first time.

President Butcher consolidated the gains of the Ikenberry era and recruited more professors with doctoral degrees. As enrollment expanded, he saw to the building of several new academic buildings, including a physical education complex (now known as the Butcher Center) and the Frank Center for Creative Arts, which enhanced the college's role as a regional cultural center. New programs included social work and nursing. The college also moved haltingly to diversify its student population and faculty.

By the beginning of the 21st century, Shepherd College had become a multipurpose liberal arts institution that served its region well as a center of learning and culture. With enrollment at about 4,000, Shepherd contemplated the new century under the presidency of David L. Dunlop. Its role in helping host peace talks between Israel and Syria in January 2000 brought it international attention.

The new century brought important institutional changes as well. The Community and Technical College separated to establish its own campus in Martinsburg. And in 2004 Shepherd College became Shepherd University.

Jerry Bruce Thomas
Shepherd University

Charles Henry Ambler, *A History of Education in West Virginia*, 1951; Millard K. Bushong, *Historic Jefferson County*, 1972; Arthur Gordon Slonaker, *A History of Shepherd College*, 1967.

Shepherdstown

Shepherdstown is located on the banks of the Potomac River in Jefferson County. Settled heavily by German immigrants and once known as Mechlenburg, it was renamed in 1798 for Thomas Shepherd, who had established a gristmill there by 1739 and later sold town lots. Shepherdstown shares honors with Romney as the oldest incorporated town in West Virginia, both receiving their charters on the same day in 1762.

Situated at Pack Horse Ford, an ancient Potomac River crossing, Shepherdstown is among West Virginia's most historic places. One contingent of the famous Bee Line March started there in 1775, as Western Virginia riflemen set out to reinforce George Washington at Boston. After the Revolution, Washington was among those interested in the steamboat tested by James Rumsey at Shepherdstown in 1787. The Civil War Battle of Antietam was fought nearby in Maryland in September 1862, with fighting spilling over into Jefferson County before and after the bloody main battle. Shepherdstown, more Northern in its allegiances than Charles Town, served as Jefferson County county seat in the aftermath of the Civil War, from 1865 to 1871. Shepherd College (now University) was established in 1871.

Shepherdstown remains a genteel country town in the early 21st century, favored by its old families as well as Washington-area commuters and retirees seeking a quiet life in settled surroundings. The U.S. Fish and Wildlife Service established the National Conservation Training Center there in 1997, and the town is also known for the annual Contemporary American Theater Festival. The Shepherdstown historic district was added to the National Register of Historic Places in 1973 and expanded in 1987. Shepherdstown's picturesque German Street is a favorite with photographers.

See also Contemporary American Theater Festival, Jefferson County, Shepherd University

Sheriff's Succession Amendment

The Sheriff's Succession Amendment, a change in the state constitution to allow a county sheriff to serve two terms, or eight years, before becoming ineligible for re-election, was ratified by the voters at a special statewide election November 6, 1973. The constitution originally provided that "the same person shall not be elected sheriff for two consecutive full terms; nor shall any person who acted as his deputy be elected successor to such sheriff, nor shall any sheriff act as deputy of his successor, nor shall he during his term of service, or within one year thereafter be eligible to any other office." The 1973 amendment, which also removed the restrictions on deputies running for sheriff, increased the influence of county sheriffs in West Virginia.

The amendment was first submitted to the voters by the legislature in 1962 but was soundly rejected by a vote of 362,884 against and 128,772 in favor. In 1973, three years after voters ratified an amendment to allow the governor to be eligible for re-election to a second term, it was one of four constitutional amendments put before the voters, and it was approved by a margin of 123,003 to 107,427. Attempts since 1973 to remove all term limitations for sheriffs have been defeated in 1982 by a vote of 320,308 to 178,713; in 1986 by a vote of 269,622 to 123,966; and in 1994 by a count of 251,924 to 131,134.

See also Constitution of West Virginia

Tom D. Miller
Huntington

Shinnston

Shinnston is located on the West Fork River at the juncture of U.S. 19 and State Route 131, in northern Harrison County. Shinns Run and Mudlick Run enter the West Fork at Shinnston.

Shinnston was settled during the Revolutionary War period by members of the Quaker Shinn family. Levi Shinn's 1778 log house is now the oldest house in Harrison County. By 1785, Shinn (1748–1807) had established a local gristmill. Asa Shinn laid out town lots in 1815. Shinnston was chartered as a town in 1852 by the Virginia General Assembly.

Shinnston grew slowly over most of the 19th century, then boomed late in the century with the exploitation of local coal, oil, and gas. The area was heavily Northern in its sentiments during the Civil War, and many local men served in the Union Army. Shinnston was raided by Confederates during the Jones-Imboden raids of 1863.

Author and state founder Granville Davisson Hall fictionalized a Shinnston tavern in his 1899 novel, *Daughter of the Elm*, and native Meredith Sue Willis (1946–) has drawn upon Shinnston memories for her novels. The Levi Shinn House is listed on the National Register of Historic Places, as is the Shinnston Historic District.

Shinnston became famous for the Shinnston Tornado of June 23, 1944, a freak storm which left 66 people dead in the town and surrounding area. The town has suffered as well from floods on the West Fork. Shinnston's population was 2,295 in 2000.

Shinnston Tornado

At the beginning of the 21st century, people in Harrison County are still telling stories about the tornado that struck Shinnston on June 23, 1944, at 8:30 p.m. Sixty-six people died in the town and surrounding area. The total number of people killed by the tornado was 103, with 430 serious injuries. After wreaking havoc in farming communities northwest of Shinnston, the twister hit hardest in a neighborhood known as Pleasant Hill, where no more than 10 houses were left standing. The tornado then continued to Shinns Run and Booths Creek, where it destroyed a large natural gas compressor station, passing on through Marion, Taylor, and Barbour counties before blowing out in Randolph County.

After the initial deaths and maiming, the greatest destruction was to property and the infrastructure. Power lines went down, including a huge tower and high-voltage transmission line near Saltwell. The two hospitals in Clarksburg had to treat victims by candle and flashlight. Phone service, however, was disrupted for only a short time, thanks to wartime emergency backup preparations. Among the many unexpected ways people helped each other were the lending of generators to the hospitals by a traveling circus and grave digging by the prison camp laborers from Gypsy, north of Shinnston. Selfless efforts were also made by elected officials, the National Guard, police, road crews, firefighters, nurses, doctors, and common citizens.

Tornadoes are rare in West Virginia, which has among the nation's lowest rates of occurrence for such storms. The Shinnston Tornado was the deadliest tornado in the history of the state. It is estimated to have been an f-4 tornado, the second highest of the rankings currently assigned to tornadoes. F-4 storms produce winds faster than 206 miles per hour, capable of leveling houses and throwing automobiles.

See also Weston

Meredith Sue Willis
South Orange, New Jersey

John L. Finlayson, *Shinnston Tornado*, 1946; Martha A. Lowther, "The Shinnston Tornado," *Goldenseal*, Summer 1998.

Shoney's Restaurants

See Alex Schoenbaum.

Short-Line Railroads

Short-line railroads were built to serve communities or industries not reached by major railroad companies. Their locomotives, trains, and people were very much a part of the places they served and retained a personal, often idiosyncratic, character that made them more like neighbors than corporations.

To cut construction and equipment costs some short lines were built as narrow gauge, usually three feet between the rails. The railroad south of Clarksburg to Glenville was narrow gauge, as was the line from Grafton to Belington. Both were acquired by the Baltimore & Ohio Railroad and converted to standard gauge in the 1890s. The West Virginia Midland served the lumber industry and the resort hotel at Webster Springs until the hotel burned; the line closed in 1930–31. The Valley River Railroad narrow track served a sawmill at Mill Creek, and carried the public to Valley Head until 1931. Most unusual was the Twin Mountain & Potomac, built 27 miles south from Keyser to serve the extensive peach orchards. Its six-year life ended in 1919. The state's last narrow gauge, the Mann's Creek Railroad, carried coal from Clifftop to coke ovens in the nearby New River Gorge until 1956.

Standard-gauge lines had the great advantage of being able to interchange cars with the main line railroads, meaning that goods did not have to be unloaded and reloaded. The Lewisburg & Ronceverte brought rail service to Lewisburg in 1907. It was converted to electric operation, but soon succumbed. There were many lines built to serve coal mines, such as Campbells Creek, Winifrede (still in operation under a different name), Kellys Creek, and Kellys Creek & Northwestern, all along the Kanawha River east of Charleston. Each was less than 25 miles long, but several had four locomotives to handle the heavy traffic. The Chesapeake & Ohio absorbed several coal railroads south of Thurmond, and others near the lumber town of Rainelle.

The Middle Creek, Buffalo Creek & Gauley, and Middle Fork railroads all connected to the Coal & Coke (later B&O) line between Charleston and Elkins. The last two were also associated with lumber companies. The Morgantown & Kingwood worked large mines with 48 miles of track and a dozen locomotives, becoming part of the B&O in 1922. Neighboring West Virginia Northern remained independent, beginning as a coal hauler in 1899 and finally quitting (as a tourist line) in 1999. The Preston Railroad, on the Maryland line, was independent until abandoned in 1960. The Dry Fork was built to carry lumber from the mill at Horton 31 miles to a Western Maryland Railroad connection, and survived until 1936.

Nearly all the state's short lines are gone, but the State Rail Authority owns two, the South Branch Valley (once B&O) south from Romney, and the West Virginia Central (formerly B&O and West-

Hugh I. Shott

Hugh Isaac "Ike" Shott, Sr., newspaper editor, businessman, and politician, was born September 3, 1866, in Staunton, Virginia, where he learned the printer's trade. Moving to Bluefield, Shott worked as a railway mail clerk on the Norfolk & Western Railway, then purchased the weekly *Bluefield Telegraph* in 1896. He began daily publication and prospered along with the bustling southern West Virginia coalfields whose news he reported.

Shott ultimately built a business empire around the Daily Telegraph Printing Company, including the morning *Daily Telegraph*, the afternoon *Sunset News* (1926–72), Telegraph Commercial Printing Company, and WHIS radio, a pioneer Appalachian station which broadcast his initials as call letters from a penthouse studio atop the West Virginian Hotel.

Long a Republican activist, Shott spent 11 years as Bluefield's postmaster, served two terms in the U.S. House of Representatives from the old Fifth District and briefly as U.S. senator in 1942. He died October 12, 1953. Shott's sons and grandsons—including three sets of male twins in the Hugh, Sr. line—presided over an extensive array of businesses after his death, adding WHIS-TV and broadcast companies in South Carolina and Iowa. The Shott family was represented on the boards of directors of many of southern West Virginia's most powerful businesses. When the Federal Communications Commission questioned the near-monopoly on public information held in Bluefield by the Shotts, the family sold many of the firms, most notably the *Telegraph*, in January 1985.

In 1984, the Shott family endowed the Hugh I. Shott Jr. Foundation, which has been influential in many of the region's philanthropic efforts and economic development activities. The Shotts hold the annual Shott breakfast community gathering, a mandatory holiday event for Bluefield's close-knit business community.

See also Bluefield Daily Telgraph, WHIS

C. Stuart McGehee
West Virginia State University

Showboats

Almost as soon as the Trans-Allegheny pioneers had settled along the navigable rivers, some type of entertainment was offered from barges or flatboats. Noah Ludlow was one of the earliest to bring professional actors and musicians to the frontier. In 1816, he bought a 25-foot flatboat with a small shelter at Olean, New York, on the Allegheny River. He named it *Ludlow's Noah's Ark* and with 11 associates floated down the Allegheny, Ohio, and Mississippi rivers, stopping to perform wherever they could.

Beginning in the 1830s, showboats regularly appeared on the inland rivers. William Chapman Sr., an Englishman, was the first person to purposely plan and build a showboat for use on the western rivers. His *Chapman Floating Theater* floated down the Ohio River from Pittsburgh in 1831. This was the first of many family showboats. In 1836, Chapman acquired a small steamboat to tow the *Floating Theater* upstream, rather than selling the showboat at New Orleans as had been the practice in years past. With this new means of moving from place to place Chapman could also travel up tributaries from the main river.

Showboats were floating theaters presenting melodramas, comedies, musical acts, and even circuses. They were towed by steamboats from landing to landing. Showboats were very popular on the Monongahela and Kanawha rivers in West Virginia. The annual visits of the showboats were a highlight of summer for river towns. Many showboats tied up for the winter at the mouths of the Little Kanawha and Kanawha rivers, because these places were safe harbors from winter ice.

Capt. Thomas J. Reynolds was among West Virginia's famous showboat operators. He was born at Point Pleasant in 1888 and started his river career by fishing for mussels. He later acquired the moving-picture boat *Illinois*. In 1917, he built his first real showboat and named it *America*. His family, which eventually included nine children, lived on the boat when they were not wintering at Point Pleasant. In 1923, he built the *Majestic,* which is now moored at Cincinnati and still operates as a showboat.

The Bryant family of Point Pleasant is West Virginia's other famous showboating family. Twenty-five-year-old Samuel and his 13-year-old wife, Violet Bryant, had come to America from England in 1884. They started a one-wagon medicine show and traveled across America. They reached the Rocky Mountains before they returned to the Ohio River and their first jobs on a showboat in 1900. Capt. Edward Price of the showboat *Water Queen* billed them as the "Four Bryants," since a son, Billy, and daughter, Florence, were a part of the act. The Bryants built the *Bryants New Showboat* in 1918 and operated it until World War II.

The Pope Dock Company of Parkersburg was the builder of some of the most famous showboats. At the mouth of the Little Kanawha River the company built the *New Grand Floating Palace* in 1901; *Eisenbarth & Henderson Floating Theatre —The New Great Modern Temple of Amusement* in 1903; *Sunny South* in 1905; and the world's largest showboat, the *Goldenrod*, in 1909, as well as many others. Like the *Majestic*, the *Goldenrod* is still in operation as a showboat, at St. Charles, Missouri. These two are among the last of the hundreds of showboats that once operated on America's rivers, and they both have West Virginia roots.

Operators such as Capt. Augustus B. French and his wife, Callie Leach French, who was the first woman to obtain a pilot's license in 1888 and the second woman to be granted a captain's license, were known for the quality of their boats and their shows.

Gerald W. Sutphin
Huntington

Phillip Graham, *Showboats*, 1951.

Shrubs

Nearly 150 shrubs grow in the various natural ecosystems in West Virginia, dominating some high mountaintops, swamps, and bogs. The evergreen rhododendron (great laurel) is our state flower and grows in dense impenetrable thickets, once called "laurel hells." Purple laurel has beautiful purple flowers and grows naturally in southeastern West Virginia. Azaleas (honeysuckles) are deciduous rhododendrons with large colorful pink, orange, red, and white flowers. The fragrance of white azaleas is exceptionally nice.

Three native roses provide showy pink flowers protected by sharp thorns. Five dogwood shrubs grow naturally in West Virginia and are known for showy clusters of white flowers and white to bluish fruits that are excellent food for wildlife. Twenty hawthorns and eight viburnums (haws) make up the largest shrub groups. Both provide important wildlife foods and are common ornamentals with showy white flower clusters.

The rarest native shrubs are woolly Hudsonia, prickly rose, common juniper, Virginia spiraea, Allegheny sloe, alderleaved and Carolina buckthorns, Canby's mountain lover, box huckleberry, and recurved fetterbush.

Blueberries, huckleberries, elderberries, hazelnuts, pawpaws, plums, serviceberries, and choke cherry provide tasty edible fruits for humans and wildlife. Holly berries are traditional Christmas decorations, spicebush was once used to flavor wild meats, bark of leatherwood was substituted for leather, and mountain laurel was carved into eating utensils. Medicinal shrubs include willows, witch hazel, St. John's wort, roses, toothache tree, wahoo, and hydrangea.

Exotic invasive shrubs, including mul-

ern Maryland) serving Elkins. Both have tourist trains as well as freight service. The Durbin & Greenbrier Valley also runs on state-owned track, south from Durbin.

See also Railroads

George Deike
Cass

tiflora rose, autumn olive, privet, winged euonymus, Japanese barberry, glossy buckthorn, and Morrow's honeysuckle are aggressive pests of pastures, roadsides, vacant lots, and open forests.

William N. Grafton
WVU Extension Service

Silver Bridge Collapse

On Friday, December 15, 1967, at about 5:00 p.m. the bridge spanning the Ohio River at Point Pleasant collapsed. The Silver Bridge, so named because it was the first bridge in the area to be painted with aluminum paint, had been designed by the J. E. Greiner Company of Baltimore. It was the first bridge built in the United States using an innovative eyebar-link suspension system rather than wire-cable suspension. The eyebar chain was a series of flat metal links held together using high-strength, heat-treated carbon steel eyebars. These eyebars were of varying lengths and about two inches thick and 12 inches wide, bolted to each other and to vertical suspension bars which descended to support the deck below. The bridge was built by the American Bridge Company of Pittsburgh and opened to traffic on May 19, 1928.

There were 31 vehicles on the bridge with 67 people in them at the time of the collapse. Of these vehicles, 24 fell into the river and six fell on the Ohio shore. Twenty-one people escaped injury or were rescued from the river. There was a total of 46 fatalities, including five killed on the Ohio shore. For 16 days federal, state, local, and private organizations conducted extensive rescue and recovery operations.

The National Transportation Safety Board later determined that the cause of the bridge collapse was a "cleavage fracture in the lower limb of the eye of eyebar 330." The crucial flaw "was inaccessible to visual inspection," it was stated, and could not have been detected by any known method without disassembly of the eyebar joint. The accident and the resulting National Transportation Safety Board's report led to the passage of legislation for a national bridge inspection and safety program.

See also Bridges

Gerald W. Sutphin
Huntington

Huntington District, U.S. Army Corps of Engineers, "Silver Bridge Collapse, after Action Report," 1968.

Robert W. Simmons

Barber Robert W. Simmons, politician and pioneer in black education, was born around 1822 at Fredericksburg, Virginia. His father, Streshley Simmons, was a free black citizen of Virginia and a veteran of the War of 1812.

While nothing is known about Simmons's upbringing, his later work as a journalist suggests some measure of formal instruction. His livelihood, however, came from barbering. This he practiced in Parkersburg which became his home in 1841 and where, in 1843, he married Susan King.

By 1858, Simmons was the father of nine children. His concern for his own children and other young African-Americans of Parkersburg propelled him in 1862 to take the lead in founding the Sumner School, a private school for the town's blacks. The tuition was one dollar per month, but children whose families were unable to pay were allowed to attend free of charge. Classes initially were housed in a dilapidated army barracks. According to legend, Simmons, on horseback, had made a long and dangerous war-time trip to Washington, where he secured the building directly from President Lincoln. The fledgling institution became a landmark in the history of education, becoming West Virginia's earliest black public school in 1866. One year later, Simmons helped to establish a black Sunday school in Parkersburg and served as its first superintendent.

Simmons was an influential Republican, and a delegate to the party's 1872 and 1876 national conventions. As a politician, who for years controlled the local African-American vote and wielded statewide power, he received many marks of recognition during the last three decades of his life. These culminated in his appointment by President Grant as U.S. consul to Haiti, which for unknown reasons Simmons declined.

Robert W. Simmons died at his Parkersburg home on January 16, 1892. In 1999, the downtown Parkersburg post office was named Simmons Station in his honor.

See also African-American Education, Sumner School

Ray Swick
Blennerhassett Island State Park

Sinks

Sinking streams, and occasional sinkholes, often simply called "sinks," are associated with the cave and karst regions of eastern and southeastern West Virginia. Sinks are points where surface water enters the ground. Sometimes called disappearing or lost rivers, sinking streams eventually return to the surface as springs or "rises." These sinks may form a "blind valley" at the base of a cliff where a surface stream enters a cave, and little or no trace of the stream is left on the land surface beyond the sink point. Many sinks are associated with large cave passages.

Examples of sinking streams include the Sinks of Gandy Creek in Randolph County, Sinks of Hills Creek in Pocahontas County, and the Sinks of Sinking Creek in Greenbrier County. Other sinking streams include Culverson Creek in Greenbrier County and Laurel Creek in Monroe County. Milligan Creek in Greenbrier County rises and sinks several times in its channel before its final rise at Davis Spring. The Lost River in Hardy County, West Virginia's largest sinking stream, sinks completely in its channel during low-flow conditions and rises as the Cacapon River.

The term sinks may also refer to sinkholes or dolines on the surface that do not necessarily capture surface streams. These sinkholes are caused by the slow dissolving of soluble underground rock strata, usually limestone. The community of Sinks Grove in Monroe County derives its name from the numerous deep sinkholes in the area.

See also Karst, Lost River, Sinks of Gandy

William K. Jones
Charles Town

Sinks of Gandy

Gandy Creek sinks under the earth at a blind valley south of Yokum Knob in eastern Randolph County. The stream then flows northeast through a large cave for about three-quarters of a mile and emerges from one of the cave's two north entrances. The cave was described in 1872 by David Hunter Strother, writing under the pen name of "Porte Crayon" in an article for *Harper's Magazine*. This account from a visit in 1854, although romanticized and fanciful, provides a remarkably accurate description of the cave itself, and his sketch of the south entrance shows the picturesque opening in the side of the hill very much as it appears today. A history of the cave by Jack Preble describes a bloody Civil War skirmish at the north exit on March 20, 1864.

The Sinks may be the most visited wild cave in West Virginia. The cave takes the entire flow of Gandy Creek and can flood suddenly following rain. An article in the *Saturday Evening Post* in 1941 by Clay Perry recounts the story of four cavers who were trapped in the cave for five hours. The cave is at the base of the Greenbrier Group limestones (Mississippian age) and has about 1.5 miles of surveyed passage.

William K. Jones
Charles Town

Jack Preble, *The Sinks of Gandy Creek*, 1969; David H. Strother, "The Mountains," *Harper's New Monthly Magazine* 45, 1872; Strother, "The Mountains," *Harper's New Monthly Magazine* 46, 1873.

Sistersville

Sistersville is located in Tyler County, on the Ohio River midway between Parkersburg and Moundsville. It is situated on State Route 2, the main north-south highway in this part of West Virginia, at the intersection with State Route 18. Sistersville is located on the famous

"Long Reach" of the Ohio, an unusual 20-mile straight stretch in the river. A toll ferry, the last in the state, conveys automobiles and passengers across the Ohio at Sistersville.

Charles Wells settled in the area about 1800, and within a few years his tavern and farm were known to travelers. Wells left his land to daughters Sarah and Delilah. They laid out town lots about 1815, and Sistersville was named for these enterprising sisters. The town was incorporated in 1839. Like some other Ohio Valley communities, Sistersville had mixed allegiances during the Civil War, with a sizable minority favoring the Confederacy.

The Ohio River Railway was built through Sistersville in 1884, and the town underwent an industrial boom with the local discovery of oil a few years later. Fortunes were made as derricks appeared even in the residential areas. Sistersville's population was estimated to have increased by more than tenfold during the boom, from about 600 in 1888 to 7,000 in 1898. The Wells Inn, a downtown landmark now listed on the National Register of Historic Places, opened as the Wells Hotel in 1895, at the height of this prosperity.

After the oil boom subsided in the early 20th century, Sistersville settled down as a quiet residential town. It remains so today, with a 2000 population of 1,588 people.

Hubert Skidmore

Hubert Skidmore was born April 11, 1909, at Laurel Mountain (Webster Springs) and later lived in Gassaway. Skidmore was a novelist who used local setting and dialect, and, often, the Depression-era lumber industry. His published works were *I Will Lift Up Mine Eyes* (1936), *Heaven Came So Near* (1938), *River Rising* (1939), *Hill Doctor* (1940), *Hawks Nest* (1941), and *Hill Lawyer* (1942), all by Doubleday. Skidmore generally depicted stoic endurance by mountain people in the face of misfortune and economic exploitation by outside interests. His twin brother Hobert (1909–69) was also a successful novelist.

Skidmore's novel *Hawks Nest* was a fictionalized treatment of what has been since described as America's worst industrial incident: the wanton disregard of workers' lives and health in the construction of the Hawks Nest Tunnel. The novel was printed and then never released from the publisher's warehouse, although an estimated 200 copies for review had been circulated. Despite rumors of corporate interference, Doubleday never officially explained the book's disappearance. Five years after the novel's suppression, Skidmore died February 2, 1946, at his Pennsylvania home. *Hawks Nest* was retrieved from oblivion by Jim Comstock in 1970, in his effort to reprint important West Virginia material, and later reprinted in a facsimile edition by Thomas In-Prints of Gauley Bridge.

See also Hawks Nest Tunnel Disaster, Literature

Gordon Simmons
Division of Culture and History
Hubert Skidmore, *Hawks Nest*, 1941.

Skiing

Modern downhill skiing was introduced to West Virginia in the mid-1950s. The first ski area was developed by the Washington Ski Club when member Bob Barton invested $15,000 in a 99-year lease for an area of Cabin Mountain known as Weiss Knob in the Canaan Valley of Tucker County. It was the first commercial ski area south of the Mason-Dixon Line. The ski complex at Canaan Valley State Park now encompasses this area. Barton is remembered as the father of West Virginia skiing.

In the 1970s, West Virginia's rugged Allegheny Mountains opened for development. Ski areas sprouted up at such a rate that the industry has now become a major component in the region's economy, bringing hundreds of thousands of skiers from all over the East each winter. With relatively high elevations, West Virginia's mountains get a good deal of natural snow, and they are within driving distance of a large part of the nation's population.

The first to see the full potential of these mountains was Tom Brigham, an Alabama dentist and developer of ski areas in North Carolina. In the early 1970s, Brigham began work on what is now Snowshoe Mountain Resort, created out of a natural bowl on Shavers Fork in Pocahontas County. Other sites soon developed, including Silver Creek in Pocahontas County (now part of Snowshoe Mountain Resort), Timberline and Canaan Valley resorts in Tucker County, and Winterplace in Raleigh County, in the southern part of the state.

At the turn of the 21st century, West Virginia's downhill skiing industry generates $200 million at the resorts in yearly revenue and attracts 800,000 skiers to the Mountain State for about 130 days of skiing each year. All the areas have more than 85 percent of their slopes equipped with snowmaking capabilities. Snowshoe's top elevation is 4,848 feet, with a 1,500-foot vertical drop served by 14 ski lifts. Canaan Valley's top elevation is 4,280 feet, with an 850-foot vertical served by three lifts. Timberline's top elevation is 4,268 with a 1,000-foot vertical served by three lifts. Winterplace's top elevation is 3,600 feet, with a 603-foot vertical drop served by nine ski lifts.

With the exception of Winterplace, the major ski resorts are open year-round, providing other recreation in the warm months.

In addition to downhill skiing and snowboarding at the major resorts, cross-country skiing areas are found throughout the eastern mountains of West Virginia. Two businesses, White Grass in Tucker County and Elk River Touring Center in Pocahontas, offer cross-country skiers the opportunity to see some of the state's wilderness areas. Other facilities, such as Blackwater Falls and Canaan Valley state parks, also offer cross-country trails and equipment rentals.

See also Tourism

Stan Cohen
Pictorial Histories

Slavery

Slavery never prospered on a widespread basis in the area that became West Virginia. On the eve of the Civil War, the entire Commonwealth of Virginia had a

Skiing at Snowshoe Mountain Resort.

A former slave looks back

"I was born in Dunbar, West Virginia, in the year 1847, and was owned by Ellis Grant . . . .

"Our homelife as slave children was hell, as we never had any playtime at all. From the time we could walk Mistress had us carrying in wood and water and we did not know what it was to get out and romp and play like children do now.

"Our quarters was pretty good, they were built out of bark logs and all the cracks were daubed with mud to keep out the cold and rain. Our beds, they were built down on the ground in one corner of our quarters out of moss, shucks and grass. Yes, we kept real warm in there all the time as we had a big rock fireplace built to keep us warm. We kept plenty wood as that and water was about all we got free.

"As slaves we done all kinds of work such as hoe tobacco, pull and dry it then, we cut rails for fences, and just anything that Mas[t]er had to do as it did not make any difference to him, he worked men or women slaves just alike. The women cooked and washed dishes while the men tended to the stock that Mas[t]er owned. Mas[t]er would give us a nickel or dime once in awhile, and we bought candy and things like that when he would give us any money, but that was seldom ever, maybe once or twice a year.

"Yes, we had plenty to eat, such as it was. We had cornbread, gathered right out of the field as we ate it grated by hand, nothing in it but water and salt. We had pork and beef cooked on the open fireplace most of the time and we called it roasted meat, it was sure good. Yes, we had plenty rabbit, possum and fish, but I never did care anything about such except fish. I sure did like fish fried good and brown on a big flat iron skillet in plenty hog grease."

—Lizzie Grant March 6, 1938

slave population of almost a half-million persons. Of these, only a relative handful resided in present West Virginia. In 1850, when the West Virginia section's slave population was at its apex, the number was 20,527 or 6.79 percent of the area's total population of 302,313. By 1860, the western section's slave population had declined both in number and as a percentage of the whole population.

The slave population was concentrated in four Western Virginia valleys: Shenandoah, South Branch, Kanawha, and Greenbrier. In 1850, only seven counties had more than 10 percent of their total population in slaves. These seven counties had 70.77 percent of all slaves in the West Virginia section of Virginia. In 1850, Jefferson County had the largest portion in number (4,341) and as a percentage (28.2) of total county population. Berkeley County had 1,956 slaves, 16.6 percent of its aggregate population. Hampshire County had the most slaves (1,433) in the South Branch region. The slave population of Kanawha County numbered 3,140, with most concentrated in Kanawha Salines. Greenbrier County had 1,317 slaves.

The great influx of slaves into the Shenandoah Valley came between 1768 and 1810, when Tidewater Virginians left their depleted tobacco plantations for new lands. These planters became wheat and general farmers and sometimes retained plantation ideals. Slaves with overseers often preceded their owners to clear and fence land and to erect housing. African-Americans cleared the forest, split rails, and removed rocks from fields. They also tended the livestock, plowed thousands of acres, harvested the crops, and hauled the produce to storage or market. Slaves supported all aspects of the household and domestic lifestyle, sometimes opulent, of the master and family. Some were skilled craftsmen. Many endlessly cut wood for cooking and for heating the huge houses. They raised, harvested, preserved, and prepared the food, and some took care of children.

The large slaveholders on the fertile South Branch soils of the Eastern Panhandle and on the limestone soils of Greenbrier and Monroe counties emulated to some degree the eastern Virginia or Shenandoah pattern of slave use. Locational and economic differences pushed slaves into occupations associated with a livestock economy and into land-clearing. The spas at western mineral springs often relied on slave labor as well.

Throughout the Trans-Allegheny, scattered slaves labored in the domestic service of well-to-do owners. Other owners in this area generally held bondsmen in single or small numbers and worked beside them on farms, in craft occupations, service enterprises, or small manufacturing operations. In the southwest, below and along the Kanawha River, slaves labored along with their masters in labor-intensive tobacco farming. The extensive industrial use of slaves in coal mining and salt manufacturing around Kanawha Valley salt furnaces was atypical.

In 1850, Kanawha saltmakers employed more than 1,500 slaves in all phases of their enterprise. These manufacturers leased more than half of the total number of bondsmen under their control. The leased slaves were usually from eastern Virginia, and some remained most of their lives on the Kanawha. Slaves at the salt furnaces worked as coal miners, teamsters, kettle-tenders, steam engine tenders, salt lifters and wheelers, general laborers, packers, blacksmiths, and cooks. Some slaves were foremen. Several saltmakers also used slaves as farmers to feed their furnace laborers.

In areas of military activity, the Civil War loosened the bonds of slave control, allowing slaves freedom and unlimited mobility. Bondsmen in remote areas generally remained with their masters and maintained the old relationships and work patterns. Fleeing slaves who remained in the state tended to congregate in towns where they could support each other. Often free persons of color supported refugees. In county seat towns in northern West Virginia, free and slave blacks engaged in a wide variety of trades and in domestic service. On the Kanawha, a greatly reduced number of blacks continued to mine coal and manufacture salt during the war.

In the Shenandoah Valley, many male slaves fled to Pennsylvania. Some labored for federal forces or enlisted in the Union army. Single black males often prospered, but the females, children, and infirm remaining on farms frequently experienced great hardship. Some large landowners encouraged the casual formation of black communities on their land to retain labor in the locality.

Although relatively uncommon in the west, slavery nonetheless greatly influenced Western Virginia's political destiny. From the American Revolution, slavery affected every political question involving the state's sections and furnished the basic source of grievances that eventually split Virginia. Even in the statehood movement, the slave issue was paramount. Because the Emancipation Proclamation applied only to areas in rebellion against the United States, and thus not to West Virginia, the Willey Amendment, which provided gradual emancipation of most but not all slaves, became a conditional requirement for statehood. A legislative enactment of February 3, 1865, that arose from consideration of ratification of the 13th Amendment actually freed the Mountain State's slaves.

See also Abolitionism, African-American Heritage

John Edmund Stealey III
Shepherd University

John E. Stealey III, "Slavery in West Virginia," *Dictionary of Afro-American Slavery*, 1997; Stealey, *The Antebellum Kanawha Salt Business and Western Markets*, 1993; Stealey, "The Freedmen's Bureau in West Virginia," *West Virginia History*, 1978.

Ada "Bricktop" Smith

Entertainer Ada Beatrice Queen Victoria Louise Virginia "Bricktop" Smith was born at Alderson, August 14, 1894. At five, red-haired little Ada made her stage debut in a performance of *Uncle Tom's Cabin* in Chicago. At 16 she performed on the vaudeville circuit. Soon afterward New York saloon keeper Barron Wilkins gave her the nickname "Bricktop" for her red hair, unusual for an African-American.

Smith performed in Paris in 1924, where Cole Porter is said to have written the song "Miss Otis Regrets She's Unable to Lunch Today" for her. In 1926, she opened a Paris club called the Music Box, soon succeeded by another club called Bricktop's.

Smith married musician Peter Ducongé in 1929. She opened a much larger Bricktop's in 1931, where Porter performed in 1932. She made radio broadcasts in France in 1938–39; then returned to the U.S. as Nazi Germany began expanding across Europe. Her only recording, "So Long, Baby," was made with Cy Coleman in 1970. Ada "Bricktop" Smith Ducongé's autobiography, *Bricktop*, co-written with James Haskins, was published in 1983, just before her death in New York City, January 31, 1984.

R. F. Hendricks
Marietta, Georgia

Agnes Smith

Author Agnes Clifford Smith was born in Clarksburg, October 18, 1906. She spent her childhood in Clarksburg and Charleston and finished high school at the Academy of St. Joseph in Brentwood, New York. She graduated from Fairmont State College (now University) with a degree in English. In 1936, Smith married Fairmont native Richard Bruce Parrish, who for many years was editor of the city's afternoon newspaper, The *West Virginian*. The couple made their home at the Parrish homestead near Worthington for more than 50 years, cultivating hay, oats, and other grains. Smith ran the farm herself while her husband served in the army during World War II.

By the age of 18, Smith had decided to devote herself to the arts, especially writing. Following graduation from college, she became active in Fairmont's Little Theatre, while pursuing her interest in writing and ceramics. Her major work, *An Edge of the Forest*, was published by Viking Press in 1959. An allegory, the book is the story of a black lamb separated from its flock and thrust into grave danger but ultimately saved by a black leopardess. *An Edge of the Forest* won the Aurianne Award of the American Library Association, a children's book award.

Smith went on to publish two additional works, *The Bluegreen Tree*, also a children's book, and a collection of essays titled *Speaking as a Writer*. She was also an accomplished sculptor, potter, and wood carver. Agnes Smith died in Fairmont, January 11, 1994.

Eleanor Mahoney
Allegheny Mountain Radio

Hulett Smith

Hulett Carlson Smith, West Virginia's 27th governor, 1965–69, was born in Beckley, October 21, 1918. He grew up in the world of business and politics. His father, Joe L. Smith, a newspaper publisher and bank president, was mayor of Beckley, a state senator, U.S. congressman, and chairman of the state Democratic Party. Hulett graduated from Woodrow Wilson High School in 1934. In 1938, he graduated from the University of Pennsylvania's Wharton School.

Smith married Mary Alice Tieche in 1942. He served in the navy in World War II, in Washington, Rhode Island, and San Francisco, where he was a logistics expert for Lt. Clark Clifford, later U.S. secretary of defense. After the war Smith returned to Beckley and the management of family businesses. He also served on the boards of Beckley and Oak Hill hospitals, as a director of the Bank of Raleigh, and vice president of Beckley College (now Mountain State University). A licensed pilot since 1940, he served on the state Aeronautics Commission from 1947 to 1959.

In 1951, Smith became chairman of Beckley's Democratic executive committee. Five years later he was named manager of Congressman Robert H. Mollohan's unsuccessful gubernatorial campaign against Republican Cecil Underwood, then became chairman of the state Democratic Party. In 1959, Smith announced his candidacy for governor, his first bid for elected office. He lost to Attorney General W. W. Barron in the Democratic primary.

In 1961, Governor Barron appointed Smith head of the new Department of Commerce. His responsibilities included economic development and promotion of tourism. He took a broad approach and was particularly proud of the department's efforts to promote traditional arts and crafts, beginning with the creation of the Mountain State Art & Craft Fair at Ripley. Smith's department was also responsible for coordinating many of the activities surrounding West Virginia's yearlong Centennial celebration in 1963.

In November 1963, he resigned to devote his energies to his second gubernatorial campaign. In the 1964 primary Smith carried 53 of the state's 55 counties, receiving more votes than his three opponents combined. In the general election he defeated former Governor Underwood.

Smith's inauguration, on a frigid January 18, 1965, was attended by 5,000 people. In his inaugural address the new governor expanded on the theme of

Governor Hulett C. Smith (1918–).

his campaign, promising that education would be his primary goal and pledging to give the state an administration with "the highest standards of ethics, integrity, and honesty . . . [and to] never tolerate incompetence or mediocrity."

During Smith's years as governor, the death penalty was abolished, new human rights legislation was passed, teachers' pay was increased, the Educational Broadcasting Authority was put on a solid footing, and the Antiquities Commission was created. One of the greatest accomplishments of Smith's administration was realized during his first year in office when the initial phase of his $32.5 million, three-year school improvement program was passed by the legislature. It included Project Head Start for preschoolers, a program actively supported by the first lady. Mrs. Smith was also the driving force behind a major restoration of the governor's mansion.

In 1966, the governor signed several important pieces of legislation into law, including a new minimum wage and hour act, but the legislature voted down a proposed constitutional amendment that would have allowed the governor to succeed himself. That same year Smith also launched one of the most important and controversial undertakings of his administration, the creation of new strip mine regulations. He regarded conservation and recreation as cornerstones of the state's economic future, and was highly critical of strip mining's devastation of West Virginia's natural beauty. He called for rigorous controls on what he referred to as "the rape of West Virginia." The governor lobbied hard, and the 1967 legislature passed what was considered the toughest strip mine legislation in the country. During the same session the legislature also passed air and stream pollution control laws, raised taxes, and expanded unemployment and workers' compensation benefits.

Smith was disappointed when legal challenges to the new environmental regulations revealed weaknesses in the stream pollution control law, although the state Supreme Court upheld the strip mine law. Then in 1968 his proposed $150 million bond issue for school construction and state facilities improvements stalled in legislative committee, and the senate refused to confirm Smith's appointee for director of the Human Rights Commission.

Despite these setbacks, the governor enjoyed several significant victories in 1968. Ground was broken for two new state office buildings. The legislature voted to place the administration's proposed $350 million road bond and modern budget amendments on the ballot. Both were approved by the voters, and the budget amendment greatly increased the power of future governors.

But 1968 was also the year when former Governor Barron, three top state officials, and two others were indicted by a federal grand jury on charges of bribery conspiracy involving state contracts. Smith immediately suspended the three officials, all holdovers from the Barron administration.

In addition to the revelations concerning Barron and his associates, several other scandals involving top officials surfaced during Smith's administration. Not long after the governor took office, his Motor Vehicles commissioner, Jack Nuckols, was indicted on fraud and related charges, and later convicted. The following year allegations of improper use of influence in the awarding of state park concessions contracts led to the resignations of two top officials from the Department of Natural Resources. Another controversy in 1966 involved State Road Commission purchasing practices.

In 1967, the governor's Alcoholic Beverage Control commissioner, Clarence C. Elmore, was indicted on charges of income tax evasion. The following year brought the Barron indictments and the indictment of a former state road equipment supervisor, Woodrow Yokum, on charges of unlawful transportation and sale of stolen government property. Elmore, Yokum, and four of those indicted with Barron were convicted. Barron was acquitted, only to later plead guilty to charges of bribing a juror.

While the U.S. Justice Department cleared Governor Smith of any involvement with the Barron case, the issue would cloud the remainder of his term and help propel Republican Arch A. Moore into the governor's office in the election later in 1968. After leaving office, Smith returned to Beckley. He resumed his activities in private business and continued his involvement with civic and philanthropic activities and in Democratic Party politics. In 1987, Smith's

Politics in the Smoke Hole

"Notwithstanding the comparative isolation from daily events, the Smoke Hole resident takes a keen interest in governmental affairs and goes to some lengths to express his political convictions at the polls.

"Along with occasional Saturday night jaunts to Petersburg or Franklin, one of his choicest entertainments consists of gathering in jeans-clad groups on Saturday and Sunday afternoons in Shreve's store, there to discuss crops, hunting, and politics. The political situation in the Smoke Hole is certainly unusual; until a few years ago it was said the Smoke Hole had 'only one Democrat and lightnin' killed him,' but recently there has been some swing of political allegiances. There are 113 registered voters in the Smoke Hole, and of these 81 are members of one of seven families, all early settlers, the Alts, Ayres, Judys, Kimbles, Selfs, Shreves, and Shirks, with the Kimble clan alone boasting 29 votes."

—*Smoke Hole and Its People* West Virginia Writers' Project (1940)

wife, Mary Alice, died. On July 14, 1990, he married the former Nancy Pat Hamilton Lewis.

In an interview with *Charleston Gazette* reporter John Morgan at the end of his term as governor, Hulett Smith said, "I like politics. It's a part of life. People who don't get involved are missing something."

See also William Wallace Barron

Margo Stafford
Clarksburg

John A. Canfield, ed., *State Papers and Public Addresses of Hulett C. Smith*, 1969; John G. Morgan, *West Virginia Governors*, 1980; Jim Wood, *Raleigh County*, 1994.

Michael W. Smith

Gospel musician Michael Whitaker Smith, born October 7, 1957, was educated at Ceredo-Kenova High School. He briefly attended Marshall University before moving to Nashville to pursue a music career. He wrote songs for Paragon-Benson Publishing Company before recording his first album, *The Michael W. Smith Project*, in 1983.

The song, "Place in this World," from a 1990 album, hit the gospel music top ten, helping Smith win New Artist of the Year at the American Music Awards in 1990. In 1992, he received an honorary doctorate of music degree from Alderson-Broaddus College. Smith founded Rocketown Ministries in 1994, and, two years later, Rocketown Records. In 1998, the contemporary Christian music magazine, *CCM*, named Smith's "Friends" the number-one song of all time. In 2001, Smith performed at the presidential inaugural prayer service and at the National Day of Prayer. In 2002, he provided the musical score for the motion picture, *Joshua*.

The singer, songwriter, and producer has written several books and appeared on numerous national television programs. Smith has been a spokesperson for Compassion International and active in Billy Graham Crusades and Samaritan's Purse, a ministry headed by Graham's son, Franklin.

As of 2004, Smith had 29 number-one songs, five platinum records, and 13 gold records. He has won the Nashville Music Award for pop album and ASCAP's Golden Note Award, as well as three Grammy Awards and 40 Dove Awards. He became a Distinguished West Virginian in 2003.

Russ Barbour
Huntington

Smoke Hole

A ruggedly scenic 18-mile canyon in Pendleton and Grant counties, the Smoke Hole was carved by the South Branch of the Potomac River between North Fork Mountain on the west and Cave Mountain on the east. Tradition holds that it received its name from a cave chamber where Indians and early settlers smoke-cured meat. Locally, Smoke Hole is often referred to in the plural, as the Smoke Holes.

The canyon's precipitous topography, underlain by complexly folded and faulted rock strata, features innumerable sandstone and limestone cliffs such as Eagle Rock, Castle Rock, Blue Rock, Bulls Head, and Ship Rock. The Nature Conservancy considers Smoke Hole and vicinity to be "one of the most biologically rich places in the East," especially valued for its rare plant communities. The Nature Conservancy included the Smoke Hole as part of the larger Smoke Hole-North Mountain Bioreserve during its "Last Great Places" campaign.

The "Big Cave" on Cave Mountain was a source of saltpeter for the production of gunpowder from the colonial period through the War of 1812. This cave, not to be confused with the commercially developed Smoke Hole Caverns on State Route 28/55 or with Smoke Hole Cave in the Smoke Hole itself, is now best known as Cave Mountain Cave. Confederates again mined there during the Civil War, until Unionist home guards destroyed the works. Smoke Hole people were overwhelmingly Unionist during the war and Republican thereafter.

Descriptions of the Smoke Hole before World War II generally emphasized its inaccessibility and the pioneer lifestyles of its inhabitants. The place also acquired renown for the production of moonshine whiskey. Many came to believe that Smoke Holers were so uncivilized and violent that it was dangerous for outsiders to enter the gorge, and that revenuers frequently disappeared there. During the 1920s, Franklin attorney H. M. Calhoun (1866–1933) became a champion of the Smoke Hole and its people.

In 1927, the boundaries of the Monongahela National Forest were extended to include the Smoke Hole. Not until 1930 was the first improved road built into the southern half of the gorge. The Civilian Conservation Corps constructed a popular recreation area in the mid-1930s. On the eve of World War II about 50 families resided in the canyon, but the war initiated out-migration and long-term population decline. In 1965, Smoke Hole became part of the Spruce Knob-Seneca Rocks National Recreation Area. The remote Smoke Hole Lodge operated in the gorge until its loss in the 1985 flood, and its replacement operated until 2001.

See also Smoke Hole Lodge

John Craft Taylor
Union College

D. Bardon Shreve, *A Place Called Smoke Hole*, 1997; Roy S. Sites, "Geology of the Smoke Hole Region of West Virginia," *Southeastern Geology*, December 1973; West Virginia Writers' Project, *Smoke Hole and Its People: A Social-Ethnic Study*, 1940.

Smoke Hole Caverns

Smoke Hole Caverns is located along State Route 28/55 about eight miles west of Petersburg in Grant County, at the western end of the North Fork Mountain water gap. The cave was opened for tours in 1940 and is one of four commercial caves in West Virginia. Smoke Hole Caverns is probably the most-visited cave in the state. The tour covers about 500 feet of the main passage; the total surveyed length is nearly 1,600 feet.

Smoke Hole Caverns developed geologically along bedding planes that have been tilted into a vertical position by the earth's tectonic movements. The cave follows a generally straight passage, tending north with a small stream flowing along the east side of the passage. The passage height reaches more than 100 feet above the floor. The cave is beautifully decorated with stalactites hanging in rows along the ceiling bedding planes. Numerous calcite flowstone draperies line the walls. The main room is called the "Room of a Million Stalactites." The cave is developed in Tonoloway limestones of Silurian age. Smoke Hole Caverns, named for the nearby Smoke Hole canyon of the South Branch Potomac,

should not be confused with the Cave Mountain Cave in the Smoke Hole.

William K. Jones
Charles Town

Smoke Hole Lodge

Located near Petersburg in Grant County, the Smoke Hole Lodge sits on the South Branch of the Potomac River in a prime natural location. The remote site is accessible only by four-wheel-drive vehicle, horse or canoe. Until it closed in 2001, the lodge offered old-fashioned accommodations to guests seeking respite from modern life.

The first lodge at Smoke Hole was originally a one-room log cabin that later served as a schoolhouse. After World War I, Wheeling industrialist Edward E. Stifel bought the property, renovated the schoolhouse, and opened the Smoke Hole Club. Other sportsmen's clubs operated in West Virginia during that time, including the Allegheny Sportsmen's Association in Pocahontas County, at Minnehaha Springs, and Cheat Mountain Club in Randolph County, west of Durbin on Shavers Fork.

The original lodge stood until November 4, 1985, when floodwaters swept it away. By 1987, Edward Stifel III had constructed a new three-story lodge. Beyond the reach of electric service, the stone-and-wood structure was furnished with gas lights, kerosene lanterns, gas refrigerators, and a wood-burning range. The lodge had five double bedrooms, two dormitory-style rooms, a living room with a stone fireplace, and a dining room. Guests could fish, hunt for small game, ride horses, canoe, help with farm animals, or take on routine chores.

Edward Stifel III sold conservation easements on the 1,126-acre property to the West Virginia Nature Conservancy in 2004 and hoped to sell the property itself to new owners who would reopen the lodge.

See also Allegheny Lodge, Cheat Mountain Club, J. L. Stifel & Sons

Nancy Buckingham, "Smoke Hole Lodge Offers the Luxury of Wondering," *Wonderful West Virginia*, March 1989.

Smoot Theatre

Built in 1926 by the Smoot Amusement Company to showcase acts on the vaudeville circuit, Parkersburg's 720-seat Smoot Theatre was packed for five shows daily during the Roaring '20s. Performers included Singer's Midgets, a troupe of miniature comedians, chorus girls, and musicians; the Hilton Sisters, Siamese twins joined at the back, playing saxophone and piano; and Guy Lombardo's big band. Silent and talking films came to the Smoot when Warner Brothers took over in 1930. During a screening of "Frankenstein," an ambulance and nurses were stationed out-

side for patrons feeling faint, and audience members, determined to get their money's worth, moved to the balcony during the flood of 1937 as water rose in the lower section.

The Smoot served as a movie theater until 1986, but its former opulence had long faded. Destined for demolition in 1989, the theater was rescued by a citizen group headed by former band director Felice Jorgeson, who led the restoration and artistic vision. The refurbished theater features gold-gilt art deco designs on the walls and ceiling; mauve, jade, blue, and beige stained-glass chandeliers; gold leaf around the proscenium; new mahogany and brass doors; and a hand-cut Austrian crystal chandelier in the lobby. In the final decade of the 20th century, the Smoot Theatre hosted performances by Wynton Marsalis, Vince Gill, Peter Nero, Tom Chapin, Preservation Hall Jazz Band, Wheeling Symphony, Vienna Boys Choir, and the Presidential Orchestra of the Russian Federation. The Smoot Theatre, located at 213 Fifth Street, was listed on the National Register of Historic Places in 1982.

H. G. Young III
WVU Parkersburg

Lisa Starcher, "Rebirth of Parkersburg's Historic Smoot Theatre," *Wonderful West Virginia*, April 1993.

Snakes

There are 22 species of snakes in West Virginia. All are cold-blooded, and their temperature approximates that of their surroundings. Ringneck snakes and black rat snakes are the most common in and around houses. The ringneck is easily identified by the yellow ring around its neck and its small size, usually less than 12 inches. They often are found on basement floors. The black rat snake is our largest. These snakes are good climbers, and adults often are found in upper rooms or rafters. They might strike when cornered but usually tame readily and make good pets. Their bite is inconsequential and painless.

The northern water snake is common around lakes and streams. It is not poisonous and will not bite unless threatened. The hognose, often called the blowing viper or puff adder, flattens its neck like a cobra and hisses loudly when threatened. It strikes with a closed mouth. If still threatened, the hognose rolls over, hangs its tongue out and plays dead. It is one of the few animals that eat toads, having an enlarged adrenal gland that allows the poisonous toad secretions to be neutralized.

Our fastest snake is the black racer, which may move four to five miles per hour, slower than a person can run.

The only two poisonous snakes in West Virginia are the copperhead and timber rattlesnake, which are pit vipers. A copperhead has a copper color with darker bands shaped like hourglasses across the back. The narrow parts of the bands are on top of the back. The bands on the back of all our other snakes are oval or rectangular-shaped, and widest on top of the back. The pupil of the eye of a copperhead is black and vertical like a cat's eye with an orange background, safely seen from a few feet away. Harmless snakes have a round pupil and often a dark background. The nonpoisonous snakes most often confused with copperheads are milk, water, and young black snakes. No snake is easily confused with a rattlesnake.

Snakes do not have eyelids and can see for only short distances, perhaps 10 to 15 feet. Lacking external ear openings, snakes pick up earthborne and airborne vibrations through their skin that are then transmitted via their spinal cord and lung to their inner ear.

Smell is the most important sense for all snakes. Molecules of odor are picked up on the constantly flicking tongue. Our poisonous snakes, the pit vipers, have heat sensing pits located on the side of each upper jaw between the eye and nostril. These enable the pit vipers to locate warm-blooded prey, such as mice, in the dark. These heat sensors also work in daylight, but sight and smell are probably as important then. The sense of smell is also important for rattlesnakes to find their den areas in the fall. If they fail to find their dens, they will likely not survive.

The bite of a copperhead or timber rattlesnake is a serious medical emergency, but deaths are rare. An estimated 30 percent to 40 percent of bites by poisonous snakes result in no venom being injected. There is no record of a death in West Virginia from a copperhead bite during the past 40 years, but there have been 13 deaths from rattlesnakes. Nine of these deaths occurred while the snakes were being handled during religious services.

Frank Jernejcic
Division of Natural Resources
N. Bayard Green and Thomas K. Pauley, *Amphibians and Reptiles in West Virginia*, 1987.

Sam Snead

Legendary golfer Samuel Jackson "Slammin' Sammy" Snead, was born May 27, 1912, at Ashwood, Virginia. A natural athlete, he excelled in sports in high school. He ran track and played baseball, basketball, football, tennis, and golf. After high school, he concentrated on golf.

In 1934, Snead became a golf professional and worked at the Upper Cascades course in Hot Springs, Virginia. After a year, he went to work as assistant golf professional at the nearby Homestead resort and then became a teaching professional at the Greenbrier resort. In 1937, he joined the Professional Golf Association tour. By 1942, he had won 29 tournaments.

Golfer Sam Snead (1912–2002).

During World War II, Snead served in the U.S. Navy. When the Greenbrier reopened as a resort in 1948, after wartime service as an army hospital, Snead returned as the golf professional. Wearing his trademark straw fedora, he continued to play on the PGA Tour, eventually winning 81 PGA events and at least 135 world tournaments. He won his last PGA event at age 52, the oldest player to do so.

In 1974, he left the Greenbrier and worked at the Homestead. In 1980, he joined the Senior PGA Tour. Upon his return to the Greenbrier in 1993, Snead was named golf professional emeritus. Highlights of his long career include three PGA championships, three Masters Tournaments, and the 1946 British Open. He was selected eight times as a member of the U.S. Ryder Cup team, and elected to the PGA Hall of Fame and the World Golf Hall of Fame. Snead published several books about golf. He split his time among the Greenbrier, his Ashwood farm, and Florida. He died at Ashwood, May 23, 2002.

See also The Greenbrier

Robert S. Conte, *The History of The Greenbrier*, 1998.

Snowshoe Mountain Resort

Snowshoe Mountain Resort in Pocahontas County is West Virginia's largest ski resort. The 234-acre, 57-slope complex rests on top of Cheat Mountain, with elevations as high as 4,848 feet.

The resort was founded in 1974 by Alabama dentist Thomas "Doc" Brigham, who had already built two ski areas in North Carolina. Looking for the snowiest location in the South, Brigham invested in the Cheat Mountain location which receives an average annual snowfall of 200 inches. The area's unusually cold weather makes it the most southerly home of snowshoe hares, which gave the resort its name. It also allows Snowshoe the longest winter in the region, with skiing from late November to mid-April.

Snowshoe differs from most ski resorts because the majority of its facilities are found at the top of the mountain, while slopes plummet to the east and west ridges. Because of the isolation of the area, the owners built an entire community which is now home to the state's highest post office. The slopes are named for the industry that preceded skiing on Cheat Mountain, logging. Names such as Skidder, Ballhooter, Whistlepunk, Gandy Dancer, and Powder Monkey are mostly logging and railroading terms. Snowshoe's famous Cupp Run and its new sister, Shay's Revenge, are the largest slopes south of New York, each boasting 1,500 vertical feet.

Snowshoe was plagued with financial woes throughout its first decade. In 1983, Silver Creek, a competing resort, opened just a half-mile down the mountain. After two bankruptcies and several changes in ownership, Snowshoe became financially stable in the mid-1980s and was able to purchase Silver Creek in 1992.

In 1995, Snowshoe became part of Intrawest Corporation, a Canadian firm and one of North America's largest resort development companies. Improvements include new slopes, increased snowmaking capacity, high-speed ski lifts, an adventure park for snowboarders, a snow tubing hill, and new lodging, condominiums, shops, and restaurant areas at its peak. Today Snowshoe Mountain receives more than a half-million visitors each year.

Connie K. Colvin
Mineral Wells

Socialist Party

The first local branch of the West Virginia Socialist Party was established in Wheeling in 1901. With the assistance of Socialist organizers from Pennsylvania and Kentucky, the West Virginia movement spread by 1908 to Huntington, Parkersburg, Clarksburg, Charleston, and a number of smaller communities throughout the state.

By 1914, several thousand West Virginians were dues-paying members of the party's 86 local branches. As early as 1910, local Socialists began to elect candidates to office, and in 1912 more than 15,000 West Virginia voters cast their ballots for Socialist Eugene Debs for president. By 1914, West Virginians had elected Socialist Party candidates to more than 40 local offices, including virtually the entire administrations of such widely scattered communities as Miami, Eskdale, Adamston, Cameron, and Hendricks. Star City, near Morgantown, would ultimately have the longest-lived Socialist municipal government in the United States. In addition, Socialists controlled Cabin Creek, Paint Creek, and Washington districts in the Kanawha County coalfields and the Falls Magisterial District of Fayette County.

To a great extent, the progress that the West Virginia Socialists achieved on the electoral front was a reflection of the party's strategy of increasing class consciousness by working with existing unions to build the power of the labor movement. The party appealed to a fairly broad cross section of wage earners. There were important concentrations among skilled craftsmen in the pottery, window glass, machine tools, cigar making, and building construction trades. Socialists from these crafts and others held leadership positions in their own unions and in a number of the state's central labor bodies. Party members had special influence in the Ohio Valley Trades and Labor Assembly, the Huntington Trades and Labor Assembly, and most important of all, the West Virginia State Federation of Labor. Socialists were especially popular with coal miners and were able by 1916 to control both District 29 and District 17 of the United Mine Workers in West Virginia.

The steady growth of West Virginia's Socialist Party also owed much to the fact that many members of the middle class were attracted to the cause. These included physicians and dentists such as Albert Bosworth of Elkins, Edgar Smith of Martinsburg, George Kline of Wheeling, and Matthew Holt of Weston, who was the party's candidate for governor in 1920. Another contingent of middle-class professionals was made up of lawyers, including George H. Duthie of Wheeling, Altha Warman of Morgantown, Samuel Webb of Saint Albans, and H. O. Davis and Harold Houston of Parkersburg. In addition, practically every major urban Socialist local branch had several businessmen who were active in the party's work, the most well known being Edward H. Kintzer, a Clarksburg real estate broker; William Blenko, the founder of Blenko Glass; Charles Boswell, a furniture dealer in Charleston; and William McMechen, a textile manufacturer and store owner whose family founded the

Northern Panhandle community that bears his name. These businessmen and professionals helped to establish the local halls, libraries, cooperative stores, and newspapers that were spreading throughout the state. Many of them served on the party's state executive committee.

Despite the progress made through 1914, the West Virginia Socialist Party experienced a precipitous fall in voting strength in 1916. Several factors combined to send the party into a rapid decline. First of all, the state legislature passed a primary law in 1915 that made it more difficult for third parties to get on the ballot. This law and the confusion it generated helped to radicalize some Socialists and drive them from the party and toward more militant action. The idea had been growing in state and national Socialist circles that militant trade unionism and direct action, not political activity, were the key to achieving a more equitable and humane society in America. These so-called "Red" Socialists were also encouraged by their participation in the bitter class warfare of the 1912–13 Paint Creek-Cabin Creek Strike.

Thus, the West Virginia Socialist Party was weakening just at the time it would face such divisive issues as America's participation in World War I and the Russian Revolution. Not until the onset of the Great Depression would the party experience a revitalization; but by then the New Deal Democrats had stolen too much of the Socialists' thunder and many of the party's issues.

See also Eugene Victor Debs, Harold Houston, Labor History

Fred A. Barkey
Marshall University Graduate College
Frederick A. Barkey, "The Socialist Party in West Virginia from 1898 to 1920: A Study in Working Class Radicalism," Ph.D. dissertation (unpublished), University of Pittsburgh, 1971; Stephen Cresswell, "When the Socialists Ran Star City," *West Virginia History*, 1993.

Soils of West Virginia

Soil is the surface layer of the earth, consisting of mineral and organic materials in which plants grow. Soil is arranged in layers known as horizons, with the cross section of all horizons known as the soil profile. The top horizon, or topsoil, is the dark-colored surface horizon where decomposed organic matter accumulates. There are five or more soil horizons, underlaid by bedrock.

The soil classification system is called soil taxonomy. This system has six categories or levels, ranging from orders at the highest level to series at the lowest. Twelve soil orders are recognized, with increasing numbers of classes added to each category from highest to lowest, so that approximately 18,000 series are now recognized in the U.S. Seven of the 12 soil

orders and about 200 series are recognized in West Virginia.

West Virginia is divided into five major land resource areas. The Eastern Panhandle is within the Northern Appalachian Ridges and Valleys, and the southeastern part of the state is within the Southern Appalachian Ridges and Valleys. Soils in the valleys have formed in limestone or shales. They are nearly level to sloping, generally well-drained, ranging from moderately deep (less than 20 inches to bedrock) on the shales to very deep (more than 60 inches to bedrock) on the limestone. Shale soils generally have medium (loamy and silty) textures, with moderate to low pH, and moderate to low fertility. Limestone soils generally have medium to fine textures (silty and clayey), moderate to high pH, and moderate to high fertility. Some of these soils are excellent for agriculture. Soils in the mountains have formed primarily from sandstone and shale. They tend to be moderately deep to deep and have loamy to sandy textures and moderate to low pH and fertility.

The Eastern Allegheny Plateau and Mountains land resource area lies just west of the Ridges and Valleys. This area has the highest elevations within the state. Most soils here formed in acid sandstone, shale, and siltstone. They are medium textured, with low pH and fertility. The geologic materials from which the soils formed have a very low nutrient content. Therefore, some of the soils at the highest elevations are the most nutrient-poor soils, in terms of calcium, magnesium, and phosphorus, found anywhere in the state. Most of the nutrients are concentrated in the vegetation and returned to the soil when vegetation dies.

In the northwestern part of the state, the Central Allegheny Plateau lies between the mountains and the Ohio River. Soils have formed on sandstone, shale, and siltstone and are moderately deep to deep, moderately well drained to well drained, with medium to fine textures. Fertility and pH of the soils vary, depending on the parent material. Some of the best agricultural soils in the state are located along the Ohio River.

The Cumberland Plateau and Mountains land resource area lies in the southern part of the state. This rugged area has a highly dissected landscape with long, steep side slopes between narrow ridgetops and narrow stream valleys. Soils are medium to fine-textured, with moderate to low fertility, and moderate to low pH.

Glaciers were never present in West Virginia, but they did affect some soils in the state. Patterned ground and other evidence of a colder climate can be found in some soils of higher elevations. Two glacial lakes were formed, one in the Teays Valley area by blockage of the ancient Teays River in present Ohio, and one in the northern part of the state formed by the blockage of the ancient Monongahela River in Pennsylvania. Remnants of terraces formed by these lakes are still present today. Soils formed from these lake sediments are moderately well-drained and normally have fine textured subsoils from the silts and clays that settled from the lake waters.

Other evidence of glacial activity may be found in the Ohio River watershed. Three unique soils occur on terraces and on west-facing hill slopes in this area. Two soils with very coarse particle sizes formed on terraces. One formed in glacial outwash. As the glaciers to the north melted, streams of water carried sediment into the Ohio Valley. The soil formed in outwash is very gravelly and sandy. Many of the gravels are granite and other types of rocks that came from the northern U.S. and Canada and are present nowhere else in the state.

The second unique soil on the terraces is a very sandy soil formed in ancient sand dunes. During the glacial period, dry times occurred. Winds from the west picked up soil materials and blew them into present West Virginia. Sands are heavier than silts and clays and are not blown as far from the source. Therefore, they tended to deposit in mounds or dunes on the eastern side of the Ohio Valley. These sandy soils can be found from the Northern Panhandle to Point Pleasant. The silty material carried by the wind moved farther east than the sands and was deposited on the western hill slopes along the valley. The soils developed in these materials have very silty textures and high pH. They are productive soils, but highly erodible.

In a mountainous area like West Virginia, erosion may have a major effect on soil development. Natural movement of soil materials is expected on steep slopes. However, when the vegetative cover is removed, accelerated erosion may decrease the thickness of the surface horizons and carry away nutrients tied up in the organic layers. Historical records recall thick organic surface layers on soils in various parts of the state that are no longer present. Logging practices around 1900 and wild fires with the ensuing erosion reduced the surface layer thickness and sometimes the fertility of soils.

It is almost impossible to find virgin soil in West Virginia because of logging, mining, fire, flooding, and construction of roads, airports, houses, and industry. By disturbing the original landscape and soil profile, humans have restarted the soil forming process. In some places these activities have produced soils of lower quality than those before the disturbance. However, in many places these soils are changing and becoming more like the original soils because of the natural soil-forming processes.

In 1997, an official state soil was designated to symbolize the crucial importance of healthy soil resources to West Virginians. This state soil is the Monongahela silt loam, a productive agricultural soil that may be found on terraces in many parts of the state and a wide surrounding region.

See also Lake Monongahela, Lake Tight, Monongahela Silt Loam

John Sencindiver
West Virginia University
USDA Soil Conservation Service, *Land Resource Regions and Major Land Resource Areas of the United States*, 1981.

Sorghum Molasses

Sorghum molasses is a thick sweet syrup made from a large grass plant known as sweet sorghum. Sorghum syrup is poured over biscuits and pancakes, and as an ingredient, the tangy syrup is added to breads, cookies, cakes, candy, and savory casseroles.

In West Virginia, as in other parts of the United States, many rural families relied on sorghum molasses as a sweetener during the late 19th and early 20th centuries. After World War II, sorghum was replaced by refined sugar as the primary sweetener, but even today, sorghum molasses has a following. It remains popular because of its long history and excellent flavor. The flavor lies between black strap molasses and light caramel syrup and is far less sweet than honey.

In West Virginia sorghum molasses has also been called molasses, lassies, and sorghums, but today, producers sometimes call their product 100 percent pure sweet sorghum syrup because of the fact that stores now sell "molasses" that are mixtures of corn syrup, flavorings, food coloring, and other additives.

On even the smallest plots, mountain farmers had enough space to plant sweet sorghum. Half an acre of land would produce from 50 to 100 gallons of syrup, and when sorghum was popular it was a valuable cash crop. Sorghum and corn are both grasses, and they grow well in the same soils and climates. Sugar cane, the source of refined sugar, requires a frost-free environment such as that found in the deep South.

Depending on the variety, sorghum grows to a height of five to 15 feet with stalks one to two inches thick. When it matures, the leaves are stripped, and the green sap is pressed from the stalks and run into evaporator pans. The pans are traditionally wood-fired on mountain farms. As moisture evaporates, the sap thickens and becomes sorghum molasses syrup. The process must be carefully attended to avoid scorching, and a green froth is skimmed away as it forms. Molasses "stir-offs" were once popular social events in mountain communities.

The making of sorghum molasses is celebrated at the West Virginia Molasses Festival held annually in late September since 1967 in Calhoun County. The three-day event is described as a "sticky time for all."

Mark F. Sohn
Pikeville College

The South Branch

The South Branch of the Potomac River, with its two major tributaries, the North Fork and South Fork, drains all of Pendleton County and parts of Grant, Hardy, Hampshire, and Morgan counties. This amounts to nearly 1,500 square miles, more than 40 percent of the eight-county Eastern Panhandle. Originating just across the state line near Monterey, Virginia, the South Branch traverses about 131 miles before joining with the North Branch near Green Spring to form the Potomac River.

With the exception of two stretches, the South Branch is easily accessible by various roads. An 11-mile section in Grant County upstream of Petersburg, known as the Smoke Hole, is accessed by no public roads; and the six miles of river known as the Trough, situated in Hardy and Hampshire counties between Moorefield and Romney, has only a railroad.

There are no large towns along the North Fork before it unites with the South Branch just upstream from Petersburg, only villages such as Circleville and Seneca Rocks. The South Fork also passes only small villages such as Sugar Grove and Brandywine before joining the South Branch at Moorefield. The South Branch itself meanders through or near sizable towns such as Franklin, Petersburg, Moorefield, and Romney.

The main use of the South Branch watershed is agricultural, but manufacturing, timbering and construction, tourism, and recreation are increasingly important. There has been a vast increase in the last decade in poultry production, primarily broiler chickens raised by growers throughout the watershed and processed mainly at plants at Moorefield. This increase in poultry production and the resulting large amounts of litter and manure have raised concerns about the water quality of the South Branch drainage.

The South Branch has long been noted for its premier smallmouth bass fishing. The smallmouth bass, not native to the South Branch, was first introduced into the C&O Canal basin at Cumberland, Maryland, in the 1850s. The fish escaped from there into the nearby North Branch of the Potomac, later spreading through the watershed. Although other stockings followed, this original stocking numbered about 30 fish. From this we have the tremendous fishery that provides recreation to countless numbers of anglers each year and has given the South Branch a respected name among fishermen in the Mid-Atlantic region. Other commonly

The South Branch of the Potomac River.

sought species are channel catfish, sunfish, and rock bass, in addition to trout (which are stocked during the spring and fall in the upper South Branch).

The Division of Natural Resources has developed several points of access to the South Branch to allow fishermen, as well as pleasure boaters and swimmers, use of the river. These access points permit float trips of various lengths, and at least two canoe rental and shuttle services are available on the river. Due to their inaccessibility by road, the Smoke Hole and Trough sections are probably the most popular floats. Although the Smoke Hole section is floatable for a shorter period of time due to its upstream location and steeper gradient, it is regarded as the most scenic and remote float on the South Branch. A float in the Trough is noteworthy because the floater almost always is ensured of seeing the majestic bald eagle. The Trough was the first known nesting site in West Virginia in modern times for the nation's symbol, and these opportunities should be available for future generations on this wonderful stream of the Eastern Panhandle.

Gerald E. Lewis
Division of Natural Resources

South Charleston

South Charleston, located on the Kanawha River southwest of Charleston, had a population of 13,390 in 2000. The city rose with the development of the chemical industry in the early 1900s.

South Charleston occupies a historic location along a buffalo trail that became the James River & Kanawha Turnpike, later known as the Midland Trail. Stagecoaches stopped at the mouth of Davis Creek, and travelers favored the dependable spring for which the South Charleston neighborhood of Spring Hill is named. The prehistoric Adena, who lived in the area from about 1000 B.C. to A.D. 200, left the second-largest burial mound in West Virginia at South Charleston.

In 1827, James Blaine built a gristmill on Blaine Island, in the Kanawha River near the present downtown. For years the area remained mostly undeveloped, however, overshadowed by its larger neighbor across the river. That changed in 1906, when former Gov. William A. MacCorkle founded the Kanawha Land Company, buying with other investors 1,800 acres on the south side of Kanawha River. Civil engineers laid out an orderly grid of streets, and the new town was named South Charleston.

In 1907, the town founders induced Banner Glass Company to relocate from Indiana. About 40 families, mostly Belgian and French, came to work at the glass factory. Other factories followed, lured by cheap coal, natural gas, and salt, and by easy access to rail, highways, and the Kanawha River.

During World War I, the town boomed as demand for chemicals and other war products grew. The federal government broke ground for the huge Naval Ordnance Plant, but the war was over by the time the plant produced its first steel in February 1921. The plant has since been put to a variety of military and civilian uses. By 1919, South Charleston had grown to more than 1,000 residents, and the state legislature officially made it a town.

The company that made South Charleston a center of industry was Union Carbide, which bought up property along the Kanawha River in 1925. "Carbide," as it was called locally, grew into one of the world's largest chemical companies, and for the next three-quarters of a century the fortunes of the company and the city were intertwined. Starting in 1949, Union Carbide developed its technical center above its South Charleston plant. The facility drew highly educated scientists from all over the world.

At its height, Union Carbide employed approximately 10,000 people in the area, and South Charleston's population peaked at 19,180 in 1960. But changing markets in the 1980s and the tragic industrial accident at its Bhopal, India, facility in 1984 undercut the company's future. Dow Corporation acquired Union Carbide in 2001 and substantially reduced employment.

With large cuts in chemical and manufacturing jobs, South Charleston has moved to diversify its economy. In the late 1990s, the city worked with developers to bring many stores to the Southridge area, which soon became the region's main shopping district. It built the area's only ice skating rink near the shopping center and several soccer fields. South Charleston is served by Thomas Memorial Hospital, which was founded in 1946 and provides health services to a wide region. The South Charleston Recreation Center opened in 1982 with an indoor pool, basketball court, racquetball courts, and weight rooms.

See also Charleston Ordnance Center, South Charleston Mound, Union Carbide

Scott Finn
Charleston Gazette

South Charleston Mound

The South Charleston, or Criel, Mound is one of the largest extant burial mounds in West Virginia, second only to Grave Creek Mound in Moundsville. The mound is located in what was the Criel family farm, now downtown South Charleston. Standing about 33 feet tall, South Charleston Mound was once surrounded by extensive earthworks that stretched for several miles on both sides of the Kanawha River. South Charleston Mound, like many conical-shaped mounds, is a prehistoric burial place. Archeologists have determined that mounds such as this were constructed by people, generally referred to as the Adena, who lived along the Ohio and Kanawha drainage systems between 1000 and 200 B.C.

South Charleston Mound was first investigated by Col. P. W. Norris of the Smithsonian Institution as part of an extensive effort to identify the builders of the numerous earthworks located west of the Appalachian Mountains. Beginning in November 1883, Norris opened a 12-foot wide shaft on top of the mound and began excavating down to the original ground surface. At depths of three and four feet, human remains were encountered in the center of the shaft. Although prehistoric, artifacts found with these upper burials indicated that they were not of Adena origin, but rather were made by later people.

Nothing more was encountered until excavators dug down 31 feet into the mound where the original interment, consisting of 11 individuals, was discovered. All of the bodies were found lying on a bark bed that had been blanketed with ashes. A second layer of bark covered the remains. Ten of the individuals surrounded the 11th, suggesting to Norris that all 11 people had been buried at the same time and that the central figure may have been someone of importance. Artifacts found only with the central figure, including shell beads and the copper remains of a headdress, further support this idea. Despite rumors that a seven-foot "giant" had been uncovered, Norris reported that all individuals buried in the mound were adults of medium size. All burials and artifacts excavated from the mound were taken to the Smithsonian Institution where they remain today.

South Charleston Mound has survived numerous historic modifications since its construction more than 2,000 years ago. Sometime prior to the Smithsonian excavations the top eight to ten feet of the mound was removed, reportedly to make room for either a bandstand or judge's stand to accompany the racetrack that once circled the mound. Erosion of the mound was hastened during its use as pasture and agricultural field in the 1800s and from episodic tree planting in the 1900s. Attempts to improve the mound include the construction of a below-ground storage facility and a sidewalk to allow visitors to reach its peak. Despite these alterations, the South Charleston Mound stands as a grand reminder of the peoples who inhabited the Kanawha Valley several hundreds of years before the arrival of Europeans. In recognition of its historic significance, South Charleston Mound was placed on the National Register of Historic Places in 1970.

See also Adena, Archeology, Mound Builders

Lora Lamarre
State Historic Preservation
Edward V. McMichael and Oscar L. Mairs, "Excavation of the Murad Mound, Kanawha County, West Virginia, and an Analysis of Kanawha Valley Mounds," *Report of Archaeological Investigations Number 1*, 1969; Cyrus Thomas, *Report on the Mound Excavations of the Bureau of Ethnology*, 1894.

Southern West Virginia Community and Technical College

Southern West Virginia Community and Technical College was founded July 1, 1971, as Southern West Virginia Community College, by joining the Marshall University branch campuses at Logan and Williamson. In 1995, the name changed to Southern West Virginia Community and Technical College. Joanne Tomblin became president of the college in November 1999.

The college is a freestanding community and technical college governed by an institutional governing board. It serves Boone, Lincoln, Logan, McDowell, Mingo, Raleigh, and Wyoming counties in West Virginia, and Martin and Pike counties in Kentucky by reciprocity agreement. It is accredited by the North Central Association of Colleges and Schools and has an open admission policy. The college is on a semester academic calendar and offers traditional classroom teaching as well as distance-learning programs.

The college's first permanent building was in Williamson and was dedicated in 1971. Sites in Mingo, Logan, and Wyoming counties were established in 1974. In 2003, the college consisted of the central administration offices located at the Earl Ray Tomblin Center, which is adjacent to the Logan campus; the Logan downtown annex; the Williamson campus; the Wyoming-McDowell campus at Saulsville; and the Boone-Lincoln campus in Danville. Satellite sites are located at the Charles Yeager Technical Center in Hamlin, Harts High School in Harts, and the Raleigh-Boone Technology Center in Pettus. The two main libraries are the Williamson campus library and the Harless Library at the Logan campus.

During the fall 2004 semester, there was a total enrollment of 2,580, equivalent to 1,781 full-time students, with 63 full-time faculty and 74 adjunct faculty. The college has 22 degree options. It offers "university parallel" curricula in Associate in Arts and Associate in Science degrees, with agreements with Bluefield State College, West Virginia University Institute of Technology, Marshall University, West Virginia State University, Concord University, and the University of Charleston, allowing Southern students to proceed to those institutions. Southern West Virginia Community and Technical College offers Associate in Applied Science degrees in 12 occupational-technical programs, and certificates in five areas.

Tanya Godfrey
Moorefield

Red Sovine

Musician Red Sovine gained country music fame for his recitations, especially those incorporating sentimental truck driver themes. Born Woodrow Wilson Sovine in Charleston, July 17, 1918, he was influenced by Frank Welling and Buddy Starcher, two local radio musicians who also delivered sentimental monologues. Sovine's earlier musical efforts brought little success at either WCHS Charleston or WWVA Wheeling. He took a factory job in the Putnam County town of Eleanor, but still did programs on local radio. After World War II, he opted for a full-time musical career in Montgomery, Shreveport, and finally Nashville. In 1949, he began recording with MGM, Decca, and eventually Starday. He joined the *Grand Ole Opry* in 1954. Although the majority of his repertoire consisted of straight country singing, his biggest hits were recitations, especially "Giddyup Go" (1965), "Phantom 309" (1967), and "Teddy Bear" (1976). Sovine remained active until his death in Nashville, April 4, 1980.

Abby Gail Goodnite
University of Rio Grande
Ivan M. Tribe, *Mountaineer Jamboree: Country Music in West Virginia*, 1984.

Spanish-American War

The 1898 Spanish-American War made the United States a world power in just a few months. West Virginia initially supplied one regiment of infantry in the call-up of federal troops. The regiment consisted of 12 companies, organized into the 1st West Virginia Volunteer Infantry and mustered into service in Kanawha City in May 1898. The regiment was sent to Camp Thomas, Georgia, to join units from throughout the east. In June a second regiment, the 2nd West Virginia Volunteer Infantry, was formed.

Both these regiments were composed of National Guardsmen from around the state. Two companies were also raised in the state for the regular army, one company from Parkersburg and one from Wheeling. They became part of the 4th U.S. Volunteer Infantry. In addition, two companies of black troops were raised for the 8th U.S. Volunteer Infantry, one from Charleston and one from Parkersburg.

A great percentage of troops raised for the Spanish-American War never got into action. The 1st West Virginia remained at camp in Georgia, and the 2nd West Virginia remained at camp in Pennsylvania. There is no record of deaths among the troops, but disease was a constant killer in the overcrowded camps in the United States and in the active campaign areas in Cuba. While no West Virginia troops actually saw combat, the state did supply one famous personality to the war, Andrew Rowan, a Monroe County native, who carried the famous "Message to Garcia" in early 1898.

See also Andrew S. Rowan

Stan Cohen
Pictorial Histories

Spencer

Spencer (population 2,352 in 2000), the county seat of Roane County, was originally chartered in 1858. The place was previously known as California, and apparently renamed for Spencer Roane, the distinguished Virginia jurist for whom the county was named. The first local settlers of European descent were Samuel Tanner and his family and Jonathan Wolfe, who moved into a cave in 1812 near present Spencer Middle School. The following spring Tanner erected a log cabin, which stood until about 1855.

Points of interest include the Robey

Theater, which opened in 1907 and is said to be the longest continuously operating movie house in the U.S.; and Heritage Park on Market and Bowman streets, featuring a restored 1920 schoolhouse; an early 1900s oil derrick; a depot museum; and a B&O caboose. Spencer annually hosts West Virginia's Black Walnut Festival and the Tour de Lake Mountain Bike Race at nearby Charles Fork Lake. On February 15, 2001, ground was broken for a new $1.35 million two-story municipal building at the corner of Church and Court streets. Spencer was traditionally known for the Spencer State Hospital, which closed in 1989. Roane County High School is located at Spencer. The town also includes the former home of singer and songwriter Tom T. Hall, who worked briefly as a disc jockey at WVRC-AM during the early 1960s, and the Heck Mansion on State Route 14, which is listed on the National Register of Historic Places. Griffith and Washington parks feature lighted tennis and basketball courts with playground and picnic areas, and Washington Park has an Olympic-sized swimming pool.

Larry Sonis
Arlington, Texas

Anne Spencer

Poet Anne Spencer was born Annie Bethel Bannister in Henry County, Virginia, February 6, 1882. In 1886, she and her mother moved to Bramwell, Mercer County, where she spent most of her childhood and adolescent years. There, she acquired a deep appreciation for nature and established lifelong and endearing relationships. The surrounding countryside nourished her creativity and influenced her writing.

Spencer received a normal-school education at Virginia Theological Seminary in Lynchburg, Virginia, from which she graduated in 1899. From the time of her enrollment until she graduated, Spencer spent summers and holidays in Bramwell. Between 1899 and 1901, Anne Spencer taught school in Maybeury and Elkhorn, West Virginia, before moving permanently to Lynchburg.

During the Harlem Renaissance, Spencer's writing was discovered by the novelist James Weldon Johnson, who in 1920 was responsible for the publication of her poem, "Before the Feast at Shushan," in *The Crisis,* the magazine of the National Association for the Advancement of Colored People. Thereafter, her poetry was applauded by critics including H. L. Mencken. Spencer's poetry was published in numerous anthologies and periodicals, including the first edition of the prestigious *Norton Anthology of Modern Poetry*.

Anne Spencer continued to write until just before her death, July 27, 1975, her last poem titled simply "1975." Her Lynch-

burg home was listed on the National Register of Historic Places in 1976.

Brucella Wiggins Jordan
Ansted

J. Lee Greene, *Time's Unfading Garden: Anne Spencer's Life and Poetry*, 1977.

Spencer State Hospital

Authorized by the legislature in 1887 to relieve overcrowding at Weston State Hospital, Spencer State Hospital was opened July 18, 1893. Its connected brick buildings, a quarter-mile in length, were sometimes referred to as the longest continuous brick building in America. Situated west of U.S. 33 on 184 acres donated to the state by Roane County, Spencer State Hospital remained in operation until June 1989. Spencer's original charter was to care for the insane and others suffering from mental illness, although its mission broadened at times to include diseases such as typhoid fever, tuberculosis, and pneumonia.

The hospital's farms were used for a dairy herd, hogs, chickens, vegetable gardens, and woodlands, providing food for patients and staff. The hospital also had its own water and power supplies. An additional 295 acres west of the facility was used for patient recreation and the hospital dam's watershed. The institution maintained an open-door policy within the hospital grounds, with patients free to come and go, but a fence was erected around the hospital to separate patients from the town. Between 1973 and 1976, the administrative building was torn down and replaced. In October 1993, the city of Spencer held an auction to dispose of most of the equipment left behind when the hospital closed. A local employer, Monarch Rubber Company (later Armacell), agreed to take possession of the Spencer State Hospital whistle so that residents could continue hearing its regular blasts morning, noon, and night.

Larry Sonis
Arlington, Texas

"Spencer State Hospital," in Jim Comstock, ed., *The West Virginia Heritage Encyclopedia*, 1976.

Sports

West Virginians of all ages play sports, from youth soccer, softball, and basketball leagues, through the Senior Olympics. More than 135 high schools compete annually in 18 championship events under the control of the Secondary School Activities Commission (SSAC). Colleges and universities in West Virginia compete at all three levels of National Collegiate Athletic Association competition. West Virginia University (Big East Conference) and Marshall University (Conference USA) field teams at the NCAA Division I level. Fourteen of the smaller public and private colleges and universities make up the West Virginia Intercollegiate Athletic

High school basketball is a popular sport.

Conference (WVIAC), which plays at the Division II level.

Professional sports include minor league teams in both baseball and hockey. Charleston, which has the state's richest tradition in baseball, is the home of the West Virginia Power, previously the Alley Cats of the South Atlantic League (Class A). The Princeton Reds and the Bluefield Orioles are long-time rivals in the Appalachian League (Rookie class). The Wheeling Nailers are members of the East Coast Hockey League. Huntington hosted a hockey team, the Huntington Blizzard, from 1993 to 2000.

Organized sports began to develop in the U.S. between 1870 and 1920. The highlight event of that era in West Virginia was an 1880 bare-knuckle boxing match between Joe Goss, the recognized champion of America, and Paddy Ryan, the challenger. Boxing was illegal, and the fight was held in Colliers, a tiny railway village in Brooke County, which was easy to get to and to get away from and conveniently close to two state lines. Ryan won the 86-round fight.

The first golf club in America was organized at Oakhurst near White Sulphur Springs in 1884. The club was established when a golf course was built on the estate of Russell Montague to entertain visiting Scottish friends. The club held Christmas Day championship matches for at least the next six years. Later, White Sulphur Springs remained the center of golf in the state when the famous Old White course was built in 1913 on the grounds of the Greenbrier resort.

College football began in West Virginia in 1891, when the team from WVU hosted Washington & Jefferson College of nearby Pennsylvania. The visitors, coming by steamboat up the Monongahela River, defeated WVU, 72-0. By the early 1900s, almost every college in the state had a football team.

During the 1920s, the explosion of spectator sports and school sports nationally also was felt in West Virginia. Three colleges began to play a national football schedule. In 1919, WVU amassed an 8-3 record, losing in close games to Pitt and to the famous "Praying Colonels" of Centre College. WVU's Ira Rodgers became the first state player to be named to the All-American team. In 1924, West Virginia Wesleyan defeated such powers as Navy (10-7), Syracuse (7-3), and Kentucky (24-7). Davis & Elkins capped an excellent 1928 season with a 7-0 win over WVU and a narrow 2-0 victory over Navy.

College and high-school competition became organized during the early 1900s. The SSAC began in 1916, although a basketball champion had been crowned since 1914 when Elkins beat Wheeling, 28-13. The segregated black high schools of the West Virginia Athletic Union held their first tournament at West Virginia State College in 1924, with Wheeling Lincoln defeating Kimball 25-24 for the championship. The WVIAC began in 1924 and the following year named Marshall as the first football champion.

Minor league baseball solidified with the development of the "farm system" during the 1920s and 1930s. The Middle Atlantic League and the Mountain States League had teams in six West Virginia cities. Amateur baseball thrived in the smaller towns and coal camps, with teams sponsored by mines and other companies. The emergence of unions and the Depression began to cut into the number of teams.

During World War II and the post-war era, West Virginia prospered and sports peaked. In football WVU dominated the Southern Conference and played in the 1953 Sugar Bowl; Marshall played in the 1949 Tangerine Bowl; and Morris Harvey College participated in the 1954 Cigar Bowl in Tampa.

Several college basketball teams reached national prominence. The 1942 WVU team won the National Invitation Tournament, defeating Western Kentucky 47-45 in the final game. Marshall, coached by the legendary Cam Henderson, won the National Association of Intercollegiate Basketball Championship in 1947 with a 73-59 win over Mankato College of Minnesota. West Virginia State College romped through an undefeated season in 1948, winning the regular season and tournament championships in the segregated Colored Intercollegiate Conference. Earl Lloyd and Bob Wilson from that team were later among the first African-Americans to play in the National Basketball Association. West Virginia State and Bluefield State integrated the previously all-white WVIAC in 1955. In

2004, the Mountain State University Cougars basketball team won the NAIA Division I national championship, defeating California's Concordia University, 74-70.

The 1950s and 1960s were the golden age of WVU basketball. Led by All-Americans Mark Workman (1952), Rod Hundley (1957), Jerry West (1958 and 1959), and Rod Thorn (1962 and 1963), the Mountaineers were a perennial Top 10 team. The apex occurred in 1959, when West led the Mountaineers into the NCAA finals against the University of California. Despite a heroic 28-point performance by West, WVU lost 71-70 on a last-second shot. Coach Gale Catlett took charge of Mountaineer basketball in the last quarter of the century, leading the team from 1978 until his retirement in the 2001–02 season.

West Virginians were also prominent in golf during the 1950s. Sam Snead, the long-time pro at the Greenbrier, was a dominant player on the PGA Tour, winning 84 tour victories from 1936 through 1965. The 1964 U.S. Amateur Championship Final matched two West Virginia golfers. Bill Campbell of Huntington (a 15-time West Virginia amateur champion) beat Ed Tutwiller of Charleston (an 11-time West Virginia amateur champion) in the match play finals.

Through the years individual athletes have stood out in worldwide competition. In the Olympics games as of 2004, West Virginians had won 11 gold medals, three silvers, and three bronzes since the Paris games of 1924, when Mountaineers first participated. In 1984, two West Virginians won top honors at the Olympics. Fairmont native Mary Lou Retton became the first American woman to win a gold medal in gymnastics, and Ed Etzel of Morgantown was a gold medalist in rifle competition. In 1992, James Jett of Shenandoah Junction was a member of the U.S. sprint relay team that captured a gold medal. Jett, who went on to a successful professional football career as a receiver for the Oakland Raiders, earned the distinction of being the fastest man in the NFL. St. Albans native Randy Barnes won the gold medal in the shot put at the 1996 Olympics after being a silver medalist in 1988.

In 1972, federal legislation mandated school and college athletic programs for girls and women. By the late 1970s, school athletic programs doubled as women's teams were begun and the WVIAC and SSAC added championship events for women.

By the mid-1980s and the 1990s, college football in West Virginia became nationally competitive. In 1980, Don Nehlen was hired as the football coach at WVU. In 1988 and 1993, he had perfect 11-0 regular season records. Although bowl losses to Notre Dame in the Fiesta Bowl and Florida in the Sugar Bowl elimi-

nated national championship hopes, those seasons marked the reestablishment of WVU football in the annual Top 25 rankings. Don Nehlen retired as coach of the WVU Mountaineers in 2000. His last game was a victory over Mississippi in the Music City Bowl.

In 1970, a tragic plane crash killed almost all the Marshall football team and coaches in the worst air disaster in college sports history. From the ashes of the crash Marshall rose to dominate NCAA Division I AA football in the 1980s and 1990s. The Thundering Herd played in seven national championship games, defeating Youngstown 31-28 in 1992 and Montana 49-29 in 1996 for national championships. In 1997, Marshall made the jump from Division I AA to Division I A, joining the Mid-American Conference (MAC). That year, led by Coach Bob Pruett, who has become Marshall's winningest football coach, the Thundering Herd became the most successful first-year I A team in history with a record of 10-3. In the years since, Marshall won four straight MAC championships and three victories in the Motor City Bowl. Marshall joined Conference USA in 2005.

C. Robert Barnett
Marshall University

Doug Huff, *Sports in West Virginia*, 1979; Kent Kessler, *Hail West Virginians!*, 1959.

Alexander Spotswood

Alexander Spotswood (1676–1740), lieutenant governor of Virginia (1710–22), had a keen interest in exploration and land speculation which inspired him to lead an expedition westward in 1716. He hoped that English settlements west of the Blue Ridge would prevent the French and Indians from expanding into the Valley of Virginia.

Spotswood crossed the mountains with a group of about 50 gentlemen and several servants, Indians, and rangers. He journeyed up the Rappahannock River and crossed over the Blue Ridge by way of Swift Run Gap into the Shenandoah Valley. Here he and his men claimed the land for King George I. Robert Brooke, a member of Spotswood's expedition and the king's surveyor general, made the first scientific observations west of the Allegheny Mountains, supposedly in present Pendleton County.

Governor Spotswood gave each one of his fellow adventurers a small golden horseshoe, some set with valuable stones, to commemorate the event, and they are remembered as "Knights of the Golden Horseshoe." Each horseshoe was inscribed "Sic juvat transcendere montes" (Thus, let him swear to cross the mountains). To encourage the study of state history, geology, geography, industry, flora and fauna, and natural resources this tradition is continued today with the presentation of a golden horseshoe to West Virginia students achieving the highest scores in their county on a test prepared by the West Virginia Department of Education.

It is believed that within a year of the Spotswood expedition settlements were established in the Shenandoah Valley. Spotswood, described as one of the "most notable" of Virginia's colonial governors by historian Virginius Dabney, is buried on his country estate near Yorktown, Virginia.

Cathy Hershberger Miller
State Archives

Spring Hill Cemetery

Spring Hill Cemetery, located on a hilltop overlooking the city of Charleston, is noted for its Victorian design and sweeping vistas of the Kanawha Valley. The burial complex is the largest in West Virginia. It totals about 175 acres, including the Mt. Olivet Catholic Cemetery, the B'nai Israel Jewish Cemetery, and the privately owned Mountain View.

Although a few farm family graves date back to 1818, Spring Hill was formally dedicated as the Charleston municipal cemetery in 1869. Intended by its Victorian planners as a park-like place for quiet walks and meditation, the roads and walkways offer breathtaking views of downtown Charleston and the capitol. Civil engineer A. J. Vosburgh, who had come to West Virginia during the Civil War, designed the elaborate Old Circle, which is the centerpiece of the cemetery's historic section. Geometric patterns distinguish Vosburgh's plan, including a quatrefoil feature that resembles a flower when seen from above.

Before Spring Hill, Charleston's first public burying ground was located on the old James River & Kanawha Turnpike, next to the Kanawha River near the present intersection of Kanawha Boulevard and Elizabeth Street. Some of the more affluent citizens arranged for their family graves to be moved from the old graveyard up to Spring Hill.

Spring Hill's classic monuments tell visitors of the history of the Kanawha Valley. Epitaphs abound, as do virtually every style of memorial from Greco-Roman to art deco. Judge James H. Brown's 35-foot obelisk is the grandest, towering above its neighbors in the Old Circle. Erected in 1900, the shining granite monument needed more than 20 horses to pull it up the cemetery hill. The cemetery's 1910 mausoleum, done in the Moorish architectural style, contains more than 500 crypts. As Charleston grew, Spring Hill gradually acquired adjoining property. Two of the larger tracts were the Wehrle and Jefferies farms in 1926.

Spring Hill holds the grave sites of many prominent citizens. They include Dr. John Peter Hale, historian, inventor,

Ornate monuments at Spring Hill Cemetery.

and businessman; Governors Atkinson, Wilson, and MacCorkle; Judge George W. Summers; and historian Julius DeGruyter. U.S. Sen. John Kenna lies within the Mt. Olivet Catholic Cemetery; merchant Moses Frankenberger in the B'nai Israel; and Gov. Walter Eli Clark of Alaska rests in the private Mountain View.

Civil War veterans are interred throughout the cemetery. Graves of the famous Confederate Kanawha Riflemen abound, and Union veterans are not uncommon, especially the 7th West Virginia. A few years ago a group of ten or more unknown Civil War graves were discovered and a monument was placed on the site in the Old Circle. Veterans of virtually all of the nation's other wars rest throughout the complex, and on Memorial Day many flags attest to their service.

In 1998, the management of the cemetery was placed in the hands of a nine-member board of commissioners. Various trees, shrubs, and flowers grace the landscaped grounds, and the natural setting has attracted numerous species of wildlife, making the cemetery a key nature preserve and greenspace.

See also Cemeteries, Charleston

Richard A. Andre
Charleston

Jim Sprouse

Judge James Marshall "Jim" Sprouse, born in Williamson, December 3, 1923, was educated at St. Bonaventure College and at Columbia University law school, where he received his law degree in 1949. He studied international law as a Fulbright Scholar at the University of Bordeaux in 1950. He served in the army infantry during World War II. He was assistant general counsel for the Displaced Persons Administration in the Truman administration and served with the Central Intelligence Agency from 1952 to 1957. He practiced law from 1957 to 1972.

Sprouse established a record of public service as a reform-minded liberal. He was elected chairman of the state Demo-

On top of West Virginia at Spruce Knob.

cratic Party in January 1965 and served until 1968, when he ran for governor, losing to Republican Arch A. Moore Jr. by 12,785 votes. He was elected to the state Supreme Court of Appeals in 1972 and resigned August 27, 1975. He was a candidate for governor again in 1976 but lost the Democratic primary to eventual governor John D. Rockefeller IV. Sprouse was appointed by President Jimmy Carter as a judge of the 4th Circuit United States Court of Appeals in 1979. He took senior status on October 31, 1992, and retired from the court in 1995. Sprouse served as state chairman of Charlotte Pritt's 1996 campaign for governor. He divided his last years between Charleston and Monroe County, dying July 3, 2004.

Tom D. Miller
Huntington

Spruce Knob

Spruce Knob, 4,861 feet at its summit and the highest point in West Virginia, is located in Pendleton County on Spruce Mountain. The mountain, a dominant feature of the West Virginia highlands which averages 4,500 feet for its 12-mile length, peaks at the knob.

Rocks at Spruce Knob are of Pottsville sandstone, dating from the Pennsylvanian age over 300 million years ago. This hard conglomerate rock is resistant to erosive weathering. Although glaciers did not reach West Virginia, the cold climate left its mark in high areas including Spruce Knob. Special rock patterns such as circles, stripes, and polygons, which are associated with cold weather freeze-thaw cycles, can still be found.

Spruce Knob was once covered with a dense forest of red spruce growing in a foot-thick layer of humus soil. Early settlers burned the original forest for pasture. Subsequent timbering and severe fires burned the rich soil and denuded the forest. In 1921, Spruce Knob was acquired by the U.S. Forest Service. The red spruce forest has grown back but regeneration has been slow, perhaps due to soil loss and harsh climate.

Spruce Knob has a climate similar to that of Newfoundland. The high altitude and cold climate have affected the vegetation, which is the Appalachian extension of the boreal or northern coniferous forest. In some areas on Spruce Knob the weather is so harsh that trees grow only shrub-high. Some plants growing around Spruce Knob, including dwarf cornel, are similar to those growing in Canada. Wildflowers include bleeding heart and fireweed. The knob offers harsh conditions for wildlife, but red fox, snowshoe hare, bobcat, ruffed grouse, raven, dark-eyed junco, and other birds are found there.

The parking area at Spruce Knob has a half-mile Whispering Spruce Trail leading around the knob with its panoramic views. The observation tower on the trail provides spectacular views. Blueberry and huckleberry bushes are abundant. Spruce Knob Lake is a 20-minute drive from the knob. Constructed as a 25-acre fishing lake in 1952, it is the state's highest lake. The lake is a good place to look for herons, kingfishers, and beavers.

Norma Jean Kennedy-Venable
Morgantown

Norma Jean Venable, *Seneca Rocks and Spruce Knob,* 1992.

Spy Rock

Spy Rock is a natural landmark with historical significance. It is located on U.S. 60, the old James River & Kanawha Turnpike, 18 miles east of Hawks Nest and about midway between Charleston and Lewisburg. The large rock ledge provided a lookout along the turnpike toward Sewell Mountain. In the early 19th century the rock was used by both Indians and whites.

During the Civil War as both Union and Confederate forces marched along the turnpike, Spy Rock was again used for observation. On September 15, 1861, in the aftermath of the Battle of Carnifex Ferry, Union forces under the command of Gen. Jacob Cox who were pursuing the defeated Confederates occupied the area of Spy Rock. During September and October, Union and Confederate forces skirmished along the turnpike as they moved into position for a battle at Sewell Mountain. Cox established his headquarters at Spy Rock and called for reinforcements from Gen. William Rosecrans to face Gen. Robert E. Lee, who had occupied Sewell Mountain.

Record rainfall in late October turned the turnpike into a sea of mud, and nothing could move. Misery, sickness, and hunger began to pile up more casualties than any fighting. At Spy Rock, Cox with more than 500 sick decided to fall back to Gauley Bridge, while Lee retreated eastward to Meadow Bluff.

See also Battle of Carnifex Ferry, Robert E. Lee

David Bard
Concord University

Harley O. Staggers Sr.

Congressman Harley Orrin Staggers Sr. served in the U.S. House of Representatives for 32 years, longer than any other West Virginian. He represented the Second District, which at the time stretched from Monongalia County to Monroe County and included the Eastern Panhandle, making it the largest congressional district east of the Mississippi River.

Staggers was born August 3, 1907, in Keyser. As a boy, he worked for a Keyser sawmill and for the B&O Railroad. After his graduation from Virginia's Emory & Henry College in 1931, he tried several professions, including farmer, teacher, and football coach. He was elected Mineral County sheriff in 1937. After his term, he entered the navy, ending World War II as a lieutenant commander. He was elected to Congress on his first attempt in 1948, defeating the incumbent Republican, Melvin Snyder of Kingwood.

Staggers was a staunch supporter of Presidents Kennedy and Johnson in the 1960s and became chairman of the powerful House Interstate and Foreign Commerce Committee in 1966. In his final term, he sponsored the Staggers Rail Act, which effectively deregulated the nation's railroad industry. Proponents of the act say it has strengthened the industry; detractors say it has led to consolidation and given rail users fewer choices.

Staggers retired from Congress in 1980; after a two-year gap, his son, Harley Staggers Jr., was elected to the seat. The younger Staggers held the seat until redistricting carved up the district in 1992.

Harley O. Staggers Sr. died August 20, 1991, and is buried in his native Mineral County.

Greg Moore
Charleston Gazette

Cherrill A. Anson, *Harley O. Staggers: Democratic Representative from West Virginia*, 1972.

Stanaford, Battle of

At dawn on Wednesday, February 25, 1903, Deputy U.S. Marshal Dan Cunningham, Raleigh County Sheriff Harvey Cook, and Howard Smith of the Baldwin-Felts Detective Agency led a posse of armed men into the village of Stanaford near Beckley. They were after striking

After the Battle of Stanaford

"I took the short trail up the hillside to Stanford [*sic*] Mountain. It seemed to me as I came toward the camp as if those wretched shacks were huddling closer in terror. Everything was deathly still. As I came nearer the miners' homes, I could hear sobbing. Then I saw between the stilts that propped up a miner's shack the clay red with blood. I pushed open the door. On a mattress, wet with blood, lay a miner. His brains had been blown out while he slept. His shack was riddled with bullets.

"In five other shacks men lay dead. In one of them a baby boy and his mother sobbed over the father's corpse. When the little fellow saw me, he said, 'Mother Jones, bring back my papa to me. I want to kiss him.'

"The coroner came. He found that these six men had been murdered in their beds while they peacefully slept; shot by gunmen in the employ of the coal company.

"The coroner went. The men were buried on the mountain side. And nothing was ever done to punish the men who had taken their lives."

—Mary Harris "Mother" Jones *The Autobiography of Mother Jones* (1925)

miners who, on the previous Saturday, had stopped Cunningham, John Laing, and Baldwin-Felts agents from serving court papers. On Tuesday, strikers had marched from Fayette County and, after an incident involving Baldwin-Felts guards at mines near Beckley, held a rally at Stanaford. The same day, Cunningham with a 30-man posse returned to Raleigh County, where he joined forces with Sheriff Cook's armed volunteers and the Baldwin-Felts men.

Both the striking miners and the posse spent the night in Stanaford. The miners were ambushed the next morning when they arose. Shots were fired into G. W. Jackson's home, where he, his wife, four small children, and eight miners were sleeping. When the firing ceased, there were three dead men in Jackson's house; one from a bullet in the back of his head. The Jacksons were an African-American family, and the men killed there were black. Elsewhere, three white miners were fatally wounded.

When a Raleigh County jury questioned the actions of the posse and its leaders, Federal Judge B. F. Keller exonerated the posse, ruling that they were acting to arrest men who had violated his August 1902 injunction and who had been indicted by a federal grand jury in January 1903.

The Battle of Stanaford was a concluding episode in the 1902 New River Coal strike, and a precursor of bloodier events to follow during the West Virginia Mine Wars.

See also Dan Cunningham, Mine Wars

Lois C. McLean
Beckley

Ken Sullivan, ed., *Goldenseal Book of the West Virginia Mine Wars*, 1991; Jim Wood, *Raleigh County, West Virginia*, 1994.

Miles Stanley

Union leader Miles Clark Stanley was one of the notable figures in 20th-century West Virginia labor history. Born in Dunbar, October 2, 1924, Stanley began his career as a machinist. After serving in the army artillery in World War II, he became a steelworker. He rose rapidly in his local union, where he was elected president in 1947. In 1954, Stanley was elected president of the Kanawha Valley Industrial Council, and three years later he was selected the first president of the West Virginia Labor Federation AFL-CIO, a position he held until his untimely death at age 49.

Recognizing the critical need for work force development in the region, Stanley organized in 1964 the AFL-CIO Appalachian Council to conduct manpower training programs in the 12 Appalachian states. In 1965, Stanley was selected as personal assistant to AFL-CIO President George Meany. In that capacity Stanley organized a federation of labor for the state of Hawaii and was adviser to the International Labor Federation. Stanley served in Washington with the national union before returning to West Virginia in 1967. He retained his position as West Virginia AFL-CIO president throughout. He was credited with making the West Virginia AFL-CIO one of the most influential political forces in the state. Acknowledged as a champion of human rights, Stanley was an adviser to the U.S. Civil Rights Commission.

Miles Stanley died May 3, 1974. The state headquarters building of the West Virginia AFL-CIO is named in Stanley's honor.

See also Labor History

Fred A. Barkey
Marshall University Graduate College

Star House

During the Great Depression, the "star house" in Hinton, a private residence, was known as a place where hungry transients could find nourishment. It is said that hobos riding trains through the busy railroad center of Hinton passed along the word that a free meal was available at the star house at any time of day or night.

The house was acquired by W. B. and Ida Skaggs in 1913, and they owned it through the Depression. It remained in the Skaggs family for many years.

Distinguished by a prominent five-point star in the gingerbread trim of the gable-end facing the street, the star house is now part of the Hinton National Historic District. Most residential development in Hinton occurred during the Victorian and Craftsman periods of American architecture. There is an abundant use of gingerbread, or pieced and patterned decorative wood trim. Built in the late 19th century on a narrow lot at 114 James Street, the star house is a Victorian vernacular two-story frame structure with clapboard siding and front porches on both tiers, a common feature in Hinton residential architecture. The star house faces Hinton's town square in which are located the War Memorial Park, Memorial Building, post office, and the red brick county courthouse.

See also Hinton

Stephen D. Trail
Hinton

Buddy Starcher

Buddy Starcher, born Oby Edgar Starcher on March 16, 1906, near Ripley, had a long career in country music. His father taught him to play rhythm guitar for square dances. Although his first radio appearances were in Baltimore, he first became popular in 1933 at WCHS Charleston, and later at WMMN Fairmont and WPDX Clarksburg.

Beginning in the early 1950s, Starcher appeared on television in Miami, Florida, and Harrisonburg, Virginia. In January 1960, he returned to Charleston and started an early morning program on WCHS-TV that enjoyed high ratings for six years. Buddy's wife, Mary Ann, Sleepy Jeffers, and others contributed to the television show's success. This program added to Starcher's popularity in West Virginia and gained him a new generation of fans in nearby states.

In 1946, Starcher cut his first recordings on Four Star, including his best-known composition, "I'll Still Write Your Name in the Sand," which became a hit in 1949. Afterward, he recorded for Columbia, Deluxe, Starday, Heart Warming, and Bluebonnet. In 1966, his recitation "History Repeats Itself" for Boone Records became a country and pop hit, causing Decca to buy the master and rush an entire Starcher album onto the market. Aspiring newcomers appreciated Starcher's encouragement, including the late star Keith Whitley.

Starcher died in Harrisonburg, Virginia, November 2, 2001.

Abby Gail Goodnite
University of Rio Grande

Ivan M. Tribe, *Mountaineer Jamboree: Country Music in West Virginia,* 1984.

Samuel W. Starks

Born in Charleston, in 1866, Samuel W. Starks became the first African-American in the United States to serve as a state librarian. Appointed to the position in 1901 by Governor White, Starks served until his death.

Outside West Virginia, Starks was best known for his work with the Knights of Pythias. A charter member of Charleston's Capitol City Lodge No. 1, Starks served 16 years as the grand chancellor of West Virginia's black Pythians. In 1897, he was elected as the supreme chancellor, the lodge's highest national office. He was reelected several times.

Under Starks's leadership, the national membership grew from 9,000 to 146,869, including 38,000 in the Order of Calanthe, the Pythians women's department. From his position as supreme chancellor, Starks promoted a concept of entrepreneurial unity and encouraged lodges to use their collective purchasing power to invest in property. To facilitate this in West Virginia, the lodge incorporated the Pythian Mutual Investment Fund in 1902.

Starks died April 3, 1908. In 1911, the Pythians erected an obelisk at his grave site in Spring Hill Cemetery in Charleston. His home in Charleston was placed on the National Register of Historic Places in 1992.

Ancella R. Bickley
Charleston

Starland Theatre

Located on U.S. 52 at Big Four, four miles east of Welch, Starland Theatre opened on July 6, 1950. In 1949, Weldon Cook of Man and Robert Livingston Russell Sr. of Bluefield formed the Cook-Russell Theater Corp. and built Starland. When completed, their drive-in had speakers for 450 cars and featured six different movies a week. Starland was McDowell County's first drive-in and one of 14 movie theaters in the county. In the mid-1950s, 76 drive-ins operated in West Virginia.

As with many drive-ins, the Starland was geared toward family entertainment, with a merry-go-round, children's train, miniature golf course, playground, and snack bar. In the early years, it was open every day from late March through mid-November. The most popular night of the season was the Fourth of July, when up to 600 cars squeezed into the drive-in, and spectators parked on U.S. 52 and at the nearby airport to view the Starland fireworks display.

McDowell County's declining coal employment and falling population, and the coming of television and later videocassettes, determined Starland's fate. The theater closed on May 31, 1986. In the 1970s and '80s, most of the other drive-ins throughout the state also closed. By 1997, fewer than 10 were open.

In May 2000, the property was sold to the county's domestic violence organization, Stop Abusive Family Environments (SAFE). The nonprofit group built low-income housing on the site, now named Starland Heights.

Michael Keller, "Going to the Drive-in," *Goldenseal,* Summer 1995.

Blaze Starr

Dancer Blaze Starr (1932–).

Entertainer Blaze Starr, "Queen of the Strippers," was born as Fanny Belle Fleming, April 10, 1932, on a farm near Wilsondale in Wayne County. One of 10 children, she left home at age 14, worked at a Logan drive-in restaurant, then caught a bus for Washington, where she found a job in a donut shop.

When a date took her to a burlesque club in Baltimore, she told the owner she could do a better job than any of the girls he had dancing. The next night she showed up to prove it. Impressed, owner Sol Goodman became her manager and rechristened her "Blaze Starr." Soon she was the star attraction at Goodman's Two O' Clock Club, part of "The Block," Baltimore's famous red-light district.

In 1959, while performing in New Orleans, she met colorful Louisiana Gov. Earl Long, the brother and successor of the populist Huey Long. Starr and Earl Long began an affair that, when it became public, horrified his friends and delighted his foes. When Long died of a heart attack, Starr returned to burlesque, bought the Two O' Clock Club from Goodman and became a Baltimore legend. Over time, she changed her style, going from vamp to comedienne. When she retired in the mid-1980s she complained that burlesque, forced to compete with pornographic movies, had become too raunchy for her tastes.

In 1974, she wrote an autobiography with co-author Huey Perry of Huntington. In 1989 the book was filmed as *Blaze*, a movie starring Paul Newman as Earl Long and Lolita Davidovich as Starr.

James E. Casto
Herald-Dispatch

Blaze Starr and Huey Perry, *Blaze Starr: My Life as Told to Huey Perry*, 1974.

State Colors

The state colors of West Virginia are blue and "old gold." The state was without official colors until its centennial year, when these colors were adopted March 8, 1963, by a concurrent resolution of the Senate and House of Delegates.

Previously, in most instances where a color scheme for the state was desired, West Virginia University's colors of blue and old gold had been used. The use of the university's colors had become almost uniform throughout the state, and many people considered them the official state colors even before the 1963 legislative action. The colors, according to the widely used Pantone color matching system, are PMS 286 (blue) and PMS 124.

State Fair

Thousands of people pour into the Greenbrier Valley every August to attend the State Fair of West Virginia in Fairlea. The origins of this multi-day event date back to smaller fairs at various locations in the 1800s. The fair now known as the West Virginia State Fair was founded by cattlemen of the Shorthorn Association as the Greenbrier Valley Fair in 1921. The state fair has other roots, as well, particularly including the big fair held on Wheeling Island in the late 19th and early 20th centuries. The Wheeling fair variously identified itself as the West Virginia State Fair and the West Virginia Exposition and State Fair and apparently was discontinued due to the periodic flooding of the island.

The 1921 Greenbrier Valley Fair was held at the site of today's fairgrounds and introduced the annual tradition of competitive exhibits from boys' and girls' 4-H agricultural clubs. Admission was 75 cents for adults that year. An old railroad track was cleared and a half-mile horse racetrack built by the Shorthorn Association. Stables, barns, a grandstand, a stage, and an exhibit building were erected over the next few years. The state legislature proclaimed the event the State Fair of West Virginia in 1941, but the fair actually is owned by local stockholders, not the state. The governor and the commissioner of agriculture are ex officio members of the 13-member board of directors.

The gates to the newly designated state fair did not reopen until 1946, after the conclusion of World War II. Because of an outbreak of measles, many parents came to the fair that year without their children.

Nationally known acts have been appearing at fairs in the Greenbrier Valley since at least 1892, when a daredevil equestrian show gave daily performances. Since the inception of the State Fair of West Virginia, entertainers have included Roy Rogers and Dale Evans, Johnny Cash and June Carter Cash, Tom Jones, Dolly Parton, Randy Travis, the Beach Boys, Alison Krauss, and others.

Today's fair continues the decades-long traditions of competitive and educational agricultural exhibits, harness racing, carnival rides and games, musical shows, fireworks and other entertainment, and concessions.

The State Fair museum is housed in Meriluco, a cottage constructed in 1928 by the Meadow River Lumber Company of Rainelle. Named from the first two letters of each word in the company's name, Meriluco was built as a sales showcase for house trim, moldings, and flooring. Over the years, the building served such functions as the fair's post office and the Greenbrier County Sheriff's headquarters at the fair. Meriluco, listed on the National Register of Historic Places in 1997, is one of many attractions on the State Fair grounds.

Belinda Anderson
Asbury

State Farm Museum

The West Virginia State Farm Museum, located on State Route 62 four miles north of Point Pleasant, is a replica of an early rural community. Begun in 1976 by Walden Roush, a retired educator, with only one building and a few farm implements, today the 50-acre site showcases 31 reconstructed buildings, including four original log structures that were moved and rebuilt. Visitors see the furnished Mission Ridge one-room schoolhouse from the 1870s and a doctor's office with period drugs and equipment. A log church recognized as the first Lutheran church west of the Allegheny Mountains is used for services. There are a blacksmith shop, country store, veterinary office, barbershop, a post office, carpenter shop, and a newspaper building with printing presses from 1895.

The State Farm Museum has large farm equipment, both horse-drawn and tractor-drawn, such as tractors, thrashers, and plows. There is a Corliss steam engine. There are numerous household items, including appliances and other furnishings. The Morgan Museum, a curiosities collection begun in Putnam County in 1905 by Sidney Morgan of Winfield and later moved to the State Farm Museum, includes a collection of stuffed birds and animals, including a two-headed calf, a golden eagle, and a Belgian draft horse. The farm includes a two-acre pond and acres of crops which are planted and harvested using 19th-century equipment and methods. A stage and picnic shelter accommodate public events.

Schools from West Virginia, Ohio, and Kentucky visit the museum for their study of Appalachian culture. Funded by the West Virginia Department of Agriculture and a small annual grant from the Mason County Commission, the West Virginia State Farm Museum is a nonprofit organization.

Olivia Miller
Memphis, Tennessee

State Flag

The West Virginia state flag was adopted by the legislature on March 7, 1929.

It is a simple design. The state's coat of arms, which is the front side of the state seal, is emblazoned in color in the center of the flag. Above the seal is a red ribbon lettered "State of West Virginia," and a wreath of rhododendron surrounds the lower part of the seal. The legislature stipulated that the proportions of West Virginia's flag be the same as those of the flag of the United States. The white field of the flag is bordered on four sides by a strip of blue. When used for parade purposes, the flag is trimmed with gold-colored fringe on three sides.

West Virginia's first state flag was authorized by the legislature on January 28, 1864, and individual flags were presented to each of the state's military regiments before the end of the Civil War. Although the details of the flag had not been designated by the legislature, all the regimental flags were similar. They were made of dark blue silk with a golden fringe. One side featured the state seal. The other side featured the national coat of arms, an eagle with a shield protecting its breast, arrows in its right talons and an olive branch in its left.

The details of the flag were apparently not standardized until the early 20th century. In 1904, officials addressed the question of a flag for the West Virginia building at the St. Louis World's Fair. A commission recommended a design that had a white field with a sprig of rhododendron flowers and leaves in the center. The state seal and the motto "Montani Semper Liberi" were on the reverse side. On February 24, 1905, the legislature adopted the design. The flag was impractical because the sides were different and the letters and the colors showed through. For the 1907 Jamestown Exposition the faults were corrected, but the flag proved expensive to produce.

Flags, unofficially made for West Vir-

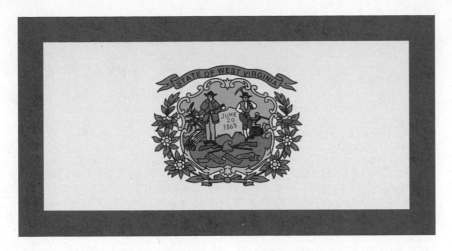

ginia's 1913 Semi-Centennial celebration at Wheeling, featured a design similar to today's flag, with a wreath of rhododendron curving upward and partly enclosing the state seal. In 1929, the legislature stipulated the proportions and design of the flag that is still in use.

State Forests

West Virginia has nine state forests encompassing a total of 78,884 acres. Seneca State Forest, the first state forest, was established in 1924. Most of the others were added in the 1930s, as state authorities worked with the Civilian Conservation Corps and other federal agencies active in that period. Two state forests were added in the 1940s, and Calvin W. Price State Forest, the youngest, was created in 1953.

State forests are similar in many respects to state parks but usually have less in the way of accommodations for visitors and are managed under a different philosophy. Whereas state parks are managed for recreation as well as conservation, the state forest system operates under a multiple-use concept including timber production (except at Kanawha State Forest, where commercial logging is prohibited by law), watershed management, wildlife management, esthetics, and recreation. State forests are important for forestry research, and for demonstrating forest management practices. State forests are open to hunting and fishing in season, subject to local regulations. Game food and cover conditions are improved as recommended by wildlife biologists from the Division of Natural Resources, working with foresters from the Division of Forestry.

The principal public attraction of state forests is for day-use and vacation recreation, as well as hunting and fishing. Cabins are available at four state forests. Tent-trailer campsites and recreational facilities are available at all of them.

Historically, the state forests of West Virginia were managed entirely by the West Virginia Division of Forestry, but their administration was transferred to the Department of Natural Resources Parks and Recreation Section in January 1978. The two agencies continue to have concurrent jurisdiction over state forests and work closely through a memorandum of understanding that was prepared the same year.

Robert Beanblossom
Division of Natural Resources

State Parks

West Virginia has a well-developed state park system. The system's 34 state parks, nine state forests, and the Greenbrier and North Bend rail trails offer hiking, biking, horseback riding, fishing, boating, downhill and cross-country skiing, camping, golfing, indoor and outdoor swimming, and nature activities. Guests can camp, occupy rustic or deluxe rental cabins, or stay in fine air-conditioned lodges with restaurants.

The state park system began in January 1925 when the Game and Fish Commission purchased 4,560 acres of second-growth timberland in Pocahontas County to develop as a wildlife and timber preserve. Later this became Watoga State Park, now West Virginia's oldest and largest state park with more than 10,000 acres.

In 1927, the legislature acted on the commission's recommendation to acquire additional areas for state parks. The goal was to secure these scenic places before they were exploited commercially and to advance the cause of conservation in West Virginia. In the years since, the state park system has evolved into a network encompassing more than 200,000 acres for recreational use by the public. Areas important to the state's history were also preserved, restored, and incorporated within the system, including Cass Scenic Railroad, Blennerhassett Island, and Droop Mountain Battlefield.

An important aspect in the formative years was the development of the "park concept," the guiding policies for preserving outstanding scenic areas and protecting them from exploitation. State park system chiefs who served from 1936 through 1948 (T. M. Cheek, Linn Wilson, R. B. Griffith, Watt Powell, and Kermit McKeever) are credited with originating these policies.

In building the early parks, the state relied extensively upon the federal work programs of President Franklin Roosevelt's New Deal. The Civilian Conservation Corps (CCC) built the backbone of the early system, and the Works Progress Administration (WPA) also provided laborers. Out-of-work engineers, planners, and architects employed in various federal programs during the Depression planned and built Babcock, Lost River, Watoga, Hawks Nest, and Grandview state parks. Skilled stone workers and hundreds of young men were housed in CCC camps often located on future park sites. Their work is still evident in these parks and still in productive use.

Family vacation cabins in natural settings received high priority in the early years, and in the 1950s planning and development of campgrounds began. In 1953, West Virginia became one of the first states to finance development of park facilities by selling bonds. This method of developing parks substantially changed traditional concepts. Building resort lodges and campgrounds became high priorities as much more money became available through the bond issues.

The rapid development and growth of the tourism industry made it necessary to develop concrete guidelines for park development. The 1958–68 Park Master Plan was the first to deal with the many facets of park usage, and is the foundation for many current practices. Later the conservation philosophy was modified to accommodate the goal of profitability in park operations, and state parks were grouped under the state's commerce bureau from 1985 to 1994. As Stonewall Jackson Lake Resort State Park was developed at century's end, another new method was pioneered as a private developer supplied funds for park facilities.

Early in the 21st century, West Virginia is a prime recreation and vacation mecca for residents and visitors alike. The state park system is a hub of the state's rapidly growing tourism industry, an important part of the West Virginia economy.

Donald R. Andrews
University of Charleston
Where People and Nature Meet: A History of West Virginia State Parks, 1988.

State Plants and Animals

West Virginia has named several plants and animals as official symbols of the state. These include the great rhododendron (state flower); cardinal (state bird); black bear (state animal); sugar maple (state tree); brook trout (state fish); golden delicious apple (state fruit); monarch butterfly (state butterfly); and honeybee (state insect).

The species chosen for such distinction are those especially familiar or meaningful to West Virginians. Often the process begins with a vote by the schoolchildren of the state, followed by governmental action in Charleston. Thus the great rhododendron, our first official state species, was designated in 1903 by a resolution of the legislature, preceded by a vote of the schoolchildren and a recommendation by Governor White. The state tree and state bird were named through a similar process in 1949. The honeybee, West Virginia's state insect, was the most recent species honored, in 2002.

Some of the species chosen, such as the cardinal, are widely beloved and the official symbol of many other states in addition to West Virginia. Designation as a state plant or animal is only symbolic, indicating the interest and affection of West Virginians, and carries no protection the plant or animal is not otherwise entitled to.

See also Black Bear, Brook Trout, Cardinal, Golden Delicious Apple, Rhododendron, Sugar Maple

State Police

Jackson Arnold, first State Police superintendent.

The West Virginia State Police was created in 1919 in response to violence arising from attempts to unionize the state's coal miners and the resulting resistence by the coal operators.

Governor Cornwell was the leading advocate of a state police force. He found sheriffs and constables ineffective, having to face periodic reelection and tending to take sides in labor struggles. Coal companies paid some deputy salaries in coalfield counties, and deputies moonlighted as private security guards. The private guard system angered workers and labor leaders, as did use of the National Guard during the bloody Paint

A state policeman recalls strike duty

"For the first year or two I was in the State Police, I didn't think there was any other kind of police work except strike duty. I was on strike duty in '24 and '25. That was in the northern part of the state, Morgantown, Clarksburg, and Fairmont, through that area. You were in the middle, you stayed in the middle, you know. The idea was to keep the peace, and of course the miners broke the peace a lot. They claimed we favored the companies, which of course I don't think we did. I didn't particularly favor any company. A matter of trying to keep down trouble. They would jump on people, beat them up—people who'd gone back to work.

"They put two of us to handle 500 strikers. They'd line up, up and down the road— we'd be up there, they'd beat somebody up down the road. We'd get back down the road, well, they'd beat somebody up up the road. Where we'd just left. So that's the way it was. Just kept you busy, you know, working almost day and night. Blowed up tipples, and they did everything. They blowed down power lines—I remember one power line they blowed down at Kilarm. That line was whipping around just like a snake. I think it was 22,000 volts. . . .

"They had a picket line, and then they ranged around and went to people's houses, even. Threaten 'em, and all of that. Some people's houses were burned down, you know. There was a lot of difficulty at times. Sometimes you had to hit somebody on the head with a riot stick."

—State Police Capt. Charles W. Ray *Goldenseal* (1980)

Creek-Cabin Creek strike of 1912–13. Besides, the process of reestablishing the National Guard after World War I did not begin until April 1921.

Labor leaders ardently opposed the police bill, but the legislature passed it anyway. Cornwell signed it into law on March 31, 1919, effective June 29. The agency was designated the Department of Public Safety. The governor appointed Jackson Arnold, grand-nephew of Gen. Thomas J. "Stonewall" Jackson and former executive officer of the 1st West Virginia Infantry, as first superintendent. Departmental headquarters was located in Charleston, and there were two field companies, with an authorized strength of 125 men. The first trooper, Sam Taylor, enlisted on July 24.

Colonel Arnold faced daunting obstacles in recruiting, uniforming, and equipping the force. Newly enlisted troopers were required to bring their World War I uniform when reporting.

Company B, commanded by Capt. James R. Brockus, was based in Williamson, the county seat of Mingo County and a center of labor troubles. The July 1920 United Mine Workers strike there continued at varying levels until October 1922. Duty in "Bloody Mingo" eventually absorbed 90 percent of State Police strength, and three troopers were killed there. The State Police also helped defend Logan County against the miners' armed march during the 1921 Battle of Blair Mountain.

Following the trouble in the south and a period battling strike violence in the state's northern coalfields, the force shifted its focus to rural law enforcement and traffic safety. Because there were few paved roads in West Virginia before World War I,

the State Police initially rode horses. But in September 1929 traffic regulation and road law enforcement became a State Police responsibility. Highway patrol quickly became the agency's major function, so automobiles and motorcycles replaced the troopers' horses. The force was also heavily engaged in enforcing Prohibition and in fighting gambling, prostitution, and illegal drug distribution.

State Police field structure grew to four companies in 1921, shrank to two in 1933, expanded to four again by 1936, and remained there until the Turnpike Division was added in 1954. A Criminal Investigation Bureau was organized in 1933 under later Capt. Charles W. Ray, to centralize arrest and conviction records. The Highway Safety Bureau and the forensic chemistry laboratory were added in 1936, and a Radio Division in 1939. FBI Director J. Edgar Hoover cited the West Virginia State Police as one of the nation's four leading law enforcement agencies in 1936.

Military leave caused a 40-percent shortfall in State Police strength during World War II. Ordinary crime and highway traffic declined during the war, but these duties were offset by war-related work such as personnel background investigations, military convoy security, and assisting selective service and ration boards.

After the war, the State Police realized a long-cherished goal by opening its academy at Institute, near Charleston, in October 1949. Captain Ray was the first director. Department headquarters relocated from the capitol building to new facilities in 1970. The first African-American trooper enlisted July 10, 1967, and resigned May 15, 1969. On May 16,

1977, the first female member enlisted, serving until 1997.

Today, the West Virginia State Police functions under the Department of Military Affairs and Public Safety.

As of 2005, there were 629 uniformed members, with 325 civilian employees performing administrative, communications, forensics, and other support tasks. In a major 1998 reorganization, "troop" designations replaced former companies. Today there are seven field troops, including one for the West Virginia Turnpike, one designated as the Bureau of Criminal Investigations, and one for Headquarters. There are 60 State Police detachments statewide.

See also State Police Academy

Merle T. Cole
Crofton, Maryland

Merle T. Cole, "Birth of the West Virginia State Police, 1919–1921," *West Virginia History*, Fall 1981; Cole, "Martial Law in West Virginia and Major Davis as 'Emperor of Tug River,'" *West Virginia History*, Winter 1982; Cole, "The Department of Special Duty Police, 1917–1919," *West Virginia History*, Summer 1983.

State Police Academy

The West Virginia State Police Academy, located at Institute, west of Charleston, began operating in 1949. Capt. Charles W. Ray, generally regarded as the father of the academy, had unsuccessfully sought funds from State Police superintendents during the 1930s. About 1943 or 1944, Col. H. Clare Hess, who had been appointed superintendent in 1941, agreed to find the necessary funds to get the project under way. Ray found the hilltop location overlooking Institute, consisting of 24 acres purchased from Kanawha County for a little more than $3,200. The original appropriation of $60,000 was obtained during the administration of Colonel Hess in the 1946 legislative session, and an additional $60,000 was received under Col. William E. Burchett in 1947.

Construction began in 1948. Although Captain Ray was the first director of the academy, the building was not completed before he retired June 30, 1949. The first class to be trained at the new facility began October 2, 1949, and graduated December 20, 1949, with 20 State Police cadets. Today the academy provides training for city police and deputy sheriffs from throughout West Virginia, as well as Division of Natural Resources officers. New state troopers are trained in the Cadet Program and later participate in annual in-service training.

The academy was extensively expanded and remodeled in the 1960s and 1970s. Building A, a new dormitory, was completed in 1969, and Building C, with additional dormitory space, offices, and a dining hall was completed in 1976. The earlier dining hall was demolished and a modern facade added to Building B, an original building, which today houses female students and a medical clinic. There are five classrooms in building A and C, and an outdoor pistol range.

See also State Police

Sharen Deitz
Charleston

State Seal

The Great Seal of West Virginia was adopted by the legislature on September 26, 1863. The seal, which has remained unchanged, was designed by Joseph H. Diss Debar. Two and a half inches in diameter, the state seal symbolizes principal pursuits and resources of West Virginia. It is used on official documents and for a variety of other purposes.

On the front or obverse side, the seal, which is also the state's coat of arms, bears the legend "State of West Virginia" along with the motto "Montani Semper Liberi." A large ivy-draped rock bearing the date of West Virginia's admission to the Union in the center of the seal symbolizes strength. At the left, representing agriculture, stands a farmer clothed in hunting garb with his right arm resting on plow handles and his left arm supporting a woodsman's ax. A sheaf of wheat and a cornstalk are next to him. On the right, to symbolize industry, stands a miner with a pickax. On his left is a partly seen anvil on which rests a sledgehammer. In front of the rock are two crossed rifles, upon which rests a Phrygian cap, or cap of liberty, indicating that freedom and liberty were won and will be maintained by the force of arms.

The seal was designed and adopted with two sides, but only the front or obverse is in common use. The reverse is encircled by a wreath of laurel and oak leaves. A wooded mountain is on the left and a slope with a log farmhouse on the right. On the side of the mountain is a representation of the Tray Run Viaduct, as an engineering feat of the time, and a train about to pass over the viaduct. A factory, fronted by a river with boats, a derrick and a shed, and a meadow with sheep and cattle grazing indicate the leading characteristics and products of the state. Above, the sun emerges from the clouds, and the rays of the sun contain the Latin phrase "Libertas E Fidelitate," which means "Freedom and Loyalty."

The reverse of the seal, which is intended to be used when the seal was suspended in the manner of a medal with both sides visible, is also the governor's official seal. The obverse of the state seal is featured in the center of the West Virginia flag.

See also Joseph H. Diss Debar, Montani Semper Liberi

E. M. Statler

Ellsworth Milton Statler, founder of the Statler Hotels chain, was born in Somerset County, Pennsylvania, October 26, 1863. A few years later, his family moved to Bridgeport, Ohio, across the Ohio River from Wheeling. As a teenager, Statler began to work as a night-time bellboy at Wheeling's leading hotel, the McLure House. He quickly rose to night desk clerk and then day clerk, helping to manage the hotel. He remained at the McLure House for nearly 20 years, leaving to open a restaurant in Buffalo, New York, in 1895.

Statler's dream was to have his own hotel, and in 1908 he opened the Buffalo Statler. He then established a chain of middle-class hotels that set standards for comfort and cleanliness at modest prices. Statler Hotel rooms had private baths, as well as radios and telephones. Statler eventually opened hotels in Boston, Cleveland, Detroit, and New York. Following his death, his widow led the company in building hotels in Washington, Dallas, Pittsburgh, Hartford, and Los Angeles. In 1954, the chain was purchased by Conrad Hilton for $111 million.

E. M. Statler died in New York City, April 16, 1928. In 1984, he was inducted into the Wheeling Hall of Fame.

Statuary

A 1992 survey identified 130 outdoor sculptures in 36 of West Virginia's 55 counties. These sculptures include free-standing figures, equestrians, busts, and bas-reliefs, shaped or assembled from

This Monroe County Confederate is a typical Civil War monument.

bronze, steel, aluminum, stone, concrete, marble, granite, ceramics, and wood.

Some are monuments to people and events before the formation of West Virginia. The frontier struggle is represented in a life-sized sculpture of Chief Logan at the Mingo County courthouse; one of the Indian fighter Levi Morgan at the Wetzel County courthouse; a similar statue of an unnamed Mingo warrior at Mingo Flats; one of another Mingo on Wheeling Hill; and one of Buckongahelas and his dying son in Buckhannon. An 84-foot obelisk with a stone sculpture of a frontiersman, dedicated in 1909, memorializes the Battle of Point Pleasant.

Remembrances to the soldiers and key figures of the Civil War are present throughout the state, with 15 freestanding statues to the Union and the Confederacy. Erected in the decades after the war, these comprise most of the oldest outdoor sculptures in the state. The Civil War statues are often near county courthouses. An exception is Monroe County's Confederate statue, which stands in a field outside the county seat.

A notable equestrian bronze sculpture of Confederate Gen. Thomas J. "Stonewall" Jackson on a polished granite base at the Harrison County courthouse is located within sight of the general's Clarksburg birthplace. There is a fine statue of Jackson afoot on the capitol grounds in Charleston. A Lincoln statue, "Lincoln Walks At Midnight" by Fred Martin Torrey, is located at the front of the capitol overlooking the Kanawha River. A Union infantryman marches to the west of Lincoln, in the place opposite Jackson.

World War I soldiers are also well represented in our state's monuments. All of these figures are life-sized and made of bronze, metal, or marble or other stone. There are nine of these monuments, with some cast as soldiers in action. A unique memorial to the Americans who gave their lives in World War I is a seven-foot bronze allegorical figure of an American airman with large bird-like wings on the campus of Linsly School in Wheeling.

Until recently there were few monuments to the soldiers of World War II and later conflicts. A statue placed in Huntington in 1980 memorialized veterans from World War II and later wars. The West Virginia Veterans Memorial in Charleston, one of the state's finest monuments, includes four figures representing a marine from the Vietnam War, a World War I soldier, a World War II sailor, and an aviator from the Korean War. Statues outside the nearby Cultural Center depict a coal miner, firefighter, and police officer.

There is a fine frontiersman statue on the east side of the capitol complex, representing the mountaineer spirit. A bronze rendition of the WVU Mountaineer mascot stands in front of the Mountainlair student center in Morgantown. There is an over-sized statue of U.S. Chief Justice John Marshall near the library at Marshall University.

The oldest sculpture found in the 1992 survey was a nine-foot wood carving of Patrick Henry, the governor of Virginia when Monongalia County was formed in 1776. Dedicated August 20, 1851, this statue was made to stand on the cupola of the courthouse in Morgantown and remained there until 1890, after which it was stored indoors. The oldest sculpture that has stood outdoors since its installation is the Soldiers and Sailors Monument in Wheeling. Erected by the Soldiers Aid Society of Wheeling in 1880 and dedicated May 30, 1883, the 16-foot stone monument incorporates three life-size carved figures. The monument has been moved to various locations and now resides in Wheeling Park.

Notable artists are represented in the state's outdoor sculpture, including the sculptor of Mount Rushmore, Gutzon Borglum. Borglum created an eight-foot bronze statue of Collis P. Huntington, founder and builder of the Chesapeake & Ohio Railroad and the founder of Huntington. The statue stands in Huntington's Heritage Village.

Charles C. Coffman
Cottageville

Staunton-Parkersburg Turnpike

The Staunton-Parkersburg Turnpike was an integral part of Virginia's early state road system, launched by the Internal Improvement Fund Act of 1816 and the Turnpike Act of 1817, which provided for the financing and organization of canal and turnpike companies.

The Staunton Turnpike was originally chartered by the General Assembly in 1817 with an anticipated terminus at Sistersville. This was amended in 1826, substituting Parkersburg at the mouth of the Little Kanawha River. The preliminary survey was made in 1823 by Col. Claudius Crozet, Virginia's chief engineer, who had once served in Napoleon's army and who had later taught at West Point. The road was laid through one of the most remote and sparsely populated sections of the state, conditions that delayed completion of the project.

Begun in 1831 at Staunton, seat of Augusta County, construction was almost immediately halted due to money problems. Serious work did not begin until the project was placed under direct control of the Board of Public Works in 1841. The road was not completed until 1847, when it finally reached Parkersburg. Today, U.S. 250 and State Route 47 generally follow its path.

While both the Staunton-Parkersburg Turnpike and the Northwestern Virginia Turnpike from Winchester to Parkersburg were intended by state authorities to compete with the National Road to the north, they themselves were rivals from the beginning. Unlike the Northwestern, which was placed under the authority of a state board of directors, the Staunton-Parkersburg route came under the supervision of each county it crossed. Thus it was subject to the whims and selfish interests of competing factions along the way. This was the principal reason the road was completed several years later than the Northwestern Turnpike, though the Staunton Road was also plagued with financing problems, labor and contractor difficulties, resistance to eminent domain, and intensely rugged terrain.

Portions of the road were open to wagon travel west of Staunton in 1841, and construction was completed to Beverly on the Tygart Valley River by 1843. With additional borrowing authorized by the Board of Public Works, the middle section was finished to Weston, on the West Fork River, in 1845. Delays in completing bridges over the Tygart, West Fork and Hughes rivers and their tributaries delayed full use of the turnpike. The western section from Weston to Parkersburg was completed in 1847, though travel from origin to terminus was impossible until 1850 when the last bridges were finished.

For the first time in the history of Virginia, a continuous road from Richmond to the Ohio River via Staunton was available. The historic highway is now commemorated by the Staunton-Parkersburg Turnpike National Scenic Byway, which follows much of the original route.

See also Claudius Crozet, Highway Development

Philip Sturm
Ohio Valley University

Charles H. Ambler, *A History of Transportation in the Ohio Valley*, 1931; I. F. Boughter, "Internal Improvements in Northwestern Virginia," Ph.D. dissertation, University of Pittsburgh, 1930.

Eleanor Steber

Singer Eleanor Steber, born in Wheeling, July 17, 1914, attended the New England Conservatory of Music, studied voice in New York City, and won the Metropolitan Opera radio auditions in 1940. In celebration of her achievements, Eleanor Steber Day was proclaimed in Wheeling, May 1, 1940, highlighted with an "Eleanor Steber Special" B&O railroad car and the first of 16 annual homecoming concerts, attended by Governor Holt.

She made her debut at the Met as Sophie in Richard Strauss's *Der Rosenkavalier*. Steber performed for USO shows, bond drives, and at veterans' hospitals during World War II; sang at the 1944 Democratic and 1948 Republican national conventions; and became a regular on NBC's *The Voice of Firestone* on radio and later television. In 1948, she commissioned and premiered Samuel Barber's *Knoxville: Summer of 1915*, for soprano and orchestra, and created and recorded the title role in Barber's opera *Vanessa* ten years later. Steber was Marie in the Met's first performance of Alban Berg's *Wozzeck*, was the first American to sing at Bayreuth after World War II as Elsa in Wagner's *Lohengrin*, and performed in musical productions of *Where's Charley?* and *The Sound of Music* at Lincoln Center.

She remained a leading soprano with the Metropolitan Opera until 1966, singing 404 performances of 33 roles, made more than 100 recordings and concertized around the world, returning to West Virginia for recitals and concerts with the Wheeling Symphony. Steber taught at the Cleveland Institute and Juilliard School and established the Eleanor Steber Music Foundation to aid young singers. She died in Langhorne, Pennsylvania, October 3, 1990, and was buried at the Greenwood Cemetery in Wheeling.

H. G. Young III
WVU Parkersburg

Eleanor Steber with Marcia Sloat, *Eleanor Steber: an autobiography*, 1992.

Steel Industry

On June 11, 1884, the West Virginia steel industry was born when the state's first Bessemer converter began operation at the Riverside Iron Works in Wheeling. Before that, Wheeling had been the center of West Virginia iron production, making so many nails from wrought iron that it became known as the "Nail City." By 1890, the state's iron production dropped to 39,223 tons; an insignificant amount compared to the 220,615 tons of steel produced that year.

Demand for canned food exploded during the 1890s, and the cans were made from tin plate, a thin-rolled steel coated with tin. The McKinley Tariff of 1890 included duties on tin plate that helped American manufacturers compete with British imports. Seeing an opportunity, local nail plants including Wheeling Corrugating and La Belle added tin plate mills between 1893 and 1895.

Unlike most of the industry, tin plate production required highly skilled steelworkers. Rolling thin gauges of steel required a keen eye and many years of experience, and the operation was still done by hand as workers passed square sheets back and forth through the rollers. Because of their scarcity, they were able to remain unionized under the Amalgamated Association of Iron, Steel, and Tin Workers long after the union's infamous defeat in Homestead, Pennsylvania, in 1892. A series of mergers between 1898 and 1900 brought several West Virginia properties including the tin mills of the La Belle Company under the ownership of the U.S. Steel Corporation. U.S. Steel methodically drove the union out of its plants, and Wheeling remained one of the last bastions of the steel union until a failed strike in 1909. Despite all the changes between 1880 and 1909, the number of West Virginia steelworkers hovered between 3,500 and 4,500 during those years.

In 1909, Ernest Weir expanded the Phillips Sheet and Tin Plate Company from Clarksburg to a 105-acre property near Holliday's Cove, now Weirton. Originally a small tin plate plant, the company would change its name to Weirton Steel and become a fully integrated steel operation, making finished products from raw materials. Company officials added a blast furnace in 1919, a melting shop and a blooming mill the following year, and another sheet plant in 1923.

With the growth of Weirton Steel and increased production during World War I, employment in the state's steelworks and rolling mills jumped from 5,348 in 1914 to 11,630 in 1919. In 1920, the incorporation of Wheeling Steel brought together the Whitaker-Glessner, Wheeling Iron & Steel, and La Belle companies, including facilities in both West Virginia and Ohio. In 1929, Weir formed the National Steel Corporation with Weirton Steel as its flagship. Meanwhile, U.S. Steel shut down six of its nine sheet plants in the Wheeling district.

In 1926, Weirton Steel was among the first companies to contract for the construction of a continuous sheet mill that would produce strips of steel a mile long. This made the hand-rolled square sheets obsolete. Wheeling Steel was not far behind, completing work on its strip mill in 1928. The era of hand-rolling sheet steel in the Wheeling district came to an end in 1943, and some 1,500 skilled rollers and their crew members had to look for jobs in other departments.

The 1930s and 1940s witnessed the rise of industrial unions in West Virginia. The old Amalgamated Association found new life, and steelworkers organized locals at both Wheeling Steel and Weirton Steel to compete with the companies' employee representation plans, known as company unions.

In the fall of 1933, Mel Moore and Billy Long led a strike at Weirton Steel that ended when Weir agreed to hold union elections. Then Weir canceled the elections, and his decision was upheld in federal court. In 1937, the National Labor Relations Board charged the company with unfair labor practices, but nonetheless employees voted overwhelmingly for the company union, the Employee Security League.

Thereafter Weirton Steel worked hard to create loyalty among its employees, and keeping employment levels high throughout the Great Depression went a long way toward that end. When the NLRB again found Weirton Steel guilty of unfairly promoting its company union in 1941, the Weirton Independent Union was created, but it, too, was declared a violation of federal labor law in 1950. That year a supervised election was held, and the Independent Steelworkers Union defeated the United Steelworkers of America by a margin of three-to-one. Weirton Steel employees never again went on strike. In the meantime, the United Steelworkers organized several locals at Wheeling Steel and signed a contract there in the spring of 1937.

During World War II, both companies converted their production lines to help with the war effort. Weirton Steel produced a large percentage of the nation's howitzer shells, helped the atom bomb project with high-precision metal-finishing, and rolled bronze and magnesium for weapons. Wheeling Steel did its part by expanding operations, producing bombs and steel drums, and breaking production records.

From the start of the war into the early 1960s was the boom time for the steel industry. Employment in West Virginia's steelworks grew from just under 13,000 in 1929 to over 15,000 by 1947. During that time West Virginia steelworkers saw their annual wages jump from an average of $1,900 to over $3,000. By 1950, primary iron and steelworkers in West Virginia numbered 22,596, with 19,181 of them in the Northern Panhandle, 1,911 in the Kanawha Valley, and 542 in the Parkersburg area. In the decade to follow, steelworkers won benefits such as pensions, health insurance, and vacation time.

The 1960s witnessed the first signs of decline. Feeling the effects of foreign competition, Wheeling Steel struggled to remain profitable. In 1968, it merged with another flagging company, Pittsburgh Steel, and became Wheeling-Pittsburgh Steel.

Both Wheeling-Pittsburgh and Weirton Steel embarked on modernization programs. Both installed basic oxygen furnaces in the 1960s, but they lagged behind European and Japanese steel producers in adopting the new technology. Weirton Steel installed continuous casters in the 1960s to further streamline production. In 1981, Wheeling-Pittsburgh began construction of its continuous casters, and the following year the employees sacrificed vacation time, holidays, and a scheduled wage increase to help finance the modernization program.

During the 1980s, the West Virginia steel industry teetered on the brink of extinction. In 1983, after National Steel announced that the Weirton plant might be shut down, workers approved a novel employee stock ownership plan to save the mill. In 1985, saddled with nearly $400 million in debt, much of it from modernization costs, Wheeling-Pittsburgh filed for bankruptcy. It emerged from bankruptcy a profitable company in the early 1990s, but global circumstances again put the local companies in peril.

In 1998, following currency devaluations in South Korea and Russia, cheap foreign steel flooded the U.S. market, and Wheeling-Pittsburgh Steel, Weirton Steel, and the steel unions lobbied to curb the imports. With mixed results from Washington, the companies found themselves in dire straits. Wheeling-Pittsburgh again filed for bankruptcy in 2000, followed by Weirton Steel in 2003. Employment dropped to levels not known since before World War I, with Weirton Steel and Wheeling-Pitt operating with greatly reduced work forces. In 2004, Weirton Steel was bought by the International Steel Group and later sold to Mittal Steel of the Netherlands. During these difficult times, steelworkers, both active and retired, faced uncertainty regarding pensions and health insurance.

See also Weirton Steel, Wheeling Steel Corporation

Lou Martin
West Virginia University

David T. Javersak, *History of Weirton, West Virginia*, 1999; James B. Lieber, *Friendly Takeover: How an Employee Buyout Saved a Steel Town*, 1995; Earl Chapin May, *Principio to Wheeling, 1715–1945: A Pageant of Iron and Steel*, 1945.

Adam Stephen

General Adam Stephen, a physician who rose rapidly to military and political prominence in Western Virginia, was born in Scotland in 1721 and lived in Martinsburg. He shared command of the frontier defenses with George Washington during the French and Indian War,

his reputation surviving the disasters of Fort Necessity and the Braddock campaign. Called to service in the Revolutionary War as a full colonel in the 4th Virginia Regiment, he was commissioned for meritorious service at Trenton as brigadier and then major general in the Continental Army. When serious errors of judgment at the 1778 Battle of Brandywine brought his military career to an abrupt close, Stephen returned to land development, medicine, and politics. Stephen played a key role in persuading the Virginia Convention to ratify the U.S. Constitution.

Stephen, who had recently moved to the area, was largely responsible for the creation of Berkeley County in February 1772, and the establishment and naming as county seat the town of Martinsburg in October 1778. He assured the town's orderly development by laying off in lots and sections 130 acres of land obtained from Col. T. B. Martin, for whom the town was named. Stephen, who served as Berkeley County's first sheriff, died July 16, 1791. His Martinsburg home, a local landmark, was named to the National Register of Historic Places on October 15, 1970.

See also Berkeley County, Martinsburg
Dallas B. Shaffer
WVU Potomac State College

James McNeil Stephenson

Lawyer, politician, and banker James McNeil Stephenson was born November 4, 1796, in Fayette County, Pennsylvania, the eldest child of Edward and Elizabeth Dils Stephenson. He came to Wood County at the age of two with an extended kinship group made up of both the Stephenson and Dils families.

In 1821, Stephenson and Henry Logan opened a tanyard at Fourth and Market streets in Parkersburg. Stephenson studied law while continuing to work as a tanner and became a successful land lawyer. He was elected as the second president of the Northwestern Bank of Virginia, forerunner of the Parkersburg National Bank, now United Bank.

In 1829, Stephenson married Agnes Miller Boreman, sister of Arthur I. Boreman, later the first governor of West Virginia. They were the parents of six children. Stephenson and Arthur Boreman shared a Parkersburg law practice for many years.

Stephenson represented Tyler, Wood, Ritchie, and Doddridge counties in the Virginia House of Delegates from 1839 to 1848. His particular interest was in improvements to benefit Western Virginia. He supported the Staunton-Parkersburg Turnpike, the Northwestern Virginia Turnpike, the James River & Kanawha Canal, the Northwestern Virginia Railroad, and the Little Kanawha Navigation Company. His political influence was evi-

denced by the fact that the Northwestern Turnpike and the Staunton-Parkersburg Turnpike converged in front of his mansion, Oakland. Stephenson helped to make Parkersburg a transportation center and regional entrepot through his tireless efforts in behalf of turnpike and railroad development and river navigation improvements.

Stephenson died April 16, 1877, at his home in Parkersburg. Oakland mansion, still a local landmark, is on the National Register of Historical Places.

Philip Sturm
Ohio Valley University

Sternwheel Regatta

The Sternwheel Regatta, Charleston's end-of-summer festival, started in 1971. That year, 12-year-old Nelson Jones, son of a prominent river family, approached Mayor John Hutchinson to suggest a race between five sternwheelers on Labor Day on the Kanawha River. Prodded by his secretary, Henrietta Cook, Hutchinson embraced the concept. Cook, herself a devoted river person, remained a major force behind the festival for many years.

Within two years, the boat races had expanded to a two-day festival centered around Charleston's downtown levee. It continued to evolve as organizers added music, fireworks, food vendors, a distance run, and numerous land-based activities. By the early 1980s, the Regatta had stretched to a week. It subsequently burgeoned to 10 days, attracting thousands of local people as well as river lovers from other states. In 1989, more than 50 boats converged on Charleston.

But the event wasn't without problems. Over the years, there was controversy over beer sales, a source of considerable revenue. Some felt crowds had become too raucous and beer sales were restricted. In 2000, festivities were scaled back to an extended weekend. Sternwheelers docked along barges moored in the Kanawha, dwarfed that year by a special guest, the grand *Delta Queen*. The legendary riverboat had made several appearances at the annual festival. Participation by sternwheelers was less in following years, and the races were discontinued in 2003.

Kay Michael
Charleston

William E. Stevenson

William Erskine Stevenson of Parkersburg, born in Warren, Pennsylvania, March 18, 1820, was West Virginia's third governor. As a young man, he became an apprentice cabinet maker in Pittsburgh. In 1856, he was elected as a member of the Pennsylvania legislature. However, he moved to Wood County, (West) Virginia, before his first term ended and bought a farm.

As the Civil War approached Stevenson

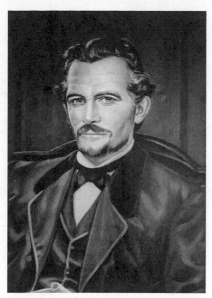

Governor William E. Stevenson (1820–83).

was a strong believer in the Union. While advocating for the cause, he was indicted by a Parkersburg grand jury for "circulating an incendiary document entitled *Helper's Impending Crisis*." He never did go to trial. Stevenson represented Wood County at the first constitutional convention of 1861. After the state of West Virginia was created, he served in the first state senate. He was elected senate president for three of the five years he was in the legislative body.

In 1868, Stevenson was elected as the third governor of the new state. Stevenson, a Republican, beat out Johnson Newlon Camden, another Parkersburg man, by about 5,000 votes in the general election.

Stevenson was the first governor to have an office in Charleston. However, he occupied the new capitol for only about three months. As governor, Stevenson encouraged the legislature to build more roads to encourage economic growth. In addition, he stood for immigration, educational opportunities for blacks, and the right to vote for former Confederates and Southern sympathizers who had been disenfranchised following the war. He and some others believed, wrongly as it happened, that if the vote were restored the Southern sympathizers would join liberal Republicans in providing moderate government in West Virginia. The Flick Amendment passed during Stevenson's term, restoring the Southern vote and ushering in a long period of Democrat rule.

Stevenson lost his bid for a second term when he was defeated by Democratic candidate John J. Jacob in the general election of 1870. Shortly after Stevenson left office, he became involved in the publication of the *State Journal*, a weekly newspaper headquartered in Parkersburg. He published the newspaper

for approximately ten years until he sold it to A. B. White (who later became governor as well). After the sale, Stevenson became associated with the West Virginia Oil and Land Company.

Stevenson worked primarily in farming, journalism, and business. He died November 29, 1883, at the age of 63. The cause of his death was believed to be cancer. He left behind his wife, the former Sarah Clotworthy of Philadelphia, and two children (a son, Orlando, and a daughter, Carrye A.). He is buried in Riverview Cemetery, which is located in Parkersburg.

S. Shuan Butcher
Parkersburg

Bernard L. Allen, *Parkersburg: A Bicentennial History*, 1985; John G. Morgan, *West Virginia Governors*, 1980.

Stifel Fine Arts Center

Located at Edemar, the Stifel family mansion on the National Road in Wheeling, the Oglebay Institute Stifel Fine Arts Center is the headquarters for Oglebay Institute's fine arts department. Exhibits of works by local, regional, and national artists and craftspeople are displayed in the center's Hart Galleries. Art and Dance workshops and classes are also held in the century old mansion.

Edward W. Stifel Sr. (1869–1947) built Edemar (named for his children Edward, Emily, and Mary) out of brick, steel, and concrete. Completed in 1912, the 39-room structure was meant to be fireproof. Formal gardens, a tennis court, fish pond, picnic area, putting green, and a swimming pool were located on the grounds of the several-acre estate. Stifel was president and chairman of J. L. Stifel & Sons, a textile manufacturing firm established by his grandfather, Johann Ludwig Stifel (1807–81), in 1835. Edward Stifel also promoted the cause of air travel and spearheaded the effort to build an airport in the Wheeling area.

In 1976, the Stifel family deeded the estate to Oglebay Institute for use as a fine arts center. Although remodeled to house galleries, craft rooms, classes and offices, the mansion, with its grand central staircase, retains much of its original character. Edemar is listed on the National Register of Historic Places.

See also J. L. Stifel & Sons, Oglebay Park

Gerry Reilly
West Virginia Independence Hall

J. L. Stifel & Sons

J. L. Stifel & Sons, founded in Wheeling by German immigrant Johann Ludwig Stifel in 1835, was an important calico printing operation and one of West Virginia's longest-lived businesses, operated by four generations of the family until its closing in December 1957. For most of its history Stifel & Sons produced indigo-dyed prints

and drills for clothing manufacturers. The company took as its trademark a boot (the literal meaning of the German word "stiefel"), and the Stifel boot was found on products sold throughout the world. At its peak, the plant in North Wheeling produced 3.5 million yards of cloth per month. The company helped introduce the process of Sanforizing (a method to prevent shrinkage) to the textile industry.

During World War II, Stifel & Sons earned the coveted Army-Navy Production Award (the "E" Award) for its role in making fatigue and battle dress for the armed forces. In the late 1930s and early 1940s, Edward E. Stifel, the grandson of Johann Ludwig, spearheaded a movement to build the Wheeling-Ohio County Airport, which opened on November 1, 1946.

By the mid-1950s, foreign competition and a domestic recession drove Stifel into the red. The company merged with Indian Head Mills, but the merger could not forestall the closing of the plant on December 17, 1957. Company President W. Flaccus Stifel wrote: "The dyeing, printing, and finishing of cotton goods just could not be done economically and competitively under present conditions."

See also Stifel Fine Arts Center

David T. Javersak
West Liberty State College

David T. Javersak, *Stifel: An Historical Perspective of the Stifel Family in Wheeling, West Virginia*, 1988.

Stone & Thomas

The first Stone & Thomas Department Store opened in 1847 on Market Street in Wheeling, as the Bee Hive. It was owned by Jacob C. Thomas and Elijah J. Stone, who later married Thomas's sister. Renamed Stone & Thomas, the store and the company prospered for well over a century. Owned and operated by the same family for five generations, Stone & Thomas grew to become West Virginia's largest independent retailer and one of the top 75 independent retail store chains in the country.

After World War II, major expansion began under Wilbur Stone Jones, great-grandson of the founder, by acquiring stores and building new stores. In the next generation, Stone & Thomas became one of the largest family-owned department store chains in the country, under the joint leadership of Wilbur Stone Jones, Jr., and Edward C. Armbrecht, Jr., his brother-in-law.

By the late 20th century, Stone & Thomas had expanded its flagship store in Wheeling to 182,000 square feet. The chain entered the Charleston market in 1941, and in 1948 opened a fine new store in the heart of downtown. At its peak Stone & Thomas had 21 stores in West Virginia, Ohio, Kentucky, and Virginia, with more than 2,000 employees. It met the needs of generations of shoppers with broad assortments in apparel and home furnishings.

Stone & Thomas closed its landmark Charleston store as the city's shopping habits changed, and in 1997 moved into Charleston's Town Center Mall. In 1998 Stone & Thomas was sold to the Elder-Beerman Company of Dayton, Ohio. Elder-Beerman renamed the stores, and the familiar Stone & Thomas name disappeared from the region's commercial landscape.

Louise Corey Palumbo
Charleston

Stonecoal Lake

Stonecoal Lake is a 550-acre lake located in Lewis and Upshur counties between Weston and Buckhannon. The lake is an impoundment of Stonecoal Creek, a tributary of the West Fork. It is surrounded by the 3,000-acre Stonecoal Lake Wildlife Management Area. The lake was built in 1972 to provide water to the Allegheny Energy's coal-fired power plant in Harrison County.

The lake is well-known for its fishing, with smallmouth bass, muskellunge, walleye, crappie, sunfish, rainbow trout, golden trout, brown trout, and channel catfish. In 1997, Anna Marsh set a state record for weight when she caught a 50.37-inch, 49.75-pound muskellunge in Stonecoal Lake. In May of 2003, Glenn Boyd of Weston set a new state record for length when he caught a 52.7-inch, 38.5-pound muskellunge in the lake. Fishing accommodations are available for physically disabled people, and each end of the lake has a concrete boat ramp. Boats are restricted to motors of 10 horsepower or less. Camping in the area is not permitted, although a private campground is located near the headwaters of the lake.

The wildlife management area around the lake is predominantly covered with hardwood forest, although it also includes some areas of brushland. Game species include deer, turkey, squirrel, and waterfowl. Stonecoal Lake is privately owned. The wildlife management area and the lake are managed for recreational purposes by the Division of Natural Resources.

Kelly Winters
Bayville, New York

Stonewall Jackson Jubilee

The Stonewall Jackson Heritage Arts & Crafts Jubilee, a celebration of the heritage of Appalachia, features craft shows, old-time music, and historic reenactments. The annual four-day festival is held on Labor Day weekend at Jackson's Mill, near Weston. Started in 1974 as a gathering of craftspeople and musicians, the event has become a showcase of traditional products, entertainment, and exhibits.

With heritage crafts and music the focus of the event, more than 150 craftsmen exhibit, sell, and demonstrate their wares, and more than 100 musicians provide entertainment at the Jubilee. In addition to stage performances, musicians and singers gather throughout each day and evening for impromptu performances on the festival grounds. Many craftsmen and musicians, along with their families, stay on the grounds, returning year after year to create a summer reunion atmosphere.

Festival events include a fine arts exhibition, photo show, quilt show, needle arts show, pie-baking contest, and glass blowing and woodchopping demonstrations. The food features traditional Appalachian favorites of cornbread and beans, roasted corn on the cob, and blackberry cobbler, as well as pork and chicken barbecue.

The Jubilee is held on the 4-H state campgrounds at Jackson's Mill. The historic youth facility, which dates to 1921, occupies the farm where Stonewall Jackson lived as a boy. A Civil War reenactment and pioneer encampment provide Jubilee visitors with a glimpse of regional life in the 18th and 19th centuries. Guests may tour the 200-year-old McWhorter cabin and the old Jackson family mill, as well as Blaker's Mill, which was moved to the site in 1985 and has been restored to working order.

See also Jackson's Mill

Stonewall Jackson Lake

Stonewall Jackson Lake lies on the West Fork River in Lewis County just off Interstate 79 near Weston. The lake and adjoining state park and wildlife management area have become a major recreational attraction. The lake's additional purposes include flood control, streamflow and water-quality augmentation, and water supply.

The concrete gravity dam has an uncontrolled spillway and five sluices through the dam. Its overall length is 620 feet, with a maximum height of 95 feet above the stream. The dam became fully operational in 1988 and creates a lake of 2,650 acres with a drainage area of 102 square miles. The winter drawdown is only five feet, so the size of the lake in winter doesn't change significantly from summer. Fishermen and boaters enjoy the lake's 26-mile length and 82-mile shoreline. The reason for its impressive size is the irregular "V" shape of the lake created by the West Fork and Skin Creek drainages.

The lake is noted for its excellent fish habitat, the result of a large amount of standing timber that was left when the lake was created. The primary fishing attractions are largemouth bass and muskies, although there are also trout in the dam tailwaters, and crappie, bluegill,

and Kentucky spotted bass in the lake. Stonewall is the premier water in the state for trophy muskellunge of 40 inches and above. Fishermen also like the several miles of no-wake zones.

Stonewall Jackson State Park and Stonewall Resort offer a full range of conference and recreational facilities, including an 18-hole golf course designed by Arnold Palmer. The park and resort cover 1,833 acres. The U.S. Army Corps of Engineers leased the land to the state for 99 years, and the state in turn contracted with private firms to develop and operate the park and resort.

Stonewall is the southernmost facility in the Pittsburgh District of the U.S. Army Corps of Engineers. The building of the lake was controversial and vigorously opposed by many who had lived in the project area.

Skip Johnson
Sutton

Stony River

The Stony River drains an area of approximately 60 square miles in northeastern West Virginia. From its headwaters near the Grant-Tucker county line to its mouth at the corner of Grant and Mineral counties, it is 25.3 miles long. The Stony is a tributary of the North Branch of the Potomac River.

Thomas Jefferson's father, Peter Jefferson, was one of the early explorers of the region. Thomas Lewis, a member of Peter Jefferson's party, left an entry in his journal on October 14, 1746, describing the stream and its rugged environs as "sufficient to strike terror into any human creature."

Full settlement of this remote wilderness occurred much later, during the logging boom of the late 1800s. Henry Gassaway Davis, an industrialist and U.S. senator, was a major landowner. He established the region's first railroads, which brought in loggers to harvest the vast stands of spruce and northern hardwoods. Coal mining began about the same time.

The Stony River is dammed in two places, both near the headwaters. Stony River Reservoir was completed in 1913 by West Virginia Pulp & Paper Company (now MeadWestvaco) to provide low flow augmentation to the North Branch Potomac to ensure plenty of water for its downstream pulp mill. A few miles below the Stony River Reservoir, Mount Storm Lake was completed in 1965 by Virginia Electric Power Company, now Dominion Power.

The Stony River once contained a healthy population of native brook trout and associated cold-water species, but early discharges of mine waste and acid water ruined much of the river. Poor water quality in Mount Storm Lake initially prevented a viable fishery from being established there. However, improvement of discharges at active mine sites and increased alkalinity of the power station's effluent have led to the establishment of a warm-water fishery. Below the dam, the heated effluent prevents the establishment of a cold-water fishery, while mine drainage from Fourmile Run and other tributaries inhibits the establishment of warm-water aquatic life.

The water quality and fauna of Stony River have been studied intensively by biologists from the West Virginia Division of Natural Resources, West Virginia Department of Environmental Protection, and Dominion Power. These groups are working to restore the environmental damage that resulted from earlier exploitation of the area's rich natural resources.

See also Mount Storm Lake

Michael A. Arcuri
Department of Environmental Protection

Storer College

Storer College, a product of the Reconstruction Era following the Civil War, was established in 1867 in Harpers Ferry by the Freewill Baptist Church to educate freed slaves in the Shenandoah Valley. The college was supported by the U.S. Bureau of Refugees, Freedmen, and Abandoned Lands and endowed by John Storer of Sanford, Maine.

Storer College was integrated and coeducational from the start. Until the establishment of West Virginia State College in 1891, it was the only college open to African-Americans in West Virginia. Frederick Douglass served on the board of trustees of Storer College and spoke on campus in 1881.

In all, more than 7,000 students from many states and countries attended the private college over the course of its history. Storer's curriculum advanced with its students. At first, students of all ages learned the rudiments of religion, reading, and ciphering. Students later studied industrial training, domestic arts, religion, and education. Storer maintained rigorous academic standards. Its graduates helped to expand educational opportunities for black children in West Virginia. Others went on to careers in medicine, law, the ministry, pharmacy, and other fields. Storer was accredited as a baccalaureate institution in 1946.

The Reverend Nathan Brackett served as president until 1897. Brackett, who continued as treasurer, died in 1910. Ernest Osgood served as president until 1899, when he was succeeded by Henry T. McDonald. Early civil rights activities took place at Storer College, including the 1906 meeting of the Niagara Movement, which brought W.E.B DuBois to the campus. The Niagara Movement was a predecessor to the National Association for the Advancement of Colored People.

In 1911, the Freewill Baptists merged into the American Baptist Convention. The governance of Storer gravitated to a private board of directors only nominally affiliated with the Baptist Church. In the 1920s, DuBois and the NAACP objected to plans for Storer College to cooperate with Confederate memorial organizations in memorializing the free black, Heyward Shepherd, a bystander who died in John Brown's 1859 raid on Harpers Ferry. President McDonald, initially opposed to the Shepherd monument, took part in its dedication in 1931, as did the Storer Col-

lege Singers. Presidents Brackett, Osgood, and McDonald were all white. Under their leadership, Storer did not hold a lasting place in the civil rights struggles of the 20th century. Increasing pressure to install a black administration led to the forced retirement of McDonald in 1944. The African-Americans Richard I. McKinney and L. E. Terrell succeeded him.

Storer College survived until 1955, when declining enrollment, financial stress, court-ordered desegregation, and racial anxieties combined to close it. Several attempts to reopen Storer failed. Alderson-Broaddus College in Philippi acquired its endowment. Storer's library and records were shared between Shepherd College and Virginia Union University in Richmond. The school's archives are housed at West Virginia University and with the National Park Service in Harpers Ferry, which owns the buildings.

See also African-American Education, Harpers Ferry, Reconstruction Era, Heyward Shepherd

Barbara Rasmussen
Fairmont State University
Barbara Rasmussen, "Sixty-Four Edited Letters of the Founders of Storer College," M.A. thesis, West Virginia University, 1986.

Strange Creek Legend

In 1795, a young greenhorn surveyor's cook, William Strange, became lost from his party in the forests near the mouth of Holly River. Hearing gunfire and fearful of Indian raiders, he ran. He and his dog scrambled for days across 40 miles of inhospitable country to the upper reaches of what was then known as Turkey Creek, near the eastern corner of present Clay County. The starving Strange settled beneath a sycamore tree to die.

Around 1835, settlers found both skeletons undisturbed, with rifle and shot. Legends say they also found, carved on the sycamore, a poem. Various versions have been quoted over time, but according to W.E.R. Byrne's *Tale of the Elk*, it read:

"Strange my name,
And strange the ground,
And strange that I
Cannot be found."

Turkey Creek was renamed Strange Creek in commemoration of the unusual event.

Peter Silitch
Strange Creek

Strauder v. West Virginia

Strauder v. West Virginia was the first decision of the U.S. Supreme Court to use the equal protection clause of the 14th Amendment to the Constitution to invalidate a state law. In doing so, the 1879 decision gave meaning to the post-Civil War amendment's ban on race discrimination.

Taylor Strauder, a black man in Wheel-

Men of Storer College gather for an outing.

ing, was convicted of murder. He argued without success to the state courts that a West Virginia law that limited jury service to white male citizens over 21 denied him equal protection of the law. He appealed to the U.S. Supreme Court, which reversed the state ruling.

The 14th Amendment, the Supreme Court explained, "was designed to assure to the colored race the enjoyment of all the civil rights that under the law are enjoyed by white persons." The West Virginia jury law violated that principle. "[T]hat colored people are singled out and expressly denied by a statute all right to participate . . . as jurors . . . is practically a brand upon them, affixed by the law, an assertion of their inferiority, and a stimulant to that race prejudice which is an impediment to securing to individuals of the race that equal justice which the law aims to secure to all others." Accordingly, Strauder's conviction was void.

Robert M. Bastress
WVU College of Law

P. D. Strausbaugh

Botanist Perry Daniel Strausbaugh, born March 21, 1886, graduated with honors from Wooster (Ohio) College in 1913. In 1920, he received his Ph.D. from the University of Chicago. While a student, he supported himself by teaching at primary and secondary schools. He taught at Wooster College from 1913 to 1923. In 1923, Strausbaugh became head of the department of botany at West Virginia University. He retired in 1948.

Strausbaugh's first challenge at WVU was to reestablish the university herbarium, which he considered essential to the study of botany. WVU's plant collection had been put into storage in 1892. Strausbaugh and his colleagues spent the summer of 1924 collecting, mounting, and filing the nucleus of a new collection.

In 1926, Strausbaugh initiated a summer field course (perhaps the first of its kind) called the botanical expedition. These summer-long excursions, renamed biological expeditions two years later when zoological studies were added, took students all around the state on an extended camping and collecting trip. Students studied plant and animal life and collected specimens for the university's herbarium and zoological collections. The expeditions continued until 1952.

Strausbaugh's most lasting legacy is the book, *Flora of West Virginia*, co-authored with his former student, Earl Core, and published in four parts from 1952 to 1964. P. D. Strausbaugh died May 3, 1965.

See also Botany, Flora of West Virginia

Scott and Nora Shalaway
Cameron

P. D. Strausbaugh and Earl L. Core, *Flora of West Virginia*, 1964.

Strawberry Festival

The West Virginia Strawberry Festival, held each May at Buckhannon, became a regular event in 1936, when Professor J. E. Judson of West Virginia Wesleyan College pointed out to the local Lions Club that the climate and soils of Upshur County were ideal for strawberries. He suggested that a festival be started to encourage strawberry production.

Soon after Judson's talk, Buckhannon and Upshur County had the first Strawberry Festival. The one-day affair was held on Wednesday, June 3, 1936, with strawberry exhibits and the coronation by Governor Kump of Queen Laura Jean Watson on the courthouse steps. More than 6,000 spectators attended the festivities, which also included a grand march parade of 30 princesses down Main Street followed by a ball held in Whitescarver Hall, a local ballroom.

Over the next six years, the Strawberry Festival grew to include a pageant, children's parade, grand parade, air show, marble tournament, and fiddlers contest. Documentary color films of the 1938, 1939, and 1940 festivals are held by the Upshur County Historical Society. In 1943, with World War II raging in Europe and the Pacific, it was decided to discontinue the festival. It was not reestablished until 1949, although the production of strawberries was promoted during the war years.

Although not as much emphasis is placed on growing and marketing strawberries today, the annual West Virginia Strawberry Festival still draws the largest late-spring crowd in Upshur County. The Strawberry Festival is held in late May each year.

Noel W. Tenney
Tallmansville

Strayer Report

The 1945 Strayer Report recommended basic reforms in the delivery of public education in West Virginia. While many of the recommendations were left undone at the time, the process entailed a thorough discussion of state and county school administration. Some key reforms were enacted later, and significant additional funds were found for the schools.

As World War II concluded, West Virginia educators reported a range of problems, including discontinuation during the war of New Deal school enrichment programs and the fact that more than 50,000 school-age youths were not enrolled for school. The state legislature appointed an interim committee to address the needs of public education. In turn, the committee hired George D. Strayer, a retired Columbia University professor, to prepare an expert report.

Strayer reported that a basic problem was the lack of sufficient funds for education, while acknowledging the unlike-

lihood of raising adequate funds under existing tax policy. A key administrative recommendation of the Strayer Report was the restructuring of the state school board as a constitutional body with an appointed, rather than elected, state school superintendent. This guaranteed the opposition of W. W. Trent, the powerful state superintendent, even to the watered-down version proposed by the legislature in a 1946 constitutional amendment. The amendment was narrowly defeated when put to the voters.

Nonetheless, important changes were made in West Virginia education in the next several years. Despite Strayer's pessimism as to resources, the legislature increased education funding by more than two-thirds in 1947. The state superintendent's job was made appointive in 1958, removing that important position from electoral politics.

See also Education, W. W. Trent

Stream Life

A large variety of plants and animals inhabit West Virginia's streams. They include a diverse community of birds. For example, cedar waxwings catch insects flying above rivers; belted kingfishers plunge from overhanging branches; green herons prowl shorelines for frogs; and ospreys hover before plummeting onto fish.

Some birds reproduce along streams. Wood duck hens lead their ducklings to slackwater nurseries. Although they nest in a variety of moist habitats, other bird species, such as the song sparrow, cerulean warbler, and Acadian flycatcher, often nest along streams.

At dusk, several species of bats, such as the little brown bat, big brown bat, and red bat echo-locate flying insects by sweeping through the open space above larger streams.

An entire streamside ecosystem, including soil, plants and animals, depends on each stream. Examples include grasses, ferns, and wildflowers in the ground cover; flowering dogwood, pawpaw, and black willow in the understory; and sycamore, silver maple, and river birch in the canopy. Such riparian plants reduce streambank erosion during high water, shed nutrient-rich leaves which power the in-stream ecosystem, and neutralize polluted runoff before it reaches the stream.

Several species of emergent plants (those plants rooted in a streambed that grow upward and out of the water with parts of their body in the air) live in West Virginia's streams. A common species is water willow. Rooted in shallow beds of gravel and cobble, water willow is adapted to a variety of water levels, including complete inundation, partial emergence, and complete exposure to air. Reproducing via runners, water willow can form large patches of many stems. While submerged, water willow stands provide cover for juvenile fish and aquatic insects. The roots of water willow secure substrate particles, an early step in the formation of islands.

In general, open, sunny, warm intermediate stretches of streams support more kinds and amounts of submerged plants than either the narrow, shaded, cool headwaters or the sluggish, muddy, deep lowest reaches. Diatoms, which are single-celled plants with shells made of silicon, and green algae cling to rocks. Adapted to swifter water, wild celery undulates in the current, whereas several species of pondweed may grow dense stands in quiet backwaters. Water stargrass's bright yellow flowers exhibit underwater pollination.

Unlike lakes, where a variety of animals live suspended in the water column, most stream-dwelling animals persist on the bottom. Pick up a six-inch rock from a healthy West Virginia stream and you will likely find several species of mayflies, stoneflies, and caddis flies. Bottom-dwelling insect communities may also include midges, black flies, hellgrammites, and riffle beetles.

Other non-insect macroinvertebrates may be found in our streams. A large variety of crayfishes and mollusks, of both snail and mussel species, may be locally numerous.

Healthy streams can host dozens of fish species, with the greatest diversity contributed by darters, minnows, suckers, and sunfishes. Stream salamanders and spring salamanders may be locally common in clean streams, while the much larger hellbenders lurk under rocks in streams draining westward, in the Ohio River watershed. Among reptiles, northern water snakes seem to be ubiquitous, while in some places painted turtles bask on sunny logs. Restricted to northeast West Virginia, the wood turtle spends about half of its time in the water and half roaming across nearby floodplains and uplands.

Several species of crepuscular mammals (those active at dawn and dusk) feed in West Virginia's streams. Raccoons fish under rocks, beavers ascend banks to whittle away tree bark to expose the nutritious underlying tissue, and white-tailed deer dunk for submerged waterweed and pondweed.

In general, human activities pose the greatest danger to West Virginia stream life, including mining and industry as well as attempts to "manage" stream flow. Dredging, channelization and other forms of habitat alteration, as well as water pollution (including excess sediment and acid mine drainage), reduce the diversity of native aquatic plants and animals while sometimes enhancing the abundance of a few pollution-tolerant forms.

George Constantz
Canaan Valley Institute

Streams

Streams are everywhere in West Virginia. Abundant precipitation coupled with hundreds of millions of years of erosion of the Allegheny Plateau combine to produce the many rivers, streams, creeks, runs, branches, forks, and rivulets on the state's landscape. There are about 10,000 named streams in West Virginia. The state has nearly 40,000 stream miles, an average of 1.65 miles of stream for every square mile of land. This is one of the highest stream densities of any region in North America.

Almost all streams in the state are part of one of two major river basins, the Potomac to the east and the Ohio to the west. (A small portion of the James River basin is found in eastern Monroe County on the Virginia border.) The Potomac River, which drains the entire Eastern Panhandle, forms the border of West Virginia and Maryland with its main stem and North Branch and ultimately flows to the Chesapeake Bay. Major rivers that are part of the upper Potomac system include the Potomac's North Branch and South Branch, the Cacapon, and the Shenandoah.

The eastern continental divide separates the Potomac River basin from the Ohio River basin. Most of West Virginia, about 80 percent of the state's area, falls west of the divide and is part of the Ohio basin. In West Virginia the Ohio watershed includes such rivers as the Guyandotte, Tug Fork, Greenbrier, New, Gauley, Elk, Coal, Kanawha, Little Kanawha, Cheat, Tygart Valley, West Fork, Monongahela, and the Ohio itself. The Ohio watershed drains to the Mississippi River and the Gulf of Mexico.

West Virginia's rivers flow in almost every direction. For example, in Pocahontas County, the "Birthplace of Rivers," five rivers originate and flow in five directions. The Greenbrier River flows south to the New; the Gauley River flows southwest to the Kanawha; the Elk River flows west to the Kanawha; and the Cheat and Tygart Valley rivers flow north and northwest to the Monongahela.

Streams come in all sizes, and there is no official standard for designating whether a particular water course should be called a creek or a river. Smaller streams tend to be named creeks, runs, forks, or branches, whereas the term "river" is reserved for larger streams. There are exceptions. For example, Middle Island Creek of Pleasants and Tyler counties is longer than the Eastern Panhandle's Stony River and far longer than Summers County's Little Bluestone River. Cultural traditions play a part in the naming of streams, as well. Runs are found mainly in the eastern and northwestern counties, for example, with such streams more likely to be called creeks or branches elsewhere in West Virginia. Such differences reflect different naming customs in the early settlers of these regions.

Basic physical and biological qualities change as streams become larger. Most streams begin as small spring seeps that may only have water for the wettest portion of the year. Often referred to as ephemeral streams, these often are cold, steep, and have a heavy shade cover. The ecosystem in small streams typically is fed by the decomposition of leaves and sticks by bacteria, fungi, and insects. As streams get larger and wider, they become lower in gradient and take a more winding path. Larger streams receive more sunlight as their banks spread apart. As a result, they are warmer, more biologically productive, and support a more diverse community of fishes, amphibians, and insects.

Streams are of great importance to the economy and the quality of life of West Virginians. Our rivers provide drinking water to major population centers in our state, including Charleston, Morgantown, and other communities, and to out-of-state cities including Pittsburgh and Washington. Our rivers also provide water for agriculture and industry. River water irrigates livestock and crops along the South Branch Potomac, for example, and meets the needs of industrial giants on the Kanawha and Ohio. Water pumped from rivers and reservoirs is used to generate steam in coal-fired power plants, and the power of rivers is directly harnessed in hydroelectric facilities on the Cheat and other rivers. West Virginia rivers have played a critical part in the nation's transportation network since early times. The Monongahela, Kanawha, Big Sandy, and Ohio rivers continue to be used for navigation, and hundreds of millions of tons of coal and chemicals are shipped on these rivers each year.

Just as important are the benefits that can be provided only by healthy stream ecosystems. The diversity of life supported by streams and rivers is both an important natural heritage and a critical component of our natural life support systems. Biodiversity enables aquatic ecosystems to assimilate our wastes, purify our water, and put fish in our creel.

In addition, recreational opportunities provided by streams, such as boating, canoeing, kayaking, and whitewater rafting provide pleasure to West Virginians and are among our valuable tourism assets.

Despite the importance of healthy streams, protection of these systems historically has been a low priority. Consequently, damage to streams and rivers from mining, industry, agriculture, and urbanization is widespread. More than 60 percent of our streams are no longer capable of providing beneficial uses such as drinking water, irrigation, fishing, or swimming. Portions of every major river in West Virginia were deemed impaired as a result of human activities by the West Virginia Division of Environmental Protection in 2004.

Nevertheless, efforts are being made to improve the condition of West Virginia streams. Researchers, citizens, industry, and political leaders across the state are attempting to find innovative ways to protect and restore creeks and rivers, while continuing to foster sustainable economic development. Nowhere are these efforts more apparent than in the citizens' watershed organizations that can be found throughout the state. From the Friends of Cheat in northeastern West Virginia to the Friends of Paint Creek in the south-central portion of the state, these groups are working to find ways to restore and protect streams, and to improve access to these valuable resources.

See also Hydroelectricity, River Transportation

Todd Petty
West Virginia University

Streetcar Lines

Although West Virginia's terrain limited the area in which streetcars could operate profitably, the state had several streetcar systems. Most were interurban lines, connecting two or more communities and offering rural people easy access to town. Interurbans filled an important need in the days before automobiles and paved roads.

The interurban movement began around 1890. As reliable electrical service became available, investors realized that electricity could be used to run locomotives or to operate single rail cars. It wasn't practical to stop a steam train at short intervals, but a single electric car, with its light weight and rapid acceleration, could stop and start quickly and frequently.

The state developed several interurban systems, some of them large. The Wheeling system began operation in 1865 with horse cars. Electric cars began to be used in 1887. Mergers produced the Wheeling Traction Company, with operations on both sides of the Ohio River. In 1933, employees bought the company and renamed it Co-operative Transit Company. It operated until 1947.

In Huntington, operation began in 1900 in the city and to nearby Ashland, Kentucky, and Ironton, Ohio. The streetcars were first operated by the Camden Interstate Railway, then Ohio Valley Electric Railway, and finally American Railways Company.

Monongahela West Penn was the biggest interurban system in West Virginia, with street railways in Clarksburg and Fairmont, a main line connecting the two cities, and branches to Mannington, Fairview, Bridgeport, and Weston. In addition to extensive passenger service, this standard-gauge rail line also served local industry from 1914 to 1938. It began as Fairmont & Clarksburg Traction in 1901. After a merger and name changes, it became Monongahela West Penn Service Company in 1934. Remaining portions became City Lines of West Virginia before operations ceased in 1947.

Parkersburg had a street railway with a 14-mile branch to Marietta, Ohio, known as the Parkersburg & Marietta Interurban and built in 1903. Although physically separated from the Clarksburg system, it later became part of Monongahela West Penn. The standard-gauge Parkersburg system interchanged freight traffic with the Baltimore & Ohio Railroad.

The Charleston Interurban Railroad operated two interurban lines, one west to St. Albans (built in 1912) and the other east to Cabin Creek (built in 1916). At a receiver's sale in 1935, the property passed into the hands of the Charleston Transit Company, which converted the entire operation to buses on June 29, 1939. Princeton and Bluefield were served by a 12-mile line which became Tri-City Traction in 1928. A six-mile line, the Lewisburg & Ronceverte Railway, connected the main line of the Chesapeake & Ohio Railroad at Ronceverte with Lewisburg. Built in 1906, it lasted until the early 1930s.

The Wellsburg, Bethany & Washington Railroad operated north of Wheeling. Despite its name, the line never reached its intended destination of Washington, Pennsylvania, but instead stopped at Bethany. Local residents incorrectly believed that the "Toonerville Trolley" comic strip was based on the antics of the WB&W. Built in 1908, it operated until 1926.

Sistersville was a hub of trolley activity. In 1903, an 11-mile line was built from Sistersville to New Martinsville. The two towns and the intervening Paden City benefited from this interurban line, which was the Union Traction Company. Also in 1903 the Parkersburg & Ohio Valley Electric Railway was built from Sistersville to Friendly, both in Tyler County. The line was five miles long. It lasted until 1918; the line from Sistersville to New Martinsville until 1925. Another line, with headquarters in Sistersville, was the Tyler Traction Company. This 13-mile standard-gauge line between Sistersville and Middlebourne was built to high standards and carried both passenger and freight traffic. Built in 1913, it ceased operation in 1930.

West Virginia streetcar and interurban lines provided cheap, frequent, and sometimes speedy transport for several decades from the early 1900s until the Depression of the 1930s. The Wheeling, Clarksburg-Fairmont, Parkersburg, and Bluefield-Princeton lines served their communities beyond the mid-1940s, and many West Virginians alive in the 21st century can recall the experiences of riding in streetcars.

Borgon Tanner
Vanceboro, Maine

Mel Street

The musician King Malachi Street, known professionally as Mel Street, had a solid career as a country honky-tonk singer in the early and mid-1970s prior to his death by suicide on his 43rd birthday. Born near Grundy, Virginia, October 21, 1935, Street gained much of his early experience on radio and television at WHIS in Bluefield, where he lived and performed for several years before making his first hit recording, "Borrowed Angel," in 1972. Moving to Nashville, he followed with 22 more hit songs, the most significant being "Lovin' On Back Streets," "Smokey Mountain Memories," and "If I Had a Cheating Heart." However, career pressures evidently took a heavy toll on Street, who died October 21, 1978.

Ivan M. Tribe
University of Rio Grande

David Hunter Strother

Artist, author, soldier, and statesman David Hunter Strother ("Porte Crayon") was born in Martinsburg, September 26, 1816. After briefly attending Jefferson College in Canonsburg, Pennsylvania, he studied art in New York City with John Gadsby Chapman and Samuel F.B. Morse. Following additional study in Europe, he returned to America and learned the craft of designing on wood for book and periodical illustration during the mid-1840s. He honed his skills on educational books and ephemeral tracts before a commission to contribute 20 illustrations to *Swallow Barn: A Sojourn in the Old Dominion* by John Pendleton Kennedy brought him critical acclaim in 1852.

In 1853, Strother was commissioned by Harper and Brothers to write and illustrate an article about a sporting expedition into the Canaan wilderness area. Submitted under the pen name "Porte Crayon" and published in *Harper's New Monthly Magazine* in December 1853, the article proved to be immensely popular. In the ensuing years Strother became a regular contributor to *Harper's Monthly* and achieved considerable renown. Among the more than two dozen illustrated travelogues he penned between December 1854 and May 1861 were "A Winter in the South," "The Dismal Swamp" and "A Summer in New England." These articles transported readers, introducing them to localities and characters from Maine to Louisiana.

When the Civil War erupted Strother remained neutral until political pressures and threats eventually induced him to join the Union army. He served as a topographer and staff officer to various generals, his intimate knowledge of the

Seneca Rocks by David Hunter Strother, about 1853.

Valley of Virginia making him a boon to the North and consequently the bane of the South. At the war's end he was appointed adjutant general of Virginia but served only briefly. Between June 1866 and April 1868, *Harper's Monthly* published 11 installments of Porte Crayon's "Personal Recollections of the War." Written with accuracy, detail, and criticism toward each side, the series contains an immediacy and an objectivity often lacking in the Civil War reminiscences of other writers.

In the years that followed, Strother continued to contribute to *Harper's Monthly* and to various other periodical publications. His most significant effort of this period was a ten-part *Harper's* series titled "The Mountains" which introduced America to the rural character and folkways of West Virginia. A staunch supporter of the fledgling state, Strother moved to Charleston briefly during the early 1870s. There he edited a newspaper and dedicated his efforts to convincing the state's leaders to invest in the infrastructure essential to West Virginia's economic well-being. Strother was one of the first writers to fully appreciate the state's dilemma in encouraging economic development while preserving its rustic beauty.

Strother's appointment and service, 1879–85, as U.S. consul general to Mexico brought his literary career to a halt. He was planning to resurrect Porte Crayon for an article focusing on Virginia's Eastern Shore when he died of pneumonia in Charles Town, March 8, 1888.

John A. Cuthbert
WVU Libraries

John A. Cuthbert and Jessie Poesch, *David Hunter Strother: "One of the Best Draughtsmen the Country Possesses,"* 1997; Cecil D. Eby, Jr., *"Porte Crayon: The Life of David Hunter Strother,"* 1960.

John Stuart

Colonel John Stuart, born March 17, 1749, in Augusta County, Virginia, was a prominent pioneer, soldier, and leader. Known as the "Father of Greenbrier County," Stuart was a surveyor in the 1769 expedition of Augusta Countians to establish a permanent settlement in the Greenbrier Valley.

At his first residence near Frankford, Stuart built the first mill in present Greenbrier County in 1770. He soon moved to the Fort Spring area near Lewisburg, where he replaced his log cabin with a large stone house in 1789. Fort Spring, a refuge during Indian raids, was built near his house and placed under his command. Stuart led a Greenbrier company at the 1774 Battle of Point Pleasant and defended Greenbrier settlements during Indian raids, including the last attack on Fort Donnally in Lewisburg in 1778. His *Memoir of Indian Wars and Other Occurrences*, written in 1799 and published in 1833, includes an account of the Battle of Point Pleasant and Cornstalk's murder.

One of Lewisburg's first city trustees, Stuart was named clerk of the county in 1780, building the first clerk's office in his own yard. As a member of the 1788 Virginia convention, he advocated ratification of the U.S. Constitution. He donated land in Lewisburg for the first courthouse and for the Old Stone Church. Stuart died August 18, 1823, and is buried in the family cemetery on his Fort Spring property.

See also Greenbrier County, Lewisburg

Debra K. Sullivan
Charleston Catholic High School

Boyd B. Stutler

Author and historian Boyd Blynn Stutler was born July 10, 1889, in Gilmer County. At 18, he became the owner, editor, and publisher of the *Grantsville News* in neighboring Calhoun County. Three years later Stutler was elected mayor of Grantsville, the Calhoun County seat. He later served as president of the board of education of the Grantsville school district. Stutler enlisted in the army in World War I, rising to the rank of sergeant and serving with distinction in the American offensives of 1918.

After the war, Stutler became chief clerk to the superintendent of public printing at the state capitol. During the 1920s, he authored several publications, became managing editor of the *West Virginia Review* magazine, and served as associate editor of the 1929 *West Virginia Encyclopedia*. In 1931, Stutler co-wrote a textbook on West Virginia history. He later served as a managing editor and director of the West Virginia Historical Education Foundation, and president of the West Virginia Historical Society. He was an avid collector of materials relating to abolitionist John Brown. In 1963, his book *West Virginia in the Civil War* was published. In 1976, Stutler's John Brown materials were acquired by the State Archives and now comprise a significant research collection.

Stutler was also active in veterans' affairs, serving as a leader at the local and national levels. He was managing editor of the American Legion magazine from 1936 until 1954. During World War II, he was a war correspondent in the Pacific, and witnessed the Japanese surrender aboard the USS *Missouri*.

Boyd B. Stutler died February 19, 1970, and was buried in Sunset Memorial Park in South Charleston.

Joe Geiger
Huntington

Joe Stydahar

Athlete Joseph Lee Stydahar was the first West Virginia University graduate elected to the Pro Football Hall of Fame. He began his career in the early years of professional football and was a member of one of its most storied teams, the Chicago Bears' famed "Monsters of the Midway."

Stydahar was born March 17, 1912, in Kaylor, Pennsylvania. He moved with his family to Harrison County and graduated from Shinnston High School. After briefly attending the University of Pittsburgh, Stydahar came to WVU, where he was a star in football and basketball.

He was the first-round selection of the Bears in the first pro draft of college players in 1936. A starter as a rookie, he was named to the All-National Football League team each year from 1937 to 1940. Early in his career, Stydahar often played without a helmet, one of the last professional players to do so. Like most players of that era, he would sometimes play all 60 minutes of a game. His teams won championships in 1940 and 1941. Stydahar joined the navy in 1943 and served through the end of World War II. The Bears won another championship in 1946, his final season.

In 1950, Stydahar was named head coach of the Los Angeles Rams, and his team won the NFL championship in 1951. He also coached the Chicago Cardinals, an NFL team. Stydahar was a charter member of WVU's athletic hall of fame. *Sports Illustrated* named him the 10th-most prominent West Virginia sports figure of the 20th century. He died March 23, 1977.

Greg Moore
Charleston Gazette

Sugar Maple

Sugar maple, one of America's most versatile and beloved trees, is the official state tree of West Virginia and several other states. Unsurpassed as a shade tree with brilliant fall colors, sugar maple also provides valuable timber and maple syrup.

Sugar maple grows in well-drained soils throughout southeastern Canada and most of the eastern United States. While more common at higher elevations, fine specimens may be found in all 55 counties of West Virginia. A tree in Bethany, 5.6 feet in diameter and 110 feet tall, was once considered the world's largest living sugar maple.

Shade-tolerant sugar maple seedlings more often mature into trees with trunk diameters of 20 to 36 inches and heights of 70 to 100 feet. Watery sap may be collected and boiled down in late winter to yield maple syrup and sugar. The heavy, hard, strong, very resilient wood is ideal for bowling alleys. Other uses include furniture, flooring, toys, and fuel. The tree's versatility, familiarity, and beauty made it an obvious choice for schoolchildren whose 1949 voting helped sugar maple become West Virginia's official state tree.

Jon Weems
West Virginia University

Leon Sullivan

The Reverend Leon Howard Sullivan, born in Charleston, October 16, 1922, was an African-American preacher and social activist who led international efforts to promote nonviolent social and economic change. A graduate of Garnet High School and West Virginia State College (1943), Sullivan received his theological training at Union Theological Seminary and Columbia University. After serving under the Reverend Adam Clayton Powell in Harlem, Sullivan began his first pastorate at a church in South Orange, New Jersey. In 1950, he began a 38-year ministry at Zion Baptist Church in Philadelphia. The church became one of the nation's largest congregations.

In 1971, Sullivan was appointed to the board of directors of General Motors, the first African-American to serve there. In 1977, Sullivan initiated the original Sullivan Principles, a code of conduct for companies operating in South Africa. GM, as well as other multinational companies, adopted the Sullivan Principles. The Principles were among the most effective efforts to end the system of apartheid or racial separation. In November 1999, the United Nations adopted the "Global Sullivan Principles" as an international corporate code of conduct.

Convinced that the oppressed need a "hand up, not a handout," Sullivan founded the Opportunities Industrialization Centers which created jobs in about 70 U.S. cities and 15 African countries, the Philippines, and Poland. He was the founder of the biennial African-American Summit, a gathering of leaders from the U.S. and African nations.

Nominated for the Nobel Peace Prize, Sullivan was awarded the Presidential Medal of Freedom in 1991 and received honorary degrees from more than 50 colleges and universities. In August 2000, the city of Charleston honored him by renaming a major thoroughfare Leon Sullivan Way. Sullivan died of leukemia in Scottsdale, Arizona, April 24, 2001.

Diana Sole
Motion Masters, Charleston
Leon H. Sullivan, *Moving Mountains: The Principles and Purposes of Leon Sullivan*, 1998.

Summers County

Summers County, located in southeastern West Virginia, encompasses 367.8 square miles. Hinton is the county seat. Summers County was established in 1871 from segments of Fayette, Greenbrier, Mercer, and Monroe counties. The county was named after George W. Summers (1804–68), a noted jurist, legislator, and one of West Virginia's founders. At the time of its formation, the county was almost entirely rural and agricultural, but the newly arrived Chesapeake & Ohio Railroad soon had a transforming effect.

Physiographically, Summers County is superimposed on folded Mississippian and Pennsylvanian rock strata, predominantly shales and sandstones. New River is the dominant stream, entering Summers County at the Virginia border and exiting below Sandstone Falls, the largest cataract on the New. Two major tributaries enter New River in Summers County, the Greenbrier and Bluestone rivers. During the mid-20th century, Bluestone Dam was constructed to control flooding on New River. This dam created Bluestone Lake, which has become a major recreational facility.

The climate is classified as continental, characterized by a wide seasonal temperature range and moderate amounts of precipitation. Summers County is heavily forested. The trees include various oaks, as well as hickory, tulip poplar, hemlock, maple, white pine, and many others. Some of the understory species are dogwood, laurel, sourwood, and rhododendron. Animals include black bear, white-tailed deer, squirrels, turkey, and many other species of birds, fish, mammals, reptiles, and amphibians.

Human habitation spans at least 10,000 years. The first inhabitants were Paleo-Indian people, and over time most Indian cultures that inhabited the eastern United States either lived in or traveled through the present county, as evidenced by their artifacts and by the interlacing trails that traversed the area.

The first European explorers probably arrived in 1671, the Batts and Fallam ex-

The New River bisects Summers County.

FAST FACTS ABOUT SUMMERS COUNTY

Founded: 1871

Land in square miles: 367.8

Population: 12,999

Percentage minorities: 3.4%

Percentage rural: 77.8%

Median age: 43.4

Percentage 65 and older: 19.9%

Birth rate per 1,000 population: 10.4

Median household income: $21,147

High school graduate or higher: 65.4%

Bachelor's degree or higher: 10.1%

Home ownership: 79.1%

Median home value: $56,100

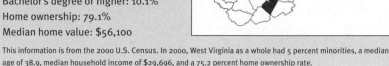

This information is from the 2000 U.S. Census. In 2000, West Virginia as a whole had 5 percent minorities, a median age of 38.9, median household income of $29,696, and a 75.2 percent home ownership rate.

pedition, which is believed to have reached present Summers County. Dr. Thomas Walker arrived in 1750. Walker's journal noted "plantations," early pioneer settlements, established on the Greenbrier River by the Greenbrier Land Company. In 1753, Andrew Culbertson settled on the floodplain of New River at Crump's Bottom, several miles upstream from present Hinton. These settlements were all erased during the French and Indian War in 1755. By about 1760, settlers had returned, but these new settlements were destroyed during Pontiac's Rebellion in 1763. By the Revolutionary War in the 1770s, permanent settlements had finally been established along the New, Greenbrier, and Bluestone. Settlement and peaceful development continued into the early 19th century.

During the Civil War, most local residents supported the Confederacy. Most men fought in either the Army of Northern Virginia or Pickett's New River Regiment, while locally formed detachments participated with other Southern units. Thurmond's Rangers, Confederate partisan irregulars, drew men from the area. Military action in present Summers County was limited to skirmishes, some of which were the bloody culmination of preceding feuds between families. Bushwhackers were common.

Pack's Ferry, at the confluence of the Bluestone and New rivers, was an important river crossing on the James River & Kanawha Turnpike. Union forces held Pack's Ferry with entrenched artillery. Mercer Saltworks on Lick Creek was another military target, only 20 miles from the Virginia border in a territory thick with Confederate sympathizers. Union troops burned and destroyed the saltworks in August 1862, under the command of Col. Rutherford B. Hayes. One of the last skirmishes of the war was fought on the lower Greenbrier River between

irregulars who were unaware of Lee's recent surrender at Appomattox. A monument to the Confederacy was erected in 1914 in Hinton.

Soon after the war, the coming of the railroad brought big changes to southern West Virginia. The legendary John Henry helped build Big Bend Tunnel at Talcott. The Chesapeake & Ohio was influential in establishing the county in 1871. Among local leaders who helped promote Summers County's formation was John Hinton. The C&O was completed through the New River Gorge in 1873, and the town of Hinton became a major railroad center. By 1900 Hinton was a boom town; in its heyday, a train stopped every 15 minutes in the Hinton yards. The New River coalfields kept the trains rolling and the economy of Hinton stable into the middle of the 20th century.

During the 1950s, a combination of factors led to the decline of the local economy. Coal mining technology changed, older mines played out, the local manufacture of coke was no longer viable, and—most importantly for Hinton—in 1954–55 the diesel locomotive replaced coal-fired steam power on the C&O. The railroad no longer required hundreds of workers for its Hinton maintenance operations. The city's population, which had stood at 6,654 in 1930 and 5,780 in 1950, fell to 2,880 by the year 2000. Summers County population peaked at 20,468 in 1930, fell to 13,213 in 1970 and remained about the same in 2000.

At the beginning of the 21st century Summers County looked toward tourism and a more diversified economy. All or parts of the Hinton National Historic District, New River Gorge National Park, Pipestem State Park, the Bluestone National Scenic River, Bluestone State Park, and Bluestone Lake are located within the county.

See also Chesapeake & Ohio Railway, Hinton

Stephen D. Trail
Hinton

James H. Miller, *History of Summers County from the Earliest Settlement to the Present Time,* 1908.

Festus Paul Summers

One of West Virginia's foremost historians, Festus Paul Summers was born at Lockwood, Nicholas County, March 2, 1895. He was a direct descendant of William Morris, who made the first permanent settlement in the upper Kanawha Valley, and his son, Henry, a prominent Nicholas County pioneer.

Summers began his teaching career in a one-room school in Clay County. He also taught in Fayette and Mercer counties, and served as superintendent of schools in Jane Lew. He attended Concord Normal School and in 1923 earned an A.B. degree at West Virginia University. After receiving an M.A. degree from the University of Chicago in 1927, Summers studied in 1927–28 at Columbia University.

From 1928 to 1931, Summers was professor of history and political science at Morris Harvey College in Barboursville. He then returned to WVU as lecturer in history and archivist. There he completed his doctorate in 1933. His academic preparation involved study under such luminaries as Charles H. Ambler, Oliver P. Chitwood, and James M. Callahan at WVU and Avery Craven, William E. Dodd, and Charlton J. H. Hayes at other institutions. At WVU he advanced to full professor in 1946, and from 1947 to 1962 he served as chairman of the history department.

Summers's interests centered around the Civil War and statehood era and late-19th century political and economic developments in the new state. His books include *The Baltimore and Ohio in the Civil War* and *William L. Wilson and Tariff Reform.* He edited *Cabinet Diary of William L. Wilson* and *A Borderland Confederate,* and co-edited with Elizabeth Cometti *The Thirty-Fifth State: A Documentary History of West Virginia.* In 1958, Summers co-authored with Charles H. Ambler the second edition of *West Virginia: The Mountain-State,* which was already regarded as a standard one-volume history of the state. In 1943–44, Summers was president of the West Virginia Historical Society, which he had helped organize a few years earlier. He died May 21, 1971.

Otis K. Rice
WVU Institute of Technology

George William Summers

Statesman George William Summers was born in Fairfax County, Virginia, March 4, 1804. The Summers family moved to Walnut Grove in present Putnam County in

1814. Following the death of his father in 1818, George went to Charleston to live with his oldest brother, Judge Lewis Summers. He attended Washington College (now Washington and Lee University), and graduated from Ohio University in 1826. Returning home, he studied law under brother Lewis and was admitted to the bar in 1827. He served three consecutive terms in the Virginia General Assembly, beginning in 1830. From 1841 to 1845 he served in the U.S. House of Representatives.

Summers was a member of the 1850–51 Constitutional Convention, where he and other westerners helped to secure reforms favoring Western Virginia. He was the candidate of the Whig Party in 1851 in the race to become the first popularly elected governor of Virginia. He was defeated by Democrat Joseph Johnson of Harrison County, most likely because Summers was perceived as an abolitionist.

In 1852, Summers was elected circuit judge of Kanawha County, an office he held for six years, resigning two years before the end of his term. He was elected by the General Assembly of Virginia as a member of the Peace Conference that assembled in Washington on February 4, 1861, to try to avert the Civil War. He was then elected a member of the Richmond secession convention of 1861, where he was recognized for his oratory skills. He opposed and voted against the Ordinance of Secession, then resigned his seat in the convention and returned home to retire from public life.

Summers married Amacetta Laidley, daughter of John Laidley of Cabell County, in February 1833. In 1857, the couple purchased from James Madison Laidley the Glenwood estate on Charleston's West Side. This brown brick edifice of vernacular Greek Revival style, now on the National Register of Historic Places, remains a local landmark. It was here that Judge Summers died September 19, 1868. In 1871, Summers County was named in his honor.

Gerald S. Ratliff
Charleston

Summersville

Summersville, the county seat of Nicholas County, is located off U.S. 19 at the intersection of State Routes 39 and 41, at an elevation of 1,894 feet.

Nicholas County was founded in 1818 and land at present Summersville was donated by John Hamilton as a site for the county seat. The town was established about 1820 and incorporated in 1860. Summersville was named for Judge Lewis Summers, who introduced the legislation in the Virginia General Assembly to create Nicholas County. The first courthouse, a two-story frame structure, served until the present stone courthouse was completed in 1898.

Summersville was located on the Weston & Gauley Bridge Turnpike, an important thoroughfare during the Civil War and heavily used by troops of both sides. Early in the war battles were fought nearby, at Keslers Cross Lanes and Carnifex Ferry. Summersville was occupied by both Northern and Southern troops late in the war, and suffered a devastating fire that destroyed much of the town. The battlefields, as well as Summersville Lake and nearby Gauley River National Recreation Area, now attract tourists to the area, especially during the warm months.

The completion of Appalachian Corridor L (U.S. 19) in the 1990s brought heavy traffic by Summersville and spawned much commercial development along the four-lane highway. Corridor L is a popular shortcut from Interstate 79 to the West Virginia Turnpike, bringing many Florida-bound Pennsylvanians, New Yorkers, and Canadians to Summersville motels and restaurants.

The 2000 population of Summersville was 3,294.

See also Nicholas County

Summersville Lake

Summersville Lake, located on the Gauley River in Nicholas County, is West Virginia's largest lake, with 2,790 surface acres at summer pool stage and 60 miles of shoreline. The dam was built between 1960 and 1966 by the U.S. Army Corps of Engineers at a cost of nearly $48 million. President Lyndon B. Johnson came on September 3, 1966, to dedicate the dam and lake.

A story is told as to the naming of the project. The Corps of Engineers normally names its dams for the nearest community, which in this case was Gad, a village near the present site of the Long Point Marina. But after brief consideration of "Gad Dam," the name Summersville was chosen instead.

Summersville Dam controls a drainage area of 803 square miles, including parts of Randolph, Nicholas, Webster, Pocahontas, and Greenbrier counties. The rock-fill dam is the second-largest of its type in the eastern United States and required 12 million cubic yards of earth and rock. The dam is 390 feet high and 2,280 feet long. Water is released downstream through a 1,555-foot long, 29-foot diameter tunnel, creating a spectacular sight from the highway that crosses the dam. Water releases during the fall lake drawdown have spawned a multimillion dollar whitewater industry on the Gauley River downstream.

With its large summer size and scenic sandstone cliffs, Summersville Lake is popular with boaters, fishermen, and other visitors. Prime recreational features include Battle Run Campground on the lake shoreline, a picnic area, Long Point overlook, Salmon Run and Long Point boat ramps, and Summersville Lake Marina. Rock climbers have established more than 50 routes around the Hughes Bridge (U.S. 19) area, and diving and hiking are also popular.

The total amount of government land at Summersville Lake is 9,346 acres, of which 5,390 acres are leased to the state for fish and wildlife management. Construction of a hydropower project at Summersville Dam began in 1999, and was completed and operating in June 2001. The two-unit powerhouse generates 217 million kilowatt-hours of electricity per year, enough for 50,000 homes.

See also Hydroelectricity, Lakes

Skip Johnson
Sutton

Sumner School

Sumner School, the first school for African-American children in West Virginia, was established as a subscription school

Long Point at Summersville Lake.

in Parkersburg in 1862. It owed its origins to a group of Parkersburg citizens who came together to find a way to educate black students. Local legend holds that barber Robert W. Simmons, a leader of the African-American community, traveled to Washington to request Abraham Lincoln's support for the school. Its board, composed of Simmons, Charles Hicks, William Sergeant, William Smith, Matthew Thomas, Robert Thomas, and Lafayette Wilson, set a $1 per month tuition fee but made provisions to accept children who could not afford to pay.

When the new state of West Virginia assumed the responsibility for schools, the black school in Parkersburg became a part of the segregated public school system in 1866. Sumner School was named for abolitionist U.S. Sen. Charles Sumner of Massachusetts. The principal teacher during the early years was S. E. Colburn, a white minister originally from New York. The school program was eventually expanded to include high school work. Sumner became the first black high school in West Virginia, graduating its first high school class of four students in 1887.

Sumner School, grades 1–12, fulfilled important educational, social, and community roles for the black population of Parkersburg. It closed in 1955 after the *Brown v. Board of Education* U.S. Supreme Court decision ordered the desegregation of public schools. First housed in temporary quarters at Fifth and Avery streets, Sumner School later moved to a permanent building farther up Avery. The school building no longer survives, although the 1926 gymnasium does. There was also a Sumner School in Martinsburg.

See also Robert W. Simmons

Ancella R. Bickley
Charleston

Sunrise

Sunrise mansion is one of Charleston's most recognizable landmarks. The Georgian structure overlooking the Kanawha River and downtown Charleston was built in 1905 by West Virginia's ninth governor, William A. MacCorkle. Sunrise was added to the National Register of Historic Places in 1974.

After leaving office in 1897, MacCorkle turned his attention to his Charleston law practice and to building a family home suitable for a man of his standing and accomplishments. He began the construction of Sunrise in 1905. The three-story stone structure has 36 rooms and a gabled roof dotted with dormers and chimneys. The paneled great room is two stories in height and features an ornate fireplace built with stones MacCorkle collected from cities around the world, including London, Rome, and Versailles, as well as places in Egypt and China. After the man-

sion's completion, MacCorkle entertained many distinguished visitors there, including Adlai Stevenson, William Jennings Bryan, and John Philip Sousa. MacCorkle died at Sunrise in 1930.

Sunrise and an adjoining mansion built by MacCorkle for his daughter were sold in 1936 by MacCorkle's heirs and acquired in 1945 by the Salvation Army. The Salvation Army sold the houses and grounds to Sunrise Foundation in 1961. The foundation operated the property as a popular museum complex. In 2003, the museum moved to a new, larger exhibition space at the Clay Center for the Arts and Sciences in downtown Charleston, and the Sunrise name was discontinued as a name for the museum. Sunrise mansion was sold back into private hands, and most of the grounds were given to the city of Charleston.

See also William Alexander MacCorkle

Eleanor Mahoney
Allegheny Mountain Radio

Supreme Court of Appeals

The Supreme Court of Appeals is West Virginia's highest court and court of last resort. West Virginia is one of only 11 states with a single appellate court. The Supreme Court of Appeals is the busiest appellate court of its type in the United States.

The Supreme Court hears appeals of decisions over matters decided in the state circuit courts, including criminal convictions affirmed by the circuit courts on appeal from magistrate court, and appeals from administrative agencies. The Court also hears appeals of domestic relations decisions decided in family court if both parties agree that they will not appeal directly to the circuit court. The Court decides which appeals it will hear, rejecting others and thereby letting the lower court decision stand.

The justices also have extraordinary writ powers and original jurisdiction in proceedings of habeas corpus, mandamus, prohibition, and certiorari. They also interpret the laws and constitutions of West Virginia and the United States.

Arguments before the Supreme Court are presented by attorneys. There are no witnesses, juries, or testimony. After justices have heard oral arguments and reviewed attorneys' written materials, known as briefs, they issue written decisions, or opinions. These opinions may be appealed only to the U.S. Supreme Court and only if federal law is involved.

There are two terms of the Supreme Court of Appeals each year, from January to July and September to December. At other times, the justices consider the emergency business that comes before the court. The court also has administrative and regulatory responsibilities over the judicial branch of state government.

The court sits in Charleston, but may travel to other locations.

The five justices are elected in partisan elections to 12-year terms. The position of chief justice is a rotating one-year position. The governor appoints justices to fill vacancies until the next election.

Democrats have dominated the membership of the modern court. Since the 1932 election, only eight Republicans have gained seats. Seven of them were appointed by Republican governors to fill vacancies. Six of these served for less than two years until Democrats won their seats in the next election, and another resigned to accept a federal appointment. Republican Brent Benjamin broke the Democratic trend in 2004, ousting Justice Warren McGraw with the aid of heavy campaign spending.

Until 2004, serious contests for seats on the court, when they occurred, were in the Democratic primary. In 1988, Margaret Workman narrowly defeated Justice Darrell McGraw in the primary and became the first woman justice and the first woman elected to statewide office in West Virginia.

For the period of the 1960s and 1970s, political scientists ranked West Virginia's court among the 12 least activist courts as regards the making of public policy. In 1976, this changed with the election of liberal justices Sam Harshbarger, Darrell McGraw, and Thomas Miller. Subsequently, the court increasingly favored claimants in decisions about workers' compensation and tort law. The court also moved from a docket overwhelmingly dominated by private law cases to deciding numerous high-profile public law cases.

Some court decisions instituted major changes in state policies regarding the prison system (*Crain v. Bordenkircher*, 1986, 1988, 1989, and 1990); the financing of public schools (*Pauley v. Kelly*, 1979, and *State ex rel. Board of Education v. Rockefeller*, 1981); and property tax assessment and appraisal methods (*Killen v. Logan County*, 1982). In 1989, the court required the legislature to redesign the system for compensating court-appointed attorneys (*Jewell v. Manard*).

The court also developed new common law doctrines. In tort claims, the court rejected the doctrine of contributory negligence that prohibited injured parties from any recovery in accidents that they themselves even partially caused (*Bradley v. Appalachian Power Co.*, 1979). In product liability suits, the court allowed recovery from damages caused by all kinds of products, not only those called inherently dangerous in the previous tort law (*Morningstar v. Black and Decker*, 1979). The 1978 *Mandolidis* case expanded an injured worker's right to sue an employer. The court also narrowed common law definition of employment at the will of the employer in ways that constrained the ability to fire workers *Cook v. Heck's*, 1986).

As of 2005, there have been 73 justices of the Supreme Court of Appeals. Two justices have served twice. In 1863, the court sat in Wheeling, the capital at the time, and consisted of three judges. Its membership was increased to four with the ratification of the current West Virginia constitution in 1872. A 1902 constitutional amendment increased the number to the present five. The longest single period of service was that of the late Frank C. Haymond of Marion County, who served as a justice for nearly 27 years. Chief Justice Joseph P. Albright and Justices Robin Jean Davis, Larry V. Starcher, Elliott E. Maynard, and Brent D. Benjamin are the members of the court in 2005.

The Supreme Court is housed on the third and fourth floors of the state capitol's east wing. The impressive court chambers are surrounded by marble Doric columns, crowned by a bronze-framed stained-glass skylight, and fitted with specially designed black walnut furniture. The capitol's architect, Cass Gilbert, was so pleased with the room that, several years later, he designed nearly identical chambers for the U.S. Supreme Court building.

See also Courts, Judicial Branch

Chuck Smith
West Virginia State University
Christopher Z. Mooney, Robert Jay Dilger, and Richard A. Brisbin, Jr., *West Virginia's State Government: The Legislative, Executive, and Judicial Branches*, 1993.

Surface Mining

Surface mining allows the removal of coal from the surface rather than through underground tunnels. It requires the stripping away of earth, rock, and vegetation (collectively known as overburden) from above the coal deposit, which can then be mined and trucked away. Often referred to as strip mining, the practice has a history of controversy due to its disturbance of the land.

The earliest recorded instances of surface mining in West Virginia occurred in 1916, and the practice became more common with the increased demand for coal during World War I. Surface mining failed to expand after the war, particularly in southern West Virginia, according to coal historian Robert F. Munn, because the rugged terrain and poor transportation made it difficult to get equipment to the coal and the coal to market. Later advances in diesel machinery, as well as improved highways and the development of large trucks, would free surface mines from the coal industry's traditional reliance on railroads and allow the development of mines with much shorter life spans than underground mines.

The West Virginia Department of Mines first reported production figures for surface mining in 1938, when the northern counties of Preston, Brooke, and Hancock produced about 200,000 tons of coal using that technique. During World War II surface mining expanded quickly. Initial mining operations could begin with relatively small capital investments and produce large amounts of coal with few men and machines. Production reached 18.4 million tons by 1947.

As early as 1939, West Virginians were concerned about the environmental impact of surface mining, and the legislature passed a bill that year to regulate the practice. As surface mining increased and its environmental impact became more apparent, more legislation to protect the environment was enacted (in 1945, 1959, 1963, and 1967), and the Department of Mines created a separate division to inspect and regulate the operations. As surface mining became a political issue Governor Smith appointed a Task Force on Strip Mining which made recommendations for major changes. A successful lobbying effort by the Citizens Task Force on Mining led to tough new restrictions in a 1967 law that provided jail sentences and fines for failure to reclaim the stripped land.

Early surface mining operations generally involved cutting a bench along the side of the mountain, exposing the coal, and pushing much of the overburden over the side. This method produced a distinctive high wall, following the elevation of the coal seam around the mountain. Coal too far back under the mountain to be exposed by the bench cut was mined by big augers, which bored into the seam and drew the coal out the same way a wood drill brings out shavings. After 1967, the benches and high walls were required to be put back to the approximate original contours of the mountain. Much coal was left in the ground by the bench-mining method.

In the 1990s, a new form of mining attracted the attention of West Virginia residents. Mountain tops, which had formerly been left intact, began to be leveled through the new process of "mountaintop removal" which gives access to coal which would be left behind by traditional strip-mining methods. Originally allowed by an exception in the 1977 Surface Mining and Reclamation Act, mountaintop removal became common by the end of the century. The process greatly changed the landscape of southern West Virginia and, for all practical purposes, eliminated the idea that stripped mountains could be returned to something approaching their original contour. Instead, gigantic amounts of earth were removed and dumped into valleys, never to be returned to contour as earlier legislation had required. Surface mining of all types accounted for 60 million tons of the total of 157 million tons of West Virginia coal production in 2001.

Regardless of technique, some West Virginians sought to eliminate strip mining altogether. They found an early ally when West Virginia's young secretary of state, John D. Rockefeller IV, announced in 1970 that he would work for the abolition of the practice. Rockefeller lost the 1972 gubernatorial election against Arch A. Moore, partly because of his stand on surface mining. Later, Rockefeller toned down his opposition and was elected governor twice, in 1976 and 1980, and then U.S. senator. No major politician has since taken so bold a stand, although the issue surfaces regularly in state politics.

As the 20th century ended, the debate over mountaintop removal escalated with lawsuits in the federal courts.

See also Coal Industry, Mountaintop Removal

Kenneth R. Bailey
WVU Institute of Technology
Kenneth R. Bailey, "Development of Surface Mine Legislation 1939–1967," *West Virginia History*, April 1969; Robert F. Munn, "The First Fifty Years of Strip Mining in West Virginia, 1916–1965," *West Virginia History*, October 1973.

Howard Sutherland

Senator Howard Sutherland, born September 8, 1865, in St. Louis County, Missouri, became the first U.S. senator from West Virginia to win election following adoption of the 17th Amendment. The amendment, adopted in 1913, required election of senators by a vote of the people rather than by state legislators as had previously been done.

Sutherland graduated from Westminster College at Fulton, Missouri, and edited a newspaper in the same town until 1890, when he moved to Washington as an official in the Census Bureau and a political ally of West Virginia Sen. Stephen B. Elkins. Elkins, who had spent much of his young life in Missouri, brought Sutherland to West Virginia, where he joined the business empire of Elkins and Henry Gassaway Davis. Sutherland remained in the town of Elkins until 1912 when he was elected to Congress after serving a single term (1909–13) as a Republican in the state senate. He was reelected to Congress two years later, then successfully contested the U.S. Senate seat of William E. Chilton in November 1916. Although Chilton afterward challenged his election, Sutherland was seated for the full term ending in 1923.

Four years before West Virginia native John W. Davis won the Democratic nomination for president in 1924, Sutherland made a bid for the presidency in 1920. At the Republican National Convention in Chicago he received the entire vote of the West Virginia delegation and one vote from Missouri. Prior to the convention Sutherland had purchased an airplane to advertise his candidacy, giving many

West Virginians their first glimpse of an airplane. The Republicans gave the presidential nomination to Ohio Sen. Warren G. Harding, and Sutherland served out the remainder of his Senate term before he was ousted by Matthew M. Neely in the election of 1922.

Sutherland returned to business in Elkins and later lived in Washington. He died March 12, 1950, and is buried in the Maplewood Cemetery, Elkins.

Paul D. Casdorph
Charleston

P. D. Casdorph, "Howard Sutherland's 1920 Bid for the Presidency," *West Virginia History,* 1973.

Sutton

Sutton, the county seat of Braxton County, was settled in 1792 by Adam O'Brien, from Bath County, Virginia. In 1809, John D. Sutton settled at the confluence of Granny's Creek and the Elk River, at the edge of the present town. The village of Suttonville, formerly known as Newville, was laid out in 1835. When Braxton County was formed in 1836 the first court was held in the home of John D. Sutton.

Sutton was situated at the juncture of major transportation routes. The Elk River was navigable at times all the way to Charleston. The Weston & Gauley Bridge Turnpike connected the Staunton & Parkersburg Turnpike to the James River & Kanawha Turnpike, via Sutton. A suspension bridge was constructed on the Weston & Gauley Bridge Turnpike across the Elk River at Sutton in 1853.

Due to its location, Sutton was embroiled in the Civil War. On September 5, 1861, the town was occupied by 5,000 Union troops. Later in 1861, General Rosecrans bivouacked 10,000 Union troops there, including future President William McKinley. On December 29, 1861, Confederate soldiers burned most of the downtown.

Sutton slowly rebuilt but remained small until the local timber industry boomed. The town then became a commercial center, and many of the banks, hotels, shops, and other historic buildings date from this 1890–1920 period. After this, Sutton once again slowed in development. Sutton Dam was built on the Elk River upstream from the town in 1961, adding a tourism component to the local economy.

Sutton is situated at a center of transportation in West Virginia. Interstate 79, a major north-south route, connects with Appalachian Corridor L (U.S. 19), another significant north-south route, just a few miles south of town. The county has two spur rail lines, serving industry in Sutton and other areas.

In 2000, Sutton had a population of 1,011.

See also Braxton County

Michael Gioulis
Sutton

Sutton Dam and Lake

The Sutton Dam, located just upstream of the Braxton County seat of Sutton, and 101 miles above Charleston, is an imposing structure. It straddles Elk River at a height of 210 feet, with a top length of 1,178 feet. The dam controls a drainage area of 537 square miles, and creates a 1,520-acre lake at summer pool stage. The summer pool depth near the dam is 112 feet.

The Army Corps of Engineers built and operates the dam for purposes of flood control, low-flow augmentation, and recreation. Planning for Sutton Dam was suspended in 1952 because of the Korean War, but was resumed in 1956 when the groundbreaking was held. The completed structure was dedicated by Governor Barron on July 8, 1961. Sutton Dam is made entirely of concrete, thus differing from its nearby neighbor, Burnsville Dam, which is of earthen and concrete composition.

Sutton Dam has tamed the floods that once plagued downstream residents and communities along Elk River, even though it has never reached more than 50 percent of its storage capacity. The lake with its 40 miles of shoreline is popular with fishermen and boaters.

There are three public campgrounds at Sutton Lake, two marinas, and a total of four boat-launching ramps. The 17,184-acre Elk River Wildlife Management Area that surrounds the lake offers hunting for squirrel, turkey, deer, and waterfowl. The Gerald R. Freeman Campground, located on the Holly River arm of the reservoir, is the largest of the three campgrounds, with 158 sites. It is named for a longtime reservoir manager.

In 1980, a high-level water outlet was added to one of Sutton Dam's five sluice gates, enabling engineers to draw warmer and clearer water from the top of the lake, thus dramatically improving downstream fishing. The colder, more turbid water released from the bottom of the lake had delayed and reduced spawning, inhibited fish growth, and cut into the populations of fish forage such as crayfish and hellgrammites in lower Elk River.

See also Lakes

Skip Johnson
Sutton

Swamps

Ecologists use the term swamp to designate a wetland dominated by woody vegetation, trees, and shrubs. Swamps are the most common type of wetland in West Virginia. They are also the most diverse and most variable and include some of the rarest plant communities in the state.

At low elevations in West Virginia, swamps are typically associated with the backwaters of river floodplains. Characteristic tree species in these swamps include red maple, silver maple, river birch, ash, sweet gum, sycamore, and pin oak. In contrast, swamps of high-elevation headwaters are more often dominated by evergreen trees such as red spruce and hemlock. Shrub swamps are found at both low and high elevations. Dominant shrub species in these habitats include alders, silky dogwood, buttonbrush, glade St. John's wort, and swamp rose.

One of West Virginia's most extensive swamps is in western Greenbrier County in the vicinity of Rupert. Here the broad floodplain of the Meadow River supports thousands of acres of pin oak forest and alder shrub swamps.

The balsam fir swamps in the Allegheny highlands of Pocahontas, Randolph, and Tucker counties are among West Virginia's most unusual and most threatened plant communities. Here at the southern extent of its distribution, balsam fir is considered rare and is mostly restricted to swamps where it grows with red spruce. Blister Swamp in Pocahontas County was named after the original balsam fir, commonly called "blister pine," but the species was eliminated from the site by grazing. Restoration of balsam fir to this site is currently being attempted, but now an insect pest, the balsam wooly adelgid, threatens the species.

Jim Vanderhorst
Division of Natural Resources

Swan Lands

James Swan, a Scots-born American officer in the Revolutionary War and a participant in the Boston Tea Party, later became one of the largest landowners in present West Virginia.

High-ranking officers and politicians had received vast grants of western land for Revolutionary service, many exceeding 50,000 acres. Officers of lower rank got smaller grants, while enlisted men got 400 acres each. Swan bought such land grants, of all sizes and in all areas of Western Virginia. His largest acquisition was a 500,000-acre tract in present Logan, McDowell, Mingo, and Wyoming counties, which had been acquired by the Philadelphia banker Robert Morris, a member of the continental congress and financier of the Revolution. Swan also acquired many tracts of 20,000 to 50,000 acres. It is estimated that he eventually owned six million acres. His dealings left him deep in debt by 1787, when he moved to France. While initially successful there, in 1808 he was imprisoned for debt in France and remained in prison until his death in 1830.

At this time the Swan lands were subdivided and assigned to various persons to sell. One of these administrators was John Peter Dumas of Paris. He employed agents such as Joseph H. Diss Debar to entice immigrants to buy and settle on Swan lands. The most successful and best-known of these ventures was in Doddridge County, now encompassing the St. Clara community and surrounding areas. Here many Germans established thriving farms.

Litigation over taxes, boundaries, ownership, and sale of the Swan lands kept courts busy for more than a century. The most important of these cases was the so-called King Case, fought to the U.S. Supreme Court between 1893 and 1910. Plaintiff Henry C. King of New York claimed title to 500,000 acres in southern West Virginia arising from the Morris-Swan claims. U.S. Supreme Court Justice Oliver Wendell Holmes ruled against King in 1910, saying that the land had been forfeited to the state because taxes had not been paid between 1883 and 1897. Other cases involving the Swan holdings clogged West Virginia courts as recently as 1934.

See also Land Ownership

Kenneth L. Carvell
Morgantown

Sweet Springs

Sweet Springs, located on State Route 3 in eastern Monroe County, is the site of a historic mineral spring resort in use since the late 1700s. The spring water, which emerges from the ground at 73 degrees F., contains a concentration of iron and carbon dioxide and has been credited with medicinal properties. The first hotel was erected in 1792 by William Lewis who developed a resort around the spring. From 1795 to 1807, a Virginia district court representing the counties of Botetourt, Greenbrier, Kanawha, and Montgomery met at the facility.

The heyday of the resort was from 1820 until the Civil War. In the 1830s, the present large brick hotel was constructed with columned porticos. Its design was long attributed to Thomas Jefferson but more recently has been accredited to a Jefferson associate. A second large building and five cottages were erected in 1857. Sweet Springs, during this period, was a day's carriage drive from eight other mineral spring resorts in what was termed the "Springs Region" of pre-Civil War Virginia. Guests would frequently make a circuit of several mineral springs resorts during the busy summer season sampling the water and social life at each. Famous visitors to Sweet Springs included George and Martha Washington, General Lafayette, Chief Justice John Marshall, Jerome Bonaparte, Patrick Henry, James and Dolley Madison, and Robert E. Lee. Presidents Pierce and Fillmore also visited the resort.

In June 1864, the resort was visited by Union forces under the command of Gen. David Hunter. His troops camped in the vicinity of the resort, but there is no record that the buildings were harmed. Sweet Springs continued to attract guests after the Civil War, but many potential visitors preferred to go to resorts that were more convenient to the rail lines.

The resort continued to operate under a succession of owners until it went into receivership in 1930. In 1945 the state of West Virginia purchased the property and established the Andrew S. Rowan Memorial Home for the aged in the old resort's buildings. A major renovation was undertaken from 1972 to 1975. The Rowan Home was closed in 1991, and the state turned the facility over to Monroe County to establish a rehabilitation center for drug addicts. This project failed, and in 1996 the former resort was sold into private hands. In 2005, the current owners hoped to reopen Sweet Springs as a hotel, spa, and conference center.

See also Architecture, Mineral Springs

Michael M. Meador
Abingdon, Virginia

The hotel building at Sweet Springs resort.

Stan Cohen, *Historic Springs of the Virginias*, 1981; Rody Johnson, "A Lewis Family Legacy: Old Sweet Springs," *Goldenseal*, Summer 2000.

Ralph Swinburn

Railroader Ralph Swinburn was one of the earliest railway men in the world and the first railroad engineer in Western Virginia. Possibly he operated the first commercial steam engine in history, because of his association with Englishman George Stephenson, builder of the famous steam locomotive, *Rocket*. In addition, Swinburn was a competent railway civil engineer.

Swinburn was born August 4, 1805, at Lamesley, England. By age 12, he was working on a small coal-hauling railway near Newcastle-upon-Tyne. There he met Stephenson, later working with him on the Stockton & Darlington Railway, the Liverpool & Manchester, and other pioneering railroads.

Deciding to emigrate to America, Swinburn sailed for New Orleans, arriving in January 1851. He traveled up the Mississippi and Ohio, during which journey he was robbed and stranded without funds in Cincinnati. Fortunately he met Charles O'Conner of the Winifrede Mining & Manufacturing Company there, and by February 1851 was employed at the company's mines on Fields Creek, in Kanawha County. Swinburn was assigned to lay out and build the first railroad in the region, a narrow-gauge line running from the mines to a barge facility on the Kanawha River. This little railroad preceded the arrival of the mainline C&O by 20 years and was literally landlocked, connecting only to the mine and the river.

Swinburn soon sent for his family, who joined him on July 4, 1851. About a year later, he left Winifrede to work for the Paint Creek Coal & Iron Mining & Manufacturing Company. Here he built a railroad up Paint Creek, extending rail facilities to a mine shaft that had been opened where a large seam of bituminous coal had been found in 1850.

After more than 40 years in railway work, Swinburn retired. In 1855, he purchased land near Ruth, cleared it, and settled down to the life of a farmer, subsequently establishing a gristmill on Davis Creek. A religious man, he was ordained a Baptist minister in 1856. Ralph Swinburn died June 7, 1895, and is buried at Graceland Cemetery at Ruth, just outside Charleston.

William H. Dean
WVU Institute of Technology

George W. Summers, "Ralph Swinburn—Pioneer in Railway Development," *West Virginia Review*, January 1934.

Swinging Bridges

Built without benefit of formal engineering design, the swinging bridge is a distinctive form of folk or "vernacular" construction, well-suited for pedestrians crossing streams in the rugged Appalachian region. Swinging bridges were common landmarks for many decades, and are still often seen in the West Virginia countryside.

Using cables, planks, and timbers, swinging bridges could be constructed quickly and cheaply to provide access to homes or farms isolated by streams. Cables composed of wire rope, or indeed, even ordinary hemp rope, were suspended from towers on each bank, with the backstays firmly anchored in the ground behind the towers. These towers, which raised and supported the cables, were made of timber, stone, or steel. The bridges reflected their environment in the materials used and the skills employed in their construction. Sometimes towers made of surplus pipe from the oil fields and used wire rope from mines and other industries formed the essential components of a swinging bridge. The wooden bridge deck was supported by ropes, wires, or rod suspenders hanging from the cables. The parallel cables themselves often formed convenient hand rails.

Although such bridges are strong enough to support foot traffic, they lack stiffness and swing from side to side and vertically under foot traffic, hence the name. Perhaps hundreds of swinging bridges once served West Virginians throughout the state, with many still in service. However, there are few records of the location and distribution, let alone the span length and other details, which are available for other bridge types. As utilitarian structures adapted specifically for their location, many swinging bridges have an appealing form, as much a part of the rural landscape as local barns, corn-cribs, tool sheds, and houses.

Emory L. Kemp
WVU Institute for the History of Technology

John Joseph Swint

Roman Catholic Bishop John Joseph Swint was a great builder of religious institutions in the Diocese of Wheeling (now the Diocese of Wheeling-Charleston). He was born in Pickens, Randolph County, December 15, 1879, the son of Peter M. and Caroline Winkler Swint. He received his education at St. Charles College in Ellicott City, Maryland, and St. Mary's Seminary in Baltimore. He was ordained to the priest-

hood in 1904 for the Diocese of Wheeling. After being trained as a missionary at the Apostolic Mission House in Washington, he established the Apostolic Mission Band for the Wheeling diocese in 1906.

In December 1922, Swint succeeded the Most Rev. Patrick J. Donahue (1849–1922) as the fourth bishop of the Diocese of Wheeling. He would serve in that role for the next 40 years. During that time, Swint oversaw tremendous growth in the diocese, whose boundaries included most of West Virginia and part of Virginia. Catholic population almost doubled from approximately 63,000 in 1922 to about 110,000 in 1962, representing more than 20 different ethnic groups. To meet the needs of this diverse and growing population, Swint initiated an aggressive building program. At the time of his death in 1962, close to 100 churches, a new cathedral, five hospitals, 43 elementary and secondary schools, one college, and one preparatory seminary had been founded under his leadership.

In 1954, on the 50th anniversary of Swint's ordination to the priesthood, Pope Pius XII bestowed the honorary title of archbishop *ad personam* on him. He also held honorary doctorates from Georgetown University and West Virginia University. Bishop Swint died at the age of 82 on November 23, 1962.

See also Diocese of Wheeling-Charleston, Roman Catholics

Tricia Pyne
St. Mary's Seminary & University, Maryland

Synthetic Rubber

On June 28, 1940, with the Japanese military threatening America's sources of natural rubber, President Franklin Roosevelt designated rubber as a strategic and critical material. In August 1940, Union Carbide Corporation was asked to investigate ways to produce butadiene and styrene, which would be used in making synthetic rubber. Within six months, Union Carbide had perfected a process, and designed equipment to convert ethyl alcohol into butadiene.

In August 1941, the U.S. Defense Plant Corporation authorized Union Carbide to build a butadiene plant at Institute, near Charleston, with a capacity of 10,000 tons per year, which was increased to 80,000 tons per year in late 1941. Union Carbide was also asked to design, build, and operate a styrene plant. The U.S. Rubber Company was asked to design,

build, and operate an adjacent rubber polymerization plant. It would consume 80,000 tons of butadiene and 25,000 tons of styrene and combine them to make 90,000 tons per year of Buna-S synthetic rubber.

Shortly after the December 7, 1941, Pearl Harbor attack, the Japanese cut off 90 percent of America's natural rubber supply. In 1942, Union Carbide and U.S. Rubber undertook to build the synthetic rubber plant in the middle of the former Wertz Air Field at Institute.

Meanwhile, construction started on the first alcohol-to-butadiene unit in April 1942. In January 1943, less than 10 months later, the first of four butadiene units started production. Construction started on two styrene units in July 1942, and the first operation began in April 1943. The construction of the three rubber polymerization units began in August 1942, and operation began seven months later. At the peak of construction, nearly 7,000 men worked around-the-clock, 12 hours a day, seven days a week, to build the synthetic rubber complex.

The first shipment of Buna-S synthetic rubber left the plant on March 31, 1943. By May 31, one million pounds of Buna-S had been produced. On June 10, government and industry dignitaries visited Institute to see the miracle plant. Institute became the largest government synthetic rubber plant and the only one whose production was totally integrated, from ethyl alcohol to the final product. In 1944, Institute produced 131,000 tons of butadiene. During World War II, the Institute plant produced 60 percent of the Buna-S made from ethyl alcohol in the United States.

After World War II ended, the government discontinued the rubber program, causing the plant to be shut down in 1946. Union Carbide purchased the butadiene, styrene, and support facilities in 1947 and began a massive conversion effort to produce other chemicals and add new facilities. The rubber facilities were purchased by B. F. Goodrich, restarted as Goodrich-Gulf Corporation, and manufactured synthetic rubber until the 1960s, when Union Carbide purchased the rubber plant.

See also Chemical Industry, Union Carbide Corporation, Wertz Field

Warren J. Woomer
Charleston

201st Field Artillery

The 201st Field Artillery (West Virginia Army National Guard) is perhaps the oldest military unit in the United States. The claim is based on the continued organization of a military company in the Eastern Panhandle since Morgan Morgan was commissioned a captain of militia on February 17, 1735. Units from this region served in the French and Indian War, Revolutionary War, War of 1812, and Mexican War. During the Civil War, local units entered both the Union and Confederate armies.

One of the first West Virginia Militia companies to reorganize after the Civil War was the Berkeley Light Infantry, commanded by Capt. Charles J. Faulkner Jr., which in the 1880s became part of the First Regiment, West Virginia National Guard. The First Regiment was activated for service in the Spanish American War and World War I. In 1926, the First Regiment was designated as the 201st Infantry. The 201st was mobilized for World War II and when the war was over, returned to state service as the 201st Artillery Battalion. The 201st Artillery Battalion was again mobilized during the Korean War and sent to Germany. The 201st Artillery Battalion was engaged in combat during the Persian Gulf War in the early 1990s and was deployed to the Iraq War in 2004.

See also West Virginia National Guard

Kenneth R. Bailey
WVU Institute of Technology
Kenneth R Bailey, *Mountaineers are Free: A History of the West Virginia National Guard,* 1978.

Tackett's Fort

Tackett's Fort was located at the mouth of the Coal River at present St. Albans. Lewis, Samuel, and Christopher Tackett and friend John Young constructed the fort about 1786. The fort was one of the first permanent settlements in the St. Albans area. The structure was erected to serve as a defense against the savage Indian raids that occurred during the late 1700s in Western Virginia.

Indian raids plagued settlers moving west into the region during this period. In spring 1790, raiding Indians attacked Fort Tackett and kidnapped several people. Later that year they struck again, this time destroying the fort. Several of the inhabitants were killed, including members of the Tackett family. The more fortunate ones eluded their attackers and escaped to Fort Lee, some 15 miles away in present Charleston.

Scott M. Kozelnik
Little Egg Harbor, New Jersey

Tamarack is a major crafts outlet.

Stan Cohen and Richard Andre, *Kanawha County Images: A Bicentennial History,* 1987; Julius DeGruyter, *The Kanawha Spectator, Vol. 1,* 1953.

Tale of the Elk

The book, *Tale of the Elk,* was written by William Easton Randolph Byrne, a lawyer and politician whose true passion was the outdoors. Bill Byrne, as he was known, practiced law in Sutton and Charleston when he wasn't fishing, hunting, and camping up and down his beloved Elk River. A favorite pastime of Byrne's was to gather friends around the campfire, telling tall tales and exchanging fish stories. His companions included both colorful local characters and prominent politicians, all of them comfortable in his company.

In 1927, Byrne began writing articles about his adventures on the Elk. From 1927 until 1931, these articles were a regular feature in *West Virginia Wild Life* magazine. In 1933, the *Braxton Democrat* newspaper in Sutton compiled and reprinted Byrne's tales. In 1940, the West Virginia Publishing Company published the stories as a book, *Tale of the Elk,* which has become a West Virginia classic.

Byrne's passion for fishing, his humor and warmth, and his love of life are immediately evident to his readers. *Tale of the Elk* follows its namesake river from headwaters to mouth in 49 chapters, with a 50th, largely Byrne's poem "Camp at the End of the World," thrown in for good measure. The book was reprinted in 1980 by Mountain State Press, and in a 1995 paperback edition by Quarrier Press. *Tale of the Elk* captures the physical beauty, political climate, and a way of life found in rural West Virginia in the late 1920s.

See also W.E.R. Byrne

Bill Clements
West Virginia Book Company

Tamarack

Tamarack is located on the West Virginia Turnpike at Beckley. The arts and crafts center, which opened in 1996, is operated by the West Virginia Parkways and Economic Development Authority. Tamarack buys and resells items fashioned by more than 2,000 West Virginians, with all work selected by expert jurors who reject roughly two-thirds of the items submitted for judging. The center retails the items to tourists and other turnpike travelers. The products sold range from glassware, pottery, and baskets to jewelry, toys, recordings, and books. Nearly 500,000 people visit Tamarack annually.

Named for the tamarack tree, which is found in some parts of West Virginia, the center is of ultramodern design with a striking roof line dominated by a series of spires jutting upward. Architect Clint Bryan of Charleston said he had a quilt pattern in mind when he came up with the design. Many visitors have said the red-roofed spires remind them of West Virginia's mountains.

The building's basic layout is circular. In addition to the retail area, the center includes studios where artists demonstrate their skills, an auditorium, and a popular food court. The center itself cost $16.2 million to build, but the expense of constructing a new turnpike exit to serve it ballooned the total outlay to nearly $33 million, prompting criticism of the project by some. A $6.5 million expansion was opened in 2003, adding banquet and conference space to Tamarack.

James E. Casto
Herald-Dispatch

William Purviance Tams Jr.

At the time of his death "Major" W. P. Tams Jr. was recognized in southern West Virginia as the last of the old-time coal barons.

Tams was born in Staunton, Virginia, May 19, 1883, and studied engineering at Virginia Polytechnic Institute in Blacksburg. He went to work for entrepreneur Samuel Dixon in the New River coalfield in 1904. With the support of Dixon and J. O. Watts of Lynchburg, Tams launched his own company, Gulf Smokeless Coal, in the new Winding Gulf coalfield in 1908. He established the company town of Tams, Raleigh County, as his headquarters, and later acquired Wyoming Coal Company in neighboring Wyoming County. He invested in other mines as well and was a leader in industry associations.

Major Tams was remarkable in a consolidating industry as a lifelong independent, selling out only at his retirement in 1955. He made Tams and Wyco into model coal camps and was remembered after his death as a benevolent paternalist. Major Tams made his modest bachelor home at Tams in a house no larger than those occupied by most of his miners, his major indulgence a sizable personal library. He authored the book, *The Smokeless Coal Fields of West Virginia*, and in his later years was often interviewed on the subject of coal history.

Tams died August 3, 1977.

Ken Sullivan
West Virginia Humanities Council
Charles Kenneth Sullivan, *Coal Men and Coal Towns*, 1989.

Tanneries

Tanning, which transforms perishable raw skins and hides into durable leather, derives its name from the use of the tannic acid found in tree bark. Tanning requires the scraping of hair and epidermis from skins, which are then impregnated by soaking in a tanning solution made of water and tanbark.

Tanning was once an important industry in West Virginia. The earliest tanneries were small enterprises. These tanners used the hides from cattle and sheep slaughtered for home consumption and the hides of wild animals, such as deer, groundhogs, and beavers. Oak and hemlock trees felled for lumber or to clear farmland provided tanbark.

By the middle of the 19th century, the first industrial tanneries appeared. Among the earliest and best-known was the Wheeling tannery founded in 1849 by John G. Hoffman. His Wheeling Centre Tannery produced heavy shoe-sole and harness leather. By 1876, the firm had become known as J. G. Hoffman and Sons. In 1870, there were 178 tanneries in West Virginia producing $840,245 worth of leather. Most remained small family firms with limited access to leather markets.

By 1880, as railroads penetrated the state, West Virginia tanneries became large operations modeled after tanneries in New York's Catskill Mountains. Now

93 tanneries produced $1.45 million in finished leather. Pennsylvania and New York tanners came to the state to open branch tanneries, or they completely moved their operations to West Virginia as tanbark disappeared in their home regions.

By the turn of the 20th century, many West Virginia tanneries were concentrated in Hampshire, Hardy, and Tucker counties. Others operated at places in the Greenbrier Valley logging district, including Frank and Marlinton, Pocahontas County. U.S. Leather, the largest producer of sole leather in the United States, had operations in Moorefield, Paw Paw, Davis, and Lost City. In Buckhannon, Pittsburgh's William Flaccus and Son in 1893 bought a tannery along the banks of the Buckhannon River and adjacent to the Baltimore & Ohio Railroad. Until it burned in 1935, the Buckhannon tannery continued to provide tanbark and finished leather to the Flaccuses' Pittsburgh operations.

West Virginia's tanneries began to disappear in the 20th century as deforestation depleted local tanbark supplies. Although chemical tanning had been introduced during the last quarter of the 19th century, it had not penetrated the tanbark regions. Demand for harness leather diminished as automobiles took over the roads, and synthetics, such as synthetic rubber, cut into the market for sole leather. The Pocahontas County tanneries closed after World War II, and Paw Paw, one of the last U.S. Leather operations, shut down in 1951.

David S. Rotenstein
Silver Spring, Maryland

Tax Limitation Amendment

The Great Depression, which commenced nationally in October 1929, had a crippling impact upon the West Virginia economy. Between 1929 and 1933 bank deposits in the state dropped from $183 million to $96 million. As banks and businesses closed their doors, many thousands of West Virginians were without work and virtually destitute. At one time 35 of the state's 55 counties were operating at a deficit.

In order to bring relief to people losing their farms or homes to tax sales, West Virginians added the Tax Limitation Amendment to the state constitution by a vote of 335,482 to 43,931 in November 1932. Under its provisions all real property in the state was placed in one of four categories and the levy rate set for each: on agricultural products and equipment, stocks, bonds, and other tangibles the maximum rate was 50 cents "on each one hundred dollars of value thereon"; on farm and residential property, $1; on all other property outside municipalities, $1.50; on all other property inside municipalities, $2. These maximum rates could

be exceeded only through voter-approved excess levies.

A series of legal challenges, the most famous being *Finlayson v. Shinnston*, before the state Supreme Court established the principle that all county tax levies had to fall under provisions of the amendment. Over time, the Tax Limitation Amendment effectively reduced the role of local governments in West Virginia by limiting local taxation authority. When it became evident that county and city governments could not function with these restrictions, the legislature implemented the county unit system of public schools, and the state assumed the funding of all public roads. In order to garner sufficient operating funds, the legislature established the sales tax to raise funds independently of property levies. Many Depression-era West Virginians long remembered the "Kump Pennies" named for incumbent Governor Kump that were required for the sales tax on retail purchases.

See also County Unit Plan, Taxation

Paul D. Casdorph
Charleston
A. S. Gatrell, "Herman Guy Kump and the West Virginia Financial Crisis of 1933," *West Virginia History,* Spring 1981.

Taxation

Before the 1930s, property taxes generally yielded more than 90 percent of total state and local revenues in West Virginia. The property tax is imposed upon the assessed value of real property and tangible personal property. Generally, an elected county assessor appraises the fair market value of all taxable property within the county as of July 1 of each year. Industrial property is appraised by the state Tax Department. In West Virginia, property is assessed at 60 percent of its appraised value. Taxes levied upon the assessed value of property are due in two installments, to be paid to the county sheriff by September 1 of the year following the year of assessment and by March 1 of the year after that.

Prior to 1921, most state tax collections came from two sources, an excise tax on corporations and an inheritance tax. The excise tax was a relatively new tax tied to the federal income tax on corporations, as approved by Congress following adoption of the 16th Amendment in 1913. The West Virginia legislature first imposed the corporate excise tax in 1915, as a replacement for liquor license fees lost when the state adopted liquor prohibition in 1914.

In 1921, the state replaced its corporate excise tax with a business gross receipts tax later referred to as the business and occupation (B&O) tax. Some had argued that the corporate excise tax unfairly singled out corporations for taxation while other businesses went untaxed. The B&O tax applied more broadly and was the state's major source of tax revenue for the next 65 years. It was eliminated for most business activities in 1987, and replaced with a severance tax imposed upon gross receipts of mining and other extractive companies and a business franchise tax imposed upon net equity of corporations and partnerships. However, many local municipalities still retain a B&O tax. For some municipalities, the B&O tax may account for up to 60 percent of total tax revenue.

The Depression had a profound effect upon government finance in West Virginia. A weakened economy depressed property values and led to a gradual decline in property tax revenue from $52 million in 1928 to $27 million in 1933. Many citizens faced the prospect of losing their property for nonpayment of taxes. This created the impetus for the 1932 Tax Limitation Amendment. This amendment to the state constitution created four classes of property, and established a maximum tax levy rate for each property class. As a result, the property tax burden for West Virginia homeowners is among the lowest in the nation.

The revenue void caused by reduced property taxes was initially filled by a new state tax on retail sales. West Virginia was one of 28 states adopting a sales tax during the 1930s. The sales tax was initially imposed at a rate of two percent, effective April 1, 1934, and was six percent in 2005. While most other states generally applied their sales tax to goods, the West Virginia consumer sales tax applied to both goods and services, with some exemptions of services.

The growth in remote interstate commerce, typically involving mail-order sales to West Virginia consumers by vendors not registered to collect the state's tax, prompted the adoption of a two-percent use tax in 1951, now six percent. The use tax is imposed upon consumer purchases bought out of state for use in West Virginia, including mail-order and Internet commerce, but is sometimes difficult to enforce. Motor vehicles are exempt from the six percent sales and use taxes, but are subject to a five percent privilege tax. This tax is paid when a vehicle is registered in West Virginia for the first time, whether purchased in the state or brought in from elsewhere. The six-percent sales and use taxes account for more than one-third of total general revenue fund collections and roughly 22 percent of total state and local tax revenue.

The education of the large post-war "baby boom" generation and the creation of Medicaid, a government health care program, placed a significant financial burden upon state and local governments in the second half of the 20th century. In response, West Virginia adopted a personal income tax in 1961 and a corporate net income tax in 1967.

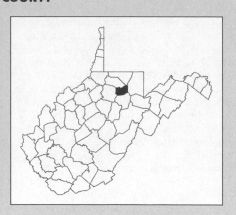

FAST FACTS ABOUT TAYLOR COUNTY

Founded: 1844

Land in square miles: 177.2

Population: 16,089

Percentage minorities: 1.9%

Percentage rural: 60.9%

Median age: 39.1

Percentage 65 and older: 15.8%

Birth rate per 1,000 population: 9.9

Median household income: $27,124

High school graduate or higher: 74.7%

Bachelor's degree or higher: 11.3%

Home ownership: 79.6%

Median home value: $61,900

This information is from the 2000 U.S. Census. In 2000, West Virginia as a whole had 5 percent minorities, a median age of 38.9, median household income of $29,696, and a 75.2 percent home ownership rate.

The starting point for the determination of the corporate net income tax is federal taxable income. The tax rate was initially set at six percent on the first $50,000 of taxable income and seven percent of taxable income in excess of $50,000. When the B&O tax was eliminated for most business activities in 1987, the corporate net income tax rate rose to 9.75 percent. Thereafter, the tax rate gradually declined to nine percent by 1993. This tax typically accounts for roughly six percent of the state's total general revenue.

The basis of the West Virginia personal income tax is the taxpayer's federal adjusted gross income, with certain modifications, minus personal exemptions. The state personal exemption equals $2,000 for each personal exemption claimed on the federal tax return. In 1961, the rate of tax was equal to six percent of the federal tax applied to West Virginia taxable income. Tax rate structures changed frequently over the years, with the most recent change in 1987. Tax rates now generally range from three percent on the first $10,000 of taxable income to 6.5 percent on taxable income in excess of $60,000. The personal income tax is now the largest source of state revenue, with a yield of more than $1 billion per year.

In fiscal year 1999–2000, West Virginia ranked 42nd in the nation with a state and local tax burden per capita of $2,413, as compared to the U.S. average of $3,100. This is largely attributable to below average economic activity in terms of gross state product, personal income, and personal consumption expenditures. Due largely to the Tax Limitation Amendment, local governments collect just 23 percent of all state and local taxes, versus a national average of 38 percent. The three major sources of state and local tax revenue (property tax, sales tax, and personal income tax) account for an average of 77 percent of total tax revenue na-

tionally, but just 63 percent of total tax revenue in West Virginia. As a result, the portion of total state and local tax revenues paid through business taxes is significantly higher in West Virginia than the national average.

Mark Muchow
Department of Tax and Revenue

Taylor County

Created by an act of the Virginia General Assembly, January 19, 1844, Taylor County was formed from parts of Barbour, Harrison, and Marion counties. The county was named in honor of U.S. Sen. John Taylor (1753–1824), a soldier-statesman from Caroline County, Virginia. Taylor County, served by U.S. routes 250, 50, and 119, is located in north-central West Virginia. The county has 177.2 square miles. Steep hillsides, V-shaped valleys, and narrow flood plains characterize the region.

Trapper John Simpson was the earliest white person known to have entered present Taylor County, in 1768. Soon afterward, settlements were established in Booths Creek in the present county's northwestern corner.

Taylor County's early economy depended upon agriculture, timbering, and transportation. The oldest towns, including Pruntytown and Fetterman, formed along the Northwestern Turnpike, which followed the path of modern U.S. 50. Pruntytown is the oldest settlement in Taylor County, dating back to the early 1770s. The town, earlier called Cross Roads and Williamsport, was located at the junction of the Northwestern Turnpike and the Booths Ferry Pike. Fetterman also lay at a commercial junction, where the turnpike crossed the Tygart Valley River. Pruntytown served as the county seat from 1844, when Taylor County was formed, until 1878. The county seat was then moved to the railroad town of Grafton, reflecting

The rolling hills of Taylor County, west of Grafton.

the nation's historic move away from turnpikes and toward railroads for commerce and transportation.

The histories of the Baltimore & Ohio Railroad, Grafton, and Taylor County are interwoven. In 1850, the Virginia legislature granted a charter to the Northwestern Virginia Railroad Company (later part of the B&O) to build a railroad from the main line of the Baltimore & Ohio to Parkersburg. A clause in the charter stipulated that the railroad should reach or cross the Tygart Valley River within three miles of Three Fork Creek, then an uninhabited area in Taylor County. Grafton, one of America's first railroad towns, emerged beside the tracks at this point in 1852. Located at the junction of the B&O main line and the branch line to Parkersburg, Grafton became an important freight and passenger hub. Today, Grafton remains an active railroad town.

Like much of West Virginia during the Civil War, Taylor County was divided in loyalty. Though most residents sided with the Grafton Guards, the local Union militia, others supported and joined the Confederate Letcher's Guard. On May 22, 1861, in a fatal encounter between these two militias, Thornsberry Bailey Brown became the first Union soldier killed in the Civil War. Control of the B&O Railroad was important for the movement of troops and supplies throughout the war. Although little military action occurred in Taylor County, there were frequent raids along the rail line, and towns in the county became hospital sites and way stations for troops. Grafton acquired a national cemetery, a federal military hospital, and a morgue. Brown is among those buried at Grafton National Cemetery.

At the beginning of the 20th century, the B&O employed about 500 men in the railroad company's repair shops in Taylor County. There were three glass factories, Tygart Valley Glass Company, Empress Glass, and the Dominion Window Glass Company. There were coal companies, including Pittsvein Coal, Wendel Coal Company, Rosemont Coal, and New York Mine. The Carr China factory in Grafton closed down in 1953 and the building was destroyed by fire in 1966.

The county's newspaper from 1870 to 1975 was the *Daily Sentinel*, published in Grafton. In 1975, it became the *Mountain Statesman*, which continues to publish three days a week.

Manufacturing, government, and public utilities are Taylor County's biggest employers today. Leading industries in the county include coal, timber, plastics, glass, horticulture, and manufactured housing. The region also benefits from its rugged beauty. Recreation and tourism are well established, with facilities including the Pleasant Creek Wildlife Management Area, Tygart Lake, Tygart Lake State Park, and Valley Falls State Park. The Tygart Valley River flows through the county, linking the two state parks. The U.S. Army Corps of Engineers completed the Tygart Dam in 1938 to provide flood protection for the region. The resulting 1,740-acre lake is a popular recreation area. Valley Falls State Park, once a lumber and gristmill community, is enjoyed for its waterfalls, scenic beauty, and West Virginia heritage.

Taylor County is the place where Mother's Day was first established and the birthplace of the "mother of Mother's Day," Anna M. Jarvis. Clair Bee, a championship college basketball coach and author of juvenile sports fiction, grew up in Grafton. The high school in his popular Chip Hilton books was named for Valley Falls.

Taylor County population peaked at 19,919 in 1940, declined to a 20th-century low of 13,878 in 1970, and rebounded to 16,089 in 2000.

See also Grafton, Pruntytown Correctional Center, Tygart Valley River

Ella Belling
Morgantown

Charles Brinkman, *A History of Taylor County*, 1989; Scott W. Daley, "From Turnpikes to Railroads: Antebellum Transportation Improvements and Community Development in Taylor County, Virginia," M.A. thesis, West Virginia University, 1999.

Grace Martin Taylor

Artist Grace Martin Frame Taylor was born February 11, 1903, in Morgantown. A painter, printmaker, collage artist, and art educator, she studied at West Virginia University and then at the Pennsylvania Academy of Fine Arts. She was a cousin of artist Blanche Lazzell, at whose invitation she visited Provincetown, Massachusetts, in 1929. She returned there frequently during the summer months for the next two decades, participating in the exhibits of the Provincetown printmakers and continuing her studies under Lazzell, Fritz Pfeiffer, and Hans Hofmann.

In addition to producing an immense body of paintings, prints, and collages in a variety of realist and abstract styles, Taylor enjoyed a lengthy career as teacher and administrator at the Mason College of Fine Arts and Music in Charleston. Beginning as an instructor in 1929, she eventually rose to the presidency of the college. When the Mason College merged with Morris Harvey College (now the University of Charleston) in 1956, she returned to the faculty until her retirement in 1968.

Taylor was a founding member of the Allied Artists of West Virginia and the group's president from 1932 to 1934. She was also a founder of the American Color Print Society. Her work has been exhibited at the National Museum of Women and the Arts, at West Virginia University, and at the West Virginia State Museum. The last two institutions own extensive collections of her work. Taylor died in Charleston, October 1, 1995.

See also Blanche Lazzell

John A. Cuthbert
WVU Libraries

John A. Cuthbert, *Early Art and Artists in West Virginia*, 2000.

Sam Taylor

The first member of the West Virginia state police, Samuel Ivan Taylor was born September 21, 1895, in Mercer County. As a state police officer, Taylor was part of the force that faced off with union miners during the 1921 Battle of Blair Mountain in Logan County. He was also stationed in Mingo County in the early 1920s, when striking miners battled coal company detectives.

Taylor had served in the U.S. Army during World War I. On his train ride home to Wayne County after the war, he met Col. Jackson Arnold, who had been assigned by Governor Cornwell to start a statewide, independent police force. Arnold, noting Taylor's gun, uniform, and enthusiastic spirit, offered him a job. Taylor took the oath to become a state policeman on July 24, 1919.

During his tenure with the State Police, Taylor tracked moonshiners and bootleggers, and helped to set up new state police detachments. His state police career ended in 1927, after a motorcycle accident while on duty caused him to lose a leg. He served as Barboursville's police chief and then worked for 30 years at ACF Industries in Huntington. Sam Taylor died on July 14, 1961, at his home in Barboursville.

See also State Police

Teachers' Strike

Thousands of public school teachers refused to go to work in March 1990 in West Virginia's first statewide teachers' strike, a result of mounting frustration with having among the lowest salaries in the nation. The 11-day strike began March 7, late in the West Virginia legislature's annual session. The strike resulted in a special session on education later in 1990 and proved to be the catalyst for several changes in the state public school system, including the establishing of faculty senates in each school.

Teachers struck after negotiations with the governor's office and legislature failed to produce agreement on a pay package. Overall, teachers in 47 of the 55 counties were involved. An end to the strike was announced March 17, when House Speaker Chuck Chambers, Senate President Keith Burdette, and teachers' union leaders announced they had reached a consensus. Legislative leaders, with the support of Governor Caperton, agreed to develop short-term and long-term plans for public education and to improve teachers' pay.

Caperton initiated a series of town meetings across the state to discuss the future of education in West Virginia. Those meetings and continuing discussions with educators helped to form the basis of the legislature's special session on education in August 1990. Teachers secured significant pay raises during the next three years and budgets were provided for faculty senates in each school, giving teachers direct input into school policies and operations. New training and support programs for teachers were developed to ensure better classroom instruction.

Elizabeth Jill Wilson
Cottageville

Bob Brunner, *The Caperton Years: 1989–1993*, 1997.

Teays River

For millions of years, the region including parts of West Virginia, Virginia, Kentucky, Ohio, Indiana, and Illinois was drained by a river system now called the Teays, after the Teays Valley of Putnam and Cabell counties. The valley itself was named for an early settler, Stephen Teays. The headwaters of the Teays River included the modern New and Gauley rivers, and the upper Kanawha River. The ancient river diverged from the modern Kanawha at present St. Albans, traveling on through Hurricane, Milton, and Huntington and westward from there. This ancestral river eventually emptied into what is now the Mississippi River near present Springfield, Illinois. Interstate 64 follows the course of the Teays River from Charleston to Huntington, where the valley is approximately one mile wide.

During the Pleistocene Epoch, commonly known as the Ice Age, beginning about two million years ago, continental ice sheets repeatedly advanced and retreated across much of northern North America. The ice never reached present West Virginia, but one of the early advances created an ice dam across the Teays River in the vicinity of Chillicothe, Ohio. The water impounded by the ice dam created what is called Lake Teays or Lake Tight, in honor of its discoverer, geologist W. G. Tight. Lake Tight occupied the valley of the Teays and its tributaries from modern Chillicothe to the vicinity of Hawks Nest State Park in Fayette County. The lake existed for about 10,000 years, during which time new drainage was being established in front of the ice. At least three additional episodes of ponding occurred subsequently.

Approximately 800,000 years ago, the Ohio River system was formed. The Teays Valley between present Nitro and Huntington was abandoned after tributaries of the Teays became the lower Kanawha River from Nitro to Point Pleasant. Hurricane Creek carries most of the surface drainage from the eastern half of the abandoned valley, and the Mud and Guyandotte rivers occupy and drain the western half of the ancestral Teays Valley.

See also Glaciation, Lake Tight

Dewey D. Sanderson
Marshall University

Teays Valley

The Teays Valley, which sweeps across western West Virginia and southern Ohio, was abandoned by the disappearance of the ancient Teays River during the Pleistocene Epoch. The broad valley, now drained by other streams, has become in its West Virginia stretches the site for major suburban development. The Putnam County section of the valley, along the Interstate 64 corridor from Scott Depot to Hurricane, has been one of the fastest growing areas of the state in recent years.

See also Teays River

Telephone Service

In 1879, three years after Alexander Graham Bell first demonstrated the telephone, West Virginia's first telephone line was strung in Wheeling. The private line connected two grocery stores. In 1880, the state's first exchange was placed in service, also in Wheeling. The new telephone system started with about 30 subscribers. At first they could make only local calls, but long-distance service was started between Wheeling and Pittsburgh in 1883.

Telephone exchanges were soon added in other cities. Switchboards were installed in Parkersburg in 1882; Charleston in 1883; Huntington in 1884; Moundsville in 1884; Martinsburg in 1886; Grafton in 1890; Clarksburg in 1891; Bluefield in 1893; Fairmont in 1894; and Morgantown in 1896. Soon after the exchanges had been established, toll lines were constructed to connect the various central offices in the state. By 1889, all of the exchanges in northern West Virginia had been interconnected.

In 1897, the American Telephone & Telegraph Company extended a long-distance line from Cuyahoga Falls, Ohio, through Point Pleasant to Charleston. The line provided a connection to the exchanges in the northern part of the state. Another long-distance line was constructed through West Virginia in 1901. With terminating points at Petersburg, Virginia, and Georgetown, Kentucky, this line provided service to Charleston and Huntington, along with other cities located along the Kanawha and Ohio rivers. Construction of toll and long-distance lines through the rest of the state soon created a network to almost every section.

Highlights in the development of telephone service include the introduction of dial service in 1925 in Huntington and direct distance dialing in Wheeling and Moundsville in 1956. In 1984, Charleston became the first city in the U.S. to be able to choose long-distance carriers other than AT&T. As the nation's test market, customers chose a company among eight serving the area with long-distance service.

In 1916, the Chesapeake & Potomac Telephone Company of West Virginia was incorporated. C&P provided the majority of telephone service throughout the state. It was part of the Bell System, whose parent was AT&T. When telephone service was deregulated, AT&T agreed in the 1980s to divest itself of the Bell operating companies that provided local service. The national telephone system was replaced by a newly structured AT&T and seven regional Bell operating companies. C&P became part of Bell Atlantic Corporation, now Verizon.

Verizon, which is the largest local telephone company in the nation, continues to serve the great majority of the state's population. Other local telephone companies in West Virginia are Frontier, which serves a sizable minority of the population, and the Armstrong, West Side, War, Spruce Knob, and Hardy telephone companies, which together serve only a small fraction of the population. By 2005, competitive local providers, such as Fibernet, had taken away many customers served by these incumbent landline companies.

Long-distance service is provided by several national carriers, such as MCI and Sprint, with AT&T still the prevalent company. However, since Verizon gained federal approval to offer long distance in 2003, more West Virginia customers are buying bundles of local and long-distance service offered by the local provider. More than 15 companies provide wireless or cellular telephone service to West Virginians. Cingular merged with AT&T Wireless in 2004 to become the largest wireless provider in the state.

Technology has dramatically changed the telephone industry. Fiber-optic cables, introduced in the 1980s, are capable of carrying much more data that conventional copper wire, and most long-distance lines are now fiber optic. The use of cellular phones has grown rapidly since they first became available in the Mountain State in the 1980s. Telecommunications companies provide service to customers in West Virginia over 1.8 million access lines. Slightly more than one million of these lines are provided by traditional landline telephone companies, while more than 700,000 lines are provided by wireless carriers. Telephone companies now also provide cable television and Internet services.

See also Verizon

Judie Smith
West Virginia Humanities Council

Television

By the late 1940s, television had come to major metropolitan areas across the United States. Sets were expensive, reception unreliable, and audiences relatively small, but national broadcasting leaders continued to champion the new medium, and entrepreneurs in West Virginia were determined to bring TV to the Mountain State.

In 1948, the Federal Communications Commission granted approval for the construction of WSAZ television in Huntington. The television station, the 72nd in the nation and the first in West Virginia, was an affiliate of WSAZ radio station. WSAZ-TV went on the air October 14, 1949, as channel 5, becoming channel 3 in 1952. Early shows included the first telecast of a Marshall College (now University) basketball game on December 3, 1949.

Radio stations in Charleston, Parkersburg, and Wheeling soon followed the lead of WSAZ radio in bringing television to their markets. In Charleston, WKNA went on the air in 1953 as channel 49. In October of that year, WTAP (channel 15) began broadcasting in Parkersburg, and WTRF (channel 7) went on the air in Wheeling. The first Charleston station, however, proved unsuccessful. As a UHF channel, WKNA required its viewers to buy special equipment, and the terrain limited reliable reception to the downtown area. Rival WCHS had acquired a permit to construct VHF channel 8, which went on the air in August 1954 while WKNA went out of business.

Four more television stations began telecasting in the 1950s: WOAY (channel 4) in Oak Hill, December 1954; WHIS (channel 6), now WVVA, in Bluefield, July 1955; WOWK (channel 13), formerly WHTN, in Huntington, October 1955; and WBOY (channel 12) in Clarksburg, November 1957. The launch in June 1960 of WJPB (channel 5), now WDTV, serving Weston-Bridgeport-Clarksburg-Fairmont was followed by a two-decade hiatus. In February 1981, WLJY (channel 46) of Clarksburg began broadcasting and, in September 1982, WVAH (channel 11, formerly 23), started transmitting from Hurricane. Since that time, additional stations have gone on the air.

Public television made its debut in West Virginia in February 1969, when WWVU (channel 24), now WNPB, of Morgantown went on the air. WMUL (channel 33), now WPBY, of Huntington followed suit in July of that year; and, in November 1970, WSWP (channel 9) of Beckley began broadcasting.

Because of its rugged topography, West Virginia was a pioneering state in the early development of cable television. In late 1949 and early 1950, commercial cable installations began operating at Piedmont in Mineral County and Cameron in Marshall County, respectively. The first coaxial cable system started carrying programming of WSAZ television to Welch in 1951. For the same reason, West Virginia also figured in the early expansion of satellite television.

Reflecting their advertising strategy, West Virginia television stations in the 1950s began producing a variety of local programming aimed at children, teens, women, and other demographic segments. Especially popular were religious shows, "hillbilly" music jamborees, wrestling matches, and guest interview broadcasts. Among the memorable personalities and programs were Farmer Bill Click, Don Wagoner the "Beachcomber," and long-time news anchor Bos Johnson (WSAZ); Dick Reid's "Lucky 8 Ranch," Marilyn Fletcher's "Romper Room," Jackie Oblinger's "Women's Page" and Katie Doonan's "Katie's Kitchen" (WCHS); Bill Hickock's "Circle 6 Ranch" and Cecil Surratt's "R.F.D. Jamboree" (WHIS); Reverend Hoover's "Message of Light" (WDTV); "Uncle Pete" for kids (WBOY); Pat Gaughan's "TV 7 Reports" (WTRF); and versatile on-air talent Shirley Love (WOAY).

Although West Virginia Media Holdings owns four stations in the state (WOWK, WBOY, WTRF, and WVNS) in 2005, other leading stations are owned by out-of-state media companies such as Sinclair Broadcast Group of Baltimore (WCHS), Emmis Communications of Indianapolis (WSAZ), Gray Television Group of Atlanta (WTAP), and Quincy Newspapers, Inc. of Illinois (WVVA).

See also Cable Television, Satellite Television

Larry Sonis
Arlington, Texas

Textile Industry

During the 19th century, the manufacturing of cloth or textiles developed into a lucrative business in some parts of West Virginia. Through the mountain counties, small, family-owned operations began to spring up and replace the household production of textile goods. These small mills usually included fulling and carding machines that made a more durable and attractive yarn than could be spun by hand, and the mills also wove cloth, blankets, linsey-woolsey, and stockings. Carding machines could be found in Wellsburg, Martinsburg, Wheeling, and a dozen other towns.

As early as 1810, Berkeley County had a sizable water-powered textile industry, and it led the state of Virginia in the production of mixed cottons. By the end of the 19th century, companies manufactured calicos in Wheeling, hosiery and woolens in Martinsburg, blankets in Charleston, and upholstery and work clothes in Huntington. J. L. Stifel & Sons operated in Wheeling from 1835 to 1957, producing calico and other cotton goods.

The country's first electric-powered textile factory was in Martinsburg, the county seat of Berkeley County. Established there in 1890–91, the Middlesex Knitting Company, later known as Interwoven, was operated by electricity from the beginning. Martinsburg became West Virginia's leader in textile manufacturing with the establishment of Middlesex, Martinsburg Worsted and Cassimere Company, and Crawford Woolen. The latter two were established by William H. Crawford of New Rochelle, New York. By the close of World War I, Crawford's interests were purchased by investors from nearby Winchester, Virginia. For the next three and a half decades, Berkeley Woolen and Dunn Woolen helped to meet the nation's demand for woolen goods.

A textile worker at Interwoven Mills, about 1950.

The two companies, along with Interwoven and Perfection Garment Company (a women's clothing company), were major elements in the Martinsburg economy. About half of the city's workers were employed at one of the textile or garment factories.

Shortly after World War I started in Europe, major changes began to occur in the textile industries. Manufacturers began turning to the use of synthetic and chemically regenerated yarns and fibers. Competition from plants at Nitro and Parkersburg which made rayon by chemically processing raw cotton and wood pulp contributed to the shift. DuPont's Belle works in Kanawha County provided vital intermediate material for the production of nylon, the first true synthetic, providing such material for the entire world production of nylon from 1937 to 1946. This trend to synthetics continued throughout the century.

World War II brought big profits and an increase in jobs to the state's textile companies, but the growth was short-lived. Companies such as Berkeley Woolen experienced serious financial difficulties and closed before the end of the 1940s. Dunn Woolen followed in the early 1950s. Employment declined in the state's textile factories, and changing ownership merely forestalled the inevitable. In 1947, 14,510 people were employed in textile-related jobs in West Virginia, but by 1967 only 7,100 people were.

In 2005, the textile industry employed fewer than 500 workers in West Virginia. They worked in mostly small shops scattered over much of the state, making yarn and fabric and such products as cur-

tains, awnings, and industrial tarps. Some embroidered, monogrammed, or silk-screened clothing.

See also Interwoven Mills, Martinsburg, J. L. Stifel & Sons

Jerra Jenrette
Edinboro University

Jerra Jenrette, "'There's No Damn Reason For It—It's Just Our Policy': Labor-Management Conflict in Martinsburg, West Virginia's Textile and Garment Industries," Ph.D. dissertation, West Virginia University, 1996.

Theatre West Virginia

Theatre West Virginia, originally the West Virginia Historical Drama Association, was founded in 1955. Its first production was the outdoor drama, *Honey in the Rock,* which opened at Cliffside Amphitheatre at Grandview State Park near Beckley in June 1961. The play by Kermit Hunter depicts the founding of the Mountain State in 1863.

In 1968, the outgoing Theatre West Virginia producer, Norman L. Fagan, suggested to the new producer, Ewel Cornett, that a show based on the famous Hatfield-McCoy Feud be added to the repertoire. Cornett commissioned West Virginia native Billy Edd Wheeler to write the feud play, and the musical drama *Hatfields and McCoys* opened June 20, 1970. *Hatfields and McCoys* was the only play produced that summer, and both plays ran in 1971 and later. The addition of the new play in combination with *Honey in the Rock* quickly doubled the attendance. The productions became a popular tourist attraction in southern West Virginia.

In 1974, Cornett assisted in reorganizing the company, forming a League of

Resident Theatres theater company and changing the corporation's name to Theatre Arts of West Virginia. This represented a professionalization of the operation. A branch called Theatre West Virginia began touring the state, performing classic theater works in community centers and schools. By the late 1970s, the troupe, including a traveling marionette theater, was touring the eastern United States from Florida to Pennsylvania. In the 1980s, the entire Theatre Arts operation began to refer to itself as Theatre West Virginia.

During the summer of 2000, Theatre West Virginia celebrated the 40th anniversary of *Honey in the Rock* and the 30th birthday of *Hatfields and McCoys*. Both plays continue to be produced each summer, in combination with popular theater standards such as *The Sound of Music, Fiddler on the Roof, Oklahoma,* and *Grease.*

Ewel Cornett
Louisville, Kentucky

"This Land is Home to Me"

"This Land is Home to Me," a pastoral letter issued by the Catholic bishops of Appalachia in 1975, was written in response to the concerns raised by the Catholic Committee of Appalachia in 1974 regarding the economic and political inequalities that characterized the Appalachian region. Over the course of the following year, members of the committee traveled throughout Appalachia, listening to individuals, community groups, and church workers. The stories that came out of these visits were then incorporated into the writing of the pastoral, which was grounded in Scripture and the teachings of the Catholic Church on social justice. The pastoral is unusual for its poetic language and the free verse style in which it is written.

The letter was signed by all 25 bishops of the Appalachian region and was promulgated on February 1, 1975, at Wheeling Jesuit University. In 1995, the Catholic Committee of Appalachia published a second pastoral message, "At Home in the Web of Life: A Pastoral Message on Sustainable Communities in Appalachia," on the observance of the 20th anniversary of "This Land is Home to Me." In this pastoral the committee advocates the creation and defense of sustainable communities in Appalachia through the responsible stewardship of the land and its resources, the most important being its people.

"This Land is Home to Me" is recognized to be one of the most significant statements to emerge from the U.S. Catholic Church and has become a model for groups all over the world that are interested in writing on matters of social justice. More than 200,000 copies of the

The bishops size up Appalachia

"The Appalachian mountains form the spiny backbone of the eastern United States. This whole stretch, which the federal government calls 'the Appalachian Region,' runs from southern New York to northern Georgia and Alabama. It contains 397 counties in 13 states, and all of West Virginia. In the region there are: mountain folk, city folk, country folk, coal miners and steel workers, union workers and non-union workers, industrial workers and service workers, farmers and farm laborers, housewives and children, teachers and health workers, ministers and rabbis and priests, artists and poets, professionals and technicians, lawyers and politicians, lobbyists and interest groups, executives and managers, little business people and big business people, coal companies and chemical companies, industrialists and bankers.

"So, you see, Appalachia is not a simple place. There are rich and poor, big and little, new and old, and lots in between."

—Appalachian Bishops "This Land is Home to Me" (1975)

pastoral are in circulation, and it has been translated into several languages.

Tricia Pyne
St. Mary's Seminary & University, Maryland

Clint Thomas

Athlete Clinton Cyrus Thomas was a star in the Negro Leagues, during the days of racial segregation in major league baseball. Thomas settled in Charleston after his playing days and made a long career in West Virginia state government.

Thomas was born November 25, 1896, in Greenup, Kentucky. He moved to Columbus, Ohio, as a teenager and joined the army when he was 18. Returning to Columbus in 1919, Thomas, who had spent his childhood playing sandlot baseball, joined a semi-pro team. The following year, he moved to New York to play for the Brooklyn Royal Giants. He joined the Lincoln Giants in 1921 and in 1922 moved to the Detroit Stars. Usually a second baseman, Thomas got the chance to play in the outfield and earned his nickname, "The Hawk," for his ability to dart across center field and pounce on anything in his vicinity.

In 1923, Thomas began a six-year stint with the Philadelphia Hilldale Giants. In his first year, he led the team with 14 home runs in 100 games, batted .374, and stole 21 bases. He was a key player in Hilldale's Eastern Colored League championship games. In 1929, Thomas began playing with the New York Black Yankees, previously the Lincoln Giants. He spoiled the 1932 unveiling of Pittsburgh's Greenlee Field by scoring the only run and making a spectacular, game-saving catch in his team's defeat of Satchel Paige and the hometown Pittsburgh Crawfords. Another highlight was when he hit a triple off Dizzy Dean and scored the game's only run in a win over a team of white all-stars in an exhibition game.

An ankle injury in 1938 interrupted Thomas's career with the Black Yankees. Attempting to return to baseball a year later, he reinjured his ankle and gave up baseball for good. In his two decades in the Negro Leagues, Thomas compiled a lifetime batting average around .350, usually hitting about 25 home runs a year.

After working at the Brooklyn Navy Yard in World War II, Thomas came to Charleston at the suggestion of his brother. He began working in the capitol in 1945 as a messenger for the Department of Mines. In 1954, he became a messenger for the state Senate. Thomas was a familiar figure at the capitol until past the age of 80, when failing eyesight forced him to retire. He died in Charleston, December 2, 1990.

Judie Smith
West Virginia Humanities Council

Frank Thomas

Aviator Frank K. "Flying Frank" Thomas was born September 16, 1921, in Lansing, Fayette County, the youngest of eight children. He earned his nickname from spending a long lifetime in the air: flying charter passengers to distant places, taking others sight-seeing over the New River Gorge, giving flight lessons, looking for downed aircraft with the Civil Air Patrol, spotting forest fires, and just about everything else connected with aviation. In 1946, he almost single-handedly built Fayette Airport, which he owned and operated. He took up one of his planes every day the weather permitted.

By the late 20th century, Thomas was an author, a poet, an artist, and a philosopher. He was an aviation legend and a colorful figure in the emergence of New River tourism, best known for his $5 tours of New River Gorge. His 1978 book, *It Is This Way with Men Who Fly*, is a fascinating history of West Virginia aviation. At an age when others had retired he said he loved flying so much that he hated to leave the field at night. Frank Thomas died March 23, 2001.

Louis E. Keefer
Reston, Virginia

Louis E. Keefer, "Flying Frank Thomas: 'Just Like a Preacher with the Calling,'" *Goldenseal*, Summer 1992; Frank Thomas, *It Is This Way with Men Who Fly*, 1978.

Thomas Memorial Hospital

The Herbert J. Thomas Memorial Hospital in South Charleston opened in December 1946. The hospital was named for a local football star killed during World War II when he threw himself on a grenade. Thomas, a U.S. Marine sergeant, was posthumously awarded the Congressional Medal of Honor for his heroism.

To remedy the Kanawha Valley's hospital bed shortage, the city of South Charleston had begun construction of the hospital in 1943. Financed with $650,000 in federal grants and loans, the building was completed in July 1945. However, the city ran out of money before the hospital could be equipped, and a group of citizens from South Charleston and surrounding communities undertook to raise the necessary funds. The Herbert J. Thomas Memorial Hospital Association, chartered in July 1946, raised $250,000 to provide money for equipment and staff. The association continues to operate the hospital, leasing from the city, which owns the property and buildings.

Originally, the hospital had 70 beds and 100 employees. Through the years, Thomas Memorial Hospital has been renovated and expanded, and in 2005 was about three times its original size, with 261 beds and more than 1,000 employees. Hospital services include a cancer center, obstetric services, behavior health services, lung center, sleep diagnostic center, physical therapy center, and a full range of imaging services.

In 2001, the Thomas emergency center expanded from 7,000 square feet to 13,000 square feet. The new facility included 20 beds on the emergency side and 10 beds in CareCenter24, which handles less serious matters. The most recent expansion at Thomas Memorial is a new four-story office building providing additional space for doctors affiliated with the hospital.

Rod Thorn

Athlete Rodney King "Rod" Thorn, born May 23, 1941, was a West Virginia University basketball All-American (1962–63). Thorn was Princeton High School's best basketball and baseball player and was heavily recruited by college teams. The straight-A student was leaning toward Duke University when the West Virginia legislature passed an unprecedented resolution declaring him a state natural resource.

At WVU, Thorn was given uniform number 44, the same as the legendary Jerry West. Though he played in the National Basketball Association, he might have been bound, too, for the major leagues to play baseball, his favorite sport. An injury, however, prevented him from playing baseball.

Thorn had an extended and distinguished career in the National Basketball Association as a player and as a team coach, general manager and president. In 1963, he was the second pick in the first round of the NBA draft and went to the Baltimore Bullets. He played with the Bullets, and later with the Detroit Pistons, St. Louis Hawks, and Seattle Supersonics. He was an assistant coach with the Sonics and the New Jersey Nets, and was head coach of the St. Louis Spirits of the old American Basketball Association before going to the Chicago Bulls as general manager. He also coached the Bulls for 30 games. As general manager, he recruited and signed Michael Jordan. He is now president and general manager of the New Jersey Nets.

Thorn was inducted into the WVU Sports Hall of Fame in 1992.

Norman Julian
Dominion Post
Norman Julian, *Legends: Profiles in West Virginia University Basketball,* 1998.

Thurmond

West Virginia's best-known boom town straddled the Chesapeake & Ohio Railway deep in the New River Gorge. Thurmond meant excitement, danger, and pleasures of the hell-raising variety to generations of miners, railroaders, and traveling men, and the Fayette County community is still remembered that way by many today.

Thurmond was founded by Capt. W. D. Thurmond in the 1880s, following local completion of the C&O in 1873. Thurmond was a railroad town, occupying a strategic site where important feeder lines came down to the main railroad from the burgeoning New River coalfield. Thanks to coal, Thurmond became a major revenue producer for the C&O, originating more freight tonnage than did Cincinnati or Richmond. The railroad located a major rail yard, water and coaling facilities for steam locomotives, and maintenance shops at Thurmond. Goods poured in while the coal rolled out, and during its heyday Thurmond was busier than the nearby county seat towns of Fayetteville and Beckley. Banks, wholesale grocers, the telephone and telegraph companies, and other key operations located themselves in Thurmond.

The bustling community attracted less reputable business, as well. But the brothels and saloons which gave Thurmond its bad name were located outside the city limits, mostly across the New River in the "Ballyhack" neighborhood. Captain Thurmond, who owned almost all Thurmond's real estate during his lifetime, was a strict Baptist who forebade riotous living within his jurisdiction.

Nonetheless, the Captain's town developed the worst sort of reputation. Thurmond was characterized as the Dodge City of the East, "hell with a river through it" where miners and their money were parted with bloody corpses the occasional byproduct. A poker game ran for 14 years at the Dunglen, before an arsonist torched the grand southside hotel. Marshal Harrison Ash, himself perhaps acquainted with both sides of the law, broke heads of individual offenders but made little headway against the overall problem.

Thurmond grew to 315 residents by 1910, the year its founder died, and peaked at 462 in 1930. Its decline began with the spread of highways through the region; historian Kyle McCormick said the rail town died of "good roads and a bad name." A series of fires reduced Thurmond's size. But the town prospered in a modest fashion through the end of steam railroading, which came in the 1950s on the C&O.

Today, Thurmond is mostly a ghost town. The trackside business block remains, however, along with the restored depot and other historic structures, providing picturesque settings for the movie *Matewan* in 1986. Thurmond is a major put-in point for whitewater rafters, and the centerpiece of National Park Service efforts to interpret the history of New River Gorge National River.

See also Harrison Ash, Matewan, New River Gorge National River, W. D. Thurmond

Ken Sullivan
West Virginia Humanities Council
Ken Sullivan, *Thurmond: A New River Community,* 1989.

W. D. Thurmond

Businessman William Dabney Thurmond, born November 11, 1820, in Amherst County, Virginia, migrated to Fayette County about 1845 as a young man with his father's family. He was a pioneer New River coal operator and founded one of the most notorious boom towns in West Virginia's industrial history.

Thurmond served as a captain during the Civil War with Thurmond's Rangers. These irregular Confederate troops were commanded by brother Philip Thurmond, who was killed in Putnam County in 1864. The guerrilla war favored by the Rangers characterized the Civil War in the mountains, and W. D. Thurmond's own family was burned out by opposing forces. According to his family, Thurmond remained an "unreconstructed Rebel" after the war, refusing to sign an oath of allegiance for the rest of his long life.

In 1873, Thurmond was commissioned to survey land on the north side of New River in the heart of New River Gorge. He accepted 73 acres as his pay, and in fol-

lowing years he built the town of Thurmond there. The town prospered with the coming of the railroad, developing at the same time a reputation as the place to let off steam in the hard-working coalfields. While W. D. Thurmond managed things within the town's narrow corporate boundaries according to his own strict Baptist beliefs, to his dismay the larger community (and the Thurmond name) became synonymous with exuberant lawlessness.

Captain Thurmond died May 14, 1910, and was buried near his home in Minden. His grandson, Walter R. Thurmond, was an important early coal operator in Logan County.

See also Thurmond, Thurmond's Rangers
Walter R. T. Witschey, *The Thurmonds of Virginia,* 1978.

Thurmond's Rangers

Thurmond's Partisan Rangers were raised for the Confederate service primarily from Fayette, Greenbrier, and Monroe counties during the spring and summer of 1862. The two companies were commanded by brothers William D. and Philip J. Thurmond of Fayette County. As other companies of rangers formed in southern West Virginia and western Virginia, these companies joined and became a battalion variously known as Thurmond's, Morris's, and Houndshell's. An estimated 650 men served with this larger unit during the war, which in late 1863 became 44th Virginia Cavalry Battalion and part of the regular army.

The mountaineers who comprised Thurmond's Rangers knew that this type of semi-independent service would allow them to remain near their homes and families. Considered by some to be nothing more than bushwhackers, partisan rangers assisted the Confederacy as scouts, spies, and raiders. They were feared and respected in this capacity. On October 26, 1864, Capt. Philip Thurmond was killed in action at Winfield, Putnam County. A postwar surveyor, coal operator, and land agent, Capt. William D. Thurmond founded the New River Gorge town of Thurmond in the 1880s. He died at age 89 on May 14, 1910.

See also W. D. Thurmond, Thurmond
Tim McKinney
Fayetteville
Jeffrey C. Weaver, *Thurmond's Partisan Rangers,* 1993; Walter R. T. Witschey, *The Thurmonds of Virginia,* 1978.

Timbering and Logging

Timbering and logging—cutting trees and transporting them to the sawmill—are the hardest parts of processing trees into lumber. In the early days trees were cut with axes and the logs were dragged to the mill by oxen, mules, or horses. As

Meadow River Lumber Company loggers at work, early 1900s.

sawmills became larger more efficient means of securing logs were needed.

In preparing a tract of land for timbering a crew of men built a rough skidroad through the trees by removing brush, stumps, and large rocks. Two sawyers then started cutting the trees adjacent to the skidroad. To direct the fall of the tree, a notch was chopped in the side of the trunk toward where it was to fall. A crosscut saw was used to fell the tree. A crosscut saw was five to seven feet long. A handle was attached to each end, and two men pulled the saw back and forth. If the tree was large, wedges were driven in the saw kerf opposite the notch. Skilled sawyers could cut a tree in a few minutes. The tree was then cleared of limbs and sawed into logs of suitable lengths. The two sawyers worked with a fitter, who notched the tree for felling and then measured the logs to be cut from it, and knot bumpers who cut the limbs from the felled tree. A six-man crew could cut and prepare about 225 logs a day.

Moving the logs out of the woods was accomplished with a team of horses. When the day's work began the teamster curried and fed his team and drove them to the skidroad. Here the skidding crew prepared a train of logs, fastening a dozen or more together end-to-end with devices called grabs. A grab was a short piece of chain with a swivel in the middle and heavy pins at each end. The pins were driven into adjacent ends of the logs to fasten them together. The teamster then hooked the horse team to the front log with special grabs and the horses pulled the train of logs to a landing located either along a stream or along the logging railroad.

If the logs were to be floated downstream to the sawmill, as was done before railroads were built into the woods, the logs were stockpiled until a flood occurred; then they were rolled into the stream and floated away. After logging railroads were built, the logs were loaded on railroad cars by steam-powered log loaders and taken to the mill by rail utilizing steam-powered geared locomotives. At the mill the logs were rolled into ponds where they floated until taken inside to be sawed.

The cutting and skidding of logs often took place miles from the mill and the town. Men working in the woods lived in camps that sometimes were large enough to accommodate 100 men. Food was hauled to the camps by the log train. The camps had their own cooks, and hearty meals were served to the hard-working men. Most stayed at camp at least a week before coming to the nearest town. Some men stayed as long as a month, and when they visited town they had a boisterous celebration making such communities as Cass roaring, wide-open places. As the original forest was depleted, logging jobs became scarce. At the same time, around the 1950s, the character of logging changed. The horse teams were replaced by caterpillar tractors, crosscut saws were replaced by chain saws, and the log train by trucks.

See also Sawmills

Roy B. Clarkson
West Virginia University

Warren E. Blackhurst, *Riders of the Flood*, 1954; Roy B. Clarkson, *Tumult on the Mountains: Lumbering in West Virginia 1770–1920*, 1964; Clarkson, *On Beyond Leatherbark: The Cass Saga*, 1990.

Timberline

Timberline Four Seasons Resort is located at Canaan Valley. The state's newest ski area opened in January 1987 and offers 36 trails on more than 91 skiable acres.

Private development of the Timberline area began in the late 1960s, corresponding with the progression of plans to create Canaan Valley State Park, which is just a few miles away. In 1985, a Philadelphia surgeon, Frederick A. Reichle, and members of his family purchased property at Timberline from the original developer to develop a ski area on Cabin Mountain. The resort opened two years later. The entire Timberline development now has about 400 houses, and rentals are available throughout the year.

Timberline offers 1,000 vertical feet of skiing, with trails for all levels of skill. Two-mile Salamander Run is the longest ski slope in the Mid-Atlantic. Three lifts accommodate 4,000 skiers an hour. The high altitude, with a 4,268-foot peak, is known for its long winters and abundant natural snowfall, which averages more than 150 inches a season. Snow-making is available for about 94 percent of the terrain. Nine trails are lighted for night skiing.

Additionally, 17 kilometers of cross-country skiing and backcountry trails are accessible from Timberline.

See also Canaan Valley, Skiing

Tobacco

Tobacco has been an important crop in West Virginia since early times. It has been a widespread social habit, and by the 20th century a major health problem. Although its economic importance as an agricultural crop dwindled over the course of the century, West Virginians' rates of tobacco consumption remained among the highest in the country.

West Virginia tobacco production peaked in 1909 at 14,400,000 pounds. By 1950, the annual crop was approximately 4,000,000 pounds, further declining to an average of 3,000,000 pounds during the 1990s. In 2002, 1,874,110 pounds of tobacco was produced in West Virginia on 544 farms. As recently as 1983, tobacco was the second most valuable farm crop in the state, with $8,922,000 in cash receipts. West Virginia producers saw tobacco receipts drop to $3,710,000 in 2003.

Virtually all tobacco produced in the state is the burley type, including the Yellow Orinoco and Sweet Roanoke varieties, maturing at a height of four to six feet. The main tobacco counties are Mason, Putnam, Lincoln, Cabell, and Jackson, although some tobacco is grown in more than a dozen other counties. West Virginia has mostly small, part-time producers who grow tobacco for extra income. The larger tobacco growers in the western part of the state typically grow 15 to 20 acres.

Raising tobacco is often a labor-intensive family enterprise, from the sowing of seed beds to transplanting, cultivating, harvesting, and stripping. In addition to weed elimination, plants must be inspected for tobacco worms and disease. Tobacco must be topped and suckered to promote root growth and larger leaves. During harvest in September the plants are cut and speared on poles and left in the field to wilt. Then the poles are hung upside down on tiered racks in open barns where the richly aromatic burley is air-cured for one to two months. Tobacco is readied for market by stripping and sorting the leaves and packing them into bales.

Some tobacco was made into "twists" and sold right off the farm well into the 20th century. Generally, however, the sale of tobacco has long been conducted through special warehouses. Shepherdstown had the first tobacco warehouse, which closed prior to the Civil War. By the late 19th century millions of pounds of burley was stored and auctioned at tobacco warehouses on the other side of West Virginia, in Cabell and Putnam counties. Warehouse operations were well established at Milton and Hurricane by the time the Huntington Tobacco Warehouse opened in 1912. It became the largest in the state and the last to remain open, closing its doors in 1998.

Opening in late November, the auction season continued until the regional crop was sold. Buyers such as Brown & Williamson, Liggett & Meyers, and others had their representatives on hand. Once the auction began, it was witty, fast-moving, and exciting with ticket markers keeping track of individual piles selling every two to three seconds. Farmers might stay in town for several days until their tobacco was sold, and the money was welcome as the holidays neared.

Tobacco farmers raise their crop within a federally regulated system of acreage allotment and price supports. Allotted quotas have decreased since the late 1990s, and many West Virginia burley growers have switched to truck crops or hay.

Wheeling is home to the better-known tobacco manufacturers in the state and was once among the nation's leading cigar producers. Marsh Wheeling Stogies made cigars in Wheeling from 1840 to 2001. Bloch Brothers began producing chewing tobacco in 1879, and the company's Mail Pouch barn signs are regional landmarks.

West Virginia has consistently ranked among the top states nationwide in adult smoking. In 2003, according to the Centers for Disease Control, 27.4 percent of adults in West Virginia smoked, compared to 22.1 percent nationally. West Virginia's rate was second only to Kentucky, which reported a rate of 30.8 percent. As the 20th century drew to a close, smokeless tobacco use in West Virginia was far above the national average, with a rate of 8.4 percent, compared to the U.S. average of 3.8 percent.

In 1994, West Virginia became the third state to file suit against the tobacco industry to recover costs for smoking-related illnesses. The 1998 settlement was expected to net the state about $1.8 billion during a 25-year time span. In 2004, West Virginia's share of the settlement was almost $63 million.

See also Bloch Brothers Tobacco Company, Mail Pouch Barns, Marsh Wheeling Stogies

Scot E. Long
Hebron, Ohio

Tolsia Highway

The portion of U.S. 52 in southern West Virginia that runs between Kenova in Wayne County and Kermit in Mingo County is often called the Tolsia Highway. The acronym is taken from the Tug-Ohio-Levisa-Sandy Improvement Association, a group of local business people and community leaders who successfully lobbied in the 1950s and 1960s to have a new roadway constructed along the Big Sandy River.

Once the new road was built, the U.S. 52 designation which previously had applied to the road connecting Huntington and Crum was moved to the new road. The old road was renumbered as U.S. 152.

In the late 1980s and early 1990s, a series of traffic fatalities, many of them involving dangerously overloaded coal trucks, prompted some West Virginians to cite the Tolsia Highway as the most dangerous road in the state. In response, state and federal officials pressed ahead with plans for upgrading it from a two-lane roadway to a four-lane divided highway.

The new, upgraded road will be built in three sections, the first from Kenova to Fort Gay, the second from Fort Gay to Crum, and the third from Crum to Kermit. Construction on the upgrade, estimated to cost more than $800 million, began in 1996 and is expected to take a decade or longer to complete.

James E. Casto
Herald-Dispatch

Joseph Tomlinson

Joseph Tomlinson, frontiersman and town founder, was born October 12, 1745, near Cumberland, Maryland. In 1770, Tomlinson moved to the Ohio River in Western Virginia, then the far frontier. He established claims to choice tracts of land at the mouth of Grave Creek (present Moundsville) and opposite the mouth of the Muskingum River (present Williamstown). In 1772, Tomlinson discovered the Grave Creek Mound.

In January 1775, Tomlinson married Elizabeth Hartness in Maryland. Soon after their return to Grave Creek, Indian incursions forced them to flee to Pennsylvania. They returned in 1783 despite continued hostilities. In April 1784, during Tomlinson's absence from home, two Wyandot warriors plundered his cabin but spared both it and his defenseless family. In gratitude, he wrote a letter thanking the tribal chief for the Indians' compassion.

Following the 1795 end of the Indian wars, Tomlinson laid out on his Grave Creek property a town he called Elizabethtown in his wife's honor, today's Moundsville. Here he died, May 30, 1825. Elizabeth survived until 1841. Her portrait now hangs in Henderson Hall near Williamstown.

Tomlinson's older brother, Samuel Tomlinson, also settled on the Ohio Valley frontier in 1770. The brothers participated jointly in some transactions. Property of theirs that was later deeded to their sister, Mrs. Isaac Williams, became the modern Williamstown.

Samuel Tomlinson, who never married, was killed when ambushed by Indians near Wheeling, August 27, 1777, at the beginning of the first siege of Fort Henry.

See also Grave Creek Mound, Moundsville

Ray Swick
Blennerhassett Island State Park

Tomlinson Run State Park

Tomlinson Run State Park is located in Hancock County, on State Route 8 near New Manchester. The park and run are named for the pioneer Tomlinson family.

The park's 1,389 acres are forested and hilly, with a lake and a gorge down to the nearby Ohio River. The gorge has sandstone cliffs, steep hills, and a trail paralleling Tomlinson Run. The park's waterways are stocked with trout in early spring, and in June the lake is stocked with catfish. Bass and bluegill fishing are also good.

While Tomlinson Run offers no individual rental cabins, the group camp is a popular feature of the park. Sleeping cabins are located near the playground, counselors' quarters, dining hall, kitchen, shower houses, and a recreation hall.

Tomlinson Run State Park started with a Civilian Conservation Corps camp in the late 1930s. Visitors can still see some of the picnic shelters built of massive stone, a hallmark throughout West Virginia of the expert handiwork of the CCC crews. The Tomlinson Run dam was built, 1940–42, by the federal Works Progress Administration (WPA).

See also State Parks

Maureen F. Crockett
St. Albans

Topography

West Virginia's land surface rises to its highest elevations in the Allegheny Mountains and Yew Mountains (a subsidiary range of the Alleghenies), which occur in the northeastern and east-central areas of the state. The highest point (4,861 feet above mean sea level) is Spruce Knob, along the crest of the Allegheny spine in Pendleton County. Most of the state's rivers begin among these high mountains. The lowest elevation in the state (247 feet) occurs at Harpers Ferry at the eastern tip of the Eastern Panhandle, where the Potomac River leaves West Virginia. To the west, the lowest elevation (approximately 620 feet) is reached at Kenova (near Huntington), the westernmost part of the state, where the Ohio River passes on to Kentucky and westward.

West Virginia is nicknamed the Mountain State because of the rugged, mountainous terrain that comprises essentially all of its area. However, the state's topographic character varies in direct association with its geology. The Eastern

The everlasting hills

"The hills are our symbol of eternity. There they stand, the evidence of things seen, as nearly everlasting and unchangeable as anything man may know. One who has dwelled within them senses that they are beyond the horizon, even when he is in the level lands. For this reassurance, all hill people will be duly thankful."

—Maurice Brooks *The Appalachians* (1965)

Panhandle lies in the Ridge and Valley province, a name that aptly describes the local topography. Long, steep, narrow, northeast-southwest trending mountain ridges are separated by relatively broad, flat-bottomed valleys. The wide, flat to gently rolling Shenandoah Valley lies in the easternmost part of the Ridge and Valley province, and extends into the northeastern part of West Virginia, culminating at Harpers Ferry.

The western boundary of the Ridge and Valley topography is distinctly marked by the Allegheny Front in the north (Mineral, Grant, and Pendleton counties), and by the St. Clair Fault in the south (Monroe and Mercer counties). Whereas most topographic boundaries within the state are transitional, this one is sharp and abrupt. Immediately west of the Ridge and Valley province is the Appalachian Plateau province, including a High Plateau subprovince. A belt of relatively broad, more massive mountain ridges makes up the High Plateau region, and includes the state's highest elevations. The High Plateau encompasses Preston, Tucker, and Randolph counties, and parts of Mineral, Grant, Pendleton and Pocahontas. The mountains exert significant influence on the weather of the region. As the typical weather pattern moves from west or southwest to east across West Virginia, the gradually rising western slope of the High Plateau induces rainfall, and receives the highest rate of precipitation of any place in the state. Conversely, the low-lying valleys just east of the abrupt Allegheny Front lie in a "rain shadow" of the high mountains, and receive the least precipitation in the state.

The western two-thirds of West Virginia lies in the Appalachian Plateau, but substantial differences in topography exist from north to south and from east to west within this province. The east-west variation is simply a transition from the broad mountains of the High Plateau to the gently rolling, small hills adjacent to the Ohio Valley. The north-south variation is less systematic. The northern part of the state exhibits broad rolling hills with often steep, narrow stream hollows. Total surface relief (the difference in elevation from highest hilltops to deepest hollows or valleys) is typically on the order of several hundred feet. The configuration of the land surface imposes relatively little restriction on residential placement, and hilltops and ridgelines

are often the settings of choice for domestic and business development.

In contrast, the southwestern part of the state (south and southwest of Charleston, in particular) has extremely rugged topography. This deeply eroded plateau exhibits narrow, winding valleys and hollows and narrow, sharp-crested ridges, with very steep slopes. Total relief commonly exceeds 1,000 feet. Cultural development is largely confined to the tight valley floors and floodplains in this area, which includes the state's rich southern coalfields.

See also Geology

Ron Mullennex
Bluefield

Tories

Tories, or Loyalists, were Americans who sided with England during the Revolutionary War. They made up a significant minority in some parts of Western Virginia, including present southern West Virginia. The Loyalist movement became a special concern for inhabitants of the Monongahela Valley and the South Branch Valley, including Hampshire and present Grant and Hardy counties. Loyalist attempts to aid the British and Indians in the Upper Ohio Valley were a major threat early in the war. The Tories of that region included Alexander McKee and Simon Girty.

In early 1781, Loyalist citizens of Hampshire County, led by John Claypool, began to resist the imposition of taxes and a military draft and refused to collect beef and clothing for the Continental Army as required by the Virginia Assembly. Claypool and his Tories were confronted by the Patriot militia, led by Gen. Daniel Morgan, on Lost River, in what is now Hardy County. The militia from nearby counties pursued the Tories into the valley of the South Branch, where they finally surrendered and were brought to trial. In June 1781, in the mountainous region of present Pendleton County, another Tory insurgency was aborted and their leaders imprisoned in Staunton.

One group of the Tories fled Hampshire County and found a haven in the eastern part of what is now Randolph County, to escape the harassment of the Patriots. Uriah Gandy, the leader of the group, established a temporary refuge on two small streams that flow into the Dry Fork River and are now identified as Big Tory and Little Tory Camp runs.

Gandy Creek, which flows into the Dry Fork River, was named for Uriah Gandy. Gandy later served as an early sheriff of Randolph County before migrating to Kentucky. His success in politics after the Revolution suggests that he managed to retain or reestablish a place of respect among his fellow citizens. Claypool's followers likewise were mostly pardoned and some served later with the Patriot forces. Historian Otis Rice suggested that "war weariness" may have been more an issue with the Tories than a commitment to the British cause.

See also Revolutionary War

Donald L. Rice
Elkins

Hu Maxwell, *History of Randolph County, West Virginia*, 1898; Oren F. Morton, *A History of Pendleton County, West Virginia*, 1910; Howard M. Wilson, *Great Valley Patriots: Western Virginia in the Struggle for Liberty*, 1976.

Fred Martin Torrey

Sculptor Fred Martin Torrey, born in Fairmont, July 29, 1884, specialized in depictions of Abraham Lincoln. Educated in the Fairmont schools, Torrey left West Virginia in 1909 to enroll at the Art Institute of Chicago. He studied there with the renowned sculptor Lorado Taft. Torrey met his wife, Mabel Landrum Torrey, also a sculptor, at the Institute.

Torrey's 1933 statue, "Lincoln Walks at Midnight," was displayed as a 29-inch bronze at the 1939 World's Fair. In 1974 a nine-and-one-half foot bronze casting of the statue as executed by Charleston artist Bernard Wiepper was erected near the West Virginia state capitol. Torrey's 42-inch plaster model of the sculpture is in the possession of the State Museum.

Torrey sculpted other historic figures as well, including Stephen Douglas, George Washington, and George Washington Carver. One of his last works was a 1965 bust of John F. Kennedy. Torrey died in Ames, Iowa, July 8, 1967.

Gladys E. Hamlin, *The Sculpture of Fred and Mabel Torrey*, 1969.

Tourism

Tourism is a big and growing business in West Virginia. In the first decade of the 21st century officials estimate that the economic impact of all tourism activities in the state exceeds $3 billion annually, representing more than eight percent of the total state economy. According to a 2001 Division of Tourism study, tourism employed over 79,000 West Virginians. West Virginia had 19.8 million visitors in 1999, and by 2002 that number had risen to 23.9 million. This growth rate was much higher than for the country as a whole, although West Virginia's visitation level remained below that of the region and nation. Visitors came mostly from the South Atlantic states and from neighboring areas of the north and midwest.

Bicycling is popular among West Virginia tourists.

Tourists come to West Virginia for a variety of reasons, including family visits, shopping, and outdoor recreation. Gambling attracts large numbers of day-trip visitors to the counties having major track and gambling facilities. Sightseeing draws many others, and West Virginia's fine park system attracts visitors at a rate far above the national average.

Some things appear to have changed little since a group of Virginia gentry mounted a fishing expedition to the Canaan Valley region in 1851 and published their travel journal as the classic book, *The Blackwater Chronicle*. Urban tourists from the eastern seaboard still make pilgrimages to the mountains, streams, and forests of West Virginia, seeking renewal in nature. Outdoor recreation remains a major attraction, though today skiing, whitewater rafting, hiking, biking, and rock climbing compete with traditional outdoor sports such as hunting and fishing. Outstanding resources such as the Monongahela National Forest, the New River Gorge National River, the many state parks and state forests, and several private ski resorts give West Virginia an advantage in attracting tourists interested in the outdoors. The second-home industry is booming, particularly in the national forest and resort areas.

While still a small part of the overall industry, cultural or heritage tourism is also growing in West Virginia. Such tourism is based upon the places, traditions, industries, and celebrations that portray the history and character of the state. West Virginia has a diversity of attractions and events to draw cultural tourists, who tend to spend more money and stay longer than other travelers. The rich industrial heritage of the timber, coal, and other industries is captured in places such as the Cass Scenic Railroad, Matewan, Thurmond, and the Wheeling National

Heritage Area. Civil War battlefields and related sites such as the Harpers Ferry National Historic Park showcase the Civil War era, while state parks at Blennerhassett Island and Point Pleasant interpret a much earlier period in the nation's history.

Visitors seek cultural experiences as well as history in West Virginia. The Contemporary American Theater Festival of Shepherdstown provides cutting-edge drama to capacity crowds each summer, while the Snowshoe Institute in Pocahontas County offers a wider cultural array. The *Wheeling Jamboree* live radio show has drawn country music lovers to the Northern Panhandle since 1933. Many thousands of people visit West Virginia's arts and crafts festivals, including the Vandalia Gathering, Stonewall Jackson Jubilee, and Mountain State Folk Festival. At Beckley, Tamarack has become one of the country's foremost outlets for fine handicrafts. The Greenbrier offers unexcelled resort accommodations.

There have been large investments in tourism in recent decades, including the building and expansion of ski resorts and of gambling facilities at state racetracks. A robust whitewater rafting industry has developed, on the New, Gauley, Cheat, and other rivers, and an extensive network of trails for all-terrain vehicles was created in the southern coalfields. State government has invested major funds, including state lottery proceeds, in the promotion of tourism. Modern highways penetrate most parts of the state, with roadside hotels and restaurants in most areas.

Tourism officials believe that more needs to be done, however. The 2001 tourism study found relatively low rates of visitor satisfaction, especially in such matters as dining and accommodations; sightseeing, by contrast, was an area of high visitor satisfaction. In attracting visitors, tourism promoters must overcome the image of West Virginia and Appalachia as a backwards region. Other challenges include overcoming the pervasive view within economic development circles that tourism as a whole is characterized by the seasonal and low wage work within some parts of the industry. Professional training programs at West Virginia University aim to equip West Virginians for management positions as well as other jobs in the industry.

T. C. Townsend

Lawyer Thomas Chasteene Townsend is most remembered for defending union coal miners on charges including treason during the 1922 trials arising from the Battle of Blair Mountain. Townsend was born in Fayette County, August 14, 1877. He grew up working in the coal mines, before saving enough money to attend West Virginia University. In 1903, Townsend opened a law office in Fayetteville.

From 1909 to 1911 and again after 1929, Townsend served as the state tax commissioner. He was elected as Kanawha County's prosecuting attorney in 1912. As tax commissioner, he worked to change the state's tax structure to remove the burden from low-income families. In addition, he drafted the legislation that put into effect the state's uniform system of accounting.

In 1921, Townsend was hired by the United Mine Workers of America to defend miners and union leaders for their part in the March on Logan and the ensuing Battle of Blair Mountain. Townsend's successful defense of Bill Blizzard and other UMWA leaders during the Charles Town trials gained him enormous prestige and secured his position with the miners' union for the rest of his life.

Townsend ran for governor on the Republican ticket in 1932 with the support of the UMWA and the West Virginia Federation of Labor, but he could not distance himself from the tarnished reputation of the Hoover administration. Herman Guy Kump defeated him by 59,665 votes. Townsend died in Charleston, November 5, 1949.

See also Battle of Blair Mountain, Mine Wars

C. Belmont Keeney
West Virginia Humanities Council

Toymaking

Folk toys are those whose designs have passed down through the generations, made by hand and not in factories. Unlike manufactured toys they are not protected by copyrights or patents, nor have they been standardized by machine production. Early folk toys were made of natural materials including wood, corncobs, and elder stalks, or of scraps of cloth, metal, and other found materials. Poplar wood

was often used because it was available, easily worked, and required no painting. Toys were considered unimportant, so little was written about them. A parent made toys for a child, or children themselves made toys. The toys often were ingenious, humorous, and used action movements. Traditionally, fathers and boys have been most interested in mechanical action toys, while mothers and girls have favored dolls and needlework.

Folk toys include action toys, models, games, puzzles, and dolls. This basic list can be enlarged to include tops, skill toys, balance toys, religious or "Sunday" toys, flying toys, shooting toys, those incorporating music or noise, and animated toys. The originator's name is lost in history, and the descriptive names given to the toys vary. Typical names include Whimmydiddle, Flipperdinger, Bullroarer, Jacob's Ladder, and Limber Jack.

Early settlers of the Appalachian region mostly came from Germany, England, Scotland, and Ireland, bringing knowledge of folk toys from their home countries. The designs often were modified in the process of handing them down, so now there are many variations. Folk toys were made throughout America but lingered longest in isolated areas such as Appalachia, which includes West Virginia. Our toys and their names vary from those elsewhere in America, because of our particular cultural influences.

The making of homemade toys waned in times of prosperity, when people could buy manufactured toys. Recently there is a new appreciation for the mountain folk toy heritage, however, and handcrafted toys are sometimes bought in preference to manufactured toys.

Dick Schnacke
New Martinsville
Dick Schnacke, *American Folk Toys*, 1973.

Toyota

Toyota, the third-largest automobile manufacturer in the world, built a $400 million engine plant on a 230-acre site in Buffalo, Putnam County, in 1997. The plant produces engines and automatic transmissions for the Japanese company's North American automobile assembly plants.

In December 1998, the Buffalo plant produced its first four-cylinder engine, with a capacity to produce 300,000 a year. By 1999, the plant had manufactured its first V-6 engine, and two years later, had started building automatic transmissions. In 2005, plant workers built four-cylinder engines for Toyota's Corolla and Matrix models, and V-6 engines for the Sienna and Lexus. Additionally, automatic transmissions were manufactured for the Camry, Solara, Lexus, and Sienna.

The state offered Toyota several incen-

tives to locate the plant in West Virginia, including $15 million in tax credits over 13 years, improvements to State Route 62, job training grants of $1,000 per employee, $2 million for site preparation and start-up expenses, exemption from property taxes on plant equipment for 10 years, and a $50,000 grant for a Saturday school for children of Japanese workers who moved to Putnam County to set up the plant.

Since the plant's opening, Toyota has announced four expansions at its West Virginia facility. At full capacity, Toyota West Virginia can produce 540,000 engines and 360,000 automatic transmissions per year. About 1,000 people, most of whom live in West Virginia, work at the plant. About 10 Toyota employees from Japan work there at any time. The Japanese workers usually take a three-year assignment, and then return home.

Trapping

The trapping of furbearing animals, a part of our traditions and once a multi-million-dollar industry in West Virginia, has declined since its last heyday in the late 1970s to early 1980s. At that time, the sale of raw pelts added almost $3 million to the state's economy each year. By the late 1990s, in part due to a rabies epidemic, that figure had dipped to less than $80,000 in one exceptional year. Rebounding in recent years, the sale of raw fur exceeded $1 million in 2005.

There were several reasons for the decline, the principal one being that the wearing of fur became less fashionable. The trapping tradition has also diminished as society has become less attuned to the land. The generations of farm boys and girls who ran traplines after school, earning pocket money by catching skunks, opossums, mink, raccoons, foxes and muskrats, have largely faded away. But there are reminders throughout West Virginia of our trapping heritage: numerous creeks, knobs, hollows, and ridges are named for furbearing wildlife species, including Coonskin Branch, Big Otter Creek, Otter Hole, Mink Shoals, Beaver Run, Fisher Run and Fox Knob.

The trapping season for furbearing animals begins in early November and runs through February, with the exception of the season for trapping fishers, which ends with January, and the season for trapping beavers, which runs through the final Saturday in March. The state Division of Natural Resources sets trapping regulations, and maintains yearly records of the fur harvest and average pelt prices. For most furbearers, the numbers were down dramatically at the end of the 1990s, but rebounded in the middle of the next decade. In 2004, high numbers of raccoon, bobcat, and coyote were trapped throughout the state. The trapping of both red and grey fox, mink, opossum, and skunk increased, while lower numbers of muskrats were reported.

The price of gray and red fox pelts, once a staple for West Virginia trappers, declined from over $40 in the late 1970s to $10–$12 as the 1990s were drawing to a close. In 2005, fox pelts sold in the $20 range. In the 21st century, raccoon pelts replaced fox as the staple fur for trappers, and the bobcat replaced fox as the top moneymaker at more than $60 per pelt.

Skip Johnson
Sutton

Cliff Brown, "Endangered Tradition," *Wonderful West Virginia,* October 1997.

Traveller

General Robert E. Lee's warhorse Traveller (1857–71), a gray gelding with black points, standing 15.3 hands, was bred and born in Greenbrier County. Of undetermined bloodlines but of Grey Eagle stock, with a hard trot, the always serviceable Traveller became a Confederate icon. A Mr. Johnson near Blue Sulphur Springs raised the colt under the name Jeff Davis, when he took top prizes in 1859 and 1860 at the Lewisburg fair.

General Lee first saw the horse when he took command of Confederate troops near Big Sewell Mountain. He immediately indicated his interest. After trial use and extensive negotiations, Lee later acquired the horse for $200, Confederate money. Lee called his new mount Greenbrier, but later changed the name. For the remainder of the war and the rest of his life, Lee rode Traveller as his primary horse with an American saddle from St. Louis. With his grey bleaching to white, Traveller died from tetanus in June 1871, about eight months after Lee had died. He is buried near his master, just outside Lee Chapel in Lexington, Virginia.

John Edmund Stealey III
Shepherd University

Traveller's Rest

A handsome limestone house located in Jefferson County, Traveller's Rest was designated a National Historic Landmark because of its association with Gen. Horatio Gates of the Revolutionary War. The house is a testament to the sturdy building practices of its time and place. It is one of the few documented works of John Ariss, a noted 18th-century architect and builder who is also credited with Col. Samuel Washington's Eastern Panhandle home, Harewood.

When Gates purchased the property early in 1773, only the eastern portion of the house, raised on a high English basement and with an asymmetrical entrance, was built. Surviving correspondence from August 1773 proves that Gates commissioned Ariss to embellish it with paneling, cornices, and mantels. Gates had little time to enjoy his new home, as his service in the Revolution kept him

Traveller's Rest is a National Historic Landmark.

constantly on the move. He was, however, able to return from time to time, and the name he gave the place indicates how much he enjoyed his sojourns there. At some time, likely after the war, he enlarged Traveller's Rest, making the facade symmetrical on each side of the entry. Inside, the addition created an additional large room on each floor. Although the house was a story and a half tall from the beginning, the dormer windows that now light the top floor postdate Gates's ownership.

Standing at the end of a private lane off Jefferson County Route 1/1, southwest of Kearneysville, Traveller's Rest is privately owned.

See also Architects and Architecture, Horatio Gates, National Historic Landmarks

S. Allen Chambers Jr.
Society of Architectural Historians

Tray Run Viaduct

The Tray Run Viaduct, located in Preston County north of Rowlesburg, was one of the most impressive early-19th-century railroad bridges in the nation and among the first modern iron railroad bridges in the United States. The original viaduct, an elevated railway consisting of a series of spans supported on arches, was constructed in the 1850s by the Baltimore & Ohio Railroad to permit passage across the Cheat River.

Building the viaduct and the tunnels and bridges on this section of railroad was a monumental undertaking given the topography of the region, and the project was unprecedented for its time. Originally designed for a single track, the curved viaduct had viewing platforms on

each side for passengers and was admired as much for its graceful form and beauty as it was respected as an engineering marvel. During the Civil War Confederate raiders and saboteurs made several attempts, including the Jones-Imboden Raid of 1863, to destroy the Tray Run Viaduct, but their efforts failed to cause any damage. The durable viaduct became a source of state pride, and the state legislature placed an image of the structure on the reverse side of the West Virginia state seal. The original stone and cast-iron structure has been replaced by two succeeding viaducts, one in 1887 and the most recent 58-foot-tall structure in 1907.

See also Baltimore & Ohio Railroad

Barry Mowell
Fort Lauderdale, Florida

Treasurer

The state treasurer is the chief financial officer of West Virginia and oversees the cash management of state government. He is responsible for receiving and depositing the state's revenue, maintaining a record of appropriations made by the legislature, endorsing state checks, and related duties.

The treasurer is a member of the executive branch, serving with the governor, auditor, secretary of state, attorney general, and commissioner of agriculture. These are West Virginia's "constitutional officers," mandated by the state constitution and elected statewide. The treasurer is elected to a four-year term, and there is no term limit. He serves on major financial boards throughout state government, including the Board of Public Works, Consolidated Public Retirement Board, Investment

Management Board, West Virginia Public Housing Fund, and Municipal Bond Commission, among others. Divisions in the treasurer's office deal with such matters as cash management, electronic government, debt management, college savings programs, unclaimed property, and other responsibilities.

West Virginia's first state treasurer, Campbell Tarr of Brooke County, served from 1863 to 1867. The treasurer in 2005, John D. Perdue, was first elected in 1996. Long-serving treasurers include Richard Talbott, who was elected in 1932 and served through 1950; and John Kelly, who was elected in 1960. Kelly served until 1975, when he resigned after being indicted in federal court on charges of bribery and extortion. He was sentenced to five years in prison.

Two of the three impeachment proceedings in West Virginia's history involve the treasurer's office. The one occasion that the state Senate sat as a court of impeachment was when it removed Treasurer John Burdett from office in 1876. After the loss of about $279 million from the state's Consolidated Investment Fund in 1987 and 1988, Treasurer A. James Manchin was impeached and resigned in 1989.

The treasurer's vault is composed of chromium steel and concrete, with walls 22 inches thick. In addition to stocks and bonds, the vault also safeguards valuables including diamonds, rare coins, and stamps, as well as state historical documents.

Treaty of Camp Charlotte

The Treaty of Camp Charlotte, negotiated with the Ohio Valley Indians after the Battle of Point Pleasant in 1774, ended Dunmore's War. Among the treaty's other terms, the Ohio River was recognized as the boundary between the Indians and whites; the Shawnees agreed to stop attacking travelers on the river; and the whites agreed not to settle in Kentucky. The treaty secured a temporary peace for Western Virginia settlers, which lasted through the early part of the American Revolution.

The October 1774 Battle of Point Pleasant, when Virginia militia under Andrew Lewis defeated the Indians led by Cornstalk, had been the major military action of the brief war. Virginia Governor Dunmore, absent from the battle, established himself with another force at Camp Charlotte, on the Scioto River south of present Columbus. It was here that the peace was negotiated at the end of the year.

Logan's Speech, one of the most important orations of the early history of Western Virginia, was delivered by an intermediary to the negotiators at Camp Charlotte. Logan, who had terrorized the frontier after his family was massacred by white frontiersmen, boycotted the peace talks.

See also Dunmore's War, Chief Logan

Ken Sullivan
West Virginia Humanities Council

Treaty of Greenville

The Treaty of Greenville was signed August 3, 1795, between the United States, represented by Gen. Anthony Wayne, and chiefs of the Indian tribes located in the Northwest Territory, including the Wyandots, Delawares, Shawnees, Ottawas, Miamis, and others. The negotiations took place at Fort Greenville on the southwestern branch of the Miami River where Greenville, Ohio, is now located. The treaty brought to an end a series of hostilities along the Ohio Valley frontier in the early 1790s which had culminated in Wayne's victory over the tribes at the Battle of Fallen Timbers, August 20, 1794. The battle and treaty were significant for the settlers of Western Virginia because they brought peace and a final end to the Indian wars in this part of the country.

Under the terms of the treaty, the Indians ceded to the United States about two-thirds of present Ohio. Prisoners held by the tribes were to be released within 90 days, and the U.S. was allowed to maintain portage sites and trade centers at places including Detroit, Michilimackinac, and the future location of Chicago. The Indians received an immediate payment of $20,000 in goods and an annual payment thereafter of $9,500 in goods. In addition, the Indians were given the right to hunt in the territorial cession and the authority to drive off or punish whites whose settlement infringed on their lands. The treaty did, however, prohibit "private revenge or retaliation" and provided instead for a mediation process.

While the treaty officially brought peace to the Ohio Valley frontier, problems continued because whites almost immediately began to breach the Indian territory to the west. Furthermore, some tribal leaders, such as Tecumseh, had not signed the treaty and did not recognize its provisions. Western Virginia settlers, however, were henceforth safe from Indian attack.

See also Battle of Fallen Timbers

Philip Sturm
Ohio Valley University

Treaty of Hard Labor

The 1768 Treaty of Hard Labor secured much of present West Virginia for white settlement. The British had won this territory as a result of the French and Indian War, but prior to the Treaty of Hard Labor the Royal Proclamation of 1763 had officially prohibited settlements west of the eastern continental divide to reduce conflict with the Indians. This divide separates the Potomac watershed, essentially the present Eastern Panhandle, from the rest of West Virginia. Many people ignored the proclamation and crossed the line, settling in territory claimed by the Cherokees. As a result, tensions between British settlers and the Cherokee claimants of the land increased. British colonies, land companies, and individual settlers demanded access to the land west of the proclamation line.

For these reasons, the British government relented and negotiated with the major Native American tribes for Trans-Appalachian land. The British and Cherokees met in Hard Labor, South Carolina, and signed the treaty in October 1768. This established a new western border for British North America, along a line extending in part from present Wytheville, Virginia, to the mouth of the Kanawha River at Point Pleasant. The only part of West Virginia not under British control after this treaty was the area southwest of the Wytheville to Point Pleasant treaty line, which ran somewhat west of and generally parallel to modern Interstate 77.

See also Frontier, Proclamation of 1763, Treaty of Lochaber

Robert T. Anderson
Howard, Pensylvania

Jack M. Sosin, *The Revolutionary Frontier, 1763–1783,* 1967.

Treaty of Lancaster

A treaty conference was held in 1744 between representatives of the colonial governments of Pennsylvania, Maryland, and Virginia and delegates from the Onondaga, Oneida, Cayuga, Seneca, and Tuscarora tribes of the Iroquois Confederation. The purpose was to settle disputes with the Iroquois over the ownership of lands at the western margin of the three colonies. The representatives from Virginia at the conference were Thomas Lee and William Beverley, with William Black as secretary.

At the conclusion of the conference, the Virginia commissioners believed they held a deed for all of the land west of Virginia to the Mississippi River and north to the Great Lakes. This included all of present West Virginia. However, the Iroquois believed that they had sold land only in Virginia south of the Potomac River and between the Blue Ridge Mountains and the Allegheny Mountains, excluding most of the present state of West Virginia. The disagreement over the land title continued until the Iroquois formally relinquished all ownership rights to the disputed territory during the Treaty of Fort Stanwix in 1768.

The Treaty of Lancaster was a milestone in the history of Western Virginia. It allowed more than 1,000 European immigrants to settle in what is now eastern West Virginia between 1745 and 1755 unopposed by the Iroquois and other tribes. These pioneers established a firm enough toehold that not all were driven away during the French and Indian War (1754–63). Those that remained after the war set the stage for the remainder of Western Virginia to be settled at a rapid pace during the last quarter of the 18th century.

Greg Adamson
Dayton, Virginia
Kenneth P. Bailey, *The Ohio Company of Virginia and the Westward Movement 1748–1792*, 1939.

Treaty of Lochaber

The 1770 Treaty of Lochaber secured for Britain, more specifically for its Virginia colony, Cherokee rights to the region of Western Virginia not covered by the 1768 Treaty of Hard Labor. The British settlers' appetite for land was not quenched with the large territory made available by the Hard Labor treaty. Their demands placed a heavy burden on the government to provide more safe western land, free from attacks by Indians seeking to protect their territory.

The two sides gathered at Lochaber, South Carolina, in October 1770. The new Cherokee land cession extended the western border of British North America to the Kentucky River in eastern Kentucky and the Holston River in eastern Tennessee. Included in this cession was most of the region of present West Virginia southwest of the line established by the Treaty of Hard Labor, which ran somewhat west of and generally parallel to modern Interstate 77.

While the treaties of Hard Labor and Lochaber extinguished Iroquois and Cherokee claims to the regions involved, they did not address the strong Shawnee claims. The Shawnees, not surprisingly, disputed the treaties. They continued a running guerrilla war for many years, first with Britain and then the United States.

See also Frontier, Indian Wars, Treaty of Hard Labor

Robert T. Anderson
Howard, Pennsylvania
Jack M. Sosin, *The Revolutionary Frontier, 1763–1783*, 1967.

Treaty of Paris

The Treaty of Paris of 1763 ended the conflict known in America as the French and Indian War and in Europe as the Seven Years War. The treaty acknowledged the French defeat, ceding all French territories on the North American continent to other powers. France gave Canada and all lands east of the Mississippi River to Great Britain, and gave Louisiana to Spain. Spain in turn gave Florida to Britain, which was left in uncontested control of the entire east coast and its hinterlands.

The Treaty of Paris had important consequences for Western Virginians and others on the Appalachian frontier. It ended a bloody frontier war, though fighting with the Indians soon resumed. The treaty also gave all of Appalachia and

neighboring regions into the possession of England and its American colonies, including areas already occupied, claimed, or coveted by colonial settlers and speculators. England attempted initially to restrict settlement to the Atlantic watershed by the King's Proclamation Line of 1763. This line, which would have excluded from settlement all of present West Virginia except the Eastern Panhandle, was soon modified by separate Indian treaties. Thus the Treaty of Paris and subsequent treaties helped to open the West, and settlement surged across present central and western West Virginia in coming decades.

Another Treaty of Paris ended the American Revolution in 1783.

See also French and Indian War, Proclamation of 1763

Trees

West Virginia's forests are made up primarily of deciduous trees. Deciduous trees are those that lose their leaves each fall. They are known as hardwoods since generally their wood is denser and harder than that of conifers. There are more than 100 species of native hardwoods, plus several introduced species.

Our hardwood forests can be grouped into northern hardwoods, mixed oak, cove hardwoods, and bottomland hardwood types.

Northern hardwood forests occur at elevations above 2,000 feet. Predominant species are sugar maple, red maple, American beech, yellow birch, and black birch. It is in these mixtures that our best black cherry is found. Other associates include mountain magnolia, buckeye, and Canadian hemlock. These stands have been a valuable source of high-quality lumber for furniture, flooring, cabinetry, and turned-wood products.

Oak mixtures predominate at moderate elevations and are typical forest cover on the drier exposures. Mixed oak stands include many species. Northern red oak is our most common species, but white oak, black oak, yellow oak, chestnut oak, and scarlet oak are all abundant throughout the state. Red and white oaks are widely used for flooring and furniture, while white oak has been the sole species suitable for making barrels for aging whiskey. Growing with these oaks are mockernut hickory, pignut and shagbark hickory, sassafras, black locust, black gum, and red maple.

Cove hardwoods mixtures, often referred to as the mixed mesophytic forest, dominate moist slopes and mountain coves at intermediate elevations. These stands may contain as many as 50 different hardwood species; however, yellow poplar is usually a major component of these stands. Other valuable species include white, northern red, and black oaks, cucumber tree, umbrella magnolia, basswood, white ash, black walnut, and occasionally butternut. Other species include sourwood, black cherry, black birch, and red and sugar maples.

Bottomland hardwood mixtures occupy the rich alluvial soils along major water courses. Among the most common of these species are box elder and silver maple. Other common trees include green ash, slippery elm, black willow, river birch, sycamore, and honey locust.

Coniferous species in West Virginia include eastern white pine, which played a major role in attracting the first large-scale forest industry to the state in the 1880s. Table mountain pine occurs only at the highest elevations and is easily identified by its large prickly cones which persist indefinitely on limbs and trunk,

Schoolchildren take the measure of the Mingo Oak.

Big trees

The first Europeans exploring present West Virginia saw giant trees of oak, maple, sycamore, hemlock, walnut, and tulip poplar. The biggest of the trees grew on deep, rich soils. Some were big enough to elicit individual notice. George Washington's journal from 1770 describes a large sycamore along the lower Kanawha River measuring 45 feet around the trunk. A large white oak tree near Lead Mine in Tucker County measured 13 feet in diameter at the top of the largest 16-foot log. This likely was the biggest tree ever known to have grown in West Virginia. The Pringle brothers lived in a large hollow sycamore near Buckhannon from about 1764 to 1767. Today a very large yellow poplar, measuring 26 feet in circumference, clings to life on Blennerhassett Island despite a top broken off by winds.

The Mingo Oak was the champion big tree when it died in 1938 at 582 years old. It was 145 feet tall and nearly 20 feet in circumference four and a half feet above the ground. The present champion is a sycamore on the Back Fork of Elk River in Webster County, with a circumference of 309 inches, which makes it more nearly 26 feet around. At 112 feet tall, it is not the tallest, however. That honor goes to a towering yellow buckeye standing 196 feet tall at Clendenin in Kanawha County.

—William N. Grafton

The top big trees in West Virginia today are as follows:

Tree	Circumference (inches)	Height (feet)	Location
Sycamore	309	112	Webster County
Sycamore	295	116	Bridgeport
Yellow Poplar	213	195	Clay County
Eastern Cottonwood	292	105	Berkeley County
Bur Oak	266	113	Mason County
Red Oak	266	106	Weston
Sycamore	247	144	Pendleton County
Yellow Poplar	188	182	Wyoming County
Yellow Poplar	201	185	Wood County
Yellow Buckeye	165	196	Kanawha County
Silver Maple	259	97	Jefferson County
Hackberry	199	118	Jefferson County

and may even be overgrown and become embedded in the wood. Virginia pine predominates on dry, recently abandoned fields, and pitch pine occurs as a scattered tree on dry ridgetops. Both are used primarily for pulpwood.

There were originally 469,000 acres of red spruce dominating elevations above 3,600 feet. These valuable stands were mixtures of red spruce and Canadian hemlock forming a dense, impenetrable forest. The large pulp mills which entered the state at the turn of the 20th century were attracted by the spruce, since at that time paper was made exclusively from spruce due to its long, strong, white fiber.

Other conifers include eastern red cedar, which is particularly common on limestone soils, as well as northern white cedar and balsam fir. Northern white cedar occurs along stream margins in the eastern counties, but only where limestone is the bedrock. This valuable tree, commonly known as arbor vitae, reaches its greatest size here at the southern part of its range, and is of great value for boat building.

West Virginia's balsam fir, restricted to a few swamps in the high mountains, is at the southern limit of its range. This strain is becoming a preferred seed source among Christmas tree growers throughout the Northeast since it has superior foliage color, good needle retention, and is resistant to disease. The trade name is "Canaan fir."

Eastern larch or tamarack, a tree of boreal forests, reaches its southern limits in Cranesville Swamp, Preston County. This large thriving colony is 150 miles south of other occurrences of this deciduous conifer. Another tree of limited occurrence is shellbark hickory or king nut which produces a very large, sweet nut, much prized by those who collect a supply of hickory nuts for winter eating. This species occurs sparingly, but is more common along the western margin of the state.

Princess-tree or paulownia, a native of the Orient, is widely scattered throughout the state. The large, heart-shaped leaves make it easily mistaken for catalpa, but the purple, trumpet-shaped flowers and brown pecan-shaped woody capsules are distinct. The wood is much in demand in China and Japan, and today West Virginia logs are exported to the Far East.

See also Flora, Timbering and Logging
Kenneth L. Carvell
Morgantown

Earl L. Core, *Vegetation of West Virginia*, 1974; P. D. Strausbaugh and Earl L. Core, "Flora of West Virginia," *West Virginia University Bulletin*, 1970; Roy B. Clarkson, *Tumult on the Mountains: Lumbering in West Virginia 1770–1920*, 1964.

W. W. Trent

Educator William Woodson Trent, known to legions of West Virginia schoolchildren from his scrawling signature on their report cards and other school documents, served as state superintendent of schools from 1933 until 1957. Born January 31, 1878, in rural Nicholas County and educated in the local schools, Marshall State Normal School (now Marshall University), and Columbia University (A.M., 1921), he rose through the teaching ranks to become secretary of the West Virginia Education Association (1919–27) and editor of the influential *West Virginia School Journal* (1923–27).

Throughout his long professional and political career, Trent maintained a close association with the state Baptist Convention, and he was often a dynamic speaker at its annual meetings. After serving as president of Broaddus College and Alderson-Broaddus College (1927–33), a Baptist institution, he ran as a Democrat for state superintendent of schools in the landmark election of 1932.

Upon assuming office, Trent almost singlehandedly oversaw implementation of the county unit system of public schools, in 1933 and 1934. A fierce, often outspoken defender of school teacher interests, he soon developed into one of the state's most formidable politicians. He was reelected as state superintendent in 1936, 1940, 1944, 1948, and 1952. In several of these elections he polled more votes statewide than the party candidate for governor. As a member of the State Board of Public Works, he was a staunch advocate of additional pay for teachers. He successfully fought off several attempts to check his powers as superintendent, including the proposed Short Ballot Amendment of 1938 and reforms proposed in the 1945 Strayer Report. When the U.S. Supreme Court handed down its decision ending segregation in the public schools, Trent worked with Governor Marland to integrate the state in a peaceful and speedy manner.

His long political career came to an end in January 1957 after Dwight D. Eisenhower and the Republicans swept the state in the election of 1956. W. W. Trent died June 15, 1960.

See also Strayer Report

Paul D. Casdorph
Charleston

William O. Trevey

Photographer William O. Trevey, born in 1879 in Virginia, left an extensive visual record of the boom years of the New River coalfields. From about 1898 until the late 1920s, Trevey and his father, E. B. Trevey, maintained a successful photography studio in the Fayette County town of Glen Jean.

Trevey operated his studio at a time when the New River coalfields were among the most prosperous in the United States. In his studio, complete with wicker chairs and bear skin rug, he made a photographic record of the variety of lifestyles in the area. His portraits feature hunters, gamblers, workers and loafers, and citizens rich and poor. From barefoot children of miners to coal barons, Trevey and his father preserved the faces of an era.

His images were not limited to studio portraits, for Trevey also traveled the area photographing coal towns, railroad communities, and mines. Trevey left his Glen Jean studio by about 1940, leaving behind hundreds of glass plate negatives in a variety of sizes. The photographic prints made from these negatives offer priceless insights into an era that now lives only in legend.

Melody Bragg
National Mine Health and Safety Academy
Melody Bragg, "The Reliable Bill Trevey: Glen Jean's Photographer," *Goldenseal*, Winter 1988.

Tri-State Airport

Located on a Wayne County hilltop just off Interstate 64 west of Huntington, Tri-State Airport offers airline service to passengers from a large area of West Virginia, Kentucky, and Ohio. The airport was dedicated November 2, 1952, with the first official landing made at 11:00 a.m. by Piedmont Airlines, followed by an Eastern Air Lines flight at 11:30.

The opening of Tri-State Airport returned regularly scheduled air service to the Huntington area for the first time since 1945, when American Airlines discontinued serving the Chesapeake Airport, a small field located just across the Ohio River from Huntington. Tri-State Airport's construction came after 30 years of effort by Huntington political and civic leaders. It is owned by a conglomerate of public and quasi-public agencies and operated by the Tri-State Airport Authority, whose members are appointed by those agencies.

The airport was the scene of a tragic crash on the night of November 14, 1970, when a chartered jet airliner carrying the Marshall University football team slammed into a hillside as it approached for landing. All 75 people aboard—players, coaches, fans, and crew—were killed.

See also Marshall Plane Crash
James E. Casto
Herald-Dispatch

Tri-State Racetrack

The Tri-State Racetrack and Gaming Center, previously known as Tri-State Greyhound Park, opened in May 1985. The facility, which is located in Cross Lanes, offers year-round greyhound racing as well as video lottery slot machines. The track installed 400 machines in 1994 under a video lottery license granted by the West Virginia Lottery Commission. The number of machines continued to grow, and as of 2005 Tri-State had 1,757 video lottery machines.

The facility, which cost $18 million, underwent a major expansion that was completed in December 2002. The $12 million Mardi Gras addition includes a new simulcast betting lounge, a full-service restaurant, a cafe, four bars, two entertainment stages, a "high-rollers" section, and a conference area. While West Virginians and residents of eastern Kentucky and southern Ohio account for most of Tri-State's visitors, a share of the market comes from as far south as Charlotte, North Carolina.

The Trough

The Trough is a narrow canyon where the South Branch of the Potomac River runs between Sawmill Ridge and River Ridge, northeast of Moorefield on the boundary of Hampshire and Hardy counties. George Washington gave as good a description as anyone, writing in his journal in 1748: "The Trough is [a] couple of Ledges of Mountains, Impassable, running side and side together for above 7 or 8 miles and ye River down between them." Washington, visiting as a young surveyor, is supposed to have raced through in a canoe. The Trough remains popular with canoeists and kayakers today, with fishermen, and with sightseeing tourists on the Potomac Eagle excursion train.

Less than a decade after Washington's visit, a bloody battle ensued at the Trough in 1756, during the French and Indian War. A large band of Shawnees defeated 18 settlers in the Battle of the Trough, killing about half of them.

Historically accessible only by water or on foot, the Trough was penetrated by a branch of the Baltimore & Ohio Railroad about 1910. The B&O's successor, the Chessie System, turned the branch line over to the West Virginia State Rail Authority in 1978. The authority continues to operate the rail lines, now known as the South Branch Valley Railroad. The Potomac Eagle operates over these rails. Passengers routinely see the train's namesake, since bald eagles reestablished themselves in the Trough in the early 1980s.

The great flood of 1985 ripped through the Trough, doing great damage to railroad facilities. Water reportedly backed up to a depth of 90 feet at the head of the canyon.

Trout Pond

Trout Pond, the only natural lake in West Virginia, is located in Hardy County 13 miles southwest of Wardensville and six miles east of Lost River. It is part of the Trout Pond Recreation Area in the George Washington National Forest. This two-acre body of water was created by springs that feed into one of the sinkholes that are common in the irregular limestone strata found in that part of the state. Water flows in on the uphill side of Trout Pond, and seeps out through the bottom of the pond. There is generally a good balance of water coming in and going out, although in drought conditions the pond becomes quite low.

Trout Pond, formerly called "Old Pond," was once stocked with trout, hence its name. It is no longer stocked because of bank erosion caused by fishermen, and also because of low water in periods of dry weather. A rustic rail fence encloses the pond, and a hiking trail circles it. Trout Pond Recreation Area and its nearby companion, Rockcliff Recreation Area, are popular for camping, picnicking, swimming, hiking, fishing, and boating. Rockcliff is located on Trout Pond Run about a quarter of a mile away from Trout Pond. Rockcliff Lake, unlike Trout Pond, is man-made.

Skip Johnson
Sutton

Tu-Endie-Wei

Tu-Endie-Wei is apparently a Wyandot Indian term meaning "place between two waters" or "where two waters meet." It has long referred to the point of land overlooking the confluence of the Ohio and Great Kanawha rivers at Point Pleasant, although it is uncertain whether the term was applied by the Indians or later whites. This is now the site of Point Pleasant Battlefield Monument State Park.

Celoron de Blainville, claiming the Ohio Valley for Louis XV of France, buried a lead plate there in 1749. On October 10, 1774, Virginia militia commanded by Andrew Lewis and Shawnees under Chief Cornstalk fought a daylong battle, the principal event of Lord Dunmore's War. In 1797, Walter Newman built a tavern that served travelers along the Ohio and Kanawha. Known today as the Mansion House, it is the oldest log structure in the Kanawha Valley. It now houses a museum.

Livia Poffenbarger and the Col. Charles Lewis chapter of the Daughters of the American Revolution campaigned for recognition of the Battle of Point Pleasant as the first battle of the Revolutionary War, a claim generally disputed by historians. An act of Congress in 1908 provided for a monument to be erected. The small state park is dominated by the 84-foot granite obelisk with its statue of a frontiersman. There are also monuments to Charles Lewis (who died in the battle), "Mad Anne" Bailey, and Cornstalk, who was murdered at nearby Fort Randolph in 1777.

Battle Days, an annual festival in October, features encampments with historical reenactments and craft demonstrations.

See also Point Pleasant

Arline R. Thorn
St. Albans

Tucker County

Tucker County lies in north-central West Virginia and includes some of the state's most rugged and mountainous terrain. The county was named for Henry St. George Tucker Sr. (1780–1848), a Virginia soldier, statesman, and jurist. The early settlers included Thomas and James Parsons, John Minear, and John Crouch. In 1778, Minear brought to what became the community of St. George, by horseback and in pieces, the machinery for the first sawmill west of the Alleghenies. Tucker County was formed from Randolph County by an act of the General Assembly of Virginia, March 7, 1856; on February 7, 1871, the legislature of West Virginia added a small portion of Barbour County to complete Tucker's 421.7 square miles. The 1860 census counted 1,428 residents in the new county.

Tucker voted for secession when Virginia left the Union, but local allegiances were deeply divided during the ensuing war. Mostly, the Civil War in Tucker County consisted of skirmishes and raids. The Battle of Corricks Ford, the best-known conflict in Tucker County, occurred July 13, 1861, when Confederates led by Gen. Robert Selden Garnett encountered U.S. troops under Brig. Gen. Thomas A. Morris. Garnett died in the battle, the first general to be killed in the Civil War.

The high plateau surrounding Davis originally had a magnificent red spruce

FAST FACTS ABOUT TUCKER COUNTY

Founded: 1856
Land in square miles: 421.7
Population: 7,321
Percentage minorities: 1.1%
Percentage rural: 100%
Median age: 42.0
Percentage 65 and older: 17.9%
Birth rate per 1,000 population: 9.0
Median household income: $26,250
High school graduate or higher: 75.5%
Bachelor's degree or higher: 10.6%
Home ownership: 82.6%
Median home value: $61,100

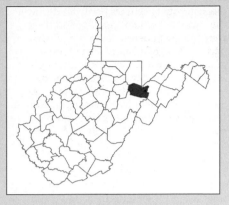

This information is from the 2000 U.S. Census. In 2000, West Virginia as a whole had 5 percent minorities, a median age of 38.9, median household income of $29,696, and a 75.2 percent home ownership rate.

and northern hardwood forest stretching mile after mile. Henry Gassaway Davis and his son-in-law, Stephen B. Elkins, both industrialists and both U.S. senators, developed plans for building a railroad into this untouched wilderness. On November 2, 1881, the first section of Davis's West Virginia Central & Pittsburg [*sic*] Railway was completed from the B&O Railroad at Piedmont to the coalfields at Elk Garden, Grant County. The track was continued into Tucker County to the town of Davis by 1884.

Development quickly followed the arrival of the railroad, when J. L. Rumbarger, a hardwood manufacturer from Indiana, began buying timber in the vicinity of Canaan Valley and built a band sawmill at Davis. He sold this mill to Albert Thompson, who formed the Blackwater Boom & Lumber Company. Under successive owners and names, this mill

cut more than one billion board feet of lumber before closing in 1924. Other major industries at Davis included a tannery, another large lumber mill owned by the Beaver Creek Lumber Company, and a huge pulp mill owned by the West Virginia Pulp & Paper Company, now MeadWestvaco. By 1924, all these operations had closed due to the depletion of the original forest.

Although Davis was the hub of the lumber industry in Tucker County, band sawmills also operated in the county at Bretz, Hambleton (two mills), Jenningston (two mills), Laneville, Parsons, Porterwood, and William. Manufacturing wood products is still the major industry in Tucker County, apart from tourism. Today, Kingsford Manufacturing Company, a manufacturer of charcoal, is the county's largest private employer, making briquettes from sawdust at its plant north of Parsons. Hinchcliff Lumber Company makes shipping pallets and in 1994 added a scragg mill to use small and marginal timber once left in the woods. The Ricottilli Lumber Company, a sawmill operating at Moore, employs about 20 people and provides income for dozens of private loggers in Tucker and surrounding counties.

Tanneries operated in the county from the late 1800s until 1975, at Davis, Hambleton, Parsons, and St. George. A planing mill opened in Parsons at the turn of the 20th century. In 1927, the building became a woolen mill, which at one time employed 270 workers. The mill closed in 1971. Parsons Footwear was next to occupy the facility, but foreign imports, local strikes, and the devastating floods of 1985 and 1996 closed that business.

The playing out of jobs in coal mines and at about 1,000 beehive coke ovens meant the loss of hundreds of Tucker County families in the mid-20th century. County population peaked at 18,675

Canaan Valley's Bear Paw Lodge is a Tucker County recreational facility.

in 1910 and fell to 7,321 in 2000. Ruth Cooper Allman's book, *Roots in Tucker County*, reports that the highest enrollment in county schools occurred during the 1919–20 school year, when there were 4,144 students. With three state parks and a good share of the West Virginia ski industry, Tucker County's leading employer today is tourism. Blackwater Falls and Canaan Valley state parks and the privately owned Timberline Resort are year-round attractions, with Canaan and Timberline among the state's top ski resorts. The tiny Fairfax Stone State Park also sees hundreds of visitors yearly. Tourism brings hundreds of thousands of visitors each year to Tucker County, and there is a thriving second-home industry.

Railroads operated for 100 years in Tucker County, from 1884 to 1984, carrying passengers as well as freight for much of that period. After the loss of rail passenger service the county was left with only narrow secondary roads. Corridor H, a modern four-lane highway, entered the county early in the 21st century.

Parsons, the county seat, is located near the juncture of Shavers Fork and Black Fork, at the head of Cheat River. The town was incorporated in 1893. It was named for Ward Parsons, the most prominent resident and largest landholder.

See also Battle of Corricks Ford, Parsons

Mariwyn McClain Smith
Parsons

Homer Floyd Fansler, *History of Tucker County, West Virginia*, 1962; Cleta M. Long, *History of Tucker County, West Virginia*, 1996.

Tug, Battle of the

In January 1920, the United Mine Workers of America launched a campaign to unionize southern West Virginia, including the Tug Fork coalfield. The local coal operators were determined to keep the UMW out. Miners who joined the union were fired, evicted from their company-owned houses, and replaced by nonunion workers. Many fought back with guns in what developed into the Battle of the Tug, or the Three Days Battle of May 1921.

Violence usually involving gunfire from the mountains at working miners in the valley, erupted sporadically through much of 1920 and into the spring of 1921. On May 12–14, 1921, bullets peppered down on about a dozen mining towns in the Matewan-Williamson area, and nonunion miners fired back. Deputy sheriffs, mine guards, the recently created West Virginia State Police, and Kentucky National Guardsmen joined the fray. Thousands of shots were fired from rifles, pistols, and even machine guns. Bullets clipped telephone wires and ripped through homes as families cowered in fear. Bridges and tipples were dyna-

mited. Businesses and schools closed. Three persons were shot and killed.

The Battle of the Tug ended on May 15 when State Police arranged a truce, with the aid of a physician who crawled under fire through the Kentucky mountains to make contact with the insurgents. During the fighting, Governor Morgan asked President Harding to send federal troops "to prevent wanton slaughter of innocent citizens." Although Morgan's request was denied, it set the stage for sending federal troops into West Virginia in September to quell the Miners' March on Mingo and Logan.

See also Mine Wars, Miners' March

Lon Savage
Salem, Virginia

Lon K. Savage, *Thunder in the Mountains*, 1990.

Tug Fork

The Tug Fork of the Big Sandy River forms the southwestern border of West Virginia for nearly 90 miles, flowing between the West Virginia counties of Mingo and Wayne and neighboring counties in Virginia and Kentucky. The stream, locally known as the Tug River, originates near the town of Jenkinjones at the corner of Mercer and McDowell counties and Tazewell County, Virginia, at an elevation of 2,450 feet. The Tug travels 126 miles in a northwesterly direction to Fort Gay. There it joins the Levisa Fork out of eastern Kentucky to form the main Big Sandy River.

In addition to Jenkinjones, McDowell County settlements along the Tug Fork include Gary, Welch, Davy, Roderfield, Iaeger, and Panther. From McDowell, the stream flows north through Mingo County, by Matewan, Williamson, Chattaroy, Nolan, and Kermit, then past the Wayne County communities of Crum, Glenhayes, and Fort Gay. The Tug forms the western boundary of Mingo and part of the western boundary of Wayne County.

The topography at the headwaters is rugged. The Tug and its tributaries have cut their channels through the sedimentary strata to produce high hogback ridges and deep V-shaped valleys. Local relief, the distance from the valley floors to the hill crests, ranges from 1,200 to 1,500 feet in McDowell County and from 600 to 1,000 feet in Mingo. Elevation above sea level at Fort Gay is 600 feet, yielding a fall of 1,875 feet along the stream's 26 miles, for an average of about 15 feet per mile. This gives the Tug Fork a rapid flow, especially in McDowell County where the rapids and falls include one section known as "the Roughs of the Tug."

The Tug Valley, one of the most remote areas of West Virginia, was among the last places in the state to be settled. Permanent settlement began about 1800, and the region was sparsely populated until the development of the coal indus-

try nearly a century later. The Hatfields, whose later feud with the McCoys is the most notorious event in Tug Valley history, were among the first settlers. Violent labor warfare rocked the valley during the early 20th century. It was at this time that the area's rich coalfields were developed, and mining continues to be the major industry.

The Tug Fork has flooded numerous times since first settlement. Historically, the river was used at flood stage to transport rafts and logs down to Kenova. Under favorable conditions merchandise was poled upriver from Kenova to Williamson in push boats.

The river is believed to have been named in 1756, during Maj. Andrew Lewis's disastrous "Sandy Creek" expedition against the Shawnee Indians in southern Ohio. Near the headwaters, the group attempted to descend the Tug River to Ohio by using canoes for the trip, but they encountered tremendous rapids and lost their supplies. The men were forced to boil and eat their boot strings or "tugs" made of buffalo hides.

Mack H. Gillenwater
Marshall University

Gladys Tuke

Sculptor Gladys Tuke was born in Linwood, Pocahontas County, November 19, 1899. She studied sculpture at the Corcoran Gallery in Washington, after which she spent about five years in Philadelphia, where she was taught by Albert Laessle at the Country School of the Pennsylvania Academy of the Fine Arts. Laessle was a noted sculptor who specialized in animals, and that, combined with Tuke's enjoyment of horseback riding, led Tuke to turn much of her work to horses.

Tuke became interested in pottery while teaching sculpture in the original art colony of the Greenbrier resort during the 1930s and soon began to combine pottery with sculpture. During World War II, she taught pottery and some sculpture at Ashford General Hospital, the U.S. Army hospital at the Greenbrier. When the war ended, she established a pottery and sculpture studio in White Sulphur Springs. In the summer of 1956, the Greenbrier art colony was reopened with her work and that of Jeanne Eleanore Coyne, a pictorial artist and teacher at Greenbrier College for Women in Lewisburg. Tuke used clay from her own land for all of her pottery and some of her sculpture. In addition to teaching, she conducted pottery demonstrations for guests of the hotel and for nearby clubs and schools.

She exhibited at the Pennsylvania Academy of the Fine Arts, the Woodmere Art Gallery in Philadelphia, the All-American Exhibition of Sculpture at the Cincinnati Museum of Art, and the Cor-

Sculptor Gladys Tuke (1899–1982) at work.

coran Gallery. Tuke died in Denmar Hospital in Pocahontas County, August 26, 1982.

Judie Smith
West Virginia Humanities Council

Tumult on the Mountains

The book *Tumult on the Mountains: Lumbering in West Virginia 1770–1920,* published in 1964, was written by Roy B. Clarkson, a native of the lumber town of Cass. Also the author of a history of Cass, *On Beyond Leatherbark* (1990), Clarkson worked at the large sawmill operation in Cass before earning a Ph.D. from West Virginia University and beginning his career as a professor of biology.

Tumult on the Mountains is a West Virginia best-seller, with more than 20,000 copies in print. The book covers the West Virginia forests from the first written accounts of George Washington in 1770 to the eventual depletion of all but a few isolated stands of virgin forest in the late 19th and early 20th centuries. Although primarily a pictorial history, the book has an extensive text that describes the plant and animal life of the early wilderness, the pioneers' impact on the land, and the coming of the timber industry to the mountains, including the impact of new technology in sawmills and railroads. Above all, *Tumult on the Mountains* is a detailed look at life in the timber camps, through photographs and interviews with loggers. It includes 257 full-page pictures from the time period. The book also includes a glossary of logging terms, a map of logging boom towns (many of which no longer exist), and an extensive bibliography.

See also Timbering and Logging

LeAnna Alderman
Allegheny Mountain Radio

Roy B. Clarkson, *Tumult on the Mountains: Lumbering in West Virginia 1770–1920,* 1964.

Turnpikes

Few reliable overland routes reached into the mountains of Western Virginia at the close of the Revolutionary era. The Virginia legislature authorized a series of roads in the 1780s, but most were neither paved nor maintained. Although public officials recognized the need for comprehensive internal improvements, poor construction techniques and difficult terrain made for slow and treacherous overland travel.

In 1808, U.S. Secretary of the Treasury Albert Gallatin outlined a national transportation plan featuring turnpikes, canals, and river improvements. After Congress failed to adopt it, individual states assumed responsibility for their own transportation improvements. The Virginia General Assembly in 1816 passed an act to establish an internal improvement fund and a Board of Public Works to charter turnpike companies. Under the board's authority, the state financed 40 percent to 60 percent of the cost for turnpikes, and private stockholders paid the rest. Varying rates of tolls were assessed, based on the size of vehicles or the number of livestock being driven, with the charges used to defray maintenance costs and, in some cases, turn a profit for investors. In reality, few stockholders expected to make money (and few did), as most settled instead for the indirect benefits of having a road linking them with outside markets.

By 1850, West Virginia had dozens of turnpikes of varying width, length, and construction, and four principal east-west routes. The National Road from Cumberland, Maryland, to Wheeling opened in 1818, while the James River & Kanawha

Turnpike was completed in 1832 from Greenbrier County to the mouth of the Big Sandy River. Completed in 1838 between Winchester and Parkersburg, the Northwestern Virginia Turnpike followed a superb line over the mountains as planned and laid out by Virginia's chief engineer, Claudius Crozet. An engineering marvel, the road opened up large sections of Western Virginia to settlement and commerce. The last of the major east-west turnpikes, the Staunton-Parkersburg, was completed in 1847. These and other turnpikes proved vital to Union and Confederate forces during the Civil War, and many clashes ensued in the struggle for their control. Shorter north to south turnpikes often provided important connections with the primary east-west thoroughfares. These included the Giles, Fayette & Kanawha Turnpike, completed from Pearisburg, Virginia, to Kanawha Falls in 1848, and the Weston & Gauley Bridge Turnpike, opened in 1858.

Despite Virginia's ambitious effort, residents beyond the mountains felt the state did not fairly allocate transportation improvements. This issue contributed to east-west sectional differences and loomed large during the statehood crisis. Western Virginia did lag behind the east in railroad construction, but records indicate that 94 of the 162 state-chartered road and turnpike companies existing in 1859 operated wholly or partly in present West Virginia. The Old Dominion chartered six new western turnpikes in 1860, but did not build any before the Civil War began.

When Virginia's turnpike era ended, the state had invested $4.8 million in 6,390 miles of toll roads. West Virginia inherited many of these routes in 1863, but the Civil War took a heavy toll on the roadways and bridges. Still, the legislature chartered 38 additional turnpike companies between 1863 and 1872. Spurred on by the incredible growth of railroads, highway traffic eventually declined, toll revenues fell off, and routes faded into oblivion or devolved into locally maintained haul roads in the late 1800s. In the automobile age many of the old turnpike routes have been revived as major secondary or interstate highways, including U.S. 60, U.S. 50, U.S. 250, and parts of Interstates 64 and 79.

In 1954, the West Virginia Turnpike opened from Charleston to Princeton, the modern successor to the great turnpikes of the century before. This two-lane toll road became the state's first high-speed expressway and ushered in a new highway era. Development of the interstate and Appalachian Corridor systems created new and faster routes through West Virginia, but the historic 19th-century turnpikes remain the basis for much of the state's existing road network.

See also Claudius Crozet, Giles, Fayette & Kanawha Turnpike, James River & Ka-

Stagecoach stop on the Northwestern Turnpike, by Joseph H. Diss Debar.

nawha Turnpike, National Road, Northwestern Virginia Turnpike, Staunton-Parkersburg Turnpike, Weston & Gauley Bridge Turnpike, West Virginia Turnpike

Billy Joe Peyton
West Virginia State University

Robert F. Hunter, "The Turnpike Movement in Virginia, 1816–1860," Ph.D. dissertation, Columbia University, 1957; Billy Joe Peyton, "To Make the Crooked Ways Straight and the Rough Ways Smooth: Surveying and Building America's First Interstate Highway," *American Civil Engineering History*, 2002.

Tuscarora Sandstone

The Tuscarora Sandstone is a prominent ridge-forming sedimentary rock in eastern West Virginia. It was named in the 1890s for exposures on Tuscarora Mountain in Pennsylvania. It is the oldest Silurian-period rock found in West Virginia and forms scenic landforms including Seneca Rocks, North Fork Mountain, Panther Knob, and Greenland Gap.

Approximately 150–200 feet thick, the Tuscarora is a quartz-rich sandstone known to geologists as arenite. The sand grains that compose the sandstone are cemented by silica, making the rock very hard and very durable. Close observation of the sandstone reveals sedimentary structures such as cross-bedding and trace fossils that indicate that the Tuscarora was most likely deposited in a shoreline environment. It was initially deposited in Early Silurian times as part of an apron of sediment shed from mountains that had formed to the east. Deep burial and cementation of the sediment (a process known as lithification) changed the sediment into the sedimentary rock we observe today.

West of the Allegheny Front the Tuscarora lies between 5,000 and 10,000 feet beneath the ground. In the western parts of the state, it has been a minor target for natural gas exploration, but only small commercial accumulations of gas have been found. Because of its strength and durability, the sandstone has little economic value except possibly as building stone. Softer sandstones, which can be crushed into sand for making glass, concrete and other purposes, are preferred.

See also Geology

David Matchen
Geological & Economic Survey

Twin Falls State Park

Twin Falls Resort State Park is located in Wyoming County between Mullens and Pineville. It is named for the two waterfalls, Foley Falls and Black Fork Falls, located in the park and within a quarter mile of each other. The park rests on 3,776 acres donated by the Western Pocahontas Corporation and Pocahontas Land Corporation in 1964 for use as a state park.

Development of the park began in the mid-1960s. In the autumn of 1967, a nine-hole golf course opened. Cabins, a swimming pool, golf pro complex, and a lodge with restaurant and gift shop opened in the spring of 1970. Several old homesteads were removed during initial development, but the park superintendent decided to reconstruct one of the oldest of these homesteads, including the restoration of the Bower cabin built in 1835. Completed in 1974 and housing live-in caretakers since 1977, the restructured pioneer farm is a piece of living history and the crown jewel of the park. In March 1981, conference and banquet facilities were completed at Twin Falls Lodge. The golf course was expanded to 18 holes in 1984. The park has picnic sheds, hiking trails, camping sites and facilities, a museum, game courts, and playgrounds.

See also Wyoming County

Shirley L. Stewart
West Virginia University

Tygart Dam and Lake

Tygart Lake is located on the Tygart Valley River three miles from Grafton, on the Taylor-Barbour county line. The dam was built during the Great Depression as part of President Franklin Roosevelt's New Deal, its construction ironically justified by both flood and drought.

Pittsburgh and other places in Pennsylvania and West Virginia had long suffered from periodic flooding of the Monongahela River, including major floods in 1888 and 1907. The Tygart Valley River is a major tributary of the Monongahela, and in 1912 Pittsburgh's Flood Commission called for a dam on the Tygart among its recommendations for watershed improvements. No action was taken on the Tygart until after the severe drought of 1930 which nearly shut down navigation on the Monongahela River. When construction began, Tygart Dam's dual purposes were to help control flooding in the Monongahela Valley and to improve low-water navigation on the Monongahela by impounding water for use in times of drought.

Authorized by the 1935 Rivers and Harbors Act, Tygart Dam was the first of 16 flood-control projects in the U.S. Army Corps of Engineers Pittsburgh District. Construction began in 1935 and was completed in 1938. The Works Progress Administration provided workers to the dam project, which employed as many as 3,000 men during construction. The dam is 1,880 feet long, 209 feet high at the spillway, and controls a watershed of 1,184 miles. The dam required 324,000 cubic yards of concrete, for years the most concrete in any dam east of the Mississippi.

The 1,740-acre lake and its surrounding land are managed by the West Virginia Division of Natural Resources. Tygart Lake State Park, located on the lake's eastern shore, offers a lodge, restaurant, cabins and camping, and a range of recreational opportunities. Pleasant Creek Wildlife Management Area occupies the opposite side of the lake. Fishermen take walleye, muskellunge, perch, and other species from Tygart Lake, which is also noted for its bass fishing.

See also Lakes, State Parks, Tygart Valley River

Tygart Valley Homesteads

The Tygart Valley Homesteads was a project of the Federal Subsistence Homesteads Corporation, created by the Roosevelt administration during the Great Depression. The idea was to provide a new start for unemployed farmers, miners, and timber workers. This was one of three resettlement projects in West Virginia, the others being at Arthurdale and Eleanor.

Initial funding in the amount of $675,000 was allocated by Congress on December 21, 1933, to acquire land in the Tygart Valley. A committee of local citizens was organized and, by 1934, land had been acquired at Dailey and Valley Bend, 10 miles south of Elkins. The plan called for the construction of 198 houses, with homesteaders to help build them. They were paid 30 cents an hour plus work credit, which could be applied to the purchase of their houses. There were 1,640 applications from families wanting to occupy the planned houses.

The first houses were ready for occupancy February 11, 1935, and by the end of 1936, 158 houses sheltered 750 people. The houses varied in size from four to six rooms, and each had from 0.9 to 2.8 acres of land. Their outbuildings included a combination garage, chicken coop, feed room, coal bin, and cellar. Ultimately, 202 houses were built or purchased and incorporated into the project.

A general supply building, a weaving center, an auto repair garage and filling station, a potato storage shed, and limestone quarry were constructed. The main industrial project was a large wood mill erected in 1937, now operated by Coastal Lumber Company. A cooperative farm, cannery, and store operated briefly. The large stone trade center building, including a bakery, restaurant, general store, barber and beauty shop, shoe repair shop, post office, and auditorium, was completed in 1937. A modern brick school building began serving the children of the homesteaders in 1939.

Eleanor Roosevelt, assisted by Congressman Jennings Randolph, promoted the homestead movement in the Tygart Valley and elsewhere. From 1934 to 1940, she made four visits to the Tygart Valley Homesteads.

The onset of World War II had an immediate impact on the settlement. Families moved elsewhere to join the war effort while men of military age left to serve the nation. By 1944, the government began to sell the homes to the settlers, and the large sawmill, trade center building, and industrial operations were soon sold to private businesses. The handsome trade center still stands as a local landmark, along with many houses and other buildings.

See also Arthurdale, Eleanor, Great Depression

Donald L. Rice
Elkins

Donald L. Rice, *Randolph 200, A Bicentennial History of Randolph County,* 1987; Thomas R. Ross, *The Tygart Valley Homesteads, Dailey and Valley Bend, W.Va.,* 1975.

FAST FACTS ABOUT TYLER COUNTY

Founded: 1814
Land in square miles: 260.1
Population: 9,592
Percentage minorities: 0.6%
Percentage rural: 72.0%
Median age: 40.8
Percentage 65 and older: 16.5%
Birth rate per 1,000 population: 10.1
Median household income: $29,290
High school graduate or higher: 75.4%
Bachelor's degree or higher: 8.5%
Home ownership: 83.7%
Median home value: $61,500

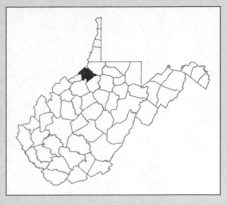

This information is from the 2000 U.S. Census. In 2000, West Virginia as a whole had 5 percent minorities, a median age of 38.9, median household income of $29,696, and a 75.2 percent home ownership rate.

Tygart Valley River

The Tygart Valley River is a major tributary of the Monongahela River. The Tygart has its source on Valley Mountain near the Randolph-Pocahontas county line. With its tributaries the Tygart drains 1,329 square miles and parts of nine counties, on its way to join the West Fork River near Fairmont, thus forming the Monongahela. The Tygart drops about 3,000 feet in the 118 miles from its source to its mouth. The greatest fall occurs in Randolph County, where the upper Tygart is a swift-flowing stream. The river bisects Randolph County from south to north, paralleled most of the way by U.S. 219-250. The river's valley includes much fine farmland, settled early in the history of Western Virginia.

The Tygart flows in a north-northwesterly course as it runs through Valley Head, Huttonsville, Mill Creek, Beverly, Elkins, Norton, Belington, Philippi, and Grafton. Northwest of Elkins, the river passes through a gap between Rich Mountain and Laurel Mountain. The main tributary of the Tygart is the Buckhannon River, which joins the Tygart upstream from Philippi.

In a reversal of the usual pattern, the Tygart Valley was named before the river, for the David Tygart family who settled with the Robert Files family south of present Beverly in 1753. The river was subsequently named for the valley and has been identified by several other names in the 250 years since its settlement. It was once frequently referred to as the East Fork of the Monongahela River.

The river valley has a long, rich history, dating from the days of early settlement and the Indian wars. The upper valley is a natural thoroughfare, occupied historically by the Staunton-Parkersburg Turnpike. The turnpike was traversed by Northern and Southern troops in the Civil War, and in 1861 a major battle was fought at nearby Rich Mountain. West Virginia's first flood-control dam was built on the Tygart Valley River near Grafton in 1935–38.

Donald L. Rice
Elkins

Tyler County

Tyler County lies on the Ohio River between Wetzel and Pleasants counties. It was formed from Ohio County on December 6, 1814, originally encompassing all of what is now Wetzel County and parts of present Doddridge and Pleasants. Tyler County was named for John Tyler, governor of Virginia (1808–11) and father of President John Tyler.

Bordered to the west by the Ohio River's Long Reach—a straight stretch in the river from Paden City to Raven Rock—Tyler County is drained largely by Middle Island Creek and its tributaries. Although there are elevations approaching 1,500 feet along Tyler's borders with Wetzel and Doddridge counties, the highest point within Tyler County is the knob known as the Owlshead at 1,444 feet above sea level. The elevation at Bens Run, on the Ohio River in the southwest corner of Tyler County, is 620 feet. Tyler County is hilly, its terrain sculpted by valleys and hollows. There are several large Ohio River islands in the county, including Williamson Island south of Paden City.

At 260.1 square miles, Tyler County has six magisterial districts: Lincoln, Union, Ellsworth, McElroy, Centerville, and Meade. In addition to Sistersville and Middlebourne, the county's communities include Friendly, Bens Run, Alma, Shirley, Josephs Mills, and Wick. In 1937, the women of Friendly were successful in their campaign to seat an all-female municipal government. The Tyler-Wetzel county line divides Paden City, which

The Tyler County Courthouse in Middlebourne.

are nearly 9,000 fewer people in Tyler County today than at the boom's peak in 1900.

Other small industries, such as gristmills and sawmills, chemicals, glass, and pottery dotted the county during the 1900s. Many residents still worked family farms or in the downsized petroleum industry. Currently, many of Tyler County's 9,592 residents work in manufacturing, often commuting across the Ohio River to plants on the Ohio side. The largest employers within the county are the Crompton Corporation chemical plant and the board of education.

Tyler County lost population throughout the first half of the 20th century, with the numbers stabilizing in the next 50 years. Today the county is a quiet, largely rural, society. Tyler Countians have a home ownership rate of 84 percent, higher than the state and much higher than the nation as a whole. Household income is about the same as for the state, and the county's poverty rate is lower then the state's.

Tyler Countians have made their mark in the larger world. Though not born there, West Virginia's first governor, Arthur I. Boreman, received his early education in Middlebourne. Pitcher Wilbur "Lefty" Cooper, who spent 12 years with the Pittsburgh Pirates, was born on Davis Run in 1892. Gov. Cecil H. Underwood was born in 1922 near Josephs Mills. Underwood, a Republican, was both the oldest and youngest governor West Virginia has had.

Today, students from all over the county attend Tyler County Consolidated Middle and High schools. Sistersville General Hospital, founded in 1908, continues to provide care for the entire county. Tyler County Speedway, at the Tyler County Fairgrounds, is one of the few dirt tracks for auto racing in the tri-state area. History buffs from across the country travel each year to Sistersville's Oil and Gas Festival, which celebrates the area's industrial heritage.

See also Middlebourne, Sistersville

Christina Myer
Wheeling

David L. McKain and Bernard L. Allen, *Where It All Began: The Story of the People and Places Where the Oil and Gas Industry Began—West Virginia and Southeastern Ohio*, 1994; Tyler County Heritage and Historical Society, *History of Tyler County, West Virginia, to 1984*, 1984.

otherwise would be the largest town in the county.

White hunters settled in what became Tyler County in 1792 near the present town of Friendly. Mainly of Scotch-Irish, English, and German descent, other settlers from the East soon flowed into the former Indian hunting grounds. By 1800 Henry Jolley established a ferry across the Ohio River at Sistersville. The Bens Run earthworks, an archeological site, is evidence of rich prehistoric activity.

Charles Wells founded the oldest of Tyler County's communities in 1802. Wells Landing was later named Sistersville, after Wells's daughters, Sarah and Deliah. It was the first county seat, and remains the largest town in Tyler County. In 1895, Charles Wells's grandson, Ephraim Wells, opened the Wells Hotel in downtown Sistersville. Still a local landmark, the red-brick hotel was added to the National Register of Historic Places in 1972.

In 1815, centrally located Middlebourne became the county seat of Tyler County. Robert Gorrell had founded Middlebourne in 1798.

The oil and gas industry transformed the region in the late 19th and early 20th centuries. In 1892, the Polecat well was drilled into one of the richest oil pools in West Virginia. In 1894, the Big Moses gas well was drilled, and became one of the largest ever found. What followed was an oil and gas rush that increased the population of Sistersville from 1,000 to 7,000 by the end of the decade, while the population of the county grew from 11,962 to 18,252. By 1910, the oil and gas boom was declining, and the effect was felt throughout the county. There

Uncle Abner

Created by writer Melville Davisson Post (1869–1930), Uncle Abner is a backwoods detective from the Harrison County area. He uses his uncanny observation coupled with a simple logic to solve mysteries that always pit the good, hardworking countryman against the unscrupulous, cowardly wrongdoer. The tales are set outdoors, the reader riding with Uncle Abner through antebellum Western Virginia, in a time of land and livestock, timber and trading, and determined men and women. Abner and the reader seek clues together and rush to a climax unexcelled by other mystery writers. The popular Uncle Abner stories appeared in the national magazines of the time, a majority of them in the *Saturday Evening Post*.

The style is dated, but Uncle Abner is still known to readers of mysteries. Most recently, John F. Suter reproduced Uncle Abner for *Ellery Queen Mystery Magazine* and also published five Abner stories in *Old Land, Dark Land, Strange Land* (University of Charleston, 1996), a collection of Suter's own short stories. Eighteen of Post's stories were published in the book, *Uncle Abner: Master of Mysteries* (Appleton, 1918). Another collection, *The Methods of Uncle Abner*, was published in 1974, and in 1977 the University of California Press issued *The Complete Uncle Abner*.

See also Melville Davisson Post

Charles F. Moore
East Tennessee State University

Underground Railroad

Neither underground nor a railroad, the Underground Railroad was a covert and loosely organized conspiracy that endeavored to aid escaped slaves on their way to Canada or safe areas in the northern states. Free African-Americans, Quakers and other white sympathizers, and other blacks still in slavery, played the most prominent role in hiding and aiding slaves as they made their way north. As the abolitionist movement gained momentum in the mid-1800s, the Underground Railroad's activity increased. Between 1840 and 1860, it is estimated that more than a thousand slaves a year were smuggled out of the South. Three crucial junctions of the Underground Railroad existed in Virginia, at Norfolk and Richmond and in Western Virginia.

Many slaves escaped through Western Virginia into Ohio. Under the fugitive slave law, slaves could be tracked and returned from anywhere in the United States, but across the Ohio River and north of the Mason-Dixon Line an es-

> ## Uncle Abner
>
> "I ought to say a word about my Uncle Abner. He was one of those austere, deeply religious men who were the product of the Reformation. He always carried a Bible in his pocket and he read it where he pleased. Once the crowd at Roy's Tavern tried to make sport of him when he got his book out by the fire; but they never tried it again. When the fight was over Abner paid Roy eighteen silver dollars for the broken chairs and the table—and he was the only man in the tavern who could ride a horse. Abner belonged to the church militant, and his God was a war lord."
>
> —Melville Davisson Post
> "The Angel of the Lord" (1911)

caped slave was in relative safety. Thus, the Ohio River symbolized the border of the "promised land" for many slaves. The river ran along the western boundary of Virginia for 277 miles, a tempting destination for slaves who could get to it.

The majority of Ohio River crossings took place in the winter, so that the slaves could cross on ice rather than swimming or finding transportation across the river. When a winter escape was not possible, abolitionists often acquired canoes, so that the slaves could paddle their way down the tributaries of the Ohio at night. The rugged mountains of Western Virginia also aided slaves as they fled north. Slave patrols usually avoided the Alleghenies and often confined their searches to central and Tidewater Virginia.

A number of stories about the Underground Railroad remain to this day. Ceredo was founded on the banks of the Ohio in 1857 by New England abolitionist Eli Thayer and populated by other abolitionists, and the Wayne County town soon actively participated in the Underground Railroad. It is said that Z. D. Ramsdell of Ceredo hid slaves in his house and smuggled them through a tunnel that led from his basement to the Ohio River. Once the slaves made it across the river, they could find sanctuary in the small town of Quaker Bottom, now Proctorville, Ohio. John Fairchild was a successful conductor in the Underground Railroad who often traveled back and forth across the Alleghenies, guiding numerous runaways from Virginia plantations to the Ohio River. Just east of Parkersburg, the Nutter Farm was an alleged stop in the Underground Railroad. Local stories persist that members of the Nutter family were murdered for their aid to runaway slaves.

At times, the history of the Underground Railroad is more legend than fact. Runaways often did not receive any assistance until they had escaped out of the

South through their own efforts. Those who offered sanctuary and aid to slaves in Virginia risked severe punishment under the law and the wrath of their slaveholding neighbors, necessitating secrecy. Therefore, no substantial evidence has endured that would give modern historians exact details as to the dimensions and organization of the Underground Railroad. Most of the surviving evidence comes from the oral histories of escaped slaves and from those who boasted that they gave the slaves aid. These oral histories often offer exaggerated accounts. Nonetheless, the Underground Railroad did exist in West Virginia and helped numerous slaves obtain their freedom in the years preceding the Civil War.

See also Abolitionism, Ceredo, Z. D. Ramsdell, Slavery

C. Belmont Keeney
West Virginia Humanities Council

Cecil Underwood

Cecil Harland Underwood, West Virginia's 25th and 32nd governor, has the distinction of having served as West Virginia's youngest and oldest chief executive. In the 40 years between his administrations, he remained active in industry and education. From the time of his election to the House of Delegates in 1944 to his sixth campaign for governor in 2000, he was one of the state's leading Republican political figures.

Born November 5, 1922, at Josephs Mills in Tyler County, Underwood was the youngest of five children of Silas and Della Underwood. While his father managed a farm and worked at other jobs, Cecil helped on the farm and studied vocational agriculture at Middlebourne High School. He graduated fifth in his class in 1940.

Underwood finished Salem College in three years, graduating in 1943 with a degree in political science. He served in the Army Reserve, although a fast pulse kept him from active duty. He began teaching high school biology in St. Marys. He won election to the House of Delegates from Tyler County in 1944, beginning a dozen years of legislative service that led to his becoming House minority leader in 1949 and, seven years later, the Republican nominee for governor. On July 25, 1948, he married Hovah Hall of Grantsville, and, in 1952, he received a master's degree in political science from West Virginia University.

By 1956, Underwood had become a leading spokesman for the Republican Party. On January 4, 1956, at the age of 33, he announced his candidacy for governor, pledging to "restore confidence and good feeling in our state government." In the primary election, Underwood narrowly defeated Charleston Mayor John T. Copenhaver for the Republican nomination. Underwood was elected governor in the gen-

Governor Cecil H. Underwood (1922–), during his first term.

eral election by a majority of 63,681 votes over opponent Robert H. Mollohan, despite a 259,000-voter Democratic registration edge in the state.

At his inauguration, January 15, 1957, Underwood pledged to hire qualified personnel, keep taxes to a minimum, reform state purchasing, improve roads, strengthen education, attract new industry, and otherwise advance the state up the ladder, a symbol of progress he had used in his campaign. To an extent beyond that of his predecessors, Underwood also promised to report regularly "via the press, radio, and television" and to "move often among the people" instead of staying at the capitol. At times during his administration, his penchant for public relations, especially the frequency of his out-of-state trips to promote West Virginia, drew criticism from opponents.

Underwood's bolder initiatives were moderated by the legislature, whose Democratic House and Senate majorities were increased in the 1958 election. In response to his call for higher taxes to finance a 10-year, $500-million road program, lawmakers were content to proceed more gradually, giving him $4.3 million of the $37 million in new annual revenue that he had sought. Among the other measures passed during his term were emergency benefits to help miners made jobless by the mechanization of the coal industry, a statewide property reappraisal, and creation of a new economic development agency.

Barred from a second consecutive term by the state constitution, Underwood in 1960 ran for the U.S. Senate. Unopposed in the Republican primary, in November he lost to Democrat Jennings Randolph by 88,240 votes, his first political defeat. In February 1961, Underwood accepted a position with Island Creek Coal Company and largely stayed out of politics for the next few years. His friends, however, were not surprised when he announced in January 1964 that he would run again for governor. He easily won the Republican primary, but lost the general election by 77,464 votes to Democrat Hulett Smith, who benefited from Lyndon Johnson's landslide victory for president.

In July 1965, Underwood took a position with Monsanto Chemical Company, and by 1967 he once more had his eye on the governor's mansion. He announced his candidacy four days before Congressman Arch Moore entered the Republican primary. On May 14, 1968, Moore defeated Underwood with 57 percent of the vote, and Underwood returned to the private sector. In 1972, after several years with a land development company he organized, Underwood was named president of Bethany College. He held the post until August 23, 1975, when he resigned in the face of discontent by some members of the faculty.

In 1976, after the state Supreme Court ruled that the gubernatorial succession amendment to the state constitution barred Governor Moore from seeking a third consecutive term, Underwood won the Republican nomination for governor. However, in the general election, he lost to Democrat John D. Rockefeller IV by 242,236 votes. Again Underwood returned to the business world, holding a variety of positions including the presidency of Princess Coal in Huntington. As Underwood pursued his career in the private sector, political circumstances created yet another opportunity for him to seek the governorship. In 1996, as a seasoned elder statesman of his party, he won the Republican nomination. The Democrats in a divisive primary nominated Charlotte Pritt of Kanawha County. In the ensuing fall campaign, Underwood defeated Pritt with 52 percent of the vote, and took office January 13, 1997, as the state's 32nd and oldest governor.

In his inaugural address, Underwood emphasized the importance of advanced technology and improvements in education and health care "as the industrial age gives way to the information age." With Democrats in control of both houses of the legislature, Underwood sought consensus. Among the accomplishments of his administration were a $565 million reduction in the workers compensation fund deficit, an aggressive road construction program, development of a high-tech partnership with Verizon telephone company, more than $1 billion in new sewer and water projects, expansion of children's programs, and assistance to help senior citizens afford prescription drugs.

In 2000, when Underwood ran for reelection, the Democrats nominated nineterm Congressman Bob Wise of Kanawha County. A majority of West Virginia voters for the first time since 1916 simultaneously gave their support to the Republican candidate for president and the Democratic nominee for governor. While George W. Bush defeated Al Gore 52 percent to 46 percent in West Virginia, Wise defeated Underwood 50 percent to 47 percent.

In his final address to the legislature on January 10, 2001, Underwood reflected on more than half a century of public life, noting that he had "come a long way from a bashful boy on a hillside farm in Tyler County."

Larry Sonis
Arlington, Texas
John G. Morgan, *West Virginia Governors 1863–1980*, 1980.

Union

Union, the county seat of Monroe County, is located in rolling limestone farm country at the intersection of U.S. 219 and State Route 3. The town, at an elevation of 2,071 feet, had a population of 548 in 2000.

Union is an old community, settled by James Alexander in 1774. Alexander later donated acreage for the town and additional land for nearby Green Hill Cemetery. Union was established by the Virginia legislature in 1800 to be the seat of government for newly established Monroe County. Some objected that the location was not central to the county, which was originally larger than it is today. Several frontier forts were located in the region, and the town received its name because it was a place where militia united for common drill during the Indian wars.

Ironically, considering its name, the people of Union and the surrounding area generally sided with the South during the Civil War. Today, Union is noted for the presence of the statue of a Confederate soldier, which stands alone in a field just outside town. The first Monroe County courthouse, built of logs, was replaced by a brick structure in 1820. The current courthouse was built in 1881. Elmwood, the ancestral home of the Caperton family, is among several historic houses in the Union area.

See also Monroe County

Union Carbide Corporation

In 1917 five companies, all related to the electric arc furnace or acetylene industry, merged to form the Union Carbide and Carbon Corporation, later the Union Carbide Corporation. In 1920, Union Carbide purchased a small refinery at Clendenin and began developing the processes for making ethylene and related chemicals. Ethylene is made from natural gas or petroleum, and the new processes gave birth to the modern petrochemical industry.

In 1925, Union Carbide purchased an

obsolete chemical plant in South Charleston to build facilities to produce the olefins ethylene and propylene. Soon chemical units covered the company acreage on the South Charleston mainland and most of the 80-acre Blaine Island in the nearby Kanawha River. Starting in the early 1930s, Union Carbide built similar plants at other locations in the U.S. and Puerto Rico, including units that supplied 100 percent of the world's ethylene.

In 1947, Union Carbide expanded to the Institute plant, west of Charleston, originally built as a part of the government's synthetic rubber program during World War II. In 1949, "Carbide," as it was called locally, built a new Technical Center in South Charleston to house research, development, and engineering facilities on an expansive campus.

The number of chemicals and plastics produced by the company increased from about 80 in 1934 to more than 400 in the early 1960s, the majority developed in South Charleston. Most of the chemicals were used by industrial customers, but some, such as Prestone antifreeze, Eveready batteries, and Sevin and Temik insecticides, were consumer products. Five basic types of plastics were produced, including phenolics (Carbide had bought the Bakelite company), epoxy, polystyrene, vinyls, and polyethylene.

Between 1946 and 1982, revenues increased from about $415 million to more than $10 billion, placing Union Carbide in the top ten companies in the United States. Worldwide employment was near 80,000, with about 12,000 in West Virginia. The company was West Virginia's largest employer for several years. But, starting in the 1950s, competition in chemicals and plastics increased substantially, while poor economic conditions resulted in decreased prices for most chemicals. Carbide's headquarters were moved from New York City to Danbury, Connecticut, in 1981.

In December 1984, an incident at the Union Carbide insecticide plant in Bhopal, India, released a large cloud of MIC, methyl isocyanate gas, which killed an estimated 3,000 people and injured thousands more. The tragedy led to new concerns about safety at chemical plants, including a Union Carbide methyl isocyanate plant in the Kanawha Valley. In 1989, the Indian government and Union Carbide reached a settlement for $470 million in the incident. Union Carbide dropped a counter-suit which argued that sabotage caused the tragic incident.

Bhopal substantially weakened the company. To avoid a hostile takeover attempt by the GAF Company, Carbide sold almost half its productive businesses. The agricultural business, which included most of the Institute plant, was sold to Rhone-Poulenc. The Consumer Products Division was sold, as was the carbon electrodes plant near Clarksburg. The electro-metallurgical plant at Alloy, whose associated hydroelectric tunnel project had claimed the lives of a multitude of workers during the construction of Hawks Nest tunnel in the early 1930s, had been sold in 1981 to the Elkem Company. In 1992, the Linde Division was split off to form a separate company, Praxair. A silicones products plant built near Sistersville in 1956 was sold in 1994.

Finally on February 6, 2001, the Dow Chemical Company acquired Union Carbide, and the company ceased to exist as a separate corporation. The Union Carbide Foundation is a contributor to *The West Virginia Encyclopedia*.

See also Chemical Industry, Hawks Nest Tunnel Disaster

> *Robert C. Hieronymus*
> *Charleston*

Robert D. Stief, *A History of Union Carbide Corporation: From the 1890s to the 1990s*, 1998.

Unitarian Universalism

Unitarian Universalism is a liberal, noncreedal religion with Judeo-Christian roots. Unitarianism is based on the unity of God, denying the Trinity; Universalism is based on the doctrine of universal salvation. The Unitarian Universalist Association, headquartered in Boston, was formed in 1961 by the consolidation of the American Unitarian Association, organized in 1825, and the Universalist Church of America, organized in 1793. The UUA represents more than 1,000 self-governing congregations and 200,000 adults and church schoolchildren in the United States and Canada.

There were five Unitarian Universalist congregations in West Virginia, with a total of 230 members in 2002.

The Ohio Valley Unitarian Universalist Congregation was founded in 1975 and chartered by the Association in 1976. It succeeded a fellowship active until the 1960s. It serves a Wheeling-area congregation, with its church building on the Ohio side of the river since 1989. The Unitarian Universalist Fellowship of Morgantown was founded in 1954. At first, the meetings were held in private homes, then in a rental building. The present church was dedicated in 1963. In Beckley, the New River Unitarian Universalist Fellowship was established in 1961 as a Sunday morning discussion forum that gathered in a local newspaper office. In 1992, the congregation purchased a meeting house. The Unitarian Fellowship of Huntington is located on Sixth Avenue.

Although the present Unitarian Universalist Fellowship of the Kanawha Valley dates back only to 1953, there was a group of Unitarians in Charleston from about 1916 to 1918, under the leadership of Julian R. Pennington, a Harvard Theological Seminary graduate. When the Reverend Pennington left the state, the group dissolved and sold its property. Unitarians regrouped in Charleston in 1953, and purchased land where the members designed and erected a building. The present building was completed and dedicated in 1994.

The Universalist Meeting House at Fork Ridge in Marshall County was erected in 1835. An additional larger building was erected in 1872. At the turn of the 20th century, two women served as ministers. This congregation was disbanded in 1998.

See also Religion

> *Jill Thompson Decker*
> *Vienna, Virginia*

John A. Buehrens and Forrest Church, *A Chosen Faith*, 1998.

United Bank

One of West Virginia's largest banks, United Bank is older than the state itself. It originated as the Northwestern Bank of Virginia, founded in 1817 in Wheeling with branches in Wellsburg, Morgantown, and Clarksburg. Virginia legislative reforms allowed an additional branch to be established in 1839 in Parkersburg. Shortly afterward, another branch was established in Jeffersonville (now Tazewell), in southwestern Virginia. After the outbreak of the Civil War, the Virginia legislature split off the Jeffersonville branch. The National Banking Act of 1864, designed to create a uniform currency in the United States and to facilitate the sale of government bonds, was amended in 1865 to allow state banks to become national banks. The Wheeling branch of the Northwestern Bank was reorganized as the National Bank of West Virginia, and the Parkersburg branch became the First National Bank of Parkersburg.

The First National Bank of Parkersburg is the direct parent of United Bank. It grew through the remaining years of the 19th century into the 20th century. In 1935, it was one of the largest national banks in West Virginia. By the 1960s, it was one of the 12 largest, and it was one of the five largest banking institutions in West Virginia in the 1980s. Legislation controlling bank expansion was relaxed in West Virginia in the early 1980s and the Parkersburg National Bank became part of United Bankshares Holding Company, which included Union Central National Bank and United National Bank. In 1985, these banks were renamed United National Bank.

In 1986, United National joined forces with InterMountain Bankshares and its subsidiary, Kanawha Banking and Trust. In 2002, United National Bank converted to a state charter, becoming United Bank. In 2005, United Bankshares, with $6.4 billion in assets, was the largest bank headquartered in West Virginia, and the second largest of all banks operating in the state. United is also the largest company of any sort headquartered in West Virginia. It has 52 offices in West Virginia, with 39 others in Virginia, Maryland, Ohio, and Washington. The company headquarters is located in Charleston with executive offices in Parkersburg. United Bank is a contributor to *The West Virginia Encyclopedia*.

See also Banking

Carrie Stollings
Charleston

Otis K. Rice, *A Centennial of Strength: West Virginia Banks*, 1991.

United Brethren

The Church of the United Brethren in Christ originated in the late 1700s among German immigrants in Pennsylvania, Maryland, and Virginia, including members of the Reformed Church and former Mennonites. The official founding of the church came in 1800, and the first general conference of clergy was held in 1815. Like the Methodists, the United Brethren emphasized the doctrine of justification by faith alone, but combined this with a strong emphasis on holy living. The major goal of the early pastors was saving souls. There was little emphasis on social gospel.

German-American settlers moving into Western Virginia from Maryland and the Shenandoah Valley either brought their United Brethren beliefs with them or were converted by traveling ministers. Church founder Philip William Otterbein made several trips into the mountains, but Christian Newcomer (1749–1830) founded and nurtured many of the churches in northern West Virginia.

D. C. Topping came from Ohio and established the church's Virginia Mission in Cabell County in 1835. Two years later it was renamed the Guyandotte Circuit. In 1836, the Virginia Conference sent Michael Moses to the vicinity of New Haven in Mason County. Moses established the Jackson Mission in Mason and Jackson counties. The first permanent UB church was built in 1847 at Sand Hill near Point Pleasant, described as a "good-sized frame church" with a side door that led to a "separate apartment for slaves."

An important early UB evangelist was Benjamin Stickley. He was converted by the preaching of Michael Moses and licensed in 1840. For years he traveled throughout present northern West Virginia establishing churches. Also in 1840, German members of Otterbein's church in Baltimore migrated to Braxton County and formed UB churches with John Engle as the pastor. In 1846, the churches in Lewis, Upshur, Barbour, and Gilmer counties were merged with those in Braxton County to form the Lewis or Buckhannon Circuit with Stickley as pastor.

In 1857, the Virginia Conference approved the creation of the Parkersburg Conference for the area now known as West Virginia. The conference initially included 11 preachers, ten charges or circuits, and 1,327 members. In 1897, the name was changed to the West Virginia Conference. By 1924, the membership had risen to 10,337.

The United Brethren were a pioneering denomination in allowing women to preach. As early as the 1850s, a few women were preaching, and at the 1889 General Conference a formal statement allowing women's ordination was made.

In 1946, the United Brethren merged with the Evangelical Association, forming the Evangelical United Brethren Church. At the time of the merger United Brethren churches existed primarily in two areas of West Virginia: the Ohio River counties of Cabell, Mason, Jackson, Wood, Pleasants, and Tyler, and the interior counties of Gilmer, Lewis, Upshur, Barbour, and Braxton. There were few, if any, south of a line from Huntington to Charleston and few in the eastern part of the state. At the time of the 1946 merger there were 261 United Brethren churches in West Virginia and only four congregations of the Evangelical Association.

In 1968 the Evangelical United Brethren Church merged with the Methodists to create the United Methodists, the largest Protestant denomination in West Virginia. At the time of the 1968 merger there were 240 EUB churches in West Virginia with a total membership of 23,911.

See also Methodists, Religion

Robert L. Frey
Miamisburg, Ohio

J. Bruce Behney and Paul H. Eller, *The History of the Evangelical United Brethren Church*, 1979; A. W. Drury, *History of the Church of the United Brethren in Christ*, 1924.

United Carbon Building

The United Carbon Building is an architecturally significant Charleston office building, designed in the streamlined modern style of the 1930s and 1940s. In 1939, Oscar Nelson, president of the United Carbon Company, commissioned Charleston architect Walter F. Martens to design the company's new headquarters.

Nelson (1879–1953), a Swedish immigrant, had begun as a laborer with the Carbon Black Company in Pennsylvania, which transferred him to a production plant in Grantsville, West Virginia. After rising to superintendent, he resigned to begin his own venture with two wealthy partners from Weston, T. F. Koblegard and Thomas A. Whelan. Under Nelson's management, the group combined a number of smaller companies in 1925 to form the United Carbon Company. By the 1930s, the company had become the world's largest producer of carbon black and a major producer of natural gas. United Carbon moved its headquarters to Charleston in the mid-1930s.

Golden brick, black alberene stone, and polished black granite clad the building's sleek sculptural form, integrating the United Carbon Company's gold and black trademark colors into the design. Sculptures including the statue of a male figure at the front of the building were designed by Martens's son, Robert, who at the time attended Michigan's Cranbrook Academy. The famous Saarinen family of Cranbrook assisted Martens in the project, seeing it as an opportunity to make a statement of their integrated approach to design. The 12th-floor penthouse suite originally had furnishings created at Cranbrook, and above Oscar Nelson's desk was a wall hanging by Eliel Saarinen's wife, Loja.

The United Carbon Building's prominence in its time is signified by its appearance in 1944 on the cover of *Pencil Points* (later *Progressive Architecture*, a major architectural magazine), where it was praised as an exemplar of integrated modern design. In 1994, barely 50 years after the building's completion, it was listed on the National Register of Historic Places. The building was owned by the Nelson family until 1978.

See also Architects and Architecture, Walter Martens

Carl Agsten Jr.
Charleston

Kenneth Reid, ed., "United Carbon Building, Charleston, West Virginia," *Pencil Points*, October 1944; Francis W. Turner and Mary Eloise, eds., "United Carbon Builds a Home," *The West Virginia Review*, October 1940.

United Mine Workers of America

On January 23, 1890, rival miners' organizations met in Columbus, Ohio, to organize the United Mine Workers of America. John B. Rae, a Scottish immigrant, became the first president. Just three months later, in Wheeling, UMWA District 17, encompassing most of West Virginia, held its first meeting, elected M. F. Moran as district president and immediately launched what became an extraordinary struggle of more than 40 years to unionize the state's coal mines.

In 1897, alarmed at the rising tonnage flooding into their markets from non-union West Virginia, the coal operators of the Central Competitive Field of the North and Midwest agreed to an uneasy peace with the union but insisted that the UMWA also organize their Mountain State competitors. In its effort to fulfill that commitment, the UMWA faced no easy task. The rugged terrain left West Virginia miners isolated and dependent upon their employers. Miners and their families lived in company housing, traded at company stores, worshiped in churches built by the company, and received part of their pay in company scrip. Ethnic and racial differences in the coal camps inhibited labor unity.

West Virginia coal operators also provided hardy resistance. Insisting that because they relied on distant markets, they could not pay union wages and continue in business, they convinced political and judicial authorities and most of the state's daily press that their struggle against the union was a battle for the state's economic survival. To carry on the fight, coal operators organized associations and hired labor spies and heavily armed mine guards, many of whom carried the force of public authority as deputy sheriffs. Operators also fought on the legal front with yellow-dog contracts—individual employment agreements that prohibited workers from joining a union—and by obtaining injunctions against union activities.

In the face of these obstacles, the UMWA's repeated efforts in the 1890s and early in the 20th century brought few West Virginia miners into the union despite support from national labor leaders, Socialist Eugene Debs and noted organizer Mary Harris "Mother" Jones. In 1912, efforts to maintain a union toehold in the Paint Creek and Cabin Creek areas of Kanawha County led to a bloody confrontation.

During World War I, coal production expanded in West Virginia, and a tenuous labor-management truce prevailed as the federal government encouraged collective bargaining. When the fighting in Europe ended, however, the Mine Wars in West Virginia resumed, resulting in pitched battles in Mingo and Logan counties in 1919–21, including the Matewan Massacre, the March on Logan, and the Battle of Blair Mountain. Martial law, the intervention of federal troops, an investigation by a U.S. Senate committee, and the arrest of state UMWA leaders C. Frank Keeney and William Blizzard on charges of treason and murder, marked these conflicts.

Although prosecutors failed to convict Blizzard and Keeney, the labor battles and treason trials enfeebled the UMWA just as the industry faced a painful readjustment. Wartime expansion had generated a mining capacity that exceeded peacetime markets. The U.S. Coal Commission, established by Congress to study the problem, concluded that there were too many mines and too many miners. During the 1920s, West Virginia operators became more determined than ever that survival required nonunion operations. Membership in the UMWA plummeted. In 1924, District 17 President Keeney and Secretary-Treasurer Fred Mooney resigned as national president John L. Lewis attempted to impose an industry-approved pay scale in West Virginia. Increasingly autocratic, Lewis then made 17 a provisional district and split its territory, creating District 31 to administer most of northern West Virginia. He also crushed district autonomy by replacing elected officials with his own appointees in many districts.

During the Great Depression, the UMWA struggled to survive and briefly faced competition from the more radical West Virginia Mine Workers Union and the National Miners Union. With Roosevelt's New Deal, the legal climate improved. New federal legislation outlawed yellow-dog contracts, placed limits on anti-union injunctions, and gave employees the right to bargain collectively. The state outlawed the mine guard system. Urged on by Lewis and led by District 17 President Van Bittner, the UMWA finally unionized the West Virginia coalfields in 1933–34, making it not only the most powerful union in the state but also for many years a political force that could make and break politicians.

By the late 1930s, productivity, employment, and wages were rising. During World War II, the industry boomed and so did the UMWA in West Virginia. Bittner served as president of District 17 until 1942, when he resigned as a result of conflicts with Lewis. Lewis again divided 17, creating District 29 to administer the low-volatile fields of southern West Virginia.

Lewis aroused much public animosity by leading the union in wartime strikes which brought repeated federal takeovers of the mines but won a captive mines agreement and portal-to-portal pay. Post-war strikes resulted in the establishment of a welfare and retirement fund. The fund eventually paid medical and retirement benefits to millions of miners and their families and in the mid-1950s built ten miners hospitals in Southern Appalachia, including hospitals at Beckley, Man, and Williamson.

After World War II, the coal industry faced growing competition from other fuels. In 1950, Lewis moved from his confrontational methods and joined forces with industry leaders to promote rapid modernization of the mines, which increased productivity and wages but decreased the number of miners and shrank union rolls. Mine mechanization also contributed to the impoverishment of Appalachia, as unemployment spread through the region. A declining membership forced the union to cut welfare and retirement fund benefits and to close or sell its medical facilities.

In the 1960s, union leadership deteriorated with the rise to the presidency of William Anthony "Tony" Boyle, a longtime Lewis assistant. After a nine-year reign of corruption, Boyle faced a challenge from reformers. They seized the initiative in coal mine health and safety issues, persuaded the West Virginia legislature to pass a black lung compensation law, and lobbied for the federal Coal Mine Health and Safety Act of 1969. The reformers sought to topple Boyle in a 1969 election, but Boyle defeated Joseph A. "Jock" Yablonski. Three weeks later Yablonski, his wife, and daughter were murdered; Boyle was eventually convicted of plotting the crime. In 1972, the reformers, organized as Miners for Democracy, elected West Virginian Arnold Miller as president. Miller's presidency fell short of the high expectations of supporters. In 1979, the union turned to a more conservative course under President Sam Church Jr., who was in turn succeeded by Richard Trumka in 1982 and in 1995 by Cecil Roberts, a West Virginian whose family had deep roots in state labor history.

As the 20th century waned, the UMWA faced an uncertain future as ever more sophisticated technologies continued to increase productivity and to reduce the mine work force. When the Pittston Company tried to abrogate commitments to the welfare and retirement fund in 1989, affected miners in West Virginia and elsewhere launched a 10-month strike that succeeded in maintaining company payments to the fund but also brought attention to the troubling dilemma facing the industry and the union as the number of retirees continued to grow in the face of rising health costs and a declining work force. The federal Coal Act in 1992 strengthened guarantees for retiree benefits, and a long strike in 1993 eventually led to a broad national agreement between the union and the Bituminous Coal Operators Association. The union nevertheless remained concerned about job security, health and safety issues, and the benefit funds. The union also feared that legislation and judicial decisions dealing with environmental issues such as sulfur emissions and mountaintop removal could further reduce mining employment. Declining numbers of active miners also brought slippage in political influence, but with large numbers of pensioners and widows the union retained considerable clout in state politics.

The decline of mines in southern West Virginia led to the elimination of District 29 in 1996, leaving most of West Virginia under Districts 17 and 31. Robert Phalen presided over historic District 17 from 1985 until retiring in 2001. Joseph Carter was elected to lead the district into the new century. Richard Eddy, elected to lead Fairmont-based District 31 in 1993, continued in office in 2005.

See also Coal Industry, Labor History, Mine Wars

Jerry Bruce Thomas
Shepherd University

Paul F. Clark, *The Miners' Fight for Democracy: Arnold Miller and the Reform of the United Mine Workers*, 1981; Melvyn Dubofsky and Warren Van Tine, *John L. Lewis: A Biography*, 1977; Maier B. Fox, *United We Stand: The United Mine Workers of America, 1890–1990*, 1990; John H.M. Laslett, ed., *The United Mine Workers of America: A Model of Industrial Solidarity?*, 1996.

University of Charleston

The University of Charleston, an independent, urban university situated on the Kanawha River opposite the state capitol, serves the greater Charleston community with a spectrum of academic and cultural opportunities. Its Arts and Sciences, Health Sciences, and Business divisions offer six associate and 29 bachelors programs, plus two masters degrees in business.

The university was founded in 1888 as Barboursville Seminary, affiliated with the Methodist Episcopal Church South. Cabell County had moved its seat of government from Barboursville to Huntington, leaving a courthouse complex that served as the school's initial campus. The early decades were ones of struggle as a series of presidents attempted to turn vision into reality. When a substantial gift from Morris Harvey, a Fayetteville coal operator, eliminated the early debt, the grateful institution changed its name to Morris Harvey College in 1901 and undertook a modest building and renovation program until Harvey's death in 1907. Although aided by periodic enrollment growth, a successful financial campaign in the early 1920s, and a bequest from the estate of Rosa M. Harvey, it could operate only as a junior college from 1909 to 1919 and entered the 1930s unable to make payment on its debt.

In the next quarter century, Leonard Riggleman, the 19th president, led the college from the depths of the Depression to its modern role as a fully accredited institution located on a permanent campus. Operating with payroll often unmet, Riggleman pursued the recurring idea of moving the college to the Charleston area. In an agonizing decision during which the Board of Trustees reversed itself three times within a week, the college accepted an invitation from the Charleston Education Center and opened in temporary quarters in downtown Charleston on September 11, 1935.

As enrollment soared, the equity in Barboursville was surrendered, civic leaders were placed on the board, and the college affiliated with Kanawha Junior College and the Mason College of Fine Arts and Music. World War II halted growth and also led the recently merged Methodist Church to decide to support only one institution in West Virginia. Rather than merge with West Virginia Wesleyan in rural Buckhannon, Morris Harvey College, in another painful decision, sought disaffiliation from the Methodist Church and became a self-governing, independent college in 1941.

Land for a permanent location was acquired during the war, and with enrollment reaching 2,000 by 1945, the college erected government surplus buildings, built a small cafeteria, and floated across the Kanawha River to its current location

The Clay Tower at the University of Charleston.

on September 8, 1947. With strong enrollments, the college set about building permanent facilities. The main administration and classroom building, appropriately named Riggleman Hall, was constructed in 1950–51. A significant turn in mission occurred in 1955 when the college built its first dormitory, and three more followed by 1966. A student union building in 1966 and a physical education building in 1969 rounded out the riverside campus.

The academic program also proceeded in stages. Although the initial accreditation attempt failed in 1953, the faculty succeeded in defining the academic goals and program for the North Central Accreditation Agency in 1958, and the institution has maintained accreditation ever since. In 1964, Morris Harvey College entered the burgeoning field of health sciences, offering an associate degree in nursing in cooperation with area hospitals.

When Dr. Riggleman retired in favor of Marshall Buckalew in 1964, the college had never been stronger. Enrollment surpassed 3,000 under Buckalew's leadership in the early 1970s, and students were living in hotels. Thereafter an alarming decline began, putting increasing pressures on a heavily indebted institution. Possible state affiliation was explored, which Riggleman returned from retirement to oppose and which ultimately was rejected by the state. In a dramatic move to change the image and fortunes of the school, new president Thomas Voss restructured programs, dismissed 16 faculty, and renamed the institution the University of Charleston in 1978. The strategy had little immediate impact, and the university faced major crises in the mid-1980s before gradually turning around.

During the 1990s, under President Edwin Welch, the university entered a new

period of strength. Budgets were consistently in surplus, new planning initiatives undertaken and accreditation standards met in program after program. Looking to the new century, the university revised its curriculum to emphasize competency-based outcomes. The Clay Tower Building, housing science labs, library and electronic classrooms—the first new structure in a quarter century—was dedicated September 7, 1997, 50 years after Morris Harvey College occupied its permanent campus. Brotherton Hall, a new dormitory, was added in August 2000, and another dormitory, New Hall, was completed in 2003. Construction began on a pharmacy school in 2005, and a third new dormitory was completed that year.

See also Morris Harvey, Leonard Riggleman

R. Eugene Harper
University of Charleston

Frank J. Krebs, *Where There Is Faith: The Morris Harvey College Story, 1888–1970*, 1974.

University of Hard Knocks

The University of Hard Knocks is an honorary society conceived by Richwood editor Jim Comstock in 1947. The society serves in a lighthearted way to recognize people who succeed in life without the benefit of a college degree. The University of Hard Knocks has its own seal, which includes a motto in Latin that translates to "Blood, Sweat and Tears." The official colors are black and blue.

Those who wish to become members of the University of Hard Knocks are either nominated by an alumnus or present their credentials to the president. A membership committee then decides who will be accepted. There is a one-time charge, and in Comstock's day the annual membership fee included a subscription to his *West Virginia Hillbilly* newspaper, where the success stories of the new graduates were printed. New members share their stories with alumni during the annual commencement weekend that takes place about the first of June on the campus of Alderson-Broaddus College in Philippi.

Amy Donaldson Arnold
Ivydale

Upshur County

Upshur County was formed in 1851 from parts of Randolph, Lewis, and Barbour counties, with Buckhannon as the county seat. Located in the north-central part of the state, Upshur County is crossed by four-lane Corridor H (U.S. 33) and is within a few miles of Interstate 79. Mining, oil and gas, timbering, farming, and small industry are the major industries. Upshur, with six magisterial districts and 354.9 square miles, is served by one high school, one middle school, and nine elementary schools. Its population was 23,404 in 2000. The county rises from rolling foothills to mountains of more than 3,000 feet in the rugged southeastern section. The Buckhannon River is the major waterway, flowing north nearly the entire length of the county.

Evidence indicates early Indian habitation. Indian Camp Rock, Ash Camp, and remnants of village sites on Hackers Creek support this conclusion. In the 1760s, John and Samuel Pringle, deserters from the British army at Fort Pitt, made their way into the area and for about three years lived in a hollow sycamore tree on the banks of the Buckhannon River. By 1770, a permanent settlement was made in the Buckhannon Valley by families named Pringle, Hacker, Cutright, Hughes, White, Jackson, Westfall, Brake, Bozarth, Strader, Post, Bush, Lorentz, Carper, Rohrbough, and others. Bush's Fort was the main defense until it was destroyed by Indians in 1782. The last Indian foray in Upshur County was the massacre of the Bozarth family in 1795.

Beginning in 1801 with Zedekiah Morgan, large numbers of New Englanders settled in Upshur County, mostly in the French Creek area. Family names from this migration included Gould, Young, Phillips, Burr, Tenney, Brooks, Bunten, Thayer, Leonard, and others. However, little of the 100,000 acres acquired by the Ruggles Woodbridge Land Company through speculation, and sold to these families, had a clear title. By 1830, more than half of these New Englanders had moved farther west, but the effect of this Yankee population can still be felt today with its influence on education, politics, and religion in Upshur County and beyond. The Brooks family especially has left a major mark on such institutions as West Virginia University, and Oglebay Park, as well as the natural sciences.

In 1810, the Methodists organized their first church here, referred to as the Car-

Wesley Chapel at West Virginia Wesleyan College is an Upshur County landmark.

per Church. Today, the United Methodists are still the dominant denomination in the county. West Virginia Wesleyan College was established in Buckhannon as the West Virginia Conference Seminary in 1887 and opened its doors in 1890. Other educational institutions included the Buckhannon Male and Female Academy, 1847–66; French Creek Academy, 1871–85; West Virginia Classical and Normal Academy, 1882–97; and the Indian Camp Normal School, 1913–18, whose building still stands today.

Throughout the Civil War, Upshur County was firmly Unionist. The only real battle in the county took place August 30, 1862, near Water Tank Hill, during the Jenkins Raid of Confederate Cavalry. Nearly three dozen Union soldiers were killed, wounded, or taken captive. That night, bonfires lighted Main Street as Confederate soldiers looted and pillaged Buckhannon. The greatest calamity to befall the county during the war was the capture of the Upshur Militia on September 12, 1863, at Centerville (now Rock

Cave). Of the 70 captives, 43 died in Southern prisons, including some at dreaded Andersonville, Georgia. They left behind 27 widows and 83 children.

The West Virginia Central & Pittsburg [*sic*] Railroad first entered Upshur County in 1883, and Henry Gassaway Davis built his Coal & Coke Railway across the county in 1904. The railroads brought industry to the area. Timbering was heavy in the southern end of the county at the turn of the 20th century. In 1901, the first coal was commercially mined, at Lorentz by the Pleasant Valley Coal Company. An explosion there in 1907 cost the lives of 12 men, the largest mining disaster in Upshur County history. Adrian developed as a major mining center with other communities following close behind. In recent times, large deep mine and strip mine operations have contributed to Upshur's economy and to its environmental problems. The county also has had a tannery, chemical company, glass plants, printing company, as well as the Corhart Refractories, Uponor

FAST FACTS ABOUT UPSHUR COUNTY

Founded: 1851

Land in square miles: 354.9

Population: 23,404

Percentage minorities: 1.8%

Percentage rural: 61.2%

Median age: 37.4

Percentage 65 and older: 14.7%

Birth rate per 1,000 population: 10.6

Median household income: $26,973

High school graduate or higher: 74.6%

Bachelor's degree or higher: 13.8%

Home ownership: 76.7%

Median home value: $70,000

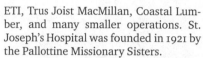

This information is from the 2000 U.S. Census. In 2000, West Virginia as a whole had 5 percent minorities, a median age of 38.9, median household income of $29,696, and a 75.2 percent home ownership rate.

ETI, Trus Joist MacMillan, Coastal Lumber, and many smaller operations. St. Joseph's Hospital was founded in 1921 by the Pallottine Missionary Sisters.

In 1936, the Central West Virginia Strawberry Festival was organized to encourage agricultural production. The festival continues at Buckhannon, with less emphasis on farming. The West Virginia Farm Bureau state headquarters is located in Buckhannon, as well as the West Virginia Department of Highways state headquarters for equipment repair and distribution, located in a landmark cutstone building on the outskirts of town. The United Methodist Annual Conference is held on the campus of Wesleyan College. The West Virginia State Wildlife Center is located at French Creek, where it was established in 1923.

Upshur County has produced many prominent individuals. Daniel D. T. Farnsworth, second governor of West Virginia, was a member of the Buckhannon family which originally owned all of the property where the city now stands. Arthur B. Waugh, native of southern Upshur County, was a Pulitzer Prize winner in journalism in 1935. Pare Lorentz was a leading documentary filmmaker of Franklin Roosevelt's New Deal. Naturalist Maurice Brooks authored the noted *The Appalachians* and much more. Jean Lee Latham received the Newbery Award for her *Carry On, Mr. Bowditch* in 1956, and modern authors Stephen Coonts and Jayne Anne Phillips are Upshur natives. Annie Latham Bartlett was well-known for her sculptural works and exhibited at the New York World's Fair in 1939. Her father, Gen. George R. Latham, served as consul to Australia in the 1860s. Warren Jackson and Laura Jackson Arnold, brother and sister to the famous Thomas T. J. "Stonewall" Jackson, both lived, died, and are buried in Upshur County.

See also Buckhannon, Pare Lorentz,

Strawberry Festival, West Virginia State Wildlife Center

Noel W. Tenney
Tallmansville

W. B. Cutright, *History of Upshur County*, 1977; French Morgan, *Yesterdays of Buckhannon and Upshur*, 1963; Noel W. Tenney, *All About Upshur County: A Bibliography*, 1993.

U.S. Army Corps of Engineers

The U.S. Army Corps of Engineers has helped to transform the face of West Virginia, converting free-flowing rivers into managed waterways for purposes of flood control and transportation. It is likely that the majority of West Virginians see the work of the Corps of Engineers every day, in the hundreds of miles of tamed and transformed streams, the floodwalls that protect cities and towns, and the lakes that attract boaters and fishermen.

The Corps of Engineers has been active in West Virginia since before the creation of the state, modifying rivers to accommodate navigation. The army was assigned this civilian work because in the early 19th century its West Point-educated engineers represented a large majority of the young nation's formally trained engineers. In 1824, Congress directed the Corps of Engineers to improve navigation on the Ohio River by removing obstructions and clearing a navigable channel. To manage this mission, the chief of engineers directed that offices be established throughout the Ohio River basin.

After 1888, division offices were established to manage the increasing navigation demands within major river basins, including the Ohio River basin. District offices were created under the division offices to manage smaller river basins, such as the Great Kanawha and the Little Kanawha basins. Since about the turn of the 20th century, West Virginia has been

included as a part of the Corps' Civil Works Program. The Huntington and Pittsburgh districts, which are part of the Great Lakes and Ohio River Division, have jurisdiction over most of the state. The Eastern Panhandle falls within the Baltimore District, which is part of the North Atlantic Division.

The Civil Works Program dealt principally with navigation improvements until the great floods of the late 1920s and the 1930s prompted Congress to direct the Corps of Engineers to develop flood-control projects. Since then, there have been ten flood-control reservoirs built in West Virginia and ten local protection projects. The flood-control dams include those at Tygart Lake, Bluestone Lake, Sutton Lake, and most recently, Stonewall Jackson Lake. Local protection projects include floodwalls around cities such as Huntington, Parkersburg, and Point Pleasant. Other such projects include emergency stream bank protection at Warwood and the snagging and clearing of Polk Creek near Weston.

The Corps of Engineers operates 13 locks and dam complexes on the Ohio, Great Kanawha, and Monongahela rivers. The entire length of the Ohio is now managed for navigation purposes, as is nearly all of the Great Kanawha and Monongahela rivers. The lower parts of the Big Sandy, Little Kanawha, and Elk are navigable, as well. Cargo originating on West Virginia rivers may travel throughout the Mississippi River and its tributaries and to the Gulf of Mexico.

The Corps' civil works responsibilities also include emergency disaster recovery assistance. Examples include involvement in recovery operations after the 1967 Silver Bridge collapse at Point Pleasant and the 1972 coal dam failure at Buffalo Creek in Logan County. As the nation's primary water resource management agency the Corps oversees the regulatory permit programs for protection of the nation's navigable waters. The Corps of Engineers has a further, indirect role in the reshaping of West Virginia's landscape as an agency in the permitting of surface mining. Section 404 of the Clean Water Act requires a permit for the filling of streams, including filling done in the course of mining, and the Corps is responsible for issuing these permits.

See also Flood Control, Lakes, Locks and Dams

Gerald W. Sutphin
Huntington

Leland R. Johnson, *The Ohio River Division, U. S. Army Corps of Engineers, The History of a Central Command*, 1992; *Water Resources Development in West Virginia*, 1981.

U.S. Coal & Coke Company

The United States Coal & Coke Company marked the entry of J. P. Morgan's United States Steel Company industrial empire into the southern West Virginia coal-fields. Outmaneuvering the Philadelphia owners of both the Norfolk & Western Railway and its subsidiary, the Flat Top Land Association property management firm, Morgan used Bank of Bramwell financier Isaac T. Mann as his intermediary. Morgan managed to force the N&W into granting a lease of about 50,000 acres of McDowell County coal-bearing land containing huge reserves of the famed "smokeless" coal from the Pocahontas No. 3 coal seam. Morgan then chartered the U.S. Coal & Coke Company in January 1902 to develop his investment, and operations were soon under way at Gary, south of Welch. Named after Morgan associate Judge Elbert Gary, the sprawling complex of a dozen company towns and coal mines and its 15,000 residents was for decades West Virginia's most productive coal operation. The company built mines and communities in Lynch, Kentucky, as well, supplying millions of tons of high-quality metallurgical fuel for the steel mills of the U.S. Steel Corporation. USX, successor to the Morgan empire, ceased all its operations in Gary in 1984.

C. Stuart McGehee
West Virginia State University
Joseph T. Lambie, *From Mine to Market: The History of Coal Transportation on the Norfolk & Western Railway*, 1954; Stuart McGehee, "Gary: A First-Class Mining Operation," *Goldenseal*, Fall 1988.

USS *Huntington*

The USS *Huntington* (ARC-5), originally the USS *West Virginia*, was the first ship named for West Virginia. An armored cruiser, one of three *Pennsylvania*-class ships authorized by Congress in 1899, it was constructed at Newport News, launched in 1903 and commissioned February 23, 1905. The vessel was 504 feet long, 70 feet wide, and displaced 13,680 tons. There was a main battery of four eight-inch guns in two turrets, with 14 six-inch guns as secondary weapons.

As the *West Virginia,* the ship spent the years before World War I in routine training and flag-showing cruises, mainly in the Pacific and Far East. In 1914 and 1916, it was on the West Coast during difficulties with Mexico. On November 11, 1916, the cruiser was renamed *Huntington* to allow transfer of the original name to a newly authorized battleship.

In 1917, the *Huntington* was equipped for early experiments in naval aviation. During World War I, it escorted convoys across the Atlantic and in coastal waters. Following the armistice, the ship was converted into a troop transport and made six roundtrips between January and July 1919, bringing home almost 12,000 soldiers. Reconverted to warship status, the *Huntington* remained in service until decommissioned in September 1920.

The USS West Virginia *was raised and rebuilt after Pearl Harbor.*

The name *Huntington* was assigned to a *Cleveland*-class light cruiser in 1941, but the ship was converted to an aircraft carrier while under construction and completed as the *Cowpens* (CVL-25). The second assignment of the name to a light cruiser was made in 1943. This *Huntington* made three tours of duty to the Mediterranean Sea before being decommissioned in 1949.

See also USS West Virginia
William P. McNeel
Marlinton

USS *West Virginia*

The USS *West Virginia* was badly damaged at Pearl Harbor, but rose from that disaster to take revenge on the Japanese navy.

The battleship was christened on November 19, 1921, the second ship to be named for West Virginia. On December 1, 1923, the *West Virginia* joined the fleet. The new battleship was 624 feet long, 94 feet wide, and had a displacement of 33,590 tons. The main battery was eight 16-inch guns in four turrets, with 12 five-inch guns as the secondary battery. Oil-fired boilers provided steam for the electrical propulsion system, which was capable of moving the ship at a maximum speed of 21 knots.

Except for training exercises in the Caribbean and visits to East Coast ports, the ship spent its entire career in the Pacific Ocean. It was one of the six battleships at Pearl Harbor on the morning of December 7, 1941, suffering massive damage from torpedoes and bombs in the surprise attack. Two officers (including Capt. Mervyn S. Bennion) and 103 crew members died.

The *West Virginia* was raised from the mud of Pearl Harbor and rebuilt in time to see service for the last year of the war. The ship went back to sea in July 1944 and joined the Seventh Fleet for the invasion of the Philippines. At the battle of Surigao Strait on October 24–25, part of the larger Battle of Leyte Gulf, *West Virginia* led the line and was the first American ship to open fire. The *West Virginia* was in Tokyo Bay on September 2, 1945, for the surrender ceremony, the only Pearl Harbor survivor present.

After the war the *West Virginia* took part in "Operation Magic Carpet," the return of troops to the United States. It was decommissioned in January 1947, then held in inactive reserve until stricken from the Navy List on March 1, 1959. On August 24 the battleship was sold for scrap.

The current USS *West Virginia* is an *Ohio* Class Trident ballistic missile submarine. The *West Virginia* is 560 feet long, 42 feet wide, and displaces 18,750 tons when submerged. Its nuclear power plant can move the submarine at more than 20 knots. As a missile submarine, the *West Virginia's* main weapons are its 24 Trident II missiles. Four torpedo tubes were also installed on the vessel. Fifteen officers and 140 enlisted personnel make up the crew.

The ship was constructed by the General Dynamics Electric Boat Division at Groton, Connecticut, and launched in 1989. Commissioning took place on October 20, 1990.

See also USS Huntington
William P. McNeel
Marlinton
Myron J. Smith Jr., *The Mountain State Battleship: USS West Virginia*, 1981.

Valley Falls State Park

Eight miles below Grafton, the Tygart Valley River drops over an impressive series of falls. In 1964, this area was acquired by the state, with a total of 1,145 acres to become Valley Falls State Park. The park offers fishing, picnicking, game courts, and hiking trails, plus stone ruins providing an insight into the past.

The history of the falls area goes back to the 18th century, when an Indian trader operated there. In 1837, W. W. Fetterman acquired the site, building a whipsaw mill that sawed logs into timbers and lumber. In 1847, a gristmill was built by Bradshaw and William Whitescarver. In 1853, the Baltimore & Ohio Railroad was completed from Grafton to Wheeling with the falls area included on the line. With this event Valley Falls underwent a boom, with a hotel, school, church, sawmills, feed mills, shoe shops, coffin factory, a Wells Fargo office, post office, and a ferry. The Civil War saw considerable activity at the falls, as the B&O moved troops and supplies through the region. In addition, many gunstocks were manufactured for the Civil War. In 1886, a fire burned much of the town, and two years later a flood destroyed many homes, buildings, bridges, and gristmills. After this, the town never fully recovered.

"Valley Falls" was given as the fictional hometown of athlete Chip Hilton and his friends, in the popular series of youth sports novels by Clair Bee, who grew up in Grafton.

Arnout Hyde Jr.
Wonderful West Virginia
David Cain, "Valley Falls State Park," *Wonderful West Virginia*, March 2000; Maureen Crockett, "Magnificent Valley Falls," *Wonderful West Virginia*, November 1991.

Andre Van Damme

Dancer Andre Benoni Van Damme, born December 16, 1919, in Belgium, was admitted to the ballet company of the Royal Opera House of Brussels shortly after his 16th birthday. When his dance career was interrupted by military service, he struck a deal with officers that allowed him to continue rehearsals while discharging his army obligation. Van Damme was recalled to military service during the mobilization of 1939. When his country fell to the Nazis, the dancer joined the underground while continuing to perform.

Meanwhile, he had been named premier *danseur étoile* by the ballet company, a title he cherished. Nevertheless, after the liberation of Europe post-war hardships took their toll. Van Damme and his family moved to America in 1947. They first settled in New York City, then were persuaded to move to West Virginia by John and Jose Hiersoux, Charleston pianists. They told Van Damme a ballet school was for sale and convinced him a living could be made in the state, and he could rehearse and tour with the Hiersouxes.

Van Damme settled in Charleston in 1948 and opened his school, which he called the American Academy of Ballet. He founded the Charleston Ballet in 1956. Van Damme remained in Charleston until his death, on February 3, 1989.

See also Charleston Ballet

Kay Michael
Charleston

Peter Godwin Van Winkle

A founder of West Virginia, U.S. Senator Peter Godwin Van Winkle was born in New York City, September 7, 1808, and died in Parkersburg, April 15, 1872. On August 4, 1863, Van Winkle was elected as one of the first two U.S. senators from the new state of West Virginia. He is best remembered for having cast the next-to-last vote that saved President Andrew Johnson from conviction on impeachment charges in 1868, one of seven Republican "recusants" who joined 12 Democrats to deny Radical Republicans the necessary two-thirds majority to remove the president from office.

The namesake falls at Valley Falls State Park.

Van Winkle moved to Parkersburg in 1835 and was soon joined by members of his wife's family, the Rathbones, who purchased 12,000 acres at Burning Springs, Wirt County, in 1840. This tract was the center of the oil boom in 1860 which altered the economy of the region for the next 75 years. Van Winkle practiced law in partnership with John Jay Jackson Sr. and served several years as president of the Parkersburg Board of Trustees. Van Winkle helped to organize the Northwestern Virginia Railroad, serving first as its secretary and later as its president, 1857 to 1870.

He served in the Second Wheeling Convention in 1861 and was a member of the Governor's Council of the Reorganized Government of Virginia, 1861–63, under Gov. Francis H. Pierpont. He represented Wood County in West Virginia's First Constitutional Convention in 1861 and 1862.

As a U.S. senator, Van Winkle was a conservative who consistently voted against civil rights and black suffrage legislation. He was the only Republican to vote with Democrats against the override of President Johnson's veto of the Second Freedman's Bureau Bill. His vote to support the president, then, was consistent with his social and political views and his antipathy to Radical Republican politics. Since he had previously announced his intention to retire in 1869 because of declining health, it is not true, as some have claimed, that he sacrificed his career to save the president.

See also Formation of West Virginia
Philip Sturm
Ohio Valley University
Philip Sturm, "Senator Peter G. Van Winkle and the Andrew Johnson Impeachment Trial: A Comprehensive View," *West Virginia History*, 1999–2000; Evert F. Whitener, "Peter Godwin Van Winkle," M.A. thesis, WVU, 1929.

Cyrus Vance

Statesman Cyrus Roberts Vance, who held several high positions during the Kennedy, Johnson, and Carter presidential administrations, was born in Clarksburg, March 27, 1917. He received his law degree at Yale in 1942. During World War II, he served in the Far East as a gunnery officer in the navy.

Vance became a partner in the New York City law firm of Simpson, Thacher and Bartlett. His first government post was counsel to Senate Majority Leader Lyndon Johnson's special committee on space and astronautics, which helped draft the law creating the National Aeronautics and Space Administration. When President Kennedy took office in 1961, Vance was named general counsel for the Department of Defense. In 1962, he became secretary of the army. He moved up to become Defense Secretary Robert McNamara's deputy secretary of defense

in 1964, and later he turned down an offer to succeed McNamara as secretary.

President Johnson dispatched Vance on trouble-shooting missions in Cyprus, Korea, and Vietnam, and to investigate police corruption in New York City and the riots following the assassination of Dr. Martin Luther King Jr. In 1977, President Carter tapped Vance as his secretary of state, where he served in quiet contrast to predecessor Henry Kissinger. In 1978, Vance was instrumental in the Camp David peace accord between Egypt and Israel and in negotiating the Panama Canal Treaty. In a much-publicized disagreement, Vance resigned his post when, over his objections, President Carter decided in 1980 to launch the ill-fated helicopter effort to rescue the hostages being held in the American Embassy in Iran.

In the 1980s and 1990s, the secretary general of the United Nations sent Vance on peace-keeping missions to Yugoslavia, South Africa, and Greece. Vance promoted reconciliation with the Soviet Union, human rights as a pillar of American foreign policy, opportunities for minorities in the court system and State Department, and patient diplomacy as an alternative to the use of force. He died January 12, 2002, in New York City.

Ken Hechler
Charleston

Jim Vance

Feudist James "Bad Jim" Vance, born about 1832, was the grandson of Tug Valley pioneer Abner Vance and the uncle of William Anderson "Devil Anse" Hatfield. Jim Vance was a leading protagonist in the Hatfield-McCoy Feud. Described by historian Otis K. Rice as a ruthless, vindictive man, he helped to keep the conflict going and took part in some of its bloodiest episodes. Vance, like Devil Anse a Confederate guerrilla during the Civil War, was suspected in the 1865 murder of Union veteran Harmon McCoy, one of the feud's precipitating events.

Vance led the 1888 New Year's Day arson attack on the McCoy family cabin, resulting in the death of Calvin and Alifair McCoy, the grown children of patriarch Randall McCoy. In this incident, Vance bludgeoned Randall's wife Sarah McCoy with a rifle butt as she tried to reach her dying daughter. A week later, on January 8, 1888, Vance and Cap Hatfield, Devil Anse's son, were surprised by a larger party of Kentuckians near Vance's Logan (now Mingo) County home. Vance was wounded in the shootout, then killed in cold blood and at close range by McCoy partisan Frank Phillips.

See also Hatfield-McCoy Feud

Vandalia Colony

Vandalia Colony was an unsuccessful idea proposed by high-placed Englishmen and prominent British Americans in

1768. England had recently won the French and Indian War, leaving it in control of North America. Settlement was proceeding rapidly in the west, including Western Virginia, in lands previously contested by the French.

A group led by Benjamin Franklin created the Great Ohio Company (known also as the Vandalia Company and not to be confused with the earlier Ohio Company) to acquire lands and organize settlement in the west. The company proposed a 14th colony, dubbing it Vandalia to curry favor with King George III through flattery of Queen Charlotte, who claimed ancestry through the ancient Vandal tribe. The proposed colony would have included almost all of West Virginia, with its capital at Point Pleasant.

Vandalia Colony might have succeeded if not for the increasingly turbulent political relations between England and its colonies. As unrest boiled over into the physical violence of the American Revolution, the new colony scheme was lost among larger events. America's birth rang the death toll for Vandalia Colony, its intended lands later becoming parts of the states of Kentucky and West Virginia. Vandalia Colony is now the namesake for Vandalia Gathering, a popular folklife festival hosted in Charleston each spring by the West Virginia Division of Culture and History in celebration of the state's cultural heritage.

Lori Henshey
Charleston
Ken Sullivan, "Vandalia at 20: What's in the Name?," *Goldenseal,* Spring 1996.

Vandalia Gathering

The Vandalia Gathering, an annual event, celebrates West Virginia's heritage of traditional music, crafts, food, folklore, and dance. The Memorial Day Weekend festival, sponsored by the West Virginia Division of Culture and History, is held at the Cultural Center and the adjoining grounds of the state capitol. Vandalia is one of West Virginia's largest festivals, attracting thousands of people each day.

Traditional musicians come from across the state to perform at Vandalia. Craftspeople demonstrate their skills and sell their products, which include wind chimes, pottery, quilts, and baskets, as well as foods such as jelly and salad dressings. Food booths offer traditional and ethnic fare, from hot dogs, hamburgers, and roasted corn, to Greek and Italian specialties and German sausages.

Highlights include old-time fiddle, banjo, and lap dulcimer competitions, flatfoot dancing demonstrations, and the liars contest, with tellers of tall tales competing to see who can create the most fanciful story. Traditional singing, instrumental performances, and dancing take place throughout the day. There are concerts on Friday and Saturday evenings, with a concluding awards concert late Sunday afternoon.

Begun in 1977 at the height of the folk arts revival, Vandalia developed a cadre of older musicians and craftspeople who returned to the festival for many years. Vandalia continues to showcase senior performers, seeking to preserve traditional forms of music and folk art and to pass the traditions on to younger generations. The Vandalia Award, which is West Virginia's highest folklife honor, is presented each year for a lifetime of contributions to the continuation of the state's folk heritage.

Vegetable Gardening

For a long time after Europeans settled here, most West Virginians were farmers. As many became miners and loggers, sawyers, and shopkeepers in the late 1800s and early 1900s, most families continued to keep a kitchen garden to supplement the wages the husband was bringing in and tide the family through the occasional short work weeks, layoffs, and strikes. By the 1950s, many West Virginians were making decent wages working in unionized mines and in steel, chemical, and glass plants, but still clung to a connection to the land. Many commuted to work from hilltop or hollow homes where they continued to run cattle, cut hay, and plant a vegetable garden. Others moved to small towns, where the house lot was often big enough to accommodate a substantial garden.

Vegetable gardens hung on in West Virginia long after most West Virginians needed them to get by. Gardening was in the culture, and families were going to plant six or eight long rows of "Irish" potatoes, some sweet potatoes, too, and a row of Late Flat Dutch cabbage. That is what their parents and grandparents had done, and they wanted to stay connected to that. They grew plenty of tomatoes, sweet peppers and hot peppers, also some sweet corn for roasting ears and cucumbers for fresh eating and pickles. They planted enormous stretches of beans, a few bush beans for early eating, and pole beans or their beloved half-runners for canning.

A kitchen was a busy and exceedingly hot place in summer as women made the pickles and sauerkraut, then canned them along with all the beans and tomatoes. West Virginians grew onions from sets, and some Black-seeded Simpson lettuce for harvest in spring. They grew a few pumpkins or winter squash for winter, and maybe they planted an extra row of sweet potatoes for storage, too. In July or August, they sowed a bed of turnips, the turnip greens for fall cooking and the turnips for storage in the root cellar beside the potatoes and canned goods.

West Virginians weren't likely to grow much eggplant, cauliflower, or aspara-

William Estler raised a great Cabell County garden in 1956.

gus, but they usually had a few rhubarb plants which returned to life each spring and made tangy stalks for pies. They sometimes planted a row of peas, and in modern times maybe some summer squash and broccoli. They weren't likely to plant blueberries, but they picked the wild raspberries and blackberries and turned them into pies and preserves. An apple tree stood beside the house, and the apples went into pies, apple sauce, and apple butter.

Over the years, gardens have shrunk in size, rendered superfluous by the continuous harvest that the modern supermarket brings in from distant lands. Gardeners have also had to work around a problem that didn't exist in the state until the mid-1970s, and in some southern counties until the mid- or late 1980s. That is the white-tailed deer. Farmers had always had to contend with the pesky groundhog, which a big dog could kill with a shake, and with the nocturnal raccoon, which fortunately ate just the roasting ears. But as deer multiplied, the entire garden became a feeding ground. Deer could ravage a garden and consume the entire crop, and the same state that declared groundhogs varmints protected deer.

Discouraged gardeners quit gardening and determined ones put up tall fences, electric fences, or seven-foot-high deer netting. Many resorted to that old standby, a good-size dog. As more West Virginians live in cities and fancy subdivisions, and as they become two or three generations removed from their rural roots, many people grow nothing edible or perhaps just a few tomato plants. Those who still want a good tomato or a sweet roasting ear patronize the truck farmers and market gardeners who raise tomatoes, corn, squash, cucumbers, and peppers and sell them along the roadside or at farmers' markets.

Bob Schwarz
Charleston Gazette

Verizon

Verizon West Virginia is the largest provider of telephone service in West Virginia. The company is a subsidiary of Verizon Communications. In West Virginia, Verizon serves about 60 percent of the state's geography and from 80 percent to 85 percent of the population.

In 1880, the first telephone exchange was established in Wheeling by the Central District Printing and Telegraph Company, the predecessor of the Chesapeake & Potomac Telephone Company of West Virginia. C&P, incorporated in 1916, was part of the Bell system, also known as AT&T, and became the dominant provider of telephone service in the state. After AT&T was broken up in 1984, C&P began independent operations as Bell Atlantic. In 2000, Bell Atlantic merged with GTE, to create Verizon Communications, America's largest local phone company with service in 29 states and the District of Columbia. Verizon's primary coverage areas are in the Northeast and Mid-Atlantic states.

After the breakup of AT&T, regional Bell companies, such as Verizon, were generally limited to providing local telephone service. In 2003, Verizon West Virginia received the Federal Communications Commission's approval to offer long-distance service in West Virginia and other mid-Atlantic and New England states. As a condition of the approval, Verizon had to open its local network to competition. By 2005, Verizon had become one of the state's largest providers of long-distance service.

Although Verizon Wireless is the nation's second-largest provider of cellular telephone services, it has a limited presence in this market in West Virginia. A joint venture of Verizon Communications and Vodafone, Verizon Wireless principally serves areas of West Virginia located within the mid-Ohio Valley. Verizon Online provides digital subscriber line (DSL) service for high-speed Internet service throughout most of the state, and the growth of the service is part of the company's transformation from a telephone company to a broad-based communications provider. Capital investments in the state have included the installation of more than 250,000 miles of optical fiber. Fiber-optic systems provide greater capacity, higher transmission speeds, and better quality for voice, video, and data transmitted over the network.

Verizon is West Virginia's eighth-largest private employer with about 2,800 workers. The company's headquarters are in Charleston. Verizon Foundation, the company's national philanthropic arm, provides technology-related grants to agencies and nonprofit organizations throughout the state, with an emphasis on literacy, work force development, and the use of technology to benefit communities. Verizon is a contributor to the *West Virginia Encyclopedia*.

See also Telephone Service

Vernacular Architecture

The term vernacular (or folk) architecture generally refers to buildings not planned by an architect but based upon regional traditions, the materials at hand, and sometimes expedience. Fred Kniffen

in the book *Folk Housing: Key to Diffusion*, suggests three source areas of building tradition in existence in America by 1790: New England, the Middle Atlantic, and the Lower Chesapeake, including Tidewater Virginia. Settlers from each of these regions carried traditional building methods associated with their particular source area as they moved westward.

The settlement of Western Virginia originated from the Middle Atlantic and Tidewater Virginia. During the 1720s the Van Meter family led a group of Dutch (German) Protestants to the South Branch Valley from northern New Jersey. Isaac Van Meter settled in the northern portion of the valley in present Hardy County in 1744. He constructed a cabin and a fort known as Fort Pleasant, near Moorefield, and each succeeding generation improved on his beginning efforts. Col. Garrett Van Meter replaced the original fort and cabin with a brick structure, and in 1832, his son, Jacob, abandoned the vernacular tradition with his house in the Greek Revival style. This progression was typical of successful families. Log houses were first-generation homes. A family's next house, usually larger and more elaborate in design, reflected its progress.

The Kanawha Valley was settled from eastern Virginia, including the Tidewater. Maj. John Hansford, born in 1765 in Orange County, acquired property on the Kanawha River and built a house below the mouth of Paint Creek. The Old Stone House at Belle was built by Samuel Shrewsbury about 1810 on Kanawha land he acquired from his father-in-law, Col. John Dickinson, of Bath County. It can best be regarded as at least a generation removed from the Tidewater source area, where stone is in scant supply, and its name, distinguishing its material, may hint at the fact that stone was not often used in early Kanawha Valley buildings.

Several building types were introduced to Western Virginia during this westward expansion. The one-room (single pen) log house with an end chimney is an early building form that could quickly expand with a second story and change appearance with the addition of weatherboarding over the logs. Many log houses were changed with such additions and alterations. Monroe County has several examples. Although much-altered, the 1810 William Clark House is one of the earliest log houses in Union, the county seat. An 1815 log house served as Union's Female Academy from 1840 to the Civil War. Even earlier, in 1790, Owen Neel II built a two-story log house near Gap Mills. It has a central doorway with rooms to each side, and two more rooms above.

In Hardy County, the Funkhouser Farm has not only a log house but also a hewn-log barn. Both buildings employ a

V notching technique to join the logs. The house dates to about 1845, the barn to about 1880. Log buildings often appear as slave quarters; for example, Altona Farm in Jefferson County includes two early-19th century clapboard-over-log quarters, each with a central chimney.

A second recognizable vernacular form is the I-house: one room deep, two rooms wide, and two stories high. Returning to Union for an example, the Byrnside-Beirne-Johnson House has an end chimney and is noted for woodwork attributed to Conrod Burgess, a prominent local builder. The house, remodeled by Beirne in the mid-19th century, incorporates a log house built by James Byrnside in 1770. Other I-houses in Union date to the 1840s.

Folk architecture is also associated with ethnic groups. For example, the shotgun house, a one-story dwelling, one room wide and several rooms deep, is identified with African-American culture. Rooms open directly into each other without a hall, and all doorways are on axis with each other. It was said that a shotgun could be fired through the front door and exit through the back door without hitting anything. In east Wheeling, groups of shotgun cottages were built prior to 1874 for workers of the Central Glass Company and the Wheeling & Elm Grove Railroad.

Other ethnic groups have also left their stamp on West Virginia's vernacular architecture. The Randolph County community of Helvetia was founded by German-speaking Swiss immigrants just after the Civil War. Second-generation buildings took advantage of Helvetia's first steam sawmill in 1887. The onion dome capping the Greek Orthodox church in Gary, McDowell County, identifies the worshipers' Eastern European origins.

A houseowner or builder might also incorporate stylistic elements copied from existing buildings or from illustrated pattern books. By the 19th century, such pattern books were used in building homes for the middle classes. The symmetrical composition of the Greek Revival style was introduced in houses such as the 1834 wood-frame Craik-Patton House in Charleston and the 1853 brick house at Fort Hill Farm in Mineral County. Wheeling's row houses illustrate decorative details of the late-19th-century Italianate style; many facades include bracketed cornices, paneled friezes, hooded windows, and colored glass windows. By the turn of the 20th century, houses took on aspects of the Queen Anne style. The twin houses that brothers A. Fremont and W. Alfred Gold built in 1908 in Mason, Mason County, are mirror images of each other, each with a wrap-around porch and incorporating elements of the Queen Anne style.

Company towns in various industries

The Byrnside-Beirne-Johnson House of Monroe County.

also exerted an influence on housing styles. At Cass, Pocahontas County, laborers at the lumber mill lived in what the company called "Class Three" houses: two-story, frame buildings with gabled facades and one-story front porches. The mill owners also provided workers with a store, school, and other buildings, all in a distinctive wood-frame style. In 1891, the Martinsburg Mining, Manufacturing and Improvement Company developed a subdivision for workers of its knitting and hosiery mills. Laid out along newly created streets, most of these houses are frame, one-and-a-half or two stories tall, and have either a side gable or end gable and a one-story front porch. By 1910, U.S. Coal & Coke built 12 individual company towns known as the Gary Works in McDowell County, with several different housing types.

By the 20th century, prefabricated buildings in popular styles could even be purchased from Sears, Roebuck and Company. Those who didn't buy might nonetheless find ideas in the catalog of Sears "Honor Bilt" homes. For example, aspects of the Sears house known as the Sheridan are reflected in the 1925 home of Benjamin Snyder, a Berkeley County concrete mason. Pre-fabricated houses were also available from West Virginia's own Minter Homes and other companies.

See also Architects and Architecture, Log Construction, Minter Homes

Susan Pierce
State Historic Preservation

Vienna

Today a community of nearly 11,000 adjoining north Parkersburg, Vienna was first settled in 1773 when Dr. John Briscoe arrived with his sons and slaves. It was an unsuccessful attempt. The eruption of Dunmore's War the following year drove the Briscoe party back to their former home in eastern Virginia.

Dr. Joseph Spencer of East Haddam, Connecticut, secured a large tract of land and permanently settled Vienna in 1794. While the origin of the name is unknown, it possibly originated from a Revolutionary War battle in which Spencer participated in Vienna, New Jersey. In 1795, the Virginia General Assembly incorporated 100 acres of the Spencer farm as a town. Like many western land speculations, it did not prosper. Few of the surveyed lots sold. Vienna failed in 1799–1800 in an attempt to become the county seat of Wood County.

Spencer and his heirs sold off his holdings, and Vienna remained mostly farms until the early 20th century. Then new means of transportation such as the Ohio River Railroad (1884), the Interurban streetcar line (1902), and improved roads encouraged the growth of both industry and population. By 1940, Vienna had five glass factories, a canning company, a silk mill, and, in 1902, West Virginia's first country club. When incorporated as a city in 1935, Vienna's population hovered around 1,500. Twenty-five years later, it had jumped to 9,300 due to a growth spurt following World War II. In 1972, Vienna became home to the Grand Central Mall, West Virginia's first shopping mall. Vienna had a population of 10,861 in 2000.

Ray Swick
Blennerhassett Island State Park

Donald F. Black, *History of Wood County, West Virginia, Volume 1: Pioneer History of Wood County, West Virginia*, 1975; *Vienna, Virginia 1794, Vienna, West Virginia 1994 Bicentennial*, 1994.

Vietnam War

Lasting from 1965 to 1973, the undeclared Vietnam War was America's longest military action. U.S. intervention began after the French withdrew in 1954 in the face of a growing Communist insurgency. During the Kennedy administration, the American military presence grew from several hundred advisers to more than 15,000. After the 1964 Gulf of Tonkin incident, Congress granted broad war powers to President Johnson, who escalated the conflict through a bombing campaign against North Vietnam.

Opposition to the war grew as the death toll increased. Many Americans resisted the draft, while college demonstrations focused youthful rebellion against the war. Nonetheless, President Nixon expanded strategic bombing raids to nearby Laos and Cambodia, before announcing a withdrawal strategy in 1970. In early 1973, the last Americans evacuated South Vietnam, which fell to the North in 1975. More than three million U.S. military personnel served in Indochina, and Americans suffered over 57,000 casualties.

As in other wars, West Virginians did more than their share in Vietnam. A total of 36,578 West Virginians served, with 1,182 killed. The Adjutant General Department estimated the state suffered a 2.75 death rate per 10,000 citizens in 1969, as compared to a national average of 1.80, while another source indicates a West Virginia death rate of 8.41 per 10,000 residents for the war as a whole compared to a national rate of 5.89. Nine West Virginians received Congressional Medals of Honor, including Thomas W. Bennett (1947–69), a conscientious objector who served as a noncombatant medic and died saving others on the battlefield. Several Vietnam memorials commemorate the sacrifices of West Virginians in Vietnam, notably the West Virginia Veterans Memorial in Charleston.

There was an active home front effort in West Virginia, as well. Charleston's Ordnance Center built armored vehicles for the U.S. Army, while ROTC programs at state colleges and universities graduated many junior officers. Many West Virginians supported the Vietnam War, while others contributed to the resistance. Students demonstrated on campuses across the state. At West Virginia University student publications reflected strong opposition from a campus generally perceived as relatively conservative. WVU demonstrations reached a tense standoff on May 7–8, 1970, after the killing by National Guard troops of student demonstrators at Kent State University. On the second day, Morgantown police brokered a truce between state troopers and activists occupying Grumbein's Island and University Avenue in the heart of the downtown campus. Protests were staged in West Virginia communities as well, including a major rally in Charleston in October 1969.

Jeffrey M. Leatherwood
West Virginia University

Vines

Nearly 30 woody and 50 herbaceous vines grow in West Virginia. They thrive in every part of the state, although some occupy only certain areas. Twenty vines are exotics, meaning they are not native and came from elsewhere. Often they are aggressive, invasive pests. Greenbrier is an example of a native woody vine that has tendrils to help it climb. Its namesakes include Greenbrier County, Greenbrier River, the Greenbrier resort, and Ronceverte (which is French for "green brier").

The larger genera of vines are grapes, dewberries, morning glories, and clematis. Climbing bittersweet, crossvine, Virginia creeper, trumpet creeper, passionflower, wild potato vine, and pipevine are excellent native ornamentals when their growth is controlled. Exotic vines, such as oriental bittersweet, porcelain berry, wisteria, akebia, climbing wintercreeper, periwinkle, Japanese clematis, and Japanese honeysuckle are showy ornamentals that have become invasive pests.

Fruits of grapes, groundnut, wild potato vine, strawberry, wild yam, and dewberries provide food for wildlife and humans. Vines of grapes, Japanese honeysuckle, kudzu, clubmosses, and bittersweets are used by craftspeople to make baskets and wreaths.

An exotic vine with a nasty reputation is kudzu, which completely overgrows forests, roadsides, and stream banks in the Kanawha Valley and southern West Virginia. Canada moonseed, bittersweets, clematis, wisteria, and Virginia creeper have poisonous fruits or seeds. Poison ivy is notorious for causing itchy skin blisters.

Wild balsam-apple is a fast-growing native vine, with small melon-like spiny fruits, that easily grows 30 feet per year. Mile-a-minute, an exotic with very sharp prickles, easily overtops brushy roadsides in the Eastern Panhandle and in Wood County and on several Ohio River islands. In contrast is creeping snowberry in mountain bogs that grows only a few millimeters per year.

See also Kudzu

William N. Grafton
WVU Extension Service

Kendall Vintroux

Cartoonist Kendall Vintroux drew for the *Charleston Gazette* newspaper. Born July 5, 1896, at Fraziers Bottom, Putnam County, he grew up on the family farm. Dropping out of high school, he helped run the farm when his father, C. E. Vintroux, became ill. Although Kendall began drawing as a boy, his career as a cartoonist began when he submitted a cartoon to the *Gazette* about the town of Poca's first paved road. Only eight feet wide, the road was the subject of many jokes.

The newspaper hired him in February 1922. By the 1930s, Vintroux began his emphasis on political cartooning, sketching national leaders such as Presidents Hoover and Roosevelt and depicting state and local topics. His cartoons of the Dog Wagon, a Charleston diner which attracted political and civic leaders, were eagerly awaited by the newspaper's readers. In his later years Vintroux shared cartooning responsibility at the *Gazette* with James Dent. After his retirement in 1968, he enjoyed seeing his work displayed in exhibits at Morris Harvey College (now the University of Charleston, which has many of his original drawings), the Truman Library, and other institutions. Vintroux died in Charleston, July 27, 1973.

Debra Basham
State Archives

The blame went both ways, according to Kendall Vintroux.

Virginia

The sternwheel steamboat *Virginia* was the middle of three almost identical steamboats built by Capt. J. Frank Ellison for the upper Ohio, the first being the *Hudson* and the last the famous *Queen City*. Most old-time boatmen will agree they were the most beautiful sternwheelers ever built. Captain Ellison, in family letters from his later years, told that the *Virginia* was his favorite of the three. It was built in Cincinnati in 1895 and came out new on New Year's Day of 1896.

The *Virginia* was probably best known for going aground on a falling Ohio River in 1910 and winding up in a cornfield at Ravenswood, Jackson County. The steamboat spent the summer a half-mile from the water and became a well-publicized tourist attraction. By fall, a house-moving company from Pittsburgh was engaged to get the *Virginia* afloat but after much maneuvering succeeded only in getting the boat to the bank, which was too soft and sandy to hold its weight. The rains came again, the river rose, and it re-floated itself. The owners refused to pay the bill, saying that their boat had been floated by an "act of God." In court the judge disagreed, ruling that in moving the *Virginia* near the river the house movers had "put the boat within God's reach."

John Hartford
Madison, Tennessee
John Hartford, *Steamboat in a Cornfield*, 1986.

Virginia Debt Question

The founders of West Virginia recognized that their state owed a share of Virginia's outstanding public debt in compensation for improvements in the counties that made up the new state. The repayment obligation was specifically included in the West Virginia constitution of 1863 and, indirectly, in the constitution of 1872.

Determining the amount to be paid was much more difficult than recognizing the obligation to pay. The issue quickly became a political matter as Virginia and West Virginia also argued over the inclusion of Berkeley and Jefferson counties in the new state. After Virginia sued to have the two counties returned to Virginia, West Virginia officials hardened their attitude about the size of the debt owed to Virginia. Many different figures were suggested, with West Virginia's calculations resulting in a smaller debt, while Virginia authorities claimed much larger sums as due from West Virginia.

The argument dragged out, without resolution, throughout the 1800s. Though the issue was politically unpopular, West Virginia state officials desired to settle the matter to improve West Virginia's bond rating in order to fund much needed new public works in the state. The matter finally was resolved in the U.S. Supreme Court, where Virginia won a judgment against West Virginia of, after continued wrangling, slightly more than $12.3 million. The 1919 West Virginia legislature created a Virginia Debt Sinking Fund to sell bonds to pay off Virginia and authorized a tax on general property to retire the debt. The tax raised sufficient funds to retire the debt in 1939.

Kenneth R. Bailey
WVU Institute of Technology
Charles H. Ambler and Festus P. Summers, *West Virginia: The Mountain State*, 1958.

Virginia v. West Virginia

Following the Civil War, Virginia sued West Virginia in the U.S. Supreme Court in the case known as *Virginia v. West Virginia*, seeking to reclaim Berkeley and Jefferson counties.

Shortly after Virginia's secession in May 1861, representatives from the northwest counties met in Wheeling and formed the Reorganized Government of Virginia which remained loyal to the Union. The Reorganized Government soon authorized a referendum on whether to form a new state out of the northwest region. Voters there endorsed the concept, and a constitutional convention ensued. Article I, Section 2 of the resulting state constitution defined the proposed state's territory as including 44 named counties and four more (Pendleton, Hardy, Hampshire, and Morgan) if the voters in those counties chose to join the new state. If they did, then the counties of Berkeley, Jefferson, and Frederick would also, upon voter approval, be included in West Virginia.

A referendum on the constitution passed in April 1862, and the first four additional counties opted to go with West Virginia. No vote was taken at the time in Berkeley, Jefferson, and Frederick because they were controlled by the Confederacy. In May, the Reorganized Government gave its consent to the formation of the new state consisting of 48 counties plus Berkeley, Jefferson, and Frederick "whenever the voters of said counties" assented. Congress agreed to the creation of West Virginia in December 1862, conditioned on a constitutional change regarding the elimination of slavery. The approval law described the new state as embracing 48 named counties, not including Berkeley or Jefferson. Meanwhile, on May 28, 1863, elections in Berkeley and Jefferson counties endorsed joining West Virginia, and those counties were included when statehood became official on June 20, 1863.

In December 1865, the Virginia legislature, now back in the hands of Old Virginia easterners, repealed its laws consenting to the admission of Berkeley and Jefferson counties into West Virginia. Then Virginia took the matter to the U.S. Supreme Court. Virginia argued that when Congress approved statehood for West Virginia, those counties were not included, and the relevant statute made no mention of their later addition. Virginia also alleged that the Berkeley and Jefferson votes to join West Virginia were fraudulent and void.

In *Virginia v. West Virginia*, the Supreme Court in 1871 rejected (7-3) Virginia's claims. It held that the statutes of the Reorganized Government regarding Berkeley and Jefferson effectively created an agreement between the two states that the counties would become part of West Virginia "whenever" voters assented. Congress had validly approved, too. The application for statehood had been carefully considered, and Congress had made admission contingent on voter approval of the constitutional change regarding slavery. An inference therefore arose that Congress "intended to consent to the admission of the State with the contingent boundaries provided for in its constitution and in the statute of Virginia . . . and in so doing [Congress] necessarily consented to the agreement of those States on that subject." As for the county referendums, the Court concluded that the certification of the elections by Virginia's own governor was conclusive on their validity. The reference was to Governor Pierpont of Reorganized Virginia.

The Court did not directly address the constitutionality of West Virginia's statehood, even though its validity had been questioned. Nevertheless, the result in *Virginia v. West Virginia* implicitly settled the matter, for all practical purposes.

See also Formation of West Virginia
Robert M. Bastress
WVU College of Law

Virginia's Chapel

Virginia's Chapel is located at Cedar Grove, just east of Kellys Creek on U.S. 60 in Kanawha County. Also known as the Little Brick Church, it was built in 1853 by William Tompkins Jr., a successful entrepreneur in the early salt and natural gas industries in the Upper Kanawha Valley. The chapel is named for Rachel and William Tompkins's daughter, Virginia.

Constructed of red bricks made on site, the original building was nearly square, with three narrow Gothic windows on each side. A few years later, new construction lengthened the chapel, adding a fourth window on each side and an octagonal cupola atop the entrance.

In its early years, the chapel was nondenominational. During the Civil War, both sides used the building at different times. Union soldiers housed their horses in it, and the Confederates converted it into a hospital. The Glasgow and Cedar Grove Methodist churches shared the chapel until the 1920s.

Over the years, the Tompkins family and community members contributed money for the chapel's upkeep. In 1975, the chapel was placed on the National Register of Historic Places. No longer an active church, Virginia's Chapel is used for weddings, funerals, a Thanksgiving service, and Easter sunrise service. Two cemeteries are located on the chapel grounds. Local white residents are buried in one, and African-American slaves are buried in the other.

Nancy Ray Adams
Pine Mountain Settlement School
Ruth Woods Dayton, *Pioneers and Their Homes on Upper Kanawha*, 1947.

Virginian Railway

Established in 1907, the Virginian Railway quickly became a serious competitor with the long-established Chesapeake & Ohio and Norfolk & Western railroads as a major transporter of coal from southern West Virginia. The Virginian allowed the development and expansion of the Winding Gulf Coalfield of Raleigh and Wyoming counties, the last of West Virginia's famous "smokeless" coalfields.

Using $30 million of his own money, Massachusetts-born business tycoon Henry Huttleston Rogers planned and built the Virginian by combining the small Deepwater Railway Company in Fayette County with the Tidewater Railway Company in Virginia. The Virginian, completed to its ocean docks in 1909, was built in the face of active opposition of the C&O and N&W. The town of Glen Rogers in Wyoming County, site of one of the largest coal mines on the Virginian line, was named in honor of Rogers, who died at age 69 just two years after the Deepwater-Tidewater merger. Col. William Nelson Page of Ansted in Fayette County was the Virginian's first president.

Known for its massive locomotives and 120-ton gondola coal cars, the Virginian moved the world's longest and heaviest coal trains through large rail yards at Mullens and Princeton to ship-loading facilities on the Atlantic Ocean at Sewalls Point, near Norfolk. Eventually the route of the Virginian from Deepwater to the ship-loading piers at Sewalls Point covered a distance of 443 miles. At its peak the port of Hampton Roads handled 88 percent of the coal exported from the United States, and the Virginian produced its share of this impressive tonnage.

The Virginian Railway began electrification of its trains in 1925 from Mullens to Clark's Gap in Virginia. The electric trains moved at twice the speed of their predecessors and could haul 6,000 tons of coal from Wyoming County to Clark's Gap. Trains with 9,000 tons of capacity were used for the remainder of the 134-mile electrified zone between Mullens and Roanoke, Virginia.

The Virginian merged with the Norfolk & Western Railroad (now Norfolk Southern) in November 1959. The rail yards at Princeton were added to the National Register of Historic Places in 2003.

See also Norfolk & Western Railway, Railroads

Karl C. Lilly III
State Senate

Virginius Island

Virginius Island, located in the Shenandoah River adjacent to Harpers Ferry, was a thriving industrial area in the decades before the Civil War. Island industry suffered devastation during the war, including the destruction and dismantling of machinery, bombardment, fire, and repeated military occupation. Over the years since then, floods and vegetation have reclaimed the structures that once dominated Virginius Island. The ruins are now preserved by the National Park Service as part of Harpers Ferry National Historic Park.

Historically an island or group of islands, Virginius was once separated from the mainland of Harpers Ferry by a natural river channel. By the 1850s, a canal had replaced the channel. Now Virginius Island is joined to the mainland. By the mid-19th century, Virginius Island was the site of a number of private industries, including a sawmill, granary, flour mill, pulp mill, tannery, iron foundry, blacksmith shop, machine shop, and cotton mills. In addition to the multi-story industrial buildings, there were 28 dwellings on the island.

James Stubblefield, the superintendent of the federal armory at Harpers Ferry, first acquired the property in 1823. It measured 13 acres, and was known then as "Stubblefield's Island." Soon afterward, in 1827 the Virginia General Assembly established the town of Virginius. The island was absorbed into the corporate boundaries of Harpers Ferry in 1851, a year before the first major flood came in 1852. The flood of 1870 proved to be even more destructive to most of Virginius Island's industrial establishments, and island industry was never able to recover.

See also Harpers Ferry

Walton Danforth Stowell Jr.
Harpers Ferry
David Gilbert, *A Walker's Guide to Harpers Ferry West Virginia*, 1995; Gilbert, *Where Industry Failed: Water Powered Mills at Harpers Ferry, West Virginia*, 1984.

VISTA

VISTA (Volunteers in Service to America) had its beginning in 1963, when President John F. Kennedy spoke of a domestic volunteer program modeled after the newly established Peace Corps. The next year, President Lyndon B. Johnson declared a "war on poverty" and signed the Economic Opportunity Act of 1964. The act created the VISTA program and housed it in the Office of Economic Development. The first VISTA members started in January 1965. In 1971, ACTION became the federal agency that oversaw both VISTA and the Peace Corps. This arrangement continued until 1993, when the federal Corporation for National and Community Service was created to oversee AmeriCorps and all domestic service programs, including VISTA.

West Virginia received its first VISTA workers in 1965. Quickly this turned into a flood of community organizers, who worked on social, environmental, and economic issues. Often called "hippies" by their detractors and sometimes denounced as meddling outsiders, by late 1968 VISTA volunteers had streamed into the most rural and hard-pressed areas of the state, frequently coming into conflict with local power brokers. Governor Moore responded with an unprecedented action requiring his approval of every VISTA assignment made in West Virginia.

These early VISTA workers came of age during a period of activism on America's college campuses, anti-war protests, the

---

What VISTA stands for

"Some youngun name of Tom Kolwlecki has showed up like he dropped out of the sky and calls hisself a VISTA worker. He told me what that VISTA stands for but I can't keep it in my head, although I can recall anything important. Nobody could figure out what Tom was here for, so I come right out and asked him. He said the VISTA is something the government thought up like the Peace Corps, only for this country. The VISTA is supposed to help end poverty. I got a hoot out of that. 'No, really,' said Tom, and he started laughing too, like he didn't believe a word of it. That started me to really wondering about him.

"Uncle Brigham is offended by the VISTA. He don't like to think we need help like they do in Africa, and he says, 'Here I am a growed man getting grayheaded and some shirttail youngun is supposed to save me? And him sent by the government and what if hit's the government I need saved from?' He asked Tom how come he didn't just stay in New Jersey where he was from, and Tom said the government likes you to go someplace different from where you grew up so you can learn new things. I reckon that is fine for the VISTAS, but I don't see where it does us much good."

—Denise Giardina *The Unquiet Earth* (1992)

Civil Rights movement, and feminism. By and large they were the children of America's middle class, well-off by the standards of rural West Virginia. Their appreciation for the arts and crafts and West Virginia folkways connected them to the back-to-the-land movement, which brought many more of their generation to the state at about the same time.

Enduring legacies in the form of environmental organizations, and Cabin Creek Quilts and other cooperatives continue into the 21st century, as does the social and political leadership by former VISTAs who stayed on to make their lives in our state. Close to 3,000 VISTA volunteers have worked in West Virginia since 1965. More than 100 were active in the state in 2005 under the program then known as AmeriCorps-VISTA. The emphasis is now on service as compared to the more controversial organizing and community development efforts of the original program.

See also Back-to-the-Land Movement
James Thibeault
Charleston

Vitrolite

Vitrolite is a trade name for structural pigmented glass, a popular building material during the first half of the 20th century. Vitrolite was a West Virginia product, manufactured after 1908 by the Meyercord-Carter Company in Vienna, Wood County. The firm reorganized in 1910 as the Vitrolite Company, and the factory was fully completed in 1914. The company's products became popular after a 1922 Washington exposition on Vitrolite. The glass giant Libbey-Owens-Ford bought the Vitrolite Company in 1935 and continued production until 1947.

Structural glass was originally developed in 1900 as a sanitary substitute for marble in wainscoting and table-top applications by the Marietta Manufacturing Company of Indianapolis, followed by Pittsburgh Plate Glass, Penn-American Plate Glass, and others. PPG's Carrara Glass and Vitrolite were the industry giants. Structural glass, applied in heavy panels, was widely used for interior and exterior siding and veneer applications, especially in rehabilitating older storefronts in many downtowns. LOF co-sponsored a "Modernize Main Street" competition with *Architectural Record* magazine in the 1930s, encouraging such use of Vitrolite.

White and black were the first colors available. In the 1930s, these gave way to other hues, including pastels and jewel tones. The material was an integral element of the Art Deco, Art Modern, and Streamlined architectural styles. The market for structural pigmented glass declined in the early 1950s with the advent of other materials.

Michael Gioulis
Sutton

Volcano

Volcano, an oil boom town between 1864 and 1897, lies in Wood County east of Parkersburg and near the Ritchie County line. The Volcanic Oil & Gas Company was formed in 1864 and purchased 2,000 acres for oil exploration. After initial strikes, oil wells were drilled as quickly as possible. The town of Volcano was founded in 1870. During its peak years there were hotels, schools, churches, saloons, an opera house, a newspaper, sawmill, barrel factory, post office, stores, and many houses at Volcano.

At first, supplies were brought in over rough roads by horse and wagon from the nearby town of Petroleum. By 1869, the Laurel Fork & Sand Hill Railroad had been constructed. It connected Volcano with the Baltimore & Ohio Railroad, a few miles away.

Disastrous fires occurred in 1879 and again in 1897. The town was never completely rebuilt. The railroad was dismantled. A pipeline then conveyed local oil to Parkersburg. Although production decreased over the years, oil continued to flow from Volcano's wells. A cable arrangement was devised to pump 50 wells still producing at the end of the 19th century. Later, the number fell to 40, and by the 1950s the cable was pumping just 25 wells. Some wells produced oil for more than 75 years.

Borgon Tanner
Vanceboro, Maine

Alexander Luark Wade

Education reformer Alexander Luark Wade was born February 1, 1832. Raised in Monongalia County, he began teaching in the rural schools at age 16. He served a decade in county government, returning to education in 1871 as principal of the Morgantown schools, shortly thereafter becoming assistant county superintendent. He was elected Monongalia County school superintendent in 1875.

By successfully reforming Monongalia County's country schools, Wade radically transformed rural elementary education. In most rural schools the students were taught in one room, regardless of age or number of years of attendance, with no structure that prepared them for higher levels of learning. Wade reorganized rural schools using a system that required progress through eight prescribed levels. Those students completing all grades and passing a public examination were recognized through graduation exercises and the receipt of a diploma. Wade implemented his plan in 1874 and held the first exams in 1876.

The graded system worked so well in Monongalia County that other counties implemented it. After the 1881 publication of Wade's *A Graduating System for Country Schools,* the plan was quickly adopted in many states. However, it was not adopted throughout West Virginia until 1891. Wade received national acclaim for his accomplishments before his death on May 2, 1904.

Harold Malcolm Forbes
WVU Libraries
Mary I. Barbe, "The Life of Alexander L. Wade," *West Virginia History,* October 1947; Alexander L. Wade, *A Graduating System for Country Schools,* 1881.

WAJR

Radio station WAJR-AM in Morgantown is one of the state's most influential stations. In 1949, it became the flagship station for a statewide network (now the Mountaineer Sports Network) distributing broadcasts of West Virginia University football and basketball games. For nearly 50 years these broadcasts featured the well-known announcer, Jack Fleming. In 1985, WAJR launched the Metronews Radio Network, which now provides daily news, talk, and sports programming via satellite to more than 60 affiliates statewide.

The West Virginia Radio Corporation has owned WAJR since it began broadcasting December 7, 1940. Founder H. C. Greer was also publisher of the Morgantown *Post* and the *Dominion News* (now the *Dominion Post*). The station was

Uncle Homer Walker plays his music.

named for the initials of Greer's wife, Agnes Jane Reeves Greer. In 1968, both radio and newspaper facilities moved into the new Greer Building. In 1976, control of the company was transferred to Greer family heirs, Richard, John, and David Raese. In 1957, the station increased power from 250 to 5,000 watts and assumed its current frequency of 1440 kHz. WAJR-FM (now WVAQ) began in 1948. WAJR's programming evolved through several music formats, and now the station offers a mix of national and local news, talk, and sports.

When the FCC relaxed ownership restrictions in the early 1990s, West Virginia Radio Corporation began acquiring additional stations in the state and now owns more than a dozen facilities in Charleston, Clarksburg, Elkins, Fairmont, and Weston. WAJR-FM, licensed at Salem, went on the air in 1999, extending the station's service into the Clarksburg market.

Ed McDonald
Keyser

Thomas Walker

Doctor Thomas Walker, born January 25, 1715, in King and Queen County, Virginia, was a physician, explorer, land speculator, farmer, merchant, legislator, and friend of famous Virginians. His skill as a physician and surgeon was widely recognized. Walker was an investor, agent, and surveyor for the Loyal Company of Virginia. In 1748, he explored Virginia's New River Valley on a journey that took him on to the Holston River in present Tennessee. In 1750, Walker led the first recorded expedition into Kentucky and named the Cumberland Gap and Cumberland River. His return route through present southern West Virginia crossed the headwaters of the Tug Fork, tra-

versed the confluence of the New and Greenbrier rivers at present Hinton, and ascended most of the Greenbrier.

In an active career of government service, Walker served in the House of Burgesses, (1752, 1756–61, and 1775–76) and the House of Delegates (1782) variously representing Albemarle, Louisa, and Hampshire counties. He served as commissary general for troops at more than 80 forts on Virginia's western frontier during the French and Indian War, 1754–63. He was with Braddock and Washington at Braddock's defeat in 1755. Walker negotiated various Indian treaties, including the Treaty of Hard Labor and the Treaty of Fort Stanwix. Appointed commissioner of Indian affairs after the Battle of Point Pleasant in 1774, he presided over treaty negotiations representing both Virginia and the Continental Congress.

Walker was a member of the Revolutionary Conventions of 1774–75, the Committee of Safety, and the Virginia Executive Council. In 1780, Walker surveyed the extension of the boundary line between Virginia and North Carolina. He died November 9, 1794, at his long-time home in Albemarle County, Virginia.

See also Exploration, Fort Stanwix Treaties, Treaty of Hard Labor
Harold Malcolm Forbes
WVU Libraries
Alexander Canady McLeod, "A Man for All Regions: Dr. Thomas Walker of Castle Hill," *The Filson Club History Quarterly,* April 1997; Keith Ryan Nyland, "Doctor Thomas Walker (1715–1794): Explorer, Physician, Statesman, Surveyor and Planter of Virginia and Kentucky," Ph.D. dissertation, Ohio State University, 1971.

Uncle Homer Walker

Musician John Homer "Uncle Homer" Walker was born February 15, 1898, in

Mercer County. He was raised in Summers County and lived much of his adult life in neighboring Glen Lyn, Virginia. He usually worked as a laborer and farm hand.

Walker played the five-string banjo in the old clawhammer style, which preceded the three-finger picking popularized by bluegrass musician Earl Scruggs. Among the last in a tradition of black Appalachian banjo players, he grew up with brothers who played guitar, fiddle, and mandolin. He started to play the banjo as a child, learning from his mother and an uncle. Walker traced his music directly back to the mid-19th century, noting that he had also learned from his maternal grandfather, who had been born a slave in Virginia.

A popular performer during the folk revival period, Walker in his later years played music at the festivals of the 1970s, including the John Henry Folk Festival in Summers County, the Vandalia Gathering in Charleston, and the Smithsonian Institution's 1976 Festival of American Folklife in Washington. He was featured in the 1972 documentary film, *Morris Family Old-Time Music Festival,* and was the subject of the 1977 film, *Banjo Man,* narrated by folk musician Taj Mahal.

Uncle Homer Walker died January 4, 1980, in Princeton.

War on Poverty

On January 8, 1964, President Lyndon B. Johnson asked Congress to declare an "unconditional war on poverty," and by August legislation was in place for a broad range of government programs under the Office of Economic Opportunity (OEO). Though the major focus was on urban poverty, the rural poverty of Appalachia and West Virginia also drew attention. Manpower training programs provided job training for workers, like many in the coal industry, whose jobs had been lost to technological change. The Job Corps offered opportunities for unemployed youth to learn marketable skills, and the Volunteers in Service to America (VISTA) called upon volunteers (who came mostly from middle-class youth) to help fight poverty in America as the Peace Corps did abroad. Head Start sought to prepare poor pre-school youngsters for the classroom. Through the Appalachian Regional Commission and other programs funding was provided for public works projects in impoverished areas. Some help also was available for struggling farmers and small businesses, and Medicare and Medicaid provided medical insurance for the elderly and the poor.

Governor Smith, a Democrat, appointed Paul L. Crabtree as the director of the state economic opportunity agency and Dr. Eugene Thoenen as chief coordinator. Elizabeth Victoria Depaulo was the first state coordinator of Project Head Start.

The most controversial part of the War on Poverty, the Community Action Program (CAP), provided funding for local antipoverty programs which were to seek "maximum feasible participation" of community people. To qualify for federal funding, counties established economic opportunity commissions which in turn were charged with organizing local people to address their problems. In West Virginia as elsewhere, established politicians found the CAP organizations threatening and complained that they undermined the elected local officials. Although federal agents of the OEO felt that many of the county organizations fell short of the agency's conceptions of what community action should be, it was precisely the counties (such as Raleigh and Mingo) with strong community action organizations that caused the greatest complaint from politicians and local authorities. In Mingo County, CAP groups campaigned for clean elections. CAP organizations challenged local school boards, county courts, and municipal governments and organized demonstrations that upset local economic and political interests.

Like their counterparts in other places, West Virginia politicians carried their complaints to Washington and to state officials. By the end of 1968, with the approval of both Washington and Charleston, counties reasserted their control over their economic opportunity commissions and community action programs.

As early as 1965, the pressures of political opposition and growing budgetary constraints imposed by the escalation of the Vietnam War led to a scaling back of plans for fighting poverty. President Richard Nixon, elected in 1968, began the dismantling of the OEO programs, and in 1974 Congress abolished the agency altogether, scattering its components throughout the federal bureaucracy.

The War on Poverty fell short of achieving its lofty goals and suffered much criticism in the more conservative decades that followed, but most of the programs established under OEO still existed at the end of the century.

See also Poverty, VISTA

Jerry Bruce Thomas
Shepherd University

Huey Perry, *They'll Cut Off Your Project: A Mingo County Chronicle,* 1972.

Ward Engineering Works

The Charles Ward Engineering Works of Charleston was an industry leader in the development of water-tube boilers and tunnel-type, screw-propelled shallow-draft river steamboats. These were the forerunners of the modern towboat.

At the request of John P. Hale, Charles Ward (1841–1915) arrived in Charleston from England in 1871 to become superintendent of the Charleston Gas Works. By 1872, Ward had begun operating his own pipe and fittings business. He developed his first boiler for Hale's packet, the *Wild Goose.* By 1880, Ward was working full-time at his own business, located first on Capitol Street, and then on the south side of the Kanawha River across from downtown. By the 1890s, Ward's patented water-tube boilers were found on both river packets and on coastal defense vessels like the USS *Monterey* of the Spanish-American War.

Ward's boilers were showcased at the 1893 Chicago World's Fair. While in Chicago, Ward defended his design before the Marine Division of the International Engineering Congress. The "battle of the boilers" was not settled until 1904 when the British Admiralty found water-tube boilers the superior choice for naval vessels.

By the early 1900s, Ward's son, Charles Edwin Ward (1867–1941), had married Governor Fleming's daughter, Gypsy, and was taking the lead in adapting the tunnel-screw design to shallow-draft vessels. In 1893 the *Mascot* was built for the U.S. Engineering Corp, followed by the *Unique* in 1901. The *James Rumsey,* built in 1902, participated with the much larger sternwheeler *D. T. Lane* in a pushing and pulling contest described by the *Pittsburgh Press* as a contest between "David and Goliath."

Ward Engineering produced a total of 89 hulls in a variety of designs including sternwheel tows, such as the *Greenbrier* (1924) and the *Scott* (1930) which later plied the Kanawha as the excursion boat *P. A. Denny.* Charles Ward Engineering closed in 1932.

Brooks F. McCabe Jr.
Charleston

George P. Parkinson Jr. and Brooks F. McCabe Jr., "Charles Ward and James Rumsey: Regional Innovation in Steam Technology on the Western Rivers," *West Virginia History,* January–April 1978; Parkinson, "Charles Ward Engineering Works: A Photo Essay," *Goldenseal,* July–August 1977.

H. Rus Warne

Architect Harry Rus Warne was born in Parkersburg, October 10, 1872. He studied at the Ohio Mechanics Institute in Cincinnati and at the Ecole des Beaux Arts in Paris. He also studied under established architects, including Richard H. Adair of Parkersburg.

After a brief practice in Parkersburg, Warne accepted a junior position in the office of the Supervising Architect, U.S. Treasury Department, Washington. Later he moved to Charleston, forming a partnership with architect Charles G. Rabenstein. The firm they established in 1902 would continue after Warne's retirement under the leadership of C. E. Silling. The century-old company, now Silling Associates, is one of the oldest continuing architectural practices in the United States.

Among Warne's most important early commissions were the 123-foot high Coal Column and the West Virginia Building, the state's two exhibits at the 1907 Jamestown Exposition in Norfolk, Virginia. The coal column has long since disappeared, but the building remains as officers' housing at a navy base. Warne also designed the West Virginia Building at the 1915 Panama-Pacific International Exposition in San Francisco.

Warne's flair for design may be seen in the Masonic Temple Building, a 1915 project which added impressive Neo-Gothic Revival details to an 1895 building that had partially burned. Warne kept his own offices in the building, still a Charleston landmark. Residential design played a key role in his work, as successful businessmen sought out Warne to design large, fashionable houses. He designed houses in Edgewood, South Hills, and Kanawha City, growing residential neighborhoods of Charleston. Many were of the Colonial Revival and Tudor Revival styles.

As his firm prospered after World War I, Warne designed many public buildings and schools. By 1921, the partnership of Warne, Tucker, and Patterson was established. Warne's buildings during this period included the State Masonic Home in Parkersburg, the main building at Greenbrier Military School in Lewisburg, and Charleston High School.

Other buildings include Edgewood Country Club (which was destroyed) and the second Edgewood Country Club; the United Fuel Gas Building; Littlepage Terrace and Washington Manor, low-cost housing; St. Marks United Methodist Church (all in Charleston); and 40 state institutional buildings, including dorms at West Virginia University. His buildings on the National Register of Historic Places include the Boone County Courthouse, Charleston City Hall, Nicholas County High School, and houses in Charleston's Grosscup Road Historic District. The Boone County Courthouse is considered the finest expression of neoclassicism in southern West Virginia.

Warne died April 25, 1954.

See also Architects and Architecture

Judie Smith
West Virginia Humanities Council

Warrior Path

The Warrior Path was one of the most important early north-south trails in eastern North America, extending from western New York to the Carolina Piedmont region by way of the Valley of Virginia. The trail passed through present West Virginia in the Eastern Panhandle, where it paralleled present Interstate 81. Several West Virginia Indian trails joined the Warrior Path in present southwest Virginia, south of the present state line. They included the Tug River Trail, the Bluestone Trail, and the Shawnee or Seneca Trail. The McCullough or Trader's Trail crossed the Eastern Panhandle to join the Warrior Path near present Winchester.

The Warrior Path followed approximately the same route as the Chesapeake Branch of the Great Indian Warpath. The trail and its branches were used for interaction among such disparate groups as the Iroquois in the Northeast, Algonquian-speaking Powhatan groups in Virginia, and the Creek and Cherokee in the Southeast. This trail was also used extensively by early traders and hunters, and by the first permanent settlers into the region.

See also Indian Trails

Darla S. Hoffman
Cultural Resource Analysts

Washington

Built at Wheeling in 1816 by the great riverman Capt. Henry M. Shreve of Brownsville, Pennsylvania, and George White and Noah Lane of Wheeling, the riverboat *Washington* was the prototype for almost every steamboat to follow.

Earlier boats had been patterned after the *New Orleans*, the first steamboat to operate on the Ohio and Mississippi rivers, built in 1811 at Pittsburgh by the Fulton, Livingston, and Roosevelt group of New York. This boat was patterned after Fulton's original Hudson River steamboat, *Clermont*, built in 1807. Based on his experience as a keelboat and steamboat captain, Shreve decided that he would build a boat and steam machinery more suitable to the western rivers. While partners White and Lane were building the hull at Wheeling using timber from historic Fort Henry, Shreve supervised the building of the high-pressure boilers and engines at Brownsville. On all of the earlier boats, low-pressure vertical boilers and engines had been placed in the hold of the boat. Shreve placed two pairs of horizontal boilers and a set of compact high-pressure engines connected to the sidewheels on the main deck of the *Washington*. This design eliminated the need for a deep hold, producing a shallow-draft vessel which floated on the water rather than in it. The *Washington* was also the first steamboat to be built with a second deck where there were cabins just for passengers.

The *Washington* soon proved that it had the power to stem the strong upstream current and maintain a regular schedule on the Mississippi and Ohio rivers, unlike its predecessors. By 1825, when Shreve replaced the first *Washington* with the *George Washington*, most of the steamboats then operating were patterned after the 1816 *Washington*.

Gerald W. Sutphin
Huntington

Edith McCall, *Conquering the Rivers: Henry Miller Shreve and the Navigation of America's Inland Waterways*, 1984.

Booker T. Washington

Educator Booker Taliaferro Washington, born a slave in Franklin County, Virginia, April 5, 1856, spent his formative years in the Kanawha Valley. Union victory in the Civil War had freed the family, and in 1865 they moved to Malden, Kanawha County, to join Washington Ferguson, Booker's stepfather, who had escaped from slavery in Franklin County during the war.

Malden afforded young Washington the opportunity to attend a one-room school for colored people. While living in Malden he came under the influence of Viola Ruffner, the wife of a salt manufacturer, who instilled in him the virtues of cleanliness and hard work. In 1871, he enrolled at Hampton Institute in Hampton, Virginia. Graduating with honors in 1875, he returned to West Virginia to begin his career as a teacher. In 1879, Washington returned to Hampton Institute as a teacher, coming home to West Virginia to work in the coal mines while school was out.

In May 1881, Washington left West Virginia. In June 1881, he opened his own educational institution, a normal school for African-Americans in Tuskegee, Alabama. The school had a humble beginning, with 37 students meeting in Butler Chapel African Methodist Episcopal Zion, a log structure with an adjoining shanty. At the close of the May 1914 term, Principal Washington's last full year as the head of the school, his Tuskegee Institute owned 110 buildings; 2,110 acres of land and more than 350 head of live-

Booker T. Washington spent his formative years in Malden.

"Wise beyond his generation"

"Booker Washington was one of the most patient and earnest and, withal, one of the ablest men whom I ever met. As a matter of fact he was one of the great men that the South has produced in twenty-five years. His theory and practice was to educate the Negro and make him a good citizen, an intelligent farmer or workman, a man, in other words, who is an intelligent voter. Of course, he was fought by the Negro who had political proclivities, and by the white man who wished to use the Negro. These two elements minimized his efforts, but he was wise beyond his generation. The intelligent people of the South respected him for his wonderful and splendid work. I was interested in him irrespective of the great question at issue because he was reared in my county of Kanawha. He was born in Franklin County, Virginia."

—Gov. William A. MacCorkle *The Recollections of Fifty Years of West Virginia* (1928)

stock; hundreds of wagons, carriages, farm implements, and other equipment valued at nearly $1.5 million; and a permanent endowment fund worth more than $2 million.

Tuskegee's success established Washington's reputation. On September 19, 1895, he delivered an address at the Atlanta Cotton States Exposition that thrust him into national prominence and made him the unofficial spokesman of the African-American people. Criticized by some as too readily accepting southern racial inequality, the speech outlined a plan for mutual cooperation among white northerners and southerners and African-Americans to bring economic prosperity to the South.

Booker T. Washington died November 14, 1915, on the Tuskegee Institute campus. He had kept up his West Virginia connections throughout his life. He was a lifelong member of African Zion Baptist Church at Malden, and returned occasionally to speak at West Virginia Colored Institute (now West Virginia State University). There is a monument to him on the grounds of the West Virginia state capitol.

Joseph Bundy
Bluefield

Louis R. Harlan, *Booker T. Washington, The Making of a Black Leader, 1856–1901,* 1972; Booker T. Washington, *Up From Slavery,* 1901.

Charles Washington

Charles Washington, for whom the Jefferson County seat of Charles Town is named, was the youngest full brother of George Washington. He was born May 2, 1738, at Hunting Creek, Virginia. Shortly after Charles's birth, his family moved to the Ferry Farm near Fredericksburg, where he spent most of his childhood. He gained prominence in this area, becoming a substantial landholder, a member of the vestry of St. George's Church, and a signer of the Westmoreland Resolutions which opposed the British Stamp Act of 1765. He married Mildred Thornton and had four children: George Augustine, Samuel, Frances, and Mildred Washington.

Charles Washington came to present Jefferson County in 1780, having inherited land from his half-brother, Lawrence. He began construction of his home, Happy Retreat, near the future site of Charles Town, the same year but did not live to see its completion. From Happy Retreat in 1786, he laid out plans for Charles Town to be built on 80 acres of his land. The town square, where the courthouse stands, was deeded by Washington as a gift to the town. The town was incorporated in January 1787. Charles Washington died September 16, 1799, and is buried in the family plot at his Jefferson County home.

William D. Theriault
Bakerton

Millard K. Bushong, *A History of Jefferson County, West Virginia,* 1941.

Washington Family

The Washington family became acquainted with the rich agricultural lands of present Jefferson County when George Washington at age 16 helped to survey lands for Lord Fairfax in 1748. Two years later, young Washington bought 550 acres of land on the South Fork of Bullskin Run, near Charles Town. Here he established his Rock Hall plantation.

George's half-brother, Lawrence, acquired several thousand acres in the Bullskin and Evitts Run area. Lawrence Washington died in 1752, leaving no children. His land went to his brother, Augustine Washington (1718–62), and to his half-brothers George Washington, who inherited Mount Vernon from Lawrence, Samuel Washington (1734–81), John Augustine Washington (1736–87), and Charles Washington (1738–99).

Samuel Washington was the first to move to present Jefferson County. He moved to the native limestone house he built and named Harewood in 1770. When Samuel died at age 47 in 1781, he left a widow and five young children. Samuel's son, George Steptoe Washington, married Lucy Payne in 1793. Lucy's widowed sister, Dolley Payne Todd, was married at Harewood to James Madison, who became president in 1809. Harewood, near Charles Town, still remains in the Washington family.

Charles Washington laid out Charles Town in 1786 on 80 acres that he had inherited from Lawrence. Charles and his wife, Mildred, resided at Happy Retreat at Charles Town. Charles had a son, Samuel, and daughter, Mildred, who married Thomas Hammond.

Cedar Lawn, near Charles Town, was built in 1825 by John Thornton Augustine Washington (1783–1841), the grandson of George's brother, Samuel Washington. Locust Hill (no longer standing) was built in 1840 by Samuel's daughter, Lucy Elizabeth Washington, who married John Bainbridge Packett on part of the original Harewood land.

John Augustine Washington did not live on the land that he inherited from Lawrence, but at his death his son, Corbin Washington, inherited the land and lived there. After the death of Corbin's wife, Hannah Lee, daughter of Richard Henry Lee, his Prospect Hill plantation in Jefferson County was divided. It consisted of 2,720 acres, 130 slaves, 15 horses, 45 horned cattle, 70 sheep, 60 hogs, and two yokes of oxen. Corbin and Hannah Washington had three sons: Richard Henry Lee Washington, who died before 1819, Bushrod Corbin (1790–1851), and John Augustine (1789–1832). When Richard Henry Lee Washington died, his land was divided among his two brothers and his sister, Mary Lee Washington Herbert, who received the Prospect Hill house, which is no longer standing. Brothers Bushrod Corbin and John Augustine Washington, the great-grandsons of George Washington's brother, married Blackburn sisters. Bushrod built Claymont Court, and John Augustine built Blakeley on the land they had inherited between 1815 and 1820. The houses, both near Charles Town, suffered major fires and were rebuilt.

There is one other well-known Washington home in Jefferson County, Beall-Air. The early section of this house was built by Thomas Beall (1748–1819) of Georgetown. His daughter, Eliza, married George Corbin Washington, who was the grandson of Augustine, the full brother of Lawrence. It was their son, Lewis William Washington (1812–71), who built the front section of the Beall-Air mansion about 1850. It was at Beall-Air on Sunday, October 16, 1859, that Lewis Washington was awakened by an armed group that took him to the fire-engine house at Harpers Ferry. There he became John Brown's hostage.

See also Blakeley, Claymont Court, Harewood, George Washington

Don C. Wood
Berkeley County Historical Society

George Washington

At the age of 16, George Washington (1732–99) ventured for the first time into the mountainous regions that later became West Virginia. Washington learned surveying at an early age, and between 1748 and 1752 he helped to survey extensive tracts of land in the Fairfax estate, which included the present Eastern Panhandle and Potomac Highlands. Compounding his income by purchasing land, he came to own more than 2,300 acres by age 20, including lands in present West Virginia.

Washington began his military career at a time in which the Appalachian interior of North America had become a battleground of France, England, and various Indian nations. As commander of Virginia militia charged with defense of the frontiers, including the present Eastern Panhandle, Washington attacked a French party before the official onset of hostilities and thus helped to bring on the global conflict known as the French and Indian or Seven Years War. His later heroism at the defeat of General Braddock near present Pittsburgh in July 1755 helped save British forces from complete destruction. As colonel of the Virginia Regiment from 1755 to 1758, Washington rose to the highest military office in Virginia before age 25. He sought to defend the western reaches of the colony with a string of forts stretched along the Appalachian Mountains, including Forts Edwards, Pearsall, and Seybert in present Hampshire and Pendleton counties.

In 1758, Washington gave up the command of the Virginia Regiment and temporarily retired to a planter's life at Mount Vernon and marriage to Virginia's wealthiest widow, Martha Dandridge Custis. During a decade spent largely in the west, he had fulfilled much of his youthful ambition for wealth and reputation. He never forgot the area and traveled there whenever possible to view his land-holdings, which ultimately exceeded 50,000 acres in the region, or to "take the waters" at Berkeley Springs. Following the French and Indian War, Washington acquired extensive lands in present West Virginia, on the Ohio River, Kanawha River, and elsewhere. In 1770, he traveled down the Ohio to view these lands and seek others.

For both personal and political reasons Washington continued to pursue the improvement and development of western lands. To open the Potomac River to commercial navigation, he helped found the Potomac Company. Placing the interests of the United States above the welfare of both native peoples and American settlers in the west, President Washington concluded numerous treaties with Indian nations and used military force to suppress political unrest during the Whiskey Rebellion. Washington understood the west and its role in the emerging nation better than most of the founding generation of political leaders, and he established the first U.S. Armory at Harp-

ers Ferry. Numerous Washington family members took up family lands in what is now the Eastern Panhandle, where their homes and properties remain landmarks today.

Warren R. Hofstra
Shenandoah University

Douglas Southall Freeman, *George Washington: A Biography*, 1948–1957; Warren R. Hofstra, ed., *George Washington and the Virginia Backcountry*, 1998; Thomas A. Lewis, *For King and Country: The Maturing of George Washington, 1748–1760*, 1993.

Lewis W. Washington

The great-grandson of Augustine Washington, who was the half-brother of George Washington, Lewis W. Washington was born November 30, 1812, in Georgetown. He lived at Beall-Air, in Jefferson County, a home built by his grandfather, Thomas Beall. Washington was visited in September 1859 by John Edwin Cook, who was scouting the countryside for abolitionist John Brown, noting the residences of slave owners and resources that would be useful in the upcoming raid on Harpers Ferry. During this visit, Washington showed Cook a sword presented by Frederick the Great to George Washington and a set of pistols given to General Washington by Lafayette.

Early on the morning after his October 16, 1859, raid on Harpers Ferry, John Brown sent a detachment into the country to collect prominent slaveholders as hostages. Washington, some of his slaves, his pistols, and sword were captured and brought to the engine house at Harpers Ferry along with other hostages. Brown carried the George Washington sword during the ensuing battle. When the engine house was taken by U.S. Marines under the command of Col. Robert E. Lee, Washington pointed out Brown to the storming party. He testified to his experiences at John Brown's trial and at the Senate subcommittee investigating the John Brown raid.

Lewis Washington died October 1, 1871, and was buried in the Zion Episcopal Church Graveyard in Charles Town.

See also John Brown, Charles Washington

William D. Theriault
Bakerton

Bushong, Millard K., *A History of Jefferson County, West Virginia*, 1941.

Samuel Washington

Samuel Washington, born November 16, 1734, at Pope's Creek, Virginia, was a younger brother of George Washington. Samuel was the first of several members of the Washington family to live in what is now the Eastern Panhandle of West Virginia. He moved to present Jefferson County in 1770, building the limestone mansion known as Harewood located near Charles Town.

Samuel Washington married five women during his 47 years and was widowed four times. Characterized by George Washington biographer James Thomas Flexner as "incompetent and improvident," Samuel was a financial drain on his famous brother. In addition to Harewood, Samuel accumulated 3,800 acres of local lands, but was privately characterized by George as being "enormously in debt." Samuel Washington served as a justice of the peace of Berkeley County, and later as the county's sheriff. He died September 26, 1781.

Harewood was inherited by Samuel's son, George Steptoe Washington. The house, which is on the National Register of Historic Places, remains in the Washington family as a private residence.

See also Harewood, Washington Family, George Washington

Water Resources

West Virginia is blessed with an abundance of water. Within the state's boundaries lie approximately 9,000 streams and rivers that total over 32,000 miles in length. In addition, there are approximately 100 public lakes and reservoirs that total over 22,000 surface acres. Over 100,000 acres of wetlands also are located within the state's borders. West Virginia's water resources are maintained by plentiful rainfall. Throughout the state rainfall averages nearly 40 inches per year, while in the higher elevations of the Allegheny Mountains, 55 inches or more per year are common.

In addition to abundant surface waters, West Virginia also possesses ample groundwater resources. The groundwater is stored within what scientists refer to as aquifers. These aquifers are water-bearing rock formations that may consist of sandstone, limestone, shale, or clay. Aquifers may be either deep or shallow.

Approximately a third of the state's population gets its household water from groundwater sources, which include public and private wells and springs. The other two-thirds gets its water from surface water sources, which include streams, rivers, lakes, and ponds. In many rural parts of the state, public water systems don't exist. In those areas, private wells or springs are used as a water source, although a small number of individuals may have a private water intake on a stream or lake.

The majority of industry in the state gets its water from surface sources.

However, groundwater is also used. Industries requiring large amounts of water typically locate along major rivers where water is abundant, but sometimes lakes are constructed as industrial water supplies. Mount Storm Lake in Grant County is one such lake, as is Cheat Lake in Monongalia County. Mount Storm Lake provides cooling and process water for the coal-fired Mount Storm Power Station,

West Virginia is blessed with abundant flowing water.

while Cheat Lake provides water for West Penn Power Company's hydroelectric power plant near Morgantown.

Protecting the state's water is largely the responsibility of the West Virginia Department of Environmental Protection. The DEP monitors the quality of the state's rivers, streams, lakes, wetlands, and groundwater. In addition, the DEP is responsible for overseeing restoration of bodies of water that have been degraded by pollution.

Although West Virginia has long had regulations for the protection of water quality, historically there have been no provisions dealing with protection of water quantity. In 2004, the state legislature passed Senate Bill 163, the Water Resources Protection Act. The act, a product of compromise with industry interests wary of regulations, marked the first attempt by the state to gather information on quantity of water used by business and industry.

Water entered the realm of political debate as a growing scarcity of water in other regions reminded West Virginians of the value and vulnerability of the resource. The Water Resources Protection Act originated over concerns that water quantity may not be adequate to satisfy demand in areas of the state that are experiencing rapid population growth and development. Another concern is the potential for out-of-state users to lay claim to state waters. The legislature, in recognizing that water is a vital public resource, agreed that it is the state's responsibility to claim and protect its waters for the use and benefit of its citizens.

The DEP is charged with overseeing implementation of the Water Resources Protection Act, which includes collecting information on: 1) location and quantity of surface and groundwater resources, 2) consumptive and nonconsumptive with-drawals, 3) threats to beneficial uses, 4) growth areas where competition for water resources may be expected, and 5) any other information that may be beneficial to assessing water availability. Detailed information is sought from the state's major water users, which are businesses and industries that use more than 750,000 gallons of water during any single month of a calendar year.

See also Waterpower

Michael A. Arcuri
Department of Environmental Protection
West Virginia DEP, "Groundwater Programs and Activities: Biennial Report to the West Virginia Legislature," 2004; West Virginia DEP, "West Virginia's Water Quality Status Assessment," 2000.

Waterford Park

See Mountaineer Race Track.

Waterpower

The combination of mountainous terrain and numerous streams has endowed West Virginia with abundant waterpower. Rivers and creeks flowing down relatively steep gradients produce the swift-moving water whose power may be converted into mechanical energy by devices as simple as an old-fashioned mill wheel or as complex as a modern industrial turbine. This energy may be used directly to power mills or mechanical equipment at the site, or converted into electricity for use at remote locations. While only a fraction of available waterpower has been harnessed in a state also blessed with plentiful fossil fuels, nonetheless waterpower has had a critical role in the story of West Virginia. Next to draft animals and human labor, waterpower was the most important and most widely used form of power in our early history.

An enduring and idyllic part of the landscape, gristmills were located on countless streams, and some streams had several. Usually these mills ground corn into meal and livestock feed. The higher-precision flour mills required a larger investment and were located primarily in the bigger towns or county seats. In Preston County alone, there were more than 50 gristmills over the years, with Bruceton Mill on Big Sandy Creek among the largest. It was likely the fifth mill to occupy the site after the first one was built there in 1792. Along the 40-mile run of Patterson Creek in Grant and Mineral counties there were 25 gristmills with just one, Lyons Mill of Williamsport, still operating after 1950.

In addition to the millstones, a gristmill's water wheel commonly powered several devices in the processing and movement of grain. These were typically operated from a common drive shaft by a variety of wooden or metal gears and leather belts. In addition to grinding grain, many gristmills also served as sawmills, using a slow-moving "up-and-down" saw. Other gristmills provided power for carding wool or operating a tannery.

Mill sites were valuable and sought-after locations, often supplying the nucleus for community development. Some mills housed the local store or post office, and many places were named for their mills or millers. For example, Thomas Shepherd built one of the state's first water mills at Shepherdstown. Built by 1739 on Town Run, a Potomac tributary, Shepherd's Mill features one of the largest overshot water wheels ever built. Thomas "Stonewall" Jackson's grandfather constructed a log gristmill in the early 1800s on the east side of the West Fork River in Lewis County, where the Civil War general worked as a boy. The place was soon known as Jackson's Mill and remains so today.

Harpers Ferry, at the confluence of the Potomac and Shenandoah rivers, was chosen as the site of the second U.S. armory because of its great waterpower potential. A munitions plant began production there in 1801 using five water-powered mills. Other 19th-century Harpers Ferry facilities driven by water included a sawmill, a flour mill, a machine shop, two cotton mills, a tannery, and an iron foundry, all of which helped establish the region as an industrial leader.

Waterpower technology was improved over the years at the Harpers Ferry munitions plant, beginning with the motion-regulating tub wheel in the 1830s, the maintenance-saving iron water wheel in the 1840s, and the higher-efficiency Boyden turbine during the 1850s. The use of waterpower continued in Harpers Ferry until the 1930s, supplying two water-powered pulp mills along the Potomac. Waterpower was used at various locations for other industrial purposes as well, including weaving. Water-powered looms were installed at Riverton, Pendleton County, and other places.

After about 1900, waterpower was harnessed for the production of electricity on several West Virginia rivers. These streams eventually included the Ohio, Cheat, Kanawha, Gauley, Potomac, Shenandoah, and New rivers. The state's oldest hydroelectric plant, at Glen Ferris on the Kanawha River, operated for more than a century before being shut down in 2002. Some dams were built specifically for the generation of electricity, including dams at Cheat Lake and at Hawks Nest on New River. In other cases, dams built primarily for navigation or flood control were later fitted for the production of hydroelectricity. A number of such projects were under way at the turn of the 21st century, although hydroelectricity still accounted for only a tiny fraction of electric power produced within the state.

See also Gristmills, Hydroelectricity, Jackson's Mill

Scot E. Long
Hebron, Ohio

Dave Gilbert, *Where Industry Failed: Water-Powered Mills at Harpers Ferry, West Virginia*, 1984; Michael Meador, "A Man and his Mill: Jim Wells Takes on the Greenville Mill," *Goldenseal*, Spring 1991; Michael Workman, "Low Tech: The Workings of a Water Mill," *Goldenseal*, Spring 1991.

Watoga Land Association

The Watoga Land Association was organized to offer African-Americans an opportunity to live among people of their race only. The separatist association was named for the community of Watoga, formerly a sawmill town, located on the Greenbrier River in southern Pocahontas County. There was a national black separatist movement in the early 1920s, led by Marcus Garvey and others. The Watoga planners may have been influenced by these ideas, although their effort seems to have been entirely a local one.

In 1921, a group from Mercer County organized the Watoga Land Association and purchased about 10,000 acres that had belonged to the Watoga Lumber Company. The site of the old sawmill town was laid off in streets and lots, and part of the cut-over timberland was divided into tracts of ten or more acres to be used for farming. A promotional article for the new town noted that blacks had built cities for others, but never a city for themselves. "Let us build us a City upon the earth," wrote the Reverend A. B. Farmer, a leader of the Watoga group.

A number of the lots and farm tracts were sold and the abandoned town reoccupied with stores, a school, and, briefly, a newspaper. However, the hopes of the Watoga Land Association for a large, viable, black community were never realized. The population was probably never more than 30 and by the late 1950s there

were no permanent residents. The reasons for the failure of the dream are not certain, but the unsuitability of the land for agriculture and the lack of other opportunities to make a living were factors, as was the isolation of the town.

Except for the town site, the association lands are now part of Watoga State Park and the Monongahela National Forest.

See also Watoga State Park

William P. McNeel
Marlinton

Watoga State Park

The largest of West Virginia's state parks, at 10,100 acres, Watoga is also among the oldest, dating back to the first land acquisitions by the West Virginia Game and Fish Commission in the 1920s. The park is located in southern Pocahontas County on the Greenbrier River. It was named for Watoga, a nearby town.

An initial 4,546 acres of former lumber company land was purchased from Watoga Land Association in January 1925 to create Watoga State Forest. The state purchased an additional 5,107 acres in August 1934 from the Maryland Lumber Company.

In 1926, a fire tower was erected. Two Civilian Conservation Corps camps were established, Camp Watoga in 1933 at the park's present maintenance area and Camp Seebert at the mouth of Island Lick Run in 1934. Also in 1934 Watoga was changed from a state forest to a state park. A third CCC camp, Camp Will Rogers, was opened in 1935. By the time the camps were closed (Seebert and Will Rogers in 1937 and Watoga in 1942), the CCC had constructed 22 cabins, a superintendent's residence, stable, restaurant-administration building, an 11-acre lake, horse and foot trails, 14 miles of roads, and a swimming pool. Deer, turkeys, raccoon, ducks, and pheasants raised at Watoga had been stocked in a seven-county area. An area for an arboretum was set aside in 1938 as a memorial to Fred E. Brooks (1868–1933), a noted naturalist.

Watoga State Park was opened to the public on July 1, 1937. Later improvements include eight additional cabins, a bathhouse, the first state park campground in West Virginia, a second campground, a recreation building, paved roads, water and sewer improvements, upgrading of the original cabins, and renovation of the arboretum.

The Civilian Conservation Corps legacy at Watoga and other state facilities is remembered in an annual CCC reunion at Watoga State Park, a museum, and a statue of a CCC enrollee.

See also Watoga Land Association

William P. McNeel
Marlinton

Clarence W. Watson

Clarence Wayland Watson, prominent coal baron and U.S. senator, was born in Fairmont, May 8, 1864, the third son of James Otis Watson and Matilda (Lamb) Watson. Clarence attended public schools in Fairmont and in 1886 graduated from Fairmont State Normal School, now Fairmont State University. In 1893, he joined his father and brothers in the family's mining enterprises.

In 1901, Clarence Watson combined the Watson mining properties with others in the Fairmont field to form the Fairmont Coal Company, which operated 28 mines and had 6,067 employees by 1902. In 1903, he played a leading role in the merger of the Fairmont Coal Company with the Consolidation Coal Company of Maryland, and was named president of the company at the time of the merger. In 1906, he headed a syndicate that purchased a majority share of the Consolidation stock. Serving as president or chairman of the board, Watson made Consolidation Coal the largest independent bituminous mining company in the nation by 1927. In 1928, he was forced out of the company, and nearly ruined by the Depression.

Watson was a Democrat who served in the U.S. Senate from 1911 to 1913, filling the unexpired term of Stephen B. Elkins. His brother-in-law, Aretas B. Fleming, was governor of West Virginia, 1890–93. In 1894, Watson married Minnie Lee Owings and moved into his father's mansion, La Grange, which he remodeled in the Spanish Mission style and renamed Fairmont Farms. Converted into apartments, the mansion still stands today. Watson bred race horses, had a private railroad car, and was an avid sportsman. He died May 24, 1940.

See also Consolidation Coal Company, Aretas Brooks Fleming, James O. Watson

Michael Edward Workman
WVU Institute for the History of Technology

Charles E. Beachley, *History of the Consolidation Coal Company 1864–1934*, 1934.

James O. Watson

Industrialist James Otis Watson, pioneer coal operator and businessman, was born May 17, 1815, at Benton's Ferry near Fairmont. The eldest son of Thomas and Rebecca Haymond Watson, James received instruction at home. He then operated a store, engaged in the cattle trade, started a brick works, and organized the construction of the Fairmont-Palatine suspension bridge. In 1852, he joined with future governor Francis H. Pierpont to open a mine in Fairmont, which exported the first coal from Western Virginia on the Baltimore & Ohio Railroad. In 1861, Watson served as a delegate to the Second Wheeling Convention, a key event in the founding of West Virginia.

After dissolving the Pierpont partner-

WATERPOWER / JAMES O. WATSON 747

ship in 1874, Watson joined his son-in-law, future governor Aretas B. Fleming, to open the Gaston mine near Fairmont. In 1886, the partners started the Montana mine, a great success which led to the opening of additional mines along the West Fork River. In 1901, the Watson mines were combined in a single corporation, the Fairmont Coal Company, the predecessor of industry giant Consolidation Coal.

A Democrat and Episcopalian, Watson built a mansion in Fairmont, La Grange, where he resided until his death, June 12, 1902. He married Matilda Lamb in 1841, and the couple had ten children. Three of his sons, James Edwin, Clarence Wayland, and Sylvanus Lamb, became prominent in the coal industry.

Son James Edwin Watson was born on January 8, 1859, at Fairmont. He learned the coal business at his father's Gaston mine, and managed the Watson coal interests until 1899. He also organized the Bank of Fairmont, and was a director of the Fairmont & Clarksburg Traction Company, the Fairmont Development Company, the Consolidation Coal Company, and other concerns. In 1909, James E. Watson built a large Tudor Revival mansion, High Gate, in Fairmont, where he resided until his death, August 2, 1926.

See also Consolidation Coal Company, Aretas Brooks Fleming, High Gate, Clarence W. Watson

Michael Edward Workman
WVU Institute for the History of Technology
James Otis Watson II, *The Valley Coal Story*, 1957; "The Fairmont Field," in Michael E. Workman, *Northern West Virginia Coal Fields: Historical Context*, 1994.

Watt Powell Park

Watt Powell Park in Charleston hosted professional baseball and all levels of amateur baseball, and some high school football games, for more than a half century after its opening on April 28, 1949. The city built the steel-and-concrete structure for $250,000 and named it for Walter B. (Watt) Powell, who died shortly before the park's opening. Powell, who grew up near Hot Springs, Virginia, had come to Charleston in 1915. He managed the Charleston Senators of the Class C Middle Atlantic League in the 1930s and ran the billiards room in the Kanawha Hotel downtown. It was Powell who convinced city officials to build a new ballpark. At the time, he worked as chief of the Division of State Parks and served on city council.

After its opening, Watt Powell Park was used for professional baseball every year except for the 1965–70 seasons and the 1984–86 seasons. In its early years, the park seated about 6,000 fans, but a reduction in the left field bleachers in the 1980s dropped capacity to about 5,000. Watt Powell Park occupied the former site of Kanawha Park, a 3,500-seat wooden structure built in 1917 to accommodate professional and amateur baseball. Kanawha Park burned in the 1940s.

On opening night in 1949, a crowd of about 8,000, including Governor Patteson, attended the city's inaugural game in the Class A Central League. Season attendance was 183,352. From 1952 through 1960, Charleston played in the Class AAA American Association, joined the AAA International League in 1961, and played in the Class A Eastern League from 1962 through 1964.

After a six-year absence from professional baseball, the park was given a refurbishing, making way for the city's return to the International League in 1971. The city continued in the I. L. through the 1983 season and in 1987 joined the Class A South Atlantic League, where it continues as a member. A favorite with generations of baseball fans who relished the cool evening breezes from nearby Mission Hollow, Watt Powell Park was replaced by the city's new Appalachian Power Park after the 2004 season. The old ballpark was demolished in 2005.

See also Baseball, Charleston

Mike Whiteford
Charleston Gazette

Watters Smith Memorial State Park

Watters Smith Memorial State Park, located in southern Harrison County, is a 532-acre historical park established through the generosity of the descendants of Watters Smith, a pioneer who settled there in the 1790s.

The park's initial 278-acre parcel, which included Watters Smith's original 112 acres, was donated to the state in 1949 upon the death of Burr Smith of Lost Creek. The bequest included land plus $50,000, the interest to be used for the park's upkeep and maintenance. The West Virginia Conservation Commission assumed control of the tract of land. In accordance with Smith's will, a memorial was erected on the site of Watters Smith's pioneer cabin on Duck Creek.

In 1975, the park expanded, thanks to Rachel Smith Hershey, another descendant of Watters Smith. She willed her farm to the park, 254 acres adjacent to Burr Smith's tract, along with several homes and their furnishings. The houses were sold and some of the furnishings are displayed in the Smith Family Residence Museum, the cabin built in 1876 by "Uncle Doc" Smith, replacing the original Watters Smith cabin. A sizable collection of antique glass is on display in the cabin museum, with early farm artifacts located in the visitors center museum and other buildings on the property.

Since its inception, in addition to the establishment of a museum and other historical outbuildings, the park has grown to include picnic areas, a swimming pool, concession stands, playgrounds, parking areas, the superintendent's house, and a log cabin relocated from Beech Fork State Park.

Debra K. Sullivan
Charleston Catholic High School

Wayne

Wayne, the county seat of Wayne County, is located on Twelvepole Creek at the junction of State Routes 37 and 152 at an elevation of 707 feet. Founded in 1842, the town came into existence at the same time as the county. The act of the Virginia General Assembly that created the county also established a place for holding court on the land of Abraham Trout. The first county government met February 24, 1842, at Trout's home.

Trout later deeded one acre on which to build a courthouse, and the town was first called Trout's Hill. It was incorporated as Fairview in 1882, but was alternately called Wayne Courthouse until 1911 when the name was officially changed to Wayne. Both the town and county were named for General "Mad Anthony" Wayne, a hero of the American Revolution and the Indian wars.

Situated near the center of the county and away from the more populous areas near Huntington, Wayne town has remained small. Its population was 1,105 in 2000. Wayne has a nonpartisan government consisting of a mayor, recorder, police judge, and a five-member council. The town clerk is appointed by council and the police chief is appointed by the mayor. Wayne is served by a branch library, a volunteer fire department, and a community park.

See also Wayne County

Tim R. Massey
Wayne

Anthony Wayne

General "Mad Anthony" Wayne (1745–96) commanded the American army that defeated the Indians at Fallen Timbers in 1794. He also played a leading role in negotiating the Treaty of Greenville in 1795 that ceded most of Ohio to the United States and ended the frontier era for Western Virginia.

Wayne, born in Pennsylvania, joined the Continental army, saw his first service in early 1776 and fought throughout the war. He then served under Nathaniel Greene in Georgia in 1781 and 1782 against the Creeks and Cherokees, his first action against Native Americans. Wayne represented Georgia in the House of Representatives from 1791 to 1792. His seat was declared vacant due to irregularities, and he declined to run again.

Meanwhile, President Washington and his cabinet, shocked by disastrous defeats of the American army by the northwestern Indians, convinced Congress to establish a larger and better organized army.

The president and his cabinet passed over Virginians Richard Henry "Lighthorse Harry" Lee and Daniel Morgan and selected Wayne, the most available of the senior revolutionary army officers, to command this newly created "legion." Wayne, although nicknamed "Mad" for his sometimes daring ways, conducted a lengthy and cautious campaign that ended with his victory at Fallen Timbers. Wayne County is named for General Wayne, who died in December 1796.

See also Battle of Fallen Timbers, Treaty of Greenville

Van Beck Hall
Pittsburgh, Pennsylvannia
Paul David Nelson, *Anthony Wayne: Soldier of the Early Republic*, 1985.

Wayne County

Wayne County was established January 18, 1842, from part of Cabell County. It was named for General "Mad Anthony" Wayne, a Revolutionary War hero who later defeated Ohio Indian tribes at the 1794 Battle of Fallen Timbers. Wayne County lies in the juncture of two of West Virginia's major rivers, the Big Sandy and the Ohio. The county occupies 517.9 square miles.

Wayne town is the county seat. Originally called Trout's Hill, the town was incorporated as Fairview in 1882 and the name changed to Wayne in 1911.

Although the southern half of the county was first to be settled, it remained sparsely populated and was slow to develop. The northern part, bordering Cabell County, expanded rapidly after the Civil War. Huntington was founded as the western terminus of the Chesapeake & Ohio Railroad in 1871 and in 1921 expanded its corporate limits westward into Wayne County.

Wayne County participated fully in the bustling post-Civil War history of the Big Sandy Valley. Steamboats plied the river on their way to headwaters towns as far east as Pikeville, Kentucky, while unpowered boats served points even farther upstream. Log drives carried the timber of three states down the Big Sandy to the Ohio River during the late 19th and early 20th centuries. The main line of the Norfolk & Western Railway was completed through Wayne County to its terminus at Kenova in 1890, and the railroad bridge across the Ohio was built two years later.

The area south of Wayne town experienced a growth spurt near the turn of the 20th century, after the Norfolk & Western Railway was completed and mining and timbering boomed in communities from East Lynn to Crum. There was a move to create a separate county that would have been called Clark or Wilson, with the county seat at Dunlow. The idea was opposed by residents in Wayne town and the northern towns of Ceredo and Kenova, and it eventually died. Another debate developed in the early 1920s when people in the north proposed to move the county seat to the Ceredo-Kenova area. A special election failed to get the required two-thirds majority.

Wayne County's population tripled from 7,852 in 1870 to 23,619 in 1900. Blessed with an abundant supply of coal, natural gas, and timber, the county population rose to a peak of 46,021 in 1980. In 2000, Wayne County had 42,903 residents.

In addition to its portion of Huntington and the town of Wayne, the county has three other incorporated communities, Fort Gay, Ceredo, and Kenova. Fort Gay, located where the Tug and Levisa forks meet to form the Big Sandy, was the first permanent settlement in Wayne County, about 1800. The town was chartered in 1875 as Cassville, and the name changed to Fort Gay in 1932.

Ceredo was founded in 1857 as an antislavery experiment by a group headed by Eli Thayer, a congressman from Massachusetts. Ceredo was the site of a Union stronghold, Fort Pierpont, during the Civil War. It was incorporated in 1866.

Kenova, located in the point between the Ohio and the Big Sandy rivers, is the westernmost town in West Virginia. It was founded in 1889 and chartered in 1894. The name is formed from the names of the three states that neighbor each other there, Kentucky, Ohio, and West Virginia. Kenova was a crossroads for competing railroads, the Baltimore & Ohio, the Chesapeake & Ohio, and the Norfolk & Western. At one time in the 1950s, it was said to have more trains passing through than any other place in America.

Wayne County has always been known for its strong family ties. A once-popular saying was that the county is "owned by the Frys, run by the Fergusons, and populated by the Adkinses." The Fry family, which was headed by state legislator Lucian Fry, acquired several thousand acres of coal and timber in southern Wayne County. The Ferguson family has long been prominent at the county courthouse. Charles W. Ferguson II (1892–1976) was circuit judge from 1928 to 1967, and his son, C. W. Ferguson III (1920–95), succeeded him, serving until 1984. Milton J. Ferguson, the brother of the elder judge and a U.S. attorney, was responsible for prosecuting Governor Barron and members of his administration. A Democrat who had served in Governor Marland's administration, Ferguson ran unsuccessfully for governor in his party's primary in 1956.

Other prominent Wayne County names include Maynard, Perry, Ross, Napier, and

FAST FACTS ABOUT WAYNE COUNTY

Founded: 1842
Land in square miles: 517.9
Population: 42,903
Percentage minorities: 1.2%
Percentage rural: 61.4%
Median age: 38.4
Percentage 65 and older: 14.9%
Birth rate per 1,000 population: 11.5
Median household income: $27,352
High school graduate or higher: 70.5%
Bachelor's degree or higher: 11.9%
Home ownership: 78.1%
Median home value: $70,900

This information is from the 2000 U.S. Census. In 2000, West Virginia as a whole had 5 percent minorities, a median age of 38.9, median household income of $29,696, and a 75.2 percent home ownership rate.

Camden Park's Big Dipper roller coaster, a Wayne County favorite.

Vinson. Sam Vinson (1833–1904) owned most of the land that became Westmoreland, the Wayne County section of Huntington. His son-in-law, Jim Hughes, was a congressman. His son, Zachary Taylor Vinson, was a well-known lawyer, and his daughter, Mary Vinson Clark, was instrumental in building Vinson High School.

Wayne County is the birthplace of the contemporary Christian singer and composer Michael W. Smith, football player Buzz Nutter, and major league pitcher Donnie Robinson. Fanny Belle Fleming, better known as Blaze Starr, a nightclub stripper in Baltimore and one-time paramour of Louisiana Gov. Earl Long, is a native Wayne Countian.

The largest companies operating in the county include Ashland Chemical Co., Sunoco Chemical, Hamer Lumber, Rockspring Development, Pen Coal Company, and Kanawha River Terminal. Wayne County has a variety of recreational areas, including Beech Fork State Park and Beech Fork Lake, East Lynn Lake, and Cabwaylingo State Forest. It also is home of Camden Park near Huntington, which is West Virginia's only surviving amusement park.

See also Ceredo, Huntington, Wayne

Tim R. Massey
Wayne

Stephen Lewis, *An Overview of the History of Wayne County,* 1997; Mildred Taylor, *History of Wayne County, West Virginia,* 1963.

WCHS

WCHS in Charleston is the third-oldest radio station in the state. The AM station went on the air as WOBU, September 15, 1927, with 50 watts at 1120 kHz. A year later it moved to 580 kHz, its present frequency, where it shared time until 1933 with WSAZ (now WRVC) in Huntington.

Walter Fredericks, owner of Charleston Radio Supply Company, started WCHS, reportedly to sell more radios. Fredericks sold the station in 1930. The call letters had changed to WCHS by early 1933, and seven years later the station was authorized to increase power to its present 5,000 watts. Early local performers included country musicians Bill Cox and the Kessinger Brothers. The *Old Farm Hour* program broadcast live country music on Friday nights from the WCHS Auditorium.

WCHS is a long-time affiliate of the CBS Radio Network. By the 1960s, network offerings were being replaced by local programming, mostly adult contemporary music, with an emphasis on news and information. Sports programming has included Cincinnati Reds baseball, high school and West Virginia University football and basketball, and the long-running *Sports Page of the Air* program, hosted for many years by Ernie Saunders.

WCHS-TV, Channel 8, was launched in 1954, and is now independent of the radio station, with separate owners. WCHS-FM (now WKWS) went on the air in 1969. West Virginia Radio Corporation acquired the station in 1992 and launched the current program format of national and local news, talk, and sports. The station's long-time location at 1111 Virginia Street East now houses facilities for the company's seven radio stations in the Charleston market.

Ed McDonald
Keyser

The Weather

The Appalachian Mountains play a big part in both the climate and daily weather of West Virginia. Elevation is the key factor in the average temperature and rain and snow variations within the state. On a daily cycle, the mountains can disrupt and weaken, or trigger and strengthen, various weather elements. Some of the heaviest rains and deepest snows have occurred in the Potomac Highland counties of Pendleton, Hampshire, and Hardy, despite this normally being one of the driest areas of the state.

West Virginia's location on the North American continent makes it susceptible to changeable weather, especially from late autumn into early spring. During this time of the year, air masses from the warm and moist Gulf of Mexico region frequently battle with the cold air from the interior of Canada, often clashing over or near West Virginia. Typically, these contrasting conditions oscillate back and forth during the winter season. It can be 65 degrees on a winter day, then snow several inches the next day. The average state temperature for the whole winter season, calculated from all the daily high and low readings, has varied from the mid-20s to the lower 40s.

Occasionally, the upper air currents settle into a stable direction for several weeks. The persistent wind from the northwest during the winter of 1976–77 led to several snowfalls and West Virginia's coldest month on record, January 1977. Terra Alta in Preston County measured 104 inches of snowfall that month, a state record. Other winters that saw prolonged cold include 1894–95, 1903–04, 1904–05, 1917–18, 1935–36, 1962–63, and 1977–78. In those years, snow cover lingered for weeks, rivers froze over, heating costs skyrocketed, transportation was curtailed, and schools closed for many days.

The coldest official temperature on record in West Virginia occurred during one of those winters. The thermometer dropped to 37 degrees below zero at Lewisburg on December 30, 1917. More recently, shorter periods of severe cold occurred in December 1989 and January 1994. In contrast were the extremely mild winters of 1889–90 and 1931–32, when a southwest wind prevailed. Trees were leafing out along the river valleys by February during those years. Communities in the lower elevations often go through mild winters without using their snow shovels. The most snow to fall from a single storm was 57 inches at Pickens during the great post-Thanksgiving storm of 1950. The most snow in a 24-hour period was 35 inches. This happened at Flat Top, on the Mercer-Raleigh county line, on January 27–28, 1998.

During the cold months, when the vegetation is dormant, widespread flooding may occur. This type of flood usually occurs when prolonged rains fall over saturated ground. Snow melt often adds to the runoff. The frequency and severity of river flooding peaked during the late 1800s and the first half of the 20th century. Widespread logging was a direct contributor to that increase in river flooding. Flood control efforts, including dams and flood walls, decreased flooding on many rivers during the last half of the 20th century. Yet, major floods still occurred, including those of November 1985 and January 1996. The Upper Ohio Valley, including Wheeling, was flooded in September 2004.

In sharp contrast to river flooding is the localized cloudburst that may flood only an isolated small creek or hollow. These are the true flash floods. They usually happen during the warm season, May through September. A stationary thunderstorm, or a train of storms passing over the same stream basin, can dump four to eight inches of rain in less than two hours. The affected creeks may rise several feet in minutes. Steep slopes can actually liquefy during these downpours, causing mud, rocks, and even trees to slide down a hillside. The increased urbanization of the state causes faster runoff into once rural streams.

The radar system operated by the National Weather Service can estimate rainfall anywhere in the state. These radars can sense small intense rotation within a thunderstorm, the key ingredient for tornado formation. Large hail can also be inferred from radar data. A network of automatic and manual rain and river gauges are positioned about the state. Nowadays, it's rare for even a flash flood to occur without some advance alert.

Droughts quietly develop over several months and typically last between one and two years. Surface water supply and wells can dry up. Major droughts came during 1894–95, 1930–31, 1953–54, 1963–64, 1965–66, 1987–88, and 1998–99. In 1930, only 9.5 inches of precipitation fell for the entire year at Upper Tract in Pendleton County. Some of the hottest temperatures have occurred during droughts. The hottest state temperature was 112 degrees. It occurred twice, once at Moorefield on August 4, 1930, then at Martinsburg on July 10, 1936.

See also Climate, Flood of 1985, Floods

Kenneth T. Batty
National Weather Service

Weaving

Even after the introduction of power looms in the 1830s, much of the fabric used by West Virginians was made at home. Items commonly produced included plain twill blankets, napkins, dish towels, clothing material, and bed coverlets. Coverlets are distinguished by their patterned overshot weave and have become prized heirlooms. Imaginatively named according to their patterns, coverlets are woven according to notation called drafts. These drafts, which look like musical notation and are often undecipherable to the uninitiated, indicate how the threads are to be set up on the loom. Handmade coverlets and other large pieces are always seamed, as the hand looms could not produce work more than about a yard wide.

Weaving was common in rural households throughout the state. The old handmade looms, generally constructed of unfinished lumber or even logs, were sturdy and well-suited to making heavier pieces, such as rag rugs. Such looms had sufficient weight to press the fibers tightly together, making a stiff rug that would lie flat and wear well.

Home weavers used cotton, wool, and, less commonly, flax in their weaving. Often children were recruited to card wool, or to tear rags into strips and sew them into lengths for their mother to weave. Sometimes children would help install the warp, or longitudinal threads, which required walking the length of the finished piece as many times as required for the desired width. The woof or weft, or cross threads, was added as the weaving proceeded.

Often the same household would raise the sheep; prepare the wool; and spin, dye, and weave it. Or wool might be acquired by purchase or barter from others. Sometimes spun thread was bought or traded for from a neighbor, perhaps for a share of the finished weaving. Cotton, which could not be grown in West Virginia, was purchased in bales of raw fiber at local stores. Some flax was grown to make linen, or to mix with wool for linsey-woolsey, despite the elaborate process required to prepare the flax fiber.

Whether wool, cotton, or flax, the fiber was spun into thread on a spinning wheel. Fibers might be dyed before spinning (thus the term, "dyed in the wool") or after it was made into thread. Natural dyes were made from pokeberry for a soft red; walnut hulls and bark for browns; marigolds for yellows; and ragweed for green. Colorfast commercial dyes were available and commonly used by the late 19th century.

Skillful itinerant weavers traveled from house to house in some areas, although this does not seem to have been a common practice in West Virginia. Such weavers used a family's own thread and loom, applying their superior skill to the work of weaving. Other weavers wove at their own homes for a fee or barter, using thread already dyed and spun by their customers.

The speed of the power loom, introduced about 1835, put some production handweavers, such as the Sloan family at Romney, out of business. Water-powered weaving mills were established at different places in Western Virginia, including Riverton in Pendleton County. The Goodwin family operated a weaving mill at Hollywood, Greenbrier County, in the late 1800s. A cousin of this family, Olive Goodwin, taught many people to weave before her death near Elkins in the 1990s.

Weaving classes were offered at the three federal homestead projects established in West Virginia as part of Franklin Roosevelt's New Deal during the Great Depression. These projects were at Arthurdale, Eleanor, and Tygart Valley, near Elkins. Eventually some of the looms were sold to women who had taken to the craft, and who continued weaving and went on to teach others.

Though no longer necessary as a home industry, weaving remains a mountain craft with a rich heritage. It is practiced today to a high level of perfection by many craftspeople. There are several guilds active in the state, and the Augusta Heritage organization in Elkins introduces new people each year to the craft while giving experienced weavers an opportunity to refine their knowledge and skills.

Kirsten Milligan
Weston

Allen H. Eaton, *Handicrafts of the Southern Highlands*, 1937; Kathleen Curtis Wilson, *Textile Art from Southern Appalachia: the Quiet Work of Women*, 2001.

Webster County

Webster County was created in 1860 from parts of Braxton, Nicholas, and Randolph counties. Named for Daniel Webster, the county occupies 558.6 square miles and is drained by the Elk, Gauley, Williams, Cranberry, Holly, and Little Kanawha rivers. The county seat is Webster Springs.

The earliest white settler was most likely Adam Stroud, who settled about 1769 near present Camden-on-Gauley on a tributary of the Gauley River now known as Strouds Creek. Three years later Stroud's family was destroyed by Indians. At about the same time, a Carpenter family sought refuge on Camp Creek from an Indian raid in what is now neighboring Braxton County. Solomon Carpenter, probably the first white child born in Webster County, was born on Camp Creek under a shelf-like cliff during this episode, an event commemorated in the traditional West Virginia fiddle tune, "Shelvin' Rock." Due to the remoteness of the area, the scarcity of tillable land, the ruggedness of terrain ranging in elevation from 1,000 feet to almost 4,000 feet, and the fear of Indians, few settlers followed until the end of the 18th century.

Since Webster County was created just before the outbreak of the Civil War, organization of the county government did not occur for several years. During this time, there was no government in the county and no taxes were collected. This lack of regular government gave birth to the so-called "Independent State of Webster," which had its own "governor" by the name of George Sawyer. In 1865, at the end of the Civil War, the formal organizing of Webster County took place, and

---

FAST FACTS ABOUT WEBSTER COUNTY

Founded: 1860
Land in square miles: 558.6
Population: 9,719
Percentage minorities: 0.8%
Percentage rural: 100%
Median age: 40.4
Percentage 65 and older: 15.2%
Birth rate per 1,000 population: 10.9
Median household income: $21,055
High school graduate or higher: 58.2%
Bachelor's degree or higher: 8.7%
Home ownership: 79.0%
Median home value: $47,500

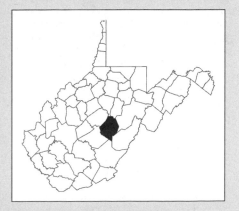

This information is from the 2000 U.S. Census. In 2000, West Virginia as a whole had 5 percent minorities, a median age of 38.9, median household income of $29,696, and a 75.2 percent home ownership rate.

A bird hunter and his dog check the brush in Webster County.

for religious, social, and institutional groups.

There were no public schools when Webster County was created in 1860. In September 1910, the first high school was opened in Webster Springs. Later, a high school was built in Cowen. In the 1970s, these high schools were consolidated into a single high school near Upper Glade.

Webster County's population peaked at 18,080 in 1940. The years following World War II saw a decline of coal industry employment and a migration of Webster Countians to factory towns in Ohio and elsewhere. This decline continued until 1970, when the county's population dropped below 10,000. The population was 9,719 in the year 2000.

With the increased interest in outdoor recreation and the construction of dams at nearby Summersville and Sutton, Webster County has become a popular destination. Since 1960, Webster County has been the site of the Woodchopping Festival. It is also the site of the Point Mountain Reunion, formerly called the Hamrick, Gregory, and Riggleman Reunion, held in August of each year.

Prominent Webster Countians include Arden Cogar (1934–), world champion woodchopper, and Eli C. "Rimfire" Hamrick (1868–1945), a renown guide and woodsman. Twin brothers Hubert (1909–69) and Hobert Skidmore (1909–46) were noted authors, Hubert producing *Hawks Nest*, the classic West Virginia novel.

See also Camp Caesar, Rimfire Hamrick, Hubert Skidmore, Webster Springs

E. Lynn Miller
Gilbert, Arizona

William C. Dodrill, *Moccasin Tracks and Other Imprints*, 1974.

Webster County Woodchopping Festival

The annual Webster County Woodchopping Festival celebrates the mountain area's timbering heritage. Each Memorial Day weekend, lumbermen from the United States and other countries participate in woodchopping and sawing events. The Webster County festival is one of three world championship woodchopping competitions.

Webster County native Arden Cogar Sr., who began competing in woodchopping events in 1956 and has won championship titles in the United States and Australia, organized the first Webster County Woodchopping Festival in 1960. Held in various places in the county in its early years, the festival was moved to its permanent location at Bakers Island Recreation Area in Webster Springs in 1965.

Cogar was the all-around champion of the Webster County Woodchopping Festival six times from 1973 to 1980. Another

county and district officials were elected. The population in 1860 was 1,555.

In the 1890s, a branch of the Baltimore & Ohio Railroad was built to the town of Cowen from Flatwoods, Braxton County. In the early 1900s, the West Virginia Midland Railroad Company built a narrow-gauge line to Webster Springs. Within a few years rails were laid through much of the county, serving the mines and sawmills. The first two decades of the 20th century were boom years for Webster County. Tourists came on the railroad to partake of the waters of the salt sulfur springs, and the coal and timber industries produced a vibrant economy. The Webster Springs Hotel was built in 1896 and enlarged in 1904. More than 11,000 people lived in Webster County by 1920.

The county had vast resources of timber and 19 seams of coal. The main employer for the timber and coal was the Pardee & Curtin Lumber Company. By the beginning of the 1940s, the timber industry was in decline, but coal mining boomed during World War II. Commercial mining had started in 1917, with an output of approximately 100,000 tons by 1929 and more than two million tons at the end of World War II. In 2004, 3.9 million tons of coal was produced in Webster County, mostly from surface mines.

The remoteness and ruggedness that had limited settlement also resulted in the preservation of areas of great scenic beauty with majestic hills and clear flowing streams. A large portion of the county is in the Monongahela National Forest. During the Roosevelt administration, several thousand acres of land near Hacker Valley was purchased by the federal Resettlement Administration, later transferred to the state, and is now Holly River State Park. In the 1920s along the Gauley River, the county established Camp Caesar, a 4-H camp which has become an important summer destination champion is Melvin Lentz, also of Webster County, who achieved the honor in 1982, 1985, 1988, and yearly from 1990 to 1994. New Zealander Jason Wynyard won the championship in 2002 and 2003, and in 2004 and 2005 it was taken by residents of New York state.

The festival has grown to include a week's worth of events, including arts and crafts, concerts, parades, car shows, a lumberjack breakfast, a 5K Run, and fireworks, but it is the Memorial Day weekend lumberjack contests that remain the highlight. Competition categories include the Jack and Jill cross cut, two-man cross cut, hot saw, solo chain saw, standing block, handicap chop, springboard chop, championship chop, and all-around champion.

See also Webster Springs

Webster Springs

Webster Springs is the county seat of Webster County. The town lies in a valley at the end of Point Mountain, at the confluence of the Back Fork and Elk River and at the junction of State Routes 15 and 20.

The saline springs, long used as a source of salt by Indians and as a salt lick by wildlife, was discovered in 1782 by early settlers John McQuirter and John Miller Sr. when they claimed a large tract of land near the site of the present town. The first permanent settler was Polly Arthur in 1860. Although the community was originally named Fork Lick, it was incorporated as Addison in 1892 in honor of Addison McLaughlin, who donated the land for the county courthouse. Since 1902, the town has been known by its postal address of Webster Springs.

The reputed medicinal qualities of the spring water attracted many visitors, and in 1890 a springhouse was constructed to provide greater access to the springs. A hotel was built about 1896 by industrialist and U.S. Sen. Johnson N. Camden and expanded into a truly grand structure by John T. McGraw by 1904. Meanwhile, a narrow-gauge railroad arrived in 1902. With ready access and fine accommodations, Webster Springs became a summer resort.

In 1926, the Webster Springs Hotel was destroyed by fire, and in 1929 the railroad was discontinued, ending a decades-long tourist boom. Webster Springs continued as the center for business activities related to the coal and timber industries as well as the government activities of the county seat, but with the loss of mining jobs in the mid-20th century the town lost much of its population. Webster Springs had 808 residents in 2000.

See also Webster County, Webster County Woodchopping Festival

E. Lynn Miller
Gilbert, Arizona

Sampson Newton Miller, *Annals of Webster County, West Virginia, Before and Since Organization, 1860,* 1969.

Webster Sycamore

West Virginia's biggest tree, a magnificent sycamore, stands along the banks of the Back Fork of Elk River, in Webster County about five miles from the town of Webster Springs. Foresters estimate its age at 350 years or more.

Also known as the American plane tree, sycamores are the largest trees native to West Virginia. Local legend says the Webster sycamore was passed by early lumbermen out of respect for its size, but perhaps it was spared because sycamore was not a valuable lumber tree or because of the lack of machinery to handle a tree of its size. The lowest limbs are more than 40 feet from the ground, and in the 1950s two hemlock trees, one 14 feet tall and one seven feet tall, were growing out of one of its dead limbs. The sycamore is estimated to be 112 feet in height, with a circumference of more than 309 inches, and a crown spread of 90 feet. While not the tallest tree in West Virginia, it receives the most points for combined height, circumference, and spread on a scale used by foresters to calculate tree size.

The sycamore, a local landmark, is the starting point for the 5K Run, which is held each year during the Webster County Woodchopping Festival. Unfortunately, the big tree, troubled by disease and recent vandalism and arson, is now considered in danger.

See also Trees

E. Lynn Miller
Gilbert, Arizona

Wedding Customs

Numerous traditional activities were practiced in West Virginia at the home of the new bride and groom on their wedding night. These widespread community practices are most often referred to as "serenade" or "serenading." Other common and historical names for the antics and social gatherings supporting the customs include "chivaree," "belling," "infare" and "wedding frolic," with the latter two more related to the gathering itself. The "race for the bottle," in older times, is another well-documented wedding custom once practiced in West Virginia.

These rituals appear to stem from Old World customs ("chivaree" comes from the French *charivari*), with most recent wedding practices being considerably more moderate than those of earlier times. Among the Scotch-Irish, for instance, the bride was physically abducted by the groom. Mock abductions continue, however, and may be found in the "serenade" customs of recent times. But most serenading customs in recent practice and memory involve the disruption

of the couple's wedding night through mischief and fun involving relatives and the community.

Typically, the bride and groom were treated to a barrage of raucous noise, in an attempt to coax them from the house. The racket might be made with cowbells, by shooting guns, detonating small charges of dynamite, banging pots and pans, and using other ingenious devices to produce harsh noise. In Braxton County, a wire was stretched from the house to a tree, rosined, and played like a giant annoying fiddle. In Randolph, a wooden box with a crank caused clappers inside to produce a loud staccato sound. Large circular saws and plow disks become noisemakers when hung on a wire and banged.

In some instances in eastern West Virginia, if the couple failed to emerge in response to the rowdy serenade, forced entry to the house was made and they were brought out. Whenever and however the couple was eventually induced outside, various misdeeds (often alluding to procreation) were carried out at the expense of the new couple. Most often, the groom is ridden on a rail. In Tucker County, a rail has been maintained through many generations in one neighborhood with the initials of all the grooms who have endured the experience carved into its length. Brides have been set in a tub of ice water and carried about. Grooms have been made to cart their new wives through town in a wheelbarrow. In Pendleton County, a couple was taken quite a ways down a muddy road, their shoes taken, and made to walk home.

Gerald Milnes
Augusta Heritage Center

Weeds

A weed is a plant growing where it is not wanted. Often a plant becomes a weed when it is brought from one place and introduced in another, becoming an exotic nuisance. This process began early in North American history and continues to the present. European colonists brought essential herbs with them. By the late 1600s, two of these, dandelion and wild carrot, were naturalized. Much later, Japanese honeysuckle was considered a lovely vine for the home garden, but it wouldn't stay behind the fence. Kudzu was first imported as a forage crop for cattle in the southern states and was once advertised as having more potential than cotton. Multiflora rose, sold as a living fence, is now one of our greatest pests.

In 1890 and 1892, C. F. Millspaugh, a botanist at West Virginia University, published three Agricultural Experiment Station bulletins on West Virginia's weeds. The second contained a list of the 25 worst weeds plus 25 others for a secondary list. It also contained botanical descriptions and ecological observations.

The "worst" list started with ox-eye daisy and followed in order with broomsedge, pasture thistle, burdock, bitterdock, wild carrot, elderberry, ironweed, yarrow, buck plantain, cockle-bur, blue thistle, ragweed, Spanish needles, whitetop, sand-briar, sorrel, wild garlic, white devil, blue devil, Canada thistle, morning glory, wild sweet potato, dog fennel, and cinquefoil. Twelve of the worst 25 were imports from Europe, one was from tropical America, and 12 were natives that had adopted the open soil of cultivated fields.

In 1975, a botanist from the state Department of Agriculture resurveyed the state's weeds. This resulted in roughly the same 50 except that wingstem, black-eyed Susan, and crabgrass had moved from the lower 25 into the top 25 and nine newly introduced weeds were found to be doing as much damage to the state's ecosystems as all 50 of the earlier ones. The nine were kudzu, multiflora rose, autumn olive, tree of heaven, Japanese honeysuckle, Japanese knotweed, coltsfoot, mile-a-minute, and purple loosestrife.

William H. Gillespie
Charleston

Ralph Weinberg

Music promoter Ralph Weinberg, born in Baltimore in 1895, moved to Bluefield after marrying Ida Effron in 1923. During the second quarter of the 20th century, Weinberg brought some of the greatest performers in the country to Bluefield and southern West Virginia. They included Fats Waller, Cab Calloway, Fats Domino, Edward "Duke" Ellington, and Frank Sinatra when he was with the Tommy Dorsey Band. Jazzman Louis Jordan's hit song, "Saltpork, West Virginia," was about a run-in Jordan had had with a Bluefield justice of the peace, Wallace W. "Squire" McNeal.

Weinberg lived in Princeton and worked out of Bluefield's Matz Hotel, promoting entertainment events throughout a wide region. He promoted sports, including boxing and wrestling, as well as music. Weinberg's Danceland Attractions provided a vital and safe conduit for African-American performers to reach audiences through the South. He established a network of theaters and dance halls and booked concert dates as far west as Texas and as far south as Birmingham. His friends recall that a young Abe Saperstein once offered him part ownership of his Harlem Globetrotters if he would handle their bookings in the South.

For the great black bands of that time, Weinberg, himself white, roped off a section where white patrons could come and enjoy the music, but the dance floor and bandstands were strictly reserved for black performers and black audiences. His concerts were noted for good music, good times, and no racial friction.

Weinberg was on a promotional visit to Columbia, South Carolina, when he died of a heart attack, April 3, 1953.

William R. Archer
Bluefield

Weirton

Weirton, located in southern Hancock and northern Brooke counties, is an industrial city dominated by Weirton Steel Company, once the largest private employer in West Virginia and the state's first billion-dollar corporation.

Incorporated in 1947, Weirton included the former communities of Hollidays Cove, Marland Heights, Weirton Heights, and Weirton. The town was named for E. T. Weir, the founder of Weirton Steel. Weirton had grown up with the steel mill, but it had previously remained unincorporated. For many years before incorporation, municipal services were provided by the Weirton Improvement Company, a subsidiary of Weirton Steel. Some of these services continued until the 1950s.

Weirton was a one-company town, but never a company town in the way many mining towns were in southern West Virginia, where the coal companies owned the entire community. Weirton Steel did own some housing, but those were barrack-like structures for unmarried men in the earliest years of the mill, before World War I. Nonetheless, the connection of company and town was close. Weirton's first mayor, Thomas Millsop, was president of Weirton Steel and later president of its successor, National Steel.

Weirton developed rapidly following the building of the steel mill in 1909. Where there had been fields of grain and orchards of fruit in 1909, Weirton became an industrial center of 8,000 people by 1920 and 18,000 by 1940. The steelworkers represented many nationalities from Europe, plus some from the Middle East, as well as a large number of African-Americans.

In its first decade after incorporation, the city built the Weirton Community Center, Weirton General Hospital, and the Mary H. Weir Library. Weirton's population peaked in 1960 at 28,201. Into the mid-1970s, Weirton reaped the blessings of the 12,000 well-paid jobs at Weirton Steel. Its citizens enjoyed one of the state's highest per capita income levels and highest percentage of home ownership.

The economic malaise of the 1970s affected Weirton, leading to a population drop to 24,736 by 1980. After National Steel sold the Weirton plant to its employees in 1984, employment at the mill and population of the city continued to drop; in 1990 Weirton's population stood at 22,124, and at 20,411 in 2000.

See also Weirton Steel

David T. Javersak
West Liberty State College
David T. Javersak, *History of Weirton, West Virginia*, 1999.

Weirton Steel

Industrialist Ernest T. Weir (1875–1957), who was born in Pittsburgh and died there, founded Phillips Sheet & Tin Plate in Clarksburg in 1905 with J. A. Phillips. After the death of Phillips, Weir moved the company to a farm just north of the village of Hollidays Cove in southern Hancock County, the site of present Weirton. On August 1, 1918, Weir's 43rd birthday, the company was renamed Weirton Steel Company.

Weir created an integrated steel mill that became West Virginia's largest employer, the state's largest taxpayer, and the world's largest tin plate producer. He created a town around his mill, and for years his Weirton Improvement Company provided Weirton's sewers, water service, garbage pickup, and other municipal services. In 1927, he took over as the chief executive officer of National Steel, of which Weirton Steel formed the keystone. In the 1930s, Weir defied Franklin Roosevelt's National Recovery Administration and National Labor Relations Board and kept national unions from organizing his mills.

Weirton Steel joined in the national recovery following the Great Depression. It converted to wartime production during World War II, producing howitzer shells and other munitions and contributing to the atom bomb project. The company shared the steel industry prosperity of the post-war years, but began to suffer the effects of foreign competition by the 1960s. Weirton modernized production during the decade but lagged behind European and Japanese producers in this regard.

During the 1970s, the American steel industry fell upon depressed times. On March 2, 1982, National Steel announced that subsidiary Weirton Steel would close unless a buyer came forward. When no corporate buyer materialized, Weirton steelworkers undertook a campaign to purchase the plant under an Employee Stock Ownership Plan or ESOP. Various constituent groups, political leaders, management, and labor joined in the innovative effort.

A plan was developed by which Weirton Steel bought the plant and its raw materials and inventory from National Steel. In September 1983, Weirton's workers approved the deal by a margin of seven to one, and in January 1984 ownership was transferred to the employees. Under the plan, the workers gave back 32 percent of their wages. All pensions before 1982 re-

Pouring molten steel at Weirton, 1970s.

the company was purchased by the International Steel Group. In 2005, International Steel sold the company to Mittal Steel of the Netherlands, which soon announced layoffs at Weirton.

See also Steel Industry, Weirton

David T. Javersak
West Liberty State College

James B. Lieber, *Friendly Takeover: How An Employee Buyout Saved a Steel Town*, 1995; John D. Ubinger, "Ernest Tener Weir: Last of the Great Steelmasters," *Western Pennsylvania Historical Magazine*, July 1975.

Weirton-Steubenville Bridge

See Cable-Stayed Bridges.

Welch

Welch, the county seat of McDowell County, is located at the confluence of Elkhorn Creek and the Tug Fork. In 1858, the first county seat was situated at Perryville, and later it was moved to other towns. In 1891, 33 years after McDowell County was created, the county seat was located at Welch.

The local topography consists of steep hills, V-shaped valleys, and sharp ridges. Welch is tucked into this rugged terrain, with the town built on the narrow valley floor of the Tug Fork and its tributaries and less than 1,000 feet wide in places. In the early 1800s, the area was settled by hunters largely from central Virginia, eastern Kentucky, and western North Carolina. In 1873, geologist Isaiah Welch, for whom the town was named, came to McDowell County to evaluate the natural resources of the area. He reported the

mained the responsibility of National; all property reverted to Weirton; and National was to receive $66 million over 15 years. What was lost in the wage giveback was later made up in profit-sharing for workers.

The rest of the 1980s were profitable years for the ESOP, with employees reaping the benefits. In 1989, to raise money for continued capital improvements, Weirton Steel stock began trading on the New York Stock Exchange. Employee ownership remained, but others could now purchase shares of the company. Some ESOP supporters objected.

In the 1990s, employment gradually fell as competition from overseas manufacturers adversely affected Weirton Steel. By the end of the century, Weirton Steel, once the largest ESOP in America, had shrunk in size, although it maintained its status as the largest industrial ESOP. Employment, however, hit a 70-year low, as Weirton and the rest of the domestic steel industry struggled with the continuing problem of steel imports. Weirton Steel declared bankruptcy in 2003, and in 2004

A 1947 Saturday afternoon, Main Street, Welch.

existence of vast amounts of timber and numerous seams of quality coal throughout the Elkhorn and Tug Fork valleys.

The report stimulated a movement of coal entrepreneurs into the county, and by 1891 the Norfolk & Western Railway Company had extended its line from Mercer County into McDowell County. Welch, the newly designated county seat, was situated on the main line of the N&W. In 1894, the 300-acre site was incorporated as the town of Welch, and in 1895 the courthouse was constructed. Entrepreneurs and mine barons quickly sought building lots in the town and constructed lavish dwellings on both bottomland and hillside lots. By the turn of the 20th century, mining towns were developing throughout the county, and Welch had become a service center for the coalfields.

Banks, stores, churches, schools, a newspaper office, and a hospital were established. The population of Welch grew steadily through the boom years of coal mining. In 1895, the estimated population was 300; by 1920, the population rose to 3,232. By 1930, the population had increased to 5,376.

As the town had boomed with the coal economy, so it suffered with the regional downturn. The population of Welch peaked at 6,603 people in 1950 and fell to 2,683 by 2000. The loss of mining jobs with the mechanization of the coal industry and the devastating floods of the late 20th and early 21st centuries contributed to the city's problems.

See also McDowell County

Mack H. Gillenwater
Marshall University

Welch Community Hospital

Welch Community Hospital, the only state-funded acute care facility in West Virginia, is the only hospital in McDowell County. The hospital originated in 1899 legislation that required the building of state hospitals for people engaged in dangerous occupations, particularly coal mining. Miners Hospital No. One opened in Welch on January 28, 1902, and miners hospitals also were built at Fairmont and McKendree. Dr. Henry Hatfield, a future governor, was a coal camp physician who helped secure funding for the miners hospitals and served on the board of directors of the Welch facility. A nursing school was established in 1914 and operated until 1944.

From its start as Miners Hospital No. One, the name changed to Welch Hospital No. One in 1912, to Welch Emergency Hospital by 1931, and to Welch Community Hospital in 2000. Today, the 124-bed facility employs about 300 people, making it McDowell County's second-largest employer.

The hospital is located on three acres within the town of Welch. The land was donated to the state in 1899 by J. J. Sperry for the purpose of building a hospital. A $12 million renovation was completed in 1984. Medical services include surgery, obstetrics, intensive care, and an emergency department. McDowell County has the highest poverty rate in West Virginia, and in 2005, operating losses at Welch Community Hospital were reported at nearly 23 percent.

See also Miners Hospitals

Isaiah Welch

Industrial promoter, land speculator, railroad developer, and Confederate veteran Isaiah Arnold Welch promoted the development of the Pocahontas coalfield in southern West Virginia. Welch was born in Doddridge County about 1825. As a young man he took part in the California Gold Rush, later returning to Western Virginia. He represented Kanawha County in the legislature of Confederate Virginia throughout the Civil War, while also attaining the rank of captain in the Confederate military service.

In cooperation with former Confederate cartographer and fellow New South industrialist Jedediah Hotchkiss, Welch surveyed the mineral reserves of the rich Pocahontas No. 3 coal seam in southern West Virginia in 1873. He published his endorsement of the investment opportunities in Hotchkiss's journal, *The Virginias*. The ensuing massive industrialization of the region by the Philadelphia capitalists who created the Norfolk & Western Railway and its subsidiary Flat Top Land Association can thus in part be attributed to Welch's influential survey report.

The city of Welch, county seat of McDowell County, is named for Isaiah Welch, who is reported to have purchased the strategic site at the confluence of Elkhorn Creek and Tug Fork for $100 and his sorrel mare. Welch died February 15, 1902, at St. Albans, Kanawha County, and is buried in Bramwell.

See also Jedediah Hotchkiss, Pocahontas No. 3 Coal Seam

C. Stuart McGehee
West Virginia State University
Joseph T. Lambie, *From Mine to Market: The History of Coal Transportation on the Norfolk & Western Railway,* 1954.

Wellsburg

Wellsburg, the county seat of Brooke County, is situated in the Northern Panhandle on the Ohio River. The town is 16 miles north of Wheeling and 40 miles west of Pittsburgh, at an elevation of 661 feet. It is served by state routes 2, 27, and 67.

Wellsburg has nine primary schools and two middle schools, with the county's consolidated high school nearby. There are also a parochial school and an alternative learning center. Brooke County Public Li-brary is located in Wellsburg. The town has a volunteer fire department, several banks, and one weekly newspaper. There are churches of various denominations. Wellsburg had a population of 2,891 in 2000. The diverse economy includes two paper mills, a glass gift outlet, several telemarketing facilities, and a factory that does metal fabrication plus plastics molding.

In 1772, the Cox brothers, Friend, Israel, and Jonathan, made tomahawk claims in the area now including Wellsburg. Their claims totaled 1,200 acres. In March 1788, Charles Prather purchased 481 acres from the Cox heirs for $3,000. In 1791, Prather petitioned Ohio County to incorporate the town of Charlestown, Virginia, naming it after himself. The original name continued until 1816, when it was changed to Wellsburg, to avoid confusion with Charles Town, Jefferson County. The new name was in honor of Alexander Wells, Charles Prather's son-in-law. Late in 1890, nearby Midway and Lazearville were annexed to Wellsburg.

Wellsburg was the home of Patrick Gass, the last surviving member of the Lewis and Clark expedition and author of a memoir of the famous journey. Here also was the home of Joseph Doddridge, author of *Notes on the Settlement and Indian Wars*. The original Grimes Golden apple tree was found just east of Wellsburg. The first glass factory in Western Virginia was built at Wellsburg in 1813.

See also Brooke County

Ruby A. Greathouse
Brooke County Historical Society
Anthony J. Cipriani Sr., *Wellsburg, West Virginia, 1791–1991,* 1991; Carlin F. Dodrill, Celia Vermillion, and William L. Young, *West Virginia Centennial Celebration, 1863–1963: Brooke County,* 1963.

Volkmar Wentzel

Photographer Volkmar Kurt Wentzel was born in Dresden, Germany, February 8, 1915. After emigrating with his family to Binghamton, New York, at age 11, he later moved to Washington on his own. He completed high school there and in Aurora, Preston County. Wentzel enlisted in the Air Force in 1941 and graduated from officer training school at Yale University.

As a teenager in West Virginia, Wentzel took up with an eclectic group of Washingtonians who had retreated to Youghiogheny Forest, a Preston County artists colony where they occupied several log cabins. While working as a helper at the colony, Wentzel established a darkroom in a pump house and began taking photographs of local scenery for postcards. Eleanor Roosevelt acquired some of his postcards on her travels through the area.

Wentzel was a writer and photographer for *National Geographic* (1937–85), and one of the magazine's most-traveled senior staffers. His articles and photographs ranged from pre-war Sweden to the wedding of African tribal royalty. He took the first photographs of little-known Nepal. One of his first major assignments was to illustrate an August 1940 article, "West Virginia, Treasure Chest of Industry." In March 1957, *National Geographic* published his second West Virginia article, "History Awakens at Harpers Ferry," illustrated by Wentzel's haunting photographs.

Wentzel's publication credits include his book of photographs, *Washington by Night*. He has won numerous awards and been decorated by Austria and knighted by Portugal, has exhibited photographs in several countries, and has been honored at the White House. Wentzel has been a Preston County property owner since his youth, and maintains a second home there.

See also Youghiogheny Forest Colony

Jeanne Mozier
Berkeley Springs

Wertz Field

The first airport in the Charleston area to offer scheduled airline service, Wertz Field, just west of West Virginia State College (now University) in Institute, opened July 4, 1930. The airport was named for Charleston Mayor W. W. Wertz, and was leased to West Virginia Airways, Inc., a group of prominent Charleston businessmen.

In October 1933, American Airlines began passenger service between Washington and Chicago via Wertz Field, and in 1935 more flights were added when Pennsylvania Central Airlines began service at the airport. Air freight service began the same year. In 1942, the federal government acquired the field and adjoining land for the construction of a plant to produce synthetic rubber for World War II. Wertz Field closed in 1942.

For much of its brief history, Wertz Field boasted a small but very modern-looking administration building where passengers awaited their flights. There were three grass runways, each just long enough to accommodate the early Douglas DC-3s and similar craft but inadequate for the larger planes coming into use by the late 1930s. Beginning in late 1939, ground school courses and flying lessons were offered at Wertz Field as part of the National Civilian Pilot Training Program designed to prepare young men for military aviation. Most of the trainees were African-American students at West Virginia State College, and several went on to become Tuskegee Airmen and to serve in the famous Army Air Corps 99th Pursuit Squadron.

Until it closed, Wertz Field was a popular place for sightseers to watch planes take off and land and to attend the occasional air show. Among the famous aviators to make stopovers were Wiley Post and Harold Gatty, who toured America following their record-breaking 1931 around-the-world flight.

Louis E. Keefer
Reston, Virginia

WesBanco

WesBanco is a multi-state bank holding company headquartered in Wheeling. It is one of the oldest banks in the state, tracing its roots back to 1870. It was first called the German Bank, the name reflecting the large German population in the area and the fact that its early officers were mostly of German descent. In 1918, with America fighting Germany in World War I, the German Bank changed its name to the Wheeling Bank & Trust Company.

In 1923, Wheeling Bank & Trust Company acquired the Bank of the Ohio Valley. A decade later, in 1933, Wheeling Bank & Trust merged with Dollar Savings & Trust to form the Wheeling Dollar Savings & Trust Company, the largest bank in West Virginia at the time, with assets exceeding $19 million. Wheeling Dollar Savings & Trust continued to acquire competitors, including Citizens Mutual (1939), National Exchange Bank (1949), and South Wheeling Bank and Trust (1964). In 1968, WesBanco was incorporated, and it became a bank holding company in 1976.

After branch banking was legalized in West Virginia in 1982, WesBanco acquired branches, primarily in the Northern Panhandle and Ohio Valley. WesBanco-owned banks could be found in Follansbee, Sistersville, Wellsburg, Elizabeth, Parkersburg, and Charleston. In July 1991, WesBanco changed all of its affiliate banks to the WesBanco name and continued to acquire other banks. WesBanco banks were now found in Fairmont, Shinnston, Bridgeport, Morgantown, and Kingwood, as well as Barnesville, Ohio.

In the 1990s, WesBanco worked to make bank operations more efficient by merging offices near each other. Universal Mortgage Company in Bridgeport was acquired in 1996, and the Hunter Insurance Agency in 1998. The Bank of Weirton, Vandalia National Corporation, Shawnee Banks of Dunbar, Commercial Bancshares of Parkersburg, and Heritage Bank of Clarksburg were also acquired during the 1990s. On January 14, 2000, WesBanco's four regional banks—Charleston, Fairmont, Parkersburg, and Wheeling—merged to form WesBanco Bank, Inc. Wheeling National Bank and Western Ohio Financial Corporation were merged with WesBanco after the turn of the 21st century.

In 2005, WesBanco Bank, Inc., operated 86 banking offices in West Virginia, Ohio, and Pennsylvania. The locations were concentrated in the Upper Ohio Valley with additional West Virginia locations in the Monongahela Valley and Preston County, and in the Charleston area.

See also Banking

Carrie Stollings
Charleston

West Augusta

Rampant land speculation and vaguely worded colonial charters resulted in conflicting claims to the territory surrounding the Monongahela Valley in the late colonial period. Pennsylvania installed the Westmoreland County government at Hanna's Town, near present Greensburg, in April 1773. In response, Virginia's governor, Lord Dunmore, asserted Virginia's jurisdiction by establishing a military presence in western Augusta County, appointing John Connolly commander of militia at Fort Pitt, in present Pittsburgh. On December 12, 1774, Dunmore ordered the Augusta County government moved from Staunton to Fort Pitt, creating the District of West Augusta by proclamation.

When revolution against the British appeared inevitable, the Virginia Convention of July 1775 supported the American cause. An act of that convention established 16 military districts, including West Augusta, granting the district two delegates and one senator in the Virginia legislature and authorizing the continuation of the county government.

In 1776, the Continental Congress was petitioned to form a new state called Westsylvania from the territory comprising West Augusta. The petitioners' grievances concerned uncertain land titles, discord between Virginia and Pennsylvania, and ineffective local government exacerbated by West Augusta's great distance from the seats of state government. However, Pennsylvania and Virginia were hostile to the creation of Westsylvania, and the Continental Congress lacked the authority to create a new state.

On October 7, 1776, the Virginia General Assembly identified the boundary of West Augusta for the first time in the very legislation that abolished it and created three new counties, Monongalia, Ohio and Yohogania. Present southwestern Pennsylvania and northern West Virginia were within the boundaries defined. The District of West Augusta's representatives and court were transferred to Yohogania County. Virginia appointed a commission to settle conflicting land claims, but its biased decisions further antagonized the Pennsylvanians. In 1784, the completion of the Mason-Dixon line survey, slicing through the center of what had been West Augusta, established the boundary between Virginia and Pennsylvania and concluded their territorial dispute.

See also Monongalia County, Ohio County, Westsylvania, Yohogania County

Harold Malcolm Forbes
WVU Libraries

Otis K. Rice, *The Allegheny Frontier: West Virginia Beginnings, 1730–1830,* 1970.

Don West

Poet and political activist Donald L. West was also a preacher, labor organizer, and educator. Born in the mountains of North Georgia, June 6, 1906, West came to West Virginia in 1965, along with his wife, Connie, to establish the Appalachian South Folklife Center at Pipestem, Summers County. West stressed the importance of respecting mountain heritage and of learning history. He wrote and spoke often against the "hillbilly" stereotype. A political radical, he was critical of the American economic system, which he felt contributed to Appalachia's poverty. Many people interested in mountain history, politics, and culture visited the 400-acre Appalachian South Folklife Center and were influenced by West's ideas. In the summers West conducted camps for low-income youth and an annual mountain music festival.

West's rural roots were deep and never forgotten. He wrote poetry that reflected his mountain background and his left-wing politics. He attended Lincoln Memorial University in the same class with Appalachian novelists Jesse Stuart and James Still, and received a divinity degree from Vanderbilt University where he was influenced by Social Gospel teachings. Studying in Denmark for a year, West discovered the Danish Folk School Movement, which also had a strong influence on him. He was a cofounder of the Highlander Folk Center in Tennessee, which was attended by many activists, including Martin Luther King and Rosa Parks. In the 1950s, West was a noncooperating witness before the House Un-American Activities Committee.

His best-known books include *O Mountaineers: A Collection of Poems* (1974) and *In a Land of Plenty: A Don West Reader* (1982). West retired from the Folklife Center in the late 1980s and lived at Cabin Creek, Kanawha County, until his death, September 29, 1992.

Yvonne Farley
National Mine Health and Safety Academy
Jeff Biggers, "The Fugitive of Southern Appalachian Literature: Reconsidering the Poetry of Don West," *Journal of Appalachian Studies,* Spring, 2000; Fred Whitehead, "Don West," *Encyclopedia of the American Left,* 1998.

West Fork River

The West Fork River joins the Tygart Valley River at Fairmont to form the Monongahela. The West Fork drains about 760 square miles, its headwaters reaching into the heart of West Virginia. The principal towns on the West Fork are Monongah, Shinnston, Lumberport, Clarksburg, and Weston. The river's length is 103 miles, and it traverses Marion, Harrison, Lewis, and Upshur counties. The

I Dare Not Say I Love the Lord

I dare not speak of God today,
A deity divine,
As if I knew Him very well -
A casual friend of mine!

I dare not speak of God like that,
It is too much for me
To see the hunger all around
And those in misery.

I saw a Negro lynched one time
By men who talk that way,
And saw a union miner killed
One sunny Sabbath day!

I dare not say I love the Lord
While children starve and freeze,
For Jesus said love first should be
Unto the least of these!

Oh Jesus spoke in simple words,
And simple truths are deep -
They who say: "We love the Lord"
Must first go feed his sheep!

—Don West (1950)

tributaries include Bingamon, Tenmile, Booths, Elk, Simpson, Lost, and Kincheloe creeks.

In 1793, Virginia chartered a company for the improvement of the river, and required owners of mill dams to install chutes for the downstream passage of boats. In 1800, the West Fork was declared a navigable public highway. Under the leadership of the Jackson family, in 1817 the Monongahela Navigation Company began efforts to construct a slackwater navigation system on the West Fork, using dams, chutes, and locks. In May 1824, the works were nearing completion when they were heavily damaged by a flood, and the project was abandoned soon after.

Flooding has been a recurring problem, with the great storm of November 1985 bringing severe flooding along the banks of the West Fork. Rain amounts of six to seven inches were measured around Weston, Clarksburg, and Fairmont during a 24-hour period that started during the predawn hours of November 4. Another severe flood, with levels probably comparable, occurred in the West Fork and Monongahela River basins in July 1888.

Plans for a West Fork flood-control dam date back to the 1930s, but disagreement between business and urban people who supported a dam and rural interests who opposed it held up construction for decades. The Stonewall Jackson Lake was finally authorized in 1966. The dam continued to be bitterly opposed and was not completed until 1988. It is located at Brownsville, about 74 miles above the West Fork's confluence with the Tygart. Today the lake is complemented by an at-

tractive state park. The smaller Stonecoal Lake is located nearby, on Stonecoal Creek, a West Fork tributary.

General Thomas J. "Stonewall" Jackson, the lake's namesake, grew up on the banks of the West Fork at Jackson's Mill. It is believed that his dying words ("Let us cross over the river and rest under the shade of the trees.") are a literal reference to the stream of his boyhood days.

See also Flood of 1985, Stonewall Jackson Lake

Wallace Venable
West Virginia University
Leland Johnson, *The Headwaters District,* 1978.

Jerry West

Basketball player Jerry Alan West, born May 28, 1938, on Cabin Creek, Kanawha County, is widely regarded as the best athlete West Virginia has produced.

West led East Bank High School to the state basketball championship in 1956 and then rewrote the record book at West Virginia University. As a sophomore, he played forward on the team that finished No. 1 in the nation at the end of the regular season in 1958. He was named most valuable player of the NCAA tournament in 1959, when he led the Mountaineers to within two points of the national championship. He was a second-team All-American in 1958 and unanimous first-team choice in 1959 and 1960. He cocaptained the undefeated U.S. Olympic team in 1960.

In his 14-year career as a player with the Los Angeles Lakers, West played in 14 all-star games and was named most valuable player in 1972. He was named to the league's first team 10 times. He was named most valuable player of the league

Jerry West during his years as a WVU Mountaineer.

playoffs in 1969. He led the league in scoring in 1970, and his 63 points in one game in 1962 stood for many years as the record for guards. West became only the third player to score more than 25,000 points, and his 29.1 scoring average in the playoffs is still among the highest in NBA history. He played a key role in the 1972 NBA championship as a player. As a Laker administrator, he had a hand in four others. He coached the Lakers for three years and was special consultant and general manager before becoming president. His silhouette appears on the NBA logo.

West played much bigger than his six foot three inches and 175 pounds. His style embodied pure shooting form, grace, intelligence, quickness, exceptional leaping ability and, above all, a determination to win that contributed to his nickname "Mr. Clutch." West was named to the Pro Basketball Hall of Fame in 1980 and to the inaugural class of the WVU Sports Hall of Fame in 1991. Also in that year he was inducted into the WVU Academy of Distinguished Alumni. West retired from the Lakers in 2000. He became president of basketball operations for the Memphis Grizzlies of the NBA in 2002, bringing him closer to friends and family in West Virginia.

Norman Julian
Dominion Post
Norman Julian, *Legends: Profiles in West Virginia University Basketball*, 1998.

West Liberty State College

On March 30, 1837, the Virginia legislature granted a charter to establish a private academy at West Liberty, north of Wheeling in Ohio County. The first class of 65 children met in the home of the Reverend Nathan Shotwell in 1838. In 1857, public-spirited citizens completed a three-story, red brick Academy Hall, which survived until the mid-1970s.

The school catalog of 1859 described a school year that lasted from early September to late June. Male students studied classical subjects such as Greek, Latin, and philosophy, and females studied such things as literature, writing, and geography. All students attended daily chapel, and public worship on the Sabbath. Students secured lodging in private homes or boarding houses. West Liberty's first dorms would not be built until 1920.

The Civil War caused enrollment declines, and by 1867, a debt of $6,000 forced the trustees to sell the school to the new state of West Virginia. The legislature passed the "Act to establish a branch Normal School at West Liberty" on March 1, 1870. For the next 61 years, the school was a teacher preparatory institution, and until 1923, also a high school.

The first 50 graduating classes, 1872–1922, totaled only 730 students. There

was no physical education department or scholastic athletics before 1921. No activity approached the popularity of the literary societies, of which the best-known were the Bryants and the Irvings, rivals from 1888 to 1925.

The post-World War I period proved unsettling. State education officials, concerned about low enrollments (134 in 1925) and weak community support, suggested moving the campus to a location nearer Wheeling. In the end, the West Liberty defenders convinced the state to permit the school to remain on its hilltop.

In 1926, John S. Bonar, Class of 1913, became president and began to expand the school. His first task was to secure money to erect Curtis and McColloch halls, the west and east wings respectively of today's Main Hall. They were completed on West Liberty's new campus, on a 100-acre farm a short distance south of Academy Hall, purchased during the presidency of John Shaw, a predecessor of Bonar. By 1931, the state changed the school name to West Liberty State Teachers College.

During the Great Depression, enrollments fell once more; appropriations shrank; and faculty salaries suffered deep cuts. Then in 1935 Paul N. Elbin, a member of the English faculty since 1928, assumed the presidency, a position he was to hold for 35 years. Elbin exploited the public works programs of the Franklin Roosevelt administration, principally the Public Works Administration and the Works Progress Administration. One grant provided money to build a boys' dorm, Fraternity (later Shotwell) Hall; another built the first faculty housing project. Other federal funds permitted the college to landscape the campus, improve roads, update sports facilities, paint the interior of its buildings, create a physics department, and install the first student union in West Virginia.

New programs were added in art, music, and home economics. The dental hygiene department opened in 1938 and quickly became one of the college's most widely respected majors. Also in 1938, a branch campus opened in Wheeling, which in 1972 became West Virginia Northern Community College. In the same momentous year, the college received the unconditional accreditation it has maintained ever since.

In 1943, the state legislature changed the name to West Liberty State College. With World War II under way, enrollments plummeted from 325 in 1939 to 212 in 1942 to only 118 in the fall of 1944. By V-E Day, a mere 100 students remained on the campus, and only eight were men.

The fall of 1945 opened with a class of 225, the largest since 1940. By the spring of 1946, the student newspaper, *Trumpet*, reported the beginnings of what was to be-

come a welcome avalanche: 52 military veterans attended classes. Ex-servicemen, taking advantage of the GI Bill, soon pushed enrollment figures to record highs. Enrollments leveled off in the early 1950s, then rose again by the mid-decade, as GIs from the Korean conflict took their places in West Liberty classrooms. By 1960, West Liberty's on-campus enrollment exceeded 1,000 for the first time.

In the 1960s, West Liberty witnessed unprecedented building to accommodate the baby-boom generation. The number of students tripled by 1970. Five new dorms opened, as did the Hall of Fine Arts, Interfaith Chapel, a remodeled and enlarged College Union, and the Paul N. Elbin Library. In 1972 West Liberty lost its Wheeling and Weirton branch campuses, which became West Virginia Northern Community College. Construction at West Liberty has been limited to a science building (Arnett Hall), a dorm (Krise Hall), Bartell Fieldhouse, and a new academic, sports and athletic complex. By the turn of the 21st century, the programs with the largest number of majors were criminal justice, elementary education, and business administration. The student population totaled 2,375 in 2004, including part-time students.

See also West Virginia Northern Community College

David T. Javersak
West Liberty State College
David T. Javersak, "West Liberty State College, 1837–1987," *Upper Ohio Valley Historical Review*, 1987; C. C. Regier, *West Liberty, Yesterday and Today*, 1939; Frank T. Reuter, *West Liberty State College: The First 125 Years*, 1963.

West Union

West Union, the county seat of Doddridge County, is located near the junction of State Route 18 and U.S. 50. West Union sits alongside Middle Island Creek, which is the longest creek in the state and one of the finest for muskie fishing.

The area was first settled in the late 1700s by James Caldwell, who owned 20,000 acres of land that included present West Union. Caldwell sold this land to Nathan Davis and his brothers about 1807. They in turn sold 16,000 acres to Lewis Maxwell, a Virginia congressman. Nearby Maxwell Ridge is said to have a cave that was later used by the Underground Railroad.

Landowner Davis supposedly suggested the name West Union, in deference to a proposed town of Union to be built on the eastern side of the creek. Union has disappeared, if it ever existed, but West Union was incorporated in 1881. It was home to Matthew M. Neely, grandfather of West Virginia's 21st governor. Gov. Neely himself was born just south of West Union.

Doddridge County's oil and gas industry was a boon to West Union. By 1906, the Ideal Glass Factory opened to take advantage of the abundant gas. It was followed by the Doddridge County Window Glass Company. The two plants employed about 300 people. In later years a garment factory opened, but closed in the 1970s. Today farming, timbering, oil and gas, and the business of county government and public education support the area, and many people commute to jobs in Salem, Clarksburg, and Parkersburg, or to the North Central Regional Jail in Greenwood.

West Union's 2000 population was 806. The town has a library, high school, the Doddridge County volunteer fire department, and two banks. The Doddridge County courthouse in West Union is listed on the National Register of Historic Places.

See also Doddridge County
Frank Engle McCallum
Good News Mountaineer Garage

West Virginia: A Guide to the Mountain State

West Virginia: A Guide to the Mountain State was part of a national guidebook series prepared by the Writers' Project of the federal Works Progress Administration during the Great Depression. Researched and written by unemployed writers hired by the WPA, the *Guide* presents a useful summary of the history, literature, and folkways of the state, as well as a list of suggested tours. Today it is regarded as a West Virginia classic.

Because some writers in the Writers' Project had radical backgrounds, including Bruce Crawford, the West Virginia director, conservatives looked upon the guidebook series with apprehension. In Washington, the House Un-American Activities Committee condemned the project. In West Virginia, Governor Holt, a conservative Democrat, sympathized with the HUAC and alleged that the West Virginia guide was "propaganda from start to finish." WPA officials, fearful that Holt might refuse to cooperate with other WPA projects, tried to address his complaints about the manuscript, eliminating photographs and sections he found distasteful, including all of the chapter on labor history.

Eventually the dispute over the West Virginia manuscript was resolved after Holt left office in 1941 to be replaced by Matthew Mansfield Neely, a Democrat more sympathetic to labor and the New Deal. With Neely's approval, the chapter on labor was restored and the West Virginia guide, one of the last of the national series to be published, finally appeared in 1941. *West Virginia: A Guide to the Mountain State* is a 559-page hardback. The book is divided into four parts. Part I provides general background on the state, Part II describes West Virginia cities, Part III offers tour ideas, and Part IV consists of a chronology with key dates in the state's history and a bibliography.

See also Bruce Crawford
Jerry Bruce Thomas
Shepherd University

West Virginia Air National Guard

See Air National Guard.

West Virginia Archeological Society

The West Virginia Archeological Society was conceived in 1948 when amateur archeologist Delf Norona invited Ralph Solecki, an archeologist with the Smithsonian Institution, to Marshall County to excavate the Natrium Mound which was in imminent danger of being destroyed. While in West Virginia, Solecki suggested the formation of a state amateur archeological society.

The society was officially incorporated in January 1949, with Joseph H. Essington as president, Oscar L. Mairs as vice-president, and Delf Norona as secretary-treasurer. Delf Norona was also editor of the society's journal, *West Virginia Archeologist*. One of the first accomplishments of the newly formed society was the creation of a museum at the Grave Creek Mound in Moundsville, which later became the Delf Norona Museum.

The goals of the new society were to encourage the study of archeology in West Virginia and prevent excavation of mounds and other prehistoric sites except where there was immediate danger of destruction, and then only with the supervision of professional archeologists using the highest standards of archeological fieldwork. The society also wanted to discourage the indiscriminate collection of Indian artifacts.

From its modest beginnings in 1949, the West Virginia Archeological Society had grown to more than 200 members in 2005, including both professional and amateur archeologists throughout the United States. There are 11 local chapters in West Virginia. An annual meeting is held to allow dissemination of information and news from the previous year. Much of what is known of the prehistory of the state has come through the efforts of society members.

Darla S. Hoffman
Cultural Resource Analysts

West Virginia Archives and History

The West Virginia Archives and History section of the Division of Culture and History is the state agency responsible for the collection, preservation, and dissemination of our state's history. Created in 1905 by the legislature as the Bureau of Archives and History, its roots extend to the West Virginia Historical and Antiquarian Society, a quasi-public organization formed in 1890. This society collected materials relating to the state's history and maintained a museum and library in the state capitol. Upon formation of the bureau, these materials were transferred to Archives and History. Prominent historian and author Virgil Lewis of Mason County was appointed the first state historian and archivist and took charge of the new agency on June 1, 1905.

Initially located in the capitol annex in downtown Charleston, the Archives and History library, state archives, and museum moved to the new state capitol in 1929 and to the adjacent Cultural Center in 1976. In 1977, Archives and History was made part of the newly formed Department (now Division) of Culture and History.

The state archives houses thousands of books and bound periodicals, pamphlets, state newspapers and newspaper clippings, and microfilm copies of state and county records. Specialized collections include manuscripts, special and archives collections, state documents, photographs, maps, architectural drawings, and audiovisual materials.

In addition to preserving these documents pertaining to the history of the state, the Archives and History section is also responsible for the administration of several programs. Unclaimed Civil War medals continue to be distributed to descendants of the state's Union soldiers under the supervision of the director of Archives and History. In 1967, the director was placed in charge of the highway historical marker program, begun in 1934. The director also serves as staff for the Records Management and Preservation Board, created in 2000 to establish programs for the management and preservation of the counties' public records. In addition, the state archives maintains the West Virginia Veterans Memorial Archives.

Each year, thousands of people consult materials in the archives library, on its website, or through research correspondence. The state archives also publishes *West Virginia History*, the state's history journal, as well as a monthly newsletter featuring articles on collections and research tips for West Virginia genealogical and historical research.

See also Virgil A. Lewis, West Virginia Historical Society

Joe Geiger
Mary Johnson
State Archives

West Virginia Athletic Union Tournament

On March 19, 1925, basketball teams from 11 of West Virginia's 24 African-American high schools took the court at West Virginia State College (now University) in Institute for the first West Virginia Athletic Union (WVAU) state basketball tournament. Lincoln High School of Wheeling defeated Kimball, 25-24, in the final game to win the championship.

The tournament grew as the number of black high schools grew. Twenty-two teams played in 1930, but by 1938 the state was divided into four regions and the winners and runners-up from each region advanced to the eight-team, single-elimination WVAU state tournament. During the early years teams from the southern part of the state, such as McDowell County's Kimball, Gary District, and Excelsior (War), and Genoa (Beckley), were dominant. That was where the heaviest concentration of black West Virginians lived.

By the 1930s and 1940s, the tournament had become the traditional end-of-the season event. The site rotated among West Virginia State College, Charleston's Garnet High School, and the Carmichael Auditorium in Clarksburg. By this time the "Midnight Classic," an informal series of games played among the players of the eliminated teams for fun and bragging rights had become a tradition, along with introduction of the "Miss" representative from each of the participating schools.

Clarksburg's Kelly Miller High School dominated the tournament from the mid-1930s to the mid-1940s, winning five championships. Kelly Miller was coached by the legendary Mark Cardwell until 1945, when he was hired to coach at West Virginia State College. By the late 1940s and early 1950s, Charleston's Garnet and Huntington's Douglass dominated the tournament. They played in the championship game nine times from 1949 to 1955, and one or the other was champion six of the seven years.

Segregation created a tight bond among players, coaches, and fans. Few hotels or restaurants would accept African-American customers, so when the teams traveled they would eat in the school cafeterias and stay in the other players' homes. "The closeness and the friendships at the tournament was what made everything so nice," said Ruth Jarrett, a student at Garnet in the 1930s and later the wife of Garnet coach Jim Jarrett.

Things changed following integration of the public schools. Uncertainty prevailed at the 1955 tournament, because no one knew how quickly integration would happen or what form it would take. In fact, the WVAU tournament continued until 1957, when Bluefield Park Central beat Byrd Prillerman 62-54 in the final game. The remaining African-American high schools played in the West Virginia Secondary Schools Activities Commission tournament (the formerly all-white high school tournament) against an increasing number of integrated schools. In 1966, Gary District became the first black high school to win the WVSSAC state championship. Williamson Liberty was the last of the African-American schools to play in the WVSSAC tournament, losing the 1966 state championship game 58-55 to an integrated Piedmont High School team.

See also Basketball Tournament, Secondary Schools Activities Commission

C. Robert Barnett
Marshall University

Robert Barnett, "The Finals: West Virginia's Black Basketball Tournament, 1925–1957," *Goldenseal*, Summer 1983; Robert Barnett and David Helmer, "The Champs," *River Cities Monthly*, March 1980.

West Virginia Baptist State Convention

The West Virginia Baptist State Convention has served traditional African-American churches of West Virginia since 1878. The convention's buildings and grounds are at Hilltop, near Oak Hill in Fayette County. This complex is used throughout the year for meetings, camps, retreats, and administrative work. The staff publishes a quarterly newspaper, *Baptist News*.

The convention's story begins with the African Zion Baptist Church at Malden, the "Mother Church of Negro Baptists" in West Virginia, where Booker T. Washington once taught Sunday School. This and other early churches developed the Mt. Olivet Missionary Baptist Association and founded the West Virginia Baptist Association in 1874. Those who helped develop the convention include Washington, I. W. Smith, James Lewis Rice, Daniel Stratton, R. J. Perkins, Nelson Barnett, I. V. Bryant, R.D.W. Meadows, and Byrd Prillerman. The convention's district associations now are Flat Top, Guyan Valley, Mt. Zion, New River, Tug River, Tygart Valley, and Winding Gulf, as well as Mt. Olivet. There are about 150 individual churches.

At the beginning of the 20th century, a West Virginia Seminary and College, founded by Rev. R. J. Perkins, occupied four acres of the present grounds of the Baptist State Convention. Fire destroyed the building in 1908, and after two years the school closed. The Jones brothers of Red Star Coal & Coke Company donated 50 acres to the seminary in 1914, largely due to the influence of Henry Jared Carter, the seminary's president. The seminary operated again from 1919 to 1926. The land was not used for 26 years.

In 1953, the convention began to meet at Hilltop during the third week of August, and the tradition continues to the present. The Women's Missionary and Education Convention and Youth Convention meet at the same time. During the year, other meetings include the Congress of Christian Education, Music Auxiliary, Laymen and Ushers, Youth Bible Bowl competition, and graduation for seminary extension students.

Convention President S. A. Abram began redevelopment of the old seminary grounds in 1952 and completed five buildings in ten years. After Executive Secretary Warren S. Lewis led the major updating in 1972, the main building, named for Abram, had a sanctuary, meeting rooms, kitchen and dining hall, offices, and sleeping quarters under one roof. The overall complex was named the Hilltop Baptist Center. It includes a picnic area, swimming pool, and semi-rustic dormitories. The newest addition is the Big Creek-Cook Dormitory, with modern rooms for guest speakers, officers, and church "messengers" or delegates.

The West Virginia Baptist State Convention is affiliated with the National Baptist Convention, USA, and supports its objectives, including foreign and home missions.

See also African Zion Baptist Church
Anna Evans Gilmer
Institute

West Virginia Beacon Digest

Benjamin Starks founded the *Beacon Journal* in Charleston in 1957. Early in the 21st century, its successor, the *West Virginia Beacon Digest*, is West Virginia's only surviving African-American newspaper. Starks ran the newspaper business from his home with the help of his family. He published the *Beacon Journal* every other month and distributed it free of charge. In its first year, circulation was approximately 500. Funds for operation were solicited from local businesses.

After Starks became ill in 1983, his son and daughter-in-law, Stephen R. and Deborah S. Starks, continued publication under the new name. To increase readership and attract new advertisers, the newspaper went to paid subscription. In 2005, the *Beacon Digest* is a weekly publication with a circulation of 30,000 subscribers throughout West Virginia and across the nation.

See also African-American Heritage
Connie Park Rice
West Virginia University

Betty L. Powell Hart, "The Black Press in West Virginia: A Brief History," in Joe William Trotter Jr. and Ancella Radford Bickley, eds., *Honoring Our Past: Proceedings of the First Two Conferences on West Virginia's Black History*, 1991.

West Virginia Central & Pittsburg Railway

The West Virginia Central & Pittsburg [*sic*] Railway evolved from a charter issued by the West Virginia legislature in 1866 under the name of the Potomac & Piedmont Coal & Railroad Company. The WVC&P culminated from Henry Gassaway Davis's ambition to develop for the world market the vast coal and timber resources in the Potomac headwaters region and the western slopes and valleys of the Allegheny Mountains.

Work commenced in April 1880, with track-laying crews building southwestward from Cumberland, Maryland. Davis, a U.S. senator (1871–83) and industrialist, formally opened his railroad on November 2, 1881. By November 1884, the WVC&P had been built to Davis, Tucker County. The rails reached Elkins in November 1889, and the first passenger train arrived on December 3. Charles M. Pepper, Davis's biographer, said that the West Virginia Central & Pittsburg "unlocked the imprisoned resources in the heart of the state."

Starting at Cumberland, the railroad followed the North Branch of the Potomac River up to its source, passing over the divide and continuing south of Backbone Mountain to Thomas. From Thomas the main line followed the waters of the Blackwater River to Dry Fork, then through the mountain gap to Parsons at the forks of Cheat River. The line then followed Shavers Fork a short distance, crossed over to Leading Creek and followed that into Elkins. From Elkins branches ran to Huttonsville, Belington, and Bemis. The Coal & Iron Railroad extending from Elkins to Durbin and the Coal & Coke Railroad from Elkins to Charleston were also built by Davis as extensions of the WVC&P. Davis sold the entire system to the Gould interests in 1902, and it became part of the Western Maryland Railway Company in 1905.

See also Henry Gassaway Davis, Railroads, Western Maryland Railway

L. Wayne Sheets
Charleston

Charles M. Pepper, *The Life and Times of Henry Gassaway Davis 1823–1916*, 1920.

West Virginia Coal Association

The West Virginia Coal Association was formed in 1915 to advance and safeguard the interests of the state's coal industry. The association has represented the majority of West Virginia's coal production since that time and has counted most large coal producers among its membership. In 2005, about 50 member companies accounted for more than 80 percent of the coal produced in the state. Another 200 associate members, consisting of non-mining companies that do business with the industry, add substantially to the strength of the West Virginia Coal Association.

Beginning in 1966, a separate organization represented the interests of West Virginia's growing surface mining industry. In 2001 this organization, the West Virginia Mining and Reclamation Association, merged with the West Virginia Coal Association. The move brought both surface and underground mining interests into the same organization.

The Coal Association was headquartered in Huntington in its early years, reflecting that city's importance as a coal industry business and banking center and its strategic location on a major coal-hauling railroad. In modern times, the West Virginia Coal Association has been located in Charleston. It maintains an active and effective lobby in the state capital and also represents West Virginia coal producers in Washington. In 2003, the Coal Association founded Friends of Coal as an independent organization of industry supporters. The two organizations continue to cooperate closely.

The West Virginia Coal Association is a nonprofit trade association. It draws its officers from the top ranks of industry leadership and maintains a paid professional staff as well. The association takes no role in labor negotiations.

West Virginia Commission on the Arts

The West Virginia Commission on the Arts was created by the legislature in 1967 as a state agency to accept and disburse federal arts dollars from the newly created National Endowment for the Arts. Originally the Governor's Council on the Arts, it was attached at the outset to the West Virginia Department of Commerce.

The organization went through a number of name changes and administrations during the 1960s and 1970s, from the West Virginia Arts and Humanities Council to the West Virginia Arts and Humanities Commission. It became a part of the West Virginia Department of Culture and History, created by the legislature in 1976. In 1988, the Department of Culture and History became a part of the larger Department of Education and the Arts, changing its name to the Division of Culture and History. The Arts and Humanities Commission became the West Virginia Commission on the Arts.

The commission has 15 members appointed by the governor to serve three-year staggered terms. Citizens from across the state are appointed based on their expertise in the arts, business, and community affairs. The commission acts as the policy board for arts funding in the state. The corresponding Arts Section of the Division of Culture and History works, under the advisement of the commission, with artists, craftspeople, arts institutions, schools, local governments, community groups, and the citizens of West Virginia to stimulate the arts throughout the state. The Arts Section administers the programs of the commission, and the two are closely connected. The director of arts for the West Virginia Division of Culture and History reports to the Division commissioner and is an ex officio member and secretary of the Commission on the Arts.

In fiscal year 2006, the Commission was to award grants totaling $810,000 from the Division of Culture and History's Education Lottery Fund budget and $193,097 from federal funds received from the National Endowment for the Arts. Additional funds from the NEA support staff and other administrative expenses and services.

Lakin Ray Cook
Clay Center for the Arts & Sciences
William M. Davis, "West Virginia Commission on the Arts: 30 years of Leadership and Service," *Artworks*, Fall 1997.

West Virginia Day

West Virginia Day is celebrated each year on June 20, the anniversary of the day West Virginia became the 35th state, June 20, 1863. The day is a legal state holiday, with time off for state employees, and is generally marked with official ceremonies in Charleston and Wheeling, the state's birthplace.

In 1963, West Virginia Day was the highpoint of a year-long celebration of the state centennial, with President John F. Kennedy speaking from the steps of the state capitol. The state enjoyed its grandest birthday party that day, beginning with a breakfast restricted to people born on June 20 and culminating with evening fireworks. A 35-layer cake was served at noon, and Kennedy's speech was followed by a 35-gun salute.

In addition to official observances, West Virginians celebrate their state's birthday with a variety of tavern toasts, family cookouts, and other unofficial acknowledgments. Long-standing customs include the creation of a special glasswork by Blenko Glass of Cabell County. Issued in a number equal to the state's age, the limited-edition piece is sold in Charleston to first-comers on the morning of West Virginia Day.

While observed informally since the state's creation, West Virginia Day became an official holiday by act of the legislature in 1927. West Virginia is one of several states to celebrate its birthday with a formal holiday.

West Virginia Distinguished Service Medal

The West Virginia Distinguished Service Medal was created by the legislature in 1939. It is awarded to former governors in their capacity as commander-in-chief of the national guard; to officers and enlisted men of the national guard for conspicuous or distinguished service in the line of duty; to West Virginians in the U.S. armed forces who distinguish themselves in the line of duty; and to any citizen for conspicuous or distinguished service to the state.

The first medals were given to West Virginians who distinguished themselves in combat through World War I. Included were Capt. Sayers L. Milliken, assistant superintendent of the Army Nurse Corps, for service during World War I, and Col. Andrew S. Rowan for delivering the famous "message to Garcia" during the Spanish-American War.

Only 128 Distinguished Service Medals have been awarded.

Among those honored later were Gen. Charles "Chuck" Yeager, who received his medal for being the first pilot to fly faster than the speed of sound; Louis Arthur Johnson, who served as an infantry officer in World War I, and as assistant secretary of war in the Roosevelt administration and secretary of defense during the Truman administration; Col. Florence A. Blanchfield, who served as chief nurse with the American Expeditionary Force in France during World War I and chief of the Army Nurse Corps during World War II; and Col. Ruby Bradley, the Army's most decorated nurse, who was captured in the Philippines after the Pearl Harbor attack, and spent 37 months as a prisoner of war.

Numerous other Distinguished Service Medals were awarded for service in the two world wars. In 1980, the 116th West Virginia Distinguished Service Medal was posthumously awarded to all deceased veterans of West Virginia who were honorably discharged from service. Sen. Robert C. Byrd was awarded the medal in 1997, for his devotion to the West Virginia National Guard. The most recent award, No. 133, was awarded to Staff Sergeant Gene Vance, West Virginia Army National Guard, who was killed while serving in Afghanistan in 2002.

A total of 225 medals were made. Of these, 128 have been awarded, and five have been used as replacements for lost medals or for display purposes.

Larry N. Sypolt
West Virginia University

West Virginia Education Association

The West Virginia Education Association was founded in 1865, just two years after the formation of West Virginia. An affiliate of the National Education Association, the WVEA is the largest education employee organization in the state with more than 17,000 members, including classroom teachers, educational support personnel, and employees of institutions of higher education, as well as retired educators and college students preparing for careers in education.

Over time, the WVEA has evolved from a professional organization often controlled by management into a powerful teachers' union. In 1863, the West Virginia legislature gave official sanction to teacher organizations in the first school law. In 1865, the state superintendent called a state convention of teachers to meet in Fairmont, and the association grew from this meeting. Thus began a period during which WVEA was under the influence of the state superintendent. The association's first recorded constitution and bylaws were drafted and adopted at its 1874 convention.

By the turn of the 20th century, teachers were beginning to look to the labor movement as a guide to meeting their needs. In 1904, for the first time, a president who was not the state superintendent of schools was elected to head the WVEA. Previously called the Education Association of West Virginia, in 1909 the name became the State Education Association. It officially became the West Virginia Education Association in 1949.

The West Virginia Education Association solidified its power in the latter half of the 20th century under strong leaders, including Phares Reeder and Kayetta Meadows. Meadows led the group during the pivotal 1990 teachers' strike, gaining significant raises and other concessions for West Virginia teachers.

See also Teachers' Strike

Jacqueline G. Goodwin
Pennsylvania State Education Association

West Virginia Folklore Society

The West Virginia Folklore Society was founded in Morgantown, July 15, 1915, by John Harrington Cox and Robert Allen Armstrong of West Virginia University and Walter Barnes of Fairmont State Normal School (now Fairmont State University). The society, which was one of the earliest state folklore societies in America, remained active until 1917, mainly collecting traditional ballads and songs that were later published in Cox's book, *Folk-Songs of the South* (1925). Cox was the society's first president.

In 1950, Barnes, along with Patrick Gainer of WVU and Ruth Ann Musick of Fairmont State College, revived the society. As president in 1951, Barnes encouraged the establishment of *West Virginia*

Folklore, the official publication of the society, which Musick edited until 1967. Gainer was president from 1959 to 1964 and directed the society's participation in the 1963 West Virginia Centennial, including publication of a song book, *The West Virginia Centennial Song Book of 100 Songs.*

The society operated intermittently in later years, with Gainer spearheading revivals during spring meetings at West Virginia University in 1970 and at Fairmont State in 1974. *West Virginia Folklore* continued to be published annually at Fairmont State until 1980. After 13 years of dormancy, in 1993, *West Virginia Folklore* was reissued under a new format and title, *Traditions: A Journal of West Virginia Folk Culture and Educational Awareness*, and is published annually at Fairmont State University. In 1998, the Folklore Society evolved into the West Virginia Folklife Center at Fairmont State University, which houses the archives of the society.

Judy Prozzillo Byers
Fairmont State University

West Virginia Geological and Economic Survey

In 1897, the legislature established the West Virginia Geological and Economic Survey to study and map the state's geology and natural resources. The agency's director, also named the state geologist, was appointed by a commission made up of the governor, state treasurer, president of West Virginia University, commissioner of agriculture, and director of WVU's Agricultural Experiment Station. The survey was based at WVU.

The first director, the pioneering geologist Israel Charles White, served from 1897 to 1927. During his tenure the survey mapped the state's topography, set up gauges on the principal rivers, charted the soils of 48 counties, and published maps and books about West Virginia geology.

In 1934, Paul H. Price was appointed director and state geologist. Under his direction, the survey began more extensive studies of the state's coal, oil, and gas reserves, and groundwater. This information was used primarily for the exploitation of mineral resources.

By 1969, when Robert B. Erwin was named director and state geologist, the agency was using computers and other high technology tools to collect and analyze data. Erwin's most important projects included a comprehensive study of the state's 117 coal seams, research on acid mine drainage, transfer of agency data onto computer programs, and publication of the *West Virginia Gazetteer of Physical and Cultural Place Names* and the 50th anniversary edition of *Springs of West Virginia*. In 1978, the survey moved its office from WVU to the Mont Chateau Research Center east of Morgantown.

In 1981, the legislature gave to the governor the authority to appoint the agency's director. Carl J. Smith has served as director since 2001. The West Virginia Geological and Economic Survey continues to do research for its mapping projects and provide educational programs for schools and the public.

See also Geology, I. C. White

West Virginia Graduate College
See Marshall University Graduate College.

West Virginia Highlands Conservancy

The West Virginia Highlands Conservancy is an activist environmental group which works to preserve forests, fragile ecosystems, and waters in the state. In several campaigns, the 1,500-member organization has helped to protect some of the state's most ecologically sensitive and pristine wilderness areas.

Formed in the mid-1960s and incorporated in 1967, the group fought to stop proposed roads through the Cranberry backcountry and the eastern highlands. Since then, the Conservancy has taken on other major campaigns. Beginning in 1970, the Conservancy worked with other groups to wage a successful, 12-year campaign to set aside 47,800 acres in the Cranberry backcountry and Laurel Fork as federal wilderness areas. The Conservancy also worked to create the 10,215-acre Dolly Sods and 20,000-acre Otter Creek National Wilderness Areas as part of the 1975 Eastern Wilderness Act. After a decades-long battle, the Conservancy helped to stop the Davis Power Plant project, which would have flooded more than 7,000 acres of wetlands in the Canaan Valley.

In recent years, the Highlands Conservancy has joined other state and national environmental groups to address mining issues, particularly mountaintop removal and acid mine drainage, and management of public lands, including timber sales in national forests. The Conservancy is also pushing legislation to regulate logging practices, and to establish the Blackwater Canyon as a national park.

The nonprofit group supports itself through membership dues and the sale of publications. Throughout the year, the Conservancy sponsors outdoor programs —hikes, canoe trips, camping, and bike trips—and public works projects such as trail maintenance in the Monongahela National Forest.

West Virginia Hillbilly

The *West Virginia Hillbilly*, a weekly newspaper (spelled "weakly" on the front-page masthead) was started in Richwood in 1957 by Jim Comstock. In its heyday, the newspaper had a circulation of 20,000 to 30,000, in 40 states and six foreign countries. Comstock also published the *Rich-*

wood News Leader, established after he returned from World War II and owned jointly with Bronson McClung.

Throughout Comstock's years as editor, the *Hillbilly* remained widely popular with West Virginia residents and native West Virginians living elsewhere ("chickened-out West Virginians," as Comstock called them). A typical issue of the tabloid-size newspaper included feature articles, columns of interest to West Virginians, book notes, and never quite enough ads to make the publication truly profitable. The most read and usually best-written section was the "Comstock Load," the editor's own column on the back page.

The paper was famous for its occasional practical jokes, once including the release of a mountain lion to trick a neighboring editor as to whether the animal was extinct in West Virginia. Curmudgeonly humorous throughout, the *West Virginia Hillbilly* conveyed Comstock's conservative politics in a good-natured way. The paper and its editor fed each other's notoriety, making Jim Comstock for many years one of the most sought-after speakers in West Virginia.

Comstock tried to sell the *Hillbilly* as early as 1976 when he hired Pete Wallace as editor and set up a plan to sell stock that Wallace could buy back and eventually own the publication. When this proved unsuccessful, Comstock in 1981 sold the *Hillbilly* to South Charleston Publishing Company. He came out of retirement on February 25, 1986, on his 75th birthday to repurchase the paper. Upon his second retirement in 1992 Comstock sold the paper to Sandy McCauley. The new owners ceased to publish the *West Virginia Hillbilly* in late 2001.

See also Jim Comstock

Tom D. Miller
Huntington

"The West Virginia Hills"

"The West Virginia Hills" is the best-known of three official state songs. On September 25, 1885, the *Glenville Crescent* published the four-verse poem, credited to Ellen Ruddell King. One account suggests that the beauty of her native hills inspired Mrs. King to write it, while another hints that the poem was actually written by her husband, Rev. David H. King; a third implies that she wrote it, and he polished it. The music was composed by Henry Everett Engle of Gilmer County who also added the words for the chorus. Engle copyrighted the music in 1886 and included it in a collection, *The West Virginia Singer,* which was published in 1913.

The movement to adopt "The West Virginia Hills" as the official state song began with the West Virginia Music Educators Association in 1960. C. Buell Agey of West Virginia Wesleyan College prepared

a definitive edition which was approved by the association's executive board and the state music consultant. This version lowered the key one step to F major and changed the word "girlhood" to "childhood" in verse two. A resolution to officially adopt the song passed the West Virginia legislature on February 3, 1961. During the year of the state's centennial, "West Virginia, My Home Sweet Home," by Col. Julian G. Hearne Jr. of Wheeling, and "This is My West Virginia" by Iris Bell of Charleston joined "The West Virginia Hills" as official state songs on February 28, 1963.

H. G. Young III
WVU Parkersburg

West Virginia Historical Education Foundation

For much of the 20th century, the West Virginia Historical Education Foundation published West Virginia history textbooks and other books pertaining to the history of West Virginia. The nonprofit organization was incorporated May 22, 1950, as the Education Foundation of West Virginia, by Phil M. Conley, Boyd B. Stutler, and associates.

The Foundation had its origins in August 1923, as Conley-Teter Publishing Company, which published the *West Virginia Review.* The company was reorganized as West Virginia Publishing Company with Phil Conley as president, editor, and general manager. The name was changed to Education Foundation, Inc., in 1956. Conley remained president until Marshall Buckalew was elected in 1979. The name was changed to West Virginia Historical Education Foundation in 1986. James Rowley was elected president at the 1992 fall board meeting. Board members who served many years include Elizabeth Hallanan, Cecil H. Underwood, Joseph C. Jefferds Jr., Edward C. Armbrecht Jr., and Otis K. Rice.

The Foundation promoted research and scholarship in literature, philosophy, and the history of West Virginia. For many years the Foundation published textbooks about West Virginia for use in the schools at both the fourth and eighth grade levels. *West Virginia Yesterday and Today* by Phil Conley, copyrighted in 1931, was officially adopted as a state textbook in 1958, but had been used by many schools before that time. Other books published by the Foundation included *West Virginia Reader: Stories of Early Days* by Phil Conley; *West Virginia in the Civil War* by Boyd B. Stutler; *Captain Matthew Arbuckle* by Joseph Jefferds Jr.; and the 1929 *West Virginia Encyclopedia.*

The Foundation has annually participated in the Golden Horseshoe contest for schoolchildren. In July 2003 it helped to create the honorary position of Historian Laureate of West Virginia. Although dissolved in 2004, the Founda-

THE WEST VIRGINIA HILLS

text by Mrs. Ellen King

music by H. E. Engle

1. Oh, the West Vir-gin-ia hills! How ma-jes-tic and how grand, With their
2. Oh, the West Vir-gin-ia hills! Where my child-hood hours were passed, Where I
3. Oh, the West Vir-gin-ia hills! How un-changed they seem to stand, With their
4. Oh, the West Vir-gin-ia hills! I must bid you now a-dieu, In my

sum-mits bathed in glo-ry, Like our Prince Im-man-uel's Land! Is it
oft-en wan-dered lone-ly, And the fu-ture tried to cast; Ma-ny
sum-mits point-ed sky-ward, To the Great Al-might-y's Land! Ma-ny
home be-yond the mount-ains, I shall ev-er dream of you; In the

a-ny won-der then, That my heart with rap-ture thrills, As I
are our vis-ions bright, Which the fu-ture ne'er ful-fills; But how
chang-es I can see, Which my heart with sad-ness fills, But no
even-ing time of life, If my Fa-ther on-ly wills, I shall

stand once more with loved ones On those West Vir-gin-ia hills? Oh, the
sun-ny were my day-dreams On those West Vir-gin-ia hills!
chang-es can be no-ticed In those West Vir-gin-ia hills!
still be-hold the vis-ion Of those West Vir-gin-ia hills!

hills. Beau-ti-ful hills, How I love those West Vir-gin-ia
Beau-ti-ful hills, Beau-ti-ful hills,

hills If o'er sea or land I roam Still I'll think of hap-py home, and my
Beau-ti-ful hills;

friends a-mong the West Vir-gin-ia hills.

Layout copyright 2005 by Mark D. Templeton.

---

tion through its individual officers and board members continues to encourage the study of West Virginia history.

The West Virginia Historical Education Foundation is a contributor to *The West Virginia Encyclopedia.*

Eileen Cain Stanley
Kenna

West Virginia Historical Society

West Virginia has had several state historical societies. The first West Virginia Historical Society existed from 1869 to 1884 and was briefly resurrected as the Trans-Allegheny Historical Society in 1901.

A state historical society with a more enduring impact was the West Virginia Historical and Antiquarian Society, established in January 1890 and incorporated a month later. In 1891, the society asked the West Virginia legislature for funding. An appropriation was forthcoming, and the quasi-private society continued to receive money from the state until the creation of West Virginia Archives and History in 1905. In addition to encouraging research and disseminating information on the state's history, the society sought to establish a library and depository for historic materials. The group's goals encompassed the preservation of Native American history in West Virginia as well, and the society attempted unsuccessfully to raise funds for the purchase of Grave Creek Mound. From 1901 to 1905, the society published *The West Virginia Historical Magazine Quarterly.*

Between 1890 and 1905, the West Virginia Historical and Antiquarian Society acquired thousands of books, pamphlets, manuscripts, museum artifacts, and other materials. At first occupying a committee room in the state capitol, the society was given larger quarters for its museum and library—the third floor armory, the capitol's largest room—in 1894. The space soon proved inadequate. In 1898, voicing concern for the safety of collections, the group's secretary suggested the state construct a fireproof building. Although the historical society was among the intended occupants of the Capitol Annex when it was designed in 1899, the collections were not moved until 1905, after the society transferred its property to the West Virginia Board of Public Works for inclusion in the newly created Archives and History. The new state historian and archivist removed the collections to Archives and History's quarters in the annex, where they served as the foundation of the agency's collections.

Separate historical societies continued to exist after the creation of Archives and History. In 1925, the legislature created another West Virginia Historical Society, an appointive body, but this short-lived society was not continued by the revised 1931 *Code of West Virginia.* The present West Virginia Historical Society was organized in October 1940 and incorporated in 1946, for the purpose of collecting, preserving, and promoting West Virginia history. The society collaborated with the State Archives in publishing *West Virginia History*, the state's official history journal, until 1979, and it continues to publish the smaller *West Virginia Historical Society Quarterly*. Since its beginning, the society has maintained a close relationship with Archives and History, and its president is an ex officio voting member of the Archives and History Commission.

See also West Virginia Archives and History

> *Mary Johnson*
> *State Archives*

West Virginia History

West Virginia History is the state journal of history, biography, bibliography, and genealogy published by the West Virginia Division of Culture and History through its Archives and History section. Legislation passed in 1925 called upon the state historian and archivist to publish a quarterly history magazine, and during the tenure of Innis C. Davis, state historian and archivist (1935–41), the publication became a reality. Davis believed such a magazine could be a vehicle both for preserving the state's history and for publicizing the state, and her agency issued the first *West Virginia History* in October 1939.

Formation of the West Virginia Historical Society in 1940 initiated a long association between Archives and the society. For many years, the society provided partial funding for *West Virginia History*, and members received the journal as part of their dues. The journal published some papers presented at society meetings as well as meeting minutes. The arrangement ended in 1979. That year brought the selection of only the third editor in the journal's 40-year history and a revamping of the editorial advisory board, first created in 1971.

The majority of articles in early issues of *West Virginia History* cover aspects of the Civil War, antebellum, and frontier eras. The Civil War remains popular, but, reflecting trends in historical study, since the late 1960s the journal has published more articles on late-19th and 20th-century industry and labor, politics, and women. Issued quarterly for many years, *West Virginia History* has been an annual publication since 1984.

See also West Virginia Archives and History

> *Mary Johnson*
> *State Archives*

West Virginia Humanities Council

Using public and private funds to provide grants and operate programs, the West Virginia Humanities Council is the principal organization promoting the humanities in West Virginia.

The Humanities Council was created June 25, 1974, at the encouragement of the National Endowment for the Humanities. Reflecting the NEH's original purposes, the council was first incorporated as the Committee for Humanities and Public Policy and focused on making grants for programs that applied the humanities to discussions of public policy by adults. Since then the council has broadened its activities, expanded the range of its target population to include all West Virginians, and diversified its sources of funding.

The council is a nonprofit corporation, not an agency of government. From modest beginnings funded entirely by federal dollars, the council has grown in 2006 to an annual budget of $1.3 million, most of which comes from public and private sources in West Virginia.

The cornerstone of the council's work continues to be the grants it awards to educational institutions, museums, public broadcasting, historical societies, and others. Major educational activities undertaken by the council itself include traveling exhibits, the enactment of historic figures, and periodic lectures. The annual Betsy K. McCreight Lecture in the Humanities features leading national scholars and authors, and the annual Charles H. Daugherty Award in the Humanities recognizes the contributions of individual West Virginians to the humanities.

The West Virginia Humanities Council is the publisher of *The West Virginia Encyclopedia*. Since 2000, the council has been headquartered at the historic MacFarland-Hubbard House in Charleston.

> *Charles H. Daugherty*
> *Charleston*

West Virginia Independence Hall

The birthplace of West Virginia, West Virginia Independence Hall is now a museum dedicated to the history of statehood and the Civil War. Located in downtown Wheeling, the three-story structure was built to be the federal custom house for the Western District of Virginia. The building also housed the post office and the federal district court.

In 1855, Ammi B. Young, supervising architect for the U.S. Treasury Department, designed the Wheeling Custom House in what he called the "Italian Palace" style, now often referred to as the Italian Renaissance Revival style. In an attempt to make government buildings fireproof and to encourage the American iron industry, Young's plans called for an innovative structural system consisting of wrought iron floor beams and hollow wrought iron box girders supported on cast iron columns. Refinements to this structural system would later lead to the development of skyscrapers.

Construction began in September 1856, and the building opened in April 1859. On June 13, 1861, the Second Wheeling Convention began in the federal courtroom on the third story of the Custom House. This convention declared the Confederate state government in Richmond illegal; created a Reorganized Government of Virginia loyal to the United States; elected Francis H. Pierpont governor of Virginia; and called for the western counties to be formed into a new state. The legislature of the Reorganized Government met in the courtroom from July 1861 to June 1863, and the constitutional convention for the new state met there in late 1861 to early 1862. Governor Pierpont and other state officials used offices on the second floor of the Custom House from June 1861 to early 1864. Thus the Wheeling Custom House served as the capitol building for Reorganized Virginia, although it was never the capitol of West Virginia.

The Custom House remained a federal building until 1907, when a new federal building was completed. An insurance company purchased the structure and over time made many changes. An addition was built on the south end and a fourth floor was added. The variety of businesses located in the building while it was in private hands include a bank, liquor store, night club, and offices for the Hazel Atlas Glass Company.

In 1964, the state purchased the building and leased it to the West Virginia Independence Hall Foundation for a dollar a year. The foundation raised funds to restore the public areas to their 1860 appearance. Original drawings from the National Archives were used to ensure the accuracy of the restoration work. In 1979, West Virginia Independence Hall was opened as a museum administered by the West Virginia Department (now Division) of Culture and History. Each year West Virginia Day is celebrated on June 20 with reenactments, music, speeches, and special programs.

> *Gerry Reilly*
> *West Virginia Independence Hall*

West Virginia Industrial Home For Youth

The West Virginia Industrial Home for Youth is located at Industrial, near Salem in Harrison County. One of two juvenile correction centers in the state, the Industrial Home is a maximum-security facility for girls and boys. The other correction center is a minimum-security facility at Davis. Additionally, West Virginia has eight juvenile detention centers.

The Industrial Home for Youth opened in 1899 as the West Virginia Industrial Home for Girls. Young females were sentenced by the juvenile courts or justices of the peace for incorrigibility and immorality, and by the criminal courts for felonies. Males were sentenced to the Industrial Home for Boys in Pruntytown, which had opened in 1891.

The change in philosophy regarding youth incarceration, which began in the 1970s, led to population declines at the industrial homes. In 1983, the Industrial School for Boys closed, and the girls' facility was redesignated as the Industrial Home for Youth. The boys from Pruntytown were moved to this institution.

In 2000, an $18 million expansion was completed at the Industrial Home for Youth, with separate wings for females, males, and sex offenders. The new building provided for greater security, in-house medical services, and treatment programs. Educational services are provided through the West Virginia Department of Education. With a capacity of 206, the correction center's population consists of males age 10 to 18 and females age 12 to 18.

See also Pruntytown Correctional Center

West Virginia Juried Exhibition

The West Virginia Juried Exhibition, a joint biennial exhibit of the West Virginia Commission on the Arts and the West Virginia Division of Culture and History, was first held at the Cultural Center in Charleston in 1979. Since then, it has become one of the state's most influential art shows. Its purpose is to encourage West Virginia artists and craftspeople and to offer the public a current view of the state of the arts and crafts as practiced in West Virginia.

The Commission on the Arts has provided $33,000 award money for the Juried Exhibition biennially since 1979. Since its inception, the awards of the exhibition include the cost of an artist's work if it is a purchase prize and the piece is to become a part of the permanent col-

lection at the State Museum at the Cultural Center.

The award structure changed over the years to accommodate larger craft works such as furniture, to allow the State Museum to purchase major artists' work, and to allow the exhibition to feature the breadth of work being done by artists and craftspeople in the state. In practice, this has meant fewer prizes of a larger average size. The Juried Exhibition now features three top Governor's Purchase Awards at $5,000 each, one of which is named the D. Gene Jordon Memorial Award in honor of the former chairman of the Commission on the Arts. In addition, there are seven $2,000 Purchase Awards and eight $500 Merit Awards.

Beginning in 1995, the Juried Exhibition expanded the statewide reach of the program through the compilation of a touring exhibit made up of the award-winning pieces to travel to smaller museums and art centers in communities across West Virginia.

Lakin Ray Cook
Clay Center for the Arts & Sciences

West Virginia Mine Workers Union

Born of a slight hope and great desperation, the West Virginia Mine Workers Union was formed March 19, 1931, as a radical alternative to the United Mine Workers of America. Southern West Virginia miners' families were starving in the hard times of the Great Depression, and many miners felt they had nothing to lose by joining the fledgling organization. The new union was socialist in its orientation and not to be confused with the communist-led National Miners Union, then active in eastern Kentucky. Frank Keeney, who had been a strong UMW leader during the 1910s and 1920s, became president of the West Virginia Mine Workers Union. The UMWA condemned the rival union.

In May 1931, the Mine Workers Union began to organize the Kanawha coalfield, and by July 6 a major strike had begun. The Conference for Progressive Labor Action, Brookwood Labor College, the League for Industrial Democracy, and many other organizations solicited and contributed substantial funds, but the cost of feeding and housing thousands of striking miners proved to be too much. The strike was called off in the middle of August.

During this time Keeney was as much revered by southern West Virginia's rank and file coal miners as was John L. Lewis in later years. The Mine Workers Union survived until 1933, but the defeat of the 1931 strike was the effective end of its power. It was not until the organizing drives by Lewis's UMWA during Franklin Roosevelt's New Deal era that labor was to regain strength in the southern West Virginia coalfields.

See also Frank Keeney, United Mine Workers of America

Gordon L. Swartz III
Cameron

David A. Corbin, *The West Virginia Mine Workers Union*, 1972; C. Belmont Keeney, "The Last Mine War: Frank Keeney and the West Virginia Mine Workers Union, 1931–33," *The Mountain Messenger*, December 2000.

West Virginia National Guard

The West Virginia National Guard traces its heritage to the 1735 militia company established in Berkeley County by Morgan Morgan. Originally formed for protection against Indian raids, militia units were quickly mobilized when necessary in war time. Militia units provided frontier service in the French and Indian War and during Dunmore's War. Men from Western Virginia fought on all fronts in the Revolutionary War. During the War of 1812, Western Virginia militia units took part in the Northwest campaigns, and one company of Cabell County troops fought alongside Andrew Jackson at the Battle of New Orleans in 1815. Cabell, Berkeley, and Jefferson counties provided infantry regiments for service in the Mexican War in 1848.

During the Civil War, West Virginia provided some 40,000 men for service in both Northern and Southern forces. Many enlisted in the regiments of bordering states, especially Kentucky, Ohio, Pennsylvania, and Virginia. These troops primarily saw service on West Virginia soil or in the Valley of Virginia. Federal and Confederate units from West Virginia were present at both the first land battle of the war at Philippi and at the Confederate surrender at Appomattox.

A few ceremonial and social militia companies were formed after the Civil War, but the state did nothing to encourage their formation. Although violence during the Great Railroad Strike of 1877 led industrialists to plead for more militia companies, organization of the militia continued to be slow due to a lack of popular and legislative support. However, national labor problems and the formation of the National Guard Association as a lobbying group resulted in federal legislation that furnished funding and material for Guard companies. In 1889, the West Virginia legislature renamed the militia the West Virginia National Guard and provided state support. The First Infantry Regiment was organized in northern West Virginia and the Second Infantry Regiment in southern West Virginia.

In 1898, the two regiments were merged into one for service in the Spanish-American War. The First West Virginia Volunteer Infantry was stationed in Georgia. Later, another regiment was formed, the Second West Virginia Volunteer Infantry, which served in Pennsylvania during the war.

Fine craftsmanship is often seen at the Juried Exhibition.

The militia or National Guard was activated for service in areas of labor unrest in 1877, 1880, 1894, 1902, and 1912. Though there were hundreds of strikes during this period, most were controlled by local police authorities. When this failed, troops were called to duty. The most prolonged service took place in 1902 when a national coal strike brought miners out in the New River Gorge, and in 1912–13 when miners struck for union recognition on Paint and Cabin creeks in Kanawha County. Martial law was declared for the strike zone in 1912, and miners and mine guards were sentenced to prison for various violations. "Mother" Jones was among those brought before the court-martial.

In 1916, the West Virginia National Guard was activated in response to President Woodrow Wilson's call for troops to pursue Pancho Villa on the Mexican border. Again, the regiments were merged and the Second West Virginia Volunteer Infantry was sent to the border. After several months the unit returned home, only to be federalized within weeks for service in World War I. The Second Regiment and a newly recruited First Regiment were absorbed into the 38th Infantry Division. The Second Regiment was reorganized and redesignated as the 150th Infantry while the First Regiment was broken up into support units. The 150th Infantry landed in Europe at the end of the war and saw no action in that conflict.

Following World War I, the 150th and 201st Infantry Regiments were organized in southern and northern West Virginia, respectively. These units were federalized in January 1941 as President Franklin D. Roosevelt prepared the nation for war. The 150th spent World War II defending the Panama Canal while the 201st provided the first line of defense for the Aleutian Islands. The National Guard was dramatically changed after World War II. Artillery units, transportation, and engineering units were added to the 150th Infantry Regiment. Probably the biggest change, however, was the addition of a combat fighter squadron, bringing an important aviation component to the Guard.

Since World War II, the Army and Air National Guard has served in a number of capacities, lending aid to West Virginians during natural disasters caused by periodic flooding and to victims of the coal refuse dam break on Buffalo Creek in 1972. As part of its military mission, elements of the West Virginia Army and Air National Guard were activated for duty during the Korean War, the war in Vietnam, the Gulf War of 1991, the Iraq War, and in support of the peacekeeping mission to Bosnia in 1997–98.

See also Air National Guard

Kenneth R. Bailey
WVU Institute of Technology

Kenneth R. Bailey, *Mountaineers are Free: A History of the West Virginia National Guard,* 1978.

West Virginia Northern Community College

West Virginia Northern Community College, a public two-year college, was created in 1972 by the West Virginia Board of Regents. It incorporated what had formerly been the Weirton and Wheeling branches of West Liberty State College, and quickly expanded to a third campus in New Martinsville in 1975. The college today offers additional courses at other sites within its service area.

West Virginia Northern offers career and technical education to the Northern Panhandle counties of Ohio, Brooke, Hancock, and Marshall, plus neighboring Wetzel and Tyler. Its mission is to develop the district work force by teaching and training students. Graduates receive two-year associate degrees, as well as certificates. An open-door policy guarantees acceptance of all adults who seek secondary education, and the college also admits high school students who are recommended by their schools for early entrance. Financial aid is readily available. The college promotes community and business development by offering continuing education programs, cultural programs, and specially designed instructional programs tailored to the needs of business. West Virginia Northern joined with the six county school systems in the district, West Liberty State College and Wheeling Jesuit University, and local businesses, industry, and labor organizations in a regional school-to-work consortium. The consortium works to create high school technical programs that lead into those at college level.

Promoting regional economic development is a priority. West Virginia Northern partnered with Weirton Steel Corporation to create the Center for Excellence in Workplace Education to provide additional training opportunities and address work force development issues. The college offers Internet courses on a variety of subjects. Campuses in New Martinsville and Wheeling are linked by interactive video and data systems. The Weirton campus built a new telecommunications classroom.

West Virginia Northern has two primary locations in Wheeling. The historic B&O Building, located at 1704 Market Street at the southern end of the business district, was originally the main terminal of the Baltimore & Ohio Railroad in the Ohio Valley. The Hazel Atlas Glass Building, at 15th and Jacob streets, was the original location of the college. The New Martinsville Regional Campus includes a classroom building and the Francis Creative Arts Center, a two-story brick structure in close proximity to the main campus facility, donated to the college by

Jack S. Francis, a local attorney. The academic facility of the Weirton Regional Campus is located at 150 Park Avenue.

The three campuses are governed by regional campus deans. Community education coordinators at each regional campus coordinate the activities at the local level. In 2004–05, 2,837 students enrolled at West Virginia Northern Community College.

Olivia Miller
Memphis, Tennessee

West Virginia Office of Miners' Health Safety and Training
See Department of Mines.

West Virginia Press Association

The West Virginia Press Association was formed in 1869 to promote journalism and the welfare of newspapers in the state. The association was organized by a group of editors and publishers who met in Parkersburg after several months of correspondence. Originally, nearly all West Virginia newspapers were represented in the association.

The Press Association became inactive sometime after 1911. The organization remained dormant for three or four years, then was revived and underwent several name changes before resuming its original name in 1954. In recent years, the association has focused on freedom of information issues involving juvenile court coverage, access to crime scenes, cameras in courtrooms, and the like. The association is headquartered in Charleston, and association lobbyists routinely visit the legislature to monitor legislation of interest to newspaper publishers. The Press Association also provides for the joint placement of advertisements in newspapers and provides other services to its members.

Over the years more than 1,300 newspapers have been published in West Virginia, with the most in existence at any one time peaking at about 150 in the late 1940s. By 2005, the number of papers in the state had declined to 24 dailies and 61 weeklies. All but one of the publications belonged to the West Virginia Press Association.

Kay Michael
Charleston

West Virginia Prison for Women

In the 1940s, the West Virginia legislature appropriated $45,000 to buy the closed resort hotel at Pence Springs, Summers County, as a state prison for women. Until 1947, female prisoners had been kept at Moundsville Penitentiary, the men's maximum-security prison. After the deserted hotel was renovated, two busloads of women and guards left Moundsville for the long trip to Pence Springs. When one of the buses overturned, all the women crowded into the other bus.

They found a place superior to their old quarters at Moundsville. The hotel lobby had become a recreation room; the ball-room became the dining room; the old casino building was used as a cannery; and the garage became a milking barn. The hotel windows had bars now, and round holes, covered by flaps, were cut in the guest room doors so that guards could check on inmates.

The women's ages ranged from 22 to 50. The most common reason for which the women had been jailed was grand larceny. The second most common crime was murder, often of a husband. Forgery was the third most common offense. Wearing bright blue jumpers and white blouses, the inmates spent their days farming, cooking, sewing, cleaning, and attending classes.

The Pence Springs prison closed in 1985, and the inmates were transferred to the Alderson Federal Prison for women. In 1988, the state's women prison inmates were moved from Alderson to the Pruntytown Correctional Center in Taylor County. In 1986, the prison property at Pence Springs was purchased and renovated as a hotel.

Today, the only all-female state prison in West Virginia is the Lakin Correctional Facility for Women, which received its first inmates in January 2003. The Mason County facility houses 240 minimum- to maximum-security adult female felons. In addition to Lakin, state female prisoners are housed at Pruntytown and the Anthony Correctional Center in Greenbrier County.

See also Pence Springs

Maureen F. Crockett
St. Albans

West Virginia Pulp & Paper Company
See Westvaco.

West Virginia Review
The *West Virginia Review* was a monthly magazine published in Charleston for nearly 25 years. Begun in October 1923 by editor Phil Conley and managing editor Dwight Teter, the magazine likely was the outgrowth of Conley's affiliation with the American Constitutional Association, for which he had worked since 1921. Conley's work led him to conclude that West Virginia suffered from a negative image. The *West Virginia Review* was designed to counteract that image, while advancing a generally conservative, pro-business viewpoint.

The magazine offered readers a mixture of history, current affairs, and literature. Articles on business were a mainstay of the publication; under Conley's editorship, the magazine printed numerous stories on the banking and coal industries, for example. The magazine also featured education and the state's scenic beauty. Articles about women ap-

peared regularly, and over the years many of the contributing authors were women.

Dwight Teter left the magazine in 1924. In subsequent years, Phil Conley was assisted by several others, among them Walter Barnes, Jennings Randolph, Cecile Goodall, Boyd Stutler, and Roy Bird Cook. Some of them also worked with Conley on the *West Virginia Encyclopedia* (1929), which, in part, relied upon the magazine's research files.

The *West Virginia Review* was published for much of its existence by Conley's West Virginia Publishing Company. Conley sold the magazine in 1937 but reacquired it late in 1942 and resumed its publication in January 1943 after a brief hiatus. Sold once again in 1946, the magazine ceased publication in 1948. Today, its issues are a valuable research source, particularly for historians interested in the business and industrial history of early 20th-century West Virginia.

See also Phil Conley

Mary Johnson
State Archives

John C. Hennen, *The Americanization of West Virginia: Creating a Modern Industrial State, 1916–1925,* 1996.

West Virginia Schools for the Deaf and Blind
After receiving a property donation from the Literary Society of Romney, the West Virginia Schools for the Deaf and the Blind, established by the legislature in 1870, opened in Romney in September of that year.

At first, many felt that one institution serving both the visually and hearing impaired was inappropriate; nonetheless, the two schools have co-existed from the beginning. Then named the West Virginia Institution for the Deaf and Dumb and Blind, the first year saw an enrollment of 25 deaf and five blind students. The enrollment grew steadily. In 1934, the first class of the deaf-blind was taught. Helen Keller, America's most famous champion of the deaf-blind, visited the school. Today the state school serves many children with multiple handicaps.

The Romney school has long advocated for the rights of the disabled. Founder Howard H. Johnson fought for benefits, including free transmission through the mails of reading material for the blind and free transportation to and from school for the pupils, at one time via a special B&O train.

The school has been a leader in teaching methodology. Early on, deaf children were taught both lip reading and sign language, some educators believing that lip reading skills would help prepare youth to function in a hearing society. The present holistic approach, known as total communication, combines speech with sign language. Computer technol-

ogy simplifies the access of print and audio-visual information for the blind and deaf. The institution's libraries provide learning materials for visually and hearing impaired individuals of all ages throughout the state.

The Romney school is an important historical site. The columned administration building, erected in 1846, originally housed the Romney Classical Institute. Other buildings date back to 1872. Later additions included a barn, bakery, gymnasium, and athletic fields. A hospital proved vital during two influenza epidemics, first during 1918 and again in 1922.

Medical advances have brought a decline in the school's traditional population. Antibiotics and immunizations against measles have greatly reduced non-congenital causes of blindness and deafness. The decline of residential students is also explained by the advent of special education programs in local public schools and the Americans with Disabilities Act which mandates access to educational and career opportunities for all disabled persons, wherever they reside. The 2005 enrollment was 180 full-time students, about half of whom reside at the institution.

Ann Warner
Shanks

Seldon Brannon, *History of the West Virginia Schools for the Deaf and Blind, 1870–1970,* 1970.

West Virginia School of Osteopathic Medicine
The West Virginia School of Osteopathic Medicine, located in Lewisburg, was chartered in December 1972 as the Greenbrier College of Osteopathic Medicine. It was housed in buildings that had been vacated by the Greenbrier Military School. The new school was founded by a small group of West Virginia osteopathic physicians who felt a need for a medical school to train primary care physicians for rural West Virginia.

Osteopathic medicine was founded in the 1870s by A. T. Still, M.D., as a response to the often ineffective and sometimes harmful medical practices of the time. Still felt that all parts of the body were interrelated and that the body should be treated as a whole. He opened the first osteopathic school of medicine in Kirksville, Missouri, in 1892. Osteopathic physicians began practicing medicine in West Virginia in the first decade of the 20th century. Osteopathic physicians are fully educated in all areas of conventional medicine, and they also receive specialized training in the manipulation of the body's musculoskeletal system to treat certain medical conditions. They may choose to specialize in any area of medicine, but a large proportion of them become primary care physicians. Upon completion of four years of osteopathic medical school, students receive the D.O. (Doctor of Osteopathy) degree.

Initial funding for the Greenbrier College of Osteopathic Medicine came from the Appalachian Regional Commission, the West Virginia legislature, and the U.S. Department of Health, Education and Welfare. Private osteopathic physicians in West Virginia also provided loans and contributions. The school opened its doors to students on October 14, 1974, with accreditation by the American Osteopathic Association. On March 6, 1975, Governor Moore signed a bill that brought the school into the state's system of higher education as the West Virginia School of Osteopathic Medicine. The first class of 33 students graduated in 1978.

In 1984, the School of Osteopathic Medicine started a postdoctoral training program in cooperation with area hospitals. A building program in the 1990s resulted in improved and expanded school facilities with the addition of a new library, clinic, science building, and alumni center. In recent years, the school has been consistently ranked by the magazine *U.S. News & World Report* as one of the top 50 medical schools in the United States for the training of primary care physicians.

In 2005, there were 362 students enrolled at the West Virginia School of Osteopathic Medicine. There were 70 graduates.

See also Greenbrier Military School, Medicine

Michael M. Meador
Abingdon, Virginia
Penny Ellis and Alayne Steiger, *The D.O.'s: Osteopathic Medicine in the Mountains,* 1986; Otis Rice, *A History of Greenbrier County,* 1986.

West Virginia State Bar

The West Virginia State Bar, established May 1, 1947, is an organization for West Virginia lawyers, and every practicing lawyer in the state must be a member. The State Bar has an unusual structure, in part official and in part independent. It is part of the judicial branch of state government since it is an administrative agency for the Supreme Court of Appeals. However, it is organized as a nonprofit corporation, governed by a board of directors elected by its members. The State Bar does not receive any taxpayer funds, relying upon dues from its members and other private sources of income.

The general purpose of the State Bar is to advance the administration of justice and to improve the legal services provided to the state's citizens, while also advancing the legal profession. The State Bar works closely with the West Virginia Supreme Court of Appeals, the West Virginia University College of Law, the voluntary statewide bar organizations, and county bar associations. The West Vir-

ginia State Bar, through the Lawyer Disciplinary Board and the Office of Disciplinary Counsel, is responsible for the discipline of lawyers.

The West Virginia State Federation of Labor

The West Virginia State Federation of Labor, an organization of labor unions, was founded in 1903. Throughout much of its existence, the federation worked to overcome serious internal divisions, sectionalism in the state, and strong employer opposition.

World War I was a time of increasing strength and financial stability for the federated labor movement at both the national and state levels, but after the war labor was again under attack. Many employers joined the "open shop" movement, which allowed nonunion workers to work alongside union workers, using the slogan, "An American Plan." Their goal was to destroy unions. The attitude of the public and employers toward labor became less tolerant, sometimes hostile. More importantly, the position of government changed from benevolence and protection to indifference and outright opposition.

After 1932, President Roosevelt's New Deal, with its favorable labor legislation, provided an opportunity for the renewed growth of the labor movement. But even growth brought its challenges. The passage under Roosevelt of the National Industrial Recovery Act and later the Wagner Act fostered the rapid unionization of factory industries, in particular. This aggravated the old issue of industrial unionism versus craft unionism, resulting in a bitter rivalry that shattered the unity of the American Federation of Labor, with which the West Virginia Federation was affiliated. In 1935, the supporters of industrial unionism, led by John L. Lewis of the United Mine Workers, organized the Committee for Industrial Organization. In 1936, the AFL suspended from its membership the unions that had affiliated with the CIO. Because the West Virginia State Federation of Labor refused to expel its CIO unions, on September 1, 1937, the AFL revoked the charter of the state federation. These unions then reorganized themselves as the West Virginia State Industrial Union Council (CIO).

In the meantime, the American Federation of Labor reestablished a West Virginia State Federation of Labor in March 1938. The rivalries and bitterness between industrial unionists and craft unionists were more pronounced than ever. For the next 19 years they raided each other's membership and often fought to organize the same workers. In politics, the two groups often supported opposing candidates. Significant numbers of unions remained unaffiliated with the federation, and it continued to be plagued by financial difficulties. Internal fights continued into the post-war period, particularly between the crafts and the United Mine Workers.

In 1955, reunification of the national labor movement occurred with the formation of the American Federation of Labor and Congress of Industrial Organizations (AFL-CIO). State groups were given two years to merge. In West Virginia, the Federation of Labor and the Industrial Union Council worked out an agreement to create the West Virginia Labor Federation, AFL-CIO, in 1957.

The West Virginia State Federation of Labor ended with the creation of the West Virginia Labor Federation in 1957.

See also Labor History

Stephen L. Cook
WVU Institute for Labor Studies
Evelyn Harris and Frank Krebs, *From Humble Beginnings: West Virginia State Federation of Labor, 1903–1957,* 1960.

West Virginia State Folk Festival

The West Virginia State Folk Festival, the most venerable of our state's folklife festivals, takes place each year on the weekend nearest June 20, West Virginia Day. This festival grew out of an Appalachian culture class taught at Glenville State College during the summer of 1950. Folklorist Patrick Gainer, who taught the class, asked his students to go out and interview someone who played a stringed instrument, sang the old ballads, or still practiced an old craft. Some of the students brought craft items back to class, and Gainer invited an antiques dealer to discuss them.

The following year the class activities spilled over into the town of Glenville, and the festival was born. Gainer set stringent guidelines which permitted only true mountain music, accompanied by acoustic instruments. He was careful not to create a commercial festival. When Gainer stopped teaching, E. G. "Fern" Rollyson took up the cause. With the assistance of volunteers, she got the West Virginia State Folk Festival officially chartered in 1961 with the charge of "preserving the pioneering traditions of West Virginia." The Belles, older women representing pioneer ways, began coming to Glenville from counties throughout the state.

Over the years, the Folk Festival became largely a music and dance event and began to attract a national audience. During the late 1960s and early 1970s, it drew huge crowds. Despite pressure for change from many directions, the festival has held to the guidelines first outlined by Gainer and then carried on for many years by Rollyson. Mack Samples served as festival president from 1979 to 1994, succeeded by Ginny Hawker. Both held the festival to its roots, and today the West Virginia State Folk Festival remains a premier event in traditional music circles.

See also Folk Arts Revival, Pat Gainer

Mack Samples
Duck

West Virginia State Medical Association

The West Virginia State Medical Association was established in 1867 as the Medical Society of West Virginia by Dr. James Edmund Reeves and colleagues. Reeves was the brother of social activist Anna Marie Reeves Jarvis. The organization's name was changed to the West Virginia State Medical Association in 1902.

In 2005, the West Virginia State Medical Association had more than 2,800 members, including practicing physicians, medical students, medical residents, and retired physicians. Sixty percent of practicing physicians in West Virginia are members of the association. The association focuses on public health issues, strives to provide a high level of continuing medical education, and advocates on behalf of the medical profession. The organization has a political action committee that presents health care issues to legislators and endorses political candidates.

The West Virginia State Medical Association oversees 30 regional medical societies within the state, which are chartered through the bylaws of the state organization. In 2002, the association established an educational and charitable organization, the West Virginia Medical Foundation, which administers various health promotion programs, including a preventive medicine conference.

The West Virginia State Medical Association, which is headquartered in Charleston, publishes the bimonthly *West Virginia Medical Journal*.

See also Medicine

West Virginia State Rail Authority

The legislature created the West Virginia State Rail Authority in 1975 to assure continued freight rail service in certain areas where service was being discontinued. A seven-member board governs the Rail Authority. The state secretary of transportation, a member ex officio, serves as chairman. The governor appoints the other six members for staggered six-year terms. The main office is in Moorefield. The Rail Authority can acquire, construct, maintain, and operate rail lines and also convert abandoned rail lines into recreational trails. It must comply with requirements of the federal Regional Rail Reorganization Act of 1973.

The Chessie System turned the South Branch Valley Railroad over to the state in October 1978 for operation by the Rail Authority, making West Virginia the first state to own and operate a commercial freight railroad. The 52-mile line, which primarily serves the poultry industry, runs from Petersburg to Green Springs, where it connects with the CSX main line. A private contract operator runs the popular Potomac Eagle excursion train over the same line.

The Rail Authority has two other rail lines, as well. Private contractors operate the freight-carrying and excursion operations of the 132-mile West Virginia Central Railroad, which passes through Barbour, Randolph, Pocahontas, and Webster counties. The five-mile recreational Durbin & Greenbrier Valley Railroad is also operated privately. The Rail Authority also provides the West Virginia station facilities for the MARC (Maryland Rapid Commuter) trains which carry Eastern Panhandle workers to jobs in metropolitan Washington.

The West Virginia State Rail Authority holds seven abandoned rail lines that total 266 miles. They are used as recreational trails, including the Greenbrier River Trail, running 78 miles from North Caldwell to Cass and Durbin; the North Bend River Trail, running 72 miles from Parkersburg to Wilsonburg and Walker; and the Caperton Trail, running 50 miles from Reedsville to the Pennsylvania line.

See also Railroads

Donald R. Andrews
St. Albans

West Virginia State Teachers' Association

The West Virginia State Teachers' Association, 1891–1954, was the professional organization for the state's black teachers. At a time when West Virginia Education Association membership was closed to them, African-American teachers began the WVSTA to facilitate their professional development and advance the education of black youth. Organized by H. B. Rice, Byrd Prillerman, and P.B. Burbridge, the first meeting of the Association was held at Simpson Methodist Church, Charleston, on Thanksgiving Day, 1891.

The State Teachers' Association met annually and published a journal titled *The Bulletin*. Membership was open to all persons engaged with school work, including elementary and secondary teachers and college faculty. The day-to-day activities of the Association were handled by the executive secretary, under the direction of a board of directors and officers.

In 1907, black teachers from northern areas such as Fairmont, Clarksburg, Elkins, Grafton, and Buckhannon formed a separate organization called the Northern Teachers' Association. No information exists as to why the northern faction was started, but it is generally surmised that geography and the personalities involved played a major part in its founding. This organization ended in 1923, and black teachers were reunited in the WVSTA.

The combination of the black and white teacher associations came with the integration of the schools. A unification ceremony held at the Municipal Auditorium, in Charleston, October 1, 1954, merged the West Virginia State Teachers' Association and the West Virginia Education Association.

See also West Virginia Education Association

Ancella R. Bickley
Charleston

Ancella R. Bickley, *History of the West Virginia State Teachers' Association*, 1979.

West Virginia State University

West Virginia State University is a public land-grant institution located at Institute, eight miles west of Charleston. It offers associate, bachelor's, and master's degree programs. West Virginia State Community and Technical College is an administratively linked, independently accredited institution on the same campus.

The university was founded as the West Virginia Colored Institute by the West Virginia Legislature on March 17, 1891. It was one of 17 black land-grant colleges established under the Second Morrill Act of 1890, which were supported (as were the previously established white land-grant colleges) by the sale of public lands owned by the United States. The first students enrolled in May 1892. Courses were offered in agriculture, mechanical arts, domestic science, teacher education, and military science. The first principal was J. Edwin Campbell.

The original goal of the Institute was to provide instruction in the trades, but the academic and normal (teacher education) curricula quickly became popular. Early campus life combined academic work, military-style discipline, manual labor, and compulsory religious services.

Byrd Prillerman, president from 1909 to 1919, expanded academic offerings and made graduation requirements more rigorous. In 1915, the legislature renamed the school the West Virginia Collegiate Institute and authorized it to grant college degrees. Over its first half-century, the institution grew from a secondary school into a national leader among public black colleges and universities. John W. Davis, a graduate of Morehouse College, became president after Prillerman and served from 1919 to 1953. Davis appointed Carter G. Woodson, noted black historian and founder of the Association for Study of Negro Life and History, as dean. Davis set out to recruit highly qualified faculty and improve the curriculum. A new administration building (now Ferrell Hall), with an auditorium, classrooms, library, and laboratories, was completed in 1925.

In 1927, the college was accredited by the North Central Association. It was the first of the original black land-grant col-

Hamblin Hall and the clock tower at West Virginia State University.

leges to be regionally accredited, and it holds the longest continuous NCA accreditation among West Virginia public colleges and universities. In recognition of this progress, the legislature in 1929 changed the name to West Virginia State College. By then the enrollment had grown to 1,000.

An historic struggle for civil rights lay ahead, bringing a great turning point in the history of the college. In 1954, the U.S. Supreme Court in *Brown v. Board of Education* declared segregated schools unconstitutional. The West Virginia Board of Education responded with a ruling that any student could attend any public school or institution of higher education regardless of race.

President William J. L. Wallace (1953–73) guided the college through desegregation. Wallace, a former professor of chemistry with degrees from the University of Pittsburgh, Columbia, and Cornell, opened the doors of West Virginia State College to white students. He faced an additional problem: enrollment had declined from a post-war high of 1,785 in 1947–48 to only 837 students by 1953–54. And in the face of desegregation, some said that West Virginia's historically black colleges—West Virginia State College and Bluefield State College—should be closed. Wallace devised a plan to recruit local adult students, which involved expanding the evening program, and promoting harmonious race relations. Harrison Ferrell, dean from 1937 to 1966, was a key figure in the success of the strategic plan. Another key figure was Edwin D. Hoffman, the first white administrator, appointed dean when Ferrell retired in 1966.

Within ten years, the college had undergone "integration in reverse" with white enrollment, mostly from Kanawha and contiguous counties, increasing to 78 percent of the student population while enrollment itself doubled. National news media spotlighted West Virginia State College as a model of peaceful racial integration.

Not all members of the college community accepted this change easily. Many worried that West Virginia State would lose all traces of its black history. Over time, as veteran faculty retired, it became difficult to recruit and retain black faculty. However, the college continues to enroll more black students (about 13 percent) than any other college in the state and in much higher proportion than the black population of the state. The faculty, staff, and administration are racially and culturally diverse. West Virginia State continued to educate students who were economically and educationally disadvantaged. Excellence in teaching and curricular innovation and reform distinguished the academic program.

A campus master plan, initiated by President Harold M. McNeill (1973–81) brought renovations and campus beautification. The community college component was established and the faculty senate was created. Thomas W. Cole was president from 1982 to 1986. During his administration, a major industrial disaster at a chemical plant in Bhopal, India, called attention to the neighboring Union Carbide plant at Institute. Cole negotiated with the chemical industry to ensure the safety of the campus and community. The Educational Network, a satellite uplink facility with an electronic classroom, began operation.

President Cole was succeeded by Hazo W. Carter, Jr. (1987–). During Carter's administration, a North Central accreditation visit in 1992 resulted in the strongest possible approval, full accreditation for ten years. West Virginia State College had lost its federal land-grant status in 1957, partly as a consequence of desegregation. After an 11-year effort on the part of President Carter and others, land-grant status was restored by Congress on October 22, 1999.

On April 4, 2004, Governor Wise signed legislation renaming the college West Virginia State University, along with name changes to three other state colleges. This legislation also restructured the community college system, making West Virginia State Community and Technical College a separate institution under the Board of Governors of West Virginia State University.

Many members of the faculty have been distinguished artists, scholars, and scientists, including musicians Harrison Ferrell, Clarence Cameron White, and P. Ahmed Williams; actor Fannin S. Belcher; artist Della Brown Taylor; poet John Matheus; the literary scholars Naomi Garrett and Sophia Nelson; and chemist Percy Julian. An outstanding alumnus is the Reverend Leon Sullivan, architect of the anti-apartheid Sullivan Principles.

In fall 2004, the enrollment (full-time equivalents) of West Virginia State University was 2,482. While the great majority of students are now white, the university remains a center of black history and culture in West Virginia. This is the legacy of an institution that takes pride in its origins as a historically black college, while it carries into a new century its mission as a "Living Laboratory of Human Relations."

Arline R. Thorn
St. Albans

Elizabeth C. Duran and James A. Duran Jr., "Integration in Reverse at West Virginia State College," *West Virginia History*, 1984; John C. Harlan, *History of West Virginia State College 1901–1965*, 1968; Dolly Withrow and Elizabeth H. Scobell, *From the Grove to the Stars: West Virginia State College 1891–1991*, 1991.

West Virginia State Wildlife Center

The West Virginia State Wildlife Center, south of Buckhannon, is a 334-acre zoological facility operated by the Division of Natural Resources. It was previously known as the French Creek Game Farm.

In 1923, the Game and Fish Commission purchased property in Upshur County and created the game farm to aid in the reestablishment of wildlife populations in the state. Species such as quail, pheasant, turkey, and deer were raised there, but the breeding programs were discontinued as farm-raised animals often failed to survive in the wild.

The facility began evolving as a zoo in 1954, when two bison and two elk, species once native to the state, were imported from Oklahoma and kept in outdoor enclosures. Other animals representing native and once-resident wildlife were kept in cages until 1986, when roomier pens making use of natural features were installed on a wooded hillside. The facility was renamed the West Virginia State Wildlife Center.

In 2005, 28 species of mammals, reptiles, fish, and birds were present at French Creek. A glass-walled snake den houses timber rattlers, black snakes, and other native serpents. Otters occupy a man-made waterfall, stream bank, and pool complex built in the 1990s. Other animals include black bears, mountain lions, wolves, coyotes, deer, elk, and bison. Birds of prey include eagles and owls. A pond equipped with an observation deck provides a home for trout, bluegill, catfish, and bass. Every Groundhog Day, visitors gather to observe whether French Creek Freddie will emerge to see his shadow.

The West Virginia Wildlife Center draws about 50,000 annual visitors, who see the animals while walking along a 1.25-mile trail leading past the enclosures. The facility is open year-round.

West Virginia Symphony Orchestra

Founded as the Charleston Civic Orchestra with William Wiant as its conductor, the symphony gave its first concert at the Municipal Auditorium on November 14, 1939. When Wiant was drafted into military service in 1942, Antonio Modarelli, conductor of the Wheeling Symphony, became conductor. The following year the name was changed to Charleston Symphony Orchestra. To attract musicians during the war years the orchestra entered into an innovative alliance with the local chemical industry, which agreed to recruit and hire chemical engineers and chemists who were also symphonic musicians. This successful partnership garnered national attention. The orchestra's first manager, Helen Thompson, a second violinist in the orchestra, was active in the founding of the American Symphony Orchestra League, became its first full-time executive secretary in 1950, and maintained the league's office in Charleston for 12 years. Following Modarelli's death, Geoffrey Hobday led the orchestra from 1954 to 1963, followed by a silver anniversary season of guest conductors (1963–64), Charles Gabor (1964–65), Charles Schiff (1965–77), and Ronald Dishinger (1977–79).

Under the leadership of board president and Charleston attorney John McClaugherty, the orchestra experienced unprecedented growth in the final two decades of the 20th century. Sidney Rothstein was appointed as conductor in 1980 and was succeeded in 1984 by Thomas Conlin, and Grant Cooper in 2001. Reflecting its expanding role throughout the state, the name was changed to the West Virginia Symphony Orchestra in 1988. The season grew to include a nine-concert subscription and three-concert pops series, establishment of a resident string quartet, staging of operatic pro-

ductions, founding of the symphony chorus, extensive statewide touring, including a second home in Parkersburg, a late summer festival at the Snowshoe resort, and groundbreaking for its new home in the Clay Center for the Arts & Sciences.

Over the years many highly recognized soloists and conductors have performed with the orchestra including Itzhak Perlman, Isaac Stern, Yo-Yo Ma, James Galway, Emanuel Ax, Marilyn Horne, Ella Fitzgerald, Doc Severinsen, Henry Mancini, Dave Brubeck, Peter Nero, Victor Borge, Arthur Fiedler, and others. The orchestra premiered several works including *Poem for Orchestra*, the orchestral debut of 17-year-old George Crumb. The West Virginia Symphony celebrated its 50th anniversary in 1989, with a five-city tour culminating at the John F. Kennedy Center for the Performing Arts in Washington.

An earlier symphony orchestra, organized by music educator W. S. Mason and others, served Charleston as early as the 1920s and perhaps before.

H. G. Young III
WVU Parkersburg

West Virginia Train

The special West Virginia exhibits train which toured the state during the summer of 1963 reached more people than any other part of the Centennial celebration. The nine-car train represented a collaboration of the Centennial Commission and the Chesapeake & Ohio, Baltimore & Ohio, Norfolk & Western, New York Central, and Pennsylvania railroads. These were the major railroads operating in West Virginia at the time, and they all contributed equipment to make up the train.

Once refurbished, the former baggage cars making up the Centennial train were outfitted with exhibits depicting West Virginia history, tourism, agriculture, resources, industry, arts and crafts, folklore, and education. The train was operated by a special train crew and staffed by rotating teams of male college students.

Starting at Washington on Memorial Day weekend, the train visited every region of West Virginia by Labor Day. More than 300,000 visitors boarded the train at its many stops, including a record 5,840 on a single day in Huntington. The exhibits were removed at the end of the summer tour, and the train cars were sold to the Montana Territorial Centennial Commission.

See also Centennial

West Virginia Turnpike

The state's only toll road originated in 1947 with the legislature's creation of the West Virginia Turnpike Commission. The commission envisioned a four-lane highway from Charleston to Princeton to

open the southern counties of the Mountain State. The route chosen varied only a few miles from a straight line between Charleston and Princeton. It was estimated the new road would cut the driving time in half, from four hours to two.

Following six years of planning, work on the West Virginia Turnpike began in 1952 and took less than two years to construct. But for the most part it was only two lanes, since prospective revenues were judged as too small to finance four lanes. Revenue bonds totaling $96 million were issued in April 1952 for the estimated $78 million project, with more bonds sold midway through construction when unexpected slides required correction at additional expense.

The commission held groundbreaking ceremonies August 29, 1952, in Mercer County and awarded the last contract for grading and bridge substructure in July 1953. Construction activity was intense, reaching a peak of one million cubic yards of earth moving per week.

With multiple ceremonies, the southern 35 miles of highway was opened in September 1954 to a first-day total of 4,000 cars by Governor Marland and Turnpike Commissioner (and former governor) Okey Patteson. When the final 51 miles between Charleston and Beckley was opened two months later, the total project had cost $133 million, averaging a nearly unheard of $1.5 million per mile.

With six miles of four lanes and 25 miles of third lanes for passing on long upgrades, the turnpike was modern for its day. As times changed, however, sections of the original concrete paving shifted, creating a "hump" between slabs, and motorists increasingly familiar with four-lane highways grew impatient with the turnpike. In 1958, the turnpike was included in the two-year-old interstate highway system, and major changes began when the Federal Highway Act of 1966 set interstate standards to require at least four lanes of traffic. After a consultant's study concluded that upgrading the turnpike to carry Interstate 77 (and later Interstate 64 between Charleston and Beckley) would be less costly than building a new highway, the 1968 Federal Highway Act included a provision permitting the use of interstate funding for the reconstruction, while the 1970 act allowed tolls to be retained.

After a slow start, reconstruction began in earnest in December 1976, aided by more than $352 million in interstate highway discretionary funds. Involving more than one-third more earth moving than the original construction, at a cost of nearly $700 million, the four-lane upgrading of the turnpike was finished in September 1987. Symbolizing the 40-year effort, the final project was a huge open cut that replaced the obsolete Memorial Tunnel and an adjacent bridge by

The West Virginia Turnpike crosses the Bluestone Gorge, 1950s.

moving 10 million cubic yards of earth from a 371-foot-high cut in the mountain to a 311-foot-deep fill in the adjoining valley.

After much public debate, the legislature in 1989 authorized the issuance of new bonds, which meant the continuation of tolls on the turnpike. The same legislation replaced the old Turnpike Commission with the West Virginia Parkways, Economic Development and Tourism Authority. In 1996, the Authority opened Tamarack, a showcase for state artisans' work, in Beckley. By its 50th anniversary, the West Virginia Turnpike had exceeded original predictions. Expected to carry more than two million vehicles in its first year and accommodating nearly five million in 1986, the last year before its entire distance became four lanes, today's turnpike carries more than 12 million vehicles annually.

See also Highway Development, Interstate Highway System, Tamarack, Turnpikes

Carol Melling
Division of Highways

West Virginia University

West Virginia University was founded February 7, 1867, by an act of the West Virginia Legislature. The school was created as a federal land-grant institution

under the Morrill Act, which Congress passed in 1862 to support agricultural colleges in each of the states through grants of public lands located mostly in the West and Midwest. Originally the university was called the Agricultural College of West Virginia.

As lawmakers debated the location of the new institution Sen. William Price of Monongalia County swayed the decision toward Morgantown when he offered the sites, buildings, and assets of the Monongalia Academy, which also encompassed the Woodburn Female Seminary. This property furnished the site for the university's historic downtown campus.

Land-grant colleges established under the Morrill Act were required to emphasize agriculture and the "mechanic arts," but other fields of study were not excluded. The legislature directed that the new institution's Board of Visitors establish "such departments in literature, science, art, and agriculture, as they may deem expedient, and as the funds under their control may warrant."

The college opened its doors in September 1867 with three instructional departments: collegiate, scientific, and agricultural. Its first class totaled 124, six at the collegiate level and 118 in prepara-

tory work. Tuition for a term of 13 weeks was $8 for the college level, $5 for preparatory school. Room and board was $3.50 a week.

The institution's first president, the Reverend Alexander Martin, stated at his inaugural in June 1867 that the true concern would be "to educate men, as men, and not as machines." The president looked forward to a time when the infant school should be to West Virginia "what Yale is to Connecticut, Harvard to Massachusetts, Charlottesville to her parent state, Ann Arbor to Michigan, or Oxford to old England—her brightest ornament and crowning glory."

To that end, Martin pushed Governor Boreman to remove the word "agricultural" from the school's title to remove the suggestion that it was a farmers' school. Thus, its name officially was changed to West Virginia University in 1868.

The legislature provided no financial support the first year. It did, however, authorize the use of $5,000 from assets received from the Monongalia Academy to acquire land contiguous to the Woodburn Seminary grounds. The seminary burned in 1873, robbing 30 students of their lodging but providing the site of

Woodburn Hall. Originally called "New Hall," Woodburn was completed in 1876 at a cost of $41,500. Wings were added in 1900 and 1911. Today, Woodburn Circle includes the university's three oldest buildings: Martin Hall, completed in 1870, Woodburn Hall, and Chitwood Hall (originally Science Hall) completed in 1893. Woodburn Circle is on the National Register of Historic Places and is the signature landmark of WVU. The university has a total of 18 buildings on the National Register.

The school faced many challenges in its early years, including interference by the legislature. Faculty turnover was high due to inadequate compensation. The university lacked statewide support, particularly among southern West Virginia legislators who believed it was too far removed to be of benefit to the rest of the state. Nevertheless, WVU showed signs of leadership and innovation. In November 1887, the first issue of the *Athenaeum*, a student literary publication, circulated. It became the *Daily Athenaeum* newspaper in 1933.

In September 1889, WVU admitted the first 10 women as degree candidates, although women had been sitting in on classes occasionally for several years. In 1891, Harriet Lyon became the first woman to receive a degree from WVU, graduating at the head of her class. The College of Law, in existence since 1878, was one of the first law schools in the nation to admit female students, graduating its first woman, Agnes Westbrook Morrison of Wheeling, in 1895. Morrison was admitted to the bar in 1896 and became one of a relatively few women at the time to practice law. Women were permitted to enter all departments and schools except the military by 1897.

The football team received its start in 1891 when two enthusiastic students raised $160 to buy uniforms and a rule book and recruited players. Four years later, the school fielded its first outstanding team, led by Fielding "Hurry Up" Yost. WVU hired its first full-time coach in 1896.

As these changes occurred, WVU was becoming more diverse academically. President Jerome Hall Raymond (1897–1901) hired the first female faculty and added art, music, and domestic science programs to attract more women. He also hired the university's first trained librarian and the first graduate students to assist faculty, and he merged individual department libraries into one main library. A summer session was established.

In 1895, Montgomery Preparatory School was established in Montgomery as a branch of WVU. It later became West Virginia Institute of Technology, an independent institution, and in the 1990s re-affiliated with WVU. Keyser was the university's second preparatory educa-

Woodburn Hall, a West Virginia University landmark.

tion site, later becoming Potomac State College of WVU. A two-year school of medicine initially operated as an affiliate of the College of Physicians and Surgeons of Baltimore, until it became an independent two-year program in 1912.

In 1904, West Virginia University reached an impressive intellectual milestone when student Charles Frederick Tucker Brooke was selected to be in the first group of Rhodes Scholars, who were chosen from around the world to train at Oxford University. As of 2005, WVU had produced 25 Rhodes Scholars, including current President David C. Hardesty Jr., and is among the top public institutions in the nation in its number of Rhodes Scholars.

By 1912, WVU's library had 46,500 books, and its agricultural roots had spread via 15 agricultural extension schools, five home economics schools, and 110 farmer institutes; 6,500 youth were enlisted in agriculture clubs throughout the state. Oglebay Hall was completed in

1918 for the College of Agriculture. In 1921, the Engineering Experimental Station was established, as was the state 4-H camp at Jackson's Mill, the nation's first.

By 1938, WVU had 3,500 students and 150 faculty. That year, the U.S. Supreme Court ruled a state's colleges must admit African-American students to graduate courses that were not available at a state's black institutions. In 1941, WVU granted a graduate degree to its first known African-American student, Kenneth Jones. Victorine Louistall became the first known African-American female to earn a graduate degree in 1945. She returned to WVU in 1966 to teach library science becoming the first known black faculty member.

Enrollment soared with the end of World War II and the establishment of the GI Bill, in which veterans were granted federal funding for educational expenses. More than 6,000 students enrolled in the fall of 1946, causing a housing crisis. Five student veterans even lived in President

Irvin Stewart's house. By 1948, enrollment was 8,069.

Stewart's tenure as president (1946–58) was an era of expansion, particularly in the medical sciences. The university acquired two farms in Morgantown that later developed into the Evansdale Campus and the Medical Center complex. Stewart originated a new approach to financing major construction by designating student fees for construction revenue bonds.

The years 1946 to 1960 were a golden era for WVU basketball, with such All-American legends as Leland Byrd, Mark Workman, "Hot Rod" Hundley, and Jerry West. West led the Mountaineers in the national championship game in 1959. The team lost by just one point, 71-70, to California. Football, too, was thriving with such stand-outs as Bob Orders, Bruce Bosley, Sam Huff, and Chuck Howley.

The School of Medicine took center stage in 1962 when Dr. Herbert Warden and his team performed the first open-heart surgery in West Virginia. The 1960s and 1970s also brought technological innovations, including WVU's first computer, an IBM. Work began on the federally funded Personal Rapid Transit System, an experimental, computer-operated, mass transit system. Twenty years after its completion, the PRT was named the best "people mover" in North America, and it still serves the university today.

Athletics again took center stage as the 1970s wore into the 1980s. The Coliseum basketball arena was completed in 1971. Governor Rockefeller made the final decision to build a new 50,000-seat football stadium, which opened in 1980. It was expanded to 63,175 seats in 1986. Other new facilities included the Shell building, which houses an indoor track, the Natatorium for water sports, and the Evansdale Library.

WVU Hospitals separated from the university to become a nonprofit corporation in 1984. The Hospitals include Ruby Memorial Hospital, which was designated the state's first level one trauma center in 1989. WVU Hospitals also include Children's Hospital, Chestnut Ridge Hospital, the Mary Babb Randolph Cancer Center, and the Jon Michael Moore Trauma Center.

During the last decade of the 20th century, WVU established a National Research Center for Coal and Energy and Mountaineer Doctor Television to link WVU physicians with patients in rural areas. The Health Sciences Center took the name of West Virginia's senior U.S. senator, Robert C. Byrd. The state's junior U.S. senator, John D. Rockefeller IV, and his family provided significant funding in 1999 to establish the Blanchette Rockefeller Neurosciences Institute, a non-profit, multimillion dollar interna-

tional medical research center and the world's only major institute focusing on human memory.

President David C. Hardesty Jr. (1996–) oversaw academic renewal as well as physical expansion in the university. Central to the effort was a $250 million building and renovation program funded from within the university and another $250 million capital campaign for private donations. Hardesty established several student-oriented programs and expanded the university's emphasis on research. WVU's research effort ranks among the top three percent of institutions in the country, earning it a prestigious national "Research Extensive" distinction, and it was one of the first 17 Truman Scholar Honor Institutions in the country.

In the new millennium, WVU's mission as a land-grant institution remains strong, with extension service programs in all 55 counties. WVU Jackson's Mill serves more than 45,000 youth and adults annually. Overall, WVU has 13 academic colleges on the Morgantown campus; three regional campuses in Parkersburg, Montgomery, and Keyser; six extended learning regional centers; a Robert C. Byrd Health Sciences Center in Charleston; and more than 160 degree programs. The university confers more than 4,700 degrees annually and enrollment exceeds 30,000 statewide.

Elizabeth Jill Wilson
Cottageville

Tony Cook and Barbara J. Howe, et al, "WVU Year-by-Year 1862–2000, *West Virginia University Alumni Magazine*, Winter 2000; William T. Doherty Jr. and Festus P. Summers, *West Virginia University: Symbol of Unity in a Sectionalized State*, 1982; Barbara J. Howe,"A People's University," *West Virginia University Alumni Magazine*, Winter 2000.

West Virginia University Hospitals

West Virginia University Hospitals include Ruby Memorial Hospital, WVU Children's Hospital, Chestnut Ridge Hospital, the Mary Babb Randolph Cancer Center, and the Jon Michael Moore Trauma Center, all on the Robert C. Byrd Health Sciences Center campus of the university in Morgantown, as well as City Hospital in Martinsburg and Jefferson Memorial Hospital in Ranson.

Ruby Memorial, which opened in 1988, is a 430-bed hospital named in honor of Hazel Ruby McQuain and J. W. Ruby. The facility includes a day surgery center, comprehensive cardiac care, and the most modern medical imaging system in the state. A 2005 addition added more patient space and six new operating rooms.

WVU Children's Hospital is located on the sixth floor of Ruby Memorial Hospital and is devoted to all aspects of care for women and children. It houses the area's only neonatal and pediatric intensive care units. More than 1,400 babies are

delivered at Children's Hospital each year, and home-like birthing rooms are available.

Chestnut Ridge Hospital, a 70-bed psychiatric and chemical dependency facility, was built in 1987. Many take advantage of the adolescent inpatient services offered at Chestnut Ridge. The WVU Departments of Behavioral Medicine and Psychiatry provide outpatient services for people of all ages at this facility.

The Jon Michael Moore Trauma Center was named in memory of the 16-year-old grandson of West Virginia's long-time U.S. senator, Robert C. Byrd. The boy died as the result of a car accident. The center is the only level one trauma center in northern West Virginia. The Health Net helicopter is dispatched from the radio center at the facility, and complex emergency surgeries are performed on a regular basis. Emergency physicians from the trauma center work together to coordinate patient care before and during their transportation from accident scenes.

In 1989, WVU Hospitals initiated the building of a Ronald McDonald House, operated by a nonprofit volunteer organization, where families can stay who sometimes have traveled long distances to be with their hospitalized, critically ill children. The Rosenbaum Family House opened in July 1999. It is located next to Ruby and houses patients who are receiving long-term care at either Ruby, the Mary Babb Randolph Cancer Center, or the trauma center, along with their families.

The Mary Babb Randolph Cancer Center offers comprehensive cancer treatment, research, and education. The cancer center includes the Betty Puskar Breast Care Center, and the WVU Blood and Marrow Transplantation Center.

The WVU Hospitals serve as a teaching hospital and training facility for the university's four health sciences schools, dentistry, medicine, nursing, and pharmacy. Nursing and medicine, particularly, use the hospital for clinical instruction of students. Some faculty have joint appointments with the hospital and the Health Sciences Center of West Virginia University, and others serve as adjunct faculty attached to the schools. WVU Hospitals operate as a nonprofit corporation affiliated with West Virginia University and belong to the West Virginia United Health System.

See also West Virginia University

Christine D. Fenn
Westover

West Virginia Water Festival

The West Virginia Water Festival, held in Summers County in mid-summer each year, had its origins in the late 1950s. The nearby Bluestone Dam and Lake had been completed in 1952, and the idea of a water show had been discussed for years. The opportunity came in 1958 when a water ski show originally scheduled for Tennessee was canceled there and moved to Hinton. The show proved successful as a reported 10,000 people watched the three-hour show on Labor Day afternoon.

Unfortunately, similar shows in 1959 and 1961 failed to draw a crowd and were financial failures. In 1961, the Hinton Jaycees decided to turn the show into a full festival with parades, a festival queen, and other events. They filed for a charter with the secretary of state in 1961 and held the first festival in the summer of 1963 in celebration of West Virginia's Centennial. Virginia Carwithen, Miss Summers County, was chosen to reign as queen. There was a Queen's Ball, as well as numerous other events and exhibits. But thousands of spectators were disappointed when boat races were canceled at the last minute for lack of equipment to get the boats in the water.

Two years later the 1965 festival was promoted as the "First Annual West Virginia Water Festival," because for the first time the queen's selection was statewide. It was an enormous success, with Sen. Jennings Randolph attending. The West Virginia Water festival has been held each year since, with the biggest event in 1971, Summers County's centennial year.

Fred Long
Hinton

West Virginia Wesleyan College

Located in Buckhannon, West Virginia Wesleyan College initially opened as the West Virginia Conference Seminary on September 3, 1890. Its founding climaxed decades of effort by the Methodist Episcopal Church to establish an educational institution within the state. In that first year, 201 men and women undertook a largely preparatory school curriculum. Gradually the school added college-level studies and awarded its first five degrees in 1905. After one year as Wesleyan University of West Virginia, the college adopted its present name in 1906, becoming one of at least 20 American institutions of higher education to be named for the founder of Methodism, John Wesley.

When the three major bodies of Methodism reunited in 1939, healing a regional split dating back to the Civil War era, the West Virginia Annual Conference decided to discontinue ties with the Southern church's college, Morris Harvey, and concentrate on building Wesleyan as a strong liberal arts college. In keeping with its historic mission, West Virginia Wesleyan still continues close affiliation with the United Methodist Church, which elects its board of trustees. The campus hosts annual meetings of the Methodist Conference and is the repository of its Commission on Archives and History.

From the first president, Bennett W. Hutchinson, until 1973, leadership was drawn from among Methodist ministers. Of the 17 presidents, Roy McCuskey (1931–41) is particularly remembered for sustaining Wesleyan through the difficult years of the Depression. Wartime brought further strain when enrollment dropped below 200, the waning numbers augmented by military training units on campus. Through these crises trustee support was guided by long-term board chairman Clyde O. Law (1933–56). As the college grew after World War II, President Stanley H. Martin (1957–72) directed a major expansion of facilities and faculty to serve an enrollment tripling that of previous years. John D. Rockefeller IV, later governor and U.S. senator and not a clergyman, became president of West Virginia Wesleyan in 1973. President William R. Haden assumed leadership in 1995 and announced retirement plans in 2005.

While its primary curriculum is that of a traditional college of liberal arts and sciences, Wesleyan has from its beginning also sought to prepare graduates in selected applied fields and is accredited by national agencies for teacher education, nursing, business, allied health, and music. Since 1986, a master's degree in business administration has been offered, primarily enrolling employed professionals, as did previous graduate courses in teacher education. A full information technology program throughout the campus provides resident students access to digital resources around the world, and distance learning courses serve those off campus.

In recent decades undergraduate enrollment has hovered around 1,500. Although students come from across the United States, West Virginians constitute about 45 percent of the graduating classes. A few international students graduated as early as 1922, but the establishment of the Dorothy Lee Scholarship in the 1940s and recent exchange arrangements have brought students from about 20 countries to Wesleyan. Foreign students make up nearly five percent of the enrollment.

The campus occupies approximately 80 acres within the city of Buckhannon. Agnes Howard Hall, built as a residence for women in 1895 and now on the National Register of Historic Places, stands alongside the slightly younger Lynch-Raine Administration Building and Annex to compose the historic heart of the campus. Campus construction since the mid-20th century has followed a unifying Georgian architectural style.

The campus centerpiece, Wesley Chapel, opened in 1966 and seats 1,800, the largest church sanctuary in the state. Inside are wooden statues of the 12 apostles, handcarved by West Virginia artist Wolfgang Flor, and the magnificent 4,244-pipe Rohrbough Memorial Organ,

connected to the 183 Shannon bells which chime the hours and play twice a day. Two features dominate the chapel's exterior: the soaring bell tower and steeple, a Buckhannon landmark, and a bronze statue of John Wesley overlooking the central campus mall.

Several buildings carry the names of benefactors of the college: the Benedum family and Claude Worthington Benedum Foundation; Edna Jenkins; the L. L. Loar family; Annie Merner Pfeiffer; and the Frank Christopher family. The first endowed professorship was established by an alumnus, Arthur Workman.

Primarily a residential college, Wesleyan offers a rich campus life program, including opportunities in choral and instrumental music, theater, and visual arts. Structured intramural and outdoor recreation activities complement the 17 varsity teams that compete in the West Virginia Intercollegiate Athletic Conference. Beginning in 1925, the Greek fraternal system replaced earlier literary societies; 11 national social organizations now have local chapters at Wesleyan. National academic and leadership societies on campus include Phi Kappa Phi, Mortar Board, Omicron Delta Kappa, and various departmental honoraries.

Wesley Chapel provides the center for an ecumenical chapel and religious life program. A long-standing student tradition of service to the community, once expressed by deputation teams working in area churches, persists in the current activities of the Community Service Center, service fraternities, and the Bonner scholarship program.

See also Methodists

Kenneth B. Welliver
Buckhannon

Kenneth M. Plummer, *A History of West Virginia Wesleyan College 1890–1965*, 1965.

West Virginian Hotel

Constructed in 1923, Bluefield's West Virginian Hotel is still the tallest building in the state south of the golden dome of the state capitol. The magnificent 12-story structure was built as a symbol of the wealth and power of the southern West Virginia coalfields.

Plans for the West Virginian began in 1918 when the Bluefield Rotary Club appointed William Jacob Cole to head a committee to undertake the development of a proper downtown hotel. Cole and his associates purchased 90,000 square feet of prime real estate at the corner of Federal and Scott streets and retained Alex B. Mahood, Bluefield's prominent architect. Respecting his city's passion for Renaissance Revival architecture, Mahood fashioned an enormous classical column of ashlar limestone, with an elegant lobby and mezzanine.

The stately West Virginian played a principal role in the community for nearly three-quarters of a century, serving as the meeting place and banquet headquarters for a wide array of civic organizations and national conventions. Every governor from Conley to Moore, as well as Vice President Nelson Rockefeller and humorist Will Rogers, enjoyed the hospitality of the elegant 240-room West Virginian. WHIS radio, among the state's pioneer stations, originally broadcast from the hotel's penthouse studio.

After serving as the centerpiece of downtown Bluefield's business community for half a century, the hotel was sold in 1977 and renovated with federal urban development funds into a retirement center for elderly tenants.

See also Bluefield, Alex Mahood
C. Stuart McGehee
West Virginia State University

Western Maryland Railway

The Western Maryland Railway, which became a major natural resources carrier in the Eastern Panhandle of West Virginia, was chartered in May 1852 as the Baltimore, Carroll & Frederick Rail Road Company. Less than a year later, the name was changed to the Western Maryland Rail Road Company. The line was opened to Union Bridge, about 45 miles west of Baltimore, in November 1862. After the Civil War it was extended to Hagerstown in 1872 and then to a nearby connection with the Chesapeake & Ohio Canal in 1873.

Meanwhile, in 1866 Henry Gassaway Davis secured a charter from the West Virginia legislature for the Potomac & Piedmont Coal & Railroad Company. Davis was president, and his son-in-law, Stephen B. Elkins, was vice president. In 1880, construction began at a point on the Baltimore & Ohio Railway near Keyser. Within the year the name of Davis's railroad was changed to the West Virginia Central & Pittsburg [*sic*], with initial construction in a southwestern direction to the coalfields around Elk Garden, Thomas, and Davis.

At first, the B&O controlled the only access to major markets for the coal and lumber shipped over the West Virginia Central. To escape this control, Davis and Elkins began a line toward Cumberland, Maryland, just across the Potomac River from West Virginia. Construction was completed to Cumberland in 1887, after near-violent opposition by the B&O.

Difficult construction through Black Fork Canyon brought the West Virginia Central to the new town of Elkins in 1889. By chartering subsidiary companies, Davis and Elkins continued to extend their railroad. In 1902, George Gould (son of the more famous railroad tycoon, Jay Gould) acquired the West Virginia Central and eventually merged it into the Western Maryland. Gould hoped to use the WM as the eastern end of a trans-

continental railroad system and needed the West Virginia Central for its coal revenues.

George Gould pledged to extend the main Western Maryland line west along the Potomac from Big Pool, Maryland, to Cumberland, paralleling the West Virginia border on the Maryland side of the Potomac River. It was no easy task because the B&O Railroad, the C&O Canal, and several highways already had taken up the best locations along the river. Nonetheless, the line was completed in 1906, connecting the Western Maryland and the West Virginia Central. Two years later, the Gould empire collapsed and the WM went into receivership. In 1909, the Western Maryland Railway Company was organized, and one month later it purchased the old Western Maryland Rail Road Company's property and equipment at a foreclosure sale. In the 1920s, the new WM purchased the Greenbrier, Cheat & Elk Railroad from the West Virginia Pulp & Paper Company. This line extended from Cheat Junction in Randolph County to Bergoo in Webster County. Acquisition of the West Virginia Midland Railway from Bergoo to Webster Springs completed the WM trackage in West Virginia.

The revitalized WM built north from Cumberland to a connection with the Pittsburgh & Lake Erie Railroad at Connellsville, Pennsylvania. This made the Western Maryland a major link between the East and the Midwest and transformed the railroad from a coal hauler to a major fast-freight line. Substantial improvements to track and terminals took place prior to World War I. John D. Rockefeller had gained a significant amount of the company's stock as a result of the Gould collapse. Eventually the B&O purchased Rockefeller's share of the Western Maryland, but the Interstate Commerce Commission determined the purchase to be in violation of the Clayton Act. Rather than give up the stock, the B&O placed it in a non-voting trust with the Chase National Bank of New York. There it remained until 1964, when the B&O, the C&O, and the WM gained permission to merge the three railroads into what became in 1972 the Chessie System and later CSX, now one of the two major rail systems operating in West Virginia.

See also CSX, Henry Gassaway Davis, Stephen B. Elkins, Railroads, West Virginia Central & Pittsburg Railway
Robert L. Frey
Miamisburg, Ohio
Roger Cook and Karl Zimmerman, *The Western Maryland Railway: Fireballs and Black Diamonds*, 1981.

Weston

Weston, founded in 1817 as the county seat of Lewis County, was initially called Preston, then Fleshersville. In 1819, Wes-

ton became the permanent name. The building of the Staunton-Parkersburg and the Weston & Gauley Bridge turnpikes spurred development, and Irish and German immigration hastened population growth. In 1858, Weston was chosen as the site for Virginia's third mental hospital; construction was under way when the Civil War began and completed in 1880. The area, alternately occupied by Union and Confederate troops, saw only skirmishes during the war.

The state hospital's economic impact cannot be overstated. Asylum-generated commerce made feasible a narrow gauge railroad connecting Weston with Clarksburg in 1879. Prosperity brought brick public schools for whites and blacks. Grand homes went up. Weston had telephones in 1885; electric lights in 1890; and a municipal water plant, sanitary and storm sewer systems, and brick-paved streets before 1900. Population quadrupled between 1865 and 1900.

Local natural gas discoveries at the turn of the century made Weston a glass-manufacturing center. Division offices for the B&O Railroad followed. Population doubled again before 1930. With a well-diversified economy, Weston suffered less than most towns during the Depression. After World War II, the strip mining of coal increased local commerce. The glass industry enjoyed its best years during the middle of the 20th century, until foreign competition encroached. Weston's population peaked at 8,945 in 1950 and had declined to 4,317 in 2000.

Closed plants and the end of mining cost Weston its rail service, but Interstate 79 and Corridor H brought new development to the outskirts of town. The building of Stonewall Jackson Dam on the West Fork eliminated flooding. New elementary, middle, and high schools were built in the 1980s and '90s. A new hospital opened in 1972. Weston State Hospital closed, but a new mental hospital was built in 1994.

See also Lewis County, Weston State Hospital

M. William Adler
Weston

Weston & Gauley Bridge Turnpike

In 1849, work began on the Weston & Gauley Bridge Turnpike, which eventually stretched nearly 110 miles through a rugged Appalachian landscape. When completed, the road connected the Staunton-Parkersburg Turnpike at Weston with the James River & Kanawha Turnpike at Gauley Bridge. It was one of the few north-south turnpikes built in the antebellum period.

The Weston & Gauley Bridge Turnpike Company was authorized by the Virginia General Assembly in March 1848 with a capital stock of $30,000. The Board of Public Works formula for financing numerous turnpike roads was to establish a private stock company, with the board subscribing three-fifths of the stock, in this case $18,000. Later, another $15,000 was authorized, bringing the total capital stock to $45,000. Local governments supplied most of the funds not provided by the state, with individuals buying only a few shares. The turnpike was built with a cleared 30-foot right of way and a road width of 15 feet, and at grades not exceeding five degrees. The Weston & Gauley Bridge Turnpike was simply an improved dirt road. The turnpike began in Weston, passed through the salt works at Bulltown, crossed the Elk River at Sutton, then traveled to Summersville, and ended on the Kanawha River at Gauley Bridge. There were notable covered bridges over the West Fork at Bendale, just south of Weston, and over the Little Kanawha River at Bulltown. The most significant structure, however, was the wire suspension bridge crossing the Elk River at Sutton. This bridge was built by Ira Hart with the wire being supplied by Bodley and Company of Wheeling. Despite problems with the construction and financing, the bridge was open for traffic in 1857 and served until 1930.

The Weston & Gauley Bridge Turnpike was completed in 1858. During the Civil War, troops from North and South reduced the road surface to a dismal state, according to contemporary accounts. In addition, it was extremely difficult to collect tolls to maintain the road during the war. Following West Virginia statehood in 1863, all of the turnpikes in the new state were turned over to the counties through which they ran. Money was scarce, and little was done to maintain these roads. It was not until the 1920s that U.S. 19, which generally follows the path of the original turnpike, was surfaced. There are a number of sections of the old road in essentially original condition, including one at Bulltown.

See also Turnpikes

Emory L. Kemp
WVU Institute for the History of Technology
Emory L. Kemp and Janet Kemp, "Building the Weston and Gauley Bridge Turnpike," *West Virginia History,* Summer 1980.

Weston State Hospital

The Weston State Hospital housed West Virginia's mentally ill from 1864 to 1994. Built on 269 acres across the West Fork River from Weston, it was authorized by the Virginia legislature in the early 1850s as the Trans-Allegheny Lunatic Asylum. Politics may have been the overriding reason in choosing its site; Lewis County, a Democratic island in a sea of Western Virginia Whigs, exercised considerable influence in Richmond.

The hospital's huge main building, two-tenths of a mile long, was designed by Richard S. Andrews of Baltimore,

Weston State Hospital is an imposing structure.

whose other work includes the south wing of the U.S. Treasury Building in Washington and the Maryland governor's mansion. A committee toured similar institutions in several states to determine what features were required. The General Assembly appropriated $50,000, and construction was under way by the end of 1858.

The Civil War interrupted the work. Virginia's Confederate government demanded unused funds be returned for state defense, but the money was saved by sending it to Wheeling. In 1862, the pro-Northern Reorganized Government of Virginia added $40,000. Work resumed and continued through the rest of the war. In 1863, the name was changed to West Virginia Hospital for the Insane, and Dr. James A. Hall was appointed its first superintendent. He was replaced by Dr. R. Hills, formerly of Columbus, Ohio, just as the first patients entered in October 1864.

By 1868, 200 patients were being cared for at the hospital. The legislature voted $110,000 in 1870 for additional buildings,

and separate rooms for black patients were added in 1873. The hospital had its own farm, dairy, waterworks, and cemetery. Ultimately, it grew to house about 1,200 patients. In 1913, the West Virginia legislature changed the name of the hospital to Weston State Hospital.

On October 3, 1935, a patient started a fire in the main building that destroyed six men's wards and caused a cupola to fall through the roof. Governor Kump, attending the Forest Festival in Elkins, rushed to the scene. The building was repaired and the hospital remained in service for nearly 60 more years. It closed in May 1994, replaced by the new $27 million William R. Sharpe Jr. Hospital. Proposals for turning the old buildings to new purposes include creating a national Civil War museum.

Gerald D. Swick
Nashville, Tennessee
Joy Gregoire Gilchrist and Charles H. Gilchrist, *Lewis County, West Virginia, A Pictorial History: The Crossroads of Central West Virginia,* 1993; Edward Conrad Smith, *A History of Lewis County, West Virginia,* 1929.

Westover

The Monongalia County town of Westover was named for its location, west of Morgantown and over the Monongahela River. Westover lies in a bend of the river, just opposite its larger neighbor. It is located at the junction of Interstate 79 and U.S. 19. The traffic of U.S. 19 is carried from Westover to Morgantown by a Monongahela River bridge, a busy entryway into the university city. Streetcar lines connected Morgantown and Westover in earlier years.

Originally farmland, Westover was settled as a suburb of Morgantown at about the turn of the 20th century, attracting families to its good school and large country-style building lots. Many early residents kept a garden, fruit trees, poultry, and livestock. Once known as the West Side, Westover was incorporated in 1911.

St. Mary's Orthodox Church, built for a congregation consisting largely of East European immigrants, was added to the National Register of Historic Places in 1988. The ornate church, with its onion-shaped golden domes, has been a Westover landmark since 1923.

Early in the 21st century Westover remains a hilly, tree-lined commercial and residential suburb, with its own park and schools and fine views of West Virginia University's historic campus. Westover is Monongalia County's second-largest municipality, with 3,941 residents in 2000.

See also Morgantown

Westsylvania

Westsylvania was an unsuccessful attempt to create a 14th state during the Revolutionary War period, the successor to several previous attempts to establish governments in the western mountains. Much of the history of trans-Allegheny Virginia (now West Virginia) was influenced by competition for control of the huge expanses of land which had been awarded to speculators. The situation was complicated by grants of the same land to groups of investors and then further complicated by "squatters" who moved into Western Virginia, western Pennsylvania, and Ohio, made improvements on the land, and then attempted to file legitimate claims on their farms.

In the 1770s, a large group of investors had tried to establish control over the region by promoting the formation of a new colony, Vandalia. That effort failed because Pennsylvania and Virginia disputed ownership of much of the region and because of the growing rift between the colonists and England which led to the Revolutionary War. A new effort to achieve the same goal was put forth in the summer of 1776 when the Continental Congress was asked to approve the creation of Westsylvania as a new commonwealth, a step toward the creation of a 14th state. The proposed state would have included all of trans-Allegheny Virginia and substantial parts of western Pennsylvania and eastern Ohio. According to historian Otis K. Rice, prime movers in the scheme were likely Benjamin Franklin, George Morgan, and Samuel and Thomas Wharton. While such investors were politically powerful, they were opposed by equally powerful interests, and once again conflicting claims from Virginia and Pennsylvania doomed the proposal.

See also Vandalia Colony

Kenneth R. Bailey
WVU Institute of Technology
Otis K. Rice, *The Allegheny Frontier: West Virginia Beginnings, 1730–1830,* 1970.

Westvaco

Westvaco, now MeadWestvaco, has a long history in West Virginia. It is a major manufacturer of paper, packaging, and specialty chemicals. Additionally, the company manages forests in West Virginia that supply timber to sawmills and paper mills.

The company began in 1888, when William Luke founded the Piedmont Pulp & Paper Company at what is now Luke, Maryland, near Piedmont in Mineral County. In 1889, Luke opened a pulp mill on an island in the North Branch Potomac opposite Piedmont and incorporated the company under the new name of the West Virginia Paper Company. The company opened its headquarters in New York City in 1894 and in 1897 consolidated various businesses to form the West Virginia Pulp & Paper Company.

In addition to the mill near Piedmont, West Virginia Pulp & Paper Company had mills in Davis, West Virginia, Tyrone, Pennsylvania, and Covington, Virginia. In 1900, West Virginia Pulp & Paper began constructing a sawmill and a new town at Cass. The company formed the Greenbrier, Cheat & Elk Railroad to connect its surrounding timberlands to the sawmill at Cass and to the C&O's Greenbrier River line. Incorporated in 1910, the logging railroad was chartered to run between Bemis, in Randolph County, and Webster Springs.

The company branched into the mining business when it opened its Hopkins Mine in Randolph County. The mine and others opened by the company were used to supply coal for locomotives and other equipment, such as log loaders and skidders.

In 1937, the company built a bleached paperboard mill in South Carolina. In 1969, the company changed its name to Westvaco, built a fine papers mill in Kentucky in 1970, began acquiring various companies, and developed international operations. The merger of Westvaco and Mead, another long-existing paper company, was approved in 2002, with headquarters in Stamford, Connecticut.

MeadWestvaco owns about 1.36 million acres of forests in the United States and Brazil, including about 214,000 acres in West Virginia. The MeadWestvaco Wildlife and Ecosystem Research Forest was established on 8,430 acres in Randolph County.

See also Cass

Wetlands

Wetlands are areas that are inundated or saturated with water for significant periods during the growing season. They may be adjacent to bodies of open water and subject to flooding, or they may be isolated and receive water from ground sources and precipitation. Plant growth is limited to those species adapted to the lack of oxygen in saturated soils, resulting in distinct wetland vegetation. Wetlands include swamps, marshes, and bogs, as well as man-made features such as shallow ponds and roadside ditches.

Although inventories of West Virginia wetlands are incomplete it is clear that they are uncommon features and unevenly distributed in the state. The total area of wetlands is estimated to comprise less than one-half percent of the state's area, the lowest in the 48 contiguous states. The small area of wetlands is a reflection of the state's mountainous topography.

The largest wetland complex in West Virginia is in Canaan Valley, Tucker County. Other important wetland areas include the upper Meadow River drainage in Greenbrier County, Cranesville Swamp in Preston County, Cranberry Glades in Pocahontas County, and the drainages of Muddelty and Little Beaver creeks in Nicholas County. Additional counties with relatively large areas of wetlands include Randolph, Grant, Barbour, Mason, Fayette, Berkeley, Jefferson, and Hampshire. Numerous small wetlands are located in every county of the state.

Wetlands have many ecological functions and provide many benefits to people. In West Virginia they are likely to be especially important for improving water quality, for wildlife habitat, and as scenic attractions. Wetlands have the capacity to improve water quality by removing nutrients and sediments and may improve the pH of acid mine run-off. In relation to their small area, wetlands contribute disproportionately to the state's biological diversity. About 40 percent of the plants and 20 percent of the vertebrates considered rare by the West Virginia Natural Heritage Program are found primarily in wetlands. Wetlands are the primary habitat for hundreds of common plants and animals and provide resources at some life stage for even more. Wetlands such as Cranberry Glades are among the state's most frequently visited tourist stops.

FAST FACTS ABOUT WETZEL COUNTY

Founded: 1846

Land in square miles: 360.5

Population: 17,693

Percentage minorities: 1.1%

Percentage rural: 53.3%

Median age: 40.4

Percentage 65 and older: 16.2%

Birth rate per 1,000 population: 11.6

Median household income: $30,935

High school graduate or higher: 77.6%

Bachelor's degree or higher: 10.4%

Home ownership: 78.5%

Median home value: $66,000

This information is from the 2000 U.S. Census. In 2000, West Virginia as a whole had 5 percent minorities, a median age of 38.9, median household income of $29,696, and a 75.2 percent home ownership rate.

More than half of the nation's original wetlands have been destroyed, with similar losses in West Virginia, although statistics are lacking. Many of the state's wetlands have been drained for agriculture and filled for industrial and residential development. Others have been flooded behind locks and dams. Large areas of wetland forests have been cleared and converted to pasture. Today, the federal government under the Clean Water Act regulates the state's wetlands, but losses continue. This has been partly compensated for by reversion of agricultural lands following failure of drainage systems and by restoration and construction of wetlands by humans and by beavers.

Jim Vanderhorst
Division of Natural Resources
Ralph W. Tiner, *West Virginia's Wetlands: Uncommon, Valuable Wildlands*, 1996.

Wetzel County

Named for Indian fighter Lewis Wetzel, Wetzel County was created in 1846. It has an area of 360.5 square miles and a population of 17,693 in 2000.

Wetzel County lies just south of the Northern Panhandle. The county fronts the Ohio River for just over 13 miles. Most of Wetzel County falls within the watershed of Fishing Creek, which joins the Ohio at New Martinsville. The Wetzel County landscape may be described as rolling to quite hilly. The county's lowest point is located in its southwestern corner on the Ohio River at 588 feet above sea level, and its highest point is at the summit of Honsocker Knob in the northeastern corner, at 1,650 feet. Wetzel is bounded on the north by Marshall County and Greene County, Pennsylvania; to the east by Monongalia, Marion, and Harrison counties; to the south by Doddridge and Tyler counties; and to the west by the Ohio River.

Wetzel was originally part of Ohio County, which was created in 1776. In 1814, Tyler County was formed from the southern part of Ohio County. Wetzel County was formed from the northern part of Tyler County in 1846.

The first white settlers were primarily of German, Swiss, Scotch-Irish, and English origin, with Edward Dulin settling New Martinsville in 1773. Reader was settled in 1788 by James Troy, and the land was later sold to the town's namesake, Benjamin Reader. Proctor was named for a fur trapper who lived in a cave on Proctor Creek and was killed by Indians in the late 1700s. John Wyatt is known to have settled Pine Grove in 1790. William Ice and Aiden Bales pioneered Grant District in 1796. Obadiah Paden, of Lancaster, Pennsylvania, settled the land of present Paden City in 1796. The William Little family settled Littleton in 1797, and Henry Church settled Hundred shortly before the turn of the 19th century. Peter Bartrug settled Burton in the early 1800s, and Wileyville was established by Shannon Wiley in the latter half of that century. Folsom was settled by Henry Talkington, and Smithfield by Aiden Bales in 1796.

The main highways in Wetzel County are State Route 2, running north and south, and State Routes 7 and 20, running east and west. Rail service is provided by CSX Transportation, and the Ohio River is a vital route for transporting goods north toward Pittsburgh and south toward the Mississippi River. A small airport is located in New Martinsville, the chief town and county seat of Wetzel County.

Natural gas, petroleum, glass, marbles, timber, livestock, fruits, and vegetables remain the county's primary industries. While no heavy industry is located within the county, many residents work at the nearby Bayer Corporation, PPG Industries, or Ormet Aluminum Corporation.

Oil and gas exploration and development began with the drilling of the first gas well in 1886 in Hundred, which is still producing. Joseph Trees and Michael Benedum, leading entrepreneurs in the industry, also developed oil and gas wells in Pine Grove, Smithfield, Folsom, and Proctor. Many of these wells continue to be active today.

Regional timber stands consist mostly of hardwoods, with oak and hickory predominating. The channel, islands, floodplain, and terraces of the Ohio River provide sand and gravel to the county.

Wetzel County has high schools at New Martinsville, Pine Grove, Paden City, and Hundred, as well as several elementary schools. The Wetzel County Board of Education employs more than 450 workers, and is the largest employer in the county.

View of New Martinsville in Wetzel County, from the Ohio shore.

Wetzel County Hospital has 68 beds with additional accommodations for skilled nursing patients, and has three operating rooms, an emergency department, and numerous outpatient services.

Wetzel County is popular with sportsmen. Deer, turkey, and squirrel hunting are common, and largemouth and smallmouth bass, hybrid bass, catfish, crappie, and walleye are caught in abundance.

New Martinsville enjoys the unusual advantage of having its own electricity generating plant. The hydroelectric facility at Hannibal locks and dam was completed in 1988. Now, it produces 37 megawatts from two units, and serves New Martinsville and one other city within the county with electricity. The nearby Veterans Memorial Bridge gives residents of Wetzel County easy access to Ohio.

See also New Martinsville

Andrea Null
New Martinsville

Lewis Wetzel

Lewis Wetzel, frontiersman, scout, and Indian fighter, was born in August 1763. He may have been born in Lancaster County, Pennsylvania, where his parents lived for several years, or along the South Branch of the Potomac, in the present Eastern Panhandle. The Wetzel family settled along Wheeling Creek, in what is now Ohio County, in 1769, along with the Zane, McColloch, and allied families.

Wetzel developed an early hatred for Indians when he and his brother, Jacob, were captured by Wyandots in 1778 while tending corn at the family homestead. In resisting, Wetzel received a gunshot wound, a superficial grazing of his breastbone. After two days in captivity, the brothers escaped and returned to Wheeling. Wetzel, his father, and brothers were among the defenders of Fort Henry when it was attacked by British and Indian forces in September 1782.

On June 19, 1786, Wetzel's father, John, and his brother, George, were killed by Indians and his brother, Martin, was wounded while on a hunting trip. Wetzel himself was the only member of the party unhurt. This experience led him to undertake a private war on all Indians. His most notorious murder was of the Seneca chief Tegunteh, who was peacefully involved in the negotiation of the Treaty of Fort Harmar (1789), near present Marietta, Ohio. Wetzel was twice arrested for this crime but never punished. He later claimed to have taken 27 scalps, but it is likely that the number of his victims was considerably higher. It is asserted that Wetzel could reload his musket while running, a rare feat among frontiersmen that enabled him to stop and fire while being pursued.

After the peace that followed the signing of the Treaty of Greenville (1795), Wetzel moved to Louisiana Territory, where he was imprisoned in New Orleans for several years on conviction of counterfeiting. He died at Rosetta, near Natchez, Mississippi Territory, in 1808. His body was later reinterred at McCreary Cemetery near Wheeling. Wetzel County was named for Lewis Wetzel.

Lewis Wetzel's role in frontier history was romanticized in the early novels of Zane Grey. More recently his exploits have been recounted in the works of Allan W. Eckert, especially *That Dark and Bloody River*.

See also Fort Henry, Indian Wars

Philip Sturm
Ohio Valley University

Clarence B. Allman, *Lewis Wetzel, Indian Fighter*, 1961; George Carroll, "Lewis Wetzel: Warfare Tactics on the Frontier," *West Virginia History*, 1991.

Kellian V. Rensalear Whaley

Congressman and Civil War officer Kellian Van Rensalear Whaley was born in Utica, New York, May 6, 1821. His family moved to Ohio, where he attended public schools, and in 1842 moved to Wayne County, near the present site of Ceredo. As an adult Whaley was engaged in the lumber business.

In keeping with his Northern roots, Whaley held strong pro-Union beliefs in the traumatic period before and after the 1860 presidential election. After Virginia adopted the secession ordinance on April 17, 1861, Whaley was elected as a Unionist to the U.S. House of Representatives on April 23, 1861, by the vote of Union loyalists from the 11th District of Virginia, replacing Albert Gallatin Jenkins, who supported the Confederacy. Whaley and four other Virginia congressmen served in the House of Representatives in the 37th Congress, representing Reorganized Virginia, which remained loyal to the United States. Under the direction of Governor Pierpont of the Reorganized Government, Whaley organized Union military recruitment in his region of the state. As a Union officer he fought, was captured, and made a remarkable escape during the Confederate raid on Guyandotte in November 1861.

Whaley was reelected to Congress in 1863 and 1865 from West Virginia as an Unconditional Unionist, but no doubt showed his true political affiliation by attending the 1864 Republican National Convention as a delegate. After his three terms, Whaley, as a loyal Union Republican, received a political appointment to serve as collector of customs in Texas. He died May 20, 1876, in Point Pleasant.

Kenneth C. Martis
West Virginia University

Billy Edd Wheeler

Songwriter, musician, playwright, humorist, and poet Billy Edd Wheeler was born in Whitesville, Boone County, De-

Coal Tattoo

Traveling down that coal town road
Listen to my rubber tires whine!
Goodbye to buckeye and white
  sycamore,
I'm leaving you behind.
I been a coal man all my life,
Layin' down track in the hole
Got a back like an ironwood
Bent by the wind,
Blood veins blue as the coal.
Blood veins blue as the coal.

Somebody said, "That's a strange
  tattoo
You have on the side of your head."
I said, "That's the blueprint left by the
  coal,
Just a little more and I'd be dead."
But I love the rumble and I love the
  dark,
I love the cool of the slate,
But it's on down the new road
Looking for a job.
This traveling and looking I hate.

I've stood for the Union, I've walked in
  the line,
I've fought against the company.
Stood for the U. M. W. of A.
Now who's gonna stand for me?
I got no house and I got no pay,
Just got a worried soul
And this blue tattoo on the side of my
  head
Left by the number nine coal.

Some day when I die and go
To heaven the land of my dreams,
I won't have to worry on losing my job
To bad times and big machines.
I ain't gonna pay my money away
And lose my hospital plans.
I'm gonna pick coal while the blue
  heavens roll
And sing with the angel bands.
And sing with the angel bands!

—Billy Edd Wheeler
Song of a Woods Colt (1969)

cember 9, 1932. After high school, he studied at Warren Wilson College for two years and received his B.A. in English from Berea College in 1955. After service in the navy he went on to the Yale School of Drama, where he studied playwriting in graduate school.

Wheeler has given hundreds of concerts ranging from churches and civic clubs to Carnegie Hall, where he has appeared twice. He has written more than 500 songs, including the top hits "Jackson," "The Reverend Mister Black," "Coward of the County," and the humorous classic, "Ode to the Little Brown Shack Out Back." His 1963 "Coal Tattoo," recorded by Wheeler and others, is a powerful evocation of life in the coalfields during the time of mine mechanization and a failing union. Wheeler's songs have been recorded by Chet Atkins, Pat Boone, Glen Campbell, Johnny Cash, Judy Collins, Merle Haggard, Richie Havens, Jerry Lee Lewis, Elvis Presley, Kenny Rogers, Hank Williams Jr., and others. In October 2000, he was inducted into the Country Music Hall of Fame.

Wheeler wrote the play "Hatfields & McCoys," performed annually by Theatre West Virginia, and 15 other plays. He authored several books of poetry, including the hauntingly beautiful *Song of a Woods Colt,* and he co-authored with Loyal Jones of Berea College a popular series of folk humor books. Wheeler lives in Swannanoa, North Carolina.

Norman L. Fagan
Red House

Wheeling

Wheeling, elevation 678 feet, population 31,419, lies 57 miles below Pittsburgh on the Ohio River. The manufacturing and commercial center of the Northern Panhandle and the county seat of Ohio County, Wheeling stretches along a narrow valley on the east bank of the Ohio, around and over the neighboring foothills, and westward across Wheeling Island. The valley of Wheeling Creek eastward is the "out-the-Pike" area, with its residential suburbs and Oglebay and Wheeling parks.

There are signs of long prehistoric habitation in this part of the Ohio Valley, including the impressive Adena mound at nearby Moundsville. The name "Wheeling" predates white settlement, deriving from a native word understood to mean "place of the head" or "place of the skull." On Wheeling Creek a white man was scalped, decapitated, and his head impaled at the creek mouth to deter further visitors.

French explorers in 1739 and 1749, the surveyor Christopher Gist in 1751, and George Washington in 1770 all came to eye the rich river valley. Celoron de Blainville buried a lead plate for the French at the mouth of Wheeling Creek in 1749. The first organized white settlement, initially called Zanesburg, dates from 1769, when Ebenezer, Silas, and Jonathan Zane emigrated from the South Branch Valley in the present Eastern Panhandle. The Zanes, their slaves, and their friends, including the Wetzels, Caldwells, Shepherds, and McCollochs, initially populated the Wheeling area.

In 1774, with the murder of Chief Logan's family, a general Indian uprising evolved into Dunmore's War, and soldiers from Fort Pitt built Fort Fincastle on a bluff near the mouth of Wheeling Creek, renamed Fort Henry for Governor Patrick Henry in 1776. Although besieged in 1777 and in 1782, when Betty Zane made her legendary gunpowder run, the community survived and prospered. In 1796, Ebenezer Zane blazed his famous trace to Maysville, Kentucky, making Wheeling an early commercial center for western pioneers. In 1797, Wheeling became the county seat, in 1806 it was chartered as a town, and in 1836 it was incorporated as a city.

In 1818, the arrival of the National Road spurred growth and fostered such enterprises as boat building, iron manufacturing, glassmaking, provision stores, blacksmith shops, hotels, and taverns. Bands of slaves arrived, leading to a slave auction block at 10th Street and also to Underground Railroad activity. Wheeling became known as the Nail City because of its enormous output of cut nails. By 1831, Wheeling was declared an inland port of entry. A handsome U.S. Custom House, now preserved as West Virginia Independence Hall, was built in 1859.

Wheeling boasted very early telegraphs, waterworks, gas lights, and electricity. It had free public schools in 1849, a hospital in 1850, and a library in 1852. In 1849, Wheeling built the first bridge across the Ohio River, which was for many years the longest suspension bridge in the world. In January of 1853, the Baltimore & Ohio Railroad reached the city.

With secession and the Civil War, Wheeling hosted the meetings that led to the creation of the unionist Reorganized Government of Virginia and then to the birth of the new state of West Virginia. Wheeling was the first capital for both. Though divided in its sentiments, Wheeling had important Union facilities during the Civil War, including Camp Carlile, a recruitment and training center; an army general hospital; and a military prison, the Atheneum.

After the war, Wheeling maintained its commercial prominence, jumping from 14,083 people in 1860 to 30,737 in 1880. The city had long offered plentiful jobs for ethnic groups such as the English, Welsh, Scotch-Irish, Irish, Germans, Italians, Poles, Slavs, and Greeks. Steel, tobacco, china and tile, textiles, breweries, and coal flourished as major industries. A strong labor heritage produced such 20th century union leaders as the Reuther brothers.

The high Victorian era saw the State Fair, which operated on Wheeling Island from 1881 to 1940, the return of the state capital (1875–85), German singing societies, rich architecture, sports, gambling, and prostitution. The 20th century brought the Wheeling Symphony, WWVA Radio, and the Capitol Theatre in the 1920s, and WWVA's *Wheeling Jamboree* country music show in 1933, but also the Great Depression and the awful 1936 flood, and the beginning of a long economic decline. Population peaked in 1930 at 61,659. The city sent its men off to World War II, and Stifel & Sons supplied uniforms. In the 1950s, Sen. Joseph McCarthy gave a famous speech in Wheeling, which began a national Red Scare, and a new city-county building and the Fort Henry Bridge were built. The 1960s saw the construction of Interstate 70 and the Wheeling Tunnel.

Times changed as heavy industry declined and outlying malls weakened the downtown. Its economy has suffered, and its population declined to 31,419 in 2000. Wheeling today has a strong educational system, low crime rate, good medical care, and fine sports, cultural, and recreational programs. The annual Festival of Lights, an expanding racetrack and gambling center on Wheeling Island, and radio station WWVA's *Jamboree USA* draw a large tourist trade. The National Heritage Area is revitalizing the historic waterfront. The city born of the "rail, road, and river" looks to its past to redefine its future.

See also Formation of West Virginia, National Road, Wheeling Island, Wheeling Suspension Bridge, Betty Zane, Ebenezer Zane

Margaret Brennan
Wheeling Area Historical Society
Doug Fetherling, *Wheeling: An Illustrated History,* 1983; Clifford M. Lewis, *Wheeling Bicentennial: 1769–1969,* 1969.

Wheeling Conventions, 1st and 2nd

See Formation of West Virginia, History of West Virginia.

Wheeling Downs

Wheeling Downs, now Wheeling Island Racetrack and Gaming Center, is a greyhound racing track and gambling center located on Wheeling Island in the city of Wheeling. In 1937, Wheeling Downs opened for harness racing as a half-mile horse track on the grounds of the State Fair Park. Races were held from late May to late June and from late August to late September. The parimutuel system of betting was used.

Wheeling Downs never was a big-money horse track, and a 1962 fire ended racing until 1968. Harness racing resumed from 1969 to 1975. The track's future was assured with the passage of a dog racing bill by the state legislature in 1975. Almost $1 million was spent to convert Wheeling Downs to dog racing, which began in 1976. Greyhound racing continues at Wheeling Downs, but the main attraction today is video slot machines. The West Virginia Lottery Commission approved the first 400 machines in 1994, and in 2004 there were 2,183 machines at the track. Video gambling provided about 85 percent of total track revenues in 2001, as compared to about 10 percent from greyhound racing. The rest came from betting on simulcast racing at other tracks.

A major expansion was completed in

2003 at a cost of $68 million. The expansion provided 30,000 more square feet for additional slot machines. In addition, the company opened a deluxe, 150-room hotel designed with a tropical theme and decor including a waterfall in the grand foyer. The hotel includes conference and meeting space. In addition, the company expanded its food service operations with the addition of a fine-dining restaurant, a casual restaurant, a food court, and a bar and lounge. The expansion included the addition of a 600-seat multipurpose showroom and a new paddock facility as well as a new off-site kennel compound.

Greyhound racing takes place year-round at Wheeling Downs.

Joseph Platania
Huntington

Wheeling Hospital

Wheeling Hospital, called the mother hospital of West Virginia because of its early founding, was chartered March 12, 1850. It was the only such medical facility between Pittsburgh and Cincinnati, and growth was swift. Its founders were the Catholic Bishop Richard Whelan and Dr. Simon Hullihen, supported by Drs. John Frissell and Matthew Houston. In 1853, the bishop brought in six Sisters of Saint Joseph from Missouri and purchased the Metcalf property, a house still standing at 110 15th Street. In 1856, the hospital outgrew this building and moved to the Michael Sweeney mansion in North Wheeling, its site for the next 119 years.

During the Civil War, in April 1864, a wing of the hospital was rented by the U.S. Army, and in July the entire institution was taken over as a general military hospital. The Sisters were hired as army nurses, treating wounded Union and Confederate soldiers side by side. The institution grew to 90 beds in 1892, and, with two new wings, to 225 beds in 1914. A nursing school was founded in 1900 and discontinued in 1975. Also designated a marine facility, the hospital served the boatmen on the Ohio River for many years.

The original hospital building was demolished and a new central portion constructed in 1933. During World War II, the institution sponsored a Cadet Nurses Corps unit and furnished doctors and nurses for the war effort. After the war, two new departments were opened: physical therapy in 1948 and outpatient in 1950. Wheeling Hospital set up the state's first intensive care unit in 1963 and the first coronary care unit in 1966.

The hospital moved from North Wheeling to a new facility in 1975 at its present location in the Clator neighborhood of Wheeling. In 1978, the region's first cardiac catheterization laboratory was opened, and a second was added in 1996. This made possible the area's first open-heart surgery in 1994. A continuous care and kidney dialysis center was dedicated in 1983. In 1994, the Howard Long Wellness Center opened, increasing innovative programs in cardiac and pulmonary disease rehabilitation. Today Wheeling Hospital, a 301-bed facility with 1,781 employees, is the umbrella organization for the Belmont Community Hospital in Bellaire, Ohio, the Wheeling Clinic, and the Visiting Nurses Association.

Margaret Brennan
Wheeling Area Historical Society

Wheeling *Intelligencer*

West Virginia's oldest continuously published daily newspaper is arguably its most famous as well. The *Wheeling Intelligencer* began in 1852, a landmark year when the tracks of the Baltimore & Ohio Railroad reached Wheeling and development blossomed. Unlike most other papers of the same era, the *Intelligencer* did not originate as a weekly or semiweekly but appeared daily from the beginning. J. H. Pendleton, one of those who established the paper, was the first editor.

In 1856, the *Intelligencer* was acquired by the city editor, Archibald Campbell (1833–1903), nephew of Alexander Campbell of nearby Bethany, the founder of the Disciples of Christ religious denomination and of Bethany College. The younger Campbell was one of the fathers of West Virginia. He favored the Republican Party and in 1860 was the only editor in Virginia to support Abraham Lincoln's candidacy for the office of president of the United States. As a reward, Archibald Campbell was appointed Wheeling's postmaster. He left the paper in 1866 but repurchased it with a new partner in 1873.

The other important figure in the early history of the *Intelligencer* was H. C. Ogden (1869–1943), who came to Wheeling in 1888 and worked as a reporter, later founding the competing *News*, an evening paper. After Campbell's death, Ogden acquired the *Intelligencer*. Under Ogden, the newspaper, previously published from a building on the north side of Quincy (now 14th) Street between Main and Market, was installed in its present home at 1500 Main Street. In 1936, Ogden merged the *News* with the *Register*, traditionally a Democratic paper, to form the *Wheeling News-Register*, which continues as an afternoon paper. The morning *Intelligencer* retains its stoutly Republican policies and pro-business slant.

The Wheeling *Intelligencer* often has been associated with important events. It strongly opposed the secession of Virginia during the Civil War and became a staunch advocate for the creation of West Virginia. The newspaper became increasingly anti-slavery and radical in its politics as the war progressed. Nearly a century later, the *Intelligencer* again found itself at the center of the national stage when it broke the news of Sen. Joe McCarthy's 1950 Wheeling speech. McCarthy's speech charged that the U.S. State Department was overrun with communists and triggered the national red scare of the early 1950s. Today, *Intelligencer* back files are an important primary source for historians, especially for the Civil War period.

Following H. C. Ogden's death, control of the paper passed to his daughter and then to her son, G. Ogden Nutting, president and publisher of Ogden Newspapers Inc., who has guided a fourth generation of his family into the business. Ogden Newspapers owns papers in 11 states, including five dailies in West Virginia, and has various other media and communications interests. Rich in tradition and loyal to its roots, the *Intelligencer* has been the early home of many journalists who have gone on to renown in larger centers.

See also Archibald W. Campbell, Herschel Coombs Ogden, Ogden Newspapers

George Fetherling
Vancouver, British Columbia

Wheeling Island

Wheeling Island is the second most heavily populated river island in the country, after New York's Manhattan. The island, located in the Ohio River between mainland Wheeling and Bridgeport, Ohio, is home to an estimated 5,000 people. It is part of the city of Wheeling. The island is 10,500 feet long and 2,265 feet wide. Ebenezer Zane is said to have bought it from the Indians for a keg of whiskey.

Though it remained undeveloped for over half a century, Wheeling Island became a fashionable place for city leaders to build riverfront mansions following the construction of Wheeling's famous suspension bridge in 1849. Development boomed following the provision of another bridge and streetcar service. The first West Virginia State Fair was held at the island fairgrounds in 1881, and later on, a racetrack, swimming pool, roller coaster, skating rink, and other recreational attractions drew big summer-long crowds well into the mid-1900s. Wheeling Downs, a greyhound racing track and gambling facility now known as Wheeling Island Racetrack and Gaming Center, is located there today. Though serious floods have taken a toll, the staunch Islanders remain, and continue to work toward restoring their neighborhood's inherent beauty.

Louis E. Keefer
Reston, Virginia

Wheeling Jamboree

Since 1933, radio station WWVA's *Wheeling Jamboree* has been West Virginia's premier live audience country music program and one of the most successful programs of its sort in the country. Over the years,

The Jamboree occupied Wheeling's beautiful Capitol Theatre for many years.

many country stars have had lengthy associations with the show, including Wilma Lee and Stoney Cooper, Hawkshaw Hawkins, Lee Moore, Doc and Chickie Williams, and Big Slim the Lone Cowboy (Harry C. McAuliffe). Major artists affiliated with the *Jamboree* for shorter periods include the Bailey Brothers, the Osborne Brothers, Hank Snow, Mac Wiseman, and Grandpa Jones. Popular regional favorites who have appeared on the program at various times include Silver Yodelin' Bill Jones, the Lilly Brothers, and the trio Cap, Andy and Flip.

The first *Jamboree* broadcast originated from the Capitol Theatre in downtown Wheeling on January 7, 1933. From December 13, 1969, through 2005 the theater was again the *Jamboree's* home. In between, the show was broadcast from several other downtown theaters. When WWVA became a 50,000-watt station in October 1942, the *Jamboree's* radio audience became much larger. From December 1942 until mid-1946, wartime shortages and a reduction in leisure travel led to the show being only a studio production, with no audience present. George Smith (d. 1946) served as WWVA program director from 1931 and provided the business leadership that made the program a success. For a time in the mid-'50s, the CBS radio network carried a portion of the *Jamboree* every third week. Initially known as the *Midnight Jamboree*, the Wheeling program soon became the *World's Original Jamboree*, and since the late 1960s the official title has been *Jamboree USA.* The commonly used name, however, always seems to have been *Wheeling Jamboree*.

In recent years, an emphasis on concert-style performances by guest stars from Nashville has tended to relegate *Jamboree* regulars to a secondary level. However, it may also have enabled the program to survive long after the golden age of radio had run its course. Today the *Jamboree* and Nashville's *Grand Ole Opry* are the only survivors of a genre that once included the *Chicago Barn Dance*, *Louisiana Hayride* and other shows. For decades the *Wheeling Jamboree* has played a significant role in the development of country music as an American art form, being especially important in reaching audiences in the rural regions north and east of Wheeling and extending into the Canadian Maritime Provinces.

See also Radio, Doc Williams, WWVA

Ivan M. Tribe
University of Rio Grande

Ivan M. Tribe, *Mountaineer Jamboree: Country Music in West Virginia*, 1984.

Wheeling Jesuit University

The youngest of the 28 Jesuit institutions of higher education in the United States, Wheeling Jesuit University is situated in the eastern part of Wheeling. It was founded by the Most Reverend John Swint, bishop of what was then the Diocese of Wheeling. In 1951, Bishop Swint asked the Maryland Province of the Society of Jesus to help him realize his dream of a Catholic college of liberal arts for West Virginia. Three years later, in September 1954, the college was incorporated, its cornerstone laid. On September 26, 1955, Wheeling College opened its doors to students. In 1988, its name was changed to Wheeling Jesuit College. It assumed university status in 1996.

In the beginning there were three modest two-story brick buildings, a student body of 90 men and women, three Jesuit administrators, nine teachers (eight of them Jesuits), and a handful of lay people as support staff. Because Swint had provided the $2.75 million start-up costs, the new college was debt free. Tuition was $215 per semester. The college had no endowment and no residence halls. Though chartered by the state of West Virginia, it had no accreditation.

By the year 2000, the 60-acre campus included six residence halls, eight additional buildings, and several athletic fields. Enrollment hovered near 1,500, and university personnel numbered 430. A substantial long-term debt, a result of the building boom of the previous 15 years, was balanced by an endowment of nearly $21 million. Wheeling Jesuit University is accredited by the North Central Association of Colleges and Schools and other agencies.

Two modern buildings, the Erma Ora Byrd Center for Educational Technologies and its companion, the Robert C. Byrd National Technology Transfer Center, represent the university's attempt to complement its traditional mission—"to integrate learning, research and economic development with classical knowledge and Christian revelation"—by new initiatives to develop the regional economy in partnership with government and business.

Between 1955 and 2005, seven Jesuit presidents served the institution. Lawrence R. McHugh, S.J. (1955–59) nursed Bishop Swint's vision to a joyful first commencement in June 1959, when 20 women and 31 men graduated. William F. Troy, S.J. (1959–66) guided the school to national accreditation in 1962. His successor, Frank R. Haig, S.J. (1966–72), presided through the turbulent years of the Vietnam era. The fourth president, Charles L. Currie, S.J. (1972–82), introduced new programs, many curricular changes, and a Bachelor of Science in Nursing degree. Rev. Thomas Acker, S.J. (1982–2000) inspired—and sometimes goaded—Wheeling Jesuit College forward. The present campus is a monument to his effort and to the substantial support of his educational initiatives by Sen. Robert Byrd and Congressman Alan Mollohan. The Reverend George Lundy, S.J., became president in 2000, and was succeeded by the Reverend Joseph R. Hacala, S.J., in 2003.

Eighteen academic departments offer 30 baccalaureate degree programs, eight pre-professional programs and five master's programs. An Adult-Evening Division offers an additional eight baccalaureate programs, including a bachelor of science degree for R.N.'s, and an English Language Institute provides instruction in English as a second language.

Instruction is provided by 73 full-time faculty members and 54 part-time colleagues. In 2004, 86 percent of the full-time faculty held doctorates or the terminal degree for their disciplines. The average class size at Wheeling Jesuit University was 18 students.

There are 14 intercollegiate sports programs. Choral performances, plays, musicals, lectures, and debates keep the Troy Theater stage occupied year-round. Twenty-two campus organizations cater to activities as diverse as wilderness camping, inner city tutoring, and celebrating African heritage. The recently acquired 545-acre Lantz farm is the university's nature center, environmental research station, and meeting center.

Fees for room, board, and tuition are close to the national average for private colleges and universities, although higher than the comparable fees at West Virginia's public colleges. But, in keeping with its specific mission to Appalachia, the university's level of student aid exceeds national averages by about 30 percent. Almost all applicants for admission qualify for assistance, and almost all receive it.

Wheeling Jesuit had 1,356 students (full-time equivalents) in fall 2004. The student body is a diverse one. In recent years between 31 percent and 37 percent of students have been West Virginians, and about two-thirds of those who acknowledged a religious affiliation were Roman Catholic. Of its 8,000-plus alumni, more than 2,000 live and work in West Virginia.

By the final years of the 20th century, in its annual surveys of America's best colleges, *U.S. News and World Report* consistently ranked Wheeling Jesuit among the 15 best universities in the southern region.

Paul Orr
St. Clairsville, Ohio
"America's Best Colleges," *U.S. News and World Report*, August 1998; *Wheeling College Catalog*, 1956–1957; Wheeling Jesuit University, *Fact Book: 2000–2001.*

Wheeling & Lake Erie Railway

The Wheeling & Lake Erie Railway connected Wheeling to Lake Erie at Toledo, opening the northeastern Ohio coalfields to both the Great Lakes and the Ohio River and offering Wheeling the best way to ship goods to Toledo, Chicago, Detroit, and Cleveland. In 1871, the W&LE was incorporated. Construction was slow because of the rugged terrain north of the Ohio River and the lack of financial re-

sources. The enterprise owed its successful completion to investments by George Gould, the son of railroad tycoon Jay Gould. Building from the Toledo end, the line was eventually completed to Martin's Ferry, Ohio, in 1891. From there, access to nearby Wheeling was provided by trackage rights on the Wheeling Bridge & Terminal Railway.

The W&LE prospered until the economic depression of the 1890s and a long strike by coal miners. The railroad entered a financial receivership in the late 1890s, and again with the collapse of the Gould empire in 1907. But the growth of the iron and steel industries of northeastern Ohio and the demand for their products in Detroit and Toledo, coupled with the demand for Ohio coal in the east, allowed the W&LE to recover and prosper. From 1920 to 1949, it did not fail to post a profit. In 1946 and 1947, the Nickel Plate Railroad purchased a majority of W&LE stock. The Wheeling & Lake Erie Railway was merged with the Nickel Plate into the Norfolk & Western Railway in 1964.

See also Railroads, Wheeling
Robert L. Frey
Miamisburg, Ohio
John A. Rehor, *The Nickel Plate Story*, 1978.

Wheeling National Heritage Area

The Wheeling National Heritage Area was created in 2000. The heritage area encompasses the central portion of Wheeling, particularly the part neighboring on the Ohio River. It includes a mixture of residential, commercial, entertainment, industrial, and government structures, with many buildings well over 100 years old. The heritage area's primary purpose is to foster economic development by exploiting Wheeling's natural, historical, and architectural assets. It is one of 24 national heritage areas in the United States, including the National Coal Heritage Area in southern West Virginia.

The ideas behind the Wheeling National Heritage Area were in large part generated by Harry Hamm, editor of the *Wheeling News-Register*, who authored the 1987 report, "Wheeling 2000." The project was supported by Wheeling businessmen and organizations, Sen. Robert C. Byrd, Congressman Alan Mollohan, the National Park Service, and the state of West Virginia. National heritage areas are designated by Congress to recognize regions making an important contribution to the history and experience of America.

One of the key elements of the plan was the formation of the Wheeling National Heritage Area Corporation on June 13, 1994. Implementation is expected to take 10 years from 2000 and to cost more than $57 million. The intent of the heritage plan is the rebirth of Wheeling as an important port of entry to the

heartland by turning the face of Wheeling back toward the Ohio River.

Gordon L. Swartz III
Cameron

Wheeling-Pittsburgh Steel

The Wheeling-Pittsburgh Steel Corporation resulted from the June 1968 merger of the Wheeling Steel and Pittsburgh Steel companies. It is the nation's sixth-largest steelmaker. Wheeling-Pitt, as it is commonly called, manufactures a wide variety of rolled steel products for industry, construction, highway and bridge building, and agriculture. With its corporate headquarters in the former Schmulbach Building in downtown Wheeling, Wheeling-Pitt is a major factor in the economy of the Upper Ohio Valley. Its plants are found in Follansbee and Beech Bottom, as well as Allenport, Pennsylvania, and four Ohio cities.

In the last quarter of the 20th century, the American steel industry steadily declined, and Wheeling-Pitt closed its works at Benwood, then sold off its La Belle Nail Works, and endured two Chapter 11 bankruptcies. There was a long, bitter labor strike in 1996–97, as union workers attempted to regain pension benefits given up during one of these bankruptcies. The company emerged from the second bankruptcy early in the 21st century, completed construction of an electric arc furnace, and experienced a significant rise in its stock prices. Employment in 2005 was approximately 3,400.

While only a sixth of the 1920 size of its predecessor companies, Wheeling-Pitt has recently expanded its interests. It is a partner with Nisshan Steel Company of Japan in the Follansbee plant, where the nation's first computerized coating facility went into operation in 1988. Wheeling-Pitt owns 50 percent of Ohio Coatings in Yorkville, Ohio, a joint operation with Dong Yang Tinplate of South Korea. In early 2005, Wheeling-Pitt entered another relationship with a foreign company, Severstal North America, a subsidiary of Russia's second-largest steelmaker. This partnership will result in the rebuilding of the Cove Works, north of Follansbee.

See also Steel Industry, Wheeling Steel, Wheeling-Pittsburgh Steel Strike

David T. Javersak
West Liberty State College

Wheeling-Pittsburgh Steel Building

The Wheeling-Pittsburgh Steel Building, originally known as the Schmulbach Building, was West Virginia's first high-rise office building. The 12-story structure was built in 1904–07 on Market Street in downtown Wheeling. Still the city's tallest office building, it remains a local landmark.

The massive H-shaped building was designed for the German immigrant brewer and industrialist, Henry Schmulbach, by Wheeling architects Millard F. Giesey and Frederick Faris. The building was taken over by the Wheeling Steel Corporation in 1921 and renamed. The first two floors of the structure are faced in granite, and the upper floors are faced in cream-colored brick.

The Wheeling-Pittsburgh Steel Building is part of the Wheeling Historic District, which was listed on the National Register of Historic Places in 1979.

See also Millard F. Giesey, Henry Schmulbach, Wheeling

Wheeling-Pittsburgh Steel Strike

A 10-month walkout by steelworkers at Wheeling-Pittsburgh Steel, beginning October 1, 1996, was the longest steel manufacturing strike on record when it concluded nearly a year later. The strike by members of the United Steelworkers of America put 4,500 workers out of work in eight plants in three states. The workers struck mainly to improve their pension benefits, which had been revised when new owners led the ailing company out of bankruptcy after 1989. By 1994, Wheeling-Pitt had been restored to a place among industry leaders, and the workers sought a readjustment of pension benefits on terms more beneficial to themselves.

The negotiations were complex and bitter. Both sides were unyielding. Seventy-eight days into the strike, negotiators for the company and the union were ordered to the Federal Mediation and Conciliation Service office in Pittsburgh, but the deadlock continued. The union with help from the AFL-CIO went after major stockholders of Wheeling-Pitt's parent, WHX Corporation of New York. In March, Sen. Jay Rockefeller convened a meeting in Washington, but again little progress was made. Another meeting was set in Pittsburgh, but the company walked out, refusing the union's offer. Finally, in August, a labor contract was ratified.

James Bowen, chief negotiator for the union and later president of the state AFL-CIO, claimed victory in the settlement, which gave workers $40 per month in pension benefits for each year of service, increasing to $44 per month on June 1, 2003. It also allowed retirement at age 55 with 30 years of service. The company achieved 850 job reductions, approximately 19 percent of the work force, mainly through attrition. The strike ended August 12, 1997, when 79 percent of the workers approved the contract.

See also Wheeling-Pittsburgh Steel

Jane Kraina
Weirton

Wheeling Steel

The Wheeling Steel Corporation was organized on June 21, 1920, when La Belle Iron Works, Whitaker-Glessner Company, and Wheeling Steel & Iron Works combined. In the 1920s, Wheeling Steel employed more than 17,000 workers and ranked as the nation's third-largest steelmaker.

Wheeling's first iron mills date to the 1830s, and for the remainder of the 19th century the city was a hub of metal working. Its most famous product was the cut nail, which was so important locally that Wheeling was once known as the "Nail City." The Whitaker-Glessner Company traces its heritage to the 1720s, when the Principio Company began production of pig iron and bar iron in Maryland. This subsidiary of Whitaker-Glessner remained in operation until 1925, when the new Wheeling Steel closed its furnaces.

During the 1880s, at the Benwood Works, Wheeling Steel produced the first steel pipe in the United States, and its Yorkville (Ohio) Works introduced the industry's first "black plate" for tinning in the 1920s. Other well-known products from Wheeling Steel included tin cans, lard pails, stoves, lunch pails, and steel plates and sheets.

Beginning in 1921, Wheeling Steel provided company housing for its coke plant workers at the East Steubenville Works at Follansbee, Brooke County. Dubbed Coketown, this community of small houses, blackened by the smoke from the coke ovens, remained intact until the 1960s, when the buildings were razed to make way for a parking lot.

By the company's 40th anniversary in 1960, Wheeling Steel plants stretched for 30 miles along the Ohio River, from Benwood, West Virginia, to Steubenville, Ohio. As an integrated operation with its own coal mines, the company lived up to its slogan, "From Mine to Market." The influence of Wheeling Steel extended beyond its various manufactured products. For eight years (1936–44), a radio program, "It's Wheeling Steel," broadcast musical entertainment to a national audience from Wheeling station WWVA.

In June 1968, Wheeling Steel merged with Pittsburgh Steel to form the Wheeling-Pittsburgh Steel Corporation.

See also La Belle Iron Works, Steel Industry, Wheeling, Wheeling-Pittsburgh Steel

David T. Javersak
West Liberty State College

Wheeling Suspension Bridge

The wire suspension bridge over the Ohio River at Wheeling was opened for traffic in October 1849 amid great public acclaim. It was the longest (1,010 feet) clear span in the world. It ushered in America's ascendancy in long-span suspension bridge building which lasted for more than a century. The bridge still serves local traffic and has been designated a national landmark by both the National Park Service and the American Society of Civil Engineers.

Charles Ellet Jr., its designer, actively promoted suspension bridges in America following his sojourn at the École des Ponts et Chaussées in Paris followed by a tour of French suspension bridges. His first success came when he was appointed chief engineer of the Fairmont Bridge (1841–42) across the Schuylkill River at Philadelphia, which served as the prototype for the Wheeling Suspension Bridge.

Ellet secured contracts for both the Wheeling and Niagara Falls suspension bridges in 1847. As a result of a dispute with the owners, Ellet was dismissed from the Niagara bridge, but successfully completed the Wheeling bridge in 1849. The distinctive features of the bridge are the main and stay cables, the vertical suspenders, massive stone towers, timber-stiffening trusses flanking the roadway, and large stone anchorages. By using drawn wrought-iron wire, a superior strength was obtained. Wheeling was a center for iron production, wire was one of many products produced in the area, and all of the components of the bridge were supplied locally. In addition, the Wheeling and Belmont Bridge Company undertook the construction, operation and maintenance of this great bridge, using local stockholders to provide the financial resources. Neither state nor federal funds were used.

With the completion of the suspension bridge, the people of Wheeling had secured a confluence of transportation systems. The bridge carried the National Road over the Ohio River, the head of summer navigation on the river was at Wheeling, and the long expected Baltimore & Ohio Railroad was due to reach Wheeling at the end of 1852. In recognition of this hub of transportation, a new U.S. Custom House was completed in 1859 to serve the port of Wheeling. It later served as the birthplace of the state of West Virginia.

In April 1854, a violent windstorm swept up the Ohio River and destroyed the deck of the bridge and threw the cables off their saddles at the tower tops. Within a few months one lane of the bridge was back in service. Under the direction of William K. McComas the bridge was rebuilt in 1860 with timber stiffening trusses and the regrouping of the six cables on each side into a pair. This altered appearance is substantially what one sees today except for the deck, with the timber flooring having been replaced with an open steel grid in 1956. Additional repairs were undertaken in 1983 and in 1999, when an overhaul was completed in time for the bridge's 150th anniversary. This bridge is not only of regional interest but also is well known by historians and engineers around the world.

See also National Road, Wheeling

Emory L. Kemp
WVU Institute for the History of Technology

Emory L. Kemp and Beverly B. Fluty, *The Wheeling Suspension Bridge: A Pictorial History*, 1999.

The Wheeling Suspension Bridge Case

The Wheeling suspension bridge case, formally known as *State of Pennsylvania v. Wheeling and Belmont Bridge Co.*, was decided by the U.S. Supreme Court in February 1852.

The Wheeling suspension bridge had opened to great fanfare in 1849. It carried the National Road (now U.S. 40) over the east channel of the Ohio River and onto Wheeling Island. With a 1,010-foot main span, it was for many years the longest bridge of its type in the world.

As Wheeling celebrated its completion, the industrialists of western Pennsylvania were quietly plotting the bridge's destruction. The bridge opponents filed an original proceeding directly with the U.S. Supreme Court to abate the bridge as a public nuisance because it obstructed passage of large steamboats, thereby impeding interstate commerce. Pennsylvania's lawyer, Edwin M. Stanton, later President Lincoln's secretary of war, told the court: "the injury occasioned by this obstruction is deep and lasting." The court referred the case to a special master, R. H. Woolworth of New York, who took testimony and reported to the court that the bridge was "an obstruction to navigation resulting in injury to packets plying waters leading to and from Pittsburgh."

The opinion of the Supreme Court was delivered in May of 1852, basically adopting the special master's conclusion. However, the majority opinion stated that the bridge could remain if it could be raised to an elevation of 111 feet above low water and maintained at that height for a distance of 300 feet. The owners of the bridge were given ten months to comply with the order. Practically speaking, this amounted to a destruction order since it was impossible to raise the structure.

The bridge owners and their supporters immediately set out to lobby Congress to declare the suspension bridge as part of a post road, entitled to special protection as a mail-carrying route. Steamboats would have to adjust their smokestacks when passing under the bridge. On August 31, 1852, this proposal became law. In 1854, a violent windstorm severely damaged the suspension bridge, and Pennsylvania returned to the Supreme Court in an attempt to stop reconstruction. The Court ultimately held that the 1852 law prevailed.

The Wheeling bridge controversy is of little interest to modern legal scholars, because the principles involved have since been absorbed fully into law. At the time, however, the original court case represented an important assumption by the Supreme Court of power to interpret the commerce clause of the U.S. Constitution. The corrective action by Congress likewise expanded the regulatory powers of the federal government, which came to fuller fruition in the Interstate Commerce Act a quarter century later.

H. John Rogers
New Martinsville

Elizabeth Brand Monroe, *The Wheeling Bridge Case*, 1992.

Wheeling Symphony

The Wheeling Symphony Orchestra, one of West Virginia's major cultural institutions, had its beginnings in a fall 1928 meeting at the home of Eleanor Caldwell. Under the leadership of Caldwell and with the support of local citizens, the Wheeling Symphony soon became a reality, appearing in its first concert on Sunday, June 30, 1929, at Oglebay Park. Under the direction of Enrico Tamburini, the new orchestra performed Mozart's *Overture to Don Juan* and Schubert's *Unfinished Symphony*, among other works.

Tamburini, the first conductor, helped to mold the fledgling group of amateurs and professionals into a cohesive ensemble. When he left in 1934, Antonio Modarelli took over, coming from the Pittsburgh Symphony. The ascension in 1947 of the able and charismatic Henry Mazer signaled a new era of professionalism for the Wheeling Symphony. Mazer had been an assistant to the outstanding conductor Fritz Reiner, at Chicago, and at Wheeling he developed an expanded program of opera, choral works, and chamber music, and performances by distinguished guest artists, such as Yehudi Menuhin, Benny Goodman, and Artur Rubinstein.

With Mazer's departure in 1960, Henry Aaron, William Steinberg's assistant in Buffalo, was appointed. He left Wheeling in 1964, and once again the symphony hired an assistant conductor of the Pittsburgh Symphony, Robert Kreis. He was a classicist, filling the winter season with traditional favorites and the summer program with popular music and show tunes. He instituted the symphony's first concert tours in 1971.

When Kreis left in 1972, a year of guest conductors followed, from whom was selected Jeff Holland Cook to be Wheeling Symphony's sixth music director, beginning with the 1973–74 season. As a former professional trombonist and conductor of the Rhode Island Philharmonic Orchestra, Cook brought extensive training and experience. He continued the effort to bring in outstanding guest artists, including Arthur Fiedler, Doc Severinsen, Itzhak Perlman, and Eleanor Steber, Wheeling's own opera diva, among others.

Rachael Worby became music director in 1986 and continued to expand on a vital tradition, increasing the number of performances each year from six to 40. She created a pops series, presented guest artists such as Eugenia Zukerman and Jean-Pierre Rampal, and led a successful touring program. Worby left in 2003, to be succeeded by Andre Raphel Smith.

The regular performance home of the symphony is Capitol Music Hall in downtown Wheeling.

Michael Ridderbusch
WVU Libraries

Edward C. Wolf and Margaret Brennan, *For the Love of Music: A 75-Year History of the Wheeling Symphony Orchestra*, 2004.

Richard Vincent Whelan

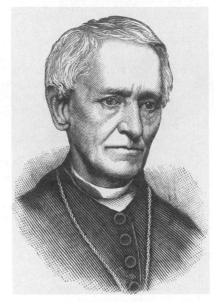

Bishop Richard V. Whelan (1809–74).

Roman Catholic Bishop Richard Vincent Whelan, founder of the Diocese of Wheeling, was born in Baltimore, January 28, 1809. He received his education at Mount St. Mary's College and Seminary in Maryland and the Seminary of St. Sulpice in France. He was ordained to the priesthood in 1831. Whelan returned to Mount St. Mary's, where he remained until 1835, serving on the faculty and as business manager for the college. He was sent to Martinsburg for his first pastoral assignment. He remained there for six years, caring for the Catholic families from Winchester to Harpers Ferry.

In 1841, at age 32, Whelan was consecrated as the second bishop of the Diocese of Richmond, which at that time comprised the entire state of Virginia, including present West Virginia. The vastness of the territory soon led him to petition the Holy See to divide the diocese along the natural barrier of the Allegheny Mountains. On July 19, 1850, Pope Pius IX erected the Diocese of Wheeling and approved Whelan's request to take over the new diocese. Whelan is thus recognized as the founding bishop. At that time, there were four churches, three chapels, six priests, and 10 women religious to serve the estimated 5,000 Catholics scattered across the Diocese of Wheeling. At his death in 1874, the diocese could claim 46 churches, seven chapels, nine schools, a seminary, a hospital, 31 priests, and 109 women religious, with a Catholic population estimated at 18,000. Bishop Whelan died in Baltimore, July 7, 1874.

See also Diocese of Wheeling-Charleston, Roman Catholics

Tricia Pyne
St. Mary's Seminary & University, Maryland

Whipple Company Store

The Whipple Company Store, located on State Route 612 south of Oak Hill, Fayette County, was built by coal operator Justus Collins in the early 20th century. As the commercial and social center for the mining town of Whipple and surrounding communities, the store housed offices for Whipple Colliery Company, the post office and doctor. The store stocked the necessities for a household, from food to furniture.

Collins started the Whipple Colliery Company in the late 1890s. In 1906, the New River Company bought several Fayette County mines, including Whipple. The Whipple store was renamed New River Company Store No. 4.

The most prominent building in town, the two-story wooden structure sits on a cut sandstone foundation. The six sided first floor is topped by an octagon-shaped second floor. An arch frames the building's main entrance, which leads to a large circular area on the first floor. From this circular space, doors allow access to smaller rooms next to the outer walls. The store building is an eye-catching landmark and a reminder of earlier times in the coalfields.

The Whipple Company Store is one of four identical stores that were built in the early 1900s in the New River area. The earliest one was constructed in 1893 in Glen Jean for the Collins Colliery Company. In 1900, the store burned and was rebuilt. The third store was constructed in Prudence. The last to be built, the Whipple store is the only one still standing.

In 1957, the Whipple mine shut down and the store closed. Reopened as a trading post, the store operated until the late 1980s, when it was used as a private residence. In 1991, the Whipple Company Store was listed on the National Register of Historic Places. In 1993, Richard Hunt bought the building and renovated it for a tourist and antiques center.

See also Justus Collins, Company Stores, New River Company

Nancy Ray Adams
Pine Mountain Settlement School

WHIS

One of West Virginia's pioneer radio stations, WHIS had its origins in the ambitions of Hugh and Jim Shott, sons of Hugh Ike Shott Sr. (1866–1953), owner of the *Bluefield Daily Telegraph* and later a congressman. The brothers made initial efforts at radio as early as 1922 and in the spring of 1929 obtained a federal license as WHIS (for the initials of Hugh Ike Shott). They went on the air as a 100-watt station on June 27 with a broadcast that featured the local Lions Club quartet. In the next few years the station increased its power to 250 watts in 1933, 500 in 1935, and 5,000 in 1948.

In 1939, WHIS affiliated with the NBC network. Local programming remained important, however, and a favorite program for many years was *The Breakfast Club* with Stuart Odell and Red Clark. Live country music also played a major role at WHIS, with groups such as the Lonesome Pine Fiddlers, Rex and Eleanor Parker, and the duo of Lynn Davis and Molly O'Day being headquartered there at various times and such well-known figures as Fiddlin' Arthur Smith there for shorter stints.

In 1948, the Shotts made a premature effort at an FM station, but later abandoned it as few of their listeners had FM radios. In 1963, they revived the station which later became WHAJ-FM (for Hugh and Jim). The family ventured into television with WHIS-TV in 1955.

By 1981, Mike Shott, Jim's grandson, had become general manager and WHIS had a "beautiful music" format while WHAJ played "adult contemporary." Pressure from the Federal Communications Commission forced the Shott family to divest themselves of their TV station in 1980 and the *Daily Telegraph* in 1985. However, Mike Shott retained WHIS and WHAJ for several years under the corporate name of Adventure Communications, Inc. In 2005, the station was owned by Triad Broadcasting and had a news and talk radio format.

See also Radio, Hugh I. Shott

Ivan M. Tribe
University of Rio Grande

Martha Jane Becker and Marilyn Fletcher, *Broadcasting in West Virginia: A History,* 1989; Ivan M. Tribe, *Mountaineer Jamboree: Country Music in West Virginia,* 1984.

Whiskey Rebellion

The Whiskey Rebellion, 1791–94, was an American frontier revolt against a federal excise tax levied upon distilled spirits. Intended to help pay off the remaining Revolutionary War debts, the tax incited civil unrest that seriously alarmed the fledgling nation's government. President George Washington mobilized a militia force nearly as large as the Continental Army and personally led the poorly trained soldiers, derisively called the "Watermelon Army," against the farmers.

The uprising began in western Pennsylvania and rapidly spread to the backcountry of New Jersey, Maryland, and Virginia. In Virginia, the counties of Ohio, Monongalia, Harrison, and Randolph each experienced uprisings associated with the Whiskey Rebellion. In Morgantown, the tax collector was intimidated into resigning, and the Ohio County excise officer was attacked. The rebellion was a serious test for the young federal government. Washington became disheartened at the military excesses that resulted, and he spoke passionately about the dangers of mobilizing soldiers against citizens.

The rebellion also pointed out ideological and moral differences among Americans. Eastern elites saw no wrong in taxing liquor, but frontiersmen considered it a harsh economic blow. To them, converting grain crops to whiskey was a prudent economic decision, since whiskey was less bulky than the grain it was made from and more easily transported over primitive roads. Frontiersmen widely believed the tax was unfairly engineered by Treasury Secretary Alexander Hamilton to shield the assets of the wealthy from taxation.

The rebellion contributed to the development of a hurtful stereotype, that of the violent hillbilly moonshiner. Prior to the tax, the spirits distilled in the mountains—especially Monongahela Rye from the area around Morgantown—was a highly prized commodity that could fetch a top price. Merchants as far away as New Orleans were anxious to acquire it. This demand gave the farmers a cash crop. Over the years, the industry became criminalized as taxation and regulation of liquor production marginalized a formerly respectable endeavor.

Barbara Rasmussen
Fairmont State University

Earl Core, *The Monongalia Story, II,* 1976; Thomas P. Slaughter, *The Whiskey Rebellion: Frontier Epilogue to the American Revolution,* 1988.

Albert Blakeslee White

Albert Blakeslee "A. B." White, West Virginia's 11th governor, 1901–05, was born September 22, 1856, in Cleveland, Ohio. He was the fourth person to serve as governor from Wood County, his adopted home.

His father, Dr. Emerson White, was president of Purdue University in Lafayette, Indiana, during six years of Albert's early boyhood and later moved the family to Columbus, Ohio. As a teenager, A. B. White was employed by his father to assist in publishing two journals, the *Ohio Educational Monthly* and the *National Teacher*. It was then that the young White acquired an interest in journalism.

Governor Albert B. White (1856–1941).

He attended Marietta College, a private liberal arts institution in Ohio just across the Ohio River from Wood County, and graduated as the valedictorian of the class of 1878. One year later, he married Agnes Ward of Marietta. The couple had five children.

Upon graduating from college, White returned to his boyhood home in Indiana as manager and part owner of a daily newspaper. He moved to Parkersburg in 1881. He purchased the *State Journal,* a weekly newspaper owned by former governor William E. Stevenson. White made several changes to the publication, turning the *State Journal* into a Republican daily newspaper and a power in state politics.

White established himself as a successful newspaper publisher. He served many years as president of the West Virginia Editorial Association and was president of the National Editorial Association in 1888. During those years, White further developed his interest in politics. He was appointed in 1889 and 1897 as an internal revenue agent, during the presidential administrations of Harrison and McKinley. In addition, he managed the successful U.S. Senate campaign of Stephen B. Elkins in 1894.

A. B. White was elected governor of West Virginia in 1900 and took office in 1901. He soundly defeated the Democratic nominee, Huntington lawyer John Homer Holt. Before taking office, White retired from journalism by selling his interest in the *State Journal.*

White was a very partisan politician and an active member of the Elkins machine. Nonetheless, he is remembered as a reform governor. During his administration he fought for changes in the election process. One law required lobby-

ists to register with the state. Governor White is most remembered for sweeping reforms in property assessment and tax laws. He appointed the industrialist and former U.S. senator, Henry Gassaway Davis, a Democrat, as chairman of the Tax Commission, which made what historian Otis Rice called a "surprisingly moderate" report despite the commission's conservative composition. Still, anti-tax forces rallied the state's railroads and key industries against tax reform, and blocked White's proposals in the legislature until Senator Elkins arranged a compromise. White worked for other progressive reforms, as well, including a food and drug act. He spoke forcefully against industrial pollution of West Virginia streams. During his term, the legislature organized the state tax commissioner's office.

White had an active public career after leaving the governor's office in 1905. He served as the state tax commissioner and in the state senate, and again as an internal revenue agent during President Harding's term. He attempted a run for the U.S. Senate but was unable to gain his party's nomination. White also was an executive in the insurance, banking, and coal industries. When the capitol building burned in January 1921, White and others organized an unsuccessful campaign to move the West Virginia state capital from Charleston to Parkersburg.

A. B. White died at the age of 84 at his Parkersburg home, July 3, 1941. He is buried in Mount Olivet Cemetery in Parkersburg.

S. Shuan Butcher
Parkersburg

Bernard L. Allen, *Parkersburg: A Bicentennial History,* 1985; John G. Morgan, *West Virginia's Governors,* 1980

Doc White

Fiddler and self-taught physician James Franklin "Doc" White was born February 5, 1889, near Ivydale, Clay County. White was a self-made man who taught himself a variety of trades through the years. He was probably best known as a fiddle player.

Doc White served the community as a doctor, dentist, and midwife, without the benefit of formal medical training. He honed his skills by apprenticing under local doctors and dentists and by reading every medical book he could get his hands on. It was estimated that White delivered more than 1,800 babies throughout the hollows of Clay County, and he routinely made house calls to residents too ill to visit his office. In addition, White served as a justice of the peace in Clay County for more than 30 years.

He was one of a long line of accomplished traditional musicians in Clay County, including Jenes Cottrell, Wilson

Douglas, Ira Mullins, Sylvia O'Brien, Minerva White, Lee Triplett, French Carpenter, and others. He was proud of his musical ability and traveled to many fairs and festivals around the state to demonstrate his talents. Doc White died on June 13, 1974, leaving behind his wife, Locie, four children, and six grandchildren.

Brad Martin
Arthurdale

Bob Heyer, "Ivydale: The Morris Family Old-Time Music Festivals," *Goldenseal,* Summer 1998.

I. C. White

Geologist Israel Charles White, born November 1, 1848, in Monongalia County, was in 1867 one of the first six students to enter the Agricultural College of West Virginia (now WVU). He earned undergraduate (1872) and master's degrees (1875) there, and received an honorary law degree in 1919. White returned to WVU to teach geology in 1877. He later worked for the Pennsylvania Geological Survey (1876–83) and the U.S. Geological Survey (1884–88). White was one of the 13 founders of the Geological Society of America.

White was noted for the practical application of geology. In 1885, in an article in the journal *Science,* he asserted his discovery, or rediscovery, of the anticlinal theory in the location of oil and gas. His application of the theory to drill producing wells provided him with financial security and put him in great demand with oil and gas companies in developing fields in Arkansas, Oklahoma, Louisiana, Texas, and Mexico.

White was West Virginia's first state geologist, appointed in 1897 and serving until his death in 1927, working without pay for all but two of those years. He took up the ambitious work of mapping the state's topography and geology and inventorying its resources. White supervised the work on the complete set of state topographic maps, as well as special resource maps, and 34 book-length reports on specific resources and single or multiple county reports. While his reputation was that of an oil and gas geologist, his work in coal geology included extensive publications on Pennsylvania and the Appalachian basin, and a 1908 report on the coal resources of Brazil.

Developing an interest in resource conservation, White was invited by the Theodore Roosevelt administration to speak at the first White House Conference on Conservation in 1908. He continued to publish articles, present speeches, and provide state leaders accounts of wasteful and unnecessary loss of resources through abusive exploitation. He advocated legislation establishing the U.S. Bureau of Mines, following the disastrous 1907 mine explosion at Monongah.

Locally, White was a promoter and developer, and an owner of businesses and residences in the Morgantown area. Many of his properties were to become part of the WVU campus, including the earlier site of the president's home. The main library and the mineral industries building stand on the site of White's former home, Cherryhurst, and the stadium and hospital are on a portion of a golf course property he helped develop. He also invested in banking and manufacturing, including brick and tin manufacturing, and the residential development of South Park. White helped to build old Mountaineer Field, as treasurer of the building committee and a major fundraiser. As WVU's oldest alumnus he wrote an invaluable memoir of the university's early years.

I. C. White died November 25, 1927, following surgery in Baltimore.

See also Geology, Natural Gas and Petroleum

Fredrick H. Armstrong
State Archives

Lloyd L. Brown, "The Life of Dr. Israel Charles White," M.A. thesis, WVU, 1946; Herman L. Fairchild, "Memorial of Israel C. White," Reprinted from *Bulletin of the Geological Society of America*, March 1928.

Jesco White

Dancer Jesse "Jesco" White, born in Boone County, July 30, 1956, became widely known with the release of the film *Dancing Outlaw* by Morgantown filmmaker Jacob Young. The award-winning 1991 documentary turned White into an unlikely national celebrity, a hillbilly ambassador whom many state residents felt only added to the stereotypes that West Virginia struggles to shake.

Gun battles and car crashes took the lives of his father and four of his 14 brothers and sisters. In the film, Jesco, who turned to religion after his father's death, spoke matter-of-factly about his drug habit and reverently about Elvis Presley. Jesco's entire trailer (and, in particular, his "Elvis Room") was festooned with all manner of Elvis paraphernalia, from many framed photographs, huge velvet paintings, and ceramic dishes to Elvis ashtrays and mirrors, a life-size bust, and a ceramic clock that played the Presley standard, "Heartbreak Hotel."

Jesco's father, D. Ray White, was a legendary Boone County dancer who was featured in *Talking Feet*, a 1992 documentary that showcased some of America's finest traditional dancers. While Jesco lacked his father's talent, he had a backwoods political incorrectness that made him quotable. Jesco's fame peaked in 1994 when he was featured in a brief cameo on the TV show *Roseanne*. Filmmaker Young followed up with the documentary, *Jesco Goes To Hollywood*.

In 2005, White lived in isolation in Boone County.

Michael Lipton
Charleston

White Sulphur Springs

The Greenbrier County town of White Sulphur Springs is named for its famous mineral springs, whose curative powers were first reported in 1778. According to one legend, in that year rheumatism sufferer Amanda Anderson was brought to the springs in a litter slung between two horses and left riding horseback after a few weeks' treatment. Her family had heard that Indians believed the strong-smelling water had healing properties. Many others came to the springs, first camping in tents then staying in rustic cabins. White Sulphur developed as one of the most fashionable of the southern spas in the antebellum period. Dr. John J. Moorman, who doctored the summer crowds from 1838 to 1883, wrote in his memoir of "the most highly medicated and efficient mineral water of its class in America, if not in the world." Modern chemical analysis shows the water to be rich in sulfate, calcium, bicarbonate and other minerals.

White Sulphur Springs is now the site of the Greenbrier resort. The community that developed around the hotel, known earlier as the "Old White," was incorporated as the town of White Sulphur Springs in 1909. The town, located east of Lewisburg on Interstate 64 at an elevation of 1,980 feet, had a population of 2,315 in 2000.

White Sulphur Springs was a Civil War battleground on August 26–27, 1863. Confederate forces under Col. George S. Patton, grandfather of the famous World War II general, forced Union troops under Gen. William W. Averell to withdraw.

Belinda Anderson
Asbury

White Sulphur Springs, Battle of

In the summer of 1863, Confederate forces reoccupied Lewisburg and began probing toward Charleston. The new state of West Virginia had just been created, and in August Union forces were dispatched from Winchester via Huntersville, Pocahontas County, to seize the Virginia state law library which had previously been established at Lewisburg for the convenience of judges and lawyers when the Virginia Supreme Court met there. The Yankees also hoped to destroy the Virginia-Tennessee Central Railroad, which traversed southwestern Virginia on its way from Richmond to Memphis. Union Gen. William Averell led a force of 1,300 mounted infantry, cavalry, and light artillery. The Confederates responded by sending 2,000 men to block the road at White Sulphur Springs, 12 miles east of Lewisburg.

On August 26, the forces collided. The Union attacked toward the west, hitting the Confederates moving east from Lewisburg. After two hours of assaults on the Confederate line, there was a lull in the fight. Union forces tried to find a weak

spot on the flanks. Twice more during the afternoon, and just before sunset, the Union attackers failed to break the Confederate line which was anchored by Col. George Patton's Virginia infantry and Edgar's militia sent from Lewisburg. On the morning of August 27, with ammunition nearly depleted, Averell decided to retreat to his base without accomplishing any of his objectives. The Union force of 1,300 sustained 218 casualties, 26 killed, 125 wounded, 67 captured. The Confederate force of 2,000 had 167 casualties, 20 killed, 129 wounded, 18 missing. The Confederates had turned back the raiders but had failed to destroy or capture the outnumbered Yankees.

David Bard
Concord University

David Bard, *Civil War: The New River Valley: 3 One-Day Driving Tours*, 2004.

Whitewater Rafting

Whitewater rafting, along with alpine skiing, anchored the rapid development of West Virginia's outdoor tourism industry in the late 20th century. Apparently the Mountain State's first rafter was Ray Moore of Alexandria, Virginia, who, along with a group of friends in the 1950s, discovered that West Virginia's rivers were among the most exciting in the nation. The group's November 1959 attempt on the Gauley River was defeated by the power of the rapids, but was a precursor of today's whitewater recreation industry.

The Cheat was the first West Virginia river to be commercially rafted, by Ralph McCarty of Monroeville, Pennsylvania. His informal weekend expeditions in the mid-1960s on West Virginia and Pennsylvania rivers grew into a company that plied a substantial portion of its business on the Cheat River each spring. A small and highly technical river, the Cheat's Class III to V whitewater has made it a favorite among some of the nation's expert paddlers.

In 1968, Jon Dragan founded Wildwater Expeditions Unlimited at Thurmond in the New River gorge, establishing the first West Virginia-based whitewater rafting company. The New River, the largest-volume whitewater river east of the Mississippi, was an ideal center for the rafting industry because of the dependability of its flows and a season that could begin as early as March and run through October. Congress named the 53-mile section between Hinton and Fayetteville the New River Gorge National River in 1978, at the urging of Congressman Nick Rahall. The lower gorge offers classic Class III to V whitewater, with Class I and II rapids in the gentle upper section.

The Gauley, divided into upper and lower sections, is among the most demanding commercially rafted white-

An exciting ride on the New River.

water streams. The section of upper Gauley beginning just below Summersville Dam is known for its five consecutive Class V rapids. The lower Gauley, beginning at Peters Creek, is slightly less rigorous than the upper. In 1988, Congress designated the 25.5 mile upper and lower Gauley and 5.5 miles of the Meadow River as the Gauley River National Recreation Area.

The Shenandoah River flows through one of the most historic and beautiful sections of the state. Its whitewater is gentle enough for families, and the scenery includes Harpers Ferry and the dramatic cliffs of the Blue Ridge where the Shenandoah joins the Potomac. The most often-rafted sections of the Tygart Valley River sport challenging Class III to V spring whitewater and magnificent scenery.

These five rivers capture most of the state's commercial rafting, although companies have occasionally offered trips on the Bluestone and Meadow rivers. At least 250,000 visitors raft in West Virginia each year; 50,000 to 60,000 of that number raft the Gauley in its 22-day fall dam release season. The Bluestone, New, Meadow, and Gauley rivers comprise the largest federally protected river system in the East. The region, along with the Nantahala River in North Carolina, and the Colorado River in the Grand Canyon, is among the top three commercial whitewater rafting centers in the United States.

Rebecca Halstead Kimmons
Charleston

Don Whitlatch

Wildlife artist Donald Jean "Don" Whitlatch was born November 11, 1931, in Parkersburg. Noted for his realistic portrayal of birds, animals, and plants, Whitlatch has published limited edition prints of his paintings for more than 30 years.

After graduation from Parkersburg High School, Whitlatch served in the U.S. Air Force and attended West Virginia University and Ohio University. He worked for an advertising company and then started his own design studio. After suffering a heart attack at 38, he left advertising and concentrated on developing his artistic abilities. His earliest works were watercolors of birds.

In the early 1990s, he accepted a four-year commission to paint scenes of Colonial Williamsburg. This was followed by orders to paint holes of famous golf courses, including the fourth hole at Cascades Course at the Homestead in Hot Springs, Virginia, the sixth at the Pete Dye Golf Club in Bridgeport, and the 16th at Augusta National, home of the Masters Tournament.

His honors include selection by the Audubon Society for the group's first art auction, one of 21 international artists chosen. A Whitlatch painting of the American bald eagle was presented to the White House during the Nixon administration. He served 17 years as the state's wildlife artist-in-residence.

Whitlatch established the first West Virginia chapters of Ducks Unlimited, National Ruffed Grouse Society, and Quail Unlimited, and donated his art to help these groups raise funds. Whitlatch lived in Parkersburg in 2005.

Jack Whittaker

Andrew Jackson "Jack" Whittaker Jr. of Putnam County won what was then the largest single lottery jackpot in history. The Putnam County contractor, already wealthy from his businesses, won $314.9 million in the Powerball lottery on Christmas Day 2002. Whittaker, who was born October 9, 1947, chose to take the cash option and netted $113,386,407.77.

Whittaker gave substantially to charity from his lottery winnings, benefiting Church of God congregations in Putnam and Summers counties, among other groups. He established the Jack Whittaker Foundation to manage his charitable giving.

Following his winning of the Powerball jackpot, Whitaker received much unwanted attention, and personal troubles culminated in the death of his granddaughter. In 2003, he was temporarily robbed of $545,000 outside a Charleston-area dance club. The theft was the first of several involving Whittaker's vehicles, office, and house in Scott Depot. Problems afflicted Whittaker, including legal charges and arrests. He was the target of lawsuits.

In an interview a year after winning the jackpot, Whittaker said, "If I had to do it all over, I'd be more secluded about it. I'd do the same things, but I'd be a little more quiet."

M. T. Whittico

African-American newspaperman Matthew Thomas Whittico was born near Martinsville, Henry County, Virginia, September 25, 1866. He graduated in 1896 from Lincoln University in Pennsylvania, returning to teach in the segregated schools of Henry and Patrick counties.

Whittico moved to Keystone, McDowell County, about 1900, joining a thriving interracial business community in the booming coal town. He purchased a local newspaper and in 1904 renamed it the *McDowell Times*, which he served as editor and publisher. Circulating well beyond McDowell County, the *Times* was for many years the state's preeminent African-American newspaper, read by black and white West Virginians interested in race issues and life in the coalfields. R. W. White was a partner in the newspaper, and T. Edward Hill, an important black leader and later a legislator, joined the venture in 1910.

Active in politics as well as business, Whittico was among the black citizens who rose to power and influence as African-Americans increased in numbers and voting strength in the southern counties during the early 20th century. He was a member of the Republican Party's state executive committee and served as a member of Keystone's city council.

The character of M. T. Whittico contributed to the development of fictional figures in Denise Giardina's 1987 coalfields novel, *Storming Heaven*, which includes an influential black newspaper editor. Whittico is credited with popularizing the phrase, "Free State of McDowell," in his work to establish African-American rights and influence in the racially diverse county. The slogan remains a rallying cry among McDowell Countians of both races. Whittico died June 21, 1939, in Bluefield, and was buried in his native Henry County, Virginia.

See also Keystone

Ken Sullivan
West Virginia Humanities Council

Thomas E. Posey, *The Negro Citizen of West Virginia*, 1934; Joe William Trotter Jr., *Coal, Class, and Color: Blacks in Southern West Virginia, 1915–32*, 1990.

Widen

Located in the rugged terrain of eastern Clay County, Widen was built as a coal company town in 1911 by the Elk River Coal & Lumber Company. The company, organized in 1905, succeeded an 1898 association of the same name composed of northern capitalists investing in central West Virginia lumber and coal lands. To extract lumber and coal, the Buffalo Creek & Gauley Railroad was built 18.6 miles out Dundon Ridge to Widen. J. G. Bradley, fresh out of Harvard Law School in 1904, came to Clay County as vice president of the railroad. L. G. Widen, the town's namesake, directed the building of the Buffalo Creek & Gauley.

Bradley soon became president of the Elk River Coal & Lumber Company, controlling more than 80,000 acres of land. Practicing "welfare capitalism" designed to attach worker loyalty to him and his company, Bradley built a solid town at Widen. Worker homes, painted company red, were well-constructed. Widen grew to possess a bank, an Elrico company store, schools, and churches, all built by the company. Eventually there appeared a YMCA, a high school, a swimming pool, and a ball diamond with company-sponsored teams.

Isolated in its early history, Widen prospered during the 1920s when West Virginia labor unions had declined. In the early 1930s, the United Mine Workers renewed its drive to unionize West Virginia miners. Strikes at Widen occurred in 1933 and 1941, the latter violent, but Bradley defeated the union. Again in 1952, a bitter strike erupted. Sixteen months later, after one man was killed and friendships and families had suffered severe disruption, the union called off the strike, but the company never recovered. Bradley sold the mines to the Clinchfield Coal Company in 1959; soon it was unionized under the new owners.

Widen continued to produce coal until 1963, when the mine and the railroad ceased operation. Now Widen is largely a ghost town where former residents gather each July on Widen Day to reminisce about both the good times and the troubles.

See also J. G. Bradley, Clay County, Company Towns

Lou Athey
Franklin & Marshall College

Betty Cantrell, Grace Phillips, and Helen Reed, "Widen: The Town J. G. Bradley Built," *Goldenseal*, January–March 1977.

John Wilburn Trial

John E. Wilburn, a coal miner and Baptist minister, was one of the few convicted of murder for his participation in the Battle of Blair Mountain of August and September, 1921.

As the march of armed miners toward Logan County converged upon Blair Mountain, Wilburn, 45, who lived in Blair, told people it was time for him to lay down his Bible, take up his rifle, and fight. On August 30, he assembled 50 to 75 armed men, including two of his sons, told them he would lead them against the enemy, and took them up the mountain toward Sheriff Don Chafin's army at the top.

After camping that night, the group ran onto Logan Deputy John Gore and two nonunion miners, all armed members of Chafin's army. On realizing they had met the enemy, both sides opened fire. All three of the Logan men and one of Wilburn's men, a black miner, were killed in the fusillade. Wilburn and his men fled back toward Blair.

Both Wilburn and his son, John, were later sentenced to 11 years in the penitentiary. Governor Morgan reduced their sentences to five years each, and Governor Gore pardoned them after they had served three years.

See also Battle of Blair Mountain, Mine Wars

Lon Savage
Salem, Virginia

Lon Savage, *Thunder in the Mountains*, 1990.

Wild Foods

In West Virginia, there are more than 500 plants, 50 animals, and several insects that can be eaten by humans. Several of the plants are introduced weeds, not native to the state.

Potherbs or boiled greens are on most wild food menus. The more common among the several dozen that can be eaten in West Virginia are ramps, spring beauties, nettles, giant chickweed, pokeweed, milkweed, dandelion, creasy greens or cress, purslane, chicory, fireweed, raceweed, lamb's quarters, and watercress. Many mushrooms can be used for food, although some others are deadly poisonous. In West Virginia, four easily recognized edible types are the morel, shaggy mane, sulfur polypore, and puffball.

Among the many wild fruits and berries are persimmons, strawberries, wild grapes, crab apples, cranberries, blueberries, huckleberries, blackberries, raspberries, dew berries, black haw, elderberries, and wild cherries. Common nuts collected in the wild are black walnuts, chinquapins, beechnuts, hickory nuts, and hazelnuts.

In the past, wild honey made from yel-

low poplar, basswood, and sourwood was often "robbed" from trees colonized by wild honeybees, but wild honeybees have now almost entirely succumbed to parasites. The sap from sugar maple is evaporated to produce maple syrup and further evaporated to make maple sugar.

There are also dozens of starchy vegetable substitutes, salad ingredients, wheat flour substitutes, tea and coffee substitutes, cool beverages, condiments, oils, and many other culinary uses of wild plants.

As with wild plants, wild animals have been a source of food since the beginning of mankind. Among the historic food animals no longer found in West Virginia are such extinct species as the passenger pigeon and woods-dwelling bison. Among those still used as food are several species of fish, crayfish, eel, beaver, black bear, frog, muskrat, opossum, rabbit, raccoon, squirrel, turtle, rattlesnake, white-tailed deer, woodchuck, ruffed grouse, wild turkey, dove, duck, and woodcock.

There is a National Wild Foods Association that meets each September at North Bend State Park near Cairo.

See also Foodways

William H. Gillespie
Charleston

William H. Gillespie, *Wild Foods of Appalachia*, 1986; L. A. Peterson, *Edible Wild Plants, Eastern/Central North America*, 1977.

Wild Turkey

The wild turkey is the largest game bird in West Virginia, and it presents one of the greatest challenges to hunters. The bird has vision much better than that of humans, and it is very wary. It is a good barometer to measure our wild lands because it needs not only open areas rich with insects to serve as food for young birds, but also large forested areas with mature food-producing trees such as oaks, beech, and black cherry.

Following the Civil War, the wild turkey population declined drastically due largely to habitat destruction, with the logging of forests and the clearing of land for agriculture. Unlike in many states, however, the wild turkey was not extirpated in West Virginia because some remote habitat survived in the eastern section of the state. Numbers reached a low point in the 1920s. Our forests slowly recovered, but as recently as 1945 there were no more than 6,000 wild turkeys in West Virginia. Most of the state was void of the magnificent bird.

The West Virginia Conservation Commission (now Division of Natural Resources) tried to reintroduce turkeys by rearing them in captivity and releasing them into the wild. This failed, and in 1950 wildlife biologists tried a different and very successful approach, trapping wild birds in the eastern mountains and moving them into other counties. From these core stockings wild turkeys expanded, and today the population has been calculated to be as high as 170,000. The trap and transfer of wild birds was responsible for reestablishing wild turkeys to 39 of our 55 counties. The return of the wild turkey to all counties in West Virginia is considered to be the state's greatest wildlife management success story.

James C. Pack
Division of Natural Resources
R. W. Bailey and K. T. Rinell, "History and Management of the Wild Turkey in West Virginia," 1968.

Wildflowers

Early spring in West Virginia, from late February to early April, signals the bonanza of wildflowers soon to come. The first flowers bloom in southern West Virginia, along stream banks. Blooming gradually migrates northward across the state, and upward to the highest peaks of the Alleghenies. Coltsfoot begins to cover roadsides with yellow, as its smaller look-alike cousin, dandelion, covers yards and fields. Dainty pink-striped flowers of spring beauties and the white and blue hepatica are a sure sign that spring is just around the corner. In cold mountain swamps, skunk cabbage produces heat to melt the ice and pushes up its quaint green cap with a purple pedestal inside. The large green leaves will flourish in the warm spring rains. Sharp eyes will spot the fragrant pink and white flowers of trailing arbutus, peeking out from under leaves flattened by winter snows.

The woods become a fascinating kaleidoscope of colors and a paradise of magnificent spring wildflowers as temperatures rise and rain showers fall. The 27 species of violets vary from white and yellow to blue. Phlox flowers range from white and blue to pink and red. White flowers of Clintonia, plumelily, anemones, mayapple, twinleaf, bloodroot, squirrel corn, Dutchman's breeches, toothworts, stonecrop, foamflower, sweet cicely, and saxifrage seem to dominate. Mayapple is recognized by the large white flower and unique umbrella-like leaves. The low-growing stonecrop has three spikes of flowers and succulent leaves similar to cactus. Dutchman's breeches look like a pair of pants hanging upside down. Its cousin, squirrel corn, has a white flower resembling a boiled kernel of corn and root bulbs that look like yellow corn.

The yellow flowers of buttercups, fawn lilies, bellworts, and golden-knees are common. Marsh marigold, also yellow, is less common and grows in wet areas in the high mountains. The rare yellow lady's slipper, with its moccasin-shaped flowers, can be found in secret haunts of the deep, rich woods.

The more common pink lady's slipper (moccasin flower) prefers dry, acid woods.

Twinleaf occurs in every county.

The showy orchis grows in rich, moist woods and has a three- to six-inch spike of delicate white and pink flowers. Shooting star flowers are pure white in southern West Virginia and deep pink elsewhere. The brightest red flower belongs to fire pink, which inhabits dry road banks and cliffs, along with red columbine flowers.

The blue flowers of dwarf iris, dwarf larkspur, wild geranium, Virginia bluebell, and blue-eyed Mary are fairly common.

Fields, meadows, and forest openings furnish habitat for many spring wildflowers. Dandelions, ragworts, and cinquefoils are common yellow flowers. Chickweeds, wild strawberries, and pussytoes are white, while florets are yellowish blue.

Leaves on trees absorb so much sunlight that summer and fall wildflowers forsake the woods for fields, roadsides, openings, and riverbanks. Canada and Turk's cap lily with large red and yellow recurved petals are two of the showiest summer wildflowers. Pasture and swamp rose flowers are showy pink and extremely fragrant. The orange flowers of butterfly weed attract numerous butterflies and insects, as do all milkweeds. Many legumes, such as wild senna, wild indigo, and partridge pea, flower with bright splashes of yellow. Goat's rue, with large yellow and purple flowers, is one of the prettiest legumes. Equal to the goat's rue is the rare wild lupine of our eastern counties, with its spike of bright blue flowers. Poison hemlock and water hemlock are two of several members of the carrot family, with large cup-shaped clusters of white flowers. Numerous mints and bedstraws with white, blue, and yellow flowers are common summer wildflowers.

Autumn, from mid-August through October, is a time of painted landscapes as tall, leafy plants of sunflowers, goldenrods, asters, and phlox provide a spectacle of flowers to match the dazzling array of fall leaf colors. Fall wildflowers generally are tall, with many leaves, and spikes or heads of flowers.

There are 22 species of goldenrods and 17 species of sunflowers that are almost all yellowish. The 30 species of asters have mostly white or blue flowers. New England aster is the showiest, with large deep violet-purple flowers, and sometimes contrasting pink or white flowers as well. Shale barren aster has lighter purple flowers but grows in very dry rocky soils and will bloom profusely until snows begin to fall. Large pink clusters of joe-pye weeds and deep purple clusters of ironweeds add to the variety of autumn colors.

Complementing all of these are the white thoroughworts and boneset, and the fuzzy pink flower heads of thistles and knapweeds. Occasionally the golden yellow foxgloves will lean outward from a road bank, or the tall white multi-spiked Culver's root will show off its glory in a wet roadside or meadow. Fall phlox and wild sweet William prefer the shady floodplains of larger streams to display their pink flower clusters. The same is true of great blue lobelia and cardinal-flower with its deep scarlet flowers, which also grow in wet road ditches. The deep blue flowers of gentians hide in dense grass and herbs where you must search for them.

We have about 2,600 plants in West Virginia. Of this number, 850 are non-native exotics, more than 100 are trees, 100 are shrubs that have inconspicuous flowers, and about 300 are grasses and sedges whose flowers are seldom noticed. An additional 200 or so herbs have very inconspicuous flowers. That leaves about 1,000 wildflowers prominent enough to be noticed by non-botanists. From cliff to swamp, mountaintop to valley, and deep woods to parking lots, there is a wildflower that grows in every niche. Some are small and hardly noticed, while others are large, bright, showy flowers suitable for the garden of a queen. Wildflowers can bloom during any month of the year, but truly spectacular flower shows occur in April and May and August through September.

See also Botany, Flora

William N. Grafton
WVU Extension Service

Wildlife

Wildlife includes those wild animals that are not domesticated and are not in captivity. At one time, the term referred only to those birds and mammals considered to be game animals. These animals were hunted for sport, such as the white-tailed deer, gray squirrel, cottontail rabbit, wild

West Virginia wildlife includes river otters.

turkey, ruffed grouse, bobwhite quail, and wood duck. Game animals also included those furbearers that were trapped, including mink, muskrat, beaver, red fox, gray fox, and raccoon. Game animals were commonly categorized as upland game animals (deer, bear, rabbits, and squirrels), upland game birds (quail, turkey, and grouse), wetland game birds (ducks, geese, and woodcock), and wetland furbearers (beaver, mink, and muskrat).

In the past, wildlife traditionally did not include fish, which were considered to be a separate group. Fish historically were classified by biologists as either game fish or commercial fish, and little research and management effort were devoted to the nearly 100 other species of fish found in West Virginia waters. Game fish were those pursued for sport, such as the bass, trout, pike, and muskie, while commercial fish were those harvested for sale, such as buffalo, carp, channel catfish, and flathead catfish.

As biologists recognized the value of animals other than the game animals and game and commercial fish, the definition of wildlife was broadened to include the hundreds of species that were not hunted, trapped, or fished. During the 1970s, a distinction was made between game and nongame wildlife. The term "nongame wildlife" was used to describe those birds, mammals, and fish that were not hunted, trapped, or fished, including such animals as songbirds, hawks, owls, bats, mice, shrews, minnows, darters, and creek chubs. It was recognized that these animals had economic, scientific, and recreational value, as well as intrinsic worth. Efforts were initiated to preserve and manage nongame birds, mammals, and fish, which throughout West Virginia

were much more numerous than were the game animals and game fish. There currently are approximately 50 species of game animals compared to 320 species of nongame animals, and approximately 25 species of game fish compared to more than 150 species of nongame fish.

By the 1980s, amphibians such as frogs, toads, and salamanders, plus reptiles such as lizards, snakes, and turtles, were also included with nongame wildlife. Thus, all vertebrates were considered to be wildlife, although fish were typically placed in a separate category of wildlife. The definition of wildlife broadened even more during the 1990s, and some of the larger and more appealing invertebrate species—butterflies, moths, mussels, and snails—were included.

An even broader definition of the term wildlife now in use encompasses not only all vertebrates, but also most invertebrate species, with small worms, insects, and spiders being included. The most liberal definition includes plants along with all kinds of animals. However, this definition has not yet received wide acceptance within the scientific community and is generally not accepted by the general public.

West Virginia's wildlife may be classified according to habitat. Wetland wildlife, forest wildlife, grassland wildlife, and wilderness wildlife are groups of animals that typically live in those specific habitats. Wetland wildlife include such animals as the beaver, muskrat, mink, wood duck, Canada goose, great-blue heron, snapping turtle, bullfrog, and spring peeper. Forest wildlife include the black bear, gray squirrel, flying squirrel, great horned owl, pileated woodpecker, and redback salamander. Grassland wildlife include the red fox, meadow vole, cot-

tontail rabbit, meadowlark, song sparrow, kestrel, garter snake, smooth green snake, and box turtle. Wilderness wildlife in West Virginia are quite rare and include the mountain lion (now absent), golden eagle, and timber rattlesnake.

Most wildlife living in West Virginia are year-round residents, but a few—primarily birds—are seasonal visitors. All fish, amphibians, reptiles, and most mammals (other than a few bats) are year-round residents, while the majority of the more than 300 bird species known to occur in West Virginia are present only during certain months. Approximately 70 species of birds spend all 12 months in the Mountain State, while many others are seasonal residents or simply pass through while migrating. Examples of permanent residents are the mallard, Canada goose, red-tailed hawk, ruffed grouse, wild turkey, great-horned owl, pileated woodpecker, blue jay, crow, raven, chickadee, and cardinal. Among the nearly 100 seasonal residents that spend the summers nesting in West Virginia are the hummingbird, flycatchers, warblers, and thrushes. Fewer than 10 birds (cormorant, rough-legged hawk, and evening grosbeak) spend only the winters in West Virginia and typically nest farther north. Many wetland birds (including many waterfowl and shorebirds) are migratory visitors and may be observed only during the fall and spring months as they migrate between northern nesting grounds and southern wintering grounds. Most invertebrates are year-round residents although a few butterflies (notably the monarch) regularly migrate through West Virginia.

There have been significant changes in the species and numbers of resident wildlife in West Virginia. Some animals that were common prior to settlement—buffalo, elk, gray wolf, and passenger pigeon—had disappeared from the state by 1900. Other common wildlife present prior to the state's settlement had become so rare by 1900 that biologists predicted they would probably disappear during the 1900s. Some of these at-risk species were the beaver, river otter, mountain lion, wood duck, black bear, and fisher. As a result of reintroduction and management by the Wildlife Resources Section of the Division of Natural Resources, however, these species are all now more numerous than they were in 1900. The notable exception is the mountain lion, believed to have been extinct in the state since the 1930s.

Certain species of wildlife that faced extinction in West Virginia during the early 1900s have recovered to levels where they are now causing serious damage. The beaver, white-tailed deer, raccoon, and Canada goose are so abundant that their numbers need to be controlled. Others—black bear and wild turkey—are currently causing problems in some areas and could become serious pests in the future. The past century has demonstrated that wildlife are much more adaptable than biologists previously imagined, and if protected from hunting and harassment, most animals can live near humans. Bald eagles, osprey, and river otter were rare in West Virginia during the 20th century, but through adaptation most likely will become relatively common in West Virginia in the future. Perhaps the mountain lion will join them.

Some wildlife that historically were never known to occur in West Virginia are now found widely scattered throughout the state. For example, coyotes expanded their geographic range from the Southwest and are now present in every county in West Virginia. Another species, the elk, was once common in West Virginia, then lost, and now seems likely to return. The native herd in Pennsylvania is growing, and elk have been sighted in southwestern West Virginia, presumably from the herd introduced into Kentucky from the West.

Canada geese and bald eagles were rare visitors to West Virginia during the early 1900s, but were not known to nest here. Canada geese now nest in most counties, and bald eagles nest along the Potomac River and the Ohio River. Selected wildlife species were intentionally introduced into North America and have spread throughout West Virginia and most of the United States. Examples of these exotic species are the English sparrow, European starling, pigeon, and carp. Other wildlife species, such as the house mouse, Norway rat, black rat, and zebra mussel, were introduced accidentally into North America, and have become serious pests throughout West Virginia and other states. In contrast, a few exotic species have been intentionally released into West Virginia because of their sporting values as game animals or game fish and are now an integral and valued part of West Virginia's wildlife, including the brown trout, rainbow trout, ring-necked pheasant, and wild boar.

Another category of wildlife present in West Virginia is the group termed feral. These are animals that have returned to an untamed state following domestication; they are free-living and do not depend on humans for food or shelter. House cats are probably the most common feral animal in West Virginia, followed by feral dogs and goats.

In contrast to those species that have increased in numbers, many other wildlife species that were common during the 1800s have experienced serious declines throughout much of West Virginia. The numbers of spadefoot toads, upland chorus frogs, timber rattlesnakes, bobwhite quail, barn owls, whippoorwills,

pink mucket pearly mussel, fanshell mussel, and clubshell mussel are now considerably lower than they were 100 years ago. The reasons for these declines are not fully understood, although loss of suitable habitat is the most likely factor.

The next 100 years will bring many noticeable changes to the wildlife of West Virginia. Some species will disappear and some will become rare, while others will become more abundant, and a few will certainly become pests. Regardless of the changes, the diversity of fascinating wildlife will be an integral part of West Virginia's natural history.

Edwin D. Michael
Morgantown

Wildlife Management Areas

West Virginia's Statewide Wildlife Management Areas Program was created to provide hunting, fishing, and related outdoor recreational opportunities throughout the Mountain State. Wildlife management activities include the establishment of wildlife habitat through tree and shrub plantings, maintenance of food plots, timber cutting, road and trail maintenance, and the use of hunting regulations to increase and control wildlife populations. These areas are managed by the Division of Natural Resources for use by the general public.

Currently there are 69 wildlife management areas that are owned by the state or leased by the Division of Natural Resources from other owners, encompassing over 336,000 acres in 50 counties. The largest state-owned areas are the Sleepy Creek WMA in Berkeley and Morgan counties and East Lynn Lake WMA in Wayne County, each more than 22,900 acres in size.

The forerunner of the WMA program was the establishment of leased wildlife refuges on privately owned land in 1922. These state-private landowner cooperative game refuges opened the way for the propagation and protection of game animals and birds. The following year the Game and Fish Commission (now Division of Natural Resources) purchased the first state-owned forest and game refuge in Pocahontas County.

In 1936, a cooperative agreement between the state of West Virginia and the U.S. Forest Service resulted in the establishment of certain areas as "game breeding ground areas" within the Monongahela National Forest. These areas later became known as wildlife management areas and now total 13 in the Monongahela, George Washington, and Jefferson national forests. The largest wildlife management area within a national forest is the Cranberry WMA (158,147 acres) in Nicholas, Webster, Pocahontas, and Greenbrier counties.

Jack I. Cromer
Beverly

Willard Hotel

Grafton's Willard Hotel was built in 1911–12 to serve travelers on the Baltimore & Ohio Railroad. Rail traffic increased as the B&O expanded, reaching 30 passenger trains a day by the 1920s. The old Grafton House, containing both hotel and depot facilities, had been built in 1857 and could no longer meet the railroad's needs.

Named in honor of B&O President Daniel Willard, the hotel was built by Grafton attorney and industrialist John T. McGraw. The contractor for both the Willard and the new B & O station was J. Walsh & Son of Baltimore, and the same granite and brick were used on both buildings. Both station and hotel were designed with entrances from the railroad and Main Street sides. The six-and-a-half-story hotel is Second Empire in style, with a mansard roof, cut stone trim, and brick corbeled quoins. The Willard was a thoroughly modern hotel for its time with all the amenities, and had one of the finest ballrooms in the area. The hotel officially opened with an elaborate banquet on April 12, 1912, attended by state and local dignitaries and railroad officials.

The Willard's heyday passed with the decline of rail passenger traffic. By the early 1960s, it had ceased to function as a hotel and was used to house train crews; by 1988 it stood vacant. In the late 1990s, the Vandalia Heritage Foundation began rehabilitation work on both the hotel and train station. The Willard is listed on the National Register of Historic Places as part of the Grafton Downtown Commercial Historic District.

See also Grafton, John T. McGraw
Margo Stafford
Clarksburg

Willey Amendment

The Willey Amendment resolved the issue of slavery in West Virginia, clearing the way to admit the new state into the Union. In 1861, voters west of the Allegheny Mountains rejected Virginia's secession from the United States, and instead opted to create a loyal Reorganized Government of Virginia. It was only a matter of time until West Virginia was created. Among the constitutional issues to be addressed was the question of slavery, which existed in parts of the proposed new state. Sentiment in the western counties was sharply divided. Some preferred to retain slavery, some favored total abolition, and some favored gradual emancipation. Still others sought to exclude blacks from the new state entirely.

The matter went before the U.S. Senate. Radical Republican Charles Sumner of Massachusetts proposed to free all slaves in West Virginia as of July 4, 1863. His proposal was defeated, and Reorganized Government of Virginia Sen. Waitman T. Willey suggested that children born to slave mothers after July 4, 1873, should be freed. This proposal in turn was not acceptable to senators wishing to eliminate slavery, a concept for which they felt the North was fighting the Civil War. Willey then managed to strike a compromise which was acceptable to a majority. The Willey Amendment to the West Virginia Statehood Bill provided that all slaves under 21 years of age on July 4, 1863, would be free on reaching that age. The compromise, later superseded by the 13th Amendment to the U.S. Constitution, led to the passage of the statehood bill and resulted in the creation of West Virginia on June 20, 1863.

See also Constitutional Convention of 1861–63, Formation of West Virginia

Kenneth R. Bailey
WVU Institute of Technology

Otis K. Rice and Stephen W. Brown, *West Virginia: A History,* 1993; Richard O. Curry, *A House Divided: A Study of Statehood Politics and the Copperhead Movement in West Virginia,* 1964.

Waitman Willey

State founder and U.S. Senator Waitman Thomas Willey, sometimes called the Father of West Virginia, was born October 11, 1811, near Farmington. Willey grew up on his family's farm and was self-taught until he entered Madison College in Uniontown, Pennsylvania, from which he graduated in 1831. He received his education as a lawyer during apprenticeships to Philip Doddridge and John C. Campbell in Wellsburg. Willey began his law practice in 1833 in Morgantown, where his career as a member of the Whig political party was launched with his election as clerk of the Monongalia County Court (1841–52). He was noted as an orator and debater. He frequently quoted Greek and Roman classics as well as the Bible in his speeches.

Willey was a delegate to the 1850–51 Virginia Constitutional Convention, where his speech "Liberty and Union" brought his first statewide recognition. He argued that "Liberty and Union are indissoluble." He was defeated as the Whig candidate for lieutenant governor of Virginia in 1859 but was selected as a delegate to the Secession Convention of 1861. His oratory against the ordinance of secession gained him many enemies. "Will you bring this desolation upon us?" he asked Virginians. "Will you expose our wives and children to the ravages of civil war?"

Virginia seceded nonetheless, and when the pro-Union Reorganized Government was established at Wheeling, Willey was elected by the legislature to a seat representing Virginia in the U.S. Senate. Although opposed to secession, Willey was not at first in favor of a new state. He gradually changed his opinion. He proposed the West Virginia Statehood Bill in the Senate and saw to its passage

State founder Waitman T. Willey (1811–1900).

and later signing by President Lincoln. He was then elected as one of West Virginia's first two U.S. senators and served from 1863 to 1871.

Although previously an owner of domestic slaves at his home in Morgantown, Willey spoke eloquently for suffrage for African-Americans at the 1872 Constitutional Convention that produced West Virginia's current constitution. "But why all this hostility to the poor Negro?" he asked. "In war we send him to the battlefront, in peace we impose on him all the burdens and duties of any other citizen. Then why should he not vote?"

Willey is remembered for the Willey Amendment, which provided for the emancipation of slaves as a precondition for the creation of West Virginia. Willey never retired from public life. He was called on for speeches at special events, such as Morgantown's centennial celebration. He died May 2, 1900, in Morgantown.

See also Formation of West Virginia, Willey Amendment

Jeanne Grimm
Morgantown

Charles H. Ambler, *Waitman Thomas Willey: Orator, Churchman, Humanitarian,* 1954.

Doc Williams

Wheeling musician Doc Williams was born Andrew John Smik of Slovak immigrant parents in Cleveland, Ohio, June 26, 1914. After growing up in the mining town of Kittaning, Pennsylvania, and gaining early radio experience in Pittsburgh, Williams and his Border Riders band came to Wheeling station WWVA in May 1937. With only slight interruption he was associated with the *Wheeling Jamboree* radio program for the rest of his performing career.

The Border Riders have at times in-

cluded Doc's fiddle-playing brother Cy (Milo Smik), blind accordionist Marion Martin, wife Chickie Williams (1919–   ) as girl vocalist, and such comedians as Froggie Cortez, William Godwin ("Hiram Hayseed"), and Smoky Pleacher. The band toured widely, especially among fans of the *Jamboree* in the Northeast and Maritime Canada.

Doc and Chickie's daughters, Barbara, Madeline, and Karen, have periodically shared in their parents' musical activity. Doc is known for such sentimental songs as "My Old Brown Coat" and "Willie Roy, the Crippled Boy," while Chickie favors old ballads and had a major hit in 1947 with "Beyond the Sunset." In more than 70 years in the business, Doc has been an advocate for maintaining a traditional country sound. He founded his own record label, Wheeling Records, and in the 1970s opened his Doc Williams Country Store across Main Street from Capitol Music Hall. The store was a Wheeling landmark until it closed in 1998.

See also Wheeling Jamboree, WWVA

Abby Gail Goodnite
University of Rio Grande

Ivan M. Tribe, *Mountaineer Jamboree: Country Music in West Virginia,* 1984.

Williams River

The Williams River rises in Pocahontas County at an elevation of almost 4,000 feet. From its source it flows 33 miles to Cowen, where it enters the Gauley River. The Williams River watershed takes in about 132 square miles of Pocahontas and Webster counties. The major tributary of the Williams is the Middle Fork, which has its source at more than 4,300 feet elevation, also in Pocahontas County.

The origin of the river's name is not certain. According to one account, it comes from William Ewing, a Revolutionary War veteran, who lived near Buckeye in Pocahontas County and is supposed to have owned land on the river's headwaters.

The remote and rugged watershed was never heavily populated. Two Dutch families who settled near the headwaters of the river in 1847 soon found the isolation overwhelming and left "Dutch Bottom" for more settled parts of Pocahontas County. One of the families, the Stultings, moved to Hillsboro, where their most noted descendant, author Pearl S. Buck, was born in 1892. The Hammonds family settled on the river before the Civil War, and in the 1960s and 1970s family members became well known due to their knowledge of traditional music.

Two resources in the Williams watershed, timber and coal, were developed. In the post-Civil War period, the timber in the watershed came to the attention of lumbermen. In the 1890s, logs were floated down the river in the flood tides of spring to a mill at Camden-on-Gauley.

Most of the timber in the Williams watershed was taken out by log train from 1905 to about 1940, to mills at Marlinton and Richwood. Coal mining activity continued on the lower Williams into the 1970s.

The isolation and ruggedness that hindered the settlement of the watershed allowed most of it to return to a near original state following the timbering, and today perhaps its most important value is for recreation. The land owned by the lumber companies went to the federal government to be included in the Monongahela National Forest, with part of the Williams River watershed now in the Cranberry Wilderness Area. For generations the river has been a popular fishing stream, and it is regarded as one of the top five trout streams in the state. It is one of the "big three" (the Cranberry, Williams, and headwaters of the Elk) that can be fished together.

William P. McNeel
Marlinton

Williamson

Williamson, the county seat of Mingo County, is located on the Tug Fork of the Big Sandy River at the junction of U.S. 119 (Appalachian Corridor G) and U.S. 52. The town is situated on the state line, just across the river from South Williamson, Kentucky, and in the heart of the rich bistate Williamson Coalfield. The Norfolk Southern Railroad runs through Williamson, which has a major rail yard.

Williamson was named for the prominent Williamson family and established on land belonging to them. The site was still farmland as late as 1890, but was transformed as the Norfolk & Western Railway (now Norfolk Southern) built its main line through the area. The county seat was located there when Mingo County was created in 1895, due to the influence of the Williamsons and other local backers. Matewan, upstream on the Tug Fork and also on the N&W line, challenged Williamson for the county seat as early as 1896. The unsuccessful bid marked the beginning of a long-term rivalry between the two towns, which are Mingo County's largest communities.

Incorporated in 1905, Williamson boomed with the growth of Mingo County and the development of the local coalfields. The city's population peaked at 8,624 in 1950. Thereafter, Williamson lost population with the decline of mining employment and the loss of railroad jobs that accompanied the shift from steam to diesel power. Williamson's population was 3,414 in 2000.

Once the victim of periodic Tug Fork flooding, Williamson has been protected by a flood wall since 1991. The Coal House, a downtown landmark built of bituminous coal in 1933, was added to the National Register of Historic Places in 1980. The nearby granite and sandstone Mingo County Courthouse was built about 1966.

See also Mingo County

Williamson Coal House

The 1,600-square-foot coal house, constructed in 1933 from 65 tons of coal, sits next to the Mingo County Courthouse in downtown Williamson, in the state's southern coalfields. Hand-sawn blocks of bituminous coal joined with black mortar form the rectangular structure's four walls and two pillars.

The landmark building was the idea of O. W. Evans, general superintendent of the fuel mines of the Norfolk & Western Railway. H. T. Hicks, an architect from Welch, designed the coal house. Local businesses and community people contributed materials and labor. The coal, taken from the Winifrede Seam, was donated by mining companies near Williamson, including Leckie Collieries, the Crystal Block Coal Company, Puritan Coal, the Sycamore Coal Company, and the Winifrede Block Coal Company.

The Tug Valley Chamber of Commerce, which maintains its office in the coal house, protects the walls of the building with periodic applications of weatherproof varnish. In 1980, the coal house was placed on the National Register of Historic Places.

See also Williamson

Nancy Ray Adams
Pine Mountain Settlement School

Williamstown

Williamstown is located on the Ohio River north of Parkersburg, at the junction of Interstate 77 and State Route 2. It is the site of one of the earliest settlements in Wood County, having been claimed in 1770 by brothers Joseph and Samuel Tomlinson. The property later passed to their sister, Rebecca Tomlinson Martin Williams. She and her husband, Isaac Williams, permanently settled the 400-acre Tomlinson tract in 1787, and Williamstown was named for them.

Williamstown is situated opposite the mouth of the Muskingum River, the present site of Marietta, Ohio, and an important and strategic point in the early history and prehistory of the Ohio Valley. Buckley Island is located in the Ohio River at Williamstown.

Once called Duncan and also Williamsport, the community was chartered as Williamstown in 1822. It was incorporated in 1921. Williamstown has long been a major Ohio River crossing point. One of Western Virginia's important early roads terminated there, and in 1800 Isaac Williams was authorized to operate a ferry to carry traffic to the Ohio shore. Early ferry flats and canoes were succeeded by a steam ferry, and a bridge was built in 1905. Today, the Interstate 77 Ohio River bridge is located nearby.

Williamstown's Tomlinson mansion, the 1839 home of Joseph Tomlinson III, was added to the National Register of Historic Places in 1974. John James Audubon was once a guest there. The Henderson Hall historic district, which neighbors Williamstown to the south, was added to the National Register in 1986. It encompasses sites associated with the Tomlinson-Henderson family and includes three Indian burial mounds within its bounds. The Fenton Art Glass Company is located at Williamstown.

Williamstown had 2,996 residents in 2000.

See also Joseph Tomlinson

Meredith Sue Willis

Author Meredith Sue Willis was born in Clarksburg on May 31, 1946. She was raised in Shinnston where her father Glenn Willis and her mother Lucille Meredith Willis were both educators. After graduating from Shinnston High School, she attended Bucknell University for two years. She dropped out to become a VISTA volunteer, later graduating from Barnard College. After a year as a recreation therapist in New York's Bellevue Hospital, she earned an MFA degree from Columbia and began to work as an artist-in-residence in New York public schools.

Willis authored three books on the teaching of writing—*Personal Fiction Writing* (1984), *Blazing Pencils* (1990), and *Deep Revision* (1993)—widely used by teachers around the country. She wrote two children's books, *The Secret Super Powers of Marco* (1994) and *Marco's Monster* (1996), published by Harper Collins. Her adult fiction, which is mainly set in West Virginia, includes *A Space Apart* (1979), *Higher Ground* (1981), *Only Great Changes* (1985), *In The Mountains of America* (1994), and *Quilt Pieces* (1991). She lives in South Orange, New Jersey, with her husband and son.

Merle Moore
Webster Springs

Patty Willis

Artist Patty Willis was born September 20, 1879, in Jefferson County and died there November 21, 1953. A painter, printmaker, designer, sculptor, and art historian, Willis studied at the Corcoran Gallery School of Art, at the Art Institute of Chicago, and at the Pratt Institute. Following World War I, she traveled extensively in Europe and the Middle East, during which period she studied with Fernand Léger at the Académie Moderne in Paris. Returning to the U.S. in the early 1920s, Willis exhibited her work at the Corcoran Gallery in 1923, and later at the Carnegie Institute, the Art Institute of Chicago, the Pennsylvania Academy of the Fine Arts, and elsewhere. During the late 1920s and 1930s, she was part of the art colony at Provincetown, Massachusetts. She exhibited with the Society of International Artists in New York in 1928, 1937, and 1938, and also exhibited at the 1939 World's Fair.

Willis resided primarily in Charles Town. She was a member of the Allied Artists of West Virginia, and exhibited with the group occasionally during the 1930s and 1940s. She frequently lectured on the history of religious art and was a pioneer in the study of West Virginia art history. Her valuable directory of Jefferson County portraits and portrait painters was published in the *Magazine of the Jefferson County Historical Society* in December 1940.

John A. Cuthbert
WVU Libraries

Willow Island Disaster

An April 27, 1978, scaffolding collapse at Willow Island in Pleasants County ranks as one of West Virginia's worst nonmining industrial disasters. Fifty-one men were at work atop the construction scaffolding when it suddenly collapsed, sending them plunging to the ground, 168 feet below. None survived.

The scaffolding had been erected for use in the construction of a new cooling tower at Monongahela Power Company's Pleasants Power Station, adjacent to the Willow Island Power Station on the Ohio River downstream from St. Marys. The men were preparing to pour a new layer of concrete when the scaffolding peeled away from the tower. The victims included a handful of supervisors who had come to the project from out of state, but most were local construction workers. Pleasants County became the focus of national media attention as grieving families buried their dead. One family counted four of five sons, a brother, two brothers-in-law, and three nephews among those killed.

The federal Occupational Safety and Health Administration levied fines against three construction companies involved in the project, charging negligence. A federal grand jury heard evidence in the case but returned no criminal indictments.

James E. Casto
Herald-Dispatch

Willow Island Sterilization Case

The 1978 "fetus protection policy" instituted by the American Cyanamid's Willow Island Plant in Pleasants County coerced five women workers to undergo surgical sterilization. Two women who chose not to be sterilized were moved to lower-paying jobs in other departments. The policy provided that women employees of child-bearing age could not hold jobs that exposed them to toxic substances at levels unsafe for fetuses. It made exception, however, for women who chose surgical sterilization.

In October 1979, the Department of Labor fined American Cyanamid $10,000. It maintained that the company's policy itself was a workplace hazard that caused serious physical harm, and that the policy thereby violated the Occupational Safety and Health Act. The company contested the fine. The Oil, Chemical and Atomic Workers International Union joined the Department of Labor as a party in the dispute. After the company won two administrative hearings, the union appealed to the U.S. Court of Appeals.

The court ruled that the company's fetus protection policy did not constitute a hazard within the meaning of the law. The union and the aggrieved women then pursued another route. They filed litigation claiming that American Cyanamid's policy was a form of sexual discrimination which violated Title VII of the Civil Rights Act of 1964. By 1984, the company agreed to settle that suit out of court. Although the suit did not establish a legal precedent, the women pioneered anti-discrimination arguments that were ultimately accepted by the U.S. Supreme Court.

Chuck Smith
West Virginia State University

Aunt Jennie Wilson

Virginia Myrtle Ellis "Aunt Jennie" Wilson was a Logan County traditional musician, considered a master of clawhammer-style banjo playing. The daughter of Huey Brian and Cinderella Lockard Ellis, she was born February 9, 1900, near Henlawson. She married James Wilson but was widowed in 1939 when he was killed in a mine accident.

Wilson's musical talent was discovered by folklorist Patrick Gainer of West Virginia University in 1958, and she became a favorite of folk festival audiences until her death. She recorded her best songs for the Library of Congress and was featured on record albums, including *A Portrait of Aunt Jennie Wilson,* produced by Billy Edd Wheeler. She left behind recorded interviews about her early life and the folk customs of Logan County.

Known for her vivid personality as well as her music, she was fond of saying, "Don't take more on your head than you can kick off your heels," meaning one should enjoy life to the utmost, which she did. She often played music with her grandson, Roger Bryant, and inspired other musicians to learn the clawhammer style. Aunt Jennie Wilson died March 2, 1992. She was a recipient of the 1984 Vandalia Award, West Virginia's highest folklife honor, for lifetime achievement in traditional music.

Robert Y. Spence
Logan

Emanuel Willis Wilson

The seventh governor of West Virginia, Emanuel Willis Wilson, was born August 11, 1844, at Harpers Ferry. His parents were English immigrants James Fitzgerald Wilson and Mariah (Spangler) Wilson, and he had two brothers and three sisters.

After public schooling and brief employment in the U.S. Armory at Harpers Ferry, Wilson studied law and was admitted to the bar in 1869. The following year he was elected as a Democrat to the West Virginia House of Delegates. In 1872, he won election to the state senate. He married Henrietta S. Cotton on April 27, 1874, and settled in Charleston. He then won two successive terms to the House of Delegates, serving from 1877 to 1881. He was elected speaker in 1880. During his legislative career Wilson sponsored legislation on behalf of mechanics and to outlaw railroad freight charge discrimination.

Although a fine stump orator, sometimes called "Windy" Wilson, he was not an effective political organizer, losing bids for Congress and attorney general. He succeeded in 1884, however, in riding a wave of rural discontent over taxes into the governorship, defeating Republican candidate Edwin Maxwell by a vote of 71,438 to 66,149.

Described by historian Otis Rice as the "most noted foe of corporate privilege" among governors of the era, Wilson represented the traditional agrarian Democrats, in contrast to the Republicans and to the pro-industry wing of his own party. He called for improvements in mine safety and the regulation of railroads. In his messages to the legislature he devoted considerable space to railroad practices that he argued had cost the state millions of dollars, and he called for both federal and state regulations. Chief among the discriminatory practices Governor Wilson sought to end was the common practice of charging more for short hauls of freight than for long hauls. He also recommended legislation to prohibit the practice by railroad companies of issuing free passes to public officials. He recommended extending corrupt practices laws to address bribery in the nomination of candidates for political office. In his 1889 message to the legislature, Wilson advocated antitrust legislation and increased immigration to the state, as well as voter registration as a way to reduce corrupt elections.

Governor at the height of the Hatfield-McCoy Feud, Wilson resisted Kentucky's request to arrest and extradite Hatfield defendants. He carried on a vigorous correspondence with the governor of Kentucky on behalf of the Hatfields, and, on his orders, West Virginia sued Kentucky for the release of a party of Hatfields carried illegally across the state line. A grate-

Governor Emanuel W. Wilson (1844–1905).

ful Devil Anse Hatfield named his youngest son in honor of Wilson.

In 1887, Governor Wilson worked with a small group of legislators to block the reelection of fellow Democrat Johnson N. Camden to the U.S. Senate; Camden represented the pro-industry faction of the party. Although Wilson's term was to have expired in March of 1889, he continued as governor for an additional 11 months until the disputed election between Republican Nathan Goff and Democrat A. B. Fleming was resolved in Fleming's favor.

After leaving office Wilson returned to the practice of law and authored a new election law in 1891. He died May 28, 1905, and was buried in Charleston.

Nicholas Burckel
Marquette University

Robert Sobel and John Raimo, *Biographical Directory of the Governors of the United States, 1789–1978,* 1978; John Alexander Williams, *West Virginia: A Bicentennial History,* 1976.

Riley Wilson

Born November 10, 1882, at Upper Falls in Kanawha County, William Edwin "Riley" Wilson became West Virginia's best known raconteur. He earned a law degree from Washington and Lee University and then went into practice with Fred Carr. Sam Chilton, Wilson's close associate, claimed that Wilson hardly ever practiced law, taking few if any cases for decades at a time. Wilson was best known for his wit and his storytelling.

Riley Wilson's best stories came out of rural West Virginia, often provided by a brother who practiced law in Lincoln County. Riley was in demand around the country as an entertainer and toastmaster. He traveled with Anna Held's theater show on the vaudeville circuit, made national radio appearances, and was considered one of the finest storytellers of his time. Riley published at least two

books, including *Reach Me the Tin* and *From Philadelphia, Pa., to Charleston, W. Va., Via Nome, Alaska.* He ran unsuccessfully for Congress in 1920, and later served Franklin Roosevelt's administration as a member of the National Bituminous Coal Administration.

Wilson became seriously ill while attending the 1949 inauguration of President Truman. He died October 6, 1952. The "Mattie Appleyard" character played by Jimmy Stewart in the 1971 movie version of the Davis Grubb novel *Fools' Parade* was based in part on Riley Wilson.

Bil Lepp
South Charleston

Ken Sullivan,"Food, Feathers, and Whiskey: Two Stories by Riley Wilson," *Goldenseal,* Summer 1982; Riley Wilson, *Reach Me The Tin,* 1932.

William Lyne Wilson

U.S. Postmaster General William Lyne Wilson, congressman, educator, and lawyer, was born May 3, 1843, in Smithfield, Jefferson County. He was educated at Charles Town Academy and graduated from Columbian College (now George Washington University) at age 17. Following graduate study at the University of Virginia, he joined the Confederate army. After serving throughout the Civil War, Wilson became professor of Latin at Columbian College, where he also studied law, graduating in 1867.

Wilson returned to Charles Town in 1871 to practice law. He prospered as a lawyer and became active in politics and education. Soon after Wilson's selection as president of West Virginia University in 1882, he accepted the Democratic nomination for House of Representatives and was elected. Continuing as WVU's president until June 1883, Wilson entered Congress, where he served six terms.

Wilson's expertise on tariff reduction, a fundamental principle of the Democratic majority, led to his appointment as chairman of the House Ways and Means Committee. Responding to the economic depression of 1893–94, Wilson prepared a revolutionary bill to reduce tariffs, but Senate modifications neutralized its effect. The failure of this legislation and the Democrats' apparent inability to deal with the depression led to the widespread defeat of Democrats, including Wilson, in the 1894 election.

Wilson joined President Cleveland's cabinet as postmaster general in 1895. In the following year, he introduced Rural Free Delivery in Jefferson County, an experiment which was quickly instituted nationwide. At the end of the Cleveland administration in March 1897, Wilson became president of Washington and Lee University. He died October 17, 1900, in Lexington, Virginia.

See also Rural Free Delivery

Harold Malcolm Forbes
WVU Libraries

Festus P. Summers, *William L. Wilson and Tariff Reform,* 1953; William L. Wilson, *A Borderland Confederate,* Festus P. Summers, ed., 1962.

Wind Power

Wind power is a developing alternative energy source in some parts of the country, including West Virginia. With enough wind, large enough windmills, and efficient turbines, wind can be harnessed to produce electrical power. Current technology commonly produces 1.5 megawatts per windmill. Multiple windmills are usually deployed in what are called wind farms. These wind farms are connected to existing power lines for distribution. In West Virginia, the sites suitable for commercial wind power development are located in the highlands of the Allegheny Mountains.

While production is small by comparison to that of certain western and midwestern states, West Virginia was listed as a leading wind power state in a study sponsored by the U.S. Department of Energy. The 2003 study identified West Virginia as one of nine states that collectively produced 95 percent of the nations's wind-generated elecricity. Within West Virginia, however, wind power provides only a small fraction of total electricity generated, less than one percent. Coal remains the undisputed champion in this field, generating 98 percent of West Virginia's large electricity production.

Wind power is regulated by the West Virginia Public Service Commission. By 2005, the PSC had approved three projects. The Mountaineer Wind Energy Center in Tucker County was the only one in operation. With 44 windmills located along Backbone Mountain, it produced 66 megawatts. Another company, Ned-Power, had PSC approval for a 300-megawatt wind farm near Mt. Storm in Grant County. U.S. Wind Force had been approved for 250 megawatts in Grant and Tucker counties near Mount Storm. In early 2006, construction had not begun on either project. A new proposal for Greenbrier County was before the PSC.

Modern wind turbines bear little resemblance to the picturesque windmills of Dutch folklore. Today's windmills look more like giant propellers. There are three blades, each about 115 feet long. These blades are mounted on a tall pylon, with electricity produced in turbines positioned directly behind the blades. The windmills swivel like weather vanes to face the wind, and the surface of the blades may be rotated or "feathered" to control their speed or stop them. Electricity is generated even at slow speeds.

Federal and state policies encourage the use of wind power as a source of renewable energy. At the federal level, there are financial incentives for both the construction of wind farms and the production of electricity from wind. In gen-

Tucker County windmills generate electricity.

people consider the windmills a form of visual pollution. Large areas of the countryside would have to be given over to windmills to replace the electricity now produced by conventional means, with nearly 2,000 of today's turbines required to replace West Virginia's largest coal-fired power plant.

The environmental community is split regarding wind power, enticed by its lack of conventional pollution but troubled by these new concerns. In 2004, Congressmen Alan Mollohan and Nick Rahall raised questions about wind power, calling for a study of its effects.

Tom Haas
Charlotte, North Carolina

Melvin Wine

Fiddler Melvin Wine was born April 20, 1909, near Burnsville. The Wine family, of German descent, has resided in Braxton County since at least 1840, having come from Rockingham County, Virginia. Melvin descended from a line of Braxton County fiddlers and singers stretching at least to his great-grandfather, Smithy Wine.

Wine, a recipient of the Vandalia Award in 1981, played his fiddle for old-time music enthusiasts throughout the nation. He was a perennial winner of ribbons at the West Virginia State Folk Festival at Glenville. He was chosen as a National Heritage Fellow in 1991 by the National Endowment for the Arts, the highest recognition given to a folk artist in the United States. He performed in concert in Washington upon accepting his award.

Wine's biggest musical influence was his father, Bob Wine, but he also acknowledged the fiddling prowess of "Un-

eral, these programs provide tax incentives and tax credits that vary with the amount of electric production. West Virginia also offers financial incentives for renewable energy and wind power. Tax incentives are available for wind power facilities in the form of reduced state business and occupation tax. Property tax relief is also available for utility-owned wind turbines through a reduction in assessed valuation.

Wind power has several advantages over conventional sources of electric generation. Wind power is a source of clean, non-polluting electricity. It does not emit greenhouse gases or the particulate matter associated with fossil fuels. Wind energy is an endlessly renewable resource.

Wind power is often unfavorably compared to conventional production as regards the current costs for the electricity produced. However, over the life cycle of the operation of a conventional power plant versus a wind farm, these costs come much closer. The cost of wind power is dropping due to technological advances, while the cost of conventional energy is rising due to the costs of energy sources and environmental issues.

Nonetheless, wind power has its problems. Earlier windmills were a source of noise pollution, but as the turbines have become more efficient they have also become quieter. One issue unresolved in the deployment of wind farms is the harmful effects on birds and bats that are injured or killed by flying into the blades. The PSC requires wind farms to comply with laws regarding endangered species, bird migration, and other environmental policies.

Another issue is the aesthetic impact on the surrounding scenery. The areas of West Virginia that have commercial wind potential are some of the most scenic areas in the eastern United States. Some

National Heritage Fellow Melvin Wine
(1909–2003).

cle Jack" McElwain of Webster County. At the beginning of the 21st century, Melvin Wine was widely recognized as one who had maintained a repertoire distinctly tied to central West Virginia and who adhered to a playing style closely linked to the 19th century. With a repertoire of more than 250 tunes, Wine's style and tunes were studied by student fiddlers at regional workshops. He directly and intensively taught three young fiddlers through the West Virginia Folk Art Apprenticeship Program.

Melvin Wine died March 16, 2003.

See also Fiddle Tradition, Uncle Jack McElwain

Gerald Milnes
Augusta Heritage Center

Winfield

Winfield is the county seat of Putnam County. When the county was founded on March 11, 1848, the town site was chosen as the seat of government because it was centrally located. The town was laid out on the banks of the Kanawha River in 1849 and named for Gen. Winfield Scott. Charles Brown, who ran the ferry, gave land, and in 1849 a two-story brick courthouse was completed. Winfield soon became a thriving village, but until the 1920s it was still the smallest county seat in the state and the only one without a paved road or a railroad leading to it. The town depended on river travel.

Red House Shoals was located in the river at Winfield. The steamboat channel through these rapids ran along the riverbank of the town. During the Civil War, the army that controlled that section of the riverfront controlled boat traffic on the upper Kanawha. This led to a skirmish that took place in the streets of Winfield on the night of October 24, 1864. Capt. Philip Thurmond, a noted Confederate partisan ranger, was mortally wounded. Before they returned, the Confederates buried their leader in an unmarked grave near the courthouse.

Winfield was incorporated in 1868. The population at that time was about 350. In 1898, the courthouse was destroyed in a terrible windstorm. Another courthouse was built in 1900, which served until it became the annex for the modern courthouse completed in 1998. In 1928, a disastrous fire destroyed an entire city block. The post office, bank, and newspaper office were all lost. A new bank was built, but it failed in 1931 during the Great Depression.

The paving of the road through town in 1926, the building of the Winfield locks and dam in 1936, and the completion of the Winfield bridge in 1957 contributed to long-term development. Finally, after Interstate 64 was completed and a number of housing developments were annexed,

FAST FACTS ABOUT WIRT COUNTY

Founded: 1848
Land in square miles: 234.4
Population: 5,873
Percentage minorities: 1.4%
Percentage rural: 100%
Median age: 37.9
Percentage 65 and older: 13.0%
Birth rate per 1,000 population: 9.5
Median household income: $30,748
High school graduate or higher: 72.4%
Bachelor's degree or higher: 9.9%
Home ownership: 83.1%
Median home value: $62,300

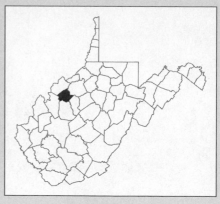

This information is from the 2000 U.S. Census. In 2000, West Virginia as a whole had 5 percent minorities, a median age of 38.9, median household income of $29,696, and a 75.2 percent home ownership rate.

the future growth of Winfield was assured. The 2000 population was 1,858.

See also Putnam County, Thurmond's Rangers

Bill Wintz
St. Albans

Winterplace

Winterplace Ski Resort is located at Flat Top south of Beckley, just off the West Virginia Turnpike (Interstate 77). Winterplace, which opened in 1983, offers 90 skiable acres with 27 trails and nine lifts. The resort is conducive to novice skiers, with 41 percent of the slopes for beginners, 44 percent for intermediate skiers, and 15 percent for advanced skiers. A nationally accredited program offers lessons for children ages four to 11. Additionally, there is a snowboard park and a 16-lane snowtubing park, which is the largest snowtubing park in West Virginia.

With a top elevation of nearly 3,600 feet and a 603-foot vertical drop, Winterplace is located at the summit of Flat Top Mountain, the southernmost range of the Allegheny Mountains, and has an annual snowfall average of about 65 inches. The resort has 100 percent snowmaking ability with a 30-million-gallon water reservoir. Night skiing is available on almost all of the slopes. The Winterplace season runs from December to March, with opening and closing dates depending on the weather.

Restaurant and food-court dining are available at Winterplace, and slopeside condominiums may be rented. Visitors also may choose other accommodations, including Glade Springs Hotel and Conference Resort, which is located several miles away. Situated by a major highway, Winterplace is West Virginia's most readily accessible ski resort. It draws skiers from a wide region of the southeast.

Jessica Smith
Charleston

Wirt County

Wirt County was created by the General Assembly of Virginia, January 19, 1848, from portions of Wood and Jackson counties. It was named for William Wirt, Virginia statesman and the presidential candidate of the Anti-Masonic Party in 1832. Located in west-central West Virginia, Wirt is bounded by Wood, Ritchie, Calhoun, Roane, and Jackson counties. It comprises 234.4 square miles and had a 2000 population of 5,873, the lowest of any county in West Virginia.

Following the creation of West Virginia in 1863, Wirt County was divided into seven districts: Elizabeth, Clay, Burning Springs, Newark, Reedy, Tucker, and Spring Creek. In addition to Elizabeth, the largest town and county seat, other communities include Newark, Freeport, Morristown, Pee Wee, Creston, Munday, Brohard, and Palestine. The county courthouse at Elizabeth is a Greek Revival structure with a clock tower. It replaced the original courthouse, which burned in 1909.

Elizabeth is centrally located along the Little Kanawha River, which divides Wirt County in half. Known originally as Beauchamp's Mills, Elizabeth was chartered by the General Assembly in 1822. It was named for Elizabeth Woodyard Beauchamp, wife of David Beauchamp, who owned and operated a mill on the site. Beauchamp was son of William Beauchamp Sr., one of the earliest settlers in the region (1799) and a notable lay minister who established the first Methodist class and organized church in the county. Other early settlers included Thomas Pribble, Isaac Enoch, Jacob Deem, Richard Lee, and William Dent at Newark; Alexander and John G. Henderson and Reuben Dye at Burning Springs; Elijah Rockhold and William Booher (who first lived in a cave) at Goose Creek; John Shepherd, John and Peter Conrad, and

John Hartley at Reedy Creek; and Barney McGraw at Spring Creek, who planted the first apple orchard in the Little Kanawha Valley in 1800. The first whites to explore the area in 1772 were frontier scouts Jesse and Elias Hughes, for whom the Hughes River was named, and their brother-in-law, William Lowther.

The history of Wirt County in the 19th century is largely the history of the local oil fields. Early settlers noticed a layer of oil on the streams and discovered the famous Burning Springs, an oil and gas spring that would ignite when fired. As early as 1819, George Lemon was extracting "sand oil" from shallow pits. Bushrod W. Creel carried on a similar operation at Oil Springs Run on the Hughes River and earned a small fortune selling petroleum. Wirt County prospered as the advent of steamboats and railroads increased the demand for oil as a lubricant for steam engines.

In 1840, William P. Rathbone, a New York City judge and alderman, along with his sons, John Castelli "Cass" Rathbone and John Valleau "Val" Rathbone, purchased 12,000 acres at Burning Springs Run. They laid out the village of Burning Springs. In 1860, a Pennsylvania promoter, Samuel D. Karnes, leased an acre from the Rathbones, and drilled an oil well that within a few weeks was producing 30 barrels a day. Following his lead, Cass Rathbone sank a well on his property and hit a gusher that produced 100 barrels a day. Others rushed to Burning Springs to make their fortune, and the Rathbones, who owned most of the adjoining tracts of land, grew wealthy.

On May 9, 1863, a Confederate raiding party under Gen. William E. Jones set fire to the Burning Springs oil field and to crude oil stored in the area. The destruction of equipment and property, along with the loss of future production, was extremely costly. The discovery of new fields elsewhere in Wirt and surrounding counties moved the center of the industry to other locations. The completion of four locks and dams by the Little Kanawha Navigation Company in 1874 enabled the county's oil and gas industry to flourish in the late 19th and early 20th centuries, since producers could ship their crude oil to Parkersburg refineries more easily. Wirt County's population peaked in 1900 at 10,284. The industry's decline after 1930 spelled economic disaster for the county.

Wirt County in the 20th century was hindered by a lack of major transportation routes. No interstate highway crosses Wirt County, which is served by state and county routes. A once thriving economy has been limited, for the most part, to retailing, farming, cattle and hog raising, logging and sawmilling. Many citizens commute to nearby Wood and Jackson counties to work.

Jessica Lynch, an early heroine of the Iraq War, is among Wirt County's best known residents.

See also Burning Springs Raid, Elizabeth, Rathbone Wells

Philip Sturm
Ohio Valley University

Jim Comstock, *Hardesty's West Virginia Counties*, 1973; Elizabeth Beauchamp Chapter, Daughters of American Pioneers, *The History of Wirt County*, 1981; David L. McKain and Bernard L. Allen, *Where It All Began: The Story of the People and Places Where the Oil & Gas Industry Began*, 1994.

Bob Wise

Elected West Virginia's 33rd governor in 2000, Robert Ellsworth "Bob" Wise Jr. was born January 6, 1948, in Washington. He grew up with his parents and two sisters in the Kanawha Valley, where his father worked for 30 years for McDonough Caperton Insurance Group. After graduating from George Washington High School in Charleston in 1966, Wise enrolled at Duke University, receiving a B.A. in 1970. After leaving Duke, Wise applied to law school and took a job in the interim as a mental health facility aide in California, relocating to Texas when he was accepted by the University of Houston. He transferred from Houston to the Tulane University School of Law in New Orleans, and worked nights as a waiter while earning a J.D.

Upon graduating in 1975, Wise returned to Charleston and opened a law practice. As a young lawyer, he represented coal miners in workers compensation cases, created a property tax reform group known as West Virginians for a Fair and Equitable Assessment of Taxes (FEAT), and became involved in community redevelopment efforts on behalf of victims of the 1972 Buffalo Creek disaster and the devastating Mingo County floods of 1978.

Wise ran for public office for the first time in 1980, challenging state Senate President W. T. Brotherton Jr. in the Kanawha County Democratic primary. As a political newcomer, Wise displayed a colorful campaign style including a willingness to jump on stage at rallies and clog for voters. With the support of the West Virginia Education Association and other labor organizations, he upset Brotherton in the primary and went on to win the November election.

Two years later, during a national economic recession, Wise decided to run for Congress. After leading a crowded field in the Democratic primary, he defeated incumbent Republican Mick Staton in November with 58 percent of the vote. He handily won the next ten elections for the House of Representatives, including an unopposed race in 1990, with majorities in his contested races ranging from 64 percent in 1994 against Republican Samuel A. Cravotta to 74 percent in 1988

Governor Bob Wise (1948–).

against Republican Paul W. Hart. Wise's electoral success was attributed to his tenacious constituent service and his maturation in office as a consensus builder with considerable political skills. The Second Congressional District Wise represented is among the largest east of the Mississippi, stretching from the Ohio River to Harpers Ferry. As a member of Congress, Wise held leadership posts including at-large whip, regional whip, and parliamentarian. He became a ranking member of the House transportation and infrastructure committee, a position that enabled him to help secure federal assistance for West Virginia road projects. West Virginia's senior senator, Robert C. Byrd, once referred to Wise as "a steam engine with britches."

While serving in Congress, Wise met and married the former Sandy Casber, who at the time was counsel to the House ways and means committee. They have a son, Robert, and a daughter, Alexandra.

After 18 years in Congress, Wise returned to West Virginia to run for governor in 2000. In the Democratic primary, he defeated Jim Lees of Scott Depot with 63 percent of the vote. The challenge facing Wise in the general election was more formidable, with the Republican incumbent, Cecil Underwood, running for reelection at a time when the state was tilting toward the GOP in the presidential race. Wise campaigned on themes including reviving the state's sluggish economy, expanding college opportunity, improving access to health care benefits, and promoting the state's energy industry while addressing environmental concerns. In a closely contested race, Wise outpolled Underwood 324,822 to 305,926, winning just over 50 percent of the vote compared with 47 percent for Underwood and 3 percent for minor candidates.

Wise was sworn into office as governor just after midnight, January 15, 2001, before a gathering of friends and family including his wife, who held the Bible while he took the oath administered by Circuit Judge Dan O'Hanlon of Huntington. At his inauguration later the same day, Wise pledged to put "cooperation over confrontation" and "practical ideas over ideology" in seeking improvements in education and health care while achieving economic gains and protecting the environment. Wise's crisis management skills as chief executive were tested early by severe flooding which caused widespread destruction. Credited for his leadership in handling the situation, he worked with the legislature to advance his agenda, including the funding of PROMISE college scholarships for all students at West Virginia colleges with at least a B average in high school and college; expanded enrollment in the federal Children's Health Insurance Program (CHIP); tax incentives for job growth and research and development investment; and prescription drug assistance for senior citizens.

With the nation's economy slowing further, Wise faced increasing fiscal pressure midway through his term. In addition to demands on state revenue for such perennial needs as teacher salaries and other school expenses, road maintenance and construction costs, and the state's general operating budget, West Virginia sought ways to continue infrastructure improvements, to address unfunded liabilities in its workers compensation insurance system, and to reduce the cost of its other long-term debt. In his State of the State address to the legislature, January 8, 2003, Wise called for a 10 percent budget cut and other measures to deal with the state's fiscal problems. Among the other issues prominent during Wise's administration were mountaintop removal mining practices, permissible weights for coal trucks operating on the state's highways, and rising medical malpractice insurance costs.

In December 2002, Wise was elected chairman of the Southern Governors Association, the first West Virginian to lead the nonpartisan organization. As a result, Charleston was designated to host the governors' annual meeting in 2003 for the first time in 40 years.

The West Virginia political landscape shifted abruptly in the spring of 2003, when Governor Wise issued a statement admitting that he had been unfaithful in his marriage. As the controversy surrounding the affair continued, he announced the following August that he would not seek reelection as governor in 2004. In 2005, Wise accepted a job in Washington as president of a nonprofit advocacy group founded to improve the nation's high schools.

Larry Sonis
Arlington, Texas

Alexander Scott Withers

Historian Alexander Scott Withers was born October 12, 1792, at Green Meadows, Fauquier County, Virginia. He attended Washington College (now Washington and Lee University) and graduated from the law department of William and Mary College. Withers practiced law at Warrenton, Fauquier County, but was hindered by a timidity in public speaking. After his father's death in 1813, he took over the management of his mother's plantation. In August 1815, he married Melinda Fisher and they had five children.

After moving to Harrison County in 1827 and accepting a teaching position, Withers began writing a history of early settlers of northwestern Virginia and frontier warfare in the Ohio Valley, drawing upon the writings of historian Hugh Paul Taylor and incorporating historical materials collected by a local judge and several venerable pioneers. He completed his manuscript while living in Lewis County, and *Chronicles of Border Warfare* was published in 1831 by Joseph Israel, a Clarksburg newspaper publisher. Israel's business failed soon afterward, and Withers received no profit from the book, which has long been regarded as a classic of West Virginia historical writing.

After his book's completion, Withers traveled to Missouri with a plan to settle and spend his remaining years, but was disappointed with the region and soon returned to Lewis County, where he engaged in farming and was appointed justice of the peace. Following the death of his wife, Withers resided with his eldest daughter, with whom he moved to Parkersburg in 1861. A supporter of the Unionist cause during the Civil War, he was selected as a delegate to the first Wheeling Convention of May 1861. Withers died at Parkersburg, January 23, 1865, and was buried in Weston.

See also Chronicles of Border Warfare
Harold Malcolm Forbes
WVU Libraries

Roy Bird Cook, *Alexander Scott Withers, Author of Chronicles of Border Warfare, A Sketch*, 1921; Alexander Scott Withers, *Chronicles of Border Warfare*, 1895.

Bill Withers

Musician William Harrison "Bill" Withers Jr., a popular 20th century rhythm and blues singer, traces his roots to a Raleigh County coal camp. Withers was born into a miner's family of 13 children in Slab Fork, July 4, 1938. His mother moved the family to Beckley when Withers was three, but he continued to spend weekends in Slab Fork.

By the time he was 15, Withers was singing with gospel groups in the Beckley area and playing baseball. He spent a summer in the 1950s playing professional baseball in the Negro League. At age 17,

he joined the U.S. Navy where he spent the next nine years.

Withers was discharged in San Jose in 1965, and moved to Los Angeles in 1968 to pursue a full-time music career. In 1970, Clarence Avant of Sussex Records introduced Withers to Booker T. Jones of the band Booker T. and the M.G.s. In 1971, Withers released his first album, *Just As I Am*, including his first Grammy-winning song, "Ain't No Sunshine." Sussex released "Lean On Me" in April 1972. It topped the charts on July 8, 1972, where it remained for three weeks.

He remains active in music through his publishing company. In addition to his Grammy in 1972 for "Ain't No Sunshine," he won a Grammy in 1982 for "Just the Two of Us," and another in 1988 for "Lean on Me," re-made that year by the band, Club Nouveau. Bill Withers was inducted into the Songwriters Hall of Fame in 2005. He lives in Los Angeles.

William R. Archer
Bluefield

The Wizard Clip

The legend of Wizard Clip is a part of Eastern Panhandle folklore. About 1800, as one version of the story goes, the Adam Livingston family took up residence near Middleway, Jefferson County. One evening a stranger asked for a night's lodging. Falling sick, the stranger told Livingston he could not live until daylight and must see a Catholic priest before he died. Livingston, or according to some accounts, his wife, refused to have a priest enter the house. In the morning the stranger was dead.

The anonymous stranger was buried nearby, and soon strange things began to happen at the Livingston place. Burning logs jumped from the fireplace and whirled around the floor. One morning, a wagoner asked Livingston why he had blocked the highway by stretching a rope across it. When the teamster drew a knife and slashed at the rope, the blade passed through without cutting the rope. The same phenomenon was experienced by other travelers. A sharp, clipping noise was heard in Livingston's house and all the family's clothes, tablecloths, and bed coverings were slit in the shape of a crescent. One lady, complimenting Mrs. Livingston on her fine flock of ducks, heard the "clip-clip" of invisible shears and saw them decapitated. Similar events followed.

One night Livingston dreamed of a man in religious garments who appeared to be conducting a ceremony, and a spirit whispered to him that this person might relieve his trouble. Local clergy were unable to help, but Father Dennis Cahill, a Catholic priest, was found, and the scissors were no longer heard after the priest visited the home. In gratitude, Livingstone deeded land to the Catholic church, and the tract known as Priest's Field now belongs to the Diocese of Wheeling-Charleston.

See also Folklore, Ghostlore

William D. Theriault
Bakerton

WJLS

Radio in Beckley began when Joe L. Smith Jr., son of Congressman Joe L. Smith and owner of the *Raleigh Register*, applied for a broadcast license in 1938. Several months later, Smith received his authorization and WJLS (for the initials of J. L. Smith) went on the air in the spring of 1939. The younger Smith served as station manager until called to military service in October 1941. His brother, Hulett C. Smith, later governor of West Virginia, took the position until he too went to the service. In June 1943, the station affiliated with the CBS network.

Local programming was important at WJLS in the early years. Several of the early country entertainers went on to significant careers in the business, notably Little Jimmy Dickens, who ultimately entered the Country Music Hall of Fame, and the Lilly Brothers, early pioneers of bluegrass music. Others associated with WJLS included Johnnie Bailes, Walter Bailes, Lynn Davis and Molly O'Day, and the Dobro pioneer and songwriter, George "Speedy" Krise.

Over the years, there were numerous changes. In 1946, WJLS added an FM affiliate that in 1953 became WBKW-FM. At the end of the 1960s, WJLS became a country station while WBKW adopted a Christian format, both stations retaining this programming for several years and the Smiths retaining control. More recently, the format has shifted again with the AM station being Southern Gospel and WJLS-FM being country. In 2005, WJLS was owned by First Media Radio of Massachusetts.

See also Radio

Ivan M. Tribe
University of Rio Grande

WMMN

Radio station WMMN of Fairmont began operations on December 22, 1928, as one of West Virginia's pioneer stations. The call letters came from the initials of Fairmont attorney and U.S. Sen. Matthew M. Neely. The station's power was increased from 500 to 1,000 watts in 1935 and to 5,000 watts in 1938. It was a long-time CBS Radio Network affiliate.

For nearly two decades beginning in 1935, WMMN was an important outlet for country and western music performers. The highlight of this era was the *Sagebrush Roundup*, a Saturday-night live-audience show which began in December 1938 and was broadcast weekly for nearly ten years. Performer Grandpa Jones was once a regular at WMMN.

As both national network and live lo-cal radio programming declined in the 1950's, WMMN began featuring more recorded popular music. It also offered regular play-by-play broadcasts of West Fairmont Senior High School and Fairmont State College sports. In October 1991, WMMN went silent when its owner, Marion Broadcast Corporation, declared bankruptcy and the station went into receivership. It was purchased the following year by Fantasia Broadcasting, Inc., a local family business which owned competing station WTCS. WMMN returned to the air in January 1993, with an all-news format from CNN Headline News.

See also Sagebrush Roundup

Ed McDonald
Keyser

George Connard Wolfe

Folk artist George Connard Wolfe, a self-trained sculptor, was born January 27, 1933, in Standard, Kanawha County. He works in stone and wood. He has been carving since about 1955, when he was discharged from the U.S. Army. Wolfe first carved stones for a wall and then made two headstones, after which he began carving in earnest. He makes his own tools from automobile leaf springs and engine valves. He was active in the craft fair revival of the 1960s and 1970s.

Wolfe's early works include a gigantic reclining nude carved from a boulder in the hills near his home and two life-sized sculptures in tree trunks, "Mountain Girl" and "Standing Christ." Both tree sculptures have been destroyed. His most famous surviving works are a bear on the campus of West Virginia Tech in Montgomery, a beaver at Bluefield High School, and a madonna and child in a Kanawha Valley church. His smaller wooden sculptures are sometimes painted but are frequently left in their natural state. Wolfe is represented in the West Virginia State Museum collection by three stone works, "Christ in Gethsemane," "Madonna and Child," and "The Kiss" from the 1970s, and two small wooden carvings made in 1994.

Wolfe lived in Standard in 2005.

James R. Mitchell
State Museum

Women's Lives

From the founding of the state to the present, most West Virginia women have lived in rural areas, a reality with many implications for their social and economic lives. In early years, most women lived on farms. Farm life involved separate but complementary roles for women and men. Women's contributions in gardening, tending chickens and small livestock, and the many activities of domestic production (spinning, sewing, weaving, canning, and so forth) were essential within the cash-poor economy of most farm households. In addition, women cared for the house and children, prepared the food which they had helped to produce, and provided home health care as needed.

Rapid industrialization during the last two decades of the 19th century dramatically altered many women's lives. Jobs in railroading, timbering, and coal mining drew men out of agriculture and into industrial work. Racial and ethnic diversity among women increased, as African-American migrants from the Deep South and immigrants from southern and eastern Europe came to West Virginia in search of the new jobs. For rural women, however, the employment opportunities were few. Unlike certain other Appalachian states, where the extensive development of textile mills offered jobs to both women and men, with some exceptions industrialization in West Virginia tended to lock women out of the paid labor force. But even as women increasingly relied on male wages to survive, so men depended on women's domestic labor to turn their wages into consumable products such as food and clothing.

Women from more affluent families sometimes achieved a measure of economic independence through professional employment. White women whose families were willing and able to support their education could attend the female seminaries and institutes that first developed during the 1830s in Western Virginia. In 1867, the West Virginia legislature authorized the establishment of normal schools to train teachers, including a school for African-Americans at Harpers Ferry. Educated black and white women saw their employment opportunities as nurses and teachers grow with the state's expanding population. However, they were often forced to choose between marriage and employment: in a majority of school districts, female teachers who married were required to resign their positions, a practice that persisted until World War II. Moreover, until the last decades of the 20th century women faced severe discrimination in more prestigious and lucrative professions such as law and medicine.

Despite these and other disadvantages, including lack of voting rights until 1920, many women in West Virginia were active political organizers who pressed for change in their workplaces, civic life, and other arenas. Working-class women joined labor unions, such as the International Ladies' Garment Workers Union, or provided organized support to men's union activities. More affluent women established local chapters of the Women's Christian Temperance Union and pressed for prison reform and women's suffrage as well as prohibition. In more recent years, women participated in groups such as the national Coal Employment Project and Women and Employment, which advocated for women's access to higher wage jobs in industries such as coal mining.

Today, women in West Virginia face many of the same obstacles, opportunities, and domestic responsibilities as women in other states. Some have benefited from the expansion of professional service employment (for example, in health and education) and the widening range of professions open to women, but many lack the education required to pursue such opportunities. Only 14 percent of West Virginia women aged 25 and over have attained a bachelor's degree or higher, compared to 22.8 percent of women across the United States. Women without higher education or technical training also experience expanded employment options, especially in the service sector, but these jobs typically offer low wages and few benefits.

In their domestic lives, West Virginia women also experience many of the same trends as women across the nation. These include a rise in female-headed families (16.1 percent of families in the state are headed by women, as compared to 18.9 percent in the U.S.), and the responsibility of caring simultaneously for older family members and younger children. The latter trend is especially prominent in West Virginia, which has the highest rate of disability of any state as well as the highest median population age. Increasingly, women are elderly themselves or care for elderly relatives even as they also care for younger family members. The majority of the state's women continue to live in rural areas where many support themselves and their families through creative subsistence strategies outside the formal labor market.

See also Family Life

Barbara Ellen Smith
University of Memphis

Women's Suffrage

In a 15-14 vote in the state senate on March 10, 1920, West Virginia became the 34th state to ratify the 19th Amendment to the U.S. Constitution, which guaranteed the right of women to vote.

Many years earlier, in 1867, just as Kansas was holding the first state referendum on women's suffrage, or the right of women to vote, Samuel Young, a minister and state senator from Pocahontas County, introduced an unsuccessful resolution calling for the enfranchisement of women in the young state of West Virginia. Reflecting a national pattern, interest in women's suffrage dissipated until the 1890s, when local suffrage clubs sprang up in the urban centers of West Virginia's northern counties, with the most active clubs in Wheeling and Fairmont.

Support had increased enough by 1913 for the House of Delegates to pass a state women's suffrage amendment, although it failed to receive the two-thirds majority needed in the Senate. Reintroduced in 1915, the amendment quickly passed the full legislature, leading to a statewide constitutional referendum in 1916. The high hopes and hard work of the suffragists were shattered, however, when the amendment failed by more than two to one, with only two of the 55 counties showing majorities in favor of giving women the vote. The suffragists blamed liquor and business interests, but voting patterns indicate that conservative social and religious beliefs were probably more influential. Anti-suffragists also had launched an effective campaign around the state.

The federal amendment for women's suffrage passed Congress in 1919. Ignoring anti-suffrage protests, Governor Cornwell included ratification on the agenda of a special legislative session called to address a tax question in late February 1920. The House of Delegates quickly ratified the amendment, but the Senate deadlocked. In a dramatic effort to end the stalemate, Sen. Jesse Bloch of Wheeling returned from a California vacation in a cross-country dash to break the tie. Thus, less than fours years after the disastrous defeat of the referendum for state suffrage, West Virginia's suffragists provided a crucial victory in the fight to win the 36 states needed to achieve women's suffrage nationally.

See also Jesse A. Bloch

Anne B. W. Effland
U.S. Department of Agriculture
Anne W. Effland, "'Exciting Battle and Dramatic Finish': The West Virginia Woman Suffrage Movement, Part I: 1867–1916," *West Virginia History*, 1985–1986; Effland, "'Exciting Battle and Dramatic Finish': West Virginia's Ratification of the Nineteenth Amendment," *West Virginia History*, 1989; Effland, "A Profile of Political Activists: Women of the West Virginia Woman Suffrage Movement," *West Virginia History*, 1990.

Wonderful West Virginia

Published by the West Virginia Division of Natural Resources, the monthly magazine *Wonderful West Virginia* promotes the state's natural beauty, wildlife, history, and tourist attractions.

Wonderful West Virginia started in 1936 as the *West Virginia Conservation Bulletin*, a mimeographed publication of news about hunting, fishing, forestry, and parks. The Conservation Commission, which later became the DNR, published the *Bulletin*. During its first four years, approximately 650 copies of the *Bulletin* were distributed monthly to sportsmen's clubs, farm leaders, newspaper editors, and outdoor enthusiasts. Among the *Bulletin's* regular features were articles about conservation education and conservation projects, and lists of those cited for hunting and fishing violations.

In 1940, the *Bulletin* began quarterly publication with a newspaper format featuring black-and-white photographs. In July 1941, after three issues as a quarterly, the *Bulletin* was renamed *West Virginia Conservation* and published monthly. In June 1942, the subscription list had increased to nearly 4,000. By the 1960s, *West Virginia Conservation* was published by the Department of Natural Resources. The magazine promoted conservation and environmental protection. Original paintings by noted wildlife artist Chuck Ripper of Huntington appeared on the covers.

In March 1967, the magazine became *Outdoor West Virginia*. The focus of *Outdoor West Virginia* changed as the state began to promote its parks and forests. Color photographs appeared for the first time. Edward R. Johnson edited the publication and photographer Arnout "Sonny" Hyde Jr. joined the staff. Monthly circulation figures averaged 20,000.

In January 1970, *Outdoor West Virginia* was renamed *Wonderful West Virginia*. Circulation increased to 36,000 and rose rapidly for the next several years. *Wonderful West Virginia* expanded its range of topics to include articles on state history, events and attractions, and arts and crafts. Color photographs added to the magazine's appeal. Hyde became editor in 1982 and continued in that position until his retirement in 1988. The number of subscriptions fell as the state reduced subsidies to the magazine. In 1997, Sonny Hyde returned as editor. In 2004, the circulation of *Wonderful West Virginia* was nearly 40,000.

See also Arnout "Sonny" Hyde Jr.

Abraham Wood

Abraham Wood (about 1615–80), who was responsible for some of the early explorations of present West Virginia, came to the Virginia colony as an indentured servant as a youth. By 1635 he was living on the Appomattox River where he began purchasing land. Wood, who was beginning to prosper as a trader, was a member of the General Assembly in 1644. For defense against the Indians a fort was built in 1646 at the falls of the Appomattox River on the southwestern frontier called Fort Henry, at present Petersburg, Virginia. Fort Henry was designated one of two places where the Indians could trade with the settlers. Wood, who eventually maintained the fort, held the important role of commander of the frontier militia.

Wood was associated with three of the four 17th-century explorations from Virginia. These explorations are often confused with trading expeditions, but they were seeking a way through the Appalachian Mountains and to the South Sea. Although trade was a result, these were first and foremost explorations. The first was the Edward Bland-Abraham Wood

FAST FACTS ABOUT WOOD COUNTY

Founded: 1798
Land in square miles: 377.8
Population: 87,986
Percentage minorities: 2.7%
Percentage rural: 27.0%
Median age: 39.3
Percentage 65 and older: 15.5%
Birth rate per 1,000 population: 11.8
Median household income: $33,285
High school graduate or higher: 81.4%
Bachelor's degree or higher: 15.2%
Home ownership: 73.4%
Median home value: $77,500

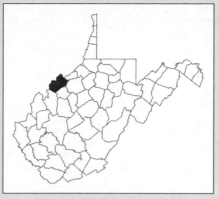

This information is from the 2000 U.S. Census. In 2000, West Virginia as a whole had 5 percent minorities, a median age of 38.9, median household income of $29,696, and a 75.2 percent home ownership rate.

exploration of 1650. Sir William Berkley, governor of Virginia, initiated the second when he sent John Lederer in 1670. For the third and fourth explorations, Wood dispatched Thomas Batts and Robert Fallam in 1671 and James Needham and Gabriel Arthur (an indentured servant) in 1673. The New River, visited by Batts and Fallam, was known for many years as the Woods River.

See also Gabriel Arthur, Batts and Fallam Expedition, Needham and Arthur Expedition

W. Eugene Cox
National Park Service

Alan Vance Briceland, *Westward From Virginia: The Exploration of the Virginia-Carolina Frontier 1650–1710*, 1987.

Wood County

Named for James Wood, Virginia's governor from 1796 to 1800, Wood County was established by the Virginia General Assembly on December 21, 1798, a little over 13 years after the first permanent white settlement (Neal's Station) had been founded in the county. The county seat is Parkersburg.

Reduced in size between 1831 and 1863 by the creation of Jackson, Roane, Ritchie, Wirt, and Pleasants counties, Wood's remaining 377.8 square miles is divided almost equally into northern and southern sectors by the Little Kanawha River. The county was in 1863 the home of four of the founders of West Virginia: Arthur Ingraham Boreman (the state's first governor), William Erskine Stevenson (the first president of the state senate), Peter Godwin Van Winkle (one of the state's first two U.S. senators), and Jacob Beeson Blair (a member of the U.S. House of Representatives). It was also the home of the state's first federal judge, John Jay Jackson Jr.

Population increased steadily in the antebellum period, due to the comple-

tion of internal improvements and several important discoveries. Wood is located at the confluence of the Ohio and

the Little Kanawha, and the introduction of the steamboat on the Ohio in 1811 increased trade through the county. The local economy was boosted by the completion of two turnpikes by 1847 and the Northwestern Virginia Railroad to Parkersburg a decade later. The discovery of petroleum in the area gave an additional spark to the economy. As a result of these developments, Wood County attracted a diverse population, including the largest Irish Catholic, German, Jewish, and African-American settlements between Wheeling and Huntington.

Within two months of the outbreak of the Civil War in 1861, federal forces were stationed in the county to protect the railroad. Later, three hospitals were established. In 1863, Fort Boreman was constructed, an installation built on a hill overlooking the point where the Little Kanawha and the Ohio meet.

After the war's end in 1865, the number of Wood County's residents increased every decade until the 1980s when the population peaked at 93,648. By 1990 it

The Wood County courthouse was built in 1899.

was the third most populous county in the state and remained so in 2000 with a population of 87,986. Its growth in 1865–1900 was fueled by the large reserves of oil and natural gas in the Mid-Ohio Valley, the construction of refineries, the completion of the Ohio River Railroad in 1884, and the development of a vigorous timber processing industry. Growth has been sustained by economic diversification and education.

Present major employers include Du-Pont, General Electric Plastics, Ames Company, the U.S. Bureau of the Public Debt, Fenton Art Glass, Wal-Mart, the Wood County Board of Education, and the Coldwater Creek mail order center. Medical care is a leading industry, with St. Joseph's Hospital, Camden-Clark Memorial Hospital, and Blue Cross-Blue Shield collectively employing more than 3,000 people. The DuPont and GE plants are situated on land once owned by George Washington.

The county ranks near the top in the state in educational leadership. In Parkersburg the first free school south of the Mason-Dixon line was established in 1862 for African-Americans, the first public high school diplomas issued in the state were awarded to Parkersburg High School graduates in 1874, and the first high school diplomas to be issued to African-Americans were granted at Sumner High School in 1887. Wood has four high schools: three public and one private. It has two baccalaureate degree-granting colleges (Ohio Valley College, established in 1957, and West Virginia University at Parkersburg, founded in 1961), as well as Mountain State Business College, which was established in 1888.

Most Wood Countians live to the west of Interstate 77, which divides the county from east to west, in Parkersburg, Vienna, Williamstown, and North Hills, the county's four incorporated communities. The county's Parks and Recreation Commission oversees several parks, including Mountwood Park, situated in the eastern section of the county adjacent to what was once the county's number one oil field boom town, Volcano, and within a mile of the county's highest point, which is 1,328 feet above sea level. Wood County has six islands, the largest of which is Blennerhassett, a part of the West Virginia State Park System.

Within the county are some of the state's finest examples of Victorian Age architecture. There are six National Register historic districts and several individual National Register historic properties.

The county's weather is generally moderate. However, on July 18, 1889, more than 19 inches of rain fell on Limestone Hill, at the southern tip of the county, in about two hours. Devastating floods hit the county almost annually before the completion of a floodwall in Parkersburg in 1950 and the construction of locks and dams on the Ohio, including one at Belleville.

Wood County has been the home of many prominent personalities. Among them are capitalists Johnson Newlon Camden, John M. Crawford, Monroe Jackson Rathbone Jr., Bernard Patrick McDonough, and Charlie O. Erickson; three governors between 1868 and 1900; U.S. diplomat William Kahn Leonhart; Admiral Felix Budwell Stump; pro-football hall of famer Alfred Earle "Greasy" Neale; college football hall of famer Floyd Schwartzwalder; the first bishop of the Episcopal Diocese of West Virginia, George William Peterkin; educator Waitman T. Barbe; entomologist Andrew Delmar Hopkins; and steamboat captain Anton Meldahl.

See also Parkersburg

Bernard L. Allen
Conway, South Carolina
Bernard L. Allen, *Parkersburg: A Bicentennial History*, 1985; Donald F. Black, *History of Wood County, West Virginia*, 1975.

Wood Products Industry

West Virginia, at the center of the Appalachian hardwoods region, is third in the nation in the percentage of land covered in forest. Large-scale logging began in the late 1800s and a century later had matured into a diversified industry. During one banner year, 1989, the West Virginia Division of Forestry reported the development of a new or expanded forest products facility each week of the year.

By the turn of the 21st century, West Virginia had attracted several of the new wood products plants being built by industry giants. Two of these, the Weyerhaeuser OSB (oriented strand board) plant at Heaters, Braxton County, and the Bruce Hardwood flooring plant at Beverly, near Elkins, are among the largest of their kind in the country. Georgia-Pacific Corporation built a new OSB plant near Mount Hope in 1995, and Columbia West Virginia, a subsidiary of Columbia Forest Products, uses all yellow poplar in producing plywood at the facility it built in Craigsville in 1992. Trus Joist, a manufacturer of engineered lumber, became the first in the world to manufacture both Micro-Lam (laminated veneer lumber) and Parallam (parallel strand lumber) under one roof when it opened a plant at Buckhannon in 1995.

The new plants use low-grade lumber for flooring, and low-grade timber that is chipped and remanufactured into four-by-eight OSB panels or sliced into veneer strips which are remanufactured into defect-free lumber. These plants, annually using hundreds of millions of board feet of low-grade lumber, have made it profitable for the first time to practice sustainable forestry within the state, as foresters remove low-value trees and replace them with vigorous specimens of the same species. In the past, these low-grade and low-value trees did not generate enough revenue to pay their way out of the woods.

The Kingsford Charcoal Plant at Parsons was once the largest briquette charcoal plant in the world and is still a major producer. In addition, American Woodmark has about 1,000 employees producing kitchen cabinet doors and fronts in two facilities at Moorefield. Appalachian Log Structures in Princeton manufactures log homes, which it merchandises globally. There are three veneer plants now operating in West Virginia, one each in Princeton, Madison, and Spencer. Wood flooring is made in Gilbert, Cowen, and Ronceverte, in addition to the Bruce Hardwood plant near Elkins.

In 2001 Coastal Lumber, Georgia Pacific Corporation, Allegheny Wood Products, International Industries, Jim C. Hamer Company, and B. A. Mullican Lumber and Manufacturing headed the list of major companies that operated 181 sawmills producing both green and kiln-dried lumber. There were another 11 companies producing pressure-treated lumber, 18 producing rustic products such as rail fencing, 58 dry kiln facilities, and at least 174 producing consumer products such as furniture and millwork.

See also Timbering and Logging

William H. Gillespie
Charleston
Dawn M. DiGiovanni, "Forest Statistics for West Virginia: 1975 and 1989," 1990; Division of Forestry, *Forest Industry of West Virginia*, 2001.

Woodhicks

"Woodhick" was a common term for loggers and woods laborers during the heyday of West Virginia logging, from about 1880 to 1920. "Lumberjack" was not commonly used in the state. The woodhicks worked in isolated, remote locations, and they made a colorful reputation for themselves. There were few settlements and sometimes not even roads in the larger tracts of timberland. The woodhicks lived in temporary shantytowns built along the narrow-gauge railroads that were used to move logs to the sawmills, which were located in larger towns such as Cass and Rainelle.

In the early decades most woodhicks came from outside West Virginia. Many were bachelors who lived in the camps for weeks at a time. Others were married men who attempted to return home at the end of each week. Some were immigrants who found jobs as loggers until they could pay off their debts and better themselves; by 1910, immigrants had become significant minorities in Randolph, Tucker, and Pocahontas counties, in the heavily timbered mountains of West Virginia. Other woodhicks were skilled loggers from Canada or from the northern states, who came to West Virginia to work

Dyed-in-the-wool loggers

"These men . . . were the true loggers, or 'wood hicks.' Theirs was an occupation taken by choice, and in it they were specialists. The camp was their home and the woods their work. They would accept no other employment and took great pride in their calling. Others might seek for work in mills and the easier life of town, but the dyed-in-the-wool logger was virtually married to the swaying softwood forests and the muddy, swirling waves of the flooded river.

"Such men as these permanent loggers were the core of each new camp. From them local men could learn the ways of the trade until all soon merged into an efficient working force. When a job 'cut out,' most of the local men would settle in other occupations, but the drifting 'hick' would move on to new forests and the familiar life of the camp. Only in few instances did one desert the bunkhouse in favor of some blue-eyed maid and the settled life of a permanent home."

—W. E. Blackhurst *Riders of the Flood* (1954)

and planned to return home when the work was done. Whatever their geographic origins, most of them had been brought up on farms before taking to the woods.

Although hard workers, most of the woodhicks had not had an opportunity to attend school, and many of the immigrants had only a slight command of the English language. The rough life of the woodsmen sparked folk tales, especially by townspeople who decried the rowdy behavior of loggers on their visits to town after being confined to a camp in the wilderness.

The origin of the term is probably self-explanatory. Loggers were looked upon as unsophisticated persons working in the woods, and since at least the 16th century the word "hick" has meant an ignorant country person. Perhaps it was for this reason West Virginia woodworkers were called woodhicks or timberhicks.

See also Timbering and Logging
William H. Gillespie
Charleston

Woodland Culture

See Prehistoric People.

Carter G. Woodson

Historian Carter Godwin Woodson, often called the "Father of Black History," spent his formative years in West Virginia. He was a historian, an author, and a publisher who began the systematic collection and dissemination of black historical information.

Born to parents who were former slaves, in Buckingham County, Virginia, December 19, 1875, Woodson spent his early life in Virginia. The family moved permanently to Huntington in 1893 after Carter and his brother, Robert, had migrated to West Virginia to work in the coal mines. Working in Fayette County, Woodson was influenced by association with Oliver Jones and other miners to whom he read books and newspapers. "In this circle the history of the race was discussed frequently, and my interest in penetrating the past of my people was

deepened and intensified," Woodson said in 1944.

Woodson attended Douglass High School in Huntington, graduating in 1896. He studied at Berea College in Kentucky, and returned to Huntington as principal of Douglass in 1900. In 1903, Woodson accepted an administrative and teaching assignment in the Philippines; during 1906–07, he traveled around the world, studied at the Sorbonne, and returned to continue his education at the University of Chicago and at Harvard, receiving a doctorate from the latter institution in 1912.

In Chicago, on September 9, 1915, Woodson and others created the Association for the Study of Negro Life and History. Using his own salary as a teacher and funds that he borrowed on his life insurance policy Woodson in 1915 also published his first book, *The Education of the Negro Prior to 1861*. This book was followed by numerous other publications, including the much-used textbook, *The Negro in Our History*. In January 1916, Woodson began the publication of the *Journal of Negro History*. Carter G. Woodson established the publishing company, Associated Publishers, in 1919, and by 1926 he inaugurated Negro History Week, which now continues as Black History Month. In 1937, he began the publication of *The Negro History Bulletin*, a journal intended for use in the schools.

From 1919 to 1920, Woodson served as the Dean of Liberal Arts at Howard University, after working as a public school teacher and principal in Washington. His final professional appointment in West Virginia was as the Dean of the West Virginia Collegiate Institute, now West Virginia State University, from 1920–22. He then returned to Washington. Though he never lived or worked in West Virginia again, Woodson maintained his family ties and came back to the state for speaking engagements and to visit in Huntington. He remained attentive to his family's needs and aided them financially for many years.

Carter G. Woodson died in Washington, April 3, 1950. In 1995, the Carter G. Woodson Memorial Foundation erected a life-sized statue of him on Hal Greer Boulevard in Huntington.

Ancella R. Bickley
Charleston

Rayford Logan, "Carter G. Woodson: Mirror and Molder of His Time," *Journal of Negro History*, January 1973; August Meier and Elliott Rudwick, "J. Franklin Jameson, Carter G. Woodson, and the Foundations of Black Historiography," *The American Historical Review*, October 1984.

Margaret Workman

Supreme Court Justice Margaret "Peggy" Workman, born May 22, 1947, in Kanawha County, received a law degree from West Virginia University in 1974, then opened a private law practice. She worked as a law clerk for the 13th Judicial Circuit and was assistant majority counsel to the U.S. Senate Public Works Committee.

In 1981, Governor Rockefeller appointed Workman to an unexpired term on Kanawha Circuit Court. She was elected to the remainder of that term in 1982, and to a full term two years later. In the election of November 1988, she simultaneously became the first woman on the West Virginia Supreme Court of Appeals and the first woman to be elected to statewide office in West Virginia.

Workman served as chief justice in 1993 and 1997. While serving on the Supreme Court, she established the task force on gender fairness in the courts, worked to establish model domestic violence programs, and formed the court-appointed special advocates for children program.

Throughout her judicial career, Workman saw herself as an advocate for children's rights. In 1993, she received the West Virginia Prosecuting Attorneys Association's Excellence in Criminal Justice Award for her work on behalf of children. She has also received the Celebrate Women Award for Government and Public Service Award, the Susan B. Anthony Award, and the WVU College of Law Women's Law Caucus Distinguished Women in the Law Award.

After resigning from the high court in August 1999, she opened a law practice in Charleston.

Kay Michael
Charleston

Works Progress Administration (WPA)

In 1935, responding to a request by President Franklin D. Roosevelt, Congress established the Works Progress Administration to provide work for the unemployed of the Great Depression. Based on the belief that direct relief payments to the able-bodied unemployed were demoralizing, the WPA sought to provide government jobs at wages higher than the dole but lower than prevailing wages in the private economy.

National WPA director Harry Hopkins appointed Frank Witcher McCullough of Huntington as the West Virginia administrator. McCullough was succeeded by Joseph Newman Alderson of Alderson in 1937. The agency ceased operations in 1942.

West Virginia was one of the handful of states in which there were serious charges of political interference with the WPA. A federal investigation in 1936 found no basis for the worst of the charges, which were made by the maverick Democratic senator, Rush D. Holt, on the floor of the U.S. Senate and on a national radio network. Both Democratic governors of the period, Guy Kump and Homer Holt, resented that control over the agency's considerable patronage rested largely in the hands of senior senator Matthew M. Neely, who was more sympathetic to New Deal programs.

Despite the bitter conflicts over the agency among the state's leading politicians, the WPA met a critical need, putting many of West Virginia's unemployed to work on a variety of projects in construction, rehabilitation, public health, recreation, conservation, rural road improvement, urban street repairs, and education. Recognizing that unemployment reached beyond blue-collar workers, WPA also generated projects for writers, teachers, artists, and musicians. For many West Virginians, WPA provided a job and hope for the future during hard times.

Although most were small projects in which most of the money would be used for wages, some of WPA's endeavors had more enduring value, such as the South Side Bridge in Charleston; a therapeutic center for the Morris Memorial Hospital for Crippled Children in Milton; an African-American high school in Morgantown, and various other public buildings around the state; the building and improvement of airports; and the writing of *West Virginia: A Guide to the Mountain State*. More capital-intensive undertakings were handled by the Public Works Administration (PWA).

Jerry Bruce Thomas
Shepherd University
William R. Brock, *Welfare, Democracy, and the New Deal*, 1988; Jerry Bruce Thomas, *An Appalachian New Deal: West Virginia in the Great Depression*, 1998.

World War I

World War I had already embroiled the imperial powers of Europe in conflict for three devastating years before the United States declared war on Germany, April 6, 1917. The war ended less than a year and a half later with only a fraction of approximately 2,150,000 American draftees and 200,000 volunteers seeing combat. Thousands of Americans arrived in France, but never saw action, and many thousands more never departed bases in the United States. Nonetheless, more than 58,000 Americans died overseas, with nearly half of them victims of the great influenza epidemic of 1918. Hostilities ended with an armistice on November 11, 1918.

West Virginia mustered 58,000 soldiers for World War I, suffering about 5,000 casualties including dead and wounded. The state's two National Guard regiments had previously been mobilized for the 1916 Punitive Expedition in Mexico. They were reorganized as the 150th and 201st Infantry Regiments, under regular army command in the 38th Division. About 27,000 West Virginians who reached the war zone were deployed across the Western Front, but others participated in the 1918 Italian Campaign and the ill-fated Russian Expedition of 1919. Between May 1917 and September 1918, three drafts were held in West Virginia.

West Virginia's casualties included 1,120 killed in action, 691 killed in training, and many wounded. Many others died of influenza and other diseases, often in camps on American soil. Among the dead, notables included aviator Louis Bennett Jr., who served with distinction with Britain's Royal Air Force, and Capt. Timothy Barber of Charleston, who organized a volunteer ambulance unit prior to gallant service as an army surgeon. Although no Congressional Medals of Honor were awarded to West Virginians during World War I, many received decorations from European allies. Sgt. Felix Hill and Marine Pvt. Raymond White, both from Moundsville, received the French Croix de Guerre. Many West Virginia soldiers lie buried in U.S. military cemeteries in France. World War I memorials may be seen at Welch, Logan, Martinsburg, and at the West Virginia Veterans Memorial in Charleston.

On the home front, World War I mobilized citizens and industry at unforeseen levels. Prior to U.S. involvement, many Americans questioned the Wilson administration's move toward war. Some newspaper editors voiced pro-German sympathy, while opposing the British naval blockade of neutral shipping to Germany and its allies. After the May 1915 sinking by the Germans of the *Lusitania*, an unarmed English passenger liner with many Americans aboard, West Virginians and other Americans turned against Germany. State colleges discontinued German language courses during the war, while several counties held "loyalty meetings." Statewide food and coal rationing went into effect during the war. Men and women volunteered as Red Cross personnel, while "Four-Minute Men" raised millions in Liberty Bonds sales across the state. Both the Charleston Ordnance Center and the Nitro gunpowder plant were built as part of the war effort, though neither saw production before the end of the war. Nitro, a Kanawha Valley community created by the war, experienced a fleeting wartime population boom of 25,000 and remains a major industrial center today.

See also Louis Bennett Jr., Nitro

Jeffrey M. Leatherwood
West Virginia University

World War II

With the Japanese bombing of Pearl Harbor on December 7, 1941, West Virginia and the nation again went to war. Hit by a bomb and seven torpedoes, the Mountain State's flagship, USS *West Virginia*, was among those sunk during the attack.

West Virginia reported the fifth-highest percentage of servicemen during the war, with 218,665 West Virginians, including 66,716 volunteers, serving in the armed forces. Of the 11,000 African-Americans representing the state, 600 came from West Virginia State College (now University). A total of 5,830 West Virginians were killed in World War II.

Mountaineers distinguished themselves throughout the war. Eleven Congressional Medals of Honor went to West Virginians for service in World War II. Hershel Woodrow "Woody" Williams earned the Medal of Honor at Iwo Jima. Silencing one Japanese gun after another, Corporal Williams was directly instrumental in neutralizing one of the best-defended strongholds on the island. In 2005, the Marion County native was West Virginia's last surviving Medal of Honor recipient from World War II.

George "Spanky" Roberts, a graduate of West Virginia State College's Civilian Pilot Program, became the first African-American cadet in the Army Air Corps. The Marion County native commanded the 99th and 332nd Pursuit Squadrons.

Charles "Chuck" Yeager became an ace in a single day by shooting down five German planes. The Lincoln County native flew 64 missions and shot down 13 enemy aircraft. A post-war test pilot, Yeager became the first person to break the sound barrier.

Felix Stump commanded the aircraft carriers *Enterprise* and *Lexington*. The Wood County native received the Silver Star, two Navy Crosses, the Army's Distinguished Service Medal, and several other awards for exceptionally meritorious service. Admiral Stump later received the Navy's Distinguished Service Medal as commander in chief of the Pacific Fleet.

Randolph County native Richard Sutherland served as chief of staff to Gen. Douglas MacArthur. It was Lieutenant General Sutherland who received the Japanese surrender of the Philippines.

Two thousand West Virginia women

Troops learned mountain climbing at Seneca Rocks during World War II.

entered military service during the war. In the navy, Hardy County native Winifred Love commanded the first contingent of WAVES to serve overseas. Dolores Dowling, of Cabell County, was among the first American nurses to land in Sicily after D-Day. Dowling was also a member of the first Mobile Army Surgical Hospital unit. Florence Blanchfield, superintendent of the Army Nurse Corps from 1943 to 1947, oversaw the growth from 1,000 to 57,000 nurses. A World War I veteran, the Jefferson County native became the first woman commissioned as a lieutenant colonel in the regular army. Colonel Blanchfield received the Distinguished Service Medal in 1945.

While a captive of the Japanese in Manila, Ruby Bradley, an army Nurse Corps administrator in the Philippines, earned the title "Angel in Fatigues." After assisting in more than 230 major operations and the delivery of 13 American babies, Bradley received two Bronze Stars. The Roane County native later received numerous medals, ribbons, and citations as a combat nurse in the Korean Conflict. Colonel Bradley is the state's most decorated female veteran.

Of 12 West Virginians applying to fly as Women Airforce Service Pilots, nine graduated. Katherine Thompson, of Pocahontas County, became the state's first WASP. Flying new and unproven aircraft within the continental United States and Canada freed male pilots for combat missions in Europe. As engineering test pilots, women often flew repaired planes that had previously crashed. These pilots trained ground crews, conducted flight instruction, performed top secret missions, and towed antiaircraft targets amid live gunfire. Frances Fortune Grimes of

Monongalia County gave her life for her country, crashing en route to deliver an airplane to its point of debarkation overseas.

Mary Lee Settle of Kanawha County, who later won the National Book Award as a novelist, wrote articles for the Office of War Information in England. Anna Norman Oates, meanwhile, cheered the Allies on to victory through poems, comic verse, and letters to soldiers. Known as "Mother Oates," the Monongalia County native reached thousands of readers and radio listeners during the war. Buckhannon native Jean Lee Latham learned to repair radio equipment for the Signal Corps. The award-winning author found herself writing directions, lectures, and course material for the inspection of radio gear.

The 201st Infantry of the West Virginia Army National Guard provided security for the Aleutian Islands during much of the war, while the 150th Infantry Regiment defended Panama, Peru, Ecuador, Guatemala, and the Galapagos Islands. Replacing National Guardsmen on active duty, state guard units protected airplanes, fought forest fires, and assisted during natural disasters on the home front.

While the army readied soldiers for northern Italy's terrain in Grant and Tucker counties, the navy groomed officers at West Virginia University and other schools around the state. The Greenbrier resort served as a detention center for German, Italian, and Japanese diplomats early in the war and, under the name of Ashford General Hospital, later treated 20,000 soldiers and veterans. General Eisenhower was among those treated there.

As well as rationing gasoline, sugar and butter, West Virginians on the home front joined the Civil Defense Corps and grew their own food. The West Virginia Farm Women's Club sold $288,997 in war bonds and collected $15,464 for the Red Cross. Children pitched in by collecting old tires, scrap metal, and other scarce materials for the war effort. Fayette County Boy Scouts, for instance, salvaged as much as 12 tons of paper in 90 days.

Mountaineers supplied more than 600 million tons of coal to fuel the war. Built in the Kanawha Valley, the world's largest synthetic rubber plant helped America to replace Japan as its primary supplier. The valley also housed the world's largest producer of steel used for battleships, tanks, and other military equipment. The U.S. Naval Ordnance Plant in Kanawha County supplied gun barrels for ships and tanks, while West Virginians built patrol boats and other ocean-going vessels on the Mason County shores of the Ohio River.

Re-floated and completely rebuilt, USS *West Virginia* returned to action in 1944. Providing considerable gun support in the Pacific, the "Wee Vee" earned five battle stars. After leading American battleships into Tokyo Bay on August 31, 1945, USS *West Virginia* was present for the formal surrender of Japan.

Russ Barbour
Huntington

Elizabeth Cometti and Festus P. Summers, *The 35th State*, 1966; L. Wayne Sheets, "Women Airforce Service Pilots of World War II," West Virginia University, 1998.

"The Wreck on the C&O"

On October 23, 1890, at 5:40 a.m., the passenger train known as the Fast Flying Virginian, pulled by engine 134, wrecked due to a rock slide three miles east of Hinton on the Chesapeake & Ohio Railway. The eastbound luxury train was traveling from Cincinnati to Washington. Its engineer, George Washington Alley, a member of a prominent railroading family, was killed while attempting to stop the train, and firemen Lewis Withrow and Robert Foster were injured.

Alley's heroic deed, which saved the lives of his passengers, became the basis for a ballad attributed to an unnamed African-American engine wiper who worked in the Hinton roundhouse, although there is no direct evidence of the song prior to about 1900. More than 80 variants have been documented, including those in John Harrington Cox's book, *Folk-Songs of the South*, but most details are historically inaccurate. The ballad's various titles include "The Wreck on the C&O," "Fatal Run," "The Brave Engineer," "George (ie) Alley" (or Allen), "Engine 143" [*sic*], and "The FFV." Recordings have been issued by the Carter Family; Lester Flatt, Earl Scruggs, and the Foggy Mountain Boys; Joan Baez; and Doc Watson.

A historical marker on State Route 3 at Bellepoint in Summers County memorializes the tragic event. Alley is buried in the Greenbrier Baptist Church cemetery in Alderson.

H. G. Young III
WVU Parkersburg
Katie Letcher Lyle, *Scalded to Death by the Steam: Authentic Stories of Railroad Disasters and the Ballads that Were Written About Them,* 1983.

WSAZ

Radio station WSAZ (now WRVC) is West Virginia's oldest continuously licensed AM radio station. It began broadcasting on October 16, 1923, in Pomeroy, Ohio, and moved to nearby Huntington in March 1927. Early downtown studio locations included the Prichard Hotel and the Keith-Albee Theater.

WSAZ's original frequency was 1160 kHz. After several changes, it moved in 1928 to 580 kHz. In 1941, it began full-time operation and assumed the permanent frequency of 930 kHz. Following World War II, the station's daytime power increased to its current 5,000 watts. The station affiliated with the Blue Network (later the ABC Radio Network) in 1943, and switched to NBC in 1957.

In 1929, WSAZ was purchased by the Huntington Publishing Company, the publisher of the *Advertiser* and *Herald-Dispatch* newspapers, which started the state's first television station with the same call letters in 1949. In 1961, both broadcast properties were sold to out-of-state owners, with the radio call letters changed to WGNT in 1970. In 1988, the station returned to local ownership. The call letters were changed briefly to WTKZ and then to WRVC, standing for "River Cities."

In addition to the network programs, WSAZ in its early years offered live programming. Musician David Miller, known as "The Blind Soldier," and his West Virginia Mockingbirds offered listeners some of the first commercial country music. Under the management of Flem Evans in the early 1940s, WSAZ listeners were treated to several other country acts, ranging from Fiddlin' Arthur Smith to the Bailes Brothers. Gene Kelly, later the radio broadcaster for the Philadelphia Phillies, served as a WSAZ announcer in the same decade.

In the 1960s, WSAZ developed a program format of adult-oriented music with an emphasis on news, sports, and community service. The music changed to country in 1983, and the 1988 ownership change introduced the current format of news, talk, and sports. In addition to local news, WRVC airs news from CNN Radio and the statewide MetroNews network. It is a long-time outlet for Cincinnati Reds baseball and for 50 years has been the flagship station for Marshall University sports.

Ed McDonald
Keyser

WVMR

Radio station WVMR is the state's only radio station owned by a cooperative, the Pocahontas Communications Cooperative. The call letters stand for West Virginia Mountain Radio. Broadcasting on 1370 AM since 1981, the non-commercial station provides the only local broadcast service to Pocahontas County. Its programming features local news and information as well as an eclectic mix of music, including live appearances by local musicians. Many of the disc jockeys are volunteers.

Pocahontas is the most sparsely populated county in the state. WVMR provides information to its 9,000 residents, who are scattered across nearly 950 square miles of rugged mountain terrain. The station's value to the county was never more evident than during the major floods of 1985 and 1996, when its round-the-clock broadcasts kept the community informed and unified.

WVMR operates by special permit near the center of a radio quiet zone mandated by the nearby National Radio Astronomy Observatory at Green Bank. The station must operate within the technical limits established by the observatory. Its AM signal is less likely than FM broadcasts to interfere with radio telescope reception of very high frequency signals from outer space.

In the mid 1990s, the cooperative helped residents of nearby Bath and Highland counties in Virginia to start their own community radio stations; neither county had had a local station before. The three stations are linked together as Allegheny Mountain Radio. Part of the day all three stations broadcast the same program, and at other times each has its own separate broadcast.

Gibbs Kinderman
Marlinton

WVU at Parkersburg

West Virginia University at Parkersburg, a state-supported, fully accredited four-year college, opened on Parkersburg's north side in 1961 as a two-year college. The college was founded through the efforts of the *Parkersburg Sentinel*, the Wood County Board of Education, Parkersburg civic and business leaders, some West Virginia University administrators, and key leaders of state government. Their goal was to provide easier access to public higher education for local students. At its founding it was the only West Virginia public college on the Ohio River between Huntington and Wheeling.

In 1963, the college became the first of a series of Appalachian Centers established by WVU President Paul A. Miller. In 1971, it was separated from WVU by the Board of Regents and converted into the state's first community college. In 1989, it was re-affiliated with WVU. The president at Parkersburg now reports to WVU's provost for academic affairs in Morgantown.

The college awarded its first associate degrees in May 1967, its first bachelor of science degrees in business administration in 1992, and its first bachelor of science degrees in elementary education in 1993. Only about 100 students were enrolled at its opening in September 1961, but the institution's enrollment grew to 5,149 full- and part-time students during the fall of 1974 before declining to about 3,800 in 2005. Some of the students are enrolled at the college's Jackson County Center, which opened in Ripley in 1973–74.

The WVU-Parkersburg main campus is situated a few miles east of Parkersburg on State Route 47 near Interstate 77, having moved there in 1969 after Wood County voters overwhelmingly approved a bond levy for construction of a modern facility. Previously the college had been located at an old elementary school on Emerson Avenue in Parkersburg. Additions were made to the new structure in 1974 and 1989. The Caperton Center for Applied Technology was dedicated in 1999.

See also West Virginia University

Bernard L. Allen
Conway, South Carolina
Bernard L. Allen, *Four Diamonds in the Rough: West Virginia University at Parkersburg.* 2000.

WVU Extension Service

The West Virginia University Extension Service provides outreach and public service programs to West Virginians statewide. WVU is a land-grant university, one of the educational institutions established in all the states and supported in part through the proceeds from the sale of public lands owned by the federal government. The land-grant institutions, first authorized by the 1862 Morrill Act, must meet certain service requirements. Since the 1914 Smith-Lever Act, these requirements include the operation of a state cooperative extension service. The WVU Extension Service now receives funds from various sources, including federal appropriations and grants, state appropriations, county commissions, county boards of education, other local government agencies, user fees, and the private sector.

The service has evolved from an organization concerned mainly with agriculture and home economics to one that also works to address economic, natural resource, workplace safety, and youth development issues. Its programs include the popular 4-H Clubs.

Every county has an extension agent, who faces a diverse agenda in the modern era. Whereas the bulk of an agent's time once was spent on coordinating the 4-H program and assisting farmers with livestock and crop problems, today's agents are involved in county economic development activities, grant writing, work force development, child care and parenting, exercise and nutrition programs, and after-school activities. During a typical day an agent might attend a 4-H meeting, visit an area garden and provide advice on insecticides and fertilizer, attend an economic development meeting, spend some time researching and writing a grant proposal for a county agency, conduct an exercise class for seniors, and assist with an after-school program. County agents continue to help farmers improve productivity and help landowners use natural resources more wisely.

The Extension Service is headquartered at WVU in Morgantown and operates the Jackson's Mill conference center and state 4-H camp, located near Weston. Historically serving as a central gathering place for youth participating in 4-H events and camps, Jackson's Mill has expanded its mission to include a variety of meetings and conferences, Elderhostel programs, a popular crafts and music festival, and other activities. It will be the new home of the state Fire Service Training Academy, where professional and volunteer firefighters will train.

The Extension Service also directs or collaborates with programs that improve economic opportunities for youth and small communities, including a summer reading program for rural low-income children, and other programs.

See also West Virginia University

Donna Colebank
WVU Extension Service

WVU Institute of Technology

The West Virginia University Institute of Technology, known as "Tech" to generations of students and alumni, is located in Montgomery, 26 miles southeast of Charleston. The college evolved from the Montgomery Preparatory School, a state institution established in 1895 to prepare students for West Virginia University.

The preparatory school was created in Montgomery because of the city's growing population, which was the result of the coal boom in surrounding Fayette and Kanawha counties; the lack of high schools in southern West Virginia; and the political influence of Thomas P. Davies, a Montgomery citizen and a leading Republican. Classes began on January 4, 1897. The work of the institution was directed by Principal Josiah Keely (1897–1907).

The need for the Montgomery Preparatory School diminished before World War I as more high schools were es-tablished. Renamed the West Virginia Trades School in 1917, the institution hoped to prosper in vocational education. The transformation was unsuccessful, however, and the school quickly returned to its earlier preparatory work.

New life was given to the institution in 1921 with its designation as the New River State School, a junior college. The name was chosen in an effort to tie the institution to the New River area, up-stream from Montgomery which itself lies on the banks of the Kanawha River. Under President Cyrus H. Martin (1921–33), the new junior college grew steadily during the 1920s, particularly as a result of its course work for elementary school teachers. During that decade and in the early 1930s, the New River State School bought land for expansion and the construction of new buildings. It awarded its first baccalaureate degree in 1929. Two years later, in 1931, the institution officially became a four-year college, New River State College. A major change was made in the curriculum with the elimination of elementary teacher education in 1934.

In 1941, the Montgomery school was renamed the West Virginia Institute of Technology. Headed by President Edwin S. Maclin (1933–45), Tech expected to become a leader in technology. The war years took their toll, with most of its male students entering the military. After the war, West Virginia Tech benefited from the GI Bill. During the presidency of M. J. Horsch (1945–53), large numbers of veterans filled the classrooms and dormitories. During the 1950s, enrollment steadily increased. By 1960, 1,000 students were enrolled at Tech. Although engineering had emerged as its primary mission, the Montgomery school remained multi-purpose in nature.

Led by President William B. Axtell (1953–61), West Virginia Tech made a number of important advances during the 1950s. Most significant was accreditation by the North Central Association of Colleges and Schools in 1956. Also, the president established the College of Engineering, directed by Leonard C. Nelson.

Tech grew dramatically during the 1960s, its enrollment climbing to nearly 2,500 at decade's end. Under President Leonard C. Nelson (1961–86), the school continued to upgrade its academic programs and the quality of its faculty. The campus underwent dramatic changes during the 1960s and early 1970s, including the addition of a new library, engineering building, student center, community and technical building, physical education building, and two student residence halls. But enrollment again declined during the 1970s and 1980s. Fewer high school graduates in the state and a declining population in Fayette and Kanawha counties were the major causes. Under President Robert C. Gillespie (1986–92), the college struggled with the twin issues of falling enrollment and tighter budgets.

Hoping to strengthen the school, President John P. Carrier (1992–99) supported the merger of West Virginia Tech with West Virginia University. The West Virginia University Institute of Technology was established on July 1, 1996, a largely career-oriented institution, emphasizing engineering, technology, nursing, and the sciences.

The school celebrated its centennial as Carrier's service drew toward its close. Tech has nurtured outstanding scholars and teachers, including West Virginia historian Otis Rice; English professors L. T. Crocker and Roscoe Vining; the historian and political scientist John Matheny; deans David Kraybill and Reed Davis; and others. The school remembers Registrar Annie L. Castle, and coaches Steve Harrick, Hugh Bosely and Neal Baisi. Successful alumni include the late judge K. K. Hall, corporate presidents Dennis Bone and W. Henry Harmon, and others.

With the retirement of Carrier in January 1999, Karen LaRoe became the WVU regional vice president and campus president at Montgomery. She was succeeded by Charles Bayless in 2005. In 2004 legislation Tech lost its community college component, which remained on the campus under separate administration, and in 2006 its relationship with WVU was again under consideration. In 2005, WVU Tech and the community college had a total enrollment of 2,003 full-time equivalents.

See also West Virginia University

Ronald R. Alexander
WVU Institute of Technology

Ronald R. Alexander, *West Virginia Tech: A History* 1992; Joseph Prudich, "History of West Virginia Institute of Technology," M.A. thesis, 1951.

WWVA

Wheeling radio station WWVA-AM began broadcasting December 13, 1926. The 50-watt station operated from the basement of John Stroebel, physics teacher and wireless pioneer, for most of its first year. By November 1927, WWVA had established broadcasting studios in a Wheeling office building and received approval to boost its power to 500 watts. Early broadcasts presented contemporary music, informal announcements, music by local amateur groups, and children's programs. Network affiliation in 1931 added national news, afternoon soap operas, and other popular shows to the schedule.

In 1933, WWVA founded the *Wheeling Jamboree* (now *Jamboree USA*), broadcasting to 17 other states and six Canadian provinces. In April 1933, the live country music show moved from the WWVA studios to the stage of the Capitol Music Hall to begin performing before an

FAST FACTS ABOUT WYOMING COUNTY

Founded: 1850

Land in square miles: 507.3

Population: 25,708

Percentage minorities: 1.4%

Percentage rural: 89.3%

Median age: 40.1

Percentage 65 and older: 13.9%

Birth rate per 1,000 population: 10.6

Median household income: $23,932

High school graduate or higher: 64.3%

Bachelor's degree or higher: 7.1%

Home ownership: 83.3%

Median home value: $47,400

This information is from the 2000 U.S. Census. In 2000, West Virginia as a whole had 5 percent minorities, a median age of 38.9, median household income of $29,696, and a 75.2 percent home ownership rate.

WWVA has been an AM station from the beginning. Now that stereo has boosted FM radio into the lead for music broadcasting, WWVA has moved into the AM market niche of news and talk, which dominate its daytime hours. Weekday evenings feature religious programs. Saturday evenings, though, country music fans do what they've done for years: they power up the clear channel of WWVA and sit back to the sounds of their favorites, performing live on *Jamboree USA*.

See also Wheeling Jamboree

Nancy Balow
Charleston

Martha Jane Becker and Marilyn Fletcher, *Broadcasting in West Virginia: A History,* 1989; John Cuthbert, "'In Steel and Song': The Wheeling Steel Radio Show," *Goldenseal,* Winter 1992; Ivan M. Tribe, *Mountaineer Jamboree: Country Music in West Virginia,* 1984.

audience. Its first performance packed the house with more than 3,000 people and turned away 1,000 more for lack of space. Over the years, the *Jamboree* has attracted the biggest stars in country music as well as a host of talented local performers led by Doc and Chickie Williams. Only Nashville's *Grand Ole Opry* rivals the *Jamboree* for broadcast power and longevity.

Although WWVA was best known for the *Jamboree*, it pioneered other live musical performances as well. On November 8, 1936, the Wheeling Steel Company's *It's Wheeling Steel* debuted on WWVA. The program included popular songs and show tunes sung and played largely by company employees. From January 2, 1938, until its last broadcast on June 18, 1944, the show was carried by many stations across the country and received national acclaim.

Wyoming County

Wyoming County, with its rugged terrain bisected by the Guyandotte River, is located in the heart of West Virginia's southern coal and natural gas producing region.

The county was formed by the Virginia General Assembly in 1850 from a part of Logan County. Only 6,247 residents were counted in the 1890 census, but the development of timbering, natural gas production, and coal mining pushed the

The homestead at Twin Falls State Park in Wyoming County.

population to 20,926 in 1930 and to a high of 37,540 in 1950. Like its neighbors, Wyoming County lost people with the loss of mining jobs. The 2000 population was 25,708.

Wyoming County has a land area of 507.3 square miles. Oceana, established in 1797 by early settler and Revolutionary War veteran John Cooke, was the seat of government until the county seat was moved to Pineville when that town was incorporated in 1907. A handsome courthouse was built in 1916 of native stone from a local quarry.

Major timbering began in 1889. Logs were floated down the Guyandotte River to its junction with the Ohio River at Huntington. The Guyandotte River originates just over the border in neighboring Raleigh County, where Winding Gulf and Devils Fork creeks come together. The Guyandotte and its tributaries drain all of Wyoming County.

Completion of the Virginian Railway in 1909 sparked the area's largest industrial boom by providing transportation of coal to ports on the Atlantic Ocean in Virginia. A large rail yard helped make Mullens the county's largest incorporated town, with a population of 3,544 in 1950. Wyoming County ranked 10th statewide in coal production, with more than 566 million tons of coal extracted, for the period between 1883 and 1998.

Financier I. T. Mann and others developed a major coal company town and mine at Itmann, near Mullens, about 1916. Today their massive cut-stone company store building remains a coalfields landmark. The first large mine was opened by Raleigh-Wyoming Coal Company at Glen Rogers in 1922 and employed nearly 1,000 men by the late 1930s. The mine was the scene of the county's worst tragedy when an underground explosion on November 6, 1923, claimed 27 lives. A total of 160 workers were killed at the Glen Rogers mine during its 40 years of operation, making it one of the most dangerous work places in West Virginia's history.

Developer C. H. Meade completed the first commercial natural gas well in 1919. The Ravencliff field, one of the state's most productive gas fields, was named after a small community in the northeastern part of the county near Bolt Mountain.

In 1964, a Wyoming County petroglyph, located near Oceana, was recorded by archeologists Oscar Mairs and Hillis Youse. Named the Luther Elkins Petroglyph, it was studied again in 1969 when archeologist Sigfus Olafson documented the site. In 1982, the petroglyph attracted widespread attention when an amateur archeologist proclaimed it to be of Irish origin with ancient markings. The claim was generally dismissed by professional archeologists.

Chief among Wyoming County's recreational facilities are Twin Falls Resort State Park, located between Pineville and Mullens, and R. D. Bailey Lake near Baileysville.

Prominent Wyoming County residents have included William C. Marland, who was elected governor in 1952; Robert D. Bailey, West Virginia secretary of state, 1965–68, and a well-known judge; Ward Wylie, a legislator and president of both the national boxing and wrestling associations in the late 1950s; and professional football star Curt Warner. Brothers Darrell V. and Warren R. McGraw both served on the West Virginia Supreme Court and in other high offices. Darrell McGraw was elected to the Supreme Court in 1977 and became state attorney general in 1993. Warren McGraw was elected to an unexpired term on the Supreme Court in 1998 and served through 2004. Warren McGraw also served in the House of Delegates from 1969 to 1972 before being elected to three terms in the state Senate. He was president of the Senate from 1981 to 1984.

See also Glen Rogers Mine Disaster, Pineville, R. D. Bailey Lake, Twin Falls State Park

Karl C. Lilly III
State Senate

Mary Keller Bowman, *Reference Book of Wyoming County History*, 1965; Bud Perry and Karl C. Lilly III, *Reopening Glen Rogers*, n.d.

Y

Yeager Airport

Commercial air service to the Charleston area started in 1930 at Wertz Field in nearby Institute. This location was deemed inadequate for the current aircraft by the late 1930s, and the search for a new location began. Coonskin Ridge, north of Charleston, was selected in 1940, but the project was delayed by World War II. Meanwhile, Wertz Field closed in 1942 for construction of a synthetic rubber plant.

With $3,000,000 in funds, construction began in October 1944 on Kanawha (now Yeager) Airport. Seven-hundred-sixty acres of land was acquired, 365 of which made up the airport proper. The leveling of three mountaintops required 2,000,000 pounds of explosives to help displace 9,000,000 cubic yards of earth and rock. Two hundred pieces of heavy equipment were used to grade the site, and a rail siding at the base of the mountain was used to shuttle in tank cars of diesel fuel. A pipeline was run to the top of the mountain to supply the 2,500 gallons of fuel used each day during construction.

Kanawha Airport was dedicated November 3, 1947, with World War I ace Capt. Eddie Rickenbacker among those present. The terminal building was finished in July 1950, and an addition was added in 1970. The runway extension to accommodate jet airliners began in 1968 and was completed December 8, 1971. The baggage claim addition was built in 1974 and major renovations to the complex took place in 1982, 1997, 2001, and 2005. Kanawha Airport was renamed Yeager Airport in honor of Brig. Gen. Chuck Yeager, a Lincoln County native, on October 14, 1985.

Kanawha Airport was home for the 167th Fighter Squadron from 1947 to 1955, when it moved to Martinsburg. The 130th Troop Carrier Squadron (now the 130th Airlift Squadron) formed in 1955, replacing the 167th at Charleston. Both were units at West Virginia Air National Guard.

The terminal, expanded in 2001 and 2005 to provide additional boarding gates and passenger seating areas, was named for U.S. Sen. Jay Rockefeller in 2003. The main lobby was remodeled to provide for a larger security presence. In 2005, Yeager Airport served 325,000 passengers annually with 80 flights daily. The airport was served by US Airways Express, Independence Air, United Express, Comair, and other regional airlines.

See also Aviation, Wertz Field, Chuck Yeager

Jack H. Smith
South Charleston

Chuck Yeager

General Charles Elwood "Chuck" Yeager, the first person to fly faster than the speed of sound, was born February 13, 1923, at Myra, on upper Mud River about seven miles from the Lincoln County seat of Hamlin. He was the second of five children born to Albert Hal and Susie Mae Sizemore Yeager. The family moved to Hamlin before young Yeager entered the first grade. In 1941, he graduated from Hamlin High School, and a statue of him now stands near the school entrance.

Yeager served in Europe during World War II and received his flight training in the military. He enlisted in the Army Air Corps in 1941 at the age of 18, starting out as an airplane mechanic, then enrolling in a flying sergeant program. He enjoyed great success as a fighter pilot, engaging the early German jets with his prop-driven P-51 Mustang. In all, he flew 64 combat missions. Yeager became "a double ace," with 13 kills, and destroyed five German planes during a single historic dogfight in November 1944. Stationed in England as a fighter pilot, he was shot down March 5, 1944, on his eighth combat mission. Yeager parachuted unharmed into German-occupied France.

He escaped across the Pyrenees into neutral Spain and later rejoined his squadron in England.

On October 14, 1947, in a Bell X-1 rocket airplane dropped from a B-29 bomber, Yeager broke the sound barrier by flying 700 miles per hour. He set another speed record on December 12, 1953, by flying two-and-a-half times the speed of sound in a Bell X-1A.

Yeager became commander of the Aerospace Research Pilot School at Edwards Air Force Base, California, in 1962. In 1968, he became a brigadier general and in 1971 was assigned as U.S. defense representative to Pakistan. He retired in 1975. Already a hero in military and aviation circles, Yeager catapulted to international celebrity with the publication in 1979 of Tom Wolfe's novel *The Right Stuff* and the popular movie which followed the book. Yeager Airport at Charleston is named after General Yeager, as is nearby Yeager Bridge on the West Virginia Turnpike. An academic program for outstanding students at Marshall University, the Yeager Scholars, is named in his honor.

Tom D. Miller
Huntington

Chuck Yeager and Leo Janos, *Yeager: An Autobiography*, 1985.

Yellow-Dog Contract

The yellow-dog contract was an anti-union device, used especially in the coal

Ace pilot Chuck Yeager (1923–).

industry. It was a contract between employer and employee by which the employee agreed as a condition of employment not to join a labor union.

In West Virginia, blank copies of yellow-dog contracts were supplied to the coal operators by their regional operators associations in both long and short versions. In the contract the coal company stated that it would not knowingly employ any member of a labor union, and the miner agreed that (in the language of one such contract) he would not "become a member of, or connected or affiliated with, or aid, assist or encourage in any way, the United Mine Workers of America, the IWW or any other labor union."

After the 1917 U.S. Supreme Court decision in *Hitchman Coal and Coke v. Mitchell*, a case arising in West Virginia, yellow-dog contracts were viewed as legal and binding by state and federal courts. That changed when the right of workers "to organize and bargain collectively through representatives of their own choosing" was codified in 1933 in section 7a of the National Industrial Recovery Act and in 1935 in the Wagner Act, both acts of federal legislation.

The language of the NIRA specifically goes on to state "that no employee and no one seeking employment shall be required as a condition of employment to join any company union or to refrain from joining . . . a labor organization of his own choosing." The outlawing of this practice was one of the factors that allowed the miners union to organize the West Virginia coalfields in a very short time in the summer of 1933.

See also Hitchman Coal and Coke v. Mitchell, et al.

Richard Fauss
State Archives

Laurence Yep

Author Laurence Michael Yep has written more than 50 works of fiction, mostly for young readers. Yep grew up in San Francisco, where he was born June 14, 1948, but has roots in West Virginia. During the Depression, Yep's maternal relatives moved from China to Ohio and then to Clarksburg, before settling in California.

Growing up hearing about his family's life in West Virginia, Yep based two of his books on those stories. The award-winning novel *The Star Fisher*, which was published in 1991, is an account of a Chinese-American family that moves to Clarksburg to open a laundry. For the book's portrayal of life in West Virginia, Yep received the West Virginia Library Association's 1995 Literary Merit Award. *Dream Soul*, a sequel, was published in 2000. Yep's autobiography, *The Lost Garden*, includes a section about his West Virginia connection.

Yep attended Marquette University for two years, earned a bachelor's degree at the University of California at Santa Cruz, and received a Ph.D. from State University of New York at Buffalo. He has taught creative writing and Asian-American Studies at the University of California at Berkeley and Santa Barbara. He lives in California.

Yohogania County

Yohogania is West Virginia's phantom county, created in the same legislative act with Monongalia and Ohio counties but later lost to history. The county arose in the early border dispute between Virginia and Pennsylvania over lands now in north-central West Virginia and the Northern Panhandle and in the adjacent southwest corner of Pennsylvania. Most of Yohogania County fell within present Pennsylvania, but its territory also included what is today Hancock County, West Virginia.

After settlers began to move into the frontier area, there was a need for local government. Disregarding Pennsylvania's claim to the land, Virginia organized the territory into the District of West Augusta. During the American Revolution, Virginia divided West Augusta into three counties, Ohio, Yohogania, and Monongalia. Early maps show that Yohogania County encompassed territory north of the present West Virginia-Pennsylvania state line and primarily east of the Allegheny River, while Monongalia County then covered much of what is now north-central West Virginia plus most of present Greene, Fayette, and Washington counties in Pennsylvania. Ohio County got most of the present panhandle and lands to the south, as well as a sliver of present Pennsylvania.

Virginia and Pennsylvania continued to dispute this territory until an agreement was reached in 1780 to extend the Mason-Dixon Line between the two states. Yohogania County quickly ceased to exist as other counties were carved from its territory. They included Fayette, Allegheny, Westmoreland, Washington, and Greene counties in Pennsylvania, and the northern tip of Ohio County (now Hancock). Ohio and Monongalia counties, covering nearly all of northwestern Virginia, themselves later contributed territory to nearly a dozen counties of present West Virginia.

See also Mason-Dixon Line

Kenneth R. Bailey
WVU Institute of Technology

Hurry-Up Yost

Coach Fielding Harris "Hurry-Up" Yost was born in Marion County, April 30, 1871. He was a tackle on West Virginia University's football team in 1895 and 1896, while earning a law degree. Best known as a college football coach, Yost was also a businessman with coal, oil, and real estate interests in West Virginia

and Tennessee. Yost was the brother-in-law of social activist Lenna Lowe Yost.

Yost began his coaching career at Ohio Wesleyan in 1897. After one season, he coached at Nebraska, Kansas, and Stanford for one year each. In 1901, Yost became coach at the University of Michigan, where he spent the remainder of his career. In his first season there, the Wolverines compiled an 11-0 record, including the 49-0 defeat of Stanford in the first Rose Bowl, and the school's first national championship. Not a single opponent scored against Michigan that season. Averaging 55 points a game, the Wolverines became known as the "point a minute" team. Yost earned the "Hurry-Up" nickname for emphasizing a fast offensive pace and is credited with inventing the no-huddle offense, the fake kick, and the position of linebacker. From 1901 to 1905, his teams were undefeated in 56 consecutive games.

In 1904, Yost's team defeated WVU 130-0, the worst defeat in the Mountaineers' history. Yost retired as Michigan's athletic director in 1941. He was inducted into the College Football Hall of Fame in 1951 and was one of the first inductees of the West Virginia Sports Hall of Fame in 1950. He was named to WVU's 1891–1917 all-time team. Yost died in Ann Arbor, Michigan, August 20, 1946.

Judie Smith
West Virginia Humanities Council

Lenna Lowe Yost

Activist Lenna Lowe Yost held key leadership roles in the woman's suffrage movement and Women's Christian Temperance Union (WCTU). She was born in Basnettville, Marion County, January 25, 1878, graduated from West Virginia Wesleyan College, and, in 1899, married Ellis Asby Yost.

Yost was the state president of the WCTU (1908–18), state legislative chair of the West Virginia Federation of Women's Clubs (1915), president of the West Virginia Equal Suffrage Association (1917–19), legislative representative for the national WCTU (1918), and Washington correspondent for the national WCTU's *Union Signal* (1919–30). She lobbied Congress to adopt the 19th Amendment, providing the vote to women, and in 1920 successfully chaired the West Virginia Equal Suffrage Association Ratification Committee.

Yost represented the United States at international congresses against alcoholism in 1921 (Switzerland) and 1923 (Denmark). She was the first woman to hold a variety of positions within the state's Republican Party, directed the Women's Division of the national Republican Party (1930–34), lobbied to build the Federal Prison for Women in Alderson, and was the first woman on the State Board of Education (1920s–'30s) and the West Virginia Wesleyan College Board of Trustees (1927–42). She spearheaded efforts to build Elizabeth Moore Hall at West Virginia University and to get the American Association of University Women to recognize the state's colleges. Yost died in Washington, May 7, 1972.

Barbara J. Howe
West Virginia University

Anne Wallace Effland, "Lenna Lowe Yost, 1878–1972," *Missing Chapters*, 1983.

Youghiogheny Forest Colony

Youghiogheny Forest Colony, a historic artists colony originally consisting of 12 log cabins, is located near the West Virginia-Maryland state line on U.S. 50 in Preston County. Initially including about 100 acres of old-growth hemlock and hardwood forest, the property was purchased in 1929 by Frank Reeves. The colony is on the headwaters of the Youghiogheny River, which originates nearby.

Reeves, born in 1886 in Fairmont, attended West Virginia University, received a Ph.D. from Johns Hopkins University (1916), and traveled the world as a geologist. He is noted for being the first to survey the famous Wolf Creek Crater in Australia. To construct the colony, Reeves worked with local craftsmen to cut timber and build the cabins and a tavern. While some of the buildings were primitive, the Gravens' cabin (designed by Clarksburg native Thomas Hood, 1940) was distinctively stylish, with a round copper-roofed kitchen and a tall glass-brick window. Constructed for summer use, the cabins were nevertheless occupied year-round during the Depression by Washington-area artists, writers, doctors, architects, and musicians. Many of them were of European origin and friends of Reeves's wife, Lottie.

The Tavern, a substantial log building, was the first structure to be built (1930). The colony's artists, including WPA muralist Robert Gates, painter Joe Goethe, architects Arved Kundzin and Thomas Hood, and photographer Volkmar Wentzel, often displayed their artwork on its walls. Eleanor Roosevelt, traveling U.S. 50 to visit Arthurdale, stopped at the Tavern. Her purchase of Wentzel's postcards inspired him to pursue his interest in photography, leading to a life-long career with *National Geographic*.

While Youghiogheny Forest Colony is still spoken of as an "artists colony," in reality this informal gathering of artists existed for only those years prior to World War II. And, while two of the original residents still lived in the 1930s log cabins in 2005, the Forest has seen many changes, including devastating fires, rebuildings, and studios abandoned to the forest's overgrowth. Volkmar Wentzel is the only artist from the 1930s to still live in the Forest. Several descendants of the 1930s residents, including the grandson and granddaughter of Frank and Lottie Reeves, make the remaining cabins their homes. Sections of the Forest have recently been timbered, and only six of the cabins remain intact.

See also Volkmar Wentzel

Michele Mouré
Aurora

Youghiogheny River

The Youghiogheny River, a major tributary of the Monongahela River, drains westernmost Maryland and a sizable portion of southwestern Pennsylvania. The Youghiogheny originates in Preston County, West Virginia, near Silver Lake, at an elevation of nearly 2,500 feet. The extreme southeastern corner of Preston County falls within the Youghiogheny watershed, including Cathedral State Forest. From here the river flows northward for about 135 miles, joining the Monongahela at McKeesport, Pennsylvania, near Pittsburgh.

The Youghiogheny River traverses historic countryside, its valley forming a passage through the mountains in frontier times. The river's upper stretches and its headwaters flow through remote, mountainous terrain, settled in the late 1700s and valued today for its recreational opportunities. Deep Creek Lake, Maryland, is located on a Youghiogheny tributary, and the fast-flowing river is popular with fishermen and whitewater rafters.

Only a tiny portion of the Youghiogheny River watershed lies within West Virginia. This rugged area, which is crossed by U.S. 50, includes the communities of Aurora and Eglon. The high ridge of Backbone Mountain separates the upper Youghiogheny from the nearby head of the North Branch of the Potomac, while the Cheat River lies just to the west.

Z

Betty Zane

Frontier heroine Elizabeth "Betty" Zane, born in the present Eastern Panhandle about 1760, was credited with saving Fort Henry in Wheeling when it was besieged in 1782, during the Revolutionary War. Conflicting reports claim that Molly Scott actually saved the fort, but Zane's role is generally accepted.

On September 10, 1782, 200 or more warriors, mostly Wyandots and Delaware with some American Loyalists and British, attacked the fort. Inside, 47 patriot civilians and militia held their ground until their gunpowder was exhausted. Betty Zane was the sister of the fort commander, Col. Silas Zane. According to a common account she volunteered to retrieve gunpowder from the Zane family cabin, perhaps as much as 60 yards away. "You have not one man to spare; a woman will not be missed in the defense of the fort," she is quoted as having said. Startled to see a young woman emerge from the fort and sprint across the open field, the British and natives held their fire. In the Zane cabin, Betty gathered a quantity of gunpowder, perhaps in her apron, and dashed back to the fort.

Betty Zane married and moved to Martin's Ferry, Ohio, where she died, probably in 1823.

Later the author Zane Grey, a collateral descendant, wrote the 1903 novel *Betty Zane* based on the incident and related events. Some historians are skeptical of the historical accuracy of Betty Zane's deed, but the legend persists. There is no mention of the heroic act in any contemporary account, including the official report by her brother to Gen. William Irvine. Its similarity to the account of Mad Anne Bailey's dash to save Fort Lee in the same decade casts additional doubt. The earliest reports of the episode are found in A. S. Withers's 1895 *Chronicles of Border Warfare* and in an early 19th-century Philadelphia newspaper account.

See also Fort Henry, Ebenezer Zane

Mary Rodd Furbee
Morgantown

Curtis Carroll Davis, "Helping to Hold the Fort, Elizabeth Zane at Wheeling, 1782: A Case Study in Renown," *West Virginia History*, Spring 1983; Norris F. Schneider and G. M. Farley, *Betty Zane: Heroine of Fort Henry*, 1970.

Ebenezer Zane

Pioneer Ebenezer Zane, the founder of Wheeling, was born on the South Branch of the Potomac River near present Moorefield in Hardy County, October 7, 1747. He married Elizabeth McColloch, sister of John and Samuel McColloch of border warfare fame.

After the 1768 Treaty of Fort Stanwix opened the frontier to the Ohio River, Zane, with his brothers Jonathan and Silas, established a settlement at the confluence of Wheeling Creek and the Ohio in 1770. He made two 400-acre claims on the site of present Wheeling, later adding other claims on both sides of the river. A colonel in the Virginia militia as well as a disbursing agent during Dunmore's War (1774), he constructed Fort Fincastle, renamed Fort Henry during the Revolutionary War, which withstood attacks by combined British-Indian forces in 1777 and 1782. The latter attack was fought after the British defeat at Yorktown.

Concerned about the state of education in Western Virginia, Zane, in 1787, helped establish Randolph Academy in Clarksburg, said to be the oldest institution of learning west of the Alleghenies. He represented Ohio County when the Virginia convention of 1788 met to consider ratification of the Constitution, which Zane supported, and he laid out the town of Wheeling in 1793. Three years later he received permission to open a road, long called Zane's Trace, from Wheeling to Limestone (now Maysville), Kentucky. The town of Zanesville, Ohio, is named for him.

Col. Ebenezer Zane, brother of the heroic Betty Zane, died in Wheeling, November 19, 1812.

See also Fort Henry, Wheeling, Betty Zane

Jack Wills
Fairmont

Wills De Hass, *History of the Early Settlement and Indian Wars of Western Virginia*, 1960; Clement L. Martzolff, *Zane's Trace*, 1904; John G. Patterson, *Ebenezer Zane: Frontiersman*, 1939.

John Zontini

Athlete John Zontini was nicknamed the "Shiek of Seth" because of his outstanding football career as a running back at Sherman High School, which is located at Seth in Boone County. He was born February 28, 1909. His rushing average per carry of 27 yards in 1929 remains a state high school record. As a junior, Zontini ran for 2,135 yards on 79 carries. He also set the state javelin record in 1931 with a throw of 172 feet, one inch.

Zontini rushed for 865 yards in 1931 as a freshman at Marshall College (now University), including 200 yards in a 60-0 win over Fairmont State. His season record of most yards per rush at 9.5 still stands at Marshall. Choosing a professional baseball career, Zontini played outfield for the Charleston Senators of the Mid-Atlantic League. He was inducted into the West Virginia Sports Writers' Hall of Fame in 1971 and the Marshall University Athletics Hall of Fame in 1984.

Sherman High School named its football facility Zontini Field in honor of John Zontini and his brothers, Red and Louis, all of whom were star athletes at Sherman and played football in college. John Zontini moved to eastern Virginia and lived there for about 40 years until his death on June 20, 1981.

ACKNOWLEDGMENTS

The West Virginia Encyclopedia was produced with the help of hundreds of West Virginians —in small towns, at colleges and universities, in state government, at libraries, and in other institutions. Other contributors came from places as far apart as Germany and British Columbia, and from across the United States. The ones recognized here are those who contributed most toward bringing this important reference work into print.

The West Virginia Humanities Council board of directors supported this project from its inception, as a group and individually. Board members, past and present, volunteered to write entries for the book and followed its progress closely. Among current board members, we especially thank Kenneth R. Bailey, Robert M. Bastress, Ronald L. Lewis, Robert F. Maslowski, James W. Rowley, and Jill Wilson.

We also recognize the special contributions of former board members Jerry Beasley, Henry Harmon, David Ice, the late Joseph Crosby "Joe" Jefferds Jr., Emory L. Kemp, Marc Harshman, J. Davitt McAteer, Jennifer Soule, and William D. Theriault.

The West Virginia Encyclopedia would not be here without its many writers. Most completed their articles as assigned. Some forgot and others stepped in to take their places. A special group served as informal consultants throughout the process. These people, experts in fields from the natural sciences and history to music and law, advised us on topics to include and the resources to get the work done. They got us through editorial sticking points with their knowledge and willingness to help. We are grateful to the following, who were with us from A to Z: Howard G. Adkins; Kenneth R. Bailey; Robert M. Bastress; Robert Beanblossom; Margaret Brennan; S. Allen Chambers Jr.; Harold Malcolm Forbes; Robert L. Frey; William N. Grafton; Skip Johnson; Ronald L. Lewis; Karl C. Lilly III; Robert F. Maslowski; and Ivan M. Tribe. A special thanks to consulting historian Otis K. Rice, who died before publication.

We appreciate the good people who offered help at all the right times. Thanks to Cathy Hershberger Miller at the State Archives, who was always there with answers to our questions; William D. Chambers, who voluntarily read the manuscript before it went to press; Kenneth R. Bailey, who served as a volunteer researcher midway through the compilation of the massive manuscript; Anna Sale, who spent much of a summer getting the contributors section under way; and Debra K. Sullivan, who called every holiday and summer break to offer fact-checking, writing, and research assistance. She helped to keep our editor sane, as well.

We are grateful to the professionals who worked with project coordinator and photo researcher Cheryl Marsh to bring together illustrations for The West Virginia Encyclopedia: Michael Keller, director of photographic services for the West Virginia Division of Culture & History; Ron Miller of Charleston Newspapers; State Archives photographer Ed Hicks; Arnout Hyde Jr., an old friend who died while our project was under way; Gary Lake; the Library of Congress; Jurgen Lorenzen; David Fattaleh and Steve Shaluta of the West Virginia Division of Tourism; Heidi Perov at the University of North Carolina Press; Roger Spencer; Volkmar Wentzel; Cornelia Alexander, John Lilly, and Gordon Simmons of Goldenseal magazine; Alan Rowe of the State Historic Preservation Office; and Stephanie Lilly and Terri Marion of the Division of Culture & History. We also thank Carol Melling and Terry Lively at the West Virginia Department of Transportation; Nanci Bross-Fregonara and Craig Stihler of the West Virginia Division of Natural Resources, Wildlife Resources Section, Elkins; John Cuthbert and Lori Hostutler of the West Virginia & Regional History Collection at WVU Libraries; and Lynn Sheehan at the University of Charleston.

Some writers did more than their own assignments, providing background for other topics as well. Some brought in photographs. Some called to ask what remained to be written. We express our appreciation to the following, who went above and beyond their contractual agreements: Richard A. Andre; Michael A. Arcuri; David Bard; Fred A. Barkey; Kenneth T. Batty; Ancella R. Bickley; Bascombe M. Blake Jr.; Judy Prozzillo Byers; Paul D. Casdorph; Roy B. Clarkson; George Constantz; Robert S. Conte; David A. Corbin; George Deike; Charles J. Denham; Howard Dorgan; Brad Douglas; Ronald D. Eller; Norman L. Fagan; Ken Fones-Wolf; William H. Gillespie; Karen Goff; Billy Jack Gregg; George W. Hammond; John Hennen; Darla Spencer Hoffman; William K. Jones; Norman Julian; Emory L. Kemp; David J. Kessler; Walter A. Lesser; Terry Lowry; David Matchen; Tim McKinney; William Price McNeel; Michael M. Meador; Gerald Milnes; James R. Mitchell; Phyllis Wilson Moore; Charles W. Morris III; Ron Mullennex; Don Page; Billy Joe Peyton; Jim Phillips; Warren Point; Gerald S. Ratliff; Gerry Reilly; H. John Rogers; Robert O. Rupp; James F. Snyder; Larry Sonis; Charles Sperow; John Edmund Stealey III; Philip Sturm; Gerald W. Sutphin; Larry N. Sypolt; Jerry Bruce Thomas; Joe William Trotter Jr.; John Alexander Williams; Warren Woomer; and H. G. Young III.

We express our thanks to those closest to the day-to-day work of producing The West Virginia Encyclopedia. Elliott Namay, Cheryl Marsh, and Keith Marsh kept the computers working smoothly. In addition, Ms. Marsh worked diligently to bring in hundreds of photographs, taking some of them herself. Humanities Council secretary Carol Nutter offered help whenever she had a free moment from her regular duties. Barbara Phillips and Judie Smith worked themselves right out of a job, as Barbara was fond of saying.

There were many others who took the difficulties in putting together a major reference work as seriously as we did. We appreciate assistance from Rosemary Jeanne Cobb at Bethany College; Tom Dixon of the C&O Historical Society in Lynchburg, Virginia; Dave Conley at the Homer Laughlin China Company; and John Walter at the Federal Reserve Back in Richmond. The Kanawha County Public Library staff, especially Joyce Williams, was extremely helpful in lending research materials. We also thank Cora P. Teel in Special Collections at Marshall University; Mary Virginia Currie and Greg Stoner at the Virginia Historical Society; Steve Hannah, Dale King, and Sandy Marinacci at the West Virginia Department of Agriculture; John Mallett and Rolland Phillips at the West Virginia Development Office; Debra Basham, Joe Geiger, Ed Hicks, Mary Johnson, and Cathy Hersberger Miller of the State Archives at the West Virginia Division of Culture & History; Matthew Dillon and Ed Murriner of the West Virginia Division of Forestry; the West Virginia Division of Natural Resources Elkins staff, especially Barbara Sargent for getting us through the common and scientific names section of this book; Lana Shaffer of the West Virginia Office of Vital Registration; Tom Tinder at the West Virginia State Bar; and Captain J. Ferda, John Hoyer, and Steve Jones of the West Virginia State Police.

We have others to thank, as well. They include Tom Allen, Lakin Ray Cook, William M. Davis, Yvonne Farley, Ken Hechler, Phoebe F. Heishman, Tina S. Holmes, Kathleen Carothers Leo, the late Herb Little, Joe Manzo, Ken Martis, the late Lewis McManus, Tom Miller, Carolyn Perry, and Leigh Taylor. Rudy Abramson provided a sympathetic ear. Dan Foster, Hilda Heady, and the late Warren Point gave advice on medical subjects. Maxwell V. Perrow offered good sources on religion in West Virginia, and Tom Rodd helped with information relating to the history of the West Virginia Supreme Court. We also thank Kathleen Curtis Wilson for her knowledge of the textile arts.

Finally, we are indebted to Ken Sullivan, our editor-in-chief. He kept us going, never losing his long-held belief that Mountain State readers are worthy of the quality of work found in the pages of The West Virginia Encyclopedia.

Deborah J. Sonis

Tom Adamich of Ohio once worked for the West Virginia Library Commission. Educated at the University of Akron and Kent State University, he belongs to the Society of Automotive Historians.

Nancy Ray Adams, director of Pine Mountain Settlement School in Kentucky, previously worked for the West Virginia Humanities Council. She was educated at Maryville College, Tennessee, and Marshall University.

Greg Adamson grew up in Pendleton County and lives in Virginia. He was educated at WVU and James Madison University. He is a geologist and a member of the Archaeological Society of Virginia, specializing in forts of the French and Indian War.

Donna Addkison-Simmons was senior adviser to the governor of Mississippi. A graduate of Mississippi University for Women, she also earned degrees from Mississippi State and Troy State universities.

Howard G. Adkins was born in Mississippi and earned a Ph.D. in geography from University of Tennessee. He is retired from the Marshall geography department and lives with his wife, Dorothy, near Ona.

John E. Adkins, a Boone County native, has degrees from West Virginia State, West Virginia Graduate College, and the University of Kentucky. Formerly with Wilbur Smith Associates of Kentucky, he is now a librarian at the University of Charleston.

Leonard M. Adkins, a Charleston native, was educated at the University of Charleston. The author of articles and books on the outdoors, he has hiked the full lengths of the Appalachian Trail four times and West Virginia's Allegheny Trail twice.

M. William Adler worked in the cable TV business before retiring. From 1982 to 1993, he wrote a weekly column for the *Weston Democrat*, chronicling the history of Weston and Lewis County. He died in 2002.

Carl Agsten Jr. is a project manager for ZMM Architects and Engineers. He earned a master's degree in the history of architecture and urban design from Cornell.

LeAnna Alderman grew up in Pocahontas County and graduated from Amherst College, Massachusetts, in 1999. She has worked as a VISTA volunteer at the Pocahontas Communications Cooperative and at the McClintic Public Library in Marlinton.

Ronald R. Alexander is an alumnus of WVU Tech with an M.A. and Ph.D. in history from the University of Kentucky. In 2003, he retired as chair of the Tech history department, where he taught for 35 years.

Bernard L. Allen was born in Harrison County. He earned an M.A. in philosophy from Southern Illinois University and a Ph.D. in history from WVU. He was professor of history and philosophy at WVU-Parkersburg until 1999.

D. J. Allen worked at the *Ritchie Gazette* for 30 years and chronicled the construction of the Hughes River dam. She lives in Cairo and owns Country Trails Bikes on the North Bend Rail Trail.

Thomas J. Allen, educated at the University of Maine, came to West Virginia in 1970 as a deer research biologist. His publications include "White-tailed Deer in West Virginia" and *The Butterflies of West Virginia and Their Caterpillars.*. Also a wildlife artist, he designed the state license plate featuring the rose-breasted grosbeak.

Belinda Anderson, a former newspaper reporter, earned an M.A. from Hollins College, Virginia, and teaches in Greenbrier County. She has written for *Goldenseal*, *Wonderful West Virginia*, and other publications.

Colleen Anderson, a Michigan native, came to West Virginia in 1970 as a VISTA volunteer. Her stories, poems, essays, articles, and songs are widely published. She lives in Charleston.

Robert T. Anderson earned a B.A. from Mercyhurst College, Pennsylvania, an M.A. from Slippery Rock University, Pennsylvania, and a history Ph.D. from WVU. He teaches at WVU-Parkersburg, specializing in the history of the upper Ohio Valley frontier.

Richard A. Andre, born in Charleston, chairs the Spring Hill Cemetery commission. Retired from the mortgage loan business, he has co-authored many articles and books on local history and produces popular pictorial features for the *Charleston Gazette*.

Donald R. Andrews earned an M.A. from Marshall. He is the former director of the Robert C. Byrd Institute for Government Studies and taught political science at the University of Charleston.

C. Michael Anslinger is CEO and vice president of operations for the West Virginia office of Cultural Resource Analysts. Educated in anthropology at Indiana State and Washington State universities, he has conducted extensive archeological research in the Kanawha Valley.

William R. Archer, educated at WVU, works as a reporter for the *Bluefield Daily Telegraph*. He has contributed to *Wonderful West Virginia* and other publications. He lives in Bluefield.

Michael A. Arcuri is a biologist-manager with the state Department of Environmental Protection's Division of Water Resources. He has a B.S. in zoology and an M.S. in biology, both from Marshall.

Fredrick H. Armstrong, state historian and archivist and director of the Archives & History section of the Division of Culture & History, was educated at WVU. With the State Archives since 1978, he is a former public school teacher and has also taught at WVU, Marshall, College of Graduate Studies, and West Virginia State.

Amy Donaldson Arnold, a Richwood native, studied biology at Bridgewater College, Virginia, and Wake Forest University. She teaches science at Charleston Catholic High School and lives in Clay County.

James Arnold, a former academic and researcher in the microscopical structure of animals and viruses, is a biological photographer. He has a particular interest in spiders. He lives in Huntington.

Martha J. Asbury, a McDowell County native and graduate of Big Creek High School, writes, directs, and performs for EcoTheater in Greenbrier County. She has been published in *Goldenseal* and other magazines, and in books of poetry.

Lou Athey, professor emeritus of history at Franklin & Marshall College in Pennsylvania, is a navy veteran who was born in the coal-fields of Illinois. He was educated at the College of New Jersey, with a Ph.D. from University of Delaware.

Kenneth R. Bailey, emeritus dean at WVU Tech, is a member of the West Virginia Humanities Council board of directors. He was educated at WVU Tech and Marshall, with a Ph.D. in history and geography from Ohio State. He has published a history of the West Virginia National Guard and articles on coal mining history.

Matthew Scott Bailey is a teacher at his alma mater, St. Marys High School. He attended WVU, where he earned undergraduate and master's degrees.

Nancy Balow lives in Charleston and works as a writer and editor for Edvantia, a private nonprofit agency for education research. She received her education at Brown University, Rhode Island, and West Virginia State.

Jay Banks lives in Monroe County, the home of his ancestors. He is a graduate of WVU and earned an M.D. from University of Arkansas in 1949. He has written many articles for the *Monroe Watchman* newspaper and two books. He chaired the Monroe County Bicentennial Commission in 1999.

Russ Barbour is co-producer and writer of *West Virginians in War*, a TV documentary. A long-time employee of West Virginia Public Broadcasting, he is a graduate of Southern West Virginia Community College and Marshall.

David Bard was educated at Ohio Wesleyan and University of Connecticut, with a Ph.D. from University of Maine. West Virginia's 2001 Professor of the Year, he retired from teaching history at Concord University in 2005.

Fred A. Barkey, a Pittsburgh native, taught for 20 years at the West Virginia College of Graduate

Studies. He was educated at Marshall and University of Pittsburgh. His history research centers on the West Virginia working class, particularly radical politics, immigration, technological change, and culture.

Jim Barnes is a social worker in Morgantown. Born in Clarksburg, he earned a B.A. from Fairmont State and an M.A. from Eastern Kentucky University. A member of the Morgantown Writers Group, he has published several short stories.

C. Robert Barnett, a professor at Marshall and a Hancock County native, has a Ph.D. from Ohio State in sports history. He has published widely on his subject and is a section editor for the *Encyclopedia of Appalachia*.

Michael Barone is a senior writer at *U.S. News & World Report* and co-author of the influential *Almanac of American Politics*. He is a graduate of Harvard and of Yale Law School. His grandmother, Minerva Buchanan Barone, grew up in Tucker County.

Rodney Bartgis, director of the West Virginia chapter of the Nature Conservancy, was educated in biology and ecology at Shepherd University and WVU. He previously worked for state natural resource agencies in Maryland and West Virginia.

Larry Bartlett, a native of Wood County, earned an M.F.A. from Tulane. A contributor to *Goldenseal*, he has worked as a teacher, college administrator, art critic, and journalist.

Debra Basham lives in Elkview and is an archivist at the State Archives. She has a B.A. from Millsaps College, Mississippi, and an M.A. from the University of Delaware.

Paul Bassett, an Ohio native educated at Duke University, is emeritus professor at Nazarene Theological Seminary in Kansas City. The author of five books as well as scholarly and popular articles, he once taught religious studies at WVU.

Robert M. Bastress, professor of law at WVU and a member of the West Virginia Humanities Council board of directors, lectures widely on constitutional law and employment law. His publications include *The West Virginia Constitution: A Reference Guide* and many articles. He was educated at Wesleyan (Connecticut) University, with a J.D. from Vanderbilt and an L.L.M. from Temple University.

Henry W. Battle, born in Charleston, was educated at Brown University in Rhode Island, University of Virginia, and University of Charleston. He is vice president of the Kay Company and president of the Kanawha Valley Historical & Preservation Society.

Jean Battlo, born in McDowell County and educated at Marshall, is a teacher, historian, and writer. Her works include a history of McDowell County and many articles.

Kenneth T. Batty was born in Philadelphia and earned B.S. and M.S. degrees in meteorology from Penn State. Since the cold winter of 1976–77, he has been a forecaster for the National Weather Service in Charleston.

Robert Beanblossom, a native of Mingo County, is a regional administrator with the Division of Natural Resources. He has written for *Goldenseal* and *Wonderful West Virginia* and volunteers to fight wildfires in West Virginia and the West.

Rachelle Bott Beckner, a WVU journalism graduate, has written for several newspapers, most recently the *Charleston Gazette*. A Morgantown native, she works for the American Lung Association of West Virginia.

Ella Belling of Morgantown directs the Tri-County Trails & Parks Information Center. She has worked with the Tygart Valley Development Authority to implement heritage tourism projects for Grafton and Taylor County.

Bruce Betler grew up in Helvetia with an interest in Swiss folk dancing, singing, fiddling, and cheese making. He graduated from Pickens School, studied at Saint Vincent College, Pennsylvania, and earned a graduate degree in theology from Catholic University, Washington. He is a monk in Germany.

Elizabeth Lawton Beury, a retired teacher, is the great-granddaughter of Col. Joe Beury, the first coal operator on the New River. She was educated at St. Mary's Junior College, North Carolina, and at WVU and the College of Graduate Studies.

Ancella R. Bickley was educated at West Virginia State, Marshall, and WVU, where she earned her Ed.D. She served on the West Virginia African-American Tourism Advisory Committee. She has written several articles and co-edited the book, *Memphis Tennessee Garrison: The Remarkable Story of a Black Appalachian Woman*.

Heather Roberts Biola, who teaches at Davis & Elkins College in her hometown of Elkins, has a Ph.D. from Georgia State University. She has written for *Goldenseal* and other publications. She is president of the Elkins Historic Landmarks Commission.

Leslie Birdwell is a resident of Huntington and a graduate of Marshall. She writes poetry, fiction, and drama.

Lyle Blackwell was professor, chairman, and dean of engineering at WVU Tech. He has produced several publications on the town of Gauley Bridge and on genealogy. He lives in retirement in Kingsport, Tennessee.

Bascombe M. Blake Jr., who studied at Waynesburg College, Pennsylvania, and WVU, has worked at the West Virginia Geological & Economic Survey since 1978. His interests include coal geology, Carboniferous stratigraphy, and Late Paleozoic paleobotany.

John M. Boback earned a B.A. from Alderson-Broaddus College and in 2005 was a doctoral student at WVU. He teaches Appalachian studies and American frontier history at Alderson-Broaddus and serves as historian and blacksmith at Pricketts Fort State Park.

Carolyn Flesher Bolovan was educated at Ohio University, Sarah Lawrence College, New York, and University of Michigan. She has served as the society editor of the *Athens* (Ohio) *Messenger* and the *Ravenswood News*.

Robert G. Bonar, a Ritchie County native now living in Grantsville, earned a B.A. and M.A. from WVU. He has worked as a Calhoun County teacher and school administrator since 1971.

Jennifer Bonnette, formerly the executive director of Arthurdale Heritage, Inc., received a B.A. from WVU in history and English. Her grandparents were the last surviving original homestead couple in Arthurdale.

David W. Bott was born in Oak Hill and lives in Westover. He has a master's degree in public administration from WVU. He was assistant director of Morgantown Municipal Airport and now works for the city of Morgantown.

Melody Bragg works at the Technical Information Center of the National Mine Health and Safety Academy, Beckley. She has written for newspapers and is the author of books dealing primarily with the coal history of the New River Gorge area.

George H. Breiding was educated at Ohio State. He worked at the Conservation Commission, forerunner to the Division of Natural Resources, as a wildlife biologist and as commissioner. Now retired, he has also been director of Oglebay Institute's nature education program and a WVU extension specialist.

Margaret Brennan, a native of Wheeling, earned a B.A. from Wheeling College and an M.A. from WVU. A local historian and president of the Wheeling Area Historical Society, she has published articles in *Goldenseal* and various scholarly publications.

Leona Gwinn Brown, a retired teacher, lives near Beckley. Her hobbies are genealogy and local history, and her articles have appeared in *Goldenseal*.

Lisle G. Brown teaches at Marshall and is curator of special collections at the university library. He has a B.A. from the University of Utah with graduate degrees from the University of Oregon and Marshall. He has published articles on Mormon history and created online computer exhibits on West Virginia history.

Stephen W. Brown, a dean at WVU Tech, was educated at Tech and Marshall, with a history Ph.D. from WVU. He is author or co-author of several publications, including *West Virginia: A History* and *The Mountain State*, both popular textbooks.

Marshall Buckalew, born in Jackson County, was educated at Morris Harvey College, WVU, and Harvard Law School. He was president of Morris Harvey, the First National Bank of South Charleston, and the West Virginia Historical Education Foundation. He died in 2002.

Nancy Bulla, who has a B.A. and M.A. from WVU, is the public relations manager and drawings manager for the West Virginia Lottery. She lives in Charleston and Lewisburg and is past president of the West Virginia Humanities Council.

Stan Bumgardner has worked for the Division of Culture & History. A native of Charleston, he earned a B.A. in history from Marshall and an M.A. in public history from WVU.

Joseph Bundy, who lives in Bluefield, is a Marshall graduate. He is an essayist, poet, and dramatist known for his Chautauqua impersonations of African-American characters.

Nicholas Burckel, dean of libraries and associate professor of history at Marquette University, was educated at Georgetown University and University of Wisconsin. He is the editor or co-author of many books, articles, and reviews. President Clinton appointed him to the National Historical Publications and Records Commission.

S. Shuan Butcher, a Parkersburg native, was educated at WVU and Marietta College. He is a member of the Wood County Historical Society and served on the Wood County Bicentennial Commission.

Janet Butler, a Minnesota native, began work at the Ohio River Islands National Wildlife Refuge in 1993. Before that, she directed the Cranberry Mountain Visitor Center in the Monongahela National Forest.

Judy Prozzillo Byers, a native of Fairmont and West Virginia's 2002 Professor of the Year, is a folklorist, storyteller, and education specialist. She teaches at Fairmont State University, where she also directs the West Virginia Folklife Center. She has a B.A. from Fairmont State and an M.A. and Ph.D. from WVU.

Becky Cain is president of the Greater Kanawha Valley Foundation and past president of the League of Women Voters of the U.S. She is a graduate of WVU with honorary degrees from Ripon College, Wisconsin, and University of Charleston.

Lloyd P. Calvert is a graduate of Marshall and Rutgers and attended WVU and the University of Charleston. He is a retired banker and former assistant director of the West Virginia Centennial Commission.

Jack Canfield, who was born in Mineral County, is a graduate of Potomac State and WVU. He was a member of the House of Delegates, 1975–77, and press spokesman for Governors Smith, Rockefeller, and Wise. He lives in Charleston.

Michael Caplinger of WVU was an industrial archeologist at the university's Institute for the History of Technology & Industrial Archaeology. He prepared the National Historic Landmark nomination for the Martinsburg Roundhouse, and helped to research the Thurmond C&O depot for the National Park Service.

Greg Carroll, originally from Fort Worth, is a historian at the State Archives. He studied at the University of Texas and Marshall.

Kenneth L. Carvell, a Massachusetts native, was educated at Harvard, Yale, and Duke. He taught forest ecology and related courses at WVU for 35 years, retiring in 1988. He has published more than 200 scientific and popular articles.

Paul D. Casdorph, a Charleston native, graduated from the universities of Texas and Kentucky. He is the author of several books and an ardent ham radio operator. Before retiring in 1994, he chaired the history department at West Virginia State.

James E. Casto, a Huntington native and Marshall graduate, is the author of three books and many magazine articles. He was associate editor of the Huntington *Herald-Dispatch* and now works at Marshall's Robert C. Byrd Institute. He makes frequent first-person presentations as railroad tycoon Collis P. Huntington.

Jack Catalano is a Kanawha County native and an employee of the Division of Highways Equipment Division in Buckhannon.

S. Allen Chambers Jr., educated at Princeton with an M.A. in architectural history from the University of Virginia, worked for the Historic American Buildings Survey in Washington. He wrote *Buildings of West Virginia*, part of the Buildings of the United States series sponsored by the Society of Architectural Historians and Oxford University Press.

Martin G. Cherniack is a medical doctor and professor of medicine at the University of Connecticut Health Center. He is the author of more than 60 scientific articles and the book *The Hawk's Nest Incident: America's Worst Industrial Disaster*.

Dan Cincotta is a fisheries biologist for the Division of Natural Resources. He has published more than 30 scientific and popular articles on the taxonomy, distribution, and biology of West Virginia fishes.

Roy B. Clarkson, born in 1926 at Cass, earned a B.S. at Davis & Elkins and an M.A. and Ph.D. from WVU. He taught 36 years at WVU, retiring in 1992. He is best known for his book *Tumult on the Mountains: Lumbering in West Virginia, 1770–1920*.

Janet L. Clayton, born in Fairmont, was educated at Marshall and Tennessee Technological University. She is a biologist at the Division of Natural Resources.

Bill Clements, a native of Mississippi, has lived in West Virginia since 1988. A book wholesaler, he distributes West Virginia books throughout the state and operates West Virginia Book Company.

Rosemary Jeanne Cobb is an archivist and coordinator of special collections at Bethany College. She is a graduate of MacMurray College, Illinois, and Central Connecticut State College.

Charles C. Coffman worked in 1992–93 as West Virginia coordinator for the Save Outdoor Sculpture (SOS) project, a nationwide effort to locate, document, and assess the condition of outdoor sculpture accessible to the public. He is a native West Virginian with a B.A. and M.A. from Marshall.

Stan Cohen, a Charleston native living in Montana, earned a B.S. in geology from WVU. He founded Pictorial Histories Publishing Company, authoring or co-authoring 66 books and publishing 250, mostly dealing with historical subjects.

Merle T. Cole, a Marshall alumnus, works for the USDA Agricultural Research Service. He has written more than 50 publications on military, naval, and police history, including a book about Baltimore's harbor defenses.

Donna Colebank is a staff writer for the WVU Extension Service. A native of Morgantown, she graduated from Fairmont State. She was a sportswriter for the *Dominion Post* in Morgantown.

Connie K. Colvin grew up in Huntington and graduated from WVU with degrees in English and Spanish. She is a former assistant editor of *Goldenseal* magazine.

Linda S. Comins is the Arts & Living editor of the *Intelligencer* and *Wheeling News-Register* newspapers. Active in the Episcopal Diocese of West Virginia, she serves on the boards of the West Virginia Independence Hall Foundation and the Bethany College Alumni Association.

Debra Conner lives in Parkersburg. Her poetry and essays are widely published. She performs as Emily Dickinson and Margaret Blennerhassett through the West Virginia Humanities Council's *History Alive!* program.

George Constantz, an ecologist at the Canaan Valley Institute, was educated at the University of Missouri and has a Ph.D. in zoology from Arizona State. He has published many research papers and a book, *Hollows, Peepers, and Highlanders: An Appalachian Mountain Ecology*.

Robert S. Conte, a California native, has been historian at the Greenbrier since 1978. He graduated from Santa Clara University, California, and earned a Ph.D. from Case Western Reserve University, Ohio. The author of *The History of The Greenbrier*, he is a frequent contributor to projects and publications about the resort.

Jeffery B. Cook, who has a Ph.D. from WVU, chairs the Department of History & Political Science at North Greenville (South Carolina) College. He has written articles and reviews and is working on a book on the war on terrorism.

Lakin Ray Cook, a Charleston native, is education manager of the Clay Center for the Arts & Sciences in Charleston. With a B.F.A. in graphic design and art history, she once directed the Arts Council staff at the Division of Culture & History.

Stephen L. Cook, director of WVU's Institute for Labor Studies & Research, has served in both houses of the legislature and as state labor commissioner. He has held leadership positions for the West Virginia Laborers' District Council, Monongalia-Preston Labor Council, and the West Virginia AFL-CIO.

David A. Corbin, a Dunbar native, was educated at Marshall and earned a Ph.D. at University of Maryland. The author of many publications, he is best known for *Life, Work, and Rebellion in the Coal Fields*. He works for Sen. Robert C. Byrd in Washington.

David H. Corcoran, an Indiana native, is editor and publisher of the *Glenville Democrat* and *Glenville Pathfinder* newspapers. He has undergraduate degrees from St. Louis University and a Ph.D. from the University of Kentucky, and was the first executive director of the Pearl Buck Birthplace Museum.

Ewel Cornett was producer and director of Theatre West Virginia, 1968–72 and 1974–80. He co-wrote the play *Hatfields and McCoys* with Billy Edd Wheeler and was the composer of 12 other works of musical theater. He died in 2002.

W. Eugene Cox, now retired, was the first chief of interpretation and visitor services at New River Gorge National River. He grew up in Southwest Virginia and graduated from Lincoln Memorial University, Tennessee.

Maureen F. Crockett, a native New Yorker who grew up in Pocahontas County, was educated at WVU. She writes about history, travel, religion, and food.

Jack I. Cromer, a Pocahontas County native with degrees from WVU and University of Michigan, served in the U.S.Marines and as a smoke jumper for the U.S. Forest Service. He is retired from the Division of Natural Resources, where he was supervisor of game management services.

Deborah Cruse works in the communications department at Potomac State College, where she graduated with a degree in journalism and English. She is a poet and the mother of four daughters.

Steve Cunningham is president of the Kanawha Valley Civil War Roundtable and webmaster of the *West Virginia in the Civil War* web site. He is writing a history of the 7th West Virginia Cavalry.

John A. Cuthbert works at WVU Libraries. With many publications on the art and cultural history of West Virginia, he is best known for the book *Early Art and Artists in West Virginia*. He was educated at Worcester State College, Massachusetts, University of Massachusetts, and WVU.

James W. Daddysman has a Ph.D. from WVU. He is professor of history and director of international studies at Alderson-Broaddus College, and chairs the Philippi Landmarks Commission. He has written *The Matamoros Trade: A Study in Confederate Commerce, Diplomacy, and Intrigue* and a number of articles.

Bob Damron grew up in Logan County and was educated in history at West Virginia State. He wrote and produced a play about Mother Jones that was performed throughout southern West Virginia. He lived in Charleston before his untimely death in 2001.

Imam Mohammad Jamal Daoudi was born in Damascus. He served in California as imam of the Islamic Center of North Valley before becoming the spiritual leader for the Islamic Association of West Virginia in 2002.

Diane Davis Darnley is a Wheeling native who studied at West Liberty State College. She is a descendant of both George Miller, the first mayor of Wheeling, and Francis Pierpont, the governor of the Reorganized State of Virginia.

Charles H. Daugherty, born in St. Louis and raised in Brazil, directed the West Virginia Humanities Council from 1976 to 1996. He earned a B.A. from Davidson College, North Carolina, an M.A. from Denver University, and a Ph.D. from Georgetown University.

George Daugherty, a West Virginia trial lawyer for nearly 50 years, is also an actor, theatrical producer, director, and songwriter. He is best known as the Earl of Elkview, performing American and Irish songs and stories, with a special emphasis on West Virginia.

Mary Lee Daugherty, an ordained Presbyterian minister, enjoyed 40 years of friendship with serpent-handling Christians. She founded the Appalachian Ministries Educational Resources Center in Berea, Kentucky, which she directed until her 1999 retirement. She died in 2004.

John David, a graduate of University of Michigan and WVU, taught with the Peace Corps in Ghana. Professor of economics and labor and chair of social sciences at WVU Tech, he is the director of the Southern Appalachian Labor School.

Shae Davidson earned an M.A. from Marshall, where he studied West Virginia labor history. He has had extensive experience in public history, including research in labor history, industrial development, and the Civil War.

Dorothy U. Davis earned bachelor's and master's degrees from WVU. She taught 37 years in Harrison County and lived in Salem. She wrote *History of Harrison County* and *John George Jackson*. She died in 2004.

Rebecca Dean grew up in St. Albans and earned three degrees at the University of Pittsburgh. She is associate professor of speech at Northampton Community College, Pennsylvania.

William H. Dean, a native of St. Albans, taught at state colleges and WVU. He earned a B.A. from Morris Harvey College and an M.A. from Marshall while working for Union Carbide, later earning a history Ph.D. from WVU. He has published many articles and book reviews.

Mary Lucille DeBerry was raised in Ritchie County and educated at WVU. She worked for public TV in Morgantown for 35 years, producing historical, cultural, and public affairs programs.

Jill Thompson Decker was born in Fayette County and raised in Charleston. Now living near Washington, she is a writer and editing consultant and former newspaper editor. She is a member of the National Press Club.

George Deike attended college in Pennsylvania and Missouri before moving to West Virginia in 1971 to pursue interests in logging, railroads, and caves. He is an officer of the Mountain State Railroad & Logging Historical Association.

Sharen Deitz, raised in Flatwoods, was educated at Glenville State College and the West Virginia College of Graduate Studies. She was the first female state trooper.

Dennis J. Deitz grew up in Greenbrier County. Educated at Rainelle High School and Glenville State College, he wrote his first book at age 70. He wrote 14 books, both historical and fiction, mostly about West Virginia. He died in 2003.

Eric Denemark, a Chicago native, is executive director of the West Virginia Motorsports Council. He is a graduate of Lawrence University, Wisconsin, with a master's degree from the University of Kentucky.

Charles J. Denham, educated at Northwestern University and Marshall University Graduate College, is a consulting chemical engineer. He is retired from the DuPont Company and edited a history of DuPont's Belle plant.

Alan J. DeYoung, a professor at University of Kentucky, specializes in the sociology of

rural schools. He spent much of the 1990s in West Virginia, working on projects for the Appalachia Educational Laboratory, the West Virginia Education Fund, and the Annenberg Rural Challenge.

Sharon Diaz, now retired, was language arts and social studies coordinator for Harrison County schools and also directed the county writing project and artist-in-residence program. She was president of the West Virginia Reading Association and the West Virginia English Language Arts Council.

Jack L. Dickinson, a West Virginia native, earned a B.A. from Marshall. He is a retired IBM systems engineer and author of five books about the Civil War, including *Tattered Uniforms & Bright Bayonets: West Virginia's Confederate Soldiers*.

Thomas W. Dixon Jr., born at Alderson, graduated from WVU. He served in the army from 1969 to 1990, retiring as lieutenant colonel. He is founder and president of the Chesapeake & Ohio Historical Society and a writer of railroad books.

Melissa May Dobbins, a native Ohioan, earned B.F.A. degrees in painting and art history from the Art Academy of Cincinnati, and an M.A. in anthropology. She directs the Pricketts Fort Memorial Foundation.

Howard Dorgan, educated at the University of Texas and Louisiana State and retired from Appalachian State University, North Carolina, is past president of the Appalachian Studies Association. He has studied Appalachian religion for many years, publishing extensively on the subject.

Brad Douglas was educated in criminal justice at West Virginia State and Marshall University Graduate College. He is a research analyst at the Division of Corrections and has authored or assisted with studies of recidivism, female offenders, and drunken driving.

John Douglas is editor of the *Morgan Messenger*, a weekly newspaper in Berkeley Springs. His mystery novels include *Shawnee Alley Fire* and *Blind Spring Rambler*, and his reporting has appeared in the *Washington Post* and many other publications.

Thomas Douglass is the editor of the *Appalachian Echoes* series from University of Tennessee Press. A graduate of Davis & Elkins, WVU, and the University of North Carolina, he has written a biography of Breece D'J Pancake.

Ora Beth Drake is an extension professor emeritus. She has degrees from Concord College and WVU, and her career included teaching and other assignments during more than 37 years with WVU Extension Service.

Bill Drennen of Shepherdstown was born and raised in Charleston. He was educated at Yale and the West Virginia College of Graduate Studies. He has worked as a producer of film and video and is past commissioner of the Division of Culture & History.

Georgia Caldwell DuBose is a freelance writer and editor from Harpers Ferry. She graduated from University of Missouri and writes for magazines and newspapers, specializing in articles about the Eastern Panhandle.

Hallie Chillag Dunlap, a native of Kanawha County who has lived in several parts of the state, works for the West Virginia Poison Control Center. She was educated in sociology at WVU and Penn State, and in 2005 was pursuing a Ph.D. in health geography at WVU.

Susan A. Eacker earned a Ph.D. from Miami University of Ohio. She taught at Morehead (Kentucky) State University, specializing in Southern women's history, oral history, and women in Appalachian music.

Stephanie Earles is a Berkeley Springs native and graduate of the University of North Carolina. She was a reporter at the *Morgan Messenger* in Berkeley Springs before moving to the West Coast.

Anne B. W. Effland earned an M.A. from WVU and a Ph.D. from Iowa State University. She has published on the West Virginia women's suffrage movement. Since leaving West Virginia, her research has turned to rural history.

Carrie Eldridge is president of Elderkin, through which she has written and published 46 genealogical books, maps, and migration atlases. Born in Kentucky, she has spent most of her life in Chesapeake, Ohio.

John Rush Elkins, a Beckley native and emeritus professor of chemistry at Concord University, does American chestnut research on his property. He is a graduate of WVU Tech and WVU, where he earned a Ph.D. His family goes back five generations in West Virginia on his father's side and six on his mother's side.

Ronald D. Eller, from southern West Virginia, is professor of history and former director of the Appalachian Center at the University of Kentucky. He earned a Ph.D. from University of North Carolina and has published more than 60 articles and books, including *Miners, Millhands, and Mountaineers*.

Bob Enoch has served as president of the Wood County Historical & Preservation Society and chairman of the Fort Boreman Historic Park Commission. He has written news articles and helped reprint items of Wood County history.

Norman L. Fagan was educated at University of Maryland, Carnegie Tech, and the Pittsburgh Playhouse School of Theater, and has a doctorate of humane letters from the West Virginia Board of Regents. Now a Putnam County farmer, he was the first commissioner of the Department of Culture & History.

Yvonne Farley, educated at Antioch College and the University of Kentucky, is library director at the National Mine Health and Safety Academy, Beckley. She has written for the *West Virginia Hillbilly*, *Goldenseal*, and other publications.

David Fattaleh is photography manager for the Division of Tourism and photo editor for HQ Publishing, which publishes *Marshall Magazine* and *Huntington Quarterly*. His photographs have appeared in the *Washington Post*, *Ohio Magazine*, *Charlotte Observer*, *Wonderful West Virginia*, and other publications.

Richard Fauss, educated at Potomac State College and WVU, compiled *A Bibliography of Labor History in Newsfilm*. He is the audio-visual archivist for the State Archives.

Christine D. Fenn, born in Cleveland and now living in Florida, moved to West Virginia in 1974 and went to work for WVU the following year. She has written for *Goldenseal*, *Pennsylvania Magazine*, and other publications.

James P. Fenton studied anthropology at University College, London, and earned a Ph.D. from Columbia. Formerly the director of the Webb Museum of Anthropology and the Office of State Archaeology at the University of Kentucky, he has excavated sites in Kentucky, Ohio, and West Virginia.

Stephen Lee Fesenmaier, educated in library science at the University of Minnesota, directed the film services division of the West Virginia Library Commission for 21 years. He co-founded the West Virginia International Film Festival and the West Virginia Filmmakers Guild.

George Fetherling, born in Wheeling, has published more than 50 books of fiction, verse, memoir, history, criticism, travel, and biography. He lives in Vancouver, British Columbia.

Scott Finn, who grew up in an Iowa farm town, has a Harvard B.A. in sociology and an M.A. in journalism from the University of Missouri. He is a statehouse reporter for the *Charleston Gazette*.

Louise Burner Flegel was raised in Morgantown and educated at WVU. She taught high school English in Pocahontas County before moving to North Carolina. She has contributed to *Wonderful West Virginia* and *Goldenseal*.

Dan B. Fleming, a St. Marys native, was educated at WVU and George Washington University, where he earned an Ed.D. A professor emeritus at Virginia Tech, he wrote *Kennedy vs. Humphrey, West Virginia, 1960* among other publications.

Dolores Atchison Fleming earned a B.A. and M.A. from WVU. She has written or edited several books, including *The Ambassadorial Diary of John W. Davis*. She was historian for the WVU School of Medicine and a member of the Archives & History Commission.

Robert B. Florian taught history at Salem International University from 1958 to 2000, retiring to pastor five small Methodist churches. Born in Connecticut, he was educated at Adrian College, Michigan, and Garrett Theological Seminary, Illinois, with a history Ph.D from WVU. He co-authored a history of United Methodism in West Virginia.

Ken Fones-Wolf, the grandson of a West Virginia steelworker, teaches history at WVU. He has a particular interest in the history of our state's glass industry.

Harold Malcolm Forbes, associate curator of the West Virginia & Regional History Collection at WVU Libraries, has been curator of West Virginia books and newspapers since 1973. Born in Morgantown, he has degrees from WVU and University of Pittsburgh.

Beri Fox is the CEO of Marble King, Inc., and president of the National Marbles Tournament board of directors. She is on the National Marbles Hall of Fame executive committee and past president of the Society of Glass Sciences & Practices.

William L. Frank, of Farmville, Virginia, earned a Ph.D. from Northwestern University. He is professor emeritus and former academic dean at Longwood University, Virginia. His books include *The Fictional World of William Hoffman*.

Claude A. Frazier is an allergist and author. He is the son of a coal mining physician and spent his childhood in West Virginia. After graduation from medical school, he established his practice in Asheville, North Carolina.

William W. French, born in Beckley, graduated from WVU and earned an M.A. and a Ph.D. from the University of Pittsburgh. He joined the WVU English department in 1967, teaching Shakespeare and drama courses until his retirement in 1999.

Robert L. Frey, a Pennsylvania native, was educated at the University of Indianapolis and Penn State, with a Ph.D. in history from University of Minnesota. He is the author or editor of six books and has written many articles. He retired as academic dean and vice president of the University of Charleston and now lives in Ohio.

Ferrell Friend from Clay County was educated at Commercial College in Charleston and the Navy School of Photography. He was a photographer and reporter at the *Charleston Gazette* for 22 years. His photographs have appeared in the *New York Times*, *Newsweek*, *Saturday Evening Post*, and in newspapers statewide.

Mary Rodd Furbee was educated at WVU and taught writing at the WVU School of Journalism. An author of nonfiction books and articles, she wrote for the *Washington Post*, *The Progressive*, *Goldenseal*, and other publications. She died in 2004.

Emmitt Maxwell Furner II, a writer of fiction and an army officer stationed in Knoxville, is also a veteran of the marines and the West Virginia Army National Guard. A Parkersburg native, he was educated at WVU and Liberty University, Virginia.

Howard P. Gamble is director of marketing and public relations at Ohio Valley Medical Center and the Ohio Valley Health Services & Education Corporation. He was educated at West Virginia Wesleyan and the WVU School of Medicine.

Harold D. Garber, a graduate of Bridgewater (Virginia) College and James Madison University, retired as superintendent of Grant County schools in 1999. He is pastor of the Moorefield Church of the Brethren.

Paul Gartner, an Ohio native, has lived in West Virginia for much of his life. He is a copy editor for the *Charleston Gazette*, where he also writes book reviews, features, and articles on traditional music. He plays guitar and banjo with an old-time string band.

Gerard W. Gawalt, a specialist in early American history at the Library of Congress, earned a Ph.D. from Clark University, Massachusetts. He has appeared on the *Today Show*, *C-Span*, and the *History Channel*, and published books on Thomas Jefferson and other subjects.

Joe Geiger was educated at Marshall. He has written several articles and a book, *Civil War* in Cabell County, West Virginia. He is assistant director and webmaster at the State Archives.

Jane Taylor Cox George, born in Roane County and educated at West Virginia State, was a leader in the folk arts revival. She was involved with the first Mountain State Art & Craft Fair, a Centennial event, and later worked in crafts development at the state Department of Commerce.

Joy Gregoire Gilchrist-Stalnaker of Horner is a writer, lecturer, genealogist, historian, and preservationist. She has served as a member and chair of the West Virginia Archives & History Commission.

Mack H. Gillenwater taught geography at Marshall. He earned a Ph.D. from University of Tennessee, focusing on the cultural and historical geography of the southern West Virginia coalfields. He has taught in China and Spain and traveled widely.

William H. Gillespie, a Webster County native, was educated at WVU. He was deputy commissioner of agriculture and state forester and has taught geology at WVU. He is widely published and has two plant genera named in his honor.

Neil Gillies, a Denver native, is executive director of the Cacapon Institute. He was educated in biology and the environment at the University of Miami and Florida International University. He plays old-time music on the hammered dulcimer.

John Gillispie, a Man native and Marshall graduate, is public relations director for the Huntington Museum of Art. He has worked for the Huntington *Herald-Dispatch*, Beckley *Register-Herald*, and *Goldenseal*.

Anna Evans Gilmer, a Charleston native, was educated at Bluefield State College. She contributes news stories to the *West Virginia Beacon Digest*.

Michael Gioulis of Sutton was educated at City University of New York and Cornell. He was a historical architect for the Department of Culture & History before becoming a historic preservation consultant.

Joseph C. Gluck served many years as vice president and dean of students at WVU. He was a Ritchie County native, educated at Bethany College, Yale, and Oxford. A former navy chaplain, he pastored the Forks of Cheat Baptist Church for 28 years. He died in 2004.

Tanya Godfrey, formerly of Moorefield, is an attorney for the Chapter 13 bankruptcy trustee in South Charleston. She attended law school at WVU.

Karen Goff, for many years reference services director at the Library Commission, is now library development director. Educated in sociology and library science at the University of Pittsburgh, she is past president of the West Virginia Library Association.

Randall S. Gooden earned B.A., M.A., and Ph.D. degrees in history from WVU. He heads the public history firm Gooden & Associates and is publisher and editor of a weekly newspaper in Ohio.

Abby Gail Goodnite, educated at Rio Grande (Ohio) College, has roots in Mason County.

She has written for *Bluegrass Unlimited*, *Buckeye Hill Country*, and *Goldenseal*.

Jacqueline G. Goodwin, educated at WVU, works for the Pennsylvania State Education Association. She was director of communications for the West Virginia Education Association for 13 years and a teacher in Parkersburg and Wirt County high schools.

Emily Grafton, a teacher and Parkersburg native, holds a B.S. in botany from Marshall and an M.A. in special education from WVU. Among other publications, she has written naturalist guides for Babcock and Blackwater Falls state parks.

William N. Grafton, a native of Fayette County, earned forestry degrees at WVU. He has worked as a specialist for the WVU Extension Service since 1967, dealing with forestry, wildlife, outdoor recreation, environmental issues, and education.

Ruby A. Greathouse retired after 29 years as secretary to the director of the United Steelworkers of America, District 23. Descended from early settlers of the Northern Panhandle, she is active in Brooke County historical and civic organizations.

Billy Jack Gregg, a lawyer and native Texan, has directed the Consumer Advocate Division at the state Public Service Commission since the office was founded. He studied at the University of Glasgow, Scotland, Austin College in Texas, and the University of Texas.

Buddy Griffin of Glenville is director of cultural events and teaches music at Glenville State College. He produces programs for public radio. He plays fiddle with *Grand Ole Opry* stars Jesse McReynolds and the Virginia Boys.

Amanda Griffith was educated in history at Shepherd College and WVU. She is executive director of Arthurdale Heritage, Inc.

Richard S. Grimes, born and raised in Wheeling, studied journalism at WVU. He was a reporter for the *Charleston Daily Mail*, covering state government for more than 30 years until his 1999 retirement. He wrote *Jay Rockefeller: Old Money, New Politics*.

Jeanne Grimm was educated at Baldwin-Wallace College, Ohio, and WVU. She prepares nominations for the National Register of Historic Places. She co-authored *Generations of Growth: A Contemporary View of West Virginia University School of Medicine*.

Gilbert Gude, born in Washington and educated at Cornell and George Washington universities, represented western Maryland in Congress. His books include *Where the Potomac Begins*, about the North Branch Valley. He chaired the 1976 Anglo-American Conference on Africa.

Tom Haas spent three years as a VISTA worker in West Virginia before graduating from Virginia Tech with a degree in biochemistry. A St. Albans native, he lives in Charlotte.

Beth Hager, educated at WVU and the University of Delaware, was curator of history at Huntington Museum of Art. She co-produced the 1995 documentary *West Virginia: A Film History* before taking a public television job in Pennsylvania. She is now at the State Museum of Pennsylvania.

Van Beck Hall, who graduated from Gassaway High School and earned a Ph.D. from the University of Wisconsin, began teaching history at the University of Pittsburgh in 1964.

George W. Hammond teaches in the Bureau of Business & Economic Research at WVU. Director of the West Virginia Economic Outlook Project, he studies the development of lagging regions and teaches in the executive M.B.A. program.

Donna Hanna-Walker is a native Charlestonian educated at Morris Harvey College and WVU. She has worked at the state workers' compensation commission and the insurance commissioner's office, where she was deputy commissioner for 11 years.

Todd A. Hanson, a Campbells Creek native, is a freelance writer and photographer. He wrote *Campbells Creek: A Portrait of a Coal Mining Community*, and his photographs have been widely published.

Andy Hansroth was a sportswriter and photographer for the *Charleston Gazette*. He studied journalism at WVU, and his work appeared in newspapers statewide. He wrote two books on hunting and fishing before his untimely death in 2005.

Clark Haptonstall has a B.A. and M.A. from Marshall. He served as Marshall's sports information director and is an assistant professor and director of the sports management program at Rice University, Texas.

W. Henry Harmon, president of Triana Energy, was educated at WVU Tech, American College, Pennsylvania, and Union Institute, where he earned a Ph.D. in economics. He is past president of the West Virginia Humanities Council.

R. Eugene Harper, educated at Wittenberg University, Ohio, and University of Pittsburgh, began teaching history at the University of Charleston in 1967. His publications include *The Transformation of Western Pennsylvania* and various articles.

Bill Harrington has a B.S. in economics from WVU. He was employed by the Secretary of State's office for 21 years where his duties included election administration.

Evelyn L. Harris, born in New York City, has taught political science and history at the University of Charleston since 1946. A graduate of Hunter College, New York, and Columbia University, she co-authored a history of the West Virginia labor movement.

Cheryl Ryan Harshman, director of the Paul N. Elbin Library at West Liberty State College, is a member of the West Virginia Humanities Council board of directors. A resident of Wheeling, she writes books for children under the name Cheryl Ryan.

Marc Harshman, a Wheeling author, poet, and storyteller, taught at a three-room school in rural Marshall County. An Indiana native educated at Bethany College, Yale Divinity School, and University of Pittsburgh, he has written many children's books.

Sarah Harshman is the daughter of Marc and Cheryl Harshman and a high school student at Mount de Chantal, Wheeling.

Daniel Hart is the son of Gary and Pam Hart of Charleston. In 2005 he was a student at George Washington High School.

John Hartford, born in New York City and raised in St. Louis, was a singer, songwriter, and TV performer. He wrote "Gentle on My Mind," which has been recorded more than 300 times, most notably by Glen Campbell in 1967. He had a particular interest in riverboats and mountain fiddlers. He died in 2001.

Ken Hechler, formerly West Virginia secretary of state and congressman, earned an A.B. from Swarthmore College, Pennsylvania, and an M.A. and Ph.D. from Columbia. He was a speech writer for President Truman and a WWII combat historian. His seven books include *Bridge at Remagen*, which was made into a motion picture with George Segal, Robert Vaughn, and Ben Gazzara.

Phoebe Heishman, who studied journalism at WVU, is editor and publisher of the *Moorefield Examiner*. She has worked for the Federal Reserve Bank of San Francisco, public TV at WVU, and U.S. Sen. Jennings Randolph. She is past president of the West Virginia Press Association.

Pat Hendricks is a non-fiction writer. She writes reviews for the *Charleston Gazette* and contributes to its Life & Style section.

R. F. Hendricks, a Parkersburg native, is a poet and publisher of children's books. His forthcoming novel, *The Long Sorrow*, is set in West Virginia. He lives in Atlanta.

John Hennen teaches history at Morehead (Kentucky) State University. A native Huntingtonian with a Ph.D. from WVU, he is the author of *The Americanization of West Virginia* and co-editor of two other books on West Virginia history.

Lori Henshey is a Charleston writer and researcher. She earned a B.A. in American history from WVU and began her career as assistant editor at *Goldenseal*.

Frank P. Herrera, a Beckley native, was educated at WVU. A photographer, he lives in Martinsburg. The recipient of many awards and fellowships, he is the author of *Decades*, a retrospective of *Life* photographer Ed Clark.

Robert C. Hieronymus, an engineering graduate of University of Illinois, made a career with Union Carbide in South Charleston, Texas, New York, and Belgium. After retiring in 1978, he was dean of business at the University of Charleston and a member of the state Air Pollution Control Commission. He died in 2005.

Mary Etta Hight grew up in Mercer County and graduated from Concord College before earning a biology Ph.D. from Wayne State University, Michigan. She teaches at Marshall and is a research associate of Carnegie Museum of Natural History.

Raymond Thomas Hill, a Missouri native, was educated at Southeast Missouri State University and George Peabody College, Tennessee. He taught geography and Appalachian studies at Concord College and was associate pastor at Concord United Methodist Church. He died in 2003.

William Hintzen is a retired schoolteacher and lifelong resident of Indiana. He has been interested in history, especially of the Wheeling area, since reading Zane Grey's *The Spirit of the Border* as a boy.

Patricia Hissom was born and raised in Kanawha County. She earned a B.S. from WVU and has been the naturalist at Blackwater Falls State Park since 1984.

Darla S. Hoffman, a Charleston native, was educated at West Virginia State and Marshall. She specializes in the visual arts and late prehistory of North America. She is a member of several archeology organizations.

Warren R. Hofstra is Stewart Bell Professor of history at Shenandoah University, Virginia. Among many other publications, he edited *George Washington and the Virginia Backcountry* and authored the recent *Planting of New Virginia,* a study of the 18th-century Shenandoah Valley.

Henry Hogmire is an extension specialist and professor of entomology at WVU. He has worked at the WVU Tree Fruit Research & Education Center in Kearneysville since 1979.

Kim Howard, a West Virginia Wesleyan graduate, was born in Buckhannon and lives there now. A freelance writer and editor, she has worked at the *Record Delta* in Buckhannon and the *Weston Democrat* in Weston.

Barbara J. Howe is director of the Center for Women's Studies at WVU, where she teaches women's history. She researches West Virginia women's history and has worked with community groups throughout the state.

Mary Hufford teaches folklore and directs the Center for Folklore & Ethnography at the University of Pennsylvania. Since the early 1990s, she has conducted fieldwork in southern West Virginia.

Basil Hurley, born in Fayette County, earned a B.A. from Ohio University and an M.A. from Ohio State. He has contributed to *Goldenseal* and lives near Toledo, Ohio.

Arnout Hyde Jr., is a subject of this book and a valued contributor. See "Arnout 'Sonny' Hyde Jr."

Lucia K. Hyde, grew up traveling West Virginia with her father, photographer Arnout Hyde Jr. Educated at Boston University, she edits *Wonderful West Virginia*.

Keith Inskeep has been professor of animal science and a researcher in the reproductive management of livestock at WVU since 1964.

Alan Jabbour is a folklorist who has studied West Virginia fiddling and related instrumental folk music. Educated at Duke, he was for many years the director of the American Folklife Center at the Library of Congress.

Kathleen M. Jacobs, a Charleston freelance writer, worked as an English teacher. She has published in *Goldenseal, Appalachian Heritage*, Charleston's *Sunday Gazette-Mail*, and elsewhere. She has an M.A. from Marshall University Graduate College.

Rick Jarrett, the son of a coal miner, studied mining engineering at West Virginia Tech and worked at several mines during the 1970s. He is compiling a history of mine disasters and fatalities in West Virginia. He lives in Kanawha County.

David T. Javersak grew up in Weirton and worked for Weirton Steel as a college student. He was educated at West Liberty State College, University of Hawaii, and WVU. He is a dean and history professor at West Liberty.

Joseph Crosby Jefferds Jr., a Charleston native and president emeritus of the West Virginia Humanities Council, graduated from the Massachusetts Institute of Technology. He served in the army during WWII before founding Jefferds Corporation, a distributor of industrial machinery. He died in 2005.

Jerra Jenrette, a North Carolina native, chairs the department of history and anthropology at Edinboro (Pennsylvania) University. She earned a Ph.D. in history from WVU.

Frank Jernejcic has been a fishery biologist with the Division of Natural Resources since 1969. He has had a lifelong interest in snakes and has raised many in captivity.

Garrett C. Jeter, of Charleston, is a graduate of Hampden-Sydney College, University of Illinois, and John Marshall Law School, Atlanta. He presents the Reverend Henry Ruffner as a Chautauqua-style character and is an active local historian.

Mary Johnson, a Charleston native, earned an M.A. from WVU. She was a contract historian for four years for Harpers Ferry National Historical Park and now works on electronic databases for the State Archives.

Skip Johnson, a native of Braxton County, is one of West Virginia's foremost outdoors writers. He retired in 1993 after more than three decades as a columnist and reporter for the *Charleston Gazette*.

William K. Jones was born in Beckley and educated at WVU and the University of Virginia. He is a consulting hydrologist, an adjunct professor at American University, Washington, and director of the Karst Waters Institute. He lives in Charles Town.

Brucella Wiggins Jordan came to West Virginia from Cleveland in 1979 and now lives in Tennessee. In 1991 she co-founded the African-American Heritage Family Tree Museum in Ansted.

Norman Jordan, a native of Ansted now living in Tennessee, co-founded the African-American Heritage Family Tree Museum. His poetry has been anthologized in many books, including *Wild Sweet Notes: Fifty Years of West Virginia Poetry*.

Katherine M. Jourdan worked for the state Historic Preservation Office. She graduated from Purdue and earned an M.A. in historic preservation from Ball State University. She lives in Indiana.

Charles A. Julian studied at Glenville State College, University of Sheffield, England, Vanderbilt, and Florida State, where he earned a Ph.D. He is a manager at the National Technology Transfer Center in Wheeling.

Norman Julian is a columnist for the *Dominion Post* in Morgantown. He is the author of four books, including a novel about Cheat River and a history of WVU basketball.

Gary Kappel graduated from Bethany College, earned an M.A. and Ph.D. from WVU, and has also studied in the Netherlands, Germany, New Zealand, and China. He is a professor of history at Bethany.

Carolyn M. Karr, a Huntington native, has degrees from Marshall and a Ph.D. from Ohio State. Her publications include articles and curriculum materials.

Louis E. Keefer, a Wheeling native now living in Virginia, graduated from Morris Harvey College and WVU. A transportation planner for more than 30 years and a WWII veteran, he has published four books and written several articles for *Goldenseal*.

C. Belmont Keeney is a writer and historian from Alum Creek. He worked as a researcher for *The West Virginia Encyclopedia* before seeking a history Ph.D. at WVU.

Michael Keller, director of photographic services for the Division of Culture & History, has had work published in *Southern Living, Los Angeles Times Magazine, Mid-Atlantic Country, Goldenseal*, and *West Virginia Magazine*. His photographs have been exhibited at the State Museum and other West Virginia locations and in Pittsburgh, Washington, and Japan.

Emory L. Kemp, founder of the Institute for the History of Technology & Industrial Archaeology at WVU and former chair of the department of civil engineering, studied at the University of Illinois and in London. He is a founding member of the Society for Industrial Archeology and first editor of its journal. He was a fellow of the American Council of Learned Societies, a Regents Fellow at the Smithsonian, a fellow at the University of Edinburgh, and member of the West Virginia Humanities Council board of directors.

Kathleen Kennedy is a native West Virginian who studied journalism as a graduate student at WVU.

Norma Jean Kennedy-Venable retired from WVU as a natural resources specialist in 1997. A New York native, she earned a B.A. from the University of Toledo. She has published widely on West Virginia natural history.

David J. Kessler has a B.A. is history. He is an administrator with the West Virginia Office of Miners' Health, Safety and Training.

Rebecca Halstead Kimmons lives in Charleston and sings with a gospel trio. Educated at WVU and the University of Iowa, she has won awards for newspaper and magazine writing and her work in media relations.

Gibbs Kinderman, of Pocahontas County, worked with the Appalachian Volunteers, the Black Lung Association, and other social action groups. He is a founder of the Pocahontas Communications Cooperative, an independent public radio broadcaster.

Brandon Ray Kirk was raised in Lincoln County. A graduate of Harts High School, he earned a B.A. from Marshall. He has been a teacher, library assistant, and reporter.

J. Steven Kite joined the WVU department of geology and geography in 1983. A native of the Shenandoah Valley, he earned a Ph.D. from University of Wisconsin. He studies the landscapes, geology, and archeology of the Appalachians.

Michael Kline earned a Ph.D. in folklore from Boston University and has been active in West Virginia folklife and music research for many years. A contributor to *Goldenseal*, where he was once assistant editor, he also co-produced an audio series on our state's traditional life.

Jerry A. Knight, a native of Fayette County, earned a B.S. in accounting from West Virginia Tech. He took a job with the Tax Department immediately upon graduation and directed the property tax division from 1993 to 2004.

Thomas J. Koon, born near Monongah in 1921, is president of the Marion County Historical Society and writes weekly historical columns for the Fairmont *Times West Virginian*. He was educated at Fairmont State and WVU.

Scott M. Kozelnik was educated in American history at WVU and Monmouth (New Jersey) University. He had a book published by Arcadia Publishing Company for its pictorial history series.

Jane Kraina was born in Weston, grew up in Morgantown, and lives in Weirton. She was educated at West Liberty State College and WVU. She works for the Library Commission and has published in *Goldenseal* and *Wonderful West Virginia*.

Gretchen Krantz-Evans, a Charleston native educated at WVU and Columbia University Law School, served as clerk to Joseph R. Goodwin, U.S. district judge for the Southern District of West Virginia.

Christine M. Kreiser, who has a public history M.A. from WVU, was a historian at the State Archives and assistant editor of *West Virginia History*. She was later managing editor of *Blues Revue* magazine, and is now a senior editor at Primedia History Magazine Group in Virginia.

Gary Lake is a freelance photographer in Morgantown. He has earned awards from the National Park Service and other organizations. His work has been included in such publications as *Sports Illustrated On Campus, TV Guide,* and the *New York Post*.

Lora Lamarre, a Cincinnati native educated in anthropology at the University of Cincinnati, is senior archeologist in the state Historic Preservation Office. She has wanted to be an archeologist since fourth grade.

Thomas Swift Landon earned an M.A. in history from WVU. He works for Workforce West Virginia, having previously worked at the state Historic Preservation Office and at Oglebay Mansion Museum.

Ron Lane, from Columbus, Indiana, is an engineering graduate of Cornell and the University of Michigan. He researches railroad folk music and railroad history, with a particular interest in the New River Gorge.

John D. Law is assistant secretary of the state Department of Health & Human Resources. A native of Fayetteville and graduate of West Virginia Tech, he has held a variety of jobs in public relations.

Rachel Nash Law learned basketmaking from her father, C. David Nash, in Alderson in the 1960s. She co-authored the book, *Appalachian White Oak Basketmaking*.

Barbara Singer and William R. Lawrence Jr. live on a small farm outside Milton. She works at the Prichard Building in Huntington and is a real estate appraiser. He is a warehouse manager for Contemporary Galleries in Charleston.

Greg Leatherman, born in Romney, founded the Stovepipe Press in 1994. He is a technical writer and writes fiction as a hobby. He lives in Hinton and serves on the board of directors for the Hinton Area Community Center.

Jeffrey M. Leatherwood, born in North Carolina, has an M.A. in history from Western Carolina University and in 2005 was a doctoral candidate at WVU. His interests include environmental, military, and world history.

Elizabeth Oliver Lee, raised in Pennsylvania, studied archeology at Bryn Mawr College, Pennsylvania, and Cambridge University. She worked as an archeologist in West Virginia and the Mid-Atlantic before returning to school to study Appalachian history at WVU.

Larry Legge of Barboursville is a lifelong West Virginian. A past president of the Upper Vandalia Historical Society, he has been an officer in the West Virginia Historical Society.

Kathleen Carothers Leo, a Michigan native, was educated in forestry and wildlife management at University of Michigan and WVU. After teaching high school in Webster County, she became a wildlife biologist for the Division of Natural Resources.

Bil Lepp is a national champion storyteller. He graduated from West Virginia Wesleyan, has a master's in theology from Duke, and is an ordained United Methodist minister.

Walter A. Lesser earned degrees from New York State Ranger School, Syracuse University, and State University of New York College of Forestry. He retired after working for more than 40 years for the state of West Virginia as a wildlife biologist.

Gerald E. Lewis, a Mineral County native, earned an M.S. in fish and wildlife management from WVU. He became a fishery biologist at the Romney office of the Division of Natural Resources in 1966.

Ronald L. Lewis holds the Stuart and Joyce Robbins Chair at the WVU history department, teaching West Virginia and Appalachian history. He is the author of *Transforming the Appalachian Countryside* and other books and articles, and a member of the West Virginia Humanities Council board of directors.

Susan E. Lewis, a freelance copy editor, was managing editor of the *Journal of Appalachian Studies*. She is a graduate of Kent State University and a native of Ohio, where she taught high school English and history before moving to Morgantown.

John Lilly is the editor of *Goldenseal* magazine. He has written for the *Encyclopedia of Country Music* and the *Encyclopedia of Appalachia*, and edited *Mountains of Music: West Virginia*

Traditional Music from Goldenseal. He was educated at Davis & Elkins College.

Karl C. Lilly III, a graduate of Beckley College (now Mountain State University), is assistant clerk of the state senate. He is a former newspaper editor and correspondent for United Press International. He is associate editor of the *West Virginia Blue Book.*

Elizabeth Johnston Lipscomb is an emeritus professor of English at Randolph-Macon Woman's College, Virginia. She was educated at Sweet Briar College, Virginia, and Harvard. She is co-editor of *The Several Worlds of Pearl S. Buck.*

Michael Lipton, born near New York City and raised in Miami, is a guitarist for the *Mountain Stage* radio show. For several years he edited *Graffiti,* of which he was a founder. His writing has appeared in the *New York Times* and *LA Weekly.*

Glade Little was educated at WVU. Before retiring, he was a newspaper reporter for the *Charleston Gazette* and an information officer for Virginia Commonwealth University.

Herb Little retired in 1985 after 39 years with the Associated Press. He spent most of his career covering state government and politics in Charleston. He was a Parkersburg native, a graduate of Marietta College, and a WWII veteran. He died in 2002.

Richard P. Lizza is a history professor and department chair at West Liberty State College. He is a former professor of social sciences at West Virginia Northern Community College and past president of the West Virginia Historical Association.

Penny Loeb reported on mountaintop removal mining for *U.S. News & World Report.* Educated at Vassar College and University of Missouri School of Journalism, she has received numerous awards and was a finalist for the Pulitzer Prize.

Fred Long, a lifelong resident of Hinton, is editor of the *Hinton News.* He is a member of the Summers County Historic Landmark Commission and a former member of the city council.

Roy C. Long, born in Covington, Virginia, lived many years in Hinton. He began working for the C&O Railroad in 1939 and retired as chief train dispatcher in 1981. In retirement, he wrote the column "Railroad Recollections" for the *Hinton News* and many articles for the C&O Historical Society magazine. He died in 1998.

Scot E. Long, who teaches cultural anthropology at Ohio University and the University of Akron, was once a reporter for the *Parkersburg News & Sentinel.* He graduated from Ohio University and earned a Ph.D. from Ohio State.

JoAnn Lough, of Fairmont, is professor emeritus at Fairmont State University. She chaired the speech and theater department and was director of theater for 17 years.

Terry Lowry of the State Archives was educated at West Virginia State and Marshall University Graduate School. Previously historian for Charleston's historic Craik-Patton House, he researches and writes on Civil War history.

M. Lois Lucas teaches history at West Virginia State University. She earned a B.A. and an M.A. from North Carolina Central University before seeking a Ph.D. in American history at the University of Kentucky.

Paul F. Lutz taught West Virginia history at Marshall. He is a graduate of Marshall and WVU, where he earned a Ph.D. He wrote a biography of Governor Marland and articles for *Goldenseal* and other publications.

Tom Lynch, who began making chairs in West Virginia in 1977, contributes to *Woodworker's Journal* and has been featured in publications including *Better Homes and Gardens* and *Country Living.* He is a master craftsman with the West Virginia Folk Arts Apprenticeship Program.

Betty L. MacQueen, educated at Potomac State College and West Virginia State, is past president of Mountain State Press and a charter member of West Virginia Writers.

Lee R. Maddex, educated at WVU and formerly of the WVU Institute for the History of Technology & Industrial Archaeology, works for an archeology firm in Pennsylvania.

Robert Franklin Maddox earned a Ph.D. at the University of Kentucky and taught history at Marshall. He published *The War Within World War II: The U.S. and International Cartels* and a biography of U.S. Sen. Harley Kilgore. He died in 2002.

Eleanor Mahoney, a graduate of Amherst now studying at Loyola University in Chicago, is a great niece of author Agnes Smith. She co-authored *Above the Smoke: A Family Album of Pocahontas County Fire Towers* while she was a VISTA volunteer at the Pocahontas Communications Cooperative.

Louis H. Manarin, who earned a B.A. from Western Maryland College and an M.A. and Ph.D. from Duke, was Virginia state archivist, 1970–95. He is the author or editor of several books on Virginia and North Carolina history of the Civil War era, including *The Wartime Papers of R. E. Lee* and *Henrico County: Field of Honor.*

Ralph Mann, a Monroe County native, was educated at Duke, with an M.A. and Ph.D. from Stanford. He teaches Civil War and U.S. social history at the University of Colorado. His research focuses on subsistence and the Civil War in Appalachia.

Christopher Marsh is the son of Keith and Cheryl Marsh of Charleston. In 2005 he was a student at George Washington High School.

Joseph F. Marsh Jr. grew up in Athens and was educated at Concord College, WVU, Dartmouth, Harvard, and Oxford. He taught economics at Dartmouth and was president of Waynesburg College, Pennsylvania, and of Concord, where his father was also president.

Paul D. Marshall, a Charleston native now retired in South Carolina, was an architect or architect's apprentice for 41 years. He has published many articles and papers, including studies of historic sites in West Virginia. His many preservation projects include Graceland, the Davis mansion in Elkins.

Brad Martin, a native of Preston County, was educated at WVU. He lives in Kingwood and teaches at South Preston Middle School.

Lou Martin was in 2005 a doctoral candidate in the history department at WVU, researching post-World War II working-class culture in the upper Ohio Valley.

Ronald Martino teaches geology at Marshall. His research includes stratigraphic and paleontological studies of sedimentary rocks in West Virginia, Ohio, and Kentucky. He earned an M.S. and Ph.D. from Rutgers.

Kenneth C. Martis earned a Ph.D. in geography from University of Michigan in 1975 and joined the faculty of WVU. In 1986 he won WVU's first Benedum Distinguished Scholar award.

Robert F. Maslowski was educated at Holy Cross College, Massachusetts, and has a Ph.D. from the University of Pittsburgh. He retired as a civilian archeologist with the Army Corps of Engineers and teaches at Concord University and Marshall University Graduate College. He is a member of the West Virginia Humanities Council board of directors.

Tim R. Massey is a native of Raleigh County. He wrote for the Huntington *Herald-Dispatch* for many years, and also the old *Baltimore News American, Charleston Gazette,* and *Raleigh Register.* He has published many magazine articles.

David Matchen, educated in geology at Juniata College, Pennsylvania, and WVU, joined the Concord University faculty in 2004. Previously with the West Virginia Geological & Economic Survey, his work includes oil field studies of the Appalachian Basin and geologic mapping in the Eastern Panhandle.

David F. Matthews, the son of Bill and Jean Matthews of Spencer, was educated at Marshall and the University of Kentucky. He is an assistant professor of library science at Fairmont State University and has been a reference librarian there since 1990.

J. Davitt McAteer of Shepherdstown, an expert on mine safety, was assistant labor secretary for mine safety and health in the Clinton administration. He has served on many advisory bodies and on the board of the West Virginia Humanities Council. He is a graduate of WVU College of Law and Wheeling Jesuit University, where he is a vice president.

Kim and Stephen McBride earned B.A.'s from Beloit College and M.A.'s and Ph.D.'s in anthropology from Michigan State. They have participated in or directed excavations in several states since 1976, including frontier forts in West Virginia. She is co-director of the Kentucky Archaeological Survey, and he directs McBride Preservation Services. Together, they have written more than 70 technical reports and co-edited a volume on historical archeology.

Brooks F. McCabe Jr., a Charleston native and state senator, is involved in downtown redevelopment with McCabe-Henley-Durbin. He earned an Ed.D. from WVU with an emphasis on planning and community development. He has published in *West*

Virginia History and the *Journal of the Society for Industrial Archeology*.

Barbara Beury McCallum, educated at Sweet Briar College, Virginia, and now retired, is the author of cookbooks, short stories, and poetry.

Frank Engle McCallum grew up in Charleston and spent summers and holidays in West Union with his grandparents. He works as garage manager at Good News Mountaineer Garage, a nonprofit organization that provides cars to low-income families.

Leslee McCarty, president of the Greenbrier River Trail Association, grew up in Cabell County. She owns a bed and breakfast inn and is active in the Greenbrier River Watershed Association and the Humane Society of Pocahontas County.

Elizabeth Ann H. McClain, a native of Pennsylvania, came to West Virginia as a student at WVU before continuing her education in Tennessee. She lives in Randolph County with her husband, Russ.

W. Russ McClain, a native West Virginian, has degrees in wildlife ecology, biology, and ornithology, working primarily in the Appalachian mountains. He has studied eastern screech-owls, songbirds, and salamanders. Formerly with the Nature Conservancy, he teaches biology at D & E College.

Brian McDonald was educated at the University of Maryland and WVU. He has worked with the Division of Natural Resources since 1979 documenting rare species and plant communities of the state.

Ed McDonald, an independent radio producer, hosts *Sidetracks,* a public radio program syndicated in West Virginia and elsewhere. Educated at Bethany College and Ohio University, he lives in Keyser.

Nicole McDonald grew up in Short Gap, Mineral County, and was educated at WVU. She worked as public relations director at Glenville State College from 2003 to 2005 and lives in Midlothian, Virginia.

Jim McGee is a folklorist, musician, and minister, with an M.A. in folklore from the University of North Carolina. He pastored churches in West Virginia and lives in Louisville, where he works as a hospital chaplain.

C. Stuart McGehee chairs the history department at West Virginia State University. He is a historian of the Appalachian coalfields and has written books and articles on the subject. A graduate of University of Tennessee at Chattanooga, he has an M.A. and Ph.D. from the University of Virginia.

William McGinley earned a B.S. and law degree from WVU, becoming general counsel for the West Virginia Education Association in 1984. He has served two terms on the Consolidated Public Retirement Board.

Bonni V. McKeown, a journalism graduate of WVU, has written for newspapers in Beckley and Charleston. She is the author of *Peaceful Patriot: The Story of Tom Bennett* and an activist on environmental and transportation issues. She is a musician in Chicago.

Tim McKinney is the author of five books on the Civil War in West Virginia, including *Robert E. Lee at Sewell Mountain*. A Fayette County native, he is past president of the West Virginia Historical Society.

Lois McLean, of Beckley, is a Mother Jones scholar. She is a member of the Raleigh County Historical Society and the West Virginia Labor History Association, and president of the Raleigh County Historic Landmarks Commission.

James McNeel, born and raised in Pocahontas County, works for the National Endowment for the Arts in Washington. He began working at the Contemporary American Theater Festival while a student at Shepherd University, where he was president of the student body.

William P. McNeel is editor of the *Pocahontas Times*. Born in Charleston and educated at Marietta College and University of Oregon, he taught school in Pocahontas County and Australia. He is the author of many publications on the history of Pocahontas County and the Greenbrier Valley.

Margaret Meador, of Princeton, was educated at West Virginia Tech and Virginia Tech. She taught home economics and science in several counties and served 25 years as a WVU extension agent in Mercer County. She helped organize the West Virginia Heritage Quilt Search.

Michael M. Meador, a Hinton native, was educated at Marshall and the West Virginia School of Osteopathic Medicine. He has written *A Walking Tour of Historic Jackson's Mill* and numerous articles for *Goldenseal.* He is a physician at the Veterans Administration Hospital in Asheville, North Carolina.

Carol Melling retired as director of public affairs after 35 years with the Division of Highways. A graduate of Syracuse University, she is past president of West Virginia Communicators.

Mary Merolle was born and raised in New York City, where she attended John Jay College of Criminal Justice. She became a West Virginian in 1997, developing an interest in our culture and history while working for the state senate.

Edwin D. Michael, born in Marion County, earned a B.S. from Marietta College and an M.S. and Ph.D. from Texas A&M. He taught at WVU for more than 25 years and has published more than 100 articles on wildlife.

Jane C. Michael is a retired teacher of science and mathematics. She grew up in Marietta, Ohio, and has lived in Morgantown since 1970.

Kay Michael, a Charleston native, was educated at West Virginia State. She worked for WCHS radio and TV news and reported for the *Charleston Gazette, Akron Beacon Journal,* and *Charleston Daily Mail.*

Mack Miles, educated at WVU, is the owner of Miles & Miles, an advertising, graphics, and exhibition design business. He designed and curated the 1985 Homer Laughlin China Company exhibit at the State Museum.

Cathy Hershberger Miller, a native West Virginian, is a library assistant at the State Archives.

She specializes in state government documents, West Virginia history, and genealogy.

Dawn Miller has written for the *Charleston Gazette* for more than a decade. She was born in Martinsburg, grew up in southern Berkeley County, and earned a history degree from WVU.

E. Lynn Miller, a Webster County native, is emeritus professor at Penn State. He is a fellow of the American Society of Landscape Architects and was the society's Congressional fellow in 1992.

Olivia Miller is an adjunct professor at the University of Memphis and a freelance writer. Her articles cover agriculture and business. She has an M.A. in journalism.

Tom D. Miller, born in Lincoln County and educated at Marshall, retired as political reporter after 38 years with the Huntington *Herald-Dispatch*. His "Under the Dome" weekly column was carried by West Virginia newspapers for more than 30 years. He is a freelance writer and public TV news reporter.

Kirsten Milligan graduated from Beloit College, Wisconsin, with a B.S. in biochemistry. She volunteers with the American Red Cross and at Sharpe Hospital in Weston.

Gerald Milnes, a fiddler, is folk arts coordinator of the Augusta Heritage Center. His works include the books *Granny Will Your Dog Bite and Other Mountain Rhymes* and *Play of a Fiddle: Traditional Music, Dance, and Folklore in West Virginia*, and three video documentaries on West Virginia folklife.

Mary Alice S. Milnes is a women's health nurse practitioner in Barbour and Randolph counties.

James R. Mitchell is the curator of the State Museum. He was educated at the University of Wisconsin, the Winterthur Program in Early American Culture at Delaware University, and Shippensburg University, Pennsylvania.

Sandra L. Moats-Burke is West Virginia coordinator for the Ohio Underground Railroad Association. She has an A.B. from Glenville State College and a J.D. from the WVU College of Law.

Stephen D. Mooney, from Dickenson County, Virginia, teaches writing, literature, and Appalachian studies at Virginia Tech. He has published many articles and reviews on Appalachian literature, history, and culture.

Charles F. Moore works at the Center for Appalachian Studies & Services at East Tennessee State University. He has written on a variety of topics, including Li'l Abner, Uncle Abner, and Robert Louis Stevenson.

Dean Moore of Cincinnati is a Ravenswood native and author of the town's first history, *Washington's Woods*. He was educated at Ohio University, Miami University of Ohio, Harvard, and the University of Cincinnati, where he earned a Ph.D.

Greg Moore is a reporter and assistant city editor for the *Charleston Gazette*. He contributed to the book *Profiles: West Virginians Who Made A Difference*. He is a native of Morgantown and attended WVU.

Merle Moore of Webster Springs was director of the Clarksburg-Harrison Library and the

National Mine Health and Safety Academy library. Educated at Glenville State, University of Pittsburgh, and WVU, she serves on the West Virginia Library Commission.

Phyllis Wilson Moore, a poet, researches the literary history of West Virginia. She is a graduate of the Fairmont General Hospital School of Nursing and Fairmont State.

John G. Morgan, a native of Charleston educated at Morris Harvey College, is a former staff writer for the *Charleston Gazette*. He is the author of *West Virginia Governors* and many articles on state history and government.

Charles W. Morris III, of Pinch, is director of collections at the State Museum. He has a B.S. from the University of Charleston, where he was a member of the basketball team.

Joyce Mott, a Marshall graduate and past director of the North House Museum in Lewisburg, has worked for more than 20 years in the publishing and museum fields. She now operates a glass and jewelry design firm in Alderson.

Michelle Mouré was educated at Maryland Institute College of Art and the University of Maryland. She lives in Aurora, where she co-founded the Aurora Project, an artists' residency and education center.

Barry Mowell, a Tennessee native with graduate degrees from East Tennessee State and the universities of Tennessee and Georgia, was in 2005 pursuing further education at Florida International University. He teaches history and geography at Broward Community College in Fort Lauderdale.

Jeanne Mozier, of Berkeley Springs, writes regularly for state and national publications. Her book *Way Out in West Virginia* is a guide to offbeat attractions.

Mark Muchow is the chief administrator for revenue operations for the state Tax Department, where he has worked since 1984. He earned an M.S. in public management and policy from Carnegie Mellon University.

Ron Mullennex, a geologist and hydrogeologist with more than 25 years experience in West Virginia and its environs, is senior vice president of a Bluefield, Virginia, geological, geophysical, and engineering firm. He is a Distinguished Alumnus of the WVU department of geology and geography.

Charles M. Murphy, formerly a student at Glenville State College, is a 20-year veteran of the U.S. Navy.

Christina Myer is the editor of the *Times-Leader* in Martins Ferry, Ohio. She has a B.A. in journalism from WVU.

Mark S. Myers was in 2005 a Ph.D. candidate and lecturer in history at WVU, specializing in Appalachian history. From Welch, he earned a B.A. from Bluefield State College and an M.A. from East Tennessee State University.

Karen N. Cartwright Nance was educated at Marshall. She owns a contracting company that specializes in historic preservation. Her areas of expertise and research are historic preservation and heritage education.

J. Todd Nesbitt is an associate professor of geography at Lock Haven University, Pennsylvania. He earned a Ph.D. in geography at WVU, specializing in Appalachian geography, regional development, and political ecology.

David S. Newhall received a Ph.D. in history from Harvard and taught at the University of Vermont and Centre College in Danville, Kentucky. He has written for other encyclopedias, including the *Encyclopedia of Appalachia*.

Gary Nicholas, educated at WVU, was raised in Calhoun County and now lives in Harrison County. He retired from the Consolidated Natural Gas System, where he was vice president and general manager of Hope Gas and West Virginia director of production for CNG Transmission Company.

Lamont D. Nottingham, a Virginia native, graduated from Randolph-Macon College, University of North Carolina, and University of Virginia. He worked at the Charleston Division of the WVU Byrd Health Sciences Center and was on the faculty of the Department of Community Medicine before his death in 2002.

Andrea Null was born in Summersville and in 2005 attended Magnolia High School in New Martinsville. She has attended the Governor's School for the Arts and the Governor's Honors Academy.

Paul J. Nyden earned a Ph.D. from Columbia University, with a dissertation on the reform movement in the United Mine Workers of America. He is a reporter for the *Charleston Gazette* and an avid baseball fan.

Ted Olson, who teaches at East Tennessee State University, has written or edited books on early country music and other subjects. He earned a Ph.D. in English from University of Mississippi. He is music editor for the *Encyclopedia of Appalachia*.

Amy H. Onken is an entomologist with the U.S. Forest Service in Morgantown. She was educated at the University of Kentucky and WVU.

Jennifer Whyte Onks, a graduate of West Virginia State University, holds a master's degree in clinical psychology from Marshall. She works for Clayman & Associates in Charleston.

Paul Orr is a graduate of Concordia College, Minnesota, McGill University, Canada, and Notre Dame, where he earned a Ph.D. He taught at Georgetown University and Wheeling Jesuit University, specializing in children's literature and Shakespeare in performance. He is writing the history of Wheeling Jesuit.

James C. Pack is a wildlife biologist with the Division of Natural Resources in Elkins. Educated at WVU and Virginia Tech, he has published more than 70 articles on wildlife. He specializes in forest ecology, wildlife habitat management, and wild turkey research.

Don Page of Beckley is a graduate of West Virginia Tech. He worked with the state Department of Commerce and the Department of Culture & History promoting the crafts industry. A charter member of the Old Mill Society, he consulted on the design and construction of the Babcock Mill.

Louise Corey Palumbo was educated at Morris Harvey College and New York University. After beginning at Saks Fifth Avenue in New York, she made a career in fashion at Stone & Thomas Department Stores. She died in 2004.

Thomas K. Pauley was educated at the University of Charleston, Marshall, and WVU, where he earned a Ph.D. He teaches biology at Marshall. He has published many articles and co-authored a book on our state's amphibians and reptiles.

Mark Payne, a banjoist and guitarist who has performed and recorded since 1973, was executive director of the Museum in the Community in Putnam County. He is program officer for the West Virginia Humanities Council.

Edward Peeks, a veteran of WWII, earned a master's degree in journalism from Northwestern University. He is a columnist for the *Charleston Gazette* and former business-labor editor. He wrote *The Long Struggle for Black Power*.

Todd Petty is an assistant professor at WVU, where he teaches and conducts research in river ecology, restoration, and management. A Virginia native, he has a B.A. in biology from the University of Virginia and an M.S. and Ph.D. in forest resources from the University of Georgia.

Billy Joe Peyton earned an M.A. and Ph.D. from WVU. He has worked at WVU's Institute for the History of Technology & Industrial Archaeology and Charleston Catholic High School and now teaches history at West Virginia State University.

Jim Phillips, a native of Princeton educated at Concord College, has been the Pipestem State Park naturalist since 1983. He is field notes editor for *Redstart*, a publication of Brooks Bird Club, and co-author of *A Guide to the Birds of the New River Gorge Area*.

Susan Pierce, an Ohio native, earned an undergraduate degree from Bryn Mawr College, Pennsylvania, and an M.S. in historic preservation from Columbia. She is West Virginia's deputy state historic preservation officer.

Joseph Platania, a Huntington native, was educated at Marshall. A freelance writer, he has contributed to *Goldenseal*, *Wonderful West Virginia*, *Huntington Quarterly*, and other publications.

Cathy Pleska, a native West Virginian, was educated at West Virginia State and Marshall University Graduate College. She has researched West Virginia's ethnic history.

William Plumley, a writer and educator at the University of Charleston for 32 years, was founding president of West Virginia Writers. He has published poetry, fiction, and critical essays and edited five anthologies of Appalachian literature.

Warren Point attended WVU and Harvard Medical School. After working at Massachusetts General Hospital, MIT, and Harvard Medical School, he returned to his native Charleston to teach at the WVU Medical Center in 1977. He chaired the department of medicine at Charleston Area Medical Center until 1990. He died in 2003.

Mary Lou Pratt is the coordinator of adult services at Cabell County Public Library. She earned a B.A. from Penn State and an M.L.S. from Clarion University, Pennsylvania. She has published in the *Wilson Library Journal* and elsewhere.

Chett Pritchett, a graduate of West Virginia Wesleyan, has done graduate study at Drew University, New Jersey, and Wesley Theological Seminary, Washington. He lives in Washington and in 2005 was a candidate for the ministry in the United Methodist Church.

Greg Proctor grew up in Pinch. He has worked as a VISTA volunteer to establish a new-reader collection at Kanawha County Public Library. He serves as para-rabbinic fellow at Temple Israel in Charleston.

Lizbeth Pyle is a geographer interested in rural places. She earned a Ph.D. in geography at the University of Minnesota and occasionally teaches geography at WVU.

Tim Pyles, a native of Weston and graduate of WVU, returned to West Virginia from Delaware to reactivate the crafts program at Cedar Lakes. He is events director at Tamarack.

Tricia Pyne, formerly the historian and archivist for the Roman Catholic Diocese of Wheeling-Charleston, is archives director at St. Mary's Seminary & University in Baltimore. She earned a B.A. from College of the Holy Cross, Massachusetts, and a Ph.D. from Catholic University, Washington.

Doris M. Radabaugh is a retired Wood County teacher. A Gilmer County native, she was educated at Tanner High School, Glenville State College, and WVU.

Paul H. Rakes, born in Fayette County, worked in the mines before taking up the life of a scholar. Educated at WVU Tech and Marshall, with a Ph.D. from WVU, he teaches history at WVU Tech. He was a researcher for *The West Virginia Encyclopedia*.

Michael Tod Ralstin, an Ohio native, was educated at Ohio State. He was a program coordinator for the West Virginia Commission on the Arts and taught English at West Virginia State.

John H. Randolph, a Harrison County native, is a storyteller, artist, and founder of Fort New Salem. He was educated at Salem College and WVU and has taught at Salem College, WVU, and Fairmont State.

Tad Randolph, born in Lafayette, Indiana, earned degrees from Indiana State University. He was a social studies teacher in Battle Creek, Michigan. He lives in Michigan and Florida.

Tracey A. Rasmer is a native of Dayton and earned her B.A. and M.A. in history from Wright State University, Ohio. She is archivist and director of the West Virginia Catholic Heritage Center at the Diocese of Wheeling-Charleston.

Barbara Rasmussen earned an M.S. and Ph.D. from WVU. Formerly a journalist, she teaches history at Fairmont State University. She is president of the Morgantown Historic Landmarks Commission. She is the author of several articles and two books.

Gerald S. Ratliff was chief photographer for *Wonderful West Virginia* magazine and the Governor's Office of Economic & Community Development, and for the book, *West Virginia: Mountain Majesty*. He is a veteran of the Air Force and the West Virginia Air National Guard.

Gerry Reilly of Wheeling earned a B.A. from John Carroll University, Ohio, and an M.A. from Case Western Reserve, Ohio, in history and museum studies. Until 2006, he was the director of West Virginia Independence Hall, our state's birthplace.

James Rentch is a forest researcher and instructor at WVU. His interests include the dynamics of oak and red spruce forests and high elevation wetlands in West Virginia.

Connie Park Rice, a Morgantown native, earned a B.A. and M.A. from WVU. She was in 2005 a Ph.D. candidate in Appalachian regional history at WVU, focusing on African-American history and religion.

Donald L. Rice was educated at Davis & Elkins and WVU. He is retired from Randolph County schools as a teacher and administrator. He has published two books, and articles in *Goldenseal*, *West Virginia Heritage Encyclopedia,* and other publications.

Otis K. Rice, West Virginia's first historian laureate, is a subject of this book and a valued contributor. See "Otis Rice."

Frank S. Riddel, a native of St. Marys, earned a B.A. and M.A. from Marshall and a Ph.D. from Ohio State. He was a professor of history at Marshall, teaching courses in West Virginia history, world civilizations, and the history of Spain.

Michael Ridderbusch is an assistant curator at the West Virginia & Regional History Collection at WVU. He was educated at the University of Washington.

Joseph C. Rieffenberger, educated at the University of Illinois, worked for 46 years as wildlife biologist for the Division of Natural Resources. He retired in 1999 as the leader of the black bear project, which helped to restore our state's bear population.

Carolanne Griffith Roberts, features editor of *Southern Living* magazine, lives in Birmingham, Alabama. She graduated from Charleston schools, Marietta College, and the West Virginia College of Graduate Studies.

James I. Robertson Jr., Alumni Distinguished Professor and director of the Virginia Center for Civil War Studies at Virginia Tech, is a leading historian of the Civil War. He is the author or editor of more than 20 books and has received every major honor in his field. His biography of Stonewall Jackson won eight national awards.

George Truett Rogers, an Indiana native who teaches part-time at WVU, has a theological degree and a B.A., M.A., and Ph.D. in history. He has published a two-volume history of Baptists in West Virginia and local church histories. He is past president of the state Baptist Historical Society.

H. John Rogers was born in Wetzel County and lives in New Martinsville, where he has practiced law since 1967. He is a graduate of WVU, Harvard Law School, the Seminary of the Immaculate Conception in New York, and Pittsburgh Theological Seminary.

Peter W. Roper, an Englishman and a chemist, had a lifelong interest in maps and mapmaking. After retiring as product development manager for a British cigarette manufacturer, he published a biography of Jedediah Hotchkiss, Stonewall Jackson's cartographer. He died in 2002.

Peggy Ross, retired after working in Cincinnati as a journalist and publicist, has written for *Goldenseal* and other publications. She lives with her husband, Tom Fortney, on their farm in Preston County which has been in his family since 1790.

Thomas Richard Ross, a WWII veteran, earned an M.A. and Ph.D. in history from Harvard. He is professor emeritus, dean emeritus, and a trustee-adviser at Davis & Elkins College. His publications include a biography of Henry Gassaway Davis and a history of the college.

David S. Rotenstein, a Maryland consulting historian with a University of Pennsylvania Ph.D., writes on the history of the American leather and livestock industries. He has conducted historical and archeological research throughout West Virginia.

Larry L. Rowe, a Malden attorney and former state senator, has a B.A., M.A., and J.D. from WVU. He was a leader in the preservation of historic Malden, where he lives with his family. He is president of the Midland Trail Scenic Highway Association and a member of the Booker T. Washington Association, Malden Historic Preservation Society, and the Cabin Creek Quilts board of trustees.

Robert Rupp, professor of history and political science at West Virginia Wesleyan, was educated at Ohio Wesleyan University and Syracuse. A member of the West Virginia Election Commission and past member of the Upshur County School Board, he frequently comments on politics in the newspapers and on public radio.

Mark A. Sadd is a Charleston lawyer and member of the city council. He earned a B.A. in history and English from the University of Virginia in 1986 and a J.D. from WVU in 1992.

Mack Samples, a fiddler and square dance caller, was educated at Glenville State College and Ohio University. He has written articles for *Wonderful West Virginia* and *Goldenseal*, and books of fiction and non-fiction. He retired from a long career in higher education.

Dewey D. Sanderson earned undergraduate degrees in geology and physics at the University of Wisconsin and a Ph.D. at Michigan State. He has taught at Marshall since 1971 and chairs the department of geology.

Lon Savage wrote *Thunder in the Mountains*, a book about the West Virginia Mine Wars. Educated at Charleston High School and Cornell University, he was a journalist with United Press International and the *Richmond Times-Dispatch*. He worked in the president's office at Virginia Tech for more than 20 years. He died in 2004.

Linda Saylor-Marchant lives in Savannah, where she works as a librarian. She has written three books.

Frances Myers Schmetzer returned to Glenville after retiring from *Reader's Digest* where she worked in the index department. Before that she taught for 16 years. She was a member of the Glenville State College board of governors until 2004.

Dick Schnacke, born in Kansas, is a graduate of Iowa State and past president of the West Virginia State Board of Education. He has been an aluminum industry engineer but is best known as a toymaker. He wrote the book *American Folk Toys*.

Mary Louise Soldo Schultz, who teaches at WVU, has received fellowships from the National Endowment for the Humanities and the West Virginia Humanities Council. She is writing a children's book on artist Blanche Lazzell.

Bob Schwarz, a native of the New York suburbs, has been a reporter at the *Charleston Gazette* since 1987.

Carter T. Seaton, a Huntington native and former executive director of Appalachian Craftsmen, lives in Huntington. She is a clay sculptor and a writer, and her sculpture has appeared in the West Virginia Juried Exhibition.

John Sencindiver earned a Ph.D. at WVU, where he is a professor of soil science. Previously, he worked for the USDA Soil Conservation Service and the Forest Service.

Dallas B. Shaffer earned a B.A. from the University of Richmond and M.A. and Ph.D. from WVU. He is a retired professor of political science at Potomac State College and an ordained Episcopal minister.

Nora Shalaway, a graduate of Marshall, was in 2005 pursuing a master's degree in literature at American University in Washington.

Scott Shalaway has a Ph.D. in wildlife ecology from Michigan State. He writes a syndicated nature column, hosts a weekly radio show in Wheeling, and contributes to *Wonderful West Virginia*. He lives on a wooded ridge in Marshall County.

Steve Shaluta, a staff photographer for the Division of Tourism, worked for 15 years as a locomotive engineer. His freelance clients include magazines, ad agencies, calendar publishers, textbook companies, and others. He has published several photographic books, including *Covered Bridges in West Virginia* and *The State Parks of West Virginia*. In 2005, he published *Wonders of West Virginia* with Jeanne Mozier and *West Virginia Impressions* with Bryan Lemasters.

D. B. Shawver, who studied at the North Carolina School of the Arts and graduated from Concord College, works for the West Virginia Coalition against Domestic Violence. She has published freelance art criticism and reviews in the *Charleston Daily Mail* and elsewhere.

L. Wayne Sheets, a native of Pocahontas County, was educated at Fairmont State with graduate study at WVU. A retired corporate pilot and air traffic controller, he freelances for newspapers and *Goldenseal*. He lives in Elkins.

Mike Shingleton is assistant chief of cold-water fish management with the Division of Natural Resources. He earned a B.S. from WVU and an M.S. from Frostburg State University, Maryland, in fisheries management.

Peter Silitch grew up near Louisville in the log house of Col. William Christian, an officer at the Battle of Point Pleasant. He earned a B.S. in philosophy and physics and is active in small-business economic development in Braxton County.

Donald C. Simmons Jr., executive director of the South Dakota Humanities Council, earned a Ph.D. from the University of Denver. He has written on Latin America and the Caribbean and on ex-Confederate settlements in British Honduras.

Gordon Simmons, who has lived in Charleston most of his life, is a well-known book man. Now an assistant editor at *Goldenseal*, he has worked as a bookseller, publisher, librarian, and adjunct instructor in philosophy at Marshall.

Jaime Simmons is a library assistant at the State Archives.

Jean Simpson of Charleston owned the General Seafood restaurant for many years, including the time it was housed in the old *Edwards Moonlight* showboat. She attended Flagler College, Florida.

Josephine Lilly Singer was born at Jumping Branch, Summers County. She lives on a small farm outside Milton, and in her 80s works as a caregiver to other seniors.

Jason Siniscalchi earned a Ph.D. in the Recreation, Parks & Tourism Resources program at WVU. He authored the Social Assessment of the Monongahela National Forest in 2004.

Janice Cale Sisler, a native of Bruceton Mills, is president of the Preston County Historical Society. Her research on the county and its people has resulted in several books, as well as articles, speeches, and storytelling.

Dean Six, a native of Ritchie County, is a graduate of WVU law school. He has written many articles and books about glass and china. He co-founded the West Virginia Museum of American Glass in Weston.

James Slack of Hurricane was an adjunct English instructor at Southern West Virginia Community College while attending Marshall University Graduate College. He is a poet and aspiring novelist.

Allison Smith, a daughter of Rob and Judie Smith of Charleston, was in 2005 a student at Charleston Catholic High School.

Barbara Smith, a writer and editor, chaired the Division of Humanities at Alderson-Broaddus College. She has published more than 300 poems, stories, and articles, and written and edited books of fiction and non-fiction.

Barbara Ellen Smith, past director of the Center for Research on Women at the University of Memphis, now holds a similar position at Virginia Tech. She earned a Ph.D. in sociology from Brandeis University, Massachusetts.

Chuck Smith, who has a Ph.D from the University of Kentucky, came to West Virginia as a VISTA worker. He teaches political science at West Virginia State University and has published on court politics, protection of religious liberty, and other subjects.

Jack H. Smith, a Charleston native, is an architectural and structural draftsman. He has worked as a motorcycle mechanic, written articles for *Fine Scale Modeler* magazine, and published four books on air force history.

Jean Edward Smith is the John Marshall Professor at Marshall University and author of *John Marshall: Definer of a Nation* and *Grant*, which was a Pulitzer Prize finalist. A Mississippi native, he taught at the University of Toronto for 33 years.

Jessica Smith, a daughter of Rob and Judie Smith of Charleston, was in 2005 a student at Charleston Catholic High School.

Judie Smith worked as a writer and researcher for *The West Virginia Encyclopedia*. Educated at Marshall and the University of Charleston, she also once worked as news editor and graphics editor of the *Charleston Daily Mail*.

Mariwyn McClain Smith, educated at Davis & Elkins College, was editor and co-publisher of the *Parsons Advocate*. She and her husband and son operate McClain Printing Company in Parsons, the publisher of many West Virginia books.

Shirley A. Smith was educated at Ohio State and Case Western Reserve, Ohio. She worked at the Kanawha County Public Library and was a field consultant for the state Library Commission.

Stephen G. Smith earned an M.A. in history from James Madison University and a Ph.D. from WVU. He has researched the Civil War in the South Branch Valley.

Anna Egan Smucker is the author of children's books, including *No Star Nights* based on her Weirton childhood. She also wrote *A History of West Virginia*, a book for adult new readers published by the West Virginia Humanities Council, and has published many poems. Educated at Carlow College, Pennsylvania, and Michigan State, she has worked as a teacher and children's librarian.

Kim Smucker is director of corporate and foundation giving and part-time teacher of German at Alderson-Broaddus College. He was educated at Michigan State and once worked as a freelance writer for MacMillan and McGraw-Hill publishing companies.

Mark A. Snell is director of the George Tyler Moore Center for the Study of the Civil War at Shepherd University, where he teaches courses on the Civil War and U.S. history. He is a retired army officer and former professor at West Point.

James F. Snyder, educated at Kent State and George Peabody College for Teachers in Tennessee, is retired from the state Department of Education. He has authored or co-authored numerous publications concerning industrial arts and technology education.

Mark F. Sohn, a Pikeville (Kentucky) College psychology professor since 1975, is also a specialist in regional foods. He has earned four degrees, including a Ph.D., and is the author of several books, including *Appalachian Home Cooking*.

Diana Sole is president of an electronic communications firm in Charleston. She was executive producer of a nationally broadcast documentary about the life of civil rights leader Leon Sullivan. A native of Weirton and graduate of Marshall, she recently produced a documentary about Sen. Robert C. Byrd.

Deborah J. Sonis, managing editor for *The West Virginia Encyclopedia*, is a native of Charleston. She was assistant editor at *Goldenseal* from 1988 to 1998 and worked previously in radio and advertising in West Virginia and Louisiana.

Larry Sonis, a Charleston native and former member of the House of Delegates, is president of Sonis Public Relations. He was a senior aide to U.S. Rep. David R. Obey and Florida Treasurer Bill Gunter. He was educated at Morris Harvey College.

J. E. Spears, born in Kentucky, has lived mostly in Elkins since 1953. She served three terms in the House of Delegates and three terms in the West Virginia Senate. She served on the visiting committee of the WVU College of Medicine.

Robert Y. Spence, a native of Logan, was educated at Marshall. The author of *Land of the Guyandot: A History of Logan County*, he contributed to *Goldenseal* and other publications that specialize in West Virginia history before his death in 2005.

Roger Spencer, who is employed by the Bayer Chemical Co. in New Martinsville, is also a freelance photographer. He is a regular contributor to *Wonderful West Virginia* and has had photographs published in calendars, travel brochures, cards, and other magazines.

Charles Sperow, a native of Berkeley County, earned a B.S. and an M.S. from WVU, where he is professor emeritus of agronomy. His 39-year career took him to all corners of the state.

Eleanor Spohr, a native New Yorker, moved to West Virginia in 1972. She lives in Huntington.

Sam Stack teaches the history and philosophy of education at WVU. He has authored numerous publications on the Arthurdale School and a biography of the progressive educator Elsie Ripley Clapp.

Margo Stafford, a former assistant editor of *Goldenseal*, was educated in theater and Medieval and Renaissance studies at WVU. She lives in Clarksburg and works for Ralph Pedersen Architect, concentrating on historic preservation.

Eileen Cain Stanley, a native of Ritchie County, is a graduate of Harrisville High School. She worked 25 years as a bookkeeper for a Charleston real estate office and later as office manager for the West Virginia Historical Education Foundation.

Teresa Statler-Keener, a native of Morgantown, is a research assistant at Old Dominion University in Norfolk. She earned a B.A. from WVU, an M.A. from Indiana University of Pennsylvania, and is completing a WVU history Ph.D.

John Edmund Stealey III, a native of Clarksburg, has a Ph.D. in history and other degrees from WVU. He has published extensively on West Virginia and Appalachia, including two books and more than 50 articles and reviews. He is a professor of history at Shepherd University.

Edward M. Steel, born in Nashville, graduated from Harvard and spent two years in the Army Air Corps before earning a Ph.D. at the University of North Carolina. He retired as a WVU history professor in 1983.

Rick Steelhammer, a reporter and columnist, has worked for the *Charleston Gazette* since 1973. He was educated at Antioch College, Ohio.

Rebecca Stelling, owner of Mountain Artisans, started the craft sales shop at the state Cultural Center in 1976 and served until 1991 as director of marketing and communications for the Division of Culture & History. She later worked for Tamarack.

Shirley L. Stewart was raised in Wyoming County. She has a B.S.J., M.S.W., and Ph.D from WVU, with a dissertation on mountain-top removal coal mining.

Craig W. Stihler coordinates endangered animal projects at the Division of Natural Resources. A Michigan native, he earned a B.S. from Michigan State and an M.S. in wildlife biology from the University of Massachusetts.

Carrie Stollings is a freelance writer living in Charleston. She has had articles published in *West Virginia MD News* and *Wonderful West Virginia* magazines.

Jerry D. Stover, a native of Boone County and president of the Clay County Historic Landmarks Commission, is a retired teacher with an interest in local history. He was the 1994 West Virginia Teacher of the Year and received the Milken Family Foundation National Teacher Award in 1997.

Walton Danforth Stowell Jr., a native of Harpers Ferry, is vice president of the local Historic Landmarks Commission. He has a master's degree in architecture from Savannah College of Art and Design and works in architecture, historic preservation, landscaping, gardening, and environmental design.

Philip Sturm is professor of history and chairs the Humanities Division at Ohio Valley University. He was West Virginia Professor of the Year in 2000. He earned a Ph.D. in American history and Appalachian studies from WVU.

Benjamin Sullivan was educated at the University of Kentucky and earned a law degree from WVU. He practices law in his native Charleston.

Debra K. Sullivan was educated at the University of Virginia and University of Pittsburgh. She moved to West Virginia in 1978 and has worked in public and private education at the classroom, school, county, and state levels. She was a lay member of the Lawyers' Disciplinary Committee and of the Visiting Committee for the WVU law school.

Ken Sullivan is editor of *The West Virginia Encyclopedia* and executive director of the West Virginia Humanities Council. He was educated in history at the University of Virginia and University of Rochester, with a Ph.D. from the University of Pittsburgh.

Gerald W. Sutphin was educated at Mullens High School and at Marshall. Formerly an army officer and a civilian employee of the Army Corps of Engineers before opening his own business, he is an expert on river history and riverboats.

David Sutton grew up in the Swiss community of Helvetia, Randolph County. He is a graduate of Davis & Elkins College and WVU, and a past archivist with the Balch Institute for Ethnic Studies in Philadelphia. He wrote a history of Helvetia.

Tommy Swaim is a Morgan County native and a building contractor. A former Morgan County sheriff, he is a county commissioner. He has traced the movements of both colonial and Civil War troops in the Eastern Panhandle.

Gordon L. Swartz III, a native West Virginian, is a coal miner and contributor to *Goldenseal*. He has written numerous articles on coal mining and other subjects and an unpublished historical novel. He has a master's degree from WVU.

John R. Swartz pastored churches in West Virginia for more than 20 years. He serves on the ministerial team at Grant County's North Fork Mennonite Church and works in curriculum development for Christian Light Publications of Virginia.

Gerald D. Swick writes a weekly history column for the Clarksburg *Exponent-Telegram* and has written for the *Encyclopedia of World War II*, as well as *Lincoln Lore* magazine and other publications. He is a Clarksburg native, educated at Fairmont.

Ray Swick, a Parkersburg native, was educated at Marietta College and the University of Virginia, with a history Ph.D. from Miami University, Ohio. He became historian for the Blennerhassett Historical Park Commission in 1979 and historian of the West Virginia state park system in 1989.

Larry N. Sypolt is a historian at the WVU Institute for the History of Technology & Industrial Archaeology. He was educated at WVU and the University of South Carolina. His publications include *Preservation Resource Guide for Public Works Managers* and a bibliography of the Civilian Conservation Corps.

I. D. "Duke" Talbott, professor emeritus at Glenville State College, earned a history Ph.D. from WVU. A student of African, African-American, and West Virginia history, he has also taught at Marshall, WVU, Fairmont State, and West Virginia Wesleyan.

Borgon Tanner, a native West Virginian, has a background in map making, printing, and photography. Retired, he collects books and gathers material about early transportation in West Virginia. He lives in rural Maine.

Pam Tarr is an attorney with the firm of Jackson Kelly. She earned her undergraduate and law degrees at WVU. She lives in Charleston.

Linda Tate, who earned a Ph.D. from University of Wisconsin and teaches English at Shepherd University, co-founded Shepherd's Appalachian Heritage Project. She was West Virginia's 2003 Professor of the Year.

Bobby Taylor is the library manager at the State Archives. He coordinates the Vandalia and Appalachian String Band Music Festival music competitions, both sponsored by the Division of Culture & History. He is a fourth-generation

West Virginia fiddler and 1977 state fiddle champion.

John Craft Taylor, a native of Pennsylvania, earned a J.D. from Duke and a history Ph.D. from Penn State. His interests include the Civil War, geography of karst in the Appalachians, and Pendleton County. He teaches at Union College, Kentucky.

Barbara Wilkie Tedford, a native of North Carolina, graduated from Maryville (Tennessee) College, University of Tennessee, and University of Pittsburgh, where she earned a Ph.D. She taught English at Davis & Elkins, Robert Morris College in Illinois, and Glenville State.

Cora P. Teel, the archivist and manuscripts librarian at Marshall University, has degrees from Marshall and University of South Carolina.

Noel W. Tenney, an Upshur County native, is a cultural specialist and instructor with the West Virginia Folklife Center at Fairmont State University. A graduate of Concord College and West Virginia Wesleyan, he is an officer of the Upshur County Historical Society.

William D. Theriault earned a Ph.D. from George Washington University. He volunteers with the Jefferson County Historic Landmarks Commission and has written extensively on local history. He has served on the West Virginia Humanities Council board of directors.

James Thibeault, born in Massachusetts and educated at the University of New Haven, Connecticut, and WVU, came to West Virginia as a VISTA worker. He founded Cabin Creek Quilts Co-op and spearheaded the Malden Historic District development.

Jerry Bruce Thomas, a professor of history at Shepherd University, earned a B.A. from WVU and a Ph.D. in U.S. history from the University of North Carolina. He wrote *An Appalachian New Deal: West Virginia in the Great Depression*.

Dean K. Thompson was senior pastor of the First Presbyterian Church of Charleston and is now president of Louisville Presbyterian Theological Seminary. He is a graduate of Marshall, and has two master's degrees and a Ph.D. in church history from Union Theological Seminary, Richmond.

Arline R. Thorn, a native of Mason County, earned a B.A. from Marshall and a Ph.D. in comparative literature from the University of Illinois. She is a professor of English at West Virginia State, a Holocaust scholar, and a poet.

Cheryl B. Torsney, who teaches English at WVU, specializes in 19th-century American literature, women writers, and cultural studies. She has written or edited books on Constance Fenimore Woolson, Henry James, and quilting.

Patrick D. Trader, born in Kansas City, was educated in anthropology at the University of Missouri. He was senior archeologist at the West Virginia Historic Preservation Unit and is now a staff archeologist at the University of Kentucky.

Stephen D. Trail, of Hinton, was educated at Marshall and Radford universities. He is the author of *History of Pence Springs Hotel* and other publications. He retired as sanitarian for Mercer and Monroe counties and now teaches at Mountain State University.

Ivan M. Tribe, who teaches at the University of Rio Grande, Ohio, earned a Ph.D. in American history from the University of Toledo. He is the author of *Mountaineer Jamboree: Country Music in West Virginia*, as well as a book on the Stoneman family musicians and many articles on early country music.

Joe William Trotter Jr., a McDowell County native, is Mellon Professor of History at Carnegie Mellon University. He was educated at Carthage College, Wisconsin, with an M.A. and a Ph.D. from University of Minnesota. His publications include *Coal, Class, and Color: Blacks in Southern West Virginia, 1915–32*.

John Unger, a Martinsburg native, represents Berkeley County in the state senate. He was educated at WVU and the University of Hong Kong, and attended Oxford as a Rhodes Scholar.

Fawn Valentine, of Greenbrier County, has lived in West Virginia since 1972. She wrote *West Virginia Quilts and Quiltmakers*, a book resulting from the West Virginia Heritage Quilt Search. She was educated at Concord College and Hollins University.

Linda Van Meter was born in Williamson and lives there today. She is a former teacher and restaurateur, and is active in the local railroad museum and historical society.

Jim Vanderhorst is an ecologist for the Division of Natural Resource's Natural Heritage Program. He works on classification, documentation, and conservation of the state's natural communities.

John C. Veasey, a Florida native, has been with the Fairmont *Times West Virginian* since graduating from WVU in 1959. He was sports editor, news editor, and managing editor before becoming editor in 1975.

Wallace Venable, born in Pittsburgh, came to West Virginia in 1964 as a doctoral student. He taught engineering mechanics at WVU for more than 30 years. He is a river enthusiast and student of glass.

Christy Venham, a graduate of WVU, works there as an archivist. She also teaches online classes on West Virginia topics through the WVU Department of Extended Learning.

Mary Dunkle Voorhees, a native West Virginian, once taught preschoolers with disabilities. She has a Ph.D. from the University of Virginia, where she teaches in the early childhood special education program.

Jim Wallace was educated in journalism at Ohio State. Now at TSG Consultants, he has worked for radio stations in Ohio and West Virginia and for the *Charleston Daily Mail*, earning awards in broadcast and print journalism.

J. W. George Wallace, a native Virginian, is editor and publisher of the *Brooke County Review* and past president of the West Virginia Press Association. He spent 30 years as a professional fundraiser before returning to the newspaper field.

Altina L. Waller teaches history at the University of Connecticut. She is best known as the author of *Feud: Hatfields, McCoys and Social Change in Appalachia*.

Barry Ward, retired from WVU, taught folklore in the English department for three decades. He has published in the areas of vernacular architecture, folk drama, folk music, and traditional arts.

Ken Ward is an award-winning investigative reporter at the *Charleston Gazette,* where he has worked since 1991. He is a native of Piedmont, Mineral County, and a graduate of WVU.

Ann Warner of Hampshire County has taught high school and college in Missouri and West Virginia. She is past president of the West Virginia English Language Arts Council.

Olive Watson, a lifelong West Virginian, is a retired schoolteacher and librarian. She is working with the National Road Alliance of West Virginia to restore the National Road to historic prominence.

Susan M. Weaver, director of library services and associate professor at Kent State University, East Liverpool (Ohio) campus, formerly worked at the Museum of Ceramics in East Liverpool.

Jon Weems, a native of Massachusetts, is an arboretum specialist at WVU. He was educated at Colby College, Maine, and WVU. A West Virginian since 1972, he has written several articles about trees and related topics.

Deborah R. Weiner, who earned a history Ph.D. at WVU, is research historian and family history coordinator at the Jewish Museum of Maryland. Her book, *Coalfield Jews: An Appalachian History*, will be published by the University of Illinois Press.

Kenneth B. Welliver is Workman Professor of Religion, emeritus, at West Virginia Wesleyan. Joining the Wesleyan faculty in 1964 after doctoral studies at Yale, he taught religion and the humanities and was vice president for academic affairs.

Sandy Wells is a Huntington native and graduate of Marshall. She is a feature writer and columnist for the *Charleston Gazette,* where she started in 1963.

Robert D. Whipkey was educated in forestry at WVU and started his career with the West Virginia Division of Forestry in 1969. In 1987 he became assistant state forester.

Paula D. White, a native of Logan County, earned an M.F.A. from Marshall with additional studio work at the Pennsylvania Academy of Fine Arts.

Mike Whiteford, a Fairmont native and Fairmont State graduate, has worked in the *Charleston Gazette* sports department since 1973, covering professional baseball and other subjects.

Cassandra Bolyard Whyte, who earned a Ph.D. from WVU, is vice president for administrative affairs at West Virginia State University. She has held various administrative and teaching positions in higher education since 1970.

Harry V. Wiant Jr., born in Burnsville, earned forestry degrees from WVU, University of Georgia, and Yale. He retired as forestry professor at WVU in 1996 and has authored many professional publications. He is the only West Virginian to have served as president of the Society of American Foresters.

Brett Williams wrote *John Henry: A Bio-Bibliography*, which includes historical and biographical background and a bibliography and discography of John Henry materials. She is an anthropologist at American University, Wahington.

Danny Williams, a Wayne County native, lives in Morgantown. He worked as folk arts specialist at the Division of Culture & History and editor at West Virginia University Press. He plays and teaches Appalachian music.

E. DeWitt Williams, a genealogist, historian, and former librarian, lives in Ripley.

John Alexander Williams attended Greenbrier County schools and earned degrees from Tulane and Yale. His books include *West Virginia: A Bicentennial History* and *Appalachia: A History*. He teaches history at Appalachian State University in North Carolina.

J. W. Williamson was editor of the *Appalachian Journal* from its founding in 1972 until his 2000 retirement. Among other publications, he wrote *Hillbillyland: What the Movies Did to the Mountains and What the Mountains Did to the Movies*.

Meredith Sue Willis grew up in Shinnston and now lives in New Jersey. A writer and teacher, she has published 14 books, including fiction for adults and children.

Jack Wills, professor emeritus at Fairmont State University, was born in Raleigh County and earned a Ph.D. from the University of Delaware. He has published articles on Byron, Charlotte Bronte, Goldsmith, Samuel Johnson, and West Virginia folklore.

Elizabeth Jill Wilson was press secretary to Governor Caperton during his second term and edited his official papers. Born in Morgantown and educated at WVU, she has worked in print and broadcast journalism for the Associated Press and others. She is past president of the West Virginia Humanities Council.

Michael K. Wilson, a Clay County native, is senior historian at the state Department of Transportation. He was educated at Glenville State College, WVU, and Marshall University Graduate College.

Rick Wilson grew up in Milton and was educated at Marshall. He is director of the American Friends Service Committee West Virginia Economic Justice Project.

Kelly Winters is the author of *Walking Home: A Woman's Pilgrimage on the Appalachian Trail*. She lives in Bayville, New York.

Jane Siers Winton, a native of Cabell County, earned a B.A. and M.A. at Marshall. She has spent 25 years in the public sector, specializing in fundraising and communications for nonprofit organizations.

Bill Wintz, a descendant of Kanawha Valley pioneers and a Union Carbide retiree, is active in historical and preservation societies. In 1979 he was honored by the American Association for State & Local History and in 1994 was named Historian of the Year by the West Virginia Historical Society.

Robert B. Wolford, a lifelong Hampshire Countian, was educated at Shepherd College and California University of Pennsylvania. He began teaching sociology at Potomac State College in 1998.

Don C. Wood, a genealogist and preservationist, studied at Shepherd College. He was a leader in the restoration of the Belle Boyd house and the Morgan Morgan cabin, and other preservation efforts. He is president of the Berkeley County Historical Society and chairman of the local Historic Landmarks Commission.

Douglas McClure Wood has a B.S. in wildlife management from WVU and has been a Department of Environmental Protection researcher since 1977.

Jim Wood, born in Wyoming County, is former editor of the Beckley *Register-Herald* and the *Raleigh Register*. Educated at Woodrow Wilson High School and the University of Kentucky, he is the author of family histories and local histories.

Bettie S. Woodward, born and raised in Lewisburg, taught at the Greenbrier College for Women for ten years. She was educated at George Peabody College for Teachers in Tennessee. She retired from Miami University of Ohio and now enjoys her Greenbrier County farm.

Warren J. Woomer, a Charleston chemical engineer and industry historian, was senior principal engineer at Union Carbide's Institute plant. He was the works manager at Bhopal, India, 1980–82, and a member of the company's investigation team after the 1984 Bhopal tragedy.

Hazel P. Wooster, now retired, was educated at West Virginia State and Marshall. At Charleston's Chandler Elementary School she taught the first special education class in Kanawha County.

Michael Edward Workman, born in Fayette County, was an underground coal miner before earning a B.A., M.A., and Ph.D. at WVU. He has worked for the National Park Service and the Institute for the History of Technology & Industrial Archaeology at WVU. His publishes on the history of the coal and steel industries, historic preservation, industrial archeology, and labor history.

Tim L. Wyatt, a Wyoming County native with an M.A. from WVU, retired after 35 years of teaching high school history in Virginia. He is the author of a history of the West Virginia boys' basketball tournament and helped to win the 1955 state championship for Mullens High School.

H. G. Young III teaches music history and theory and conducts the college chorale at WVU-Parkersburg. A Clendenin native, he earned a B.S. from West Virginia Wesleyan, an M.A. from WVU, and a Ph.D. from the University of Florida.

Richard K. Zimmerman is an extension specialist in horticulture and a professor of plant sciences at WVU. He joined the Extension Service in 1972 and works at the WVU Tree Fruit Research & Education Center in Kearneysville.

ILLUSTRATION CREDITS

We thank those who supplied the many photographs and other illustrations used in *The West Virginia Encyclopedia*. Our abbreviations are as follows: Charleston Newspapers (CN); State Historic Preservation Office (SHPO); West Virginia Division of Culture & History (WVDC&H); West Virginia Division of Natural Resources (WVDNR); West Virginia Division of Tourism (WVDT); West Virginia State Archives (WVSA); West Virginia & Regional History Collection (WV&RHC); West Virginia University Libraries (WVU Libraries).

A: p.1, courtesy David H. Martin / p.2, photo by James Harding, courtesy SHPO / p.5, photo by Steve Shaluta, WVDT / p.8, courtesy WV Air National Guard / p.11, photo by Craig Stihler, courtesy WVDNR / p.13, from T. C. Crawford, *An American Vendetta* (New York, Chicago & San Francisco: Belford, Clarke & Co., 1889) / p.14, Thomas Anshutz, 1880, oil on canvas, courtesy Fine Arts Museums of San Francisco, gift of Mr. and Mrs. John D. Rockefeller III / p.21, photo by Michael Keller, WVDC&H / p.22, from Edward V. McMichael, *Introduction to West Virginia Archeology* (Morgantown: WV Geological & Economic Survey, 1968) / p.25, photo by Tim Sinn, courtesy SHPO / p.25, photo by Michael Keller, courtesy SHPO / p.27, courtesy Arthurdale Heritage, Inc. / p.28, courtesy Maryland Historical Society / p.33, courtesy Junior Meadows.

B: p.34, courtesy Larry Levine / p.35, courtesy Ivan Tribe and *Goldenseal* (July–Sept. 1977) / p.37, photo by William Trevey, courtesy George Bragg / p.38, photo by J. J. Young, courtesy *Goldenseal* (Summer 2001) / p.39, photo by Pam Hutton, courtesy *Goldenseal* (Fall 1989) / p.40, courtesy Doug Bumgardner / p.43, photo by David Fattaleh, WVDT / p.44, courtesy WVSA / p.47, courtesy American Media, Inc., reprinted by permission / p.50, courtesy Bettijane Burger / p.51, courtesy Hollins University / p.53, courtesy SHPO / p.55, photo by Steve Shaluta, WVDT / p.57, photo by Michael Keller, courtesy *Goldenseal* (Fall 1992) / p.59, courtesy Maslowski Wildlife Productions / p.61, courtesy Maslowski Wildlife Productions / p.63, photo by Steve Shaluta, WVDT / p.64, map by Heidi Perov / p.65, photo by Michael Keller, WVDC&H / p.66, photo by Steve Shaluta, WVDT / p.67, courtesy WVSA, Blizzard Collection / p.69, courtesy Eastern Regional Coal Archives / p.71, photo by Gerald S. Ratliff, courtesy WVSA, Department of Commerce Collection / p.74, photo by Michael Keller, WVDC&H / p.75, courtesy WVSA / p.76, from P. D. Strausbaugh & Earl L. Core, *Flora of West Virginia* (Reprint, Morgantown: Seneca Books, 1993) / p.81, photo by Steve Shaluta, WVDT / p.83, photo by David Bowen, courtesy WV Division of Highways / p.84, artwork by Duane

Raver, U.S. Fish & Wildlife Service / p.86, courtesy WV&RHC, WVU Libraries, Strother Collection / p.87, courtesy WVSA, Emil Varney Collection / p.90, photo by Earl Benton / p.91 courtesy *Charleston Gazette* / p.94, photo by Thomas J. Allen, courtesy WVDNR / p.95, courtesy office of Sen. Robert C. Byrd.

C: p.98, photo by Michael Keller, WVDC&H / p.102, courtesy WVSA / p.103, courtesy The Greenbrier / p.104, photo by Michael Keller, WVDC&H / p.108, courtesy WVSA / p.110, photo by Roger Spencer / p.113, map by Heidi Perov / p.113, courtesy WVSA, Carpenter Family Collection / p.115, courtesy WVSA / p.117, photo by Steve Shaluta, WVDT / p.118, photo by Ed McCarthy / p.119, courtesy Wheeling Civic Center / p.119, photo by Michael Keller, WVDC&H / p.123, photo by David Fattaleh, WVDT / p.124, photo by Steve Shaluta, WVDT / p.128, photo by Thomas K. Pauley, Marshall University / p.130, photo by William E. Barrett, 1978, courtesy Historic American Engineering Record, Library of Congress / p.131, courtesy WVSA, Gauley Bridge Historical Society Collection / p.132, courtesy CSX Transportation / p.134, courtesy CN / p.138, from *Harper's Weekly* (July 1861), courtesy WVSA / p.142, photo by Michael Keller, courtesy Clay Center / p.144, photo by Tim Sinn, courtesy SHPO / p.144, courtesy Franklin Cleckley / p.147, courtesy Norfolk Southern [nw189] Digital Library & Archives, University Libraries, Virginia Polytechnic Institute & State University / p.151, photo by Melvin Grubb, Grubb Photo Service / p.154, courtesy CN / p.156, from National Archives, Records of the Solid Fuels Administration for War [ARC identifier 540275] courtesy Mark Crabtree / p.157, photo by Red Ribble, courtesy Mark Crabtree / p.157, photo by Doug Chadwick, courtesy *Goldenseal* (Jan.–Mar. 1980) / p.158, courtesy Concord University / p.160, courtesy WVSA / p.166, photo by Ken Cobb, courtesy Contemporary American Theater Festival / p.169, courtesy WVSA / p.173, courtesy WVSA, Carpenter Glassplates Collection / p.175, courtesy WV State University Library Archives / p.176, courtesy Historic American Engineering Record, Library of Congress / p.177, photo by Michael Keller, courtesy *Goldenseal* (Winter 1994) / p.181, photo by William Crumb.

D: p.184, cover *Life* (July 16, 1951), courtesy Getty Images / p.185, used with permission of Davis & Elkins College / p.186, courtesy WVSA / p.187, courtesy WVSA / p.192, courtesy Bureau of Business & Economic Research, WVU / p.194, photographer unknown, courtesy *Goldenseal* (Winter 1990) / p.198, photo by Michael Keller, WVDC&H / p.199, photo by David Fattaleh, WVDT / p.201, photo by Michael Keller, courtesy *Goldenseal* (Summer 1986) / p.203,

map by Heidi Perov / p.205, from Irvin Dugan Papers, Special Collections, James E. Morrow Library, Marshall University / p. 206, courtesy *Wheeling News-Register* and *Goldenseal*.

E: p.208, photo by Melvin Grubb, Grubb Photo Service / p.209, photo by Steve Shaluta, WVDT / p.212, courtesy WVSA, Marion County Historical Society Collection / p.215, courtesy WVSA / p.217, photo by David Fattaleh, WVDT / p.219, courtesy Maslowski Wildlife Productions.

F: p.225, photo by Gerald S. Ratliff, courtesy WVSA & *Goldenseal* (Fall 1997) / p.227, photo by Gary Lake / p.230, courtesy CN / p.231, courtesy WVSA / p.233, photo by Steve Shaluta, WVDT / p.236, from P.D. Strausbaugh & Earl L. Core, *Flora of West Virginia* (Reprint, Morgantown: Seneca Books, 1993) / p.238, National Archives [16-G-278-1-S-6757-C] courtesy WVU Libraries / p.238, photo by Michael Keller, WVDC&H / p.240, photo by Michael Keller, courtesy *Goldenseal* (Spring 1987) / p.241, photo by David Fattaleh, WVDT / p.243, courtesy WVSA / p.245, courtesy AP/Wide World Photos / p.249, photo by Michael Keller, courtesy *Goldenseal* (Spring 1999) / p.254, copyright 1971, Columbia Pictures, courtesy *Goldenseal* (Summer 1995) / p.255, courtesy WVSA, U.S. Forest Service Collection / p.259, courtesy WVSA / p.263, courtesy WVSA.

G: p.268, photo by Richard Phillips, courtesy WV State Folk Festival & *Goldenseal* (Summer 2000) / p.269, courtesy Ohio University Press, publishers of Ancella R. Bickley & Lynda Ann Ewen, eds., *Memphis Tennessee Garrison: The Remarkable Story of a Black Appalachian Woman* (Athens, 2001) / p.280, courtesy Gary Coberly / p.280, courtesy WVDNR / p.281, photo by Steve Shaluta, WVDT / p.282, courtesy WVSA / p.284, courtesy WVSA / p.287, courtesy *Goldenseal* (Spring 1996) / p.288, courtesy WVSA / p.289, photo by David Fattaleh, WVDT / p.291, photo by Michael Keller, WVDC&H / p.293, photo by David Fattaleh, WVDT / p.295, courtesy WVSA, Mary Behner Christopher Collection / p.299, photo by Steve Shaluta, WVDT / p.302, courtesy The Greenbrier / p.304, by M. D. Arnold, 1928 [No. 110478] USDA Pomological Watercolor Collection, Special Collections, National Agricultural Library.

H: p.307, courtesy WVSA / p.310, photo by Steve Shaluta, WVDT / p.312, photo by Steve Shaluta, WVDT / p.315, photo by Steve Shaluta, WVDT / p.317, photo by Roger Spencer / p.319, photo by Roger Spencer / p.320, courtesy WVSA / p.321, courtesy WVSA / p.325, courtesy WVSA, Union Carbide Collection / p.326, photo by Michael Keller, WVDC&H / p.328, courtesy WVSA, Walter Aegerter Collection / p.329, photo by Michael Keller, courtesy *Goldenseal* (Summer

1996) / p.331, photo by James E. Harding, courtesy SHPO / p.335, from *Harper's Weekly* (July 6, 1861), courtesy WVSA / p.339, courtesy WVSA / p.341, courtesy WVSA, Bollinger Collection / p.345, photo by Michael Keller, courtesy *Goldenseal* (Winter 1984) / p.346, courtesy WVSA / p.349, photo by Jurgen Lorenzen, courtesy Bill Hopen / p.349 map by Jedediah Hotchkiss, from Peter W. Roper, *Jedediah Hotchkiss: Rebel Mapmaker and Virginia Businessman* (Shippensburg, PA: White Mane Publishers, 1992) / p.354, photo by Michael Keller, courtesy Jerry Shaffer & *Goldenseal* (Winter 2000) / p.355, photo by David Fattaleh, WVDT / p.357, courtesy WVSA, Union Carbide Collection.

I: p.359, Library of Congress, Prints & Photographs Division [LC-DIG-cwpb-06349] / p.363 courtesy WVDNR / p.365, photo by Steve Shaluta, WVDT / p.368, photo by Michael Keller, WVDC&H / p.370, photo by David Fattaleh, WVDT / p.371, photo by Michael Keller, WVDC&H.

J: p.372, photo by Ed Connors Jr. / p.373, courtesy WVSA / p.376, courtesy WVSA / p.379, photo by David Fattaleh, WVDT / p.382, courtesy *Goldenseal* (Spring 1990) / p.385, Library of Congress, Prints & Photographs Division [LC-F82-1234] / p.386, photo by Tom Screven, courtesy *Goldenseal* (Apr.–Sept. 1978) / p.386, map by Heidi Perov.

K: p.391, courtesy CN / p.392, courtesy State Museum / p.393, photo by Cheryl R. Marsh / p.395, courtesy WVSA / p.397, courtesy WVSA, Coal Life Collection / p.399, courtesy CN / p.401, courtesy WVSA / p.405, courtesy WVSA.

L: p.408, courtesy WVSA, Coal Life Collection / p.411, photo by Michael Keller, WVDC&H / p.413, courtesy *Goldenseal* (Spring 1982) / p.414, courtesy WVSA, Paul Skaff Collection / p.417, photo by Steve Shaluta, WVDT / p.417, courtesy Smithsonian American Art Museum / p.419, photo by Steve Shaluta, WVDT / p.421, photo by David Fattaleh, WVDT / p.425, photo by Ric MacDowell / p.427, with permission of Louis D. & Virginia Steele Grubb, courtesy *Goldenseal* (Summer 1985) / p.428, with permission of Diane Goode, artist, from Cynthia Rylant, *When I Was Young in the Mountains* (New York: E. P. Dutton, 1982) / p.429, courtesy WVSA, Robert Knotts Collection / p.433, photo by Steve Shaluta, WVDT / p.435, photo by Steve Shaluta, WVDT.

M: p.439, from William A. MacCorkle, *The Recollections of Fifty Years of West Virginia* (New York: G. P. Putnam's Sons, 1928) / p.440, photo by Steve Shaluta, WVDT / p.442, photo by Steve Shaluta, WVDT / p.443, photo by Rick Lee, courtesy office of Gov. Joe Manchin III / p.448, photo by Steve Shaluta, WVDT / p.449, courtesy WVSA / p.454, photo by Rick Haye, courtesy Marshall University / p.457, courtesy Marx Toy Museum / p.458, photo by Roger Spencer / p.460, photo by LeRoy Schultz / p.462, courtesy WVSA / p.464, courtesy WVSA / p.465, photo by

Michael Keller, WVDC&H / p.469, courtesy WVSA / p.470, courtesy WVSA / p.473, photo by David Fattaleh, WVDT / p.477, courtesy *Goldenseal* (Spring 1985) / p.481, photo by Michael Keller, WVDC&H / p.484, courtesy WVSA, Coal Life Collection / p.486, courtesy WVSA / p.488, photo by Volkmar Wentzel, courtesy Volkmar Wentzel Collection / p.490, photo by Roger Spencer / p.494, photo by Roger Spencer / p.496, courtesy WVSA / p.499, courtesy WVSA / p.501, photo by Gary Lake / p.502, courtesy *Huntington Quarterly* / p.506, photo by Michael Keller, courtesy *Goldenseal* (Summer 1995) / p.510, courtesy WVU Photographic Services / p.514, photo by Steve Shaluta, WVDT.

N: p.517, courtesy WVSA / p.519, photo by Steve Shaluta, WVDT / p.521, courtesy WVSA / p.526, courtesy WVSA / p.529, photo by Gary Lake / p.531, photo by Roger Spencer / p.535, photo by Steve Shaluta, WVDT / p.536, photo by Steve Shaluta, WVDT / p.539, courtesy E. I. du Pont de Nemours & Company, Belle.

O: p.541, photo by Michael Keller, courtesy *Goldenseal* (Fall 1989) / p.543, photo by David Fattaleh, WVDT / p.546, photo by Roger Spencer / p.548, photo by Lewis Hine, Library of Congress, Prints & Photographs Division [LC-USZ62-29142] / p.550, photo by Roger Spencer.

P: p.552, courtesy Richard Ammar / p.553, courtesy WVSA, Coal Life Collection / p.556, courtesy WVSA / p.557, courtesy WVSA / p.559, photo by Roger Spencer / p.563, photo by Steve Shaluta, WVDT / p.568, from P. D. Strausbaugh & Earl L. Core, *Flora of West Virginia* (Reprint, Morgantown: Seneca Books, 1993) / p.569, photo by Roger Spencer / p.571, photo by Roger Spencer / p.573, photo by David Fattaleh, WVDT / p.575, courtesy *Goldenseal* (July–Sept. 1979) / p.579, photo by Mark Turner / p.581, courtesy Agricultural Extension Division, WVU / p.585, photo by Roger Spencer / p.586, courtesy WVSA / p.588, courtesy CN / p.590, courtesy WVSA / p.592, photo by Cheryl R. Marsh.

Q: p.594, courtesy State Museum.

R: p.595, photo by Roger Spencer / p.597, photo by Jay Potter, courtesy *Goldenseal* (Fall 2004) / p.599, courtesy Glade Springs Hotel & Conference Resort / p.601, photo by Steve Shaluta, WVDT / p.602, courtesy CN / p.606, photo by Steve Shaluta, WVDT / p.608, photo by Michael Keller, WVDC&H / p.610, courtesy United Methodist Foundation of WV / p.613, courtesy WVSA, Cecil Underwood Collection / p.616, photo by Steve Shaluta, WVDT / p.617, map by Heidi Perov / p.619, photo by Roger Spencer / p.621, photo by C. R. Neale III, courtesy Madison Coal & Supply Company / p.623, photo by Jeff Fetty / p.625, courtesy WVSA / p.628, courtesy WV&RHC, WVU Libraries / p.631, courtesy Harrison Rural Electrification Association & *Goldenseal* (Summer 1989).

S: p.632, photo by Roger Spencer / p.634, courtesy *Goldenseal* (Spring 1983) / p.635, photo by Michael Keller, courtesy *Goldenseal* (Summer 1988) / p.638, photo by Gary Lake / p.640, courtesy WVSA, Meadow River Lumber Company Collection / p.642, courtesy CN / p.644, courtesy State Museum / p.648, photo by Gary Lake / p.650, courtesy Mary Lee Settle / p.653, courtesy *Goldenseal* (Spring 1988) / p.656, photo by Michael Keller, WVDC&H / p.660, photo by David Fattaleh, WVDT / p.662, courtesy WVSA / p.665, courtesy CN / p.668, courtesy Steve Shaluta, WVDT / p.670, courtesy *Charleston Daily Mail* / p.672, photo by Michael Keller, WVDC&H / p.673, photo by Gary Lake / p.675, courtesy *Goldenseal* (Winter 1991) / p.678, courtesy WVSA, WV State Police Collection / p.680, photo by Michael Keller, WVDC&H / p.683, courtesy WVSA / p.685, courtesy Harpers Ferry National Historical Park [Ref. #HF-1095] & *Goldenseal* (Spring 1990) / p.689, courtesy WV&RHC, WVU Libraries / p.690, photo by Steve Shaluta, WVDT / p.692, photo by Steve Shaluta, WVDT / p.696, courtesy SHPO.

T: p.698, photo by Roger Spencer / p.701, photo by Steve Shaluta, WVDT / p.704, courtesy WVSA, G. Walter Kibler Collection / p.707, courtesy WVSA, Meadow River Lumber Company Collection / p.710, photo by David Fattaleh, WVDT / p.712, courtesy SHPO / p.714, courtesy WVSA / p.717, photo by Steve Shaluta, WVDT / p.719, courtesy The Greenbrier / p.720, courtesy WVSA, Joseph H. Diss Debar Collection / p.722, photo by Michael Keller, WVDC&H.

U: p.724, courtesy WVSA / p.728, courtesy University of Charleston / p.729, photo by Duane Carpenter, courtesy WV Wesleyan / p.731, courtesy CN.

V: p.732, photo by Steve Shaluta, WVDT / p.734, photographer unknown, courtesy *Goldenseal* (Summer 1994) / p.736, courtesy SHPO / p.737, courtesy Morris Harvey Archives, University of Charleston.

W: p.741, photo by Steve Payne, courtesy *Goldenseal* (July–Sept. 1980) / p.743, courtesy Library of Congress, Prints & Photographs Division [LC-USZ62-49568] / p.746, photo by Roger Spencer / p.749, photo by Rick Lee, courtesy Camden Park / p.752, photo by David Fattaleh, WVDT / p.755, courtesy Weirton Steel & WVSA / p.755, photo by Russell Lee, courtesy National Archives, Records of the Solid Fuels Administration for War [ARC Identifier, 541004] / p.758, courtesy WVU Photographic Services / p.763, courtesy WVSA / p.767, courtesy WVDC&H / p.772, photo by Steve Shaluta, WVDT / p.774, courtesy WVSA, WV Turnpike Collection / p.775, courtesy WVU Photographic Services / p.779, photo by Michael Keller, WVDC&H / p.781, photo by Kim Berger / p.785, photo by Steve Shaluta, WVDT / p.788, from George W. Atkinson & Alvaro F. Gibbens, *Prominent Men of West Virginia* (Wheeling: W. L. Callin, 1890) / p.790, courtesy WVSA / p.792, photo by Steve Shaluta, WVDT / p.794, from P. D. Strausbaugh & Earl L. Core, *Flora of West Virginia* (Reprint, Morgantown: Seneca Books, 1993) / p.795, photo by Ron Snow / p.797, courtesy WVSA / p.800, courtesy WVSA / p.801, photo by Michael Keller, WVDC&H / p.801, photo by Michael Keller, WVDC&H / p.803, courtesy CN / p.807, photo by Michael Keller, WVDC&H / p.811, photo by A. Aubrey Bodine, copyright Jennifer B. Bodine / p.814, photo by David Fattaleh, WVDT.

Y: p.816, courtesy CN.

SIDEBAR CREDITS

A: p.4, **Coming to the new state**, from Booker T. Washington, *Up From Slavery* (New York: Doubleday, 1901) / p.15, "**Appalachia**," from *Appalachia* (Charleston: MHC Publications, 1977). Reprinted by permission / p.23, **Excavating the South Charleston mound**, from John P. Hale, *History of the Great Kanawha Valley* (Madison, WI: Brant, Fuller & Co. 1891) / p.29, "**This country will require much work**," from "Selections from the Journals of a Circuit Rider: The Reverend Francis Asbury," 1788, in Ronald L. Lewis & John C. Hennen Jr., eds., *West Virginia: Documents in the History of A Rural-Industrial State* (Dubuque, IA: Kendall/Hunt Pub. Co., 1991). Reprinted by permission.

B: p.36, "**Ballad of Mad Ann Bailey**," from Louise McNeill, *Gauley Mountain* (New York: Harcourt, Brace & Co., 1939) / p.47, **Batts and Fallam discover the New River**, from "The Expedition of Batts and Fallam," 1671, in Ronald L. Lewis and John C. Hennen Jr., eds., *West Virginia: Documents in the History of a Rural-Industrial State* (Dubuque, IA: Kendall/Hunt Pub. Co., 1991). Reprinted by permission / p.52, "**To give service to my country**," from Bonni V. McKeown, *Peaceful Patriot: The Story of Tom Bennett* (Charleston: Mountain State Press, 1980). Reprinted by permission / p.58, **Southern dead at the Battle of Bartow**, from "A Bivouac of the Dead," 1903, in *Ambrose Bierce's Civil War* (Chicago: Gateway Editions, 1956) / p.62, **Crusading for black lung reform**, from B. L. Dotson-Lewis, *Appalachia: Spirit Triumphant* (West Conshohocken, PA : Infinity, 2004). Reprinted by permission.

C: p.106, **Canaan comes back**, from Maurice Brooks, *The Appalachians* (Boston: Houghton Mifflin, 1965) / p.114, **Squirrelly Bill, Elk River fisherman**, from W.E.R. Byrne, *Tale of the Elk* (Charleston: West Virginia Pub. Co., 1940) / p.124, **Choosing the capital city**, from Booker T. Washington, *Up From Slavery* (New York: Doubleday, 1901) / p.153, **The medical situation is primitive**, from Helen B. Hiscoe, *Appalachian Passage* (Athens, GA: University of Georgia Press, 1991). Reprinted by permission / p.180, "**Claude Crozet**," from Louise McNeill, *Gauley Mountain* (New York: Harcourt, Brace & Co., 1939).

D: p.193, **Worse in Morgantown**, from James F. Dent, *The Dog with the Cold Nose* (Charleston: Jalamap, 1981). Reprinted by permission / p.193, **Contrary to the law of the land**, from Justice Marmaduke Dent, *Williams v. Board of Education*, 1898 / p.195, "**West Virginia, My Home**," Hazel Dickens (copyright Happy Valley Music, 1976). Reprinted by permission.

E: p.219, **King Coal**, from Thomas Dunn English, "The Three Kings," in *American Ballads* (New York: Harper & Brothers, 1879) / p.222, "**Be worthy of your game**," from George Bird Evans, *The Upland Shooting Life* (New York: Alfred A. Knopf, 1971).

F: p.235, **Split-rail fences**, from "The Mystery at Hillhouse," 1928, Melville Davisson Post, *Country Gentleman* (May & June, 1928) / p.250, **Singing was part of their lives**, from B. B. Maurer, ed., *Mountain Heritage* (Ripley: Mountain State Art & Craft Fair, 1974) / p.253, **Dinnertime at a mountain home**, from Gov. William A. MacCorkle, *The Recollections of Fifty Years of West Virginia* (New York: G. P. Putnam's Sons, 1928) / p.266, **On the border**, from "A Twilight Adventure," 1914, Melville Davisson Post, *Uncle Abner: Master of Mysteries* (New York: Appleton, 1918).

G: p.271, **Poke greens**, from Delmer Robinson, *Appalachian Hill Country Cook Book* (Charleston: Jalamap Pub., 1980). Reprinted by permission / p.278, **A thirsty ghost**, from Ruth Ann Musick, "The Glass Jug," in *Telltale Lilac Bush & Other West Virginia Ghost Tales* (Lexington: University of Kentucky Press, 1965). Reprinted by permission / p.282, "**It takes feeling for glass**," from A. O. Barnette, "A Practical Man's View of Glass Making," *Goldenseal* (Spring 1996).

H: p.323, **Murderland**, from T. C. Crawford, *An American Vendetta* (New York, Chicago & San Francisco: Belford, Clarke & Co., 1889) / p.333, **What is a hillbilly?** by Jim Comstock, Chesapeake & Potomac Telephone Company of West Virginia advertisement / p.351, **Not ready to change flags**, letter from Chester Hubbard to Waitman Willey, 1861, courtesy West Virginia & Regional History Collection, WVU Libraries.

K: p.398, **Last visit to Senator Kenna**, from Gov. William A. MacCorkle, *The Recollections of Fifty Years of West Virginia* (New York: G. P. Putnam's Sons, 1928).

L: p.428, *When I Was Young in the Mountains*, Cynthia Rylant (New York: E. P. Dutton, 1982). Reprinted by permission / p.432, **Logan's speech**, from Thomas Jefferson, *Notes on the State of Virginia*.

M: p.449, **Governor William C. Marland proposes the severance tax**, from Governor Marland, *State Papers and Public Addresses of William C. Marland*, Message to the 51st Legislature, January 22, 1953 / p.476, "**More than a thousand babies**," from Gretchen Moran Laskas, *The Midwife's Tale* (New York: Bantam Dell, 2003). Reprinted by permission / p.485, "**A rebellious and treasonous**

enterprise**,**" editorial, *Charleston Daily Mail*, 9/1/1921.

N: p.524, "**The best place to live**," from Phyllis Reynolds Naylor, *Shiloh* (New York: Atheneum Books for Young Readers, 1991). Reprinted by permission.

P: p. 578, **Twilight in the hills**, from "A Twilight Adventure," 1914, Melville Davisson Post, *Uncle Abner: Master of Mysteries* (New York: Appleton, 1918).

R: p.610, "**A call to preach**," from Booker T. Washington, *Up From Slavery* (New York: Doubleday, 1901) / p.614, **A revenuer remembers a busy year**, from "Gazette Special," *Charleston Gazette*, 1904.

S: p.643, **A Scotch-Irishman speaks of his own**, from Gov. William A. MacCorkle, *The Recollections of Fifty Years of West Virginia* (New York: G. P. Putnam's Sons, 1928) / p.661, **A former slave looks back**, from "Lizzie Grant: Narrative of a Former Slave," 1938, in Ronald L. Lewis & John C. Hennen Jr., eds., *West Virginia Documents in the History of a Rural-Industrial State* (Dubuque, IA: Kendall/Hunt Pub. Co., 1991). Reprinted by permission / p.663, **Politics in the Smoke Hole**, from West Virginia Writers' Project, Works Projects Administration, *Smoke Hole And Its People* (Charleston, 1940) / p.674, **After the Battle of Stanaford**, from Mary Field Parton, ed., *Autobiography of Mother Jones* (Chicago: C. H. Kerr & Co., 1925) / p.678, **A State Policeman recalls strike duty**, from "To Keep the Peace: Captain Charles W. Ray, State Policeman," *Goldenseal* (Oct.–Dec. 1980).

T: p.705, **The bishops size up Appalachia**, from "This Land Is Home To Me," (Prestonsburg, KY: Catholic Committee of Appalachia, 1975). Reprinted by permission / p.709, **The everlasting hills**, from Maurice Brooks, *The Appalachians* (Boston: Houghton Mifflin, 1965) / p. 715, **Big Trees**, courtesy William N. Grafton, WVU Extension Service.

U: p.723, **Uncle Abner**, from "The Angel of the Lord," 1911, Melville Davisson Post, *Uncle Abner: Master of Mysteries* (New York: Appleton, 1918).

V: p.739, **What VISTA stands for**, from Denise Giardina, *The Unquiet Earth* (New York: W. W. Norton & Co., 1992). Reprinted by permission.

W: p. 744, "**Wise beyond his generation**," from Gov. William A. MacCorkle, *The Recollections of Fifty Years of West Virginia* (New York: G. P. Putnam's Sons, 1928) / p.758, **I Dare Not Say I Love the Lord**, 1950, from Don West, *In the Land of Plenty* (Los Angeles: West End Press, 1982) / p. 765, "**The West Virginia Hills**" (Layout

copyright 2005 by Mark D. Templeton) / p.782,
Coal Tattoo, from Billy Edd Wheeler, *Song of a
Woods Colt* (Anderson, SC: Droke House, 1969).
Reprinted by permission / p.809, **Dyed-in-the-
wool loggers**, from W. E. Blackhurst, *Riders of
the Flood* (Parsons: McClain Pub., 1954).

The names of wild plants and animals included in articles in *The West Virginia Encyclopedia* are listed below. They are alphabetized by the common name, in English to the left, with the scientific name in Latin to the right. Some show more than one scientific name because the common name is shared by more than one species.

The list of scientific names is based on the most current information available and was reviewed and corrected by Barbara Sargent of the Wildlife Resources Section of the West Virginia Division of Natural Resources in Elkins.

COMMON NAME	SCIENTIFIC NAME
Acadian flycatcher	*Empidonax virescens*
adder's tongue fern	*Ophioglossum vulgatum; O. pusillum*
akebia	*Akebia quinata*
alder	*Alnus spp.*
alder-leaved buckthorn	*Rhamnus alnifolia*
alfalfa	*Medicago sativa ssp. sativa*
Allegheny flyback grass	*Danthonia compressa*
Allegheny wild onion	*Allium alleghieniense*
Allegheny Menziesia	*Menziesia pilosa*
Allegheny sloe	*Prunus alleghaniensis*
Allegheny woodrat	*Neotoma magister*
American beech	*Fagus grandifolia*
American bison	*Bos bison*
American chestnut	*Castanea dentata*
American crow	*Corvus brachyrhynchos*
American eel	*Anguilla rostrata*
American lily-of-the-valley	*Convallaria majuscula*
American toad	*Bufo americanus*
anemone	*Anemone spp.*
aphid	*Homoptera*
Appalachia darter	*Percina gymnocephala*
Appalachian blue violet	*Viola appalachiensis*
Appalachian cottontail	*Sylvilagus obscurus*
Appalachian oak fern	*Gymnocarpium appalachianum*
arbor-vitae	*Thuja occidentalis*
ash	*Fraxinus spp.*
aspen	*Populus grandidentata; P. tremuloides*
Atlantis fritillary	*Speyeria atlantis*
autumn olive	*Elaeagnus umbellata var. parviflora*
azalea	*Rhododendron spp.*
bald eagle	*Haliaeetus leucocephalus*
balsam fir	*Abies balsamea*
balsam squaw-weed	*Packera paupercula*
banded darter	*Etheostoma zonale*
Barbara's buttons	*Marshallia grandiflora*
bark beetle	*Coleoptera*
barn owl	*Tyto alba*
Bartram's serviceberry	*Amelanchier bartramiana*
basswood	*Tilia americana var. americana*
beaked hazelnut	*Corylus cornuta var. cornuta*
beaked rush	*Rhynchospora alba; R. recognita; R. capitellata*
beaver	*Castor canadensis*
bedstraw	*Galium spp.*
bellwort	*Uvularia spp.*
belted kingfisher	*Ceryle alcyon*
big bluestem	*Andropogon gerardii*
big brown bat	*Eptesicus fuscus*
bigmouth chub	*Nocomis platyrhynchus*
bird-foot violet	*Viola pedata*
bishop's cap	*Mitella diphylla*
bitter-dock	*Rumex obtusifolius*
bitternut	*Carya cordiformis*
bittersweet	*Solanum dulcamara var. dulcamara*
black ash	*Fraxinus nigra*
black bear	*Ursus americanus*

COMMON NAME	SCIENTIFIC NAME
black birch	*Betula lenta*
black bullhead	*Ameiurus melas*
black cherry	*Prunus serotina*
black chokeberry	*Photinia melanocarpa*
black cohosh	*Actaea racemosa var. racemosa*
black crappie	*Pomoxis nigromaculatus*
black elderberry	*Sambucus nigra spp. canadensis*
black gum	*Nyssa sylvatica*
black haw	*Viburnum prunifolium*
black huckleberry	*Gaylussacia baccata*
black kingsnake	*Lampropeltis getula niger*
black locust	*Robinia pseudoacacia*
black morel	*Morchella elata*
black oak	*Quercus velutina*
black racer	*Coluber constrictor constrictor*
black raspberry	*Rubus occidentalis*
black rat	*Rattus rattus*
black snake (black rat snake)	*Elaphe alleghaniensis*
black walnut	*Juglans nigra*
black willow	*Salix nigra*
black-eyed susan	*Rudbeckia hirta*
blackberry	*Rubus spp.*
blackfly	*Simuliidae*
blacknose dace	*Rhinichthys atratulus*
blackside darter	*Percina maculata*
Blanchard's cricket frog	*Acris crepitans blanchardi*
bleeding heart	*Dicentra eximia*
bloodroot	*Sanguinaria canadensis*
blue ash	*Fraxinus quadrangulata*
blue beech	*Carpinus caroliniana ssp. virginiana*
blue cohosh	*Caulophyllum thalictroides*
blue devil	*Echium vulgare*
blue hepatica	*Hepatica nobilis*
blue jay	*Cyanocitta cristata*
blue thistle	*Echium vulgare*
blue violet	*Viola sororia*
blue-eyed Mary	*Collinsia verna*
blueberry	*Vaccinium angustifolium; V. Corymbosum V. myrtilloides; V. pallidum*
bluegill	*Lepomis macrochirus*
Bluestone sculpin	*Cottus sp.*
bobcat	*Lynx rufus*
bobwhite quail	*Colinus virginianus*
bog clubmoss	*Lycopodiella inundata*
bog goldenrod	*Solidago uliginosa*
bog rosemary	*Andromeda polifolia var. glaucophylla*
boneset	*Eupatorium perfoliatum var. perfoliatum*
bottlebrush grass	*Elymus hystrix var. hystrix*
box elder	*Acer negundo*
box huckleberry	*Gaylussacia brachycera*
box turtle	*Terrapene carolina*
bracken	*Pteridium aquilinum*
bristly rose	*Rosa acicularis ssp. sayi*
broad beech fern	*Phegopteris hexagonoptera*
broad-winged hawk	*Buteo platypterus*

COMMON NAME	SCIENTIFIC NAME	COMMON NAME	SCIENTIFIC NAME
broadheaded skink	*Eumeces laticeps*	clubmoss	*Lycopodium spp.; Lycopodiella spp.;*
brook trout	*Salvelinus fontinalis*		*Huperzia spp.*
brookside alder	*Alnus serrulata*	clubshell mussel	*Pleurobema clava*
broom-sedge	*Andropogon virginicus*	cobblestone tiger beetle	*Cicindela marginipennis*
brown thrush	*Toxostoma rufum*	cockle-bur	*Xanthium spinosum*
brown trout	*Salmo trutta*	coltsfoot	*Tussilago farfara; Hexastylis virginica*
buck plantain	*Plantago lanceolata*	columbine	*Aquilegia canadensis*
buckbean	*Menyanthes trifoliata*	common cinquefoil	*Potentilla simplex*
buckeye	*Aesculus flava; A. glabra*	common clubmoss	*Lycopodium clavatum*
buckwheat	*Fagopyrum esculentum*	common garden	*Fragaria x ananassa var. ananassa*
buffalo	*Bos bison*	strawberry	
buffalo sucker	*Ictiobus bubalus; I. cyprinellus; I. niger*	common juniper	*Juniperus communis var. depressa*
bullfrog	*Rana catesbeiana*	common spring peeper	*Pseudacris crucifer crucifer*
bunch-flower	*Melanthium spp.*	cooper's milkvetch	*Astragalus neglectus*
bunchberry	*Cornus canadensis*	cormorant	*Phalacrocorax auritus*
burdock	*Arctium minus*	cottongrass	*Eriophorum virginicum*
buttercup	*Ranunculus spp.*	cottontail rabbit	*Sylvilagus floridana*
butterfly weed	*Ascelepias tuberosa*	cottonwood	*Populus deltoides ssp. deltoides*
butternut (white walnut)	*Juglans cinerea*	Cow Knob salamander	*Plethodon punctatus*
buttonbrush	*Cephalanthus occidentalis*	coyote	*Canis latrans*
caddisfly	*Trichoptera*	crab apple	*Malus coronaria var. coronaria*
Canada goose	*Branta canadensis*	crabgrass	*Digitaria sanguinalis*
Canada hemlock	*Tsuga canadensis*	cranberry	*Vaccinium macrocarpon; V. oxycoccos*
Canada honeysuckle	*Lonicera canadensis*	crappie	*Pomoxis spp.*
Canada lily	*Lilium canadense*	crayfish	*Fallicambarus spp.; Cambarus spp.;*
Canada mayflower	*Maianthemum canadense*		*Orconectes spp.*
Canada moonseed	*Menispermum canadense*	creasy or cress	*Lepidium campestre*
Canada thistle	*Cirsium arvense*	creek chub	*Semotilus atromaculatus*
Canada violet	*Viola canadensis*	crested coralroot	*Hexalectris spicata*
Canada yew	*Taxus canadensis*	cricket frog	*Acris crepitans*
Canby's mountain-lover	*Paxistima canbyi*	crossbill	*Loxia spp.*
candy darter	*Etheostoma osburni*	crossvine	*Bignonia capreolata*
carpet moss	*Bryophyta*	cucumber tree	*Magnolia acuminata*
catamount	*Puma concolor*	Culver's root	*Veronicastrum virginicum*
cardinal-flower	*Lobelia cardinalis*	currant	*Ribes spp.*
Carey's saxifrage	*Saxifraga careyana*	cushion moss	*Bryophyta*
carnivorous sundew	*Drosera rotundifolia var. rotundifolia*	damselfly	*Odonata*
Carolina lily	*Lilium michauxii*	dandelion	*Taraxacum officinale*
carp	*Cyprinus carpio*	dark-eyed junco	*Junco hyemalis*
carp sucker	*Carpiodes spp.*	darter	*Percidae*
catchfly	*Silene spp.*	deerberry	*Vaccinium stamineum*
cattail	*Typha spp.*	deerfly	*Diptera*
cave cricket	*Orthoptera*	dewberry	*Rubus spp.*
cave salamander	*Eurycea lucifuga*	diatoms	*Bacillariophyceae*
cedar waxwing	*Bombycilla cedrorum*	dittany	*Cunila origanoides*
Centennial Golden Trout	*Oncorhynchus mykiss*	dock	*Rumex spp.*
centipede	*Chilopoda*	dog fennel	*Eupatorium capillifolium*
cerulean warbler	*Dendroica cerulea*	dogwood	*Cornus florida*
channel catfish	*Ictalurus punctatus*	doll's-eye	*Actaea pachypoda*
channel shiner	*Notropis wickliffi*	dove	*Zenaida macroura; Columba livia*
cheat grass	*Bromus secalinus*	downy arrowwood	*Viburnum rafinesquianum*
Cheat Mountain salamander	*Plethodon nettingi*	downy woodpecker	*Picoides pubescens*
chestnut oak	*Quercus prinus*	dragonfly	*Odonata*
chickadee	*Poecile atricapilla; Poecile carolinensis*	dry-land fish	*Morchella esculenta*
chickaree	*Tamiasciurus hudsonicus*	duck	*Anatinae*
chickweed	*Caryophyllaceae*	Dutchman's breeches	*Dicentra cucullaria*
chicory	*Cichorium intybus*	Dutchman's pipe (pipevine)	*Aristolochia macrophylla*
chinquapin	*Castanea pumila var. pumila*	dwarf apple	*Malus pumila*
chinquapin oak	*Quercus muehlenbergii*	dwarf cornel	*Cornus canadensis*
choke cherry	*Prunus virginiana var. virginiana*	dwarf ginseng	*Panax trifolius*
Christmas fern	*Polystichum acrostichoides*	dwarf hawthorn	*Crataegus uniflora*
chub	*Cyprinidae*	dwarf hackberry	*Celtis tenuifolia*
cinnamon fern	*Osmunda cinnamomea var. cinnamomea*	dwarf iris	*Iris cristata*
cinquefoil	*Potentilla spp.*	dwarf larkspur	*Delphinium tricorne*
clematis	*Clematis spp.*	dwarf trillium	*Trillium pusillum var. virginianum*
climbing fern	*Lygodium palmatum*	early coralroot	*Corallorhiza trifida*
climbing wintercreeper	*Euonymus fortunei*	earthworm	*Haplotaxida*

COMMON NAME	SCIENTIFIC NAME	COMMON NAME	SCIENTIFIC NAME
eastern bluebird	*Sialia sialis*	grasshopper	*Orthoptera*
eastern chipmunk	*Tamias striatus*	gray bat	*Myotis grisescens*
eastern cottontail	*Sylvilagus floridana*	gray beardtongue	*Penstemon canescens*
eastern fence lizard	*Sceloporus undulatus*	gray catbird	*Dumetella carolinensis*
eastern larch	*Larix laricina*	gray fox	*Urocyon cinereoargenteus*
eastern phoebe	*Sayornis phoebe*	gray squirrel	*Sciurus caolinensis*
eastern tent caterpillar	*Malacosoma americanum*	gray wolf	*Canis lupus*
eastern tiger swallowtail	*Papilio glaucus*	great blue heron	*Ardea herodias*
eel	*Anguilla rostrata*	great blue lobelia	*Lobelia siphilitica var. siphilitica*
elderberry	*Sambucus spp.*	great horned owl	*Bubo virginianus*
elk	*Cervus elaphus*	green algae	*Chlorophyaceae*
elm	*Ulmus spp.*	green ash	*Fraxinus pensylvanica*
emerald shiner	*Notropis atherinoides*	green heron	*Butorides virescens*
English sparrow	*Passer domesticus*	green sunfish	*Lepomis cyanellus*
European rose chalcid	*Megastigmus aculeatus*	greenbrier	*Smilax spp.*
European starling	*Sturnus vulgaris*	greenside darter	*Etheostoma blennioides*
evening grosbeak	*Coccothraustes vespertinus*	ground pine	*Lycopodium spp.*
fall phlox	*Phlox paniculata*	ground skink	*Scincella lateralis*
fallfish	*Semotilus corporalis*	ground-cherry	*Physalis heterophylla*
false rue-anemone	*Enemion biternatum*	groundnut	*Apios americana*
fameflower	*Talinum teretifolium*	Guyandotte beauty	*Synandra hispidula*
fanshell	*Cyprogenia stegaria*	gypsy moth	*Lymantria dispar*
fantail darter	*Etheostoma flabellare*	haircap moss	*Bryophyta*
fawn lily	*Erythronium americanum ssp. americanum*	hairgrass	*Agrostis hyemalis; Muhlenbergia capillaris var. capillaris*
fern moss	*Bryophyta*		
field mouse (deer mouse)	*Peromyscus maniculatus*	hairy forked chickweed	*Paronychia fastigiata*
filmy fern	*Trichomanes boschianum*	hairy lip fern	*Cheilanthes lanosa*
fire pink	*Silene virginica var. robusta*	harperella	*Ptilimnium fluviatile*
fireweed	*Epilobium angustifolium*	harvest mouse	*Reithrodontomys humulis*
fisher	*Martes pennanti*	hawthorn	*Crataegus spp.*
five-lined skink (blue-tailed lizard)	*Eumeces fasciatus*	hay-scented fern	*Dennstaedtia punctilobula*
		hazelnut	*Corylus americana*
flame azalea	*Rhododendron calendulaceum*	heartworm	*Dirofilaria immitis*
flat-spired three-toothed land snail	*Triodopsis platysayoides*	hellbender	*Cryptobranchus alleganiensis*
		hellebore	*Helleborus viridis*
flathead catfish	*Pylodictis olivaris*	hellgrammite	*Corydalidae*
flatworm	*Polycladida*	hemlock	*Tsuga canadensis*
fluke	*Trematoda*	hemlock woolly adelgid	*Adelges tsugae*
flycatcher	*Tyrannidae*	hermit thrush	*Catharus guttatus*
foamflower	*Tiarella cordifolia*	hickory chicken	*Morchella esculenta*
four-toed salamander	*Hemidactylium scutatum*	hobblebush	*Viburnum lantanoides*
Fowler's toad	*Bufo fowleri*	hog sucker	*Hypentelium nigricans*
fox squirrel	*Scirus niger*	holly	*Ilex opaca var. opaca*
foxglove	*Aureolaria spp.*	honey comb	*Morchella spp.*
Fraser's sedge	*Cymophyllus fraserianus*	honey locust	*Gleditsia triacanthos*
freshwater drum	*Aplodinotus grunniens*	honeysuckle	*Lonicera spp.*
fringed loosestrife	*Lysimachia ciliata*	hookworm	*Necator americanus*
garter snake	*Thamnophis sirtalis*	hornwort	*Ceratophyllum echinatum; C. demersum*
gaywings	*Polygala paucifolia*	horsebrier	*Smilax rotundifolia*
gentian	*Gentiana spp.*	horsefly	*Diptera*
giant chickweed	*Myosoton aquaticum*	house finch	*Carpodacus mexicanus*
ginger	*Asarum canadense*	house mouse	*Mus musculus*
ginseng	*Panax quinquefolius*	huckleberry	*Vaccinium stamineum*
gizzard shad	*Dorosoma cepedianum*	hummingbird	*Archilochus colubris*
glade spurge	*Euphorbia purpurea*	hybrid striped bass	*Morone chrysops x M. saxatilis*
goat's rue	*Tephrosia virginiana*	Indian cucumber root	*Medeola virginiana*
golden club	*Orontium aquaticum*	Indian grass	*Sorghastrum nutans*
golden eagle	*Aquila chrysaetos*	Indian hemp	*Apocynum cannabinum*
golden mouse	*Ochrotomys nuttalli*	Indian turnip	*Arisaema triphyllum*
golden redhorse	*Moxostoma erythrurum*	Indiana bat	*Myotis sodalis*
golden-knees	*Chrysogonum virginianum var. virginianum*	indigo bunting	*Passerina cyanea*
goldenrod	*Solidago spp.*	intermediate wood fern	*Dryopteris intermedia*
goldenseal (yellowroot)	*Hydrastis canadensis*	interrupted fern	*Osmunda claytoniana*
Goldie's shield fern	*Dryopteris goldiana*	ironweed	*Vernonia novaboracensis*
goldthread	*Coptis trifolia*	jack-in-the-pulpit	*Arisaema triphyllum*
gooseberry	*Ribes uva-crispa var. sativum*	Jacob's ladder	*Polemonium vanbruntiae*
goshawk	*Accipiter gentilis*	James spiny mussel	*Pleurobema collina*
grass pink	*Calopogon tuberosus var. tuberosus*	Japanese clematis	*Clematis terniflora*

COMMON NAME	SCIENTIFIC NAME	COMMON NAME	SCIENTIFIC NAME
Japanese honeysuckle	*Lonicera japonica*	mosquito	*Diptera*
Japanese knotweed	*Polygonum cuspidatum*	mosspink	*Phlox subulata*
Japanese loosestrife	*Lysimachia japonica*	mottled sculpin	*Cottus bairdi*
Jerusalem artichoke	*Helianthus tuberosus*	mountain ash	*Sorbus americana*
jewelweed	*Impatiens capensis; I. pallida*	mountain bellwort	*Uvularia puberula*
joe-pye weed	*Eupatorium fistulosum*	mountain dusky	*Desmognathus ochrophaeus*
johnny darter	*Etheostoma nigrum*	salamander	
Juneberry	*Amelanchier arborea var. arborea*	mountain fetterbush	*Pieris floribunda*
Kanawha darter	*Etheostoma kanawhae*	mountain harebell	*Campanula rotundifolia*
Kanawha minnow	*Phenacobius teretulus*	mountain holly	*Ilex ambigua; I. montana*
Kates Mountain clover	*Trifolium virginicum*	mountain laurel	*Kalmia latifolia*
Kentucky spotted bass	*Micropterus punctulatus*	mountain lily-of-the-valley	*Convallaria majuscula*
kestrel	*Falco sparverius*	mountain lion	*Puma concolor*
knapweed	*Centaurea nigra*	(eastern cougar, panther)	
kudzu	*Pueraria montana var. lobata*	mountain magnolia	*Magnolia fraseri*
lamb's quarters	*Chenopodium album var. album*	mountain mint	*Pycnanthemum spp.*
lamprey	*Lampetra spp.; Ichthyomyzon spp.*	mountain pimpernel	*Taenidia montana*
large flowered trillium	*Trillium grandiflorum*	mountain wood fern	*Dryopteris campyloptera*
largemouth bass	*Micropterus salmoides*	mourning warbler	*Oporornis philadelphia*
least shrew	*Cryptotis parva*	mulberry	*Morus spp.*
least weasel	*Mustela nivalis*	multiflora rose	*Rosa multiflora*
leatherwood	*Dirca palustris*	muskellunge	*Esox masquinongy*
lichen	*Lecanorales*	muskrat	*Ondatra zibethicus*
little bluestem	*Schizachyrium scoparium var. scoparium*	mussel	*Bivalvia*
little brown bat	*Myotis lucifugus*	nannyberry	*Viburnum lentago*
liverwort	*Jungermmaniales*	Nashville warbler	*Vermivora ruficapilla*
locust (jar fly)	*Cicadidae*	netted chainfern	*Woodwardia areolata*
logperch	*Percina caprodes*	nettle	*Urtica spp.*
long beech fern	*Phegopteris connectilis*	New England aster	*Symphyotrichum novae-angliae*
long-stalked holly	*Ilex collina*	New Jersey tea	*Ceanothus americanus*
long-tailed weasel	*Mustela frenata*	New River shiner	*Notropis scabriceps*
longear sunfish	*Lepomis megalotis*	New York fern	*Thelypteris noveboracensis*
longnose dace	*Rhinichthys cataractae*	ninebark	*Physocarpus opulifolius var. opulifolius*
longnose gar	*Lepisosteus osseus*	nodding wild onion	*Allium oxyphilum*
maize	*Zea mays ssp. mays*	northeastern bulrush	*Scirpus ancistrochaetus*
mallard	*Anas platyrhynchos*	northern cardinal	*Cardinalis cardinalis*
mammoth	*Mammuthus primigenius*	northern flying squirrel	*Glaucomys sabrinus fuscus*
mandarin	*Prosartes maculata*	northern red salamander	*Pseudotriton ruber ruber*
manna grass	*Torreyochloa pallida var. pallida; Glyceria acutiflora; G. laxa; T. pallida var. fernaldii; G. melicaria*	northern water shrew	*Sorex palustris punctulatus*
		northern watersnake	*Nerodia sipedon sipedon*
		Norway rat	*Rattus norvegicus*
marsh fern	*Thelypteris palustris var. pubescens*	Norway spruce	*Picea abies*
marsh marigold	*Caltha palustris var. palustris*	nuthatch	*Sitta spp.*
masked shrew	*Sorex cinereus*	opossum	*Didelphis virginiana*
mayapple	*Podophyllum peltatum*	oriole	*Icterus spp.*
mayfly	*Ephemeroptera*	osage orange	*Maclura pomifera*
maygrass	*Phalaris caroliniana*	osprey	*Pandion haliaetus*
McDowell sunflower	*Helianthus dowellianus*	Oswego tea	*Monarda didyma*
meadow jumping mouse	*Zapus hudsonius*	ox-eye daisy	*Leucanthemum vulgare; Heliopsis helianthoides var. helianthoides*
meadow vole	*Microtus pennsylvanicus*		
meadowlark	*Sturnella magna*		
midges	*Chironomidae*	paddlefish	*Polyodon spathula*
mile-a-minute	*Polygonum perfoliatum*	painted trillium	*Trillium undulatum*
milkweed	*Asclepias syriaca*	panicled bellflower	*Campanula divaricata*
millipede	*Diploda*	partridge pea	*Chamaecrista fasciculata var. fasciculata*
mimic shiner	*Notropis volucellus*	passion-flower	*Passiflora incarnata*
mink	*Mustela vison*	pasture rose	*Rosa carolina var. carolina*
minnow	*Cyprinidae*	pasture thistle	*Cirsium vulgare*
mistletoe	*Phoradendron leucarpum*	paulownia (empress tree)	*Paulownia tomentosa*
mockernut hickory	*Carya alba*	pawpaw	*Asimina triloba*
mockingbird	*Mimus polyglottos*	pearly everlasting	*Anaphalis margaritacea*
mole	*Talpidae*	pennyroyal	*Hedeoma pulegioides*
mollusk	*Mollusca*	perch	*Perca flavescens*
monarch	*Danaus plexippus*	peregrine falcon	*Falco peregrinus*
monkey flower	*Mimulus ringens var. ringens*	periodical cicada	*Magicicada spp.*
mooneye	*Hiodon tergisus*	periwinkle	*Vinca minor*
morel mushroom	*Morchella spp.*	persimmon	*Diospyros virginiana*
morning glory	*Ipomoea purpurea*	pheasant	*Phasianus colchicus*
		pickerel frog	*Rana palustris*

COMMON NAME	SCIENTIFIC NAME	COMMON NAME	SCIENTIFIC NAME
pigeon	*Columba livia*	red-backed vole	*Clethrionomys gapperi*
pignut hickory	*Carya glabra*	red-bellied turtle	*Pseudemys rubriventris*
pileated woodpecker	*Dryocopus pileatus*	red-eyed vireo	*Vireo olivaceus*
pin oak	*Quercus palustris*	red-headed woodpecker	*Melanerpes erythrocephalus*
pine snake	*Pituophis melanoleucus melanoleucus*	red-shouldered hawk	*Buteo lineatus*
pine squirrel	*Tamiasciurus hudsonicus*	red-tailed hawk	*Buteo jamaicensis*
pink lady's slipper (moccasin flower)	*Cypripedium acaule*	redback salamander	*Plethodon cinereus*
		redbud	*Cercis canadensis*
pink mucket pearly mussel	*Lampsilis abrupta*	redhorse sucker	*Moxostoma spp.*
pink-edged sulphur butterfly	*Colias interior*	redroot	*Ceanothus herbaceus*
		redtop	*Agrostis gigantea*
pipestem	*Spiraea alba*	reindeer moss	*Cladina spp.*
pipsissewa	*Chimaphila umbellata ssp. cisatlantica*	rhododendron (mountain rosebay)	*Rhododendron maximum*
pitch pine	*Pinus rigida*		
pitcher plant	*Sarracenia purpurea ssp. gibbosa*	riffle beetle	*Coleoptera*
planaria	*Tricladida*	ring-necked pheasant	*Phasianus colchicus*
plume lily	*Maianthemum racemosum ssp. racemosum*	river birch	*Betula nigra*
poison hemlock	*Conium maculatum*	river otter	*Lutra canadensis*
poison ivy	*Toxicodendron radicans*	riverbank goldenrod	*Solidago simplex ssp. randii var. racemosa*
poison sumac	*Toxicodendron vernix*	riverbank grape	*Vitis riparia*
poke	*Phytolacca americana*	robin	*Turdus migratorius*
polypody	*Polypodium spp.*	rock bass	*Ambloplites rupestris*
pondweed	*Potamogeton spp.*	rock vole	*Microtus chrotorrhinus*
porcelain berry	*Ampelopsis brevipedunculata*	rockcress	*Arabis spp.*
post oak	*Quercus stellata*	rocktwist	*Draba ramosissima*
prairie cordgrass	*Spartina pectinata*	rose pogonia	*Pogonia ophioglossoides*
prairie ragwort	*Packera plattensis*	rosyface shiner	*Notropis rubellus*
prairie vole	*Microtus ochrogaster*	rough-legged hawk	*Buteo lagopus*
prickly ash	*Zanthoxylum americanum*	roundleaf dogwood	*Cornus rugosa*
prickly pear cactus	*Opuntia humifusa var. humifusa*	roundworm	*Nematoda*
prickly rose	*Rosa acicularis*	ruffed grouse	*Bonasa umbellus*
princess pine	*Lycopodium obscurum*	running buffalo clover	*Trifolium stoloniferum*
prothonotary warbler	*Protonotaria citrea*	rusty woodsia	*Woodsia ilvensis*
puffball mushroom	*Calvatia gigantea*	St. Johns wort	*Hypericum spp.*
purple avens	*Geum rivale*	sand-briar	*Solanum carolinense*
purple clematis	*Clematis occidentalis*	sand cherry	*Prunus pumila var. depressa*
purple cliffbrake	*Pellaea atropurpurea*	sassafras	*Sassafras albidum*
purple finch	*Carpodacus purpureus*	saxifrage	*Boykinia aconitifolia; Saxifraga michauxii; S. careyana; S. caroliniana*
purple fringed orchid	*Platanthera grandiflora*		
purple laurel	*Rhododendron catawbiense*	sauger	*Stizostedion canadense*
purple loosestrife	*Lythrum salicaria*	saw brier	*Smilax glauca*
purple stonecrop	*Sedum telephium ssp. telephium*	scarlet oak	*Quercus coccinea var. coccinea*
purple-stem aster	*Symphyotrichum puniceum var. puniceum*	scarlet tanager	*Piranga olivacea*
purslane	*Portulaca oleracea*	scouring rush	*Equisetum hyemale*
pussytoes ragwort	*Packera antennariifolia*	scrub oak	*Quercus ilicifolia*
pygmy shrew	*Sorex hoyi*	serviceberry (shad bush)	*Amelanchier spp.*
quail	*Colinus virginianus*	shagbark hickory	*Carya ovata*
raccoon	*Procyon lotor*	shaggy mane mushroom	*Coprinus comatus*
raceweed	*Galinsoga quadriradiata*	shale barren aster	*Symphyotrichum oblongifolium*
Rafinesque's big-eared bat	*Corynorhinus rafinesquii*	shale barren evening-primrose	*Oenothera argillicola*
ragweed	*Ambrosia artemisiifolium*		
ragwort	*Packera spp.*	shale barren goldenrod	*Solidago arguta var. harrisii*
rainbow trout	*Oncorhynchus mykiss*	shale barren pussytoes	*Antennaria virginica*
ramp	*Allium tricoccum*	shale barren rockcress	*Arabis serotina*
rattlesnake orchid	*Goodyera repens; G. pubescens*	shale bindweed	*Calystegia spithamaea ssp. purshiana*
raven	*Corvus corax*	shale skullcap	*Scutellaria parvula var. missouriensis*
recurved fetterbush	*Leucothoe recurva*	sharp-shinned hawk	*Accipiter striatus*
red bat	*Lasiurus borealis*	sheep sorrel	*Rumex acetosella*
red cedar	*Juniperus virginiana var. virginiana*	shellbark hickory	*Carya laciniosa*
red chokeberry	*Photinia pyrifolia*	shiner	*Cyprinidae*
red elderberry	*Sambucus racemosa var. racemosa*	shooting star	*Dodecatheon meadia ssp. meadia*
red fox	*Vulpes vulpes*	short-tailed shrew	*Blarina brevicauda*
red hickory	*Carya ovalis*	showy orchis	*Galearis spectabilis*
red maple	*Acer rubrum var. trilobum*	shrew	*Soricidae*
red oak	*Quercus rubra*	shrubby yellowroot	*Xanthorhiza simplicissima*
red pine	*Pinus resinosa*	Shumard oak	*Quercus shumardii*
red spruce	*Picea rubens*	side-oats grama	*Bouteloua curtipendula var. curtipendula*
red squirrel	*Tamiasciurus hudsonicus*	silky cornel	*Cornus amomum*

COMMON NAME	SCIENTIFIC NAME	COMMON NAME	SCIENTIFIC NAME
silky dogwood	*Cornus obliqua*	stoneroller minnow	*Campostoma anomalum*
silky willow	*Salix sericea*	stonecrop	*Sedum ternatum*
silver maple	*Acer saccharinum*	stonefly	*Plecoptera*
silver shiner	*Notropis photogenis*	stream salamander	*Caudata*
silver-spotted skipper	*Epargyreus clarus*	striped bass	*Morone saxatilis*
silverjaw minnow	*Notropis buccata*	striped maple	*Acer pensylvanicum*
silvery nailwort	*Paronychia argyrocoma*	striped shiner	*Luxilus chrysocephalus*
silvery spleenwort	*Deparia acrostichoides*	striped skunk	*Mephitis mephitis*
skipjack herring	*Alosa chrysochloris*	sucker	*Catstomidae*
skunk cabbage	*Symplocarpus foetidus*	sugar maple	*Acer saccharum var. saccharum*
skunk currant	*Ribes glandulosum*	sulfur polypore mushroom	*Polyporus sulphureus*
slippery elm	*Ulmus rubra*	sumac	*Rhus spp.*
small-whorled pogonia	*Isotria medeoloides*	summer grape	*Vitis aestivalis var. bicolor*
smallmouth bass	*Micropterus dolomieu*	sundew	*Drosera rotundifolia var. rotundifolia*
smartweed	*Polygonum spp.*	sunfish	*Lepomis spp.*
Smoke Hole bergamot	*Monarda fistulosa ssp. brevis*	sunflower	*Helianthus spp.*
smoky shrew	*Sorex fumeus*	Swainson's thrush	*Catharus ustulatus*
smooth arrowwood	*Viburnum recognitum*	swamp rose	*Rosa palustris*
smooth azalea	*Rhododendron arborescens*	sweet cicely	*Osmorhiza claytonii; O. longistylis*
smooth green snake	*Opheodrys vernalis*	sweet gum	*Liquidambar styraciflua*
smooth rose	*Rosa blanda var. blanda*	sweet white violet	*Viola blanda var. blanda*
smooth serviceberry	*Amelanchier laevis*	sweetfern	*Comptonia peregrina*
smooth sunflower	*Helianthus laevigatus*	switch grass	*Panicum virgatum var. virgatum*
snail-hunting ground beetle	*Coleoptera*	swordleaf phlox	*Phlox buckleyi*
		sycamore	*Platanus occidentalis*
snapping turtle	*Chelydra serpentina*	Table mountain pine	*Pinus pungens*
snowberry	*Gaultheria hispidula; Symphoricarpos albus var. albus*	tapeworm	*Cestoda*
		tasselrue	*Trautvettaria caroliniensis*
snowshoe hare	*Lepus americanus*	teaberry	*Gaultheria procumbens*
soft maple	*Acer negundo var. negundo; A. rubrum; A. saccharinum*	thistle	*Cirsium vulgare; C. muticum*
		three-toothed cinquefoil	*Sibbaldiopsis tridentata*
Solomon's seal	*Polygonatum biflorum var. commutatum; P. pubescens*	tick	*Ixodida*
		tiger beetle	*Cicindelidae*
song sparrow	*Melospiza melodia*	timber rattlesnake	*Crotalus horridus*
sorrel	*Rumex acetosella*	timber wolf	*Canis lupus*
sourwood	*Oxydendrum arboreum*	toothache tree	*Zanthoxylum americanum*
southeastern shrew	*Sorex longirostris*	toothwort	*Cardamine spp.*
southern flying squirrel	*Glaucomys volans*	touch-me-not	*Impatiens spp.*
southern loosestrife	*Lysimachia tonsa*	trailing arbutus	*Epigaea repens*
southern mountain cranberry	*Vaccinium erythrocarpum*	tree frog	*Hyla spp.*
		tree of heaven	*Ailanthus altissima*
spadefoot toad	*Scaphiopus holbrookii*	tree squirrel	*Sciuridae*
Spanish needles	*Bidens bipinnata*	trillium	*Trillium spp.*
speckled alder	*Alnus incana ssp. rugosa*	trumpet-creeper	*Campsis radicans*
sphagnum moss	*Sphagnum spp.*	tulip poplar	*Liriodendron tulipfera*
spicebush	*Lindera benzoin*	turk's cap lily	*Lilium superbum*
spinulose wood fern	*Dryopteris carthusiana*	turkeybeard	*Xerophyllum asphodeloides*
spleenwort	*Asplenium spp.*	twayblade	*Listera spp.*
spotfin shiner	*Cyprinella spiloptera*	twinflower	*Linnaea borealis ssp. americana*
spotted bass	*Micropterus punctulatus*	twinleaf	*Jeffersonia diphylla*
spotted skunk	*Spilogale putorius*	two-eyed partridge berry	*Mitchella repens*
spotted turtle	*Clemmys guttata*	two-leaved toothwort	*Cardamine diphylla*
spreading pogonia	*Cleistes bifaria*	umbrella magnolia	*Magnolia tripetala*
spring beauty	*Claytonia virginica var. virginica*	upland chorus frog	*Pseudacris feriarum feriarum*
spring cress	*Barbarea verna*	variegate darter	*Etheostoma variatum*
spring iris	*Iris verna var. smalliana*	viburnum (haw)	*Viburnum spp.*
spring peeper	*Pseudacris crucifer crucifer*	Virginia big-eared bat	*Corynorhinus townsendii virginianus*
spring salamander	*Gyrinophilus spp.*	Virginia bluebell	*Mertensia virginica*
squirrel corn	*Dicentra canadensis*	Virginia creeper	*Parthenocissus quinquefolia*
staghorn sumac	*Rhus typhina*	Virginia nailwort	*Paronychia virginica*
starling	*Sturnus vulgaris*	Virginia pine (scrub pine)	*Pinus virginiana*
star-nosed mole	*Condylura cristata*	Virginia spiraea	*Spiraea virginiana*
star tickseed	*Coreopsis pubescens var. pubescens*	wake robin	*Trillium erectum*
star-violet	*Dalibarda repens*	walking fern	*Asplenium x ebenoides*
stiff aster	*Ionactis linariifolius*	walleye	*Stizostedion vitreum*
stiff clubmoss	*Lycopodium annotinum*	warbler	*Parulidae*
stiff goldenrod	*Oligoneuron rigidum var. rigidum*	water hemlock	*Cicuta maculata var. maculata*
stinging nettle	*Urtica dioica ssp. dioica*	water stargrass	*Heteranthera dubia*

COMMON NAME	SCIENTIFIC NAME	COMMON NAME	SCIENTIFIC NAME
water willow	*Justicia americana*	wild onion	*Allium cernuum var. cernuum*
watercress	*Rorippa nasturtium-aquaticum*	wild pink	*Silene caroliniana*
weasel	*Mustela spp.*	wild plum	*Prunus americana*
West Virginia spring salamander	*Gyrinophilus subterraneus*	wild senna	*Senna marilandica*
		wild strawberry	*Fragaria virginiana ssp. virginiana*
whip-poor-will	*Caprimulgus vociferus*	wild sweet potato	*Ipomoea pandurata*
white ash	*Fraxinus americana*	wild sweet William	*Phlox maculata*
white azalea	*Rhododendron viscosum*	wild turkey	*Meleagris gallopavo*
white cedar	*Thuja occidentalis*	wild yam	*Dioscorea villosa*
white clintonia	*Clintonia umbellulata*	wineberry	*Rubus phoenicolasius*
white coralberry	*Symphoricarpos albus*	wingstem	*Verbesina alternifolia*
white crappie	*Pomoxis annularis*	winterberry	*Ilex verticillata*
white devil	*Aster pilosus*	wisteria	*Wisteria frutescens*
white hepatica	*Hepatica acutiloba forma albiflora*	witch hazel	*Hamamelis virginiana*
white monkshood	*Aconitum reclinatum*	wood duck	*Aix sponsa*
white oak	*Quercus alba*	wood lily	*Lilium philadelphicum var. philadelphicum*
white pine	*Pinus strobus*	wood nettle	*Laportea canadensis*
white sucker	*Catostomus commersoni*	wood turtle	*Insculpta*
white thoroughwort	*Eupatorium album; E. leucolepis*	wood warbler	*Parulidae*
white violet	*Viola blanda var. blanda*	woodchuck	*Marmota monax*
white wood sorrel	*Oxalis montana*	woodcock	*Scolopax minor*
white-flowered alumroot	*Heuchera alba*	wood bison	*Bos bison*
white-footed mouse	*Peromyscus leucopus*	woolly adelgid	*Adelges spp.*
white-tailed deer	*Odocoileus virginianus*	woolly hudsonia	*Hudsonia tomentosa*
white-top	*Erigeron annus*	wrinkled thimble cap	*Verpa bohemica*
whitehaired leather flower	*Clematis albicoma*	yarrow	*Achillea millefolium var. occidentalis*
wild balsam-apple	*Echinocystis lobata*	yellow birch	*Betula alleghaniensis var. alleghaniensis*
wild blue phlox	*Phlox divaricata*	yellow buckwheat	*Eriogonum allenii*
wild boar	*Sus scrofa*	yellow clintonia	*Clintonia borealis*
wild carrot	*Daucus carota; D. pusillus*	yellow fawn lily	*Erythronium americanum ssp. americanum*
wild celery	*Apium graveolens var. dulce*	yellow lady's slipper	*Cypripedium parviflorum var. pubescens; C. parviflorum var. parviflorum*
wild garlic	*Allium vineale ssp. vineale*		
wild geranium	*Geranium maculatum*	yellow morel	*Morchella esculenta*
wild ginger	*Asarum canadense*	yellow nailwort	*Paronychia virginica*
wild grape	*Vitis spp.*	yellow oak	*Quercus velutina*
wild indigo	*Baptisia tinctoria*	yellow poplar	*Liriodendron tulipfera*
wild lily-of-the-valley	*Maianthemum canadense*	yellow violet	*Viola pubescens*
wild lupine	*Lupinus perennis ssp. perennis*	zebra mussel	*Dreissena polymorpha*
wild mint	*Mentha arvensis*		

BIBLIOGRAPHY & CITATIONS

Our goal in compiling *The West Virginia Encyclopedia* is to provide as much information as possible while directing the interested reader to additional information outside the pages of this book. Thus, the text of many articles is followed by one or more sources, intended as a "further reading" suggestion for those wanting to learn more on the subject in question. The citations in this section offer a fuller documentation for most of the articles in *The West Virginia Encyclopedia*.

The bibliography preceding the citations lists the books and other publications cited most frequently in *The West Virginia Encyclopedia*. It is not intended as a full bibliography of West Virginia studies, but rather as a list of the books found most useful by our writers in preparing their articles. These books are abbreviated in the citations which follow, using the abbreviations indicated to the right of each item in the bibliography. Books cited with less frequency are not abbreviated, although their publishers may be abbreviated as indicated in the "Publishers and other organizations" list which follows. Certain frequently cited magazines and newspapers are also abbreviated, as indicated below.

The citations following the bibliographic abbreviations are listed in alphabetical order. Article titles, given in bold type, are identical to those used in the text of the book.

BOOKS	ABBREVIATIONS
Ambler, Charles H. & Festus P. Summers. *West Virginia: The Mountain State*. Englewood Cliffs, NJ: Prentice-Hall, 1958.	Ambler & Summers
Ambler, Charles H. *A History of Education in West Virginia: From Early Colonial Times to 1949*. Huntington: Standard Printing & Publishing, 1951.	Ambler–*Education*
Byrne, W.E.R. *Tale of the Elk*. Charleston: West Virginia Publishing Company, 1940. Reprint, Charleston: Quarrier Press, 1995.	Byrne–*Tale*
Clarkson, Roy B. *Tumult on the Mountains: Lumbering in West Virginia 1770–1920*. Parsons: McClain, 1964.	Clarkson–*Tumult*
Cohen, Stan & Richard Andre. *Kanawha County Images*. Charleston: Pictorial Histories Publishing Company & Kanawha County Bicentennial, 1987.	Cohen–*Kanawha Images*
Cometti, Elizabeth & Festus P. Summers. *The Thirty-Fifth State: A Documentary History of West Virginia*. Morgantown: West Virginia University Library, 1966.	Cometti–*Thirty-Fifth*
Comstock, Jim, ed. *West Virginia Heritage Encyclopedia*. Richwood: Jim Comstock, 1967–73/ 1974/ 1976.	Comstock–*Encyclopedia*
Conley, Phil, ed. *West Virginia Encyclopedia*. Charleston: West Virginia Publishing, 1929.	Conley–*Encyclopedia*
Corbin, David A. *Life, Work, and Rebellion in the Coal Fields: The Southern West Virginia Miners, 1880–1922*. Urbana: University of Illinois Press, 1981.	Corbin–*Life, Work*
Hardesty's Historical and Geographical Encyclopedia. Chicago: H. H. Hardesty, 1883. Reprint, Richwood: Comstock, *Hardesty's West Virginia Counties*, 8 vols., 1973.	Hardesty's
Kercheval, Samuel. *A History of the Valley of Virginia*. Winchester: S. H. Davis, 1833. Reprint, Shenandoah Publishing, 1973.	Kercheval–*Valley*
Lee, Howard B. *Bloodletting in Appalachia*. Morgantown: West Virginia University, 1969.	Lee–*Bloodletting*
McMichael, Edward V. *Introduction to West Virginia Archeology*. Morgantown: West Virginia Geological & Economic Survey, 1968.	McMichael–*Archeology*
Miller, Thomas Condit, and Hu Maxwell. *West Virginia and Its People*. 3 vols. New York: Lewis Historical Publishing, 1913.	Miller & Maxwell
Morgan, John G. *West Virginia Governors, 1863–1980*. Charleston: Charleston Newspapers, 1980.	Morgan–*Governors*
Rice, Otis K. *The Allegheny Frontier: West Virginia Beginnings, 1730–1830*. Lexington: University Press of Kentucky, 1970.	Rice–*Allegheny Frontier*
Rice, Otis K. *A History of Greenbrier County*. Parsons: McClain, 1986.	Rice–*Greenbrier County*
Rice, Otis K. & Stephen W. Brown. *West Virginia: A History*. Lexington: University Press of Kentucky, 1993.	Rice & Brown
Savage, Lon. *Thunder in the Mountains*. Pittsburgh: University of Pittsburgh Press, 1990.	Savage–*Thunder*
Stutler, Boyd. *West Virginia in the Civil War*. Charleston: Education Foundation, 1966.	Stutler–*Civil War*
Sullivan, Charles Kenneth. *Coal Men and Coal Towns: Development of the Smokeless Coalfields of Southern West Virginia, 1873–1923*. New York: Garland Publishing, 1989.	Sullivan–*Coal Men*
Thomas, Jerry Bruce. *An Appalachian New Deal: West Virginia in the Great Depression*. Lexington: University Press of Kentucky, 1998.	Thomas–*New Deal*
Tribe, Ivan M. *Mountaineer Jamboree: Country Music in West Virginia*. Lexington: University Press of Kentucky, 1984.	Tribe–*Jamboree*
West Virginia Writers' Project. *West Virginia: A Guide to the Mountain State*. New York: Oxford University Press, 1941.	WPA–*Guide*
West Virginia Atlas & Gazetteer. Yarmouth, ME: Delorme, 1997.	Delorme–*Atlas*
West Virginia Blue Book. Senate Clerk, State of West Virginia. Charleston, 1916–2003.	Blue Book
Where People and Nature Meet: A History of West Virginia State Parks. Charleston: Pictorial Histories Publishing Company, 1988.	*History of State Parks*
Williams, John Alexander. *West Virginia and the Captains of Industry*. Morgantown: West Virginia University Library, 1976.	Williams–*Captains*
Withers, Alexander Scott. *Chronicles of Border Warfare*. Cincinnati: Robert Clarke, 1895. Reprint, McClain, 1994.	Withers–*Chronicles*

MAGAZINES	
West Virginia Archeologist	*WV Archeologist*
West Virginia History	*WVH*
Wonderful West Virginia	*WWV*

NEWSPAPERS	
Bluefield Daily Telegraph	*Daily Telegraph*
Charleston Daily Mail	*Daily Mail*
Charleston Gazette	*Gazette*
Huntington *Herald-Dispatch*	*Herald-Dispatch*
Morgantown *Dominion Post*	*Dominion Post*

PUBLISHERS AND OTHER ORGANIZATIONS

Eastern Regional Coal Archives, Craft Memorial Library, Bluefield	Eastern Regional Archives	University of Virginia Press	UVA Press
Louisiana State University Press	LSU Press	University Press of Kentucky	UPK
McClain Printing Company	McClain	West Virginia & Regional History Collection, WVU Libraries	WV&RHC
Pictorial Histories Publishing Company	PHPC	West Virginia Department of Transportation	WVDOT
United States Geological Survey	USGS	West Virginia Division of Culture & History	WVDC&H
United States Government Printing Office	GPO	West Virginia Division of Highways	WVDOH
University of Illinois Press	UI Press	West Virginia Division of Natural Resources	WVDNR
University of North Carolina Press	UNC Press	West Virginia Geological & Economic Survey	WVGES
University of Pennsylvania Press	UP Press	West Virginia Library Commission	WVLC
University of Pittsburgh Press	UPP	West Virginia University Libraries	WVU Libraries
University of Tennessee Press	UT Press	West Virginia University Press	WVU Press

---

Patch Adams: Burnside, Mary W. "Patched Together." *Gazette*, 12/24/1998 • Kempley, Rita. "The Doctor is Out. Way Out." *Washington Post*, 12/25/1998.

Adena: Dragoo, Don W. *Mounds for the Dead: An Analysis of the Adena Culture*. Pittsburgh: Carnegie Museum, 1963 • Webb, William S. & Raymond S. Baby. *The Adena People, No. 2*. Columbus: Ohio Historical Society, 1957.

Walter Aegerter: Sutton, David H. *One's Own Hearth Is Like Gold: A History of Helvetia*. New York: Peter Lang, 1990 • Sutton. *Portrait of a Community: The Aegerter Photographs of Helvetia*. Permanent exhibit. Helvetia Community Hall. Helvetia • Sutton. "A West Virginia Swiss Community: The Aegerter Photographs of Helvetia, Randolph County." *Goldenseal* (Apr.–June 1980).

African Methodist Episcopal Church: Gregg, Howard D. *History of the African Methodist Episcopal Church*. Nashville: AMEC Sunday School Union, 1980 • Lincoln, Eric C. & Lawrence H. Mamiya. *The Black Church in the African American Experience*. Durham: Duke University Press, 1990.

African Zion Baptist Church: Bickley, Ancella R., ed. *Our Mount Vernons: Historic Register Listings of Sites Significant to the Black History of West Virginia*. Huntington: Carter G. Woodson Memorial Foundation & Drinko Academy, 1997 • Cohen–*Kanawha Images* • Comstock–*Encyclopedia*, vol. 1, 1976.

African-American Coal Miners: Corbin–*Life, Work* • Lewis, Ronald L. *Black Coal Miners in America*. Lexington: UPK, 1987 • Salzman, Jack, et al., eds., *Encyclopedia of African American Culture and History*. New York: Macmillan Pub., 1996 • Trotter, Joe William Jr. *Coal, Class, and Color: Blacks in Southern West Virginia, 1915–32*. Urbana: UI Press, 1990.

African-American Education: Bickley, Ancella R. "Black Education in West Virginia." *WV&RHC Newsletter* (Summer 1989) • Bickley. *History of the West Virginia State Teachers' Association*. Washington: National Education Assn., 1979 • Hight, Joel E. "History of Negro Secondary Education in McDowell County, West Virginia." M.E. thesis, University of Cincinnati, 1946 • Woodson, Carter G. *Early Negro Education in West Virginia*. Institute: WV Collegiate Institute, 1921.

African-American Heritage: Corbin–*Life, Work* • Lewis, Ronald L. *Black Coal Miners in America*. Lexington: UPK, 1987 • Posey, Thomas E. *The Negro Citizen of West Virginia*. Institute: Press of WV State College, 1934 • Trotter, Joe William Jr. *Coal, Class, and Color: Blacks in Southern West Virginia, 1915–1932*. Urbana: UI Press, 1990 • Trotter. "West Virginia," in Jack Salzman, et al., eds., *Encyclopedia of African American Culture and History*. New York: Macmillan Pub., 1996 • Turner, William H. & Edward Cabbell, eds. *Blacks in Appalachia*. Lexington: UPK, 1985.

Agriculture: Ambler & Summers • Diss Debar, Joseph H. *The West Virginia Hand-book and Immigrant's Guide*. Parkersburg: Gibbons Brothers, 1870 • Rice & Brown • WV Agricultural Statistics Service, Annual Bulletin, no. 30, 1999. WV Dept. of Agriculture & U.S. Dept. of Agriculture, 2000.

Department of Agriculture: Ambler & Summers • Barns, William D. *The West Virginia State Grange, The First Century, 1873–1973*. Morgantown Printing & Binding, 1973 • *Blue Book*, 1998.

Air National Guard: Smith, Jack H. *The Coonskin Boys*. Charleston: PHPC, 1987 • Smith. *Mountaineer Sabres*. Charleston: PHPC, 1988 • Smith. *Mustangs and Unicorns*. Charleston: PHPC, 1997 • Smith. *West Virginia Air Power*. Charleston: PHPC, 1992.

Akro Agate Company: Hardy, Roger & Claudia Hardy. *Akro Agate Price Guide*. Clarksburg, 1998 • Sweeney, Edwin. "Marbles and Pressed Glass." *Goldenseal* (Summer 1984).

Alderson-Broaddus College: Withers, Richard & Martha Rose Roy. *Light on the Hill: A Pictorial History of Alderson-Broaddus College*. Virginia Beach: Donning Co., 1995.

Allegheny Front: Fenneman, Nevin M. *Physiography of Eastern U.S.* New York: McGraw-Hill, 1938 • USGS Maps, Scale 1:250,000. Bluefield, Charleston, Charlottesville & Cumberland quadrangles • Delorme–*Atlas*.

Allegheny Lodge: Brown, Leona G. "Allegheny Lodge." *Goldenseal* (Fall 1991).

Allegheny Mountain, Battle of: Geiger, Joe. "Holding the Line: Confederate Defense of the Parkersburg-Staunton Turnpike." M.A. thesis, Marshall University, 1995 • Stutler–*Civil War*.

Allegheny Mountains: Fenneman, Nevin M. *Physiography of Eastern U.S.* New York: McGraw-Hill, 1938 • USGS Maps, Scale 1:250,000. Charlottesville & Cumberland quadrangles • Delorme–*Atlas*.

Allegheny Plateau: Fenneman, Nevin M. *Physiography of Eastern U.S.* New York: McGraw-Hill, 1938 • Hunt, Charles B. *Physiography of the U.S.* San Francisco: W. H. Freeman & Co., 1967 • USGS Maps, Scale 1:250,000. Bluefield, Canton, Charleston, Charlottesville, Clarksburg, Cumberland, Huntington & Jenkins quadrangles.

Allegheny Trail: Adkins, Leonard M. "Along the Allegheny." *Gazette*, 7/25/1985 • Bird, Fred & Doug Wood. *Hiking Guide to the Allegheny Trail*. Charleston: WV Scenic Trails Assn., 1983.

Allegheny Woodrat: Castleberry, Steven Bryan. "Conservation and Management of the Allegheny Woodrat in the Central Appalachians." Ph.D. diss., WVU, 2000 • WVDNR. "A Closer Look at One of West Virginia's Rare Mammals." *WV Wildlife* (Fall 2001).

Walter Allen: Savage–*Thunder*.

Alpha Psi Omega: Garner, Dwight. "50 Years of Alpha Psi Omega." *The Playbill* (Oct. 1975) • Opp, Paul F. "Alpha Psi Omega Sponsors Formation of Two New Honor Societies." *The Playbill* (Sept. 1929).

Amphibians and Reptiles: Green, N. B. & T. K. Pauley. *Amphibians & Reptiles in West Virginia*. Pittsburgh: UPP, 1987.

Amtrak: Edmonson, Harold A. *Journey to Amtrak*. Milwaukee: Kalmbach Pub., 1972.

Andrews Methodist Episcopal Church: National Register of Historic Places Nomination, ms., WVDC&H, 1970 • Wolfe, Howard H. *Mother's Day and the Mother's Day Church*. Kingsport, TN: Kingsport Press, 1962.

Thomas Anshutz: Cuthbert, John A. *Early Art and Artists in West Virginia*. Morgantown: WVU Press, 2000.

Appalachia: Eller, Ronald D. *Miners, Millhands, and Mountaineers*. Knoxville: UT Press, 1982 • Shapiro, Henry. *Appalachia on our Mind*. Chapel Hill: UNC Press, 1978 • Williams, John Alexander. *Appalachia: A History*. Chapel Hill: UNC Press, 2002.

Appalachian Basin: Janssen, Raymond E. *Earth Science: A Handbook on the Geology of West Virginia*. Clarksburg: Educational Marketers, 1973.

Appalachian Bible College: Coberly, Fern Hanlin. *Appalachian Bible College, 1950–2000*. Virginia Beach: Donning Co., 2000.

Appalachian Mountains: Fenneman, Nevin M. *Physiography of Eastern U.S.* New York: McGraw-Hill, 1938 • Hunt, Charles B. *Physiography of the U.S.* San Francisco: W. H. Freeman & Co., 1967 • Janssen, Raymond E. *Earth Science: A Handbook on the Geology of West Virginia*. Clarksburg: Educational Marketers, 1973.

Appalachian Orogeny: Dott, Robert H. Jr. & Donald R. Prothero. *Evolution of the Earth*. New York: McGraw-Hill, 1994 • Hatcher, R. D. Jr., W. A. Thomas & G. W. Viele, eds. *The Appalachian-Ouachita Orogen in the United States*. Boulder: Geological Society of America, 1989 • "In Suspect Terrane," in John McPhee, *Annals of the Former World*. New York: Farrar, Straus & Giroux, 1998 • Woodrow, Donald L. & William D. Sevon, eds. *The Catskill Delta*. Boulder: Geological Society of America, 1985.

Appalachian Regional Commission: *Appalachia: Journal of the Appalachian Regional Commission* (Winter-Spring 1995) • Appalachian Regional Commission, 1997 Annual Report. Washington: ARC, 1998 • Bradshaw, Michael J. *The Appalachian Regional Commission: Twenty-five Years of Government Policy*. Lexington: UPK, 1992.

Appalachian Regional Hospitals: Krajcinovic, Ivana. *From Company Doctors to Managed Care: The United Mine Workers' Noble Experiment*. Ithaca, NY: ILR Press, 1997.

The Appalachian Trail: Adkins, Leonard M. *The Appalachian Trail*. Birmingham: Menasha Ridge Press, 1998 • Albright, Jack, ed. *Appalachian Trail Guide to Central Virginia*. Harpers Ferry: Appalachian Trail Conference, 1994 • Golightly, Jean C., ed. *Appalachian Trail Guide to Maryland and Northern Virginia*. Vienna, VA: Potomac Appalachian Trail Club, 1995.

Apples: Pollan, Michael. *The Botany of Desire*. New York: Random House, 2001.

John W. M. Appleton: Bailey, Kenneth R. "One of the Famous 54th Massachusetts: A Short Biography of General John W. M. Appleton." *WVH* (Apr. 1970).

Aracoma Hotel: "Great Hotel to be Built in the City." *Logan Democrat*, 8/3/1916 • Spence, Robert Y. *The Land of the Guyandot*. Detroit: Harlo Press, 1976 • "U.S. Troops Now Enroute to Logan." *Logan Banner*, 9/2/1921.

Matthew Arbuckle: Jefferds, Joseph C. Jr. *Captain Matthew Arbuckle: A Documentary Biography*. Charleston: Education Foundation, 1981.

Arbuckle's Fort: Jefferds, Joseph C. Jr. *Captain Matthew Arbuckle: A Documentary Biography*. Charleston: Education Foundation, 1981 • McBride, W. Stephen & Kim A. McBride. "Forting Up on the Greenbrier: Archaeological Investigations of Arbuckle's Fort," Report no. 252. Lexington: University of Kentucky, 1993 • McBride, W. Stephen, Kim A. McBride & J. David McBride. "Frontier Defense of the Greenbrier and Middle New River Country," Report no. 375. Lexington: University of Kentucky, 1996 • Rice–*Greenbrier County*.

Archeology: Davis, R. P. Stephen Jr. *Bibliography of West Virginia Archeology*. Morgantown: WVGES, 1978 • Mayer-Oakes, William J. *Prehistory of the Upper Ohio Valley*. Pittsburgh: Carnegie Museum, 1955 • McMichael–*Archeology*.

Arthurdale: *Arthurdale: A First Lady's Legacy*. Documentary. Morgantown: WNPB, 1988 • Cook, Blanche Wiesen. *Eleanor Roosevelt: Vol. Two, 1933–1938*. New York: Viking, 1999 • Ward, Bryan, ed. *A New Deal for America*. Arthurdale: Arthurdale Heritage, 1995.

The Artists' Excursion: Davis, Julia. *The Shenandoah*. New York: Farrar & Rinehart, 1945 • Strother, David Hunter. "Artists' Excursion over the Baltimore & Ohio Rail Road." *Harper's* (June 1859).

Francis Asbury: Rudolph, L. C. *Francis Asbury*. Nashville: Abingdon Press, 1966.

Ashford General Hospital: Keefer, Louis E. "The West Virginia WWII Home Front: Ashford General Hospital: The Greenbrier Goes to War." *Goldenseal* (Fall 1993) • Keefer. *Shangri-La for Wounded Soldiers*. Reston, VA: COTU Pub., 1995.

Atheneum Prison: Phillips, Edward. *The Atheneum*. Wheeling, 1999.

Mary Meek Atkeson: Comstock–*Encyclopedia*, vols. 10–11, 1974 • *Who's Who of American Women*, vol. 1. Chicago: Marquis, 1958.

George W. Atkinson: Atkinson, George W. & Alvaro F. Gibbins. *Prominent Men of West Virginia*. Wheeling: W. L. Callin, 1890 • Callahan, James M. *History of West Virginia, Old and New*, vol. 3. Chicago & New York: American Historical Society, 1923 • Morgan–*Governors*.

Audra State Park: *History of State Parks • Wild and Wonderful: West Virginia State Parks & Forests*. Charleston: Chapman Printing, 2000.

Auger Mining: *Annual Report & Directory of Mines 1951*. WV Dept. of Mines, 1952 • *Dictionary of Mining Terms*. U.S. Bureau of Mines, 1976.

Augusta County, Virginia: Peyton, John Lewis. *History of Augusta County, Virginia*. Staunton: S. M. Yost & Son, 1882 • Robinson, Morgan P. *Virginia Counties: Those Resulting from Virginia Legislation*. Richmond: Superintendent of Public Printing, 1916 • Waddell, Joseph Addison. *Annals of Augusta County*. Staunton: C. Russell Caldwell Pub., 1902.

Averell's Raid: Averell, William Woods. *Ten Years in the Saddle: The Memoirs of William Woods Averell*. Edward K. Eckert & Nicholas J. Amato, eds. San Rafael, CA: Presidio Press, 1978 • "Averell's Raid in West Virginia," in *The War of the Rebellion: A Compilation of the Official Records of the Union and Confederate Armies*. Series I, vol. 29, part 1. Washington: GPO, 1890.

Aviation: Bickley, Ancella R. "Dubie, Spanky, and Mr. Death: West Virginia's Pioneering Black Airmen." *Goldenseal* (Summer 1997) • Furbee, Mary R. "I was Never Afraid of Anything: Pilot Rose Rolls Cousins." *Goldenseal* (Summer 1997) • Graham, O. R. "First Flight over West Virginia." *WV Review* (Feb. 1945) • Keefer, Louis E. "Wings over Glen Dale." *Goldenseal* (Winter 1991) • Lohmann, Beatrice, "Wings over West Virginia." *WV Review* (Sept. 1939) • McLaughlin, J. Kemp. *The Mighty Eighth in WWII*. Lexington: UPK, 2000 • Yeager, Chuck & Leo Janos. *Yeager: An Autobiography*. New York: Bantam Books, 1985.

The Bailes Brothers: Tribe–*Jamboree*.

Cleve Bailey: Wilson, Michael K. "Cleveland M. Bailey: Mountaineer Congressman." M.A. final project, Marshall University Graduate College, 1999.

"Mad Anne" Bailey: Hall, Grace McCartney. "Anne Bailey in West Virginia Tradition." *WVH* (Oct. 1955).

R. D. Bailey: "Mighty Oak has Fallen, Judge Bailey Funeral Rites Held Thursday." Pineville *Independent Herald*, 10/27/1961 • Miller, Bob. "Brush with Death." *Gazette*, 3/12/1995 • "R. D. Bailey, Former Mingo Judge Dies." *Williamson Daily News*, 10/25/1961.

Newton Diehl Baker: Comstock - *Encyclopedia*, vol. 2, 1976 • Cramer, Clarence. *Newton D. Baker, a Biography*. Cleveland: World Pub., 1961 • Wintz, William D. *Nitro: World War I Boom Town*. Charleston: Jalamap, 1985.

The Baldwin-Felts Detective Agency: Hadsell, Richard & William Coffey. "From Law and Order to Class Warfare: Baldwin-Felts Detectives in the Southern West Virginia Coal Fields." *WVH* (Spring 1979) • McDaniel, Brenda. "Guns, Thugs, and Heroes." *The Roanoker* (July–Aug. 1979) • Savage–*Thunder* • U.S. Senate. Committee on Education & Labor. *Conditions in the Paint Creek Coal Fields of West Virginia*. 63rd Congress, first session, 3 vols. Washington: GPO, 1913 • U.S. Senate. *West Virginia Coal Fields*. Hearings before the Committee on Education & Labor. 67th Congress, first session, 2 vols. Washington: GPO, 1921–22.

Dr. Maggie Ballard: Parkinson, George. "Interview with the Revered Monroe Countian Dr. Margaret Byrnside Ballard: 1900–1976." *Goldenseal* (Apr.–June 1977).

Baltimore & Ohio Railroad: Hungerford, Edward. *The Story of the Baltimore & Ohio Railroad*. New York: G.P. Putnam's Sons, 1928 • Stover, John F. *History of the Baltimore & Ohio Railroad*. West Lafayette, IN: Purdue University Press, 1987.

Harry Hill Bandholtz: Laurie, Clayton L. "The United States Army and the Return to Normalcy in Labor Dispute Interventions: The Case of the West Virginia Coal Mine Wars." *WVH* (1991) • *National Cyclopaedia of American Biography*, vol. 19. New York: James T. White & Co., 1926 • Savage–*Thunder*.

Banjo: Conway, Cecelia. *African Banjo Echoes in Appalachia: A Study of Folk Traditions*. Knoxville: University of Tennessee, 1995.

Banking: Rice, Otis & Stephen Brown. *A Centennial of Strength: West Virginia Banks*. Charleston: WV Bankers Assn., 1991.

Baptists: McNeel, Isaac. "History of the Baptist Churches," (unpub. ms.). WV&RHC, ca. 1937 • Rogers, Truett. *West Virginia Baptist History, 1770–1865*. Terra Alta: Headline Books, 1990 • Rogers. *West Virginia Baptist History, 1865–1965*. Terra Alta: Headline Books, 1994 • Semple, Robert B. *A History of the Rise and Progress of the Baptists in Virginia*. Richmond: Pitt & Dickinson, 1894 • Torbet, Robert G. *A History of the Baptists*. Valley Forge: Judson Press, 1969.

Barbour County: Barbour County Historical Society. *Barbour County*. Philippi, 1979 • Maxwell, Hu. *History of Barbour County*. Morgantown: Acme Pub. Co., 1899 • *The War of the Rebellion: A Compilation of the Official Records of the Union and Confederate Armies*. Series I, vol. 2. Washington: GPO, 1890 • U.S. Census, 2000 • *Blue Book*, 2002.

Barger Springs: Cohen, Stan. *Historic Springs of the Virginias*. Charleston: PHPC, 1981 • Miller, James H. *History of Summers County*. Hinton: J. H. Miller, 1908 • Price, Paul, et al. *Springs of West Virginia*. Morgantown: WVGES, 1936.

Gray Barker: Interviews by author. 1970–80 • Story, Ronald D., ed. *The Encyclopedia of UFOs*. Garden City, NY: Dolphin Books, 1980.

The *Barnette* Case: Manwaring, David R. *Render Unto Caesar: The Flag Salute Controversy*. Chicago: University of Chicago Press, 1962.

Barns: Biola, Heather R. "Barn Builder: The Working Wisdom of Lawson Kimbrew." *Goldenseal* (Winter 1987) • Milnes, Gerald C. "The Barns of Pendleton County." *Goldenseal* (Spring 1998) • Montell, Lynwood W. & Michael L. Morse. *Kentucky Folk Architecture*. Lexington: UPK, 1976 • Noble, Allen G. *The Old Barn Book: A Field Guide to North American Barns and Other Farm Structures*. New Brunswick: Rutgers University Press, 1996 • Shultz, Leroy G. "The Barns of West Virginia." *Goldenseal* (Apr.–Sept. 1978).

William Wallace Barron: Morgan–*Governors*.

Annie Latham Bartlett: Eaton, Allen H. *Handicrafts of the Southern Highlands*. New York: Dover Publications, 1973 • Phillips, Michael. "Annie Latham Bartlett." *Upshur County Historical Society Newsletter* (Winter 1999–2000).

Baseball: Johnson, Lloyd & Miles A. Wolff, eds. *The Encyclopedia of Minor League Baseball*. Durham: Baseball America, 1993.

Basket Making: Irwin, John Rice. *Baskets and Basket Makers in Southern Appalachia*. Exton, PA: Schiffer, 1982 • Law, Rachel N. & Cynthia W. Taylor. *Appalachian White Oak Basketmaking*. Knoxville: UT Press, 1991 • Leffler, Susan. "Ballads and Baskets: The Clyde Case Story." *Goldenseal* (Fall 1991) • Milnes, Gerald. "Thank You, Homer: Preserving a Basket Making Tradition." *Goldenseal* (Summer 1993) • Stephenson, Sue H. *Basketry of the Appalachian Mountains*. New York: Van Nostrand Reinhold, 1977.

Basketball Tournament: Wyatt, Tim L. *The Final Score*. Woodbridge, VA: T. Wyatt, 1999.

Bats: Barbour, R. W. & W. H. Davis. *Bats of America*. Lexington: UPK, 1969 • Harvey, Michael J. *Bats of the Eastern U.S.* Little Rock: Arkansas Game & Fish Commission, 1992 • Tuttle, Merlin D. *America's Neighborhood Bats*. Austin: University of Texas Press, 1988.

Gordon Battelle: Blazier, George J. "The Pioneer Battelles and their Contributions to the Building of Ohio and West Virginia." *WVH* (Apr. 1954).

Batts and Fallam Expedition: Summers, Lewis P. *History of Southwest Virginia, 1746–1786, Washington County, 1777–1870*. Johnson City: Overmountain Press, 1989.

Bear Rock Lakes: "Bear Rocks Lakes Wildlife Management Area," Pamphlet. WVDNR, 1993 • "West Virginia Small Impoundment Fishing Guide," Pamphlet. WVDNR, 1983.

Tony Beaver: Cober, Mary E. *The Remarkable History of Tony Beaver, West Virginian*. New York: David McKay Co., 1953 • Montague, Margaret Prescott. *Up Eel River*. Freeport: Books for Libraries Press, 1928 • Musick, Ruth Ann, ed. "A Man of West Virginia." *WV Folklore Journal* (Fall 1954) • Rector, Laura J. "Prose Legends of West Virginia." M.A. thesis, Ohio University, 1943.

Beckley: Klaus, Fran & Pauline Haga. *Looking Back: A Pictorial History of Beckley*. Beckley: Beckley Main Street, 1991 • Warren, Harlow. *Beckley U.S.A.* Beckley, 1955.

Beckley Register-Herald: Wood, Jim. *Raleigh County*. Beckley: J. Wood, 1994.

Clair Bee: McCallum, Jack. "A Hero for all Times." *Sports Illustrated* (1/7/1980) • McAvoy, Rogers. "Mr. Basketball: The Clair Bee Story." *Goldenseal* (Winter 1991).

Bee Line March: Bushong, Millard Kessler. *Historic Jefferson County*. Boyce, VA: Carr Pub., 1972 • Dandridge, Danske. *Historic Shepherdstown*. Charlottesville: Michie Pub., 1910.

Beech Fork Lake: *History of State Parks* • "Beech Fork," Pamphlet. WVDNR.

Beech Fork State Park: Miller, Tom. "Beech Fork Lodge Sites Down to Two." *Herald-Dispatch*, 9/15/1994 • *Blue Book*, 1997.

Mary Behner: Burger, Bettijane. "Mary Elizabeth Behner Christopher," in *Missing Chapters II: West Virginia Women in History*. Charleston: WV Women's Commission, 1986 • Kreiser, Christine M., ed. "'I Wonder Whom God Will Hold Responsible': Mary Behner and Scotts Run." *WVH* (1994).

Belgians: Barkey, Frederick. *Cinderheads in the Hills: The Belgian Window Glass Workers of West Virginia*. Charleston: WV Humanities Council, 1988.

Belsnickling: Barrick, Mac. E. *German-American Folklore*. Little Rock: August House, 1987 • Cline, Ruth H. "Belsnickles and Shanghais." *Journal of American Folklore* (Apr.–June 1958) • Milnes, Gerald C. "Old Christmas and Belsnickles." *Goldenseal* (Winter 1995).

Michael L. Benedum: Mallison, Sam T. *The Great Wildcatter*. Charleston: Education Foundation, 1953.

Jesse Bennet: Poling, Dorothy. "Jesse Bennet." *WVH* (Jan. 1951).

Louis Bennett Jr.: Bennett, Louis Jr. "Louis Bennett Jr. Papers." WV&RHC • Sheets, L. Wayne. "Able Courage: The Monumental Sallie Maxwell Bennett." *Goldenseal* (Spring 2000).

Tom Bennett: McKeown, Bonni V. *Peaceful Patriot: The Story of Tom Bennett*. Charleston: Mountain State Press, 1980 • Ryan, F. Evelyn. "Memorial to Honor Local Vietnam War Casualty." *Dominion Post*, 7/31/1988 • "Vietnam Vet to be Honored." *WVU Alumni News* (Apr. 1990).

Bens Run Earthworks: Bailey, Douglas L. "Archaeological Localities at the Bens Run Earthworks Site," Report. Charleston: Strategic Environmental, 1993 • Fowler, Daniel B. "Ancient Ruins," (unpub. ms.). WV Collections Management Facility, Moundsville, 1974 • Riggs, George P. & Nikola Riggs. "Shrouded in Mystery are the Great Prehistoric Ruins at Bens Run, West Virginia," (unpub. ms.). WV Collections Management Facility, Moundsville, 1927.

Benwood Mine Disaster: Various newspaper accounts, *Wheeling Intelligencer*, Apr.–May 1924.

Berkeley Castle: Newbraugh, Fred. *Berkeley Castle*. Shippensburg, PA: Beidle Printing House, 1988.

Berkeley County Riflemen: Conley, Phil. *West Virginia Yesterday and Today*. Charleston: WV Review Press, 1931 • Lewis, Virgil A. *History and Government of West Virginia*. New York: American Book, 1912 • "Morgan, Daniel." *Encyclopedia Americana*, International ed., vol. 19. Danbury, CT: Grolier, 1999.

Bethany College: Cummins, D. Duane. *The Disciples Colleges: A History*. St. Louis: CBP Press, 1987 • Gresham, Perry. *Campbell and the Colleges*. Nashville: Disciples of Christ Historical Society, 1973 • McAllister, Lester. *Bethany: The First 150 Years*. Bethany College Press, 1991.

Beverly: Baxter, Phyllis & Donald L. Rice. *Historic Beverly: A Guide Book*. Elkins: Tom's Printing, 1993 • Bosworth, Albert S. *History of Randolph County*. Parsons: McClain, 1975 • Maxwell, Hu. *History of Randolph County*. Morgantown: Acme Pub., 1898.

Ambrose Bierce: Carpenter, Charles. "West Virginia People and Places," Comstock - *Encyclopedia*, vol. 22, 1974 • Faust, Patricia L., ed. *Historical Times Illustrated Encyclopedia of the Civil War*. New York: Harper Collins, 1986 • McCann, William, ed. *Ambrose Bierce's Civil War*. Washington: Regnery Gateway, 1956.

Big Sandy River: Crowe-Carraco, Carol. *The Big Sandy*. Lexington: UPK, 1979.

Birds: Buckelew, Albert R. Jr. *West Virginia Breeding Bird Atlas*. Pittsburgh: UPP, 1994 • Bullard, James W., ed. *Birding Guide to West Virginia*. Wheeling: Brooks Bird Club, 1998 • Hall, George A. *West Virginia Birds*. Pittsburgh: Carnegie Museum of Natural History, 1983.

Van Bittner: Fox, Maier B. *United We Stand*. Washington: UMWA, 1990 • Thomas–*New Deal* • Zieger, Robert H. *The CIO, 1935–1955*. Chapel Hill: UNC Press, 1995.

The Black Hand: Belanger, Ruth. "Thomas and its Opera House." *Goldenseal* (Oct.–Dec. 1980) • Comstock - *Encyclopedia*, vol. 3, 1976 • Davis, Dorothy. *History of Harrison County*. Clarksburg, 1970.

Black Knight Country Club: Conley, Phil. "A Man of Vision . . . a Builder." *WV Review* (Sept. 1930).

Black Lung Disease: Smith, Barbara E. *Digging our Own Graves: Coal Miners and the Struggle over Black Lung Disease*. Philadelphia: Temple University Press, 1987.

Black Lung Movement: Hume, Brit. *Death in the Mines: Rebellion and Murder in the United Mine Workers*. New York: Grossman Pub., 1971 • Seltzer, Curtis. *Fire in the Hole: Miners and Managers in the American Coal Industry*. Lexington: UPK, 1985 • Smith, Barbara E. *Digging our*

Own Graves: Coal Miners and the Struggle over Black Lung Disease. Philadelphia: Temple University Press, 1987.

Sam Black: Comstock–*Encyclopedia,* vol. 3, 1976 • Rice & Brown • WPA–*Guide.*

W. E. Blackhurst: Foreword by G. A. Bowling, in Warren E. Blackhurst, *Afterglow.* Parsons: McClain, 1972 • Pocahontas County Historical Society. *History of Pocahontas County.* Marlinton, 1981.

The Blackwater Chronicle: Kennedy, Philip P. *The Blackwater Chronicle.* New York: Radford, 1853. Reprint, WVU Press, 2002.

Blackwater Falls: Kennedy, Philip P. *The Blackwater Chronicle.* New York: Radford, 1853. Reprint, WVU Press, 2002 • Ludlum, John & Thomas Arkle. *Blackwater Falls State Park and Canaan Valley State Park.* Morgantown: WVGES, 1971 • Smith, J. Lawrence. *Blackwater Country.* Parsons: McClain, 1972.

Blackwater River: Reger, David B, WVGES. *Tucker County.* Wheeling News Litho. Co., 1923 • USGS Maps, 7.5 Minute Series, WV quadrangles: Blackwater Falls, Davis & Mozark Mountain.

Blaine Island: Laidley, W.S. *History of Charleston and Kanawha County.* Chicago: Richmond-Arnold Pub. Co., 1911 • Cohen–*Kanawha Images* • Poe, J. Alfred & Albert Giles. *The History of South Charleston.* South Charleston History Book Publications Committee, 1995.

Jacob Beeson Blair: *Biographical Directory of the U.S. Congress.* Washington: GPO, 1989 • Conley, Phil. *West Virginia Reader.* Charleston: Education Foundation, 1970 • Conley–*Encyclopedia.*

Blair Mountain, Battle of: Corbin–*Life, Work* • Savage–*Thunder.*

Blenko Glass: Eige, Eason & Rick Wilson. *Blenko Glass 1930–1953.* Marietta, OH: Antique Publications, 1987 • Wilson, Rick. "We're in for it: Early Days at Blenko Glass." *Goldenseal* (Fall 1987).

Harman Blennerhassett: Fitch, Raymond E. ed. *Breaking with Burr: Harman Blennerhassett's Journal, 1807.* Athens: Ohio University Press, 1988 • Swick, Ray. *An Island Called Eden: An Historical Sketch of Blennerhassett Island near Parkersburg, West Virginia, 1798–1807.* Parkersburg Printing, 1996 • Swick. "Harman Blennerhassett: An Irish Aristocrat on the American Frontier." Ph.D. diss., Miami University, 1978 • Swick. "Harman Blennerhassett: Irish Aristocrat and Frontier Entrepreneur." M.A. thesis, University of Virginia, 1971.

Blennerhassett Island: Bennett, Emerson. *The Traitor or the Fate of Ambition.* Cincinnati: U.P. James, 1860 • Lowther, Minnie Kendall. *Blennerhassett Island in Romance and Tragedy.* Rutland, VT: Tuttle Pub., 1939 • Swick, Ray. "Harman Blennerhassett: An Irish Aristocrat on the American Frontier." Ph.D. diss., Miami University, 1978.

Margaret Agnew Blennerhassett: Swick, Ray. *An Island Called Eden: An Historical Sketch of Blennerhassett Island.* Parkersburg Printing, 1996.

Blizzard Treason Trial: Corbin–*Life, Work* • Davidson, Shae. "'The Boys'll Listen to Me:' The Labor Career of William Blizzard." M.A. thesis, Marshall University, 1998.

Blue Book: Blue Books, 1928, 1933, 1997.

Blue Jacket: "Blue Jacket." *American National Biography.* New York: Oxford University Press, 1999 • Johnson, Louise F. "Testing Popular Lore: Marmaduke Swearingen a.k.a. Blue Jacket." *National Genealogical Quarterly* (Sept. 1994) • Sugden, John. *Blue Jacket: Warrior of the Shawnees.* Lincoln: University of Nebraska Press, 2000 • "Van Swearingen, Marmaduke." Comstock–*Encyclopedia,* vol. 22, 1976.

Blue Sulphur Springs: Cohen, Stan. *Historic Springs of the Virginias.* Charleston: PHPC, 1981.

Bluefield: McGehee, C. Stuart. *Bluefield, West Virginia 1889–1989: A Centennial History.* City of Bluefield, 1990 • Rankin, John. *Early History and Development of Bluefield.* Radford, VA: Commonwealth, 1976.

Bluefield State College: McGehee, C. Stuart & Frank Wilson. *A Centennial History of Bluefield State College.* Tazewell, VA: Clinch Valley Press, 1995 • *Upward through the Years: Semi-Centennial Bulletin.* Bluefield State College, 1945 • Wilson, Frank E. *Historical Highlights.* Columbus: Continental Printing.

Bluegrass Music: Larkin, Colin, ed. *The Virgin Encyclopedia of Country Music.* London: Virgin Pub., 1998.

Blues Revue: Cryser, Julie R. "Technology, Low Overhead Overcome Drawbacks of Doing Business in W.Va." *Gazette,* 11/19/1996 • Miller, Chris. "Doddridge Man Spreads Passion for Blues." *Gazette,* 12/23/1992.

Bluestone Dam and Lake: "Bluestone Lake," Pamphlet. U.S. Army Corps of Engineers, 1999 • Casto, James E. "Bluestone Dam Celebrates 50 Years." *WWV* (1999).

Bluestone River: Reger, David B., WVGES. *Mercer, Monroe, and Summers Counties.* Wheeling News Litho. Co., 1926.

Board of Control: "Oldest State Board Heads for Oblivion Next June 30." *Daily Mail,* 3/21/1957 • "The State Institutions as seen by Investigating Committee; its Report." *Daily Mail,* 2/16/1909.

Bogs: Darlington, H. C. "Vegetation and Substrate of Cranberry Glades, WV." *Botanical Gazette* (1943) • Watts, W. A. "Late Quaternary Vegetation of Central Appalachia and the New Jersey Coastal Plain." *Ecological Monographs* (1979).

Bollman Truss Bridge: Harwood, Herbert H. Jr. *Impossible Challenge: The Baltimore and Ohio Railroad in Maryland.* Baltimore: Barnard, Roberts & Co., 1979.

Boone County: *Boone County.* Madison: Boone County Genealogical Society, 1990.

Daniel Boone: Draper, Lyman C. *The Life of Daniel Boone.* Mechanicsburg, PA: Stackpole Books, 1998 • Faragher, John Mack. *Daniel Boone: The Life and Legend of an American Pioneer.* New York: Holt, 1992 • Hale, John P. *History of the Great Kanawha Valley.* Madison, WI: Brant, Fuller & Co., 1891. Reprint, Gauley & New River Pub., 1994.

Arthur Ingraham Boreman: Ambler & Summers • Morgan–*Governors* • Woodward, Isaiah A. "Arthur Ingraham Boreman." *WVH* (July & Oct. 1970).

Alexander Robinson Boteler: Adams, Charles S., ed. *Alexander Boteler, Wheel Horse of Whiggery, Stonewall's Courier.* Shepherdstown: Charles S. Adams, 1998 • Boteler Papers, Duke University • Pendleton, Helen Boteler, "Alexander Robinson Boteler–A Nineteenth Century Romantic." *Shepherdstown Register,* 12/14, 21/1933; 1/11, 18, 25/1934; 2/1, 8, 14/1934.

The Boundary of West Virginia: Puetz, C. J. *West Virginia County Maps.* Lyndon Station, WI: Thomas Pub. • USGS Maps, Scale 1:250,000. Baltimore, Bluefield, Canton, Charlottesville, Clarksburg, Cumberland, Huntington & Jenkins quadrangles • Van Zandt, Franklin K. "Boundaries of the United States and the Several States," Bulletin 1212. USGS. Washington: GPO, 1976 • Delorme–*Atlas*

Bounty Lands: Abernethy, Thomas Perkins. *Western Lands and the American Revolution.* New York: Appleton-Century-Crofts, 1937 • Cook, Roy Bird. *Washington's Western Lands.* Strasburg, VA: Shenandoah Pub. House, 1931 • Rice–*Allegheny Frontier.*

Bourbon Democrats: Ambler & Summers • Rice & Brown • Williams–*Captains* • Williams, John Alexander. "The New Dominion and the Old: Ante-Bellum Statehood Politics as the Background of West Virginia's Bourbon Democracy." *WVH* (July 1972).

Belle Boyd: Sigaud, Louis A. *Belle Boyd: Confederate Spy.* Richmond, VA: Dietz Press, 1945.

Jennings Boyd: Hypes, Larry. "Decade Saw Blue Demons Set National Championship Record." *Daily Telegraph,* 12/31/1989 • Hypes. "Northfork, Boyd Began Legendary Run 25 Years Ago." *Daily Telegraph,* 12/27/1998 • Marino, Rose. *Welch and its People.* Marceline, MO: Walsworth Pub., 1985 • Murphy, Jody. "Boyd Recalls Glory Days." Beckley *Register-Herald,* 3/16/2000.

Nathan Cook Brackett: Rasmussen, Barbara. "Sixty-Four Edited Letters of the Founders of Storer College." M.A. thesis, WVU, 1986 • Riley, Wayne. *Sarah Jane Foster: Teacher of Freedmen.* Charlottesville: UVA Press, 1990 • Storer College Archives. WV&RHC.

Braddock's Road: Ansel, William H. Jr. *Frontier Forts along the Potomac and its Tributaries.* Parsons: McClain, 1984 • Hough, Walter. *Braddock's Route through the Virginia Colony.* Winchester, VA: Winchester-Frederick County Historical Society, 1970.

J. G. Bradley: Cantrell, Betty, Grace Phillips & Helen Reed. "Widen: The Town J. G. Bradley Built." *Goldenseal* (Jan.–Mar. 1977) • Stewart, C. C. "Strike Duty: A State Trooper Recalls Trouble in the Coalfields." *Goldenseal* (Winter 1995).

Ruby Bradley: Hedges, David. "Military Heroine Passes Away." *Times Record,* 5/30/2002 • "Ruby Bradley. Most Decorated Woman in U.S. Military History." Interview by Bob Dotson. *NBC Nightly News.* 2/23/2000.

Bramwell: *Daily Telegraph*, 11/1/1896 • Hager, Beth A. "Millionaires' Town: The Houses and People of Bramwell." *Goldenseal* (Winter 1982) • Sullivan, Kenneth. "Coal Men of the Smokeless Coalfields." *WVH* (Winter 1980).

Harry Brawley: Brawley, Harry M. *Twenty Years on an Oasis in the Vast Wasteland.* Charleston: Education Foundation, 1981 • *Harry Brawley: Making a Difference.* Documentary. Huntington: WBPY, 1993.

Braxton County: Sutton, John D. *History of Braxton County and Central West Virginia.* Parsons: McClain, 1967 • *Blue Book*, 1997.

Braxton County Rune Stone: "Graven Stone Key to Mound Builders." *Daily Mail*, 4/21/1940 • Stradonwold, Olaf. "Notes on the Grave Creek and Braxton County Rune Stones," in *Upper Ohio Valley Pioneer* (Mar. 1946).

Bretz Coke Ovens: "Elkins Coal & Coke Company Historic District." National Register of Historic Places Nomination, ms.,WVDC&H, 1978.

Brick Industry: Hayes, E. L. *Illustrated Atlas of the Upper Ohio River and Valley from Pittsburgh, PA. to Cincinnati, OH.* Philadelphia: Titus, Simmons & Titus, 1877 • McCue, John B., et al. *Clays of West Virginia.* Charleston: WVGES, 1948 • *New Cumberland, West Virginia: People and Places, 150 Years, 1839–1989.* New Cumberland: Hancock Courier Printing, 1989 • Welch, Jack. *History of Hancock County.* Wheeling News Litho. Co., 1963.

Bridges: Cohen, Stan. *West Virginia's Covered Bridges.* Charleston: PHPC, 1992 • Kemp, Emory L. *West Virginia's Historic Bridges.* Morgantown: WVU, 1984.

Brooke County: Conley–*Encyclopedia.* • Dodrill, Carlin F., Celia Vermillion & William L. Young. *West Virginia Centennial Celebration, 1863–1963, Brooke County.* Follansbee Review Press, 1963 • Newton, J. H., G. G. Nichols & A. G. Sprankle. *History of the Pan-Handle.* Wheeling: Caldwell, 1879.

A. B. Brooks: Boone, Weldon. *History of Botany in West Virginia.* Parsons: McClain, 1974 • Conley–*Encyclopedia* • Conley, Phil & William T. Doherty. *West Virginia History.* Charleston: Education Foundation, 1974.

William T. Brotherton Jr.: WV Legislature. *Senate Journal*, 4/8/1997.

Izetta Jewell Brown: "Izetta Jewell Brown Miller." Comstock - *Encyclopedia*, vol. 22, 1974 • *New York Times*, 11/15/1978.

John Brown: Finkelman, Paul, ed. *His Soul Goes Marching On.* Charlottesville: UVA Press, 1995 • Oates, Stephen B. *To Purge this Land with Blood.* New York: Harper & Row, 1970.

Browns Island: Doyle, Joseph. *20th Century History of Steubenville and Jefferson County and Representative Citizens.* Richmond: Arnold, 1910 • Kraina, Jane. "In Time and the River: The Story of Browns Island." *Goldenseal* (Winter 1989) • Pietranton, Frank A. *History of Weirton and Holliday's Cove and Life of J. C. Williams.* Weirton: Frank Pietranton, 1936 • Welch, Jack. *History of Hancock County.* Wheeling News Litho. Co., 1963.

The Bruen Lands Feud: Harmon, Dale L. *Kanawha County, West Virginia, Bruen Property Land Purchases from 47,000 Acre Sheba Tract 1850–1908.* Durham: Dale Harmon, 1984 • Johnson, Ludwell H. "'The Horrible Butcheries of West Virginia': Dan Cunningham on the Hatfield-McCoy Feud." *WVH* (1985–86) • *The Vandalia Journal* (July 1966).

Brush Creek Falls: Kesecker, C. L. "Brush Creek Falls Once Operated as Grist and Woolen Mill." *Princeton Observer*, 12/28/1950 • McCormick, Kyle. *The Story of Mercer County.* Charleston Printing, 1957 • Meador, Michael. "Factories Operated at Brush Creek Falls." *Daily Telegraph*, 3/25/1984.

Pearl S. Buck: Buck, Pearl S. *My Mother's House.* Richwood: Appalachian Press, 1965 • Conn, Peter. *Pearl S. Buck: A Cultural Biography.* New York: Cambridge University Press, 1996 • Doyle, Paul A. *Pearl S. Buck.* Boston: Twayne Pub., 1980.

Buckhannon: Comstock - *Encyclopedia*, vol. 4, 1976 • Cutright, W. B. *History of Upshur County.* Parsons: McClain, 1977 • Crampton, Norm. *Making your Move to One of America's Best Small Towns.* New York: M. Evans & Co., 2000.

Buckhannon River: *Hardesty's*, vol. 2.

Buckongahelas: Comstock–*Encyclopedia*, vol. 12–13, 1976 • McWhorter, J. C. *The Scout of the Buckongehanon.* Boston: Christopher Pub., 1927 • McWhorter, Lucullus Virgil. *The Border Settlers of Northwestern Virginia.* Hamilton, OH: Republican Pub. Co., 1915. Reprint, Comstock, 1974.

Buffalo Academy: *Hardesty's*, vol. 1 • "History of Buffalo," Bicentennial Pamphlet, 1976 • *Vandalia Journal* (July 1976).

Buffalo Archeological Site: Broyles, Bettye J. "A Late Archaic Component at the Buffalo Site, Putnam County, WV." *Report of Archeological Investigations*, no. 6. Morgantown: WVGES, 1976 • Hanson, Lee H. Jr. "The Buffalo Site: A Late 17th Century Indian Village Site in Putnam County, West Virginia." *Report of Archeological Investigations*, no. 5. Morgantown: WVGES, 1975 • Maslowski, Robert F. "Protohistoric Villages in Southern West Virginia." *Upland Archeology in the East, Symposium 2.* Harrisonburg, VA: James Madison University, 1984.

Buffalo Creek Flood: "The Buffalo Creek Flood and Disaster." *Official Report from the Governor's Ad Hoc Commission of Inquiry.* Aug. 1972 • Erikson, Kai T. *Everything in its Path.* New York: Simon & Schuster, 1976 • Lindsay, Cliff, Steve Hoyle & John Fredland. "The Buffalo Creek Disaster." *Joseph A. Holmes Safety Association Bulletin* (July–Aug. 2002).

Buffalo Mask: Brain, Jeffrey P. & Philip Phillips. *Shell Gorgets: Styles of the Late Prehistoric and Protohistoric Southeast.* Cambridge, MA: Peabody Museum, Harvard University, 1996 • Brashler, Janet G. & Ron W. Moxley. "Late Prehistoric Engraved Shell Gorgets of West Virginia." *WV Archeologist* (Spring 1990) • Hoffman, Darla S. "From the Southeast to Fort Ancient: A Survey of Shell Gorgets in West Virginia." *WV Archeologist* (Spring & Fall 1997).

Buffington Island: Hayes, E. L. *Illustrated Atlas of the Upper Ohio River and Valley from Pittsburgh, PA. to Cincinnati, OH.* Philadelphia: Titus, Simmons & Titus, 1877 • "Justice to Whom Justice is Due." Wheeling *Daily Intelligencer*, 2/25/1863 • Robinson, Bob. "Shifts in Ohio River Start Paper War over Islands." *Daily Mail*, 4/16/1979 • Smith, Myron J. Jr. "Gunboats at Buffington." *WVH* (Winter 1983).

Lew Burdette: *Baseball Encyclopedia.* New York: Macmillan Pub., 1996 • Driver, David. "The Pride of Nitro." *Goldenseal* (Fall 1998) • Porter, David, ed. *Biographical Dictionary of American Sports: Baseball.* Westport, CT: Greenwood Press, 1999.

Burial Customs: Crissman, James K. *Death and Dying in Central Appalachia.* Urbana: UI Press, 1994 • Stannard, David E., ed. *Death in America.* Philadelphia: UP Press, 1975.

Burning Springs: "Burning Springs." *Kanawha Banner*, 1/21/1831 • Cook, Roy Bird. "The Burning Springs Land." *Washington's Western Lands.* Strasburg, VA: Shenandoah Pub., 1930 • Ruffner, Lewis. "American Salt." *Kanawha Republican*, 11/12/1842.

Burning Springs Oil Field: Comstock–*Encyclopedia*, vol. 4, 1976 • Lee, Howard B. *The Burning Springs and Other Tales of the Little Kanawha.* Morgantown: WVU, 1968 • Reed, Louis. "Conflict and Error in the History of Oil." *WVH* (Oct. 1963).

Burning Springs Raid: Cole, Scott. *34th Battalion Virginia Cavalry.* Lynchburg: H. E. Howard, 1993 • Moore, George E. *A Banner in the Hills.* New York: Appleton-Century-Crofts, 1963.

Burr Conspiracy: Abernethy, Thomas P. "Aaron Burr in Mississippi." *Journal of Southern History* (1949) • Blackwood, Stephen A. "The Aaron Burr Conspiracy." M.A. thesis, UNC at Greensboro, 1979 • Lomask, Milton. *Aaron Burr: The Conspiracy and Years of Exile 1805–1836.* New York: Farrar, Straus, Giroux, 1982 • Reed, V. B. & J. D. Williams, eds. *The Case of Aaron Burr.* Boston: Houghton Mifflin, 1960 • Smith, Jean Edward. *John Marshall: Definer of a Nation.* New York: Henry Holt & Co., 1996.

Bushwhackers: Jones, Virgil Carrington. *Ranger Mosby.* Chapel Hill: UNC Press, 1944 • Stutler–*Civil War.*

Butterflies: Allen, Thomas J. *The Butterflies of West Virginia and their Caterpillars.* Pittsburgh: UPP, 1997.

Betsy Byars: Byars, Betsy. *The Moon and I.* Englewood Cliffs, NJ: Simon & Schuster, 1991 • Commire, Anne, ed. *Something About the Author*, vol. 46. Detroit: Gale Research, 1986 • Hile, Kevin, ed. *Something About the Author*, vol. 80. Detroit: Gale Research, 1995 • McMahon, Thomas, ed. *Authors & Artists for Young Adults*, vol. 19. Detroit: Gale Research, 1996.

W.E.R. Byrne: Comstock–*Encyclopedia*, vol. 4, 1976 • Laidley, W. S. *History of Charleston and Kanawha County.* Chicago: Richard-Arnold Pub., 1911 • Sullivan, Ken. "W.E.R. Byrne: A Fishing Lawyer." *Goldenseal* (Spring 1996).

Cabell County: Dilger, Robert J. *Cabell County History.* Morgantown: Dept. of Political Science, WVU, 2000 • KYOWVA Genealogical Society. *Cabell County Heritage: 1809–1996.* Huntington, 1996 • Wallace, George Selden. *Cabell County Annals and Families.* Richmond: Garrett & Massie, 1935.

Cabell Huntington Hospital: Casto, James E. *Huntington: An Illustrated History*. Huntington: Chapman Printing, 1997 • Cosco, Kathy M. "Cabell Huntington Hospital: Historical Progress," Report. 1997 • Kennedy, Nicole. "Hospitals get OK to Affiliate." *Herald-Dispatch*, 6/25/1998.

William H. Cabell: Wallace, George S. *Cabell County Annals and Families*. Richmond: Garrett & Massie, 1935.

Cabwaylingo State Forest: Woods, John H. "CCC Days in West Virginia." *WWV* (Mar. 1988).

Cacapon River: Ansel, W. H. Jr. *Frontier Forts along the Potomac and its Tributaries*. Parsons: McClain, 1984 • Constantz, George, N. Ailes & D. Malakoff. *Portrait of a River: The Ecological Baseline of the Cacapon River*. High View: Pine Cabin Run Ecological Laboratory, 1993 • Constantz, George & J. Matheson. "Science, Grass Roots, and the Cacapon River." *WWV* (Oct. 1989) • Wirtz, W. *Capon Valley Sampler*. Silver Spring, MD: Bartleby Press, 1990.

Calhoun County: Cuthbert, John. "Riverboat Days on the Little Kanawha River." *WWV* (Jan. 1996) • Elliott, Mae Stump. "Navigation on the Little Kanawha River." *Calhoun County Lines and Links* (Apr. 1980) • Calhoun County Historical & Genealogical Society. *History of Calhoun County*. Grantsville, 1990 • Holiday, Harry. "Early History of the Oil and Gas Industry in Calhoun County," (unpub. ms.) • Mathews, A. G. "Transportation in Calhoun County." *Grantsville News*, 8/9/1956 • Murphy, James M. "Transportation on the Little Kanawha River." M.A. thesis, WVU, 1950.

Johnson Newlon Camden: Chernow, Ron. *Titan: The Life of John D. Rockefeller Sr.* New York: Random House, 1998 • Lewis, Ronald L. *Transforming the Appalachian Countryside*. Chapel Hill: UNC Press, 1998 • Summers, Festus P. *Johnson Newlon Camden*. New York: G. P. Putnam's Sons, 1937 • Williams–*Captains*.

Camden Park: Platania, Joseph. "The Sign of the Happy Clown: Looking Back at Camden Park," *Goldenseal* (Summer 1987) • Platania. "Camden Park." *WWV* (July 1996).

Camp Ashford: Keefer, Louis E. "Prisoners of War at Camp Ashford." *Goldenseal* (Spring 1993) • Keefer. "The West Virginia WWII Home Front: Ashford General Hospital: The Greenbrier Goes to War." *Goldenseal* (Fall 1993).

Camp Brock: "Happy Negro Children Enjoy Life at State Camp." *Gazette*, 8/11/1935 • Thomas–*New Deal* • Withrow, Dolly. *From the Grove to the Stars: West Virginia State College 1891–1991*. Charleston: PHPC, 1991.

Camp Caesar: Woods, Wilson. "A Man Called Jack." *Webster Echo*, 3/9/1994 to 6/8/1994.

Camp Dawson: Keefer, Louis E. "The West Virginia WWII Home Front: POW: The Italian Prisoners at Camp Dawson." *Goldenseal* (Spring 1993) • "Welcome to the Army Training Site," Pamphlet. WV National Guard.

Camp Fairchance: Beehler, William N. *Relief, Work and Rehabilitation*, Report. WV Relief Administration. Charleston: Matthews Printing & Litho., Co., 1934 • *Gazette*, 10/28/1934 & 5/17/1936 • Dept. of Public Welfare, Biennial Report. 1936 • Thomas–*New Deal*.

Camp Good Luck: Stewart, Guy H. *A Touch of Charisma: A History of the 4-H Club Program in West Virginia*. Morgantown, 1969 • Wegman, Werner. "History of the First 4-H Camp in the World." *Magazine of History and Biography* (Sept. 1942). Elkins: Randolph County Historical Society.

Camp Piatt: Belle Woman's Club. *Bicentennial Belle, West Virginia: 1776–1976*. Belle, 1976 • Rice, Otis K. *Charleston and the Kanawha Valley: An Illustrated History*. Woodland Hills, CA: Windsor Pub., 1981.

Camp Woodbine: Peyton, Billy Joe & Pamela B. Redmond. "Cultural Resource Survey, Monongahela National Forest, CCC Camps, Fire Towers, Administrative Sites," (unpub. ms.). Monongahela National Forest, U.S. Forest Service, Elkins • *Woodland News*, Official Paper of CCC Co. 521, Richwood. Chicago: Center for Research Libraries.

Alexander Campbell: Campbell, Selina H. *Home Life and Reminiscences of Alexander Campbell*. St. Louis: John Burns, 1882 • Richardson, Robert. *Memoirs of Alexander Campbell*. Philadelphia: J. B. Lippincott, 1868–70 • Smith, Benjamin L. *Alexander Campbell*. St. Louis: Bethany Press, 1930.

Archibald W. Campbell: Cometti–*Thirty-Fifth*.

Canaan Valley: *History of State Parks* • Venable, Norma Jean. *Canaan Valley*. Morgantown: WVU, 1989.

Canaan Valley State Park: Allman, Ruth C. *Canaan Valley and the Black Bear*. Parsons: McClain, 1976 • *History of State Parks*.

Cannel Coal: Ashley, George H. "Cannel Coal in the U.S.," Bulletin 659. USGS. Washington: GPO, 1918 • Laing, James. "The Early Development of the Coal Industry in the Western Counties of Virginia, 1800–1865." *WVH* (Jan. 1966) • Rice, Otis K. "Coal Mining in the Kanawha Valley to 1861." *Journal of Southern History* (Nov. 1965).

Cap, Andy, and Flip: Tribe–*Jamboree*.

Allen Taylor Caperton: Morton, Oren F. *A History of Monroe County*. Staunton, VA: McClure, 1916 • Wakelyn, Jon L. *Biographical Dictionary of the Confederacy*. Westport, CT: Greenwood Press, 1977.

William Gaston Caperton III: Brunner, Bob. *The Caperton Years: 1989–1993*. Beckley: BJW Printing, 1997 • Rice, Otis K. & Stephen W. Brown. *The Mountain State: An Introduction to West Virginia*. Cincinnati: C. J. Krehbiel, 1997 • Wilson, Elizabeth Jill. *The Caperton Years: 1993–1997*, 2 vols. Charleston: Chapman Printing, 2005.

Capital Punishment: Bumgardner, Stan & Christine Kreiser, "'Thy Brother's Blood': Capital Punishment in West Virginia." *WV Historical Society Quarterly* (Mar. 1996).

The Capitol: Damron, Bob. "Building the Capitol." *Goldenseal* (Summer 1982).

Capon Springs Resort: Earls, Stephanie. "A King-Sized Reunion: Capon Springs Resort." *Goldenseal* (Spring 1997) • Wirtz, Willard. *Capon Valley Sampler*. Silver Spring, MD: Bartleby Press, 1990.

Captain Bull: Hyer, William H. & Benton B. Boggs Jr. *The Bulltown Country*. no. 10. Charleston: WV Writers' Program, 1940 • McWhorter, Lucullus. *The Border Settlers of Northwestern Virginia from 1768–1795*. Hamilton, OH: Republican Pub. Co., 1915. Reprint, Comstock, 1974. Reprint, Baltimore: Genealogical Pub. Co., 1975 • Parkman, Francis. *The Conspiracy of Pontiac and the Indian War*. Lincoln: University of Nebraska Press, 1994 • Withers–*Chronicles*.

John S. Carlile: Ambler, Charles H. *Waitman Thomas Willey*. Huntington: Standard Printing & Pub., 1954 • Moore, George E. *A Banner in the Hills*. New York: Appleton-Century-Crofts, 1963 • Stutler–*Civil War* • *West Virginia Biographical Dictionary*. St. Clair Shores, MI: Somerset Pub., 1999.

Carnegie Hall: Montgomery, John F. "Carnegie Hall." *Journal of the Greenbrier Historical Society* (1984).

Carnegie Libraries: Javersak, David T. "One Place on this Great Green Planet Where Andrew Carnegie Can't Get a Monument with his Money." *WVH* (Fall 1979) • Julian, Charles A. "An Analysis of the Historical Growth and Development of the West Virginia State Library Association." Ph.D. diss., Florida State University, 1990.

Carnifex Ferry, Battle of: Bard, David. *Civil War: The New River Valley*. Charleston: Quarrier Press, 2004 • Lowry, Terry. *September Blood: The Battle of Carnifex Ferry*. Charleston: PHPC, 1985.

Carnifex Ferry Battlefield State Park: *History of State Parks* • *Blue Book*, 1998.

Carpenter Family: Carpenter, Ernie. *Elk River Blues*. Augusta Heritage Records, AHR 003, Davis & Elkins College, Elkins, 1986 • Milnes, Gerald. *Play of a Fiddle*. Lexington: UPK, 1999 • Milnes, Gerald & Michael Kline. "Ernie Carpenter: Tales of the Elk River Country." *Goldenseal* (Summer 1986) • Sutton, John D. *History of Braxton County and Central West Virginia*. Sutton, 1919.

"Squirrelly Bill" Carpenter: Byrne -*Tale* • Milnes, Gerald. *Play of a Fiddle*. Lexington: UPK, 1999 • Milnes, Gerald & Michael Kline. "Ernie Carpenter: Tales of the Elk River Country." *Goldenseal* (Summer 1986).

Carr China Company: Taylor County Historical & Genealogical Society. *A History of Taylor County*. Grafton, 1986.

Fannie Cobb Carter: "Fannie Cobb Carter (1872–1973)," in *Missing Chapters: West Virginia Women in History*. Charleston: WV Women's Commission & the Humanities Foundation of WV, 1983.

George L. Carter: Sisson, Sebert L. "George L. Carter: Mountain Capitalist." *Mountain Laurel* (Oct. 1989).

Cass: Clarkson, Roy B. *On Beyond Leatherbark: The Cass Saga*. Parsons: McClain, 1990 • Clarkson–*Tumult* • WV Pulp & Paper Co. Records. WV&RHC.

Cass Scenic Railroad: Clarkson, Roy B. *On Beyond Leatherbark: The Cass Saga*. Parsons: McClain, 1990.

Castle Rock: Hennen, Ray V. & Robert W. Gawthorp, WVGES. *Wyoming and McDowell Counties*. Wheeling News Litho. Co., 1915 • *Pineville, Where Wyoming Trails Cross*. Charleston: WV Writers' Program, 1940.

The Casto Hole: Powers, Hoyt O. "The Casto Hole." *Jackson County History and Folklore*. Ripley: Jackson County Historical Society, 1983 • Comstock–*Encyclopedia*, 1976.

Cathedral State Park: Venable, Norma Jean. *Cathedral State Park*. Morgantown: WVU.

Gale Catlett: Julian, Norman. *Legends: Profiles in West Virginia University Basketball*. Morgantown: Trillium Pub., 1998 • *WVU Basketball Media Guide*, 1998–1999.

Catlette v. United States: Smith, Chuck. "Jehovah's Witnesses and the Castor Oil Patriots: A West Virginia Contribution to Religious Liberty." *WVH* (1998).

Caudy's Castle: Comstock–*Encyclopedia*, vol. 4, 1976 • Maxwell, Hu & H. L. Swisher. *History of Hampshire County*. Morgantown: A. B. Boughner, 1897. Reprint, McClain, 1972 • White, I. C., WVGES. *Hampshire and Hardy Counties*. Morgantown Printing & Binding, 1927.

Caves: Davies, W. E. *Caverns of West Virginia*. Morgantown: WVGES, 1965 • Jones, W. K. *Karst Hydrology Atlas of West Virginia*. Charles Town: Karst Waters Institute, 1997.

Cedar Lakes Conference Center: Jackson, Debby Sonis. "Building Cedar Lakes." *Goldenseal* (Fall 1990).

Celeron de Blainville: Cometti- *Thirty-Fifth* • WPA–*Guide*.

Cemeteries: Crissman, James K. *Death and Dying in Central Appalachia*. Urbana: UI Press, 1994 • West Virginia Cemeteries, Calendar. State Historic Preservation Office, WVDC&H, 2004 • Little, M. Ruth. *Sticks and Stones: Three Centuries of North Carolina Gravemarkers*. Chapel Hill: UNC Press, 1998.

Central City: Gorczyca, Beth. "Central City Days." *Herald-Dispatch*, 6/12/2000 • "The Heart of Central City in History," Pamphlet. Cabell-Huntington Convention & Visitors Bureau, 2001.

Don Chafin: Comstock–*Encyclopedia*, vol. 5, 1976 • *Gazette*, 8/10/1954 • Lee–*Bloodletting*.

Chair Making: Alexander, John D. *Make a Chair from a Tree: An Introduction to Working Green Wood*. Newtown, CT: Taunton Press, 1978 • Di Bartolomeo, Robert E. & Cherry G. Di Bartolomeo. "Wheeling's Chairs and Chairmakers 1828–1864." *Spinning Wheel* (May 1970) • Milnes, Gerald. "West Virginia Split Bottom: The Seat of Choice." *Goldenseal* (Fall 1986).

Champe Rocks: Judy, E. L. *History of Grant and Hardy Counties*. Charleston Printing, 1951 • Morton, Oren F. *A History of Pendleton County*. Dayton, VA: Ruebush-Elkins, 1910 • WPA–*Guide*.

Louis Watson Chappell: Cameron, Kenneth W. "WVU Sixty Years Ago and Memories of Louis Watson Chappell." *West Virginia & Regional History Collection Newsletter* (1988) • Chappell, Louis W. *John Henry: A Folk-Lore Study*. Jena, Germany: Frommannsche Verlag, W. Biederman, 1933. Reprint, Kennikat Press, 1968 • Chappell. *Folk-Songs of Roanoke and the Albemarle*. Morgantown: Ballad Press, 1939 • Cuthbert, John A. *West Virginia Folk Music*. Morgantown: WVU Press, 1982.

Charles Town Opera House: Hartgroves, Jean. "Old Opera House 20th Year Anniversary Celebration." Speech. WV&RHC • "The Old Opera House, Established 1910, Reopened 1976." Program. WV&RHC.

Charles Town Races: Theriault, William D. "For Love and Money: Jefferson County Horse Racing." *Goldenseal* (Spring 1989).

Charleston Area Medical Center: *Birth of a Medical Center: A History of CAMC*. Charleston: PHPC, 1988 • Fleming, Dolores. *The Southern Pylons*. Morgantown: Robert C. Byrd Health Sciences Center, 1997.

Charleston Gazette: Morgan, John G. "Gazette Gains First Century Milestone." *Gazette*, 4/30/1973.

Charleston National Bank: Rice, Otis K. & Stephen W. Brown. *A Centennial of Strength: West Virginia Banks*. Charleston: WV Bankers Assn., 1991.

Charleston Town Center: Maurice, Johanna. "Design of Mall Influenced by Works of Masters." *Daily Mail*, 9/2/1983 • Maurice. "Developer's Road to Town Center Began in Lumberyard." *Daily Mail*, 11/4/1983.

Cheat Lake: Callahan, James M. *History of the Making of Morgantown, West Virginia: A Type Study in Trans-Appalachian Local History*. Morgantown Printing & Binding, 1926 • Core, Earl L. *The Monongalia Story*, 5 vols. Parsons: McClain, 1974–84 • Core. *The Westover Observer*, 10/4/1956.

Cheat Mountain: Clarkson, Roy B. *On Beyond Leatherbark: The Cass Saga*. Parsons: McClain, 1990 • Price, Paul H., WVGES. *Pocahontas County*.

Wheeling News Litho, Co. 1929 • Reger, David B., WVGES. *Randolph County*. Morgantown: WVU, 1931.

Cheat Mountain, Battle of: Cohen, Stan. *Civil War in West Virginia*. Charleston: PHPC, 1979 • Moore, George E. *A Banner in the Hills*. New York: Appleton-Century-Crofts, 1963.

Cheat Mountain Salamander: Green, N. B. & T. K. Pauley. *Amphibians & Reptiles in West Virginia*. Pittsburgh: UPP, 1987.

Cheat River: Brooks, A. B. *West Virginia Geographical Survey*. Morgantown: Acme Pub., 1910 • Brooks, Maurice. *The Appalachians*. Boston: Houghton Mifflin, 1965. Reprint, Seneca Books, 1975 • Comstock–*Encyclopedia*, vol. 5, 1976 • Core, Earl L. *The Monongalia Story*, 5 vols. Parsons: McClain, 1974–84.

Chemical Industry: "The Salt Industry in the Kanawha Valley." South Charleston: FMC, 1976 • Wintz, William D. *Nitro: World War I Boom Town*. Charleston: Jalamap, 1985 • Woomer, Warren J. *The Institute Site from George Washington to the World of Chemicals*. Institute: Aventis Crop Science, 2000.

Lemuel Chenoweth: Downey, Virginia Y. "Lemuel Chenoweth–Bridge Builder," in Eva Margaret Carnes, ed., *Centennial History of the Philippi Covered Bridge, 1852–1952*. Philippi: Barbour County Historical Society, 1952 • Jackson, Debby Sonis. "Lemuel Chenoweth." *Goldenseal* (Summer 1988) • Maxwell, Claude W. "Lemuel Chenoweth." *Magazine of History and Biography* (Dec. 1954). Elkins: Randolph County Historical Society • Rice, Donald L. "Lemuel Chenoweth." *Randolph 200*. Elkins: Randolph County Historical Society, 1987.

Cherokees: Dowd, Gregory E. *A Spirited Resistance. The North American Indian Struggle for Unity*. Baltimore: Johns Hopkins University Press, 1992 • McLoughlin, William G. *Cherokee Renascence in the New Republic*. Princeton University Press, 1986 • Perdue, Theda. *Cherokee Women*. Lincoln: University of Nebraska Press, 1998.

Chesapeake & Ohio Railway: Turner, Charles W., et al. *Chessie's Road*. Alderson: C&O Historical Society, 1986.

Chessie System: Turner, Charles W., et al. *Chessie's Road*. Alderson: C&O Historical Society, 1986.

Chestnut Blight: Comstock–*Encyclopedia*, vol. 5, 1976 • Griffin, Lucille. "Battling the Blight." *Goldenseal* (Winter 1995) • Roane, Martha K., Gary J. Griffin & John R. Elkins. *Chestnut Blight, Other Endothia Diseases, and the Genus Endothia*. St. Paul: American Phytopathological Society Press, 1986.

Children's Home Society of West Virginia: Bumgardner, Stan. *Children's Home Society of West Virginia: Children–Yesterday, Today, Tomorrow*. Charleston: Children's Home Society, 1996.

William Edwin Chilton: Ambler & Summers • Cohen–*Kanawha Images* • MacCorkle, William A. *The Recollections of Fifty Years of West Virginia*. New York: G. P. Putnam's Sons, 1928 • Morgan, John G. "Gazette Gains First Century Milestone." *Gazette*, 4/30/1973.

Christian Church (Disciples of Christ): Garrison, Winfred E. & Alfred T. DeGroot. *The Disciples of Christ*. St. Louis: Bethany Press, 1948 • McAllister, Lester G. & William E. Tucker. *Journey in Faith: A History of the Christian Church (Disciples of Christ)*. St. Louis: Bethany Press, 1975.

Christian Panoply: Ambler & Summers • Harvey, Sir Paul. *Oxford Companion to English Literature*. Oxford, England: Clarendon Press, 1967 • Kunitz, Stanley J. & Howard Haycraft, eds. *British Authors before 1800: A Biographical Dictionary*. New York: Wilson, 1952.

Chronicles of Border Warfare: Cook, Roy Bird. *Alexander Scott Withers, Author of Chronicles of Border Warfare*. 1921 • Hesseltine, William B. *Pioneer's Mission: The Story of Lyman Copeland Draper*. Madison: State Historical Society of Wisconsin, 1954 • Turk, David S. "Hugh Paul Taylor, Historian and Mapmaker." *WVH* (1997).

Cicadas: Shalaway, Scott. "Periodical Cicadas." *WWV* (June 1999) • "The Periodical Cicada in West Virginia," Pamphlet. WV Dept. of Agriculture, 1999.

Civil Rights: Peeks, Edward. *The Long Struggle for Black Power*. New York: Charles Scribner's Sons, 1971 • Posey, Thomas E. *The Negro Citizen of West Virginia*. Institute: Press of WV State College, 1934 • Randall, James D. & Anna E. Gilmer. *Black Past*. Charleston, 1989.

Civil War: Curry, Richard O. *A House Divided: Statehood Politics & the Copperhead Movement in West Virginia*. Pittsburgh: UPP, 1964 • McPherson, James. *Battle Cry of Freedom*. New York: Oxford University Press, 1988 • Sauers, Richard A. *The Devastating Hand of War: Romney,*

West Virginia during the Civil War. Glen Ferris: Gauley Mount Press, 2000.

Civil Works Administration: Beehler, William N. *Relief, Work and Rehabilitation*, Report. WV Relief Administration. Charleston: Matthews Printing & Litho., Co., 1934 • Thomas–*New Deal*.

Civilian Conservation Corps: Cohen, Stan. *The Tree Army: A Pictorial History of the Civilian Conservation Corps, 1933–1942.* Missoula, MT: PHPC, 1980 • Harr, Milton. *The CCC Camps in West Virginia.* Charleston: Milton Harr, 1992 • Merrill, Perry. *Roosevelt's Forest Army: A History of the Civilian Conservation Corps, 1933–1942.* Montpelier, VT: P. H. Merrill, 1981.

Clarksburg: "Clarksburg Downtown Historic District." National Register of Historic Places Nomination, ms., WVDC&H, 1981 • Comstock–*Encyclopedia*, vol. 5, 1976 • Davis, Dorothy. *History of Harrison County.* Clarksburg: American Assn. of University Women, 1970 • Pool, James M. ed. *Clarksburg: A Bicentennial Album, 1785–1985.* Salem: Don Mills, Inc., 1986.

Clarksburg Education Convention: Rice & Brown.

Roy B. Clarkson: Clarkson–*Tumult*.

Claude Worthington Benedum Foundation: *In the Company of Extraordinary People: A Special Report upon the Occasion of the 50th Anniversary of the Claude Worthington Benedum Foundation.* Benedum Foundation, 1994 • Mallison, Sam. *The Great Wildcatter.* Charleston: Education Foundation, 1953.

Clay County: Conley–*Encyclopedia* • North, E. Lee. *The 55 West Virginias.* Morgantown: WVU Press, 1998.

Clay County Wild Man: *Hickory and Lady Slippers: Life and Legend of Clay County People,* vol. 3. Clay County High School, 1985 • Wilson, Jill. "Wild Man Still Startling Passers-by." *Sunday Gazette-Mail,* 9/30/1984.

Clay Mining: Hayes, E. L. *Illustrated Atlas of the Upper Ohio River and Valley from Pittsburgh, PA. to Cincinnati, OH.* Philadelphia: Titus, Simmons & Titus, 1877 • McCue, John B., et al. *Clays of West Virginia.* Charleston: WVGES, 1948 • *New Cumberland, West Virginia: People and Places.* New Cumberland: Hancock Courier Printing, 1989 • Welch, Jack. *History of Hancock.* Wheeling News Litho. Co., 1963.

Claymont Court: Bushong, Millard K. *A History of Jefferson County, West Virginia.* Charles Town: Jefferson Pub. Co., 1941 • Fairbairn, Charlotte J. *Washington Homes of Jefferson County.* Ranson: Whitney & White, 1946.

Clendenin Family: Clendenen, John F. & Harriet M. Clendenen. *Charles Clendenin of Virginia: His parents, his son Alexander, some of Alexander Clendinen's descendants,* vols. 1–4. San Luis Obispo, CA: Poor Richard's Press, 2000–2001 • Handley, Harry H. "The Clendenin Massacre." *Journal of Greenbrier Historical Society* (1970).

George Clendenin: DeGruyter, Julius A. *Kanawha Spectator.* Charleston: Jarrett Printing, 1953 • Morgan, John G. & Robert J. Byers. *Charleston 200.* Charleston: *Gazette,* 1994 • Rice, Otis K. *Charleston and the Kanawha Valley: An Illustrated History.* Woodlands Hills, CA: Windsor Pub., 1981.

J. R. Clifford: Evans, Willis F. *History of Berkeley County.* Martinsburg: Willis Evans, 1928 • Simmons, William J. *Men of Mark.* Chicago: Johnson Pub., 1970.

Cliftonville Mine Battle: Zwierzchowski, Mary. "The Cliftonville Riot." *Goldenseal* (Summer 1994).

Clover Archeological Site: Adams, John J. "A Fluted Point from Cabell County." *WV Archeologist* (1960) • Adams, John J. & S. F. Durrett. "Fort Ancient Art in Cabell and Mason Counties." *WV Archeologist* (1952) • Griffin, James B. *The Fort Ancient Aspect.* Ann Arbor: University of Michigan Press, 1943 • Maslowski, Robert F. "Protohistoric Villages in Southern West Virginia." *Upland Archeology in the East, Symposium 2.* Harrisonburg, VA: James Madison University, 1984.

Coal: *Annual Report and Directory of Mines 2000.* WV Office of Miners' Health, Safety & Training, 2001 • Barlow, James A. "Coal and Coal Mining in West Virginia." Coal Geology Bulletin. WVGES, 1974 • Headlee, A. J. & John P. Nolting Jr. "Characteristics of Minable Coals of West Virginia," Report 13. WVGES, 1940 • Repine, Thomas E., Bascombe M. Blake Jr., et al. "Regional and Economic Geology of Pennsylvanian Age Coal Beds of West Virginia." *International Journal of Coal Geology.* (1993).

Coal & Coke Railway: Callahan, James M. *History of West Virginia, Old and New.* Chicago: American Historical Society, 1923 • Pepper, Charles

M. *Life and Times of Henry Gassaway Davis.* New York: Century, 1920 • Ross, Thomas R. *Henry Gassaway Davis.* Parsons: McClain, 1994.

Coal Industry: Bailey, Kenneth R. "A Judicious Mixture: Negroes and Immigrants in the West Virginia Mines, 1880–1917." *WVH* (Jan. 1973) • Dix, Keith. *What's a Coal Miner to Do?* Pittsburgh: UPP, 1988 • Eller, Ronald D. *Miners, Millhands, and Mountaineers.* Knoxville: UT Press, 1982 • Ford, Thomas R., ed. *The Southern Appalachian Region: A Survey.* Lexington: UPK, 1962 • Isserman, Andrew M. "Where are the West Virginians?" *West Virginia Demographic Monitor* (Feb. 1995) • Sullivan, Kenneth. "Coal Men of the Smokeless Coalfields." *WVH* (Winter 1980).

Coal Mine Disasters: Cohen, Stan. *King Coal.* Charleston: PHPC, 1984 • Dillon, Lacy A. *They Died for King Coal.* Winona, MN: Apollo Books, 1985 • Dillon. *They Died in the Darkness.* Parsons: McClain, 1976 • MSHA. *Report of Investigation, Underground Coal Mine Explosion, Blacksville No.1 Mine.* Washington: U.S. Dept. of Labor, 1993 • WV Dept. of Mines, Annual Report. 1886 • WV Dept. of Mines, Annual Report. 1894 • WV Dept. of Mines. *Report of Major Coal Mine Fire, Blacksville. No. 1 Mine.* 1972 • WV Office of Miners' Health, Safety & Training, Annual Report. 1996.

Coal Mine Health and Safety Legislation: Finley, Joseph E. *The Corrupt Kingdom.* New York: Simon & Schuster, 1972 • Hume, Brit. *Death and the Mines.* New York: Grossman Pub., 1971 • Lockard, Duane. *Coal.* Charlottesville: UVA Press, 1998 • Sinclair, Ward. "Lone Ranger of Mine Safety." *Louisville Courier-Journal,* 1/4/1970.

Coal Mine Mechanization: Dix, Keith. *What's a Coal Miner to Do?* Pittsburgh: UPP, 1988 • Hotchkiss, Willard E., et al. *Mechanization, Employment, and Output Per Man in Bituminous Coal Mining.* Philadelphia: Work Projects Administration, 1939.

Coal River: Dean, William H. "Steamboat Whistles on the Coal." *WVH* (July 1971) • Dean. "When Steamboats Plied the Coal," in St. Albans Historical Society, *St. Albans History.* Marceline, MO: Walsworth Pub., 1993 • WVDNR, Division of Water Resources. *Comprehensive Survey of the Coal River Basin.* 1978.

Coal River Navigation Company: Gamble, J. Mack. "When Steamboats Plied the Coal River." *S&D Reflector* (Dec. 1966) • Johnson, Leland R. *Men, Mountains, and Rivers.* Washington: GPO, 1977.

Coalfield Doctors: Frazier, Claude A. & F. K. Brown. *Miners and Medicine: West Virginia Memories.* Norman: University of Oklahoma Press, 1992.

Arden Cogar Sr.: Comstock–*Encyclopedia,* vol. 5, 1976 • "Team USA Wins First International Competition." *Webster Republican,* 5/30/2001 • "Woodchopping Contest Best Ever." *Webster Echo,* 6/4/1969.

Coke Making: Workman, Michael E. *Northern West Virginia Coal Fields.* Morgantown: Institute for the History of Technology & Industrial Archaeology, 1994.

Columbia Energy Group: Dawson, Albert F. *Columbia System: A History.* New York: J. J. Little & Ives, 1938.

Company Stores: Athey, Louis L. "The Company Store in Coal Town Culture." *Labor's Heritage* (Jan. 1990) • Corbin–*Life, Work* • Fishback, Price V. "Did Coal Miners 'Owe their Souls to the Company Store'?" *Journal of Economic History* (1986) • Johnson, Ole. *The Industrial Store: Its History, Operations, and Economic Significance.* Atlanta: Foote & Davies, 1952 • Shifflett, Crandall A. *Coal Towns: Life, Work, and Culture in Company Towns of Southern Appalachia, 1880–1960.* Knoxville: UT Press, 1991.

Company Towns: Eller, Ronald D. *Miners, Millhands, and Mountaineers.* Knoxville: UT Press, 1982 • Gillenwater, Mack H. "Cultural and Historical Geography of Mining Settlements in the Pocahontas Coal Field." Ph.D. diss., University of Tennessee, 1972 • Sullivan–*Coal Men* • Tams, W. P. *The Smokeless Coal Fields of West Virginia.* Morgantown: WVU Libraries, 1964.

Jim Comstock: "Famed Hillbilly Editor Dies at 85." *Marshall Journalism School AlumNews.* Huntington: Wayne Co. Pub. 1996 • Kelly, Richard A. *Outstanding West Virginians.* Charleston: Bold Enterprises, 1969.

Confederate Soldiers in West Virginia: Dickinson, Jack L. *Tattered Uniforms and Bright Bayonets: West Virginia's Confederate Soldiers.* Huntington: Marshall University Foundation, 1995 • Howard, Harold E. *The Virginia Regimental Histories Series.* Appomattox, VA: H. E. Howard, 1996 • Linger, James Carter. "Confederate Military Units of West Virginia," ms., State Archives, 1989 • "Compiled Service Records of

Confederate Soldiers Who Served in Organizations from the State of Virginia." Microfilm publication #324. National Archives.

Congressional Medal of Honor: U.S. Senate. Committee on Veterans Affairs. *Medal of Honor Recipients, 1863–1978.* Washington: GPO, 1979.

Congressional Representation: *Biographical Directory of the American Congress, 1774–1989.* Washington: GPO, 1989 • Martis, Kenneth C. *The Historical Atlas of Political Parties in the U.S. Congress: 1789–1989.* New York: Macmillan, 1989 • Martis, Kenneth C. & Gregory Elmes. *The Historical Atlas of State Power in Congress: 1790–1990.* Washington: Congressional Quarterly Press, 1993.

William Gustavus Conley: Morgan–*Governors* • Thomas–*New Deal* • Williams, John Alexander. *West Virginia: A History.* New York: W. W. Norton & Co., 1976. Reprint, 1984.

Conservation Movement: Carvell, Kenneth L. & William R. Maxey. *Protectors of the Forest Resources: A History of the West Virginia Division of Forestry, 1909–1998.* Charleston: WV Division of Forestry, 1998 • Clarkson-*Tumult* • Stephenson, Steven L., ed. *Upland Forests of West Virginia.* Parsons: McClain, 1993.

Consolidated Bus Lines: Craft, James Elliott. *Wheels on the Mountain.* Parsons: McClain, 1969.

Consolidation Coal Company: Cook, Jeffery B. "The Ambassador of Development: Aretas Brooks Fleming." Ph.D. diss., WVU, 1998 • Massay, Glenn F. "Coal Consolidation: Profile of the Fairmont Field." Ph.D. diss., WVU, 1970 • Williams-*Captains* • Workman, Michael E. "Political Culture and the Coal Economy in the Upper Monongahela Region: 1774–1933." Ph.D. diss., WVU, 1995.

Constitution of 1830: Peterson, Merrill D., ed. *Democracy, Liberty, and Property: The State Constitutional Conventions of the 1820's.* New York: Bobbs-Merrill, 1966 • *Proceedings and Debates of the Virginia State Convention of 1829–30.* Richmond: S. Shepherd & Co., 1830 • Pulliam, David L. *Constitutional Conventions of Virginia.* Richmond: John T. West, 1901 • Williams–*Captains*.

Constitution of 1851: Pulliam, David L. *Constitutional Conventions of Virginia.* Richmond: John T. West, 1901 • *Register of Debates and Proceedings of the Virginia Reform Convention.* Richmond, 1851 • Van Schreeven, William J. *The Conventions and Constitutions of Virginia 1776–1966.* Richmond: Virginia State Library, 1967.

The Constitution of West Virginia: Bastress, Robert M. *The West Virginia State Constitution.* Westport, CT: Greenwood Press, 1995 • *Debates and Proceedings of the First Constitutional Convention of West Virginia.* Huntington: Gentry Brothers, 1939 • Rice & Brown.

Constitutional Convention of 1861–63: Ambler, Charles H., Frances H. Atwood & William B. Mathews, eds. *Debates and Proceedings of the First Constitutional Convention of West Virginia.* Huntington: Gentry Brothers, 1939 • Ambler & Summers • Rice & Brown.

Constitutional Convention of 1872: Bastress, Robert M. *The West Virginia State Constitution.* Westport, CT: Greenwood Press, 1995 • *Journal of Constitutional Convention, Assembled at Charleston, West Virginia, Jan. 16, 1872.* Charleston: Henry S. Walker, Printer, 1872.

Coon Hunting: Blisard, John. "Coondog Heaven." *Goldenseal* (Winter 2000) • Rogers, Rich. "West Virginia's Hunting Hound Heritage." *WWV* (Nov. 1990).

Samuel Cooper: Meyer, Simon, ed. *One Hundred Years: An Anthology of Charleston Jewry.* Charleston: Jones Printing, 1972 • Shinedling, Abraham. *West Virginia Jewry: Origins and History, 1850–1958.* Philadelphia: Maurice Jacobs, 1963.

Wilma Lee and Stoney Cooper: Tribe–*Jamboree*.

Coopers Rock State Forest: Carvell, Kenneth L. "Heartstone of Coopers Rock State Forest." *WWV* (Mar. 1975) • Core, Earl L. *The Monongalia Story*, 5 vols. Parsons: McClain, 1974–84 • Rodd, Judith. *A Guide to Coopers Rock State Forest.* Moatsville: Barn Echo Press, 1994.

Copperhead Movement: Curry, Richard O. *A House Divided: A Study of Statehood Politics & the Copperhead Movement in West Virginia.* Pittsburgh: UPP, 1964.

Corncribs: Schultz, LeRoy G. "West Virginia Cribs and Granaries." *Goldenseal* (Winter 1983) • Wright, Ray. "More to the New Corncrib than Meets the Eye." *News from the Frontier Culture Museum,* vol. 17, no. 2, Staunton, VA, 2002.

Cornstalk: Hodge, Fredrick W., ed. *Handbook of American Indians North of Mexico, Part 1.* New York: Pageant Books, 1959 • Kellogg, Louise Phelps.

"Cornstalk." *Dictionary of American Biography.* New York: Scribner, 1946–1958 • Morgan–*Governors* • Rice–*Allegheny Frontier*.

John Jacob Cornwell: Fisher, Lucy L. "John J. Cornwell, Governor of West Virginia, 1917–1921." *WVH* (Apr. & July 1963) • Hennen, John. *The Americanization of West Virginia.* Lexington: UPK, 1996 • Morgan-*Governors*.

Corricks Ford, Battle of: Cohen, Stan. *Civil War in West Virginia.* Charleston: PHPC, 1979 • Moore, George E. *A Banner in the Hills.* New York: Appleton-Century-Crofts, 1963.

Jenes Cottrell: Screven, Tom. "Remembering Jenes Cottrell." *Goldenseal* (Apr.–June 1981).

Country Doctors: Hale, John P. "Dr. Jesse Bennet," in *History of the Great Kanawha Valley.* Madison, WI: Brant, Fuller & Co., 1891. Reprint, Gauley & New River Pub., 1994 • Joy, James E. "'Get Yourself a Good Horse': Dr. James Dye of Calhoun County." *Goldenseal* (Spring 1982) • Prichard, Arthur C. "Phoebia G. Moore, M.D." *Goldenseal* (Oct.–Dec. 1979).

"Country Roads": Burnside, Mary Wade. "Take Me Home." *Gazette,* 8/5/1999 • Denver, John. *Poems, Prayers, and Promises.* RCA recording 0445, 1971; reissued on CD, RCA 5189-2-R • Denver, John, Bill Danoff & Taffy Danoff. "Take Me Home, Country Roads." Port Chester, NY: Cherry Lane Music, 1971.

County Poor Farms: Brammer, Richard. "A Home for the Homeless." *Goldenseal* (Fall 1994) • Cosco, Joe. "Cabell County Poor Farm, 1853–1929." *Goldenseal* (Apr.–June 1979) • Thomas–*New Deal*.

County Unit Plan: Ambler–*Education* • Ambler & Summers • Thomas–*New Deal*.

The Courts: Brisbin, Richard A. Jr. "The West Virginia Judiciary," in Christopher Z. Mooney, et al. *West Virginia's State Government: The Legislative, Executive, and Judicial Branches.* Morgantown: WVU Institute for Public Affairs, 1993.

Rose Agnes Rolls Cousins: Furbee, Mary Rodd. "'I was Never Afraid of Anything': Pilot Rose Rolls Cousins." *Goldenseal* (Summer 1997) • Withrow, Dolly. *From the Grove to the Stars: West Virginia State College 1891–1991.* Charleston: PHPC, 1991.

Covered Bridges: Allen, Richard Sanders. *Covered Bridges of the Mid-Atlantic States.* Brattleboro, VT: Stephen Green Press, 1959 • Auvil, Myrtle. *Covered Bridges of West Virginia.* Parsons: McClain, 1972 • Cohen, Stan. *West Virginia's Covered Bridges.* Charleston: PHPC, 1992.

Billy Cox: Tribe–*Jamboree*.

John Harrington Cox: Cox, John Harrington. *Folk-Songs Mainly from West Virginia.* New York: National Service Bureau, 1939 • Cox. *Folk-Songs of the South.* Cambridge: Harvard University Press, 1925 • Cox. *Traditional Ballads Mainly from West Virginia.* New York: National Service Bureau, 1939.

Cranberry Glades: Brooks, Maurice G. *The Appalachians.* Boston: Houghton Mifflin, 1965. Reprint, Seneca Books, 1975 • Core, Earl L. *Vegetation of West Virginia.* Parsons: McClain, 1974 • Darlington, H. Clayton. "Vegetation and Substrate of Cranberry Glades." *Botanical Gazette* (1943).

Cranesville Swamp: Browning, Meshach. *Forty-four Years of the Life of a Hunter.* Philadelphia: Lippincott, 1859 • Venable, Norma Jean. *Cranesville Swamp.* Morgantown: WVU, 1991.

Bruce Crawford: Papers of the WV Writers' Program. WV&RHC • Prichard, Arthur C. "'In West Virginia I Had More Freedom': Bruce Crawford's Story." *Goldenseal* (Spring 1984) • Thomas, Jerry Bruce. "'The Nearly Perfect State': Governor Homer Adams Holt, the WPA Writers' Project and the Making of *West Virginia: A Guide to the Mountain State.*" *WVH* (1993).

William Crawford: Butterfield, C. W. *The Washington-Crawford Letters.* Cincinnati: R. Clarke & Co., 1877 • Eckert, Allan W. *That Dark and Bloody River.* New York: Bantam Books, 1995 • Scholl, Allen W. *The Brothers Crawford: Colonel William, 1722–1782, and Valentine Jr., 1724–1777.* Westminster, MD: Heritage Books, 1995.

Michael Cresap: Jacob, John J. *A Biographical Sketch of the Life of the Late Captain Michael Cresap.* Cumberland, MD: J. M. Buchanan, 1826. Reprint, McClain, 1971.

Crime: FBI-Uniform Crime Report Statistics, 1960–2003 • Harrison, Paige M. & Allen J. Beck. "Prisoners in 2001," Bulletin. Bureau of Criminal Justice Services, July 2002.

Croatian Cultural Club: Kline, Michael. "The Music Made Everything Okay." *Goldenseal* (Summer 1982).

Claudius Crozet: Couper, William. *Claudius Crozet: Soldier–Sailor–Educator–Engineer (1789–1864)*. Charlottesville: Historical Pub., 1936 • Hunter, Robert F. & Edwin L. Dooley Jr. *Claudius Crozet*. Charlottesville: UVA Press, 1989.

George Crumb: Crumb, George. *Echoes of Time and the River: Four Processionals for Orchestra*. 1967. The Louisville Orchestra, Jorge Mester, conductor, Louisville S-711 • Gillespie, Don, ed. *George Crumb: Profile of a Composer*. New York: C. F. Peters, 1986.

CSX: Turner, Charles W., et al. *Chessie's Road*. Alderson: Chesapeake & Ohio Historical Society, 1986.

Cultural Center: Griffith, Carolanne. "For a Tour of West Virginia's New Science & Culture Center." *WWV* (Dec. 1976).

The Cultural Landscape: Glassie, Henry. *Pattern in the Material Folk Culture of the Eastern United States*. Philadelphia: UP Press, 1968 • Hart, John Fraser. *The Rural Landscape*. Baltimore: Johns Hopkins University Press, 1998 • Jackson, John Brinkerhoff. *Discovering the Vernacular Landscape*. New Haven, CT: Yale University Press, 1984 • Noble, Allen G. *To Build in a New Land: Ethnic Landscapes in North America*. Baltimore: Johns Hopkins University Press, 1992.

Dan Cunningham: Bailey, Kenneth R. "The Murder of John Harless," in *Proceedings of the New River Symposium*, 1991 • Johnson, Ludwell H. "'The Horrible Butcheries of West Virginia:' Dan Cunningham on the Hatfield-McCoy Feud." *WVH* (1985–86) • Mylott, James P. *A Measure of Prosperity: A History of Roane County*. Charleston: Mountain State Press, 1984.

Richard Currey: Douglas, Thomas W. "Interview: Richard Currey." *Appalachian Journal* (Summer 1993).

Phyllis Curtin: *Current Biography Yearbook: 1964*. New York: H. W. Wilson, 1964 • Floyd, Carlisle. *Susannah*. New Orleans Opera with Phyllis Curtin in the Title Role, 1962. VAI Audio 1115.

Daughters of the American Revolution: Baker, Juliette B. *West Virginia State History of the Daughters of the American Revolution*. West Virginia State Society, DAR, 1928 • Spearman, Maxine P. *West Virginia State History of the Daughters of the American Revolution*. West Virginia State Society, DAR, 1982.

Davis & Elkins College: Ross, Thomas Richard. *Davis & Elkins College: The Diamond Jubilee History*. Parsons: McClain, 1980.

Henry Gassaway Davis: Pepper, Charles M. *The Life and Times of Henry Gassaway Davis*. New York: Century, 1920 • Ross, Thomas Richard. *Henry Gassaway Davis*. Parsons: McClain, 1994 • Williams–*Captains*.

John W. Davis: Harbaugh, William H. *Lawyer's Lawyer: The Life of John W. Davis*. New York: Oxford University Press, 1973. Reprint, UVA Press, 1990.

John Warren Davis: Harlan, John C. *History of West Virginia State College*. Dubuque, IA: Wm. C. Brown, 1968 • John W. Davis Papers. Drain-Jordan Library, WV State University • Stoner, John C. "John W. Davis," in *Encyclopedia of African American Culture and History*, vol. 2. New York: Simon & Schuster, 1996.

Julia Davis: Davis, Julia. *The Embassy Girls*. Morgantown: WVU Press, 1992 • Davis. *The Shenandoah*. New York: Farrat & Rinehart, 1945.

Rebecca Harding Davis: Davis, Rebecca Harding. *Life in the Iron Mills: With a Biographical Interpretation by Tillie Olsen*. Old Westbury, NY: Feminist Press, 1972 • Harris, Sharon M. *Rebecca Harding Davis and American Realism*. Philadelphia: UP Press, 1991.

William M. O. Dawson: Burckel, Nicholas C. "Publicizing Progressivism: William M. O. Dawson." *WVH* (Spring–Summer 1981) • Morgan–*Governors* • Rice & Brown.

Mack Day: Battlo, Jean. "Booger Man: Recalling Revenuer Mack Day." *Goldenseal* (Summer 1996).

Alston G. Dayton: Lunt, Richard D. *Law and Order vs. the Miners*. Charleston: Appalachian Editions, 1992 • Rice & Brown • Williams–*Captains*.

Wills De Hass: De Hass, Wills. *History of the Early Settlement and Indian Wars of Western Virginia*. Philadelphia: H. Hoblitzell, 1851 • Norona, Delf. "Skeletal Material from the Grave Creek Mounds." *WV Archeologist* (Feb. 1953) • *Who's Who in America, 1901–1902*. Chicago: A. N. Marquis, 1901.

Eugene Victor Debs: Corbin, David A. "Betrayal in the West Virginia Coal Fields: Eugene V. Debs and the Socialist Party of America, 1912–1914."

Journal of American History (1978) • Fagge, Roger. "Eugene Debs in West Virginia, 1913: A Reappraisal," *WVH* (1993).

Declaration of Rights of the People of Virginia: Ambler & Summers • Hall, Granville Davisson. *The Rending of Virginia*. Chicago: Mayer & Miller, 1902 • Lewis, Virgil A. *How West Virginia was Made*. Charleston: News-Mail, 1909.

Deer Season: Allen, Tom & Jack Cromer. "White-tailed Deer in West Virginia," Bulletin. WVDNR, 1977.

Deforestation: Eller, Ronald D. *Miners, Millhands, and Mountaineers*. Knoxville: UT Press, 1982 • Lewis, Ronald L. *Transforming the Appalachian Countryside*. Chapel Hill: UNC Press, 1998.

Martin Robison Delany: Delany, Martin R. *The Condition, Elevation, Emigration and Destiny of the Colored People of the United States*. Philadelphia, 1852. Reprint, Ayer, 1988 • Levine, Robert S., ed. *Martin R. Delany: A Documentary Reader*. Chapel Hill: UNC Press, 2003. • Rollin, Frank A. *The Life and Public Service of Martin R. Delany*. Boston: Lee & Shepard, 1883. Reprint, Ayer, 1970 • Sterling, Dorothy. *The Making of An Afro-American: Martin Robison Delany*. New York: Da Capo Press, 1996.

Democratic Party: Brisbin, Richard A. Jr., et al. *West Virginia Politics and Government*. Lincoln: University of Nebraska Press, 1987 • Fenton, John F. *Politics in the Border States*. New Orleans: Hauser Press, 1957 • Peirce, Neil R. *The Border South States: People, Politics, and Power in the Five States of the Border South*. New York: W. W. Norton, 1975.

Demography: Lego, Brian. "West Virginia: A 20th Century Perspective on Population Change," ms. Morgantown: WVU, 1999 • Rice & Brown.

James Dent: "Gazetteer James F. Dent Dead at 63." *Gazette*, 7/18/1992 • Knight, Wallace E. "James F. Dent: An Appreciation." *Charlestonian Magazine* (Spring 1993).

Marmaduke H. Dent: Reid, John Phillip. *An American Judge: Marmaduke Dent of West Virginia*. New York: NYU Press, 1968.

The Department of West Virginia: Lang, Theodore. *Loyal West Virginia from 1861 to 1865*. Baltimore: Deutsch Pub., 1895 • Stutler–*Civil War*.

DeSales Heights: Goodwin, Jacqueline G. "Faith and Works: The Sisters of DeSales Heights." *Goldenseal* (Winter 1990)

Dialect: Dial, Wylene P. "Language," in B. B. Maurer, ed., *Mountain Heritage*. Ripley: Mountain State Art & Craft Fair, 1974 • Montgomery, Michael B. & Joseph S. Hall. *Dictionary of Smoky Mountain English*. Knoxville: UTP, 2004 • Williams, Cratis D. *Southern Mountain Speech*. Berea, KY: Berea College Press, 1992 • Wolfram, Walt & Donn Christian. *Appalachian Speech*. Arlington, VA: Center for Applied Linguistics, 1976.

Diamond Department Store: Wells, Sandy. "Remembering the Diamond." *Gazette*, 2/1/1996.

Hazel Dickens: Rosenberg, Neil, Alice Gerrard & Hazel Dickens. *Hazel Dickens and Alice Gerrard: Pioneering Women of Bluegrass*, liner notes, 1996 • Straw, Richard. "Hazel Dickens & Mike Seeger," in J. W. Wilson & Edwin T. Arnold, eds., *Interviewing Appalachia*. Knoxville: UT Press, 1994 • Wolfe, Charles. *Hazel and Alice*, liner notes, 1995.

Little Jimmy Dickens: Tribe–*Jamboree*.

John Quincy Dickinson: Drennen, Bill. *One Kanawha Valley Bank: A History*. Charleston, 2001 • "J. Q. Dickinson Loses Battle Against Death." *Gazette*, 11/27/1925 • Miller & Maxwell, vol. 2.

Dickinson Family: Drennen, Bill. *One Kanawha Valley Bank: A History*. Charleston, 2001 • Gallaher, DeWitt C. *Genealogical Notes of the Miller-Quarrier-Shrewsbury-Dickinson Families*. Charleston: Tribune Printing Co., 1917 • Miller & Maxwell, vol. 2.

Joseph H. Diss Debar: Stutler, Boyd B. "Joseph H. Diss Debar–Prophet, Colonizer." *WV Review* (Dec. 1931) • Wilson, Donald Edward. "Joseph H. Diss Debar in West Virginia." M.A. thesis, WVU, 1961.

Doddridge County: Doddridge County Historical Society. *The History of Doddridge County*. Dallas: Taylor Pub., 1979 • *Hardesty's*, vol. 2.

Joseph Doddridge: Ambler, Charles H. *West Virginia: Stories and Biographies*. New York: Rand McNally, 1937 • Ambler. *West Virginia: The Mountain State*. New York: Prentice-Hall, 1940 • Doddridge, Joseph. *Notes on the Settlement and Indian Wars of the Western Parts of Virginia*. Wellsburgh, VA: Office of the Gazette, 1824. Reprint, New Werner, 1912.

Philip Doddridge: Ambler & Summers • Lambert, Oscar D. *Pioneer Leaders of Western Virginia*. Parkersburg: Scholl Printing, 1935.

Dolly Sods: "Dolly Sods Wilderness and Surrounding Area," Pamphlet. U.S. Forest Service, 1988 • Venable, Norma Jean. *Dolly Sods.* Morgantown: WVU, 2001.

Donaghho Pottery: Baker, Stanley W. "Crocks and Churns: A. P. Donaghho and Parkersburg Stoneware." *Goldenseal* (Summer 1985) • Grimsley, G. P., WVGES. *Clays, Limestones and Cements.* Wheeling News Litho. Co., 1906 • Smith, Elmer L. *Pottery.* Lebanon, PA: Applied Arts Publishers, 1972.

Shirley Donnelly: Fayette County Chamber of Commerce. *History of Fayette County.* Marceline, MO: Heritage House, 1993 • Shawkey, Morris. *West Virginia: In History, Life, Literature and Industry,* 5 vols. Chicago: Lewis Pub., 1928.

Douglass High School: Bickley, Ancella R. "Douglass High School, 1892–1961." *Douglass High School Centennial Reunion Book.* Huntington: Franklin Printing, 1993 • Gould, Alan. "Nomination of Douglass High School to the National Register of Historic Places," in Ancella R. Bickley, ed., *Our Mount Vernons: Historic Register Listings of Sites Significant to the Black History of West Virginia.* Huntington: Carter G. Woodson Memorial Foundation & Drinko Academy, 1997 • Meadows, Floyd P., Novella Gipson & Aubrey Gipson. "The History of Douglass School, 1892–1961." *Douglass High School Reunion Souvenir Program Book.* Huntington: Franklin Printing, 1973.

Dolores I. Dowling: Kelly, Richard A. *Outstanding West Virginians of 1969–70.* Charleston: Bold Enterprises, 1969 • Comstock–*Encyclopedia,* vol. 7, 1976.

Draft Animals: Campbell, Bob, producer. "Echoes from the Hills: West Virginia Draft Animals." Videotape. WVDC&H, Archives & History Section, 1999 • Clark, Nancy. "Midland Trail." *WWV* (Dec. 1979) • Dickens, Dennis. "I Hated to Tend that New-ground." From the sound recording, *Tending the Commons: Folklife and Landscape in Southern West Virginia.* American Folklife Center, Library of Congress, 2000 • Goodwin, Jacqueline. "Gentle Giants: The Draft Horse Revival." *Goldenseal* (Summer 1986) • Millimet, Lisa Gray. "'All They Knew was to Pull and Get It': Daniel Richmond about Then and Now." *Goldenseal* (Summer 1997).

Draper Collection: Hesseltine, William B. *Pioneer's Mission: The Story of Lyman Copeland Draper.* Madison: State Historical Society of Wisconsin, 1954.

Muriel Miller Dressler: "Behold the Land." Documentary. Beckley: WSWP-TV, 1974 • Gaskins, Avery. "Notes on the Poetry of Muriel Miller Dressler," in William Plumley, et al., ed., *Things Appalachian.* Charleston: MHC Publications, 1977.

Elizabeth Simpson Drewry: Byrd, Robert C., to Elizabeth Drewry, 12/1/1954. Elizabeth Drewry Collection, Eastern Regional Archives • McGehee, C. Stuart. "Politics and Education in the 'Free State:' Elizabeth Simpson Drewry, Pioneer African-American Politician." Paper presented at the 6th annual WV Black History Conference, Marshall University, 1993.

Droop Mountain: Lowry, Terry. *Last Sleep: The Battle of Droop Mountain.* Charleston: PHPC, 1996 • Pocahontas County Historical Society. *History of Pocahontas County.* Marlinton, 1981 • USGS Maps, 7.5 Minute Series, WV quadrangle: Droop • Delorme–*Atlas.*

Droop Mountain, Battle of: Lowry, Terry. *Last Sleep: The Battle of Droop Mountain.* Charleston: PHPC, 1996.

Drovers and Livestock Drives: Henlein, Paul C. *Cattle Kingdom in the Ohio Valley 1783–1860.* Lexington: UPK, 1959 • MacMaster, Richard K. "The Cattle Trade in Virginia, 1760–1830," in Robert D. Mitchell, ed., *Appalachian Frontiers.* Lexington: UPK, 1991 • Whitcomb, Robert & Judith Whitcomb. "Mountain Cattle Drives." *Goldenseal* (Summer 1998).

Joanne Dru: *Gazette,* 2/2/1947 • *Gazette,* 9/12/1996 • *Wheeling News-Register,* 9/12/1996.

Anne S. Dudley: Rasmussen, Barbara. "Sixty-Four Edited Letters of the Founders of Storer College." M.A. thesis, WVU, 1986.

Dulcimer: Smith, L. Allen. *A Catalogue of Pre-Revival Appalachian Dulcimers.* Columbia: University of Missouri Press, 1983.

Dun Glen Hotel: Cox, William E. *Life on the New River.* Philadelphia: Eastern National Park & Monument Assn., 1984.

Ellis Dungan: Dungan, Ellis with Barbara D. Smik. *A Guide to Adventure: An Autobiography.* Pittsburgh: Dorrance Pub., 2002 • Smik, Barbara D., "Ready, Wheeling, and Able." *Goldenseal* (Fall 1996).

Dunmore's War: Lewis, Virgil A. *History of the Battle of Point Pleasant.*

Charleston: Tribune Printing, 1909. Reprint, C. J. Carrier Co., 1974 • Rice & Brown • Thwaites, Reuben Gold & Louise Phelps Kellogg. *Documentary History of Dunmore's War, 1774.* Madison, WI: Wisconsin Historical Society, 1905.

DuPont Belle Works: Denham, Charles J., ed. *Sentimental Journey: The DuPont Belle Works: A 75-Year History 1926–2001.* Charleston: E. I. du Pont de Nemours & Co., 2001.

East Lynn Lake: "East Lynn Lake," Pamphlet. U.S. Army Corps of Engineers.

East River: Reger, David B., WVGES. *Mercer, Monroe and Summers Counties.* Wheeling News Litho. Co., 1926 • WV Department of Transportation. *General Highway Map, Mercer County.* 1992.

East River Mountain: Reger, David B., WVGES. *Mercer, Monroe and Summers Counties.* Wheeling News Litho. Co., 1926.

Eastern Orthodox Christianity: Durkit, Leonty. "The Orthodox Voyage: A History of Holy Dormition Church, Elkhorn, West Virginia, 1895–1995." *100th Anniversary Commemorative Booklet.* 1995 • Morris, John W. "Antiochian Orthodox Christian Church," in B. B. Maurer & Keith A. Muhleman, eds., *Mission in the Mountain State.* Charleston: WV Council of Churches, 1981 • Tamoush, Philip, ed. *Directory of Orthodox Parishes and Institutions in North America, 1998.* Grand Isle, VT: Oakwood Publications, 1998.

Eastern Panhandle: Rice & Brown • WPA–*Guide* • Delorme–*Atlas.*

Easton Roller Mill: Venable, Norma Jean. *Easton Roller Mill.* Morgantown: Monongalia Historical Society, 1994.

Eccles Mine Explosions: Dillon, Lacy A. *They Died in the Darkness.* Parsons: McClain, 1976 • Humphrey, H. B. *Historical Summary of Coal-Mine Explosions in the U.S., 1810–1958.* Washington: GPO, 1960 • WV Department of Mines, Annual Report. 1914.

John Echols: McKinney, Tim. *Civil War in Fayette County.* Charleston: PHPC, 1988 • Warner, Ezra. *Generals in Gray.* Baton Rouge: LSU Press, 1959.

The Economy: *WV Business and Economic Review* (Winter 2001). Morgantown: WVU College of Business & Economics.

EcoTheater: French, William W. *Maryat Lee's EcoTheater.* Morgantown: WVU Press, 1998 • Lee, Maryat. "To Will One Thing." *Drama Review* (Winter 1983).

Edgewood Country Club: Norris, James H. Interview by author. 8/19/1999 • *Rules of Membership, Edgewood Country Club.* Charleston, 1910 & 1999.

Education: Ambler–*Education* • Ambler & Summers • Rice & Brown.

Department of Education: *Master Plan for Public Education in West Virginia.* Charleston: WV Dept. of Education, 1983 • Wright, J. Zeb. *200 Years of Public Education in West Virginia.* Charleston: WV Dept. of Education, 1976.

William Henry Edwards: Ambler & Summers • Conley, Phil. *History of the West Virginia Coal Industry.* Charleston: Education Foundation, 1960 • Conley–*Encyclopedia* • Miller & Maxwell, vol. 3.

Eleanor: Wilson, Rick. "Happy to Have a Chance: The Founding of Eleanor." *Goldenseal* (Spring 1988).

Elizabeth: Puetz, C. J. *West Virginia County Maps.* Lyndon Station, WI: Thomas Pub. • Reed, Louis. *Warning in Appalachia: A Study of Wirt County.* Morgantown: WVU Library, 1967.

Elk River: Byrne–*Tale* • "Elk River Basin Plan," Pamphlet. WVDNR, 1985 • Johnson, Skip. *Woods & Waters.* Sutton: Quality Printing, 1993.

Elkins: Holmes, Charles J. & Justin M. Kunkle, eds. *Elkins, West Virginia, November Nineteen Six.* Elkins: Board of Trade, 1906 • Rice, Donald L. *Elkins Centennial Album.* Parsons: McClain, 1990 • Rice. *Randolph 200.* Elkins: Randolph County Historical Society, 1987.

Hallie Davis Elkins: Lambert, Oscar Doane. *Stephen Benton Elkins: American Foursquare.* Pittsburgh: UPP, 1955 • Ross, Thomas Richard. *Henry Gassaway Davis.* Parsons: McClain, 1994.

Stephen B. Elkins: Holmes, Charles J. & Justin M. Kunkle, eds. *Elkins, West Virginia: Its Past, Present, and Future.* Elkins: Board of Trade, 1906 • Lambert, Oscar D. *Stephen Benton Elkins: American Foursquare.* Pittsburgh: UPP, 1955.

Elkinsia Polymorpha: Gillespie, William H., Gar W. Rothwell & Stephen E. Scheckler. "The Earliest Seeds." *Nature* (1981) • Rothwell, Gar W., Stephen E. Scheckler & William H. Gillespie. "*Elkinsia* gen. nov., a Late Devonian Gymnosperm with Cupulate Ovules." *Botanical Gazette* (1989)

• Serbert, Rudolph & Gar W. Rothwell. "Characterizing the Most Primitive Seed Ferns. 1. A Reconstruction of *Elkinsia polymorpha*." *International Journal of Plant Sciences* (1992).

End of the World: Byrne–*Tale* • Jones, James Gay. *Haunted Valley and More Folk Tales of Appalachia*. Parsons: McClain, 1979.

Endangered Species: Fact Sheet. Elkins: WVDNR.

Thomas Dunn English: Ambler & Summers • Spence, Bob. "The Poet of Lawnsville." *Goldenseal* (July–Sept. 1979) • WPA–*Guide*.

Episcopal Church: Hamilton, Eleanor Meyer. "The Flair & the Fire." Charleston: Diocese of WV, 1977.

Etam Earth Station: Richelson, Jeffrey. "Desperately Seeking Signals." *Bulletin of the Atomic Scientists* (Mar.–Apr. 2000) • Steelhammer, Rick. "Easy Listening: Government has its Ear on You via Satellite." *Gazette*, 4/9/2000.

Ethnic Life: "An Introduction to West Virginia Ethnic Communities." Charleston: WVDC&H, 1999 • Fones-Wolf, Ken & Ronald L. Lewis, eds. *Transnational West Virginia*. Morgantown: WVU Press, 2002 • "Profile of General Demographic Characteristics: Geographic Area West Virginia 2000." U.S. Census Bureau • Schwarz, Bob. "Muslim in America." *Gazette*, 12/7/2001.

George Bird Evans: Evans, George Bird. *Grouse on the Mountain*. Brandonville, WV: Old Hemlock, 1994 • Evans. *Troubles with Bird Dogs*. New York: Winchester Press, 1975 • Harper, Catherine A. *George Bird Evans: Life of a Shooting Gentleman*. Minocqua, WI: Willow Creek Press, 1999.

Everettville Mine Disaster: Dillon, Lacy A. *They Died in the Darkness*. Parsons: McClain, 1976 • McCaa, G. S. & H. C. Howarth. "Report on a Gas and Dust Explosion at the Federal Number Three Mine." 1928.

The Executive Branch: Morgan–*Governors* • *Blue Book*, 1998.

Exploration: Alvord, Clarence W. & Lee Bidgood. *The First Explorations of the Trans-Allegheny Region by the Virginians, 1650–1674*. Cleveland: Arthur H. Clark, 1912 • Briceland, Alan Vance. *Westward from Virginia: The Exploration of the Virginia-Carolina Frontier, 1650–1710*. Charlottesville: UVA Press, 1987 • Cumming, William P. *The Discoveries of John Lederer*. Charlottesville, 1958.

Extension Homemaker Clubs: Humphreys, Gertrude. *Adventures in Good Living*. Parsons: McClain, 1972.

4-H: Meador, Michael M. "'Part P. T. Barnum and Part Billy Sunday': Jim Morris Remembers 'Teepi' Kendrick." *Goldenseal* (Summer 1984) • Stewart, Guy H. *A Touch of Charisma: A History of the 4-H Club Program in West Virginia*. Morgantown, 1969 • Wessel, Thomas & Marilyn Wessel. *4-H: An American Idea 1900–1980*. Chevy Chase: National 4-H Council, 1982.

Ferdinando Fairfax: Cartmell, T. K. *Shenandoah Valley Pioneers and their Descendants: A History of Frederick County*. Berryville, VA: Chesapeake Book Co., 1963 • Jefferson County Historical Society. *Between the Shenandoah and the Potomac: Historic Homes of Jefferson County*. Winchester, VA: Winchester Printers, 1990 • Washington, John A. "Jefferson County Personal Property Tax List, 1800." *Magazine of the Jefferson County Historical Society* (Dec. 1967).

George William Fairfax: Brown, Stuart E. Jr. *Virginia Baron*. Berryville, VA: Chesapeake Book Co., 1965.

Fairfax Lands: Brown, Stuart E. Jr. *Virginia Baron*. Berryville, VA: Chesapeake Book Co., 1965 • Morrison, Charles. *The Fairfax Line*. Parsons: McClain, 1970.

Fairfax Stone: Fansler, Homer Floyd. *History of Tucker County*. Parsons: McClain, 1962 • Morrison, Charles. *The Fairfax Line*. Parsons: McClain, 1970 • Morrison. *The Western Boundary of Maryland*. Parsons: McClain, 1976 • USGS Maps, 7.5 Minute Series, WV quadrangle: Davis.

William Fairfax: Brown, Stuart E. Jr. *Virginia Baron*. Berryville, VA: Chesapeake Book Co., 1965.

Fairmont: Koon, Thomas J. & Oce Smith. *Marion County—A Pictorial History*. Virginia Beach: Donning Co., 1995 • Lough, Glenn D. *Now and Long Ago: A History of the Marion County Area*. Morgantown Printing & Binding, 1969 • Marion County Historical Society. *A History of Marion County*. Fairmont, 1985.

Fairmont High Level Bridge: Condit, Carl W. *American Building Art: the 19th Century*. New York: Oxford University Press, 1960 • National Register of Historic Places Nomination, ms., WVDC&H, 1991.

Fairmont State University: Lough, Jo Ann. "Fairmont State College Occasional Papers Number 5, A Legacy: Cause and Effect." Fairmont: Fairmont State College, 1994 • Turner, William P. *A Centennial History of Fairmont State College*. Fairmont State College, 1970.

Family Life: Maurer, B. B. *Mountain Heritage*. Ripley: Mountain State Art & Craft Fair, 1974 • "Quickfacts 2000." U.S. Census Bureau • Weller, Jack E. *Yesterday's People: Life in Contemporary Appalachia*. Lexington: UPK, 1965.

Farm Security Administration: Mertz, Paul E. *New Deal Policy and Southern Rural Poverty*. Baton Rogue: LSU Press, 1978 • Thomas–*New Deal*.

Farmington Mine Disaster: Braithwaite, John. *To Punish or Persuade: Enforcement of Coal Mine Safety*. Albany: State University of New York Press, 1985 • Hume, Brit. *Death and the Mines: Rebellion and Murder in the UMW*. New York: Grossman Pub., 1971 • Lewis, Ronald L. & John C. Hennen Jr., eds. *West Virginia: Documents in the History of a Rural-Industrial State*. Dubuque, IA: Kendall-Hunt Pub., 1991.

Daniel D. T. Farnsworth: Bailey, Guy F. *The Farnsworth Family*, (unpub. ms.). Central WV Genealogy & History Library, Horner • Comstock–*Encyclopedia*, vol. 7, 1976 • Morgan–*Governors*.

Fasnacht: Mailloux, Eleanor Fahrner. *Oppis guet's vo Helvetia*. Helvetia: Alpen Rose Garden Club, 1969 • Milnes, Gerald, producer. *Helvetia: The Swiss of West Virginia*. Video. 1993 • Sutton, David. *One's Own Hearth is Like Gold: A History of Helvetia*. New York: Peter Lang, 1990.

Charles James Faulkner: Keesecker, Guy L. *Marriage Records of Berkeley County, Virginia, 1781–1854*. Martinsburg, 1969 • McVeigh, Donald Rusk. "Charles James Faulkner: Reluctant Rebel." Ph.D. diss., WVU, 1954 • Rice & Brown.

Fayette County: Cherniack, Martin. *The Hawk's Nest Incident: America's Worst Industrial Disaster*. New Haven: Yale University Press, 1986 • Fayette County Chamber of Commerce. *History of Fayette County*. Oak Hill, 1993 • Lane, Ron & Ted Schnepf. *Sewell: A New River Community*. Philadelphia: Eastern National Park & Monument Assn., 1989 • McKinney, Tim. *The Civil War in Fayette County*. Charleston: PHPC, 1988 • Peters, J. T. & H. B. Carden. *History of Fayette County*. Charleston: Jarrett Printing, 1926 • Sullivan, Ken. *Thurmond: A New River Community*. Oak Hill: Eastern National Park & Monument Assn., 1989.

Fayetteville: Fayette County Chamber of Commerce. *History of Fayette County, West Virginia: 1993*. Oak Hill, 1993 • Peters, J. T. & H. B. Carden. *History of Fayette County*. Charleston: Jarrett Printing, 1926.

Fences: Jordan, Terry G. & Matti Kaups. *The American Backwoods Frontier*. Baltimore: Johns Hopkins University Press, 1989 • Lewin, Jeff L. "The Silent Revolution in West Virginia's Law of Nuisance." *WV Law Review* (Winter 1989–90) • Lewis, Ronald L. *Transforming the Appalachian Countryside*. Chapel Hill: UNC Press, 1998.

Fenton Art Glass Company: Heacock, William. *Fenton Glass: The First 25 Years*. Williamstown, 1978.

Harrison H. Ferrell: Ferrell, Grazia B. *The Dean: Harrison H. Ferrell*. Charleston, 1981 • Obituary. *Sunday Gazette-Mail*, 11/20/1977.

Ferries: Leahy, Ethel C. *Who's Who on the Ohio River*. Cincinnati: E. C. Leahy Pub., 1931 • Snively, W. D. Jr. & Louanna Furbee. *Satan's Ferryman: A True Tale of the Old Frontier*. New York: Frederick Unger Pub., 1968.

Feuds: Fischer, David Hackett. *Albion's Seed: Four British Folkways in America*. New York: Oxford University Press, 1989 • Pearce, John Ed. *Days of Darkness: The Feuds of Eastern Kentucky*. Lexington: UPK, 1994 • Rice, Otis K. *The Hatfields and the McCoys*. Lexington: UPK, 1982.

Fiddle Tradition: Milnes, Gerald. *Play of a Fiddle*. Lexington: UPK, 1999.

Fiestaware: Huxford, Bob & Sharon Huxford. *The Collector's Encyclopedia of Fiesta*. Paducah, KY: Collector Books, 1992.

Filmmaking: Boyd, Danny; Carenbauer, Beth; Dungan, Ellis; Fesenmaier, Steve; Gates, Bob; & Nakashima, John. Telephone conversations with author Bill Drennen, 1999–2001.

Fish: Page, L. M. & B. M. Burr. *A Field Guide to Freshwater Fishes of North America North of Mexico*. Boston: Houghton Mifflin, 1991 • Stauffer, Jay R. Jr., Jeffrey Boltz & Laura White. *The Fishes of West Virginia*. Philadelphia: Academy of Natural Sciences of Philadelphia, 1995.

Susanne Fisher: Ewen, David. *Living Musicians*. New York: H. W. Wilson, 1940 • Sabin, Robert, ed. *The International Cyclopedia of Music and Musicians*. New York: Dodd, Mead & Co., 1964 • "Obituaries." *Opera News*, vol. 55, no. 2 (1990).

Flat Top Mountain: Adkins, Howard G. & Mack H. Gillenwater. "The Coal Road," Report. Economic Development Administration, U.S. Dept. of Commerce, 1989 • Conley, Phil. *History of the West Virginia Coal Industry*. Charleston: Education Foundation, 1960 • Rice & Brown • USGS Maps, 7.5 Minute Series, WV quadrangles: Crumpler, Flat Top, Matoaka, Odd, Rhodell & Shady Spring • USGS Maps, Scale 1:250,000. Bluefield quadrangle.

Flatwoods Monster: Barker, Gray. *They Knew Too Much About Flying Saucers*. New York: University Books, 1956 • Jones, James Gay. *Appalachian Ghost Stories and Other Tales*. Parsons: McClain, 1975.

Aretas Brooks Fleming: Cook, Jeffery B. "The Ambassador of Development: Aretas Brooks Fleming." Ph.D. diss., WVU, 1998 • Morgan–*Governors* • Williams–*Captains* • Workman, Michael E. "Political Culture and the Coal Economy in the Upper Monongahela Region: 1774–1933." Ph.D. diss., WVU, 1995.

Jack Fleming: Fleming, Jack. Interviews by author. 1995 & 1999.

Flick Amendment: Ambler & Summers • Callahan, James M. *Semi-Centennial History of West Virginia*. Charleston: Semi-Centennial Commission, 1913 • Rice & Brown.

Flood Control: Casto, James E. *Towboat on the Ohio*. Lexington: UPK, 1995 • Johnson, Leland R. *Men, Mountains, and Rivers*. Washington: GPO, 1977.

Flood of 1985: Bittinger, Wayne, ed. *The Flood of November 4–5, 1985, in Tucker, Preston, Grant and Hardy Counties*. Parsons: McClain, 1985 • Newmark, Todd. "Looking Back Ten Years Later: The Flood of 1985." *Goldenseal* (Fall 1995) • Teets, Bob & Shelby Young, eds. *Killing Waters: The Great Flood of 1985*. Terra Alta: Cheat River Pub., 1985.

Floods: Bittinger, Wayne, ed. *The Flood of November 4–5, 1985, in Tucker, Preston, Grant and Hardy Counties*. Parsons: McClain, 1985 • Davies, W. E., J. F. Bailey & B. K. Donovan. "West Virginia's Buffalo Creek Flood: A study of the Hydrology and Engineering Geology," Circular 667. USGS, 1972 • Grover, N. C. *Floods of Ohio and Mississippi Rivers, Jan.– Feb. 1937*. Washington: GPO, 1938 • Janssen, Quinith. *Harpers Ferry Floods!* Shepherdstown: Specialty Binding & Printing, 1985 • Teets, Bob & Shelby Young. *Killing Waters: The Great Flood of 1985*. Terra Alta: Cheat River Pub., 1985 • "What Happened on Buffalo Creek," in Peter Briggs, *Rampage*. New York: David McKay, 1973.

Flora: Core, Earl L. *Vegetation of West Virginia*. Parsons: McClain, 1966 • Keener, C. S. "Distribution and Biohistory of the Endemic Flora of the Mid-Appalachian Shale Barrens." *Botanical Review* (1983) • Strausbaugh, P. D. & Earl L. Core. *Flora of West Virginia*. Morgantown, 1964. Second edition, 4 vols. Morgantown: WVU, 1970–77.

Flora of West Virginia: Core, Earl L. *Vegetation of West Virginia*. Parsons: McClain, 1966 • Strausbaugh, P. D. & Earl L. Core. *Flora of West Virginia*, 2nd edition, 4 vols. Morgantown: WVU, 1970–77.

John B. Floyd: Osborne, Randall & Jeffrey C. Weaver. *The Virginia State Rangers and State Line*. Lynchburg: H. E. Howard, 1994 • Warner, Ezra. *Generals in Gray*. Baton Rouge: LSU Press, 1959.

Russ Fluharty: Sullivan, Ken. "Russell Fluharty, the Dulcimer Man." *Goldenseal* (Winter 1986).

Fokker Aircraft Plant: Keefer, Louis E. "Wings over Glen Dale." *Goldenseal* (Winter 1991).

Folk Dance: Botkin, Benjamin A. *American Play-Party Song*. Lincoln: University of Nebraska, 1937. Reprint, Ungar, 1963 • Dalsemer, Robert G. *West Virginia Square Dances*. New York: Country Dance & Song Society of America, 1982 • Kurath, Gertrude P. "Dance: Folk and Primitive," in Maria Leach, ed., *Funk & Wagnalls Standard Dictionary of Folklore, Mythology, and Legend*. New York: Funk & Wagnalls, 1949 • Seeger, Mike & Ruth Pershing. *Talking Feet: Buck, Flatfoot and Tap: Solo Southern Dance of the Appalachian, Piedmont and Blue Ridge Mountain Regions*. Berkeley, CA: North Atlantic Books, 1992.

Folk Medicine: Crellin, John K. & Jane Philpott. *Trying to Give Ease*. Durham: Duke University Press, 1990 • Hand, Wayland. *American Folk Medicine*. Berkeley, CA: University of California Press, 1976.

Folk Music: Cox, John Harrington. *Folk-Songs of the South*. Cambridge: Harvard University Press, 1925 • Gainer, Patrick W. *Folk Songs from the West Virginia Hills*. Grantsville: Seneca Books, 1975 • Milnes, Gerald. *Play of a Fiddle*. Lexington, UPK, 1999.

Follansbee: Caldwell, Nancy. *A History of Brooke County*. Wellsburg: Brooke County Historical Society, 1975 • *Follansbee, West Virginia Polk City Directory*. Richmond: R. L. Polk & Co., 1997 • McIntosh, Eura Cox Ulrich, ed. *Diamond History of Follansbee*. Marceline, MO: Walsworth Pub., 1984.

Food Preservation: Robe-Terry, Anna Lee. *Bootstraps and Biscuits: 300 Wonderful Wild Food Recipes from the Hills of West Virginia*. Fairmont: A. L. Robe-Terry, 1997 • Sohn, Mark F. *Mountain Country Cooking: A Gathering of the Best Recipes from the Smokies to the Blue Ridge*. New York: St. Martin's Press, 1996.

Foodways: "Foods and Things: West Virginia Grown," Pamphlet. WV Dept. of Agriculture, 1999 • Sohn, Mark F. *Hearty Country Cooking: Savory Southern Favorites*. New York: St. Martin's Press, 1998 • Sohn. *Mountain Country Cooking: A Gathering of the Best Recipes from the Smokies to the Blue Ridge*. New York: St. Martin's Press, 1996.

Fools' Parade: Bunting, Camilla. "When Hollywood Came to Moundsville: Filming Davis Grubb's *Fools' Parade*." *Goldenseal* (Summer 1995) • Grubb, Davis. *Fools' Parade*. New York: World Pub. Co., 1969 • Welch, Jack. "Davis Grubb: A Vision of Appalachia." Ph.D. diss., Carnegie Mellon University, 1980.

Foreman Massacre: Cranmer, G. L. *History of Wheeling City and Ohio County*. Chicago: Biographical Pub., 1902 • Newton, J. H. *History of the Pan-Handle*. Wheeling: Caldwell, 1879 • *Wheeling Daily News*, 9/26/1933.

Forestry: Brooks, A. B. *Forestry and Wood Industries*. Morgantown: WVGES, 1910 • Williams, Michael. *Americans & their Forests: A Historical Geography*. Cambridge, England: Cambridge University Press, 1989.

Division of Forestry: Widner, Ralph R. *Forests and Forestry in the American States*. Washington: National Assn. of State Foresters, 1968.

Forests: Brooks, A. B. *Forestry and Wood Industries*. Morgantown: WVGES, 1910 • DiGiovanni, Dawn M. *Forest Statistics for West Virginia: 1975 and 1989*. Radnor, PA: U.S. Forest Service Northeastern Forest Experiment Station, 1989 • Gillespie, William H. & Earl L. Core. *Forest Trees of West Virginia*. Charleston: WV Division of Forestry, 1976.

Forks of Cheat: Core, Earl L. *The Monongalia Story*, 5 vols. Parsons: McClain, 1974–84 • Janssen, Quinith & William Fernbach. *West Virginia Place Names*. Shepherdstown: J & F Enterprises, 1984 • Kenny, Hamill. *West Virginia Place Names*. Piedmont: Place Name Press, 1945 • Weltner, Fred Hamilton & Harry LeRoy Jeffries, eds. *The Stewartstown Story*. Morgantown Printing & Binding Co., 1971 • WPA–*Guide* • Wiley, Samuel T. *History of Monongalia County*. Kingwood: Preston Pub. Co., 1883.

Formation of West Virginia: Ambler, Charles H. *Francis H. Pierpont: Union War Governor of Virginia and Father of West Virginia*. Chapel Hill: UNC Press, 1937 • Crofts, Daniel W. *Reluctant Confederates: Upper South Unionists and the Secession Crisis*. Chapel Hill: UNC Press, 1989 • Williams, John Alexander. "The Birth of a State: West Virginia and the Civil War," in Altina Waller, ed., *True Stories from the American Past*. New York: McGraw Hill, 1994.

Fort Ancient Culture: Griffin, James B. *The Fort Ancient Aspect*. Ann Arbor: University of Michigan Press, 1943 • McMichael–*Archeology*.

Fort Ashby: Abbot, W. W., ed. *The Papers of George Washington*. Charlottesville: UVA Press, 1984 • Ansel, William H. *Frontier Forts along the Potomac and its Tributaries*. Parsons: McClain, 1984 • McBride, W. Stephen & Kim Arbogast McBride. *Frontier Forts in West Virginia*. Charleston: WVDC&H, 2003 • *The Official Records of Robert Dinwiddie, Lieutenant Governor of the Colony of Virginia, 1751–1758*. Richmond: The Virginia Historical Society, 1883–84.

Fort Boreman: Matheny, H. E. *Wood County W. Va. in Civil War Times*. Parkersburg: Trans-Allegheny Books, 1987.

Fort Edwards, Battle of: Abbot, W. W., ed. *The Papers of George Washington*. Charlottesville: UVA Press, 1984 • McBride, W. Stephen & Kim Arbogast McBride. *Frontier Forts in West Virginia*. Charleston: WVDC&H, 2003.

Fort Henry: Cranmer, Gibson Lamb, ed. *History of Wheeling City and Ohio County, West Virginia*. Chicago: Biographical Pub. Co., 1902 • Newton, J. H. *History of the Pan-Handle*. Wheeling: Caldwell, 1879 • Rice & Brown.

Fort Lee: Cook, Roy Bird. *Annals of Fort Lee*. Charleston: WV Review Press, 1935.

Fort Maidstone: Abbot, W. W., ed. *The Papers of George Washington*. Charlottesville: UVA Press, 1984 • Ansel, William H. *Frontier Forts along* *the Potomac and its Tributaries*. Parsons: McClain, 1984 • Mason, Hughlett A. *The Journal of Charles Mason and Jeremiah Dixon*. Philadelphia: American Philosophical Society, 1969.

Fort Pleasant: Abbot, W. W., ed. *The Papers of George Washington*. Charlottesville: UVA Press, 1984 • Ansel, William H. *Frontier Forts along the Potomac and its Tributaries*. Parsons: McClain, 1984 • Kercheval–*Valley*.

Fort Randolph: Callahan, James M. *History of West Virginia*, vol. 1. Chicago: American Historical Society, 1923 • Conley, Phil & William T. Doherty. *West Virginia History*. Charleston: Education Foundation, 1974 • Rice & Brown.

Fort Savannah: Dayton, Ruth W. *Lewisburg Landmarks*. Charleston: Education Foundation, 1957 • Lewis, Virgil A. *Life and Times of Anne Bailey*. Charleston: Butler Printing Co., 1891 • McBride, W. Stephen & Kim A. McBride. "An Archaeological Survey of Frontier Forts, in the Greenbrier and Middle New River Valleys of West Virginia." Report no. 252. Lexington: University of Kentucky, 1991 • McBride, W. Stephen, Kim A. McBride & J. David McBride. "Frontier Defense of the Greenbrier and Middle New River Country," Report no. 375, Lexington: University of Kentucky, 1996 • Rice–*Greenbrier County*.

Fort Seybert: Ansel, William H. *Frontier Forts along the Potomac and its Tributaries*. Parsons: McClain, 1984 • Kercheval–*Valley* • Morton, Oren. *A History of Pendleton County*. Dayton: Ruebush-Elkins Co., 1910 • Morton. *A Centennial History of Alleghany County, Virginia*. Dayton: J. K. Ruebush Co., 1923. Reprint, C. J. Carrier Co., 1986 • Talbot, Mary Lee. *The Dyer Settlement: The Fort Seybert Massacre*. Chicago: Larson-Dingle Printing, 1937 • Weslager, C. A. *The Delaware Indians: A History*. New Brunswick: Rutgers University Press, 1972.

Fort Stanwix Treaties: "Fort Stanwix." *The Encyclopedia Americana*, vol. 11. New York: Americana Corp., 1955 • Lewis, Virgil A. *History and Government of West Virginia*. New York: American Book, 1912.

Fort Upper Tract: Abbot, W. W. *The Papers of George Washington*. Charlottesville: UVA Press, 1984 • Ansel, William H. *Frontier Forts along the Potomac and its Tributaries*. Parsons: McClain, 1984 • Chalkley, Lyman. *Chronicles of the Scotch-Irish Settlement in Virginia 1745–1800*. Rosslyn, VA: The Commonwealth Printing Co., 1912. Reprint, Genealogical Pub., 1989.

Forting: Bond, Donovan H. "Frontier Forts of Monongalia County," in Earl L. Core, *The Monongalia Story*, 5 vols. Parsons: McClain, 1974–84 • Cook, Roy Bird. "Virginia Frontier Defenses, 1719–1795." *WVH* (Jan. 1940) • Doddridge, Joseph. *Notes on the Settlement and Indian Wars of the Western Parts of Virginia and Pennsylvania, 1763–1783*. Wellsburgh, VA: Office of the Gazette, 1824. Reprint, New Werner, 1912.

Fossils: Cardwell, D. H. *Geologic History of West Virginia*. Morgantown: WVGES, 1975 • Gillespie, W. H., J. A. Clendening & H. W. Pfefferkorn. *Plant Fossils of West Virginia and Adjacent Areas*. Morgantown: WVGES, 1978 • Happ, S. & H. Alexander. "Footprints from the Permian of West Virginia." *Journal of Geology* (1938) • Lund, R., E. R. Garton & D. B. Weishampel. "Fossil Vertebrates of the Pennsylvanian System of West Virginia," in *Proposed Pennsylvanian System Stratotype, Virginia and West Virginia*. 1979 • Lund, et al. "Vertebrate Fossil Zonation and Correlation of the Dunkard Basin," in J. A. Barlow, ed., *The Age of the Dunkard*. Proceedings of the 1st I. C. White Memorial Symposium. Morgantown: WVGES, 1975 • Martino, R. L. "*Limnopus* trackways from the Conemaugh Group (Late Pennsylvanian), southern West Virginia." *Journal of Paleontology*, vol. 65 • McClelland, S. W. "Fossil Footprints Unearthed in Eastern Panhandle," in *Mountain State Geology*. WVGES, 1988 • Sandberg, F. A., et al. "Upper Carboniferous Amphibian Trackways from the Bluefield Formation, West Virginia, USA." *Ichnos*, vol. 1 (1990).

Ruel E. Foster: "Farewell, Dr. Foster." WVU English Dept. Newsletter (Feb. 2000) • Lofstead, Becky. "Joys of Retiring in Morgantown." *WVU Alumni Magazine* (Summer 1984) • *Dominion Post*, 11/11/1999.

Fostoria Glass: Kerr, Ann. *Fostoria: An Identification and Value Guide*. Paducah, KY: Collector Books, 1994 • Long, Milbra & Emily Seate. *Fostoria Stemware: The Crystal for America*. Paducah, KY: Collector Books, 1995 • Pina, Leslie. *Fostoria: Serving the American Table 1887–1986*. Atglen, PA: Schiffer Pub., 1995.

Fox Hunting: Cone, Carl B., ed. *Hounds in the Morning: Sundry Sports of Merry England*. Lexington: UPK, 1981 • Hufford, Mary T. *Chaseworld*.

Philadelphia: UP Press, 1992 • Longrigg, Roger. *The History of Foxhunting*. New York: Clarkson N. Potter, 1975 • Milnes, Gerald C. "Listen to that Beautiful Music: Fox Chasing in the Mountain State." *Goldenseal* (Summer 1996) • Watson, J.N.P. *The Book of Foxhunting*. New York: Arco Pub., 1977.

Franklin: Boggs, Elsie B. *A History of Franklin*. Staunton, VA: McClure Printing, 1960 • Morton, Oren. *A History of Pendleton County*. Dayton: Ruebush-Elkins Co., 1910 • Pendleton County Commission. *Pendleton County, West Virginia, Past and Present*. Waynesville, NC: Don Mills Inc., 1991.

Frederick County, Virginia: Cartmell, Thomas Kemp. *Shenandoah Valley Pioneers and their Descendants: A History of Frederick County, Virginia*. Winchester: Eddy Press Corp., 1909 • Glass, William Wood. "An Outline of the History of Frederick County." *Virginia and the Virginia County* (Mar. 1950) • Norris, J. E., ed. *History of the Lower Shenandoah Valley Counties of Frederick, Berkeley, Jefferson and Clarke*. Chicago: A. Warner & Co., 1890.

Frederick Hotel: Dial, Becky. "The Frederick." Huntington *Herald-Advertiser*, 7/1/1973 • "Three Injured After Elevator Dives 5 Floors." *Herald-Dispatch*, 8/19/1989.

Freedmen's Bureau: Stealey, John E. III. "The Freedmen's Bureau in West Virginia." *WVH* (Jan.–Apr. 1978) • Stealey. "Reports of Freedmen's Bureau Operations in West Virginia." *WVH* (Fall 1980–Winter 1981) • Stealey. "Reports of Freedmen's Bureau District Officers on Tours and Surveys in West Virginia." *WVH* (Winter 1982).

French and Indian War: Hurt, R. Douglas. *The Ohio Frontier: Crucible of the Old Northwest, 1720–1830*. Bloomington: Indiana University Press, 1996 • Rice–*Allegheny Frontier* • Ward, Matthew C. *Breaking the Backcountry: The Seven Years' War in Virginia and Pennsylvania*. Pittsburgh: UPP, 2003.

Friars Hole Cave: Baker, L., et al. "The Friars Hole System," Bulletin 1. Capitol Area Cavers, 1982 • Dougherty, P. H., et al. "Karst Regions of the Eastern U.S. with Special Emphasis on the Friars Hole Cave System," in Yuan Daozian & Liu Zaihua, eds., *Global Karst Correlation*. New York: Science Press, 1998 • Storrick, G. D. "The Caves and Karst Hydrology of Southern Pocahontas County and the Upper Spring Creek Valley," Bulletin 10. WV Speleological Survey, 1992.

Lynette "Squeaky" Fromme: "Fromme Transferred to Kentucky Prison." *Gazette*, 6/5/1988 • Sifakis, Carl. *Encyclopedia of Assassinations*. New York: Facts on File, 1991.

The Frontier: Caruso, John A. *The Appalachian Frontier*. Indianapolis: Bobbs-Merrill, 1959 • Rice–*Allegheny Frontier* • Rice & Brown • Sturm, Philip W. *Kinship Migration to Northwestern Virginia*. Morgantown: WVU Press, 2004.

Frontier Defense: Cook, Roy Bird. "Virginia's Frontier Defenses, 1719–1795." *WVH* 1 (1940) • Koontz, Louis K. *The Virginia Frontier, 1754–1763*. Baltimore: Johns Hopkins University Press, 1925 • McBride, W. Stephen, Kim A. McBride & J. David McBride. "Frontier Defense of the Greenbrier and Middle New River Country," Report no. 375. Lexington: University of Kentucky, 1996 • Rice–*Allegheny Frontier* • Titus, James. *The Old Dominion at War: Society, Politics, and Warfare in Late Colonial Virginia*. Columbia: University of South Carolina Press, 1991.

Stella Fuller: Platania, Joseph. "Actions Louder than Words: Remembering Stella Fuller." *Goldenseal* (Fall 1986) • Platania. "Angel of Huntington: The Stella Fuller Story." *Huntington Quarterly* (Autumn 1993) • Whear, Nancy. "Stella Lawrence Fuller," in *Missing Chapters: West Virginia Women in History*. Charleston: WV Women's Commission & the Humanities Foundation of WV, 1983.

Pat Gainer: Gainer, Patrick W. *Folk Songs of the Allegheny Mountains*, two records, Folk Heritage Recordings, 1963 • Gainer. *Folk Songs from the West Virginia Hills*. Grantsville: Seneca Books, 1975 • Gainer. "Music," in B. B. Maurer, ed., *Mountain Heritage*. Ripley: Mountain State Art & Craft Fair, 1974 • Gainer. *Witches, Ghosts and Signs*. Morgantown: Seneca Books, 1975 • *West Virginia Centennial Book of 100 Songs, 1863–1963*. Morgantown, 1963.

John S. Gallaher: *Spirit of Jefferson*, 10/17/1957 • *Virginia Free Press*, 1/14/1869 & 2/10/1877.

Game Laws: Slone, Frank B. "History of Conservation Law Enforcement," (unpub. ms.) WVDNR, revised by Charles Costilow, 1974.

Garnet High School: Bickley, Ancella. *History of the West Virginia State Teachers' Association.* Washington: National Education Assn., 1979 • Randall, James. "The Way We Were." Charleston: Garnet High School, 1978.

Memphis Tennessee Garrison: Bickley, Ancella & Lynda Ann Ewen. *Memphis Tennessee Garrison: The Remarkable Story of a Black Appalachian Woman.* Athens: Ohio University Press, 2001 • *Black Women in America: An Historical Encyclopedia.* Bloomington: Indiana University Press, 1993 • Thomas, Dolores. "Memphis Tennessee Garrison: The Real Gains of a Life 1890–1988." *West Virginia Beacon Digest,* 8/30– 9/7/1988.

Gary: Clipping files, Hornick Collection & USX records, Eastern Regional Archives • McGehee, Stuart. "Gary: A First-Class Operation." *Goldenseal* (Fall 1988).

Patrick Gass: Jacob, J. G. *The Life and Times of Patrick Gass.* Wellsburg: Jacob & Smith Publishers, 1859 • McGirr, Newman F. "Patrick Gass and his Journal of the Lewis and Clark Expedition." *WVH* (1941–42) • MacGregor, Carol L., ed. *The Journals of Patrick Gass.* Missoula, MT: Mountain Press Pub. Co., 1997.

Henry Louis Gates Jr.: Gates, Henry Louis. *Colored People: A Memoir.* New York: Knopf, 1994.

Gaudineer Knob: Breiding, George H. "Where North Meets South." *Bird Watcher's Digest* (May–June 1995) • Carvell, Kenneth L. "Gaudineer Knob." *WWV* (Sept. 1999) • "Gaudineer Scenic Area," Pamphlet. U.S. Forest Service, Monongahela National Forest.

Gauley Mountain: de Hart, A. & Bruce Sundquist. *Monongahela National Forest Hiking Guide.* Charleston: WV Highlands Conservancy, 1993 • Kenny, Hamill. *West Virginia Place Names.* Piedmont: Place Name Press, 1945 • Lewis, Virgil A. *First Biennial Report of the Department of Archives and History of the State of West Virginia.* Charleston: Tribune Pub., 1906 • USGS Maps, 7.5 Minute Series, WV quadrangles: Ansted, Gauley Bridge, Webster Springs Southeast, Webster Springs Southwest & Woodrow • Delorme–*Atlas.*

Gauley Mountain: McNeill, Louise. *Gauley Mountain.* New York: Harcourt, Brace & Co., 1939.

Geography: Fenneman, Nevin M. *Physiography of Eastern U.S.* New York: McGraw-Hill, 1938 • Hill, Raymond, T. "The Physical Regions of West Virginia," in Howard G. Adkins, et al., ed., *West Virginia and Appalachia: Selected Readings.* Dubuque, IA: Kendall-Hunt Pub., 1977 • Lee, Chang & Raymond T. Hill. "Land Slope in West Virginia." *West Virginia Agriculture & Forestry* 6 (1976).

Frank George: Meador, Michael M. "Grandpaw Got Me Started." *Goldenseal* (Spring 1983).

German Dunkards: Brumbaugh, Martin. *A History of the German Baptist Brethren in Europe and America.* Mt. Morris: Brethren Pub. House, 1961 • Wust, Klaus. *The Saint-Adventurers of the Virginia Frontier.* Edinburg, VA: Shenandoah History Pub., 1977.

Germans: Ambler & Summers • Rice & Brown.

Germany Valley: Calhoun, H. M. *'Twixt North and South.* Franklin: McCoy Pub., 1974 • Carvell, Kenneth L. "Germany Valley." *WWV* (Sept. 2000) • Perry, William J. Jr. *The Wills Mountain Anticline.* Morgantown: WVGES, 1978.

Denise Giardina: Ballard, Sandra. "Political and Spiritual Dimensions of the Work of Denise Giardina." *Carson-Newman Studies* (1997) • "Denise Giardina Issue." *Iron Mountain Review* (1999).

Cass Gilbert: Cohen, Stan & Richard Andre. *Capitols of West Virginia.* Charleston: PHPC, 1989 • Comstock–*Encyclopedia,* vol. 9, 1976 • Irish, Sharon. *Cass Gilbert, Architect: Modern Traditionalist.* New York: Monacelli Press, 1999.

Giles, Fayette & Kanawha Turnpike: *Acts of the General Assembly of Virginia.* Richmond: Thomas Ritchie, Printer to the Commonwealth, 1837 • Callahan, James M. *Semi-Centennial History of West Virginia.* Semi-Centennial Commission, 1913 • GAI Consultants. *Phase Ia Archaeological Reconnaissance and Historic Survey of Route 19/16 Fayetteville Interchange.* Charleston: WVDOH, 1995.

Gilmer County: Gilmer County Historical Society. *History of Gilmer County, West Virginia, 1845–1989.* Marceline, MO: Walsworth Pub., 1994 • Moss, Margaret Knisley. *Gilmer County One-Room Schools, 1873–1955.* Glenville, 1998 • Wells, Nelson L. & Charles Holt. *Lighthouse on the Hill: Glenville State College, 1872–1997.* Virginia Beach: Donning Co., 1997.

Ginseng: Epler, John W. *All about Ginseng.* Hastings, NE: Cornhusker Press, 1985 • Harding, A. R. *Ginseng and Other Medicinal Plants.* Columbus: A. R. Harding, 1972 • Parsons, W. Scott. *American Ginseng: Green Gold.* Asheville: Bright Mountain Books, 1994.

Christopher Gist: Ambler, Charles H. *West Virginia: The Mountain State.* New York: Prentice-Hall, 1940 • Bailey, Kenneth P. *Christopher Gist.* Hamden, CT: Archon Books, 1976.

Glaciation: Fenneman, Nevin M. *Physiography of Eastern U.S.* New York: McGraw-Hill, 1938 • Janssen, Raymond E. *Earth Science: A Handbook on the Geology of West Virginia.* Clarksburg: Educational Marketers, 1973 • WPA–*Guide.*

Glass Industry: Barkey, Frederick. *Cinderheads in the Hills: The Belgian Window Glass Workers of West Virginia.* Charleston: WV Humanities Council, 1988 • Fones-Wolf, Ken. "Work, Culture and Politics in Industrializing West Virginia: The Glassworkers of Clarksburg and Moundsville, 1891–1919." *WVH* (1999–2000).

William Ellsworth Glasscock: Comstock–*Encyclopedia,* vol. 9, 1976 • Jones, Mary Harris. Speech on capitol steps, in David Alan Corbin's *West Virginia Mine Wars.* Charleston: Appalachian Editions, 1990 • Lee–*Bloodletting* • Morgan–*Governors* • *National Cyclopedia of American Biography,* vol. 23. New York: James T. White & Co., 1933 • Rice, Otis. *Charleston and the Kanawha Valley.* Woodland Hills, CA: Windsor Pub., 1981.

Glen Rogers Mine Disaster: Dillon, Lacy. *They Died in the Darkness.* Parsons: McClain, 1976 • *Historical Summary of Mine Disasters in the United States.* U.S. Mine Safety & Health Administration, 1998.

"Little Sleepy" Glenn: Julian, Norman. *Legends: Profiles in West Virginia University Basketball.* Morgantown: Trillium Pub., 1998 • *WVU Basketball Media Guide,* 1998–99 • *WVU Football Media Guide,* 1999.

Glenville: Gilmer County Historical Society. *History of Gilmer County, West Virginia, 1845–1989.* Marceline, MO: Walsworth Pub., 1994 • *Hardesty's,* vol. 7. • "History of Gilmer County," Folder. Robert F. Kidd Library, Glenville State College • WPA Writers' Project. *Gilmer: The Birth of a County.* Charleston: 1940.

Joseph C. Gluck: Hepler, Linda. "The Preacher and the Bear: A Monongalia Church Celebrates an Unusual Tradition." *Goldenseal* (Spring 1991) • Spitznogle, Laura. "The Man of a Thousand Stories." *WVU Alumni Magazine* (Fall 1998).

Nathan Goff Jr.: Atkinson, George W. & Alvaro F. Gibbens. *Prominent Men of West Virginia.* Wheeling: W. L. Callin, 1890 • Smith, G. Wayne. "Nathan Goff in the Civil War." *WVH* (Jan. 1953).

Goldenseal: Sullivan, Ken. "A Fond Farewell." *Goldenseal* (Spring 1997) • Sullivan. "Our Founder." *Goldenseal* (Winter 1994).

Good Roads Movement: Ambler & Summers • Thomas–*New Deal.*

Howard Mason Gore: Ambler & Summers • "Howard M. Gore Taken by Death." *Fairmont West Virginian,* 6/20/1947 • "Howard Gore, Former State Governor, Dies." *Fairmont Times,* 6/21/1947 • Morgan–*Governors.*

Goss-Ryan Heavyweight Fight: Barnett, Bob. "Coming to Scratch." *Sports Heritage* (Sept.–Oct. 1987) • *National Police Gazette,* 6/12/1880.

Governors of West Virginia: Conley–*Encyclopedia* • Morgan–*Governors.*

Graceland: Belanger, Ruth. "Graceland: the Past and Future of an Elkins Landmark." *Goldenseal* (July–Sept. 1979) • Marshall, Paul D. "Graceland, Home of Henry Gassaway Davis, 1823–1916," First Phase of Historic Structures Report. Elkins, 1979 • Pepper, Charles M. *The Life and Times of Henry Gassaway Davis 1823–1916.* New York: Century Co., 1920.

Grafton: Brinkman, Charles. *A History of Taylor County.* Grafton: Taylor County Historical & Genealogical Society, 1989 • Carvell, Kenneth. "Grafton Then and Now." *WWV* (Oct. 2000) • McDevitt, Wayne F. "Grafton and the B&O Railroad," in *A History of Taylor County.* Parsons: McClain, 1986.

Grand Army of the Republic: Dearing, Mary R. *Veterans in Politics: The Story of the G.A.R.* Baton Rouge: LSU Press, 1952 • Grand Army of the Republic, Dept. of WV. *Proceedings of the Annual Encampments, 1883– 1927.* State Archives • McConnell, Stuart. *Glorious Contentment: The Grand Army of the Republic, 1865–1900.* Chapel Hill: UNC Press, 1992.

Grandview Park: Wood, Jim. *Raleigh County.* Beckley: J. Wood, 1994.

The Grange: Ambler & Summers • Conley–*Encyclopedia* • Martin, Edward Winslow. *History of the Grange Movement.* New York: Augustus M. Kelley, 1969 • Rice & Brown.

Grantsville: Cuthbert, John. "Riverboat Days on the Little Kanawha River." *WWV* (Jan. 1996) • Calhoun County Historical & Genealogical Society. *History of Calhoun County.* Grantsville, 1990 • Hamilton, L. C. "Early Court Held in Various Locations." *Calhoun Chronicle,* 8/25/1997 • Reed, Louis. "A Brief History of Grantsville." *Grantsville News,* 3/19/1944 • White, Helen M. "County Seat Debate Costly for Calhoun." *Parkersburg News,* 3/9/1969.

Grave Creek Mound: Hemmings, E. Thomas. "Investigations at Grave Creek Mound 1975–1976." *WV Archeologist* (1984) • McMichael– *Archeology* • Norona, Delf. *Moundsville's Mammoth Mound.* Moundsville: WV Archeological Society, 1954. Reprint, WV Archeological Society, 1998.

Grave Creek Tablet: Barnhart, Terry A. "Curious Antiquity? The Grave Creek Controversy Revisited." *WVH* (1985–86) • Norona, Delf. *Moundsville's Mammoth Mound.* Moundsville: WV Archeological Society, 1954. Reprint, WV Archeological Society, 1998.

Gravely Tractor: Marra, John L. "Ben Gravely's Garden Tractor." *Goldenseal* (Summer 1997).

Catfish Gray: Green, Ted & Allen Bennett. "Catfish: The Work and Ways of an Herb Doctor." *Goldenseal* (July–Sept. 1977).

Great Bend Tunnel: Dixon, Thomas W. Jr. *Chesapeake & Ohio Alleghany Subdivision.* Alderson: C&O Historical Society, 1985 • Turner, Charles W. *Chessie's Road.* Alderson: C&O Historical Society, 1986.

The Great Depression: Coffey, William E. "Rush Dew Holt, the Boy Senator, 1905–1942." Ph.D. diss., WVU, 1970 • Gatrell, Albert Steven. "Herman Guy Kump: A Political Profile." Ph.D. diss., WVU, 1967 • Haid, Stephen Edward. "Arthurdale: An Experiment in Community Planning." Ph.D. diss., WVU, 1975 • Olson, James S. "The Depths of the Great Depression: Economic Collapse in West Virginia, 1932–1933." *WVH* (Apr. 1977) • Salstrom, Paul. *Appalachia's Path to Dependency: Rethinking a Region's Economic History, 1730–1940.* Lexington: UPK, 1994 • Thomas– *New Deal.*

Daniel Greathouse: Cranmer, G. L. *History of the Upper Ohio Valley.* Madison, WI: Brant, Fuller & Co., 1891 • Rice, Otis. "Introduction," in John J. Jacobs, *A Biographical Sketch of the Life of the Late Captain Michael Cresap.* Parsons: McClain, 1971 • Wayne, Audra Rickey & Barbara Ellen Wayne. *The Greathouse Family of West Virginia,* Booklet. Wheeling, 1977.

Greathouse Party Massacre: Cranmer, G. L. *History of the Upper Ohio Valley.* Madison, WI: Brant, Fuller & Co., 1891 • Jefferson, Thomas. *Notes on the State of Virginia.* Richmond: J. W. Randolph, 1853 • Withers– *Chronicles.*

Greeks: Davis, Dorothy. *History of Harrison County.* Clarksburg: American Assn. of University Women, 1970 • Makricosta, Pamela. "A Bundle of Treasures: Greeks in West Virginia." *Goldenseal* (Winter 1997) • Stafford, Margo. "All Greek and all Hard Workers." *Goldenseal* (Fall 1982).

Green Bottom: National Register of Historic Places Nomination, ms., WVDC&H, 1978.

Greenbrier: Kenny, Hamill. *West Virginia Place Names.* Piedmont: Place Name Press, 1945.

Greenbrier College for Women: Graybill, Henry B. *A Brief History of Greenbrier College.* Lewisburg: Greenbrier College, 1949.

Greenbrier Company: Rice–*Allegheny Frontier.*

Greenbrier Division: McNeel, William P. *The Durbin Route: The Greenbrier Division of the Chesapeake & Ohio Railway.* Charleston: PHPC, 1995.

Greenbrier Ghost: Deitz, Dennis J. *The Greenbrier Ghost and Other Strange Stories.* South Charleston: Mountain Memories Books, 1990.

Greenbrier Limestone: Bathurst, R. G. *Carbonate Sediments and their Diagenesis.* New York: Elsevier Publishers, 1976 • Davies, W. E. *Caverns of West Virginia.* Morgantown: WVGES, 1958 • Smosna, R. "Play Mgn: Upper Mississippian Greenbrier/Newman Limestones," in J. B. Roen & B. J. Walker, eds., *The Atlas of Major Appalachian Gas Plays.* Morgantown: WVGES, 1996.

Greenbrier Military School: Rice–*Greenbrier County.*

Greenbrier State Forest: Brooks, Fred C. "Welcome to Greenbrier State Forest." *WWV* (Aug. 1976).

The Greenbrier: Conte, Robert S. *The History of The Greenbrier.* Charleston: PHPC, 1998.

Greene Line: Way, Frederick. "Greenland." *S&D Reflector,* vol. 14 (1977) • Way. *The Saga of the Delta Queen.* Cincinnati: Young & Klein, Inc., 1951.

Greenwood Cemetery: Crammer, Gibson Lamb. *History of Wheeling City and Ohio County.* Chicago: Biographical Pub., 1902 • "Greenwood Cemetery Tour," Pamphlet. Greenwood Cemetery Assn., 1991.

Hal Greer: Moffatt, Charles H. *Marshall University: An Institution Comes of Age, 1837–1980.* Huntington: Marshall University Alumni Assn., 1981.

Grenadier Squaw: Jefferds, Joseph C. Jr. *Captain Matthew Arbuckle: A Documentary Biography.* Charleston: Education Foundation, 1981 • Thwaites, Reuben Gold & Louise Phelps Kellogg, eds. *Frontier Defense on the Upper Ohio 1777–1778.* Madison, WI: Wisconsin Historical Society, 1912.

Perry Epler Gresham: Carty, James W. Jr. *The Gresham Years.* Athens, OH: Lawhead Press, 1970 • Gresham, Perry E. *Growing Up in the Ranchland.* Simla, CO: Gaddy Printing, 1993 • Marty, Corie. "Noted College President, Dr. Gresham, Dies." *Wheeling Sunday News-Register,* 9/11/1994.

Grimes Golden: Calhoun, Creighton Lee Jr. *Old Southern Apples.* Blacksburg, VA: McDonald & Woodward Pub., 1995 • Comstock– *Encyclopedia,* vols. 10–12 & 21, 1974.

Gristmills: Gilbert, Dave. *Where Industry Failed: Water-Powered Mills at Harpers Ferry, West Virginia.* Charleston: PHPC, 1984 • Miller & Maxwell, vol. 1 • Stine, Oscar C. *The Shepherd Grist Mill.* Shepherdstown: O. C. Stine, 1964 • Workman, Michael. "Low Tech: The Workings of a Water Mill." *Goldenseal* (Spring 1991).

Davis Grubb: Bunting, Camilla. "When Hollywood Came to Moundsville." *Goldenseal* (Summer 1995).

Felix Grundy: Ewing, Frances Howard. "The Senatorial Career of the Honorable Felix Grundy," in *Dictionary of American Biography,* vol. 4. New York, 1931–32 • Parks, Joseph Howard. *Felix Grundy: Champion of Democracy.* Baton Rouge: LSU Press, 1940.

Guineas: Gaskins, Avery F. "An Introduction to the Guineas: West Virginia's Melungeons." *Appalachian Journal* (Autumn 1973) • Ward, Barry J. "Going Yander: The West Virginia Guineas' View of Ohio." *Goldenseal* (Apr.–June 1976).

Guyandotte: Wallace, George S. *Cabell County Annals and Families.* Richmond: Garrett & Massie, 1935.

Guyandotte, Battle of: Geiger, Joe Jr. *Civil War in Cabell County.* Charleston: PHPC, 1991 • Geiger. "Tragic Fate of Guyandotte." *WVH* (1995) • Stutler–*Civil War.*

Guyandotte River: Johnson, Leland R. *Men, Mountains, and Rivers.* Washington: GPO, 1977.

Gypsies: Kraina, Jane & Mary Zwierzchowski. "Death of a Gypsy King." *Goldenseal* (Winter 1998) • "Strange Rites over Body of Gypsy King." *Weirton Daily Times,* 11/21/1931 • Sway, Marlene. *Familiar Strangers: Gypsy Life in America.* Urbana: UI Press, 1988.

John P. Hale: Cohen–*Kanawha Images* • Laidley, W. S. *History of Charleston and Kanawha County.* Chicago: Richmond-Arnold Pub. Co., 1911.

Granville Davisson Hall: Atkinson, George W. & Alvaro F. Gibbens. *Prominent Men of West Virginia.* Wheeling: W. L. Callin, 1890 • Comstock–*Encyclopedia,* vol. 10, 1976 • Davis, Dorothy. *History of Harrison County.* Clarksburg: American Assn. of University Women, 1960.

Halliehurst Mansion: Cohen, Stan B. & Michael J. Pauley. *Historic Sites of West Virginia.* Charleston: PHPC, 1985 • Holmes, Charles J. & Justin M. Kunkle, eds. *Elkins, West Virginia: Its Past, Present and Future.* Elkins: Board of Trade, 1906 • National Register of Historic Places Nomination, ms., WVDC&H, 1969 • Pepper, Charles M. *The Life and Times of Henry Gassaway Davis, 1823–1916.* New York: Century Co., 1920.

Hamlin: Brisco, Alta B. & Gladys B. Smart. *Records of Hamlin, WV, Post Office 1857–1861.* State Archives • *Ceredo Advance,* 11/11/1886 • *Gazette,* 8/3/1978 • *Hardesty's,* vol. 7 • F. B. Lambert Collection, Special Collections, Morrow Library, Marshall University, Huntington, WV • *Lincoln Republican,* 1/12/1918 & 11/6/1930 • *The Llorrac: The Yearbook of the Carroll High School of Hamlin,* 1926.

Edden Hammons: Cuthbert, John & Alan Jabbour, eds. *Edden Hammons Collection,* vols. 1–2, compact disc. Morgantown: WVU Press, 1999–2000 • Milnes, Gerald. *Play of a Fiddle.* Lexington: UPK, 1999.

Hammons Family: Cuthbert, John & Alan Jabbour, eds. *Edden Hammons Collection,* vols. 1–2, compact disc. Morgantown: WVU Press, 1999–2000 • Fleischhauer, Carl & Alan Jabbour, eds. *The Hammons Family: The*

Traditions of a West Virginia Family and their Friends. Rounder CD 1504/05, 1998 • Milnes, Gerald. *Play of a Fiddle.* Lexington: UPK, 1999.

Hampshire County: Brannon, Selden W. *Historic Hampshire.* Parsons: McClain, 1976 • *Historic Romney, 1762–1937.* Romney: WV Writers' Project, 1937 • Maxwell, Hu & H. L. Swisher. *History of Hampshire County.* Morgantown: A. B. Boughner, 1897. Reprint, McClain, 1972.

Hampshire Review: Moulden, Bill. "In The Family: A Hundred Years at the Hampshire Review." *Goldenseal* (Spring 1990).

Rimfire Hamrick: Comstock–*Encyclopedia,* vol. 10, 1976 • Sturm, Harry P. & H. G. Rhawn. *Rimfire: West Virginia's Typical Mountaineer.* Parsons: McClain, 1967 • "Nephew of Hamrick Brothers Says Ellis was Subject for Sculptor." *Daily Mail,* 7/14/1946.

Hancock County: Boyd, Peter. *History of Northern West Virginia Panhandle.* Topeka, KS: Historical Pub. Co., 1927 • Javersak, David T. *History of Weirton.* Virginia Beach: Donning Co., 1999.

Handcrafts: Eaton, Allen H. *Handicrafts of the Southern Highlands.* New York: Russell Sage Foundation, 1937. Reprint, Dover, 1973 • Law, Rachel Nash & Cynthia W. Taylor. *Appalachian White Oak Basketmaking.* Knoxville: University of Tennessee Press, 1991.

Hanging Rock Observatory: Davis, J. Ray. *The Redstart,* vol. 65, no. 2 • Hurley, George. *The Redstart,* vol. 37, no.3; vol. 42, no. 4; vol. 54, no. 3; vol. 64, no. 4.

Nancy Hanks: Baber, Adin. *Nancy Hanks.* Kansas, IL: Adin Baber, 1963 • Briggs, Harold E. *Nancy Hanks Lincoln: A Frontier Portrait.* New York: Bookman Associates, 1952 • Steers, Edward Jr. "Nancy Hanks, West Virginian." *Lincoln Herald* (Summer 1998).

Alberta Pierson Hannum: Ambler & Summers • Bowden, Jane A., ed. *Contemporary Authors.* Detroit: Gale Research, 1977.

Hardy County: Duffey, J. W. *Two Generals Kidnapped,* Booklet. Moorefield: *Moorefield Examiner,* 1944 • MacMaster, Richard K. *The History of Hardy County 1786–1986.* Moorefield: Hardy County Public Library, 1986 • Moore, Alvin E. *History of Hardy County of the Borderland.* Parsons: McClain, 1963.

"John Hardy": Chappell, Louis W. *John Henry: A Folk-Lore Study.* Port Washington, NY: Kennikat Press, 1932 • Comstock–*Encyclopedia,* vol. 23, 1974 • Cox, John Harrington. *Folk-Songs of the South.* Cambridge: Harvard University Press, 1925 • Ramella, Richard. "John Hardy: The Man and the Song." *Goldenseal* (Spring 1992).

Minnie Buckingham Harper: *Blue Book,* 1928.

Harpers Ferry Armory and Arsenal: Brown, Stuart E. Jr. *The Guns of Harpers Ferry.* Berryville, VA: Virginia Book, 1968 • Gilbert, Dave. *Where Industry Failed: Water-Powered Mills at Harpers Ferry, West Virginia.* Charleston: PHPC, 1984 • Gluckman, Arcadi. *Identifying Old U.S. Muskets, Rifles, and Carbines.* Harrisburg, PA: Stackpole Books, 1959 • Theriault, William D. *A History of Eastern Jefferson County.* Bakerton: Jefferson County Oral & Visual History Assn., 1988.

Harpers Ferry Civil War Campaign: Hearn, Chester G. *Six Years of Hell.* Baton Rouge: LSU Press, 1996 • Moulton, Charles H. *Fort Lyon to Harpers Ferry.* Shippensburg, PA: White Mane Pub. Co., 1987.

Harpers Ferry National Historic Park: Frye, Dennis E. "Harpers Ferry Park," in *Harpers Ferry National Historic Park 50th Anniversary Commemorative Program.* Washington: National Park Service, 1994.

Thomas Maley Harris: Bak, Richard. *The Day Lincoln was Shot.* Dallas: Taylor Pub., 1998 • Comstock–*Encyclopedia,* vol. 10, 1976 • Conley–*Encyclopedia* • Harris, Thomas Maley. *The Assassination of Lincoln: A History of the Great Conspiracy.* Boston: American Citizen Co., 1892 • Matheny, H. E. *Major General Thomas Maley Harris.* Parsons: McClain, 1963.

Harrison County: Davis, Dorothy. *History of Harrison County.* Clarksburg: American Assn. of University Women, 1970.

Harrisville: Lowther, Minnie Kendall. *Ritchie County in History and Romance.* Wheeling News Litho. Co., ca. 1911. Reprint, McClain, 1990 • Ritchie County Historical Society. *The History of Ritchie County.* Harrisville, 1980

Morris Harvey: Hill, Mildred Haptonstall. "Morris Harvey." *WVH* (Jan. 1951).

William "Coin" Harvey: Harvey, William Hope. *Coin's Financial School.* Cambridge, MA, 1963 • Rice & Brown • WPA–*Guide.*

Devil Anse Hatfield: Hatfield, Coleman & Robert Y. Spence. *The Tale of the Devil: The Biography of Devil Anse Hatfield.* Chapmanville: Woodland Press, 2003 • Rice, Otis K. *The Hatfields & the McCoys.* Lexington: UPK, 1982 • Waller, Altina L. *Feud: Hatfields, McCoys, and Social Change in Appalachia, 1860–1900.* Chapel Hill: UNC Press, 1988.

Hatfield Family: Hatfield, Elliott. *The Hatfields.* Stanville, KY: Big Sandy Valley Historical Society, 1974 • Rice, Otis K. *The Hatfields & the McCoys.* Lexington: UPK, 1982.

Henry D. Hatfield: Burckel, Nicholas C. "Progressive Governors in the Border States: Reform Governors of Missouri, Kentucky, West Virginia, and Maryland." Ph.D. diss., University of Wisconsin, 1971 • Karr, Carolyn. "A Political Biography of Henry Hatfield." *WVH* (Oct. 1966, Jan. 1967) • Penn, Neil S. "Henry D. Hatfield and Reform Politics." Ph.D diss., Emory University, 1977.

Sid Hatfield: Savage–*Thunder* • U.S. Senate. *West Virginia Coal Fields.* Hearings before the Committee on Education & Labor. U.S. Senate, 67th Congress, first session, 2 vols. Washington: GPO, 1921–22.

The Hatfield-McCoy Feud: Rice, Otis K. *The Hatfields & the McCoys.* Lexington: UPK, 1982 • Waller, Altina L. *Feud: Hatfields, McCoys, and Social Change in Appalachia, 1860–1900.* Chapel Hill: UNC Press, 1988.

Hamilton Hatter: Caldwell, A. B., ed. *History of the American Negro,* vol. 7: WV Edition. Atlanta: A. B. Caldwell Pub. Co., 1923 • Reports of the Board of Regents of Bluefield Colored Institute, 1903–1906, Biennial Reports • Storer College Catalogs, 1877–1906.

Hawks Nest Strike: Bailey, Kenneth R. "Hawk's Nest Coal Company Strike." *WVH* (July 1969).

Hawks Nest Tunnel Disaster: Cherniack, Martin G. *The Hawk's Nest Incident: America's Worst Industrial Disaster.* New Haven: Yale University Press, 1986 • "476 Graves." Comstock–*Encyclopedia,* vol. 7, 1972 • Skidmore, Hubert C. *Hawk's Nest.* Reprint, Comstock–*Encyclopedia,* vol. 4, 1970 • U.S. Congress. House. Committee on Labor. *An Investigation Relating to Health Conditions of Workers Employed in the Construction and Maintenance of Public Utilities.* Hearings on House Joint Resolution 449. 74th Congress, second session. Washington: GPO, 1936.

Hawkshaw Hawkins: Tribe–*Jamboree.*

Hazel Atlas Glass Company: Algeo, J. S. *A Story of the Hazel-Atlas Glass Company,* Booklet. WV&RHC, 1956 • Weatherman, Hazel Marie. *Colored Glassware of the Depression Era II.* Springfield, MO: Weatherman Glassbooks, 1974 • Welker, John & Elizabeth Welker. *Pressed Glass in America.* Ivyland, PA: Antique Acres Press, 1985.

He-Man Club: Concord Archives, Concord University Library, Athens.

Ken Hechler: Hechler, Ken. *The Bridge at Remagen.* New York: Ballantine Books, 1957 • Hechler. *Working with Truman.* New York: G. P. Putnam's Sons, 1982 • Moffat, Charles H. *Ken Hechler: Maverick Public Servant.* Charleston: Mountain State Press, 1987.

Helvetia: Cometti, Elizabeth. "Swiss Immigration to West Virginia." *Mississippi Valley Historical Review* (June 1960) • Sutton, David H. *One's Own Hearth Is Like Gold: A History of Helvetia.* New York: Peter Lang, 1990.

Cam Henderson: Clagg, Sam. *The Cam Henderson Story.* Parsons: McClain, 1981 • Toothman, Fred R. *Wild Wonderful Winners: Great Football Coaches of West Virginia.* Huntington: Vandalia Book Co., 1991.

John Henry: Chappell, Louis. *John Henry: A Folk-Lore Study.* Port Washington, NY: Kennikat Press, 1968 • Johnson, Guy B. *John Henry: Tracking Down a Negro Legend.* New York: AMS Press, 1969 • Williams, Brett. *John Henry: A Bio-Bibliography.* Westport, CT: Greenwood Press, 1983.

Frank Hereford: Ambler & Summers • Summers, Festus P. *Johnson Newlon Camden.* New York: G. P. Putnam's Sons, 1937.

High Gate: National Register of Historic Places Nomination, ms., WVDC&H, 1982 • Williams–*Captains.*

Historic Preservation: Lamarre, Lora. *Preserving our Mountaineer Heritage: West Virginia Statewide Historic Preservation Plan, 2002–2006.* Charleston: WVDC& H, 2001.

Hitchman Coal & Coke v. Mitchell et al: Bernstein, Irving. *The Lean Years.* Boston: Houghton Mifflin, 1960 • Lunt, Richard D. *Law and Order vs. the Miners.* Charleston: Appalachian Editions, 1992.

Joist Hite: Hofstra, Warren R. "Land, Ethnicity, and Community at the Opequon Settlement, Virginia, 1730–1800." *Virginia Magazine of History & Biography* (July 1990) • Kerns, Wilmer L. *Frederick County, Virginia: Settlement and Some First Families of Back Creek Valley.* Baltimore: Gateway Press, 1995.

Hollidays Cove: Ferguson, Mary Shakley. *History of Hollidays Cove.* Weirton, 1976 • Javersak, David T. *History of Weirton.* Virginia Beach: Donning Co., 1999.

Holly Grove: Cohen–*Kanawha Images* • Dayton, Ruth Woods. *Pioneers and their Houses on Upper Kanawha.* Charleston: WV Pub., 1947 • Morgan, John G. & Robert J. Byers. *Charleston 200. Gazette,* 1994.

Holly River State Park: Anderson, Stanley "Judd." *The Kanawha Head Project: A History of Holly River State Park.* Utica, KY: McDowell Pub., 1993 • *History of State Parks.*

Rush Holt: Coffey, William E. "Isolationism and Pacifism: Senator Rush D. Holt and American Foreign Policy." *WVH* (1992).

Homer Adams Holt: *Gazette,* 1/17/1976 • Morgan–*Governors* • Rice, Otis K. *West Virginia: A History.* Lexington: UPK, 1985.

Homer Laughlin China Company: Cunningham, Jo. *Homer Laughlin: A Giant Among Dishes 1873–1939.* Atglen, PA: Schiffer Pub., 1998 • Gates, William C. & Dana E. Ormerod. "The East Liverpool, Ohio, Pottery District," in Ronald E. Michael, ed., *Historical Archaeology.* (Mar., Oct. 1982) • Page, Bob, Dale Frederiksen & Dean Six. *Homer Laughlin: Decades of Dinnerware.* Greensboro, NC: Page/Frederiksen Pub., 2003 • Welch, Jack. "The Homer Laughlin China Company." *Goldenseal* (Spring 1985).

Homestead Exemption: *Michie's West Virginia Code, Annotated, Volume 4,* Chapter 11, Article 6B. Charlottesville: Lexis Pub. • *Michie's West Virginia Code, Annotated, Volume 4A,* Chapter 11, Article 21. Charlottesville: Lexis Pub. • *Michie's West Virginia Code, Annotated, Volume 1,* Article 10. Charlottesville: Lexis Pub. • House Joint Resolution No. 1, Extraordinary Session, 1982 • House Joint Resolution No. 30, Regular Session, 1980 • House Joint Resolution No. 7, Regular Session, 1973.

Hopemont Sanitarium: Crockett, Maureen. "Hopemont: Curing Tuberculosis in Preston County." *Goldenseal* (Spring 1986).

Jedediah Hotchkiss: Roper, Peter W. *Jedediah Hotchkiss: Rebel Mapmaker and Virginia Businessman.* Shippensburg, PA: White Mane Pub., 1992.

House of Delegates: Atkinson, George W. "Legislative History of West Virginia," in James M. Callahan, ed., *Semi-Centennial History of West Virginia.* Charleston: Semi-Centennial Commission, 1913 • *Blue Book,* 2001.

Harold Houston: Barkey, Fred. "Fritz Merrick." *WVH* (1998) • Barkey. "West Virginia Socialist Party, 1898–1920." Ph.D diss., University of Pittsburgh, 1971 • Lane, Winthrop D. *Civil War in West Virginia.* New York: B.W. Huebsch, Inc., 1921 • Lee–*Bloodletting.*

Sam Huff: *Gazette,* 12/9/1973.

Jesse Hughes: McWhorter, Lucullus Virgil. *The Border Settlers of Northwestern Virginia from 1768 to 1795: Embracing the Life of Jesse Hughes.* Hamilton, OH: The Republican Pub. Co., 1915. Reprint, Comstock, vols. 12–13, 1974 • Withers–*Chronicles.*

Hughes River: Erwin, Robert B. *West Virginia Gazetteer of Physical and Cultural Place Names.* Morgantown: WVGES, 1986 • Lowther, Minnie Kendall. *History of Ritchie County.* Wheeling News Litho. Co., 1911.

Milton W. Humphreys: McKinney, Tim. *The Civil War in Fayette County.* Charleston: PHPC, 1988 • Scott, John L. *Lowry's, Bryan's and Chapman's Batteries of Virginia Artillery.* Lynchburg: H. E. Howard, 1988.

Hot Rod Hundley: Julian, Norman. "Hundley Credits his Success to Start at WVU." *Dominion Post,* 1/28/1996.

Hungarians: Bailey, Kenneth R. "A Judicious Mixture: Negroes and Immigrants in the West Virginia Mines, 1880–1917." *WVH* (Jan. 1973) • Barkey, Fredrick A. "Immigration and Ethnicity in West Virginia," in Ronald L. Lewis & John C. Hennen Jr. eds., *West Virginia History: Critical Essays on the Literature.* Dubuque, IA: Kendall-Hunt Pub., 1993 • *14th Census of the U.S.: Population 1920.* Washington: GPO, 1922.

Hunting: Allen, Thomas & Jack Cromer. "White-tailed Deer in West Virginia," Bulletin. WVDNR, 1977 • Stone, Frank & Charles Costilow. *History of Conservation Law Enforcement in West Virginia.* Charleston: WVDNR, 1974.

Huntington: Casto, James E. *Huntington: An Illustrated History.* Northridge, CA: Windsor Pub., 1985 • Miller, Doris C. *A Centennial History of Huntington.* Huntington: Huntington Centennial Commission, 1971 • Wallace, George S. *Huntington through 75 Years.* Huntington, 1947.

Collis P. Huntington: Evans, Cerinda W. *Collis Potter Huntington.* Newport News: Mariners' Museum, 1954 • Lavender, David. *The Great Persuader.* Garden City, NY: Doubleday, 1970.

Hurricane: Shanklin, Harry L. "History of Hurricane," in William D. Wintz & Ivan M. Hunter, eds., *History of Putnam County.* Charleston: Upper Vandalia Historical Society, 1967.

Frank Hutchison: "A Real Fine Looking Man." *Goldenseal* (Spring 1984). • Tribe–*Jamboree.*

Huttonsville Correctional Center: Comstock–*Encyclopedia,* vol. 11, 1976 • Kek, Anna D. *Randolph County Profile, 1976: A Handbook of the County.* Parsons: McClain, 1976 • *Blue Book,* 1972.

Ices Ferry Ironworks: Moreland, James R. *The Early Cheat Mountain Iron Works.* Morgantown: Monongalia Historical Society, 1992.

George W. Imboden: Beckelheimer, Christine. "George W. Imboden," in *History of Fayette County.* Fayetteville: Fayette County Chamber of Commerce, 1993 • Delauter, Roger U. Jr. *18th Virginia Cavalry.* Lynchburg: H. E. Howard, 1985 • Peters, J. T. & H. B. Carden. *History of Fayette County.* Charleston: Jarrett Printing, 1926 • Woodward, Harold R. Jr. *Defender of the Valley: Brigadier General John D. Imboden, CSA.* Berryville, VA: Rockbridge Publications, 1996.

John D. Imboden: Delauter, Roger. *The 62nd Virginia Mounted Infantry.* Lynchburg: H. E. Howard, 1988 • Faust, Patricia L., ed. *Historical Times Illustrated Encyclopedia of the Civil War.* New York: Harper & Row, 1986.

Immigration Commissioner: Bailey, Kenneth R. "West Virginia and the Alien Contract Labor Law," in *New River Symposium Proceedings,* 1993 • Harris, Evelyn K. & Frank J. Krebs. *From Humble Beginnings: The West Virginia State Federation of Labor, 1903–1957.* Charleston: WV Labor History Pub. Fund, 1960.

Indian Mound Cemetery: Fowkes, Gerald. "Archeological Investigations in the James and Potomac Valleys," Bulletin 23. Washington: Bureau of American Ethnology, 1894 • Maxwell, Hu & H. L. Swisher. *History of Hampshire County.* Morgantown: A. B. Boughner, 1897. Reprint, McClain, 1972.

Indian Trails: Myer, William E. *Indian Trails of the Southeast.* Washington: Bureau of American Ethnology, 1928 • Rice & Brown • Riddel, Frank S. *Historical Atlas of West Virginia,* (unpub. ms.) • Sturtevant, William C., ed. *Handbook of North American Indians. Northeast,* vol. 15. Washington: Smithsonian Institution, 1978.

Indian Wars: Carroll, George. "Lewis Wetzel: Warfare Tactics on the Frontier." *WVH* (1991) • Doddridge, Joseph. *Notes on the Settlement and the Indian Wars.* Pittsburgh: John S. Ritenour & Wm. T. Lindsay, 1912 • Dowd, Gregory E. *A Spirited Resistance: The North American Indian Struggle for Unity, 1745–1815.* Baltimore: Johns Hopkins University Press, 1992.

Indians: Logan, Michael H. "My Great Grandmother was a Cherokee Indian Princess: Ethnic Forgery or Darwinian Reality." *Tennessee Anthropologist* (Spring 1990) • Smith, Joanne J., Florence K. Barnett & Lois K. Croston. "We, the People of Chestnut Ridge: A Native Community in Barbour County." *Goldenseal* (Fall 1999) • Sturtevant, William C., ed. *Handbook of North American Indians: Northeast,* vol. 15. Washington: Smithsonian Institution, 1978 • Washburn, Wilcomb E., ed. *Handbook of North American Indians: History of Indian-White Relations.* Washington: Smithsonian Institution, 1990.

The Influenza Epidemic of 1918: Chamberlain, Lorna. "The Flu Epidemic of 1918." *Goldenseal* (Winter 1990) • Persico, Joseph. "The Great Swine Flu Epidemic of 1918." *American Heritage* (June 1976) • Report of the State Health Dept. Charleston, 7/1/1918–6/30/1919, Annual Report.

Insects: Allen, Thomas J. *The Butterflies of West Virginia and their Caterpillars.* Pittsburgh: UPP, 1997 • Constantz, George. *Hollows, Peepers, and Highlanders.* Missoula, MT: Mountain Press, 1994 • Stephenson, Steven L. *Upland Forests of West Virginia.* Parsons: McClain, 1993 • Wagner, David L., et al. *Caterpillars of Eastern Forests.* Morgantown: USDA., 1997.

Instant Libraries: "Public Library Construction." Charleston: WVLC, 1976.

Integration: Johnson, Paul. "Integration in West Virginia Since 1954." M.A. thesis, WVU, 1959 • Smith, Douglas. "In Quest of Equality: The West Virginia Experience." *WVH* (Apr. 1978) • *Southern School News.* Nashville, TN: Southern Education Reporting Service, 1954–1965.

Interstate Highway System: Melling, Carol. "Across the State in '88 (The Completion of the Interstate System in West Virginia)," Pamphlet. WVDOH, 1988 • *Blue Book,* 1997.

Interwoven Mills: Jenrette, Jerra, "'There's No Damn Reason for It–It's Just our Policy': Labor-Management Conflict in Martinsburg, West

Virginia's Textile and Garment Industries." Ph.D. diss., WVU, 1996 • Johnston, Wilbur. *Weaving a Common Thread: A History of the Woolen Industry in the Top of the Shenandoah Valley*. Winchester: Winchester-Frederick County Historical Society, 1990 • Rice & Brown.

Invertebrates: Buchsbaum, Ralph & L. Milne. *The Lower Animals: Living Invertebrates of the World*. Garden City: Doubleday, 1960 • Dindall, D. L. *Soil Biology Guide*. New York: John Wiley & Son, 1990 • Jezerinac, R. F. et al. "The Crayfishes of West Virginia," Bulletin 10. Ohio Biological Survey, 1995 • Levi, H. & L. Levi. *Spiders and their Kin*. New York: Golden Press, 1968 • Pennak, R. W. *Fresh-Water Invertebrates of the U.S.* New York: Ronald Press, 1989.

Irish: Allen, Bernard L. Newspaper series. *Parkersburg News*, July–Sept. 1989 • Callahan, James M. *History of West Virginia*, vol. 1. Chicago: American Historical Society, 1923 • Pyne, Tricia T. *Faith in the Mountains: A History of the Diocese of Wheeling-Charleston, 1850–2000*. Strasbourg, France: Editions du Signe, 2000.

Irish Mountain: Brown, Leona G. "Recalling an Irish Mountain Family." *Goldenseal* (Spring 1991) • McLean, Lois C. "Irish Mountain." *Goldenseal* (Spring 1991) • Index to Deeds & Wills, Books 10, 17 & 29. Birth Records, 1860–1899. Raleigh County Courthouse, Beckley • Baptismal & Marriage Records, 1874–1907. St. Patrick Church, Hinton • U.S. Census, 1860–1880, 1900–1920 • Wood, Jim. *Raleigh County*. Beckley: J. Wood, 1994.

The Irish Tract: Hurley, Basil. "Tales from the Irish Tract." *Goldenseal* (Spring 1998).

Ironmaking: Grimsley, G. P., WVGES. *Iron Ore, Salt and Sandstones*. Morgantown: Acme Pub., 1909 • Maddex, Lee R. "Furnaces in Blast along the Chesapeake & Ohio Railroad." *Canal History and Technology Proceedings*, vol. 15. Easton, PA: Hugh Moore Park & Museum, 1996 • Moreland, James R. *Early Cheat Mountain Iron Works*. Morgantown: Monongalia Historical Society, 1992 • Scott, Henry Dickerson. *Iron and Steel in Wheeling*. Toledo, OH: Caslon Co., 1929 • Theriault, William D. "Friend's Orebank and the Keep Triste Furnace." *WVH* (1989).

Iroquois: Richter, Daniel K. *The Ordeal of the Longhouse: The Peoples of the Iroquois League in the Era of European Colonization*. Chapel Hill: UNC Press, 1992.

Italian Heritage Festival: "Italian Heritage Festival," Programs. 1979–1998.

Italian Prisoners of War: Keefer, Louis E. *Italian Prisoners of War in America*. New York: Praeger, 1992 • Keefer. "The West Virginia World War II Home Front: POW: The Italian Prisoners at Camp Dawson." *Goldenseal* (Spring 1993).

Italians: Bailey, Kenneth. "A Judicious Mixture: Negroes and Immigrants in the West Virginia Mines, 1880–1917." *WVH* (Jan. 1973) • Barkey, Fred. "Here Come the Boomer 'Talys: Italian Immigrants and Industrial Conflict in the Upper Kanawha Valley, 1903–1917," in Ken Fones-Wolf & Ronald L. Lewis, eds., *Transnational West Virginia*. Morgantown: WVU Press, 2002 • Davis, Dorothy. *History of Harrison County*. Clarksburg: American Assn. of University Women, 1970 • Klaus, William. "Uneven Americanization: Italian Immigration to Marion County," in Ken Fones-Wolf & Ronald L. Lewis, eds., *Transnational West Virginia*. Morgantown: WVU Press, 2002 • Wood, Jim. *Raleigh County*. Beckley: J. Wood, 1994.

Itmann Company Store: Bower, Charles H. "Itmann," (unpub. ms.) • National Register of Historic Places Nomination, ms., WVDC&H, 1990 • Pocahontas Operators Assn. Collection, Eastern Regional Archives.

It's Wheeling Steel: Cuthbert, John A. "'In Steel and Song': The Wheeling Steel Radio Show." *Goldenseal* (Winter 1992).

Jackson County: Jackson County Historical Society. *Jackson County, West Virginia, Past and Present*. Waynesville, NC: Don Mills, Inc., 1990 • Moore, Dean W. *Washington's Woods*. Parsons: McClain, 1971.

Jackson Family: Cook, Roy Bird. *Family and Early Life of Stonewall Jackson*. Charleston: Education Foundation, 1963 • Davis, Dorothy. *History of Harrison County*. Clarksburg: American Assn. of University Women, 1970 • Jackson, John C. *Shadow on the Tetons: David E. Jackson and the Claiming of the American West*. Missoula, MT: Mountain Press, 1993 • Miller & Maxwell, vol 3.

Jacob Beeson Jackson: Ambler & Summers • Miller & Maxwell, vol. 3 • Morgan–*Governors*.

John George Jackson: Brown, Stephen W. *Voice of the New West: John G.*

Jackson, his Life and Times. Macon, GA: Mercer University Press, 1985 • Davis, Dorothy. *John George Jackson*. Parsons: McClain, 1976.

John Jay Jackson Jr.: Baas, Jacob C. Jr. "John Jay Jackson Jr.: His Early Life and Public Career, 1824–1870." Ph.D. diss., WVU, 1975 • Brown, Stephen W. "John George Jackson: A Biography." Ph.D. diss., WVU, 1975.

John Jay Jackson Sr.: Baas, Jacob C. Jr. " John Jay Jackson Jr.: His Early Life and Public Career, 1824–1870." Ph.D. diss., WVU, 1975 • Brown, Stephen W. *Voice of the New West: John G. Jackson, his Life and Times*. Macon, GA: Mercer University Press, 1985.

Lily Irene Jackson: Cuthbert, John A. *Early Art and Artists in West Virginia*. Morgantown: WVU Press, 2000 • Matheny, H. E. *Wood County W. Va. in Civil War Times*. Parkersburg: Trans-Allegheny Books, 1987 • *Parkersburg State Journal*, 2/22/1887, 1/10 & 6/17/1891, 6/12/1897 • *Parkersburg Sentinel*, 12/10/1928 • Will Book, Wood County Courthouse, Parkersburg.

Mudwall Jackson: Faust, Patricia L., ed. *Historical Times Illustrated Encyclopedia of the Civil War*. New York: Harper Perennial, 1991 • Lowther, Minnie K. *Ritchie County in History and Romance*. Wheeling News Litho. Co., 1911. Reprint, McClain, 1990 • Matheny, H. E. *Wood County W. Va. in Civil War Times*. Parkersburg: Trans-Allegheny Books, 1987.

Stonewall Jackson: Robertson, James I. Jr. *Stonewall Jackson*. New York: MacMillan Library Reference, USA, 1997.

Jackson's Mill: Cook, Roy Bird. *Family and Early Life of Stonewall Jackson*. Charleston Printing, 1948 • Meador, Michael M. *Historic Jackson's Mill: A Walking Tour*. Parsons: McClain, 1991 • Stewart, Guy H. *A Touch of Charisma: A History of the 4-H Club Program in West Virginia*. Morgantown, 1969.

John Jeremiah Jacob: *Encyclopaedia of Contemporary Biography of West Virginia*. New York: Atlantic Pub. & Engraving, 1894 • Morgan–*Governors* • "West Virginia's Fourth Governor." *WV Review* (Apr. 1945).

Elmer Forrest Jacobs: Fleming, Dolores. "Architect Elmer Jacobs." *Panorama, Dominion Post*, 5/8/1988.

T. D. Jakes: Caldwell, Deborah Kovach. "Bishop Jakes Believes He Can Help Heal Hurts." *Dallas Morning News*, 7/10/1997 • Copeland, Libby. "With Gifts from God." *Washington Post*, 3/25/2001 • Jackson, Martha. "Jakes Hiked Long Road to Success." *Daily Mail*, 11/18/1995.

James Gang: Platania, Joseph. "Tracking the James Gang: Folklore of the Great Huntington Bank Robbery of 1875." *Goldenseal* (Fall 1983) • *Huntington Quarterly* (Winter 1989–90) • KYOWVA Genealogical Society. *Cabell County Heritage 1809–1996*. Huntington, 1996 • Platania, Joseph. "The 1875 Huntington Bank Robbery." *WWV* (Jan. 1995)

James River & Kanawha Canal: Johnson, Leland R. *Men, Mountains, and Rivers*. Washington: GPO, 1977 • Kemp, Emory. *Great Kanawha Navigation*. Morgantown: WVU Institute for the History of Technology, 1998.

James River & Kanawha Turnpike: Dunaway, Wayland Fuller. *History of the James River and Kanawha Company*. New York: Columbia University, 1922.

Anna Jarvis: Pomroy, Estella R. "Anna Maria Reeves Jarvis, 1832–1905," in *Missing Chapters II: West Virginia Women in History*. Charleston: WV Women's Commission, 1986 • Wolfe, Howard H. *Mother's Day and the Mother's Day Church*. Kingsport, TN: Kingsport Press, 1962.

Jefferson County: Bushong, Millard K. *A History of Jefferson County, West Virginia*. Charles Town: Jefferson Pub.Co., 1941 • Magazine of the Jefferson County Historical Society, 1935 to present.

Jefferson National Forest: Sarvis, Will. "History of the Jefferson National Forest," (unpub. ms.). Roanoke, VA: U.S. Forest Service, 1992.

Jefferson Rock: Gilbert, David. *A Walker's Guide to Harpers Ferry, West Virginia*. Harpers Ferry: Harpers Ferry Historical Assn., 1995.

Jehovah's Witnesses v. Pittsburgh Plate Glass Company: Smith, Chuck. "Paul Schmidt: A Workingman's Tenacious Pursuit of Religious Liberty." *Journal of Law and Religion*. (1999–2000) • Smith. "War Fever and Religious Fervor: The Firing of Jehovah's Witnesses Glassworkers in West Virginia and Administrative Protection of Religious Liberty." *American Journal of Legal History* (1999) • Smith. "West Virginia Jehovah's Witnesses and the Expansion of Legal Protection for Religious Liberty," in James R. Forrester, *Government and Politics in West Virginia*. Boston: Pearson Custom Pub., 2000.

Albert Gallatin Jenkins: Dickinson, Jack L. *Jenkins of Greenbottom.* Charleston: PHPC, 1988 • Geiger, Joe Jr. *Civil War in Cabell County.* Charleston: PHPC, 1991 • Hechler, Ken. Newspaper series. Huntington *Herald-Advertiser*, 1961 • McManus, Howard Rollins. *The Battle of Cloyds Mountain: The Virginia & Tennessee Railroad Raid.* Lynchburg: H. E. Howard, 1989.

Jenkins Raid: Dickinson, Jack. *The 8th Virginia Cavalry.* Lynchburg: H. E. Howard, 1985 • McKinney, Tim. *The Civil War in Fayette County, West Virginia.* Charleston: PHPC, 1988.

Jenny Lind House: Sullivan, Ken. "Cheap, Quick and Drafty: The Jenny Lind House." *Goldenseal* (Spring 1990).

Jews: Alexander, Irving. "Jewish Merchants in the Coalfields." *Goldenseal* (Spring 1990) • Meador, Michael. "Faith, Knowledge and Practice: The Jews of Southern West Virginia." *Goldenseal* (Summer 1985) • Meyer, Simon, ed. *One Hundred Years: An Anthology of Charleston Jewry.* Charleston: Jones Printing, 1972 • Shinedling, Abraham I. *West Virginia Jewry: Origins and History, 1850–1958.* Philadelphia: Maurice Jacobs, 1963 • Weiner, Deborah R. "The Jews of Clarksburg: Community Adaptation and Survival, 1900–60." *WVH* (1995).

Fanny Kemble Johnson: Frazier, Kitty B. *West Virginia Women Writers, 1822–1979.* Charleston: Kitty Frazier, 1979. • "West Virginia Women and the Arts," Pamphlet. WVU Public History Program & WVU Center for Women's Studies. Morgantown, 1990.

Johnnie Johnson: Fitzpatrick, Travis. *Father of Rock & Roll: The Story of Johnnie "B. Goode" Johnson.* Houston: Thomas, Cooke & Co., 1999.

Joseph Johnson: Atkinson, George W. & Alvaro F. Gibbens. *Prominent Men of West Virginia.* Wheeling: W. L. Callin, 1890 • Clark, Catherine J. P. "Governor Joseph Johnson." *Southern Magazine* 2 (1936) • Kester, Bart Earl. "Joseph Johnson, Governor of Virginia." M.A. thesis, WVU, 1939.

Frances Benjamin Johnston: Daniel, Pete & Ray Smock. *A Talent for Detail: The Photographs of Miss Frances Benjamin Johnston.* New York: Harmony Books, 1974.

Jones Diamond: Clark, Nancy. "Horseshoe Pitchers Discover Huge Diamond in the Rough. *WWV* (Dec. 1981) • Hyde, Arnout Jr. *New River: A Photographic Essay.* Charleston: Cannon Graphics, 1991 • Motley, Charles B. *Gleanings of Monroe County.* Radford, VA: Commonwealth Press, 1973.

Harriet B. Jones: *West Virginia Women.* Comstock–*Encyclopedia*, vol. 25, 1974 • Howe, Barbara J. "West Virginia Women's Organizations, 1880s–1930." *WVH* (1990).

Mother Jones: Fetherling, Dale. *Mother Jones: The Miners' Angel.* Carbondale, IL: Southern Illinois University Press, 1974 • Gorn, Elliott J. *Mother Jones: The Most Dangerous Woman in America.* New York: Hill & Wang, 2001 • Jones, Mary. *The Autobiography of Mother Jones.* Chicago: Charles Kerr, 1925 • Steel, Edward M. *Correspondence of Mother Jones.* Pittsburgh: UPP, 1985.

S. L. Jones: Lampell, Ramona & Millard Lampell. *O, Appalachia: Artists of the Southern Mountains.* New York: Stewart, Tabori & Chang, 1989 • Yelen, Alice Rae. *Passionate Visions of the American South: Self-Taught Artists from 1940 to the Present.* New Orleans: New Orleans Museum of Art, 1995.

Jones-Imboden Raid: Cohen, Stan. *The Civil War in West Virginia.* Charleston: PHPC, 1976 • Stutler–*Civil War* • Swick, Gerald D. "Confederate raiders rampage along the Monongahela." *Clarksburg Exponent Telegram*, 3/8/1998.

Joy Loading Machine: Dix, Keith. *What's a Coal Miner to Do?* Pittsburgh: UPP, 1988.

Judicial Branch: Hagan, John Patrick. "Political Activism in the West Virginia Supreme Court of Appeals, 1930–1985." *WV Law Review* (Fall 1986) • Kilwein, John C. "The West Virginia Judicial System at the Crossroads of Change." *Public Affairs Reporter* (Fall 1999) • Mason, John W. "The Origin and Development of the Judicial System of West Virginia," in James M. Callahan, ed., *Semi-Centennial History of West Virginia.* Charleston: Semi-Centennial Commission, 1913.

Jug of Middle Island Creek: Gregg, Gladys. "The Jug," in *History of Tyler County.* Marceline, MO: Walsworth Pub., 1984 • *Hardesty's*, vol. 1.

Kamp Kump: Thomas–*New Deal.*

Kanawha County: Cohen–*Kanawha Images* • Laidley, W. S. *History of Charleston and Kanawha County.* Chicago: Richmond-Arnold Pub. Co., 1911 • Rice, Otis K. *Charleston and the Kanawha Valley.* Woodland Hills, CA: Windsor Pub., 1981.

Kanawha County Textbook Controversy: *Kanawha County, West Virginia: A Textbook Study in Cultural Conflict.* Washington: National Education Assn., 1975 • Moffett, James. *Storm in the Mountains.* Carbondale, IL: Southern Illinois University Press, 1989 • Parker, Franklin. *The Battle of the Books: Kanawha County.* Bloomington, IN: Phi Delta Kappa Education Foundation, 1975.

Kanawha Falls: Comstock–Encyclopedia, vols. 10 & 11, 1974.

Kanawha Madonna: Hale, John P. *History and Mystery of the Kanawha Valley.* Charleston: Butler Printing Co., 1897 • Pepper, George H. *A Wooden Image from Kentucky.* New York: Museum of the American Indian, 1921.

Kanawha Riflemen: Cohen–*Kanawha Images* • Cohen, Stan, Richard Andre & William D. Wintz. *Bullets and Steel.* Charleston: PHPC, 1995 • Lowry, Terry. *The Battle of Scary Creek.* Charleston: PHPC, 1982 • Lowry. *22nd Virginia Infantry.* Lynchburg: H. E. Howard, 1988.

Kanawha River: Johnson, Leland R. *Men, Mountains, and Rivers.* Washington: GPO, 1977 • Sutphin, Gerald W. & Richard A. Andre. *Sternwheelers on the Great Kanawha River.* Charleston: PHPC, 1991 • Wintz, William D. *Annals of the Great Kanawha.* Charleston: PHPC, 1993.

Kanawha Salines: Stealey, John E. III. *The Antebellum Kanawha Salt Business and Western Markets.* Lexington: UPK, 1993.

Kanawha Salt Company: Stealey, John E. III. *The Antebellum Kanawha Salt Business and Western Markets.* Lexington: UPK, 1993 • Stealey, ed. *Kanawhan Prelude to Nineteenth-Century Monopoly in the United States: The Virginia Salt Combinations.* Richmond: Virginia Historical Society, 2000.

Kanawha Trail: Hale, John P. *Trans-Allegheny Pioneers.* Cincinnati: Graphic, 1886. Reprint, R. I. Steele, 1971 • Myer, William E. "Indian Trails of the Southeast," in *Bureau of Ethnology 42nd Annual Report, 1924–1925.* Washington: GPO, 1928 • Rice–*Allegheny Frontier.*

Kanawha Valley Bank: Drennen, Bill. *One Kanawha Valley Bank, A History.* Charleston, 2001 • Baronner, Robert; Morrison, Holmes; Pauley, Don; Ratrie, Mary Price. Interviews by author, 1997–2000.

Kanawha Valley Hospital: *Birth of a Medical Center: A History of CAMC.* Charleston: PHPC, 1988.

Karst: Jones, W. K. *Karst Hydrology Atlas of West Virginia.* Charles Town: Karst Waters Institute, 1997 • McColloch, Jane S. *Springs of West Virginia.* Morgantown: WVGES, 1986 • White, W. B. *Geomorphology and Hydrology of Karst Terrains.* New York: Oxford University Press, 1988.

Kates Mountain: Rice–*Greenbrier County.*

Kaymoor: Athey, Lou. *Kaymoor: A New River Community.* Philadelphia: Eastern National Park & Monument Assn., 1986 • Athey. "The Company Store in Coal Town Culture." *Labor's Heritage* (Jan. 1990).

Elizabeth Kee: Hardin, William H. "Elizabeth Kee, 1899–1975," in *Missing Chapters II: West Virginia Women in History.* Charleston: WV Women's Commission, 1986.

Benjamin F. Kelley: Delauter, Roger U. *McNeill's Rangers.* Lynchburg: H. E. Howard, 1986 • Warner, Ezra. *Generals in Blue.* Baton Rouge: LSU Press, 1964.

Kelly Axe and Tool Company: Goodall, Elizabeth J. "The Charleston Industrial Area: Development, 1797–1937." *WVH* (Oct. 1968).

Teepi Kendrick: Hartley, L. S. *"Teepi": A Brief Account of the Early Life and Ancestry of William H. Kendrick.* Morgantown Pub., 1982 • Meador, Michael M. *Historic Jackson's Mill: A Walking Tour.* Parsons: McClain, 1991 • Stewart, Guy H. *A Touch of Charisma: A History of the 4-H Program in West Virginia.* Morgantown, 1969.

John F. Kennedy: Fleming, Dan B. *Kennedy vs. Humphrey, West Virginia, 1960.* Jefferson, NC: McFarland & Co., 1992.

Kennedy-Humphrey Primary: Fleming, Dan B. *Kennedy vs. Hunphrey, West Virginia, 1960.* Jefferson, NC: McFarland & Co., 1992 • White, Theodore H. *The Making of the President, 1960.* New York: Atheneum, 1961.

Kenova: Platania, Joseph. "Wayne County's Twin Cities." *WWV* (Feb. 1994) • Rice & Brown • Rice, Otis K. *West Virginia: The State and its People.* Parsons: McClain, 1972 • Thomson, C. W. *History of Ceredo and Kenova.* Ceredo, 1958.

Simon Kenton: Clark, Thomas D. *Simon Kenton: Kentucky Scout.* Ashland, KY: Jesse Stuart Foundation, 1998.

Samuel Kercheval: Kercheval–*Valley* • Wayland, John W. *Twenty-five Chapters on the Shenandoah Valley, to which is Appended a Concise*

History of the Civil War in the Valley. Strasburg, VA: Shenandoah Pub., 1957.

Clark Kessinger: *The Kessinger Brothers: Complete Recorded Works in Chronological Order*, vols. 1–3, Document DOCD 8010-8012 • *The Legendary Clark Kessinger*. County CD 2713 • Wolfe, Charles. "Clark Kessinger: Pure Fiddling." *Goldenseal* (Fall 1997) • Wolfe. *The Devil's Box: Masters of Southern Fiddling*. Nashville: Vanderbilt University Press & Country Music Foundation, 1997.

Keslers Cross Lanes, Battle of: Lowry, Terry. *September Blood: The Battle of Carnifex Ferry*. Charleston: PHPC, 1985 • McKinney, Tim. *The Civil War in Fayette County*. Charleston: PHPC, 1988.

Kettle Bottom: Chase, Frank E. & Gary P. Sames. *Kettlebottoms: Their Relation to Mine Roof and Support*. Washington: U.S. Bureau of Mines, 1983.

Keystone: Battlo, Jean. "Cinder Bottom: A Coalfields Red-Light District." *Goldenseal* (Summer 1994) • "Community Profile: Keystone." *Daily Telegraph*, 12/15/1968 • Lee–*Bloodletting* • Matthews, Garrett. "Ashes, Memories Have Settled on Keystone's Cinder Bottom." *Daily Telegraph*, 5/26/1975 • Virginia Lad. (pseudonym) *Sodom and Gomorrah of Today, or the History of Keystone, West Virginia*. 1912.

Harley Kilgore: Maddox, Robert Franklin. *The War Within World War II: The U.S. and International Cartels*. Westport, CT: Praeger, 2001 • Maddox. *The Senatorial Career of Harley Martin Kilgore*. New York: Garland, 1981 • *Memorial Services Held in the Senate and House of Representatives of the United States, Together with Remarks Presented in Eulogy of Harley Martin Kilgore, a Late Senator from West Virginia*. 84th Congress, 2nd Session, 1956.

Killbuck: Ansel, William H. *Frontier Forts along the Potomac and its Tributaries*. Parsons: McClain, 1984 • Kercheval–*Valley* • "Turmoil in Ohio," in C. A. Weslager, *The Delaware Indians: A History*. New Brunswick: Rutgers University Press, 1972.

Kimball War Memorial: Bickley, Ancella R., ed. *Our Mount Vernons: Historic Register Listings of Sites Significant to the Black History of West Virginia*. Huntington: Carter G. Woodson Memorial Foundation & Drinko Academy, 1997 • Pedersen, Ralph. "Restoration and Rehabilitation of the Kimball Memorial Building." Feasibility Study for the McDowell County Commission, 1985 • Stone, Greg. "Time Honored: McDowell Trying to Rally Support for War Memorial." *Gazette*, 6/22/1998.

Kingwood Tunnel: Rice, Otis K. *West Virginia: The State and its People*. Parsons: McClain, 1972 • Thomas, Charles A. *Images of America: Preston County*. Charleston, SC: Arcadia Pub., 1998 • Wiley, S. T. *History of Preston County*. Parsons: McClain, 1968.

Kinnan, Mary: Phelps, McKinnie L. *The Indian Captivity of Mary Kinnan, 1791–1794*. Boulder: Pruett Press, 1967.

Knights of Labor: Fox, Maier B. *United We Stand*. Washington: UMWA, 1990 • Harris, Evelyn K. & Frank J. Krebs. *From Humble Beginnings: The West Virginia State Federation of Labor, 1903–1957*. Charleston: WV Labor History Pub. Fund, 1960.

Don Knotts: "From Mayberry to Charleston." *Gazette*, 4/29/1993.

John Knowles: Brenni, Vito J. *West Virginia Authors: A Bibliography*. 2nd ed., rev. by Joyce Binder. Morgantown: WVU Library, 1968 • Bryant, H. B. *A Separate Peace: The War Within*. Boston: Twayne Pub., 1990.

Korean War: Hastings, Max. *The Korean War*. New York: Simon & Schuster, 1987 • Singlaub, John K. with Malcolm McConnell. *Hazardous Duty: An American Soldier in the 20th Century*. New York: Summit Books, 1991.

Tom Kromer: Gray, Frances. "Waiting for Nothing: Tom Kromer, 1906–1969." Ph.D. diss., State University of New York at Stony Brook, 1978 • Kromer, Tom. *Waiting for Nothing and Other Writings*. Athens, GA: University of Georgia Press, 1986. • "Tom Kromer." *West Virginia Hillbilly*, 11/23/1968.

Ku Klux Klan: Chalmers, David. *Hooded Americanism: The History of the Ku Klux Klan*. Durham: Duke University Press, 1987 • Newton, Michael & Judy Newton. *The Ku Klux Klan: An Encyclopedia*. New York: Garland, 1991 • Southern Poverty Law Center. Intelligence Report. Montgomery: Southern Poverty Law Center, 1999.

Herman Guy Kump: Gatrell, Albert Steven. "Herman Guy Kump: A Political Profile." Ph.D. diss., WVU, 1979 • Kump, Herman Guy. *State Papers and Public Addresses*. Charleston: Jarrett Printing, 1937 • Morgan–*Governors* • Thomas–*New Deal*.

Kyashuta: Darlington, William M. *Christopher Gist's Journals*. Pittsburgh: J. R. Weldin & Co., 1893 • Jackson, D., ed. *The Diaries of George Washington. Vol. II 1766–70*. Charlottesville: UVA Press, 1939 • Sipe, C. Hale. *The Indian Chiefs of Pennsylvania*. Butler, PA: Ziegler Printing Co., 1927. Reprint, Wennawoods Pub., 1997.

La Belle Ironworks: May, Earl Chapin. *From Principio to Wheeling, 1715 to 1945: A Pageant of Iron and Steel*. New York: Harper & Brothers, 1945 • Scott, Henry Dickerson. *Iron & Steel in Wheeling*. Toledo, OH: Caslon, 1929.

Division of Labor: "Department of Labor 1889–1964," 75th Annual Report. Beckley: Biggs, Johnston, Withrow, 1964.

Labor History: Ambler & Summers • Anson, Charles P. "A History of the Labor Movement in West Virginia." Ph.D. diss., University of North Carolina, Chapel Hill, 1940 • Corbin–*Life, Work*.

Lake Monongahela, Lake Tight: Clendening, John A., John J. Renton & Barbara M. Parsons. "Preliminary Palynological and Mineralogical Analyses of a Lake Monongahela (Pleistocene) Terrace Deposit at Morgantown," Circular C4. Morgantown: WVGES, 1967 • Cross, Aureal T. & Mart P. Schemel. "Geology of the Ohio River Valley in West Virginia," in Aureal T. Cross, et al. *Geology and Economic Resources of the Ohio River Valley in West Virginia*. Morgantown: WVGES, 1956 • Gillespie, William H. & John A. Clendening. "A Flora from Proglacial Lake Monongahela." *Castanea* (Dec. 1968) • Rhodehamel, Edward C. & Charles W. Carlston. "Geologic History of the Teays Valley in West Virginia," Bulletin. Geological Society of America, Mar. 1963.

Lakes: "Water Resources Development in West Virginia," Report. Washington: GPO, 1999 • "West Virginia State Parks & Forests," Pamphlet. WVDNR, 1981 • "West Virginia Fishing Regulations," Pamphlet. WVDNR, 2004.

Daniel Lamb: Atkinson, George W. *Bench and Bar of West Virginia*. Charleston: Virginia Law Book Co., 1919 • Atkinson, George W. & Alvaro F. Gibbens. *Prominent Men of West Virginia*. Wheeling: W. L. Callin, 1890.

Land Ownership: Rasmussen, Barbara. *Absentee Landowning and Exploitation in West Virginia, 1760–1920*. Lexington: UPK, 1994 • Rice–*Allegheny Frontier* • Williams–*Captains*.

Last Public Hanging: Goodwin, Jacqueline G. "I Remember Well: Events Surrounding the Last Public Hanging in West Virginia." *Goldenseal* (Spring 1990).

George Robert Latham: Comstock–*Encyclopedia*, vol. 13, 1976.

Jean Lee Latham: Ambler & Summers • Evory, Ann, ed. *Contemporary Authors: A Bio-Bibliographical Guide*. Detroit: Gale Research, 1982.

Laurel Lake: Erwin, Robert B. *West Virginia Gazetteer of Physical and Cultural Place Names*. Morgantown: WVGES, 1986.

Layland Mine Explosion: Humphrey, H. B. *Historical Summary of Coal-Mine Explosion in the U.S., 1810–1958*. Washington: GPO, 1960 • Report of the Department of Mines. Annual Report, 1915.

John Lederer: Carrier, Lyman. "The Veracity of John Lederer." *William & Mary Quarterly* (Oct., 1939) • Cunz, Dieter. "John Lederer, Significance and Evaluation." *William & Mary Quarterly* (Apr. 1942) • Lederer, John. *The Discoveries of John Lederer*. Charlottesville: UVA Press, 1958.

Charles Lee: Alden, John Richard. *General Charles Lee: Traitor or Patriot?* Baton Rouge: LSU Press, 1951 • Billias, George Athan, ed. *George Washington's Generals*. New York: William Morrow, 1964 • Thayer, Theodore. *The Making of a Scapegoat: Washington and Lee at Monmouth*. Port Washington, NY: Kennikat Press, 1976.

Howard B. Lee: Lee–*Bloodletting*.

Maryat Lee: Fitzgerald, Sally, ed. *The Habit of Being: The Correspondence of Flannery O'Connor*. New York: Farrar, Straus, Giroux, 1979 • French, William W. *Maryat Lee's EcoTheater*. Morgantown: WVU Press, 1998 • Lee, Maryat. "To Will One Thing." *Drama Review* (Winter 1983).

Robert E. Lee: McKinney, Tim. *Robert E. Lee at Sewell Mountain: The West Virginia Campaign*. Charleston: PHPC, 1990 • Warner, Ezra. *Generals in Gray*. Baton Rouge: LSU Press, 1959.

Jay Legg: Byrne–*Tale* • Jones, James Gay. *Haunted Valley & More Folk Tales*. Parsons: McClain, 1979.

Legislature: Forrester, James R., ed. *Government and Politics in West Virginia*. Needham Heights, MA: Ginn Press, 1989 • Morgan–*Governors* • *Michie's West Virginia Code*. Charlottesville: Lexis Pub.

Lewis and Clark Expedition: Ambrose, Stephen E. *Undaunted Courage: Meriwether Lewis, Thomas Jefferson, and the Opening of the American West*. New York: Simon & Schuster, 1996 • Jackson, Donald, ed. *Letters of the Lewis & Clark Expedition with Related Documents, 1783–1854*. Urbana: UI Press, 1962 • Moulton, Gary, ed. *The Journals of the Lewis & Clark Expedition*. Lincoln: University of Nebraska Press, 1989.

Andrew Lewis: DeHass, Wills. *History of the Early Settlement and Indian Wars of Western Virginia*. Philadelphia: H. Hoblitzell, 1851 • Lewis, Virgil A. *History of the Battle of Point Pleasant*. Charleston: Tribune Printing, 1909 • Poffenbarger, Livia Nye Simpson. *The Battle of Point Pleasant, October 19, 1774*. Point Pleasant: State Gazette, 1909.

John L. Lewis: Alinsky, Saul D. *John L. Lewis*. New York: Vintage Books, 1970 • Fox, Maier B. *United We Stand*. Washington: UMWA, 1990.

Virgil A. Lewis: Atkinson, George W. & Alvaro F. Gibbens. *Prominent Men of West Virginia*. Wheeling: W. L. Callin, 1890 • *Gazette*, 12/6/1912 • Shawkey, Morris. *West Virginia: In History, Life, Literature and Industry*, 5 vols. Chicago: Lewis Pub. Co., 1928.

Lewisburg: Benjamin, J. W. "Rutherford B. Hayes Stayed in Lewisburg in 1863." *West Virginia Daily News*, 3/3/1976 • Lindsley, Helen. "Ah. . . The Shanghai," in Bicentennial Committee, *Come, Walk with Me: A Nostalgic View of Lewisburg*. Parsons: McClain, 1982 • Montgomery, John F. "An Introduction to Lewisburg," & "Glimpses of Lewisburg through the Years," in Bicentennial Committee, *Come, Walk with Me: A Nostalgic View of Lewisburg*. Parsons: McClain, 1982 • Swope, Kenneth D. "The Great Lewisburg Fire: August 3, 1897." *The Journal of the Greenbrier Historical Society*, vol. 4, no. 1. (1981) • Turley, C. E. "The Lewisburg Historic District." *The Journal of the Greenbrier Historical Society*, vol. 4, no. 1. (1981).

Lewisburg, Battle of: Bard, David. *Civil War: The New River Valley*. Charleston: Quarrier Press, 2004 • Long, E. B. *The Civil War Day by Day: An Almanac, 1861–1865*. Garden City, NY: Doubleday, 1971 • Welcher, Frank J. *The Union Army, 1861–1865: Organization and Operations*. Bloomington: Indiana University Press, 1989.

Libraries: Blasingame, Ralph. *Library Services in West Virginia*. Charleston: WVLC, 1960 • Julian, Charles Anthony. "An Analysis of the Historical Growth and Development of the Library Association." Ph.D. diss., WVU, 1991 • Noon, Paul A. T. & Mildred W. Sandoe. *West Virginia Library Survey*. Charleston: WVLC, 1960.

"Life in the Iron Mills": Blain, Virginia, et al., eds., *The Feminist Companion to Literature in English: Women Writers from the Middle Ages to the Present*. New Haven & London: Yale University Press, 1990 • Davis, Rebecca Harding. *Life in the Iron Mills: With a Biographical Interpretation by Tillie Olsen*. Old Westbury, NY: Feminist Press, 1972.

Joseph A. J. Lightburn: McKinney, Tim. "Miscellaneous Papers on the Life of J.A.J. Lightburn." Speech delivered to Fayette County Historical Society, 1984 • Sifakis, Stewart. *Who Was Who in the Civil War*. New York: Facts on File, 1988.

Lilly Brothers: Tribe–*Jamboree*.

Cousin Abe Lilly: *Beckley Post-Herald*, 6/22/1956.

Lilly Family: Lilly, Jack. *Lilly Family History*. Canton, OH: J. Lilly, 1997.

Limestone Glades: Bartgis, Rodney L. "The Limestone Glades and Barrens of West Virginia." *Castanea* (June 1993).

Linsly School: Ross, Philip. *Forward and No Retreat: The Linsly Story*. Wheeling: Linsly School, 1994 • *Wheeling Intelligencer*, 9/1/1859.

Little Bluestone River: Lilly, Jack. "The Lost Village of Lilly." *Goldenseal* (Summer 1998) • Mathes, M. V., et al. *Drainage Areas of the Kanawha River Basin*. Charleston: WVGES, 1982 • Sanders, William. *A New River Heritage*. Parsons: McClain, 1992.

Little Kanawha River: Gilchrist, Joy Gregoire. "It was Crowded up There." *Goldenseal* (Summer 1994) • Gilchrist. "Riverboats: A Scrapbook of Various Articles." Hackers Creek Pioneer Descendants, Horner • Murphy, James M. "Transportation on the Little Kanawha River in Gilmer County." M.A. thesis, WVU, 1950 • Sypolt, Larry & Emory Kemp. "The Little Kanawha Navigation." *Canal History and Technology Proceedings*, 1991.

C. E. Lively: Savage–*Thunder*.

Livestock: Eller, Ronald D. *Miners, Millhands, and Mountaineers*. Knoxville: UT Press, 1982 • Lewis, Ronald L. *Transforming the Appalachian Countryside*. Chapel Hill: UNC Press, 1998 • MacMaster, Richard K. "The Great Cattle Trade in Western Virginia," in Robert

Mitchell, ed. *Appalachian Frontiers: Settlement, Society, and Development in the Preindustrial Era*. Lexington: UPK, 1991 • Waller, Altina L. *Feud: Hatfields, McCoys, and Social Change in Appalachia, 1860–1900*. Chapel Hill: UNC Press, 1988.

Locks and Dams: Johnson, Leland R. *Men, Mountains, and Rivers*. Washington: GPO, 1977 • Johnson. *The Headwaters District: A History of the Pittsburgh District, U.S. Army Corps of Engineers*. Washington: GPO, 1979 • Sutphin, Gerald W. & Richard A. Andre. *Sternwheelers on the Great Kanawha River*. Charleston: PHPC, 1991.

Log Construction: McRaven, Charles. *Building the Hewn Log House*. New York: Thomas Y. Crowell, 1978 • Milnes, Gerald. "The Barns of Pendleton County." *Goldenseal* (Spring 1998) • Montell, Lynwood & Michael Lynn Morse. *Kentucky Folk Architecture*. Lexington: UPK, 1976 • Sloane, Eric. *A Museum of Early American Tools*. New York: Ballantine Books, 1964.

Log Driving and Rafting: Blackhurst, W. E. *Riders of the Flood*. Parsons: McClain, 1954 • Clarkson–*Tumult* • Lewis, Ronald L. *Transforming the Appalachian Countryside*. Chapel Hill: UNC Press, 1998.

Chief Logan: Jacob, John J. *A Biographical Sketch of the Life of the Late Captain Michael Cresap*. Cumberland, MD: J. M. Buchanan, 1826. Reprint, McClain, 1971 • Kehoe, Vincent J. R. *Virginia-1774*. Malaga, Spain: Ricardo Sanchez, 1958 • Sawvel, Franklin B. *Logan the Mingo*. Boston: Richard G. Badger, Gorham Press, 1921.

Logan County: Spence, Robert Y. *Land of the Guyandot*. Detroit: Harlo, 1976.

Lonesome Pine Fiddlers: Tribe–*Jamboree*.

Pare Lorentz: Barnouw, Erik. *Documentary: A History of the Non-Fiction Film*. New York: Oxford University Press, 1974 • Lorentz, Elizabeth. Telephone conversations with author. 1992–98 • Lorentz, Pare. *FDR's Moviemaker*. Reno: University of Nevada Press, 1992 • Lorentz, Pare. Telephone conversations with author. 1990–92 • Lorentz, Pare. Videotape interview by author. *Cultural Conversations*. Charleston: WVLC, Mar. 1990. • Lorentz, Pare Jr. Telephone conversations with author. 1998 • Wade, Bess Lorentz. *Lest We Forget*. White Plains, NY: Murphy Printing, 1968.

Lost River: Conley–*Encyclopedia* • Powell, N. *What to See and Do in the Lost River and South Branch Valleys*. Lost River: Lost River Educational Foundation, 1997 • Tilton, J. L., et al. WVGES. *Hampshire and Hardy Counties*. Morgantown Printing & Binding, 1927.

Louie Glass Company: "Louie: Salesman and Glass-Manufacturer." *WV Review* (Oct. 1931) • "Louie: Noted Industrialist." *WV Review* (Nov. 1936) • Six, Dean. "Weston Glass." *Glass Collector's Digest* (Dec.–Jan. 1994).

Minnie Kendall Lowther: Minnie Kendall Lowther Papers. WV&RHC • Minnie Kendall Lowther Papers. Blennerhassett Island Historical State Park archives, Parkersburg • "Miss Lowther Taken by Death." *Parkersburg Sentinel*, 9/19/1947.

Daniel Bedinger Lucas: Atkinson, George W. & Alvaro F. Gibbens. *Prominent Men of West Virginia*. Wheeling: W. L. Callin, 1890 • Conley–*Encyclopedia* • Williams–*Captains*.

Lumberjack Contests: *North American Axmen's News*, vol. 8. (2001) • Stafford, Thomas F. "The First Mountain State Forest Festival." *Goldenseal* (July–Sept. 1979).

Luna Park: Bing, Louise. "Remembering Luna Park." *Goldenseal* (Fall 1982) • Wells, Sandy. "Rollee Coaster Operator Recalls Luna Park Heyday." *Gazette*, 8/6/1985.

Lutherans: Cassell, C. W., et al., ed., *History of the Lutherans in Virginia and East Tennessee*. Strasburg, VA: Shenandoah Pub., 1930 • Maurer, Beryl B. "Unto the Hills," in *Proceedings: Twelfth Annual Assembly West Virginia-Western Maryland Synod*, 1999 • Maurer, B. B. & Mary Miller Strauss. *Lutherans on the Mountaintop*. Fairmont: West Virginia-Western Maryland Synod, 1992 • Nelson, E. Clifford, ed. *The Lutherans of North America*. Philadelphia: Fortress Press, 1975 • Weirick, George C. *The Lutheran Church in Mason and Jackson Counties*. Ravenswood, 1992 • *The West Virginia Synod: An Interpretation*. Keyser: Keyprint, 1962 • *Proceedings of the Eighth Annual Assembly of West Virginia-Western Maryland Synod*, 1995.

William Alexander MacCorkle: MacCorkle, William A. *The Recollections of Fifty Years of West Virginia*. New York: G. P. Putnam's Sons, 1928 • Morgan–*Governors*.

Alex Mahood: Hedrick, Charles B. *Official Blue Book of Mercer County*. Princeton: Mercer County Blue Book Assn., 1931 • Mahood, Alex Jr. "The

Mahood Family History," in Mercer County Historical Society, *Mercer County History 1984*. Marceline, MO: Walsworth Pub., 1985.

Mail Pouch Barns: Harvey, Tom. "Treat Yourself to the Best." *Goldenseal* (Oct.–Dec. 1976).

Sam Mallison: Mallison, Sam T. *The Great Wildcatter*. Charleston: Education Foundation of West Virginia, 1953 • Mallison. *Let's Set a Spell*. Charleston: Education Foundation of West Virginia, 1961.

A. James Manchin: Comstock–*Encyclopedia*, vol. 13, 1976 • Icenhower, Greg. *A. James Manchin: A Biography of Controversy*. Terra Alta: Headline Books, 1990.

Mandolidis Case: Miller, Tom. "Mandolidis Plan in Limelight Early." *Herald-Dispatch*, 4/6/1983.

I. T. Mann: Lambie, Joseph T. *From Mine to Market: The History of Coal Transportation on the Norfolk & Western Railway*. New York: NYU Press, 1954 • Miller & Maxwell, vol. 3 • Obituary. *Daily Telegraph*, 5/19/1932 • Sullivan–*Coal Men* • Tams, W. P. *The Smokeless Coal Fields of West Virginia: A Brief History*. Morgantown: WVU Library, 1963 • Toothman, Fred R. *Great Coal Leaders of West Virginia*. Huntington: Vandalia Book Co., 1988.

Maple Syrup: Hauser, Susan Carol. *Sugartime: The Hidden Pleasure of Making Maple Syrup*. New York: Lyons Press, 1997 • Lawrence, James M. & Rux Martin. *Sweet Maple: Life, Lore and Recipes from the Sugarbush*. Montpelier: Vermont Life/Chapters, 1993 • Sutton, Mary Lee. "Sweet Pickens: Looking Back at Maple Harvest Time." *Goldenseal* (Spring 1988).

Maps, Atlases, and Gazetteers: Lessing, Peter & Nora L. Simcoe. *Catalog of West Virginia Maps*. Morgantown: WVGES, 1988 • McKee, Marianne M. "A Selected Bibliography of Map Books and Periodicals, Many of Which Relate to Virginia" [electronic resource]. Feb. 2000 • Norona, Delf. "Cartography of West Virginia, Parts 1 and 2." *WVH* (Jan. & Apr. 1948).

Marijuana Cultivation: *Michie's West Virginia Code*, Chapter 60A. Charlottesville: Lexis Pub. • National Drug Intelligence Center. "West Virginia Drug Threat Assessment," Report. 2004 • The National Organization for the Reform of Marijuana Laws. "1998 Marijuana Crop Report." Washington: NORML and NORML Foundation • Office of National Drug Control Policy. "The National High Intensity Drug Trafficking Area Program," Annual Report. 2004 • U.S. Department of Justice Drug Enforcement Administration. "West Virginia Fact Sheet." GPO: Washington, 2005.

Marion County: Balderson, Walter L. *Fort Prickett Frontier and Marion County*. Fairmont, 1977 • Dunnington, George A. & Richard P. Lott. *History and Progress of the County of Marion*. Fairmont: G. A. Dunnington, 1880. Reprint, Marion County Historical Society, 1992 • Koon, Thomas J. & Oce Smith. *Marion County*. Virginia Beach: Donning Co., 1995 • Lough, Glenn D. *Now and Long Ago: A History of the Marion County Area*. Morgantown Printing & Binding, 1969 • Marion County Historical Society. *A History of Marion County*. Fairmont, 1985.

The *Market Bulletin*: Douglass, Gus. "Welcome to the Fair!," in the *Market Bulletin*, Special Edition, Aug. 1999 • Ross, Peggy. "Market Bulletin Smaller Yet Thriving." *Dominion Post*, 4/5/1992 • Ross. "The Farmer's Friend: The West Virginia *Market Bulletin*." *Goldenseal* (Summer 1993).

William Casey Marland: Lutz, Paul F. *From Governor to Cabby*. Huntington: Marshall University Library Associates, 1995.

Catherine Marshall: Marshall, Catherine. *Light in my Darkest Night*. Old Tappan, NJ: Chosen Books, 1989 • Marshall. *Meeting God at Every Turn*. Carmel, NY: Guideposts, 1980.

Marshall County: Brantner, J. H., compiler. *Historical Collections of Moundsville*. Moundsville: Marshall County Historical Society, 1947. Reprint, Closson Press, 2000 • Marshall County Historical Society. *History of Marshall County*. Moundsville, 1984 • Powell, Scott. *History of Marshall County, from Forest to Field*. Moundsville, 1925. Reprint, Closson Press, 1997.

John Marshall: Smith, Jean Edward. *John Marshall: Definer of a Nation*. New York: Henry Holt & Co., 1996.

Marshall Plane Crash: Hardin, Jack. "Marshall Team, Coaches, Fans Die in Plane Crash." Huntington *Herald-Advertiser*, 11/15/1970 • National Transportation Safety Board. "A Report on the Marshall Plane Crash." Washington: GPO, 1971 • Peyton, Dave. "10 Years Later, Huntington Still Remembers." *Herald-Dispatch*, 11/9/1980.

Marshall University: Moffat, Charles Hill. *Marshall University: An Institution Comes of Age 1837–1980*. Huntington: Marshall University Alumni Assn., 1981 • Toole, Robert Chase. "A History of Marshall College, 1837 to 1915." M.A. thesis, Marshall College, 1951.

Marshall University Graduate College: Jacobs, Kathleen M. "History of the Graduate College," in *West Virginia Graduate College: Celebrating 25 Years of Service to West Virginia*, 1995.

Walter Martens: Clark, Walter E., ed. *West Virginia Today*. New Orleans: West Virginia Editorial Assn., 1941 • Collins, Rodney. "Walter F. Martens, FAIA," (unpub. ms.) • Shearer, Connie. "Homeland." *Gazette*, 5/28/1986 • "New Civic Center." *The Architectural Record* (Nov. 1956) • "United Carbon Building, Charleston, West Virginia." *Pencil Points* (Oct. 1944).

Martin v. Hunter's Lessee: Brown, Stuart E. Jr. *Virginia Baron*. Berryville, VA: Chesapeake Book Co., 1965 • Smith, Jean Edward. *John Marshall: Definer of a Nation*. New York: Henry Holt & Co., 1996.

Louis Marx & Company: Pinsky, Maxine A. *Greenberg's Guide to Marx Toys, 1923–1950*. Sykesville, MD: Greenberg, 1988–1990 • Pinsky. *Marx Toys: Robots, Space, Comic, Disney & TV Characters, with Values*. Atglen, PA: Schiffer, 1996 • Smith, Michelle L. *Marx Toys Sampler: A History & Price Guide*. Iola, WI: Krause, 2000.

Mason College of Music and Fine Arts: Wells, Sandy. "An Audible Oasis of Culture." *Gazette*, 4/25/1991.

Mason County: Comstock–*Encyclopedia*, vol. 14, 1976 • Conley–*Encyclopedia* • *Hardesty's*, vol. 5 • Lewis, Virgil A. *History and Government of West Virginia*. New York: American Book Co., 1912 • Rice, Otis K. *West Virginia: The State and its People*. Parsons: McClain, 1972 • Williams, John Alexander. *West Virginia: A Bicentennial History*. New York: Norton, 1976.

Mason-Dixon Line: *Encyclopaedia Brittanica* CD, 1997 • USGS Maps, 7.5 Minute Series, WV quadrangle: East Liverpool North • Wiley, Samuel T. *History of Monongalia County, West Virginia, from its First Settlements to the Present Time*. Kingwood: Preston Pub. Co., 1883 • Wilford, John Noble. *The Mapmakers*. New York: Alfred A. Knopf, 1981.

Material Culture: Eller, Ronald D. *Miners, Millhands, and Mountaineers*. Knoxville: UT Press, 1982 • Glassie, Henry H. *Pattern in the Material Folk Culture of the Eastern U.S.* Philadelphia: UP Press, 1969 • Glassie, Henry. "Folk Art," in Richard M. Dorson, ed., *Folklore and Folklife*. Chicago: University Press of Chicago, 1972 • Raitz, Karl B. & Richard Ulack. *Appalachia, A Regional Geography*. Boulder: Westview Press, 1984 • Roberts, Warren E. "Folk Craft," in Richard M. Dorson, ed., *Folklore and Folklife*. Chicago: University of Chicago Press, 1972 • Wigginton, Eliot, ed. *The Foxfire Book*. Garden City, NY: Doubleday, 1972.

Matewan Massacre: Lee–*Bloodletting* • Savage–*Thunder* • U.S. Senate. *West Virginia Coal Fields*. Hearings before the Committee on Education & Labor. United States Senate. 67th Congress, first session, 2 vols. Washington: GPO, 1921–22.

Henry Mason Mathews: Malone, Dumas, ed. *Dictionary of American Biography*. New York: Charles Scribner's Sons, 1933 • Morgan–*Governors* • Sobel, Robert & John Raimo, eds. *Biographical Directory of the Governors of the U.S., 1789–1978*. Westport, CT: Meckler Books, 1978.

Kathy Mattea: Tribe–*Jamboree*.

Hu Maxwell: Comstock–*Encyclopedia*, vol. 14, 1976 • Turner, Ella May. *Stories and Verse of West Virginia*. Scottdale, PA: Mennonite Pub., 1925.

May Moore Mound: McMichael–*Archeology* • Thomas, Cyrus. *Report on the Mound Explorations of the Bureau of Ethnology*. Washington: GPO, 1894. Reprint, Smithsonian Institution Press, 1985.

Joseph E. McCarthy's Wheeling Speech: Moore, Greg. "Wheeling Speech Set McCarthy on his Path." *Sunday Gazette-Mail*, 2/6/2000 • Reeves, Thomas C. *The Life and Times of Joe McCarthy*. New York: Stein & Day, 1982 • Rovere, Richard H. *Senator Joe McCarthy*. New York: Harcourt, Brace & Co., 1959.

John McCausland: Pauley, Michael J. *Unreconstructed Rebel: The Life of General John McCausland CSA*. Charleston: PHPC, 1993 • Robertson, James I. "John McCausland," in Patricia L. Faust, ed., *Historical Times Illustrated Encyclopedia of the Civil War*. New York: Harper & Row, 1986 • Stutler–*Civil War*.

McColloch's Leap: Newton, J. H. *History of the Pan-Handle*. Wheeling: Caldwell, 1879.

Kyle McCormick: Obituary. *Daily Telegraph*, 11/3/1971.

Charlie McCoy: Tribe–*Jamboree*.

McCoy's Mill: Jacobs, Kathleen M. "Home to the Hofeckers: A Story of Bridge Building, Inn Keeping and Fine Furniture." *Goldenseal* (Spring 1993).

McDowell County: Battlo, Jean. *McDowell County in West Virginia and American History*. Parsons: McClain, 1998 • Corbin–*Life, Work* • Tams, W. P. *The Smokeless Coal Fields of West Virginia*. Morgantown: WVU Press, 1963.

Uncle Jack McElwain: Milnes, Gerald. *Play of a Fiddle*. Lexington: UPK, 1999.

Frank Duff McEnteer: Kemp, Janet K. & Emory L. Kemp. "Frank Duff McEnteer," in American Public Works Assn., *Reporter* (Feb. 1984).

Bill McKell: Bragg, Melody E. "Glen Jean, Echo of an Empire." *Goldenseal* (Winter 1988) • Sullivan–*Coal Men*.

McKendree Hospital: Cox, William E. "McKendree No. 2: The Story of West Virginia's Miners Hospitals." *Goldenseal* (Fall 1981) • Nyden, Paul. "Mabel Gwinn, New River Nurse." *Goldenseal* (Fall 1981).

McKinley's Palace: National Register of Historic Places Nomination, ms., WVDC&H, 1983.

Irene McKinney: Anderson, Colleen. "Coming Home Again-And Again." *Gazette*, 6/2/1989 • "New State Poet Laureate Chosen." *Gazette*, 12/2/1993.

J. Kemp McLaughlin: McLaughlin, J. Kemp. *The Mighty Eighth in WWII: A Memoir*. Lexington: UPK, 2000.

McLure Hotel: Lewis, Clifford M., ed. *Wheeling Bicentennial: 1769–1969*. Wheeling, 1969 • *Wheeling News-Register*, 3/9/1977.

Louise McNeill: McNeill, Louise, *The Milkweed Ladies*. Pittsburgh: UPP, 1988 • McNeill. *Hill Daughter: New & Selected Poems*. Pittsburgh: UPP, 1991 • McNeill. *Gauley Mountain*. New York: Harcourt, Brace & Co., 1939.

McNeill's Rangers: Blue, John. *Hanging Rock Rebel*. Dan Oates, ed. Shippensburg, PA: Burd Street Press, 1994 • Jones, Virgil C. *Gray Ghosts and Rebel Raiders*. New York: Holt, 1956 • Stanchak, John E. "McNeils's Rangers," in Patricia L. Faust, ed., *Historical Times Illustrated Encyclopedia of the Civil War*. New York: Harper & Row, 1986.

Mechanization Agreement: David, John P. "Earnings, Health, Safety, and Welfare of Bituminous Coal Miners Since the Encouragement of Mechanization by the U.M.W.A." Ph.D. diss., WVU, 1972.

Medicine: Bureau of Health Professions, National Center for Health Workforce Analysis. "HRSA State Health Workforce Profiles: West Virginia," Report. Washington: U.S. Dept. Health & Human Services, 2000 • Hill, Nancy. "WVSMA Historical Monument in Rivesville Restored: Replica Placed at WVSMA Office." *West Virginia Medical Journal* (July–Aug. 2000) • Nottingham, Lamont & Michael Lewis. "Back to Rurality: AHEC in West Virginia." *Journal of Rural Health* (Spring 2003) • Point, Warren. "The Country Doctor," (unpub. ms.). Robert C. Byrd Health Sciences Center of WV, Charleston Division, 2001.

Memorial Day: Crissman, James K. *Death and Dying in Central Appalachia*. Urbana: UI Press, 1994.

Mennonites: Brunk, Harry A. *History of the Mennonites in Virginia, 1727–1900*. Staunton: McClure Printing, 1959 • Brunk. *History of the Mennonites in Virginia 1900–1960*. Verona: McClure Printing, 1972.

Mercer County: Hedrick, Charles B. *Official Blue Book of Mercer County*. Princeton: Mercer County Blue Book Assn., 1931 • Johnston, David E. *A History of Middle New River Settlements and Contiguous Territory*. Huntington: Standard Co., 1906 • McCormick, Kyle. *The Story of Mercer County*. Charleston Printing, 1957 • McGehee, C. Stuart. *Bluefield, West Virginia: Centennial History: 1889–1989*. City of Bluefield, 1990 • "Mercer County." *WV Review* (Aug. 1944) • "Mercer County Centennial." *WV Review* (Aug. 1937) • Mercer County Historical Society. *Mercer County History 1984*. Marceline, MO: Walsworth Pub., 1985 • "Mercer County History," (unpub. ms.). WPA Writers' Project, WV&RHC.

Mercer Healing Springs: "Hotel at Mercer Healing Springs is Burned Down." *Princeton Evening Press*, 5/12/1922 • Cohen, Stan. *Historic Springs of the Virginias*. Charleston: PCPC, 1983 • Meador, Michael M. "Taking the Waters: The Mercer Healing Springs Resort." *Goldenseal* (Fall 1982).

Methodists: Brucke, Emory S., ed. *The History of American Methodism in Three Volumes*. Nashville: Abingdon Press, 1964 • Maurer, B. B. & Keith A. Muhleman. *Mission in the Mountain State*. Parsons: McClain, 1981 • Norwood, Frederick A. *The Story of American Methodism*. Nashville:

Abingdon Press, 1974 • Smeltzer, Wallace Guy. *Methodism in the Headwaters of the Ohio*. Nashville: Parthenon Press, 1951.

Metropolitan Theater: Callahan, James M. Jr. "Morgantown 1925–1950." M.A. thesis, WVU, 1953 • Core, Earl L. *The Monongalia Story*, 5 vols. Parsons: McClain, 1974–84 • Morgantown Historic Landmarks Commission. Notes on Historic Downtown Morgantown. Monongalia Historical Society, 2001.

Middlebourne: Tyler County Heritage & Historical Society. *History of Tyler County*. Marceline, MO: Walsworth Pub., 1984.

Midwifery: Beckman, I. Lynn. "Home Delivery: Amy Mildred Sharpless, Mountaintop Midwife." *Goldenseal* (Winter 1993) • Belanger, Ruth. "Midwives' Tales." *Goldenseal* (Oct.–Dec. 1979) • Bickley, Ancella. "Midwifery in West Virginia." *WVH* (1990) • Gibbs, Judith. "Nature Always Worked: Opal Freeman, Moatsville Midwife." *Goldenseal* (Spring 1984).

Migration: Coles, Robert C. *The South Goes North: Volume III of Children of Crisis*. Boston: Little Brown & Co., 1971 • Feather, Carl E. *Mountain People in a Flat Land: A Popular History of Appalachian Migration to Northeast Ohio, 1940–1965*. Athens: Ohio University Press, 1998 • Gregory, James N. "The Southern Diaspora and the Urban Dispossessed: Demonstrating the Census Public Use Samples." *Journal of American History* (June 1995).

Mill Point Prison Camp: Crockett, Maureen. "Doing Time on Kennison Mountain: Pocahontas County's Forgotten Prison." *Goldenseal* (Spring 1985).

James H. Miller: Comstock–*Encyclopedia*, vol. 15, 1976 • Keller, Barbara, ed. *Summers County, West Virginia Historical Society: Cemetery Book*. Beckley, 1996 • Miller, James H. *History of Summers County*. Hinton: J. H. Miller, 1908 • "Pioneer Citizen of this County Died at Home in Bellepoint Saturday Night." *Hinton Daily News*, 2/11/1929.

Mrs. Alex. McVeigh Miller: Comstock–*Encyclopedia*, vol. 15, 1976 • Rice–*Greenbrier County* • "To be Continued in our Next," (unpub. ms.). Mrs. Alex. McVeigh Miller Papers. Greenbrier Historical Society. Lewisburg, 1986.

Okey Mills: Haga, Pauline A. *Tribute to the Police Officer*, Booklet. Crab Orchard: Pauline Haga, 1993 • Mills, Nettie. Interview by author. 6/26/2000 • Mills, Okey. Interview by author. 6/22/2000 • *Post Herald*, 12/25/1975 • *Raleigh Herald*, 1/20/1986 • Warren, Harlow. *Beckley USA*, vol. 3. Beckley: Warren Harlow, 1955 • Wood, Jim. *Raleigh County*. Beckley: J. Wood, 1994.

Mine Safety: Graebner, William. *Coal-Mining Safety in the Progressive Period*. Lexington: UPK, 1976 • Massay, Glenn F. "Legislators, Lobbyists and Loopholes." *WVH* (Apr. 1971) • Todd, Alden. "December 6, 1907–50 Years Ago: The Horror at Monongah." *UMW Journal* (Dec. 1957).

The Mine Wars: Corbin–*Life, Work* • Lunt, Richard D. *Law and Order vs. the Miners: West Virginia, 1907–1933*. Hamden, CT: Archon Books, 1979 • Savage–*Thunder*.

Mineral County: Canfield, Jack. *A Penny for Coming Back*. Charleston: Jack Canfield, 1995 • Gilbert, Gude. *Where the Potomac Begins: A History of the North Branch Valley*. Cabin John, MD: Seven Locks Press, 1984 • Mineral County Heritage Society. *Mineral County, West Virginia*. Dallas: Taylor Pub., 1980 • *Mineral County Illustrated*. Keyser: Mountain Echo, 1913.

Mineral Springs: Cohen, Stan. *Historic Springs of the Virginias*. Charleston: PHPC, 1981.

Miners Health Plan: Fox, Maier B. *United We Stand*. Washington: UMWA, 1990 • Seltzer, Curtis. *Fire in the Hole: Miners and Managers in the Coal Industry*. Lexington: UPK, 1985 • Ward, Ken Jr. "Miner's Widow is One of 120,000 Who are Facing the Loss of Health Insurance." *Gazette*, 2/23/1992.

Mingo County: Smith, Nancy Sue. *History of Logan and Mingo Counties*. Williamson: Williamson Printing, 1960 • Waller, Altina. *Feud: Hatfields, McCoys, and Social Change in Appalachia, 1860–1900*. Chapel Hill: UNC Press, 1988 • Williamson Chamber of Commerce. *Williamson, West Virginia: "Heart of the Billion Dollar Coal Field."* Williamson, 1931.

Mingo Indians: Richter, Daniel K. *The Ordeal of the Longhouse: The Peoples of the Iroquois League in the Era of European Colonization*. Chapel Hill: UNC Press, 1992 • Wallace, Paul A. W. *Conrad Weiser, 1696–1760: Friend of Colonist and Mohawk*. Philadelphia: UP Press, 1945.

Mining Methods in the Hand-Loading Era: Dix, Keith. *What's a Coal Miner to Do?* Pittsburgh: UPP, 1988 • Tams, W. P. *The Smokeless Coal Fields of West Virginia.* Morgantown: WVU Press, 1963.

Minter Homes: Cammack, Lucius H. *Huntington.* Huntington Chamber of Commerce, 1912 • *Huntington Lumber & Supply Co. Catalogue Number 101.* Huntington Lumber & Supply Co., 1916 • Wintz, William D. *Nitro: World War I Boom Town.* Charleston: Jalamap, 1985.

Billy Mitchell: Maurer, Maurer & Calvin F. Senning. "Billy Mitchell, the Air Service and the Mingo War." *WVH* (Oct. 1968) • *The National Cyclopaedia of American Biography.* New York: James T. White & Co., 1937.

Mildred Mitchell-Bateman: West Virginia Women's Commission. *American Sampler: West Virginia's African-American Women of Distinction, Vol. 1.* Charleston: Printing Press, Ltd., 2002.

Moccasin Rangers: Calhoun County Historical & Genealogical Society. *History of Calhoun County.* Grantsville, 1990 • Stutler–*Civil War.*

Modern Budget Amendment: Citizens Advisory Commission on the Legislature of West Virginia. "Recommendations for Strengthening the West Virginia Legislature," Final Report. Charleston: Jarrett Printing, 1968 • Davis, Claude J., et al. *State and Local Government.* Morgantown Printing & Binding, 1963 • West Virginia Constitution, Article 6, Section 51, in *Michie's West Virginia Code, Annotated, Vol. 1.* Charlottesville: Lexis Pub.

Monongah Mine Disaster: Graebner, William. *Coal-Mining Safety in the Progressive Period.* Lexington: UPK, 1976 • "The Greatest Coal-Mine Disaster in our History." *American Review of Reviews* (Feb. 1908) • *New York Times,* 12/7/1907 • Todd, Alden. "December 6, 1907—50 Years Ago: The Horror at Monongah." *UMW Journal* (Dec. 1957).

Monongahela Culture: Johnson, William C. "The Protohistoric Monongahela and the Case for an Iroquois Connection," in David S. Brose, et al., ed., *Societies in Eclipse: Archaeology of the Eastern Woodlands Indians, A.D. 1400–1700.* Washington: Smithsonian Institution Press, 2001 • Means, Bernard K. "Circular Reasoning: Ring-Shaped Village Settlements in the Late Prehistoric Southwestern Pennsylvania and Beyond." *Journal of Middle Atlantic Archaeology* (2001).

Monongahela National Forest: Cohen, Stan. *The Tree Army: A Pictorial History of the Civilian Conservation Corps, 1933–1942.* Charleston: PHPC, 1980 • de Hart, Allen & Bruce Sundquist. *Monongahela National Forest Hiking Guide.* Charleston: West Virginia Highlands Conservancy, 1999 • U.S. Forest Service. "USDA Forest Service Interim Strategic Outreach Plan." U.S. Dept. of Agriculture, April 2000.

Monongahela Power Company: "Bit by Bit, Monongahela Grew from a Few Arc Lights to an Integrated Power Network." *Monongahela News: Special 75th Anniversary Edition.* Fairmont: Monongahela Power Co., 12/1/1965 • *Chronology of the Development of Electricity in Monongahela Power Territory.* Fairmont: Monongahela Power Co., 1987.

Monongahela River: Core, Earl L. *The Monongalia Story,* 5 vols. Parsons: McClain, 1974–1984 • Gillespie, William H. & John A. Clendening. "A Flora from Proglacial Lake Monongahela." *Castanea* (Dec. 1968).

Monongalia County: Callahan, James M. *History of the Making of Morgantown.* Morgantown Printing & Binding, 1926 • Core, Earl L. *The Monongalia Story,* 5 vols. Parsons: McClain, 1974–84 • WVU Public History Option. *Morgantown: A Bicentennial History.* Morgantown Historical Society, 1985.

Monroe County: Banks, James W. *200 Years from Good Hope.* Parsons: McClain, 1983 • Cometti–*Thirty-Fifth* • *West Virginia Women.* Comstock–*Encyclopedia,* vol. 25, 1974 • Conley, Phil. *West Virginia Reader.* Charleston: Education Foundation, 1970 • Miller, James H. *History of Summers County.* Hinton: J. H. Miller, 1908 • Morton, Oren. *History of Monroe County.* Staunton, VA: McClure, 1916.

Margaret Prescott Montague: Ambler & Summers • Conley–*Encyclopedia.*

Montani Semper Liberi: Hale, J. P. *The Historical Magazine Quarterly* (Jan. 1901) • Shankle, George, ed. *State Names, Flags, Seals, Songs, Birds, Flowers and Other Symbols.* Westport, CT: Greenwood Press, 1970 • Wheeling *Intelligencer,* 9/28/1863.

Fred Mooney: Corbin–*Life, Work* • Mooney, Fred. *Struggle in the Coal Fields: The Autobiography of Fred Mooney.* Morgantown, WVU Library, 1967.

Moonshine: Dabney, Joseph Earl. *Mountain Spirits: A Chronicle of Corn Whiskey.* New York: Charles Scribner's Sons, 1974 • Sohn, Mark F. *Mountain Country Cooking: A Gathering of the Best Recipes.* New York: St. Martin's Press, 1996.

Sara Jane Moore: "Attempt to Assassinate Ford like Invitation to Mrs. Moore." *Gazette,* 9/26/1975 • Sifakis, Carl. *Encyclopedia of Assassinations.* New York: Facts on File, 1991.

Moorefield: Moore, Alvin Edward. *History of Hardy County of the Borderland.* Parsons: McClain, 1963.

Moorefield, Battle of: Powell, Nancy H. *What to See and Do in the Lost River and South Branch Valleys.* Lost River: Lost River Educational Foundation, 1997 • Reed, Paula & Associates & Michael Baker Jr., Inc. *Middle South Branch Valley Rural Historic District and Study Area: Architectural and Historical Documentation.* Charleston: WVDOT, WVDOH, Apr. 1998 • Smith, Stephen G. *The First Battle of Moorefield: Early's Cavalry is Routed.* Danville, VA: Blue & Gray Education Society, 1998.

Morel: Fisher, David W. & Alan E. Bessette. *Edible Wild Mushrooms of North America.* Austin: University of Texas Press, 1992 • Kluger, Marilyn. *The Wild Flavor.* New York: Henry Holt & Co., 1973.

Morgan County: Newbraugh, Frederick T. *Warm Springs Echoes: About Berkeley Springs and Morgan County.* Berkeley Springs: Morgan Messenger, 1967.

Ephraim Franklin Morgan: Hennen, John. *The Americanization of West Virginia.* Lexington: UPK, 1996 • Laurie, Clayton D. "The U.S. Army and the Return to Normalcy in Labor Dispute Interventions: The Case of the West Virginia Coal Mine Wars, 1920–1921." *WVH* (1991) • Morgan–*Governors* • Rice & Brown.

Morgan Morgan: Conley, Phil. *West Virginia Yesterday and Today.* Charleston: WV Review Press, 1931 • Genealogical & clipping files, Berkeley County Historical Society • Morgan, French. *A History and Genealogy of the Family of Col. Morgan Morgan.* Washington, 1950.

Zackquill Morgan: *Descendants of First Lot Owners, Morgan's Town, 1785.* Morgantown Bicentennial Descendants Committee, 1985 • Morgan, French. *A History and Genealogy of the Family of Col. Morgan Morgan.* Washington, 1950 • WVU Public History Option. *Morgantown: A Bicentennial History.* Morgantown Historical Society, 1985.

Morgantown: Core, Earl L. *The Monongalia Story,* 5 vols. Parsons: McClain, 1974–84 • Rice, Connie Park. *Our Monongalia.* Terra Alta: Headline Books, 1999 • WVU Public History Option. *Morgantown: A Bicentennial History.* Morgantown Historical Society, 1985.

The *Morgantown Weekly Post*: Core, Earl L. *The Monongalia Story,* 5 vols. Parsons: McClain, 1974–84 • Forbes, Harold M. *West Virginia Newspapers, 1790–1990: A Union List.* Morgantown: WVU Libraries, 1989.

Morgantown Glass Works: Gallagher, Jerry. *A Handbook of Old Morgantown Glass.* J. Gallagher, 1995 • Six, Dean. "Morgantown: The Factory and Growth." *Old Morgantown Topics* (Spring 1991) • Snyder, Jeffrey B. *Morgantown Glass: From Depression Glass through the 1960s.* Atglen, PA: Schiffer Pub., 1998.

Mormons: *Deseret News 2004 Church Almanac.* Salt Lake City: Deseret News, 2003 • Zimmerman, Diane Hill. *"Almost Heaven:" A History of the Church of Jesus Christ of Latter-Day Saints in West Virginia.* Parsons: McClain, 1998.

Dwight Whitney Morrow: Howland, Hewitt H. *Dwight Whitney Morrow: A Sketch in Admiration.* New York: Century Co., 1930 • Lopez, Lorenzo C. "Morrow, Dwight W.," in Werner, Michael, ed., *Encyclopedia of Mexico.* Chicago: Fitzroy Dearborn, 1997 • Ostendarp, Anne. *Dwight W. Morrow Papers Microfilm.* Amherst, MA: Amherst College, 1991.

Mosses: Conard, H. S. *The Mosses and Liverworts.* Dubuque, IA: Wm. C. Brown Co., 1956 • Crum, Howard A. & Lewis E. Anderson. *Mosses of Eastern North America.* New York: Columbia University Press, 1981 • Grout, A. J. *Mosses with a Hand-lens.* Newfane, VT, 1947.

Mother's Day: Krythe, Maymie R. *All About American Holidays.* New York: Harper & Brothers, 1962 • Taylor County Historical & Genealogical Society. *A History of Taylor County.* Parsons: McClain, 1986 • Wolfe, Howard H. *Mother's Day and the Mother's Day Church.* Kingsport, TN: H. H. Wolfe, 1962.

Mothman: Keel, John A. *The Mothman Prophecies.* New York: Saturday Review Press, 1975 • Sergent, Donnie Jr. & Jeff Wamsley. *Mothman: The Facts Behind the Legend.* Point Pleasant: Mothman Lives Pub., 2001.

Mound Builders: McMichael–*Archeology* • Norona, Delf. *Moundsville's Mammoth Mound*. Moundsville: WV Archeological Society, 1954. Reprint, WV Archeological Society, 1998 • Willey, Gordon R. & Jeremy A Sabloff. *A History of American Archaeology*. London: Thames & Hudson, 1980.

Moundsville: Brantner, J. H., compiler. *Historical Collections of Moundsville*. Moundsville: Marshall County Historical Society, 1947 • Marshall County Historical Society. *History of Marshall County*. 1984 • Smith, R. J. *A Glimpse of Moundsville, West Virginia in Words and Pictures*. Moundsville: Moundsville Chamber of Commerce.

Moundsville Penitentiary: Clipping File 1, State Archives.

Mount Carbon Prehistoric Site: Atkinson, George Wesley. *A History of Kanawha County*. Charleston: WV Journal, 1876 • Hale, John P. *Some Local Archaeology*. Charleston, 1898 • Smithsonian Institution. *12th Annual Report of the Bureau of Ethnology* (July 1981).

Mount Nebo Gospel Sings: Samsell, James. "Singing on the Mountain." *Goldenseal* (Summer 1982).

Mount Olive Prison: *Blue Book*, 1998.

Mountain Boy: Sutphin, Gerald W. & Richard A. Andre. *Sternwheelers on the Great Kanawha River*. Charleston: PHPC, 1991.

Mountain Cove Spiritualist Community: Carroll, Bret E. "Spiritualism and Community in Antebellum America: The Mountain Cove Episode." *Communal Societies* (1992) • Peters, J. T. & H. B. Carden. *History of Fayette County*. Charleston: Jarrett Printing, 1926.

Mountain Lion: Russell, Kenneth R. "Mountain Lion," in John L. Schmidt & Douglass L. Gilbert, eds., *Big Game of North America*. Harrisonburg, VA: Stackpole Books, 1978.

Mountain State Forest Festival: Stell, Harold. *History of the Festival*, Booklet • Whetsell, Robert. *Elkins, West Virginia: The Metropolis Revisited*. Parsons: McClain, 1994.

Mountain State University: Wood, Jim. *Raleigh County*. Beckley: J. Wood, 1994.

Mountaintop Removal Mining: Loeb, Penny. "Shear Madness." *U.S. News & World Report* (8/11/1997) • Ward, Ken. Newspaper series. *Gazette*, Apr. 1998–June 2001 • Warrick, Joby. "'Mountaintop Removal' Shakes Coal State." *Washington Post*, 8/31/1998.

Karl Dewey Myers: Conley, Phil M. "Karl Myers, Poet, Philosopher." *WV Review* (Apr. 1925) • Fansler, Homer Floyd. *History of Tucker County*. Parsons: McClain, 1962 • "Karl Dewey Myers Dies December 4." *Parsons Advocate*, 12/6/1951.

Walter Dean Myers: Bishop, Rudine Sims. *Presenting Walter Dean Myers*. Boston: Twayne Pub., 1991 • Commire, Anne, ed. *Something About the Author*, vol 71. Detroit: Gale Research, 1993 • McMahon, Thomas, ed. *Authors & Artists for Young Adults*, vol. 4. Detroit: Gale Research, 1998 • Trosky, Susan, ed. *Contemporary Authors*, vol. 42. Gale Research, 1994.

The Mystery Hole: "Magical Mystery Hole Tour: West Virginia Loses an Icon and a Roadside Attraction with Creator's Death." *Gazette*, 3/1/1998.

John Forbes Nash Jr.: Nasar, Sylvia. *A Beautiful Mind*. New York: Simon & Schuster, 1998.

National Conservation Training Center: Cohn, Jeffrey P. "Unique Facility Provides a Host of Benefits for Fish and Wildlife Pros and Others." *Bioscience* (2000).

National Forests: McKim, C. R. *50 Year History of the Monongahela National Forest*. 1970.

National Hillbilly News: Tribe–*Jamboree*.

National Park Service in West Virginia: *The National Parks: Index 1995*. Washington: U.S. Dept. of the Interior, 1995 • *The National Parks: Shaping the System*. Washington: U.S. Dept. of the Interior, 1991.

National Radio Astronomy Observatory: Pocahontas County Historical Society. *History of Pocahontas County*. Marlinton, 1981 • *Information About the National Radio Astronomy Observatory*. Charlottesville: NRAO.

National Register of Historic Places: Chambers, S. Allen. *Buildings of West Virginia*. Oxford, NY: Oxford University Press, 2004 • State Historic Preservation Office. *Historic West Virginia: The National Register of Historic Places*. WVDC&H, 2000.

National Road: Raitz, Karl, ed. *The National Road*. Baltimore: Johns Hopkins University Press, 1996 • Searight, Thomas B. *The Old Pike: A History of the National Road*. Uniontown, PA: Thomas B. Searight, 1894.

Natural Gas and Petroleum: Ambler & Summers • Cardwell, D. H & K. L. Avary. "Oil and Gas Fields of West Virginia, Geological Survey." 1982 •

Haught, O. L. "Oil and Gas in West Virginia, Geological Survey." 1964 • McKain, David L. & Bernard L. Allen. *Where it all Began: The Story of the People and Places Where the Oil and Gas Industry Began*. Parkersburg: David L. McKain, 1994 • Rice & Brown • Thoenen, Eugene D. *History of the Oil and Gas Industry in West Virginia*. Charleston: Education Foundation, 1964.

Phyllis Reynolds Naylor: *Authors & Artists for Young Adults*, vol. 29. Detroit: Gale Research, 1990 • Naylor, Phyllis. *How I Came to be a Writer*. New York: Antheneum, 1978. Reprint, Aladdin, 1987 • Naylor, Phyllis. Telephone interview by author. 8/13/1998 • Stover, Lois T. *Presenting Phyllis Reynolds Naylor*. New York: Twayne Pub., 1997.

Church of the Nazarene: Greathouse, William M. *What is the Church of the Nazarene?* Kansas City: Nazarene Pub. House, 1984 • *Manual of the Church of the Nazarene*. Kansas City: Nazarene Pub. House, 1997 • Parrott, Leslie. *Introducing the Nazarenes*. Kansas City: Nazarene Pub. House, 1969 • Smith, Timothy L. *Called Unto Holiness: The Story of the Nazarenes—The Formative Years*. Kansas City: Nazarene Pub. House, 1962.

Needham and Arthur Expedition: Briceland, Alan Vance. *Westward from Virginia: The Exploration of the Virginia-Carolina Frontier 1650–1710*. Charlottesville: UVA Press, 1987.

Matthew Mansfield Neely: Morgan–*Governors* • *Blue Book*, 1940.

The Negro Citizen of West Virginia: Posey, Thomas E. *The Negro Citizen of West Virginia*. Institute: Press of WV State College, 1934.

Don Nehlen: Smith, Bill. *I'm Nobody Special*. South Charleston: Jalamap, 1984 • *WVU Football Media Guide*, 1998.

New Cumberland: New Cumberland Area Chamber of Commerce. "Good People Make a Good Town," Pamphlet • Newton, J. H. *History of the Pan-Handle*. Wheeling: Caldwell, 1879.

New Deal: Haid, Stephen Edward. "Arthurdale: An Experiment in Community Planning." Ph.D. diss., WVU, 1975 • Salstrom, Paul. *Appalachia's Path to Dependency: Rethinking a Region's Economic History, 1730–1940*. Lexington: UPK, 1994 • Thomas–*New Deal*.

New River: Cox, William E. *Life on the New River*. Philadelphia: Eastern National Park & Monument Assn., 1984 • Hyde, Arnout Jr. *New River: A Photographic Essay*. Charleston: Cannon Graphics, 1991.

New Vrindaban: Hubner, John. *Monkey on a Stick: Murder, Madness, and the Hare Krishnas*. New York: Harcourt Brace Jovanovich, 1988 • *Prabhupada's Palace of Gold*. Moundsville: New Vrindaban Community, 1986.

New York Central: Harlow, Alvin F. *The Road of the Century*. New York: Creative Age Press, 1947.

Newspapers: Forbes, Harold M. *West Virginia Newspapers, 1790–1990: A Union List*. Morgantown: WVU Libraries, 1989 • Norona, Delf & Charles Shetler. *West Virginia Imprints, 1790–1863: A Checklist of Books, Newspapers, Periodicals and Broadsides*. Moundsville: WV Library Assn., 1958 • Rice, Otis K. "West Virginia Printers and their Work, 1790–1830." *WVH* (July 1953).

Niagara Movement: "Address to the Country," in David Levering Lewis, ed., *W.E.B. DuBois: A Reader*. New York: Henry Holt & Co., 1995 • Lewis, David Levering. *W.E.B. DuBois: Biography of a Race, 1868–1919*. New York: Henry Holt & Co., 1993 • Quarles, Benjamin. *Allies for Freedom: Blacks and John Brown*. New York: Oxford University Press, 1974 • Rudwick, Elliott M. "The Niagara Movement." *Journal of Negro History* (July 1957).

Night of the Hunter: Grubb, Davis. Interviews by author. 1977–80 • Pickard, Roy. *The Oscar Movies*. New York: Facts on File, 1994.

Nitro: Harper, R. Eugene. "Wilson Progressives vs. DuPont: Controversy in Building the Nitro Plant." *WVH* (1989) • Wintz, William D. *Nitro: World War I Boom Town*. Charleston: Jalamap, 1985.

Norfolk & Western Railway: Lambie, Joseph T. *From Mine to Market: The History of Coal Transportation on the Norfolk & Western Railway*. New York: NYU Press, 1954 • Striplin, E. F. Pat. *The Norfolk & Western: A History*. Roanoke: Norfolk & Western Railway, 1981.

Normal Schools: Ambler–*Education* • Rice, Otis K. "West Virginia Educational Historiography: Status and Needs," in Ronald L. Lewis & John C. Hennen Jr., eds., *West Virginia History: Critical Essays on the Literature*. Dubuque, IA: Kendall-Hunt Pub., 1993.

Delf Norona: Comstock–*Encyclopedia*, vol. 16, 1976.

North Fork Mountain: de Hart, Allen & Bruce Sundquist. *Monongahela National Forest Hiking Guide*. Charleston: WV Highlands Conservancy, 1999 • Smith, J. Lawrence. *The Potomac Naturalist: The Natural History of the Headwaters of the Historic Potomac*. Parsons: McClain, 1968 • Trianosky, Paul. "Saving North Fork Mountain." *WWV* (Sept. 1997).

North House Museum: Montgomery, John F. "Lewisburg in Stagecoach Days," in Bicentennial Committee, *Come, Walk with Me: A Nostalgic View of Lewisburg*. Parsons: McClain, 1982.

The North-South Game: Keefer, Louis E. "North-South: The Big Game of '43." *Goldenseal* (Fall 1994).

Northern Panhandle: North, E. Lee. *The 55 West Virginias*. Morgantown: WVU Press, 1985 • Puetz, C. J. *West Virginia County Maps*. Lyndon Station, WI: Thomas Pub. • Rice & Brown • WPA–*Guide*.

Northfork Basketball: Boyd, Jennings. Interview by author. 4/13/1999 • Wyatt, Tim L. *The Final Score*. Woodbridge, VA: T. Wyatt, 1999.

Northwestern Virginia Turnpike: Ambler, Charles H. *A History of Transportation in the Ohio Valley*. Glendale, CA: Arthur H. Clark, 1932 • Boughter, I. F. "Internal Improvements in Northwestern Virginia." Ph.D. diss., University of Pittsburgh, 1930 • Taylor, George R. *The Transportation Revolution*. New York: Rinehart, 1951.

Norwalk Motor Car: Friend, Daniel J. "The Norwalk: Martinsburg's Motor Car." *Goldenseal* (Summer 2003) • Platania, Joseph. "The Elusive Jarvis-Huntington: Early Automobiles of West Virginia." *Goldenseal* (Fall 1999).

John Nugent: Harris, Evelyn K. & Frank J. Krebs. *From Humble Beginnings: The West Virginia State Federation of Labor, 1903–1957*. Charleston: WV Labor History Pub. Fund, 1960 • U.S. Senate. Committee on Education & Labor. *Conditions in the Paint Creek Coal Fields of West Virginia*. 63rd Congress, first session, 3 vols. Washington: GPO, 1913.

Lawrence William Nuttall: Boone, Weldon. *A History of Botany in West Virginia*. Parsons: McClain, 1965 • Core, Earl. "Lawrence William Nuttall." *Castanea* (Dec. 1952).

Eldora Marie Bolyard Nuzum: Vaughan, Gail. "Eldora–Crusading Editor, Working Mother." *Dominion Post*, 6/25/1970.

Nylon: Denham, Charles J., ed. *Sentimental Journey: The DuPont Belle Works: A 75-Year History 1926–2001*. Charleston: E. I. du Pont de Nemours & Co., 2001 • McAllister, John F. *The First Nylon Plant*. Washington: American Chemical Society, 1995.

Oak Hill: Donnelly, Shirley. *History of Oak Hill, West Virginia*. Charleston: Jarrett Printing, 1953 • Peters, J. T. & H. B. Carden. *History of Fayette County*. Charleston: Jarrett Printing, 1926 • Posey, Thomas E. *The Negro Citizen of West Virginia*. Institute: Press of WV State College, 1934.

Oak Park: Ross, Peggy. "Echoes of Things Past: Preston County's Oak Park." *Goldenseal* (Summer 1994) • Thomas, Charles A. *Images of America: Preston County*. Charleston, SC: Arcadia Pub., 1998.

Oakhurst Links: Asbury, Martha J. "Oakhurst Links: A Romance with Golf." *WWV* (Jan. 1998) • Bedell, Tom. "Time Travel at Oakhurst Links." *Diversion* (Mar. 2000).

Sylvia O'Brien: O'Brien, Sylvia. Interview by author. 10/8/1997 • Sullivan, Ken. "'We Lived Good Back Then': Vandalia Award Winner Sylvia O'Brien." *Goldenseal* (Fall 1989).

Molly O'Day and Lynn Davis: Goodnite, Abby Gail & Ivan M. Tribe. "'Living the Right Life Now': Lynn Davis & Molly O'Day." *Goldenseal* (Spring 1998).

Herschel Coombs Ogden: DeFrancis, Robert. "H. C. Ogden," (unpub. ms.). 1994 • *Wheeling News-Register*, 2/1–3/1943.

Earl Oglebay: Shawkey, Morris. *West Virginia: In History, Life, Literature and Industry*, 5 vols. Chicago: Lewis Pub., 1928.

Oglebay Park: Fetherling, Doug. *Wheeling: An Illustrated History*. Woodland Hills, CA: Windsor Pub., 1983 • Weir, Ralph H. *The Story of Oglebay Park, Wheeling, West Virginia, and the History of Oglebay Institute and the Oglebay Family*. Columbus, OH: F. J. Heer Printing Co., 1963.

Ohio Company: Bailey, Kenneth P. *The Ohio Company of Virginia and the Westward Movement*. Glendale, CA: Arthur H. Clark Co., 1939.

Ohio County: Comstock–*Encyclopedia*, vol. 16, 1976 • Conley–*Encyclopedia* • Newton, J. H. *History of the Pan-Handle*. Wheeling: Caldwell, 1879.

Ohio River: Banta, R. E. *The Ohio*. New York: Rinehart, 1949.

Ohio Valley University: Sturm, Philip W. *Dreams and Visions: The Silver Anniversary History of Ohio Valley College*. Parkersburg: Silver Anniversary Committee of Ohio Valley, 1985.

Ohio Valley Trades and Labor Assembly: Javersak, David T. "The Ohio Valley Trades and Labor Assembly." Ph.D. diss., WVU, 1977 • Javersak. "Response of the O.V.T.&L.A. to Industrialism." *The Journal of the West Virginia Historical Association* (Spring 1980).

Sigfus Olafson: "Archaeologist Sigfus Olafson Dies at 90." *Gazette*, 3/2/1987 • Youse, Hillis. *WV Archeologist* (Spring 1987).

Old Appalachia: Fenneman, Nevin M. *Physiography of Eastern United States*. New York: McGraw-Hill, 1938 • Hunt, Charles B. *Physiography of the United States*. San Francisco: W. H. Freeman, 1967 • Janssen, Raymond E. *Earth Science: A Handbook on the Geology of West Virginia*. Clarksburg: Educational Marketers, 1973 • WPA–*Guide*.

The Old Farm Hour: Tribe–*Jamboree*.

Old-Growth Forests: Carvell, Kenneth L. "Virgin Timber Stands: Why Were They Spared?" *WWV* (July 1996) • Davis, Mary Byrd, ed. *Eastern Old-growth Forests: Prospects for Rediscovery and Recovery*. Washington: Island Press, 1996.

Old Stone Presbyterian Church: Montgomery, John F. *History of Old Stone Presbyterian Church*. Parsons: McClain, 1983.

Old-time Music: Boette, Marie. *Singa Hipsy Doodle and other Folk Songs of West Virginia*. Parsons: McClain, 1971 • Conway, Cecelia. *African Banjo Echoes in Appalachia: A Study of Folk Traditions*. Knoxville: UT Press, 1995 • Milnes, Gerald. *Play of a Fiddle*. Lexington: UPK, 1999.

John Hunt Oley: Geiger, Joe Jr. *Civil War in Cabell County*. Charleston: PHPC, 1991 • Wallace, George S. *Cabell County Annals and Families*. Richmond: Garrett & Massie, 1935 • *Wheeling Intelligencer*, 3/1888.

The One-Room School: Lutz, Paul F. "One Room was Enough." *Goldenseal* (Fall 1996).

Organ Cave: Baker, L., et al. "The Friars Hole System," Bulletin 1. Capital Area Cavers, 1982 • Dougherty, P. H., et al. "Karst Regions of the Eastern U.S. with Special Emphasis on the Friars Hole Cave System, West Virginia," in Y. Daixuan & L. Zaihua, *Global Karst Correlation*. New York: Science Press, 1998 • Jones, W. K. *Karst Hydrology Atlas of West Virginia*. Charles Town: Karst Waters Institute, 1997 • Stevens, Paul J. "Caves of the Organ Cave Plateau," Bulletin. WV Speleological Survey, 1988 • Storrick, G. D. "The Caves and Karst Hydrology of Southern Pocahontas County and the Upper Spring Creek Valley," Bulletin 10. WV Speleological Survey, 1992.

Oriskany Sandstone: Bruner, Katherine R. "Depositional Environments, Petrology, and Diagenesis of the Oriskany Sandstone in the Subsurface in West Virginia." Ph.D. diss., WVU, 1991 • Harper, J. A. & D. G. Patchen. "Play Dos: Lower Devonian Oriskany Sandstone Structural Play," in J. B. Roen & B. J. Walker, eds., *Atlas of Major Appalachian Gas Plays*. Morgantown: WVGES, 1996.

Osage and Pursglove Mine Disasters: Humphrey, H. B. *Historical Summary of Coal-Mine Explosions in the U.S., 1810–1958*. Washington: GPO, 1960 • Rakes, Paul H. "Casualties on the Homefront: Scotts Run Mining Disasters during World War II." *WVH* (1994).

Michael Owens: Barkey, Fred. "Mike Owens' Glass Company." *Goldenseal* (Spring 1996) • Davis, Pearce. *Development of the American Glass Industry*. Cambridge: Harvard University Press, 1949 • Scoville, Warren C. *Revolution in Glassmaking*. Cambridge: Harvard University Press, 1948 • Zembala, Dennis. "Machines in the Glasshouse: The Transformation of Work in the Glass Industry, 1820–1915." Ph.D. diss., George Washington University, 1984.

Pack Peddlers: Alexander, Irving. "Wilcoe: People of a Coal Town." *Goldenseal* (Spring 1990) • Bennett, Chessie Clay. "These Times Stand Out in Memory." *Goldenseal* (Spring 1989) • Dietz, Elizabeth Jane. "As We Lived a Long Time Ago." *Goldenseal* (Fall 1981) • Farley, Yvonne Snyder. "To Keep their Faith Strong: The Raleigh Orthodox Community." *Goldenseal* (Summer 1992) • Prichard, Arthur C. "Two Hundred Pounds or More: The Lebanese Community in Mannington." *Goldenseal* (Apr. 1978) • Semrau, Ronda G. "Roxie Gore: Looking Back in Logan County." *Goldenseal* (Summer 1990) • Sutton, Clive B. "We Toiled and Labored and Grew Up: Looking Back in Ritchie County." *Goldenseal* (Fall 1990).

William Nelson Page: Athey, Louis L. "William Nelson Page." *WVH* (1985–86) • Page, William Nelson. W. N. Page Papers. University of Virginia, Alderman Library, Charlottesville • Page. *A Fossil Fern and Other Poems*. Boston: Boston Stratford Co., 1925 • Peters, J. T. & H. B. Carden. *History of Fayette County*. Charleston: Jarrett Printing, 1926.

Painted Trees: Olafson, Sigfus. "The Painted Trees and the War Road, Paint Creek, Fayette County." *The West Virginia Archeologist* (Sept. 1958) • Sturtevant, William C., ed. *Handbook of North American Indians: Northeast,* vol. 15. Washington: Smithsonian Institution, 1978 • Warhus, Mark. *Another America: Native American Maps and the History of our Land.* New York: St. Martins Press, 1997.

Breece D'J Pancake: Douglass, Thomas E. *A Room Forever: The Life, Work and Letters of Breece D'J Pancake.* Knoxville: UT Press, 1998.

Panther State Forest: Beanblossom, Robert. "Panther State Forest: Recreational Jewel of McDowell County." *WWV* (Aug. 1987).

Pardee & Curtin Lumber Company: Brown, D. D. Collection. WV&RHC • Hennen, Ray V., WVGES. *Braxton and Clay Counties.* Wheeling News Litho. Co., 1917 • Reger, David B, WVGES. *Nicholas County.* Wheeling News Litho. Co., 1921.

Rex and Eleanor Parker: Dorgan, Howard. *The Airwaves of Zion: Radio & Religion in Appalachia.* Knoxville: UT Press, 1993 • Tribe–*Jamboree.*

Parkersburg: Allen, Bernard L. *Parkersburg: A Bicentennial History.* Parkersburg Bicentennial Commission, 1985 • Marsh, Nancy & Mrs. Albert Moellendick. *The Story of Parkersburg.* Parkersburg: Union Trust & Deposit Co., 1953 • *Blue Book,* 1993.

Phoeba Parsons: Taped interviews & musical recordings. Hutchins Library, Augusta Collection, Davis & Elkins College, Elkins.

Okey L. Patteson: Morgan–*Governors.*

Paw Paw: Morgan County Historical Society. *Morgan County, West Virginia and its People.* Berkeley Springs, 1981 • Papers of the C&O Canal Co. National Archives, Washington.

Pawpaws: Peterson, R. N. "Genetic Resources of Temperate Fruit and Nut Crops." *Acta Horticulturae* (Feb. 1991) • Reich, Lee. *Uncommon Fruits Worthy of Attention.* Reading, MA: Addison-Wesley, 1991.

Christopher H. Payne: Posey, Thomas E. *The Negro Citizen of West Virginia.* Institute: WV State College Press, 1934.

Pence Springs: Cohen, Stan. *Historic Springs of the Virginias.* Charleston: PHPC, 1981 • Miller, James H. *History of Summers County.* Hinton: J. H. Miller, 1908 • O'Malley, Nancy. *Prehistory along the Greenbrier: Archaeological Investigations at Pence Springs, Summers County, West Virginia.* Lexington: UPK, 1985.

Pendleton County: Boggs, Elsie Byrd. *A History of Franklin: The County Seat of Pendleton County.* Staunton, VA: McClure Printing, 1960 • Calhoun, H. M. *'Twixt North and South.* Franklin: McCoy Pub., 1974 • Morton, Oren F. *A History of Pendleton County.* Franklin: Oren F. Morton, 1910. Reprint, Regional Pub. Co., 1974.

Pentecostalism: McCaulcy, Deborah V. *Appalachian Mountain Religion: A History.* Urbana: UI Press, 1995.

Pepperoni Rolls: Mozier, Jeanne. *Way Out in West Virginia.* Charleston: Quarrier Press, 1999.

Peter Tarr Furnace: Welch, Jack. *History of Hancock County.* Wheeling News Litho. Co., 1963.

George William Peterkin: Carnes, Eva M. "George W. (Bishop) Peterkin at Valley Mountain." *Magazine of History & Biography* (1961). Elkins: Randolph County Historical Society • Comstock–*Encyclopedia,* vol. 17, 1976 • Peterkin, George W. *A History and Record of the Protestant Episcopal Church in the Diocese of West Virginia.* Charleston: Tribune Co. Printers, 1902.

Peters Mountain: Reger, David B., WVGES. *Mercer, Monroe and Summers Counties.* Wheeling News Litho. Co., 1926.

Petroglyphs: Braley, Dean. *Shaman's Story: The West Virginia Petroglyphs.* St. Albans: St. Albans Pub., 1993 • Brashler, Janet G. "An Application of the Method of Multiple Working Hypotheses to Two West Virginia Petroglyph Sites." *WV Archeologist* (Spring 1989) • Richardson, James B. III & James L. Swauger. "The Petroglyphs Speak: Rock Art and Iroquois Origins." *Journal of Middle Atlantic Archaeology* (1996).

Philippi Covered Bridge: Carnes, Margaret. *Centennial History of the Philippi Covered Bridge.* Philippi: Barbour County Historical Society, 1952 • Cohen, Stan. *A Pictorial Guide to West Virginia's Civil War Sites.* Charleston: PHPC, 1992 • Cohen. *West Virginia's Covered Bridges.* Charleston: PHPC, 1992 • Kemp, Emory L. *West Virginia's Historic Bridges.* Morgantown: WVU, 1984 • Kemp, Emory L. & Paul D. Marshall. "Rebuilding the Historic Philippi Covered Bridge in West Virginia." *APT Bulletin,* vol. 24. (1992).

Philippi Mummies: Lipton, Michael. "Have You Saw the Mummies?" *Gazette,* 10/29/1989 • Smith, Barbara. "'Preserved until Judgment Day': The Philippi Mummies." *Goldenseal* (Fall 2001).

Jayne Anne Phillips: "'Black Tickets' State Writer's Debut." *Panorama, Dominion Post,* 11/3/1979 • *Contemporary Authors.* Detroit: Gale Research, 1988 • Douglass, Thomas. "Jayne Anne Phillips." *Appalachian Journal* (Winter 1994).

Pickens Leper: Sheets, Wayne L. "The Pickens Leper." *Goldenseal* (Fall 1997).

Francis Harrison Pierpont: Ambler, Charles H. *Francis H. Pierpont.* Chapel Hill: UNC Press, 1937 • Francis H. Pierpont Papers. WV&RHC.

Pigeon's Roost, Battle of: Bard, David. *Civil War: The New River Valley.* Charleston: Quarrier Press, 2004 • Johnston, David E. *History of the Middle New River Settlement and Contiguous Territory.* Huntington: Standard Printing & Pub. Co., 1906. Reprint, Commonwealth Press, 1969 • Mercer County Historical Society. *Mercer County History: Sesquicentennial Year, 1987.* Princeton, 1991 • Moore, Frank. *The Rebellion Record.* New York: G. P. Putnam & Sons, 1867 • Straley, Harrison. *Memoirs of Old Princeton.* Princeton, 1925. Reprint, Mercer County Historical Society, 1975.

Pilgrim Glass: Eige, G. Eason. "Pilgrim's New Cameo Glass," Bulletin. National Early American Glass Club, 1992 • McKeand, Robert G. & Thomas O'Connor. "A Formula for Success: The Pilgrim Glass Story." *Glass Collector's Digest* (Oct.–Nov. 1990).

Pinch Reunion: Elk-Blue Creek Historical Society. *Elk River Communities in Kanawha County: A Continuing History.* Cleveland: Typemasters, 1993 • Chambers, W. W., grandson of W. W. Wertz. Telephone conversation with author. 12/26/2000 • Shepherd, Blaine. Telephone conversation with author. 11/19/2000 • "West Virginians of 1934–1935." *Wheeling Intelligencer,* 1935.

Pipestem Resort State Park: Strausbaugh, P. D. & Earl L. Core. *Flora of West Virginia,* 2nd edition, 4 vols. Morgantown: WVU, 1970–77 • Summers County Historical Society. *The History of Summers County.* Salem, 1984.

Pittston Strike: Brisbin, Richard A. *A Strike Like No Other Strike: Law and Resistance during the Pittston Coal Strike of 1989–1990.* Baltimore: Johns Hopkins University Press, 2002 • Sessions, Jim. "Singing across Dark Spaces: The Union/Community Takeover of Pittston's Moss 3 Plant," in Stephen L. Fisher, ed., *Fighting Back in Appalachia: Traditions of Resistance and Change.* Philadelphia: Temple University Press, 1993.

Place Names: Alotta, Robert I. *Signpost and Settlers: The History of Place Names in the Middle Atlantic States.* Chicago: Bonus Books, 1992 • Hill, Raymond T. "The Toponymy of the Lower New River." *Proceedings of the New River Symposium,* 1990 • Hill. "Toponymy of Southern West Virginia." *Proceedings, The Seventh Biennial Conference on Appalachian Geography,* 1992 • Fernbach, William & Quinith Janssen. *West Virginia Place Names: Origins and History.* Shepherdstown: J&F Enterprises, 1984 • Kenny, Hamill. *West Virginia Place Names.* Piedmont: Place Name Press, 1945.

Pleasants County: Pemberton, Robert L. *A History of Pleasants County.* St. Marys: Oracle Press, 1929 • Pleasants County Historical Society. *History of Pleasants County to 1980.* Dallas: Taylor Pub., 1980.

Pocahontas Land Corporation: Sullivan–*Coal Men.*

Pocahontas No. 3 Coal Seam: Lambie, Joseph T. *From Mine to Market: The History of Coal Transportation on the Norfolk & Western Railway.* New York: NYU Press, 1954 • McCulloch, Gayle H. "'Poky 3' World's Finest, Coal Geologist Argues." *Welch Daily News,* 2/24/1984 • Pocahontas Operators Assn. Collection. Eastern Regional Archives • Rehbein, Edward A., C. Douglas Henderson & Ronald Mullennex. "No. 3 Pocahontas Coal in Southern West Virginia–Resources and Depositional Trends," Bulletin B-38. WVGES, 1981 • Stow, Audley H. "Mining in the Pocahontas Field." *Coal Age* (4/19/1913).

Livia Simpson Poffenbarger: "'Manufactured History': Re-Fighting the Battle of Point Pleasant." *WVH* (1997) • Whear, Nancy. "Livia Simpson Poffenbarger, 1862–1937," in *Missing Chapters II: West Virginia Women in History.* Charleston: WV Women's Commission, 1986.

Point Pleasant: *Point Pleasant Register. Bicentennial Souvenir Edition,* 10/6–13/1974 • Simmons, Ethel C. "Historic Point Pleasant," in *John B. Rogers Producing Company Presents and Directs the Historical Pageant and Homecoming.* Point Pleasant Kiwanis Club, 1925 • *Blue Book,* 1997.

Point Pleasant, Battle of: Lewis, Virgil A. *History of the Battle of Point Pleasant.* Charleston: Tribune Printing Co., 1909. Reprint, C. J. Carrier Co., 1974 • Thwaites, Reuben Gold & Louise Phelps Kellogg. *Documentary History of Dunmore's War, 1774.* Madison, WI: Wisconsin Historical Society, 1905.

Dick Pointer: Bice, David A. *A Panorama of West Virginia II.* South Charleston: Jalamap, 1985 • Lewis, Virgil A. *History of West Virginia in Two Parts.* Philadelphia: Hubbard Brothers, 1889 • Rice & Brown.

Poles: Barkey, Frederick A. "Immigration and Ethnicity in West Virginia: A Review of the Literature," in Ronald L. Lewis & John Hennen Jr., eds., *West Virginia History: Critical Essays on the Literature.* Dubuque, IA: Kendall-Hunt, 1993 • Fones-Wolf, Ken & Ronald L. Lewis, eds. *Transnational West Virginia.* Morgantown: WVU Press, 2002 • Rice, Otis. *Charleston and the Kanawha Valley.* Woodland Hills, CA: Windsor Pub., 1981.

Pontiac's Rebellion: Peckham, Howard Henry. *Pontiac and the Indian Uprising.* Princeton: Princeton University Press, 1947 • Tanner, Helen H., ed. *Atlas of Great Lakes Indian History.* Norman: University of Oklahoma Press, 1986.

Population: Lego, Brian. "West Virginia: A 20th Century Perspective on Population Change," ms. Morgantown: WVU, 1999 • Rice & Brown.

Port Amherst: Hanson, Todd A. *Campbell's Creek.* Charleston: PHPC, 1989.

Melville Davisson Post: Anderson, Jack Sandy. "Melville Davisson Post." *WVH* (July 1967) • Brady, James Francis (Brother James Damian, F.M.S.). "The Life and Work of Melville Davisson Post." M.A. thesis, St. John's University, 1954 • Norton, Charles A. *Melville Davisson Post.* Bowling Green, OH: Bowling Green University Popular Press, 1973.

Potomac Highlands: Rice & Brown • USGS Maps, Scale 1:250,000. Charlottesville & Cumberland quandrangles.

Potomac River: Gutheim, Frederick. *The Potomac.* Baltimore: Johns Hopkins University Press, 1986 • Ator, Scott W., et al. "Water Quality in the Potomac River Basin, 1992–1996," Circular 1166. Denver: USGS, 1998 • Hyde, Arnout Jr. & Ken Sullivan. *The Potomac: A Nation's River.* Charleston: Cannon Graphics, 1993.

Potomac State College: Ambler–*Education* • Conley–*Encyclopedia* • Courrier, Dinah. "Summary of the History of Potomac State College," (unpub. ms.). Mar. 2000.

Potomak Guardian: Rice, Otis K. "West Virginia Printers and their Work, 1790–1830." *WVH* (July 1953).

Pottery Industry: Barber, Edwin Atlee. *Pottery and Porcelain of the United States.* New York: G. P. Putnam's Sons, 1901 • Ramsay, John. *American Potters and Pottery.* Ann Arbor: Ars Ceramica, 1976 • Thorn, C. Jordan. *Handbook of Old Pottery and Porcelain Marks.* New York: Tudor Pub., 1947.

Poultry: Hyre, H. M. & B. W. Moore. *The West Virginia Poultry Association: 1934–1984.* Moorefield: WV Poultry Assn., 1985 • Office of WV Agricultural Statistics. Annual Bulletin No. 31. 2000.

Joe Powell: McElhinny, Brad. "Powell Will Miss the Job." *Daily Mail,* 8/19/1997 • Seiler, Fanny. "Union Leader to Retire." *Gazette,* 8/19/1997.

Harry Powers: Bumgardner, Stan & Christine Kreiser. "'Thy Brother's Blood': Capital Punishment in West Virginia." *WV Historical Society Quarterly.* (Mar. 1996) • Clipping files. State Archives.

Prehistoric People: Maslowski, Robert F. "Protohistoric Villages in Southern West Virginia." *Upland Archeology in the East, Symposium* 2. Harrisonburg, VA: James Madison University, 1984. • Mayer-Oakes, William J. "Prehistory of the Upper Ohio Valley." *Annals of Carnegie Museum,* vol. 34. Pittsburgh: Carnegie Museum, 1955 • McMichael–*Archeology.*

Presbyterians: Ellis, Dorsey D. *Look Unto the Rock.* Parsons: McClain, 1982 • *History of the Presbytery of Kanawha, 1895–1956.* Charleston: Jarrett Printing, 1956 • Montgomery, John F. *History of Old Stone Presbyterian Church, 1783–1983.* Parsons: McClain, 1983 • Thompson, Ernest T. *Presbyterians in the South,* 3 vols. Richmond: John Knox Press, 1963–73.

Preston County: Funk, Terri L., Assessor of Preston County. "General Information," Pamphlet. 2001 • Preston County Historical Society. *Preston County, West Virginia, History.* Kingwood, 1979 • Wiley, S. T. *History of Preston County.* Kingwood: Journal Printing, 1882.

Cal Price: Pocahontas County Historical Society. *History of Pocahontas County.* Marlinton, 1981.

The Pride of West Virginia: Wilcox, Don. Interview by author. 1/2000.

Princeton: Mercer County Historical Society. *Mercer County History 1984.* Marceline, MO: Walsworth Pub., 1985 • Reger, David B., WVGES. *Mercer, Monroe and Summers Counties.* Wheeling News Litho. Co., 1926.

Pringle Tree: Cutright, W. B. *The History of Upshur County.* Buckhannon, 1907. Reprint, McClain, 1977.

Proclamation of 1763: Rice & Brown.

Progressive Miners of America: Brophy, John. *A Miner's Life.* Madison, WI: University of Wisconsin Press, 1964 • Harris, Evelyn K. & Frank J. Krebs. *From Humble Beginnings: The West Virginia State Federation of Labor, 1903–1957.* Charleston: WV Labor History Pub. Fund, 1960.

Prohibition: Conley–*Encyclopedia* • Report of the State Commissioner of Prohibition, 1921–22, 4th Biennial Report • Rice & Brown • Report of the State Commissioner of Prohibition, 1925–26, 6th Biennial Report • State Dept. of Prohibition Bulletins. Apr. & Nov.–Dec. 1930; Jan. 1931.

Public Health: "A Century of Progress: Public Health in West Virginia," Report. WV Department of Health, 1981 • "West Virginia County Profiles-2000." WV Bureau for Public Health, 2001.

Board of Public Works: Citizens Advisory Commission on the Legislature of West Virginia. "Recommendations for Strengthening the West Virginia Legislature," Final Report. Charleston: Jarrett Printing, 1968 • Davis, Claude J., et al. *State and Local Government.* Morgantown Printing & Binding, 1963 • *Blue Book,* 1960.

Daniel Boardman Purinton: Core, Earl L. *The Monongalia Story,* 5 vols. Parsons: McClain, 1974–84 • Doherty, William T. Jr. & Festus P. Summers. *West Virginia University.* Morgantown: WVU Press, 1982.

Putnam County: Hale, John P. *History of the Great Kanawha Valley.* Madison, WI: Brant, Fuller & Co., 1891. Reprint, Gauley & New River Pub., 1994 • *Hardesty's,* vol. 1 • *Vandalia Journal* (July 1965) • *Vandalia Journal* (Apr. 1967) • *Vandalia Journal* (July 1991) • Wintz, William D. *Annals of the Great Kanawha.* Charleston: PHPC, 1993 • Wintz. *History of Putnam County, Volume 1.* St Albans: PHPC, 1999 • Wintz. *Nitro: World War I Boom Town.* Charleston: Jalamap, 1985.

Quiltmaking: Valentine, Fawn. *West Virginia Quilts and Quiltmakers: Echoes from the Hills.* Athens, OH: Ohio University Press, 2000.

R. D. Bailey Lake: Tidman, Ginevra. "R. D. Bailey Lake Dedicated August 10." *WWV* (Oct. 1980).

Radio: Becker, Martha J. & Marilyn Fletcher. *Broadcasting in West Virginia: A History.* Charleston: WV Broadcasters Assn., 1989.

Dyke Raese: Julian, Norman. *Legends: Profiles in West Virginia University Basketball.* Morgantown: Trillium Pub., 1998 • *WVU Basketball Media Guide,* 1998–99.

Railroad Strike of 1877: Bailey, Kenneth R. *Mountaineers are Free: A History of the West Virginia National Guard.* St. Albans: Harless Printing, 1978 • Bruce, Phillip V. *1877, Year of Violence.* Indianapolis: Bobbs-Merrill, 1959 • Hungerford, Edward. *The Story of the Baltimore and Ohio Railroad, 1827–1927.* New York: G. P. Putnam's Sons, 1928.

Raleigh County: County Court, Circuit Court & Land Book records. Raleigh County Courthouse, Beckley • WV Department of Mines. Annual Reports • Wood, Jim. *Raleigh County.* Beckley: J. Wood, 1994.

Ramps: McCallum, Barbara B. *Mom & Ramps Forever.* Charleston: Mountain State Press, 1983.

Z. D. Ramsdell: McClintic, Elizabeth K. "Ceredo: An Experiment in Colonization." M.A. thesis, Harvard-Radcliffe, 1937 • Napier, Mose A. *Ceredo: Its Founders and Families.* Ceredo: Phoenix Systems, 1989.

Randolph County: Bosworth, Albert S. *History of Randolph County.* Elkins, 1916 • Kek, Anna D., ed. *Randolph County Profile-1976.* Parsons: McClain, 1976 • Maxwell, Hu. *History of Randolph County.* Morgantown: Acme Pub., 1898 • Rice, Donald L. *Randolph 200: A Bicentennial History of Randolph County, West Virginia.* Elkins: Randolph County Historical Society, 1987.

Donald L. Rasmussen: Derickson, Alan. *Black Lung.* Ithaca, NY: Cornell University Press, 1998.

Ravenswood Strike: Juravich, Tom & Kate Bronfenbrenner. *Ravenswood: The Steelworkers' Victory and the Revival of American Labor.* Ithaca, NY: Cornell University Press, 1999.

Rebel Records: *Rebel Records: 1960–1995.* Roanoke, VA: Rebel Records, 1997.

The Recollections of Fifty Years of West Virginia: MacCorkle, William A. *The Recollections of Fifty Years of West Virginia*. New York: G. P. Putnam's Sons, 1928.

Red Ash, Rush Run Explosions: Dillon, Lacy A. *They Died in the Darkness*. Parsons: McClain, 1976 • Donnelly, Clarence Shirley. *Notable Mine Disasters of Fayette County, West Virginia*. Oak Hill: Fayette County Historical Society, 1951 • WV Department of Mines, Annual Reports. 1900 & 1905.

Red House Shoal: Johnson, Leland R. *Men, Mountains, and Rivers*. Washington: GPO, 1977 • Sutphin, Gerald W. & Richard A. Andre. *Sternwheelers on the Great Kanawha River*. Charleston: PHPC, 1991.

Red Robin Inn: Kline, Michael. "The Coon Dog Truth: Charlie Blevins at the Red Robin Inn." *Goldenseal* (Winter 1982).

Red Sulphur Springs: Cohen, Stan. *Historic Springs of the Virginias*. Charleston: PHPC, 1981 • Morton, Oren. *A History of Monroe County*. Staunton, VA: McClure, 1916 • Motley, Charles B. *Gleanings of Monroe County*. Radford, VA: Commonwealth Press, 1973.

Redeemers: Rice & Brown • Williams, John Alexander. "The New Dominion and the Old." *WVH* (July 1972).

Blind Alfred Reed: Tribe–*Jamboree*.

Nat Reese: Kline, Michael. "Something to Give: Nat Reese's Early Life and Music." *Goldenseal* (Winter 1987).

Reforestation: Clarkson–*Tumult*.

Rehoboth Church: King James Version. *The Holy Bible*. Cleveland: The World Pub. Co. • Motley, Charles B. *Gleanings of Monroe County*. Radford, VA: Commonwealth Press, 1973.

Religion: Daugherty, Mary Lee. "Serpent-Handling as Sacrament." *Theology Today* (Oct. 1976) • Manfred O. Meitzen, "West Virginia," in Samuel S. Hill, ed., *Religion in the Southern States*. Macon, GA: Mercer University Press, 1983 • Rice & Brown.

Religious Broadcasting: Armstrong, Ben. *The Electric Church*. New York: Thomas Lenson Publishers, 1989 • Dorgan, Howard. *Airwaves of Zion: Radio & Religion in Appalachia*. Knoxville: UT Press, 1993 • Tribe–*Jamboree* • Tribe, Ivan M. & John W. Morris. *Molly O'Day, Lynn Davis, and the Cumberland Mountain Folks: A Bio-Discography*. Los Angeles: University of California Press, 1975.

The Rending of Virginia: Stealey, John E. III. "Introduction," in Granville Davisson Hall, *The Rending of Virginia*. Knoxville: UT Press, 2000.

Jesse L. Reno: Cullum, George Washington. *Biographical Register of the Officers and Cadets of the U.S. Military Academy at West Point*. Boston: Houghton-Mifflin, 1891 • Sears, Stephen W. *Landscape Turned Red: The Battle of Antietam*. New Haven & New York: Ticknor & Fields, 1983 • Waugh, John C. *The Class of 1846, from West Point to Appomattox*. New York: Warner Books, 1994.

Reorganized Government of Virginia: Ambler, Charles H. *West Virginia: The Mountain State*. Englewood Cliffs, NJ: Prentice-Hall, 1940 • Curry, Richard O. *A House Divided: A Study of Statehood Politics & the Copperhead Movement in West Virginia*. Pittsburgh: UPP, 1964.

Mary Lou Retton: Simms, J. T. "Women Have Long Sports History." *Daily Mail*, 7/6/1999.

William Chapman Revercomb: Price, Samuel W. Jr. "A Stalwart Conservative in the Senate: William Chapman Revercomb." M.A. thesis, Marshall University, 1978 • "William Chapman Revercomb, 1895–1979." *Biographical Directory of the U.S. Congress, 1774–Present*. [electronic resource] Washington: The Congress, 2002.

The Revolutionary War: Curry, Richard O. "Loyalism in Western Virginia during the American Revolution." *WVH* (Apr. 1953).

Alexander Welch Reynolds: Jordan, Weymouth T. Jr., et al. *Soldier of Misfortune: Alexander Welch Reynolds of the U.S., Confederate and Egyptian Armies*. Lewisburg: Greenbrier Historical Society, 2001.

Frederick Hurten Rhead: Huxford, Bob & Sharon Huxford. *Collector's Encyclopedia of Fiesta*. Paducah: Collector Books, 1992.

The Rhododendron: Calvert, Lloyd P. "Here Comes the Showboat." *Travel West Virginia* (Summer 1963) • Final Report of the West Virginia Centennial Commission, 1963.

Rich Mountain, Battle of: Cox, Jacob D. "McClellan in West Virginia," in Robert Johnson & Clarence Buel, eds., *Battles and Leaders of the Civil War*, vol. 1. New York: Century Co., 1884–87 • Stutler–*Civil War*.

Richwood: Comstock–*Encyclopedia*, vol. 19, 1976 • Craig, A. L. "City of Richwood." Reprint, *Clarksburg Exponent Telegram*, 5/8/1927 • Farley,

Yvonne S. "A Good Part of Life: Remembering the Civilian Conservation Corps." *Goldenseal* (Jan.–Mar. 1981) • Harr, Milton. *The CCC Camps in West Virginia*. Charleston: Milton Harr, 1992 • *Blue Book*, 1998.

Ridge and Valley Province: Fenneman, Nevin M. *Physiography of Eastern United States*. New York: McGraw-Hill, 1938 • USGS Maps, Scale 1:250,000. Baltimore, Bluefield, Charleston, Charlottesville & Cumberland quadrangles • Delorme–*Atlas*.

Leonard Riggleman: Garrett, Mark. *Sincerely Yours: The Life and Work of Leonard Riggleman*. Charleston, 1980 • Krebs, Frank J. *Where There is Faith: The Morris Harvey College Story, 1888–1970*. Charleston: MHC. Publications, 1974.

Ritchie County: Hendricks, Ronald F. "Mole Hill or Mountain?" *Parkersburg News*, 10/17/1999 • Lowther, Minnie Kendall. *History of Ritchie County*. Wheeling News Litho. Co., 1911 • Puetz, C. J. *West Virginia County Maps*. Lyndon Station, WI: Thomas Pub. • Ritchie County Historical Society. *The History of Ritchie County, West Virginia to 1980*. Harrisville, 1980.

Ritchie Mines: Lowther, Minnie K. *History of Ritchie County*. Wheeling News Litho. Co., 1911 • Ritchie County Historical Society. *A Photographic History of Ritchie County*. 1989.

Charles Lloyd Ritter: "C. L. Ritter Sr., 80-Year-Old Realty Owner, Taken by Death." Huntington *Advertiser*, 12/23/1945 • "C. L. Ritter's Funeral is Set for Thursday." *Herald-Dispatch*, 12/24/1945 • Comstock–*Encyclopedia*, vol. 19, 1976 • Wallace, George S. *Huntington through 75 Years*. Huntington: Standard Printing & Pub., 1947.

Ritter Park: Casto, James E. *Huntington: An Illustrated History*. Huntington: Chapman Printing, 1997 • Ridenour Associates, *Master Development Plan for Ritter Park*. Pittsburgh, 1992 • Wallace, George S. *Huntington through 75 Years*. Huntington: Standard Printing & Pub., 1947.

William M. Ritter: Bailey, Kenneth R. "A Temptation to Lawlessness: Peonage in West Virginia, 1903–1908." *WVH* (1991) • Reedy, Dennis E. *W. M. Ritter Lumber Company Family History Book*. William M. Ritter Lumber Collection. Western Carolina University Library, Cullowee, North Carolina • "Ritter, Pioneer Lumber, Coal Operator, Dies in Capital." *Daily Mail*, 5/22/1952.

River Transportation: Hulbert, Archer Butler. *Waterways of Westward Expansion: The Ohio River and its Tributaries*. Cleveland: Arthur H. Clark Co., 1903 • Hunter, Louis C. *Steamboats on the Western Rivers*. Cambridge, MA: Harvard University Press, 1949 • Leahy, Ethel C. *Who's Who on the Ohio River*. Cincinnati: E. C. Leahy Pub., 1931.

Roadside Historical Markers: *Marking our Past: West Virginia's Historical Highway Markers*. Charleston: State Archives, 2002.

Roane County: Comstock–*Encyclopedia*, vol. 19, 1976 • Mylott, James P. *A Measure of Prosperity: A History of Roane County*. Charleston: Mountain State Press, 1984.

Spanky Roberts: Bickley, Ancella R. "Dubie, Spanky, and Mr. Death: West Virginia's Pioneering Black Airmen." *Goldenseal* (Summer 1997) • George S. Roberts Papers. Drain-Jordan Library, WV State University, Institute.

Rock Climbing: Barnes, Tony. "Little Big Mountain: Seneca." *Climbing* (Oct.–Nov. 1993) • Barnes. *Seneca: The Climber's Guide*. Helena, MT: Falcon, 1995 • Cater, Steve. *New River Gorge and Summersville Lake: Rock Climber's Guide Book*. Fayetteville: King Coal Propaganda, 1999 • Darmi, Peter. "Letting Go: New River Moderates." *Rock & Ice* (Mar.–Apr. 1995) • "New River Gorge." *Rock & Ice* (Apr.–May 2001) • Shull, Harrison. "The Old School: If You Can Climb at Seneca, You Can Climb Anywhere." *Rock & Ice* (June 1998) • Thompson, Rick. *New River Rock*. Helena, MT: Falcon, 1997.

Rat Rodgers: Kessler, Kent. *Hail West Virginians!* Weston: George L. Bland, 1959.

Rosbys Rock: Cometti–*Thirty-Fifth* • Sedosky, Dorothy Dakan. "Rosbys Rock," in *History of Marshall County*. Moundsville: Marshall County Historical Society, 1984.

William Starke Rosecrans: *American National Biography*. New York: Oxford University Press, 1999 • Lamers, William M. *The Edge of Glory: A Biography of General William S. Rosecrans*. New York: Harcourt, Brace & World, 1961 • Thomas, Emory H. *Robert E. Lee*. New York: W. W. Norton, 1995.

Benjamin L. Rosenbloom: Conley–*Encyclopedia* • Postal, Bernard & Lional Lippman. *American Jewish Landmarks: A Travel Guide and History*. New York: Fleet Press, 1977 • Shinedling, Abraham I. *West Virginia Jewry*. Philadelphia: Maurice Jacbos, Inc., 1963 • *West Virginia Biographical Dictionary*. St. Clair Shores, MI: Somerset Pub., 1999 • *Who's Who in West Virginia*. Chicago: Marquis Co., 1939 • *Blue Books*, 1918, 1924.

Andrew S. Rowan: Hubbard, Elbert. "A Message to Garcia." East Aurora, NY: Roycrofters, 1899 • Motley, Charles B. *Gleanings of Monroe County*. Radford, VA: Commonwealth Press, 1973 • Rowan, Andrew Summers. *How I Carried the Message to Garcia*. San Francisco: W. D. Harney, 1922.

Anne Newport Royall: Jackson, George S. *Uncommon Scold: The Story of Anne Royall*. Boston: Bruce Humphries, 1937 • James, Bessie R. *Anne Royall's U.S.A.* New Brunswick, NJ: Rutgers University Press, 1972 • Maxwell, Alice S. & Marion B. Dunlevy. *Virago! The Story of Anne Newport Royall (1769–1854)*. Jefferson, NC: McFarland, 1985 • Porter, Sarah H. *The Life and Times of Anne Royall*. Cedar Rapids, IA: Torch Press Book Shop, 1908.

Ruffner Family: Morgan, John G. & Robert J. Byers. *Charleston 200*. Charleston: *Gazette*, 1994 • "The Ruffner Family of Kanawha." *Kanawha Gazette*, 7/23, 7/30 & 8/6, 1884 • Zimmerman, Marcellus W. "Rev. Henry Ruffner, D. D., LL.D. and General Lewis Ruffner." *Greenbrier Independent*, 8/28/1884.

Henry Ruffner: Britt, Samuel Jr. "Henry Ruffner, 19th Century Educator." Ed.D. diss., University of Arizona, 1962 • Ruffner, Henry. *Address to the People of West Virginia*. Bridgewater, VA: The Green Bookman, 1933 • Ruffner. *Judith Bensaddi. Seclusaval*. J. Michael Pemberton, ed. Baton Rouge: LSU Press, 1984.

James Rumsey: Beltzhoover, George M. "James Rumsey, Inventor of the Steamboat." Charleston: West Virginia Historical & Antiquarian Society, 1900 • Curtis, Darwin O. "The Rumseian Experiment." Shepherdstown: Rumseian Society, 1987 • Flexner, James T. *Steamboats Come True*. Boston: Little, Brown & Co., 1978 • Newbraugh, Frederick T. "My God, She Moves." *Valleys of History*, vol. 6. Hagerstown, MD, 1970.

Rural Electrification: Ellison, Helen S. "Electricity Comes to the Country." *Goldenseal* (Summer 1989) • Thomas–*New Deal*.

Rural Free Delivery: Comstock–*Encyclopedia*, vol. 19, 1976 • Fuller, Wayne E. *RFD: The Changing Face of America*. Bloomington: Indiana University Press, 1965 • Scheele, Carl H. *A Short History of the Mail Service*. Washington: Smithsonian Institution Press, 1970 • Stafford, Margo. "RFD: A West Virginia First." *Goldenseal* (Summer 1983) • "Wilson, William." Comstock–*Encyclopedia*, vol. 23, 1976.

Cynthia Rylant: *Something About the Author*, vol. 76. Detroit: Gale Research, 1994.

Sagebrush Roundup: Tribe–*Jamboree*.

St. Albans: Davisson, Russell L., ed. *A Century with St. Albans: WV Centennial, 1863–1963*. St. Albans: Harless Printing, 1963 • St. Albans Historical Society. *St. Albans History*. Marceline, MO: Walsworth Pub., 1993 • Wintz, William D. *Annals of the Great Kanawha*. Charleston: PHPC, 1993 • Rust, Mary Jane. *Recollections & Reflections of Mollie Hansford*. Charleston: PHPC, 1996.

St. Albans Archeological Site: Brashler, Janet G., et al. "Recent Research at the St. Albans Site," in William S. Dancey, ed., *The First Discovery of America*. Ohio Archaeological Council, 1994 • Broyles, Bettye J. "Preliminary Report: The St. Albans Site, Kanawha County, West Virginia." *WV Archeologist* (Fall 1966) • "Second Preliminary Report: The St. Albans Site, Kanawha County, West Virginia." Archaeological Investigation 3, WVGES, 1971.

St. Francis Hospital: *70 Years, St. Francis Hospital*, Booklet. Charleston, 1983 • Special Dedication Issue, *St. Francis Hospital Messenger* (June 1986).

St. George's Chapel: "Old Norborne Parish." *Magazine of the Jefferson County Historical Society* (1976 & 1979).

St. Joseph Settlement: Cometti–*Thirty-Fifth* • Sedosky, Dorothy. "Rosbys Rock," in *History of Marshall County*. Marshall County Historical Society, 1984.

St. Marys: Pemberton, Robert L. *A History of Pleasants County*. St. Marys: Oracle Press, 1929 • Pleasants County Historical Society. *History of Pleasants County to 1980*. Dallas: Taylor Pub., 1980.

Salem International University: Bond, S. Orestes. *The Light of the Hills*. Charleston: WV Education Foundation, 1960 • Smith, Myron J. *100 Years of Opportunity: A Pictorial History of Salem College*. Marceline, MO: Walsworth Press, 1988.

John Peter Salling: Batman, Richard. "The Odyssey of John Peter Salley." *Virginia Cavalcade* (Summer 1981) • Harrison, Fairfax. "The Virginians on the Ohio and the Mississippi in 1742." *Virginia Magazine of History and Biography* (Apr. 1922).

Salt Industry: Stealey, John E. III. *The Antebellum Kanawha Salt Business and Western Markets*. Lexington: UPK, 1993 • Stealey. "Virginia's Mercantile-Manufacturing Frontier: Dickinson & Shrewsbury and the Great Kanawha Salt Industry." *Virginia Magazine of History and Biography* (Oct. 1993) • Stealey, ed. *Kanawhan Prelude to Nineteenth-Century Monopoly in the United States: The Virginia Salt Combinations*. Richmond: Virginia Historical Society, 2000.

Salt Sulphur Springs: Cohen, Stan. *Historic Springs of the Virginias*. Charleston: PHPC, 1981 • Morton, Oren F. *A History of Monroe County*. Staunton, VA: McClure, 1916. Reprint, Regional Pub. Co., 1974.

Saltpeter Mining: Comstock–*Encyclopedia*, vol. 19, 1976 • Hauer, Peter. "Saltpeter Mining in West Virginia." *Goldenseal* (July–Sept. 1975).

Salvation Army: Satterlee, Allen. *Sweeping through the Land: A History of the Salvation Army in the Southern United States*. Atlanta: The Salvation Army Supplies, 1989 • Salvation Army District & Regional Records. The Salvation Army Archives & Research Center. Salvation Army National Headquarters, Alexandria, VA.

Sandy Creek Expedition: "Preston's Journal of the Sandy Creek Expedition." Draper mss., IQQ 96–123, State Historical Society of Wisconsin. Reprinted in Cometti–*Thirty-Fifth*.

Chris Sarandon: Terman, Tim. "Distinguished Alumni Recall WVU." *WVU Alumni Magazine* (Summer 1998).

Abel Morgan Sarjent: Eddy, Richard. *Universalism in America*, vol. 1. Boston: Universalist Pub., 1886 • Hildreth, Samuel P. "Biographical Sketches of the Early Physicians of Marietta, Ohio." *The New England Historical & Genealogical Register*, vol. 2 (1849) • Hildreth. "Outlines for Biography of Dr. McIntosh." Manuscript Collection, Slack Research Collections, Dawes Memorial Library, Marietta College, Marietta, OH • *The Holy Bible*. London, 1698. Blennerhassett Island Historical State Park archives, Parkersburg (Personal bible of the Rev. Sarjent with extensive autobiographical & genealogical entries in his hand).

Savage Grant: Collections. James E. Morrow Library, Marshall University, Special Collections Dept. • DeHass, Wills. *History of the Early Settlement and Indian Wars of Western Virginia*. Philadelphia: H. Hoblitzell, 1851 • Wallace, George S. *Cabell County Annals and Families*. Richmond: Garrett & Massie, 1935.

Sawmills: Brooks, A. B. *Forestry and Wood Industries*. Morgantown: WVGES, 1910 • Clarkson–*Tumult*.

Scary Creek, Battle of: Lowry, Terry. *The Battle of Scary Creek*. Charleston: PHPC, 1982.

Fred Schaus: Julian, Norman. *Legends: Profiles in West Virginia University Basketball*. Morgantown: Trillium Pub., 1998 • *WVU Basketball Media Guide*, 1998–99.

Scotch-Irish: Kennedy, Billy. *The Scots-Irish in the Shenandoah Valley*. Londonderry, England: Causeway Press, 1996 • Leyburn, James G. *The Scotch-Irish: A Social History*. Chapel Hill: UNC Press, 1962. Reprint, Chapel Hill, UNC, 1978 • Rice–*Allegheny Frontier*.

Scotts Run: Ward, Brian, ed. *A New Deal for America*. Arthurdale: Arthurdale Heritage, Inc., 1995 • Scotts Run edition. *WVH* (1994) • Lewis, Ronald L. "'Why Don't You Bake Bread?' Franklin Trubee and the Scotts Run Reciprocal Economy." *Goldenseal* (Spring 1989).

Scrip: Athey, Lou. "The Company Store in Coal Town Culture." *Labor's Heritage* (Jan. 1990) • Massay, Glenn F. "Legislators, Lobbyists and Loopholes: Coal Mining Legislation in West Virginia, 1875–1901." *WVH* (Apr. 1971).

Secondary School Activities Commission: Carter, Warren, WVSSAC Exec. Sec. Interview by author. 4/7/1999 • Secondary School Activities Commission. *Rules & Regulations Handbook*, 1998.

Sectionalism and the Virginias: Ambler, Charles Henry. "The Cleavage Between Eastern and Western Virginia." *American Historical Review* (1909–1910) • Ambler. *Sectionalism in Virginia from 1776 to 1861*. Chicago: University of Chicago Press, 1910 • Gaines, Francis P. Jr. "The Virginia Constitutional Convention of 1850–51." Ph.D. diss., University of Virginia, 1950.

Senate: Atkinson, George W. "Legislative History of West Virginia," in James M. Callahan, ed., *Semi-Centennial History of West Virginia*. Charleston: Semi-Centennial Commission, 1913 • *Blue Book*, 2001.

Seneca: Richter, Daniel K. *The Ordeal of the Longhouse: The Peoples of the Iroquois League in the Era of European Colonization*. Chapel Hill: UNC Press, 1992 • Wallace, Anthony F. C. *The Death and Rebirth of the Seneca*. New York: Knopf, 1969.

Seneca Glass Company: Page, Bob & Dale Frederiksen. *Seneca Glass Company 1891–1983*. Greensboro, NC: Page-Frederiksen Pub., 1995 • Six, Dean. "Decorating Techniques at Seneca Glass." *Glass Collector's Digest* (Apr.–May 1991).

Seneca Rocks: Venable, Norma Jean. *Seneca Rocks and Spruce Knob*. Morgantown: WVU Extension Service, 1992.

The Seneca Trail: Cobb, William H. *Indian Trails, Frontier Forts, Revolutionary Soldiers and Pioneers of Randolph County*. Elkins, 1923 • Fansler, Homer F. *History of Tucker County*. Parsons: McClain, 1962 • Maxwell, Hu. "The Seneca Indian Trail." *Magazine of History & Biography* (1954). Elkins: Randolph County Historical Society.

Serpent Handling: Leonard, Bill, ed. *Christianity in Appalachia*. Knoxville: UT Press, 1999 • Daugherty & Ambrose, producers. "Saga of the Serpent Handlers," three videos. Cultural Center Library, Charleston. WVLC Series, 1981.

Mary Lee Settle: Garrett, George P. *Understanding Mary Lee Settle*. Columbia: University of South Carolina Press, 1988 • Rosenberg, Brian. *Mary Lee Settle's Beulah Quintet: The Price of Freedom*. Baton Rouge: LSU Press, 1991 • Settle, Mary Lee. *Addie: A Memoir*. Columbia: University of South Carolina Press, 1998.

Seventh Day Baptists: Randolph, Corliss Fitz. *A History of Seventh Day Baptists in West Virginia*. Plainfield, NJ: American Sabbath Tract Society, 1905. Reprint, Heritage Books, 1997 • Wardin, Albert. *Baptists Around the World: A Comprehensive Handbook*. Nashville: Broadman & Holmes Pub., 1995.

Sewell Mountain: Clarkson–*Tumult* • USGS Maps, 7.5 Minute Series, WV quadrangles: Corliss, Danese, Fayetteville, Meadow Bridge, Meadow Creek, Rainelle, Thurmond & Winona.

Shale Barrens: Core, Earl L. *Vegetation of West Virginia*. Parsons: McClain, 1966 • Keener, C. S. "Distribution and Biohistory of the Endemic Flora of the Mid-Appalachian Shale Barrens." *Botanical Review* 49 (1983).

Shannondale Springs: Theriault, William D. "Shannondale." *WVH* (1998)

Shape-Note Singing: Cabbell, Edward. "Where Could I Go but to the Lord? Shape-note Singing Among Blacks in Southern West Virginia." *Goldenseal* (Winter 1981) • Jackson, George Pullen. *White Spirituals in the Southern Uplands: The Story of the Fasola Folk*. Chapel Hill: UNC Press, 1933. Reprint, Dover, 1965 • Welch, Jack & Alice F. Welch. "Shape-note Singing in Appalachia." *Goldenseal* (Apr.–Sept. 1978).

Sam Shaw: Obituary. *Moundsville Daily Echo*, 12/23 & 26/1995.

Shawnee: Clark, Jerry E. *The Shawnee*. Lexington: UPK, 1993 • Dowd, Gregory Evans. *A Spirited Resistance: The North American Indian Struggle for Unity, 1745–1815*. Baltimore: Johns Hopkins University Press, 1992 • Howard, James H. *Shawnee! The Ceremonialism of a Native Indian Tribe and its Cultural Background*. Athens, OH: Ohio University Press, 1981.

Sheltering Arms Hospital: Rice, Otis & Wayne Williams. *The Sheltering Arms Hospital*. Charleston: WV Educational Services, 1990.

Shenandoah Bloomery: "Iron Industry in Jefferson County." *Jefferson County Historical Society Magazine* (Dec. 1964) • Wayland, John W. *Hopewell Friend History, 1734–1934, Frederick County, Virginia*. Strasburg, VA: Shenandoah Pub. House, 1936.

Shenandoah River: Davis, Julia. *The Shenandoah*. New York: Farrar & Rinehart, 1945 • Strother, David Hunter. "Artists' Excursion over the Baltimore & Ohio Rail Road." *Harper's* (June 1859).

Heyward Shepherd: Johnson, Mary. "An 'Ever Present Bone of Contention': The Heyward Shepherd Memorial." *WVH* (1997).

Shepherd University: Ambler–*Education* • Bushong, Millard K. *Historic Jefferson County*. Boyce, VA: Carr Pub., 1972 • Slonaker, Arthur Gordon. *A History of Shepherd College*. Parsons: McClain, 1967.

Shinnston Tornado: Finlayson, John L. *Shinnston Tornado*. New York: Hobson Book Press, 1946 • Lowther, Martha A. "The Shinnston Tornado." *Goldenseal* (Summer 1998) • Poling, Lena E. *A History of the City of Shinnston*. Parsons: McClain, 1975.

Hugh I. Shott: Clipping file, Eastern Regional Archives • *Daily Telegraph Semi-Centennial Edition*, 12/12/1939 • Matthews, Garret. "The Shott

Family," (unpub. ms.). Eastern Regional Archives • Mercer County Historical Society. *Mercer County History 1984*. Marceline, MO: Walsworth Pub., 1985 • Miller & Maxwell, vol. 2 • Obituary. *Daily Telegraph*, 10/13/1953 • Shott Papers. WV&RHC.

Showboats: Graham, Phillip. *Showboats*. Austin: University of Texas Press, 1951.

Silver Bridge Collapse: "Silver Bridge Collapse, after Action Report." Huntington District, U.S. Army Corps of Engineers. 1968.

Robert W. Simmons: Ambler–*Education* • "Children Skated at 5th and Market Sts." *Parkersburg Sentinel*, 9/12/1954 • "Death of Robert Simmons." *Parkersburg Daily Sentinel*, 1/16/1892 • *Hardesty's*, vol. 8 • Lacy, Ellen C., great-granddaughter of Robert W. Simmons. Interview by author. 6/21/1983.

Sinks of Gandy: Preble, Jack. *The Sinks of Gandy Creek*. Parsons: McClain, 1969 • Strother, David H. "The Mountains." *Harper's* 45 (1872) • Strother. "The Mountains." *Harper's* 46 (1873) • Strother. Jim Comstock, ed. *Porte Crayon Sampler*. Richwood, 1974.

Hubert Skidmore: Brenni, Vito J. *West Virginia Authors: A Bibliography*. 2nd ed., rev. by Joyce Binder. Morgantown: WVU Library, 1968 • Comstock–*Encyclopedia*, vol. 20, 1976 • Skidmore, Hubert. *Hawks Nest*. New York: Doubleday/Doron & Co., 1941.

Slavery: Stealey, John E. III. "Slavery in West Virginia," in Randall M. Miller & John D. Smith, eds. *Dictionary of Afro-American Slavery*. Westport, CT: Praeger, 1997 • Stealey. *The Antebellum Kanawha Salt Business and Western Markets*. Lexington: UPK, 1993 • Stealey. "The Freedmen's Bureau in West Virginia." *WVH* (Jan.–Apr. 1978).

Hulett Carlson Smith: Canfield, John A., ed. *State Papers and Public Addresses of Hulett C. Smith*. Charleston, 1969 • Morgan–*Governors* • Rice & Brown • Wood, Jim. *Raleigh County*. Beckley: J. Wood, 1994.

Ada "Bricktop" Smith: *Black Women in America: An Historical Encyclopedia*. Bloomington: Indiana University Press, 1993 • *Newsweek* (2/13/1984) • Smith, Ada & James Haskins. *Bricktop*. New York: Atheneum 1983.

Smoke Hole: Calhoun, H. M. "A Trip through Smoke Hole." *WV Review* (Oct. 1926) • Shreve, D. Bardon. *A Place Called Smoke Hole*. Fredericksburg, VA: Fredericksburg Press, 1997 • Sites, Roy S. "Geology of the Smoke Hole Region of West Virginia." *Southeastern Geology* (Dec. 1973) • WV Writers' Project. *Smoke Hole and its People: A Social-Ethnic Study*. Charleston: WPA, 1940.

Smoke Hole Lodge: Buckingham, Nancy. "Smoke Hole Lodge Offers the Luxury of Wondering." *WWV* (Mar. 1989).

Smoot Theatre: Starcher, Lisa. "Rebirth of Parkersburg's Historic Smoot Theatre." *WWV* (Apr. 1993).

Snakes: Green, N. B. & T. K. Pauley. *Amphibians & Reptiles in West Virginia*. Pittsburgh: UPP, 1987 • "Snakes of West Virginia," Pamphlet. WVDNR, Elkins.

Sam Snead: Conte, Robert S. *The History of The Greenbrier*. Charleston: PHPC, 1998.

Snowshoe Mountain Resort: Deike, George H. III. *Logging South Cheat: The History of the Snowshoe Resort Lands*. Youngstown, OH: Trebco, 1978.

Socialist Party: Barkey, Frederick A. "The Socialist Party in West Virginia from 1898 to 1920: A Study in Working Class Radicalism." Ph.D. diss. (unpub.), University of Pittsburgh, 1971 • Cresswell, Stephen. "When the Socialists Ran Star City." *WVH* (1993).

Soils of West Virginia: General Soil Map of West Virginia. USDA Soil Conservation Service. Morgantown, 1979 • *Soil Taxonomy: A Basic System of Soil Classification for Making and Interpreting Soil Surveys*. Agricultural Handbook No. 436, USDA Natural Resources Conservation Service. Washington: GPO, 1999 • *Land Resource Regions and Major Land Resource Areas of the United States*. Agricultural Handbook 296, USDA Soil Conservation Service. Washington: GPO, 1981.

Sorghum Molasses: Davidson, Alan. *The Oxford Companion to Food*. Oxford: Oxford University Press, 1999.

The South Branch: Henshall, James A. *Book of the Black Bass*. Cincinnati: Caxton Press, 1923 • Hyde, Arnout Jr. & Ken Sullivan. *The Potomac: A Nation's River*. Charleston: Cannon Graphics, 1993.

South Charleston Mound: McMichael, Edward V. & Oscar L. Mairs. "Excavation of the Murad Mound, Kanawha County, West Virginia, and an Analysis of Kanawha Valley Mounds," in *Report of Archaeological Investigations No. 1*. Morgantown: WVGES, 1969 • Thomas, Cyrus.

Report on the Mound Excavations of the Bureau of Ethnology. Washington: Smithsonian Institution Press, 1894. Reprint, 1985.

Southern West Virginia Community and Technical College: Rice & Brown.

Red Sovine: Tribe–*Jamboree*.

Spanish-American War: Cohen, Stan. *Images of the Spanish-American War*. Missoula, MT: PHPC, 1998.

Anne Spencer: Greene, J. Lee. *Time's Unfading Garden: Anne Spencer's Life and Poetry*. Baton Rouge: LSU Press, 1977.

Spencer State Hospital: "Spencer State Hospital." *Roane County Journal* (Winter 1994) • Comstock–*Encyclopedia*, vol. 20, 1976 • Walbrown, Donna J. *Roane County, West Virginia Family History 1989*. Marceline, MO: Walsworth Pub., 1990.

Sports: Huff, Doug. *Sports in West Virginia*. Virginia Beach: Donning Co., 1979 • Kessler, Kent. *Hail West Virginians!* Weston: George L. Bland, 1959.

Alexander Spotswood: Conley, Phil & William Doherty. *West Virginia*. Charleston: Education Foundation, 1974 • Dodson, Leonidas. *Alexander Spotswood: Governor of Colonial Virginia, 1710–1722*. Philadelphia: UP Press, 1932 • Lewis, Virgil A. *History of West Virginia in Two Parts*. Philadelphia: Hubbard Brothers, 1889.

Spruce Knob: Venable, Norma Jean. *Seneca Rocks and Spruce Knob*. Morgantown: WVU Extension Service, 1992.

Harley O. Staggers Sr.: Anson, Cherrill A. *Harley O. Staggers*. Washington: Grossman Pub., 1972 • "Ex-Congressman Staggers Dies at 84." *Gazette*, 8/21/1991 • *Blue Book*, 1980.

Stanaford, Battle of: Jones, Mary Harris. *The Autobiography of Mother Jones*. Chicago: Charles Kerr Pub., 1925 • Sullivan, Ken, ed. *Goldenseal Book of the West Virginia Mine Wars*. Charleston: PHPC, 1991 • Wood, Jim. *Raleigh County*. Beckley: J. Wood, 1994.

Buddy Starcher: Tribe–*Jamboree*.

Samuel Starks: Bickley, Ancella R. "From Samuel W. Starks to the Sojourners." *Daily Mail*, 2/27/1987 • *Charleston Advocate* 7/11/1907, 2/14/1907, 4/7/1908, 1/27/1910, 11/23/1911 • Collins, Rodney. "Nomination of the Starks House to the National Register of Historic Places," in Ancella R. Bickley, ed., *Our Mount Vernons: Historic Register Listings of Sites Significant to the Black History of West Virginia*. Huntington: Carter G. Woodson Memorial Foundation & Drinko Academy, 1997.

Starland Theatre: Keller, Michael. "Going to the Drive-in." *Goldenseal* (Summer 1995) • Tuckwiller, Tara. "Living in Starland." *Sunday Gazette-Mail*, 7/1/2001.

Blaze Starr: Starr, Blaze & Huey Perry. *Blaze Starr: My Life*. New York: Praeger Publishers, 1974.

State Fair: Anderson, Belinda. "Going to the State Fair with the Tuckwillers." *Goldenseal* (Summer 1999) • "State Fair of West Virginia: 75 Years: West Virginia's Finest Tradition Continues." *WWV* (Aug. 1999).

State Parks: Harr, Milton. *The CCC Camps in West Virginia*. Charleston: Milton Harr, 1992 • *History of State Parks*.

State Police: Cole, Merle T. "Birth of the West Virginia State Police, 1919–1921." *WVH* (Fall 1981) • Cole. "The Department of Special Deputy Police, 1917–1919." *WVH* (Summer 1983) • Cole. "Martial Law in West Virginia." *WVH* (Winter 1982) • *Michie's West Virginia Code*, Chapter 15, Article 2. Charlottesville: Lexis Pub. • Powers, Senior Trooper Jay C., WVSP Public Affairs Officer. Interview by author. 5/6/2002.

Staunton-Parkersburg Turnpike: Ambler, Charles H. *A History of Transportation in the Ohio Valley*. Westport, CT: Greenwood Press, 1931 • Boughter, I. F. "Internal Improvements in Northwestern Virginia." Ph.D. diss., University of Pittsburgh, 1930 • Taylor, George R. *The Transportation Revolution*. New York: Rinehart, 1951.

Eleanor Steber: Steber, Eleanor, with Marcia Sloat. *Eleanor Steber: An Autobiography*. Ridgeway, NJ: Wordsworth, 1992 • Barber, Samuel. *Vanessa*, op. 32. Metropolitan Opera with Eleanor Steber in the Title Role, 1958. RCA Victor Gold Seal, CD 7899-2-RG.

Steel Industry: Javersak, David T. *History of Weirton*. Virginia Beach: Donning Co., 1999 • Lieber, James B. *Friendly Takeover: How an Employee Buyout Saved a Steel Town*. New York: Viking, 1995 • May, Earl Chapin. *Principio to Wheeling, 1715–1945: A Pageant of Iron and Steel*. New York: Harper & Brothers, 1945 • Martin, Louis C. "Causes and Consequences of the 1909–1910 Steel Strike in the Wheeling District." M.A. thesis, WVU, 1999.

Adam Stephen: Doherty, William T. *Berkeley County U.S.A.: A Bicentennial History*. Parsons: McClain, 1972 • Evans, Willis F. *History of Berkeley County*. Martinsburg, 1928 • West Virginia Antiquities Commission. Annual Report. 1972.

James McNeil Stephenson: Miller & Maxwell, vol. 3 • Sturm, Philip W. *A River to Cross: Bicentennial History of Wood County*. State College, PA: Jostens Printing Co., 1999.

William E. Stevenson: Allen, Bernard L. *Parkersburg: A Bicentennial History*. State College, PA: Jostens Printing Co., 1985 • Casdorph, Paul D. "The 1872 Liberal Republican Campaign in West Virginia." *WVH* (July 1968) • Morgan–*Governors* • *National Cyclopaedia of American Biography*. New York: J. T. White, 1892.

J. L. Stifel & Sons: Javersak, David T. *Stifel: An Historical Perspective of the Stifel Family in Wheeling*. Wheeling: J. L. Stifel & Sons, 1988.

Stony River: Clarkson–*Tumult* • Lewis, Gerald. "Status of Stony River Watershed, Grant County, West Virginia," Report. WVDNR, 1970 • Lewis, Thomas. *The Fairfax Line: Thomas Lewis's Journal of 1746*. New Market, VA: Henkel Press, 1925.

Storer College: Baxter, Norman. *History of the Freewill Baptist Church*. Rochester, NY: American Baptist Historical Society, 1957 • Mongin, Alfred. "A College in Secessia." *WVH* (July 1962) • Rasmussen, Barbara. "Sixty-Four Edited Letters of the Founders of Storer College." M.A. thesis, WVU, 1986.

Strange Creek Legend: Bell, C. W. "A Strange Man in a Strange Land." *Braxton Democrat*, 1/6/1927. Reprinted, 10/2/1987 • Byrne–*Tale* • Sutton, John D. *History of Braxton County and Central West Virginia*. Sutton: Sutton Press, 1919. Reprint, McClain, 1967.

P. D. Strausbaugh: Strausbaugh, P. D. & Earl L. Core. *Flora of West Virginia*. Morgantown, 1964. 2nd edition, 4 vols. Morgantown: WVU, 1970–77.

Strawberry Festival: Tenney, Noel W. "Strawberry Festival Begins in 1936." "Historically Speaking Sesquicentennial Celebration Column," *Record Delta*, 9/14/01.

Streetcar Lines: Ellifritt, Duane. "Early Engineering in the Hills." *West Virginia Hillbilly*, 7/1/1978 • Hilton, George W. & John F. Due. *The Electric Interurban Railways in America*. Stanford, CA: Stanford University Press, 1960. Reprint, Stanford University, 2000 • Maguire, Steve. "The Last Interurbans." *Railroad Magazine* (Feb. 1955) • O'Connell, John. *Popular Mechanics Railroad Album*. Chicago: Popular Mechanics, 1954.

Mel Street: Tribe–*Jamboree*.

David Hunter Strother: Cuthbert, John A. & Jessie Poesch. *David Hunter Strother: "One of the Best Draughtsmen the Country Possesses."* Morgantown: WVU Press, 1997 • Eby, Cecil D. Jr. *"Porte Crayon: The Life of David Hunter Strother."* Chapel Hill: UNC Press, 1960 • Eby, ed. *A Virginia Yankee in the Civil War: The Diaries of David Hunter Strother*. Chapel Hill: UNC Press, 1961 • Poesch, Jessie. "David Hunter Strother: Mountain People, Mountain Images," in Judy L. Larsen, ed., *Graphic Arts in the South: Proceedings of the 1990 American Print Conference*. Fayetteville, AK: University of Arkansas Press, 1993.

John Stuart: Cole, J. R. *History of Greenbrier County*. Lewisburg: J. R. Cole, 1917 • Cometti–*Thirty-Fifth* • Hale, John P. *Trans-Allegheny Pioneers*. Cincinnati: Graphic, 1886. Reprint, R. I. Steele, 1971 • Rice & Brown.

Boyd B. Stutler: Boyd Stutler Collection, State Archives • *WV Review* (Jan. 1937).

Joe Stydahar: Halas, George Stanley. *Halas*. New York: McGraw-Hill, 1979.

Leon Sullivan: Sullivan, Leon H. *Alternatives to Despair*. Valley Forge: Judson Press, 1972 • Sullivan. *America is Theirs and Other Poems*. New York: Sayle & Wimmer, 1948 • Sullivan. *Build, Brother, Build*. Philadelphia: Macae Smith Co., 1969 • Sullivan. *Moving Mountains: The Principles and Purposes of Leon Sullivan*. Valley Forge: Judson Press, 1998.

Summers County: Applegarth, J. D., et al. *Bulletin of the Society for Pennsylvania Archaeology* (May 1978) • Lively, Lester. *History of Summers County*. Hinton, ca. 1963 • Miller, James H. *History of Summers County*. Hinton: J. H. Miller, 1908.

George William Summers: "Biographical Sketch of Judge George W. Summers," in George W. Atkinson, *History of Kanawha County*. Charleston: *WV Journal*, 1876 • "Biographical Sketch of Judge George W.

Summers," in W. S. Laidley, *History of Charleston and Kanawha County*. Chicago: Richmond-Arnold Pub., 1911 • Ryon, Ann Isabell. "The Summers Family." *Historical Magazine* (July 1903).

Sumner School: Browne, Rae. "Sumner School," in Friends of Blennerhassett, *The Island Packet* (Fall 1995) • "A Prominent Parkersburger of Civil War Times," in H. E. Matheny, *Wood County W. Va. in Civil War Times*. Parkersburg: Trans-Allegheny Books, 1987.

Supreme Court of Appeals: Mooney, Christopher Z., et al. *West Virginia's State Government: The Legislative, Executive, and Judicial Branches*. Morgantown: WVU Institute for Public Affairs, 1993.

Surface Mining: Bailey, Kenneth R. "Development of Surface Mine Legislation 1939–1967." *WVH* (Apr. 1969) • Munn, Robert F. "The First 50 Years of Strip Mining in West Virginia, 1916–1965." *WVH* (Oct. 1973).

Howard Sutherland: Casdorph, P. D. "Howard Sutherland's 1920 Bid for the Presidency." *WVH* (Oct. 1973) • *Biographical Directory of the American Congress, 1774–1961*. Washington: GPO, 1961.

Swan Lands: Carvell, Kenneth L. "The German Settlement at St. Clara." *WWV* (Apr. 2000) • Stutler, Boyd B. "Joseph H. Diss Debar–Prophet, Colonizer." *WV Review* (Dec. 1931) • Summers, George W. "Owned a Sixth of W. Va., Died in Prison for Debt," in "Pages from the Past." Comstock–*Encyclopedia*, vol. 21, 1974.

Sweet Springs: Cohen, Stan. *Historic Springs of the Virginias*. Charleston: PHPC, 1981 • Johnson, Rody. "A Lewis Family Legacy: Old Sweet Springs." *Goldenseal* (Summer 2000) • Morton, Oren. *A History of Monroe County*. Staunton, VA: McClure, 1916 • Price, Paul, et al. *Springs of West Virginia*. Morgantown: WVGES, 1936.

Swinburn, Ralph: *The Baptist Banner*, 6/26/1895 • Summers, George W. "Ralph Swinburn–Pioneer in Railway Development," *WV Review* (Jan. 1934).

Synthetic Rubber: "Butadiene and Styrene for Buna S Synthetic Rubber from Grain Alcohol." Carbide & Carbon Chemicals Corp., Union Carbide & Carbon Corp., NY, 1943 • "Synthetic Times–In the Great Kanawha Valley." United States Rubber Co., Institute, WV, 1943 • "Report on the Rubber Program, 1940–1945." Rubber Reserve Co., Washington, 1945.

201st Field Artillery/Infantry: Bailey, Kenneth R. *Mountaineers are Free: A History of the West Virginia National Guard*. St. Albans: Harless Printing, 1978 • Lineage & Honors, 201st Artillery (First West Virginia). U.S. Dept. of the Army.

Tackett's Fort: Cohen–*Kanawha Images* • DeGruyter, Julius. *Kanawha Spectator*, vol. 1. Charleston: Jarrett Printing, 1953.

William Purviance Tams Jr.: Sullivan–*Coal Men*.

Tanneries: Hoover, Edgar M. *Location Theory and the Shoe and Leather Industry*. Cambridge, MA: Harvard University Press, 1937 • "Tanning in the Virginias." *The Shoe & Leather Reporter*, 2/25/1892.

Tax Limitation Amendment: Casdorph, P. D. *Youth Education in West Virginia*. Charleston, 1975 • Gatrell, A. S. "Herman Guy Kump and the West Virginia Financial Crisis of 1933." *WVH* (Spring 1981).

Taxation: Due, John F. & John L. Mikesell. *Sales Taxation State and Local Structure and Administration*. Washington: Urban Institute Press, 1994 • Fox, Fred L. *Fifteenth Biennial Report, State Tax Commissioner*. Charleston: Jarrett Printing, 1934 • Hall, Grant P. *Tenth Biennial Report, State Tax Commissioner*. Charleston: Jarrett Printing, 1924 • *Michie's West Virginia Code, Annotated, Volume 4*. Chapter 11, Article 1–130. Charlottesville: Lexis Pub., 1999 • "State and Local Government Finances: 1997–1998." U.S. Census Bureau, 2001 • State of Washington Dept. of Revenue. *Comparative State and Local Taxes: 1998*. Olympia, 2001 • WV Dept. of Tax & Revenue, Research Division. "A History of Taxation by the State of West Virginia Fiscal Years 1970–1989," (unpub. ms.) • WV Legislative Auditor's Office. *Digest of Revenue Sources in West Virginia*. Charleston, 2000.

Taylor County: Brinkman, Charles. *A History of Taylor County*. Grafton: Taylor County Historical & Genealogical Society, 1989 • Daley, Scott W. "From Turnpikes to Railroads: Antebellum Transportation Improvements and Community Development in Taylor County, Virginia." M.A. thesis, WVU, 1999 • Shingleton, George A. *Grafton and Taylor County during the Civil War Days and Points of Interest*. Grafton: Taylor County Historical & Genealogical Society, 1961.

Grace Martin Taylor: Cuthbert, John A. *Early Art and Artists in West Virginia*. Morgantown: WVU Press, 2000.

Sam Taylor: Wells, Sandy. "A Gun, a Uniform and a Love of Adventure." *Gazette*, 12/26/1993.

Teachers' Strike: Brunner, Bob. *The Caperton Years: 1989–1993*. Beckley: BJW Printing, 1997 • *Gazette*, 3/1990 • Rice, Otis K. & Stephen W. Brown. *The Mountain State: An Introduction to West Virginia*. Charleston: WV Historical Education Foundation, 1997.

Teays River: Fleshman, Nikki & Dewey D. Sanderson. "The Ancestral and Modern Mud River Valley," in *Proceedings of the West Virginia Academy of Science*, 1998 • Melhorn, Wilton N. & John P. Kempton, eds. *Geology and Hydrogeology of the Teays-Mahomet Bedrock Valley System*. Boulder: Geological Society of America, 1991 • Tight, W. G. *Drainage Modifications in Southeastern Ohio and Adjacent Parts of West Virginia and Kentucky*. USGS Professional Paper 12. USGS, 1903.

Textile Industry: Jenrette, Jerra. "'There's No Damn Reason for It–It's Just our Policy': Labor-Management Conflict in Martinsburg, West Virginia's Textile and Garment Industries." Ph.D. diss., WVU, 1996 • Johnston, Wilbur. *Weaving a Common Thread: A History of the Woolen Industry in the Top of the Shenandoah Valley*. Winchester: Winchester-Frederick County Historical Society, 1990 • Rice & Brown.

Frank Thomas: Keefer, Louis E. "Flying Frank Thomas: 'Just Like a Preacher with the Calling.'" *Goldenseal* (Summer 1992) • Thomas, Frank. *It is this Way with Men Who Fly*. Parsons: McClain, 1978.

Rod Thorn: Julian, Norman. *Legends: Profiles in West Virginia University Basketball*. Morgantown: Trillium Pub., 1998 • *WVU Basketball Media Guide*, 1998–99.

Thurmond: Sullivan, Ken. *Thurmond: A New River Community*. Glen Jean: Eastern National Park & Monument Assn., 1989.

W. D. Thurmond: Witschey, Walter R. T. *The Thurmonds of Virginia*. Richmond: Gatewood Co., 1978.

Thurmond's Rangers: Weaver, Jeffrey C. *Thurmond's Partisan Rangers*. Lynchburg: H. E. Howard, 1993 • Witschey, Walter R. T. *The Thurmonds of Virginia*. Richmond: Gatewood Co., 1978.

Timbering and Logging: Blackhurst, Warren E. *Riders of the Flood*. New York: Vantage Press, 1954 • Clarkson, Roy B. *On Beyond Leatherbark: The Cass Saga*. Parsons: McClain, 1990 • Clarkson–*Tumult*.

Tobacco: Conley, Phil & Boyd B. Stutler. *West Virginia: Yesterday and Today*. Charleston: Education Foundation, 1952 • Sullivan, Ken "We Lived Good Back Then." *Goldenseal* (Fall 1989) • "West Virginia's Tobacco Heritage: Nourished with Pride," Pamphlet. Washington: Tobacco Institute, ca. 1981.

Joseph Tomlinson: Bartlett, Margaret W. H. "The Joseph Tomlinson Family." *The Pioneer Daughter* (Apr. 1902) • Hildreth, Samuel P. "Biographical Sketch of Isaac Williams." *The American Pioneer* (1842) • Thomas, Virginia H., comp. "Miscellaneous Notes of the Tomlinson Family." Henderson Family Papers. Henderson Hall, Williamstown, WV • Tomlinson, A. B. "American Antiquities at Grave Creek." *The American Pioneer* (1843) • Tomlinson. "First Settlement of Grave Creek." *The American Pioneer* (1843) • Tomlinson. "Mr. Tomlinson's Letter." *The American Pioneer* (1843).

Tories: Maxwell, Hu. *History of Randolph County*. Morgantown: Acme Pub., 1898 • Morton, Oren F. *A History of Pendleton County*. Dayton, VA: Ruebush-Elkins Co., 1910 • Wilson, Howard M. *Great Valley Patriots: Western Virginia in the Struggle for Liberty*. Verona, VA: McClure Press, 1976.

Fred Martin Torrey: Hamlin, Gladys E. *The Sculpture of Fred and Mabel Torrey*. Alhambra, CA: Borden Pub. Co., 1969.

Tourism: Fitsch, A. *Ecotourism in Appalachia*. Lexington: UPK, 2004 • Hollenhorst, S. & P. Salstrom. " Keeping the wild in Wonderful West Virginia." *West Virginia Public Affairs Reporter* (Summer 1994) • Wang, T., et al. "Growing Heritage Tourism in the Mountain State." *West Virginia Public Affairs Reporter* (Winter 2001).

Toymaking: Comstock–*Encyclopedia*, vol. 1., 1976 • Schnacke, Dick. *American Folk Toys*. Baltimore: Penguin Books, 1973 • Wigginton, Eliot. *Foxfire 6*. Garden City, NY: Anchor Press/Doubleday, 1980.

Toyota: Finn, Scott. "Toyota Makes it Official: Buffalo Plant to Expand at Friday Announcement." *Gazette*, 1/27/2001 • Ward, Ken Jr. "Toyota Looks at Site in Putnam for Plant." *Gazette*, 1/1/1996.

Trapping: Brown, Cliff. "Endangered Tradition." *WWV* (Oct. 1997).

Traveller: Broun, Thomas. "General Robert E. Lee's War Horse," in Southern Historical Society, *Southern Historical Society Papers*, vol. 35.

Richmond: Virginia Historical Society, 1907 • Craven, Avery, ed. *To Markie: The Letters of Robert E. Lee to Martha Custis Williams*. Cambridge: Harvard University Press, 1934 • Rhinesmith, W. Donald. "Traveller: 'Just the Horse for General Lee.'" *Virginia Cavalcade* (Summer 1983) • Stealey, John E. III. "Traveller." ms., 1962.

Tray Run Viaduct: Plowden, David. *Bridges: Spans of North America*. New York: W. W. Norton & Co., 2001 • Wiley, S. & A. Frederick. *A History of Preston County*. Baltimore: Genealogy Warehouse, 1998.

Treaty of Camp Charlotte: Downes, Randolph C. *Council Fires on the Upper Ohio: A Narrative of Indian Affairs in the Upper Ohio Valley until 1795*. Pittsburgh: UPP, 1968.

Treaty of Greenville: Bird, Harrison. *War for the West, 1790–1813*. New York: Oxford University Press, 1971.

Treaty of Hard Labor: Sosin, Jack M. *The Revolutionary Frontier, 1763–1783*. New York: Holt, Rinehart & Winston, 1967.

Treaty of Lancaster: Bailey, Kenneth P. *The Ohio Company of Virginia and the Westward Movement 1748–1792*. Glendale, CA: Arthur H. Clark Co., 1939. Reprint, Wennawoods Pub., 2000 • Mulkearn, Lois, ed. *George Mercer Papers Relating to the Ohio Company of Virginia*. Pittsburgh: UPP, 1954.

Treaty of Lochaber: Sosin, Jack M. *The Revolutionary Frontier, 1763–1783*. New York: Holt, Rinehart & Winston, 1967.

Treaty of Paris: Anderson, Fred. *Crucible of War: The Seven Years' War and the Fate of Empire in British North America*. New York: Knopf, 2000.

Trees: Clarkson–*Tumult* • Core, Earl L. *Vegetation of West Virginia*. Parsons: McClain, 1974 • Strausbaugh, P. D. & Earl L. Core. "Flora of West Virginia." *WVU Bulletin*. 1970.

W. W. Trent: Casdorph, P. D. *Youth Education in West Virginia*. 1975 • Trent, W. W. *Mountaineer Education: A Story of Education in West Virginia*. Charleston: Jarrett Printing, 1960.

William O. Trevey: Bragg, Melody. "The Reliable Bill Trevey: Glen Jean's Photographer." *Goldenseal* (Winter 1988).

The Trough: Kercheval–*Valley* • MacMaster, Richard K. *The History of Hardy County*. Moorefield: Hardy County Public Library, 1986 • Moore, Alvin Edward. *History of Hardy County of the Borderland*. Moorefield: *Moorefield Examiner*, 1963.

Tu-Endie-Wei: Anderson, Colleen. *The New West Virginia One-Day Trip Book*. McLean, VA: EPM Publications, 1998 • Comstock–*Encyclopedia*, vols. 10–11, 1976 • WPA–*Guide*.

Tucker County: Fansler, Homer Floyd. *History of Tucker County*. Parsons: McClain, 1962 • Long, Cleta M. *History of Tucker County*. Parsons: McClain, 1996.

Tug, Battle of the: *New York Times*, 5/1921 • *Gazette*, 5/1921 • Savage–*Thunder* • U.S. Senate. *West Virginia Coal Fields*. Hearings before the Committee on Education & Labor. United States Senate. 67th Congress, first session, 2 vols. Washington: GPO, 1921–22.

Tumult on the Mountains: Clarkson–*Tumult*.

Turnpikes: Hunter, Robert F. "The Turnpike Movement in Virginia, 1816–1860." Ph.D. diss., Columbia University, 1957 • Peyton, Billy Joe. "To Make the Crooked Ways Straight and the Rough Ways Smooth: Surveying and Building America's First Interstate Highway." *American Civil Engineering History*. Washington: American Society of Civil Engineers Committee on History & Heritage, 2002.

Tuscarora Sandstone: Avary, K. L. "Play Sts: The Lower Silurian Tuscarora Sandstone Fractured Anticlinal Play," in J. B. Roen & B. J. Walker, eds., *Atlas of Major Appalachian Gas Plays*. Morgantown: WVGES, 1996 • Pettijohn, F. J., et al. "A Basic Discussion of Sedimentation," in *Sand & Sandstone*. Berlin: Springer-Verlag, 1973.

Tygart Dam and Lake: Johnson, Leland R. *The Headwaters District–A History of the Pittsburgh District*. U.S. Army Corps of Engineers, Pittsburgh District, 1978.

Tygart Valley Homesteads: Harris, Macel K. "The Tygart Valley Homesteads." *Davis & Elkins Historical Magazine* (Mar. 1950) • Rice, Donald L. *Randolph 200: A Bicentennial History*. Marceline, MO: Walsworth Pub., 1987 • Ross, Thomas R. *The Tygart Valley Homesteads, Dailey and Valley Bend*. Elkins: Randolph County Creative Arts Council, 1975.

Tygart Valley River: Heinz, H. J. *Report of Flood Commission*. Pittsburgh: State of Pennsylvania, 1912 • Reger, David B., WVGES. *Randolph County*. Morgantown: WVU, 1912.

Tyler County: Griffin, Dot R. *The First Petticoat Government*. Emory, VA: Granny Lavender Press, 1990 • McKain, David L. & Bernard L. Allen. *Where it all Began: The Story of the People and Places Where the Oil and Gas Industry Began*. Parkersburg: David L. McKain, 1994 • Tyler County Heritage & Historical Society. *History of Tyler County, West Virginia, to 1984*. Marceline, MO: Walsworth Pub., 1984.

Cecil H. Underwood: Morgan–*Governors* • *Stateline: A Newsletter for West Virginia State Government Employees*. (Feb. 1998).

Union Carbide Corporation: Daniels, George H., comp. "Timeline-A Chronology of Significant Events Relating to the History of Union Carbide Corporation." Danbury, CT: Carbide Retiree Corps, 1998 • Stief, Robert D. *A History of Union Carbide Corporation*. Danbury, CT: Union Carbide Retiree Corps, 1998.

Unitarian Universalism: Buehrens, John A. & F. Forrest Church. *A Chosen Faith*. Boston: Beacon Press, 1998.

United Bank: Rice, Otis K. *A Centennial of Strength: West Virginia Banks*. Charleston: WV Bankers Assn., 1991.

United Brethren: Behney, J. Bruce & Paul H. Eller. *The History of the Evangelical United Brethren Church*. Nashville: Abingdon Press, 1979 • Drury, A. W. *History of the Church of the United Brethren in Christ*. Dayton, OH: United Brethren Pub. House, 1924.

United Carbon Building: Reid, Kenneth, ed. "United Carbon Building, Charleston, West Virginia." *Pencil Points* (Oct. 1944) • Turner, Francis W. & Mary Eloise, eds. "United Carbon Builds a Home." *WV Review* (Oct. 1940).

United Mine Workers of America: Clark, Paul F. *The Miners' Fight for Democracy: Arnold Miller and the Reform of the United Mine Workers*. Ithaca, NY: Cornell Studies in Industrial & Labor Relations, 1981 • Dubofsky, Melvyn & Warren Van Tine. *John L. Lewis: A Biography*. New York: Quadrangle, 1977 • Fox, Maier B. *United We Stand*. Washington: UMWA, 1990 • Laslett, John H. M., ed. *The United Mine Workers of America: A Model of Industrial Solidarity?* University Park, PA: The Pennsylvania State University Press, 1996.

University of Charleston: Henderson, Mildred L. "Birth of a College." *WV Review* (Sept. 1942) • Knight, Frank A. "Morris Harvey: College with a Future." *WV Review* (Feb.–Mar. 1947) • Krebs, Frank J. *Where There is Faith: The Morris Harvey College Story, 1888–1970*. Charleston: Morris Harvey College, 1974.

Upshur County: Cutright, W. B. *History of Upshur County*. Buckhannon, 1907. Reprint, McClain, 1977 • Hornbeck, Betty. *Upshur Brothers of the Blue and the Gray*. Buckhannon: *Republican-Delta*, 1961. Reprint, McClain, 1967 • McWhorter, Lucullus Virgil. *The Border Settlers of Northwestern Virginia*. Hamilton, OH: Republican Pub. Co., 1915. Reprint, Comstock, 1974 • Morgan, French. *Yesterdays of Buckhannon and Upshur*. Buckhannon: *Republican-Delta*, 1963 • Tenney, Noel W. *From Camp Rock and Cabin to Courthouse*. Buckhannon: Upshur County Historical Society, 1984 • Tenney. "Historic Upshur County," Poster. Buckhannon: Upshur County Historical Society, 1991 • Tenney. *All About Upshur County: A Bibliography*. Buckhannon: Upshur County Historical Society, 1993.

U.S. Army Corps of Engineers: Johnson, Leland R. *Men, Mountains, and Rivers*. Washington: GPO, 1977 • Johnson. *The Ohio River Division, U.S. Army Corps of Engineers: The History of a Central Command*. Cincinnati: U.S. Army Corps of Engineers, Ohio River Division, 1992 • *Water Resources Development in West Virginia, 1981*. Cincinnati: U.S. Army Corps of Engineers, Ohio River Division, 1981.

U.S. Coal & Coke Company: Hornick, Mike. "United States Coal & Coke Company Begins." *Welch Daily News*, 6/2/1983 • Lambie, Joseph T. *From Mine to Market: The History of Coal Transportation on the Norfolk & Western Railway*. New York: NYU Press, 1954 • McGehee, Stuart. "Gary: A First-Class Mining Operation." *Goldenseal* (Fall 1988).

USS *West Virginia*: Smith, Myron J. Jr. *The Mountain State Battleship: USS West Virginia*. Richwood: WV Press Club, 1981.

Valley Falls State Park: Cain, David. "Valley Falls State Park."*WWV* (Mar. 2000) • Crockett, Maureen. "Magnificent Valley Falls." *WWV* (Nov. 1991).

Peter Godwin Van Winkle: Atkinson, George W. & Alvaro F. Gibbens. *Prominent Men of West Virginia*. Wheeling: W. L. Callin, 1890 • Miller & Maxwell, vol. 3 • Sturm, Philip. "Senator Peter G. Van Winkle and the Andrew Johnson Impeachment Trial: A Comprehensive View." *WVH*

(1999–2000) • Whitener, Evert F. "Peter Godwin Van Winkle." M.A. thesis, WVU, 1929.

Vandalia Colony: Sullivan, Ken. "Vandalia at 20: What's in the Name?" *Goldenseal* (Spring 1996).

Vernacular Architecture: Dell, Upton & John Michael Vlach. *Common Places: Readings in American Vernacular Architecture.* Athens, GA: University of Georgia Press, 1986 • McAlester, Virginia & Lee McAlester. *A Field Guide to American Houses.* New York: Knopf, 1986 • Nolin, Elizabeth, ed. *Wheeling Port of Entry: An Industrial Guide.* Fairmont Printing Co., 1988.

Vienna: Black, Donald F. *History of Wood County.* Marietta, OH: Richardson Printing, 1975 • "Lewis Summers' Journal of a Tour from Alexandria, Virginia, to Gallipolis, Ohio, in 1808." *Southern Historical Magazine* (Feb. 1892) • Vienna Historical Committee. *Vienna, Virginia 1794, Vienna, West Virginia 1994 Bicentennial.* Parsons: McClain, 1994.

Vietnam War: Doherty, William T. & Festus P. Summers. *West Virginia University: Symbol of Unity in a Sectionalized State.* Morgantown: WVU Press, 1982 • Fullerton, Robert. "One Man's Relevancy: The Case of Tom Bennett." *WVU Magazine* (Spring 1971) • Simons, Donald L. *I Refuse: Memories of a Vietnam War Objector.* Trenton, NJ: Broken Rifle Press, 1992 • Snyder, Dorothy B. *Not to be Forgotten: Prestonians Who Died in Vietnam 1965–1970.* Dover, DE: Dorothy B. Snyder, 2001 • *West Virginia Casualties in Vietnam.* Charleston: State Adjutant General's Office, 6/30/1969 • *West Virginia Casualties in Vietnam* [supplement]. Charleston: State Adjutant General's Office, 12/31/1971 • *West Virginia University Magazine.* (Spring & Summer 1969, Summer & Winter 1970) • Young, Marilyn B. *The Vietnam Wars 1945–1990.* New York: Harper-Collins, 2001.

Virginia: Hartford, John. *Steamboat in a Cornfield.* New York: Crown, 1986.

Virginia Debt Question: Ambler & Summers.

Virginia's Chapel: Dayton, Ruth Woods. *Pioneers and their Homes on Upper Kanawha.* Charleston: WV Pub. Co., 1947.

Virginian Railway: Perry, Bud & Karl C. Lilly III. *Reopening Glen Rogers.* Sissonville: PAL Productions • Reid, H. *The Virginian Railway.* Milwaukee: Kalmbach Pub. Co., 1961 • "Virginian Railway Feature." *Sam R. Pennington's Feature Stories Magazine.* (June 1933).

Virginius Island: Gilbert, David. *A Walker's Guide to Harpers Ferry.* Charleston: PHPC, 1983. Reprint, Harpers Ferry Historical Society, 1995 • Gilbert. *Where Industry Failed: Water Powered Mills at Harpers Ferry, West Virginia.* Charleston: PHPC, 1984.

Volcano: Callahan, James M. *History of West Virginia.* Chicago & New York: American Historical Society, 1923 • Leavengood, Betty. "'I'm the One Who Stayed': Walter Taitt's 99 years in Volcano." *Goldenseal* (Winter 2002) • Pepper, Brooks. "Volcano, West Virginia's Most Eruptive Town." *West Virginia Hillbilly,* 10/11/1969.

Alexander Luark Wade: Ash, Irvin O. *West Virginia Educators.* Shepherdstown: Irvin O. Ash, 1936 • Barbe, Mary I. "The Life of Alexander L. Wade." *WVH* (Oct. 1947) • Wade, Alexander L. *A Graduating System for Country Schools.* Boston: New England Pub., 1881.

Thomas Walker: Henderson, Archibald. "Dr. Thomas Walker and the Loyal Company of Virginia," in *Proceedings of the American Antiquarian Society,* 1931 • McLeod, Alexander C. "A Man for all Regions: Dr. Thomas Walker of Castle Hill." *Filson Club History Quarterly* (Apr. 1997) • Nyland, Keith R. " Doctor Thomas Walker (1715–1794): Explorer, Physician, Statesman, Surveyor and Planter of Virginia and Kentucky." Ph.D. diss., Ohio State University, 1971.

War on Poverty: "Hulett Carlson Smith," in Morgan–*Governors* • Mutsow, Allen J. *The Unraveling of America: A History of Liberalism in the 1960s.* New York: Harper & Row, 1984 • Perry, Huey. *They'll Cut Off your Project: A Mingo County Chronicle.* New York: Praeger, 1972.

Ward Engineering Works: Parkinson, George P. Jr. "Charles Ward Engineering Works." *Goldenseal* (July–Aug. 1977) • Parkinson, George P. Jr. & Brooks F. McCabe Jr. "Charles Ward and James Rumsey: Regional Innovation in Steam Technology on the Western Rivers." *WVH* (Jan.–Apr. 1978) • "Through the Lens: Pioneering Steam Propeller Towboats." *Egregious Steamboat Journal* (Nov.–Dec. 1993).

Warrior Path: Myer, William E. "Indian Trails of the Southeast." *Bureau of American Ethnology 42nd Annual Report.* Washington: GPO, 1928 • Rice–*Allegheny Frontier.*

Washington: Gould, E. W. *Fifty Years on the Mississippi; or Gould's History of River Navigation.* St. Louis: Nixon-Jones, 1889 • McCall, Edith. *Conquering the Rivers: Henry Miller Shreve and the Navigation of America's Inland Waterways.* Baton Rouge: LSU Press, 1984 • Mitchell, C. Bradford & Kenneth R. Hall. *Merchant Steam Vessels of the United States, 1790–1868.* Staten Island, NY: Steamship Historical Society of America, 1975 • Way, Frederick Jr. *Way's Packet Directory, 1848–1983.* Athens, OH: Ohio University Press, 1983.

Booker T. Washington: Harlan, Louis R. *Booker T. Washington: The Making of A Black Leader, 1856–1901.* New York: Oxford University Press, 1972 • Harlan. *Booker T. Washington: The Wizard of Tuskegee.* New York: Oxford University Press, 1983 • Lantz, Virginia. *Booker T. Washington and the Adult Education Movement.* Gainesville, FL: University Press of Florida, 1993 • Washington, Booker T. *Up From Slavery.* New York: Doubleday, 1901.

Charles Washington: Bushong, Millard K. *A History of Jefferson County, West Virginia.* Charles Town: Jefferson Pub. Co., 1941.

George Washington: Freeman, Douglas Southall. *George Washington: A Biography,* 5 vols. New York: Charles Scribner's Sons, 1948–1957 • Hofstra, Warren R., ed. *George Washington and the Virginia Backcountry.* Madison, WI: Madison House, 1998 • Lewis, Thomas A. *For King and Country: The Maturing of George Washington, 1748–1760.* New York: Harper Collins, 1993.

Lewis W. Washington: Bushong, Millard K. *A History of Jefferson County, West Virginia.* Charles Town: Jefferson Pub. Co., 1941.

Water Resources: West Virginia DEP. "Groundwater Programs and Activities: Biennial Report to the West Virginia Legislature." 2004 • West Virginia DEP. "West Virginia's Water Quality Status Assessment Report." 2000.

Waterpower: Gilbert, Dave. *Where Industry Failed: Water-Powered Mills at Harpers Ferry, West Virginia.* Charleston: PHPC, 1984 • Meador, Michael. "A Man and his Mill: Jim Wells Takes on the Greenville Mill." *Goldenseal* (Spring 1991).

Clarence W. Watson: Beachley, Charles E. *History of the Consolidation Coal Company.* New York: Consolidation Coal Co., 1934 • Caudill, Harry M. *Theirs be the Power: The Moguls of Eastern Kentucky.* Chicago: UI Press, 1983 • Watson, James O. *The Valley Coal Story.* Fairmont Printing Co., 1957.

James O. Watson: Caudill, Harry M. *Theirs be the Power: The Moguls of Eastern Kentucky.* Chicago: UI Press, 1983 • Watson, James O. *The Valley Coal Story.* Fairmont Printing Co., 1957 • "The Fairmont Field," in Michael E. Workman, *Northern West Virginia Coal Fields: Historical Context.* Morgantown: Institute for the History of Technology & Industrial Archaeology, 1994.

Watt Powell Park: Whiteford, Mike. "Alley Cats to Celebrate Park's 50th Anniversary." *Gazette,* 3/24/1999.

Wayne: Comstock–*Encyclopedia,* vol. 7, 1974 • Kirby, Wesley D. *History of Wayne Community.* Morgantown: Agricultural Extension Division, 1926 • Lewis, Stephen. *An Overview of the History of Wayne County.* Wayne, 1997 • Taylor, Mildred. *History of Wayne County.* Wayne: Taylor, 1963 • "Wayne, our Town," Pamphlet. Wayne Chamber of Commerce & the Woman's Club of Wayne, 1975. (updated in 2000).

Anthony Wayne: Kohn, Richard H. *Eagle and Sword: The Federalists and the Creation of the Military Establishment in America.* New York: Free Press, 1991 • Nelson, Paul David. *Anthony Wayne: Soldier of the Early Republic.* Bloomington, IN: Indiana University Press, 1985.

Wayne County: Lewis, Stephen. *An Overview of the History of Wayne County.* Wayne, 1997 • Taylor, Mildred. *History of Wayne County.* Wayne: Taylor, 1963.

Weaving: Davison, Marguerite P. *A Handweaver's Pattern Book.* Swarthmore: Marguerite P. Davison, 1944 • Eaton, Allen H. *Handicrafts of the Southern Highlands.* New York: Russell Sage Foundation, 1937. Reprint, Dover, 1973 • Armentrout, Jocie, 9/14/90; Coffman, Bernice, 3/10/92; Goddin, Sadavoie & Hinkle, Willetta, 2/19/92; Goodwin, Olive, 11/12/90; Hofer, Genevieve, 3/16/92; Marstiller, Rebecca, 2/20/92; Teets, Kate & Roy, 2/24/92; Thompson, Dorothy, 4/20/90; Whetsell, Grace, 10/6/92. Interviews by Gerry Milnes, Augusta Heritage Center, Davis & Elkins College, Elkins • Wilson, Kathleen Curtis. *Textile Art from Southern Appalachia: The Quiet Work of Women.* Johnson City, TN: Overmountain Press, 2001.

Webster County: Dodrill, William C. *Moccasin Tracks and Other Imprints.* Parsons: McClain, 1974 • Miller, Sampson N. Sr. *Annals of Webster County.* Orlando: Golden Rule Press, 1969.

Webster Springs: Miller, Sampson N. Sr. *Annals of Webster County.* Orlando: Golden Rule Press, 1969.

Weeds: Millspaugh, C. F. "Your Weeds and your Neighbors," Bulletin 22, Part 2. WV Agricultural Experiment Station • Uva, Richard H., et al. *Weeds of the Northeast.* Ithaca, NY: Cornell University Press, 1997.

Weirton: Javersak, David T. *History of Weirton.* Virginia Beach: Donning Co., 1999.

Weirton Steel: Lieber, James B. *Friendly Takeover: How An Employee Buyout Saved a Steel Town.* New York: Viking/Penguin Group, 1995 • Ubinger, John D. "Ernest Tener Weir." *Western Pennsylvania Historical Magazine* (July 1975).

Isaiah Welch: Hotchkiss, Jedediah. "The Great Flat-Top Coal-Field." *The Virginias* (June 1882) • Lambie, Joseph T. *From Mine to Market: The History of Coal Transportation on the Norfolk & Western Railway.* New York: NYU Press, 1954 • Roper, Peter W. *Jedediah Hotchkiss: Rebel Mapmaker and Virginia Businessman.* Shippensburg, PA: White Mane Publishers, 1992 • Welch, Isaiah A. "The Pocahontas-Flat-Top Coal Field." *Daily Telegraph,* 11/1/1896.

Wellsburg: Cipriani, Anthony J. Sr. *Wellsburg, West Virginia, 1791–1991.* Wellsburg: Any Forms & Checks, 1991 • Dodrill, Carlin F., et al. *West Virginia Centennial Celebration, 1863–1963: Brooke County.* Follansbee Review Press, 1963 • Newton, J. H. *History of the Pan-Handle.* Wheeling: Caldwell, 1879.

Wertz Field: Cohen–*Kanawha Images* • Withrow, Dolly. *From the Grove to the Stars: West Virginia State College 1891–1991.* Charleston: PHPC, 1991.

West Augusta: Crumrine, Boyd. *History of Washington County, Pennsylvania, with Biographical Sketches.* Philadelphia: L. H. Everts & Co, 1882. Reprint, Apollo, 1980 • Rice–*Allegheny Frontier* • Veech, James. *The Monongahela of Old; or, Historical Sketches of South-western Pennsylvania to the Year 1800.* Pittsburgh: Mrs. E. V. Blaine, 1858–1892. Reprint, McClain, 1971.

Don West: Biggers, Jeff. "The Fugitive of Southern Appalachian Literature: Reconsidering the Poetry of Don West." *Journal of Appalachian Studies* (Spring 2000) • West, Don. *In a Land of Plenty: A Don West Reader.* Minneapolis: West End Press, 1982 • Whitehead, Fred. "Don West," in Mario Jo Buhle, et al., eds., *Encyclopedia of the American Left.* New York: Oxford University Press, 1998.

West Fork River: Johnson, Leland R. *The Headwaters District: A History of the Pittsburgh District.* U.S. Army Corps of Engineers, Pittsburgh District, 1978.

Jerry West: Julian, Norman. *Legends: Profiles in West Virginia University Basketball.* Morgantown: Trillium Pub., 1998 • *WVU Basketball Media Guide,* 1999–2000.

West Liberty State College: Javersak, David T. "West Liberty State College, 1837–1987." *Upper Ohio Valley Historical Review* (Fall–Winter 1987) • Regier, C. C. *West Liberty, Yesterday and Today.* Wheeling News Litho. Co., 1939 • Reuter, Frank T. *West Liberty State College: The First 125 Years.* West Liberty State College, 1963.

West Virginia: A Guide to the Mountain State: Pritchard, Arthur C. "In West Virginia I Had More Freedom: Bruce Crawford's Story." *Goldenseal* (Spring 1984) • Thomas–*New Deal* • Thomas, Jerry Bruce. "'The Nearly Perfect State': Governor Homer Adams Holt, The WPA Writers' Project and the Making of *West Virginia: A Guide to the Mountain State*." *WVH* (1993) • WPA–*Guide* • WV Writers' Program Papers. WV&RHC.

West Virginia Archives and History: Reports of Archives & History, 1905–72, Annual Reports • Reports of Culture & History, 1977–2003, Annual Reports.

West Virginia Athletic Union Tournament: Barnett, C. Robert. "The Finals: West Virginia's Black Basketball Tournament, 1925–1957." *Goldenseal* (Summer 1983) • Barnett, C. Robert & David Helmer. "The Champs." *River Cities Monthly* (Mar. 1980).

West Virginia Beacon Digest: Hart, Betty L. Powell. "The Black Press in West Virginia: A Brief History," in Joe W. Trotter & Ancella R. Bickley, eds., *Honoring our Past: Proceedings of the First Two Conferences on West Virginia's Black History.* Charleston: Alliance for the Collection, Preservation & Dissemination of West Virginia's Black History, 1991.

West Virginia Central & Pittsburg Railway: Fansler, Homer F. *History of Tucker County.* Parsons: McClain, 1962 • Henry Gassaway Davis Papers. WV&RHC • Pepper, Charles M. *The Life and Times of Henry Gassaway Davis.* New York: Century Co., 1920.

West Virginia Commission on the Arts: Davis, William M. "West Virginia Commission on the Arts: 30 Years of Leadership and Service." *Artworks* (Fall 1997).

West Virginia Distinguished Service Medal: Carlton Custer Pierce Papers. A&M 1674. WV&RHC • West Virginia Adjutant General Reports, 1939–1990, Annual Reports. • *Journal of the House of Delegates.* H.B. no. 82. 44th Legislature of West Virginia, Regular Session, 1939.

West Virginia Education Association: Lord, Charles A. *Years of Decision: A History of an Organization.* Charleston: Education Assn., 1965.

West Virginia Hillbilly: Anthony, Ted. "Comstock Country." Charleston: Associated Press, 1/4/1993 • Comstock, Jay, son of Jim Comstock. Interview by author. 11/4/1998.

"West Virginia Hills": "Research Shows State Song 'West Virginia Hills' a Product of Gilmer County." *Glenville Democrat,* 1/25/1973.

West Virginia Historical Society: Reports & Publications of the West Virginia Historical & Antiquarian Society, 1891–1905 • Reports of the Department of Archives & History, 1905–1906 & 1938–1942, Annual Reports.

West Virginia History: Atkinson, Robert. "West Virginia's Historical Magazine." *WV Review* (Oct. 1940).

West Virginia Independence Hall: Curry, Richard O. *A House Divided: A Study of Statehood Politics & the Copperhead Movement in West Virginia.* Pittsburgh: UPP, 1964 • *West Virginia Independence Hall.* Wheeling: WV Independence Hall Foundation, 2001.

West Virginia Mine Workers Union: Corbin–*Life, Work* • Corbin, David A. *The West Virginia Mine Workers Union.* Articles reprinted from *Labor Age,* Apr. to Dec., 1931. Huntington: Appalachian Movement Press, 1972 • Keeney, C. Belmont. "The Last Mine War: Frank Keeney and the West Virginia Mine Workers Union, 1931–33." *The Mountain Messenger* (Dec. 2000) • Wilson, Edmund. *The American Jitters.* New York: Charles Scribner's Sons, 1932.

West Virginia National Guard: Bailey, Kenneth R. *Mountaineers are Free: A History of the West Virginia National Guard.* St. Albans: Harless Printing, 1978.

West Virginia Review: Hennen, John C. *The Americanization of West Virginia.* Lexington: UPK, 1996 • Penix, Jan. "West Virginia: A Matter of Pride." *West Virginia Illustrated* (Aug.–Sept. 1971).

West Virginia School of Osteopathic Medicine: Ellis, Penny & Alayne Steiger. *The D. O.'s: Osteopathic Medicine in the Mountains.* Charleston: WV Society of Osteopathic Medicine, 1986 • Rice–*Greenbrier County.*

West Virginia Schools for the Deaf and Blind: Brannon, Seldon. *History of the West Virginia Schools for the Deaf & Blind 1870–1970.* Romney: West Virginia Schools for the Deaf & Blind, 1970.

West Virginia State Federation of Labor: Harris, Evelyn K. & Frank J. Krebs. *From Humble Beginnings: West Virginia State Federation of Labor, 1903–1957.* Charleston: WV Labor History Pub. Fund, 1960.

West Virginia State Teachers' Association: Bickley, Ancella R. *History of the West Virginia State Teachers' Association.* Washington: National Education Assn., 1979 • Sheeler, J. Reuben. "The First Ten Years of the West Virginia State Teachers' Association," (unpub. ms.). Drain-Jordan Library, WV State University, Institute • Whiting, Gregory W. "History of the West Virginia State Teachers' Association," (unpub. ms.). Drain-Jordan Library, WV State University, Institute.

West Virginia State University: Duran, Elizabeth C. & James A. Duran Jr. "Integration in Reverse at West Virginia State College." *WVH* (1984) • Harlan, John C. *History of West Virginia State College 1901–1965.* Dubuque, IA: William C. Brown, 1968 • Thorn, Arline R. "West Virginia State College: A Brief History." Institute: WV State College Foundation, 1988 • Withrow, Dolly. *From the Grove to the Stars: West Virginia State College 1891–1991.* Charleston: PHPC, 1991.

West Virginia Symphony Orchestra: Blachley, Frederick J. O. "Grass Roots Symphony." *Musical America* (Feb. 1947). Condensed as "Music by and for the Whole Town," *Reader's Digest,* (June 1947) • Furry, Shirley. "Charleston Symphony Orchestra," in Robert Craven, ed., *Symphony Orchestras of the United States: Selected Profiles.* New York: Greenwood

Press, 1986 • Griffith, Ann B. *West Virginia Symphony 50th Anniversary Commemorative Issue*, Booklet. West Virginia Symphony, 1989.

West Virginia University: Cook, Tony & Barbara J. Howe, et al. "WVU Year-by-Year 1862–2000." *WVU Alumni Magazine* (Winter 2000) • Doherty, William T. Jr. & Festus P. Summers. *West Virginia University: Symbol of Unity in a Sectionalized State*. Morgantown: WVU Press, 1982 • Howe, Barbara J. "A People's University." *WVU Alumni Magazine* (Winter 2000).

West Virginia Wesleyan College: Plummer, Kenneth M. *A History of West Virginia Wesleyan College 1890–1965*. Buckhannon: West Virginia Wesleyan College Press, 1965.

West Virginian Hotel: McGehee, C. Stuart. "Bluefield's Biggest: The Grand West Virginian Hotel." *Goldenseal* (Summer 1993) • Clipping file & Alex Mahood papers, Eastern Regional Archives.

Western Maryland Railway: Cook, Roger & Karl Zimmerman. *The Western Maryland Railway: Fireballs and Black Diamonds*. San Diego: Howell-North Books, 1981.

Weston & Gauley Bridge Turnpike: Kemp, Emory L. *Links in a Chain: The Development of Suspension Bridges, 1801–1870*. London: Institution of Structural Engineers, 1979 • Kemp. "Charles Ellet Jr. and the Wheeling Suspension Bridge," in *Proceedings of an International Conference on Historic Bridges*. Morgantown: WVU Press, 1999 • Kemp. "Roebling, Ellet and the Wire Suspension Bridge," in Margaret Latimer, et al., eds., *Bridge to the Future: A Centennial of the Brooklyn Bridge*. New York: Academy of Sciences, 1984 • Kemp, Emory L. & Beverly B. Fluty. *The Wheeling Suspension Bridge*. Charleston: PHPC, 1999 • Kemp, Emory L. & Janet Kemp. "Building the Weston and Gauley Bridge Turnpike." *WVH* (Summer 1980).

Weston State Hospital: Gilchrist, Joy G. & Charles H. Gilchrist. *Lewis County, West Virginia*. Virginia Beach: Donning Co., 1993 • Smith, Edward C. *A History of Lewis County*. Weston: Edward C. Smith, 1929.

Westsylvania: Rice–*Allegheny Frontier*.

Wetlands: McDonald, Brian R., ed. *Proceedings of the Symposium on Wetlands of the Unglaciated Appalachian Region*. Morgantown: WVU, 1982 • Tiner, Ralph W. *West Virginia's Wetlands*. Charleston: WVDNR, 1996.

Lewis Wetzel: Allman, Clarence B. *Lewis Wetzel, Indian Fighter*. New York: Devin-Adair Co., 1961. Reprint, Devin-Adair Co., 1977 • Carroll, George. "Lewis Wetzel: Warfare Tactics on the Frontier." *WVH* (1991) • Hintzen, William. *A Sketchbook of the Border Wars of the Upper Ohio Valley, 1769–1794*. Manchester, CT: Precision Shooting, Inc., 1999.

Wheeling: Fetherling, Doug. *Wheeling: An Illustrated History*. Woodland Hills, CA: Windsor Pub., 1983 • Lewis, Clifford M., ed. *Wheeling Bicentennial: 1769–1969*. Wheeling, 1969 • WPA–*Guide*.

Wheeling Hospital: *From Lincoln to Laser: The Wheeling Hospital Story*. 1987 • "The Spirit of Healing for 150 Years." *Wheeling Intelligencer* & *Wheeling News-Register*, 3/9/2000.

Wheeling Island: Keefer, Louis E. "The Island: Surrounded by Water in Wheeling." *Goldenseal* (Spring 1995).

Wheeling Jamboree: Tribe–*Jamboree*.

Wheeling Jesuit University: "America's Best Colleges-1999." *U.S. News & World Report*. (8/31/1998) • *Fact Book: 2000–2001*. Wheeling Jesuit University Archives • Wheeling College. *Wheeling College Catalog: 1956–1957*.

Wheeling & Lake Erie Railway: Rehor, John A. *The Nickel Plate Story*. Milwaukee: Kalmbach Pub., 1978.

Wheeling-Pittsburgh Steel: Boyd, Peter. *History of the Northern West Virginia Panhandle*. Topeka: Historical Pub. Co., 1927 • May, Earl C. *Principio to Wheeling: A Pageant of Iron and Steel*. New York & London: Harper & Brothers, 1945 • Stamp, Andy. "W-P Completes a Significant Year." Supplement to the *Intelligencer* & *News-Register*, 2/24/2005.

Wheeling-Pittsburgh Steel Strike: Baker, Stephen. "'Why this Steel Chief has Such an Iron Will." *Business Week* (5/19/1997) • Bernstein, Aaron. "'Working Capital': Labor's New Weapon." *Business Week* (9/29/1997) • Greenwald, John & David Jackson. "A Nearly Silent Steel Strike." *Time* (7/ 21/1997) • "Pension Change." *Business Insurance* (8/25/1997).

Wheeling Suspension Bridge: Kemp, Emory L. & Beverly B. Fluty. *The Wheeling Suspension Bridge*. Charleston: PHPC, 1999.

The Wheeling Suspension Bridge Case: Monroe, Elizabeth Brand. *The Wheeling Bridge Case*. Boston: Northeastern Univ. Press, 1992.

Wheeling Symphony: "History of Wheeling Symphony." Wheeling Symphony Collection. WV&RHC • Wolf, Edward C. & Margaret Brennan. *For the Love of Music: A 75-Year History of the Wheeling Symphony Orchestra*. Wheeling, 2004 • The Wheeling Symphony Society. *The Wheeling Symphony Society, Fiftieth Anniversary*. Wheeling, 1979.

Whipple Company Store: National Register of Historic Places Nomination, ms. WVDC&H, 1991.

WHIS: Becker, Martha Jane & Marilyn Fletcher. *Broadcasting in West Virginia: A History*. South Charleston: West Virginia Broadcasters Assn., 1989 • Tribe–*Jamboree*.

Whiskey Rebellion: Core, Earl L. *The Monongalia Story*, 5 vols. Parsons: McClain, 1974–84 • Mayola, Peter L. "Whiskey Insurrection of 1794 in Fayette County, Pennsylvania." M.A. thesis, WVU, 1949 • Slaughter, Thomas P. *The Whiskey Rebellion*. New York: Oxford University Press, 1988.

Albert Blakeslee White: Allen, Bernard L. *Parkersburg: A Bicentennial History*. Parkersburg Bicentennial Commission, 1985 • Morgan–*Governors*.

Doc White: Clay County History Book Committee. *History of Clay County, 1989*. Salem: Don Mills, Inc., 1989 • Clay County History Book Committee. *History of Clay County, Vol. II*. Salem: Don Mills, Inc., 1994 • Heyer, Bob. "Ivydale: The Morris Family Old-Time Music Festivals." *Goldenseal* (Summer 1998).

I. C. White: Brown, Lloyd L. "The Life of Dr. Israel Charles White." M.A. thesis, WVU, 1946 • Fairchild, Herman L. "Memorial of Israel C. White." Reprinted from *Bulletin of the Geological Society of America* (3/30/1928) • Hennen, Ray V. "Israel Charles White Memorial." Reprinted from Bulletin of the American Assn. of Petroleum Geologists (Mar. 1928) • Papers of Israel C. White, 1867–1941. WV&RHC • Price, Paul H. "Israel Charles White, Geologist (1848–1927)." Manuscript copy presented to Upsilon Chapter, Morgantown, Feb. 5, 1958 • White, I. C. "The Waste of our Fuel Resources." Address of I.C. White, State Geologist of WV, at the Conference of Natural Resources, the White House, May 13, 1808 • White, I. C. "The Geology of Natural Gas," *Science* (June & July 1885) • White, I. C. "Stratigraphy of the Bituminous Coal Field of Pennsylvania, Ohio and West Virginia," Bulletin 65. USGS. Washington: GPO, 1891.

White Sulphur Springs: Moorman, John J. "The Memoir of Dr. John J. Moorman." *Journal of the Greenbrier Historical Society*, vol. 3, no. 6 (1980) • Olcott, William. *The Greenbrier Heritage*. Philadelphia: Arndt, Preston, Chapin, Lamb & Keen, Inc., 1967.

White Sulphur Springs, Battle of: Bard, David. *Civil War: The New River Valley*. Charleston: Quarrier Press, 2004 • Stutler–*Civil War*.

M. T. Whittico: Posey, Thomas E. *The Negro Citizen of West Virginia*. Institute: Press of WV State College, 1934 • Trotter, Joe William Jr. *Coal, Class, and Color: Blacks in Southern West Virginia, 1915–1932*. Urbana: UI Press, 1990.

Widen: Cantrell, Betty, et al. "Widen: The Town J. G. Bradley Built." *Goldenseal* (Jan.–Mar. 1977) • Stewart, C. C. "Strike Duty: A State Trooper Recalls Trouble in the Coalfields." *Goldenseal* (Winter 1995) • Yeager, Barbara. "Mostly Work: Making a Home in Widen." *Goldenseal* (Jan.–Mar. 1977).

John Wilburn Trial: Savage–*Thunder*.

Wild Foods: Gillespie, William H. *Wild Foods of Appalachia*. Morgantown: Seneca Books, 1986 • McNight, Kent H. & Vera B. Kent. *Mushrooms of North America*. Norwalk, CT: Easton Press, 1988 • Peterson, L. A. *Edible Wild Plants, Eastern/Central North America*. Norwalk, CT: Easton Press, 1977.

Wild Turkey: Bailey, R. W. & K. T. Rinell. "History and Management of the Wild Turkey in West Virginia," Bulletin No. 6. WVDNR, 1968 • Pack, James C. "Life History of the Wild Turkey." *WWV* (Oct. 1994) • Pack. "We Did It!" *WWV* (May 1989).

Willard Hotel: Brinkman, Charles. "History of Taylor County." Newspaper Series. Published in the 1930s. Collected & bound. Taylor County Public Library, Grafton • Potter, Janet G. *Great American Railroad Stations*. New York: John Wiley & Sons, 1996 • Potter, Jay. "Grafton, West Virginia." *CTC Board Railroads Illustrated*. (Nov. 1997) • Taylor County Historical & Genealogical Society. *A History of Taylor County*. Parsons: McClain, 1986.

Willey Amendment: Curry, Richard O. *A House Divided: A Study of Statehood Politics & the Copperhead Movement in West Virginia.* Pittsburgh: UPP, 1964 • Rice & Brown.

Waitman Willey: Ambler, Charles H. *Waitman Thomas Willey: Orator, Churchman, Humanitarian.* Huntington: Standard Printing & Pub. Co., 1954.

Doc Williams: Tribe–*Jamboree.*

Williamson Coal House: "Coal House Subject of English Magazine Article." *Mingo Republican* 4/5/1940 • State Historic Preservation Office. *Historic West Virginia: The National Register of Historic Places.* WVDC&H, 2000 • "Williamson Coal House." *Goldenseal* (Spring 2002).

Meredith Sue Willis: Willis, Meredith Sue. Interview by author. 9/29/1998.

Willow Island Sterilization: *Oil, Chemical & Atomic Workers International Union v. American Cyanamid Company.* 741 Federal Reports 2nd 444. (3rd Cir. 1984).

Emmanuel Willis Wilson: Morgan–*Governors* • Sobel, Robert & John Raimo. *Biographical Directory of the Governors of the United States, 1789–1978,* vol. 4. Westport: Meckler Books, 1978 • Williams, John Alexander. *West Virginia: A Bicentennial History.* New York: W. W. Norton, 1976.

Riley Wilson: Chilton, Sam. Interview by author. ca. 1970 • Sullivan, Ken. "Food, Feathers, and Whiskey: Two Stories by Riley Wilson." *Goldenseal* (Summer 1982) • Wilson, Riley. *From Philadelphia, Pa., to Charleston, W. Va., via Nome, Alaska.* Charleston: Rose City Press, 1932 • Wilson. *Reach Me the Tin.* Charleston: Rose City Press, 1932.

William Lyne Wilson: Summers, Festus P. *William L. Wilson and Tariff Reform.* New Brunswick, NJ: Rutgers University Press, 1953 • Wilson, William L. *A Borderland Confederate.* Edited by Festus P Summers. Pittsburgh: UPP, 1962 • Wilson. *The Cabinet Diary of William L. Wilson, 1896–1897.* Edited by Festus P. Summers. Chapel Hill: UNC Press, 1957.

Melvin Wine: Beisswenger, Donald A. "Fiddling Way Out Yonder: Community and Style in the Music of Melvin Wine." Ph.D. diss., University of Memphis, 1997 • Leffler, Susan. "Melvin Wine." *Goldenseal* (Summer 1991) • Wine, Melvin. *Hannah at the Springhouse.* Marimac AHS-2 • Wine. *Vintage Wine.* Marimac AHS-6 • Wine. *Cold Frosty Morning.* Poplar LP1 • Wine. *Old-Time Fiddling of Braxton County,* vol. 2, Augusta Heritage Records, AHR-013.

Wirt County: *The History of Wirt County.* Elizabeth: Elizabeth Beauchamp Chapter, Daughters of American Pioneers, 1981 • *Hardesty's,* vol. 6 • McKain, David L. & Bernard L. Allen. *Where it all Began: The Story of the People and Places Where the Oil and Gas Industry Began.* Parkersburg: David L. McKain, 1994.

Bob Wise: "Bob Wise Celebrates his Victory." *Gazette,* 11/3/1982 • Cauchon, Dennis. "Forging Alliances with Little Flash." *USA Today,* 11/8/2000 • Eyre, Eric. "Candidates Differ on School Consolidation." *Sunday Gazette-Mail,* 10/8/2000 • O'Hanlon, Dan. "the hq interview." *Huntington Quarterly Magazine* (Winter–Spring 2001) • *Biographical Directory of the United States Congress.* Washington: GPO, 1990.

Alexander Scott Withers: Cook, Roy Bird. *Alexander Scott Withers.* 1921 • McWhorter, Lucullus Virgil. *The Border Settlers of Northwestern Virginia.* Hamilton, OH: Republican Pub. Co., 1915. Reprint, Comstock, 1974 • Withers–*Chronicles.*

The Wizard Clip: "The Legend of Wizard Clip," in Joseph Barry, *The Strange Story of Harpers Ferry.* Martinsburg: Thompson Brothers, 1903.

WJLS: Becker, Martha J. & Marilyn Fletcher. *Broadcasting in West Virginia: A History.* South Charleston: West Virginia Broadcasters Assn., 1989 • Tribe–*Jamboree.*

Women's Lives: Howe, Barbara J. "West Virginia Women's Organizations, 1880s–1930." *WVH* (1990) • Maggard, Sally W. "From Farm to Coal Camp to Back Office and McDonald's." *Journal of the Appalachian Studies Association* (1994) • Oberhauser, Ann M. "Industrial Restructuring and Women's Homework in Appalachia: Lessons from West Virginia." *Southeastern Geographer* (May 1993).

Women's Suffrage: Effland, Anne W. "'Exciting Battle and Dramatic Finish': The West Virginia Woman Suffrage Movement, Part I: 1867–1916." *WVH* (1985–1986) • Effland. "'Exciting Battle and Dramatic Finish': West Virginia's Ratification of the Nineteenth Amendment." *WVH* (1989) • Effland. "A Profile of Political Activists: Women of the West Virginia Woman Suffrage Movement." *WVH* (1990).

Abraham Wood: Briceland, Alan Vance. *Westward from Virginia: The Exploration of the Virginia-Carolina Frontier 1650–1710.* Charlottesville: UVA Press, 1987.

Wood County: Allen, Bernard L. *Parkersburg: A Bicentennial History.* Parkersburg: Parkersburg Bicentennial Commission, 1985 • Black, Donald F. *History of Wood County,* vol. 1. Parkersburg: Donald F. Black, 1975 • Fisher, Francis P. "PHS Class of 1874 to be Memorialized," in *Echoes from the Hills.* Charleston: West Virginia Assn. of Retired School Employees, 1976 • Libbey, Marie M., ed. *West Virginia Statistical Abstract 1995–1996.* Morgantown: College of Business & Economics, WVU, 1995 • Paul Liston, WVGES. Interview by author. 1998 • Matheny, H. E. *Wood County W. Va. in Civil War Times.* Parkersburg: Trans-Allegheny Books, 1987.

Wood Products Industry: DiGiovanni, Dawn M. "Forest Statistics for West Virginia–1975 & 1989." *Northeastern Forest Experiment Station Bulletin NE-114.* Radnor, PA: U.S. Forest Service, 1990 • WV Division of Forestry. *Forest Industry of West Virginia,* Booklet. Charleston, 2001.

Carter G. Woodson: Logan, Rayford. "Carter G. Woodson: Mirror and Molder of his Time." *Journal of Negro History* (Jan. 1973) • Meier, August & Elliott Rudwick. "J. Franklin Jameson, Carter G. Woodson, and the Foundations of Black Historiography." *American Historical Review* (Oct. 1984) • Wesley, Charles R. "Carter G. Woodson as a Scholar." *Journal of Negro History* (1951) • Woodson, Carter G. "My Recollections of Veterans of the Civil War." *Negro History Bulletin* (Feb. 1944).

Works Progress Administration (WPA): Brock, William R. *Welfare, Democracy, and the New Deal.* Cambridge: Cambridge University Press, 1988 • Thomas–*New Deal.*

World War I: Harper, R. Eugene. "Wilson Progressives vs. DuPont: Controversy in Building the Nitro Plant." *WVH* (1989) • Monongalia Post of the American Legion. Souvenir program, July 4, 1919. WV&RHC • Saunders, Eugene F. "West Virginia Editorial Opinion on U.S. Entry into World War I." M.A. thesis, WVU, 1950 • Schaefer, Christina K. *The Great War: A Guide to the Service Records of all the World's Fighting Men and Volunteers.* Baltimore: Genealogical Pub. Co., 1998 • Smith, R. J., ed. *War Work of Marshall County, WV: The Fighting Forces and the Inner Lines.* Marshall County: War Activity Committee, Nov. 1919 • Sprague, D. D. *Charleston's Roll of Honor.* Charleston: Charleston Printing Co., 1919 • U.S. War Department to West Virginia Adjutant General. Revised List of Deceased Soldiers [of the] World War. Charleston: Department of Veterans Affairs, 1922. Reprint, 1961.

World War II: Ambler & Summers • Cometti–*Thirty-Fifth* • Conley, Phil & William T. Doherty. *West Virginia History.* Charleston: Education Foundation, 1974 • Conte, Robert S. *The History of The Greenbrier.* Charleston: PHPC, 1998 • Hopson, C. F. "Report of Bureau of Negro Welfare & Statistics." Charleston: Jarrett Printing, 1946 • Mooney, James L. *Dictionary of American Naval Fighting Ships.* U.S. Navy, Naval Historical Center • Office of Controller. "Selected Data on Participants of World War II." Washington: Veterans Administration, 1975 • Sheets, L. Wayne. "Women Airforce Service Pilots of World War II." Morgantown: WVU, 1998 • Wells, Sandy. "Just an Army Nurse." *Gazette,* 9/7/1999 • Yeager, Chuck & Leo Janos. *Yeager: An Autobiography.* New York: Bantam Books, 1985.

"The Wreck on the C&O": Cohen, Norm. *Long Steel Rail: The Railroad in American Folksong.* Urbana: UI Press, 2000 • Frankenstein, Alfred. "George Alley: A Study in American Folk Lore." *Musical Courier* (Apr. 16, 1932) • Lyle, Katie Letcher. *Scalded to Death by the Steam.* Chapel Hill: Algonquin Books, 1983.

WVU at Parkersburg: Allen, Bernard L. *Four Diamonds in the Rough-West Virginia University at Parkersburg.* Parkersburg: WVU at Parkersburg, 2000.

WVU Extension Service: Berry, Ann & Larry Cote. "The Power of Partnership: WVU Extension Service Strategic Plan 2000–2005," Report. 2000 • WVU Extension Service. "Building Greatness. Campaign: West Virginia." Morgantown: WVU Extension Service, 2000.

WVU Institute of Technology: Alexander, Ronald R. *West Virginia Tech.* Charleston: PHPC, 1992 • Prudich, Joseph. "History of West Virginia Institute of Technology." M.A. thesis, WVU, 1951 • Riggio, Suzanne. "Course of Events." *West Virginia Tech Catalog,* 1971–72.

WWVA: Becker, Martha Jane & Marilyn Fletcher. *Broadcasting in West Virginia: A History.* Charleston: WV Broadcasters Assn., 1989 • Cuthbert,

John A. "'In Steel and Song': The Wheeling Steel Radio Show." *Goldenseal* (Winter 1992) • Tribe–*Jamboree* • Tribe, Ivan M. "West Virginia Country Music during the Golden Age of Radio." *Goldenseal* (Apr. 1978).

Wyoming County: Bowman, Mary K. *Reference Book of Wyoming County History*. Parsons: McClain, 1965 • National Register of Historic Places Nomination, ms., Mullens Historic District. WVDC&H, 1993 • Perry, Bud & Karl C. Lilly III. *Reopening Glen Rogers*. Sissonville: PAL Productions • *Blue Book*, 2000.

Chuck Yeager: Yeager, Chuck & Leo Janos. *Yeager*. New York: Bantam Books, 1985 • *World Book Encyclopedia* • Wolfe, Tom. *The Right Stuff*. New York: Farrar, Straus, Giroux, 1979.

Yohogania County: Board of Trustees of the Carnegie Institute. *Annals of the Carnegie Museum*. Pittsburgh: Carnegie Institute, 1902 • Crumrine, Boyd, ed. *History of Washington County, Pennsylvania*. Philadelphia: L. H. Everts & Co., 1882.

Lenna Lowe Yost: Effland, Anne Wallace. "Lenna Lowe Yost, 1878–1972," in *Missing Chapters*. Charleston: WV Women's Commission & the Humanities Foundation of WV, 1983.

Betty Zane: Conley–*Encyclopedia* • Davis, Curtis Carroll. "Helping to Hold the Fort: Elizabeth Zane at Wheeling, 1782." *WVH* (Spring 1983) • Hintzen, William. "Betty Zane, Lydia Boggs, and Molly Scott: The Gunpowder Exploits at Fort Henry." *WVH* (1996) • Schneider, Norris F. & G. M. Farley. *Betty Zane: Heroine of Fort Henry*. Williamsport, MD: The Zane Grey Collector, 1970 • Withers–*Chronicles*.

Ebenezer Zane: De Hass, Wills. *History of the Early Settlement and Indian Wars of Western Virginia*. Philadelphia: H. Hoblitzell, 1851. Reprint, McClain, 1960 • Martzolff, Clement L. *Zane's Trace*. Columbus: Heer, 1904 • Patterson, John G. *Ebenezer Zane: Frontiersman*. Charlottesville: UVA Press, 1939.

INDEX

Most topics that are the subjects of articles in *The West Virginia Encyclopedia* are not included in this index. To find those topics you should consult the contents of the book, which are arranged alphabetically.

A. T. Massey coal strike, 278
Aaron, Henry, 788
Aaron, Marcus, 347
Abandoned Mine Land Reclamation Fund, 483, 484
Abbs Valley Anticline, 566
Abraham, Paul K., 451
Abram, S. A., 761
Acadian Orogeny, 18
Accoville, 89
Acheson, Dean, 384, 463
Acker, Thomas, 785
Acme Carbon, 198
Act of Darkness (Bishop), 122, 144
Adair, Richard H., 25
Adams, Ben, 425
Adams, Herbert Baxter, 101
Adams, John, 147, 452
Adams, John Quincy, 381
Adams, Sandy, 34
Adams, William McMillan, 187
Adamston, 51, 283, 666
Addis, Bob, 436
Adell Polymers, 293
Adkins, Cain, 425
Adkins, Greg, 70
Admiralty Coal Company, 292
Adolph, 602
Adrian, 729
Advantage Foods, 581
Advocate, 530
Affleck, Ben, 269
Age of Reason, An (Paine), 135
Agee, James, 532
Agey, C. Buell, 764
Aide's, 414
Ailes, John, 311
Airways Development Act, 33
Airy, John, 26
Akron, Canton & Youngstown Railroad, 533
Akzo-Nobel, 130
Albert, Charles, 185
Albert, Robert, 403
Albertazzi, Ralph D., 33
Albright, Joseph P., 694
Alcan company, 372
Alden, 480
Alder Run Bog, 73
Alderson, Emma, 8
Alderson, J., 92
Alderson, John, Jr., 40
Alderson, Joseph Newman, 810
Alderson bridge, 467
Alderson-Broaddus College, **8–9**, 41, 42, 157, 299, 562, 610
Alexander, James, 493, 724

Alexander, Robert, 536
Alexander, William Davis, 304
All American Aviation, 32–33
All Saints Church (South Charleston), 220
Allard, H. A., 76
Alleghany College, 69
Alleghenian Orogeny, 18
Allegheny Ballistics Laboratory, 481
Allegheny coal formation, 147
Allegheny College, 213
Allegheny Energy, 491–92, 569, 684
Allegheny National Forest, 139
Allegheny Power, 631
Allegheny River, 266, 492
Allegheny Sportsmen's Association, 664
Allegheny Wood Products, 293, 559, 808
Allen, David K., 185
Allen, James E., 185, 454
Allen, John J., 373
Allen, Leroy, 70
Allen, Richard, 2
Alley, George Washington, 811
Alley Agate Manufacturing Company, 446, 635
Alliance for the Collection, Preservation, and Dissemination of West Virginia's Black History, 5
Allied Egry, 293
Allman, C. B., 452
Allman, Ruth Cooper, 718
Alloy, 324, 725
Alpena, 602
Alston, Walter, 45
Altamont, 28
Altmeyer, John, 490
Alton, 88
Altona Farm, 735
Altona-Piedmont Marsh, 77, 455
Alvord, Clarence W., 223
Amalgamated Association of Iron, Steel, and Tin Workers, 681
Amalgamated Transit Union, 450, 451
Amberson (Emerson), John, 90
America First Day, 499
American Academy of Ballet, 125
American Airlines, 757
American Automobile Association, 476
American Baptist Churches in the USA, 41
American Baptist Conference Center, 373
American Baptist Missionary Union, 41
American Brewing Company, 237
American Chestnut Cooperators' Foundation, 133
American Chestnut Foundation, 133
American Constitutional Association, 160, 170, 499, 769
American Cyanamid, 130, 569, 799
American Federation of Labor (AFL), 210, 340, 408, 420, 613, 770
American Flint Glass Workers Union, 282, 283, 551
American Fork and Hoe Company, 398
American Motors Corporation, 128
American Queen (ship), 302

American Railways Company, 688
American Sheet and Tin Plate Company, 500
American Telephone & Telegraph (AT&T), 702, 703, 735
American Viscose, 129, 555
American Woodmark, 497, 808
Ames Company, 808
Amherst Fuel Company, 577
Amherst Industries, 215
Amherstdale, 89
Amistad case, 305
Ammar Brothers, 414
Ammons, Nelle, 76, 248
Amos, Frank, 61
Anawalt, 383, 466
Anderson, Amanda, 791
Anderson, Donald D., 438
Anderson, Gillian, 239
Anderson, M. E., 25
Anderson, Maggie, 427, 469
Anderson, S. R., 128
Anderson, Tom, 210
Anderson, William, 210
Andrews, Earle T., 283
Andrews, Edward Gayer, 14
Andrews, Hale E., 283
Andrews, R. Carl, 346, 526
Andrews, Richard Snowden, 24, 779
Angel, Charlotte, 239
Angel, Dan, 454
Angel, Florette, 177, 248, 507
Anglins Creek, 470
Angsman, Elmer, 286
Anna furnace, 492
Ansted, 57, 234, 462
Ansted, David T., 166
Ansted National Bank, 553
Anthonys Creek, 300, 546
Antietam Formation, 261
Antiquities Act (1906), 334
Apache Indians, 362
Appalachia, **15–16**; Cherokee in, 130; speech characteristics in, 194; conservation in, 265; travel difficulties in, 471; natural history of, 522, 546; federal definition of, 582
Appalachian Bible College, **16–17**, 49, 600
Appalachian Blacksmiths Association, 177
Appalachian Log Structures, 808
Appalachian Plateau, 522, 709
Appalachian Regional Development Act (1965), 19, 296, 603
Appalachian Regional Healthcare, 19
Appalachian String Band Music Festival, 104
Appalachian Timber Services, 81
Appalachians, The (M. Brooks), 106, 522, 709
Apple Grove, 130, 459
Appleseed, Johnny, 20, 304, 548
Arbutis, John, 268
Arch Minerals, 215
Arco, 130
Argand (steamboat), 58
Argiro, Frank "Cheech," 560

Argiro, Giuseppe "Joseph," 560
Ariss, John, 316, 712
Armbrecht, Edward C., Jr., 683, 764
Armco Steel, 215
Armstrong, 583
Armstrong, Louis, 202, 378, 566
Armstrong, Neil, 509
Armstrong, Robert Allen, 43, 763
Arnold, Benedict, 122
Arnold, Boyd Harrison "Slim," 510
Arnold, Jackson, 678, 702
Arnold, Laura Jackson, 57, 88, 730
Arnold, Phyllis, 395
Arnold family, 276
Art Glass Company, 120
Arthur, Chester A., 77
Arthur, Polly, 753
Arthur, Richard, 27
Asbury Academy, 47
Asbury Church, 139
Ash Camp, 729
Ashby, John, 258
Ashby, Turner, 77
Ashcraft, C. A., 126
Ashford, Bailey K., 29, 102
Ashland Chemical Company, 750
Ashley, John, 622
Associated Dry Goods, 195
Athens, 473, 588
Athey, Robert, 23
Athey, Willliam, 23
Atiouandaron group, 491
Atkeson, Thomas Clark, 29, 30, 292
Atkeson, Willis, 30
Atkinson, George Wesley, **29–30**, 109, 182, 341, 427, 505, 672
Atkinson, Robert Poland, 221
Atkinson family, 82
Atlantic & Danville Railroad, 533
Atlantic, Mississippi & Ohio Railroad, 533
Atzerodt, George, 318
Auburn, 274, 548
Auden, W. H., 60
Audubon, John James, 344, 630, 798
Aurora (German Settlement), 585
Austin, Lou, 111
Austin, Pat, 137
Austin, Virginia, 111
Autry, Gene, 184, 626
Avalon, Frankie, 370
Avampato Discovery Museum, 141, 512
Avampato, Charles M., 143
Avant, Clarence, 804
Aventis, 130
Averell, William Woods, 32, 203, 497, 791
Avtex Fibers, 129
Ax, Emanuel, 773
Axis Sally, 8
Axtell, William B., 813
Ayres, Robert, 474
Aztec Indians, 362

B. A. Mullican Lumber and Manufacturing, 808
Bache, Charles, 23
Back Allegheny Mountain, 10, 115
Back Creek, 584
Back Fork, 216
Backbone Mountain, 10, 127, 226, 818
Bacon's Rebellion, 336
Baer, Charles, 76

Baez, Joan, 812
Bailey, Dallas, 636
Bailey, Emery, 547
Bailey, Ernest L., 332
Bailey, J. Earl, 637
Bailey, James, 35
Bailey, John, 36
Bailey, Kenneth P., 281
Bailey, Walter, 565, 805
Bailey Brothers, 785
Baines, Dunbar, 205
Baird, Jane, 376
Baisi, Neal, 813
Baker, Ann, 379
Baker, Betty H., 417
Baker, Joshua, 297
Baker, Michael, Jr., 528
Baker, Newton Diehl, Jr., 54
Baker, Richard, 95
Baker's Bottom, 297
Bakewell, Selina Huntington, 105
Bald Knob, 116, 242, 273
Baldwin, William G., 37
Bales, Aiden, 781
Ball, John, 35
Ballantyne family, 82
Ballengee, Isaac, 334
Ballintyne, Julia, 396
Balsama, George, 509
Bambrick, Joseph, 312
Bampfield, Samuel J., 193
Bancroft (Energetic), 593
Bane family, 276
Bank of Bramwell, 371, 444
Bank of the Ohio Valley, 757
Bank of the West, 307
Bank of Weirton, 757
Bank One, 126, 127
Banks, George, 137
Banks, J. E., 225
Banner Glass Company, 668
Baptist State Association, 4
Barber, Daniel, 125
Barber, Mike, 536
Barber, Timothy L., Sr., 125, 395
Barbour, James, 42
Barbour, Philip Pendleton, 41, 562, 567
Barbour County, **41–42**, 148, 305, 780; Grange in, 292; integration in, 364; Mennonites in, 473
Barboursville Clay Manufacturing Company, 143
Barker, Jesse, 109
Barker, John, 454
Barker, Stonie, 370
Barker's Bottom, 258
Barnes, Joseph, 630
Barnes, Randy, 671
Barnet, Charlie, 379
Barnett, Nell M., 224
Barnett, Nelson, 761
Barnette, A. O., 282
Baronner, Robert F., 395
Barrackville covered bridge, 83, *130*, *175*, *176*
Barrackville mine, 150
Barrett, James Lee, 253
Barrett & Thompson, 112
Barron, William Wallace, **44–45**, 316, *399*, 489, 602, 695; corrupt practices of, 191, 290, 575, 576, 624, 641, 663, 749; folk arts promoted

by, 248, 251, 316; public broadcasting promoted by, 595; electoral record of, 662
Bartgis, Rodney, 77
Bartlett, George R., 730
Bartlett, Leonidas, 45
Bartley, 150
Barton, Benjamin, 75
Barton, Bob, 660
Barton, William E., 313
Bartow, 132, 570
Bartrug, Peter, 781
Baruch, Bernard, 621
Bascom, Henry, 136, 474
Basie, Count, 379
Bass, Lillian, 167
Bassell, Ellen G. "Nell," 186
Bateman, William L., 489
Bates, C. W., 475
Bates, Edward, 257
Bates, L. E., 204
Bath, 498
Battle of Antietam, 138, 159, 435
Battle of Barboursville, 42, 97
Battle of Belington, 41
Battle of Brandywine (1778), 682
Battle of Buffington Island, 91, 372, 603
Battle of Cedar Creek, 359
Battle of Cloyd's Mountain, 463
Battle of First Manassas, 138, 159, 210
Battle of Fisher's Hill, 359
Battle of Gettysburg, 138, 159
Battle of Greenland Gap, 293, 386
Battle of Kernstown, 210
Battle of Lewisburg, 547
Battle of Lundy's Lane, 270
Battle of Monmouth, 415
Battle of Mucklow, 480
Battle of New Market, 138, 210, 359
Battle of New Orleans, 359, 767
Battle of Second Manassas, 138, 159, 612
Battle of the Monongahela, 265, 361, 647
Batts, Thomas, 47, 68, 223, 266, 336, 690–91, 807
Baughman's Fort, 494
Bava, John, 177, 611
Bavely, Ernest, 12
Baxter, Anne, 253
Bayer Corporation, 130, 277, 781
Bayless, Charles, 813
Beach Boys, 676
Beale, Clyde, 35
Bealin, John, 41
Beall, Eliza, 744
Beall, John Y., 437
Beall, Thomas, 744, 745
Beard, Jacob, 598
Beasley, Jerry Lynn, 157, 158
Beauchamp, Alfred, 216
Beauchamp, David, 216, 802
Beauchamp, Elizabeth Woodland, 216, 802
Beauchamp, Manlove, 216
Beauchamp, William, 216, 802
Beaumont Glass, 377
Beaver Creek Lumber Company, 717
Beaver Pond, 473
Becco, 89
Beck, George, 26
Becker, Mary, 302
Beckett, James, 479
Beckley, **48–49**, 343; health care in, 19, 727;

baseball in, 45; in Civil War, 116, 599; integration in, 364; Jews in, 383; Lebanese and Syrians in, 414; Orthodox Christians in, 550; broadcasting in, 595, 703; climate in, 600; Unitarians in, 725

Beckley, Henry M., 434

Beckley Correctional Center, 506

Beckley Exhibition Coal Mine, 49

Bedinger, Caroline Dane, 184

Bedinger, Henry, 184

Bee Knob, 271, 272

Beech Bottom Mound, 23

Beech Bottom, 84, 537

Beech Fork Dam, 244

Beecher, Henry Ward, 204

Beelor, Christopher, 401

Beiderbecke, Bix, 566

Belcher, Fannin S., 772

Belcher, Red, 423

Belington, 41

Bell, Alexander Graham, 333, 702

Bell, Bernard, 573

Bell, Emily Miriam Grazia, 236

Bell, Iris, 379, 764

Belldina's Bottoms, 491

Belle, 129, 340, 391

Belle Alkali Company, 129

Belle Works, 539

Belmont, 569

Belpre Island, 66

Belvedere Apartments, 456

Belvoir, 225

Bendale, 419

Bender, Albert K., 42

Bender, Chester R., 82

Bender, Lonnie, 426

Benedum, Sarah, 141

Benedum Airport, 140

Benedum-Trees Company, 441

Benét, Stephen Vincent, 272, 469

Benfield, William A., Jr., 584

Benford, Tommy, 379

Benjamin, Brent D., 693, 694

Bennett, Charles J. C., 228

Bennett, Gordon L., 422

Bennett, Harold, 76

Bennett, Jonathan M., 328

Bennett, Louis, 284, 285

Bennett, Nelson M., 285

Bennett, Sallie Maxwell, 52

Bennett's Fort, 270

Bennion, Mervyn S., 731

Benny, Jack, 475

Bens Run, 129, 335, 721, 722

Benwood, 83, 340, 367, 452, 787

Benwood mine, 150

Beradelli, Francisco, 61

Bergoo, 554

Berkeley, Norborne, 53

Berkeley, William, 223, 415

Berkeley Club Beverages, 77

Berkeley County, 53–54, 225, 226; farming in, 6, 7, 549; population of, 18, 577; in French and Indian War, 79; clay mining in, 143; formation of, 165, 171, 209, 257, 264, 273, 682, 738; religious life in, 171; in Dunmore's War, 207; flora in, 219; forestation in, 256, 715; Freedmen's Bureau in, 264; settlement of, 274, 336, 456; Germans in, 277; legislative representation of, 350; integration in, 364; natural features of, 395, 455; slavery in, 661; industry in, 703; Mexican War and, 767; wetlands in, 780; Wildlife Management Area in, 796

Berkeley Glass Sand Company, 283

Berkeley Intelligencer, 530

Berkeley Springs, 20, 24, **55**, 77, 482, 745

Berkley, Ashby, 558

Berkley, William, 807

Berle, Milton, 184

Berlin, 277

Bernstein, Leonard, 183

Berry, A. M., 56

Berry, C. H., 303

Berry, Chuck, 383

Berthy, J. N., Sr., 103

Beta Theta Pi, 56

Bethany, 84, 688

Bethany College, 24, **56–57**, 84, 112, 191, 213, 303–04, 543, 590, 610, 724

Bethel A.M.E. Church of Philadelphia, 2

Bethlehem Steel Corporation, 82

Better Government Amendment, 165–66

Better Highways Amendment (1973), 266

Better Roads Amendment (1964), 366, 496

Beulah Quintet (Settle), 427

Beverley, William, 713

Beverly-Fairmont Turnpike, 130, 563

Bevins, James, 321

Beyer, Frank, 563

Bhaktipada, Kirtanananda Swami (Keith Gordon Ham), 529

Bickel, "Wig," 277

Bickley, George W. L., 22

Bidgood, Lee, 223

Big Bend Tunnel, 691

Big Clear Creek, 470

Big Coal River, 27, 152

Big Creek, 132

Big Moses gas well, 722

Big Ridge Mountain, 435

Big Run Bog, 73, 247

Big Sandy Creek, 216

Big Sandy River, **58**, 152, 544; as boundary, 77, 431; fish species in, 240; flooding of, 244; navigability of, 273, 687, 730; damming of, 339; navigation on, 622

Big Sandy Trail, 360

Big Schloss, 276

Big Sewell Mountain, 628

Big Two Run, 118

Big Ugly Creek, 424, 425

Biggs, Thomas, 294

Bill Knob, 272

Billheimer, John, 428

Bingamon Creek, 758

Birch, John, 426

Birch Boom & Lumber Company, 59

Bird, Brandon, 222

Bird, Elmer, 39, 547

Birke, William D., 330

Bishop, 150

Bituminous Coal Operators Association, 471, 485, 567, 727

"Bivouac of the Dead" (Bierce), 58

Black, George W., 451

Black, William, 713

Black Fork Falls, 720

Black Minqua (Massawomeck) Indians, 491

Blackbeard, 514

Blackberry City, 480

Blackberry Creek, 322

Blackfoot Indians, 362

Black's Cabin, 542

Blacksville No. 1 mine, 150

Blackwater Boom & Lumber Company, 717

Blagrove, C., 135

Blaine, Charles, 63

Blair, James (miller), 668

Blair, James G. (school principal), 228

Blake, Basil, 205

Blake, Fred "Sheriff," 152, 153

Blake, John, 379

Blaker's Mill, 304, 376, 453, 684

Bland, Edward, 806

Bland, William Thomas, 373

Bland Hills, 277

Blankenship, Don, 487

Blasingame, Ralph, 422

Blenko, Marian, 65

Blenko, Richard, 65

Blenko, William H., 65, 666

Blenko, William H., Jr., 65

Blenko, William John, 65, 189

Blevins, Charlie, 606

Blister Swamp, 247, 695

Blizzard's Fort, 260

Bloch, Aaron, 67

Bloch, Samuel, 67

Bloch, Thomas, 67

Bloch family, 277

Bloodletting in Appalachia (Lee), 415

Bloomery, 311, 368

Blue Creek, 216, 521

Blue Ridge Tunnel, 180

Blue Rock, 663

Blueboy to Holiday—Over (Flagg), 242

Bluefield, 37, **69**; architecture in, 25, 440; baseball in, 45, 46, 670; Carnegie grant to, 112; racial and religious strife in, 137, 381; Italians in, 371; Jews in, 383; Druse in, 414; development of, 473–74, 572; Orthodox Christians in, 550; radio in, 595; streetcars in, 688; telephone service in, 702; television in, 703

Bluefield coal formation, 147

Bluefield Colored Institute, 69, 79, 324

"Bluegrass Belt," 198

Blue's Gap, 310

Bluestone Baptist Church, 429

Bluestone coal formation, 147

Bluestone Gorge, 473

Bluestone Lake, 60, 409

Bluestone Trail, 743

B'nai Israel Synagogue, 189

Boarman, Andy, 39

Boarman, Charles, 54, 72

Boch-Metsch Porcelain Company, 580

Bodley and Company, 779

Boette, Marie, 251, 277, 316

Boettner, Si, 647

Boggs, Annis, 215

Boggs, Edward, 215

Boggs, Elsie Byrd, 464

Boggs, James, 559

Boggs, John (18th-century captain), 655

Boggs, John (Civil War soldier), 559

Boggs, Lacy Ann, 73

Boggs, Neil, 143

Boggs, Ruth, 652

Boldt, Charles, 551

Boley, Donna Jean, 416
Boley, J. C., 281
Bolling School, 299
Bollman, Wendel, 73, 83
Bolton, Frances Payne, 65
Bombardier, 33
Bomkamp, Robert, 565
Bonaparte, Jerome, 696
Bonar, John S., 759
Bond, John C., 350
Bond, S. Orestes, 635
Bone, Dennis, 813
Booher, William, 802
Boomer, 370, 371
Boone, James H., 549
Boone, Joel T., 483
Boone, Weldon, 76
Boone County, **73–74**, 424, 447; natural
    resources in, 10, 148, 152, 196, 577; water
    supply for, 216; farming in, 281; racial
    tensions in, 364; fauna in, 441; housing stock
    in, 445; courthouse of, 743
Boone Timber Company, 74
Boonesborough, 400
Booth, Catherine, 638
Booth, J. D., 202
Booth, James, 448
Booth, John Wilkes, 318
Booth, William, 638
Boothby, R. L., 650
Booths Creek, 657, 700
Border Rangers, 97
Borderland, 480
Boreman, Agnes Miller, 682
Boreman, Arthur Ingraham, **75**, 107, 258, 308,
    722, 807; as Unionist, 189, 338, 555; electoral
    record of, 231, 290, 612, 647; state peniten-
    tiary built by, 505; as industrialist, 521;
    religious views of, 610; law practice of, 682;
    education policies of, 774
Boreman, Herbert S., 556
Borge, Victor, 184, 773
Borglum, Gutzon, 355, 680
Bosely, Hugh, 813
Bosley, Bruce, 352, 776
Boswell, Charles, 666
Bosworth, Albert, 666
Bosworth, J. W., 288
Boudon, David, 26
Bowden Hatchery, 241
Bowen, James, 787
Bower (historic home), 184
Bowers, Hubert, 405
Bowers Pottery, 580
Bowles, Lori Lee, 546
Bowman, Frank, 602
Boyd, Benjamin R., 78
Boyd, Charles Wesley, 269
Boyd, Daniel, 239
Boyd, Elisha, 95, 231
Boyd, Glenn, 684
Boyd, J. N., 228
Boyd, Mary W., 231
Boydville, 232
Boyers, Jacob Edgar, 646
Boyle, Albert J., 123
Boylin, James P., 102
Brackens Creek, 470
Braddock, Edward, 22, 36, 79, 179, 265, 281, 336,
    406, 415, 418, 557, 638, 745

Bradley, 17
Bradley, Joseph P., 79
Bradt, Paul, 624
Brady, Samuel, 202, 361
Brady, Spates, 405
Braeholm, 89
Bragg, Patricia, 511
Bragg, Rick, 438
Braham, Rich, 536
Brake, Annie, 476
Bramwell, J. Herbert, 80
Brandeis, Louis, 134
Brandonville, 274, 585
Brandywine, 18, 273
Brannon, Henry, 412
Bransfield, Michael J., 627
Brant, Joseph, 406
Braxton, Carter, 80
Braxton County, **80–81**, 142, 447; Indians in, 111;
    natural features of, 216; Civil War in, 338;
    wedding customs in, 753
Brazie, Charles, 432
Brazie, William, 432
Breckenridge, John, 22, 36
Breezemont, 453
Bretz, 155, 717
Breuer, Marcel, 26
Brewster, Marianne, 596
Briar Hill Coal Company, 149
Briceland, Alan, 223
Bridgeport, 140, 580, 688, 715
Bridgeport Civic Center, 52
Bridgeport Methodist Church, 52
Briery Mountain, 10
Brigham, Thomas "Doc," 660, 665
Brinkley, David, 83
Brisban, Richard, 191
Briscoe, John, 54, 500, 736
Bristle, Keith, 504
British United Turkeys of America, 420, 580
Britt Bottom, 491
Britton, Max, 504
Broaddus Hospital, 41
Broaddus, William F., 8
Broadway Pottery Company, 580
Brock, George D., 102
Brockenbrough, John W., 437, 461
Brockus, James R., 678
Brockway Glass Company, 326
Brooke, Charles Frederick Tucker, 775
Brooke, Lena T., 437
Brooke, Robert, 84, 671
Brooke Academy, 212
Brooke County, **84–85**, 542; labor unrest in, 146;
    mining disasters in, 150; religious life in, 199;
    poverty in, 581; strip mining in, 694
Brooks, Dale, 177
Brooks, Earle, 59, 60, 76, 85
Brooks, Elisha, 123, 390, 629, 636
Brooks, Fred E., 76, 85, 178, 747
Brooks, Maurice, 178
Brookside Resort, 116
Brothers, William H., 70
Brotherton, William, 478
Brown, A. H., 137
Brown, Bonn, 641
Brown, Charles, 802
Brown, James H., 390, 672
Brown, John K., 421–22

Brown, Margaret, 105
Brown, Maude, 188
Brown, Melvin, 76
Brown, Orval Elijah, 143
Brown, R. (potter), 580
Brown, Richard (Revolutionary soldier), 87
Brown, Richard L. (artist), 248
Brown, Russell, 76
Brown, Scott M., 269
Brown, Stephen D., 278
Brown, Stephen W., 617
Brown, Thornsberry Bailey, 291
Brown, Tony, 269, 391
Brown, Willard, 137
Brown, William Gay, 86, 159, 585
Brown & Williamson, 708
Brown Lumber Company, 552
Brown v. Board of Education, 4, 5, 137, 213, 339,
    363, 364, 449, 693, 772
Broyles, Bettye J., 23
Brubaker, Jacob Clement, 264
Brubeck, Dave, 379, 773
Bruce Hardwood, 808
Bruceton Mill, 746
Bruen, Matthias, 87
Brumfield, Allen, 237, 425
Brumfield, Charley, 425
Brumfield, Paris, 425
Brumfield, William W., 168, 424
Brumfield-McCoy Feud, 425
Brunner, Bob, 108
Brush Creek, 524
Brushy Knob, 618
Brushy Run, 559
Bryan, Clint, 698
Bryan, Elton "Butch," 575
Bryan, William Jennings, 320, 478, 603, 626,
    693
Bryant, Billy, 658
Bryant, Florence, 658
Bryant, I. V., 761
Bryant, Morgan, 53
Bryant, Roger, 799
Bryant, Samuel, 658
Bryant, Violet, 658
Bucci, Guy, 122
Buchanan, James, 54
Buchanon, John, 88
Buck, Ed, 353
Buck, John Lossing, 87
Buckalew, Marshall, 728, 764
Buckalew, Ralph, 44
Buckelew, Albert, Jr., 85
Buckeye, 473
Buckhannon Male and Female Academy, 729
Buckhorn Knob, 208
Buckley Island, 798
Buckskin Area Council Boy Scout Museum, 512
Buell, John, 52
Buffalo, 84, 89, 258, 583, 593
Buffalo Creek, 132, 141, 216, 245, 341, 433, 434
Buffalo Creek Farmer's Library, 422
Buffalo Site, 23
Buffington, Joel, 90
Buffington, Jonathan, 640
Buffington, Peter Cline, 354
Buffington, Thomas, 305, 640
Buffington, William, 639–40
Bull Creek, 569

Bull Moose Party, 91
Bullard, James, 85
Bullitt, Cuthbert, 145, 259
Bullitt, Thomas, 123, 266
Bullock, Laurane Tanner, 75
Bulls Head, 663
Bullskin, 584
Bullskin Run, 144
Bunker Hill, 54, 209, 220, 266, 336, 500
Bunker Hill Mill, 304
Bunnell, John, 619
Bunning, Jim, 46
Burbridge, P. B., 771
Burchett, William E., 679
Burdett, John S., 168, 350, 647, 713
Burdett, Swinton, 291
Burdette, Harry Atlee, 109
Burdette, Keith, 702
Burdette, Larry, 239
Bureau of Alcohol, Tobacco and Firearms, 95
Burgess, Conrod, 735
Burgoyne, John, 270, 415
Burke, William, 607
Burkett, Jesse, 543
Burks, Cynthia, 137
Burnet, Daniel, 654
Burnet, J. J., 132
Burnette, Walter, 43
Burns, John, 81, 93
Burns, Robert, 526
Burnside, Ambrose, 612
Burnside, Katherine, 26
Burnsville Lake, 60
Burr, Aaron, 65, 66, 93, 555
Burr, Theodore, 130, 176
Burton, Phillip, 151
Bush Creek Falls, 72
Bush, Eleanor, 76
Bush, George W., 96, 160, 613, 724
Bush's Fort, 729
Buskirk, Louisa, 596
Buster, George Washington, 68
Butcher, James A., 656
Butler, Mary Cuthbert, 44
Butters, Samuel, 580
Byars, Edward, 94
Byers, Judy, 251
Byers, R. Charles, 5
Byrd, Leyland, 776
Bye-Stander, 530
Byrd, Nancy McNeal, 637
Byrd, Richard E., 95, 184
Byrd, Robert C., 41, **95–96**, 596, 600, 776; 167th
    Fighter Squadron saved by, 8; transportation
    policies of, 17, 112; conservation and preser-
    vation policies of, 106, 318, 786; electoral
    record of, 108, 475, 602; honors to, 131, 349,
    763, 776; longevity of, 159; film biography of,
    239; political influence of, 342, 490
Byrd, Titus Dalton, 95
Byrd, Vlurma, 95
Byrd, William, 95
Byrnside, James, 735

C&O Canal, 498
C&P Telephone, 133
CB&T Financial Corporation, 516
Cabela's, 543
Cabell County, **97–98**, 424, 433, 447; farming in,

6, 708; crafts in, 17; petroglyphs in, 22; state
    park in, 50; clay mining in, 143; manufactur-
    ing in, 274; courthouse of, 354; landowning
    in, 638; settlement of, 640; Mexican War
    and, 767
Cabin Creek, 132, 385, 391, 396, 553, 666
Cabot, Godfrey L., 100, 293, 521
Cabot Corporation, 569
Cacapon Mountains, 498
Cahill, Dennis, 804
Cain, Becky, 391
Cairo, 619, 620
Cairo & Kanawha (Calico) railroad, 620
Caldwell, Eleanor, 788
Caldwell, James, 197, 759
Calhoun, 293
Calhoun, H. M., 664
Calhoun, John C., 100, 637
Calhoun County, 34, **100–101**, 250; carbon black
    industry in, 521; alcohol sales in, 589
Callaghan, David, 248
Callahan, Maude Fulcher, 101
Calloway, Cab, 56, 379, 402, 754
Cambrian Period, 261, 482
Camcare, 125
Camden, Gideon D., 328
Camden, Johnson Newlon, **102**, 808; as indus-
    trialist, 149, 162, 243, 410, 467, 521, 555, 570,
    603, 607, 753; electoral record of, 330, 376,
    555, 683, 800; questionable ethics of, 575;
    conservatism of, 576
Camden, Myra, 30
Camden Interstate Railway, 688
Cameron, 99, 150, 666
Cameron, Nancy R., 228
Cameron, Simon, 79
Camp Bartow, 9, 10
Camp Buffalo, 445
Camp Chase, 29, 557
Camp Cranberry, 617
Camp Hill Cemetery, 557
Camp Price, 203
Camp Rim Rock, 100
Camp Seebert, 747
Camp Watoga, 747
Camp Will Rogers, 747
Campbell, A. B., 131
Campbell, Alexander, Jr., 57
Campbell, Bill, 671
Campbell, Bob, 239
Campbell, David, 213
Campbell, J. Edwin, 771
Campbell, Jane, 105
Campbell, John C. (lawyer), 797
Campbell, John C. (physician), 172
Campbell, John E. (newspaperman), 572
Campbell, Sida, 279
Campbell, Thomas, 105, 135
Campbell, William Camrock, 221
Campbell's Creek Coal Company, 577
Campbells Creek, 390, 396, 483
Campbell's Creek Railroad, 597, 657
Canebrake, 568
Canfield, James B., 572
Cannelton, 107, 390, 511
Cantrell, Tommy, 546
Capehart, Harry J., 5, 137
Caperton, Alice B., 330
Caperton, William Gaston, III, **108**, 402; state
    parks and, 50; appointments of, 144; Better

Government Amendment backed by, 165–
    66; preservation policies of, 168; progres-
    sivism of, 191, 342; education policies of, 214,
    642; electoral record of, 223, 290, 443, 576,
    588; administrative reorganization by, 407;
    family business interests of, 498–99; labor
    unrest and, 567, 702
Caperton Rail Trail, 501
Capito, "Gus," 239
Caplan, Fred, 383
Caplinger, Warren, 107, 546
Capon Springs, 77, 309, 482
Carbide and Carbon Chemicals Corporation, 129
Carden, Isaac, 42
Cardwell, Mark, 761
Carelink, 125
Carey, Michael, 575
Cargill, Lucy, 464
Carlile, John Snyder, 1, 103, **112**, 140, 168, 189,
    318, 338, 564, 612
Carlisle, 197, 574
Carlisle, Bill, 546
Carlisle, Cliff, 546
Carlsen, Jack, 447
Carlsen, Vause, 447
Carlyle, John, 654
Carnegie, Andrew, 545
Carnegie Gas, 198
Carney, E. M., 558
Carolina and Northwestern Railroad, 533
Carolina, Clinchfield & Ohio Railroad, 115
Carpenter, Benjamin, 113
Carpenter, Ernie, 114, 547
Carpenter, Frances, 396
Carpenter, Hiram A., 570
Carpenter, Jeremiah, 113, 114
Carpenter, Kate, 396
Carpenter, Mary Chapin, 508
Carpenter, Nicholas, 396
Carpenter, Shelt, 114
Carpenter, Solomon "Old Solly" (settler), 113,
    751
Carpenter, Solomon "Devil Sol" (fiddler), 114,
    142
Carpenter, Tom, 114
Carr, Fred, 800
Carr, Robert, 647
Carr, Thomas, 114
Carrico, James, 529
Carrier, John P., 813
Carroll, Bill, 604
Carroll, Jim O'Dell, 626
Carrollton, 175, 176
Carry the Tiger to the Mountain (Lee), 166
Carter, Benny, 56, 379
Carter, Emory, 115
Carter, Hazo W., Jr., 772
Carter, Henry Jared, 761
Carter, James, 115, 292
Carter, Jimmy, 140, 509, 673, 733
Carter, Joseph, 727
Carter, Phil, 137
Carter, Robert "King," 226
Carter, Thomas, 258
Carter Family, 316, 811–12
Carter Oil, 198
Caruthers, Isaac, 637
Carvell, Kenneth, 76
Carver, George Washington, 104, 710
Carwithen, Virginia, 777

Casber, Sandy, 803
Case, E. Lewis, 545
Casey, Peter, Jr., 402
Cash, Johnny, 676
Cash, June Carter, 676
Cassella, Billy, 504
Cassiano, Dick, 286
Cassville (Fort Gay), 749
Cast Thy Bread, 154
Castle, Annie L., 813
Castle Brook Carbon, 198
Casto, Nicholas, 116
Catholic Knights of America, 506
Catlette, Martin, 117
Catskill Delta, 18
Catt, Carrie Chapman, 414
Caudy, James, 118
Cavalier Apartments, 456
Cave Mountain Gap, 208
Cave Mountain, 424
Cayuga Indians, 369, 713
Cedar Grove (Kellys Creek), 378, 393
Cedarton coal seam, 148
Center for Professional Development, 108
Center Point, 175, 176, 198
Centerville (Rock Cave), 729
Centner, Lewis, 633
Central Glass Company, 643, 735
Central Pacific Railroad, 355
Central West Virginia Racing Association, 504
Centralia (Laurel Fork), 113, 114, 129, 491
Century Aluminum, 372
Ceredo Crescent, 530
Chaddock, Floyd "Budd," 504
Chafin, Levicy, 320
Chalakaatha Indians, 653
Chambers, Ed, 37, 322, 350, 429–30, 480
Chambers, Geraldine Kiser, 122
Chambers, James E., 122
Chambers, John, 125
Chambers, Robert Charles "Chuck," **122**, 702
Chambers, Sally, 350
Champe, John, 122
Champion Glass, 446
Chapin, Dewey, 649
Chapin, Tom, 664
Chapline, Hanson, 542
Chapman, John (Hancock County settler), 527
Chapman, John Gadsby (artist), 688
Chapman, William, Sr., 658
Chapmanville, 4, 433
Charles I, king of England, 336, 578
Charles II, king of England, 225, 336
Charles Town Academy, 225
Charleston, **123–25**, 145, 274, 577; black education in, 3, 4; as capital, 25, 26, 110, 341, 376, 391; baseball in, 45, 46, 670; bridges in, 83; Carnegie grant to, 112; industry in, 211, 282, 283, 340, 703; water plant in, 216; public works in, 296; ferries in, 307; African-Americans in, 334, 390; labor movement in, 340; integration in, 364; Irish in, 367; Jews in, 382, 383; Lebanese and Syrians in, 414; Muslims in, 513; Orthodox Christians in, 550, 611; in Civil War, 584; Presbyterians in, 584; broadcasting in, 595, 703, 741, 750; climate in, 600; Rotary in, 629; hotels in, 630; as county seat, 655–56; socialism in, 665; streetcars in, 688; telephone service in, 702; Unitarians in, 725; architecture in, 735, 742

Charleston Art Association, 11
Charleston, Clendenin & Sutton Railroad, 148
Charleston Industrial Corporation, 532
Charleston Middle Ferry, 238
Charleston Renaissance Corporation, 141
Charleston United Church Women, 364
Charleston Vitreous Clay Products Company, 143
Charleston Women's Club, 456
Charlestown Gazette, 530
Charlotte, queen of England, 733
Charlton, Armstrong, 580
Charlton, Cornelius, 159
Chase, O. G., 330
Chase, Salmon P., 257
Chase, William Merritt, 413
Chatham Convention, 191
Cheat Neck, 129
Cheat River, 10, **128–29**, 256, 492; natural features of, 10, 256; covered bridges across, 83; damming of, 127, 233, 357, 747; endangered species near, 219; flooding of, 244, 245; industry along, 329; navigability of, 431, 432, 710
Cheek, T. M., 677
Chelyan, 98
Chemical Workers Union, 408
Chen, Ai Qiu, 349
Chenoweth, Eli, 563
Chernoff, Howard, 595
Cherokee Sue, 632
Cherry Grove, 559
Cherry River, 273
Cherry River Boom & Lumber Company, 178, 532, 617
Chesapeake & Ohio Canal, 317, 535, 578
Chester, 311, 348, 536, 625
Chestnut Flat, 271
Chestnut Mountain, 10
Chestnut Ridge, 492
Chickerneo, John, 286
Child, Francis, 268
Childers, Bazel, 569
Childers, Dave, 422
Childers Site, 583
Chillers (film), 239
Chilson, Ernest, 61
Chilton, Elizabeth, 126
Chilton, Joseph E., 126
Chimney Top, 535
Chinn, Susan, 400
Chipley, J. J., 497
Choctaw Indians, 90, 362
Christensen, Martin, 447
Christian Commission, 456
Christman, Paul, 286
Christopher, David, 51
Christopher, Frank, 777
Church, Henry, 781
Church, Sam, Jr., 727
Church of the Good Shepherd (Kanawha City), 221
Church of the Good Shepherd (Parkersburg), 221
Cincinnati Gas and Electric Company, 155
Cincinnati, Portsmouth & Virginia Railroad, 533
Cinder Bottom, 401
Cingular, 703
Citizens Mutual, 757
City Holding Company, 136, 137
City Hospital Training School for Nurses, 545

City Net, 137
Civic Interest Progressives, 137
Civil Aeronautics Act, 33
Civil Air Patrol, 33
Civil Rights Act (1964), 364, 603, 624, 799
Civil War, **137–38**, 338–39, 767; farming disrupted by, 5; Battle of Allegheny Mountain, 9–10; Averell's Raid, 32; railroads in, 37; Jefferson County in, 38, 380; churches in, 41; Beckley in, 48, 116, 599; Berkeley County in, 54; Berkeley Springs in, 55; Bethany College in, 57; Beverly in, 57; Battle of Blair Mountain, 64; Blue Ridge in, 68; espionage in, 78, 320; Bulltown in, 91; Morgantown in, 92, 386; Bushwhackers in, 94; Monroe County in, 94, 493, 494; Cabell County in, 97; Calhoun County in, 100; camps in, 104; Battle of Carnifex Ferry, 112–13, 615; Jackson County in, 116, 372; caves used in, 118; Ceredo in, 121, 530; Charleston in, 123–24, 584; Battle of Cheat Mountain, 128, 628; Clarksburg in, 140; Clay County in, 142; coal industry in, 148; Confederate soldiers in West Virginia in, 158–59; Department of West Virginia in, 193–94; Doddridge County in, 197–98; Eastern Panhandle in, 209; Echols as officer in, 210; Wirt County in, 216; Flat Top Mountain in, 242; Floyd as officer in, 248; West Virginia formed during, 257; Wood County in, 258; Gauley River in, 273; Glen Ferris Inn in, 284; veterans' organizations and, 291; Grant County in, 293; Greenbrier County in, 299; Guyandotte in, 305, 381; Hampshire County in, 310; Hancock County in, 312; Hardy County in, 314; Harpers Ferry in, 316, 317; Harris as officer in, 318; Logan County in, 338, 433; Nicholas County in, 338, 531–32; Fairmont in, 386; Kanawha County in, 390–91; Keyser in, 401; Lewis County in, 419; Lewisburg in, 420, 421; Lightburn as officer in, 423; Lincoln County in, 424; Logan Wildcats in, 434; Loring Raid in, 435; Mannington in, 445; Martinsburg in, 456; Mercer County in, 473; Mineral County in, 481; Moccasin Rangers in, 489; Monongalia County in, 492–93; Battle of Moorefield, 497; Morgan's Raid, 500; newspapers in, 530; Northwestern Turnpike in, 538; Ohio County in, 543; Parkersburg in, 555; Pendleton in, 559; Battle of Philippi, 562–63; Battle of Pigeon Roost, 565; Pocahontas County in, 570; Presbyterians in, 584; Preston County in, 585; Princeton in, 588; Putnam County in, 592; Raleigh County in, 599; Randolph County in, 601; Ravenswood in, 603; Battle of Rich Mountain, 617; Romney in, 627; Rosecrans as general in, 628; saltpeter mining during, 637, 663; Shepherdstown in, 656; Shinnston in, 657; Summers County in, 691; Sutton in, 695; Taylor County in, 701; Tucker County in, 717; Upshur County in, 729
Civilian Pilot Training Act, 33
Clark, Andrew, 101
Clark, Edward C., 350
Clark, George Rogers, 31, 140, 202, 259, 318, 400
Clark, Hyre D., 228
Clark, J. B. "Champ," 57
Clark, J. F. J., 269
Clark, Joe, 73
Clark, Mary Vinson, 750

Clark, Red, 789
Clark, T. S., 126
Clark, Walter Eli, 126, 672
Clark, William, 418
Clarke-McNary Act (1924), 161, 517
Clarksburg Convention, 112
Clarksburg Fuel Company, 162
Clarkson, John, 305
Clay, Buckner W., 126, 143
Clay, Cecil, 508, 634
Clay, Henry, 68, 141, 142, 299, 301, 344, 630, 655
Clay, Lyell B., 126, 143
Clay County, **142–43**, 250; industry in, 80;
    natural features of, 216; apples in, 287
Claypool, John, 709, 710
Clayton, John, 48, 75
Clayton Anti-Trust Act (1904), 186
Clean Air Act, 511
Clean Water Act, 511, 730, 781
Clear Channel Communications, 596
Clear Fork, 152
Clearon Corporation, 130
Clem, William H., 422
Clemens, Sherrard, 1, 168
Clendenin, 129, 145, 216, 391, 724
Clendenin, Alexander, 145, 259
Clendenin, Ann, 145
Clendenin, Archibald, 145
Clendenin, Archibald, Jr., 145
Clendenin, Charles, 123, 145
Clendenin, Jane, 145
Clendenin, John, 145
Clendenin, Mary Ellen, 145
Clendenin, Robert, 145
Clendenin, William, 145, 259
Clere, Slim, 546
Cleveland, Grover, 77, 800
Click, Farmer Bill, 703
Clifford, Clark, 662
Clifford, Isaac, 145
Clifford, Saltipa Kent, 145
Cliffside Amphitheater, 292
Clifton, 146, 459
Clifton Heights, 562
Clinch Mountain Clan, 70, 146, 167, 604
Clinchfield Coal Company, 90, 793
Cline, Charlie, 70, 434
Cline, Ezra, 70, 434
Cline, Ned, 70, 434
Cline, Patsy, 239, 324
Cline, Perry, 323, 464
Cline, W. P., 438
Clinton, Bill, 122, 151, 326, 333, 383, 475
Clover, 258, 583
Clover Bottom, 473
Clover Complex, 583
Clover Phase, 23
Clovic, E. E., 349
Clovis, Jesse, 76
CMI Inc., 263
Coal Act (1992), 483, 484, 596
Coal & Iron Railroad, 300
Coal Employment Project, 805
Coal Fork, 396
Coal Heritage Trail, 371
Coal River & Western Railroad, 132
Coal River Mining & Lumber Company, 74
Coal River Trail, 360
Coal Siding, 554
Coal Valley (Montgomery), 45, 233, 234, 324

Coalburg, 215, 367
Coalfield Fuel Company, 161
Coalfields Expressway, 600
Coalwood, 115
Coastal Lumber Company, 82, 721, 730, 808
Cobb, Fleming, 63
Coburn, Nellie R., 85
Coffin Hollow (Musick), 251
Coffindaffer, Billy, 70
Coffman (Kauffman), Isaac, 472
Cogar, Arden, Jr., 437
Cogar, Paul, 437
Colasessano, Filippo, 560
Colasessano, Spider, 560
Colburn, S. E., 693
Cole, Samuel, 152
Cole, Thomas W., 772
Cole, William Jacob, 777
Coleman, Cy, 662
Coleman, John V., 5
Colfax Brick Company, 143
Colgate-Palmolive, 436
Colin Anderson Center, 569
Collier, John, 230
Colliers, 150, 670
Collins Colliery Company, 155, 789
Colston, Sophie Hunter, 417
Columbia Gas Transmission (United Fuel Gas
    Company), 155, 521
Columbia Natural Resources, 521
Columbia West Virginia, 808
Colyer, Dale, 410
Cometti, Elizabeth, 691
Commerce Bank, 516
Commercial Bancshares, 757
Community Action Program (CAP), 742
Comuntzis brothers, 475
ConAgra, 497, 581
Concord University (College), 70, 76, **157–58**,
    326, 474, 533
Concrete Steel Bridge Company, 83
Concrete Steel Engineering Company, 227
Conelly (Manchin), Gayle, 443
Conemaugh coal formation, 147
Confederate Mountaineers, 70
Conference of Appalachian Governors, 19
Congress of Industrial Organizations (CIO), 60,
    407, 408, 420, 613, 770
Congress of Racial Equality (CORE), 137
Conley, Perry, 320, 489
Conley, William Gustavus, 61, **160–61**, 313;
    appointments of, 103; lynchings deplored by,
    137; financial crisis under, 295
Conlin, Thomas, 773
Connell, Dudley, 70
Conner, Carolyn, 143
Conner, James, 356
Connolly, John, 757
Conrad, Clyde, 280
Conrad, John, 802
Conrad, Peter, 802
Conrad, Ulrich, Sr., 464, 559
Conservation Fund, 265
Consol No. 9 mine, 150
Consolidated Natural Gas Transmission, 293, 521
Continental Can Corporation, 325, 326
Continental Clay Products, 143
Conway, Archie, 434
Cook (general), 299
Cook, Douglas, 327

Cook, Harvey, 674
Cook, Henrietta, 682
Cook, Jeff Holland, 788
Cook, John Edwin, 745
Cook, W. H., 566
Cook, Weldon, 675
Cooke, George Esten, 26
Cooke, John (settler), 815
Cooke, John Esten (novelist), 513
Cooke, Roy Lee, 626
Cook-Hayman Pharmacy Museum, 512
Coolidge, Calvin, 36, 139, 186, 288, 341, 502
Coolidge, William H., 369
Coon, Ralph, 43
Coonskin Park, 124
Coonskin Ridge, 816
Cooper, Chris, 461
Cooper, Edward, 80
Cooper, Grant, 773
Cooper, Wilbur "Lefty," 722
Co-operative Transit Company, 688
Coopers, 72, 473
Cooper's Mill, 304
Copas, Cowboy, 324, 356
Copeland, Leonard, 153
Copely oil well, 521
Copenhaver, John T., 723
Coppola, Francis Ford, 239
Corbett, James "Gentleman Jim," 66
Corbly, John, 40, 256
Corbly, Lawrence J., 453
Core, Andrew S., 534
Corhart Refractories, 729
Cornett, Ewel, 323, 704
Corning Glass, 54
Cornplanter (Seneca chief), 361, 647
Cornwallis, Charles, Marquess, 270
Cornwell, John Jacob, 52, **169–70**, 341; Capitol
    fire and, 110; as banker, 111; electoral record
    of, 187, 191; grave of, 311, 360; in Mine Wars,
    499; state police force backed by, 678, 702;
    women's suffrage and, 806
Cornwell, William, 311
Corrin, Frazer, 540
Cortez, Froggie, 797
Corum, William (Billy Denver), 504
Costello, Vincent, 383
Cotiga Development Corporation, 411
Cottle, John Brooks, 501
Cotton, Henrietta S., 799
Cottrell, Noah, 101, 242, 556
Cottrell, O. B., 504
Coughlin, Cornelius, 368
Council for Community and Economic Develop-
    ment, 108
Council For West Virginia Archaeology, 24
Council of the Southern Mountains, 20
County Unit Plan (1933), 339
Covington & Ohio Railroad, 131
Cox, Benjamin, 372
Cox, Donald, 76
Cox, Friend, 756
Cox, Isaac, 252
Cox, Israel, 756
Cox, Jacob D., 42, 391, 421, 565, 628, 641, 673–74
Cox, Jonathan, 756
Cox, Kenyon, 413
Cox, Robert, 159
Coyne, Jeanne Eleanore, 718
Crabtree, Paul L., 742

Craft, James Elliott "Jack," 162
Craig, Neville, 49
Craig, Wick, 546
Craig-Botetourt Electric Cooperative, 631
Craik, James, 155, 179, 266, 372, 458, 535
Cramblet, T. E., 57
Cramblet, W. H., 57
Cramer, William, 61
Cranberry, 197, 491
Cranberry Summit, 28
Cranberry Wildlife Management Area, 796, 798
Craneco, 89
Cranny Crow, 435
Craven, Avery, 691
Cravotta, Samuel A., 803
Crawford, John M., 808
Crawford, Theron C., 13–14, 321, 323
Crawford, William (captain), 259, 361, 372
Crawford, William H. (textile entrepreneur), 703
Crawford Woolen Company, 457, 703
Cree Indians, 362
Creek Indians, 90
Creel, Alexander H., 569, 635
Creel, Bushrod W., 803
Cresap Mound, 23
Cresap, Thomas, 542
Crescent Manufacturing Company, 29
Cresswell, Nicholas, 294
Creston, 429
Crichlow, B. A., 193
Cricket (sternwheeler), 58
Criss, Howard Paul, Jr., 437, 487
Criswell, Benjamin C., 159
Crites, 89
Crocker, Charles, 355
Crocker, L. T., 813
Croghan, George, 65
Crompton, 130
Crompton Corporation, 722
Cromwell, Oliver, 336
Crook, George, 194, 314, 397, 420, 421, 469, 587
Crooked Creek Church of Christ, 269
Crosby, Bing, 475
Cross Creek, 84
Cross Lanes, 136, 716
Cross Roads (Pruntytown), 580, 589, 700
Crouch, Jackson, 104
Crouch, John, 717
Crow, Burton "Irish," 510
Crowley, John B., 437 633
Crown, 89
Cruger, Daniel, 655
Crump's Bottom, 473
Crystal Block Coal Company, 798
Culbertson, Andrew, 691
Culverson Creek, 395, 659
Culverson Creek Cave, 118
Cumberland, 38
Cumberland Road, 520
Cumberland Valley Railroad, 54
Cummins, D. Duane, 57
Cunningham, James L., 564
Cunningham, John, 632
Cunningham, Nathan, 87, 182
Cunningham-Skinner farm, 81, 82
Cuppy, John, 527
Currence's Fort, 600
Currie, Charles L., 785
Curry, Hugh, 395
Curry, Richard O., 168

Curtin, George W., 554
Curtis, Charles, 215
Cusick, Allison, 76
Custer, George Armstrong, 159
Custer, Philander, 298
Custis, Mary, 415
Cutlip, Odiem, 241
Czolgosz, Leon, 391

D. E. McNichol China, 580
D. F. Mohler and Sons, 74
D. George Harris & Associates, 283
Dabney, Virginius, 672
Dahle family, 199
Dahle, Johann, 277
Dailey, 26, 601, 628, 721
Dalhart, Vernon, 59, 283
Dancing Outlaw (film), 239
Dandridge, A. B., 184
Daniels, 133
Danner, Ray, 642
Danoff, Bill, 172
Darby, Abraham, 154
Darke, William, 54
Darlington, H. C., 76
Darrow, Clarence, 404
Darst, John, 109
Daugherty, George, 508
Daugherty, Jeanie Caldwell, 404
Davenport, Frances Isabel, 158
Davidovich, Lolita, 676
Davidson(-Stevenson) Porcelain Company, 580
Davidson, Donald, 262
Davidson, Ken, 392
Davidson's Ferry, 237
Davies, Thomas P., 813
Davies, William E., 117
Davis, 10, 438, 699, 717
Davis, Andy, 447
Davis, Edwin H., 22, 504–05
Davis, H. O., 666
Davis, Hannibal, 76
Davis, Henry Gassaway, **185–86**, 290, 518, 564,
    575, 601, 602; orphanage financed by, 133; as
    industrialist, 148, 217, 218, 341, 410, 467, 535,
    570, 607, 684, 694, 717, 729, 761–62, 778;
    electoral record of, 398, 481; conservatism
    of, 576; as tax commissioner, 790
Davis, Homer, 624
Davis, Innis C., 766
Davis, James Edward, 26–27
Davis, Jefferson, 210, 384
Davis, Jim, 447
Davis, John J., 1, 168
Davis, Joseph, 197
Davis, Lemuel Clarke, 187
Davis, Leonard "Lynn," 423, 541, 789, 805
Davis, Mary Louise, 217
Davis, Nathan, 197, 759
Davis, Reed, 813
Davis, Richard Harding, 187
Davis, Robert Jean, 694
Davis, Thomas B., 370, 579
Davis, Thomas E., 439
Davis, Thomas Jefferson, 478
Davis, Tyreeca, 76
Davis, William, 197
Davis & Elkins College, **185**, 217, 218, 290, 601–02;
    folklore archive at, 251; athletics at, 329, 671;

founding of, 350; architecture of, 456; festivals
    at, 509; Presbyterian ties of, 584, 610
Davis Child Shelter, 133
Davis furnace, 492
Davis Spring, 395
Davis Twins, 546
Davisson, Daniel, 140, 318, 578
Dawson, Daniel Boone, 470, 526
Dawson, William Mercer Owens, 103, **187–88**,
    290; appointments of, 160, 420, 479; elec-
    toral record of, 169; as "Elkins governor," 341
Day, Elisha, 580
Day, William, 580
Dayton, Arthur (Charleston lawyer), 11
Dayton, Arthur Spencer (Barbour County
    lawyer), 188
Dayton, Ruth Woods, 42
Dayton, Spencer, 188
Daywood Foundation, 42
de Graffenreid, Christopher, 68, 223, 266, 336, 476
de la Renta, Oscar, 507
Dean, Dizzy, 705
Dean, E. Keith, 189
Dean, S. Brooks, 189
Decker, John, 84, 252
Decker, Thomas, 276
Decker, Tobias, 492
Deckers Creek, 493, 500
Dedmon, Donald, 454
Deem, Jacob, 802
Deepwater Railway Company, 359, 739
Deer Creek, 300
Deer Hunter, The (film), 239
Deitz, Dennis, 278
Delaware Indians, 131, 259, 264, 265, 267, 361,
    369, 402, 406, 481, 576, 653, 713
Delf Norona Museum, 23
Delmore Brothers, 546
Delta Psi Omega, 11, 12
Dempsey, Jack, 184
Dempwolf, Fred, 468
Denmar Correctional Center, 506
Denmar, 192, 349, 591
Dennis, Henry E., 269
Denny, Reginald, 397
Dent, Marshall Mortimer, 193
Dent, William, 802
Dents Run, 175, 176
Denver, Billy (William Corum), 504
Denver, John, 172
Depaulo, Elizabeth Victoria, 742
Derrick Herald, 530
Derrick, W. R., 2
Despard, Laura E., 286
Dessalines, Jean-Jacques, 461
Devil Creek, 490
Devon, William "Babe," 133
Devonian Era, 18, 147, 261, 300, 549
Devonian Shales, 520
Dewey, John, 28, 139
Dewey, Thomas E., 384
Dewing, W. S., 128
DeWitt, Joyce, 403
DeYoung, Jerry, 472
DiCaprio, Leonardo, 269
Dickason, Henry Lake, 70
Dickey, James, 333
Dickey, M. Lizzie, 228
Dickinson, Angia M., 359
Dickinson, Henry Clay, 196, 394

Dickinson, John L., 196, 395
Dickinson, John, 196, 629, 735
Dickinson, William, Jr., 196, 394
Dickinson, William, Sr., 196
Different Drummer (film series), 239
Diggs, Mary Appolonia, 194
Diller, Dwight, 309
Dillion, "Quince," 607
Dillon, J. C., 68
Dillon, Josiah, 228
DiMaggio, Joe, 370
Dingell-Johnson Act, 162
Dingess Creek, 132
Dingess, Hugh, 425
Dingess, James, 434
Dinsmoor, James, 569
Dinwiddie, Robert, 78, 336, 638
DiOrio, Rene, 426
Disciples of Christ, 56, 105, 135
Dishinger, Ronald, 773
Dixon Rock Shelter, 23
Dixon, Archilles, 204
Dixon, Ellen, 204
Dixon, Jeremiah, 459
Dixon, "King" Samuel, 234, 699
D-Mac Industries, 407
Dobbin Ridge, 226
Dobbin Slashing, 247
Dobson, Helen, 611
Dodd, William E., 691
Doddridge County, **197-98**; Grange in, 292;
    Swan lands in, 696
Doddridge County Window Glass Company, 198,
    760
Dodrill, William C., 51, 463
Doe Run, 198
Dole, Elizabeth, 483, 567
Dollar Savings & Trust Company, 643
Doll's Run, 493
Dolly Ridge, 277
Dominion Power, 506–07, 684, 685
Dominion Resources, 293, 521
Dominion Transmission Corporation, 348
Dominion Window Glass Company, 701
Domino, Fats, 754
Donaghho, A. P., 580
Donahue, Florence, 368
Donahue, John, 368
Donahue, Patrick J., 610, 627, 633, 697
Donnally, Andrew, 394
Donnally, Moses W., 125, 126
Donnally family, 266
Donnally's Fort, 267
Doonan, Katie, 703
Dope! (Lee), 415
Dornblazer, George, 509
Dorsey, Tommy, 379
Dos Passos, John, 179
Douglas, Christopher, 534
Douglas, Isaac R., 314
Douglas, John, 428
Douglas, Joshua, 320
Douglas, Stephen, 710
Douglas, Wilson, 114, 143, 238, 547, 790
Douglass, Frederick, 191, 685
Douglass, Gus R., 7, 223
Dow, Herbert, 200
Dowling, Dolores, 811
Downs, George, 489
Dragan, Jon, 791

Dragoo, Don, 23
Drake, Frank, 519
Drake, Laurie Boggs, 416
Dramatics (periodical), 12
Draper, Dorothy, 302
Draper, Lyman Copeland, 135, 202, 361, 426
Dreiser, Theodore, 179, 423
Drennen, William "Bill," 24, 239, 427
Dressler, Lester, 202
Driesell, Lefty, 116
Drinker, John, 26
Drinko, John Deaver, 570
Driscol, John, 488
Droddy, Charles, 622
Droddy's Mills (Droddyville; Walton), 622
Droop Mountain Bog, 178, 247
Dry Branch, 553
Dry Fork Railroad, 657
Dry Fork, 466
Dry Forks River, 127, 129
DuBois, Henry, 152
DuBois, W. E. B., 137, 531, 655, 685
Ducongé, Peter, 662
Duffie, Alfred N., 203
Dugger, Jerold O., 70
Duhring, 72, 473
Dulin, Edward, 527, 781
Dumas, John Peter, 197, 695
Dumont, Ebenezer, 562
Dunbar Fairgrounds, 503, 504
Dunbar Flint Glass, 205
Dunbee-Combex Ltd, 457
Duncan, Edwin S., 135
Dunkard Bottom, 266, 276
Dunkard coal formation, 147
Dunkard Fork Lake, 409
Dunkards, 129
Dunlap (captain), 261
Dunlop, David L., 656
Dunloup Branch Railroad, 205
Dunn Woolen, 703, 704
DuPont Corporation, 54, 124, 129, 130, 207, 211,
    391, 408, 473, 532, *539*, 555, 704, 808
Duppstadt, Homer, 76
Duquesne Bottle Factory, 552
Durand, Asher B., 28
Durante, Jimmy, 626
Durbin and Greenbrier Valley Railroad, 146, 658,
    771
Durgan, Andrew, 611
Durian, Vicki, 598
Duskey, Daniel, 489
Dutch Hollow Wine Cellars, 453
Duthie, George H., 666
Duval, Harding H., 146
Dye, James, 172
Dye, Reuben, 802
Dye, W. T. W., 172
Dylan, Bob, 464

Eades Fort, 100
Eades Mill, 72
Eagan, Ellen, 30
Eagle, William, 208
Earl Ray Tomblin Conference Center, 133
Early, Jubal, 210, 293, 469, 497
Easley, Walter, 536
East Lynn Dam, 244
East Ohio Gas Company, 348

East Steubenville, 583
Eastern States Archaeological Federation, 23
Eastern West Virginia Regional Airport, 32
Eastern Wilderness Act (1975), 550, 764
Eaton, Allen, 45
Eccles, 150, 152, 210, 341
Eccleston, J. H., 221
Echelon network, 221
Echols, Harriet, 107
Eckarly brothers, 10
Eckerlin, Gabriel, 266, 276
Eckerlin, Israel, 266, 276
Eckerlin, Samuel, 266, 276
Eckert, Allan W., 782
Eckstine, Billy, 379
Economy Tumbler, 501
Eddy, Richard, 727
Edemar, 683
Edison, Thomas, 128
Edmundton, 601
Edray Hatchery, 241
Education Reform Act, 108
Edwards, William S., 367
Edwards Run, 310
Edworthy, Z. B., 171
Effron, Ida, 754
Egan, Michael, 367
Egnor, Virginia Ruth, 184
Eicher, Asta, 582
Eightmile Island, 145
Eisenhower, Dwight D., 65, 131, 291, 301–02, 341,
    715, 811
Eisenhower Interstate Highway System, 332
Eisenstaedt, Alfred, 184
Elbin, Paul N., 759
Eldridge, Roy, 56, 379
Elinipsico, 169, 260
Elizabethan English, 195
Elizabethtown, 505
Eljer Company, 580
Elk Creek, 140, 318, 758
Elk Garden, 481
Elk Lick Run, 236
Elk Milling and Produce Company, 396
Elk Mountain (Pocahontas County), 10
Elk Mountain (Randolph County), 10
Elk Refining Company, 521
Elk River Coal & Lumber Company, 79–80, 90,
    146, 793
Elk River, 10, **216–17**; naming of, 113;
    navigability of, 141, 730; logging and, 142;
    damming of, 233, 430; fishing in, 241
Elk River Touring Center, 660
Elkem Metals Corporation, 284, 325, 725
Elkford Lake, 409
Elkhorn Creek, 466
Elkhorn Tunnel, 533
Elkins, Barbara, 649
Elkins, Davis, 217
Elkins, Robert, 649
Elkins, Stephen Benton, 185, **218**, 308, 518, *575*,
    602, 747; tax hikes opposed by, 30; as indus-
    trialist, 82, 217, 502, 601, 694, 717, 778; as
    senator, 159, 186, 188, 790; as power broker,
    284, 286, 341, 576, 612; rumors surrounding,
    377; death of, 644, 647
Elkins Coal & Coke Company, 82, 540
Elkins Industries, 444
Elkins Speedway, 504

Elko Chemical, 129
Elk-Poca, 549
Elkwater, 128, 601
Ellet, Charles Jr., 787
Ellicott, Andrew, 359
Ellicott brothers, 329, 359
Ellington, Duke, 70, 379, 566, 754
Elliot, William, 261
Elliott, Lloyd H., 143
Ellis, Brooks F., 570
Ellis, James M., 233, 540
Ellis, Lester, 327
Ellis, Thomas, 327
Ellison, J. Frank, 738
Elmore, Clarence C., 663
Ely-Thomas mill, 654
Emerson (Amberson), John, 90
Emigrant Aid Company, 121
Emmert, Howard H., 55
Empire Bank, 140
Empire Savings and Loan Company, 396
Employees Security League, 408, 681
Empress Glass, 701
Endicott Johnson Shoes, 465
Energetic (Bancroft), 593
Engle, Henry Everett, 279, 764
Engle, John, 726
English (town), 465
Enoch, Isaac, 802
Erickson, Charlie O., 808
Erie Indians, 544
Erskine, William, 637
Erwin, Robert B., 763
Escoffier, Auguste, 498
Eskdale, 553, 666
Eskew, Stanley, 509
Essington, Joseph H., 23, 760
Estep, Cesco, 91
Estep, Speedy, 504
Esterow, Milton, 348
Etam, 586
Etzel, Ed, 671
Euclid Manufacturing Company, 552
Eureka Art Glass Company, 65
Evangelical Association (EV), 475
Evans, 504
Evans, Angus, 152
Evans, Dale, 676
Evans, Dan, 76
Evans, Dana, 76
Evans, Flem, 812
Evans, John (lieutenant governor of Delaware), 500
Evans, John (settler), 256
Evans, O. W., 798
Evans, Vincent, 120
Evans, Virginia B., 26
Evans, Walker, 230
Evansdale, 501
Even the Heavens Weep (film), 239
Everett, John, 479
Everett, Nathan, 479
Everettville, 150
Evergreen, 548
Everhart, Catherine, 513
Everhart, George, 513
Eversole, Robyn, 428
Evick, Francis, 263
Ewen-Purcell Horn Antenna, 519
Ewing, William, 797

Excel Homes, 445
Exhibition Coal Mine and Coal Camp, 512
Eye, Osbra, 76

Fagan, Norman L., 248, 287, 323, 704
Fairchance, 583
Fairchild, John, 723
Fairfax, Bryan, 225, 226
Fairfax, Joseph Sinclair, 25, 505
Fairfax, Robert, 226
Fairlea, 133, 676
Fairmont, 93, 227; baseball in, 45; railway bridge
    at, 83; craft unions in, 340; Jews in, 383; in
    Civil War, 386; mansions in, 448; miners
    hospital in, 484; streetcars in, 491, 688;
    industry in, 551; broadcasting in, 595, 741;
    telephone service in, 702
Fairmont and Clarksburg Traction Company,
    491, 748
Fairmont Coal Company, 149, 150, 162, 227, 243,
    747, 748
Fairmont Electric Light and Power, 491
Fairmont Male and Female Seminary, 213
Fairmont, Morgantown & Pittsburgh Railroad,
    501, 502
Fairmont True Virginian, 530
Fairmont-Wheeling Turnpike, 130
Fall Rock, 429
Fall Run, 344
Fallam, Robert, 47, 68, 223, 266, 336, 690–91,
    807
Falling Rock Creek, 107
Falling Waters, 53, 584
Family Lines, 181
Fanco, 89
Faris, Frederic F., 25, 278, 787
Farley Branch Trail, 103
Farley, Francis, 599
Farmer, A. B., 747
Farmer, Bill, 608
Farmers' Advocate, 530
Farmers' Alliance, 292
Farmington, 150, 151, 341, 448, 480
Farnsworth, Daniel Duane Tompkins, 88, 231,
    290; accession of, 647; family background
    of, 730
Farrow, Ernest, 379
Fast, Richard E., 462
Faulconer, John, 334
Faulconer, Tom, 334
Faulkner, Charles James, Jr., 232, 437, 596, 698
Faulkner, William, 427
Fayette County, 233–34; architecture in, 26;
    industry in, 34, 369; coal mining in, 150, 155,
    157, 166, 192, 196, 574; courthouse of, 278;
    farming in, 281; labor disputes in, 346; Irish
    in, 368; scenic roads through, 378; fauna in,
    442; wetlands in, 780
Fayette County Jail and Law Enforcement
    Museum, 512
Fayette Station, 528
FayRal Development Corp., 17
Feaster, Eaton K., 228
Federal-Aid Highway Acts (1944, 1956), 332
Federal Airport Act, 33
Federal Highway Acts, 332, 773
Federal Hill (Mole Hill; Mountain), 619
Federal No. 3 mine, 150
Federal Subsistence Homesteads Corporation,
    720

Federation of Flat Glass Workers, 283
Feeney, Immaculate, 633
Fell, Barry, 562
Felts, Al, 37, 461
Felts, Lee, 37, 461
Felts, Thomas L., 37
Fenton, John, 191
Ferguson, C. W., III, 749
Ferguson, Charles W., II, 749
Ferguson, Everett, 87
Ferguson, James H., 410
Ferguson, Milton J., 749
Ferguson, Washington, 743
Fernow, Bernhard E., 236
Ferrell, Dick, 434
Ferrin, Frank, 207
Ferrin, Richard, 636
Fetterman, 554, 700
Fetterman, W. W., 732
Fetzer, Elmer W., 23
Fiedler, Arthur, 773, 788
Fields, James, 187
54th Massachusetts Infantry, 21
Fike Chemical, 129
Files (Foyles), Robert, 266, 600, 721
Fillmore, Millard, 268, 652, 696
Fincastle County, 31, 206
Findlay, Fred, 61
Fink, Albert, 83, 457
Finnegan, David, 151
Finney, Ross Lee, 180
Fire Creek, 467
Fireco, 152
Firestone, Harvey, 128
First Baptist Church of Charleston, 5
First Congregational Church (Huntington), 354
First Huntington National Bank, 126
First National Bank of Morgantown, 516
First Presbyterian Church (Southern), 584
Fish, Dominic, 371
Fish Creek, 175, 176
Fisher, Francis, 508
Fisher, Jake, 288
Fisher, Melinda, 804
Fisher, Ralph E., 497
Fitzgerald, Ella, 773
Fitzgerald, F. Scott, 60
Flaccus, William, 699
Flagg, George H., 631
Flambeau Products Company, 206
Flannery, William, 350
Flat Fork, 572
Flat Top, 57, 72, 473
Flat Top Coal Company, 80
Flat Top coalfield, 148, 571
Flat Top Land Association, 270, 444, 533, 731
Flatt and Scruggs, 35, 70, 423
Flatwoods, 81
Fleischhauer, Carl, 251
Fleming, Aretas Brooks, 227, 243, 448, 742, 747,
    800; flexibility of, 78; as industrialist, 149,
    748; electoral record of, 286
Fleming, Boaz, 227, 448
Fleming, Gypsy, 742
Fleming, Julian, 501
Fleming, R. E., 497
Fleming, William, 260, 574
Flesher, Henry, 418
Fletcher Enamel, 205

Fletcher, 175, 176
Fletcher, Marilyn, 703
Fletcher, William, 465
Flexner, James Thomas, 745
Flexsys, 130
Flick, H. H., 244, 559
Flight of the Intruder (Coonts), 167
Flikke, Julia, 65
Flint Glass Workers, 209
Flipping, 72
Flood, Eleanor Bolling, 95
Flor, Wolfgang, 777
Floyd, Carlisle, 183
Floyd, Charles, 270
Floyd, John, 531, 628
FMC, 129, 391
Fogelsong, Robert "Doc," 487
Fogelsong, Roma, 7
Foggy Mountain Boys, 70, 812
Fokker, Anthony H. G., 33, 248
Folded, Doc, 504
Foley Falls, 720
Foley, Scott, 269
Foley, Terence, 368
Folio, Armando, 371
Folk Songs from the West Virginia Hills, 251
Follow The River (Thom), 363
For Liberty and Union (film), 239
Forbes, John, 179, 265, 337
Ford, Gerald R., 183, 265, 291, 307, 308, 497, 509
Ford, Henry, 128, 538
Fore Knobs, 388
Foreman, William, 254
Forestry and Wood Industries (A. B. Brooks), 522
Forks of Cacapon, 117
Forks of Cheat (film), 239
Forrestal, James V., 384
Fort Blair, 260, 458, 573
Fort Butler, 585
Fort Capon, 310
Fort Cocke, 258
Fort Cox, 79, 310
Fort Donnally, 22, 260, 303, 615, 688
Fort Duquesne, 36, 79, 258, 418
Fort Edwards, 267, 310, 745
Fort Enoch, 79
Fort Frederick, 638
Fort Fuller, 401, 579
Fort Gay (Cassville), 749
Fort Harmar, 361
Fort Henry Club, 263
Fort Le Boeuf, 336
Fort Lewis, 31
Fort Logan, 258
Fort Mill Ridge, 310
Fort Milroy, 128
Fort Moore, 279
Fort Morris, 585
Fort Necessity, 264, 418, 682
Fort Niagara, 647
Fort Pearsall, 310, 627, 745
Fort Pierpont, 749
Fort Pitt, 31, 88, 265, 318, 336, 361, 576
Fort Shepherd, 24
Fort Spring, 395, 689
Fort Tomlinson, 254
Fortney, C. P., 332
Fortney, Ronald, 76
Fortney, William Este, 652

Forty-Four Years of the Life of a Hunter
   (Browning), 86
Foster, Chester L., 70
Foster, Jodie, 239
Foster, Robert, 811
Foulke Pottery, 580
Fourmile Run, 685
Fowke, Gerard, 23
Fowler, Daniel B., 23
Fowler, John, 204
Fowler, Thaddeus Mortimer, 262
Fowlersville, 20
Fox, John G., 364
Foyles (Files), Robert, 266, 600, 721
Fraley, Annadeene, 307
Fraley, J. P., 307
Francis, Jack S., 768
Francis, James Draper, 370
Frank (town), 571, 699
Frank, Larry, 504
Frank A. Knight Memorial Fund, 296
Frankenberger, Moses, 672
Frankenberger Gallery, 11
Franklin, Benjamin, 263, 630, 733, 780
Franklin, John Hope, 70
Fraser, John, 75
Frazer, Hugh, 159
Frazier, Claude "Cowboy," 504
Frazier, James, 535
Frederick the Great, 745
Frederick William IV, King, 634
Fredericks, Jay, 193
Fredericks, Walter, 750
Freeburn, 480
Freedom Cabin, 512
Freeland, Richard, 604
Freeman, 473
Freeman, David, 604
Freeman, John, 148
Freewill Baptist Church, 3, 685
Freidin, Nicholas, 147
Frémont, John C., 293, 420, 469, 628
French, Augustus B., 658
French, Callie Leach, 658
French, James Harvey, 157, 158
French Creek Academy, 729
French's Mill, 304
"Fresh Start Salt Village," 3
Frey, Clarence, 432
Friend, Lloyd, 579
Friend, Nanya, 126
Friendly, 721
Friends of Coal, 762
Friend's Orebank, 379
Friendship Gap, 10
Frissell, John, 303, 784
Frog Creek, 572
Fry, Lucian, 749
Fry, Lucy Clayton, 461
Fugitive Slave Act (1851), 191, 338
Fulk, Ludwick, 261
Fuller, Elmer, 267
Fulton, Robert, 630, 743
Funkhouser, Raymond J., 64, 144
Future Farmers of America, 118, 119, 173, 177
Future Homemakers of America, 118, 119, 177

Gabor, Charles, 773
Gabriel Brothers, 414
Gad, 692

Gadd, Cyrus, 396
GAF Company, 725
Gainer, Glen B., Jr., 30, 223
Gainer, Glen, B., III, 223
Gallatin, Albert, 520, 719
Gallipolis Locks and Dam, 459
Galway, James, 773
Galyean, Jerry, 239
Gandee, Sarah, 622
Gandy, Uriah, 709–10
Gannett Company, 330
Garcia, Calixto, 629
Gardiner, Theodore, 635
Gardner, Don, 545
Gardner, John, 549
Gardner, Ty, 239
Garfield, James A., 57, 351, 600
Garner, Erroll, 379
Garner, Francis, 622
Garnet, Henry Highland, 269
Garnett, Robert Selden, 41, 170, 617, 652, 717
Garretson, Catherine, 500
Garrett, John W., 38
Garrett, Naomi, 772
Garrison, Olive, 398
Garrison, William Melvin, 269
Garvey, Marcus, 4, 747
Gary Works, 736
Gary, Elbert, 731
Gassaway City Building, 189
Gassaway, 81, 148, 216
Gates, Anna Johnson, 416
Gates, Robert, 239, 325, 818
Gatty, Harold, 757
Gaughan, Pat, 703
Gaujot, Antoine (Tony), 159
Gaujot, Julien, 159
Gauley Mountain Coal Company, 359, 552
Gay, Harry S., 387
Geary, Wehrle B., 176, 195
General Davis Cave, 13
General Electric, 130, 808
General Motors, 54, 690
General Porcelain, 580
Genesis Affiliated Health Services, 635
George, Jane Cox, 177, 248, 249, 275-76
George, Tom, 432
George, W. Franklin, 392
George III, king of England, 588, 733
George Washington (ship), 338
Georgia Pacific Corporation, 90, 411, 470, 598, 620, 808
Gere, Richard, 503
German Bank, 641
German Settlement (Aurora), 585
Gerrard, Alice, 195
Gerrardstown, 53, 584
Gess, Perry, 536
Gesundheit! Institute, 1
Getz, Stan, 379
Getzendanner, H. C., 652
Ghiz, Harvey, 21
Gibbon, Edward, 135
Gibbons, Euell, 534
Gibson, Ann M., 231
Gibson, Harry C., 631
Gibson, John, 433
Gideon, Dave, 330
Giffen, Frank, 404
Gihon Park, 504

Gilbert, 486
Gilbert, Cass, Jr., 471
Gilchrist, James, 303
Gill, Joseph H., 306
Gill, Vince, 664
Gillespie, Dizzy, 56, 70
Gillespie, James, 76
Gillespie, Robert C., 813
Gillespie, William, 76
Gilley, J. Wade, 70, 454
Gilliam, Frank, 76
Gilmer, Paul, 624
Gilmer, Ripley & Ohio Turnpike, 622
Gilmer, Thomas W., 279
Gilmer County, **279–80**, 447; back-to-the-land
    movement in, 34; Calhoun County created
    from, 100; Cedar Creek State Park in, 118;
    148; folk music in, 250
Gilmer Station, 429
Gilmore (hunter), 260
Gilmore, Elizabeth, 137
Gingrich, Newt, 296
Girty, Simon, 400, 531, 709
Gish, Lillian, 532
Givens, Marguerite, 248
Glackens, William, 14
Glade Creek bridge, 365
Glade Creek, 242, 281, 470
Glade Springs Resort, 242, 599
Glady Fork, 11, 129
Glasgow Site, 583
Glass Bottle Blowers Association, 282, 283
Glasscock, William Ellsworth, 9, **283–84**, 434;
    Paint Creek-Cabin Creek Strike and, 189,
    340, 553; legislative stalemate and, 321, 647;
    as "Elkins governor," 341
Glazer, Frederic J., 363, 422
Gleason, Joanna Hall, 639
Gleizes, Albert, 413
Glen Dale, 248, 457
Glen Ferris Dam, 357, 747
Glen Jean, 205, 383, 467, 716, 789
Glen Rogers, 150, 739, 815
Glen White, 480
Glenville State College, 255, 280, **285–86**, 364,
    533
Glenwood, 453
Glenwood Athletic Club, 211
Globe Hill, 23, 583
Glover, Leonard H., 200
Gluck, Margaret Hannah, 286
Goddard, Clarence "Hank," 554
Goddin, Margaret Purdum, 185
Gods and Generals (film), 239
Godwin, William, 797
Goering, Hermann, 327
Goethe, Joe, 818
Goff, Nathan, Jr., **286**, 319; newspaper owned
    by, 140; as gubernatorial candidate, 243,
    462, 800; as U.S. senator, 284
Goff Building, 140, 319
Goheen, Michael, 368
Goins, Melvin, 70, 434, 604
Goins, Ray, 70, 434, 604
Gold, A. Fremont, 735
Gold, W. Alfred, 735
Golden, W. W. "Ben," 564
Goldovsky, Boris, 183
Goldsmith, Paul, 504
Goldstone, Duke, 206, 239

Go-Mart, 81
Gompers, Samuel, 340, 420
Good, E. L., 567
Good Children's Zoo, 512, 542
Goodall, Cecile, 769
Goodman, Benny, 202, 788
Goodman, Sol, 675
Goodrich Corporation, 494, 697
Goodwill, 473
Goodwill, Philip, 80
Goodwin, Joseph R., 511
Goodwin, Olive, 751
Goodyear, 130
Gore, Al, 724
Gore, Howard Mason, 41, 140, **288**, 290, 319,
    793; appointments of, 316, 441, 466, 514
Gore, John, 793
Gore, Truman, 641
Gormania, 293
Gorrell, Robert, 476, 722
Goshorn, Belle, 439
Goshorn's Ferry, 237
Goss, Joe, 288, 670
Gould, George, 778, 786
Gould, Jay, 778, 786
Grafton, John, 291
Grafton, William, 76
Graham, Billy, 663
Graham, Franklin, 663
Graham, Frederick Poe, 373
Graham, J. A., 620
Graham, J. L., 620
Graham, John W., 334
Graham, Little John, 632
Graham Station, 459
Grand Ohio Company, 31
Grand Ole Opry, 35, 70, 196
Grant, Arvid, 99
Grant, George, 540
Grant, Lizzie, 661
Grant, Ulysses S., 100, 112, 186, 286, 292, 293,
    600, 659
Grant County Mulch, 293
Grant County, 225, 226, 276, **292–93**; turkey
    production in, 6; fauna in, 13, 128; rainfall in,
    146; formation of, 171–72, 185, 209, 310, 314;
    flood of 1985 in, 245; flora in, 246; settlement
    of, 336; industry in, 368; natural features of,
    424, 578; Potomac and, 535; Tories in, 709;
    wetlands in, 780
Grape Island, 271
Grapevine Creek, 323
Gravatt, William Loyall, 221
Grave Creek, 505
Graves, Michael, 26
Gray, Asa, 75
Gray, Howard, 470
Graybill, H. B., 651
Graziano, Rocky, 370
Great Awakening, 28
Great Cacapon, 498
Great Gettin' Up Mornin' (Flagg), 242
Great Indian Warpath, 360, 743
Great Wagon Road, 535
Greater Cumberland Regional Airport, 32
Greater Kanawha Valley Science Center, 142
Greathouse, Harmon, 297, 312, 344
Greathouse, Jacob, 297
Green, Henry S., 316

Green Bank, 44, 571
Green Bottom Swamp, 455
Green Bottom Wildlife Management Area, 146
Green Hills of Magic (Musick), 251
Green Lime Company, 559
Green Revolution (newsletter), 34
Greenbrier Boys, 70
Greenbrier & Elk River Railroad, 115
Greenbrier Coal & Coke, 155
Greenbrier Conference, 28, 609
Greenbrier County, 8, 34, 233, **298–99**; fauna in,
    12; in Revolutionary War, 22; architecture in,
    24; natural features of, 118, 395, 455, 695;
    racial tensions in, 137, 364; formation of, 165,
    689; flora in, 219; fossils in, 261; farming in,
    281; Irish in, 367, 368; scenic roads through,
    378; religious life in, 473, 584, 587; slavery in,
    661
Greenbrier Male Academy, 299
Greenbrier Railway Company, 132
Greenbrier River, 9, 10, **300–301**, 618; industry
    along, 115; settlements along, 145, 691;
    aquatic life and fishing in, 241; flooding of,
    244, 245; forts along, 267; navigability of,
    431; railroad along, 558
Greenbrier Valley Airport, 32
Greenbrier Weekly Era, 530
Greene, Chloe, 410
Greene, Chris, 302
Greene, Gordon C., 302
Greene, Jimmy, 410
Greene, Mary B. "Maw," 302
Greene, Nathaniel, 748
Greene, Tom, 302
Greenfield, David, 126
Greenland (ship), 302
Greenman, Emerson F., 82
Greenmont, 500
Greenspace Coalition, 501
Greenup Locks and Dam, 431
Greenway Court, 226
Greer Industries, 596
Greer Lime Company, 277
Greer, Agnes Jane Reeves, 501, 741
Greer, Herbert Chester, 501, 741
Greever, Robert O., 432
Gregg, George, 388
Gregg, Kathy, 76
Greigsville, 367
Grey, Zane, 447, 782, 819
Griffin, Buddy, 70
Griffin, Daniel, 368
Griffin, James B., 23, 147
Griffith, Alexander, 424
Griffith, Andy, 403
Griffith, Holly, 253
Griffith, R. B., 677
Griffithsville, 424, 425
Grigsby, Benjamin, 547
Grimes, Frances Fortune, 811
Grimes, Thomas, 20, 287, 304
Grimm, J. W., 476
Groce, Larry, 508
Groll, Albert, 417
Gropius, Walter, 26, 324, 356, 512
Grove, Lefty, 45
Groves, S. J., 99
Gruenewald, Guido, 132
Gue Farm, 258

Guelich, Robert, 16
Guerilla, 530
Guerin, Charles, 413
Gulf Smokeless Coal, 699
Guthrie, Roland, 76
Guyan, Henry, 3-6
Guyandot Valley Railroad, 132
Guyandotte Navigation Company, 431
Guyandotte Trail, 360
Guyer, Barbara, 454
Gwinn, John, 367
Gypsy, 306

H. K. Bedford (ship), 302
H. R. Wyllie China, 580
Hacala, Joseph R., 785
Hacker, John, 135, 277, 418, 429
Hackers Creek, 135, 277
Haddad, Fred, 327, 391, 414
Hadden family, 266
Hadden's Fort, 600
Haden, William R., 777
Hager, Robert, 1
Haggerty, Thomas, 589
Haig, Frank R., 785
Haley, Lawrence, 307
Haley, Milt, 425
Half-King (Tanacharison), 485
Hall, D. Ray, 295
Hall, George A., 85
Hall, James A., 779
Hall, John (political leader), 165, 458
Hall, John H. (inventor), 316
Hall, Mrs. Cyrus W., 456
Hall, Tom T., 670
Hall (town), 88
Hall (Underwood), Hovah, 723
Hall's Rifle Works, 316, 317
Hall's Run, 319
Hallanan, Imogene Burns, 308
Halltown Union Colored Sunday School, 519
Halltown, 122
Hambleton, 717
Hamer Lumber, 750
Hamilton (hunter), 260
Hamilton, Alexander, 93, 789
Hamilton, Floyd "Scotty," 596
Hamilton, Henry, 614
Hamilton, John, 531, 692
Hamilton Farm, 562
Hamlin, Leonidas, 308, 424
Hamm, Harry, 786
Hammer, Armand, 370
Hammer, Keith, 504
Hammer on the Slammer (film), 239
Hammon, Betty Shaffer, 309
Hammond, John Swainston, 78
Hammond, John, 379
Hammond, Philip, 260, 303
Hammond, Thomas, 744
Hammond, William, 574
Hammond Fire Brick Company, 143
Hammonds, Brother, 649
Hammonds, Minnie, 476
Hammons, Burl, 309, 547
Hammons, Jesse, 309, 547
Hammons, Sherman, 309, 547
Hamner, Earl, 202
Hampshire County, 111, 161, 226, **309–11**, 314;
    farming in, 6, 7, 430, 549; in French and
Indian War, 79, 258; natural features of, 99,
    276, 535, 578; formation of, 165, 171, 172, 209,
    738; in Dunmore's War, 207; settlement of,
    266, 336; integration in, 364; industry in,
    368, 699; religious life in, 473; railroads and,
    481; Presbyterians in, 584; slavery in, 661;
    Tories in, 709; weather in, 750; wetlands in,
    780
Hampshire Southern Railway, 293
Hampton, Lionel, 56, 379
Hampton Normal Institute, 3
Hamrick, Ellis, 311
Hamrick, Graham, 563
Hamrick, J. Edward, 524
Hancock, John, 312
Hancock County, **311–12**; industry in, 11, 274,
    340, 368, 694; clay mining in, 143, 144;
    ethnic makeup of, 297; formation of, 542,
    817; demographic and economic character-
    istics of, 577, 581
Hancock Works, 293
Hand, George W., 228
Handlan, John W., 85
Handley, Charles, Sr., 85
Handsome Lake (Seneca chief), 647
Hanger, James, 563
Hanger Prosthetics, 563
Hanging Rocks, 209, 310
Hank the Cowhand (David Stanford), 177, 632
Hankins, Mark A., 276
Hanks, Festus, 373
Hanks, Jarvis, 26
Hanks, Joseph, 313
Hanna, Homer, Sr., 449
Hanna, John, 26
Hannaman, William, 372
Hannibal Dam, 357, 528
Hannis, Henry, 456
Hannon, Thomas, 97
Hannum, Robert Fulton, 313
Hanover Shoe, 559
Hansford, 125, 583
Hansford, John, 735
Hanway, Samuel, 368
Harder, Pat, 286
Hardesty, David C., Jr., 775, 776
Harding, Rebecca Blaine, 187
Harding, Warren G., 38, 64, 480, 484, 499, 695,
    718, 790
Hardinge, Samuel Wylde, Jr., 78
Hardway, Wendell G., 70
Hardy, John, 250
Hardy, Samuel, 314
Hardy County, 161, 226, **314–15**; farming in, 6,
    274, 430, 581; vernacular architecture in, 26,
    735; natural features of, 99, 276, 395, 424,
    578; formation and accession of, 209, 310,
    738; flora in, 219, 276; settlement of, 266,
    336; industry in, 368, 699; religious life in,
    472, 473, 584; electrification of, 631; Tories
    in, 709; weather in, 750
Hare Krishna Palace of Gold, 26, 452, 529
Hargis, Henry, 73
Harless, Budd, 504
Harless, James H. "Buck," 487
Harless, John, 182
Harman, Lydia, 465
Harman, Mathias, 465
Harman Hills, 277
Harmar, Josiah, 68
Harmon, Thomas, 479
Harmon, W. Henry, 813
Harned, Joseph, 76
Harper Gap, 277
Harper, E. Howard, 5, 316
Harper, John, Jr., 248
Harper, Lee, 7
Harrick, Steve, 813
Harris, J., 2
Harris, John T., 67, 320, 416
Harris, Kay, 222
Harris, Lou, 399
Harris, Major, 527
Harris, Mary B., 8
Harris, Paul P., 629
Harris, Thomas (settler), 319, 619
Harris, Thomas Lake (mystic), 507
Harris, Virgie, 185
Harrison, Benjamin, 186, 218, 318, 384, 518, 607,
    790
Harrison, P. M., 467
Harrison, William Henry, 564
Harrison County, 197, **318–19**, 448; cattle indus-
    try in, 6; Black Hand in, 61; formation of,
    140; settlement of, 266; Grange in, 292;
    ethnic makeup of, 297, 305, 370; legislative
    representation of, 350
Harrison-Marion Regional Airport (Tri-County
    Airport), 32
Harrison Riflemen, 383
Harrison Rural Electrification Association, 631
Harrisville Southern Railroad, 320, 620
Harshbarger, Sam, 85, 444, 478, 693
Harshman, Marc, 427, 428
Hart, David, 617
Hart, Ira, 779
Hart, John, 130
Hart, Nancy Ann, 130
Hart, Paul W., 803
Hart, Walter L. "Bill," 501
Harte, Richard, 121
Hartford, 359
Hartley, John, 803
Hartman, Dolly, 402
Hartman, G. E., 509
Hartness, Elizabeth, 708
Harvey, 197
Harvey, Harold, 421
Harvey, Henry, 172
Harvey, Nicholas, 607
Harvey, Paul, 193
Harvey, Rosa M., 728
Harvey, Roy, 153
Harvey, Vera Andrews, 316
Hashinger, W. Roy, 438
Haskins, James, 662
Hass, Brandon, 116
Hassam, Childe, 356
Hatfield, Anderson "Preacher Anse," 320
Hatfield, Anna Musick, 321
Hatfield, Elias, 322
Hatfield, Ellison, 321, 322, 464
Hatfield, Ephraim, 321
Hatfield, Floyd, 322, 464
Hatfield, Henry Drury, 210, **321–22**, 432, 466;
    appointments of, 188, 499; in Mine Wars,
    189, 284, 340, 396, 553, 480; electoral record
    of, 288, 346; medical background of, 290,
    484, 591, 756; progressivism of, 341, 576;

Virginia Debt Suit appealed by, 423; as Sen-
ate president, 647
Hatfield, Johnse, 321, 322, 464
Hatfield, Willis, 323
Hathawikila Indians, 653
Haught, James F., 624
Havaco (Jed), 150
Haviland, Charles, 195
Hawker, Ginny, 770
Hawkins, Coleman, 56
Hawks Nest, 57, 233, 272, 324, 340, 396, 452, 467,
725
Hawks Nest (Skidmore), 427, 752
Hawks Nest Coal Company, 552
Hawse, Lee, 556
Hawthorne, Nathaniel, 66
Hayes, Charlton J. H., 691
Hayes, Helen, 475
Hayes, Lester, Jr., 241
Hayes, Raymond, 649
Hayes, Robert B., 454
Hayes, Rutherford B., 104, 286, 420, 462, 565,
597, 599, 600, 691
Haymes, Dick, 204
Haymond, Daniel, 619
Haymond, John, 636
Haymond, William, 492, 500, 619
Hays City, 285
Hazelton Mill, 586
Hazelwood, Haney Davis, 200
Hazleton, 10
Healy, Charles P., 187
Hearne, Julia G., Jr., 764
Heaton Agate, 446
Heatwole, Potter John, 472
Heck Mansion, 670
Hecker, James, 511
Hedges, Dan, 412, 604
Hedgesville, 584
Hedrick, Clinton, 159
Hedrick, E. H., 600
Hedrick, Grover C., 509
Heflin, Harry B., 286
Heifetz, Jascha, 404
Heishman, David, 497
Heishman, Phoebe Fisher, 497
Heizer Creek, 572
Held, Anna, 800
Helen, 152
Hemphill, Herbert Wade, Jr., 385
Hendershot oil field, 569
Henderson, Alexander, 802
Henderson, David English, 26
Henderson, Fletcher, 56, 378
Henderson, John G., 802
Hendricks, 666
Henkel, Paul, 438
Hennis, Anne, 36
Henri, Robert, 14
Henry, Patrick, 212, 259, 260, 543, 622, 680, 696,
783
Henry House Hill, 138
Hensley, Amanda, 649
Hensley, George, 649
Hensley, James, 649
Henson, E. Bennett, 125
Herbert, Mary Lee Washington, 744
Hercules Powder, 532
Herendeen, Ed, 166
Herford, Sydenham, 172

Heritage Bank, 757
Herman, Woody, 379
Hermanson, Gordon E., 185
Herns Mill, 175, 176
Hershey, Rachel Smith, 748
Hess (general), 299
Hess, H. Clare, 679
Hester Industries, 497, 581
Heth, Henry, 420, 421
Heywood, Eddie, 379
Hiawatha, 369
Hickock, Bill, 703
Hickory Grove, 548
Hicks, Charles, 693
Hicks, Hassel T., 402, 798
Hicks, Thomas, 28
Hiersoux, John, 732
Hiersoux, Jose, 732
Hiett's Run, 536
Higgs, Augustus Ferzard, 264
High, Nathaniel, 78
High Gate Carriage House, 453
High Knob, 618
High Plateau, 275
Highland, Cecil B., 140
Highland, Cecil B., Jr., 141
Hildreth, Eugene A., 303
Hill, Bonner, 91
Hill, Felix, 810
Hill, Lawson, 510
Hill, T. Edward, 791
Hill, William Lee, 33
Hills, R., 779
Hills Creek, 265, 395
Hillsboro, 584
Hilltop, 4
Hilton, Chip, 50, 732
Hinchcliff Lumber Company, 717
Hindman, Sam, 126
Hiner, Ralph M., 559
Hines, Jerome, 404
Hines, John, 299
Hinkle, Hannah, 260
Hinkle, John Justus, 277
Hinkle family, 276
Hinkle Gap, 277
Hinkle's Fort, 559, 643
Hinton, John, 691
Hinton coal formation, 147
Hiscoe, Bonta, 153
*History of the Early Settlement and Indian Wars
of Western Virginia* (De Hass), 426
History of the Valley of Virginia (Kercheval), 402
Hitchcock, Chip, 239
Hitchman Coal and Coke Company, 407
Hite, Abraham, 260
Hite, George, 225
Hite, Jacob, 54, 582
Hite, John W., 453
Hoard, Charles B., 121
Hobbs, Cliff, 176
Hobday, Geoffrey, 773
Hoblitzell, John, 602
Hocking Valley Railroad, 132
Hodel, Emile, 49
Hodel, George, 49
Hodel, John, 49
Hodges, Thomas E., 453
Hoffman, Edwin D., 772

Hoffman, John S., 328
Hoffman, Nimrod Nelson, 501
Hoffman, William, 427, 428
Hoffman and Sons Tannery, 293, 699
Hoffmann, John G., 699
Hofmann, Hans, 414, 701
Hogan, Bill, 239
Hoge, Isaac, 634
Hoge, Rachel, 634
Hogg, Elizabeth, 52
Hogg, Peter, 52, 458
Hokes Mill, 175, 176
Holden, 369, 370, 433
Holden, Albert F., 369, 370
Holden, Carol, 352
Holden, Guy, 426
Hole (cave), 118
Holiday, Billie, 8, 566
Holliday, John, 312, 344
Holliday, Robert, 109
Hollow Rock String Band, 392
Holmes, Darrell E., 68
Holmes, Oliver Wendell, Jr., 696
Holston Conference, 136
Holt, Homer Adams, 96, 234, 299, 316, **345–46**,
681; conservatism of, 174, 179, 191, 295, 449,
526, 760; New Deal and, 527, 810
Holt, J. Howard, 109
Holt, John Homer, 790
Holt, Matthew S., 499, 666
Holy Family School, 635
Homewood Pottery, 580
Hominy Falls, 554
Hood, Thomas, 818
Hoover, Herbert C., 131, 184, 405, 737
Hoover, J. Edgar, 678
Hope, Bob, 184, 475
Hopkins Mine, 780
Hopkins, Andrew Delmar, 373, 522, 607, 808
Hopkins, Harry, 810
Hopkins, Mark, 355
Horan, Marvin, 392
Horn, Bessie, 326
Hornbook, Tryphena, 303
Horne, Marilyn, 773
Horne, Terry, 126
Hornor, Robert, 555
Horsch, M. J., 813
Horse Creek, 548
Horseneck, 569
Horwitz, Elinor, 615
Hospital Corporation of America, 211
Hot Rize, 71
Houston, Matthew, 784
Houston, Sam, 344, 630
Howard Creek, 300
Howard, C. D., 103
Howard, John, 224, 390, 636
Howard, Josiah, 636
Howard, Oliver Otis, 264
Howatt, Alexander, 588
Howdyshell, Roger, 446
Howe, William, 176
Howells, William Dean, 351
Howell's Gristmill, 304
Hubbard, Don, 624
Hubbard, Elbert, 629
Hubbard, William, 188
Huff Knob, 242
Huffman, Darryl, 611

Huffman, John L., 635
Hughart, William, 574
Hughes, Edwin Holt, 452
Hughes, Elias, 352, 803
Hughes, Jim, 750
Hughes, Langston, 70
Hughes, Randy, 324
Hughes, Sara, 614
Hughes, Thomas, 352
Hughes Farm Site, 491
Hull, Arlie, 12
Hullihen, Simon, 784
Humphrey, Hubert H., 44, 83, 95, 131, 341, 398, 399, 509, 574
Humphreys, Gertrude, 224
Hunsaker's Ferry, 130
Hunt, Nancy P., 507
Hunt, Richard, 789
Hunt, William, 153
Hunter, Alberta, 566
Hunter, David (general), 77, 696
Hunter, David (landowner), 456
Hunter, Henry Harrison, 283
Hunter, Kermit, 292, 348, 704
Hunter, Robert M. T., 12
Hunter Insurance Agency, 757
Huntington, 97, 133, 274, **355–56**, 577; architecture in, 25; sports in, 45, 46, 670; bridges in, 83, 99; Carnegie grant to, 112; annexation by, 120, 749; organizations in, 121, 629; railroads and, 131–32, 148; black schooling in, 200; industry in, 211, 237, 244, 282, 340, 551; public works in, 296; religious life in, 382, 383, 550, 725; Lebanese and Syrians in, 414; flood protection for, 595, 730; broadcasting in, 595, 703; health care in, 591, 634–35; socialism in, 665; streetcars in, 688; telephone service in, 702
Huntington, Henry E., 355
Huntington Banks, 516
Huntington Tobacco Warehouse, 708
Hurley, James, 368
Hurley, K. Duane, 635
Hurley, Thomas, 368
Hurricane Bridge, 592
Hutchinson, Bennett W., 777
Hutchinson, John, 127, 682
Hutton, E. E., 76
Huttonsville, 381, 584, 601
Huttonsville Presbyterian Church, 130
Hyde, Anthony J., 248
Hyde, Lucia K., 357
Hyer, Tommy, 243
Hylton, Charles D., 334
Hylton, Tony, 334
Hyman, A. B., 397
Hyman, S. J., 397
Hyre, Hazel, 416

Ice, Frederick, 276
Ice, William, 781
Ices Ferry, 127, 129, 276, 492
Ideal Glass, 198, 760
Ikenberry, Oliver S., 656
Illinois County, 31
Impartial Observer, 530
In Memory of the Land and People (film), 239
Independent Bankers Association, 40
Independent Baptist Church (Pettus), 16
Independent Steelworkers Union, 408, 681

Indian Camp Normal School, 729
Indian Camp Rock, 729
Indian Creek, 175, 176
Indian Grove Mountain, 242
Indiana Territory, 31
Industrial Home for Youth, 590
Industrial Union Council, 210
Infinity Broadcasting, 596
Ingalls, Huntley, 265
Ingalls, Melville E., 132
Ingles, Thomas, 363
Ingles, William, 362, 639
Internal Revenue Service, 54, 95, 614
International Association of Machinists, 408
International Industries, 808
International Ladies' Garment Workers Union, 805
International Mother's Day Shrine Commission, 14
International Nickel Company, 97
International Steel Group, 341, 369, 682, 755
International Sunday School Association, 171
International Thespian Society, 11, 12
Interstate Highway Act (1956), 365
Intrawest Corporation, 665
Inwood, 7
Ioxy, 370
Ireland, Betty, 646
Ireland, John, 204
Ireland, Mary J., 231
Irish Hill, 456
Irish Ridge, 367
Irvine, William, 819
Islamic Center of West Virginia, 414, 513
Island Creek, 258
Israel, Joseph, 135, 804
Itmann, 444, 815
ITT, 283

Jabbour, Alan, 251, 608
Jabo Inc., 446–47
Jackling, Daniel J., 532
Jackson, Andrew Gardner, 373
Jackson, Andrew, 68, 344, 372, 374, 630, 652
Jackson, Cummins, 376
Jackson, David E., 373
Jackson, Edward Brake, 373
Jackson, Edward, 373, 375
Jackson, Elizabeth Cummins, 373
Jackson, G. W., 674
Jackson, George, 373, 374
Jackson, H. R., 128
Jackson, Jacob Beeson, 78, **373–74**, 555
Jackson, James Madison, 373
Jackson, James Monroe, 373
Jackson, Jesse, 567
Jackson, John, 373
Jackson, Jonathan, 376
Jackson, Laura, 376
Jackson, Lloyd, 425, 444
Jackson, Mary Payne, 140
Jackson, Robert H., 43
Jackson, Samuel, 359, 368
Jackson, Thomas Moore, 373
Jackson, Tom, 137
Jackson, Warren, 730
Jackson, William "Buckwheat," 510
Jackson, William Wirt, 374
Jackson County Fairgrounds, 504

Jackson County, 87, 118, **372–73**; tobacco farming in, 6, 708; in Civil War, 116; Land Wars in, 182; courthouse of, 189; feuding in, 237
Jackson Sheet and Tin Plate Company (Phillips Sheet and Tin Plate Company), 140, 681
Jaco, Luke, 198
Jacob, John J., 376
Jacob, John Jeremiah, 311, **376–77**; electoral record of, 290, 338, 683; grave of, 360
Jacob, Susan McDavitt, 376
Jacobs, William, 501
James, Charles H., 377
James, Charles, II, 377
James, Charles, III, 377
James, E. L., 377
James (Byrd), Erma Ora, 95
James, Francis, 377
James, Frank, 377
James I, king of England, 335
James River, 15, 240, 377–78
Jamestown Exposition, 25
Jamison No. 9 mine, 150
Jane Lew, 318, 376, 419, 691
Jane Lew Brick and Drain Tile Company, 143
Jansky, Karl G., 519
Jarrett, Jim, 761
Jarrett, John W., 125, 126
Jarrett, Ruth, 761
Jarrett-Aim Communications, 136
Jarvis, Granville E., 378
Jarvis, Warren, 554
Jawbone Park, 89
Jed (Havaco), 150
Jefferds, Joseph C., Jr., 764
Jeffers, Sleepy, 546, 675
Jefferson, Othella, 137
Jefferson, Peter, 684
Jefferson, Thomas, 24, 49, 65, 93, 179, 212, 379, 381, 383, 433, 520, 696
Jefferson County, 18, 172, 226, **379–80**, 577, 615; farming in, 6, 7, 549; architecture in, 24, 93, 144, 735; in Civil War, 38, 380; boundary dispute and, 78; in French and Indian War, 79; formation of, 122, 165, 209, 225, 257, 273, 738; schools in, 140, 213; religious life in, 171; governance of, 173, 289; forestation in, 256, 715; fossils in, 261; Freedmen's Bureau in, 264; Germans in, 277; settlement of, 336; legislative representation of, 350; integration in, 364; industry in, 368; natural features of, 395, 455, 655; libraries in, 422; Presbyterians in, 584; second homes in, 645; slavery in, 661; Mexican War and, 767; wetlands in, 780
Jehovah's Witnesses, 43
Jenifer, Walter, 588
Jenkins, Edna, 777
Jenkins, William, 297
Jenningston, 717
Jett, James, 671
Jim and Jesse, 70
Jim C. Hamer Company, 808
Job Prickett House, 512, 587
Joel's Branch, 548
John Andross (Rebecca Harding Davis), 187
John Birch Society, 392
John Boch pottery, 580
John E. Amos Plant, 12, 358
John F. Casey Company, 227
John Henry: A Folklore Study (Chappell), 251

John Henry: Tracking Down a Negro Legend (G. B. Johnson), 251
John K. Skidmore Development, Inc., 81
John Wesley Methodist Church, 299
Johnkoski, Vincent J., 641
John's Creek, 58
Johnson, Andrew, 348, 565, 732, 733
Johnson, Bos, 703
Johnson, Bradley, 497
Johnson, Clara, 422
Johnson, Dolores, 427
Johnson, Edward (colonel), 10
Johnson, Edward R. (editor), 806
Johnson, Guy B., 251, 330
Johnson, Herman, 218
Johnson, Howard H., 769
Johnson, Hugh S., 519
Johnson, James Weldon, 670
Johnson, Jess, 153
Johnson, Jesse, 508
Johnson, Jimmy D., 87
Johnson, John W., 87
Johnson, Joshua, 26
Johnson, Junior, 504
Johnson, Louis A. (assistant secretary of war), 140
Johnson, Louis Arthur (infantry officer), 762
Johnson, Lyndon B., 120, 184, 532, 648, 674, 692; Appalachian Regional Commission and, 19; war on poverty waged by, 20, 342, 434, 582, 739, 742; as Senate majority leader, 95, 733; Great Society and, 296; landslide reelection of, 724; Vietnam War waged by, 736
Johnson, Robert L., 19
Johnson, W. R., 330
Johnson, Wallace, 422
Johnson, William, 111, 261, 588
Johnson Creek, 572
Johnson ironworks, 329
Johnson Mountain Boys, 70
Johnson Shoals, 393
Johnston, Benjamin, 87
Johnston, Joseph E., 210
Jolley, Henry, 722
Joncaire, Louis, 647
Jones, Absalom, 2
Jones, Annie, 384
Jones, Booker T., 804
Jones, Brereton, 573
Jones, C. Joy, 545
Jones, Charles T., 540
Jones, Claude, 159
Jones, George, 554
Jones, Grandpa, 632, 785, 805
Jones, Grover, 384
Jones, Henry Smith, 200
Jones, Hugh Bolton, 26
Jones, James Earl, 461
Jones, James Gay, 278, 463
Jones, Jenkin, 148
Jones, Kenneth, 775
Jones, Kojo, 427
Jones, Loyal, 783
Jones, Nelson, 682
Jones, Oliver, 809
Jones, Robert Trent, Jr., 100
Jones, Samuel, 32
Jones, Silver Yodelin' Bill, 785
Jones, Tom, 676
Jones, Virgil Carrington, 323

Jones, Wilbur Stone, 683
Jones, Wilbur Stone, Jr., 683
Jones, William "Punch," 384
Jones, William E. "Grumble," 92–93, 302, 375, 386, 492, 603, 803
Jordache Enterprises, 327
Jordan, Andrew, 479
Jordan, Louis, 637, 754
Jordan, Michael, 706
Jordan, Thomas, 121
Jorgeson, Felice, 664
Joseph, Ken, 215
Joy, Joseph Francis, 386–87
Judd, Kirk, 427
Judds, 554
Judelson Dryer Company, 452
Judson, J. E., 686
Judy Rocks, 208, 277
Julian, Percy, 772
Juliet Museum of Art, 141–42
Juniata Formation, 18
Justice, Dick, 153
Justice, Scott, 432

Kaemmerling, S. Maude, 106
Kaiser Aluminum and Chemical Corporation, 372
Kaleem, Musa, 379
Kalm, Peter, 75
Kanawha and Gallipolis Packet Company, 507
Kanawha & Michigan Railroad, 148, 339, 391, 529, 597
Kanawha Boulevard, 296
Kanawha Church of Charleston, 584
Kanawha City, 551
Kanawha coal formation, 147, 148
Kanawha County, 36, 87, 97, 123, 233, 372, **390–91**, 424, 433, 447, 577; Ku Klux Klan in, 4; coal mining in, 21, 196; schools in, 115, 140, 213; clay mining in, 143; formation of, 145; saltworks in, 148, 192; natural features of, 152; water supply for, 216; industry in, 274; farming in, 281; legislative representation of, 350; scenic roads through, 378; Presbyterians in, 584; slavery in, 661; forestation in, 715
Kanawha, Glen Jean & Eastern Railway, 468
Kanawha Land Company, 439, 668
Kanawha Presbyterian Church, 25, 584
Kanawha Ring, 134, 391, 398, 439
Kanawha River Terminal, 750
Kanawha River, 18, 92, 119, 123, 124, 145, 217, 233, 272, **393**, 544; prehistoric settlements along, 1, 89, 504, 583; industry along, 12, 148, 274, 432; damming of, 220, 244, 339, 357, 409, 430, 523, 747; navigation on, 236, 237, 273, 302, 622; aquatic life and fishing in, 240, 513; flooding of, 245; waterfall at, 392; oil and gas reserves along, 520; saltworks on, 636–37; showboats on, 658
Kanawha Salines Church, 584
Kanawha Sand & Gravel, 465
Kanawha Valley Star, 530
Kane, J. J., 368
Karnes, Samuel D., 92, 521, 603, 803
Karst Waters Institute, 118
Kasdan, Lawrence, 239
Kauffman (Coffman), Isaac, 472
Kaufman, Paul, 20, 62
Kautz, Charles, 453

Kayser-Roth, Inc., 366
Kee, Jim, 69, 396
Kee, John, 69, 396
Keel, John, 503
Keely, Josiah, 813
Keenan, Edward, 609
Keeney, John, 22
Keeney family, 266
Keep Tryst Furnace, 368
Keim, N. G., 218
Kell, Lula, 525
Kellar, James H., 23, 505
Keller, B. F., 182, 674
Keller, Helen, 769
Keller, Lewis, Sr., 540
Keller-Cook Company, 166
Kelley, Jack K., 421
Kelley, Jonah, 159
Kelley, Walter, 390
Kellogg, Louise Phelps, 202
Kelly, Benjamin, 314
Kelly, Gene, 812
Kelly, John, 622, 713
Kelly, Shannon, 613
Kelly, Walter, 266
Kelly, William C., 397
Kellys Creek (Cedar Grove), 378, 393
Kellys Creek & Northwestern Railroad, 657
Kellys Creek Railroad, 657
Kemp, Emory, 24
Kemp, Julianne, 125
Kenhawa Spectator, 530
Kennedy, Bob, 58
Kennedy, Bruce Lee, **290–91**
Kennedy, Edward M., 95, 451
Kennedy, George, 253
Kennedy, Jacqueline, 184, 501, 507
Kennedy, John Pendleton, 688
Kennedy, Patricia L., 584
Kennedy, Philip Pendleton, 63, 522
Kennedy, Robert F., 22
Kenney, Jacob, 465
Kennison Mountain, 478
Kennison, Charles, 203
Kenny, Izetta Jewell, 86
Kenton, Stan, 379
Kenton Corporation, 123, 654
Kentucky River, 1
Kerens, R. C., 218
Kermit, 486
Kern, Michael, 501
Kerns Fort, 492
Kerr, S. M., 19
Kerry, John, 626
Kessel, Oliver, 118
Kessell, Samuel D., 632
Kessinger, Luches, 400
Kessinger Brothers, 750
Key, V. O., 613
Key Bancshares, 40
Keyser, William, 401
Keyser family, 276
Keyser Pottery Company, 580
Kickapoo Indians, 576
Kidd, William, 514
Kile Knob, 535
Kilham, Dixie, 333
Kimball, 383, 466, 572
Kimball, Frederick J., 350, 533, 571

Kimm Products, 580
Kin, Matthias, 75
Kincheloe Creek, 758
Kinder, Chuck, 427
King, Angie, 584
King, David H., 764
King, Ellen Ruddell, 279, 285, 764
King, Henry C., 696
King, Jerrold, 504
King, Martin Luther, Jr., 327, 624, 733, 758
King, Susan, 659
King Pharmaceuticals, 514
Kings Creek, 337, 536, 561
Kingsford Manufacturing Company, 717, 808
Kingston Trio, 316
Kingsville, 602
Kinnan, Joseph, 402
Kintzer, Edward H., 666
Kishpoko Indians, 653
Kiss, Robert "Bob," 350
Kissinger, Henry, 733
Kistler, 89
Kittredge, George Lyman, 177
Kiwanivista Park, 97
Kizer, John, 575
Klaus, William, 371
Kline, George, 666
Kline, Michael, 556
Kline family, 276
Klipstein, E. C., 129
Klusmeyer, Mike, 221
K-Mart, 327
Knapps Creek, 300, 450
Knapsack, 530
Kniffen, Fred, 735
Knight, Charles Landon, 403
Knight, Frank, 536
Knight, Leah, 187
Knights of St. George, 506
Knights of the Golden Horseshoe, 266
Knights of the South Branch, 315
Knobler, Alfred, 565
Knutti, John G., 656
Koblegard, T. F., 726
Kochenderfer, Jim, 236
Koger, Lisa, 427
Kolibash, William, 575
Kolwiecki, Tom, 739
Konrad, Karel, 565
Koontz, Arthur B., 499
Koontz, Henry, 210
Koontz Bend, 546
Krause, Arthur E., 328
Krauss, Alison, 508, 676
Kraybill, David, 813
Kreis, Robert, 788
Kreisler, John Philip, 404
Krieg, Wallace & McQuaide Company, 166
Krise, George "Speedy," 805
Kroger, 211
Krug, Julius, 483
Kruk, John, 580
Kump, Herman Guy, 311, 390, **405**, 602, 686, 779; conservation policies of, 162, 523; education and library policies of, 174, 422; electoral record of, 295, 401, 711; New Deal and, 341, 527, 810; fiscal policies of, 346, 699; conservatism of, 526
Kundzin, Arved, 818
Kunkle, Justin M., 501

Kurtz, Dave, 504
Kuykendall, Nathaniel, 537
Kyle, Darwin, 159

L. S. Good House, 278
La Galissonnière, Roland-Michel Barrin, Marquis de, 119
La Salle, René Robert Cavelier, Sieur de, 97, 119, 223, 372, 544
Laessle, Albert, 718
Lafayette, Marie-Joseph, Marquis de, 233, 316, 696, 745
Laidley, Amacetta, 692
Laidley, James Madison, 439, 692
Laidley, John, 97, 453, 692
Laing, John, 674
Lake Lynn Power Plant, 127
Lake Shawnee, 473
Lake Stephens, 49
Lakeview, 127
Lakin, J. W., 579
Lakin Correctional Facility for Women, 769
Lakota Indians, 362
Lamb, Leonard, 329
Lamb, Thomas W., 397
Lambie, R. M., 210
Lancaster Colony Corporation, 262
Landis family, 276
Landry, Tom, 351
Lane, Lawrence, 603
Lane, Levi, 35
Lane, Noah, 743
Lane, Warden M., 523
Laneville, 717
Langham, Red, 504
LaPoe Site, 491
Larenium, 651
Larkin brothers, 580
LaRoe, Karen, 813
LaRue, Isaac, 569, 635
LaRue, Jacob, 569, 635
Laska, Gretchen, 427
Last Forest, The (McNeill), 522
Late Silurian Era, 18
Lateef, Yusef, 379
Latrobe, 89
Latrobe, Benjamin, 537
Laughlin, Homer, 347, 580
Laughlin, Shakespeare, 347
Laughton, Charles, 532
Laurel Creek, 175, 216, 303, 494, 659
Laurel Fork (Centralia), 113, 114, 129, 491
Laurel Hill, 601, 617
Laurel Mountain, 10, 41
Laurie, Clayton, 499
Law, Clyde O., 777
Lawson, Anthony, 432
Lawson, Mont, 434
Lawson, Sherman, 153, 356
Layland, 150
Leaberry, John, 575
Leadbelly, 316
Leadclad Wire Company, 452
Leading Creek, 367
Leatherbark Creek, 115
Leatherman family, 276
Leckie Collieries, 798
Lee, Carl, 536
Lee, Grace Davis, 291
Lee, Richard (settler), 802

Lee, Richard Henry "Light Horse Harry," 259, 314, 415, 435, 744, 749
Lee, Thomas, 542, 713
Lee, Wilma, 70, 167, 785
Lee Cabin, 435
Lee Sulphur Spring, 314, 435, 482
Leeper, Harry, 12
Lees, Jim, 444, 803
Léger, Fernand, 413, 798
Legg, Sarah Ann, 416
Legg, Susan, 416
Legg Fork, 572
Lemke, Dorothy, 582
Lemon, Eugene, 242
Lemon, Frederick, 619, 620
Lemon, George, 521, 619, 803
Lentz, Melvin, 437, 753
Leonhart, William Kahn, 808
LeSourd, Leonard E., 451
Lessel, John, 552
Lester, Jerry, 184
Letart, 458
Letcher, John, 158
Letter Gap, 285
Levassor, Clara, 197, 198
Levisa Fork, 431
Lewin, Max, 509
Lewis, Angelo, 184
Lewis, Art "Pappy," 352
Lewis, Benjamin, 420
Lewis, Carlos, 611
Lewis, Charles, 298, 418, 458, 574
Lewis, Grover, 152
Lewis, Jacob, 403
Lewis, Jennie, 184
Lewis, John, 31, 298, 418, 420, 437, 450
Lewis, John Dickinson, 196
Lewis, Laurie, 347
Lewis, Letitia Preston Floyd, 633
Lewis, Meriwether, 418
Lewis, Nancy Pat Hamilton, 663
Lewis, Raymond, 66
Lewis, Robert, 298
Lewis, Ronald L., 430
Lewis, Samuel, 205, 260, 303
Lewis, Thomas (Greenbrier County settler), 420
Lewis, Thomas (Mason County settler), 458
Lewis, Thomas (Stony River explorer), 684
Lewis, Thomas (surveyor), 75
Lewis, Warren S., 761
Lewis, William Lynn, 633
Lewis, William, 298, 696
Lewis County, 80, 197, **418–19**, 447; agriculture in, 6, 292; glass industry in, 11; clay mining in, 143; Irish in, 367; oil and gas in, 521; as Democratic stronghold, 779
Lewis family, 266
Lewis Spring, 260
Lewisburg Academy, 212, 298, 584
Lewisburg & Ronceverte Railway, 657, 688
Lewisburg Female Institute, 112, 298, 299
Ley, William C., 210
Libbey, Edward, 282, 551
Libbey-Owens-Ford Company, 124, 282, 367, 391, 740
Libert, Hazel, 476
Library Services Act (1956), 422
Lieber, Maxim, 404

Liggett & Myers, 708
Lilly, Bob, 351
Lilly, Charles Everett, 423
Lilly, Everett, 70
Lilly, Goff P., 424
Lilly, Jiles, 423
Lilly, John (editor), 287
Lilly, John (settler), 423
Lilly, John H., 424
Lilly, Lois Elaine, 401
Lilly, Mark, 423
Lilly, Mary Frances Moody, 429
Lilly, Mitchell Burt "Bea," 70, 423
Lilly, Robert (settler), 423, 429
Lilly, Robert G. (university administrator), 509
Lilly (village), 71, 423, 429
Lilly Fork, 142
Limber's Ridge, 116
Lincoln, Abraham, 286, 659, 693; emancipation
    clause backed by, 1; West Virginia statehood
    backed by, 64, 120, 257, 338, 612, 797; Civil
    War outbreak and, 137; appointments by,
    373, 374, 105–06; iconography of, 680, 710;
    local support for, 784
Lincoln, Thomas, 313
Lincoln County, 34, 99, 152, 424–25, 447;
    tobacco farming in, 6, 708; crafts in, 17;
    formation of, 171–72; schools in, 215; water
    supply for, 216; housing stock in, 445
"Lincoln County Crew," 237
Lindbergh, Anne Morrow, 502
Lindbergh, Charles, 502
Lindsay, David, 241
Lindside, 580
Linger, James G., 425, 426
Linger, Waitman T., 425
Linsly, Noah, 212, 426
List, W. M., 303
Literary Fund, 494
Little, K. Carl, Jr., 177
Little, William, 781
Little Buffalo Creek, 133
Little Clear Creek, 470
Little Coal River, 152, 430
Little Kanawha Craft House, 178
Little Kanawha Navigation Company, 429, 430,
    803
Little Kanawha River, 10, 216, 352, 429, 544;
    damming of, 81, 93, 233, 339; oil and gas
    reserves along, 92, 107, 520, 521; commercial
    traffic on, 100, 285, 293; ferries across, 236;
    aquatic life in, 240, 442; flooding of, 244,
    245; navigability of, 273, 280, 730; as power
    source, 279; showboats on, 622, 658
Little Kanawha Trail, 360
Little Laurel Run, 546
Little Levels, 439
Little Sandy Creek, 216
Little Sewell Creek, 470
Little Switzerland Brewing Company, 237
Little Turtle (Indian chief), 68, 229
Little Two Run, 118
Littlepage Terrace (Charleston), 743
Lively, Cecil, 59
Lively, Charles, 68
Livingston, Adam, 804
Livingston, John A., 85
Lloyd, Earl, 671
Loar, L. L., 777
Lockhart, Basil, 426

Lockheed Martin, 33, 319
Lockridge, H. M., 9
Lockwood, John, 91
Locust Creek, 175, 176, 395
Logan, Henry, 682
Logan, James, 432
Logan, Tex, 70
Logan County, 36, 233, 424, 433–34, 447, 577;
    Ku Klux Klan in, 4; labor movement in, 74,
    121, 340, 397, 484; mining in, 74, 89, 121, 148,
    150, 484; natural features of, 152; company
    towns in, 157; politics in, 191, 269, 596;
    schools in, 215; farming in, 281; Hatfield-
    McCoy Feud in, 322; in Civil War, 338; Hun-
    garians in, 353; industry in, 369, 466; land
    ownership in, 410; fauna in, 441
Logging Sediment Control Act, 255
Lomax (lieutenant), 261
Lomax, Alan, 316
Lomax, John, 316
Lombardi, Vince, 352
Lombardo, Guy, 184, 626, 664
London (W. Va.), 357
Long, Billy, 681
Long, Cleta M., 556
Long, Earl, 675
Long, Edward, 330
Long, Hilda, 330
Long, Huey, 675
Long, John, 258
Long, Kate, 347
Long, Stephen H., 176
Long, Walker, 330
Long, Ware, 622
Longacre, 370
Loop Creek Colliery, 552
Lopez, Joseph, 580
Lorado, 89
Loring, William Wing, 10, 128, 279, 381, 391, 435,
    628
Lost City, 699
Lost Creek, 319, 548, 758
Lost Highway (Currey), 428
Loudin, Thelma Brand, 228
Louis, Joe, 70
Louis Berkman Company, 252
Louisa, 58
Louistall, Victorine, 775
Louisville Coal & Coke Company, 155
Loup Creek Colliery, 359
Loury, Samuel B., 572
Love, Francis J., 463, 526
Love, Shirley, 540, 703
Love, Winifred, 811
Loveberry, 367
Lovett, Joe, 511
Lovett, Lyle, 508
Lovett, Sarah, 333
Lovett, Thomas, 333
Lovett, William, 333
Low, A. A., 396
Low Gap, 104
Low Moor Iron Company, 396
Lowe, John W., 641
Lower Kittaning/No. 5 Block coal seam, 148
Lowther, William, 803
Lubeck, 277
Lucas, Boney, 425
Lucas, John W., 631

Lucite, 207
Ludlow, Noah, 658
"Ludlow Massacre," 37
Luke, John G., 115
Luke, William, 780
Lunceford, Jimmie, 379
Lundale, 89
Lundy, George, 785
Lunk, William A., 76, 248
Lunsford, Alexander M., 269
Lutz, Carl E., 328
Lynch, Tom, 426
Lyng, Richard, 560
Lynn, Albert M., 127
Lynn, John, 254
Lyon, Florence A., 592
Lyon, Harriet, 582, 775
Lyon's Mill, 746
Lyondell, 130

M&G Polymers, 130
Ma, Yo-Yo, 773
Maben, 621
MacArthur, Douglas, 810
McBeth mine, 150
MacConkey, Dorothy I., 185, 584
MacCorkle, Isabelle, 439
MacCorkle, William Alexander, 9, 114, 187, 290,
    316, 439, 566; flexibility of, 78; as business-
    man, 126, 668; appointments of, 134, 523;
    recollections of, 141, 253, 427, 604–05, 643,
    672, 744; as member of Kanawha Ring, 398;
    charitable efforts of, 638; mansion built by,
    693
MacCorkle, William G., 439
Maccrady coal formation, 147
MacDonald mine, 197
MacDonald, Angus W., 212, 259
Mace, 127
Mace, Chester, 120
Mack, Alexander, Jr., 276
MacKaye, Benton, 20
Mackey family, 82
MacLean, John P., 23
MacLeish, Archibald, 60
MacLeod, Alexander, 540
MacLeod, Roderick, 540
Maclin, Edwin S., 813
MacMaster, Richard K., 430
MacQueen, George A., 395
Maddy, John, 303
Mader, Dave, Jr., 504
Madison, Dolley Payne Todd, 24, 140, 316, 318,
    374, 696, 744
Madison, James (bishop), 446
Madison, James (president), 24, 140, 163, 199,
    305, 316, 374, 439, 696
Madison, William, 22, 36
Madison Coal and Supply, 577
Mahan, William, 252
Mahonegon, 88
Mahood, Alex, Jr., 440
Mahood, Belva, 440
Mahood, John, 440
Maier Foundation Hall, 141
Maier, William J., Jr., 125
Mail Pouch Chewing Tobacco, 67
Maillard, Keith, 427
Main Island Creek, 432
Main Street West Virginia, 334

Mairs, Oscar L., 23, 463, 562, 760, 815
Mallery, Garrick, 23
Man (town), 19, 258, 433, 726
Manassas Gap Railroad, 38
Manchin, Joe, III, **443–44**, 448; electoral record
 of, 588, 646
Mancini, Henry, 773
Manhattan Jazz Quartet, 379
Manila Creek, 572
Mann, G. Thomas, 185
Mann, Jacob, 303
Mann, John, 303
Manning, Carlos, 21
Manning, Charles F., 445
Manningsville, 152
Mann's Creek Railroad, 657
Manolidis, James, 444
Mansell, L. R., 650
Mansfield, Mike, 95
Marbon Chemical, 555
Marche, Thomas B., 631
Marcus, Aaron, 447
Margolin, A. S., 248
Marietta Manufacturing Company, 459, 573, 740
Marion, Francis, 448
Marion County, **448–49**; mining in, 143, 150, 155,
 156; courthouse in, 227; folk music in, 250;
 Grange in, 292; legislative representation of,
 350; ethnic makeup of, 353, 370, 371, 574;
 integration in, 364
Marion County in the Making, 251
Marks, Zeke, 306
Marland, William Casey, 285, 290, **449–50**, 640–
 41, 773, 815; desegregation under, 137, 213,
 364, 715; tax policies of, 191; electoral record
 of, 346, 602, 614; alcoholism of, 557
Marland Heights, 344, 754
Marlin, Jacob, 266, 450, 570
Marlin's Bottom, 450, 570
Marmac Company, 465
Marmet, 125, 258, 357, 584
Marple, Jorea, 467
Marsalis, Wynton, 664
Marsh Fork, 152
Marsh, Anna, 241, 684
Marsh, Joseph Franklin, Jr., 158
Marsh, Joseph Franklin, Sr., 157, 158
Marsh, Mifflin, 451
Marsh, William, 451
Marshall, George Preston, 352
Marshall, Hezekiah B., 572
Marshall, Humphrey, 565
Marshall, James, 456
Marshall, Peter, 451
Marshall, T. Marcellus, 280, 285
Marshall County, 150, **451–52**; early education
 in, 213; representation of, 350
Marshall University, 97, 158, 354, **453–54**, 487,
 548, 656; archeology at, 24, 147; botany at,
 76; civil rights activism at, 137; job training
 at, 211; origins of, 212, 213, 339, 533, 534;
 athletics at, 303, 329, 502, 670, 671; library
 training by, 422; mascot of, 447; medical
 school at, 471; journalism school at, 566;
 radio at, 595; Rahall Transportation Institute
 at, 596; accreditation of, 652–53
Martens, Robert, 26, 456, 726
Martin, Clarence E., 346, 526
Martin, Cyrus H., 813
Martin, Denny, 456

Martin, Ella, 519
Martin, Joseph (compiler), 446
Martin, Joseph E., Jr. (physician), 61
Martin, Marion, 797
Martin, Presley, 527
Martin, Stanley H., 777
Martin, Strother, 253
Martin, Thomas Bryant, 54, 456, 682
Martin family, 276
Martinsburg, 54, 133, 209, **456–57**, 577; black
 education in, 3; baseball in, 45; as county
 seat and prospective capital, 110, 341, 682;
 Germans in, 277; labor in, 340, 596–97; Jews
 in, 383; libraries in, 422; telephone service
 in, 702; industry in, 703–04
Martinsburg & Potomac Railroad, 456
Martinsburg Formation, 482
Martinsburg Mining, Manufacturing, and
 Improvement Company, 457, 736
Martinsburg Worsted and Cassimere Company,
 703
Marvel, Gary, 379
Marx, Louis, 457
Maryland Heights, 318
Maryland Lumber Company, 192, 747
Mash Fork, 103
Mason, 458, 459
Mason, Charles, 459
Mason, George, 212, 458
Mason, Matilda, 458
Mason, Salina Hite, 453
Mason, Samuel, 464
Mason, William Sandheger "Sandy," 458, 773
Mason County, 18, 213, 372, 447, **458–59**; cattle
 industry in, 6; corn production in, 6; tobacco
 farming in, 6, 11, 708; crafts in, 17; formation
 of, 52, 145; legislative representation of, 350;
 Lutherans in, 438; prehistoric peoples in,
 583; forestation in, 715; vernacular architec-
 ture in, 735; wetlands in, 780
Masonic Temple Building (Charleston), 743
Massawomeck (Black Minqua) Indians, 491
Massey Energy, 487
Massie, Nancy, 470
Master Marble, 446
Masters, Edgar Lee, 469
Masters, Frankie, 379
Matewan Missionary Baptist Church, 189
Matheny, John, 813
Mathers, William, 351
Mathews, Albert G., 311
Mathews, Alex, 298
Mathews, Henry Mason, 299, **461–62**; as "Bour-
 bon" governor, 78, 607; strikes and, 324,
 596–97
Mathews, Mason, 461
Matthews, Sutton, 107
Matthews International Corporation, 402
Mauch Chunk coal formation, 147
Maurer, Beryl B., 268, 438
Maxwell, Edwin, 799
Maxwell, Haymond, 56
Maxwell, Lewis, 759
Maxwell, Robert, 475
Maxwell, Sarah Bonnifield, 462
May, Clark W., 425
May, Kathleen, 242
May, Teddy, 242
May Moore, 583
Mayberry, Thomas, 337, 654

Mayer-Oakes, William J., 23
Mayflower Vehicle Systems, 128
Maynard, Elliott E., 487, 694
Maynard, Lee, 427
Mayo, William, 401
Mayse, Budge, 632
Mayse, Fudge, 632
Mazer, Henry, 788
McAteer, J. Davitt, 151
McAuliffe, William C., 785
McCarthy, Joseph R., 463, 783, 784
McCarty, Patrick, 401, 481
McCarty, Ralph, 791
McCauley, G. W., 497
McCauley, Sandy, 157, 764
McClain, Faith Reynolds, 463
McClain, Ken, 463
McClaugherty, John, 773
McClellan, George B., 138, 435, 503, 562, 563,
 601, 612, 617, 628, 641
McClintock, Mabel, 620
McClung, Bronson, 764
McClung, C. H., 324
McClung, James, 381
McClure, Lucy, 43
McClure, Simon, 422
McColloch, Elizabeth, 819
McColloch, Samuel, 463–64
McComas, 473
McComas, William K., 787
McComas family, 424
McCoy, Alifair, 321, 323, 733
McCoy, Calvin, 321, 323, 733
McCoy, Daniel, 464
McCoy, Francis, 508
McCoy, Gen. William, 464–65
McCoy, Green, 425
McCoy, Harmon, 320, 322
McCoy, Katherine, 497
McCoy, Margaret, 464
McCoy, Paris, 322
McCoy, Pharmer, 322
McCoy, Randolph, Jr., 322
McCoy, Rose Anna, 321, 322, 464
McCoy, Sam, 322
McCoy, Samuel Alexander, 497
McCoy, Sarah, 321, 323, 464, 733
McCoy, Selkirk, 322
McCoy, Tolbert, 322
McCoy, William (merchant), 465, 559
McCue, John, 584
McCullough, Dave, 447
McCullough, Frank Witcher, 810
McCullough (Trader's) Trail, 743
McCuskey, John, 490
McCuskey, Roy, 777
McDade, James, 372
McDavid, John E., 516
McDermot, John F., 105
McDonald, Astynax, 434
McDonald, Henry T., 318, 685
McDonald, J. E., 625
McDonald, Julia Leavell, 186
McDowell, Andrew N., 191
McDowell, James, 465
McDowell County, 162, 447, **465–66**, 577; archi-
 tecture in, 24, 25, 735, 736; coal and coke in,
 150, 155, 157, 192, 233, 369; cockfighting in,
 154; formation of, 165; schools in, 215; fores-
 tation in, 256, 608–09; farming in, 281; labor

disputes in, 346; Hungarians in, 353; integration in, 364; Italians in, 370; during World War I, 402; land ownership in, 410; literacy in, 426; poverty in, 591; Primitive Baptists in, 587

McDowell Times, 4, 5, 401, 530

McElhenney, John, 298, 299, 547, 584

McElhenney, Rebecca, 584

McElroy mine, 150, 452

McFarland, Ezekiel, 603

McGee, Fred, 333

McGee, John F., 126

McGill, Daniel, 584

McGillicuddy, Cornelius, 368

McGinley, Patrick, 511

McGovern, George, 134

McGowan Mountain, 127

McGraw, Barney, 803

McGraw, Gene, 153

McGraw, Warren R., 62, 467, 693, 815

McGraw, Warren, II, 467

McGraw, Willard, 153

McGrew, James, 585

McGuire Park, 419

McHugh, Lawrence R., 785

McHugh, Thomas, 412

McKee, Alexander, 709

McKell, John, 467

McKell, Thomas Gaylord, 205, 467

McKendree, 591

McKinley, Agra Bennett, 468

McKinley, Johnson Camden, 468

McKinley, William, 104, 167, 565, 599, 612, 629, 695, 790

McKinney, Howard W., 137

McKinney, John C., 61

McKinney, O. S, 228

McKinney, Richard I., 685

McKinney's Cotton Pickers, 378

McLaglen, Andrew V., 253

McLaughlin, Addison, 753

McManus, Lew, 350

McMechen, 452, 615, 666

McMechen, William, 666

McMichael, Edward V., 23, 89

McMilan (McMullen), Mary, 86

McMillan, William A., 125

McMullen (McMilan), Mary, 86

McMurran, Joseph, 656

McNamara, Robert S., 733

McNeal, Wallace W. "Squire," 637, 754

McNeel, William Price, 572, 586

McNeil, Meade, 76

McNeill, Daniel, 497

McNeill, G. D., 309, 469, 522

McNeill, Harold M., 772

McNeill, Jesse, 314, 469

McNeill, John Hanson, 314, 397, 469

McNeill, Robert B., 584

McOlgin, David, 142

McOlgin farm, 141

McPherson, Hugh, 379

McPherson, James Alan, 554

McPherson, James Lowell, 316

McQuade, Marian Herndon, 291, 292, 344

McQuain, Hazel Ruby, 776

McQuirter, John, 753

McVeigh, Timothy, 564

Meade, C. H., 815

Meade, Gus, 307

Meador, Josiah, 429

Meador, Rufus G., 474

Meadow Creek, 470

Meadows, Clarence Watson, 41, 49, **470–71**, 600; appointments of, 316, 325, 556

Meadows, Joe, 70

Meadows, Josiah, 423

Meadows, Kayetta, 763

Meadows, Marion, 379

Meadows, R. D. W., 761

Meadows Stone & Paving, 81

Meanor and Handloser, 397

Meany, George, 674

Meeks, Cleburne, 59

Megowen, Dorothy, 248

Meigs, Jonathan, Jr., 374

Meigs, Mary Sophia, 374

Meigs, Montgomery C., 180

Meitzen, Manfred, 611

Meldahl, Anton, 808

Melungeons, 305, 362

Mencken, H. L., 670

Menuhin, Yehudi, 788

Menz, Clifford, 241

Mequashake Indians, 653

Mercer, Hugh, 458, 473, 567, 588

Mercer, John, 258, 259

Mercer Academy, 584

Mercer County Airport, 32

Mercer County, **473–74**; Ku Klux Klan in, 4; natural features of, 87, 208–09; formation of, 165; county farms in, 174; African-American miners in, 192; flora in, 246; fossils in, 261; labor disputes in, 346; integration in, 364; fauna in, 442

Mercer Saltworks, 691

Mercury Coal & Coke Company, 82

Meriluco, 676

Merrimac, 480

Mesozoic Era, 17, 546

Mestrezat, Walter, 587

Meyercord-Carter Company, 740

Miami, 666

Miami Indians, 544, 576, 713

Michaux, Andre, 75

Michel, Franz Louis, 68, 223, 266, 336

Michels, Don, 447

Mid-Atlantic of West Virginia, 446

Middelburg, Ferdinand, 322

Middle Creek Railroad, 657

Middle Creek, 58

Middle Fork Railroad, 657

Middle Fork, 89, 572

Middle Island Creek, 198, 388, 476, 687

Middle Mountain, 10

Milam, Charlotte June, 188

Miles, Butch, 379

Miles End, 374

Military Reconstruction Act (1867), 565

Mill Creek Baptist Church, 40

Mill Creek Cannel Coal Company, 21

Mill Creek Coal & Coke, 57

Mill Island, 315

Miller, Alexander McVeigh, 478

Miller, David, 812

Miller, Glenn, 202

Miller, Hugh, 86

Miller, Izetta Jewell, 86

Miller, Jane Tompkins, 478

Miller, John (orchardman), 54

Miller, John, Sr. (settler), 753

Miller, Orville Q., 546

Miller, Paul A., 812

Miller, Priscilla Ann, 307

Miller, Rosa Lee, 558

Miller, Thomas Condit, 462

Miller, Thomas E. (Supreme Court justice), 412, 444, 693

Miller, Tom (journalist), 410

Miller, William (religious leader), 650

Miller, William S. (orchard farmer), 548–49

Miller site, 258

Milligan Creek, 395, 659

Milliken, Sayers L., 762

Mills, Howard, 76

Mills, Lou, 116

Millsop, Thomas, 754

Milnes, Gerald, 251, 547

Milroy, Robert H., 9–10

Miltenberger, James, 172

Minden, 540

Minear, John, 277, 717

Mineral County, 226, 336, **481–82**; courthouse in, 25; formation of, 172, 185, 310; poultry farming in, 209; integration in, 364; industry in, 368; Potomac and, 535; fruit production in, 549; natural features of, 578; Presbyterians in, 584; vernacular architecture in, 735

Mineral Wells, 504

Mingo Company, 74

Mingo County, 99, 157, 447, **486–87**, 577; coal reserves in, 148; formation of, 172, 433; schools in, 215; farming in, 281; labor movement in, 340, 397; industry in, 369; in Mine Wars, 484; prehistoric mounds in, 504; in war on poverty, 742; growth of, 798

Mingo Flats, 602

Minter, William E., 488

Mississippi Queen, 302

Mississippi Valley Historical Association, 12

Mississippian Period, 147, 218, 261–62, 265, 300, 303, 436, 482, 520, 638

Mitchell, John, 407

Mitchum, Robert, 532

Mittal Steel, 755

Mobay company, 452

Modarelli, Antonio, 773, 788

Moffat, Jessie Thornton, 67

Mohawk Indians, 369

Mohawk, 429, 480

Mole Hill (Federal Hill; Mountain), 619

Mollohan, Robert H., 101, 294, 352, 448, 489, 496, 662, 724

Monarch Rubber Company, 670

Monongah, 150, 341, 383, 448, 490

Monongah Glass, 227

Monongahela coal formation, 147

Monongahela Indians, 583

Monongahela Iron and Steel Company, 552

Monongahela Navigation Company, 374, 431, 492, 758

Monongahela River, 10, 17, 18, 129, 161, 220, 227, 256, 275, 431, **492**, 622; fish species in, 240; flooding of, 244; as route of settlement, 266, 500; navigability of, 273, 687, 720; industry along, 274; in prehistory, 281, 408; damming of, 339, 409, 523, 730; damage to, 513; showboats on, 658

Monongahela River Railroad, 38, 493

Monongahela West Penn, 688

Monongalia Academy, 774
Monongalia County, 448, **492–93**, 615; schools in, 4; natural features of, 127; coal and coke in, 139, 150, 155; formation of, 171, 757, 817; demography of, 192; settlement of, 266; legislative representation of, 350; industry in, 359, 368; integration in, 364; Italians in, 370; literacy in, 426
Monongalia Gazette, 530
Monroe, Bill, 39, 70, 508
Monroe, James, 49, 163, 199, 374, 493, 652
Monroe County, 34, 35, **493–95**, 615; farming in, 6; fauna in, 13; architecture in, 24, 735; boundary dispute and, 78; in Civil War, 94; natural features of, 118, 161, 276, 380, 395, 523; religious life in, 136, 473, 474–75; schools in, 140; formation of, 165; 4-H movement in, 225; flora in, 246; fossils in, 261; Presbyterians in, 584; electrification of, 631; slavery in, 661
Monsanto Company, 129, 130, 391
Montague, Russell, 540, 670
Montana Mining Company, 148
Montcalm, 72
Montgomery, James C., 234
Montgomery, Samuel B., 499
Montgomery (Coal Valley), 45, 233, 234, 324
Montgomery Preparatory School, 775
Montgomery Ward, 488
Moody, James, 379
Moore, Alice, 391, 392
Moore, Alvin E., 314
Moore, Arch Alfred, Jr., 131, 181, 291–92, 378, 452, **495–96**, 770; electoral record of, 35, 108, 166, 223, 290, 443, 603, 613, 625, 626, 663, 673, 694, 724; black lung movement and, 62; Buffalo Creek Flood and, 90; criticism of, 134; judiciary reorganized under, 388, 416; budgetary powers increased under, 489; criminal trials of, 575, 576, 613; VISTA reined in by, 739
Moore, Ben, 137, 449
Moore, Billy, 379
Moore, Blaine Free, 29
Moore, C. Forrest, 572
Moore, Conrad, 497
Moore, Eli Herdman, 172
Moore, F. T., 496
Moore, Fleecie, 637
Moore, H. B., 300
Moore, James, 175, 176
Moore, John Trotwood, 202
Moore, Lee, 785
Moore, Louis, 447
Moore, Mel, 681
Moore, O'Brien, 126
Moore, Phoebia, 172
Moore, Ray, 791
Moore, Robert, 70
Moore, Sam (filmmaker), 239
Moore, Sam (rock climber), 624
Moore-Keppel company, 146
Moorehouse, Mary Frances, 541
Moorman, John J., 791
Moran, M. F., 726
Moran, Thomas, 417
Moretti, Alessandro, 565
Moretti, Roberto, 565
Morgan, Caroline, 303
Morgan, Daniel, 50, 54, 264, 314, 498, 709, 749

Morgan, David, 448, 500
Morgan, Ephraim Franklin, 4, 227, 289, 448, **499–500**; appointments of, 214; in Mine Wars, 64, 385, 484, 485, 718, 793
Morgan, George, 780
Morgan, Henry M., 501
Morgan, John (reporter), 556, 663
Morgan, John (settler), 456
Morgan, John F. (murderer), 410, 618
Morgan, John Hunt (general), 90–91, 372, 500
Morgan, John Pierpont (financier), 132, 270, 339, 444, 533, 730
Morgan, Joseph, 456
Morgan, Levi, 680
Morgan, Morgan, II, 500
Morgan, Sidney, 676
Morgan, William S., 448
Morgan, Zedekiah, 729
Morgan County, 226, **498–99**, 577; apple and peach production in, 7, 549; natural features of, 99; formation of, 209, 738; settlement of, 336; Poles in, 574; Wildlife Management Area in, 796
Morgan Orchard, 21
Morgantown, 133, 381, **500–501**, 577; basketball in, 46; bridges in, 83; in Civil War, 92, 386; industry in, 283, 580, 625; labor movement in, 340; Jews in, 383; libraries in, 422; Orthodox Christians in, 550, 611; Presbyterians in, 584; broadcasting in, 595, 703; telephone service in, 702; Unitarians in, 725
Morgantown Female Collegiate Institute, 492
Morrill Act (1862), 75, 339, 492, 774, 812
Morrill Act (1890), 771
Morris, Edmund, 479
Morris, Henry, 531, 691
Morris, Isaac, 210
Morris, John (Cabell County settler), 479
Morris, John (musician), 143, 145, 547
Morris, Peter, 531
Morris, Robert, 465, 695
Morris, Ruby, 327
Morris, Thomas A., 170, 717
Morris, Tusca, 61
Morris, Will, 61
Morris, William, 266, 390, 531, 691
Morris, William, Jr., 531
Morris Brothers Old-time Music Festival (film), 251
Morris family, 393
Morrison, Agnes Westbrook, 775
Morrison, C. M., 176
Morrison, J. Holmes, 395
Morrison, O. J., 373
Morrison, Sandy, 515
Morrison, Will, 515
Morrow, James Elmore, 502
Morrow, Nancy R. Cameron, 228
Morse, Larry, 76
Morse, Samuel F. B., 688
Morton, Jelly Roll, 379
Morton, Levi, 607
Morton, Oren F., 637
Morton, Quinn, 91
Morzani, T. W., 176
Moser family, 276
Moses, Michael, 726
Moss, John W., 555
Moss-Bennett Bill, 23
Mother Jones (magazine), 107

Mother's Pension Law, 326
Mothershed, Gay, 584–85
Mothes, Gordon, 265
Mothman Prophecies (film), 239
Mott, Charles T., 308
Mount Carbon, 258, 335
Mt. Carbon Company, 552
Mount Hope, 233, 234
Mt. Lookout, 381
Mount Nebo, 250
Mount Storm, 293, 506
Mountain (Federal Hill; Mole Hill), 619
Mountain Brook mine, 150, 485
Mountain Heritage (Maurer), 250, 251, 268
Mountain House, 111
Mountain State Business College, 555, 808
Mountain State Hospital, 125
Mountain State University (Beckley College, College of West Virginia), 49, **509**, 600
Mountaineer, The (film series), 239
Mountaineer Gas Company, 155, 491
Mountaineer Wind Energy Center, 800
Mountaineer Woodturners, 177
Mountaintop Vacationland, 12
Mounts, Arden, 504
Mounts, Ellison "Cottontop," 323, 486
Mower Lumber Company, 115, 128
Mowrey, J. R. S., 650
MTR Gaming Group, 510
Muck, Karl, 404
Mucklow, 91, 340, 480, 553
Mud (town), 511
Mud River Covered Bridge, 175, 176
Muddy Creek, 22, 300
Mulligan, James A., 293
Mullins, Anderson, 287
Mullins, Bewel, 287
Mullins, Ira, 143, 238, 547, 790
Muncy, Will, 153
Mundell, Luella Raab, 228
Munn, Robert F., 694
Murphy, Elsie Bogardus, 144
Murphy, Kelsey, 565
Murphy tract, 547
Murray, Eddie, 46
Murrow, Edward R., 184
Muscia, Jim, 432
Muse, George, 458
Museum of Radio and Technology, 512
Musial, Stan, 45, 152
Music, Dorothy, 76
Muskingum War, 400
Myer, William E., 360, 394
Myers, Bob, 422
Myers, Greg, 185
Myers, Hu, 9
Myers, Hubert "Bumps," 379
Myers, John, 513

NAACP Legal Defense Fund, 187
Nadenbousch distillery, 456
Nader, Ralph, 151
Nail City Brewery, 641
Nakashima, John, 239
Napoleon I, 180
Nash, James H., 344
Nathaniel Mountain, 310
National Academy of Design, 14
National Academy of Peace, 603

National Aeronautics and Space Administration (NASA), 95, 733
National Air and Space Museum, 33
National Alliance, 564
National Association for the Advancement of Colored People (NAACP), 4, 137, 144, 146, 269, 655, 685
National Aviation Day, 33
National Banking Act (1864), 725
National Baptists, 41
National Bituminous Coal Wage Agreement (1950), 20, 471
National Carbon Company, 319
National Commerce Bancorp, 516
National Exchange Bank, 757
National Historic Preservation Act (1966), 15, 23, 334, 519
National Industrial Recovery Act (1933), 27, 341, 407, 420, 519, 770, 817
National Labor Relations Act (1932), 149, 519
National Miners Union, 767
National Organization for the Reform of Marijuana Laws, 447
National Parks and Recreation Act (1978), 518
National Passenger Railroad Act, 13
National Rifle Association, 443
National Science Foundation, 401
National Steel Corporation, 369, 681, 682, 754–55
National Thespian Society, 11
National Trust for Historic Preservation, 334
National Youth Administration, 296
Native American Graves Protection and Repatriation Act, 24
Natrium Mound, 23, 760
Navaho Indians, 362
Nave, Jessie Campbell, 105
Naylor, Rex V., 524
Neal, James, 266
Neal, Teddy, 243
Neal, Will E., 327
Neale, Julia, 376
Neal's Landing, 258
NedPower, 800
Needham, James, 27, 525, 807
Neel, Charles, 639
Neel, Owen, II, 735
Neely, Alfred R., 526
Neely, Corrine, 526
Neely, Harold, 44
Neely, John Champ, 526
Neely, Matthew Mansfield, 227, 448, **525–26**, 636, 759, 805; appointments of, 35, 288, 470; electoral record of, 159, 322, 346, 401, 614, 695; labor support for, 191, 341, 576; early career of, 198; New Deal backed by, 295, 296, 405, 449, 527, 760, 810; death of, 450, 602
Neely, Nettie Mae, 479
Neely, Richard, 389, 412
Neff, Lucy, 188
Neill, A. D., 648
Nelson, Bobby, 444
Nelson, Jordan, 572
Nelson, Leonard C., 70, 813
Nelson, Morgan, 409
Nelson, Oscar, 726
Nelson, Roland, 454
Nelson, Sophia, 772
Nelson, Steve, 626

Nelson Rocks, 277
Nemacolin (Delaware chief), 65
Nemours, 473
Neolin (Delaware chief), 576, 653
Nero, Peter, 664, 773
Nesselroade, John, 603
New England Fuel and Transportation Company, 222
New Haven, 233, 459
New Howard, 480
New Kanawha Power Company, 324
New Manchester, 312
New Orleans (steamboat), 621
New River, 15, 76, 208, 272, **528**, 544; formation of, 10, 17, 335; settlements along, 18, 233, 274, 583, 691; exploration of, 47, 223; damming of, 71, 72, 244, 324, 357, 409, 690, 747; railroads along, 132; ferries across, 237; aquatic life and fishing in, 240, 241; flooding of, 245, 690; preservation of, 327; waterfall at, 392; commercial traffic on, 431, 622; rafting on, 710, 791
New River & Pocahontas Consolidated Coal Company, 413
New River coal formation, 147, 148
New River coalfield, 155, 197, 233, 467, 529
New River Gorge, 233, 234, 273, 468, 528, 597, 599, 657, 706
New River Gorge Heritage Festival, 234
New River Pocahontas Coal Company, 396
New River Regiment, 691
New York Mine, 701
Newburg, 150, 585
Newcomer, Christian, 726
Newell, 312, 340, 347, 348, 536, 580
Newell, Hugh, 417
Newman, Claudeis "Chip," 646
Newman, Dora Lee, 251
Newman, Paul, 676
Newman, Walter, 573, 716
Newton, James, 507
NGK Sparkplugs, 538
NiSource, 155, 521
Nicholas, Wilson Cary, 297, 465
Nicholas Chronicle, 531
Nicholas County, 80, 142, 216, 233, **531–32**; coal reserves in, 148; courthouse of, 189; folk music in, 250; in Civil War, 338; prehistoric mounds in, 504; industry in, 554; forestation in, 715
Nicholson, Hugh G., 395
Nicholson, Tom, 239
Nickel Plate Railroad, 132, 533, 786
Nickerson, Henry, 159
Nighbert, James Andrew, 369, 433, 434, 596
Nightingale, Jack H., 407
99th Pursuit Squadron, 33
Nitro Pencil Company, 129
Nitro Soap Factory, 129
Nittany apple, 21
Nitzschke, Dale F., 454
Nivert, Taffy, 172
Nixon, Richard M., 33, 95, 151, 291, 308, 398, 404, 509, 736, 742
No Drums, No Bugles (film), 239
Nogay (Carenbauer), Beth, 239
Noland, 480
Nonhelema, 169, 260
Noon, A. T., 422
Norman, John Clavon, Sr., 534

Norris, Milton, 285
Norris, P. W., 22–23, 505, 668–69
North, John A., 535
North Bend Lake, 409
North River Mountain, 309
Northcott, Robert Saunders, 140
Northeast Rail Reorganization Act (1981), 161
Northern Neck, 226
Northern Teachers' Association, 771
Northfork, 133, 383, 537, 572
Northrup Grumman, 319
Northwest Territory, 31
Northwestern Academy, 212
Northwestern Virginia Academy, 47
Norton, 601
Norton, David Z., 541–42
Notes on the Settlement . . . (J. Doddridge), 199, 202, 426
Notes on the State of Virginia (Jefferson), 381, 432
Nourse, James, 633
Nuckols, Jack, 663
No. 2 gas seam, 148
Nunley, Neal, 243
Nuttall, John, 234, 538
Nuttall, Thomas, 52, 75
Nutter, Buzz, 750
Nutter, T. G., 5, 137
Nutter's Fort, 318
Nutting, George Ogden, 457, 541, 784
Nuzum, Jack Robert, 539

O. Ames Company, 465, 555
Oakes, J. W., 507
Oakland, 92
Oakvale, 473, 474
Oakwood, 197
Oates, Anna Norman, 811
Oblinger, Jackie, 703
O'Brien, Adam, 695
O'Brien, Edward C., 109
O'Brien, Emmett J., 563
O'Brien, John, 427
O'Brien, Thomas, 367
O'Brien, Tim, 70
O'Brien, William Smith, 223, 646
Occidental Petroleum Company, 370
Oceana, 566, 815
O'Conner, Charles, 696
O'Connor, Simon, 368
October Sky (film), 239
Odell, Stuart, 789
O'Donovan, William Rudolf, 26
Office of Economic Opportunity (OEO), 742
Ogden, Dunbar H., 584
Ogle (captain), 254
Oglebay Glass Museum, 512
Oglebay Mansion, 263, 512
O'Hanlon, Dan, 804
Ohio Apex Chemical, 129
Ohio County, **542–43**; schools in, 140; formation of, 171, 492, 757, 817; religious life in, 199; schools in, 213; ethnic makeup of, 297; legislative representation of, 350; housing stock in, 445
Ohio Fuel Supply Company, 155
Ohio River, 77, 93, 492, **543–44**; settlements along, 1, 145, 266, 274, 491, 504, 583, 609,

653; industry along, 12, 148, 283, 609; formation of, 17, 275, 281, 335, 408; agricultural land along, 18; bounty lands along, 78; bridges across, 83, 99; islands in, 90; commercial traffic on, 129, 622; damming of, 220, 233, 339, 357, 523, 730, 747; exploration of, 223; ferries across, 237; aquatic life and fishing in, 240, 241, 513, 687; flooding of, 244, 245, 354, 394; navigability of, 211, 273, 430, 431, 536, 807; sand and gravel in, 523; deforestation along, 608; saltworks on, 637; wildlife along, 796

Ohio River Railroad, 38, 808

Ohio Valley China Company, 580

Ohio Valley University (College), **544–45**, 555, 610, 808

Ohio Valley Electric Railway, 688

Ohio Valley Refining Company, 569, 635

Ohio Valley Speedway, 504

Ohl, Ronald, 636

Oil, Chemical and Atomic Workers International Union, 408, 799

Oil Spring Run, 521

Old Ben Coal Corporation, 285

Old Fields, 209, 260

Old Flag, 530

"Old Red Brick," 216

Old Rehoboth Church Museum, 512

Oldham, Will, 461

Olin Chemical Company, 130

Oliverio, Mike, 444

Omaha Indians, 544

Omar, 433

Omnibus Parks and Public Lands Management Act (1996), 516

Ona, 504

130th Troop Carrier Squadron, 33

167th Fighter Squadron, 33, 54

Onego Mill, 281

Oneida Indians, 369, 713

O'Neill, Eugene, 404

O'Neill, Thomas P. "Tip," 596

Onondaga Indians, 369, 713

Opequon Creek, 267

Opequon, 209, 264

Opp, Paul F., 11–12

Orbison, Roy, 464

Orchard, 258, 584

Orders, Bob, 776

Ordovician Period, 261

Ormet Aluminum Corporation, 781

Orrel Coal Company, 585

Osage, 364, 550

Osborne, Bob, 434

Osborne, Richard, 432

Osborne Brothers, 785

Osgood, Ernest, 685

Ottawa Indians, 576, 713

Otter Creek Boom & Lumber Company, 550

Otterbein, Philip William, 726

Our Lady of Grace (Wheeling), 574

Our Lady of Lebanon Church (Wheeling), 414, 451

Overhill, 131

Overseas National Airway, 302

Owen, Robert, 351

Owens, Ted, 116

Owings, Minnie Lee, 747

Owlshead, 721

Ozanic, Joe, 588

Pack, Cowboy Loye, 632

Packett, John Bainbridge, 744

Packette, Annie G., 122

Packhorse Ford, 209

Pack's Ferry, 691

Paden, Obadiah, 552, 781

Paden City Pottery Company, 580

Page, Don, 177, 248, 281

Page, "Hot Lips," 379

Paige, Satchel, 705

Paine, Thomas, 135

Paint Creek, 91, 215, 233, 385, 391, 553, 666

Paint Creek Trail, 360

Painter, Fred Clifford, 109

Palace Furniture Company, 466

Palace of Gold, 537

Palatine, 227

Paleozoic Era, 16, 17, 261, 262, 272, 274, 482, 618

Palladium of Virginia and the Pacific Monitor, 530

Pallister, Sarah, 351

Palmer, Arnold, 684

Palmer, Phoebe, 638

Palmer Lumber Company, 344

Palmer mill, 554

Palmer Shoe Company, 396

Pancake, Breece D'J, 272, 427

Panhandle Railroad, 84

Panorama Overlook, 498

Panther Knob, 273, 524, 535, 618, 720

Paradise Park (film), 239

Paramount Glass, 635

Parchment Valley, 373

Pardee, 89

Pardee, Barton, 554

Parham, Charles Fox, 560

Parker, Alexander, 555

Parker, Alston, 481

Parker, Conizene, 555

Parker, Granville, 1

Parker, Maggie Hammons, 309

Parker, Rexana, 555

Parker Creek, 429

Parkersburg, 133, **555**, 577; black education in, 3; architects in, 25; as transportation center, 38, 682; baseball in, 45; Unionists in, 75; bridges in, 83; Carnegie grant to, 112, 422; Chamber of Commerce in, 121; industry in, 211, 340, 521, 580; settlement of, 266; Germans in, 277; labor movement in, 340; Irish in, 367; Jail House riots in, 375; Jews in, 382, 383; Lebanese and Syrians in, 414; motor racing in, 504; broadcasting in, 595, 703; electrification of, 630; socialism in, 665; streetcars in, 688; telephone service in, 702; flood protection in, 730

Parkersburg Rig and Reel Company, 555

Parkersburg Trades and Labor Assembly, 210

Parks, Dora Ruth, 422

Parks, Rosa, 758

Parks Corporation, 128

Parral mine, 150, 197, 233

Parrish, Richard Bruce, 662

Parsons, James, 717

Parsons, Thomas, 717

Parsons, Ward, 555, 718

Parsons, William, 372, 618

Parsons Footwear, 717

Partlow, Ira J., 449, 466

Parton, Dolly, 676

Patric, James H., 236

Patrick, Mason Mathews, 299

Patrick, Spicer, 307, 390

Patterson, Andrew, 107, 546

Patterson, John B., 316

Patterson, Johnny, 504

Patterson, Milton, 107

Patterson, William, 418

Patterson Creek, 209, 226, 258, 267, 302, 746

Patteson, Henry, 113

Patteson, Okey L., 35, 234, 348, **556–57**, 748; park improvements under, 113; appointments of, 449; as gubernatorial aide, 470–71; as turnpike commissioner, 470–71

Patton, George S. (Civil War colonel), 124, 138, 155, 391, 392–93, 641, 791

Patton, George S. (World War II general), 124, 155, 393

Patton, William Howe, 25

Patton family, 203

Paul VI, Pope, 197, 626

Paul Wissmach Glass Company, 552

Pauley, Janet, 604

Pauley, Kim, 125

Paull, Morgan, 253

Pax, 553

Paxton, Nancy, 500

Payne, Gloria, 185

Payne, Lucy, 316, 744

Payne, Mary, 374

Peale, Charles Willson, 77

Pearsall, Job, 627

Pearsall, John, 627

Pearsall's Flats, 310, 627

Pease, Roger, 469

Petersburg Hatchery, 240, 241

Pechiney Rolled Products, 372

Peck, L. T., 399

Pedneau, Dave, 428

Peeryville, 465

Pegram, John, 170, 601, 617

Pekowi Indians, 653

Pelham, Rosa, 53

Pelligrino, Carmine, 371

Peltier, Sellers, 446

Pelurie, Frank, 77

Pemberton, James B., 126

Pen Coal Company, 750

Pence, Andrew S., 558

Pence, John W., 228

Pendleton, Edmund, 558

Pendleton, Fred, 607

Pendleton, J. H., 784

Pendleton, W. H., 561

Pendleton County, 263, **558–60**; poultry farming in, 6, 274, 581; fauna in, 13, 47, 128, 219; natural features of, 18, 118, 122, 161, 276, 424, 578, 618; weather in, 146, 245, 750; formation of, 165, 209, 310, 738; libraries in, 422; livestock production in, 430; religious life in, 472, 473; Tories in, 709; wedding customs in, 753

Penn-American Plate Glass, 740

Penn National Gaming, 123

Penney, Katherine, 286

Pennington, Julian R., 725

Pennsboro, 504

Pennsboro & Harrisville Railroad, 320, 620

Pennsylvania Academy of the Fine Arts, 14

Pennsylvania Drake Well, 107
Pennsylvania Glass Sand Company, 283
Pennsylvania Railroad, 38, 82, 132, 529
Pennsylvanian Period, 16, 18, 147, 218, 262, 272,
    300, 455, 482
Pennzoil (South Penn Oil Company), 198, 521
Peoples Bank of Martinsburg, 516
Pepper, Charles M., 762
Perdue, 580, 581
Perdue, John D., 713
Pere Marquette Railroad, 132
Perfection Garment Company, 704
Perkins, R. J., 761
Perkovic, John, 180
Perkovic, Mike, 180
Perkowski, Harry, 152
Perlman, Itzhak, 788
Perry, Clay, 659
Perry, Huey, 196, 676
Perry, Oliver, 312, 359, 561
Perry Ridge, 548
Pershing, John J., 36
Pet Milk, 54
Peters, Jacob, 561
Peters Creek, 273
Peters Falls, 223
Peterson, Roger Tory, 85
Peterson family, 276
Peterstown, 20
Petroleum (town), 521, 619
Pettus, 16
Petty, Lee, 504
Peyton, William Madison, 107, 152, 439
Peytona, 107, 152
Pfeiffer, Annie Merner, 777
Pfeiffer, Fritz, 701
Pfost, Alice, 410
Pfost, Matilda, 410
Phalen, Robert, 727
Phelps, John M., 458
Philadelphia Company, 198
Philip Sporn Plant, 18, 459
Philips, William B., 24
Phillips Sheet and Tin Plate Company (Jackson
    Sheet and Tin Plate Company), 140, 297, 681
Phillips, Frank, 323, 733
Phillips, J. A., 754
Phillips, Violet, 76
Piatt, Abraham, 104
Pickaway, 584
Pickenpaugh, Estella Ley, 210
Pickens, 10, 18, 246, 273
Pickens, Hugh, 569
Pickett, George, 138
Picklesimer, Hayes, 395
Pierce, Carleton C., 103
Pierce, Franklin, 268, 696
Pierpont, Francis Harrison, 227, 386, 448, **564–
    65**, 733, 738; election of, 103, 766; Lincoln
    and, 105, 612; troops raised by, 257, 547, 612,
    782; First Wheeling Convention and, 338,
    563; as industrialist, 747
Pierson, Joseph, 374
Pierson Hollow, 546
Pigeon Roost, 565
Pike Island, 536
Pikeville, 58
Pilgrim's Pride, 497, 580, 581
Pilot Knob, 242

Pine Run School, 118
Pinecrest, 49, 591
Piney Creek, 132
Piney River & Paint Creek railroad, 197
Pingley, Clara, 587
Pink, Berry, 446
Piper, Edwin Ford, 512
Pipkin, Lester E., 16
Pisgah Methodist Episcopal Church, 383
Pittman-Robertson Act, 162
Pittsburgh & West Virginia Railroad, 533
Pittsburgh Plate Glass Company, 282, 452, 740
Pittsburgh, Wheeling & Kentucky Railroad, 351
Pittston Corporation, 89–90, 278, 434, 483, 485,
    497, 567, 624, 727
Pittsvein Coal, 701
Pius IX, Pope, 196, 626, 788
Pius XII, Pope, 697
Pleacher, Smoky, 797
Pleasant Hill, 657
Pleasant Valley Coal Company, 729
Pleasant Valley Hospital, 635
Pleasants, James, 569
Pleasants County, **569–70**; oil fields in, 521;
    St. Marys in, 635; Willow Island Disaster in,
    799; American Cyanamid, 799
Pleistocene Epoch, 275, 281, 408, 482, 544, 702
Plessy v. Ferguson (1896), 363–64
Plow That Broke the Plains, The (film), 239, 434
Plumley, William, 509
Plymale, Lewis, 76
Pocahontas coal formation, 147, 148
Pocahontas coalfield, 57, 155, 473, 533
Pocahontas County, 1, 34, 120, **570–71**; sheep
    farming in, 6; natural features of, 10, 118,
    127, 129, 216, 395, 687; flora and fauna in, 13,
    128, 115, 607, 695, 796; architecture in, 26;
    state park in, 48; Bierce in, 58; settlement of,
    145, 266; coal reserves in, 147; formation of,
    165, 559; courthouse of, 278; religious life in,
    473, 584; second homes in, 645; tanning in,
    699; vernacular architecture in, 736
Pocahontas Development Corporation, 467, 572
Pocahontas Fuel Company, 371, 444
Pocatalico Creek, 572
Poe, Edgar Allan, 219, 514
Poffenbarger, George, 412, 572, 573
Point, Mittie Frances Clarke, 478
Point Man for God (film), 239
Point Pleasant Register, 530
Polan, Barbara Faith, 73
Poland, C. F., 311
Poling, Eleanor, 166
Polk, Charles (university president), 509
Polk, Charles Peale (painter), 26
Polk, James K., 305
Pollack, Augustus, 303
Pollard, John Garland, 405
Pollock, Abigail, 14
Polsley, Daniel, 458, 573
Polson, John, 458
Pomeroy, Ralph, 159
Pompeys Knob, 272
Pond Creek No. 1 mine, 150
Pond Creek Pocahontas Coal Company, 45
Pond Fork, 152
Pond Lick Mountain, 127
Pontiac (Indian chief), 336, 576
Poole, Charlie, 153
Pope Dock Company, 658

Poplar Forest, 178
Porter, Cole, 662
Porter family, 82
Porterfield, George A., 41, 562, 563
Porterwood, 717
Posey, Thomas E., 526
Post, Wiley, 757
Potawatomi Indians, 576
Poteat, Patricia L., 57
Poteet, John, 636
Potomac Academy, 212
Potomac Edison Company, 491
Potomac River, 99, 122, 146, 209, 430, 523, 534–
    35, **578–79**, 687; exploration of, 68, 223;
    pollution and, 220; fish species in, 240, 667–
    68; flooding of, 244, 245; navigability of,
    273, 745; damming of, 357, 747; prehistoric
    mounds along, 504; wildlife along, 796
Potomoke, 336
Pound, Ezra, 60
Powell, Adam Clayton, 690
Powell, E. L., 137
Powell, James Marvin, 545
Powell, Walter B. (Watt), 677, 748
Powell, William, 353
Powell Mountain, 353
Powers, Elihugh, 116
Powers, Michael, 368
PPG Industries, 781
Prabhupada, Srila, 529
Prather, Charles, 756
Pratt & Whitney, 33, 319
Preast, Elsie, 649
Preble, Jack, 659
Preservation Alliance of West Virginia, 334
Preservation Hall Jazz Band, 664
President's Appalachian Regional Commission
    (PARC), 19
Presley, Elvis, 184
Prestera, Michael, 453
Preston, James Patton, 585
Preston, William, 207, 260, 261
Preston County, 12, 225, 226, **585–86**, 615;
    schools in, 4, 139; farming in, 6; natural fea-
    tures of, 10; homesteads in, 26, 27–28; fores-
    tation in, 116, 715; coal and coke in, 155, 694;
    flora in, 246; settlement of, 266; legislative
    representation of, 350; Italians in, 370;
    gristmills in, 746
Preston Railroad, 657
Pribble, Thomas, 802
Price, Andrew, 572, 586
Price, David, 422
Price, Edward, 658
Price, Eugenia, 391
Price, James (fiddler), 70
Price, James (newspaperman), 572, 586
Price, John R., 16
Price, Norman, 572
Price, Paul H., 23, 763
Price, William (anthologist), 278
Price, William (state senator), 774
Price, William T. (newspaperman), 572, 586
Price coal formation, 147
Price Hill, 197
Prickett, Jacob, 448, 587
Prince, Edwin, 49
Princess Coal, 724
Princess House, 436

Principled Man, A (film), 239
Pringle, John, 88, 588, 729
Pringle, Samuel, 88, 588, 729
Prisk, Dennis P., 455
Probert, Lionel, 132
Progressive Bankers Association, 40
Project Ozma, 519
Property Tax Limitation and Homestead Exemption Amendment (1982), 348
Prosperity, 197
Protohistoric Clover Phase, 146–47
Pruntytown (Cross Roads), 580, 589, 700
Pryor, John, 260, 303
Public Broadcasting Act (1967), 595
Public Utility Holding Company Act (Wheeler-Rayburn; 1935), 155
Public Utility Regulatory Policy Act (1982), 357
Pudden'head Wilson (film), 239
Pughtown, 584
Punkin Center, 548
Puopolo, L. A., 239
Purdue, Rissie, 35
Purdum, Raymond R., 185
Purdy, Jedediah, 427
Purdy, Simeon, 505
Pure Oil Company, 521
Puritan Coal, 798
Purnell, William "Keg," 379
Pursglove mines, 150, 550
Pursh, Frederick, 75
Puskar, Milan, 514
Putnam, Israel, 592
Putnam County, 87, 424, 577, **592–93**; tobacco farming in, 6, 11, 708; natural features of, 152; water supply for, 216; literacy in, 426; affluence of, 581
Putney, James, 172
Putney, Richard Ellis, 172
Pyles, Tim, 176
Pythian Building, 29

Quad Graphics, 54
Quaker Oats Company, 457
Quaker State, 521
Quebecor Printing, 54
Quinlan, John, 367
Quinnimont, 57, 368, 396, 523
Quirk, Thomas, 367

R. D. Bailey Dam, 244, 486
Rabenstein, Charles G., 742
Racetrack Video Lottery Act (1994), 510
Rae, John B., 726
Raese, David A., 501, 741
Raese, John, 596, 741
Raese, Richard, 741
Rafinesque, Constantine, 75
Rain People, The (film), 239
Raine, John, 470, 598
Raine, Thomas, 470, 598
Raine Lumber Company, 648
Raleigh Coal & Coke, 61
Raleigh County Memorial Airport, 32
Raleigh County, 196, 577, **598–600**; formation of, 48, 233; coal mining in, 150, 157, 739; natural features of, 152; logging in, 201; flora in, 246; farming in, 281; labor disputes in, 346; fauna in, 441, 442
Raleigh General Hospital, 49
Raleigh-Wyoming Mining Company, 285, 815

Ralsten, Murrill, 453
Ramage, Alberta C., 526
Ramps, 271, **600**
Rampal, Jean-Pierre, 788
Ramsdell House, 121
Randolph, Beverley, 57
Randolph, Edmund, 145, 212, 601
Randolph, Ernest, 602
Randolph, Jennings, 41, 131, 292, 319, 382, **602–03**, 636, 651, 769, 777; Appalachian Regional Commission and, 17; as aviation pioneer, 33; longevity of, 159; as publicist, 185; national parks and, 318, 380; as sports writer, 441; electoral record of, 450, 496, 724; homestead movement backed by, 721
Randolph, Jesse, 602, 635
Randolph, Peyton, 260
Randolph Academy, 140, 212, 819
Randolph County, **600–602**; livestock production in, 6, 430; natural features of, 10, 118, 129, 148, 216, 509; fauna in, 13, 128, 508; Bierce in, 58; timberland in, 115, 607, 695; settlement of, 266; farming in, 281; Italians in, 370; religious life in, 472; Tories in, 709; wedding customs in, 753; wetlands in, 780
Rankin, James, 561
Ranson, 209
Rapid America Corporation, 123
Rashid, Charley, 564
Rashid, George, 564
Rathbone, John Castelli "Cass," 92, 521, 603, 803
Rathbone, John Valleau "Val," 603, 803
Rathbone, Monroe Jackson, Jr., 808
Rathbone, William Palmer, 92, 102, 521, 603, 803
Ravenswood Aluminum Corporation, 372, 603–04
Ravenswood Novelty Works, 446
Ravenswood Porcelain, 580
Rawl, 480
Ray, Charles W., 678, 679
Rayburn, Sam, 509
Raymond, Henry Jarvis, 28
Raymond, Jerome Hall, 775
Reader, Benjamin, 781
Reagan, Ronald, 62, 296, 308
Reber, Grote, 519
Reber Radio Telescope, 518, 519
Rebrook, Ed, 575
Rece, Abia, 479
Rece, Joseph, 479
Rece, Milton, 479
Recht, Arthur M., 214, 412, 425, 505, 604
Reckart's Mill, 304
Reckless (film), 239
Rector College, 213
Red Hawk (Shawnee subchief), 169, 260
Red Jacket Consolidated Coal and Coke Company, 620, 621
Red Jacket, 480
Red Lick Mountain, 10
Red Oak Knob, 272
Redd, Marie E., 417
Reddish Knob, 276
Redman, Don, 378–79
Redstone Conference, 136
Reed, Arville, 607
Reeder, Phares, 763
Reeds Creek Hatchery, 241

Reedy, 622
Reedy, Wilford, 143
Reese, Lee, 131
Reeves, James Edmund, 472, 771
Reger, Jacob, 277
Rehoboth Chapel, 136
Reichle, Frederick A., 707
Reid, Dick, 703
Reiner, Fritz, 404, 788
Reinhart, K. G., 236
Relihan, Michael, 368
Renick, 584
Renick, William, 361
Renick family, 266
Renzie, Maggie, 461
Reuther, Valentine, 545, 613
Reuther, Victor, 613
Revercomb, Chapman, 602
Reynolds, Debbie, 184
Reynolds, Joseph J., 128
Reynolds, Thomas Jr., 658
Reynolds Memorial Hospital, 221, 452
Rheinbraun (firm), 162
Rhoads, Charles, 555
Rhode, Ruth Bryan Owen, 478
Rhone-Poulenc, 130, 725
Riccards, Michael, 166
Rice Field, 20
Rice, Glen, 333
Rice, H. B., 771
Rice, James Lewis, 761
Rich, Marc, 604
Rich Creek, 384, 494
Rich Knob, 242
Rich Mountain, 10, 57, *601*, 617
Richards, John, 525
Richardson, Billy, 58–59
Richardson, Dan, 239
Richardson, Larry, 434
Richland Coal Company, 146
Richmond, Daniel, 201
Richmond, William, 260, 599
Richwood City Hall, 189
Rickenbacker, Eddie, 509, 816
Ricketts House, 189
Ricotilli Lumber Company, 717
Ridenour, Andy, 508
Ridge Hatchery, 240
Ridgeley, 482
Ridgley, Duke, 447
Riley, 89
Riley, Frieda Joy, 626
Riley, Thomas, 367
Rinehart and Dennis, 324
Ripken, Cal, Jr., 46, 474
Ripley, Harry, 372, 618
Ritchie, Thomas, 12, 619
Ritchie, W. S., Jr., 333
Ritchie County, **619–20**; glass industry in, 11; back-to-the-land movement in, 34; Doddridge County formed from, 197; Harrisville in, 319; oil fields in, 521
Ritchie Democrat, 530
Rittenhouse, David, 359
Ritter, Anita Bell, 621
Ritter, George, 475–76
Ritter, Paul D., 621
Ritter, William R., Jr., 264
Ritz, Harold A., 221
Ritz, Helen Ruffner, 221

River, The (film), 239, 434
River Knobs, 277, 388
Rivers and Harbors Act (1935), 720
Riverside Iron Works, 681
Riverside Potteries Company, 580
Riverton Rocks, 277
Roads Development Amendment (1968), 266, 496
Roane, Spencer, 622, 669
Roane County, 182, 237, **622–23**; agriculture in, 6; back-to-the land in, 34; Bruen Lands Feud in, 87; bushwhackers in, 94; Elk River in, 216
Roaring Creek, 148, 473
Roaring Creek & Belington Railroad, 148
Roaring Creek & Charleston Railroad, 148
Roaring Mennonite Church, 473
Roaring Plains, 247
Robert C. Byrd Locks and Dam, 459
Roberts, Justin B., 545
Robertson, Dana, 624
Robertson, Edward, 407
Robertson, Julia Augusta, 564
Robertson, Richard, 407
Robey Theater, 669–70
Robinette, 89
Robinson, Carson J., 59
Robinson, Craig, 62
Robinson, Delmer, 271
Robinson, Donnie, 750
Robinson, Ira E., 42, 169, 423
Robinson, J. W. (schools supervisor), 364
Robinson, James (soldier), 574
Rock (town), 72, 567
Rock Cave (Centerville), 729
Rock Cliff Lake, 314
Rock Dome, 77
Rock Forge, 368
Rock Oak, 536
Rockcastle Creek, 116, 566
Rockefeller, John D., 102, 149, 162, 348, 521, 541, 778
Rockefeller, John D. "Jay," IV, 50, 108, 131, 223, 402, 475, 510, 560–61, 603, **625–26**, 816; banking reform backed by, 40; veterans home opened by, 42; progressivism of, 191, 576; electoral record of, 290, 496, 596, 646, 673, 724; appointments of, 316, 469, 809; strip mining opposed by, 342, 694; workers compensation and, 444; Coal Act backed by, 483; Pittston strike and, 567; construction projects of, 776; as college president, 777; labor disputes and, 787
Rockefeller, Nelson, 778
Rockefeller, Sharon Percy, 177, 507, 625
Rocket Boys (Hickam), 115, 330–31, 427
Rockhold, Elijah, 802
Rockingham Poultry Marketing Cooperative, 581
Rockne, Knute, 248
Rockspring Development, 750
Rocky Fork, 572
Rocky Gap, 32
Rocky Mountain Fur Company, 373
Roderfield, 480
Rogers, Henry Huttleston, 552, 739
Rogers, John, 549
Rogers, Roy, 626, 676
Rogers, Will, 778
Rogers, William Barton, 350
Rohde, Borge, 626
Rohr Rock Shelter, 23

Rohrbough, Edward G., 35, 285
Rolfe Lee, 258, 583
Roller, Jane W., 248
Rollin Chemical Company, 129
Rollyson, E. G. "Fern," 770
Romayne, Sally, 402
Romeo, Patricia Ann, 79
Ronceverte School, 299
Ronceverte, 132, 276, 570, 634
Roney's Fort, 600
Roosevelt Year, 1933, The, 239
Roosevelt, Franklin D., 103, 241, 509, 627; labor unions and, 20, 60; activism of, 56, 191, 341; public works efforts of, 71, 809; opposition to, 95, 186, 346, 499; CCC and, 99, 139, 161, 405; appointments of, 140, 384, 800; depictions of, 204, 434, 737; West Virginia vote for, 295, 527, 602; monuments created by, 318; papers of, 327; conservation policies of, 380; NIRA backed by, 420, 519; during World War II, 697, 768
Roosevelt, Franklin D., Jr., 19, 399
Roosevelt, Theodore, 199, 627; appointments of, 30, 284, 558; electoral record of, 91, 188, 481; progressivism of, 244, 480, 490, 790
Rootes, P., 135
Rose, Fred, 541
Rose, Willie, 626
Roseberry Farm, 257, 258
Rosebrake, 184
Rosemont Coal, 701
Rosenman, Samuel I., 327
Rosier, Joseph, 228, 346, 526, 636
Ross, Alexander, 53
Ross, Melinda, 596
Ross, Thomas R., 185
Rossbach, George, 76
Rosser, Thomas Lafayette, 130, 497
Rosser's Raid, 57
Rossetter, George, 89
Rossey, Christopher Columbus, 326
Rossiter, Thomas, 28
Rothstein, Arthur, 230
Rothstein, Sidney, 773
Rotruck family, 276
Roush family, 438
Roush, John, 458
Roush, Waldon, 676
Rowlesburg, 245, 367, 432
Rowley, Edythe L., 373
Rowley, James, 70, 455, 764
Royal, 599
Royal Coal and Coke Company, 396
Royall, William 629
Rubinstein, Artur, 788
Ruby, Hazel, 12
Ruby, J. W., 12, 776
Rucker, Edward P., 466
Ruffner, A. L., 630
Ruffner, Abraham, 629
Ruffner, Ann Brumbach, 629
Ruffner, Daniel, 629–30
Ruffner, David, 394, 584, 629, 636
Ruffner, Eve, 629
Ruffner, Joseph, Jr., 629
Ruffner, Joseph, Sr., 394, 629, 636
Ruffner, Lewis, 441, 629
Ruffner, Meredith, 630
Ruffner, Samuel, 629
Ruffner, Tobias, 629

Ruffner, Viola Knapp, 629, 743
Ruffner, William Henry, 629
"Ruffner Pamphlet," 1, 337, 629, 630
Ruggles Woodbridge Land Company, 729
Rum Creek, 132
Rumbarger, J. L. 717
Runner, Elaine, 206
Runyon, John W., 425
Rupert, 470
Rupp, Adolph, 116
Rural Arts and Crafts Cooperative, 177
Rush, Benjamin, 52
Russell, Effie Schriver, 14
Russell, Kurt, 253
Russell, Richard, 95
Russell, Robert Livingston, Sr., 675
Rust, Albert, 128
Ruth, Babe, 131
Rutherford, Carl, 153
Rutherford, M. R. "Slim," 504
Rutherford, Robert, 379
Rutland, Georgia Slim, 307
Ryan, Cheryl, 428
Ryan, Paddy, 288, 670
Ryan, Tom, 182
Ryburn, Frank McCutchan, 584
Rydberg, Per Axel, 76

Saad, Roger, 451
Saarinen, Eliel, 26
Sabbath School Union, 171
Sabraton, 500, 501
Sacred Heart Church (Bluefield), 25
Sacred Heart Church (Spring Dale), 368
Sacred Heart Hospital, 635
Sacred Heart of Mary (Weirton), 574
Saddle Site, 491
Sago, 88
Sago mine disaster, 150, 480
St. Clair Fault, 275, 709
St. Clair, Arthur, 361
St. Clara, 198, 277, 696
St. Colman's Catholic Church, 367, 368
St. George, 172, 717
St. George Orthodox Church (Charleston), 414, 415, 550
St. John's Episcopal Church (Charleston), 220, 221, 520
St. Joseph, 277
St. Joseph Cathedral, 25
St. Joseph's Seminary, 545
St. Ladislaus Catholic Church (Wheeling), 574
St. Luke's on the Island (Wheeling), 221
St. Mark's Methodist Church, 176, 743
St. Mary Carpatho-Russian Orthodox Church (Bluefield), 550
St. Marys Glass, 635
St. Mary's Orthodox Church (Westover), 780
St. Matthew's Church (Wheeling), 221, 545
St. Michael's Roman Catholic Church (Burnsville), 81
St. Patrick's Church (Hinton), 367, 368
St. Peter Claver, 4
St. Peter's Lutheran Church, 438
St. Phillips Academy, 4
St. Phillips Episcopal Church, 4
Sale, Cornelius Calvin, Jr., 95
Sale, William H., 111
Salem, 283, 319
Salem, Fred, 202

Salem International University, 41, 319, 602, 610, **635–36**, 650
Salem Raid, 32
Salt Rock, 562
Salvati, James, 370
Samels, Mark, 239
Samples, Mack, 770
Sanborn, Isaac, 650
Sanborn Company, 446
Sand Fork, 367, 521
Sand Hill & Laurel Fork Railroad, 620
Sandburg, Carl, 404
Sandcrest Farms, 221
Sanders, Martha Green, 638
Sanders, W. W. (civil rights figure), 137
Sanders, William (landowner), 638
Sandoe, Mildred W., 422
Sandon, Mario, 565
Sands, Harry S., 221
Sandy Ridge, 276
Santomero, Nancy, 598
Saperstein, Abe, 754
Sarandon, Susan, 639
Sarvis Fork, 175, 176
Satterwaite, Linton, Jr., 23
Saunders, 89
Saunders, Ernie, 750
Saunders, John W., 509
Saurburn, Peter, 489
Savage, George, 401
Savage, John, 639–40
Save the Children, 582
Sawyer, George, 751
Sayles, John, 239, 461
Scarbro, 197, 540
Scary Creek, 138, 381, 392, 393, 592, 641
Schiff, Charles, 773
Schiffler, A. C., 526
Schmidt, Paul, 381
Schmitt, Bernard W., 627
Schmitt, Tom, 432
Schofield, John, 565
School Building Authority, 108
Schoolcraft, Henry Rowe, 294
Schoolfield, Ann Bloomfield Gamble, 578
Schott Scientific Glass, 277
Schramm, David, 348
Schroath, Fred, 641
Schulte, Francis B., 627
Schuyler, Philip, 261
Schwartzwalder, Floyd, 808
Schwietering, Joseph F., 218
Scioto River, 1
Scioto-Monongahela Trail, 360
Scioto Valley Railway, 533
SCM Corporation, 293
Scott Hollow, 118
Scott, Barbara, 21
Scott, Edna, 405
Scott, James L., 507
Scott, Molly, 655, 819
Scott, Pearl, 160
Scott, Walter, 105
Scott, William, 21
Scott, Winfield, 415, 592, 802
Scott Depot, 593
Scott Field, 504
Scout of the Buckongehanon, The (McWhorter), 470
Scrafford, E. J., 70

Screven, Tom, 287
Scruggs, Earl, 39, 316, 423, 742, 812
Seaboard Coast Line, 132, 181
Seabrooke, Brenda, 428
Sears, Roebuck, 488
Sears, Upton "Uppie," 437, 487
Seckar, Alvena, 427
Second Creek, 300, 494
Second Great Awakening, 1, 475, 507, 610
Second Presbyterian Church, 189
See, Clyde, 496, 497
Seeger, King, 507
Seeger, Pete, 316
Seely Pine Furniture, 498–99
Sellers, Gary, 151
Sellers, Jim, 476
Sellers, John, 258
Semple, John, 368
Seneca, 500
Seng Camp Run, 271
Separate Peace, A (Knowles), 403, 427
Sergeant, William, 693
Sesse, Eddie, 447
Setzler, Frank, 23
Seventh Day Baptists, 41
Severinsen, Doc, 773, 788
Sevier, Valentine, 574
Sevy, Albert G., 540
Seward, William H., 231–32
Sewell, 234, 467, 528
Sewell, Stephen, 266, 450, 528, 570, 598, 651
Sewell coal seam, 148
Sewell Creek, 450, 470, 651
Sewell Lumber, 146
Seybert, Jacob, 260
Seymour, William J., 560
Shadle Farm, 258
Shadrick, Kenneth, 404
Shahn, Ben, 230
Shannon Hill, 225
Shannondale, 225, 226
Sharp, Cecil, 249, 250, 316
Sharp, Jane Price, 572, 586
Sharp, Summers H., 346
Sharples Massacre, 341
Shattuck Park, 503
Shattuck, Charles H., 521
Shaver Mountain, 10
Shaver, Dusty, 177
Shaver, Ronald, 242–43
Shaw, Charles G., 537
Shaw, James David, 652
Shaw, John, 759
Shaw, Robert G., 21
Shaw, Samuel Craig, 652
Shawhan, H. W., 523
Shawnee Banks, 757
Shawnee (Seneca) Trail, 743
Shearer, Richard E., 9
Sheen, Martin, 239
Shelby, Isaac, 574
Sheldon, John, 76
Shelton College, 632
Shelton, Harry, 185
Shelton, Mary Ann, 91
Shenandoah, The (Davis), 427
Shenandoah Hotel, 137
Shenandoah Mountain, 276
Shenandoah Pants Company, 457
Shenandoah Valley Electric Cooperative, 631

Shenandoah Valley Railroad, 533
Shepherd (colonel), 254
Shepherd, John, 802
Shepherd, Moses, 24, 655
Shepherd, Rezin Davis, 655
Shepherd, Stephen, 580
Shepherd, Thomas, 304, 656, 746
Shepherd Field (Eastern West Virginia Regional Airport), 32
Shepherd University (College), 77, 166, 293, 380, 533, **655–56**
Shepherd's Mill, 746
Shepherdstown Chronicle, 541
Sheridan, Philip H., 32, 194
Shikellamy (Oneida chief), 432, 495
Shingas (Delaware chief), 258–59
Shinn, Asa, 136, 474, 657
Shinn, Levi, 657
Shinn, Samuel, 318
Shinns Run, 657
Ship Rock, 663
Shipman, J. Versus, 104, 225
Shoemaker Mine, 452
Shoney's, 642
Shonk, Donald, 136
Shore, Dinah, 626
Short Ballot Amendment, 346, 715
Short Mountain Wetlands, 455
Short Mountain, 310
Shorthorn Association, 676
Shott, Hugh Ike, Jr., 69, 474, 789
Shott, James H., 69, 789
Shott, Mike, 789
Shotwell, Nathan, 759
Shreve, Dan, 239
Shreve, Henry M., 259, 337, 743
Shrewsbury, Joel, 196
Shrewsbury, John, 196
Shrewsbury, Samuel, 196, 735
Shriver, David, 520
Shriver, Samuel Sprigg, 303
Shroyer, D. K., 509
Shue, Edward, 300
Shue, Zona Heaster, 300
Shuman, John, 280
Shumate, H. K., 596
Shupe, Walt, 344
"Shupe's Chute," 344
Siber, Edward, 433
Siers, Sherman, 626
Significant Statistic, A (Flagg), 242
Silence of the Lambs, The (film), 239
Silling, C. E., 181, 742
Silurian Period, 261
Silurian Salina Formation, 483
Simmons, Gary, 239
Simmons, Streshley, 659
Simmons, William K., 286
Simms, Nathaniel, 347
Simms, Phil, 349
Simms, Walter, 308
Simon, Winston "Spree," 444
Simonton Windows, 620
Simpson, Grant, 202
Simpson, John, 140, 266, 700
Simpson Creek Baptist Church, 40
Simpson Creek, 175, 176, 383, 758
Simpson Methodist Episcopal Church, 139
Sims, Edgar B., 223

Sims, Robert Page, 69–70
Sinatra, Frank, 184, 754
Sinclair, Charles, 636
Singa Hipsy Doodle and Other Folk Songs of West Virginia (Boette), 251
Sinnett Branch, 142
Sino Swearingen, 33, 54
Sinsel, Columbia May, 188
Sisters of St. Joseph, 331
Sistersville Oil Review, 530
Siviter, Anna Pierpont, 12
Skaggs, Ida, 675
Skaggs, Ricky, 508
Skaggs, W. B., 675
Skelt, 344
Skidmore, Hobert, 427, 752
Skidmore, Linda Howell, 218
Skidmore, Owings & Merrill, 26, 623
Sky Chief Restaurant, 137
Slack, John M., Jr., 157
Slash, Joseph A., 200
Slate, Joseph, 428
Slaty Mountain, 77, 524, 651
Sleepy Creek Wildlife Management Area, 796
Slider Brothers Cement Block Company, 552
Sloan, Howard, 525
Sloan, John, 14
Sly, John Fairfield, 405
Small, John K., 396
Smillie, Thomas William, 384
Smith, Aaron, 619
Smith, Andre Raphael, 788
Smith, Barbara, 427
Smith, Barnes, 619
Smith, Bessie, 56, 566
Smith, Blaine, 632
Smith, Burr, 748
Smith, C. A. (developer), 625
Smith, C. Alphonso (folklorist), 251
Smith, C. L., 228
Smith, Carl J., 764
Smith, Chuck, 34
Smith, Clay, 236
Smith, E. F., 523
Smith, Edgar, 666
Smith, Ephraim, 383
Smith, Fannie, 3
Smith, Fiddlin' Arthur, 789, 812
Smith, George (printer), 463
Smith, George (radio executive), 785
Smith, George W. (landowner), 542
Smith, Gerrit, 204
Smith, Glen, 547
Smith, Howard W. (detective), 674
Smith, Howard Willis (artist), 42
Smith, Hulett Carlson, 49, 313, 348, 467, 600, 641, **662–63**; as commerce commissioner, 44, 248; capital punishment repealed by, 109; folk arts promoted by, 251; on Kennedy campaign, 398; surface mining and, 694; electoral record of, 724; in war on poverty, 742; in broadcasting, 805
Smith, I. W., 761
Smith, J. Lawrence, 76
Smith, Jedediah, 373
Smith, Jennie, 379
Smith, Joe L., Jr., 805
Smith, Joe L., Sr., 509, 600, 662, 805
Smith, John (captain), 578
Smith, John (Methodist leader), 136, 474

Smith, John H. (Episcopal leader), 221
Smith, Jonas, 573
Smith, Joseph, 502
Smith, Kenneth E., 463
Smith, Mariwyn, 463
Smith, Phyllis, 183
Smith, Robert L. (botanist), 76
Smith, Robert L., Jr. (newspaper publisher), 126
Smith, Robert L., Sr. (newspaper publisher), 126
Smith, Sallie (wife of "Uncle Dyke" Garrett), 269
Smith, Sarah (Sallie; wife of Joseph Johnson), 383, 384
Smith, Stewart H., 454
Smith, Watters, 748
Smith, William (board member), 693
Smith, William (landowner), 588
Smith, William Prescott (railroad executive), 28
Smith-Hughes Act, 579
Smith-Lever Act (1914), 225, 812
Smithburg, 198
Smithers, 370, 371
Smucker, Anna Egan, 428
Snedegars Cave, 265
Snidow, 584
Snow, Hank, 785
Snyder, Benjamin, 736
Snyder, Melvin, 674
Social Security Act (1935), 405, 527
Sole, Diana, 239
Solecki, Ralph, 23, 760
Solow, Robert, 516
Solutia, 130
Somerset Coal Company, 149, 162
Sonntag, William L., 26
Soper, Abraham D., 165
Soul of the Senate (film), 239
Sousa, John Philip, 404, 693
South Branch Creek, 226
South Branch Intelligencer, 311, 530
South Branch Mountain, 309
South Branch of the Potomac, 208, 209, 293
South Branch Valley Railroad, 293, 315, 581, 657
South Branch Valley, 6, 310
South Branch Vocational Technical Center, 293
South Burns Chapel, 549
South Charleston Crusher Company, 439
South Charleston Stamping and Manufacturing Company (SCSM), 128
South Mountain, 316
South Park, 500
South Penn Oil Company (Pennzoil), 198, 521
South Wheeling Bank and Trust, 757
Southern Appalachian Botanical Club, 168
Southern Baptist Convention, 41
Southern Carbon, 198
Southern Cult, 147
Southern Merchant Tailoring Company, 457
Southern Pacific Railroad, 355
Southern Railway System, 181, 533, 598
Southern States Cooperative, 229
Southside, 258
Southwestern Community Action Council, 17
Space Preachers (film), 239
Spanishburg, 72
Sparrow, Kathleen, 440
Speer, Noah, 283
Speidel Site, 23
Spencer, Allie, 525
Spencer, Joseph, 736
Spencer, Junior, 504

Spencer, Robert A., 49
Sperry, J. J., 756
Spicelick Creek, 429
Spillers, Lee, 496
Spirit of Jefferson, 530
Spradling, Owen, 504
Sprague, 197
Sprague, P. W., 197
Sprigg, 480
Sprigg, Amelia Hay McElheran, 303
Sprigg, Zachariah, 542
Spring Creek, 300, 395, 584
Spring Gap Mountain, 79
Spring Run hatchery, 120, 241
Springer, Drusilla, 500
Springfield, 310
Spruce Fork, 152
Spruce Mountain, 10, 388
Spurr, B. M., 452
Squier, Ephraim G., 22, 294, 504
Staats Mill, 175, 176
Stafford, Tony, 371
Stage Struck (film), 239
Staggers, Harley, Jr., 490, 674
Stalnaker, Salathiel, 279
Stalnaker, Samuel, 638
Stalnaker family, 266
Stam, James, 636
Standard Oil, 348, 521
Stanford, David (Hank the Cowhand), 177, 632
Stanford, Leland, 355
Stanhagen, William, 333
Stanley, Jerrel, 434
Stanley, Ralph, 70, 146, 434, 604
Stanley Brothers, 70, 434
Stansbury, Harry, 46
Stanton, Edwin M., 788
Stanwix, John, 261
Star City, 51, 283, 666
Starcher, Jacob, 372
Starcher, Larry V., 694
Starcher, Mary Ann, 675
Starcher, Phillip, 100
Stark, William, 258
Stark Brothers' Nursery, 21, 287
Starks, Benjamin, 761
Starks, Deborah S., 761
Starks, Stephen R., 761
Starvaggi, Michael, 87
State Farm and Homemakers Council, 224
State Industrial School for Colored Boys, 590
State Masonic Home (Parkersburg), 743
State Temporary Employment Program (STEP), 570
Staton, Bill, 322
Staton, Mick, 803
Staunton, Frederick M., 126
Staunton conventions (1816, 1825), 337, 374
Stebbins, Harold, 286
Steel Workers Organizing Committee (United Steelworkers of America), 408, 681
Steele, Pauline, 618
Steele brothers, 394
Steffens, Lincoln, 404
Stein, Gertrude, 427
Stelling, Rebecca, 178
Stephens, Alexander, 21
Stephens, Andrew, 458
Stephens, Robert W., Jr., 545
Stephenson, David, 308, 424

Stephenson, George, 145, 696
Stephenson, Hugh, 50, 54
Stephenson, Steve, 76
Steptoe and Pixley (Steptoe and Johnson), 384
Stern, Isaac, 773
Sterrett, James, 368
Steubenville, 83
Stevenson, Adlai E., 327, 509, 693
Stevenson, Richard, 654
Stevenson, William Erskine, 290, 555, **682–83**,
    807; electoral record of, 231, 376; newspaper
    owned by, 790
Stewart, Bert, 117
Stewart, Blaine, 632
Stewart, Charlie, 504
Stewart, Irvin, 168, 776
Stewart, James (architect), 264
Stewart, James H. (agriculture commissioner),
    449
Stewart, Jimmy, 253, 800
Stewart, Robert, 259
Stewart, Virgil Harvey, 158
Stewart, William, 256
Stewartstown, 129, 256
Stickley, Benjamin, 726
Stieren, H., 459
Stifel, Edward E., 664, 683
Stifel, Edward W., Sr., 683
Stifel, Edward, III, 664
Stifel, Johann Ludwig, 683
Still, A. T., 769
Still, James, 758
Stockton, Aaron, 107, 284, 392
Stockton, Frank R., 144
Stockton, Richard, 284
Stockton coal seam, 148
Stoker, Smokey, 504
Stokowski, Leopold, 404
Stone, Barton Warren, 105, 135
Stone, Elijah J., 683
Stone, W. J., 650
Stonecoal Creek, 758
Stonega Coal Company, 210
Stonewall Jackson Dam, 244, 419
Stoney Gap Sandstone, 566
Stony Creek Mill, 281
Stop Abusive Family Environments (SAFE), 675
Storer, John, 685
Storming Heaven (Giardina), 401, 427
Story, Joseph, 456
Stotler, Shirley Anne, 624
Stotts, E. Keith, 545
Stover, Don, 39, 70, 423
Stowe, 89
Strader, George, 123
Straight, Ross, 89
Straight, Roy, 329
Straight Run, 116
Strange, William, 685
Straton, "Major" John William, 433
Stratosphere Balloon Cave, 648
Stratton, Daniel, 761
Strauder, Taylor, 685–86
Strauss, Ferdinand, 457
Strauss, Lewis L., 277
Strauss, Richard, 404
Strayer, George D., 471, 686
Strickland, William "Flip," 107, 546
Strider, Edward Lee, 221
Strider, I. Keyes, 631

Strider, Melvin T., 631
Stroebel, John, 813
Strother, James A., 465
Stroud, Adam, 96, 111, 751
Strunk, William F., 248
Stuart family, 266
Stuart mine, 150
Stuart, 197
Stuart, J. E. B., 77
Stuart, Jane, 586
Stuart, Jesse, 262, 758
Stubblefield, James, 739
Stuebe, L. F. W., 455
Stull, Minnie, 595
Stull, Paul, 43
Stump, E. Turner, 11
Stump, Felix Budwell, 808, 810
Stumpy Bottom, 306
Sturdevant, George, 87
Sturgis, John H., 263
Sturgis, Samuel, 612
Sturgiss, George C., 373
Suarez, Benjamin, 467
Sublette, William, 373
Suck Creek, 429
Sugar Camp Run, 118
Sugar Grove, 221, 559
Suit, Samuel Taylor, 53
Sullivan, Carl R., 120
Sullivan, Charles, 26
Sullivan, Ken, 287
Sullivan, Maurice, 367, 368
Sullivan's Knob, 367
Summers, Lewis, 53, 390, 692
Summers County, 34, 35, **690–91**; demography
    of, 192; formation of, 233, 368, 473, 493
Summersville Dam, 244, 273, 357, 595, 752
Summersville Memorial Hospital, 532
Summit Point Raceway Orchards, 21
Summit Point, 138
Sumner, Charles H., 693, 796
Suncrest, 501
Sunday, Billy, 22
Sunnyside, 500
Sunoco Chemical, 750
Sunrise Museum of Charleston, 141
Superior Pocahontas Coal, 155
Surface Mining Control and Reclamation Act
    (1977), 511, 694
Surratt, Cecil, 703
Surratt, Mary, 318
Susquehannock (White Minqua) Indians, 226,
    361, 491, 544
Suter, John F., 428
Sutherland, Jock, 286
Sutherland, Richard, 810
Sutherland, Woodford, 7
Sutton, Isaac, 40
Sutton, James, 40
Sutton, John (minister), 40
Sutton, John D. (settler), 81, 695
Swami (film), 239
Swan, James, 695
Swandale, 80, 90
Swann, F. R., 125
Swann, Thomas, 537
Swanson, Gloria, 239, 528
Sweeney, Andrew J., 303
Sweet Dreams (film), 239

Swinton, John, 785
Switchback, 152
Switzer, Rufus, 620
Sycamore Coal Company, 798
Sylvester, 16
Symms Gap Meadow, 20

Table Rock, 562
Tabor, Trigg, 465
Tackett, Christopher, 632, 698
Tackett, John, 424
Tackett, Lewis, 632, 698
Tackett, Samuel, 698
Taconic Orogeny, 18
Taft, Lorado, 710
Taft, William Howard, 384
Talbot, Benton, 185
Talbott, Richard E., 223, 713
Talkington, Henry, 781
Tallman, Gene, 504
Tamburini, Enrico, 788
Tams, 152, 699
Tanacharison (Half-King), 485
Tanner, Grace, 352
Tanner, Preston, 73
Tanner, Samuel, 372, 622, 669
Tarr, Campbell, 713
Tarr, Peter, 561
Tassey, Morrison and Company, 329
Tate, Allen, 60
Tate Lohr Hatchery, 241
Taylor County, 226, **700–701**; Guineas in, 305;
    integration in, 364
Taylor, Alfred, 161
Taylor, Della Brown, 772
Taylor, Hugh Paul, 135, 804
Taylor, Jake, 632
Taylor, John, 700
Taylor, Loretta, 611
Taylor, Peter, 554
Taylor, Zachary, 268
Taylor-Ide, Daniel, 507
Teays, Stephen, 702
Tech Center, 129
Tecumseh (Shawnee chief), 653, 713
Teedyuscung (Delaware chief), 111
Teets, John L. "Bugs," 131
Tegunteh (Seneca chief), 782
Telford, Robert L., 298
Telltale Lilac Bush, The (Musick), 251, 278
Temple, David G., 223
Tenmile Creek, 758
Tennant, Natalie, 510
Tennessee River, 15
Tennyson, William, Jr., 637
Tenskwatawa (Shawnee chief), 653
Terra Alta, 10
Terrell, L. E., 685
Testerman, Cable C., 322, 461
Teter, Dwight, 769
Teter family, 276
Tetrick, Guy, 141
Textile Workers of America, 366
Thaxton, Gussie, 525
Thayer, Eli, 1, 121, 337, 600, 723, 749
Theatre Communications Group, 166
Thibeault, James, 177
Thirteenth Amendment, 4
Thoenen, Eugene, 742
Thom, James Alexander, 363

Thomas Speedway, 504
Thomas, Cyrus, 22, 23, 462
Thomas, Frederick, 125
Thomas, Herbert, 159
Thomas, Jacob C., 303, 683
Thomas, James, 564
Thomas, Jerry Bruce, 526
Thomas, Lowell, 404
Thomas, Matthew, 693
Thomas, Robert, 693
Thomas, W. H., 80
Thompson, Albert, 717
Thompson, Bob, 379
Thompson, Carlene, 428
Thompson, Ernest Trice, 584
Thompson, Frank, 182
Thompson, French W., 298
Thompson, Helen, 773
Thompson, Jimmy, 504
Thompson, John W., 680
Thompson, Katherine, 811
Thompson, Phillip R., 632
Thompson Lumber Company, 34
Thomson Newspapers, 126, 143, 228
Thorn Creek, 464, 559
Thornton, Mildred, 744
Thornton, Robert, 555
Thorpe, Jim, 525
Thrasher, Leslie, 26
302nd Fighter Squadron, 33
3M Corporation, 54
Thurmond, Philip J., 706, 802
Thurmond, Strom, 96
Thurmond, W. D., 94, 706
Thurmond, Walter R., 706
Thurston, Charles, 458
Thwaites, Reuben Gold, 135, 202
Tick Ridge, 99
Tieche, Mary Alice, 662
Tiger Aircraft, 33
Tight, W. G., 702
Tilton, J. C., 450
Timber and Watershed Lab, 236
Timmons Farm, 562
Tobacco Workers Union, 67
Tokyo Rose, 8
Tolbert, James, 137
Tolley, Rick, 453
Tomahawk, 53
Tomato Festival, 20
Tomblin, Earl Ray, 647
Tomblin, Joanne, 669
Tomlinson, Abelard, 294
Tomlinson, Elizabeth Harkness, 505
Tomlinson, James, 505
Tomlinson, Joseph, III, 798
Tomlinson, Samuel, 505, 708–09, 798
Tompkins, William, 92, 337, 738
Tonkovich, Dan, 575, 647
Top Mill, 369
Top of Allegheny, 570
Topping, D. C., 726
Torme, Mel, 379
Torrey, Mabel Landrum, 710
Torrin, Lionel, 540
Towers, George, 318
Trace Fork, 424
Traden, John, 654
Trader's (McCullough) Trail, 743

Traditional Ballads, Mainly from West Virginia
    (Cox), 251
Trans-Allegheny Pioneers (Hale), 426
Transforming the Appalachian Countryside
    (Lewis), 430
Travis, Randy, 676
Trbovich, Mike, 483
Treaty of Albany, 209
Treaty of Fort Harmar (1789), 782
Treaty of Fort Wayne (1803), 88
Treaty of Pittsburgh (1775), 260
Treaty of Utrecht (1713), 369
Treaty of Vincennes (1804), 88
Trees, Joseph, 781
Trenle Blake China Company, 580
Trevey, E. B., 716
Triangle Conduit Company, 452
Trianosky, Paul, 77
Tri-City Traction, 688
Tri-County Airport, 32
Trimble, George R., Jr., 236
Trinity Church (Huntington), 221
Triplett, George, 325
Triplett, Lee, 143, 238, 547, 790
Triplett, Sinnett, 142
Tri-State Glass Manufacturing Company, 565
Tross, Clarence, 39
Trotter, Richard, 36
Trotter, William (son of Anne Bailey), 36
Trotter, William Monroe (activist), 531
Trout, Abraham, 748
Trout Pond, 276, 314, 409
Trout Rock, 559
Troy, James, 781
Troy, William F., 785
True (village), 71
True Temper (Kelly Axe), 124, 398, 574
Truman, Harry S., 120, 131, 140, 184, 204,
    327, 509, 539; coal mining and, 150, 483;
    universal health care backed by, 296; elec-
    toral record of, 384, 556; as senator, 401
Trumbauer, Horace, 25, 331
Trumka, Richard L., 567, 624, 727
Trus Joist, 730, 808
Tucker, Henry St. George, Sr., 717
Tucker, Larry, 575, 647
Tucker County, 5, 172, 225, 226, 717–18; natural
    features of, 10; flora and fauna in, 13, 106,
    128, 246, 607; timberland in, 24, 695; settle-
    ment of, 336; Italians in, 370; religious life
    in, 472; Potomac and, 535; second homes in,
    645; tanning in, 699; wedding customs in,
    753; wind power in, 800
Tucker's Riffle, 216
Tug River Lumber Company, 620
Tug River Trail, 743
Tug Valley, 321, 322, 486
Tunnelton, 367
Tuohy, Walter J., 132
Turkey Creek, 494, 685
Turkey Gap, 473
Turkey Mountain, 311
Turkeybone Mountain, 10
Turner, C. A. P., 227
Turner, Ella Mae, 383
Turner, Francis Wheeler, 174
Turner, Frederick Jackson, 12
Turner, Joe, 649
Turner, John Roscoe, 600
Turner, Myrtle, 649

Tuscarora, 53, 584
Tuscarora Indians, 209, 369, 713
Tuskegee Airmen, 186, 757
Tuskegee Institute, 3, 743–44
Tutwiller, Ed, 671
Twain, Mark, 239, 333
"Twelve Apostles," 165
Twelvepole Creek, 99, 533
Twin Creeks, 488
Twin Mountain & Potomac Railroad, 657
Two Run, 141
Twohig, Richard, 368
Tygart, David, 266, 600, 721
Tygart Valley Glass Company, 701
Tyler, Erastus B., 400
Tyler, H. E., 2
Tyler, John (governor of Virginia), 721
Tyler, John (president), 199, 301
Tyler, T. Texas, 546
Tyler County, 197, 542, 721–22; industry in, 129;
    oil fields in, 521
Tyler Mountain Water, 77
Tyler Star News, 531
Tyler Traction Company, 688
Tyree, Frank, 182
Tyree, Mary Frances, 359

Underwood, Cecil H., 356, 492, 576, 636, 722,
    723–24, 764; sales tax rejected by, 44; as col-
    lege president, 57; electoral record of, 223,
    290, 341, 346, 444, 449, 489, 588, 613, 625,
    662, 803; appointments of, 308, 464, 602,
    641; strip mining and, 511
Underwood (Hall), Hovah, 723
Unger, John, 283
Union Bank, 140
Union Pacific-Central Pacific, 131, 355
Union Presbyterian Church, 584
Union Stopper Company, 377
Union Traction Company, 688
United Clay Products, 143
United Fuel Gas Building, 743
United Fuel Gas Company (Columbia Gas Trans-
    mission), 155, 521
United Hospital Center, 319
U.S. Borax & Chemical Company, 283
U.S. Coal & Oil Company, 369
U.S. Defense Plant Corporation, 697
U.S. Freedmen's Bureau, 3
U.S. Leather, 699
U.S. Navy Radio Station, 221
U.S. Rubber Corporation, 129, 697
U.S. Silica, 498, 499
United States Stamping Company, 452
U.S. Steel, 270, 528, 681
U.S. Wind Force, 800
United Steelworkers of America (Steel Workers
    Organizing Committee), 408, 681
United Textile Workers, 55
United Woolen Mills, 189
United Zinc Smelting Corporation, 452
Universal Mortgage Insurance Company, 757
Universal Negro Improvement Association, 4
Unto the Least of These (Flagg), 242
Up from Slavery (B. T. Washington), 124, 610
Uponor ETI, 729–30
Upper Ohio Valley Archeological Survey, 23
Upper Painted Trees, 554

Upper Tract, 261
Upshur County, 148, 231, **729–30**; agriculture in, 6, 292; artisans in, 17; natural features of, 88; folk music in, 250
Upton, Thomas, 63
Usery, William J., Jr., 567
Uvilla, 122

Vale, Jerry, 370
Valley Bend, 721
Valley Mountain, 10, 128, 601
Valley River Railroad, 657
Van Bibber, John, 92
Van Bibber, Peter, 92
Van Buren, Martin, 301, 305, 652
Vance Memorial Presbyterian Church, 263
Vance, Abner, 321, 733
Vance, Gene, 763
Vance, John C., 168
Vance, Nancy, 321
Vandal, Abraham, 234
Vandalia Company, 31, 542
Vandalia National Corporation, 757
Vandalia Sampler (film series), 239
Vanderbilt, Cornelius, 339
Vandergrift, James B., 506
VanKirk, Fred, 333
Van Meter, Abraham, 379
Van Meter, Garrett, 735
Van Meter, Henry, 260, 266
Van Meter, Isaac, 53, 264, 266, 735
Van Meter, Jacob, 735
Van Meter, John, 53, 264, 266
Van Meterford bridge, 83
Van Swearingen, Marmaduke, 68
Van Sweringen, Mantis J., 132
Van Sweringen, Otis P., 132
Vasquez de Allyon, Lucas, 514
Vaucluse, 569
Vaughan, Sarah, 379
Vaughn, Viola, 525
Veasey, Oscar, 150
Venable, Charles, 479
Venable, M. W., 110
Vestal, William, 368, 654
Vezner, Jon, 462
Via, E. G., 102
Via, Jenny, 517
Via, Orville, 517
Victoria Iron Furnace, 552
Vienna Boys Choir, 664
Vienna Racing Association, 504
Viking Glass Company, 527
Villa, Pancho, 768
Vining, Roscoe, 813
Vinson, Sam, 750
Vinson, Zachary Taylor, 369, 750
Viquesney, J. A., 9
Virginia Boys, 70
Virginia Central Railroad, 131
Virginia Electric Power, 293
Virginia Military Institute, 138
Virginia Pottery, 580
Virginia: A Geographical and Political Summary (Hotchkiss), 350
Virginia Republican, 530
Virship, Richard, 425–26
Vitro Agate, 446–47
Vivian, C. T., 624
Volcano Lubricator, 530

Volcano oil field, 521, 555, 740
Volstead Act (1919), 589
von Neumann, John, 516
Von Schlegell, Max, 457
Vorel, Bob, 71
Vosburgh, A. J., 672
Voss, Thomas, 728

Wabash railroad, 132, 533
Waddington Farm, 542
Waggener, Andrew, 458
Waggener, Charles B., 458
Waggoner, J. D., 422
Waggoner, Thomas, 260
Wagner Act (1935), 408, 770, 817
Wagoner, Don "the Beachcomber," 703
Waiting for Nothing (Kromer), 404, 427
Waldo Hotel, 140, 319, 635
Waldron, Cliff, 604
Walker Studio Theater, 141
Walker, Albert, 70
Walker, Ben, 425
Walker, John H., 589
Walker, "Pistol" Nell, 234
Walker, Romie, 125
Walker, W. F., 125
Walkersville, 148, 175, 176, 419
Wall, Robert D., 170
Wallace, George C. (governor of Alabama), 44
Wallace, George S. (historian), 639
Wallace, Peter, 509, 764
Wallace, William J. L., 772
Waller, Fats, 70, 379, 754
Walling, Florence, 525
Walloons, 51
Walls, Winston, 379
Wal-Mart, 98, 211, 327, 532
Walnut Gap, 271
Walpole Company, 31
Walsh, Richard, 88
Walton (Droddy's Mills; Droddyville), 622
Wampler-Longacre, 581
Wanamaker, John, 631
Wandering Soldier, 530
War (town), 150
War Creek, 56
War Eagle, 480
War Memorial Building (Wetzel County), 278
Ward, Agnes, 790
Ward, Charles Edwin, 742
Ward, Charles, 742
Ward, Monty, 504
Ward Engineering, 215
Warden, Dorothy R. "Bebe" (Reuter), 557
Warden, Herbert, 776
Warden, Jacob, 314
Warden, Karl, 556
Wardensville, 246, 314
Ware, Cheryl, 428
Ware, Clyde, 239
Ware, Thomas, 474
Warfield Anticline, 483
Waring, Fred, 468
Warm Springs Ridge, 283, 498
Warman, Altha, 666
Warner, Curt, 536, 815
Warner, Monty, 444
Warner-Klipstein Chemical Company, 129
Warren, George, 125

Warren, James, 176
Warren, Phyllis C., 160
Warren, Robert Penn, 262
Warrick, Harley, 441
Warwick Pottery Company, 114
Warwood Fire Station, 278
Washington, Augustine, 542, 744
Washington, Bushrod Corbin, 64, 144, 744
Washington, Corbin, 744
Washington, George Corbin, 744
Washington, George Steptoe, 316, 744, 745
Washington, Hannah Lee, 744
Washington, John Augustine, 744
Washington, John Augustus, 744
Washington, John Augustus, II, 64, 144
Washington, John Augustus, III, 64, 128
Washington, John Thornton Augustine,
Washington, Lawrence, 226, 744
Washington, Lucy Elizabeth, 744
Washington, Martha Dandridge Cus... 696, 745
Washington, Mildred (daughter),
Washington, Mildred (mother), 7
Washington, Richard B., II, 64
Washington, Richard Henry Lee,
Washington, Samuel (son of Cl...s Washington), 744
Washington, Willi...,
Washington Bottom, 179
Washington Manor (Charleston), 743
Water Resources Protection Act (2004), 746
Water Tank Hill, 759
Watkins, Evan, 289
Watkins, Hays T., Jr., 132
Watne, Ross, 239
Watson Farm, 23, 583
Watson, Carrie M., 243
Watson, Clarence Wayland, 748
Watson, Doc, 812
Watson, James Edward, 25, 227, 331, 448
Watson, James Edwin, 748
Watson, Richard, 135
Watson, Sylvanus Lamb, 748
Watts, Cornelius C., 30
Watts, J. O., 699
Waugh, Arthur B., 730
Wayne County, 99, 424, 447, **749–50**; abolitionism in, 1; artisans in, 17; natural features of, 50; Wildlife Management Area in, 796
Weatherford, Dorothy Dembosky, 177, 507
Weatherford, Teddy, 379
Weaver, Eldridge, 210
Webb, Bob, 239
Webb, Charles B., 126
Webb, Samuel, 666
Webb-Kenyon Act (1913), 589
Weber, Edward J., 25
Webster, Daniel, 199, 751
Webster, John, 619
Webster County, **751–52**; coal deposits in, 148; woodchopping festival in, 154; natural features of, 216; forestation in, 256, 608–09, 715; lumber industry in, 554
Weekly World News, 46–47
Weeks Act (1911), 254, 491, 492, 517
Weir, Ernest T., 312, 344, 681, 754
Weirick, George C., 438
Weirton Daily Times, 541
Weirton Heights, 344, 584, 754

Upper Tract, 261
Upshur County, 148, 231, **729–30**; agriculture in, 6, 292; artisans in, 17; natural features of, 88; folk music in, 250
Upton, Thomas, 63
Usery, William J., Jr., 567
Uvilla, 122

Vale, Jerry, 370
Valley Bend, 721
Valley Mountain, 10, 128, 601
Valley River Railroad, 657
Van Bibber, John, 92
Van Bibber, Peter, 92
Van Buren, Martin, 301, 305, 652
Vance Memorial Presbyterian Church, 263
Vance, Abner, 321, 733
Vance, Gene, 763
Vance, John C., 168
Vance, Nancy, 321
Vandal, Abraham, 234
Vandalia Company, 31, 542
Vandalia National Corporation, 757
Vandalia Sampler (film series), 239
Vanderbilt, Cornelius, 339
Vandergrift, James B., 506
VanKirk, Fred, 333
Van Meter, Abraham, 379
Van Meter, Garrett, 735
Van Meter, Henry, 260, 266
Van Meter, Isaac, 53, 264, 266, 735
Van Meter, Jacob, 735
Van Meter, John, 53, 264, 266
Van Meterford bridge, 83
Van Swearingen, Marmaduke, 68
Van Sweringen, Mantis J., 132
Van Sweringen, Otis P., 132
Vasquez de Allyon, Lucas, 514
Vaucluse, 569
Vaughan, Sarah, 379
Vaughn, Viola, 525
Veasey, Oscar, 150
Venable, Charles, 479
Venable, M. W., 110
Vestal, William, 368, 654
Vezner, Jon, 462
Via, E. G., 102
Via, Jenny, 517
Via, Orville, 517
Victoria Iron Furnace, 552
Vienna Boys Choir, 664
Vienna Racing Association, 504
Viking Glass Company, 527
Villa, Pancho, 768
Vining, Roscoe, 813
Vinson, Sam, 750
Vinson, Zachary Taylor, 369, 750
Viquesney, J. A., 9
Virginia Boys, 70
Virginia Central Railroad, 131
Virginia Electric Power, 293
Virginia Military Institute, 138
Virginia Pottery, 580
Virginia: A Geographical and Political Summary (Hotchkiss), 350
Virginia Republican, 530
Virship, Richard, 425–26
Vitro Agate, 446–47
Vivian, C. T., 624
Volcano Lubricator, 530

Volcano oil field, 521, 555, 740
Volstead Act (1919), 589
von Neumann, John, 516
Von Schlegell, Max, 457
Vorel, Bob, 71
Vosburgh, A. J., 672
Voss, Thomas, 728

Wabash railroad, 132, 533
Waddington Farm, 542
Waggener, Andrew, 458
Waggener, Charles B., 458
Waggoner, J. D., 422
Waggoner, Thomas, 260
Wagner Act (1935), 408, 770, 817
Wagoner, Don "the Beachcomber," 703
Waiting for Nothing (Kromer), 404, 427
Waldo Hotel, 140, 319, 635
Waldron, Cliff, 604
Walker Studio Theater, 141
Walker, Albert, 70
Walker, Ben, 425
Walker, John H., 589
Walker, "Pistol" Nell, 234
Walker, Romie, 125
Walker, W. F., 125
Walkersville, 148, 175, 176, 419
Wall, Robert D., 170
Wallace, George C. (governor of Alabama), 44
Wallace, George S. (historian), 639
Wallace, Peter, 509, 764
Wallace, William J. L., 772
Waller, Fats, 70, 379, 754
Walling, Florence, 525
Walloons, 51
Walls, Winston, 379
Wal-Mart, 98, 211, 327, 532
Walnut Gap, 271
Walpole Company, 31
Walsh, Richard, 88
Walton (Droddy's Mills, Droddyville), 622
Wampler-Longacre, 581
Wanamaker, John, 631
Wandering Soldier, 530
War (town), 150
War Creek, 56
War Eagle, 480
War Memorial Building (Wetzel County), 278
Ward, Agnes, 790
Ward, Charles Edwin, 742
Ward, Charles, 742
Ward, Monty, 504
Ward Engineering, 215
Warden, Dorothy R. "Bebe" (Reuter), 557
Warden, Herbert, 776
Warden, Jacob, 314
Warden, Karl, 556
Wardensville, 246, 314
Ware, Cheryl, 428
Ware, Clyde, 239
Ware, Thomas, 474
Warfield Anticline, 483
Waring, Fred, 468
Warm Springs Ridge, 283, 498
Warman, Altha, 666
Warner, Curt, 536, 815
Warner, Monty, 444
Warner-Klipstein Chemical Company, 129
Warren, George, 125

Warren, James, 176
Warren, Phyllis C., 160
Warren, Robert Penn, 262
Warrick, Harley, 441
Warwick Pottery Company, 114
Warwood Fire Station, 278
Washington, Augustine, 542, 744
Washington, Bushrod Corbin, 64, 144, 744
Washington, Corbin, 744
Washington, George Corbin, 744
Washington, George Steptoe, 316, 744, 745
Washington, Hannah Lee, 744
Washington, John Augustine, 744
Washington, John Augustus, 744
Washington, John Augustus, II, 64, 144
Washington, John Augustus, III, 64, 128
Washington, John Thornton Augustine, 744
Washington, Lawrence, 226, 744
Washington, Lucy Elizabeth, 744
Washington, Martha Dandridge Custis, 225, 696, 745
Washington, Mildred (daughter), 744
Washington, Mildred (mother), 744
Washington, Richard B., II, 64
Washington, Richard Henry Lee, 744
Washington, Samuel (son of Charles Washington), 744
Washington, William, 55
Washington Bottom, 179
Washington Manor (Charleston), 743
Water Resources Protection Act (2004), 746
Water Tank Hill, 729
Watkins, Evan, 259
Watkins, Hays T., Jr., 132
Watne, Ross, 239
Watson Farm, 23, 583
Watson, Carrie M., 243
Watson, Clarence Wayland, 748
Watson, Doc, 812
Watson, James Edward, 25, 227, 331, 448
Watson, James Edwin, 748
Watson, Richard, 135
Watson, Sylvanus Lamb, 748
Watts, Cornelius C., 30
Watts, J. O., 699
Waugh, Arthur B., 730
Wayne County, 99, 424, 447, **749–50**; abolitionism in, 1; artisans in, 17; natural features of, 50; Wildlife Management Area in, 796
Weatherford, Dorothy Dembosky, 177, 507
Weatherford, Teddy, 379
Weaver, Eldridge, 210
Webb, Bob, 239
Webb, Charles B., 126
Webb, Samuel, 666
Webb-Kenyon Act (1913), 589
Weber, Edward J., 25
Webster, Daniel, 199, 751
Webster, John, 619
Webster County, **751–52**; coal deposits in, 148; woodchopping festival in, 154; natural features of, 216; forestation in, 256, 608–09, 715; lumber industry in, 554
Weekly World News, 46–47
Weeks Act (1911), 254, 491, 492, 517
Weir, Ernest T., 312, 344, 681, 754
Weirick, George C., 438
Weirton Daily Times, 541
Weirton Heights, 344, 584, 754

Weise, Suzanne, 511
Weiss Knob, 107, 660
Welch, Alexander, 615
Welch, Edwin, 728
Welch, Frances Hunter Lawrence Arbuckle, 615
Welcome Mound, 23
Welling, Frank, 669
Wells, Alexander, 252, 756
Wells, Charles, 660, 722
Wells, Delilah, 660
Wells, Ephraim, 722
Wells, Hawey A., Jr., 61, 62, 89, 151, 603
Wells, Richard "Greybeard," 84
Wells, Sarah, 660
Wells, W. E., 347
Wellsburg, Bethany & Washington Railroad, 688
Wenberg, Thomas James, 325
Wendel Coal Company, 701
Wertz, William W., 565, 757
Wesley, Charles, 560
Wesley, John, 28, 136, 474, 560, 638, 777
West, John, 458
West, Paul, 187
West, S. B., 2
West Fairmont, 227
West Liberty, 584
West Penn Power Company, 491, 746
West Virginia: A Film History, 239
West Virginia-American Water Company, 216
West Virginia Association of Museums, 512
West Virginia Bar Association, 413
West Virginia Brick Company, 143
West Virginia Broadcasters Association, 595
West Virginia Centennial Book of 100 Songs (Gainer), 251
West Virginia Central & Pittsburg [*sic*] Railway, 186, 217, 218, 344, **761**
West Virginia Classical and Normal Academy, 729
West Virginia Coal Company, 82
West Virginia Committee on Native American and Archaeological Burial Policies, 24
West Virginia Conference Seminary, 729
West Virginia Derby, 510
West Virginia Draft Horse and Mule Association, 201
West Virginia Eagle Coal Company, 161
West Virginia Educational Broadcasting Authority, 595
West Virginia Enterprise, 558
West Virginia Federation of Teachers, 214
West Virginia Folk Art Apprenticeship Program, 32
West Virginia Homemakers Council, 224
West Virginia Human Rights Commission, 364
West Virginia Institute of Technology, 775
West Virginia Midland Railroad, 345, 657, 752
West Virginia Mining and Reclamation Association, 762
West Virginia Motor Speedway, 504
West Virginia Motor Sports Council, 504
West Virginia Mountain State Gospel Singers Corporation, 506
West Virginia Northern Railroad, 657
West Virginia Oil and Land Company, 683
West Virginia Poetry Society, 316
West Virginia Porcelain, 580
West Virginia Preparatory School, 579
West Virginia Public Health Association, 591
West Virginia Scenic Trails Association, 11

West Virginia Society of Osteopathic Medicine, 472
West Virginia Spring Water Company, 77
West Virginia State Farm Museum, 512
West Virginia State Normal School, 533
West Virginia State Poultry Association, 581
West Virginia University, 211, 579–80, **774–76**; industrial archeology at, 24; botany at, 45, 76, 141, 168, 247, 479, 686; governance of, 72, 213, 214; creation of, 75, 339, 492, 500; athletics at, 116–17, 120, 349, 352, 509–10, 670, 671, 758; medical school of, 125, 471, 493, 556–57; forestry at, 167, 255; fraternities at, 191; regional history holdings at, 251; architecture of, 377, 440; law school of, 412; mascot of, 510–11; transit system of, 561; public health at, 591; experimental farms at, 615; antiwar sentiment at, 737
West Virginia Walking Beam, 530
West Virginia Wildlife Center, 512
West Virginia Writers' Project, 179
West Virginians for Life, 443
West's Fort, 318
Western Ohio Financial Corporation, 757
Western Pocahontas Corporation, 720
Western Star, 530
Westfall, Joel, 231
Westfall family, 266
Westfall's Fort, 267, 601
Westinghouse Electric, 227
Weston Brick and Coal Company, 143
Weston College, 213
Weston Democrat, 531
Wetzel, George, 782
Wetzel, Jacob, 782
Wetzel, John, 277, 451, 782
Wetzel, Martin, 782
Wetzel, Ray, 379
Wetzel Chronicle, 541
Wetzel County, 542, **781–82**; oil fields in, 521; New Martinsville in, 527; Paden City in, 552; county named for, 782
Wexler, Haskell, 461
Weyerhaeuser, 81, 808
Wharton, Samuel, 780
Wharton, Thomas, 780
Wheeler-Rayburn (Public Utility Holding Company Act; 1935), 155
Wheeling, **783**; black education in, 3; architecture in, 24; as capital, 25, 124, 341, 376, 391; prison in, 29; bridges in, 38, 83; sports in, 45, 670; Indian attacks on, 88; Carnegie grant to, 112; Unionism in, 113; Chamber of Commerce in, 121; industry in, 211, 297, 337, 369, 371, 407, 537, 580, 610, 681, 703; Germans in, 277; labor in, 340; Irish in, 367; Italians in, 371; Jews in, 382, 383; Lebanese and Syrians in, 414; libraries in, 422; Lutherans in, 438; as inland port, 520; as county seat, 542–43; Orthodox Christians in, 550, 611; Poles in, 574; population rank of, 577; Presbyterians in, 584; broadcasting in, 595, 703; Catholics in, 626, 627; Rotary in, 629; streetcars in, 688; telephone service in, 702, 734–35; as tobacco center, 708; Unitarians in, 725; vernacular architecture in, 735; flooding in, 750; founding of, 819
Wheeling Artisan Center, 178
Wheeling Bridge Company, 641
Wheeling Centre Tannery, 699

Wheeling Corrugating, 681
Wheeling Creek, 119, 266, 542
Wheeling Daily News, 541
Wheeling Dollar Savings & Trust, 757
Wheeling Female Academy, 505
Wheeling Hill, 464
Wheeling Iron and Steel, 407, 681
Wheeling Jesuit University, 543, 610, 627, **785–86**, 768
Wheeling Metal and Manufacturing Company, 452
Wheeling National Bank, 757
Wheeling Pottery Company, 580
Wheeling (News-)Register, 541
Wheeling Repository, 530
Wheeling Sanitary Manufacturing Company, 580
Whelan, Thomas A., 726
When I Was Young in the Mountains (Rylant), 427–28
When the Line Goes Through (film), 239
Wherry, Edgar, 76
Whetsell, Harry, 185
Whipple, 540, 574
Whipple Mine, 155
Whitaker-Glessner Company, 369, 407, 681, 787
White, Albert Blakeslee, **789–90**; tax commission appointed by, 188; 290; as "Elkins governor," 341, 555; Samuel W. Starks appointed by, 675; *State Journal* sold to, 683
White, Bob, 463
White, Catherine Jackson, 376
White, Clarence Cameron, 461, 772
White, Cora, 137
White, D. Ray, 791
White, Emerson, 789
White, George, 743
White, H. B., 137
White, H. S., 182
White, Lewis, 137
White, Minerva, 790
White, R. W. (newspaperman), 792
White, Raymond (war hero), 810
White, Robert (lawyer), 376
White, Theodore H., 399, 574
White, W. H. S., 656
White, William (captain), 88
White, William Ryland (minister), 213, 214, 264
White Grass, 660
White Minqua (Susquehannock) Indians, 226, 361, 491, 544
White Oak Railroad, 197
White Pantry Restaurant, 137
White Pole Meeting House, 570
White Sulphur Springs Company, 462
White Top Mountain, 272
Whitehead, John Lyman, 33
Whitehead, Mary, 179
White's Draft, 651
Whitescarver, Bradshaw, 732
Whitescarver, William, 732
Whiting, Gregory W., 70
Whitley, Keith, 675
Whitman, Walt, 66
Whitten, Rex, 365
Whittredge, T. Worthington, 26
Wiant, W. T. (Civil War captain), 279
Wiant, William (conductor), 773
Wickham, William C., 131
Widen, L. G., 793

Wieboldt, Tom, 76
Wilcox, Don, 587
Wilcox, Opal Marie, 44
Wildcat Branch, 562
Wildwood, 49
Wiles Hill, 500
Wiley, Shannon, 781
Wilkins, Barron, 662
Willard, Daniel, 38, 796
Willebrandt, Mabel Walker, 8
Willett, John T., 318
William, 717
William Penn Association, 506
Williams, Barbara, 797
Williams, Chickie, 785, 797, 814
Williams, Cy, 797
Williams, Hank, 474, 541
Williams, Hershel Woodrow "Woody," 159, 810
Williams, Isaac, 266, 798
Williams, John Alexander, 102, 373, 437, 576, 607, 643
Williams, John D., 454
Williams, Karen, 797
Williams, Leroy, 4
Williams, Madeline, 797
Williams, Mrs. Isaac, 709
Williams, Norman, 100
Williams, P. Ahmed, 772
Williams, Paul, 434
Williams, Rebecca Tomlinson Martin, 798
Williams, Vincent, Jr., 402
Williamsburg School, 299
Williamson, Arnold, 356
Williamson, Irving, 356
Williamson Island, 721
Williamsport (Pruntytown), 580, 589, 700
Willis, Edward Jefferson, 8
Willis, Nathaniel, 580
Willis, Sue, 319
Willis, Todd C., 68
Willis Branch, 480
Willkie, Wendell, 184
Willow Glen, 468
Willow Island, 130, 569
Wills Mountain, 328, 388, 535, 642, 648
Wilson, Andrew, 168
Wilson, Benjamin, 601, 636
Wilson, Blaine, 82
Wilson, Bob, 671
Wilson, David, 623
Wilson, Donald, 514–15
Wilson, Emmanuel Willis "Windy," **799–800**; flexibility of, 78; activism of, 191, 576; disputed election of 1888 and, 243, 286, 647; Hatfield-McCoy Feud and, 323; striking miners defended by, 324; appointments of, 407, 437; grave of, 672
Wilson, Garland, 379
Wilson, Hack, 45
Wilson, James Keys, 24
Wilson, Lafayette, 693
Wilson, Linn, 677
Wilson, Mark, 307
Wilson, Quentin, 626
Wilson, Rachel, 187

Wilson, Teddy, 56
Wilson, Virginia Myrtle "Aunt Jennie" Ellis, 356, 434
Wilson, Woodrow, 36, 54, 137, 189, 244, 333, 378, 495, 503, 768, 810
Wilson family, 266
Wilson-Woodrow-Mytinger House, 311
Wilson's Fort, 600
Win a Date with Tad Hamilton (film), 239
Winchester, 264
Winchester & Potomac Railroad, 73, 316
Winding Gulf, 48, 155, 385, 699, 739
Windom, William, 253
Windsor Heights, 84
Wine, Bob, 801
Wine, Smithy, 547, 801
Winfield Bridge, 593
Winifrede Block Coal Company, 798
Winifrede Railroad, 597, 657
Winter Festival of Lights, 537
Winters, Shelley, 532
Winton, Norma, 517
Wirt, William, 802
Wirt County, 577, **802–03**; tobacco farming in, 6; in Civil War, 93; formation of, 216; carbon black industry in, 521
Wirtz, Willard, 100
Wise, Bob, 96, 290, 444, 504, **803–04**; electoral record of, 85, 724; education policies of, 214, 589, 772
Wise, Henry A., 248, 437, 575, 628, 641
Wiseman, Mac, 785
Witcher, John S., 425
Witches, Ghosts and Signs (Gainer), 251
Withrow, Lewis, 811
Witt, James, 260
WLR Foods, 497, 580, 581
Wohinc, Louie, 436
Wohinc, Margaret,
Wolcott, Marion Post, 230
Wolf Creek, 494
Wolfe, Jonathan, 622, 669
Wolfe, Tom, 33, 816
Wolfram, Judd, 103
Wolverton, John M., 294
Women and Employment, 805–06
Women's Christian Temperance Union (WCTU), 385, 805, 817
Wood, C. V., 204
Wood, Isabel, 346
Wood, James, 264
Wood, Thomas, 47
Wood County Airport, 32
Wood County, **807–08**; beef cattle in, 6; glass industry in, 11; Fort Boreman in, 258; 274; 372; Vienna in, 736
Woodard, Prince, 455
Woodburn Female Seminary, 492, 500, 774
Woodchopping Festival, 154
Woodgrove furnace, 492
Woodland Indians, 335
Woodland, Elizabeth, 216
Woodrum Home Outfitting Company, 327
Woodrum, June, 154

Woods, Mrs. Henry, 616
Woods, Robert, 552
Woods, Tom Jack, 466
Woodward, Stimpson H., 303
Woolworth, R. H., 788
Worby, Rachael, 108, 788
Workman, Arthur, 777
Workman, James, 322
Workman, Joseph, 322
Workman, Mark, 671, 776
Wright, Oscar, 39
Wright, Peter, 561
Wright, Stephen J., 70
Wriston, Emory N. "Pop," 239, 254
WVU at Parkersburg, 455, 555, **812**
WVU Institute of Technology, 234, 391, **813**
Wyandot Indians, 259, 260, 406, 576, 713
Wyant, Alexander, 26
Wyatt, John, 781
Wyco, 699
Wyeth, Andrew, 356
Wylie, Ward, 815
Wyllie, Harry R., 9
Wynyard, Jason, 753
Wyoming Coal Company, 699
Wyoming County, 715, **814–15**; coal mining in, 150, 369, 371; fauna in, 441; courthouse in, 566

Yankee, 530
Yarbrough, Herman, 546
Yates, Alexander, 291
Yeager, John, 123
Years Are Even, The (Skidmore), 427
Yew Mountains, 709
Yokum, Woodrow, 663
Yost Law, 470, 589
Youghiogheny Forest, 756
Young, Ammi B., 24, 766
Young, Frank, 631
Young, G. O., 523
Young, Jacob, 239, 791
Young, John, 698
Young, Keziah, 632
Young, Robert R., 132
Young, Samuel, 806
Younger, Cole, 218, 377
Youngstown Sheet & Tube, 115
Youse, Hillis, 562, 815
Youth Museum of Southern West Virginia, 49, 512
Yukon mine, 150

Zabeau, Rene, 283
Zane, Jonathan, 783, 819
Zane, Mary Lovely Chapline, 303
Zane, Noah, 135
Zane, Silas, 783, 819
Zane's trace, 520, 819
Zerex antifreeze, 207
Ziebold, William, Sr., 125
Ziegler, John, 121
Zion Church (Charles Town), 220, 221
Zola, Emile, 423, 461
Zukerman, Eugenia, 788

WEST VIRGINIA

PEN

OHIO

KENTUCKY

New Cumberland
HANCOCK
Weirton
Wellsburg
BROOKE
Wheeling OHIO
Moundsville
MARSHALL
Monongahela River
79
119
Cheat Lake
MONONGALIA
Morgantown
MARION
Kingwood
Fairmont
PRES
Grafton
HARRISON
TAYLOR
Tygart Lake
New Martinsville
WETZEL
Middlebourne
TYLER
St. Marys
PLEASANTS
West Union
DODDRIDGE
Clarksburg
BARBOUR
Philippi
TU
Parkersburg
Harrisville
RITCHIE
119
Weston
250
Buckhannon
WOOD
77
Elizabeth
WIRT
GILMER
LEWIS
119
UPSHUR
Elkins
JACKSON
Glenville
33
Stonewall Jackson Lake
219
RAND
Point Pleasant
Ripley
33
Spencer
Grantsville
Glenville
79
19
Buckhannon River
MASON
ROANE
CALHOUN
BRAXTON
Sutton
Burnsville Lake
WEBSTER
250
35
PUTNAM
Winfield
119
Sutton Lake
Tygart Valley River
POCAHONTAS
Huntington
CABELL
KANAWHA
Elk River
Webster Springs
Elk River
64
60
Charleston
Clay
NICHOLAS
Gauley River
Marlinton
Beech Fork Lake
Hamlin
CLAY
Summersville
Wayne
LINCOLN
WEST
River
Summersville Lake
WAYNE
East Lynn Lake
Madison
64
Fayetteville
GREENBRIER
Guyandotte River
BOONE
VIRGINIA
FAYETTE
60
119
New River
Lewisburg
MINGO
Logan
LOGAN
RALEIGH
Beckley
64
Williamson
19
Hinton
Union
119
WYOMING
R.D. Bailey Lake
SUMMERS
Bluestone Lake
219
MONROE
52
Pineville
TURNPIKE
Welch
MERCER
McDOWELL
Princeton
460
Bluefield
77
19